ZIP CODE FINDER

The information in the *ZIP Code Finder* was collected directly from the Rand McNally *1999 Commercial Atlas & Marketing Guide* and other Rand McNally products.

The Rand McNally *ZIP Code Finder* and its contents are not affiliated with the U.S. Postal Service.

Printed in the United States of America

ZIP Code Finder

Table of Contents

Introduction / The Meaning of Your ZIP Code ....p. 5

Using the ZIP Code Finder ....p. 6

Standard Address Abbreviations ....p. 7

Toll-Free Reservation Numbers ....p. 8

Telephone Area Code / Time Zone Tables ....p. 9 – 11

Telephone Area Code / Time Zone Map ....p. 12 – 13

Mailing Information ....p. 14 – 18

U.S. Postal Service Business Centers ....p. 19 – 22

Basic Listings and 3-Digit ZIP Code Maps

State/City	3-Digit Map	Listings
Alabama	24-25	23
Alaska	34-35	36
Arizona	38-39	40
Phoenix		41
Arkansas	44-45	46
California	52-53	51
Los Angeles		59
Riverside		63
Sacramento		63
San Diego		63
San Francisco		63
San Jose		66
Colorado	70-71	69
Denver		69
Connecticut	76-77	75
Hartford		78
Delaware	180-181	80
District of Columbia	180-181	82
Washington		82
Florida	84-85	86
Jacksonville		89
Miami		90
Orlando		92
St. Petersburg		94
Tampa		95
Georgia	98-99	97
Atlanta		97
Hawaii	108-109	107
Honolulu		107
Idaho	112-113	111
Illinois	116-117	115
Chicago		119
Indiana	132-133	131
Indianapolis		136
Iowa	144-145	143
Kansas	150-151	149
Kansas City		152
Kentucky	156-157	155
Louisville		161
Louisiana	166-167	168
New Orleans		171
Maine	174-175	173

Basic Listings and 3-Digit ZIP Code Maps, continued

State/City	3-Digit Map	Listings
Maryland	180-181	179
Baltimore		179
Massachusetts	190-191	192
Boston		192
Michigan	198-199	200
Detroit		201
Minnesota	210-211	209
Minneapolis		213
St. Paul		215
Mississippi	218-219	220
Missouri	226-227	225
Kansas City		230
St. Louis		232
Montana	234-235	236
Nebraska	238-239	240
Nevada	242-243	244
Las Vegas		244
New Hampshire	246-247	245
New Jersey	250-251	249
New Mexico	256-257	258
New York	262-263	261
Albany		261
Buffalo		264
New York City		270
Rochester		274
North Carolina	278-279	280
North Dakota	290-291	289
Ohio	294-295	293
Cincinnati		296
Cleveland		297
Columbus		297

State/City	3-Digit Map	Listings
Oklahoma	308-309	310
Oklahoma City		312
Oregon	314-315	316
Portland		317
Pennsylvania	320-321	319
Philadelphia		335
Pittsburgh		335
Rhode Island	76-77	343
Providence		343
South Carolina	344-345	346
South Dakota	350-351	352
Tennessee	354-355	356
Memphis		361
Nashville		362
Texas	368-369	367
Dallas		371
Houston		375
San Antonio		381
Utah	386-387	385
Salt Lake City		388
Vermont	390-391	389
Virginia	394-395	393
Norfolk		401
Richmond		403
Washington	406-407	408
Seattle		411
West Virginia	414-415	413
Wisconsin	422-423	421
Milwaukee		426
Wyoming	430-431	432

Major Cities with 5-Digit ZIP Code Maps

City	5-Digit Map
Atlanta, GA	100
Baltimore, MD	182
Boston, MA	193
Chicago, IL	120
Dallas, TX	372
Detroit, MI	202
Houston, TX	376
Kansas City, KS	153
Los Angeles, CA	60

City	5-Digit Map
Miami, FL	91
Minneapolis, MN	214
New York, NY	271/272
Philadelphia, PA	336
Phoenix, AZ	42
San Diego, CA	64
San Francisco, CA	65
St. Paul, MN	216
Washington, DC	83

Introduction

The Rand McNally *ZIP Code Finder* is a complete and convenient reference containing ZIP Code listings for approximately 120,000 places in the United States. Arranged alphabetically by state, these listings enable you to quickly and easily find ZIP Codes. The *ZIP Code Finder's* listings are visually enhanced by a detailed three-digit ZIP Code map for each state; these maps show the location of towns and cities within the three-digit ZIP Code Service Areas.

Listings for 50 major U.S. cities include ZIP Codes for selected colleges/universities, financial institutions, hospitals, hotels/motels, and military installations. Additionally the Washington, DC listing includes ZIP Codes for government offices.

For each multiple ZIP Code city, the *ZIP Code Finder* displays the toll-free telephone number that can be called to determine which of the city's ZIP Codes you need. Listings for cities with only two ZIP Codes, one for the delivery **area** and one for **post office boxes**, do not include telephone numbers. Instead, a footnote designates which ZIP Code is for the delivery area (*), and which ZIP Code is for post office boxes (†). Five-digit ZIP Code maps display ZIP Code boundaries for each of eighteen multiple ZIP Code cities

The Rand McNally *ZIP Code Finder* saves you time and money. Information provided on mailing rates and regulations, plus the locations of U.S. Postal Service business offices, helps you mail economically and efficiently. Convenient listings of toll-free numbers for car rentals, airline reservations and hotel/motel accommodations place these services at your fingertips. In addition, telephone area code lists provide a helpful reference when placing long-distance calls.

The Meaning of Your ZIP Code

ZIP Codes, set up by the U.S. Postal Service to improve mail distribution, define areas within the U.S.

The country is divided into ten geographic regions that consist of three or more states. Each of these regions is assigned a number from 0 to 9. This number is the first digit of your ZIP Code.

Within the ten geographic regions, states are further divided into smaller geographic units. The second and third digits of your ZIP Code identify these units.

Together, the first three digits of your ZIP Code identify either a particular Processing and Distribution Center or multi-coded city. A Processing and Distribution Center, usually located at the natural center of local transportation, is a large post office serving many smaller post offices. The multi-coded city is a main city post office which serves its stations and branches.

The final two digits of your ZIP Code identify the post offices served by the Processing and Distribution Center or branches and stations served by the main city post office.

The example below further illustrates the meaning of a five-digit ZIP Code:

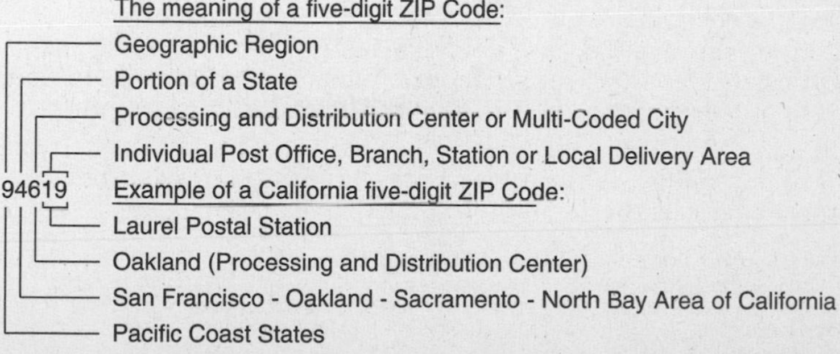

Using the ZIP Code Finder

Using the Rand McNally *ZIP Code Finder* is easy. If you have the name of a city or town, but don't know its ZIP Code, check the basic listings. The basic listings are organized by state. Cities and towns are arranged alphabetically within each state.

Since it is not uncommon for the name of a city or town to occur more than once within a state, the *ZIP Code Finder* differentiates between such cities or towns in several ways. First, if a city or town has the same name as another city or town, but is located in a different county, the *ZIP Code Finder* will list the county in which the city or town is located. The county will be listed in *italic type* following the name of the city or town for all places that have a name which is identical to the name of another place within the same state.
For example:

Country Acres, *La Salle* 61360
Country Acres, *St. Clair* 62220

In most cases, listing the county in which a city or town is located will differentiate between places with the same name. However, since the *ZIP Code Finder* also lists townships and "towns,"[1] places that are "part of" other places, Census Designated Places (noted with a "♦"), postal stations ("‡"), and several other types of localities, additional differentiation may be shown in parenthesis following the name of the place.
For example:

Ashford 06278
Ashford (Town) 06250

In this case, the first listing refers to a single community that has the same name as the larger civil division which contains it and several other communities or places as well. The ZIP Code for the larger civil division is shown in the second listing.

For places with more than one ZIP Code, the *ZIP Code Finder* provides the *range* of ZIP Codes as shown below:

Oak Park 60301-04
For specific ZIP Codes
call (888) 275-8777, or
your local postmaster.

In this example, the hyphenated numbers indicate the ZIP Code range for Oak Park. To obtain the ZIP Code for a specific address within this multi-coded city, telephone the toll-free number shown or your local postmaster. (Listings for cities with only two ZIP Codes, one for the delivery **area** and one for **post office boxes**, include footnotes that designate the nature of the ZIP Code, * and † respectively.)

In addition to the telephone number for ZIP Code information, a five-digit ZIP Code map is provided for eighteen of the largest cities in the U.S. The five-digit ZIP Code map appears on the first full page following the beginning of the listing for each of these cities. For a list of these cities see the Table of Contents, page 4.

The *ZIP Code Finder* also provides three-digit ZIP Code maps for the fifty states and the District of Columbia. More detailed inset maps of the three-digit Service Areas around major urban areas are included on the maps. In addition to selected cities and towns, all state capitals, counties, county seats and Service Areas are shown on the maps. These maps include a population key based on Census population figures, and Processing and Distribution Centers are indicated by a circle around the population symbol. (Arrows show that a Service Area is served by a Processing and Distribution Center located in another Service Area.)

ZIP Codes for selected hospitals, military installations, hotels/motels, financial institutions, and colleges/universities are also listed for fifty of America's largest cities.

---

[1] In certain states, the civil divisions know as "townships" or "towns" have significant local importance. These civil divisions frequently include several distinct communities or places, and one of these places may bear the same name as the civil division. In the *ZIP Code Finder*, townships are included in the listings for Illinois, Indiana, Michigan, Ohio, New Jersey and Pennsylvania, and towns are included for Connecticut, Maine, Massachusetts, New Hampshire, New York, Rhode Island, Vermont and Wisconsin.

Standard Abbreviations for Addresses

Listed below are two-letter state abbrevations which can be used in addressing mail:

Alabama . . . . AL
Alaska . . . . AK
Arizona . . . . AZ
Arkansas . . . . AR
California . . . . CA
Colorado . . . . CO
Connecticut . . . . CT
Delaware . . . . DE
District of Columbia . . . DC
Florida . . . . FL
Georgia . . . . GA
Hawaii . . . . HI
Idaho . . . . ID
Illinois IL
Indiana . . . . IN
Iowa . . . . IA
Kansas . . . . KS
Kentucky . . . . KY
Louisiana . . . . LA
Maine . . . . ME
Maryland . . . . MD
Massachusetts . . . . MA
Michigan . . . . MI
Minnesota . . . . MN
Mississippi . . . . MS
Missouri . . . . MO
Montana . . . . MT
Nebraska . . . . NE
Nevada . . . . NV
New Hampshire . . . . NH
New Jersey . . . . NJ
New Mexico . . . . NM
New York . . . . NY
North Carolina . . . . NC
North Dakota . . . . ND
Ohio . . . . OH
Oklahoma . . . . OK
Oregon . . . . OR
Pennsylvania . . . . PA
Rhode Island . . . . RI
South Carolina . . . . SC
South Dakota . . . . SD
Tennessee . . . . TN
Texas . . . . TX
Utah . . . . UT
Vermont . . . . VT
Virginia . . . . VA
Washington . . . . WA
West Virginia . . . . WV
Wisconsin . . . . WI
Wyoming . . . . WY

Listed below are additional abbreviations that may be useful in addressing mail:

Avenue . . . . Ave
Boulevard . . . . Blvd
Bypass . . . . Byp
Causeway . . . . Cswy
Center . . . . Ctr
Circle . . . . Cir
Court(s) . . . . Ct(s)
Cove Cv
Drive . . . . Dr
Estates . . . . Est
Expressway . . . . Expy
Extension . . . . Ext
Freeway . . . . Fwy
Gardens . . . . Gdns
Grove . . . . Grv
Heights . . . . Hts
Highway . . . . Hwy
Hill(s) . . . . Hls(s)
Island(s) . . . . Is(s)
Junction . . . . Jct
Key . . . . Ky
Lake(s) . . . . Lk(s)
Lane . . . . Ln
Loop . . . . Loop
Manor . . . . Mnr
Mountain . . . . Mtn
Park . . . . Park
Parkway . . . . Pky
Pass . . . . Pass
Path . . . . Path
Pike . . . . Pike
Place . . . . Pl
Plaza . . . . Plz
Point . . . . Pt
Port . . . . Prt
Prairie . . . . Pr
Ridge . . . . Rdg
River . . . . Riv
Road . . . . Rd
Rural . . . . R
Shore . . . . Shr
Spring(s) . . . . Spg(s)
Square . . . . Sq
Station . . . . Sta
Street . . . . St
Terrace . . . . Ter
Trace . . . . Trce
Trail(s) . . . . Trl(s)
Turnpike . . . . Tpke
Valley . . . . Vly
View . . . . Vw
Village . . . . Vlg
Walk . . . . Walk
Way . . . . Way

Selected Toll–Free Reservation Numbers

To save you time and facilitate your reservations needs, the following toll-free reservation numbers are provided for selected lodging accommodations, car rental services and major airlines. (All numbers listed were effective at the time of publication.)

AIRLINES

America West
800-235-9292

American
800-433-7300

Continental
800-525-0280

Delta
800-221-1212

Northwest - KLM
800-225-2525

Southwest
800-435-9792

TWA
800-221-2000

United
800-241-6522

U.S. Airways
800-428-4322

HOTELS/MOTELS

Best Western International, Inc.
800-528-1234

Days Inn
800-325-2525

Doubletree and Redline
800-424-2900

Embassy Suites
800-EMBASSY

Fairmont Hotels
800-527-4727

Harley Hotels
800-321-2323

Helmsley Hotels
800-221-4982

Holiday Inns
800-HOLIDAY

Howard Johnson's Motor Lodges
800-654-2000

Hyatt Hotels Corp.
800-228-9000

ITT Sheraton Hotels & Motor Inns
800-325-3535

Marriott
800-228-9290

Omni Hotels
800-843-6664

Preferred Hotels
800-323-7500

Quality Inns
800-228-5151

Radisson Hotels Int'l.
800-333-3333

Ramada Inns, Inc.
800-228-2828

Regent International Hotels
800-545-4000

Renaissance Hotels & Resorts
800-HOTELS-1

Westin Hotels
800-228-3000

CAR RENTAL COMPANIES

Alamo Rent-A-Car
800-327-9633

Avis Reservations Center
800-331-1212 *(Domestic)*
800-331-1084 *(International)*

Budget Rent-A-Car
800-527-0700

Dollar Rent-A-Car
800-800-4000

Enterprise Rent-A-Car
800-325-8007

Hertz Corporation
800-654-3131

National Car Rental
800-328-4567

Payless Car Rental
800-PAYLESS

Sears Car and Truck Rental
800-527-0770

Thrifty Car Rental
800-367-2277

Telephone Area Code and Time Zone Information

The following tables list telephone area codes used in the United States. The first table is arranged in alphabetical order by state. The second table lists telephone area codes in numerical order.

The United States (including Alaska and Hawaii) is divided longitudinally into six time zones. If you were traveling from east to west, you would pass through the time zones in the following order: Eastern Standard Time (EST), Central Standard Time (CST), Mountain Standard Time (MST), Pacific Standard Time (PST), Alaska Time (AK), and Hawaii Time (HI). Each time you enter a new time zone, it becomes one hour earlier. When it is 5 p.m. Eastern Standard Time (EST), it is 4 p.m. Central Standard Time (CST), 3 p.m. Mountain Standard Time (MST), etc. For your convenience, the appropriate time zone is listed in parentheses after each area code below. The map on pages 12 and 13 details the time zone boundaries.

ALPHABETICAL LIST OF TELEPHONE AREA CODES

Alabama	
Birmingham (CST)	205
Huntsville (CST)	256
Montgomery (CST)	334
Alaska (AK-HI)	907
Juneau (AK)	907
Arizona	
Phoenix (MST)	602
Tucson (MST)	520
Arkansas	
Little Rock (CST)	501
Pine Bluff (CST)	870
California	
Anaheim (PST)	714
Bakersfield (PST)	805
Concord (PST)	925
Escondido (PST)	760
Eureka (PST)	707
Fresno (PST)	559
La Jolla (PST)	858
Long Beach (PST)	562
Los Angeles (PST)	213, 323
Los Angeles-Suburban (PST)	626, 818
Mission Viejo (PST)	949
Oakland (PST)	510
Redding (PST)	530
Riverside (PST)	909
Sacramento (PST)	916
Salinas (PST)	831
San Diego (PST)	619
San Francisco (PST)	415
San Jose (PST)	408
San Mateo (PST)	650
Santa Monica (PST)	310, 424
Stockton (PST)	209
Colorado	
Colorado Springs (MST)	719
Denver (MST)	303, 720
Fort Collins (MST)	970
Connecticut	
Bridgeport (EST)	203
Hartford (EST)	860
Delaware	302
Dover (EST)	302
District of Columbia	202
Washington (EST)	202
Florida (CST, EST)	
Ft. Lauderdale (EST)	954
Gainesville (EST)	352
Jacksonville (EST)	904
Lakeland (EST)	941
Miami (EST)	305
Orlando (EST)	407
St. Petersburg (EST)	727
Tallahassee (EST)	850
Tampa (EST)	813
West Palm Beach (EST)	561
Georgia	
Atlanta (EST)	404, 678
Columbus (EST)	706
Marietta (EST)	678, 770
Savannah (EST)	912
Hawaii (HI)	808
Honolulu (HI)	808
Idaho (MST, PST)	208
Boise (MST)	208
Illinois	
Chicago (CST)	312, 773
Chicago-North Suburban (CST)	224, 847
Chicago-South Suburban (CST)	708
Chicago-West Suburban (CST)	630
Peoria (CST)	309
Rockford (CST)	815
Springfield (CST)	217
West Frankfort (CST)	618
Indiana (CST, EST)	
Evansville (EST)	812
Indianapolis (EST)	317
Muncie (EST)	765
South Bend (EST)	219
Iowa	
Council Bluffs (CST)	712
Des Moines (CST)	515
Dubuque (CST)	319
Kansas (CST, MST)	
Kansas City (CST)	913
Topeka (CST)	785
Wichita (CST)	316
Kentucky (CST, EST)	
Covington (EST)	606
Frankfort (EST)	502
Louisville (EST)	502
Louisiana	
Baton Rouge (CST)	225
New Orleans (CST)	504
Shreveport (CST)	318
Maine	207
Augusta (EST)	207
Maryland	
Annapolis (EST)	410, 443
Rockville	240, 301
Massachusetts	
Boston (EST)	617
Lowell (EST)	978
Lynn (EST)	781
Springfield (EST)	413
Worcester (EST)	508
Michigan (CST, EST)	
Ann Arbor (EST)	734
Detroit (EST)	313

Telephone Area Code and Time Zone Information, continued

Alphabetical List of Telephone Area Codes, continued

Escanaba (EST) ... 906
Grand Rapids (EST) ... 616
Lansing (EST) ... 517
Pontiac (EST) ... 248
Warren (EST) ... 810
Minnesota
Duluth (CST) ... 218
Minneapolis (CST) ... 612
Rochester (CST) ... 507
St. Cloud (CST) ... 320
St. Paul (CST) ... 651
Mississippi
Gulfport (EST) ... 228
Jackson (CST) ... 601
Missouri
Jefferson City (CST) ... 573
Kansas City (CST) ... 816
St. Louis (CST) ... 314
Sedalia (CST) ... 660
Springfield (CST) ... 417
Montana ... 406
Helena (MST) ... 406
Nebraska (CST, MST)
Lincoln (CST) ... 402
North Platte (CST) ... 308
Omaha (CST) ... 402
Nevada
Carson City (PST) ... 775
Las Vegas (PST) ... 702
New Hampshire ... 603
Concord (EST) ... 603
New Jersey
Edison (EST) ... 732
Elizabeth (EST) ... 908
Jersey City (EST) ... 201
Newark (EST) ... 973
Trenton (EST) ... 609
New Mexico ... 505
Santa Fe (MST) ... 505
New York
Albany (EST) ... 518
Binghamton (EST) ... 607
Buffalo (EST) ... 716
Hempstead (EST) ... 516
New York (Manhattan) (EST) ... 212, 917
New York (Bronx, Brooklyn, Queens, Richmond)(EST) ... 718, 917
Syracuse (EST) ... 315
White Plains (EST) ... 914
North Carolina
Asheville (EST) ... 828
Charlotte (EST) ... 704
Fayetteville (EST) ... 910
Greensboro (EST) ... 910
Raleigh (EST) ... 919
Rocky Mount (EST) ... 252
North Dakota (CST, MST) ... 701
Bismark (CST) ... 701
Ohio
Akron (EST) ... 330
Cincinnati (EST) ... 513
Cleveland (EST) ... 216
Columbus (EST) ... 614
Dayton (EST) ... 937
Lorain (EST) ... 440
Newark (EST) ... 740
Toledo (EST) ... 419
Oklahoma
Lawton (CST) ... 580
Oklahoma City (CST) ... 405
Tulsa (CST) ... 918
Oregon (MST, PST)
Eugene (PST) ... 541
Portland (PST) ... 503
Salem (PST) ... 503
Pennsylvania
Allentown (EST) ... 610
Erie (EST) ... 814
Harrisburg (EST) ... 717
New Castle (EST) ... 724
Philadelphia (EST) ... 215
Pittsburgh (EST) ... 412
Rhode Island ... 401
Providence (EST) ... 401
South Carolina
Charleston (EST) ... 843
Columbia (EST) ... 803
Greenville (EST) ... 864
South Dakota (CST, MST) ... 605
Pierre (CST) ... 605
Tennessee (CST, EST)
Clarksville (CST) ... 931
Knoxville (EST) ... 423
Memphis (CST) ... 901
Nashville (CST) ... 615
Texas (CST, MST)
Abilene (CST) ... 915
Amarillo (CST) ... 806
Austin (CST) ... 512
Baytown (CST) ... 281
Beaumont (CST) ... 409
Dallas (CST) ... 214
Del Rio (CST) ... 830
Fort Worth (CST) ... 817
Garland (CST) ... 972
Houston (CST) ... 713
Laredo (CST) ... 956
San Antonio (CST) ... 210
Tyler (CST) ... 903
Waco (CST) ... 254
Wichita Falls (CST) ... 940
Utah
Logan (MST) ... 435
Salt Lake City (MST) ... 801
Vermont ... 802
Montpelier (EST) ... 802
Virginia
Alexandria (EST) ... 703
Richmond (EST) ... 804
Roanoke (EST) ... 540
Virginia Beach (EST) ... 757
Washington
Bellingham (PST) ... 360
Everett (PST) ... 425
Olympia (PST) ... 360
Seattle (PST) ... 206
Spokane (PST) ... 509
Tacoma (PST) ... 253
West Virginia ... 304
Charleston (EST) ... 304
Wisconsin
Eau Claire (CST) ... 715
Green Bay (CST) ... 920
Madison (CST) ... 608
Milwaukee (CST) ... 414
Wyoming ... 307
Cheyenne (MST) ... 307

Telephone Area Code and Time Zone Information, continued

NUMERICAL LIST OF TELEPHONE AREA CODES

Area Code	Location (Time Zone)
201	New Jersey (EST)
202	District of Columbia (EST)
203	Connecticut (EST)
205	Alabama (CST)
206	Washington (PST)
207	Maine (EST)
208	Idaho (MST, PST)
209	California (PST)
210	Texas (CST)
212	New York (EST)
213	California (PST)
214	Texas (CST)
215	Pennsylvania (EST)
216	Ohio (EST)
217	Illinois (CST)
218	Minnesota (CST)
219	Indiana (CST, EST)
224	Illinois (CST)
225	Louisiana (CST)
228	Mississippi (CST)
240	Maryland (EST)
248	Michigan (CST)
252	North Carolina (EST)
253	Washington (PST)
254	Texas (CST)
256	Alabama (CST)
281	Texas (CST)
301	Maryland (EST)
302	Delaware (EST)
303	Colorado (MST)
304	West Virginia (EST)
305	Florida (EST)
307	Wyoming (MST)
308	Nebraska (CST, MST)
309	Illinois (CST)
310	California (PST)
312	Illinois (CST)
313	Michigan (EST)
314	Missouri (CST)
315	New York (EST)
316	Kansas (CST, MST)
317	Indiana (EST)
318	Louisiana (CST)
319	Iowa (CST)
320	Minnesota (CST)
323	California (PST)
330	Ohio (EST)
334	Alabama (CST)
336	North Carolina (EST)
352	Florida (EST)
360	Washington (PST)
401	Rhode Island (EST)
402	Nebraska (CST, MST)
404	Georgia (EST)
405	Oklahoma (CST)
406	Montana (MST)
407	Florida (EST)
408	California (PST)
409	Texas (CST)
410	Maryland (EST)
412	Pennsylvania (EST)
413	Massachusetts (EST)
414	Wisconsin (CST)
415	California (PST)
417	Missouri (CST)
419	Ohio (EST)
423	Tennessee (CST, EST)
424	California (PST) *effective 7/17/99*
425	Washington (EST)
435	Utah (MST)
440	Ohio (EST)
443	Maryland (EST)
501	Arkansas (CST)
502	Kentucky (CST, EST)
503	Oregon (PST)
504	Louisiana (CST)
505	New Mexico (MST)
507	Minnesota (CST)
508	Massachusetts (EST)
509	Washington (PST)
510	California (PST)
512	Texas (CST)
513	Ohio (EST)
515	Iowa (CST)
516	New York (EST)
517	Michigan (EST)
518	New York (EST)
520	Arizona (MST)
530	California (PST)
540	Virginia (EST)
541	Oregon (MST, PST)
559	California (PST)
561	Florida (EST)
562	California (PST)
573	Missouri (CST)
580	Oklahoma (CST)
601	Mississippi (CST)
602	Arizona (MST)
603	New Hampshire (EST)
605	South Dakota (CST, MST)
606	Kentucky (EST)
607	New York (EST)
608	Wisconsin (CST)
609	New Jersey (EST)
610	Pennsylvania (EST)
612	Minnesota (CST)
614	Ohio (EST)
615	Tennessee (CST)
616	Michigan (EST)
617	Massachusetts (EST)
618	Illinois (CST)
619	California (PST)
626	California (PST)
630	Illinois (CST)
650	California (PST)
651	Minnesota (CST)
660	Missouri (CST)
678	Georgia (EST)
701	North Dakota (CST, MST)
702	Nevada (PST)
703	Virginia (EST)
704	North Carolina (EST)
706	Georgia (EST)
707	California (PST)
708	Illinois (CST)
710	U.S. Govenment
712	Iowa (CST)
713	Texas (CST)
714	California (PST)
715	Wisconsin (CST)
716	New York (EST)
717	Pennsylvania (EST)
718	New York (EST)
719	Colorado (MST)
720	Colorado (MST)
724	Pennsylvania (EST)
727	Florida (EST)
732	New Jersey (EST)
734	Michigan (CST,EST)
740	Ohio (EST)
757	Virginia (EST)
760	California (PST)
765	Indiana (EST)
770	Georgia (EST)
773	Illinois (CST)
775	Nevada (PST)
781	Massachusetts (EST)
785	Kansas (CST)
800	800 Service
801	Utah (MST)
802	Vermont (EST)
803	South Carolina (EST)
804	Virginia (EST)
805	California (PST)
806	Texas (CST)
808	Hawaii (HI)
810	Michigan (EST)
812	Indiana (CST, EST)
813	Florida (EST)
814	Pennsylvania (EST)
815	Illinois (CST)
816	Missouri (CST)
817	Texas (CST)
818	California (PST)
828	North Carolina (EST)
830	Texas (EST)
831	California (PST)
843	South Carolina (EST)
847	Illinois (CST)
850	Florida (CST)
858	California (PST) *effective 6/12/99*
860	Connecticut (EST)
864	South Carolina (EST)
877	877 Service
888	888 Service
900	900 Service
901	Tennessee (CST)
903	Texas (CST)
904	Florida (CST,EST)
906	Michigan (CST, EST)
907	Alaska (AK-HI)
908	New Jersey (EST)
909	California (PST)
910	North Carolina (EST)
912	Georgia (EST)
913	Kansas (CST, MST)
914	New York (EST)
915	Texas (CST, MST)
916	California (PST)
917	New York (EST)
918	Oklahoma (CST)
919	North Carolina (EST)
920	Wisconsin (CST)
925	California (PST)
931	Tennessee (CST)
937	Ohio (EST)
940	Texas (CST)
941	Florida (EST)
949	California (PST)
954	Florida (EST)
956	Texas (CST)
970	Colorado (MST)
972	Texas (CST)
973	New Jersey (EST)
978	Massachusetts (EST)

Pacific Time Zone
Mountain Time Zone
Central Zone
Pacific Ocean
Gulf of California
BRITISH COLUMBIA
ALBERTA
SASKATCHEWAN
MANITOBA
CANADA
MEXICO
867 YUKON NORTHWEST TER.
907 ALASKA
808 HAWAII
WASHINGTON
OREGON
CALIFORNIA
NEVADA
IDAHO
MONTANA
WYOMING
UTAH
COLORADO
ARIZONA
NEW MEXICO
NORTH DAKOTA
SOUTH DAKOTA
NEBRASKA
KANSAS
OKLAHOMA
TEXAS
NEW AREA CODES - CALIFORNIA
424 Overlays area code 310 - In effect 7/17/99
858 In effect 6/12/99
SCALE IN MILES
0 25 50 100 200 300
To copy or reproduce this copyrighted map, or any portion thereof, by any method, including office copying machines, for personal or company use or resale without written permission is illegal.
99-1

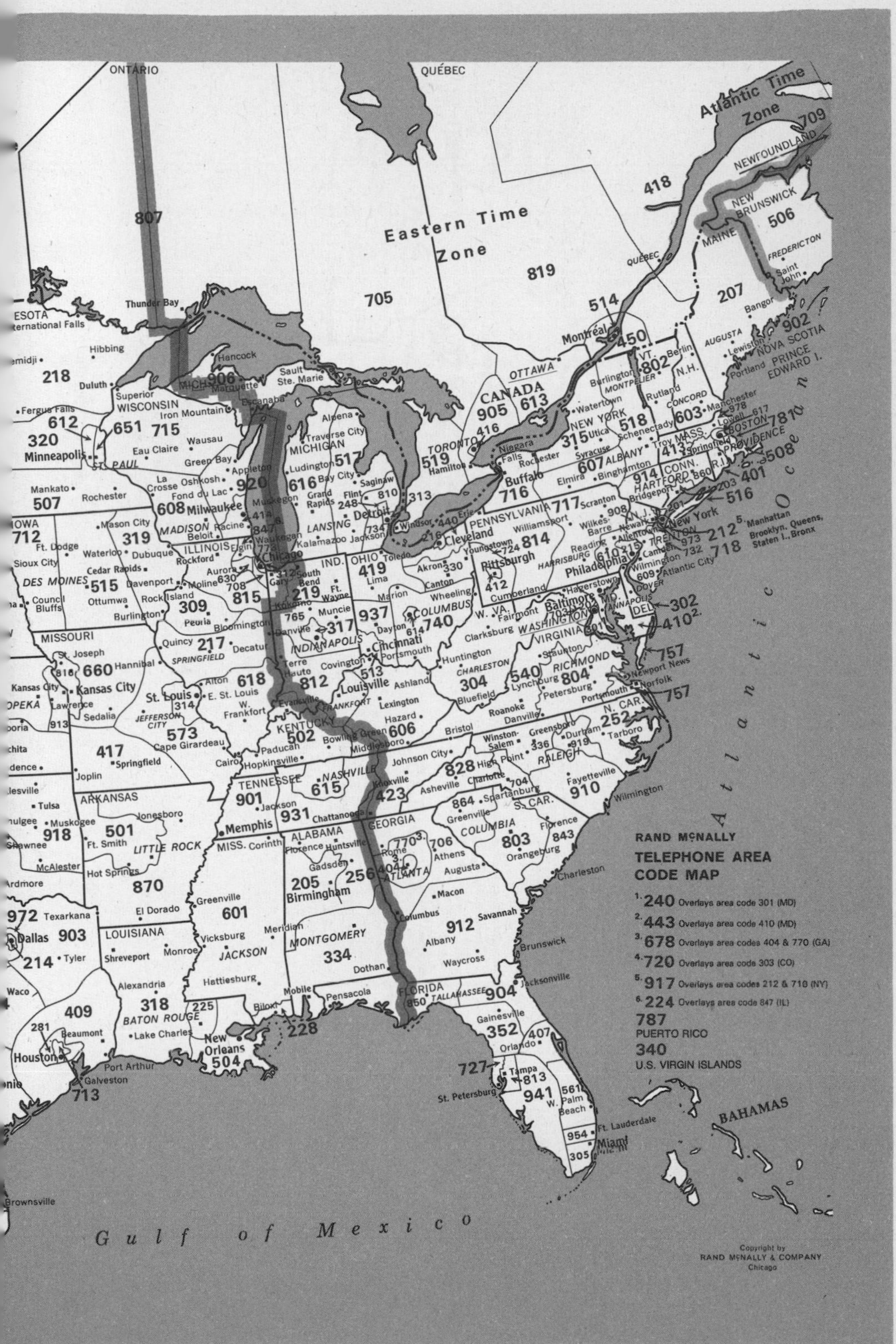
Eastern Time Zone
Atlantic Time Zone
Gulf of Mexico
Atlantic Ocean
ONTARIO
QUÉBEC
CANADA
NEWFOUNDLAND
NEW BRUNSWICK
NOVA SCOTIA
PRINCE EDWARD I.
BAHAMAS
807
705
819
418
709
506
902
514
450
905
613
416
519
Thunder Bay
Montréal
OTTAWA
TORONTO
Hamilton
FREDERICTON
Saint John
218
612
320
651
715
507
712
319
515
608
920
414
262
847
773
312
630
708
815
309
217
618
906
616
517
810
248
313
734
219
765
317
812
419
216
440
330
937
614
740
513
502
606
304
540
804
757
716
315
518
607
914
717
814
724
412
610
215
908
201
973
732
212
718
516
860
203
413
617
781
978
508
401
603
802
207
301
240
410
443
302
816
660
314
573
913
417
918
501
870
972
903
214
409
281
713
318
225
504
601
228
901
931
615
423
828
336
704
919
252
910
864
803
843
205
256
334
706
770
404
678
912
904
850
352
407
727
813
941
561
954
305
Minneapolis
ST. PAUL
Duluth
Hibbing
Rochester
Mankato
WISCONSIN
Superior
Eau Claire
Wausau
Green Bay
Appleton
Oshkosh
Fond du Lac
La Crosse
Milwaukee
MADISON
Racine
Beloit
Waukegan
Chicago
ILLINOIS
Rockford
Elgin
Aurora
Moline
Rock Island
Peoria
Bloomington
Decatur
SPRINGFIELD
Quincy
Alton
E. St. Louis
MICHIGAN
Marquette
Escanaba
Iron Mountain
Sault Ste. Marie
Hancock
Alpena
Traverse City
Ludington
Muskegon
Grand Rapids
Bay City
Saginaw
Flint
Detroit
LANSING
Kalamazoo
Jackson
Windsor
IOWA
Ft. Dodge
Sioux City
Waterloo
Dubuque
Cedar Rapids
DES MOINES
Davenport
Council Bluffs
Ottumwa
Burlington
Mason City
MISSOURI
St. Joseph
Kansas City
Hannibal
St. Louis
JEFFERSON CITY
Sedalia
Cape Girardeau
Springfield
Joplin
IND.
South Bend
Gary
Ft. Wayne
Kokomo
Muncie
Danville
INDIANAPOLIS
Terre Haute
Evansville
OHIO
Toledo
Lima
Marion
Akron
Canton
Cleveland
Youngstown
COLUMBUS
Dayton
Cincinnati
Portsmouth
KENTUCKY
Covington
Louisville
FRANKFORT
Lexington
Ashland
Hazard
Paducah
Hopkinsville
Bowling Green
Middlesboro
PENNSYLVANIA
Erie
Pittsburgh
Williamsport
Scranton
Wilkes-Barre
Allentown
Reading
HARRISBURG
Philadelphia
Cumberland
Hagerstown
W. VA.
Wheeling
Fairmont
Clarksburg
CHARLESTON
Huntington
Bluefield
VIRGINIA
Staunton
RICHMOND
Lynchburg
Petersburg
Roanoke
Danville
Norfolk
Portsmouth
Newport News
WASHINGTON
Baltimore
MD.
ANNAPOLIS
DEL.
DOVER
Wilmington
N.J.
TRENTON
Camden
Atlantic City
Newark
New York
Manhattan
Brooklyn, Queens, Staten I., Bronx
NEW YORK
Buffalo
Niagara Falls
Rochester
Syracuse
Utica
Watertown
Elmira
Binghamton
ALBANY
Schenectady
Troy
CONN.
HARTFORD
Bridgeport
R.I.
PROVIDENCE
MASS.
Springfield
BOSTON
Lowell
VT.
MONTPELIER
Burlington
Rutland
N.H.
CONCORD
Manchester
Berlin
MAINE
AUGUSTA
Lewiston
Portland
Bangor
N. CAR.
Winston-Salem
Greensboro
High Point
Durham
RALEIGH
Tarboro
Charlotte
Fayetteville
Wilmington
Asheville
Johnson City
Bristol
S. CAR.
Greenville
Spartanburg
COLUMBIA
Florence
Orangeburg
Charleston
TENNESSEE
Jackson
NASHVILLE
Knoxville
Chattanooga
Memphis
GEORGIA
Rome
ATLANTA
Athens
Augusta
Macon
Columbus
Albany
Savannah
Waycross
Brunswick
ALABAMA
Florence
Huntsville
Gadsden
Birmingham
MONTGOMERY
Dothan
Mobile
MISS.
Corinth
Greenville
Meridian
Vicksburg
JACKSON
Hattiesburg
Biloxi
ARKANSAS
Jonesboro
Ft. Smith
LITTLE ROCK
Hot Springs
El Dorado
Texarkana
LOUISIANA
Shreveport
Monroe
Alexandria
BATON ROUGE
Lake Charles
New Orleans
Tulsa
Muskogee
McAlester
Ardmore
Dallas
Tyler
Waco
Houston
Beaumont
Port Arthur
Galveston
Brownsville
FLORIDA
TALLAHASSEE
Pensacola
Jacksonville
Gainesville
Orlando
Tampa
St. Petersburg
W. Palm Beach
Ft. Lauderdale
Miami
RAND McNALLY
TELEPHONE AREA CODE MAP
1. 240 Overlays area code 301 (MD)
2. 443 Overlays area code 410 (MD)
3. 678 Overlays area codes 404 & 770 (GA)
4. 720 Overlays area code 303 (CO)
5. 917 Overlays area codes 212 & 718 (NY)
6. 224 Overlays area code 847 (IL)
787
PUERTO RICO
340
U.S. VIRGIN ISLANDS
Copyright by RAND McNALLY & COMPANY Chicago

U.S. Postal Service Rates

Listed below are U.S. Postal Service rates for First-Class, Periodicals, Standard Mail (A), and Express Mail. (All rates shown were current at the time of publication.)

FIRST-CLASS MAIL

Letters

11 ozs. or less .... first oz. 33¢

.... each additional oz. 22¢

Over 11 ozs. .... use Priority Mail, see page 15

Post Cards .... 20¢

EXPRESS MAIL

Packages that are taken to a postal facility offering Express Mail Service, and addressed to an area which also has Express Mail Service, will be delivered next day to the addressee in most areas.

½ lb. or less $11.75

Over ½ lb. and up to 2 lbs.* $15.75

Over 2 lbs. and up to 3 lbs. $18.50

Over 3 lbs. and up to 4 lbs. $21.25

Over 4 lbs. and up to 5 lbs. $24.00

Over 5 lbs. and up to 70 lbs. .... consult postmaster

For additional rate and schedule information, call your local Post Office.

* The two-pound rate applies to mail sent in the "flat rate" envelopes provided by the U.S. Postal Service.

PERIODICALS *(Formerly known as "Second-Class Mail".)*

For newspapers and periodicals issued on a regular (at least quarterly) basis. Consult your Postmaster for information.

STANDARD MAIL (A) *(Formerly known as "Third-Class Mail".)*

For circulars, books, catalogs, and other printed matter not legally required to be sent First-Class. Designed primarily for bulk mailings with a minimum of 200 pieces or 50 pounds. Consult your Postmaster for details.

STANDARD MAIL (B) *(Formerly known as "Fourth-Class Mail" or Parcel Post".)*

Includes printed matter, merchandise, and parcels weighing 16 ounces or more. Standard Mail (B) does not promise the quick delivery times offered by Express and Priority mail, but is significantly less costly, particularly for heavy parcels. There are special rates for books, films, and catalogs, as well as a special library rate. Consult your Postmaster for information.

Small Parcel Rates and Information

Ground service rates for packages of 1 to 20 pounds are shown for the United States Postal Service (USPS), United Parcel Service (UPS), and Roadway Package System (RPS). Information on air service is also shown for selected air freight companies. (All information shown was current at the time of publication.)

In order to use the ground zone rate charts presented below for the USPS, UPS, and RPS, you will need to contact the carrier of your choice and request the zone chart that applies to your specific geographic location. This chart will enable you to determine the zone which corresponds to the destination of your parcel. Contact your local post office or UPS office; RPS may be contacted by calling the toll-free number which appears beneath the RPS Ground Zones Chart.

GROUND SERVICE

United States Postal Service (USPS) — Priority Mail*

Single-Piece Rates: all First-Class Mail weighing over 11 ozs. Maximum weight is 70 lbs.; size is limited to 108 inches in combined length and girth. (Mail weighing less than 15 lbs., but measuring more than 84 inches in combined length and girth, will be charged at the 15 lb. rate.)

Weight over 11 ozs. and not exceeding	Zones Local, 1,2 & 3	4	5	6	7	8
1 lb(s).	$ 3.20	$ 3.20	$ 3.20	$ 3.20	$ 3.20	$ 3.20
2	3.20	3.20	3.20	3.20	3.20	3.20
3	4.30	4.30	4.30	4.30	4.30	4.30
4	5.40	5.40	5.40	5.40	5.40	5.40
5	6.50	6.50	6.50	6.50	6.50	6.50
6	6.60	6.90	7.10	7.45	7.70	8.25
7	6.70	7.30	7.70	8.40	8.90	10.00
8	6.80	7.70	8.30	9.35	10.10	11.75
9	6.90	8.10	8.90	10.30	11.30	13.50
10	7.00	8.50	9.50	11.25	12.50	15.25
11	7.20	9.15	10.30	12.20	13.45	16.50
12	7.40	9.80	11.05	13.10	14.45	17.80
13	7.75	10.40	11.80	14.05	15.50	19.10
14	8.10	11.05	12.55	14.95	16.50	20.40
15	8.50	11.70	13.30	15.85	17.50	21.70
16	8.85	12.30	14.00	16.75	18.55	23.00
17	9.20	12.95	14.75	17.70	19.55	24.30
18	9.60	13.60	15.50	18.60	20.60	25.60
19	9.95	14.20	16.25	19.50	21.60	26.95
20	10.35	14.85	17.00	20.40	22.65	28.20

For additional rate information call your local Post Office.

* Priority Mail service is similar to First-Class Mail in that it may be transported by a combination of ground and air service.

Small Parcel Rates and Information, continued

United Parcel Service (UPS) — Commercial deliveries only.

Weight not to exceed	Ground Zones 2	3	4	5	6	7	8
1 lb(s).	$ 2.82	$ 3.00	$ 3.18	$ 3.23	$ 3.36	$ 3.43	$ 3.52
2	2.88	3.06	3.38	3.49	3.79	3.88	4.12
3	2.95	3.21	3.57	3.73	4.01	4.18	4.57
4	3.07	3.35	3.75	3.95	4.22	4.43	4.87
5	3.20	3.48	3.92	4.15	4.42	4.63	5.12
6	3.33	3.59	4.06	4.33	4.61	4.83	5.37
7	3.46	3.70	4.17	4.47	4.79	5.03	5.62
8	3.59	3.81	4.28	4.57	4.95	5.33	6.02
9	3.72	3.92	4.37	4.66	5.11	5.68	6.42
10	3.85	4.03	4.46	4.81	5.29	6.03	6.87
11	3.98	4.15	4.56	4.96	5.53	6.48	7.40
12	4.10	4.27	4.66	5.08	5.81	6.93	7.93
13	4.21	4.40	4.73	5.19	6.13	7.36	8.46
14	4.31	4.54	4.81	5.30	6.49	7.79	9.00
15	4.40	4.69	4.89	5.54	6.86	8.22	9.54
16	4.49	4.85	5.04	5.81	7.23	8.65	10.09
17	4.58	5.02	5.24	6.08	7.60	9.08	10.64
18	4.68	5.20	5.44	6.35	7.97	9.51	11.19
19	4.79	5.38	5.65	6.62	8.34	9.94	11.74
20	4.91	5.56	5.86	6.89	8.71	10.37	12.29

For additional rate information, contact your local UPS office, or visit the UPS web site at www.ups.com.

Roadway Package System (RPS) — Commercial deliveries only.

Weight not to exceed	Ground Zones 2	3	4	5	6	7	8
1 lb(s).	$ 2.82	$ 3.00	$ 3.18	$ 3.23	$ 3.36	$ 3.43	$ 3.52
2	2.88	3.06	3.38	3.49	3.79	3.88	4.12
3	2.95	3.21	3.57	3.73	4.01	4.18	4.57
4	3.07	3.35	3.75	3.95	4.22	4.43	4.87
5	3.20	3.48	3.92	4.15	4.42	4.63	5.12
6	3.33	3.59	4.06	4.33	4.61	4.83	5.37
7	3.46	3.70	4.17	4.47	4.79	5.03	5.62
8	3.59	3.81	4.28	4.57	4.95	5.33	6.02
9	3.72	3.92	4.37	4.66	5.11	5.68	6.42
10	3.85	4.03	4.46	4.81	5.29	6.03	6.87
11	3.98	4.15	4.56	4.96	5.53	6.48	7.40
12	4.10	4.27	4.66	5.08	5.81	6.93	7.93
13	4.21	4.40	4.73	5.19	6.13	7.36	8.46
14	4.31	4.54	4.81	5.30	6.49	7.79	9.00
15	4.40	4.69	4.89	5.54	6.86	8.22	9.54
16	4.49	4.85	5.04	5.81	7.23	8.65	10.09
17	4.58	5.02	5.24	6.08	7.60	9.08	10.64
18	4.68	5.20	5.44	6.35	7.97	9.51	11.19
19	4.79	5.38	5.65	6.62	8.34	9.94	11.74
20	4.91	5.56	5.86	6.89	8.71	10.37	12.29

For additional rate information, call 800-ROADPAK, or visit the RPS web site at www.shiprps.com.

Small Parcel Rates and Information, continued

AIR SERVICE

Most private carriers offer a variety of services, including next-flight-out, next-day and second-day delivery. Most provide free envelopes and shipping containers and offer discounts for drop-offs by the sender.

All of the private carriers listed provide pickup as well as delivery. Most have drop-off boxes available in convenient locations. Pickup and delivery times vary by carrier.

For your convenience in obtaining information on costs, other levels of service, multiple shipments and frequent shipper discounts, toll-free telephone numbers and world-wide-web addresses have been included. (All rates, service levels and delivery times are subject to change without notice.) Rates depend on package weight and the distance it is being sent. All carriers offer service to all fifty states and international destinations.

United Parcel Service (UPS)
Domestic locations: 800-742-5877; SonicAir service: 800-451-4550; international service: 800-782-7892. Web address: www.ups.com/. Specific size and weight limitations. Packages weighing 70–150 pounds require a special label.

<u>SonicAir Service</u>
Next-flight-out service between any U.S. and most international destinations, 24 hours a day, 7 days a week.

<u>Next Day Air Early A.M.</u>
Guarantees delivery by 8:00 a.m. to major U.S. cities; by 8:30 a.m. to most other U.S. cities (9:00 a.m. or 9:30 a.m. on Saturday).

<u>Next Day Air</u>
Guarantees delivery by 10:30 a.m. or end of the next business day, depending on destination (noon or 1:30 p.m. on Saturday).

<u>Next Day Air Saver</u>
Guarantees next business day delivery by 3:00 or 4:30 p.m. in the 48 contiguous states.

<u>2nd Day Air A.M.</u>
Guarantees second business day delivery before noon to most metro addresses in the 48 contiguous states.

<u>2nd Day Air</u>
Guarantees delivery by end of second business day to every address in the U.S. and Puerto Rico.

Federal Express (FedEx) 800-463-3339. Web address: www.fedex.com/

<u>Same Day</u>
Guarantees delivery the same day you call, 24 hours a day, 7 days a week. Maximum weight 70 lbs.; maximum size: 48″ in length, 90″ in length and girth combined.

Federal Express continued

Small Parcel Rates and Information, continued

Federal Express continued

First Overnight

Delivery by 8:00 a.m. the next business day to 90 major U.S. markets (except Hawaii). Maximum weight, 150 lbs.

Priority Overnight

Next business day delivery by 10:30 a.m. to thousands of U.S. cities, by noon to most other areas, and by 4:30 to remote locations. Maximum weight: 150 lbs.; maximum size: 119″ in length, 165″ in length and girth combined. Monday-Saturday pickup and delivery; Sunday delivery limited to selected ZIP codes in 50 metro areas.

Standard Overnight

Next business day delivery by 3:00 p.m. to thousands of U.S. cities; by 4:30 p.m. to many other areas. Same size and weight limits as Priority Overnight. Monday-Friday pickup and delivery; Saturday pickup only.

2Day

Delivery by 4:30 p.m. of second business day to most areas within U.S.; by 7 p.m. for residential deliveries. Same size and weight limits as Priority Overnight. Monday-Saturday pickup and delivery.

Airborne Express 800-247-2676; Same-Day/Next-Flight-Out Service: 800-336-3344
Web address: www.airborne-express.com/

Same-Day/Next-Flight-Out Service

Sky Courier same-day service, with door-to-door delivery to any U.S. city, 24 hours a day, 7 days a week.

Overnight Air Express Service

Door-to-door delivery of packages weighing up to 150 lbs. to thousands of U.S. cities and metro areas, usually by 10:30 the next business day.

Next Afternoon Service

For smaller packages and documents that can afford a later delivery time. Shipments weighing up to 5 lbs. are delivered by 3:00 p.m. the next day in many areas.

Second Day Service

Shipments weighing up to 150 lbs. are delivered by 5:00 p.m. the second business day.

Heavy-Weight Packages

These carriers have no weight or size restrictions for most categories of service.

Emery Worldwide
800-714-8779 for Expedite! Air next-flight-out service; 800-946-5393 for Gold Priority Daylight, Gold Standard, Gold Plus and other services.
Web address: www.emeryworld.com/

BAX Global (formerly Burlington Air Express)
800-225-5229. Web address: www.baxworld.com/
First Arrival, Overnight, Airport-to-Airport and other services.

U.S. Postal Service Business Centers

The following is a list of the 115 Postal Business Centers that operate nationwide. In the event that you have questions about mailing procedures, rates or regulations, contact the appropriate Center. The listings below were current at the time of publication.

ALABAMA

Birmingham (205) 521-0364
351 24th St. N
Birmingham, AL 35203-9691

ALASKA

Anchorage (907) 564-2823
3201 C St., Suite 505
Anchorage, AK 99503-9611

ARIZONA

Phoenix (602) 223-3535
1441 E. Buckeye Rd., Room 200
Phoenix, AZ 85034-9621

ARKANSAS

Little Rock (501) 228-4300
11324 Arcade Dr., Suite 4
Little Rock, AR 72212-4309

CALIFORNIA

Long Beach (562) 986-7300
2300 Redondo Ave.
Long Beach, CA 90809-9694

Los Angeles (213) 586-1843
7001 S. Central Ave., Room 264
Los Angeles, CA 90052-9602

Oakland (510) 251-3073
201 13th St., Room 103B
Oakland, CA 94612-9351

Petaluma (707) 778-5234
20113th St., Room 103B
Petaluma, CA 94612-9351

Sacramento (916) 923-4357
2035 Hurley Way, Suite 200
Sacramento, CA 95825-3209

San Diego (619) 674-0272
11251 Rancho Carmel Dr.
Room 304
San Diego, CA 92199-9621

San Francisco (415) 550-5600
P.O. Box 193000
San Francisco, CA 94119-3000

San Jose (408) 723-6262
P.O. Box 50014
San Jose, CA 95150-0014

Santa Ana (714) 662-6213
3101 W. Sunflower Ave.
Santa Ana, CA 92799-9323

Van Nuys (805) 294-6910
28201 Franklin Pkwy.
Santa Clarita, CA 91383-9682

COLORADO

Denver (303) 313-5555
1745 Stout St., Suite 101
Denver, CO 80266-9617

CONNECTICUT

Hartford (860) 610-3108
77 Hartland St., Suite 108
East Hartford, CT 06108-9631

New Haven (203) 782-7198
50 Brewery St.
New Haven, CT 06511-9631

Stamford (203) 326-2132
427 West Ave.
Stamford, CT 06910-9631

DELAWARE

Wilmington (302) 323-3733
147 Quigley Blvd.
New Castle, DE 19720-9998

DISTRICT OF COLUMBIA

The District of Columbia is served by the Postal Business Center in Silver Spring, Maryland.

FLORIDA

Fort Lauderdale (954) 527-6981
1900 W. Oakland Park Blvd.,
Suite 211
Fort Lauderdale, FL 33310-9600

Jacksonville (904) 858-6539
P.O. Box 40005
Jacksonville, FL 32203-0005

Miami (305) 470-0803
8525 NW 53rd Ter., Suite 101
Miami, FL 33166-4538

Orlando (407) 893-3800
P.O. Box 53810
Orlando, FL 32853-8100

Tampa (813) 354-6245
2203 N. Lois Ave., Suite 1162
Tampa, FL 33607-7162

West Palm Beach (561) 697-2180
3200 Summit Blvd., Suite 111
West Palm Beach, FL 33406-9602

GEORGIA

Macon (912) 752-8709
451 College St., Room 325
Macon, GA 31213-9300

North Metro (770) 935-2371
P.O. Box 599332
Duluth, GA 30026-9332

HAWAII

Honolulu (808) 423-3761
3600 Aolele St., Room 106
Honolulu, HI 96820-9623

IDAHO

Idaho is served by the Postal Business Center in Spokane, Washington.

ILLINOIS

Aurora (630) 978-4455
3900 Gabrielle Lane
Aurora, IL 60599-9601

Carol Stream (630) 260-5518
500 E. Fullerton Ave.
Carol Stream, IL 60199-9661

Chicago (312) 983-8440
433 W. Harrison St., 2nd Floor
Chicago, IL 60607-9601

Peoria (309) 671-8916
95 State St.
Peoria, IL 61601-9602

U.S. Postal Service Business Centers, continued

INDIANA

Fort Wayne (219) 427-7253
1501 S. Clinton St.
Fort Wayne, IN 46802-9341

Gary (219) 886-8093
1499 Martin Luther King Dr.
Gary, IN 46401-9601

Indianapolis (317) 464-6010
125 W. South St., Room 325
Indianapolis, IN 46206-9631

IOWA

Des Moines (515) 251-2336
P.O. Box 189996
Des Moines, IA 50318-9605

KANSAS

Wichita (316) 946-4528
7117 W. Harry St.
Wichita, KS 67276-9600

KENTUCKY

Louisville (502) 473-4200
P.O. Box 31660
Louisville, KY 40231-9660

LOUISIANA

New Orleans (504) 589-1366
701 Loyola Ave., Suite 10210
New Orleans, LA 70113-9680

MAINE

Portland (207) 871-8567
125 Forest Ave.
Portland, ME 04101-9600

MARYLAND

Baltimore (410) 347-4358
900 E. Fayette St., Room 502
Baltimore, MD 21233-9661

Silver Spring (301) 565-2177
8455 Colesville Rd., Suite 950
Silver Spring, MD 20910-3319

MASSACHUSETTS

Boston (617) 654-5725
25 Dorchester Ave., Room 1000
Boston, MA 02205-9602

Springfield (413) 731-0306
1883 Main St.
Springfield, MA 01101-9600

Woburn (781) 938-1450
P.O. Box 2236
Woburn, MA 01888-0336

MICHIGAN

Birmingham (248) 546-1321
P.O. Box 9630
Birmingham, MI 48009-9630

Detroit (313) 226-8600
1927 Rosa Parks Blvd.
Detroit, MI 48216-9620

Grand Rapids (616) 776-6147
P.O. Box 999661
Grand Rapids, MI 49599-9661

MINNESOTA

Minneapolis (612) 349-6360
100 S. First St., Room 117
Minneapolis, MN 55401-9617

MISSISSIPPI

Jackson (601) 351-7100
401 E. South St., Suite 100
Jackson, MS 39201-9825

MISSOURI

Kansas City (816) 374-9613
315 W. Pershing Rd., Room 104
Kansas City, MO 64108-9623

St. Louis (314) 534-2678
2665 Scott Ave.
St. Louis, MO 63103-3048

MONTANA

Billings (406) 255-6432
2602 First Ave. N, Suite 133
Billings, MT 59101-2300

Missoula (406) 329-2231
1100 W. Kent Ave.
Missoula, MT 59801-9625

NEBRASKA

Omaha (402) 573-2100
5303 N. 91st Ave.
Omaha, NE 68134-9600

NEVADA

Las Vegas (702) 361-9318
1001 E. Sunset Rd., Room 1006
Las Vegas, NV 89199-9605

NEW HAMPSHIRE

Manchester (603) 644-3838
955 Goffs Falls Rd., Suite 671
Manchester, NH 03103-9671

NEW JERSEY

Bellmawr (609) 933-6000
P.O. Box 9001
Bellmawr, NJ 08099-9996

Edison (908) 819-3600
21 Kilmer Rd.
Edison, NJ 08899-9610

Newark (973) 468-7066
494 Broad St., Room 223
Newark, NJ 07102-9333

NEW MEXICO

Albuquerque (505) 245-9480
1135 Broadway Blvd. NE, Room 147
Albuquerque, NM 87101-9601

NEW YORK

Albany (518) 464-7475
30 Old Karner Rd.
Albany, NY 12288-9653

Brooklyn (718) 348-3624
1050 Forbell St., Room 20117
Brooklyn, NY 11256-9621

Buffalo (716) 846-2581
1200 William St., Room 100
Buffalo, NY 14240-9661

Flushing (718) 321-5700
142-02 20th Ave., Room 123B
Flushing, NY 11351-9621

New York, continued

U.S. Postal Service Business Centers, continued

New York, continued

Melville (516) 755-2900
65 Maxess Rd.
Melville, NY 11747-3158

New York (212) 330-3809
421 8th Ave., Room 4202H
New York, NY 10199-9619

Rochester (716) 272-7220
P.O. Box 22908
Rochester, NY 14692-2908

Syracuse (315) 452-3636
5640 E. Taft Rd.
Syracuse, NY 13220-9610

White Plains (914) 697-7294
P.O. Box 9211
White Plains, NY 10610-9211

NORTH CAROLINA

Charlotte (704) 393-4481
2901 S. I-85 Service Rd.
Charlotte, NC 28228-9975

Greensboro (910) 665-9740
P.O. Box 27499
Greensboro, NC 27498-9661

Raleigh (919) 420-5165
P.O. Box 9603
Raleigh, NC 27676-9603

OHIO

Akron (216) 996-9721
675 Wolf Ledges Pkwy.
Akron, OH 44309-9600

Cincinnati (513) 723-9900
990 Dalton Ave.
Cincinnati, OH 45203-9601

Cleveland (216) 443-4401
2400 Orange Ave., Room 23
Cleveland, OH 44101-9604

Columbus (614) 469-4336
850 Twin Rivers Dr.
Columbus, OH 43216-9601

Dayton (937) 227-3901
1111 E. 5th St., Room 317
Dayton, OH 45401-9601

Toledo (419) 245-6926
435 S. Saint Clair St.
Toledo, OH 43601-9611

Youngstown (330) 740-8951
99 S. Walnut St.
Youngstown, OH 44501-9601

OKLAHOMA

Oklahoma City (405) 720-2675
7101 NW Expressway St., Suite 325
Oklahoma City, OK 73132-1598

OREGON

Portland (503) 294-2306
715 NW Hoyt St., Room 4101
Portland, OR 97208-9996

PENNSYLVANIA

Erie (814) 878-0018
1314 Griswold Plaza, Room 111
Erie, PA 16501-9631

Harrisburg (717) 257-2108
1425 Crooked Hill Rd.
Harrisburg, PA 17107-9601

Lancaster (717) 396-8795
1400 Harrisburg Pike
Lancaster, PA 17604-9601

Lehigh Valley (610) 882-3227
17 S. Commerce Way
Lehigh Valley, PA 18002-9601

Philadelphia (215) 895-8046
P.O. Box 13416
Philadelphia, PA 19101-3416

Pittsburgh (412) 359-7601
1001 California Ave., Room 1007
Pittsburgh, PA 15290-9652

Southeastern (610) 964-6441
1000 W. Valley Rd.
Southeastern, PA 19399-9604

PUERTO RICO

San Juan (787) 793-0444
1510 Ave FD Roosevelt, Suite 160
Guaynabo, PR 00968-9600

RHODE ISLAND

Providence (401) 276-5038
24 Corliss St., Room 355
Providence, RI 02904-9602

SOUTH CAROLINA

Charleston (803) 760-5315
P.O. Box 239601
Charleston, SC 29423-9601

Columbia (803) 926-6310
P.O. Box 929641
Columbia, SC 29292-9641

Greenville (864) 282-8357
600 W. Washington St.
Greenville, SC 29602-9600

SOUTH DAKOTA

Sioux Falls (605) 357-5049
320 S. 2nd Ave.
Sioux Falls, SD 57104-7574

TENNESSEE

Knoxville (423) 558-4600
1237 E. Weisgarber Rd.
Knoxville, TN 37950-9604

Memphis (901) 576-2020
1 N. Front St., Room 313
Memphis, TN 38103-2157

Nashville (615) 885-9399
525 Royal Pky., Room 315
Nashville, TN 37229-9601

Chattanooga (423) 893-0102
6050 Shallowford Rd.
Chattanooga, TN 37421-9624

TEXAS

Austin (512) 494-2350
510 Guadalupe St.
Austin, TX 78701-9623

Dallas (972) 393-6701
951 W. Bethel Rd.
Coppell, TX 75099-9681

Fort Worth (817) 317-3600
4600 Mark IV Pky., Room 180K
Fort Worth, TX 76161-9681

Houston (713) 226-3349
P.O. Box 250001
Houston, TX 77202-9610

North Houston (281) 985-4108
4600 Aldine Bender Rd., Room 227
North Houston, TX 77315-9610

Lubbock (806) 762-7874
515 Avenue G
Lubbock, TX 79402-9681

San Antonio (210) 368-8578
10410 Perrin Beitel Rd., Room 1069
San Antonio, TX 78284-9623

U.S. Postal Service Business Centers, continued

UTAH

Salt Lake City (801) 974-2503
1760 W. 2100 S
Salt Lake City, UT 84199-9625

VERMONT

(800) 230-2370

Vermont is served by the Postal Business Center in Springfield, Massachusetts.

VIRGINIA

Merrifield (703) 207-6800
8409 Lee Hwy.
Merrifield, VA 22081-9621

Norfolk (757) 855-6259
2600 Eltham Ave., Suite 109
Norfolk, VA 23513-2504

Richmond (804) 775-6224
1801 Brook Rd., Room 303
Richmond, VA 23232-9610

Roanoke (540) 985-8861
419 Rutherford Ave. NE
Roanoke, VA 24022-9996

WASHINGTON

Seattle (206) 652-2100
4735 E. Marginal Way S
Seattle, WA 98134

Spokane (509) 626-6733
707 W. Main Ave., Suite 600
Spokane, WA 99299-9641

WEST VIRGINIA

Charleston (304) 340-4233
P.O. Box 59661
Charleston, WV 25350-9661

Clarksburg (304) 623-7705
200 Cava Dr.
Clarksburg, WV 26301-9996

WISCONSIN

Madison (608) 246-1245
P.O. Box 14750
Madison, WI 53714-0750

Milwaukee (414) 287-2522
P.O. Box 5008
Milwaukee, WI 53201-5008

WYOMING

Wyoming is served by the Postal Business Center in Denver, Colorado.

Place	ZIP
Abanda	36276
Abbeville	36310
Abel	36258
Abercrombie	35042
Aberfoil	36089
Abernant	35440
Abernathy	36264
Acipcoville (Part of Birmingham)	35207
Ackerville	36768
Acmar	35004
Active	36793
Ada	36069
Adamsburg	35967
Adams Crossroads	35960
Adamsville	35005
Addison	35540
Adger	35006
Adler	36779
Aimwell	36782
Airport Highlands (Part of Birmingham)	35206
Airport Station (Part of Mobile)‡	36608
Akron	35441
Alabama City (Part of Gadsden)‡	35904
Alabama Fork	35614
Alabama Port	36523
Alabama Shores	35660
Alabaster	35007
Alaga	36343
Alberta	36720
Alberta City (Part of Tuscaloosa)	35401
Alberton	36453
Albertville	35950-51
For specific ZIP Codes call (888) 275-8777, or your local postmaster.	
Alder Springs	35951
Aldrich	35115
Aldridge	35580
Aldridge Grove	35650
Alexander City	35010*
	35011†
Alexandria	36250
Alexis	35960
Aliceville	35442
Allen	36419
Allens Crossroads	35175
Allenton	36768
Allenton Station	36768
Allenville	36738
Allgood	35013
Allsboro	35616
Allsop	36272
Alma	36501
Almeria	36089
Almond	36276
Almont	35115
Alpha Springs	36022
Alpine	35014
Alta	35546
Altadena Valley	35243
Alton	35015
Altoona	35952
America	35580
Andalusia	36420
Anderson, *Etowah*	35901
Anderson, *Lauderdale*	35610
Andrews Chapel	35619
Angel	36265
Annemanie	36721
Anniston	36201-07
For specific ZIP Codes call (888) 275-8777, or your local postmaster.	
Anniston Army Depot	36201
Ansley	36079
Antioch, *Calhoun*	36253
Antioch, *Covington*	36420
Antioch, *Pike*	36079
Appleton	36426
Aqua Vista	35645
Aquilla	36558
Arab	35016
Ararat	36921
Arbacoochee	36264
Arbor Acres (Part of Huntsville)	35810
Arcola	36742
Ardell	35053
Ardilla (Part of Dothan)	36301
Ardmore	35739
Argo	35173
Argo Heights	35550
Arguta	36360
Ariton	36311
Arkadelphia	35033
Arkdell	35648
Arkwright (Part of Vincent)	35178
Arley	35541
Arlington	36722
Armstead	35121
Armstrong	36089
Aroney	36067
Arrowhead (Part of Montgomery)	36109
Arrowwood (Part of Tuscaloosa)	35405
Asberry	36272
Asbury, *Dale*	36360
Asbury, *Marshall*	35951
Ashbank	35578
Ashby	35035
Ashford	36312
Ashland, *Clay*	36251
Ashland, *Madison*	35811
Ashridge	35565
Ashville	35953
Askea Grove	35016
Aspel	35768
Atkinson	36784
Atmore	36502-04
For specific ZIP Codes call (888) 275-8777, or your local postmaster.	
Attalla	35954
Atwood	35571
Auburn	36830-32
For specific ZIP Codes call (888) 275-8777, or your local postmaster.	
Auburn University (Part of Auburn)	36849
Augustin	36701
Aurora	35956
Aurora Springs	35616
Austinville (Part of Decatur)	35601
Autaugaville	36003
Avalon Park (Part of Hueytown)	35020
Avant	36033
Avery (Part of Stevenson)	35772
Avon	36312
Avondale (Part of Birmingham)	35222
Avondale Mill (Part of Alexander City)	35010
Avondale Village (Part of Pell City)	35125
Avon Park (Part of Birmingham)	35234
Awin	36768
Axis	36505
Ayres	35126
Babbie	36420
Bacon Level	36274
Bagley	35062
Bailey Cove (Part of Huntsville)‡	35802
Bailey Springs	35634
Baileyton	35019
Baileytown	35019
Baker Hill	36027
Bald Hill	36375
Balkum	36345
Ballplay	35903
Bangor	35079
Bankhead, *DeKalb*	35984
Bankhead, *Walker*	35580
Banks	36005
Bankston	35542
Barachias (Part of Montgomery)	36064
Barber	36312
Barfield	36266
Barlow	36558
Barlow Bend	36545
Barnes	36311
Barnesville	35570
Barnett Chapel	35572
Barnett Crossroads	36426
Barney	35550
Barnisdale Forest (Part of Birmingham)	35215
Barnwell	36532
Barrytown	36908
Barton	35616
Basham	35601
Bashi	36784
Basin	36323
Bass	35772
Bassetts Creek	36585
Batesville	36053
Battelle	35989
Battens Crossroads	36316
Battleground	35179
Battles Wharf	36532
Bauxite	35960
Bay Minette	36507
Bayou La Batre	36509
Bay Shore Junction (Part of Prichard)	36610
Bayside (Part of Decatur)	35603
Bayside (Part of Mobile)‡	36605
Bay Springs	35960
Bayview	35005
Bazemore	35559
Beachwood Park (Part of Birmingham)	35212
Beamon	36360
Bean Rock	35175
Bear Creek	35543
Bear Point (Part of Orange Beach)	36561
Beasons Mill	36264
Beatrice	36425
Beaty Crossroads (Part of Ider)	35981
Beauregard	36804
Beaverton	35544
Beaver Town	35442
Beck	36420
Beda	36483
Beehive	36865
Bel Air (Part of Birmingham)	35210
Bel Air (Part of Mobile)‡	36616
Bel Air Mall (Part of Mobile)	36606
Belchers	35184
Belforest	36526
Belgreen	35653
Belk	35545
Bellamy	36901
Bellefontaine	36567
Bellefonte	35752
Bellefountaine	36582
Bellemeade	35634
Belle Mina	35615
Belleville	36401
Bellevue (Part of Gadsden)	35904
Bell Springs	35622
Bellview	36726
Bellwood, *Geneva*	36313
Bellwood (Part of Fairfield)	35064
Belmont	35470
Beloit	36759
Beltline (Part of Decatur)‡	35601
Belview Heights (Part of Tuscumbia)	35674
Bemiston (Part of Talladega)	35160
Bendale (Part of Birmingham)	35217
Benevola	35466
Benoit	35550
Bentley Hills (Part of Mountain Brook)	35216
Benton	36785
Ben Vines Gap (Part of Maytown)	35118
Berkley	35748
Berlin	35055
	35058
For specific ZIP Codes call (888) 275-8777, or your local postmaster.	
Bermuda, *Conecuh*	36401
Bermuda, *Monroe*	36460
Berney Points (Part of Birmingham)	35211
Berry	35546
Bertha	36353
Bessemer	35020-23
For specific ZIP Codes call (888) 275-8777, or your local postmaster.	
Bessemer Gardens (Part of Hueytown)	35020
Bessemer Homestead (Part of Bessemer)	35020
Bessie	35005
Bessie Junction	35005
Bethel, *Barbour*	36311
Bethel, *Cullman*	35057
Bethel, *Limestone*	35620
Bethlehem	36046
Bethsaida	35654
Beulah, *Covington*	36467
Beulah, *Greene*	35469
Beulah, *Lee*	36854
Beverly Station (Part of Birmingham)	35211
Bexar	35570
Bibbville	35188
Biddle Crossroads (Part of Henagar)	35978
Bigbee	36558
Big Creek	36301
Big Oak	35645
Big Tussle	35033
Billingsley	36006
Billy Goat Hill	35960
Bingham	36093
Birdine	36740
Birdsong	35058
Birmingham	35201-66
	35283
For specific ZIP Codes call (888) 275-8777, or your local postmaster.	
Birmingham Green (Part of Birmingham)‡	35237
Birwat (Part of Tarrant)	35217
Bishop	35616
Biven	35214
Black	36314
Blackankle	35768
Black Bottom	35077
Black Diamond	35023
Black Pond	35553
Black Rock	36042
Blacksher	36507
Blackwood	36345
Bladon Springs	36919
Blanche	35973
Blanton	36854
Bleecker	36874
Blossburg	35073
Blount Springs	35079
Blountsville	35031
Blow Gourd	35049
Blue Creek	35023
Blue Creek Junction (Part of Bessemer)	35020
Blue Mountain	36201
Blue Pond	35959
Blue Ridge♦	36093
Blues Old Stand	36061
Blue Spring (Part of Huntsville)	35810
Blue Springs, *Barbour*	36017
Blue Springs, *Blount*	35031
Blue Springs, *Covington*	36467
Blue Springs Garden	35811
Bluff	35555
Bluff Park (Part of Hoover)	35226
Bluff Spring	36251
Bluff Springs	36323
Bluffton	30138
Boar Tush	35565
Boaz	35956-57
For specific ZIP Codes call (888) 275-8777, or your local postmaster.	
Boaz Factory Outlet Center (Part of Boaz)	35957
Bobo, *Fayette*	35594
Bobo, *Madison*	35773
Boiling Spring	36728
Boiling Springs	36271
Boldo	35504
Boley Springs	35546
Boligee	35443
Bolinger	36919
Bolivar	35740
Bolling	36033
Bomar	35960
Bon Air	35032
Bonita	36749
Bonnie Doone	35611
Bonny Brook	36265
Bon Secour	36511
Booth	36008
Boot Hill	36048
Boozer Heights (Part of Oxford)	36203
Borden Springs	36262
Borden Wheeler Springs	36262
Boromville	36860
Boston (Part of Brilliant)	35548
Boswell	36081
Bowden Grove	36266
Bowles	36401
Bowmans Crossroads	35744
Boyd	35470
Boykin, *Escambia*	36426
Boykin, *Wilcox*	36723
Boyles (Part of Birmingham)	35217
Boylston (Part of Montgomery)‡	36110
Boys Ranch	36761
Bradford	35089
Bradley	36483
Bradleyton	36041
Braggs	36761
Branchville	35120
Brandontown (Part of Huntsville)	35805
Brannon Stand (Part of Dothan)	36305
Brantley, *Crenshaw*	36009
Brantley, *Dallas*	36703
Brantleyville	35114
Bread Tray Hill	36089
Bremen	35033
Brent	35034
Brewersville	35470
Brewton	36426*
	36427†
Briar Hill	36035
Brick	35660
Bridgeport	35740
Bridgeville	35442
Bridlewood Forest Estates	35215
Brierfield	35035
Brighton	35020
Bright Star	35980
Brilliant	35548
Brisco Store	35772
Broadmoor (Part of Bessemer)	35020
Bromley	36507
Brompton	35004
Brookhurst (Part of Birmingham)	35215
Brookhurst (Part of Huntsville)	35810
Brookley (Part of Mobile)	36605
Brooklyn, *Coffee*	36453
Brooklyn, *Conecuh*	36429
Brooklyn, *Cullman*	35083
Brooks	36456
Brookside	35036
Brooksville, *Blount*	35031
Brooksville, *Morgan*	35670
Brookwood	35444
Brookwood Forest (Part of Athens)	35613
Brookwood Village (Part of Homewood)	35209
Broomtown	35973
Broughton	36274
Browns	36759
Brownsboro	35741
Browns Corner	35773

*** Area Zip Code** † **Post Office Boxes** ‡ **Postal Station** ♦ **Census Designated Place** *Italic Type* **County**

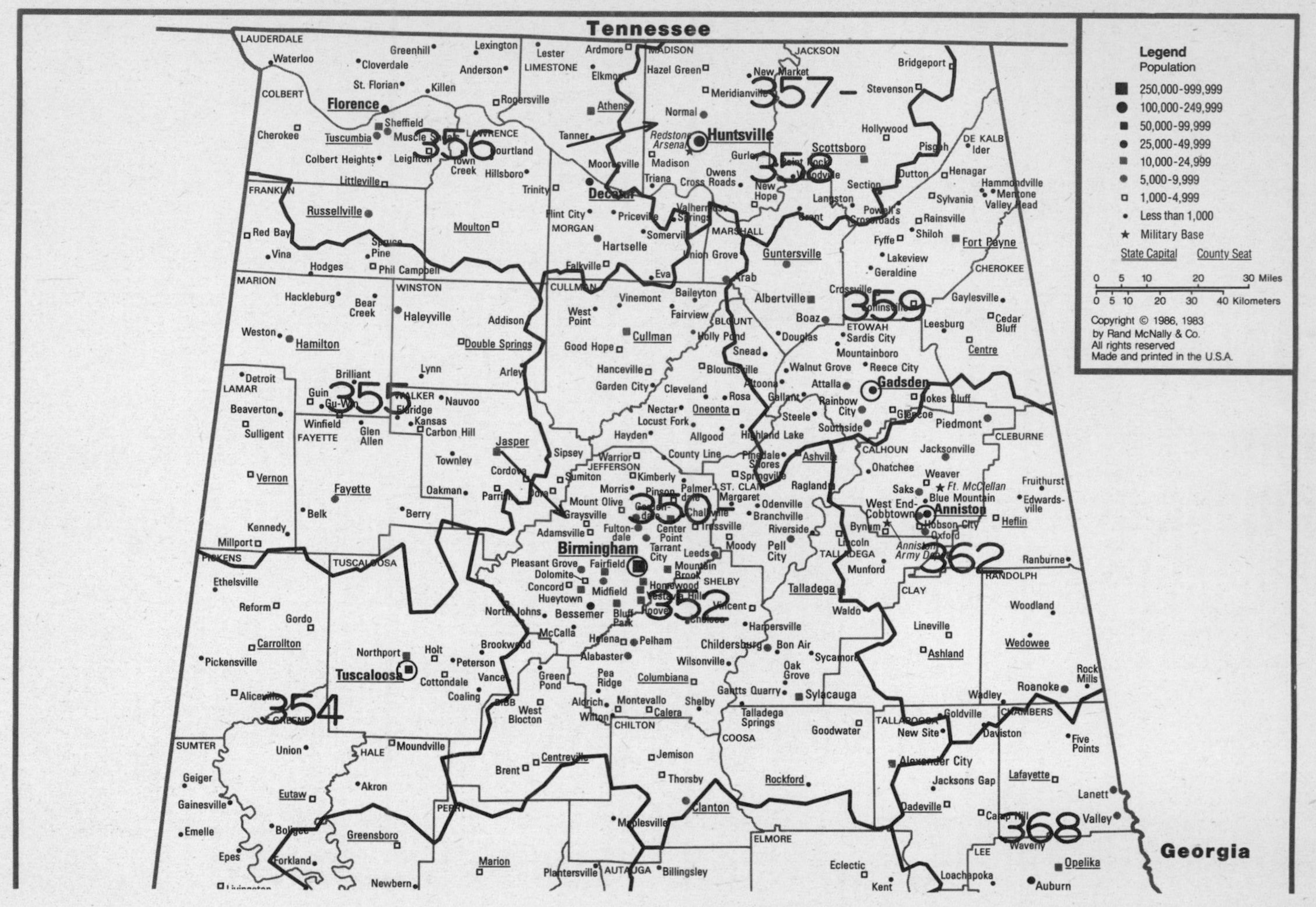
Tennessee
Georgia
Legend
Population
250,000-999,999
100,000-249,999
50,000-99,999
25,000-49,999
10,000-24,999
5,000-9,999
1,000-4,999
Less than 1,000
Military Base
State Capital
County Seat
0 5 10 20 30 Miles
0 5 10 20 30 40 Kilometers
Copyright © 1986, 1983
by Rand McNally & Co.
All rights reserved
Made and printed in the U.S.A.
Huntsville
Birmingham
Gadsden
Anniston
Tuscaloosa
Florence
Decatur
Cullman
Jasper
357 -
358
359
356
355
350 -
352
362
354
368

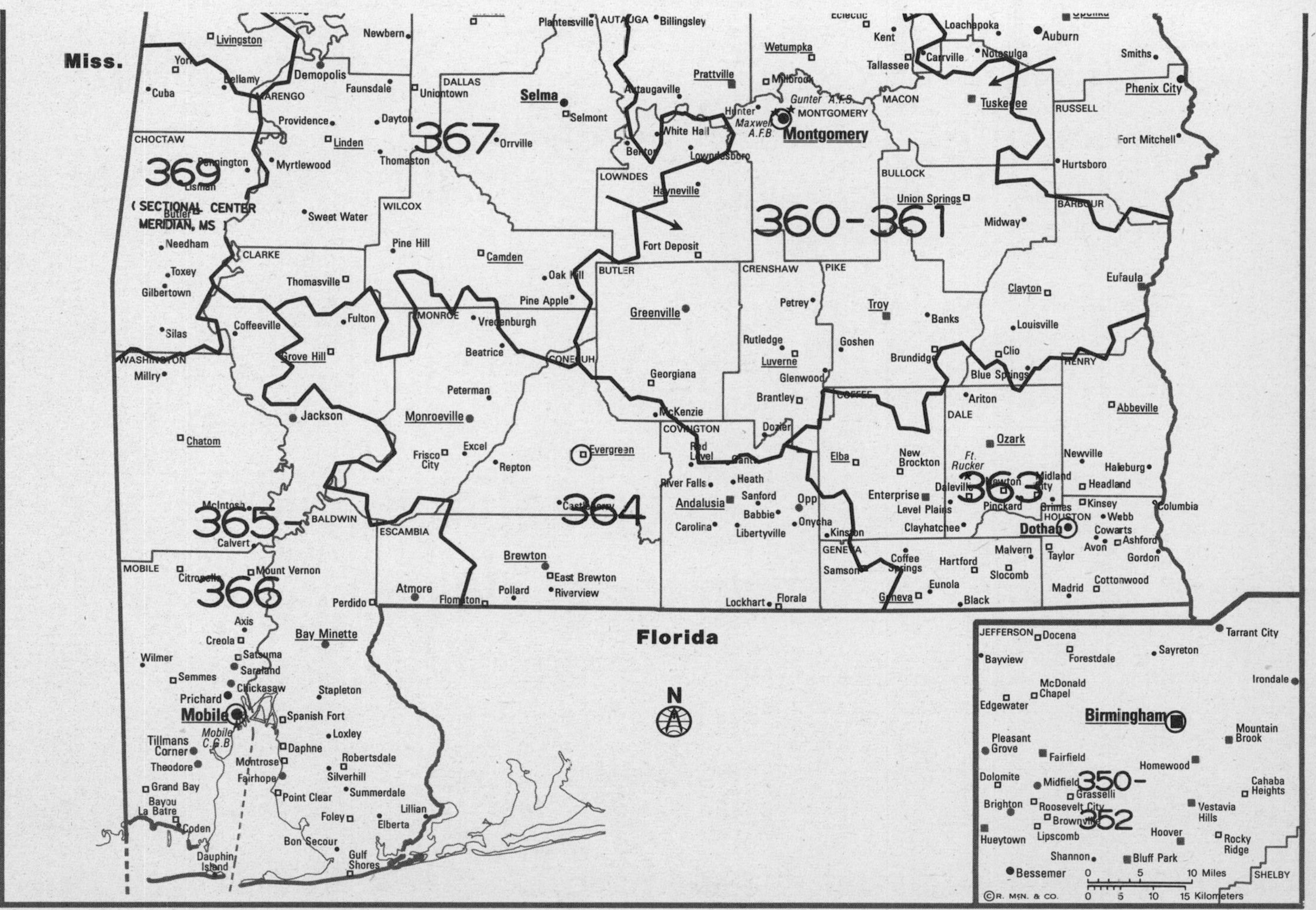
Miss.
Florida
N
Montgomery
Selma
Mobile
Dothan
Birmingham
Tuskegee
Phenix City
Eufaula
Troy
Greenville
Andalusia
Enterprise
Ozark
Evergreen
Brewton
Monroeville
Jackson
Demopolis
Livingston
Linden
Camden
Prattville
Wetumpka
Union Springs
Clayton
Abbeville
Luverne
Elba
Geneva
Chatom
Grove Hill
Bay Minette
Hayneville
Atmore
Auburn
Smiths
Fort Mitchell
Hurtsboro
Midway
Louisville
Clio
Blue Springs
Ariton
Banks
Brundidge
Goshen
Petrey
Glenwood
Rutledge
Brantley
Dozier
Heath
Sanford
Babbie
Libertyville
Opp
Onycha
Kinston
Samson
Coffee Springs
Eunola
Hartford
Slocomb
Malvern
Black
Taylor
Madrid
Cottonwood
Gordon
Ashford
Cowarts
Webb
Avon
Kinsey
Columbia
Headland
Haleburg
Newville
Midland City
Pinckard
Clayhatchee
Level Plains
Daleville
New Brockton
Fort Deposit
Lowndesboro
White Hall
Benton
Autaugaville
Billingsley
Plantersville
Selmont
Orrville
Uniontown
Dayton
Faunsdale
Newbern
Thomaston
Pine Hill
Oak Hill
Pine Apple
Vredenburgh
Beatrice
Peterman
Excel
Frisco City
Repton
Georgiana
McKenzie
River Falls
Carolina
Lockhart
Florala
East Brewton
Riverview
Pollard
Flomaton
Perdido
Stapleton
Spanish Fort
Loxley
Robertsdale
Silverhill
Summerdale
Lillian
Elberta
Foley
Gulf Shores
Bon Secour
Point Clear
Fairhope
Montrose
Daphne
Chickasaw
Saraland
Satsuma
Creola
Axis
Prichard
Semmes
Wilmer
Tillmans Corner
Theodore
Grand Bay
Bayou La Batre
Coden
Dauphin Island
Mount Vernon
Calvert
McIntosh
Citronelle
Millry
Silas
Coffeeville
Fulton
Thomasville
Sweet Water
Myrtlewood
Providence
Pennington
Lisman
Butler
Needham
Toxey
Gilbertown
Cuba
York
Bellamy
Tallassee
Kent
Loachapoka
Notasulga
Carrville
Maxwell A.F.B.
Gunter A.F.S.
Hunter
Millbrook
AUTAUGA
DALLAS
MARENGO
CHOCTAW
WILCOX
CLARKE
WASHINGTON
MOBILE
BALDWIN
ESCAMBIA
MONROE
CONECUH
BUTLER
LOWNDES
CRENSHAW
PIKE
COVINGTON
COFFEE
DALE
GENEVA
HOUSTON
HENRY
BARBOUR
BULLOCK
RUSSELL
MACON
MONTGOMERY
SECTIONAL CENTER MERIDIAN, MS
369
367
360-361
363
364
365-366
350-352
JEFFERSON
SHELBY
Tarrant City
Irondale
Mountain Brook
Cahaba Heights
Sayreton
Forestdale
Docena
Bayview
Edgewater
McDonald Chapel
Pleasant Grove
Fairfield
Homewood
Vestavia Hills
Rocky Ridge
Hoover
Bluff Park
Dolomite
Midfield
Grasselli
Roosevelt City
Brownville
Lipscomb
Brighton
Hueytown
Bessemer
Shannon
10 Miles
15 Kilometers
©R. McN. & CO.

Browns Crossroad 36310
Browns Crossroads 36360
Brownsville 35072
Browntown, *Jackson* .. 35978
Brown Town, *Mobile* .. 39451
Brownville, *Conecuh* .. 36401
Brownville (Part of Birmingham) 35211
Brownville, *Tuscaloosa* 35475
Bruceville 36089
Brundidge 36010
Brunnet Heights (Part of Tarrant) 35217
Brushy Creek 36033
Brushy Pond 35033
Bryant 35958
Bryant's Lower Landing 36579
Bryce Hospital (Part of Tuscaloosa) 35401
Buchanan Peninsula .. 35616
Buckhorn, *Madison* 35761
Buckhorn, *Pike* 36005
Buck Island Shores 35976
Bucks 36512
Bucksnort 35747
Bucksville 35111
Buena Vista 36425
Buena Vista Highlands (Part of Homewood).. 35209
Buffalo 36862
Buggs Chapel (Part of New Hope) 35763
Buhl 35446
Bull City 35468
Bull Gap 36267
Bullock 36009
Burchfield 35444
Burgreen Gin 35756
Burks Gardens (Part of Tuscaloosa) 35401
Burkville 36752
Burl 36753
Burlington 36078
Burningtree Estates (Part of Decatur) 35603
Burningtree Mountain (Part of Decatur) 35603
Burns 36272
Burnsville 36703
Burnt Corn 36431
Burntout 35593
Burnwell 35038
Burstall (Part of Bessemer) 35020
Butler 36904
Butler Springs 36030
Buttston 36853
Buyck 36080
Bynum♦ 36253
Caddo 35673
Caffee Junction 35111
Cahaba 36767
Cahaba Heights♦ 35243
Cahaba Hills (Part of Leeds) 35094
Cahaba River Estates.. 35244
Calcis 35178
Caldwell 35146
Caledonia 36753
Calera 35040
Calhoun 36047
Calumet 35580
Calvert 36513
Camden 36726
Camelot (Part of Huntsville) 35803
Cameronsville 35772
Campbell, *Chilton* 35085
Campbell, *Clarke* 36727
Campbells Crossroads 36266
Campbell Springs 36266
Campbellville 35063
Camp Branch 35007
Camp Hill 36850
Camp Oliver 35130
Canoe 36502
Cantebury Heights (Part of Mobile) 36609
Cantelous Spur 36113
Canton Bend 36726
Capitol Heights (Part of Montgomery)‡ 36107

Capps 36353
Capshaw 35742
Carbon Hill 35549
Cardiff 35041
Carlisle 35956
Carlowville 36761
Carlton 36515
Carns 35746
Carolina 36420
Carolyn (Part of Montgomery)‡ 36106
Carpenter 36507
Carriger 35611
Carr Mill 36251
Carrollton 35447
Carrville (Part of Tallassee) 36078
Carson 36548
Carter Grove 35750
Carterville 35967
Cartwright 35620
Carver Court (Part of Tuskegee) 36088
Casemore 36742
Casey 36701
Castleberry 36432
Catalpa 36081
Catherine 36728
Cavalry Hill (Part of Huntsville) 35805
Cave Spring, *Etowah* .. 35954
Cave Spring, *Madison* 35763
Cave Springs 35674
Cecil 36013
Cedar Bluff 35959
Cedar Cove 35453
Cedar Fork 36482
Cedar Grove, *Baldwin* 36542
Cedar Grove, *Covington* 36420
Cedar Grove, *Jackson* 35772
Cedar Hill, *Fayette* 35555
Cedar Hill, *Limestone* .. 35739
Cedar Hill Estates 35674
Cedar Plains 35622
Cedar Point 35760
Cedar Springs 36265
Cedrum 35549
Center 35565
Centercrest 35215
Centergrove 35670
Center Hill, *Chilton* 35085
Center Hill, *Cullman* 35077
Center Hill, *Lauderdale* 35648
Center Hill, *Limestone* 35773
Center Point, *Clarke* 36524
Center Point, *Jefferson*♦ 35215
Center Point Gardens 35215
Center Springs 35172
Center Star 35645
Centerville 36401
Centerwood Estates .. 35215
Central, *Cullman* 35057
Central, *Elmore* 36024
Central, *Jackson* 35978
Central City 36330
Central Heights 35633
Central Highlands (Part of Birmingham) 35206
Central Mills 36773
Centre 35960
Centreville 35042
Century Plaza (Part of Birmingham) 35210
Ceramic (Part of Phenix City) 36867
Chalkville 35215
Chalybeate Springs 35643
Champion 35121
Chance 36751
Chancellor 36316
Chandler Mountain 35987
Chandler Springs 35160
Chapel Hill, *Chambers* 36862
Chapel Hill (Part of Hoover) 35216
Chapman 36015

Chapman Heights (Part of Huntsville) 35810
Chase 35811
Chastang 36560
Chatom 36518
Chelsea (Part of Huntsville) 35801
Chelsea, *Shelby*♦ 35043
Cherokee 35616
Cherokee Bluffs 36078
Cherokee Forest (Part of Mountain Brook) .. 35223
Cherry Grove 35611
Chesson 36029
Chesterfield 30731
Chestnut 36425
Chestnut Grove 36010
Chetopa 35073
Chickasaw 36611
Chigger Hill 35971
Childersburg 35044
Chilton 36451
China 36401
China Grove 36081
Chinneby 36268
Chisholm (Part of Montgomery) 36110
Choccolocco 36254
Choctaw Bluff 36545
Choctaw City 36904
Choctaw Corner (Part of Thomasville) 36784
Christiana 36258
Chrysler 36480
Chulafinnee 36264
Chulavista 35125
Chunchula 36521
Circlewood (Part of Tuscaloosa) 35405
Citronelle 36522
Claiborne 36470
Clairmont Springs 35160
Clanton 35045-46
For specific ZIP Codes call (888) 275-8777, or your local postmaster.
Clarksville 36524
Claud 36024
Clay 35048
Clay City 36532
Clayhatchee 36322
Clayhill 36784
Claysville 35976
Clayton 36016
Clearview, *Covington* .. 36028
Clearview, *Crenshaw* .. 36041
Cleveland, *Blount* 35049
Cleveland, *Fayette* 35542
Cleveland Crossroads 35072
Cliff Haven (Part of Sheffield) 35660
Clift Acres (Part of Madison) 35758
Clinton 35448
Clintonville 36351
Clio 36017
Clisby Park (Part of Montgomery) 36104
Clopton 36317
Cloverdale (Part of Birmingham) 35215
Cloverdale, *Lauderdale* 35617
Cloverdale, *Mobile* 36541
Cloverdale (Part of Tuscaloosa) 35401
Cloverdale Heights 35633
Cloverland (Part of Montgomery)‡ 36105
Clowers Crossroads .. 36010
Clubview Heights (Part of Gadsden) 35901
Coal Bluff 36769
Coalburg (Part of Birmingham) 35068
Coal City 35131
Coal Fire 35481
Coaling 35449
Coalmont 35114
Coal Valley 35579
Coatopa 35470
Cobb City (Part of Glencoe) 35905
Cobbs Ford 36025

Cobb Town 36201
Cochrane 35442
Coden 36523
Cody 35555
Coffee Springs 36318
Coffeeville 36524
Cohasset 36474
Coker 35452
Colbert Heights 35674
Cold Springs, *Cullman* 35033
Cold Springs, *Elmore* .. 36022
Coldwater, *Calhoun* 36260
Coldwater, *Covington* 36420
Cole Spring 35622
Coleta 36267
Collbran 35967
Collins Chapel 35045
Collinsville 35961
Collirene 36785
Colonial Gardens 35759
Colonial Heights (Part of Tuscumbia) 35674
Colony 35077
Columbia 36319
Columbiana 35051
Columbus City 35976
Colwell 35905
Comer 36053
Concord, *Fayette* 35555
Concord, *Jefferson* 35023
Congo 35959
Consul 36728
Cook Springs 35052
Cool Springs 35953
Coon Creek 35063
Coopers 35046
Coosa Court (Part of Childersburg) 35044
Coosada 36020
Coosa River 36022
Copeland 36558
Copeland Bridge 35961
Copeland Ferry 35130
Copper Springs 35120
Coppinville (Part of Enterprise) 36330
Corcoran (Part of Troy) 36081
Cordova 35550
Corinth, *Bullock* 36081
Corinth, *Cullman* 35179
Corinth, *Randolph* (mail Wadley) 36276
Corinth, *Randolph* (mail Wedowee) 36278
Corner 35180
Cornerstone 36089
Cornhouse 36274
Cornwall Furnace 35959
Corona 35579
Cortelyou 36585
Cotaco 35670
Cottage Grove 35089
Cottage Hill (Part of Pleasant Grove) 35127
Cottage Hill (Part of Mobile)‡ 36609
Cotton 36024
Cottondale 35453
Cottonton 36851
...... 36859
For specific ZIP Codes call (888) 275-8777, or your local postmaster.
Cottontown 35646
Cotton Valley 36083
Cottonville 35747
Cottonwood 36320
Country Club Acres (Part of Athens) 35611
Country Club Estates (Part of Huntsville) 35201
Country Club Estates (Part of Mobile) 36608
Country Club Village (Part of Mobile) 36608
Country Estates, *Jefferson* 35215
Country Estates, *Montgomery* 36108
County Line, *Blount* 35172
County Line, *Covington* 36453

County Line, *Cullman* .. 35019
County Line, *Pike* 36034
Courtland 35618
Covin 35555
Cowarts 36321
Cox Beach (Part of Satsuma) 36572
Coxey 35611
Coy 36435
Cragford 36255
Crane Hill 35053
Crawford (Part of Mobile) 36608
Crawford, *Russell* 36869
Creek Stand 36089
Creeltown 35063
Creola 36525
Crescent Heights (Part of Lipscomb) 35020
Crestline (Part of Mountain Brook) 35213
Crestline Gardens (Part of Birmingham) 35210
Crestline Heights (Part of Mountain Brook) .. 35213
Crestline Park (Part of Birmingham) 35213
Crestview (Part of Mobile) 36609
Crestview Gardens (Part of Pell City) 35125
Crestwood (Part of Huntsville) 35807
Creswell 35078
Crews 35586
Crichton (Part of Mobile)‡ 36607*
...... 36670†
Crocker Junction 35117
Cromwell 36906
Crooked Oak 35674
Cropwell (Part of Pell City) 35054
Crosby 36343
Cross Key 35620
Crossroads, *Baldwin* .. 36507
Crossroads (Part of Guntersville) 35976
Crosston 35126
Crossville, *DeKalb* 35962
Crossville, *Lamar* 35592
Crudup (Part of Reece City) 35954
Crumley Chapel 35214
Cuba 36907
Cullman 35055-58
For specific ZIP Codes call (888) 275-8777, or your local postmaster.
Cullman Shopping Center (Part of Cullman) 35055
Cullomburg 36919
Cunningham, *Clarke* .. 36727
Cunningham, *Pickens* 35442
Curry, *Talladega* 36268
Curry, *Walker* 35504
Currytown 36350
Curtis 36323
Curtiston (Part of Attalla) 35954
Cusseta 36852
Cypress 35474
Cyril 36912
Dadeville 36853
Daisey City 35214
Daleville 36322
Dallas, *Blount* 35172
Dallas (Part of Huntsville) 35801
Damascus, *Coffee* 36323
Damascus, *Escambia* 36426
Dancy 35442
Dancy Quarter (Part of Decatur) 35603
Danley Crossroads 36323
Danville 35619
Danway 36852
Daphne 36526
Dargin 35040
Darlington 36726
Darwin Downs (Part of Huntsville) 35801

*** Area Zip Code** **† Post Office Boxes** **‡ Postal Station** **♦ Census Designated Place** *Italic Type* **County**

Dauphin Island 36528
Davis Hills (Part of Huntsville) 35805
Daviston 36256
Davisville 36083
Dawes 36601
Dawson 35963
Dawsons Mill 36749
Dayton 36731
De Armanville 36257
Deason Hill 35550
Deatsville 36022
Deavertown 35049
Decatur 35601-09
For specific ZIP Codes call (888) 275-8777, or your local postmaster.
Deerhurst 35124
Deer Park 36529
DeFoor 35565
Delchamps 36523
Delmar 35551
Delta 36258
Demopolis 36732
Dempsey 35653
Deposit 35761
Detroit 35552
Devenport 36047
Dexter 36092
Diamond 35976
Dickert 36276
Dickinson 36436
Dillard 36360
Dilworth 35063
Dime 35581
Dixiana 35126
Dixie 36420
Dixie Springs 35579
Dixon Corner 36544
Dixon Shop 35983
Dixons Mills 36736
Dixonville 36426
Docena 35060
Dock 36037
Dodge City 35057
Dog Town, *DeKalb* 35967
Dogtown, *Walker* 35549
Dogwood 35115
Dolcito (Part of Tarrant) 35217
Doliska (Part of Dora) 35130
Dolomite (Part of Birmingham) 35061
Dolonah (Part of Bessemer) 35022
Dora 35062
Doster 36311
Dothan 36301-05
For specific ZIP Codes call (888) 275-8777, or your local postmaster.
Double Bridges (Part of Ashland) 35951
Double Bridges, *Henry* 36310
Double Bridges, (mail Albertville) *Marshall* 35950
Double Bridges, (mail Boaz) *Marshall* 35957
Doublehead 36862
Double Springs 35553
Douglas (Part of Fort Payne) 35967
Douglas, *Marshall* 35964
Douglasville (Part of Birmingham) 35207
Downing 36052
Downs 36039
Downtown (Part of Huntsville)‡ 35801*
35804†
Downtown (Part of Montgomery)‡ 36101-04
For specific ZIP Codes call (888) 275-8777, or your local postmaster.
Downtown (Part of Tuscaloosa)‡ 35401
Dozier 36028
Drewry 36460
Drummond 35063
Dry Forks 36726
Dry Valley, *Shelby* 35115
Dry Valley (Part of Lincoln) 35096
Dublin 36036
Duck Nest Springs 36268
Duck Springs 35954
Dudley 35490
Dudleyville 36850
Duke 36279
Duncan 35010
Duncan Crossroads 35771
Duncanville 35456
Dundee 36344
Dunn 36081
Dunns 36420
Dupree 36312
Dutton 35744
Duval (Part of Opp) 36467
Dyas 36507
Dyers Crossroads 35058
Eady City (Part of Valley) 36854
Eagle 35540
Earlytown 36453
Eastaboga 36260
East Birmingham (Part of Birmingham) 35204
East Boyles (Part of Birmingham) 35217
East Brewton 36426
Eastbrook (Part of Montgomery)‡ 36109
East Brookwood 35444
Eastdale Mall (Part of Montgomery) 36123
Eastern Hills 35453
Eastern Valley 35020
East Gadsden (Part of Gadsden)‡ 35903
East Hampton (Part of Athens) 35611
East Haven 35215
East Irondale (Part of Irondale) 35210
East Killen (Part of Killen) 35645
East Lake Roebuck (Part of Birmingham)‡ 35206
East Point 35055
35058
For specific ZIP Codes call (888) 275-8777, or your local postmaster.
Eastside (Part of Tuscaloosa)‡ 35404
East Tallassee (Part of Tallassee) 36023
East Thomas (Part of Birmingham) 35204
Eastwood (Part of Oneonta) 35121
Eastwood (Part of Birmingham) 35224
Eastwood Mall (Part of Birmingham) 35234
Ebenezer 35179
Echo 36350
Echola 35457
Echols Crossroads 35670
Echols Hills (Part of Huntsville) 35801
Eclectic 36024
Eddings Town 35115
Eddy (Part of Arab) 35016
Eden (Part of Pell City) 35125
Edgefield, *Barbour* 36016
Edgefield, *Jackson* 35772
Edgemont (Part of Homewood) 35209
Edgemont Park (Part of Homewood) 35209
Edgewater 35224
Edmonton Heights (Part of Huntsville) 35810
Edna 36922
Edwardsville 36261
Edwin 36317
Egypt, *Etowah* 35952
Egypt, *Marshall* 35016
Eight Mile (Part of Prichard) 36613
Elamville 36311
Elba 36323
Elberta 36530
Eldridge 35554
Elgin 35652
Eliska 36480
Elkmont 35620
Elkwood 35773
Ellards 35034
Elliotsville (Part of Alabaster) 35007
Ellisville, *Baldwin* 36551
Ellisville, *Cherokee* 35960
Elmore 36025
Elrod 35458
Elsanor 36567
Elsmeade (Part of Montgomery) 36116
Elting (Part of Florence)‡ 35630
Elyton (Part of Birmingham) 35204
Emelle 35459
Emerald Shores 35634
Empire 35063
Englewood 35405
English Village (Part of Mountain Brook) 35223
English Village (Part of Huntsville) 35802
Enon, *Bullock* 36053
Enon, *Cullman* 35179
Enon, *Houston* 36376
Enon, *Pike* 36005
Ensley (Part of Birmingham)‡ 35218
Enterprise, *Chilton* 36091
Enterprise, *Coffee & Dale* 36330*
36331†
Eoda 36420
Eoline 35042
Epes 35460
Equality 36026
Erin 36266
Escatawpa 36584
Estelle 36726
Estes Crossroads 36272
Estillfork 35745
Ethelsville 35461
Euclid Estates (Part of Mountain Brook) 35217
Eufaula 36027*
36072†
Eulaton 36201
Eunola 36340
Eureka 35772
Eutaw 35462
Eva 35621
Evansville 35441
Evergreen, *Autauga* 36006
Evergreen, *Conecuh* 36401
Ewell 36360
Excel 36439
Exie 36272
Exmoor 36782
Fabius 35966
Fackler 35746
Fadette 36375
Fairdale (Part of Centreville) 35042
Fairfax (Part of Valley) 36854
Fairfield, *Covington* 36420
Fairfield, *Jefferson* 35064
Fairfield, *Lawrence* 35650
Fairfield Highlands (Part of Midfield) 35064
Fairford 36553
Fairhope 36532*
36533†
Fairmont 35611
Fairnelson 36401
Fairoaks 35477
Fairview, *Chilton* 35045
Fairview, *Coffee* 36323
Fairview, *Conecuh* 36401
Fairview, *Cullman* 35058
Fairview, *DeKalb* 35963
Fairview (Part of Birmingham)‡ 35208
Fairview, *Limestone* 35611
Fairview, *Marion* 35564
Fairview, *Mobile* 36587
Fairview (Part of Decatur) 35601
Fairview, *Pickens* 35466
Fairview, *St. Clair* 35131
Fairview, *Winston* 35540
Fairview West 35077
Falco 36483
Falkville 35622
Falls City 35553
Fannie 36441
Farill 35959
Farley (Part of Huntsville) 35802
Farmersville 36761
Farmville 36801
Fatama 36726
Faunsdale 36738
Fayette 35555
Fayetteville 35151
Fergusons Cross Roads 35972
Fernbank 35576
Fernland 36541
Fernwood Estates 35215
Fieldstown (Part of Gardendale) 35071
Fig Tree 36749
Finchburg 36444
Finley Crossing 36784
Fisher Crossroads (Part of Fort Payne) 35967
Fish Pond 35643
Fish River 36555
Fisk 35750
Fitzpatrick 36029
Five Points, *Blount* 35049
Five Points, *Chambers* 36855
Five Points, *Cleburne* 36264
Five Points, *Dale* 36352
Five Points, *Dallas* 36767
Five Points, *Elmore* 36025
Five Points (Part of Madrid) 36320
Five Points, *Lawrence* 35619
Five Points, *Madison*‡ 35801
Five Points, *Marshall* 35755
Five Points, *Walker* 35503-04
For specific ZIP Codes call (888) 275-8777, or your local postmaster.
Five Points East (Part of Irondale) 35210
Five Points West Shopping City (Part of Birmingham) 35208
Flat Creek 35130
Flat Rock (Part of Lineville) 36266
Flat Rock, *Conecuh* 36401
Flat Rock, *Jackson* 35966
Flat Top 35062
Flatwood, *Montgomery* 36110
Flatwood, *Walker* 35549
Flatwood, *Wilcox* 36728
Flatwoods 36032
Flea Hop 36078
Fleetwood 35453
Fleming Meadows (Part of Huntsville) 35802
Flemington Heights (Part of Huntsville) 35802
Fleta 36043
Flint City (Part of Decatur) 35601
Flintridge Center (Part of Fairfield 35064
Flomaton 36441
Florala 36442
Floral Crest 35774
Florence 35630-34
For specific ZIP Codes call (888) 275-8777, or your local postmaster.
Florette 35670
Flower Hill 35643
Foley 36535*
36536†
Ford City 35660
Forest 35461
Forest Brook Estates 35226
Forestdale‡ 35214
Forester Chapel 36276
Forest Hill (Part of Mobile) 36608
Forest Hills (Part of Childersburg) 35044
Forest Hills (Part of Fairfield) 35064
Forest Hills (Part of Florence) 35630
Forest Hills (Part of Oxford) 36203
Forest Home 36030
Forest Park (Part of Birmingham) 35222
Forest Park (Part of Mobile) 36608
Forkland 36740
Forkville 35565
Forney 35960
Fort Benning 31905
Fort Dale 36037
Fort Davis 36031
Fort Deposit 36032
Fort McClellan 36205
Fort Mitchell 36856
Fort Morgan 36542
Fort Payne 35967-68
For specific ZIP Codes call (888) 275-8777, or your local postmaster.
Fort Rucker 36362
Fosheeton 35010
Fosters 35463
Fostoria 36761
Fountain 36460
Fountain Heights (Part of Birmingham) 35204
Four Mile 35186
Four Roads 35984
Four Wing Lake 35007
Fowlers Crossroads 35542
Fowl River 36582
Fox 35401
Foxwood 36064
Frances Heights (Part of Fultondale) 35068
Francisco 37345
Francis Mill 36271
Frankfort 35653
Franklin, *Macon* 36083
Franklin, *Monroe* 36444
Frankville 36538
Fredonia 36855
Freemanville 36502
Fremont 36749
French Mill 35613
Fridays Crossing 35121
Friendship, *Butler* 36033
Friendship, *Covington* 36467
Friendship, *Elmore* 36078
Friendship, *Marshall* 35016
Friendship, *Montgomery* 36036
Frisco 36010
Frisco City 36445
Frisco Quarters (Part of Jasper) 35501
Frog Mountains 36272
Frost (Part of Centreville) 35042
Fruitdale 36539
Fruithurst 36262
Fry 35016
Fullers Crossroads 36049
Fullerton 35973
Fulton 36446
Fulton Bridge (Part of Hamilton) 35570
Fultondale 35068
Fulton Springs (Part of Fultondale) 35068
Furman 36741
Fyffe 35971
Gadsden 35901-05
35907
35999
For specific ZIP Codes call (888) 275-8777, or your local postmaster.
Gadsden Mall (Part of Gadsden) 35901
Gainer 36477
Gainestown 36540
Gainesville 35464
Gallant 35972
Galleria (Part of Hoover)‡ 35244
Gallion 36742
Gamble 35503

Place	ZIP
Gandys Cove	35622
Gann Crossroad	35981
Gantt	36038
Gantts Junction (Part of Sylacauga)	35151
Gantts Quarry	35151
Garden	35442
Garden City	35070
Gardendale	35071
Garden Highlands (Part of Birmingham)	35211
Gardiners Gin	35550
Garland	36456
Garth	35764
Gary Springs	35042
Garywood (Part of Birmingham)	35023
Gasque	36542
Gastonburg	36728
Gate City (Part of Birmingham)	35212
Gaylesville	35973
Gay Meadows (Part of Montgomery)	36111
Geiger	35459
General Mail Facility (Part of Montgomery)‡	36119
Genery	35020
Geneva	36340
Gentilly Forest (Part of Vestavia Hills)	35216
Georgetown	36521
Georgia (Part of Hartselle)	35640
Georgiana	36033
Gerald (Part of Level Plains)	36322
Geraldine	35974
Germania (Part of Birmingham)	35211
Gibson Crossroads	35971
Gibsonville	36251
Gilbert Crossroads	35963
Gilbertown	36908
Gilbertsboro	35647
Giles	35188
Gilliam Springs (Part of Arab)	35016
Gipsy	35620
Girard (Part of Phenix City)	36869
Glades	36267
Gladstone	35806
Glascow	35005
Glass (Part of Valley)	36854
Gleandean (Part of Auburn)	36830
Glen Allen	35559
Glen City (Part of Pell City)	35128
Glencoe, Etowah	35905
Glencoe (Part of Mountain Brook)	35213
Glen Hills (Part of Bessemer)	35020
Glen Mary	35577
Glenn Acres	36608
Glen Oaks (Part of Fairfield)	35064
Glenville	36871
Glenwood	36034
Gnatville	36272
Godwin Estates	35215
Goldbranch	35183
Golden Springs (Part of Anniston)	36207
Gold Mine	35548
Gold Ridge, *Cullman*	35058
Gold Ridge, *Lee*	36879
Gold Ridge, *Randolph*	36263
Goldville	36255
Gonce	35772
Good Hope, *Cullman*	35055
Good Hope, *Elmore*	36024
Goodman	36330
Good Spring	35593
Good Springs, *Limestone*	35610
Goodsprings, *Walker*	35560
Goodwater	35072
Goodway	36449
Goodyear (Part of Gadsden)	35903
Goose Pond Crossroads (Part of Scottsboro)	35769
Gordo	35466
Gordon	36343
Gordon Heights (Part of Lipscomb)	35020
Gordonsville	36785
Gorgas	35580
Goshen	36035
Gosport	36482
Gourdsville	35647
Graball (Part of Abbeville)	36310
Grace	36456
Grady	36036
Graham	36263
Grand Bay♦	36541
Grangeburg	36343
Grant	35747
Grantley	36272
Granttown	36268
Grasmere	35014
Grasselli (Part of Birmingham)	35211
Grassy, *Lauderdale*	35648
Grassy, *Marshall*	35016
Gravel Hill (Part of Russellville)	35653
Gravelly Springs	35633
Gray Hill	35184
Graymont (Part of Birmingham)	35204
Grays Chapel	35745
Grayson	35572
Graystone	35013
Graysville	35073
Grayton	36271
Green Acres (Part of Birmingham)	35228
Greenbrier (Part of Florence)	35630
Greenbrier, *Limestone*	35756
Green Chapel	35971
Greenhill	35634
Green Lantern (Part of Montgomery)‡	36111
Green Pond	35074
Greensboro	36744
Greens Chapel	35049
Greensport	35953
Green Springs (Part of Homewood)‡	35219
Green Street	36401
Green Valley (Part of Southside)	35903
Green Valley (Part of Hoover)	35216
Greenville	36037
Greenwood, Clarke	36451
Greenwood (Part of Bessemer)	35020
Greenwood (Part of Tuskegee)	36088
Greenwycke Village (Part of Huntsville)	35802
Griffith Bend	35160
Grimes	36303
Grove Hill	36451
Groveoak	35975
Grove Park (Part of Homewood)	35209
Grove Park (Part of Childersburg)	35044
Grovewood Estates	36108
Guerryton	36860
Guest (Part of Fyffe)	35971
Guin	35563
Guinea	35474
Gulf Crest	36521
Gulf Shores	36542*
	36547†
Gum Pond	35621
Gum Spring	35640
Gum Springs	35031
Gunter Air Force Station	36114-15
For specific ZIP Codes call (888) 275-8777, or your local postmaster.	
Guntersville	35976
Gurley	35748
Guthery Crossroads	35053
Gu-Win	35563
Hackleburg	35564
Hackneyville	35010
Hacoda	36477
Hagler	35456
Haleburg	36319
Haleyville	35565
Half Acre	36763
Halls Crossroads, *Bullock*	36089
Halls Crossroads, *Monroe*	36445
Halltown	35582
Halsell	36912
Halso Mill	36037
Hamburg, *Perry*	36759
Hamburg, *Wilcox*	36768
Hamilton	35570
Hamilton Crossroads	36010
Hammondville	35989
Hamner	35460
Hampden	36722
Hanceville	35077
Hancock Crossroads	35771
Hannah (Part of Athens)	35611
Hannon	36860
Hanover	35136
Hardaway	36039
Hardwick	35120
Harkins Crossroads	36251
Harlem Heights (Part of Hueytown)	35023
Harmon	35042
Harmony, *Covington*	36420
Harmony, *Lawrence*	35650
Harper Hill	35474
Harpersville	35078
Harrell	36759
Harriman Park (Part of Birmingham)	35207
Harrisburg, Bibb	35034
Harrisburg (Part of Pell City)	35125
Harrisville	35952
Hartford	36344
Hartselle	35640
Harvest	35749
Hassell Gap	36266
Hatchechubbee	36858
Hatton, *Colbert*	35646
Hatton, *Lawrence*	35672
Havana	35474
Hawk	36280
Hawthorn	36585
Hayden	35079
Haynes	36067
Haynes Crossing	35772
Haynes Crossroad	36258
Hayneville	36040
Haysland (Part of Huntsville)‡	35802-03
	35815
For specific ZIP Codes call (888) 275-8777, or your local postmaster.	
Haysland Estates (Part of Huntsville)	35802
Hays Mill	35620
Haywood	36280
Hazel Green♦	35750
Hazen	36767
Headland	36345
Healing Springs	36558
Heath	36420
Hebron, *Bibb*	35184
Hebron, *Marshall*	35747
Hector	36029
Heflin	36264
Heiberger	36756
Helena	35080
Helicon, *Crenshaw*	36036
Helicon, *Winston*	35541
Henagar	35978
Henderson	36035
Hendrick Mill	35121
Hendrix	35121
Hendrixville	35961
Henryville	35976
Henson Springs	35544
Herbert	36401
Heron Bay	36523
Hester Heights (Part of Russellville)	35653
Hickory	35442
Hickory Flat	36274
Hickory Grove	35651
Hickory Hills (Part of Florence)	35630
Hickory Hills (Part of Decatur)	35603
Hidden Forest	36093
Hidden Valley	35151
Hideaway Hills	35645
Higdon	35979
High Bluff	36344
Highfalls	36344
Highland, *Chilton*	35045
Highland (Part of Lineville)	36266
Highland Home	36041
Highland Lake	35121
Highland Park (Part of Montgomery)	36107
Highmound	35980
Highnote	36314
High Pine	36267
High Point, *DeKalb*	35989
High Point, *Marshall*	35950
High Ridge	36089
Hightogy	35592
Hightower	36263
Hillandale (Part of Huntsville)	35805
Hillard	35587
Hillman Gardens	35020
Hillman Park	35020
Hillsboro, *Lawrence*	35643
Hillsboro, *Madison*	35761
Hillsdale (Part of Jasper)	35504
Hilltop (Part of Bessemer)	35020
Hillview	35214
Hinton	39355
Hirsch	36871
Hissop	35089
Hobbs Island	35803
Hobgood	35674
Hoboken (Part of Eufaula)	36027
Hoboken, *Marengo*	36782
Hobson	36518
Hobson City	36201
Hodge	35744
Hodges	35571
Hodgesville	36301
Hodgewood	36921
Hogglesville	35474
Hog Jaw	35016
Hokes Bluff	35903
Holiday Homes (Part of Huntsville)	35807
Holiday Park Estates	35215
Holland Gin	35620
Holley Crossroads	36272
Hollins	35082
Hollis Crossroads	36264
Holly Grove	35587
Holly Pond	35083
Holly Springs	35146
Hollytree	35751
Hollywood, *Jackson*	35752
Hollywood (Part of Homewood)	35209
Holman, *Escambia*	36503
Holman, *Tuscaloosa*	35466
Holmes Gap	35179
Holt♦	35404
Holt Junction (Part of Tuscaloosa)	35401
Holtville	36022
Holy Trinity	36859
Homewood	35209
Honoraville	36042
Hoods Crossroads	35121
Hooks	36871
Hooks Crossroads	36089
Hoover, *Jefferson*	35236
Hoover, *Madison*	35749
Hope Hull (Part of Montgomery)	36043
Hopewell, *Blount*	35016
Hopewell, *Cherokee*	35959
Hopewell, *Cleburne*	36264
Hopewell, *DeKalb*	35974
Hopewell (Part of Bessemer)	35020
Hoppes	36535
Hornady	36083
Horn Hill	36467
Horton	35980
Hortons Mill	35121
Houston	35572
Houstontown	35645
Howard	35549
Howells Cross Roads	35960
Howelton	35952
Howton	35453
Hubbard	35085
Hubbertville (Part of Glen Allen)	35555
Hudson Gardens (Part of Lipscomb)	35020
Hudson Settlement	35503
Hueytown	35023
Hueytown Crest (Part of Hueytown)	35020
Huffman (Part of Birmingham)	35215
Huffman Gardens (Part of Birmingham)	35215
Hugo	36783
Huguley♦	36854
Hulaco	35087
Hull (Part of Sumiton)	35063
Humpton	35747
Hunter (Part of Montgomery)	36108
Hunters Crossroads	36319
Huntsville	35801-24
For specific ZIP Codes call (888) 275-8777, or your local postmaster.	
Huntsville Park (Part of Huntsville)	35807
Hurricane	36507
Hurtsboro	36860
Hustleville	35951
Huxford	36543
Hyatt	35980
Hybart	36481
Hytop	35768
Idaho	36251
Ider	35981
Independence	36067
Indian Creek	36061
Indian Forest (Part of Indian Springs Village)	35124
Indian Hill (Part of Childersburg)	35044
Indian Springs, *Lauderdale*	35634
Indian Springs, *Mobile*	36613
Indian Springs Village	35124
Indian Valley	35244
Industrial City (Part of Hueytown)	35023
Industry	36033
Ingate	35042
Inglenook (Part of Birmingham)	35217
Ingram	35474
Inland	35121
Inmanfield	35540
Ino	36453
Institute	36778
Interburan Heights (Part of Fairfield)	35064
Inverness, *Bullock*	36089
Inverness, *Shelby*♦	35242
Ironaton	36268
Iron City	36207
Irondale	35210
Irvington	36544
Isabella	36750
Isbell	35653
Ishkooda (Part of Birmingham)	35211
Isney	36919
Ivalee	35954
Ivanhoe (Part of Birmingham)	35222
Jachin	36910
Jack	36346
Jackson	36545
Jackson Heights (Part of Mobile)	36609
Jackson Oak	36526
Jacksons Gap	36861
Jacksonville	36265
Jack Springs	36502

*** Area Zip Code** **† Post Office Boxes** **‡ Postal Station** **♦ Census Designated Place** *Italic Type* **County**

Place	ZIP
Jamback	36005
Jamestown	35973
Jamesville	36879
Jarrett (Part of Valley)	36854
Jasper	35501-04
For specific ZIP Codes call (888) 275-8777, or your local postmaster.	
Java	36010
Jeddo	36480
Jeff	35806
Jefferson	36745
Jefferson Hills (Part of Birmingham)	35217
Jefferson Park	35210
Jefferson Station	36745
Jemison	35085
Jena	35480
Jenifer	36268
Jericho	36756
Jernigan	36851
Jerusalem Heights	35405
Joe Wheeler Dam	35672
Johnsons Crossing	35077
Johnstonville	36401
Jones	36749
Jonesboro, *Baldwin*	36526
Jonesboro, *Franklin*	35653
Jonesboro (Part of Bessemer)	35020
Jones Chapel	35057
Jones Crossroads	35611
Jones Valley (Part of Birmingham)	35211
Jones Valley Estates (Part of Huntsville)	35802
Joppa	35087
Joquin	36035
Jordan, *Elmore*	36092
Jordan, *Washington*	36518
Jordans Mill	35593
Josephine	36530
Joseph Springs	36207
Josie	36005
Kahatchee	35044
Kansas	35573
Kaolin (Part of Phenix City)	36869
Kaulton (Part of Tuscaloosa)	35401
Keego	36426
Keener	35954
Kellerman	35468
Kelly	36322
Kelly Chapel	35769
Kellys Crossroads	35136
Kelly Springs (Part of Dothan)	36303
Kellyton	35089
Kendale Gardens	35634
Kennedy	35574
Kent, *Elmore*	36045
Kent, *Pike*	36035
Kenwood	35226
Ketona (Part of Tarrant)	35217
Key	35960
Keyno	35089
Keys Mill	35761
Keystone (Part of Pelham)	35007
Keyton	36330
Kilby (Part of Montgomery)	36114
Kilgore	35062
Killen	35645
Killough Springs (Part of Birmingham)	35235
Kilpatrick	35951
Kimberly	35091
Kimbrel	35111
Kimbrough	36769
Kincheon	35045
Kings Landing, *Baldwin*	36574
Kings Landing, *Dallas*	36775
Kingston (Part of Birmingham)	35234
Kingsway Terrace (Part of Birmingham)	35206
Kingtown	35652
Kingville	35574
Kinsey	36303
Kinston	36453
Kinterbish	36907
Kirbytown	35755
Kirk	35466
Kirkland	36426
Kirklands Crossroads	36345
Kirks Grove	35960
Klein	35078
Knightens Crossroads	36272
Knoxville	35469
Koenton	36558
Kowaliga Beach	35010
Krafton (Part of Prichard)	36610
Kyles	35746
Kymulga	35014
Laceys Chapel	35020
Laceys Spring	35754
Lacon	35622
Ladiga	36272
Ladonia♦	36869
Lafayette	36862
Lake Coves	35634
Lake Drive Estates (Part of Homewood)	35209
Lake Forest	36526
Lake Purdy♦	35242
Lakeside Acres	35645
Lakeside Highlands (Part of Florence)	35630
Lakeview, *DeKalb*	35971
Lakeview (Part of Guntersville)	35976
Lakeview Highlands (Part of Muscle Shoals)	35660
Lakewood (Part of Birmingham)	35234
Lakewood (Part of Athens)	35611
Lakewood (Part of Huntsville)	35810
Lakewood Estates (Part of Bessemer)	35020
Lamison	36728
Land	36904
Landersville	35650
Lands Crossroads (Part of Rainsville)	35986
Lane Springs	35616
Lanett	36863
Langdale (Part of Valley)	36854
Langston	35755
Langtown	35650
Laniers	35014
Lapine	36046
La Place	36075
Larkinsville	35768
Larkwood	35215
Lasca	36784
Latham	36579
Lathamville	35962
Lattiwood	35950
Lauderdale Beach	35634
Laurendine	36582
Lavaca	36904
Lawley	36793
Lawrence	35959
Lawrence Cove	35621
Lawrence Mill	35555
Lawrenceville	36310
Leatherwood	36201
Lebanon, *Cleburne*	36269
Lebanon, *DeKalb*	35961
Lebanon, *Morgan*	35640
Lecta	36264
Leeds	35094
Leeds Mineral Well (Part of Leeds)	35094
Leesburg	35983
Leesdale (Part of Falkville)	35622
Leggtown	35620
Le Grand	36105
Leighton	35646
Lenlock (Part of Anniston)	36201
Lenox	36454
Leon	36028
Leroy	36548
Lester	35647
Letcher	35776
Letchers	36201
Letohatchee	36047
Level Plains	36322
Levelroad	36276
Levert	36779
Lewis	36350
Lewisburg (Part of Birmingham)	35207
Lewiston	35462
Lexington	35648
Liberty, *Blount*	35031
Liberty, *Butler*	36037
Liberty, *DeKalb*	35957
Liberty, Pickens	35461
Liberty City	36866
Liberty Highlands	35210
Liberty Hill, *Franklin*	35581
Liberty Hill, *Jackson*	35966
Libertyville	36420
Lickskillet	35967
Lightwood	36022
Ligon Springs	35654
Lillian	36549
Lily Flag (Part of Huntsville)	35802
Lime	36274
Lime Kiln	35616
Limestone	36460
Lim Rock	35776
Lincoln (Part of Huntsville)	35810
Lincoln, *Talladega*	35096
Lincoya Estates (Part of Vestavia Hills)	35216
Lindbergh	35073
Linden	36748
Lineville	36266
Linn Crossing	35073
Linwood	36081
Lipscomb	35020
Lisman	36912
Little Oak	36079
Little River, *Baldwin*	36550
Little River, *Cherokee*	35959
Little Rock	36502
Little Shawmut (Part of Lanett)	36863
Little Texas	36083
Littleton, *Etowah*	35954
Littleton, *Jefferson*	35073
Littleville, *Colbert*	35654
	35674
For specific ZIP Codes call (888) 275-8777, or your local postmaster.	
Littleville, *Winston*	35565
Live Oak Landing	36507
Livingston	35470
Loachapoka	36865
Loango	36474
Locke Crossroads	35620
Lockhart	36455
Lock Six	35645
Lock Three	35652
Locust Fork	35097
Loflin	36859
Logan	35098
Logton	36081
Lola City	35173
Lomax	35045
London, *Conecuh*	36432
London, *Montgomery*	36052
Long Island	35958
Longleaf Estates (Part of Decatur)	35603
Longview, *Cullman*	35179
Longview, *Shelby*	35137
Longwood (Part of Huntsville)	35801
Loop, *Cherokee*	35959
Loop (Part of Mobile)‡	36606
Loree	36401
Lott	36613
Lottie	36502
Louisville	36048
Love Hill	36312
Lovelace Crossroads	35633
Loveless	35967
Loveless Park	35020
Lovick	35173
Lower Peach Tree	36751
Lowery	36453
Lowerytown	35184
Low Gap	35120
Lowndesboro	36752
Lowry Mill	36346
Loxley	36551
Loxley Heights	36551
Lucille	35184
Lugo	36027
Lumbull (Part of Bear Creek)	35543
Lupton	35578
Luttrell	35971
Luverne	36049
Lydia	35968
Lyeffion	36401
Lynn	35575
Lynndale (Part of Montgomery)	36105
Lynn Haven (Part of Tuscaloosa)	35404
Lynns Park	35550
Lytle	36477
Mabson	36360
McCalla	35111
McClure Town	36081
McCollum	35501
McCord Crossroads	35960
McCulley Hill	35184
McCullough	36502
McDonald Chapel	35224
McDowell	35470
Macedonia, *Cleburne*	36273
Macedonia, *Jackson*	35771
Macedonia (Part of Montgomery)	36036
Macedonia, *Pickens*	35461
Macedonia, *Walker*	35503
McElderry	36268
McFarland Mall (Part of Tuscaloosa)	35405
McGhees Bend	35960
McGinty (Part of Valley)	36854
McIntosh	36553
McKenzie	36456
McKestes	35963
Mackey	35983
McKinley	36728
McLarty	35980
McLendon	36851
McMullen	35442
Macon	36271
McQueen	36066
McShan	35471
McVay	36451
McVille	35951
McWilliams	36753
Madison	35756-58
For specific ZIP Codes call (888) 275-8777, or your local postmaster.	
Madison Crossroads	35772
Madison Square Mall (Part of Huntsville)	35806
Madrid	36320
Magazine (Part of Mobile)	36610
Magnolia	36754
Magnolia Beach (Part of Fairhope)	36532
Magnolia Shores	36041
Magnolia Springs	36555
Magnolia Terminal	36722
Mahrt	36851
Majestic	35116
Malbis	36526
Malcolm	36556
Mall, The (Part of Huntsville)	35801
Malone	36276
Malta	36502
Malvern	36349
Mamie	36052
Manack	36752
Manchester, *Marshall*	35976
Manchester, *Walker*	35503
Manila	36545
Manningham	36037
Mansion View	35633
Mantua	35462
Maple Hill	35773
Mapleville	36750
Maplewood (Part of Leeds)	35094
Maplewood (Part of Madison)	35758
Marble City Heights (Part of Sylacauga)	35150
Marble Valley	35151
Marbury	36051
Marcoot	36862
Margarot	35112
Margerum	35616
Marietta	35579
Marion	36756
Marion Junction	36759
Markeeta	35094
Marl	36477
Marley Mill (Part of Ozark)	36360
Marlow	36580
Marshall	35957
Mars Hill, *Chilton*	35085
Mars Hill (Part of Florence)	35630
Martins (Part of Birmingham)	35208
Martintown	35752
Martinville	36502
Martling	35950
Marvel	35115
Marvyn	36804
Marylee	35504
Maryville	35954
Massey	35619
Masterson Mill	35650
Mastin Lake (Part of Huntsville)‡	35810-11
For specific ZIP Codes call (888) 275-8777, or your local postmaster.	
Mathews	36052
Mattawana	35121
Maud	35616
Mauville	36613
Maxine	35130
Maxwell	35401
Maxwell Air Force Base (Part of Montgomery)	36112-13
For specific ZIP Codes call (888) 275-8777, or your local postmaster.	
Maxwellborn	36272
Maxwell Heights (Part of Montgomery)	36113
Mayfair (Part of Homewood)	35209
Mayfair (Part of Huntsville)	35801
Maylene (Part of Alabaster)	35114
Maynards Cove	35768
Mays Crossroads, *Clarke*	36570
Mays Crossroads, *Etowah*	35903
Maysville	35741
Maytown	35118
McCall	36426
Meadowbrook♦‡	35242
Meadow Hills (Part of Huntsville)	35810
Meadows Crossroads	36874
Mechanicsville	36874
Meeksville	36081
Megargel	36457
Mellow Valley	36255
Melrose, *Conecuh*	36401
Melrose, *Pickens*	35471
Melton	36776
Meltonsville	35755
Melvin	36913
Memphis	39341
Mentone	35984
Mercury	35811
Meridianville♦	35759
Merrell Beach	35143
Merry	36064
Mertz (Part of Mobile)	36606
Mexboro	36445
Mexia	36458
Mexia Crossing	36458
Micaville	36264
Middle Brooks Cross Roads	36879
Middleton	36271
Midfield	35228
Midland City	36350
Midtown (Part of Mobile)‡	36604
Midway, *Bullock*	36053

Midway, *Butler* 36042
Midway, *Chilton* 36051
Midway (Part of Lineville) 35072
Midway, *Lawrence* 35650
Midway, *Monroe* 36768
Midway, *Tallapoosa* 36861
Miflin 36530
Mignon♦ 35150
Miles (Part of Fairfield) 35064
Millbrook 36054
Miller 36748
Millers Ferry 36726
Millertown 36613
Millerville 36267
Millport 35576
Millry 36558
Mills Quarter's 36535
Milltown 36862
Mill Village (Part of Guntersville) 35976
Milstead 36075
Milton 36749
Mineral Springs 35085
Minooka 35040
Minor 35224
Minor Terrace (Part of Childersburg) 35044
Minter 36761
Minvale (Part of Fort Payne) 35967
Mitchell 36029
Mitchell Crossroads 36804
Mitchell Town 35645
Mobile 36601-12
36615-95
For specific ZIP Codes call (888) 275-8777, or your local postmaster.
Mobile Festival Centre (Part of Mobile) 36608
Mobile Junction 35022
Moffett 36587
Mollie 36906
Molloy 35586
Mon Louis 36523
Monroeville 36460*
36461†
Monrovia 35806
Montague 35740
Monterey 36030
Monterey Heights 36877
Monte-Sano (Part of Birmingham) 35228
Montevallo 35115
Monte Vista (Part of Gadsden) 35904
Montgomery 36601-25
For specific ZIP Codes call (888) 275-8777, or your local postmaster.
Montgomery Mall (Part of Montgomery) 36116
Monticello 36005
Montrose 36559
Moody 35004
Moontown 35741
Moorefield 36862
Moores Bridge 35475
Moores Crossroad 35971
Moores Crossroads, *Randolph* 36274
Moores Crossroads, *Shelby* 35115
Moores Mill 35811
Moores Valley 36769
Mooresville 35649
Moreland 35572
Morgan (Part of Bessemer) 35020
Morgan City 35175
Moriah 35136
Morningside 35215
Morris 35116
Morrows Grove 35462
Morvin 36762
Moshat 35960
Mosses 36040
Mossy Grove 36079
Mostellers 35143
Motley 36276
Moulton 35650
Moulton Heights (Part of Decatur) 35601
Moundville 35474
Mountainboro 35957
Mountain Brook, *Jefferson* 35223
Mountain Brook (Part of Huntsville) 35801
Mountain Brook Village (Part of Mountain Brook) 35223
Mountain Chest (Part of Guntersville) 35976
Mountain Creek 36051
Mountain Gap 35976
Mountain Grove 35031
Mountain Home 35673
Mountain Park (Part of Birmingham) 35217
Mountain Star 35654
Mountain View (Part of Guntersville) 35976
Mountain Woods (Part of Vestavia Hills) 35216
Mountain Woods Park (Part of Vestavia Hills) 35216
Mount Andrew 36053
Mount Carmel, *Jackson* 35740
Mount Carmel, *Marshall* 35976
Mount Carmel, *Montgomery* 36046
Mount Hebron, *Greene* 35443
Mount Hebron, *Marshall* 35957
Mount Hester 35616
Mount Hilliard 36089
Mount Hope 35651
Mount Ida 36009
Mount Jefferson 36801
Mount Meigs 36057
Mount Nebo 36785
Mount Olive, *Coosa* 35072
Mount Olive, *Jefferson* 35117
Mount Pleasant, *Coffee* 36330
Mount Pleasant, *Monroe* 36480
Mount Rozell 35647
Mount Sinai 36113
Mount Sterling 36904
Mount Union 36401
Mount Vernon, *Cullman* 35179
Mount Vernon, *DeKalb* 35967
Mount Vernon, *Fayette* 35555
Mount Vernon, *Mobile* 36560
Mount Willing 36032
Mount Zion 36069
Movico 36560
Mt. Lebanon 35759
Mt. Olive 35452
Mt. Pleasant 35661
Mt. Tabor 35640
Muck City 35650
Mud Creek, *Jackson* 35752
Mud Creek, *Jefferson* 35006
Mulberry 36003
Mulga 35118
Mulga Mine 35118
Munford 36268
Murphree Crossroads 35957
Murphy Crossroads 35677
Murrays Chapel 35146
Muscadine 36269
Muscadine Junction 36269
Muscle Shoals 35661*
35662†
Muscoda 35020
Mynot 35616
Myrick Chapel 36022
Myrtlewood 36763
Nadawah 36726
Naftel 36046
Nanafalia 36764
Nances Creek 36272
Napier Field 36303
Napoleon 36280
Nat (Part of Woodville) 35776
Natchez 36425
Nathan (Part of Arley) 35541
Natural Bridge 35577
Nauvoo 35578
Navco (Part of Mobile) 36605
Nebo (Part of Huntsville) 35758
Nebo, *Madison* 35760
Nectar 35049
Needham 36915
Needmore, *Marshall* 35957
Needmore, *Pike* 36081
Needmore, *Winston* 35565
Neel 35640
Neenah 36726
Nellie 36726
Neman 36078
Neshota (Part of Mobile) 36605
Nesmith, *Cullman* 35057
Ne Smith, *Lawrence* 35672
Nettleboro 36436
Newbern 36765
Newberry Crossroads 35960
New Brockton 36351
Newburg 35654
New Castle 35119
New Center 35640
New Dora (Part of Dora) 35062
Newell 36270
New Georgia 35540
New Haven 35758
New Hill (Part of Lipscomb) 35020
New Home 35978
New Hope, *Coffee* 36010
New Hope, *Cullman* 35083
New Hope, *Jackson* 35768
New Hope, *Madison* 35760
New Hope, *Marion* 35594
New Hope (Part of Indian Springs Village) 35243
New Hopewell 36264
New Jagger 35587
New Lexington 35546
New London 35054
New Market♦ 35761
New Moon 35973
New Mt. Hebron 35443
New Prospect, *Autauga* 36051
New Prospect, *Hale* 35441
New Sharon 35750
New Site 35010
Newsome (Part of Rainsville) 35986
Newton, *Dale* 36352
Newton (Part of Dothan) 36301
Newtonville 35555
Newtown (Part of Russellville) 35653
New Town (Part of Stevenson) 35772
Newville 36353
New West Greene 35462
Nichburg 36475
Nicholsville 36784
Nitrate City 35660
Nixburg 36026
Nix Mill 35581
Nixons Chapel 35980
Noah 35960
Nokomis 36502
Nolandale (Part of Madison) 35758
Nolan Hills (Part of Madison) 35758
Normal (Part of Huntsville) 35762
Normandale Shopping Center (Part of Montgomery) 36111
North Arab (Part of Arab) 35016
North Athens (Part of Athens) 35611
North Bibb (Woodstock) 35188
North Birmingham (Part of Birmingham)‡ 35207
North Courtland 35618
North Daye Hill 35749
North Elmore 36025
North Florence (Part of Florence)‡ 35630
North Highlands (Part of Hueytown) 35020
North Johns 35006
North Mobile (Part of Chickasaw) 36611
Northport 35473
35475-76
For specific ZIP Codes call (888) 275-8777, or your local postmaster.
Northside (Part of Dothan)‡ 36304
Northside Acres 35806
Northside Mall (Part of Dothan) 36303
North Smithfield Estates 35214
North Smithfield Manor (Part of Birmingham) 35207
North Vinemont 35179
North Walter 35055
Northwood Hills (Part of Florence) 35630
Norton, Etowah 35954
Norton, Madison 35803
Norwood (Part of Birmingham) 35234
Notasulga 36866
Nottingham 35014
Nuckols 36856
Nymph 36401
Oak 36542
Oak Bowery 36862
Oak Crossing (Part of Leeds) 35094
Oakdale 35613
Oakdale Acres 35613
Oak Grove, *Autauga* 36067
Oak Grove, *Chilton* 35085
Oak Grove, *Franklin* 35654
Oak Grove, *Geneva* 36314
Oak Grove, *Hale* 36742
Oak Grove, *Jefferson* 35006
Oak Grove, *Limestone* 35739
Oak Grove, *Madison* 35760
Oak Grove, *Marshall* 35768
Oak Grove, *Mobile* 36613
Oak Grove, *Talladega* 35150-51
For specific ZIP Codes call (888) 275-8777, or your local postmaster.
Oak Hill, *DeKalb* 35962
Oak Hill, *Wilcox* 36766
Oakhurst (Part of Birmingham) 35207
Oakland 35633
Oakleigh Estates (Part of Gadsden) 35901
Oak Level 36262
Oakley 36792
Oakley Grove 36353
Oakman 35579
Oakmulgee 36793
Oak Ridge, *Morgan* 35640
Oak Ridge (Part of Pell City) 35125
Oak Ridge Park (Part of Birmingham) 35212
Oakville (Part of Birmingham) 35206
Oakville, *Lawrence* 35619
Oakwood (Part of Bessemer) 35020
Oakwood College 35896
Oakworth (Part of Decatur) 35601
Oaky Streak 36037
Ocampo 35040
Octagon 36748
Odena 35150
Oden Ridge 35621
Odenville 35120
Odom 36456
Ofelia 36266
Ohatchee 36271
Okomo 35143
Old Bethel 35646
Old Burleson 35593
Old Davistown 36201
Old Fabius 35966
Oldfield (Part of Sylacauga) 35150
Old Jonesboro 35215
Old Kingston 36067
Old Maylene (Part of Alabaster) 35114
Old Mill Trace 35453
Old Monrovia 35806
Old Nauvoo 35653
Old Samuel 36908
Old Sparta 36401
Old Spring Hill 36742
Old Texas 36768
Old Town, *Conecuh* 36401
Old Town, *Dallas* 36785
Oleander 35175
Oliver 35652
Ollie 36460
Olney 35442
Omaha 36274
O'Neal 35614
Oneonta 35121
Onycha 36467
Opelika 36801-04
For specific ZIP Codes call (888) 275-8777, or your local postmaster.
Opine, *Clarke* 36784
Opine, *Covington* 36467
Opp 36467
Orange Beach 36561
Orchard (Part of Mobile) 36618
Ord (Part of Gadsden) 35901
Orion 36081
Orrville, *Dallas* 36767
Orrville, *Limestone* 35671
Osanippa (Part of Valley) 36854
Osborn 36779
Oswichee 36856
Our Town 35010
Overbrook 35150
Overton 35210
Owassa 36401
Owens Cross Roads 35763
Owenton (Part of Birmingham) 35204
Oxford 36203
Oxford Lake (Part of Oxford) 36203
Oxmoor 35211
Oyster Bay 36542
Ozark 36360*
36361†
Painter 35962
Paint Rock 35764
Palestine 36262
Palmerdale 35123
Palmers Crossroads 36480
Palmetto 35481
Palmetto Beach 36542
Palos 35130
Panola, *Crenshaw* 36046
Panola, *Sumter* 35477
Pansey 36370
Paran 36274
Park City 36526
Parkdale 35072
Parker Springs 36483
Park Hill (Part of Pell City) 35125
Parkland (Part of Jasper) 35501
Parkway City (Part of Huntsville) 35801
Parkway Estates (Part of Huntsville) 35802
Parkwood 35020
Parrish 35580
Partridge Crossroads 35180
Patsburg 36049
Patton 35579
Patton Chapel (Part of Hoover) 35216
Paul 36401
Pauls Hill 35020
Pawnee 35217

*** Area Zip Code** **† Post Office Boxes** **‡ Postal Station** **♦ Census Designated Place** *Italic Type* **County**

Peachburg 36089
Peacock 36451
Pearces Mills 35570
Pea Ridge, *Escambia* .. 36426
Pea Ridge, *Fayette* 35546
Pea Ridge (Part of Huntsville) 35801
Pea Ridge, *Marion* 35563
Pea Ridge, *Shelby* 35115
Pearson 35456
Pebble 35565
Peckerwood 36861
Peeks Corner 35961
Peeks Hill 36271
Peets Corner 35611
Pelham 35124
Pelham Heights (Part of Anniston) 36201
Pell City 35125
.... 35128
For specific ZIP Codes call (888) 275-8777, or your local postmaster.
Penfield Heights (Part of Birmingham) 35217
Penn 35619
Pennington 36916
Pennsylvania (Part of Satsuma) 36572
Penton 36862
Pentonville 35136
Pepperell (Part of Opelika) 36801
Perdido 36562
Perdido Beach 36530
Perdue Hill 36470
Perote 36061
Perry Store 36453
Perryville 36701
Peterman 36471
Peterson 35478
Petersville‡ 35633
Petrey 36062
Petronia 36785
Pettusville 35620
Peytonia Points 35660
Phelan 35055
Phenix City 36867-70
For specific ZIP Codes call (888) 275-8777, or your local postmaster.
Phil Campbell 35581
Phillips Estates (Part of Bessemer) 35020
Phillipsville 36507
Phoenixville (Part of Birmingham) 35221
Pickensville 35447
Piedmont, *Calhoun* 36272
Piedmont (Part of Huntsville) 35801
Piedmont Springs 36272
Pigeon Creek 36037
Pike Road 36064
Pikeville 35768
Pilgrims Rest (Part of Southside) 35907
Pinckard 36371
Pinder Hill 35772
Pine Apple 36768
Pine Beach 36542
Pinebelt 36767
Pinecrest 36541
Pine Dale, *Limestone* .. 35739
Pinedale (Part of Montgomery) 36116
Pinedale Acres, *Lauderdale* 35645
Pinedale Acres (Part of Athens) 35611
Pinedale Shores 35953
Pine Flat 36022
Pine Grove, *Baldwin* 36507
Pine Grove, *Bullock* 36053
Pine Grove, *Cherokee* 35960
Pine Grove, *Lee* 36804
Pine Grove, *Pickens* 35401
Pine Grove, *Tallapoosa* 36850
Pine Grove Village 35143
Pine Hill, *Randolph* 36263
Pine Hill, *Wilcox* 36769
Pine Level, *Autauga* 36022
Pine Level, *Coffee* 36323

Pine Level, *Montgomery* 36065
Pine Mountain 35133
Pine Orchard 36471
Pine Ridge 35968
Pineview, *Escambia* 36426
Pineview (Part of Irondale) 35210
Pinewood Terrace (Part of Childersburg) 35044
Piney 35960
Piney Bend 35593
Piney Chapel 35614
Piney Grove, *Geneva* .. 36477
Piney Grove, *Lawrence* 35619
Piney Grove, *Marion* .. 35548
Piney Woods 36262
Pinkeyville 35072
Pinkney City 35214
Pinnell 36850
Pinson 35126
Pintlala 36043
Pisgah, *Jackson* 35765
Pisgah, *Limestone* 35773
Pisgah, *Montgomery* .. 36036
Pittsview 36871
Plainview, *Cleburne* 36264
Plainview (Part of Rainsville) 35986
Plantation Hills 36526
Plant City (Part of Lanett) 36863
Plantersville, *Dallas* 36758
Plantersville, *Talladega* 35014
Plateau (Part of Mobile) 36610
Plaza De Malaga (Part of Mobile)‡ 36685
Pleasant Acres 35811
Pleasant Gap 36272
Pleasant Grove, *Chilton* 35085
Pleasant Grove, *Jefferson* 35127
Pleasant Grove, *Marshall* 35950
Pleasant Groves 35772
Pleasant Hill, *Barbour* .. 36027
Pleasant Hill, *Choctaw* 36908
Pleasant Hill, *Dallas* 36701
Pleasant Hill, *Escambia* 36502
Pleasant Hill, *Franklin* .. 35585
Pleasant Hill, *Jefferson* 35020
Pleasant Hill, *Winston* 35553
Pleasant Home 36420
Pleasant Plains 36312
Pleasant Ridge, *Franklin* 35654
Pleasant Ridge, *Greene* 35462
Pleasant Ridge, *Marion* 35570
Pleasant Ridge, *Pike* .. 36034
Pleasant Site 35582
Pletcher 36750
Plevna 35761
Poarch 36502
Poarch Creek Indian Reservation 36502
Pocahontas 35549
Pogo 35582
Point Clear♦ 36564
Polk 36785
Pollard 36441
Pollards Bend 35983
Ponderosa Estates 36575
Ponders 36853
Pondville 35034
Pooles Crossroads 36274
Pools Crossroads 35045
Pope 36769
Poplar Ridge 35760
Poplar Springs, *Marshall* 35951
Poplar Springs, *Winston* 35578
Port Birmingham 35118
Porter 35005

Portersville 35961
Posey Mill 35565
Poseys Crossroads, *Autauga* 36067
Poseys Crossroads, *Chilton* 35085
Postoak 36089
Potash 36274
Potter 36701
Powderly (Part of Birmingham) 35211
Powderly Hills (Part of Birmingham) 35211
Powell 35971
Powers 35474
Powhatan 35118
Powledge 36874
Praco 35130
Prairie 36728
Prairieville 36742
Pratt City (Part of Birmingham) 35214
Pratts 36016
Prattville 36066-68
For specific ZIP Codes call (888) 275-8777, or your local postmaster.
Prescott 35125
Preston 35769
Prestwick 36548
Priceville 35603
Prichard 36610
Pride 35674
Primitive Ridge 35184
Princeton 35766
Pronto 36081
Prospect 35578
Providence, *Butler* 36033
Providence, *Cullman* .. 35179
Providence, *Marengo* .. 36742
Providence, *Walker* 35579
Pruitton 35634
Pulaski Pike (Part of Huntsville)‡ 35810
Pulltight 35548
Pumpkin Center (Part of Fort Payne) 35967
Pumpkin Center, *Morgan* 35619
Pumpkin Center, *Walker* 35130
Pushmataha 36912
Putnam 36784
Pyriton 36266
Queenstown 35173
Quintard Mall (Part of Oxford) 36203
Quinton 35130
Quintown 35130
Rabb 36401
Rabbittown, *Calhoun* .. 36272
Rabbit Town, *Marshall* 35950
Rabbittown, *Winston* .. 35565
Rabun 36507
Ragland 35131
Raimund 35020
Rainbow (Part of Huntsville) 35758
Rainbow City 35906
Rainbow Mountain Heights 35758
Rainsville 35986
Ralph 35480
Ramer 36069
Ranburne 36273
Randolph 36792
Range 36473
Rash 35772
Rayburn (Part of Guntersville) 35976
Read's Mill 36279
Red Bank 35672
Red Bay 35582
Reddock Springs 36037
Red Hill, Blount 35063
Red Hill, *Elmore* 36078
Red Hill, *Marshall* 35976
Redland Heights (Part of Valley) 36854
Red Level 36474
Redmont Park (Part of Mountain Brook) 35213
Red Ore 35020
Red Rock 35674
Red Rock Junction 35616

Redstone Arsenal 35808-09
For specific ZIP Codes call (888) 275-8777, or your local postmaster.
Redtown 36502
Reece City 35954
Reeds Ferry 35130
Reedtown (Part of Russellville) 35653
Reeltown 36078
Reform 35481
Regency Square (Part of Florence) 35630
Regency (Part of Florence)‡ 35630
Regent Forest 35226
Rehobeth 36301
Rehoboth 36720
Reid 35611
Remlap 35133
Renfroe 35160
Repton 36475
Republic 35214
Reynolds Mill 35014
Rhoades 36453
Rhodesville 35634
Rice 35201
Richmond 36761
Richmond Hills (Part of Tuscumbia) 35674
Richville 35136
Rideout Village (Part of Huntsville) 35806
Riderville 36790
Riderwood 36904
Ridgecrest (Part of Montgomery) 36105
Ridgeville, *Butler* 36030
Ridgeville, *Etowah* 35954
Ringgold 35973
Ripley 35611
Riverbend 35184
Riverdale (Part of Mentone) 35984
River Falls 36476
Rivermont (Part of Sheffield) 35660
Rivermont, *Lauderdale* 35634
River Oaks Center (Part of Decatur) 35603
River Park, *Baldwin* 36532
River Park, *DeKalb* 35984
Riverside, *Blount* 35031
Riverside, *Cullman* 35077
Riverside, *St. Clair* 35135
Riverton 35616
Riverview (Part of Valley)‡ 36854
Riverview, *Escambia* .. 36426
Riverview (Part of Tuscaloosa) 35401
Riverwood (Part of Tuscaloosa) 35406
Roanoke 36274
Roanoke Junction (Part of Opelika) 36801
Roba 36089
Robbins Crossroads .. 35062
Roberta 35040
Roberts 36420
Robertsdale 36567
.... 36574
For specific ZIP Codes call (888) 275-8777, or your local postmaster.
Robinsons 36752
Robinson Springs 36025
Robinsonville 36502
Robinwood 35217
Rock City, *Jackson* 35771
Rock City, *Marion* 35594
Rock Creek, *Escambia* 36483
Rock Creek, *Winston* .. 35553
Rockdale 35020
Rocket 35808
Rockford 35136
Rock Hill 36426
Rockledge 35954
Rock Mills 36274
Rock Run 36272
Rock Spring (Part of Glencoe) 35905

Rock Spring Quarry (Part of Glencoe) 35905
Rock Springs, *Blount* .. 35031
Rock Springs, *Choctaw* 36904
Rock Stand 36274
Rockville 36545
Rockwest 36726
Rockwood 35653
Rocky Head 36311
Rocky Hill 35672
Rocky Hollow 35550
Rocky Ridge (Part of Vestavia Hills) 35243
Rodentown 35957
Roebuck (Part of Birmingham) 35206
Roebuck Crest Estates (Part of Birmingham) 35215
Roebuck Forest (Part of Birmingham) 35235
Roebuck Gardens (Part of Birmingham) 35235
Roebuck Park (Part of Birmingham) 35215
Roebuck Plaza 35235
Roebuck Springs (Part of Birmingham) 35206
Roebuck Terrace (Part of Birmingham) 35206
Roeton 36010
Rogersville 35652
Rolling Hills (Part of Decatur) 35603
Rollins 36022
Romar Beach 36561
Rome 36420
Romulus 35446
Roper 35173
Rosa 35121
Rosalie 35765
Roseboro 37328
Rosebud 36766
Rosedale (Part of Homewood) 35209
Rose Hill, *Covington* 36028
Rose Hill, *Jefferson* 35210
Rosehill, *Walker* 35578
Rosemont (Part of Birmingham) 35221
Rose Park (Part of Florence) 35630
Rosinton 36567
Rossland City 35555
Round Hill 36784
Rowells Crossroad 36879
Roxana 36879
Royal 35031
Ruffner (Part of Irondale) 35210
Russell Heights (Part of Leeds) 35094
Russell Mill (Part of Alexander City) 35010
Russell Village (Part of Decatur) 35603
Russellville 35653-54
For specific ZIP Codes call (888) 275-8777, or your local postmaster.
Rutan 36518
Ruth 35016
Rutherford 36860
Rutledge 36071
Rutledge Heights (Part of Midfield) 35064
Rutledge Heights (Part of Huntsville) 35816
Ryan 35115
Ryan Crossroads 35087
Ryland 35767
Saco 36081
Safford 36773
Saginaw 35137
Sahama Village (Part of Tuscaloosa) 35401
St. Bernard 35055
St. Clair 36752
St. Clair Springs 35146
St. Elmo 36568
St. Florian 35634
Saints Crossroads 35654
St. Stephens 36569

Saks	36201
Salem, *Dallas*	36767
Salem, *Fayette*	35546
Salem, *Lee*	36874
Salem, *Limestone*	35620
Salitpa	36570
Samantha	35482
Samson	36477
Samuels Chapel	35952
Sand Cut	36432
Sandfield	36081
Sandfort	36875
Sandhurst Park (Part of Huntsville)	35802
Sand Rock	35961
Sandtown	35546
Sandusky (Part of Birmingham)	35214
Sandy Creek	36850
Sandy Ridge	36047
Sanford	36420
Sanie	35120
San Souci Beach (Part of Bayou La Batre)	36509
Santuck	36092
Sapps	35447
Saragossa	35578
Saraland	36571
Saratoga (Part of Albertville)	35950
Sardine	36441
Sardis, *Bullock*	36089
Sardis, *Crenshaw*	36041
Sardis, *Dallas*	36775
Sardis, *Walker*	35550
Sardis City	35956
Sardis Springs	35613
Satsuma	36572
Saucer	36030
Saville	36041
Sawyerville	36776
Sayre	35139
Scant City	35016
Scarce Grease	35647
Scenic Heights (Part of Gadsden)	35904
Schmidts Mill	35096
Schuster Springs	36768
Scotland	36471
Scotrock (Part of Alabaster)	35007
Scott City (Part of Leeds)	35094
Scottland	36089
Scottsboro	35768-69
For specific ZIP Codes call (888) 275-8777, or your local postmaster.	
Scranage	36502
Scranton	36313
Screamer	36310
Scyrene	36436
Seaboard	36583
Seacliff (Part of Fairhope)	36532
Seale	36875
Sealy Springs (Part of Cottonwood)	36320
Searight	36028
Searles	35444
Section	35771
Sedgefield	36089
Segco	35580
Selbrook	36108
Selfville	35133
Sellers	36046
Sellersville	36318
Selma	36701-03
For specific ZIP Codes call (888) 275-8777, or your local postmaster.	
Selma Mall (Part of Selma)	36703
Selmont	36703
Seman	36024
Seminole	36567
Semmes	36575
Service	36919
Seven Hills	36601
Seymour Bluff	36542
Shacklesville	36033
Shades Crest Estates	35226
Shady Grove, *Clay*	35072
Shady Grove, *Coffee*	36323
Shady Grove, *Franklin*	35581
Shady Grove, *Jefferson*	35005
Shady Grove, *Pike*	36035
Shady Lane (Part of Huntsville)	35810
Shakespeare (Part of Montgomery)‡	36117
Shanghai	35611
Shannon	35142
Shawmut (Part of Valley)	36854
Shawnee	36726
Sheffield	35660
Shelby	35143
Shelby Shores	35143
Shellhorn	36081
Shepardville	36761
Sherman Heights (Part of Anniston)	36201
Sherwood Forest (Part of Florence)	35630
Sherwood Park (Part of Huntsville)	35206
Shiloh, *DeKalb*	35968
Shiloh, *Marengo*	36754
Shiloh, *Pike*	36005
Shinebone	36266
Shoals Acres	35645
Shopton	36029
Short Creek	35118
Shorter	36075
Shorterville	36373
Shortleaf (Part of Demopolis)	36732
Shottsville	35570
Shreve	36456
Shuster Springs	36768
Sico	35150
Siddonsville	36738
Sidney	35976
Sigma	36319
Sigsbee	35967
Sikesville	36276
Silas	36919
Siloam	36907
Siluria (Part of Alabaster)	35144
Silver Cross	36538
Silverhill	36576
Silver Run	36268
Simcoe	35058
Simmons Crossroads	36850
Simmsville	35043
Sims Chapel	36553
Simsville	36089
Single Spring	35593
Sipsey	35584
Six Mile	35035
Six Way	35603
Skaggs Corner (Part of Ider)	35978
Skeggs Crossroads	35072
Skinem	35750
Skinnerton	36401
Skipperville	36374
Skirum	35963
Skyland (Part of Tuscaloosa)	35407
Skyline	35768
Skyline Acres	35758
Skyline Estates	35226
Sky Ranch (Part of Hoover)	35226
Skyview (Part of Bessemer)	35020
Slackland	35901
Slicklizzard	35578
Slocomb	36375
Smithfield (Part of Birmingham)	35204
Smith Hill	35184
Smith Institute	35956
Smiths	36877
Smiths Crossroads (Part of Glencoe)	35905
Smithson	35020
Smithsonia	35634
Smithtown	36613
Smoke Rise♦	35180
Smut Eye	36061
Smyer	36727
Smyrna	36303
Snead	35952
Snoddy	35462
Snowdoun	36105
Snow Hill, *Dale*	36360
Snow Hill, *Wilcox*	36778
Snowtown	35062
Socapatoy	35089
Society Hill	36804
Soleo	35072
Somerville	35670
South, Covington	36474
South (Part of Montgomery)‡	36116
South Calera (Part of Calera)	35040
South Gadsden (Part of Gadsden)	35904
Southgate Mall (Part of Muscle Shoals)	35660
South Guntersville (Part of Guntersville)	35976
South Haleyville (Part of Haleyville)	35565
South Highland (Part ofBirmingham)‡	35205
South Lowell	35503
Southmont (Part of Montgomery)	36105
South Park Estates (Part of Huntsville)	35802
South Sheffield (Part of Tuscumbia)	35674
Southside	35907
Southtown (Part of Guntersville)	35976
Southwood (Part of Homewood)	35209
Souwilpa	36919
Spanish Fort	36527
Speake	35619
Speed	36026
Speeds Water Mill	35466
Speigener	36022
Spivey's	36535
Sprague	36069
Springbrook (Part of Tuscaloosa)	35405
Spring Creek	35143
Springdale (Part of Tarrant)	35217
Springdale Mall (Part of Mobile)	36606
Springfield, *Clarke*	36784
Springfield, *Lauderdale*	35652
Springfield, *Randolph*	36274
Spring Garden	36275
Spring Hill, *Barbour*	36053
Springhill, *Clay*	36251
Spring Hill, *Conecuh*	36401
Spring Hill, *Escambia*	36426
Spring Hill (Part of Mobile)‡	36608
Spring Hill, *Pike*	36079
Spring Hill, *Walker*	35549
Spring Valley, *Colbert*	35674
Spring Valley (Part of Montgomery)	36116
Springville	35146
Springville Lake Estates	35146
Sprott	36779
Spruce Pine	35585
Stafford	35461
Standard (Part of Parrish)	35580
Standing Rock	36855
Stanley	36420
Stansel	35481
Stanton	36790
Stapleton	36578
Star	35576
Starlington	36033
State Line	36320
Statesville	36703
Steele	35987
Steele Crossing	37328
Steelwood	36551
Steenson Hollow (Part of Muscle Shoals)	35660
Steiner (Part of Montgomery)	36111
Sterrett	35147
Stevenson	35772
Stewart	35441
Stewarts	35125
Stewartsville	35151
Stills Crossroad	36081
Stockdale	36268
Stockton	36579
Stokeley (Part of Andalusia)	36420
Stokes	35456
Stoney Point	36022
Stotesville	35184
Stough	35555
Straight Mountain	35121
Strata	36046
Straughn	36420
Strawberry	35016
Stroud	36855
Studdards Crossroads	35549
Sturdivant Creek	36861
Sturkie	36862
Sugar Creek	35079
Suggsville	36482
Sulligent	35586
Sulphur Springs, *Blount*	35079
Sulphur Springs, *Calhoun*	36271
Sulphur Springs, *Cullman*	35053
Sulphur Springs, *DeKalb*	30738
Sulphur Springs, *Jackson*	35966
Sulphur Springs, *Madison*	35761
Sumiton	35148
Summerdale	36580
Summerfield	36701
Summit	35031
Summit Farm	35022
Sumterville	35460
Sunflower	36581
Sunny Cove	36582
Sunny South	36769
Sunset Cove (Part of Huntsville)	35802
Sunset Mill Village (Part of Selma)	36701
Sunset Shores	36535
Sun Valley	35215
Surginer	36754
Susan Moore	35952
Suspension	36089
Suttle	36701
Swaim	35764
Swancott	35756
Swearengin	35769
Sweet Water	36782
Sycamore	35149
Sylacauga	35150-51
For specific ZIP Codes call (888) 275-8777, or your local postmaster.	
Sylvan Grove	36350
Sylvania	35988
Sylvan Springs	35118
Tabernacle, *Coffee*	36351
Tabernacle (Part of Taylor)	36301
Tabor	35904
Taft	35973
Taits Gap	35121
Talladega	35160-61
For specific ZIP Codes call (888) 275-8777, or your local postmaster.	
Talladega Springs	35151
Tallahatta Springs	36784
Tallapoosa City (Part of Tallassee)	36078
Tallassee	36078
Tallaweka (Part of Tallassee)	36078
Talucah	35775
Tannehill	35111
Tanner	35671
Tanner Crossroads	35671
Tanner Heights (Part of Hartselle)	35640
Tanner Williams	36587
Tanyard, *Bullock*	36061
Tanyard, *St. Clair*	35125
Tarentum	36010
Tarpley (Part of Birmingham)	35211
Tarrant	35217
Tarrant Heights (Part of Tarrant)	35217
Tasso	36767
Tattlersville	36524
Taylor	36301
Taylors Crossroads	36274
Taylorville	35405
Teals Crossroads	36311
Teasleys Mill	36052
Tecumseh	30138
Teddy	36426
Ten Broeck (Part of Lakeview)	35971
Tennala	35960
Tennant	36274
Tennille	36010
Tensaw	36579
Terese (Part of Eufaula)	36027
Terry Heights (Part of Huntsville)	35805
Texasville	36016
Thach	35503
Tharptown	35654
Thatch	35620
The Cedars (Part of Florence)	35630
The Highlands (Part of Gadsden)	35901
The Highlands (Part of Huntsville)	35810
Theodore♦	36582*
	36590†
The Ridge	36460
Thomas, *Autauga*	36067
Thomas (Part of Birmingham)	35214
Thomas Acres (Part of Bessemer)	35020
Thomas Hill (Part of Sylacauga)	35150
Thomaston	36783
Thomasville	36784
Thompson	36089
Thornhill	35565
Thornton	36853
Thorntontown	35652
Thorsby	35171
Three Notch	36053
Threet	35617
Thurston	36340
Tibbie	36583
Tilden	36761
Tiller Crossroads	36850
Tillery Crossroads	36854
Tillmans Corner‡	36619
Tinela	36481
Tishabee	35443
Titus	36080
Toadvine	35020
Toddtown	36451
Tompkinsville	36916
Toney	35773
Toonersville	35652
Toulminville (Part of Mobile)	36610
Town Creek	35672
Towne West (Part of Mobile)‡	36618
Townley	35587
Toxey	36921
Trade	35053
Trafford	35172
Travis Bridge	36401
Tredegar	36265
Trenton	35774
Triana	35756
Trickem	36785
Trimble	35057
Trinity	35673
Trotwood Park (Part of Birmingham)	35206
Troy	36079
	36081
For specific ZIP Codes call (888) 275-8777, or your local postmaster.	
Trussville	35173
Tuckabatchie	36078
Tuckahoe Heights (Part of Gadsden)	35904
Tucker	35594
Tucker Crossroads	35959
Tumbleton	36345

*** Area Zip Code** **† Post Office Boxes** **‡ Postal Station** **♦ Census Designated Place** *Italic Type* **County**

Tunnel Springs	36471
Tupelo	35768
Turkestan	36768
Turkey Branch	36555
Turkeytown	35901
Turner Crossroads	36351
Tuscaloosa	35401-07
	35485-86
For specific ZIP Codes call (888) 275-8777, or your local postmaster.	
Tuscumbia	35674
Tuskegee	36083
Tuskegee Institute	36087†
	36088*
Twilley Town	35130
Twin	35563
Twin Oaks (Part of Montgomery)	36123
Twinsprings	36027
Tyler	36785
Tyler Crossroads	36048
Tyson	36043
Tysonville	36075
Uchee	36858
Underwood, *Lauderdale*	35633
Underwood, *Shelby*	35115
Underwood Crossroads	35646
Union, *Clay*	36258
Union, *Etowah*	35957
Union, *Greene*	35462
Union, *Henry*	36310
Union, *Morgan*	35670
Union, *Tallapoosa*	36853
Union Grove, *Chilton*	35085
Union Grove, *Cullman*	35083
Union Grove, *Jefferson*	35005
Union Grove, *Marshall*	35175
Union Hill, *Cleburne*	36273
Union Hill, *Limestone*	35610
Union Hill, *Morgan*	35754
Union Springs	36089
Uniontown	36786
Unity, *Autauga*	36006
Unity, *Coosa*	35183
Unity, *Tuscaloosa*	35401
Universal Heights	35404
University (Part of Tuscaloosa)‡	35486
University Mall (Part of Tuscaloosa)	35401
University of Montevallo (Part of Montevallo)‡	35115
University of South Alabama (Part of Mobile)‡	36608
Upper Coalburg (Part of Birmingham)	35068
Upper Green Hill	35634
Upshaw	35540
Uriah	36480
Valdosta (Part of Tuscumbia)	35674
Valhermoso Springs	35775
Valley	36854*
	36872†
Valley Creek	35020
Valley Creek Junction	36758
Valley Grande	36703
Valley Head	35989
Valley Junction	35115
Valley View	35640
Vance	35490
Vanderbilt (Part of Birmingham)	35204
Vandiver	35176
Vangale	36782
Vaughn	36579
Vaughn Corners	35757
Verbena	36091
Verlie (Part of Alabaster)	35007
Vernledge	36049
Vernon	35592
Vernontown	35184
Vestavia Hills	35216
Vestavia Hills Centre (Part of Vestavia Hills)	35216
Vesthaven (Part of Vestavia Hills)	35216
Veterans Hospital (Part of Tuscaloosa)	35401
Veto	35620
Vick (Part of Centreville)	35042
Victoria	36323
Vida	36067
Vidette	36049
Vienna	35442
Viewpoint	35974
Vigo	36272
Village Creek (Part of Birmingham)	35207
Village Springs	35126
Villula	36871
Vina	35593
Vincent	35178
Vinegar Bend	36584
Vine Hill	36758
Vineland	36784
Vineland Park (Part of Hueytown)	35020
Vinemont	35179
Vinesville (Part of Birmingham)	35208
Virginia (Part of Hueytown)	35020
Virginia Shores	36660
Vocation	36543
Volanta (Part of Fairhope)	36532
Vredenburgh	36481
Vulcan City (Part of Birmingham)	35207
Waco	35654
Wacoochee Valley	36874
Wadley	36276
Wadsworth	36022
Wagar	36585
Wagarville	36585
Wahouma (Part of Birmingham)	35206
Walco (Part of Sylacauga)	35150
Waldo	35160
Walker Chapel (Part of Fultondale)	35068
Walkers Corner	35055
	35058
For specific ZIP Codes call (888) 275-8777, or your local postmaster.	
Walker Springs	36586
Wallace	36426
Walley	36584
Wallsboro	36092
Wall Street, *Limestone*	35756
Wallstreet, *Tallapoosa*	36078
Walnut Grove	35990
Walnut Hill	36853
Walnut Park (Part of Gadsden)	35904
Walter	35077
Wannville	35752
Ward, *Bibb*	35042
Ward, *Sumter*	36922
Ware	36078
Warrenton	35976
Warrior	35180
Warriorstand	36089
Warsaw	35477
Waterford (Part of Newton)	36352
Waterloo	35677
Water Valley	36908
Watson, *Cherokee*	35973
Watson, *Jefferson*	35181
Watsonville	36753
Watts Crossroads	36266
Wattsville	35182
Waugh	36109
Waverly	36879
Wawbeek	36502
Waxahatchee	35143
Wayne	36782
Wayside	35594
Weatherly Heights (Part of Huntsville)	35802
Weaver	36277
Webb	36376
Webster Chapel	36279
Wedgewood	36108
Wedgworth	36776
Wedowee	36278
Weed	36009
Weeden Heights (Part of Florence)	35630
Weeks	36453
Wegra	35130
Wehadkee	36274
Wellington	36279
Welti	35055
Wende	36860
Wenonah (Part of Birmingham)	35211
Weogufka	35183
Weoka	36092
Wessington	35040
West (Part of Huntsville)‡	35805-08
For specific ZIP Codes call (888) 275-8777, or your local postmaster.	
West Alexandria	36250
West Bend	36524
West Blocton	35184
West End, Calhoun	36201
West End (Part of Birmingham)‡	35211
West End (Part of Montgomery)	36104
West Ensley (Part of Birmingham)	35224
Western Hills (Part of Mobile)	36618
Western Hills Estates	35749
Western Hills Mall (Part of Fairfield)	35064
West Greene	35491
West Highlands (Part of Hueytown)	35023
West Huntsville (Part of Huntsville)	35807
West Jefferson	35130
West Lake Highlands (Part of Bessemer)	35020
Westlake Mall (Part of Bessemer)	35020
Westlawn (Part of Huntsville)	35807
West Monroeville (Part of Monroeville)	36460
Weston (Part of Hamilton)	35570
Westover	35185
West Point	35057
West Pratt (Part of Dora)	35062
West Sayre	35062
West Selmont	36703
West Side (Part of Bessemer)	35020
West Side (Part of Montgomery)‡	36108
West Wellington	36279
Westwood	35005
Wetumpka	36092-93
For specific ZIP Codes call (888) 275-8777, or your local postmaster.	
Whatley	36482
Wheat	35053
Wheeler	35618
Wheelerville (Part of Mobile)	36608
Whistler (Part of Prichard)	36612
White City, *Autauga*	36051
White City, *Cullman*	35077
White Hall	36040
Whitehead	35652
Whitehouse	35565
Whitehouse Forks	36507
Whiteoak, *Colbert*	35646
White Oak, *Henry*	36310
Whiteoak (Part of Albertville)	35950
White Plains, *Calhoun*	36207
White Plains, *Chambers*	36862
Whites Bluff	36767
Whitesboro	35956
Whitesburg (Part of Huntsville)‡	35802
Whites Chapel (Part of Moody)	35173
Whites Gap	36265
Whitesville	35957
Whitfield	36925
Whitney (Part of Ashville)	35953
Whiton	35962
Whorton	35960
Wicksburg	36352
Wiggins (Part of Babbie)	36420
Wigginsville	35611
Wiginton	35564
Wiley (Part of Montgomery)	36105
Wiley, *Tuscaloosa*	35501
Wilkes (Part of Midfield)	35064
Wilkinstown	36346
Williams, *Calhoun*	36265
Williams, *Houston*	36319
Williamsburg	35005
Williamstown	35580
Willowbrook (Part of Huntsville)	35802
Willow Point Country Club	35010
Willow Springs	36093
Wills Crossroads	36310
Wills Valley	35967-68
For specific ZIP Codes call (888) 275-8777, or your local postmaster.	
Wilmer	36587
Wilson Bend	35541
Wilson Lake Shores	35660
Wilson Quarters	36303
Wilsonville	35186
Wilton	35187
Wimberly	36921
Winburn	35176
Wind Creek Farms	35010
Windham Springs	35546
Windsor Highlands (Part of Homewood)	35209
Winfield	35594
Wing	36483
Wingard	36035
Wininger	35776
Winn	36545
Winslow	36003
Winterboro	35014
Winton	35670
Wolf Creek	35128
Wolf Springs	35672
Womack Hill	36908
Woodaire Estates	35215
Woodbluff	36727
Wooddale (Part of Pelham)	35124
Woodland, *Macon*	36866
Woodland, *Randolph*	36280
Woodland Forest (Part of Tuscaloosa)	35405
Woodland Lake	35111
Woodlawn (Part of Birmingham)‡	35212
Woodlawn Heights (Part of Russellville)	35653
Woodlawn Heights (Part of Birmingham)	35212
Woodley Park (Part of Montgomery)	36116
Woodmeadow (Part of Hoover)	35226
Woodmont (Part of Hueytown)	35020
Woodstock (North Bibb)	35188
Woodstock Junction	35188
Woodville	35776
Woodward	35020
Wooltolk	36268
Wren	35650
Wright	35677
Wright Crossroads	36830
Wyatt	35130
Wylam (Part of Birmingham)‡	35224
Wynn Drive (Part of Huntsville)‡	35816
Wynnville	35952
Yantley	36912
Yarbo	36558
Yelling Settlement	36526
Yellow Bluff	36769
Yellow Creek Falls	35959
Yellow Pine	36539
Yerkwood	35130
York	36925
Youngblood	36079
Yucca	35966
Yupon	36555
Zimco	36451
Zion, *Montgomery*	36047
Zion, *Pickens*	35466
Zion City (Part of Birmingham)	35207
Zion Heights (Part of Birmingham)	35207
Zip City	35634
Zoar	36323

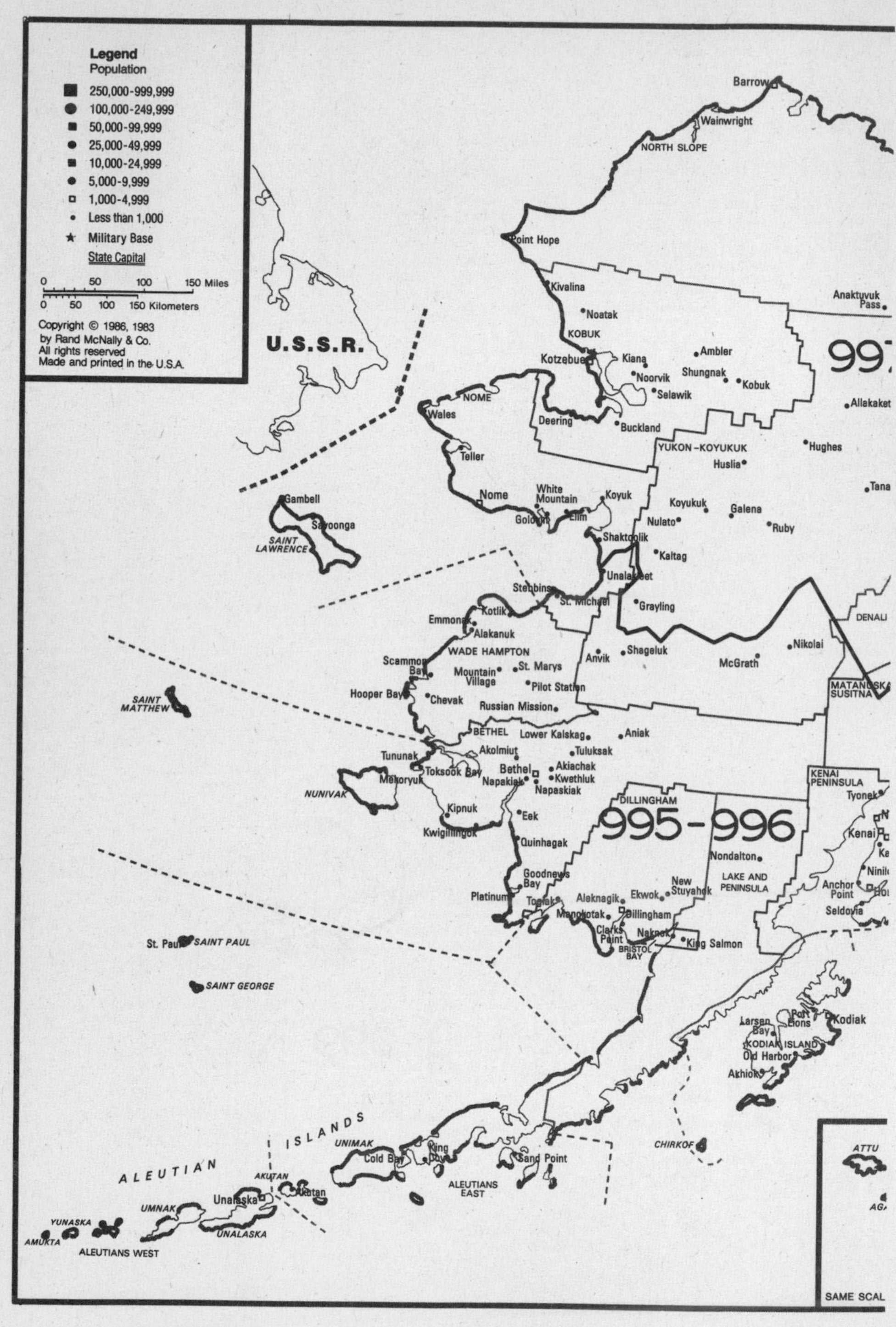

Legend
Population
250,000-999,999
100,000-249,999
50,000-99,999
25,000-49,999
10,000-24,999
5,000-9,999
1,000-4,999
Less than 1,000
Military Base
State Capital
0 50 100 150 Miles
0 50 100 150 Kilometers
Copyright © 1986, 1983 by Rand McNally & Co. All rights reserved Made and printed in the U.S.A.
U.S.S.R.
Barrow
Wainwright
NORTH SLOPE
Point Hope
Kivalina
Noatak
KOBUK
Anaktuvuk Pass
Kotzebue
Kiana
Ambler
Shungnak
Kobuk
Noorvik
Selawik
Allakaket
NOME
Wales
Deering
Buckland
YUKON-KOYUKUK
Hughes
Huslia
Teller
Tana
Nome
White Mountain
Koyuk
Golovin
Elim
Koyukuk
Galena
Nulato
Ruby
Gambell
Savoonga
SAINT LAWRENCE
Shaktoolik
Kaltag
Unalakleet
Stebbins
St. Michael
Grayling
DENALI
Kotlik
Emmonak
Alakanuk
Nikolai
WADE HAMPTON
Anvik
Shageluk
Scammon Bay
Mountain Village
St. Marys
McGrath
Hooper Bay
Pilot Station
MATANUSKA SUSITNA
SAINT MATTHEW
Chevak
Russian Mission
BETHEL
Lower Kalskag
Aniak
Akolmiut
Tuluksak
Tununak
Akiachak
Bethel
Kwethluk
Toksook Bay
Mekoryuk
Napakiak
Napaskiak
KENAI PENINSULA
NUNIVAK
DILLINGHAM
Tyonek
Kipnuk
Eek
995-996
Kwigillingok
Kenai
Quinhagak
Nondalton
Goodnews Bay
New Stuyahok
LAKE AND PENINSULA
Platinum
Togiak
Aleknagik
Ekwok
Anchor Point
Manokotak
Dillingham
Seldovia
Clarks Point
Naknek
King Salmon
BRISTOL BAY
St. Paul
SAINT PAUL
SAINT GEORGE
Larsen Bay
Port Lions
Kodiak
KODIAK ISLAND
Old Harbor
Akhiok
ALEUTIAN ISLANDS
UNIMAK
King Cove
Cold Bay
Sand Point
CHIRKOF
ATTU
AKUTAN
Akutan
ALEUTIANS EAST
Unalaska
UMNAK
YUNASKA
AMUKTA
UNALASKA
ALEUTIANS WEST
SAME SCAL

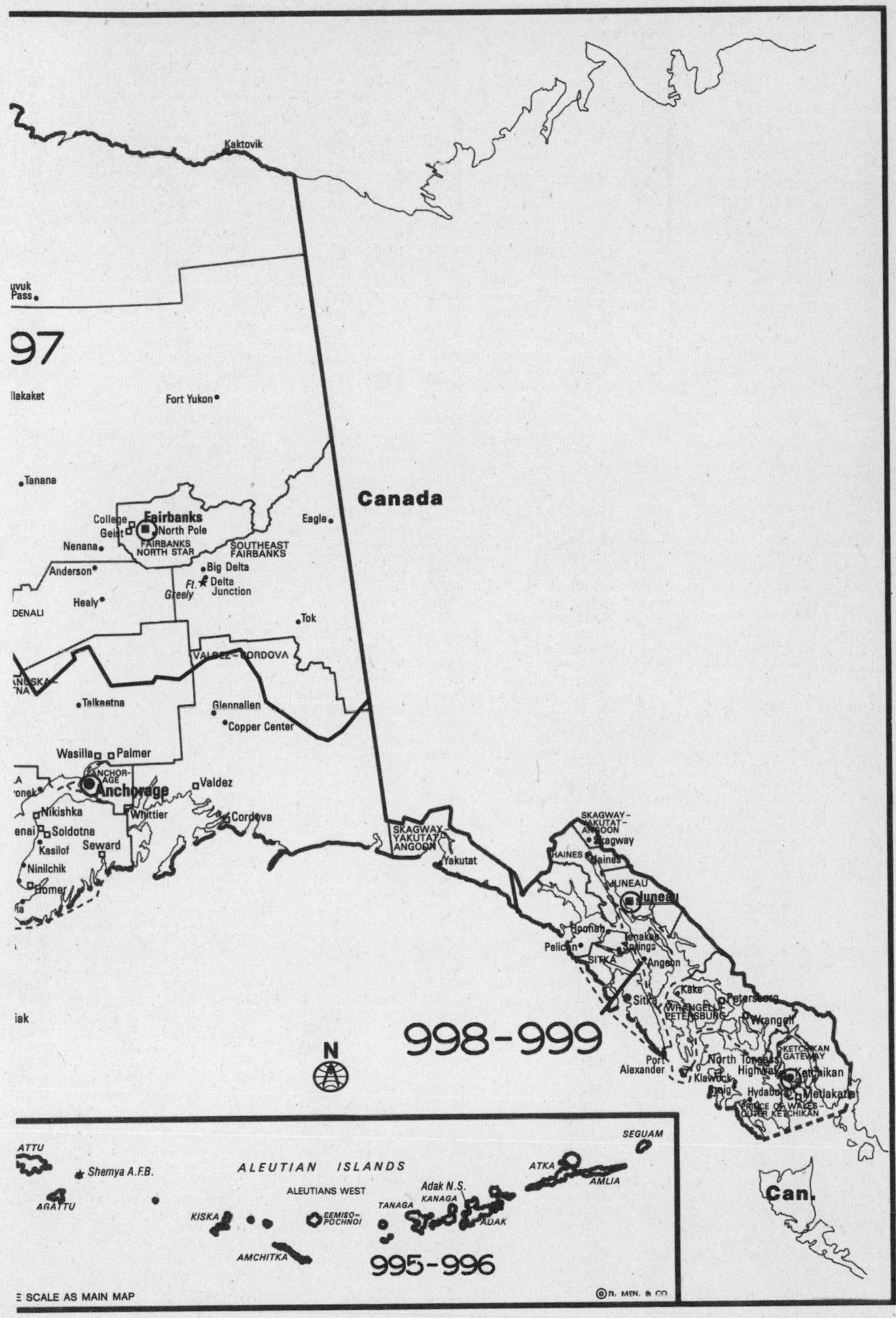

Kaktovik
Pass
97
Fort Yukon
Tanana
Canada
College
Fairbanks
North Pole
FAIRBANKS NORTH STAR
Eagle
Nenana
SOUTHEAST FAIRBANKS
Anderson
Big Delta
Ft. Greely
Delta Junction
Healy
DENALI
Tok
VALDEZ-CORDOVA
Talkeetna
Glennallen
Copper Center
Wasilla
Palmer
Anchorage
Valdez
Nikishka
Whittier
Cordova
Soldotna
Kasilof
Seward
Ninilchik
Homer
SKAGWAY-YAKUTAT-ANGOON
Yakutat
Skagway
HAINES
Haines
JUNEAU
Juneau
Hoonah
Pelican
Tenakee Springs
SITKA
Angoon
Kake
Sitka
Petersburg
WRANGELL-PETERSBURG
Wrangell
998-999
Port Alexander
North Tongass Highway
KETCHIKAN GATEWAY
Ketchikan
Klawock
Craig
Hydaburg
Metlakatla
PRINCE OF WALES-OUTER KETCHIKAN
N
SEGUAM
ATTU
Shemya A.F.B.
ALEUTIAN ISLANDS
ATKA
AMLIA
ALEUTIANS WEST
Adak N.S.
KANAGA
AGATTU
TANAGA
KISKA
SEMISOPOCHNOI
ADAK
Can.
AMCHITKA
995-996
SCALE AS MAIN MAP
©R. MCN. & CO

Adak	99546
Adak Station♦	99546
Akhiok	99615
Akiachak	99551
Akiak	99552
Akutan	99553
Alakanuk	99554
Alatna (Part of Allakaket)	99720
Aleknagik	99555
Alexander	99695
Alitak	99697
Allakaket	99720
Ambler	99786
Amchitka♦	99501
Amook	99697
Anaktuvuk Pass	99721
Anchorage	99501-04
	99507-24
	99599
For specific ZIP Codes call (888) 275-8777, or your local postmaster.	
Anchorage 5th Avenue Shopping Center (Part of Anchorage)	99501
Anchor Point♦	99556
Anderson	99744
Angoon	99820
Aniak	99557
Annette♦	99926
Anvik	99558
Arctic Village♦	99722
Atka	99547
Atmautluak	99559
Atqasuk	99791
Attu	99502
Auke Bay (Part of Juneau)	99821
Aurora (Part of Fairbanks)	99701
Aurora Lodge	99701
Baranof (Part of Sitka)	99835
Barrow	99723
Bartlett Cove	99826
Beaver♦	99724
Bell Island Hot Springs	99901
Beluga	99695
Bethel	99559
Bettles Field	99726
Big Delta♦	99737
Big Horn	99701
Big Lake♦	99652
Birch Creek♦	99740
Birch Estates	99701
Birchwood (Part of Anchorage)	99567
Bird (Part of Anchorage)	99540
Bjerremark (Part of Fairbanks)	99701
Black Sand	99689
Bluff	99762
Border	99780
Boswell Bay	99574
Boundary	99780
Brevig Mission	99785
Broadmoor Acres	99701
Brooks Lodge	99613
Browerville (Part of Barrow)	99723
Buckland	99727
Butte♦	99645
Campbell (Part of Anchorage)	99517
Candle	99752
Cantwell♦	99729
Cape Lisburne	99766
Cape Newenham	99576
Cape Newenham Air Force Station	99576
Cape Pole	99901
Cape Romanzof Air Force Station	99559
Cape Yakataga	99695
Carlanna (Part of Ketchikan)	99901
Central♦	99730
Chalkyitsik♦	99788
Chandalar	99701
Charcoal Point (Part of Ketchikan)	99901
Chase♦	99676
Chatanika	99712
Chatham (Part of Sitka)	99803
Chefornak	99561
Chena Hot Springs	99701
Chenega♦	99693
Chernofski	99685
Chevak	99563
Chickaloon	99674
Chicken	99732
Chignik	99564
Chignik Lagoon♦	99565
Chignik Lake♦	99548
Chisana	99780
Chistochina♦	99586
Chitina♦	99566
Chuathbaluk	99557
Chugiak (Part of Anchorage)	99567
Circle♦	99733
Circle Hot Springs Station♦	99730
Clam Gulch♦	99568
Clark's Point	99569
Clear	99704
Clearwater Ranch	99737
Clover Pass	99901
Coffman Cove	99918
Cohoe	99610
Cold Bay	99571
Coldfoot	99701
College	99708
College Village (Part of Anchorage)	99504
Collegiate Park	99701
Colorado	99695
Cooper Landing♦	99572
Copper Center♦	99573
Cordova	99574
Cosna	99756
Cottonwood	99654
Council	99762
Craig	99921
Crooked Creek♦	99575
Crown Point♦	99631
Cube Cove	99850
Deadhorse♦	99734
Debarr Shopping Center (Part of Anchorage)	99504
Deering	99736
Delta Junction	99737
Denali National Park♦	99755
Derby Tract (Part of Fairbanks)	99701
Dillingham	99576
Dimond Center (Part of Anchorage)	99515
Dora Bay♦	99901
Dot Lake♦	99737
Douglas (Part of Juneau)	99824
Downtown (Part of Anchorage)‡	99501*
	99510†
Downtown (Part of Fairbanks)‡	99707
Driftwood Bay	99695
Duncan Canal	99833
Dutch Harbor	99692
Eagle	99738
Eagle River (Part of Anchorage)	99577
Eagle Village♦	99738
Eastchester (Part of Anchorage)‡	99520
Edna Bay	99901
Eek	99578
Egegik♦	99579
Eielson Air Force Base	99702
Eklutna (Part of Anchorage)	99567
Eklutna Housing Project (Part of Anchorage)	99645
Ekuk	99695
Ekwok	99580
Elfin Cove♦	99825
Elim	99739
Ellamar	99695
Emmonak	99581
English Bay♦	99603
Eska	99674
Ester♦	99725
Eureka (Matanuska-Susitna Borough)	99645
Eureka (Yukon-Koyukuk Census Division)	99756
Evansville♦	99726
Excursion Inlet	99850
Eyak♦	99574
Fairbanks	99701
	99706-12
	99775
For specific ZIP Codes call (888) 275-8777, or your local postmaster.	
False Pass	99583
Farewell	99627
Ferry♦	99743
Fire Lake (Part of Anchorage)	99577
Fishhook Junction	99645
Flat	99584
Fort Greely	96508
Fort Wainwright	99703
Fortymile Roadhouse	99737
Fort Yukon	99740
Four Corners	99645
Fox♦	99701
Freshwater Bay (Part of Sitka)	99803
Fritz Cove (Part of Juneau)	99801
Fritz Creek♦	99603
Funter Bay	99850
Gakona♦	99586
Galena	99741
Gambell	99742
Ganes Creek	99675
Girdwood (Part of Anchorage)	99587
Glennallen♦	99588
Gold Creek	99695
Golovin	99762
Goodnews Bay	99589
Goodnews Mining Camp	99651
Graehl (Part of Fairbanks)	99701
Granite Mountain	99762
Grayling	99590
Gulkana	99695
Gustavus♦	99826
Haines	99827
Halibut Cove♦	99603
Hamilton Acres (Part of Fairbanks)	99701
Happy Valley	99556
Hawk Inlet	99850
Haycock	99753
Healy♦	99743
Healy Lake♦	99737
Herring Cove	99901
Hobart Bay	99850
Hogatza	99701
Hollis	99901
Holy Cross	99602
Homer	99603
Hoonah	99829
Hooper Bay	99604
Hope♦	99605
Houston	99694
Huffman (Part of Anchorage)‡	99511
Hughes	99745
Huslia	99746
Hydaburg	99922
Hyder♦	99923
Icy Bay	99695
Igiugig♦	99613
Iliamna♦	99606
Indian (Part of Anchorage)	99540
Indian River	99720
Island Homes (Part of Fairbanks)	99701
Ivanof Bay♦	99695
Jakolof Bay♦	99695
Jennie M.	99701
Johnston (Part of Fairbanks)	99701
Juneau	99801-11
For specific ZIP Codes call (888) 275-8777, or your local postmaster.	
Kachemak	99603
Kake	99830
Kako	99657
Kaktovik	99747
Kalifonsky♦	99610
Kalskag	99607
Kaltag	99748
Kanakanak	99576
Kantishna	99755
Karluk♦	99608
Kasaan	99901
Kashegelok	99668
Kasigluk	99609
Kasilof♦	99610
Kasitsna Bay	99695
Kenai	99611
Kenai Lake	99572
Kenai Packers Cannery (Part of Kenai)	99611
Kennicott	99588
Kenny Cove	99695
Ketchikan	99901
Kiana	99749
King Cove	99612
King Salmon♦	99613
Kipnuk♦	99614
Kitoi Bay	99697
Kivalina	99750
Klawock	99925
Klukwan♦	99827
Knik	99654
Knudson Cove	99901
Kobuk	99751
Kodiak	99615-19
For specific ZIP Codes call (888) 275-8777, or your local postmaster.	
Kokhanok♦	99606
Kokrines	99768
Koliganek♦	99576
Kongiganak♦	99559
Kotlik	99620
Kotzebue	99752
Koyuk	99753
Koyukuk	99754
Kupreanof	99833
Kustatan	99682
Kwethluk	99621
Kwigillingok♦	99622
Lake Minchumina♦	99757
Lake Otis (Part of Anchorage)‡	99511
Lakloey Hill	99701
Larsen Bay	99624
Lawing	99664
Lemeta (Part of Fairbanks)	99701
Lemon Creek (Part of Juneau)	99801
Lena Cove (Part of Juneau)	99801
Levelock♦	99625
Liberty	99738
Lignite♦	99743
Lime Village♦	99627
Little Diomede	99762
Little Port Walter	99835
Livengood	99701
Long	99768
Long Island	99654
Lost River (Nome Census Division)	99762
Lost River (Yakutat Borough)	99689
Lower Kalskag	99626
Lower Mendenhall Valley (Part of Juneau)	99801
McCarthy♦	99695
McGrath	99627
Mack	99701
McKinley Acres	99701
Main Office (Part of Anchorage)‡	99519
Manley Hot Springs♦	99756
Manokotak	99628
Mansfield Village	99760
Marshall	99585
Marvel Creek	99557
Mary's Igloo	99778
Matanuska	99645
May Creek	99695
Meade River	99791
Medfra	99627
Meekins Roadhouse	99645
Meier	99737
Mekoryuk	99630
Mendeltna Lodge	99645
Mendenhall (Part of Juneau)‡	99803
Mendenhall Flats (Part of Juneau)	99801
Mentasta Lake♦	99780
Metlakatla♦	99926
Meyers Chuck♦	99903
Midtown (Part of Anchorage)‡	99503
Minto♦	99758
Montana	99688
Moose Creek♦	99701
Moose Pass♦	99631
Moser Bay	99697
Mountain Point	99901
Mountain View (Part of Anchorage)‡	99508
Mountain Village	99632
Mount Edgecumbe (Part of Sitka)	99835
Mud Bay	99901
Muldoon (Part of Anchorage)‡	99504
Nabesna	99586
Naknek♦	99633
Nancy	99688
Napaimute	99557
Napakiak	99634
Napaskiak	99559
Nelson Lagoon♦	99571
Nenana	99760
Nenana Native Village (Part of Nenana)	99760
Newhalen	99606
New Stuyahok	99636
Newtok	99559
Nightmute	99690
Nikiski♦	99635
Nikolai	99691
Nikolski♦	99638
Ninilchik♦	99639
Noatak♦	99761
Nome	99762
Nondalton	99640
Noorvik	99763
North Douglas (Part of Juneau)	99801
North Pole	99705
Northway♦	99764
Northway Junction♦	99764
Northway Village♦	99764
Nuiqsut	99789
Nulato	99765
Nunaka Valley (Part of Anchorage)	99504
Nunapitchuk	99641
Nyac	99557
Okagamute	99607
Old Andreafski	99658
Old Harbor	99643
Olnes	99701
Olsonville	99576
Oscarville♦	99559
Ouzinkie	99644
Palmer	99645
Paradise Hill	99602
Parks	99697
Paxson♦	99737
Pederson Point	99633
Pedro Bay♦	99647
Pelican	99832
Peninsula Point	99901
Pennock Island	99901
Perryville♦	99648
Petersburg	99833
Peters Creek (Part of Anchorage)	99567
Pilot Point	99649
Pilot Station	99650
Pitkas Point♦	99658
Pittman	99654
Platinum	99651
Pleasant Valley♦	99701
Point Baker♦	99927
Point Barrow DEW Station	99723
Point Higgins	99901
Point Hope	99766
Point Lay♦	99759
Point Whiteshed	99574
Poorman	99768
Portage (Part of Anchorage)	99587

Portage Creek	99695
Port Alexander	99836
Port Alice♦	99901
Port Alsworth♦	99653
Port Armstrong	99836
Port Ashton	99695
Port Bailey	99697
Port Clarence♦	99790
Port Graham♦	99603
Port Heiden	99549
Port Lions	99550
Portlock	99663
Port Moller	99571
Port Protection	99901
Port Walter	99835
Port Williams	99697
Potter (Part of Anchorage)	99501
Primrose♦	99631
Prudhoe Bay♦	99734
Quartz Creek	99572
Queen	99576
Quinhagak	99655
Rainbow (Part of Anchorage)	99501
Rampart♦	99767
Red Devil♦	99656
Red Mountain	99603
Red Salmon	99633
Rego	99701
Rodman (Part of Sitka)	99835
Rogers Park (Part of Anchorage)	99508
Rowan Bay	99835
Ruby	99768
Russian Jack (Part of Anchorage)‡	99514
Russian Mission	99657
St. George Island	99591
St. Mary's	99658
St. Marys Mission (Part of St. Mary's)	99658
St. Michael	99659
St. Paul Island	99660
Salamatof♦	99611
Salcha♦	99714
Salmon Creek (Part of Juneau)	99801
Sand Lake (Part of Anchorage)‡	99522
Sand Point	99661
Savoonga	99769
Saxman	99901
Saxman East (Part of Saxman)	99901
Scammon Bay	99662
Scow Bay	99833
Seal Bay	99697
Selawik	99770
Seldovia	99663
Seward	99664
Shageluk	99665
Shaktoolik	99771
Shanley (Part of Fairbanks)	99701
Sheldon Point	99666
Shemya Air Force Base	99501
Shemya Station	99501
Shishmaref	99772
Shungnak	99773
Sitka	99835
Situk	99689
Skagway	99840
Skwentna♦	99667
Slana♦	99586
Slaterville (Part of Fairbanks)	99701
Sleetmute♦	99668
Snowball	99701
Snug Harbor	99572
Soldotna	99669
Solomon	99790
Sourdough	99586
South (Part of Anchorage)	99511
South Bjerremark	99701
South Naknek♦	99670
Spenard (Part of Anchorage)‡	99509
Sprucewood	99701
Squaw Harbor	99661
Starr Hill (Part of Juneau)	99801
Stebbins	99671
Steele Creek	99738
Steese	99710
Sterling♦	99672
Stevens Village♦	99774
Stony River♦	99557
Strelna	99566
Summit	99729
Summit Lodge	99586
Sunnyside	99832
Sunshine	99695
Suntrana	99743
Sutton♦	99674
Takotna♦	99675
Talkeetna♦	99676
Tanacross♦	99776
Tanana	99777
Tatalina	99627
Tatitlek♦	99677
Taylor	99762
Tee Harbor (Part of Juneau)	99801
Telida	99695
Teller	99778
Tenakee Springs	99841
Terror Bay	99697
Tetlin♦	99779
Tetlin Junction	99779
Thane (Part of Juneau)	99801
Thorne Bay	99919
Tiekel	99686
Tin City	99783
Togiak	99678
Tok♦	99780
Tokeen	99901
Toksook Bay	99637
Tonsina♦	99573
Totem Bight	99901
Totem Park	99701
Trapper Creek	99683
Tuluksak	99679
Tuntutuliak♦	99680
Tununak	99681
Turnagain (Part of Anchorage)	99517
Turnagain by-the-Sea (Part of Anchorage)	99517
Turnagain Heights (Part of Anchorage)	99517
Twin Hills♦	99576
Two Rivers♦	99716
Tyonek♦	99682
Uganik	99697
Ugashik	99613
Umiat	99701
Unalakleet	99684
Unalaska	99685
Ungalik	99684
University Center (Part of Anchorage)	99503
University Park	99701
Upper Mendenhall Valley (Part of Juneau)	99801
Upper Nickeyville (Part of Ketchikan)	99901
U.S. Coast Guard Station	99619
Usibelli	99743
Valdez	99686
Vank Island	99929
Venetie♦	99781
View Cove	99901
Wainwright	99782
Wales	99783
Ward Cove	99928
Wasilla	99654*
	99687†
Waterfall	99901
West Fairwest	99701
Westgate (Part of Fairbanks)	99701
West Juneau (Part of Juneau)	99801
West Point	99697
Westwood	99701
Whale Pass	99901
White Mountain	99784
Whites Crossing	99688
Whitney (Part of Anchorage)	99501
Whittier	99693
Wilcox	99701
Wilcox Estates	99701
Wild Lake	99726
Willow♦	99688
Wiseman	99790
Woodland Park (Part of Anchorage)	99517
Wood River	99576
Wrangell	99929
Yakutat	99689
Yankee Creek	99675
Zachar Bay	99697

* **Area Zip Code** † **Post Office Boxes** ‡ **Postal Station** ♦ **Census Designated Place**

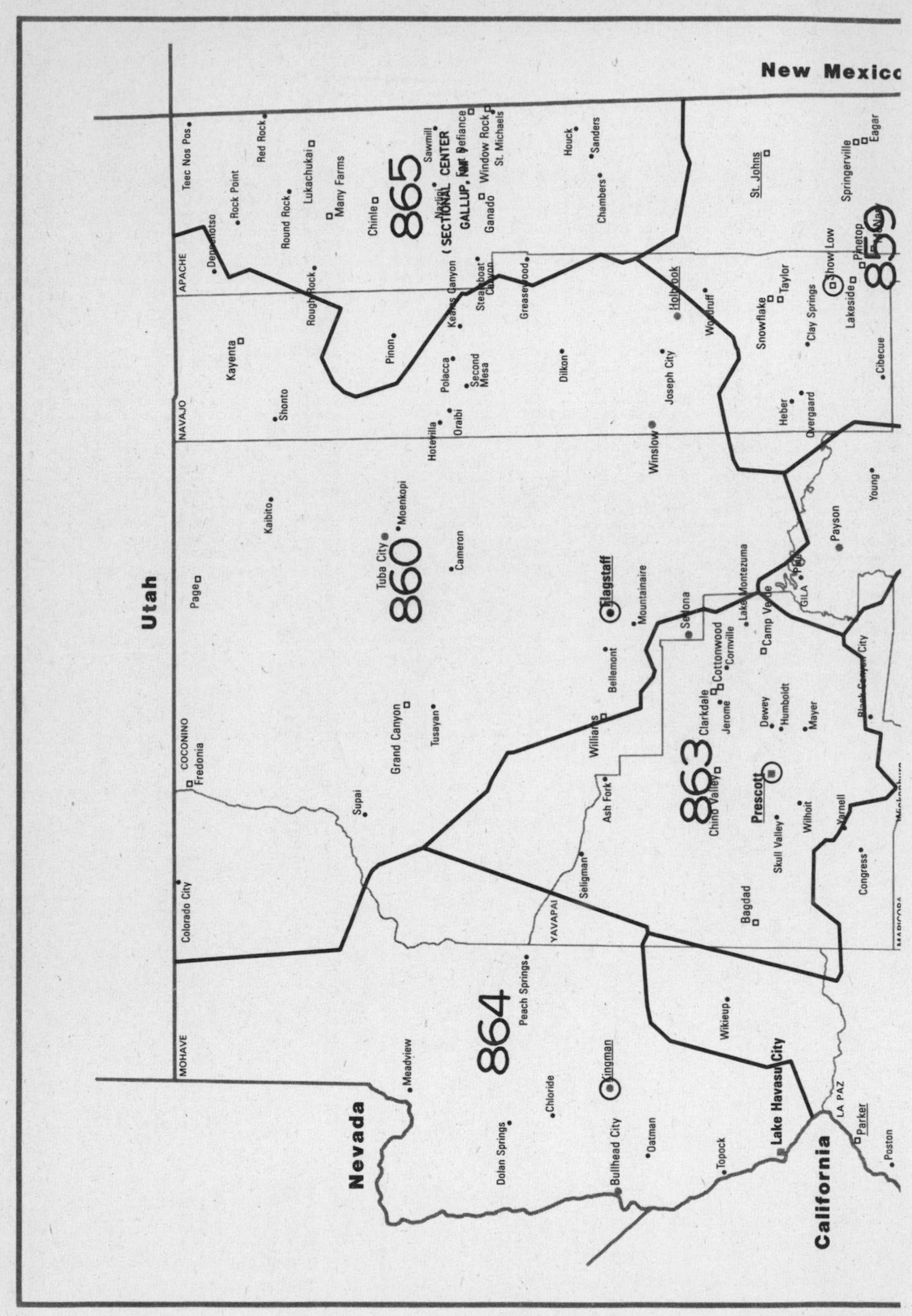

Utah
New Mexico
Nevada
California
APACHE
NAVAJO
COCONINO
MOHAVE
YAVAPAI
GILA
LA PAZ
865
860
863
864
859
(SECTIONAL CENTER
GALLUP, NM)
Teec Nos Pos
Red Rock
Rock Point
Lukachukai
Round Rock
Many Farms
Dennehotso
Chinle
Sawmill
Fort Defiance
Window Rock
St. Michaels
Nazlini
Ganado
Houck
Sanders
Chambers
St. Johns
Springerville
Eagar
Kayenta
Rough Rock
Pinon
Keams Canyon
Steamboat Canyon
Greasewood
Polacca
Second Mesa
Shonto
Hotevilla
Oraibi
Dilkon
Holbrook
Woodruff
Joseph City
Winslow
Snowflake
Taylor
Show Low
Clay Springs
Lakeside
Pinetop
Cibecue
Heber
Overgaard
Young
Kaibito
Tuba City
Moenkopi
Cameron
Page
Flagstaff
Mountainaire
Sedona
Lake Montezuma
Camp Verde
Payson
Cottonwood
Cornville
Clarkdale
Jerome
Bellemont
Dewey
Humboldt
Mayer
Black Canyon City
Williams
Grand Canyon
Tusayan
Fredonia
Supai
Chino Valley
Prescott
Ash Fork
Wilhoit
Yarnell
Skull Valley
Seligman
Congress
Bagdad
Colorado City
Peach Springs
Wikieup
Meadview
Kingman
Lake Havasu City
Chloride
Dolan Springs
Bullhead City
Oatman
Topock
Parker
Poston

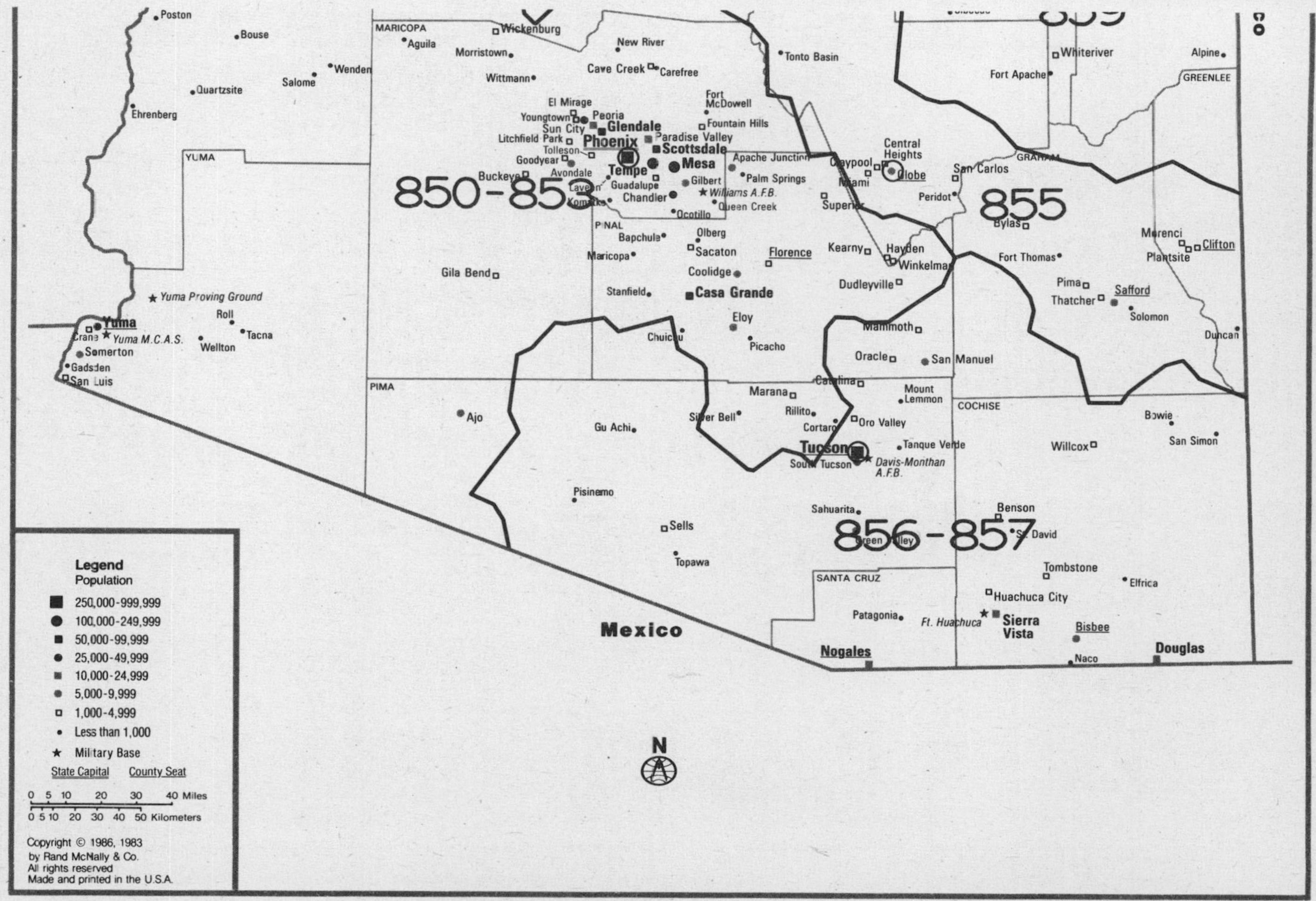
850-853
855
856-857
MARICOPA
YUMA
PIMA
PINAL
GREENLEE
GRAHAM
COCHISE
SANTA CRUZ
Mexico
N
Phoenix
Glendale
Scottsdale
Mesa
Tempe
Chandler
Tucson
South Tucson
Yuma
Casa Grande
Florence
Globe
Safford
Clifton
Bisbee
Nogales
Douglas
Sierra Vista
Legend
Population
250,000-999,999
100,000-249,999
50,000-99,999
25,000-49,999
10,000-24,999
5,000-9,999
1,000-4,999
Less than 1,000
Military Base
State Capital
County Seat
0 5 10 20 30 40 Miles
0 5 10 20 30 40 50 Kilometers
Copyright © 1986, 1983
by Rand McNally & Co.
All rights reserved
Made and printed in the U.S.A.

Acres Foothills	85614
Adamana	86025
Adamsville	85232
Agua Caliente	85333
Agua Linda	85640
Aguila	85320
Ahwatukee‡	85044-45
	85048
	85076
For specific ZIP Codes call (888) 275-8777, or your local postmaster.	
Airpark (Part of Scottsdale)‡	85260
Ajo♦	85321
Akchin	85634
Ak-Chin Village♦	85239
Alamo Crossing	85357
Alchesay Flat	85941
Ali Chuk	85634
Ali Molina	85634
Allentown	86506
Alpine	85920
Amado	85645
Ames Acres	86047
Andersen Springs (Part of Chandler)‡	85224
Anegam	85634
Apache	88056
Apache Grove	85534
Apache Ho (Part of Apache Junction)	85220
Apache Junction	85217-20
	85278
For specific ZIP Codes call (888) 275-8777, or your local postmaster.	
Apache Wells (Part of Mesa)	85215
Araby	85364
Aravaipa	85292
Aravaipa Canyon	85292
Arcadia (Part of Phoenix)‡	85018
	85060
For specific ZIP Codes call (888) 275-8777, or your local postmaster.	
Arcosanti	86333
Arivaca	85601
Arizola	85222
Arizona City♦	85223
Arizona Shores	85344
Arlington	85322
Arrowhead (Part of Glendale)‡	85318
Arrowhead Town Center (Part of Glendale)‡	85308
Artesa	85634
Artesia	85546
Ash Fork	86320
Avondale	85323
Aztec	85333
Baby Rock	86033
Bacobi	86030
Bagdad♦	86321
Bakerville (Part of Bisbee)	85603
Bald Mesa (Unit 1)	86024
Bald Mesa (Unit 2)	86024
Bapchule	85221
Beardsley	85373
Beautys Estates (Part of Nogales)	85621
Beaver Dam	86432
Beaver Valley Estates	85541
Bella Vista Estates (Part of Sierra Vista)	85635
Bellemont	86015
Benson	85602
Beyerleville	85621
Biltmore Fashion Park (Part of Phoenix)	85016
Bisbee	85603
Bisbee Junction	85603
Bitahochee	86031
Bitter Springs	86036
Black Canyon City	85324
Black Hills (Part of Clarkdale)	86324
Blackwater♦	85228
Blue	85922
Blue Gap	86520
Blue Ridge	86024
Bonita	85643
Bonita Creek	85541
Bouse	85325
Bowie	85605
Boys Ranch (Part of Queen Creek)	85242
Braemer (Part of Peoria)	85345
Branding Iron	85701
Brenda	85348
Bridge Canyon Country Estates	86337
Bridgeport	86326
Briggs Townsite (Part of Bisbee)	85603
Bryce	85543
Buckeye	85326
Buckhorn	85205
Buena Vista	85546
Bullhead City	86429-30
	86439
	86442
For specific ZIP Codes call (888) 275-8777, or your local postmaster.	
Bumble Bee	86333
Burnt Water	86512
Bushman Acres	86047
Bylas♦	85530
Cactus (Part of Phoenix)‡	85032
	85046
	85078
For specific ZIP Codes call (888) 275-8777, or your local postmaster.	
Cactus Flat	85546
Cactus Forest	85232
Calva	85530
Cameron♦	86020
Camp Creek	85331
Camp Verde	86322
Camp Verde Indian Reservation	86322
Cane Beds	86022
Canelo	85611
Canoa Estates	85614
Canyon (Part of Mesa)‡	85201
Canyon Day♦	85941
Canyon Sights	86301
Capitol (Part of Phoenix)‡	85005
	85009
For specific ZIP Codes call (888) 275-8777, or your local postmaster.	
Carefree	85377
Carmen	85640
Carrizo	85901
Casa Adobes (Part of Tucson)‡	85737
	85739-40
For specific ZIP Codes call (888) 275-8777, or your local postmaster.	
Casa Blanca	85221
Casa Grande	85222*
	85230†
Casa Paloma I	85614
Casa Paloma II	85614
Casas Adobes	85704
Cascabel	85602
Cashion (Part of Avondale)	85329
Castle Canyon Mesa	86301
Castle Hot Springs	85342
Castle Rock Shores	85344
Catalina♦	85738
Catalina Foothills	85718
Cave Creek	85327†
	85331*
Cedar Creek	85941
Cedar Ridge	86020
Centerville (Part of Clarkdale)	86324
Central	85531
Central Heights	85501
Chambers	86502
Chandler	85224-26
	85244
	85246
	85248-49
For specific ZIP Codes call (888) 275-8777, or your local postmaster.	
Chandler Heights	85227
Chaparral (Part of Chandler)‡	85224
Cherry	86327
Chevelon	86001
Chiawuli Tak	85634
Chilchinbito	86033
Childs	85321
Chinle♦	86503
Chino de Manana (Part of Chino Valley)	86323
Chino Heights	86323
Chino Meadows (Part of Chino Valley)	86323
Chino Ranches	86323
Chino Valley	86323
Chloride	86431
Choulic	85634
Christopher Creek	85541
Chris-Town Center (Part of Phoenix)	85015
Chuichu♦	85222
Cibecue♦	85911
Cibola	85328
Cienega Springs	85344
Circle City	85342
Citrus Gardens	85201
Clarkdale	86324
Claypool♦	85532
Clay Springs	85923
Cleator	86333
Clifton	85533
Coal Mine Mesa	86045
Cobblestone Village (Part of Peoria)	85381
Cochise	85606
Cocopah Indian Reservation	85350
Colcord Estates	85541
College (Part of Tucson)	85722
Colorado City	86021
Colorado River Indian Reservation	85344
Commerce (Part of Phoenix)‡	85030
Comobabi	85634
Concho	85924
Concho Valley	85924
Congress	85332
Continental	85614
Continental Vistas	85614
Coolidge	85228
Coolidge Dam	85542
Co-op Village	85339
Copper Mine	86040
Copper Queen (Part of Bisbee)‡	85603
Cordes	86333
Cordes Juntion	86333
Cordes Lakes	86333
Cork	85536
Cornfields	86505
Cornville♦	86325
Coronada Foothills Estates	85718
Corona de Tucson	85747
Coronado (Part of Tucson)‡	85711*
	85732†
Cortaro	85652
Cottonwood	86326
Cottonwood Station	86503
Country Club Estates (Part of Sierra Vista)	85650
Country Club Estates, *Pima*	85614
Country Club Vistas I, II, III	85614
Country Life	85201
Cove	87420
Covered Wells	85634
Cowlic	85634
Cow Springs	86044
Crane	85364
Craycroft (Part of Tucson)	85712
Crestview (Part of Bisbee)	85603
Cross Canyon	86511
Crown King	86343
Cuckelbur	85222
Curley Horn Ranch	85629
Cutter	85501
Dam View	85344
Date	85332
Dateland	85333
Davis Dam (Part of Bullhead City)	86430
Davis-Monthan Air Force Base	85702
Del Rio	86323
Del Sol	85364
Dennehotso♦	86535
Desert (Part of Mesa)‡	85206
	85208
	85216
For specific ZIP Codes call (888) 275-8777, or your local postmaster.	
Desert Air	85364
Desert Carmel	85222
Desert Foothills‡	85718*
	85728†
Desert Harbor (Part of Peoria)	85381
Desert Hills, *Mohave*‡	86403
Desert Hills, *Pima*	85614
Desert Meadows I	85614
Desert Meadows II	85614
Desert Meadows III	85614
Desert Sands (Part of Mesa)	85208
Desert Shadows	86438
Desert Steppes (Part of Tucson)	85710
Desert View	86023
Dewey	86327
Diamond Point	85541
Diamond Valley	86301
Dilkon	86047
Discovery at the Orchard (Part of Peoria)	85381
Dobson (Part of Mesa)‡	85202
	85272
	85274
For specific ZIP Codes call (888) 275-8777, or your local postmaster.	
Dolan Springs♦	86441
Dome	85365
Don Luis (Part of Bisbee)	85603
Dos Cabezas	85643
Double Adobe	85617
Douglas	85607-08
	85655
For specific ZIP Codes call (888) 275-8777, or your local postmaster.	
Downtown (Part of Flagstaff)‡	86001
Downtown (Part of Kingman)‡	86402
Downtown (Part of Phoenix)‡	85001-04
	85007
For specific ZIP Codes call (888) 275-8777, or your local postmaster.	
Downtown (Part of Tempe)‡	85281
Downtown (Part of Tucson)‡	85701*
	85702†
Downtown (Part of Yuma)‡	85364*
	85366†
Dragoon	85609
Drake	86334
Dreamland Villa	85205
Drexel Heights	85746
Drippings Springs	85292
Dudleyville♦	85292
Dugas	86333
Duncan	85534
Eagar	85925
Eagle Creek	85533
East Flagstaff (Part of Flagstaff)‡	86001
East Fork♦	85941
East Plantsite (Part of Clifton)	85540
Eden	85535
Ehrenberg♦	85334
El Con Regional Shopping Center (Part of Tucson)	85716
Eleven Mile Corner	85222
Elfrida	85610
Elgin	85611
Ellison Creek	85541
El Mirage (mobile home park)	85201
El Mirage	85335
Eloy	85231
El Pueblecito (Part of Yuma)	85364
El Rio (Part of Tucson)	85745
Emery Park (Part of Tucson)	85706
Empire Landing	85344
Fairbank	85621
Fairways I	85614
Fairways II	85614
Fairways III	85614
Falcon Field (Part of Mesa)‡	85205
	85207
	85215
	85277
For specific ZIP Codes call (888) 275-8777, or your local postmaster.	
Falcon Estates (Part of Mesa)	85203
Fiesta Mall (Part of Mesa)	85202
Fiesta Park	85201
Fishers Landing	85365
Flagstaff	86001-04
For specific ZIP Codes call (888) 275-8777, or your local postmaster.	
Flecha Caida Estates	85718
Florence	85232*
	85279†
Florence Junction	85219
Flowing Wells♦	85705
Floy	85924
Foothills North	85364
Forbing Park (Part of Prescott)	86305
Forest Lakes	85931
Fort Apache	85926
Fort Apache Indian Reservation	85941
Fort Apache Junction	85941
Fort Defiance♦	86504
Fort Lowell (Part of Tucson)‡	85712
	85715
	85749
For specific ZIP Codes call (888) 275-8777, or your local postmaster.	
Fort McDowell	85264
Fort McDowell Indian Reservation	85264
Fort Mohave Indian Reservation	86427
Fort Rock	86337
Fort Thomas	85536
Fortuna Heights	85364
Fortuna Hills	85364
Fountain East	85201
Fountain Hills	85268*
	85269†
Fountain of the Sun (Part of Mesa)	85208
Foxfire (Part of Peoria)	85381
Foxwood (Part of Peoria)	85381
Franklin	85534
Fredonia	86022
Fresnal Canyon	85634
Friendly Corners	85231
Fry (Part of Sierra Vista)	85635
Gadsden	85336
Galena (Part of Bisbee)	85603
Ganado♦	86505
Geronimo	85536
Gibson	85321
Gila Acres	85364
Gila Bend	85337
Gila Bend Indian Reservation	85634
Gila Crossing	85339
Gila River Indian Reservation	85247
Gilbert	85233-34
	85296
	85299
For specific ZIP Codes call (888) 275-8777, or your local postmaster.	
Gisela	85541
Gladden	85320
Gleeson	85610
Glendale	85301-08
	85310-12
	85318
For specific ZIP Codes call (888) 275-8777, or your local postmaster.	
Glen Ilah	85362
Globe	85501*
	85502†
Gold Canyon	85219
Golden Shores	86436
Goldfield	85219
Goodwin (Part of Prescott)‡	86303
Goodyear	85338

Goodyear Farms (Part of Litchfield Park) 85340
Gordon Canyon Estates 85541
Graham 85552
Grand Canyon♦ 86023
Grand Canyon Caverns 86434
Grandview 86301
Grandview Estates 86301
Granite Dells 86301
Granite Oaks 86305
Grasshopper Junction 86401
Gray Mountain 86016
Greasewood, *Apache* 86507
Greasewood, *Navajo*♦ 86505
Greaterville 85637
Greenback Valley 85553
Green Valley♦ 85614*
 85622†
Greenway (Part of Glendale)‡ 85306*
 85312†
Greer 85927
Gripe 85546
Groom Creek 86303
Guadalupe 85283
Gunsight 85634
Gu Oidak 85634
Guthrie 85533
Gu Vo 85634
Hacienda De Valencia 85201
Hackberry 86411
Haivana Nakya 85634
Hamilton Corner 85248
Hannagan Meadow 85922
Hano 86042
Happy Jack 86024
Harcuvar 85348
Harmony Villa 85201
Hassayampa 85343
Havasupai Indian Reservation 86435
Hawkins 85332
Hawley Lake 85930
Hayden 85235
Hayden Junction 85235
Heber 85928
Hereford 85615
Hereford Hills 86323
Hermits Rest 86023
Hickiwan 85634
Hidden Springs 86020
Highland Park 85603
Highland Pines 86305
Higley 85236
Hillcrest 85546
Hillside 86301
Hilltop 85632
Ho Kay Gan 86305
Holbrook 86025
Holiday 85344
Holiday Hills 86301
Hollywood 85546
Hon Dah 85935
Hope 85348
Hopi (Part of Scottsdale)‡ 85258*
 85261†
Hopi Indian Reservation 86039
Horn 85333
Horse Mesa 85219
Horse Thief 86333
Hotason Vo 85634
Hotevilla♦ 86030
Houck 86506
Huachuca City 85616
Huachuca Terrace (Part of Bisbee) 85603
Hualapai 86412
Hualapai Indian Reservation 86434
Hubbell 86505
Humboldt 86329
Hunt 85924
Hunters Point 86511
Hyder 85333
Immanuel Mission 86514
Indian Gardens 86336
Indian Ridge Estates 85715
Indian School (Part of Phoenix)‡ 85014
Indian Wells 86031
Inscription House 86044
Inspiration 85532
Iron Springs 86330

Jackrabbit 85222
Jackson Acres 86301
Jacob Lake 86022
Jade Park North (Part of Phoenix) 85308
Jakes Corner 85541
Jeddito 86034
Jerome 86331
Johnson 85609
Joseph City 86032
Juniper Heights 86301
Kachina Gardens 86047
Kaibab 86022
Kaibab Indian Reservation 86022
Kaibab Lodge 86022
Kaibito♦ 86053
Kaihon Kug 85634
Kaka 85321
Kansas Settlement 85643
Katherine 86429
Kayenta♦ 86033
Keams Canyon♦ 86034
Kearny 85237
Kelvin 85237
Kerwo 85634
Kingman 86401*
 86402†
Kings Ranch 85217
Kingswood 86305
Kinlichee 86505
Kino (Part of Tucson)‡ 85703†
 85705*
Kino Hills (Part of Nogales) 85621
Kino Springs 85621
Kinsley Ranch 85640
Kirkland 86332
Kirkland Junction 86332
Klagetoh 86505
Klondyke 85644
Kohatk 85634
Kohls Ranch 85541
Komatke♦ 85339
Ko Vaya 85634
Kykotsmovi Village♦ 86039
La Canada Norte 85629
Lake Havasu City 86403-06
For specific ZIP Codes call (888) 275-8777, or your local postmaster.
Lake Mead City 86444
Lake Mead Rancheros 86401
Lake Mohave 86430
Lake Montezuma♦ 86342
Lakeside, *La Paz* 85344
Lakeside (Part of Pinetop-Lakeside) 85929
Lampliter Village (Part of Clarkdale) 86324
La Palma 85222
La Quintas de Santo Tomas 85629
La Quintas Serenas 85629
Las Ligas (Part of Avondale) 85323
Laveen 85339
Leche-e Chapter 86040
Lees Ferry 86036
Leisure World 85206
Leupp♦ 86035
Leupp Corner 86047
Liberty 85326
Ligurta 85356
Litchfield Greens (Part of Litchfield Park) 85340
Litchfield Park 85340
Little Acres 85501
Littlefield 86432
Little Tucson 85634
Lizard Acres 85373
Lochiel 85624
Loma Linda 85619
Loma Linda Estates 85533
Lone Star 85546
Long Valley 86001
Los Arcos Mall (Part of Scottsdale) 85257
Los Gatos 85255
Lowell (Part of Bisbee) 85603
Lower Miami 85539
Low Mountain 86503
Lukachukai♦ 86507
Luke Air Force Base 85309
Lukeville 85341
Lupton 86508
Lynx Estates 86301

McDowell (Part of Phoenix)‡ 85008*
 85010†
McGees Settlement 85736
McGuireville 86335
McNary♦ 85930
McNeal 85617
Madera Canyon 85706
Mammoth 85618
Many Farms♦ 86538
Marana 85653
Marble Canyon 86036
Maricopa 85239
Maricopa (Ak-Chin) Indian Reservation 85239
Maricopa Village 85339
Marine Corps Air Station 85369
Mariposa Manor (Part of Nogales) 85621
Martinez Lake 85365
Maryvale (Part of Phoenix)‡ 85019
 85063
For specific ZIP Codes call (888) 275-8777, or your local postmaster.
Mayer 86333
Meadow Brook (Part of Yuma) 85364
Meadview 86444
Mennonite Mission 86505
Mesa 85201-16
 85240
 85274-77
For specific ZIP Codes call (888) 275-8777, or your local postmaster.
Mesa del Caballo 85541
Mesa Del Oro 85219
Mesa del Sol 85364
Mescal 85602
Metrocenter (Part of Phoenix) 85051
Mexican Town 85321
Mexican Water 86514
Miami 85539
Miami Gardens 85539
Middle Verde (Part of Camp Verde) 86322
Midland City 85501
Miller Valley (Part of Prescott) 86301
 86305
For specific ZIP Codes call (888) 275-8777, or your local postmaster.
Miracle Valley 85615
Miramonte Acres (Part of Bisbee) 85603
Mishongnovi 86043
Mission (Part of Tucson)‡ 85706
 85714
 85734
For specific ZIP Codes call (888) 275-8777, or your local postmaster.
Mobile 85239
Moccasin 86022
Moenave 86045
Moenkopi♦ 86045
Mohave Valley♦ 86440*
 86446†
Morenci 85540
Mormon Lake 86038
Morristown 85342
Mountainaire 86001
Mountain Club 86301
Mountain View (Part of Bisbee) 85603
Mountain View (Part of Mesa)‡ 85203
 85213
 85275
For specific ZIP Codes call (888) 275-8777, or your local postmaster.
Mountain View, *Navajo* 85935
Mountain View (Part of Tucson)‡ 85741*
 85752†
Mountain View Acres 85629
Mount Elden (Part of Flagstaff) 86001
Mount Lemmon 85619
Mumurva 86030
Munds Park 86017
Na-Ah-Tee Canyon 86025

Naco 85620
Navajo 86502
Navajo Depot Activity 86015
Navajo Indian Reservation 86515
Navajo Mountain 86044
Navajo Spring 86036
Navajo Station 86505
Nazlini 86540
Nelson 86434
New Hope 85201
New Oraibi 86039
New River 85027
New Tucson (Part of Tucson) 85747
Nicksville 85615
Nogales 85621
 85628
 85662
For specific ZIP Codes call (888) 275-8777, or your local postmaster.
Nogales West (Part of Nogales) 85621
Nolia 85634
Normal Junction (Part of Tempe) 85281
Northeast (Part of Phoenix)‡ 85016*
 85064†
Northern Hills 85704
North Komelik 85634
Northridge Park 86314
North Rim 86052
Northwest (Part of Phoenix)‡ 85015
 85017
 85061
 85079
For specific ZIP Codes call (888) 275-8777, or your local postmaster.
Nortons Corner (Part of Chandler) 85225
Nutrioso 85932
Oak Knoll Village 86301
Oak Springs 86511
Oasis Park (Part of Apache Junction) 85220
Oatman 86433
Ocotillo 85248
Ocotillo Ranch 85629
Octave 85332
Olberg 85247
Old Columbine 85546
Oracle♦ 85623
Oracle Foot Hill Estates 85704
Oracle Junction 85737
Oraibi 86039
Orange Grove Estates 85704
Oro Valley 85737
Osborn‡ 85012-13
 85067
For specific ZIP Codes call (888) 275-8777, or your local postmaster.
Overgaard 85933
Page 86040
Page Springs 86325
Palm Springs (Part of Apache Junction) 85219
Palominas 85615
Palo Verde 85343
Pan Tak 85634
Papago (Part of Scottsdale)‡ 85257
Papago Indian Reservation 85634
Paradise 85632
Paradise Valley 85253
Paradise Valley Mall (Part of Phoenix) 85032
Park Central Mall (Part of Phoenix) 85013
Parker 85344
Park Mall (Part of Tucson) 85711
Parks 86018
Pascua Yaqui Indian Reservation 85746
Patagonia 85624
Paulden 86334
Paul Spur 85607
Payson 85541*
 85547†
Peach Springs♦ 86434
Pearce 85625
Peeples Valley 86332

Peoria 85345
 85380-82
For specific ZIP Codes call (888) 275-8777, or your local postmaster.
Peralta Estates 85219
Peridot♦ 85542
Perkinsville 86323
Perryville 85326
Petrified Forest National Park 86028

Phoenix

 85001-86
For specific ZIP Codes call (888) 275-8777, or your local postmaster.

Colleges & Universities

American Indian Coll 85021
Arizona Coll of the Bible 85021
Arizona State Univ West 85069
DeVry Inst of Technol 85021
Grand Canyon Univ 85017
Southwestern Coll 85032
Univ of Phoenix 85072
Western International Univ 85021

Financial Institutions

Bank of America, NTSA 85003
Bank One, NA 85004
Norwest Bank, NA 85012
Wells Fargo Bank, NA 85008

Hospitals

Arizona State Hosp 85008
Carl T Hayden Veterans Affairs Med Ctr 85012
Good Samaritan Regional Med Ctr 85062
Maricopa Med Ctr 85010
St Joseph's Hosp & Med Ctr 85001

Hotels/Motels

Ambassador Inn 85018
Crowne Plaza 85004
Days Inn, Airport 85008
Doubletree Guest Suites 85008
Hyatt Regency at Civic Plaza 85004
Phoenix Airport Hilton 85034
The Pointe Hilton Resort at Squaw Peak 85020
The Pointe Hilton Resort on South Mountain 85044
The Pointe Hilton Resort at Tapatio Cliffs 85020
Premier Inns MetroCenter 85051
Quality Hotel & Resort 85013
The Ritz-Carlton 85016
Sheraton Crescent 85021
Wyndham MetroCenter 85051

Military Installations

Arizona Air Nat Guard, FB6021, Sky Harbor International Airport 85034
Directorate of Logistics for Arizona 85008

Phoenix Pecos (Part of Phoenix)‡ 85048*
 85070†
Pia Oik 85634
Picacho 85241
Pima 85543
Pine 85544
Pinedale 85934
Pine Lake, *Apache* 85924
Pine Lake, *Mohave* 86401
Pine Lake, *Yavapai* 86305
Pine Springs 86506
Pinetop (Part of Pinetop-Lakeside) 85935
Pinetop Country Club 85935
Pinetop Lake Country Club 85935
Pinetop-Lakeside 85935

*** Area Zip Code** **† Post Office Boxes** **‡ Postal Station** **♦ Census Designated Place** *Italic Type* **County**

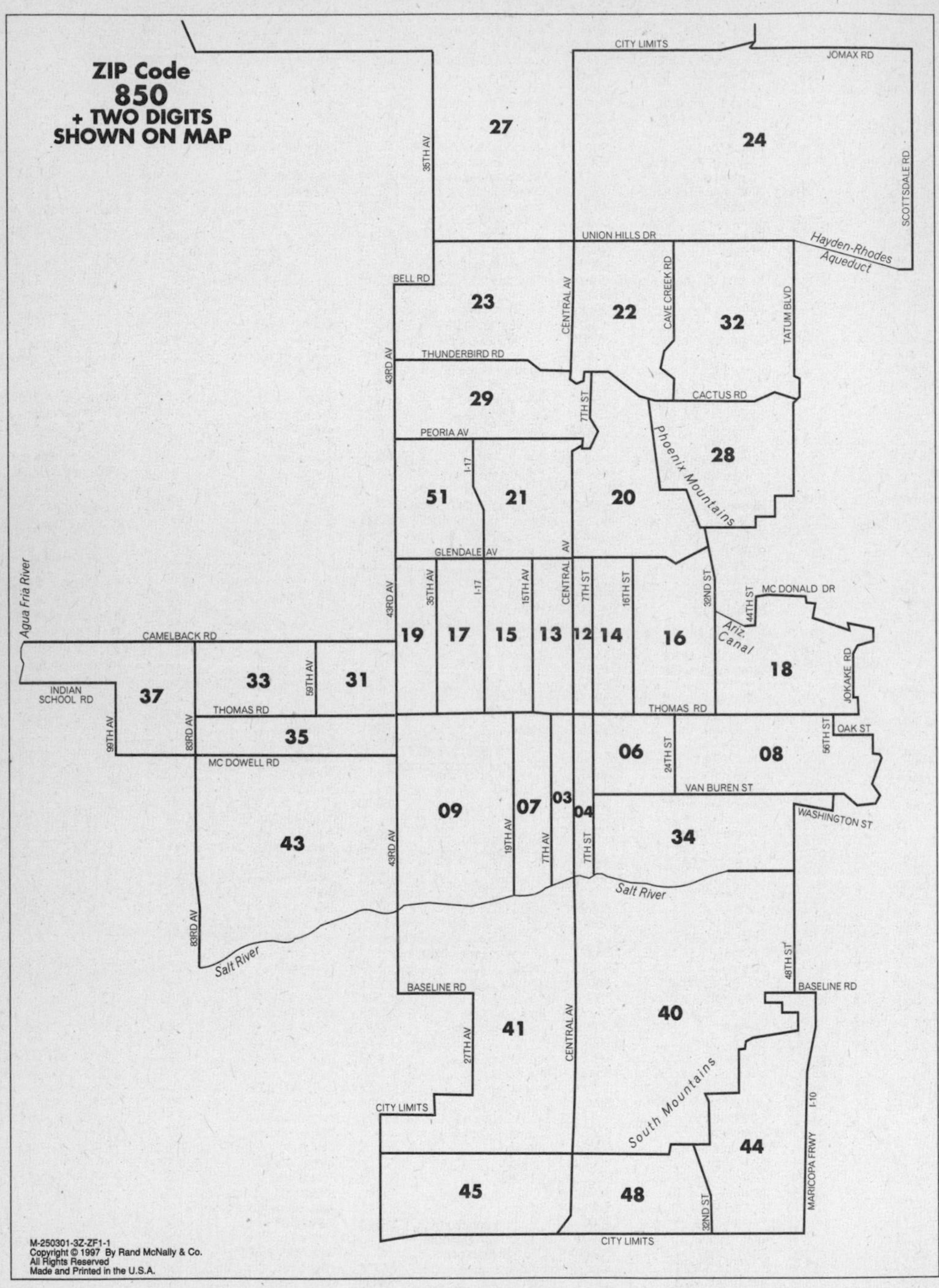
ZIP Code
850
+ TWO DIGITS
SHOWN ON MAP
CITY LIMITS
JOMAX RD
27
24
35TH AV
SCOTTSDALE RD
UNION HILLS DR
Hayden-Rhodes Aqueduct
BELL RD
23
CENTRAL AV
22
CAVE CREEK RD
32
TATUM BLVD
THUNDERBIRD RD
43RD AV
29
7TH ST
CACTUS RD
PEORIA AV
Phoenix Mountains
28
I-17
51
21
20
GLENDALE AV
Agua Fria River
35TH AV
15TH AV
16TH ST
32ND ST
44TH ST
MC DONALD DR
CAMELBACK RD
19
17
15
13
12
14
16
Ariz. Canal
18
JOKAKE RD
INDIAN SCHOOL RD
37
33
59TH AV
31
THOMAS RD
99TH AV
83RD AV
35
56TH ST
OAK ST
06
24TH ST
08
MC DOWELL RD
VAN BUREN ST
09
07
03
04
WASHINGTON ST
43
19TH AV
7TH AV
34
Salt River
BASELINE RD
48TH ST
41
40
27TH AV
South Mountains
I-10
CITY LIMITS
44
45
48
32ND ST
MARICOPA FRWY
CITY LIMITS

Pinion Pine Estates 86401
Pinnacle Peak Village‡ 85255
Pinon♦ 86510
Pioneer (Part of Mesa)‡ 85210
Pirtleville♦ 85626
Pisinemo♦ 85634
Plantsite 85540
Plaza Del Rio (Part of Peoria) 85381
Polacca♦ 86042
Poland Junction 86333
Pomerene 85627
Ponderosa Park 86301
Ponderosa Springs 85541
Portal 85632
Porter Creek Estates 85929
Porter Mountain Estates 85929
Poston♦ 85371
Potato Patch 86301
Prescott 86301-05
... 86313
For specific ZIP Codes call (888) 275-8777, or your local postmaster.
Prescott Canyon Estates 86301
Prescott Country Club 86301
Prescott Riviera 86301
Prescott Valley 86312†
... 86314*
Presidential Estates 85616
Pueblo del Sol (Part of Sierra Vista) 85635
Pueblo del Sol Village I (Part of Sierra Vista) 85650
Pueblo Estates 85614
Pumpkin Center 85553
Quartzsite 85346
... 85359
For specific ZIP Codes call (888) 275-8777, or your local postmaster.
Queen Creek 85242
Queen Valley 85219
Querino 86506
Rainbow Valley 85326
Ranch del Sol 85296
Rancho Buena Vista 85629
Rancho del Rio 85344
Ranchos Carmela (Part of Sierra Vista) 85635
Rancho Verde 85364
Rancho Vista Hills 86301
Randolph 85222
Reata Pass (Part of Scottsdale) 85255
Redington 85602
Red Mesa 86514
Red Rock, *Apache* 87420
Red Rock, *Pinal* 85245
Red Valley 86544
Rillito 85654
Rimrock 86335
Rincon, *Pima* 85634
Rincon (Part of Tucson)‡ 85710*
... 85731†
Rio Rico 85648
Rio Salado (Part of Phoenix)‡ 85006
Rio Verde 85263
Riverside 85237
Riviera (Part of Bullhead City) 86439
... 86442
For specific ZIP Codes call (888) 275-8777, or your local postmaster.
Rock Point 86545
Rock Springs 85026
Roll 85347
Rolling Hills Country Club Estates (Part of Tucson) 85710
Roosevelt 85545
Roosevelt Estates 85545
Roosevelt Resort 85545
Rough Rock♦ 86503
Round Rock 86547
Royal Estates (Part of Nogales) 85621
Royal Oaks 86305
Rye 85541
Sacate 85221
Sacaton♦ 85247
Sacaton Flats 85247
Sacred Mountain 86001
Safford 85546*
... 85548†
Saginaw (Part of Bisbee) 85603
Sahuarita 85629
Sahuarita Heights 85629
St. David♦ 85630
St. Johns 85936
St. Michaels♦ 86511
Salado 85936
Salina 86503
Salome 85348
Salt River Indian Reservation 85256
Salt River Powder District Camp 85545
San Carlos♦ 85550
San Carlos Indian Reservation 85550
Sanchez 85546
Sanders 86512*
Sand Springs 86039
San Jose (Part of Bisbee) 85603
San Jose, *Graham* 85546
San Lucy Village 85337
San Luis, *Pima* 85634
San Luis, *Yuma* 85349
San Manuel♦ 85631
San Miguel 85634
San Pedro 85634
San Rafael Terrace (Part of Bisbee) 85603
San Simon 85632
Santa Cruz 85221
Santa Maria 85009
Santan♦ 85247
Santa Rita 85640
Santa Rosa♦ 85634
Santo Tomas 85629
Santo Tomas del Norte 85629
Santo Tomas Village 85629
San Xavier 85746
San Xavier Indian Reservation 85634
Sasabe 85633
Sawmill♦ 86549
Schuchk 85634
Schuchuli 85634
Scottsdale 85250-52
... 85254-62
... 85264-67
... 85271
For specific ZIP Codes call (888) 275-8777, or your local postmaster.
Scottsdale Fashion Square (Part of Scottsdale) 85251
Scottsdale Galleria (Part of Scottsdale) 85251
Seba Dalkai 86047
Second Mesa♦ 86043
Sedona 86336
... 86339-41
... 86351
For specific ZIP Codes call (888) 275-8777, or your local postmaster.
Seligman 86337
Sells♦ 85634
Sentinel 85333
Seven Springs 85331
Shadow Meadows 86323
Shaw Butte (Part of Phoenix)‡ 85029
Sheldon 85534
Sherwood (Part of Mesa)‡ 85204*
... 85214†
Shipolovi 86043
Shongopovi♦ 86043
Shonto♦ 86054
Shopishk 85634
Show Low 85901*
... 85902†
Shumway 85901
Sichomovi 86042
Sierra Adobe‡ 85023-24
... 85027
... 85050
... 85053-54
... 85080
For specific ZIP Codes call (888) 275-8777, or your local postmaster.
Sierra Bonita 85643
Sierra Vista 85635-36
... 85650
... 85671
For specific ZIP Codes call (888) 275-8777, or your local postmaster.
Sierra Vista Estates (Part of Sierra Vista) 85650
Sil Nakya 85634
Silverbell (Part of Tucson)‡ 85745*
... 85754†
Site Six (Part of Lake Havasu City) 86403
Skull Valley 86338
Skyline Del Aire Estates 85718
Skyway Village 85205
Smoke Signal 86503
Snowflake 85937
Solomon 85551
Somerton 85350
Sonoita 85637
Sonora Town 85233
South Bisbee 85603
South Central (Part of Phoenix)‡ 85040*
... 85066†
South Komelik 85634
South Santan 85247
South Tucson 85713*
... 85725†
Springerville 85938
Spring Valley 86333
Sprucedale 85922
Stagecoach Acres 86301
Stanfield 85272
Stanton 85332
Stargo 85540
Starlight Pines 86024
Star Valley 85541
Steamboat Canyon 86505
Stoneman Lake 86024
Strawberry 85544
Sun (Part of Tucson)‡ 85717
... 85719
... 85733
For specific ZIP Codes call (888) 275-8777, or your local postmaster.
Sun City♦ 85351
... 85372-73
For specific ZIP Codes call (888) 275-8777, or your local postmaster.
Sun City Rancho Vistoso 85738
Sun City West♦ 85375*
... 85376†
Sunflower 85201
Sunizona 85625
Sun Lakes♦ 85248
Sunnyslope (Part of Phoenix)‡ 85020
... 85022
... 85068
For specific ZIP Codes call (888) 275-8777, or your local postmaster.
Sunrise, *Coconino* 86047
Sunrise (Part of Chino Valley) 86323
Sunrise Springs 86505
Sunset 85643
Sunset Acres 85603
Sunshine Acres (Part of Mesa) 85201
Sunsites 85625
Suntown (Part of Peoria) 85345
Sun Valley 86029
Supai♦ 86435
Superior 85273
Superstition Estates (Part of Apache Junction) 85220
Superstition Springs Center (Part of Mesa) 85206
Supi Oidak 85634
Surprise 85378-79
... 85387
For specific ZIP Codes call (888) 275-8777, or your local postmaster.
Sweet Acres 86301
Sweetwater, *Apache* 87401
Sweetwater, *Maricopa* 85326
Sweetwater, *Pinal* 85221
Swift Trail Junction♦ 85546
Tacna 85352
Tall Pines (Part of Show Low) 85935
Tapco 86324
Tat Momoli 85634
Tatria Toak 85634
Taylor 85939
Teec Nos Pos♦ 86514
Tees To 86047
Tempe 85280-87
For specific ZIP Codes call (888) 275-8777, or your local postmaster.
Temple Bar Marina 86443
Tes Nez Iah 86033
Thatcher 85552
Theba 85337
The Foothills 85364
The Gap 86020
The Summit Estates (Part of Sierra Vista) 85635
Three Points♦ 85714
Three Way 85534
Tintown (Part of Bisbee) 85603
Tolani 86047
Tolleson 85353
Toltec (Part of Eloy) 85231
Tombstone 85638
Tonalea 86044
Tonkawa 86305
Tonopah 85354
Tonto Basin 85553
Tonto Hills 85331
Tonto Village 85541
Topawa 85639
Topock 86436
Toreva 86043
Tortilla Flat 85290
Totopitk 85634
Tovrea (Part of Phoenix) 85034
Tower Plaza Mall (Part of Phoenix) 85018
Town and Country (Part of Sierra Vista) 85635
Toyei 86505
Tremaine 85225
Tri-City Mall (Part of Mesa) 85201
Truxton 86434
Tsaile♦ 86556
Tubac 85646
Tuba City 86045
Tucson 85701-37
... 85739-54
For specific ZIP Codes call (888) 275-8777, or your local postmaster.
Tucson Country Club Estates 85715
Tucson Mall, The (Part of Tucson) 85705
Tucson National Estates 85741
Tumacacori 85640
Turkey Flat 85546
Tusayan 86023
Tusconita 85706
Twin Arrows 86001
Twin Buttes 85629
Twin Knolls 85207
Two Story 86511
University of Arizona (Part of Tucson) 85717
Upper Wheatfields 86556
Utting 85348
Vahki 85221
Vail 85641
Vaiva Vo 85634
Valencia (Part of Buckeye) 85326
Valentine 86437
Valle Verde del Norte 85629
Valley Farms 85291
Vamori 85634
Vandenberg Village 85708
Vaya Chin 85634
Velda Rose Estates 85205
Velda Rose Gardens 85201
Ventana 85634
Ventana Lakes (Part of Peoria) 85382
Venture Out 85201
Verde Lee Estates 85533
Verde Valley 85364
Verde Village (Part of Cottonwood) 86326
Vernon 85940
Vicksburg 85348
Vicksburg Junction 85348
Village Meadows (Part of Sierra Vista) 85635
Village of Oak Creek 86341
Villages of Green Valley 85614
Vista Grande (Part of Chino Valley) 86323
Vista Linda 85546
Waddell 85355
Wagoner 86332
Wahak Hotrontk 85634
Wahweap 86040
Walker 86301
Walnut Grove 86332
Walpi 86042
Warren (Part of Bisbee)‡ 85603
Washington (Part of Phoenix)‡ 85021
... 85051
... 85069
For specific ZIP Codes call (888) 275-8777, or your local postmaster.
Washington Camp 85624
Washington Park 85541
Wellton 85356
Wenden 85357
Westbrook Village (Part of Peoria) 85382
West Chandler (Part of Chandler) 85224
Westfield (Part of Peoria) 85345
Westgate 85611
Westgreen Estates (Part of Peoria) 85345
Westridge (Part of Phoenix) 85075
Westridge Mall (Part of Phoenix) 85033
West Sedona (Part of Sedona) 86340
Westward Quest 85201
Wheatfields 86515
Whipple (Part of Prescott)‡ 86313
Whippoorwill 86510
Whispering Hills (Part of Sierra Vista) 85635
Whispering Pines 85541
White Clay 86504
White Cone 86025
White Mountain Lake 85912
White Mountain Summer Homes 85935
Whiteriver 85941
White Tanks 85326
Why 85321
Wickenburg 85358†
... 85390*
Wide Ruin 86502
Wikieup 85360
Wildwood Estates 86305
Wilhoit 86332
Willcox 85643*
... 85644†
Williams 86046
Williamson Valley 86305
Willow Beach 86445
Willow Canyon 85619
Willow Valley Estates♦ 86440
Window Rock♦ 86515
Winkelman 85292
Winona 86001
Winslow 86047
Winslow West 86047
Winwood 85603
Wittmann 85361
Woodruff 85942
Woodsprings 86505
Wrangler Ranch 85629
Yaqui (Part of Tucson) 85746
Yarnell 85362
Yava 86301
Yavapai Indian Reservation 86301
York 85534
Young 85554
Youngtown 85363
Yucca 86438
Yuma 85364-69
For specific ZIP Codes call (888) 275-8777, or your local postmaster.
Yuma East 85364
Yuma Proving Ground 85365

*** Area Zip Code** **† Post Office Boxes** **‡ Postal Station** **♦ Census Designated Place** *Italic Type* **County**

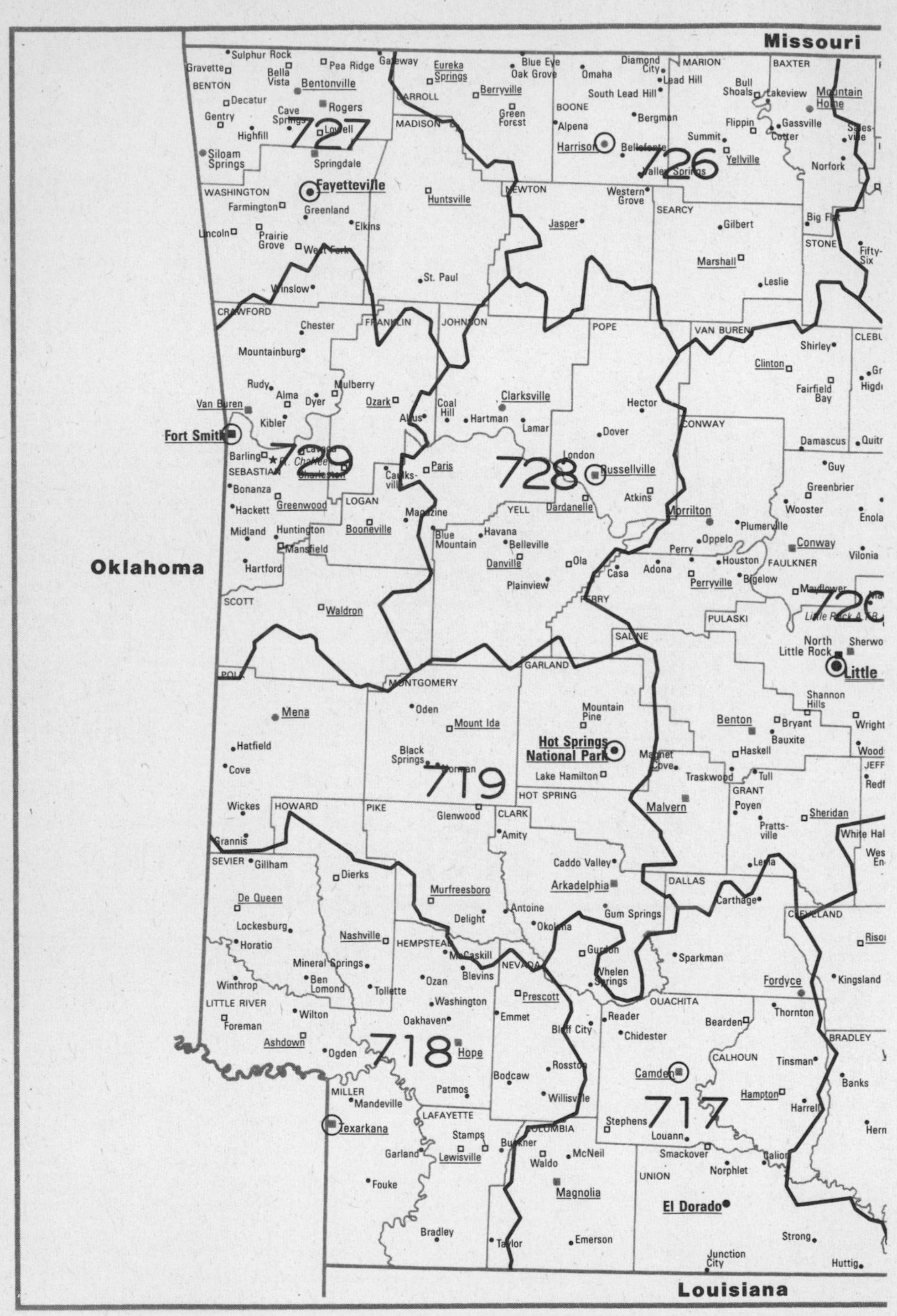
Missouri
Oklahoma
Louisiana
727
726
729
728
719
718
717
Sulphur Rock
Gravette
Bella Vista
Pea Ridge
Gateway
Eureka Springs
Blue Eye
Oak Grove
Omaha
Diamond City
MARION
BAXTER
BENTON
Bentonville
Berryville
Lead Hill
Bull Shoals
Lakeview
Mountain Home
Decatur
Rogers
CARROLL
Green Forest
South Lead Hill
BOONE
Gentry
Cave Springs
Highfill
Lowell
MADISON
Alpena
Bergman
Flippin
Gassville
Cotter
Summit
Siloam Springs
Springdale
Harrison
Bellefonte
Yellville
Norfork
Valley Springs
WASHINGTON
Fayetteville
Huntsville
NEWTON
Western Grove
Farmington
Greenland
SEARCY
Elkins
Jasper
Gilbert
Big Flat
Lincoln
Prairie Grove
West Fork
STONE
Fifty-Six
Marshall
St. Paul
Leslie
Winslow
CRAWFORD
FRANKLIN
JOHNSON
POPE
VAN BUREN
Chester
Shirley
Mountainburg
Clinton
Mulberry
Fairfield Bay
Rudy
Alma
Dyer
Ozark
Clarksville
Van Buren
Coal Hill
Hector
Kibler
Altus
Hartman
Lamar
CONWAY
Fort Smith
Dover
Damascus
London
Barling
Paris
Russellville
Guy
SEBASTIAN
Greenbrier
Atkins
Bonanza
Greenwood
LOGAN
YELL
Dardanelle
Morrilton
Wooster
Hackett
Magazine
Plumerville
Enola
Midland
Huntington
Booneville
Havana
Oppelo
Conway
Mansfield
Blue Mountain
Belleville
Perry
Houston
Vilonia
FAULKNER
Hartford
Danville
Ola
Casa
Adona
Perryville
Bigelow
Plainview
SCOTT
Waldron
PERRY
PULASKI
SALINE
North Little Rock
POLK
GARLAND
MONTGOMERY
Shannon Hills
Oden
Mountain Pine
Mena
Mount Ida
Benton
Bryant
Bauxite
Hot Springs National Park
Hatfield
Black Springs
Haskell
Cove
Lake Hamilton
Traskwood
Tull
HOT SPRING
GRANT
Wickes
HOWARD
PIKE
Glenwood
CLARK
Malvern
Poyen
Sheridan
Amity
Pratts-ville
Grannis
SEVIER
Gillham
Caddo Valley
Dierks
Arkadelphia
DALLAS
Murfreesboro
De Queen
Antoine
Carthage
Delight
Gum Springs
Lockesburg
Okolona
Horatio
Nashville
HEMPSTEAD
Sparkman
McCaskill
Gurdon
Mineral Springs
Blevins
NEVADA
Whelen Springs
Fordyce
Kingsland
Winthrop
Ben Lomond
Tollette
Ozan
Prescott
OUACHITA
LITTLE RIVER
Washington
Thornton
Wilton
Emmet
Reader
Bearden
Foreman
Oakhaven
Bluff City
Chidester
BRADLEY
Ashdown
Ogden
Hope
CALHOUN
Tinsman
Rosston
Camden
Banks
Bodcaw
MILLER
Patmos
Hampton
Mandeville
Willisville
Harrell
LAFAYETTE
Stephens
Texarkana
COLUMBIA
Stamps
Buckner
Louann
Lewisville
Garland
Waldo
McNeil
Smackover
Norphlet
UNION
Fouke
Magnolia
El Dorado
Bradley
Taylor
Emerson
Strong
Junction City
Huttig

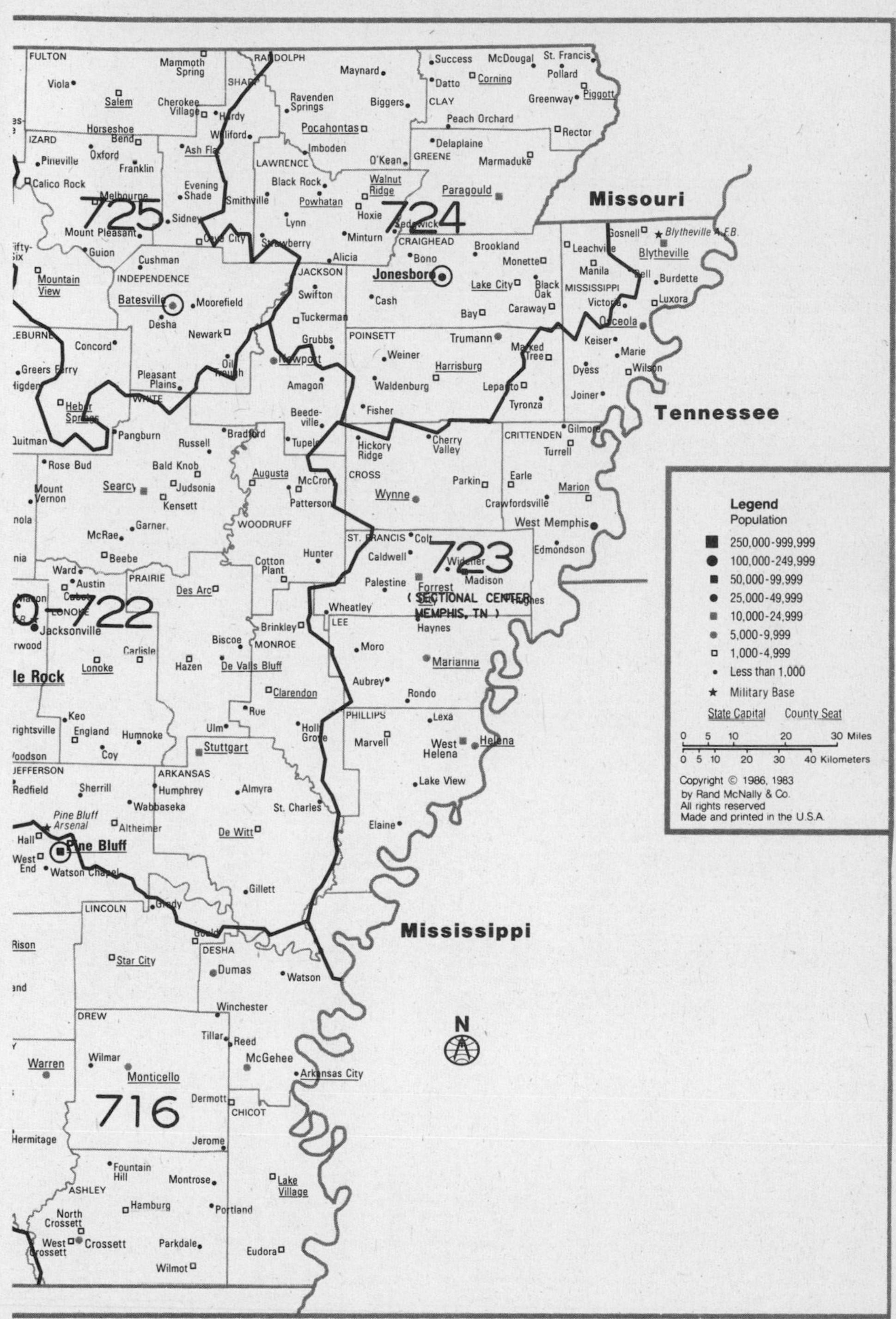
Missouri
Tennessee
Mississippi
725
724
723
722
716
(SECTIONAL CENTER MEMPHIS, TN)
Jonesboro
Paragould
Blytheville
Batesville
Newport
Searcy
Wynne
West Memphis
Forrest City
Marianna
Helena
West Helena
Stuttgart
Pine Bluff
Jacksonville
Monticello
McGehee
Dumas
Crossett
Warren
Legend
Population
250,000-999,999
100,000-249,999
50,000-99,999
25,000-49,999
10,000-24,999
5,000-9,999
1,000-4,999
Less than 1,000
Military Base
State Capital
County Seat
0 5 10 20 30 Miles
0 5 10 20 30 40 Kilometers
Copyright © 1986, 1983
by Rand McNally & Co.
All rights reserved
Made and printed in the U.S.A.

Abbott 72944
Aberdeen 72134
Acorn 71953
Ada 72001
Adkins Lake 71601
Adona 72001
Agnos 72513
Alabam 72740
Albert Pike (Part of Hot Springs)‡ 71913
Albion 72143
Alco 72610
Alexander, *Greene* 72450
Alexander, *Pulaski* 72002
Algoa 72112
Alicia 72410
Alix 72820
Allbrook 71851
Alleene 71820
Allison 72560
Allport 72046
Alma 72921
Almond 72550
Almyra 72003
Alpena 72611
Alpine 71920
Alread 72031
Altheimer 72004
Alto 72354
Altus 72821
Aly 72857
Amagon 72005
Amanca 72376
Amboy (Part of North Little Rock) 72118
Amity 71921
Amy 71701
Andy 72376
Annieville 72434
Antioch, *Perry* 72070
Antioch, *White* 72012
Antoine 71922
Aplin 72126
Appleton 72823
Apt 72401
Arbor Grove 72433
Ard 72834
Arden 71822
Arkadelphia 71923
Arkana 71826
Arkansas City 71630
Arkinda 71836
Arkola 72940
Arlberg 72031
Armorel 72310
Armstrong 72482
Armstrong Springs 72143
Artesian 71744
Artist Point 72946
Ashdown 71822
Asher, *Madison* 72727
Asher (Part of Little Rock)‡ 72204
Ash Flat 72513
Athelstan 72370
Athens 71971
Atkins 72823
Atlanta 71740
Attica 72455
Aubrey 72311
Augsburg 72847
Augusta 72006
Aurelle 71765
Aurora 72740
Austin, *Conway* 72031
Austin, *Lonoke* 72007
Auvergne 72112
Avilla 72002
Avoca 72711
Avon 71832
Back Gate 71639
Baker 72482
Balch 72005
Bald Knob 72010
Baldwin (Part of Fayetteville) 72701
Ballard 72513
Band Mill 72517
Banks 71631
Banner 72523
Barber 72927
Barcelona 72955
Bard 72450
Bardstown 72350
Barfield 72315
Barling 72923
Barney 72047
Barton 72312
Barton Eddins 72312
Bashe (Part of Fort Smith) 72901
Bass 72655
Bassett 72313
Batavia 72601

Batchelor 72366
Bates 72924
Batesville 72501*
72503†
Battlefield 71801
Baucum 72117
Bauxite 72011
Baxter 71638
Bay 72411
Bayou Meto, *Arkansas* 72160
Bayou Meto, *Lonoke* 72086
Bay Village 72324
Bear Creek Springs 72601
Bearden 71720
Beaver 72613
Beaver Shores 72756
Beck 72348
Becton 72036
Beebe 72012
Bee Branch 72013
Beech Grove, *Dallas* 71742
Beech Grove, *Greene* 72412
Beedeville 72014
Beirne 71721
Bellaire 71638
Bella Vista♦ 72714-15
For specific ZIP Codes call (888) 275-8777, or your local postmaster.
Bellefonte 72601
Belle Meade 72348
Belleville 72824
Bells Chapel 72823
Bellville 71846
Belton 71852
Ben 72530
Ben Gay 72466
Ben Hur 72856
Ben Lomond 71823
Benton 72015
72018
For specific ZIP Codes call (888) 275-8777, or your local postmaster.
Bentonville 72712
Bergman 72615
Berryville 72616
Beryl 72032
Best 72756
Bethany 71833
Bethel 72450
Bethel Heights 72764
Bethesda 72501
Beulah 72017
Bevis Corners 72142
Bexar 72515
Bidville 72959
Bigelow 72016
Big Flat 72617
Big Fork 71953
Biggers 72413
Big Lake 72442
Big Springs 72657
Billingsley's Corner 71866
Billstown 71958
Bingen 71852
Birdell 72455
Birdeye 72314
Birdsong 72386
Birdtown 72157
Birta 72853
Biscoe 72017
Bismarck 71929
Blackburn 72959
Blackfish 72346
Black Fork 71953
Black Oak, *Craighead* 72414
Black Oak, *Poinsett* 72386
Black Rock 72415
Black Springs 71960
Blackton 72069
Blackville, *Conway* 72823
Blackville, *Jackson* 72112
Blakely 71949
Blakemore 72046
Blevins 71825
Bloomer 72933
Bloomfield 72734
Blossom 72392
Blue Ball 72833
Blue Eye 65611
Blue Hill 72118
Blue Mountain 72826
Blue Springs 71909
Blue Springs Village 72764
Bluff City 71722
Bluffton 72827
Blytheville 72315-19
For specific ZIP Codes call (888) 275-8777, or your local postmaster.

Board Camp 71932
Bodcaw 71858
Bogg Springs 71944
Bolding 71747
Boles 72926
Bonanza 72916
Bondsville 72354
Bonnerdale 71933
Bono, *Craighead* 72416
Bono, *Faulkner* 72058
Booker 72117
Booneville 72927
Booster 72645
Boothe 72927
Boston 72752
Boswell 72516
Botkinburg 72031
Boughton 71857
Bowen 71940
Bowman 72437
Boxley 72740
Boyd 71837
Boydell 71658
Boyd Hill 71845
Boydsville 72461
Boynton 72438
Bradford 72020
Bradley 71826
Brady (Part of Little Rock)‡ 72205
Bragg City 71726
Brakebill 72478
Branch 72928
Brasfield 72017
Bredlow Corner 72046
Brentwood 72959
Brewer 72044
Brickeys 72320
Briggsville 72828
Brighton 72450
Bright Star 71834
Brightwater 72756
Brinkley 72021
Brister 71740
Brockett 72455
Brockwell 72517
Brookland 72417
Brown's Crossing 71640
Brown Springs 72104
Brownstown 71846
Brownsville 72067
Bruins 72348
Brumley 72032
Brummitt 72160
Bruno 72682
Brush Creek 72084
Bryant 72022*
72089†
Bryant Addition 72857
Buckeye 72438
Buckner 71827
Buck Range 71851
Buckville 71956
Buena Vista 71764
Buffalo City 72653
Buie 72129
Bullfrog Valley 72837
Bull Shoals 72619
Bunney 72414
Burdette 72321
Burg 71833
Burlington 72662
Burnville 72936
Buroak 72650
Burtsell 71962
Busch 72631
Bussey 71860
Butlerville 72176
Butterfield 72104
Byron 72576
Cabanol 72616
Cabot 72023
Caddo Gap 71935
Caddo Valley 71923
Cain 72946
Calamine 72466
Caldwell 72322
Cale 71828
Caledonia 71749
Calhoun 71753
Calico Rock 72519
Calion 71724
Calmer 71665
Calumet 72315
Camark 71701
Camden 71701*
71711†
Cammack Village 72207
Camp 72520
Campbell Station 72473
Camp Joseph T. Robinson 72118
Canaan 72650
Canal Gardens 72348

Cane Creek 72150
Canehill 72717
Caney, *Faulkner* 72032
Caney, *Hot Spring* 71929
Caney Valley 71921
Canfield 71845
Cantwell 72422
Capps 72601
Capps City 71069
Caraway 72419
Carbon City 72855
Carden Bottoms 72834
Careyville 71765
Carlile Highland 72653
Carlisle 72024
Carmel 71671
Carmi 72438
Carolan 72927
Carpenter 71642
Carpenter Addition 71655
Carroll's Corner 72442
Carrollton 72611
Carryville 72454
Carson 72370
Carter Cove Use Area 72857
Carthage 71725
Casa 72025
Cash 72421
Cass 72949
Casscoe 72026
Catalpa 72854
Catcher 72956
Catholic Point 72027
Cathy Lake 72396
Cato 72114
Catron 72367
Caulksville 72951
Cauthron, *Logan* 72927
Cauthron, *Scott* 72958
Cavanaugh (Part of Fort Smith) 72901
Cave City 72521
Cave Creek 72501
Cave Springs 72718
Cecil 72930
Cedar Creek 72950
Cedar Grove 72534
Cedarville 72932
Center 72542
Center Hill (Part of Paragould)‡ 72450
Center Hill, *White* 72143
Center Point, *Clark* 71743
Center Point, *Hempstead* 71801
Center Point, *Howard* 71852
Center Point, *Prairie* 72064
Center Ridge, *Clark* 71921
Center Ridge, *Cleburne* 72543
Center Ridge, *Conway* 72027
Centerton 72719
Center Valley 72802
Centerville, *Faulkner* 72058
Centerville, *Hempstead* 71835
Centerville, *Yell* 72829
Central, *Clark* 71923
Central, *Cross* 72396
Central, *Hot Spring* 72104
Central, *Sevier* 71842
Central Baptist College (Part of Conway) 72032
Central City (Part of Hot Springs)‡ 71913
Central City, *Sebastian* 72941
Central Mall (Part of Fort Smith) 72903
Cerrogordo 71866
Chambersville 71766
Chapel Hill 71832
Charleston 72933
Charlotte 72522
Chasewood Landing 71969
Chatfield 72348
Chelford 72386
Cherokee City 72734
Cherokee Village 72525
72529
For specific ZIP Codes call (888) 275-8777, or your local postmaster.
Cherry Hill, *Perry* 72126
Cherry Hill, *Polk* 71953
Cherry Valley 72324
Chester 72934
Chickalah 72834
Chicot Junction 71640
Chidester 71726

Childress 72447
Chimes 72645
Chismville 72943
Choctaw 72028
Choctaw Acres 72031
Christy Acres 72015
Chula 72857
Cincinnati 72769
Clarendon 72029
Clarkedale 72325
Clarkridge 72623
Clarks Corner 72394
Clarksville 72830
Clay 72143
Clear Lake, *Grant* 72150
Clear Lake, *Mississippi* 72315
Clear Point 72756
Clear Spring 71962
Cleveland 72030
Clifty 72756
Clinton 72031
Clover Bend 72433
Clow 71855
Clyde 72717
Coaldale 74937
Coal Hill 72832
Coffeeville 72020
Coffman, *Greene* 72450
Coffman, *Lawrence* 72433
Coldwater 72373
Coleman 71655
Colfax 72653
College City 72476
Collegehill 71752
College Station 72053
Collegeville 72002
Collins 71638
Colt 72326
Columbus 71831
Combs 72721
Cominto 71655
Compton 72624
Concord 72523
Congo 72015
Connells Point 72366
Conway 72032*
72033†
Copper Mine 72756
Cord 72524
Corinth 72824
Corley 72855
Cornerstone 72004
Cornerville 71667
Corning 72422
Cotter 72626
Cotterneck 71742
Cottonbelt 71720
Cotton Plant 72036
Cottonshed 71851
Cottonwood Corner, *Craighead* 72447
Cottonwood Corner, *Mississippi* 72370
Council 72320
Cove 71937
Cowell 72856
Cowlingsville 71846
Coy 72037
Cozahome 72639
Crabapple Point 71724
Crabtree 72031
Cravens 72949
Crawfordsville 72327
Creigh 72366
Crigler 71667
Crockett 72454
Crocketts Bluff 72038
Crosses 72701
Crossett 71635
Crossroads, *Cleburne* 72131
Cross Roads, *Hot Spring* 71933
Crossroads, *Izard* 72566
Crossroads (Part of Newport) 72112
Cross Roads, *Little River* 71866
Cross Roads, *Logan* 72863
Cross Roads, *Madison* 72738
Crossroads, *Prairie* 72040
Crows 72015
Crumpler 72644
Crumrod 72328
Crystal Hill 72118
Crystal Springs 71968
Crystal Springs Landing 71968
Cullendale (Part of Camden)‡ 71701
Culpeper 72031
Cumi 72544

*** Area Zip Code** **† Post Office Boxes** **‡ Postal Station** **♦ Census Designated Place** *Italic Type* **County**

Place	ZIP
Curtis	71728
Cushman	72526
Cypert	72366
Cypress Valley	72156
Dabney	72110
Daisy	71950
Dalark	71923
Dallas	71953
Dalton	72455
Damascus	72039
Danville	72833
Dardanelle	72834
Datto	72424
Davis Creek	72120
Dawn Hill Country Club	72761
Dayton	72940
DeAnn	71801
Deans Market	72921
Dean Springs	72921
Decatur	72722
Deckerville	72386
Deep Elm	71653
Deer	72628
Deerfield	72328
Delaney	72727
Delaplaine	72425
Delaware	72835
Delfore	72438
Delight	71940
Dell	72426
De Luce	72042
Denmark	72020
Dennard	72629
Denning	72821
Denton	72458
Denver	72638
Denwood	72386
De Queen	71832
Dermott	71638
De Roche	71929
Des Arc	72040
Desha	72527
Detonti	72011
De Valls Bluff	72041
Dewey, *Chicot*	71638
Dewey, *White*	72121
De Witt	72042
Dialion	71665
Diamond Bay	72531
Diamond City	72630
Diamondhead	71913
Dian (Part of Prescott)	71857
Diaz	72043
Dickey Heights	72768
Dicus	72476
Dierks	71833
Dillen	72854
Dixie, *Craighead*	72437
Dixie (Part of North Little Rock)	72114
Dixie, *Woodruff*	72006
Doddridge	71834
Dogtown	71832
Dogwood (Part of Blytheville)	72315
Dogwood Acres	71957
Dollarway (Part of Pine Bluff)	71602
Dolph	72528
Donaldson	71941
Dongola	72650
Doniphan	72143
Dora	72956
Double Bridges	72358
Douglas	71643
Dover	72837
Dowdy	72524
Downtown (Part of Little Rock)‡	72201
Drakes Creek	72740
Drasco	72530
Driggs	72943
Dripping Springs	72955
Driver	72329
Dryden	72404
Dryfork	72740
Dublin	72863
Duff	72675
Dumas	71639
Durham	72727
Dutch Mills	72744
Dutton	72760
Dyer	72935
Dyess	72330
Eagle Mills	71720
Eagle Point	72531
Eagleton	71953
Earle	72331
East Black Oak	72386
East Camden	71701
East End	72065
Eastview	72351
Eaton	72458
Ebenezer	71764
Ebony	72364
Echo	72927
Economy	72823
Eden Isle	72543
Edgemont	72044
Edmondson	72332
Eglantine	72153
Egypt	72427
Elaine	72333
El Dorado	71730*
	71731†
Elevenpoint	72455
Elgin	72112
Elizabeth	72531
Elkins	72727
Elk Ranch	72631
Elliott	71701
Ellison	72152
Elm Springs	72728
Elm Store	65778
Elmwood	72601
Elnora	72455
El Paso	72045
Emerson	71740
Emmet	71835
Empire	71661
Enders	72131
Engelberg	72455
England	72046
English	72004
Enola	72047
Enterprise	72901
Eros	72633
Erwin	72112
Ethel	72048
Etna	72949
Etowah	72428
Euclid Heights (Part of Hot Springs)	71901
Eudora	71640
Eula	72675
Eureka Springs	72631-32
For specific ZIP Codes call (888) 275-8777, or your local postmaster.	
Evansville	72729
Evening Shade, *Hempstead*	71801
Evening Shade, *Scott*	72958
Evening Shade, *Sharp*	72532
Evening Star	72422
Everton	72633
Excelsior	72936
Fairbanks	72131
Fairfield (Part of Little Rock)	72209
Fairfield Bay	72088
Fairmont	72160
Fair Oaks	72397
Fairview, *Chicot*	71653
Fairview, *Lonoke*	72086
Fairview, *Marion*	72650
Fairview (Part of Camden)	71701
Fairview, *Sevier*	71841
Fairwood	71913
Falcon	71827
Falls Chapel	71846
Fallsville	72854
Fancy Hill	71935
Fannie	71970
Farelly Lake	72160
Fargo	72021
Farmington	72730
Farmville	71671
Farville	72417
Fayetteville	72701-04
For specific ZIP Codes call (888) 275-8777, or your local postmaster.	
Felsenthal	71747
Felton	72360
Fender	72476
Fendley	71921
Fenter	72167
Ferguson	72328
Ferguson Crossroads	71837
Fern	72946
Ferndale	72208
Fianna (Part of Fort Smith)‡	72908
Fifty-Six	72533
Figure Five	72956
Finch	72450
Fisher, *Craighead*	72421
Fisher, *Poinsett*	72429
Fitzgerald (Part of Diaz)	72112
Fitzgerald Crossing	72396
Fitzhugh	72006
Fivemile	72530
Flag	72645
Flat Rock	72847
Flint Springs	72583
Flippin	72634
Floodway	72442
Floral	72534
Florence	71655
Floyd	72143
Fomby	71822
Fontaine	72416
Fordyce	71742
Foreman	71836
Forest Grove, *Columbia*	71740
Forest Grove, *Lafayette*	71861
Forest Park (Part of Little Rock)‡	72207
Formosa	72031
Forrest City	72335*
	72336†
Fort Chaffee	72905
Fort Douglas	72854
Fort Lynn	71837
Fort Smith	72901-18
For specific ZIP Codes call (888) 275-8777, or your local postmaster.	
Fortune	72373
Forty Four	72585
Forum	72740
Fouke	71837
Fountain Hill	71642
Fountain Lake	71901
Fourche	72016
Fourche Junction	72857
Fourche Valley	72827
Fourmile Hill	72143
Fox	72051
Francis	72601
Franklin	72536
Free Hope	71753
Frenchmans Bayou	72338
Frenchport	71701
Fresno	71643
Friendship, *Cleveland*	71665
Friendship, *Columbia*	71860
Friendship, *Hot Spring*	71942
Friley	72752
Fritz	72461
Fryatt	72554
Frys Mill	72386
Fulton	71838
Furlow	72086
Gaines Landing	71653
Gainesville	72450
Gainsboro	72501
Gaither	72601
Galla Rock	72823
Gallatin	72761
Galloway	72117
Gamaliel	72537
Gammon	72364
Gardner	71765
Garfield	72732
Garland City	71839
Garland Springs	72111
Garner	72052
Garner's Farm	71742
Garnett	71667
Garret Grove	72368
Garrett	72846
Garrett Bridge	71639
Gassville	72635
Gateway	72733
Gaylor	72657
Geneva	71832
Genoa	71840
Gentry	72734
George Creek	72687
Georgetown, *Madison*	72773
Georgetown, *Pope*	72847
Georgetown, *White*	72143
Gepp	72538
Geridge	72046
Gethsemane	72004
Gibbs	71969
Gibson, *Craighead*	72404
Gibson, *Pulaski*♦	72120
Gieseck	72373
Gifford	72104
Gilbert	72636
Gilchrist	72358
Giles Spur	72476
Gilkey	72853
Gillett	72055
Gillham	71841
Gilmore	72339
Gin City	71826
Gladden	72331
Gleason	72032
Glemore	72802
Glencoe	72539
Glendale	71667
Glen Rose	72104
Glenview (Part of North Little Rock)	72117
Glenwood	71943
Gobblers Point	72080
Gobell	72366
Gold Creek	72032
Golden City	72927
Golden Lake	72395
Gold Lake Estates	72032
Goobertown	72417
Good Hope	71726
Goodwin	72340
Goose Camp	72840
Goshen	72735
Gosnell	72315
Gould	71643
Gourd	71639
Gourd Neck	72101
Grady	71644
Grand Glaise	72020
Grandview	72601
Grange	72521
Grannis	71944
Grapevine	72057
Graphic	72921
Grassy Lake Bottom	72331
Gravel Hill, *Van Buren*	72030
Gravel Hill, *White*	72136
Gravelly	72838
Gravelridge, *Bradley*	71631
Gravel Ridge, *Pulaski*♦	72076
Graves Chapel	71846
Gravesville	72039
Gravette	72736
Gray Rock	72855
Grays	72101
Grayson	72927
Greasy Corner	72346
Green Acres	72758
Greenbrier	72058
Greene High	72450
Greenfield	72432
Green Forest	72638
Green Hill	71675
Greenland	72737
Green Tree	72031
Greenway	72430
Greenwich Village	71854
Greenwood, *Franklin*	72949
Greenwood, *Sebastian*	72936
Greers Ferry	72067
Gregory	72059
Grider	72370
Griffith Spring	71667
Griffithtown	71923
Griffithville	72060
Grubbs	72431
Guernsey	71801
Guion	72540
Gum Corner	71640
Gum Log	72802
Gum Springs, *Clark*	71923
Gum Springs, *Newton*	72641
Gurdon	71743
Guy	72061
Hackett	72937
Hagarville	72839
Half Moon	72315
Halley	71638
Halley Junction	71638
Halliday	72443
Hamburg	71646
Hamil	72460
Hamilton	72024
Hampton	71744
Hampton's Landing	72041
Hancock	72419
Hanna	71640
Hannaberry	72160
Hanover	72560
Happy	72143
Happy Bend	72823
Happy Corners	72438
Hardin	71602
Hardy	72542
Hargrave Corner	72461
Harlow	71766
Harmon, *Boone*	72601
Harmon, *Washington*	72704
Harmontown	72501
Harmony, *Columbia*	71753
Harmony, *Johnson*	72830
Harmony, *Madison*	72740
Harmony, *White*	72143
Harmony Grove	71701
Harness	72645
Harp	72104
Harrell	71745
Harriet	72639
Harrisburg	72432
Harrison	72601*
	72602†
Hartford	72938
Hartman	72840
Hartwell	72740
Harvey	72841
Haskell	72015
Hasty	72640
Hatchie Coon	72472
Hatfield	71945
Hattieville	72063
Hatton	71946
Havana	72842
Hayley	72040
Haynes	72341
Hazen	72064
Heafer	72331
Healing Springs	72712
Heart	72539
Heber Springs	72543
Hebron	71660
Hector	72843
Helena	72342
Helena Crossing (Part of Helena)	72342
Helena Junction	72342
Hempwallace	71964
Henderson	72544
Henderson College (Part of Arkadelphia)‡	71923
Hendrix College (Part of Conway)‡	72032
Hensley	72065
Herbine	71665
Hergett	72404
Heritage Estates	72653
Herman	72404
Hermitage, *Bradley*	71647
Hermitage (Part of Little Rock)	72206
Herndon	72404
Hervey	71854
Heth	72346
Hickeytown	72847
Hickman	72315
Hickoria	72422
Hickory Creek	72745
Hickory Flat	72121
Hickory Hill	72110
Hickory Plains	72066
Hickory Ridge	72347
Hickory Valley	72521
Hicks	72366
Hicks Station	72394
Hicksville	72366
Hidden Valley	72542
Higden	72067
Higgins (Part of Little Rock)	72206
Higginson	72068
Highfill	72734
Highland	72542
Highland Estates	72745
Hill Creek	72127
Hillcrest, *Johnson*	72830
Hillcrest (Part of Little Rock)‡	72205
Hilleman	72101
Hilltop	72482
Hilo	71647
Hindsville	72738
Hiram	72179
Hiwasse	72739
Hobbs Spur	72952
Holiday Hills	72531
Holiday Island	72631
Holland	72173
Hollis	72857
Holly Grove	72069
Holly Hills	72501
Holly Island	72461
Holly Ridge	71640
Holly Springs, *Dallas*	71763
Holly Springs, *White*	72143
Hollywood	71923
Holman	72846
Holub	72360
Homan	71854
Homewood	72025
Hon	72958
Hooker	72450
Hope	71801*
	71802†
Hopeville	71766
Hopewell, *Cleburne*	72137
Hopewell, *Greene*	72443
Hopewell, *Lawrence*	72433

*** Area Zip Code** **† Post Office Boxes** **‡ Postal Station** **♦ Census Designated Place** *Italic Type* **County**

Hopper 71935
Horatio 71842
Horseshoe 72112
Horseshoe Bend 72512
Horseshoe Lake, *Crittenden* 72348
Horseshoe Lake, *Woodruff* 72006
Horton 72326
Hot Springs (Hot Springs National Park) 71901-14
71951
For specific ZIP Codes call (888) 275-8777, or your local postmaster.
Hot Springs Mall (Part of Hot Springs) 71913
Hot Springs Village 71909
Houston 72070
Howell 72071
Hoxie 72433
Hudspeth 71638
Huff 72501
Huffman 72315
Hughes 72348
Hulbert (Part of West Memphis) 72301
Humnoke 72072
Humphrey 72073
Hunt 72840
Hunter 72074
Huntington 72940
Huntsville 72740
Hurricane Grove 71957
Hutchinson 72534
Huttig 71747
Hydrick 72324
Ida 72546
Imboden 72434
Immanuel 72003
Index 71854
Indian Bay 72069
Indiandale (Part of Hot Springs)‡ 71901
Indianhead Lake Estates (Part of North Little Rock) 72116
Indian Meadows 65733
Indian Springs 72002
Industrial (Part of Little Rock)‡ 72209
Ingalls 71647
Ingleside 72112
Ingram 72478
Ink 71953
Ione 72927
Iron Springs 72206
Island Town 72112
Iuka 72519
Ivan 71748
Ivesville (Part of Little Rock) 72207
Ivy 71725
Jabb 72046
Jackson Heights (Part of Jacksonville) 72076
Jacksonport 72075
Jacksonville 72076-78
72099
For specific ZIP Codes call (888) 275-8777, or your local postmaster.
Jamestown, *Independence* 72501
Jamestown, *Johnson* 72830
Japton 72740
Jarrett 72444
Jasmine 72060
Jasper 72641
Jefferson 72079
Jefferson Square (Part of Pine Bluff) 71601
Jeffersonville 72360
Jeffrey 72118
Jennette 72327
Jennie 71649
Jenny Lind 72916
Jenson 72937
Jericho 72327
Jerome 71650
Jersey 71651
Jerusalem 72080
Jessieville 71949
Jesup 72466
Joan 71923
Johnson 72741
Johnson Addition 72411
Johnstown 72112
Johnsville 71647
Joiner 72350
Jolliff Store 72442
Jonesboro 72401-03
For specific ZIP Codes call (888) 275-8777, or your local postmaster.
Jones Mills 72105
Jonesville 71837
Jonquil 72346
Joplin 71957
Jordan 72519
Joy 72143
Joyce City 71762
Joyland Park 72927
Judd Hill 72472
Judsonia 72081
Julius 72327
Jumbo 72556
Junction City 71749
Kansas 71772
Kearney 72132
Kedron 71665
Keiser 72351
Kellum 71832
Kelso 71674
Kenova 71762
Kensett 72082
Kent 71701
Kentucky 72015
Kenwood 72823
Keo 72083
Kerlin 71753
Kerr 72142
Kibler 72956
Kimberley 71958
Kindall 72374
King 71841
Kingsland 71652
Kingston, *Madison* 72742
Kingston, *Yell* 72853
Kingswood Estates 72653
Kingtown 72366
Kirby 71950
Kirkland 71751
Knob 72436
Knobel 72435
Knoxville 72845
Koch Ridge 72031
Lacey 71655
Laconia 72379
LaCrosse 72584
Ladd 71601
Ladelle 71655
Lafe 72436
Lafferty 72561
La Grange 72352
Lake Bull Shoales Estates 72687
Lake Catherine 71901
Lake City 72437
Lake Dick 72004
Lake Elmdale 72764
Lake Francis 72761
Lake Hamilton♦ 71913
Lake Poinsett 72432
Lakeport 71653
Lakeside (Part of Hot Springs) 71901
Lakeside, *Ouachita* 71701
Lakeside Country Club 72065
Lakeside Terrace 72653
Lakeview, *Baxter* 72642
Lakeview, *Conway* 72110
Lake View, *Craighead* 72437
Lake View, *Phillips* 72342
Lakeview Estates 71970
Lake Village 71653
Lakeway 72687
Lakewood, *Jefferson* 72004
Lakewood (Part of North Little Rock) 72116
Lakewood Estates 75501
Lakewood Village (Part of North Little Rock) 72116
Lamar 72846
Lamartine 71770
Lambert 71929
Lambrook 72353
Landers 72472
Landis 72650
Laneburg 71844
Langford 72004
Langley 71952
Lanieve 72416
Lansing 72327
Lanty 72063
Lapile 71765
La Plaza Acres 72143
Larkin 72584
Larue 72756
Latour 72355
Lauratown 72433
Lavaca 72941
Lawson 71750
Lazy Acres 65733
Leachville 72438
Lead Hill 72644
Lebanon 71846
Lee Creek 72934
Lehi 72364
Leitner (Part of Pine Bluff) 71601
Leola 72084
Leonard 72461
Lepanto 72354
Leslie 72645
Lester 72437
Letona 72085
Levy (Part of North Little Rock) 72118
Lewisville 71845
Lexa 72355
Lexington 72031
Liberty 72835
Liberty Hall 72834
Liberty Valley 72010
Lick Mountain 72027
Light 72439
Limedale 72501
Limestone 72628
Lincoln 72744
Linder 72058
Lisbon 71730
Little Bay 71766
Little Flock 72756
Little Garnett 71667
Little Italy 72016
Little Red 72121
Little River 72442
Little River Country Club 71866
Little Rock 72201-07
72209-95
For specific ZIP Codes call (888) 275-8777, or your local postmaster.
Little Rock Air Force Base 72099
Locke 72946
Lockesburg 71846
Locust Bayou 71701
Locust Grove 72550
Lodge Corner 72160
Lodi 71943
Logan 72761
Lollie 72106
London 72847
Lonelm 72947
Lone Pine 72650
Lono 72084
Lonoke 72086
Lonsdale 72087
Lookout, *Benton* 72756
Lookout, *Monroe* 72134
Lorado 72401
Lorine 72455
Lost Bridge Village 72732
Lost Cane 72442
Lost Corner 72080
Louann 71751
Louise 72376
Lowell 72745
Lower Boydsville 72461
Lower Poplar Ridge 72414
Lower White Oak Lake 71726
Low Gap 72641
Luber 72560
Lucas 72927
Ludwig 72830
Lumber 71770
Luna 71653
Lundell 72367
Lunenburg 72556
Lunsford 72437
Lurton 72856
Lutherville 72846
Luxora 72358
Lynch (Part of North Little Rock) 72117
Lynn 72440
Mabelvale (Part of Little Rock) 72103
McAlmont 72117
McArthur 71654
McBrides 65733
McCain Mall (Part of North Little Rock) 72116
McCaskill 71847
McClelland 72006
McCormick 72472
McCreanor 72024
McCrory 72101
McDonald 72373
McDougal 72441
Macedonia, *Columbia* 71753
Macedonia, *Conway* 72063
McElroy 72396
McEntre 72476
Macey 72447
McFadden 72347
McGehee 71654
McGintytown 72058
McGregor 72036
McHue 72501
McJester 72121
McKamie 71860
Macks 72112
McMilan Corner 71653
McNab 71838
McNeil 71752
McNutt 72476
Macon 72076
Macon Lake 71653
McRae 72102
Madding 72004
Madison 72359
Magazine 72943
Magic Springs 72650
Magness 72553
Magnet Cove 72104
Magnolia 71753*
71754†
Main Street (Part of North Little Rock)‡ 72119
Mallet Town 72157
Mallory Spur 72348
Malvern 72104
Mammoth Spring 72554
Mandalay 72442
Mandeville 75501
Manfred 71935
Mangrum 72414
Manila 72442
Manning 71763
Mansfield 72944
Many Island 72554
Maple 72616
Maple Corner 72374
Maple Grove 72472
Maple Springs 72571
Marble 72740
Marble Falls 72648
Marcella 72555
Marche 72118
Marc Lyn Estates 72687
Marianna 72360
Marie 72395
Marion 72364
Marked Tree 72365
Marmaduke 72443
Marsden 71647
Marsena 72650
Marshall 72650
Mars Hill 71860
Martindale 72210
Martinville 72204
Marvell 72366
Marvinville 72842
Marysville 71753
Mason Valley 72712
Masonville 71654
Massard (Part of Fort Smith) 72901
Maumee 72675
Maumelle‡ 72113
Maxville 72521
Mayfield 72703
Mayflower 72106
Maynard 72444
Maysville 72747
Mazarn 71933
Meadow Cliff 72335
Meeks Settlement 71962
Melbourne 72556
Mellwood 72367
Melrose 72550
Mena 71953
Menifee 72107
Meridian 71635
Meroney 71643
Merrivale (Part of Little Rock) 72209
Mesa 72041
Metalton 72601
Middlebrook 72444
Middleton 72027
Midland (Part of Fort Smith)‡ 72904
Midland, *Sebastian* 72945
Midway, *Baxter* 72651
Midway, *Hot Spring* 71941
Midway, *Howard* 71852
Midway, *Jackson* 72479
Midway, *Lafayette* 71845
Midway, *Logan* 72865
Midway, *Nevada* 71857
Midway, *White* 72568
Midway Corner 72376
Milford 71846
Mill Creek, *Pope* 72802
Mill Creek (Part of Fort Smith) 72901
Mill Creek Estates 72687
Milligan Ridge 72442
Milltown 72936
Milo 71646
Mimosa Circle 72513
Mineral 71841
Mineral Springs 71851
Minorca 72444
Minturn 72445
Mist 71646
Mitchell 72583
Mitchellville 71639
Mixon 72927
Moark 72422
Mohawk 71740
Moko 72557
Monarch 72687
Monette 72447
Monkey Run 72635
Monnie Springs 72135
Monroe 72108
Montana 72840
Monte Ne Shores 72758
Monterey 72373
Monticello 71655*
71657†
Montongo 71655
Montreal 72940
Montrose 71658
Moore 72856
Moore Camp 71822
Moorefield 72501
Moreland 72802
Morgan 72118
Morganton 72013
Morning Star, *Garland* 71901
Morning Star, *Searcy* 72650
Morning Sun 72143
Moro 72368
Morobay 71651
Morrilton 72110
Morris 71828
Morrison Bluff 72863
Morriston 72576
Morrow 72749
Morton 72101
Mosby 72328
Moscow 71659
Mosley 72834
Mossville 72641
Mounds, *Crittenden* 72376
Mounds, *Greene* 72461
Mountainburg 72946
Mountain Crest 72727
Mountain Fork 71953
Mountain Harbor 71957
Mountain Home 72653*
72654†
Mountain Pine 71956
Mountain Springs 72023
Mountain Top 72949
Mountain Valley 71901
Mountain View 72560
Mount Elba 71660
Mount Elba Edition 71665
Mount Gayler 72959
Mount George 72833
Mount Hersey 72685
Mount Holly 71758
Mount Ida 71957
Mount Judea 72655
Mount Moriah 71958
Mount Olive, *Bradley* 71647
Mount Olive, *Conway* 72127
Mount Olive, *Izard* 72556
Mount Olive, *Washington* 72727
Mount Pisgah 72143
Mount Pleasant, *Izard* 72561
Mount Pleasant, *Miller* 71854
Mount Sherman 72641
Mount Tabor 71956
Mount Vernon, *Faulkner* 72111
Mount Vernon, *Johnson* 72840
Mozart 72051
Muddyfork 71852
Mulberry 72947
Mull 72687
Murfreesboro 71958
Murphys Corner 72112
Mustin Lake 71701
Myron 72513
Nady 72166
Nail 72628
Nance 72087
Nashville 71852

* **Area Zip Code** † **Post Office Boxes** ‡ **Postal Station** ♦ **Census Designated Place** *Italic Type* **County**

Nathan 71852
Natural Dam 72948
Natural Steps 72135
Naylor 72173
Neal Springs 71842
Nebo 71667
Needham 72437
Needmore 72958
Nella 71953
Nelsonville 72466
Nettleton (Part of Jonesboro)‡ 72402
Neuhardt 72376
Newark 72562
New Augusta (Part of Augusta) 72006
New Blaine 72851
Newburg 72556
New Dixie 72016
New Edinburg 71660
Newell 71730
New Gascony 72004
New Hope, *Dallas* 71763
New Hope, *Drew* 71655
New Hope, *Hempstead* 71801
New Hope, *Independence* 72501
Newhope, *Pike* 71959
New Hope, *Pope* 72802
New London 71765
Newnata 72680
Newport 72112
New Spadra 72830
New Summit (Part of Benton) 72011
New Town, *Crawford* 72921
Newtown, *Jefferson* 72004
Nimmo 72143
Nimmons 72461
Nimrod 72126
Nine Elms 72761
Noble Lake 71601
Nodena 72395
Noland 72455
Norfolk Lake Estates 72544
Norfork 72658-59
For specific ZIP Codes call (888) 275-8777, or your local postmaster.
Norfork Village 72658
Norman 71960
Norphlet 71759
Norristown (Part of Russellville) 72802
North Bingen 71852
North Cedar (Part of Pine Bluff)‡ 71601
North Crossett♦ 71635
North Dardanelle 72802
Northern Ohio 72365
North Heights (Part of Texarkana) 71854
North Hughes 72348
North Little Rock 72113-20
72124
72190
For specific ZIP Codes call (888) 275-8777, or your local postmaster.
Northpoint 72135
Northwest Arkansas Mall (Part of Fayetteville) 72703
Norvell (Part of Earle) 72331
Nuckles 72020
Number Nine 72315
Nunley 71953
Oak Bower 71929
Oak Forest, *Lee* 72360
Oak Forest (Part of Little Rock) 72205
Oak Grove, *Carroll* 72660
Oak Grove, *Clark* 71728
Oak Grove, *Hot Spring* 72104
Oak Grove, *Little River* 71822
Oak Grove, *Lonoke* 72007
Oak Grove, *Nevada* 71858
Oak Grove, *Perry* 72070
Oak Grove, *Pope* 72802
Oak Grove, *Pulaski* 72118
Oak Grove, *Sevier* 71846
Oak Grove, *Washington* 72764
Oak Grove Heights 72450
Oakhaven 71801
Oak Hill 71822
Oakland 72661
Oaklawn (Part of Hot Springs) 71901

Oak Park (Part of Pine Bluff)‡ 71603
Oark 72852
Oden 71961
O'Donnell Bend 72358
Ogden 71853
Ogemaw 71764
Oil Trough 72564
O'Kean 72449
Okolona 71962
Ola 72853
Old Alabam 72740
Old Austin 72007
Old Grand Glaise 72020
Old Hickory 72063
Old Jenny Lind 72901
Old Joe 72658
Old Town 72389
Old Union 71730
Old Weona 72472
Olio 72958
Oliver 72958
Olmstead 72076
Olvey 72601
Olyphant 72020
Oma 71964
Omaha 72662
Omega, *Carroll* 72616
Omega, *Yell* 72834
Onda 72774
One Horse Store 72160
Oneida 72369
Onia 72663
Onyx 72857
Opal, *Polk* 71953
Opal, *White* 72012
Oppelo 72110
Optimus 72519
Orion 72132
Orlando 71660
Osage 72638
Osage Mills 72712
Osage Village 72531
Osceola 72370
Ott 65626
Otto 72173
Otwell 72404
Ouachita 71763
Ouachita College (Part of Arkadelphia)‡ 71923
Overcup, *Conway* 72110
Overcup, *Woodruff* 72101
Owensville 72087
Oxford 72565
Oxley 72645
Ozan 71855
Ozark 72949
Ozark Acres, *Baxter* 72635
Ozark Acres, *Sharp* 72482
Ozark Lithia 71901
Ozone 72854
Pace City 71751
Palestine 72372
Palmyra 71667
Pangburn 72121
Pankey (Part of Little Rock) 72212
Panther Forest 71653
Paradise Landing 72106
Paragould 72450*
72451†
Paraloma 71846
Paris 72855
Parkdale 71661
Parkers 72206
Parkers Chapel 71730
Park Grove 72029
Park Hill (Part of North Little Rock)‡ 72116
Parkin 72373
Park Place 72320
Park Plaza (Part of Little Rock) 72205
Parks 72950
Parma 72044
Parmenter Addition 72315
Parnell 72023
Paron 72122
Parthenon 72666
Pastoria 72152
Patmos 71801
Patrick 72727
Patsville 71647
Patterson 72123
Pawheen 72438
Payneway 72472
Peach Orchard 72453
Pearcy 71964
Pea Ridge, *Benton* 72751
Pea Ridge, *Desha* 71674
Pearson 72131
Pecan Point 72350
Peel 72668

Pelsor 72856
Pencil Bluff 71965
Pendleton 71639
Penjur 72348
Pennington 72005
Pennys 71846
Penrose 72101
Peppers Landing 72041
Perla 72104
Perry 72125
Perrytown 71801
Perryville 72126
Peter Pender 72933
Peter Rock Acres 72031
Pettigrew 72752
Pettus 72086
Pettyville 72442
Pfeiffer 72501
Philadelphia 72401
Philander Smith College (Part of Little Rock) 72202
Phillips Bayou 72360
Phoenix Village (Part of Fort Smith) 72901
Pickens, *Desha* 71662
Pickens, *White* 72143
Pickering 71730
Piercetown 72641
Piggott 72454
Pike 71958
Pilgrims Rest 72764
Pindall 72669
Pine Bluff 71601-13
For specific ZIP Codes call (888) 275-8777, or your local postmaster.
Pine Bluff Arsenal 71602
Pine Bluff Southeast (Part of Pine Bluff) 71601
Pine City 72069
Pine Grove 71763
Pine Grove Valley 72944
Pine Ridge 71966
Pine Tree 72326
Pineville 72566
Piney, *Garland*♦ 71913
Piney, *Johnson* 72847
Piney Grove 71845
Pinnacle 72135
Pisgah, *Pike* 71940
Pisgah, *Yell* 72834
Pitman 72444
Pitts 72421
Plainfield 71740
Plainview, *White* 72081
Plainview, *Yell* 72857
Plant 72031
Pleasant Grove, *Craighead* 72401
Pleasant Grove, *Stone* 72567
Pleasant Grove, *Van Buren* 72030
Pleasant Hill, *Crawford* 72947
Pleasant Hill, *Cross* 72396
Pleasant Hill, *Garland* 71901
Pleasant Hill, *Nevada* 71857
Pleasant Plains 72568
Pleasant Ridge 72632
Pleasant Valley, *Carroll* 72616
Pleasant Valley, *Faulkner* 72058
Pleasant Valley, *Izard* 72519
Pleasant Valley, *Lafayette* 71826
Pleasant Valley, *Perry* 72016
Pleasant Valley, *Pope* 72837
Pleasant View, *Conway* 72110
Pleasant View, *Franklin* 72949
Pleasure Heights 72745
Plumerville 72127
Plunketts 72017
Pocahontas 72455
Point Cedar 71921
Pollard 72456
Ponca 72670
Ponders 72476
Pontoon 72025
Poplar Grove 72374
Portia 72457
Portland 71663
Posey 72392
Possum Grape 72020
Postelle 72366
Post Oak 71658
Potter 71953
Potter Junction 71953
Pottsville 72858

Poughkeepsie 72569
Powhatan 72458
Poyen 72128
Prairie Creek♦ 72756
Prairie Grove 72753
Prairie View 72863
Prattsville 72129
Prescott 71857
Preston 72032
Preston Ferry 72134
Price Place 65729
Prim 72130
Princedale 72373
Princeton 71725
Process City 71832
Proctor 72376
Promised Land, *Mississippi* 72315
Promised Land, *Poinsett* 72472
Providence 72081
Provo 71846
Pruitt 72648
Pumpkin Bend 72101
Pyatt 72672
Quarry Heights 72826
Quinn 71730
Quitman 72131
Raggio 72320
Ragtown 72069
Rainbow Island 72121
Ralph 72687
Rambo Riveria 72756
Ramsey 71742
Ramsey Hill 72501
Ranger 72824
Ratcliff 72951
Ratio 72333
Ravanna 75556
Ravenden 72459
Ravenden Springs 72460
Rawlison 72348
Ray Lee Addition 72802
Reader 71726
Readland 71640
Rea Valley 72634
Rector 72461
Redfield 72132
Redland 71857
Red Leaf 71653
Red Onion 72447
Red Springs 71743
Red Star 72752
Red Wing 71832
Reed 71670
Reedville 71639
Relfs Bluff 71667
Remmel 72112
Rena 72956
Republican 72058
Revel 72006
Rex 72031
Reydell 72133
Reyno 72462
Rich 72021
Richardson 72004
Richland View 72727
Richmond 71822
Richwood 72476
Richwoods 71923
Ridgeway 72601
Rio Vista 72010
Risher 72421
Rison 71665
Rivercliff Estates 72756
Riverdale 72941
River Mountain 72835
Riverside 72101
Rivervale 72377
Riverview 72110
Riverview Addition 72501
Rixey (Part of North Little Rock) 72117
Robertsville 72063
Robinson 72761
Rob Roy 72004
Rock Hill 71846
Rockport 72104
Rock Springs 71675
Rockwell 71913
Rocky 71953
Rocky Hill 72629
Rocky Mound, *Hempstead* 71801
Rocky Mound, *Miller* 71837
Rodney 72519
Roe 72134
Rogers 72756-58
For specific ZIP Codes call (888) 275-8777, or your local postmaster.
Rogers Avenue (Part of Fort Smith)‡ 72903

Rohwer 71666
Roland 72135
Rolla 72104
Romance 72136
Rondo, *Lee* 72355
Rondo, *Miller* 71854
Rosa 72358
Rosboro 71921
Rose Bud 72137
Rose City (Part of North Little Rock)‡ 72117
Rose Hill 71655
Roseland 72442
Rose Meadow (Part of Little Rock) 72206
Roseville 72949
Rosie 72571
Ross 72846
Rosston 71858
Ross Van-Ness 71640
Rotan 72370
Round Pond 72394
Rover 72828
72860
For specific ZIP Codes call (888) 275-8777, or your local postmaster.
Rowell 71665
Roy 71852
Royal 71968
Royal Oak 72103
Rubicon 72015
Ruddell Hill 72501
Rudy 72952
Rule 72638
Rumley 72645
Rupert 72031
Rushing 72051
Russell 72139
Russellville 72801-02
72811-12
For specific ZIP Codes call (888) 275-8777, or your local postmaster.
Rutherford 72501
Rye 71665
Sacred Heart 72840
Saddle 72554
Saffell 72572
Sage 72573
Saginaw 71941
St. Charles 72140
St. Francis 72464
St. Joe 72675
St. Matthews 71752
St. Paul 72760
St. Vincent 72063
Salado 72575
Salem, *Fulton* 72576
Salem, *Lee* 72368
Salem, *Pike* 71943
Salem, *Saline*♦ 72015
Salesville 72653
Saltillo 72032
Salus 72854
Sand Hill 72040
Sandtown 72501
Sandy Bend 71765
Sandyland 71762
Sandy Ridge 72315
Sans Souci 72370
Sarassa 71644
Saratoga 71859
Sardis 72011
Savoy 72704
Schaal 71851
Schaberg 72946
Schooley 71851
Schug 72450
Scotland 72141
Scott 72142
Scottsville 72837
Scott Valley 72360
Scranton 72863
Screeton 72064
Searcy 72143*
72145†
Seaton 72046
Seaton Dump 72046
Sedgwick 72465
Sellers Store 72542
Selma 71670
Seyppel 72348
Shady 71953
Shady Grove, *Faulkner* 72058
Shady Grove, *Fulton* 72583
Shady Grove, *Johnson* 72830
Shady Grove, *Mississippi* 72442
Shady Grove, *Nevada* 71857

Place	ZIP Code
Shady Grove, *Poinsett*	72472
Shakertown	71923
Shannon	72455
Shannondale	72348
Shannon Hills	72103
Shannonville	72331
Sharman	71860
Sharum	72455
Shaw	72015
Shearerville	72346
Shelbyville	72521
Shell Lake	72346
Sheppard	71838
Sheridan	72150
Sherrill	72152
Sherwood	72120
Sherwood Hills	72105
Shiloh, *Howard*	71851
Shiloh, *Pope*	72802
Shippen	72351
Shirley	72153
Shoffner	72112
Shover Springs	71801
Sidney	72577
Sidon	72137
Signal Hill	72560
Siloam Springs	72761
Silver	71957
Silver Hill	72675
Silver Ridge, *Cleburne*	72530
Silver Ridge, *Sevier*	71846
Sims	71969
Simsboro	72348
Sitka	72482
Skunkhollow	72032
Slaytonville	72937
Slonikers Mill	72372
Slovak	72160
Smackover	71762
Smale	72021
Smearney	71647
Smithdale	72373
Smiths Corner	72368
Smithville, *Lawrence*	72466
Smithville, *Miller*	71834
Snow	72687
Snowball	72650
Snow Hill	71751
Snow Lake	72379
Snyder	71658
Social Hill	72104
Solgohachia	72156
Sonora	72764
South Bend	72076
South Crossett (Part of Crossett)	71635
Southern Hills	72601
Southern State College (Part of Magnolia)‡	71753
South Fort Smith (Part of Fort Smith)‡	72906
South Jacksonville (Part of Jacksonville)	72076
Southland, *Craighead*	72437
Southland, *Phillips*	72355
South Lead Hill	72644
South Lewisville	71845
South Ozark	72949
South Sheridan	72150
South Shore Park	72543
South Side, *Independence*	72501
South Side (Part of Little Rock)‡	72206
Southside, *Van Buren*	72013
Spadra	72830
Sparkman	71763
Spence Junction	72856
Spirit Lake	71845
Springdale	72762-66
For specific ZIP Codes call (888) 275-8777, or your local postmaster.	
Springfield	72157
Springhill, *Faulkner*	72058
Spring Hill, *Hempstead*	71801
Spring Lake Estates	72653
Springtown	72734
Spring Valley (Part of Little Rock)	72210
Spring Valley, *Independence*	72501
Spring Valley, *Washington*	72764
Sprudel	71838
Stacy, *Crittenden*	72384
Stacy, *Poinsett*	72472
Stamps	71860
Standard-Umsted	71762
Stanford	72450
Star City	71667
State Capitol (Part of Little Rock)‡	72201
State Line, *Columbia*	71740
State Line, *Lafayette*	71861
State University (Part of Jonesboro)	72467
Staves	71665
Stelltown	71940
Stephens	71764
Steprock	72159
Stevens Creek	72010
Stevens Landing	72472
Stokes	72455
Stonewall	72450
Stony Point	72070
Story	71970
Strangers Home	72410
Strawberry, *Johnson*	72846
Strawberry, *Lawrence*	72469
Stringtown	71842
Strong	71765
Stump City	72346
Sturkie	72578
Stuttgart	72160
Subiaco	72865
Success	72470
Sugar Grove	72927
Sugarloaf Lake	72937
Sulphur City	72701
Sulphur Rock	72579
Sulphur Springs, *Benton*	72768
Sulphur Springs, *Jefferson*	71603
Sulphur Springs, *Johnson*	72830
Sulphur Springs, *Yell*	72834
Summers	72769
Summerville	71744
Summit	72677
Sumpter	71647
Sunnydale	72081
Sunny Hill (Part of Searcy)	72143
Sunset, *Crittenden*	72364
Sunset, *Washington*	72959
Sunshine, *Ashley*	71661
Sunshine, *Garland*	71968
Supply	72444
Sutton	71835
Swain	72628
Swan Lake	72004
Sweden	72004
Sweethome, *Montgomery*	71957
Sweet Home (Part of Little Rock)	72164
Swifton	72471
Sycamore Bend	72348
Sylamore	72556
Sylvan Hills (Part of Sherwood)	72116
Sylvania	72176
Sylverino	71854
Tafton	72183
Talley	71740
Tall Trees	72322
Tamo	71644
Tanglewood	72756
Tannenbaum	72530
Tarry	71667
Tate	72927
Tates Bluff	71726
Taylor	71861
Tech (Part of Russellville)‡	72801
Tennessee	71655
Texarkana	71854
Thebes	71658
Thida	72165
Thompson Grove	72348
Thornburg	72126
Thorney	72727
Thornton	71766
Three Brothers	72653
Three Creeks	71749
Three Way	72370
Tichnor	72166
Tie Plant Spur (Part of North Little Rock)	72117
Tillar	71670
Tilly	72679
Tilton	72347
Timber Lake Manor	72531
Timber Lane	71833
Timbo	72657
	72680
For specific ZIP Codes call (888) 275-8777, or your local postmaster.	
Tinsman	71767
Toad Suck	72016
Togo	72373
Tokio	71852
Toledo	71665
Tollette	71851
Tollville	72041
Toltec	72142
Tomahawk	72675
Tomato	72381
Tomberlin	72046
Toneyville (Part of Jacksonville)	72076
Tongin	72320
Tontitown	72770
Trammellville	72461
Traskwood	72167
Treasure Hills, *Faulkner*	72032
Treasure Hills (Part of Little Rock)‡	72207
Treat	72854
Trenton	72374
Troy	71764
Trumann	72472
Tucker	72168
Tuckerman	72473
Tuckertown	72321
Tulip	71725
Tull	72015
Tully	72472
Tulot	72472
Tumbling Shoals	72581
Tupelo	72169
Turkey Scratch	72366
Turner	72383
Turrell	72384
Tuttle	72727
Twentythree	72010
Twin Groves	72039
Twin Lakes (Part of Little Rock)	72205
Twin Springs	72211
Twist	72331
Tyro	71639
Tyronza	72386
Ulm	72170
Umpire	71971
Union, *Fulton*	72576
Union, *Sevier*	71832
Union Hill	72020
Uniontown	72955
Unionville	71665
Unity	71852
University Mall (Part of Little Rock)‡	72205
University of Arkansas at Monticello (Part of Monticello)	71655
University of Central Arkansas (Part of Conway)‡	72032
Uno	72421
Upper White Oak Lake	71726
Urbana	71768
Urbanette	72601
Ursula	72933
Vaden	71923
Vail	72438
Valley Gin	71837
Valley Springs	72682
Valley View	72404
Van	72042
Van Buren	72956*
	72957†
Vandervoort	71972
Vanndale	72387
Vaughn	72712
Velvet Ridge	72010
Vendor	72683
Verona	72682
Vesta	72933
Vick	71647
Victoria	72370
Village	71769
Vilonia	72173
Vimy Ridge	72002
Vincent	72327
Vine Prairie	72947
Vineyard	72360
Viney Grove	72753
Vinity Corner	72143
Viola	72583
Violet Hill	72584
Vista Shores	72732
Wabash	72389
Wabbaseka	72175
Wakefield Village (Part of Little Rock)	72209
Walcott	72474
Waldenburg	72475
Waldo	71770
Waldron	72958
Walker, *Columbia*	71753
Walker, *White*	72143
Walker's Corner	72142
Walkers Creek	71861
Walkerville	71740
Wallace	71836
Walnut	72854
Walnut Corner, *Greene*	72416
Walnut Corner, *Phillips*	72312
Walnut Grove, *Clay*	72435
Walnut Grove, *Independence*	72524
Walnut Grove, *Van Buren*	72031
Walnut Grove, *Washington*	72730
Walnut Grove, *Yell*	72842
Walnut Hill	71826
Walnut Ridge	72476
Walnut Springs	71842
Walters	72438
Waltreak	72833
Ward	72176
Wardell	72350
War Eagle	72756
Warm Springs	72478
Warner	71701
Warren	71671
Washburn	72936
Washington	71862
Washita	71957
Watalula	72949
Waterloo	71858
Watkins Corner	72366
Watson	71674
Watson Chapel (Part of Pine Bluff)	71601
Wattensaw	72086
Waveland	72842
Waverly	72376
Wayton	72628
Webb City	72949
Weber	72166
Wedington	72704
Wedington Woods	72704
Weiner	72479
Welcome	71861
Welcome Home	72650
Weldon	72112
Wellford	71640
Weona	72472
Wesley	72773
Wesley Chapel	72110
Wesson	71749
West (Part of Springdale)‡	72762
	72766
For specific ZIP Codes call (888) 275-8777, or your local postmaster.	
West Camden Heights (Part of Camden)	71701
West Crossett♦	71635
West End (Part of Pine Bluff)	71601
Western Grove	72685
West Fork	72774
West Gum Springs (Part of Gum Springs)	71923
West Hartford	72938
West Helena	72390
West Line	74734
West Marche	72118
West Memphis	72301*
	72303†
West Pangburn	72121
West Point, *Benton*	72734
West Point, *White*	72178
West Ridge	72391
Westside (Part of Little Rock)‡	72211
Westville	72956
Westwood (Part of Little Rock)	72204
Wharton	72740
Wheatley	72392
Wheeler	72703
Wheeling	72576
Whelen Springs	71772
Whispering Springs	72067
Whistleville	72442
Whitaker	72432
White	71635
White Cliffs	71846
White Hall, *Drew*	71655
White Hall, *Jefferson*	71602*
	71612†
Whitehall, *Lee*	72320
Whitehall, *Poinsett*	72432
Whiteoak	72949
White Oak Bluff	71665
White Rock	72701
Whitetown	71961
Whiteville	72635
Whitmore	72394
Whitton	72386
Wickes	71973
Wideman	72585
Widener	72394
Wiederkehr Village	72821
Wilburn	72179
Wild Cherry	72576
Wildwood	72346
Williamson	71842
Williford	72482
Willisville	71864
Willow	72084
Wilmar	71675
Wilmot	71676
Wilson, *Mississippi*	72395
Wilson, *Pope*	72823
Wilton	71865
Winchester	71677
Windamere (Part of Little Rock)	72201
Winesburg	72404
Winfield	72958
Winfrey	72959
Wing	72860
Winslow	72959
Winston Terrace (Part of Little Rock)	72201
Winthrop	71866
Wirth	72554
Wiseman	72587
Witcherville	72940
Witherspoon	71923
Witter	72776
Wittsburg	72396
Witts Springs	72686
Wiville	72101
Wolf Bayou	72530
Wonderview	72063
Woodberry	71744
Woodland	72830
Woodland Corner	72315
Woodland Heights (Part of Little Rock)	72212
Woodland Hills, *Fulton*	72542
Woodland Hills, *Saline*	72002
Woodlawn, *Cleveland*	71665
Woodlawn, *Lonoke*	72007
Woodrow	72130
Woodson	72180
Wooster	72181
Worden	72010
Wright	72182
Wrights Corner	72010
Wrightsville	72183
Wycamp	72390
Wye	72016
Wyman	72701
Wynne	72396-97
For specific ZIP Codes call (888) 275-8777, or your local postmaster.	
Wyola	72959
Yale	72752
Yancopin	71674
Yancy	71855
Yarbro	72315
Yardelle	72685
Y City	72926
Yellow Bayou	71653
Yellville	72687
Yocana	71953
Yoestown	72921
Yorktown	71678
Zachery	72366
Zent	72021
Zinc	72601
Zion	72556
Zion Hill	72110

A (Part of Berkeley)‡ 94702
A (Part of Buena Park)‡ 90621
A (Part of Eureka)‡ 95502
A (Part of Richmond)‡ 94808
A (Part of Vallejo)‡ 94590
A (Part of Walnut Creek)‡ 94596
Aberdeen 93526
Acacia Acres 93291
Academy 93611
Acampo 95220
Actis Gardens 93501
Acton♦ 93510
Adams Springs 95426
Adelaida 93446
Adelanto 92301
Adin 96006
Adobe Corners 92392
Aerial Acres 93523
Aetna Springs 94567
Afton 95920
Agate Bay 96140
Ager 96064
Agnew (Part of Santa Clara)‡ 95054*
95056†
Agoura (Part of Agoura Hills) 91301
Agoura Hills, *Los Angeles* 91301*
91376†
Agua Caliente 95476
Agua Caliente Indian Reservation 92262
Agua Dulce 91350
Aguanga 92536
Ahwahnee 93601
Airbase (Part of Santa Maria) 93455
Airport (Part of Oakland)‡ 94614
Alabama Hills 93545
Alameda 94501-02
For specific ZIP Codes call (888) 275-8777, or your local postmaster.
Alamo 94507
Alamo Oaks (Part of Danville) 94526
Alamorio 92227
Albany 94706
Alberhill 92530
Albion 95410
Albrae (Part of Fremont) 94538
Alcatraz (Part of San Francisco) 94123
Alderbrook Tract (Part of Cupertino) 95014
Aldercroft Heights 95033
Alderpoint 95511
Alder Springs 93602
Alessandro (Part of Riverside) 92508
Alexander Valley 95441
Alhambra 91801-04
91896
91899
For specific ZIP Codes call (888) 275-8777, or your local postmaster.
Alhambra Valley 94553
Alisal (Part of Salinas)‡ 93905
Aliso Viejo♦ 92656
Alleghany 95910
Allendale 95688
Allensworth 93219
Alliance (Part of Arcata) 95521
Allied Gardens (Part of San Diego) 92120
Almaden Plaza (Part of San Jose) 95118
Almaden Valley (Part of San Jose)‡ 95120
Almanor 96020
Almonte 94941
Alondra‡ 90249
Alpaugh 93201
Alpine♦ 91901*
91903†
Alpine Forest 93561
Alpine Heights 91901
Alpine Meadows 96146
Alpine Village, *Riverside* 92262
Alpine Village, *Tulare* 93265
Alta 95701
Altadena♦ 91001-03
For specific ZIP Codes call (888) 275-8777, or your local postmaster.

Alta Heights (Part of Napa) 94559
Alta Hill 95945
Al Tahoe (Part of South Lake Tahoe) 96151
Alta Loma (Part of Rancho Cucamonga) 91701
91737
For specific ZIP Codes call (888) 275-8777, or your local postmaster.
Alta Sierra, *Kern* 93285
Alta Sierra, *Nevada*♦ 95949
Altaville (Part of Angels Camp) 95221
Alta Vista 93514
Alto (Part of Mill Valley) 94941
Alton 95540
Alturas 96101
Alvarado (Part of Union City)‡ 94587
Alviso (Part of San Jose) 95002
Amador City 95601
Amarillo Beach (Part of Malibu) 90265
Ambassador (Part of Los Angeles)‡ 90005
Ambler Park 93901
Amboy 92304
Ambrose 94565
American Canyon 94589
American House 95981
Anaheim 92801-25
For specific ZIP Codes call (888) 275-8777, or your local postmaster.
Anaheim Hills (Part of Anaheim)‡ 92807-08
For specific ZIP Codes call (888) 275-8777, or your local postmaster.
Anaheim Plaza (Part of Anaheim) 92801
Ana Verde (Part of Palmdale) 93551
Anchor Bay 95445
Anderson 96007
Anderson Springs 95461
Andrew Jackson (Part of San Diego)‡ 92115
Angels Camp 95222
Angelus Oaks 92305
Angiola 93212
Angora Highlands 96150
Angwin♦ 94508
Annapolis 95412
Annex Three (Part of Los Angeles)‡ 91405-06
For specific ZIP Codes call (888) 275-8777, or your local postmaster.
Antelope 95843
Antelope Acres 93536
Antelope Valley Mall (Part of Palmdale) 93550
Antioch 94509*
94531†
Antonio 93437
Anza 92539
Applegate 95703
Apple Valley 92307-08
For specific ZIP Codes call (888) 275-8777, or your local postmaster.
Aptos♦ 95001†
95003*
Arbolada (Part of Ojai) 93023
Arbuckle♦ 95912
Arcade (Part of Los Angeles)‡ 90052
Arcade, *Sacramento* 95821
Arcadia 91006-07
91066
91077
For specific ZIP Codes call (888) 275-8777, or your local postmaster.
Arcata 95518†
95521*
Arch Beach Heights (Part of Laguna Beach) 92651
Arden‡ 95825
Arden Fair Mall (Part of Sacramento) 95815
Arden Town 95825
Ardmore (Part of South Gate) 90280
Arena 95301
Argus 93562

Arlanza Village (Part of Riverside) 92505
Arleta (Part of Los Angeles) 91331
Arlington (Part of Riverside)‡ 92503*
92513†
Arlington Heights Estate 95934
Arlynda Corners 95536
Armistead 93527
Armona♦ 93202
Army Point 94510
Army Terminal (Part of Oakland)‡ 94626
Arnold♦ 95223
Arnold Heights 92508
Aromas♦ 95004
Arrowbear Lake 92382
Arrowhead Highlands 92325
Arroyo Grande 93420*
93421†
Arroyo Vista (Part of Dublin) 94566
Artesia 90701*
90702†
Artois 95913
Arvin 93203
Arvin (labor camp) 93308
Ash Creek 96057
Ashland♦ 94541
Asian Village (Part of Westminster) 92683
Asilomar (Part of Pacific Grove) 93950
Aspendell 93514
Asti 95425
Atascadero 93422*
93423†
Athens 90047
Atherton 94027
Athlone 95333
Atlanta 95366
Atlantic Plaza (Part of Pittsburg)‡ 94565
Atlantic Richfield Plaza (Part of Los Angeles)‡ 90071
Atwater 95301
Atwood (Part of Placentia) 92811
Auberry♦ 93602
Auburn 95602-04
For specific ZIP Codes call (888) 275-8777, or your local postmaster.
Avalon 90704
Avalon Village (Part of Carson) 90745
Avenal 93204
Avery 95224
Avila Beach 93424
Avocado Heights♦ 91746
Azusa 91702
B (Part of Oakland)‡ 94612
Baden (Part of South San Francisco) 94080
Badger 93603
Bailey (Part of Whittier)‡ 90601
Baker 92309
Baker Ranch 95631
Bakersfield 93301-90
For specific ZIP Codes call (888) 275-8777, or your local postmaster.
Bakersfield East (Part of Bakersfield) 93305
Bakersfield Plaza (Part of Bakersfield) 93308
Bakersfield South (Part of Bakersfield) 93304
Balance Rock 93260
Balboa (Part of Los Angeles)‡ 91316*
91426†
Balboa (Part of Newport Beach)‡ 92661
Balboa Bay Shores (Part of Newport Beach) 92663
Balboa Island (Part of Newport Beach)‡ 92662
Balch Camp 93602
Balderson Station 95634
Baldwin Hills Regional Shopping Mall (Part of Los Angeles) 90008
Baldwin Lake 92314
Baldwin Park 91706
Baldy Mesa 92371
Ballarat 93562
Ballard 93463
Ballico 95303

Ballou (Part of Ontario) 91761
Balls Ferry 96007
Baltimore Park (Part of Larkspur) 94939
Bandini (Part of Commerce) 90040
Bangor 95914
Bankhead Springs 91934
Banner 92036
Banning 92220
Banta 95304
Barber City (Part of Westminster) 92683
Bard 92222
Bardsdale 93015
Barona 92040
Barona Indian Reservation 92040
Barrett 91917
Barrington (Part of Los Angeles)‡ 90049
Barron Park (Part of Palo Alto) 94306
Barstow, *Fresno* 93705
Barstow, *San Bernardino* 92311*
92312†
Barton (Part of Fresno)‡ 93702
Base Line (Part of San Bernardino) 92410
Bassett 91746
Bassetts 96125
Bass Lake 93604
Bass Lake Height 93644
Batavia 95620
Baumberg (Part of Hayward) 94545
Baxter 95701
Bay (Part of Big Bear Lake)‡ 92315
Bay (Part of Newport Beach)‡ 92659†
92663*
Bay Cities Annex (Part of El Segundo)‡ 90245
Bay Fair Mall (Part of San Leandro) 94578
Bayliss 95943
Bayo Vista 94572
Bay Park (Part of San Diego) 92110
Bay Point 94565
Bayshore (Part of Brisbane) 94005
Bayshore Mall (Part of Eureka) 95501
Bayside, *Humboldt* 95524
Bayside (Part of San Jose)‡ 95131
95134
95164
For specific ZIP Codes call (888) 275-8777, or your local postmaster.
Bayview, *Humboldt*♦ 95503
Bayview (Part of San Francisco)‡ 94124
Bayview Park 94806
Baywood Park 93402
Beach Center (Part of Huntington Beach)‡ 92648
Beale Air Force Base 95903
Bear Creek Estates 95006
Bear River Lake 95666
Bear River Pines 95945
Bear Valley, *Alpine* 95223
Bear Valley, *Mariposa* 95338
Bear Valley Springs♦ 93561
Beaumont 92223
Beckwourth 96129
Bee Rock 93426
Bel Air (Part of Los Angeles) 90024
Bel Aire Estates (Part of Tiburon) 94920
Belden 95915
Bell, *Los Angeles* 90201
Bell (Part of Merced)‡ 95341
Bella Vista, *Contra Costa* 94565
Bella Vista, *Kern* 93283
Bella Vista (Part of Los Angeles) 90022
Bella Vista, *Shasta* 96008
Belle Haven (Part of Menlo Park) 94025
Belleview 95370
Bellflower 90706*
90707†
Bell Gardens 90202

Bell Mountain 92392
Belltown 92509
Bel Marin Keys 94947
Belmont 94002*
94003†
Belmont Shore (Part of Long Beach)‡ 90803
Belridge Farms 93251
Belvedere, *Los Angeles* 90022
Belvedere, *Marin* 94920
Belvedere Gardens 90022
Belvedere-Tiburon (Part of Belvedere) 94920
Belvernon Gardens (Part of Tiburon) 94920
Benbow 95542
Bend 96080
Ben Hur 93653
Benicia 94510
Ben Lomond♦ 95005
Benton 93512
Berenda 93637
Berkeley 94701-05
94707-12
For specific ZIP Codes call (888) 275-8777, or your local postmaster.
Bermuda Dunes♦ 92201
Bernal (Part of San Francisco)‡ 94110
Berry Creek 95916
Berryessa (Part of San Jose)‡ 95132
Berryessa Highlands 94558
Berryessa Park 94558
Berteleda 95531
Bertsch Terrace 95531
Bethany Park (Part of Scotts Valley) 95066
Bethel Island♦ 94511
Betteravia 93455
Beverly (Part of Beverly Hills)‡ 90212
Beverly Center (Part of Los Angeles) 90048
Beverly Hills 90209-13
For specific ZIP Codes call (888) 275-8777, or your local postmaster.
Bicentennial (Part of Los Angeles)‡ 90048
Bieber 96009
Big Bar 96010
Big Basin 95006
Big Bear City♦ 92314
Big Bear Lake 92315
Big Bend 96011
Big Chief 96161
Big Creek 93605
Big Eddy Estates 96028
Biggs 95917
Big Lagoon Park 95570
Big Meadows 95223
Big Oak Flat 95305
Big Pine♦ 93513
Big Pine Indian Reservation 93513
Big River♦ 92242
Big Springs 96064
Big Sur 93920
Big Trees 95018
Bijou (Part of South Lake Tahoe)‡ 96156
Bijou Park (Part of South Lake Tahoe) 96156
Binghamton 95620
Biola 93606
Birch Hill 92060
Birch Meadow Acres 95945
Birdcage Walk 95610
Bird Rock (Part of San Diego) 92037
Birds Landing 94512
Bishop 93514*
93515†
Bishop Acres 93263
Bishop Indian Reservation 93514
Bitterwater 93930
Bixby (Part of Long Beach)‡ 90807
Bixby Knolls (Part of Long Beach) 90807
Black Bear 96031
Black Meadow Landing 92267
Black Point 94947
Blackrock 93526
Blackstone (Part of Fresno)‡ 93710
Blackwells Corner 93249
Blairsden 96103
Blanco 93901

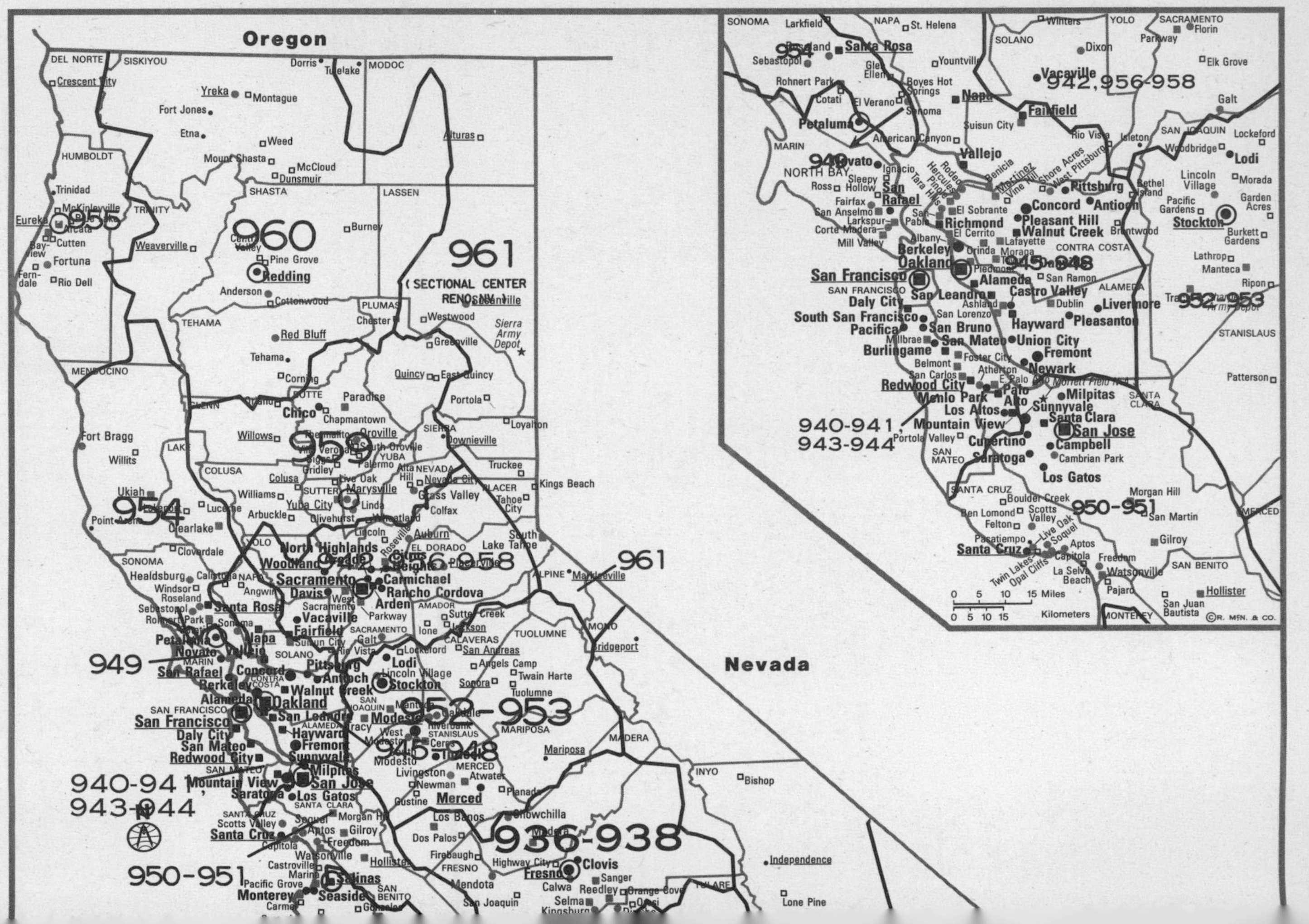

Oregon
Nevada
960
961
954
955
959
949
940-941
943-944
950-951
952-953
936-938
942, 956-958
945-948
(SECTIONAL CENTER RENO, NV)
Sierra Army Depot
NORTH BAY
Crescent City
Yreka
Alturas
Weaverville
Redding
Red Bluff
Eureka
Fortuna
Ukiah
Fort Bragg
Chico
Oroville
Willows
Colusa
Yuba City
Marysville
Quincy
Susanville
Downieville
Auburn
Placerville
Sacramento
Davis
Vacaville
Fairfield
Napa
Santa Rosa
Petaluma
Novato
San Rafael
San Francisco
Daly City
Oakland
Berkeley
Richmond
Vallejo
Concord
Walnut Creek
Pleasant Hill
Antioch
Pittsburg
Hayward
Fremont
San Mateo
Redwood City
Palo Alto
Mountain View
Sunnyvale
San Jose
Santa Clara
Los Gatos
Saratoga
Cupertino
Campbell
Milpitas
Livermore
Pleasanton
Stockton
Lodi
Modesto
Merced
Mariposa
Fresno
Clovis
Santa Cruz
Monterey
Seaside
Salinas
Hollister
Gilroy
Bishop
Independence
Lone Pine
Bridgeport
Markleeville
South Lake Tahoe
San Andreas
Sonora
Jackson
Kilometers
Miles
©R. MFN. & CO.

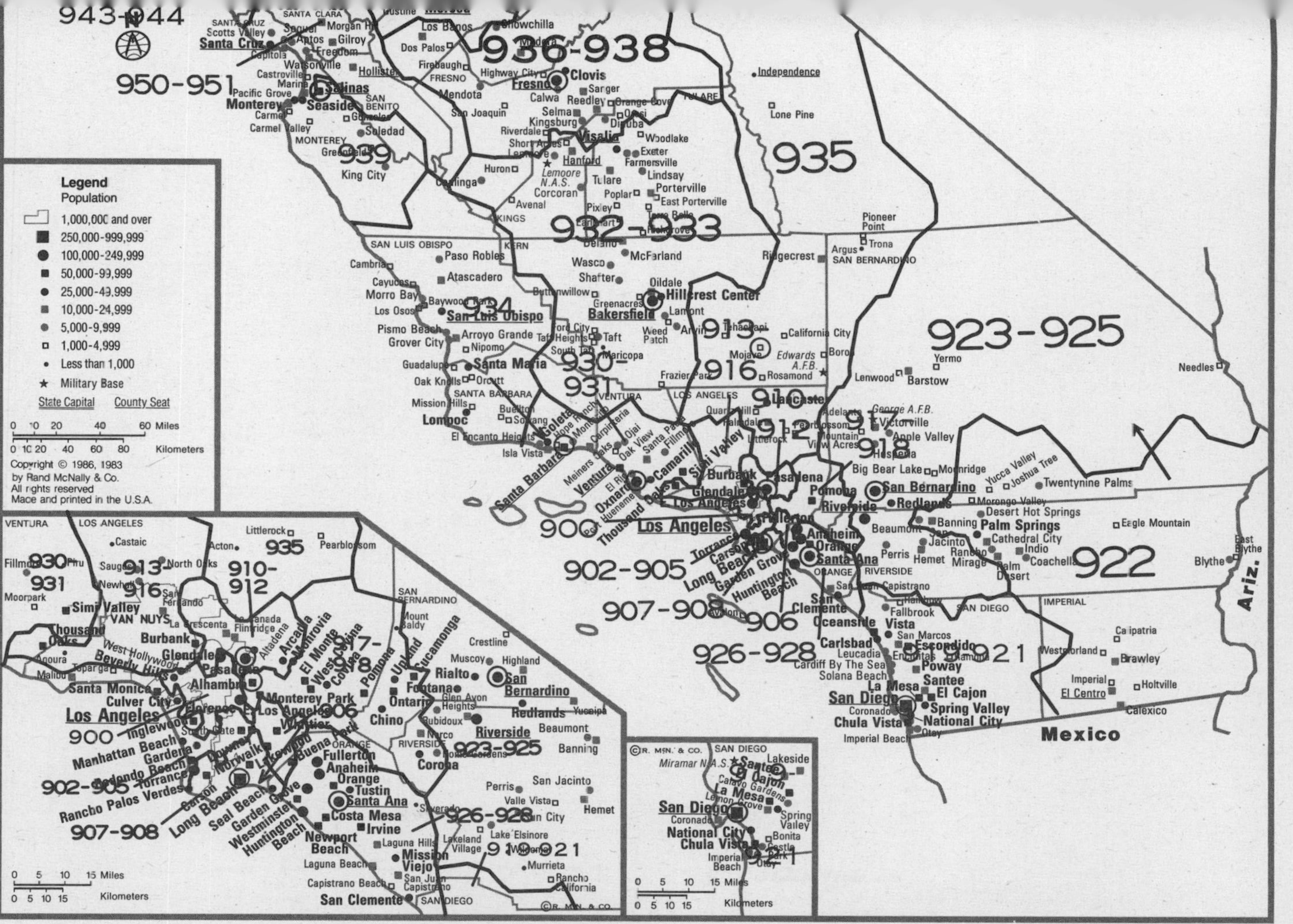
Legend
Population
1,000,000 and over
250,000-999,999
100,000-249,999
50,000-99,999
25,000-49,999
10,000-24,999
5,000-9,999
1,000-4,999
Less than 1,000
Military Base
State Capital
County Seat
0 10 20 40 60 Miles
0 10 20 40 60 80 Kilometers
Copyright © 1986, 1983
by Rand McNally & Co.
All rights reserved
Made and printed in the U.S.A.
943-944
950-951
936-938
939
935
932-933
934
930-931
913-916
910
912
917
918
909
923-925
922
900
902-905
907-908
906
926-928
919-921
Mexico
Ariz.

- Blocksburg 95514
- Bloomfield 94952
- Bloomfield Acres (Part of Arcata) 95521
- Bloomington♦ 92316
- Blossom Hill (Part of San Jose)‡ 95123
- Blossom Valley (Part of Mountain View)‡ 94040
- Blue Canon 95715
- Blue Hills (Part of Saratoga) 95070
- Blue Jay 92317
- Blue Lake 95525
- Blue Lakes 95493
- Bluewater♦ 92242
- Bluff Creek 95546
- Blythe 92225* 92226†
- Bodega 94922
- Bodega Bay 94923
- Bodfish♦ 93205
- Bolinas♦ 94924
- Bolsa (Part of Westminster)‡ 92683
- Bolsa Knolls 93906
- Bombay Beach 92257
- Bonadelle Ranchos 93637
- Bonds Corner 92250
- Bonita, *Madera* 93637
- Bonita, San Diego♦ 91902* 91908†
- Bonny Doon 95060
- Bonnyview (Part of Redding) 96001
- Bonsall♦ 92003
- Boonville 95415
- Boron♦ 93516* 93596†
- Borosolvay 93562
- Borrego Springs♦ 92004
- Borrego Wells 92004
- Bostonia‡ 92021
- Boulder Creek♦ 95006
- Boulder Oaks 91962
- Boulder Park 91934
- Boulevard 91905
- Bowman 95604
- Box Springs 92507
- Boyes Hot Springs♦ 95416
- Boyle (Part of Los Angeles)‡ 90033
- Boyle Heights (Part of Los Angeles)‡ 90033
- Boys Republic (Part of Chino Hills) 91710
- Brackney 95005
- Bradbury 91010
- Bradford (Part of Hayward)‡ 94541
- Bradley 93426
- Bradley International (Part of Los Angeles)‡ 90045
- Brandeis 93064
- Brannan Street Station (Part of San Francisco)‡ 94107
- Branscomb 95417
- Brawley 92227
- Bray 96058
- Brea 92621-23 For specific ZIP Codes call (888) 275-8777, or your local postmaster.
- Brea Mall (Part of Brea) 92821
- Brentwood 94513
- Briceburg 95345
- Briceland 95542
- Bridgehead 94509
- Bridgeport, *Mariposa* 95338
- Bridgeport, *Mono* 93517
- Bridgeport, *Nevada* 95977
- Bridgeville 95526
- Brisbane 94005
- Bristol (Part of Santa Ana)‡ 92703
- Broadmoor♦ 94015
- Broadway (Part of Burlingame) 94010
- Broadway (Part of Sacramento)‡ 95818
- Broadway Manchester (Part of Los Angeles)‡ 90003
- Broadway Plaza (Part of Walnut Creek) 94596
- Brockway 96143
- Broderick (Part of West Sacramento) 95605
- Brookdale 95007
- Brookhurst Center (Part of Anaheim)‡ 92804* 98214†
- Brooks 95606
- Brookside Park (Part of Portola Valley) 94028
- Browns Corner (Part of Woodland) 95695
- Browns Valley 95918
- Brownsville 95919
- Bruceville 95758
- Brundage (Part of Bakersfield)‡ 93307* 93387†
- Brush Creek 95916
- Bryant (Part of Long Beach)‡ 90815
- Bryant Street Annex (Part of San Francisco)‡ 94103
- Bryn Mawr (Part of Loma Linda) 92318
- Bryson 93426
- Bryte (Part of West Sacramento) 95605
- Buckeye, *El Dorado* 95634
- Buckeye (Part of Redding) 96003
- Buckhorn Lodge 95666
- Buckingham Park 95451
- Buck Meadows 95321
- Bucks Bar 95667
- Bucks Lake 95971
- Bucks Lake Lodge 95971
- Bucktail 96052
- Buellton 93427
- Buena (Part of Vista) 92083
- Buena Park 90620-22 90624 For specific ZIP Codes call (888) 275-8777, or your local postmaster.
- Buena Park Mall (Part of Buena Park) 90620
- Buenaventura Plaza (Part of Ventura) 93003
- Buena Vista, *Amador* 95640
- Buena Vista, *Sonoma* 95476
- Buffalo Hill 95634
- Buhach 95340
- Bummerville 95255
- Bunker Hill (Part of Los Angeles)‡ 90071
- Burbank, *Los Angeles* 91501-10 For specific ZIP Codes call (888) 275-8777, or your local postmaster.
- Burbank, *Santa Clara*♦ 95128
- Burkett Acres (Part of Stockton) 95215
- Burkett Gardens 95205
- Burlingame 94010-12 For specific ZIP Codes call (888) 275-8777, or your local postmaster.
- Burlingame Annex (Part of Burlingame)‡ 94011
- Burlingame Hills (Part of Burlingame) 94010
- Burney♦ 96013
- Burnt Ranch 95527
- Burrel 93607
- Burrough 93667
- Burson 95225
- Butano Canyon 94060
- Butte City 95920
- Butte Creek 95928
- Butte Meadows 95942
- Buttonwillow♦ 93206
- Byron 94514
- Byron Rumford (Part of Oakland)‡ 94612
- Cabazon♦ 92230
- Cabazon Indian Reservation 92201
- Cabin Cove 93271
- Cabrillo (Part of Long Beach)‡ 90810
- Cabrillo Estates 93402
- Cache Creek 93501
- Cachuma Village 93101
- Cadiz 92319
- Cahuilla 92539
- Cahuilla Estates 92539
- Cahuilla Hills 92260
- Cahuilla Indian Reservation 92543
- Cairns Corner 93247
- Cajon Junction 92403
- Calabasas 91302* 91372†
- Calabasas Highlands 91302
- Calabasas Hills 91301
- Calabasas Park 91302
- Calaveras (Part of Stockton)‡ 95207
- Calaveras Yacht and Country Club Estates 95204
- Calaveritas 95249
- Calavo Gardens 91941
- Calexico 92231* 92232†
- Calexico Lodge 91905
- Calico 92398
- Cal-Ida 95922
- Caliente 93518
- California City 93504† 93505*
- California Hot Springs 93207
- California Rehabilitation Center (Part of Norco) 91760
- California Valley 93453
- Calimesa 92320
- Calipatria 92233
- Calistoga 94515
- Calla 95336
- Callahan 96014
- Calpella 95418
- Calpine 96124
- Calville 95519
- Calwa (Part of Fresno)‡ 93725
- Camanche Lake 95640
- Camarillo 93010-12 For specific ZIP Codes call (888) 275-8777, or your local postmaster.
- Camarillo Heights (Part of Camarillo) 93010
- Cambria♦ 93428
- Cambrian Park‡ 95124
- Cambridge (Part of Palo Alto)‡ 94306
- Camden 93242
- Camellia (Part of Sacramento)‡ 95819
- Cameo Acres (Part of Danville) 94526
- Cameron Corners 91906
- Cameron Creek Colony 93223
- Cameron Park♦ 95682
- Camino 95709
- Camino Heights 95709
- Camino Media (Part of Bakersfield) 93390
- Campbell 95008-09 95011 For specific ZIP Codes call (888) 275-8777, or your local postmaster.
- Campbell Hot Springs 96126
- Camp Connell 95223
- Camp Evers (Part of Scotts Valley) 95066
- Camp Meeker 95419
- Camp Nelson 93208
- Campo 91906
- Campo Indian Reservation 91906
- Campo Seco 95226
- Camp Pendleton 92055
- Camp Pendleton Marine Corps Base 92055
- Camp Richardson 96150
- Camp Sierra 93664
- Camp St. Michael 95585
- Camp Ten 95634
- Camptonville 95922
- Camp Wishon 93265
- Camulos 93040
- Canby 96015
- Canebrake 93255
- Cannery Row (Part of Monterey)‡ 93942
- Canoga Annex (Part of Los Angeles)‡ 91304
- Canoga Park 91303-05 91307-09 For specific ZIP Codes call (888) 275-8777, or your local postmaster.
- Cantil 93519
- Cantua Creek 93608
- Canyon 94516
- Canyon Acres (Part of Laguna Beach) 92651
- Canyon Country (Part of Santa Clarita) 91351* 91386†
- Canyon Crest (Part of Riverside)‡ 92507* 92517†
- Canyon Crest Heights (Part of Riverside) 92507
- Canyondam 95923
- Canyon Lake 92587
- Capay, *Glenn* 95963
- Capay, *Yolo* 95607
- Capetown 95536
- Capistrano Beach (Part of Dana Point) 92624
- Capistrano Highlands (Part of Laguna Hills) 92653
- Capital Hill (Part of Paso Robles) 93446
- Capitola 95010
- Capitol Square (Part of San Jose) 95133
- Capuchino (Part of Burlingame)‡ 94010* 94011†
- Carbona 95376
- Carbon Beach (Part of Malibu) 90265
- Carbon Canyon (Part of Chino Hills) 91710
- Cardiff By The Sea (Part of Encinitas) 92007
- Cardwell (Part of Fresno)‡ 93704
- Caribou 95915
- Carlotta 95528
- Carlsbad 92008-09 92018 For specific ZIP Codes call (888) 275-8777, or your local postmaster.
- Carlton Hills (Part of Santee) 92071
- Carmel 93921-23 For specific ZIP Codes call (888) 275-8777, or your local postmaster.
- Carmel By The Sea (Part of Carmel)‡ 93921
- Carmel Highlands 93923
- Carmel Hills 93923
- Carmel Mountain Plaza (Part of San Diego) 92128
- Carmel Point 93923
- Carmel Valley♦ 93924
- Carmel Woods 93923
- Carmenita (Part of Santa Fe Springs) 90670
- Carmet 94923
- Carmichael♦ 95608* 95609†
- Carnelian Bay 96140
- Carpinteria 93013* 93014†
- Carquinez Heights (Part of Vallejo) 94590
- Carriage Hills 91977
- Carrick Addition 96094
- Carson 90745-46 90749 For specific ZIP Codes call (888) 275-8777, or your local postmaster.
- Carson Heights Mesa 93550
- Carson Hill 95222
- Carson Mall (Part of Carson) 90746
- Cartago 93549
- Caruthers♦ 93609
- Carvin Creek Homesites 96126
- Casa Blanca (Part of Riverside) 92504
- Casa Conejo♦ 91359
- Casa Correo (Part of Concord)‡ 94521
- Casa de Oro‡ 91976† 91977*
- Casa Grande (Part of Petaluma)‡ 94952
- Cascadel Woods 93643
- Casitas Springs 93001
- Casmalia 93429
- Caspar 95420
- Cassel 96016
- Castaic 91310† 91384*
- Castella 96017
- Castellammare (Part of Los Angeles) 90272
- Castle Air Force Base 95342
- Castle Garden 95301
- Castle Park (Part of Chula Vista) 91911
- Castle Rock Springs 95461
- Castlewood 94588
- Castro (Part of Mountain View) 94042
- Castro Valley♦ 94546 94552 For specific ZIP Codes call (888) 275-8777, or your local postmaster.
- Castroville♦ 95012
- Catalina (Part of Pasadena)‡ 91116
- Cathedral City 92234* 92235†
- Catheys Valley 95306
- Cawelo 93308
- Cayucos♦ 93430
- Cazadero 95421
- Cecilville 96031
- Cedar (Part of Lancaster)‡ 93534* 93584†
- Cedarbrook 93641
- Cedar Crest 93605
- Cedar Flat 96140
- Cedar Glen 92321
- Cedar Grove, *El Dorado* 95709
- Cedar Grove, *Fresno* 93633
- Cedarpines Park 92322
- Cedar Ridge, *Nevada* 95924
- Cedar Ridge, *Tuolumne* 95370
- Cedar Slope 93265
- Cedar Stock 96052
- Cedar Valley 93644
- Cedarville 96104
- Center Avenue (Part of Huntington Beach)‡ 92605
- Centerpoint Mall (Part of Oxnard) 93033
- Centerville (Part of Fremont) 94536
- Centerville, *Fresno* 93657
- Central City Mall (Part of San Bernardino) 92401
- Centre (Part of Sacramento)‡ 95860
- Century City (Part of Los Angeles)‡ 90067
- Century City Shopping Center (Part of Los Angeles) 90067
- Ceres 95307
- Cernon (Part of Vacaville)‡ 95688
- Cerritos 90703
- Cerro Villa Heights (Part of Villa Park) 92861
- Chalfant 93514
- Challenge 95925
- Challenger (Part of Los Angeles)‡ 91303* 91305†
- Chambless 92319
- Champagne Fountain (Part of Saratoga) 95070
- Chandler (Part of Los Angeles)‡ 91603
- Channel Islands‡ 93030
- Chapmantown (Part of Chico) 95928
- Chapman Woods 91107
- Chappo 92055
- Charter Oak♦ 91724
- Chatsworth 91311-13 For specific ZIP Codes call (888) 275-8777, or your local postmaster.
- Chatsworth Lake Manor 91311
- Chawanakee 93602
- Cheeseville 96037
- Chemehuevi Indian Reservation 92363
- Chemeketa Park 95033
- Cherokee, *Butte* 95965
- Cherokee, *Nevada* 95959
- Cherokee Strip 93263
- Cherry Creek Acres 95949
- Cherry Valley♦ 92223
- Chester♦ 96020
- Chestnut (Part of South San Francisco)‡ 94080
- Chicago Park 95712
- Chico 95926-28 95973 For specific ZIP Codes call (888) 275-8777, or your local postmaster.
- Chilcoot 96105
- Childs Meadows 96061
- Chili Bar 95667
- China (Part of San Francisco) 94108
- China Camp 94901

China Lake (Part of Ridgecrest) 93555
China Lake Naval Weapons Center 93555
Chinatown (Part of San Francisco)‡ 94108
Chinese Camp 95309
Chino ..... 91708†
..... 91710*
Chino Hills 91709
Chinowths Corner (Part of Visalia) 93277
Chinquapin 95389
Chiquita Lake 95634
Chiriaco Summit 92201
Cholame 93461
Chowchilla 93610
Christian Valley 95602
Christofferson 93610
Chrome 95963
Chualar 93925
Chula Vista 91909-15
..... 91921
For specific ZIP Codes call (888) 275-8777, or your local postmaster.
Chula Vista Shopping Center (Part of Chula Vista) 91910
Cima 92323
Cimarron (Part of Los Angeles)‡ 90018
Circle Oaks 94558
Cisco 95728
Citrus Heights♦ 95610-11
..... 95621
For specific ZIP Codes call (888) 275-8777, or your local postmaster.
City Hall (Part of San Francisco)‡ 94102
City Heights (Part of San Diego)‡ 92105
City of Industry 91714-16
For specific ZIP Codes call (888) 275-8777, or your local postmaster.
City Shopping Center, The (Part of Orange) 92868
City Terrace 90063
Civic Center (Part of Fresno)‡ 93721
Civic Center (Part of La Habra)‡ 90633
Civic Center (Part of Los Angeles)‡ 91401
Civic Center (Part of Oakland)‡ 94612
Civic Center (Part of Santa Ana)‡ 92701
Clairemont (Part of San Diego) 92117
Clam Beach 95519
Claremont 91711
Clarksburg 95612
Clarksville 95682
Clay 95638
Clayton 94517
Clayton Street Station (Part of San Francisco)‡ 94117
Clear Creek, *Lassen* 96137
Clear Creek, *Siskiyou* 96039
Clearlake 95422
Clearlake Oaks♦ 95423
Clearlake Park (Part of Clearlake) 95424
Clearlake Riviera 95451
Clements 95227
Cleone 95437
Cliff Haven (Part of Newport Beach) 92663
Clifton 90277
Clingans Junction 93675
Clinter (Part of Fresno)‡ 93703
Clinton 95642
Clio 96106
Clipper Gap 95603
Clipper Mills 95930
Cloverdale, *Shasta* 96007
Cloverdale, *Sonoma* 95425
Clovis 93611-13
For specific ZIP Codes call (888) 275-8777, or your local postmaster.
Clyde 94520
Coachella 92236
Coalinga 93210
Coarsegold 93614
Coarsegold Creek Ranch 93614
Coarsegold Highlands 93614
Coast Guard Island (Part of Alameda)‡ 94501
Cobb♦ 95426
Cockatoo Grove (Part of Chula Vista) 91910
Coddington Center (Part of Santa Rosa) 95401
Coddingtown (Part of Santa Rosa)‡ 95401
Codora 95970
Coffee Creek 96091
Cohasset 95973
Coit 93040
Cold Fork 96080
Cole (Part of West Hollywood) 90025
..... 90046
For specific ZIP Codes call (888) 275-8777, or your local postmaster.
Coleville 96107
Colfax 95713
College City 95931
College Grove Center (Part of San Diego) 92115
College Heights (Part of Bakersfield) 93305
College Heights, *San Bernardino* 91786
College Heights, *Santa Cruz* 95003
College Park (Part of Thousand Oaks) 91360
College Plaza (Part of Oceanside)‡ 92056
Collegeville 95206
Collier (Part of Los Angeles)‡ 91307
Collierville 95220
Collinsville 94585
Colma 94014
Coloma 95613
Colonial (Part of Sacramento)‡ 95820
Colonial Juarez (Part of Fountain Valley) 92708
Colonnade (Part of San Jose)‡ 95172
Colony 92363
Colorado (Part of Santa Monica)‡ 90404-05
..... 90411
For specific ZIP Codes call (888) 275-8777, or your local postmaster.
Colorado River Indian Reservation 85344
Colton 92313
..... 92324
For specific ZIP Codes call (888) 275-8777, or your local postmaster.
Columbia♦ 95310
Columbus (Part of Bakersfield)‡ 93306
Colusa 95932
Commerce 90040
Commonwealth (Part of Fullerton)‡ 92832*
..... 92836†
Community Center (Part of Simi Valley) 93065
Comptche 95427
Compton 90220-24
For specific ZIP Codes call (888) 275-8777, or your local postmaster.
Concepcion 93436
Concord 94518-22
..... 94524
..... 94527
For specific ZIP Codes call (888) 275-8777, or your local postmaster.
Concord Naval Weapons Station 94520
Conejo 93662
Conejo Valley (Part of Thousand Oaks)‡ 91358
Confidence 95383
Convict Lake 93514
Cool 95614
Copco 96004
Copper Cove 95228
Copperopolis 95228
Copperwood (Part of Oceanside)‡ 92054
Copsey Creek 95457
Corbin Village (Part of Los Angeles)‡ 91364
Corcoran 93212
Cordelia 94585
Cornell 91301
Corning 96021
Corona 91718-20
For specific ZIP Codes call (888) 275-8777, or your local postmaster.
Corona Del Mar (Part of Newport Beach) 92625
Coronado 92118*
..... 92178†
Coronado Naval Amphibious Base 92155
Corona Mall (Part of Corona) 91720
Coronita 91720
Corral Beach (Part of Malibu) 90265
Corralitos♦ 95076
Corte Madera 94925*
..... 94976†
Coso Junction 93549
Costa Mesa 92626-28
For specific ZIP Codes call (888) 275-8777, or your local postmaster.
Cosumnes 95683
Cotati 94931
Coto de Caza♦ 92679
Cottage Springs 95223
Cotton Center 93257
Cottonwood♦ 96022
Coulterville 95311
Country Club (Part of Moraga)‡ 94556
Country Club Acres 93644
Country Club Centre 95825
Country Club Estates 93401
Country Club Plaza 95825
Country Modern 93501
County East Mall (Part of Antioch) 94509
Court (Part of Martinez)‡ 94553
Courtland 95615
Covelo♦ 95428
Covina 91722-24
For specific ZIP Codes call (888) 275-8777, or your local postmaster.
Covington Mill 96052
Cowan Heights 92705
Cowell (Part of Concord) 94518
Coy Flat 93208
Coyote (Part of San Jose) 95013
Craf 92359
Crafton 92359
Crenshaw (Part of Los Angeles)‡ 90008
Crenshaw-Imperial (Part of Inglewood)‡ 90303
Crescent (Part of Beverly Hills)‡ 90213
Crescent City 95531
Crescent Mills 95934
Cressey 95312
Crest 92021
Crestline♦ 92325
Crestmore 92316
Crestmore Heights 92509
Creston 93432
Crest Park 92326
Crestview Village 95608
Crockett♦ 94525
Cromberg 96103
Crossroads (Part of Santa Rosa)‡ 95401
Crossroads Plaza (Part of Pico Rivera)‡ 90661
Crowley Lake (Part of Mammoth Lakes) 93546
Crown Point (Part of San Diego) 92109
Crows Landing 95313
Crutcher (Part of Paramount) 90723
Crystal Court (Part of Costa Mesa) 92626
Crystal Cove 92651
Cucamonga 91729-30
..... 91739
For specific ZIP Codes call (888) 275-8777, or your local postmaster.
Cudahy 90201
Cuesta-by-the-Sea 93402
Culver City 90230-33
For specific ZIP Codes call (888) 275-8777, or your local postmaster.
Cummings 95454
Cunningham 95472
Cupertino 95014-16
For specific ZIP Codes call (888) 275-8777, or your local postmaster.
Curry Village 95389
Curtiss Heights (Part of Arcata) 95521
Curtner (Part of Fremont) 94539
Cutler♦ 93615
Cutten♦ 95534
Cuyama 93254
Cypress 90630
Cypress South (Part of Cypress)‡ 90630
D (Part of Oakland)‡ 94612
D (Part of San Jose)‡ 95116
Daggett 92327
Dairyland 93610
Dairyville 96080
Dales 96080
Daly City 94014-17
For specific ZIP Codes call (888) 275-8777, or your local postmaster.
Dana 96028
Dana Point 92629
Danby 92332
Danville 94506
..... 94526
For specific ZIP Codes call (888) 275-8777, or your local postmaster.
Danville Square (Part of Danville)‡ 94526
Daphnedale Park 96101
Dardanelle 95314
Darrah 95338
Darwin 93522
Daulton 93637
Davenport 95017
Davis 95616*
..... 95617†
Davis Creek 96108
Day 96056
Dayton 95928
Day Valley♦ 95076
Dearborn Park 94060
Death Valley 92328
Death Valley Junction 92328
Decoto (Part of Union City) 94587
Deep Springs 89010
Deer Creek 96061
Deer Lick Springs 96076
Deer Park, *Napa*♦ 94576
Deer Park, *Santa Cruz*‡ 95003
Del Aire 90250
Del Amo (Part of Torrance)‡ 90503
Del Amo Fashion Center (Part of Torrance) 90503
Delano 93215*
..... 93216†
Del Dios 92029
Delevan 95988
Delft Colony 93618
Delhi♦ 95315
Delkern 93307
Dell (Part of Campbell)‡ 95032
Delleker 96122
Del Loma 96010
Del Mar, *San Diego* 92014
Del Mar, *Santa Cruz* 95060
Del Mesa 94904
Del Monte Heights (Part of Seaside) 93955
Del Monte Park (Part of Pacific Grove)‡ 93950
Del Monte Shopping Center (Part of Monterey) 93940
Del Paso Heights (Part of Sacramento)‡ 95838
Del Rey♦ 93616
Del Rey Oaks 93940
Del Rio Woods 95448
Del Rosa (Part of San Bernardino)‡ 92404
Del Sur (Part of Lancaster) 93536
Delta (Part of Stockton)‡ ..... 95201†
..... 95202*
De Luz 92028
Del Valle (Part of Los Angeles)‡ 90015
Delways 95695
Democrat Hot Springs 93301
Denair♦ 95316
Denny 95527
Denverton 94585
Derby Acres 93224
Descanso 91916
Desert 92364
Desert Beach 92254
Desert Center 92239
Desert Hot Springs 92240-41
For specific ZIP Codes call (888) 275-8777, or your local postmaster.
Desert Lake 93516
Desert Shores 92274
Desert View Highlands♦ 93550
Des Moines (Part of La Habra) 90631
Devils Den 93204
Devore 92407
Devore Heights 92407
Diablo 94528
Diamond (Part of Santa Ana)‡ 92704
Diamond Bar 91765
Diamond Heights (Part of San Francisco)‡ 94131
Diamond Springs♦ 95619
Diamond Springs Heights 95619
Di Giorgio 93203
Dillon Beach 94929
Dimond (Part of Oakland)‡ 94602
Dinkey Creek 93664
Dinsmore 95526
Dinuba 93618
Disneyland (Part of Anaheim) 92802
Dixieland 92273
Dixon 95620
Dobbins 95935
Dockweiler (Part of Los Angeles)‡ 90007
..... 90018
For specific ZIP Codes call (888) 275-8777, or your local postmaster.
Dogtown, *Calaveras* 95249
Dogtown, *Marin* 94924
Dollar Ranch (Part of Walnut Creek)‡ 94595
Dolomite 93545
Dominguez (Part of Carson) 90810
Donlon (Part of Oxnard) 93030
Donner (Part of Truckee)‡ 96162
Donner Lake 96161
Don Pedro Camp 95329
Dorrington 95223
Dorris 96023
Dos Palos 93620
Dos Palos Y 93661
Dos Rios 95429
Douglas City 96024
Douglas Flat 95229
Downey 90239-42
For specific ZIP Codes call (888) 275-8777, or your local postmaster.
Downieville 95936
Downtown (Part of Auburn)‡ 95603
Downtown (Part of Bakersfield)‡ 93302-03
For specific ZIP Codes call (888) 275-8777, or your local postmaster.
Downtown (Part of Burbank)‡ 91502*
..... 91503†
Downtown (Part of Eureka)‡ 95501
Downtown (Part of Long Beach)‡ ..... 90801†
..... 90802*
Downtown (Part of Manhattan Beach)‡ 90266
Downtown (Part of Ontario)‡ 91761
Downtown (Part of Redding)‡ 96001
Downtown (Part of Redwood City)‡ 94064
Downtown (Part of Riverside)‡ 92501*
..... 92502†

Downtown (Part of San Bernardino)‡ 92401*
...... 92402†
Downtown (Part of San Diego)‡ 92101*
...... 92112†
Downtown (Part of Sonora)‡ 95370
Downtown Plaza (Part of Sacramento) 95814
Doyle, *Lassen* 96109
Doyle (Part of Porterville)‡ 93258
Drakesbad 96020
Dryden Flight Research Center 93523
Drytown 95699
Duarte ...... 91009†
...... 91010*
Dublin 94568
Ducor 93218
Dulzura 91917
Duncans Mills 95430
Dunlap 93621
Dunlap Acres (Part of Yucaipa) 92399
Dunmovin 93549
Dunneville Corners 95023
Dunnigan 95937
Dunsmuir 96025
Durham 95938
Dustin Acres 93268
Dutch Flat 95714
E (Part of Oakland)‡ 94661
Eagle Lake Resort 96130
Eagle Mountain 92239
Eagle Rock (Part of Los Angeles)‡ 90041
Eagle Rock Plaza (Part of Los Angeles) 90041
Eagle Station (Part of Susanville) 96130
Eagle Tree 95690
Eagleville 96110
Earlimart♦ 93219
Earp 92242
East (Part of Downey)‡ 90239
East Applegate 95703
East Bakersfield (Part of Bakersfield)‡ 93305*
...... 93385†
East Baldy Mesa 92371
East Bluff (Part of Newport Beach) 92660
East Blythe♦ 92225
East Compton (Part of Compton) 90221
East Downey (Part of Downey)‡ 90239
East Foothills♦ 95127
East Fresno (Part of Fresno)‡ 93727
Eastgate (Part of Beverly Hills)‡ 90211
East Gridley 95948
East Guernewood 95446
East Hemet♦ 92544
East Highlands 92346
East Irvine (Part of Irvine)‡ 92650
Eastlake (Part of Chula Vista)‡ 91914
Eastland Shopping Center (Part of West Covina) 91791
East Linda 95901
East Long Beach (Part of Long Beach)‡ 90804
East Los Angeles♦ 90022
East Lynwood (Part of Lynwood)‡ 90262
Eastmont (Part of Oakland)‡ 94605
Eastmont Mall (Part of Oakland) 94605
East Nicolaus 95659
Easton♦ 93706
East Palo Alto 94303
East Pasadena♦‡ 91107*
...... 91117†
East Porterville♦ 93257
East Quincy 95971
East Richmond Heights♦ 94805
Eastridge (Part of San Jose)‡ 95122*
...... 95173†
East San Diego (Part of San Diego)‡ 92105
East San Gabriel♦ 91775
East San Pedro (Part of Los Angeles) 90731

East Santa Cruz (Part of Santa Cruz)‡ 95060
Eastside Acres 93622
Eastside Ranch 93622
East Sonora♦ 95370
East Stockton (Part of Stockton)‡ 95205
...... 95215
For specific ZIP Codes call (888) 275-8777, or your local postmaster.
East Tustin 92705
East Vallejo (Part of Vallejo) 94590
East Ventura (Part of Ventura)‡ 93003*
...... 93006†
Eastview (Part of Rancho Palos Verdes)‡ 90734
Echo Lake 95721
Echo Park (Part of Los Angeles) 90026
Edendale (Part of Los Angeles)‡ 90026
Edgemar (Part of Pacifica) 94044
Edgemont (Part of Moreno Valley) 92508
Edgemont Acres 93523
Edgewater Estates 91977
Edgewood 96094
Edison 93220
Edmundson Acres 93203
Edwards 93523*
...... 93524†
Edwards Air Force Base‡ 93523
Edwards Estates 93523
Edwards Palisades 93523
Eel Rock 95554
Eighteenth Street Station (Part of San Francisco)‡ 94114
Eight Mile House 95709
El Bonita 95446
El Cajon 92019-22
For specific ZIP Codes call (888) 275-8777, or your local postmaster.
El Camino 96035
El Camino North Shopping Center (Part of Oceanside) .. 92054
El Casco Lake 92373
El Centro 92243*
...... 92244†
El Cerrito, *Contra Costa* 94530
El Cerrito, *Riverside*♦ .. 91720
El Cerrito Plaza (Part of El Cerrito) 94530
Elders Corner 95603
Elderwood 93286
El Dorado 95623
El Dorado Hills♦ 95762
Eldridge♦ 95431
El Encanto Heights 93117*
...... 93118†
El Granada♦ 94018
Elizabeth Lake 93532
Elk 95432
Elk Creek 95939
Elk Grove♦ 95624
...... 95758-59
For specific ZIP Codes call (888) 275-8777, or your local postmaster.
Elkhorn♦ 95012
Elk River 95503
Elk River Corners 95503
Ellwood 93118
El Macero (Part of Davis) 95618
Elmhurst (Part of Oakland) 94603
Elmira 95625
El Mirador 93247
El Mirage 92301
El Modena (Part of Orange)‡ 92859
...... 92862
...... 92869
For specific ZIP Codes call (888) 275-8777, or your local postmaster.
El Monte (Part of Concord) 94521
El Monte, *Los Angeles* 91731-32
...... 91734
For specific ZIP Codes call (888) 275-8777, or your local postmaster.

El Monte Park 92040
Elm View 93609
Elmwood (Part of Berkeley)‡ 94705
El Nido 95317
El Portal 95318
El Porto Beach (Part of Manhattan Beach) 90266
El Pueblo 94565
El Rio♦ 93030
El Rio Villa 95694
El Segundo 90245
El Sereno (Part of Los Angeles)‡ 90032
El Sobrante♦ 94803*
...... 94820†
El Sueno 93110
El Toro 92610
...... 92630
For specific ZIP Codes call (888) 275-8777, or your local postmaster.
El Toro Marine Corps Air Station 92709
El Verano♦ 95433
Elverta 95626
El Viejo‡ ...... 95353†
...... 95354*
Emandal 95490
Embarcadero Postal Center (Part of San Francisco)‡ 94105
Emerald Bay 92651
Emerald Lake Hills♦ 94062
Emeryville 94608*
...... 94662†
Emigrant Gap 95715
Empire 95319
Encanto (Part of San Diego)‡ 92114
Encinal (Part of Sunnyvale)‡ 94087
...... 94090
For specific ZIP Codes call (888) 275-8777, or your local postmaster.
Encinitas ...... 92023†
...... 92024*
Encino (Part of Los Angeles) 91316
...... 91416
...... 91426
...... 91436
For specific ZIP Codes call (888) 275-8777, or your local postmaster.
Enterprise (Part of Redding) 96001
Erwin Lake 92386
Escalle (Part of Larkspur) 94939
Escalon 95320
Escondido 92025-27
...... 92029-33
...... 92046
For specific ZIP Codes call (888) 275-8777, or your local postmaster.
Escondido Junction (Part of Oceanside) .. 92054
Escondido Village Mall (Part of Escondido) .. 92027
Esparto♦ 95627
Esplanade, The 93030
Essex 92332
Estrella 93451
Estudillo (Part of San Leandro)‡ 94577
Etiwanda (Part of Rancho Cucamonga) 91739
Etna 96027
Ettersburg 95542
Eucalyptus Hills 92040
Eugene 95230
Eureka 95501-03
For specific ZIP Codes call (888) 275-8777, or your local postmaster.
Excelsior Station (Part of San Francisco)‡ 94112
Exeter 93221
Fairfax, *Kern* 93307
Fairfax, *Marin* 94930*
...... 94978†
Fairfield 94533
Fairhaven 95564
Fairmead 93610
Fairmont 93534
Fairmont Hospital 94578
Fairmont Terrace 94577
Fairmount (Part of El Cerrito)‡ 94530

Fair Oaks, *Sacramento*♦ 95628
Fair Oaks (Part of Stockton) 95205
Fairview, *Alameda*♦ 94542
Fairview, *Trinity* 96052
Fairview, *Tulare* 93238
Fairway Park (Part of Hayward) 94544
Falk 95503
Fallbrook♦ 92028*
...... 92088†
Fallbrook Junction 92055
Fallbrook Mall (Part of Los Angeles) 91307
Fallen Leaf 96151
Falling Springs 91702
Fallon 94971
Fall River Mills 96028
Fallsvale 92339
Famoso 93250
Fancher 93727
Farmers Market (Part of Los Angeles) 90036
Farmersville 93223
Farmington 95230
Fashion Valley (Part of San Diego)‡ 92168
Fawnskin 92333
Fay Creek 93283
Feather Falls 95940
Feather River 96020
Feather River Inn 96103
Feather River Park 96103
Federal (Part of Anaheim)‡ 92805*
...... 92815†
Federal (Part of Covina)‡ 91723
Federal (Part of Los Angeles)‡ 90012-13
...... 90053
For specific ZIP Codes call (888) 275-8777, or your local postmaster.
Federal Building (Part of Lawndale)‡ 90261
Federal Building (Part of Oxnard)‡ 93030
Federal Building (Part of San Francisco)‡ 94102
Federal Terrace (Part of Vallejo) 94590
Fellows 93224
Felterwood 95531
Felton 95018
Felton Grove 95018
Fernbridge 95540
Fernbrook 92065
Ferndale 95536
Fern Valley 92549
Fernwood 90290
Fetters Hot Springs 95476
Fickle Hill 95521
Fiddletown 95629
Fieldbrook 95519
Fields Landing 95537
Fig Garden (Part of Fresno) 93704
Fig Garden Village (Part of Fresno) 93704
Figueroa (Part of Los Angeles)‡ 91001
Fillmore 93015*
...... 93016†
Financial Plaza (Part of Palm Springs)‡ 92264
Fine Gold 93643
Finley 95435
Firebaugh 93622
Fire Mountain 96061
Firestone (Part of South Gate)‡ 90280
Firestone Park 90001
First Street (Part of Oceanside)‡ ...... 92049†
...... 92054*
Fish Camp 93623
Fish Springs 93513
Fisk (Part of San Francisco)‡ 94122
Fitchburg (Part of Oakland) 94621
Five Brooks 94950
Five Mile Terrace 95667
Five Points, *Fresno* 93624
Five Points (Part of San Diego) 92110
Flamingo Heights 92284
Flinn Springs 92021
Flint (Part of Los Angeles) 90057

Flintridge (Part of La Canada Flintridge) 91011
Florence 90001
Florin♦‡ 95828-29
For specific ZIP Codes call (888) 275-8777, or your local postmaster.
Florin Mall (Part of Sacramento) 95823
Floriston 96111
Flosden Acres (Part of Vallejo) 94590
Flournoy 96029
Fly in Acres 95223
Folsom 95630*
...... 95763†
Folsom Junction (Part of Folsom) 95630
Fontana 92334-37
For specific ZIP Codes call (888) 275-8777, or your local postmaster.
Foothill Farms‡ 95841
Forbestown 95941
Ford City♦ 93268
Forest 95910
Foresta 95389
Forest Falls 92339
Forest Glen 96041
Foresthill♦ 95631
Forest Home, *Amador* 95669
Forest Home, *San Bernardino* 92339
Forest Knolls 94933
Forest Lake 95426
Forest Park 95006
Forest Ranch 95942
Forest Springs, *Nevada* 95949
Forest Springs, *Santa Cruz* 95006
Forestville♦ 95436
Forks of Salmon 96031
Forrest Park 91350
Fort Baker 94965
Fort Barry 94965
Fort Bidwell 96112
Fort Bidwell Indian Reservation 96112
Fort Bragg 95437
Fort Cronkhite 94965
Fort Dick 95538
Fort Goff 96086
Fort Hunter Liggett 93928
Fort Independence Indian Reservation 93526
Fort Irwin 92310
Fort Jones 96032
Fort MacArthur (Part of Los Angeles)‡ 90731
Fort Mason (Part of San Francisco) 94123
Fort Miley (Part of San Francisco) 94121
Fort Mohave Indian Reservation 92363
Fort Ord Village (Part of Seaside) 93955
Fort Seward 95511
Fort Sutter (Part of Sacramento)‡ 95816
Fortuna 95540
Fort Yuma 85366
Fort Yuma Indian Reservation 92283
Foster City 94404
Fountainhead Springs 93257
Fountain Valley 92708*
...... 92728†
Four Corners, *Madera* 93637
Four Corners (Part of Twentynine Palms) 92277
Four Corners, *San Bernardino* 93516
Fouts Springs 95979
Fowler 93625
Fox Creek 95528
Fox Hills (Part of Culver City)‡ 90233
Fox Hills Mall (Part of Culver City) 90230
Fox Plaza (Part of San Francisco)‡ 94102
Foy (Part of Los Angeles)‡ 90017
...... 90057
For specific ZIP Codes call (888) 275-8777, or your local postmaster.
Franciscan Park (Part of Daly City) 94014

Franklin (Part of Napa)‡ 94559
Franklin, *Sacramento* 95758
Frazier Park♦ 93222†
93225*
Fredericksburg 96120
Freedom♦ 95019
Freeman Junction 93527
Freestone 95472
Fremont 94536-39
94555
For specific ZIP Codes call (888) 275-8777, or your local postmaster.
Fremont Hub Shopping Center (Part of Fremont) 94538
French Camp♦ 95231
French Corral 95960
French Gulch 96033
Fresh Pond 95726
Freshwater 95503
Freshwater Corners 95503
Fresno 93650
93701-94
93844
93888
For specific ZIP Codes call (888) 275-8777, or your local postmaster.
Fresno Fashion Fair (Part of Fresno) 93710
Friant 93626
Friendly Hills 92252
Fruitland 95554
Fruitridge 95820
Fruitvale (Part of Oakland)‡ 94601
Fruitvale, *Kern* 93308
Fruto 95988
Fullerton 92831-38
For specific ZIP Codes call (888) 275-8777, or your local postmaster.
Fulton 95439
Gabilan (Part of Salinas) 93906
Gabilan Acres 93906
Galleria at South Bay, The (Part of Redondo Beach)‡ 90277
Galleria at Tyler (Part of Riverside) 92503
Gallinas 94903
Galt 95632
Garberville 95542
Garden (Part of San Jose)‡ 95155
Gardena 90247-49
For specific ZIP Codes call (888) 275-8777, or your local postmaster.
Garden Acres 95205
Garden Farms 93422
Garden Gate Village (Part of Cupertino) 95014
Garden Grove 92640-46
For specific ZIP Codes call (888) 275-8777, or your local postmaster.
Garden Valley 95633
Garden Village (Part of Daly City) 94015
Garey 93454
Garfield 93205
Garlock 93554
Gasoline Alley 95603
Gas Point 96022
Gasquet 95543
Gateway (Part of Culver City)‡ 90232
Gateway (Part of Truckee) 96161
Gateway Station (Part of San Francisco)‡ 94126
Gaviota 93117
Gazelle 96034
Geary (Part of San Francisco)‡ 94121
Gene 92267
Genesee 95983
Genesee Plaza (Part of San Diego) 92111
Georgetown 95634
George Washington (Part of San Diego)‡ 92103
Gerber 96035
Geyserville 95441
Gilman Hot Springs 92583
Gilroy 95020*
95021†
Glamis 92227
Glassell (Part of Los Angeles) 90065
Glen Arbor 95005
Glen Avon♦ 92509
Glenbrook, *Lake* 95461
Glenbrook, *Nevada* 95945
Glenburn 96028
Glencoe 95232
Glencove (Part of Vallejo) 94590
Glendale, *Humboldt* 95519
Glendale, *Los Angeles* 91201-10
91221-22
91225-26
For specific ZIP Codes call (888) 275-8777, or your local postmaster.
Glendale Galleria (Part of Glendale) 91210
Glendora 91740-41
For specific ZIP Codes call (888) 275-8777, or your local postmaster.
Glen Ellen♦ 95442
Glenhaven 95443
Glen Martin 92305
Glenn 95943
Glennville 93226
Glenoaks (Part of Burbank)‡ 91504
Glenshire-Devonshire♦ 96161
Glenview, *Los Angeles* 90290
Glenview, *San Diego* 92021
Glenwood 95066
Glorietta (Part of Orinda) 94563
Goffs 92332
Golden Gate (Part of San Francisco)‡ 94159
Golden Hill (Part of San Diego) 92102
Golden Hills, *Calaveras* 95249
Golden Hills, *Kern*♦ 93561
Golden Valley (Part of Santa Clarita)‡ 91350
Gold Flat 95959
Gold Gulch 95018
Gold Hill 95667
Gold River 95670
Gold Run 95717
Goleta 93116-18
For specific ZIP Codes call (888) 275-8777, or your local postmaster.
Gonzales 93926
Goodyears Bar 95944
Gorda 93920
Gordon Valley 94585
Gorman 93243
Goshen 93227
Graeagle 96103
Graham 90002
Granada Hills (Part of Los Angeles) 91344
Grand Avenue (Part of Santa Ana)‡ 92705
Grand Central (Part of Glendale)‡ 91201*
91221†
Grand Lake (Part of Oakland)‡ 94610
Grand Terrace 92313
Grandview 92311
Grangeville 93230
Granite Bay 95746
Granite Hill (Part of Grass Valley) 95945
Granite Hills♦ 92019
Graniteville 95959
Grantville (Part of San Diego)‡ 92120
Grapevine 93243
Grass Valley 95945
95949
For specific ZIP Codes call (888) 275-8777, or your local postmaster.
Graton♦ 95444
Grayson 95363
Greeley 93307
Greeley Hill 95311
Green (Part of Los Angeles)‡ 90037
Greenacres♦ 93308
Greenbrae 94904
Greenbrook (Part of Danville) 94526
Greenfield 93927
Greenmead (Part of Los Angeles)‡ 90059
Green Meadows (Part of Davis) 95616
Greenspot 92359
Green Valley 91350
Green Valley Estates 94585
Green Valley Lake 92341
Greenview 96037
Greenview Acres (Part of Arcata) 95521
Greenville♦ 95947
Greenwich Village (Part of Thousand Oaks) 91360
Greenwood 95635
Grenada 96038
Gridley 95948
Griffith (Part of Los Angeles)‡ 90039
Grimes 95950
Grizzly Flats 95636
Grossmont (Part of La Mesa)‡ 91942
Groveland 95321
Grover Beach 93433*
93483†
Guadalupe 93434
Gualala 95445
Guasti (Part of Ontario) 91743
Guatay 91931
Guerneville♦ 95446
Guernewood Park 95446
Guernsey 93230
Guinda 95637
Gustine 95322
Hacienda (Part of Pleasanton)‡ 94588
Hacienda, *Sonoma* 95436
Hacienda Heights♦ 91745
Haiwee 93549
Halcyon 93420
Hales Grove 95585
Half Moon Bay 94019
Hall (Part of Union City) 94587
Halloran Springs 92364
Halls Corner 93245
Hallwood 95901
Hamburg 96050
Hamilton‡ 94301*
94302†
Hamilton City♦ 95951
Hammer Ranch (Part of Stockton)‡ 95209
95219
95269
For specific ZIP Codes call (888) 275-8777, or your local postmaster.
Hammil 93514
Hammonton 95901
Hancock (Part of Los Angeles)‡ 90044
Hanford 93230-32
For specific ZIP Codes call (888) 275-8777, or your local postmaster.
Happy Camp 96039
Harbin Springs 95461
Harbin Springs Annex 95461
Harbison Canyon♦ 92020
Harbor City (Part of Los Angeles) 90710
Harbor Island (Part of Newport Beach) 92660
Harbor Side (Part of Chula Vista) 91911
Hardman Center (Part of Riverside)‡ 92504*
92514†
Hardwick 93230
Harlem Springs (Part of Highland) 92346
Harmony 93435
Harmony Grove 92029
Harris 95542
Harrison Park 92036
Hartland 93603
Harvard 92398
Harvest (Part of Irvine)‡ 92612
Haskell Creek Homesites 96124
Haskins Resort 95971
Hat Creek 96040
Hathaway Pines 95233
Hatton Fields 93923
Havasu Lake 92363
Havilah 93518
Hawaiian Gardens 90716
Hawkins Bar 95563
Hawkinsville 96097
Hawthorne 90250*
90251†
Hawthorne Plaza (Part of Hawthorne) 90250
Hayfork♦ 96041
Hayward 94540-45
94557
For specific ZIP Codes call (888) 275-8777, or your local postmaster.
Hayward Highlands (Part of Hayward) 94542
Hazard 90063
Healdsburg 95448
Heather Glen 95703
Heber♦ 92249
Helena 96048
Helendale 92342
Helm 93627
Hemet 92543-46
For specific ZIP Codes call (888) 275-8777, or your local postmaster.
Henderson (Part of Porterville)‡ 93258
Henderson (Part of Eureka)‡ 95501
Henderson Village 95240
Henley 96044
Henleyville 96021
Herald 95638
Hercules 94547
Heritage Ranch 93446
Heritage Village (Part of Campbell)‡ 95009
Herlong 96113
Hermosa Beach 90254
Hernandez 95023
Herndon (Part of Fresno) 93711
Hesperia 92340†
92345*
Heyer 94546
Hickman 95323
Hidden Hills 91302
Hidden Lake Estate 93637
Hidden Lakes Estates 93626
Hidden Meadows♦ 92025
Hidden Valley 95650
Hidden Valley Lake♦ 95457
Highgrove♦ 92507
Highland 92346
Highland Park, *Kern* 93308
Highland Park (Part of Los Angeles)‡ 90042
Highway City (Part of Fresno) 93706
Highway Highlands (Part of Glendale) 91214
Hilarita (Part of Tiburon) 94920
Hildreth 93645
Hillcrest (Part of Los Angeles)‡ 90301
Hillcrest (Part of San Diego)‡ 92103
Hillcrest Center (Part of Bakersfield)‡ 93306*
93386†
Hillcrest Park 94590
Hillsborough 94010
Hillsdale (Part of San Mateo)‡ 94403
Hillsdale Shopping Center (Part of San Mateo) 94403
Hills Flat (Part of Grass Valley) 95945
Hilltop (Part of Richmond) 94806
Hilltop, *Kern* 93307
Hillview (Part of San Jose)‡ 95121
Hilmar♦ 95324
Hilt 96044
Hilton 95436
Hinkley 92347
Hiouchi Valley 95531
Hirschdale 96161
Hi Vista 93535
Hoaglin 95595
Hobart (Part of Vernon) 90058
Hobart Mills 96161
Hobergs 95426
Hodge 92311
Holiday (Part of Anaheim)‡ 92802*
92812†
Holiday Lake (Part of Morgan Hill) 95037
Hollister 95023*
95024†
Hollydale (Part of South Gate)‡ 90280
Hollydale, *Sonoma* 95436
Hollywood 90027-28
90038
90068
90078
For specific ZIP Codes call (888) 275-8777, or your local postmaster.
Hollywood Beach 93035
Hollywood by the Sea 93035
Hollywood Riviera (Part of Torrance) 90277
Holmes 95569
Holt 95234
Holtville 92250
Holy City 95026
Home Garden♦ 93239
Home Gardens♦ 91720
Homeland♦ 92548
Homestead, *Kern* 93527
Homestead, *Riverside* 92539
Homestead (Part of Stockton)‡ 95206
Homestead Valley 94941
Homewood 96141
Honby 91350
Honcut 95965
Honeydew 95545
Hood 95639
Hooker 96022
Hookston (Part of Pleasant Hill) 94523
Hoopa 95546
Hoopa Valley Indian Reservation 95546
Hope Ranch 93105
Hopeton 95369
Hope Valley 96120
Hopland 95449
Hornbrook 96044
Hornitos 95325
Horse Creek 96050
Horseshoe Bar 95650
Horton Plaza (Part of San Diego) 92101
Howard Landing 95690
Howest (Part of Burlingame) 94010
Hub City (Part of Compton)† 90220
Hudson‡ 95355-57
For specific ZIP Codes call (888) 275-8777, or your local postmaster.
Hughes (Part of Fresno)‡ 93705
Hughson 95326
Humboldt Bay CGAS 95521
Hume 93628
Humphreys Station 93611
Hunters Valley 95325
Huntington (Part of Huntington Beach)‡ 92646
Huntington Beach 92605
92615
92646-49
For specific ZIP Codes call (888) 275-8777, or your local postmaster.
Huntington Center (Part of Huntington Beach) 92647
Huntington Harbor (Part of Huntington Beach) 92649
Huntington Lake 93629
Huntington Park 90255
Huron 93234
Hyampom 96046
Hyde Park (Part of Los Angeles) 90043
Hydesville♦ 95547
Ida Jean Haxton (Part of Huntington Beach)‡ 92647
Idlewild 93260
Idria 95023
Idyllwild 92549
Ignacio 94947
Igo 96047
Imperial 92251
Imperial Beach 91932*
91933†
Imperial Crest (Part of Norwalk) 90650
Incline 95318
Independence 93526
Indian Beach 95443
Indian Falls 95934
Indian Hill Mall (Part of Pomona) 91767
Indian Lakes Estates 93614
Indian Mission 93602

Indianola 95503
Indian Springs 93644
Indian Wells, *Kern* 93527
Indian Wells, *Riverside* 92210
Indio 92201-03
For specific ZIP Codes call (888) 275-8777, or your local postmaster.
Industrial (Part of Santa Ana)‡ 92705
Inglenook 95437
Ingleside (Part of San Francisco) 94112
Inglewood 90301-12
For specific ZIP Codes call (888) 275-8777, or your local postmaster.
Ingot 96008
Inland Center (Part of San Bernardino) 92408
Inskip 95978
Inverness♦ 94937
Inverness Park 94956
Inwood 96088
Inyokern 93527
Ione 95640
Iowa Hill 95713
Irish Beach 95459
Iron Mountain 92242
Irvine 92602-04
92606
92612
92614
92616-23
92650
92709-10
For specific ZIP Codes call (888) 275-8777, or your local postmaster.
Irvington (Part of Fremont)‡ 94538
Irwin 95324
Irwindale 91706
Irwin Estates 92311
Island Mountain 95542
Isla Vista♦ 93117
Isleton 95641
Ivanhoe♦ 93235
Ivanpah 92364
Jacinto Grange 95943
Jackie Robinson‡ 91103-04
For specific ZIP Codes call (888) 275-8777, or your local postmaster.
Jackson 95642
Jackson Gate (Part of Jackson) 95642
Jacumba 91934
Jalama 93436
Jamesburg 93924
Jamestown♦ 95327
Jamul♦ 91935
Janesville 96114
Japan Center (Part of San Francisco) 94115
Jarbo 95965
Jelly 96080
Jenner 95450
Jenny Lind 95252
Jesmond Dene 92026
Jimtown 95448
Johannesburg 93528
John Adams (Part of San Diego)‡ 92116
Johnsondale 93238
Johnson Park 96013
John Steinbeck (Part of Salinas)‡ 93901
Johnstonville 96130
Johnstown 92021
Johnsville 96103
Jolon 93928
Jonesville 95942
Joshua Hills (Part of Palmdale) 93550
Joshua Tree♦ 92252
Julian♦ 92036
Junction City 96048
June Lake 93529
June Lake Junction 93529
Juniper Hills 93543
Juniper Lake Resort 96020
Juniper Springs 92548
Jurupa 92509
Kaiser Center (Part of Oakland)‡ 94612
Kaiser Eagle Mountain 92239
Kaweah 93237
Keddie 95971
Keeler 93530
Keene 93531
Kelly 96020
Kelsey 95667
Kelseyville♦ 95451
Kelso 92309
Kennedy Meadow 95370
Kennedy Ranch 95449
Kensington♦ 94707-08
For specific ZIP Codes call (888) 275-8777, or your local postmaster.
Kensington Park (Part of San Diego) 92116
Kentfield♦ 94914
Kentwood-In-The Pines 92036
Kent Woodlands 94904
Kenwood 95452
Keough Hot Springs 93514
Kerman 93630
Kern City (Part of Bakersfield) 93309
Kern Homes 93308
Kernvale 93240
Kernville♦ 93238
Keswick 96001
Kettleman City♦ 93239
Kevet (Part of Santa Paula) 93060
Keyes♦ 95328
Kilkare Woods 94586
King (Part of Santa Ana)‡ 92706
King City 93930
King Island 95219
King Salmon 95503
Kings Beach♦ 96143
Kingsburg 93631
Kings Mall (Part of Hanford) 93230
Kingvale 95728
Kirkville 95645
Kirkwood, *Alpine* 95646
Kirkwood, *Tehama* 96021
Kit Carson 95644
Klamath♦ 95548
Klamath Glen 95548
Klamath River 96050
Klinefelter 92363
Kneeland 95549
Knightsen 94548
Knights Ferry 95361
Knights Landing 95645
Knob 96076
Knotts Berry Farm (Part of Buena Park) 90620
Knowles 93653
Konocti 95451
Kono Tayee 95443
Korbel 95550
Krug (Part of St. Helena) 94574
Kyburz 95720
La Barr Meadows 95949
La Canada (Part of La Canada Flintridge) 91011
La Canada Flintridge 91011*
91012†
La Costa (Part of Malibu)‡ 90265
La Costa, *San Diego*‡ 92008
La Costa Beach (Part of Malibu) 90265
La Crescenta 91214*
91224†
La Cresta, *Kern* 93305
La Cresta, *San Diego* 92020
La Cumbre Plaza (Part of Santa Barbara) 93105
Ladera 94028
Ladera Heights‡ 90045
Lafayette 94549
La Grange 95329
Laguna Beach 92651*
92652†
Laguna Creek 95758
Laguna Hills 92653*
92654†
Laguna Hills Mall (Part of Laguna Hills) 92653
Laguna Lake (Part of San Luis Obispo) 93405
Laguna Niguel 92607
92677
For specific ZIP Codes call (888) 275-8777, or your local postmaster.
Laguna West 95832
Lagunitas 94938
La Habra 90631-33
For specific ZIP Codes call (888) 275-8777, or your local postmaster.
La Habra Fashion Square (Part of La Habra) 90631
La Habra Heights 90631
La Honda 94020
Lairport (Part of El Segundo) 90245
La Jolla (Part of Placentia) 92870
La Jolla (Part of San Diego) 92037-39
92092-93
For specific ZIP Codes call (888) 275-8777, or your local postmaster.
La Jolla Indian Reservation 92025
Lake Almanor 96137
Lake Alpine 95223
Lake Arrowhead 92352
Lake Christopher (Part of South Lake Tahoe) 96150
Lake City 96115
Lake Earl 95531
Lake Elsinore 92530-32
For specific ZIP Codes call (888) 275-8777, or your local postmaster.
Lake Forest, *Orange* 92630
Lake Forest, *Placer* 96145
Lakehead 96051
Lake Henshaw 92070
Lake Hills Estates 95762
Lake Hughes 93532
Lake Isabella♦ 93240
Lake Kirkwood 95646
Lakeland Village‡ 92530
Lake Los Angeles 93550
Lake Madera Country Estates 93637
Lake Marie Estates 93455
Lake Mary 93546
Lake Morena Village 91906
Lake Murray (Part of San Diego) 92119
Lake Nacimiento♦ 93446
Lake of the Pines♦ 95603
Lake of the Woods 93225
Lake Pillsbury Homesites 95469
Lake Pillsbury Resort 95469
Lakeport 95453
Lake San Marcos♦ 92069
Lakeshore 93634
Lakeshore Lodge 95971
Lakeside♦ 92040
Lakeside Farms 92040
Lake Tamarisk 92239
Lakeview, *Kern* 93307
Lakeview, *Riverside*♦ 92567
Lakeview, *San Diego* 92040
Lake View Terrace (Part of Los Angeles) 91342
Lakeville 94954
Lake Williams Estates 92386
Lakewood 90711-15
For specific ZIP Codes call (888) 275-8777, or your local postmaster.
Lakewood Center Mall (Part of Lakewood) 90712
La Loma (Part of Modesto) 95354
Lamanda Park (Part of Pasadena) 91107
La Mesa 91941-44
For specific ZIP Codes call (888) 275-8777, or your local postmaster.
La Mirada 90637†
90638*
La Mirada Mall (Part of La Mirada) 90638
Lamont♦ 93241
Lanare 93656
Lancaster 93534-39
93584-86
For specific ZIP Codes call (888) 275-8777, or your local postmaster.
Landers 92285
Land Park (Part of Sacramento)‡ 95822
Landscape (Part of Berkeley)‡ 94707
Lansdale (Part of San Anselmo) 94960
La Palma 90623
La Panza 93432
La Patera 93117
La Porte 95981
La Puente 91744
91746-47
91749
For specific ZIP Codes call (888) 275-8777, or your local postmaster.
La Quinta 92253
Larabee 95569
La Riviera♦ 95826
Larkfield 95403
Larkspur 94939*
94977†
Larson Tract 93240
Larwin Plaza (Part of Vallejo)‡ 94590
Las Cruces 93117
La Selva Beach 95076
Las Flores (Part of Malibu) 90265
Las Flores, *Tehama* 96035
La Sierra (Part of Riverside)‡ 92505*
92515†
La Sierra Heights (Part of Riverside) 92505
Las Lomas♦ 95076
Las Posas Estates 93010
Lathrop 95330
La Tijera (Part of Los Angeles)‡ 90043
Laton♦ 93242
Latrobe 95682
Laurel (Part of Oakland)‡ 94619
Laurel Canyon‡ 91605-06
For specific ZIP Codes call (888) 275-8777, or your local postmaster.
Laurel Plaza (Part of Los Angeles) 91606
Laurelwood (Part of Los Angeles) 91604
La Verne 91750
La Vina 93637
Lawndale 90260-61
For specific ZIP Codes call (888) 275-8777, or your local postmaster.
Lawrence (Part of Danville) 94506
Laws 93514
Layman 96103
Laytonville♦ 95454
Lazy Acre 93311
Lebec 93243
Lee 96020
Lee Vining 93541
Leggett 95585
Le Grand♦ 95333
Leisure Acres 93643
Leisure Town (Part of Vacaville) 95687
Leisure World (Part of Seal Beach) 90740
Leliter 93527
Lemoncove 93244
Lemon Grove 91945*
91946†
Lemon Heights 92705
Lemoore 93245
Lemoore Naval Air Station 93245
Lennox♦ 90304
Lenwood♦ 92311
Leona Valley 93551
Leucadia (Part of Encinitas)‡ 92023†
92024*
Lewiston♦ 96052
Liberty Acres 90250
Liberty Farms 95620
Libfarm 95620
Lido Isle (Part of Newport Beach) 92663
Likely 96116
Lily Valley 95255
Limco 93060
Lincoln 95648
Lincoln Acres 91947
Lincoln Heights (Part of Los Angeles)‡ 90031
Lincoln Village (Part of Carson) 90810
Lincoln Village, *San Joaquin*♦ 95207
Linda♦ 95901
Linda Mar (Part of Pacifica)‡ 94044
Linda Vista (Part of Pasadena) 91103
Linda Vista (Part of San Diego)‡ 92111
Linda Vista, *Santa Clara* 95127
Lind Cove 93221
Linden, *San Joaquin*♦ 95236
Linden (Part of South San Francisco)‡ 94080
Lindenwood (Part of Menlo Park) 94027
Lindsay 93247
Lingard 95333
Linnell 93292
Linns Valley 93226
Litchfield 96117
Little Lake 93542
Little Norway 95721
Little Reed Heights (Part of Tiburon) 94920
Littleriver 95456
Littlerock♦ 93543
Little Saigon (Part of Westminster) 92683
Little Shasta 96064
Little Valley 96053
Live Oak, *Santa Cruz* 95062
Live Oak, *Sutter* 95953
Live Oak Acres, *Tehama* 96080
Live Oak Acres, *Ventura* 93022
Live Oak Canyon 91750
Live Oak Springs 91905
Livermore 94550-51
For specific ZIP Codes call (888) 275-8777, or your local postmaster.
Livingston 95334
Llano 93544
Lobitos 94019
Lobo (Part of Stanton) 90680
Loch Lomond 95461
Locke 95690
Lockeford♦ 95237
Lockhart 92347
Lockwood 93932
Lodge Pole 93262
Lodi 95240-42
For specific ZIP Codes call (888) 275-8777, or your local postmaster.
Lodoga 95979
Logan Heights (Part of San Diego) 92113
Loleta 95551
Loma (Part of Long Beach)‡ 90814
Loma Linda 92354
Loma Mar 94021
Loma Portal (Part of San Diego) 92110
Loma Rica 95901
Lomas Santa Fe (Part of Solana Beach) 92075
Loma Verda (Part of Novato) 94949
Lomita 90717
Lomita Park (Part of San Bruno) 94066
Lompico 95018
Lompoc 93436-38
For specific ZIP Codes call (888) 275-8777, or your local postmaster.
London♦ 93618
Lone Pine♦ 93545
Lone Pine Indian Reservation 93545
Long Barn 95335
Long Beach 90801-53
For specific ZIP Codes call (888) 275-8777, or your local postmaster.
Long Beach Plaza (Part of Long Beach) 90802
Longvale 95490
Lonoak 93930
Lonoke (Part of Gilroy) 95020
Lookout 96054
Lookout Ranchettes 96054
Loomis 95650
Loomis Corners 96003
Loraine 93518
Loree Estates 95014
Los Alamitos 90720*
90721†
Los Alamitos Naval Air Station 90720
Los Alamos 93440
Los Altos 94022-24
For specific ZIP Codes call (888) 275-8777, or your local postmaster.
Los Altos Hills 94022

Los Altos Shopping Center (Part of Long Beach) 90815
Los Amigos (Part of Downey)‡ 90240

Los Angeles

.... 90001-68
.... 90070-99
.... 90101
For specific ZIP Codes call (888) 275-8777, or your local postmaster.

Colleges & Universities

American Film Inst, Ctr for Advanced Film & Television Studies 90027
California State Univ 90032
Loyola Marymount Univ 90045
Mount Saint Mary's Coll 90049
Occidental Coll 90045
Otis Coll of Art & Design 90045
Southern California Inst of Architecture 90066
Univ of California 90024
Univ of Judaism 90077
Univ of Southern California 90089

Financial Institutions

Cathay Bank 90012
General Bank 90017
Manufacturers Bank 90071
Tokai Bank 90071
Union Bank of California 90071

Hospitals

California Hosp Med Ctr 90015
Cedars-Sinai Med Ctr 90048
Childrens Hosp 90027
Kaiser Foundation Hosp 90027
L A County, Univ of Southern California Med Ctr 90033
L A County-King-Drew Med Ctr 90059
Queen of Angels-Hollywood Presbyterian Med Ctr 90027
St Vincent Med Ctr 90057
Univ of California L A Med Ctr 90095
Veterans Affairs Med Ctr-West L A 90073
White Memorial Med Ctr 90033

Hotels/Motels

Continental Plaza, L A Airport 90045
Crowne Plaza 90045
Doubletree, LAX 90045
Holiday Inn, L A Airport 90045
Hyatt Regency 90017
Inter-Continental 90012
L A Airport Hilton & Towers 90045
Marriott, Airport 90045
The New Otani Hotel & Garden 90012
Omni Hotel & Centre 90017
Radisson Wilshire Plaza 90010
Regal Biltmore Hotel 90071
Renaissance Hotel, Airport 90045
Sheraton Gateway 90045
Hotel Sofitel 90048
Westin Bonaventure & Suites 90071
Wyndham Hotel at L A Airport 90045

Military Installations

Air Mobility Command 90045
U S Army Corps of Engineers 90053

Los Banos 93635
Los Berros 93420
Los Cerritos Center (Part of Cerritos) 90703
Los Coyotes Indian Reservation 92086
Los Deltos 93622
Los Feliz (Part of Los Angeles)‡ 90027
.... 90029
For specific ZIP Codes call (888) 275-8777, or your local postmaster.
Los Gatos 95030-33
For specific ZIP Codes call (888) 275-8777, or your local postmaster.
Los Molinos♦ 96055
Los Nietos 90606
Los Olivos 93441
Los Osos 93402*
.... 93412†
Los Ranchitos 94903
Los Serranos♦ 91709
Lost Hills♦ 93249
Lost Lake 92225
Los Trancos Woods 94028
Los Tules 92086
Lotus 95651
Lovelock 95954
Lower Echo Lake 95721
Lower Lake♦ 95457
Lowrey 96080
Loyalton 96118
Loyola♦ 94024
Lucas Valley 94903
Lucerne♦ 95458
Lucerne Valley 92356
Lucia 93920
Ludlow 92338
Lugo (Part of Los Angeles)‡ 90023
Lugonia (Part of Redlands)‡ 92375
Lunada Bay (Part of Palos Verdes Estates) 90274
Lundy 93541
Lushmeadows Mountain Estates 95338
Luther Burbank (Part of Santa Rosa)‡ 95402
Lyman Springs 96075
Lynwood 90262
Lynwood Gardens (Part of Lynwood) 90262
Lyons‡ 91321*
.... 91322†
Lytle Creek 92358
Lytton 95448
McArthur 96056
McBride (Part of Santa Rosa)‡ 95403
McCann 95569
McClellan Air Force Base 95652
McCloud♦ 96057
Macdoel 96058
McFarland 93250
McHie 96080
McIntyre Park 92225
McKeon 95631
McKinleyville♦ 95519
McKittrick 93251
McKnight Acres 94590
Mc Laren (Part of San Francisco)‡ 94134
McMillan Manor (Part of Oxnard) 93030
McVittie Annex (Part of Richmond)‡ 94804
Macy's Postal Store (Part of Los Angeles) 90081
Madeline 96119
Madera 93637-39
For specific ZIP Codes call (888) 275-8777, or your local postmaster.
Madera Acres♦ 93637
Madera Country Club Estates 93637
Madera Highlands 93637
Madera Ranchos 93637
Madison 95653
Madonna Road Plaza (Part of San Luis Obispo) 93405
Mad River 95552
Madrone (Part of Morgan Hill) 95037
Magalia 95954
Magnolia, *Imperial* 92227
Magnolia (Part of Santa Barbara) 93111
Magnolia Avenue (Part of Riverside) 92506
Magnolia Center (Part of Riverside)‡ 92506*
.... 92516†
Magnolia Park (Part of Burbank)‡ 91505
Main Office (Part of Oakland)‡ 94623
MainPlace/Santa Ana (Part of Santa Ana) 92701
Malaga 93725
Malibu 90263-65
For specific ZIP Codes call (888) 275-8777, or your local postmaster.
Malibu Beach (Part of Malibu) 90265
Malibu Bowl (Part of Malibu) 90265
Malibu Canyon Homes 91302
Malibu Junction (Part of Agoura Hills) 91301
Mall of Orange, The (Part of Orange) 92865
Mammoth Lakes 93546
Manchester 95459
Manchester Center (Part of Fresno) 93726
Manhattan Beach 90266*
.... 90267†
Manhattan Village (Part of Manhattan Beach) 90266
Manila 95521
Manka's Corners 94585
Manlove 95826
Manor (Part of Fairfax) 94930
Manteca 95336-37
For specific ZIP Codes call (888) 275-8777, or your local postmaster.
Manton 96059
Manzana 95444
Manzanita 95948
Manzanita Indian Reservation 91905
Maple Creek 95550
Maravilla Park 90022
Marcelina (Part of Torrance)‡ 90501
March Air Force Base 92518
Marcus Foster (Part of Oakland)‡ 94624
Maricopa 93252
Marina, *Monterey* 93933
Marina (Part of San Francisco)‡ 94123
.... 94147
For specific ZIP Codes call (888) 275-8777, or your local postmaster.
Marina Del Rey♦ 90292*
.... 90295†
Marin City 94965
Marin Country Club Estates (Part of Novato) 94949
Marine Corps Logistics Support Base, Pacific‡ 92311
Marine Corps Supply Center, West Yermo Area 92398
Mariner (Part of Seal Beach)‡ 90740
Marinwood 94903
Mariposa♦ 95338
Market (Part of Los Angeles)‡ 90021
Marketplace At The Grove (Part of San Diego)‡ 92115
Markleeville 96120
Marloma (Part of Rolling Hills Estates) 90274
Marne (Part of City of Industry) 91743
Marshall 94940
Marshall Station 93611
Martell 95654
Martinez 94553
Martins Beach 94019
Mar Vista (Part of Los Angeles)‡ 90066
Marysville 95901
Massack 95971
Maxwell 95955
Mayflower Village♦ 91016
Maywood 90270
Meadowbrook 92570
Meadowbrook Woods 92326
Meadow Lake Park (Part of Truckee) 96161
Meadow Lakes 93602
Meadowsweet (Part of Corte Madera) 94925
Meadow Valley 95956
Meadow Vista♦ 95722
Mead Valley 92570
Mecca♦ 92254
Media City Center (Part of Burbank) 91505
Medicine Lake Lodge 96134
Meeks Bay 96142
Meiners Oaks♦ 93023
Melody Oaks 95642
Meloland 92243
Melvin (Part of Clovis) 93611
Mendocino 95460
Mendota 93640
Menifee 92584
Menlo Park 94025-26
.... 94029
For specific ZIP Codes call (888) 275-8777, or your local postmaster.
Mentone♦ 92359
Merced 95340-41
.... 95344
.... 95348
For specific ZIP Codes call (888) 275-8777, or your local postmaster.
Merced Falls 95369
Merced Mall (Part of Merced) 95348
Meridian 95957
Mesa Center (Part of Costa Mesa)‡ 92627
Mesa Grande 92070
Mesa Verde 92225
Metro (Part of Sacramento)‡ 95814
Metropolitan, *Humboldt* 95540
Metropolitan (Part of Los Angeles)‡ 90014
Mettler 93301
Mexican Colony 93263
Meyers (Part of South Lake Tahoe) 96155
Michigan Bluff 95631
Michillinda 91107
Mid City (Part of Stockton)‡ 95202
Midco (Part of Santa Maria) 93458
Middlefield Road 94061
Middle River 95234
Middletown 95461
Midpines 95345
Midtown (Part of Chico)‡ 95928
Midtown (Part of Woodland)‡ 95695
Midway 96088
Midway City 92655
Mikon (Part of West Sacramento) 95605
Milford 96121
Millbrae 94030*
.... 94031†
Millbrae Meadows (Part of Millbrae) 94030
Mill City 93546
Mill Creek 96061
Mill Creek Park 92359
Millers Corners 93637
Mills College (Part of Oakland)‡ 94613
Mill Valley 94941*
.... 94942†
Millville 96062
Milo 93265
Milpas (Part of Santa Barbara)‡ 93103
Milpitas 95035*
.... 95036†
Milton 95230
Mineral 96063
Mineral King 93271
Minkler 93657
Mint Canyon (Part of Santa Clarita) 91350
Mirabel Heights 95436
Mirabel Park 95436
Miracle Hot Springs 93301
Miracle Manor 93501
Miracle Mile (Part of Los Angeles)‡ 90036
Miraleste (Part of Rancho Palos Verdes) 90274
Mira Loma♦ 91752
Miramar 94018
Mira Mesa (Part of San Diego)‡ 92126
Miramonte, *Fresno* 93641
Mira Monte, *Ventura*♦ 93023
Miranda 95553
Mira Vista (Part of Richmond)‡ 94805
Mission (Part of San Luis Obispo)‡ 93406
Mission (Part of Santa Clara)‡ 95051
Mission Beach (Part of San Diego) 92109
Mission City Annex (Part of Los Angeles)‡ 91346
Mission Highlands 95476
Mission Hills (Part of Los Angeles) 91345*
.... 91346†
Mission Hills (Part of San Diego) 92103
Mission Hills, *Santa Barbara*♦ 93436
Mission Rafael (Part of San Rafael)‡ 94901
Mission San Jose (Part of Fremont)‡ 94539
Mission Station (Part of San Francisco)‡ 94110
Mission Valley Center (Part of San Diego) 92108
Mission Viejo 92690-92
For specific ZIP Codes call (888) 275-8777, or your local postmaster.
Mission Viejo Mall (Part of Mission Viejo) 92691
Missouri Triangle 93251
Mitchell Mill 95257
Mitchells Corner 93203
Mi-Wuk Village♦ 95346
Moccasin 95347
Mococo (Part of Martinez) 94553
Modesto 95350-58
For specific ZIP Codes call (888) 275-8777, or your local postmaster.
Modjeska 92867
Modoc Recreational Estates 96101
Moffett Field 94035
Mohave Manor 92311
Mojave♦ 93501*
.... 93502†
Mojave Heights (Part of Victorville) 92392
Mojave Knolls 93501
Mokelumne Hill 95245
Monarch Bay (Part of Laguna Niguel) 92677
Monmouth 93725
Mono Hot Springs 93642
Mono Lake 93541
Mono Village 93517
Mono Vista♦ 95372
Monrovia 91016*
.... 91017†
Monson 93618
Montague 96064
Montair (Part of Danville) 94526
Montalvin Manor 94806
Montalvo (Part of Ventura) 93003*
.... 93005†
Montara♦ 94037
Monta Vista (Part of Cupertino) 95014
Montclair 91763
Montclair Plaza (Part of Montclair) 91763
Montebello 90640
Montebello Gardens (Part of Pico Rivera) 90660
Montebello Hills (Part of Montebello)‡ 90640
Montebello Town Center (Part of Montebello) 90640
Montecito 93108
Monte Nido 91302
Monterey 93940-44
For specific ZIP Codes call (888) 275-8777, or your local postmaster.
Monterey Park 91754-55
For specific ZIP Codes call (888) 275-8777, or your local postmaster.
Monte Rio♦ 95462
Monte Rosa 95446
Montesano 95446
Monte Sereno 95030
Monte Toyon 95003

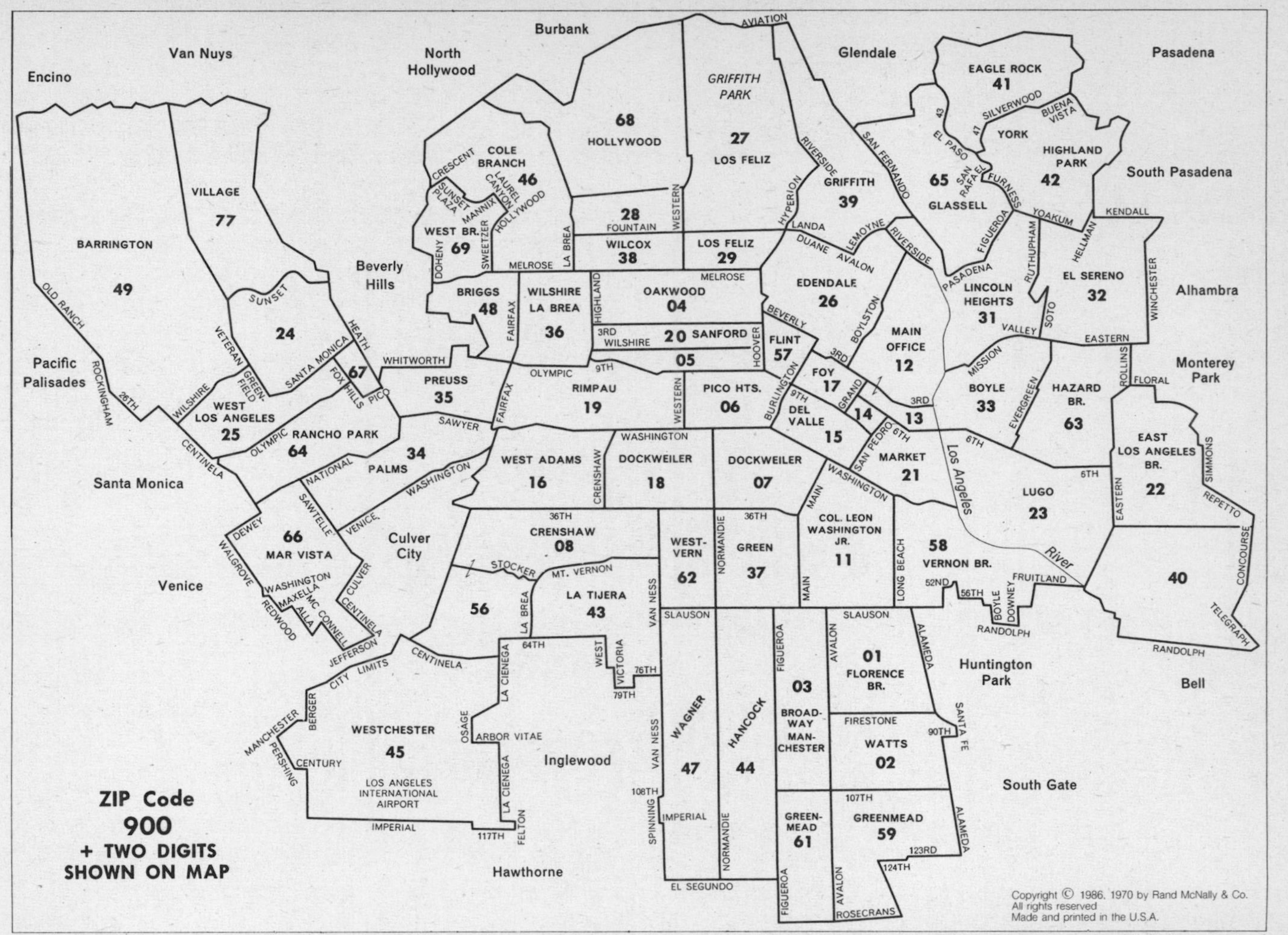
Encino
Van Nuys
North Hollywood
Burbank
Glendale
Pasadena
South Pasadena
Alhambra
Monterey Park
Beverly Hills
Pacific Palisades
Santa Monica
Culver City
Venice
Inglewood
Hawthorne
Huntington Park
South Gate
Bell
BARRINGTON 49
VILLAGE 77
24
WEST LOS ANGELES 25
RANCHO PARK 64
67
PREUSS 35
PALMS 34
MAR VISTA 66
COLE BRANCH 46
WEST BR. 69
BRIGGS 48
WILSHIRE LA BREA 36
HOLLYWOOD 68
28
WILCOX 38
GRIFFITH PARK
27 LOS FELIZ
LOS FELIZ 29
OAKWOOD 04
20 SANFORD
05
RIMPAU 19
PICO HTS. 06
WEST ADAMS 16
DOCKWEILER 18
DOCKWEILER 07
CRENSHAW 08
56
LA TIJERA 43
WEST-VERN 62
GREEN 37
WESTCHESTER 45
LOS ANGELES INTERNATIONAL AIRPORT
WAGNER 47
HANCOCK 44
GRIFFITH 39
EDENDALE 26
FLINT 57
FOY 17
DEL VALLE 15
14
13
MAIN OFFICE 12
MARKET 21
COL. LEON WASHINGTON JR. 11
03
BROAD-WAY MAN-CHESTER
GREEN-MEAD 61
01 FLORENCE BR.
WATTS 02
GREENMEAD 59
58 VERNON BR.
EAGLE ROCK 41
YORK
HIGHLAND PARK 42
65 GLASSELL
LINCOLN HEIGHTS 31
EL SERENO 32
BOYLE 33
HAZARD BR. 63
LUGO 23
EAST LOS ANGELES BR. 22
40
Los Angeles River
OLD RANCH
ROCKINGHAM
26TH
WILSHIRE
VETERAN
GREEN-FIELD
SUNSET
SANTA MONICA
HEATH
FOX HILLS
PICO
WHITWORTH
OLYMPIC
CENTINELA
NATIONAL
SAWYER
SAWTELLE
VENICE
WASHINGTON
DEWEY
WALGROVE
MAXELLA
MC CONNELL
ALLA
REDWOOD
CULVER
JEFFERSON
CITY LIMITS
MANCHESTER
PERSHING
BERGER
CENTURY
IMPERIAL
117TH
FELTON
LA CIENEGA
OSAGE
ARBOR VITAE
64TH
LA BREA
STOCKER
MT. VERNON
WEST
VICTORIA
76TH
79TH
VAN NESS
108TH
SPINNING
EL SEGUNDO
NORMANDIE
FIGUEROA
AVALON
ROSECRANS
124TH
123RD
ALAMEDA
107TH
90TH
SANTA FE
FIRESTONE
SLAUSON
MAIN
LONG BEACH
52ND
56TH
BOYLE
DOWNEY
FRUITLAND
RANDOLPH
TELEGRAPH
CONCOURSE
REPETTO
SIMMONS
EASTERN
6TH
FLORAL
ROLLINS
WINCHESTER
KENDALL
HELLMAN
YOAKUM
RUTHUPHAM
SOTO
VALLEY
MISSION
EVERGREEN
3RD
SAN PEDRO
GRAND
9TH
BURLINGTON
BOYLSTON
BEVERLY
HOOVER
WESTERN
HIGHLAND
3RD
WILSHIRE
MELROSE
FAIRFAX
CRENSHAW
36TH
FOUNTAIN
DOHENY
SWEETZER
CRESCENT
SUNSET PLAZA
LAUREL CANYON
MANNIX
HOLLYWOOD
AVIATION
RIVERSIDE
HYPERION
LANDA
DUANE
AVALON
LEMOYNE
SAN FERNANDO
PASADENA
FIGUEROA
FURNESS
SAN RAFAEL
EL PASO
43
47
SILVERWOOD
BUENA VISTA
ZIP Code
900
+ TWO DIGITS
SHOWN ON MAP

Place	ZIP Code
Montgomery Creek	96065
Montgomery Village (Part of Santa Rosa)‡	95405
Montrose	91020*
	91021†
Moody (Part of Cypress)	90630
Moonridge (Part of Big Bear Lake)‡	92315
Moonstone	95570
Moorpark	93020†
	93021*
Moorpark Home Acres	93021
Morada♦	95212
Moraga	94556
	94570
	94575
For specific ZIP Codes call (888) 275-8777, or your local postmaster.	
Morena	92040
Moreno‡	92554†
	92555*
Moreno Valley	92551-57
For specific ZIP Codes call (888) 275-8777, or your local postmaster.	
Moreno Valley Mall at Towngate (Part of Moreno Valley)	92508
Morgan Hill	95037*
	95038†
Mormon Bar	95338
Morningside Park (Part of Inglewood)‡	90305
Morongo Indian Reservation	92220
Morongo Valley♦	92256
Morro Bay	93442*
	93443†
Morro Palisades	93402
Moss Beach♦	94038
Mossdale	95330
Moss Landing	95039
Mountain Center	92561
Mountain Gate	96003
Mountain House, *Alameda*	95376
Mountain House, *Butte*	95916
Mountain Meadow	96091
Mountain Mesa♦	93240
Mountain Pass	92366
Mountain Ranch, *Calaveras*	95246
Mountain Ranch, *Madera*	93638
Mountain Rest	93664
Mountain Spring	91934
Mountain View, *Kern*	93307
Mountain View, *Santa Clara*	94039-43
For specific ZIP Codes call (888) 275-8777, or your local postmaster.	
Mountain View Acres♦	92392
Mount Aukum	95656
Mount Baldy	91759
Mount Bullion	95338
Mount Eden (Part of Hayward)	94557
Mount Hamilton	95140
Mount Hannah Lodge	95451
Mount Hebron	96058
Mount Helix	91941
Mount Hermon	95041
Mount Laguna	91948
Mount Shasta	96067
Mount Signal	92231
Mount View	94553
Mount Whitney	93545
Mount Wilson	91023
Mt. Roberta	95066
Mugginsville	96032
Muir (Part of Willits)	95490
Muir Beach	94965
Murietta	93640
Murphys♦	95247
Murray Park (Part of Larkspur)	94939
Murrieta	92562-64
For specific ZIP Codes call (888) 275-8777, or your local postmaster.	
Murrieta Hot Springs♦	92563
Muscoy♦	92405
Myers Flat	95554
Myrtletown♦	95501
Nadeau	90001
Napa	94558-59
	94581
For specific ZIP Codes call (888) 275-8777, or your local postmaster.	
Napa Junction	94590
Naples (Part of Long Beach)	90803
Napoleon Street (Part of San Francisco)‡	94124
Nashville	95623
National City	91950*
	91951†
Navajo (Part of San Diego)‡	92119
Naval Air Facility‡	92243
Naval Air Station (Part of Lemoore)	93245
Naval Air Station Miramar‡	92145
Naval Amphibious Base‡	92155
Naval Base (Part of Port Hueneme)	93043
Naval Regional Medical Center	92055
Naval Station (Part of San Diego)‡	92136
Naval Weapons Station, *Contra Costa*	94520
Naval Weapons Station, *Orange*	90740
Navarro	95463
Navelencia	93654
Nebo	92311
Needles	92363
Nelson	95958
Nestor (Part of San Diego)	92153
Nevada City	95959
New Almaden	95042
Newark	94560
New Auberry	93602
Newberry Springs	92365
Newburg	95540
Newbury Park	91319†
	91320*
Newcastle	95658
New Cuyama	93254
Newell	96134
Newhall	91321*
	91322†
Newhall Ranch (Part of Santa Clarita)	91350
New Helvetia (Part of Sacramento)	95815
Newman	95360
New Monterey (Part of Monterey)	93940
New Park Mall (Part of Newark)	94560
New Pine Creek	97635
Newport Beach	92657-63
For specific ZIP Codes call (888) 275-8777, or your local postmaster.	
Newport Center Fashion Island (Part of Newport Beach)	92660
Newport Heights (Part of Newport Beach)	92663
Newport Island (Part of Newport Beach)	92663
Newtown, *El Dorado*	95667
Newtown, *Nevada*	95959
Newville	95963
Nicasio	94946
Nice♦	95464
Nichols	94565
Nicolaus	95659
Nightingale	92561
Niguel Terrace (Part of Laguna Niguel)	92677
Niland♦	92257
Niles (Part of Fremont)‡	94536
Niles Junction (Part of Fremont)	94536
Nimshew	95954
Nipinnawassee	93001
Nipomo♦	93444
Nipton	92364
Nob Hill (Part of San Francisco)	94108
Noe Valley (Part of San Francisco)‡	94114
No Mirage	92259
Norco	91760
Nord	95973
Norden	95724
Normal Heights (Part of San Diego)	92116
North Beach (Part of San Francisco)‡	94133
North Belridge	93429
North Berkeley (Part of Berkeley)‡	94709
North Bloomfield	95959
North Clairemont (Part of San Diego)	92117
North Columbia	95959
North County Fair (Part of Escondido)	92025
Northcrest (Part of Crescent City)	95531
North Downey (Part of Downey)‡	90240
Northeast Modesto (Part of Modesto)	95355
North Edwards‡	93523
North Elsinore (Part of Lake Elsinore)	92530
North Fair Oaks♦	94025
North Fork	93643
Northgate Mall (Part of San Rafael)	94903
North Glendale (Part of Glendale)‡	91202*
	91222†
North Highlands♦	95660
North Hills (Part of Los Angeles)	91343
North Hollywood	91601-03
	91605-06
	91609
	91615-16
For specific ZIP Codes call (888) 275-8777, or your local postmaster.	
North Inglewood (Part of Inglewood)‡	90302
North Island Naval Air Station‡	92135
North Lakeport	95453
North Loma Linda (Part of Loma Linda)	92354
North Long Beach (Part of Long Beach)‡	90805
North Modesto (Part of Modesto)	95356
North Oakland (Part of Oakland)‡	94609
North Palm Springs	92258
Northpark (Part of San Bernardino)‡	92427
North Park (Part of San Diego)‡	92104
North Redondo Beach (Part of Redondo Beach)‡	90278
North Richmond	94804
Northridge	91324-28
For specific ZIP Codes call (888) 275-8777, or your local postmaster.	
Northridge Center (Part of Salinas)	93906
Northridge Fashion Center (Part of Los Angeles)	91324
North Sacramento (Part of Sacramento)	95815
North San Juan	95960
North Shore	92254
Northside (Part of Palm Desert)‡	92260
North Torrance (Part of Torrance)‡	90504
North Valley Plaza (Part of Chico)	95926
North Whittier	91746
North Whittier Heights	91745
Norwalk	90650-52
For specific ZIP Codes call (888) 275-8777, or your local postmaster.	
Norwalk Manor (Part of Norwalk)	90650
Novato	94945
	94947-49
For specific ZIP Codes call (888) 275-8777, or your local postmaster.	
Noyo	95437
Nubieber	96068
Nuevo♦	92567
Number Twenty Three (Part of San Francisco)‡	94123
Nummi (Part of Fremont)	94538
Nut Tree (Part of Vacaville)	95696
Nyland Acres	93030
Oak Bottom	96095
Oakdale	95361
Oak Glen (Part of Yucaipa)	92399
Oak Grove (Part of Oroville)	95966
Oak Grove, *San Diego*	92536
Oak Grove (Part of Menlo Park)‡	94025
Oakhills	93907
Oakhurst♦	93644
Oak Knoll Hills (Part of Cupertino)	95014
Oak Knolls	93455
Oakland	94601-07
	94609-19
	94621-61
For specific ZIP Codes call (888) 275-8777, or your local postmaster.	
Oakley♦	94561
Oakmont (Part of Santa Rosa)	95409
Oak Park (Part of Paso Robles)	93446
Oak Park (Part of Sacramento)‡	95817
Oak Park, *Ventura*♦	91301
Oak Park Estates	95249
Oakridge (Part of Stockton)	95207
Oakridge Mall (Part of San Jose)	95123
Oak Run	96069
Oaks (Part of Arroyo Grande)‡	93420
Oaks, The (Part of Thousand Oaks)	91360
Oak Shores	93426
Oak View♦	93022
Oakville	94562
Oakwood (Part of Los Angeles)‡	90004
Oasis	89010
O'Brien	96070
Occidental	95465
Ocean Beach (Part of San Diego)‡	92107
Oceano♦	93445
Ocean Park (Part of Santa Monica)‡	90405*
	90409†
Oceanside	92049-58
	92068
For specific ZIP Codes call (888) 275-8777, or your local postmaster.	
Ocean View (Part of Huntington Beach)	92647
Ocean View (Part of San Francisco)	94112
Ocean View, *Sonoma*	94923
Ockenden	93664
Ocotillo	92259
Ocotillo Wells	92004
Odd Fellows Park	95446
Oildale‡	93308*
	93388†
Ojai	93023*
	93024†
Olancha	93549
Old Fort Jim	95667
Old Gilroy	95020
Old Hopland	95449
Old Mammoth (Part of Mammoth Lakes)	93546
Old River	93309
Old San Diego (Part of San Diego)	92110
Old Station	96071
Old Town, *Madera*	93643
Old Town (Part of Temecula)‡	92593
Old Towne (Part of Tehachapi)	93582
Oleander	93725
Olema	94950
Oleum	94572
Olinda (Part of Brea)	92821
Olinda, *Shasta*	96007
Olive (Part of Orange)‡	92857†
	92865*
Olivehurst♦	95961
Olivenhain (Part of Encinitas)	92024
Olympia	95018
Olympic (Part of Beverly Hills)‡	90212
Olympic Valley	96146
Omo Ranch	95684
O'Neals	93645
One Hundred Palms	92274
Ono	96047
Ontario	91758
	91761-62
	91764
	91798
For specific ZIP Codes call (888) 275-8777, or your local postmaster.	
Ontario Mail Facility (Part of Ontario)‡	91761
Onyx	93255
Opal Cliffs♦	95062
Ophir	95603
Orange	92856-69
For specific ZIP Codes call (888) 275-8777, or your local postmaster.	
Orange Center (Part of Riverside)	92501
Orange Cove	93646
Orangefair Mall (Part of Fullerton)	92832
Orange Glen (Part of Escondido)‡	92027
Orange Heights (Part of Upland)	91786
Orangehurst (Part of Fullerton)‡	92833*
	92837†
Orange Park Acres	92869
Orangevale♦	95662
Orangewood (Part of Pasadena)‡	91115
Orchard Farms (Part of San Jose)‡	95170
Orcutt	93455*
	93457†
Ordbend	95943
Oregon City	95965
Oregon House	95962
Orick	95555
Orinda	94563
Orinda Village (Part of Orinda)	94563
Orland	95963
Orleans	95556
Ormand	92509
Oro Fino	96032
Oro Grande	92368
Oro Loma	93622
Orosi	93647
Oroville	95965-66
For specific ZIP Codes call (888) 275-8777, or your local postmaster.	
Osbourne (Part of Los Angeles)‡	90028
Otay (Part of Chula Vista)	91911
Otay Mesa‡	92153†
	92154*
Otterbein	91748
Outingdale	95684
Oval (Part of Visalia)‡	93291
Oxnard	93030-35
For specific ZIP Codes call (888) 275-8777, or your local postmaster.	
Oxnard Beach	93035
Pabrico (Part of Union City)	94587
Pachappa	92506
Pacheco♦	94553
Pacific (Part of Long Beach)‡	90806
Pacifica	94044*
	94045†
Pacific Beach (Part of San Diego)‡	92109*
	92169†
Pacific Gardens	95204
Pacific Grove	93950
Pacific Grove Acres (Part of Pacific Grove)	93950
Pacific House	95726
Pacific Manor (Part of Arcata)	95521
Pacific Manor (Part of Pacifica)	94044
Pacific Missile Test Center-Point Mugu	93042
Pacific Palisades (Part of Los Angeles)	90272
Pacific Shores	95531
Pacific Valley	93920
Pacoima	91331-34
For specific ZIP Codes call (888) 275-8777, or your local postmaster.	
Paddison Square (Part of Norwalk)‡	90652

*** Area Zip Code** **† Post Office Boxes** **‡ Postal Station** **♦ Census Designated Place** *Italic Type* **County**

Paicines 95043
Paintersville 95615
Pajaro♦ 95076
Pala 92059
Pala Indian Reservation 92059
Pala Mesa Village 92028
Palermo♦ 95968
Palm City (Part of Palm Desert) 92211
Palmdale 93550-52
93590-91
For specific ZIP Codes call (888) 275-8777, or your local postmaster.
Palm Desert 92211
92255
92260-61
For specific ZIP Codes call (888) 275-8777, or your local postmaster.
Palm Desert Town Center (Part of Palm Desert) 92260
Palmer Creek 95540
Palms (Part of Los Angeles)‡ 90034
Palm Springs 92262-64
92292
For specific ZIP Codes call (888) 275-8777, or your local postmaster.
Palm Springs Mall (Part of Palm Springs) 92262
Palo Alto 94301-10
For specific ZIP Codes call (888) 275-8777, or your local postmaster.
Palo Cedro 96073
Paloma 95252
Palomar Mountain 92060
Palomar Park 94062
Palos Verdes Estates 90274-75
For specific ZIP Codes call (888) 275-8777, or your local postmaster.
Palos Verdes Peninsula (Part of Rolling Hills Estates) 90274-75
For specific ZIP Codes call (888) 275-8777, or your local postmaster.
Palo Verde 92266
Palo Vista (Part of Vista)‡ 92083
Panoche 95043
Panorama City (Part of Los Angeles) 91402*
91412†
Panorama Heights, *Orange* 92705
Panorama Heights, *Tulare* 93260
Panorama Mall (Part of Los Angeles)‡ 91402
Pappas 93640
Paradise, *Butte* 95967†
95969*
Paradise (Part of Modesto)‡ 95351
95358
For specific ZIP Codes call (888) 275-8777, or your local postmaster.
Paradise Cay (Part of Tiburon) 94920
Paradise Estates 93514
Paradise Hills (Part of San Diego)‡ 92139
Paradise Park 95060
Paraiso Springs 93960
Paramount 90723
Parchers Camp 93514
Park (Part of Berkeley)‡ 94702
Park Central (Part of Alameda)‡ 94501
Parker Dam 92267
Parkfield 93451
Parkmoor (Part of San Jose)‡ 95128*
95159†
Parkside (Part of San Francisco)‡ 94116
Park Siding (Part of Petaluma) 94952
Park Village 92328
Parkway 95823
Parkway Plaza (Part of El Cajon) 92020
Parkwood♦ 93637
Parlier 93648
Pasadena 91101-07
91109-17
For specific ZIP Codes call (888) 275-8777, or your local postmaster.
Pasatiempo 95060
Paskenta 96074
Paso Robles 93446*
93447†
Patata (Part of South Gate) 90280
Patrick Creek 95543
Patricks Point 95570
Patterson, *Stanislaus* 95363
Patterson, *Tulare* 93291
Patton Village 96113
Pauma Indian Reservation 92061
Pauma Valley 92061
Paxton 95971
Paynes Creek 96075
Paynesville 96120
Peanut 96041
Pearblossom 93553
Peardale 95945
Pearland (Part of Palmdale) 93550
Pearsonville 93527
Pebble Beach 93953
Pechanga Indian Reservation 92590
Pecwan 95546
Pedley♦ 92509
Pedro Valley (Part of Pacifica) 94044
Peninsula Center (Part of Rolling Hills Estates)‡ 90274
Peninsula Village 96137
Penngrove 94951
Pennington 95953
Penn Valley♦ 95946
Penryn 95663
Pentz 95965
Pepperwood 95565
Peralta Hills 92867
Perkins‡ 95826-27
For specific ZIP Codes call (888) 275-8777, or your local postmaster.
Perris 92570-72
For specific ZIP Codes call (888) 275-8777, or your local postmaster.
Perry (Part of Whittier) 90603
Pescadero 94060
Petaluma 94952-55
94975
94999
For specific ZIP Codes call (888) 275-8777, or your local postmaster.
Peters 95236
Petrolia 95558
Phelan 92329†
92371*
Phillipsville 95559
Philo 95466
Phoenix Lake Country Club Estates 95370
Pico (Part of Pico Rivera)‡ 90660
Pico Heights (Part of Los Angeles)‡ 90006
Pico Rivera 90660-62
For specific ZIP Codes call (888) 275-8777, or your local postmaster.
Piedmont 94620
Piedra 93649
Pierce Lake Estates 93644
Piercy 95587
Pierpoint Springs 93208
Pike 95960
Pilot Hill 95664
Pine Cove, *Riverside* 92549
Pine Cove, *Trinity* 96052
Pinecrest 95364
Pinedale (Part of Fresno) 93650
Pine Flat, *Fresno* 93649
Pine Flat, *Tulare* 93207
Pine Grove, *Amador* 95665
Pine Grove, *Lake* 95426
Pine Grove, *Mendocino* 95437
Pine Grove, *Shasta* 96079
Pine Hills, *Humboldt* 95503
Pine Hills, *San Diego* 92036
Pinehurst 93641
Pine Mountain Club‡ 93222
Pine Mountain Lake 95321
Pineridge 93602
Pine Street (Part of San Francisco)‡ 94109
Pine Valley♦ 91962
Pinnacles 95043
Pinole 94564
Pinon Hills 92372
Pinon Pines Estates 93225
Pinyon Crest 92262
Pinyon Pines 92561
Pioneer 95666
Pioneer Point 93562
Pioneertown 92268
Piru♦ 93040
Pismo Beach 93448†
93449*
Pittsburg 94565
Pittville 96056
Pixley♦ 93256
Placentia 92670
Placerville 95667
Plainsburg 95333
Plainview 93267
Planada♦ 95365
Planehaven 95652
Plantation 95421
Plaster City 92243
Platina 96076
Playa (Part of Laguna Beach)‡ 92652
Playa Del Rey (Part of Los Angeles) 90293*
90296†
Playa Vista (Part of Los Angeles)‡ 90094
Playmor (Part of Chula Vista) 91911
Plaza (Part of Orange)‡ 92856†
92666*
Plaza (Part of Pasadena)‡ 91102
Plaza (Part of Sunnyvale)‡ 94086
Plaza Camino Real (Part of Carlsbad) 92008
Plaza Center (Part of Ontario)‡ 91762
Plaza Pasadena (Part of Pasadena) 91101
Pleasant Grove 95668
Pleasant Hill 94523
Pleasanton 94566
94588
For specific ZIP Codes call (888) 275-8777, or your local postmaster.
Pleasant Valley 95667
Pleasant View 93260
Plymouth 95669
Poinsettia Tract 94565
Point Arena 95468
Point Dume‡ 90264†
90265*
Point Loma (Part of San Diego)‡ 92106
Point Pleasant 95758
Point Reyes Station 94956
Point Richmond (Part of Richmond)‡ 94807
Poker Flat 95228
Pollock Pines♦ 95726
Pomona 91766-69
For specific ZIP Codes call (888) 275-8777, or your local postmaster.
Pond 93280
Ponderosa Sky Ranch 96075
Pondosa 96057
Pope Valley 94567
Poplar♦ 93258
Port Chicago 94520
Port Costa 94569
Porter Ranch 91326*
91327†
Porterville 93257*
93258†
Porterville West (Part of Porterville) 93257
Port Hueneme 93041*
93044†
Port Kenyon 95536
Portola 96122
Portola Valley 94028
Port San Luis 93424
Portuguese Bend (Part of Rancho Palos Verdes) 90274
Posey 93260
Poso Park 93260
Postal Avenue‡ 92556†
92557*
Post Office Annex (Part of Burlingame)‡ 94010
Potrero, *San Diego* 91963
Potrero (Part of San Francisco) 94110
Potter Valley 95469
Poway 92064*
92074†
Power Tract 93283
Pozo 93453
Prather 93651
Prattville 95923
Presidential Heights (Part of San Clemente) 92672
Presidio (Part of San Francisco)‡ 94129
Preston Heights (Part of Arcata) 95521
Preuss (Part of Los Angeles)‡ 90035
Priest Valley 93210
Princeton, *Colusa* 95970
Princeton, *San Mateo* 94019
Proberta 96078
Project City 96079
Promenade Mall (Part of Los Angeles) 91367
Prosser Lakeview Estates 96161
Prunedale♦ 93907
Pudding Creek 95437
Puente Junction (Part of City of Industry) 91744
Puerco Beach (Part of Malibu) 90265
Pulga 95965
Pumpkin Center 93309
Quail Valley♦ 92587
Quaking Aspen 93265
Quartz Hill♦ 93551
Quincy 95971
Quintette 95634
Quito (Part of Saratoga) 95070
Rackerby 95972
Radec 92543
Rafael Village (Part of Novato) 94949
Rail Road Flat 95248
Rainbow♦ 92028
Raisin 93652
Ralph 95370
Ramirez (Part of Los Angeles)‡ 90037
90082
For specific ZIP Codes call (888) 275-8777, or your local postmaster.
Ramona♦ 92065
Ramona Acres 93432
Ramona Woods 95006
Ramos Village 95336
Rancheria 95449
Ranch House 92055
Ranchita 92066
Rancho Bernardo (Part of San Diego)‡ 92128
Rancho Buena 96022
Rancho California (Part of Temecula) 92590
Rancho Cordova♦ 95670
95741-42
For specific ZIP Codes call (888) 275-8777, or your local postmaster.
Rancho Cucamonga 91729
91730
91739
For specific ZIP Codes call (888) 275-8777, or your local postmaster.
Rancho Del Mar 94590
Rancho Del Rey (Part of Chula Vista)‡ 91909†
91911*
Rancho Los Amigos (Part of Downey)‡ 90242
Rancho Mirage 92270
Rancho Murieta 95683
Rancho Palos Verdes 90275
Rancho Park (Part of Los Angeles)‡ 90064
Rancho Penasquitos (Part of San Diego)‡ 92129
Rancho Rinconada♦ 95014
Rancho San Diego♦ 91941
Rancho Santa Fe 92067†
92091*
Rancho Santa Margarita♦ 92688
Randall Island 95615
Randolph 96126
Randsburg 93554
Ravendale 96123
Ravenswood (Part of East Palo Alto) 94303
Rawhide 95370
Rawson 96080
Raymond 93653
Raynor Park (Part of Sunnyvale) 94087
Red Bank 96080
Red Bluff 96080
Redcrest 95569
Redding 96001-03
96049
96099
For specific ZIP Codes call (888) 275-8777, or your local postmaster.
Red Hill 92705
Redlands 92373-75
For specific ZIP Codes call (888) 275-8777, or your local postmaster.
Red Mountain 93558
Redondo Beach 90277-78
For specific ZIP Codes call (888) 275-8777, or your local postmaster.
Reds Meadow 93546
Red Top 95340
Redway♦ 95560
Redwood City 94059
94061-65
For specific ZIP Codes call (888) 275-8777, or your local postmaster.
Redwood Estates 95044
Redwood Grove 95006
Redwood Lodge 95437
Redwood Retreat 95020
Redwood Shores (Part of Redwood City) 94065
Redwood Terrace 94020
Redwood Valley 95470
Reedley 93654
Relief 95959
Requa 95548
Rescue 95672
Reseda 91335-37
For specific ZIP Codes call (888) 275-8777, or your local postmaster.
Rheem (Part of San Pablo) 94801
Rheem Valley (Part of Moraga) 94570
Rialto 92376*
92377†
Rice 92280
Richardson Springs 95973
Richfield 96021
Richgrove♦ 93261
Richmond, *Contra Costa* 94801-02
94804-05
94807-08
94850
For specific ZIP Codes call (888) 275-8777, or your local postmaster.
Richmond (Part of San Francisco) 94118
Richvale 95974
Ridgecrest 93555*
93556†
Rimcrest (Part of Palm Springs) 92264
Rimforest 92378
Rimpau (Part of Los Angeles)‡ 90019
Rimrock 92268
Rincon 92061
Rincon Center (Part of San Francisco)‡ 94119
Rincon Indian Reservation 92025
Rincon Valley (Part of Santa Rosa) 95409
Rio Bonito 95917
Rio Bravo‡ 93306
Rio Dell, *Humboldt* 95562
Rio Dell, *Sonoma* 95436
Rio del Mar♦ 95003
Rio Linda♦ 95673
Rio Nido 95471
Rio Oso 95674
Rio Vista 94571
Ripley 92225
Ripon 95366
Ripperdan 93637
Ritter Ranch 93551
Rivera (Part of Pico Rivera) 90660
Riverbank 95367
Riverbank Army Ammunition Plant 95367

Riverdale♦ 93656
River Kern 93238
River Oaks 95045
River Pines 95675
River Road (Part of Modesto) 95351
Riverroad Estates 93637

Riverside, *Riverside*
92501-17
92519
For specific ZIP Codes call (888) 275-8777, or your local postmaster.

Colleges & Universities
California Baptist Coll 92504
La Sierra Univ 92515
Univ of California 92521

Financial Institutions
Bank of America Nat Trust 92501
Union Bank of California 92501
Wells Fargo Bank, NA 92501

Hospitals
Kaiser Foundation Hosp 92505
Parkview Community Hosp 92503
Riverside Community Hosp 92501

Hotels/Motels
Holiday Inn, Riverside Convention Ctr 92501

Riverside Grove 95006
Riverside Park 95528
Riverside Plaza (Part of Riverside) 92506
Rivertown (Part of Antioch)‡ 94509
Riverview 92040
Riverview Farms 92040
Riviera Cliff 95204
Roads End 93238
Robbins 95676
Robertsville (Part of San Jose)‡ 95118
Robinsons Corner 95965
Robles Del Rio 93924
Rob Roy Junction 95003
Rockaway Beach (Part of Pacifica) 94044
Rock Creek 95965
Rock Crest 95980
Rock Haven 93664
Rocking Horse Ranchos (Part of Rancho Palos Verdes) 90731
Rocklin 95677
95765
For specific ZIP Codes call (888) 275-8777, or your local postmaster.
Rockport 95488
Rockridge (Part of Oakland) 94618
Rockville 94585
Rodeo♦ 94572
Rodgers Flat 95980
Rogina Heights 95482
Rohnert Park 94927†
94928*
Rohnerville 95540
Rolinda 93706
Rolling Hills, *Los Angeles* 90274
Rolling Hills, *Madera* 93637
Rolling Hills, *Riverside* 92539
Rolling Hills Estates, Los Angeles 90274
Rolling Hills Estates, San Luis Obispo 93401
Rolling Hills Plaza (Part of Torrance) 90505
Rolling Hills Riviera (Part of Rancho Palos Verdes) 90731
Rollingwood 94806
Romie Lane (Part of Salinas)‡ 93901
Romoland♦ 92585
Roosevelt Corner 93534
Roosevelt Terrace 94590
Rosamond♦ 93560
Rose Bowl (Part of Pasadena)‡ 91103
Rosedale 93308
Roseland‡ 95407
Rosemead 91770
Rosemead Square (Part of Rosemead) 91770
Rosemont, *Sacramento*♦ 95826
Rosemont, *San Diego* 92065
Roseville 95661
95678
95747
For specific ZIP Codes call (888) 275-8777, or your local postmaster.
Rosewood (Part of Eureka) 95503
Ross 94957
Ross Corner 92222
Rossmoor♦ 90720
Rossmoor Business Center (Part of Seal Beach) 90740
Rossmoor Highlands (Part of Los Alamitos) 90720
Rough And Ready 95975
Round Hill Country Club 94507
Round Mountain 96084
Round Valley 93514
Round Valley Indian Reservation 95428
Rovana 93514
Rowland (Part of City of Industry) 91743
Rowland Heights♦ 91748
Rubidoux 92509*
92519†
Rucker 95020
Rumsey 95679
Running Springs♦ 92382
Rupert 95901
Russell (Part of Hayward) 94541
Russian River Terrace 95436
Ruth 95526
Rutherford 94573
Ryde 95680
Sabre City 95678

Sacramento
94203-99
95801-42
95851-66
For specific ZIP Codes call (888) 275-8777, or your local postmaster.

Colleges & Universities
California State Univ 95819
Univ of the Pacific-McGeorge School of Law 95817

Financial Institutions
Bank of America, NTSA 95814
Sanwa Bank 95814
Union Bank of California 95814
U S Bank, NA 95814
Wells Fargo Bank, NA 95814

Hospitals
Mercy General Hosp 95819
Sutter General Hosp 95816
Sutter Memorial Hosp 95819
Univ of California, Davis Med Ctr 95817

Hotels/Motels
Fountain Suites 95814
Hilton 95815
Holiday Inn, Capitol Plaza 95814
Hyatt Regency at Capitol Pk 95814
Radisson 95815
Red Lion Inn 95815

Military Installations
U S Army Corps of Engineers 95814

Sacramento Area Mail Processing Center 95798-99
For specific ZIP Codes call (888) 275-8777, or your local postmaster.
Sacramento South 95820
Sage 92544
Sage Valley 96113
St. Bernard 96061
St. Francis Heights (Part of Daly City) 94015
St. Helena 94574
St. James Park (Part of San Jose)‡ 95113
St. Johns 93286
St. Marys College (Part of Moraga)‡ 94575
St. Matthew (Part of San Mateo)‡ 94401
94405
For specific ZIP Codes call (888) 275-8777, or your local postmaster.
Salida♦ 95368
Salinas 93901-15
93962
For specific ZIP Codes call (888) 275-8777, or your local postmaster.
Salinas Resort 95451
Salmon Creek 94923
Salton City 92275
Salton Sea Beach 92274
Saltus 92304
Salvador (Part of Napa) 94558
Salyer 95563
Samoa 95564
San Andreas♦ 95249
San Anselmo 94960*
94979†
San Anselmo, *Marin* 94979
San Antonio Heights♦ 91784
San Antonio Shopping Center (Part of Mountain View) 94040
San Ardo 93450
San Benito 95043
San Bernardino 92401-27
For specific ZIP Codes call (888) 275-8777, or your local postmaster.
San Bruno 94066-67
94096-99
For specific ZIP Codes call (888) 275-8777, or your local postmaster.
San Carlos (Part of San Diego) 92119
San Carlos, *San Mateo* 94070*
94071†
San Clemente 92672-74
For specific ZIP Codes call (888) 275-8777, or your local postmaster.
Sand City 93955
Sanderson (Part of Hemet)‡ 92545
Sand Hill 94561

San Diego
92101-17
92119-42
92145-72
92174-77
92182-99
For specific ZIP Codes call (888) 275-8777, or your local postmaster.

Colleges & Universities
The Advertising Arts Coll 92121
California School of Professional Psychology 92121
California Pacific Univ 92131
California Western School of Law 92101
Design Institute 92121
ITT Technical Institute 92123
Newschool of Architecture 92101
Point Loma Nazarene Coll 92106
San Diego State Univ 92182
United States International Univ 92131
Univ of San Diego 92110

Financial Institutions
Bank of America, NTSA 92101
Comerica Bank 92101
General Bank 92111
Manufacturer's Bank 92101
Sanwa Bank 92101
The Sumitomo Bank 92101
Union Bank of California 92120
Wells Fargo Bank, NA 92111

Hospitals
Mercy Health Ctr-Hillcrest 92103
Naval Med Ctr 92134
Sharp Memorial Hosp 92123
Univ of California Med Ctr 92103
Veterans Affairs Med Ctr 92161

Hotels/Motels
Bahia Hotel 92109
Best Western Hanalei 92108
Best Western Seven Seas 92108
Catamaran Resort 92109
Clarion Bay View 92101
Embassy Suites 92101
Hilton Beach & Tennis Resort 92109
Holiday Inn, Mission Bay/Sea World 92108
Holiday Inn on the Bay 92101
Hyatt Islandia on Mission Bay 92109
Hyatt Regency 92101
Marriott Hotel & Marina 92101
Marriott, Mission Valley 92108
Mission Valley Hilton 92108
Paradise Point 92109
Radisson Harbor View 92101
Sheraton 92101
Town & Country 92108
Wyndham Emerald Plaza 92101

Military Installations
Coast Guard Air Sta 92101
Defense Distribution Depot 92136
Defense Fuel Support Point, Point Loma 92132
Fleet & Industrial Supply Ctr 92132
Fleet & Industrial Supply Ctr, Fuel Dept, Point Loma Annex 92132
Fleet & Industrial Supply Ctr, Regional Contracts Dept 92132
Marine Corps Air Station, Miramar 92145
Marine Corps Recruiting Depot 92140
Naval Air Sta, North Island 92135
Naval Amphibious Base, Coronado 92155
Naval Command, Control & Ocean Surveillance Ctr 92152
Naval Hosp 92134
Naval Recruiting Dist 92133
Supervisor of Shipbuilding, Conversion & Repair 92136

San Diego Country Estates♦ 92065
San Dimas 91773
Sandy Korner 92274
San Felipe 95023
San Fernando 91340*
91341†
Sanford (Part of Los Angeles)‡ 90005
90010
90020
90075-76
For specific ZIP Codes call (888) 275-8777, or your local postmaster.

San Francisco
94101-88
For specific ZIP Codes call (888) 275-8777, or your local postmaster.

Colleges & Universities
Academy of Art Coll 94105
American Conservatory Theatre 94108
California Institute of Integral Studies 94109
Golden Gate Univ 94105
Lincoln Univ 94118
Louise Salinger Academy of Fashion 94105
New Coll of California 94102
San Francisco Art Institute 94133
San Francisco Conservatory of Music 94122
San Francisco State Univ 94132
Saybrook Institute 94133
Univ of California 94143
Univ of California-Hastings Coll of Law 94102
Univ of San Francisco 94117

Financial Institutions
Bank of America, NTSA 94104
Manufacturer's Bank 94104
Sanwa Bank 94111
The Sumitomo Bank 94104
Tokai Bank 94111
Union Bank of California 94104
Wells Fargo Bank, NA 94104

Hospitals
California Pacific Med Ctr 94120
General Hosp Med Ctr 94110
Kaiser Med Ctr 94115
Univ of California SF Med Ctr 94143
Veterans Affairs Med Ctr 94121

Hotels/Motels
ANA Hotel 94103
Cathedral Hill Quality Hotel 94109
Fairmont Hotel 94108
Grand Hyatt on Union Square 94108
Hilton & Towers 94102
Holiday Inn, Financial District 94108
Holiday Inn, Fisherman's Wharf 94133
Holiday Inn, Golden Gateway 94109
Holiday Inn, Union Square 94108
Hyatt Regency 94111
The Mark Hopkins Inter-Continental 94108
Marriott 94103
Hotel Nikko 94102
Parc Fifty Five 94102
Ramada Plaza 94103
Renaissance, Stanford Court 94108
Sheraton at Fisherman's Wharf 94133
Sir Francis Drake 94102
The Westin St Francis 94102

Military Installations
Naval Sta, Treasure Island 94130
U S Army Corps of Engineers 94105

San Francisco Shopping Centre (Part of San Francisco) 94103
San Gabriel 91775-78
For specific ZIP Codes call (888) 275-8777, or your local postmaster.
Sanger 93657
San Geronimo 94963
San Gregorio 94074
San Jacinto 92581-83
For specific ZIP Codes call (888) 275-8777, or your local postmaster.
San Joaquin 93660
San Joaquin River Club 95385

San Jose
95101-39
95141-96
For specific ZIP Codes call (888) 275-8777, or your local postmaster.

Colleges & Universities
San Jose Christian Coll 95108

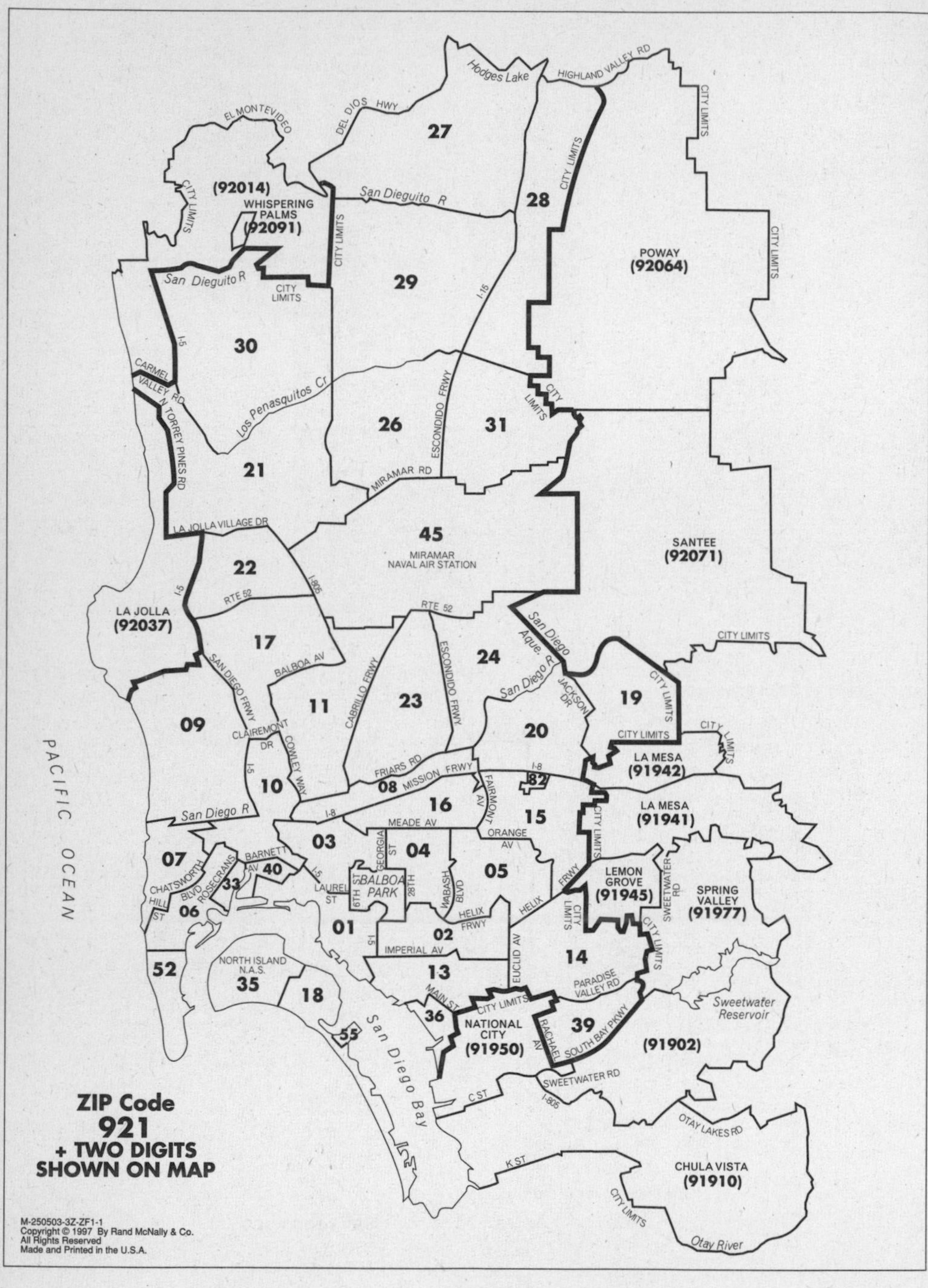

ZIP Code
921
+ TWO DIGITS
SHOWN ON MAP
PACIFIC OCEAN
San Diego Bay
LA JOLLA
(92037)
(92014)
WHISPERING
PALMS
(92091)
POWAY
(92064)
SANTEE
(92071)
LA MESA
(91942)
LA MESA
(91941)
LEMON
GROVE
(91945)
SPRING
VALLEY
(91977)
NATIONAL
CITY
(91950)
(91902)
CHULA VISTA
(91910)
MIRAMAR
NAVAL AIR STATION
NORTH ISLAND
N.A.S.
BALBOA
PARK
Hodges Lake
Sweetwater
Reservoir
Otay River
San Dieguito R
San Diego R
Los Penasquitos Cr
San Diego Aque.
CITY LIMITS
M-250503-3Z-ZF1-1

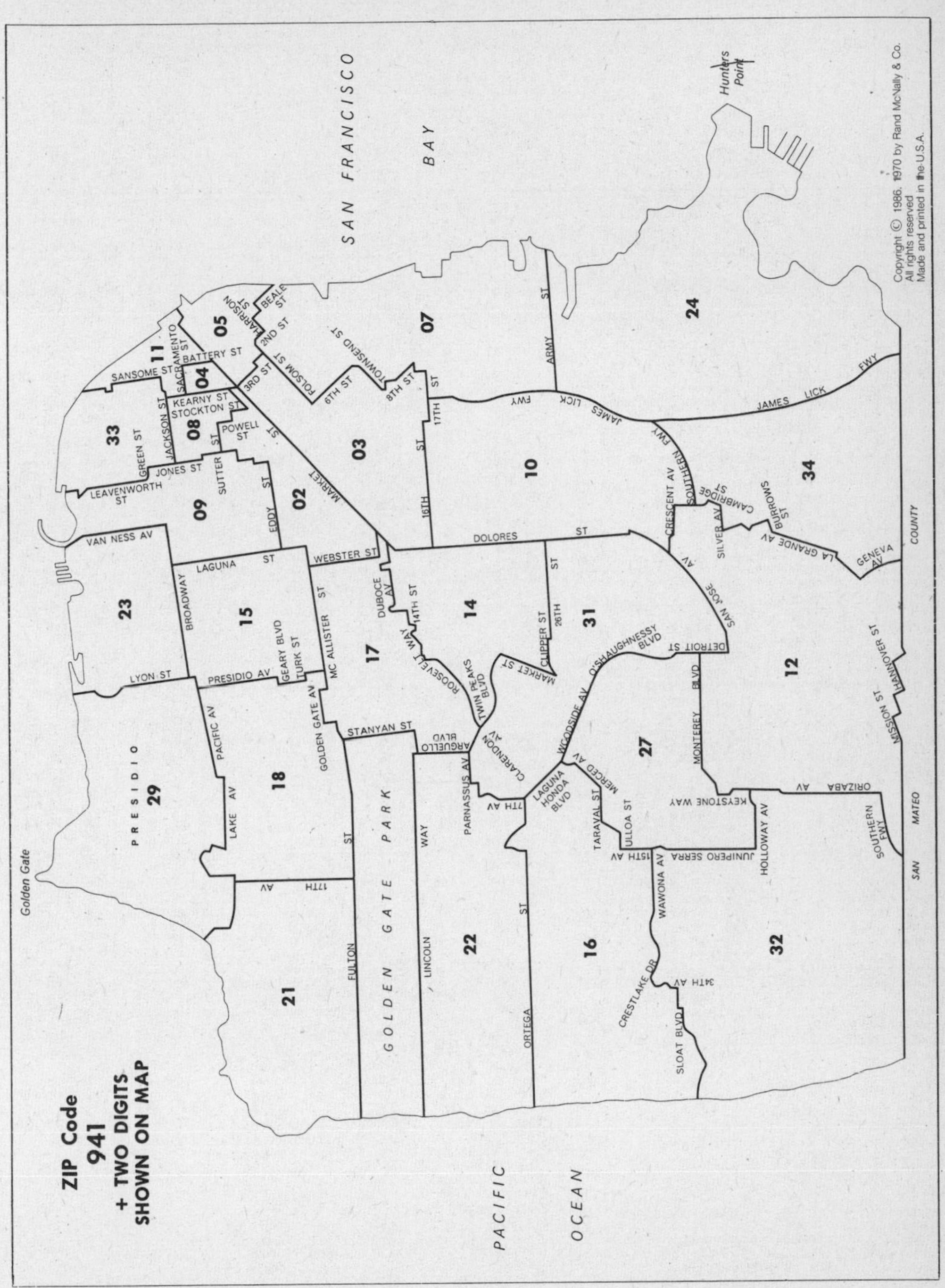
ZIP Code
941
+ TWO DIGITS
SHOWN ON MAP
SAN FRANCISCO
BAY
PACIFIC
OCEAN
Golden Gate
PRESIDIO
GOLDEN GATE PARK
Hunters Point
SAN MATEO
COUNTY
11
05
04
08
33
09
02
03
07
23
15
17
14
10
24
34
31
12
29
18
27
21
22
16
32
VAN NESS AV
LEAVENWORTH ST
JONES ST
GREEN ST
JACKSON ST
SANSOME ST
SACRAMENTO ST
BATTERY ST
KEARNY ST
STOCKTON ST
POWELL ST
SUTTER ST
EDDY ST
MARKET ST
3RD ST
2ND ST
BEALE ST
HARRISON ST
FOLSOM ST
TOWNSEND ST
6TH ST
8TH ST
17TH ST
16TH ST
ARMY ST
JAMES LICK FWY
LAGUNA ST
WEBSTER ST
BROADWAY
GEARY BLVD
TURK ST
MC ALLISTER ST
PRESIDIO AV
LYON ST
DUBOCE AV
14TH ST
ROOSEVELT WAY
DOLORES ST
26TH ST
CLIPPER ST
MARKET ST
TWIN PEAKS BLVD
O'SHAUGHNESSY BLVD
DETROIT ST
SAN JOSE AV
CRESCENT AV
SOUTHERN FWY
CAMBRIDGE ST
BURROWS ST
SILVER AV
LA GRANDE AV
GENEVA AV
PACIFIC AV
LAKE AV
GOLDEN GATE AV
STANYAN ST
ARGUELLO BLVD
CLARENDON AV
PARNASSUS AV
7TH AV
WOODSIDE AV
LAGUNA HONDA BLVD
MERCED AV
MONTEREY BLVD
MISSION ST
HANNOVER ST
KEYSTONE WAY
ORIZABA AV
HOLLOWAY AV
JUNIPERO SERRA
15TH AV
TARAVAL ST
ULLOA ST
WAWONA AV
CRESTLAKE DR
34TH AV
SLOAT BLVD
17TH AV
FULTON ST
LINCOLN WAY
ORTEGA ST
SOUTHERN FWY

San Jose State Univ.... 95192
Univ of Phoenix-Northern California Campus 95134

Financial Institutions

Bank of America, NTSA 95113
Cathay Bank 95122
Comerica Bank 95113
Sanwa Bank 95113
The Sumitomo Bank 95112
Union Bank of California 95110
Wells Fargo Bank, NA 95113

Hospitals

Good Samaritan Hosp 95124
Santa Clara Valley Med Ctr 95128

Hotels/Motels

Doubletree 95110
The Fairmont 95113
Hilton & Towers 95110
Hyatt at San Jose Airport 95112
Wyndham 95112

San Jose Recreation Camp 95321
San Juan Bautista 95045
San Juan Capistrano 92675*
92693†
San Juan Plaza (Part of San Juan Capistrano)‡ 92675
San Lawrence Terrace 93451
San Leandro 94577-79
For specific ZIP Codes call (888) 275-8777, or your local postmaster.
San Lorenzo♦ 94580
San Lorenzo Park 95006
San Lorenzo Woods 95006
San Lucas 93954
San Luis Obispo 93401
93403-10
For specific ZIP Codes call (888) 275-8777, or your local postmaster.
San Luis Rey (Part of Oceanside) 92068
San Luis Rey Heights 92028
San Marcos 92069*
92079†
San Marin (Part of Novato) 94945
San Marino 91108*
91118†
San Martin♦ 95046
San Mateo 94401-09
For specific ZIP Codes call (888) 275-8777, or your local postmaster.
San Mateo Fashion Island (Part of San Mateo) 94404
San Miguel♦ 93451
San Onofre 92672
San Pablo 94806
San Pasqual Indian Reservation 92082
San Pedro 90731-34
For specific ZIP Codes call (888) 275-8777, or your local postmaster.
San Quentin 94964†
94974*
San Rafael 94901-03
94912-13
94915
For specific ZIP Codes call (888) 275-8777, or your local postmaster.
San Ramon 94583
San Ramon Village (Part of Dublin) 94568
San Roque (Part of Santa Barbara)‡ 93105
San Simeon 93452
San Simeon Acres 93452
Santa Ana 92701-07
92711-12
92799
For specific ZIP Codes call (888) 275-8777, or your local postmaster.
Santa Ana Heights 92707
Santa Ana Marine Corps Air Facility 92709
Santa Anita Fashion Park (Part of Arcadia) 91007

Santa Barbara 93101-11
93120-90
For specific ZIP Codes call (888) 275-8777, or your local postmaster.
Santa Clara 95050-56
For specific ZIP Codes call (888) 275-8777, or your local postmaster.
Santa Clarita 91350
91380
91382-83
For specific ZIP Codes call (888) 275-8777, or your local postmaster.
Santa Cruz 95060-65
For specific ZIP Codes call (888) 275-8777, or your local postmaster.
Santa Cruz Gardens 95062
Santa Fe Plaza‡ 90605
Santa Fe Springs 90670*
90671†
Santa Margarita 93453
Santa Maria 93454-58
For specific ZIP Codes call (888) 275-8777, or your local postmaster.
Santa Maria Town Center (Part of Santa Maria) 93454
Santa Monica 90401-11
For specific ZIP Codes call (888) 275-8777, or your local postmaster.
Santa Monica Canyon (Part of Los Angeles) 90402
Santa Monica Place (Part of Santa Monica) 90401
Santa Nella 95322
Santa Paula 93060*
93061†
Santa Rita (Part of Salinas) 93906
Santa Rita, *Santa Barbara* 93436
Santa Rita Park 93661
Santa Rosa 95401-09
For specific ZIP Codes call (888) 275-8777, or your local postmaster.
Santa Rosa Indian Reservation, *Kings* 93245
Santa Rosa Indian Reservation, *Riverside* 92543
Santa Rosa Island Air Force Station 93041
Santa Rosa Plaza (Part of Santa Rosa) 95401
Santa Susana (Part of Simi Valley) 93063
Santa Venetia♦ 94901
Santa Western (Part of Los Angeles)‡ 90072
Santa Ynez♦ 93460
Santa Ysabel 92070
Santa Ysabel Indian Reservation 92070
Santee 92071*
92072†
San Ysidro (Part of San Diego) 92143†
92173*
Saranap 94595
Saratoga 95070*
95071†
Saratoga Springs 95493
Sather Gate (Part of Berkeley)‡ 94704
Saticoy (Part of Ventura)‡ 93004*
93007†
Sattley 96124
Saugus (Part of Santa Clarita) 91350
Sausalito 94965*
94966†
Saviers (Part of Oxnard)‡ 93033
Sawyers Bar 96027
Scenic Brook Estates 95370
Scenic Center (Part of Modesto) 95355
Scheideck 93252
Schellville 95476
Scotia 95565
Scotland 92358
Scott Bar 96085
Scotts Valley 95066*
95067†
Seacliff 95003

Seahaven 94937
Seal Beach 90740
Seal Beach Naval Weapons Station 90740
Seal Cove 94038
Seaside 93955
Sebastiani (Part of Sonoma) 95476
Sebastopol, *Nevada* 95960
Sebastopol, *Sonoma* 95472*
95473†
Sedco Hills♦ 92530
Seeley♦ 92273
Seiad Valley 96086
Selby 94525
Selma 93662
Seneca 95923
Sepulveda (Part of Los Angeles) 91343
Sequoia Crest 93265
Sequoia Mall (Part of Visalia) 93277
Sequoia National Park 93262
Serena Park 93013
Serene Lakes 95728
Serra (Part of Dana Point) 92624
Serra Mesa (Part of San Diego)‡ 92123
Serramonte (Part of Daly City) 94015
Serramonte Center (Part of Daly City) 94015
Sespe 93015
Seven Oaks 92305
Seven Pines 93526
Seville 93291
Shadow Hills 95461
Shady Glen 95713
Shafter 93263
Shandon 93461
Sharon Heights (Part of Menlo Park) 94025
Sharpe Army Depot 95296
Sharp Park (Part of Pacifica) 94044
Shasta 96087
Shasta Forest Village 96088
Shasta Lake 96019
96079
For specific ZIP Codes call (888) 275-8777, or your local postmaster.
Shaver Lake 93664
Shaver Lake Heights 93664
Shaver Lake Point 93664
Sheepranch 95250
Sheldon 95624
Shell Beach (Part of Pismo Beach)‡ 93449
Shelter Cove, *Humboldt* 95589
Shelter Cove (Part of Pacifica) 94044
Sheridan 95681
Sherman Oaks (Part of Los Angeles) 91403
91413
91423
For specific ZIP Codes call (888) 275-8777, or your local postmaster.
Sherman Oaks Galleria (Part of Los Angeles) 91403
Sherwood (Part of Salinas)‡ 93906
Sherwood Forest 94803
Sherwood Mall (Part of Stockton) 95207
Shingle Springs♦ 95682
Shingletown 96088
Shinn (Part of Fremont) 94536
Shively 95565
Shore Acres 94565
Short Acres (Part of Hanford) 93230
Shoshone 92384
Sierra (Part of Fresno)‡ 93703
Sierra Army Depot 96113
Sierra Brooks 96118
Sierra Cedars 93664
Sierra City 96125
Sierra Heights 93247
Sierra Lake Estates 93644
Sierra Madre 91024*
91025†
Sierra Pines 89439
Sierra Sky Park (Part of Fresno) 93722

Sierra Village No.1 95346
Sierraville 96126
Signal Hill 90804
90806-07
For specific ZIP Codes call (888) 275-8777, or your local postmaster.
Silverado 92676
Silver City 93271
Silver Fork 95720
Silver Lake 95666
Silver Strand 93035
Simi Valley 93062-63
93065
93093
For specific ZIP Codes call (888) 275-8777, or your local postmaster.
Simmler 93453
Simms (Part of San Rafael)‡ 94901
Simms, *San Joaquin* 95366
Sisquoc 93454
Sites 95979
Skaggs Island‡ 95476
Skyforest 92385
Skyhigh 95223
Skyline East 92311
Skyline North 92311
Sky Londa (Part of Woodside) 94062
Sky Valley 92241
Slawson (Part of Pico Rivera)‡ 90662
Sleepy Hollow, *Marin* 94960
Sleepy Hollow (Part of Chino Hills) 91710
Slide Inn 95335
Sloat 96103
Sloughhouse 95683
Smartville 95977
Smiley Heights (Part of Redlands) 92373
Smiley Park 92382
Smithflat 95667
Smith River 95567
Smoke Tree (Part of Palm Springs)‡ 92262
Snelling 95369
Snow Creek 92282
Snowline 95709
Soboba Hot Springs 92583
Soboba Indian Reservation 92583
Soda Bay 95451
Soda Springs 95728
Solana Beach 92075
Solano Mall (Part of Fairfield) 94533
Soledad 93960
Solemint (Part of Santa Clarita) 91350
Solvang 93463*
93464†
Somerset 95684
Somes Bar 95568
Somis 93066
Sonoma 95476
Sonoma Vista 95476
Sonora 95370
Sonora Junction 93517
Soquel♦ 95073
Sorensen (Part of Hayward) 94544
Sorensens 96120
Sorrento Valley (Part of San Diego)‡ 92191
Soto (Part of Huntington Park)‡ 90255
Soulsbyville♦ 95372
South (Part of Los Angeles)‡ 90061
South Alhambra (Part of Alhambra)‡ 91803
South Bakersfield (Part of Bakersfield)‡ 93304*
93384†
Southbay Pavilion‡ 90745-46
For specific ZIP Codes call (888) 275-8777, or your local postmaster.
South Belridge 93251
South Berkeley (Part of Berkeley)‡ 94703
South Coast Plaza (Part of Costa Mesa) 92626
South Corona (Part of Corona) 91718
South Dos Palos♦ 93665
South Downey (Part of Downey)‡ 90242
Southeastern (Part of San Diego)‡ 92113

South El Monte 91733
South Fontana (Part of Fontana) 92337
South Fork, *Humboldt* 95569
South Fork, *Madera* 93643
South Fork, *Mariposa* 95318
South Gardena (Part of Gardena)‡ 90248
South Gate 90280
South Hills (Part of West Covina)‡ 91791
South Laguna (Part of Laguna Beach) 92677
South Lake♦ 93240
South Lake Tahoe 96150-58
For specific ZIP Codes call (888) 275-8777, or your local postmaster.
Southland Shopping Center (Part of Hayward) 94545
South Leggett 95585
South Los Angeles (Part of Los Angeles) 90061
South Main (Part of Santa Ana)‡ 92707
South Modesto (Part of Modesto) 95350
South Oroville 95965
South Pasadena 91030*
91031†
Southport (Part of West Sacramento) 95691
South San Francisco 94080-83
For specific ZIP Codes call (888) 275-8777, or your local postmaster.
South San Gabriel‡ 91770
South San Jose Hills♦ 91744
South San Leandro (Part of San Leandro)‡ 94578
South Shafter 93263
South Shore Shopping Center (Part of Alameda) 94501
South Taft♦ 93268
South Whittier♦ 90605
South Whittier Heights 90605
South Yuba City♦ 95991
Spanish Flat, *El Dorado* 95633
Spanish Flat, *Napa* 94558
Spanish Hills 91720
Spanish Ranch 95956
Spaulding 96130
Spicer City 93206
Spreckels 93962
Spring Creek Tract 96158
Springfield 95370
Spring Garden 95971
Spring Hill (Part of Grass Valley) 95945
Springstowne (Part of Vallejo)‡ 94591
Spring Valley♦ 91976-79
For specific ZIP Codes call (888) 275-8777, or your local postmaster.
Spring Valley Casa de Oro (Part of Spring Valley)‡ 91976†
91977*
Spring Valley Lake (Part of Apple Valley) 92392
Springville 93265
Spruce Point 95503
Spurgeon‡ 92701*
92702†
Squaw Valley♦ 93675
Squirrel Mountain Valley 93240
Stadium (Part of Anaheim)‡ 92825
Stafford 95565
Stallion Springs 93561
Stamoules 93640
Standard 95373
Standish 96128
Stanford♦ 94305
Stanford Shopping Center (Part of Palo Alto) 94304
Stanton 90680
Starlight 93514
Starlite Pines 96088
State Capitol (Part of Sacramento)‡ 95814

Stateline (Part of South Lake Tahoe)‡ 96157
State Street (Part of Huntington Park)‡ 90255
Station A (Part of Long Beach)‡ 90822
Steele Park 94558
Steinbeck (Part of Salinas)‡ 93901
Steiner Street Station (Part of San Francisco)‡ 94115
Stent 95370
Stephens (Part of Santa Fe Springs) 90670
Sterling Park (Part of Daly City) 94017
Stevenson Ranch (Part of Santa Clarita) 91381
Stevinson 95374
Stewarts Point 95480
Stewart Springs 96094
Stine Station (Part of Bakersfield) 93309
Stinson Beach 94970
Stirling City 95978
Stockdale (Part of Bakersfield)‡ 93309
Stockton 95201-19
95267-69
For specific ZIP Codes call (888) 275-8777, or your local postmaster.
Stonegate (Part of Portola Valley) 94028
Stonehurst (Part of Oakland) 94603
Stone Lagoon 95570
Stoneman (Part of Alhambra) 91801
Stonestown (Part of San Francisco)‡ 94132
Stonewood Shopping Center (Part of Downey) 90241
Stonyford 95979
Storrie 95980
Stovepipe Wells 92328
Stratford 93266
Strathmore♦ 93267
Strawberry, *El Dorado* 95720
Strawberry, *Marin*♦ 94941
Strawberry, *Tuolumne* 95375
Strawberry Valley 95981
Stuart 92054
Studebaker (Part of Norwalk) 90650
Studio City (Part of Los Angeles) 91604*
91614†
Suburban Acres 96080
Sugarloaf 92386
Sugarloaf Mountain Park 93260
Sugar Pine, *Madera* 93644
Sugar Pine, *Tuolumne* 95383
Suisun City 94585
Sulphur Springs 93060
Sultana 93666
Summer Home 95336
Summerhome Park 95436
Summerland 93067
Summit 92345
Summit City 96089
Sumner Hill 93637
Sun City 92585-87
For specific ZIP Codes call (888) 275-8777, or your local postmaster.
Sunfair 92252
Sunkist (Part of Anaheim)‡ 92806*
92816†
Sunland 91040*
91041†
Sunny Brae (Part of Arcata) 95521
Sunnybrook 95640
Sunny Hills (Part of Fullerton)‡ 92635*
92838†
Sunnymead (Part of Moreno Valley) 92551
Sunnyside, *Fresno* 93727
Sunnyside, *Placer* 96145
Sunnyside, *San Diego* 91902
Sunnyslope, *Butte* 95914
Sunnyslope, *Riverside*♦ 92509
Sunnyvale 94086-91
For specific Zip Codes call (888) 275-8777, or your local postmaster.
Sunnyvale Town Center (Part of Sunnyvale) 94086
Sunny Vista (Part of Chula Vista) 91910
Sunol 94586
Sunrise Mall 95610
Sunrise Vista 95451
Sunset (Part of Arcata) 95521
Sunset (Part of San Francisco)‡ 94122
94172
For specific ZIP Codes call (888) 275-8777, or your local postmaster.
Sunset Beach, *Orange* 90742
Sunset Beach, *Santa Cruz* 95076
Sunset Cliffs (Part of San Diego) 92107
Sunset Hills 91745
Sunset Terrace 93402
Sunset Tract 93022
Sunset View 95945
Sunset Whitney Ranch (Part of Rocklin) 95677
Sunshine Homes 91350
Sunshine Summit 92536
Sunvalley (Part of Concord) 94520
Sun Valley 91352*
91353†
Sun Village (Part of Palmdale) 93550
Surf 93436
Surfside (Part of Seal Beach) 90743
Susana Knolls (Part of Simi Valley) 93063
Susanville 96127†
96130*
Sutter♦ 95982
Sutter Creek 95685
Sutter Hill 95685
Sutter Island 95615
Sutter Street (Part of San Francisco)‡ 94104
Swall Meadows 93514
Swanton 95017
Sweet Brier 96017
Sweetwater 95451
Sycamore, *Colusa* 95957
Sycamore (Part of Danville) 94526
Sylmar (Part of Los Angeles) 91342
Sylvia Park 90290
Table Bluff 95551
Taft 93268
Taft Heights♦ 93268
Tahoe City 96145
Tahoe Keys (Part of South Lake Tahoe) 96154
Tahoe Paradise (Part of South Lake Tahoe)‡ 96155
Tahoe Pines 96141
Tahoe Valley (Part of South Lake Tahoe)‡ 96158
Tahoe Vista♦ 96148
Tahoma 96142
Talica (Part of Oceanside) 92054
Talmage 95481
Tamalpais Valley 94941
Tamarack 95223
Tanforan (Part of South San Francisco) 94080
Tanforan Park (Part of San Bruno) 94066
Tangair 93437
Tanglewood 95018
Tara Hills♦ 94564
Tarpey (Part of Fresno) 93727
Tarzana 91356*
91357†
Tassajara Hot Springs 93924
Taurusa 93291
Taylorsville 95983
Tecate 91980
Tecnor 96058
Tecopa 92389
Tecopa Hot Springs 92389
Tehachapi 93561
93581-82
For specific Zip Codes call (800) 275-8777, or your local postmaster.
Tehama 96090
Temecula 92589-93
For specific ZIP Codes call (888) 275-8777, or your local postmaster.
Temelec♦ 95476
Temple City 91780
Templeton♦ 93465
Tennant 96058
Tent City (Part of Coronado) 92118
Terminal Annex (Part of Los Angeles)‡ 90054
Terminous 95240
Termo 96132
Terra Bella♦ 93270
Terra Linda (Part of San Rafael)‡ 94903
Textile (Part of Los Angeles)‡ 90015
90055
90079
For specific ZIP Codes call (888) 275-8777, or your local postmaster.
The Falls 93604
The Forks, *Madera* 93604
The Forks, *Mendocino* 95482
The Geysers 95425
The Hermitage 95585
The Oaks 95945
The Pines 93604
Thermal 92274
Thermalito♦ 95965
The Sea Ranch 95497
Thomas Mountain 92561
Thornton 95686
Thousand Oaks 91358-60
91362
For specific ZIP Codes call (888) 275-8777, or your local postmaster.
Thousand Palms♦ 92276
Three Arch Bay (Part of Dana Point) 92677
Three Point 93532
Three Rivers 93271
Three Rocks 93608
Tiburon 94920
Tierra Buena♦ 95991
Tierra del Sol 91905
Tionesta 96134
Tipton♦ 93272
Tivy Valley 93657
Tobin 95965
Tocaloma 94950
Todd Valley 95631
Todos Santos (Part of Concord)‡ 94522
Tollhouse 93667
Toluca Lake (Part of Los Angeles) 91610
Tomales 94971
Toms Place 93514
Tonyville 93247
Tooleville 93221
Topanga 90290
Topanga Beach (Part of Malibu) 90265
Topanga Oaks 90290
Topanga Park 90290
Topanga Plaza (Part of Los Angeles) 91303
Topaz 96133
Top of the World (Part of Laguna Beach) 92651
Tormey 94525
Torrance 90501-10
For specific ZIP Codes call (888) 275-8777, or your local postmaster.
Torres-Martinez Indian Reservation 92274
Torrey Pines Homes (Part of San Diego) 92037
Tower (Part of Fresno)‡ 93728
Town and Country (Part of Moreno Valley) 92551
Town and Country, *Sacramento*‡ 95821
Town Center (Part of Palmdale)‡ 93550
Town Center (Part of Visalia)‡ 93291
Town Center Corte Madera (Part of Corte Madera) 94925
Town Square (Part of Palmdale)‡ 93550
Trabuco Canyon 92678†
92679*
Trabuco Highlands♦ 92691
Tracy 95376-78
For specific ZIP Codes call (888) 275-8777, or your local postmaster.
Trade Center‡ 90831*
90832†
Tranquillity 93668
Traver 93673
Treasure Island (Part of San Francisco)‡ 94130
Tres Pinos 95075
Trevarno (Part of Livermore) 94550
Trigo 93637
Trimmer 93657
Trinidad 95570
Trinity Alps 96052
Trinity Center 96091
Trinity Village 95527
Triple R Estates 93257
Trona 93562*
93592†
Tropico, *Kern* 93560
Tropico (Part of Glendale)‡ 91204-05
91208
For specific ZIP Codes call (888) 275-8777, or your local postmaster.
Trowbridge 95659
Truckee 96160-62
For specific ZIP Codes call (888) 275-8777, or your local postmaster.
Tujunga 91042*
91043†
Tulare 93274*
93275†
Tulelake 96134
Tule River Indian Reservation 93257
Tunitas 94019
Tuolumne♦ 95379
Tuolumne Meadows 95389
Tupman 93276
Turlock 95380-82
For specific ZIP Codes call (888) 275-8777, or your local postmaster.
Turner 95336
Tustin 92780-82
For specific ZIP Codes call (888) 275-8777, or your local postmaster.
Tustin Marine Corps Air Station 92710
Tuttle 95340
Tuttletown 95370
Tuxedo Country Club Estates 95204
Tuxedo Park (Part of Stockton)‡ 95204
T.V. Bell (Part of Merced)‡ 95340
Twain 95984
Twain Harte♦ 95383
Twenty-Fifth Avenue Station (Part of San Mateo)‡ 94403
Twentynine Palms 92277-78
For specific ZIP Codes call (888) 275-8777, or your local postmaster.
Twentynine Palms Marine Corps Base 92278
Twentytwo Mile House 93637
Twin Bridges 95735
Twin Creeks 95120
Twin Lakes, *Lake* 95457
Twin Lakes, *Mono* 93517
Twin Lakes, *Santa Cruz*♦ 95060
Twin Oaks 92069
Twin Peaks 92391
Two Rock Coast Guard Station‡ 94952
Ukiah 95482
Ulmar (Part of Livermore) 94550
Union (Part of Napa) 94558
Union City 94587
Union Hill 95945
Universal City (Part of Los Angeles) 91608
91618
For specific ZIP Codes call (888) 275-8777, or your local postmaster.
University (Part of Irvine)‡ 92716
University, *Santa Barbara* 93106-07
For specific ZIP Codes call (888) 275-8777, or your local postmaster.
University City (Part of San Diego)‡ 92122
University of Santa Clara (Part of Santa Clara)‡ 95050
University Towne Centre (Part of San Diego) 92122
Upland 91784-86
For specific ZIP Codes call (888) 275-8777, or your local postmaster.
Upper Lake 95485
Uptown (Part of San Bernardino)‡ 92405*
92406†
Vaca (Part of Vacaville)‡ 95687
Vacation 95446
Vacaville 95687-88
95696
For specific ZIP Codes call (888) 275-8777, or your local postmaster.
Valencia 91354-55
91385
For specific ZIP Codes call (888) 275-8777, or your local postmaster.
Valinda♦ 91744
Valla (Part of Santa Fe Springs) 90670
Vallco Fashion Park (Part of Cupertino) 95014
Vallecito 95251
Vallecitos Town Center (Part of San Marcos) 92069
Vallejo 94589-92
For specific ZIP Codes call (888) 275-8777, or your local postmaster.
Vallemar (Part of Pacifica) 94044
Valle Vista (Part of Hayward) 94541
Valle Vista, *Riverside*♦ 92544
Valley Acres 93268
Valley Center♦ 92082
Valley Estates 93283
Valley Fair (Part of San Jose) 95128
Valley Ford 94972
Valley Home 95361
Valley Lake Ranchos 93637
Valley of Enchantment‡ 92325
Valley of the Moon 92325
Valley Plaza (Part of Bakersfield) 93304
Valley Plaza (Part of Los Angeles)‡ 91606*
91616†
Valley Springs 95252
Valley View Park 92325
Valley Village (Part of Los Angeles) 91607
Valona 94525
Val Verde Park♦ 91350
Valyermo 93563
Vandenberg Air Force Base 93437
Vandenberg Village♦ 93436
Van Nuys (Part of Los Angeles) 91401
91404-11
For specific ZIP Codes call (888) 275-8777, or your local postmaster.
Vanowen (Part of Los Angeles)‡ 91405
Vasona (Part of Los Gatos) 95032
Venice (Part of Los Angeles) 90291*
90294†
Ventucopa 93252
Ventu Park (Part of Thousand Oaks) 91320
Ventura 93001-09
For specific ZIP Codes call (888) 275-8777, or your local postmaster.
Verdemont 92402
Verdi 89439

Verdugo City (Part of Glendale) 91046
Verdugo Viejo (Part of Glendale)‡ 91206-08
91226
For specific ZIP Codes call (888) 275-8777, or your local postmaster.
Vermont (Part of Los Angeles)‡ 90029
Vernalis 95385
Vernon 90058
Vernon Landing 95659
Verona 95659
Veteran Heights 94508
Veterans Administration (Part of Los Angeles) 90073
Veterans Bureau Hospital (Part of Palo Alto)‡ 94304
Veterans Home (Part of Yountville)‡ 94599
Victor 95253
Victoria Court (Part of Santa Barbara)‡ 93101
Victoria Park (Part of Carson) 90746
Victorville 92392-94
For specific ZIP Codes call (888) 275-8777, or your local postmaster.
Victory Center (Part of Los Angeles)‡ 91609
Vidal 92280
Vidal Junction 92280
Viejas Indian Reservation 91901
View Park 90043
Viking (Part of Long Beach)‡ 90808
Village (Part of Saratoga)‡ 95071
Village Station (Part of Los Angeles)‡ 90024
90067
For specific ZIP Codes call (888) 275-8777, or your local postmaster.
Villa Grande 95486
Villa Park 92861
Villa Verona 95965
Vina 96092
Vineburg 95487
Vine Hill♦ 94553
Vintage Faire Mall (Part of Modesto) 95356
Vinton 96135
Vinvale (Part of South Gate) 90280
Viola 96088
Virginia Colony 93021
Virner 95634
Visalia 93277-79
93291-92
For specific ZIP Codes call (888) 275-8777, or your local postmaster.
Visalia Mall (Part of Visalia) 93277
Visitacion (Part of San Francisco)‡ 94134
Vista 92083-85
For specific ZIP Codes call (888) 275-8777, or your local postmaster.
Vista Del Mar (Part of San Clemente)‡ 92672
Vista del Morro 93402
Vista Grande, *Madera* 93637
Vista Grande (Part of Daly City)‡ 94014
94016
For specific ZIP Codes call (888) 275-8777, or your local postmaster.
Vista La Mesa (Part of La Mesa) 91941
Vista Park 93307
Volcano 95689
Volcanoville 95634
Volta 93635
Vorden 95690
Waddington 95536
Wagner Branch (Part of Los Angeles)‡ 90047
Wagy Flats 93240
Walerga 95660
Walker (Part of Bell) 90201
Walker, *Mono* 96107
Walker Landing 95690
Wallace 95254
Walnut 91788†
91789*
Walnut Creek 94595-98
For specific ZIP Codes call (888) 275-8777, or your local postmaster.
Walnut Creek West 94596
Walnut Grove 95690
Walnut Heights 94596
Walnut Park♦ 90255
Walteria (Part of Torrance)‡ 90505
Warm Springs (Part of Fremont)‡ 94539
Warner Ranch (Part of Moreno Valley) 92551
Warner Springs 92086
Wasco 93280
Washington (Part of Los Angeles)‡ 90011
Washington (Part of Pasadena)‡ 91114
Washington, *Nevada* 95986
Washington Manor (Part of San Leandro)‡ 94579
Waterford 95386
Waterloo 95215
Waterman Gardens (Part of San Bernardino) 92410
Watson (Part of Carson) 90745
Watsonville 95076*
95077†
Watsonville Junction 95076
Watts (Part of Los Angeles)‡ 90002
Watts Valley 93667
Waukena 93282
Waverly Heights (Part of Thousand Oaks) 91360
Wawona 95389
Weaverville♦ 96093
Weberstown Mall (Part of Stockton) 95207
Webster Street (Part of Alameda)‡ 94501
Weed 96094
Weedpatch♦ 93241
Weimar 95736
Weitchpec 95546
Weldon 93283
Wendel 96136
Weott 95571
West Adams (Part of Los Angeles)‡ 90016
West Arcadia (Part of Arcadia)‡ 91006
West Athens♦ 90247
West Butte 95953
West Carson♦ 90502
Westchester (Part of Los Angeles)‡ 90045
90083
For specific ZIP Codes call (888) 275-8777, or your local postmaster.
West Covina 91790-93
For specific ZIP Codes call (888) 275-8777, or your local postmaster.
Westend 93562
Western Pacific Mole (Part of Oakland) 94607
Western Village 93501
West Escondido (Part of Escondido) 92029
West Garden Grove (Part of Garden Grove)‡ 92845*
92846†
Westgate (Part of San Jose)‡ 95117
Westgate Mall (Part of San Jose) 95129
West Guernewood 95446
Westhaven, *Fresno* 93245
Westhaven, *Humboldt* 95570
West Hills 91307*
91308†
West Hollywood 90069
Westlake (Part of Daly City)‡ 94014-15
For specific ZIP Codes call (888) 275-8777, or your local postmaster.
Westlake Shopping Center (Part of Daly City) 94015
Westlake Village, *Los Angeles* 91359†
91361*
Westlake Village (Part of Thousand Oaks) 91361
West Lane (Part of Stockton)‡ 95208
Westley 95387
West Los Angeles (Part of Los Angeles) 90025
West Menlo Park♦ 94025
Westminster 92683-85
For specific ZIP Codes call (888) 275-8777, or your local postmaster.
Westminster Mall (Part of Westminster) 92683
West Modesto (Part of Modesto) 95351
Westmont♦ 90044
Westmorland 92281
West Palm Springs 92282
West Parlier (Part of Parlier) 93648
West Point 95255
Westport 95488
West Portal (Part of San Francisco)‡ 94127
94169
For specific ZIP Codes call (888) 275-8777, or your local postmaster.
West Puente Valley♦ 91744
West Sacramento 95691
95798-99
For specific ZIP Codes call (888) 275-8777, or your local postmaster.
West Saticoy (Part of Ventura) 93004
Westside (Part of San Bernardino)‡ 92411
Westside Pavilion (Part of Los Angeles) 90064
Westvern (Part of Los Angeles)‡ 90062
West Whittier 90606
Westwood, *Lassen*♦ 96137
Westwood (Part of Los Angeles) 90024
Westwood Manor 96001
Westwood Village (Part of Arcata) 95521
Westwood Village (Part of Los Angeles) 90024
Wheatland 95692
Wheeler Ridge 93301
Wherry Housing 93523
Whiskeytown 96095
Whispering Pines, *Lake* 95461
Whispering Pines, *San Diego* 92036
White Hall 95726
White Oak (Part of Los Angeles)‡ 91416
White Pines 95223
White River 93257
White Rock 95630
Whitethorn 95589
White Water 92282
Whitewood (Part of Whittier)‡ 90603
Whitley Gardens 93446
Whitlow 95554
Whitmore 96096
Whitmore Hot Springs 93546
Whitner Heights (Part of Parlier) 93648
Whittier 90601-10
For specific ZIP Codes call (888) 275-8777, or your local postmaster.
Whittier Quad Shopping Center (Part of Whittier) 90605
Whittwood Mall (Part of Whittier)‡ 90603
Wiest 92227
Wilbur Springs 95987
Wilcox (Part of Los Angeles)‡ 90038
Wildflower 93662
Wildomar♦ 92595
Wildwood, *Santa Cruz* 95006
Wildwood, *Trinity* 96076
Wilfred 95401
Wilkerson 93514
Willaura Estates 95949
Williams 95987
William Taft (Part of San Diego)‡ 92117
Willits 95490
Willowbrook‡ 90222*
90223†
Willow Creek, *Humboldt*♦ 95573
Willow Creek, *Plumas* 96020
Willow Glen (Part of San Jose)‡ 95125
Willow Ranch 96108
Willows 95988
Willow Springs, *Kern* 93560
Willow Springs, *Mono* 93517
Willow Springs, *Tuolumne* 95372
Will Rogers (Part of Santa Monica)‡ 90402*
90408†
Wilmar (Part of Rosemead) 91770
Wilmineton 90748
Wilmington (Part of Los Angeles) 90744*
90748†
Wilmington Park (Part of Los Angeles) 90744
Wilseyville 95257
Wilsona 93535
Wilson Acres 96080
Wilsona Gardens 93534
Wilsonia 93633
Wilton 95693
Winchester♦ 92596
Windsor 95492
Windsor Hills 90052
Windy Acres 93283
Winnetka (Part of Los Angeles) 91306*
91396†
Winter Gardens 92040
Winterhaven 92283
Winters 95694
Wintersburg (Part of Huntington Beach) 92647
Winterwarm 92028
Winton♦ 95388
Wise (Part of El Segundo) 90245
Wiseburn (Part of Hawthorne) 90250
Wishon 93669
Witch Creek 92065
Witter Springs 95493
Wofford Heights♦ 93285
Wolf 95603
Wonderland 96003
Wonder Valley 93649
Woodacre♦ 94973
Woodbridge♦ 95258
Woodcrest♦ 92504
Woodfords 96120
Woodlake 93286
Woodland 95695
95776
For specific ZIP Codes call (888) 275-8777, or your local postmaster.
Woodland Hills 91364-67
For specific ZIP Codes call (888) 275-8777, or your local postmaster.
Woodleaf 95925
Woodruff Avenue (Part of Bellflower) 90706
Woodside 94062
Woodside Glens (Part of Woodside) 94062
Woodside Plaza Station (Part of Redwood City)‡ 94061
Woodson Bridge Estates 96021
Woodville♦ 93258
Woodward Park (Part of Fresno)‡ 93710
93720
93729
For specific ZIP Codes call (888) 275-8777, or your local postmaster.
Woody 93287
Workman (Part of South Gate) 90280
Worldway Postal Center (Part of Los Angeles)‡ 90009
90080
For specific ZIP Codes call (888) 275-8777, or your local postmaster.
Wrights Lake 95720
Wrightwood♦ 92397
Wyandotte 95965
Wynola 92070
Wyntoon 96091
Yale (Part of Hemet)‡ 92544
Yankee Hill 95965
Yankee Jims 95631
Yerba Buena Island (Part of San Francisco) 94130
Yermo 92398
Yettem 93670
Ygnacio Valley (Part of Walnut Creek)‡ 94598
Yolanda (Part of San Anselmo) 94960
Yolo 95697
Yorba (Part of Pomona)‡ 91767
Yorba Linda 92685-87
For specific ZIP Codes call (888) 275-8777, or your local postmaster.
York (Part of Los Angeles)‡ 90050
Yorkville 95494
Yosemite Forks 93644
Yosemite Lodge 95389
Yosemite National Park 95389
Yosemite West 95389
Yountville 94599
Yreka 96097
Yuba City 95991-93
For specific ZIP Codes call (888) 275-8777, or your local postmaster.
Yuba City Farm Labor Center 95991
Yucaipa 92399
Yucca Valley 92284*
92286†
Yurok Indian Reservation 95546
Zamora 95698
Zayante 95018
Zenia 95595

Acres Green 80124
Adams 80022
Adams City (Part of Commerce City)‡ 80022
Agate 80101
Aguilar 81020
Airport Mail Facility (Part of Denver)‡ 80207
Akron 80720
Alameda (Part of Lakewood) 80215
Alamosa 81101
Alamosa East♦ 81101
Alcott (Part of Denver)‡ 80212
Allenspark 80510
Allison 81137
Alma 80420
Almont 81210
Alpine, *Chaffee* 81236
Alpine, *Rio Grande* 81154
Altura (Part of Aurora) 80011
Altura Annex (Part of Aurora)‡ 80011
American City 80427
Ames 81426
Amherst 80721
Andersonville (Part of Fort Collins) 80521
Angel Acres 80433
Antares (Part of Colorado Springs)‡ 80909*
80932†
Antelope Hills 81230
Antlers 81650
Anton 80801
Antonito 81120
Apache City 81089
Apex 80403
Appleton 81501
Applewood 80401
Arabian Acres 80816
Arapahoe 80802
Arapahoe East (Part of Greenwood Village) 80112
Arboles 81121
Arickaree 80812
Aristocrat Ranchettes 80621
Arlington 81021
Aroya 80862
Arriba 80804
Arriola 81323
Arvada 80001-07
For specific ZIP Codes call (888) 275-8777, or your local postmaster.
Aspen (Part of Fort Collins)‡ 80527
Aspen 81611-12
For specific ZIP Codes call (888) 275-8777, or your local postmaster.
Aspen-Gerbaz 81611
Aspen Park 80433
Association Camp 80511
Atwood 80722
Ault 80610
Aurora 80010-19
80040-47
For specific ZIP Codes call (888) 275-8777, or your local postmaster.
Aurora Mall (Part of Aurora) 80012
Austin (Part of Orchard City) 81410
Avon 81620
Avondale 81022
Bailey 80421
Bakersville 80476
Baldwin 81230
Balltown 81228
Barnesville 80624
Barr 80601
Bartlett 81090
Barton 81041
Basalt 81621
Battlement Mesa 81636
Baxterville 81132
Bayfield 81122
Beacon Hill 80860
Bear Valley (Part of Denver)‡ 80227
80232
80235-36
For specific ZIP Codes call (888) 275-8777, or your local postmaster.

Bear Valley Shopping Center (Part of Denver) 80227
Beaver Ridge 80440
Bedrock 81411
Beecher Island 80758
Belle Plain (Part of Pueblo) 81001
Bellvue 80512
Belmar (Part of Lakewood) 80226
Belmont (Part of Pueblo)‡ 81001
Bendemeer Valley 80439
Bennett 80102
Bergen Park 80439
Berthoud, *Larimer* 80513
Berthoud, *Weld* 80513
Berthoud Falls 80438
Berthoud Pass 80452
Bethune 80805
Beulah 81023
Beverly Heights (Part of Golden) 80401
Beverly Hills 80104
Big Bend 81092
Big Elk Meadows 80540
Black Forest♦ 80908
Black Hawk 80422
Blanca 81123
Blende 81006
Blue Mountain 81610
Blue Mountain Estates 80403
Blue Ridge 80424
Blue River 80424
Blue Valley 80452
Bonanza 81155
Boncarbo 81024
Bond 80423
Bondad 81301
Boone 81025
Boulder 80301-08
For specific ZIP Codes call (888) 275-8777, or your local postmaster.
Boulder Heights 80302
Boulder Mail Handling Facility (Part of Boulder)‡ 80501
Bountiful 81140
Bovina 80818
Bowie 81428
Bow Mar 80123
Boxelder Estates 80521
Boyero 80806
Bracewell 80631
Brandon 81071
Branson 81027
Breckenridge 80424
Breen 81326
Brewster 81226
Briargate (Part of Colorado Springs) 80920
Brigadoon Glen 80503
Briggsdale 80611
Brighton 80601
Bristol 81047
Broadmoor (Part of Colorado Springs) 80906
Broadway Estates 80120
Broken Arrow Acres 80433
Brook Forest 80439
Brook Forest Estates 80439
Brookridge 80120
Brookside 81212
Brookvale 80439
Broomfield 80020-21
80038
For specific ZIP Codes call (888) 275-8777, or your local postmaster.
Brownlee 80480
Brownsville 80026
Brush 80723
Buckeye 80549
Buckingham (Part of Fort Collins) 80521
Buckingham Square (Part of Aurora) 80012
Buda 80513
Buena Vista 81211
Buffalo Creek 80425
Buffalo Park Estates 80439
Buford 81641
Burdett 80720
Burland Ranchettes 80470
Burlington 80807
Burns 80426
Burnt Mill 81005

Byers♦ 80103
Caddoa 81044
Cadet‡ 80841
Cahone 81320
Calhan 80808
Camp Bird 81427
Camp George West 80401
Campion 80537
Campo 81029
Canfield 80026
Canon 81120
Canon City 81212-15
81246
For specific ZIP Codes call (888) 275-8777, or your local postmaster.
Capitol Hill (Part of Denver)‡ 80218
Capulin 81124
Carbondale 81623
Cardiff 81601
Carr 80612
Cascade 80809
Castle Rock 80104
Castlewood, *Arapahoe* 80120
Castlewood, *Douglas* 80116
Cattle Creek 81623
Cedar Cove 80537
Cedaredge 81413
Center 81125
Centerville 81236
Central City 80427
Chaddsford (Part of Aurora) 80014
Chama 81126
Chambers Square (Part of Aurora)‡ 80011
Chapel Hills 80907
Chatfield Estates 80128
Chautauqua (Part of Boulder) 80302
Cheraw 81030
Cherry Creek (Part of Denver)‡ 80206
Cherry Creek Shopping Center (Part of Denver) 80206
Cherry Hills Crest 80120
Cherry Hills Manor 80120
Cherry Hills Village 80110-11
For specific ZIP Codes call (888) 275-8777, or your local postmaster.
Cherry Knolls 80120
Cherry Park 80110
Cherry Valley 80116
Cherrywood Village 80120
Cheyenne Canon (Part of Colorado Springs) 80906
Cheyenne Wells 80810
Chimney Rock 81127
Chipita Park 80809
Chivington 81036
Chromo 81128
Chula Vista 80403
Cimarron 81220
Cinderella City (Part of Englewood) 80110
Citadel, The (Part of Colorado Springs) 80909
Clark 80428
Clark Farms (Part of Parker) 80134
Clifton♦ 81520
Climax 80429
Coal Creek 81221
Coaldale 81222
Coalmont 80430
Cokedale 81082
Collbran 81624
College Heights (Part of Durango)‡ 81301
Colona 81401
Colorado City (Part of Colorado Springs) 80904
Colorado City, *Pueblo*♦ 81019
Colorado Mountain Estates 80816
Colorado Sierra 80403
Colorado Springs 80901-70
For specific ZIP Codes call (888) 275-8777, or your local postmaster.
Columbine, *Jefferson* 80128
Columbine, *Routt* 80428
Columbine Hills‡ 80128
Columbine Knolls South 80128
Columbine Manor 80128

Columbine Valley 80123
Commerce City 80022*
80037†
Como 80432
Conejos 81129
Conifer 80433
Conifer Mountain 80433
Conifer Park 80433
Cope 80812
Copper Mountain 80443
Copper Spur 80423
Cornelia 81054
Cornish 80611
Coronado 80229
Cortez 81321
Cory (Part of Orchard City) 81414
Cotopaxi 81223
Country Acres 80534
Country Club Estates 80521
Country Club Park 80303
Cowdrey 80434
Cozy Corner 80234
Cragmor (Part of Colorado Springs) 80907
Craig 81625*
81626†
Cranor Acres (Part of Gunnison) 81230
Crawford 81415
Creede 81130
Crescent 80403
Crested Butte 81224*
81225†
Crested Butte South 81224
Crestmoor (Part of Glendale) 80222
Crestone 81131
Crestview Village 80403
Crestwoods 80424
Crews 80911
Cripple Creek 80813
Crisman 80302
Crook 80726
Crossroads Mall (Part of Boulder) 80301
Crowley 81033
Crystola 80863
Cuchara 81055
Cuerna Verde 81069
Dacono 80514
Dailey 80728
De Beque 81630
Deckers 80135
Deer Creek Valley Ranchos 80470
Deer Park 80467
Deer Trail 80105
Delhi 81059
Del Norte 81132
Delta 81416

Denver

80201-14
80216-25
80227
80229
80231
80233-95
For specific ZIP Codes call (888) 275-8777, or your local postmaster.

Colleges & Universities

Coll for Financial Planning 80237
Denver Conservative Baptist Seminary 80250
Denver Technical Coll 80224
Iliff School of Theology 80210
Regis Univ 80221
Rocky Mountain Coll of Art & Design 80224
Metropolitan State Coll 80217
Univ of Colorado 80217
Univ of Colorado Health Sciences Ctr 80262
Univ of Denver 80208

Financial Institutions

Bank One, NA 80202
KeyBank 80206
Norwest Bank 80274
USBank, NA 80202
Wells Fargo Bank 80270

Hospitals

Exempla St Joseph Hosp 80218
Porter Adventist Hosp 80210
Rose Med Ctr 80220
St Anthony Central Hosp 80204
Univ Hosp 80262
Veterans Affairs Med Ctr 80220

Hotels/Motels

Adam's Mark 80202
Cherry Creek Inn 80222
Embassy Suites, Downtown 80202
Executive Tower Inn 80202
Holiday Inn, Denver International Airport 80239
Holiday Inn, Downtown 80202
Holiday Inn, North/Coliseum 80216
Hyatt Regency, Downtown 80202
Hyatt Regency, Tech Ctr 80237
Marriott, City Center 80202
Marriott, Southeast 80222
Marriott, Tech Ctr 80237
Regency 80216
Renaissance 80207
Stapleton Plaza Hotel & Fitness Center 80207
The Westin, Tabor Center 80202
Wyndham Garden Hotel 80222

Military Installations

Defense Finance & Accounting Serv 80279
General Services Administration, Denver Forward Supply Point 80225

Denver Merchandise Mart 80216
Derby Junction 80426
Devine 81001
Dillon 80435
Dinosaur 81610
81633
For specific ZIP Codes call (888) 275-8777, or your local postmaster.
Divide 80814
Dolores 81323
Dome Rock 80433
Dorey Lakes 80403
Dotsero 81637
Dove Creek 81324
Downieville 80436
Downtown (Part of Colorado Springs)‡ 80903
Downtown (Part of Denver) 80201*
80202†
Downtown (Part of Englewood)‡ 80110
Downtown (Part of Loveland)‡ 80537
Doyleville 81239
Drake 80515
Drakes (Part of Fort Collins) 80521
Dream House Acres 80120
Dry Creek Basin 81431
Dumont 80436
Dupont 80024
Durango 81301*
81302†
Durango West 81301
Dyke 81147
Eads 81036
Eagle 81631
Eagle-Vail♦ 81620
Eastlake, *Adams* 80614
Eastlake (Part of Pueblo) 81004
Eastonville 80831
East Portal 80474
Eastridge (Part of Aurora) 80014
East Weston 81091
Eastwood (Part of Pueblo) 81001
Eaton 80615
Echo Lake 80452
Eckert (Part of Orchard City) 81418

*** Area Zip Code** **† Post Office Boxes** **‡ Postal Station** **♦ Census Designated Place** *Italic Type* **County**

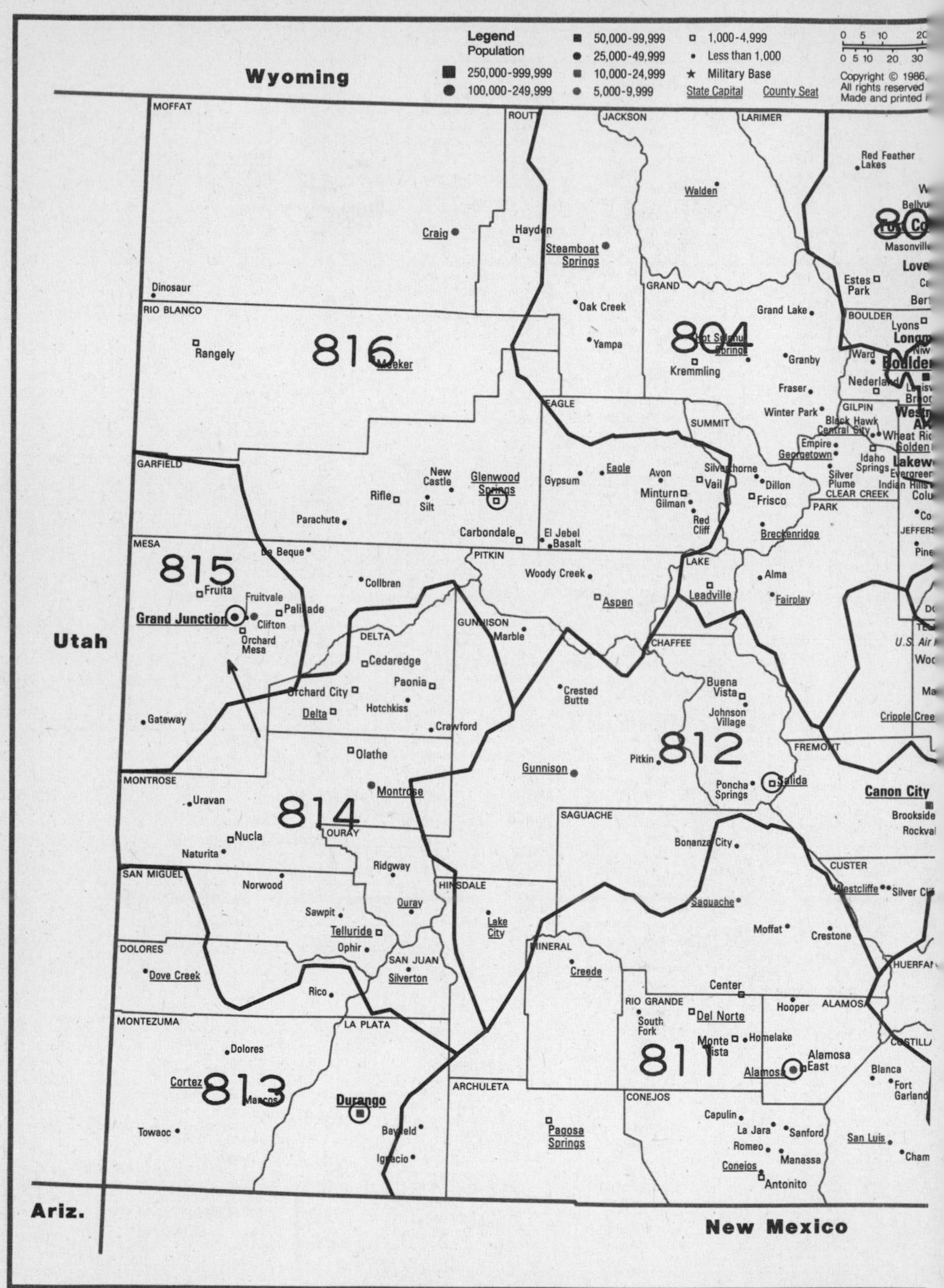
Legend
Population
250,000-999,999
100,000-249,999
50,000-99,999
25,000-49,999
10,000-24,999
5,000-9,999
1,000-4,999
Less than 1,000
Military Base
State Capital
County Seat
Wyoming
Utah
Ariz.
New Mexico
MOFFAT
ROUTT
JACKSON
LARIMER
Red Feather Lakes
Walden
Craig
Hayden
Steamboat Springs
Masonville
Dinosaur
Estes Park
GRAND
Oak Creek
Grand Lake
RIO BLANCO
BOULDER
Lyons
Rangely
816
Meeker
Yampa
804
Hot Sulphur Springs
Kremmling
Granby
Ward
Nederland
Fraser
EAGLE
GILPIN
Winter Park
Black Hawk
Central City
SUMMIT
Empire
Georgetown
Idaho Springs
GARFIELD
Silverthorne
Silver Plume
Avon
Vail
Dillon
CLEAR CREEK
New Castle
Glenwood Springs
Gypsum
Eagle
Minturn
Gilman
Frisco
Rifle
Silt
PARK
Parachute
Red Cliff
Breckenridge
Carbondale
El Jebel
Basalt
MESA
De Beque
PITKIN
LAKE
815
Woody Creek
Alma
Collbran
Fruita
Fruitvale
Palisade
Leadville
Aspen
Fairplay
Grand Junction
Clifton
DELTA
GUNNISON
Orchard Mesa
Marble
CHAFFEE
Cedaredge
Paonia
Crested Butte
Buena Vista
Orchard City
Hotchkiss
Johnson Village
Delta
Crawford
Gateway
FREMONT
Olathe
Pitkin
812
MONTROSE
Gunnison
Salida
Poncha Springs
Canon City
Uravan
Montrose
814
SAGUACHE
OURAY
Bonanza City
Nucla
Naturita
Ridgway
CUSTER
SAN MIGUEL
Norwood
HINSDALE
Westcliffe
Ouray
Saguache
Sawpit
Lake City
Telluride
Moffat
Crestone
Ophir
MINERAL
DOLORES
SAN JUAN
Silverton
Dove Creek
Creede
Center
HUERFANO
Rico
RIO GRANDE
Hooper
ALAMOSA
South Fork
Del Norte
MONTEZUMA
LA PLATA
Monte Vista
Homelake
Dolores
811
Alamosa East
Alamosa
Blanca
Fort Garland
Cortez
813
Mancos
ARCHULETA
Durango
CONEJOS
Capulin
La Jara
Sanford
Towaoc
Bayfield
Pagosa Springs
Romeo
San Luis
Manassa
Ignacio
Conejos
Antonito

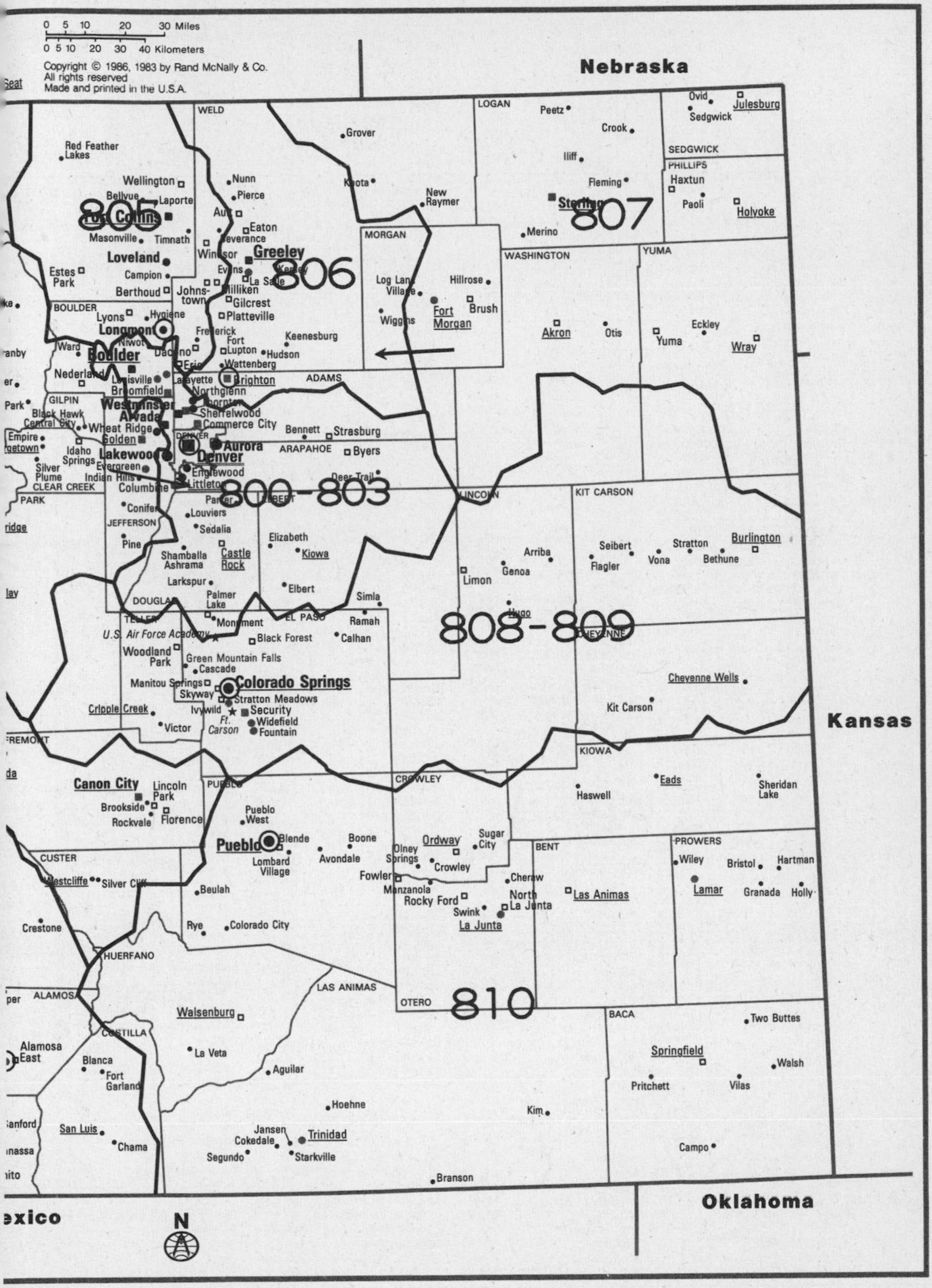

0 5 10 20 30 Miles
0 5 10 20 30 40 Kilometers

Nebraska

Kansas

Oklahoma

exico

N

805
806
807
800–803
808–809
810

WELD
LOGAN
SEDGWICK
PHILLIPS
MORGAN
WASHINGTON
YUMA
BOULDER
GILPIN
ADAMS
DENVER
ARAPAHOE
CLEAR CREEK
PARK
JEFFERSON
DOUGLAS
ELBERT
LINCOLN
KIT CARSON
TELLER
EL PASO
CHEYENNE
FREMONT
KIOWA
PUEBLO
CROWLEY
CUSTER
BENT
PROWERS
OTERO
HUERFANO
LAS ANIMAS
ALAMOSA
COSTILLA
BACA

Red Feather Lakes
Wellington
Nunn
Pierce
Grover
Bellvue
Laporte
Fort Collins
Ault
Eaton
Severance
Timnath
Masonville
Windsor
Greeley
Kersey
Loveland
Evans
La Salle
Campion
Estes Park
Berthoud
Johnstown
Milliken
Gilcrest
Platteville
Lyons
Hygiene
Longmont
Niwot
Frederick
Fort Lupton
Keenesburg
Hudson
Ward
Boulder
Dacono
Erie
Wattenberg
Nederland
Louisville
Lafayette
Broomfield
Northglenn
Brighton
Thornton
Westminster
Arvada
Sherrelwood
Commerce City
Black Hawk
Central City
Wheat Ridge
Golden
Bennett
Strasburg
Byers
Empire
Georgetown
Idaho Springs
Lakewood
Aurora
Denver
Silver Plume
Evergreen
Indian Hills
Englewood
Littleton
Columbine
Deer Trail
Conifer
Parker
Louviers
Sedalia
Pine
Shamballa Ashrama
Castle Rock
Elizabeth
Kiowa
Larkspur
Elbert
Palmer Lake
Simla
Monument
Ramah
U.S. Air Force Academy
Black Forest
Calhan
Woodland Park
Green Mountain Falls
Cascade
Manitou Springs
Colorado Springs
Skyway
Stratton Meadows
Ivywild
Security
Ft. Carson
Widefield
Fountain
Cripple Creek
Victor
Kiota
New Raymer
Peetz
Crook
Iliff
Fleming
Sterling
Merino
Ovid
Julesburg
Sedgwick
Haxtun
Paoli
Holyoke
Log Lane Village
Hillrose
Fort Morgan
Brush
Wiggins
Akron
Otis
Yuma
Eckley
Wray
Limon
Arriba
Genoa
Hugo
Seibert
Flagler
Stratton
Vona
Bethune
Burlington
Cheyenne Wells
Kit Carson
Canon City
Lincoln Park
Brookside
Rockvale
Florence
Pueblo West
Pueblo
Blende
Lombard Village
Boone
Avondale
Olney Springs
Ordway
Sugar City
Crowley
Fowler
Manzanola
Rocky Ford
Swink
La Junta
North La Junta
Cheraw
Las Animas
Haswell
Eads
Sheridan Lake
Wiley
Lamar
Bristol
Granada
Hartman
Holly
Westcliffe
Silver Cliff
Beulah
Crestone
Rye
Colorado City
Walsenburg
La Veta
Aguilar
Alamosa East
Blanca
Fort Garland
San Luis
Chama
Sanford
Manassa
Hoehne
Jansen
Cokedale
Trinidad
Segundo
Starkville
Branson
Kim
Two Buttes
Springfield
Walsh
Pritchett
Vilas
Campo
Seat
Granby
Ridgway
Salida

Place	ZIP
Eckley	80727
Eden	81003
Edgemont (Part of Lakewood)	80401
Edgewater	80214
Edison	80864
Edith	81128
Edler	81073
Edwards	81632
Egnar	81325
Elba	80720
Elbert	80106
Eldora	80466
Eldorado Springs	80025
Elephant Park	80439
Eleven Mile Village	80827
Elizabeth	80107
El Jebel	81628
Elk Creek Acres	80470
Elk Creek Highlands	80421
Elkdale	80478
Elkhorn Acres	80470
Elk Springs	81633
Elkton	80860
Ellicott	80808
El Moro	81082
El Rancho	80401
El Vado	80302
Elwell	80534
Emma	81621
Empire	80438
Englewood	80110-12
	80150-55
For specific ZIP Codes call (888) 275-8777, or your local postmaster.	
Erie	80516
Erie Air Park (Part of Erie)	80516
Escalante Forks	81416
Espinosa	81141
Estes Park	80511†
	80517*
Estrella	81101
Evans	80620
Evanston	80530
Evergreen	80437
	80439
For specific ZIP Codes call (888) 275-8777, or your local postmaster.	
Evergreen Highlands	80439
Ever Green Hills	80439
Evergreen Meadows	80439
Evergreen Meadows West	80439
Evergreen Park Estates	80439
Evergreen West	80439
Fairplay	80440
Fairview	81069
Fairview Estates	80128
Fairway Estates	80521
Falcon	80908
Falcon Estates	80920
Falfa	81301
Fall Creek	81430
Farisita	81089
Farmers	80631
Federal Heights	80221
Fenders	80465
Ferncliff	80510
Firestone	80520
First View	80810
Flagler	80815
Fleming	80728
Fletcher (Part of Aurora)‡	80010*
	80040†
Flintwood Hills	80116
Florence	81226
Florissant	80816
Florissant Heights	80816
Fondis	80106
Foothills Fashion Mall (Part of Fort Collins)	80525
Forest Hills	80403
Fort Carson	80913
Fort Collins	80521-28
For specific ZIP Codes call (888) 275-8777, or your local postmaster.	
Fort Garland	81133
Fort Logan (Part of Sheridan)	80236
Fort Lupton	80621
Fort Morgan	80701
	80705
For specific ZIP Codes call (888) 275-8777, or your local postmaster.	
Fountain	80817
Fountain Valley School	80911
Fowler	81039
Fox Creek	81120
Foxfield	80016
Foxton	80433
Franktown	80116
Fraser	80442
Frederick	80530
Friendship Ranch	80470
Frisco	80443
Fruita	81521
Fruitvale♦	81504
Fulton Heights (Part of Pueblo)	81003
Galeton	80622
Garcia	81134
Garden City	80631
Gardner	81040
Gateway (Part of Aurora)‡	80014*
	80044†
Gateway, *Douglas*♦	80126
Gateway, *Mesa*	81522
Gato	81147
Gaynor Lakes	80501
Gem Village	81122
Genesee♦	80401
Genoa	80818
Georgetown	80444
Gilcrest	80623
Gill	80624
Gilman	81645
Glade Park	81523
Glen Comfort	80515
Glendale	80222
Glendevey	82063
Gleneagle♦	80132
Glen Eden	80428
Glenelk	80470
Glen Haven	80532
Glen Isle	80421
Glen Park (Part of Palmer Lake)	80133
Glenwood Springs	81601*
	81602†
Goat Hill	81006
Golden	80401-03
For specific ZIP Codes call (888) 275-8777, or your local postmaster.	
Golden Mail Handling Unit (Part of Golden)‡	80401
Goldfield	80860
Gold Hill	80302
Goodnight	81005
Goodrich	80653
Gould	80480
Granada	81041
Granby	80446
Grand Junction	81501-06
For specific ZIP Codes call (888) 275-8777, or your local postmaster.	
Grand Lake	80447
Grand Mesa	81413
Grandview	81301
Grandview Estates	80134
Granite	81228
Grant	80448
Gray's Mary Greenwood	81069
Great Divide	81625
Greeley	80631-34
For specific ZIP Codes call (888) 275-8777, or your local postmaster.	
Greeley Mall (Part of Greeley)	80631
Green Gables (Part of Lakewood)	80232
Greenhorn	81019
Greenland	80118
Green Mountain (Part of Lakewood)	80228
Green Mountain Camp	80498
Green Mountain Estates (Part of Lakewood)	80228
Green Mountain Falls	80819
Green Mountain Village (Part of Lakewood)	80228
Green Towers	81069
Green Valley Acres	80433
Greenway Park	80020
Greenwood, *Custer*	81253
Greenwood, *Pueblo*	81069
Greenwood Village	80121
Greystone	81640
Greystone Lodge	80439
Grover	80729
Guadalupe	81129
Guffey	80820
Gulnare	81042
Gunbarrel	80501
Gunbarrel Estates	80503
Gunbarrel Greens	80301
Gunnison	81230
	81247
For specific ZIP Codes call (888) 275-8777, or your local postmaster.	
Gypsum	81637
Hahns Peak	80428
Hale	80735
Halfway House	81220
Hamilton	81638
Hanover	80909
Happy Canyon	80104
Hardin	80644
Harmony (Part of Fort Collins)	80521
Harris Park (Part of Westminster)	80036
Harris Park, *Park*	80470
Hartman	81043
Hartsel	80449
Hasty	81044
Haswell	81045
Hawley	81067
Haxtun	80731
Hayden	81639
Hazeltine Heights	80640
Heather Ridge (Part of Aurora)	80014
Heatherwood	80301
Heeney	80498
Henderson	80640
Hereford	80732
Heritage Dells	80401
Heritage Place	80110
Hermosa	81301
Herzman Mesa	80439
Hesperus	81326
Hiawatha	82901
Hidden Valley	80439
Hideaway Park (Part of Winter Park)	80482
High Chateau Ranches	80816
Highland Acres	80631
Highland Hills	80634
Highland Lake	80651
Highland Lakes	80814
Highland Park	80470
Highland Pines	80470
Highlands (Part of Denver)	80211
Highlands Ranch	80126*
	80163†
High-Mar (Part of Boulder)‡	80303*
	80307†
Hi-Land Acres	80601
Hill N' Park	80631
Hillrose	80733
Hillside	81232
Hilltop	80134
Hiwan Hills	80439
Hoehne	81046
Hoffman Heights (Part of Aurora)‡	80012
Holiday Acres	81147
Holiday Hills	80863
Holland Park (Part of Colorado Springs)	80907
Holly	81047
Holyoke	80734
Homelake	81135
Hooper	81136
Hotchkiss	81419
Hot Sulphur Springs	80451
Howard	81233
Howells (Part of Littleton)‡	80120
Hoyt	80654
Hudson	80642
Hugo	80821
Husted	80840
Hyde	80743
Hygiene	80533
Hyland Hills	80439
Hyland Knolls	80634
Idaho Springs	80452
Idalia	80735
Idledale	80453
Ignacio	81137
Iliff	80736
Ilse	81212
Indian Creek	80816
Indian Creek Ranch	80135
Indian Head	81239
Indian Hills	80454
Indian Springs Village	80470
Indian Tree‡	80006-07
For specific ZIP Codes call (888) 275-8777, or your local postmaster.	
Ione	80621
Irondale	80022
Ivywild (Part of Colorado Springs)‡	80906
	80926
	80960
For specific ZIP Codes call (888) 275-8777, or your local postmaster.	
Jacks Cabin	81210
Jamestown	80455
Jansen	81082
Jaroso	81138
Jefferson	80456
Jefferson Heights	80456
Joes	80822
Johnson Village	81211
Johnstown	80534
Juanita	81147
Julesburg	80737
Kahler	80513
Karval	80823
Kearns	81147
Keenesburg	80643
Kelim	80537
Kelker (Part of Colorado Springs)	80906
Kellytown	80125
Ken Caryl	80127
Keota	80729
Kersey	80644
Keystone	80435
Kim	81049
Kingsborough (Part of Aurora)	80017
Kingsborough South (Part of Aurora)	80012
Kings Corner	80537
Kiowa	80117
Kipling Hills	80123
Kipling Villas	80123
Kirk	80824
Kit Carson	80825
Kittredge	80457
Kline	81326
Knaus	80634
Knob Hill (Part of Colorado Springs)	80910
Koen	81041
Kornman	81052
Kremmling	80459
Kuhlmann Heights	80403
Kutch	80832
Lafayette	80026
La Garita	81132
Laird	80758
La Jara	81140
La Junta	81050
La Junta Gardens (Part of La Junta)	81050
Lakeborough	80235
Lake City	81235
Lake George	80827
Lakeside	80212
Lake View	80403
Lakewood	80215
	80226
	80228
	80232
For specific ZIP Codes call (888) 275-8777, or your local postmaster.	
Lamar	81052
La Montana Mesa	80816
Laporte	80535
La Posta	81301
Lariat (Part of Monte Vista)	81144
Larkspur	80118
La Salle	80645
Las Animas	81054
Lasauses	81151
Las Mesitas	81120
Last Chance	80757
La Valley	81152
La Veta	81055
Lawson	80452
Lay	81625
Lazear	81420
Leadville	80461
Leadville North♦	80461
Leawood	80128
Lebanon	81323
Leisure Living	80516
Lewis	81327
Leyden	80007
Liberty Bell Village	81435
Lime	81005
Limon	80828
Lincoln Park♦	81212
Lindon	80740
Littleton	80120-28
	80160-63
For specific ZIP Codes call (888) 275-8777, or your local postmaster.	
Livengood Hills	80138
Livermore	80536
Lobatos	81120
Lochbuie	80601
Lochwood (Part of Lakewood)	80232
Log Lane Village	80705
Loma	81524
Loma Linda	81301
Lombard Village	81006
Lone Pine Estates	80465
Lone Star	80743
Lonetree	81147
Longmont	80501-04
For specific ZIP Codes call (888) 275-8777, or your local postmaster.	
Longview	80433
Lookout Mountain	80401
Loretto Heights (Part of Denver)	80236
Los Fuertes	81152
Louisville	80027
Louviers	80131
Loveland	80537-39
For specific ZIP Codes call (888) 275-8777, or your local postmaster.	
Loveland Heights	80515
Lubers	81057
Lucerne	80646
Ludlow	81082
Lyons	80540
Lyons Park Estates	80540
McClave	81057
McClellands (Part of Fort Collins)	80521
McCoy, *Chaffee*	81201
McCoy, *Eagle*	80463
Mack	81525
Mad Creek	80487
Madison Hill (Part of Westminster)	80030
Madrid	81082
Magnolia	80466
Maher	81421
Mail Handling Center (Part of Englewood)‡	80111
Manassa	81141
Mancos	81328
Mandalay Gardens	80021
Manitou Springs	80829
Manzanola	81058
Marble	81623
Marshall	80302
Marshdale Park	80439
Marvel	81329
Mary Jane	80480
Maryvale	80442
Mason Corner	80631
Masonic Park	81154
Masonville	80541
Massadona	81610
Masters	80649
Matheson	80830
Maxeyville	81144
Maybell	81640
Mayday	81326
Maysville	81201
May Valley	81052
Mead	80542
Meadow Brook Heights	80120
Meadowood (Part of Aurora)	80013
Medina Plaza	81091

Place	ZIP Code
Meeker	81641
Meeker Park	80510
Merchant Station (Part of Denver)‡	80202
Meredith	81642
Merino	80741
Mesa, Mesa	81643
Mesa (Part of Pueblo)	81006
Mesa Lakes	81643
Mesa Verde National Park	81330
Mesita	81152
Messex	80741
Midtown (Part of Pueblo)‡	81003
	81008
For specific ZIP Codes call (888) 275-8777, or your local postmaster.	
Mile High (Part of Denver)‡	80204
Milliken	80543
Milner	80487
Mineral Hot Springs	81143
Minnequa (Part of Pueblo)	81004
Minnequa Heights (Part of Pueblo)	81004
Minturn	81645
Mirage	81143
Mission Viejo (Part of Aurora)	80013
Model	81059
Moffat	81143
Mogote	81120
Molina	81646
Monarch	81227
Montbello (Part of Denver)‡	80239
	80249
For specific ZIP Codes call (888) 275-8777, or your local postmaster.	
Montclair (Part of Denver)‡	80220
Monte Vista	81144
Monte Vista Estates	80104
Montezuma	80435
Montrose	81401*
	81402†
Monument	80132
Monument Lake Park	81091
Moore Dale	80421
Morgan	81140
Morrison	80465
Mosca	81146
Mountain View, *Jefferson*	80212
Mountain View, *Larimer*	80521
Mountain View Acres	81101
Mountain View Lakes	80470
Mount Crested Butte‡	81225
Mount Massive Lakes	80461
Mount Princeton Hot Springs	81236
Mount Vernon Club Place	80401
Mutual	81089
Nast	81642
Nathrop	81236
Naturita	81422
Nederland	80466
Nevadaville	80427
New Castle	81647
New Raymer	80742
Nighthawk	80135
Nine Mile Corner	80026
Niwot♦	80544
Nob Hill	80122
North Avondale	81022
North Cherry Creek Valley	80231
North Delta	81416
North End (Part of Colorado Springs)‡	80907*
	80933†
Northglenn	80233
Northglenn Mall (Part of Northglenn)	80234
North La Junta (Part of La Junta)	81050
North Pecos‡	80221
North Pole‡	80809
North Valley Shopping Center (Part of Thornton)	80229
North Washington Heights	80229
North Yard (Part of Denver)	80221
Norwood	81423
Nucla	81424
Numa	81063
Nunn	80648
Nutria	81147
Oak Creek	80467
Oak Grove	81401
Oehlmann Park	80433
Ohio	81237
Olathe	81425
Old Town Station (Part of Fort Collins)‡	80522
Olney Springs	81062
Olympus Heights	80515
Ophir	81426
Orchard	80649
Orchard City	81410
Orchard Mesa♦	81501
Ordway	81063
Ormandale	81005
Ortiz	81120
Otis	80743
Ouray	81427
Ovid	80744
Oxford	81137
Pactolus	80403
Padroni	80745
Pagosa Springs	81147
	81157
For specific ZIP Codes call (888) 275-8777, or your local postmaster.	
Paisaje	81120
Palisade	81526
Palmer Lake	80133
Palos Verdes	80123
Palos Verdes East	80110
Pandora	81435
Panorama Heights	80401
Panoview Park (Part of Gunnison)	81230
Paoli	80746
Paonia	81428
Parachute	81635*
	81636†
Paradox	81429
Paragon Estates	80303
Park Center	81212
Park City	80420
Parker	80134
	80138
For specific ZIP Codes call (888) 275-8777, or your local postmaster.	
Park Hill (Part of Denver)‡	80207
Park Vista Estates	80908
Parlin	81239
Parshall	80468
Peaceful Valley	80540
Peagreen	81416
Peak Seven West	80424
Pearl	80434
Peckham	80645
Peetz	80747
Penitentiary (Part of Canon City)	81212
Penrose	81240
Peyton	80831
Pheasant Run (Part of Aurora)	80015
Phippsburg	80469
Piedra	81147
Pierce	80650
Pine	80470
Pinebrook Hills	80302
Pinecliffe	80471
Pine Crest (Part of Palmer Lake)	80133
Pinehaven	81055
Pine Hills	80132
Pine Junction	80470
Pine Nook	80135
Pine Park Estates	80465
Pinewood Springs	80540
Pinnacle Park	80631
Pinon	81008
Pinon Acres	81301
Pinon Canyon	81059
Pinon Hills	81201
Pitkin	81241
Placerville	81430
Plateau City	81624
Platner	80743
Platoro	81144
Platteville	80651
Plaza	81132
Pleasant Valley (Part of Colorado Springs)	80904
Pleasant View, *Jefferson*	80401
Pleasant View, *Montezuma*	81331
Poncha Springs	81242
Ponderosa	80424
Ponderosa Hills	80138
Ponderosa Park	80107
Poudre Park	80521
Powderhorn	81243
Powder Wash	82901
Pritchett	81064
Proctor	80736
Prospect Heights	81212
Prospect Valley	80643
Prowers	81052
Pryor	81089
Pueblo	81001-08
For specific ZIP Codes call (888) 275-8777, or your local postmaster.	
Pueblo Army Depot	81001
Pueblo Dam	81003
Pueblo Mall (Part of Pueblo)	81008
Pueblo West♦	81007
Punkin Center	80821
Quincy (Part of Aurora)	80015
Radium	80423
Ragged Mountain	81434
Rainbow Valley	80814
Ramah	80832
Rand	80473
Rangely	81648
Rangeview Estates, *Boulder*	80501
Range View Estates, *Weld*	80631
Rattlesnake Buttes	81089
Raymond	80540
Read	81416
Red Cliff	81649
Red Feather Lakes	80545
Redlands♦	81503
Redmesa	81326
Red Rock Ranch	80132
Redstone	81623
Redvale	81431
Red Wing	81066
Rezago	81082
Richfield	81140
Rico	81332
Ridgeview Hills	80122
Ridgway	81432
Rifle	81650
Rinn	80504
Rio Blanco	81650
Riverside	80540
Roberta	81050
Rockrimmon (Part of Colorado Springs)‡	80908
	80919
	80949
	80962
For specific ZIP Codes call (888) 275-8777, or your local postmaster.	
Rockvale	81244
Rocky Ford	81067
Rocky Mountain Arsenal	80022
Rocky Mountain Station (Part of Denver)‡	80249
Rogers Mesa	81419
Roggen	80652
Roland Valley	80470
Rollinsville	80474
Romeo	81148
Rosedale, *Jefferson*	80439
Rosedale (Part of Garden City)	80631
Rosita	81252
Roswell (Part of Colorado Springs)	80907
Rowena	80455
Roxborough Park	80125
Royal Gorge	81246
Royal Ranch	80421
Ruedi	81621
Rulison	81635
Rush	80833
Russell Gulch	80427
Russelville	80116
Rustic	80512
Rye	81069
Rye Ranchettes	81069
Sable (Part of Aurora)	80011
Saguache	81149
Saint Charles Mesa	81006
St. Elmo	81236
St. Petersburg	80728
Salida	81201
Salina	80302
Salt Creek (Part of Pueblo)	81006
San Acacio	81151
San Antonio	81120
Sandown (Part of Denver)	80216
Sanford	81151
Sangre De Cristo Ranches	81133
San Isabel	81069
San Juan	81082
San Luis	81152
San Pablo	81152
Santa Fe (Part of Denver)‡	80204
Santa Fe (Part of Pueblo)‡	81003
Sapinero	81247
Sarcillo	81091
Sarcillo Canon	81091
Sargents	81248
Sargents School	81144
Sawpit	81430
Security‡	80911
	80925
	80931
For specific ZIP Codes call (888) 275-8777, or your local postmaster.	
Sedalia	80135
Sedgwick	80749
Segundo	81082
Seibert	80834
Severance	80546
Shadow Mountain, *Grand*	80447
Shadow Mountain, *Jefferson*	80433
Shadows North	80424
Shaffers Crossing	80433
Shamballa Ashrama	80135
Shaw Heights	80030
Shaw Heights Mesa	80030
Shawnee	80475
Sheridan	80110
Sheridan Lake	81071
Sherrelwood	80221
Sherrelwood Estates	80221
Silt	81652
Silver Cliff	81249
Silver Creek	80446
Silver Heights	80104
Silver Plume	80476
Silver Shekel	80424
Silver Springs	80470
Silver Spruce	80301
Silverthorne	80498
Silverton	81433
Simla	80835
Singleton	80475
Skyland	81224
Skyland Village (Part of Westminster)	80030
Skyline	80222
Sky Village	80465
Skyway (Part of Colorado Springs)	80906
Skyway, *Mesa*	81643
Skyway Estates (Part of Colorado Springs)	80906
Skyway Park (Part of Colorado Springs)	80906
Slater	81653
Slick Rock	81325
Smeltertown	81201
Smith Hill	80403
Smoky Hill (Part of Aurora)‡	80015*
	80046†
Snowmass	81654
Snowmass Village	81615
Snow Mountain Ranch	80446
Snyder	80750
Somerset	81434
South Canon (Part of Canon City)	81212
South Denver (Part of Denver)‡	80209
Southern Ute Indian Reservation	81137
South Fork	81154
Southglenn	80122*
	80161†
South Golden Road Station (Part of Golden)‡	80403
South Park City (Part of Fairplay)	80440
South Platte	80433
South Roggen	80652
Southwind	80120
Southwood	80120
Spanish Peaks	81055
Spanish Village	80631
Sparks	82901
Sphinx Park	80470
Spivak (Part of Lakewood)	80214
Springfield	81073
Spring Valley	80814
Sprucedale	80439
Stanley Park	80439
Starkville	81074
Station #1 (Part of Grand Junction)‡	81501
Station #2 (Part of Grand Junction)‡	81505
Station #3 (Part of Grand Junction)‡	81503
Station #4 (Part of Grand Junction)‡	81506
Steamboat Plaza (Part of Steamboat Springs)	80488
Steamboat Springs	80477
	80487-88
For specific ZIP Codes call (888) 275-8777, or your local postmaster.	
Steamboat Village (Part of Steamboat Springs)	80487
Stem Beach	81005
Sterling	80751
Stockyards (Part of Denver)‡	80216
Stonegate (Part of Parker)	80134
Stoneham	80754
Stoner	81323
Stonewall	81091
Stonington	81075
Strasburg	80136
Stratmoor	80906
Stratmoor Hills	80906
Stratton	80836
Stratton Meadows (Part of Colorado Springs)	80906
Stratton Park (Part of Colorado Springs)	80907
Stringtown	80461
Stroh Ranch	80134
Sugar City	81076
Sugarloaf	80302
Sullivan (Part of Denver)‡	80231
	80237
For specific ZIP Codes call (888) 275-8777, or your local postmaster.	
Summit Cove	80435
Summitville	81132
Sunbeam	81640
Sundance Plaza Station (Part of Steamboat Springs)‡	80487
Sunnyside, *Boulder*	80466
Sunnyside (Part of Denver)‡	80211
Sunnyside, *La Plata*	81301
Sunnyslopes	80020
Sunset (Part of Pueblo)‡	81004-05
For specific ZIP Codes call (888) 275-8777, or your local postmaster.	
Sunshine	80302

Place	ZIP
Superior	80027
Surrey Ridge	80104
Sutank	81623
Swallows	81003
Swede Corners	81149
Sweetwater	81637
Swink	81077
Swissvale	81201
Switzerland Village	80470
Tabernash	80478
Tallahassee School	81212
Tamarron (Part of Colorado Springs)	80919
Tamarron, *La Plata*	81301
Tanglewood Acres	81252
Tarryall	80827
Taylor Park	81210
Telluride	81435
Templeton (Part of Colorado Springs)‡	80936
Ten Mile Vista	80424
Tennyson Heights (Part of Fort Collins)	80521
Texas Creek	81223
Thatcher	81059
The Meadows	80127
The Mesa	80904
The Pinery	80134
The Shadows	80424
Thomasville	81642
Thornton	80229
Thurman	80801
Tiffany	81137
Timbers (Part of Aurora)	80014
Timnath	80547
Timpas	81050
Tincup	81210
Tiny Town	80465
Tolland	80474
Toltec	81089
Tomichi Heights (Part of Gunnison)	81230
Toponas	80479
Tordal Estates	80424
Torres, *Las Animas*	81091
Torres, *Rio Grande*	81144
Towaoc♦	81334
Towner	81071
Tranquil Acres	80863
Trimble	81301
Trinchera	81081
Trinidad	81082
Trout Haven	80814
Trout Lake	81426
Truckton	80864
Trujillo	81147
Trumbull	80135
Twin Crossing	81301
Twin Forks	80454
Twin Lakes	81251
Twin Rock	80816
Twin Spruce	80403
Two Buttes	81084
Tyrone	81059
Unaweep	81527
Uncompahgre	81401
Union	80750
Union Stock Yards (Part of Denver)	80216
United States Air Force Academy♦	80840*
	80841†
University (Part of Boulder)	80309
University Hills Mall (Part of Denver)	80222
University Park (Part of Denver)‡	80210*
	80250†
Upper San Juan River	81147
Uravan	81422
Ute Heights	81201
Ute Mountain Indian Reservation	81334
Utleyville	81064
Vail	81657*
	81658†
Valdez	81082
Vallecito	81122
Valley of Blue	80424
Vancorum	81422
Velasquez Plaza	81091
Venetian Village (Part of Colorado Springs)	80907
Vernon	80755
Victor	80860
Viejo San Acacio	81151
Vigil	81091
Vilas	81087
Village East (Part of Aurora)	80012
Village Seven (Part of Colorado Springs)	80917
Villa Grove	81155
Villa Italia Center (Part of Lakewood)	80226
Villegreen	81049
Vineland	81001
Virginia Dale	80536
Vista Grande (Part of Colorado Springs)	80918
Vista Verde	80120
Vollmar	80621
Vona	80861
Vroman	81067
Waconda Hills	80132
Wagner Manor	80302
Wagon Wheel Gap	81154
Wahatoya	81055
Wah Keeney Park	80439
Wahketa Village	80701
Walden	80480
Wallstreet	80302
Walnut Hills	80112
Walsenburg	81089
Walsh	81090
Waltonia	80515
Walts Corner	81027
Wamblee Park	80433
Wamblee Valley	80433
Wandcrest Park	80470
Ward	80481
Waterton	80125
Watkins	80137
Wattenberg	80621
Waverly	81101
Welby	80229
Weldona	80653
Wellington	80549
Wellshire (Part of Denver)‡	80222
	80224
For specific ZIP Codes call (888) 275-8777, or your local postmaster.	
Wellsville	81201
West (Part of Greeley)	80634
Westcliffe	81252
West End (Part of Colorado Springs)‡	80904*
	80934†
Western Hills	80221
West Farm	81052
Westland Center (Part of Lakewood)	80215
Westminster	80030-31
	80035-36
For specific ZIP Codes call (888) 275-8777, or your local postmaster.	
Westminster East♦	80221
Westminster Mall (Part of Westminster)	80030
Weston	81091
Westridge	80634
West Vail (Part of Vail)	81657
Westwood (Part of Denver)‡	80219
Westwood Lake	80863
Wetmore	81253
Wheat Ridge	80033*
	80034†
Wheeler	80403
White Pine	81248
Whitewater	81527
Widefield	80911
Wiggins	80654
Wild Horse, *Cheyenne*	80862
Wild Horse, *Pueblo*	81001
Wiley	81092
Willard	80741
Williamsburg, *Fremont*	81226
Williamsburg, *Jefferson*	80127
Willis Heights	80501
Willowbrook	80465
Willow Creek	80110
Willow Gulch	81423
Wilmot	80439
Wilson Lake Estates	80816
Windsor	80550
Windsor Gardens (Part of Denver)	80231
Winter Park	80482
Wolcott	81655
Wondervu	80403
Woodglen (Part of Thornton)	80233
Woodland Acres	81069
Woodland Park	80863*
	80866†
Woodmar Village	80123
Woodrow	80757
Woody Creek	81656
Wray	80758
Yampa	80483
Yellow Jacket	81335
Yoder	80864
Yorkborough (Part of Thornton)	80229
Yuma	80759
Yuma Camp of the Rockies (Part of Estes Park)‡	80511

Abington	06230
Addison	06033
Agua Vista (Part of Danbury)	06810
Aljen Heights	06339
Allerton Farms (Part of Naugatuck)	06770
Allingtown (Part of West Haven)	06516
Almyville	06354
Alpine	06810
Amenia Union	06069
Amesville	06031
Amity (Part of New Haven)‡	06525
Amston	06231
Andover	06232
Ann Street (Part of Hartford)‡	06103
Ansonia	06401
Ashford (Town)	06250
Ashford	06278
Ashford Lake	06250
Aspetuck	06880
Atlantic Street (Part of Stamford)‡	06901
Attawan Beach	06357
Attawaugan	06241
Atwoodville	06250
Avery Heights	06776
Avery Hill	06339
Avon	06001*
Baileyville	06455
Bakersville	06057
Ballouville	06233
Ball Pond	06812
Baltic	06330
Banksville	06830
Bantam	06750
Barkhamsted	06063
Barnum (Part of Bridgeport)‡	06605
Barry Place (Part of Stamford)‡	06902
Barry Square (Part of Hartford)‡	06134
Bartlett Corners	06375
Bayview (Part of Milford)	06460
Bayview Station (Part of Bridgeport)‡	06610
Beacon Falls	06403
Beardsley (Part of Bridgeport)‡	06606
Beaverbrook (Part of Danbury)	06810
Becketville (Part of Danbury)	06810
Bedlam Corner	06256
Bel Aire Estates	06355
Belden (Part of Norwalk)‡	06850
Belle Haven	06830
Bell Island (Part of Norwalk)	06853
Belltown (Part of Stamford)	06906
Berkshire	06482
Berkshire Estates	06488
Berkshire Shopping Center (Part of Danbury)	06810
Berlin	06037
Beseck Lake	06455
Bethany	06524
Bethel	06801
Bethlehem	06751
Birch Groves	06776
Birch Hill	06757
Birch Meadow	06479
Birchwood	06095
Birdland	06082
Bishop	06374
Bishops Corner	06137
Bissell‡	06074
Black Point	06357
Black Point Beach Club	06357
Bloomfield	06002
Blue Hills, Hartford♦	06002
Blue Hills (Part of Hartford)‡	06132
Boardman Manor	06776
Boardmans Bridge	06776
Bolton	06043
Bolton Center	06040
Borough (Part of Groton)‡	06340
Boston	06875
Botsford	06404
Boulder Lake	06413
Bozrah	06334
Branchville	06829
Branford	06405
Branford Hills	06405
Branhaven Shopping Center	06405
Brendan Heights	06076
Bretton Heights (Part of Middletown)	06457
Bridgeport	06601-10
	06650
For specific ZIP Codes call (888) 275-8777, or your local postmaster.	
Bridgewater	06752
Brighton Beach	06371
Bristol	06010*
	06011 †
Bristol Terrace (Part of Naugatuck)	06770
Broad Brook	06016
Bromica	06757
Brookfield	06804
Brookfield Center	06804
Brooklyn	06234
Brook Valley (Part of Naugatuck)	06770
Browns Corner	06057
Bruce Park	06830
Brush Island	06820
Buckingham	06033
Buckland‡	06040
Buckland Hills Mall	06040
Bucks Corners	06073
Bulls Bridge	06785
Bunker Hill (Part of Waterbury)	06708
Burlington (Town)	06085
Burlington	06013
Burnside	06108
Burrville (Part of Torrington)	06790
Burwells Beach (Part of Milford)	06460
Byram	06830
Byram Shore	06830
Camp Bethel	06438
Camptown (Part of Derby)	06418
Canaan (Town)	06031
Canaan♦	06018
Candlewood Echoes	06784
Candlewood Hill	06441
Candlewood Hills	06812
Candlewood Isle	06812
Candlewood Knolls	06810
Candlewood Lake Club	06804
Candlewood Lake Estates	06784
Candlewood Orchards	06804
Candlewood Point	06776
Candlewood Shores	06804
Candlewood Springs	06776
Candlewood Trails	06776
Cannondale	06897
Canterbury	06331
Canton	06019
Canton Center	06020
Carmel Hill	06751
Castle Hill	02891
Cedar Beach (Part of Milford)	06460
Cedar Heights (Part of Danbury)	06810
Cedarhurst	06482
Cedar Knolls	06776
Cedar Lake (Part of Bristol)	06010
Cedar Land	06488
Center	06611
Centerbrook	06409
Center Groton	06340
Centerville	06518
Central (Part of Hartford)‡	06103
Central Village	06332
Chaffeeville	06268
Chalkers Beach	06475
Chapel Square (Part of New Haven)	06510
Chaplin	06235
Chapman Beach	06498
Charcoal Ridge	06812
Cherry Brook	06020
Cherry Hill	06796
Cherrywood	06479
Cheshire	06410
Chester	06412
Chestnut Hill	06237
Chickahominy	06830
Chippens Hill (Part of Bristol)	06010
Christy Hill Estates	06335
Churchwood	06357
Clarks Corner	06256
Clarks Falls	06359
Clarks Village	02891
Clearview Heights	06076
Clinton	06413
Clinton Beach	06413
Clintonville	06473
Cobalt	06414
Codfish Hill	06801
Colburn Hill	06076
Colchester	06415
Colebrook	06021
Collinsville♦	06022
Columbia	06237
Compo Beach	06880
Compo Hill	06880
Conantville	06226
Congamond Lakes	06093
Connecticut Post Mall (Part of Milford)	06460
Conning Towers	06340
Copaco Shopping Center	06002
Cornwall	06753
Cornwall Bridge	06754
Cornwall Center	06796
Cornwall Hollow	06031
Cos Cob	06807
Cottage Grove	06002
Coventry	06238
Cranbury (Part of Norwalk)	06851
Cranska Village	06354
Crescent Beach	06357
Cromwell	06416
Cromwell Hills	06416
Crystal Lake♦	06029
Damascus	06405
Danbury	06810-11
	06813
For specific ZIP Codes call (888) 275-8777, or your local postmaster.	
Danbury Fair Mall (Part of Danbury)	06810
Danbury Shopping Center (Part of Danbury)	06810
Danielson	06239
Darien	06820
Dayville	06241
Dean Corners	06753
Deep River	06417
Deer Island	06758
Deer Run Shores	06784
Derby	06418
Derby Junction (Part of Derby)	06418
Derby Neck (Part of Derby)	06418
Devon (Part of Milford)‡	06460
Diamond Lake	06033
Dickerman's Corner	06479
Doanville	06365
Dodgingtown	06470
Dolphin Gardens	06340
Double Beach	06405
Dowd's Corner	06019
Downersville	02891
Drakeville (Part of Torrington)	06790
Durham	06422
Durham Center	06422
Eagleville	06268
East Berlin	06023
East Bristol (Part of Bristol)	06010
East Brooklyn♦	06239
East Canaan	06024
East Cornwall	06759
East Derby (Part of Derby)	06418
East End (Part of Waterbury)‡	06705
Eastern Point (Part of Groton)	06340
East Farmington Heights	06032
East Farms (Part of Waterbury)	06705
Eastford	06242
East Glastonbury	06025
East Granby	06026
East Great Plain (Part of Norwich)	06360
East Haddam	06423
East Haddam Landing	06423
East Hampton	06424
East Hampton Center	06424
East Hartford	06108
	06118
	06128
	06138
For specific ZIP Codes call (888) 275-8777, or your local postmaster.	
East Hartland	06027
East Haven	06512
East Hill	06019
East Killingly	06243
East Litchfield	06759
East Lyme	06333
East Meriden	06450
East Morris	06763
East Mountain (Part of Waterbury)	06706
East New London (Part of New London)	06320
East Norwalk (Part of Norwalk)	06855
Easton	06612
East Plymouth	06786
East Port Chester	06830
East Putnam	06260
East River	06443
East Street	06796
East Thompson	06277
East Village	06468
East Wallingford	06492
East Willington	06279
East Windsor (Town)	06016
East Windsor	06088
East Windsor Hill	06028
East Woodstock	06244
Ebbs Corner	06093
Edgewood	06830
Edgewood (Part of Bristol)	06010
Edgewood (Part of Stafford Springs)	06076
Ekonk	06354
Ellington	06029
Elliot	06259
Ellsworth	06069
Elm Hill	06111
Elmville	06241
Elmwood	06133
Elys Ferry	06371
Emmons Corners	06796
Enfield	06082*
	06083†
Enfield Square	06082
Enfield Street‡	06082
Essex♦	06426
Ethel Acres	06351
Ettadore Park (Part of Milford)	06460
Fairfield	06430-32
For specific ZIP Codes call (888) 275-8777, or your local postmaster.	
Fairground (Part of Norwich)	06360
Fair Haven (Part of New Haven)‡	06513
Fair Lawn (Part of Waterbury)	06705
Fairmount (Part of Waterbury)	06706
Fairy Lake	06370
Fall Mountain (Part of Bristol)	06010
Fall Mountain Lake	06786
Falls Switch (Part of Norwich)	06360
Falls Village	06031
Farmington	06032*
	06034†
Far View Beach (Part of Milford)	06460
Federal (Part of New Haven)‡	06510
Fenwick	06475
Fenwood	06475
Ferris Estates	06776
Ferry Point	06475
Ferry View Heights	06335
Field Crest Estates	06355
Firetown	06070
Five City Plaza Shopping Center	06032
Five Points, *Fairfield*	06876
Five Points, *Hartford*	06035
Flanders	06757
Flax Hill (Part of Norwalk)	06850
Floral Park	06475
Floydville	06035
Forbes Village	06108
Forest Glen	06475
Forest Heights (Part of Milford)	06460
Forest Hills	06489
Forest Park	06248
Forestville (Part of Bristol)‡	06010
Fort Hill	06776
Fort Trumbull Beach (Part of Milford)	06460
Fox Den	06001
Foxon	06512
Franklin	06254
Franklin Square (Part of Norwich)	06360
Furnace Hollow	06076
Gales Ferry	06335
Gaylordsville	06755
Georgetown, *Fairfield*♦	06829
Georgetown, *Hartford*	06479
Germantown (Part of Danbury)	06810
Giants Neck	06357
Giants Neck Heights	06357
Gildersleeve	06480
Gilead	06248
Gilman	06336
Glasgo	06337
Glastonbury	06033
Glenbrook (Part of Stamford)‡	06906
Glenville‡	06830
Golden Spur	06385
Good Hill, *Litchfield* (Kent Township)	06757
Good Hill, *Litchfield* (Woodbury Township)	06783
Good Hill, *New Haven*	06478
Goodrich Heights	06416
Goodsell Point	06405
Goshen, *Litchfield*	06756
Goshen, *New London*	06385
Goshen Hills	06249
Governor's Hill	06478
Granby	06035
Granite Bay	06405
Grant Hill	06002
Grappaville	06750
Grassy Hill	06798
Grassy Plain	06801
Great Hammock	06475
Great Harbor	06437
Great Meadows	06810
Greenfield Hill	06430
Greenhaven Shores	02891
Green Manorville	06082
Greens Farms	06436
Greenville (Part of Norwich)	06360
Greenwich	06830-36
For specific ZIP Codes call (888) 275-8777, or your local postmaster.	
Greystone	06786
Griswold (Town)	06351
Griswoldville	06109
Grosvenor Dale	06246
Groton	06340-49
For specific ZIP Codes call (888) 275-8777, or your local postmaster.	
Groton Heights (Part of Groton)	06340
Groton Lake Shores	06357

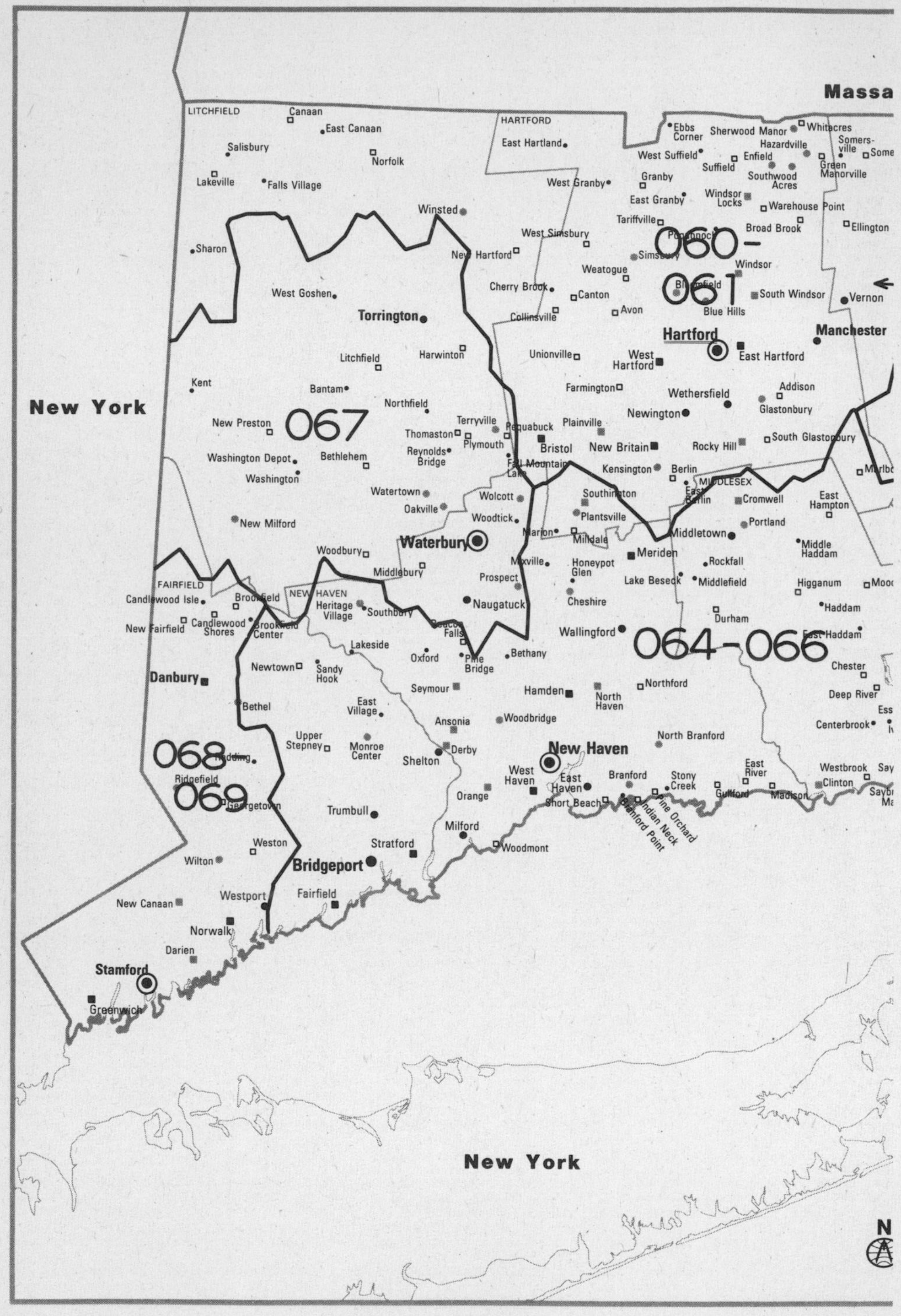
Massa
New York
LITCHFIELD
HARTFORD
FAIRFIELD
NEW HAVEN
MIDDLESEX
060-
061
067
064-066
068-
069
Canaan
East Canaan
Salisbury
Norfolk
Lakeville
Falls Village
Winsted
Sharon
West Goshen
Torrington
Litchfield
Harwinton
Kent
Bantam
Northfield
New Preston
Terryville
Thomaston
Plymouth
Reynolds Bridge
Washington Depot
Bethlehem
Washington
Watertown
Oakville
Wolcott
Woodtick
New Milford
Waterbury
Woodbury
Middlebury
Prospect
Naugatuck
Candlewood Isle
Brookfield
Heritage Village
Southbury
New Fairfield
Candlewood Shores
Brookfield Center
Lakeside
Oxford
Pine Bridge
Bethany
Danbury
Newtown
Sandy Hook
Seymour
Bethel
East Village
Ansonia
Woodbridge
Upper Stepney
Monroe Center
Derby
Shelton
Ridgefield
Georgetown
Trumbull
Orange
Weston
Stratford
Milford
Wilton
Bridgeport
Woodmont
Westport
Fairfield
New Canaan
Norwalk
Darien
Stamford
Greenwich
East Hartland
West Granby
West Simsbury
New Hartford
Cherry Brook
Canton
Weatogue
Simsbury
Collinsville
Avon
Unionville
Farmington
Bristol
Plainville
Fall Mountain Lake
Southington
Plantsville
Marion
Milldale
Honeypot Glen
Cheshire
Meriden
Wallingford
Hamden
North Haven
New Haven
West Haven
East Haven
Short Beach
Branford
Stony Creek
Pine Orchard
Indian Neck
Branford Point
Guilford
Madison
East River
North Branford
Northford
Durham
Middlefield
Rockfall
Lake Beseck
Middletown
Portland
Cromwell
East Berlin
Berlin
Kensington
New Britain
Rocky Hill
Newington
Wethersfield
West Hartford
Hartford
East Hartford
Manchester
Blue Hills
Bloomfield
Windsor
South Windsor
Vernon
Ellington
Broad Brook
Warehouse Point
Windsor Locks
East Granby
Granby
Tariffville
West Suffield
Suffield
Ebbs Corner
Sherwood Manor
Hazardville
Enfield
Southwood Acres
Whitacres
Somersville
Green Manorville
Glastonbury
Addison
South Glastonbury
East Hampton
Middle Haddam
Higganum
Haddam
East Haddam
Chester
Deep River
Centerbrook
Westbrook
Clinton
Milldale
Mixville
N

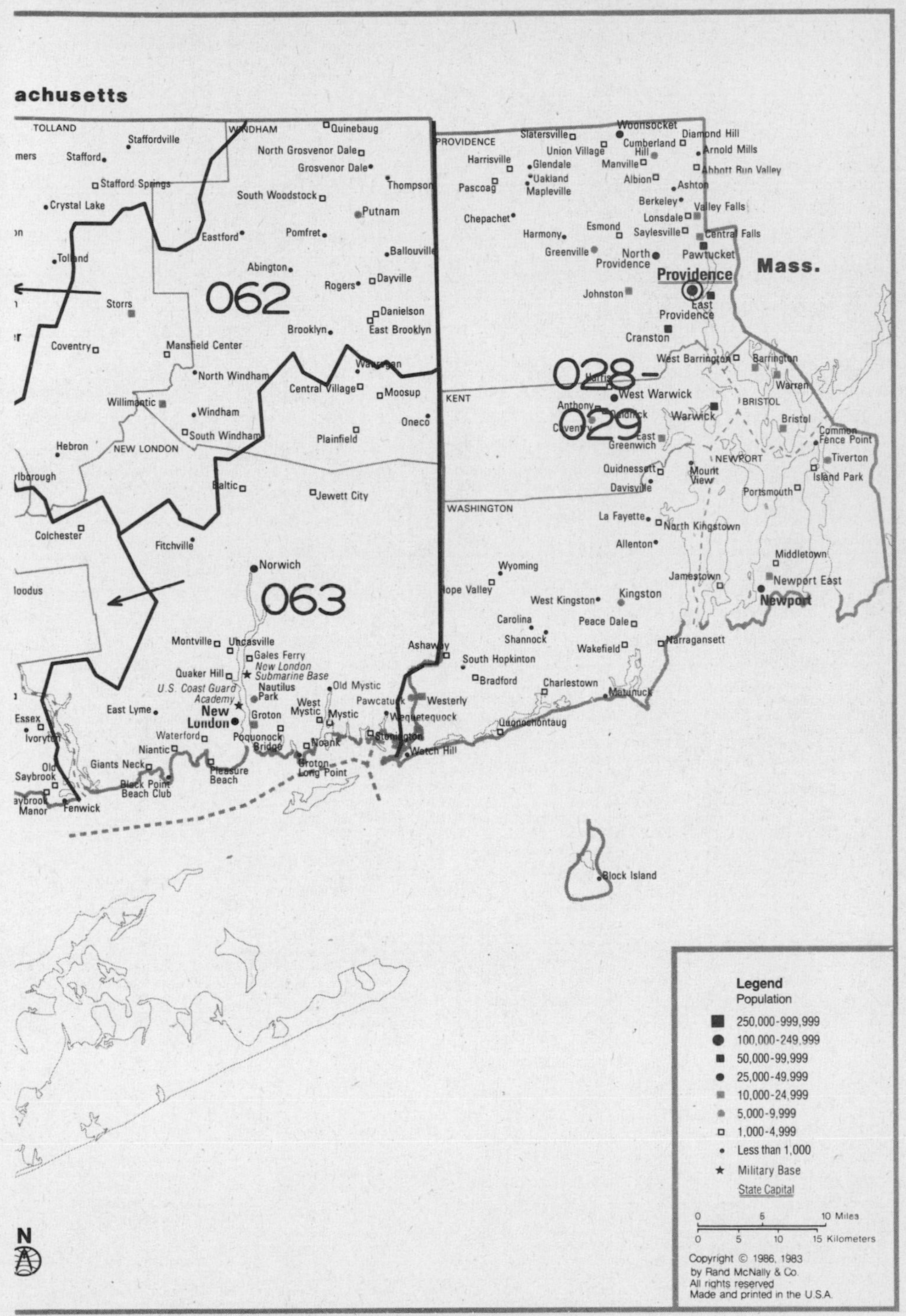
achusetts
Mass.
062
063
028-
029
Providence
Woonsocket
Pawtucket
Cranston
Warwick
West Warwick
Newport
New London
Norwich
Westerly
Putnam
Storrs
Willimantic
Danielson
Block Island
TOLLAND
WINDHAM
NEW LONDON
PROVIDENCE
KENT
WASHINGTON
BRISTOL
NEWPORT
Legend
Population
250,000-999,999
100,000-249,999
50,000-99,999
25,000-49,999
10,000-24,999
5,000-9,999
1,000-4,999
Less than 1,000
Military Base
State Capital
0 5 10 Miles
0 5 10 15 Kilometers
N

Groton Long Point 06340
Groton Naval Base‡ 06349
Grove Beach 06413
Gugliotti 06479
Guilford 06437
Guilford Lake 06437
Gurleyville 06268
Haddam 06438
Haddam Neck 06424
Hadlyme 06439
Hale Court 06880
Halls Hill 06415
Hallville 06365
Hamburg 06371
Hamden 06514
...... 06517-18
For specific ZIP Codes call (888) 275-8777, or your local postmaster.
Hamden Plaza 06514
Hammertown 06079
Hampton 06247
Hank Hills 06268
Hanover 06350
Happyland 06365
Harborview (Part of Norwalk) 06853
Harbor View, *Middlesex* 06413
Harrisons 06375
Harrisville 06281

Hartford

...... 06101-06
...... 06112-15
...... 06120-26
...... 06132
...... 06134
...... 06140-99
For specific ZIP Codes call (888) 275-8777, or your local postmaster.

Colleges & Universities

Hartford Seminary 06105
Rensselaer at Hartford 06120
Trinity Coll 06106

Financial Institutions

BankBoston, NA 06103
First Union Bank 06103
Fleet Nat Bank 06115

Hospitals

Hartford Hosp 06106
Saint Francis Hosp Med Ctr 06105

Hotels/Motels

Holiday Inn, Downtown Civic Ctr 06120
Sheraton 06103

Military Installations

U S Property & Fiscal Off for Connecticut 06105

Hartland (Town) 06027
Harwinton (Town) 06790
Harwinton♦ 06791
Hawks Nest Beach 06371
Hawleyville 06440
Hawthorne Terrace (Part of Danbury) 06810
Hayden 06095
Hayestown (Part of Danbury) 06810
Hazardville 06082
Headquarters 06759
Hebron 06248
Heritage Village♦ 06488
Hidden Lake 06441
Higganum♦ 06441
Highland Park 06040
Hi-Ho Shopping Mall (Part of Bridgeport) 06604
Hitchcock Lake 06716
Holiday Homes (Part of Colchester) 06415
Hollywyle Park 06810
Honeypot Glen 06410
Hopeville (Part of Waterbury) 06706
Hopeville, *New London* 06351
Horton Hill (Part of Naugatuck) 06770
Hotchkissville 06798
Huckleberry Hill 06001
Hungary Hill 06377
Huntington (Part of Shelton)‡ 06484
Huntsville 06031
Hydeville 06075
I-91 Exit 8 Mall (Part of New Haven) 06515
Indian Cove 06437
Indian Neck 06405
Ivoryton 06442
Jericho Hill 06371
Jewett City 06351
Joyceville 06079
Kellogg Corners 06796
Kelly Corner 06756
Kelseytown 06413
Kensington♦ 06037
Kent 06757
Kent Furnace 06757
Kenyonville 06282
Kilby (Part of New Haven)‡ 06519
Killingly (Town) 06239
Killingly Center 06241
Killingworth 06419
Kings Corner 06088
Knollcrest 06810
Knollwood 06475
Lake Bashan 06469
Lake Bungee 06282
Lake Garda 06013
Lake Hayward 06415
Lake Plymouth 06782
Lake Pocotopaug♦ 06424
Lakeside, *Litchfield* 06758
Lakeside, *New Haven* 06488
Lakeview Terrace 06076
Lakeville 06039
Lakewood (Part of Waterbury) 06704
Lanesville 06776
Lattins Landing (Part of Danbury) 06810
Laurel (Part of Middletown) 06457
Laurel Beach (Part of Milford) 06460
Laurel Glen 06359
Laurel Hill (Part of Norwich) 06360
Laysville 06371
Lebanon 06249
Ledyard 06339
Leesville 06469
Leetes Island 06437
Leffingwell 06360
Liberty Hill 06249
Lime Rock 06039
Lisbon 06351
Litchfield 06759
Little City 06441
Long Hill, *Fairfield* 06611
Long Hill (Part of Middletown) 06457
Long Hill (Part of Waterbury) 06704
Long Hill, *New London* 06340
Long Ridge (Part of Stamford) 06901
Lordship 06615
Lords Point 06378
Lower Merryall 06776
Lydallville 06040
Lyme 06371
Lyons Plains 06880
Macedonia 06757
Madison 06443
Main Street (Part of Danbury)‡ 06813
Manchester 06040
...... 06045
For specific ZIP Codes call (888) 275-8777, or your local postmaster.
Manchester Green 06040
Manchester Parkade 06040
Mansfield (Town) 06250
Mansfield Center 06250
Mansfield City 06268
Mansfield Depot 06251
Mansfield Four Corners 06268
Mansfield Hollow 06250
Maple Hill 06111
Maple Hallow 06057
Maplewood (Part of Derby) 06418
Marble Dale 06777
Margerie Manor (Part of Danbury) 06810
Marion 06444
Marlborough 06447
Maromas (Part of Middletown) 06457
Mashantucket Pequot Indian Reservation 06339
Mashapaug 06076
Mason Island 06355
Massapeag 06382
Mayberry Village 06108
Meads Point 06830
Mechanicsville 06277
Melrose 06049
Melville Village 06430
Meriden 06450-51
For specific ZIP Codes call (888) 275-8777, or your local postmaster.
Meriden Square (Part of Meriden) 06450
Merrow 06251
Mianus 06807
Middle Beach 06443
Middlebury 06762
Middlefield 06455
Middle Haddam 06456
Middletown 06457
Midway 06340
Mill Brook, *Litchfield* 06098
Milbrook, *New Haven* 06830
Milford 06460
Milford Lawns (Part of Milford) 06460
Millbrook 06518
Milldale 06467
Millington 06423
Mill Plain (Part of Danbury) 06810
Mill Plain (Part of Waterbury) 06705
Millville (Part of Naugatuck) 06770
Milton 06759
Mitchelltown 06069
Mixville 06410
Mohegan 06382
Momauguin 06512
Monroe 06468
Monroe Center 06468
Montowese 06473
Montville 06353
Montville Manor 06370
Moodus♦ 06469
Moosup♦ 06354
Morningside (Part of Milford) 06460
Morris 06763
Morris Cove 06512
Mount Carmel 06518
Mount Hope 06250
Murphy Road Annex (Part of Hartford)‡ 06114
Murray 06430
Myrtle Beach (Part of Milford) 06460
Mystic♦ 06355
Naugatuck 06770
Naugatuck Gardens (Part of Milford) 06460
Naugatuck Valley Mall (Part of Waterbury) 06705
Nautilus Park 06340
Nepaug 06057
Newberry Corner (Part of Torrington) 06790
New Britain 06050-53
For specific ZIP Codes call (888) 275-8777, or your local postmaster.
New Canaan 06840
Newent 06351
New Fairfield (Town) 06810
New Fairfield 06812
Newfield (Part of Stamford) 06607
Newfield Heights (Part of Middletown) 06457
Newhallville (Part of New Haven) 06511
New Hartford 06057
New Haven 06501-11
...... 06513
...... 06515
...... 06519-21
...... 06530-36
For specific ZIP Codes call (888) 275-8777, or your local postmaster.
Newington 06111*
...... 06131†
Newington Junction 06111
New London 06320
New Milford 06776
New Preston♦ 06777
New Preston-Marble Dale 06777
Newtown 06470
New Village 06374
Niantic♦ 06357
Nichols 06611
Noank‡ 06340
Noble (Part of Bridgeport)‡ 06608
Norfolk 06058
Noroton‡ 06820
Noroton Heights‡ 06820
North Ashford 06282
North Bloomfield 06002
North Branford 06471
North Bridgeport (Part of Bridgeport) 06601
North Canaan (Town) 06018
North Canton 06059
North Cornwall 06796
North End (Part of Waterbury) 06704
North Farms 06471
Northfield 06778
Northford 06472
North Franklin 06254
North Glenwood 06335
North Goshen 06756
North Granby 06060
North Grosvenor Dale♦ 06255
North Guilford 06437
North Haven 06473
North Kent 06757
North Madison 06443
North Mianus 06807
North Norfolk 06058
North Plain 06423
North Sterling 06377
North Stonington 06359
North Thompsonville 06082
Northville 06776
North Westchester 06474
North Wilton 06897
North Windham 06256
Norwalk 06850-56
For specific ZIP Codes call (888) 275-8777, or your local postmaster.
Norwich 06360
Norwichtown (Part of Norwich) 06360
Nut Plains 06437
Oakdale 06370
Oakdale Heights 06370
Oakdale Manor 06488
Oakland Gardens 06032
Oakville♦ 06779
Oakwood Acres 06812
Occum (Part of Norwich) 06360
Old Greenwich 06870
Old Lyme 06371
Old Lyme Shores 06371
Old Mystic 06372
Old Saybrook 06475
Old Saybrook Shopping Center 06475
Old State House (Part of Hartford)‡ 06123
Oneco 06373
Orange 06477
Orcutts 06076
Ore Hill 06039
Oronoke (Part of Waterbury) 06708
Oronoque 06614
Oswegatchie 06385
Overlook (Part of Waterbury) 06710
Owenoke 06880
Oxford 06478
Ox Hill (Part of Norwich) 06360
Pachaug 06351
Palestine 06470
Palmertown 06353
Paradise Green 06614
Parcel Post (Part of Milford)‡ 06460
Park Lane 06776
Parkville (Part of Hartford) 06106
Pavilion at Buckland Hills, The 06040
Pawcatuck♦ 06379
Pemberwick 06830
Pequabuck 06781
Perkins Corner 06226
Phoenixville 06235
Pine Bridge 06403
Pine Grove, *Litchfield* 06031
Pine Grove, *New London* 06357
Pine Meadow 06061
Pine Orchard 06405
Pine Rock Park (Part of Shelton) 06484
Plainfield 06374
Plainville 06062
Plantsville 06479
Platts Mills (Part of Waterbury) 06706
Plaza (Part of Waterbury)‡ 06704
Pleasant Acres (Part of Danbury) 06810
Pleasant Valley 06063
Pleasure Beach 06385
Plymouth 06782
Point Beach (Part of Milford) 06460
Point O'Woods 06376
Pomfret 06258
Pomfret Center 06259
Pomfret Landing 06259
Pond Point (Part of Milford) 06460
Ponset 06441
Pootatuck Park 06482
Poquetanuck 06365
Poquonock 06064
Poquonock Bridge♦ 06340
Portland 06480
Presidential 06082
Preston 06365
Prospect 06712
Prospect Beach (Part of West Haven) 06516
Puddle Town 06022
Putnam 06260
Putnam Heights 06260
Putney 06614
Quaddick 06277
Quaker Farms 06478
Quaker Hill 06375
Quarryville 06040
Quebec 06239
Quinebaug♦ 06262
Quinnipiac 06492
Rawson 06247
Redding 06896
Redding Center 06875
Redding Ridge 06876
Ridgebury 06877
Ridgefield 06877
Ridgeway Shopping Center (Part of Stamford)‡ 06905
Ridgewood 06413
Ridgewood Park 06385
Rising Corner 06093
Rivercliff (Part of Milford) 06460
River Glen 06032
Riverside, *Fairfield* (Newton Township) 06482
Riverside, *Fairfield* (Greenwich Township) 06878
Riverside, *New Haven* 06478
Riversville 06830
Riverton 06065
Robertsville 06065
Rockfall 06481
Rock Ridge 06830
Rocky Hill 06067
Rogers 06263
Round Hill 06830

*** Area Zip Code** **† Post Office Boxes** **‡ Postal Station** **♦ Census Designated Place** *Italic Type* **County**

Place	ZIP Code
Rowayton (Part of Norwalk)‡	06853
Roxbury	06783
Roxbury Falls	06783
Sachem Head	06437
Sadds Mill	06029
Salem	06420
Salisbury	06068
Samp Mortar‡	06430
Sandy Beach	06758
Sandy Hook	06482
Sanfordtown	06896
Saugatuck‡	06880
Saugatuck Shores	06880
Saunders Point	06357
Savin Rock (Part of West Haven)	06516
Saybrook Manor♦	06475
Saybrook Point	06475
Scantic	06088
Scitico	06082
Scotland	06264
Seaview Beach	06443
Secret Lake	06001
Seymour	06483
Shady Rest	06482
Shailerville	06438
Sharon	06069
Sharon Valley	06069
Shelton	06484
Sherman	06784
Sherman Corner	06256
Sherwood Manor♦	06082
Shippan Point (Part of Stamford)	06902
Short Beach‡	06405
Silver Beach (Part of Milford)	06460
Silver Lane	06138
Simsbury	06070
Skiff Mountain	06757
Somers (Town)	06071
Somersville	06072
Sound View	06371
South Britain	06487
Southbury	06488
South Canaan	06031
South Coventry♦	06238
South Ellsworth	06069
South End (Part of Stamford)	06902
South End, *New Haven*	06512
South Farms (Part of Middletown)	06457
Southford	06488
South Glastonbury	06073
South Glenwoods	06335
Southington	06489
South Kent	06785
South Killingly	06239
South Lyme	06376
South Manchester	06040
South Meriden (Part of Meriden)	06451
South Norfolk	06058
South Norwalk (Part of Norwalk)	06854
Southport	06490
South Wethersfield	06109
South Willington	06265
South Windham♦	06266
South Windsor	06074
Southwood Acres♦	06082
South Woodstock♦	06267
Sport Hill	06612
Sprague (Town)	06330
Springdale (Part of Stamford)‡	06907
Spring Hill	06268
Spring Lake Village	06489
Stafford	06075
Stafford Springs	06076
Staffordville	06077
Stamford	06901-12
For specific ZIP Codes call (888) 275-8777, or your local postmaster.	
Stamford Town Center (Part of Stamford)	06901
Stanwich	06830
State Line, *Litchfield*	06039
State Line, *Tolland*	06076
Station A (Part of Hartford)‡	06126
Station A (Part of Meriden)‡	06450
Stepney	06448
Sterling	06377
Sterling Hill	06377
Stetson Corner	06234
Stevenson	06491
Still River	06776
Stonington	06378
Stony Corners	06001
Stony Creek‡	06405
Storrs♦	06268
Straitsville (Part of Naugatuck)	06770
Stratfield	06432
Stratford	06497
	06614-15
For specific ZIP Codes call (888) 275-8777, or your local postmaster.	
Stratmore Farms	06492
Suburban Enfield Mall	06082
Suffield	06078
Summer Hill	06492
Sunrise Hill	06525
Taconic	06079
Taft Station (Part of Norwich)	06360
Taftville (Part of Norwich)	06380
Talcott Village	06032
Talcottville‡	06066
Talmadge Hill	06840
Tariffville♦	06081
Terminal (Part of New Haven)‡	06511
Terryville♦	06786
Thamesville (Part of Norwich)	06360
The Cedars	06039
Thompson	06277
Thompsonville	06082
Timber Trails	06784
Titicus	06877
Tokeneke	06820
Tolland	06084
Torringford (Part of Torrington)	06790
Torrington	06790
Town Hill	06057
Town Plot Hill (Part of Waterbury)	06708
Trails Corner	06340
Trumbull (Town)	06612
Trumbull♦	06611
Trumbull Shopping Center	06611
Trumbull Shopping Park	06611
Turn of River (Part of Stamford)	06901
Turnpike‡	06066
Twin Lakes	06079
Tyler Lake Heights	06756
Uncasville	06382
Union	06076
Union City (Part of Naugatuck)‡	06770
Unionville	06085
Unity Plaza (Part of Hartford)‡	06140
Upper Merryall	06776
Upper Stepney	06468
Vernon	06066
Vernon Center	06066
Versailles	06383
Versailles Station	06383
Village Hill	06249
Voluntown	06384
Wailacks Point (Part of Stamford)	06902
Wallingford	06492
Walnut Beach (Part of Milford)	06460
Walnut Hill	06333
Wamphassuc Point	06378
Wapping	06074
Warren (Town)	06753
Warren	06754
Warrenville	06278
Washington (Town)	06793
Washington Depot	06793-94
For specific ZIP Codes call (888) 275-8777, or your local postmaster.	
Washington Green‡	06793
Washington Hill	06059
Washington Square (Part of Norwich)	06360
Waterbury	06701-10
	06720-26
For specific ZIP Codes call (888) 275-8777, or your local postmaster.	
Waterbury Plaza Shopping Center (Part of Waterbury)	06704
Waterford (Town)	06385
Waterside (Part of Stamford)	06901
Watertown	06795
Waterville (Part of Waterbury)	06704
Wauregan♦	06387
Wauwecus Hill (Part of Norwich)	06360
Weatogue♦	06089
Webster Square Shopping Center	06037
Welles Village	06033
Wells Quarter Village	06109
Wellsville	06776
Wequetequock	02891
Wesleyan (Part of Middletown)‡	06457
West Ashford	06250
West Avon	06001
Westbrook	06498
Westchester	06415
West Cornwall	06796
West End (Part of Bristol)	06010
Westfarms	06032
West Farms Village (Part of New Britain)	06050
Westfield (Part of Middletown)	06457
Westford	06278
West Goshen	06756
West Granby	06090
West Hartford	06107
	06110
	06117
	06119
	06127
	06133
	06137
For specific ZIP Codes call (888) 275-8777, or your local postmaster.	
West Hartland	06091
West Haven	06516
West Lakes	06437
West Mystic♦	06388
West Norfolk	06058
West Norwalk (Part of Norwalk)	06851
Weston (Town)	06880
Weston	06883
Westport♦	06880*
	06881†
West Putnam Avenue‡	06830
West Redding	06896
West Shore (Part of West Haven)	06516
West Side (Part of Norwich)	06360
West Side Hill (Part of Waterbury)	06708
West Simsbury♦	06092
West Stafford	06076
West Suffield	06093
West Thompson	06277
West Torrington (Part of Torrington)	06790
Westville (Part of New Haven)‡	06515
West Wauregan	06387
Westwood Park (Part of Norwich)	06360
West Woods	06069
West Woodstock	06282
Wethersfield♦	06109*
	06129†
Wethersfield Shopping Center	06109
Wheeler Farms (Part of Milford)	06460
Whigville	06013
Whipstick	06877
White Oaks	06488
White Sands Beach	06371
Whitneyville	06517
Wildermere Beach (Part of Milford)‡	06460
Williams Crossing	06249
Willimantic♦	06226
Willington	06279
Willington Hill	06279
Willow Point	06388
Wilsonville	06255
Wilton	06897
Winchester (Town)	06094
Winchester Center	06094
Windermere	06029
Windham	06280
Windham Center	06280
Winding Lanes	06001
Windsor	06095
Windsor Locks	06096
Windsorville	06016
Winnipauk (Part of Norwalk)	06851
Winsted♦	06098
Winthrop	06417
Wolcott	06716
Woodbridge	06525
Woodbury	06798
Woodlake	06798
Woodmont‡	06460
Woodstock	06281
Woodstock Valley	06282
Woodtick	06716
Woodville	06777
Wormwood Hill	06268
Yale (Part of New Haven)‡	06520
Yalesville‡	06492
Yantic (Part of Norwich)	06389
Yelping Hill	06796
Zoar	06482

Adams Crossroads	19950
Adamsville	19950
Afton	19810
Alapocas	19803
Albertson Park	19808
Analine Village (Part of Claymont)	19703
Andrewville	19950
Anglesey	19807
Angola	19971
Angola by the Bay	19971
Anne Acres	19971
Arden	19810
Ardencroft	19810
Ardentown	19810
Argos Corner	19963
Arundel	19808
Ashbourne Hills	19703
Ashland	19807
Ashley	19804
Atlanta	19933
Atlanta Estates	19973
Augustine Beach	19731
Bacons	19940
Bakers Choice	19946
Bayard	19945
Bay Berry Dunes	19930
Bay View Beach	19709
Bay View Park	19930
Bayville	19975
Bay Vista	19971
Bear	19701
Beaver Brook Apartments	19720
Beaverdam Heights	19973
Bellefonte	19809
Bellemoor	19804
Bellevue Manor	19809
Belltown	19958
Belvedere	19804
Bestfield	19804
Bethany Beach	19930
Bethany Dunes	19930
Bethany Village	19930
Bethel	19931
Big Mills Bridge (Part of Laurel)	19956
Big Oak Corners	19977
Big Pine	19950
Big Stone Beach	19963
Binns Village (Part of Newark)	19711
Birchwood Park	19713
Blackbird	19977
Blackiston	19938
Blackwater Village	19939
Blades	19973
Blue Hen Mall (Part of Dover)	19901
Bowers Beach	19946
Boxwood	19804
Brackenville	19707
Brack-Ex	19805
Brandywine	19810
Brandywine Estates	19703
Brandywine Hills (Part of Wilmington)	19802
Brandywine Springs	19808
Brandywood	19810
Breezewood, *Kent*	19943
Breezewood, *New Castle*	19713
Breeze Wood, *Sussex*	19971
Brenford	19977
Briar Park	19904
Bridgeville	19933
Broad Acres	19973
Broad Creek	19956
Broadkill Beach	19968
Brookbend	19713
Brookdale Heights	19934
Brookhaven	19711
Brookland Terrace	19805
Brookside	19713
Brownsville	19952
Bull Pine Corners	19947
Bunting	19975
Cabbage Corner	19947
Camden	19934
Camden Wyoming (Part of Wyoming)	19934
Cannon	19933
Canterbury	19943
Capitol Green (Part of Dover)	19901
Capitol Park	19901
Cardiff	19810
Carlisle Village	19904
Carrcroft	19803
Carrcroft Crest	19803
Carter	19901
Castle Hills	19720
Catalina Gardens (Part of Newark)	19713
Cave Colony	19968
Cedar Beach	19963
Cedarbrook Acres	19977
Cedar Heights	19804
Centerville	19807
Chalfonte	19810
Channin	19803
Chapel Hill	19711
Chatham	19810
Chelsea Estates	19720
Chestnut Grove	19904
Chestnut Hill Estates	19713
Cheswold	19936
Christiana	19702
Christiana Acres	19720
Christine Manor	19711
Clarksville	19970
Claymont	19703
Clayton	19938
Clearfield	19703
Cleland Heights	19805
Cocked Hat	19933
College Park (Part of Newark)	19711
Collins Park	19720
Colmar Manor	19977
Colonial Heights	19805
Columbia	19940
Concord	19973
Concord Mall	19803
Cool Spring	19968
Cooper Farm	19808
Cotton Patch Hills	19930
Country Club Estates	19963
Country Living	19966
Coventry	19720
Coverdale Crossroads	19933
Covered Bridge Farms	19711
Covey Creek	19958
Cowgills Corner	19901
Craigs Mill	19973
Cranston Heights	19808
Crossgates (Part of Dover)	19904
Cross Keys	19966
Dagsboro	19939
Darley Woods	19810
Dartmouth Woods	19810
Deerhurst	19803
Delaneys Corner	19938
Delaplane Manor	19711
Delaware City	19706
Delaware Heights	19807
Del Haven Estates	19962
Delmar	19940
Del Park Manor	19808
Devon	19810
Devonshire	19810
Devonshire Woods	19973
Dewey Beach	19971
Diamond Acres	19939
Dobbinsville (Part of New Castle)	19720
Dover	19901-05
For specific ZIP Codes call (888) 275-8777, or your local postmaster.	
Dover Air Force Base Housing Annex	19901
Dover Base Housing♦	19902
Dover Mall (Part of Dover)	19901
Downs Chapel	19938
Drummond North	19711
Dublin Hill	19933
Dunleith	19801
Dunlinden Acres	19808
Dupont Manor	19901
Du Ross Heights	19720
Dutch Acres	19958
Eastman Heights	19963
Eberton	19901
Eden Park	19720
Edge Hill (Part of Dover)	19901
Edgehill Acres (Part of Dover)	19901
Edgemoor	19802
	19809
For specific ZIP Codes call (888) 275-8777, or your local postmaster.	
Edgemoor Gardens	19802
Edgemoor Terrace	19802
Edgewater	19958
Edgewater Acres	19975
Edgewood Hills	19802
Edwardsville	19943
Ellendale	19941
Elmhurst	19804
Elsmere	19805
English Village	19711
Fairfax	19803
Fairfield Farms	19901
Fairmount	19966
Fairwinds	19701
Farmington	19942
Faulkland	19808
Faulkwoods	19808
Federal (Part of Newark)‡	19711
Felton	19943
Felton Heights	19943
Fenwick Island	19944
Fieldsboro	19734
Flemings Corners	19952
Flemings Landing	19734
Forest Brook Glen	19804
Forest Hills Park	19803
Four Seasons	19702
Foxhall Courtside	19904
Fox Hollow	19958
Frankford	19945
Frederica	19946
Garfield Park	19720
Georgetown	19947
Ginns Corner	19734
Glasgow	19702
Glasgow Court	19702
Glasgow Pines	19702
Glen Berne Estates	19804
Glendale	19702
Glenville	19804
Gordon Heights	19802
Gordy Estates	19804
Granogue	19807
Gravel Hill	19947
Graylyn Crest	19803
Green Acres	19803
Greenbrier	19720
Greentree	19703
Greenview	19901
Greenville, *Kent*	19952
Greenville, *New Castle*	19807
Greenville Place	19807
Greenwood	19950
Gulls Nest	19930
Gumboro	19945
Guyencourt	19807
Gwinhurst	19809
Hall Estates	19963
Hamilton Park	19720
Hanby Corners	19810
Harbeson	19951
Hardscrabble	19973
Harmony Hills	19711
Harrington	19952
Hartly	19953
Haven Lake Acres	19963
Hayden Park	19804
Hazlettville	19953
Hearns Crossroads	19956
Hearns Mill	19973
Heather Woods	19702
Henlopen Acres	19971
Heritage Village	19973
Hickman	19950
Hickory Hill	19966
Hickory Ridge	19977
Highland Acres, *Kent*	19901
Highland Acres, *Sussex*	19958
Highland West	19808
High Point Park	19946
Hillcrest	19809
Hill N Dale	19973
Hillside Acres	19943
Hillside Heights	19713
Hilltop Manor	19809
Hitchens Crossroads	19956
Hockessin	19707
Holiday Acres	19939
Hollandsville	19943
Holletts Corners	19938
Holloway Terrace	19720
Holly Oak, *New Castle*	19809
Holly Oak, *Sussex*	19973
Holly Oak Terrace	19809
Hollyville	19951
Houston	19954
Huntley	19901
Hyde Park	19808
Indian Beach	19971
Indian River Acres	19939
Iron Hill Apartments	19702
Ivy Ridge	19720
Jefferson Farms	19720
Jimtown	19958
Johnson	19975
Johnstown	19950
Jones Crossroads	19956
Keen-Wik	19975
Keenwick Sound	19975
Keenwick West	19975
Kenmore Park	19973
Kent Acres	19901
Kenton	19955
Kiamensi	19804
Kirkwood	19708
Kitts Hummock	19901
Lake Pines	19956
Lamatan	19711
Lancashire	19810
Lancaster Avenue Station (Part of Wilmington)‡	19805
Lancaster Village	19805
Laurel	19956
Lebanon	19901
Leedom Estates	19720
Leipsic	19901
Lewes	19958
Lewes Beach (Part of Lewes)	19958
Liftwood	19803
Limestone Acres	19808
Limestone Gardens	19808
Lincoln	19960
Lindamere	19809
Little Creek	19961
Little Heaven	19946
Llangollen Estates	19720
London Village	19962
Long Neck♦	19966
Longview Farms	19810
Loveville	19808
Lowe	19956
Lowes Crossroads	19966
Lumbrook (Part of Newark)	19711
Lynch Heights	19963
Lyndalia	19804
Lynnfield	19803
McClellandville	19711
McDaniel Heights	19803
Magnolia	19962
Manor	19720
Manor Park	19720
Maplecrest	19808
Marabou Meadows	19702
Marshallton	19808
Marvels Crossroads	19952
Marydel	19964
Masseys Landing	19966
Mastens Corner	19943
Mayfair (Part of Dover)	19904
Mayfield	19803
Meadowbrook	19804
Meadowbrook Acres	19962
Meadowood	19711
Mechanicsville	19711
Meeting House Hill	19711
Melody Meadows	19702
Mendenhall Village	19711
Middleford	19973
Middlesex Beach	19930
Middletown	19709
Midvale	19720
Midway	19971
Milford	19963
Milford Crossroads	19711
Millpond Acres	19958
Millsboro	19966
Milltown	19808
Millville	19967
Milton	19968
Minquadale	19720
Mispillion Light	19963
Mission	19966
Montchanin	19710
Morris Estates (Part of Dover)	19901
Mount Cuba	19807
Mount Pleasant	19709
Naamans Corner	19703
Naamans Gardens	19810
Naamans Manor	19810
Nanticoke Acres	19973
Nassau	19969
Newark	19702
	19711-17
For specific ZIP Codes call (888) 275-8777, or your local postmaster.	
New Castle	19720
New Castle Manor (Part of New Castle)	19720
Newport	19804
Newport Heights	19804
Northcrest	19810
North Hills	19809
Northridge	19977
North Seaford Heights	19973
Northshire	19810
North Shore	19963
North Shores, *Sussex* (mail Rehoboth Beach)	19971
North Shores, *Sussex* (mail Seaford)	19973
North Star	19711
Northwest Dover Heights (Part of Dover)	19904
Northwood	19803
Nottingham Green (Part of Newark)	19711
Oak Forest Estates	19953
Oak Grove (Part of Dover)	19901
Oak Grove, *Sussex*	19973
Oak Hill	19805
Oak Lane Manor	19803
Oakley	19941
Oakmont	19801
Oak Orchard	19966
Ocean View	19970
Ocean Village	19930
Odessa	19730
Ogletown	19711
Old Furnace	19947
Omar	19945
Orchard Acres	19943
Overbrook Shores	19958
Overview Gardens	19720
Owens	19950
Owls Nest Estates	19807
Paris Villa	19962
Pearsons Corner	19904
Pembrey	19803
Penarth	19803
Penn Acres	19720
Pennrock	19809
Penny Hill	19809
Pepper	19956
Pepperbox	19956
Perth	19803
Petersburg	19943
Phillips Hill	19966
Pickering Beach	19901
Pike Creek♦	19711
	19808
For specific ZIP Codes call (888) 275-8777, or your local postmaster.	
Pinetown	19958
Pine Tree Corners	19734
Piney Grove	19947
Pleasant Hill	19711
Pleasanton Acres	19901
Pleasantville	19720
Plymouth	19943
Porter	19701
Port Mahon	19901
Port Penn	19731
Portsville	19956
Primehook Beach	19963
Quaker Heights	19958
Radnor Green	19703
Rambleton Acres	19720
Ramblewood	19810
Redden	19947
Redden Crossroads	19947
Red Lion	19701
Reeves Crossing	19943
Rehoboth Beach	19971
Reliance	19973
Richardson Park	19805
Rising Sun	19934
Riverdale	19966
Riverview Gardens	19703
Riverview, *Kent*♦	19946
Riverview, *Sussex*	19966
River Village	19966
Robscott Manor	19713
Rockland	19732

*** Area Zip Code** **† Post Office Boxes** **‡ Postal Station** **♦ Census Designated Place** *Italic Type* **County**

Place	ZIP
Rodney Square (Part of Wilmington)‡	19801*
	19899†
Rodney Village	19904
Rodric Village	19901
Rogers Haven	19970
Rogers Manor	19720
Rolling Hills	19804
Rolling Park	19703
Rose Gate	19720
Roselle	19805
Roseville Park	19711
Roxana	19945
Rutherford	19713
St. Georges	19733
Sand Dunes Village	19958
Sandtown	19943
Sandy Brae	19958
Scottfield	19713
Scotts Corner	19933
Seabreeze	19971
Sea Air	19971
Sea Del Estates	19930
Seaford	19973
Seaford Heights	19973
Sedgley Farms	19807
Seeneytown	19938
Selbyville	19975
Shady Lane	19901
Shaft Ox Corner	19966
Sharpley	19803
Shawnee Acres	19963
Shell Bridge	19956
Shellburne	19803
Sherwood (Part of Dover)	19904
Sherwood Acres	19945
Sherwood Forest	19713
Sherwood Park	19808
Shipley Heights	19803
Shortly	19947
Silverbrook	19805
Silverside Heights	19809
Silview	19804
Simonds Gardens	19720
Slaughter Beach	19963
Smyrna	19977
Smyrna Landing (Part of Smyrna)	19977
Snug Harbor	19973
South Bethany	19930
South Bowers	19946
Southwood	19707
Springfield Crossroads	19947
Spruance City	19977
Stanton	19804
Star Hill	19901
Staytonville	19952
Stockdale	19703
Stockley	19947
Stoneybrook Apartments	19703
Stratford	19720
Summit Bridge	19709
Surrey Park	19803
Sussex Shores	19930
Swain Acres (Part of Georgetown)	19947
Swann Keys	19975
Swanwyck	19720
Swanwyck Estates	19720
Swanwyck Gardens	19720
Sycamore	19956
Sycamore Gardens	19711
Talleyville	19803
Tarleton	19810
Tavistock	19803
Taylor Estates	19901
Taylors Bridge	19734
The Cedars	19808
The Island	19973
The Timbers	19803
Thomas Landing	19734
Thompsonville	19963
Tidbury Manor	19901
Todd Estates	19713
Towne Point (Part of Dover)	19901
Townsend	19734
Tuxedo Park	19804
Twin Eagle Farms	19938
Tybrook	19808
Van Dyke Village (Part of New Castle)	19720
Varlano	19702
Vernon	19952
Village of Drummond Hill	19711
Villa Monterey	19809
Viola	19979
Voshell Cove	19901
Ward	19940
Warwick	19966
Warwick Park	19966
Washington Heights	19971
Webster Farms	19803
Wedgewood	19720
Wellington Woods	19702
Welshire	19803
West Beach	19939
Westfield	19804
West Haven	19807
West Meadow	19711
Westover Hills	10807
West Park	19807
Westview	19804
Westwood Manor	19810
Whaleys Corners	19956
Whaleys Crossroads	19956
Whiteleysburg	19943
White Oak Farms (Part of Dover)	19901
Whitesville	19940
Williamsville, *Kent*	19954
Williamsville, *Sussex*	19975
Willow Grove	19934
Willow Run	19805
Wilmington	19801-99
For specific ZIP Codes call (888) 275-8777, or your local postmaster.	
Wilmington Manor	19720
Wilmington Manor Gardens	19720
Wilmont	19803
Windermer	19804
Windsor Hills	19803
Windy Bush	19810
Windy Hills	19711
Winterthur	19735
Woodbine	19810
Woodbrook (Part of Dover)	19901
Woodbrook, *New Castle*	19803
Woodbury	19943
Woodcrest (Part of Dover)	19904
Woodcrest, *New Castle*	19804
Wooddale	19807
Woodenhawk	19950
Woodland, *New Castle*	19805
Woodland, *Sussex*	19973
Woodland Beach	19977
Woodshade	19702
Woods Haven	19963
Woodside	19980
Woods Manor	19901
Workmans Corners	19947
Wyoming	19934
York Beach (Part of South Bethany)	19930
Yorklyn	19736

Parts of Washington

Anacostia‡ 20020
Barnaby Terrace 20032
Barnaby Woods 20015
Bellevue 20032
Benjamin Franklin‡ 20004
Benning‡ 20019
Benning Heights 20019
Blue Plains 20032
Bolling Air Force Base‡ 20336
Brightwood‡ 20011*
20040†
Brightwood Park 20011
Brookland‡ 20017
Burleith 20007
Calvert‡ 20007
Cleveland Park‡ 20008
Colonial Village 20012
Columbia Heights‡ 20009-10
For specific ZIP Codes call (888) 275-8777, or your local postmaster.
Congress Heights‡ 20032
Congress Park 20032
Customs House‡ 20018
Douglas Dwellings 20020
Deanewood 20019
Eckington 20002
Fairfax Village 20020
Farragut‡ 20033
Fort Davis‡ 20020
Fort Lincoln New Town 20018
Fort McNair 20319
Foxhall Village 20007
Friendship‡ 20007-08
20016
20088
For specific ZIP Codes call (888) 275-8777, or your local postmaster.
Garfield Heights 20020
Georgetown‡ 20007
Georgetown Park 20007
Glover Park 20007
Good Hope 20020
Greenway 20019
Hawthorne 20015
Hillcrest 20020
Ivy City 20002
Kalorama‡ 20009
Kendall Green‡ 20002
Kenilworth 20019
Kent 20016
Knox Hill Dwellings 20020
Lamond 20011
Lamond-Riggs Station‡ 20039
Langdon 20018
Le Droit Park‡ 20001
L'Enfant Plaza‡ 20024
McLean Gardens 20016
Macpherson 20038
Manor Park 20011
Marshall Heights 20019
Martin Luther King, Jr.‡ 20043
Mid City‡ 20005
Mount Pleasant 20010
National Capitol‡ 20013
Naval Research Laboratory 20375
Naylor Gardens 20020
Northeast‡ 20002
North Gate 20012
Northwest 20015
Palisades‡ 20016
Park View 20010
Petworth‡ 20011
Potomac Heights 20016
Randle‡ 20020
River Terrace 20019
Southeast‡ 20003
Southwest‡ 20024
Spring Valley 20016
Techworld‡ 20091
Temple Heights‡ 20009
Tenleytown 20016
Terra Cotta 20011
The Palisades 20016
Trinidad 20002
T Street‡ 20009
Twentieth Street‡ 20036
Twining 20020
Walter Reed‡ 20012
Ward Place‡ 20036-37
For specific ZIP Codes call (888) 275-8777, or your local postmaster.
Washington General Mail Facility‡ 20066
Washington Highlands 20032
Washington Square‡ 20035-36
For specific ZIP Codes call (888) 275-8777, or your local postmaster.
Watergate‡ 20037
Wesley Heights 20016
Woodley Park 20008
Woodridge 20018

Washington

20001-99
20101-04
20201-99
20301-34
20336
20501-99
For specific ZIP Codes call (888) 275-8777, or your local postmaster.

Colleges & Universities

American Univ 20016
Catholic Univ of America 20064
Corcoran School of Art 20006
Gallaudet Univ 20002
Georgetown Univ 20057
George Washington Univ 20052
Howard Univ 20059
Mount Vernon Coll 20007
Southeastern Univ 20024
Strayer Coll 20005
Trinity Coll 20017
Univ of the District of Columbia 20008
Wesley Theological Seminary 20016

Financial Institutions

Crestar Bank 20036
First Union Nat Bank 20005
Riggs Bank, NA 20005

Government Offices

Administrative Off of the U S Courts 20544
Advisory Council on Historic Preservation 20004
African Development Foundation 20005
Agency for International Development 20523
American Battle Monuments Cmsn 20314
Appalachian Regional Cmsn 20235
Architect of the Capitol 20515
Architectural & Transportation Barriers Compliance Bd 20004
Ballistic Missile Defense Org 20301
Bureau of Alcohol, Tobacco & Firearms 20226
Bureau of Engraving & Printing 20228
Bureau of Prisons 20534
Bureau of the Public Debt 20239
Central Intelligence Agcy 20505
Citizens' Stamp Advisory Cmte 20260
Commission of Fine Arts 20001
Committee for the Implementation of Textile Agreements 20230
Committee on Foreign Investment in the U S 20220
Commodity Futures Trading Cmsn 20581
Congressional Budget Off 20515
Coordinating Council on Juvenile Justice & Delinquency Prevention 20531
Corporation for National & Community Serv 20525
Council of Economic Advisors 20502
Council on Environmental Quality 20503
Defense Legal Servs Agcy 20301
Delaware River Basin Cmsn 20001
Dept of Agriculture 20250
Dept of Commerce 20230
Dept of Defense 20301
Dept of Education 20202
Dept of Energy 20585
Dept of Health & Human Servs 20201
Dept of Justice 20530
Dept of Labor 20210
Dept of State 20520
Dept of the Air Force 20330
Dept of the Army 20310
Dept of the Interior 20240
Dept of the Navy 20350
Dept of the Treasury 20220
Dept of Transportation 20590
Dept of Veterans Affairs 20420
Drug Enforcement Admin 20537
Endangered Species Cmte 20240
Equal Employment Opportunity Cmsn 20507
Export Admin Review Bd 20230
Export-Import Bank of the U S 20571
Fed Aviation Admin 20591
Fed Bureau of Investigation 20535
Fed Communications Cmsn 20554
Fed Financial Institutions Examination Council 20037
Fed Financing Bank 20220
Fed Highway Admin 20590
Fed Housing Finance Bd 20006
Fed Interagcy Cmte on Education 20202
Fed Judicial Ctr 20002
Fed Library & Information Ctr Cmte 20540
Fed Maritime Cmsn 20573
Fed Mediation & Conciliation Serv 20427
Fed Mine Safety & Health Review Cmsn 20006
Fed Railroad Admin 20590
Fed Reserve System 20551
Fed Trade Cmsn 20580
Fed Transit Admin 20590
Financial Management Serv 20227
Foreign Claims Settlement Cmsn of the U S 20579
Franklin Delano Roosevelt Memorial Cmsn 20510
Gallaudet Univ 20002
General Accounting Off 20548
Graduate School, U S Dept of Agriculture 20250
Harry S Truman Scholarship Foundation 20006
Health Care Financing Admin 20201
House of Representatives 20515
Howard Univ 20059
Immigration & Naturalization Serv 20536
Indian Arts & Crafts Bd 20240
Industrial College of the Armed Forces 20319
Information Resources Management College 20319
Interagcy Cmte on Employment of People with Disabilities 20507
Inter-American Development Bank 20577
Internal Revenue Serv 20224
International Boundary Cmsn, U S & Canada 20037
Japan-U S Friendship Cmsn 20005
Joint Board for the Enrollment of Actuaries 20224
Legal Servs Corp 20002
Library of Congress 20540
Maritime Admin 20590
Merit Systems Protection Bd 20419
Migratory Bird Conservation Cmsn 20240
Nat Aeronautics & Space Admin 20546
Nat Capital Planning Cmsn 20576
Nat Cmsn on Libraries & Information Science 20005
Nat Council on Disability 20004
Nat Credit Union Admin 22314
Nat Defense Univ 20319
Nat Endowment for the Arts 20506
Nat Endowment for the Humanities 20506
Nat Highway Traffic Safety Admin 20590
Nat Labor Relations Bd 20570
Nat Mediation Bd 20572
Nat Oceanic & Atmospheric Admin 20230
Nat Park Foundation 20036
Nat Railroad Passenger Corp (AMTRAK) 20002
Nat Security Council 20506
Nat Transportation Safety Bd 20594
Nat War College 20319
Nuclear Regulatory Cmsn 20555
Occupational Safety & Health Review Cmsn 20036
Off of Admin 20503
Off of Management & Budget 20503
Off of Science & Technol Policy 20502
Off of Special Counsel 20036
Off of the U S Trade Representative 20508
Off of the Vice President of the U S 20501
Org of American States 20006
Overseas Private Investment Corp 20527
Panama Canal Cmsn 20006
Peace Corps 20526
Pension Benefit Guaranty Corp 20005
Permanent Cmte for the Oliver Wendell Holmes Devise 20540
Postal Rate Cmsn 20268
President's Cmte on Employment of People with Disabilities 20004
President's Council on Integrity & Efficiency 20503
President's Foreign Intelligence Advisory Bd 20502
Saint Lawrence Seaway Development Corp 20590
Securities & Exchange Cmsn 20549
Senate 20510
Smithsonian Institution 20560
Supreme Court of the U S 20543
Textile Trade Policy Group 20508
Trade & Development Agency 20523
Trade Policy Cmte 20508
U S Botanic Garden 20024
U S Coast Guard 20593
U S Customs Serv 20229
U S Information Agcy 20547
U S International Development Cooperation Agcy 20523
U S Marine Corps 20380
U S National Central Bureau-International Criminal Police Org (INTERPOL-Washington) 20530
U S Off of Special Counsel 20036
U S Postal Serv 20260
U S Secret Serv 20223
U S Sentencing Cmsn 20002
U S Tax Court 20217
White House Cmsn on Presidential Scholars 20202
White House Off 20500

Hospitals

DC General Hosp 20003
Georgetown Univ Med Ctr 20007
George Washington Univ Hosp 20037
Greater Southeast Community Hosp 20032
Howard Univ Hosp 20060
Providence Hosp 20017
Sibley Memorial Hosp 20016
Walter Reed Army Med Ctr 20307
Washington Hosp Ctr 20010

Hotels/Motels

ANA Hotel 20037
The Capital Hilton 20036
Grand Hyatt at Washington Center 20001
Hilton & Towers 20009
Holiday Inn, Capitol 20024
Holiday Inn on the Hill 20001
Hotel Washington 20004
Hyatt Regency on Capitol Hill 20001
Loew's L'enfant Plaza 20024
The Madison 20005
Marriott 20037
Marriott Metro Center 20005
Omni Shoreham 20008
Renaissance Mayflower 20036
Renaissance, Washington DC 20001
Sheraton 20008
Sheraton, City Centre 20037
The Willard Inter-Continental 20004

Military Installations

Armed Forces Inst of Pathology 20306
Bolling Air Force Base 20332
Coast Guard Headquarters 20593
Defense Fuel Support Point Anacostia 20011
Fort Lesley J McNair/ Military Dist of Washington, DC 20319
Walter Reed Army Medical Ctr 20307

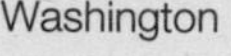

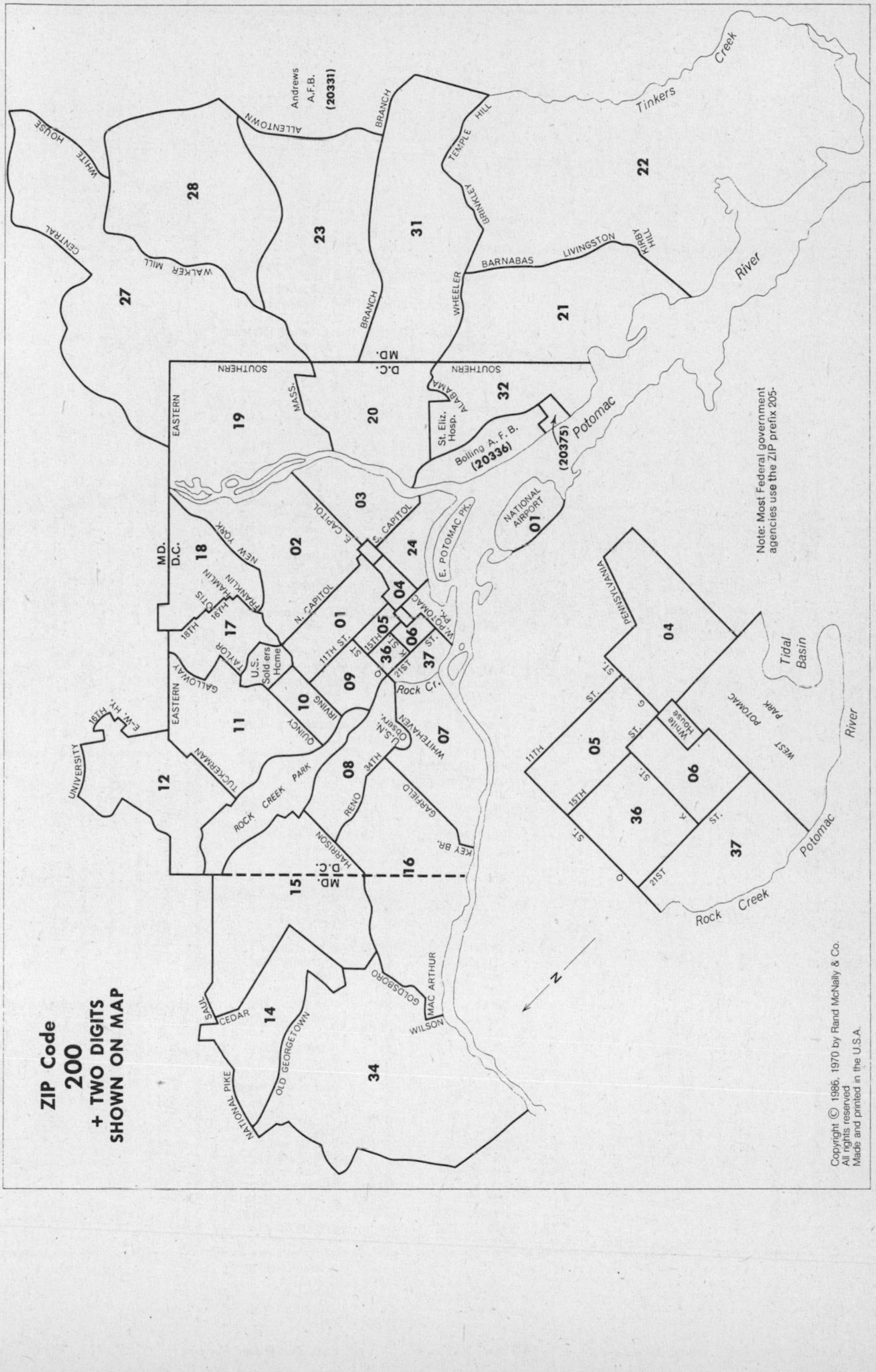

ZIP Code 200 + TWO DIGITS SHOWN ON MAP

Note: Most Federal government agencies use the ZIP prefix 205-

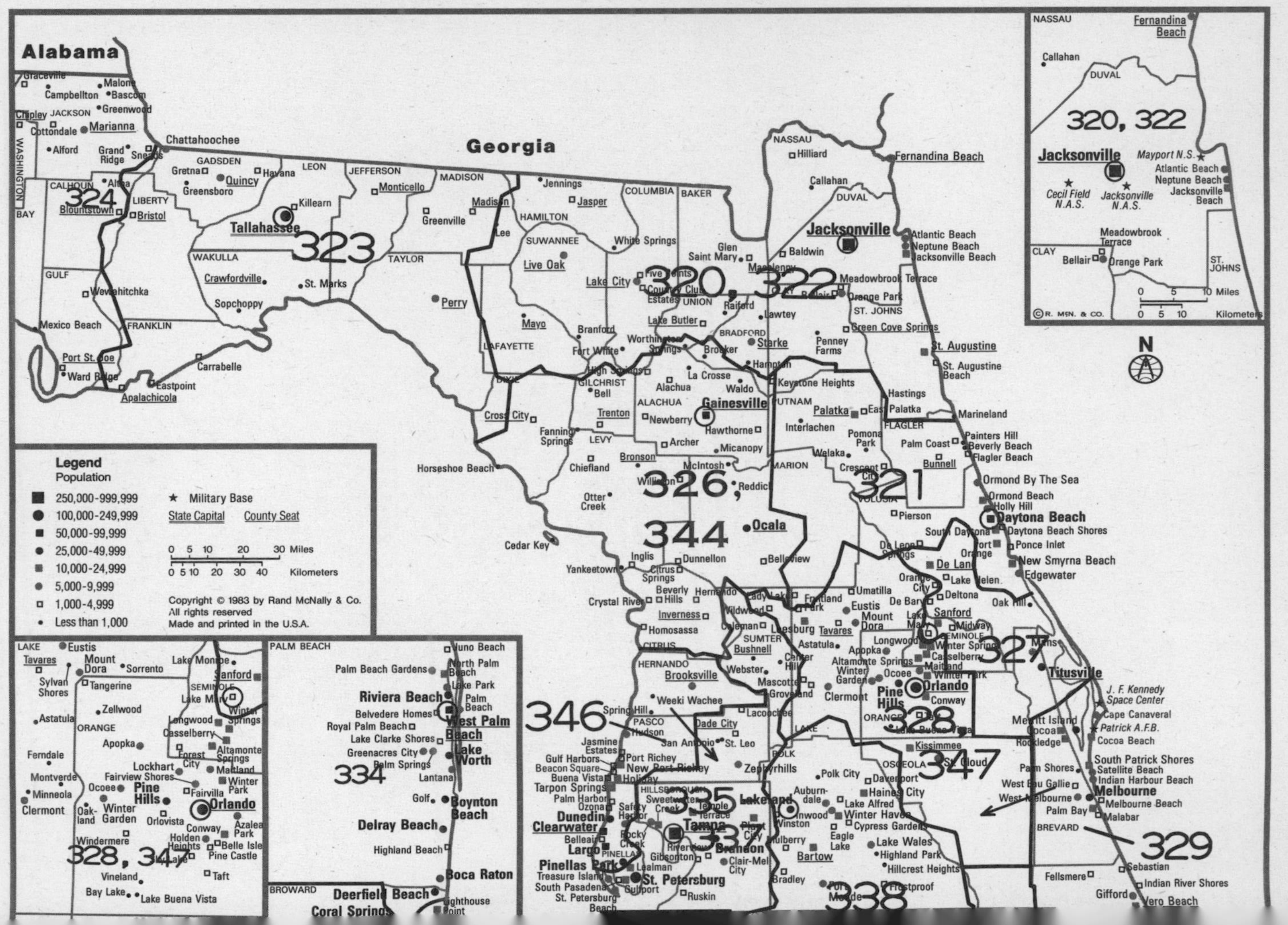

Alabama
Georgia
Legend
Population
250,000-999,999
100,000-249,999
50,000-99,999
25,000-49,999
10,000-24,999
5,000-9,999
1,000-4,999
Less than 1,000
★ Military Base
State Capital
County Seat
0 5 10 20 30 Miles
0 5 10 20 30 40 Kilometers
Copyright © 1983 by Rand McNally & Co.
All rights reserved
Made and printed in the U.S.A.
Campbellton
Malone
Bascom
Greenwood
Marianna
Cottondale
Alford
Grand Ridge
Chattahoochee
Gretna
Quincy
Havana
Greensboro
Killearn
Tallahassee
Monticello
Madison
Greenville
Jennings
Jasper
White Springs
Live Oak
Lake City
Crawfordville
St. Marks
Sopchoppy
Perry
Mayo
Wewahitchka
Mexico Beach
Port St. Joe
Ward Ridge
Carrabelle
Eastpoint
Apalachicola
Blountstown
Bristol
Jacksonville
Fernandina Beach
Hilliard
Callahan
Baldwin
Atlantic Beach
Neptune Beach
Jacksonville Beach
Meadowbrook Terrace
Orange Park
Green Cove Springs
Penney Farms
St. Augustine
St. Augustine Beach
Starke
Lawtey
Raiford
Lake Butler
Keystone Heights
Hastings
Palatka
East Palatka
Interlachen
Marineland
Palm Coast
Bunnell
Painters Hill
Beverly Beach
Flagler Beach
Gainesville
Alachua
La Crosse
Waldo
Newberry
Hawthorne
Archer
Micanopy
McIntosh
Reddick
Trenton
Bell
Fanning Springs
Chiefland
Bronson
Otter Creek
Cedar Key
Horseshoe Beach
Cross City
Ocala
Belleview
Dunnellon
Inglis
Yankeetown
Crystal River
Inverness
Homosassa
Brooksville
Weeki Wachee
Spring Hill
Hudson
Dade City
San Antonio
St. Leo
Zephyrhills
Bushnell
Webster
Wildwood
Coleman
Leesburg
Tavares
Eustis
Mount Dora
Umatilla
Ormond By The Sea
Ormond Beach
Holly Hill
Daytona Beach
Daytona Beach Shores
Ponce Inlet
New Smyrna Beach
Edgewater
Oak Hill
Pierson
De Land
Orange City
Deltona
Sanford
Titusville
Orlando
Pine Hills
Conway
Clermont
Kissimmee
St. Cloud
J. F. Kennedy Space Center
Cape Canaveral
Patrick A.F.B.
Cocoa Beach
Cocoa
Rockledge
Merritt Island
Palm Shores
South Patrick Shores
Satellite Beach
Indian Harbour Beach
Melbourne
Melbourne Beach
West Melbourne
Palm Bay
Malabar
Sebastian
Indian River Shores
Vero Beach
Gifford
Fellsmere
Lakeland
Polk City
Davenport
Haines City
Lake Alfred
Winter Haven
Cypress Gardens
Eagle Lake
Bartow
Lake Wales
Highland Park
Hillcrest Heights
Frostproof
Mulberry
Bradley
Tampa
Brandon
Temple Terrace
Plant City
Ruskin
St. Petersburg
Gulfport
Pinellas Park
Largo
Clearwater
Dunedin
Tarpon Springs
Palm Harbor
Port Richey
New Port Richey
Treasure Island
South Pasadena
St. Petersburg Beach
Juno Beach
North Palm Beach
Lake Park
Palm Beach
Palm Beach Gardens
Riviera Beach
West Palm Beach
Lake Worth
Lantana
Boynton Beach
Delray Beach
Highland Beach
Boca Raton
Deerfield Beach
Coral Springs
Lighthouse Point
Sorrento
Tangerine
Zellwood
Apopka
Lake Monroe
Winter Springs
Longwood
Casselberry
Altamonte Springs
Maitland
Winter Park
Fairvilla
Lockhart
Ocoee
Winter Garden
Oakland
Windermere
Orlovista
Azalea Park
Belle Isle
Pine Castle
Taft
Vineland
Bay Lake
Lake Buena Vista
Minneola
Montverde
Ferndale
Astatula

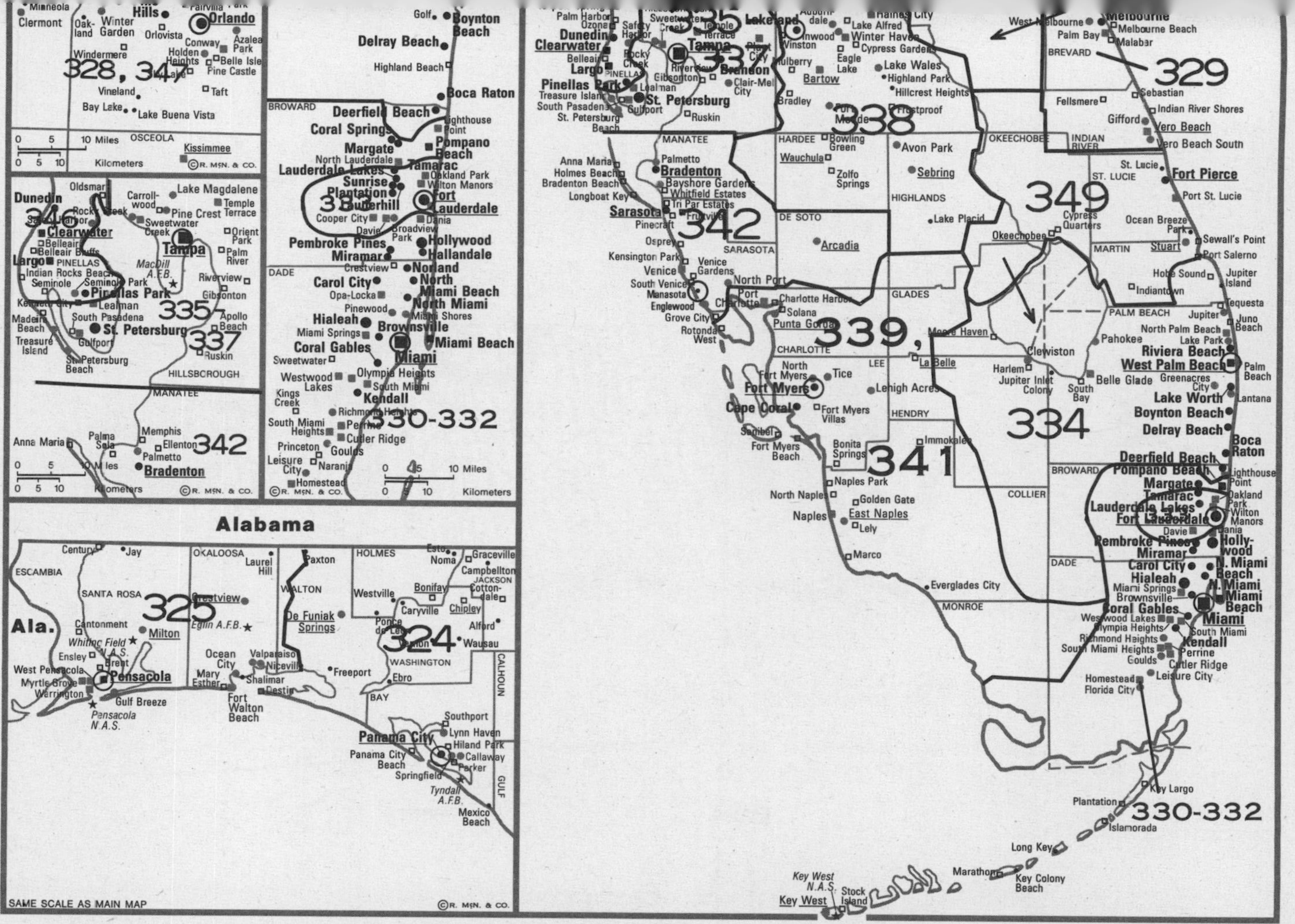
328, 347
Orlando
Kissimmee
335
337
342
Alabama
325
324
Ala.
Pensacola
Milton
Panama City
De Funiak Springs
SAME SCALE AS MAIN MAP
330-332
Boynton Beach
Delray Beach
Boca Raton
Deerfield Beach
Coral Springs
Pompano Beach
Fort Lauderdale
Hollywood
Hallandale
Pembroke Pines
Miramar
Carol City
Hialeah
Coral Gables
Miami
Miami Beach
Kendall
329
Melbourne
Vero Beach
Fort Pierce
349
Stuart
West Palm Beach
Riviera Beach
Lake Worth
334
338
Lakeland
Tampa
Clearwater
Dunedin
Largo
Pinellas Park
St. Petersburg
Bradenton
Sarasota
Arcadia
Sebring
339,
341
Fort Myers
Cape Coral
Punta Gorda
Naples
East Naples
Everglades City
Key Largo
Islamorada
Marathon
Key West
©R. MCN. & CO.

A (Part of Palm Beach)‡ 33480
Aberdeen 33437
Abe Springs 32424
Acline 33950
Adams Beach 32347
Adamsville, *Hillsborough* 33534
Adamsville, *Sumter* 34785
Airport Siding (Part of Jacksonville) 32229
Alachua 32615*
... 32616†
Aladdin City 33187
Alamana 32168
Alderman Park (Part of Jacksonville) 32211
Alford 32420
Allandale 32119
Allanton 32404
Allapattah (Part of Miami)‡ 33142*
... 33242†
Allentown 32570
Alliance 32448
Alligator Point 32327
Aloma (Part of Winter Park) 32792*
... 32793†
Alpine Heights 32433
Altamonte Mall (Part of Altamonte Springs)‡ 32701
Altamonte Springs 32701
... 32714-16
For specific ZIP Codes call (888) 275-8777, or your local postmaster.
Altha 32421
Alton 32066
Altoona 32702
Alturas 33820
Alumni Village (Part of Tallahassee) 32310
Alva♦ 33920
Amelia City 32034
Amelia Island Plantation‡ 32034
American Beach 32034
Anclote 34691
Andalusia 32110
Andover Golf Estates 33169
Andover Lake Estates 33169
... 33179
For specific ZIP Codes call (888) 275-8777, or your local postmaster.
Andrews 32046
Angel City 32952
Angler Park 33037
Angus Valley 33544
Anna Maria 34216
Anthony 32617
Antioch 33565
Apalachee Ridge (Part of Tallahassee) 32301
Apalachicola 32320*
... 32329†
Apollo Beach♦ 33572
Apopka 32703-04
... 32712
For specific ZIP Codes call (888) 275-8777, or your local postmaster.
Aquarina 32951
Araquey 32095
Arbor Hills (Part of Tallahassee) 32308
Arcadia 34265†
... 34266*
Archer 32618
Argyle 32422
Aripeka 34679
Arlington (Part of Jacksonville)‡ 32211
... 32239
... 32277
For specific ZIP Codes call (888) 275-8777, or your local postmaster.
Arlington Hills (Part of Jacksonville) 32211
Arlingwood (Part of Jacksonville) 32211
Armstrong 32033
Arran 32327
Arredondo 32608
Asbury Lake♦ 32043
Ashton 34771
Ashville 32331
Astatula 34705
Astor♦ 32102
Astor Park 32102
Astronaut Trail (Part of Titusville)‡ 32782
Athena 32347
Atlantic (Part of Coral Springs) 33077
Atlantic Beach 32233
Atlantic Boulevard Estates (Part of Jacksonville) 32225
Atlantic Heights (Part of Miami Beach) 33139
Atlantis 33462
Auburn 32536
Auburndale 33823
Aucilla 32344
Audubon 32952
Aurantia 32754
Autumn Woods 34683
Avalon Beach 32583
Aventura♦ 33160
... 33180
For specific ZIP Codes call (888) 275-8777, or your local postmaster.
Aventura Mall (Part of Aventura) 33180
Avenues, The (Part of Jacksonville) 32256
Avondale (Part of Jacksonville) 32205
Avon Park 33825*
... 33826†
Avon Park Air Force Base 33825
Avon Park Estates 33825
Avon Park Lakes 33825
Azalea Park♦ 32807
Babson Park♦ 33827
Bagdad♦ 32530
Bahia Oaks 34474
Bahia Shores (Part of St. Pete Beach) 33706
Baker 32531
Baker Settlement 32464
Bakersville 32092
Bal-Alex Estates 32561
Baldwin 32234
Bal Harbour 33154
Bal Harbour Shops (Part of Bal Harbour) 33154
Ballantine Manor 34243
Ballast Point (Part of Tampa) 33611
Balm 33503
Bamboo 34748
Barberville 32105
Bardin 32177
Bardmoor 33771
Bare Beach 33440
Barefoot Bay 32976
Barrineau Park 32577
Barth 32577
Bartow 33830*
... 33831†
Bascom 32423
Basinger 34972
Baskin♦ 33774
... 33778
For specific ZIP Codes call (888) 275-8777, or your local postmaster.
Bassville Park♦ 34788
Basswood Estates 34972
Baum 32308
Bay Acres 34229
Bayard (Part of Jacksonville) 32256
Bay Crest Park 33615
Bay Grove 32439
Bay Harbor Islands 33154
Bayhead, *Bay* 32466
Bay Head, *Pasco* 33523
Bay Hill♦ 32819
... 34786
For specific ZIP Codes call (888) 275-8777, or your local postmaster.
Bay Lake 34736
Bayonet Point♦ 34667
Bayou George 32405
Bay Pines♦ 33744
Bay Point, *Bay* 32411
Bay Point (Part of Miami) 33137
Bayport 34607
Bayridge 32703
Bayshore 33917
Bayshore Gardens♦ 34207
Bayshore Manor 33917
Bay Springs 32568
Bayview 32401
Bay Vista (Part of North Miami) 33181
Bay Vista (Part of St. Petersburg)‡ 33712
Bayway (Part of St. Petersburg) 33715
Baywood 32140
Baywood Village 34683
Beach‡ 32963*
... 32964†
Beach Haven 32507
Beach Highlands 32459
Beach Park (Part of Tampa) 33609
... 33629
For specific ZIP Codes call (888) 275-8777, or your local postmaster.
Beachside‡ 32175†
... 32176*
Beachville 32071
Beachwood (Part of Jacksonville) 32246
Beacon Beach 32403
Beacon Groves 34683
Beacon Hill 32456
Beacon Hills (Part of Jacksonville) 32225
Beacon Lakes 34691
Beacon Light (Part of Lighthouse Point) 33064
Beacon Square 34691
Bealsville 33567
Bean City 33440
Bear Creek 32401
Bear Lake 32703
Bearss Plaza‡ 33612
Beauclere Gardens (Part of Jacksonville) 32257
Beaver Creek 32531
Becker 32097
Beckhamtown 32640
Beeghly Heights (Part of Jacksonville) 32218
Bee Ridge♦ 34233
Bel-Air (Part of Sanford) 32771
Belair Beach 32408
Bell 32619
Bellair 32073
Bellair Plaza (Part of Daytona Beach) 32118
Belleair 33756
Belleair Beach 33786
Belleair Bluffs 33770
Belleair Shore 33786
Belle Glade 33430
Belle Glade Camp♦ 33430
Belle Isle 32809
... 32812
For specific ZIP Codes call (888) 275-8777, or your local postmaster.
Belleview 34420-21
For specific ZIP Codes call (888) 275-8777, or your local postmaster.
Belleview Heights 34420
Bellview♦ 32506
... 32526
For specific ZIP Codes call (888) 275-8777, or your local postmaster.
Bellwood 32780
Belvedere Homes 33409
Benbow 33440
Bennett 32466
Bent Tree Village 34241
Ben White Raceway (Part of Orlando) 32810
Beresford 32720
Berkshire Estates 34241
Berry 33868
Berrydale 32565
Bertha 32792
Bethany 34251
Bethel 32327
Bethlehem 32425
Bethune Beach 32169
Betmar Acres 33541
Betton Hills (Part of Tallahassee) 32312
Beulah, *Escambia* 32526
Beulah, *Orange* 34787
Beverly Beach 32136
Beverly Hills♦ 34464-65
For specific ZIP Codes call (888) 275-8777, or your local postmaster.
Beverly Hills (Part of Jacksonville) 32208
Beverly Terrace 34234
Bevilles Corner 33513
Big Bayou (Part of St. Petersburg)‡ 33705*
... 33739†
Big Coppitt Key♦ 33040
Big Cypress Seminole Indian Reservation 33440
Big Pine Key♦ 33043
Big Scrub 32179
Biltmore (Part of Jacksonville) 32254
Biltmore Beach 32408
Bird Key (Part of Sarasota) 34236
Biscayne Gardens 33168-69
For specific ZIP Codes call (888) 275-8777, or your local postmaster.
Biscayne One (Part of Miami)‡ 33111†
... 33131*
Biscayne Park 33161
Biscayne Plaza Shopping Center (Part of Miami) 33138
Bithlo♦ 32807
Black Creek 32439
Black Jacks 32680
Blackman 32531
Black Rock 32097
Bland 32615
Blanton 33523
Blichton 34482
Bloomingdale 33594
Blountstown 32424
Bloxham 32310
Blue Gulf Beach 32459
Blue Lake 32720
Blue Mountain Beach 32459
Blue Springs 34797
Bluff Springs 32535
Boardman 32633
Boca Grande 33921
Boca Pointe♦ 33433
Boca Raton 33427-29
... 33431-34
... 33481
... 33486-88
... 33496-98
For specific ZIP Codes call (888) 275-8777, or your local postmaster.
Boca West♦ 33434
Bogia 32568
Bokeelia 33922
Bonaventure 33326
Bonifay 32425
Bonita Beach 34134
Bonita Shores 34134
Bonita Springs 33959
... 34134-36
For specific ZIP Codes call (888) 275-8777, or your local postmaster.
Bonnie Loch 33064
Bookertown 32771
Bostwick 32007
Boulougne 32046
Bowden (Part of Jacksonville) 32216
Bowling Green 33834
Boyd 32347
Boyette 33547
Boynton Beach 33424-26
... 33435-37
... 33474
For specific ZIP Codes call (888) 275-8777, or your local postmaster.
Boynton Beach Mall (Part of Boynton Beach) 33426
Boys Ranch 32060
Braden Castle (Part of Bradenton) 34208
Braden River 34201-03
... 34208
For specific ZIP Codes call (888) 275-8777, or your local postmaster.
Bradenton 34201-10
... 34280-82
For specific ZIP Codes call (888) 275-8777, or your local postmaster.
Brandon Town Center 33511
Bradenton Beach 34217
Bradfordville 32312
Bradley 33835
Bradshaw Acres 34711
Brandon♦ 33509-11
For specific ZIP Codes call (888) 275-8777, or your local postmaster.
Brandon Town Center 33511
Branford 32008
Brannonville 32401
Bratt 32535
Brent♦ 32503
... 32505
For specific ZIP Codes call (888) 275-8777, or your local postmaster.
Brentwood (Part of Jacksonville) 32206
Brentwood, *Sarasota* 34232
Brickell Postal Store (Part of Miami) 33231
Bright (Part of Hialeah)‡ 33013
Brighton 34972
Brighton Seminole Indian Reservation 33471
Briny Breezes 33435
Bristol 32321
Britton Plaza (Part of Tampa) 33611
Broadview Park♦ 33317
Broadwater (Part of St. Petersburg) 33711
Brock Crossroad 32463
Bronson 32621
Brooker 32622
Brooklyn (Part of Jacksonville) 32204
Brookridge♦ 34613
Brooksville 34601-05
... 34609-10
... 34613-14
For specific ZIP Codes call (888) 275-8777, or your local postmaster.
Browardale♦ 33311
Broward Mall (Part of Plantation) 33388
Brownsdale 32565
Brownsville, *Dade*♦ 33142
Brownsville, *Escambia* 32505
Browntown 32440
Brownville 34266
Bruce 32455
Bruceville 34488
Bryant 33439
Bryceville 32009
Brynwood 33912
Buccaneer Estates 33054
Buchanan 33890
Buckhead Ridge♦ 34974
Buckhorn 32358
Buckingham 33905
Buckingham West 32601
Buena Ventura Lakes♦ 34743
Buena Vista (Part of Miami)‡ 33137
Buena Vista, *Jackson* 32460
Buena Vista, *Orange* 32830
Buena Vista, *Pasco* 34691
Buffalo 32189
Bunche Park♦ 33054
Bunker, *DeSoto* 34266
Bunker, *Walton* 32459
Bunnell 32110
Burbank 32134
Burnett's Lake (Part of Alachua) 32615
Bushnell 33513
Butler Beach♦ 32084
Byrneville 32535
Callahan 32011
Callaway 32404
Camellia Gardens 32809
Camelot Park (Part of Tallahassee) 32301
Cameron City 32771
Campbell 34746
Campbellton 32426
Camps Mine 34601
Campton 32567
Campville 32640
Canaan 32771
Canal Point 33438
Candler 32111
Cannon Town 32531
Canoe Creek 34990
Cantonment 32533
Cape Canaveral 32920

Cape Canaveral Air Station 32920
Cape Coral 32904
33909-10
33914-15
33990-91
For specific ZIP Codes call (888) 275-8777, or your local postmaster.
Cape Coral Central‡ (Part of Cape Coral) 33915
Cape Haze 33946
Capital Hills (Part of Tallahassee) 32308
Capitola 32311
Capps 32336
Capri Isle (Part of Treasure Island) 33706
Captiva 33924
Carleton 32640
Carl Fisher (Part of Miami Beach) 33239
Carlson 33538
Carlton Village 32159
Carol City♦ 33055-56
For specific ZIP Codes call (888) 275-8777, or your local postmaster.
Carr 32421
Carrabelle 32322
Carrabelle Beach 32322
Carraway 32177
Carrollwood♦ 33618
33624
33688
For specific ZIP Codes call (888) 275-8777, or your local postmaster.
Carters Corner 33823
Carver (Part of Jacksonville)‡ 32209
Carver Manor (Part of Jacksonville) 32209
Carver Ranches 33023
Caryville 32427
Casa Bianco 32344
Casey Key 34275
Cason Inglis Acres 34449
Cassadaga (Part of Deltona) 32706
Casselberry 32707
32718
32730
For specific ZIP Codes call (888) 275-8777, or your local postmaster.
Cassia 32726
Causeway (Part of Ft. Lauderdale)‡ 33316*
33346†
Causeway Isles (Part of St. Petersburg) 33707
Cedar Creek 34488
Cedar Grove 32401
32405
For specific ZIP Codes call (888) 275-8777, or your local postmaster.
Cedar Hammock 34207
Cedar Hills Estates (Part of Jacksonville) 32210
Cedar Key 32625
Cedar Lake Estates 34428
Cedar Point (Part of Jacksonville) 32226
Cedar Shores (Part of Ocala) 34471
Center Hill 33514
Centerville Station (Part of Tallahassee)‡ 32308
32312
32317
For specific ZIP Codes call (888) 275-8777, or your local postmaster.
Central (Part of St. Petersburg)‡ 33713-14
33784
For specific ZIP Codes call (888) 275-8777, or your local postmaster.
Central Shopping Plaza (Part of Miami) 33126
Century 32535
Century Village♦ 33417
Century Village 33434
Cerrogordo 32464
Chain O'Lakes 32767
Chaires 32311
Charlotte Beach 33927

Charlotte Harbor♦ 33980
Charlotte Park♦ 33950
Chaseville (Part of Jacksonville) 32276
Chason 32421
Chassahowitzka 34447
Chatmar 34432
Chattahoochee 32324
Cherry Lake, *Madison* 32340
Cherry Lake, *Sumter* 32159
Chester 32097
Chestnut Hill Ranches 34482
Chiefland 32626*
32644†
Chipley 32428
Chipola 32421
Chipola Terrace 32448
Choctaw 32459
Choctaw Beach 32439
Chokoloskee 34138
Christina 33813
Christmas 32709
Chuluota♦ 32766
Chumuckla 32571
Cinco Bayou 32548
Cisky Park 34748
Citra 32113
Citronelle 34433
Citrus (Part of Inverness)‡ 34450
Citrus Center 33471
Citrus Park 33624
Citrus Springs♦ 34433
Clair-Mel City 33619
Clarcona 32710
Clark 32643
Clarksville 32430
Clear Springs, *Okaloosa* 32567
Clear Springs, *Walton* 32567
Clearwater 33755-67
For specific ZIP Codes call (888) 275-8777, or your local postmaster.
Clearwater Beach (Part of Clearwater)‡ 33767
Clearwater Coast Guard Air Station 33762
Clearwater Mall (Part of Clearwater) 33764
Clermont 34711*
34712†
Cleveland 33982
Cleveland Street (Part of Clearwater)‡ 33755*
33757†
Clewiston 33440
Clifton (Part of Jacksonville) 32211
Clinton Heights 33525
Cloud Lake 33406
Cluster Springs 32433
Coastland Center (Part of Naples) 34102
Cobbtown 32565
Cocoa 32922-24
32926-27
For specific ZIP Codes call (888) 275-8777, or your local postmaster.
Cocoa Beach 32931*
32932†
Cocoa West♦ 32922
Coconut Creek 33063
33066
33073
33097
For specific ZIP Codes call (888) 275-8777, or your local postmaster.
Coconut Grove‡ 33133-34
33233
For specific ZIP Codes call (888) 275-8777, or your local postmaster.
Cody 32344
Colee (Part of Fort Lauderdale)‡ 33301*
33303†
Coleman 33521
College Park (Part of Jacksonville) 32209
College Park (Part of Ocala) 34474
College Park (Part of Orlando)‡ 32804
College Point 32444
Collier City (Part of Pompano Beach) 33069
Colonial Gables 34232

Colonial Hills 34652
Colonial Manor (Part of Jacksonville) 32207
Colonial Plaza Mall (Part of Orlando) 32803
Colonialtown (Part of Orlando)‡ 32803
Columbia 32055
Commerce (Part of Tampa)‡ 33602
Compass Lake 32420
Compass Lake Hills 32420
Conch Key 33050
Concord 32333
Conner 34488
Connersville 33830
Conway 32812
Cooks Hammock 32066
Cooper City 33226
33228
33230
For specific ZIP Codes call (888) 275-8777, or your local postmaster.
Copeland 34137
Copeland Settlement 32609
Coquina Key (Part of St. Petersburg) 33705
Cora 32565
Coral Cove 34231
Coral Gables 33114
33124
33143-44
33146
33156
33158
33234
For specific ZIP Codes call (888) 275-8777, or your local postmaster.
Coral Gardens 34997
Coral Ridge Mall (Part of Fort Lauderdale)‡ 33306*
33339†
Coral Springs 33065
33167
33171
33175-76
For specific ZIP Codes call (888) 275-8777, or your local postmaster.
Coral Square (Part of Coral Springs) 33071
Coral Way Village 33155
Coralwood Mall (Part of Cape Coral) 33904
Cordova (Part of Pensacola) 32503
Cordova Lakes (Part of Bradenton) 34209
Cordova Mall (Part of Pensacola) 32504
Corkscrew 34142
Corley Island 34748
Cornwell 33857
Coronet 33566
Corry Station Naval Training Center 32511
Cortez 34215
Cortez Road (Part of Bradenton)‡ 34210
Cottage Hill 32533
Cottondale 32431
Cotton Plant 34474
Country Club Acres 33484
Country Club Estates, *Columbia* 32055
Country Club Estates, *Polk* 33801
Country Club Manor (Part of Sanford) 32771
Countryside, *Marion*‡ 34481
Countryside (Part of Clearwater) 33761
Countryside Mall (Part of Clearwater) 33761
Countryway 33635
Courtenay 32952
Cove (Part of Panama City)‡ 32401
Cox 32424
Coytown (Part of Orlando)‡ 32803
Crackertown (Part of Inglis) 34449
Crandall 32097
Crawford 32009
Crawfordville 32326†
32327*
Crescent Beach, *St. Johns*♦ 32086

Crescent Beach, *Sarasota* 34242
Crescent City 32112
Crescent Shores Heights 32157
Crestview 32536
32539
For specific ZIP Codes call (888) 275-8777, or your local postmaster.
Crewsville 33890
Crooked Lake Park♦ 33853
Croom-A-Coochee 33597
Cross City 32628
Cross County Mall 33409
Cross Creek 32640
Crossroads‡ 33709-10
33743
For specific ZIP Codes call (888) 275-8777, or your local postmaster.
Crows Bluff 32720
Crystal Beach 34681
Crystal Lake 32409
Crystal River 34423-29
For specific ZIP Codes call (888) 275-8777, or your local postmaster.
Crystal Springs 33524
Cudjoe 33042
Cunningham Acres 33541
Curlew 34683
Curtis Mill 32358
Cutler Ridge 33157
33189
For specific ZIP Codes call (888) 275-8777, or your local postmaster.
Cypress (Part of Pompano Beach)‡ 33060
Cypress, Jackson 32432
Cypress Creek 33850
Cypress Gardens 33884
Cypress Lake Estates 33919
Cypress Point 32131
Cypress Quarters♦ 34972
Cyprus Village‡ 33014
Dade City 33525*
33526†
Dade City North♦ 33523
Dadeland Mall 33156
Dalkeith 32465
Dallas 34491
Dames Point (Part of Jacksonville) 32226
Dania 33004
Danks Corner 34491
Darby 33525
Darlington 32464
Davenport 33836†
33837*
Davie 33312
33314
33317
33324-25
33328-32
33355
For specific ZIP Codes call (888) 275-8777, or your local postmaster.
Davis Islands (Part of Tampa) 33606
Day 32013
Daytona Beach 32114-27
For specific ZIP Codes call (888) 275-8777, or your local postmaster.
Daytona Beach Shores 32116
Daytona Highbridge Estates 32114
Daytona Mall (Part of Daytona Beach) 32114
Daytona Park Estates 32720
DeBary 32713
Deerfield Beach 33441-43
For specific ZIP Codes call (888) 275-8777, or your local postmaster.
Deerfield Lakes 32011
Deerfield Mall (Part of Deerfield Beach) 33442
Deering Bay 33158
Deerland 32536
Deer Park 32901
Deer Point 32405
Deerwood (Part of Jacksonville) 32256
De Funiak Springs 32433*
32435†
Dekle Beach 32347

DeLand 32720-21
32723-24
For specific ZIP Codes call (888) 275-8777, or your local postmaster.
DeLand Highlands 32720
De Leon Springs♦ 32130
Delespine 32927
Dellwood, *Jackson* 32442
Dellwood (Part of Tallahassee) 32303
Delray Beach 33444-48
33482-84
For specific ZIP Codes call (888) 275-8777, or your local postmaster.
Delray Beach Mall (Part of Delray Beach) 33483
Delray Garden Estates 33484
Del Rio♦ 33617
Deltona 32725
32728
32738-39
For specific ZIP Codes call (888) 275-8777, or your local postmaster.
Deltona Pines (Part of Deltona) 32738
Del Tura 33903
Denaud 33935
Denver 32112
De Soto Acres 34235
De Soto City 33870
Desoto Lakes♦ 34235
DeSoto Square 34205
Destin 32540†
32541*
Devils Garden 33440
Dickerson City 32583
Dills 32344
Dinsmore (Part of Jacksonville)‡ 32219
Diplomat Mall (Part of Hallandale)‡ 33009
Dirego Park 32405
Dixie Heights 32962
Dixieland (Part of Lakeland)‡ 33803*
33806†
Dixie Ranch Acres 34972
Dixie Village (Part of Orlando)‡ 32806
Doctor Phillips♦ 32819
Doctors Inlet 32030
Dogtown 32351
Dogwood Estates 34601
Dogwood Heights 32446
Dogwood Lake Estates 32425
Dona Vista 32784
Dorcas 32539
Douglas City 32351
Douglas Crossroads 32455
Dover♦ 33527
Dover Shores (Part of Orlando)‡ 32806
Dowling Park 32060
Downtown (Part of Boca Raton)‡ 33429†
33432*
Downtown (Part of Boynton Beach)‡ 33435
Downtown (Part of Brooksville)‡ 34601
Downtown (Part of Daytona Beach)‡ 32115
32118
For specific ZIP Codes call (888) 275-8777, or your local postmaster.
Downtown (Part of Delray Beach)‡ 33444
Downtown (Part of Fort Myers)‡ 33901*
33902†
Downtown (Part of Fort Pierce)‡ 34950
Downtown (Part of Gainesville)‡ 32601
Downtown (Part of Jacksonville)‡ 32202
Downtown (Part of Lakeland)‡ 33802
Downtown (Part of Milton)‡ 32570
Downtown (Part of Naples)‡ 34106

Downtown (Part of Orlando)‡ 32801*
32802†
Downtown (Part of Pensacola)‡ 32501
Downtown (Part of Sarasota)‡ 34236
Downtown (Part of Tampa)‡ 33601-02
For specific ZIP Codes call (888) 275-8777, or your local postmaster.
Downtown (Part of West Palm Beach)‡ 33401*
33402†
Downtown Station (Part of Panama City)‡ 32402
Drayton Island 32139
Dreamworld (Part of Sanford) 32771
Drew Park (Part of Tampa) 33614
Drifton 32344
Dr. M. L. King, Jr.‡ 33147*
33247†
Druid Hills 32751
Duck Key 33050
Duette 33834
Dundee 33838
Dune Allen Beach 32459
Dunedin 34697†
34698*
Dunedin Isles (Part of Dunedin) 34698
Dunnellon 34430-34
For specific ZIP Codes call (888) 275-8777, or your local postmaster.
Dupont 32110
Dupont Center 32086
Durant 33530
Durham 32424
Duval (Part of Jacksonville) 32218
Dyal 32011
Eagle Lake 33839
Eagle Ridge 33912
Eagles Nest 33852
Earleton 32631
East Avenue (Part of Sarasota)‡ 34237
Eastbrook 32792
Eastern Shores (Part of North Miami Beach) 33160
Eastgate (Part of Tallahassee) 32308
Eastgate (Part of Winter Park)‡ 32792
East Hill (Part of Pensacola)‡ 32503
East Lake 33610
East Lake Harris Estates 34705
Eastlake Square 33610
Eastlake Weir 32133
East Lake Woodlands 34677
East Milton 32583
East Naples♦ 34112
East Orlando Estates 32822
East Palatka♦ 32131
Eastpoint♦ 32328
East Port Plaza (Part of Port St. Lucie) 34952
East Rockland Key 33040
East Side (Part of Altamonte Springs)‡ 32715
East Silver Springs Shores 32179
East Tampa 33619
East Williston 32696
Eaton Park 33840
Eatonville 32751
Eau Gallie (Part of Melbourne)‡ 32934-36
32940
For specific ZIP Codes call (888) 275-8777, or your local postmaster.
Ebb 32331
Ebro 32437
Edgar 32149
Edgewater (Part of Miami) 33137
Edgewater, *Volusia* 32132
32141
For specific ZIP Codes call (888) 275-8777, or your local postmaster.
Edgewater Gulf Beach (Part of Panama City Beach) 32407
Edgewood 32809
32839
For specific ZIP Codes call (888) 275-8777, or your local postmaster.
Edgewood Manor (Part of Jacksonville) 32209
Edison 33547
Edison Center (Part of Miami)‡ 33151
Edison Mall (Part of Fort Myers) 33901
Eglin Air Force Base 32542
Eglin Village 32544
Egypt Lake♦ 33614
El Chico 33040
Elder Springs 32773
Electra 32179
Elfers 34680
El Jobean 33927
Elkton 32033
Ellaville, *Jackson* 32426
Ellaville, *Suwannee* 32060
Ellinor Village (Part of Ormond Beach) 32175
Ellison Acres 32168
Ellisville 32055
Ellzey 32683
Eloise 33880
Eloise Woods 33884
El Portal 33138
33150
For specific ZIP Codes call (888) 275-8777, or your local postmaster.
Elsi De Monde Heights 32448
Elwood Park 34208
Empire Point (Part of Jacksonville) 32207
Emporia 32180
Englewood (Part of Jacksonville) 32207
Englewood 34223-24
34295
For specific ZIP Codes call (888) 275-8777, or your local postmaster.
Englewood Beach 34223
Englewood Isles 34223
English Estates 32730
Enon 32568
Enterprise 32725
Eppes Heights (Part of Tallahassee) 32304
Eridu 32331
Erin Park 33872
Errol Estates 32712
Escambia Farms 32531
Espanola 32110
Esperenza 32131
Estero 33928
Estiffanulga 32321
Esto 32425
Eucheeanna 32433
Euclid (Part of St. Petersburg)‡ 33704*
33734†
Eureka 32134
Eustis 32726-27
32736
For specific ZIP Codes call (888) 275-8777, or your local postmaster.
Eva 33809
Evans Village 32808
Everglades City 34139
Evergreen, *Martin* 34990
Evergreen, *Nassau* 32097
Evinston 32633
Facil 32096
Factory Outlet World-Orlando (Part of Orlando) 32819
Fairbanks 32601
Fairfield 32634
Fair Meadows (Part of Tallahassee) 32304
Fairmont (Part of St. Petersburg) 33711
Fairview Shores 32804
Fairvilla 32804
Fairway Village 33624
Fairyland 32952
Falls, The 33176
Falmouth 32060
Fanlew 32344
Fanning Springs 32680
Fashion Mall, The (Part of Plantation) 33324
Favorita 32110
Feather Sound♦ 33762
Federal Point 32131
Fedhaven 33854
Felda 33930
Fellowship 34482
Fellsmere 32948
Fenholloway 32347
Fernandina Beach 32034*
32035†
Ferndale 34729
Fern Park♦ 32730
Ferry Pass♦ 32504
32514
For specific ZIP Codes call (888) 275-8777, or your local postmaster.
Festus 32344
Fiddlesticks 33912
Fidelis 32565
Fiesta Key 33001
Fisher Island (Part of Miami Beach) 33109
Fisherman's Cove 34997
Fishermans Road 32767
Fish Lake 34744
Five Points (Part of Cocoa)‡ 32922*
32924†
Five Points, *Columbia*♦ 32055
Five Points, *Washington* 32427
Flagami (Part of Miami) 33126
Flagler (Part of Miami)‡ 33101
33128-32
33136
For specific ZIP Codes call (888) 275-8777, or your local postmaster.
Flagler (Part of Key West)‡ 33040
33045
For specific ZIP Codes call (888) 275-8777, or your local postmaster.
Flagler Beach 32136
Flagler Estates 32145
Flagler-Tamiami (Part of Miami) 33126
33144
For specific ZIP Codes call (888) 275-8777, or your local postmaster.
Flamingo 33034
Flamingo Bay 33956
Flamingo Plaza (Part of Hialeah) 33010
Flemington 32686
Fletcher 33612*
33695†
Florahome 32140
Floral Bluff (Part of Jacksonville) 32211
Floral City♦ 34436
Floral Park 33462
Florence Lake 33881
Florence Villa (Part of Winter Haven)‡ 33881
33885
For specific ZIP Codes call (888) 275-8777, or your local postmaster.
Florida A and M University (Part of Tallahassee)‡ 32307
Florida City 33034
Florida Gardens 33460
Floridana Beach 32951
Florida Ridge 32962
Florida State University (Part of Tallahassee)‡ 32313
Florosa 32569
Flowersville 32567
Fluffy Landing 32439
Footman 32952
Forest City 32714
Forest Heights (Part of Tallahassee) 32303
Forest Hills (Part of Tampa)‡ 33612
33682
For specific ZIP Codes call (888) 275-8777, or your local postmaster.
Forest Hills, *Lake* 32720
Forest Hills, *Pasco* 34690
Forest Hills, *Volusia* 32174
Forest Lakes, *Pinellas* 34677
Forest Lakes (Part of Sarasota) 34232
Forest Lakes Park 32179
Forest Ridge Village (Part of Fernandina Beach) 32034
Formosa (Part of Orlando) 32804
Fort Basinger 34972
Fort Caroline Club Estates (Part of Jacksonville) 32277
Fort Drum 34972
Fort George Island (Part of Jacksonville) 32226
Fort Green 33834
Fort Green Springs 33834
Fort King Acres 33541
Fort Lauderdale 33101-26
33128-94
For specific ZIP Codes call (888) 275-8777, or your local postmaster.
Fort Lonesome 33547
Fort McCoy 32134
Fort Meade 33841
Fort Myers 33901-03
33905-08
33911-13
33916-19
33994
For specific ZIP Codes call (888) 275-8777, or your local postmaster.
Fort Myers Beach♦ 33931*
33932†
Fort Myers Shores 33905
Fort Myers Villas 33912
Fort Ogden 34267
Fort Pierce 34945-51
34954
34979-82
For specific ZIP Codes call (888) 275-8777, or your local postmaster.
Fort Pierce Beach (Part of Fort Pierce) 34949
Fort Pierce Shores 34949
Fort Taylor (Part of Key West) 33040
Fort Union 32060
Fort Walton Beach 32547-49
For specific ZIP Codes call (888) 275-8777, or your local postmaster.
Fort White 32038
Fountain 32438
Four Mile Village 32459
Fowler Bluff 32626
Foxcroft (Part of Tallahassee) 32308
Fox Town 33809
Francis 32177
Franklin Park 33916
Franklintown 32034
Freeport 32439
Frink 32430
Frontenac 32927
Frostproof 33843
Fruit Cove 32259
Fruitland 32112
Fruitland Park 34731
Fruitville 34232
Fuller Heights 33860
Fussels Corner 33823
Gainesville 32601-14
32627
32641
32653
For specific ZIP Codes call (888) 275-8777, or your local postmaster.
Gainesville Mall (Part of Gainesville) 32601
Galleria at Fort Lauderdale, The (Part of Fort Lauderdale) 33304
Galliver 32564
Galloway 33810
Galt City 32583
Galt Ocean Mile (Part of Fort Lauderdale) 33308
Garden City (Part of Jacksonville) 32218
Garden City, Okaloosa 32536
Garden Grove Estates 34609
Gardens, The (Part of Palm Beach Gardens) 33410
Gardenville 33534
Gardner 33890
Gaskin 32433
Gateway (Part of Fort Lauderdale)‡ 33338
Gateway Center (Part of Jacksonville) 32208
Gateway Mall (Part of St. Petersburg)‡ 33702*
33742†
Gator Creek Estates 34241
General Mail Facility (Part of Cedar Grove)‡ 32401
General Mail Facility (Part of Daytona Beach)‡ 32114
General Mail Facility (Part of Gainesville)‡ 32608
General Mail Facility (Part of Jacksonville)‡ 32203
General Mail Facility (Part of Miami)‡ 33152
General Mail Facility (Part of Pensacola)‡ 32522-23
For specific ZIP Codes call (888) 275-8777, or your local postmaster.
Geneva 32732
Georgetown, *Madison* 32340
Georgetown, *Putnam* 32139
Georgiana 32952
Gibson 32333
Gibsonia♦ 33809-10
For specific ZIP Codes call (888) 275-8777, or your local postmaster.
Gibsonton 33534
Gifford♦ 32960-61
32967
For specific ZIP Codes call (888) 275-8777, or your local postmaster.
Gilberts Mill 32428
Gillette 34221
Gilmore (Part of Jacksonville) 32276
Glencoe 32168
Glendale (Part of Tallahassee) 32303
Glendale, *Walton* 32433
Glen Oaks (Part of Sarasota) 34232
Glen Ridge 33406
Glen Saint Mary 32040
Glenvar Heights 33143
Glenwood, *Nassau* 32097
Glenwood, *Volusia* 32722
Glory 32351
Glynlea Park (Part of Jacksonville) 32216
Golden Beach 33160
Golden Gate, *Collier*♦ 34116
34119
For specific ZIP Codes call (888) 275-8777, or your local postmaster.
Golden Gate, *Martin* 34997
Golden Gate Estates 34117
34119-20
For specific ZIP Codes call (888) 275-8777, or your local postmaster.
Golden Hills 34482
Golden Isles (Part of Hallandale) 33009
Golden Lakes♦ 33411
Goldenrod 32733
Golden Shores (Part of Aventura) 33160
Golfview 33406
Golfview Park 33853
Gomez 33455
Gonzalez♦ 32560
Goodbys (Part of Jacksonville) 32257
Good Hope 32531
Goodland 34140
Gopher Ridge 32145
Gordon 32433
Gordon Chapel 32640
Gordonville 33830
Gotha 34734
Goulding♦ 32501
Goulds♦ 33170
Governor's Square Mall (Part of Tallahassee) 32301
Graceville 32440

Graham 32042
Grahamsville 34488
Grand Crossing (Part of Jacksonville) 32209
Grandin 32138
Grand Island 32735
Grand Park (Part of Jacksonville) 32209
Grand Ridge 32442
Grandview 32131
Grangers Mill 32055
Grant 32949
Grassy Key 33050
Gratigny (Part of North Miami) 33168
Grayton Beach 32459
Greenacres 33413, 33415, 33463, 33467
For specific ZIP Codes call (888) 275-8777, or your local postmaster.
Greenbriar 32771
Green Cove Springs 32043
Greenhead 32428
Green Hills 32438
Greenland (Part of Jacksonville) 32256, 32258
For specific ZIP Codes call (888) 275-8777, or your local postmaster.
Greensboro 32330
Greenville 32331
Greenwood, *Jackson* 32443
Greenwood, *Santa Rosa* 32565
Grenelefe 33844
Gretna 32332
Griffin 33810
Gross 32097
Grove City♦ 34224
Groveland 34736
Grove Park, *Alachua* 32640
Grove Park (Part of Jacksonville) 32216
Grove Park (Part of Lakeland) 33801
Gulf Beach 32507
Gulf Beach Heights 32507
Gulf Breeze 32561-62, 32566
For specific ZIP Codes call (888) 275-8777, or your local postmaster.
Gulf City 33570
Gulf Gate Estates♦ 34231
Gulf Gate Mall 34231
Gulf Hammock 32639
Gulf Harbors 34652
Gulf Pines 32459
Gulfport 33307*, 33337†
Gulf Resort Beach (Part of Panama City Beach) 32407
Gulf Stream 33483
Gulfwinds (Part of St. Petersburg)‡ 33711*, 33747†
Hague 32601
Haines City 33844*, 33845†
Hainesworth 32615
Hallandale 33008†, 33009*
Hamilton (Part of Pompano Beach) 33072
Hammock 32137
Hammocks♦ 33196
Hampton 32044
Hanson 32340
Harbinwood Estates 32303
Harbor Bluffs♦ 33770
Harbor Oaks 32127
Harbor Shores 34748
Harbor View, *Charlotte* 33980
Harbor Vew (Part of Jacksonville) 32209
Harbour Heights♦ 33983
Hardaway 32324
Hardeetown (Part of Chiefland) 32626
Hardin Heights 32324
Harlem♦ 33440
Harmony Heights 34946
Harold 32563
Harshaw (Part of St. Petersburg) 33713
Hastings 32145
Hatchbend 32008
Havana 32333
Haverhill 33415, 33417
For specific ZIP Codes call (888) 275-8777, or your local postmaster.
Hawthorne 32640
Heathrow 32746
Hedges 32097
Heilbronn 32091
Henderson Creek 34114
Heritage Estates 32960
Hernando♦ 34442
Hernando Beach♦ 34607
Hernando City Heights 34442
Hernando Ridge 33523
Herndon (Part of Orlando)‡ 32803
Hero 32097
Hesperides 33853
Hialeah 33002, 33010-18
For specific ZIP Codes call (888) 275-8777, or your local postmaster.
Hialeah Gardens 33010
Hialeah Lakes‡ 33014-15, 33018
For specific ZIP Codes call (888) 275-8777, or your local postmaster.
Hiawasee 32808
Hibernia 32043
Hibiscus 32757
Hickory Hill 32464
Hidden Lake Villas (Part of Sanford) 32773
Hidden Oaks 33173
Hidden River 34240
Highland 32058
Highland Beach 33487
Highland City♦ 33846
Highland Lakes 34684
Highland Park, *Franklin* 32320
Highland Park, *Polk* 33853
Highland Park (Part of Sanford) 32771
Highlands (Part of Jacksonville) 32218
Highlands Lakes 33825
Highlands Park Estates 33852
Highland View 32456
Highpoint 33759-60
For specific ZIP Codes call (888) 275-8777, or your local postmaster.
High Springs 32643*, 32655†
Highway Park 33852
Hiland Park 32405
Hildreth 32008
Hillcrest Heights 33827
Hilldale (Part of Tampa)‡ 33614*, 33684†
Hilliard 32046
Hill N Dale 34602
Hillsboro Beach 33062
Hinson 32333
Hinson Crossroads 32427
Hobe Sound 33455*, 33475†
Hog Valley 32134
Holden Heights 32805
Holder 34445
Holiday♦ 34690-91
For specific ZIP Codes call (888) 275-8777, or your local postmaster.
Holiday Harbor (Part of Jacksonville) 32224
Holiday Heights 33037
Holiday Manor 33844
Holland Crossroads 32425
Holley 32561
Holliday Hills (Part of Jacksonville) 32216
Hollister 32147
Holly Ford (Part of Jacksonville) 32218
Holly Hill 32117
Holly Hills (Part of Tallahassee) 32303
Holly Point (Part of Orange Park) 32073
Hollywood 33019-29, 33081, 33083-84
For specific ZIP Codes call (888) 275-8777, or your local postmaster.
Hollywood Beach 32413
Hollywood Beach Gardens (Part of Hollywood) 33021
Hollywood Fashion Center (Part of Hollywood) 33023
Hollywood Hills (Part of Hollywood)‡ 33021*, 33081†
Hollywood Mall (Part of Hollywood) 33021
Hollywood Seminole Indian Reservation 33024
Holmes Beach 34218
Holmes Valley 32462
Holopaw 32901
Holt 32564
Homeland 33847
Homestead 33030-35, 33039, 33090-92
For specific ZIP Codes call (888) 275-8777, or your local postmaster.
Homestead Ridge 32308
Homosassa♦ 34446, 34448, 34487
For specific ZIP Codes call (888) 275-8777, or your local postmaster.
Homosassa Springs 34447
Honeyville 32465
Hooker Point, Hendry 33440
Hooker Point (Part of Tampa) 33605
Hopewell, *Hillsborough* 33566
Hopewell, *Madison* 32340
Horseshoe Beach 32648
Hosford 32334
Houston 32060
Howard 33176
Howard Creek 32465
Howey-in-the-Hills 34737
Hudson♦ 36467, 36469, 36474
For specific ZIP Codes call (888) 275-8777, or your local postmaster.
Hull 34266
Hunt Club 32703
Huntington 32112
Huntington Estates 32303
Huntington Woods (Part of Tallahassee) 32303
Hurlburt Field 32544
Hyde Grove (Part of Jacksonville) 32210
Hyde Park (Part of Jacksonville) 32210
Hyde Park (Part of Tampa) 33606, 33609
For specific ZIP Codes call (888) 275-8777, or your local postmaster.
Hyde Park, *Wakulla* 32327
Hypoluxo 33462
Iddo 32331
Immokalee♦ 34142*, 34143†
Imperial Lakes 33860
Imperial Point 33774
Indialantic 32903
Indian Bluff 32466
Indian Bluff Island 34683
Indian Creek 33154
Indian Harbour Beach 32937
Indian Head Acres (Part of Tallahassee) 32301
Indian Hills (Part of Cocoa)‡ 32922
Indian Lake Estates 33855
Indian Mound Village 32771
Indianola 32952
Indian Pass 32456
Indian River City (Part of Titusville)‡ 32780
Indian River Estates♦ 34982
Indian River Shores 32963
Indian Rocks Beach 33785
Indian Shores 33785
Indiantown♦ 34956
Indian Wells 34746
Indrio 34946
Inglis 34449
Inlet Beach 32413
Innerarity Point 32507
Innisbrook 34684
Interbay (Part of Tampa)‡ 33611*, 33681†
Intercession City 33848
Interlachen 32148*, 32149†
Inverness 34450-53
For specific ZIP Codes call (888) 275-8777, or your local postmaster.
Inverrary (Part of Lauderhill) 33319
Inwood, *Jackson* 32460
Inwood, *Polk*♦ 33881
Iona 33908
Irvine 32686
Islamorada♦ 33036
Island Estates (Part of Clearwater) 33767
Island Grove 32654
Islandia 33131
Isleboro (Part of New Smyrna Beach) 32168
Isle of Palms (Part of Jacksonville) 32250
Isle of Palms (Part of Treasure Island) 33706
Isle of Palms South (Part of Jacksonville) 32250
Isles of Capri 34113
Isleworth 34786
Istachatta 34636
Istokpoga Shores 33857
Ivan 32327
Ives Estates 33179
Izagora 32427

Jacksonville

32201-32, 32234-47, 32254-60, 32267, 32276-77
For specific ZIP Codes call (888) 275-8777, or your local postmaster.

Colleges & Universities

Edward Waters Coll 32209
Jacksonville Univ 32211
Jones Coll 32211
Trinity Baptist Coll 32254
Univ of North Florida 32224

Financial Institutions

AmSouth Bank 32257
Barnett Bank, NA 32202
First Union Nat Bank 32202
NationsBank, NA 32256
SouthTrust Bank, NA 32223

Hospitals

Baptist Med Ctr 32207
Memorial Hosp 32216
St Vincent's Med Ctr 32203
Univ Med Ctr 32209

Hotels/Motels

Holiday Inn, Airport 32229
Holiday Inn, Bay Meadows 32256
Marriott 32256
Omni 32202
Radisson Riverwalk 32207
Ramada Conference Ctr 32211

Military Installations

Defense Distribution Depot 32212
Defense Fuel Support Point 32218
Fleet & Industrial Supply Ctr 32212
Fleet & Industrial Supply Ctr, Fuel Dept 32218
Florida Air Nat Guard, FB6091, Jacksonville International Airport 32218
Naval Air Sta 32212
Naval Air Sta, Cecil Field 32215
Naval Sta, Mayport 32228
Supervisor of Shipbuilding, Conversion & Repair 32228
U S Army Corps of Engineers 32202

Jacksonville Air Transfer Office (Part of Jacksonville)‡ 32229
Jacksonville Beach 32240†, 32250*
Jacksonville Heights (Part of Jacksonville) 32210
Jacob City 32431
Jamaica Bay 33912
Jan Phyl Village♦ 33880
Jarrott 32344
Jasmine Estates♦ 34668
Jasper 32052
Jay 32565
Jena 32359
Jennings 32053
Jensen Beach♦ 34957*, 34958†
Jerome 34137
Jessamine 33523
John's Lake 34787
Johnson 32640
Johnson's Corner 32767
Jonathan's Landing 33477
Jonesville 32669
Judson 32693
Julington Forest (Part of Jacksonville) 32258
June Park♦ 32901
Jungle (Part of St. Petersburg) 33710
Juniper 32330
Juno Beach 33408
Jupiter 33458, 33468-69, 33477-78
For specific ZIP Codes call (888) 275-8777, or your local postmaster.
Jupiter Inlet Colony 33469
Jupiter Island 33455
Kathleen♦ 33849
Keaton Beach 32347
Kenansville 34739
Kendall 33156*, 33256†
Kendrick 34475
Kennedy Space Center 32815
Kenneth City 33709
Kensington Park♦ 34235
Kerr City 32134
Keuka 32148
Key Biscayne 33149
Key Colony Beach 33051
Key Largo♦ 33037
Key Largo Park 33037
Key Largo Village 33037
Keystone Heights 32656
Keystone Islands (Part of North Miami) 33181
Keysville 33547
Key West 33040-41, 33045
For specific ZIP Codes call (888) 275-8777, or your local postmaster.
Key West Naval Air Station 33040
Killarney 34740
Killearn Acres 32308
Killearn Estates (Part of Tallahassee) 32308
Killearn Lakes 32312
Kinard 32449
Kincaid Hills 32601
Kings Bay 33158
Kings Ferry 32046
Kingsley Lake 32091
Kingsley Village 32091
Kings Road (Part of Jacksonville) 32254
Kingswood Manor 32804
Kissimmee 34741-47, 34758-59
For specific ZIP Codes call (888) 275-8777, or your local postmaster.
Kissimmee Park 34772
Knights 33565
Korona 32110
Kossuthville 33823
Kynesville 32431
La Belle 33935*, 33975†
Lackawana Estates 32640
Lacoochee♦ 33537
La Crosse 32658

Lady Lake 32158†
32159*
La Gorce Island (Part of Miami Beach) 33141
La Grange 32796
Laguna Beach♦ 32413
Lake Alfred 33850
Lake Ashby Shores 32168
Lake Bird 32347
Lake Brantley 32750
Lakebreeze 32303
Lake Bryant 32179
Lake Buena Vista 32830
Lake Butler 32054
Lake Cain Hills 32805
Lake Charm (Part of Oviedo) 32765
Lake City 32024-25
32055-56
For specific ZIP Codes call (888) 275-8777, or your local postmaster.
Lake Clarke Shores 33406
Lake Como 32157
Lake Crescent Estates 32112
Lake Forest, *Broward* 33023
Lake Forest (Part of Jacksonville)‡ 32208
Lake Forest Hills (Part of Jacksonville) 32208
Lake Frances (Part of Tavares) 32778
Lake Garfield 33830
Lake Geneva 32160
Lake Hamilton 33851
Lake Harbor 33459
Lake Harris Shores 32778
Lake Haven Estates 33872
Lake Helen 32744
Lake Jem 32745
Lake Joanna 32726
Lake Josephine 33872
Lake Kathryn Heights 32720
Lakeland 33801-13
For specific ZIP Codes call (888) 275-8777, or your local postmaster.
Lakeland Square (Part of Lakeland) 33810
Lake Letta 33825
Lake Lindsey 34601
Lake Lotela 33825
Lake Lucerne 33056
33169
For specific ZIP Codes call (888) 275-8777, or your local postmaster.
Lake Lucina (Part of Jacksonville) 32277
Lake Mack Park 32720
Lake Magdalene♦ 33612-13
For specific ZIP Codes call (888) 275-8777, or your local postmaster.
Lake Marian Highlands 34739
Lake Mary 32746*
32795†
Lake Mendelin Estates 32703
Lake Miona Heights 34785
Lake Monroe 32747
Lakemont 33825
Lake Mystic 32321
Lake of the Hills 33853
Lake Panasoffkee♦ 33538
Lake Park 33403
Lake Pasadena Heights 33525
Lake Placid 33852*
33862†
Lakeport 33471
Lake Sarasota 34241
Lake Saunders 32757
Lake Shore (Part of Jacksonville)‡ 32210*
32238†
Lakeshore Mall 33870
Lakeside Green♦ 33417
Lakeside Hills 32140
Lakes Mall (Part of Lauderdale Lakes) 33319
Lake St. George‡ 34684
Lake Tarpon 34684
Lake Wales 33853*
33859†
Lake Weir 32179
Lake Winnott 32640
Lakewood (Part of Jacksonville) 32207
Lakewood, Walton 32433
Lakewood Heights (Part of Tallahassee) 32311
Lakewood Park♦ 34951
Lakewood Village 32303
Lake Worth 33454
33460-67
For specific ZIP Codes call (888) 275-8777, or your local postmaster.
Lamont 32336
Lamplighter (Part of Gainesville) 32609
Lam Smith Crossroads 32425
Lanark Village 32323
Land O'Lakes♦ 34639
Lane (Part of Jacksonville) 32254
Lantana 33462*
33465†
Lantana Homes 33463
Largo 33770-71
33773-74
33777-79
For specific ZIP Codes call (888) 275-8777, or your local postmaster.
Largo Mall (Part of Largo) 33771
Larkin Fish Camp 32321
Lauderdale-by-the-Sea 33308
Lauderdale Lakes 33309
33311
33313
33319
For specific ZIP Codes call (888) 275-8777, or your local postmaster.
Lauderhill 33313
33319
33351
For specific ZIP Codes call (888) 275-8777, or your local postmaster.
Lauderhill Mall (Part of Lauderhill) 33313
Laurel 34272
Laurel Grove (Part of Orange Park) 32073
Laurel Hill 32567
Laurel Park, *Escambia* 32505
Laurel Park, *Orange* 32809
Lawtey 32058
Lazy Lagoon 33982
Lazy Lake 33305
Lealman♦ 33714
Lebanon 34431
Lecanto♦ 34460-61
For specific ZIP Codes call (888) 275-8777, or your local postmaster.
Lee 32059
Lee Cypress 34137
Leesburg 34748-49
34788-89
For specific ZIP Codes call (888) 275-8777, or your local postmaster.
Lehigh (Part of Tallahassee) 32301
Lehigh Acres♦ 33936
33970-72
For specific ZIP Codes call (888) 275-8777, or your local postmaster.
Leisure City♦ 33033
Leisure Lakes 33852
Lely♦ 34113
Lemon Bluff 32764
Lemon City (Part of Miami) 33127
33137
For specific ZIP Codes call (888) 275-8777, or your local postmaster.
Lemon Grove 33873
Leon Station (Part of Tallahassee)‡ 32303*
32315†
Leonards 32424
Leonia 32464
Leonton 32344
Lessie 32046
Liberty 32433
Liberty City (Part of Miami) 33142
Liberty Square (Part of Miami) 33147
Lido Key (Part of Sarasota) 34239
Lighthouse Point, *Broward* 33064*
33074†
Lighthouse Point, *Martin* 34994
Lily 33865
Limestone, *Hardee* 33865
Limestone, *Jefferson* 32344
Limona 33510
Lincoln City 32091
Lincoln Estates (Part of Gainesville) 32601
Lincoln Road Mall (Part of Miami Beach) 33139
Linden 33597
Lisbon 34788
Lithia 33547
Little Acres 34736
Little Gasparilla 33946
Little Havana (Part of Miami) 33125
Little Hollywood 32976
Little Lake City 32619
Little River (Part of Miami)‡ 33138*
33238†
Little River Springs 32071
Little Torch Key 33042
Live Oak, *Suwannee* 32060*
32064†
Live Oak, *Washington* 32462
Live Oak Island 32327
Lloyd 32337
Lochloosa 32662
Lochmoor 33903
Lock Arbor (Part of Sanford) 32773
Lockhart♦ 32810
Londonderry (Part of Orlando) 32808
Longboat Key 34228
Long Key 33001
Longwood, *Okaloosa* 32579
Longwood, *Seminole* 32579
32750
32752
32779
32791
For specific ZIP Codes call (888) 275-8777, or your local postmaster.
Lorida 33857
Lotus 32952
Loughman♦ 33858
Lovedale 32423
Lovett 32331
Lovewood 32431
Lowell 32663
Lower Clay Landing 32626
Lower Matecumbe Key 33036
Loxahatchee 33470
Lucerne Avenue (Part of Lake Worth)‡ 33460
Lucerne Park (Part of Winter Haven) 33881
Ludlam (Part of Miami) 33155*
33255†
Lullwater Beach (Part of Panama City Beach) 32407
Lulu 32061
Lumberton 33540
Lundy 32177
Luraville 32060
Lutz♦ 33548†
33549*
Lynne 34488
Lynn Haven 32444
Lyonsboro (Part of Coconut Creek) 33067
33073
33076
For specific ZIP Codes call (888) 275-8777, or your local postmaster.
Mabel 33514
Mabry Manor (Part of Tallahassee) 32310
McAlpin 32062
Macclenny 32063
Macclenny II 32063
McDavid 32568
Macedonia 32424
McGregor♦ 33919
McIntosh 32664
McKinnon 32568
McLellen 32570
McMeekin 32640
Madeira Beach 33708*
33738†
Madison 32340*
32341†
Magnolia Beach 32408
Magnolia Gardens (Part of Jacksonville) 32209
Magnolia Springs 32043
Mainland (Part of Ormond Beach)‡ 32174
Mainlands Center (Part of Pinellas Park)‡ 33782
Main Street (Part of Gainesville)‡ 32601-02
32605
32611
32613
32627
For specific ZIP Codes call (888) 275-8777, or your local postmaster.
Maitland 32751
32794
For specific ZIP Codes call (888) 275-8777, or your local postmaster.
Malabar 32950
Malone 32445
Manalapan 33462
Manasota 34260
Manatee (Part of Bradenton)‡ 34208
Mandarin (Part of Jacksonville)‡ 32223*
32241†
Mango 33550
Mango Hills 33584
Mangonia Park 33407
Marathon♦ 33050
Marathon Shores 33052
Maravilla (Part of Fort Pierce) 34982
Marco♦ 33145*
33146†
Margate 33063
33068
33093
For specific ZIP Codes call (888) 275-8777, or your local postmaster.
Marianna 32446-48
For specific ZIP Codes call (888) 275-8777, or your local postmaster.
Marietta (Part of Jacksonville) 32220
Marineland 32086
Mariner Mall 32505
Mariner Sands 34997
Marion Oaks 34473
Market Square Mall (Part of Jacksonville) 32207
Martel 34475
Martin 32617
Martin Downs 34990
Mary Esther 32569
Masaryktown 34609
Mascotte 34753
Matlacha 33909
Maxcy Quarters 33843
Maximo Moorings (Part of St. Petersburg) 33711
Maxville (Part of Jacksonville) 32234
Mayfair in the Grove (Part of Miami) 33133
Mayo 32066
Mayo Junction 32066
Mayport (Part of Jacksonville)‡ 32233*
32267†
Mayport Naval Station 32227*
32228†
Meadowbrook 32808
Meadowbrook Terrace 32073
Meadowlawn (Part of St. Petersburg) 33702
Meadowlea on the River 32713
Meadow Wood♦ 32824
Mecca 32771
Medart 32327
Medley 33178
Medulla♦ 33811
Melbourne 32901-02
32904
32934-36
32940-41
For specific ZIP Codes call (888) 275-8777, or your local postmaster.
Melbourne Beach 32951
Melbourne Shores 32951
Melbourne Square Mall (Part of Melbourne) 32904
Melbourne Village 32904
Melody Hills (Part of Tallahassee) 32308
Melrose 32666
Melrose Park, *Broward*♦ 33312
Melrose Park, *Columbia* 32055
Memphis♦ 34221
Memphis Heights 34221
Merritt Island♦ 32952-54
For specific ZIP Codes call (888) 275-8777, or your local postmaster.
Merritt Square Mall 32952
Metro Mall (Part of Fort Myers) 33916
Mexico Beach 32410

Miami

33101-47
33150-99
33201-99
For specific ZIP Codes call (888) 275-8777, or your local postmaster.

Colleges & Universities

Carribean Center for Advance Studies, Miami Institute of Psychology 33166
Florida International Univ 33199
Jones Coll 33143
Trinity International Univ 33132

Financial Institutions

First Union Nat Bank 33126
NationsBank, NA 33131
Northern Trust Bank, NA 33131
Ocean Bank 33126
Republic Nat Bank 33126
SunTrust Bank, NA 33131

Hospitals

Baptist Hosp 33176
Cedars Med Ctr 33101
Heart Institute 33141
Jackson Memorial Hosp 33136
Mercy Hosp 33133
North Shore Med Ctr 33150
South Miami Hosp 33143
Veterans Affairs Med Ctr 33125

Hotels/Motels

Best Western Beach Resort 33140
Castillo del Mar Resort 33140
Crowne Plaza 33132
Dadeland Marriott 33156
Doral Golf Resort & Spa 33178
Dupont Plaza 33131
Eden Roc Resort & Spa 33140
Embassy Suites, Airport 33142
The Everglades 33132
Fontainebleau Hilton Resort & Towers 33140
Hyatt Regency 33131
Inter-Continental 33131
Marriott 33126
Marriott, Biscayne Bay 33132
The Miami Airport Hilton 33126
Newport Beach Crowne Plaza 33160
Radisson Mart Plaza 33126
Ramada Resort, Deauville 33141
Seville Beach 33140
Sheraton, Biscayne Bay 33131
Sheraton Gateway 33142
South Beach Hotel 33139
Turnberry Isle Resort & Club 33180
Westin Resort 33140

Military Installations

7th Coast Guard Dist Off 33131

* Area Zip Code † Post Office Boxes ‡ Postal Station ♦ Census Designated Place *Italic Type* County

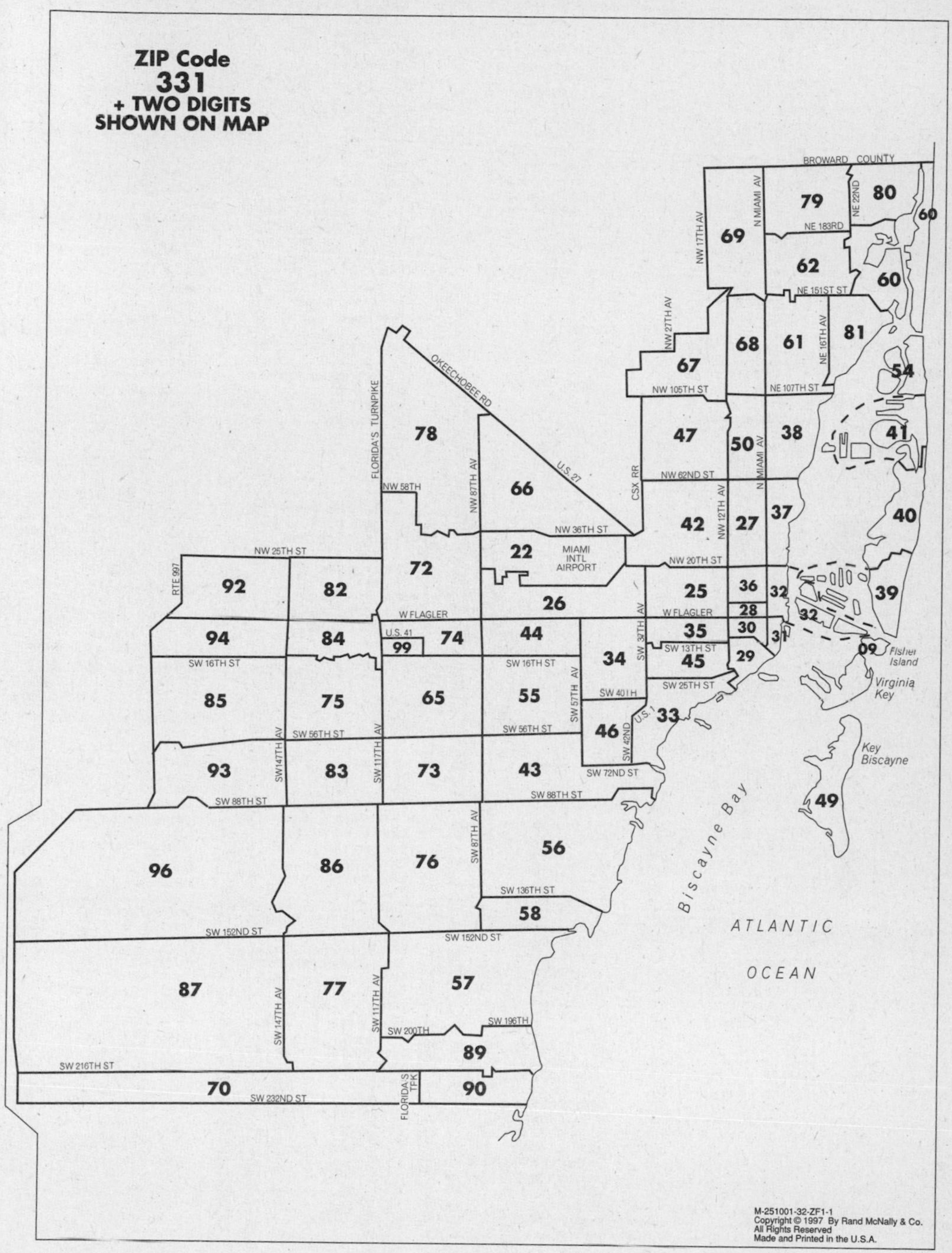
ZIP Code
331
+ TWO DIGITS
SHOWN ON MAP
BROWARD COUNTY
79
80
60
N MIAMI AV
NE 22ND
NE 183RD
69
NW 17TH AV
62
60
NE 151ST ST
NW 27TH AV
68
61
81
NE 16TH AV
67
54
NW 105TH ST
NE 107TH ST
OKEECHOBEE RD
78
47
50
38
41
N MIAMI AV
FLORIDA'S TURNPIKE
U.S. 27
NW 87TH AV
CSX RR
NW 62ND ST
NW 58TH
66
42
NW 12TH AV
27
37
40
NW 36TH ST
NW 25TH ST
22
MIAMI INTL AIRPORT
NW 20TH ST
72
RTE 997
92
82
25
36
32
39
26
W FLAGLER
W FLAGLER
28
32
94
84
U.S. 41
74
44
35
30
31
99
SW 13TH ST
09
Fisher Island
SW 16TH ST
SW 16TH ST
34
SW 32TH AV
45
29
SW 57TH AV
SW 25TH ST
Virginia Key
85
75
65
55
SW 40TH
U.S. 1
33
SW 56TH ST
SW 56TH ST
46
SW 147TH AV
SW 117TH AV
SW 42ND
Key Biscayne
93
83
73
43
SW 72ND ST
SW 88TH ST
SW 88TH ST
49
Biscayne Bay
SW 87TH AV
56
96
86
76
SW 136TH ST
58
SW 152ND ST
SW 152ND ST
ATLANTIC
OCEAN
87
77
57
SW 147TH AV
SW 117TH AV
SW 200TH
SW 196TH
89
SW 216TH ST
70
90
SW 232ND ST
FLORIDA'S TPK
M-251001-32-ZF1-1

Miami Beach 33109
33119
33139-41
For specific ZIP Codes call (888) 275-8777, or your local postmaster.
Miami Coast Guard Station 33054
Miami Gardens (Part of Hialeah)‡ 33015*
33017†
Miami Lakes♦ 33014
33016
For specific ZIP Codes call (888) 275-8777, or your local postmaster.
Miami Shores 33138
33150
33153
For specific ZIP Codes call (888) 275-8777, or your local postmaster.
Miami Springs 33166*
33266†
Micanopy 32667
Micco 32958
Miccosukee 32309
Miccosukee Hills (Part of Tallahassee) 32308
Miccosukee Indian Reservation 33440
Middle (Part of Lake Mary) 32799
Middleburg♦ 32050†
32068*
Mid Town Plaza (Part of Sarasota)‡ 34239
Midway, *Gadsden* 32343
Midway, *Hillsborough* 33565
Midway, *Seminole* 32771
Millcreek 32092
Millers Ferry 32462
Milligan 32537
Millview 32506
Millville (Part of Panama City) 32401
Milton 32570-72
32583
For specific ZIP Codes call (888) 275-8777, or your local postmaster.
Mi-Lu Estates 32159
Mims 32754
Mineral Springs 32565
Minneola 34755
Miracle City Mall (Part of Titusville) 32780
Miracle Mile (Part of Fort Myers)‡ 33901
Miracle Mile (Part of Coral Gables) 33234
Miramar 33023
33025
33027
33029
For specific ZIP Codes call (888) 275-8777, or your local postmaster.
Miramar Beach♦ 32541
Miramar Terrace (Part of Jacksonville) 32207
Mission Bay 33428
33498
For specific ZIP Codes call (888) 275-8777, or your local postmaster.
Mission City 32168
Mission Hills (Part of Clearwater) 33759
Mission Plaza (Part of Largo)‡ 33773
Moffitt 33890
Molino♦ 32577
Molino Crossroads 32577
Monroes Corner 34491
Montbrook 32696
Montclair 34748
Monteocha 32609
Monterey (Part of Jacksonville) 32211
Monticello 32344*
32345†
Montverde 34756
Monument (Part of Jacksonville) 32225
Monument Lakes (Part of Jacksonville) 32225
Moon Lake Estates 34654
Moore Haven 33471
Moreland Park 34785

Morningside (Part of Miami) 33137
Morningside Park 32809
Morrison Bluff 32102
Morriston 32668
Morse Shores♦ 33905
Mosley Hall 32331
Moss Bluff 32179
Moss Town 33537
Mossy Head 32434
Moultrie 32086
Mountain Park 34601
Mount Carmel 32565
Mount Dora 32756†
32757*
Mount Pleasant 32352
Mount Plymouth♦ 32776
Mount Royal 32193
Mulberry 33860
Munson 32570
Murat Hills (Part of Tallahassee) 32304
Murdock 33938
Murray Hill (Part of Jacksonville)‡ 32205
32226
32254
For specific ZIP Codes call (888) 275-8777, or your local postmaster.
Myakka City 34251
Myakka Head 33865
Myakka Valley Ranchos 34241
Myrtis 32055
Myrtle Grove♦ 32506*
32516†
Nalcrest 33856
Naples 34101-20
For specific ZIP Codes call (888) 275-8777, or your local postmaster.
Naples Manor 34113
Naples Park♦ 34108
Naranja♦ 33032-33
For specific ZIP Codes call (888) 275-8777, or your local postmaster.
Narcoossee 34771
Nash 32336
Nashua 32189
Nassau Village 32011
Nassauville 32034
National Gardens 32174
Naval Air Station 32508
Naval Coastal Systems Lab 32407
Naval Regional Medical Clinic‡ 33040
Naval Training Center Annex 32824
Navarre 32566
Navy Point 32507
Neptune Beach 32266
Neptune Shores 34744
New Berlin (Part of Jacksonville) 32226
Newberry 32669
Newburn 32060
New Eden 34771
New Harmony 32433
New Hope, *Holmes* 32464
New Hope, *Washington* 32462
Newmans Lake Homesites 32601
Newport, *Monroe* 33037
Newport, *Wakulla* 32327
New Port Richey 34652-56
For specific ZIP Codes call (888) 275-8777, or your local postmaster.
New River‡ 33301*
33302†
New Smyrna Beach 32168-70
For specific ZIP Codes call (888) 275-8777, or your local postmaster.
New Zion 33865
Niceville 32578*
32588†
Nichols 33863
Nobles (Part of Pensacola)‡ 32504
32514
For specific ZIP Codes call (888) 275-8777, or your local postmaster.
Nobleton 34661
Nocatee 34268

Nokomis♦ 34274†
34275*
Noma 32452
Norland♦ 33169
33179
For specific ZIP Codes call (888) 275-8777, or your local postmaster.
Normandy (Part of Miami Beach) 33141
Normandy (Part of Jacksonville) 32205
Normandy Mall (Part of Jacksonville) 32254
Normandy Manor (Part of Jacksonville) 32221
Normandy Village (Part of Jacksonville) 32221
North Babcock (Part of Melbourne)‡ 32901
North Bay Village 33141
North Beach 32095
North Biscayne (Part of North Miami) 33161
Northcliffe 32561
Northcrest 32703
Northdale 33624
North Fort Myers 33903*
33918†
North Jacksonville (Part of Jacksonville)‡ 32218
32226
For specific ZIP Codes call (888) 275-8777, or your local postmaster.
North La Belle 33935
North Lauderdale 33068
North Meadowbrook Terrace 32073
North Miami 33161
33167-68
33179
33181
33261
For specific ZIP Codes call (888) 275-8777, or your local postmaster.
North Miami Beach 33161
33167-68
33179
33181
33261
For specific ZIP Codes call (888) 275-8777, or your local postmaster.
North Naples♦ 34108
34110
For specific ZIP Codes call (888) 275-8777, or your local postmaster.
North Oak Hill (Part of Jacksonville) 32210
North Palm Beach 33408
North Port 34286-87
For specific ZIP Codes call (888) 275-8777, or your local postmaster.
North Redington Beach 33708
North River Shores♦ 34994
North Shore (Part of Jacksonville) 32208
North Side (Part of Panama City)‡ 32406
Northwest St. Johns‡ 32259*
32260†
Northwood (Part of West Palm Beach)‡ 33407
Northwood Centre (Part of Tallahassee) 32303
Northwood Pines (Part of Gainesville) 32605
Northwood Plaza (Part of Clearwater)‡ 33761
Norwood (Part of Jacksonville) 32208
Nubbin Ridge 32531
Nutall Rise 32336
Oak 34479
Oakbrook (Part of Ocala)‡ 34470
Oak Crest, *Alachua* 32640
Oakcrest (Part of Ocala)‡ 34479
Oakdale 32448
Oak Forest 34436
Oak Grove, *Escambia* 32568
Oak Grove, *Gadsden* 32324

Oak Grove, *Gulf* 32456
Oak Grove, *Hardee* 33873
Oak Grove, *Lake* 32159
Oak Grove, *Okaloosa* 32531
Oak Grove, *Sumter* 33597
Oak Harbor (Part of Jacksonville) 32233
Oakhaven (Part of Jacksonville) 32211
Oak Hill 32759
Oak Hill Park (Part of Jacksonville) 32244
Oakhurst 33776
Oakland 34760
Oakland Park, *Broward* 33306-09
33311
33334
For specific ZIP Codes call (888) 275-8777, or your local postmaster.
Oakland Park, *Lake*♦ 32757
Oakland Shores 32751
Oak Run 34481
Oak Street (Part of Kissimmee)‡ 34741
34746-47
For specific ZIP Codes call (888) 275-8777, or your local postmaster.
Oak Terrace 33860
Oakwood 34488
Oakwood Hills 32433
Oakwood Villa (Part of Jacksonville) 32211
O'Brien 32071
Ocala 34470-83
For specific ZIP Codes call (888) 275-8777, or your local postmaster.
Ocala Highlands (Part of Ocala) 34471
Ocala Highlands Estates 34482
Ocala Park Ranch 34482
Ocala Ridge 34474
Ocala Waterway 34474
Ocala West 34474-75
For specific ZIP Codes call (888) 275-8777, or your local postmaster.
Ocean Breeze Park 34957
Ocean City♦ 32547-48
For specific ZIP Codes call (888) 275-8777, or your local postmaster.
Ocean Reef Club 33037
Ocean Ridge 33435
Ocean View (Part of Miami Beach) 33140
Oceanway (Part of Jacksonville) 32218
Ocheesee 32442
Ochopee 34141
Ocoee 34761
Odessa 33556
Ojus♦ 33163
33179-80
For specific ZIP Codes call (888) 275-8777, or your local postmaster.
Okahumpka 34762
Okaloosa Island 32548
Okeechobee 34972-74
For specific ZIP Codes call (888) 275-8777, or your local postmaster.
Oklawaha 32179*
32183†
Old Fernandina (Part of Fernandina Beach) 32034
Old Myakka 34240
Oldsmar 34677
Old Town 32680
Olga 33905
Olustee 32072
Olympia Heights 33163*
33265†
Omni International of Miami (Part of Miami) 33132
Ona 33865
Oneco 34203
O'Neil 32034
On Top of the World 34481
Opa-Locka 33054-56
For specific ZIP Codes call (888) 275-8777, or your local postmaster.

Open Air (Part of St. Petersburg)‡ 33701
33731-32
For specific ZIP Codes call (888) 275-8777, or your local postmaster.
Orange 32321
Orange Avenue (Part of Fort Pierce)‡ 34954
Orange Bend 34788
Orange Blossom (Part of Orlando)‡ 32805
Orange Blossom Estates 33872
Orange Blossom Gardens 32159
Orange Blossom Hills 34491
Orange Blossom Hills South 32159
Orange Blossom Mall (Part of Fort Pierce) 34947
Orange City 32763*
32774†
Orange City Hills 32763
Orange City Terrace 32763
Orangedale, *Polk* 33809
Orangedale, *St. Johns* 32092
Orange Harbor 33905
Orange Heights 32640
Orange Hill 32428
Orange Home 34785
Orange Lake 32681
Orange Mills 32131
Orange Park 32065
32067
32073
For specific ZIP Codes call (888) 275-8777, or your local postmaster.
Orange River Hills 33905
Orange Springs 32182
Orchid 32960
Orient Park 33619
Oriole Beach 32561

Orlando

32801-78
For specific ZIP Codes call (888) 275-8777, or your local postmaster.

Colleges & Universities
Orlando Coll 32810
Univ of Central Florida 32816

Financial Institutions
AmSouth Bank 32801
Barnett Bank, NA 32801
First Union Nat Bank of Florida 32803
NationsBank, NA 32801
STI Capital Management, NA 32802
SunTrust Bank, Central Florida, NA 32802

Hospitals
Florida Hosp 32803
Lucerne Med Ctr 32801
Orlando Regional Med Ctr 32806

Hotels/Motels
Best Western Plaza International 32819
Caribe Royale Resort Suites 32821
Clarion Plaza 32819
Days Inn & Lodge, Florida Mall 32809
Days Inn, Lakeside 32819
Delta Resort at Universal Studios 32819
Holiday Inn/ International Drive Resort 32819
Hyatt Regency, Grand Cypress Resort 32836
Hyatt Regency, Orlando International Airport 32827
Marriott, Orlando 32819
Marriott, Orlando Airport 32822
Marriott's Orlando World Center 32821
Omni Rosen 32819
The Peabody 32819
Quality Inn International 32819
Quality Inn Plaza 32819
Radisson Twin Towers, Hotel & Conference Ctr 32819

Sheraton World Resort 32821

Military Installations

Naval & Marine Corps Readiness Ctr 32803
Naval Training Ctr 32813
Naval Undersea Warfare Ctr 32856

Orlando Fashion Square (Part of Orlando) 32803
Orlo Vista♦ 32811
32835
32861
For specific ZIP Codes call (888) 275-8777, or your local postmaster.
Ormond Beach 32173-76
For specific ZIP Codes call (888) 275-8777, or your local postmaster.
Ormond By The Sea♦ 32174
Ortega (Part of Jacksonville)‡ 32210
Ortega Farms (Part of Jacksonville) 32210
Ortega Forest (Part of Jacksonville) 32210
Ortega Hills (Part of Jacksonville) 32244
Ortega Terrace (Part of Jacksonville) 32210
Osceola Heights (Part of Tallahassee) 32301
Osprey 34229
Osteen 32764
Otter Creek 32683
Overstreet 32456
Oviedo 32762
32765-66
For specific ZIP Codes call (888) 275-8777, or your local postmaster.
Owens 34266
Oxford 34484
Ozello 34429
Ozona 34660
Pace♦ 32571
Paddock Mall (Part of Ocala) 34474
Page Field (Part of Ft. Myers)‡ 33906†
33907*
Page Park 33907
Pahokee 33476
Painters Hill 32136
Paisley 32767
Palatka 32177*
32178†
Palma Ceia (Part of Tampa)‡ 33609
33629
33690
For specific ZIP Codes call (888) 275-8777, or your local postmaster.
Palma Sola 34209*
34280†
Palma Sola Park 34209
Palm Bay 32905-11
For specific ZIP Codes call (888) 275-8777, or your local postmaster.
Palm Bay West (Part of Palm Bay) 32707-11
For specific ZIP Codes call (888) 275-8777, or your local postmaster.
Palm Beach 33480
Palm Beach Gardens 33410
33418
33420
For specific ZIP Codes call (888) 275-8777, or your local postmaster.
Palm Beach Mall (Part of West Palm Beach) 33401
Palm Beach Shores 33404
Palm City 34990*
34991†
Palm Coast♦ 32135
32137
32142
32164
For specific ZIP Codes call (888) 275-8777, or your local postmaster.
Palmdale 33944
Palmetto 34220*
34221†

Palmetto Lakes (Part of Hialeah)‡ 33014
Palm Grove Colony 34607
Palm Harbor 34682-85
For specific ZIP Codes call (888) 275-8777, or your local postmaster.
Palm Plaza 34233
Palm River, *Collier*♦ 34110
Palm River, *Hillsborough* 33619
Palm Shores 32935
32940
For specific ZIP Codes call (888) 275-8777, or your local postmaster.
Palm Springs 33461
Palm Springs Mile Shopping Center (Part of Hialeah) 33012
Palm Springs North♦ 33015
Palms West (Part of Royal Palm Beach) 33421
Palm Valley♦ 32082
Palm View 34221
Palm Village (Part of Hialeah)‡ 33012
Panacea 32346
Panacea Park 32346
Panacoochee Retreats 33538
Panama City 32401-09
32411-17
For specific ZIP Codes call (888) 275-8777, or your local postmaster.
Panama City Beach 32407-08
32411
32413
32417
For specific ZIP Codes call (888) 275-8777, or your local postmaster.
Panama City General Mail Facility (Part of Panama City)‡ 32412
Panama City Mall (Part of Panama City) 32405
Panama Park (Part of Jacksonville) 32208
Paola 32771
Paradise Bay 34210
Paradise Beach 32506
Paradise Heights 32703
Paradise Island (Part of Treasure Island) 33706
Paradise Palms (Part of Boca Raton) 33486
Paradise Park 34946
Paradise Point (Part of Crystal River) 34429
Park Avenue Station (Part of Tallahassee)‡ 32302
Parker 32404
Parkland 33067
33076
For specific ZIP Codes call (888) 275-8777, or your local postmaster.
Parkside (Part of Tallahassee) 32303
Parmalee 34251
Parramore 32423
Parrish 34219
Pasadena Shores 33525
Pass-a-Grille Beach (Part of St. Pete Beach) 33706*
33741†
Patersonville 32131
Patrick Air Force Base 32925
Paxton 32538
Peaceful Acres 34431
Peace River Shores 33982
Peach Orchard 32618
Pecan Park (Part of Jacksonville) 32218
Pedro 34491
Pelican Bay 34108
Pelican Lake 33438
Pembroke Lakes Mall (Part of Pembroke Pines) 33024
Pembroke Park 33009
33023
For specific ZIP Codes call (888) 275-8777, or your local postmaster.
Pembroke Pines 33023-29
33084
For specific ZIP Codes call (888) 275-8777, or your local postmaster.

Peniel 32177
Peninsula (Part of Tampa)‡ 33609*
33679†
Peninsula (Part of Daytona Beach)‡ 32118
Penney Farms 32079
Pennsuco 33010
Pensacola 32501-26
32534
32573-76
32581-82
32589-98
For specific ZIP Codes call (888) 275-8777, or your local postmaster.
Pensacola Beach 32561
Pensacola Heights (Part of Pensacola) 32503
Pensacola Naval Air Station 32508
Peppertree Bay 34231
Perdido Bay 32507
Perrine♦ 33157*
33257†
Perry 32347*
32348†
Pettis Springs 32331
Pheasant Walk 33487
Phillipi Gardens 34231
Pickettville (Part of Jacksonville) 32254
Picnic 33547
Picolata 32092
Piedmont (Part of Tallahassee) 32312
Piedmont, Orange 32703
Pierce 33860
Pierson 32180
Pine Castle♦ 32809
32839
32859
For specific ZIP Codes call (888) 275-8777, or your local postmaster.
Pinecraft 34239*
34278†
Pinecrest 33547
Pineda 32935
Pine Dale 33860
Pine Forest 32506
Pine Grove, *Osceola* 34771
Pine Grove, *Suwannee* 32060
Pine Hill Estates 32601
Pine Hills, *Lake* 32736
Pine Hills, *Orange* 32808
32818
For specific ZIP Codes call (888) 275-8777, or your local postmaster.
Pine Hills Center 32808
Pine Island, *Calhoun* 32424
Pine Island, *Hernando* 34607
Pine Island Center 33945
Pine Island Ridge, *Broward*♦ 33324
Pine Island Ridge, *Lee* 33922
Pine Island Ridge Plaza (Part of Davie) 33324
Pine Lakes 32736
Pineland 33945
Pineland Gardens (Part of Jacksonville) 32216
Pine Level 34266
Pinellas Park 33780-82
For specific ZIP Codes call (888) 275-8777, or your local postmaster.
Pinellas Square (Part of Pinellas Park) 33781
Pine Log 32437
Pine Manor 33907
Pineola 34436
Pine Ridge 34108
Pine Ridge Country Estates 34465
Pine Run 34481
Pine Shores 34231
Pinesville 32618
Pinetta 32350
Pineville 32568
Pinewood Park 33147
33150
For specific ZIP Codes call (888) 275-8777, or your local postmaster.
Pinland 32347
Pipers Landing 34990

Pirate Harbor 33955
Pirates Wood 32097
Pittman, *Holmes* 32427
Pittman, *Lake* 32702
Placida 33946-47
For specific ZIP Codes call (888) 275-8777, or your local postmaster.
Placid Lakes♦ 33852
Plantation, *Broward* 33313
33317-18
33322-25
For specific ZIP Codes call (888) 275-8777, or your local postmaster.
Plantation, *Monroe*♦ 33036
Plantation, *Sarasota*♦ 34293
Plant City 33564-67
For specific ZIP Codes call (888) 275-8777, or your local postmaster.
Playland Estates (Part of Hollywood) 33021
Playland Isles 33312
Pleasant Grove, *Escambia* 32507
Pleasant Grove, *Hillsborough* 33530
Pleasant Grove, *Walton* 32567
Pleasant Ridge 32433
Plummer (Part of Jacksonville) 32219
Plymouth 32768
Poinciana 33467
Poinciana Park 32962
Poinciana Place♦ 34758-59
For specific ZIP Codes call (888) 275-8777, or your local postmaster.
Poinciana Village 34105
Point Baker 32570
Point Brittany (Part of St. Petersburg) 33715
Point O' Rocks 34242
Point Washington 32454
Polk City 33868
Polly Town (Part of Jacksonville) 32218
Pomona Park 32181
Pompano Beach 33060-69
33071-77
33093-97
For specific ZIP Codes call (888) 275-8777, or your local postmaster.
Pompano Beach Highlands 33064
Pompano Park 33319
Pompano Square (Part of Pompano Beach) 33062
Ponce de Leon 32455
Ponce Inlet 32127
Ponte Vedra 32082
Ponte Vedra Beach 32004†
32082*
Poplar Head 32425
Port Charlotte♦ 33948-49
33952-54
33980-81
For specific ZIP Codes call (888) 275-8777, or your local postmaster.
Port Charlotte Town Center 33948
Port Everglades (Part of Fort Lauderdale)‡ 33316
Port Hatchineha 33844
Port La Belle♦ 33935
Portland 32439
Port Malabar (Part of Palm Bay) 32905
Port Mayaca 33438
Port Orange 32129
Port Richey 34668*
34673†
Port Salerno♦ 34992
Port Sewall 34996
Port St. Joe 32456*
32457†
Port St. John 32927
Port St. Lucie 34952-53
34983-88
For specific ZIP Codes call (888) 275-8777, or your local postmaster.
Port Tampa City (Part of Tampa)‡ 33616

Pottsburg (Part of Jacksonville)‡ 32216
32245-46
For specific ZIP Codes call (888) 275-8777, or your local postmaster.
Powell 34609
Princeton 33032*
33092†
Produce (Part of Tampa)‡ 33610*
33680†
Progress Village 33619
Prospect Road (Part of Oakland Park)‡ 33309
Prosperity 32464
Providence, Polk 33809
Providence, Union 32054
Pumpkin Center 34797
Punta Gorda 33950-51
33955
33982-83
For specific ZIP Codes call (888) 275-8777, or your local postmaster.
Punta Gorda Isles (Part of Punta Gorda) 33950
Punta Rassa♦ 33908
Putnam Hall 32185
Quail Heights 33170
33177
33187
33189-90
33197
For specific ZIP Codes call (888) 275-8777, or your local postmaster.
Queens Cove 34947
Quincy 32351*
32353†
Raccoon Key 33040
Raiford 32083
Rainbow Lakes, *Marion* 34431
Rainbow Lakes, *Palm Beach*♦ 33437
Rainbow Springs 34432
Raleigh 32696
Ramblewood (Part of Sanford) 32773
Ramrod Key 33042
Ratliff 32011
Ravenna Park 32771
Recruit Training Command 32893
Red Bay 32455
Reddick 32686
Red Head 32437
Redington Beach 33708
Redington Shores 33708
Redland 33031
Red Level 34428
Regal Oaks 34744
Regal Park 34475
Regency (Part of Jacksonville)‡ 32211
Regency Park (Part of Jacksonville) 32225
Regency Square Mall (Part of Jacksonville) 32225
Resota Beach 32409
Rex 32640
Ribault Manor (Part of Jacksonville) 32208
Rice Creek 32177
Rich Bay 32333
Richland 33540
Richloam 33597
Richmond Heights♦ 33176
Richter Crossroads 32440
Ridge Harbor 33982
Ridge Manor♦ 33523
Ridgeway 33903
Ridgewood 32065
Ridgewood Estates 34232
Rio♦ 34957
Riomar (Part of Vero Beach) 32063
Riverdale, *Hernando* 33525
Riverdale, *St. Johns* 32095
River Forest (Part of Jacksonville) 32211
Riverhaven Village 34447
River Isles (Part of Bradenton) 34208
River Park 34983
River Ranch 33867
River Retreats 34431
Riverside (Part of Miami)‡ 33135

Riverside (Part of Jacksonville) 32204
River Trails 33917
Riverview (Part of Jacksonville) 32208
Riverview, *Hillsborough* 33568†
33569*
Riviera Beach 33404*
33419†
Robin Hill 32701
Robinson Heights 32667
Robinwood 32808
32818
For specific ZIP Codes call (888) 275-8777, or your local postmaster.
Rochelle 32601
Rock Bluff 32321
Rock Harbor 33037
Rock Hill, *Okaloosa* 32531
Rock Hill, *Walton* 32433
Rock Hill, *Washington* 32428
Rockledge 32955*
32956†
Rocksprings, *Marion* 34431
Rock Springs, *Orange* 32703
Rocky Creek 33615
Rocky Point 32608
Roeville 32583
Ro-Len Lake Gardens (Part of Hallandale) 33009
Rolling Acres 34602
Rolling Hills (Part of Jacksonville) 32221
Rolling Hills, *Marion* 34474
Rolling Hills, *Polk* 33860
Rolling Ranches 34431
Romeo 34432
Rosedale 32324
Roseland♦ 32957
Rosewood 32625
Round Lake 32420
Royal 34785
Royal Gardens Estates 34209
Royal Palm Beach 33411
Royal Palm Village 33908
Royals Cross Roads 32464
Royal Terrace (Part of Jacksonville) 32209
Rubonia 34221
Runnymeade 32303
Ruskin♦ 33570
Russell 32043
Rutland 33538
Sabal Palm Estates 33319
33368
For specific ZIP Codes call (888) 275-8777, or your local postmaster.
Sabal Palm Postal Store‡ 33319*
33359†
Saddlebunch Keys 33040
Saddle Creek 34241
Safety Harbor 34695
St. Andrews (Part of Panama City)‡ 32401
St. Armands (Part of Sarasota)‡ 34236
St. Augustine 32084-86
32092
32095
For specific ZIP Codes call (888) 275-8777, or your local postmaster.
St. Augustine Beach 32086
St. Augustine Shores♦ 32086
St. Augustine South♦ 32086
St. Catherine 33513
St. Cloud 34769-73
For specific ZIP Codes call (888) 275-8777, or your local postmaster.
St. George Island 32328
Saint James 32358
St. James City♦ 33956
Saint Joe Beach 32456
St. Johns Park (Part of Jacksonville) 32210
St. Johns Park, *Flagler* 32110
St. Johns River Estates, *Putnam* 32189
Saint Johns River Estates, *Seminole* 32771
Saint Josephs 32771
St. Leo 33574
St. Lucie 34946
St. Marks 32355
St. Nicholas (Part of Jacksonville) 32207
St. Pete Beach 33706*
33736†

St. Petersburg

33701-43
33747
33784
For specific ZIP Codes call (888) 275-8777, or your local postmaster.

Colleges & Universities

Eckerd Coll 33711

Financial Institutions

AmSouth Bank 33715
Barnett Bank, NA 33701
First Union Nat Bank 33702
NationsBank, NA 33713
Northern Trust Bank 33701
SouthTrust Bank, NA 33701

Hospitals

Bayfront Med Ctr 33701
Edward White 33713
General Hosp 33710
St. Anthony's Hosp 33705

Hotels/Motels

Bayfront Hilton 33701
Isla Del Sol 33715
Renaissance Vinoy Resort 33701

Military Installations

Coast Guard Sta 33701

St. Teresa 32358
Salem 32356
Salt Springs 32134
Samoset♦ 34208
Sampson City 32091
Samsula 32168
San Antonio 33576
San Blas 32456
San Carlos Park♦ 33912
Sandalwood (Part of Jacksonville) 32246
Sand Cut 33438
Sanderson 32087
Sandestin 32541
Sand Lake (Part of Orlando) 32819
32821
32836-37
32869
For specific ZIP Codes call (888) 275-8777, or your local postmaster.
Sandlefoot Cove 33428
Sandy 34251
Sandy Point 32008
Sanford 32771-73
For specific ZIP Codes call (888) 275-8777, or your local postmaster.
Sanibel 33957
San Jose (Part of Jacksonville) 32217
San Marco (Part of Jacksonville) 32207
San Mateo (Part of Jacksonville) 32218
San Mateo, *Putnam* 32187
San Souci Estates (Part of North Miami) 33181
San Souci Lakes 33917
Sans Souci, *Charlotte* 33982
Sans Souci (Part of Jacksonville) 32216
Santa Fe 32615
Santa Monica 32413
Santa Rosa Beach 32459
Santa Rosa Mall (Part of Mary Esther) 32569
Santos 34474
Sarasota 34230-43
34276-78
For specific ZIP Codes call (888) 275-8777, or your local postmaster.
Sarasota Heights (Part of Sarasota) 34239
Sarasota Main Plaza (Part of Sarasota) 34236
Sarasota Springs♦ 34232
Sarasota Square Mall 34238
Saratoga 32189
Sarno Plaza (Part of Melbourne)‡ 32935
Sasafrass Acres 32038
Satellite Beach 32937
Satsuma 32189
Saufley Field 32509
Sawdust 32351
Sawgrass♦ 32082
Sawgrass Mills (Part of City of Sunrise) 33323
Scenic Heights (Part of Tallahassee) 32303
Scotland 32333
Scotts Ferry 32424
Scottsmoor 32775
Seaglades 32507
Seagrove Beach 32459
Sea Ranch Lakes 33062
Searstown Mall (Part of Titusville) 32780
Seascape 32541
Seaside 32459
Sebastian 32958
32976-78
For specific ZIP Codes call (888) 275-8777, or your local postmaster.
Sebastian Highlands (Part of Sebastian) 32958
Sebring 33870-72
For specific ZIP Codes call (888) 275-8777, or your local postmaster.
Sebring Country Estates 33870
Sebring Hills 33872
Sebring Hills South 33870
Sebring Ridge 33870
Sebring Shores 33870
Seffner 33583†
33584*
Seminole, *Okaloosa* 32578
Seminole, *Pinellas* 33772
33775-76
For specific ZIP Codes call (888) 275-8777, or your local postmaster.
Seminole Heights (Part of Tampa)‡ 33603*
33673†
Seminole Mall (Part of Seminole) 33772
Seminole Manor (Part of Tallahassee) 32310
Seminole Manor, *Palm Beach* 33460
Seminole Park 33777
Seminole Plaza (Part of Casselberry) 32707
Seven Springs 34655
Seville 32190
Sewall's Point 34996
Shadeville 32327
Shadow Run 33569
Shady 34474
Shady Grove, *Jackson* 32442
Shady Grove, *Taylor* 32357
Shalimar 32579
Shamrock 32628
Shangri La 33584
Shannon Forest (Part of Tallahassee) 32308
Shannon Woods 32607
Sharpes 32959
Shawnee 33440
Shell Point 32327
Shenandoah (Part of Miami)‡ 33245
Sheridan Plaza (Part of Hollywood) 33021
Sherman 34974
Sherwood Forest (Part of Jacksonville) 32219
Sherwood Forest, *Osceola* 34746
Sherwood Park (Part of Delray Beach) 33445
Shockley Heights 32702
Shockley Hills 32702
Shore Acres (Part of St. Petersburg) 33705
Siesta Key♦ 34242
Siesta Lago 34746
Silver Beach Heights 32784
Silver Sands (Part of Panama City Beach) 32407
Silver Springs, *Marion* 34488-89
For specific ZIP Codes call (888) 275-8777, or your local postmaster.
Silver Springs, *Okaloosa* 32536
Silver Springs Shores♦ 34472
Simmons Point 32346
Singer Island (Part of Riviera Beach) 33404
Sink Creek 32448
Sirmans 32331
Skycrest (Part of Clearwater) 33755
Sky Lake♦ 32809
Skylake Mall 33162
Skyland Meadows 34442
Skyline Hills (Part of Lady Lake) 32159
Slavia 32765
Slones Ridge 34736
Sneads 32460
Snell Isle (Part of St. Petersburg) 33705
Snow Hill 32765
Socrum 33810
Solana♦ 33950
Sopchoppy 32358
Sorrento 32776
Sorrento Shores 34229
Sorrento Shores South 34275
South Apopka 32703
South Bay 33493
South Beach (Part of Miami Beach) 33139
Southboro (Part of West Palm Beach)‡ 33405
South Bradenton♦ 34205
South Clermont 34711
South Clinton Heights 33525
South Daytona 32121
South Florida (Part of Pembroke Pines)‡ 33082
Southgate‡ 34239*
34277†
South Gate Plaza (Part of Sarasota) 34239
South Gate Ridge 34233
South Jacksonville (Part of Jacksonville)‡ 32207*
34247†
South Merritt Estates 32952
South Miami 33143
33155
33243
For specific ZIP Codes call (888) 275-8777, or your local postmaster.
South Miami Heights 33157
33177
For specific ZIP Codes call (888) 275-8777, or your local postmaster.
South Mulberry 33860
South Palm Beach 33480
South Pasadena 33707
South Patrick Shores♦ 32937
South Pine Lakes 32736
Southpoint (Part of Jacksonville)‡ 32256
South Ponte Vedra Beach 32082
Southport, *Bay* 32409
South Port, *Osceola* 34746
South Punta Gorda Heights 33955
Southside (Part of Fort Lauderdale)‡ 33315-16
33335
For specific ZIP Codes call (888) 275-8777, or your local postmaster.
Southside (Part of Lakeland) 33807
33811
33813
For specific ZIP Codes call (888) 275-8777, or your local postmaster.
Southside Estates (Part of Jacksonville) 32246
South Venice♦ 34293
South Weeki Wachee 34606
Southwood 32809
Sparr 32192
Spring Creek 32327
Springfield, *Bay* 32401
Springfield (Part of Jacksonville) 32206
Spring Glen (Part of Jacksonville) 32207
Springhead 33566
Springhill, *Columbia* 32071
Spring Hill, *Hernando*♦ 34606-08
34611
For specific ZIP Codes call (888) 275-8777, or your local postmaster.
Spring Lake, *Hernando* 34602
Spring Lake, *Highlands* 33870
Spring Oaks (Part of Altamonte Springs) 32714
Springside 32177
Springs Plaza (Part of Longwood) 32779
Spruce Creek 32119
Spuds 32033
Starke 32091
State Capitol (Part of Tallahassee)‡ 32399
State Line 32426
Station A (Part of Daytona Beach)‡ 32122
Station F (Part of Jacksonville)‡ 32206
Steinhatchee 32359
Stetson University (Part of De Land) 32720
Stock Island♦ 33040
Stuart 34994-97
For specific ZIP Codes call (888) 275-8777, or your local postmaster.
Stucky Still 34736
Sugar Loaf Shores 33044
Sugar Mill, *Hillsborough* 33624
Sugar Mill, *Volusia* 32168
Sugarmill Woods 34446
Sulphur Springs (Part of Tampa)‡ 33604*
33674†
Sumatra 32335
Summerbrooke (Part of Tallahassee) 32312
Summerfield, *Hillsborough* 33569
Summerfield, *Marion* 34491-92
For specific ZIP Codes call (888) 275-8777, or your local postmaster.
Summer Haven 32086
Summerland Key 33042
Summer Place 32960
Summerport Beach 34786
Sumner 32625
Sumterville 33585
Sun City 33586
Sun City Center♦ 33571†
33573*
Suncoast Estates♦ 33917
Sun Haven 34231
Suniland 33156
Sunlake 32735
Sunland Estates 32771
Sunland Gardens 34947
Sunniland, *Collier* 34142
Sunniland, *Dade* 33156
Sun 'n Lake Acres 33852
Sun 'n Lake Estates 33852
Sun 'n Lakes 33870
Sunny Breeze Harbour 34266
Sunny Hills 32428
Sunny Isles♦ 33160
Sunnyland 34233
Sunnyside, *Bay* 32461
Sunnyside, *Lake* 34748
Sun Ray Homes 33843
Sunrise, *Broward* 33313
33322-23
33325-26
33338
33345
33351
For specific ZIP Codes call (888) 275-8777, or your local postmaster.
Sunrise (Part of Fort Lauderdale) 33304
Sunset Harbor 34491
Sunset Islands (Part of Miami Beach) 33140
Sunshine Mall (Part of Clearwater) 33756
Suntree 32940
Sun Valley♦ 33437
Surf 32346
Surfside 33154
Survey Creek 34136

Suwannee 32692
Suwannee Gardens 32680
Suwannee River Park Estates 32060
Suwannee Springs 32060
Suwannee Valley 32055
Svea 32567
Sweet Gum Head 32464
Sweetwater, *Dade* 33172
... 33174
For specific ZIP Codes call (888) 275-8777, or your local postmaster.
Sweetwater, *Liberty* 32321
Sweetwater Creek 33615
Sweetwater Oaks 32750
Switzerland 32043
Sycamore 32351
Sydney 33587
Sylvania 32462
Sylvan Shores, *Highlands*♦ 33852
Sylvan Shores, *Lake* 32757
Taft 32824
Talisman Estates 33523
Tallahassee 32301-04
... 32306-08
... 32310-17
... 32399
For specific ZIP Codes call (888) 275-8777, or your local postmaster.
Tallahassee Mall (Part of Tallahassee) 32303
Tallevast 34270
Talleyrand (Part of Jacksonville) 32206
Tamarac 33320-21
For specific ZIP Codes call (888) 275-8777, or your local postmaster.
Tamiami (Part of Miami)‡ 33144

Tampa

... 33601-97
For specific ZIP Codes call (888) 275-8777, or your local postmaster.

Colleges & Universities

Education America-Tampa Technical Institute Campus 33612
International Academy of Merchandising & Design 33634
ITT Technical Institute 33634
Tampa Coll 33614
Univ of South Florida 33620
Univ of Tampa 33606

Financial Institutions

AmSouth Bank 33602
Barnett Bank 33602
First Union 33602
NationsBank, NA 33602
SouthTrust Bank, NA 33609
SunTrust Bank, Tampa Bay 33602

Hospitals

James A Haley Veterans Hosp 33612
St Joseph's Hosp 33607
Tampa General Healthcare 33613
Univ Community Hosp 33613

Hotels/Motels

Best Western, Busch Gardens 33612
The Camberley Plaza, Sabal Park 33610
Crowne Plaza 33609
Days Inn, Airport/Stadium 33607
Days Inn, Busch Gardens North 33612
Doubletree Guest Suites, Tampa Airport 33607
Holiday Inn, Busch Gardens 33612
Hyatt Regency at City Ctr 33602
Hyatt Regency, Westshore on Tampa Bay 33607
Marriott, Airport 33607
Marriott, Westshore 33607
Radisson Bay Harbor Inn 33607
Ramada, Airport Hotel & Conference Ctr 33609
Sheraton Grand Westshore 33609
Wyndham, Harbour Island Hotel 33602

Military Installations

Defense Fuel Support Point 33686
MacDill Air Force Base 33621
Marine Corps Res Training Ctr 33611

Tampa Bay Center (Part of Tampa) 33607
Tangelo Park♦ 32819
Tangerine 32777
Tang-O-Mar Beach 32541
Tarpon Lake Village 34685
Tarpon Springs 34688†
... 34689*
Tarpon Woods 34685
Tarrytown 33597
Tavares 32778
Tavernier♦ 33070
Taylor 32087
Taylor Creek♦ 34974
Tee and Green Estates 33982
Telogia 32360
Temple Terrace 33617*
... 33687†
Tenille 32356
Tensulate (Part of Jacksonville) 32209
Tequesta 33469
Terra Ceia 34250
The Forest 33908
The Fountains 33467
The Hamptons 33434
The Landings, *Lee* 33919
The Landings, *Sarasota* 34231
The Meadows, *Clay* 32065
The Meadows, *Lake* 32702
The Meadows, *Sarasota*♦ 34235
Theressa 32091
The Vineyards 34119
Thomas City 32344
Thompson Estates 32778
Thonotosassa 33592
Three Rivers 32322
Three Rivers Estates 32038
Tice♦ 33905
Tierra Verde‡ 33715
Tiger Point 32561
Tildenville 34787
Timberline Estates 34461
Timberwood Estates 34785
Tisonia (Part of Jacksonville) 32218
Titusville 32780-83
... 32796
For specific ZIP Codes call (888) 275-8777, or your local postmaster.
Tocoi 32033
Tommytown (Part of Dade City) 33523
Tomoka Estates 32174
Torchlite 34711
Torrey 33834
Tower Shops (Part of Davie) 33314
Town and Country Plaza 32505
Town and River Estates 33919
Town Center at Boca Raton (Part of Boca Raton) 33431
Town & Country Center 33183
Town 'n' Country 33615
... 33635
For specific ZIP Codes call (888) 275-8777, or your local postmaster.
Town Park Estates 33165
... 33174
For specific ZIP Codes call (888) 275-8777, or your local postmaster.
Trailer Estates 34281
Trailer Haven (Part of Melbourne)‡ 32901
Trapnell 33567
Treasure Island (Part of North Bay Village) 33141
Treasure Island, *Lake* 34788
Treasure Island, *Pinellas* 33706
Trenton 32693
Triangle Acres 32757
Trilby 33593
Tri Par Estates 34234
Tropic 32952*
... 32965†
Tropical Acres 33569
Tropical Farms 34990
Tropical Gulf Acres 33955
Tropical Shores Manor 32778
Tropic Palms (Part of Delray Beach) 33444
Tropic Vista 33469
Truckland 33908
Turkey Creek 33567
Turner River 34141
Turquoise Beach 32459
Tuscanooga 34736
Tuskawilla (Part of Winter Springs) 32708
Twin City Mall (Part of North Palm Beach) 33408
Two Egg 32423
Tyndall Air Force Base 32403
Tyrone Square (Part of St. Petersburg) 33710
Uleta 33164
Umatilla 32784
Union Park♦ 32817*
... 32867†
University‡ 32603*
... 32604†
University Mall (Part of Pembroke Pines) 33024
University Mall (Part of Pensacola) 32504
University Mall, *Hillsborough* 33612
University of Miami (Part of Coral Gables) 33124
University of Tampa (Part of Tampa) 33606
University Park (Part of Jacksonville) 32277
University Park, *Manatee* 34201
University Park, *Orange* 32817
University Plaza 33612
University West♦ 33612-13
For specific ZIP Codes call (888) 275-8777, or your local postmaster.
USAF Hospital‡ 32542
Useppa Island 33924
Valdez 32713
Valkaria 32905
Valparaiso 32580
Valrico 33594*
... 33595†
Vamo♦ 34231
Venetia (Part of Jacksonville) 32210
Venetian Islands (Part of Miami Beach) 33139
Venetian Isles (Part of St. Petersburg) 33705
Venetian Isles, *Santa Rosa* 32561
Venetia Terrace (Part of Jacksonville) 32244
Venice 34284-86
... 34292-93
For specific ZIP Codes call (888) 275-8777, or your local postmaster.
Venice Acres 34292
Venice East 34293
Venice Gardens♦ 34293
Venus 33960
Verdie 32009
Vermont Heights 32033
Verna 34251
Vernon 32462
Vero Beach 32960-69
For specific ZIP Codes call (888) 275-8777, or your local postmaster.
Vero Beach Highlands 32962
Vero Lake Estates 32967
Vero Shores 32962
Vicksburg 32401
Viera 32940
Vilano Beach♦ 32095
Vilas 32334
Village (Part of Deerfield Beach)‡ 33442
Village Green (Part of Rockledge)‡ 32955
Village Green (Part of Bradenton) 34209
Village of Golf 33436
Village of Pine Run 32174
Villages of Oriole♦ 33446
Villa Sabine 32561
Villa Tasso 32578
Vina del Mar (Part of St. Pete Beach) 33706
Virginia Gardens 33166
Volusia 32102
Volusia Mall (Part of Daytona Beach) 32114
Wabasso♦ 32970
Wacahotta 32667
Waccasassa Lake 32693
Wacissa 32361
Wadesboro 32308
Wahneta♦ 33880
Wahoo 33513
Wakulla 32327
Wakulla Gardens 32327
Wakulla Springs 32305
Waldo 32694
Wallace 32571
Walnut Hill 32568
Walsingham 33774
Walton 34957
Wannee 32619
Ward Ridge 32456
Warm Mineral Springs♦ 34287
Warrington♦ 32507
Washington Lake Estates (Part of Jacksonville) 32218
Washington Park♦ 33311
Washington Shores (Part of Orlando) 32805
Waters Lake 32693
Watertown 32055
Waterway Estates 33903
Wauchula 33873
Wauchula Hills 33873
Waukeenah 32344
Wausau 32463
Waverly♦ 33877
Waverly Hills (Part of Tallahassee) 32312
Weathersfield 32714
Webster 33597
Weeki Wachee 34606
Weeki Wachee Acres♦ 34606
Weeki Wachee Gardens♦ 34607
Weirsdale 32195
Wekiva Springs 32779
... 32791
For specific ZIP Codes call (888) 275-8777, or your local postmaster.
Wekiwa Acres 32703
Welaka 32193
Welcome 33547
Wellborn 32094
Wellington‡ 33414
Wesconnett (Part of Jacksonville) 32244
Wesley Chapel 33543-44
For specific ZIP Codes call (888) 275-8777, or your local postmaster.
Wesley Manor‡ 32223
West Atlantic (Part of Coral Springs) 33071*
... 33077†
West Bay 32413
West Bradenton♦ 34209
Westchester 33144
... 33155
... 33165
... 33174
For specific ZIP Codes call (888) 275-8777, or your local postmaster.
West End, *Calhoun* 32424
West End (Part of Marianna)‡ 32446
Western Acres 33903
West Farm 32340
West Frostproof 33843
Westgate (Part of Bradenton)‡ 34205
Westgate, *Palm Beach* 33409
West Holly Hill 32117
West Hollywood (Part of Pembroke Pines) 33023*
... 33083†
West Jacksonville (Part of Jacksonville) 32254
West Kendall 33296
Westland Mall (Part of Hialeah) 33012
Westland Promenade (Part of Hialeah) 33014
West Lantana (Part of Lantana) 33462
West Melbourne 32904*
... 32912†
West Miami 33144
... 33155
For specific ZIP Codes call (888) 275-8777, or your local postmaster.
Weston 33326
West Palm Beach 33401-07
... 33409-20
For specific ZIP Codes call (888) 275-8777, or your local postmaster.
West Palmetto Park (Part of Boca Raton)‡ 33427†
... 33486*
West Panama City Beach (Part of Panama City Beach) 32413
West Pensacola♦ 32505
Westridge 33433
West Scenic Park 33853
West Shore Plaza (Part of Tampa) 33609
West Tampa (Part of Tampa)‡ 33607*
... 33677†
West Town Corners (Part of Altamonte Springs) 32714
Westville 32464
Westwood (Part of Jacksonville) 32244
Westwood, *Orange* 32808
Westwood Acres 34474
Westwood Lakes♦ 33165
Wewahitchka 32465
Whiskey Creek♦ 33919
Whispering Pines, *Madison* 32340
Whispering Pines, *Okeechobee* 34972
Whispering Pines, *Putnam* 32139
Whisper Walk 33496
White City, *Gulf* 32465
White City, *St. Lucie*♦ 34981
Whitehouse (Part of Jacksonville)‡ 32220
White Springs, *Hamilton* 32096
White Springs, *Liberty* 32321
Whitfield Estates 34243
Whiting Field 32570
Whitney 34748
Whitney Beach (Part of Longboat Key) 34228
Wilbur-By-The-Sea 32127
Wilcox 32693
Wildwood 34785
Williamsburg♦ 32821*
... 32823†
Williams Point 32959
Willis Landing 32465
Williston 32696
Williston Highlands 32696
Willow Oak♦ 33860
Wilson Corner 33597
Wilson Neck 32097
Wilton Manors 33305-06
... 33311
... 33334
For specific ZIP Codes call (888) 275-8777, or your local postmaster.
Wimauma♦ 33598
Windermere 34786
Winding Lakes 33428
Windsor 32601
Winfield 32055
Winston 33811
Winter Beach 32971

Winter Garden 34777-78
.... 34787
For specific ZIP Codes call (888) 275-8777, or your local postmaster.
Winter Haven 33880-85
For specific ZIP Codes call (888) 275-8777, or your local postmaster.
Winter Haven Mall (Part of Winter Haven) 33880
Winter Park 32789-90
..................................32792-93
For specific ZIP Codes call (888) 275-8777, or your local postmaster.
Winter Park Estates 32792
Winter Park Mall (Part of Winter Park) 32789
Winter Springs 32708*
.... 32719†
Wiscon 34609
Woodland (Part of Boca Raton)‡ 33431*
.... 33448†
Woodland Drives (Part of Tallahassee) 32301
Woodlawn, Bay 32407
Woodlawn (Part of St. Petersburg).......... 33704
Woodlawn, *St. Johns*.. 32095
Woodlawn Beach 32561
Woodmont (Part of Tamarac) 33321
Woods........................ 32321
Woods and Lakes 32179
Woodville♦................. 32362
Woodward Avenue (Part of Tallahassee)‡ 32304*
.... 32316†
Worthington Springs .. 32697
Wright♦ 32547
Wulfert (Part of Sanibel) 33957
Wynnehaven Beach.... 32569
Wynwood (Part of Miami) 33127
Wynwood (Part of Sanford)................... 32771
Yacht Club Colony...... 33917
Yalaha♦ 34797
Yankeetown................ 34498
Ybor City (Part of Tampa)‡ 33605*
.... 33675†
Yeehaw Junction 34972
Yellow Pine 32340
Yelvington 32131
York........................... 34474
Youmans 33566
Youngstown 32466
Yukon (Part of Jacksonville) 32244
Yulee .... 32041†
.... 32097*
Yulee Heights............. 32097
Yulee Woods 32097
Zellwood 32798
Zephyrhills 33539-44
For specific ZIP Codes call (888) 275-8777, or your local postmaster.
Zolfo Springs 33890
Zuber.......................... 34475

Aaron	30450
Abba	31750
Abbeville	31001
Abbott	30094
Abbottsford	30240
Aberdeen (Part of Peachtree City)	30269
Acree	31791
Acworth	30101-02
For specific ZIP Codes call (888) 275-8777, or your local postmaster.	
Adairsville	30103
Adams Park (Part of Atlanta)	30311
Adams Park, *Twiggs*	31020
Adamsville (Part of Atlanta)	30331
Adasburg	30673
Adel	31620
Adgateville	31038
Adrian	31002
Agnes	30817
Agnes Scott College (Part of Decatur)‡	30030
Agricola	30820
Ailey	30410
Air Line	30516
Airport Mail Facility (Part of Atlanta)‡	30320
Akers Mill‡	30339*
	31139†
Akin	30415
Alamo	30411
Alapaha	31622
Albany	31701-08
For specific ZIP Codes call (888) 275-8777, or your local postmaster.	
Albion Acres	30906
Alcovy	30014
Alcovy Shores	31064
Aldora	30204
Alexander	30456
Alfords	31791
Aline	30420
Allendale, *Gwinnett*	30045
Allendale (Part of Columbus)	31909
Allenhurst	31301
Allentown	31003
Allenville	31639
Allenwood	31061
Allie	30222
Alma	31510
Almon	30014
Almond Park (Part of Atlanta)	30318
Alpharetta	30004-05
	30009
	30022-23
For specific ZIP Codes call (888) 275-8777, or your local postmaster.	
Alpine	30731
Alps Road (Part of Athens)‡	30604
Alston	30412
Altamaha	30453
Alta Vista (Part of Columbus)	31907
Altman	30467
Alto	30510
Alto Park	30165
Alvaton	30218
Amboy	31714
Ambrose	31512
Americus	31709
Amity	30817
Amos Mill	35967
Amsterdam	31734
Anderson City	31744
Andersonville	31711
Andrew Wood (Part of Columbus)	31903
Anguilla	31525
Ansley	30828
Ansley Estates	30274
Anthony Terrace (Part of Macon)	31206
Antioch, *Polk*	30125
Antioch, *Troup*	30240
Aonia	30673
Apalachee	30650
Apple Valley	30529
Appling	30802
Arabi	31712
Aragon	30104
Aragon Park	30901
Arcade	30549
Arch City	30701
Arco	31520
Arcola	30415
Ardick	31331
Ardmore	31329
Ardsley Park (Part of Savannah)	31405
Argyle	31623
Arkwright	31204
Arlington	31713
Arlington (Part of Macon)‡	31217
Arlington Park (Part of Macon)	31204
Armuchee	30105
Arnco Mills	30263
Arnoldsville	30619
Arp	31783
Arrowhead Village	30236
Ascalon	30738
Ashburn	31714
Ashford Park	30319
Ashintilly	31331
Ashland	30521
Athens	30601-13
For specific ZIP Codes call (888) 275-8777, or your local postmaster.	
Atkinson	31543

Atlanta

	30301-94
	31101-56
For specific ZIP Codes call (888) 275-8777, or your local postmaster.	

Colleges & Universities

American Intercontinental Univ	30326
Atlanta Coll of Art	30309
Beulah Heights Bible Coll	30316
Clark Atlanta Univ	30314
Emory Univ	30322
Georgia Institute of Technology	30332
Georgia State Univ	30303
Interdenominational Theological Ctr	30314
Morehouse Coll	30314
Morehouse School of Medicine	30310
Morris Brown Coll	30314
Oglethorpe Univ	30319
Spelman Coll	30314

Financial Institutions

First Union Nat Bank	30309
NationsBank, NA	30303
The Prudential Bank & Trust Co	30346
SouthTrust Bank, NA	30308
SunTrust Bank	30303
Wachovia Bank, NA	30303

Hospitals

Crawford Long Hosp of Emory Univ	30365
Emory Univ Hosp	30322
Georgia Baptist Med Ctr	30312
Georgia Mental Health Institute	30306
Grady Memorial Hosp	30335
Northside Hosp	30342
Piedmont Hosp	30309
Saint Joseph's Hosp	30342

Hotels/Motels

Crowne Plaza, Ravinia	30346
Hilton & Towers, Atlanta	30303
Holiday Inn, Airport North	30344
Hyatt Regency in Peachtree Ctr	30303
Marriott, Atlanta Airport	30337
Marriott Marquis	30303
Marriott Northwest	30339
Marriott, Perimeter Ctr	30346
Omni at CNN Ctr	30335
Radisson	30303
Ramada, Downtown	30303
Renaissance, Atlanta Hotel-Concourse	30354
Renaissance, Downtown	30308
Renaissance Waverly	30339
The Ritz-Carlton	30303
The Ritz-Carlton, Buckhead, Uptown	30326
Sheraton Colony Square	30361
Sheraton Gateway	30337
The Westin Peachtree Plaza	30303

Military Installations

U S Army Corps of Engineers, South Atlantic Div	30335
U S Property & Fiscal Off for Georgia	30316

Atlanta Naval Air Station	30060
Attapulgus	31715
Attapulgus Station	31715
Attica	30607
Auburn	30011
Audubon	30735
Augusta	30901-19
For specific ZIP Codes call (888) 275-8777, or your local postmaster.	
Aumond Heights	30909
Aumond Place	30909
Auraria	30534
Austell	30106
	30168
For specific ZIP Codes call (888) 275-8777, or your local postmaster.	
Autreyville	31768
Autumn Forest	30236
Avallon	30328
Avalon (Part of Savannah)	31419
Avalon, *Stephens*	30557
Avans	30752
Avants	30411
Avera	30803
Avert Acres	31705
Avery	30115
Avondale, *Bibb*	31216
Avondale, *McDuffie*	30814
Avondale (Part of Columbus)	31903
Avondale Estates	30002
Avondale Heights (Part of Columbus)	31903
Avondale Park (Part of Savannah)	31404
Axson	31624
Ayersville	30577
Azalea Park (Part of Macon)	31204
Babcock	31737
Bachlott	31553
Baconton	31716
Bainbridge	31717*
	31718†
Bairdstown	30669
Baker Village (Part of Columbus)‡	31903
Baldwin	30511
Baldwin Park (Part of Savannah)	31401
Baldwinville	31812
Ball Ground, *Cherokee*	30107
Ball Ground, *Murray*	30705
Baltimore (Part of Washington)	30673
Banks Crossing	30529
Banning	30185
Bannockburn	31639
Barksdale	31082
Barnesville	30204
Barnett	30821
Barnett Shoals	30605
Barney	31625
Barneyville	31647
Barnhill	30457
Barnsley	30145
Barrett Parkway (Part of Kennesaw)‡	30144
Barretts	31605
Barrettsville	30534
Barrow Heights	30680
Bartletts Ferry	31808
Barton Village	30906
Bartonwoods	30307
Bartow	30413
Barwick	31720
Bascom	30467
Bass Crossroads	30230
Batesville	30523
Bath	30805
Battery Point	31404
Battle Forest (Part of Decatur)	30034
Baughs Crossroads	31833
Baxley	31513*
	31515†
Bay	31756
Bay Branch	30467
Bayview	31316
Beach	31554
Beachton	31792
Beacon Heights	30650
Beallwood (Part of Columbus)‡	31904
Beaulieu	31406
Beaumont	30736
Beaverdale	30721
Bedingfield (Part of Macon)	31206
Beechwood Shopping Center (Part of Athens)	30606
Belair	30907
Belair Hills Estates	30909
Belfast	31324
Bellemeade	30906
Bellton (Part of Lula)	30554
Bellville	30414
Bellville Bluff	31331
Belmont, *DeKalb*	30086
Belmont, *Hall*	30507
Belmont Hills Shopping Center (Part of Smyrna)	30080
Belvedere	30032
Belvins Acres	30736
Bemiss	31605
Benedict	30125
Benevolence	31740
Ben Hill (Part of Atlanta)‡	30331*
	31131†
Benning Hills (Part of Columbus)	31903
Bentley Place	30741
Benton	30165
Bent Tree	30143
Berckman Hills	30909
Berckman Village	30909
Berkeley Lake	30096
Berkshire Woods (Part of Savannah)	31419
Berlin	31722
Berner	31029
Berryton	30747
Berzelia	30814
Bethany	31762
Bethel, *Jasper*	31064
Bethel, *Randolph*	31740
Bethesda, *Chatham*	31406
Bethesda, *Greene*	30669
Bethesda, *Gwinnett*	30045
Bethlehem	30620
Between	30656
Beulah, *Hancock*	31087
Beulah, *Lincoln*	30668
Beulah, *Paulding*	30153
Beulah Heights (Part of Atlanta)	30312
Beverly Hills	30741
Boxton	30259
Bibb City‡	31904
Bibb Mills	31029
Bickley	31554
Big Canoe	30143
Big Creek	30041
Big Springs	30241
Billarp	30187
Bingville (Part of Savannah)‡	31405
Birdie	30223
Birmingham	30004
Bishop	30621
Blackjack	30276
Blackshear	31516
Blackshear Place	30507
Blacksville♦	30253
Blackville	30457
Blackwells	30066
Blackwood	30701
Blaine	30175
Blairsville	30512*
	30514†
Blair Village (Part of Atlanta)	30354
Blakely	31723
Blandford	31326
Bland Villa	31015
Blandy (Part of Milledgeville)	31061
Blitchton	31308
Bloomfield Gardens (Part of Macon)	31216
Bloomingdale	31302
Blount	31029
Blowing Springs	30725
Blue Ridge	30513
Blue Spring	30736
Blue Springs, *Dougherty*	31707
Blue Springs, *Screven*	30446
Bluffton	31724
Blun	30401
Blundale	30401
Blythe	30805
Bogart	30622
Bold Spring	30656
Bolingbroke	31004
Bolton (Part of Atlanta)	30318
Bona Bella	31406
Bonair	30907
Bonaire	31005
Bonanza♦	30238
Bond	30633
Boneville	30806
Bonny Brook Estates (Part of Atlanta)	30311
Booker Washington Heights (Part of Columbus)	31909
Boozeville	30147
Boston	31626
Bostwick	30623
Bowden Hills (Part of Macon)	31217
Bowdon	30108
Bowdon Junction	30109
Bowens Mill	31750
Bowersville	30516
Bowman	30624
Box Springs	31801
Boyd Highlands	30736
Boydville	30577
Boykin	31737
Boynton	30736
Boys Estate	31523
Bradley	31032
Branchville	31730
Brantley	31803
Braselton	30517
Braswell	30153
Bremen	30110
Brent	31029
Brentwood, *Dougherty*	31707
Brentwood, *Wayne*	31555
Brentwood (Part of Atlanta)	30331
Brest	31716
Brewton	31021
Briarcliff (Part of Atlanta)‡	30329
Briarwood (Part of Savannah)	31408
Briarwood, *Columbia*	30907
Briarwood (Part of East Point)	30344
Briarwood, *Rockdale*	30094
Briar Wood Estates	30068
Brick Store	30025
Bridgeboro	31705
Bridgeman Heights	31217
Brighton	31794
Brighton Woods (Part of Pooler)	31322
Brinson	31725
Brisbon	31324
Bristol	31518
Bristol Forest (Part of Macon)	31217
Bristol Woods	30094
Broad	30668
Broadhurst	31545
Broadview (Part of Atlanta)‡	30324
Brockton	30549
Bronco	30728
Bronwood	31726
Brookfield	31727
Brookfield West	30907
Brookhaven, *Bibb*	31206
Brookhaven, *DeKalb*	30319
Brookhaven (Part of Columbus)	31906
Brooklet	30415

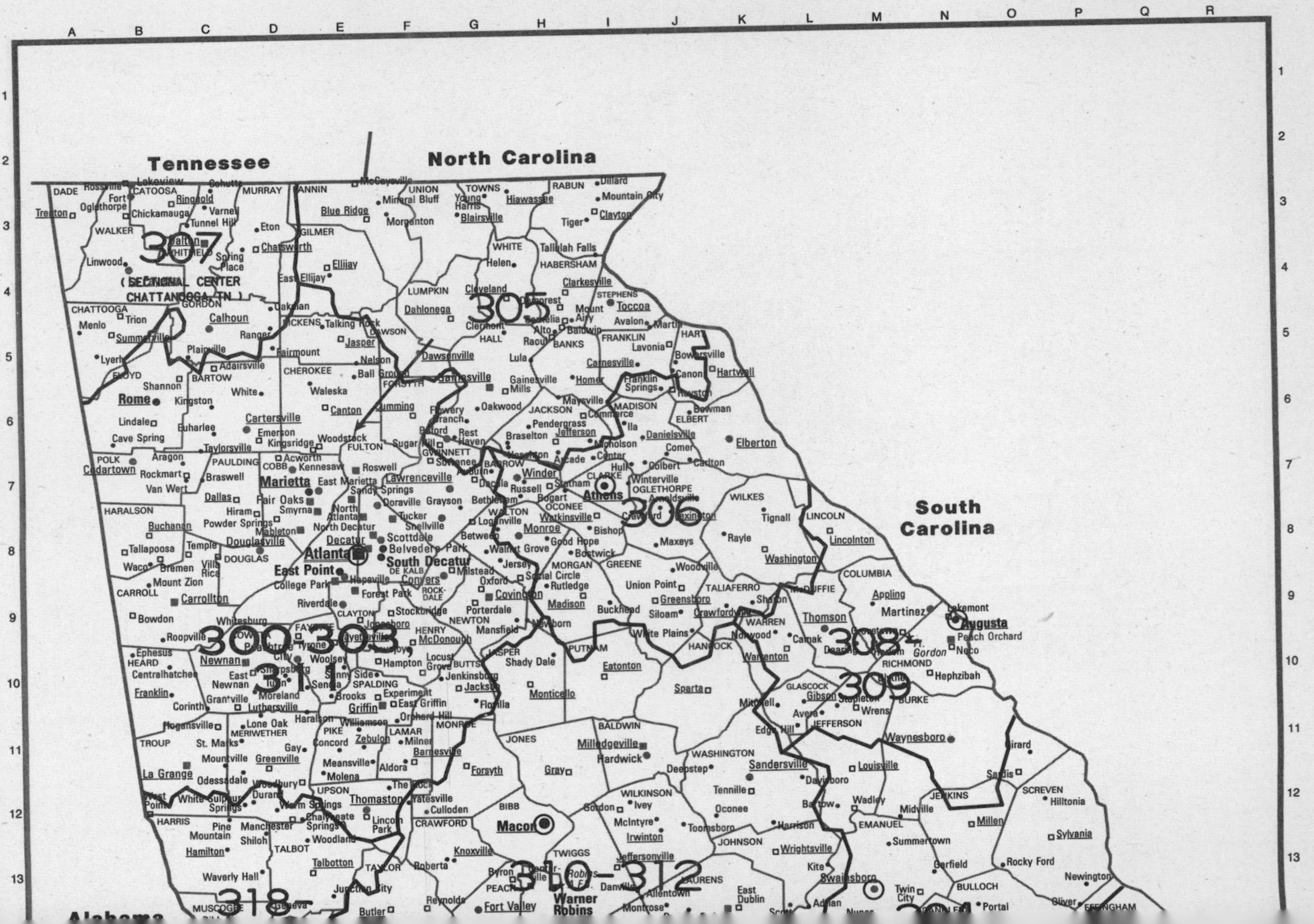
Tennessee
North Carolina
South Carolina
(SECTIONAL CENTER
CHATTANOOGA, TN)
307
305
306
300 303,
311
308
309
310-312
318
Rome
Dalton
Calhoun
Cartersville
Marietta
Atlanta
East Point
Decatur
South Decatur
Carrollton
Newnan
La Grange
Griffin
Thomaston
Gainesville
Toccoa
Athens
Elberton
Washington
Augusta
Thomson
Waynesboro
Milledgeville
Sandersville
Macon
Warner Robins
Fort Valley
Swainsboro

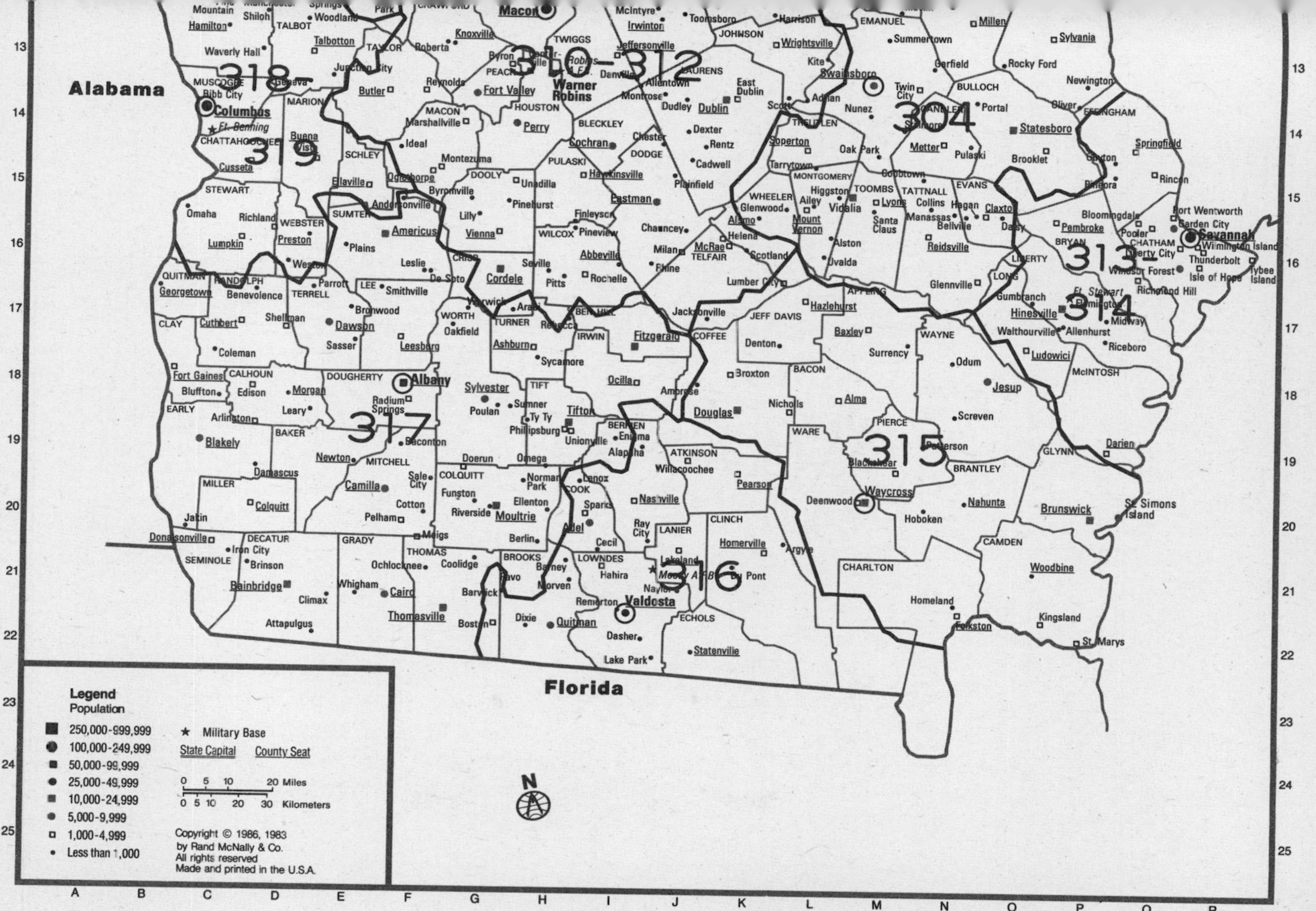
Alabama
Florida
Columbus
Macon
Warner Robins
Albany
Valdosta
Waycross
Savannah
Brunswick
Legend
Population
250,000-999,999
100,000-249,999
50,000-99,999
25,000-49,999
10,000-24,999
5,000-9,999
1,000-4,999
Less than 1,000
★ Military Base
State Capital
County Seat
0 5 10 20 Miles
0 5 10 20 30 Kilometers
Copyright © 1986, 1983
by Rand McNally & Co.
All rights reserved
Made and printed in the U.S.A.

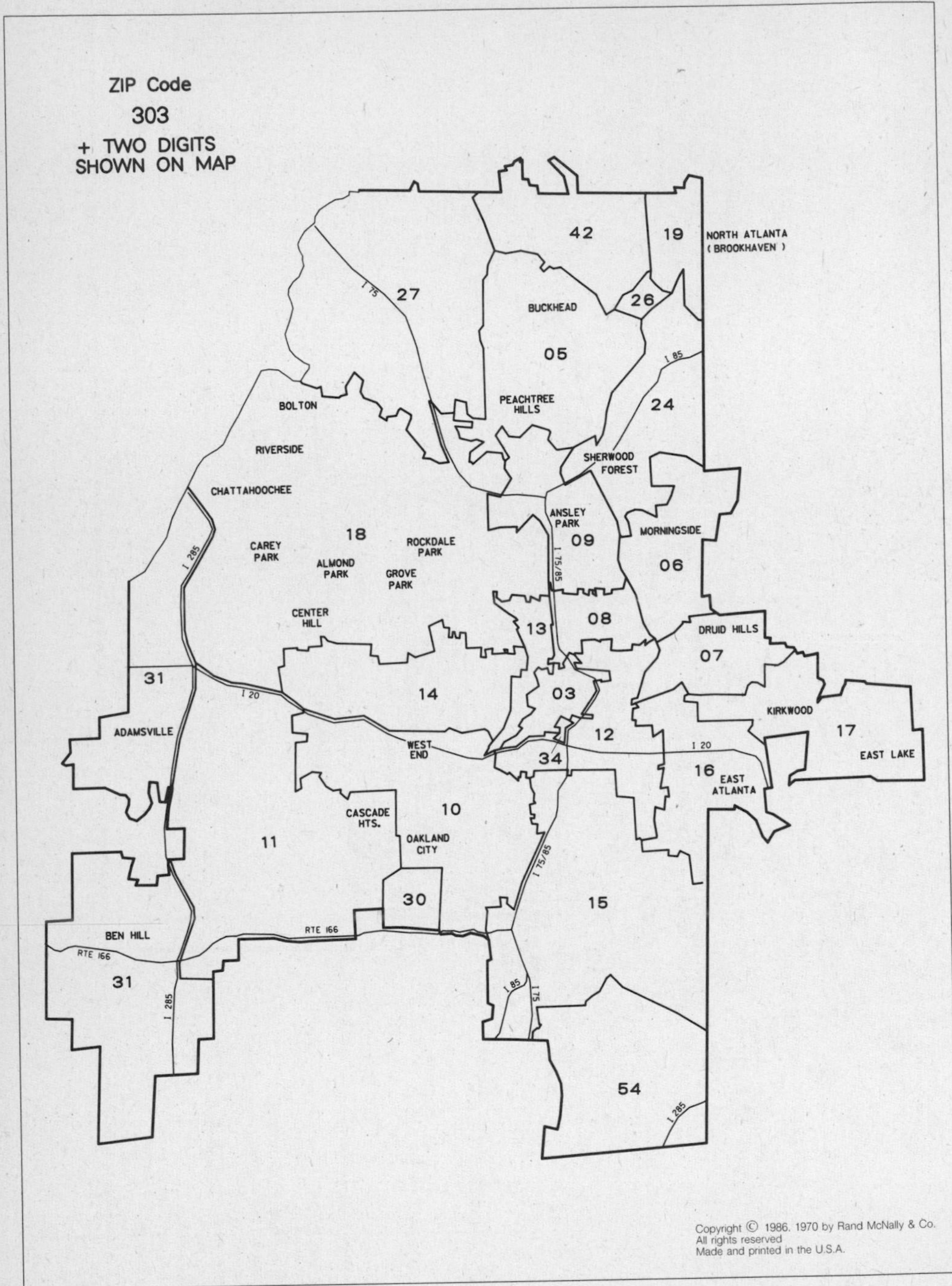
ZIP Code
303
+ TWO DIGITS
SHOWN ON MAP
42
19
NORTH ATLANTA
(BROOKHAVEN)
27
26
BUCKHEAD
05
PEACHTREE HILLS
24
BOLTON
RIVERSIDE
SHERWOOD FOREST
CHATTAHOOCHEE
ANSLEY PARK
18
MORNINGSIDE
CAREY PARK
ROCKDALE PARK
09
ALMOND PARK
GROVE PARK
06
CENTER HILL
08
13
DRUID HILLS
07
31
03
14
KIRKWOOD
ADAMSVILLE
12
17
WEST END
34
EAST LAKE
16
EAST ATLANTA
10
CASCADE HTS.
11
OAKLAND CITY
30
15
BEN HILL
RTE 166
31
54
I 75
I 85
I 285
I 20
I 75/85

Brooklyn 31825
Brooks 30205
Brookstone (Part of Acworth)‡ 30101
Brookstone (Part of Columbus) 31904
Brookstore Place 30342
Brooksville 31740
Brookton 30506
Brookvale Estates 30736
Brookview 31406
Brookwood, *Forsyth* 30005
Brookwood (Part of Dublin) 31021
Brookwood, *Richmond* 30909
Browndale 31036
Browns, *Baldwin* 31061
Browns, *Dade* 30752
Brownsville 30133
Browntown 31543
Brownwood 30650
Broxton 31519
Brunswick 31520-21
31523-25
For specific ZIP Codes call (888) 275-8777, or your local postmaster.
Brynwood 30909
Buchanan 30113
Buckhead (Part of Atlanta)‡ 30326*
31126†
Buckhead, Morgan 30625
Bucktown 30108
Budapest 30176
Buena Vista 31803
Buffington 30114
Buford 30515
30518-19
For specific ZIP Codes call (888) 275-8777, or your local postmaster.
Bullard 31020
Bulloch Crossroads 31816
Bumphead 31806
Bunker Hill 30512
Burning Bush 30736
Burnside 31406
Burnside Island 31406
Burroughs 31405
Burwell 30117
Bushnell 31533
Butler, *Dougherty* 31705
Butler, *Taylor* 31006
Butler Manor 30905
Butts 30442
Byers Crossroads 30185
Byne Crossroads 31763
Byromville 31007
Byron 31008
Cabaniss 31029
Cadley 30821
Cadwell 31009
Cagle 30143
Cairo 31728
Caleb 30058
Calhoun 30701-03
For specific ZIP Codes call (888) 275-8777, or your local postmaster.
Callaway 30660
Calvary 31729
Camak 30807
Camellia Terrace (Part of Savannah) 31404
Camelot, *Clarke* 30606
Camelot, *Clayton* 30236
Cameron 30467
Camilla 31730
Campania 30814
Campbellton 30213
Campton 30655
Campus (Part of Athens) 30605
Canal Lake 30512
Candler 30507
Cannon Crossing 30742
Cannon Gate 30907
Cannonville 30240
Canon 30520
Canoochee 30471
Canton 30114-15
For specific ZIP Codes call (888) 275-8777, or your local postmaster.
Canton Plaza (Part of Marietta)‡ 30066
Capel 31728

Capitol Hill (Part of Atlanta)‡ 30334
Captola 30467
Carbondale 30721
Carey Park (Part of Atlanta) 30318
Carl 30011
Carlton 30627
Carmichael Crossroads 30115
Carnegie 31740
Carnes Creek 30577
Carnesville 30521
Carnigan 31319
Carns Mill 30175
Caroline Park (Part of Columbus) 31904
Carrollton 30116-17
For specific ZIP Codes call (888) 275-8777, or your local postmaster.
Carrs 31087
Carsonville 31006
Cartecay 30540
Carter Acres (Part of Columbus) 31903
Carters 30705
Carters Grove 30660
Cartersville 30120-21
For specific ZIP Codes call (888) 275-8777, or your local postmaster.
Carver Heights (Part of Columbus) 31906
Carver Village (Part of Savannah) 31415
Cary 31014
Cascade Heights (Part of Atlanta)‡ 30311
Cascade Hills (Part of Columbus) 31904
Cash 30701
Cassandra 30707
Cassville 30123
Castle Park (Part of Valdosta)‡ 31604
Castlewood (Part of Columbus) 31907
Cataula 31804
Catlett 30728
Cave Spring 30124
Cecil 31627
Cedar Creek 30274
Cedar Creek Park 30605
Cedar Crossing 30436
Cedar Grove (Part of Savannah) 31419
Cedar Grove, *DeKalb* 30288
30294
For specific ZIP Codes call (888) 275-8777, or your local postmaster.
Cedar Grove, *Fulton* 30213
Cedar Grove, *Laurens* 31021
Cedar Grove, *Walker* 30707
Cedar Hammock 31406
Cedar Hills (Part of Columbus) 31907
Cedar Point 31332
Cedar Springs 31732
Cedartown 30125
Celeste 30673
Cenchat 30707
Centennial 30663
Center, Bartow 30121
Center, Jackson 30601
Center, Toombs 30474
Center Hill, *Colquitt* 31768
Center Hill (Part of Atlanta) 30318
Center Point 30179
Centerpost 30728
Centerville, *Elbert* 30635
Centerville, *Gwinnett* 30058
Centerville, *Houston* 31028
Centerville, *Talbot* 31812
Central City (Part of Atlanta)‡ 30303
Central City Retail (Part of Atlanta)‡ 30302
Centralhatchee 30217
Central Junction (Part of Garden City) 31408
Century 31763
Chalybeate Springs 31816
Chamberlain 30728
Chamblee‡ 30341
Chambliss 31709
Chapel Hill 30134
Chappel 30257

Charing 31058
Charles, *Stewart* 31815
Charles, *Toombs* 30474
Charleston South 30906
Charlotteville 30473
Charter Oaks (Part of Columbus) 31909
Chaserville 31647
Chastain 31738
Chatham City (Part of Garden City) 31408
Chatham Villa (Part of Garden City) 31408
Chatsworth 30705
Chattahoochee (Part of Atlanta) 30318
Chattahoochee Plantation 30067
Chatterton 31554
Chattoogaville 30730
Chauncey 31011
Checkero 30525
Chelsea 30731
Chennault 30668
Cherokee (Part of Macon) 31204
Cherokee Forest 30188
Cherrylog 30522
Cheshire Bridge (Part of Atlanta) 30324
Chestatee 30040
Chester 31012
Chestnutflat 30728
Chestnut Mountain 30502
Chickamauga 30707
Chickasawhatchee 31742
Chicopee 30507
China Hill 31077
Chippewa Terrace (Part of Savannah) 31406
Choestoe 30512
Chubbtown 30124
Chula 31733
Cinderella Hills 30736
Cisco 30708
Civic Center (Part of Atlanta)‡ 30308
Clarkdale 30111
Clarke Dale 30605
Clarkesville 30523
Clarksboro 30607
Clarkston 30021
Clarkview (Part of Macon) 31204
Claxton 30417
Clayfields 31054
Clayton 30525
Clearview (Part of Savannah) 31415
Clem 30116
Clermont 30527
Cleveland 30528
Cliftondale 30337
Climax 31734
Clinchfield 31013
Clinton 31032
Cloudland 30731
Cloverdale 30738
Clubview Heights (Part of Columbus) 31906
Clyattville 31601
Clyo 31303
Coal Mountain 30040
Cobb 31735
Cobbtown 30420
Cochran 31014
Coffee 31551
Coffee Bluff Plantation (Part of Savannah) 31419
Cogdell 31634
Cohutta 30710
Cohutta Springs 30711
Colbert 30628
Cole City 30752
Coleman 31736
Colemans Lake 30441
Colesburg 31569
College (Part of Fort Valley)† 31030
College Heights, *Dougherty* 31705
College Heights (Part of Columbus) 31906
College Park‡ 30337
Collins 30421
Collinsville 30058
Colomokee 31723
Colonial Oaks (Part of Savannah) 31419
Colonial Place 31705
Colonial Village (Part of Savannah) 31406

Colony Park 30909
Colquitt 31737
Columbia Heights 30907
Columbus 31901-04
31906-94
For specific ZIP Codes call (888) 275-8777, or your local postmaster.
Columbus Heights (Part of Macon) 31204
Columbus Square (Part of Columbus) 31906
Colwell 30541
Comer 30629
Commerce 30529-30
For specific ZIP Codes call (888) 275-8777, or your local postmaster.
Concord, *Jasper* 31064
Concord, *Pike* 30206
Concord, *Schley* 31806
Concord, *Sumter* 31709
Coney 31015
Conley♦ 30288
Constitution 30316
Conyers 30012-13
30094
For specific ZIP Codes call (888) 275-8777, or your local postmaster.
Cooksville 30230
Cooktown 31737
Coolidge 31738
Cool Spring 31771
Cooper Creek Park (Part of Columbus) 31907
Cooper Heights 30707
Coopers 31031
Coosa 30165
Copeland 31077
Cordele 31010†
31015*
Corinth 30230
Cornelia 30531
Cotton 31739
Cotton Hill 31767
Council 31631
Country Club Estates♦ 31520
Country Club Hills (Part of Augusta) 30904
Country Park 30906
Country Place 30809
Country Side (Part of Savannah) 31406
County Line, *Barrow* 30680
County Line, *DeKalb* 30032
Court Square (Part of Dublin)‡ 31021
Covena 30401
Coverdale 31714
Covington 30014-16
For specific ZIP Codes call (888) 275-8777, or your local postmaster.
Covington Mills (Part of Covington) 30014
Cox 31331
Coxs Crossing 30321
Crabapple 30004
Crandall 30711
Craneeater 30701
Cravey 31060
Crawford 30630
Crawfordville 30631
Crescent 31304
Crest 30286
Cresthill 31406
Crest Hill Gardens (Part of Savannah) 31406
Crestview 31713
Crestwell Heights 31204
Crosland 31771
Cross Keys (Part of Macon) 31217
Crossroads, *Hart* 30516
Crossroads, *Liberty* 31323
Crossroads at Stewart Lakewood, The (Part of Atlanta) 30315
Cruse 30045
Crystal Springs, *Bibb* 31217
Crystal Springs, *Floyd* 30105
Crystal Valley (Part of Columbus) 31907
Culloden 31016
Culverton 31087
Cumming 30028
30040-41
30130
For specific ZIP Codes call (888) 275-8777, or your local postmaster.
Curryville 30701

Curtis 30513
Cusseta 31805
Cuthbert 31740
Cypress Mills 31520
Dacula 30019
Daffin Heights (Part of Savannah) 31404
Dahlonega 30533
Daisy 30423
Dakota 31714
Dallas 30132
Dallas Heights 30906
Dallondale 30741
Dalton 30719-22
For specific ZIP Codes call (888) 275-8777, or your local postmaster.
Damascus, *Early* 31741
Damascus, *Gordon* 30701
Dames Ferry 31046
Danburg 30668
Daniel 31324
Daniel Springs 30669
Danielsville 30633
Danville 31017
Darien 31305
Dasher 31601
Davisboro 31018
Davis Crossroads 30707
Dawesville 31792
Dawnville 30721
Dawson 31742
Dawsonville 30534
Days Crossroads 31751
Dearing 30808
Decatur 30030-37
30089
For specific ZIP Codes call (888) 275-8777, or your local postmaster.
Deenwood 31503
Deepstep 31082
Deer Run 30094
Deerwood Forest 30906
Deerwood Park 30032
Delhi 30668
Dellwood 30401
DeLowe (Part of East Point) 30344
Demorest 30535
30544
For specific ZIP Codes call (888) 275-8777, or your local postmaster.
Denmark 30415
Dennis 31024
Denton 31532
Denver 30217
Deptford (Part of Savannah) 31404
De Soto 31743
De Soto Park 30161
Desser 31745
Devereux 31087
Dewberry 30741
Dewy Rose 30634
Dexter 31019
Dial 30513
Dialtown 30054
Diamond Hill 30628
Dickey 31746
Digbey 30205
Dillard 30537
Dillon 31757
Dinglewood (Part of Columbus) 31906
Dixie, *Brooks* 31629
Dixie, *Newton* 30014
Dixie Heights (Part of Albany) 31705
Dixie Union 31503
Dobbins Air Force Base‡ 30069
Dock Junction♦ 31520
Doctortown 31545
Doerun 31744
Doles 31791
Donald 31316
Donalsonville 31745
Donegal 30461
Donovan 31096
Doogan 30708
Dooling 31063
Doraville 30340
Dorchester, *Liberty* 31320
Dorchester, *Richmond* 30909
Dot 30108
Double Branches 30817
Doublegate 31707
Double Run 31072
Dougherty 30534

*** Area Zip Code** **† Post Office Boxes** **‡ Postal Station** **♦ Census Designated Place** *Italic Type* **County**

Douglas 31533-35
For specific ZIP Codes call (888) 275-8777, or your local postmaster.
Douglasville 30133-35
30154
For specific ZIP Codes call (888) 275-8777, or your local postmaster.
Dove Creek 30635
Dover 30424
Doverel 31742
Downs 31018
Downtown (Part of Columbus)‡ 31901
Doyle 31803
Drakes Still 31745
Draketown 30179
Dranesville 31803
Drayton 31092
Dresden 30263
Drew 30040
Druid Hills‡ 30322
Dry Branch, *Jenkins* 30822
Dry Branch, *Twiggs* 31020
Dry Pond 30529
Dublin 31021*
31040†
Dubois 31014
Ducktown 30040
Dudley 31022
Due West 30064
Duffee 31730
Dugdown 30113
Duluth 30026
30029
30095-97
For specific ZIP Codes call (888) 275-8777, or your local postmaster.
Dumas 31824
Dunaire‡ 30032
Duncan Park 37412
Dunwoody‡ 30338
Du Pont 31630
Durand 31830
Dutch Island 31406
Eagle Cliff 30725
Eagle Grove 30520
Eason 31757
East Albany (Part of Albany) 31701
Eastanollee 30538
East Armuchee 30728
East Athens 30683
East Atlanta (Part of Atlanta)‡ 30316
East Boynton 30736
East Cobb (Part of Marietta)‡ 30068
East Columbus 31907
East Dublin 31021
East Edgewood (Part of Columbus) 31907
East Ellijay 30539
East Griffin♦ 30223
East Highlands (Part of Columbus) 31901
East Juliette 31046
East Lake (Part of Decatur) 30030
Eastman 31023
East Marietta 30062
East Meadow 30605
East Newnan♦ 30263
East Point 30344
East Savannah (Part of Savannah) 31404
East Side (Part of Dalton)‡ 30719
East Thomasville (Part of Thomasville)‡ 31757
East Town (Part of Albany) 31705
East Trion (Part of Trion) 30753
Eastville 30621
Eastwood, *DeKalb*‡ 30316
Eastwood (Part of Atlanta) 30317
Eatonton 31024
Ebenezer 30279
Echeconnee 31008
Echota 30701
Eden 31307
Edge Hill 30810
Edgemoor East 30236
Edgemoor West 30236
Edgewater (Part of Savannah) 31406
Edgewater Park (Part of Savannah) 31406
Edgewood, *Columbia* 30907
Edgewood (Part of Columbus)‡ 31907
Edison 31746
Edith 31631
Ednaville 30517
Egypt 31329
Elberta 31093
Elberton 30635
Elder 30677
Eldora 31308
Eldorado 31794
Eldorendo 31737
Eleanor Village 31705
Elim 31316
Elizabeth (Part of Marietta) 30060
Elko 31025
Ellabell 31308
Ella Gap 30540
Ellaville 31806
Ellenton 31747
Ellenwood 30294
Ellerslie 31807
Ellijay 30540
Elliotts Bluff 31558
Ellwood 30805
Elmodel 31770
Elza 30453
Embry Hills‡ 30341
Emerson 30137
Emerson Park 31503
Emit 30458
Emma 30534
Emmalane 30442
Empire 31014
Englewood (Part of Columbus) 31907
Enigma 31749
Enon Grove 30217
Enterprise 30627
Ephesus 30217
Epworth 30541
Epworth Acres 31522
Eric 30411
Esom Hill 30138
Etna 30125
Eton 30724
Euharlee 30120
Eulonia 31331
Evans♦ 30809
Evansville 30240
Everett 31523
31525
For specific ZIP Codes call (888) 275-8777, or your local postmaster.
Everett Springs 30105
Evergreen 31707
Excelsior 30439
Executive Park‡ 30347
Experiment 30212
Faceville 31717
Fairburn 30213
Fairchild 31745
Fairfax 31552
Fairfield (Part of Savannah) 31404
Fairlawn Acres (Part of Fort Oglethorpe) 30741
Fairmount 30139
Fair Oaks‡ 30060
Fairplay, *Douglas* 30187
Fairplay, *Morgan* 30663
Fairview, *Franklin* 30553
Fairview, *Habersham* 30535
Fairview, *Jackson* 30567
Fairview, *Walker* 30741
Fairway Oaks (Part of Savannah) 31406
Fairway Village 30906
Fancy Hall 31324
Fantasy Hills 30725
Fargo 31631
Farmdale 30467
Farmers High 30117
Farmington 30638
Farmville 30701
Farrar 31085
Fashion 30705
Faulkner 30107
Fayette Pavillion 30214
Fayetteville 30214-15
For specific ZIP Codes call (888) 275-8777, or your local postmaster.
Federal Reserve (Part of Atlanta)‡ 30303
Federal Station (Part of Albany)‡ 31702
Fellwood Homes (Part of Savannah) 31415
Felton 30140
Fernwood (Part of Savannah) 31404
Ficklin 30673
Ficklings Mill 31006
Fidele 30735
Fife 30213
Fincherville 30233
Findlay 31070
Finleyson 31071
Fish Creek 30125
Fitzgerald 31750
Fitzgerald Cotton Mill 31750
Fitzpatrick 31044
Five Forks, *Gwinnett* 30045
Five Forks, *Thomas* 31626
Fivemile Still 31634
Five Points (Part of Atlanta) 30303
Five Points, *Lowndes* 31602
Five Points, *Macon* 31063
Five Points, *Marion* 31803
Five Points, *Randolph* 31786
Five Points, *Taylor* 31006
Five Points, *Treutlen* 30457
Five Springs 30721
Flat Rock (Part of Columbus) 31907
Flat Rock, *Putnam* 31024
Flat Shoals 30516
Fleetwood (Part of Savannah) 31404
Fleming 31309
Fleming Heights 30906
Flemington 31313
Flint 31716
Flint Hill 31826
Flint River 31711
Flint River Estates 30238
Flintside 31735
Flintstone 30725
Flintwood 30274
Flippen 30253
Floral Hill 30668
Florence 31821
Flovilla 30216
Flowery Branch 30542
Floyd 30126
Floyd Springs 30105
Folkston 31537
Folsom 30103
Forest Estates 30909
Forest Hills (Part of Columbus) 31907
Forest Hills (Part of Augusta) 30909
30919
For specific ZIP Codes call (888) 275-8777, or your local postmaster.
Forest Lake (Part of Macon) 31210
Forest Park, *Clayton* 30297*
30298†
Forest Park, *Dougherty* 31701
Forest Park, *Richmond* 30904
Forest River Farms (Part of Savannah) 31406
Forrest Hills (Part of Savannah) 31404
Forsyth 31029
Fort Benning 31905
Fort Gaines 31751
Fort Gillem‡ 30297
Fort Gordon 30905
Fort Lamar 30633
Fort McAllister 31324
Fort Oglethorpe 30742
Fort Screven (Part of Tybee Island) 31328
Fortson (Part of Columbus) 31808
Fortsonia 30635
Fort Stewart 31314-15
For specific ZIP Codes call (888) 275-8777, or your local postmaster.
Fort Valley 31030
Foster Hills 30736
Fosters Mills 30161
Four Points (Part of Albany)‡ 31705
Four Seasons 30094
Fowlstown 31752
Fox (Part of Rome) 30161
Foxboro 31602
Frances Hollow 30094
Franklin 30217
Franklin Springs 30639
Franklinton 31020
Frazier 31014
Free Home 30115
Friendship, *Polk* 30125
Friendship, *Sumter* 31709
Frolona 30217
Fruitland 31630
Fry 30555
Fullwood Springs 30125
Funston 31753
Furniture City 30126
Gabbettville 30240
Gaddistown 30572
Gaillard 31078
Gaines School‡ 30605
Gainesville 30501
30503-07
For specific ZIP Codes call (888) 275-8777, or your local postmaster.
Gainesville Mills♦ 30501
Galloway 30513
Garden Acres Estates (Part of Pooler) 31322
Garden City 31408
Garden Lakes 30165
Garden Valley 31041
Gardi 31545
Gardner (Part of Oconee) 31067
Garfield 30425
Garland 30533
Garnersville 31767
Garretta 31021
Gasco (Part of Atlanta) 30301
Gates City (Part of Atlanta)‡ 30312
Gateway (Part of Thomasville) 31792
Gay 30218
Geneva 31810
Gentian (Part of Columbus) 31907
Georgetown, *Chatham*♦ 31405
Georgetown, *Quitman* 31754
Georgetown Estates 30906
Georgia Pacific Sru (Part of Atlanta)‡ 30303
Georgia Southern (Part of Statesboro)‡ 30460
Georgia Southwestern College (Part of Americus) 31709
Georgia University (Part of Athens)‡ 30612
Germany 30525
Gibson 30810
Gill 30668
Gillis Springs 30457
Gillsville 30543
Girard 30426
Gladesville 31064
Gladys 31622
Glasgow 31626
Gleason Heights (Part of Pooler) 31322
Glencliff 30286
Glen Haven 30032
Glenloch 30217
Glenloch Village (Part of Peachtree City) 30269
Glenmore 31503
Glenn 30219
Glenn Hills 30906
Glennville 30427
Glenridge (Part of Atlanta)‡ 30342
Glenwood, *Floyd* 30165
Glenwood, *Wheeler* 30428
Glenwood Hills 30032
Glory 31622
Gloster 30045
Glynn Haven 31522
Goat Town 31082
Gobblers Hill 31805
Gober 30107
Godfrey 30650
Godwinsville 31023
Goggins 30204
Golden Isle 31410
Goldmine 30520
Goldsboro 31014
Goldson 31006
Goodes 30268
Good Hope 30641
Goolsby 31064
Gordon 31031
Gordon Springs 30740
Gordonston (Part of Savannah) 31404
Gordy 31791
Gore 30747
Goss 30635
Gough 30811
Graball 30668
Gracewood 30812
Grady 30153
Graham 31513
Grandview 30143
Grange 30434
Granite Hill 31087
Grantville 30220
Gratis 30655
Graves 31742
Gray 31032
Gray Hill 31833
Graymont (Part of Twin City) 30471
Grays 31404
Grayson 30017
Graysville 30726
Great Southwest Industrial Park (Part of Atlanta) 30336
Green Acres (Part of Fort Oglethorpe) 30741
Green Acres (Part of Savannah) 31404
Green Acres, *Clarke* 30605
Green Acres Estate (Part of Dublin) 31021
Greenbriar (Part of Atlanta) 30331
Green Island Hills (Part of Columbus) 31904
Greenough 31716
Greensboro 30642
Greens Cut 30906
Greenville 30222
Greenville Street (Part of Newman)‡ 30264
Greenway, *Emanuel* 30441
Greenway, *Fulton* 30075
Greenwood, *Henry* 30253
Greenwood, *Lanier* 31649
Greenwood, *Mitchell* 31730
Greenwood Forest 31649
Gregorys Mill 30711
Gresham Park♦ 30316
Gresham Road (Part of Marietta)‡ 30067
Greshamville 30650
Gresston 31023
Griffin 30223
30224
For specific ZIP Codes call (888) 275-8777, or your local postmaster.
Grimball Park 31406
Griswoldville 31217
Grizzletown 30101
Grooverville 31626
Grovania 31036
Groveland, *Bryan* 31321
Groveland (Part of Savannah) 31405
Grove Park (Part of Savannah) 31406
Grove Park, *Chatham* 31406
Grove Park (Part of Atlanta) 30318
Grove Point 31405
Grovetown 30813
Gumbranch 31313
Gumlog, *Towns* 30582
Gum Log, *Union* 30512
Guysie 31510
Guyton 31312
Gwinnett Mall Corners (Part of Duluth)‡ 30095†
30096*
Habersham 30544
Haddock 31033
Hagan 30429
Haggards Crossroads 30633
Hahira 31632
Halcyondale 30467
Hale Gap 30752
Halfmoon Landing 31320
Halls 30145
Halls Crossing 31018
Hallwood 31024
Halycon Bluff 31401
Hamilton 31811
Hammett 31078
Hampton 30228

* Area Zip Code † Post Office Boxes ‡ Postal Station ♦ Census Designated Place *Italic Type* County

Handy 30263
Hanes Manor (Part of Atlanta) 30305
Haney 30124
Hannah 30187
Hannahs Mill 30286
Hannatown 31717
Hansell 31765
Hapeville 30354
Haralson 30229
Harbins 30620
Harbor Creek 31410
Hard Cash 30634
Hardwick 31034
Hardwicke 31324
Harlem 30814
Harmony 31024
Harmony Church‡ 31905
Harp 30215
Harper Mill (Part of Lake City) 30260
Harrietts Bluff 31569
Harrington 31522
Harrisburg 30747
Harris City 30222
Harrison 31035
Harrisonville 30230
Harrock Hall 31406
Hartford 31036
Harts 30810
Hartsfield 31756
Hartwell 30643
Harvest 30523
Haskins Crossing 31022
Hassier Mill 30740
Hatcher 31754
Hatcher's Store 30830
Hatley 31015
Hawkinsville 31036
Haylow 31630
Hayneville 31036
Hayston 30055
Hazlehurst 31539
Head River 30731
Heardville 30040
Hebardville 31503
Helen 30545
Helena 31037
Hemp 30560
Henderson 31025
Hentown 31723
Hephzibah 30815
Herndon 30441
Herod 31742
Hiawassee 30546
Hickory Bluff 31565
Hickory Flat, *Banks* 30554
Hickory Flat, *Cherokee* 30115
Hickory Level 30116
Hickory Ridge (Part of Macon) 31204
Hickox 31553
Hicks Circle 30012
Hidden Acres 30094
Hidden Lake (Part of Savannah) 31419
Higdon 30541
Higgston 30410
Highfalls 30233
Highgate 30909
Highland Circle (Part of Macon) 31211
Highland Heights 31709
Highland Mills 30223
Highland Park (Part of Savannah) 31406
Highland Pines (Part of Columbus) 31909
High Point, *Newton* 30016
High Point, *Walker* 30707
High Shoals 30645
Hightower 30040
Hill City 30735
Hillcrest 30240
Hillcrest Heights (Part of Macon) 31204
Hillman 30631
Hillsboro 31038
Hillsdale 31794
Hillside (Part of La Grange) 30241
Hilltonia 30467
Hilton 31723
Hilton Heights (Part of Columbus) 31906
Hinesville 31310†
.... 31313*
Hinkles 30738
Hinsonton 31765
Hinton 30143
Hiram 30141
Hi Roc Shores 30012
Hobby 31714
Hoboken 31542
Hogansville 30230
Hoggard Mill 31770
Hog Hammock 31327
Holbrook 30040
Holcomb Bridge (Part of Roswell)‡ 30076
Holland 30730
Hollingsworth 30510
Hollis 31778
Hollonville 30292
Holly Hills (Part of Columbus) 31906
Holly Springs, *Cherokee* 30142
Holly Springs, *Jackson* 30558
Hollywood 30523
Holt 31798
Homeland 31537
Homer 30547
Homerville 31634
Honey Creek 30094
Hooker 30752
Hopeful 31730
Hopeulikit 30458
Hopewell, *Cherokee* 30115
Hopewell, *Harris* 31822
Horns 31078
Hornsby 30901
Horseleg Estates 30165
Hortense 31543
Hoschton 30548
Houston Lake 31047
Howard 31039
Howell 31636
Howell Mill (Part of Atlanta)‡ 30325
Howells Transfer (Part of Atlanta) 30301
Howell Tower (Part of Atlanta) 30318
Huber 31217
Hubert 30415
Huffer 31533
Hughland 30438
Hulett 30116
Hull 30646
Hunter 30467
Hunters Point (Part of Columbus) 31909
Huntington 31709
Hunts Corner 30701
Hurst 30560
Hutchins 30630
Ideal 31041
Ila 30647
Imlac 30293
Imperial 31024
Inaha 31790
Indian Hills 30236
Indianola 31602
Indian Springs, *Butts* 30216
Indian Springs, *Catoosa*♦ 30736
Industrial (Part of Atlanta)‡ 30336
Industrial City 30705
Ingleside (Part of Macon) 31204
Inman 30232
Iron City 31759
Irondale♦ 30238
Irwins Crossroads 31089
Irwinton 31042
Irwinville 31760
Isabella 31791
Islandwood 31410
Isle of Hope 31406
Ivey 31031
Ivy Log 30512
Jackson 30233
Jacksons Crossroads 30668
Jacksons Store 30668
Jacksonville, *Telfair* 31544
Jacksonville, *Towns* 30582
Jake 30182
Jakin 31761
Jamaica Estates 30907
James 31032
Jamestown 31503
Jarrell 31006
Jasper 30143
Jay Bird Springs 31011
Jefferson 30549
Jeffersonville 31044
Jekyll Island 31527
Jenkinsburg 30234
Jersey 30018
Jerusalem, *Camden* 31568
Jerusalem, *Pickens* 30143
Jesup 31545-46
.... 31598
For specific ZIP Codes call (888) 275-8777, or your local postmaster.
Jewell 31045
Jewtown 31522
Jinks 31717
Johnson Corner 30436
Johnson Crossroads 31822
Johnstonville 30204
Jolly 30292
Jones 31323
Jones Acres 31217
Jonesboro 30236-38
For specific ZIP Codes call (888) 275-8777, or your local postmaster.
Jones Creek 30512
Jones Crossroads 31822
Jonesville 30108
Jordan 30411
Jordan City (Part of Columbus) 31904
Jot Em Down Store 31516
Joy Lake 30260
Juliette 31046
Junction City 31812
Juniper 31801
Juno 30534
Kansas 30182
Kathleen 31047
Keith 30755
Keithsburg 30114
Keller 31324
Kelley Hill 31905
Kelleytown 30252
Kelly 31085
Kemp 30401
Kenilworth 30909
Kennesaw 30144
.... 30152
For specific ZIP Codes call (888) 275-8777, or your local postmaster.
Kensington 30707
Kensington Park (Part of Savannah) 31405
Kenwood, *Fayette* 30214
Kenwood (Part of Columbus) 31909
Keysville 30816
Kibbee 30474
Kiker 30540
Kildare 30446
Killarney 31761
Kimbrough 31825
Kinderlou 31601
Kings 30016
Kings Bay 31547
Kingsboro 31811
Kingsland 31547
Kingsridge 30188
Kingston, *Bartow* 30145
Kingston (Part of Columbus) 31904
Kingston, *Richmond* 30909
Kings Wood, *Chatham* 31401
Kingswood, *Clarke* 30606
Kings Wood (Part of Augusta) 30904
Kirkland, *Atkinson* 31642
Kirkland, *Jeff Davis* 31539
Kirkwood (Part of Atlanta) 30317
Kirkwood (Part of Columbus) 31904
Kirkwood (Part of Moultrie) 31768
Kite 31049
Klondike, *DeKalb* 30058
Klondike, *Houston* 31036
Knott 30241
Knoxville 31050
Kramer 31001
Lacrosse 31806
La Fayette 30728
Lafayette Plaza (Part of Albany)‡ 31707
LaGrange 30240-41
.... 30261
For specific ZIP Codes call (888) 275-8777, or your local postmaster.
Lake 30125
Lake Arrowhead 30183
Lake Capri Estates 30058
Lake Cindy 30228
Lake City 30260
Lake Creek 30125
Lake Hills 30263
Lake Howard 30728
Lake Jodeco 30236
Lakeland 31635
Lake Lanier Islands 30518
Lake Lucerne 30047
Lakemont, *Rabun* 30552
Lakemont, *Richmond* 30901
Lake Park 31636
Lakeshore Estates (Part of Gainesville) 30501
Lakeshore Mall (Part of Gainesville) 30501
Lakeside Hills (Part of Macon) 31217
Lakeside Park 31406
Lake Talmadge 30228
Lake Tara 30236
Lakeview, *Bleckley* 31014
Lakeview, *Catoosa*♦ 30741
Lakeview, *Peach* 31030
Lakeview Estates♦ 30012
Lakewood, *Clarke* 30605
Lakewood (Part of Atlanta)‡ 30315
Lakewood Heights (Part of Atlanta) 30315
Lamar 31709
Lamara Heights (Part of Savannah) 31405
Lamarville (Part of Savannah) 31405
Landrum 30534
Lanier 31321
Laroche Park (Part of Savannah) 31404
Lashley 31005
Lathemtown 30115
Laurel Hills (Part of Columbus) 31904
Lavender 30165
La Vista 30329
Lavonia 30553
Lawrenceville 30042-46
.... 30227
For specific ZIP Codes call (888) 275-8777, or your local postmaster.
Lax 31774
Leaf 30528
Leafmore 30033
Leah 30802
Leary 31762
Leathersville 30817
Lebanon 30146
Lee (Part of Lake City) 30260
Leefield 30415
Lee Pope 31030
Leesburg 31763
Lees Crossing (Part of La Grange) 30240
Lees Mill 30214
Leland 30126
Leliaton 31650
Lena 30101
Lenox 31637
Leslie 31764
Lewis 30467
Lewis Corner 30701
Lewiston 30809
Lexington 30648
Lexsy 30401
Liberty 30678
Liberty City (Part of Savannah) 31405
Liberty Hill 30257
Lifsey 30295
Lilburn 30047*
.... 30048†
Lilly 31051
Lillypond 30701
Limestone, *Bleckley* 31014
Limestone (Part of Gainesville)‡ 30501
Lincoln Hills (Part of Columbus) 31909
Lincoln Park 30286
Lincolnton 30817
Lindale♦ 30147
Lindbergh Plaza (Part of Atlanta) 30324
Lindsey Creek (Part of Columbus)‡ 31907*
.... 31917†
Lindsley Park (Part of Macon) 31216
Linesville 30631
Linton 31087
Linwood (Part of La Fayette) 30728
Lions Gate 30327
Listonia 31015
Lithia Springs♦ 30122
Lithonia 30038
.... 30058
For specific ZIP Codes call (888) 275-8777, or your local postmaster.
Little Five Points (Part of Atlanta)‡ 31107
Little Hope 31745
Little Miami 31601
Livingston 30161
Lizella 31052
Loco 30817
Locust Grove 30248
Loftin 31816
Loganville 30052
Lollie 31021
Lone Oak 30230
Long Cane 30240
Lookout Mountain 30750
Lorane 31210
Lorenzo 31329
Lorwood (Part of Savannah) 31406
Lost Mountain 30127
Lothair 30457
Lotts 31519
Louise 30230
Louisville 30434
Louvale 31814
Lovejoy 30250
Lovett 31021
Loving 30560
Lowell 30116
Lowry 30215
Lucile 31723
Lucius 30522
Ludowici 31316
Ludville 30175
Luella 30248
Lula 30554
Lulaton 31553
Lumber City 31549
Lumpkin 31815
Lundberg 30673
Luthersville 30251
Luvdale 31701
Luxomni 30047
Lyerly 30730
Lyn Hills (Part of Columbus) 31909
Lynhurst 31406
Lynmore Estates (Part of Macon) 31216
Lynn 31717
Lynnwood 30741
Lyons 30436
Lytle 30707
Mableton 30126
McAfee 30032
McBean 30906
McCaysville 30555
McCollum 30263
McDaniels 30701
McDonald Acres 30741
McDonough 30252-53
For specific ZIP Codes call (888) 275-8777, or your local postmaster.
Macedonia, *Cherokee* 30115
Macedonia, *Towns* 30546
McElroys Mill 30052
McGregor 30410
Machen 31064
McIntosh 31320
McIntosh Mill Village 30263
McIntyre 31054
McKinnon 31545
Macland 30127
Macon 31201-21
.... 31297-98
For specific ZIP Codes call (888) 275-8777, or your local postmaster.
Macon Mall (Part of Macon)‡ 31216
McPherson 30132
McRae 31055
McWhorter 30134
Madison 30650
Madola 30541
Madras 30263
Madray Springs 31545
Magby Gap 30752
Magnet 30013
.... 30094
For specific ZIP Codes call (888) 275-8777, or your local postmaster.
Magnolia (Part of Savannah) 31406
Magnolia (Part of Atlanta) 30318
Magruder 30441
Mallorysville 30668

Manassas 30438
Manchester 31816
Manningtown 31545
Manor 31550
Mansfield 30055
Manta 31805
Marblehill 30148
Maretts 30553
Margret 30572
Maridale Estates (Part of Columbus) 31904
Marietta 30006-08
30060-69
For specific ZIP Codes call (888) 275-8777, or your local postmaster.
Marietta Campground 30062
Marine Corps Supply Center 31704
Marion 31020
Marketplace at North DeKalb (Part of Decatur) 30033
Marlborough 30238
Marlow 31312
Marshallville 31057
Mars Hill 30101
Martech (Part of Atlanta)‡ 30318
Martin 30557
Martinez 30907
Massee 31620
Matt 30040
Matthews 30818
Mattox 31537
Mauk 31058
Maura Estates 30906
Maxeys 30671
Maxim 30817
Maxwell 31085
Mayday 31636
Mayfair (Part of Savannah) 31406
Mayfield 31087
Mayhaw 31723
Maysville 30558
Meadowbrook (Part of Macon) 31204
Meadow Grove 30906
Meansville 30256
Mechanicsville 30340
Meeks 31049
Meigs 31765
Meinhard (Part of Port Wentworth) 31407
Meldrim 31318
Melrose 31636
Memorial (Part of Stone Mountain)‡ 30083
Mendes 30427
Menlo 30731
Mercer University (Part of Macon) 31204
Meridian 31319
Merrillville 31738
Mershon 31551
Mesena 30819
Metasville 30673
Metcalf 31792
Metter 30439
Mica 30107
Middleton 30635
Midland (Part of Columbus) 31820
Midtown (Part of Atlanta)‡ 30309
Midville 30441
Midway, *Catoosa* 30741
Midway, *Clinch* 31634
Midway, *Liberty* 31320
Midway, *Tattnall* 30427
Milan 31060
Miles Park 30906
Milford 31762
Mill Creek 30740
Mill Creek Estates 30506
Milledgeville 31061
Millen 30442
Millers Mill 30281
Millhaven 30467
Millwood 31552
Milner 30257
Milstead 30012
Mineola 31602
Mineral Bluff 30559
Minish 30646
Minnesota 31744
Mission Ridge (Part of Rossville) 30741
Mitchell, *Dodge* 31023
Mitchell, *Glascock* 30820
Mize 30577
Mizell 31006
Mock Road (Part of Albany)‡ 31705
Modoc 30401
Molena 30258
Moncrief 32301
Moniac 31646
Monroe 30655-56
For specific ZIP Codes call (888) 275-8777, or your local postmaster.
Montclair 30907
Monteith (Part of Port Wentworth) 31407
Montevideo 30635
Montezuma 31063
Montgomery 31406
Monticello, *Jasper* 31064
Monticello, *Richmond* 30906
Montreal 30033
Montrose 31065
Moody Air Force Base 31699
Moons 30725
Moores 31021
Mora 31650
Moreland 30259
Morgan, *Calhoun* 31766
Morgan, *Haralson* 30110
Morganton 30560
Morganville 30757
Morningside (Part of Atlanta) 30306
Morningside (Part of Columbus) 31909
Morningside Hills 30501
Morris 31767
Morris Brown (Part of Atlanta)‡ 30314
Morris Estates 30736
Morris Siding (Part of Atlanta) 30301
Morrow 30260
30287
For specific ZIP Codes call (888) 275-8777, or your local postmaster.
Mortons 31405
Morven 31638
Mossy Creek 30528
Moultrie 31768*
31776†
Mountainbrook (Part of Pine Mountain) 31822
Mountain City 30562
Mountain Hill 31811
Mountain Park, *Fulton* 30075
Mountain Park, *Gwinnett*‡ 30087
Mountaintown 30540
Mountain View, *Clayton* 30321
Mountain View, *Walker* 30741
Mount Airy 30563
Mount Berry 30149
Mount Bethel 30068
Mount Carmel 30728
Mount Olivet 30643
Mount Pleasant, *Banks* 30547
Mount Pleasant, *Wayne* 31543
Mount Vernon, *Montgomery* 30445
Mount Vernon, *Walton* 30655
Mount Vernon, *Whitfield* 30740
Mountville 30261
Mount Zion 30150
Moxley 30477
Mulberry 30680
Mulberry Grove 31804
Mulberry Heights (Part of Albany) 31705
Mulberry Street (Part of Macon)‡ 31201
Munnerlyn 30830
Murphy 31738
Murray Hills 30909
Murrays Crossroads 31806
Murrayville 30564
Musella 31066
Myrtle Grove 31324
Mystic 31769
Nahunta 31553
Nails Creek 30521
Nance Springs 30721
Nankipooh (Part of Columbus) 31909
Naomi 30728
Nashville 31639
National Hills 30904
Naylor 31641
Neal 30206
Nebo 30132
Needmore 31631
Neese 30646
Nelson 30151
Nevils 31321
Newark 31757
Newborn 30056
New Branch 30436
New Elm 31768
New England 30752
New Era 31709
New Georgia 30132
New Holland 30501
New Home 30752
New Hope, *Gilmer* 30540
New Hope, *Gwinnett* 30045
New Hope, *Lincoln* 30817
New Hope, *Paulding* 30132
Newington 30446
Newnan 30263-65
30271
For specific ZIP Codes call (888) 275-8777, or your local postmaster.
New Point 31780
New Salem 30547
Newton 31770
Newtown, *Fulton* 30023
New Town, *Gordon* 30701
New Town, *Wilkes* 30673
New York (Part of Aragon) 30153
Neyami 31763
Nicholasville 31713
Nicholls 31554
Nicholson 30565
Nickelsville 30701
Nicklesville 31042
Nickleville 31797
Nickville 30634
Noah's Station 30818
Noble 30728
Noonday 30066
Norcross 30003
30010
30071
30091-93
For specific ZIP Codes call (888) 275-8777, or your local postmaster.
Norman 30668
Norman Park 31771
Normantown 30474
Norris 30828
Norristown 30447
North Atlanta 30319
North Canton 30114
North Decatur♦ 30033
North Druid Hills 30033
North Dublin (Part of Dublin) 31021
North Elberton 30635
Northgate (Part of Columbus) 31907
North Highland (Part of Atlanta)‡ 31106
North Highlands (Part of Columbus) 31904
North High Shoals 30645
Northlake‡ 30345
North Point Mall (Part of Alpharetta) 30023
Northridge (Part of Conyers) 30012
North Roswell (Part of Roswell) 30075
Northside (Part of Warner Robins)‡ 31093
North West Point 31833
Norton Acres 30906
Norwood 30821
Note 31024
Nuberg 30634
Nunez 30448
Oakdale (Part of Savannah) 31405
Oakdale, *Cobb* 30080
Oakfield 31772
Oak Forest, *Chatham* 31404
Oak Forest, *Clayton* 30236
Oak Grove, *Carroll* 30117
Oak Grove, *Cherokee* 30102
Oak Grove, *DeKalb* 30033
Oak Grove, *Troup* 31822
Oakhaven 31707
Oak Hill, *Gilmer* 30540
Oak Hill, *Newton* 30016
Oakhurst (Part of Savannah) 31406
Oakland 30218
Oakland City (Part of Atlanta) 30301
Oakland Heights 30121
Oakland Park (Part of Savannah) 31404
Oakland Park (Part of Columbus) 31903
Oaklawn 30263
Oakleaf Plantation 30067
Oakman 30732
Oak Mountain 31826
Oak Park 30401
Oakwood 30566
Oasis 30513
Oatland Island 31410
Ocee 30023
Ochillee 31905
Ochlocknee 31773
Ochwalkee 30428
Ocilla 31774
Oconee 31067
Oconee Heights 30607
Odessadale 30222
Odum 31555
Offerman 31556
Ogeechee 30467
Ogeechee Farms 31405
Ogeechee Road 31405
Ogeecheeton (Part of Savannah) 31415
Oglethorpe (Part of Savannah)‡ 31406
Oglethorpe, *Macon* 31068
Oglethorpe Mall (Part of Savannah) 31406
Oglethorpe Park (Part of Savannah) 31406
Oglethorpe University 30319
Ogletree Woods (Part of Columbus) 31909
Ohoopee 30436
Okefenokee 31503
Ola 30252
Old Damascus 31741
Old National (Part of Atlanta)‡ 30349
Old South 30236
Olive Branch 31827
Oliver 30449
Olney 31308
Omaha 31821
Omega 31775
Oostanaula 30701
Ophir 30107
Orange 30115
Orchard Hill 30266
Orchard Hills 30741
Orianna, *Laurens* 31002
Orianna, *Treutlen* 30457
Orland 30457
Ormewood Sta. (Part of Atlanta) 30312
Oscarville 30506
Osierfield 31750
Other 30132
Ottawa Estates (Part of Bloomingdale) 31302
Owen 31516
Owensboro 31079
Owltown 30512
Oxford 30054
Pace 30014
Pachitta 31740
Padena 30560
Palalto 31064
Palmetto, *Fulton* 30268
Palmetto, *Oglethorpe* 30627
Palmyra 31763
Pancras 31061
Panhandle 31076
Pannell 30655
Panola 30058
Pantertown 30559
Panthersville♦ 30032
Paoli 30629
Paradise Park (Part of Savannah) 31406
Paradise Park, *Wayne* 31545
Paradise Valley 30607
Parhams 30521
Parkchester (Part of Columbus) 31906
Park City (Part of Fort Oglethorpe) 30741
Parkers 30467
Parkersburg 31406
Parkerville 31744
Park Hill (Part of Gainesville) 30501
Parkwood (Part of Savannah) 31404
Parrott 31777
Pateville 31015
Patillo 30233
Patten 31626
Patterson 31557
Pavo 31778
Payne, *Bibb* 31201
Payne, *Cherokee* 30102
Peach Orchard 30906
Peachtree Center (Part of Atlanta)‡ 30343
Peachtree City 30269
Peachtree Hills (Part of Atlanta) 30305
Peachtree Mall (Part of Columbus) 31909
Pearly 31021
Pearson 31642
Pebble City 31784
Pedenville 30206
Pelham 31779
Pembroke 31321
Pendergrass 30567
Pendley Hills 30032
Penfield 30669
Penia 31015
Pennick 31525
Pennington 30650
Pennville 30747
Peoples Still 31797
Pepperton (Part of Jackson) 30233
Perkins 30822
Perry 31069
Persimmon 30525
Petross 30474
Pharr Road (Part of Atlanta) 30305*
30355†
Phelps 30720
Phillipsburg♦ 31794
Philomath 30660
Phinizy 30802
Phipps Plaza (Part of Atlanta) 30326
Phoenix (Part of Atlanta)‡ 30301
Phoenix, *Putnam* 31024
Pickard 30286
Piedmont, *Jasper* 31064
Piedmont, *Lamar* 30204
Pierceville 37317
Pineboro 31768
Pine Chapel 30701
Pine Gardens (Part of Savannah) 31404
Pine Grove 31513
Pine Harbor 31331
Pine Hill (Part of Columbus) 31903
Pinehurst, *Dooly* 31070
Pinehurst, *Henry* 30281
Pine Lake 30072
Pineland 31631
Pine Log 30171
Pine Mountain, *DeKalb* 30058
Pine Mountain, *Harris* 31822
Pine Mountain, *Rabun* 29664
Pine Mountain Valley 31823
Pineora 31312
Pine Park 31728
Pine Valley, *Cook* 31620
Pine Valley, *Richmond* 30904
Pineview 31071
Pinewood Shores 30094
Piney Bluff 31565
Piney Grove 31808
Pin Point 31406
Pinson 30161
Pio Nono (Part of Macon)‡ 31206
Pirkle Woods 30040
Pitts 31072
Pittsburg 30084
Plainfield 31073
Plains 31780
Plainview, *Franklin* 30521
Plainview, *Whitfield* 30720
Plainville 30733
Planter 30646
Plaza Way (Part of Marietta)‡ 30064

Pleasant Hill, *Fulton* 30337
Pleasant Hill, *Gwinnett* 30096
Pleasant Hill, *Talbot* 31836
Pleasant Hill, *Terrell* 31742
Pleasant Valley, *Bartow* 30103
Pleasant Valley, *Dooly* 31092
Pocataligo 30633
Pointe South 30238
Point Peter 30627
Pollards Corner 30802
Pomona 30223
Pond Spring 30707
Pooler 31322
Pope City 31079
Popes Ferry 31046
Poplar Springs, *Haralson* 30113
Poplar Springs, *Oconee* 30677
Portal 30450
Porter 31014
Porterdale 30070
Porter Springs 30533
Portland 30104
Port Royal 31324
Port Wentworth 31407
Port Wentworth Junction (Part of Port Wentworth) 31407
Postell 31217
Potterville 31076
Poulan 31781
Powder Springs 30127
Powell Place 31701
Powelton 31087
Powers Lake 30327
Powersville 31008
Prather 30673
Prattsburg 31827
Presley 30546
Preston 31824
Pretoria 31701
Price 30506
Pridgen 31519
Primrose 30222
Princeton (Part of Athens) 30601
Pringle 31096
Prior 30125
Pritchetts 31744
Privette Heights 30008
Prospect 31064
Pulaski 30451
Pumpkin Center 30814
Putnam 31803
Putney 31782
Pyles Marsh 31525
Pyne 30240
Queensland 31750
Quitman 31643
Rabbit Hill 31324
Rabun Gap 30568
Race Pond 31537
Radium Springs 31702
Raines 31015
Raleigh 30293
Ramhurst 30705
Randall 31815
Ranger 30734
Raoul♦ 30510
Raulerson, *Brantley* 31557
Raulerson, *Pierce* 31557
Ravenwood 30907
Raybon 31553
Ray City 31645
Rayle 30660
Raymond 30265
Raytown 30631
Rebecca 31783
Rebie 31012
Recovery 32324
Redan 30074
Redbud 30701
Red Clay 30710
Red Hill, *Franklin* 30521
Red Hill, *Stewart* 31825
Red Lane 30501
Red Oak 30272
Red Rock, *Paulding* 30101
Red Rock, *Worth* 31791
Red Stone 30549
Red Store Crossroads 31770
Reed Creek♦ 30643
Reese 30828
Reeves 30701
Regency Mall (Part of Augusta) 30904
Register 30452
Rehoboth 30033

Reidsboro 30292
Reidsville 30453
Reka 31321
Relay 30125
Remerton 31601
Renfroe 31805
Reno 31728
Rentz 31075
Reo 30740
Resaca 30735
Resseaus Crossroads 31024
Rest Haven 30518
Retreat 31323
Rex 30273
Reynolds 31076
Reynoldsville 31745
Rhine 31077
Riceboro 31323
Richfield (Part of Savannah) 31405
Richland 31825
Richmond Hill 31324
Richwood 31092
Rico 30268
Riddleville 31018
Ridgefield Heights (Part of Columbus) 31907
Ridgeville 31331
Ridgewood 30909
Rincon 31326
Ringgold 30736
Rio 30223
Rio Vista, *Chatham* 31406
Rio Vista (Part of Albany) 31705
Rising Fawn 30738
Riverdale 30274
30296
For specific ZIP Codes call (888) 275-8777, or your local postmaster.
Riverland Terrace (Part of Columbus) 31903
River Oaks 31410
River Road 31707
Rivers End (Part of Savannah) 31406
Riverside (Part of Macon)‡ 31204
Riverside, *Colquitt* 31768
Riverside, *Floyd* 30161
Riverside (Part of Atlanta) 30318
Rivertown 30213
Riverturn 31745
Riverview (Part of Macon) 31204
Rivoli Park (Part of Macon) 31210
Roanoke Acres 31750
Roberta 31078
Robertstown 30545
Robertsville 30707
Robins Air Force Base 31098
Robinson 30669
Rochelle 31079
Rock Branch 30635
Rock Chapel 30058
Rockdale (Part of Atlanta) 30318
Rock Hill 31723
Rockingham 31510
Rockledge 30454
Rockmart 30153
Rock Spring 30739
Rockville 31024
Rocky Creek 30701
Rocky Face 30740
Rocky Ford 30455
Rocky Mount 30251
Rocky Plains 30016
Roddy 31014
Rogers 30530
Rolling Green 30094
Rolling Meadows 30905
Rome 30161-65
For specific ZIP Codes call (888) 275-8777, or your local postmaster.
Roopville 30170
Roosterville 30170
Roper 31539
Ropers Crossroads 30809
Roscoe 30263
Rosebud 30052
Rosedale 30701
Rose Dhu 31406
Rose Hill (Part of Savannah) 31406
Rose Hill, *Pike* 30256

Rose Hill Heights (Part of Columbus) 31904
Rosemont 30802
Rosemont Park 30161
Rosier 30434
Rossignol Hill (Part of Garden City) 31408
Rossville 30741
Roswell 30075-77
For specific ZIP Codes call (888) 275-8777, or your local postmaster.
Round Oak 31038
Roundtop 30540
Rover 30292
Rowena 31713
Roxanna 30132
Royston 30662
Ruckersville 30635
Rudden 31024
Rupert 31081
Russell 30680
Russellville 31016
Rutledge 30663
Rydal 30171
Ryo 30139
Saginaw 31554
St. Charles 30259
St. Clair 30816
St. George 31646
St. Marks 30230
St. Marys 31558
St. Marys Hills (Part of Columbus) 31906
St. Simons Island♦ 31522
Sale City 31784
Salem Arms 30906
Sanborn 31705
Sandalwood 31701
Sand Bed 31047
Sandersville 31082
Sandfly 31406
Sand Hill, *Brooks* 31778
Sand Hill, *Carroll* 30180
Sand Hill, *Muscogee* 31905
Sand Hills 30904
Sandtown 30673
Sandy Cross, *Franklin* 30662
Sandy Cross, *Oglethorpe* 30627
Sandy Plains 30075
Sandy Springs 30328
Sanford, *Madison* 30646
Sanford, *Stewart* 31815
Sangrena Woods (Part of Pooler) 31322
Santa Claus 30436
Sapelo Island 31327
Sapp 31014
Sardis 30456
Sargent 30275
Sasser 31785
Satolah 30525
Sautee-Nacoochee 30571
Savannah 31401-99
For specific ZIP Codes call (888) 275-8777, or your local postmaster.
Savannah Gardens (Part of Savannah) 31404
Savannah Mall (Part of Savannah) 31401
Sawdust 30814
Sawhatchee 31723
Scarboro 30442
Scarbrough Cross Roads 30294
Scarlet 31569
Schatulga (Part of Columbus) 31820
Schlatterville 31501
Schley 31768
Scotland 31083
Scott 31002
Scottdale♦ 30079
Scottsboro 31061
Screven 31560
Screven Fork 31320
Screvens Point 31410
Seabrook 31320
Seagraves 30646
Sea Island 31561
Sea Palms 31522
Sells 30548
Seney 30104
Senoia 30276
Sessoms 31554
Seville 31084
Shady Dale 31085
Shake Rag 30174

Shannon♦ 30172
Sharon 30664
Sharon Park (Part of Garden City) 31408
Sharpe 30728
Sharphagen 31745
Sharpsburg 30277
Sharps Spur 30410
Sharp Top 30114
Shawnee 31329
Sheffield 30909
Shell Bluff 30830
Shellman 31786
Shellman Bluff 31331
Shelly 31778
Shenandoah 30265
Sheppards 30467
Sherwood, *Clayton* 30236
Sherwood, *Richmond* 30904
Sherwood Forest (Part of Macon) 31216
Sherwood Forest, *Coweta* 30263
Sherwood Forest, *DeKalb* 30032
Sherwood Forest, *Floyd* 30161
Shields Crossroads 30707
Shiloh, *Harris* 31826
Shiloh, *Lowndes* 31634
Shiloh, *Madison* 30633
Shiloh, *Sumter* 31709
Shingler 31781
Shirley Hills (Part of Macon) 31211
Shirley Park (Part of Savannah) 31404
Shoal Creek 30553
Shoals 30820
Shurlington (Part of Macon)‡ 31211
Sigsbee 31744
Silco 31537
Silica Hills 31705
Silk Hope 31401
Silk Mills 30635
Siloam 30665
Silver City 30506
Silver Creek 30173
Silver Crest 30906
Silver Pines 31216
Simpson 30217
Six Mile 30165
Skipperton 31216
Skyland 30319
Skyland Terrace (Part of Savannah) 31401
Sky Valley 30525
Smarr 31086
Smiths Crossroads, *Harris* 31823
Smiths Crossroads, *Troup* 30240
Smithsonia 30628
Smithville 31787
Smyrna 30080-82
For specific ZIP Codes call (888) 275-8777, or your local postmaster.
Snake Nation 30513
Snapfinger 30058
Snapping Shoals 30016
Snead 30809
Snellville 30039
30078
For specific ZIP Codes call (888) 275-8777, or your local postmaster.
Snipesville 31532
Snow Spring 31091
Snug Harbor Estates 30504
Soapstick 30701
Social Circle 30025
Sofkee 31216
Somerset Park (Part of Savannah) 31419
Sonoraville 30701
Soperton 30457
South Base (Part of Warner Robins) 31098
South Cobb 30106
Southdale 30906
South Decatur 30034
South DeKalb Mall 30034
Southern Tech (Part of Marietta)‡ 30062
Southgate Villa 30906
South Glen 30236
Southlake Mall (Part of Morrow) 30260
Southland 30906

South Macon (Part of Macon)‡ 31205-06
31216
For specific ZIP Codes call (888) 275-8777, or your local postmaster.
South Moultrie (Part of Moultrie) 31768
South Nellieville 30901
South Newport 31323
Southover (Part of Savannah) 31405
South Pooler 31322
Southside (Part of Savannah)† 31419
Spalding 31063
Spanish Trace 30906
Spann 31096
Sparks 31647
Sparta 31087
Spence 31779
Spencer Hills 30741
Split Silk 30052
Spout Spring Crossroads 30542
Spring Bluff 31565
Springfield 31329
Spring Hill (Part of Savannah) 31404
Spring Hill, *Wheeler* 30411
Spring Lake (Part of Columbus) 31909
Spring Place 30705
Springvale 31767
Springvale Station 31767
Spring Valley (Part of Columbus) 31909
Springview Acres (Part of Gainesville) 30501
Staley Heights (Part of Savannah) 31405
Stanleys Store 30436
Stanton Woods 30094
Stapleton 30823
Stark 30233
Starr 30094
Starrs Mill 30215
Starrsville 30014
State College 31404
Statenville 31648
Statesboro 30458-61
For specific ZIP Codes call (888) 275-8777, or your local postmaster.
Statham 30666
Staunton 31637
Steadham Store 31717
Steadman 30176
Steam Mill 31745
Steffen Wood Estates (Part of Pooler) 31322
Stellaville 30833
Stephens 30667
Stephensville 30752
Sterling 31525
Stevens Pottery 31031
Stewart 30016
Stewart Town 30752
Stilesboro 30120
Stillmore 30464
Stillwell 31329
Stilson 30415
Stockbridge 30281
Stockton 31649
Stockwood 30188
Stone Mountain 30083
30086-88
For specific ZIP Codes call (888) 275-8777, or your local postmaster.
Stonewall (Part of Union City) 30349
Stoney Point 30170
Stovall (Part of Cornelia) 30531
Stovall, *Meriwether* 30222
Strategic Weapons Facility Atlantic, Kings Bay 31547
Stratford (Part of Atlanta) 30311
Strouds 31016
Stuckey 30428
Subligna 30747
Suches 30572
Sudie 30132
Sugar Hill, *Gwinnett* 30518
Sugar Hill, *Hall* 30507
Sugartown 30755
Sugar Valley 30746

Place	ZIP
Sulphur Springs	30738
Sulphur Springs Station	30752
Sumach	30705
Summertown	30466
Summerville	30747
Summit (Part of Twin City)	30471
Sumner	31789
Sumter	31709
Sunbury	31320
Sunny Acres	31701
Sunnydale Acres (Part of Macon)	31217
Sunny Side, *Spalding*	30284
Sunnyside, *Ware*♦	31501
Sunset	31768
Sunset Heights (Part of Gainesville)	30501
Sunset Park (Part of Savannah)	31404
Sunset Village	30286
Sunshine Acres (Part of Columbus)	31909
Sunsweet	31794
Surrency	31563
Sutalee	30184
Suttles Mill	30728
Suttons Corner	31724
Suwanee	30024
Swainsboro	30401
Swan Lake	30281
Swords	30625
Sybert	30817
Sycamore	31790
Sylvan Hills (Part of Atlanta)	30310
Sylvania	30467
Sylvester	31791
Tails Creek	30540
Talahi Island	31410
Talbotton	31827
Talking Rock	30175
Tallapoosa	30176
Tallulah Falls	30573
Tallulah Lodge	30573
Talmo	30575
Talona	30175
Tanglewood, *Clarke*	30606
Tanglewood, *Richmond*	30909
Tarboro	31568
Tarrytown	30470
Tarver	31631
Tarversville	31020
Tate	30177
Tate City	30525
Tatumsville (Part of Savannah)	31405
Tax	31826
Taylorsville	30178
Tazewell	31803
Teloga	30747
Temperance	31077
Temple	30179
Temple Grove	30711
Tennga	30751
Tennille	31089
Terrace Manor	30906
Terrell	31789
Texas	30217
Thalmann	31523
The Hill (Part of Augusta)‡	30904
The Landings	31411
The Rock	30285
Thomasboro	30455
Thomaston	30286
Thomasville (Part of Atlanta)	30315
Thomasville, *Thomas*	31757
	31792
	31799
For specific ZIP Codes call (888) 275-8777, or your local postmaster.	
Thomas Woods	30906
Thompson	31601
Thompsonville	30738
Thomson	30824
Thornhedge	30274
Thornton Estates	30236
Thrift	30442
Thunderbolt	31404
Thurmock	30567
Thurston	30642
Thyatira	30549
Ticknor	31744
Tifton	31793†
	31794*
Tiger	30576
Tignall	30668
Tilton	30720
Timothy Estates	30606
Tippettville	31092
Tison	30427
Titus	30546
Toccoa	30577
Toccoa Falls	30598
Toco Hills	30329
Toledo	31646
Tom	31049
Toms Creek	30557
Toney Valley	30032
Toomsboro	31090
Topeka Junction	30285
Town and Country	30815
Town and Country Acres	31707
Town and Country Shopping Center (Part of Marietta)	30060
Towns	31055
Townsend	31331
Traders Hill	31537
Tranquilla Woods (Part of Savannah)	31419
Trans	30728
Travisville	31634
Tremont, *Crisp*	31015
Tremont, *Richmond*	30907
Tremont Park (Part of Savannah)	31405
Trenton	30752
Trice	30286
Trickum	30755
Trimble	30230
Trion	30753
Troutman	31740
Trudie	31557
Tucker	30084*
	30085†
Tugaloo (Part of Tallulah Falls)	30573
Tulakes (Part of Columbus)	31904
Tunnel Hill	30755
Turin	30289
Turner City (Part of Albany)	31705
Turners Corner	30528
Turners Rock	31406
Turnerville	30580
Tusculum	31329
Tuxedo (Part of Atlanta)	30342
Twin City	30471
Twin Lakes	31636
Tybee Island	31328
Tyler	31064
Tyrone, *Fayette*	30290
Tyrone, *Wilkes*	30673
Ty Ty	31795
Tyus	30108
Unadilla	31091
Union, *Marion*	31803
Union, *Paulding*	30179
Union, *Quitman*	31767
Union, *Stewart*	31821
Unionburg	31794
Union City	30291
Union Hill	30004
Union Point	30669
Unionville (Part of Macon)	31204
Unionville, *Tift*♦	31794
Unity	30521
University Heights	30605
Upatoi (Part of Columbus)	31829
Upton	31533
Uptonville	31537
Uvalda	30473
Vada	31734
Valdosta	31601-06
For specific ZIP Codes call (888) 275-8777, or your local postmaster.	
Valley Forge	30906
Valley View	30725
Valona	31332
Vanceville	31794
Vandiver Heights	30066
Vanna	30662
Vans Valley	30161
Van Wert	30153
Varnell	30756
Vaughn	30223
Veal	30108
Veazey	30642
Vega	30256
Veribest	30627
Vernonburg	31406
Vernon View	31406
Vesta	30627
Veterans Hospital (Part of Augusta)	30909
Victoria	30189
Victory	30108
Victory Heights (Part of Savannah)	31404
Vidalia	30474*
	30475†
Vidette	30434
Vienna	31092
View	30531
Villanow	30728
Villa Rica	30180
Vineland	30909
Vineville (Part of Macon)	31204
Vinings	30339
Vinson Village (Part of Macon)	31216
Vista-Grove	30033
Vulcan	30738
Waco	30182
Wadley	30477
Wagon Wheel	31647
Wahoo	30533
Walden	31216
Waleska	30183
Walker Park	30655
Walkersville	31516
Wallace	31036
Wallaceville	30707
Walls Crossing	31806
Walnut Grove, *Walker*	30728
Walnut Grove, *Walton*	30014
Walnut Square (Part of Dalton)	30720
Walthourville	31333
Waresboro	31564
Wares Crossroads	30240
Waresville	30217
Waring	30720
Warm Springs	31830
Warner Robins	31088
	31093
	31095
	31098-99
For specific ZIP Codes call (888) 275-8777, or your local postmaster.	
Warren Terrace	30741
Warrenton	30828
Warsaw	30005
Warthen	31094
Warwick	31796
Washington	30673
Waterloo	31733
Waterport	30052
Waters	30467
Watkinsville	30677
Waverly, *Camden*	31565
Waverly, *Richmond*	30909
Waverly Hall	31831
Waverly Heights (Part of Macon)	31216
Waverly Park	30741
Wax	30104
Wayback	31746
Waycross	31501-03
For specific ZIP Codes call (888) 275-8777, or your local postmaster.	
Waynesboro	30830
Waynesville	31566
Wayside	31032
Webb	30004
Webb Bridge (Part of Alpharetta)	30023
Weber	31639
Welcome	30263
Welcome Hill	30753
Wenona	31015
Weracoba Heights (Part of Columbus)	31906
Wesley, *Emanuel*	30401
Wesley, *Taylor*	31812
Wesleyan College (Part of Macon)‡	31210
Wesleyan Estates	31204
Wesleyan Woods (Part of Macon)	31210
West Bainbridge (Part of Bainbridge)‡	31717
West Brow	30738
West Crossing	30176
West Dublin (Part of Dublin)	31021
West End (Part of Rome)‡	30165
West End (Part of Atlanta)‡	30310
Westgate (Part of Albany)	31707
Westgate Mall (Part of Macon)	31216
Westgate Park	30607
West Georgia College (Part of Carrollton)‡	30118
West Green	31567
Westhampton	30907
West Hills	30907
Westmont	30907
Westoak	30062
Weston	31832
West Point	31833
West Rome (Part of Rome)	30164
West Savannah (Part of Savannah)	31401
Westside, *Catoosa*	30741
Westside, *Hall*♦	30501
West Valdosta	31601
West Vidalia (Part of Vidalia)	30474
Westwick	30909
Westwood	31750
Wexwood	30274
Wheat Hill (Part of Garden City)	31408
Wheeler Heights	31217
Whigham	31797
Whistleville	30680
Whitaker	31543
White	30184
White Bluff (Part of Savannah)	31406
White City	30187
White Hall	30605
Whitehouse	30252
Whitemarsh Island♦	31404
White Oak	31568
White Plains	30678
Whitesburg	30185
Whitestone	30175
White Sulphur Springs	31822
Whitesville	31833
Whitworth	30553
Wilbanks Store	30711
Wildwood	30757
Wiley	30581
Willacoochee	31650
Willard	31024
Williamsburg Manor (Part of Savannah)	31419
Williamson	30292
Wilmington Island‡	31410
Wilmington Park	31410
Wilshire (Part of Savannah)	31419
Wilshire Estates (Part of Savannah)	31419
Wilsons Church	30558
Wilsonville	31554
Wimberly on the Marsh	31406
Wimbish Woods (Part of Macon)	31210
Winchester	31057
Winchester Hills	30012
Winder	30680
Windermere	30904
Windsor	30052
Windsor Estates	30263
Windsor Forest (Part of Savannah)	31419
Windsor Forest, *Richmond*	30904
Windsor Park, *Lowndes*	31601
Windsor Park (Part of Columbus)‡	31909
Windward (Part of Savannah)	31419
Windy Hill (Part of Marietta)‡	30006
Windy Ridge	30559
Winfield	30824
Winokur	31537
Winona Park	31503
Winship Gardens (Part of Macon)	31204
Winston	30187
Winterville	30683
Withers	31630
Woodbine	31569
Woodbury	30293
Woodcliff	30467
Woodgate	30909
Woodlake	30906
Woodlake Landing	30274
Woodland	31836
Woodland Hills, *Laurens*	31021
Woodland Hills, *Walker*	30741
Woodlawn (Part of Savannah)	31406
Woodlawn Estates (Part of Columbus)	31907
Woodlawn Terrace (Part of Garden City)	31406
Woodridge Estates	31410
Woods Grove	30582
Wood Station	30736
Woodstock	30188-89
For specific ZIP Codes call (888) 275-8777, or your local postmaster.	
Woodville (Part of Savannah)	31415
Woodville, *Greene*	30669
Woolsey	30215
Wooster	30218
Wormsloe	31406
Worth	31714
Worthville	30233
Wray	31798
Wrayswood	30677
Wrens	30833
Wright Landing	30236
Wright Square (Part of Savannah)‡	31401
Wrightsville	31096
Wymberly	31406
Wynngate	30907
Wynnton (Part of Columbus)‡	31906
Yahoola	30533
Yates	30263
Yatesville	31097
Yellow Bluff Fishing Village	31320
Yeomans	31742
Yonah	30510
Yonkers	31014
Yorktown (Part of Columbus)	31907
Yorkville	30132
Youngcane	30512
Young Harris	30582
Youngs	30125
Youngstown	30512
Youth	30052
Zaidee	30457
Zebina	30833
Zebulon	30295
Zeigler	30467
Zenith	31078
Zetella	30223-24
For specific ZIP Codes call (888) 275-8777, or your local postmaster.	
Zetto	31751
Zingara	30094

Ahualoa 96727
Ahuimanu 96744
Aiea 96701
Aiea Heights 96701
Aiea Shopping Center 96701
Aikahi‡ 96734
Aina Haina‡ 96821*
96824†
Akasaki Camp 96774
Alabama Village 96784
Ala Moana Center (Part of Honolulu)‡ 96814
Alewa Heights (Part of Honolulu) 96819
Aliamanu♦ 96818
Amauulu Camps 96720
Anahola♦ 96703
Andrade Camp 96783
Barbers Point Housing♦ 96862
Barbers Point Coast Guard Air Station 96862
Brigham Young University-Hawaii‡ 96762
Camp 106 96727
Camp H.M. Smith Marine Corps Base 96861
Captain Cook♦ 96704
Chinatown (Part of Honolulu)‡ 96817
96827
For specific ZIP Codes call (888) 275-8777, or your local postmaster.
Chin Chuck 96710
Coconut Grove 96734
Coral Gardens 96744
Crestview 96797
Downtown (Part of Hilo)‡ 96720
Downtown (Part of Honolulu)‡ 96801-13
For specific ZIP Codes call (888) 275-8777, or your local postmaster.
Downtown (Part of Lahaina)‡ 96767
Dowsett Highlands (Part of Honolulu) 96817
Eight and One-half Mile Camp 96749
Eightmile Camp 96749
Eleele 96705
Elevenmile Homestead 96760
Ewa‡ 96706
Ewa Beach♦ 96706*
96709†
Ewa Gentry♦ 96706
Fernandez Village 96706
Ford Island‡ 96818
Fort Shafter‡ 96819
Foster Village 96818
Glenwood 96771
Haaheo 96720
Haena 96714
Haiku 96708
Haina 96727
Hakalau 96710
Halaula♦ 96755
Halawa, *Hawaii* 96755
Halawa, *Maui* 96748
Halawa Heights 96701
Halawa Hills 96701
Haleiwa♦ 96712
Halepalaoa Landing 96763
Haliimaile♦ 96768
Hamoa 96713
Hana♦ 96713
Hanalei♦ 96714
Hanamaulu♦ 96715
Hanapepe♦ 96716
Hanapepe Heights 96716
Haou 96713
Happy Valley 96793
Hauula♦ 96717
Hawaiian Beaches♦ 96778
Hawaiian Ocean View♦ 96704
Hawaiian Paradise Park♦ 96778
Hawaii Kai (Part of Honolulu)‡ 96825
Hawaii National Park 96718
Hawaii State Hospital 96744
Hawi♦ 96719
Heeia♦ 96744
Hickam Air Force Base 96853
Hickam Housing♦ 96818
Highway Village 96728
Hilo♦ 96720*
96721†
Hoaeae 96797
Hokamahoe House Lot 96764
Holualoa♦ 96725
Honalo♦ 96750
Honaunau 96726
Honohina 96710
Honokaa♦ 96727
Honokahua 96761
Honokai Hale 96707
Honokohau 96725
Honokowai 96761

Honolulu

96801-39
96850
For specific ZIP Codes call (888) 275-8777, or your local postmaster.

Colleges & Universities

Chaminade Univ 96816
Hawaii Pacific Univ 96813
International Coll & Graduate School 96817
Univ of Hawaii at Manoa 96822

Financial Institutions

Bank of Hawaii 96813
Central Pacific Bank 96813
First Hawaiian Bank 96813

Hospitals

Kapiolani Med Ctr for Women & Children 96826
Queen's Med Ctr 96813
Tripler Army Med Ctr 96859

Hotels/Motels

Ala Moana 96814
Hawaii Prince Waikiki 96815
Hawaiian Regent 96815
Hawaiian Waikiki Beach 96815
Hilton Hawaiian Village 96815
Hyatt Regency Waikiki Resort 96815
The Ilikai Hotel Nikko Waikiki 96815
Outrigger Hobron 96815
Outrigger Maile Sky Court 96815
Outrigger Prince Kuhio 96815
Outrigger Reef on the Beach 96815
Outrigger Waikiki on the Beach 96815
Outrigger West 96815
Pacific Beach Hotel 96815
Royal Hawaiian 96815
Sheraton Moana Surfrider 96815
Sheraton Princess Kaiulani 96815
Sheraton Waikiki 96815
Waikiki Beachcomber 96815

Military Installations

Fort Shafter 96819
Honolulu Coast Guard Base 96817
Tripler Army Medical Center 96819

Honomakau 96755
Honomu♦ 96728
Honouliuli 96706
Honuapo 96772
Hookena 96704
Hoolehua 96729
Hoopuloa 96726
Huehue 96725
Huelo 96708
Iroquois Point♦ 96706
Iwasaki Camp 96760
Iwilei (Part of Honolulu) 96817
Kaaawa♦ 96730
Kaahumanu Center 96732
Kaalaea 96744
Kaalawai 96821
Kaanapali♦ 96761
Kaapahu 96776
Kaapoko Homesteads 96781
Kaauhuhu Homesteads 96719
Kaawanui Village 96769
Kahakuloa 96793
Kahala Mall 96816
Kahaluu, *Hawaii* 96725
Kahaluu, *Honolulu*♦ 96744
Kahana, *Honolulu* 96717
Kahana, *Maui* 96761
Kahei Homesteads 96719
Kahua 96755
Kahuku, *Hawaii* 96772
Kahuku, *Honolulu*♦ 96731
Kahului♦ 96732*
96733†
Kaiaakea 96773
Kaieie Homesteads 96781
Kailua, *Honolulu*♦ 96734
Kailua, *Maui* 96708
Kailua Kona♦ 96740*
96745†
Kai Malino 96704
Kaimu 96778
Kaimuki (Part of Honolulu)‡ 96816
Kainaliu 96750
Kainalu 96748
Kaiwiki 96720
Kalae 96757
Kalaheo♦ 96741
Kalamaula 96748
Kalaoa 96740
Kalaoa Homesteads 96725
Kalapana 96778
Kalauao 96701
Kalaupapa 96742
Kalepolepo 96753
Kalihi (Part of Honolulu) 96819
Kalihi Kai (Part of Honolulu) 96818
Kalihi Shopping Center (Part of Honolulu) 96819
Kalihiwai♦ 96754
Kaluaaha 96748
Kamaili 96778
Kamalo 96748
Kamehameha Heights (Part of Honolulu) 96819
Kamiloloa 96748
Kamooloa 96791
Kamuela♦ 96743
Kaneohe♦ 96744
Kaneohe Station♦ 96863
Kaniahiku Village 96778
Kapaa♦ 96746
Kapaau♦ 96755
Kapahulu (Part of Honolulu) 96815
Kapaia 96766
Kapaka 96747
Kapalama (Part of Honolulu)‡ 96817
Kapehu 96780
Kapoho 96778
Kapolei‡ 96707*
96709†
Kapulena 96727
Kaumakani♦ 96747
Kaumalapau 96763
Kaumana 96720
Kaunakakai♦ 96748
Kaupakalua 96708
Kaupo 96713
Kawaihae‡ 96743
Kawaihua 96746
Kawailoa 96712
Kawailoa Beach 96712
Kawainui 96783
Kawela, *Honolulu*♦ 96731
Kawela, *Maui* 96748
Keaau♦ 96749
Keaau Camp 96749
Keaau Ranch 96749
Kealakehe Homesteads 96740
Kealakekua♦ 96750
Kealia 96751
Keanae 96708
Keauhou 96739
Keaukaha 96720
Keawakapu 96753
Keehia 96774
Keei 96726
Kehena 96778
Kekaha♦ 96752
Kelawea 96761
Keokea, *Hawaii* 96704
Keokea, *Maui* 96790
Koolu Hills 96734
Kihei♦ 96753
Kilauea♦ 96754
Kilauea Military Camp 96718
Kilauea Settlement 96785
Kipahulu 96713
Kipu, *Kauai* 96766
Kipu, *Maui* 96757
Koali 96713
Koele 96763
Kokee 96752
Kokohahi 96744
Kokomo 96708
Kolekole Beach Park 96710
Kolo 96704
Koloa♦ 96756
Kualapuu♦ 96757
Kualoa 96730
Kuhio Village 96743
Kuhua 96761
Kukaiau 96776
Kukui 96771
Kukuihaele♦ 96727
Kukuiula 96756
Kukui Village 96774
Kula 96790
Kumukumu 96703
Kunia 96759
Kupolo 96766
Kurtistown♦ 96760
Lahaina♦ 96761*
96767†
Lahaina Shopping Center 96761
Laie♦ 96762
Lalakoa 96763
Lanai City♦ 96763
Lanikai 96734
Lanikai Heights 96734
Laupahoehoe♦ 96764
Laupahoehoe Point 96764
Lawai♦ 96765
Lihue♦ 96766
Lihue Shopping Center 96766
Lower Paia 96779
Lower Village 96706
Lualualei 96792
Lualualei Homesteads 96792
Maalaea♦ 96793
McGerrow Village 96784
McGrew Point 96701
Maili♦ 96792
Makaha♦ 96792
Makaha Valley♦ 96792
Makakilo City♦ 96706
Makapala 96755
Makawao♦ 96768
Makaweli♦ 96769
Makena 96753
Makiki‡ 96822-23
96826
For specific ZIP Codes call (888) 275-8777, or your local postmaster.
Makiki Heights (Part of Honolulu) 96822
Mana 96752
Mark Twain Estates 96772
Maulua 96780
Maunalani Heights (Part of Honolulu) 96816
Maunaloa♦ 96770
Maunalua 96816
Maunawili 96734
Mililani Town♦ 96789
Milolii 96726
Milo Village 96774
Moanalua (Part of Honolulu) 96819
Moiliili (Part of Honolulu)‡ 96814*
96828†
Mokuleia♦ 96791
Momilani Estates 96782
Mountain View♦ 96771
Muolea 96713
Naalehu♦ 96772
Nanakuli♦ 96792
Napili 96761
Napoopoo 96704
Navy Cantonment (Part of Honolulu)‡ 96818
Navy Terminal (Part of Honolulu)‡ 96818
Nawiliwili 96766
Newtown Estates 96701
Nine Miles 96749
Ninole 96773
Niulii 96755
Niumalu 96766
Niu Valley (Part of Honolulu) 96821
Niu Valley Shopping Center (Part of Honolulu) 96821
Niu Village 96774
Numila 96705
Olinda 96768
Olomana 96734
Olowalu 96761
Omao♦ 96756
Omapio 96790
Onomea 96781
Ookala 96774
Opihikao 96778
Orpheum Village 96779
Paauhau 96775
Paauhau Mauka 96727
Paauilo♦ 96776
Pacific Heights (Part of Honolulu) 96817
Pacific Palisades 96782
Pahala♦ 96777
Pahoa♦ 96778
Pahoehoe 96704
Paia♦ 96779
Palama (Part of Honolulu) 96817
Palani Junction 96725
Panaewa 96720
Papa 96704
Papaaloa 96780
Papaikou♦ 96781
Paukaa♦ 96720
Paukukalo 96793
Paumalu 96712
Pauwela 96708
Pearl City 96782
Pearl City Heights 96782
Pearl Harbor Naval Base and Shipyard 96860
Pepeekeo♦ 96783
Pepeekeo Mill 96783
Pihana 96793
Piihonua 96720
Pohakea Homesteads 96776
Pohakupu 96734
Pohoiki 96778
Poipu♦ 96756
Pomoho 96786
Port Allen 96705
Portlock 96825
Prince Kuhio Plaza 96720
Puako♦ 96743
Pualaea Homestead 96764
Pua Loke 96766
Puhi♦ 96766
Pukalani♦ 96788
Pukoo 96748
Pulehu 96790
Punaluu, *Hawaii* 96777
Punaluu, *Honolulu*♦ 96717
Puohala Village 96744
Pupukea 96712
Puuanahulu 96725
Puueo 96720
Pu'uhonua o Honaunau National Historical Park 96726
Puu Hue 96719
Puuiki 96713
Puunene 96784
Puunoa 96761
Puunui (Part of Honolulu) 96819
Puuohala 96793
Puu Waawaa 96740
Puuwai 96769
Renton Village 96706
Royal Hawaiian (Part of Honolulu)‡ 96815
St. Louis Heights (Part of Honolulu) 96816
Schofield Barracks‡ 96786
Spreckelsville 96779
Submarine Base‡ 96818
Sunset Beach 96712
Tantalus (Part of Honolulu) 96822
Tenney 96706
Timber Town (Part of Honolulu) 96826
Ualapue 96748
Ulumalu 96708
Ulupalakua 96790
Umikoa 96776
Union Mill 96719
University‡ 96822
Upolu Point 96719
Uptown (Part of Honolulu)‡ 96837
Varona Village 96706
Village Park♦ 96797
Village Seven 96705
Volcano♦ 96785
Wahiawa, *Honolulu*♦ 96786
Wahiawa, *Kauai* 96705
Waiahole 96744
Waiaka 96743

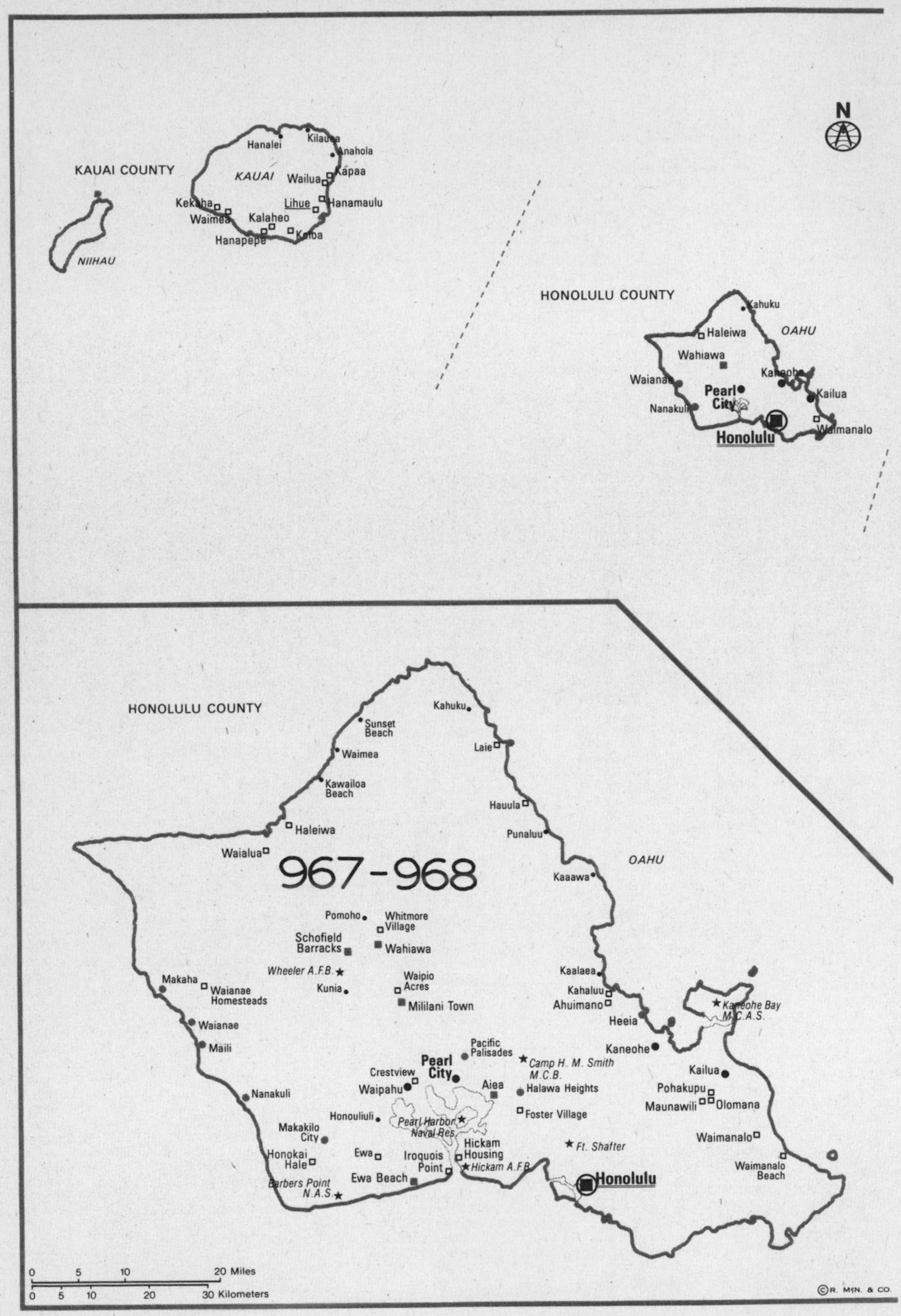

KAUAI COUNTY
NIIHAU
KAUAI
Hanalei
Kilauea
Anahola
Wailua
Kapaa
Kekaha
Lihue
Hanamaulu
Waimea
Kalaheo
Hanapepe
Koloa
HONOLULU COUNTY
OAHU
Kahuku
Haleiwa
Wahiawa
Waianae
Kaneohe
Pearl City
Kailua
Nanakuli
Honolulu
Waimanalo
N
HONOLULU COUNTY
Kahuku
Sunset Beach
Laie
Waimea
Kawailoa Beach
Hauula
Haleiwa
Punaluu
Waialua
OAHU
967-968
Kaaawa
Pomoho
Whitmore Village
Schofield Barracks
Wahiawa
Wheeler A.F.B.
Waipio Acres
Kaalaea
Makaha
Waianae Homesteads
Kunia
Kahaluu
Mililani Town
Ahuimano
Kaneohe Bay M.C.A.S.
Waianae
Heeia
Maili
Pacific Palisades
Kaneohe
Camp H. M. Smith M.C.B.
Pearl City
Crestview
Kailua
Waipahu
Aiea
Halawa Heights
Pohakupu
Nanakuli
Maunawili
Olomana
Honouliuli
Foster Village
Makakilo City
Pearl Harbor Naval Res.
Waimanalo
Hickam Housing
Ft. Shafter
Honokai Hale
Ewa
Iroquois Point
Hickam A.F.B.
Waimanalo Beach
Barbers Point N.A.S.
Ewa Beach
Honolulu
0 5 10 20 Miles
0 5 10 20 30 Kilometers
©R. McN. & CO.

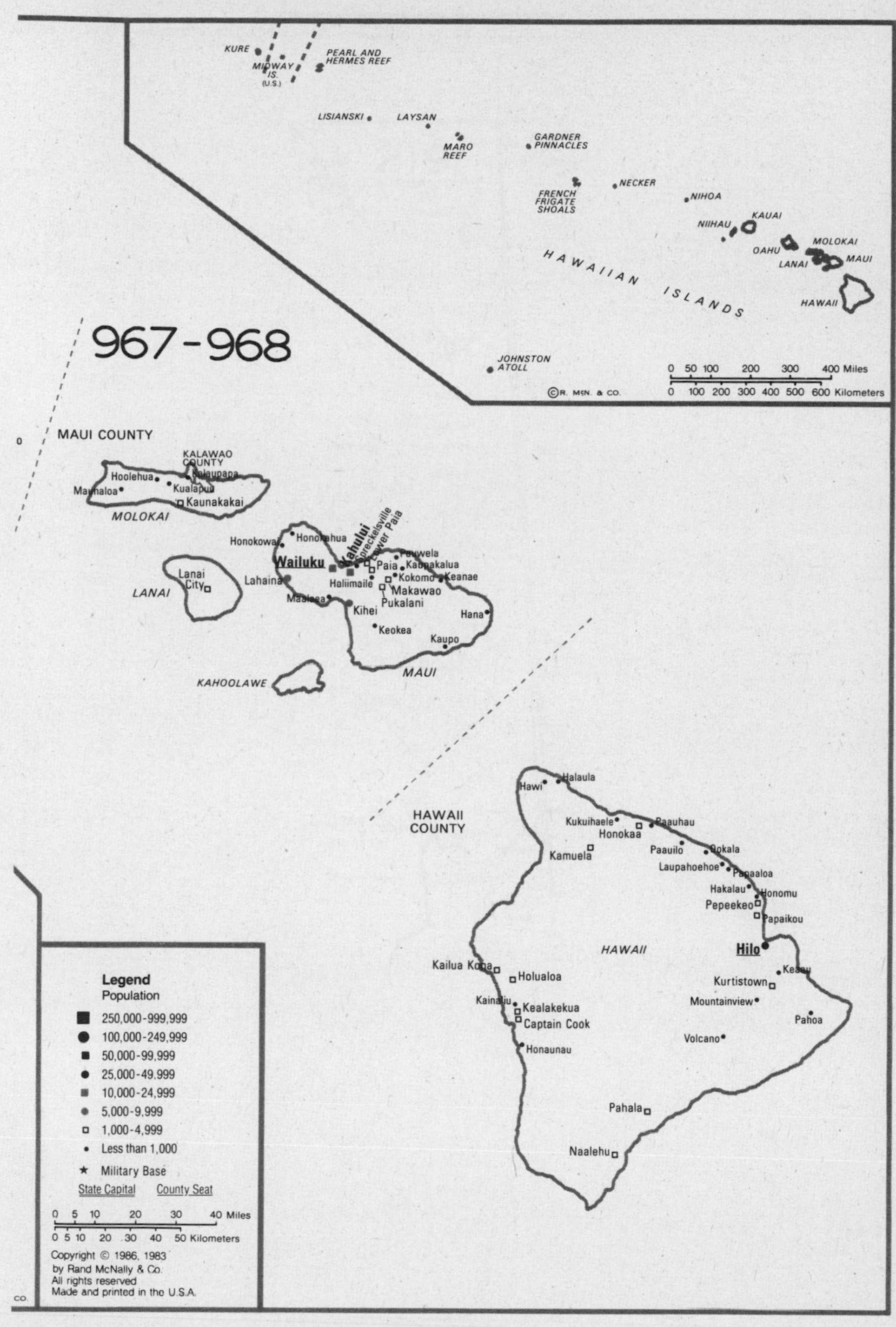
KURE
MIDWAY IS. (U.S.)
PEARL AND HERMES REEF
LISIANSKI
LAYSAN
MARO REEF
GARDNER PINNACLES
FRENCH FRIGATE SHOALS
NECKER
NIHOA
KAUAI
NIIHAU
OAHU
MOLOKAI
LANAI
MAUI
HAWAII
HAWAIIAN ISLANDS
JOHNSTON ATOLL
0 50 100 200 300 400 Miles
0 100 200 300 400 500 600 Kilometers
©R. McN. & CO.
967-968
MAUI COUNTY
KALAWAO COUNTY
Hoolehua
Kalaupapa
Kualapuu
Maunaloa
Kaunakakai
MOLOKAI
Honokowai
Honokahua
Kahului
Spreckelsville
Lower Paia
Wailuku
Pauwela
Paia
Kaupakalua
Lanai City
Lahaina
Haliimaile
Kokomo
Keanae
Makawao
Pukalani
LANAI
Maalaea
Kihei
Hana
Keokea
Kaupo
MAUI
KAHOOLAWE
HAWAII COUNTY
Hawi
Halaula
Kukuihaele
Paauhau
Honokaa
Kamuela
Paauilo
Ookala
Laupahoehoe
Papaaloa
Hakalau
Honomu
Pepeekeo
Papaikou
HAWAII
Hilo
Kailua Kona
Holualoa
Keaau
Kurtistown
Mountainview
Kainaliu
Kealakekua
Captain Cook
Pahoa
Volcano
Honaunau
Pahala
Naalehu
Legend
Population
250,000-999,999
100,000-249,999
50,000-99,999
25,000-49,999
10,000-24,999
5,000-9,999
1,000-4,999
Less than 1,000
Military Base
State Capital
County Seat
0 5 10 20 30 40 Miles
0 5 10 20 30 40 50 Kilometers
Copyright © 1986, 1983
by Rand McNally & Co.
All rights reserved
Made and printed in the U.S.A.

Waiakea...................... 96720
Waiakea Camps 96720
Waialae-Kahala (Part of Honolulu)‡ 96816
Waialua, *Honolulu*♦ 96791
Waialua, *Maui* 96748
Waialua Mill 96791
Waianae...................... 96792
Waianae Homesteads 96792
Waiau 96782
Waiau View Estates 96782
Waiehu 96793
Waiehu Village 96793
Waihee 96793
Waikane♦ 96744
Waikapu♦ 96793
Waikele 96797
Waikiki (Part of Honolulu)‡ 96815*
.... 96830¶
Waikoloa♦ 96738
Wailea 96710
Wailea-Makena♦ 96753
Wailua, *Kauai*♦........... 96746
Wailua, *Maui* 96708
Wailua Homesteads♦.. 96746
Wailuku♦ 96793
Wailupe 96821
Waimalu...................... 96701
Waimanalo♦............... 96795
Waimanalo Beach♦ 96795
Waimea, *Honolulu* 96712
Waimea, *Kauai*♦......... 96796
Wainaku♦ 96720
Wainee 96761
Wainiha 96714
Waiohinu 96772
Waipahu♦ 96797
Waipio 96727
Waipio Acres♦ 96786
Waipouli...................... 96746
Waipunalei Homesteads 96764
Wharf.......................... 96761
Wheeler Army Airfield♦ 96854
Whitmore Village♦ 96786
Wilhelmina Rise (Part of Honolulu) 96816
Woodlawn (Part of Honolulu) 96822
Wood Valley................ 96777

Place	ZIP
Aberdeen	83210
Acequia	83350
Ahsahka	83520
Alameda (Part of Pocatello)‡	83201
Albion	83311
Aldape Heights (Part of Boise)	83701
Algoma	83860
Almo	83312
Alpha	83611
Alton	83254
American Falls	83211
Ammon	83404
Anderson Dam	83647
Annis	83442
Apple Valley	83660
Arbon	83212
Archer	83440
Arco	83213
Argora	83423
Arimo	83214
Artesian City	83344
Ashton	83420
Athol	83801
Atlanta	83601
Atomic City	83215
Avery	83802
Avon	83823
Baker	83467
Bancroft	83217
Banida	83263
Banks	83602
Bannock (Part of Pocatello)‡	83204
Basalt	83218
Basin	83346
Bates	83422
Bayview	83803
Beachs Corner	83401
Bear	83612
Bellevue	83313
Belmont	83801
Bench	83241
Benewah	83861
Bennington	83254
Berger	83301
Bern	83220
Big Creek	83677
Big Little Acres	83338
Big Springs (Part of Island Park)	83433
Blackfoot	83221
Black Lake	83861
Blackrock	83245
Blaine	83843
Blanchard	83804
Bliss	83314
Bloomington	83223
Boise	83701-88
For specific ZIP Codes call (888) 275-8777, or your local postmaster.	
Boise Airport (Part of Boise)‡	83715
Boise Town Square (Part of Boise)	83701
Boles	83522
Bone	83427
Bonners Ferry	83805
Borah (Part of Boise)‡	83702
Bovill	83806
Bowmont	83686
Box Canyon (Part of Island Park)	83429
Bradley (Part of Kellogg)	83837
Bridge	83342
Bruneau	83604
Bruneau Valley	83604
Buhl	83316
Buist	83243
Bunn	83873
Burgdorf	83638
Burke	83873
Burley	83318
Burmah	83349
Burton	83440
Butler Bay	83861
Butte City	83213
Cabinet	83811
Cache	83452
Calder	83808
Caldwell	83605*
	83606†
Caldwell Labor Camp	83605
Cambridge, *Bannock*	83234
Cambridge, *Washington*	83610
Cameron	83537
Cardiff	83546
Care-Free Estates	83318
Carey	83320
Careywood	83809
Carlin Bay	83833
Carmen	83462
Cascade	83611
Castleford	83321
Cataldo	83810
Cathedral Pines	83340
Cavendish	83537
Central	83217
Central Cove	83676
Challis	83226
Chapin	83455
Chatcolet	83851
Cherry Creek	83252
Cherry Lane (Part of Boise)	83705
Chester	83421
Chesterfield	83217
Chilco	83801
Chubbuck	83202
Churchill	83318
Clagstone	83856
Clark Fork	83811
Clarkia	83812
Clawson	83452
Clayton	83227
Clearwater	83539
Clementsville	83436
Cleveland	83263
Cliffs	97910
Clifton	83228
Clover	83316
Coats	83350
Cobalt	83229
Cocolalla	83813
Coeur d'Alene	83814-16
For specific Zip Codes call (888) 275-8777, or your local postmaster.	
Coeur d'Alene Indian Reservation	83851
Colburn	83865
Cole Village (Part of Boise)‡	83704
Collister (Part of Boise)‡	83703
Coltman	83401
Columbus Park (Part of Boise)	83705
Conda	83230
Conkling Park	83876
Conner	83342
Coolin	83821
Cooperville	83554
Corral	83322
Cotterel	83323
Cottonwood	83522
	83538
For specific ZIP Codes call (888) 275-8777, or your local postmaster.	
Council	83612
Country Club Mall (Part of Idaho Falls)	83401
Country Club Manor (Part of Boise)	83705
Country Club Terrace (Part of Boise)	83705
Craigmont	83523
Crescent	83537
Crouch	83622
Crystal	83672
Culdesac	83524
Culver	83865
Cuprum	83612
Curry	83328
Dalton Gardens	83815
Daniels	83252
Darlington	83231
David Taylor Research Center, Acoustic Research Detachment	83803
Davis Acres (Part of Garden City)	83704
Dayton	83232
Deary	83823
Declo	83323
Deep Creek, *Oneida*	83252
Deep Creek, *Twin Falls*	83316
Delta	83873
Dent	83544
Denton (Part of Boise)	83704
Denver	83530
Desmet	83824
Dietrich	83324
Dingle	83233
Dixie	83525
Doles	83605
Donnelly	83615
Dover	83825
Downey	83234
Driggs	83422
Drummond	83420
Dubois	83423
Duck Valley Indian Reservation	89832
Dudley	83810
Eagle, Ada	83616
Eagle, Shoshone	83874
Eagle Rock (Part of Idaho Falls)‡	83402
Easley Hot Springs	83340
East Hope	83836
East Kamiah	83536
East Lewiston (Part of Lewiston)	83501
Eastport	83826
Eaton	83672
Echo Beach	83858
Eddiville	83814
Eden	83325
Edgemere	83856
Edmonds	83440
Elgin	83445
Elba	83326
Elk City	83525
Elk River	83827
Ellis	83235
Elmira	83862
Emida	83861
Emmett	83617
Enaville	83839
Enkraft	83350
Enrose	83605
Evergreen	83654
Excelsior Beach	83858
Fairfield	83327
Fairview, *Franklin*	83263
Fairview, *Twin Falls*	83316
Fall Creek, *Elmore*	83647
Fall Creek, *Idaho*	83530
Falls City	83338
Featherville	83647
Felt	83424
Fenn	83531
Ferdinand	83526
Fernan Lake Village	83814
Fernwood	83830
Filer	83328
Firth	83236
Fish Haven	83287
Florence	83542
Fort Hall	83203
Fort Hall Indian Reservation	83203
Fox Creek	83455
Franklin (Part of Boise)	83704
Franklin, Franklin	83237
Franklin Park (Part of Boise)	83704
Fraser	83544
Freedom	83120
Frisco	83873
Fruitland	83619
Fruitvale	83620
Galena	83340
Gannett	83313
Gardena	83629
Garden City‡	83714
Garden Valley	83622
Garfield	83442
Garwood	83835
Gem	83873
Genesee	83832
Geneva	83238
Georgetown	83239
Gibbonsville	83463
Gibson	83221
Gibson City (Part of Pinehurst)	83850
Gifford	83541
Glendale	83263
Glengary	83864
Glenns Ferry	83623
Glenwood (Part of Orofino)	83544
Glenwood, *Idaho*	83536
Golden	83530
Gooding	83330
Goodrich	83612
Goshen	83274
Grace	83241
Grand Teton Mall (Part of Idaho Falls)	83401
Grandview, *Bingham*	83210
Grand View, *Owyhee*	83624
Grangemont	83544
Grangeville	83530
Granite	83801
Grant	83442
Grasmere	83604
Gray	83276
Greencreek	83533
Greenleaf	83626
Greenwood	83335
Greer	83544
Gross	83657
Groveland	83221
Gwenford	83252
Hagerman	83332
Hailey	83333
Hamer	83425
Hammett	83627
Hampton	83857
Hansen	83334
Harpster	83539
Harrison	83833
Harvard	83834
Hatch	83217
Hatwai	83501
Hauser	83854
Havens	83221
Hayden	83835
Hayden Lake	83835
Hazelton	83335
Headquarters	83546
Heglar	83211
Heise	83443
Helmer	83823
Heman	83445
Henry	83230
Heyburn	83336
Hibbard	83440
Highlands (Part of Boise)	83702
Hill City	83337
Hillview (Part of Ammon)	83401
Holbrook	83243
Hollister	83301
Home Acres (Part of Boise)	83704
Homedale	83628
Honeysuckle Hills	83835
Hop (Part of Greenleaf)	83626
Hope	83836
Hornet	83612
Horseshoe Bend	83629
Hot Spring Landing	83333
Hot Springs	83604
Howe	83244
Hoyt	83802
Huckleberry Bay	83821
Huetter	83854
Hulen Meadows	83340
Humphrey	83446
Hunt	83325
Huston	83630
Idaho City	83631
Idaho Falls	83401-06
For specific ZIP Codes call (888) 275-8777, or your local postmaster.	
Idahome	83323
Idmon	83423
Indian Cove	83627
Indian Hills (Part of Pocatello)	83204
Indian Valley	83632
Inkom	83245
Iona	83427
Irwin	83428
Island Park	83429
Jackson	83350
Jacques	83524
Jamestown	83274
Jerome	83338
Joel	83843
Johnny Creek (Part of Pocatello)	83204
Jonathan	83672
Joseph	83522
Judge Town	83546
Juliaetta	83535
Juniper	84336
Kamiah	83536
Karcher Mall (Part of Nampa)	83651
Kellogg	83837
Kendrick	83537
Ketchum	83340
Keuterville	83538
Kidder	83539
Kilgore	83423
Kimball	83236
Kimberly	83341
King Hill	83633
Kings Corner	83686
Kingston	83839
Knowlton Heights	83605
Kooskia	83539
Kootenai	83840
Kuna	83634
Labelle	83442
Laclede	83841
Lake Creek	83876
Lake Fork	83635
Lakeview	83803
Lamb Creek	83856
Lamont	83420
Lanark	83254
Lancaster Terrace (Part of Boise)	83702
Lane	83810
Lapwai	83540
Lardo (Part of McCall)	83638
Last Chance Resort (Part of Island Park)	83429
Lava Hot Springs	83246
Leadore	83464
Leland	83537
Lemhi	83465
Lenore	83541
Leslie	83255
Letha	83636
Lewiston	83501
Lewiston Orchards (Part of Lewiston)	83501
Lewisville	83431
Liberty	83254
Lidy Hot Springs	83423
Lincoln	83401
Linrose	83286
Lone Pine	83464
Lorenzo	83442
Lost River, *Butte*	83255
Lost River, *Custer*	83255
Lowell	83539
Lower Stanley	83278
Lowman	83637
Lucile	83542
Lund	83217
Lyman	83440
McArthur	83847
McCall	83638
McCammon	83250
Mace	83873
McGuires (Part of Post Falls)	83854
Mackay	83251
Macks Inn (Part of Island Park)	83433
Magic City	83313
Magic Resort	83352
Malad City	83252
Malta	83342
Mapleton	83263
Marble Creek	83808
Marion	83346
Marley (Part of Richfield)	83349
Marshcenter	83234
Marsing	83639
Marysville	83420
May	83253
Meadow Creek	83805
Meadows	83654
Meadowville	83276
Medimont	83842
Melba	83641
Menan	83434
Meridian	83642*
	83680†
Mesa	83643
Mica	83814
Midas	83864
Middleton	83644
Midvale	83645
Midway	83651
Miller Creek Settlement	89832
Milltown	83861
Milo	83401
Minidoka	83343
Minkcreek	83263
Mohler	83523
Montana Junction (Part of Pocatello)	83201
Monteview	83435
Montour	83617
Montpelier	83254
Moore	83255
Mora	83634
Moravia	83805

*** Area Zip Code** **† Post Office Boxes** **‡ Postal Station** **♦ Census Designated Place** *Italic Type* **County**

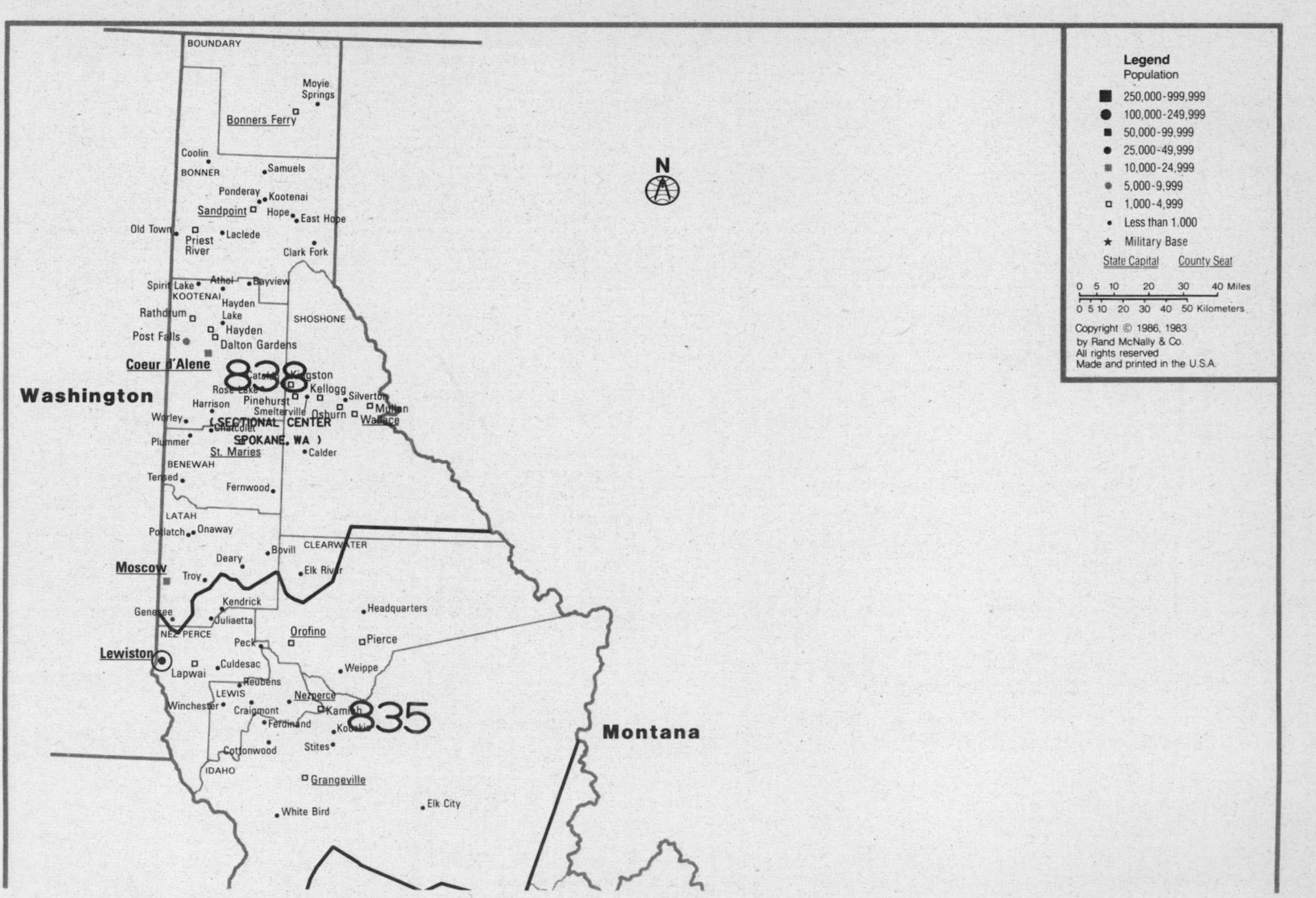
Legend
Population
250,000-999,999
100,000-249,999
50,000-99,999
25,000-49,999
10,000-24,999
5,000-9,999
1,000-4,999
Less than 1,000
Military Base
State Capital
County Seat
0 5 10 20 30 40 Miles
0 5 10 20 30 40 50 Kilometers
Copyright © 1986, 1983
by Rand McNally & Co.
All rights reserved
Made and printed in the U.S.A.
N
Washington
Montana
BOUNDARY
Moyie Springs
Bonners Ferry
Coolin
BONNER
Samuels
Ponderay
Kootenai
Sandpoint
Hope
East Hope
Old Town
Priest River
Laclede
Clark Fork
Athol
Bayview
KOOTENAI
Hayden Lake
Rathdrum
Post Falls
Hayden
Dalton Gardens
SHOSHONE
Coeur d'Alene
838
Kellogg
Harrison
Pinehurst
Silverton
Smelterville
Osburn
Mullan
Wallace
Worley
SECTIONAL CENTER
SPOKANE, WA
Plummer
St. Maries
Calder
BENEWAH
Fernwood
LATAH
Onaway
Bovill
CLEARWATER
Deary
Moscow
Troy
Elk River
Kendrick
Juliaetta
Headquarters
Orofino
Pierce
Peck
Lewiston
Culdesac
Lapwai
Weippe
Reubens
LEWIS
Nezperce
Winchester
Craigmont
Ferdinand
835
Stites
Cottonwood
IDAHO
Grangeville
White Bird
Elk City

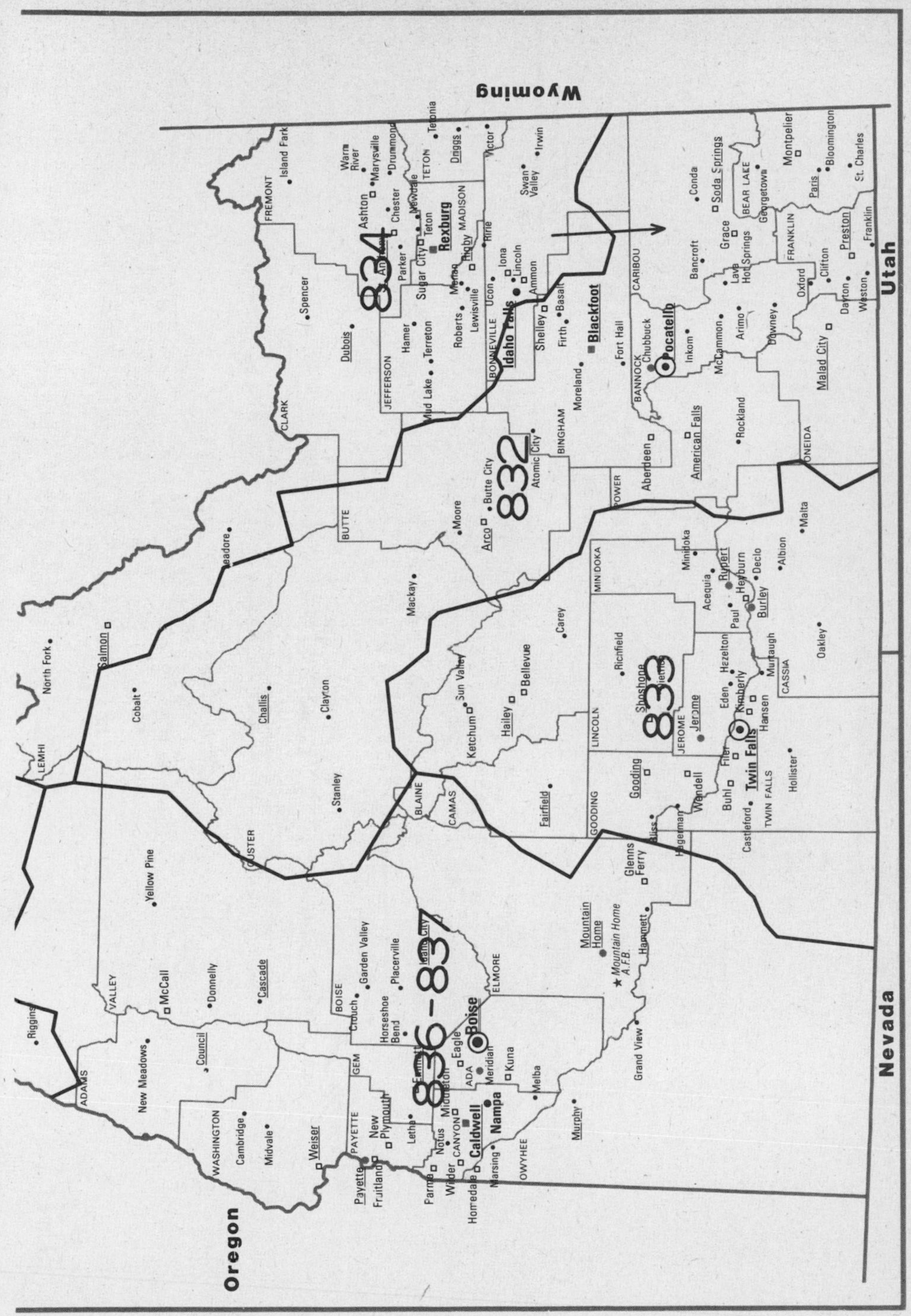
Wyoming
Oregon
Nevada
Utah
834
832
833
836-837
FREMONT
CLARK
JEFFERSON
MADISON
TETON
BONNEVILLE
BINGHAM
BUTTE
CARIBOU
BANNOCK
POWER
BEAR LAKE
FRANKLIN
ONEIDA
MINIDOKA
CASSIA
JEROME
LINCOLN
GOODING
TWIN FALLS
BLAINE
CAMAS
CUSTER
LEMHI
VALLEY
ADAMS
WASHINGTON
PAYETTE
GEM
BOISE
ADA
CANYON
ELMORE
OWYHEE
Island Park
Spencer
Dubois
Ashton
Warm River
Marysville
Drummond
Chester
Newdale
Tetonia
Driggs
Victor
Irwin
Swan Valley
Rexburg
Teton
Sugar City
Parker
Rigby
Ririe
Menan
Lewisville
Roberts
Hamer
Terreton
Mud Lake
Ucon
Iona
Lincoln
Ammon
Idaho Falls
Shelley
Basalt
Firth
Blackfoot
Moreland
Fort Hall
Chubbuck
Pocatello
Inkom
McCammon
Arimo
Downey
Bancroft
Grace
Lava Hot Springs
Conda
Soda Springs
Georgetown
Montpelier
Paris
Bloomington
St. Charles
Preston
Franklin
Oxford
Clifton
Dayton
Weston
Malad City
American Falls
Aberdeen
Rockland
Atomic City
Butte City
Arco
Moore
Mackay
Leadore
Salmon
North Fork
Cobalt
Challis
Clayton
Stanley
Sun Valley
Ketchum
Hailey
Bellevue
Carey
Fairfield
Minidoka
Rupert
Acequia
Heyburn
Paul
Burley
Declo
Albion
Malta
Oakley
Richfield
Shoshone
Dietrich
Jerome
Eden
Hazelton
Murtaugh
Kimberly
Hansen
Twin Falls
Filer
Buhl
Castleford
Hollister
Wendell
Gooding
Hagerman
Bliss
Glenns Ferry
Hammett
Mountain Home
Mountain Home A.F.B.
Grand View
Murphy
Melba
Kuna
Meridian
Boise
Eagle
Nampa
Caldwell
Middleton
Emmett
Horseshoe Bend
Placerville
Idaho City
Garden Valley
Crouch
Cascade
Donnelly
McCall
Yellow Pine
Riggins
New Meadows
Council
Cambridge
Midvale
Weiser
Payette
Fruitland
New Plymouth
Letha
Notus
Parma
Wilder
Homedale
Marsing

Moreland 83256
Morgans Alley (Part of Lewiston)‡ 83501
Moscow 83843
Mountain Home 83647
Mountain Home Air Force Base 83648
Mountain View (Part of Boise)‡ 83704
Mount Idaho 83530
Moyie Springs 83845
Mud Lake 83450
Mullan 83846
Murphy 83650
Murray 83874
Murtaugh 83344
Myrtle 83535
Naf 83342
Nampa 83651-53
83686-87
For specific ZIP Codes call (888) 275-8777, or your local postmaster.
Naples 83847
Naval Administration Unit, Idaho Falls 83401
Neeley 83211
New Centerville 83631
Newdale 83436
New Meadows 83654
New Plymouth 83655
New Sweden 83402
Nezperce 83543
Nez Perce Indian Reservation 83540
Niter 83241
Nordman 83848
Norland 83343
North Fork 83466
North Lewiston (Part of Lewiston) 83501
North Shoshone 83352
Northside (Part of Boise)‡ 83702
Northside (Part of Emmett)‡ 83617
North Avenue (Part of Coeur d'Alene)‡ 83815
Notus 83656
Nounan 83254
Nuclear Power Training Unit, Idaho Falls 83401
Oakley 83346
Obsidian 83340
Ola 83657
Oldtown 83822
Onaway 83855
Oreana 83650
Orofino 83544
Orogrande 83525
Osburn 83849
Osgood 83402
Outlet Bay 83856
Ovid 83254
Oxford 83263
Page 83868
Palisades 83428
Palmetto (Part of Eagle) 83616
Palouse Empire Mall (Part of Moscow) 83843
Paradise Hot Springs 83647
Paris 83261
Park 83823
Parker 83438
Parma 83660
Patterson 83253
Paul 83347
Payette 83661
Pearl 83616
Peck 83545
Pedee (Part of Chatcolet) 83851
Pegram 83254
Pella 83318
Picabo 83348
Pierce 83546
Pine 83647
Pinehurst, *Adams* 83654
Pinehurst, *Shoshone* 83850
Pine Ridge 83612
Pine Ridge Mall (Part of Pocatello) 83201
Pingree 83262
Pinto Point 83821
Pioneerville 83631
Placerville 83666
Plano 83440
Pleasantview 83252
Plummer 83851
Pocatello 83201-02
83204-06
For specific ZIP Codes call (888) 275-8777, or your local postmaster.
Polaris (Part of Osburn) 83849
Pollock 83547
Ponderay 83852
Ponds Resort (Part of Island Park) 83429
Porthill 83853
Post Falls 83854*
83877†
Potlatch 83855
Potlatch Junction 83855
Prairie 83647
Preston 83263
Prichard 83873
Priest River 83856
Princeton 83857
Raft River 83211
Ramsdell (Part of Chatcolet) 83851
Rathdrum 83858
Raymond 83114
Redfish Lake 83278
Red River Hot Springs 83525
Reno 83423
Reubens 83548
Rexburg 83440
Reynolds 83650
Richfield 83349
Riddle 83604
Rigby 83442
Riggins 83549
Ririe 83443
Riverdale 83263
Riverside, *Bingham* 83221
Riverside, *Canyon* 83605
Riverside (Part of Orofino) 83544
Roberts 83444
Robin 83214
Rock Creek 83334
Rockford 83221
Rockford Bay 83814
Rockland 83271
Rocky Bar 83647
Rocky Point (Part of Chatcolet) 83851
Rocky Point, *Bonner* 83821
Rogerson 83302
Rose 83221
Roseberry 83615
Rose Lake 83810
Roseworth 83321
Roswell 83660
Roy 83271
Rupert 83350
Sagle 83860
St. Anthony 83445
St. Charles 83272
St. Joe 83861
St. John 83252
St. Leon 83401
St. Maries 83861
Salem 83440
Salmon 83467
Samaria 83252
Samuels 83862
Sanders 83870
Sandpoint 83864
Sandy Shores Addition 83821
Santa 83866
Selle 83864
Setters 83876
Sharon 83254
Shelley 83274
Shelton 83401
Sherwood Beach 83821
Shoshone 83352
Shoup 83469
Silver City 83650
Silver Creek Plunge 83602
Silver Sands Beach 83858
Silverton 83867
Skyline (Part of Idaho Falls)‡ 83402
Slate Creek 83554
Slickpoo 83524
Small 83423
Smelter Heights (Part of Kellogg) 83837
Smelterville 83868
Smiths Ferry 83611
Soda Springs 83276
Soldier 83327
Soldiers Home (Part of Boise) 83704
South Boise (Part of Boise) 83706
South Gate Plaza (Part of Lewiston) 83501
South Park (Part of Pocatello) 83204
Southside (Part of Boise)‡ 83706
Southwick 83537
Spalding 83551
Spencer 83446
Spirit Lake 83869
Springdale 83318
Springfield 83277
Squirrel 83447
Standrod 83342
Stanley 83278
Star 83669
Starkey 83620
Starrhs Ferry 83318
State Line 83854
Sterling 83210
Stites 83552
Stoddard 83686
Stone 83280
Sugar City 83448
Sunbeam 83278
Sunnydell 83440
Sunnyside 83864
Sunnyslope 83605
Sun Valley 83353-54
For specific ZIP Codes call (888) 275-8777, or your local postmaster.
Swan Falls 83634
Swanlake 83281
Swan Valley 83449
Sweet 83670
Sweetwater 83540
Syringa 83539
Taber 83221
Talache 83860
Tamarack 83612
Taylor 83401
Teakean 83541
Tendoy 83468
Tenmile 83642
Tensed 83870
Terreton 83450
Teton 83451
Tetonia 83452
Thatcher 83283
Thomas 83221
Thomas Junction 83221
Thornton 83440
Three Creek 83301
Topaz 83246
Transfer (Part of Lewiston) 83501
Treasureton 83263
Trestle Creek 83836
Triumph 83333
Troy 83871
Turner Bay 83833
Tuttle 83314
Twin Falls 83301*
83303†
Twin Groves 83445
Twin Lakes 83858
Twinlow 83858
Tyhee 83201
Ucon 83454
Unity 83318
University (Part of Moscow)‡ 83843
Ustick 83713
Valley View Heights (Part of Lewiston) 83501
Victor 83455
View 83318
Viola 83872
Virginia 83234
Waha 83501
Wallace 83873
Wapello 83221
Wardboro 83254
Wardner 83837
Warm Lake 83611
Warm River 83420
Warren 83671
Washoe 83661
Wayan 83285
Webb 83540
Weippe 83553
Weiser 83672
Weitz 83605
Wendell 83355
Westgate Acres (Part of Boise) 83704
Westlake 83526
Westmond 83860
Westmoreland (Part of Boise) 83704
West Mountain 83611
Weston 83286
Whiskeyjack 83864
White Bird 83554
Whitney (Part of Boise)‡ 83705
Whitney, Franklin 83263
Wilder 83676
Wilford 83445
Winchester 83555
Winder 83263
Winona 83539
Wolf Lodge 83814
Wolverine 83236
Woodland 83536
Woodland Park 83873
Woodruff 83252
Woodville 83274
Worley 83876
Yellow Pine 83677

*** Area Zip Code** **† Post Office Boxes** **‡ Postal Station** **♦ Census Designated Place** *Italic Type* **County**

A (Part of Champaign)‡ 61820
Abingdon 61410
Abington (Twp) 61476
Acacia Acres 60525
Acme Station (Part of Bartonville) 61607
Adair 61411
Adams, *La Salle* (Twp) 60531
Adams, *Adams* 62347
Adams Corner 62410
Addieville 62214
Addison 60101
Adeline 61047
Aden 62895
Adrian 62310
Aero Estates 60564
Aetna, *Logan* (Twp) 61749
Aetna, *Coles* 61938
Afolkey 61018
Afton (Twp) 60115
Agnew 61081
Air Mail Facility O'Hare (Part of Chicago) 60666
Airport 61074
Airport Heights 61607
Akin 62805
Akron (Twp) 61559
Alan Dale 62035
Alba (Twp) 61235
Albany 61230
Albany Park (Part of Chicago) 60625
.... 60630
For specific ZIP Codes call (888) 275-8777, or your local postmaster.
Albers 62215
Albion 62806
Albright Acres 62018
Alden 60001
Aldridge 62998
Aledo 61231
Alexander 62601
Alexis 61412
Algonquin 60102
Algonquin Shores 60102
Algonquin Trails (Part of Mount Prospect) 60056
Alhambra 62001
Allen, *La Salle* (Twp) 60470
Allen, *Mason* 62682
Allen, *Whiteside* 61071
Allendale 62410
Allens Corners 60140
Allens Grove (Twp) 62682
Allentown 61568
Allenville 61951
Allerton 61810
Allin (Twp) 61774
Allison (Twp) 62439
Alma 62807
Almora 60123
Almora Heights 60123
Alorton 62207
Alpha 61413
Alsey 62610
Alsip 60803
Alsip Woods (Part of Alsip) 60803
Alta 61614
Altamont, *Effingham* 62411
Altamont (Part of Godfrey 62035
Alto (Twp) 60553
Alton 62002
Altona 61414
Alton Square (Part of Alton) 62002
Alto Pass 62905
Altorf 60914
Alvin 61811
Alworth 61088
Amboy 61310
Amenia 61856
America 62996
Americana Village (Part of Glendale Heights) 60139
Ames 62277
Amity (Twp) 61319
Anchor 61720
Anchorage (Part of Glenview) 60026
Ancient Tree (Part of Northbrook) 60062
Ancona 61311
Andalusia 61232
Anderman Acres 60544
Anderson (Twp) 62441
Anderson Lake 61501

Andersonville (Part of Chicago) 60640
Andover 61233
Andres 60468
Andrew 62707
Anna 62906
Annapolis 62413
Annawan 61234
Antioch 60002
Appanoose (Twp) 62354
Apple Canyon Lake 61001
Applegate (Part of Schaumburg) 60193
Apple River 61001
Appleton 61428
Appletree (Part of Country Club Hills) 60478
Appolaloosa West 60119
Aptakisic 60069
Arboretum East 60137
Arboretum Villages (Part of Lisle) 60532
Arboretum West 60137
Arbor Trails (Part of Park Forest) 60466
Arbury Hills 60448
Arcadia 62650
Archer 62707
Archer Heights (Part of Chicago) 60632
Archie 61876
Arcola 61910
Arenzville 62611
Argenta 62501
Argo (Part of Summit) 60501
Argo Fay 61053
Argyle 61011
Arispie (Twp) 61368
Arlington 61312
Arlington Heights 60004-06
For specific ZIP Codes call (888) 275-8777, or your local postmaster.
Arlington Ridge (Part of Arlington Heights) 60004
Armington 61721
Armour Square (Part of Chicago) 60609
.... 60616
For specific ZIP Codes call (888) 275-8777, or your local postmaster.
Armstrong 61812
Arnold 62650
Aroma (Twp) 60901
Aroma Park 60910
Aroma Park Northwest 60901
Arrington (Twp) 62886
Arrowhead, *DuPage* 60187
Arrowhead, *Kankakee* 60914
Arrowhead Hills 60543
Arrowsmith 61722
Arrow Wood 62035
Artesia (Twp) 60918
Arthur 61911
Asbury (Twp) 62871
Ashburn (Part of Chicago)‡ 60652
Ash Grove, *Iroquois* (Twp) 60953
Ash Grove, *Shelby* (Twp) 61957
Ashkum 60911
Ashland 62612
Ashley 62808
Ashmore 61912
Ashton 61006
Assumption 62510
Astoria 61501
Athens 62613
Athensville 62082
Atkinson 61235
Atlanta 61723
Atlas 62370
Atlee Ogles 62223
Atterbury 62675
Attila 62974
Atwater 62511
Atwood 61913
Atwood Heights (Part of Alsip) 60803
Auburn, *Clark* (Twp) 62441
Auburn, *Sangamon* 62615
Auburn Gresham (Part of Chicago) 60620
Auburn Park (Part of Chicago)‡ 60620
Auburn Woods (Part of Palatine) 60067
Audubon (Twp) 62075
Augsburg 62885
Augusta 62311

Aurora (Twp) 60505
Aurora 60504-07
.... 60598
For specific ZIP Codes call (888) 275-8777, or your local postmaster.
Aurora East (Part of Aurora)‡ 60598
Austin, *Macon* (Twp) 62573
Austin (Part of Chicago)‡ 60644
Austin View (Part of Alsip) 60803
Aux Sable (Twp) 60447
Ava 62907
Avalon Park (Part of Chicago) 60617
.... 60019
For specific ZIP Codes call (888) 275-8777, or your local postmaster.
Avena 62458
Avery Hill 62223
Aviston 62216
Avoca (Twp) 61739
Avon, *Lake* (Twp) 60030
Avon, *Fulton* 61415
Avondale (Part of Chicago) 60618
.... 60641
For specific ZIP Codes call (888) 275-8777, or your local postmaster.
Ayers (Twp) 61816
Babcock 61244
Babson (Part of St. Charles) 60175
Babylon 61431
Baden Baden (Part of Pierron) 62275
Bader 62624
Baileyville 61007
Bainbridge (Twp) 62639
Baker 60531
Baker Lake 60010
Bakerville 62864
Balcom 62906
Bald Bluff (Twp) 61476
Bald Hill (Twp) 62883
Baldwin 62217
Baldwin Beach 62644
Bales Lake 60948
Ball (Twp) 62629
Ballou 60481
Banner, *Effingham* (Twp) 62461
Banner, *Fulton* 61520
Bannister 62881
Bannockburn 60015
Barclay 62561
Bardolph 61416
Bargerville 62960
Barnard Mill 60097
Barnett, *De Witt* (Twp) 61727
Barnett, *Montgomery* 62056
Barnhill 62809
Barr, *Macoupin* (Twp) 62674
Barr, *Sangamon* 62613
Barren (Twp) 62812
Barrington (Twp) 60010
Barrington 60010*
.... 60011†
Barrington Center (Part of Barrington Hills) 60010
Barrington Downtown‡ 60010*
.... 60011†
Barrington Highlands 60010
Barrington Hills 60010
Barrington Square (Part of Hoffman Estates) 60195
Barrington Woods 60074
Barrenville 60012
Barrow 62082
Barry 62312
Barstow 61236
Bartolco 62218
Bartlett 60103
Bartonville 61607
Basco 62313
Base (Part of Rantoul) 61866
Batavia 60510
Batchtown 62006
Bates 62670
Batestown 61834
Bath 62617
Bay City 62938
Bayle 62080
Baylestown 62033
Baylis 62314

Bay View Gardens 61611
Beach Park 60099
Beacon Hill (Part of Chicago Heights) 60411
Bear Creek, *Christian* (Twp) 62556
Bear Creek, *Hancock* (Twp) 62313
Beardstown 62618
Bear Grove (Twp) 62471
Bearsdale 62526
Beason 62512
Beau Bien (Part of Lisle) 60532
Beaucoup 62263
Beaver (Twp) 60931
Beaver Creek, *Hamilton* (Twp) 62887
Beaver Creek, *Bond* 62246
Beaver Valley, *Boone* 61008
Beaver Valley, *Cook* 60467
Beaverville 60912
Beckemeyer 62219
Bedford, *Wayne* (Twp) 62823
Bedford, *Pike* 62361
Bedford Park 60499
Beecher 60401
Beecher City 62414
Beechville 62006
Beecreek 62361
Beh Lake Estates 61038
Belgium 61883
Belgium Row 61858
Belknap 62908
Bellair 62449
Belle Prairie (Twp) 61731
Belle Prairie City 62828
Belle Rive 62810
Belleview 62355
Belleville 62220-23
.... 62226
For specific ZIP Codes call (888) 275-8777, or your local postmaster.
Bellevue 61604
Bellflower 61724
Bellmont 62811
Bell Plain (Twp) 61541
Bell Ridge 61944
Belltown 62092
Bellwood (Part of Glenview) 60025
Bellwood, *Cook* 60104
Bel-Mar Estates 61008
Belmont, *Iroquois* (Twp) 60970
Belmont (Part of Downers Grove) 60515
Belmont Acres 60970
Belmont-Cragin (Part of Chicago) 60634
.... 60649
.... 60641
For specific ZIP Codes call (888) 275-8777, or your local postmaster.
Belmont Road (Part of Downers Grove) 60515
Belmont Village (Part of Godfrey) 62035
Beltrees 62022
Belvidere 61008
Belvidere Mall (Part of Waukegan) 60085
Bement 61813
Benedale Green (Part of Lisle) 60532
Benevolent Heights 62220
Benld 62009
Bennington, *Marshall* (Twp) 61369
Bennington, *Edwards* 62476
Bensenville 60106
Benson 61516
Bentley 62321
Benton, *Lake* (Twp) 60096
Benton, *Franklin* 62812
Benton Park 62812
Ben Town 61701
Bent Tree Village (Part of Elgin) 60120
Berdan 62016
Bergen 53525
Berkeley 60163
Berkland Heights 61341
Berlin, *Bureau* (Twp) 61312
Berlin, *Sangamon* 62670
Bernadotte 61441
Bernice (Part of Lansing) 60438
Berreman (Twp) 61053
Berry, *Wayne* (Twp) 62850

Berry, *Sangamon* 62563
Berryville, *Richland* 62419
Berryville, *Union* 62952
Bertinetti Lake 62568
Berwick 61417
Berwyn 60402
Bethalto 62010
Bethany 61914
Bethel, *McDonough* (Twp) 61415
Bethel, *Morgan* 62628
Bethel, *Vermilion* 61870
Bethlehem 62411
Beulah Heights (Part of Eldorado) 62930
Be-Ver Kreek 61008
Beverly, *Adams* 62312
Beverly (Part of Chicago) 60620
.... 60643
For specific ZIP Codes call (888) 275-8777, or your local postmaster.
Beverly Manor (Part of Washington) 61571
Beyers Lake Addition 62557
Bible Grove 62858
Biddleborn 62257
Big Bay 62960
Big Foot 60033
Big Grove (Twp) 60541
Biggs 62633
Biggsville 61418
Big Hollow 60041
Big Mound (Twp) 62837
Bigneck 62349
Big Rock 60511
Big Spring (Twp) 62447
Billett 62439
Bingham 62011
Binghampton 61310
Binney 62074
Bird (Twp) 62630
Birds 62415
Birkbeck 61727
Birmingham 62367
Bishop, *Effingham* (Twp) 62424
Bishop, *Mason* 61532
Bishop Hill 61419
Bishop Quarter Lane (Part of Oak Park) 60302
Bismarck 61814
Bissell 62707
Black 62806
Blackberry (Twp) 60119
Blackberry Heights 60538
Blackberry Woods 60554
Blackhawk (Part of Elgin) 60120
Blackhawk (Twp) 61264
Blackhawk Heights (Part of Clarendon Hills) 60514
Blackhawk Island 61102
Black Hawk Springs 60545
Blackstone 61313
Blaine 61065
Blair, *Clay* (Twp) 62858
Blair, *Livingston* 60961
Blair, *Randolph* 62286
Blairsville, *Hamilton* 62859
Blairsville, *Williamson* 62918
Blandinsville 61420
Blissville (Twp) 62894
Block 61877
Blodgett (Part of Highland Park) 60035
Blodgett, *Will* 60421
Bloom (Twp) 60411
Bloomfield, *Edgar* 61924
Bloomfield, *Johnson* 62995
Bloomfield, *Scott* 62694
Bloomingdale 60108
Bloomingdale Court (Part of Bloomingdale) 60108
Bloomington 61701-04
For specific ZIP Codes call (888) 275-8777, or your local postmaster.
Bloomington Heights 61704
Blossom Hill (Part of Cary) 60013
Blount (Twp) 61834
Blue Island 60406
Blue Island Junction (Part of Blue Island) 60406
Blue Island Junction (Part of Chicago) 60617
Blue Mound, *McLean* (Twp) 61730

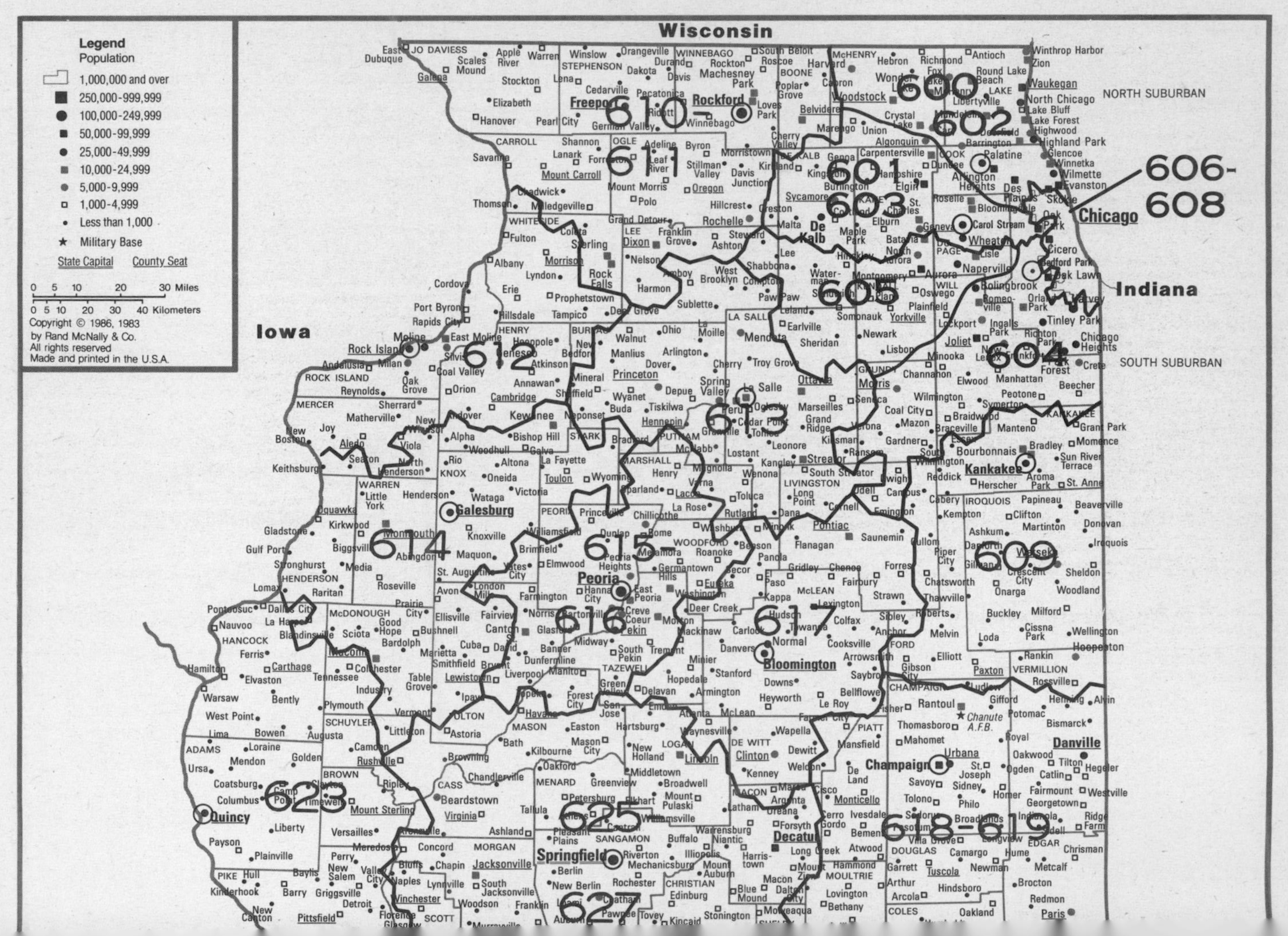
Wisconsin
Iowa
Indiana
NORTH SUBURBAN
SOUTH SUBURBAN
Chicago
606-608
600
602
601
603
604
605
609
610-611
612
613
614
615
616
617
618-619
623
625
627
Legend
Population
1,000,000 and over
250,000-999,999
100,000-249,999
50,000-99,999
25,000-49,999
10,000-24,999
5,000-9,999
1,000-4,999
Less than 1,000
Military Base
State Capital
County Seat
0 5 10 20 30 Miles
0 5 10 20 30 40 Kilometers
Copyright © 1986, 1983
by Rand McNally & Co.
All rights reserved
Made and printed in the U.S.A.

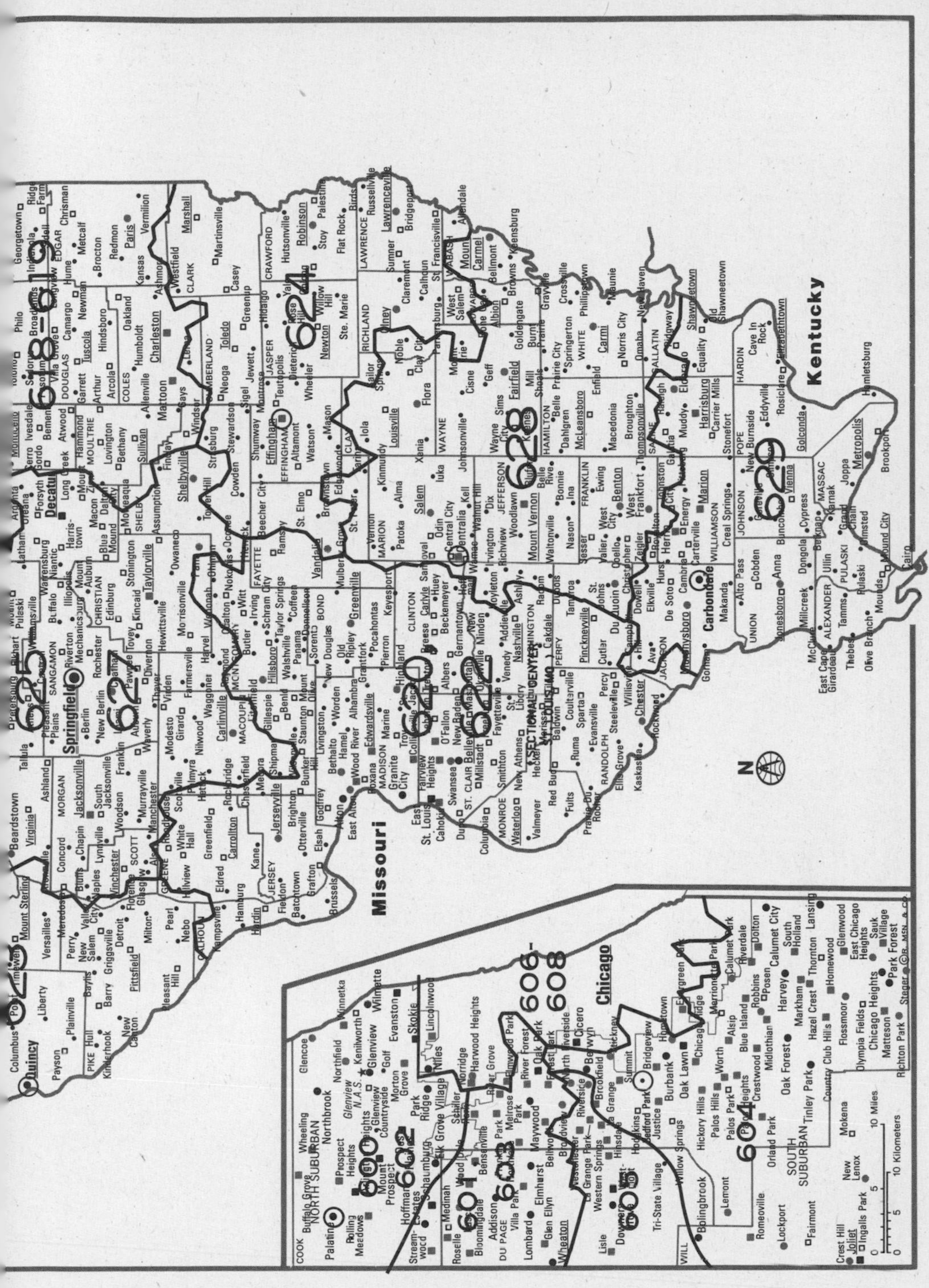
Kentucky
Missouri
Chicago
Springfield
Carbondale
Decatur
Quincy
Effingham
NORTH SUBURBAN
SOUTH SUBURBAN
10 Miles
10 Kilometers
N
618-619
624
625
627
628
629
620
622
600
601
602
603
604
605
606-608

Blue Mound, *Macon* (Twp) 62514
Blue Mound, *Macon* 62513
Blue Point 62401
Blue Ridge 61854
Bluff City, *Fayette* 62471
Bluff City, *Schuyler* 62624
Bluffdale, *Greene* (Twp) 62027
Bluffdale, *Henderson* 61437
Bluff Hall 62360
Bluffs 62621
Bluffside 62236
Bluff Springs 62622
Bluff View Park (Part of Caseyville) 62232
Bluford 62814
Blyton 61477
Boaz 62956
Boden 61281
Bogota 62448
Bohleysville 62260
Bois d'Arc (Twp) 62533
Boles 62909
Bolingbrook 60440
 60490
For specific ZIP Codes call (888) 275-8777, or your local postmaster.
Boling Green (Part of Bolingbrook) 60440
Bolivia 62545
Bolo (Twp) 62808
Bolton 61032
Bond (Twp) 62439
Bondville 61815
Bone Gap 62815
Bonfield 60913
Bongard 61864
Bonnie 62816
Bonnie Brea 60441
Bonpas (Twp) 62419
Bonus (Twp) 61038
Boody 62514
Boone (Twp) 61012
Boos 62448
Booster Station 62269
Borton 61917
Boskydell 62901
Boulder 62283
Boulder Hill♦ 60538
Boulevard Manor (Part of Cicero) 60804
Bourbon 61953
Bourbonnais 60914
Bowdre (Twp) 61910
Bowen 62316
Bowes 60123
Bowlesville (Twp) 62984
Bowling (Twp) 61264
Bowling Green (Twp) 62422
Boyd 62830
Boyleston 62837
Boynton (Twp) 61734
Braceville 60407
Bradbury 62468
Bradford, *Lee* (Twp) 61006
Bradford, *Stark* 61421
Bradfordton 62707
Bradley, *Jackson* (Twp) 62907
Bradley, *Grundy* 60450
Bradley, *Kankakee* 60915
Braeside (Part of Highland Park) 60035
Braidwood 60408
Branding 62013
Brandywine 60181
Branigar Estates 60007
Breckenridge 62563
Breeds 61520
Breese 62230
Bremen, *Cook* (Twp) 60426
Bremen, *Randolph* 62233
Brementowne Mall (Part of Tinley Park) 60477
Brenton (Twp) 60959
Brentwood (Part of Des Plaines) 60016
Brentwood Estates 60074
Brereton 61520
Briar Bluff 61240
Briarbrook Village (Part of Wheaton) 60187
Briarcliffe (Part of Wheaton) 60187
Briarcliffe Knolls (Part of Wheaton) 60187
Briarcliff Estates (Part of Bourbonnais) 60914
Briarwick 61938
Briarwoods Estates (Part of Deerfield) 60015
Briarwood Trace 62901
Brickman Manor (Part of Mount Prospect) 60056
Brickyard, The (Part of Chicago) 60635
Bridgelane 61265
Bridgeport (Part of Chicago) 60608
 60616
For specific ZIP Codes call (888) 275-8777, or your local postmaster.
Bridgeport, *Lawrence* 62417
Bridgeview 60455
Bridgeway Addition (Part of Moline) 61265
Bridle Creek Estates 60175
Brierwood 60175
Bright Oaks (Part of Cary) 60013
Brighton 62012
Brighton Park (Part of Chicago) 60632
Brimfield 61517
Brisbane 60451
Bristol 60512
Bristol Lake 60560
Bristol Ridge 60560
Broadlands 61816
Broadmoor 61421
Broadview 60153
Broadview Village Square 60153
Broadwell 62634
Brocton 61917
Brooke Estates (Part of Highland Park) 60035
Brookeridge 60515
Brookfield, *La Salle* (Twp) 60470
Brookfield, *Cook* 60513
Brook Forest (Part of Oak Brook) 60523
Brookforest North 60435
Brookhaven 61277
Brookhaven Manor (Part of Darien) 60561
Brookhill 60048
Brooklyn, *Lee* (Twp) 61318
Brooklyn, *Schuyler* 62367
Brookport 62910
Brooks 62040
Brookside, *Clinton* (Twp) 62801
Brookside, *Kane* 60175
Brooks Isle 61061
Brookview 61614
Brookville 61064
Brookwood (Part of Prospect Heights) 60070
Brookwood (Part of Rolling Meadows) 60008
Brookwood, *Kane* 60174
Brookwood Estates (Part of Wood Dale) 60191
Brothers 61858
Broughton, *Livingston* (Twp) 60934
Broughton, *Hamilton* 62817
Brouilletts Creek (Twp) 61924
Brown (Twp) 61845
Brownfield 62938
Browning, *Franklin* (Twp) 62812
Browning, *Schuyler* 62624
Browns 62818
Brownstown 62418
Brownsville 62821
Brownwood 61747
Brubaker 62881
Bruce, *La Salle* (Twp) 61364
Bruce, *Moultrie* 61951
Brunning 60441
Brushy (Twp) 62935
Brushy Mound (Twp) 62033
Brussels 62013
Bryant 61519
Bryce 60953
Bryn Mawr (Part of Chicago) 60649
Buck (Twp) 61944
Buckeye (Twp) 61013
Buckhart, *Christian* (Twp) 62531
Buckhart, *Sangamon* 62545
Buckheart (Twp) 61563
Buckhorn (Twp) 62375
Buckhorn 62353
Buckingham 60917
Buckley 60918
Buckner 62819
Bucks 61777
Buda 61314
Budd 61313
Buena Vista, *Schuyler* (Twp) 62681
Buena Vista (Part of Harrisburg) 62946
Buena Vista, *Stephenson* 61032
Buffalo, *Ogle* (Twp) 61064
Buffalo, *Sangamon* 62515
Buffalo Grove, *Cook* 60089
Buffalo Grove, *Ogle* 61064
Buffalo Hart 62515
Buffalo Prairie 61237
Bull Creek 60048
Bullock Addition 61241
Bull Valley 60098
Bulpitt 62517
Buncombe 62912
Bungay 62887
Bunker Hill 62014
Bunkum (Part of Fairview Heights) 62208
Bunsenville 61846
Burbank 60459
Burches 60914
Bureau (Twp) 61379
Bureau 61315
Burgess, *Bond* (Twp) 62275
Burgess, *Mercer* 61231
Burksville 62298
Burlington 60109
Burnham 60633
Burnham Mill (Part of Elgin) 60123
Burns (Twp) 61443
Burnside (Part of Chicago) 60619
Burnside, *Hancock* 62318
Burnside's Lakewood (Part of Richton Park) 60471
Burnt Prairie (Twp) 62821
Burnt Prairie 62820
Burritt (Twp) 61088
Burr Oak (Part of Blue Island) 60406
Burr Oaks (Part of Joliet) 60435
Burrowsville 61929
Burr Ridge 60521
Burt 61721
Burton, *McHenry* (Twp) 60081
Burton, *Adams* 62301
Burtons Bridge 60050
Burtonview 62656
Bush, *Jackson* 62924
Bush, *Williamson* 62924
Bushnell 61422
Bushton 61920
Butler, *Vermilion* (Twp) 60960
Butler, *Montgomery* 62015
Butler Grove (Twp) 62015
Butterfield 60148
Butterfield West 60137
Button (Twp) 60960
Buysse Addition 61240
Buzzville 62644
Byron 61010
Byron Hills, *Ogle* 61010
Byron Hills, *Rock Island* 61275
Cabery 60919
Cable 61281
Cache 62913
Cadiz 62931
Cadwell 61911
Cahokia, *Macoupin* (Twp) 62023
Cahokia, *St. Clair* 62206
Cairo 62914
Caledonia 61011
Calhoun 62419
Calumet, *Cook* (Twp) 60406
Calumet (Part of East Hazel Crest) 60429
Calumet City 60409
Calumet Harbor (Part of Chicago) 60633
Calumet Heights (Part of Chicago) 60617
Calumet Park 60643
Calumet Yard (Part of Chicago) 60617
Calvin 62827
Camargo 61919
Cambria 62915
Cambridge, *Henry* 61238
Cambridge (Part of Libertyville) 60048
Camden 62319
Camelot, *Effingham* 62401
Camelot, *Will* 60431
Cameron 61423
Campbell Hill 62916
Campbells Island 61244
Camp Epworth 61038
Camp Grant (Part of Rockford) 61102
Camp Ground 62864
Camp Grove 61424
Camp Logan 60099
Camp Point 62320
Campton (Twp) 60183
Campus 60920
Campus Walk (Part of Elgin) 60120
Camridge West (Part of Mundelein) 60060
Candlewood Estates 61853
Canoe Creek (Twp) 61257
Canteen (Twp) 62204
Cantera Village (Part of Warrenville) 60555
Canterbury Lane (Part of Glenview) 60025
Canterbury Shopping Center (Part of Markham) 60426
Canton 61520
Cantrall 62625
Capitol (Part of Springfield)‡ 62701
Capri Gardens 60074
Capri Village 60074
Capron 61012
Carbon (Part of O'Fallon) 62269
Carbon Cliff 61239
Carbondale (Twp) 62901
Carbondale 62901-03
For specific ZIP Codes call (888) 275-8777, or your local postmaster.
Carbon Hill 60416
Cardiff 60420
Carle Springs 61777
Carlinville 62626
Carlock 61725
Carlsburg 62069
Carlyle 62231
Carlysle (Part of Schaumburg) 60194
Carman 61425
Carmi 62821
Carol Stream 60188
 60197-99
For specific ZIP Codes call (888) 275-8777, or your local postmaster.
Carol Stream Main‡ 60197-98
For specific ZIP Codes call (888) 275-8777, or your local postmaster.
Carpenter 62025
Carpentersville 60110
Carriage Creek (Part of Richton Park) 60471
Carriage Park 60543
Carriage Way Court 60074
Carrier Mills 62917
Carrigan, *Marion* (Twp) 62875
Carrigan, *Clinton* 62231
Carroll (Twp) 61870
Carroll Addition, *Champaign* 61802
Carroll Addition, *Ford* 60936
Carrollton 62016
Carson (Twp) 62080
Carterville 62918
Carthage 62321
Carthage Lake 61425
Cartter 62853
Cartwright (Twp) 62677
Cary 60013
Casey 62420
Caseyville 62232
Casner, *Jefferson* (Twp) 62898
Casner, *Macon* 62552
Cass (Twp) 61477
Castellean Lower 61021
Castellean Upper 61021
Castleton 61426
Catatoga 60123
Catatoga 2 60123
Catlin 61817
Cave (Twp) 62890
Cave-In-Rock 62919
Cayuga 61764
Cazenovia 61545
Cedar (Twp) 61410
Cedar Glen 60543
Cedar Grove 62959
Cedar Island 60020
Cedar Meadows 62269
Cedar Park 62040
Cedar Point 61316
Cedar Run (Part of Wheeling) 60090
Cedarville 61013
Centaur Estate 61008
Center Hill 61053
Centerville, *Calhoun* 62036
Centerville, *Macoupin* 62685
Centerville, *Piatt* 61884
Centerville, *White* 62821
Central (Twp) 62246
Central City, *Grundy* 60407
Central City, *Marion* 62801
Centralia 62801
Central Park 61832
Central Street (Part of Evanston) 60201
Centre of Park Forest, The (Part of Park Forest) 60466
Centreville 62207
Century Oaks (Part of Elgin) 60123
Century Oaks West (Part of Elgin) 60123
Cerro Gordo 61818
Chadwick 61014
Chalfin Bridge 62244
Chalmers (Twp) 61455
Chambersburg 62323
Chambord (Part of Oak Brook) 60523
Chamness Town 62932
Champaign (Twp) 61820
Champaign 61820-26
For specific ZIP Codes call (888) 275-8777, or your local postmaster.
Chana 61015
Chandlerville 62627
Channahon 60410
Channel Lake♦ 60002
Chantilly (Part of Highland Park) 60035
Chapin 62628
Chapman 62032
Charleston 61920
Charlestowne Mall (Part of St. Charles) 60174
Charlotte 60921
Charlotte Hills 62274
Charter Grove 60178
Chasco 62923
Chateau Terrace 62221
Chatham (Part of Chicago) 60619
Chatham, *Sangamon* 62629
Chatham Manor (Part of Buffalo Grove) 60089
Chatsworth 60921
Chatton 62346
Chauncey 62466
Chautauqua 62028
Chautauqua Park, *Mason* 62644
Chautauqua Park, *Menard* 62675
Chebanse (Twp) 60927
Chebanse 60922
Checkrow 61415
Chelsea Cove (Part of Wheeling) 60090
Cheltenham (Part of Chicago) 60649
Chemung 60033
Cheneys Grove (Twp) 61770
Cheneyville 60942
Chenoa 61726
Chenot Place 62221
Cherry 61317
Cherry Grove-Shannon (Twp) 61046
Cherry Hill 60431
Cherry Hills, *Champaign* 61822
Cherry Hills (Part of Aurora) 60506
Cherry Point 61924
Cherryvale Mall (Part of Cherry Valley) 61112
Cherry Valley 61016
Cherrywood, *Christian* 62568
Cherrywood (Part of Bolingbrook) 60440
Chesney Shores 60046
Chester, *Logan* (Twp) 62656
Chester, *Randolph* 62233

Chesterfield 62630
Chesterville 61911
Chestline 62314
Chestnut, *Knox* (Twp) 61544
Chestnut, *Logan* 62518
Chestnut Street (Part of Chicago)‡ 60610

Chicago

60601-26
60626-41
60643-49
60651-64
60701
60799
For specific ZIP Codes call (888) 275-8777, or your local postmaster.

Colleges & Universities

Adler School of Professional Psychology 60601
American Academy of Art 60604
American Schools of Professional Psychology 60603
Catholic Theological Union 60615
Chicago School of Professional Psychology 60605
Chicago State Univ 60628
Chicago Theological Seminary 60637
Columbia Coll 60605
De Paul Univ 60604
DeVry Institute of Technology 60618
Dr William M Scholl Coll of Podiatric Medicine 60610
East-West Univ 60605
Harrington Institute of Interior Design 60605
Illinois Coll of Optometry 60616
Illinois Institute of Technology 60616
International Academy of Merchandising & Design 60602
John Marshall Law School 60604
Loyola Univ 60611
McCormick Theological Seminary 60637
Moody Bible Institute 60610
NAES Coll 60659
Northeastern Illinois Univ 60625
North Park Univ & Theological Seminary 60625
Robert Morris Coll 60601
Roosevelt Univ 60605
Rush Univ 60612
Saint Xavier Univ 60655
School of the Art Institute 60603
Spertus Coll 60605
Univ of Chicago 60637
Univ of Illinois 60607
VanderCook Coll of Music 60616

Financial Institutions

American Nat Bank & Trust Co 60690
Cole Taylor Bank 60607
Firstar Bank 60602
First Chicago NBD 60670
Harris Trust & Svgs Bank 60603
LaSalle Nat Bank 60603
LaSalle Nat Bank 60657
LaSalle Bank, NA 60641
Northern Trust 60675
USBank, NA 60611

Hospitals

Children's Memorial Hosp 60614
Columbia Michael Reese Hosp & Med Ctr 60616
Columbus Hosp 60614
Cook County Hosp 60612
Holy Cross Hosp 60629
Illinois Masonic Med Ctr 60657
Mercy Hosp & Med Ctr 60616
Mt Sinai Hosp Med Ctr 60608
Northwestern Memorial Hosp 60611
Ravenswood Hosp Med Ctr 60640
Resurrection Med Ctr 60631
Rush-Presbyterian-St Luke's Med Ctr 60612
Saint Mary of Nazareth Hosp Ctr 60622
St Joseph Health Ctr & Hosp 60657
Swedish Covenant Hosp 60625
University Hosps 60637
Univ of Illinois Med Ctr 60612
Veterans Affairs Lakeside Med Ctr 60611
Veterans Affairs West Side Med Ctr 60612

Hotels/Motels

The Allerton 60611
Clarion Executive Plaza 60601
Days Inn, Lakeshore Drive 60611
The Drake 60611
The Fairmont 60601
Hilton & Towers 60605
Holiday Inn City Centre 60611
Holiday Inn Mart Plaza 60654
Hyatt Regency on Chicago's Riverwalk 60601
Inter-Continental 60611
Marriott, Downtown 60611
Palmer House Hilton 60603
The Ramada Congress 60605
Renaissance 60601
The Ritz-Carlton 60611
Sheraton Hotel & Towers 60611
Swissotel 60601
The Westin 60611
The Westin, River North 60610

Military Installations

U S Army Corps of Engineers 60606

Chicago Bulk Mail Center (Part of Forest Park)‡ 60799
Chicago Heights 60411*
60412†
Chicago Lawn (Part of Chicago)‡ 60629
Chicago Ridge 60415
Chicago Ridge Mall (Part of Chicago Ridge) 60415
Chicken Bristle 61953
Childers Acres 61068
Chili 62380
Chillicothe 61523
Chilon Chalet (Part of Chicago Heights) 60411
China (Twp) 61310
Chinatown (Part of Chicago) 60616
Chinatown (Part of Maryville) 62062
Chippendale (Part of Barrington) 60010
Chippewa 60803
Chippewa Ridge (Part of Alsip) 60803
Chittenden (Part of Gurnee) 60031
Chittyville (Part of Herrin) 62948
Chouteau (Twp) 62040
Chrisman 61924
Christopher 62822
Christy (Twp) 62466
Churchill (Part of Hoffman Estates) 60195
Churchville (Part of Bensenville) 60126
Cicero 60804
Cimic (Part of Divernon) 62530
Cincinnati, *Pike* (Twp) 62343
Cincinnati, *Tazewell* (Twp) 61554
Cincinnati Landing 62356
Cinnamon Creek (Part of Bolingbrook) 60440
Circle Drive 61364
Circle Park 62565
Cisco 61830
Cisne 62823
Cissna Park 60924
Citation Lake Estates 60062
Clank 62988
Clare 60111
Claremont 62421
Clarence 60960
Clarendon Hills 60514
Clarion (Twp) 61330
Clark Center 62441
Clarksburg 62565
Clarksdale 62556
Clarksville, *Clark* 62441
Clarksville, *McLean* 61753
Clarmin 62257
Clay City 62824
Clays Prairie 61944
Clayton, *Woodford* (Twp) 61516
Clayton, *Adams* 62324
Claytonville 60926
Clearing (Part of Chicago)‡ 60638
Clear Lake, *Cass* 62622
Clear Lake, *Sangamon* 62707
Cleburne 62865
Clement (Twp) 62252
Clements 62638
Cleone 62442
Cleveland 61241
Clifton 60927
Clifton Terrace (Part of Godfrey) 62035
Clifty Heights 62959
Clinch 62832
Clinton, *DeKalb* (Twp) 60556
Clinton, *De Witt* 61727
Clintonia (Twp) 61727
Clover (Twp) 61490
Cloverdale, *DuPage* 60103
Cloverdale (Part of East Peoria) 61611
Cloverleaf, *Madison* 62060
Clyde, *Whiteside* (Twp) 61270
Clyde (Part of Cicero) 60650
Coach Homes of Willow Bend (Part of Rolling Meadows) 60008
Coach Light Manor (Part of Mount Prospect) 60056
Coal City 60416
Coal Hollow 61356
Coalton 62075
Coal Valley 61240
Coatsburg 62325
Cobblestone 60025
Cobblewood (Part of Northbrook) 60062
Cobden 62920
Coe (Twp) 61275
Coello 62825
Coffeen 62017
Colby Point 60050
Colchester 62326
Coldbrook (Twp) 61401
Coldbrook 61423
Cold Spring (Twp) 62571
Colehour (Part of Chicago) 60617
Coleman 60177
Coles 61938
Coleta 61017
Colfax, *Champaign* (Twp) 61851
Colfax, *McLean* 61728
College Green (Part of Elgin) 60123
College Hills Mall (Part of Normal) 61761
College Park (Part of Elgin) 60123
College View 60441
Collins, *Will* 60544
Collins, *Winnebago* 61080
Collinsville 62234
Collison 61831
Colmar 62367
Coloma (Twp) 61071
Colona 61241
Colonial Gardens (Part of Machesney Park) 61115
Colonial Manor (Part of Mount Prospect) 60056
Colonial Ridge 60016
Colonial Village, *Madison* 62035
Colonial Village (Part of Bolingbrook) 60440
Colonial Village (Part of Rockford) 61108
Colony Grove 61853
Colony Park (Part of Carol Stream) 60188
Colony Point (Part of Deerfield) 60015
Colp 62921
Columbia 62236
Columbia Heights 61430
Columbia Village 61802
Columbus (Twp) 62320
Columbus 62328
Columbus Manor (Part of Oak Lawn) 60452
Colusa 62329
Colvin Park 60145
Como 61081
Compromise (Twp) 61862
Compton 61318
Compton Pines 60175
Comstock 62025
Conant 62274
Concord, *Adams* (Twp) 62324
Concord, *Bureau* (Twp) 61361
Concord, *Iroquois* (Twp) 60945
Concord, *Morgan* 62631
Condit (Twp) 61840
Confidence 62418
Congerville 61729
Congress Park (Part of Brookfield) 60513
Conlogue 61944
Conover 60560
Conrad 62036
Continental Village (Part of Waukegan) 60085
Cooks Mills 61931
Cooksville 61730
Cooper, *Sangamon* (Twp) 62563
Cooper, *Tazewell* 61571
Cooperstown 62353
Copley (Twp) 61485
Cora 62280
Coral (Twp) 60180
Coral 60152
Coral Gable (Part of O'Fallon) 62269
Cordova 61242
Corinth 62890
Cornell 61319
Cornerville 62935
Cornland 62519
Cornwall (Twp) 61235
Cortese 60901
Cortland 60112
Corwin (Twp) 62666
Cottage (Twp) 62946
Cottagegrove 62930
Cottage Hills 62018
Cotton Hill (Twp) 62563
Cottonwood, *Cumberland* (Twp) 62468
Cottonwood, *Gallatin* 62871
Coulterville 62237
Council Hill 61075
Council Hill Station 61075
Country Acres, *La Salle* 61360
Country Acres, *St. Clair* 62220
Country Aire, *Jefferson* 62864
Country Aire (Part of Elgin) 60120
Country Club 61938
Country Club Acres 62626
Country Club Heights 61938
Country Club Hills 60478
Country Club Manor (Part of Country Club Hills) 60478
Country Club Place 62223
Country Club Terrace 62220
Country Courts 61265
Country Estates 61254
Country Fair (Part of Champaign) 61821
Country Gardens (Part of Prospect Heights) 60070
Country Heights (Part of Mount Vernon) 62864
Country Knolls (Part of Elgin) 60123
Country Knolls, *Knox* 61410
Country Lake 60563
Country Lake Estates 62613
Country Manor, *Coles* 61938
Country Manor, *Effingham* 62401
Country Manor (Part of Geneseo) 61254
Country Oaks 61745
Country Orchard 61938
Countryside, *Cook* 60525
Countryside, *Kane* 60560
Countryside (Part of Yorkville) 60560
Countryside Estates 60922
Countryside Lake 60060
Countryside Manor 60048
Country Squire (Part of Urbana) 61801
Country Squire Estates 61032
Countryview Estates, *Kane* 60118
Country View Estates, *Will* 60564
Covel 61704
Coventry (Part of Crystal Lake) 60014
Coventry East (Part of Crystal Lake) 60014
Covington 62271
Covington Manor, (Part of Buffalo Grove) 60089
Cow Bell Lane 62274
Cowden 62422
Cowling 62863
Crab Orchard 62959
Crab Orchard Estates 62901
Cragin (Part of Chicago)‡ 60639
Craig Manor (Part of Des Plaines) 60016
Crainville 62918
Cramer 61529
Crane Creek (Twp) 62633
Cravat 62801
Crawford Countryside (Part of Matteson) 60443
Creal Springs 62922
Creek (Twp) 61750
Creekside (Part of Matteson) 60443
Creekside (Part of Rolling Meadows) 60008
Creekwood 60439
Crenshaw 62959
Crescent (Twp) 60953
Crescent City 60928
Cress Creek (Part of Naperville) 60563
Crest Haven (Part of Fairview Heights) 62221
Crest Hill 60435
Creston 60113
Crestview 60970
Crestview Terrace (Part of Fairfield) 62837
Crestwood 60445
Crestwood Estates 62959
Crete 60417
Creve Coeur 61610
Cricket Hill (Part of Matteson) 60443
Crisp 62895
Crittenden (Twp) 61880
Crocketts Estates 60041
Crook (Twp) 62859
Crooked Creek, *Cumberland* (Twp) 62428
Crooked Creek, *Jasper* (Twp) 62432
Crooked Lake 60046
Cropsey 61731
Cross County Mall (Part of Mattoon) 61938
Crossroads, *Johnson* 62995
Crossroads (Part of Fairview Heights) 62232
Crossroad Terrace (Part of Fairview Heights) 62232
Crossville 62827
Crouch (Twp) 62895
Cruger 61530
Crystal Gardens (Part of Crystal Lake) 60014
Crystal Lake, *Jersey* 62012
Crystal Lake, *McHenry* 60012
60014
60039
For specific ZIP Codes call (888) 275-8777, or your local postmaster.
Crystal Lake, *Madison* 62035

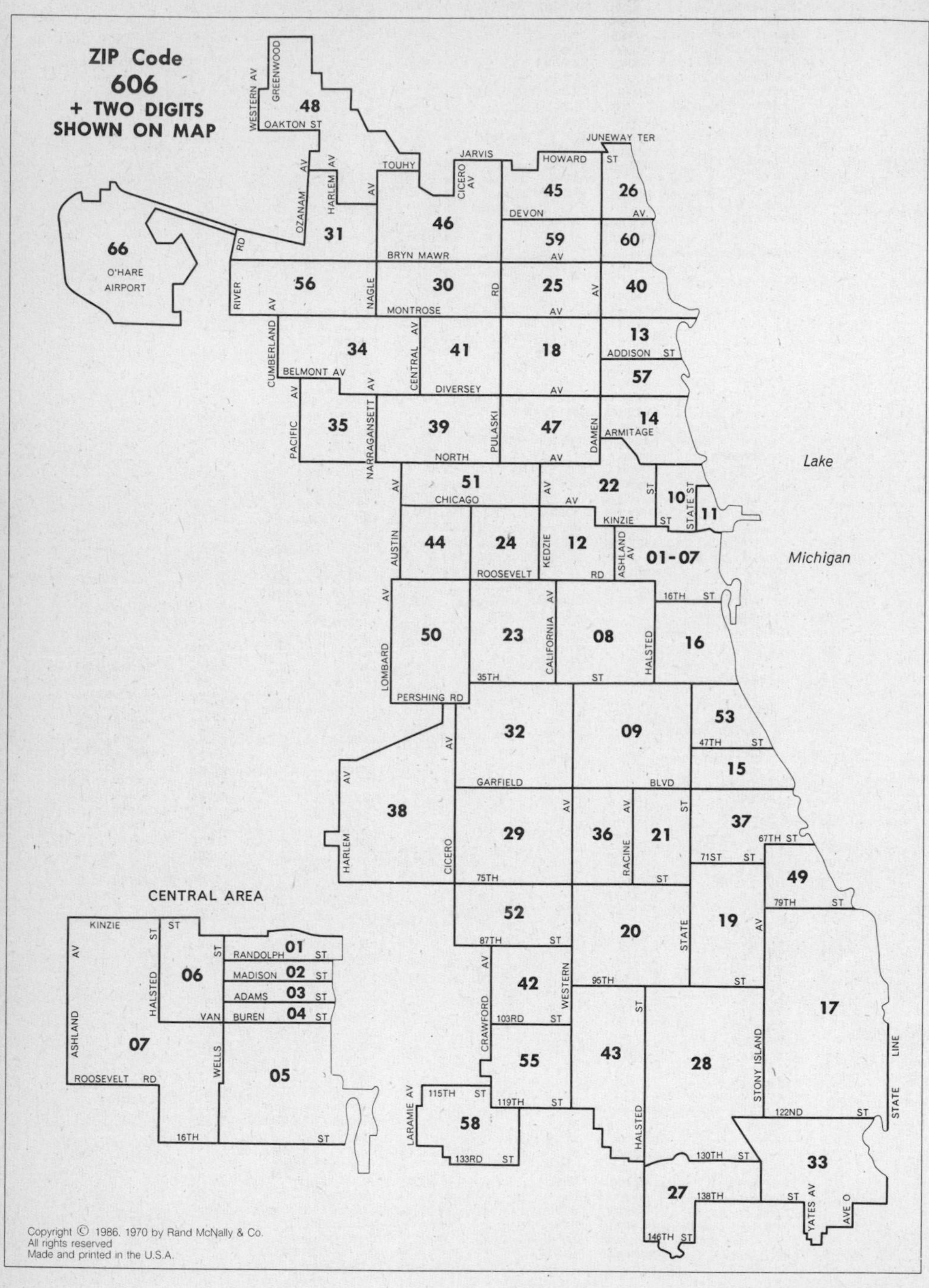
ZIP Code
606
+ TWO DIGITS
SHOWN ON MAP
CENTRAL AREA
Lake
Michigan
O'HARE AIRPORT
01-07
01 02 03 04 05 06 07 08 09 10 11 12 13 14 15 16 17 18 19 20 21 22 23 24 25 26 27 28 29 30 31 32 33 34 35 36 37 38 39 40 41 42 43 44 45 46 47 48 49 50 51 52 53 55 56 57 58 59 60 66
WESTERN AV
GREENWOOD
OAKTON ST
OZANAM AV
HARLEM AV
TOUHY AV
JARVIS
CICERO AV
HOWARD ST
JUNEWAY TER
DEVON AV.
BRYN MAWR AV
RIVER RD
NAGLE
MONTROSE AV
CUMBERLAND AV
CENTRAL AV
ADDISON ST
BELMONT AV
DIVERSEY AV
PACIFIC AV
NARRAGANSETT AV
PULASKI RD
DAMEN AV
ARMITAGE
NORTH AV
CHICAGO AV
STATE ST
KINZIE ST
AUSTIN
KEDZIE
ASHLAND AV
ROOSEVELT RD
16TH ST
LOMBARD AV
CALIFORNIA AV
HALSTED
35TH ST
PERSHING RD
47TH ST
GARFIELD BLVD
HARLEM AV
CICERO AV
RACINE AV
67TH ST
71ST ST
75TH ST
79TH ST
87TH ST
STATE
WESTERN
95TH ST
CRAWFORD AV
103RD ST
115TH ST
119TH ST
LARAMIE AV
133RD ST
HALSTED ST
STONY ISLAND AV
122ND ST
STATE LINE
130TH ST
138TH ST
146TH ST
YATES AV
AVE O
KINZIE ST
HALSTED ST
RANDOLPH ST
MADISON ST
ADAMS ST
VAN BUREN ST
ASHLAND AV
ROOSEVELT RD
WELLS
16TH ST

Place	ZIP Code
Crystal Lake Estates	60014
Crystal Lawns♦	60435
Crystal Manor (Part of Crystal Lake)	60014
Crystal Point Mall (Part of Crystal Lake)	60014
Crystal Vista (Part of Crystal Lake)	60014
Cuba, *Lake* (Twp)	60010
Cuba, *Fulton*	61427
Cullom	60929
Cumberland (Part of Des Plaines)	60016
Cumberland Green (Part of St. Charles)	60174
Cumberland Heights (Part of Fairfield)	62837
Cumberland Highlands (Part of Des Plaines)	60016
Cunningham (Twp)	61801
Cunningham Courts (Part of Palatine)	60067
Curran	62670
Custer (Twp)	60481
Custer Park	60481
Cutler	62238
Cypress	62923
Cypress Gardens	62901
D'Adrian Gardens	62035
Daggetts	61053
Dahinda	61428
Dahlgren	62828
Dailey	61862
Dakota	61018
Dale, *McLean* (Twp)	61772
Dale, *Hamilton*	62829
Dale Valley	61853
Dallasania	62917
Dallas City	62330
Dalton City	61925
Dalzell	61320
Damiansville	62215
Dana	61321
Danada North (Part of Wheaton)	60187
Danada West (Part of Wheaton)	60187
Danforth	60930
Danley	62261
Danvers	61732
Danville	61832*
	61834†
Danville Junction (Part of Danville)	61832
Danway	61341
Darien	60561
Darmstadt	62255
Darrow	60966
Darwin	62477
David Acres	62012
Davis	61019
Davis Junction	61020
Dawson, *McLean* (Twp)	61737
Dawson, *Sangamon*	62520
Dawson Park	60953
Daysville	61061
Dayton, *Henry*	61241
Dayton, *La Salle*	61350
Decatur (Twp)	62521
Decatur	62521-26
For specific ZIP Codes call (888) 275-8777, or your local postmaster.	
Decker (Twp)	62868
Decorra	61480
Deep Lake	60046
Deep Woods (Part of Mundelein)	60060
Deerbrook Mall (Part of Deerfield)	60015
Deer Creek	61733
Deerfield, *Fulton* (Twp)	61431
Deerfield, *Lake* (Twp)	60035
Deerfield, *Lake*	60015
Deer Grove	61243
Deering (Part of Chicago)	60610
Deering City	62896
Deer Lake	60010
Dee Road (Part of Park Ridge)	60068
Deer Park, *La Salle* (Twp)	61348
Deer Park, *Lake*	60010
Deer Plain	62013
Deer Run	60175
Deerwood Estates	62471
Degognia (Twp)	62950
De Kalb	60115
Delafield	62859
De Land	61839
Delavan	61734
Del-Bar	61520
Delhi	62052
Dellwood Highlands	60441
Del Mar Woods	60015
DeLong	61436
Del Rey	60968
Delwood	62946
Dement (Twp)	61068
Denison (Twp)	62460
Denmark	62238
Denning (Twp)	62896
Dennison	62423
Denny	62832
Denver, *Richland* (Twp)	62868
Denver, *Hancock*	62321
De Pue	61322
Derby, *Ford*	60936
Derby, *Saline*	62947
Derinda (Twp)	61028
Derinda Center	61028
Derry (Twp)	62312
Deselm	60950
De Soto	62924
Des Plaines	60016-18
For specific ZIP Codes call (888) 275-8777, or your local postmaster.	
Des Plaines Manor (Part of Des Plaines)	60016
Des Plaines Terrace (Part of Des Plaines)	60016
Detroit	62332
Devereux Heights (Part of Springfield)	62707
Devonshire (Part of Des Plaines)	60018
Dewey	61840
De Witt	61735
Dewmaine	62918
Dexter	62411
Diamond	60416
Diamond City	62859
Diamond Lake	60060
Diamond Town	62274
Dieterich	62424
Dillon	61568
Dillsburg	61866
Dimmick (Twp)	61301
Diona	62428
Disco	61450
Diswood	62988
Divernon	62530
Divido	62889
Division Street (Part of Chicago)‡	60651
Dix, *Ford* (Twp)	60933
Dix, *Jefferson*	62830
Dixmoor	60406
Dixon	61021
Dixon Springs	62943
Dobbins Downs	61821
Dodds (Twp)	62864
Doddsville	61452
Dollville	62571
Dolson (Twp)	61944
Dolton	60419
Dongola	62926
Donnellson	62019
Donovan	60931
Dora (Twp)	61925
Dorans	61938
Dorchester (Twp)	62009
Dorchester	62033
Dorr (Twp)	60098
Dorris Heights (Part of Harrisburg)	62946
Dorsey	62021
Douglas (Part of Chicago)	60616
Douglas, *Clark* (Twp)	62441
Douglas, *Effingham* (Twp)	62401
Douglas, *Iroquois* (Twp)	60938
Douglas, *Knox*	61572
Douglas, *St. Clair*	62243
Douglas Park	61081
Dover (Twp)	61356
Dover	61323
Dow	62022
Dowell	62927
Downers Fairview (Part of Downers Grove)	60515
Downers Grove (Twp)	60559
Downers Grove	60515-17
For specific ZIP Codes call (888) 275-8777, or your local postmaster.	
Downers Grove Estates	60515
Downey (Part of North Chicago)	60064
Downs	61736
Downtown (Part of Bloomington)‡	61701
Downtown (Part of Carbondale)‡	62901
Downtown (Part of Des Plaines)‡	60016
Downtown (Part of Glen Ellyn)‡	60137
Downtown (Part of La Salle)‡	61301
Downtown (Part of Springfield)‡	62701*
	62705†
Downtown (Part of Villa Park)	60181
Dozaville	63673
Drake	62092
Dresden Acres	60450
Drexel (Part of Cicero)	60804
Drivers	62898
Druce Lake	60046
Drummer (Twp)	60936
Drury (Twp)	52761
Dry Grove (Twp)	61732
Dry Point (Twp)	62422
Dubois	62831
Duck Lake Woods	60041
Dudley	61944
Dudleyville	62246
Duncan, *Mercer* (Twp)	61231
Duncan, *Stark*	61559
Duncans Mills	61542
Duncanville	62454
Dundas	62425
Dundee (Part of West Dundee)	60118
Dunfermline	61524
Dunham (Twp)	60033
Dunhurst (Part of Wheeling)	60090
Dunkel	62557
Dunlap	61525
Dunlap Lake (Part of Edwardsville)	62025
Dunleith (Twp)	61025
Dunn	61951
Dunning (Part of Chicago)‡	60634
Du Page (Twp)	60441
Dupo	62239
Du Quoin	62832
Durand	61024
Durham	62330
Durley Camp	62246
Dutch Creek Woodlands	60050
Dutch Hollow (Part of Belleville)‡	62223
Duvall	62565
Dwight	60420
Dykersburg	62987
Eagarville	62023
Eagle (Twp)	61364
Eagle Creek (Twp)	62934
Eagle Heights	60123
Eagle Lake	60401
Eagle Park	62060
Eagle Point (Twp)	61064
Eagle Point Bay	62939
Earl (Twp)	60518
Earl Estates	60554
Earlville	60518
East Alton	62024
East Bend (Twp)	61840
East Brooklyn	60474
East Cape Girardeau	62957
East Carondelet	62240
East Clinton	61252
East Dubuque	61025
East Dundee	60118
East Eldorado (Twp)	62930
Eastern (Twp)	62812
East Fork, *Clinton* (Twp)	62283
East Fork, *Montgomery* (Twp)	62017
East Fulton	61252
East Galena (Twp)	61036
East Galesburg	61430
Eastgate	62881
East Gillespie	62033
East Grove (Twp)	61349
East Hannibal	62343
East Hardin	62031
East Hazel Crest	60429
East Keokuk (Part of Hamilton)	62341
Eastland Mall (Part of Bloomington)	61701
East Lincoln (Twp)	62656
East Loon Lake	60002
East Lynn	60932
East Marion (Twp)	62959
East Meadowbrook	62067
East Meadowview (Part of Bradley)	60915
East Moline	61244
East Nelson (Twp)	61951
East Newbern	62022
East Oakland (Twp)	61943
Easton	62633
East Peoria	61611
East River	60964
East Rockford (Part of Rockford)‡	61110
East Side (Part of Chicago)	60617
East Side, *Kankakee*	60954
East St. Louis	62201-07
For specific ZIP Codes call (888) 275-8777, or your local postmaster.	
East Wenona	61377
Eastwood Manor	60050
Eaton	62454
Eberle	62424
Echo Lake	60047
Eckard	62644
Eco Park (Part of DeKalb)	60115
Eddyville	62928
Edelstein	61526
Eden, *La Salle* (Twp)	61370
Eden, *Peoria*	61536
Eden, *Randolph*	62286
Edens Plaza (Part of Wilmette)	60091
Edford (Twp)	61254
Edgar (Twp)	60118
Edgar	61924
Edgebrook (Part of Chicago)‡	60646
Edgebrook (Part of De Kalb)	60178
Edgemont (Part of East St. Louis)‡	62203
Edgewater (Part of Chicago)	60640
Edgewater Beach	62231
Edgewood, *Champaign*	61802
Edgewood, *Effingham*	62426
Edgewood Heights	61008
Edgington	61284
Edinburg	62531
Edison Park (Part of Chicago)	60648
Edison Square (Part of Waukegan)‡	60085
Edwards	61528
Edwardsville	62025
Effingham	62401
Effner	60966
Egan	61047
Egyptian Hills	62922
Egyptian Shores	62922
Eight Mile Prairie	62918
Eiker Addition	61448
Eileen (Part of Coal City)	60416
Ela (Twp)	60047
Elam Lake	61951
Elba, *Knox* (Twp)	61489
Elba, *Gallatin*	62871
Elba Center	61572
Elbridge	61944
Elburn	60119
Elco	62988
El Dara	62312
Eldena	61324
Elderville	62313
Eldorado, *McDonough* (Twp)	61411
Eldorado, *Saline*	62930
Eldred	62027
Eleanor	61453
Eleroy	61027
Elgin (Twp)	60120
Elgin	60120-23
For specific ZIP Codes call (888) 275-8777, or your local postmaster.	
Elgin Estates	60123
Eliza	61272
Elizabeth	61028
Elizabethtown	62931
Elk (Twp)	62932
Elk Grove (Twp)	60007
Elk Grove Village	60007*
	60009†
Elkhart	62634
Elkhorn (Twp)	62353
Elkhorn Grove (Twp)	61051
Elk Prairie (Twp)	62816
Elk Ridge Villa (Part of Mount Prospect)	60056
Elkton	62268
Elkville	62932
Ellery	62833
Ellington	62301
Elliott	60933
Elliottstown	62424
Ellis	61865
Ellis Grove	62241
Ellison (Twp)	61478
Ellisville	61431
Ellsworth	61737
Ellwood Greens	60135
Elm Grove (Twp)	61554
Elmhurst	60126
Elmira	61483
Elmore	61451
El Morro (Part of Oak Forest)	60452
Elm River (Twp)	62842
Elmwood	61529
Elmwood Park	60707
El Paso	61738
El-Rancho	60901
Elsah	62028
Elsdon (Part of Chicago)‡	60632
El Sierra (Part of Downers Grove)	60515
Elva	60115
Elvaston	62334
Elvira	62912
El Vista (Part of Oak Forest)	60452
El Vista (Part of Peoria)‡	61604
Elwin	62532
Elwood, *Vermilion* (Twp)	61870
Elwood, *Will*	60421
Embarrass (Twp)	61949
Emden	62635
Emerald Green (Part of Warrenville)	60555
Emerald Park	60050
Emerald Terrace	62226
Emerson	61081
Emerson City	62883
Eminence (Twp)	61721
Emington	60934
Emma	62834
Emmet (Twp)	61455
Empire (Twp)	61752
Empire Hills	60175
Enchanted Forest	61604
Energy	62933
Enfield	62835
Engelmann (Twp)	62258
England Heights	62901
Englewood (Part of Chicago)‡	60621
English (Twp)	62052
Enion	62644
Enos	62626
Enright	61738
Enterprise	62823
Eola	60519
Eppards Point (Twp)	61764
Epworth	62821
Equality	62934
Erie	61250
Erienna (Twp)	60450
Erin (Twp)	61027
Erontenac	60118
Esmen (Twp)	60460
Esmond	60129
Essex, *Stark* (Twp)	61491
Essex, *Kankakee*	60935
Estate Lane (Part of Glenview)	60025
Etherton	62966
Euclid Lake (Part of Mount Prospect)	60056
Eureka	61530
Evans	61377
Evanston	60201-04
For specific ZIP Codes call (888) 275-8777, or your local postmaster.	
Evanston North (Part of Evanston)‡	60201
Evanston South (Part of Evanston)‡	60202
Evansville	62242
Evarts	61067

*** Area Zip Code** **† Post Office Boxes** **‡ Postal Station** **♦ Census Designated Place** *Italic Type* **County**

Evergreen Park 60642
60805
For specific ZIP Codes call (888) 275-8777, or your local postmaster.
Evergreen Plaza (Part of Evergreen Park) 60805
Ewbanks 62301
Ewing 62836
Exeter 62621
Exline 60901
Expo Park (Part of Hoffman Estates) 60192
Eylar 61769
Ezra 62896
Fairbanks 61937
Fairbury 61739
Fair City 62952
Fairdale 60146
Fairfield, *Bureau* (Twp) 61283
Fairfield, *Lake* 60047
Fairfield, *Wayne* 62837
Fairfield Heights 61032
Fair Grange 61920
Fair Haven 61014
Fairland 61956
Fairman 62882
Fairmont♦ 60441
Fairmont City 62201
Fairmount, *Pike* (Twp) 62314
Fairmount (Part of Godfrey) 62035
Fairmount, *Massac* 62960
Fairmount, *Vermilion* 61841
Fair Oaks (Part of Streamwood) 60107
Fair Oaks, *DuPage* 60185
Fair Oaks, *Kane* 60175
Fairview (Part of Fairview Heights) 62232
Fairview, *Fulton* 61432
Fairview (Part of Taylorville) 62568
Fairview Addition 62930
Fairview Gardens (Part of Mount Prospect) 60056
Fairview Heights 62208
Fairway 61401
Fairway Estates (Part of Orland Park) 60462
Fairway Estates (Part of Wheaton) 60187
Fall Creek 62360
Fall River (Twp) 61350
Falmouth 62448
Fancher 62444
Fancy Creek (Twp) 62684
Fancy Prairie 62613
Fandon 62326
Fargo 62375
Farina 62838
Farmer City 61842
Farmers (Twp) 61482
Farmersville 62533
Farmingdale, *DuPage* 60561
Farmingdale, *Sangamon* 62677
Farmingdale South (Part of Darien) 60561
Farmingdale Terrace (Part of Darien) 60561
Farmingdale Village (Part of Darien) 60561
Farmington, *Coles* 62440
Farmington, *Fulton* 61531
Farmington, *Kane* 60174
Farmington (Part of Kildeer) 60047
Farm Ridge (Twp) 61325
Farmsted (Part of Naperville) 60565
Farnsworth (Part of Waukegan) 60088
Farrington (Twp) 62814
Farrow 61605
Fayette, *Livingston* (Twp) 61775
Fayette, *Greene* 62044
Fayetteville 62258
Fayville 62990
Feehanville (Part of Mount Prospect) 60056
Felix (Twp) 60416
Felker (Part of Washington) 61571
Fenton 61251
Fergestown 62959
Ferrel 61944
Ferrin 62231
Ferris 62336
Fiatt 61433
Ficklin 61953
Fiday View 60435
Fidelity 62030
Field (Twp) 62889
Fieldcrest (Part of Oak Forest) 60452
Fieldon 62031
Fields West 61822
Fillmore 62032
Filson 61910
Findlay 62534
Finley Square Mall (Part of Downers Grove) 60515
Finney Heights 62801
Fisher 61843
Fishhook 62314
Fithian 61844
Five Islands Park 60177
Flag Center 61068
Flagg 61068
Flamingo Estates 62286
Flanagan 61740
Flannigan (Twp) 62890
Flat Branch (Twp) 62550
Flat Rock 62427
Flatville 61878
Flat Woods 62985
Fletcher 61730
Flickerville 60914
Flint (Twp) 62340
Flora, *Boone* (Twp) 61008
Flora, *Clay* 62839
Floraville 62298
Florence, *Will* (Twp) 60481
Florence, *Pike* 62363
Florence, *Stephenson* 61032
Florid 61327
Flossmoor 60422
Flossmoor Highlands (Part of Flossmoor) 60422
Floyd (Twp) 61423
Fondulac, *Tazewell* (Twp) 61611
Fon-Du-Lac, *Will* 60544
Foosland 61845
Ford City Shopping Center (Part of Chicago) 60652
Fordham (Part of Chicago) 60619
Ford Heights 60411
Forest Acres 62201
Forest City 61532
Forest Estates 60067
Forest Gardens 60084
Forest Glen (Part of Chicago) 60646
Foresthaven 60045
Forest Heights (Part of Chicago Heights) 60411
Forest Hill (Part of Chicago) 60652
Forest Hills Estates 62471
Forest Homes 62018
Forest Lake♦ 60047
Forest Manor 60441
Forest Park 60130
Forest Park Mall (Part of Forest Park) 60130
Forest River 60056
Forest View 60402
Forest View Hills (Part of Oak Forest) 60452
Forman 62908
Forrest 61741
Forrestal Village (Part of North Chicago) 60088
Forreston 61030
Forsyth 62535
Fort Dearborn‡ 60610-11
For specific ZIP Codes call (888) 275-8777, or your local postmaster.
Fort Gage 62241
Fort Russell (Twp) 62010
Foss Acres (Part of Waukegan) 60088
Foster, *Madison* (Twp) 62002
Foster, *Marion* (Twp) 62807
Fosterburg 62010
Foster Pond 62298
Fountain 62295
Fountain Bluff (Twp) 62950
Fountain Creek 60942
Fountain Gap 62236
Fountain Green 62321
Four Lakes 60532
Four Mile (Twp) 62895
Fowler 62338
Fox, *Jasper* (Twp) 62448
Fox, *Kendall* 60560
Fox Chase (Part of St. Charles) 60174
Foxcroft 60137
Foxfield 60175
Fox Lake 60020
Fox Lake Hills♦ 60046
Fox Lake Vista 60081
Fox Lawn 60560
Fox Point (Part of Barrington) 60010
Fox River Bluffs 2 60118
Fox River Commons (Part of Aurora) 60540
Fox River Estates 60174
Fox River Gardens 60560
Fox River Grove 60021
Fox River Heights 60174
Fox River Valley Gardens 60010
Fox Valley Center (Part of Aurora)‡ 60504
Fox Valley Mail Processing Center‡ 60598†
60599*
Fox Valley East (Part of Aurora)‡ 60505
Fox Valley Villages (Part of Aurora) 60505
Frankfort, *Franklin* (Twp) 62896
Frankfort, *Will* 60423
Frankfort Heights (Part of West Frankfort) 62840
Frankfort Square♦ 60423
Franklin, *DeKalb* (Twp) 60146
Franklin, *Morgan* 62638
Franklin Grove 61031
Franklin Park 60131
Franklin Square 60423
Franklinville 60098
Frederick 62639
Freeburg 62243
Freedom, *Carroll* (Twp) 61046
Freedom, *La Salle* (Twp) 61350
Freeman Spur 62841
Freeport 61032
Fremont (Twp) 60060
Fremont Center 60060
Fremont Junction (Part of Hanover Park) 60103
Frenchman's Cove (Part of Arlington Heights) 60004
French Village (Part of Fairview Heights) 62208
Frentress Lake 61025
Friends Creek (Twp) 62501
Friendsville 62863
Frisco 62836
Frog City 62914
Frogtown, *Clinton* 62231
Frogtown, *Washington* 62271
Frontenac 60563
Frost 62901
Fruit 62025
Fruitland 61265
Fuller Park (Part of Chicago) 60609
Fulton 61252
Fults 62244
Funkhouser 62401
Funks Grove 61754
Future City 62914
Fyre Lake 61281
Gage Park (Part of Chicago) 60629
60632
For specific ZIP Codes call (888) 275-8777, or your local postmaster.
Gages Lake♦ 60030
Galatia 62935
Gale 62990
Galena 61036
Galena Oaks 61028
Galesburg (Twp) 61401
Galesburg 61401*
61402†
Galesville 61854
Gallagher 62450
Galnipper Place 62047
Galt 61037
Galton 61910
Galva 61434
Ganeer (Twp) 60954
Ganntown 62943
Garber 60936
Gardena (Part of East Peoria) 61611
Garden Heights 62946
Garden Hill (Twp) 62899
Garden Hills (Part of Champaign) 61821
Garden of Eden 60954
Garden Plain 61252
Garden Prairie 61038
Garden Quarter (Part of Elgin) 60123
Gardner, *Sangamon* (Twp) 62677
Gardner, *Grundy* 60424
Gards Point 62863
Garfield, *Grundy* (Twp) 60424
Garfield, *La Salle* 61377
Garfield Park (Part of Chicago)‡ 60624
Garfield Ridge (Part of Chicago) 60638
Garland 61917
Garrett 61913
Gary Gardens 60188
Gateway Yard (Part of East St. Louis) 62207
Gays 61928
Geff 62842
Genesee (Twp) 61270
Geneseo 61254
Geneseo Hills 61254
Geneva 60134
Genoa 60135
Gent City 62959
Gentry Acres 62918
Georgetown, *Carroll* 61046
Georgetown, *McDonough* 61455
Georgetown, *Vermilion* 61846
Gerald 61812
Gerlaw 61435
German (Twp) 62421
German Corner 61238
Germantown 62245
Germantown Hills 61548
German Valley 61039
Germanville (Twp) 60921
Gibson City 60936
Gibsonia 62954
Gifford 61847
Gila 62445
Gilberts 60136
Gilchrist 61486
Gilead 62006
Gillespie 62033
Gillespie Lakes 62033
Gillum 61704
Gilman 60938
Gilmer (Twp) 62328
Gilmore 62443
Gilmore Lake 62236
Gilson 61436
Ginger Creek (Part of Oak Brook) 60523
Ginger Hill (Part of Milan) 61264
Girard 62640
Givins (Part of Chicago) 60620
Gladstone 61437
Gladstone Park (Part of Chicago) 60630
Glasford 61533
Glasgow 62694
Glass Works (Part of Alton) 62002
Glen Acres (Part of Rosemont) 60018
Glenarm 62536
Glen Arms 60041
Glenavon 61724
Glenayre Gardens (Part of Glenview) 60025
Glenbard South♦ 60532
Glenbrook Countryside 60062
Glenburn 61858
Glen Carbon 62034
Glencoe 60022
Glendale, *Pope* 62985
Glendale (Part of Silvis) 61282
Glendale Gardens (Part of Wood River) 62024
Glendale Heights 60139
Glen Ellyn 60137*
60138†
Glen Ellyn Countryside 60137
Glen Ellyn Downtown (Part of Glen Ellyn)‡ 60138
Glen Ellyn Woods 60137
Glengarry (Part of Geneva) 60134
Glen Hill (Part of Glendale Heights) 60139
Glenn 62280
Glen Oak 60137
Glen Park 60551
Glen Ridge (Part of Matteson) 60443
Glenshire (Part of Glenview) 60025
Glenview, *Cook* 60025
Glen View (Part of O'Fallon) 62269
Glenview Countryside 60025
Glenview Estates 60025
Glenview Naval Air Station 60026
Glenview Terrace (Part of Glenview) 60025
Glenview Woodlands (Part of Glenview) 60025
Glenwood 60425
Glenwood Estates (Part of Glenwood) 60425
Godfrey 62035
Godley 60407
Golconda 62938
Gold (Twp) 61344
Golden 62339
Golden Acres (Part of Glenview) 60025
Golden Eagle 62036
Golden Gardens (Part of Centreville) 62206
Goldengate 62843
Golden Highridge (Part of Des Plaines) 60016
Golden Manor (Part of Des Plaines) 60016
Gold Hill (Twp) 62984
Golena Knolls 61523
Golf 60029
Golf Mill Center (Part of Niles) 60714
Golfview Hills 60521
Goode (Twp) 62884
Goodenow 60401
Goodfarm (Twp) 60424
Goodfield 61742
Good Hope 61438
Goodings Grove♦ 60441
Goodrich 60913
Goodwine 60939
Goofy Ridge 61567
Goose Creek (Twp) 61839
Goose Lake (Twp) 60444
Gordons 62454
Goreville 62939
Gorham 62940
Goshen (Twp) 61483
Gossett 62869
Graceland (Part of Chicago) 60657
Grafton, *McHenry* (Twp) 60142
Grafton, *Jersey* 62037
Grand Chain 62941
Grand Crossing (Part of Chicago)‡ 60619
Grand Detour 61021
Grand Prairie (Twp) 62898
Grand Rapids (Twp) 61325
Grand Ridge 61325
Grand Tower 62942
Grandview, *Carroll* 61285
Grandview, *Edgar* 61944
Grandview, *Sangamon* 62702
Grandview, *Woodford* 61611
Grandview Park (Part of Oak Lawn) 60453
Grandville (Twp) 62481
Grandwood Park♦ 60031
Granite City 62040
Grant, *Lake* (Twp) 60041
Grant, *Vermilion* (Twp) 60942
Grantfork 62249
Grant Park 60940
Grantsburg 62943
Granville 61326
Grape Creek 61834
Grass Lake 60002
Grassy (Twp) 62958
Gray (Twp) 62844
Graymont 61743
Graymoor (Part of Olympia Fields) 60461
Grays Lake 60030
Grays Siding 61858
Grayville 62844
Green Acres, *McDonough* 61455
Green Acres, *Sangamon* 62707
Greenbriar (Part of New Lenox) 60451
Greenbriar Addition 62918

Greenbrook Country (Part of Hanover Park) ... 60103
Greenbush ... 61415
Greene, *Mercer* (Twp) ... 61486
Greene, *Woodford* (Twp) ... 61516
Greenfield, *Grundy* (Twp) ... 60474
Greenfield, *Greene* ... 62044
Green Garden (Twp) ... 60423
Greenleaf Hills ... 61842
Green Meadows (Part of Streamwood) ... 60107
Green Oak ... 61356
Green Oaks ... 60048
Greenpond ... 62361
Green River ... 61241
Green Rock ... 61241
Greentree (Part of Libertyville) ... 60048
Greenup ... 62428
Green Valley (Part of Lombard) ... 60148
Green Valley, *Tazewell* ... 61534
Greenview ... 62642
Greenville, *Bureau* (Twp) ... 61376
Greenville, *Bond* ... 62246
Greenwich ... 60901
Greenwood, *Christian* (Twp) ... 62546
Greenwood, *McHenry* ... 60098
Greenwood Acres ... 61840
Greenwood Meadows ... 62035
Greer ... 60973
Gresham (Part of Chicago) ... 60620
Gridley ... 61744
Grigg ... 62278
Griggsville ... 62340
Grimes Addition ... 61081
Grimsby ... 62940
Grinnell ... 62908
Grisham (Twp) ... 62077
Griswold ... 60929
Gromers Woods ... 60120
Gross ... 62931
Grove (Twp) ... 62448
Grove, The (Part of Downers Grove) ... 60516
Grove City ... 62531
Groveland, *La Salle* (Twp) ... 61358
Groveland, *Tazewell* ... 61535
Grover (Twp) ... 62837
Grupe ... 62401
Guilford (Twp) ... 61028
Guilford ... 61036
Gulf Port ... 52601
Gurnee ... 60031
Gurnee Mills (Part of Gurnee) ... 60031
Guthrie ... 60936
Hadley ... 62312
Haegers Bend ... 60102
Hafer ... 62918
Hagaman ... 62630
Hagarstown ... 62247
Hagener (Twp) ... 62618
Hahnaman (Twp) ... 61283
Hahnaman ... 61243
Haines (Twp) ... 62853
Hainesville ... 60030
Haldane ... 61030
Hale (Twp) ... 61462
Half Day ... 60069
Hall (Twp) ... 61362
Hallidayboro ... 62932
Hallock, *Peoria* (Twp) ... 61526
Hallock, *Iroquois* ... 60973
Hallville ... 61727
Halsey Village (Part of Waukegan) ... 60088
Hamburg, *Bond* ... 62284
Hamburg, *Calhoun* ... 62045
Hamel ... 62046
Hamilton, *Lee* (Twp) ... 61349
Hamilton, *Hancock* ... 62341
Hamlet ... 61231
Hamletsburg ... 62944
Hammond ... 61929
Hampshire ... 60140
Hampton ... 61256
Hampton Court (Part of Country Club Hills) ... 60478
Hancock (Twp) ... 62321
Hanna (Twp) ... 61254
Hanna City ... 61536
Hannon (Part of Taylorville) ... 62568
Hanover, *Cook* (Twp) ... 60103
Hanover, *Jo Daviess* ... 61041
Hanover Highlands (Part of Hanover Park) ... 60103
Hanover Park ... 60103
Hanover Square (Part of Hanover Park) ... 60103
Hanson ... 62080
Happy Hollow Lake ... 61428
Harbor Estates ... 60010
Harco ... 62935
Hardin, *Pike* (Twp) ... 62355
Hardin, *Calhoun* ... 62047
Harding ... 60518
Hardinville ... 62449
Harlem, *Stephenson* (Twp) ... 61032
Harlem, *Winnebago* ... 61111
Harlem-Irving Plaza (Part of Chicago) ... 60634
Harmon ... 61042
Harmony, *Hancock* (Twp) ... 62321
Harmony, *Jefferson* ... 62814
Harmony, *McHenry* ... 60140
Harmony Village (Part of Wheeling) ... 60090
Harp (Twp) ... 61727
Harper ... 61030
Harpster ... 61845
Harris, *Fulton* (Twp) ... 61459
Harris, *Piatt* ... 61842
Harrisburg ... 62946
Harrison, *Jackson* ... 62966
Harrison, *Winnebago* ... 61072
Harrisonville, *Grundy* ... 60416
Harrisonville, *Monroe* ... 62295
Harristown ... 62537
Harter (Twp) ... 62839
Hartford ... 62048
Hartland ... 60098
Hartsburg ... 62643
Harvard ... 60033
Harvard Hills ... 61571
Harvel ... 62538
Harvey ... 60426
Harwood (Twp) ... 61847
Harwood Heights ... 60656
Hastings ... 61876
Hatcher Woods ... 60450
Hatton ... 62477
Havana ... 62644
Haw Creek (Twp) ... 61458
Hawthorn Center (Part of Vernon Hills) ... 60061
Hawthorne, *White* (Twp) ... 62821
Hawthorne (Part of Chicago)‡ ... 60623
Hawthorne (Part of Cicero) ... 60650
Hawthorn Woods ... 60047
Hawthrone Hills ... 62864
Hayes ... 61953
Hayford (Part of Chicago) ... 60652
Haymarket (Part of Chicago)‡ ... 60606
Haypress ... 62027
Hazel Crest ... 60429
Hazelcrest Highlands (Part of Hazel Crest) ... 60429
Hazel Dell ... 62428
Hazelgreen (Part of Alsip) ... 60482
Hazelhurst ... 61064
Hazelwood ... 61254
Hazelwood Heights ... 61254
Hazelwood West ... 61254
Headyville ... 62424
Heapsville ... 61425
Heartland Meadows (Part of South Elgin) ... 60177
Heartville ... 62401
Heathercrest (Part of Northbrook) ... 60062
Heatherfield ... 60450
Heatherlea (Part of Palatine) ... 60074
Heathsville ... 62427
Hebron ... 60034
Hecker ... 62248
Hegeler ... 61834
Hegewisch (Part of Chicago)‡ ... 60633
Helena ... 62466
Helmar ... 60541
Helvetia (Twp) ... 62249
Heman ... 62573
Henderson, *Knox* ... 61439
Henderson, *Macoupin* ... 62033
Henderson Grove ... 61401
Hendryx Manor ... 61614
Hennepin ... 61327
Henning ... 61848
Henry ... 61537
Hensley (Twp) ... 61820
Henton ... 62565
Herald ... 62845
Heralds Prairie (Twp) ... 62869
Herbert ... 60145
Herborn ... 62465
Heritage Estates (Part of Bourbonnais) ... 60914
Hermon ... 61458
Hermosa (Part of Chicago) ... 60639
Herod ... 62947
Herrick ... 62431
Herrin ... 62948
Herscher ... 60941
Hersman ... 62353
Hervey City ... 62549
Hettick ... 62649
Hewittville ... 62568
Heyworth ... 61745
Hickory (Twp) ... 62624
Hickory Falls ... 60097
Hickory Grove ... 62301
Hickory Hill (Twp) ... 62895
Hickory Hills, *Cook* ... 60457
Hickory Hills, *Piatt* ... 61884
Hickory Hollow ... 60118
Hickory Point, *Macon* (Twp) ... 62535
Hickory Point, *Shelby* ... 62565
Hickoryville ... 63673
Hicks ... 62947
Hidalgo ... 62432
Hidden Creek ... 60074
Hidden Hill ... 60123
Hidden Hills ... 61455
Higginsville ... 61865
High Knob ... 60187
High Lake ... 60185
Highland, *Grundy* (Twp) ... 60437
Highland, *Madison* ... 62249
Highlander ... 62901
Highland Glen (Part of Elgin) ... 60123
Highland Haven ... 60123
Highland Hills ... 60148
Highland Lake ... 60030
Highland Park, *Lake* ... 60035
Highland Park, *Marion* ... 62881
Highlands (Part of Chicago Heights) ... 60411
Highlands (Part of Hinsdale) ... 60521
Highlands-Clarks ... 60543
Highland Shores ... 60097
Highlawn (Part of Riverdale) ... 60827
High Meadows ... 61607
High Point (Part of Hoffman Estates) ... 60195
Highway Village (Part of East Peoria) ... 61611
Highwood ... 60040
Highwood Terrace (Part of Belleville) ... 62221
Hilcrest ... 62089
Hildreth ... 61876
Hillcrest, *Calhoun* ... 62355
Hillcrest, *Douglas* ... 61953
Hillcrest (Part of Geneseo) ... 61254
Hillcrest, *Ogle* ... 61068
Hillcrest (Part of Taylorville) ... 62568
Hilldale Villages (Part of Hoffman Estates) ... 60195
Hillerman ... 62941
Hillery ... 61834
Hillsboro ... 62049
Hillsdale ... 61257
Hillside, *Cook* ... 60162
Hillside Manor ... 60901
Hill Top, *McLean* ... 61753
Hill Top, *Menard* ... 62675
Hillview ... 62050
Hillyard (Twp) ... 62076
Himrod ... 61883
Hinckley ... 60520
Hindsboro ... 61930
Hinsdale ... 60521*
... 60522†
Hinswood (Part of Darien) ... 60561
Hire (Twp) ... 62326
Hitt ... 61051
Hittle (Twp) ... 61721
Hodgetown ... 62865
Hodgkins ... 60525
Hoffman ... 62250
Hoffman Estates ... 60194-95
For specific ZIP Codes call (888) 275-8777, or your local postmaster.
Hoffmann Edition ... 60924
Holbrook (Part of Chicago Heights) ... 60411
Holcomb ... 61043
Holcombville Corners ... 60012
Holder ... 61736
Holiday Hills ... 60050
Holiday Shores ... 62025
Holland ... 62414
Hollandia ... 62221
Hollenback ... 60460
Hollendale (Part of South Holland) ... 60473
Holliday ... 62414
Hollis (Twp) ... 61607
Hollowayville ... 61356
Hollydale (Part of Homewood) ... 60430
Hollywood Heights ... 62232
Holmes Center ... 61523
Homberg ... 62938
Home Gardens (Part of Danville) ... 61832
Homer, *Will* (Twp) ... 60441
Homer, *Champaign* ... 61849
Homestead (Part of O'Fallon) ... 62269
Hometown ... 60456
Homewood, *Cook* ... 60430
Homewood (Part of Moline) ... 61265
Homewood Acres ... 60430
Homewood Shores (Part of Homewood) ... 60430
Homewood Terrace (Part of Homewood) ... 60430
Honegger ... 61741
Honey Bend ... 62056
Honey Creek, *Adams* (Twp) ... 62325
Honey Creek, *Crawford* (Twp) ... 62427
Honey Creek, *Ogle* ... 61015
Honey Point (Twp) ... 62056
Hononegah Heights ... 61073
Hoodville ... 62859
Hookdale ... 62284
Hoopeston ... 60942
Hooppole ... 61258
Hoosier (Twp) ... 62858
Hope, *La Salle* (Twp) ... 61334
Hope, *Vermilion* ... 61812
Hopedale ... 61747
Hopewell (Twp) ... 61540
Hopewell ... 61565
Hop Hollow ... 62035
Hopkins (Twp) ... 61081
Hopkins Park ... 60944
Hopper ... 61480
Horace ... 61924
Horatio Gardens ... 60069
Hord ... 62858
Hornsby ... 62056
Horseshoe ... 62934
Houston, *Adams* (Twp) ... 62339
Houston, *Randolph* ... 62286
Howardton ... 62942
Howe Terrace ... 60010
Hoyleton ... 62803
Hubbard Woods (Part of Winnetka)‡ ... 60093
Hubbard Woods, *Marion* ... 62801
Hubly ... 62642
Hudgens ... 62959
Hudson ... 61748
Huegely ... 62803
Huey ... 62252
Hugh's Addition ... 62684
Hugo ... 61953
Hull ... 62343
Humboldt ... 61931
Humbolt Park (Part of Chicago) ... 60651
Hume, *Whiteside* (Twp) ... 61071
Hume, *Edgar* ... 61932
Humm Wye ... 62938
Humrick ... 61870
Hunt City ... 62480
Hunter, *Boone* ... 61011
Hunter, *Edgar* ... 61944
Hunter Trail (Part of Oak Brook) ... 60523
Huntington (Part of Naperville) ... 60540
Huntington Commons (Part of Mount Prospect) ... 60056
Huntington Park (Part of Elgin) ... 60120
Huntinton Park ... 62035
Huntley ... 60142
Huntsville ... 62344
Hurlbut (Twp) ... 62634
Hurricane (Twp) ... 62080
Hurst ... 62949
Hutchins Park ... 61103
Hutsonville ... 62433
Hutton ... 61920
Hyde Park (Part of Chicago)‡ ... 60615
... 60653
For specific ZIP Codes call (888) 275-8777, or your local postmaster.
Idaville Corner ... 60924
Ideal ... 61285
Idlewild ... 60030
Idlewood ... 62864
Iliana ... 47982
Illiana Heights ... 60954
Illini (Twp) ... 62573
Illinois Center (Part of Marion) ... 62959
Illinois City ... 61259
Illinois Veterans Home (Part of Quincy)‡ ... 62301
Illiopolis ... 62539
Imbs ... 62240
Imperial ... 60048
Ina ... 62846
Inclose ... 61933
Independence, *Saline* (Twp) ... 62946
Independence, *Pike* ... 62363
Indian Creek, *White* (Twp) ... 62869
Indian Creek, *Lake* ... 60061
Indian Grove (Twp) ... 61739
Indian Head Park ... 60525
Indian Hill (Part of Naperville) ... 60563
Indian Hill (Part of Winnetka) ... 60093
Indian Hills (Part of Sauk Village) ... 60411
Indian Hills, *Jo Daviess* ... 61025
Indian Oaks, *Kankakee* ... 60914
Indian Oaks (Part of Bolingbrook) ... 60440
Indianola ... 61850
Indian Point, *Knox* (Twp) ... 61410
Indian Point, *Lake* ... 60002
Indian Point, *Menard* ... 62613
Indian Prairie (Twp) ... 62823
Indian Ridge, *McHenry* ... 60097
Indian Ridge, *Piatt* ... 61884
Indiantown (Twp) ... 61421
Indian Trail Estates ... 60015
Industrial Park ... 62864
Industry ... 61440
Ingalls Park♦ ... 60431
Ingalton ... 60185
Ingleside, *Lake* ... 60041
Ingleside (Part of Fox Lake) ... 60041
Ingleside Shores ... 60041
Ingraham ... 62434
Ingram Hill ... 62946
International Village (Part of Bolingbrook) ... 60440
International Village (Part of Schaumburg) ... 60173
Inverness ... 60067
Inverness on the Ponds (Part of Inverness) ... 60067
Iola ... 62847
Ipava ... 61441
Irene ... 61016
Irishtown (Twp) ... 62253
Irondale (Part of Chicago) ... 60617
Iroquois (Twp) ... 60928
Iroquois ... 60945
Irving ... 62051
Irving Park (Part of Chicago)‡ ... 60641
Irvington ... 62848
Irwin ... 60901
Isabel, *Fulton* (Twp) ... 61542
Isabel, *Edgar* ... 61943

*** Area Zip Code** **† Post Office Boxes** **‡ Postal Station** **♦ Census Designated Place** *Italic Type* **County**

- Island Grove, *Sangamon* (Twp) 62677
- Island Grove, *Jasper* 62467
- Island Lake 60042
- Israelite Farm 62992
- Itasca 60143
- Itasca Ranchettes 60143
- Iuka 62849
- Ivanhoe (Part of Bolingbrook) 60440
- Ivanhoe, *Lake* 60060
- Ivanhoe Estates 61802
- Ivesdale 61851
- Ivy Glen (Part of Aurora) 60506
- Ivy Heights (Part of Wood River) 62024
- Jackson, *Effingham* (Twp) 62401
- Jackson, *Will* (Twp) 60421
- Jackson Park (Part of Chicago)‡ 60637
- Jacksonville 62650*
- 62651†
- Jacob 62950
- Jalapa 62054
- Jamaica 61841
- Jamesburg 61865
- Jamestown, *Clinton* 62275
- Jamestown, *Perry* 62238
- Janesville 62435
- Jarvis (Twp) 62294
- Jasper (Twp) 62837
- Jefferson (Twp) 61062
- Jefferson Park (Part of Chicago)‡ 60630
- Jefferson Square Mall (Part of Joliet) 60435
- Jeffries 62951
- Jeiseyville 62568
- Jenkins 61727
- Jerome 62704
- Jersey (Twp) 62052
- Jerseyville 62052
- Jewett 62436
- Johannisburg 62214
- Johnsburg 60050
- Johnson, *Christian* (Twp) 62568
- Johnson, *Clark* (Twp) 62420
- Johnsonville 62850
- Johnston City 62951
- Johnstown 62440
- Joliet (Twp) 60431
- Joliet 60431-36
  For specific ZIP Codes call (888) 275-8777, or your local postmaster.
- Jonathan Creek (Twp) 61911
- Jones, *Coles* 61938
- Jonesboro 62952
- Jones Ridge 62280
- Jonesville 61348
- Joppa 62953
- Jordan (Twp) 61081
- Joshua (Twp) 61432
- Joslin 61257
- Joy 61260
- Joywood Farms Estates 62028
- Jubilee (Twp) 61559
- Junction 62954
- Junction City 62882
- Justice 60458
- Kampsville 62053
- Kane 62054
- Kaneville 60144
- Kangley 61364
- Kankakee 60901
- Kankakee Valley 60964
- Kansas, *Woodford* (Twp) 61725
- Kansas, *Edgar* 61933
- Kappa 61738
- Karbers Ridge 62955
- Karnak 62956
- Kasbeer 61328
- Kaskaskia, *Fayette* (Twp) 62892
- Kaskaskia, *Randolph* 63673
- Kaskaskia Heights 62217
- Kaskaskia River 62231
- Kaufman 62001
- Kedron 62934
- Kedzie Grace (Part of Chicago)‡ 60618
- Keene (Twp) 62349
- Keenes 62851
- Keeneyville 60172
- Keensburg 62852
- Keith (Twp) 62878
- Keithsburg 61442
- Kell 62853
- Kellart Lake 60924
- Kellerville 62324
- Kelleyville (Part of Westville) 61883
- Kelly (Twp) 61412
- Kemp 61910
- Kemper 62063
- Kempton 60946
- Kendall (Twp) 60560
- Kendall Hills 62024
- Keneddy 61080
- Kenilwicke (Part of Palatine) 60067
- Kenilworth 60043
- Kenney 61749
- Ken Rock 61109
- Kensington (Part of Chicago) 60628
- Kensington Junction (Part of Chicago) 60628
- Kent 61044
- Kenton (Part of Chicago) 60644
- Kentucky 61944
- Kenwood (Part of Champaign) 61821
- Kenwood (Part of Chicago) 60615
- Keptown 62411
- Kernan 61364
- Kerr (Twp) 61847
- Kerton (Twp) 62644
- Kewanee 61443
- Keyesport 62253
- Keyesport Landing 62253
- Kickapoo 61528
- Kidd 62277
- Kidley 61924
- Kilbourne 62655
- Kildeer 60047
- Kimball Farms 60110
- Kimberly Heights (Part of Oak Forest) 60452
- Kincaid 62540
- Kinderhook 62345
- King (Twp) 62546
- Kingdom 61021
- Kingman 62463
- Kings 61068
- Kings Cove (Part of Deerfield) 60015
- Kings Island (Part of Fox Lake) 60020
- Kings Park (Part of Bolingbrook) 60440
- Kingston, *Adams* 62312
- Kingston, *DeKalb* 60145
- Kingston Mines 61539
- Kingswood 60175
- Kinkaid (Twp) 62907
- Kinmundy 62854
- Kinsman 60437
- Kirkland 60146
- Kirksville 61951
- Kirkwood 61447
- Kishwaukee Glen 61109
- Klein Acres (Part of Rantoul) 61866
- Klendworth Addition 61250
- Klines Corner 62837
- Klondike, *Alexander* 62914
- Klondike, *Lake* 60002
- Klondyke 62466
- Knapp's Noll 61072
- Knight Prairie (Twp) 62859
- Knolle Hill 62036
- Knollwood, *Christian* 62568
- Knollwood, *Lake* 60044
- Knollwood (Part of Lake Zurich) 60047
- Knollwood, *Sangamon* 62684
- Knottingham (Part of Downers Grove) 60515
- Knox (Twp) 61448
- Knoxville 61448
- Kortcamp (Part of Schram City) 62049
- Kraft Addition 62812
- Kriegh Addition 61448
- Kristal Lake Ranch 61032
- Kuhn 62025
- Kumler 61724
- La Clede 62426
- Lacon 61540
- La Crosse 61450
- Ladd 61329
- Laenna (Twp) 62548
- Lafayette, *Coles* (Twp) 61938
- Lafayette, *Ogle* (Twp) 61006
- La Fayette, *Stark* 61449
- La Fontaine (Part of Glenview) 60025
- Lafox 60147
- Lagrange, *Bond* (Twp) 62019
- La Grange, *Brown* 62378
- La Grange, *Cook* 60525-26
  For specific ZIP Codes call (888) 275-8777, or your local postmaster.
- La Grange Highlands 60525
- La Grange Park 60526
- La Grange Road (Part of La Grange) 60525
- Laguna Woods 60462
- La Harpe 61450
- La Hogue 60938
- Lake (Twp) 62801
- Lake 62283
- Lake Barrington 60010
- Lake Bluff 60044
- Lake Boulevard Addition 61834
- Lake Bracken 61401
- Lake Briarwood (Part of Arlington Heights) 60005
- Lake Camelot 61547
- Lake Carlinville 62626
- Lake Catherine♦ 60002
- Lake Centralia 62801
- Lake Charleston 61920
- Lake Charlotte 60174
- Lake City 61937
- Lake Creek (Twp) 62959
- Lakecrest, *Montgomery* 62049
- Lake Crest, *Williamson* 62922
- Lake Estates 62959
- Lake Forest 60045
- Lake Forest Estates (Part of Belleville) 62221
- Lake Fork (Twp) 62548
- Lake Fork 62541
- Lake Holiday 60548
- 60552
  For specific ZIP Codes call (888) 275-8777, or your local postmaster.
- Lakehurst Shopping Center (Part of Waukegan) 60085
- Lake in the Hills 60102
- Lake in the Woods 60515
- Lake Iroquois 60948
- Lake Ka-Ho 62069
- Lake Killarney 60013
- Lake Lancelot 61547
- Lakeland Hills, *Jackson* 62901
- Lakeland Hills, *St. Clair* 62221
- Lakeland Park (Part of McHenry) 60050
- Lake Lawrence 62439
- Lake Louise 61010
- Lake Lynwood (Part of Lynwood) 60411
- Lake Lynwood, *Henry* 61262
- Lake Mantero 60950
- Lake Marie 60002
- Lake Marion 60110
- Lake Mattoon 62447
- Lakemoor 60050
- Lake Oakland 61943
- Lake of the Winds (Part of Wheeling) 60090
- Lake of the Woods 61525
- Lake Pana 62557
- Lake Park‡ 61822
- Lake Park Estates 60067
- Lake Park Forest 60067
- Lake Petersburg 62675
- Lake Piasa 62012
- Lake Sara 62401
- Lakeshore Acres 62231
- Lakeside Knolls 62049
- Lakeside Villas (Part of Wheeling) 60090
- Lake Summerset♦ 61019
- Lake Tacoma 62901
- Lake Tara Estates 60118
- Lake Thunderbird 61560
- Laketown (Part of Springfield) 62703
- Lakeview (Part of Chicago)‡ 60613
- 60657
  For specific ZIP Codes call (888) 275-8777, or your local postmaster.
- Lakeview Acres 62234
- Lakeview Estate 62881
- Lakeview Estates, *Jefferson* 62864
- Lake View Estates, *Williamson* 62958
- Lake Villa, *Clinton* 62283
- Lake Villa, *Lake* 60046
- Lake Wildwood 61375
- Lake Williamson 62626
- Lakewood, *DuPage* 60185
- Lakewood, *McHenry* 60014
- Lakewood (Part of Glen Carbon) 62035
- Lakewood (Part of Richton Park) 60471
- Lakewood, *Shelby* 62438
- Lakewood Park 62901
- Lakewood Shores♦ 60481
- Lake Zurich 60047
- Lamard (Twp) 62842
- Lamb 62919
- La Moille (Twp) 61349
- La Moille 61330
- Lamoine (Twp) 61415
- Lamotte (Twp) 62451
- Lamplighter (Part of Towanda) 61776
- Lanark 61046
- Lancaster, *Stephenson* (Twp) 61032
- Lancaster, *Wabash* 62855
- Landers (Part of Chicago) 60652
- Landes 62466
- Landings, The (Part of Lansing) 60438
- Lane 61750
- Lanesville 62515
- Langleyville 62568
- Lansdowne (Part of East St. Louis) 62204
- Lansing 60438
- Laona (Twp) 61024
- La Place 61936
- La Prairie, *Marshall* (Twp) 61523
- La Prairie, *Adams* 62346
- La Prairie Center 61565
- Larchland 61462
- Larkdale (Part of Decatur) 62521
- Larkdale (Part of Wauconda) 60084
- Larkinsburg (Twp) 62426
- La Rose 61541
- La Salle 61301
- Latham 62543
- Latona 62479
- Laura 61451
- Lawndale, *McLean* (Twp) 61728
- Lawndale (Part of Chicago) 60623
- Lawndale, *Logan* 61751
- Lawn Ridge 61526
- Lawrence, *Lawrence* (Twp) 62439
- Lawrence, *McHenry* 60033
- Lawrenceville 62439
- Leaf River 61047
- Leaverton Park 62451
- Lebanon 62254
- Leclaire (Part of Edwardsville) 62025
- Ledford 62946
- Lee, *Brown* (Twp) 62375
- Lee, *Fulton* (Twp) 61470
- Lee, *Lee* 60530
- Lee Center 61331
- Leech (Twp) 62833
- Leeds 61377
- Leef (Twp) 62249
- Leepertown (Twp) 61315
- Leesburg 61501
- Leesville 60964
- Lehigh 60901
- Leisure Lea 60543
- Leisure Village (Part of Fox Lake) 60020
- Leland 60531
- Leland Grove 62704
- Leland Lake 62650
- Lemont 60439
- Lena 61048
- Lenox (Twp) 61462
- Lenzburg (Twp) 62257
- Lenzburg 62255
- Leonard 60938
- Leon Corners 61277
- Leonore 61332
- L'Erable 60927
- Lerna 62440
- Le Roy, *Boone* (Twp) 61012
- Le Roy, *McLean* 61752
- Levan (Twp) 62966
- Levee (Twp) 62343
- Leverett 61822
- Lewistown 61542
- Lewood 60544
- Lexington 61753
- Leyden (Twp) 60131
- Liberty, *Effingham* (Twp) 62414
- Liberty, *Adams* 62347
- Liberty, *Saline* 62946
- Liberty Acres 60048
- Liberty Hill 62428
- Liberty Lake (Part of Libertyville) 60048
- Liberty Park 60559
- Libertyville (Twp) 60048
- Libertyville 60048*
- 60092†
- Lick 62629
- Lick Creek 62912
- Licking (Twp) 62449
- Lidice (Part of Crest Hill) 60435
- Lightsville 61047
- Lilac Circle Homes (Part of Lombard) 60148
- Lilly 61755
- Lily Cache 60544
- Lily Cache Acres 60544
- Lily Lake 60151
- Lilymoor 60050
- Lima 62348
- Limestone, *Kankakee* (Twp) 60901
- Limestone, *Peoria* (Twp) 61604
- Limestone (Part of Bartonville) 61607
- Lincoln, *Ogle* (Twp) 61064
- Lincoln, *Logan* 62656
- Lincoln Addition (Part of Wood River) 62095
- Lincoln Estates 60423
- Lincoln Gardens (Part of Alton) 62002
- Lincoln Hills 60137
- Lincoln Mall (Part of Matteson) 60443
- Lincoln Park (Part of Chicago)‡ 60614
- 60657
  For specific ZIP Codes call (888) 275-8777, or your local postmaster.
- Lincolnshire, *Lake* 60069
- Lincolnshire (Part of Crete) 60417
- Lincolnshire Fields 61822
- Lincoln Square (Part of Chicago) 60625
- Lincolnwood 60645
- 60659
  For specific ZIP Codes call (888) 275-8777, or your local postmaster.
- Lincolnwood Hills 60451
- Lincolnwood Town Center (Part of Lincolnwood) 60645
- Lindenhurst 60046
- Lindenhurst Estates (Part of Lindenhurst) 60046
- Lindenwood 61049
- Linder (Twp) 62016
- Linn, *Woodford* (Twp) 61570
- Linn, *Wabash* 62410
- Linrose Heights 62216
- Lintner 61929
- Lioncrest (Part of Richton Park) 60471
- Lis 62448
- Lisbon 60541
- Lisbon Center 60541
- Lisle 60532
- Litchfield 62056
- Literberry 62660
- Little America 61542
- Little Indian 62691
- Little Mackinaw (Twp) 61759
- Little Rock 60545
- Little Swan Lake 61415
- Littleton 61452
- Little York 61453
- Lively Grove 62268
- Liverpool 61543
- Livingston, *Clark* 62441
- Livingston, *Madison* 62058
- Loami 62661
- Loch Lomond (Part of Mundelein) 60060

- Lockhaven 62035
- Lockport 60441
- ... 60446
  For specific ZIP Codes call (888) 275-8777, or your local postmaster.
- Locust (Twp) 62555
- Loda 60948
- Lodge 61856
- Logan, *Peoria* (Twp) 61536
- Logan, *Edgar* 61924
- Logan, *Franklin* 62856
- Logan Square (Part of Chicago)‡ 60647
- Lomax 61454
- Lombard 60148
- Lombardville 61421
- London Mills 61544
- Lone Grove (Twp) 62880
- Lone Tree 61368
- Long Branch (Twp) 62935
- Long Creek 62521
- Long Grove 60047
- Long Lake♦ 60041
- Long Meadow (Part of Downers Grove) 60515
- Long Point 61333
- Longview 61852
- Longview Addition 61745
- Longwood Farms (Part of Chicago Heights) 60411
- Longwood Manor 60563
- Loogootee 62857
- Looking Glass (Twp) 62265
- Lookout Point 60097
- Loon Lake 60002
- Loop (Part of Chicago)‡ 60601-05
  For specific ZIP Codes call (888) 275-8777, or your local postmaster.
- Loraine, *Henry* (Twp) 61277
- Loraine, *Adams* 62349
- Loran 61062
- Lords' Park Manor (Part of Elgin) 60120
- Lorenzo 60481
- Loretto 60460
- Lorraine Park (Part of Wheaton) 60187
- Lostant 61334
- Lost Lake 61070
- Lost Nation 61021
- Lotus 61845
- Lotus Woods 60081
- Lou Del 62298
- Loudon (Twp) 62414
- Louis Joliet Mall (Part of Joliet) 60435
- Louisville 62858
- Love (Twp) 61870
- Lovejoy, *Iroquois* (Twp) 60973
- Lovejoy, *St. Clair* 62059
- Loves Park 61111
- ... 61130-32
  For specific ZIP Codes call (888) 275-8777, or your local postmaster.
- Lovington 61937
- Lowder 62662
- Lowe (Twp) 61911
- Lowell 61370
- Lowpoint 61545
- Loxa 61938
- Lucas (Twp) 62424
- Ludlow 60949
- Lukin (Twp) 62417
- Lumaghi Heights 62234
- Luther 62664
- Lyman (Twp) 60962
- Lynchburg (Twp) 62617
- Lyndon 61261
- Lynn, *Henry* (Twp) 61262
- Lynn, *Knox* (Twp) 61414
- Lynn Center 61262
- Lynn Gardens 60901
- Lynnville, *Ogle* (Twp) 61049
- Lynnville, *Morgan* 62650
- Lynnwood (Part of Lynwood) 60411
- Lynnwood, *Kendall* 60543
- Lynnwood, *La Salle* 61354
- Lynwood 60411
- Lynwood Estates 61285
- Lyons, *Cook* (Twp) 60525
- Lyons, *Cook* 60534
- Lyons (Part of Belgium) 61883
- McCall 62321
- McClellan (Twp) 62894
- McClure 62957
- McClusky 62052
- McConnell 61050
- McCook 60525
- McCormick 62987
- McCullom Lake 60050
- McCully 61764
- McDowell 61764
- Macedonia 62860
- McGirr 60556
- McHenry (Twp) 60050
- McHenry 60050*
- ... 60051†
- McHenry Shores (Part of McHenry) 60050
- Machesney Park 61115
- Machesney Park Mall (Part of Machesney Park) 61111
- MacIntoch 61364
- McIntosh 60123
- McKee (Twp) 62347
- McKeen 62441
- McKendree (Twp) 61834
- Mackinaw 61755
- McKinley Park (Part of Chicago) 60608
- Mackler Heights (Part of Chicago Heights) 60411
- McLean 61754
- McLeansboro 62859
- McNabb 61335
- Macomb (Twp) 61438
- Macomb 61455
- Macon, *Bureau* (Twp) 61314
- Macon, *Macon* 62544
- Macoupin 62676
- McQueen 60185
- McVey 62640
- Madison, *Richland* (Twp) 62450
- Madison, *Madison* 62060
- Madonnaville 62298
- Maeystown 62256
- Magnet 61938
- Magnolia 61336
- Mahomet 61853
- Maine, *Cook* (Twp) 60016
- Maine, *Grundy* (Twp) 60444
- Main Street (Part of Evanston) 60202
- Makanda 62958
- Malden 61337
- Malibu Village 62901
- Malone (Twp) 61534
- Malta 60150
- Malvern 61270
- Manchester, *Boone* (Twp) 61011
- Manchester, *Scott* 62663
- Manhattan 60442
- Manito 61546
- Manlius, *La Salle* (Twp) 61360
- Manlius, *Bureau* 61338
- Mannheim (Part of Franklin Park) 60131
- Mannon 61272
- Mansfield 61854
- Manteno 60950
- Manville 61319
- Maplebrook (Part of Naperville) 60565
- Maple Grove 62476
- Maple Hill (Part of Warrenville) 60555
- Maple Lane 61081
- Maple Park 60151
- Maple Point 62428
- Maples Mill 61520
- Mapleton 61547
- Maplewood (Part of Cahokia) 62206
- Maplewood (Part of Chicago) 60647
- Maplewood Estates 61520
- Maquon 61458
- Marblehead 62301
- Marcelline 62376
- Marcoe 62864
- Mardell Manor 61607
- Marengo 60152
- Marietta 61459
- Marigold 62242
- Marina Terrace 60543
- Marina Village 60543
- Marine 62061
- Marion, *Lee* (Twp) 61310
- Marion, *Ogle* (Twp) 61015
- Marion, *Williamson* 62959
- Marion Circle 60554
- Marion Country Club 62959
- Marion Hills (Part of Darien) 60561
- Marissa 62257
- Mark 61340
- Market Place (Part of Champaign) 61820
- Markham, *Cook* 60426
- Markham, *Morgan* 62628
- Markham City (Part of Bluford) 62814
- Marley, *Edgar* 61944
- Marley, *Will* 60448
- Marlow 62872
- Marnico Village 62650
- Maroa 61756
- Marquette Heights 61554
- Marrowbone (Twp) 61914
- Mars (Part of Chicago) 60639
- Marseilles 61341
- Marshall 62441
- Marston 61279
- Martin, *Crawford* (Twp) 62454
- Martin, *McLean* (Twp) 61728
- Martinsburg 62363
- Martinsville 62442
- Martinton 60951
- Mary Crest (Part of Country Club Hills) 60478
- Mary Crest (Part of Joliet 60436
- Marydale 62231
- Marydale Manor (Part of Dolton) 60419
- Maryland (Twp) 61007
- Maryland 61064
- Mary Meadows 60175
- Maryville 62062
- Mascoutah 62258
- Mason 62443
- Mason City 62664
- Massbach 61028
- Massilon (Twp) 62883
- Matanzas Beach 62644
- Matherville 61263
- Matteson 60443
- Mattoon 61938
- Maud 62863
- Maunie 62861
- Maxwell (Twp) 62661
- May, *Christian* (Twp) 62567
- May, *Lee* (Twp) 61367
- Mayberry (Twp) 62817
- Mayfair (Part of Chicago) 60630
- Mayfair, *Tazewell* 61550
- Mayfield (Twp) 60178
- Maynard Lake 61822
- Mays 61944
- Maysville 62340
- Maytown 61310
- Mayview 61802
- Maywood 60153
- Mazon 60444
- Meacham (Twp) 62854
- Meadowbrook, *McDonough* 61455
- Meadowbrook, *Madison* 62010
- Meadowbrook (Part of Wheeling) 60090
- Meadow Heights (Part of Collinsville) 62234
- Meadowlake 61821
- Meadows 61726
- Meadows Town Mall (Part of Rolling Meadows) 60008
- Meadowview, *Kane* 60175
- Meadowview (Part of Kankakee) 60901
- Mechanicsburg 62545
- Medalist Park (Part of Palatine) 60067
- Media 61460
- Medina (Twp) 61523
- Medinah♦ 60157
- Medinah on the Lake (Part of Bloomingdale) 60108
- Medora 62063
- Meeks 61846
- Meersman 61244
- Melrose, *Adams* (Twp) 62301
- Melrose, *Clark* 62477
- Melrose Park 60160-61
- ... 60164
  For specific ZIP Codes call (888) 275-8777, or your local postmaster.
- Melville (Part of Godfrey) 62035
- Melvin 60952
- Memorial (Part of Decatur)‡ 62526
- Menard 62259
- Mendon 62351
- Mendota 61342
- Menominee 61025
- Meppen 62013
- Mercer (Twp) 61231
- Merchandise Mart (Part of Chicago)‡ 60654
- Meredosia 62665
- Meriden 61342
- Meridian (Twp) 62283
- Meridian Heights (Part of Mounds) 62964
- Mermet 62908
- Merna 61758
- Merriam 62837
- Merrimac 62295
- Merrionette Park 60655
- Merritt 62650
- Merry Oaks 61244
- Mesa Lake 62863
- Metamora 61548
- Metcalf 61940
- Metropolis 62960
- Mettawa 60048
- Meyer, *Adams* 62379
- Meyer, *Kankakee* 60901
- Meyerbrook 60545
- Meyers Bay (Part of Fox Lake) 60020
- Michael 62065
- Middlebury (Part of Barrington Hills) 60010
- Middle Creek, *Hancock* 62367
- Middlecreek, *Kane* 60175
- Middlefork (Twp) 61865
- Middle Grove 61531
- Middleport (Twp) 60970
- Middlesworth 62565
- Middletown 62666
- Midland City 61727
- Midland Hills 62958
- Midlothian 60445
- Midway, *Madison* 62067
- Midway, *Massac* 62960
- Midway, *Tazewell* 61554
- Midway, *Vermilion* 61883
- Midwest (Part of Chicago)‡ 60612
- Midwest Club (Part of Oak Brook) 60523
- Milam (Twp) 62544
- Milan, *DeKalb* (Twp) 60550
- Milan, *Rock Island* 61264
- Mildred 62707
- Miles Station 62012
- Milford 60953
- Milks Grove (Twp) 60941
- Millbrook, *Peoria* (Twp) 61451
- Millbrook, *Kendall* 60536
- Millburn 60083
- Mill Creek, *Jersey* 62022
- Mill Creek, *Union* 62961
- Milledgeville 61051
- Miller (Twp) 61360
- Miller Addition 61250
- Miller City 62962
- Miller Lake 62864
- Millersburg (Twp) 61260
- Millersburg 61231
- Millersville 62557
- Miller Woods, (Part of Chicago Heights 60411
- Millhurst 60545
- Millington 60537
- Mills (Twp) 62246
- Mill Shoals 62862
- Mill Spring 62035
- Millstadt 62260
- Milmine 61855
- Milo 61421
- Milton, *DuPage* (Twp) 60187
- Milton, *Pike* 62352
- Mindale 62344
- Mineral 61344
- Minier 61759
- Minonk 61760
- Minooka 60447
- Missal 61364
- Mission (Twp) 60551
- Mission Hills 60062
- Mississippi (Twp) 62022
- Missouri (Twp) 62353
- Mitchell 62040
- Mitchellsville 62917
- Mitchie 62295
- Mobet Meadows 61275
- Mobile City 61401
- Moccasin 62411
- Mode 62444
- Modena 61491
- Modesto 62667
- Modoc 62261
- Moecherville 60505
- Mokena 60448
- Moline (Twp) 61265
- Moline 61265*
- ... 61266†
- Momence 60954
- Mona (Twp) 60964
- Monee 60449
- Money Creek (Twp) 61753
- Monica 61559
- Monmouth 61462
- Monroe (Twp) 61052
- Monroe Center 61052
- Monroe City 62298
- Mont 62034
- Montague Forest 60123
- Mont Clare (Part of Chicago) 60639
- Montebello (Twp) 62341
- Monterey 61520
- Monterey Village (Part of University Park) 60466
- Montezuma 62361
- Montgomery, *Crawford* (Twp) 62427
- Montgomery, *Woodford* (Twp) 61733
- Montgomery, *Kane* 60538
- Monticello 61856
- Montmorency (Twp) 61071
- Montrose 62445
- Moon Lake Village (Part of Hoffman Estates) 60194
- Moonshine 62442
- Moores Prairie (Twp) 62810
- Mooseheart 60539
- Moraine Valley Facility (Part of Bridgeview) 60455
- Morea 62451
- Morehaven 61073
- Morgan (Twp) 61943
- Morgan Park (Part of Chicago)‡ 60643
- Morgan's Gate 60067
- Moriah 62420
- Moro 62067
- Morris 60450
- Morris Hills (Part of Collinsville) 62234
- Morrison 61270
- Morrisonville 62546
- Morristown 61274
- Morseville 61085
- Mortimer 61924
- Morton 61550
- Morton Grove 60053
- Morton Park (Part of Cicero) 60804
- Moser Highlands (Part of Naperville) 60540
- Moses Lake 62812
- Mosquito (Twp) 62547
- Mossville 61552
- Mound, *Effingham* (Twp) 62411
- Mound, *McDonough* (Twp) 61455
- Mound City 62963
- Mounds 62964
- Mountain (Twp) 62946
- Mountain Glen 62920
- Mount Auburn 62547
- Mount Carbon 62966
- Mount Carmel 62863
- Mount Carroll 61053
- Mount Clair 62035
- Mount Clare 62033
- Mount Erie 62446
- Mount Greenwood (Part of Chicago)‡ 60655
- ... 60658
  For specific ZIP Codes call (888) 275-8777, or your local postmaster.
- Mount Hope (Twp) 61754
- Mount Joy 61723
- Mount Morris 61054
- Mount Olive 62069
- Mount Palatine 61334
- Mount Pleasant, *Whiteside* (Twp) 61270
- Mount Pleasant, *Union* 62912
- Mount Prospect 60056
- Mount Prospect Gardens (Part of Mount Prospect) 60056

*** Area Zip Code** **† Post Office Boxes** **‡ Postal Station** **♦ Census Designated Place** *Italic Type* **County**

Place	ZIP Code
Mount Prospect Plaza (Part of Mount Prospect)	60056
Mount Pulaski	62548
Mount Sterling	62353
Mount Vernon	62864
Mount Zion	62549
Moweaqua	62550
Mozier	62070
Mozier Landing	62045
Mt. Vernon	61025
Muddy	62965
Mulberry Grove	62262
Mulkeytown	62865
Muncie	61857
Mundelein	60060
Mundelein Ridge Estates (Part of Mundelein)	60060
Munson (Twp)	61238
Munster	61364
Murdock	61941
Murphy Acres	60435
Murphysboro	62966
Murrayville	62668
Myers Lake	62568
Mylith Park	60050
Myrtle	61047
Na-Au-Say (Twp)	60560
Nachusa	61057
Nameoki, *Madison* (Twp)	62040
Nameoki (Part of Granite City)‡	62040
Nantucket Cove (Part of Schaumburg)	60193
Naperville	60540
	60563-67
For specific ZIP Codes call (888) 275-8777, or your local postmaster.	
Naplate	61350
Naples	62665
Nashville	62263
Nason	62866
Natalie Estates (Part of Oak Forest)	60452
National Stock Yards	62071
Natrona	62682
Nauvoo	62354
Navajo Hills (Part of Palos Heights)	60463
Neadmore	62442
Near North Side (Part of Chicago)	60610-11
For specific ZIP Codes call (888) 275-8777, or your local postmaster.	
Near South Side (Part of Chicago)	60616
Nebo	62355
Nebraska (Twp)	61740
Neelys	62621
Neil Street (Part of Champaign)‡	61820
Nekoma	61490
Nelson	61058
Neoga	62447
Neponset	61345
Nerska (Part of Chicago)	60632
Nettle Creek (Twp)	60541
Neunert	62950
Nevada (Twp)	60460
Nevins	61944
Newark	60541
New Athens	62264
New Baden	62265
New Bedford	61346
New Berlin	62670
Newbern	62022
New Blossom Hill (Part of Cary)	60013
New Boston	61272
Newburg, *Pike* (Twp)	62363
Newburg, *Macon*	62501
New Burnside	62967
Newby	61938
New Camp	62921
New Canton	62356
Newcastle	62987
New Century Town (Part of Vernon Hills)	60061
New City (Part of Chicago)	60609
New City, *Sangamon*	62563
New Columbia	62943
Newcomb (Twp)	61853
New Delhi	62052
New Dennison	62959
New Douglas	62074
Newell (Twp)	61834
New Hanover	62298
New Hartford	62363
New Haven	62867
New Hebron	62454
New Holland	62671
New Lebanon	60140
New Lenox	60451
New Liberty	62910
Newman	61942
Newmansville	62612
New Memphis	62266
New Milford	61109
New Minden	62263
New Palestine	62297
New Philadelphia	61459
Newport, *Lake* (Twp)	60083
Newport (Part of Madison)	62060
New Salem, *McDonough* (Twp)	61482
New Salem, *Pike*	62357
Newton, *Whiteside* (Twp)	61250
Newton, *Jasper*	62448
Newtown, *Livingston* (Twp)	61311
Newtown, *Vermilion*	61858
New Trier (Twp)	60093
New Virginia	62951
New Windsor	61465
Niantic	62551
Niles (Twp)	60076
Niles	60714
Nilwood (Twp)	62640
Nilwood	62672
Nineteenth Avenue (Part of Melrose Park)‡	60160
Niota	62358
Nippersink Terrace	60081
Nixon (Twp)	61882
Nixon's Greenwood-Central	60025
Noble	62868
Nokomis	62075
Nora	61059
Nordic Park	60143
Nordic Woods	61010
Normal	61761
Norman (Twp)	60450
Normandale	61554
Normandy	61376
Normandy Heights	62864
Normandy Hill (Part of Northbrook)	60062
Normandy Villa (Part of Chicago Heights)	60411
Norpaul (Part of Franklin Park)	60131
Norridge	60634
	60656
For specific ZIP Codes call (888) 275-8777, or your local postmaster.	
Norris	61553
Norris City	62869
North Alton (Part of Alton)	62002
North Arm	61944
North Aurora	60542
North Barrington	60010
Northbelt Homesites (Part of Belleville)	62221
Northbrook	60062*
	60065†
Northbrook Court (Part of Northbrook)	60062
Northbrook Downtown (Part of Northbrook)‡	60062
Northbrook Knolls (Part of Northbrook)	60062
Northbrook West	60062
North Center (Part of Chicago)	60618
North Chicago	60064
North Chillicothe (Part of Chillicothe)	61523
North Dixon (Part of Dixon)	61021
Northeast (Twp)	62339
Northern (Twp)	62860
Northern Heights	61010
Northern Hills	61032
Northfield, *Cook* (Twp)	60025
Northfield, *Cook*	60093
Northfield, *Grundy*	60450
North Fork (Twp)	62979
Northgate (Part of Hanover Park)	60103
Northgate Shopping Center (Part of Aurora)	60506
North Glen Ellyn	60137
North Hampton	61523
North Henderson	61466
North Hills	60060
Northlake	60164
North Lakewood	62881
Northland Mall (Part of Sterling)	61081
North Libertyville Estates	60048
North Litchfield (Twp)	62056
Northmore (Part of Godfrey)	62035
Northmore Heights (Part of Effingham)	62401
North Mounds	62964
North Muddy (Twp)	62479
North Okaw (Twp)	61938
North Oregon	61061
North Otter (Twp)	62690
North Palmyra (Twp)	62667
North Park (Part of Chicago)	60659
North Park (Part of Machesney Park)	61115
North Park Mall (Part of Villa Park)	60181
North Pekin	61554
North Plato	60140
Northpoint Estates (Part of Bourbonnais)	60914
Northpoint Shopping Center (Part of Arlington Heights)	60004
North Prairie Acres	61953
North Riverside	60546
North Riverside Park Mall (Part of North Riverside)	60546
North Shore (Part of Crystal Lake)	60014
North Shoreland	62959
North Suburban Facility (Part of River Grove)	60199
Northtown (Part of Chicago)‡	60645
	60659
For specific ZIP Codes call (888) 275-8777, or your local postmaster.	
North University (Part of Peoria)‡	61614
North Venice (Part of Venice)	62090
Northville (Twp)	60551
Northwood	61802
Northwoods, *DeKalb*	60135
North Woods, *DuPage*	60185
Northwoods (Part of O'Fallon)	62269
Northwoods Place (Part of East Alton)	62024
Northwoods Shopping Center (Part of Peoria)	61613
Norton (Twp)	60917
Nortonville	62668
Norway	60551
Norwood, *Mercer*	61412
Norwood, *Peoria*	61604
Norwood Park, *Cook* (Twp)	60656
Norwood Park (Part of Chicago)‡	60631
Nottingham Park (Part of Bridgeview)	60638
Nottingham Woods	60119
Novak Park	60175
Nubbin Ridge	62835
Nunda (Twp)	60012
Nutwood	62031
Oak	62947
Oak Bluff Estates	61038
Oak Brook, *DuPage*	60523
Oakbrook, *Macoupin*	62626
Oakbrook Shopping Center (Part of Oak Brook)	60523
Oakbrook Terrace	60181
Oakdale (Part of Chicago)	60619
Oakdale, *Washington*	62268
Oakdale Woods	60106
Oakford	62673
Oak Forest	60452
Oak Grove	61264
Oak Hill	61517
Oak Hills	62232
Oak Hills Estates	61008
Oak Knolls	60118
Oakland (Part of Chicago)	60653
Oakland, *Schuyler* (Twp)	62681
Oakland, *Coles*	61943
Oak Lawn, *Cook*	60453*
	60454†
Oaklawn (Part of Danville)	61832
Oakley	62552
Oak Manor	60545
Oak Meadows	60185
Oak Park	60301-04
For specific ZIP Codes call (888) 275-8777, or your local postmaster.	
Oak Park South (Part of Oak Park)‡	60304
Oak Ridge	61548
Oak Run	61428
Oak Spring Woods	60048
Oakwood (Part of Westmont)	60559
Oakwood, *Henderson*	61437
Oakwood, *Peoria*	61605
Oakwood, *Vermilion*	61858
Oakwood Acres (Part of Geneseo)	61254
Oakwood Hills	60013
Oakwood Shores	60097
Obed	62510
Oblong	62449
Oconee	62553
Ocoya	61764
Odell	60460
Odgen	62863
Odin	62870
O'Fallon	62269
Ogden	61859
Ogden Park (Part of Chicago)‡	60636
Oglesby	61348
O'Hare Mail Processing Facility (Part of Chicago)	60701
Ohio	61349
Ohio Grove (Twp)	61231
Ohlman	62076
Oil Center (Part of Centralia)	62801
Oilfield	62420
Okaw (Twp)	62534
Okawville	62271
Oklahoma Addition	62451
Old Camp	62921
Old Du Quoin	62832
Oldenburg	62024
Olde Salem (Part of Hanover Park)	60103
Old Farm (Part of Naperville)	60565
Old Gilchrist	61231
Old Kane	62054
Old Marissa (Part of Marissa)	62257
Old Mill Creek	60083
Old Orchard Shopping Center (Part of Skokie)‡	60077
Old Pearl	62361
Old Ripley	62086
Old Shawneetown	62984
Old Stonington	62567
Oldtown, *McLean* (Twp)	61701
Oldtown, *Saline*	62987
Olena	61480
Olio (Twp)	61530
Olive (Twp)	62058
Olive Branch	62969
Oliver	62441
Olivet	61846
Olmsted	62970
Olney	62450
Olympia Fields	60461
Olympia Gardens (Part of Flossmoor)	60411
Olympic Terrace (Part of Naperville)	60565
Olympic Village (Part of Chicago Heights)	60411
Omaha	62871
Omega	62854
Omphghent (Twp)	62097
Onarga	60955
Oneco	61060
Oneida	61467
One Schaumburg Place (Part of Schaumburg)	60195
Ontario (Twp)	61467
Ontario Street (Part of Chicago)‡	60611
Ontarioville	60103
Opdyke	62872
Ophiem	61468
Ophir (Twp)	61342
Oquawka	61469
Ora (Twp)	62971
Oran (Twp)	62512
Orange, *Clark* (Twp)	62442
Orange, *Knox* (Twp)	61436
Orange Prairie	61614
Orangeville	61060
Oraville	62971
Orchard (Twp)	62850
Orchard Acres	60014
Orchard Estates	60187
Orchard Heights	62450
Orchard Mines	61607
Orchard Valley	60031
Orchardville	62899
Oreana	62554
Oregon	61061
Oregon-Nashua (Twp)	61061
Orel (Twp)	62895
Orient	62874
Orion, *Fulton* (Twp)	61520
Orion, *Henry*	61273
Orland (Twp)	60462
Orland Hills, *Cook*	60462
Orland Hills (Westhaven)	60477
Orland Park	60462
	60467
For specific ZIP Codes call (888) 275-8777, or your local postmaster.	
Orland Park Place (Part of Orland Park)	60462
Orland Square (Part of Orland Park)	60462
Orleans	62601
Orleans Terrace (Part of Addison)	60101
Orvil (Twp)	62635
Orville H. Browning (Part of Quincy)‡	62301
Osage, *La Salle* (Twp)	61377
Osage, *Franklin*	62983
Osbernville	62513
Osborn	61257
Osceola (Twp)	61421
Osceola	61345
Osco (Twp)	61274
Osco	61274
Oskaloosa	62899
Osman	61843
Ospur	61727
Ossami Lake (Part of Morton)	61550
Oswego	60543
Otego (Twp)	62418
Ottawa	61350
Otter Creek, *Jersey* (Twp)	62052
Otter Creek, *La Salle* (Twp)	61364
Otterville	62037
Otto	60922
Otto Mall (Part of Chicago Heights)‡	60411
Ottville	61362
Outter Creek	62031
Owaneco	62555
Owego (Twp)	61764
Owen (Twp)	61103
Oxford (Twp)	61413
Oxville	62621
Ozark	62972
Pacesetter Park (Part of South Holland)	60473
Paderborn	62298
Padua	61737
Painesville	62948
Palatine (Twp)	60067
Palatine	60067
	60074
	60078
	60094-95
For specific ZIP Codes call (888) 275-8777, or your local postmaster.	
Palatine Processing & Distribution Center (Part of Palatine)‡	60095
Palermo	61876
Palestine, *Woodford* (Twp)	61771
Palestine, *Crawford*	62451
Palmer	62556
Palmyra, *Lee*	61021
Palmyra, *Macoupin*	62674

Place	ZIP Code
Paloma	62359
Palos (Twp)	60464
Palos Heights	60463
Palos Hills	60465
Palos Park	60464
Palos Westgate (Part of Palos Heights)	60463
Palsgrove	61053
Pam Anne Estates (Part of Glenview)	60025
Pana	62557
Panama	62077
Pankeyville	62946
Panola	61738
Panther Creek (Twp)	62627
Papineau	60956
Paradise	61938
Paradise Acres	62918
Paris	61944
Park City	60085
Parker, *Clark* (Twp)	62474
Parker, *Johnson*	62922
Parkersburg	62452
Parkfield Terrace	62206
Park Forest	60466
Park Hills (Part of Effingham)	62401
Parkhome (Part of Cicero)	60804
Park Lane	60964
Park Meadows (Part of Rolling Meadows)	60008
Park Ridge	60068
Parkville	61872
Parkway (Part of North Riverside)	60546
Parkwood (Part of Elgin)	60120
Parkwood Village (Part of Elgin)	60120
Parnell	61842
Parrish	62890
Parrish Addition	62930
Partridge (Twp)	61545
Partridge Hill (Part of Hoffman Estates)	60194
Passport	62868
Patoka	62875
Patterson	62078
Patterson Heights (Part of Godfrey)	62035
Patterson Springs	61919
Patton, *Ford* (Twp)	60957
Patton, *Wabash*	62863
Pattonsburg	61309
Paulton	62959
Pavillion	60560
Pawnee	62558
Paw Paw, *DeKalb* (Twp)	60518
Paw Paw, *Lee*	61353
Paxton	60957
Paynes Point	61015
Payson	62360
Peach Orchard (Twp)	60952
Pea Ridge (Twp)	62375
Pearl (Twp)	62361
Pearl	62361
Pearl City	61062
Pecan Grove	62031
Pecatonica	61063
Peerless	60544
Pekin (Twp)	61554
Pekin	61554*
	61555†
Pekin Heights (Part of Pekin)	61554
Pekin Mall (Part of Pekin)	61554
Pella (Twp)	60959
Pembroke (Twp)	60964
Pendleton (Twp)	62810
Penfield	61862
Penn, *Shelby* (Twp)	62550
Penn, *Stark* (Twp)	61421
Pennsylvania (Twp)	62664
Penrose	61081
Peoria	61601-07
	61612-56
For specific ZIP Codes call (888) 275-8777, or your local postmaster.	
Peoria Heights	61614
Peotone	60468
Pepper Tree	60067
Pequot (Part of Coal City)	60416
Percy	62272
Perdueville	60957
Perks	62973
Perry	62362
Perryton (Twp)	61279
Perryville	61016
Persifer (Twp)	61436
Peru	61354
Peru Mall (Part of Peru)	61354
Pesotum	61863
Petersburg, *Menard*	62675
Petersburg (Part of O'Fallon)	62269
Peters Creek	62931
Petite Lake	60002
Petrolia	62417
Petty (Twp)	62466
Pheasant Creek (Part of Northbrook)	60062
Pheasant Hollow	60187
Pheasant Meadows	60401
Pheasant Ridge (Part of Mokena)	60448
Pheasant Ridge, *Will*	60544
Phelps	62240
Phenix (Twp)	61254
Philadelphia	62612
Phillips (Twp)	62827
Phillipstown	62827
Philo	61864
Phinney	61821
Phoenix	60426
Piasa, *Jersey* (Twp)	62012
Piasa, *Macoupin*	62079
Piasa Hills	62035
Picadilly Terrace	60514
Pickaway (Twp)	61914
Pierce (Twp)	60151
Pierceburg	62449
Pierron	62273
Pierson	61929
Piety Hill	61348
Pigeon Grove (Twp)	60924
Pike, *Livingston* (Twp)	61726
Pike, *Pike*	62370
Pilot, *Kankakee* (Twp)	60941
Pilot, *Vermilion* (Twp)	61831
Pilot Grove (Twp)	62318
Pilot Knob (Twp)	62263
Pilsen (Part of Chicago)‡	60608
Pinckneyville	62274
Pine Creek (Twp)	61064
Pinecrest	60435
Pine Meadow (Part of Bolingbrook)	60440
Pine Ridge	61254
Pine Rock (Twp)	61015
Pingree Grove	60140
Pinkstaff	62439
Pin Oak (Twp)	62025
Pioneer Acres	61025
Pioneer Terrace	60115
Piopolis	62859
Piper City	60959
Pisgah	62650
Pistakee Bay	60050
Pistakee Heights (Part of Fox Lake)	60050
Pistakee Highlands	60050
Pistakee Hills	60050
Pistaqua Heights	60050
Pitchin	60924
Pitman (Twp)	62572
Pittsburg, *Fayette*	62471
Pittsburg, *Williamson*	62974
Pittsfield	62363
Pittwood	60970
Pixley (Twp)	62868
Plainfield	60544
Plainfield Acres	60544
Plainview	62676
Plainville	62365
Plano	60545
Plato (Twp)	60123
Plato Center	60170
Plattville	60560
Playfield (Part of Crestwood)	60445
Plaza (Part of Belleville)	62223
Pleasant (Twp)	61441
Pleasant Dale (Part of Burr Ridge)	60525
Pleasantdale Estates	60439
Pleasant Grove, *Coles* (Twp)	62440
Pleasant Grove, *Johnson*	62912
Pleasant Hill, *DuPage*	60188
Pleasant Hill, *Jackson*	62901
Pleasant Hill, *McLean*	61753
Pleasant Hill, *Pike*	62366
Pleasant Hills	60172
Pleasant Mound	62284
Pleasant Plains	62677
Pleasant Ridge, *Livingston* (Twp)	61741
Pleasant Ridge, *Madison*	62062
Pleasant Run (Part of Wheeling)	60090
Pleasant Vale (Twp)	62356
Pleasant Valley (Twp)	61085
Pleasant View, *Macon* (Twp)	62513
Pleasant View, *Schuyler*	62681
Plumfield	62896
Plum Grove Countryside (Part of Palatine)	60067
Plum Grove Estates	60007
Plum Grove Hills (Part of Rolling Meadows)	60008
Plum Grove Village (Part of Rolling Meadows)	60008
Plum Grove Woods	60067
Plum Hill	62214
Plum Hollow	61021
Plymouth	62367
Plymouth Farms (Part of Vernon Hills)	60061
Poag	62025
Pocahontas	62275
Point Pleasant (Twp)	61473
Polk (Twp)	62626
Polo	61064
Pomona	62975
Pond	62995
Pontiac, *Livingston*	61764
Pontiac (Part of Fairview Heights)	62232
Pontiac Station (Part of Fairview Heights)	62208
Pontoon Beach	62040
Pontoosuc	62330
Pope (Twp)	62875
Poplar City	62633
Poplar Grove, *Boone*	61065
Poplar Grove, *Rock Island*	61244
Portage Park (Part of Chicago)	60641
Port Byron	61275
Portland	61277
Port Ridge (Part of Lockport)	60441
Posen, *Cook*	60469
Posen, *Washington*	62263
Posey	62231
Post Oak	62418
Potomac	61865
Pottawatawi Highlands (Part of Tinley Park)	60477
Pottstown	61614
Powder Creek	62223
Powder Mill Woods	62220
Powellton	62358
Prairie, *Crawford* (Twp)	62442
Prairie, *Edgar* (Twp)	61924
Prairie, *Hancock* (Twp)	62321
Prairie, *Shelby* (Twp)	62463
Prairie, *Randolph*	62278
Prairie Center	61350
Prairie City	61470
Prairie Creek (Twp)	62635
Prairie Du Long (Twp)	62243
Prairie du Pont	62240
Prairie du Rocher	62277
Prairie Estates	62675
Prairie Green (Twp)	60942
Prairie Grove	60050
Prairie Home	62550
Prairieton (Twp)	62550
Prairietown	62097
Prairie View	60069
Prairie View Plaza (Part of Morton Grove)	60053
Prairieville	61021
Preemption	61276
Prentice	62612
Presswood Hills	62274
Prestbury	60506
Preston, *Richland* (Twp)	62450
Preston, *Randolph*	62242
Preston Heights♦	60431
Prestwick	60423
Prickett (Part of Edwardsville)	62025
Princeton	61356
Princeville	61559
Proctor	60936
Prophetstown	61277
Prospect	61866
Prospect Heights	60070
Prospect Meadows (Part of Mount Prospect)	60056
Prospect Park (Part of Fairview Heights)	62208
Providence	61368
Provincetown (Part of Country Club Hills)	60478
Proving Ground	61074
Proviso (Twp)	60160
Prudential Plaza (Part of Chicago)‡	60601
Pruett	62458
Pulaski	62976
Pulleys Mill	62939
Pullman (Part of Chicago)	60628
Pullman Junction (Part of Chicago)	60617
Putman (Twp)	61427
Putnam	61560
Quarry (Twp)	62037
Quatoga	62035
Quincy	62301-06
For specific ZIP Codes call (888) 275-8777, or your local postmaster.	
Quincy Mall (Part of Quincy)	62301
Quiver (Twp)	62644
Quiver Beach	62644
Raccoon (Twp)	62801
Raddle	62950
Radford	62550
Radnor (Twp)	61525
Radom	62876
Rainbow Hills	60174
Rakers Addition	62216
Raleigh	62977
Ramona Place (Part of Godfrey)	62035
Ramsey	62080
Randall Ridge (Part of Elgin)	60123
Randhurst (Part of Mount Prospect)	60056
Randolph	61745
Range	62864
Rankin	60960
Ransom	60470
Ransom Ridge Estates (Part of Park Ridge)	60068
Rantoul	61866
Rapatee	61544
Rapids City	61278
Rardin	61920
Raritan	61471
Rasmussen Addition	60936
Raven	61924
Ravenswood (Part of Chicago)‡	60625
Ravinia (Part of Highland Park)‡	60035
Ravinia Park (Part of Highland Park)	60035
Rawalts	61520
Rawlins (Twp)	61036
Ray	62681
Raymond, *Champaign* (Twp)	61852
Raymond, *Montgomery*	62560
Reader	62630
Reading	61311
Rector (Twp)	62930
Red Bud	62278
Reddick	60961
Redmon	61949
Red Oak	61032
Red Oak Terrace (Part of Highland Park)	60035
Reed (Twp)	60408
Reed City	61547
Reeds Station	62924
Rees	62638
Reevesville	62943
Regency Grove	60515
Regency Terrace (Part of Bloomingdale)	60108
Reilly	60960
Reily Lake	62241
Rellswood Hills	61008
Renault	62279
Renchville	61523
Rend City	62812
Reno	62246
Rentchler	62221
Reseda (Part of Palatine)	60067
Resthaven	60481
Reynolds, *Lee* (Twp)	61006
Reynolds, *Rock Island*	61279
Reynoldsburg	62991
Reynoldsville	62952
Rice, *Jo Daviess* (Twp)	61036
Rice, *Perry*	62274
Rice Lake	61401
Rich (Twp)	60471
Richards, *Grundy*	60450
Richards, *La Salle*	61364
Richardson	60151
Richardson Estates	61802
Richfield	62365
Richland, *La Salle* (Twp)	61334
Richland, *Marshall* (Twp)	61570
Richland, *Shelby* (Twp)	62465
Richland, *Sangamon*	62677
Richland Grove (Twp)	61281
Richmond	60071
Richton Hills (Part of Richton Park)	60471
Richton Park	60471
Richview	62877
Richwood (Twp)	62031
Richwoods, *Peoria* (Twp)	61614
Richwoods, *Crawford*	62451
Ricks (Twp)	62546
Riddle Hill	62707
Ridge (Twp)	62565
Ridgecrest	60450
Ridge Farm	61870
Ridgefield	60012
Ridgeland (Twp)	60968
Ridgemoor (Part of Willowbrook)	60521
Ridge Prairie Heights (Part of O'Fallon)	62269
Ridgeville	60955
Ridgewood (Part of Western Springs)	60558
Ridgewood East	60452
Ridgewood West (Part of Oak Forest)	60452
Ridgway	62979
Ridott	61067
Rieuf's Meadows	61341
Riffel	62858
Riggston	62694
Riley (Twp)	61038
Riley Center	60152
Rinard	62878
Ring Neck	60543
Ringwood	60072
Rio	61472
Ripley	62353
Rising Sun	62821
Ritchason Addition	62896
Ritchie	60481
Riverair	62035
Rivercrest Center (Part of Crestwood)	60607
Riverdale, *Cook*	60827
Riverdale, *Winnebago*	61073
River Forest	60305
River Glen	60010
River Grange Lakes	60175
River Grove	60171
River Heights (Part of Danville)	61832
River Isle	60954
River Oaks Center (Part of Calumet City)	60409
River Reach	61008
River Ridge	60560
River Road	61067
Riverside, *Adams* (Twp)	62301
Riverside, *Cook*	60546
Riverside Island (Part of Fox Lake)	60020
Riverside Lawns	60546
Riverside Park	60050
Riverton	62561
Riverview, *Carroll*	61285
Riverview, *Lee*	61021
Riverview, *Whiteside*	61071
Riverview Heights	60543
Riverwoods	60015
Rivoli (Twp)	61465
Roaches	62898
Roachtown	62260
Roanoke	61561
Robbins	60472
Robbs	62985
Robein (Part of East Peoria)	61611
Roberts, *Marshall* (Twp)	61375
Roberts, *Ford*	60962

*** Area Zip Code** **† Post Office Boxes** **‡ Postal Station** **♦ Census Designated Place** *Italic Type* **County**

Robin Hill (Part of Joliet) 60431
Robinson 62454
Rob Roy Country Club (Part of Prospect Heights) 60070
Roby 62545
Rochelle 61068
Rochester, *Sangamon* 62563
Rochester, *Wabash* 62863
Rock 62938
Rockbridge 62081
Rock City 61070
Rock Creek, *Hancock* (Twp) 62321
Rock Creek, *Hardin* 62919
Rock Creek-Lima (Twp) 61046
Rockdale 60436
Rockdale Junction (Part of Crest Hill) 60436
Rock Falls 61071
Rockford 61101-10
61112-14
61125-26
For specific ZIP Codes call (888) 275-8777, or your local postmaster.
Rockford Broadway (Part of Rockford)‡ 61106
Rockford Downtown (Part of Rockford)‡ 61101
Rockford Main (Part of Rockford)‡ 61125
Rockgate Estates 62035
Rock Grove 61070
Rock Island (Twp) 61201
Rock Island 61201-04
For specific ZIP Codes call (888) 275-8777, or your local postmaster.
Rock Island Arsenal 61299
Rockport 62370
Rock River Terrace 61010
Rock Run (Twp) 61019
Rockton 61072
Rockvale (Twp) 61061
Rock Vale Heights 61061
Rockville (Twp) 60950
Rockwell (Part of La Salle) 61301
Rockwood 62280
Rocky Run (Twp) 62379
Rodden 61041
Rogers (Twp) 60946
Rogers Park (Part of Chicago)‡ 60626
60660
For specific ZIP Codes call (888) 275-8777, or your local postmaster.
Rohrer 62692
Rolling Acres (Part of Peoria)‡ 61614
Rolling Acres (Part of Rantoul) 61866
Rolling Green 61938
Rolling Hills, *Clinton* 62293
Rolling Hills, *Piatt* 61884
Rolling Meadows 60008
Rollo 60518
Rome, *Jefferson* (Twp) 62830
Rome, *Peoria*♦ 61562
Rome Heights 61523
Romeoville 60446
Romine (Twp) 62849
Rondout 60044
Ron Lee 60431
Roodhouse 62082
Rooks Creek (Twp) 61764
Rooney Heights 60435
Roosevelt Road (Part of Chicago) 60607
Roots 62261
Root Spring 60013
Ropers Landing 62938
Rosamond 62083
Roscoe 61073
Rose (Twp) 62565
Rosebud 62938
Rosecrans 60083
Rosedale 62031
Rosefield (Twp) 61529
Rose Hill (Part of Chicago) 60640
Rose Hill, *DuPage* 60515
Rose Hill, *Jasper* 62432
Rose Lake (Part of Fairmont City) 62201
Roseland (Part of Chicago)‡ 60628
Roselle 60172

Rosemont, *Cook* 60018
Rosemont (Part of Washington Park) 62204
Roseville 61473
Rosiclare 62982
Roslyn 62462
Ross, *Edgar* (Twp) 61924
Ross, *Pike* (Twp) 62366
Ross, *Vermilion* (Twp) 60963
Rossville 60963
Round Barn (Part of Champaign)‡ 61821
Round Grove, *Livingston* (Twp) 60420
Round Grove, *Whiteside* 61270
Round Knob 62960
Round Lake 60073
Round Lake Beach 60073
Round Lake Heights 60073
Round Lake Park 60073
Round Prairie 62823
Rountree (Twp) 62094
Rowe 61764
Roxana 62084
Roxanne 62901
Roxbury 61353
Royal 61871
Royal Lake Resort, *Bond* 62262
Royal Lake Resort, *Clinton* 62231
Royal Lakes, *Macoupin* 62685
Royal Lakes, *Marion* 62870
Royal Oaks 61032
Royalton 62983
Rozetta (Twp) 61447
Rozetta 61469
Rubicon (Twp) 62044
Rudement 62946
Ruma 62278
Rural, *Rock Island* (Twp) 61240
Rural, *Shelby* (Twp) 62510
Rush (Twp) 61085
Rushville 62681
Russell (Twp) 47591
Russell 60075
Russellville 62439
Rutland, *Kane* (Twp) 60120
Rutland, *La Salle* (Twp) 61341
Rutland, *La Salle* 61358
Rutledge (Twp) 61752
Ruyle (Twp) 62063
Sabina 61722
Sacramento 62835
Sadorus 61872
Sag Bridge 60439
Saidora 62627
Sailor Springs 62879
St. Albans (Twp) 62380
St. Anne 60964
St. Anne Woods 60964
St. Augustine 61474
St. Charles 60174-75
For specific ZIP Codes call (888) 275-8777, or your local postmaster.
St. Clair (Twp) 62221
St. Clair Square (Part of Fairview Heights) 62208
St. David 61563
St. Elmo 62458
St. Francis (Twp) 62467
St. Francisville 62460
St. George 60914
St. Jacob 62281
St. James 62857
St. James Estates (Part of Sauk Village) 60411
St. Joe 62298
St. Johns 62832
St. Joseph 61873
St. Joseph's 60557
St. Libory 62282
Ste. Marie 62459
St. Mary 62367
St. Marys 62401
Saint Morgan 62293
St. Paul 62885
St. Peter 62880
St. Regis (Part of Lombard) 60148
St. Rose (Twp) 62293
St. Rose 62230
Salem, *Carroll* (Twp) 61046
Salem, *Knox* (Twp) 61572
Salem, *Marion* 62881
Salina (Twp) 60913
Saline (Twp) 62249

Saline Landing 62919
Saline Mines 62984
Salisbury 62677
Salt Creek (Twp) 62664
Samoth 62943
Samsville 62476
Sand Barrens 62460
Sandburg Mall (Part of Galesburg) 61401
Sandburg Village (Part of Chicago) 60610
Sandoval 62882
Sandpebble Walk (Part of Wheeling) 60090
Sand Prairie (Twp) 61534
Sandra Heights (Part of Chicago Heights) 60411
Sand Ridge 62940
Sandusky 62988
Sandwich 60548
Sangamon, *Piatt* (Twp) 61884
Sangamon, *Macon* 62521
Sangamon Heights 61853
Sangamon Valley (Twp) 62618
San Jose 62682
Santa Anna (Twp) 61842
Santa Fe (Twp) 62218
Santa Fe Park 60521
Saratoga, *Grundy* (Twp) 60450
Saratoga, *Marshall* (Twp) 61537
Saratoga, *Union* 62906
Sargent (Twp) 61943
Sato 62907
Sauganash (Part of Chicago) 60646
Sauget 62201
Sauk Village 60411
Saunemin 61769
Savanna 61074
Savoy 61874
Sawyerville 62085
Say Brook (Part of Naperville) 60563
Saybrook, *McLean* 61770
Scales Mound 61075
Scarboro 60553
Schaeferville 61554
Schapville 61028
Schaumburg 60159
60168
60173
60192-95
For specific ZIP Codes call (888) 275-8777, or your local postmaster.
Schaumburg Green (Part of Schaumburg) 60194
Scheller 62883
Schiller Park 60176
Schoper 62686
Schram City 62049
Schrodt 62863
Schuline 62286
Schwer 60953
Sciota 61475
Scioto Mills 61076
Scotland, *McDonough* (Twp) 61455
Scotland, *Edgar* 61924
Scotsboro 62959
Scott, *Champaign* (Twp) 61875
Scott, *Ogle* (Twp) 61020
Scott Air Force Base 62225
Scottsburg 61422
Scottswood 61801
Scottville 62683
Seaton 61476
Seatonville 61359
Seco Park 60115
Secor 61771
Seeger (Part of Des Plaines) 60016
Seehorn 62343
Sefton 62418
Selby 61322
Selmaville 62881
Seminary, *Fayette* (Twp) 62471
Seminary, *Richland* 62450
Senachwine (Twp) 61560
Seneca, *McHenry* (Twp) 60098
Seneca, *La Salle* 61360
Sepo 61542
Serena 60549
Sesser 62884
Seven Hickory (Twp) 61920
Seville 61477

Seward, *Kendall* (Twp) 60447
Seward, *Winnebago* 61077
Sexson Corner 61928
Seymour 61875
Shabbona 60550
Shabbona Grove 60518
Shadetree (Part of Oak Forest) 60452
Shadow Lawn 60954
Shady Acres 62665
Shady Beach 61254
Shady Grove 62910
Shady Hill 60010
Shafter 62471
Shakerag 62951
Shale City 61231
Shanghai City 61412
Shangrila 61068
Shannon 61078
Sharon (Twp) 62080
Sharp Rock Falls 62907
Sharpsburg 62568
Shattuc 62283
Shaw 60073
Shawnee (Twp) 62984
Shawneetown 62984
Shaws 61310
Shaws Point (Twp) 62511
Sheffield 61361
Sheffield Park (Part of Schaumburg) 60194
Shelbyville 62565
Sheldon 60966
Sheldons Grove 62624
Shepherd 62343
Sherburnville 60940
Sheridan, *Logan* (Twp) 62671
Sheridan, *La Salle* 60551
Sheridan Village (Part of Peoria)‡ 61614
Sherman, *Mason* (Twp) 62633
Sherman, *Sangamon* 62684
Sherrard 61281
Sherwood Forest (Part of Peoria) 61614
Sherwood Forest (Part of Wood Dale) 60191
Sherwood Oaks 60120
Shields, *Lake* (Twp) 60045
Shields, *Jefferson* 62851
Shiloh, *Edgar* (Twp) 61917
Shiloh, *Jefferson* (Twp) 62864
Shiloh, *St. Clair* 62221
62269
For specific ZIP Codes call (888) 275-8777, or your local postmaster.
Shiloh Hill 62916
Shiloh Valley (Twp) 62221
Shipman 62685
Shippingsport 61348
Shires of Inverness (Part of Inverness) 60067
Shirland 61079
Shirley 61772
Shoal Creek (Twp) 62086
Shobonier 62885
Shokokon 61425
Shore Acres 61071
Shore Heights Manor 60543
Shore Hills 60097
Shores of Shining Waters (Part of Carol Stream) 60188
Shorewood, *Kankakee* 60964
Shorewood, *Will* 60435
Shull's Urban Estates (Part of Rantoul) 61866
Shumway 62461
Sibley 61773
Sicily 62558
Sidell 61876
Sidney 61877
Sigel 62462
Signal Hill 62223
Silver Creek (Twp) 61032
Silver Lake 60013
Silver Ridge 61061
Silvis 61282
Silvis Heights (Part of Silvis) 61282
Simpson, *Johnson* 62985
Simpson, *White* 62827
Sims 62886
Sims Western Acres 62707
Sinclair 62650
Six Mile (Twp) 62999
Sixty Six Court 60452
Skokie 60076-77
For specific ZIP Codes call (888) 275-8777, or your local postmaster.

Slap Out 62849
Sleepy Hollow 60118
Smallwood (Twp) 62448
Smithboro 62284
Smithfield 61477
Smithshire 61478
Smithton 62285
Smithville 61536
Snicarte 62617
Sollitt 60401
Solon Mills 60080
Somer (Twp) 61820
Somerset, *Jackson* (Twp) 62966
Somerset (Part of Crystal Lake) 60014
Somerset (Part of Hinsdale) 60521
Somerset, *Saline* 62946
Somonauk 60552
Songer (Twp) 62899
Sonora (Twp) 62354
Sorento 62086
South Addison (Part of Villa Park) 60181
South Barrington 60010
South Beloit 61080
South Chicago (Part of Chicago)‡ 60617
South Chicago Heights 60411
South Crouch (Twp) 62859
South Danville (Part of Danville) 61832
South Deering (Part of Chicago) 60617
South Dixon (Twp) 61021
South Elgin 60177
Southern (Twp) 62939
Southern Hills 62901
Southern View 62703
South Fillmore (Twp) 62032
South Flannigan (Twp) 62890
South Fork (Twp) 62540
South Grove (Twp) 60146
South Holland 60473
South Homer (Twp) 61849
South Hurricane (Twp) 62011
South Jacksonville 62650
South Litchfield (Twp) 62056
South Lockport (Part of Lockport) 60441
South Macon (Twp) 62544
South Moline (Twp) 61244
South Moline Gardens (Part of Moline) 61265
Southmore (Part of Godfrey) 62035
Southmore Heights 62411
South Mounds (Part of Mounds) 62964
South Muddy (Twp) 62448
South Ottawa (Twp) 61350
South Otter (Twp) 62674
South Palmyra (Twp) 62674
Southpark Mall (Part of Moline) 61265
South Pekin 61564
Southport 61517
South Rock Island (Twp) 61201
South Rome 61523
South Ross (Twp) 61848
South Roxana 62087
South Shore (Part of Chicago)‡ 60649
South Standard 62686
South Streator 61364
South Twigg (Twp) 62817
South Waukegan (Part of North Chicago) 60064
Southwest (Twp) 62466
Southwest Station (Part of Springfield)‡ 62704
South Wheatland (Twp) 62532
South Wilmington 60474
Space Valley 60521
Spankey 62031
Sparks Hill 62931
Sparland 61565
Sparta, *Knox* (Twp) 61488
Sparta, *Randolph* 62286
Spaulding, *Cook* 60120
Spaulding, *Sangamon* 62561
Speer 61479
Spencer 60451
Spencer Heights 62964
Spillertown 62959
Spin Lake 61732
Sportsman Lake 62881
Spring (Twp) 61008

Spring Arbor Lake 62901
Spring Bay 61611
Spring Creek (Twp) 62355
Springerton 62887
Springfield (Twp) 62702
Springfield 62701-94
For specific ZIP Codes call (888) 275-8777, or your local postmaster.
Spring Garden 62846
Spring Grove, *Warren* (Twp) 61412
Spring Grove, *McHenry* 60081
Springhaven (Part of Godfrey) 62035
Spring Hill 61250
Spring Hill Mall (Part of West Dundee) 60118
Spring Lake, *Champaign* 61853
Spring Lake, *Tazewell* 61546
Spring Point (Twp) 62462
Spring Valley 61362
Squaw Grove (Twp) 60520
Squaw Prairie Estate 61008
Stable 62918
Stainfield 60545
Staley 61822
Standard 61363
Standard City 62686
Stanford, *Clay* (Twp) 62824
Stanford, *McLean* 61774
Stanton (Twp) 61873
Stanton Point 60041
Stark 61559
Starks 60140
Starnes 62702
State Line 62423
State Park Place 62201
State Street (Part of Chicago) 60628
Station No.5 (Part of Joliet)‡ 60435
Staunton 62088
Stavanger 61360
Steel City 62812
Steeleville 62288
Steeple Run 60540
Steger 60475
Stelle 60919
Sterling 61081
Sterling Place (Part of Caseyville) 62232
Steuben (Twp) 61565
Stevenson (Twp) 62881
Steward 60553
Stewardson 62463
Stickney 60402
Stillman Valley 61084
Stillmeadow 60119
Stillwell 62380
Stiritz 62896
Stites (Twp) 62059
Stockland 60967
Stockton 61085
Stock Yards (Part of Chicago)‡ 60609
Stolletown 62231
Stone 62931
Stone Church 62214
Stonefort, *Saline* (Twp) 62987
Stonefort, *Williamson* 62987
Stonehenge 60178
Stonelake (Part of Woodstock) 60098
Stone Park 60165
Stoneyville 61350
Stonington 62567
Stookey (Twp) 62221
Storeyland 62035
Storybrook 60512
Stoy 62464
Strasburg 62465
Stratford 61064
Stratford Park 61821
Stratford Square (Part of Bloomingdale) 60108
Stratton, *Edgar* (Twp) 61944
Stratton, *Jefferson* 62814
Strawberry Hill 61270
Strawn 61775
Streamwood 60107
Streator 61364
Streator Junction (Part of Eureka) 61530
Stringtown 62450
Stronghurst 61480
Stubblefield 62246
Sublette 61367
Suburban Estates 60515
Suburban Heights 62801
Suez (Twp) 61412
Sugar Brook (Part of Bolingbrook) 60440
Sugar Creek (Twp) 62293
Sugar Grove, *Kane* 60554
Sugar Grove, *Mercer* 61231
Sugar Island 60922
Sugar Loaf, *St. Clair* (Twp) 62240
Sugar Loaf (Part of Dupo) 62240
Sullivan, *Livingston* (Twp) 60929
Sullivan, *Moultrie* 61951
Sullivant (Twp) 61773
Summerdale (Part of Chicago) 60640
Summerfield 62289
Summerhill (Part of Northbrook) 60062
Summer Hill (Part of Elgin) 60120
Summer Hill, *Pike* 62363
Summerlakes (Part of Warrenville) 60555
Summersville (Part of Mount Vernon) 62864
Summerville 62063
Summit, *Effingham* (Twp) 62461
Summit, *Cook* 60501
Summit-Argo (Part of Summit) 60501
Summit Heights 62089
Summum 61501
Sumner, *Kankakee* (Twp) 60940
Sumner, *Warren* (Twp) 61453
Sumner, *Lawrence* 62466
Sumpter (Twp) 62468
Sunbeam 61231
Sunbury 61313
Sunfield 62832
Sunny Acres, *Champaign* 61853
Sunny Acres, *Kankakee* 60950
Sunny Crest 60430
Sunnydale 61021
Sunny Hill 61273
Sunny Hills Estates 60515
Sunnyland (Part of Washington) 61571
Sunny Land (Part of Crest Hill) 60435
Sunnyside (Part of Johnsburg) 60050
Sunnyside (Part of Herrin) 62948
Sunnyside Acres 62531
Sunrise Ridge (Part of Romeoville) 60441
Sun River Terrace 60964
Sunset Acres, *Lake* 60048
Sunset Acres, *Stephenson* 61032
Sunset Harbor 62959
Sunset Hills 60172
Sunset Lake 62640
Sutter 62373
Sutton 60010
Sutton Point (Part of Northbrook) 60062
Swan (Twp) 61473
Swan Creek 61473
Swansea 62221
Swanwick 62237
Swedona 61262
Sweetwater 62642
Swiss Valley (Part of Crete) 60417
Swissville (Part of Dixon) 61021
Swygert 61764
Sycamore 60178
Sylvan Hill 60462
Sylvan Lake 60060
Symerton 60481
Symmes (Twp) 61944
Table Grove 61482
Tabor 61778
Taggert Woods 62626
Talbott 61546
Talkington (Twp) 62692
Tall Trees (Part of Glenview) 60025
Tallula 62688
Tamalco 62253
Tamarac (Part of Flossmoor) 60422
Tamaroa 62888
Tamms 62988
Tampico 61283
Tanbark (Part of Tinley Park) 60477
Tanglewood (Part of Hanover Park) 60103
Tate (Twp) 62935
Tatumville 62988
Taylor (Twp) 61021
Taylor Ridge 61284
Taylor Springs 62089
Taylorville 62568
Techny (Part of Northbrook) 60082
Teheran 62664
Temple Hill 62938
Tenerelli 60511
Tennessee 62374
Terra Cotta 60014
Terre Haute 61454
Teutopolis 62467
Texas (Twp) 61727
Texas City 62930
Texico 62889
Thackeray 62859
Thawville 60968
Thayer 62689
Thebes 62990
Thebes Junction (Part of Thebes) 62990
The Burg 61318
The Clusters (Part of Bolingbrook) 60440
The Covered Bridges (Part of Carol Stream) 60188
The Fairway of Country Lakes (Part of Naperville) 60563
The Greens of Woodgate (Part of Matteson) 60443
The Grove Shopping Center (Part of Elk Grove Village) 60007
The Knolls 60175
The Laurels (Part of Justice) 60458
The Ledges 61073
The Meadows 60532
The Old Farm 61021
The Quarry (Part of Hodgkins) 60525
Third Lake 60046
Thomas 61283
Thomasboro 61878
Thomas Addition 61364
Thomasville 62533
Thompson (Twp) 61001
Thompson Addition 61241
Thompsonville 62890
Thomson 61285
Thornhill (Part of Carol Stream) 60188
Thornton 60476
Thornton Junction (Part of South Holland) 60473
Thornwilde (Part of Warrenville) 60555
Thunderbird Lake 62012
Tice 62675
Ticona 61370
Tierra Grande (Part of Country Club Hills) 60478
Tilden 62292
Tilton 61833
Timber (Twp) 61533
Timberbrook 61254
Timbercrest (Part of Schaumburg) 60194
Timber Lake, *Carroll* 61053
Timber Lake, *Lake* 60010
Timberlake Estate 62568
Timberlake Estates 60521
Timberlake Village (Part of Mount Prospect) 60056
Timber Lane 61008
Timberline 60435
Timber Ridge 60190
Timber Terrace 60115
Timber Trails (Part of Oak Brook) 60523
Timber View 61801
Timberview 61853
Time 62363
Timewell 62375
Timothy 62428
Tinley Park 60477
Tinley Terrace (Part of Tinley Park) 60477
Tioga 62351
Tipton 62298
Tiskilwa 61368
Todds Mill 62274
Todds Point 61914
Toledo 62468
Tolono 61880
Toluca 61369
Tomahawk Bluff 61301
Tompkins (Twp) 61447
Toms Prairie 62837
Tonica 61370
Tonti 62881
Topeka 61567
Toronto 62707
Toulon 61483
Tovey 62570
Towanda 61776
Tower Hill 62571
Tower Lakes 60010
Town and Country 62901
Towne Oaks 61535
Tradewinds 60115
Trago Lake 62839
Tremont, *Madison* 62035
Tremont, *Tazewell* 61568
Trenton 62293
Trenton Corners 61428
Trilla 62469
Trimble 62454
Triple Lance Heights 62901
Tri-State Village 60521
Triumph 61371
Triumvera 60025
Trivoli 61569
Trout Valley 60013
Trowbridge 62447
Troxel 60151
Troy, *Will* (Twp) 60435
Troy, *Madison* 62294
Troy Grove 61372
Tru Lock Acres 61455
Trumbull 62821
Truro (Twp) 61489
Tullamore (Part of Mundelein) 60060
Tunbridge (Twp) 61749
Tunnel Hill 62991
Turnberry 60014
Tuscarora 61607
Tuscola 61953
Twelvemile Corner 61318
Twenty-Second Street (Part of Chicago)‡ 60616
Twigg (Twp) 62829
Twilight Terrace 62221
Twin City (Part of Champaign) 61801
Twin Grove 61704
Twin Lakes 62294
Twin Oaks (Part of Joliet) 60431
Tyrone (Twp) 62822
Udina 60123
Ulah 61238
Ullin 62992
Union, *Cumberland* (Twp) 62428
Union, *Effingham* (Twp) 62424
Union, *Fulton* (Twp) 61415
Union, *Livingston* (Twp) 60460
Union, *Logan* 62635
Union, *McHenry* 60180
Union Center 62428
Union Grove 61270
Union Hill, *Kankakee* 60969
Union Hill (Part of Fairview Heights) 62232
Union Stock Yards (Part of Chicago) 60609
Uniontown 61531
Unionville, *Massac* 62910
Unionville, *Vermilion* 61883
Unionville, *Whiteside* 61270
Unity, *Piatt* (Twp) 61913
Unity, *Alexander* 62993
University (Part of Urbana)† 61801
University Heights (Part of Charleston) 61920
University Mall (Part of Carbondale) 62901
University Park 60466
Upper Alton (Part of Alton)‡ 62002
Uptown (Part of Chicago)‡ 60640
Urbain 62865
Urban (Part of Taylorville) 62568
Urbana 61801-03
For specific ZIP Codes call (888) 275-8777, or your local postmaster.
Urbandale 62914
Ursa 62376
Ustick (Twp) 61270
Utica (Twp) 61373
Utica 61373
Vale Vue Acres 62650
Valier 62891
Valley (Twp) 61491
Valley City 62340
Valley Creek (Part of Elgin) 60123
Valley Lo (Part of Glenview) 60025
Valley View, *DeKalb* 60145
Valley View, *DuPage* 60137
Valley View, *Kane* 60174
Valley View (Part of East Peoria) 61611
Valmeyer 62295
Van Burensburg 62032
Vance (Twp) 61841
Vandalia 62471
Van Orin 61374
Varna 61375
Velma 62568
Venedy 62214
Venetian Village 60046
Venice 62090
Venice Crossing (Part of Venice) 62090
Vera 62080
Vergennes 62994
Vermilion, *La Salle* (Twp) 61370
Vermilion, *Edgar* 61955
Vermilion Grove 61870
Vermilion Heights 61834
Vermilionville 61370
Vermillion Estates 61764
Vermont 61484
Vernon, *Lake* (Twp) 60069
Vernon, *Marion* 62892
Vernon Hills 60061
Verona 60479
Versailles 62378
Versailles-on-the-Lake (Part of Schaumburg) 60173
Vets Row 61523
Vevay Park 62420
Vicic (Part of East Peoria) 61611
Victor (Twp) 60556
Victoria 61485
Vienna, *Grundy* (Twp) 60479
Vienna, *Johnson* 62995
Village Crossing Shopping Center (Part of Skokie) 60076
Village Green (Part of Warrenville) 60555
Village Mall (Part of Danville) 61832
Village Square, *DuPage* 60515
Village Square (Part of Northbrook) 60062
Villa Grove 61956
Villa Grove Junction (Part of Villa Grove) 61956
Villa Hills 62223
Villa Marie (Part of Godfrey) 62035
Villa Park 60181
Villa Ridge 62996
Villas Salceda (Part of Northbrook) 60062
Villa Verde (Part of Buffalo Grove) 60089
Villa West (Part of Palos Park) 60464
Vincennes Trail 60954
Vinegar Hill (Twp) 61036
Viola, *Lee* (Twp) 61318
Viola, *Mercer* 61486
Virden 62690
Virgil 60182
Virginia 62691
Volo 60073
Vonachen Knolls 61523
Voorhies 61813
Vulcan (Part of East Carondelet) 62240
Wabash (Twp) 62441
Wacker, *Carroll* 61053
Wacker, *Kendall* 60560
Wacker Drive (Part of Chicago)‡ 60607
Waddams (Twp) 61050

Waddams Grove 61048
Wade, *Clinton* (Twp).... 62231
Wade, *Jasper* (Twp).... 62448
Wadsworth 60083
Waggoner 62572
Wakefield 62448
Waldo (Twp) 61744
Walker, *Hancock* (Twp) 62313
Walker, *Macon* 62544
Walkerville 62050
Wall (Twp) 60948
Wallace (Twp) 61350
Walla Walla 62428
Wallingford 60442
Walnut 61376
Walnut Grove, *Knox* (Twp) 61414
Walnut Grove, *McDonough* (Twp) 61438
Walnut Grove, *McDonough* 61470
Walnut Hill 62893
Walnut Park 62231
Walnut Prairie 62477
Walpole 62817
Walsh 62297
Walshville 62091
Waltham 61373
Walton 61021
Waltonville 62894
Wamac 62801
Wanda 62025
Wanlock 61231
Wapella 61777
Wards Grove (Twp) 61048
Ware 62952
Warner 61273
Warren, *Lake* (Twp) 60031
Warren, *Jo Daviess* 61087
Warrenhurst (Part of Warrenville) 60555
Warren Park (Part of Cicero) 60804
Warrensburg 62573
Warrenville 60555
Warrington 61933
Warsaw 62379
Wartburg 62298
Wartrace 62943
Wasco 60183
Washburn 61570
Washington, *Carroll* (Twp) 61074
Washington, *Will* (Twp) 60401
Washington, *Tazewell* 61571
Washington Heights (Part of Chicago) 60620
.... 60643
For specific ZIP Codes call (888) 275-8777, or your local postmaster.
Washington Park (Part of Chicago) 60615
Washington Park, *St. Clair* 62204
Washington Square Mall (Part of Homewood) 60430
Wasson 62930
Wataga 61488
Waterford, *Fulton* (Twp) 61542
Waterford (Part of Willowbrook) 60521
Waterloo 62298
Waterman 60556
Water Tower Place (Part of Chicago) 60611
Watertown (Part of East Moline) 61244
Watervalley 62920
Watseka 60970
Watson 62473
Wauconda 60084
Waukegan 60079
.... 60085-87
For specific ZIP Codes call (888) 275-8777, or your local postmaster.
Wauponsee (Twp) 60450
Waverly 62692
Waycinden Park 60018
Wayne (Twp) 60185
Wayne 60184
Wayne Center 60185
Wayne City 62895
Waynesville 61778
Wayside 62939
Weathersfield (Part of Schaumburg) 60194
Weaver 62423
Webber (Twp) 62814
Webster 62321
Webster Park (Part of Spring Valley) 61362
Wedgewood Estates .. 62293
Wedron 60557
Weedman 61842
Wee-Ma-Tuk Hills 61427
.... 61520
For specific ZIP Codes call (888) 275-8777, or your local postmaster.
Weldon 61882
Welge 62288
Weller (Twp) 61238
Wellington 60973
Wellington Heights 60435
Wells 62871
Wendelin 62448
Wenona 61377
Wenonah 62075
Wentworth Avenue (Part of Calumet City)‡ 60409
Wesley, *Will* (Twp) 60481
Wesley (Part of Creve Coeur) 61611
West, *Effingham* (Twp) 62458
West, *McLean* (Twp) .. 61722
Westaway 60506
Westbrook 61853
Westbrook Estates (Part of O'Fallon) 62269
West Brooklyn 61378
Westbury (Part of Bolingbrook) 60440
Westchester 60154
West Chicago 60185*
.... 60186†
West City 62812
West Clinton Estates .. 62265
Westdale Gardens 60126
West Deerfield (Twp) .. 60015
West Dundee 60118
West Elsdon (Part of Chicago) 60629
.... 60632
For specific ZIP Codes call (888) 275-8777, or your local postmaster.
West End 62890
West Englewood (Part of Chicago) 60636
Western (Twp) 61273
Western Knolls 62707
Western Mound (Twp) 62630
Western Springs 60558
Westervelt 62565
Westfield, *Bureau* (Twp) 61312
Westfield, *Clark* 62474
Westfield (Part of Joliet) 60431
West Frankfort 62896
West Frankfort Lake.... 62896
West Galena (Twp) 61036
Westgate 62959
West Glen (Part of Peoria)‡ 61614
West Glenview 60025
West Hallock 61526
West Hinsdale (Part of Hinsdale) 60521
West Jersey 61483
West Kankakee (Part of Kankakee) 60901
West Lake, *Crawford* .. 62454
Westlake (Part of Glendale Heights) 60139
West Lake Forest (Part of Lake Forest) .. 60045
West Lawn (Part of Chicago) 60629
West Liberty 62475
West Lincoln (Twp) 62656
West Marion (Twp) 62959
West Meadowview (Part of Kankakee) 60901
West Miltmore 60046
Westmont 60559
Westmore (Part of Lombard) 60148
Westmoreland (Part of Rockford) 61102
Weston 61726
West Peoria 61604
West Point, *Stephenson* (Twp) 61048
West Point, *Hancock* .. 62380
West Point, *Morgan* 62650
West Point Center (Part of Hillside) 60162
Westport, *Knox* 61401
Westport, *Lawrence*.... 62439
West Pullman (Part of Chicago) 60628
West Ridge (Part of Chicago) 60659
West Ridge, *Douglas* .. 61953
West Salem 62476
West Sandford 61944
West Side (Part of Chicago) 60607
.... 60612
For specific ZIP Codes call (888) 275-8777, or your local postmaster.
West Town (Part of Chicago) 60622
West Union 62477
Westview Center (Part of Hanover Park) 60107
Westville 61883
Westwood (Part of Addison) 60101
West York 62478
Wetaug 62926
Wethersfield (Twp) 61277
Wetzel 61944
Wheatfield (Twp) 62231
Wheatland, *Bureau* (Twp) 61368
Wheatland, *Fayette* (Twp) 62418
Wheatland, *Will* (Twp).. 60544
Wheatland View 60564
Wheaton 60187*
.... 60189†
Wheaton Center (Part of Wheaton) 60187
Wheaton South (Part of Wheaton)‡ 60187
Wheeler 62479
Wheeling 60090
Whiskey Corners 60071
Whiskey Creek 60185
Whispering Hills 60050
Whispering Oaks (Part of Lake Forest) 60045
Whitaker 60940
Whiteash 62959
White City 62069
White Cliffs 62035
Whitefield 61537
Whitehall (Part of Mount Prospect) 60056
White Hall, *Greene* 62092
White Heath 61884
White Oak, *McLean* (Twp) 61725
White Oak, *Mason* 62644
White Oaks 61021
White Oaks Bay 60097
White Oaks Mall (Part of Springfield) 62704
White Pigeon 61270
White Pines 60106
White Post 62093
White Rock, *Lee* 61021
White Rock, *Ogle* 61068
Whites Addition 61244
Whitley (Twp) 61928
Whitmore (Twp) 62501
Whittington 62897
Wichert 60964
Wicker Park (Part of Chicago)‡ 60622
Wickmore 62035
Wideview 60175
Wieisbrook 62918
Wilbern 61570
Wilberton (Twp) 62885
Wilbur Heights 61822
Wilcox (Twp) 62379
Wildrose 60174
Wildwood, *Kane* 60506
Wildwood, *Lake* 60030
Wildwood Addition (Part of Moline) 61265
Wildwood Valley 60123
Will (Twp) 60468
Willard, *Alexander* 62962
Willard, *St. Clair* 62269
Willeys 62568
Williams (Twp) 62693
Williamsburg 61937
Williamsfield 61489
Williamson 62088
Williams Park 60084
Williams Place 62035
Williamsville 62693
Willisville 62997
Willow 61085
Willoway (Part of Naperville) 60540
Willoway Manor (Part of Willowbrook) 60521
Willow Branch (Twp) .. 61830
Willowbrook, *DuPage*.. 60521
Willowbrook, *Kendall* .. 60512
Willowbrook, *Will*♦ 60417
Willow Brooke 61080
Willow Creek (Twp) 60530
Willow Estates, *DeKalb* 60135
Willow Estates, *Iroquois* 60912
Willow Hill 62480
Willow Springs 60480
Willow Wood (Part of Palatine) 60067
Wilmette 60091
Wilmington 60481
Wilshire Bluffs Estate .. 61008
Wilsman 61364
Wilson (Twp) 61777
Wilson Heights 62234
Wilsonville 62093
Wilton (Twp) 60442
Wilton Center 60442
Winchester 62694
Winden Oak 60119
Windham Manor (Part of Northbrook) 60062
Windings 60175
Windsor 61957
Windsor Estates West (Part of Mount Prospect) 60056
Windsor Park, *Champaign* 61822
Windsor Park (Part of Chicago) 60649
Windsor Square (Part of Peoria)‡ 61614
Wine Hill 62288
Winfield (Twp) 60185
Winfield 60190
Wing 61741
Winkle 62237
Winnebago 61088
Winneshiek 61032
Winnetka 60093
Winslow 61089
Winston Hills (Part of Woodridge) 60515
Winston Park (Part of Palatine) 60067
Winston Park Northwest (Part of Palatine) 60067
Winston Park South (Part of Country Club Hills) 60478
Winston Plaza Shopping Center (Part of Melrose Park) 60160
Winston Village (Part of Bolingbrook) 60440
Winston Woods (Part of Bolingbrook) 60440
Winterrowd 62424
Winthrop Harbor 60096
Wireton (Part of Blue Island) 60406
Witt 62094
Woburn 62246
Wolf Lake 62998
Womac 62626
Wonder Lake 60097
Wonder View 60097
Wonder Woods 60097
Woodbine 61085
Woodborough (Part of Homewood) 60430
Woodbridge (Part of Elgin) 60123
Woodburn 62014
Woodbury 62445
Wood Dale, *DuPage* 60191
Wooddale, *Peoria* 61607
Wooded Shores 60097
Woodfield (Part of Schaumburg)‡ .... 60159†
.... 60173*
Woodfield Village Green (Part of Schaumburg) 60173
Woodford 61760
Woodford Heights 61548
Woodgate 60178
Woodgate Estate 62012
Woodhill Estates 61038
Woodhull 61490
Woodland, *Carroll* (Twp) 61053
Woodland, *Fulton* (Twp) 61501
Woodland, *Iroquois* 60974
Woodland, *Kankakee* .. 60954
Woodland Addition 61350
Woodland Heights (Part of Streamwood) 60107
Woodland Hills (Part of Batavia) 60510
Woodland Lake 61817
Woodland Shores 61021
Woodlawn (Part of Chicago) 60637
Woodlawn, *Jefferson* .. 62898
Woodlawn Heights 61081
Woodlawn Acres 61068
Woodmere (Part of Libertyville) 60048
Woodridge 60517
Wood River 62095
Woods Edge 61802
Woodside (Twp) 62703
Woodside Estates (Part of Oak Brook) .. 60523
Woodson 62695
Woodstock, *Schuyler* (Twp) 62681
Woodstock, *McHenry* 60098
Woodview Manor (Part of Prospect Heights) 60070
Woodville (Twp) 62027
Woodworth 60953
Woody 62016
Woodyard, *Edgar* 61924
Woodyard, *Fayette* 62885
Wooster Lake 60041
Woosung 61091
Worden 62097
Worth, *Woodford* (Twp) 61548
Worth, *Cook* 60482
Wrights 62098
Wrights Corner 62414
Wyanet 61379
Wynoose 62868
Wyoming, *Lee* (Twp) .. 61353
Wyoming, *Stark* 61491
Wysox (Twp) 61051
Wythe (Twp) 62379
Xenia 62899
Yale 62481
Yankee Ridge 61802
Yantisville 62534
Yard Center (Part of Dolton) 60419
Yates (Twp) 61726
Yates City 61572
Yatesville 62612
Yellowhead (Twp) 60940
Yeoward Addition 61071
York, *Carroll* (Twp) 61285
York, *DuPage* (Twp).... 60181
York, *Clark* 62477
York Center♦ 60148
Yorkfield 60126
Yorkshire Woods (Part of Oak Brook) 60523
Yorktown, *Henry* (Twp) 61277
Yorktown, *Bureau* 61283
Yorktown Shopping Center (Part of Lombard) 60148
Yorkville 60560
Young America (Twp).. 61940
Young Hickory (Twp) .. 61544
Youngstown 61473
Zanesville (Twp) 62572
Zearing 61337
Zeigler 62999
Zenith 62899
Zif (Twp) 62824
Zion, *Carroll* 61074
Zion, *Lake* 60099
Zuma (Twp) 61257
Zurich Heights (Part of Lake Zurich) 60047

* **Area Zip Code** † **Post Office Boxes** ‡ **Postal Station** ♦ **Census Designated Place** *Italic Type* **County**

Aberdeen 47040
Abington 47330
Aboite (Twp) 46804
Aboite 46783
Abydel 47454
Acme 47274
Acton (Part of Indianapolis) 46259
Adams, *Allen* (Twp) 46806
.... 46816
For specific ZIP Codes call (888) 275-8777, or your local postmaster.
Adams, *Carroll* (Twp) 47960
Adams, *Cass* (Twp) 46988
Adams, *Decatur* (Twp) 47272
Adams, *Hamilton* (Twp) 46069
Adams, *Madison* (Twp) 46056
Adams, *Morgan* (Twp) 46151
Adams, *Parke* (Twp) 47872
Adams, *Ripley* (Twp) 47041
Adams, *Warren* (Twp) 47975
Adams, *Decatur* 47240
Adams, *Morgan* 46151
Adamsboro 46947
Adams Lake 46795
Adams Mill 46920
Addison (Twp) 46176
Addmore (Part of Clarksville) 47129
Ade 47922
Advance 46102
Aetna (Part of Gary) 46402
Ainsworth 46342
Air Mail Field (Part of Indianapolis)‡ 46251
Akron 46910
Alamo 47916
Albany 47320
Albion 46701
Aldine 46366
Alert 47283
Alexandria 46001
Alfont 46040
Alford 47567
Alfordsville 47553
Algiers 47567
Alida 46391
Allen, *Miami* (Twp) 46951
Allen, *Noble* (Twp) 46710
.... 46755
For specific ZIP Codes call (888) 275-8777, or your local postmaster.
Allendale 47802
Allens Acres 46077
Allensville 47011
Allisonville (Part of Indianapolis) 46250
Allman 46158
Alpine 47331
Alquina 47331
Alta 47854
Alto 46902
Alton 47137
Altona 46738
Alvarado 46742
Amberley 47201
Amber Valley 47803
Ambia 47917
Amboy 46911
Americus 47905
Amity 46131
Amo 46103
Anderson, *Madison* (Twp) 46016
Anderson, *Perry* (Twp) 47586
Anderson, *Rush* (Twp) 46156
Anderson, *Warrick* (Twp) 47630
Anderson, *Madison* 46011-18
For specific ZIP Codes call (888) 275-8777, or your local postmaster.
Andersonville 47024
Andrews 46702
Angola 46703
Annandale Estates 47448
Annapolis 47832
Anoka 46947
Ansley Acres 46804
Anthony 47303
Antioch 46041
Antiville 47371
Apache Acres 47805
Arba 47355
Arcadia 46030
Arcana 46952

Arcola 46704
Arctic Springs (Part of Jeffersonville) 47130
Arda 47567
Ardmore 46628
Argos 46501
Ari 46723
Arlington, *Monroe* 47404
Arlington, *Rush* 46104
Arlington Park 46835
Armstrong 47720
Armuth Acres 47203
Arney 47431
Aroma 46031
Arrowhead Park 46580
Art 47834
Arthur 47598
Artic 46721
Ashboro 47840
Asherville 47834
Ash Grove 47920
Ashland, *Morgan* (Twp) 46151
Ashland, *Henry* 47362
Ashley 46705
Athens 46912
Atherton 47874
Atlanta 46031
Attica 47918
Atwood 46502
Atwood Lake 46795
Aubbeenaubbee (Twp) 46975
Auburn 46706
Auburn Junction 46706
Augusta (Part of Indianapolis) 46268
Augusta, *Pike* 47598
Aultshire (Part of Muncie) 47303
Aurora 47001
Austin 47102
Avalon Hills (Part of Indianapolis) 46220
Avery 46041
Avilla 46710
Avoca 47420
Avon 46234
Avondale 46952
Ayrshire 47598
Azalia 47232
B (Part of Anderson)‡ 46015
Babcock 46304
Bacon (Part of Indianapolis)‡ 46205
.... 46220
For specific ZIP Codes call (888) 275-8777, or your local postmaster.
Baileys Corner 47978
Bainbridge, *Dubois* (Twp) 47546
Bainbridge, *Putnam* 46105
Baker (Twp) 47433
Bakers Corner 46069
Bakertown 46701
Balbec 47369
Baldwin Heights (Part of Princeton) 47670
Ball Lake 46742
Bandon 47514
Banquo 46940
Banta 46106
Bar-Barry Heights (Part of West Lafayette) 47906
Barbee 46562
Bargersville 46106
Barkley (Twp) 47978
Barnaby Acres 47201
Barnard 46172
Barr (Twp) 47558
Barrick Corner 47841
Bartlettsville 47421
Bartley 47805
Barton (Twp) 47660
Bartonia 47390
Bass Lake 46534
Batesville 47006
Bath 47010
Battle Ground 47920
Baugh City 47610
Baugo (Twp) 46514
Bayfield 46562
Beacon Heights (Part of New Albany) 47150
Beal 47591
Bean Blossom, *Monroe* (Twp) 47429
Bean Blossom, *Brown* 46160

Bear Branch 47018
Bearcreek (Twp) 47326
Beard 46041
Beardstown 46996
Bear Lake 46701
Beattys Corner 46360
Beaver, *Newton* (Twp) 47963
Beaver, *Pulaski* (Twp) 46996
Beaver City 47922
Beaver Dam Lake 46510
Becks Grove 47235
Becks Mill 47167
Bedford 47421
Beecamp 47250
Beech Brook 46176
Beech Creek (Twp) 47459
Beech Grove, *Marion* 46107
Beech Grove, *Morgan* 46151
Beechwood 47137
Bee Ridge 47834
Bellefountain 47371
Belle Union 46120
Belleview 47250
Belleville 46118
Bellmore 47830
Bell Rohr Park 46538
Belmont, *Brown* 47448
Belmont (Part of New Castle) 47362
Belshaw 46356
Ben Davis (Part of Indianapolis) 46241
Bengal 46131
Benham 47042
Bennetts Switch 46901
Bennettsville 47143
Bennington 47011
Benton, *Monroe* (Twp) 47408
Benton, *Elkhart* 46526-28
For specific ZIP Codes call (888) 275-8777, or your local postmaster.
Bentonville 47322
Benwood 47834
Berlien 46703
Berne 46711
Bethany 46151
Bethel, *Posey* (Twp) 47616
Bethel, *Wayne* 47341
Bethel Village 47201
Bethlehem, *Cass* (Twp) 46947
Bethlehem, *Clark* 47104
Between-the-Lakes Park 46538
Beverly Shores 46301
Bicknell 47512
Big Bass Lake 46307
Big Creek (Twp) 47929
Bigger (Twp) 47265
Big Lake 46701
Big Springs 46069
Billingsville 47353
Billtown 47834
Billville 47834
Bippus 46713
Birdseye 47513
Birmingham 46951
Black (Twp) 47620
Blackhawk, *Allen* 46815
Blackhawk, *Vigo* 47866
Blackhawk Beach 46383
Blackhawk Forest 46815
Blackman Lake 46795
Black Oak (Part of Gary) 46406
Blaine 47371
Blairsville 47638
Blanford 47831
Blocher 47138
Bloomer 46011
Bloomfield, *Lagrange* (Twp) 46761
Bloomfield, *Greene* 47424
Bloomfield, *Spencer* 47611
Bloomingdale 47832
Blooming Grove 47012
Bloomingport 47355
Bloomington (Twp) 47408
Bloomington 47401-08
For specific ZIP Codes call (888) 275-8777, or your local postmaster.
Blountsville 47354
Blue Creek 46772
Blue Lake 46723
Blue Ridge 46176
Blue Ridge Estates (Part of Bloomington) 47408

Blue River, *Hancock* (Twp) 46140
Blue River, *Harrison* (Twp) 47115
Blue River, *Henry* (Twp) 47360
Blue River, *Johnson* (Twp) 46124
Bluff Creek 46106
Bluff Point 47371
Bluffs 46151
Bluffton 46714
Bobtown 47274
Bogard (Twp) 47501
Boggstown 46110
Bogle Corner 47438
Bolivar (Twp) 47970
Bonnell 47022
Bono 47446
Boon (Twp) 47601
Boone, *Cass* (Twp) 46978
Boone, *Crawford* (Twp) 47137
Boone, *Dubois* (Twp) 47546
Boone, *Harrison* (Twp) 47135
Boone, *Madison* (Twp) 46036
Boone, *Porter* (Twp) 46341
Boone Grove 46302
Boonville 47601
Borden 47106
Boston 47324
Boswell 47921
Boundary City 47371
Bourbon 46504
Bowers 47940
Bowerstown 46750
Bowling Green 47833
Bowman 47567
Bowman Acres (Part of Greenfield) 46140
Boxley 46069
Boyleston 46057
Bracken 46750
Bradford 47107
Bradford Park (Part of Yorktown) 47396
Brairwood 46737
Bramble 47553
Branchville 47514
Brandywine, *Hancock* (Twp) 46140
Brandywine, *Shelby* (Twp) 46126
Braytown 47043
Brazil 47834
Breezewood 46952
Breezewood Park 47302
Breezy Point 47960
Bremen 46506
Brems 46534
Brendan Wood (Part of Lebanon) 46052
Brendonwood (Part of Indianapolis) 46226
Brent Woods (Part of Shelbyville) 46176
Bretzville 47542
Brewersville 47265
Brewington Woods 47303
Briarwood 46157
Brice 47371
Brick Chapel 46135
Bridgeport (Part of Indianapolis) 46231
Bridgeton 47836
Brierwood Hills 46804
Bright♦ 47025
Brighton 46746
Brightwood (Part of Indianapolis)‡ 46218
Brimfield 46720
Brinckley 47340
Bringhurst 46913
Bristol 46507
Bristow 47515
Broadlands 47805
Broad Ripple (Part of Indianapolis)‡ 46220
.... 46230
For specific ZIP Codes call (888) 275-8777, or your local postmaster.
Broadview, *Grant* 46952
Broadview, *Monroe* 47403
Bromer 47452
Brook 47922
Brookfield 46126
Brookhaven 46953
Brooklyn 46111
Brookmoor 46158

Brooks 46060
Brooksburg 47250
Brookside Estates, *Allen* 46805
Brookside Estates, *Vigo* 47802
Brookston 47923
Brookville 47012
Brookville Heights 46163
Broom Hill 47106
Brown, *Hancock* (Twp) 46186
.... 47384
For specific ZIP Codes call (888) 275-8777, or your local postmaster.
Brown, *Hendricks* (Twp) 46112
Brown, *Montgomery* (Twp) 47933
Brown, *Morgan* (Twp) 46158
Brown, *Ripley* (Twp) 47250
Brown, *Washington* (Twp) 47108
Brownsburg 46112
Browns Crossing 46151
Brownstown, *Crawford* 47118
Brownstown, *Jackson* 47220
Browns Valley 47933
Brownsville 47325
Bruce Lake 46939
Bruceville 47516
Brummitt Acres 46304
Brunswick, *Lake* 46303
Brunswick (Part of Gary)‡ 46406
Brushy Prairie 46761
Bryant 47326
Bryantsburg 47250
Bryantsville 47446
Buck Creek, *Hancock* (Twp) 46140
Buck Creek, *Tippecanoe* 47924
Buckeye 46792
Buckskin 47647
Bucktown 47838
Bud 46131
Buddha 47421
Buena Vista 47024
Buffalo 47925
Buffaloville 47550
Buffington (Part of Gary)‡ 46406
Bufkin 47620
Bullocktown 47601
Bunker Hill, *Fayette* 47331
Bunker Hill, *Knox* 47591
Bunker Hill, *Miami* 46914
Bunker Hill, *Washington* 47167
Burdick 46304
Burket 46508
Burlington 46915
Burlington Beach 46383
Burnett 47805
Burnettsville 47926
Burney 47240
Burns City 47553
Burns Harbor 46304
Burnsville 47201
Burr Oak, *Marshall* 46511
Burr Oak, *Noble* 46701
Burrows 46916
Busseron 47561
Butler, *De Kalb* (Twp) 46763
Butler, *Franklin* (Twp) 47012
Butler, *Miami* (Twp) 46970
Butler, *De Kalb* 46721
Butler Center 46738
Butlerville 47223
Byrneville 47122
Byron 46350
Caborn 47620
Cadiz 47362
Caesar Creek (Twp) 47018
Cain (Twp) 47949
Cairo 47906
Cale 47581
California (Twp) 46534
Calumet (Twp) 46408
Calvertville 47424
Cambria 46041
Cambridge City 47327
Camby (Part of Indianapolis) 46113
Camden 46917
Cammack 47302
Campbell, *Jennings* (Twp) 47223

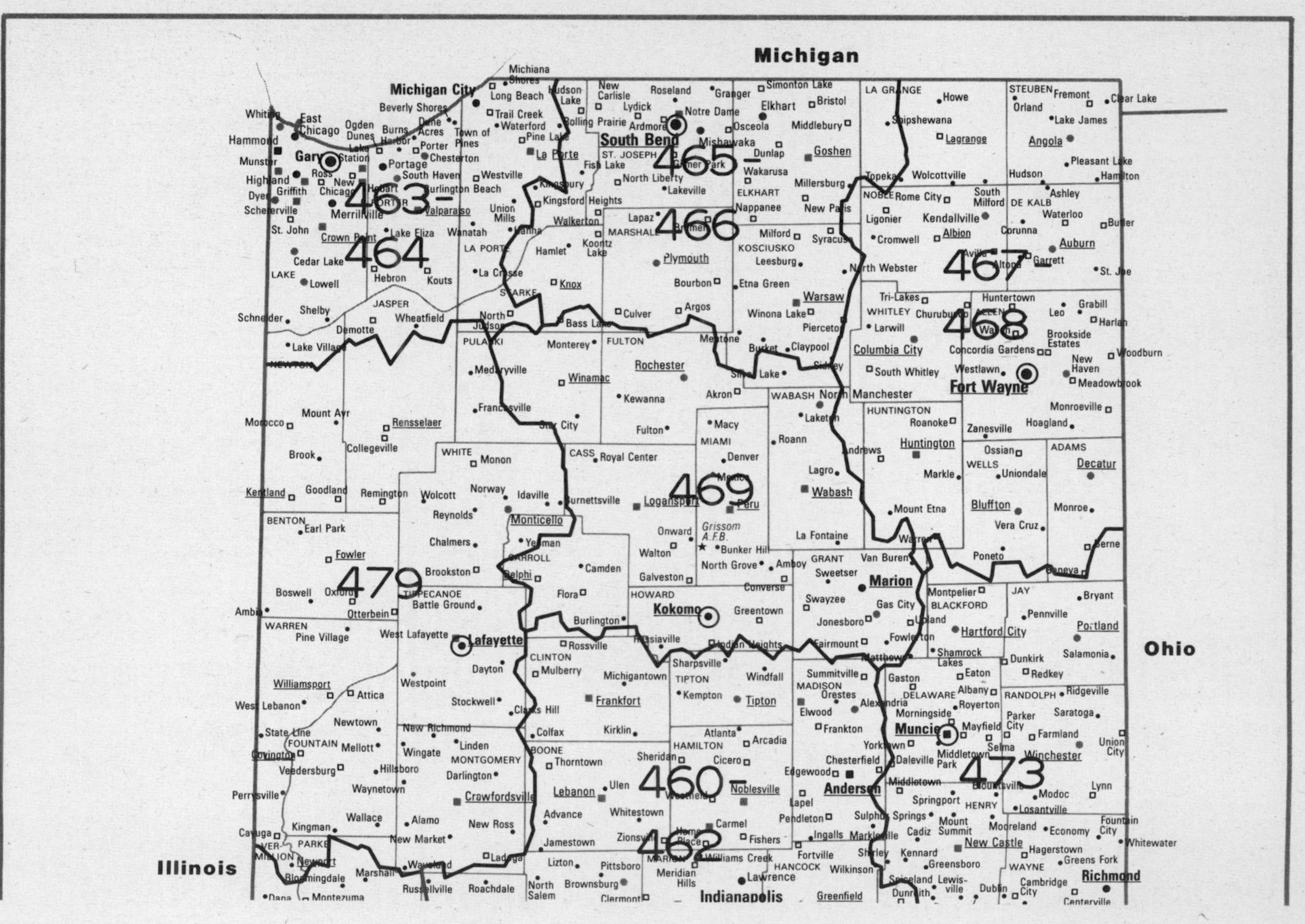
Michigan
Ohio
Illinois
463
464
465
466
467
468
469
460
462
473
479
Michigan City
Gary
South Bend
La Porte
Valparaiso
Crown Point
Goshen
Elkhart
Warsaw
Plymouth
Fort Wayne
Huntington
Wabash
Peru
Logansport
Kokomo
Marion
Muncie
Anderson
Richmond
New Castle
Indianapolis
Noblesville
Lebanon
Frankfort
Lafayette
Crawfordsville
Rochester
Monticello
Rensselaer
Tipton
Bluffton
Decatur
Portland
Winchester
Hartford City
Auburn
Angola
Lagrange
Columbia City
Albion
Knox
Winamac
Delphi
Williamsport
Covington
Fowler
Kentland
Greenfield

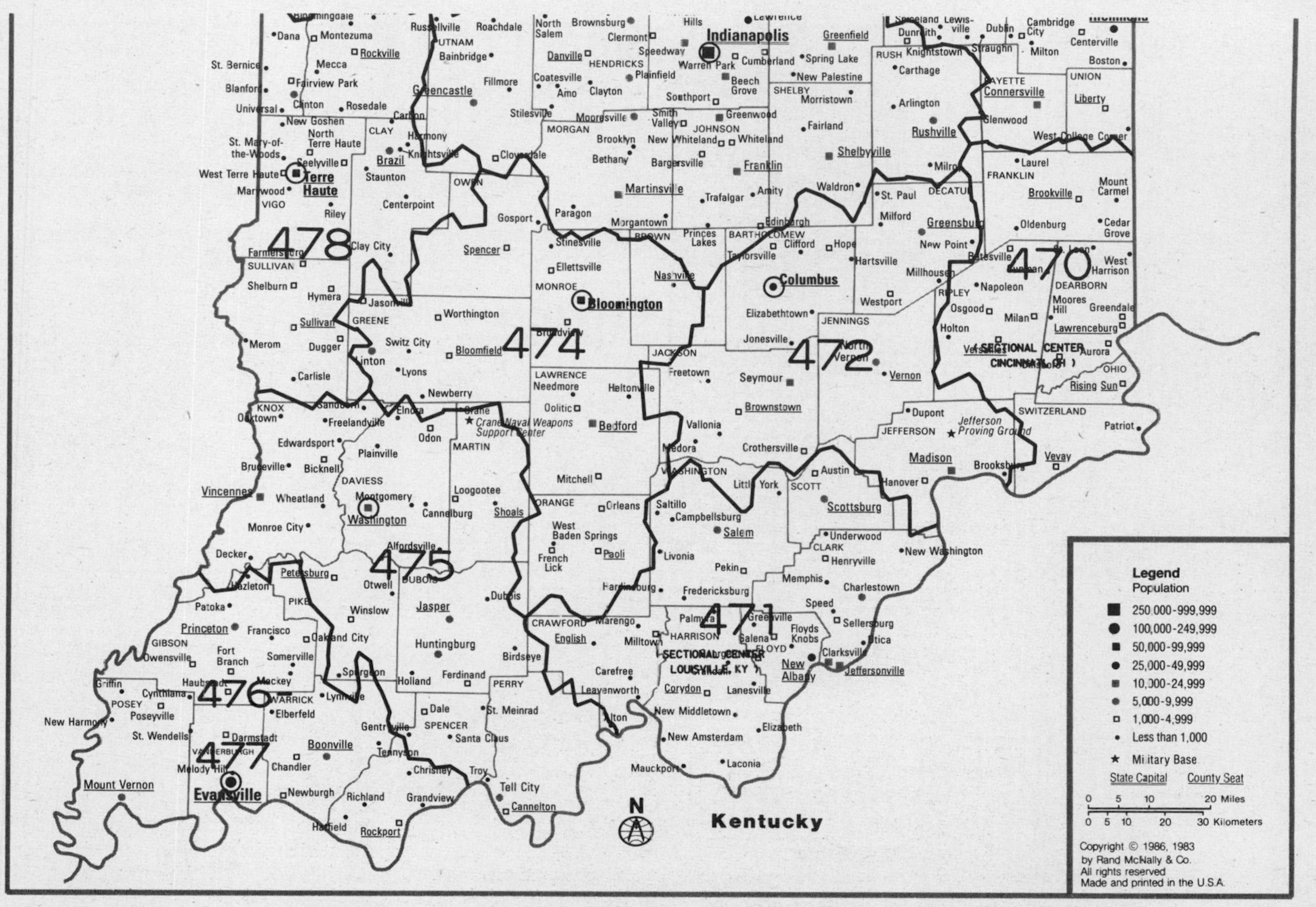
Legend
Population
250,000-999,999
100,000-249,999
50,000-99,999
25,000-49,999
10,300-24,999
5,000-9,999
1,000-4,999
Less than 1,000
Military Base
State Capital
County Seat
0 5 10 20 Miles
0 5 10 20 30 Kilometers
Copyright © 1986, 1983
by Rand McNally & Co.
All rights reserved
Made and printed in the U.S.A.
Kentucky
N
470
471
472
474
475
476
477
478
SECTIONAL CENTER CINCINNATI, OH
SECTIONAL CENTER LOUISVILLE, KY
Indianapolis
Bloomington
Columbus
Evansville
Terre Haute
Jefferson Proving Ground
Crane Naval Weapons Support Center
UNION
FAYETTE
RUSH
SHELBY
FRANKLIN
DECATUR
DEARBORN
RIPLEY
OHIO
SWITZERLAND
JEFFERSON
JENNINGS
BARTHOLOMEW
JOHNSON
HENDRICKS
MORGAN
BROWN
MONROE
JACKSON
SCOTT
CLARK
WASHINGTON
FLOYD
HARRISON
LAWRENCE
ORANGE
CRAWFORD
PERRY
SPENCER
MARTIN
DUBOIS
DAVIESS
GREENE
OWEN
CLAY
VIGO
SULLIVAN
KNOX
PIKE
GIBSON
WARRICK
VANDERBURGH
POSEY
PUTNAM
Greenfield
Shelbyville
Rushville
Connersville
Liberty
Brookville
Lawrenceburg
Rising Sun
Vevay
Madison
Versailles
Greensburg
Vernon
Scottsburg
Jeffersonville
New Albany
Corydon
Salem
Brownstown
Franklin
Martinsville
Nashville
Bedford
Paoli
English
Shoals
Jasper
Washington
Bloomfield
Spencer
Sullivan
Brazil
Greencastle
Rockville
Danville
Vincennes
Petersburg
Princeton
Boonville
Rockport
Cannelton
Mount Vernon

Campbell, *Warrick* (Twp) 47610
Campbellsburg 47108
Campbelltown 47598
Canaan 47224
Candleglo Village 46176
Candle Light Village (Part of Columbus) 47201
Cannelburg 47519
Cannelton 47520
Canton 47167
Capilano by the Lake 47906
Carbon 47837
Carbondale 47993
Cardonia 47834
Carefree 47137
Carlisle 47838
Carlos 47355
Carmel 46032-33
46082
For specific ZIP Codes call (888) 275-8777, or your local postmaster.
Cammack 47304
Carp 47460
Carpenter (Twp) 47977
Carpentersville 46172
Carr, *Clark* (Twp) 47106
Carr, *Jackson* (Twp) 47260
Carriage Estates (Part of Columbus) 47201
Carriage Estates, *Hancock* 46163
Carrollton (Twp) 46929
Carrollton, *Carroll* 46913
Carrollton, *Hancock* 46129
Carter (Twp) 47523
Cartersburg 46114
Carthage 46115
Carwood 47106
Cascade (Part of Bloomington) 47401
Cass, *Clay* (Twp) 47868
Cass, *Dubois* (Twp) 47541
Cass, *Greene* (Twp) 47449
Cass, *La Porte* (Twp) 46390
Cass, *Ohio* (Twp) 47040
Cass, *Pulaski* (Twp) 47957
Cass, *White* (Twp) 47960
Cass, *Sullivan* 47848
Cassville 46901
Castleton (Part of Indianapolis) 46250
Castleton Square 46250
Cataract 47460
Cates 47952
Catlin 47872
Cato 47598
Cavanaugh (Part of Gary) 46406
Cayuga 47928
Cedar Canyons 46741
Cedar Creek, *Allen* (Twp) 46741
Cedar Creek, *Lake* (Twp) 46356
Cedar Creek, *De Kalb* 46738
Cedar Grove 47016
Cedar Lake, *Lake* 46303
Cedar Lake, *Whitley* 46725
Cedar Point 47960
Cedar Shores 46741
Cedarville (Part of Leo-Cedarville) 46741
Celestine 47521
Cemar Estates 47805
Cementville (Part of Jeffersonville) 47129
Centenary 47842
Centennial (Part of Fort Wayne)‡ 46808
46825
46895
For specific ZIP Codes call (888) 275-8777, or your local postmaster.
Centennial, *Fountain* 47952
Center, *Benton* (Twp) 47944
Center, *Boone* (Twp) 46052
Center, *Clinton* (Twp) 46041
Center, *Dearborn* (Twp) 47001
Center, *Delaware* (Twp) 47302
Center, *Gibson* (Twp) 47649
Center, *Grant* (Twp) 46952
Center, *Greene* (Twp) 47424
Center, *Hancock* (Twp) 46140
Center, *Hendricks* (Twp) 46122
Center, *Howard* (Twp) 46901-02
For specific ZIP Codes call (888) 275-8777, or your local postmaster.
Center, *Jennings* (Twp) 47265
Center, *Lake* (Twp) 46307
Center, *La Porte* (Twp) 46350
Center, *Marion* (Twp) 46204
Center, *Marshall* (Twp) 46563
Center, *Martin* (Twp) 47553
Center, *Porter* (Twp) 46383
46385
For specific ZIP Codes call (888) 275-8777, or your local postmaster.
Center, *Posey* (Twp) 47638
Center, *Ripley* (Twp) 47037
Center, *Rush* (Twp) 46148
Center, *Starke* (Twp) 46534
Center, *Union* (Twp) 47353
Center, *Vanderburgh* (Twp) 47710-11
For specific ZIP Codes call (888) 275-8777, or your local postmaster.
Center, *Wayne* (Twp) 47330
Center, *Howard* 46902
Center, *Jay* 47371
Center, *Warrick* 47601
Center Point 47840
Center Square 47043
Centerton 46151
Center Valley 46158
Centerville, *Spencer* 47611
Centerville, *Wayne* 47330
Central 47110
Central Barren 47161
Centre (Twp) 46614
Centre East (Part of Indianapolis) 46229
Century Consumer Mall (Part of Merrillville) 46410
Ceylon 46740
Chain O'Lakes 46628
Chalmers 47929
Chambersburg 47454
Champlin Meadows (Part of Martinsville) 46151
Chandler 47610
Chapel Bluff (Part of Columbus) 47201
Chapel Creek 47150
Chapel Hill (Part of Indianapolis) 46214
Chapel Hill, *Monroe* 47436
Charlestown 47111
Charle Sumac Estates (Part of Indianapolis) 46259
Charlottesville 46117
Chase 47921
Chelsea 47138
Cherokee Heights 47150
Cherokee Terrace 47130
Cherry Grove 47933
Chester, *Wabash* (Twp) 46962
Chester, *Wells* (Twp) 46781
Chester, *Wayne* 47374
Chesterfield 46017
Chesterton, *Hamilton* 46280
Chesterton, *Porter* 46304
Chesterville 47032
Chestnut Hill (Part of Chesterton) 46304
Chestnut Ridge 47274
Chicago Avenue (Part of East Chicago)‡ 46312
Chili 46926
China 47250
Chippewa‡ 46613-14
For specific ZIP Codes call (888) 275-8777, or your local postmaster.
Chrisney 47611
Christiansburg 47201
Churubusco 46723
Cicero, *Tipton* (Twp) 46031
Cicero, *Hamilton* 46034
Cicero Heights 46072
Cincinnati 47424
Circle City (Part of Indianapolis)‡ 46202
Circle Park 46742
Circleville 46173
Clare 46060
Clark, *Johnson* (Twp) 46142
Clark, *Montgomery* (Twp) 47954
Clark, *Perry* (Twp) 47515
Clarksburg 47225
Clarks Hill 47930
Clarks Landing 46742
Clarksville, *Clark* 47129
Clarksville, *Hamilton* 46060
Clay, *Bartholomew* (Twp) 47203
Clay, *Carroll* (Twp) 46923
Clay, *Cass* (Twp) 46947
Clay, *Dearborn* (Twp) 47018
Clay, *Decatur* (Twp) 47240
Clay, *Hamilton* (Twp) 46032-33
For specific ZIP Codes call (888) 275-8777, or your local postmaster.
Clay, *Hendricks* (Twp) 46121
Clay, *Howard* (Twp) 46901
Clay, *Kosciusko* (Twp) 46510
Clay, *Lagrange* (Twp) 46761
Clay, *Miami* (Twp) 46914
Clay, *Morgan* (Twp) 46151
Clay, *Owen* (Twp) 47460
Clay, *Pike* (Twp) 47640
Clay, *St. Joseph* (Twp) 46637
Clay, *Spencer* (Twp) 47550
Clay, *Wayne* (Twp) 47345
Clay City, *Clay* 47841
Clay City, *Spencer* 47550
Claypool 46510
Claysville 47108
Clayton 46118
Clear Creek, *Huntington* (Twp) 46750
Clear Creek, *Monroe* (Twp) 47401
Clear Creek, *Monroe* 47426
Clear Creek Estates 47403
Clear Lake 46737
Clearspring, *Lagrange* (Twp) 46571
Clear Spring, *Jackson* 47220
Clermont (Part of Indianapolis) 46234
Clermont Heights 46112
Cleveland, *Elkhart* (Twp) 46514
Cleveland, *Whitley* (Twp) 46787
Cleveland, *Hancock* 46140
Clifford 47226
Clifton 47353
Clifty (Twp) 47203
Clifty Village 47203
Clinton, *Boone* (Twp) 46052
Clinton, *Cass* (Twp) 46947
Clinton, *Decatur* (Twp) 47240
Clinton, *Elkhart* (Twp) 46528
Clinton, *La Porte* (Twp) 46382
Clinton, *Putnam* (Twp) 46135
Clinton, *Vermillion* 47842
Clinton Falls 46135
Cloud Crest Hills 47448
Cloverdale 46120
Cloverland 47834
Clover Village 46126
Clunette 46538
Clymers 46947
Coal Bluff 47874
Coal City 47427
Coal Creek, *Montgomery* (Twp) 47967
47994
For specific ZIP Codes call (888) 275-8777, or your local postmaster.
Coal Creek, *Fountain* 47932
Coalmont 47845
Coatesville 46121
Cobbler's Corner 47150
Cochran (Part of Aurora) 47001
Coe 47598
Coesse 46725
Coffey 47448
Colburn, *Tippecanoe* 47905
Colburn, *St. Joseph* 46536
Cold Springs, *Dearborn* 47032
Cold Springs, *Steuben* 46742
Coldwater Crossing (Part of Fort Wayne) 46801
Colfax, *Newton* (Twp) 46349
Colfax, *Clinton* 46035
Collamer 46787
College Corner 47371
College Mall (Part of Bloomington) 47407
College Meadows 46280
College Park (Part of Indianapolis) 46268
Collegeville♦ 47978
Collett 47371
Collins 46725
Coloma 47872
Colonial Park 47802
Colonial Village 46040
Columbia, *Dubois* (Twp) 47527
Columbia, *Gibson* (Twp) 47660
Columbia, *Jennings* (Twp) 47265
Columbia, *Whitley* (Twp) 46725
Columbia, *Fayette* 47331
Columbia City 46725
Columbus 47201-03
For specific ZIP Codes call (888) 275-8777, or your local postmaster.
Commiskey 47227
Como 47371
Concord, *De Kalb* (Twp) 46785
Concord, *Elkhart* (Twp) 46517
Concord, *De Kalb* 46706
Concord, *Tippecanoe* 47905
Concordia Gardens (Part of Fort Wayne) 46825
Connersville 47331
Continental Camp 47616
Converse 46919
Cook (Part of Cedar Lake) 46303
Cook Acres 47303
Coolspring (Twp) 46360
Cope 46151
Copperfield 47711
Cordry Lake 46164
Cornettsville 47568
Correct 47042
Cortland 47228
Corunna 46730
Cory 47846
Corydon 47112
Cosperville 46794
Cottage Grove 47353
Cotton (Twp) 47043
Country Charm 47905
Country Club Gardens 46804
Country Club Heights 46011
Country Club Meadows (Part of Evansville) 47710
Countryside Estates 48615
Country Terrace 47303
Country Trace 47715
Country View 47905
Country Village 47303
Courter 46970
Coveyville 47421
Covington 47932
Covington Dells 46804
Cowan 47302
Coxton 47421
Coxville 47874
Craig (Twp) 47043
Craigville 46731
Crandall 47114
Crane 47522
Crane Naval Depot 47522
Crane Naval Weapons Support Center 47522
Crawfordsville 47933
Cree Lake 46755
Crest Manor (Part of South Bend) 46614
Crestmoor (Part of Shelbyville) 46176
Creston 46356
Crestview (Part of New Albany) 47150
Crestwood (Part of Fort Wayne) 46825
Crete 47355
Critchfield 46143
Crocker (Part of Portage) 46383
Crompton Hill 47842
Cromwell 46732
Crooked Lake, *Steuben* 46703
Crooked Lake, *Whitley* 46725
Cross Plains 47017
Crothersville 47229
Crown Center 46157
Crown Colony 46816
Crown Point 46307*
46308†
Crows Nest (Part of Indianapolis) 46228
Crump Estates (Part of Columbus) 47201
Crumstown 46554
Crystal 47527
Cuba, *Allen* 46741
Cuba (Part of Edinburgh) 46124
Cuba, *Owen* 47460
Culver 46511
Culver Military Academy (Part of Culver) 46511
Cumback 47501
Cumberland (Part of Indianapolis) 46229
Cunot 46120
Curby 47118
Curry (Twp) 47879
Curryville, *Adams* 46731
Curryville, *Sullivan* 47879
Curtisville 46036
Cutler 46920
Cuzco 47432
Cyclone 46041
Cynthiana 47612
Cypress 47712
Dabney 47023
Daggett 47427
Daisy Hill 47106
Dale 47523
Daleville 47334
Dallas (Twp) 46702
Dallas Lake 46795
Dalton 47346
Dana 47847
Danville 46122
Darlington 47940
Darmstadt 47711
Darrough Chapel 46901
Davis, *Fountain* (Twp) 47918
Davis, *Starke* (Twp) 46532
Davis (Part of Michigan City) 46360
Daylight 47711
Dayton 47941
Dayville 47630
Deacon 46994
De Camp Gardens 46516
Decatur, *Marion* (Twp) 46241
Decatur, *Adams* 46733
Decker 47524
Deedsville 46921
Deep River 46342
Deer Creek, *Carroll* (Twp) 46923
Deer Creek, *Cass* (Twp) 46932
Deer Creek, *Miami* (Twp) 46959
Deer Creek, *Carroll* 46917
Deerfield (Part of Columbus) 47201
Deerfield, *Randolph* 47380
Deerfield, *Vigo* 47802
Deers Mills 47989
De Fries Landing 46538
De Gonia 47601
Delaware, *Delaware* (Twp) 47320
Delaware, *Hamilton* (Twp) 46060
Delaware, *Ripley* 47037
Delong 46922
Delp 47905
Delphi 46923
Deming 46034
Deming Woods (Part of Terre Haute) 47803
Democrat (Twp) 46920
Demotte 46310
Denham 46996
Denmark 47427
Denver 46926
Depauw 47115
Deputy 47230
Derby 47525
Desoto 47303
Devonshire (Part of Indianapolis) 46226
Dewey (Twp) 46348
Diamond 47874
Diamond Lake, *Kosciusko* 46982
Diamond Lake, *Noble* 46794

* **Area Zip Code** † **Post Office Boxes** ‡ **Postal Station** ♦ **Census Designated Place** *Italic Type* **County**

Diamond Valley (Part of Evansville)‡ 47710-11
47724
For specific ZIP Codes call (888) 275-8777, or your local postmaster.
Dick Johnson (Twp) 47834
Dillman 46792
Dillsboro 47018
Diplomat Plaza (Part of Fort Wayne)‡ 46806
Disko 46982
Dixon 46773
Doans 47424
Dodd 47520
Dodds Bridge 47849
Dogwood 47135
Dolan 47408
Domestic 46714
Donaldson 46513
Dongola 47660
Doolittle Mills 47118
Door Village 46350
Dover, *Boone* 46052
Dover, *Dearborn* 47022
Dover Hill 47581
Dovers View 46072
Dowden Acres 47802
Downtown (Part of Gary)‡ 46402
Downtown (Part of Lafayette)‡ 47901*
47902†
Downtown (Part of Muncie)‡ 47305
47308
For specific ZIP Codes call (888) 275-8777, or your local postmaster.
Downtown (Part of Valparaiso)‡ 46383
Dresden 47453
Dresser 47885
Drexel Gardens (Part of Indianapolis) 46241
Driftwood (Twp) 47281
Dublin 47335
Dubois 47527
Dubois Crossroads 47527
Duck Creek (Twp) 46036
Dudley (Twp) 47387
Dudleytown 47274
Duff 47542
Dugger 47848
Dundee 46001
Dune Acres 46304
Duneland Beach 46360
Dunfee 46804
Dunkirk, *Cass* 46947
Dunkirk, *Jay* 47336
Dunlap 46516
Dunlapsville 47353
Dunn 47944
Dunnington 47944
Dunns Bridge 46380
Dunreith 47337
Dupont 47231
Durbin 46060
Dyer 46311
Eagle (Twp) 46077
Eagle Creek, *Lake* (Twp) 46341
Eagle Creek (Part of Indianapolis) 46214
Eagle Hollow 47250
Eagletown 46074
Eagle Village 46077
Eaglewood Estates 46077
Earle 47711
Earlham (Part of Richmond)‡ 47374
Earl Park 47942
East Cedar Lake (Part of Cedar Lake) 46303
East Chicago 46312
East Clifford 47203
East Columbus (Part of Columbus) 47201
East Enterprise 47019
Eastern Heights (Part of Bloomington) 47408
Eastgate (Part of Columbus) 47201
Eastgate (Part of Jeffersonville) 47130
Eastgate, *Hancock* 46040
Eastgate (Part of Indianapolis)‡ 46219
Eastgate Consumer Mall (Part of Indianapolis) 46219
East Germantown 47370
East Glenn 47803
East Lake Estates (Part of Elkhart) 46514
Eastland Gardens (Part of Fort Wayne) 46816
Eastland Mall (Part of Evansville) 47715
East Monticello 47960
East Mount Carmel 47665
East Oolitic 47421
East Park (Part of Frankfort) 46041
Eastridge Manor 47203
East Shelburn (Part of Shelburn) 47879
East Union 46031
Eastwich (Part of Lafayette) 47905
Eastwood 46017
Eaton 47338
Echo Crest 46280
Eckerty 47116
Economy 47339
Eden, *Lagrange* (Twp) 46571
Eden, *Hancock* 46140
Edgerton 46797
Edgewater 46383
Edgewood (Part of Columbus) 47201
Edgewood (Part of Indianapolis) 46227
Edgewood, *Madison* 46011
Edgewood Park 46818
Edinburgh 46124
Edison Park (Part of South Bend)‡ 46615
Edna Mills 46065
Edwardsport 47528
Edwardsville 47150
Eel (Twp) 46947
Eel River, *Allen* (Twp) 46723
Eel River, *Hendricks* (Twp) 46165
Ege 46763
Ehrmandale 47805
Ekin 46031
Elberfeld 47613
El Dorado 46143
Elizabeth 47117
Elizabethtown 47232
Elizaville 46052
Elkhart, *Elkhart* (Twp) 46526
Elkhart, *Noble* (Twp) 46794
Elkhart, *Elkhart* 46514-17
For specific ZIP Codes call (888) 275-8777, or your local postmaster.
Elkhart Market Center (Part of Goshen) 46526
Elkinsville 47448
Elk Pointe (Part of Jeffersonville) 47130
Ellettsville 47429
Ellis 47848
Elliston 47424
Elmdale 47933
Elmhurst (Part of Anderson) 46011
Elmira 46761
Elmore (Twp) 47529
Elmwood (Part of Peru) 46970
Elmwood, *Boone* 46052
Elnora 47529
Elrod 47018
Elston 47905
Elwood 46036
Elwren 47403
Emerald Glen 46012
Eminence 46125
Emison 47561
Emma 46571
Emporia 46011
Enchanted Hills 46732
Englewood (Part of Bedford) 47421
English 47118
English Lake 46366
Enochsburg 47240
Enos 47963
Enos Corners 47660
Enterprise 47635
Epsom 47568
Epworth Forest 46555
Erie 46970
Ervin (Twp) 46901
Etna, *Kosciusko* (Twp) 46524
Etna, *Whitley* 46725
Etna Green 46524
Etna-Troy (Twp) 46725
Eugene 47928
Eureka, *Lawrence* 47421
Eureka, *Spencer* 47635
Evanston 47531
Evansville 47701-37
For specific ZIP Codes call (888) 275-8777, or your local postmaster.
Evergreen Acres (Part of Clarksville) 47129
Everroad Park (Part of Columbus) 47203
Everton 47331
Ewing (Part of Brownstown) 47220
Exchange 46158
Fair Acres (Part of Salem) 47167
Fairbanks 47849
Fairfax (Part of Anderson) 46012
Fairfield, *De Kalb* (Twp) 46730
Fairfield, *Franklin* (Twp) 47012
Fairfield, *Tippecanoe* (Twp) 47905
Fairland♦ 46126
Fairlawn (Part of Columbus) 47201
Fairmount 46928
Fair Oaks 47943
Fair Oaks Mall (Part of Columbus) 47201
Fairplay (Twp) 47424
Fairview, *Fayette* 47331
Fairview, *Randolph* 47373
Fairview, *Switzerland* 47011
Fairview Park 47842
Fairwood Hills (Part of Indianapolis) 46256
Falcon Ridge (Part of New Albany) 47150
Fall Creek, *Hamilton* (Twp) 46038
Fall Creek, *Henry* (Twp) 47356
Fall Creek, *Madison* (Twp) 46064
Falmouth 46127
Farlen 47562
Farmers 47431
Farmersburg 47850
Farmers Retreat 47018
Farmersville 47620
Farmland 47340
Farrabee 47167
Farrville 46952
Fayette, *Vigo* (Twp) 47885
Fayette, *Boone* 46052
Fayetteville 47421
Fenn Haven (Part of Tell City) 47586
Ferdinand 47532
Ferguson Hill 47885
Fewell Rhoades 46151
Fiat 47326
Fickle 46041
Fields 46158
Fifteenth Avenue (Part of Gary)‡ 46407
Fillmore 46128
Fincastle 46172
Finchland (Part of New Albany) 47150
Finley (Twp) 47170
Fishers 46038
Fishersburg 46051
Fish Lake, *Lagrange* 46761
Fish Lake, *La Porte* 46574
Fiskville (Part of Crawfordsville) 47933
Five Points (Part of Indianapolis) 46239
Five Points, *Allen* 46797
Five Points, *Morgan* 46158
Five Points, *Whitley* 46725
Flat Rock, *Bartholomew* (Twp) 47203
Flat Rock, *Shelby* 47234
Flat Rock Park 47203
Fleming 47274
Fletcher Lake 46939
Flint 46703
Flintwood (Part of Columbus) 47201
Flora 46929
Florence 47020
Florida, *Parke* (Twp) 47874
Florida, *Madison* 46011
Floyd (Twp) 46121
Floyds Knobs 47119
Folsomville 47614
Fontanet 47851
Foraker 46526
Foresman 47922
Forest 46039
Forest Hill (Part of Evansville) 47711
Forest Hill, *Decatur* 47240
Forest Park (Part of Columbus) 47203
Forest Park Beach 46742
Forest Park Heights 47404
Forest Ridge 46952
Forest Ridge Estates 46804
Forrest Hills Estates 46036
Fort Branch 47648
Fort Ritner 47430
Fortville 46040
Fort Wayne 46801-99
For specific ZIP Codes call (888) 275-8777, or your local postmaster.
Foster 47932
Fountain 47918
Fountain City 47341
Fountain Park, *Jasper* 47977
Fountain Park, *Steuben* 46742
Fountain Square (Part of Indianapolis) 46203
Fountaintown 46130
Fowler 47944
Fowlerton 46930
Fox Hill 46113
Fox Lake 46703
Fox Ridge (Part of Greencastle) 46135
Francesville 47946
Francisco 47649
Frankfort 46041
Franklin, *De Kalb* (Twp) 46721
Franklin, *Floyd* (Twp) 47150
Franklin, *Grant* (Twp) 46952
Franklin, *Harrison* (Twp) 47136
Franklin, *Hendricks* (Twp) 46180
Franklin, *Henry* (Twp) 47352
Franklin, *Kosciusko* (Twp) 46539
Franklin, *Marion* (Twp) 46239
Franklin, *Montgomery* (Twp) 47940
Franklin, *Owen* (Twp) 47460
Franklin, *Pulaski* (Twp) 46996
Franklin, *Putnam* (Twp) 46172
Franklin, *Randolph* (Twp) 47380
Franklin, *Ripley* (Twp) 47031
Franklin, *Washington* (Twp) 47167
Franklin, *Wayne* (Twp) 47374
Franklin, *Johnson* 46131
Franklin, *Wayne* 47346
Frankton 46044
Fredericksburg 47120
Fredonia 47137
Freedom 47431
Freeland Park 47944
Freelandville 47535
Freeman 47460
Freeport 46161
Freetown 47235
Fremont 46737
French, *Adams* (Twp) 46714
French, *Ohio* 47001
French Lake 47802
French Lick 47432
Frenchtown 47115
Friendship 47021
Friendswood 46113
Fritchton 47591
Fruitdale 46160
Fritz Terrace (Part of Bloomington) 47404
Fugit (Twp) 47240
Fulda 47536
Fulton, *Fountain* (Twp) 47952
Fulton, *Fulton* 46931
Furnace 47424
Furnessville 46304
Gadsden 46052
Galena, *La Porte* (Twp) 46371
Galena, *Floyd*♦ 47119
Galveston 46932
Gambill 47848
Gar Creek 46774
Garden Acres, *Boone* 46071
Garden Acres, *Monroe* 47403
Garden City 47201
Garden Village 46514
Garfield (Part of Indianapolis)‡ 46203
Garrett 46738
Gary 46401-09
For specific ZIP Codes call (888) 275-8777, or your local postmaster.
Gasburg 46158
Gas City 46933
Gaston 47342
Gatchel 47586
Gatesville 46164
Gateway Shopping Center (Part of Richmond) 47374
Gaynorsville 47240
Geetingsville 46041
Gem 46140
Geneva, *Jennings* (Twp) 47273
Geneva, *Adams* 46740
Geneva, *Shelby* 47234
Gentry Estates 47401
Gentryville 47537
Georgetown, *Allen* 46741
Georgetown, *Cass* 46947
Georgetown, *Floyd* 47122
Georgetown, *Randolph* 47340
Georgetown, *St. Joseph*♦ 46637
Georgia 47446
Gerald 47520
German, *Bartholomew* (Twp) 47203
German, *Marshall* (Twp) 46506
German, *St. Joseph* (Twp) 46628
German, *Vanderburgh* (Twp) 47720
Germantown 47272
Gessie 47974
Gibson (Twp) 47170
Gifford 47978
Gilboa (Twp) 47944
Gilead 46951
Gill (Twp) 47861
Gillam (Twp) 46378
Gilman 46001
Gilmer Park 46624
Gilmour 47438
Gingrich 47960
Gings 46173
Giro 47640
Glen Aire 47803
Glenbrook Square (Part of Fort Wayne) 46805
Glendale 47558
Glendale Center (Part of Indianapolis) 46220
Glendale Lake 46953
Glen Eden 46703
Glenhall 47992
Glenns Valley (Part of Indianapolis) 46217
Glen Park East (Part of Gary)‡ 46409
Glenview 47203
Glenwood 46133
Glenwood Acres 47620
Glenwood Park (Part of Fort Wayne) 46815
Glezen 47567
Glyn Ellen (Part of Anderson) 46012
Gnaw Bone 47448
Goblesville 46750
Goff 46953
Golden Hill 47960
Golden Lake 46779
Goldsmith 46045
Golfview Estates 47130
Goodland 47948
Goose Lake 46725

*** Area Zip Code** **† Post Office Boxes** **‡ Postal Station** **♦ Census Designated Place** *Italic Type* **County**

Goshen, *Elkhart* 46526-28
For specific ZIP Codes call (888) 275-8777, or your local postmaster.
Goshen, *Scott* 47170
Gosport 47433
Gowdy 46173
Grabill 46741
Grafton 47620
Graham (Twp) 47230
Graham Woods 46304
Grammer 47236
Grandview (Part of Anderson) 46011
Grandview (Part of Bloomington) 47408
Grandview, *Spencer* 47615
Grandview Lake 47201
Grandview Village 47150
Granger♦ 46530
Grant, *Benton* (Twp) 47921
Grant, *De Kalb* (Twp) 46793
Grant, *Greene* (Twp) 47465
Grant, *Newton* (Twp) 47948
Grant City 47384
Grantsburg 47123
Granville 47338
Grass (Twp) 47611
Grass Creek 46935
Grassy Fork (Twp) 47274
Gravel Beach 46795
Gravelton 46542
Grayford 47265
Graysville 47852
Green, *Grant* (Twp) 46986
Green, *Hancock* (Twp) 46140
Green, *Madison* (Twp) 46048
Green, *Marshall* (Twp) 46501
Green, *Morgan* (Twp) 46151
Green, *Noble* (Twp) 46701
Green, *Randolph* (Twp) 47340
Green, *Wayne* (Twp) 47393
Green Acres 46410
Greenbriar 46135
Greenbriar Hills 47710
Greenbrier, *Orange* 47454
Greenbrier, *Warrick* 47601
Greencastle 46135
Green Center 46701
Greendale 47025
Greene, *Jay* (Twp) 47371
Greene, *Parke* (Twp) 47989
Greene, *St. Joseph* (Twp) 46614
Greenfield, *Lagrange* (Twp) 46746
Greenfield, *Orange* (Twp) 47118
Greenfield, *Hancock* 46140
Greenfield Estates 46952
Greenfield Mills 46746
Green Hill 47970
Greenleaf Manor (Part of Elkhart) 46514
Green Meadows, *Shelby* 46126
Green Meadows, *Tippecanoe* 47906
Green Oak 46975
Green River Estates 47711
Greensboro 47362
Greensburg 47240
Greensfork, *Randolph* (Twp) 47355
Greens Fork, *Wayne* 47345
Greentown 46936
Green Tree Mall (Part of Clarksville) 47129
Greenvalley Estates (Part of New Albany) 47150
Greenville 47124
Greenwood, *Johnson* 46142-43
For specific ZIP Codes call (888) 275-8777, or your local postmaster.
Greenwood, *Lagrange* 46795
Greenwood Place (Part of Indianapolis) 46227
Greenwood Park Mall (Part of Greenwood) 46142
Greer (Twp) 47613
Gregg (Twp) 46151
Greybrook Lake 47868
Griffin 47616
Griffith 46319
Groomsville 46049
Groveland 46105
Grovertown 46531

Guilford, *Hendricks* (Twp) 46168
Guilford, *Dearborn* 47022
Guion 47872
Gurley Corner 47038
Guthrie (Twp) 47421
Guthrie 47421
Guy 46936
Gwynneville 46144
Hacienda Village 46815
Hackleman 46928
Haddon (Twp) 47838
Hadley 46121
Hagerstown 47346
Haglund (Part of Burns Harbor) 46304
Halbert (Twp) 47581
Haleysbury 47281
Hall, *Dubois* (Twp) 47546
Hall, *Morgan* 46157
Hamblen (Twp) 46164
Hamburg, *Clark* 47172
Hamburg, *Franklin* 47024
Hamilton, *Delaware* (Twp) 47302
Hamilton, *Jackson* (Twp) 47274
Hamilton, *Sullivan* (Twp) 47882
Hamilton, *Clinton* 46058
Hamilton, *Madison* 46011
Hamilton, *Steuben* 46742
Hamilton Park 47303
Hamilton Village 47303
Hamlet 46532
Hammond, *Spencer* (Twp) 47615
Hammond, *Lake* 46320-27
For specific ZIP Codes call (888) 275-8777, or your local postmaster.
Hamor Heights 47203
Hancock Chapel 47115
Handy 47401
Hanfield 46952
Hanging Grove (Twp) 47978
Hanna 46340
Hanover, *Lake* (Twp) 46303
Hanover, *Shelby* (Twp) 46161
Hanover, *Jefferson* 47243
Hanover Beach 47243
Happy Hollow Heights (Part of West Lafayette) 47906
Harbison (Twp) 47527
Harbor (Part of East Chicago)‡ 46312
Hardinsburg, *Dearborn* 47025
Hardinsburg, *Washington* 47125
Hardscrabble 46051
Harlan 46743
Harmony, *Posey* (Twp) 47631
Harmony, *Union* (Twp) 47331
Harmony, *Clay* 47853
Harper 47283
Harris (Twp) 46530
Harrisburg 47331
Harris City 47240
Harrison, *Bartholomew* (Twp) 47201
Harrison, *Blackford* (Twp) 47359
Harrison, *Boone* (Twp) 46052
Harrison, *Cass* (Twp) 46950
Harrison, *Clay* (Twp) 47841
Harrison, *Daviess* (Twp) 47501
Harrison, *Dearborn* (Twp) 47060
Harrison, *Delaware* (Twp) 47304
Harrison, *Elkhart* (Twp) 46526
Harrison, *Fayette* (Twp) 47331
Harrison, *Harrison* (Twp) 47112
Harrison, *Henry* (Twp) 47384
Harrison, *Howard* (Twp) 46902
Harrison, *Knox* (Twp) 47557
Harrison, *Kosciusko* (Twp) 46580
Harrison, *Miami* (Twp) 46911
Harrison, *Morgan* (Twp) 46151
Harrison, *Owen* (Twp) 47433
Harrison, *Pulaski* (Twp) 46996

Harrison, *Spencer* (Twp) 47532
Harrison, *Union* (Twp) 47353
Harrison, *Vigo* (Twp) 47807
Harrison, *Wayne* (Twp) 47327
Harrison, *Wells* (Twp) 46714
Harrison Hills (Part of Columbus) 47201
Harrison Lake 47201
Harristown 47167
Harrisville 47390
Harrodsburg 47434
Hart (Twp) 47619
Hartford, *Adams* (Twp) 46740
Hartford, *Ohio* 47001
Hartford City 47348
Hartford Place (Part of Columbus) 47201
Hartleyville 47421
Hartsville 47244
Hartzel 46795
Harveysburg 47952
Hashtown 47424
Haskell 46390
Haskell Heights 46390
Hastings 46542
Hatfield 47617
Haubstadt 47639
Haw Creek (Twp) 47246
Hawthorne Hills 46307
Hayden 47245
Haysville 47546
Hazelrigg 46052
Hazelwood (Part of Fort Wayne)‡ 46805
Hazelwood, *Hendricks* 46118
Hazleton 47640
Headlee 47960
Heather Heights (Part of Columbus) 47201
Heaton Lake 46514
Hebron 46341
Hedrick 47993
Heilman 47523
Helmcrest (Part of Fortville) 46040
Helmer 46747
Helmsburg 47435
Helt (Twp) 47847
Heltonville 47436
Hemlock 46937
Hemlock Lakes 47952
Henderson 46173
Hendricks, *Shelby* (Twp) 46176
Hendricks, *Johnson* 46142
Hendricksville 47459
Henry, *Fulton* (Twp) 46910
Henry, *Henry* (Twp) 47362
Henryville 47126
Hensley (Twp) 46181
Herbst 46952
Heritage Hills 47150
Heritage Lake 46121
.... 46128
For specific ZIP Codes call (888) 275-8777, or your local postmaster.
Herr 46052
Hessen Cassel 46819
Hesston 46350
Hessville (Part of Hammond)‡ 46323
Heth (Twp) 47142
Heusler 47712
Hibbard 46511
Hibernia 47111
Hibernia 47933
Hickory Grove (Twp) 47917
Hidden Lake Estates 47130
Hidden Valley♦ 47025
Hideaway Lake 47952
Highbanks 46555
High Lake 46701
Highland, *Franklin* (Twp) 47012
Highland, *Greene* (Twp) 47424
Highland, *Vermillion* (Twp) 47974
Highland, *Lake* 46322
Highland, *Vanderburgh*♦ 47710
Highland, *Vermillion* 47854
Highland Grove (Part of Highland) 46322
Highland Meadows 46952
Highland Village (Part of Bloomington) 47403
Highwoods (Part of Indianapolis) 46222

Hiker Trace (Part of Columbus) 47201
Hildebrand Village 46176
Hillcrest (Part of Anderson) 46012
Hillcrest (Part of Columbus) 47201
Hillcrest (Part of Corydon) 47112
Hillcrest (Part of Fort Wayne) 46816
Hillcrest, *Porter* 46383
Hillendale 47006
Hillham 47432
Hillisburg 46041
Hills And Dales 47383
Hillsboro, *Fountain* 47949
Hillsboro, *Henry* 47362
Hillsdale, *Vanderburgh* 47711
Hillsdale, *Vermillion* 47854
Hillview Estates 47201
Hindostan Falls 47581
Hindustan 47408
Hitchcock 47167
Hi-View (Part of South Bend) 46624
Hoagland 46745
Hobart 46342
Hobbieville 47462
Hobbs 46047
Hoffman Lake 46580
Hogan (Twp) 47001
Hogtown 47140
Holaday Hills and Dales 46032
Holiday Lakes 46738
Holiday Park 46902
Holland 47541
Hollandsburg 47872
Hollybrook Lake 47433
Holton 47023
Home Corner 46952
Home Place 46280
Homer 46146
Homestead (Part of Greendale) 47025
Honey Creek, *Howard* (Twp) 46979
Honey Creek, *Vigo* (Twp) 47802
Honey Creek, *White* (Twp) 47980
Honey Creek, *Henry* 47356
Honey Hills 47802
Honeyville 46571
Hoosier Acres (Part of Bloomington) 47401
Hoosier Highlands 47868
Hoosierville 47834
Hoover 46947
Hope 47246
Hopewell, *De Kalb* 46706
Hopewell, *Johnson* 46131
Horace 47240
Horseshoe Lake 46350
Hortonville 46069
Houston 47235
Hovey 47620
Howard, *Howard* (Twp) 46901
Howard, *Parke* (Twp) 47859
Howard, *Washington* (Twp) 47167
Howard, *Parke* 47952
Howe 46746
Howell (Part of Evansville) 47712
Howesville 47438
Hubbell 47427
Hubbells Corner 47041
Hudson, *La Porte* (Twp) 46552
Hudson, *Steuben* 46747
Hudson Lake 46552
Hudsonville 47558
Huff (Twp) 47615
Huffman 47588
Hull Addition 46072
Hunter Lake 46540
Huntersville (Part of Batesville) 47006
Huntertown 46748
Huntingburg 47542
Huntington 46750
Huntsville, *Madison* 46064
Huntsville, *Randolph* 47358
Hurlburt 46341
Huron 47437
Hyde Park 47302
Hymera 47855

Idaho (Part of Terre Haute)‡ 47802
Idaville 47950
Ijamsville 46962
Imperial Gardens 46835
Imperial Hills (Part of Greenwood) 46142
Independence 47918
Independence Hill (Part of Merrillville) 46410
Indiana Beach 47960
Indiana Oaks 47172

Indianapolis

..........46201-90
For specific ZIP Codes call (888) 275-8777, or your local postmaster.

Colleges & Universities

Butler Univ 46208
Christian Theological Seminary 46208
Indiana Univ-Purdue Univ 46202
ITT Technical Institute 46268
Marian Coll 46222
Martin Univ 46218
Univ of Indianapolis 46227

Financial Institutions

Bank One, NA 46277
The Fifth Third Bank of Central Indiana 46204
National City Bank 46255
NBD Bank, NA 46266

Hospitals

Community Hosps 46227
Indiana Univ Med Ctr 46202
Methodist Hosp of Indiana 46202
William N Wishard Memorial Hosp 46202

Hotels/Motels

Adam's Mark 46241
Crowne Plaza, Union Sta 46225
Embassy Suites 46204
Holiday Inn Select, Airport 46241
Holiday Inn Select at the Pyramids 46268
Hyatt Regency at State Capitol 46204
Marriott 46219
Omni Severin 46225
Radisson, City Ctr 46204
Ramada, Indianapolis Airport 46241
University Place/ Doubletree 46202
The Westin 46204

Military Installations

Naval Air Warfare Ctr Aircraft Division 46219
Defense, Finance & Accounting Serv, Indianapolis Ctr 46249
Unit Training & Equipment Site, Camp Atterbury, Indiana Army Nat Guard 46241
U S Property & Fiscal Off for Indiana 46241

Indianapolis Union Stockyards (Part of Indianapolis) 46241
Indian Creek, *Lawrence* (Twp) 47421
Indian Creek, *Monroe* (Twp) 47403
Indian Creek, *Pulaski* (Twp) 46985
Indian Heights♦ 46902
Indian Hills (Part of Columbus) 47203
Indian Lake (Part of Lawrence) 42636
Indianola 46795
Indian Springs 47581
Indian kVillage (Part of Fort Wayne) 46809
Indian Village, *Noble* 46732
Indian Village, *St. Joseph* 46637
Industry (Part of Muncie) 47302
Ingalls 46048

Inglefield (Part of Darmstadt) 47618
Innisdale 46001
Inverness 46703
Inwood 46563
Iona 47591
Ireland 47545
Irondale (Part of Anderson) 46016
Ironton 47581
Iroquois (Twp) 47922
Island Park, *Kosciusko* 46580
Island Park, *Steuben* 46742
Iva 47564
Ivanhoe (Part of Indianapolis) 46219
Ivy Hills (Part of Indianapolis) 46250
Jackson, *Allen* (Twp) 46773
Jackson, *Bartholomew* (Twp) 47201
47274
For specific ZIP Codes call (888) 275-8777, or your local postmaster.
Jackson, *Blackford* (Twp) 47348
Jackson, *Boone* (Twp) 46147
Jackson, *Brown* (Twp) 47448
Jackson, *Carroll* (Twp) 46917
Jackson, *Cass* (Twp) 46932
Jackson, *Clay* (Twp) 47834
Jackson, *Clinton* (Twp) 46041
Jackson, *Dearborn* (Twp) 47041
Jackson, *Decatur* (Twp) 47283
Jackson, *De Kalb* (Twp) 46706
Jackson, *Dubois* (Twp) 47542
Jackson, *Elkhart* (Twp) 46553
Jackson, *Fayette* (Twp) 47331
Jackson, *Fountain* (Twp) 47949
Jackson, *Greene* (Twp) 47462
Jackson, *Hamilton* (Twp) 47030
Jackson, *Hancock* (Twp) 46140
Jackson, *Harrison* (Twp) 47161
Jackson, *Howard* (Twp) 46936
Jackson, *Huntington* (Twp) 46783
Jackson, *Jackson* (Twp) 47274
Jackson, *Jay* (Twp) 47326
Jackson, *Kosciusko* (Twp) 46510
Jackson, *Madison* (Twp) 46011
Jackson, *Miami* (Twp) 46919
Jackson, *Morgan* (Twp) 46151
Jackson, *Newton* (Twp) 47963
Jackson, *Orange* (Twp) 47432
Jackson, *Owen* (Twp) 46120
Jackson, *Parke* (Twp) 47872
Jackson, *Porter* (Twp) 46304
Jackson, *Putnam* (Twp) 46172
Jackson, *Randolph* (Twp) 47390
Jackson, *Ripley* (Twp) 47037
Jackson, *Rush* (Twp) 46113
Jackson, *Shelby* (Twp) 46176
Jackson, *Spencer* (Twp) 47537
Jackson, *Starke* (Twp) 46534
Jackson, *Steuben* (Twp) 46703
Jackson, *Sullivan* (Twp) 47879
Jackson, *Tippecanoe* (Twp) 47905
Jackson, *Washington* (Twp) 47165
Jackson, *Wayne* (Twp) 47327
Jackson, *Wells* (Twp) 46991
Jackson, *White* (Twp) 47926
Jacksonburg 47327
Jackson Hill 47879
Jalapa 46952
Jamestown, *Boone* 46147
Jamestown, *Elkhart* 46517
Jamestown, *Steuben* 46703
Jasonville 47438
Jasper 47546*
47547†
Jay City 47326
Jefferson, *Adams* (Twp) 46711
Jefferson, *Allen* (Twp) 46773-74
For specific ZIP Codes call (888) 275-8777, or your local postmaster.
Jefferson, *Boone* (Twp) 46052
Jefferson, *Carroll* (Twp) 47960
Jefferson, *Cass* (Twp) 46947
Jefferson, *Dubois* (Twp) 47513
Jefferson, *Elkhart* (Twp) 46528
Jefferson, *Grant* (Twp) 46989
Jefferson, *Greene* (Twp) 47471
Jefferson, *Henry* (Twp) 47386
Jefferson, *Huntington* (Twp) 46792
Jefferson, *Jay* (Twp) 47371
Jefferson, *Kosciusko* (Twp) 46550
Jefferson, *Miami* (Twp) 46970
Jefferson, *Morgan* (Twp) 46151
Jefferson, *Newton* (Twp) 47951
Jefferson, *Noble* (Twp) 46701
Jefferson, *Owen* (Twp) 47427
Jefferson, *Pike* (Twp) 47564
Jefferson, *Pulaski* (Twp) 46996
Jefferson, *Putnam* (Twp) 46120
Jefferson, *Sullivan* (Twp) 47838
Jefferson, *Switzerland* (Twp) 47043
Jefferson, *Tipton* (Twp) 46072
Jefferson, *Washington* (Twp) 47108
Jefferson, *Wayne* (Twp) 47346
Jefferson, *Wells* (Twp) 46777
Jefferson, *Whitley* (Twp) 46725
Jefferson, *Clinton* 46041
Jeffersonville 47130*
47131†
Jennings, *Crawford* (Twp) 47137
Jennings, *Fayette* (Twp) 47331
Jennings, *Owen* (Twp) 46120
Jennings, *Scott* (Twp) 47102
Jericho 47848
Jerome 46936
Jessup 47874
Jewell Village 47201
Jockey 47637
Johnsburg 47542
Johnson, *Clinton* (Twp) 46041
Johnson, *Crawford* (Twp) 47116
Johnson, *Gibson* (Twp) 47639
Johnson, *Knox* (Twp) 47591
Johnson, *Lagrange* (Twp) 46795
Johnson, *La Porte* (Twp) 46574
Johnson, *Ripley* (Twp) 47042
Johnson, *Scott* (Twp) 47170
Johnson, *Gibson* 47665
Johnsonville 47993
Johnstown, *Greene* 47471
Johnstown, *Knox* 47512
Jolietville 46069
Jonesboro 46938
Jonestown 47842
Jonesville 47247
Joppa 46158
Jordan, *Jasper* (Twp) 47978
Jordan, *Warren* (Twp) 47993
Jordan, *Owen* 47868
Judah 47421
Judson, *Howard* 46901
Judson, *Parke* 47856
Judyville 47993
Julietta (Part of Indianapolis) 46239
Kalorama Park 46538
Kankakee, *Jasper* (Twp) 46392
Kankakee, *La Porte* (Twp) 46350
Kasson 47712
Keener (Twp) 46310
Kellerville 47527
Kelso (Twp) 47022
Kempton 46049
Kendallville 46755
Kennard 47351
Kent, *Warren* (Twp) 47932
Kent, *Jefferson* 47250
Kentland 47951
Kentwood (Part of Frankfort) 46041
Kenwood 47885
Kersey 46310
Kewanna 46939
Keyser (Twp) 46738
Keystone 46759
Killbuck Terrace 46012
Kilmore 46041
Kimberly Estates 47906
Kimmell 46760
Kinder 46106
Kingman 47952
Kingsbury 46345
Kingsford Heights 46346
Kingsland 46777
Kingston 47240
Kingswood Terra 47802
Kirkland (Twp) 46733
Kirklin (Twp) 46050
Kirklin 46050
Kirkpatrick 47955
Kirksville 47403
Kitchel 47353
Klemmes Corner 47012
Klondyke 47842
Knapp Lake 46732
Knight (Twp) 47711
47714-15
For specific ZIP Codes call (888) 275-8777, or your local postmaster.
Knighthood Grove 46176
Knighthood Village 46176
Knightstown 46148
Knightsville 47857
Kniman 46392
Knob Hill 47711
Knox, *Jay* (Twp) 47371
Knox, *Starke* 46534
Kokomo 46901-04
For specific ZIP Codes call (888) 275-8777, or your local postmaster.
Kokomo Mall (Part of Kokomo) 46902
Koleen 47439
Koontz Lake♦ 46574
Kossuth 47167
Kouts 46347
Kramer 47918
Kreitsburg 46311
Kriete Corners 47274
Kurtz 47249
Kyana 47575
Kyle 47001
Laconia 47135
La Crosse 46348
Ladoga 47954
Lafayette, *Allen* (Twp) 46783
Lafayette, *Floyd* (Twp) 47119
Lafayette, *Madison* (Twp) 46011
Lafayette, *Owen* (Twp) 47460
Lafayette, *Tippecanoe* 47901-05
For specific ZIP Codes call (888) 275-8777, or your local postmaster.
Lafayette Place (Part of Indianapolis 46254
Lafayette Square (Part of Indianapolis) 46254
La Fontaine 46940
Lagrange 46761
Lagro 46941
Lake, *Allen* (Twp) 46818
Lake, *Kosciusko* (Twp) 46982
Lake, *Newton* (Twp) 46349
Lake Bodona 46158
Lake Bruce 46939
Lake Cicott 46942
Lake Dalecarlia♦ 46356
Lake Dilldear 47018
Lake Edgewood 46151
Lake Eliza 46385
Lake Everett 46818
Lake Hart 46158
Lake Hills 46375
Lake Holiday, *Lake* 46307
Lake Holiday, *Montgomery* 47933
Lake James 46703
Lake Latonka 46511
46563
For specific ZIP Codes call (888) 275-8777, or your local postmaster.
Lake Manitou 46975
Lake Maxine 47456
Lake McCoy 47240
Lake Mohee 47348
Lake Noji 47802
Lake of the Woods 46506
Lake Park 46552
Lake Santee 47240
Lake Shores (Part of Fort Wayne) 46819
Lakeside Park (Part of Warsaw) 46580
Lakes of the Four Seasons 46307
Lake Station 46405
Lake Sullivan 47882
Laketon 46943
Lakeview, *Franklin* 47024
Lakeview, *Lagrange* 46795
Lake Village 46349
Lakeville 46536
Lake Wood, *Grant* 46952
Lakewood, *Vigo* 47802
Lakewood, *White* 47960
Lakewood Hills (Part of Evansville) 47711
Lamar 47550
Lamb 47043
Lamb Lake 46181
Lamong 46069
Lancaster, *Wells* (Twp) 46714
Lancaster, *Huntington* 46750
Lancaster, *Jefferson* 47250
Lancaster Park 47403
Landess 46991
Lane (Twp) 47637
Lanesville 47136
Lantana Estate (Part of Shelbyville) 46176
Lantern Park 47304
Laotto 46763
Lapaz 46537
La Paz Junction 46563
Lapel 46051
La Porte 46350-52
For specific ZIP Codes call (888) 275-8777, or your local postmaster.
Lapping Park Estates (Part of Clarksville) 47130
Larimer Hill 47885
Larwill 46764
Laud 46725
Laughery (Twp) 47041
Lauramie (Twp) 47930
Laurel (Twp) 47024
Laurel 47024
Lawndale (Part of Evansville)‡ 47715-16
For specific ZIP Codes call (888) 275-8777, or your local postmaster.
Lawrence 46226
46256
For specific ZIP Codes call (888) 275-8777, or your local postmaster.
Lawrenceburg 47025
Lawrenceport 47446
Lawrenceville 47041
Lawton 46996
Layton Mills 47240
Leases Corner 46950
Leavenworth 47137
Lebanon 46052
Lee 47978
Leesburg 46538
Leesville 47421
Leininger Acres 46072
Leipsic 47452
Leisure 46036
Leiters Ford 46945
Lena 47834
Leo (Part of Leo-Cedarville) 46765
Leo-Cedarville 46741
46765
For specific ZIP Codes call (888) 275-8777, or your local postmaster.
Leopold 47551
Leota 47170
Leroy 46355
Letts 47240
Letts Corner 47240
Lewis, *Clay* (Twp) 47438
Lewis, *Vigo* 47858
Lewisburg 46970
Lewis Creek 47234
Lewisville, *Henry* 47352
Lewisville, *Morgan* 46120
Lexington, *Carroll* 46920
Lexington, *Scott* 47138
Liber 47371
Liberty, *Carroll* (Twp) 46917
Liberty, *Crawford* (Twp) 47140
Liberty, *Delaware* (Twp) 47383
Liberty, *Fulton* (Twp) 46931
Liberty, *Grant* (Twp) 46928
Liberty, *Hendricks* (Twp) 46118
Liberty, *Henry* (Twp) 47362
Liberty, *Howard* (Twp) 46901
Liberty, *Parke* (Twp) 47952
Liberty, *Porter* (Twp) 46383
Liberty, *St. Joseph* (Twp) 46554
Liberty, *Shelby* (Twp) 46182
Liberty, *Tipton* (Twp) 46068
Liberty, *Wabash* (Twp) 46940
Liberty, *Warren* (Twp) 47918
Liberty, *Wells* (Twp) 46766
Liberty, *White* (Twp) 47960
Liberty, *Union* 47353
Liberty Center 46766
Liberty Hills 46804
Liberty Mills 46946
Liberty Park 46307
Libertyville 47885
Licking (Twp) 47348
Liggett 47885
Lighthouse Place (Part of Michigan City) 46360
Ligonier 46767
Lilly Dale 47586
Lima (Twp) 46746
Limberlost Hills 47803
Limedale 46135
Lincoln, *Hendricks* (Twp) 46112
Lincoln, *La Porte* (Twp) 46365
Lincoln, *Newton* (Twp) 46310
Lincoln, *St. Joseph* (Twp) 46574
Lincoln, *White* (Twp) 47950
Lincoln, *Cass* 46994
Lincoln City 47552
Lincoln Heights (Part of Clarksville) 47129
Lincoln Hills 46385
Lincoln Park (Part of Clarksville) 47129
Lincolnshire (Part of Fort Wayne) 46807
Lincolnshire (Part of Terre Haute) 47803
Lincoln Village (Part of Merrillville) 46410
Lincolnville 46992
Lindbergh Estates 46012
Linden 47955
Lindenwood (Part of Indianapolis) 46227
Linkville 46563
Linn Grove 46769
Linnsburg 47933
Linton, *Vigo* (Twp) 47802
Linton, *Greene* 47441
Linwood, *Madison* 46001
Linwood (Part of Indianapolis)‡ 46201
Lisbon 46755
Little 47567
Little Acre 47274
Little Cedar Lake 46725
Little Point 46180
Little Saint Louis 47115
Little York 47139
Liverpool (Part of Lake Station) 46805
Livonia 47108
Lizton 46149

Place	ZIP
Locke	46550
Lockhart (Twp)	47585
Lockport	47926
Lodi	47952
Logan, *Fountain* (Twp)	47918
Logan, *Pike* (Twp)	47567
Logan, *Dearborn*	47060
Logansport	46947
Logansport Mall (Part of Logansport)	46947
Lomax	46374
London	46126
London Heights	46126
Long Beach	46360
Long Lake, *Steuben*	46737
Long Lake, *Wabash*	46962
Long Lake Island	46383
Loogootee	47553
Lookout	47041
Loon Lake	46725
Lorane	46725
Loree	46914
Losantville	47354
Lost Creek (Twp)	47803
Lost River (Twp)	47581
Lottaville (Part of Merrillville)	46410
Lotus	47353
Lovett	47265
Lowell, *Bartholomew*	47201
Lowell, *Lake*	46356*
	46399†
Lower Sunset Park	47960
Luce (Twp)	47634
Lucerne	46950
Ludwig Park (Part of Fort Wayne)	46825
Lukens Lake	46974
Luray	47386
Luther	46787
Lutheran Lake	47201
Lydick	46628
Lyford	47874
Lynn, *Posey* (Twp)	47620
Lynn, *Randolph*	47355
Lynnhurst (Part of Indianapolis)	46241
Lynnville	47619
Lynwood Estates	47404
Lyons	47443
Lyonsville	47331
McCarty	46142
McClellan (Twp)	47963
Mc Col Place (Part of Salem)	47167
McCordsville	46055
McCoysburg	47978
McCutchanville	47711
McDaniel	46151
Mace	47933
Mac-Fair-Mar	46947
McGrawsville	46911
Mackey	47654
McKinley	47108
McKinley Town and Country Shopping Center (Part of Mishawaka)	46545
McNatts	47359
Macy	46951
Madison, *Allen* (Twp)	46773
Madison, *Carroll* (Twp)	46923
Madison, *Clinton* (Twp)	46058
Madison, *Daviess* (Twp)	47562
Madison, *Dubois* (Twp)	47546
Madison, *Jay* (Twp)	45846
Madison, *Montgomery* (Twp)	47933
Madison, *Morgan* (Twp)	46158
Madison, *Pike* (Twp)	47567
Madison, *Putnam* (Twp)	46135
Madison, *St. Joseph* (Twp)	46614
Madison, *Tipton* (Twp)	46072
Madison, *Washington* (Twp)	47108
Madison, *Jefferson*	47250
Magley	46733
Magnet	47520
Mahalasville	46151
Mahon	46750
Majenica	46750
Malden	46383
Maltersville	47542
Manchester	47001
Manhattan	46135
Manilla	46150
Manor Woods	46804
Mansfield	47872
Manson	46041
Manville	47250
Maplecrest Plaza (Part of Kokomo)	46902
Maple Lane	46635
Maples	46816
Mapleton (Part of Indianapolis)‡	46208
	46228
For specific ZIP Codes call (888) 275-8777, or your local postmaster.	
Maple Valley	46186
Maplewood, *Hendricks*	46122
Maplewood, *Vigo*	47885
Maplewood Park (Part of Fort Wayne)	46815
Marco	47443
Marengo	47140
Mariah Hill	47556
Marietta	46176
Marineland Gardens	46567
Marion, *Allen* (Twp)	46745
Marion, *Boone* (Twp)	46069
Marion, *Decatur* (Twp)	47240
Marion, *Dubois* (Twp)	47546
Marion, *Hendricks* (Twp)	46122
Marion, *Jasper* (Twp)	47978
Marion, *Jennings* (Twp)	47230
Marion, *Lawrence* (Twp)	47446
Marion, *Owen* (Twp)	47455
Marion, *Pike* (Twp)	47590
Marion, *Putnam* (Twp)	46128
Marion, *Grant*	46952-53
For specific ZIP Codes call (888) 275-8777, or your local postmaster.	
Marion, *Shelby*	46176
Marion Heights	47885
Markland	47020
Markland Mall (Part of Kokomo)	46902
Markle	46770
Markleville	46056
Marlin Hills	47401
Marquette Mall (Part of Michigan City)‡	46360
Marrs (Twp)	47620
Marrs Center	47620
Marshall, *Lawrence* (Twp)	47421
Marshall, *Parke*	47859
Marshfield	47993
Mars Hill (Part of Indianapolis)	46241
Marshtown	46939
Martin Heights (Part of Salem)	47167
Martinsburg	47165
Martinsville	46151
Martz	47841
Maryland	47802
Marysville, *Clark*	47141
Marysville, *Pike*	47598
Marywood	47802
Matlock Heights (Part of Bloomington)	47408
Matthews	46957
Mattix Corner	46041
Mauckport	47142
Maumee (Twp)	46797
Mauzy	46173
Max	46052
Maxinkuckee	46511
Maxville	47340
Maxwell, *Hancock*	46154
Maxwell, *Morgan*	46151
Mayfield (Part of Muncie)	47302
Mays	46155
Maysville	47501
Maywood (Part of Indianapolis)	46241
Meadowbrook (Part of Anderson)	46014
Meadowbrook, *Allen*	46774
Meadowbrook, *Tippecanoe*	47905
Meadowood Estates	46036
Meadowview	46947
Mead Village (Part of Columbus)	47201
Mecca	47860
Mechanicsburg, *Boone*	46050
Mechanicsburg, *Decatur*	47263
Mechanicsburg, *Henry*	47356
Medaryville	47957
Medford	47302
Medina (Twp)	47970
Medora	47260
Meiks	46176
Mellott	47958
Melody Hill♦	47711
Meltzer	46176
Memphis	47143
Mentone	46539
Mentor	47513
Meridian Hills (Part of Indianapolis)	46260
Merom Station	47861
Merriam	46701
Merrillville	46410*
	46411†
Metamora	47030
Metea	46950
Metz	46703
Mexico♦	46958
Miami, *Cass* (Twp)	46947
Miami, *Miami*	46959
Miami Bend	46947
Miami Trails Addition	46614
Michaelsville	46953
Michiana Shores	46360
Michigan, *Clinton* (Twp)	46057
Michigan, *La Porte* (Twp)	46360
Michigan City	46360*
	46361†
Michigantown	46057
Mickleyville (Part of Indianapolis)	46241
Middle (Twp)	46167
Middleboro	47374
Middlebury	46540
Middlefork, *Clinton*	46041
Middlefork, *Jefferson*	47231
Middletown, *Henry*	47356
Middletown, *Shelby*	46182
Middletown Park	47302
Midland	47445
Midway (Part of Goshen)	46526
Midway, *Jefferson*	47250
Midway, *Spencer*	47601
Mier	46919
Mifflin	47118
Milan, *Allen* (Twp)	46774
Milan, *Ripley*	47031
Milan Center	46774
Milford, *Lagrange* (Twp)	46795
Milford, *Decatur*	47240
Milford, *Kosciusko*	46542
Milford Junction	46542
Mill (Twp)	46933
Millcreek, *Fountain* (Twp)	47952
Mill Creek, *La Porte*	46365
Milledgeville	46052
Miller, *Dearborn* (Twp)	47025
Miller (Part of Gary)‡	46403
Millersburg, *Elkhart*	46543
Millersburg, *Hamilton*	46030
Millersburg, *Orange*	47454
Millersville (Part of Indianapolis)	46220
Millgrove, *Steuben* (Twp)	46776
Mill Grove, *Blackford*	47348
Millhousen	47261
Milligan	47872
Millport	47281
Milltown	47145
Millville	47362
Milo	46991
Milroy, *Jasper* (Twp)	47978
Milroy, *Rush*	46156
Milton, *Jefferson* (Twp)	47250
Milton, *Ohio*	47018
Milton, *Wayne*	47357
Mineral City	47424
Mineral Springs	46538
Mishawaka	46544-46
For specific ZIP Codes call (888) 275-8777, or your local postmaster.	
Mitchell	47446
Mitcheltree (Twp)	47581
Mixerville	47010
Moberly	47115
Modesto	47408
Modoc	47358
Mohawk	46140
Mongo	46771
Monitor	47905
Monmouth	46733
Monon	47959
Monoquet	46580
Monroe, *Adams* (Twp)	46711
Monroe, *Allen* (Twp)	46773
Monroe, *Carroll* (Twp)	46929
Monroe, *Clark* (Twp)	47126
Monroe, *Delaware* (Twp)	47302
Monroe, *Grant* (Twp)	46952
Monroe, *Howard* (Twp)	46979
Monroe, *Jefferson* (Twp)	47250
Monroe, *Kosciusko* (Twp)	46580
Monroe, *Madison* (Twp)	46001
Monroe, *Morgan* (Twp)	46157
Monroe, *Pike* (Twp)	47598
Monroe, *Pulaski* (Twp)	46996
Monroe, *Putnam* (Twp)	46135
Monroe, *Randolph* (Twp)	47340
	47368
For specific ZIP Codes call (888) 275-8777, or your local postmaster.	
Monroe, *Washington* (Twp)	47167
Monroe, *Adams*	46772
Monroe, *Tippecanoe*	47905
Monroe City	47557
Monroe Manor	46350
Monroeville	46773
Monrovia	46157
Montclair	46149
Monterey	46960
Monterey Village (Part of Noblesville)	46060
Montezuma	47862
Montgomery, *Gibson* (Twp)	47665
Montgomery, *Jennings* (Twp)	47230
Montgomery, *Owen* (Twp)	47460
Montgomery, *Daviess*	47558
Monticello	47960
Montmorenci	47962
Montpelier	47359
Moonlight Bay	46779
Moonville	46001
Moore	46721
Moorefield (Part of Indianapolis)	46222
Moorefield, *Switzerland*	47043
Mooreland	47360
Moores Hill	47032
Mooresville	46158
Moral (Twp)	46126
Moran	46041
Morgan, *Harrison* (Twp)	47164
Morgan, *Owen* (Twp)	47868
Morgan, *Porter* (Twp)	46383
Morgan Park (Part of Chesterton)	46304
Morgantown	46160
Morningside (Part of Muncie)	47302
Morocco	47963
Morris	47033
Morristown	46161
Morton	46135
Moscow	46156
Mott Station	47161
Mound (Twp)	47932
Mounds Mall (Part of Anderson)	46016
Mount Auburn, *Shelby*	46124
Mount Auburn, *Wayne*	47327
Mount Ayr	47964
Mount Carmel, *Franklin*	47012
Mount Carmel, *Washington*	47108
Mount Comfort	46140
Mount Etna	46750
Mount Healthy	47201
Mount Liberty	47448
Mount Meridian	46135
Mount Olympus	47640
Mount Pisgah	46761
Mount Pleasant, *Delaware* (Twp)	47396
Mount Pleasant, *Delaware*	47302
Mount Pleasant, *Johnson*	46131
Mount Pleasant, *Martin*	47553
Mount Pleasant, *Perry*	47520
Mount Sinai	47032
Mount Sterling	47043
Mount Summit	47361
Mount Vernon, *Posey*	47620
Mount Vernon, *Wabash*	46940
Mount Zion	46792
Mud Center (Part of Evansville)	47712
Mudlavia Springs	47918
Mulberry	46058
Mull	47394
Muncie	47302-08
For specific ZIP Codes call (888) 275-8777, or your local postmaster.	
Muncie Mall (Part of Muncie)	47303
Munster	46321
Muren	47598
Murray	46714
Nabb	47147
Napoleon	47034
Nappanee	46550
Nashville	47448
Navilleton	47119
Nead	46970
Nebraska	47262
Needham	46162
Needmore, *Brown*	47448
Needmore, *Lawrence*	47421
Negangards Corner	47031
Nevada	46068
Nevada Mills	46703
Nevins (Twp)	47805
New Albany (Twp)	47150
New Albany	47150*
	47151†
New Alsace	47022
New Amsterdam	47110
Newark	47459
New Augusta (Part of Indianapolis)	46268
New Bellsville	47201
Newbern	47201
Newberry	47449
New Boston, *Harrison*	47117
New Boston, *Spencer*	47531
New Britton	46038
New Brunswick	46052
Newburgh	47629†
	47630*
New Burlington	47302
Newbury (Twp)	46565
New Carlisle	46552
Newcastle, *Fulton* (Twp)	46975
New Castle, *Henry*	47362
New Chicago	46342
New Columbus	46011
New Corydon	47326
New Durham (Twp)	46350
New Elizabethtown	47274
New Elliott	46319
New Fairfield	47012
New Farmington	47274
New Frankfort	47170
New Garden (Twp)	47341
New Goshen	47863
New Harmony	47631
New Haven	46774
Newland	47978
New Lebanon	47864
New Lisbon, *Henry*	47366
New Lisbon, *Randolph*	47390
New London	46979
New Marion	47023
New Market, *Clark*	47141
New Market, *Montgomery*	47965
New Maysville	46172
New Middletown	47160
New Mount Pleasant	47371
New Palestine	46163
New Paris♦	46553
New Pennington	47240
New Philadelphia	47167
New Pittsburg	47390
Newpoint	47263

Newport 47966
New Richmond 47967
New Ross 47968
New Salem 46173
New Salisbury 47161
New Santa Fe 46970
Newton (Twp) 47978
Newtonville 47615
Newtown 47969
New Trenton 47035
New Unionville 47408
Newville 46721
New Washington 47162
New Waverly 46961
New Whiteland 46184
New Winchester 46122
Nibbyville 46507
Niles (Twp) 47338
Nine Mile 46809
Nineveh 46164
Nisbet 47639
Noble, *Cass* (Twp) 46947
Noble, *Jay* (Twp) 47371
Noble, *La Porte* (Twp) 46382
Noble, *Noble* (Twp) 46701
Noble, *Rush* (Twp) 46173
Noble, *Shelby* (Twp) 47234
Noble, *Wabash* (Twp) 46992
Noblesville 46060*
46061†
Noblitt Falls (Part of Columbus) 47201
Nora (Part of Indianapolis) 46240
Nora Plaza (Part of Indianapolis) 46240
Norland Park 46706
Norma Jean 47905
Normal 46986
Norman 47264
Normanda 46072
Norristown 47234
North, *Lake* (Twp) 46312
North, *Marshall* (Twp) 46563
North Anderson (Part of Anderson) 46012
Northaven (Part of Jeffersonville) 47130
North Bend (Twp) 46534
Northcliff 47203
North Columbus (Part of Columbus) 47203
Northcrest (Part of Fort Wayne) 46825
Northcrest Shopping Center (Part of Fort Wayne) 46805
North Crows Nest (Part of Indianapolis) 46228
North Delphi (Part of Delphi) 46923
Northeast (Twp) 47452
Northern Meadows 46077
Northfield 46077
Northfield Village (Part of Lebanon) 46052
North Gate 47201
North Grove 46911
North Hayden 46356
North Highland (Part of Fort Wayne) 46808
North Judson 46366
North Liberty 46554
North Madison (Part of Madison)‡ 47250
North Manchester 46962
North Oaks 46714
North Ogilville 47201
North Park, *Bartholomew* 47280
North Park Mall (Part of Marion) 46952
North Ridge Village 46280
North Salem 46165
North Terre Haute 47805
North Vernon 47265
North Webster 46555
Northwest (Twp) 47469
Northwood (Part of Nappanee) 46550
Northwood, *Lagrange* 46761
Northwood, *Vigo* 47805
Northwood Hills 46033
North Wood Park 46383
Norton 47432
Nortonburg 47203
Norway 47960
Notre Dame 46556
Nottingham 47359
Nulltown 47331
Numa 47874
Nyesville 47872
Nyona Lake 46951
Oakcrest 47203
Oakdale (Part of Peru) 46970
Oakford 46965
Oak Forest 47012
Oak Grove, *Benton* (Twp) 47971
Oak Grove, *Starke* 46511
Oak Grove, *Vigo* 47802
Oak Hill 47660
Oakland City 47660
Oaklandon (Part of Lawrence) 46235-36
For specific ZIP Codes call (888) 275-8777, or your local postmaster.
Oaklawn Terrace (Part of Jeffersonville) 47130
Oak Park 47130
Oaktown 47561
Oakville 47367
Oakwood 46742
Oakwood Park (Part of Syracuse) 46567
Oakwood Shores 46742
Oatsville 47567
Ober 46534
Occident 46115
Ockley 46923
Odell 47918
Odon 47562
Ogden 46148
Ogden Dunes 46368
Ogilville 47201
Ohio, *Bartholomew* (Twp) 47201
Ohio, *Crawford* (Twp) 47137
Ohio, *Spencer* (Twp) 47635
Ohio, *Warrick* (Twp) 47610
Oil (Twp) 47576
Old Bargersville 46106
Old Bath 47012
Oldenburg 47036
Old Milan 47031
Old Romney Heights 47905
Old Tip Town 46570
Oldtown (Part of Lawrenceburg) 47025
Olean 47042
Olive, *Elkhart* (Twp) 46573
Olive, *St. Joseph* (Twp) 46552
Oliver 47620
Oliver Lake 46795
Olive Street (Part of South Bend)‡ 46619
Omega 46030
Ontario 46746
Onward 46967
Oolitic 47451
Ora 46968
Orange, *Noble* (Twp) 46784
Orange, *Rush* (Twp) 46173
Orange, *Fayette* 47331
Orangeville 47452
Orchard Heights 47905
Orchard Heights Addition 46614
Orchard Park 46280
Oregon, *Clark* (Twp) 47141
Oregon, *Starke* (Twp) 46574
Oregon Heights (Part of Hobart) 46405
Orestes 46063
Oriole 47551
Orland 46776
Orleans 47452
Orleans Southwest 46902
Ormas 46725
Osborn Landing 46580
Osceola 46561
Osgood 47037
Osolo (Twp) 46514
Ossian 46777
Oswego 46538
Otis 46391
Otisco 47163
Otsego (Twp) 46742
Otterbein 47970
Otter Creek, *Ripley* (Twp) 47023
Otter Creek, *Vigo* (Twp) 47805
Otter Lake 46703
Otto 47162
Otwell 47564
Owasco 46065
Owen, *Clark* (Twp) 47111
Owen, *Clinton* (Twp) 46041
Owen, *Jackson* (Twp) 47220
Owen, *Warrick* (Twp) 47637
Owensburg 47453
Owensville 47665
Oxford 47971
Packerton 46510
Paint Mill Lake 47802
Palestine, *Franklin* 47012
Palestine, *Kosciusko* 46539
Palmer 46307
Palmyra, *Knox* (Twp) 47591
Palmyra, *Harrison* 47164
Panama 46703
Paoli 47454
Papakeechie Lake 46567
Paradise 47630
Paradise Lakes 46151
Paragon 46166
Paris 47270
Paris Crossing 47270
Parish Grove (Twp) 47944
Park 47424
Parker City 47368
Parkersburg 47954
Parkers Settlement 47638
Park Fletcher 46241*
46242†
Park Forest Estates (Part of Columbus) 47201
Park Ridge (Part of Bloomington) 47408
Park Ridge East (Part of Bloomington) 47408
Parkside (Part of Columbus) 47203
Parkview (Part of Terre Haute) 47805
Park View Heights (Part of Peru) 46970
Parkway Hills 46804
Parkwood 47129
Parr 47978
Patoka, *Crawford* (Twp) 47175
Patoka, *Dubois* (Twp) 47542
Patoka, *Gibson* (Twp) 47670
Patoka, *Pike* (Twp) 47598
Patoka, *Gibson* 47666
Patricksburg 47455
Patriot 47038
Patronville 47635
Patton 47960
Patton Hill 47421
Patton Lake 46151
Paw Paw (Twp) 46974
Paxton 47865
Paynesville 47243
Peabody 46725
Pearsontown 47140
Peerless 47421
Pekin 47165
Pelzer 47601
Pence 47993
Pendleton 46064
Penn, *Jay* (Twp) 47369
Penn, *Parke* (Twp) 47832
Penn, *St. Joseph* (Twp) 46544
46561
For specific ZIP Codes call (888) 275-8777, or your local postmaster.
Penn Meadows 46545
Penn Park 46742
Penntown 47041
Pennville, *Jay* 47369
Pennville, *Wayne* 47327
Peoga 46181
Peoria, *Franklin* 45056
Peoria, *Miami* 46970
Peppertown 47030
Perkinsville 46011
Perry, *Allen* (Twp) 46748
46845
For specific ZIP Codes call (888) 275-8777, or your local postmaster.
Perry, *Boone* (Twp) 46052
Perry, *Clay* (Twp) 47846
Perry, *Clinton* (Twp) 46035
Perry, *Delaware* (Twp) 47302
Perry, *Lawrence* (Twp) 47462
Perry, *Marion* (Twp) 46227
Perry, *Martin* (Twp) 47553
Perry, *Miami* (Twp) 46970
Perry, *Monroe* (Twp) 47401
Perry, *Noble* (Twp) 46767
Perry, *Tippecanoe* (Twp) 47905
Perry, *Vanderburgh* (Twp) 47712
Perry, *Wayne* (Twp) 47339
Perry Manor (Part of Indianapolis) 46227
Perrysburg 46951
Perrysville 47974
Pershing, *Fulton* 46975
Pershing (Twp) 47235
Perth 47837
Peru 46970
Petersburg 47567
Peterson 46733
Peters Switch 47274
Petersville 47203
Petroleum 46778
Pettit 47905
Pheasant Run 46819
Philadelphia 46140
Philomath 47325
Phlox 46936
Pickard 46050
Pierce (Twp) 47167
Pierceton 46562
Pierceville 47039
Pierre Moran Mall (Part of Elkhart)‡ 46514
Pierson (Twp) 47802
Pigeon, *Vanderburgh* (Twp) 47710-11
47713
47720
For specific ZIP Codes call (888) 275-8777, or your local postmaster.
Pigeon, *Warrick* (Twp) 47523
Pike, *Jay* (Twp) 47371
Pike, *Marion* (Twp) 46254
Pike, *Ohio* (Twp) 47018
Pike, *Warren* (Twp) 47991
Pike, *Boone* 46052
Pikes Peak 47201
Pikeville 47590
Pilot Knob 47140
47145
For specific ZIP Codes call (888) 275-8777, or your local postmaster.
Pimento 47866
Pine, *Benton* (Twp) 47944
Pine, *Porter* (Twp) 46360
Pine, *Warren* (Twp) 47975
Pine Grove Estates 47006
Pine Lake 46350
Pine Valley 47454
Pine Village 47975
Pinhook, *La Porte* 46350
Pinhook, *Lawrence* 47421
Pinola 46350
Pipe Creek, *Madison* (Twp) 46036
Pipe Creek, *Miami* (Twp) 46970
Pittsboro 46167
Pittsburg 46923
Plain (Twp) 46538
46580
For specific ZIP Codes call (888) 275-8777, or your local postmaster.
Plainfield 46168
Plainville 47568
Plano 46151
Plato 46761
Plattsburg 47281
Pleasant, *Allen* (Twp) 46798
46819
For specific ZIP Codes call (888) 275-8777, or your local postmaster.
Pleasant, *Grant* (Twp) 46952
Pleasant, *Johnson* (Twp) 46142
Pleasant, *La Porte* (Twp) 46350
Pleasant, *Porter* (Twp) 46347
Pleasant, *Steuben* (Twp) 46703
Pleasant, *Wabash* (Twp) 46962
Pleasant, *Switzerland* 47224
Pleasant Gardens 46171
Pleasant Lake 46779
Pleasant Mills 46780
Pleasant Plain 46792
Pleasant Run (Twp) 47436
Pleasant Valley 46561
Pleasant View 46126
Pleasant View Village 46124
Pleasantville 47838
Pleasure Valley 46182
Plevna 46901
Plummer 47424
Plum Tree 46792
Plymouth 46563
Poe 46819
Point (Twp) 47620
Point Commerce 47471
Point Idalawn 47468
Point Isabel 46928
Poland 47868
Polk, *Huntington* (Twp) 46750
Polk, *Marshall* (Twp) 46574
Polk, *Monroe* (Twp) 47436
Polk, *Washington* (Twp) 47165
Poneto 46781
Pontiac 47837
Pony Express (Part of Evansville)‡ 47710
Popcorn 47462
Portage, *St. Joseph* (Twp) 46619
46628
For specific ZIP Codes call (888) 275-8777, or your local postmaster.
Portage, *Porter* 46368
Porter (Twp) 46383
Porter 46304
Portersville 47546
Portland 47371
Portland Mills 46135
Posey, *Clay* (Twp) 47834
Posey, *Fayette* (Twp) 47331
Posey, *Franklin* (Twp) 47024
Posey, *Harrison* (Twp) 47117
Posey, *Rush* (Twp) 46104
Posey, *Switzerland* (Twp) 47038
Posey, *Washington* (Twp) 47120
47125
For specific ZIP Codes call (888) 275-8777, or your local postmaster.
Poseyville 47633
Pottawattomie Park 46360
Potters Hollow 47905
Pottersville 47460
Powers 47371
Prairie, *Henry* (Twp) 47362
Prairie, *Kosciusko* (Twp) 46580
Prairie, *La Porte* (Twp) 46340
Prairie, *Tipton* (Twp) 46049
Prairie, *Warren* (Twp) 47921
Prairie, *White* (Twp) 47923
Prairie City 47834
Prairie Creek 47869
Prairieton 47870
Prairie Village 47802
Prather 46151
Preble (Twp) 46733
Preble 46782
Prescott 46176
Presidential Village 46774
Pretty Lake, *Lagrange* 46795
Pretty Lake, *Mashall* 46563
Prince's Lakes 46164
Princeton, *White* (Twp) 47995
Princeton, *Gibson* 47670
Progress 47302
Progress Acres 47805
Prospect 47469
Providence 46106
Publico (Part of New Albany) 47150
Puckett 46953
Pulaski 46996
Pumpkin Center 47170
Purcell 47591
Putnamville 46170
Pyrmont 46923
Queensville 47265
Quercus Grove 47040
Quincy 47456
Raber 46725
Raccoon, *Parke* (Twp) 47874
Raccoon, *Putnam* 46172
Radioville 47957
Radley 46938
Radnor 46923
Raglesville 47562
Ragsdale 47573
Railroad (Twp) 46374
Rainbow (Part of Indianapolis)‡ 46222
Rainsville 47918
Raleigh 46173

Place	ZIP Code
Ramsey	47166
Randolph, *Ohio* (Twp)	47040
Randolph, *Tippecanoe* (Twp)	47985
Raub	47976
Ravenswood (Part of Indianapolis)	46240
Ravinamy	47906
Ray, *Franklin* (Twp)	47036
Ray, *Morgan* (Twp)	46166
Ray, *Steuben*	46737
Raymond	47010
Rays Crossing	46176
Raysville	46148
Red Bank (Part of Evansville)	47712
Red Bush	47630
Redding (Twp)	47274
Reddington	47274
Red Hill	47462
Redkey	47373
Redmond Park	46567
Reed	47304
Reelsville	46171
Reeve (Twp)	47553
Rego	47125
Reiffsburg	46714
Remington	47977
Reno	46121
Rensselaer	47978
Reo	47635
Republican (Twp)	47250
Reserve (Twp)	47862
Retreat	47229
Rexville	47250
Reynolds	47980
Riceville	47513
Richey Park	47960
Rich Grove (Twp)	46996
Richland, *Benton* (Twp)	47942
Richland, *De Kalb* (Twp)	46730
Richland, *Fountain* (Twp)	47958
	47969
For specific ZIP Codes call (888) 275-8777, or your local postmaster.	
Richland, *Fulton* (Twp)	46975
Richland, *Grant* (Twp)	46952
Richland, *Greene* (Twp)	47424
Richland, *Jay* (Twp)	47336
	47373
For specific ZIP Codes call (888) 275-8777, or your local postmaster.	
Richland, *Madison* (Twp)	46011
Richland, *Miami* (Twp)	46970
Richland, *Monroe* (Twp)	47429
Richland, *Steuben* (Twp)	46742
Richland, *Whitley* (Twp)	46764
Richland, *Rush*	46173
Richland, *Spencer*	47634
Richmond	47374*
	47375†
Richmond Square (Part of Richmond)	47374
Richvalley	46992
Riddle	47118
Ridgemede (Part of Bloomington)	47401
Ridgeport	47424
Ridgeview (Part of Peru)	46970
Ridgeview Heights	46806
Ridgeville	47380
Ridgeway	46809
Ridinger Lake	46562
Rigdon	46036
Riley	47871
Rileysburg	47932
Riley Village (Part of Shelbyville)	46176
Ripley, *Montgomery* (Twp)	47933
Ripley, *Rush* (Twp)	46115
Ripley, *Pulaski*	46996
Rising Sun	47040
Risse (Part of Frankfort)	46041
Rivare	46733
River City (Part of Evansville)‡	47714
	47728
For specific ZIP Codes call (888) 275-8777, or your local postmaster.	
River Falls Mall (Part of Clarksville)	47129
River Forest	46011
Riverhaven	46803
Riverside, *Clark*	47129-30
For specific ZIP Codes call (888) 275-8777, or your local postmaster.	
Riverside, *Fountain*	47918
Riverton	47861
Rivervale	47446
Riverview	47849
Riverview Acres (Part of Columbus)	47203
Riverwood	46060
Roachdale	46172
Roann	46974
Roanoke	46783
Robb (Twp)	47633
Robertsdale (Part of Hammond)	46394
Robinson (Twp)	47638
Robinwood	47803
Roble Woods	46383
Rob Roy	47918
Rochester	46975
Rock Creek, *Bartholomew* (Twp)	47232
Rock Creek, *Carroll* (Twp)	46923
Rockcreek, *Wells* (Twp)	46714
Rock Creek, *Huntington*	46750
Rockdale	47060
Rockfield	46977
Rockford, *Jackson*	47274
Rockford, *Wells*	46714
Rock Lake	46910
Rocklane	46143
Rockport	47635
Rockville	47872
Rocky Ripple (Part of Indianapolis)	46208
Roland	47469
Roll	47348
Rolling Fields (Part of Jeffersonville)	47130
Rolling Hill Estates (Part of Schererville)	46375
Rolling Hills, *Allen*	46804
Rolling Hills, *Grant*	46952
Rolling Hills, *Tippecanoe*	47905
Rolling Prairie	46371
Rolling Ridge (Part of Shelbyville)	46176
Rome	47574
Rome City	46784
Romney	47981
Romona	47460
Root (Twp)	46733
Rose (Part of Terre Haute)‡	47803
Roseburg, *Grant*	46953
Roseburg, *Union*	47353
Rosedale	47874
Rosedale Hills (Part of Indianapolis)	46227
Roseland	46637
Roselawn	46372
Rosewood	47117
Ross, *Clinton* (Twp)	46065
Ross, *Lake* (Twp)	46410
Ross, *Lake*	46408
Rossburg	47240
Rosston	46077
Rosstown	47201
Rossville	46065
Roth Park	47960
Round Grove (Twp)	47923
Round Lake, *Noble*	46755
Round Lake, *Whitley*	46725
Royal Center	46978
Royal Oaks	46815
Royalton	46077
Royal View	47201
Royer Lake	46761
Royerton	47303
Royerton Park	47303
Rugby	47246
Rural	47394
Rushville	46173
Russell (Twp)	46172
Russell Lake	46077
Russellville	46175
Russels Point	46742
Russiaville	46979
Rustic Hills	47630
Rutherford (Twp)	47553
Rutland	46563
Rykers Ridge	47250
Sagers Lake	46383
St. Anthony	47575
St. Bernice	47875
St. Croix	47576
St. Henry	47532
St. James	47639
St. Joe	46785
St. John	46373
St. Johns	46738
St. Joseph, *Allen* (Twp)	46835
St. Joseph, *Vanderburgh*	47720
St. Leon	47060
St. Louis	47246
St. Louis Crossing	47201
St. Marks, *Dubois*	47575
St. Marks, *Perry*	47586
St. Mary-of-the-Woods	47876
St. Marys, *Adams* (Twp)	46733
St. Marys, *Floyd*	47119
St. Marys, *Franklin*	47006
St. Marys, *St. Joseph*	46556
St. Maurice	47240
St. Meinrad	47577
St. Omer	47272
St. Paul	47272
St. Peter	47012
St. Philip	47620
St. Thomas	47591
St. Wendel	47712
	47720
For specific ZIP Codes call (888) 275-8777, or your local postmaster.	
Salamonia	47381
Salamonie (Twp)	46792
Salem, *Adams*	46772
Salem, *Delaware* (Twp)	47334
Salem, *Pulaski* (Twp)	47946
Salem, *Steuben* (Twp)	46747
Salem, *Jay*	47390
Salem, *Washington*	47167
Salem Center	46747
Salem Heights	46350
Saline City	47840
Salt Creek, *Decatur* (Twp)	47240
Salt Creek, *Franklin* (Twp)	47024
Salt Creek, *Jackson* (Twp)	47235
Salt Creek, *Monroe* (Twp)	47401
Saltillo	47108
Saluda	47243
Samaria	46181
Sandborn	47578
Sand Creek, *Bartholomew* (Twp)	47232
Sand Creek, *Decatur* (Twp)	47283
Sand Creek, *Jennings* (Twp)	47265
Sandcut	47805
Sanders	47401
Sandford	47885
Sand Ridge	47635
Sandusky	47240
Sandy Beach	47960
Sandy Hook (Part of Columbus)	47201
Sandytown	47842
San Jacinto	47223
San Pierre	46374
Santa Claus	47579
Santa Fe	46970
Saratoga	47382
Sardinia	47283
Saugany Lake	46371
Savah	47620
Scenic Heights (Part of Tell City)	47586
Scenic Hill	47553
Schaefer Lake	47246
Schererville	46375
Schneider	46376
Schnellville	47580
Scipio, *Allen* (Twp)	45813
Scipio, *La Porte* (Twp)	46350
Scipio, *Franklin*	47012
Scipio, *Jennings*	47273
Scircleville	46041
Scotchtown	47848
Scotland	47457
Scott, *Kosciusko* (Twp)	46550
Scott, *Montgomery* (Twp)	47933
Scott, *Steuben* (Twp)	46703
Scott, *Vanderburgh* (Twp)	47711
Scott, *Lagrange*	46565
Scott City	47879
Scottsburg, *Pike*	47660
Scottsburg, *Scott*	47170
Scottsdale Mall (Part of South Bend)	46612
Scottsville	47106
Sedalia	46067
Sedan	46793
Seelyville	47878
Sellersburg	47172
Sellers Lake	46562
Selma	47383
Selvin	47523
Servia	46980
Sevastopol	46510
Seward (Twp)	46510
Sexton	46173
Seymour	47274
Shadeland, *Grant*	46952
Shadeland, *Tippecanoe*	47905
Shady Hills	46952
Shady Lawn (Part of Crown Point)	46307
Shady Nook	46795
Shaffer Woods	47303
Shamrock Lakes	47348
Shannondale	47933
Sharon	46929
Sharpsville	46068
Shawnee (Twp)	47987
Shawswick (Twp)	47421
Shawville	47805
Sheddfield (Part of Hammond)	46320
Sheffield (Twp)	47905
Sheffield Woods	46809
Shelburn	47879
Shelburne	46151
Shelby, *Jefferson* (Twp)	47250
Shelby, *Ripley* (Twp)	47250
Shelby, *Shelby* (Twp)	46176
Shelby, *Tippecanoe* (Twp)	47906
Shelby, *Lake*	46377
Shelbyville	46176
Shepardsville	47880
Sheridan, *Hamilton*	46069
Sherwood Forest (Part of Indianapolis)	46240
Shideler	47338
Shields	47274
Shipshewana	46565
Shirkieville	47885
Shirley	47384
Shoals	47581
Shoe Lake	46538
Shordon Estates	46805
Shoreland Hills	46360
Shorewood Forest	46383
Shriner Lake	46725
Siberia	47515
Sidney	46566
Silver Creek (Twp)	47172
Silver Hills (Part of New Albany)	47150
Silver Lake	46982
Silver Lakes Estates	47129
Silverville	47470
Silverwood	47952
Simonton Lake♦	46514
Sims (Part of Columbus)	47201
Sims, *Grant*	46986
Sitka	47960
Skelton (Twp)	47637
Skinner Lake	46701
Sleepy Hollow	46182
Sleeth	46923
Sloan	47993
Smartsburg	47933
Smedley	47108
Smith, *Greene* (Twp)	47471
Smith, *Posey* (Twp)	47612
Smith, *Whitley* (Twp)	46723
Smithfield, *De Kalb* (Twp)	46793
Smithfield, *Delaware*	47383
Smithland	46176
Smithson	47980
Smith Valley	46142-43
For specific ZIP Codes call (888) 275-8777, or your local postmaster.	
Smithville	47458
Smyrna, *Decatur*	47240
Smyrna, *Jefferson*	47250
Snow Hill	47394
Solitude	47620
Solsberry	47459
Somerset	46984
Somerville	47683
South Bend	46601-80
For specific ZIP Codes call (888) 275-8777, or your local postmaster.	
South Bethany	47201
South Boston	47167
South Calumet Avenue (Part of Hammond)‡	46324
South Center	46532
Southeast (Twp)	47140
Southeast Grove	46341
Southeast Manor	46126
South Edgewood (Part of Edgewood)	46011
Southern Estates	47150
Southern View	47905
Southgate (Part of Fort Wayne)‡	46806
South Gate, *Franklin*	47060
South Haven♦	46385
South Lake	47885
Southlake Mall (Part of Merrillville)	46410
South Milford	46786
South Mud Lake	46951
South Park	46567
South Peru (Part of Peru)	46970
Southport, *Marion*	46217
Southport, *Owen*	47460
South Raub	47905
South Salem	47390
Southtown Mall (Part of Fort Wayne)	46816
South Wanatah	46390
South Washington	47501
Southwest	46526
South Whitley	46787
Southwick Village	46816
Southwood, *Vigo*	47802
Spades	47041
Sparksville	47260
Sparta, *Noble* (Twp)	46732
Sparta, *Dearborn*	47032
Spartanburg	47355
Spearsville	46181
Speed	47172
Speedway	46224
Speicherville	46992
Spelterville	47805
Spencer, *De Kalb* (Twp)	46788
Spencer, *Harrison* (Twp)	47115
Spencer, *Jennings* (Twp)	47265
Spencer, *Owen*	47460
Spencerville	46788
Spiceland	47385
Spice Valley (Twp)	47437
Spraytown	47274
Springersville	47325
Springfield, *Allen* (Twp)	46741
Springfield, *Franklin* (Twp)	47012
Springfield, *La Porte* (Twp)	46360
Springfield, *Lagrange* (Twp)	46761
Springfield, *Posey*	47620
	47638
For specific ZIP Codes call (888) 275-8777, or your local postmaster.	
Spring Grove	47374
Spring Grove Heights (Part of Spring Grove)	47374
Spring Hill Estates	47802
Spring Hills (Part of Indianapolis)	46228
Spring Lake	46140
Springport	47386

Springville, *La Porte* 46350
Springville, *Lawrence* 47462
Springwood 47805
Spurgeon 47584
Spurgeons Corner 47235
Stacer 47639
Stafford, *De Kalb* (Twp) 46721
Stafford, *Greene* (Twp) 47441
Stampers Creek (Twp) 47454
Stanford 47463
Star City 46985
Starlight 47106
State Line 47885
State Line City 47982
Station #1 (Part of Michigan City)‡ 46360
Staunton 47881
Stavetown 47012
Stearleyville 47834
Steele (Twp) 47501
Steen (Twp) 47597
Steeplechase 47130
Steinbarger Lake 46794
Stendal 47585
Sterling, *Crawford* (Twp) 47118
Steuben, *Steuben* (Twp) 46779
Steuben, *Warren* (Twp) 47993
Steubenville 46705
Stevenson 47610
Stewart 47993
Stewartsville 47633
Stilesville 46180
Stillwell 46350
Stinesville 47464
Stockdale 46974
Stockton (Twp) 47441
Stockwell 47983
Stone 47394
Stonebluff 47987
Stoneburner Landing 46580
Stonecrest 46953
Stone Head 47448
Stones Crossing 46143
Stoney Creek, *Henry* (Twp) 47360
Stoney Creek, *Randolph* (Twp) 47368
Stonington 47446
Stony Creek (Twp) 46051
Stony Lonesome 47201
Story 47448
Stratford Hills (Part of Terre Haute) 47802
Straughn 47387
Strawtown 46060
Stringtown (Part of Evansville) 47711
Stringtown, *Boone* 46052
Stringtown, *Hancock* 46140
Stroh 46789
Stoutsburg 46392
Sugar Creek, *Boone* (Twp) 46071
Sugar Creek, *Clinton* (Twp) 46050
Sugar Creek, *Hancock* (Twp) 46163
Sugar Creek, *Montgomery* (Twp) 47933
Sugar Creek, *Parke* (Twp) 47859
Sugar Creek, *Shelby* (Twp) 46110
Sugar Creek, *Vigo* (Twp) 47885
Sugar Creek, *Shelby* 46126
Sugar Ridge (Twp) 47840
Sullivan 47882
Sulphur 47174
Sulphur Springs 47388
Suman 46383
Sumava Resorts 46379
Summit Grove 47842
Summit Ridge (Part of Fort Wayne) 46815
Summitville 46070
Sundown Manor 46158
Sunman 47041
Sunnybrook Acres 46805
Sunnymede, *Allen* 46803
Sunnymede (Part of Wabash) 46992
Sunnymede Woods 46803
Sunny Slopes 47401
Sunset Parkway (Part of Seymour) 47274

Sunset Village 47111
Sunshine Gardens (Part of Indianapolis) 46217
Sunview 46040
Surprise 47274
Swan 46763
Swanington 47944
Swayzee 46986
Sweetser 46987
Sweetwater Lake 46164
Switz City 47465
Sycamore 46936
Sycamore Hills 46036
Sycamore Knolls 47802
Sycamore Park 47885
Sylvan Hills 46953
Sylvania 47832
Sylvan Manor 46385
Syndicate 47842
Syracuse 46567
Tab 47917
Talbot 47984
Tall Timbers 46952
Talma 46975
Tampico 47220
Tangier 47952
Tarry Park 47421
Taswell 47175
Taylor, *Greene* (Twp) 47424
Taylor, *Harrison* (Twp) 47117
Taylor, *Howard* (Twp) 46902
Taylor, *Owen* (Twp) 47460
Taylorsville♦ 47280
Tecumseh (Part of Lafayette) 47905
Tecumseh, *Vigo* 47885
Teegarden 46574
Tee Lake 46350
Tefft 46380
Tell City 47586
Temple 47118
Templeton 47986
Tennyson 47637
Terhune 46069
Terrace Bay 47960
Terrace Lake (Part of Columbus) 47201
Terre Haute 47801-08
For specific ZIP Codes call (888) 275-8777, or your local postmaster.
Terre Town (Part of Terre Haute) 47805
Terre Vista (Part of Terre Haute) 47803
Tetersburg 46072
Texas (Part of Aurora) 47001
Thayer 46381
The Hamlet 47303
The Meadows 47130
Thomas Lake 46135
Thomaston 46390
Thorncreek (Twp) 46725
Thornhope 46985
Thorntown 46071
Thurman 46774
Tilden 46112
Tillman 46773
Timbercrest, *Allen* 46804
Timbercrest, *Cass* 46947
Timberhurst 46795
Tiosa 46975
Tippecanoe, *Carroll* (Twp) 46923
Tippecanoe, *Kosciusko* (Twp) 46555
Tippecanoe, *Pulaski* (Twp) 46960
Tippecanoe, *Tippecanoe* (Twp) 47906
Tippecanoe, *Marshall* 46570
Tippecanoe Mall (Part of Lafayette) 47905
Tipton, *Cass* (Twp) 46994
Tipton, *Tipton* 46072
Tipton Park (Part of Columbus) 47201
Toad Hop 47885
Tobin (Twp) 47520
Tobinsport 47520
Tocsin 46777
Toledo 46750
Tolleston (Part of Gary)‡ 46404
Toll Gate Heights (Part of Bluffton) 46714
Topeka 46571
Toto 46534
Townley 46773
Town of Pines 46360

Tracy 46532
Traders Point (Part of Indianapolis) 46278
Trafalgar 46181
Trail Creek 46360
Travisville 46714
Treaty 46992
Tremont 46304
Trenton 47348
Trevlac 47448
Trier Ridge Park (Part of Fort Wayne 46816
Tri-Lakes♦ 46725
Trinity 47326
Trinity Springs 47581
Troy, *De Kalb* (Twp) 46721
Troy, *Fountain* (Twp) 47932
Troy, *Perry* 47586
Tulip 47424
Tunker 46787
Tunnel Hill 47118
Tunnelton 47467
Turkey Creek (Twp) 46567
Turkey Creek Meadows (Part of Merrillville) 46410
Turkey Track 46151
Turman (Twp) 47882
Turner 47834
Twelve Mile 46988
Twelve Points (Part of Terre Haute)‡ 47804
Twin Brooks (Part of Indianapolis) 46227
Twin Crest 47203
Twin Lakes 46563
Twin Oaks Lake 46160
Tyner 46572
Ulen 46052
Underwood 47177
Underwood Meadows 46036
Union, *Adams* (Twp) 46733
Union, *Benton* (Twp) 47944
Union, *Boone* (Twp) 46069
Union, *Clark* (Twp) 47143
Union, *Clinton* (Twp) 46041
Union, *Crawford* (Twp) 47123
Union, *De Kalb* (Twp) 46706
Union, *Delaware* (Twp) 47303
Union, *Elkhart* (Twp) 46550
Union, *Fulton* (Twp) 46939
Union, *Gibson* (Twp) 47648
Union, *Hendricks* (Twp) 46149
Union, *Howard* (Twp) 46936
Union, *Huntington* (Twp) 46750
Union, *Jasper* (Twp) 47943
Union, *Johnson* (Twp) 46106
Union, *La Porte* (Twp) 46346
Union, *Madison* (Twp) 46011
Union, *Marshall* (Twp) 46511
Union, *Miami* (Twp) 46926
Union, *Montgomery* (Twp) 47933
Union, *Ohio* (Twp) 47001
Union, *Parke* (Twp) 47872
Union, *Perry* (Twp) 47520
Union, *Porter* (Twp) 46342
Union, *Randolph* (Twp) 47355
47358
For specific ZIP Codes call (888) 275-8777, or your local postmaster.
Union, *Rush* (Twp) 46173
Union, *St. Joseph* (Twp) 46536
Union, *Shelby* (Twp) 46176
Union, *Tippecanoe* (Twp) 47905
Union, *Union* (Twp) 47003
Union, *Vanderburgh* (Twp) 47712
Union, *Wells* (Twp) 46777
Union, *White* (Twp) 47960
Union, *Whitley* (Twp) 46725
Union, *Pike* 47640
Union Center 46532
Union City 47390
Uniondale 46791
Union Mills 46382
Unionport 47340
Uniontown, *Jackson* 47229
Uniontown, *Perry* 47515
Unionville (New Unionville) 47401
Unionville 47468
Universal 47884

University Farms (Part of West Lafayette) 47906
University Heights (Part of Indianapolis) 46227
University Park Mall (Part of Mishawaka) 46545
Upland 46989
Upper Long Lake 46701
Upper Sunset Park 47960
Upton 47620
Urbana 46990
Urbandale 46902
Urmeyville 46131
Utah (Part of Aurora) 47001
Utica 47130
Valeene 47125
Valentine 46761
Valley Acres 46953
Valley Brook (Part of Wabash) 46992
Valley City 47110
Valley Mills (Part of Indianapolis) 46241
Vallonia 47281
Valparaiso 46383-85
For specific ZIP Codes call (888) 275-8777, or your local postmaster.
Van Bibber Lake 46135
Van Blaricum 47201
Van Buren, *Brown* (Twp) 47448
Van Buren, *Clay* (Twp) 47834
Van Buren, *Daviess* (Twp) 47562
Van Buren, *Fountain* (Twp) 47987
Van Buren, *Kosciusko* (Twp) 46542
Van Buren, *Lagrange* (Twp) 46565
Van Buren, *Madison* (Twp) 46070
Van Buren, *Monroe* (Twp) 47403
Van Buren, *Pulaski* (Twp) 46985
Van Buren, *Shelby* (Twp) 46176
Van Buren, *Grant* 46991
Van Buren Park 47403
Vandalia 47460
Vanmeter Park 46996
Vawter Park 46567
Veale (Twp) 47501
Veedersburg 47987
Velpen 47590
Vera Cruz 46714
Vermillion (Twp) 47966
Vermont 46901
Verne 47591
Vernon, *Hancock* (Twp) 46040
Vernon, *Jackson* (Twp) 47229
Vernon, *Washington* (Twp) 47108
Vernon, *Jennings* 47282
Versailles 47042
Veterans Administration Medical Center (Part of Marion) 46952
Vevay 47043
Vicksburg 47441
Victor 47403
Vienna 47170
Vigo (Twp) 47512
Vilas 47460
Vincennes 47591
Virgie 47978
Vistula 46507
Volga 47250
Wabash, *Adams* (Twp) 46740
Wabash, *Fountain* (Twp) 47932
Wabash, *Gibson* (Twp) 47665
Wabash, *Jay* (Twp) 47326
Wabash, *Parke* (Twp) 47872
Wabash, *Tippecanoe* (Twp) 47906
Wabash, *Wabash* 46992
Wabash Shores (Part of West Lafayette) 47906
Wadena 47944
Wadesville 47638
Wakarusa 46573
Wakefield Village 46755
Wakeland 46166
Wake Robin Fields 46304

Walden 46815
Waldron 46182
Waldron Lake 46794
Walesboro 47201
Walford Manor 47130
Walker, *Jasper* (Twp) 47978
Walker, *Rush* (Twp) 46173
Walker Park 46538
Walkerton 46574
Walkerville (Part of Shelbyville) 46176
Wallace 47988
Wall Lake 46776
Walnut, *Montgomery* (Twp) 47933
Walnut, *Marshall* 46501
Walnut Gardens 47960
Walnut Grove 46030
Walnut Heights 47421
Walnut Ridge 47265
Walton 46994
Waltz (Twp) 46992
Wanamaker (Part of Indianapolis) 46239
Wanatah 46390
Wantland Manor 46012
Ward (Twp) 47380
Warren, *Clinton* (Twp) 46039
Warren, *Huntington* (Twp) 46750
Warren, *Marion* (Twp) 46219
Warren, *Putnam* (Twp) 46135
Warren, *St. Joseph* (Twp) 46528
Warren, *Warren* (Twp) 47918
Warren, *Huntington* 46792
Warren Park (Part of Indianapolis) 46219
Warrenton 47639
Warrington 46186
Warsaw 46580*
46581†
Washington, *Adams* (Twp) 46733
Washington, *Allen* (Twp) 46818
Washington, *Blackford* (Twp) 47348
Washington, *Boone* (Twp) 46071
Washington, *Brown* (Twp) 47448
Washington, *Carroll* (Twp) 46947
Washington, *Cass* (Twp) 46947
Washington, *Clark* (Twp) 47162
Washington, *Clay* (Twp) 47833
Washington, *Clinton* (Twp) 46041
Washington, *Dearborn* (Twp) 47001
Washington, *Decatur* (Twp) 47240
Washington, *Delaware* (Twp) 47342
Washington, *Elkhart* (Twp) 46507
Washington, *Gibson* (Twp) 47640
Washington, *Grant* (Twp) 46952
Washington, *Greene* (Twp) 47443
Washington, *Hamilton* (Twp) 46074
Washington, *Harrison* (Twp) 47110
Washington, *Hendricks* (Twp) 46122
Washington, *Jackson* (Twp) 47274
Washington, *Knox* (Twp) 47516
Washington, *Kosciusko* (Twp) 46562
Washington, *La Porte* (Twp) 46350
Washington, *Marion* (Twp) 46220
46260
For specific ZIP Codes call (888) 275-8777, or your local postmaster.
Washington, *Miami* (Twp) 46970
Washington, *Monroe* (Twp) 47408

*** Area Zip Code** **† Post Office Boxes** **‡ Postal Station** **♦ Census Designated Place** *Italic Type* **County**

Place	ZIP Code
Washington, *Morgan* (Twp)	46151
Washington, *Newton* (Twp)	47922
Washington, *Noble* (Twp)	46562
	46725
For specific ZIP Codes call (888) 275-8777, or your local postmaster.	
Washington, *Owen* (Twp)	47460
Washington, *Parke* (Twp)	47859
Washington, *Pike* (Twp)	47567
Washington, *Porter* (Twp)	46383
Washington, *Putnam* (Twp)	46171
Washington, *Randolph* (Twp)	47394
Washington, *Ripley* (Twp)	47042
Washington, *Rush* (Twp)	46127
Washington, *Shelby* (Twp)	47234
Washington, *Starke* (Twp)	46534
Washington, *Tippecanoe* (Twp)	47905
Washington, *Warren* (Twp)	47993
Washington, *Washington* (Twp)	47167
Washington, *Wayne* (Twp)	47357
Washington, *Whitley* (Twp)	46725
Washington, *Daviess*	47501
Washington Center	46725
Washington Place (Part of Indianapolis)	46219
Washington Square (Part of Indianapolis)	46229
Washington Square Mall (Part of Evansville)	47715
Waterford	46360
Waterford Mills	46526
Waterloo, *De Kalb*	46793
Waterloo, *Fayette*	47331
Waterloo, *Johnson*	46106
Waterswolde	46825
Wathen Heights	47130
Watson	47130
Waugh	46075
Wauhob Lake	46383
Waveland	47989
Waverly	46151
Waverly Woods	46151
Wawaka	46794
Wawpecong	46901
Waymansville	47201
Wayne, *Allen* (Twp)	46809
Wayne, *Bartholomew* (Twp)	47201
Wayne, *Fulton* (Twp)	46939
Wayne, *Hamilton* (Twp)	46060
Wayne, *Henry* (Twp)	46148
Wayne, *Huntington* (Twp)	46940
Wayne, *Jay* (Twp)	47371
Wayne, *Kosciusko* (Twp)	46590
Wayne, *Marion* (Twp)	46224
	46241
For specific ZIP Codes call (888) 275-8777, or your local postmaster.	
Wayne, *Montgomery* (Twp)	47990
Wayne, *Noble* (Twp)	46755
Wayne, *Owen* (Twp)	47433
Wayne, *Randolph* (Twp)	47390
Wayne, *Starke* (Twp)	46366
Wayne, *Tippecanoe* (Twp)	47992
Wayne, *Wayne* (Twp)	47374
Waynedale (Part of Fort Wayne)‡	46804
	46809
For specific ZIP Codes call (888) 275-8777, or your local postmaster.	
Waynesburg	47244
Waynesville	47201
Waynetown	47990
Wea (Twp)	47905
Webster, *Harrison* (Twp)	47112
Webster, *Wayne*	47392
Wegan	47220
Weisburg	47041
Wellington Heights (Part of Shelbyville)	46176
Wellsboro	46382
Wellsburg	46714
West (Twp)	46563
Westacres	47304
West Baden Springs	47469
West Brook Downs	47404
Westchester (Part of Fort Wayne)	46816
Westchester, *Porter* (Twp)	46304
Westchester, *Jay*	47371
West College Corner	47003
West Creek (Twp)	46356
West Elwood	46036
Western Acres (Part of Chesterton)	46304
Western Village (Part of Anderson)	46011
Westfield, *Hamilton*	46074
Westfield, *St. Joseph*	46619
West Fork	47118
West Franklin	47620
West Harrison	47060
West Haven	46580
West Hill	46383
West Indianapolis (Part of Indianapolis)‡	46221
West Lafayette	47906-07
	47996
For specific ZIP Codes call (888) 275-8777, or your local postmaster.	
Westlawn	46804
West Lebanon	47991
West Liberty	46936
West Middleton	46995
Westmoor (Part of Fort Wayne)	46804
West Newton (Part of Indianapolis)	46183
West Noblesville (Part of Noblesville)	46060
West Petersburg (Part of Petersburg)	47567
Westphalia	47596
West Point, *White* (Twp)	47980
West Point, *Howard*	46901
Westpoint, *Tippecanoe*	47992
Westport	47283
Westside (Part of Aurora)	47001
West Terre Haute	47885
Westville	46391
West Wabash (Part of Evansville)‡	47708
	47712
	47719
For specific ZIP Codes call (888) 275-8777, or your local postmaster.	
Westwood	47362
Wheatfield	46392
Wheatland	47597
Wheatonville	47613
Wheeler	46393
Wheeling, *Carroll*	46929
Wheeling, *Delaware*	47342
Wheeling, *Gibson*	47649
Whiskey Run (Twp)	47145
Whitaker	46166
Whitcomb	47012
Whitcomb Heights	47885
White Cloud	47112
Whitehall	47404
Whiteland	46184
Whiteoak	47598
White Post (Twp)	47957
White Ridge	46952
White River, *Gibson* (Twp)	47666
White River, *Hamilton* (Twp)	46034
White River, *Johnson* (Twp)	46142
White River, *Randolph* (Twp)	47394
White Rose	47441
Whitestown	46075
Whitesville	47933
Whitewater, *Franklin* (Twp)	47060
Whitewater, *Wayne*	47374
Whitfield	47553
Whiting	46394
Wickliffe	47116
Widner (Twp)	47561
Wilbur	46151
Wildcat (Twp)	46076
Wilders	46348
Wildwood	46703
Wildwood Lake	47454
Wilfred	47879
Wilhelm	46350
Wilkinson	46186
Williams, *Adams*	46733
Williams, *Lawrence*	47470
Williamsburg	47393
Williams Creek (Part of Indianapolis)	46240
Williamsport	47993
Williamstown	47240
Willisville	47567
Willow Branch	46186
Willowbrook Estates	46151
Willow Valley	47581
Wills (Twp)	46371
Wilmington, *Dearborn*	47001
Wilmington, *De Kalb* (Twp)	46721
Wilmot	46562
Wilshire (Part of Frankfort)	46041
Wilshire Plaza (Part of Mishawaka)	46545
Wilson	47106
Wilson Corner	46176
Wilson Lake	46725
Winamac	46996
Winchester	47394
Windemere Lake	47885
Windfall	46076
Windom	47581
Windsor	47368
Windsor Village (Part of Indianapolis)	46219
Winfield	46307
Wingate	47994
Winona	46534
Winona Lake	46590
Winslow	47598
Winthrop	47918
Wirt	47250
Witmer Lake	46795
Witmer Manor	46795
Witts Station	47353
Wolcott	47995
Wolcottville	46795
Wolff	46151
Wolflake	46796
Wonder Lake	47802
Wood (Twp)	47106
Woodbridge (Part of Bloomington)	47407†
	47408*
Woodburn	46797
Woodbury	46055
Woodcrest	46151
Woodgate	47802
Woodgate East	47802
Woodland	46614
Woodland Heights	46952
Woodland Hills (Part of New Albany)	47150
Woodland Hills, *Lagrange*	46761
Woodland Lake	46160
Woodland Park, *Delaware*	47303
Woodland Park, *Lagrange*	46795
Woodlawn Heights	46011
Woodridge	47803
Woodruff	46795
Woodruff Place (Part of Indianapolis)	46201
Woodville	46304
Wooster, *Kosciusko*	46562
Wooster, *Scott*	47138
Worth (Twp)	46075
Worthington	47471
Wright (Twp)	47438
	47441
For specific ZIP Codes call (888) 275-8777, or your local postmaster.	
Wrights Corners	47001
Wyandotte	47137
Wyatt	46595
Wynnedale (Part of Indianapolis)	46228
Yankeetown	47630
Yeddo	47952
Yellowbanks	46555
Yellow Creek Lake	46510
Yeoman	47997
Yockey	47446
Yoder	46798
York, *Benton* (Twp)	47942
York, *Dearborn* (Twp)	47022
York, *Elkhart* (Twp)	46507
York, *Noble* (Twp)	46701
York, *Steuben* (Twp)	46703
York, *Switzerland* (Twp)	47020
York, *Steuben*	46737
Yorktown	47396
Yorkville	47022
Young	46158
Young America	46998
Youngs Corner	47012
Youngs Creek	47454
Youngstown	47802
Youngstown Meadows	47802
Yountsville	47933
Zanesville	46799
Zelma	47264
Zenas	47223
Zephyr	47201
Zionsville	46077
Zoar	47541
Zulu	46773

Place	ZIP Code
Abingdon	52533
Ackley	50601
Ackworth	50001
Adair	50002
Adaza	50050
Adel	50003
Adelphi	50237
Afton	50830
Agency	52530
Ainsworth	52201
Akron	51001
Albaton	51055
Albert City	50510
Albia	52531
Albion	50005
Alburnett	52202
Alden	50006
Alexander	50420
Algona	50511
Alleman	50007
Allendorf	51330
Allerton	50008
Allison	50602
Alpha	52171
Alta	51002
Alta Vista	50603
Alton	51003
Altoona	50009
Alvord	51230
Amana	52203
Amber	52205
Amboy	50208
Ames	50010-14
For specific ZIP Codes call (888) 275-8777, or your local postmaster.	
Amish	52247
Anamosa	52205
Anderson	51652
Andover	52701
Andrew	52030
Anita	50020
Ankeny	50021
Anthon	51004
Aplington	50604
Arcadia	51430
Archer	51231
Aredale	50605
Argyle	52619
Arion	51520
Arispe	50831
Arlington	50606
Armstrong	50514
Arnolds Park	51331
Artesian	50677
Arthur	51431
Asbury	52002
Ashton	51232
Aspinwall	51432
Atalissa	52720
Athelstan	50836
Atkins	52206
Atlantic	50022
Attica	50138
Auburn	51433
Audubon	50025
Augusta	52658
Aurelia	51005
Aureola	50653
Aurora	50607
Austinville	50608
Avery	52531
Avoca	51521
Avon	50047
Avon Lake	50047
Ayrshire	50515
Badger	50516
Bagley	50026
Baldwin	52207
Balltown	52073
Bancroft	50517
Bangor	50258
Bankston	52045
Barnes City	50027
Barnum	50518
Bartlett	51654
Bassett	50645
Batavia	52533
Battle Creek	51006
Baxter	50028
Bayard	50029
Beacon	52534
Beaconsfield	50074
Beaman	50609
Beaver	50031
Beaverdale (Part of Des Moines)‡	50310
Beckwith	52556
Bedford	50833
Beebeetown	51546
Beech	50225
Bel Air Beach	50588
Belknap	52537
Bellefountain	50143
Belle Plaine	52208
Bellevue	52031
Belmond	50421
Beloit	51240
Bennett	52721
Benton	50835
Bentonsport	52565
Berkley	50220
Bernard	52032
Bertram	52401
Berwick	50032
Bethlehem	50238
Bettendorf	52722
Bevington	50033
Big Rock	52745
Bingham	51601
Birmingham	52535
Bladensburg	52501
Blairsburg	50034
Blairstown	52209
Blakesburg	52536
Blanchard	51630
Blencoe	51523
Blockton	50836
Bloomfield	52537
Blue Grass	52726
Bluff Park (Part of Montrose)	52639
Bluffton	52101
Bode	50519
Bolan	50448
Bonair	52155
Bonaparte	52620
Bondurant	50035
Boone	50036-37
For specific ZIP Codes call (888) 275-8777, or your local postmaster.	
Booneville	50038
Botna	51454
Bouton	50039
Boxholm	50040
Boyd	50659
Boyden	51234
Boyer	51448
Braddyville	51631
Bradford	50041
Bradgate	50520
Brainard	52141
Brandon	52210
Brayton	50042
Brazil	52574
Breda	51436
Bremer	50677
Bridgewater	50837
Brighton	52540
Bristow	50611
Britt	50423
Bronson	51007
Brooklyn	52211
Brooks	50841
Browns Station	52731
Brunsville	51008
Brushy	50532
Bryant	52727
Bryantsburg	50641
Buchanan	52772
Buckcreek	50674
Buckeye	50043
Buck Grove	51528
Buckingham	50612
Buffalo	52728
Buffalo Center	50424
Buffalo Heights	52728
Burchinal	50469
Burlington	52601
Burnside	50521
Burr Oak	52131
Burt	50522
Bussey	50044
Cairo	52738
Calamus	52729
Calhoun	51555
California Junction	51555
Callender	50523
Calmar	52132
Calumet	51009
Camanche	52730
Cambria	50060
Cambridge	50046
Camp Dodge	50131
Canby	50048
Canton	52309
Cantril	52542
Capitol Heights	50317
Capitol Square (Part of Des Moines)‡	50393
Carbon	50839
Carl	50841
Carlisle	50047
Carmel	51247
Carnarvon	51437
Carnes	51003
Carney	50021
Carnforth	52347
Carpenter	50426
Carroll	51401
Carson	51525
Carter Lake	51510
Cartersville	50469
Cascade	52033
Casebeer	50009
Casey	50048
Casino Beach	50588
Castalia	52133
Castana	51010
Cedar	52543
Cedar Bluff	52772
Cedar Crest Woods	52401
Cedar Falls	50613
Cedar Rapids	52401-11
For specific ZIP Codes call (888) 275-8777, or your local postmaster.	
Cedar Terrace	52401
Cedar Valley	52358
Cedar View	50616
Centerdale	52776
Center Grove (Part of Dubuque)	52003
Center Junction	52212
Center Point	52213
Centerville, *Appanoose*	52544
Centerville, *Boone*	50036
Central (Part of Davenport)‡	52801
Central City	52214
Central College (Part of Pella)‡	50219
Central Heights (Part of Mason City)	50401
Centralia	52068
Chapin	50427
Chariton	50049
Charles City	50616
Charleston	52619
Charlotte	52731
Charter Oak	51439
Chatsworth	51011
Chelsea	52215
Cherokee	51012
Chester	52134
Chickasaw	50645
Chillicothe	52548
Church	52151
Churchville	50211
Churdan	50050
Cincinnati	52549
Clare	50524
Clarence	52216
Clarinda	51632
Clarion	50525
Clarkdale	52544
Clarksville	50619
Clayton	52049
Clayton Center	52043
Clearfield	50840
Clear Lake	50428
Cleghorn	51014
Clemons	50051
Clermont	52135
Cleves	50601
Climbing Hill	51015
Clinton	52732*
	52733†
Clio	50052
Clive	50325
Cloverdale	51249
Cloverhills (Part of West Des Moines)	50265
Clutier	52217
Coalville	50501
Coburg	51566
Coggon	52218
Coin	51636
Colesburg	52035
Colfax	50054
College Springs	51637
College Square (Part of Cedar Falls)	50613
Collins	50055
Colo	50056
Colonial Village (Part of West Des Moines)	50266
Columbia	50057
Columbus City	52737
Columbus Junction	52738
Colwell	[illegible]
Commerce (Part of West Des Moines)	50265
Conesville	52739
Confidence	52569
Conger	50240
Conover	52132
Conrad	50621
Conroy	52220
Conway	50833
Cool	50125
Coon Rapids	50058
Cooper	50059
Coppock	52654
Coralville	52241
Corley	51537
Cornelia	50525
Cornell	50585
Corning	50841
Correctionville	51016
Corwith	50430
Corydon	50060
Cosgrove	52322
Cotter	52738
Cottonville	52054
Coulter	50431
Council Bluffs	51501-03
For specific ZIP Codes call (888) 275-8777, or your local postmaster.	
Country Estate Acres	52401
Country Rock Estates	52341
Covington	52324
Craig	51017
Cranston	52754
Crawfordsville	52621
Crescent	51526
Cresco	52136
Creston	50801
Crestview Acres	52401
Crestwood (Part of Windsor Heights)	50311
Crestwood Acres	52401
Crocker	50226
Cromwell	50842
Crossroads Center (Part of Waterloo)	50702
Crossroads Mall (Part of Fort Dodge)	50501
Croton	52626
Crystal Lake	50432
Cumberland	50843
Cumming	50061
Curlew	50527
Cushing	51018
Cylinder	50528
Dahlonega	52501
Dakota City	50529
Dallas (Part of Melcher-Dallas)	50163
Dallas Center	50063
Dana	50064
Danbury	51019
Danville	52623
Darbyville	52544
Davenport	52801-09
For specific ZIP Codes call (888) 275-8777, or your local postmaster.	
Davis City	50065
Dawson	50066
Dayton	50530
Daytonville	52356
Dean	52572
Decatur	50067
Decorah	52101
Dedham	51440
Deep River	52222
Deer Lake Estates	52401
Defiance	51527
Delaware	52036
Delhi	52223
Delmar	52037
Deloit	51441
Delphos	50860
Delta	52550
Denison	51442
Denmark	52624
Denver	50622
Depew	50528
Derby	50068
Des Moines	50301-95
For specific ZIP Codes call (888) 275-8777, or your local postmaster.	
De Soto	50069
Dewar	50623
Dewey	50853
De Witt	52742
Dexter	50070
Diagonal	50845
Dickens	51333
Dike	50624
Dillon	50158
Dinsdale	50669
Dixon	52745
Dodge Park (Part of Council Bluffs)	51501
Dodgeville	52650
Dolliver	50531
Donahue	52746
Donnan	52142
Donnellson	52625
Doon	51235
Dorchester	52140
Douds	52551
Dougherty	50433
Douglas	52175
Dow City	51528
Downey	52358
Downtown (Part of Cedar Rapids)‡	52401
Dows	50071
Drakesville	52552
Dubuque	52001-04
For specific ZIP Codes call (888) 275-8777, or your local postmaster.	
Duck Creek Plaza (Part of Bettendorf)	52722
Dumont	50625
Dunbar	50158
Duncan	50423
Duncombe	50532
Dundee	52038
Dunkerton	50626
Dunlap	51529
Durango	52039
Durant	52747
Durham	50119
Dutchman Landing	50219
Dutchtown	52057
Dyersville	52040
Dysart	52224
Eagle Center	50701
Eagle Grove	50533
Eagle Point (Part of Dubuque)	52001
Earlham	50072
Earling	51530
Earlville	52041
Early	50535
East Amana	52203
East Des Moines (Part of Des Moines)‡	50309
East Fourteenth Street (Part of Des Moines)‡	50316
East Pleasant Plain	52540
Eddyville	52553
Edgewood	52042
Edgewood Park (Part of Bettendorf)	52722
Edna	51246
Egralharve	51360
Elberon	52225
Eldon	52554
Eldora	50627
Eldorado	52175
Eldridge	52748
Elgin	52141
Elkader	52043
Elkhart	50073
Elk Horn	51531
Elkport	52044
Elk Run Heights	50701
Elliott	51532
Ellston	50074
Ellsworth	50075
Elma	50628
Elon	52170
Elrick Junction	52653
Elvira	52732
Elwood	52226
Ely	52227
Emeline	52207
Emerson	51533
Emery	50401
Emmetsburg	50536
Enterprise	50073
Epworth	52045
Essex	51638
Estherville	51334
Evans	52577
Evansdale	50707
Evanston	50532
Evergreen (Part of Buffalo)	52804
Everlou Heights	52401

* **Area Zip Code** † **Post Office Boxes** ‡ **Postal Station** ♦ **Census Designated Place** *Italic Type* **County**

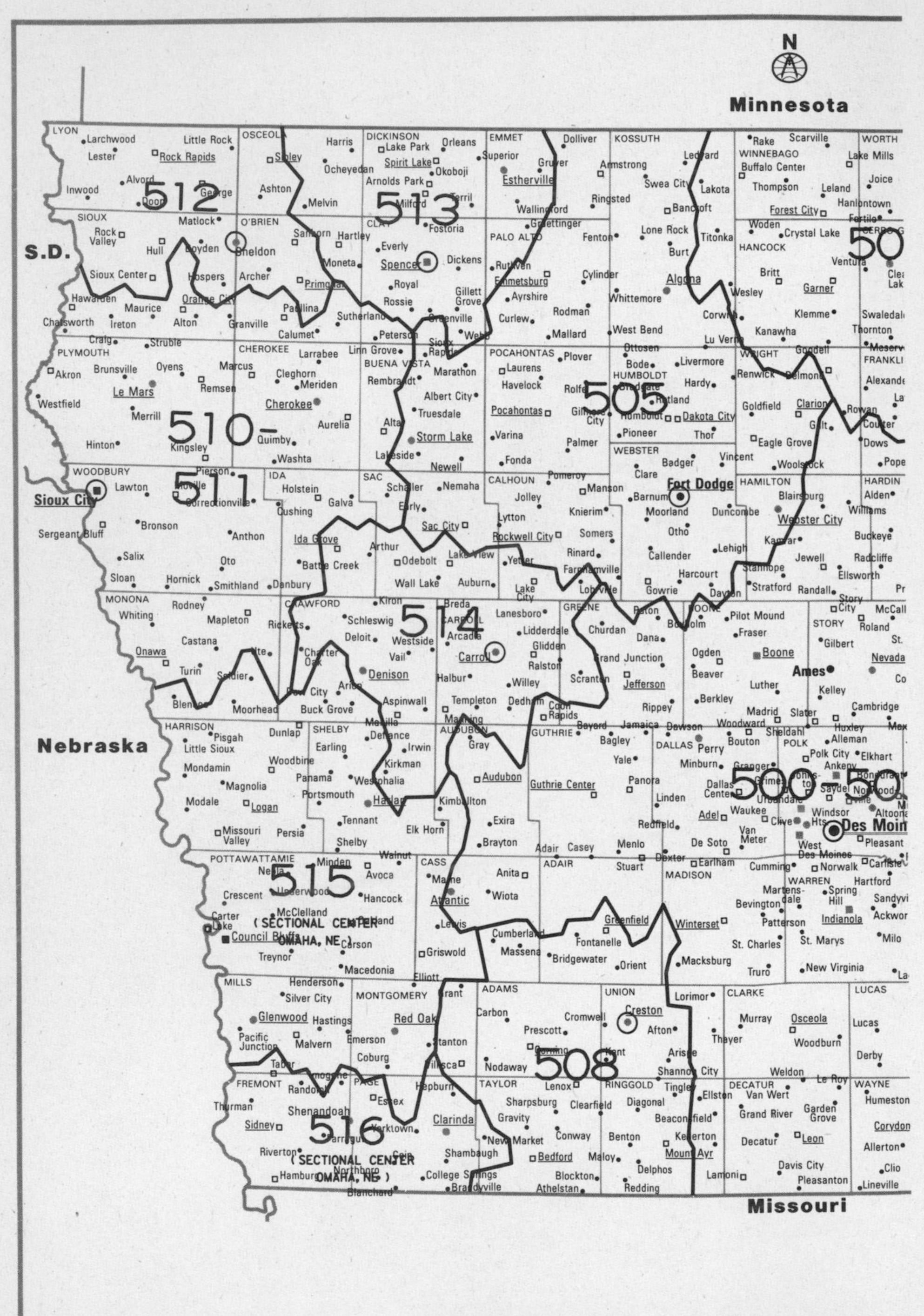
N
Minnesota
S.D.
Nebraska
Missouri
512
513
505
510-
511
514
515
500-50
508
516
50
LYON
Larchwood
Little Rock
Lester
Rock Rapids
Alvord
Inwood
George
Doon
OSCEOLA
Sibley
Ashton
Harris
Ocheyedan
Melvin
DICKINSON
Lake Park
Spirit Lake
Orleans
Okoboji
Arnolds Park
Milford
Terril
EMMET
Superior
Estherville
Gruver
Dolliver
Wallingford
Gruettinger
Ringsted
Armstrong
KOSSUTH
Ledyard
Swea City
Lakota
Bancroft
WINNEBAGO
Rake
Scarville
Buffalo Center
Thompson
Leland
Forest City
WORTH
Lake Mills
Joice
Hanlontown
Fertile
SIOUX
Matlock
Rock Valley
Hull
Boyden
O'BRIEN
Sheldon
Sanborn
Hartley
CLAY
Everly
Fostoria
Spencer
Dickens
Moneta
PALO ALTO
Ruthven
Emmetsburg
Ayrshire
Fenton
Lone Rock
Burt
Titonka
Algona
Woden
Crystal Lake
HANCOCK
Britt
Ventura
Garner
Wesley
Sioux Center
Hospers
Archer
Primghar
Orange City
Hawarden
Maurice
Chatsworth
Ireton
Alton
Granville
Paullina
Royal
Rossie
Gillett Grove
Greenville
Sutherland
Calumet
Peterson
Webb
Curlew
Cylinder
Whittemore
Rodman
Mallard
West Bend
Corwith
Kanawha
Klemme
Swaledale
Thornton
Lu Verne
Craig
Struble
PLYMOUTH
Akron
Brunsville
Oyens
Marcus
CHEROKEE
Larrabee
Cleghorn
Meriden
Remsen
Le Mars
Westfield
Merrill
Cherokee
Aurelia
Linn Grove
Sioux Rapids
BUENA VISTA
Rembrandt
Marathon
Albert City
Truesdale
Alta
Storm Lake
Lakeside
Newell
POCAHONTAS
Laurens
Havelock
Plover
Rolfe
Pocahontas
Gilmore City
Varina
Fonda
Palmer
Ottosen
Bode
HUMBOLDT
Livermore
Hardy
Rutland
Humboldt
Dakota City
Pioneer
Thor
WRIGHT
Goodell
Renwick
Belmond
Goldfield
Clarion
Rowan
Galt
Eagle Grove
Woolstock
FRANKLIN
Alexander
Coulter
Dows
Meservey
Hinton
Kingsley
Quimby
Washta
Pierson
WOODBURY
Lawton
Moville
Sioux City
Correctionville
IDA
Holstein
Galva
Cushing
Ida Grove
SAC
Schaller
Nemaha
Early
Sac City
CALHOUN
Jolley
Lytton
Rockwell City
Pomeroy
Manson
Knierim
Somers
Rinard
WEBSTER
Clare
Badger
Vincent
Fort Dodge
Barnum
Moorland
Duncombe
Otho
Lehigh
Callender
Harcourt
HAMILTON
Blairsburg
Webster City
Kamrar
Jewell
Stanhope
Stratford
Randall
HARDIN
Alden
Williams
Buckeye
Radcliffe
Ellsworth
Pope
Sergeant Bluff
Bronson
Anthon
Salix
Oto
Sloan
Hornick
Smithland
Danbury
Battle Creek
Arthur
Odebolt
Lake View
Wall Lake
Auburn
Yetter
Lake City
Farnhamville
Lohrville
Gowrie
Dayton
Story City
McCallsburg
MONONA
Whiting
Rodney
Mapleton
CRAWFORD
Kiron
Schleswig
Ricketts
Deloit
Westside
Breda
CARROLL
Arcadia
Lanesboro
Lidderdale
GREENE
Churdan
Paton
Dana
Boxholm
BOONE
Pilot Mound
Fraser
STORY
Roland
Gilbert
Nevada
Castana
Onawa
Turin
Soldier
Ute
Charter Oak
Vail
Denison
Carroll
Glidden
Ralston
Grand Junction
Ogden
Boone
Ames
Beaver
Jefferson
Scranton
Halbur
Willey
Templeton
Dedham
Coon Rapids
Luther
Kelley
Berkley
Rippey
Blencoe
Moorhead
Buck Grove
Dow City
Arion
Aspinwall
Manning
Madrid
Slater
Cambridge
Woodward
Sheldahl
HARRISON
Pisgah
Little Sioux
Dunlap
SHELBY
Earling
Manilla
Defiance
Irwin
AUDUBON
Gray
GUTHRIE
Bayard
Bagley
Jamaica
Dawson
DALLAS
Perry
Bouton
Huxley
Alleman
POLK
Polk City
Elkhart
Ankeny
Mondamin
Woodbine
Kirkman
Yale
Minburn
Granger
Panama
Westphalia
Audubon
Guthrie Center
Panora
Magnolia
Portsmouth
Dallas Center
Grimes
Urbandale
Modale
Logan
Harlan
Kimballton
Linden
Waukee
Clive
Windsor Heights
Altoona
Des Moines
Tennant
Exira
Redfield
Adel
Missouri Valley
Persia
Elk Horn
Shelby
Brayton
Adair
Casey
Menlo
De Soto
Van Meter
West Des Moines
Pleasant Hill
Walnut
POTTAWATTAMIE
Neola
Minden
Avoca
CASS
Marne
Anita
ADAIR
Stuart
Dexter
Earlham
MADISON
Cumming
Norwalk
Carlisle
WARREN
Hartford
Crescent
Underwood
Hancock
Atlantic
Wiota
Martensdale
Spring Hill
Bevington
Sandyville
Carter Lake
Council Bluffs
McClelland
(SECTIONAL CENTER OMAHA, NE)
Oakland
Carson
Treynor
Macedonia
Lewis
Griswold
Cumberland
Massena
Greenfield
Fontanelle
Bridgewater
Orient
Winterset
Patterson
Indianola
Ackworth
St. Charles
St. Marys
Milo
Macksburg
Truro
New Virginia
Elliott
MILLS
Henderson
Silver City
MONTGOMERY
Grant
ADAMS
Carbon
UNION
Creston
Lorimor
CLARKE
LUCAS
Glenwood
Hastings
Red Oak
Prescott
Cromwell
Afton
Thayer
Murray
Osceola
Lucas
Pacific Junction
Malvern
Emerson
Stanton
Corning
Kent
Arispe
Woodburn
Derby
Coburg
Villisca
Nodaway
Shannon City
Weldon
Tabor
Imogene
Randolph
FREMONT
PAGE
Essex
Hepburn
TAYLOR
Lenox
RINGGOLD
Tingley
Ellston
DECATUR
Van Wert
Le Roy
WAYNE
Humeston
Thurman
Shenandoah
Sharpsburg
Clearfield
Diagonal
Grand River
Garden Grove
Sidney
Farragut
Yorktown
Clarinda
Gravity
Beaconsfield
Corydon
Riverton
Coin
New Market
Conway
Benton
Kellerton
Decatur
Leon
Allerton
Shambaugh
Bedford
Maloy
Mount Ayr
Hamburg
Northboro
College Springs
Blockton
Delphos
Lamoni
Davis City
Clio
Blanchard
Braddyville
Athelstan
Redding
Pleasanton
Lineville

Wisconsin
Illinois
500
503
504
506
507
520
521
522-524
525
526
527-528
SECTIONAL CENTER ROCK ISLAND, IL
Des Moines
Cedar Rapids
Davenport
Dubuque
Waterloo
Iowa City
Burlington
Ottumwa
Mason City
Clinton
Marshalltown
Muscatine
Fort Madison
Keokuk
Decorah
Cedar Falls
Newton
Oskaloosa
Knoxville
Fairfield
Mount Pleasant
Centerville
Independence
Charles City
Waverly
Oelwein
Manchester
Maquoketa
Anamosa
Vinton
Marengo
Washington
Sigourney
Bloomfield
Keosauqua
Albia
Chariton
Toledo
Grinnell
Montezuma
Tipton
Wapello
Elkader
Waukon
Cresco
New Hampton
West Union
Osage
Allison
Grundy Center
Iowa Falls
MITCHELL
HOWARD
WINNESHIEK
ALLAMAKEE
FLOYD
CHICKASAW
FAYETTE
CLAYTON
BUTLER
BREMER
GRUNDY
BLACK HAWK
BUCHANAN
DELAWARE
DUBUQUE
TAMA
BENTON
LINN
JONES
JACKSON
MARSHALL
CLINTON
JASPER
POWESHIEK
IOWA
JOHNSON
CEDAR
MUSCATINE
MARION
MAHASKA
KEOKUK
WASHINGTON
LOUISA
MONROE
WAPELLO
JEFFERSON
HENRY
DES MOINES
APPANOOSE
DAVIS
VAN BUREN
LEE
BOONE
STORY
POLK
DALLAS
WARREN
Ankeny
West Des Moines
Urbandale
Altoona
0 5 10 Miles
0 5 10 Kilometers
©R. McN. & CO.
Legend
Population
250,000-999,999
100,000-249,999
50,000-99,999
25,000-49,999
10,000-24,999
5,000-9,999
1,000-4,999
Less than 1,000
State Capital
County Seat
0 5 10 20 30 Miles
0 5 10 20 30 40 Kilometers
Copyright © 1986, 1983
by Rand McNally & Co.
All rights reserved
Made and printed in the U.S.A.

Place	ZIP
Everly	51338
Ewart	50171
Exira	50076
Exline	52555
Fairbank	50629
Fairfax	52228
Fairfield	52556
Fair Ground (Part of Dubuque)	52002
Fairmount Park (Part of Council Bluffs)	51503
Fairport	52761
Fairview	52205
Farley	52046
Farlin	50129
Farmersburg	52047
Farmington	52626
Farnhamville	50538
Farragut	51639
Farrar	50161
Farson	52563
Faulkner	50601
Fayette	52142
Fenton	50539
Ferguson	50078
Fern	50665
Fernald	50201
Fertile	50434
Festina	52144
Fillmore	52033
Finchford	50647
Fiscus	50025
Five Points	52073
Flagler	50138
Florenceville	52136
Floris	52560
Floyd	50435
Folletts	52730
Fonda	50540
Fontanelle	50846
Forbush	52544
Forest City	50436
Fort Atkinson	52144
Fort Dodge	50501
Fort Dodge Junction (Part of Fort Dodge)	50501
Fort Madison	52627
Fostoria	51340
Four Corners	52635
Franklin	52625
Frankville	52162
Fraser	50036
Fredericksburg	50630
Frederika	50631
Fredonia	52738
Freeman	50401
Freeport	52101
Fremont	52561
Frenh Creek	52151
Froelich	52047
Fruitland	52749
Fulton	52060
Galesburg	50232
Galland	52639
Galt	50101
Galva	51020
Garber	52048
Garden City	50102
Garden Grove	50103
Gardiner	50039
Garnavillo	52049
Garner	50438
Garrison	52229
Garry Owen	52079
Garwin	50632
Gaza	51245
Geneva	50633
George	51237
Georgetown	52531
Germantown	51046
German Valley	50480
Germanville	52540
Giard	52157
Gibson	50104
Gifford	50259
Gilbert	50105
Gilbertville	50634
Gillett Grove	51341
Gilman	50106
Gilmore City	50541
Gladbrook	50635
Glasgow	52556
Glendon	50164
Glenwood	51534
Glidden	51443
Goddard	50054
Goldfield	50542
Goodell	50439
Goose Lake	52750
Gowrie	50543
Grace Hill	52353
Graettinger	51342
Graf	52073
Grafton	50440
Grand Junction	50107
Grand Mound	52751
Grand River	50108
Grandview	52752
Granger	50109
Granger Homesteads	50109
Granite	51241
Grant	50847
Grant Wood (Part of Bettendorf)	52722
Granville	51022
Gravity	50848
Gray	50110
Greeley	52050
Green Castle	50054
Greene	50636
Greenfield	50849
Greenfield Plaza	50315
Green Island	52064
Green Mountain	50632
Greenville	51343
Greenwood Acres	50021
Grimes	50111
Grinnell	50112
Griswold	51535
Grundy Center	50638
Gruver	51344
Guernsey	52221
Gunder	52162
Guss	50857
Guthrie Center	50115
Guttenberg	52052
Halbur	51444
Hale	52362
Hamburg	51640
Hamill	52625
Hamilton	50116
Hamlin	50117
Hampton	50441
Hancock	51536
Hanford	50401
Hanley	50240
Hanlontown	50444
Hanover	51002
Hansell	50441
Harcourt	50544
Hardy	50545
Harlan	51537
	51593
For specific ZIP Codes call (888) 275-8777, or your local postmaster.	
Harper	52231
Harpers Ferry	52146
Harris	51345
Harrisburg	52620
Hartford	50118
Hartley	51346
Hartwick	52232
Harvard	50008
Harvey	50119
Haskins	52201
Hastings	51540
Hauntown	52732
Havelock	50546
Haven	52339
Haverhill	50120
Hawarden	51023
Hawkeye	52147
Hawleyville	51632
Hawthorne	51566
Hayesville	52562
Hayfield	50438
Hazleton	50641
Hedrick	52563
Henderson	51541
Hepburn	51632
Herndon	50128
Herrold	50131
Hesper	52101
Heytmans Station	52151
Hiawatha	52233
High Amana	52203
Highland Center	52501
Highland Park (Part of Des Moines)‡	50313
Highlandville	52149
High Point	50103
Highview	50595
Hills	52235
Hillsboro	52630
Hillsdale	51534
Hinton	51024
Hiteman	52531
Hobarton	50511
Hocking	52531
Holbrook	52325
Holiday Lake	52211
Holland	50642
Holly Springs	51026
Holmes	50525
Holmes Morse	52401
Holstein	51025
Holy Cross	52053
Homer	50595
Homestead	52236
Honey Creek	51542
Hopeville	50174
Hopkinton	52237
Hornick	51026
Horton	50677
Hospers	51238
Houghton	52631
Hubbard	50122
Hudson	50643
Hull	51239
Humboldt	50548
Humeston	50123
Huntington	51334
Hurstville	52060
Hutchins	50423
Huxley	50124
Iconium	52571
Ida Grove	51445
Imogene	51645
Independence	50644
Indian Creek (Part of Marion)	52302
Indianola	50125
Industry	50540
Inwood	51240
Ionia	50645
Iowa Army Ammunition Plant	52638
Iowa Center	50161
Iowa City	52240
	52242-46
For specific ZIP Codes call (888) 275-8777, or your local postmaster.	
Iowa Falls	50126
Iowa State University	50011-13
For specific ZIP Codes call (888) 275-8777, or your local postmaster.	
Ira	50127
Ireton	51027
Ironhills	52060
Irving	52208
Irvington	50560
Irwin	51446
Ivy	50009
Jackson Junction	52171
Jacksonville	51537
Jamaica	50128
James	51108
Jamison	50210
Janesville	50647
Jefferson	50129
Jerico	50659
Jerome	52544
Jesup	50648
Jewell	50130
Johnston	50131
Johnston Station (Part of Johnston)	50131
Joice	50446
Jolley	50551
Jordan	50036
Julien	52003
Juniata	50588
Kalo	50569
Kalona	52247
Kamrar	50132
Kanawha	50447
Kellerton	50133
Kelley	50134
Kellogg	50135
Kendallville	52136
Kennedy Mall (Part of Dubuque)	52001
Kensett	50448
Kent	50851
Keokuk	52632
Keomah Village	52577
Keosauqua	52565
Keota	52248
Kesley	50649
Keswick	50136
Keystone	52249
Key West (Part of Dubuque)	52003
Kilbourn	52535
Killduff	50137
Kimballton	51543
Kingsley	51028
Kingston	52637
Kinross	52335
Kirkman	51447
Kirkville	52566
Kiron	51448
Klemme	50449
Klinger	50668
Knapp Garden	50109
Knierim	50552
Knittel	50668
Knoke	50575
Knoxville	50138
Knoxville Estates	50138
Konigsmark	52401
Kossuth	52637
Koszta	52208
Lacelle	50213
Lacey	50207
Lacona	50139
Ladora	52251
La Fayette	52202
Lake Canyada	52804
Lake City	51449
Lake Mills	50450
Lake Park	51347
Lakeside	50588
Lake View	51450
Lakewood	50211
Lakota	50451
Lambs Grove	50208
Lamoille	50158
Lamoni	50140
Lamont	50650
La Motte	52054
Lanesboro	51451
Langdon	51301
Langworthy	52252
Lansing	52151
Lanyon	50544
La Porte City	50651
Larchwood	51241
Larrabee	51029
Latimer	50452
Laurel	50141
Laurens	50554
Lawler	52154
Lawn Hill	50206
Lawton	51030
Leando	52551
Lebanon, *Sioux*	51250
Lebanon, *Van Buren*	52565
Le Claire	52753
Ledyard	50556
Leeds (Part of Sioux City)‡	51108
Le Grand	50142
Lehigh	50557
Leighton	50143
Leland	50453
Le Mars	51031
Lenox	50851
Leon	50144
Le Roy	50123
Lester	51242
Letts	52754
Lewis	51544
Liberty	50210
Liberty Center	50145
Libertyville	52567
Lidderdale	51452
Lime City	52778
Lime Springs	52155
Linby	52580
Lincoln	50652
Lincoln Center	50841
Lindale Mall (Part of Cedar Rapids)	52402
Linden	50146
Lineville	50147
Linn Grove	51033
Linwood (Part of Buffalo)	52805
Lisbon	52253
Liscomb	50148
Little Cedar	50454
Littleport	52055
Little Rock	51243
Little Sioux	51545
Littleton	50648
Little Turkey	52154
Livermore	50558
Livingston	52549
Lockridge	52635
Logan	51546
Logansport	50036
Lohrville	51453
Lone Rock	50559
Lone Tree	52755
Long Grove	52756
Lorah	50022
Lorimor	50149
Loring	50161
Lost Nation	52254
Lourdes	50628
Loveland	51555
Lovilia	50150
Lovington	50322
Lowden	52255
Lowell	52645
Low Moor	52757
Luana	52156
Lucas	50151
Lundstrom Heights	50021
Luther	50152
Luther Manor (Part of Bettendorf)	52722
Luton	51052
Lu Verne	50560
Luxemburg	52056
Luzerne	52257
Lyman	51535
Lynnville	50153
Lyons (Part of Clinton)‡	52732
Lyons, *Linn*	52302
Lytton	50561
McCallsburg	50154
McCausland	52758
McClelland	51548
Macedonia	51549
McGregor	52157
McIntire	50455
Macksburg	50155
McNally	51027
Macy	50601
Madison (Part of Council Bluffs)	51503
Madrid	50156
Magnolia	51550
Malcom	50157
Mallard	50562
Mall of the Bluffs (Part of Council Bluffs)	51503
Malone	52742
Maloy	50836
Malvern	51551
Manawa (Part of Council Bluffs)	51501
Manchester	52057
Manilla	51454
Manly	50456
Manning	51455
Manson	50563
Maple Heights (Part of Charles City)	50616
Maple Hill	50514
Maple River	51401
Mapleton	51034
Maquoketa	52060
Marathon	50565
Marble Rock	50653
Marcus	51035
Marengo	52301
Marietta	50158
Marion	52302
Mark	52537
Marne	51552
Marquette	52158
Marquisville	50313
Marsh	52659
Marshalltown	50158
Marshalltown Mall (Part of Marshalltown)	50158
Martelle	52305
Martensdale	50160
Martinsburg	52568
Martinstown	52544
Marysville	50116
Mason City	50401*
	50402†
Masonville	50654
Massena	50853
Massey	52003
Massillon	52255
Matlock	51244
Maurice	51036
Maxwell	50161
May City	51349
Maynard	50655
Maysville	52773
Mechanicsville	52306
Mederville	52043
Mediapolis	52637
Medora	50125
Melbourne	50162
Melcher (Part of Melcher-Dallas)	50163
Melcher-Dallas	50163
Melrose	52569

*** Area Zip Code** **† Post Office Boxes** **‡ Postal Station** **♦ Census Designated Place** *Italic Type* **County**

Place	ZIP
Meltonville	50472
Melvin	51350
Menlo	50164
Meriden	51037
Merle Hay Mall (Part of Des Moines)	50310
Meroa	50461
Merrill	51038
Meservey	50457
Methodist Camp	51360
Meyer	50455
Middle Amana	52307
Middleburg	51041
Middle River	50273
Middletown	52638
Midlands Mall (Part of Council Bluffs)	51503
Midway	52302
Miles	52064
Milford	51351
Miller	50438
Millersburg	52308
Millerton	50165
Millville	52052
Milnerville	51062
Milo	50166
Milton	52570
Minburn	50167
Minden	51553
Mineola	51554
Minerva	50005
Mingo	50168
Missouri Valley	51555
Mitchell	50461
Mitchellville	50169
Modale	51556
Moingona	50036
Mona	50472
Mondamin	51557
Moneta	51346
Monmouth	52309
Monona	52159
Monroe	50170
Monteith	50115
Monterey	52537
Montezuma	50171
Montgomery	51360
Monti	52218
Monticello	52310
Montour	50173
Montpelier	52759
Montrose	52639
Mooar	52632
Moorhead	51558
Moorland	50566
Moran	50276
Moravia	52571
Morley	52312
Morningside (Part of Sioux City)‡	51106
Morning Sun	52640
Morrison	50657
Morse	52240
Morton Mills	50864
Moscow	52760
Moulton	52572
Mount Auburn	52313
Mount Ayr	50854
Mount Carmel	51401
Mount Etna	50841
Mount Joy	52804
Mount Pleasant	52641
Mount Sterling	52573
Mount Union	52644
Mount Vernon	52314
Mount Zion	52565
Moville	51039
Munterville	52536
Murphy	50677
Murray	50174
Muscatine	52761
Muscatine Mall (Part of Muscatine)	52761
Mystic	52574
Napier	50014
Nashua	50658
Nashville	52060
Nemaha	50567
Neola	51559
Neptune	51031
Nevada	50201
Nevinville	50801
New Albin	52160
New Boston	52619
Newburg	50112
Newell	50568
New Era	52761
Newhall	52315
New Hampton	50659
New Hartford	50660
New Haven	50461
Newkirk	51238
New Liberty	52765
New London	52645
New Market	51646
New Providence	50206
New Sharon	50207
Newton	50208
New Vienna	52065
New Virginia	50210
Nichols	52766
Noble	52641
Nodaway	50857
Nora Springs	50458
Nora Springs Junction (Part of Nora Springs)	50458
Northboro	51647
North Branch	50002
North Buena Vista	52066
Northeast (Part of Cedar Rapids)‡	52402
North English	52316
North Grand (Part of Ames)	50010
North Liberty	52317
Northpark Mall (Part of Davenport)	52806
North Side (Part of Sioux City)‡	51104
North Wall Lake (Part of Wall Lake)	51466
North Washington	50661
Northwest (Part of Cedar Rapids)‡	52405
Northwest (Part of Davenport)‡	52804
Northwood	50459
Norwalk	50211
Norway	52318
Norwich	51601
Norwood	50151
Norwoodville	50317
Numa	52544
Nyman	51566
Oakdale (Part of Coralville)	52319
Oakland	51560
Oakland Acres	50112
Oakland Mills	52641
Oakley	50049
Oak Valley	52401
Oakville	52646
Oakwood	50653
Oasis	52358
Ocheyedan	51354
Odebolt	51458
Oelwein	50662
Ogden	50212
Okoboji	51355
Old Balltown	52073
Olds	52647
Old Town	51351
Olin	52320
Olivet	50143
Ollie	52576
Onawa	51040
Oneida	52057
Onslow	52321
Ontario (Part of Ames)	50014
Oralabor	50021
Oran	50664
Orange (Part of Waterloo)	50701
Orange City	51041
Orchard	50460
Orient	50858
Orilla	50061
Orleans	51360
Osage	50461
Osborne	52043
Osceola	50213
Osgood	50536
Oskaloosa	52577
Ossian	52161
Osterdock	52035
Otho	50569
Otley	50214
Oto	51044
Otranto	50472
Otter Creek	52079
Otterville	50644
Ottosen	50570
Ottumwa	52501
Ottumwa Junction (Part of Ottumwa)	52501
Owasa	50126
Oxford	52322
Oxford Junction	52323
Oxford Mills	52323
Oyens	51045
Pacific Junction	51561
Packard	50619
Packwood	52580
Painted Rock	50214
Palmer	50571
Palm Grove	50501
Palmyra	50047
Palo	52324
Panama	51562
Panora	50216
Panorama Park	52722
Paralta	52336
Paris, *Davis*	52552
Paris, *Linn*	52214
Parkersburg	50665
Park Hills	50214
Park View♦	52748
Parnell	52325
Paton	50217
Patterson	50218
Paullina	51046
Payne	51640
Pekin	52580
Pella	50219
Peoria	50219
Peosta	52068
Percival	51648
Perkins	51239
Perlee	52556
Perry	50220
Pershing	50138
Persia	51563
Peru	50222
Petersburg	52040
Peterson	51047
Petersville	52731
Pierceville	52565
Pierson	51048
Pilot Grove	52648
Pilot Mound	50223
Pioneer	50541
Piper	50579
Pisgah	51564
Pittsburg	52565
Pitzer	50072
Plainfield	50666
Plain View	52773
Plano	52581
Plaza Hills (Part of Windsor Heights)	50311
Pleasant Grove	52645
Pleasant Hill	50317
Pleasanton	50065
Pleasant Plain	52540
Pleasant Prairie	52761
Pleasant Valley	52767
Pleasantville	50225
Plover	50573
Plymouth	50464
Pocahontas	50574
Polk City	50226
Pomeroy	50575
Popejoy	50227
Portland	50401
Portsmouth	51565
Postville	52162
Powersville	50636
Prairieburg	52219
Prairie City	50228
Prairie Grove	52655
Prescott	50859
Preston	52069
Primghar	51245
Primrose	52625
Princeton	52768
Prole	50229
Promise City	52583
Prospect Hill (Part of Burlington)	52601
Protivin	52163
Pulaski	52584
Quarry	50158
Quasqueton	52326
Quimby	51049
Radcliffe	50230
Rake	50465
Ralston	51459
Randalia	52164
Randall	50231
Randolph	51649
Rands	50579
Rathbun	52544
Raymar	50701
Raymond	50667
Readlyn	50668
Reasnor	50232
Redding	50860
Redfield	50233
Red Line	51447
Red Oak	51566
Red Rock Lakeview	50138
Reinbeck	50669
Rembrandt	50576
Remsen	51050
Renwick	50577
Rhodes	50234
Riceville	50466
Richards	50579
Richland	52585
Richmond	52247
Rickardsville	52073
Ricketts	51460
Ridgeport	50036
Ridgeway	52165
Higgs	52731
Rinard	50587
Ringsted	50578
Rippey	50235
Rising Sun	50317
Ritter	51201
Riverdale	52722
River Heights	52240
River Junction	52755
Riverside, *Washington*	52327
Riverside (Part of Sioux City)	51109
River Sioux	51545
Riverton	51650
Roberts	50569
Robertson	50601
Robins	52328
Robinson	52330
Rochester	52772
Rockdale (Part of Dubuque)	52003
Rock Falls	50467
Rockford	50468
Rock Rapids	51246
Rock Valley	51247
Rockwell	50469
Rockwell City	50579
Rodman	50562
Rodney	51051
Roelyn	50566
Roland	50236
Rolfe	50581
Rome	52642
Rose Hill	52586
Roselle	51401
Ross	50025
Rosserdale	50164
Rossie	51357
Rossville	52159
Rowan	50470
Rowley	52329
Royal	51357
Rubio	52585
Rudd	50471
Runnells	50237
Russell	50238
Ruthven	51358
Rutland	50582
Ryan	52330
Sabula	52070
Sac and Fox Indian Reservation	52339
Sac City	50583
Sageville	52001
St. Ansgar	50472
St. Anthony	50239
St. Benedict	50511
St. Catherine	52003
St. Charles	50240
St. Donatus	52071
St. Joseph	50519
St. Lucas	52166
St. Marys	50241
St. Olaf	52072
St. Paul	52657
Salem	52649
Salina	52556
Salix	51052
Sanborn	51248
Sand Springs	52237
Sandusky	52632
Sandyville	50001
Santiago	50169
Saratoga	52155
Saude	52154
Savannah	52537
Sawyer	52627
Saydel	50313
Saylorville♦	50313
Scarville	50473
Schaller	51053
Schleswig	51461
Schley	52136
Sciola	50864
Scotch Grove	52310
Scotch Ridge	50047
Scranton	51462
Searsboro	50242
Selma	52588
Selser's	52228
Seneca	50539
Seney	51031
Sergeant Bluff	51054
Sewal	50060
Sexton	50483
Seymour	52590
Shaffton	52730
Shambaugh	51651
Shannon City	50861
Sharon Center	52240
Sharpsburg	50862
Shawondasse	52003
Sheffield	50475
Shelby	51570
Sheldahl	50243
Sheldon	51201
Shell Rock	50670
Shellsburg	52332
Shenandoah	51601
	51693
For specific ZIP Codes call (888) 275-8777, or your local postmaster.	
Sheridan	50157
Sherrill	52073
Sherwood	50579
Shipley	50201
Shueyville	52404
Siam	50833
Sibley	51249
Sidney	51652
Sigourney	52591
Silver City	51571
Sinclair	50665
Sioux Center	51250
Sioux City	51101-11
For specific ZIP Codes call (888) 275-8777, or your local postmaster.	
Sioux Rapids	50585
Six Mile	52732
Slater	50244
Slifer	50543
Sloan	51055
Smithland	51056
Soldier	51572
Solon	52333
Somers	50586
South Amana	52334
South Des Moines (Part of Des Moines)‡	50315
South English	52335
Southern Hills Mall (Part of Sioux City)	51106
South Muscatine (Part of Muscatine)	52761
South Ottumwa (Part of Ottumwa)	52501
Southridge Mall (Part of Des Moines)	50315
Spaulding	50801
Spencer	51301
Sperry	52650
Spillville	52168
Spirit Lake	51360
Spragueville	52074
Springbrook	52075
Springdale	52358
Spring Green Estates	52411
Spring Grove	52601
Spring Hill	50125
Springville	52336
Spruce Hills Village (Part of Bettendorf)	52722
Stacyville	50476
Stanhope	50246
Stanley	50671
Stanton	51573
Stanwood	52337
Stanzel	50849
State Center	50247
Steamboat Rock	50672
Stennett	51566
Sterling	52070
Stiles	52537
Stilson	50423
Stockport	52651
Stockton	52769
Stone City	52205
Storm Lake	50588
Story City	50248
Stout	50673
Strahan	51540
Stratford	50249
Strawberry Point	52076
Stringtown	50851

Struble 51057
Stuart 50250
Suburban Heights 52556
Sully 50251
Sulphur Springs 50588
Summerset 50125
Summitville 52632
Sumner 50674
Sunbury 52778
Sunshine 52544
Superior 51363
Sutherland 51058
Sutliff 52253
Swaledale 50477
Swan 50252
Swea City 50590
Swedesburg 52652
Sweetland Center 52761
Swisher 52338
Tabor 51653
Taintor 50207
Talleyrand 52248
Tama 52339
Tara 50501
Teeds Grove 52771
Templar Park 51360
Templeton 51463
Ten Mile 52727
Tennant 51574
Tenville 50864
Tenville Junction 50864
Terril 51364
Thayer 50254
Thirty 52544
Thompson 50478
Thor 50591
Thornburg 50255
Thornton 50479
Thorpe 52057
Thurman 51654
Ticonic 51010
Tiffin 52340
Timber Creek 52401
Timberland Heights (Part of Ames) 50014
Tingley 50863
Tipton 52772
Titonka 50480
Toddville 52341
Toeterville 50481
Toledo 52342
Toolesboro 52653
Toronto 52777
Tower Terrace 52233
Tracy 50256
Traer 50675
Trenton 52641
Treynor 51575
Triboji Beach 51360
Tripoli 50676
Troy 52537
Troy Mills 52344
Truax 52553
Truesdale 50592
Truro 50257
Turin 51059
Turkey River 52052
Twin Knolls 52401
Twin Lakes Estates 52401
Twin View Heights 52333
Udell 52593
Ulmer 51450
Underwood 51576
Union 50258
Union Center 51031
Union Mills 50207
Unionville 52594
University Heights 52246
University Park 52595
University Place (Part of Des Moines)‡ 50311
Urbana 52345
Urbandale 50322
Ute 51060
Utica 52651
Vail 51465
Valeria 50054
Valley West Mall (Part of West Des Moines) 50266
Van Cleve 50162
Vandalia 50228
Van Horne 52346
Van Meter 50261
Van Wert 50262
Varina 50593
Ventura 50482
Ventura Heights 50482
Vernon 52565
Vernon Springs 52136
Vernon View 52401
Veterans Administration Medical Center (Part of Knoxville) 50138
Victor 52347
Villa Hermosa 52401
Villisca 50864
Vincennes 52619
Vincent 50594
Vining 52348
Vinton 52349
Viola 52350
Volga 52077
Volney 52159
Voorhies 50643
Wadena 52169
Wahpeton 51351
Walcott 52773
Wales 51533
Walford 52351
Walker 52352
Wallingford 51365
Wall Lake 51466
Walnut 51577
Walnut City 52574
Wapello 52653
Ware 50546
Washburn 50706
Washington 52353
Washta 51061
Waterloo 50701-07
For specific ZIP Codes call (888) 275-8777, or your local postmaster.
Waterville 52170
Watkins 52354
Waubeek 52214
Waucoma 52171
Waukee 50263
Waukon 52172
Waukon Junction 52146
Waupeton 52073
Waverly 50677
Wayland 52654
Webb 51366
Webster 52355
Webster City 50595
Welch Avenue (Part of Ames)‡ 50014
Weldon 50264
Wellman 52356
Wellsburg 50680
Welton 52774
Wesley 50483
West Ackley (Part of Ackley) 50601
West Amana 52203
West Bend 50597
West Branch 52358
West Broadway (Part of Council Bluffs) 51501
West Burlington 52655
West Chester 52359
Westdale Mall (Part of Cedar Rapids) 52404
West Des Moines 50265-66
For specific ZIP Codes call (888) 275-8777, or your local postmaster.
Western College 52404
Westfield 51062
Westgate 50681
West Grove 52538
West Le Mars 51031
West Liberty 52776
West Okoboji 51351
Weston 51576
Westphalia 51578
West Point 52656
West Post Estates 52404
Westside 51467
West Spencer 51301
West Storm Lake (Part of Storm Lake) 50588
West Suburban (Part of Des Moines)‡ 50325
West Union 52175
Westwood 52641
Wever 52658
What Cheer 50268
Wheatland 52777
White Oak 50073
Whiting 51063
Whittemore 50598
Whitten 50269
Whittier 52336
Wichita 50115
Wick 50240
Wildwood 52341
Wildwood Camp 52756
Willey 51401
William Penn College (Part of Oskaloosa)‡ 52577
Williams 50271
Williamsburg 52361
Williamson, *Adams* 50859
Williamson, *Lucas* 50272
Williamstown 52247
Wilton 52778
Windham 52322
Windsor Heights 50311
Winfield 52659
Winnebago Heights 50401
Winterset 50273
Winthrop 50682
Wiota 50274
Wiscotta 50233
Woden 50484
Wood 52042
Woodbine 51579
Woodburn 50275
Woodland, *Decatur* 50103
Woodland, *Polk* 50237
Woodward 50276
Woolstock 50599
Worthington 52078
Wright 52577
Wyman 52621
Wyoming 52362
Yale 50277
Yarmouth 52660
Yetter 51433
Yorktown 51656
Zaneta 50643
Zearing 50278
Zion 50858
Zook Spur 50156
Zwingle 52079

Place	ZIP Code
Abbyville	67510
Abilene	67410
Ada	67467
Adams	67128
Adams Corner	67561
Admire	66830
Aetna	67071
Agenda	66930
Aggieville (Part of Manhattan)	66502
Aggieville Shopping Center (Part of Manhattan)	66502
Agra	67621
Agricola	66871
Akron	67156
Alamota	67839
Albert	67511
Alden	67512
Alexander	67513
Aliceville	66093
Allen	66833
Alma	66401
Almena	67622
Altamont	67330
Alta Vista	66834
Alton	67623
Altoona	66710
Americus	66835
Ames	66901
Amy	67850
Andale	67001
Andover	67002
Angelus	67738
Angola	67337
Anna	66701
Anness	67106
Anson	67152
Antelope	66858
Anthony	67003
Antioch	66083
Antonino	67601
Arcadia	66711
Arcola	67425
Argentine (Part of Kansas City)‡	66106
Argonia	67004
Arkansas City	67005
Arlington	67514
Arma	66712
Armourdale (Part of Kansas City)	66105
Arnold	67515
Arrington	66436
Arthur Heights (Part of Bel Aire)	67220
Arvonia	66523
Asherville	67420
Ash Grove	67481
Ashland, Clark	67831
Ashland, Riley	66502
Ashton	67051
Assaria	67416
Atchison	66002
Atchison Mall (Part of Atchison)	66002
Athol	66932
Atlanta	67008
Attica	67009
Atwood	67730
Aubry	66085
Auburn	66402
Augusta	67010
Aulne	66861
Aurora	67417
Aurora Park (Part of Bel Aire)	67220
Axtell	66403
Baileyville	66404
Bala	66531
Baldwin City	66006
Bancroft	66428
Barclay	66523
Barker (Part of Kansas City)	66104
Barnard	67418
Barnes	66933
Bartlett	67332
Basehor	66007
Bassett	66749
Bavaria	67401
Baxter Springs	66713
Bayard	66039
Bazaar	66845
Bazine	67516
Beagle	66064
Beardsley	67730
Beattie	66406
Beaumont	67012
Beaver	67525
Beech	67207
Beeler	67518
Bel Aire	67220
Bellaire	66952
Belle Plaine	67013
Belleville	66935
Belmont	67068
Beloit	67420
Belpre	67519
Belvidere	67028
Belvue	66407
Bendena	66008
Benedict	66714
Bennington	67422
Bentley	67016
Benton	67017
Bern	66408
Berryton	66409
Berwick	66534
Beulah	66743
Beverly	67423
Big Bow	67855
Big Springs	66050
Bird City	67731
Birmingham	66436
Bismarck Grove (Part of Lawrence)	66044
Bison	67520
Black Wolf	67490
Blaine	66549
Blair	66090
Blakeman	67730
Bloom	67865
Bloomington, *Butler*	67010
Bloomington, *Osborne*	67473
Blue Hills (Part of Manhattan)	66502
Blue Mound	66010
Blue Rapids	66411
Blue Valley (Part of Overland Park)	66213
Bluff City	67018
Bogue	67625
Boicourt	66075
Bolton	67301
Bonita	66061
Bonner Springs	66012
Bonnie Brae (Part of Wichita)	67207
Bonnie Ridge	67401
Boyle	66088
Bradford	66423
Brainerd	67154
Brazilton	66743
Bremen	66412
Brenham	67059
Brenner Heights (Part of Kansas City)	66104
Brewster	67732
Bridgeport	67416
Bronson	66716
Brookhaven Estates	67230
Brookridge (Part of Overland Park)	66212
	66282
For specific ZIP Codes call (888) 275-8777, or your local postmaster.	
Brookville	67425
Brookwood Shopping Center (Part of Topeka)	66614
Brownell	67521
Browns Spur	67068
Buckeye	67410
Bucklin	67834
Bucyrus	66013
Buffalo	66717
Buhler	67522
Bunker Hill	67626
Burden	67019
Burdett	67523
Burdick	66838
Burlingame	66413
Burlington	66839
Burns	66840
Burr Oak	66936
Burrton	67020
Busby	67352
Bush City	66032
Bushong	66833
Bushton	67427
Buxton	66736
Byers	67021
Cadmus	66026
Cairo	67035
Caldwell	67022
Calista	67035
Callahan (Part of Wichita)	67209
Calvert	67622
Cambridge	67023
Camp Fifty	66712
Camp Forsyth♦	66442
Camp Funston	66442
Camp Naish	66111
Campus	67748
Camp Whiteside	66442
Canada	66861
Caney	67333
Canton	67428
Capaldo	66762
Carbondale	66414
Carlton	67448
Carlyle	66749
Carneiro	67425
Carona	66773
Cassoday	66842
Castleton	67501
Catharine	67627
Cato	66711
Cave	67952
Cawker City	67430
Cedar, *Johnson*	66018
Cedar, *Smith*	67628
Cedar Bluffs	67749
Cedar Point	66843
Cedar Vale	67024
Centerview	67552
Centerville	66014
Centralia	66415
Centropolis	66067
Chanute	66720
Chapman	67431
Charleston	67853
Chase	67524
Chautauqua	67334
Cheney	67025
Cherokee	66724
Cherryvale	67335
Chetopa	67336
Chicopee	66762
Child's Acres	67101
Chiles	66071
Chisholm (Part of Wichita)‡	67213
Cicero	67152
Cimarron	67835
Circleville	66416
Civic Center (Part of Kansas City)‡	66101
Claflin	67525
Clare	66061
Claudell	66951
Clay Center	67432
Clayton	67629
Clearfield	66025
Clearview City	66019
Clearwater	67026
Clements	66843
Cleveland	67068
Clifton	66937
Climax	67137
Clinton	66049
Clonmel	67149
Cloverdale	67024
Clyde	66938
Coalvale	66711
Coats	67028
Codell	67663
Coffeyville	67337
Colby	67701
Coldwater	67029
Collyer	67631
Colony	66015
Columbus	66725
Colwich	67030
Concordia	66901
Conway	67460
Conway Springs	67031
Coolidge	67836
Copeland	67837
Corbin, *Montgomery*	67335
Corbin, *Sumner*	67032
Corinth Square (Part of Prairie Village)	66208
Corning	66417
Corporate Hills (Part of Wichita)‡	67207
Corwin	67061
Cottonwood Falls	66845
Council Grove	66846
Countryside	66202
County Acres (Part of Wichita)	67212
Courtland	66939
Covert	67651
Cow Town (Part of Wichita)	67203
Coyville	66727
Craig	66215
Crestline	66728
Croweburg	66756
Cruppers Corner	67501
Crystal Springs	67058
Cuba	66940
Cullen Village (Part of Topeka)	66619
Cullison	67124
Culver	67484
Cummings	66016
Cunningham	67035
Curranville	66756
Dalton	67152
Damar	67632
Danville	67036
Dartmouth	67530
Dearing	67340
Deerfield	67838
Deerhead	67071
De Graff	66840
Delano (Part of Wichita)‡	67209
Delavan	67449
Delia	66418
Dellvale	67654
Delphos	67436
Denison	66419
Denmark	67455
Dennis	67341
Densmore	67645
Denton	66017
Dentonia	66941
Derby	67037
Dermot	67954
De Soto	66018
Detroit	67410
Devon	66701
Dexter	67038
Diamond Springs	66838
Dighton	67839
Dillwyn	67557
Dispatch	67430
Dodge City	67801
Doniphan	66002
Dorrance	67634
Douglass	67039
Dover	66420
Downs	67437
Downtown (Part of Topeka)‡	66601*
	66603†
Downtown (Part of Wichita)‡	67201-03
For specific ZIP Codes call (888) 275-8777, or your local postmaster.	
Dresden	67635
Drury	67022
Dubuque	67634
Duluth	66521
Dunavant	66088
Dundee	67530
Dunkirk	66762
Dunlap	66846
Duquoin	67058
Durham	67438
Dwight	66849
Earlton	66720
East Bank (Part of Iola)	66749
Eastborough	67206-07
For specific ZIP Codes call (888) 275-8777, or your local postmaster.	
East Forbes	66620
Eastgate Plaza (Part of Wichita)	67207
Easton	66020
Eastshore	66861
Edgerton	66021
Edmond	67645
Edna	67342
Edson	67733
Edwardsville	66113
Effingham	66023
Elbing	67041
El Dorado	67042
Elgin	67361
Elk City	67344
Elk Falls	67345
Elkhart	67950
Ellinwood	67526
Ellis	67637
Ellsworth	67439
Elmdale	66850
Elmhurst (Part of Overland Park)	66204
Elmo	67451
Elmont	66618
Elsmore	66732
Elwood	66024
Elyria	67460
Emmeram	67671
Emmett	66422
Empire City (Part of Galena)	66739
Empire Junction (Part of Galena)	66739
Emporia	66801
Englevale	66756
Englewood	67840
Ensign	67841
Enterprise	67441
Erie	66733
Esbon	66941
Eskridge	66423
Eudora	66025
Eureka	67045
Eureka City Lake	67045
Everest	66424
Ewell	67031
Fairfax (Part of Kansas City)‡	66115
Fairmount	66048
Fairport	67665
Fairview	66425
Fairway	66205
Fall Leaf	66052
Fall River	67047
Falun	67442
Fanning	66087
Farlington	66734
Farlinville	66014
Farmington	66023
Faulkner	67336
Fellsburg	67552
Fleming	66762
Floral	67156
Florence	66851
Flush	66535
Fontana	66026
Ford	67842
Forest Hills (Part of Wichita)	67206
Forest Lake (Part of Edwardsville)	66113
Formoso	66942
Fort Dodge	67801
Fort Leavenworth	66027
Fort Riley	66442
Fort Scott	66701
Fostoria, *Osage*	66413
Fostoria, *Pottawatomie*	66426
Four Corners	66537
Fowler	67844
Fox Town	66756
Frankfort	66427
Franklin	66735
Frederick	67444
Fredonia	66736
Freemount	67456
Freeport	67049
Friend	67871
Frontenac	66763
Fulton	66738
Furley	67147
Gage Center (Part of Topeka)‡	66604
Galatia	67565
Galena	66739
Galesburg	66740
Galva	67443
Garden City	67846
Garden Plain	67050
Gardner	66030
Gardner Lake	66030
Garfield	67529
Garland	66741
Garnett	66032
Gas	66742
Gaylord	67638
Gem	67734
General Mail Facility (Part of Wichita)‡	67209
Geneseo	67444
Gerlane	67104
Geuda Springs	67051
Girard	66743
Glade	67639
Glasco	67445
Glendale	67425
Glen Elder	67446
Glen Park (Part of Kansas City)	66102
Glenville (Part of Wichita)	67217
Globe	66006
Goddard	67052
Goessel	67053
Goff	66428
Golden Belt Spur (Part of Salina)	67401
Goodland	67735
Goodrich	66072
Gordon	67010
Gorham	67640
Gove	67736
Grainfield	67737
Granada	66550
Grand Summit	67023
Grandview (Part of Bonner Springs)	66012
Grandview Plaza	66441
Grantville	66429
Great Bend	67530
Greeley	66033
Green	67447
Greenbush	66743

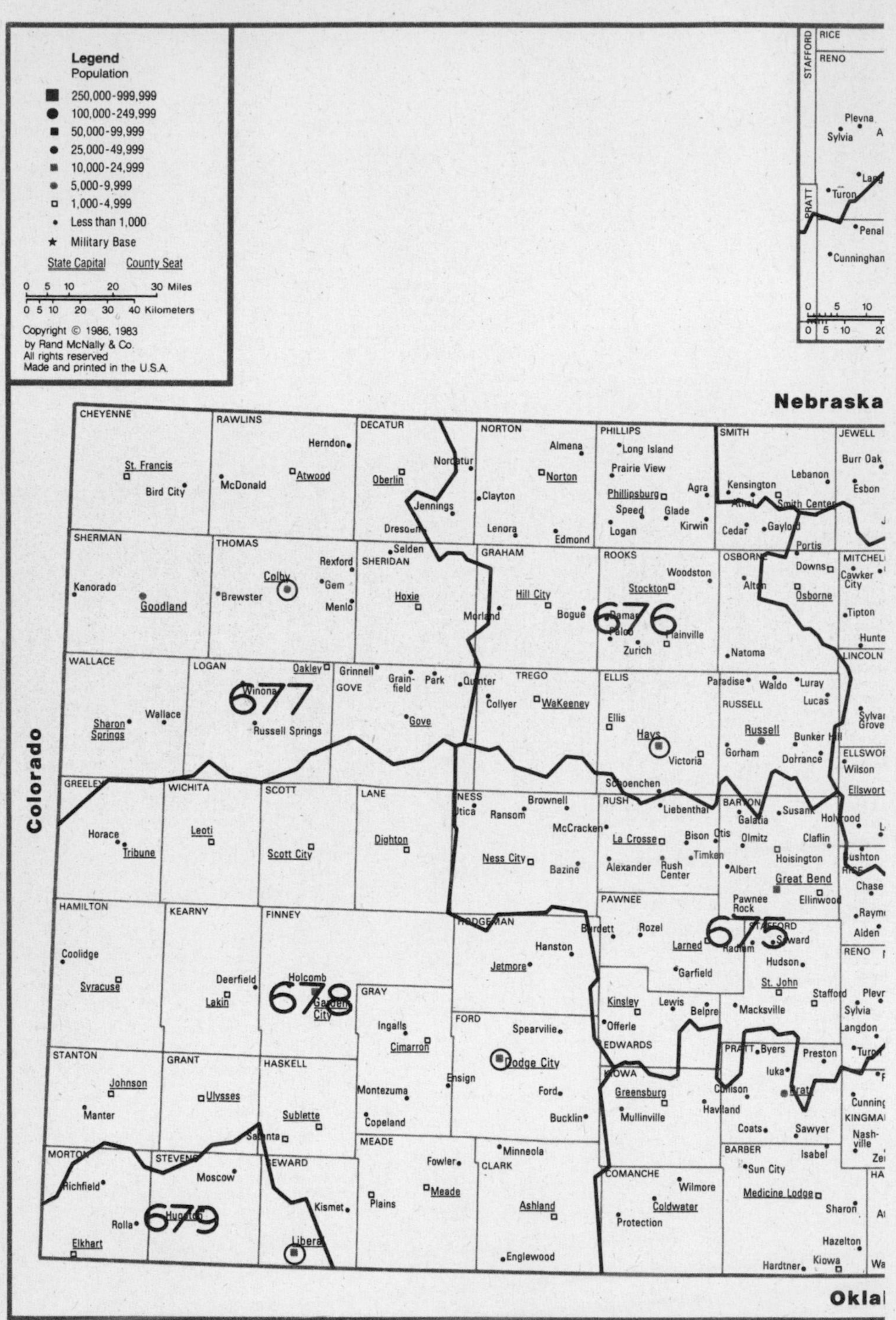
Legend
Population
250,000-999,999
100,000-249,999
50,000-99,999
25,000-49,999
10,000-24,999
5,000-9,999
1,000-4,999
Less than 1,000
Military Base
State Capital
County Seat
0 5 10 20 30 Miles
0 5 10 20 30 40 Kilometers
Copyright © 1986, 1983
by Rand McNally & Co.
All rights reserved
Made and printed in the U.S.A.
Nebraska
Colorado
Okla
676
677
678
679
675
CHEYENNE
St. Francis
Bird City
RAWLINS
Herndon
McDonald
Atwood
DECATUR
Oberlin
Jennings
NORTON
Almena
Norton
Clayton
Lenora
Edmond
PHILLIPS
Long Island
Prairie View
Phillipsburg
Agra
Speed
Glade
Logan
Kirwin
SMITH
Kensington
Lebanon
Smith Center
Cedar
JEWELL
Burr Oak
Esbon
SHERMAN
Kanorado
Goodland
THOMAS
Colby
Brewster
Rexford
Gem
Menlo
SHERIDAN
Selden
Hoxie
GRAHAM
Hill City
Morland
Bogue
ROOKS
Woodston
Stockton
Zurich
Plainville
OSBORNE
Alton
Downs
Osborne
Portis
MITCHELL
Cawker City
Tipton
Natoma
LINCOLN
WALLACE
Wallace
Sharon Springs
LOGAN
Oakley
Winona
Russell Springs
Grinnell
GOVE
Grainfield
Park
Gove
Quinter
Collyer
TREGO
WaKeeney
ELLIS
Ellis
Hays
Victoria
Schoenchen
Paradise
Waldo
Luray
Lucas
RUSSELL
Russell
Gorham
Bunker Hill
Dorrance
Wilson
Sylvan Grove
Ellsworth
GREELEY
Horace
Tribune
WICHITA
Leoti
SCOTT
Scott City
LANE
Dighton
NESS
Utica
Ransom
Brownell
McCracken
Ness City
Bazine
RUSH
La Crosse
Alexander
Rush Center
Bison
Otis
Timken
Liebenthal
BARTON
Galatia
Susank
Olmitz
Claflin
Hoisington
Albert
Great Bend
Ellinwood
Holyrood
Chase
HAMILTON
Coolidge
Syracuse
KEARNY
Deerfield
Lakin
FINNEY
Holcomb
Garden City
HODGEMAN
Hanston
Jetmore
PAWNEE
Burdett
Rozel
Larned
Garfield
Pawnee Rock
STAFFORD
Seward
Hudson
St. John
Stafford
Alden
RENO
GRAY
Ingalls
Cimarron
FORD
Spearville
Dodge City
Ensign
Ford
Bucklin
Kinsley
Lewis
Belpre
Offerle
EDWARDS
Macksville
PRATT
Byers
Preston
Iuka
Pratt
STANTON
Johnson
Manter
GRANT
Ulysses
HASKELL
Sublette
Satanta
Montezuma
Copeland
KIOWA
Greensburg
Mullinville
Haviland
Coats
Sawyer
KINGMAN
Nash-ville
MORTON
Richfield
Rolla
Elkhart
STEVENS
Moscow
Hugoton
SEWARD
Kismet
Liberal
MEADE
Plains
Meade
Fowler
CLARK
Minneola
Ashland
Englewood
COMANCHE
Wilmore
Coldwater
Protection
BARBER
Sun City
Medicine Lodge
Isabel
Sharon
Hazelton
Hardtner
Kiowa
STAFFORD
RICE
RENO
Plevna
Sylvia
Turon
PRATT
Cunningham

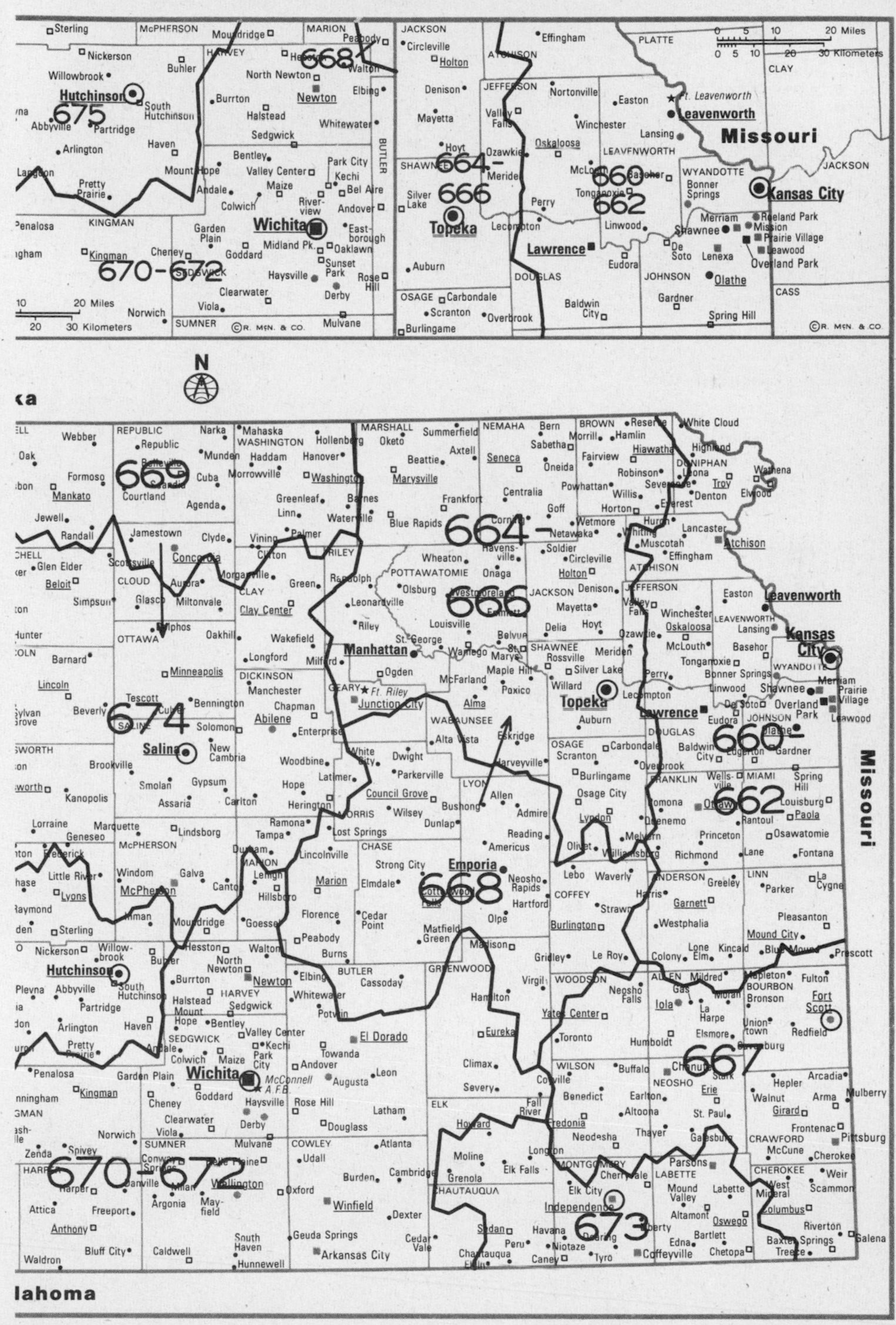
Sterling
McPHERSON
Moundridge
MARION
Peabody
Nickerson
Buhler
HARVEY
Hesston
668
Walton
Willowbrook
Hutchinson
North Newton
Elbing
675
South Hutchinson
Burrton
Newton
Abbyville
Partridge
Halstead
Whitewater
Sedgwick
Arlington
Haven
Bentley
Valley Center
Park City
Kechi
Mount Hope
Andale
Maize
Bel Aire
Pretty Prairie
Colwich
River-view
Andover
BUTLER
Penalosa
KINGMAN
Garden Plain
Wichita
East-borough
Oaklawn
Kingman
Cheney
Goddard
Midland Pk.
Sunset Park
670-672
SEDGWICK
Haysville
Rose Hill
Clearwater
Derby
20 Miles
Norwich
Viola
30 Kilometers
SUMNER
Mulvane
©R. McN. & CO.
JACKSON
Circleville
Holton
Denison
Mayetta
Hoyt
SHAWNEE
664-
666
Silver Lake
Topeka
Auburn
OSAGE
Carbondale
Scranton
Burlingame
Overbrook
Effingham
ATCHISON
JEFFERSON
Nortonville
Valley Falls
Ozawkie
Meriden
Oskaloosa
Perry
Lecompton
Lawrence
DOUGLAS
Baldwin City
PLATTE
0 5 10 20 Miles
0 5 10 20 30 Kilometers
CLAY
Ft. Leavenworth
Leavenworth
Missouri
Easton
Winchester
Lansing
LEAVENWORTH
McLouth
Basehor
660-
662
Tonganoxie
WYANDOTTE
Bonner Springs
Kansas City
JACKSON
Linwood
Merriam
Roeland Park
Mission
Shawnee
Prairie Village
Leawood
Overland Park
De Soto
Lenexa
Eudora
JOHNSON
Olathe
Gardner
Spring Hill
CASS
©R. McN. & CO.
N
ka
Webber
REPUBLIC
Republic
Narka
Mahaska
WASHINGTON
Hollenberg
Munden
Haddam
Hanover
669
Cuba
Morrowville
Washington
Formoso
Mankato
Courtland
Agenda
Greenleaf
Barnes
Linn
Waterville
Jewell
Randall
Jamestown
Clyde
Vining
Palmer
Concordia
Clifton
Glen Elder
Beloit
Scottsville
CLOUD
Aurora
Morganville
Simpson
Glasco
Miltonvale
CLAY
Clay Center
Delphos
Oakhill
OTTAWA
Wakefield
Barnard
Longford
Minneapolis
DICKINSON
Manchester
Lincoln
Tescott
Culver
Bennington
674
Chapman
Abilene
Beverly
Solomon
Enterprise
SALINE
Salina
New Cambria
Woodbine
Brookville
Smolan
Gypsum
Hope
Kanopolis
Assaria
Carlton
Lorraine
Marquette
Lindsborg
Geneseo
McPHERSON
Durham
MARION
Little River
Windom
Galva
Lehigh
Lyons
McPherson
Canton
Hillsboro
Inman
Moundridge
Goessel
Sterling
Nickerson
Willow-brook
Hesston
Walton
Hutchinson
North Newton
Buhler
Burrton
Newton
Plevna
Abbyville
South Hutchinson
HARVEY
Halstead
Sedgwick
Partridge
Mount Hope
Bentley
Arlington
Haven
Valley Center
SEDGWICK
Kechi
Pretty Prairie
Andale
Colwich
Maize
Park City
Penalosa
Garden Plain
Wichita
McConnell A.F.B.
Kingman
Goddard
Cheney
Haysville
Clearwater
Derby
Viola
Norwich
SUMNER
Mulvane
Zenda
Spivey
Conway Springs
Belle Plaine
670-672
Harper
Danville
Milan
Wellington
Argonia
Mayfield
Attica
Freeport
Anthony
Bluff City
South Haven
Caldwell
Waldron
Hunnewell
lahoma
MARSHALL
Oketo
Summerfield
NEMAHA
Bern
BROWN
Reserve
White Cloud
Sabetha
Morrill
Hamlin
Axtell
Beattie
Seneca
Oneida
Fairview
Hiawatha
Highland
DONIPHAN
Marysville
Powhattan
Robinson
Severance
Troy
Wathena
Elwood
Centralia
Willis
Denton
Frankfort
Everest
Goff
Horton
Blue Rapids
664-
Corning
Wetmore
Netawaka
Huron
Lancaster
Whiting
Muscotah
Atchison
Havensville
Soldier
RILEY
Wheaton
Circleville
Effingham
Randolph
POTTAWATOMIE
Onaga
Holton
ATCHISON
Olsburg
666
Westmoreland
JACKSON
Denison
JEFFERSON
Leonardville
Emmett
Mayetta
Valley Falls
Winchester
Easton
Leavenworth
Louisville
Hoyt
Oskaloosa
Riley
St. George
Belvue
Delia
Ozawkie
LEAVENWORTH
Lansing
Kansas City
Manhattan
Wamego
St. Marys
SHAWNEE
Rossville
Meriden
McLouth
Basehor
Tonganoxie
Milford
Maple Hill
Silver Lake
Perry
Bonner Springs
WYANDOTTE
Ogden
McFarland
Paxico
Willard
Topeka
Lecompton
Linwood
Shawnee
Merriam
Prairie Village
GEARY
Ft. Riley
Junction City
Alma
Lawrence
Eudora
De Soto
Overland Park
Leawood
WABAUNSEE
Auburn
JOHNSON
Olathe
Alta Vista
Eskridge
OSAGE
Carbondale
DOUGLAS
660-
White City
Dwight
Scranton
Baldwin City
Edgerton
Gardner
Harveyville
Overbrook
Parkerville
Burlingame
Wellsville
MIAMI
Spring Hill
LYON
Latimer
Council Grove
Osage City
FRANKLIN
662
Louisburg
Allen
Bushong
Herington
MORRIS
Wilsey
Admire
Lyndon
Pomona
Ottawa
Paola
Rantoul
Dunlap
Quenemo
Ramona
Lost Springs
Reading
Princeton
Osawatomie
Tampa
Americus
Melvern
Olivet
Williamsburg
Richmond
Lane
Fontana
Lincolnville
CHASE
Strong City
Emporia
Lebo
Waverly
ANDERSON
LINN
La Cygne
Marion
Elmdale
Neosho Rapids
Greeley
Parker
668
Cottonwood Falls
Hartford
COFFEY
Harris
Garnett
Florence
Cedar Point
Olpe
Strawn
Pleasanton
Burlington
Westphalia
Peabody
Matfield Green
Mound City
Burns
Madison
Lone Elm
Kincaid
Blue Mound
Prescott
Gridley
Le Roy
Colony
Elbing
BUTLER
Cassoday
GREENWOOD
ALLEN
Mildred
Mapleton
Fulton
Virgil
WOODSON
Gas
Moran
BOURBON
Whitewater
Neosho Falls
Iola
Bronson
Hamilton
Potwin
Yates Center
La Harpe
Fort Scott
El Dorado
Eureka
Elsmore
Union-town
Redfield
Toronto
Savonburg
Towanda
Humboldt
667
Andover
Climax
WILSON
Buffalo
Chanute
Leon
Augusta
Coyville
NEOSHO
Stark
Severy
Benedict
Earlton
Erie
Hepler
Arcadia
Rose Hill
Walnut
Arma
Mulberry
Fall River
Altoona
Girard
Latham
ELK
Douglass
Howard
Fredonia
St. Paul
Thayer
Frontenac
Neodesha
Galesburg
Pittsburg
COWLEY
CRAWFORD
Atlanta
McCune
Udall
Longton
Cherokee
Moline
Elk Falls
MONTGOMERY
Parsons
Cambridge
Cherryvale
LABETTE
CHEROKEE
Weir
Burden
Grenola
Mound Valley
Labette
West Mineral
Scammon
Oxford
Elk City
CHAUTAUQUA
Independence
Columbus
Winfield
Altamont
Oswego
Dexter
673
Riverton
Sedan
Havana
Liberty
Bartlett
Baxter Springs
Galena
Cedar Vale
Peru
Niotaze
Dearing
Edna
Geuda Springs
Chautauqua
Caney
Tyro
Coffeyville
Chetopa
Treece
Arkansas City
Elgin
Missouri

Place	ZIP
Greenleaf	66943
Greensburg	67054
Greenwich	67055
Greenwich Heights	67207
Grenola	67346
Gretna	67661
Gridley	66852
Grigston	67871
Grinnell	67738
Gross	66711
Grove	66539
Groveland	67546
Gypsum	67448
Hackney	67156
Haddam	66944
Haggard	67835
Hale	67344
Half Mound	66088
Halford	67701
Hallowell	66725
Halls Summit	66871
Halstead	67056
Hamilton	66853
Hamlin	66434
Hammond	66701
Hanover	66945
Hanston	67849
Hardtner	67057
Harlan	66967
Harper	67058
Harris	66032
Hartford	66854
Harveyville	66431
Haskell (Part of Lawrence)‡	66044
Havana	67347
Haven	67543
Havensville	66432
Haverhill	67010
Haviland	67059
Hays	67601
Haysville	67060
Hazelton	67061
Healy	67850
Hedville	67401
Heizer	67530
Hepler	66746
Herington	67449
Heritage Hills	66002
Herkimer	66508
Herndon	67739
Hesper	66025
Hessdale	66401
Hesston	67062
Hewins	67024
Hiattville	66701
Hiawatha	66434
Hickok	67880
Hickory Acres	66512
Hicrest (Part of Topeka)‡	66605
Hidden Lakes (Part of Wichita)	67212
Highland	66035
Highland Park (Part of Topeka)	66605
Hill City	67642
Hillsboro	67063
Hillsdale	66036
Hillside (Part of Wichita)	67208
Hill Top	66860
Hitschmann	67525
Hoge	66086
Hoisington	67544
Holcomb	67851
Holland	67410
Hollenberg	66946
Holliday (Part of Shawnee)	66218
Holliday Square Shopping Center (Part of Topeka)	66611
Hollis	66901
Holton	66436
Holyrood	67450
Home	66438
Homewood	66095
Hope	67451
Hopewell	67557
Horace	67879
Horton	66439
Howard	67349
Hoxie	67740
Hoyt	66440
Hudson	67545
Hugoton	67951
Humboldt	66748
Hunnewell	67140
Hunter	67452
Huron	66041
Huscher	66901

Place	ZIP
Hutchinson	67501-04
For specific ZIP Codes call (888) 275-8777, or your local postmaster.	
Hutchinson Mall (Part of Hutchinson)	67501
Idana	67432
Imes	66079
Independence	67301
Indian Creek (Part of Overland Park)	66207
Indian Junior College (Part of Lawrence)	66044
Indian Ridge	66512
Indian Springs Shopping Center (Part of Kansas City)‡	66102
Indian Valley	66608
Indian Village	67337
Industry	67410
Ingalls	67853
Inman	67546
Iola	66749
Ionia	66949
Iowa Indian Reservation	66094
Iowa Point	66035
Isabel	67065
Iuka	67066
Jacobs Creek Landing	66854
Jamestown	66948
Jarbalo	66048
Jayhawk (Part of Lawrence)‡	66046
Jefferson	67301
Jennings	67643
Jetmore	67854
Jewell	66949
Jingo	66040
Johnson	67855
Junction City	66441
Juniata	67423
Kackley	66948
Kalvesta	67856
Kanona	67749
Kanopolis	67454
Kanorado	67741

Kansas City

66101-19

For specific ZIP Codes call (888) 275-8777, or your local postmaster.

Colleges & Universities

Place	ZIP
Donnelly Coll	66102
Univ of Kansas Med Ctr	66160

Hospitals

Place	ZIP
Bethany Med Ctr	66102
Providence Med Ctr	66112
Univ of Kansas Med Ctr	66160

Place	ZIP
Kansas State University of Agriculture and Applied Science (Part of Manhattan)	66506
Kanwaka	66049
Keats	66503
Kechi	67067
Keene	66423
Kellogg	67156
Kelly	66538
Kelso	66846
Kendall	67857
Kennekuk	66439
Kenneth	66223
Kensington	66951
Kickapoo	66048
Kickapoo Indian Reservation	66439
Kimball	66733
Kimeo	66943
Kincaid	66039
Kingman	67068
Kingsdown	67865
Kinsley	67547
Kiowa	67070
Kipp	67401
Kirkwood	66762
Kiro	66539
Kirwin	67644
Kismet	67859
Labette	67356
La Crosse	67548
La Cygne	66040
Lafontaine	66736
La Harpe	66751
Lake Chaparral	66056
Lake City	67071
Lake Dabanawa	66054
Lake Kahola	66846

Place	ZIP
Lakeland Estates	67047
Lake of the Forest (Part of Bonner Springs)	66012
Lake Quivira	66106
Lake Shore, *Ellsworth*	67454
Lake Shore, *Jefferson*	66070
Lakeshore, *Shawnee*	66605
Lakeside Acres Addition	67208
Lakeside Village	66070
Lake View	66049
Lakeview Heights	67230
Lake Wabaunsee	66401
Lakewood Hills	66070
Lakin	67860
Lamont	66855
Lancaster	66041
Lane	66042
Langdon, *Crawford*	66762
Langdon, *Reno*	67583
Langley	67464
Lansing	66043
Larkinburg	66436
Larned	67550
Latham	67072
Latimer	67449
Lawrence	66044-47
	66049
For specific ZIP Codes call (888) 275-8777, or your local postmaster.	
Lawton	66781
Leavenworth	66048
Leawalk	66781
Leawood	66206
	66209
	66211
For specific ZIP Codes call (888) 275-8777, or your local postmaster.	
Lebanon	66952
Lebo	66856
Lecompton	66050
Lehigh	67073
Le Loup	66092
Lenape	66052
Lenexa	66210
	66215-17
	66219-20
	66227
For specific ZIP Codes call (888) 275-8777, or your local postmaster.	
Lenora	67645
Leon	67074
Leona	66532
Leonardville	66449
Leoti	67861
Leoville	67757
Lerado	67583
Le Roy	66857
Levant	67743
Lewis	67552
Liberal	67901-05
For specific ZIP Codes call (888) 275-8777, or your local postmaster.	
Liberty	67351
Liebenthal	67553
Lillis	66544
Lincoln	67455
Lincolnville	66858
Lindsborg	67456
Linn	66953
Linn Valley Lakes	66040
Linwood	66052
Little River	67457
Logan	67646
Lone Elm	66039
Lone Star, *Crawford*	66762
Lone Star, *Douglas*	66046
Longford	67458
Long Island	67647
Longton	67352
Loretta	67520
Lorraine	67459
Lost Springs	66859
Louisburg	66053
Louisville	66450
Lovewell	66942
Lowell	66713
Lowemont	66020
Lucas	67648
Ludell	67744
Luray	67649
Lydia	67861
Lyle	67653
Lyndon	66451
Lyons	67554
McConnell Air Force Base	67221
McCracken	67556
McCune	66753
McDonald	67745

Place	ZIP
McFarland	66501
Macksville	67557
McLouth	66054
McPherson	67460
Macyville	66901
Madison	66860
Mahaska	66955
Maize	67101
Manchester	67410
Manhattan	66502-06
For specific ZIP Codes call (888) 275-8777, or your local postmaster.	
Manhattan Town Center (Part of Manhattan)	66502
Mankato	66956
Manning	67871
Manter	67862
Maple City	67102
Maple Hill	66507
Mapleton	66754
Marienthal	67863
Marietta	66518
Marion	66861
Marion County Lake	66861
Marmaton	66701
Marquette	67464
Marysville	66508
Matfield Green	66862
Mayetta	66509
Mayfield	67103
Meade	67864
Meadowview (Part of Wichita)	67212
Mecca Acres	67230
Medicine Lodge	67104
Medina	66073
Medora	67502
Melrose	67336
Melvern	66510
Menlo	67753
Mentor	67401
Mercier	66439
Meriden	66512
Merriam	66202-04
For specific ZIP Codes call (888) 275-8777, or your local postmaster.	
Metcalf South Shopping Center (Part of Overland Park)	66212
Michigan	66528
Midland, *Douglas*	66044
Midland (Part of Wichita)‡	67216
Midland Park	67216
Midway, *Kingman*	67111
Midway, *Rawlins*	67739
Milan	67105
Milberger	67665
Mildred	66039
Milford	66514
Millbrook (Part of Wichita)	67212
Miller	66868
Milton	67106
Miltonvale	67466
Mingo	67701
Minneapolis	67467
Minneola	67865
Mission	66201-02
	66205
	66222
For specific ZIP Codes call (888) 275-8777, or your local postmaster.	
Mission Hills	66208
Mission Shopping Center (Part of Mission)	66222
Mission Woods	66205
Mitchell	67554
Modoc	67863
Moline	67353
Monmouth	66753
Monrovia	66023
Montana	67356
Montara	66619
Montezuma	67867
Monticello (Part of Shawnee)	66218*
	66286†
Mont Ida	66091
Montrose	66956
Monument	67747
Moolight	67431
Moran	66755
Moray	66087
Morehead	66776
Morganville	67468
Morland	67650
Morrill	66515

Place	ZIP
Morrowville	66958
Morse	66061
Moscow	67952
Mound City	66056
Moundridge	67107
Mound Valley	67354
Mount Hope	67108
Mount Vernon	67025
Mulberry	66756
Mullinville	67109
Mulvane	67110
Muncie (Part of Kansas City)‡	66111
Munden	66959
Munger (Part of Wichita)‡	67208
Munjor	67601
Murdock	67111
Muscotah	66058
Narka	66960
Nashville	67112
Natoma	67651
Navarre	67451
Neal	66863
Nekoma	67559
Neodesha	66757
Neosho Falls	66758
Neosho Rapids	66864
Ness City	67560
Netawaka	66516
Neuchatel	66521
Neutral	66725
New Albany	66759
New Almelo	67645
Newbury	66526
New Cambria	67470
New Gottland	67460
New Lancaster	66040
Newman	66073
New Salem	67156
Newton	67114
Nickerson	67561
Nicodemus	67625
Niles	67480
Niotaze	67355
Norcatur	67653
Northbranch	66936
Northern Hills	66608
North Newton	67117
North Osage City (Part of Osage City)	66523
North Topeka (Part of Topeka)‡	66608
North Wichita (Part of Wichita)‡	67204
Norton	67654
Nortonville	66060
Norway	66961
Norwich	67118
Oakhill	67432
Oakland (Part of Topeka)	66616
Oaklawn	67216
Oakley	67748
Oak Park Commons (Part of Lenexa)	66215
Oak Park Mall (Part of Overland Park)	66214
Oak Valley	67352
Oatville	67060
Oberlin	67749
Ocheltree	66083
Odense	66772
Odin	67525
Offerle	67563
Ogallah	67656
Ogden	66517
Oketo	66518
Olathe	66051
	66061-63
For specific ZIP Codes call (888) 275-8777, or your local postmaster.	
Olathe East‡	66062*
	66063†
Olivet	66856
Olmitz	67564
Olpe	66865
Olsburg	66520
Onaga	66521
Oneida	66522
Opolis	66760
Orchard Park (Part of Parsons)	67357
Oronoque	67654
Osage City	66523
Osawatomie	66064
Osborne	67473
Oskaloosa	66066
Ost	67108
Oswego	67356
Otego	66936
Otis	67565
Ottawa	66067

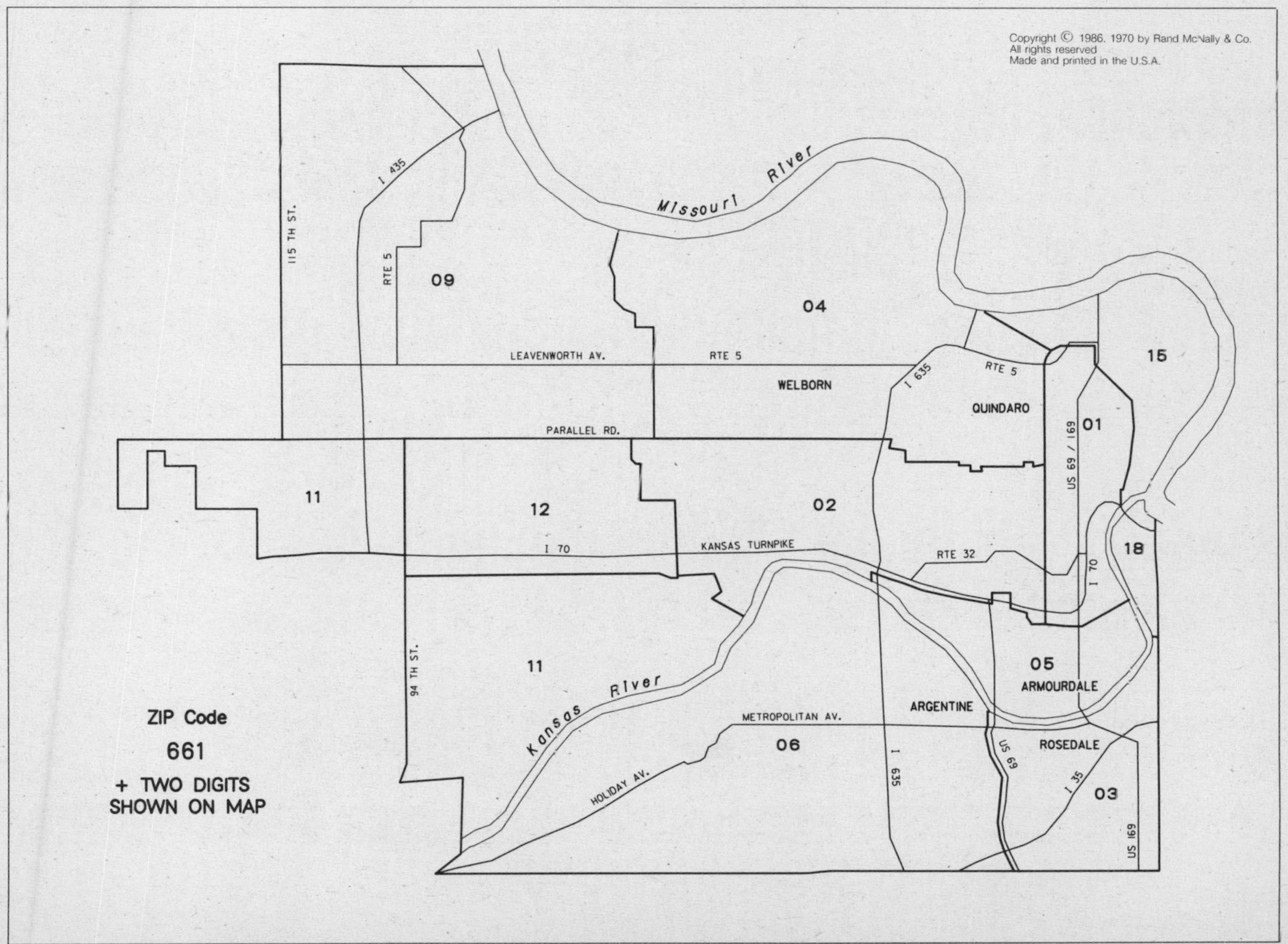

Copyright © 1986, 1970 by Rand McNally & Co.
All rights reserved
Made and printed in the U.S.A.
ZIP Code
661
+ TWO DIGITS
SHOWN ON MAP
Missouri River
Kansas River
09
04
15
01
18
11
12
02
05
06
03
11
WELBORN
QUINDARO
ARMOURDALE
ARGENTINE
ROSEDALE
115 TH ST.
94 TH ST.
I 435
RTE 5
LEAVENWORTH AV.
PARALLEL RD.
I 635
US 69 / 169
I 70
KANSAS TURNPIKE
RTE 32
METROPOLITAN AV.
HOLIDAY AV.
US 69
I 35
US 169

Ottumwa 66839
Overbrook 66524
Overland Park 66204
66207
66209-14
66221
66223-25
For specific ZIP Codes call (888) 275-8777, or your local postmaster.
Oxford 67119
Ozawkie 66070
Packers (Part of Kansas City)‡ 66109
Padonia 66434
Page City 67764
Palco 67657
Palermo 66090
Palmer 66962
Paola 66071
Paradise 67658
Park 67751
Park City 67219
Park East 67208
Parker 66072
Parkerville 66846
Parklane Shopping Center (Part of Wichita) 67218
Parsons 67357
Partridge 67566
Patterson 67020
Pauline (Part of Topeka) 66619
Pawnee Plaza Mall (Part of Wichita) 67211
Pawnee Rock 67567
Paxico 66526
Peabody 66866
Pearl 67431
Peck 67120
Peck Addition 66605
Penalosa 67035
Pence 67871
Pen Dennis 67839
Penokee 67659
Peoria 66067
Perry 66073
Perth 67152
Peru 67360
Petrolia 66720
Pfeifer 67660
Phillipsburg 67661
Pickrell Corner 67010
Piedmont 67122
Pierceville 67868
Pilsen 66861
Piper 66109
Piqua 66761
Pittsburg 66762
Plains 67869
Plainville 67663
Pleasant Grove 66046
Pleasanton 66075
Plevna 67568
Plymell 67846
Plymouth 66801
Pomona 66076
Portis 67474
Portland 67140
Potawatomi Indian Reservation 66436
Potter 66077
Potwin 67123
Powhattan 66527
Prairie View 67664
Prairie Village 66207-08
For specific ZIP Codes call (888) 275-8777, or your local postmaster.
Prairie Village Shopping Center (Part of Prairie Village) 66208
Pratt 67124
Prescott 66767
Preston 67583
Pretty Prairie 67570
Princeton 66078
Prospect 67042
Prospect Park 67215
Protection 67127
Purcell 66041
Quenemo 66528
Quincy 66870
Quinter 67752
Radium 67550
Radley 66762
Rago 67128
Ramona 67475
Ranch Mart Shopping Center (Part of Leawood) 66206
Randall 66963

Randolph 66554
Ransom 67572
Rantoul 66079
Raymond 67573
Reading 66868
Reager 67654
Redel 66085
Redfield 66769
Red Onion 66756
Redwing 67544
Reece 67045
Reno 66086
Republic 66964
Reserve 66434
Rexford 67753
Rice 66901
Richfield 67953
Richland 66409
Richmond 66080
Richter 66067
Riley 66531
Ringer (Part of Wichita) 67212
Ringo 66743
River City (Part of Wichita)‡ 67216
Riverdale 67152
Riverside (Part of Wichita) 67203
Riverton 66770
Riverview 67204
Robert L. Roberts (Part of Kansas City)‡ 66104
Robinson 66532
Rock 67131
Rock Creek 66512
Rocky Ford 66502
Roeland Park 66205
Rolla 67954
Rolling Hills (Part of Wichita) 67212
Rome 67152
Roper 66714
Rosalia 67132
Rose 66783
Rosedale (Part of Kansas City)‡ 66103
Rose Hill 67133
Roseland 66773
Rosewood (Part of Parsons) 67357
Rossville 66533
Roxbury 67476
Rozel 67574
Ruleton 67735
Runnymede 67058
Rush Center 67575
Russell 67665
Russell Springs 67755
Sabetha 66534
Sac and Fox Indian Reservation 66434
Saffordville 66801
St. Benedict 66538
St. Francis 67756
St. George 66535
St. John 67576
St. Joseph 66938
St. Leo 67112
St. Mark 67030
St. Marys, *Pottawatomie* 66536
Saint Marys, *Sedgwick* 67050
St. Mary's College (Part of Leavenworth)‡ 66048
St. Pats 66002
St. Paul 66771
St. Peter 67650
Salina 67401*
67402†
Sand Spring 67410
Sanford 67550
Sarcoxie 66052
Satanta 67870
Saunders 67862
Savonburg 66772
Sawyer 67134
Saxman 67579
Scammon 66773
Scandia 66966
Schoenchen 67667
Schulte 67215
Scipio 66032
Scott City 67871
Scottsville 67420
Scranton 66537
Sedan 67361
Sedgwick 67135
Seguin 67740
Selden 67757
Selkirk 67861
Selma 66039
Seneca 66538

Severance 66087
Severy 67137
Seward 67576
Shady Bend 67455
Shady Brook 67449
Shaffer 67575
Shallow Water 67871
Sharon 67138
Sharon Springs 67758
Sharpe 66871
Shaw 66733
Shawnee 66203
66216-18
66226
For specific ZIP Codes call (888) 275-8777, or your local postmaster.
Shawnee Mission 66201-86
For specific ZIP Codes call (888) 275-8777, or your local postmaster.
Sherman 67356
Sherwin 66725
Sherwood Estates 66604
Shields 67839
Sibleyville 66044
Silverdale 67005
Silver Lake 66539
Simpson 67478
Sitka 67831
Skiddy 66872
Skidmore 66773
Smith Center 66967
Smolan 67456
Soldier 66540
Solomon 67480
Somerset 66071
South Dodge (Part of Dodge City) 67801
Southeast (Part of Wichita)‡ 67218
South Haven 67140
South Hoisington 67544
South Hutchinson 67505
South Mound 67357
South Radley 66762
South Seneca Gardens(Part of Wichita) 67217
Sparks 66035
Spearville 67876
Speed 67661
Spivey 67142
Springdale, *Leavenworth* 66020
Springdale, *Sedgwick* 67230
Spring Grove (Part of Galena) 66739
Spring Hill 66083
Stafford 67578
Stanley 66221
66223-24
66283
For specific ZIP Codes call (888) 275-8777, or your local postmaster.
Stanton 66064
Stark 66775
State House (Part of Topeka)‡ 66612
Sterling 67579
Stilwell 66085
Stippville 66725
Stockton 67669
Stony Point (Part of Kansas City) 66111
Strauss 66753
Strawn 66839
Strong City 66869
Studley 67740
Stull 66050
Stuttgart 67670
Sublette 67877
Suburban Heights (Part of Independence) 67301
Sugar Valley 66056
Summerfield 66541
Sun City 67143
Sunnydale 67147
Sunset Lakes 67581
Sunset Park (Part of Haysville) 67060
Suppesville 67106
Susank 67544
Sutphen 67431
Sycamore 67363
Sylvan Grove 67481
Sylvia 67581
Syracuse 67878
Talmage 67482
Talmo 66935
Tampa 67483
Tanglewood Lake 66040
Tasco 67740

Tecumseh 66542
Terra Heights (Part of Topeka) 66609
Tescott 67484
Thayer 66776
The Dell (Part of Wichita) 67209
Thompsonville 66073
Thrall 67045
Timken 67575
Tipton 67485
Toledo 66801
Tonganoxie 66086
Topeka 66601-86
For specific ZIP Codes call (888) 275-8777, or your local postmaster.
Toronto 66777
Towanda 67144
Town Center Plaza (Part of Leawood) 66209
Towne East Square (Part of Wichita) 67207
Towne West Square (Part of Wichita) 67209
Trading Post 66075
Traer 67749
Travel Air 67206
Treece 66778
Trego Center 67672
Tribune 67879
Trousdale 67059
Troy 66087
Turck 66725
Turner (Part of Kansas City) 66106
Turon 67583
Twin Lakes Shopping Center (Part of Wichita) 67203
Tyro 67364
Udall 67146
Ulysses 67880
Union Stock Yards (Part of Wichita) 67219
Uniontown 66779
University (Part of Lawrence) 66044
University (Part of Pittsburg)‡ 66762
Upland 67431
Urbana 66720
Utica 67584
V.A. Hospital (Part of Topeka)‡ 66622
Valeda 67337
Valencia 66604
Valley Center 67147
Valley Falls 66088
Varner 67068
Vassar 66543
Venango 67464
Verdi 67480
Vermillion 66544
Vernon 66783
Vesper 67455
Victoria 67671
Vilas 66720
Village Square Mall (Part of Dodge City) 67801
Vine Creek 67458
Vining 66937
Vinland 66006
Viola 67149
Virgil 66870
Vliets 66544
Voda 67631
Wabaunsee 66547
Waco 67060
Wagon Wheel Ranch 67010
Wagstaff 66071
Wakarusa 66546
WaKeeney 67672
Wakefield 67487
Waldo 67673
Waldron 67150
Walker 67674
Wallace 67761
Walnut 66780
Walton 67151
Wamego 66547
Washburn University (Part of Topeka)‡ 66621
Washington 66968
Waterloo 67111
Waterville 66548
Wathena 66090
Watson 66542
Wauneta 67024
Waverly 66871
Wayne 66930
Wayside 67301
Wea 66013
Webber 66970

Webster 67669
Wego-Waco 67060
Weir 66781
Welborn (Part of Kansas City) 66104
Welda 66091
Wellington 67152
Wells 67467
Wellsford 67059
Wellsville 66092
Weskan 67762
Wesleyan (Part of Salina) 67401
Westboro (Part of Topeka) 66604
West Coffeyville 67337
Westfall 67455
Westlink Shopping Center (Part of Wichita) 67212
Westlink Village (Part of Wichita) 67212
West Mineral 66782
Westmoreland 66549
Westphalia 66093
Westport (Part of Wichita) 67217
West Ridge Mall (Part of Topeka) 66604
West Shore 66512
Westwood 66205
Westwood Hills 66205
Wetmore 66550
Wheaton 66551
Wheatridge Addition (Part of Wichita) 67212
Wheeler 67756
White Church (Part of Kansas City) 66109
White City 66872
White Cloud 66094
White Lakes Mall (Part of Topeka) 66611
Whitewater 67154
Whiting 66552
Wichita 67201-20
67223-78
For specific ZIP Codes call (888) 275-8777, or your local postmaster.
Wichita Mall (Part of Wichita) 67218
Wichita State University (Part of Wichita) 67208
Wilburton 67950
Wilder Junction 66226
Willard 66604
Williamsburg 66095
Williamstown 66073
Willis 66434
Willowbrook 67501
Willowdale 67142
Wilmore 67155
Wilmot 67156
Wilroads Gardens 67801
Wilsey 66873
Wilson 67490
Winchester 66097
Windom 67491
Windsor Park 67207
Windthorst 67876
Winfield 67156
Winifred 66427
Winona 67764
Winway (Part of Parsons) 67357
Wolcott (Part of Kansas City) 66109
Womer 66952
Wonsevu 66840
Woodbine 67492
Woodlawn 66534
Woodruff 67661
Woods 67951
Woodston 67675
Worden 66006
Wright 67882
Wyandotte West‡ 66111-12
For specific ZIP Codes call (888) 275-8777, or your local postmaster.
Xenia 66716
Yaggy 67501
Yale 66762
Yates Center 66783
Yocemento 67601
Yoder 67585
Zarah (Part of Shawnee) 66218
Zeandale 66502
Zenda 67159
Zenith 67578
Zook 67550
Zurich 67663

Place	ZIP Code
Aaron	42602
Abbott	40006
Abegall	41044
Aberdeen	42201
Absher	42728
Access	41164
Acorn	42501
Acorn Village (Part of Henderson)	42420
Acton	42718
Acup	41751
Adaburg	42347
Adair	42348
Adairville	42202
Adams	41230
Adamson	41517
Add	41224
Addison	40143
Adeline	41129
Aden	41142
Adolphus	42120
Aetnaville	42368
Aflex	41514
Ages	40801
Ages-Brookside	40801
Air Mail Facility-Standiford Field (Amf-Sdf) (Part of Louisville)‡	40221
Airport Gardens	41701
Airview Estates	42701
Akersville	42133
Albany	42602
Alberta	40370
Alcalde	42501
Alcorn	40447
Alexandria	41001
Algonquin Manor (Part of Louisville)	40211
Alhambra	41055
Aliceton	40328
Allais (Part of Hazard)	41701
Allegre	42203
Allen	41601
Allendale	42782
Allen Springs	42122
Allensville	42204
Allock	41773
Almo	42020
Almo Heights	42020
Alonzo	42120
Alpha	42603
Alphoretta	41619
Alpine	42519
Alton	40342
Alton Station	40342
Altro	41339
Alumbaugh	40336
Alum Springs	40440
Alva	40863
Alvaton	42122
Amandaville	42711
Amba	41635
Amburgey	41773
Ammie	40962
Ammons	40170
Amos	42153
Anchorage	40223
	40245
For specific ZIP Codes call (888) 275-8777, or your local postmaster.	
Anco	41759
Andyville	40157
Anna	42270
Anneta	42754
Annville	40402
Ano	42501
Ansel	42553
Anthoston	42420
Antioch	41003
Antioch Shores	42519
Anton	42431
Apex	42464
Aqua Shores	40065
Arat	42717
Arch	42724
Argillite	41121
Argo	41568
Argyle	42516
Arista	42718
Arjay	40902
Arkansas	41649
Arkansas Creek	41649
Arkle	40734
Arlington, Carlisle	42021
Arlington (Part of Richmond)	40475
Arlington Heights (Part of Frankfort)	40601
Armstrong Hill	41164
Arnett	41314
Arnold	42349
Arnold Ridge Estates (Part of Frankfort)	40601
Arrington Corner	42348
Artemus	40903
Arthurmable	41465
Artville	40387
Arvel	40447
Ary	41712
Ashbyburg	42456
Ashcamp	41512
Asher	40803
Ashers Fork	40962
Ashland	41101-05
For specific ZIP Codes call (888) 275-8777, or your local postmaster.	
Ashland Park (Part of Lexington)	40502
Ashland Town Center (Part of Ashland)	41101
Ashlock	42717
Ashville	40291
Askin	42343
Atchison	42718
Athens (Part of Lexington)	40509
	40515
For specific ZIP Codes call (888) 275-8777, or your local postmaster.	
Athertonville	42748
Athol	41307
Atkinstown	40434
Atoka	40422
Atwood	41063
Auburn	42206
Audobon Acres (Part of Owensboro)	42301
Audubon Park	40213
Augusta	41002
Ault	41164
Aurora	42048
Austerlitz	40361
Austin	42123
Auxier	41602
Avawam	41713
Avoca	40223
Avon (Part of Lexington)	40516
Avondale (Part of Paducah)‡	42001
Axtel	40143
Azalea Hills	42420
Bachelors Rest	41040
Backusburg	42054
Bagdad	40003
Bailey Creek	40828
Baileys Switch	40906
Bainbridge	42215
Baizetown	42349
Baker Branch	41263
Bakerton	42711
Bald Hill	41041
Baldrock	40744
Baldwin	40475
Ballard	40342
Ballardsville	40014
Balltown, *Nelson*	40051
Balltown (Part of Williamsburg)	40769
Balmoral (Part of Henderson)	42420
Baltimore	42066
Bancroft, *Jefferson*	40222
Bancroft, *Muhlenberg*	42345
Bandana	42022
Bandy	42567
Bank Lick	41094
Banner	41603
Baptist	41301
Barbourmeade	40222
Barbourville	40906
Barcreek	40972
Bardo	40831
Bardstown	40004
Bardstown Junction	40165
Bardwell	42023
Barefoot	40311
Bark Camp	40701
Barlow	42024
Barnesburg	42501
Barnetts Creek	41256
Barnrock	41219
Barnsley	42431
Barnyard	40935
Barrallton	40165
Barren River	42101
Barrier	42633
Barr Street (Part of Lexington)‡	40501
	40507
	40584-96
For specific ZIP Codes call (888) 275-8777, or your local postmaster.	
Barterville	40311
Barthell	42647
Barwick	41339
Bascom	41171
Bashford Manor Mall (Part of West Buechel)	40218
Baskett	42402
Bass	42733
Bath	41836
Battle	40040
Battle Run	41039
Battletown	40104
Baughman	40906
Baughman Heights (Part of Danville)	40422
Baxter, *Harlan*	40806
Baxter (Part of Louisville)‡	40204
Bayfork	42122
Bayou	42081
Bays	41310
Bays Branch	41216
Bealers Knob	42371
Beals	42451
Bear Branch	41714
Beartown	41164
Bearville	41740
Bear Wallow	42127
Beattyville	41311
Beaumont	42124
Beaumont Park (Part of Lexington)	40504
Beauty	41203
Beaver	41604
Beaver Bottom	41522
Beaver Dam	42320
Beaverlick	41094
Becknerville	40391
Beckton	42141
Beda	42347
Bedford	40006
Beech	41339
Beech Bottom	42539
Beechburg	41093
Beech Creek	42321
Beech Grove, *Bullitt*	40150
Beech Grove, *Carter*	41143
Beech Grove, *McLean*	42322
Beechland	42256
Beechmont (Part of Louisville)‡	40214
Beechmont, Muhlenberg	42323
Beechville	42129
Beechwood	40359
Beechwood Village	40207
Beechy	41175
Beefhide	41537
Beelerton	42041
Bee Lick	40419
Bee Spring	42207
Beetle	41143
Bel-Air (Part of Winchester)	40391
Belcher	41513
Belcourt	42456
Belcraft	41858
Belfry	41514
Belknap	41342
Belknap Beach	40059
Bell City (Part of Sandy Hook)	41171
Bell City, *Graves*	42040
Bellefonte	41101
Bellemeade	40222
Bellepoint (Part of Frankfort)	40601
Belleview	41005
Bellevue	41073
Bellewood	40207
Bell Farm	42647
Bells Run	42378
Belltown	40033
Bellview (Part of Frankfort)	40601
Belmont, *Bullitt*	40150
Belmont (Part of Cynthiana)	41031
Belton	42324
Ben Bow	41230
Bengal	42718
Benham	40807
Benito	40849
Bennettstown	42236
Benson	40601
Bent	42501
Benton	42025
Bentwoods	40601
Berea	40403-04
For specific ZIP Codes call (888) 275-8777, or your local postmaster.	
Berea College (Part of Berea)‡	40404
Berkley	42021
Berlin	41043
Bernice	40932
Bernstadt	40741
Berry	41003
Berrytown	40223
Bethanna	41465
Bethany	41313
Bethel, *Bath*	40374
Bethel, *Jessamine*	40356
Bethelridge	42516
Bethesda	42633
Bethlehem	40007
Betsey	42633
Betsy Layne	41605
Beulah, *Hickman*	42039
Beulah, *Hopkins*	42408
Beulah Heights	42653
Beverly	40913
Beverly Hills (Part of Danville)	40422
Bevier	42337
Bevinsville	41606
Bewleyville	40146
Biddle	40324
Big Bear Creek	42025
Big Bone	41091
Big Branch	41522
Big Clifty	42712
Big Creek	40914
Big Eddy	40601
Big Fork	41777
Biggs	41524
Bighill	40405
Big Laurel	40808
Big Rock	41777
Big Sandy Junction (Part of Catlettsburg)	41129
Big Spring	40106
Bigstone	41171
Big Woods	40387
Bimble	40915
Birdie	40342
Birdsville	42081
Birk City	42301
Birmingham	42044
Black Bottom	40828
Blackey	41804
Blackford	42403
Black Gnat	42718
Black Gold	42285
Black Jack	42134
Black Mountain	40847
Black Rock	42754
Black Snake	40845
Blackwater	40744
Bladeston	41004
Blaine	41124
Blair	40823
Blairs Mills	41472
Blair Town	41501
Blanche	40902
Blanchet	41010
Blandville	42087
Blaze	41472
Bledsoe	40810
Blevins	41124
Blincoe	40037
Blood	42071
Bloomfield	40008
Bloomingdale	40391
Bloomington, *Grayson*	42754
Bloomington, *Magoffin*	41465
Bloss	40456
Blowing Spring	42743
Bluebank	41041
Blue Diamond	41719
Blue Grass (Part of Lexington)‡	40503
	40523-24
For specific ZIP Codes call (888) 275-8777, or your local postmaster.	
Bluegrass Estates (Part of Danville)	40422
Blue Heron	42647
Bluehole	40962
Blue John	42519
Blue Level	42274
Blue Lick Springs	40311
Blue Moon	41655
Blue Ridge Manor	40223
Blue River	41607
Blue Spring	42211
Bluestone	40351
Blue Water Estates	42211
Bluff Boom	42743
Bluff City	42420
Board Tree	41528
Boatwright	42071
Boaz	42027
Bobs Creek	40815
Bobs Fork	41714
Bobtown	40403
Bohon	40330
Boiling Spring	42101
Boldman	41501
Boles	42167
Boltsfork	41168
Bolyn	41630
Bon	40769
Bon Air Hills	40601
Bonanza	41653
Bon Ayr	42160
Bond	40402
Bondurant	42050
Bondville	40372
Boneyville	40484
Bon Haven (Part of Winchester)	40391
Bonnie Brae	40065
Bonnieville	42713
Bonnyman	41719
Booker	40069
Boone	40403
Boone Aire	41042
Boone Heights	40906
Boonesboro	40475
Boonesborough	40475
Booneville	41314
Boons Camp	41204
Bordley	42404
Boreing	40740
Borowick Farms	40031
Boston, *Butler*	42256
Boston, *Nelson*	40107
Boston, *Pendleton*	41006
Botland	40004
Botto	40944
Bourbon Downs (Part of Bardstown)	40004
Bourbon Furnace	40360
Bourne	40444
Bow	42717
Bowen	40309
Bowling Green	42101-04
For specific ZIP Codes call (888) 275-8777, or your local postmaster.	
Boyce	42122
Boyd	41003
Boyds Crossing	42782
Boydsville	42079
Boydtown	40324
Bracht	41030
Bracktown (Part of Lexington)	40510
Bradford	41043
Bradfordsville	40009
Bradley	41465
Bradshaw	40434
Brady (Part of Morehead)	40351
Brainard	41465
Bramlett	42743
Brandenburg	40108
Brandenburg Station	40108
Brandy	40351
Brandykeg	41653
Brassfield	40385
Braxton	40330
Breadens Creek	40927
Breckinridge	41031
Breeding	42715
Bremen	42325
Brentsville	40361
Brentwood (Part of Madisonville)	42431
Brewers	42025
Briartown (Part of Springfield)	40069
Briarwood	40222
Briarwood Manor (Part of Bowling Green)	42103
Bridgeport	40601
Bridge Street (Part of Paducah)‡	42003
Bridgeville	41004
Briensburg	42025
Brighton (Part of Lexington)	40505
Brightshade	40962
Brinegar	41164
Brinkley	41822
Bristow	42101
Britmart	42220

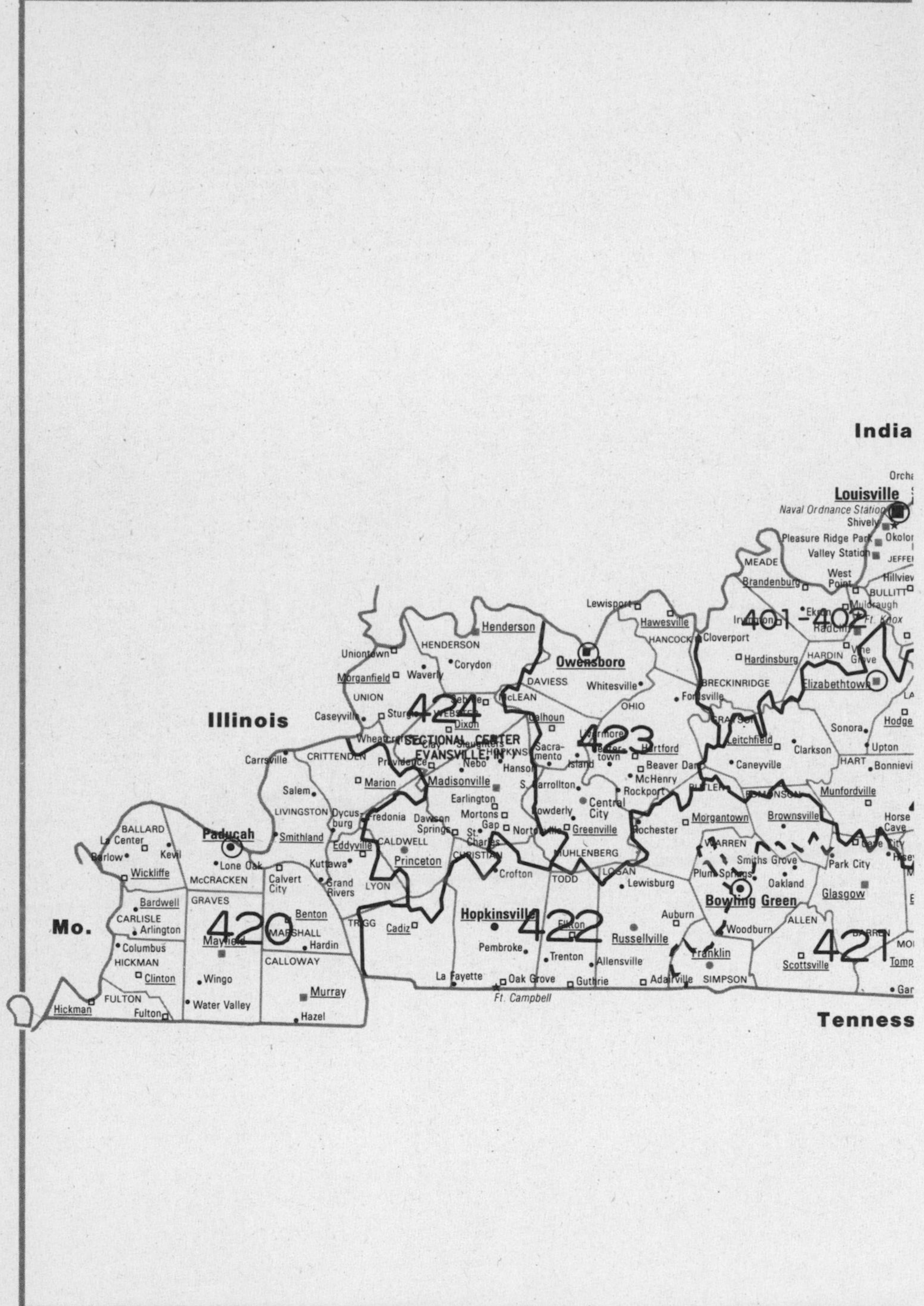
India
Louisville
Naval Ordnance Station
Shively
Pleasure Ridge Park
Valley Station
MEADE
Brandenburg
West Point
Hillview
BULLITT
Muldraugh
Ft. Knox
Lewisport
Hawesville
HANCOCK
Cloverport
Irvington
Ekron
Radcliff
401-402
Henderson
HENDERSON
Corydon
Uniontown
Morganfield
Waverly
UNION
Owensboro
DAVIESS
Whitesville
Hardinsburg
HARDIN
Vine Grove
BRECKINRIDGE
Elizabethtown
McLEAN
Calhoun
OHIO
Fordsville
Illinois
Caseyville
Sturgis
424
Dixon
SECTIONAL CENTER EVANSVILLE, IN
423
Livermore
Hartford
Leitchfield
Clarkson
Sonora
Hodgenville
Upton
Carrsville
CRITTENDEN
Providence
Nebo
Hanson
Sacramento
Island
Beaver Dam
McHenry
Rockport
Caneyville
HART
Bonnieville
Salem
Marion
Madisonville
S. Carrollton
Central City
Munfordville
Earlington
LIVINGSTON
Dycusburg
Fredonia
Dawson Springs
Mortons Gap
Nortonville
Drakesboro
Greenville
Rochester
Morgantown
Brownsville
Horse Cave
Cave City
BALLARD
La Center
Barlow
Kevil
Paducah
Smithland
Eddyville
CALDWELL
Princeton
St. Charles
CHRISTIAN
MUHLENBERG
WARREN
Smiths Grove
Park City
Wickliffe
Lone Oak
McCRACKEN
Calvert City
Kuttawa
Grand Rivers
LYON
Crofton
TODD
LOGAN
Lewisburg
Plum Springs
Bowling Green
Oakland
Glasgow
Bardwell
CARLISLE
Arlington
GRAVES
420
Benton
MARSHALL
Hardin
TRIGG
Cadiz
Hopkinsville
422
Elkton
Russellville
Auburn
Woodburn
ALLEN
BARREN
421
Mo.
Columbus
HICKMAN
Clinton
Mayfield
CALLOWAY
Pembroke
Trenton
Allensville
Franklin
Scottsville
Tompkinsville
Wingo
Murray
La Fayette
Oak Grove
Guthrie
Adairville
SIMPSON
FULTON
Hickman
Fulton
Water Valley
Hazel
Ft. Campbell
Tenness

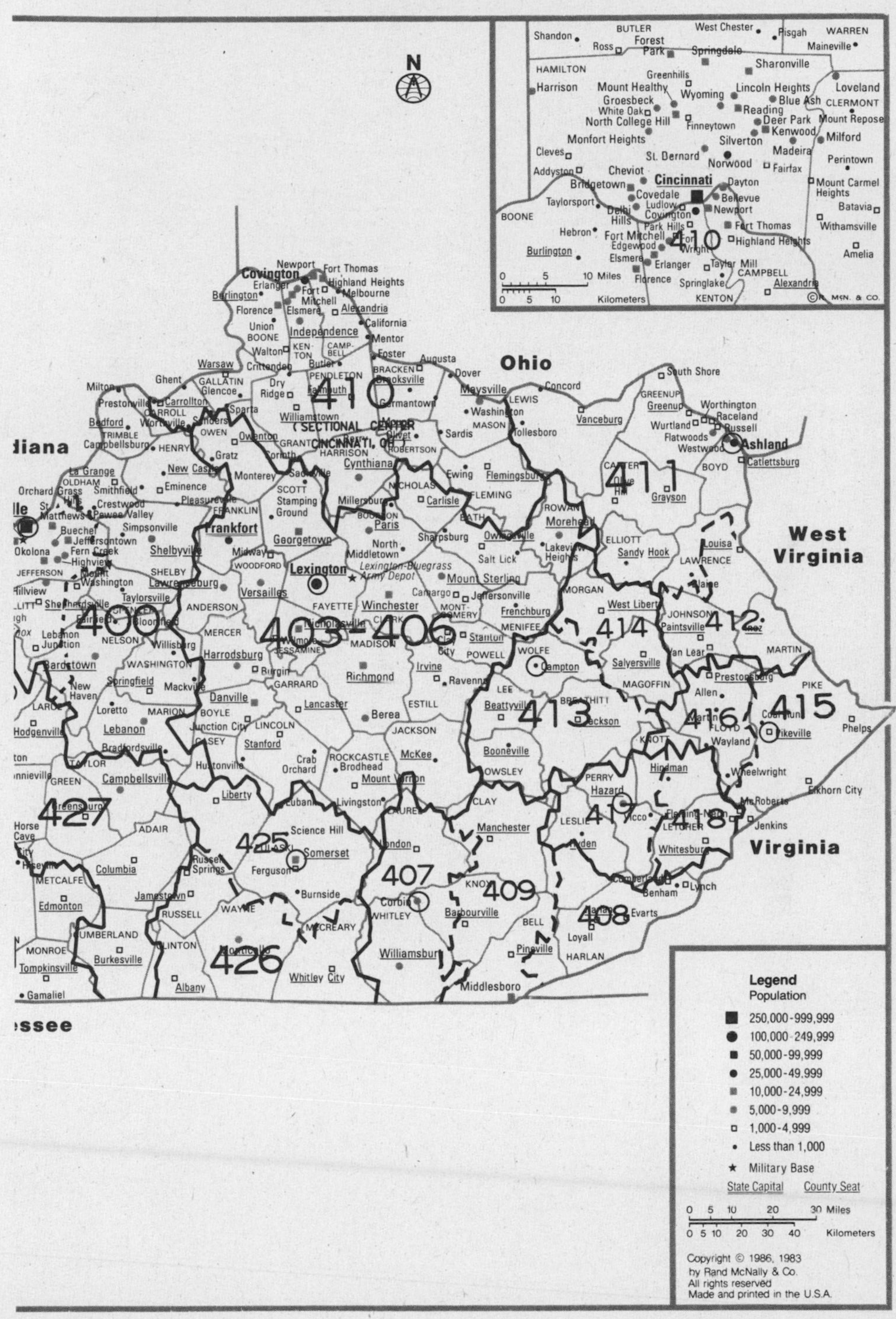
N
Shandon
BUTLER
Forest Park
West Chester
Pisgah
WARREN
Maineville
Ross
Springdale
Sharonville
HAMILTON
Greenhills
Harrison
Mount Healthy
Wyoming
Lincoln Heights
Loveland
Blue Ash
CLERMONT
Groesbeck
Reading
White Oak
North College Hill
Finneytown
Deer Park
Mount Repose
Kenwood
Milford
Monfort Heights
Silverton
Madeira
Cleves
St. Bernard
Norwood
Perintown
Fairfax
Addyston
Cheviot
Cincinnati
Dayton
Mount Carmel Heights
Bridgetown
Covedale
Bellevue
Taylorsport
Ludlow
Batavia
Delhi Hills
Covington
Newport
BOONE
Park Hills
Fort Thomas
Withamsville
Hebron
Fort Mitchell
Edgewood
Highland Heights
Burlington
Elsmere
Amelia
Erlanger
Taylor Mill
CAMPBELL
Florence
Springlake
Alexandria
KENTON
410
0 5 10 Miles
0 5 10 Kilometers
© R. McN. & Co.
Ohio
Indiana
West Virginia
Virginia
Tennessee
Covington
Newport
Fort Thomas
Highland Heights
Melbourne
Alexandria
Independence
California
Mentor
Foster
Augusta
Dover
Maysville
Washington
Concord
South Shore
Vanceburg
Greenup
Worthington
Raceland
Russell
Flatwoods
Westwood
Ashland
Catlettsburg
Grayson
Louisa
Sandy Hook
Paintsville
Salyersville
Prestonsburg
Pikeville
Phelps
Elkhorn City
Jenkins
Whitesburg
Hazard
Hindman
Hyden
Benham
Lynch
Evarts
Harlan
Loyall
Pineville
Middlesboro
Barbourville
Corbin
Williamsburg
London
Manchester
Booneville
Beattyville
Jackson
Campton
Stanton
Irvine
Richmond
Berea
McKee
Mount Vernon
Somerset
Burnside
Monticello
Albany
Whitley City
Jamestown
Russell Springs
Columbia
Edmonton
Burkesville
Tompkinsville
Gamaliel
Campbellsville
Greensburg
Lebanon
Springfield
Bardstown
Danville
Harrodsburg
Stanford
Lancaster
Liberty
Versailles
Lexington
Winchester
Paris
Georgetown
Frankfort
Shelbyville
Lawrenceburg
Taylorsville
Shepherdsville
Cynthiana
Carlisle
Flemingsburg
Owingsville
Morehead
Mount Sterling
Frenchburg
West Liberty
Falmouth
Williamstown
Owenton
Carrollton
Warsaw
Bedford
La Grange
New Castle
Lexington-Bluegrass Army Depot
SECTIONAL CENTER CINCINNATI, OH
400
403-406
407
408
409
410
411
412
413
414
415
416
417
418
425
426
427
Legend
Population
250,000-999,999
100,000-249,999
50,000-99,999
25,000-49,999
10,000-24,999
5,000-9,999
1,000-4,999
Less than 1,000
Military Base
State Capital
County Seat
0 5 10 20 30 Miles
0 5 10 20 30 40 Kilometers

Place	ZIP Code
Broadbent Subdivision	42211
Broad Bottom	41501
Broad Fields	40207
Broad Ford	42726
Broadview Manor	40601
Broadway	42207
Broadwell	41031
Brodhead	40409
Broeck Pointe	40201
Bromley, *Kenton*	41016
Bromley, *Owen*	41086
Bromo	40456
Bronston	42518
Brookhaven (Part of Lexington)	40503
Brooklyn	42209
Brooks♦	40109
Brookside	40801
Brooksville	41004
Broughtentown	40419
Browder	42326
Browning	42274
Browning Corner	41040
Brownsboro	40014
Brownsboro Farm	40222
Brownsboro Village	40207
Browns Crossroads	42602
Browns Fork	41701
Browns Grove	42071
Browns Valley	42376
Brownsville, *Edmonson*	42210
Brownsville, *Fulton*	42050
Brownwood Manor	42303
Bruin	41171
Brushart	41144
Brush Grove	40040
Brutus	40972
Bryan	42629
Bryants Store	40921
Bryantsville	40410
Buchanan	41129
Buckettown	40475
Buckeye	40444
Buck Grove	40117
Buckhorn	41721
Buckingham	41636
Buckner	40010
Buechel♦	40218
	40228
	40261
For specific ZIP Codes call (888) 275-8777, or your local postmaster.	
Buel	42327
Buena Vista, *Garrard*	40444
Buena Vista, *Harrison*	41031
Buena Vista, *Lewis*	41179
Buena Vista, *Marshall*	42044
Buffalo, *Larue*	42716
Buffalo, *Trigg*	42211
Buford	42376
Bug	42602
Bugtussle	42140
Bulan	41722
Bull Creek	41653
Bullittsville	41005
Burdick	42718
Burdine (Part of Jenkins)	41517
Burfield	42633
Burgin	40310
Burke	41171
Burkes Spring	40037
Burkesville	42717
Burkhart	41301
Burk Hollow	40769
Burkshire Terrace	40214
Burlington	41005
Burna	42028
Burnaugh	41129
Burnetta	42544
Burning Fork, *Magoffin*	41465
Burning Fork, *Pike*	41501
Burning Springs	40962
Burnside	42519
Burnwell	41514
Burr	40456
Burton	41612
Burtonville	41189
Bush	40724
Bushtown	40330
Buskirk, *Morgan*	41332
Buskirk, *Pike*	41544
Busseyville	41230
Busy	41723
Butler (Part of Frankfort)	40601
Butler, *Pendleton*	41006
Butterfly	41719
Buttimer Hill (Part of Frankfort)	40601
Buttonsberry	42350
Bybee	40385
Bypro	41612
Cabell	42633
Cabot	42343
Caddo	41040
Cadentown (Part of Lexington)	40505
Cadiz	42211
Cains Store	42544
Cairo	42420
Caldwell Manor (Part of Danville)	40422
Caleast	40475
Caledonia	42211
Calf Creek	41224
Calhoun	42327
California	41007
Calla	40336
Callaway	40977
Calloway	40456
Calvary	40033
Calvert City	42029
Calvin	40813
Camargo	40353
Cambridge	40220
Cambridge Shores	42044
Campbellsburg	40011
Campbellsville	42718*
	42719†
Camp Dick Robinson	40444
Camp Dix	41127
Camp Grounds	40701
Camp Kennedy	40444
Camp Nelson (rural)	40356
Camp Nelson	40444
Camp Pleasant	40601
Camp Springs	41059
Camp Taylor (Part of Louisville)	40213
Campton	41301
Canada	41519
Canby	41010
Cane Creek	40744
Cane Valley	42720
Caney	41472
Caneyville	42721
Canmer	42722
Cannel City	41408
Cannon	40923
Cannonsburg	41102*
	41105†
Canoe	41339
Canton	42211
Canton Heights Estates	42211
Canyon Falls	41311
Capital Estates	40601
Capito	40965
Carbondale	42408
Carbon Glow	41832
Carcassonne	41804
Cardinal Hill	40004
Cardinal Hills (Part of Frankfort)	40601
Cardinal Valley (Part of Lexington)	40503
Cardwell	40330
Carlisle	40311
Carntown	41006
Carpenter	40906
Carr Creek	41847
Carrie	41725
Carrollton	41008
Carrsville	42081
Carter	41128
Carthage	41007
Cartwright	42602
Carver	41465
Cary	40977
Casey Creek	42728
Caseyville	42459
Cash	42784
Casky	42240
Catalpa	41129
Catawba	41040
Cat Creek	40380
Catlettsburg	41129
Causey	41777
Cave City	42127
Cavehill	42274
Cave Ridge	42129
Cave Spring	42265
Cawood	40815
Cayce	42041
Cecil	42001
Cecilia	42724
Cedar Bluff	42445
Cedar Brook	41031
Cedar Flats	42129
Cedar Grove	42220
Cedar Hill Heights	42518
Cedar Knoll Galleria (Part of Ashland)	41101
Cedar Run Creek	40601
Cedar Spring	42160
Cedar Springs	42164
Cedarville	40456
Center	42214
Centerfield	40014
Center Point	42167
Center Ridge	42071
Centertown	42328
Centerview	40145
Centerville	40324
Central Avenue (Part of Paducah)	42001
Central City	42330
Ceralvo	42369
Cerulean	42215
Chad	40823
Chalybeate	42171
Chambers	42348
Chance	42728
Chandlers Chapel	42206
Chandlerville	41257
Chapel Hill	42120
Chaplin	40012
Chapman	41230
Chappell	40816
Charleston	42408
Charleswood	40229
Charley	41230
Charters	41179
Chatham	41002
Chavies	41727
Chenault	40170
Chenoa	40977
Chenowee	41339
Cherokee (Part of Louisville)‡	40205*
	40255†
Cherokee, *Lawrence*	41180
Cherry	42071
Cherrywood Village	40207
Chesnutburg	40962
Chestnut Gap	41314
Chestnut Grove	40065
Chevrolet	40831
Chevy Chase (Part of Lexington)	40502
Chicken Bristle	40484
Chilesburg (Part of Lexington)	40509
Chloe	41501
Choateville	40601
Christianburg	40065
Christine	42728
Christopher	41701
Church Hill	42240
Cinda	41776
Cinderella Estates	40229
Cisco	41410
Cisselville	40069
Clabber Bottom	40324
Clare	42134
Clarence	42567
Clark	40023
Clark Hill	41164
Clarksburg	41179
Clarkson	42726
Clark Street (Part of Paducah)	42001
Claryville	41001
Claxton	42408
Clay	42404
Clay City	40312
Clayhole	41317
Clay Lick	40337
Claymour	42220
Claypool	42103
Claysville	41031
Clay Village	40065
Clear Creek Springs	40977
Clearfield	40313
Cleaton	42332
Clementsville	42539
Clemons	41719
Cleopatra	42327
Clermont	40110
Cliff (Part of Prestonsburg)	41653
Clifford	41230
Clifton	40383
Clifty	42216
Climax	40456
Clinton	42031
Clintonville	40361
Clio	40769
Closplint	40927
Clover Bottom	40447
Cloverdale (Part of Frankfort)	40601
Clover-Darby	40927
Cloverport	40111
Clovertown	40831
Cloyds Landing	42717
Clutts	40823
Coakley	42743
Coalgood	40818
Coal Run	41501
Coalton	41168
Cobb	42445
Cobhill	40336
Coburg	42743
Codyville (Part of Hardinsburg)	40143
Cofer	42129
Colby	40391
Colby Hills	40391
Coldiron	40819
Cold Spring	41076
Cold Spring-Highland Heights (Part of Highland Heights)	41076
Coldstream	40202
Coldwater	42071
Coleman	41553
Colemansville	41003
Colesburg	40150
Coletown (Part of Lexington)	40515
Colfax	41049
College (Part of Berea)‡	40403
College Farm	41501
College Heights (Part of Bowling Green)‡	42101
College Hill	40385
College Park (Part of Frankfort)	40601
Collins	41501
Collista	41222
Colmar	40965
Colonial Terrace	40222
Colony (Part of Frankfort)	40601
Colson	41858
Columbia	42728
Columbus	42032
Colville	41031
Combs	41729
Comer	42327
Concord, *Fleming*	41041
Concord, *Lewis*	41179
Concord, *Pendleton*	41040
Concordia	40157
Conder	41514
Confederate	42038
Confederate Estates	40056
Confluence	41730
Congleton, *Lee*	41311
Congleton, *McLean*	42327
Conley	41465
Connersville	41031
Conoloway	42726
Consolation	40003
Constance	41048
Constantine	40140
Conway	40456
Cooktown	42123
Coolbrook	40601
Cool Springs	42320
Cooper	42633
Co-Operative	42647
Cooperstown	42276
Coopersville	42633
Copebranch	41339
Copland	41339
Copperfield	40223
Coral Hill	42141
Coral Ridge	40118
Corbin	40701*
	40702†
Cordell	41124
Cordia	41701
Cordova	41010
Corey	41142
Corinth, *Grant*	41010
Corinth, *Logan*	42276
Cork	42129
Corn Creek	40006
Corners	40146
Cornette	40729
Cornettsville	41731
Cornishville	40330
Corydon	42406
Costelow	42276
Cote	40828
Cottageville	41179
Cottle	41472
Cottonburg	40475
Country Club Estates	40475
Country Club Heights (Part of Frankfort)	40601
Country Club Heights (Part of Maysville)	41056
Country Lane Estates	40601
Country Manor	40065
Countryside	40059
Country Village	40014
Counts Crossroads	41164
Covedale	41179
Covington	41011-18
For specific ZIP Codes call (888) 275-8777, or your local postmaster.	
Cowan	41039
Cow Creek, *Estill*	40472
Cowcreek, *Owsley*	41314
Cox Bend	42519
Coxs Creek	40013
Coxton	40831
Crab Orchard	40419
Cracker	41649
Crailhope	42214
Craintown	41041
Crane Nest	40906
Cranks	40820
Cranston	40351
Crawford	41719
Crayne	42033
Craynor	41635
Creal	42764
Creekmore	42649
Creekside	40222
Creekville	40962
Creelsboro	42629
Crenshaw	40071
Crescent Hill (Part of Louisville)	40206
Crescent Park	41017
Crescent Springs	41017
Cressmont	41311
Crest	42701
Crestmoor (Part of Bowling Green)	42101
Creston	42539
Crestview	41076
Crestview Hills	41017
Crestview Hills Mall (Part of Crestview Hills)	41017
Crestwood (Part of Lexington)	40503
Crestwood (Part of Frankfort)	40601
Crestwood, *Oldham*	40014
Creswell	42411
Crider	42445
Crittenden	41030
Crix	40313
Croakes	40069
Crockett	41413
Crocus	42728
Crofton	42217
Croley	42031
Cromona	41810
Cromwell	42333
Cropper	40057
Crossgate	40222
Cross Keys	40065
Crossland	42049
Crown	41858
Crowtown (Part of Princeton)	42445
Crummies	40815
Crutchfield	42041
Crystal	40336
Crystal Lake	40031
Cuba	42066
Cubage	40856
Cub Run	42729
Culver	41171
Culvertown	40051
Cumberland	40823
Cumberland City	42602
Cumberland College (Part of Williamsburg)‡	40769
Cumberlane Estates (Part of Campbellsville)	42718
Cumminsville	41004
Cundiff	42728
Cunningham	42035
Cupio	40177
Curdsville, *Daviess*	42334
Curdsville, *Mercer*	40330
Curt	41339
Custer	40115
Cutshin	41776
Cutuno	41465
Cuzick	40475
Cyclone	42166
Cynthiana	41031
Dabney	42501

Place	ZIP
Dabolt	40421
Dahl	42501
Daisy	41731
Dal	40769
Dalesburg, *Breathitt*	41314
Dalesburg, *Fleming*	41041
Dalton	42445
Dan, *Menifee*	40387
Dan, *Ohio*	42349
Dana	41615
Danby	42276
Daniel Boone	42442
Daniels Creek	41265
Danleytown	41144
Dant	40037
Danville	40422*
	40423†
Darfork	41701
Darkmont	40828
Davella	41214
David	41616
Davis	40370
Davisburg	40977
Davis Cross Roads	42256
Davison Station	42361
Davisport	41262
Davistown, *Garrard*	40444
Davistown, *Woodford*	40347
Dawson Springs	42408
Day	41858
Dayhoit	40824
Daylight	42408
Daysboro	41332
Daysville	42276
Dayton	41074
Deane	41812
Deatsville	40013
Debord	41214
Decker	42721
DeCoursey (Part of Taylor Mill)	41015
Decoy	41339
Dee Acres	42366
Deep Springs (Part of Lexington)	40505
Deepwood (Part of Hopkinsville)	42240
Deer Lick	42256
Defeated Creek	41833
Defiance	41760
Defoe	40057
Defries	42722
Dehart	41472
Dekoven	42459
Delafield (Part of Bowling Green)	42101
Delaplain	40324
Delaware	42373
Delia	41097
Delmer	42544
Delphia	41735
Delta	42633
Delville	40011
Delvinta	41311
Dema	41859
Democrat	41858
De Mossville	41033
Demplytown	40014
Denney	42633
Dennis	42276
Denniston	40316
Denton	41132
Denver	41215
Depoy	42345
Derby Hills	40383
Dermont	42303
Desda	42602
Devon	41042
Devondale (Part of Graymoor-Devondale)	40222
Dewdrop	41171
Dewitt	40930
Dexter	42036
Dexterville	42261
Diablock	41701
Diamond	42404
Dice	41736
Dietz Acres	40121
Dillon	40865
Dimple	42261
Dingus	41472
Dione	40823
Dishman Springs	40906
Disputanta	40456
Dix Fork	41564
Dixie, *Henderson*	42406
Dixie (Part of Lakeside Park)	41017
Dixie Bend	42558
Dixie Manor Shopping Center	40258
Dixie Plantation (Part of Lexington)	40505
Dixon	42409
Dix River Estates	40484
Dixville	40330
Dizney	40825
Dobson	41228
Dock	41653
Doddy	42164
Doe Creek	40336
Doe Valley Estates	40108
Dogtown	42025
Dog Walk, *Lincoln*	40409
Dogwalk, *Ohio*	42721
Dogwood	42051
Donaldson	42211
Donansburg	42743
Donerail (Part of Lexington)	40511
Dongola	41858
Dorton	41520
Dorton Branch	40977
Do Stop	42721
Dot	42202
Douglas	41560
Douglass Hills	40243
Dover	41034
Downtown (Part of Bowling Green)‡	42101
Downtown (Part of Louisville)‡	40201†
	40203*
Doylesville	40475
Dozier Heights	42431
Draffenville	42025
Draffin	41522
Drake	42128
Drakesboro	42337
Draper (Part of Evarts)	40828
Drennon Springs	40011
Dressen (Part of Harlan)	40831
Dreyfus	40385
Drift	41619
Dripping Spring	42171
Drip Rock	40336
Dr. Martin Luther King Jr. (Part of Louisville)‡	40211*
	40251†
Druid Hills	40207
Drum	42501
Dry Creek	41862
Dry Fork, *Barren*	42141
Dry Fork, *Pike*	41561
Dryhill	41749
Dry Ridge	41035
Dublin	42039
Dubre	42731
Duckers	40347
Duckrun	40769
Duco	41465
Duff	42754
Duganville	40330
Dukedom	42085
Dukes	42348
Dulaney	42445
Duluth	40403
Dunbar	42219
Duncan, *Casey*	40442
Duncan, *Mercer*	40330
Dundee	42338
Dunham (Part of Jenkins)	41537
Dunlap	41524
Dunleary	41522
Dunmor	42339
Dunnville	42528
Dunraven	41754
Durbin	41129
Durbintown	41003
Duval	40324
Dwale	41621
Dwarf	41739
Dycusburg	42037
Dyer	40115
Dykes	42501
Eadsville	42633
Eagle Creek	41098
Eagle Hill	41046
Eagle Station	41083
Earlington	42410
East Bernstadt	40729
Easterday	41008
Eastern	41622
East Fork	42129
East Hickman	40356
East Jenkins (Part of Jenkins)	41537
Eastland	40004
Eastland Park (Part of Lexington)	40505
Eastland Park (Part of Bowling Green)	42104
Eastland Shopping Center (Part of Lexington)	40505
East McDowell	41647
Easton	42343
East Pineville	40977
East Point	41216
East Union	40311
East View	42732
Eastwood	40018
Ebenezer, *Mercer*	40372
Ebenezer, *Monroe*	42167
Ebenezer, *Muhlenberg*	42337
Echo	42154
Echols	42320
Echo Point	42518
Echo Valley	40031
Eddyville	42038
Eddyville Shores	42038
Edenton	40475
Edgewater	41534
Edgewood, *Franklin*	40601
Edgewood, *Kenton*	41017
Edgewood (Part of Bardstown)	40004
Edgewood (Part of Louisville)	40213
Edmonton	42129
Edna	41419
Edwards	42256
Eglon	40447
Egypt	40486
Eighty Eight	42130
Ekron	40117
Elamton	41472
Elba	42327
Elcomb	40831
Eldridge	41149
Eli	42642
Elihu	42501
Elizabeth Station	40361
Elizabethtown	42701*
	42702†
Elizaville	41037
Elkatawa	41339
Elk Creek	40023
Elkfork	41421
Elk Horn	42733
Elkhorn City	41522
Elk Lake Shores	40359
Elkton	42220
Ella	42728
Ellington	42717
Elliottville	40317
Ellisburg	40437
Elliston, *Grant*	41035
Elliston, *Madison*	40475
Ellisville	40311
Ellmitch	42343
Elwood	41538
Elmburg	40057
Elmer Davis Lake	40359
Elmrock	41640
Elmville	40601
Elna	41219
Elsie	41422
Elsinore	40601
Elsmere	41018
Elswick	41538
Elva	42082
Elys	40939
Emanuel	40734
Emerson	41135
Eminence	40019
Emlyn	40730
Emma	41653
Emmalena	41740
Empire	42442
Endicott	41653
End of Line	41667
Engle	41727
English	41008
Ennis	42337
Ensor	42366
Enterprise	41164
Eolia	40826
Epleys	42276
Epperson	42003
Epson	41465
Epworth	41189
Equality	42328
Erline	40962
Erlanger	41018
Ermine	41815
Erose	40935
Essie	40827
Estesburg	40489
Estill	41666
Esto	42642
Ethridge	41095
Etna	42567
Etoile	42131
Etterwood	40324
Etty	41572
Eubank	42567
Eunice	42728
Evanston	41339
Evarts	40828
Eveleigh	42754
Ever	41465
Everett	42256
Evergreen	40601
Eversole	41314
Ewing	41039
Ewingford	40006
Ewington	40353
Exie	42743
Ezel	41425
Faber	40701
Fagan	40322
Fairbanks, *Graves*	42079
Fairbanks, *Owen*	40359
Fairdale	40118
Fairdealing	42025
Fairfield, *Breckinridge*	40144
Fairfield, *Nelson*	40020
Fairland	42602
Fairmeade	40207
Fairmont, *Jefferson*	40291
Fairmont, *Webster*	42404
Fairplay	42735
Fairview, *Anderson*	40342
Fairview, *Boyd*	41101
Fairview, *Christian*	42221
Fairview, *Edmonson*	42210
Fairview, *Fleming*	41039
Fairview, *Kenton*	41015
Fairview, *Lyon*	42038
Fairview, *Whitley*	40769
Fairview Heights (Part of Frankfort)	40601
Fairview Hill	41146
Fairway (Part of Lexington)	40502
Falcon	41426
Fall Rock	40932
Fallsburg	41230
Falls of Rough	40119
Falmouth	41040
Fancy Farm	42039
Fannin	41171
Fariston	40744
Farler	41774
Farmdale	40601
Farmers	40351
Farmers Mill	40831
Farmersville	42445
Farmington	42040
Farraday	41855
Farristown	40403
Faubush	42544
Faulconer	40422
Faxon	42071
Faye	41171
Fayette Mall (Part of Lexington)	40503
Faywood	40383
Fearisville	41179
Fearsville	42240
Feathersburg	42733
Fedscreek	41524
Feliciana	42085
Felty	40962
Fentress Lookout	40119
Fenwick (Part of Lexington)	40516
Ferguson, *Logan*	42276
Ferguson, *Pulaski*	42533
Ferguson Creek (Part of Pikeville)	41501
Fern Creek	40291
Ferndale	40977
Fernleaf	41034
Ferrells Creek	41513
Fiddle Bow	42408
Fielden	41171
Fillmore	41311
Fincastle	40222
Finchville	40022
Finley	42718
Finley Addition	42420
Finney	42141
Firebrick	41137
Firmantown	40383
Fisherville	40023
Fishtrap	41557
Fiskburg	41033
Fisty	41743
Fitch	41164
Fitchburg	40472
Five Forks	41230
Fivemile	41339
Fixer	41397
Flag Fork	40601
Flag Spring	41007
Flaherty	40175
Flat	41301
Flat Fork	41427
Flatgap	41219
Flat Lick	40935
Flat Rock, *Caldwell*	42411
Flat Rock, *McCreary*	42653
Flat Rock, *Rockcastle*	40460
Flat Rock, *Simpson*	42170
Flatwoods	41139
Fleming (Part of Fleming-Neon)	41840
Fleming-Neon	41840
Flemingsburg	41041
Flemingsburg Junction	41041
Flener	42261
Flingsville	41030
Flint Springs	42349
Flintville	41348
Flippin	42167
Floral	42348
Florence	41022†
	41042*
Florence Mall (Part of Florence)	41042
Florence Square (Part of Florence)	41042
Florress	41472
Flournoy	42437
Floyd	42567
Floydsburg	40014
Fogertown	40962
Folsom	41035
Folsomdale	42051
Fonde	40940
Fonthill	42642
Foraker	41465
Ford	40392
Fords Branch	41526
Fordsville	42343
Forest Grove	40391
Forest Hills, *Jefferson*	40299
Forest Hills, *Pike*	41527
Forest Hills (Part of Campbellsville)	42718
Forest Hills (Part of Paducah)	42003
Forks of Elkhorn	40601
Forkton	42167
Forrest Park (Part of Winchester)	40391
Fort Campbell	42223
Fort Garrett	40383
Fort Knox	40121
Fort Mitchell	41017
Fort Spring (Part of Lexington)	40510
	40513
For specific ZIP Codes call (888) 275-8777, or your local postmaster.	
Fort Thomas	41075
Fort Wright	41011
Foster	41043
Fount	40999
Fountain Run	42133
Fourmile	40939
Four Oaks	41040
Fourseam	41701
Fox	40336
Fox Chase	40165
Fox Creek	40342
Foxport	41093
Foxtown	40447
Frakes	40940
Frances	42064
Francisville	41048
Frankfort	40601-04
For specific ZIP Codes call (888) 275-8777, or your local postmaster.	
Franklin	42134*
	42135†
Franklin Cross Roads	42724
Franklinton	40057
Frazer	42633
Fraziertown	40056
Fredericktown	40069
Fredonia	42411
Fredville	41465
Freeburn	41528
Freedom, *Barren*	42157
Freedom, *Russell*	42629
Free Union	42409
Fremont	42003
Frenchburg	40322
Fresh Meadows	40824
Friendly Hills	40219
Frisby	42633

*** Area Zip Code** **† Post Office Boxes** **‡ Postal Station** **♦ Census Designated Place** *Italic Type* **County**

Place	ZIP
Fritz	41465
Frogtown	40033
Frogue	42717
Frontier Village (Part of Henderson)	42420
Frozen Creek	41339
Fruit Hill	42217
Fry	42743
Fryer	42445
Fuget	41219
Fulgham	42031
Fulton	42041
Fultz	41143
Funston	42634
Furnace	40472
Fusonia	41774
Future City	42053
Gabbard	41364
Gabe	42743
Gadberry	42728
Gage	42056
Gainesville	42164
Gainesway (Part of Lexington)	40502
Gallup	41230
Galveston	41635
Gamaliel	42140
Gapcreek	42603
Gap in Knob	40165
Gapville	41433
Gardenside (Part of Lexington)‡	40504
	40533
	40544
For specific ZIP Codes call (888) 275-8777, or your local postmaster.	
Garden Springs (Part of Lexington)	40504
Garden Village	41501
Gardnersville	41033
Garfield	40140
Garlin	42728
Garner, *Boyd*	41168
Garner, *Knott*	41817
Garrard	40941
Garrett, *Floyd*	41630
Garrett, *Meade*	40117
Garrettsburg	42236
Garrison	41141
Garvin Ridge	41164
Gascon	42129
Gaskill (Part of Jenkins)	41537
Gasper	42206
Gates	40351
Gatewood	42348
Gatliff	40769
Gatun	40806
Gausdale	40906
Gaybourn	40383
Gays Creek	41745
Geddes	42134
General Mail Facility (Part of Owensboro)‡	42304
Geneva, *Henderson*	42406
Geneva, *Lincoln*	40437
Gentrys Mill	42728
Georgetown, *Harlan*	40843
Georgetown, *Scott*	40324
Germantown, *Bracken*	41044
Germantown (Part of Louisville)	40217
Gertrude	41004
Gesling	41128
Gest	40057
Gethsemane	40051
Ghent	41045
Gibbs	40906
Gifford	41465
Gilbertsville	42044
Gillem Branch	41219
Gilley	41819
Gillmore	41301
Gilpin	42539
Gilreath	42635
Gilstrap	42349
Gimlet	41164
Girdler	40943
Girkin	42101
Gishton	42325
Glasgow	42141*
	42142†
Gleanings	40052
Glenarm	40014
Glencoe	41046
Glendale	42740
Glendale Junction	42740
Glen Dean	40119
Glengary	40118
Glensboro	40342
Glens Fork	42741
Glen Springs	41179
Glenview, *Jefferson*	40025
Glenview, *Shelby*	40065
Glenview Hills	40222
Glenview Manor	40222
Glenville	42376
Glenwood	41230
Glo	41666
Globe	41164
Glomawr	41701
Goddard	41093
Goering	42348
Goffs Corner	40391
Goforth	41040
Goins	40763
Goldbug	40769
Gold City	42134
Golden Ash	40831
Golden Pond	42211
Golo	42054
Goochtown	42567
Goodluck	42129
Goodnight	42127
Goodwater	42501
Goody	41514
Goose Creek	40222
Goose Rock	40944
Gordon	41819
Gordon Ford	41472
Gordonsville	42276
Goshen	40026
Gotts	42103
Grab	42743
Grace	40962
Gracey	42232
Gradyville	42742
Graefenburg	40601
Graham	42344
Graham Hill	42420
Grahamville	42086
Grahn	41142
Gra-Mor	40004
Grancer	42287
Grand Rivers	42045
Grandview (Part of Tompkinsville)	42167
Grandview Heights (Part of Frankfort)	40601
Grange City	41049
Grangertown	42459
Grants Lick	41001
Grant Wood Hills	42420
Grapevine	42431
Grassy Creek	41332
Grassy Lick	40353
Gratz	40359
Gravel Switch	40328
Gray	40734
Gray Hawk	40434
Graymoor (Part of Graymoor-Devondale)	40222
Graymoor-Devondale	40222
Grays Branch	41144
Grays Knob	40829
Grayson	41143
Grayson Springs	42726
Graysville	40146
Greasy Creek	41562
Great Crossing	40324
Greear	41472
Green	41164
Green Acres (Part of Danville)	40422
Green Acres (Part of Lexington)	40511
Greenbriar, *Daviess*	42303
Greenbriar, *Marion*	40033
Greenbriar, *Oldham*	40031
Greenbrier	40489
Greencastle	42270
Greendale (Part of Lexington)	40511
Green Fields Estates	40391
Green Grove	42717
Green Hall	41314
Green Hill, *Jackson*	40402
Greenhill, *Warren*	42103
Green Hills	42728
Greenland Park	40065
Greenmount	40741
Green Road	40946
Greensburg	42743
Green Spring	40222
Greenup	41144
Greenview	41042
Greenville	42345
Greenwood, *McCreary*	42634
Greenwood, *Pendleton*	41006
Greenwood (Part of Bowling Green)	42104
Greenwood Mall (Part of Bowling Green)	42104
Gregory	42633
Gregoryville	41143
Gresham	42743
Grethel	41631
Grider	42717
Griderville	42127
Griffin	42633
Griffith	42301
Griffytown	40243
Grigsby	41722
Grove Center	42437
Grundy	42501
Guage	41339
Gubser Mill	41007
Guerrant	41339
Guffie	42327
Gullett	41465
Gulnare	41501
Gulston	40830
Gum Sulphur	40419
Gum Tree	42167
Gunlock	41632
Guston	40142
Guthrie	42234
Guy	42101
Gwinn Island	40422
Gypsy	41464
Habit	42366
Haddix	41339
Hadensville	42234
Hadley	42235
Hager	41465
Hagerhill	41222
Hail	42501
Halcom	41171
Haldeman	40329
Halfway	42150
Halifax	42164
Hall, *Jessamine*	40356
Hall, *Knott*	41840
Hallie	41821
Halls Gap	40489
Halls Store	42276
Halo	41606
Hamlin	42046
Hammackville	42286
Hammond	41240
Hammonville	42757
Hampton	42047
Hampton Manor (Part of Winchester)	40391
Handshoe	41640
Hanly	40356
Hannah	41124
Hansford	40456
Hanson	42413
Happy	41746
Happy Acre	42642
Happy Landing	40403
Harbor Village	40324
Hardburly	41747
Hardin	42048
Hardinsburg	40143
Hardin Springs	42783
Hardmoney	42003
Hardshell	41348
Hardwick	42633
Hardy	41531
Hardyville	42746
Hare	40729
Hargett	40336
Harlan	40831
Harlan Crossroads	42167
Harlan Gas	40831
Harmony	40359
Harmony Lake Estates	40059
Harmony Village	40059
Harned	40144
Harold	41635
Harper	41465
Harreldsville	42256
Harrington Mill Estates	40065
Harris	41179
Harris Grove	42071
Harrisonville	40076
Harrodsburg	40330
Harrods Creek	40027
Harrods Hills (Part of Lexington)	40513
Hart	40741
Hartford	42347
Hartley	41572
Harveyton	41719
Harvy	42025
Haskingsville	42743
Hatcher	42718
Hatfield	41514
Hatton	40601
Hawesville	42348
Hawkeegan Point	40601
Hayes	41040
Haynesville	42368
Hays	42171
Hays Crossing	40351
Hayward	41173
Haywood	42141
Hazard	41701*
	41702†
Hazel	42049
Hazel Green	41332
Hazel Patch	40729
Head of Grassy	41135
Headquarters	40311
Hearin	42404
Heath	42086
Hebbardsville	42420
Hebron	41048
Hebron Estates	40165
Hecla	42410
Hector	40962
Hedgeville	40444
Heekin	41097
Heenon	41501
Heflin	42347
Hegira	42717
Heidelberg	41333
Heidrick	40949
Heiner	41722
Helechawa	41332
Helena	41055
Hellier	41534
Helton	40840
Hemp Ridge	40076
Henderson	42419†
	42420*
Hendricks	41465
Hendron	42001
Henrietta	41240
Henry Clay (Part of Lexington)‡	40502*
	40522†
Henry Clay, *Pike*	41542
Henryville	40311
Henshaw	42437
Hensley, *Breckinridge*	40146
Hensley, *Clay*	40962
Herbert	42368
Herd	40486
Heritage Village (Part of Campbellsville)	42718
Hermitage Hills (Part of Lexington)	40505
Hermon	42234
Herndon	42236
Herron Hill	41189
Heselton	41179
Hesler	40359
Hestand	42151
Hi Acres (Part of Lexington)	40505
Hickman	42050
Hickory	42051
Hickory Flat	42134
Hickory Grove, *Cumberland*	42717
Hickory Grove, *McCreary*	42638
Hickory Hill	40222
Hickory Hills (Part of Frankfort)	40601
Hidalgo	42633
Hide-A-Way Hills	40359
High Bridge	40390
High Falls	41301
Highgrove	40013
High Knob	40402
Highland, *Lincoln*	40484
Highland, *Simpson*	42134
Highland Heights	41076
Highland Park (Part of Louisville)	40209
Highland Park (Part of Williamsburg)	40769
Highlands (Part of Lexington)	40511
Highlands (Part of Louisville)	40206
High Plains	40106
High Point	42086
Highsplint	40828
Hightop	40744
Highview, *Jefferson*	40228
Highview, *Ohio*	42320
Highway	42602
Hignite	40965
Hi Hat	41636
Hikes Point (Part of Louisville)‡	40220*
	40250†
Hilda	40351
Hillcrest	40475
Hillendale	41095
Hill-N-Dale	40065
Hill Ridge	40299
Hills and Dales	40222
Hillsboro	41049
Hillsdale	42134
Hillside	42330
Hill Top, *Fleming*	41039
Hilltop, *Grant*	41097
Hilltop, *Logan*	42202
Hill Top, *McCreary*	42647
Hillview, *Bullitt*	40229
Hillview, *Edmonson*	42207
Hima	40951
Himyar	40906
Hinda Heights (Part of Lexington)	40502
Hindman	41822
Hinkle	40953
Hinkleville	42056
Hinton	41010
Hinton Hills	40143
Hippo	41653
Hiram	40823
Hisel	40447
Hiseville	42152
Hislope	42544
Hitchins	41146
Hite	41649
Hitesville	42437
Hobson	42718
Hode	41267
Hodgenville	42748
Hogue	42553
Holbrook	41097
Holiday Hills (Part of Lexington)	40504
Holifield	42088
Holland	42153
Holliday	41472
Hollonville	41301
Holloway Hills	42420
Hollow Bill	42256
Hollow Creek	40228
Hollybush	41844
Hollyhill	42635
Hollyvilla	40118
Holmes Mill	40843
Holt	42332
Holy Cross	40037
Homer	42276
Homestead	40383
Honaker	41603
Honeybee	42634
Honey Fork	41513
Honey Grove	42240
Honeysuckle Estates	40342
Hooktown	41031
Hootentown	40391
Hope	40334
Hopeful Heights	41042
Hopewell, *Greenup*	41144
Hopewell, *Jefferson*	40299
Hopkinsville	42240*
	42241†
Hopson	42445
Horntown	42642
Horse Branch	42349
Horse Cave	42749
Horton	42320
Hoskinston	40844
Houston	41314
Houston Acres	40220
Hovious Ridge	42728
Howard Mills	40334
Howardstown	40051
Howel	42262
Howe Valley	42724
Hubble	40444
Hubbs	40921
Huddy	41535
Hudgins	42782
Hudson	40145
Hueys Corners	41091
Hueysville	41640
Huff	42210
Hulen	40845
Humble	42642
Hummel	40492
Hunnewell	41121
Hunt	40391
Hunter	41655
Hunter Hill	40258
Hunters Hollow	40229
Hunters Trace	40216
Huntersville	42602
Hunter Town	40383
Hunting Creek (Part of Hopkinsville)	42240
Huntington Woods	40601
Huntsville	42251
Hurley	40447
Hurricane Hills	40107

Hurstbourne 40222
Hurstbourne Acres 40220
Hustonville 40437
Hutch 40965
Hutchison 40361
Hyattsville 40444
Hyden 41749
Hydro 42171
Iberia 42726
Ibex 41164
Ice 41858
Ida 42602
Ida May 41311
Idle Hour (Part of Lexington) 40502
Idlewild 41005
Ilsley 42408
Independence 41051
Index (Part of West Liberty) 41472
Indian Fields 40391
Indian Hills, *Carroll* 41008
Indian Hills, *Jefferson* 40207
Indian Hills, *Russell* 42642
Indian Hills (Part of Bowling Green) 42103
Indian Hills (Part of Elizabethtown) 42701
Indian Hills (Part of Frankfort) 40601
Indian Hills (Part of Georgetown) 40324
Indian Hills (Part of Hopkinsville) 42240
Indian Hills Cherokee Section 40207
Indian Lake 42348
Inez 41224
Ingle 42544
Ingleside 42053
Ingram 40955
Insco 42276
Insko 41332
Inverness Estates (Part of Frankfort) 40601
Iron Hill, *Carter* 41143
Iron Hill, *Lyon* 42055
Ironville 41102
Ironworks Estates 40324
Iroquois (Part of Louisville)‡ 40209
40214
For specific ZIP Codes call (888) 275-8777, or your local postmaster.
Iroquois Heights 40214
Irvine 40336
Irvington 40146
Irvins Store 42642
Island 42350
Island City 41338
Isom 41824
Isonville 41149
Iuka 42045
Ivel 41642
Ivis 41822
Ivor 41007
Ivy Grove 40939
Ivyton 41444
Jabez 42544
Jackhorn 41825
Jackson 41339
Jacksonville, *Bourbon* 40361
Jacksonville, *Shelby* 40003
Jackstown 40311
Jacktown 40009
Jacobs 41150
Jamboree 41553
Jamestown 42629
Jarvis 40906
Jason 41714
Jasper Bend 42519
Jeff 41751
Jeffersontown 40269†
40299*
Jeffersonville 40337
Jeffrey 42157
Jellico 40769
Jellico Creek 40769
Jenkins 41537
Jenkinsville 40040
Jenson 40977
Jeptha 41472
Jeremiah 41826
Jericho, *Henry* 40068
Jericho, *Larue* 42748
Jerico 42256
Jessietown 40033
Jetson 42252
Jett 40601
Jetts Creek 41314
Jewell City 42456
Jimtown (Part of Lexington) 40505
Jimtown, *Washington* 40069
Jinks 40336
Job 41224
Jock 42207
Johnetta 40460
Johns Creek 41265
Johnsontown 40272
Johnsport (Part of Campbellsville) 42718
Johns Run 41143
Johnsville 41043
Jonancy 41538
Jonesville, *Grant* 41052
Jonesville, *Hart* 42757
Joppa 42728
Jordan 42050
Josephine 40370
Joy 42047
Judio 42717
Judson 40444
Judy 40334
Judyville 40311
Julien 42232
Julip 40769
Jumbo 40484
Junction City 40440
Juniper Hill (Part of Frankfort) 40601
Justell 41605
Justice 42256
Justiceville 41501
Kaler 42051
Kaliopi 41749
Kansas 42069
Karlus 42629
Katharyn 40177
Kavanaugh 41129
Kayjay 40906
Keaton 41226
Keavy 40737
Keefer 41010
Keene 40339
Keeneland 40223
Kehoe 41141
Keith 40806
Kelat 41003
Kellacey 41472
Kelly 42240
Kellyville 42728
Keltner 42761
Ken Acres 40065
Kenawood (Part of Lexington) 40505
Kendall Springs 40360
Kennianna 42046
Keno 42558
Kensee 40769
Kenshores 42046
Kentenia 40873
Kenton 41053
Kenton Hills (Part of Covington) 41011
Kentontown 41064
Kenton Vale 41015
Kentucky Dam Village 42044
Kentucky Heights 41166
Kentucky Oaks Mall (Part of Paducah) 42001
Kenvir 40847
Kenwood (Part of Louisville) 40214
Kerby Knob 40447
Kernie 41465
Kessinger 42765
Keswick 40769
Kettle 42717
Kettlecamp 41522
Kettle Island 40958
Kevil 42053
Keysburg 42204
Keyser Heights 41501
Kidder 42518
Kidds Crossing 42611
Kidds Store 40437
Kiddville 40353
Kildav 40828
Kilgore 41168
Kimbrell 40336
Kimper 41539
Kinchloes Bluff 42330
Kingbee 42516
Kings Creek 41858
Kings Forest 40165
Kingsley 40205
Kings Mountain 40442
Kingston (Part of Lexington) 40505
Kingston, *Madison* 40403
Kingswood 40144
Kinniconick 41179
Kino 42141
Kirbyton 42023
Kirk 40143
Kirkmansville 42220
Kirksey 42054
Kirksville 40475
Kirkwood 40372
Kirkwood Springs 42408
Kite 41828
Kitts 40831
Knifley 42753
Knob Lick 42154
Knottsville 42366
Knowlton 40380
Knoxfork 40906
Knoxville 41097
Kodak 41773
Kona 41858
Korea 40387
Kragon 41339
Krypton 41754
Kuttawa 42055
Kyrock 42285
Labascus 42539
La Center 42056
Lacey 41465
Lacie 40075
Lackey 41643
Lacon 42726
Laden 40865
La Fayette 42254
La Grange 40031
Lair 41031
Lake 40744
Lake Carnico 40311
Lake City 42045
Lake Dreamland 40216
Lake Louisvilla 40014
Lakeside Park 41017
Lakeview (Part of Fort Wright) 41011
Lakeview Heights 40351
Lakeview-Mt. Tabor (Part of Lexington) 40502
Lakeview-Woodspoint (Part of Lexington) 40509
Lakeville 41465
Lakeway Shore 42071
Lakewood Acres (Part of Lexington) 40502
Lamasco 42038
Lamb 42141
Lambric 41340
Lamero 40445
Lamont, *McCracken* 42053
Lamont, *Perry* 41727
Lancaster 40444
Lancelot Estates 40324
Lancer (Part of Prestonsburg) 41653
Landsaw 41301
Langdon Place 40222
Langley 41645
Langnau 40741
Lanhamtown 42539
Lansdowne (Part of Lexington) 40502
Larkslane 41817
Latonia (Part of Covington) 41015
Latonia Lakes 41015
Laura 41250
Laurel Creek 40962
Laurel Fork 40940
Laurel Ridge 42259
Lawhorn Hill 42539
Lawrenceburg 40342
Lawrenceville 41010
Lawson 41339
Lawton 41164
Layman 40819
Leafdale 42748
Leander 41228
Leatha 41465
Leatherwood 41731
Lebanon 40033
Lebanon Junction 40150
Leburn 41831
Leckieville 41514
Lecta 42141
Ledbetter 42058
Ledocio 41230
Lee City 41342
Leeco 41301
Leesburg 41031
Lees Lick 41031
LeGrande 42749
Leighton 40336
Leitchfield 42754*
42755†
Leitchfield Crossing (Part of Munfordville) 42765
Lejunior 40849
Lemon 42327
Lenarue 40818
Lenore 40013
Lenox 41472
Lenoxburg 41040
Leon 41143
Lerose 41344
Lesbas 40744
Leslie 42717
Letcher 41832
Levee 40337
Level Green 40456
Levi 41314
Levias 42064
Lewisburg, *Logan* 42256
Lewisburg, *Mason* 41056
Lewisport 42351
Lexington 40501-96
For specific ZIP Codes call (888) 275-8777, or your local postmaster.
Lexington-Bluegrass Army Depot (Headquarters), Fayette 40511
Lexington-Bluegrass Army Depot, *Madison* 40475
Lexington Mall (Part of Lexington) 40502
Liberty, *Casey* 42539
Liberty, *Webster* 42409
Liberty, *Whitley* 40769
Liberty Heights (Part of Lexington) 40505
Liberty Heights, *Nicholas* 40311
Liberty Road (Part of Morgan) 41472
Liberty Road (Part of Lexington)‡ 40505*
40555†
Lick Branch 41472
Lickburg 41465
Lick Creek 41540
Lick Fork 40313
Licking River 41472
Lickskillet, *Logan* 42265
Lickskillet, *Meade* 40175
Lida 40744
Liggett 40831
Ligon 41604
Liletown 42743
Lily 40740
Limaburg 41005
Limestone 41164
Limestone Springs 40165
Limeville 41175
Lincoln 40962
Lincolnshire 40220
Lindseyville 42257
Linefork 41833
Linton 42211
Linwood, *Grayson* 42726
Linwood, *Hart* 42757
Lionilli 41537
Lisletown 40391
Lisman 42404
Litsey 40069
Littcarr 41834
Little 41339
Little Barren 42743
Little Bear Creek 42044
Little Creek 40902
Little Cypress 42029
Little Dixie 41501
Little Georgetown (Part of Lexington) 40513
Little Hickman 40356
Little Mount 40071
Little Needmore 40422
Little Rock 40311
Little Sandy 41171
Little Tar Springs 42348
Little Texas (Part of Lexington) 40513
Littleton 40962
Littrell 42717
Livermore 42352
Livia 42327
Livingston 40445
Lloyd 41156
Load 41144
Lockards Creek 40941
Lockport 40036
Lockwood Estates 40014
Locust 41008
Locust Grove, *Clark* 40391
Locust Grove, *Pendleton* 41040
Locust Hill 40144
Lodiburg 40146
Logana 40356
Logansport 42261
Logantown 40484
Log Lick 40391
Log Mountain 40977
Logville 41465
Lola 42078
Lombard 40380
London 40741-45
For specific ZIP Codes call (888) 275-8777, or your local postmaster.
Lone 41347
Lone Oak 42003
Lone Star 42713
Lone Way Acres 42718
Long Fork 41572
Longlick 40379
Long Ridge 40359
Long Run 40245
Long View 42701
Longview Estates 40422
Lookout 41542
Loradale (Part of Lexington) 40505
Loretto 40037
Lost Creek 41348
Lot 40769
Lothair (Part of Hazard) 41701
Lotus 40013
Louden 40769
Louellen 40828
Louisa 41230

Louisville

40201-99
For specific ZIP Codes call (888) 275-8777, or your local postmaster.

Colleges & Universities

Bellarmine Coll 40205
Louisville Presbyterian Theological Seminary 40205
The Southern Baptist Theological Seminary 40280
Spalding Univ 40203
Sullivan Coll 40205
Univ of Louisville 40292

Financial Institutions

Bank of Louisville 40202
Bank One 40232
The Fifth Third Bank 40202
Nat City Bank 40202
PNC Bank, Inc 40202

Hospitals

Alliant Hosps 40202
Audubon Med Ctr 40217
Baptist Hosp East 40207
Jewish Hosp 40202
Suburban Hosp 40207
Univ of Louisville Hosp 40202
Veterans Affairs Med Ctr 40206

Hotels/Motels

The Camberley Brown 40202
Executive Inn 40209
Executive West 40209
The Galt House 40202
Holiday Inn Downtown 40202
Holiday Inn Hurstbourne 40222
Holiday Inn South Airport 40213
Hyatt Regency 40202
Marriott East 40299
Seelbach 40202

Military Installations

Kentucky Air Nat Guard, FB6161 Standiford Field 40213
U S Army Corps of Engineers 40201

Lovelaceville 42060
Lovely 41231
Lowell 40461
Lower Kings Addition 41175
Lower Pompey 41501
Lowes 42061
Lowmansville 41232
Loyall 40854
Lucas 42156
Lucastown 41855

Lucky Fork 41364
Lucky Stop (Part of Jeffersonville) 40337
Ludlow 41016
Luner 40456
Lusby's Mill 40359
Luzerne 42345
Lykins 41465
Lynch 40855
Lyndale 40391
Lyndon 40222
40241-42
40252
For specific ZIP Codes call (888) 275-8777, or your local postmaster.
Lynn 41144
Lynn City 42372
Lynn Grove 42071
Lynnview 40213
Lynnville 42063
Lyons 40051
Lytten 41171
Mac 42718
McAfee 40330
McAndrews 41543
McBrayer 40342
McCarr 41544
McClure 41250
McCombs 41501
McCreary 40444
McDaniels 40152
McDowell 41647
Macedonia, *Christian* 42217
Macedonia, *Jackson* 40447
Maceo 42355
McGowan 42445
McHenry 42354
McKee 40447
McKinney 40448
McKinneysburg 41040
Mackville 40040
McQuady 40153
McRoberts♦ 41835
McVeigh 41546
McVille 41005
McWhorter 40741
Madison Hills (Part of Richmond) 40475
Madisonville 42431
Madrid 42754
Magan 42343
Maggard 41465
Magnolia 42757
Magoffin 41465
Majestic 41547
Major 41314
Malaga 41301
Mallard Point 40324
Mallie 41836
Mall in St. Matthews, The (Part of St. Matthews) 40207
Malone 41451
Maloneton 41175
Mammoth Cave 42259
Manchester 40962
Mangum 42516
Manila 41238
Manitou 42436
Mannington 42217
Mannsville 42758
Manor Creek 40222
Man O' War Place (Part of Lexington) 40509
Manse 40461
Manton, *Floyd* 41649
Manton, *Washington* 40037
Maple Grove 42211
Maple Mount 42356
Maplesville 40741
Marcellus 40444
Marcum 40962
Marcus 41003
Maretburg 40456
Mariba 40322
Marion 42064
Mark 42501
Marksbury 40444
Marlowe 41858
Marrowbone 42759
Marshall, *Marshall* 42044
Marshall, *Mason* 41056
Marshallville 41452
Marshes Siding 42631
Martha 41159
Martin 41649
Martinsville 42159
Mary 41301
Mary Alice 40964
Marydell 40751
Maryhill Estates 40207
Mashfork 41465
Mason, *Grant* 41054
Mason, *Magoffin* 41465
Masonic Home (Part of Louisville) 40041
Masonville 42376
Massac 42001
Matanzas 42328
Matlock 42104
Matthew 41472
Mattingly 40111
Mattoon 42064
Mattoxtown (Part of Lexington) 40505
Maud 40069
Maulden 40486
Mavity 41129
Maxine 42776
Maxwell 42376
Mayfield 42066
Mayflower 41501
Mayking 41837
Maynard 42164
Mayo 40330
Mayo Village (Part of Pikeville) 41501
Mays Lick 41055
Maysville 41056
Maytown 41472
Maywood 40484
Mazie 41160
Meador 42164
Meadowbrook (Part of Winchester) 40391
Meadowbrook, *Shelby* 40065
Meadowbrook Farm 40223
Meadow Creek 40759
Meadowrun 40065
Meadows (Part of Frankfort) 40601
Meadows (Part of Lexington) 40505
Meadowthorpe (Part of Lexington) 40511
Meadow Vale 40222
Meadowview Estates 40220
Meads 41101
Mealy 41234
Means 40346
Medora 40272
Meece 42501
Meeting Creek 42732
Melber 42069
Melbourne 41059
Meldrum 40965
Mell 42743
Melody Lake 40051
Melvin 41650
Memphis Junction 42101
Mentor 41007
Meredith 42754
Merewood (Part of Versailles) 40383
Meridian 41006
Merrick Place (Part of Lexington) 40502
Merrimac 40009
Merrittstown 42240
Merry Oaks 42171
Mershons 40729
Meshack 42167
Meta 41501
Mexico 42064
Midas 41640
Middleburg 42541
Middlesboro 40965
Middlesboro Mall (Part of Middlesboro) 40965
Middleton 42134
Middleton Heights (Part of Shelbyville) 40065
Middletown, *Jefferson* 40243*
40253†
Middletown (Part of Berea) 40403
Midland, *Bath* 40371
Midland, *Muhlenberg* 42325
Midway, *Calloway* 42049
Midway, *Crittenden* 42064
Midway, *Meade* 40142
Midway, *Woodford* 40347
Milburn 42070
Mildred 40447
Milford 41061
Millard 41562
Mill Creek 41055
Milledgeville 40437
Miller, *Fulton* 42050
Miller, *Nicholas* 40311
Millersburg 40348
Millers Creek 40472
Millerstown 42726
Million 40475
Mill Pond 40962
Millport 42372
Mills 40935
Millseat 41101
Mill Springs 42632
Millstone 41838
Milltown, *Adair* 42761
Milltown, *Nicholas* 40350
Millville 40601
Millwood 42762
Milner 40383
Milo 41262
Milton 40045
Mima 41472
Minerva 41062
Minnie 41651
Minor Lane Heights 40219
Minorsville 40379
Mintonville 42539
Miracle 40856
Mistletoe 41351
Mitchell Hill (Part of Madisonville) 42431
Mitchellsburg 40452
Mize 41352
Moberly 40475
Mockingbird Valley 40207
Moct 41385
Modoc 42717
Molus 40819
Monford 42252
Monica 41362
Monica Gardens 40065
Monitor 40006
Monkeys Eyebrow 42056
Monroe 42746
Montclair (Part of Lexington) 40502
Montclair, *Shelby* 40067
Monterey 40359
Montgomery 42211
Montgomerys Mill 42743
Monticello 42633
Monticello Estates (Part of Lexington) 40503
Montpelier 42728
Montrose (Part of Lexington) 40516
Montrose Park (Part of Frankfort) 40601
Mooleyville 40143
Moon 41472
Moon Lake Estates 40324
Moorefield 40350
Moore Hill 40701
Moores Creek 40402
Moores Ferry 40371
Mooresville 40069
Moorland 40223
Moorman 42330
Moranburg 41056
Morehead 40351
Moreland 40437
Morgan 41040
Morganfield 42437
Morgantown 42261
Morning Glory 41031
Morning View 41063
Morrill 40447
Morris Fork 41314
Mortiner Station 42202
Mortons Gap 42440
Mortonsville 40383
Moscow 42031
Moseleyville 42301
Mossy Bottom 41501
Motley 42103
Mount Aerial 42128
Mountain Ash 40769
Mountain Top 41164
Mountain Valley 41385
Mount Auburn 41006
Mount Carmel, *Fleming* 41041
Mount Carmel, *Hopkins* 42464
Mount Eden 40046
Mount Gilead, *Green* 42743
Mount Gilead, *Monroe* 42167
Mount Hermon 42157
Mount Lebanon 40356
Mount Olive, *Casey* 42539
Mount Olive, *Lee* 41311
Mount Olivet 41064
Mount Pisgah 42633
Mount Pleasant, *Ohio* 42333
Mount Pleasant, *Trimble* 40006
Mount Salem 40437
Mount Sherman 42764
Mount Sterling 40353
Mount Tabor, *Larue* 42716
Mount Tabor, *Todd* 42220
Mount Union 42120
Mount Vernon, *Rockcastle* 40456
Mount Vernon (Part of Georgetown) 40324
Mount Victor 42104
Mount Victory 42501
Mount Washington 40047
Mount Zion, *Allen* 42164
Mount Zion, *Grant* 41035
Mount Zion, *Pulaski* 42553
Mousie 41839
Moutardier 42754
Mouthcard 41548
Moxley 40363
Mozelle 40858
Mud Camp 42717
Muddy Ford 40324
Mud Lick 42167
Muir (Part of Lexington) 40516
Mulberry 40065
Muldraugh 40155
Mulfordtown 42459
Mullikin Junction 42028
Mullins 40456
Mummie 40486
Munfordville 42765
Murl 42633
Murphyfork 41332
Murphysville 41056
Murray 42071
Murray Hill 40222
Muses Mills 41065
Music 41168
Myers 40311
Myra 41549
Mystic 40146
Nada 40380
Nancy 42544
Naomi 42544
Napfor 41754
Naples 41102
Napoleon 41046
Narrows 42347
Narvel 42602
Nashtown 41189
Natlee 41010
Natural Bridge 40376
Nazareth 40048
Neafus 42721
Neave 41040
Nebo, *Hopkins* 42441
Nebo, *Muhlenberg* 42345
Ned 41317
Needmore, *Boyle* 40422
Needmore, *Butler* 42261
Needmore, *Caldwell* 42445
Nelse 41501
Nelson 42330
Nelsonville 40107
Neon (Part of Fleming-Neon) 41840
Neon Junction 41840
Neosheo 42134
Nepton 41039
Nerinx 40049
Nero 41265
Netty 41465
Nevada 40330
Nevelsville 42653
Nevin 40342
Nevisdale 40754
New 40359
New Allen 41601
Newburg 40213
40218-19
For specific ZIP Codes call (888) 275-8777, or your local postmaster.
Newby 40475
New Camp 41503
New Castle 40050
New Columbus 41010
Newcombe 41149
New Concord 42076
New Cypress, *Hickman* 42031
New Cypress, *Muhlenberg* 42345
Newfound 40972
Newfoundland 41171
Newgarden‡ 40121
New Haven 40051
New Hope 40052
New Liberty 40355
Newman 42301
New Market 40033
Newport 41071-72
41076
For specific ZIP Codes call (888) 275-8777, or your local postmaster.
Newport Shopping Center (Part of Newport) 41071
New Providence 42049
New Roe 42120
New Salem 40437
Newstead 42240
Newt 42743
Newtown 40324
New Zion, *Jackson* 40447
New Zion, *Scott* 40324
Niagara 42420
Nicholasville 40340†
40356*
Nichols, *Bullitt* 40177
Nichols, *Hickman* 42031
Nicholson, *Kenton* 41051
Nicholson, *Trigg* 42215
Nickell 41332
Nigh Siding 41524
Nina 40444
Nineteen 42320
Ninevah 40342
Nippa 41240
Noble 41317
Nobob 42166
No Creek 42347
Noctor 41339
Node 42214
Noetown (Part of Middlesboro) 40965
Nolansburg 40870
Nolin 42776
Nolin Lake Estates 42726
Nonesuch 40383
Nonnel 42337
Nora 42602
Norbourne Estates 40207
Norfleet 42544
Normal (Part of Ashland) 41101
Normandy 40071
North Corbin♦ 40701
Northfield 40222
North Irvine 40336
North Middletown 40357
Northtown 42749
Norton Branch 41168
Nortonville 42442
Norwood, *Jefferson* 40222
Norwood, *Pulaski* 42553
Nuckols 42352
Nugent Cross Roads 40383
Nugym 40902
Number One 42633
Oakbrook 41042
Oakdale, *Breathitt* 41339
Oakdale (Part of Louisville) 40215
Oakdale, *McCracken* 42003
Oak Forest 42164
Oak Grove, *Christian* 42262
Oak Grove, *Ohio* 42333
Oak Hill, *Hopkins* 42442
Oak Hill, *Pulaski* 42501
Oakland 42159
Oakland Mills 40311
Oaklawn Estates 41222
Oak Level 42025
Oakley 40729
Oak Ridge, *Edmonson* 42207
Oak Ridge (Part of Independence) 41051
Oaks, *Bell* 40856
Oaks, *McCracken* 42003
Oaks, *Ohio* 42343
Oakton 42031
Oakville 42276
Oakwood (Part of Lexington) 40511
O'Bannon 40223
Oddville 41031
Odessa 40360
Offutt 41240
Ogle 40962
Oil City 42141
Oil Springs 41238
Oil Valley 42633
Okolona♦ 40219
40229
40259
For specific ZIP Codes call (888) 275-8777, or your local postmaster.
Olaton 42361
Olcott 40977
Old Brownsboro Place 40222

* Area Zip Code † Post Office Boxes ‡ Postal Station ♦ Census Designated Place *Italic Type* County

Place	ZIP
Old Christianburg	40003
Old Flat Lick	40935
Oldham Acres	40059
Old Landing	41311
Old Olga	42629
Old Orchard	40447
Old Pine Grove	40391
Old Stephensburg	42724
Old Taylor Place	40026
Oldtown	41144
Old Volney	42265
Olga	42629
Olin	40447
Olive	42025
Olive Branch, *Fleming*	41041
Olive Branch, *Shelby*	40065
Olive Hill	41164
Ollie	42259
Olmstead	42265
Olney	42408
Olympia	40358
Olympia Springs	40358
Omaha	41843
Oneida	40972
Oneonta	41007
Ono	42642
Onton	42455
Open Gates (Part of Lexington)	40503
Ophir	41459
Orangeburg	41056
Orchard Grass Hills	40014
Ordinary	41171
Oregon	40372
Orkney	41647
Orlando	40460
Orr	41180
Ortiz	42455
Orville	40057
Osborn	41635
Oscaloosa	41858
Oscar	42056
Otia	42167
Ottawa	40409
Ottenheim	40489
Otter Pond	42445
Oven Fork	40823
Overlook (Part of Eddyville)	42038
Ovesen Heights	42748
Owensboro	42301-04
For specific ZIP Codes call (888) 275-8777, or your local postmaster.	
Owensboro East (Part of Owensboro)	42303
Owensboro West (Part of Owensboro)	42301
Owenton	40359
Owingsville	40360
Owsley	41501
Oxford	40324
Oxmoor Center (Part of Louisville)	40222
Ozark	42728
Pactolus	41143
Paddock Place	40383
Paducah	42001-03
For specific ZIP Codes call (888) 275-8777, or your local postmaster.	
Paint Lick	40461
Paintsville	41240
Palestine	41091
Palma	42025
Palmer	40336
Panama	41472
Panco	40972
Panola	40385
Panorama Shores	42071
Panther	42376
Paragon Park (Part of Henderson)	42420
Paris	40361*
	40362†
Park City	42160
Parkers Lake	42634
Park Hills (Part of Lexington)	40502
Park Hills, *Kenton*	41011
Park Hills, *Rowan*	40351
Park Lake	41093
Parkland (Part of Louisville)	40211
Parksville	40464
Parkview Shores No. 1	42164
Parkview Shores No. 2	42164
Parkway Village	40207
Parmleysville	42633
Parnell	42633
Parrot	40447
Partridge	40862
Partridge Run (Part of Henderson)	42420
Pascal	42746
Patesville	42348
Pathfork	40863
Patrick	41230
Patsey	40380
Pauley (Part of Pikeville)	41501*
	41502†
Paw Paw	41553
Paxton	41385
Payne Gap	41537
Paynes Depot	40324
Payneville	40157
Payton	41332
Peabody	40914
Peach Grove	41006
Peach Orchard	41230
Peak	40324
Peaks Mill	40601
Pea Ridge, *Scott*	40379
Pea Ridge, *Todd*	42220
Pearl	40940
Pearman	42726
Peasticks	40360
Pebble	40360
Pebworth	41314
Peden Mill	42134
Peedee	42236
Pelfrey	40313
Pellville	42364
Pellyton	42728
Pembroke	42266
Pence	41313
Pendleton	40055
Penile	40272
Penny, *Calloway*	42071
Penny, *Pike*	41501
Pennyrile Mall (Part of Hopkinsville)	42240
Penrod	42365
Peonia	42726
Peoples	40467
Perry Park	40363
Perryville	40468
Persimmon Grove	41001
Persimon	42167
Petersburg	41080
Petersville	41179
Petra	41004
Petrie	42348
Petroleum	42120
Petros	42274
Pettit	42301
Pewee Valley	40056
Peytona	40065
Peyton Creek	41501
Peytonsburg	42717
Peytons Store	40437
Peytontown	40475
Phelps	41553
Phillipsburg	42718
Philpot	42366
Phyllis	41554
Pickett	42761
Pickway (Part of Lexington)	40503
Pierce	42743
Pig	42171
Pigeon	41501
Pigeonroost	40962
Pike View	42757
Pikeville	41501*
	41502†
Pilgrim	41250
Pilot Oak	42085
Pilot View	40391
Pinchem, *Clark*	40391
Pinchem, *Todd*	42234
Pinckard	40383
Pinckneyville	42078
Pine Bluffs	42046
Pine Grove, *Clark*	40391
Pine Grove, *Laurel*	40740
Pine Hill	40456
Pine Knob	42721
Pine Knot♦	42635
Pine Meadows (Part of Lexington)	40504
Pine Mountain	40810
Piner	41063
Pine Ridge	41360
Pine Top	41843
Pineville	40977
Piney Fork	42064
Piney Grove	42501
Pink	40356
Pinnacle	41311
Pinson	41543
Pinsonfork	41555
Pioneer	41005
Pioneer Village	40165
Pippa Passes	41844
Piqua	41064
Pisgah	40383
Piso	41501
Pitts	40472
Pittsburg	40755
Plainview (Part of Jeffersontown)	40224
Plank	40962
Plano	42104
Plantation	40222
Plato	42501
Pleasant Grove Hill	42240
Pleasant Hill, *Butler*	42273
Pleasant Hill, *Mercer*	40330
Pleasant Hill, *Pendleton*	41006
Pleasant Home	40359
Pleasant Ridge	42376
Pleasant Valley, *Nicholas*	41039
Pleasant Valley (Part of Pikeville)	41501
Pleasant View	40769
Pleasure Ridge Park	40258*
	40268†
Pleasureville, *Fleming*	41093
Pleasureville, *Henry*	40057
Plum	40361
Plummers Landing	41081
Plummers Mill	41093
Plum Springs	42101
Plumville	41056
Plymouth Village	40207
Poindexter	41031
Pointer	42544
Point Leavell	40444
Point Pleasant	42718
Polksville	40371
Polkville	42159
Polly	41858
Pomeroyton	40387
Pomp	41472
Ponderosa	42726
Pondsville	42171
Pongo	40456
Poole	42444
Poortown	40356
Pope	42128
Poplar	41128
Poplar Corner	40033
Poplar Flat	41189
Poplar Grove, *Fleming*	41041
Poplar Grove, *McLean*	42372
Poplar Grove, *Owen*	41046
Poplar Highlands	41169
Poplar Hills	40213
Poplar Plains	41041
Poplarville	42501
Porter	40370
Portland, *Adair*	42761
Portland (Part of Louisville)	40212
Portland, *Pendleton*	41033
Port Royal	40058
Portsmouth	41339
Possum Trot	42029
Potters	41230
Potters Fork	41537
Pottsville, *Graves*	42051
Pottsville, *Washington*	40069
Powderly	42367
Powells Creek	41501
Powersburg	42633
Powersville	41004
Prairie Village	40272
Prater	41164
Pratt	42455
Preachersville	40419
Premium	41845
Prentiss	42320
Presidential	40004
Press	41339
Preston	40366
Preston Estates	41240
Prestonia (Part of Louisville)	40213
Prestonsburg	41653
Prestonville	41008
Price	41636
Prices Mill	42134
Pricetown, *Casey*	42539
Pricetown (Part of Lexington)	40509
Priceville	42765
Pride	42404
Primrose	41362
Princess	41102
Princeton	42445
Printer	41655
Pritchardsville	42141
Privett	40486
Proctor	41311
Prospect	40059
Prosperity	42207
Providence, *Jessamine*	40503
Providence, *Knox*	40906
Providence, *Simpson*	42134
Providence, *Trimble*	40011
Providence, *Webster*	42450
Provo	42267
Pruden	37851
Pryorsburg	42066
Pryse	40336
Public	42501
Pueblo	42633
Pulaski	42567
Pumpkin Center	42445
Puncheon	41828
Purdy	42728
Putney	40865
Pyles	42058
Pyramid	41653
Quail	40409
Quality	42256
Quicksand	41339
Quincy	41166
Quinton	42518
Rabbit Hash	41005
Rabbit Ridge	42441
Raccoon	41557
Raceland	41169
Radcliff (Part of Lexington)	40505
Radcliff	40159†
	40160*
Ragland	42053
Railton	42171
Randolph	42129
Ransom	41531
Rapids	42134
Raven‡	41861
Ravenna	40472
Raymond	40176
Raywick	40060
Ready	42721
Rectorville	41056
Redbud	40828
Redbush	41219
Red Cross	42160
Redfox	41847
Red Hill, *Allen*	42164
Red Hill, *Daviess*	42376
Redhouse	40475
Red Lick	42129
Red River	42202
Redwine	41477
Reed	42451
Reeds Crossing	40475
Reedville	41143
Reedyville	42275
Regina	41559
Region	42275
Reidland	42003
Reid Village	40353
Relief	41472
Rella	40902
Renaker	41003
Render	42320
Renfro Valley	40473
Renfrow	42349
Repton	42064
Revelo	42638
Rex	42746
Rexville	41332
Reynolds Station	42368
Reynoldsville	40374
Rhea	40806
Rheber	42528
Rhoda	42210
Rhodelia	40161
Ribolt	41189
Rice Station	40336
Ricetown	41364
Riceville (Part of Fulton)	42041
Riceville, *Johnson*	41240
Richardson	41230
Richardsville	42270
Richelieu	42206
Richland	42431
Richlawn	40207
Richmond	40475*
	40476†
Richmond Mall (Part of Richmond)	40475
Rich Pond	42104
Richwood	41094
Ridgeview Estates (Part of Frankfort)	40601
Ridgeview Heights (Part of Independence)	41051
Ridgeway	40849
Riley	40328
Rileyville	40927
Rineyville	40162
Ringgold	42503
Ringos Mills	41049
Rio Vista (Part of Loyall)	40854
Risner	41649
Ritchie	41701
Ritner	42633
Rivals	40071
River	41254
River Bluff	40059
Riverfront (Part of Louisville)‡	40270
River Oaks	42765
River Park (Part of Lexington)	40502
River Ridge	40828
Riverside	42270
Riverside Gardens	40216
Riverview	42003
Riverview Estates (Part of Harrodsburg)	40330
Riverwood	40207
Road Junction	41522
Roaring Spring	42211
Roark	40979
Robards	42452
Robinson	41031
Robinson Creek	41560
Robinsville	40475
Robinswood	40207
Robinwood Estates (Part of Lexington)	40503
Rob Roy	42320
Rochester	42273
Rockbridge	42167
Rockcastle	42211
Rockdale, *Boyd*	41102
Rockdale, *Owen*	40359
Rockfield	42274
Rock Haven	40175
Rockholds	40759
Rockhouse	41561
Rockland	42101
Rockport	42369
Rock Springs	42406
Rockybranch	42633
Rocky Hill, *Barren*	42141
Rocky Hill, *Edmonson*	42163
Rodburn	40351
Roff	40178
Rogers	41365
Rogers Chapel	40380
Rogers Gap	40324
Rolling Acres (Part of Frankfort)	40601
Rolling Fields	40207
Rolling Hills	40222
Rollington (Part of Pewee Valley)	40056
Rome	42301
Romine	42718
Rookwood (Part of Lexington)	40505
Roscoe	41171
Rose Crossroads	42629
Rosefork	41301
Rose Hill, *Carter*	41164
Rose Hill, *Mercer*	40330
Rose Terrace	40121
Rosetta	40146
Roseville, *Barren*	42141
Roseville, *Hancock*	42368
Rosewood	42345
Rosine	42370
Ross	41059
Rossland	40734
Rosslyn	40380
Rosspoint	40806
Rothwell	40322
Roundhill, *Edmonson*	42275
Round Hill, *Madison*	40475
Roundstone	40456
Rouse (Part of Covington)‡	41014
Rousseau	41366
Routt	40299
Rowdy	41367
Rowena	42629
Rowland	40484
Rowletts	42765
Roxana	41848
Royalton	41464
Royrader	40402
Royville	42642
Ruckerville	40391

- Ruddels Mills 40361
- Ruin 41171
- Rumsey 42371
- Rural 41514
- Rush 41168
- Russell 41169
- Russell Heights (Part of Russell) 41169
- Russell Springs 42642
- Russellville 42276
- Ruth 42501
- Rutherford 40927
- Rutland 41031
- Ryan 41093
- Ryland 41015
- Ryland Heights 41015
- Sacramento 42372
- Sadieville 40370
- Sadler 42754
- St. Catharine 40061
- St. Charles 42453
- St. Dennis 40216
- St. Elmo 42266
- St. Francis 40062
- St. Helens 41368
- St. John 42701
- St. Johns 42001
- St. Joseph, *Daviess* 42301
- St. Joseph, *Marion* 40060
- St. Mary 40063
- St. Matthews 40206-07, 40222, 40257

  For specific ZIP Codes call (888) 275-8777, or your local postmaster.
- St. Paul, *Grayson* 42754
- St. Paul, *Lewis* 41170
- St. Regis Park 40220
- St. Vincent 42437
- Saldee 41339
- Salem, *Livingston* 42078
- Salem, *Russell* 42642
- Salleeton 40033
- Salmons 42134
- Saloma 42718
- Salt Gum 40935
- Salt Lick 40371
- Salt River (Part of Shepherdsville) 40165
- Salt Well 40311
- Salvisa 40372
- Salyersville 41465
- Sample 40143
- Samuels 40013
- Sandefur Crossing 42320
- Sanders 41083
- Sandgap 40481
- Sand Hill, *Estill* 40336
- Sand Hill (Part of Cumberland) 40823
- Sand Hill, *Warren* 42101
- Sand Springs, *Jackson* 40447
- Sand Springs, *Rockcastle* 40456
- Sandy 42325
- Sandy Hook 41171
- Sano 42728
- Sarah 41171
- Saratoga 42445
- Sardis 41056
- Sassafras 41759
- Sassafras Ridge 42050
- Sasser 40744
- Saul 40981
- Savage 42602
- Savage Branch 41129
- Savoy 40769
- Savoyard 42749
- Sawyer 42634
- Saxton 40769
- Saylor 40840
- Scale 42025
- Scalf 40982
- Schley 42202
- Schochoh 42202
- Schultztown 42320
- Schweizer 42134
- Science Hill 42553
- Scottown 42320
- Scottsburg 42445
- Scotts Station 40065
- Scottsville 42164
- Scoville 41314
- Scranton 40322
- Scuddy 41760
- Seatonville 40299
- Seaville 40078
- Sebastians Branch 41314
- Sebree 42455
- Seco 41849
- Sedalia 42079
- Segal 42210
- Seitz 41465
- Select 42333
- Seminary 42602
- Seminary Village (Part of Louisville) 40207
- Semiway 42371
- Seneca Gardens 40205
- Senterville 41522
- Se Ree 40164
- Sergent 41858
- Settle 42164
- Settlers Point 40059
- Seventy Six 42602
- Sewell 41385
- Sewellton 42629
- Sextons Creek 40983
- Seymour 42749
- Shadeland (Part of Lexington) 40502
- Shady Grove, *Crittenden* 42064
- Shady Grove, *McCracken* 42003
- Shady Grove, *Metcalfe* 42214
- Shady Nook 41031
- Shafter 42501
- Sha Lawn Village 42718
- Shannon 41055
- Sharer 42235
- Sharkey 40351
- Sharon 41002
- Sharondale 41514
- Sharon Grove 42280
- Sharpe 42025
- Sharpsburg 40374
- Sharpsville 40330
- Shawhan 40361
- Shawnee (Part of Louisville) 40212
- Shawnee Estates (Part of Bowling Green) 42104
- Shearer Valley 42633
- Shelbiana 41562
- Shelby (Part of Louisville)‡ 40217
- Shelby City (Part of Junction City) 40422
- Shelby Gap 41563
- Shelbyville 40065*, 40066†
- Shepherdsville 40165
- Shepola 42544
- Sherburne 41041
- Sheridan 42064
- Sherman 41035
- Sherwood Shores 42044
- Shetland 40383
- Shields 40849
- Shiloh 42071
- Shipley 42602
- Shively 40216*, 40256†
- Shopville 42501
- Shore Acres 40601
- Short Creek 42721
- Short Town 40828
- Shoulderblade 41339
- Shreve 42343
- Shrewsbury 42721
- Sibert 40962
- Sidell 40962
- Sideview 40353
- Sideway 41164
- Sidney 41564
- Siler, *Knox* 40701
- Siler, *Whitley* 40763
- Silerville 42649
- Silica 41164
- Siloam 41175
- Silver City 42261
- Silver Creek 40403
- Silver Grove 41085
- Silverhill 41472
- Silver Lake Farm (Part of Frankfort) 40601
- Simmons 42354
- Simpson 41301
- Simpsonville 40067
- Sims Fork 40902
- Sinai 40342
- Sinking Fork 42240
- Sirocco 40108
- Sitka 41255
- Sizerock 41762
- Skillman 42348
- Skinnersburg 40379
- Skycrest (Part of Lexington) 40504
- Skylight 40026
- Skyline 41821
- Slade 40376
- Slat 42633
- Slate Lick 40403
- Slater 42087
- Slate Valley 40360
- Slaughters 42456
- Slavans 42653
- Slemp 41763
- Slickford 42633
- Slick Rock 42141
- Sligo 40055
- Sloans Valley 42555
- Smilax 41764
- Smile 40351
- Smith 40815
- Smithfield 40068
- Smithland 42081
- Smith Mills 42457
- Smiths Creek 41164
- Smiths Grove 42171
- Smith Town 42647
- Smithview 42721
- Smithwood 42076
- Smoky Valley 41164
- Smyrna 40219
- Snell 42501
- Snow 42602
- Snow Hill 40065
- Soft Shell 41831
- Soldier 41173
- Somerset 42501-03, 42564

  For specific ZIP Codes call (888) 275-8777, or your local postmaster.
- Sonora 42776
- Sorgho 42301
- South 42754
- South Buffalo 42716
- South Campbellsville (Part of Campbellsville) 42718
- South Carrollton 42374
- Southdown 41815
- South Elkhorn (Part of Lexington) 40503
- Southern Hills (Part of Richmond) 40475
- South Fork, *Lincoln* 40437
- Southfork, *Owsley* 41314
- Southgate 41071
- South Higginsport 41002
- South Highlands 42066
- South Hill 42261
- South Irvine 40336
- Southland (Part of Lexington) 40503
- South Marshall 42025
- South Park 40118
- South Park View 40219
- Southport (Part of Lexington) 40503
- South Portsmouth 41174
- South Ripley 41034
- South Shore 41175
- South Shores 40065
- South Union 42283
- Southville 40065
- South Wallins♦ 40873
- South Williamson 41503
- Southwire 42348
- Spa 42256
- Spann 42633
- Sparksville 42728
- Sparta 41086
- Spears 40502
- Speck 42728
- Speedwell 40475
- Speight 41572
- Spence (Part of Newport)‡ 41071
- Spencer 40353
- Spider 41843
- Spindletop 40324
- Spiro 40456
- Spottsville 42458
- Spring Creek 40962
- Springfield 40069
- Spring Grove 42437
- Springhill, *Hickman* 42031
- Springhill, *Nelson* 40004
- Springhill (Part of Bowling Green) 42101
- Spring Hill Estates 40601
- Springlake 41015
- Springlee 40207
- Spring Lick 42721
- Spring Mill 40228
- Spring Station 40347
- Spring Valley 40222
- Sprout 40350
- Spruce Pine 40874
- Sprule 40906
- Spurlington 42718
- Spurlock 40972
- Squib 42501
- Squiresville 40359
- Stab 42501
- Stacy Fork 41472
- Staffordsburg 41051
- Staffordsville 41256
- Stambaugh 41257
- Stamping Ground 40379
- Stanfill 40831
- Stanford 40484
- Stanley 42375
- Stanton 40380
- Stanville 41659
- Stark 41164
- Star Mills 42740
- Stateland (Part of Richmond) 40475
- State Line 42050
- Static 42602
- Station Camp 40336
- Station No. 1 (Part of Tompkinsville)‡ 42167
- Stay 41364
- Stearns 42647
- Steele 41566
- Steff 42721
- Stella, *Calloway* 42071
- Stella, *Magoffin* 41465
- Stephens 41171
- Stephensburg 42724
- Stephensport 40170
- Stepstone 40360
- Steubenville 42633
- Stewart 40330
- Stewartsville 41097
- Stiles 40051
- Stillwater 41301
- Stinnett 40868
- Stinnettsville 40146
- Stinson 41143
- Stockholm 42259
- Stone 41567
- Stonegate 40383
- Stone Hedge Estates 40324
- Stonestreet 40272
- Stonewall, *Bracken* 41004
- Stonewall, *Scott* 40370
- Stonewall Estates (Part of Lexington) 40503
- Stonewall Estates, *Franklin* 40601
- Stoney Fork 40988
- Stoney Point 41034
- Stony Fork Junction (Part of Middlesboro) 40965
- Stony Point 40361
- Stop 42633
- Stopover 41568
- Stormking 41701
- Stovall 42160
- Straight Creek 40977
- Strait Creek 41132
- Strathmoor Gardens (Part of Strathmoor Village) 40205
- Strathmoor Manor 40205
- Strathmoor Village 40205
- Straw 42259
- Strawberry 42501
- Stricklett 41179
- Stringtown, *Anderson* 40342
- Stringtown, *Boone* 41048
- Stringtown, *Fleming* 41049
- Stringtown, *Grant* 41003
- Stringtown, *Lawrence* 41230
- Stringtown, *McLean* 42372
- Stringtown, *Madison* 40475
- Stringtown, *Magoffin* 41465
- Stringtown, *Mercer* 40330
- Stringtown, *Muhlenberg* 42372
- Strunk 42649
- Stubblefield 42088
- Sturgeon 41314
- Sturgis 42459
- Sublett 41465
- Sublimity City 40744
- Subtle 42129
- Sudith 40371
- Sugar Creek 41095
- Sugar Grove 42261
- Sugar Hill 42501
- Sugartit 41042
- Sullivan 42460
- Sulphur 40070
- Sulphur Lick 42166
- Sulphur Springs 42347
- Sulphur Well, *Jessamine* 40356
- Sulphur Well, *Metcalfe* 42129
- Summer Shade 42166
- Summersville 42782
- Summit, Boyd 41102
- Summit, Hardin 42783
- Summit Hills Heights (Part of Edgewood) 41017
- Sumpter 42633
- Sunfish 42210
- Sunny Acres (Part of Taylor Mill) 41015
- Sunnybrook 42633
- Sunny Corner 42348
- Sunnydale 42347
- Sunnyside 42101
- Sunrise 41031
- Sunset 41049
- Sunshine, *Greenup* 41175
- Sunshine, *Harlan* 40831
- Susie 42633
- Sussex Estates 40356
- Suterville 40379
- Sutherland 42376
- Sutton 41562
- Suwanee 42055
- Swallowfield 40601
- Swamp Branch 41240
- Swampton 41465
- Swanee Shores 41097
- Swan Lake 40906
- Swanpond 40906
- Sweeden 42285
- Sweeneyville 42718
- Sweet Owen 40359
- Switzer 40601
- Sycamore 40223
- Sycamore Estates 40383
- Sylvandell 41031
- Sylvania 40258
- Symbol 40729
- Symsonia 42082
- Tabernacle 42220
- Tablow 40330
- Tacky Town 40988
- Taffy 42347
- Taft 41314
- Talbert 41377
- Talcum 41722
- Tallega 41311
- Talmage 40330
- Tanbark 42717
- Tanglewood (Part of Frankfort) 40601
- Tanksley 40962
- Tanner 42748
- Tar Fork 40111
- Tar Hill 42754
- Tarryon No 1 42055
- Tates Creek Estates 40356
- Tateville 42558
- Tatham Springs 40078
- Tattersail Trails Estates 40701
- Tatumsville 42044
- Taulbee 41385
- Taylor Mill 41015
- Taylor Mines 42320
- Taylorsport 41048
- Taylors Store 42049
- Taylorsville 40071
- Teaberry 41660
- Tedders 40906
- Teddy 42539
- Teetersville 40831
- Teges 40972
- Temperance 42134
- Temple Hill 42141
- Ten Broeck 40222
- Ten Spot 40828
- Teresita 40359
- Terrapin 40330
- Terryville 41159
- Texas 40069
- Texola 40336
- Thealka 41240
- The Colony (Part of Lexington) 40504
- The Colony, *Woodford* 40383
- Thelma 41260
- The Moors 42044
- The Ridge 41171
- Thistleton Heights (Part of Frankfort) 40601
- Thixton 40291
- Thomas 41653
- Thompsonville 40069
- Thorn Hill (Part of Frankfort) 40601
- Thornhill, *Jefferson* 40222
- Thornton 41855
- Thorobred East Subdivision No. 2 42301

*** Area Zip Code** **† Post Office Boxes** **‡ Postal Station** **♦ Census Designated Place** *Italic Type* **County**

Thousandsticks 41766
Threeforks, *Martin* 41224
Three Forks, *Warren* 42159
Threelinks 40456
Three Mile 41144
Three Point 40815
Three Springs, *Hart* 42746
Three Springs, *Warren* 42104
Thruston 42301
Thurlow 42743
Tierra Linda (Part of Frankfort) 40601
Tierra Linda III (Part of Frankfort) 40601
Tilden 42409
Tilford 42721
Tiline 42083
Tilton 41041
Timber Lake 42518
Timberwood Lake Shores 41010
Tina 41740
Tinsley 40977
Tiny Town 42234
Tiptop 41465
Todds Point 40065
Toddville 40444
Toler 41569
Toliver 41332
Tollesboro 41189
Tolliver Town 41810
Tolu 42084
Tomahawk 41262
Tompkinsville 42167
Tonieville 42748
Toonerville 41548
Topmost 41862
Topton 40741
Torrent 41301
Totz 40870
Toulouse 41723
Touristville 42633
Tousey 40119
Town and Country, *Daviess* 42301
Town and Country, *Logan* 42276
Towne Mall (Part of Elizabethtown) 42701
Towne Square Mall (Part of Owensboro) 42301
Tracy 42133
Trailwood Lakes 40003
Tram 41663
Trammel 42164
Trapp 40391
Trappist 40051
Travellers Rest 41314
Treasure Island 40229
Tremont 40873
Trent 41301
Trenton 42286
Tress Shop 42220
Tribbey 41722
Tribune 42064
Tri City 42040
Trigg Furnace 42211
Trimble 42544
Trinity 41179
Trisler 42343
Trosper 40995
Troublesome 41712
Troy 40383
Tuckertown 42159
Tuggleville 40845
Tunnel Hill 42701
Turfland Mall (Part of Lexington) 40504
Turkey 41314
Turkey Creek 41514
Turkey Foot 40370
Turkeytown 40419
Turners Station 40075
Turnersville 40484
Turnertown, *Butler* 42256
Turnertown, *Simpson* 42134
Tutor Key 41263
Tuttle 40744
Tway (Part of Harlan) 40831
Twentysix 41472
Twila 40873
Twin Lakes 41091
Twin Oaks (Part of Lexington) 40503
Two Creeks 40601
Tyewhoppety 42216

Tyner 40486
Typo 41701
Tyrone 40342
Ula 42501
Ulvah 41731
Ulysses 41264
Union 41091
Union City 40475
Union Hall 40472
Union Mills 40356
Union Ridge 42365
Union Star 40171
Uniontown 42461
University Estates 42701
University Heights (Part of Hopkinsville) 42240
Uno 42749
Upchurch 42602
Upper Kings Addition 41175
Upper Tygart 41164
Upton 42784
Urban 40962
Utica 42376
Utility 42348
Uttingertown (Part of Lexington) 40516
Vada 41311
Valeria 41301
Valley Downs 40272
Valley Gardens 40258
Valley Hill 40069
Valley Oak 42501
Valley Station 40258
…… 40272
For specific ZIP Codes call (888) 275-8777, or your local postmaster.
Valley View, *Bracken* 41002
Valley View, *Madison* 40475
Valley Village 40272
Van 41858
Vanarsdell 40330
Vanceburg 41179
Vancleve 41385
Vanderburg 42409
Vandetta 42413
Vanhook 42501
Van Lear 41265
Van Voorhis Manor 40121
Vanzant 40119
Varilla 40813
Varney 41571
Vooch 40022
Venters 41522
Verda 40828
Verna Hills 40391
Verne 40769
Vernon 42151
Verona 41092
Versailles 40383
Vertrees 42724
Vest 41772
Vester 42728
Vicco 41773
Victory 40729
Village Center (Part of Harlan) 40831
Villa Hills 41017
Vincent 41386
Vine Grove 40175
Vineyard 40356
Viola 42051
Viper 41774
Virden 40312
Virgie 41572
Visalia 41015
Volga 41219
Vortex 41301
Wabaco 41701
Wabash 42713
Wabd 40456
Waco 40385
Waddy 40076
Wadesboro 42048
Wagersville 40336
Wago 42602
Wait 42603
Wakefield 40071
Walden 40701
Waldo 41632
Wales 41572
Walker 40997
Walkertown (Part of Hazard) 41701
Wallaceton 40461
Wallingford 41093

Wallins Creek 40873
Wallonia 42211
Walltown 40489
Walnut Grove, *Allen* 42120
Walnut Grove, *Caldwell* 42411
Walnut Grove, *Marshall* 42025
Walnut Grove, *Pulaski* 42501
Walsh 41175
Waltersville 40312
Walton 41094
Waltz 40351
Wanamaker 42455
Waneta 40488
Warbranch 40874
Warco 41645
War Creek 41339
Warfield 41267
Warnock 41144
Warren 40906
Warsaw 41095
Washington (Part of Maysville) 41096
Wasioto 40977
Watauga 42602
Watch 40701
Waterford 40071
Watergap 41653
Waterloo 41005
Water Valley 42085
Waterview 42786
Watkinsville 40379
Watterson Park 40213
…… 40218
For specific ZIP Codes call (888) 275-8777, or your local postmaster.
Watts 41348
Waverly 42462
Waverly Hills 40272
Wax 42726
Wayland 41666
Waynesburg 40489
Weaverton (Part of Henderson) 42420
Webbs 42743
Webbs Cross Roads 42642
Webbville 41180
Weberstown 42364
Webster 40176
Wedonia 41055
Weeksbury 41667
Weir 42345
Welborn 42501
Welchs Creek 42287
Welcome 42261
Weldon 40108
Wellhope 40456
Wellington, *Jefferson* 40205
Wellington, *Menifee* 40387
Wellington Place (Part of Bardstown) 40004
Wells 42330
Wellsburg 41043
Wells Landing 40422
Wendover 41775
Wentz 41731
Wesco 42431
Wesleyan Park (Part of Winchester) 40391
Wesleyville 41164
Westbend 40312
West Brook 42240
West Buechel 40218
West Clifty 42754
West Danville (Part of Danville) 40422
Western 42050
West Fairview 41101
West Future City 42053
West Garrett 41630
Westgate (Part of Frankfort) 40601
West Irvine 40336
West Liberty 41472
West Louisville 42377
Weston 40311
West Paducah 42086
Westplains 42051
West Point 40177
Westport 40077
West Prestonsburg (Part of Prestonsburg) 41668

West Russell (Part of Flatwoods) 41169
Westside Station (Part of Frankfort)‡ 40604
West Somerset (Part of Somerset)‡ 42564
West Van Lear 41268
Westview 40178
Westwood, *Boyd*♦ 41101
Westwood, *Jefferson* 40222
Westwood Park (Part of Frankfort) 40601
Wheatcroft 42463
Wheatley 40359
Wheel 42061
Wheeler 40906
Wheelersburg 41465
Wheelwright 41669
Whick 41390
Whipps Millgate 40223
Whitaker, *Floyd* 41216
Whitaker, *Letcher* 41849
Whitco 41858
White City, *Hopkins* 42464
White City, *Larue* 42748
White Hall 40475
Whitehouse 41240
White Lily 42501
White Mills 42788
White Oak, *Garrard* 40444
White Oak, *Morgan* 41472
White Oak Junction 42647
White Plains (Part of Scottsville) 42164
White Plains, *Hopkins* 42464
Whitepost 41514
White Run 42349
Whitesburg 41858
White Sulphur, *Caldwell* 42411
White Sulphur, *Scott* 40324
Whitesville 42378
White Tower 41051
White Villa 41063
Whitewood 42743
Whitfield 40047
Whitley City♦ 42653
Wiborg 42653
Wickliffe 42087
Wicks Well 42431
Widecreek 41311
Wilbur 41124
Wild Cat 40962
Wilder 41071
…… 41076
For specific ZIP Codes call (888) 275-8777, or your local postmaster.
Wilderness Road 42259
Wildie 40492
Wildwood 40223
Wilhurst 41385
Willailla 40409
Willard 41181
Williams 41472
Williamsburg 40769
Williamsport 41271
Williamstown 41097
Willisburg 40078
Willow, *Bracken* 41004
Willow, *Lee* 41311
Willowcrest 40601
Willow Grove 41043
Willow Shade 42166
Willowtown 42718
Willow Tree 40472
Wilmore 40390
Wilson 42406
Wilsonville, *Boyle* 40422
Wilsonville, *Spencer* 40023
Wilstacy 41339
Wilton 40771
Winburn Estates (Part of Lexington) 40511
Winchester 40391*
…… 40392†
Wind Cave 40447
Winding Falls 40207
Windsor 42565
Windy 42633
Windy Hill 42349
Windy Hills 40207
Windyville 42210
Wingo 42088
Winifred 41219
Winlow Park 42064

Winston 40495
Winston Park (Part of Taylor Mill) 41015
Winwright 41501
Wiscoal 41759
Wisconsin 41759
Wisdom 42129
Wisemantown 40336
Wises Landing 40006
Wiswell 42071
Wittensville 41274
Witt Springs 40336
Wofford 40769
Wolf 41164
Wolf Coal 41339
Wolf Creek 40104
Wolfpit 41522
Wolverine 41339
Wonder 41653
Wonnie 41465
Woodbine 40771
Woodburn 42170
Woodbury 42288
Woodford Village (Part of Versailles) 40383
Woodlake 40601
Woodland Estates 41240
Woodland Hills 40243
Woodland Park (Part of Hazard) 41701
Woodlands (Part of Frankfort) 40601
Woodlawn, *Campbell* 41071
Woodlawn, *McCracken* 42003
Woodlawn, *Nelson* 40004
Woodlawn Park, Anderson 40342
Woodlawn Park, Jefferson 40207
Woodman 41568
Woods 41653
Woodsbend 41472
Woodson Bend 42518
Woodsonville 42765
Woodstock 42501
Woodville 42086
Wooleyville 42718
Woollum 40999
Wooton 41776
Worthington 41183
Worthington Hills 40223
Worthville 41098
Wray Gap 42633
Wrights 42718
Wrightsburg 42327
Wrigley 41477
Wurtland 41144
Wyett 41171
Wyman 42327
Yaden 40769
Yancey 40831
Yatesville 41230
Yeaddiss 41777
Yeager 41501
Yeaman 42361
Yellow Rock 41311
Yelvington 42355
Yerkes 41778
Yesse 42164
Yocum 41472
York 41175
Yosemite 42566
Younger Creek 42701
Youngs Creek 40701
Yuma 42733
Zachariah 41301
Zag 41472
Zandale (Part of Lexington) 40503
Zebulon 41501
Zelda 41129
Zion, *Henderson* 42420
Zion, *Todd* 42234
Zion Hill 40347
Zion Station 41035
Zoe 41397
Zoneton (Part of Pioneer Village) 40165
Zula 42603

*** Area Zip Code** **† Post Office Boxes** **‡ Postal Station** **♦ Census Designated Place** *Italic Type* **County**

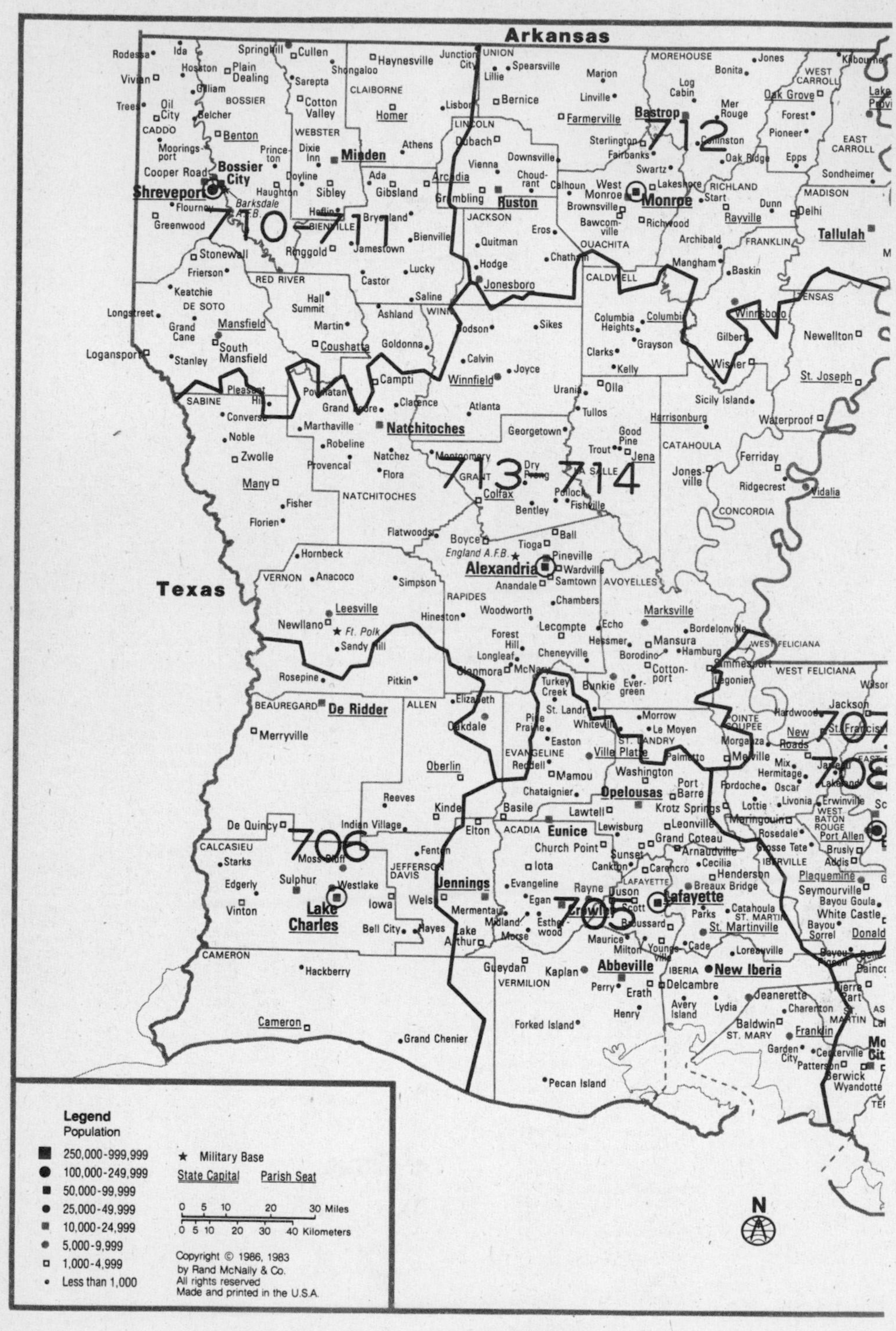
Arkansas
Texas
710-711
712
713-714
706
705
Shreveport
Bossier City
Barksdale A.F.B.
Minden
Ruston
Monroe
West Monroe
Bastrop
Farmerville
Homer
Tallulah
Rayville
Oak Grove
Delhi
Winnsboro
Jonesboro
Columbia
St. Joseph
Harrisonburg
Jena
Winnfield
Natchitoches
Mansfield
Coushatta
Many
Colfax
Alexandria
Pineville
England A.F.B.
Marksville
Vidalia
Leesville
Ft. Polk
De Ridder
Oberlin
Ville Platte
Opelousas
Eunice
New Roads
Port Allen
Jennings
Lake Charles
Crowley
Lafayette
St. Martinville
Abbeville
New Iberia
Franklin
Cameron
Plaquemine
Donald
Elton
Kinder
Oakdale
Sulphur
Westlake
Vinton
Moss Bluff
De Quincy
Hackberry
Grand Chenier
Forked Island
Pecan Island
Kaplan
Gueydan
Erath
Delcambre
Jeanerette
Morgan City
Patterson
Berwick
Breaux Bridge
Henderson
Cecilia
Arnaudville
Grand Coteau
Sunset
Carencro
Scott
Broussard
Youngsville
Maurice
Milton
Rayne
Duson
Iota
Church Point
Mamou
Basile
Washington
Port Barre
Melville
Krotz Springs
Leonville
Bunkie
Cottonport
Mansura
Simmesport
Jackson
St. Francisville
Ferriday
Jonesville
Newellton
Waterproof
Lake Providence
Jones
Bonita
Mer Rouge
Collinston
Oak Ridge
Epps
Sondheimer
Start
Dunn
Mangham
Baskin
Archibald
Richwood
Calhoun
Choudrant
Downsville
Dubach
Vienna
Grambling
Arcadia
Gibsland
Athens
Haynesville
Junction City
Spearsville
Bernice
Lillie
Marion
Linville
Sterlington
Swartz
Springhill
Cullen
Sarepta
Shongaloo
Cotton Valley
Plain Dealing
Hosston
Ida
Rodessa
Vivian
Oil City
Belcher
Benton
Haughton
Doyline
Sibley
Heflin
Ringgold
Bienville
Castor
Saline
Hall Summit
Stonewall
Keatchie
Logansport
Converse
Zwolle
Florien
Fisher
Provencal
Robeline
Campti
Clarence
Goldonna
Sikes
Calvin
Joyce
Olla
Tullos
Urania
Georgetown
Pollock
Ball
Tioga
Boyce
Flatwoods
Hornbeck
Anacoco
Simpson
Woodworth
Lecompte
Forest Hill
Glenmora
McNary
Pitkin
Rosepine
Merryville
Reeves
Iowa
Welsh
Lake Arthur
Mermentau
Egan
Estherwood
Morse
Legend
Population
250,000-999,999
100,000-249,999
50,000-99,999
25,000-49,999
10,000-24,999
5,000-9,999
1,000-4,999
Less than 1,000
★ Military Base
State Capital
Parish Seat
0 5 10 20 30 Miles
0 5 10 20 30 40 Kilometers
Copyright © 1986, 1983
by Rand McNally & Co.
All rights reserved
Made and printed in the U.S.A.
N

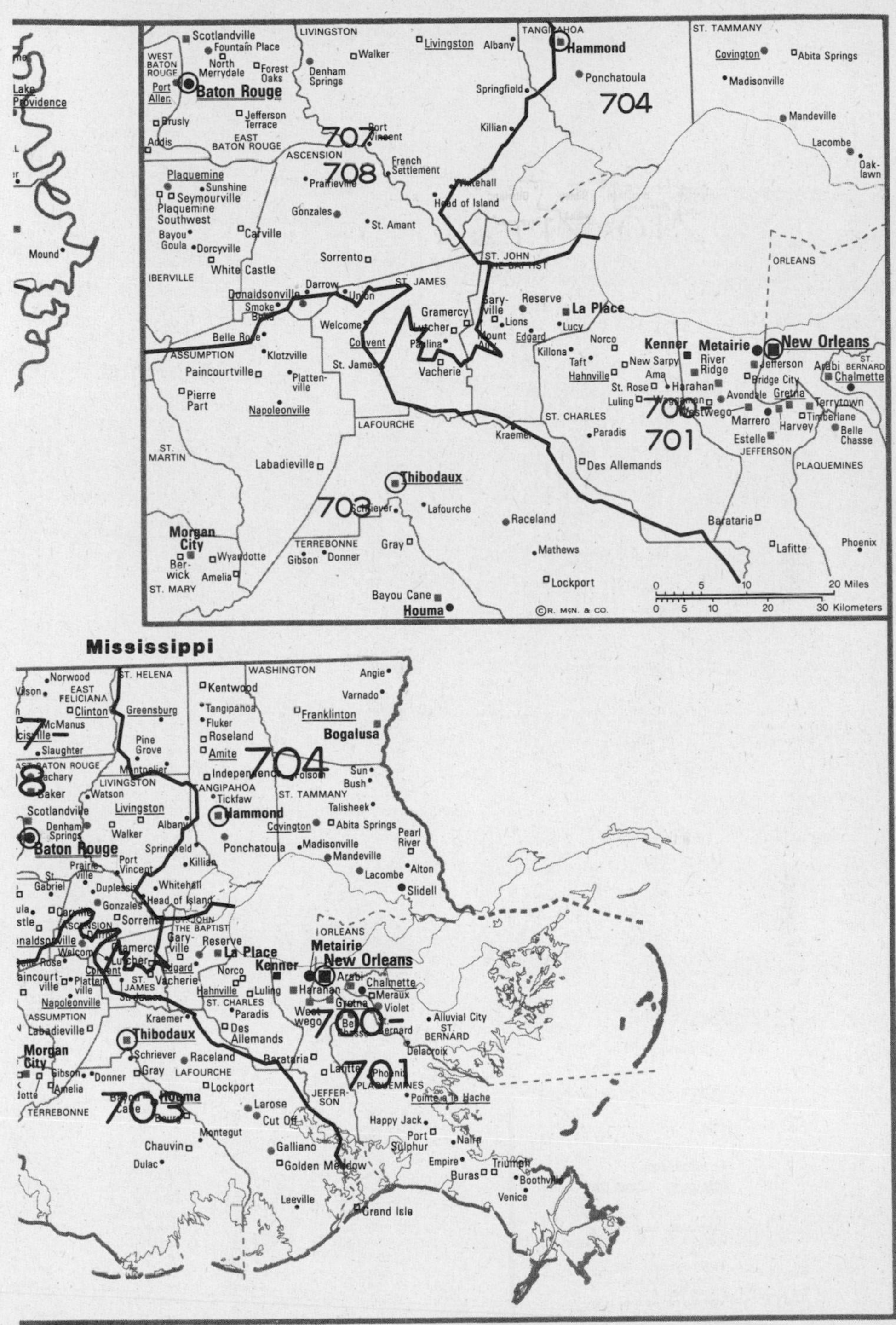

Mississippi
Baton Rouge
Hammond
Ponchatoula
Thibodaux
Houma
New Orleans
Metairie
Kenner
La Place
Morgan City
Bogalusa
Slidell
704
707
708
703
700-
701
©R. McN. & CO.
20 Miles
30 Kilometers

A (Part of Metairie)‡ 70055
Abbeville 70510*
70511†
Abby Plantation 70301
Aben 70346
Abington 71052
Abita Springs 70420
Acadia 70301
Acadia Academy 70535
Acme 71316
Acy 70774
Ada 71080
Addis 70710
Adeline 70544
Adner 71037
Advance (Part of Hodge) 71247
Afton 71282
Aimwell 71401
Airline Park 70003
Airview Terrace (Part of Alexandria) 71301
Ajax 71450
Akers 70421
Albania 70544
Albany 70711
Alberta 71016
Alco 71446
Alden Bridge 71006
Alexandria 71301-15
For specific ZIP Codes call (888) 275-8777, or your local postmaster.
Alexandria Mall (Part of Alexandria) 71301
Alfalfa 71409
Alfords 70720
Algiers (Part of New Orleans) 70114
Alice B 70538
Alice C 70538
Allemand 70360
Allen 71469
Allendale 70767
Alliance 70037
Allon 70760
Alluvial City 70085
Aloha 71417
Aloysia 70788
Alsen 70807
Alto 71269
Alton 70458
Alvin Callender 70037
Ama 70031
Amelia♦ 70340
Amite 70422
Anacoco 71403
Anandale 71301
Andrew 70548
Andrew Guillot Subdivision 70301
Angelina 70076
Angie 70426
Annadale 70788
Ansley 71270
Antioch, *Claiborne* 71040
Antioch, *Lincoln* 71275
Antonia 71467
Antonio 70767
Antrim 71064
Arabi♦ 70032
Ararat 70601
Arbroth 70720
Arcadia 71001
Archibald 71218
Archie 71343
Arcola 70456
Ardoyne 70360
Argo 71343
Argyle 70360
Arizona 71040
Arklatex (Part of Mooringsport) 71060
Arlington 70808
Armistead 71019
Arnaudville 70512
Ashland, *Natchitoches* 71002
Ashland, *Terrebonne* 70360
Ashley 71282
Ashton 70538
Athens 71003
Atlanta 71404
Attakapas Landing 70390
Audubon (Part of Baton Rouge)‡ 70806
Audubon Terrace 70808
Augusta, *Iberville* 70788
Augusta, *Plaquemines* 70037
Avalon 70392
Avandale 71366
Avery Island 70513
Avondale♦ 70094
Aycock 71001
Azucena 71375
Bagdad 71417
Bains 70775
Baker 70704†
70714*
Baldwin 70514
Ball 71405
Bancroft 70653
Bankers 70582
Banks 70807
Banks Springs 71418
Baptist 70403
Barataria♦ 70036
Barber Spur 70586
Bardel 71269
Barnet Springs (Part of Ruston) 71270
Barron 71328
Barton 70346
Basile 70515
Baskin 71219
Baskinton 71219
Bastrop 71220*
71221†
Batchelor 70715
Baton Rouge 70801-98
For specific ZIP Codes call (888) 275-8777, or your local postmaster.
Batree 70090
Bawcomville 71292
Bayou Barbary 70754
Bayou Blue 70360
Bayou Cane♦ 70359
Bayou Chicot 70586
Bayou Crab 70390
Bayou Current 71353
Bayou Gauche 70030
Bayou Goula 70716
Bayou Pigeon 70764
Bayou Sale 70538
Bayou Sorrel 70764
Baywood 70739
Beach Grove 71277
Beachview (Part of Kenner) 70062
Bear Creek 71008
Bear Skin 71266
Beaver 71463
Bee Bayou 71269
Beech Springs 71247
Beekman 71220
Beggs 71322
Bel 70658
Belah 71371
Belair 70040
Belair Cove 70586
Belcher 71004
Bell City 70630
Belle Amie 70345
Belle Chasse♦ 70037
Belledeau 71341
Belle Place 70552
Belle Point 70084
Belle River 70339
Belle Rose 70341
Belle Terre, *Assumption* 70346
Belle Terre, *Iberville* 70764
Belleview 70570
Bellevue, *Bossier* 71037
Bellevue, *Caldwell* 71418
Bellfontaine 70815
Bell Helene 70734
Bellwood 71468
Belmont, *Sabine* 71406
Belmont, *St. James* 70743
Belmont, *West Baton Rouge* 70767
Benson 71419
Bentley 71407
Benton 71006
Bermuda 71456
Bernice 71222
Bertie 70390
Bertrand (Part of Lafayette)‡ 70596
Bertrandville, *Assumption* 70390
Bertrandville, *Plaquemines* 70040
Berwick 70342
Bethany 71007
Bienville 71008
Big Bend 71355
Big Branch 70445
Big Cane 71356
Big Creek 71219
Big Island 71328
Big Woods 70668
Billeaud 70518
Bissonnet 70003
Bivens 70653
Blackburn 71038
Black Hawk 71373
Blade 71342
Blanchard 71009
Blanche 71433
Blanks 70717
Blankston 71202
Blond 70435
Bluff Creek 70722
Bob Acres 70560
Bodcau 71037
Bodoc 71329
Bogalusa 70427-29
For specific ZIP Codes call (888) 275-8777, or your local postmaster.
Bohemia 70082
Bolden 71358
Boleyn 71450
Bolinger 71064
Bolivar 70444
Bonaire 70808
Bond 71463
Bonfouca 70458
Bonita 71223
Bon Marche Mall (Part of Baton Rouge) 70806
Bon Secour 70086
Book 71343
Boone's Corner 70607
Boothville 70038
Bordelonville 71320
Borodino 71355
Bosco 71201
Boscoville 70570
Bossier City 71111-13
71171-72
For specific ZIP Codes call (888) 275-8777, or your local postmaster.
Boston 70533
Boudreaux Canal 70344
Bourg 70343
Boutte 70039
Boyce 71409
Braithwaite 70040
Branch 70516
Breard (Part of Monroe) 71203
Breaux Bridge 70517
Breezy Hill 71467
Brewton's Mill 71031
Bridge City 70094
Brignac 70737
Bristol 70584
Brittany 70718
Broadmoor (Part of New Orleans) 70125
Broadmoor, *Terrebonne* 70360
Broadview (Part of Baton Rouge)‡ 70815
Brooks 70760
Brouillette 71351
Broussard 70518
Brown 71016
Brownell 71295
Brownfields♦ 70811
Brown Heights 70714
Brownlee 71111
Brownville, *Caldwell* 71418
Brownville, *Ouachita* 71291
Brule 70372
Brule Guillot 70301
Bruly La Croix 70788
Bruly Saint Martin 70341
Brusle Saint Vincent 70390
Brusly 70719
Bryant (Part of New Iberia) 70560
Bryceland 71008
Buckeye 71328
Buckner 71269
Bueche 70720
Buhler 70663
Bull Run 70395
Bunkie 71322
Buras 70041
Burkplace 71016
Burr Ferry 71403
Burroughs 71418
Burrwood 70091
Burton Lane 70086
Bush 70431
Bushes 71295
Bywater (Part of New Orleans)‡ 70117
Caddo (Part of Oil City) 71061
Caddo Station 71082
Cade 70519
Cadeville 71238
Caernarvon 70040
Caffery 70538
Calcasieu, *Allen* 71433
Calcasieu, *Rapides* 71433
Calhoun 71225
Calumet 70392
Calvin 71410
Camelia Gardens (Part of Alexandria) 71301
Cameron♦ 70631
Camp Beauregard 71360
Camperdown 70538
Campti 71411
Cancienne 70390
Canebrake 71334
Caney 71446
Cankton 70584
Cannonburg 70788
Capitan 70592
Capitol (Part of Baton Rouge)‡ 70804
Caplis 71111
Carencro 70520
Carlisle 70042
Carlton 71225
Carlyss♦ 70665
Carmel 71052
Caroline 70552
Carrollton (Part of New Orleans)‡ 70118
Carrollton Central Plaza (Part of New Orleans) 70118
Carrolwood 70068
Carterville 71064
Carthage Bluff Landing 70462
Cartwright 71227
Carville (Part of St. Gabriel) 70721
Caspiana 71115
Castle Village 71301
Castor 71016
Catahoula 70582
Catherine 70716
Cat Island 71418
Catuna 71052
Cavett 71004
Cecile 71105
Cecilia♦ 70521
Cedar Crest 70816
Cedar Glen 70811
Cedar Grove, *Assumption* 70372
Cedar Grove (Part of Shreveport) 71106
Cedar Grove, *Plaquemines* 70037
Cedarton 71227
Centenary (Part of Shreveport)‡ 71104
Center Point 71323
Centerville, *Evangeline* 71367
Centerville, *St. Mary* 70522
Central, *East Baton Rouge* 70818
Central, *St. James* 70723
Central, *Terrebonne* 70360
Chacahoula 70395
Chackbay 70301
Chalmette♦ 70043*
70044†
Chalmette Vista 70043
Chamale Cove (Part of Slidell) 70460
Chamberlin 70767
Chambers 71346
Chandler Park (Part of Alexandria) 71301
Charenton♦ 70523
Charles Park (Part of Alexandria) 71301
Charlotte 70560
Chase 71324
Chataignier 70524
Chateau Village (Part of Kenner) 70065
Chatham 71226
Chatman Town 70090
Chauvin♦ 70344
Chef Menteur (Part of New Orleans)‡ 70126
Cheneyville 71325
Cheniere 71291
Cherokee Court 70123
Cherokee Village (Part of Alexandria) 71301
Cherry Grove 70655
Chesbrough 70444
Chestnut 71070
Chickama 71346
Chickasaw 71263
Chinchuba 70448
Chipola 70441
Chitimacha Indian Reservation 70523
Chloe 70647
Choctaw, *Iberville* 70767
Choctaw, *Lafourche* 70301
Chopin 71447
Choudrant 71227
Choupique, *Lafourche* 70301
Choupique, *St. Mary* 70538
Chula 70372
Church Point 70525
Church Spur 70390
Cinclare 70767
Cindy Park 70075
Claiborne, *Ouachita* 71291
Claiborne, *St. Tammany* 70433
Claibourne Gardens 70094
Clare 71429
Clarence 71414
Clarks 71415
Clay 71270
Clayton 71326
Clayton Junction (Part of Clayton) 71326
Clearview Shopping Center 70002
Clearwater 71325
Clifton, *Rapides* 71455
Clifton, *Washington* 70438
Clinton 70722
Clio 70449
Clotilda 70394
Cloutierville 71416
Clovelly Farms 70345
Cocodrie 70344
Cocoville 71350
Coker 71052
Coleman 71282
Colfax 71417
Colgrade 71483
College (Part of Hammond)‡ 70401
Collinsburg 71064
Collinston 71229
Colonial Heights 71109
Colquitt 71038
Columbia, *Caldwell* 71418
Columbia, *St. John the Baptist* 70049
Columbia Heights 71418
Commerce Park (Part of Baton Rouge)‡ 70810
Como 71295
Concession 70037
Concord 71263
Constance Beach 70631
Consuella 71375
Contreras 70085
Convent 70723
Converse 71419
Conway 71260
Coon 70715
Cooper Road 71107
Coopers 71446
Copenhagen 71418
Cora 71444
Corbin (Part of Walker) 70785
Corey 71202
Corinth 71235
Cornerview 70737
Cornor 39669
Cortana Mall (Part of Baton Rouge) 70815
Coteau Holmes 70582
Coteau Rodaire 70512
Cotton Plant 71435
Cottonport 71327
Cotton Valley 71018
Couchwood 71018
Coulon Plantation 70301
Country Club Subdivision 70301
Coushatta 71019
Covington 70433-35
For specific ZIP Codes call (888) 275-8777, or your local postmaster.

Covington Country Club Estates	70433
Cow Island	70510
Cravens	70656
Creedmoor	70085
Creole	70632
Crescent, *Iberville*	70764
Crescent, *Terrebonne*	70360
Creston	71070
Crew Lake	71269
Crews	71454
Crichton	71019
Cross-Road	71435
Crossroads, *Lincoln*	71235
Cross Roads, *Red River*	71019
Crowley	70526*
	70527†
Crown Point	70072
Crowville	71230
Crozier	70360
Cullen	71021
Curry	71483
Curtis	71112
Cut Off♦	70345
Cypremort	70538
Cypress, *Natchitoches*	71457
Cypress, *Ouachita*	71291
Cypress Gardens, *St. Bernard*	70075
Cypress Gardens, *Terrebonne*	70360
Cypress Island	70582
Daigleville (Part of Houma)	70360
Dalcour	70040
Danville	71008
D'Arbonne	71227
Darlington	70441
Darnell	71266
Darrow	70725
Daspit	70560
Davant	70046
Dean	71260
Dean Chapel	71291
De Broeck Landing	71106
Deerford	70791
Deer Park	71373
Dehlco	71269
Delacroix, *St. Bernard*	70085
Delacroix, *St. Martin*	70582
Del Bueno Park	70075
Delcambre	70528
Delhi	71232
Delta	71233
Delta Farms	70374
Denham Springs	70726*
	70727†
Dennis Mills	70726
Denson	70449
Dent Terrace	70808
DeQuincy	70633
DeRidder	70634
Derry	71416
Des Allemands♦	70030
De Selle	71301
Dess	71429
Destrehan♦	70047
Devalls	70767
Deville	71328
Dewdrop	71220
Diamond	70083
Dixie	71107
Dixie Acres	71280
Dixie Gardens	71105
Dixie Inn	71055
Dodson	71422
Donaldsonville	70346
Donner	70352
Dorcyville	70788
Douglas	71227
Downsville	71234
Downtown (Part of Alexandria)‡	71309
Downtown (Part of Baton Rouge)‡	70821
Downtown (Part of Monroe)‡	71201*
	71210†
Downtown (Part of Morgan City)‡	70380
Downtown (Part of Shreveport)‡	71101
Doyle (Part of Livingston)	70754
Doyline	71023
Drew (Part of Lake Charles)‡	70602†
	70605*
Drew, *Ouachita*	71291

Drusilla (Part of Baton Rouge)‡	70809
Dry Creek	70637
Dry Prong	71423
Dubach	71235
Dubberly	71024
Duckroost	70774
Dufresne	70070
Dukedale	71006
Dulac	70353
Dunbarton	71334
Dunn	71232
Duplessis	70728
Dupont, *Avoyelles*	71329
Dupont, *Pointe Coupee*	70783
Duson	70529
Dutch Town	70734
Dykesville	71038
Easleyville	70441
Eastgate Plaza (Part of Shreveport)	71108
East Hammond (Part of Hammond)	70401
East Hodge	71247
East Natchitoches (Part of Natchitoches)‡	71457
Easton	70586
East Point	71025
East Side (Part of Lake Charles)‡	70615*
	70616†
Eastside Columbia	71418
Eastwood♦	71037
Ebenezer	70526
Echo	71330
Eden	71371
Edgard	70049
Edgefield	71019
Edgerly	70668
Edna	70648
Effie	71331
Egan	70531
Elam	71378
Elba	71353
Eliza	70764
Elizabeth	70638
Ellendale	70360
Ellis	70526
Ellsworth	70360
Elmer, *Lafourche*	70301
Elmer, *Rapides*	71424
Elmfield	70390
Elm Grove	71051
Elm Hall	70390
Elm Hall Junction	70390
Elm Park	70775
Elmwood	70123
Elton	70532
Empire	70050
Encalade	70083
Energy Center (Part of Lafayette)‡	70598
Englewood	71282
English Turn	70040
Enola	70390
Enon	70438
Enterprise, *Catahoula*	71425
Enterprise (Part of Jeanerette)	70544
Eola	71322
Epps	71237
Erath	70533
Eros	71238
Erwinville	70729
Essen Heights	70808
Estelle♦	70072
Esther	70510
Estherwood	70534
Ethel	70730
Eunice	70535
Eureka	71234
Eva	71354
Evangeline	70537
Evans	70639
Evelyn	71052
Evergreen, *Avoyelles*	71333
Evergreen, *Webster*	71055
Extension	71243
Fairbanks	71240
Fairlane	70360
Fairmont	71417
Fairview	71373
Farmer Spur (Part of Vienna)	71270
Farmerville	71241
Faubourg	70589
Felixville	70722
Fellowship	71371

Fenris	70554
Fenton	70640
Ferriday	71334
Ferry Lake	71061
Fields	70653
Fifth Ward	71351
Fillmore	71037
Fisher	71426
Fishville	71467
Fiske	71263
Five Forks	71483
Flat Creek	71479
Flatwoods	71427
Flora	71428
Florence	70538
Florien	71429
Florissant	70085
Flournoy	71109
Floyd	71266
Fluker	70436
Foley, *Allen*	70655
Foley, *Assumption*	70390
Folsom	70437
Fondale	71201
Forbing	71106
Fordoche	70732
Foreman	70815
Forest	71242
Forest Glen	70445
Forest Hill	71430
Forest Oaks	70815
Forest Park	71291
Forked Island	70510
Forksville	71225
Fort De Russy	71351
Fort Jesup	71449
Fort Necessity	71243
Fort Polk	71459
Fosters (Part of Bossier City)	71111
Fosters Canal	70083
Foules	71326
Fourborge	70586
Four Corners	70538
Four Forks, *Caddo*	71046
Four Forks, *Richland*	71259
Fowler	71240
Francis Place	70075
Franklin	70538
Franklinton	70438
Fred	70791
Freetown, *Assumption*	70390
Freetown, *St. Mary*	70538
French Settlement	70733
Frenier	70068
Friendship	71008
Frierson	71027
Frisco	70755
Frogmore	71334
Frost	70754
Frost Town	71234
Fryeburg	71039
Fullerton	70642
Fulton	70657
Funston	71049
Gaars Mill	71422
Gahagan	71019
Galbraith	71447
Galion	71223
Galliano♦	70354
Galva	70421
Galvez	70769
Gandy	71429
Gansville	71422
Garden City	70540
Gardere♦	70810
Gardner	71431
Garland	71322
Garyville♦	70051
Gassoway	71254
Gateway (Part of Baton Rouge)‡	70835
Gayles	71105
Ged	70668
Geismar	70734
Gentilly (Part of New Orleans)‡	70122
Georgetown	71432
Georgeville	70443
Georgia	70390
Getty Camp	70091
Gheens	70355
Gibbstown	70630
Gibsland	71028
Gibson	70356
Gilark	71055
Gilbert	71336
Gilleyville	71269
Gilliam	71029
Gillis	70611

Girard	71269
Glade	71343
Glencoe	70538
Glen Dale	70049
Glenmora	71433
Glenwild	70342
Glenwood	70390
Gloria	70037
Gloster	71030
Glynn	70736
Godchaux	70394
Godchaux Community	70068
Gold Dust	71322
Golden Meadow	70357
Golden Star Plantation	70090
Goldman	71375
Goldonna	71031
Goldridge	70788
Gonzales	70707†
	70737*
Goodbee	70433
Good Hope	70079
Good Pine	71342
Goodwill	71263
Goodwood	71353
Gordon	71038
Gorum	71434
Goudeau	71333
Gouldsboro (Part of Gretna)	70053
Grambling	71245
Gramercy	70052
Grand Bayou	71052
Grandbois	70343
Grand Caillou	70360
Grand Cane	71032
Grand Chenier	70643
Grand Coteau	70541
Grand Ecore	71457
Grand Isle	70358
Grand Lake	70607
Grand Point	70763
Grand Prairie	70589
Grand River	70764
Grangeville	70422
Grant	70644
Gray♦	70359
Gray Point	70586
Grayson	71435
Green Acres, *Concordia*	71373
Green Acres, *East Baton Rouge*	70811
Green Acres, *St. Charles*	70030
Green Gables	71360
Greenlaw	70444
Green Lawn (Part of Kenner)	70065
Green Lawn Terrace (Part of Kenner)	70065
Greensburg	70441
Greenwell Springs	70739
Greenwood, *Caddo*	71033
Greenwood (Part of Morgan City)	70380
Greenwood, *Terrebonne*	70356
Greenwood Park	71108
Gretna	70053-54
	70056
For specific ZIP Codes call (888) 275-8777, or your local postmaster.	
Grosse Tete	70740
Gueydan	70542
Gulf Outport (Part of New Orleans)	70146
Gullett	70422
Gum Ridge	71264
Gurley	70730
Haaswood	70452
Hackberry♦	70645
Hacketts Corner	70630
Hackley	70438
Hagewood	71457
Hahnville♦	70057
Haile	71260
Haire	70548
Half Way, *Assumption*	70346
Halfway, *Red River*	71019
Hall Summit	71034
Hamburg	71339
Hammet	71373
Hammond	70401-04
For specific ZIP Codes call (888) 275-8777, or your local postmaster.	
Hanna	71019

Hanson City (Part of Kenner)	70062
Happy Jack	70083
Harahan	70123
Hardwood	70775
Hargis	71454
Hargrove	70633
Harlem, *Plaquemines*	70046
Harlem (Part of Abbeville)	70510
Harmon	71036
Harrisonburg	71340
Harvey	70058*
	70059†
Hathaway	70532
Haughton	71037
Hawthorne	71446
Hayes	70646
Haynesville	71038
Hazelwood	70577
Head of Island	70449
Hearn Island	71418
Hebert	71418
Hecker	70647
Heflin	71039
Helena	71366
Henderson	70517
Henfer Park	70123
Henry	70533
Hermitage	70749
Hessmer	71341
Hester	70743
Hewes	70762
Hickory, *Avoyelles*	71327
Hickory, *St. Tammany*	70452
Hickory Grove	71328
Hickory Valley	71473
Hicks	71446
Hico	71235
Higginbotham	70525
Highland Acres	70123
Highland Park (Part of Monroe)	71201
Highland Park (Part of West Monroe)	71291
Highland Park, *Terrebonne*	70360
Highland Park Heights	70808
Highland Road‡	70808
Highway Park (Part of Kenner)	70065
Hillaryville	70725
Hillsdale	70422
Hilltop	71268
Hilly	71235
Hineston	71438
Hobart	70769
Hodge	71247
Hohen Solms	70788
Holden	70744
Holiday Park	70502
Holloway	71328
Holly	71032
Holly Beach	70631
Hollybrook	71254
Holly Grove	71378
Holly Ridge, *Richland*	71269
Holly Ridge, *Tensas*	71375
Hollywood (Part of Sulphur)	70663
Hollywood, *Terrebonne*	70360
Hollywood, *West Feliciana*	70775
Holmwood	70647
Holum	71435
Home Place	70083
Homer	71040
Hopedale	70085
Hope Villa	70808
Hornbeck	71439
Horse Bluff Landing	70462
Hosston	71043
Hotwells	71409
Houltonville	70447
Houma	70360-64
For specific ZIP Codes call (888) 275-8777, or your local postmaster.	
Howard	71105
Hubertville (Part of Jeanerette)	70544
Hudson	71422
Hughes	71006
Humphreys	70356
Hundley	70535
Hunter	71052
Huntington (Part of Shreveport)‡	71129
Huron	70512

*** Area Zip Code** **† Post Office Boxes** **‡ Postal Station** **♦ Census Designated Place** *Italic Type* **Parish**

Hurricane 71003
Husser 70442
Hutton 71446
Hyde (Part of Simmesport) 71369
Hymel 70090
Iberville 70776
Ida 71044
Idlewild, *St. Mary* 70392
Idlewild, *Terrebonne* 70364
Ikes 70634
Independence 70443
Indian Bayou 70578
Indian Mound 70739
Indian Village, *Allen* 70648
Indian Village, *Ouachita* 71225
Industrial (Part of Shreveport)‡ 71107
Ingleside 70390
Innis 70747
Inniswold♦ 70809
International Trade Mart (Part of New Orleans)‡ 70130
Intracoastal City 70510
Iota 70543
Iowa 70647
Irish Bend 70538
Irma 71457
Ironton 70083
Isabel 70427
Isle Labbe 70582
Istrouma (Part of Baton Rouge)‡ 70805
Ivan 71006
Jackson 70748
Jackson Road 70748
Jacoby 70753
Jamestown 71045
Janie 71447
Jarreau 70749
Jay 70374
Jeanerette 70544
Jean Lafitte 70067
Jefferson, Jefferson♦ 70121
Jefferson (Part of Lafayette)‡ 70501*
.... 70502†
Jefferson Island 70560
Jefferson Terrace 70808
Jena 71342
Jennings 70546
Jesuit Bend 70037
Jewella (Part of Shreveport)‡ 71109
Jigger 71249
Johnson, *St. John the Baptist* 70049
Johnson, *St. Mary* 70538
Johnson Ridge 70301
Johnson's Bayou 70631
Johnson Street (Part of Metairie)‡ 70001*
.... 70004†
Jones 71250
Jonesboro 71251
Jonesburg 71269
Jones Park (Part of Kenner) 70065
Jonesville 71343
Jordan Hill 71483
Joyce 71440
Junction 70653
Junction City 71749
Kadesh 71454
Kahns 70767
Kaplan 70548
Katy 70538
Keatchie 71046
Kedron 70422
Keithville 71047
Kelly 71441
Kellys 71270
Kendale 70062
Kendrick's Ferry 71336
Kenilworth 70085
Kenmore 70757
Kennedy Heights 70094
Kenner 70062-65
For specific ZIP Codes call (888) 275-8777, or your local postmaster.
Kenner Junction (Part of Kenner) 70062
Kentwood 70444
Kickapoo 71030
Kilbourne 71253
Killian 70462
Killona 70066
Kinder 70648
King Hill 71019
Kingston 71032
Kingsville 71360
Kiroli Woods 71291
Kisatchie 71468
Kleinpeter 70808
Klondyke 70343
Klotzville 70341
Kolin 71360
Kolter (Part of Keatchie) 71046
Koran 71037
Kraemer 70371
Krotz Springs 70750
Kurthwood 71443
Laark 71250
Labadieville♦ 70372
Labarre 70751
Lacamp 71444
Lacassine 70650
Lachute 71115
Lacombe♦ 70445
Lacour 70715
Lafayette 70501-09
.... 70596-98
For specific ZIP Codes call (888) 275-8777, or your local postmaster.
Lafayette Square (Part of New Orleans)‡ 70130
Lafayette Woods 70360
Lafitte♦ 70067
Lafourche 70301
Lagan 70086
Lagonda♦ 70380
Lake 70769
Lake Arthur 70549
Lake Bruin 71366
Lake Charles 70601-16
For specific ZIP Codes call (888) 275-8777, or your local postmaster.
Lake End 71019
Lake Forest (Part of New Orleans)‡ 70127
Lake Judge Perez 70083
Lakeland 70752
Lake Providence 71254
Lakeshore 71203
Lakeside, *Cameron* 70542
Lakeside, *Rapides* 71360
Lakeside Shopping Center 70002
Lakeview, *Caddo* 71107
Lakeview, *Natchitoches* 71456
Lakeview (Part of New Orleans)‡ 70124
Lamar 71232
Lamourie 71346
Lampman (Part of Abbeville) 70510
Landay Gautreaux Subdivision 70301
Lapine 71291
La Place♦ 70068*
.... 70069†
Laran 71765
La Reusitte 70037
Larose♦ 70373
La Rosen (Part of Shreveport) 71118
Larto 71343
Latanier 71346
Laurel Grove 70301
Laurel Hill 39669
Laurel Lea 70808
Laurel Ridge 70788
Laurel Valley Plantation 70301
Lawhon 71045
Lawtell 70550
Lazy Acres 70360
Leander 71438
Lebeau 71345
Le Blanc 70651
Le Bleu 70615
Lecompte 71346
Lee Bayou 71326
Lee Heights 71360
Lees Creek 70427
Lees Landing 70454
Leesville 71446*
.... 71496†
Leeville 70357
Legonier 70753
Leighton 70301
Leland 71368
Leleux 70560
Lemannville 70346
Le Moyen 71356
Lena 71447
Leonville 70551
Leroy 70555
Leton 71072
Lettsworth 70753
Levert 70582
Levins 71334
Lewisburg, *St. Landry* 70525
Lewisburg, *St. Tammany* 70448
Lewiston 70444
Lewistown 70394
Liberty 71225
Liberty Hill 71008
Libuse 71348
Liddieville 71295
Lillie 71256
Linda Lee 70706
Lindsay 70748
Link 70516
Linton 71006
Linville 71260
Linwood 70514
Lions 70068
Lisbon 71048
Lismore 71343
Litroe 71260
Little Caillou 70344
Little Creek 71371
Little Prairie 70769
Little Texas 70390
Live Oak 70037
Live Oak Hills 70447
Live Oak Manor 70094
Liverpool 70441
Livingston 70754
Livonia 70755
Lobdell 70767
Lockhart 71277
Lockport 70374
Lockport Heights 70374
Locust Ridge 71366
Logansport 71049
Log Cabin 71220
Logtown 71202
Lonepine 71367
Lone Star, *Iberville* 70788
Lone Star, *St. Charles*♦ 70070
Longbridge, *Avoyelles* 71327
Long Bridge, *Lafayette* 70501
Longlake 71418
Longleaf 71448
Long Straw 71227
Longstreet 71049
Longview 71295
Longville 70652
Longwood, *Caddo* 71060
Longwood, *East Baton Rouge* 70780
Loranger 70446
Loreauville 70552
Lorelein 71336
Lottie 70756
Louisiana Army Ammunition Plant 71102
Louisiana Tech (Part of Ruston)‡ 71272
Louisville (Part of Monroe)‡ 71207
Lower Bonne Idee 71264
Lower Texas 70390
Loyds Bridge 71325
Lozes 70560
Lucas 71105
Lucky 71008
Lucy 70049
Ludington (Part of De Ridder) 70634
Ludvine 70374
Lukeville 70719
Lula 71052
Luling♦ 70070
Luna 71291
Lunita 70661
Lutcher 70071
Lydia♦ 70569
Lynbrook (Part of Shreveport)‡ 71106
Lyons Point 70526
McBride 70360
McCall 70346
McClendon 70438
McCrea 70715
McDade 71051
McDonoghville (Part of Gretna) 70053
McGinty 71250
McIlhenny 70513
McIntyre 71055
McKneeley 70732
McLeod 70374
McManus 70748
McNary 71433
McNeely 71417
McNeese University (Part of Lake Charles)‡ 70609
Madewood 70390
Madisonville 70447
Magda 71301
Magnolia, *Assumption* 70341
Magnolia, *East Baton Rouge* 70739
Magnolia, *Livingston* 70744
Magnolia, *Natchitoches* 71456
Magnolia, *Plaquemines* 70083
Magnolia, *Terrebonne* 70360
Magnolia Park 71417
Magnolia Woods (Part of Baton Rouge) 70808
Maitland 71326
Major (Part of New Roads) 70760
Mallard Junction 70647
Mamou 70554
Manchester 70647
Mandalay 70360
Mandeville 70448
.... 70470
.... 70471
For specific ZIP Codes call (888) 275-8777, or your local postmaster.
Mangham 71259
Manifest 71343
Mansfield 71052
Mansura 71350
Many 71449
Maplewood (Part of Sulphur) 70663
Marcel 70560
Marco 71447
Maringouin 70757
Marion 71260
Marksville 71351
Marrero♦ 70072*
.... 70073†
Marsalis 71003
Mars Hill 71404
Marthaville 71450
Martin 71019
Martin Park (Part of Alexandria) 71301
Mason 71295
Mathews 70375
Maurepas 70449
Maurice 70555
Maxie 70526
Mayfair (Part of Baton Rouge) 70808
Mayna 71343
Meadowbrook 70056
Meadow Park Heights 71108
Meaux 70510
Mechanicsville (Part of Houma) 70360
Meeker 71346
Melder 71433
Melrose 71452
Melville 71353
Meraux♦ 70075
Mermentau 70556
Mer Rouge 71261
Merryville 70653
Messick 71019
Metairie♦ 70001-11
.... 70033
.... 70055
For specific ZIP Codes call (888) 275-8777, or your local postmaster.
Methvin 71019
Michoud (Part of New Orleans)‡ 70129
Mid City (Part of New Orleans)‡ 70119
Midland 70559
Midway, *Bossier* 71006
Midway, *La Salle*♦ 71342
Midway, *Rapides* 71430
Midway, *St. Mary* 70538
Midway, *Webster* 71071
Milldale 70791
Millerton 71038
Millerville, *Acadia* 70543
Millerville, *East Baton Rouge* 70815
Millikin 71254
Milly Plantation 70764
Milton 70558
Mimosa Park♦ 70070
Minden 71055-58
For specific ZIP Codes call (888) 275-8777, or your local postmaster.
Mineral Springs, *Lincoln* 71235
Mineral Springs, *Ouachita* 71225
Minerva 70360
Minorca 71334
Mira 71044
Mire 70578
Mitchell 71419
Mittie 70654
Mix 70760
Modeste 70376
Moisant Airport (Part of Kenner)‡ 70141
Moncla 71351
Monette Ferry 71447
Monroe 71201-13
For specific ZIP Codes call (888) 275-8777, or your local postmaster.
Montcalm 71275
Montegut♦ 70377
Monterey 71354
Montgomery 71454
Monticello, *East Baton Rouge*♦ 70815
Monticello, *East Carroll* 71254
Montpelier 70422
Montrose 71457
Montz 70068
Mooringsport 71060
Mora 71455
Morbihan 70560
Moreauville 71355
Moreland 71301
Morgan City 70380*
.... 70381†
Morganza 70759
Morningside (Part of Shreveport)‡ 71108
Morrisonville 70764
Morrow 71356
Morse 70559
Morvant 70301
Morville 71373
Moss Bluff‡ 70611*
.... 70612†
Moss Lake 70665
Mossville 70663
Mot 71064
Mound 71282
Mount Airy 70076
Mount Carmel 71429
Mount Hermon 70450
Mount Lebanon 71028
Mount Moriah 71226
Mount Olive 71268
Mount Sinai 71038
Mount Union 71277
Mount Zion, *Lincoln* 71235
Mount Zion, *Winn* 71454
Mowata 70535
Mudville 71432
Mulberry 70360
Myrtle Grove (Part of Plaquemine) 70764
Myrtle Grove, *Plaquemines* 70083
Naborton 71052
Nairn 70041
Naomi 70037
Napoleonville 70390
Napoleonville Junction (Part of Thibodaux) 70301
Naquin 70301
Natalbany♦ 70451
Natchez 71456
Natchitoches 71457*
.... 71458†
Neal Landing 70462
Nebo 71342
Negreet 71460
Nesser 70815
Newellton 71357
New Era 71354
Newhope 71266
New Iberia 70560-63
For specific ZIP Codes call (888) 275-8777, or your local postmaster.

New Light, *Richland* 71259
Newlight, *Tensas* 71357
New Llano 71461

New Orleans

70101-90
For specific ZIP Codes call (888) 275-8777, or your local postmaster.

Colleges & Universities

Dillard Univ 70122
Louisiana State Univ Medical Ctr 70112
Loyola Univ 70118
New Orleans Baptist Theological Seminary 70126
Notre Dame Seminary, Graduate School of Theology 70118
Our Lady of Holy Cross Coll 70131
Southern Univ 70126
Tulane Univ 70118
Univ of New Orleans 70148
Xavier Univ 70125

Financial Institutions

Bank One 70170
First Nat Bank of Commerce 70112
Hibernia Nat Bank 70130
Regions Bank 70130
Whitney Nat Bank 70130

Hospitals

Medical Ctr of Louisiana 70112
Memorial Med Ctr 70115
Ochsner Foundation Hosp 70121
Veterans Affairs Med Ctr 70146

Hotels/Motels

Chateau Sonesta 70112
Crowne Plaza 70130
Doubletree 70130
Fairmont 70112
Hilton, Riverside 70140
Holiday Inn Downtown-Superdome 70112
Holiday Inn French Quarter 70130
Hyatt Regency at Superdome 70113
Inter-Continental 70130
Marriott 70130
Le Meridien 70130
The Monteleone 70140
Omni Royal Orleans 70140
Radisson 70112
Royal Sonesta 70140
Sheraton 70130
The Westin, Canal Place 70130
Windsor Court 70130

Military Installations

Coast Guard Integrated Support Command 70110
Louisiana Air Nat Guard, FB6171, NAS New Orleans, Joint Res Base 70143
MTMC 1314th Medium Port Command 70146
Naval Air Sta, New Orleans, Joint Res Base 70143
Naval Support Activity 70142
Supervisor of Shipbuilding, Conversion and Repair 70142
U S Army Corps of Engineers 70160
U S Property and Fiscal Off for Louisiana 70146
8th Marine Corps Dist 70142
926th Fighter Wing (AFRES), NAS New Orleans, Joint Res Base 70143

New Orleans Centre (Part of New Orleans) 70112
New Roads 70760
New Rockdale 71052
New Sarpy♦ 70078
Newton 70601
New Verda 71404
Nibletts Bluff 70668
Nicholas 70560
Nicholls University (Part of Thibodaux)‡ 70301
Nickel 71465
Ninock 71051
Noble 71462
Noles Landing 71073
Norah 70374
Norco♦ 70079
Normandy Park 70094
Norris Springs 71368
Northeast Louisiana University (Part of Monroe) 71209
North 18th Street (Part of Monroe)‡ 71201
Northgate Mall (Part of Lafayette) 70501
North Hodge 71247
North Kenner (Part of Kenner)‡ 70065
North Merrydale 70812
North Monroe 71201
North Plaquemine (Part of Plaquemine) 70764
North Shore 70458
North Shore Beach 70458
Northside (Part of Monroe)‡ 71207
North Slidell (Part of Slidell) 70458
Northwestern (Part of Natchitoches)‡ 71457
Norton Shop 71072
Norwood 70761
Notleyville 70512
Notnac 71357
Numa 70560
Nunez 70548
Oakdale 71463
Oak Forest 70356
Oak Grove, *Ascension* 70769
Oak Grove, *Cameron* 70643
Oak Grove, *Grant* 71417
Oak Grove, *Lincoln* 71275
Oak Grove, *Sabine* 71419
Oak Grove, *West Carroll* 71263
Oak Hills Place♦ 70808
Oakland 71260
Oaklawn, *St. Mary* 70538
Oaklawn, *St. Tammany* 70445
Oakley 70390
Oak Manor 70815
Oaknolia 70777
Oak Ridge 71264
Oaks 71038
Oakshire Manor 70364
Oakville 70037
Oakwood Center (Part of Gretna) 70053
Oberlin 70655
Oil Center (Part of Lafayette)‡ 70501
Oil City 71061
Okaloosa 71238
Old Athens 71003
Oldfield 70785
Old Hammond‡ 70815-19
For specific ZIP Codes call (888) 275-8777, or your local postmaster.
Old Jefferson♦ 70816
Old Lafitte 70067
Old Shongaloo 71072
Olive Branch 70777
Oliver (Part of Hammond) 70401
Olivier 70560
Olla 71465
Ollie 70037
Omega 71276
Opelousas 70570*
70571†
Orange Grove Plantation 70301
Oretta 70633
Oscar 70762
Ossun 70583
Ostrica 70041
Otis 71466
Ouachita City 71280
Oubre (Part of Loreauville) 70552
Oxford, *De Soto* 71052
Oxford, *St. Mary* 70538
Pace 71055
Packton 71483
Paincourtville♦ 70391
Palmetto 71358
Palo Alto 70346
Panchoville 70532
Panola 71254
Paradis 70080
Paradise 71360
Paradise Manor 70123
Parhams 71343
Park Manor‡ 70003
Parks 70582
Parkside Manor 70123
Park Vista (Part of Opelousas) 70570
Patoutville 70544
Patterson 70392
Paulina 70763
Pearl River 70452
Peason 71429
Pecan Grove 70094
Pecaniere 70512
Pecan Island 70548
Pecan Place 70764
Peck 71368
Pelican 71063
Perkins 70633
Perry 70575
Perryville 71220
Phoenix 70042
Pickering 71446
Pierre Bossier Mall (Part of Bossier City) 71112
Pierre Part Settlement 70339
Pilottown 70081
Pine 70438
Pine Coupee 71427
Pine Grove, *Ouachita* 71201
Pine Grove, *St. Helena* 70453
Pine Island 70532
Pine Oak Terrace (Part of Shreveport) 71108
Pine Prairie 70576
Pineville 71360*
71361†
Pioneer 71266
Pitkin 70656
Pitreville 70525
Plain Dealing 71064
Plains 70791
Plainview 70427
Plaisance 70570
Plantation Acres (Part of Alexandria) 71301
Plantation Station (Part of Bossier City)‡ 71112
Plaquemine 70764*
70765†
Plaquemine Southwest (Part of Plaquemine) 70764
Plattenville 70393
Plaucheville 71362
Plaza, The (Part of New Orleans) 70127
Pleasant Hill, *Bienville* 71028
Pleasant Hill, *Sabine* 71065
Pleasant Hills 70811
Pleasant Valley 71234
Plettenberg 70775
Point 71234
Point Au Chien 70377
Point Blue 70586
Pointe a la Hache 70082
Pointe Coupee 70760
Point Pleasant 71220
Poland 71301
Pollock 71467
Ponchatoula 70454
Ponchatoula Beach 70454
Pontchartrain Beach (Part of New Orleans) 70122
Pontchartrain Shores (Part of New Orleans) 70122
Poole 71051
Poplar Grove 70767
Portage 70512
Port Allen 70767
Port Barre 70577
Port Barrow (Part of Donaldsonville) 70346
Port Eads 70091
Porters Curve 70450
Porterville 71071
Port Fourchon 70357
Port Gardner 70791
Port Hickey 70791
Port Manchac 70421
Port of West Saint Mary 70538
Port Sulphur♦ 70083
Port Vincent 70726
Potash 70083
Pot Cove 70586
Poufette 70560
Powhatan 71066
Poydras♦ 70085
Prairie Ronde 70570
Prairieville 70769
Pratt 71028
Presque Isle 70363
Pride 70770
Prien Lake Mall (Part of Lake Charles) 70601
Princeton 71067
Promised Land 70040
Prospect, *Grant* 71423
Prospect, *St. Charles* 70078
Provencal 71468
Providence 70062
Puckett 70791
Pumpkin Center 70403
Punkin Center 71247
Quaid 71343
Quimby 71282
Quitman 71268
Raceland♦ 70394
Ragley 70657
Ramah 70757
Rambin 71063
Randolph 71256
Rapides 71409
Ratliff 70390
Rattan 71429
Rayne 70578
Rayville 71269
Readhimer 71070
Red Chute 71037
Reddell 70580
Red Gum 71334
Redland, *Bossier* 71064
Redland, *Evangeline* 70554
Red Oaks 70815
Reeves 70658
Reggio 70085
Reids 70656
Remy 70763
Reserve♦ 70084
Rhinehart 71363
Rhymes 71269
Riceville 70542
Richard 70525
Richardson 70438
Richmond 71282
Richohoc 70538
Richwood 71201
Rideau Settlement 71358
Ridge 70578
Ridgecrest 71334
Ridgewood 70739
Rienzi Plantation 70301
Ringgold 71068
Rio 70427
Risinger Woods 71107
Riverlands 70068
River Ridge♦ 70123
Riverton 71418
Riverwood 70433
Roanoke 70581
Robeline 71469
Robert 70455
Robson 71105
Rock 71447
Rock Hill 71423
Rocky Branch 71241
Rocky Mount 71064
Rodessa 71069
Rogers 71342
Romeville 70723
Roosevelt 71276
Rosa 71345
Rosedale, *Assumption* 70390
Rosedale, *Iberville* 70772
Rosefield 71435
Roseland 70456
Rosepine 70659
Rougon 70773
Rousseau 70394
Roxana 71301
Roy 71016
Ruby 71365
Rum Center 71256
Ruple 71038
Rural Park 70123
Ruston 71270-73
For specific ZIP Codes call (888) 275-8777, or your local postmaster.
Ruth 70517
Rynella 70560
Sadie 71260
Sadou 70529
Sailes 71028
St. Amant 70774
St. Benedict 70457
St. Bernard 70085
St. Bernard Grove 70075
St. Charles 70301
St. Clair 70040
St. Claude Heights 70032
St. Elmo 70725
St. Francisville 70775
St. Gabriel 70776
St. Genevieve 71373
St. Gertrude 70435
St. James 70086
St. Joe 70452
St. John 70301
St. Joseph 71366
St. Landry 71367
St. Martinville 70582
St. Maurice 71471
St. Rosalie 70037
St. Rose♦ 70087
St. Tammany 70445
St. Thomas 70390
Saline 71070
Samstown 70788
Samtown 71301
Sandy Hill 71446
Sardis, *Sabine* 71419
Sardis, *Winn* 71483
Sarepta 71071
Satsuma 70754
Savoy 70535
Scarsdale 70040
Schriever♦ 70395
Scotlandville (Part of Baton Rouge) 70807*
70874†
Scott 70583
Searcy 71371
Sebastapol 70085
Sellers 70079
Selma 71432
Sentell 71107
Serena 71343
Seymourville 70764
Shadyside 70538
Shamrock 71469
Sharon 71235
Sharon Hills 70811
Sharp 71447
Shaw 71373
Shelburn 71254
Shelton 71220
Shenandoah♦ 70816
Sherburne 70750
Sheridan 70438
Sherwood 71435
Shiloh, *Tangipahoa* 70422
Shiloh, *Union* 71222
Shongaloo 71072
Shreve City Shopping Center (Part of Shreveport) 71105
Shreveport 71101-10
71115-66
For specific ZIP Codes call (888) 275-8777, or your local postmaster.
Shrewsbury 70121
Shuteston 70570
Sibley, *Lincoln* 71227
Sibley, *Webster* 71073
Sicard (Part of Monroe) 71201
Sicily Island 71368
Siegle 71291
Sieper 71472
Sikes 71473
Sikes Ferry 71072
Silverwood 70546
Simmesport 71369
Simms 71467
Simpson 71474
Simsboro 71275
Singer 70660
Siracusaville 70380
Slacks 70757
Slagle 71475
Slaughter 70777
Slidell 70458-61
70469
For specific ZIP Codes call (888) 275-8777, or your local postmaster.
Sligo 71112

*** Area Zip Code** **† Post Office Boxes** **‡ Postal Station** **♦ Census Designated Place** *Italic Type* **Parish**

Place	ZIP Code
Smithfield	70767
Smith Ridge	70344
Smoke Bend	70346
Socola	70083
Soileau	70655
Somerset	71357
Sondheimer	71276
Soniat	70788
Sorrell	70544
Sorrento	70778
South Acres	70663
South Bend	70538
Southdown	70360
Southeast (Part of Baton Rouge)‡	70808
Southern	70813
Southfield (Part of Shreveport)‡	71105
South Fort Trailer Park	71459
South Kenner	70094
South Lafourche	70357
South Mansfield	71052
South Park (Part of Alexandria)‡	71301
South Park (Part of Shreveport)‡	71118
South Park Mall (Part of Shreveport)	71118
South Pass	70091
Southport	70121
South Sherwood (Part of Baton Rouge)‡	70816
South Vacherie♦	70090
Southwestern University (Part of Lafayette)‡	70504
Spaulding	71441
Spearsville	71277
Spencer	71280
Spillman	70748
Splane Place (Part of West Monroe)	71291
Spokane	71334
Springcreek	70444
Springfield	70462
Spring Hill, *Jackson*	71251
Springhill, *Washington*	70438
Springhill, *Webster*	71075
Spring Ridge, *Caddo*	71047
Spring Ridge, *Sabine*	71065
Springville, *Livingston*	70754
Springville, *Red River*	71019
Standard	71465
Stanley	71049
Star	70037
Starhill	70748
Staring (Part of Baton Rouge)	70801
Starks	70661
Start	71279
State Line	70438
Stella	70040
Stephensville	70380
Sterlington	71280
Stevensdale	70815
Stevenson	71220
Stonewall	71078
Stoney Point	70438
Stonypoint	70739
Stumpf's Westside Shopping Center (Part of Gretna)	70053
Sugarcreek	71001
Sugartown	70662
Sulphur	70663-65
For specific ZIP Codes call (888) 275-8777, or your local postmaster.	
Summerfield	71079
Summer Grove (Part of Shreveport)	71118
Summerville	71465
Sun	70463
Sunnybrook	70814
Sunny Hill	70438
Sunrise	70767
Sunset	70584
Sunshine	70780
Sun Spur	71232
Supreme♦	70390
Susan Park (Part of Kenner)	70062
Swampers	71295
Swartz♦	71281
Sweet Lake	70630
Swords	70525
Taconey	71373
Taft	70057
Talisheek	70464
Talla Bena	71276
Tallulah	71282-84
For specific ZIP Codes call (888) 275-8777, or your local postmaster.	
Tangipahoa	70465
Tanglewood, *East Baton Rouge*	70811
Tanglewood, *Rapides*	71301
Tannehill	71422
Tate Cove	70586
Taylor	71080
Taylor Hill	71447
Taylortown, *Bossier*	71051
Taylortown, *Union*	71277
Tchefuncte Estates	70433
Temple	71474
Tendal	71282
Terry	71263
Terrytown♦	70053
Theriot	70397
The Rock	71417
Thibodaux	70301-10
For specific ZIP Codes call (888) 275-8777, or your local postmaster.	
Thomas	70438
Thomastown	71282
Thornwell	70549
Three Oaks	70032
Three Rivers Heights	70447
Tickfaw	70466
Tidewater Camp	70091
Tigerville	70049
Timberlane	70053
Timber Trails	71360
Tioga	71477
Toca	70085
Toomey	70668
Topsy	70601
Torbert	70781
Toro	71429
Torras	70753
Tower Park (Part of Leesville)‡	71446
Town and Country	71201
Transylvania	71286
Trees	71082
Tremont	71227
Trenton	71052
Trinity, *Catahoula*	71343
Trinity (Part of Rosedale)	70772
Triumph	70041
Tropical Bend	70050
Trout	71371
Truxno	71260
Tullos	71479
Tunica	70782
Turkey Creek	70585
Turnerville (Part of Plaquemine)	70764
Twin Oaks	71223
Uncle Sam	70792
Union	70723
Union Church	71268
Union Hill, *Rapides*	71433
Union Hill, *Winn*	71483
Union Landing	70754
Union Springs	71419
Unionville	71235
University (Part of Baton Rouge)‡	70803
Upland	71220
Upstream	70123
Uptown (Part of New Orleans)‡	70115
Urania	71480
Utility	71343
Vacherie♦	70090
Valmar	70075
Valverda	70757
Vanceville	71111
Varnado	70467
Vatican	70520
Vaughn	71220
Velma	70422
Venice	70091
Ventress	70783
Verda	71481
Verdun	70754
Verdunville	70538
Vernon	71270
Verret	70085
Veterans Administration Hospital (Part of Shreveport)	71101
Vick	71331
Vidalia	71373
Vidrine	70586
Vienna	71270
Vieux Carre (Part of New Orleans)‡	70112
Village East	70360
Village St. George♦	70808
Ville Platte	70586
Vincent Landing	70665
Vincent Park	70075
Vinton	70668
Vista Village Regional Shopping Center (Part of Opelousas)	70570
Vivian	71082
Vixen	71418
Voorhies	71355
Vowells Mill	71469
Wadesboro	70454
Waggaman	70094
Wakefield	70784
Waldheim	70435
Walker, *Jackson*	71251
Walker, *Livingston*	70785
Wallace	70049
Wallace Ridge	71343
Walls	70720
Walters	71343
Ward	71463
Warden	71232
Wardview	71064
Wardville, *Morehouse*	71220
Wardville, *Rapides*	71360
Warnerton	70438
Warsaw Landing	70462
Washington	70589
Waterloo	70783
Waterproof, *Tensas*	71375
Waterproof, *Terrebonne*	70360
Watson	70786
Waverly	71232
Waxia	70589
Weil	71301
Welcome	70086
Weldon	71222
Welsh	70591
Wemple	71052
Westdale	71105
Western Kraft	71411
Westfield	70390
Westlake	70669
Westminster♦	70809
West Monroe	71291-94
For specific ZIP Codes call (888) 275-8777, or your local postmaster.	
Weston	71251
Westover	70767
West Pointe a la Hache	70083
Westport	70656
Westside (Part of Alexandria)‡	71301*
	71315†
West Slidell (Part of Slidell)‡	70460
Westwego	70094*
	70096†
Weyanoke	70787
Whatley Landing	71371
Wheeling	71454
White	70301
White Castle	70788
Whitehall, *La Salle*	71342
Whitehall, *Livingston*	70449
White Hall, *St. James*	70723
White Hills	70714
White Sulphur Springs	71371
Whiteville	71322
Whittington	71301
Wickland Terrace	70815
Wickliffe	70783
Wildsville	71377
Wildwood, *Assumption*	70390
Wildwood, *East Baton Rouge*	70808
Willhite	71234
Williams	71105
Williana	71423
Willow Glen	71301
Wills Point	70040
Wilmer	70444
Wilshire Park	71301
Wilson	70789
Wilsona	71366
Wilson Point	71301
Wilton Subdivision	71107
Winnfield	71483
Winnsboro	71295
Wisner	71378
Womack, *Jackson*	71226
Womack, *Red River*	71068
Woodardville	71068
Woodhaven	70466
Woodland	70083
Woodlawn (Part of Baton Rouge)‡	70816-17
For specific ZIP Codes call (888) 275-8777, or your local postmaster.	
Woodlawn, *Assumption*	70390
Woodlawn, *Jefferson Davis*	70647
Woodlawn, *Plaquemines*	70040
Woodlawn, *Terrebonne*	70360
Woodside	71353
Woodville	71270
Woodworth	71485
Wyandotte	70380
Wyatt	71251
Yellow Pine	71073
Youngsville	70592
Zachary	70791
Zebedee	71269
Zenoria	71371
Zion	71432
Zion City (Part of Baton Rouge)	70811
Zwolle	71486
Zylks	71069

* Area Zip Code † Post Office Boxes ‡ Postal Station ♦ Census Designated Place *Italic Type* **Parish**

- Abbot (Town) 04406
- Abbotts Mill 04219
- Abbot Village 04406
- Acton 04001
- Addison 04606
- Admiralty Village 03904
- Agamenticus Village 03902
- Airport Mall (Part of Bangor) 04401
- Albion 04910
- Alexander 04694
- Alfred 04002
- Alfred Mills 04002
- Allagash 04774
- Allens Mills 04938
- Alna 04535
- Alna Center 04535
- Alton 04468
- Amherst 04605
- Amity (Town) 04471
- Andover 04216
- Anson 04911
- Appleton 04862
- Areys Corners 04444
- Argyle 04468
- Aroostook Farm (Part of Presque Isle) 04769
- Arrowsic 04530
- Arundel 04046
- Ashdale 04565
- Ashland 04732
- Ash Point 04854
- Ashville 04607
- Athens 04912
- Atkinson (Town) 04426
- Atkinson Corner 04426
- Atkinson Mills 04426
- Atlantic 04685
- Auburn 04210-12
  For specific ZIP Codes call (888) 275-8777, or your local postmaster.
- Auburn Mall (Part of Auburn) 04210
- Auburn Plains (Part of Auburn) 04210
- Augusta 04330-38
  For specific ZIP Codes call (888) 275-8777, or your local postmaster.
- Aurora 04408
- Avon 04966
- Back Narrows 04537
- Bailey Corner 04345
- Bailey Island 04003
- Baileyville (Town) 04694
- Baker Corner 04062
- Balch Pond 03830
- Bald Head 03902
- Bald Mountain 04970
- Baldwin (Town) 04024
- Bancroft 04497
- Bangor 04401*
  04402†
- Bangor Mall (Part of Bangor) 04401
- Bar Harbor♦ 04609
- Baring 04694
- Bar Mills 04004
- Barretts (Part of Caribou) 04736
- Bartlett Mills 04043
- Basin Mills 04473
- Bass Harbor 04653
- Batchelders Crossing 04350
- Bath 04530
- Bay Point 04548
- Bayside, *Hancock* 04605
- Bayside, *Waldo* 04849
- Bayview (Part of Saco) 04072
- Bayville 04536
- Beals 04611
- Beans Corner 04225
- Beaver Cove (Town) 04441
- Beddington (Town) 04622
- Beech Hill Pond 04605
- Beech Ridge 03909
- Belfast 04915
- Belgrade 04917
- Belgrade Lakes 04918
- Belmont (Town) 04952
- Belmont Corner 04952
- Benedicta 04733
- Benton 04901
- Benton Falls 04901
- Benton Station 04901
- Bernard 04612
- Berry Mills 04224
- Berwick 03901
- Bethel 04217
- Biddeford 04005*
  04007†
- Biddeford Pool (Part of Biddeford) 04006
- Bigelow 04947
- Big Lake Campground 04668
- Bingham♦ 04920
- Birch Harbor 04613
- Birch Island 04011
- Birch Point 04747
- Blackstrap 04105
- Blaine 04734
- Blaisdell Corners 04027
- Blake Corner 04250
- Blanchard 04406
- Blanchard Corner 04666
- Blue Hill 04614
- Blue Hill Falls 04615
- Blue Point 04074
- Bolsters Mills 04040
- Bonny Eagle 04093
- Boothbay 04537
- Boothbay Harbor (Town) 04538
- Boothbay Park (Part of Saco) 04072
- Bowdoin (Town) 04008
- Boudoin Center 04008
- Bowdoinham 04008
- Bowerbank (Town) 04426
- Boyd Lake 04463
- Bradburys 04743
- Bradford 04410
- Bradford Center 04410
- Bradley 04411
- Bremen (Town) 04551
- Brewer 04412
- Brewer Lake 04474
- Bridgewater 04735
- Bridgton♦ 04009
- Briggs Corner 03905
- Brighton 04912
- Bristol 04539
- Brixham 03909
- Brixham Lower Corners 03909
- Broad Cove 04572
- Brookhaven 04062
- Brooklin 04616
- Brooks 04921
- Brooksville 04617
- Brookton 04413
- Brown Corner, *Aroostook* 04750
- Brown Corner, *Waldo* 04849
- Brownfield 04010
- Brownville 04414
- Brownville Junction 04415
- Brunswick♦ 04011
- Brunswick Naval Air Station 04011
- Bryant Pond 04219
- Bryants Corner (Part of Belfast) 04915
- Buckfield 04220
- Bucks Harbor 04655
- Bucksport♦ 04416
- Bucksport Center 04416
- Bunganuc Landing 04011
- Bunkers Harbor 04613
- Burkettville 04862
- Burlington 04417
- Burnham 04922
- Burnt Meadow Pond 04041
- Bustins Island 04013
- Buxton 04093
- Buxton Center 04093
- Byron 04275
- Calais 04619
- Caldwel Corner 04270
- Cambridge 04923
- Camden♦ 04843
- Camp Ellis (Part of Saco) 04072
- Canaan 04924
- Canton 04221
- Canton Point 04221
- Cape Cottage 04107
- Cape Elizabeth 04107
- Cape Neddick 03902
- Cape Porpoise 04014
- Capitol Island 04538
- Caratunk 04925
- Cardville 04418
- Caribou 04736
- Caribou Road (Part of Presque Isle) 04769
- Carmel 04419
- Carrabassett 04947
- Carrabassett Valley (Town) 04947
- Carroll 04487
- Carson 04786
- Carthage 04224
- Cary 04471
- Carys Mills 04730
- Casco 04015
- Cash Corner (Part of South Portland) 04106
- Castine 04421
- Castle Hill (Town) 04757
- Caswell (Town) 04750
- Caswell Plantation 04750
- Cathance 04086
- Center Lebanon 04027
- Center Lovell 04016
- Center Minot 04258
- Center Montville 04941
- Center Vassalboro 04989
- Centerville 04623
- Central Aroostook (Town) 04760
- Central Hancock (Town) 04640
- Central Somerset (Town) 04920
- Chamberlain 04541
- Chapman 04757
- Charles Chase Corner 04090
- Charleston 04422
- Charlotte (Town) 04666
- Chases Pond 03909
- Chatham 04037
- Chebeague Island 04017
- Chelsea (Town) 04345
- Chelsea 04330
- Cherryfield 04622
- Chester 04457
- Chesterville 04938
- Chesuncook 04441
- Chicopee 04093
- China 04926
- Chisholm♦ 04239
- Christmas Cove 04568
- Cider Hill 03909
- City Point (Part of Belfast) 04915
- Clark Island 04859
- Clarks Mills 04042
- Clay Hill 03902
- Clayton Lake 04737
- Cleveland 04772
- Cliff Island (Part of Portland) 04019
- Clifton 04428
- Clinton♦ 04927
- Cobbs Bridge 04260
- Coburn Gore 04936
- Codyville 04490
- Colby 04736
- Colby College (Part of Waterville)‡ 04901
- Cold Brook 04401
- Coles Corner 04496
- Columbia (Town) 04623
- Columbia Falls 04623
- Concord 04920
- Concordville 03910
- Connor (Town) 04736
- Convene 04029
- Cooks Corner, *Cumberland* 04011
- Cooks Corner, *Waldo* 04987
- Cooks Mills 04015
- Cooper 04638
- Coopers Corner 04043
- Coopers Mills 04341
- Coplin (Town) 04982
- Corea 04624
- Corinna 04928
- Corinna Center 04928
- Corinth (Town) 04427
- Cornish 04020
- Cornville 04976
- Costigan 04423
- Cote Corner 04750
- Country Living 04073
- Cousins Island 04096
- Coventry North 04048
- Cranberry Isles 04625
- Cranes Corner 03903
- Crawford (Town) 04619
- Crescent Beach 04854
- Crescent Lake 04015
- Criehaven (Town) 04851
- Crockett Corner 04021
- Crossman Corner 04252
- Crouseville 04738
- Crystal 04747
- Cumberland (Town) 04021
- Cumberland Center♦ 04021
- Cumberland Foreside 04110
- Cumberland Mills (Part of Westbrook) 04092
- Cundys Harbor 04011
- Curtis Corner 04263
- Cushing 04563
- Cushing Island (Part of Portland) 04109
- Cutler 04626
- Cutts Island 03905
- Cyr (Town) 04785
- Daigle 04743
- Dallas (Town) 04970
- Damariscotta 04543
- Damariscotta Mills 04553
- Damascus 04419
- Danforth 04424
- Danville (Part of Auburn) 04223
- Dark Harbor 04848
- Davenport Cove 04424
- Davis Island 04556
- Days Ferry 04579
- Dayton (Town) 04005
- Deblois 04622
- Dedham 04429
- Deep Cut 04011
- Deering (Part of Portland) 04103
- Deering (Part of Presque Isle) 04769
- Deer Isle 04627
- Delano Park 04106
- Denmark 04022
- Dennistown (Town) 04945
- Dennysville 04628
- Derby 04463
- Detroit 04929
- Dexter♦ 04930
- Dickey 04774
- Dickvale 04290
- Dirego Corner 04358
- Dixfield♦ 04224
- Dixfield Center 04224
- Dixmont 04932
- Dixmont Center 04932
- Dog Corner 04038
- Dog Island Corner (Part of Belfast) 04915
- Dogtown, *Somerset* 04967
- Dog Town, *Washington* 04630
- Dorman 04643
- Douglas Hill 04029
- Dover-Foxcroft♦ 04426
- Dover South Mills 04426
- Downtown (Part of Portland)‡ 04101*
  04112†
- Drake Corner 04849
- Drakes Island 04090
- Dresden (Town) 04342
- Dresden Mills 04342
- Drew (Town) 04497
- Dryden 04225
- Dry Mills 04039
- Ducktrap 04849
- Dunkertown 04270
- Dunns Corner 04355
- Durgintown 04041
- Durham 04222
- Dyer Brook 04747
- Dyer Cove 04011
- E (Town) 04758
- Eagle Lake 04739
- East Andover 04226
- East Auburn (Part of Auburn) 04210
- East Baldwin 04024
- East Benton 04910
- East Bethel 04217
- East Blue Hill 04629
- East Boothbay 04544
- Eastbrook 04634
- East Brownfield 04010
- East Buckfield 04220
- East Central Franklin (Town) 04947
- East Central Penobscot (Town) 04423
- East Central Washington (Town) 04628
- East Corinth 04427
- East Deering (Part of Portland) 04103
- East Denmark 04022
- East Dixfield 04227
- East Dixmont 04932
- East Dover 04426
- East Eddington 04428
- East Edgecomb 04556
- East Eliot 03903
- East End (Part of Portland) 04101
- East Exeter 04427
- East Franklin 04634
- East Friendship 04547
- East Fryeburg 04037
- East Gray 04039
- East Hampden 04444
- East Hancock (Town) 04408
- East Harpswell 04011
- East Hebron 04238
- East Hiram 04041
- East Holden 04429
- East Knox 04986
- East Lamoine 04605
- East Lebanon 04027
- East Limington 04049
- East Livermore 04228
- East Lowell 04493
- East Lyndon (Part of Caribou) 04736
- East Machias 04630
- East Madison 04950
- East Millinocket♦ 04430
- East Monmouth 04259
- East Newport 04933
- East New Portland 04961
- East Northport 04849
- Easton 04740
- Easton Center 04740
- Easton Station 04740
- East Orland 04431
- East Orrington 04474
- East Otisfield 04270
- East Palermo 04354
- East Parsonsfield 04028
- East Peru 04290
- East Pittston 04345
- East Poland 04230
- Eastport 04631
- East Raymond 04071
- East Sebago 04029
- East Stoneham 04231
- East Sullivan 04607
- East Sumner 04220
- East Surry 04605
- East Thorndike 04986
- East Troy 04987
- East Union 04862
- East Vassalboro 04935
- East Warren 04864
- East Waterboro 04030
- East Waterford 04088
- East Wilton 04234
- East Winn 04455
- East Winthrop 04343
- Eaton 04424
- Eddington 04428
- Eden 04672
- Edes Falls 04055
- Edgecomb 04556
- Edinburg (Town) 04448
- Edmunds 04628
- Eggemoggin 04650
- Egypt 04605
- Eight Corners 04074
- Eliot 03903
- Ellingwood Corner 04496
- Ellis Pond 04275
- Ellsworth 04605
- Ellsworth Falls (Part of Ellsworth) 04605
- Elmore 04860
- Elms 04090
- Elmwood 04084
- Embden 04958
- Embden Pond 04958
- Emerson Corner 04967
- Emery Mills 04076
- Emerys Bridge 03908
- Emerys Corner 04048
- Emory Corner 04004
- Enfield 04493
- English (Part of Presque Isle) 04769
- Epping 04623
- Estcourt Station 04743
- Estes Lake 04073
- Etna 04434
- Etna Center 04434
- Eugley Corner 04572
- Eustis 04936
- Exeter 04435
- Exeter Center 04435
- Exeter Corners 04435

*** Area Zip Code** **† Post Office Boxes** **‡ Postal Station** **♦ Census Designated Place** *Italic Type* **County**

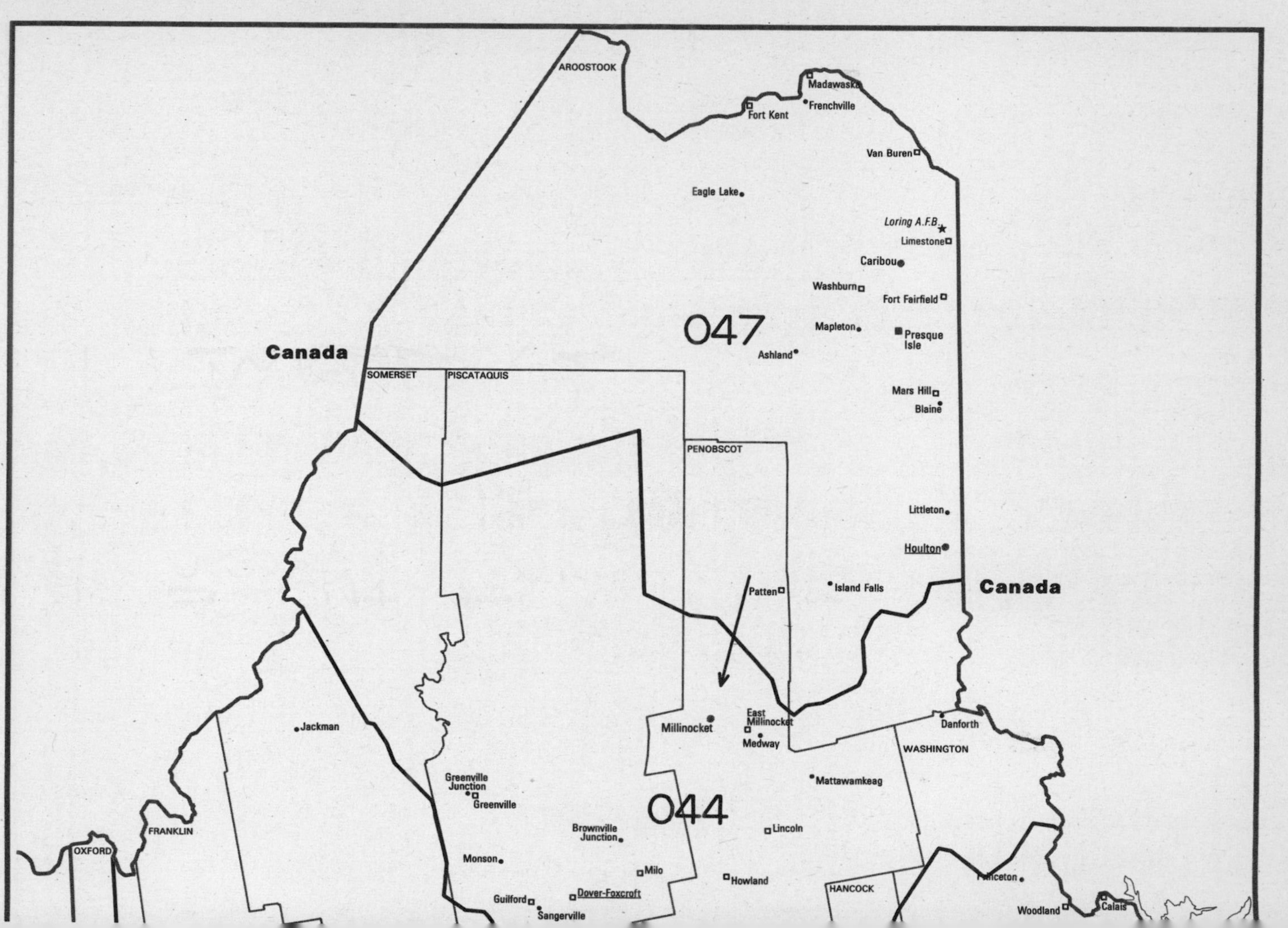
AROOSTOOK
Madawaska
Frenchville
Fort Kent
Van Buren
Eagle Lake
Loring A.F.B.
Limestone
Caribou
Washburn
Fort Fairfield
047
Mapleton
Presque Isle
Ashland
Canada
SOMERSET
PISCATAQUIS
Mars Hill
Blaine
PENOBSCOT
Littleton
Houlton
Patten
Island Falls
Canada
East Millinocket
Millinocket
Medway
Danforth
Jackman
WASHINGTON
Mattawamkeag
Greenville Junction
Greenville
044
FRANKLIN
Brownville Junction
Lincoln
OXFORD
Monson
Milo
Howland
HANCOCK
Guilford
Dover-Foxcroft
Sangerville
Woodland
Calais

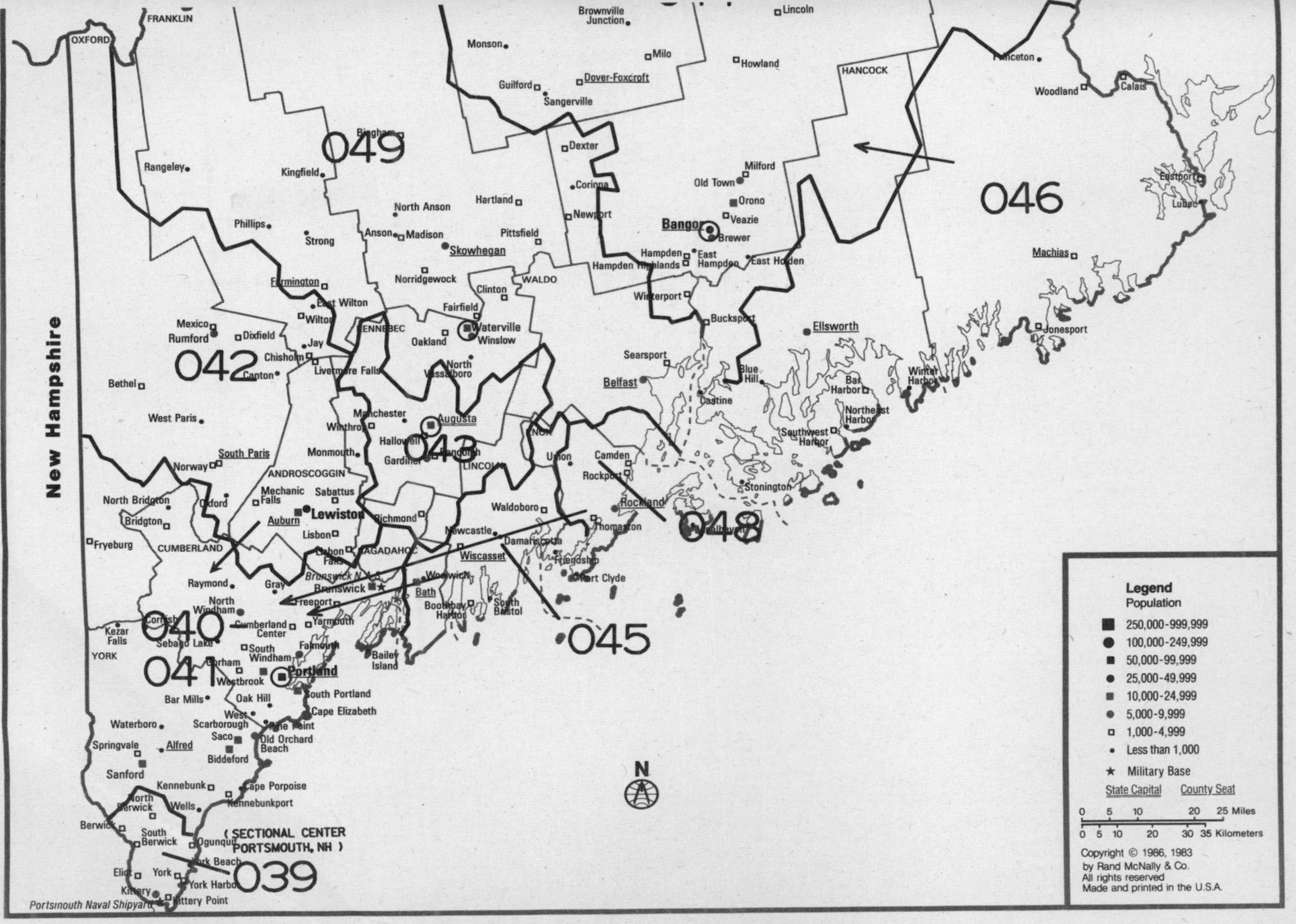
New Hampshire
OXFORD
FRANKLIN
HANCOCK
WALDO
KENNEBEC
LINCOLN
SAGADAHOC
ANDROSCOGGIN
CUMBERLAND
YORK
049
046
042
043
048
040
041
045
039
(SECTIONAL CENTER
PORTSMOUTH, NH)
Brownville Junction
Lincoln
Monson
Milo
Howland
Guilford
Dover-Foxcroft
Sangerville
Woodland
Calais
Eastport
Lubec
Machias
Jonesport
Winter Harbor
Bar Harbor
Northeast Harbor
Southwest Harbor
Ellsworth
Stonington
Blue Hill
Castine
Bucksport
Dexter
Corinna
Newport
Milford
Old Town
Orono
Veazie
Bangor
Brewer
Hampden
East Hampden
Hampden Highlands
East Holden
Winterport
Searsport
Belfast
Camden
Rockport
Rockland
Thomaston
Port Clyde
Friendship
Union
Waldoboro
Damariscotta
South Bristol
Newcastle
Wiscasset
Boothbay Harbor
Woolwich
Bath
Bailey Island
Rangeley
Kingfield
Bingham
North Anson
Hartland
Anson
Madison
Pittsfield
Skowhegan
Phillips
Strong
Farmington
Norridgewock
Clinton
Fairfield
Waterville
Winslow
Oakland
North Vassalboro
East Wilton
Wilton
Mexico
Rumford
Dixfield
Jay
Chisholm
Canton
Livermore Falls
Bethel
West Paris
Manchester
Augusta
Winthrop
Hallowell
Gardiner
Monmouth
South Paris
Norway
Mechanic Falls
Sabattus
Lewiston
Auburn
Lisbon
Lisbon Falls
Richmond
North Bridgton
Bridgton
Oxford
Fryeburg
Raymond
Gray
Brunswick
Freeport
North Windham
Cumberland Center
Yarmouth
Kezar Falls
Sebago Lake
South Windham
Falmouth
Gorham
Westbrook
Portland
South Portland
Cape Elizabeth
Bar Mills
Oak Hill
West Scarborough
Pine Point
Waterboro
Springvale
Alfred
Saco
Old Orchard Beach
Biddeford
Sanford
Kennebunk
Cape Porpoise
Kennebunkport
North Berwick
Wells
Berwick
South Berwick
Ogunquit
York Beach
Eliot
York
York Harbor
Kittery
Kittery Point
Portsmouth Naval Shipyard
N
Legend
Population
250,000-999,999
100,000-249,999
50,000-99,999
25,000-49,999
10,000-24,999
5,000-9,999
1,000-4,999
Less than 1,000
Military Base
State Capital
County Seat
0 5 10 20 25 Miles
0 5 10 20 30 35 Kilometers
Copyright © 1986, 1983
by Rand McNally & Co.
All rights reserved
Made and printed in the U.S.A.

Place	ZIP
Exeter Mills	04427
Fairbanks	04938
Fairfield♦	04937
Fairfield Center	04937
Fairmount	04742
Falmouth	04105
Falmouth Foreside♦	04105
Farmingdale♦	04344
Farmington♦	04938
Farmington Falls	04940
Farwells Corner	04988
Fayette	04349
Fayette Corner	04349
Felch Corner	04048
Ferry Beach (Part of Saco)	04072
Fish Street	04037
Five Corners, *Androscoggin*	04256
Five Corners, *York*	03906
Five Islands	04548
Five Mile Corners	04431
Fletchers Landing	04605
Forest City	04413
Fort Fairfield♦	04742
Fort Kent♦	04743
Fort Kent Mills	04744
Fort Kent Village	04743
Fortunes Rocks (Part of Biddeford)	04005
Fosters Corner, *Cumberland*	04062
Fosters Corner, *Waldo*	04921
Four Corners, *Aroostook*	04750
Four Corners, *York*	04043
Fournier	04756
Frankfort	04438
Franklin	04634
Franklin Road	04606
Freedom	04941
Freeport♦	04032
Frenchboro	04635
Frenchville (Ashland Town)	04732
Frenchville (Frenchville Town)	04745
Friendship	04547
Frye	04275
Fryeburg♦	04037
Fryeburg Center	04037
Fryeburg Harbor	04037
Frye Island	04071
Gardiner	04345
Garfield (Town)	04732
Garland	04939
Georgetown	04548
Gerrishville	04693
Ghent	04973
Gilbertville	04221
Gilead	04217
Glantz Corner	04062
Glenburn (Town)	04401
Glenburn Center	04401
Glen Cove	04846
Glendon	04572
Glenmere	04860
Glenwood (Town)	04497
Goodings (Part of Presque Isle)	04769
Good Will-Hinckley School	04944
Goodwins Mills	04005
Goose Rocks Beach	04046
Gorham♦	04038
Gotts Island	04653
Gould Corner	03903
Gould Landing	04401
Gouldsboro	04607
Grand Beach	04074
Grand Isle	04746
Grand Lake Stream	04637
Granite Hill (Part of Hallowell)	04347
Grass Corner	04750
Gray	04039
Grays Corner	04676
Great Diamond Island (Part of Portland)	04109
Great East Lake	04001
Great Falls (Part of Auburn)‡	04210*
....	04212†
Great Pond	04408
Great Works (Part of Old Town)	04468
Great Works, *York*	03908
Greeley Landing	04426
Green Acre	03903
Greenbush	04467
Greene	04236
Greenfield	04423
Green Lake	04429
Greens Corner	04988
Greenville	04441
Greenville Junction	04442
Greenwood	04289
Grimes Mill (Part of Caribou)	04736
Grindstone	04460
Grindstone Neck	04693
Grove	04638
Groveville	04093
Growstown	04011
Guerette	04783
Guilford♦	04443
Guillemette	04073
Hackett Mills	04258
Halldale	04941
Hallowell	04347
Hall Quarry	04660
Hamilton Station	04672
Hamlin	04785
Hammond (Town)	04730
Hampden	04444
Hampden Center	04444
Hampden Highlands	04444
Hancock	04640
Hancock Point	04640
Hanover	04237
Harborside	04642
Harding	04011
Harfords Point	04442
Harmon Beach	04084
Harmony	04942
Harpswell (Town)	04079
Harpswell Center	04079
Harrington	04643
Harrington Corner	04555
Harrison	04040
Hartford	04221
Hartland♦	04943
Haskell Corner (Part of Auburn)	04210
Hatchs Corner	04342
Haven	04616
Hayden Corner	04901
Haynesville	04497
Head of the Tide (Part of Belfast)	04915
Head Tide	04535
Hebron	04238
Hermon	04401
Hermon Center	04401
Hermond Pond	04401
Heron Island	04568
Herricks	04617
Hersey (Town)	04765
Hibberts (Town)	04348
Higgins Beach	04074
Higginsville	04450
Highland (Town)	04961
Highland Lake (Part of Westbrook)	04092
Highpine	04090
Hills Beach (Part of Biddeford)	04005
Hillside	04029
Hinckley	04944
Hiram	04041
Hodgdon	04730
Hodgdon Corner	04901
Holden (Town)	04429
Holden Center	04429
Hollis (Town)	04042
Hollis Center	04042
Holmes Bay	04691
Holmes Mill (Part of Belfast)	04915
Hope	04847
Houghton	04275
Houlton♦	04730
Howes Corner	04282
Howland, *Penobscot*	04448
Hoyttown	04654
Hudson	04449
Hulls Cove	04644
Hunnewell Hill	04074
Hunts Corner	04217
Hutchins Corner	04942
Indian Island	04468
Indian Point	04660
Indian River	04606
Industrial (Part of Presque Isle)	04769
Industry (Town)	04938
Ingall's Hill	04009
Intervale	04260
Ireland Corner	04062
Irish Settlement	04424
Island Falls	04747
Isle au Haut	04645
Isle of Springs	04549
Islesboro	04848
Islesford	04646
Jackman	04945
Jackson	04921
Jackson Corner	04479
Jackson Corners	04921
Jacksonville	04630
Jay	04239
Jefferson	04348
Jemtland	04783
Jewett	03908
Jonesboro	04648
Jonesport	04649
Jordan Mills	04459
Kalers Corner	04572
Keegan	04785
Keenes Corner	04263
Kendalls Corner	04915
Kenduskeag	04450
Kennard Corner	03903
Kennebago Lake	04970
Kennebec	04654
Kennebunk♦	04043
Kennebunk Beach	04043
Kennebunk Landing	04043
Kennebunk Pond	04002
Kennebunkport♦	04046
Kents Hill	04349
Kezar Falls	04047
Kingfield	04947
Kingman	04451
Kingsbury	04942
Kinney Shores (Part of Saco)	04072
Kittery♦	03904
Kittery Foreside	03904
Kittery Point♦	03905
Knights Landing	04414
Knightville (Part of South Portland)	04106
Knowles Corner	04780
Knox (Town)	04986
Knox Center	04986
Knox Corner	04986
Knox Station	04986
Kokadjo	04441
Lagrange	04453
Lake Arrowhead Estates	04061
Lake City	04843
Lake Moxie	04985
Lake View	04463
Lakeville (Town)	04487
Lakewood	04950
Lambert Lake	04454
Lambs Corner	04901
Lamoine Beach	04605
Lamoine Corner	04605
Land of Nod	04062
Larone	04937
Larrabee	04655
Lawry	04547
Lebanon (Town)	04027
Lee	04455
Leeds	04263
Leeds Junction	04263
Levant	04456
Lewiston	04240-43
For specific ZIP Codes call (888) 275-8777, or your local postmaster.	
Lewiston Junction (Part of Auburn)	04210
Lewiston Mall (Part of Lewiston)	04240
Libby Hill (Part of Gardiner)	04345
Liberty	04949
Lille	04746
Lily Bay	04441
Limerick	04048
Limerick Mills	04048
Limestone♦	04750
Limington	04049
Lincoln, *Oxford* (Town)	03579
Lincoln, *Penobscot*♦	04457
Lincoln Center	04457
Lincoln Mills	04928
Lincolnville	04849
Lincolnville Center	04850
Linekin	04544
Linneus	04730
Lisbon	04250
Lisbon Center	04252
Lisbon Falls♦‡	04252
Litchfield	04350
Litchfield Corners	04350
Litchfield Plains	04350
Little Deer Isle	04650
Little Diamond Island (Part of Portland)	04109
Little Falls	04038
Littlefield Corner (Part of Auburn)	04210
Littlejohn Island	04096
Little Machias	04626
Littleton	04730
Livermore	04253
Livermore Falls♦	04254
Locke Mills	04255
Long Beach, *Cumberland*	04084
Long Beach, *York*	03910
Long Cove	04857
Long Island	04050
Long Pond	04945
Lookout	04645
Lovell	04051
Lowell	04493
Lower Dennysville	04628
Lubec	04652
Lucerne-In-Maine	04429
Ludlow	04730
Lyman (Town)	04002
Lynchville	04231
McFarlands Corner	04941
McGraw (Part of Caribou)	04736
Machias♦	04654
Machiasport	04655
Mackworth Island	04105
Mackworth Point	04105
MacMahan	04548
Macwahoc	04451
Madawaska♦	04756
Madawaska (Part of Caribou)	04736
Madawaska Lake	04783
Madison♦	04950
Madrid	04966
Magalloway (Town)	03579
Maine (Part of Caribou)	04736
Maine Mall (Part of South Portland)	04106
Mainstream	04942
Manchester	04351
Manset	04679
Maple Grove	04742
Mapleton	04757
Maplewood	04095
Mariaville	04605
Marion	04628
Marlboro	04605
Marrtown	04548
Marshfield	04654
Mars Hill	04758
Marshville	04643
Marston Corner (Part of Auburn)	04210
Martin	04547
Martinsville	04860
Masardis	04759
Mason Bay	04649
Mast Landing	04032
Matinicus	04851
Matinicus Isle (Town)	04851
Mattawamkeag	04459
Maxfield (Town)	04453
Mayberry Hill	04015
Maysville (Part of Presque Isle)	04769
Mayville	04217
Mechanic Falls♦	04256
Meddybemps (Town)	04657
Meddybemps	04657
Medford	04453
Medford Center	04453
Medomak	04551
Medway	04460
Melvin Heights	04843
Mercer	04957
Merepoint	04011
Merrill (Town)	04780
Mexico♦	04257
Middle Dam	04216
Middle Intervale	04217
Milbridge	04658
Milford♦	04461
Milliken Mills	04064
Millinocket♦	04462
Milltown (Part of Calais)‡	04619
Milo♦	04463
Milton	04219
Minot	04258
Minturn	04685
Molunkus	04451
Monarda	04776
Monhegan	04852
Monmouth	04259
Monroe	04951
Monroe Center	04951
Monson	04464
Monticello	04760
Montsweag	04579
Montville (Town)	04941
Moody	04054
Moody Beach	04054
....	04090
For specific ZIP Codes call (888) 275-8777, or your local postmaster.	
Moody Point	04090
Moosehead	04442
Moose River	04945
Morgan Beach	04493
Moro (Town)	04780
Morrill	04952
Morris Corner	04750
Morrison Corner	04927
Morse Corners	04928
Moscow	04920
Mountainview	04964
Mount Chase (Town)	04765
Mount Desert	04660
Mount Pisgah	04538
Mount Vernon	04352
Mousam Lake	04076
Murphys Corner	04579
Muscongus	04551
Naples	04055
Nashville (Town)	04732
Naskeag	04616
Naval Computer and Telecommunications Center, Cutler	04630
Nequasset	04579
Newagen	04552
New Auburn (Part of Auburn)	04210
Newburgh (Town)	04444
Newburgh Center	04444
Newburgh Village	04444
New Canada (Town)	04743
Newcastle	04553
Newfield	04056
New Gloucester	04260
Newhall	04062
New Harbor	04554
New Limerick	04761
New Meadows	04530
Newport♦	04953
New Portland	04954
Newry	04261
New Sharon	04955
New Sweden	04762
Newtown (Part of Biddeford)	04005
New Vineyard	04956
Nickerson Lake	04730
Nobleboro	04555
Nobles Corner	04268
Norcross	04462
Norridgewock♦	04957
North Alfred	04002
North Amity	04471
North Anson	04958
North Appleton	04862
North Auburn (Part of Auburn)	04210
North Augusta (Part of Augusta)	04330
North Baldwin	04024
North Bancroft	04424
North Bangor (Part of Bangor)	04401
North Bath (Part of Bath)	04530
North Belgrade	04917
North Berwick♦	03906
North Blue Hill	04614
North Bradford	04410
North Brewer (Part of Brewer)	04412
North Bridgton	04057
North Brooklin	04616
North Brooksville	04617
North Buckfield	04220
North Bucksport	04416
North Castine	04421
North Chatham	04037
North Chesterville	04938
North Cushing	04563
North Cutler	04630
North Deering (Part of Portland)	04103

Place	ZIP Code
North Deer Isle	04627
North Dexter	04930
North Dixmont	04932
North East Carry	04478
Northeast Harbor	04662
Northeast Piscataquis (Town)	04462
Northeast Somerset (Town)	04920
North Edgecomb	04556
North Ellsworth (Part of Ellsworth)	04605
Northern Maine Junction	04401
North Fairfield	04937
North Falmouth	04105
Northfield	04654
North Franklin (Town)	04936
North Fryeburg	04037
North Gorham	04075
North Gray	04039
North Guilford	04443
North Harpswell	04079
North Haven	04853
North Hermon	04401
North Hollis	04042
North Islesboro	04848
North Jay	04262
North Jefferson	04348
North Lamoine	04605
North Lebanon	04027
North Leeds	04263
North Limington	04049
North Lincoln	04457
North Livermore	04254
North Lovell	04051
North Lubec	04652
North Lyndon (Part of Caribou)	04736
North Monmouth	04265
North Monroe	04951
North Newcastle	04553
North New Portland	04961
North Newry	04261
North Norway	04268
North Orrington	04474
North Oxford (Town)	03579
North Palermo	04354
North Paris	04289
North Parsonsfield	04047
North Penobscot, Penobscot (Town)	04462
North Penobscot, *Hancock*	04476
North Perry	04667
Northport	04849
North Pownal	04069
North Raymond	04071
North Scarborough	04074
North Searsmont	04973
North Searsport	04974
North Sebago	04029
North Sedgwick	04676
North Shapleigh	04076
North Sidney	04330
North Sullivan	04664
North Turner	04266
North Vassalboro	04962
North Wade	04786
North Waldoboro	04572
North Washington (Town)	04686
North Waterboro	04061
North Waterford	04267
North Wayne	04284
Northwest Aroostook (Town)	04788
Northwest Bethel	04217
Northwest Hancock (Town)	04408
Northwest Piscataquis (Town)	04441
Northwest Somerset (Town)	04945
North Whitefield	04353
North Windham	04062
North Windsor	04363
North Woodstock	04219
North Yarmouth (Town)	04021
Norway♦	04268
Norway Center	04268
Norway Lake	04268
Notre Dame	04746
Number Four	04051
Oakdale (Part of Portland)	04101
	04103
For specific ZIP Codes call (888) 275-8777, or your local postmaster.	
Oakfield	04763
Oak Hill, *Androscoggin*	04274
Oak Hill, *Cumberland*	04074
Oakland♦	04963
Oak Point	04605
Oak Ridge (Part of Biddeford)	04005
Oaks Pond	04976
Oak Terrace	03904
Ocean Park	04063
Ocean Point	04544
Oceanview Harbor	04074
Oceanville	04681
Ogontz	04478
Ogunquit	03907
Olamon	04467
Olde Mill Brook	04074
Old Orchard Beach♦	04064
Old Town	04468
Onawa	04443
Oquossoc	04964
Orffs Corner	04572
Orient	04471
Orland	04472
Orono♦	04473
Orrington	04474
Orrington Center	04474
Orrs Island	04066
Osborn (Town)	04605
Otis	04605
Otisfield	04270
Otter Creek	04665
Owls Head	04854
Oxbow	04764
Oxford♦	04270
Paine Corner	04281
Paines Corner	04901
Palermo	04354
Palmyra	04965
Paris	04271
Parker Head	04562
Parkhurst (Part of Presque Isle)	04769
Parkman	04443
Parsonfield (Town)	04028†
	04047*
Parsonsfield	04047
Passadumkeag	04475
Passamaquoddy Indian Township Reservation	04668
Patten	04765
Pauls (Part of Caribou)	04736
Peaks Island (Part of Portland)	04108
Pea Ridge	04457
Pejepscot	04086
Pelton Hill (Part of Augusta)	04330
Pemaquid	04558
Pemaquid Beach	04554
Pemaquid Harbor	04558
Pemaquid Point	04554
Pembroke	04666
Penley's Corner (Part of Auburn)	04210
Penobscot	04476
Penobscot Indian Island Reservation	04468
Perham	04766
Perkins (Town)	04357
Perry (Part of Presque Isle)	04769
Perry, *Washington*	04667
Perrys Corner	04048
Peru	04290
Peter Dana Point	04668
Phair (Part of Presque Isle)	04769
Phillips	04966
Phippsburg	04562
Pigeon Hill	04658
Pike Corner	04015
Pine Cliff	04576
Pine Hill	03902
Pine Park	04064
Pine Point	04074
Pinkhams Cove	04917
Pishon Ferry	04944
Pittsfield♦	04967
Pittston	04345
Pittston Farm	04478
Plaisted	04739
Pleasant Beach	04858
Pleasantdale (Part of South Portland)	04106
Pleasant Hill (mail Freeport)	04032
Pleasant Hill (mail Scarborough)	04074
Pleasant Hill (mail Portland)	04105
Pleasant Lake	04694
Pleasant Point	04563
Pleasant Point Indian Reservation	04667
Pleasant Pond	04925
Pleasant Ridge	04920
Plummer Island	04074
Plymouth	04969
Poland	04274
Poland Spring	04274
Pond Cove	04107
Poors Mills (Part of Belfast)	04915
Popham Beach	04562
Portage	04768
Portage Lake (Town)	04768
Port Clyde	04855
Porter	04068
Porterfield	04047
Porter Landing	04032
Portland	04101-04
	04109
	04112
For specific ZIP Codes call (888) 275-8777, or your local postmaster.	
Portsmouth Naval Shipyard	03801
Pownal (Town)	04069
Pownal Center	04069
Pratt Corner	04281
Prentiss	04487
Presque Isle	04769
Prides Corner (Part of Westbrook)	04092
Princeton	04668
Promenade Mall (Part of Lewiston)	04240
Promised Land	04274
Prospect	04981
Prospect Ferry	04981
Prospect Harbor	04669
Prouts Neck‡	04074
Pulpit Harbor	04853
Pumpkin Valley	04009
Quimby	04770
Quoddy (Part of Eastport)	04631
Randolph♦	04346
Rangeley	04970
Raymond	04071
Rayville	04270
Razorville	04574
Reach	04627
Readfield	04355
Readfield Depot	04355
Red Beach (Part of Calais)	04619
Redding	04292
Red Rock Corner	04672
Reed (Town)	04497
Reeds	04966
Remick Corners	03904
Reynolds Corner	04922
Richmond♦	04357
Richmond Corner	04357
Richmond Mill	04284
Richville	04084
Ridge	04652
Ridlonville	04257
Riley	04239
Ripley, *Somerset*	04930
Ripley, *Washington*	04643
Riverside	04330
Riverton (Part of Portland)	04103
Riverview (Part of Presque Isle)	04769
Robbinston	04671
Roberts (Part of Caribou)	04736
Roberts Corner	04093
Robinhood	04548
Robinson	04758
Robinson Corner	04240
Robyville	04450
Rockland	04841
Rockport	04856
Rockville	04856
Rockwood	04478
Rogers Corners	04987
Rome	04957
Rome Corner	04957
Roque Bluffs	04654
Rosemont (Part of Portland)	04103
Ross Corner	04087
Round Pond	04564
Rowe Corner (Part of Auburn)	04210
Roxbury	04275
Rumford♦	04276
Rumford Center	04278
Rumford Corner	04219
Rumford Point	04279
Sabattus	04280
Sabbathday Lake	04260
Saco	04072
St. Agatha	04772
St. Albans	04971
St. David	04773
St. Francis	04774
St. George	04857
St. John	04743
Salom	04903
Salmon Falls	04004
Salsbury Cove	04672
Sanderson Corners	04349
Sandhill Corner	04341
Sandy Beach	04401
Sandy Creek	04009
Sandy Point	04972
Sandy River (Town)	04970
Sandy River Beach	04649
Sanford♦	04073
Sangerville	04479
Saponac	04417
Sargentville	04673
Saunders (Part of Presque Isle)	04769
Scarborough♦	04074
Schoodic Lake	04623
Scituate	03909
Scotland, *Cumberland*	04062
Scotland, *York*	03909
Scott (Part of Presque Isle)	04769
Scribners Mill	04040
Seabury	03909
Seal Cove	04674
Seal Harbor	04675
Searsmont	04973
Searsport♦	04974
Seawall	04679
Sebago	04029
Sebago Lake	04075
Sebasco	04565
Sebasco Estates	04565
Sebec	04481
Sebec Corners	04426
Sebec Lake	04482
Seboeis	04448
Seboomook	04478
Seboomook Lake (Town)	04478
Sedgwick	04676
Shady Nook	03830
Shaker Village	04260
Shapleigh	04076
Shaw Mills	04084
Shawmut	04975
Sheepscot	04578
Sheridan	04775
Sherman	04776
Sherman Mills	04776
Shermans Corner	04949
Shermans Corner (Part of Belfast)	04915
Sherman Station	04777
Shin Pond	04765
Shirley (Town)	04485
Shirley Mills	04485
Shy Corner	04254
Sibley Pond	04924
Sidney	04330
Sidney Center	04330
Silver Ridge	04776
Simonton Corners	04856
Simpson Corners	04856
Sinclair	04779
Skillings Corner	04282
Skowhegan♦	04976
Slab City, *Oxford*	04051
Slab City, *Waldo*	04849
Small Point	04567
Small Point Beach	04567
Smithfield	04978
Smithville	04680
Smyrna (Town)	04780
Smyrna Center	04780
Smyrna Mills	04780
Soldier Pond	04781
Solon	04979
Somerville	04348
Somersville	04660
Sorrento	04677
Sound	04660
South Acton	04001
South Addison	04606
South Andover	04216
South Arm	04216
South Aroostook (Town)	04730
South Berwick	03908
South Blue Hill	04615
South Brewer (Part of Brewer)	04412
South Bridgton	04009
South Bristol	04568
South Brooksville	04617
South Buxton	04038
South Casco	04077
South China	04358
South Corinth	04427
South Deer Isle	04681
South Dover	04426
South Durham	04222
Southeast Piscataquis (Town)	04463
South Eliot♦	03903
South Exeter	04435
South Franklin (Town)	04224
South Freeport	04078
South Gardiner (Part of Gardiner)	04359
South Gorham	04038
South Gouldsboro	04607
South Gray	04039
South Hancock	04605
South Harpswell (Harpswell)	04079
South Hiram	04041
South Hollis	04042
South Hope	04847
South Jefferson	04553
South Lagrange	04453
South Lebanon	04027
South Levant	04456
South Lewiston (Part of Lewiston)‡	04240
South Liberty	04949
South Limington	04049
South Lincoln	04457
South Livermore	04254
South Lubec	04652
South Monmouth	04259
South Montville	04949
South Newcastle	04553
South Orland	04472
South Orrington	04474
South Oxford (Town)	04267
South Paris♦	04281
South Parsonsfield	04047
South Penobscot	04476
Southport	04576
South Portland	04106*
	04116†
South Portland Heights (Part of South Portland)	04106
South Princeton	04668
South Rangeley	04964
South Rumford	04276
South Sanford♦	04073
South Sebec	04481
South Side	03909
South Springfield	04487
South Strong	04983
South Surry	04684
South Thomaston	04858
South Trescott	04652
South Union	04864
South Vasselboro	04989
South Waldoboro	04572
South Warren	04864
South Waterford	04081
Southwest Harbor	04679
Southwest Harbor Coast Guard Base	04679
South Windham	04082
South Windsor	04363
South Woodstock	04289
South Woodville	04457
Spears Corner	04345
Spooners Mill	04930
Spragueville (Part of Presque Isle)	04769
Springfield	04487
Springvale♦	0408
Spruce Head	048
Spruce Head Island	0
Spruce Point	
Spruce Shores	
Squa Pan	
Square Lake (Town)	
Square Pond	
Squirrel Island	
Stacyville	

* Area Zip Code † Post Office Boxes ‡ Postal Station ♦ Census Designated Place *Italic Type* Co

Place	ZIP
Standish	04084
Stanwood Park (Part of South Portland)	04106
Starboard	04655
Starks	04911
State Road	04757
Station A (Part of Portland)‡	04101
Stebbins	04742
Steep Falls	04085
Stetson	04488
Steuben	04680
Stevens Corner	03830
Stevensville	04742
Stickney Corner	04574
Stillwater (Part of Old Town)	04489
Stockholm	04783
Stockton Springs	04981
Stoneham (Town)	04231
Stonington	04681
Stover Corner	04617
Stow	04037
Stratton	04982
Strickland	04263
Strong	04983
Stroudwater (Part of Portland)	04102
Sugar Hill	04735
Sullivan	04664
Summerhaven (Part of Augusta)	04330
Sumner (Town)	04292
Sunset	04683
Sunset Park (Part of Portland)	04106
Sunshine	04627
Surfside	04064
Surry	04684
Sutton Island	04662
Swan Pond	04002
Swans Island	04685
Swanville	04915
Sweden, *Oxford* (Town)	04040
Sweden, *Aroostook*	04762
Tacoma	04350
Tainter Corner	04224
Tallwood	04355
Talmadge (Town)	04492
Tatnic	04090
Tattle Corner (Part of Biddeford)	04005
Tea Kettle Corner (Part of Biddeford)	04005
Temple	04984
Temple Heights	04849
Tenants Harbor	04860
The Forks	04985
The Highlands	04441
The Kingdom	04941
Thomaston♦	04861
Thompson Point	04055
Thorndike	04986
Thornton Heights (Part of South Portland)	04106
Tibbettstown	04623
Tobeys Corner	03903
Topsfield	04490
Topsham♦	04086
Tory Hill	04093
Toulouse Corner	04937
Town Farm Hill	04040
Town Hill	04609
Tracy Corners	04606
Trainor Corner	04345
Trap Corner	04289
Trefethen (Part of Portland)	04108
Tremont	04605
Tremont (Town)	04653
Trenton	04605
Trevett	04571
Troutdale	04985
Troy	04987
Troy Center	04987
Turbats Creek	04046
Turner	04282
Turner Center	04283
Turners Corner	04572
Turnpike Mall (Part of Augusta)	04330
Twelve Corners	04254
Twombly (Town)	04417
Two Trails	04084
Union	04862
Unionville	04622
Unity, *Kennebec* (Town)	04988
Unity, *Waldo*	04988
University Bookstore‡	04473
Upper Abbot	04406
Upper Frenchville	04745
Upper Gloucester	04260
Upton	04261
Van Buren♦	04785
Vanceboro	04491
Vassalboro	04989
Veazie	04401
Verona	04416
Verona Park	04416
Vienna	04360
Viking Village	04217
Vinalhaven	04863
Virginia	04276
Wade (Town)	04786
Waite	04492
Waldo	04915
Waldoboro♦	04572
Wales (Town)	04280
Wales Center	04280
Wales Corner	04280
Wallagrass	04781
Walnut Hill (N. Yarmouth)	04097
Walpole	04573
Waltham	04605
Wards Cove	04075
Wardtown	04032
Warren	04864
Warren Station	04864
Washburn	04786
Washington	04574
Waterboro	04087
Waterboro Center	04087
Waterford	04088
Waterman Beach	04858
Water Street (Part of Augusta)‡	04330*
	04338†
Waterville	04901*
	04903†
Waverly	04967
Wayne	04284
Webb Hill	04459
Webster (Town)	04487
Webster	04473
Webster Corner	04250
Weeks Mills	04358
Welchville	04270
Weld	04285
Wellington	04942
Wells	04090
Wells Beach	04090
Wells Branch	04090
Wesley	04686
West Appleton	04862
West Athens	04912
West Auburn (Part of Auburn)	04210
West Baldwin	04091
West Bath (Town)	04530
West Bethel‡	04217
West Boothbay Harbor	04575
West Bowdoin	04287
West Bridgton	04009
Westbrook	04092*
	04098†
West Brooklin	04616
West Brooksville	04617
West Buxton	04093
West Central Franklin (Town)	04285
West Charleston	04422
West Corinth	04427
West Cumberland	04021
West Denmark	04022
West Durham	04069
West Ellsworth (Part of Ellsworth)	04605
West End (Part of Portland)	04102
West Enfield	04493
West Falmouth Corner	04105
West Farmington	04992
Westfield	04787
West Forks	04985
West Franklin	04634
West Fryeburg	04037
West Gardiner (Town)	04345
West Georgetown	04548
West Gorham	04038
West Gouldsboro	04607
West Gray	04039
West Hampden	04444
West Harpswell	04079
West Harrington	04643
West Hollis	04042
West Jonesport	04649
West Kennebunk	04094
West Lebanon	04027
West Leeds	04263
West Levant	04456
West Lubec	04652
Westmanland (Town)	04783
West Mills	04938
West Minot	04288
West Mount Vernon	04352
West Newfield	04095
West Old Town (Part of Old Town)	04468
Weston	04424
West Palmyra	04965
West Paris	04289
West Pembroke	04666
West Penobscot	04476
West Peru	04290
West Point	04565
West Poland	04291
Westport	04578
West Pownal (Pownal)	04069
West Princeton	04668
West Ripley	04930
West Rockport	04865
West Scarborough	04070
West Seboois	04462
West Sidney	04330
West Southport	04576
West Stonington	04681
West Sullivan	04664
West Sumner	04292
West Tremont	04690
West Trenton	04605
West Waldoboro	04572
West Washington	04574
West Winterport	04496
Wheelock	04743
Whitefield	04353
White Oak Corner	04864
White Rock	04038
White School Corner	04950
Whites Corner	04260
Whiting	04691
Whitlocks Mill	04619
Whitney (Town)	04487
Whitney Corner	04864
Whitneyville	04654
Wildes District	04046
Wildwood Park	04110
Wiley Corner	04861
Willimantic	04443
Wilson Corner (Part of Ellsworth)	04605
Wilsons Mills	03579
Wilton	04294
Windham♦	04062
Windham Center	04062
Windham Hill	04062
Windemere	04988
Windsor	04363
Winn	04495
Winnecook	04922
Winnegance	04562
Winslow♦	04901
Winslows Mills	04572
Winter Harbor	04693
Winterport♦	04496
Winterville	04788
Winthrop♦	04364
Winthrop Center	04364
Wiscasset♦	04578
Wonsqueak Harbor	04613
Woodfords (Part of Portland)‡	04101
Woodland, *Aroostook* (Town)	04736
Woodland, *Washington*♦	04694
Woodland Junction	04694
Woodmans Mills	04973
Woodstock (Town)	04219
Woodville (Town)	04457
Woolwich	04579
Worthley Pond	04290
Wyman, *Franklin* (Town)	04982
Wyman, *Washington*	04658
Wytopitlock	04497
Yarmouth♦	04096
York Corner	03911
York Village	03909
York Beach‡	03910
York Cliffs	03902
York Harbor	03911
York Heights	03909
Youngs Corner (Part of Auburn)	04210
Youngtown	04850

Abell 20606
Aberdeen 21001
Aberdeen Proving Ground 21005
Abingdon 21009
Academy Heights 21228
Academy Junction 21113
Accident 21520
Accokeek♦ 20607
Accokeek Acres 20607
Accokeek Groves 20607
Acco Park 20607
Adamstown 21710
Adams Woods 20783
Adelina 20678
Adelphi 20783
Adelphi Hills 20783
Adelphi Manor 20783
Ady 21154
Aero Acres 21220
Aikin (Part of Perryville) 21903
Airey 21613
Albantown 21074
Albeth Heights 21163
Aldino 21001
Alesia 21107
Allanwood 20906
Allegany Grove 21502
Allen 21810
Allenford 21042
Allens Fresh 20632
Allentown Mall‡ 20748
Allenwood 21801
Allenwood Acres 20748
Allview 21045
Allview Estates 21046
Alpha 21104
Alpine Beach 21122
Altamont 21561
Alta Vista 20817
Alta Vista Gardens 20814
Alta Vista Terrace 20814
Amberly 21401
Amberly of Kings Court 21237
Amber Meadows (Part of Bowie) 20716
Amcelle Acres 21502
American Cities‡ 21044
American Corners 21632
Ammendale 20705
Anchorage (Part of Annapolis) 21403
Ancient Oak 20878
Ancient Oak North 20878
Andersontown 21629
Andover Estates 20692
Andrew Hills 20748
Andrews 21626
Andrews Air Force Base 20762
Andrews Estates 20746
Andrews Manor 20746
Annapolis 21401-05
For specific ZIP Codes call (888) 275-8777, or your local postmaster.
Annapolis Junction 20701
Annapolis Rock 21797
Anneslie 21212
Antietam 21782
Apple Green 20754
Apple Grove 20744
Appleton Acres 21921
Appliance Park-East (Part of Baltimore) 21045
Appolds 21778
Aquasco 20608
Aragona Village 20744
Arden-on-the-Severn♦ 21032
Ardmore 20785
Ardwick 20785
Argonne Hills 20755
Argyle Park 20901
Arlington (Part of Baltimore)‡ 21215
Armagh 21204
Arnold 21012
Arnold Heights 20746
Arnoldtown 21755
Arrowhead, *Howard* 21046
Arrow Head, *Montgomery* 20879
Arrowood 20817
Arundel Gardens 21225
Arundel Hills 21090
Arundel on the Bay 21403
Arundel Plaza 21146
Arundel View 21054
Arundel Village 21225

Asbury Methodist Home (Part of Gaithersburg)‡ 20877
Ashburton 20817
Asher Glade 21531
Ashton 20861
Ashton Pond 20861
Asleigh 20817
Aspen Hill 20906
Aspen Hill Park 20853
Aspen Knolls 20853
Athol 21837
Atholton 21045
Atholton Manor 21045
Augusta 21758
Aurora Hills 21108
Auth Village 20746
Autrey Park (Part of Rockville) 20850
Autumn Hill 21043
Avalon Shores 20764
Avenue 20609
Avilton 21539
Avondale Grove 20782
Ayrlawn 20814
Back Bay Beach 20778
Back River Highlands 21221
Baden 20613
Bainbridge Naval Training Center 21904
Bakersville 21713
Bald Eagle 20613
Baldwin 21013
Baldwin Hill 21108
Baldwin Hills South 21032
Ballard Gardens 21220
Ballenger Creek♦ 21701

Baltimore

.... 21201-03
.... 21205-06
.... 21209-19
.... 21222-26
.... 21229-33
.... 21239-40
.... 21270-85
.... 21297
For specific ZIP Codes call (888) 275-8777, or your local postmaster.

Colleges & Universities

Baltimore Hebrew Univ 21215
Coll of Notre Dame of Maryland 21210
Coppin State Coll 21216
Johns Hopkins Univ 21218
Loyola Coll 21210
Maryland Institute Coll of Art 21217
Morgan State Univ 21239
Ner Israel Rabbinical Coll 21208
Peabody Institute of Johns Hopkins Univ 21202
Saint Mary's Seminary & Univ 21210
Sojourner-Douglass Coll 21205
Univ of Baltimore 21201
Univ of Maryland 21201

Financial Institutions

Crestar Bank 21202
The First Nat Bank 21201
First Union Nat Bank 21224
Mercantile-Safe Deposit 21201
Provident Bank 21202

Hospitals

Franklin Square Hosp Ctr 21237
Greater Baltimore Med Ctr 21204
Harbor Hosp Ctr 21225
Johns Hopkins Bayview Med Ctr 21224
Johns Hopkins Hosp 21287
Mercy Med Ctr 21202
St Agnes Health Care 21229
Sinai Hosp 21215
Union Memorial Hosp 21218
Univ of Maryland Med System 21201

Hotels/Motels

BWI Airport Marriott 21240
Hyatt Regency, Inner Harbor 21202
Marriott, Inner Harbor 21201
Omni, Inner Harbor 21201
Renaissance, Harborplace 21202
Sheraton, Inner Harbor 21201
Sheraton North 21204

Military Installations

Air Force Publishing Distribution Ctr 21220
Coast Guard Yard, Curtis Bay 21226
Defense Fuel Support Point 21226
Maryland Air Nat Guard, FB6191, Martin State Airport 21220
MTMC Baltimore Outport 21227
U S Army Corps of Engineers 21203
U S Army Publications Distribution Ctr 21220

Baltimore Corner 21640
Baltimore Highlands 21227
Banks O'Dee 20664
Bannockburn 20814
Bannockburn Estates 20817
Bannockburn Heights 20817
Barclay 21607
Barefoot Acres 20619
Bar Harbor 21122
Bark Hill 21791
Barksdale 21921
Barnaby Manor 20744
Barnaby Run Estates 20745
Barnaby Village 20745
Bar Neck 21671
Barnes Corner 21917
Barnesville 20838
Barrelville 21545
Barstow 20610
Bartholows 21771
Barton 21521
Bartonsville 21701
Battery Park 20814
Battle Grove 21222
Bayberry 21012
Bay City 21666
Bay Highlands 21403
Baynesville 21204
Bay Ridge 21403
Bayside Beach 21122
Bay View, Cecil 21901
Bay View (Part of Baltimore) 21224
Bay View Estates 21919
Beachville 20684
Beachwood Forest 21122
Beachwood Grove 21122
Beachwood on the Burley 21401
Beacon Heights 20737
Beacon Hill 21401
Beale Manor 21403
Beall Estates 20716
Beallsville 20839
Beantown 20601
Bear Creek Junction 21222
Beaufort Park 20759
Beauty Beach 21061
Beauvue 20650
Beaver Creek 21740
Beaver Dam 21851
Beaver Dam Estates 20785
Beaver Heights 20743
Beckleysville 21074
Bedford 20708
Bedfordshire 20854
Bel Air, *Allegany* 21502
Bel Air, *Harford* 21014-15
For specific ZIP Codes call (888) 275-8777, or your local postmaster.
Belair (Part of Bowie) 20715
Bel Air Acres, *Charles* 20601
Bel Air Acres, *Harford* 21014
Belair Buckingham (Part of Bowie) 20715
Belair Chapel Forge (Part of Bowie) 20715
Belair Foxhill (Part of Bowie) 20715
Belair Heather Hills (Part of Bowie) 20715

Belair Idlewild (Part of Bowie) 20715
Belair Kenilworth (Part of Bowie) 20715
Belair Longridge (Part of Bowie) 20715
Belair Overbrook (Part of Bowie) 20715
Belair Rockledge (Part of Bowie) 20715
Belair Shopping Center (Part of Bowie) 20715
Belair Somerset (Part of Bowie) 20715
Belair Tulip Grove (Part of Bowie) 20715
Belair White Hall (Part of Bowie) 20715
Belair Yorktown (Part of Bowie) 20715
Bel Alton 20611
Belcamp 21017
Belhaven 21122
Belleair Estates 20744
Belle Farm Estates 21208
Bellefonte 20735
Belle Grove 21766
Bellemead 20784
Belleview Estates 21146
Bellevue 21662
Bellevue Estates 20607
Bells Mill Village 20854
Belmar 21206
Bel Pre Estates 20906
Bel Pre Park 20906
Bel Pre Woods 20853
Beltsville .... 20704†
.... 20705*
Beltsville Heights 20705
Beltway Plaza (Part of Greenbelt) 20770
Belvedere Heights 21012
Bembe Beach 21403
Benedict 20612
Benevola 21713
Bennsville 20603
Ben Oaks 21146
Benson 21018
Bentley Springs 21120
Bentons Pleasure 21619
Berkley 21034
Berkshire 20746
Berlin 21811
Berrett 21784
Berry 20603
Berrywood 21146
Berwyn (Part of College Park) 20740
Berwyn Heights‡ 20740
Bestgate 21401
Bethany Manor 21042
Bethel, *Carroll* 21048
Bethel, *Cecil* 21915
Bethel, *Frederick* 21702
Bethel, *Garrett* 21550
Bethesda♦ 20813-14
.... 20816-17
.... 20824
.... 20827
For specific ZIP Codes call (888) 275-8777, or your local postmaster.
Bethgate 21043
Bethlehem 21609
Betterton 21610
Beulah 21643
Beverly Beach 21106
Beverly Farms 20854
Big Pines 20850
Big Pool 21711
Big Spring 21722
Bigwoods 21678
Billingsley Forest 20616
Birchwood City 20745
Birchwood Gardens 20708
Birdlawn 20744
Bird River Beach 21220
Birdsville 20776
Birmingham Estates 20705
Birmingham Terrace 20705
Bishop 21813
Bishops Head 21672
Bishopville 21813
Bitter Sweet 21403
Bittinger 21522
Bivalve 21814
Black Horse 21161
Blackrock Estates 20874
Blacks Corner 21157

Blackwater 21622
Bladensburg 20710
Bladenwoods (Part of Bladensburg) 20710
Blair 20910
Blenheim 21131
Bloomfield 21702
Blooming Rose 21531
Bloomington 21523
Bloomsbury 21228
Blossom Hills 21122
Blueball 21921
Blueberry Hills 20855
Blue Hill (Part of Hancock) 21750
Blue Mount 21111
Blue Mountain, *Frederick* 21788
Blue Mountain, *Washington* 21740
Blue Ridge Manor 20902
Blue Ridge View 21157
Blythedale 21903
Bolivar Heights 21769
Bolton 20603
Bond Mill Park 20707
Bonds 20607
Bon Haven 21401
Bonnie Acres 21043
Bonnie Brae 21784
Bonnie Brook 21613
Bonnie Knob (Part of Woodsboro) 21798
Bonnie Ridge 21209
Boonsboro 21713
Borden Shaft 21532
Boring 21020
Boulevard Heights 20743
Boulevard Park on the Magothy 21122
Bowens 20678
Bowie 20715-21
For specific ZIP Codes call (888) 275-8777, or your local postmaster.
Bowleys Quarters♦ 21220
Bowling Green 21502
Bowlings Alley 20622
Boxhill North 21009
Boxiron 21829
Boxwood Village (Part of Greenbelt) 20770
Boyds 20841
Boyer Mill Heights 21775
Bozman 21612
Bradbury Heights 20743
Bradbury Park 20746
Braddock 21702
Braddock Estates (Part of Frostburg) 21532
Braddock Heights♦ 21714
Bradley Farms 20854
Bradley Hills 20817
Bradley Hills Grove 20817
Bradley Woods 20817
Bradshaw 21021
Brady 21502
Braebrook Village 20770
Branchville (Part of College Park) 20740
Brandwine Farms 21047
Brandywine♦ 20613
Brandywine Country 20772
Brandywine Heights 20613
Breathedsville 21713
Breezewood Farms 21163
Breezy Point 20732
Breezy Point Beach 21221
Brentwood 20722
Breton Beach 20650
Briarcrest Heights 21755
Briarwood, Charles 20601
Briarwood, *Prince George's* 20708
Briddletown 21811
Bridgeport, *Frederick* 21787
Bridgeport, *Washington* 21742
Bridgetown 21636
Bright Oaks 21015
Brighton, *Baltimore* 21244
Brighton, *Montgomery* 2080
Brightview Woods 21
Brightwood Acres ....
Brinkleigh ....
Brinkleigh Manor ....
Brinkley Manor ....
Brinklow ....
Bristol
Broad Cr
Broadm

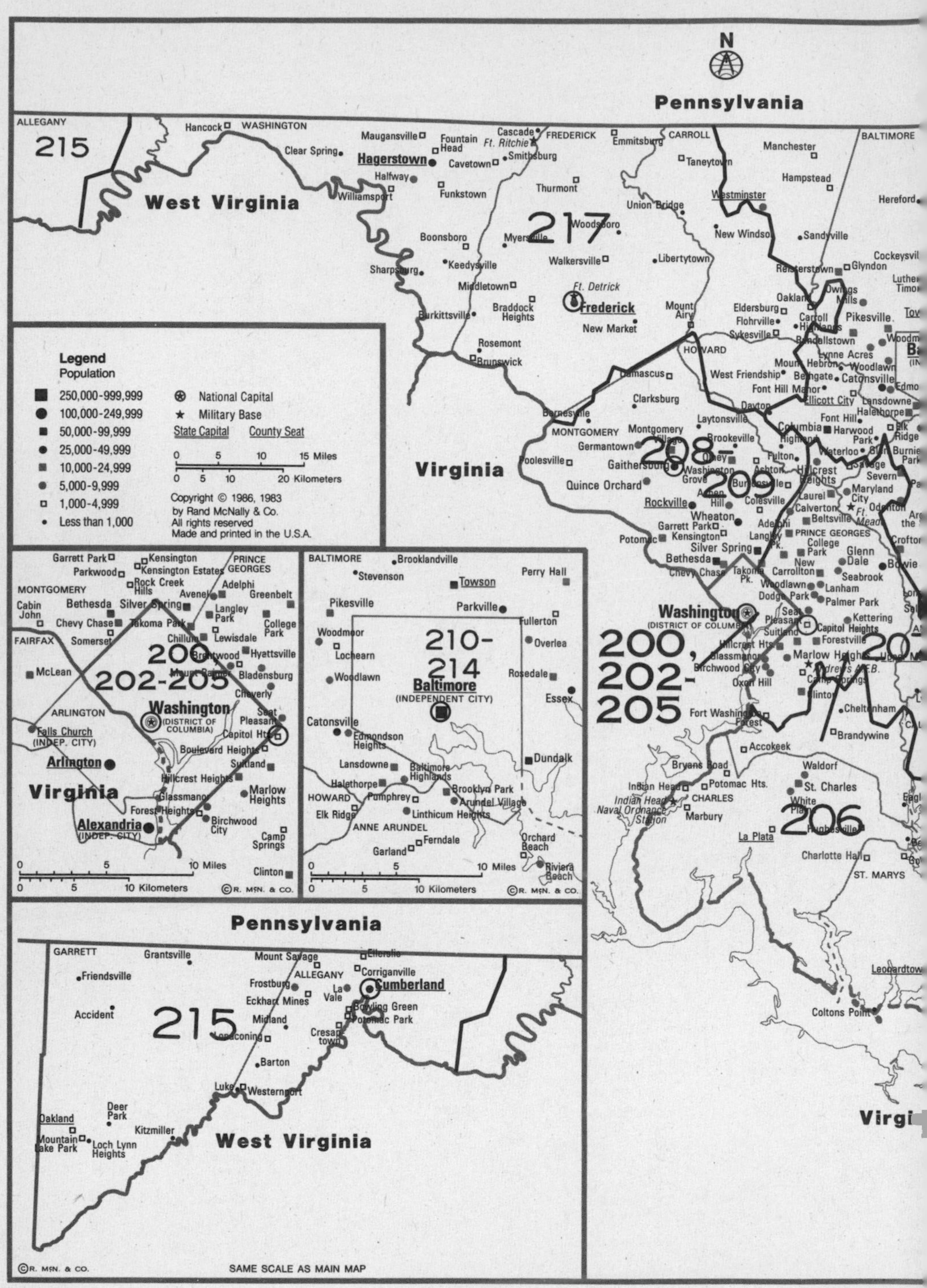
N
Pennsylvania
ALLEGANY
215
Hancock
WASHINGTON
Clear Spring
West Virginia
Maugansville
Fountain Head
Cascade
Ft. Ritchie
FREDERICK
Emmitsburg
CARROLL
Manchester
BALTIMORE
Hagerstown
Cavetown
Smithsburg
Taneytown
Hampstead
Halfway
Williamsport
Funkstown
Thurmont
Westminster
Hereford
217
Union Bridge
Woodsboro
Boonsboro
Myersville
New Windsor
Sandyville
Sharpsburg
Keedysville
Walkersville
Libertytown
Reisterstown
Glyndon
Cockeysville
Middletown
Ft. Detrick
Owings Mills
Burkittsville
Braddock Heights
Frederick
Mount Airy
Eldersburg
Flohrville
Carroll Highlands
Pikesville
New Market
Sykesville
Randallstown
Rosemont
HOWARD
Lynne Acres
Brunswick
Damascus
West Friendship
Mount Hebron
Woodlawn
Catonsville
Font Hill Manor
Ellicott City
Lansdowne
Halethorpe
Clarksburg
Dayton
Font Hill
Barnesville
Laytonsville
Columbia
Harwood Park
Elk Ridge
MONTGOMERY
Montgomery Village
Brookeville
Highland
Germantown
Poolesville
Gaithersburg
208-209
Olney
Fulton
Waterloo
Washington Grove
Ashton
Hillcrest Heights
Severn
Virginia
Quince Orchard
Aspen Hill
Burtonsville
Maryland City
Rockville
Colesville
Laurel
Ft. Meade
Wheaton
Calverton
Beltsville
Odenton
Garrett Park
Adelphi
Potomac
Kensington
Langley Pk.
PRINCE GEORGES
College Park
Crofton
Silver Spring
Glenn Dale
Bowie
Bethesda
New Carrollton
Chevy Chase
Takoma Pk.
Seabrook
Woodlawn
Lanham
Dodge Park
Palmer Park
Washington
(DISTRICT OF COLUMBIA)
Seat Pleasant
Kettering
Suitland
Capitol Heights
Forestville
200, 202-205
Hillcrest Hts.
Glassmanor
Marlow Heights
Birchwood City
Andrews A.F.B.
Oxon Hill
Camp Springs
Clinton
Fort Washington Forest
Cheltenham
Brandywine
Accokeek
Bryans Road
Waldorf
Indian Head
Potomac Hts.
St. Charles
Indian Head Naval Ordnance Station
CHARLES
White Plains
Marbury
206
La Plata
Hughesville
Charlotte Hall
ST. MARYS
Leonardtown
Coltons Point
Legend
Population
250,000-999,999
100,000-249,999
50,000-99,999
25,000-49,999
10,000-24,999
5,000-9,999
1,000-4,999
Less than 1,000
National Capital
Military Base
State Capital
County Seat
0 5 10 15 Miles
0 5 10 20 Kilometers
Copyright © 1986, 1983 by Rand McNally & Co.
All rights reserved
Made and printed in the U.S.A.
Garrett Park
Kensington
PRINCE GEORGES
Parkwood
Kensington Estates
Rock Creek Hills
Adelphi
MONTGOMERY
Avenel
Greenbelt
Cabin John
Bethesda
Silver Spring
Langley Park
Chevy Chase
Takoma Park
College Park
FAIRFAX
Somerset
Chillum
Lewisdale
200, 202-205
Brentwood
Hyattsville
McLean
Mount Rainier
Bladensburg
Cheverly
ARLINGTON
Washington
(DISTRICT OF COLUMBIA)
Seat Pleasant
Falls Church
(INDEP. CITY)
Capitol Hts.
Boulevard Heights
Arlington
Suitland
Hillcrest Heights
Virginia
Glassmanor
Marlow Heights
Forest Heights
Birchwood City
Alexandria
(INDEP. CITY)
Camp Springs
0 5 10 Miles
0 5 10 Kilometers
Clinton
©R. McN. & CO.
BALTIMORE
Brooklandville
Stevenson
Perry Hall
Towson
Pikesville
Parkville
Fullerton
Woodmoor
210-214
Overlea
Lochearn
Woodlawn
Rosedale
Baltimore
(INDEPENDENT CITY)
Essex
Catonsville
Edmondson Heights
Dundalk
Lansdowne
Baltimore Highlands
Halethorpe
Brooklyn Park
HOWARD
Pumphrey
Arundel Village
Elk Ridge
Linthicum Heights
ANNE ARUNDEL
Ferndale
Orchard Beach
Garland
Riviera Beach
0 5 10 Miles
0 5 10 Kilometers
©R. McN. & CO.
Pennsylvania
GARRETT
Grantsville
Mount Savage
Ellerslie
Friendsville
ALLEGANY
Corriganville
Frostburg
La Vale
Cumberland
Eckhart Mines
Accident
215
Midland
Bowling Green
Potomac Park
Lonaconing
Cresaptown
Barton
Luke
Westernport
Deer Park
Oakland
Kitzmiller
Mountain Lake Park
Loch Lynn Heights
West Virginia
©R. McN. & CO.
SAME SCALE AS MAIN MAP

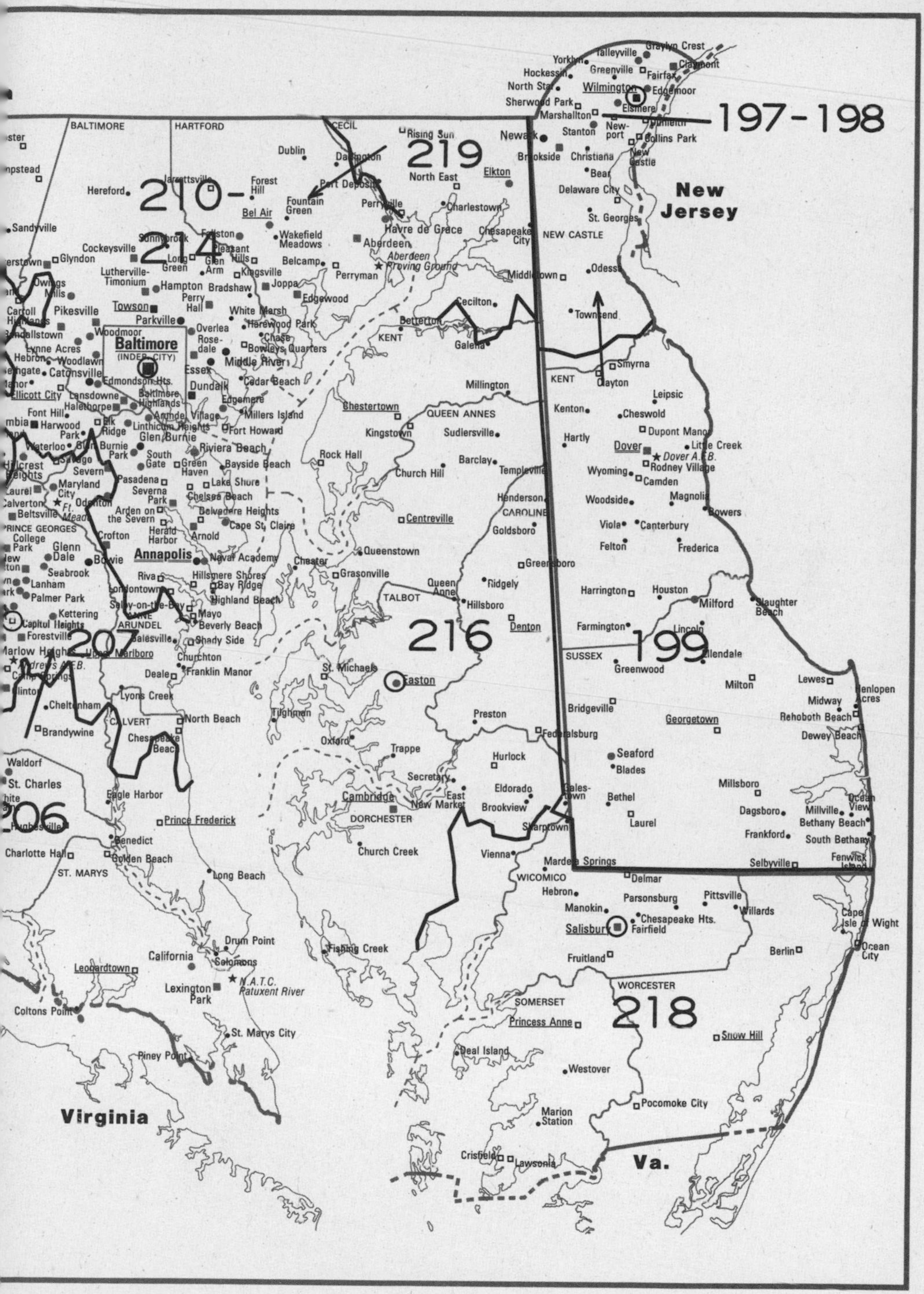

197-198
219
210-
214
216
199
207
206
218

BALTIMORE
HARTFORD
CECIL
KENT
QUEEN ANNES
TALBOT
CAROLINE
DORCHESTER
WICOMICO
SOMERSET
WORCESTER
NEW CASTLE
SUSSEX
ANNE ARUNDEL
PRINCE GEORGES
CALVERT
ST. MARYS

New Jersey
Virginia
Va.

Yorklyn
Talleyville
Graylyn Crest
Claymont
Hockessin
Greenville
Fairfax
North Star
Wilmington
Edgemoor
Sherwood Park
Elsmere
Marshallton
Newark
Stanton
New-port
Collins Park
Brookside
Christiana
New Castle
Bear
Delaware City
St. Georges
Middletown
Odessa
Townsend
Smyrna
Clayton
Leipsic
Kenton
Cheswold
Dupont Manor
Hartly
Dover
Little Creek
Dover A.F.B.
Rodney Village
Wyoming
Camden
Woodside
Magnolia
Bowers
Viola
Canterbury
Felton
Frederica
Harrington
Houston
Milford
Slaughter Beach
Farmington
Lincoln
Ellendale
Greenwood
Milton
Lewes
Henlopen Acres
Midway
Rehoboth Beach
Dewey Beach
Bridgeville
Georgetown
Seaford
Blades
Millsboro
Bethel
Laurel
Dagsboro
Millville
Ocean View
Bethany Beach
Frankford
South Bethany
Selbyville
Fenwick Island
Delmar

Rising Sun
Dublin
Darlington
North East
Elkton
Port Deposit
Perryville
Charlestown
Havre de Grace
Chesapeake City
Aberdeen
Aberdeen Proving Ground
Perryman
Cecilton
Betterton
Galena
Millington
Chestertown
Kingstown
Sudlersville
Rock Hall
Barclay
Templeville
Church Hill
Henderson
Goldsboro
Centreville
Queenstown
Greensboro
Grasonville
Chester
Ridgely
Queen Anne
Hillsboro
Denton
St. Michaels
Easton
Tilghman
Preston
Federalsburg
Oxford
Trappe
Hurlock
Secretary
Eldorado
Cambridge
East New Market
Galestown
Brookview
Sharptown
Church Creek
Vienna
Mardela Springs
Hebron
Parsonsburg
Pittsville
Willards
Manokin
Salisbury
Chesapeake Hts.
Fairfield
Fruitland
Cape Isle of Wight
Ocean City
Berlin
Fishing Creek
Princess Anne
Snow Hill
Deal Island
Westover
Pocomoke City
Marion Station
Crisfield
Lawsonia

Hereford
Jarrettsville
Forest Hill
Fountain Green
Bel Air
Fallston
Wakefield Meadows
Sandyville
Sunnybrook
Pleasant Hills
Cockeysville
Glyndon
Long Green
Glen Arm
Kingsville
Belcamp
Lutherville-Timonium
Hampton
Bradshaw
Joppa
Edgewood
Owings Mills
Pikesville
Towson
Perry Hall
White Marsh
Carroll Highlands
Parkville
Overlea
Harewood Park
Randallstown
Woodmoor
Rosedale
Chase
Baltimore (INDEP. CITY)
Bowleys Quarters
Lynne Acres
Hebron
Woodlawn
Middle River
Essex
Catonsville
Edmondson Hts.
Cedar Beach
Dundalk
Ellicott City
Lansdowne
Baltimore Highlands
Edgemere
Halethorpe
Arundel Village
Millers Island
Font Hill
Harwood
Elk Ridge
Linthicum Heights
Fort Howard
Glen Burnie
Riviera Beach
Waterloo
Burnie Park
South Gate
Green Haven
Bayside Beach
Hillcrest Heights
Savage
Severn
Pasadena
Lake Shore
Maryland City
Severna Park
Chelsea Beach
Laurel
Calverton
Odenton
Ft. Meade
Beltsville
Arden on the Severn
Belvedere Heights
Herald Harbor
Cape St. Claire
College Park
Crofton
Arnold
Glenn Dale
Annapolis
Naval Academy
Bowie
Seabrook
Lanham
Riva
Hillsmere Shores
Bay Ridge
Palmer Park
Londontown
Highland Beach
Kettering
Selby-on-the-Bay
Mayo
Capitol Heights
Forestville
Beverly Beach
Galesville
Shady Side
Marlow Heights
Upper Marlboro
Churchton
Andrews A.F.B.
Camp Springs
Deale
Franklin Manor
Clinton
Lyons Creek
Cheltenham
North Beach
Brandywine
Chesapeake Beach
Waldorf
St. Charles
Eagle Harbor
Prince Frederick
Hughesville
Benedict
Charlotte Hall
Golden Beach
Long Beach
Drum Point
California
Solomons
Leonardtown
Lexington Park
N.A.T.C. Patuxent River
Coltons Point
St. Marys City
Piney Point

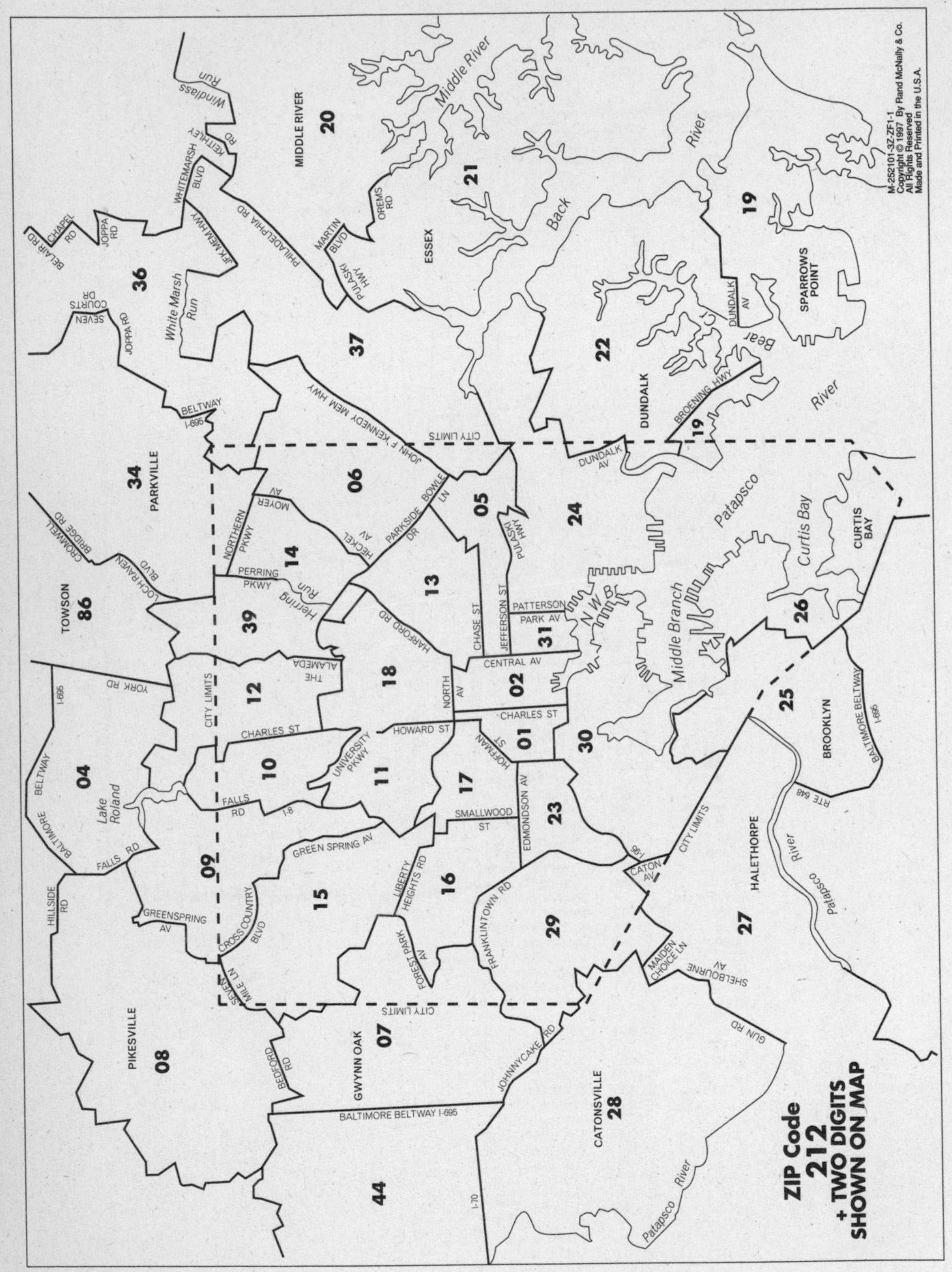

ZIP Code
212
+ TWO DIGITS
SHOWN ON MAP
M-252101-3Z-ZF1-1
Copyright © 1997 By Rand McNally & Co.
All Rights Reserved
Made and Printed in the U.S.A.
PIKESVILLE
08
09
04
Lake Roland
TOWSON
86
34
PARKVILLE
36
MIDDLE RIVER
20
21
ESSEX
37
22
DUNDALK
19
SPARROWS POINT
06
05
14
13
39
12
10
18
31
02
01
11
17
15
16
23
30
24
26
CURTIS BAY
25
BROOKLYN
27
HALETHORPE
29
07
GWYNN OAK
28
CATONSVILLE
44
CITY LIMITS
BALTIMORE BELTWAY I-695
Middle River
Back River
Bear
Patapsco River
Curtis Bay
Middle Branch
N W B
Herring Run
White Marsh Run
Windlass Run

Broad Run 21755
Broadview 20748
Broadview Acres 21701
Broadwater Estates 20744
Broadwater Point 20733
Broadwood Manor (Part of Rockville) 20851
Brock Bridge 20708
Brock Hall 20774
Brock Hall Estates 20774
Brock Hall Gardens 20774
Brock Hall Manor 20774
Brookdale 20815
Brookdale Heights 21804
Brooke-Jane Manor 20735
Brooke Manor 20745
Brookemanor Estates 20853
Brookeville 20833
Brook Hill 21702
Brooklandville 21022
Brooklyn (Part of Baltimore) 21225
Brooklyn Park 21225
Brookmead 20874
Brookmead North 20874
Brookmont 20816
Brookside Forest 20901
Brookside Manor 20782
Brookview 21659
Brookville Knolls 20833
Brookwood 20772
Brookwood Estates 20695
Broomes Island 20615
Browns Corner 21617
Brownsville, *Queen Anne's* 21617
Brownsville, *Washington* 21715
Browns Woods Villa 21401
Bruceville, *Carroll* 21757
Bruceville, *Talbot* 21673
Brunswick 21716
Bryans Road 20616
Bryantown, *Charles* 20617
Bryantown, *Queen Anne's* 21658
Bryant Square 21044
Bryant Woods 21044
Buckeystown 21717
Buckingham View 21157
Buck Lodge 20783
Bucktown 21613
Budds Creek 20659
Buena Vista 20678
Buffalo Run 21531
Burgundy Estates (Part of Rockville) 20851
Burgundy Knolls (Part of Rockville) 20850
Burgundy Village (Part of Rockville) 20850
Burkittsville 21718
Burning Tree Estates 20817
Burning Tree Manor 20817
Burns Corner (Part of Aberdeen) 21001
Burnt Mills 20901
Burnt Mills Hills 20901
Burnt Mills Knolls 20901
Burnt Mills Manor 20901
Burnt Mills Village 20901
Burrisville 21617
Burrsville 21629
Burtner 21713
Burtonsville♦ 20866
Bush 21009
Bushs Corner 21132
Bushwood 20618
Butler 21023
Butlertown 21678
Buttercup Estates 21794
Buttonwood Beach 21919
Byforde 20895
Bynum 21050
Bynum Ridge 21050
Byrdtown 21817
Cabin Creek 21643
Cabin John 20818
Cabin John Park 20818
Cactus Hill 20607
Cadillac Homes 21060
California 20619
Callaway 20620
Caltor Manor 20744
Calvary 21028
Calvert, *Cecil* 21901
Calvert (Part of Baltimore)‡ 21202
Calvert Beach 20685
Calvert Manor 20607
Calverton♦ 20705
Cambria 21131
Cambridge 21613
Cambridge Estates 20735
Camden (Part of Baltimore) 21230
Camden (Part of Salisbury) 21810
Camelback Village 20832
Camelot, *Harford* 21015
Camelot, *Prince George's* 20769
Camotop 20854
Campbell 21813
Campbelltown 21813
Camp Springs‡ 20748
Camp Springs Forest 20748
Campus Hills 21286
Canal 21904
Candlewood Park 20855
Cannon Acres 21613
Canton (Part of Baltimore) 21224
Cape Anne 20733
Cape Arthur 21146
Cape Estate 21012
Cape Isle of Wight 21842
Cape Loch Haven 21037
Cape May Beach 21221
Cape St. Claire 21401
Cape St. John 21401
Capital Estates 20695
Capital Plaza (Part of Landover Hills)‡ 20784
Capitol Heights 20731
 20743
 20791
For specific ZIP Codes call (888) 275-8777, or your local postmaster.
Capitol Hills 21061
Capitol View Park 20910
Capri Estate 21012
Captains Hill 21842
Carderock Springs 20817
Cardiff 21160
Carea 21161
Carleton East 20706
Carlson Spring 20747
Carmichael 21658
Carmody Hills 20743
Carney 21234
Carney Grove 21234
Carney Heights 21234
Carole Highlands 20782
Carpenter Point 21903
Carroll (Part of Baltimore)‡ 21229
Carroll County Trails 21048
Carroll Heights (Part of Hagerstown) 21740
Carroll Highlands 21784
Carroll Island 21220
Carroll Knolls 20910
Carroll Manor (Part of Takoma Park) 20912
Carrollton 21784
Carrollton Manor 21146
Carrollwood 21220
Carrollwood Estate 21771
Carsins Run 21001
Carsondale 20706
Carter Hill (Part of Rockville) 20850
Carvel Beach 21226
Carver Heights 20653
Cascade 21719
Cashell Estates 20855
Casselman 21536
Castle Marina 21619
Castleton 21034
Catchpenny 21856
Catoctin 21716
Catoctin Furnace 21788
Catoctin View 21771
Catonsville♦ 21228
Catonsville Heights 21228
Catonsville Manor 21207
Cavalier Country 20754
Cavetown 21720
Cayots 21915
Cearfoss 21740
Cecilton 21913
Cedar Acres 21044
Cedar Beach 21221
Cedar Grove 20876
Cedar Grove Beach 21631
Cedar Hall 21851
Cedar Haven 20608
Cedar Heights 20743
Cedarhurst, *Anne Arundel* 20764
Cedarhurst, *Carroll* 21048
Cedarhurst Acres 21830
Cedarhurst-on-the-Bay 20764
Cedar Lawn 21740
Cedarmere 21117
Cedar Park (Part of Annapolis) 21401
Cedar Spring 21015
Cedartown 21863
Cedarville 20613
Centennial 21042
Centennial Estates 21042
Center Court 20879
Centerville 21754
Centreville 21617
Ceresville 21701
Chadwick Manor 21244
Chalfone Manor 21228
Chalk Point 20778
Champ 21853
Chance 21821
Chaney 20754
Chaneyville 20736
Chaneyville Farm Estates 20736
Chapel 21601
Chapel Gate 21113
Chapel Hill 20744
Chapel Hill Estates 20610
Chapel Oaks 20743
Chapelview 21043
Chaptico 20621
Charles Manor 21047
Charlesmont 21222
Charlestown, *Allegany* 21539
Charlestown, *Cecil* 21914
Charlestown Manor Beach 21901
Charlesville 21702
Charlotte Hall 20622
Charlton 21722
Charred Oak Estates 20817
Chartley 21136
Chartridge 21146
Chartwell 21146
Chase 21027
Chateau Valley 21042
Chatham 20783
Chattolanee 21117
Chelsea Beach 21122
Chelsea Woods (Part of Greenbelt) 20770
Cheltenham 20623
Cheltenham Forest 20735
Chelten Park 20735
Cherry Hill, *Cecil* 21921
Cherry Hill, *Harford* 21154
Cherry Hill, *Prince George's* 20705
Cherry Hill (Part of College Park) 20740
Cherrywalk 21830
Chesaco Park 21237
Chesapeake Beach 20732
Chesapeake City 21915
Chesapeake Estates 21666
Chesapeake Heights 21804
Chesapeake Isle 21901
Chesapeake Landing 21620
Chesapeake Ranch Estates 20657
Chesapeake Terrace 21222
Cheshaven 21919
Chester 21619
Chesterfield 21032
Chesterfield Gardens 21122
Chester Harbor 21620
Chester River Beach 21638
Chestertown 21620
Chesterville 21651
Chesterville Forest 21651
Chestnut Grove, *Frederick* 21701
Chestnut Grove, *Washington* 21756
Chestnut Hill, *Baltimore* 21286
Chestnut Hill, *Harford* 21050
Chestnut Hill, *Howard* 21043
Chestnut Hill Estates 21043
Chestnut Hills 20705
Chestnut Ridge, *Baltimore* 21117
Chestnut Ridge, *Prince George's* 20737
Cheverly 20784
Cheverly Manor 20785
Chevy Chase♦ 20815
Chevy Chase Lake 20815
Chevy Chase Manor 20815
Chevy Chase Section Five 20815
Chevy Chase Section Three 20815
Chevy Chase Terrace 20815
Chevy Chase View 20895
Chevy Chase Village 20815
Chewsville 21721
Chicamuxen 20640
Childs 21916
Chillum 20782
Chillum Estates 20783
Chillum Heights 20783
Chillum Manor 20783
Chingville 20620
Choptank 21655
Christs Rock 21613
Church Creek 21622
Church Hill, *Frederick* 21773
Church Hill, *Queen Anne's* 21623*
 21656†
Churchill Town Sector 20874
Churchton 20733
Churchville 21028
Cinnamon Ridge 20774
Cissel Farms 20777
Claggettsville 20872
Claiborne 21624
Claremont (Part of Baltimore) 21223
Clarksburg 20871
Clarks Landing 20636
Clarksville 21029
Clarksville Ridge 21029
Clarysville 21532
Clearfield 21157
Clear Spring 21722
Clearview 21040
Clearview Manor 20745
Clearview Village 21122
Clearwater Beach 21226
Clements 20624
Clifford (Part of Baltimore) 21230
Cliffs City 21620
Clifton 21702
Clifton-East End (Part of Baltimore)‡ 21213
Clifton on the Potomac 20664
Clifton Park 20901
Clinton 20735
Clinton Acres 20613
Clinton Estates 20735
Clinton Gardens 20735
Clinton Grove 20735
Clinton Hills 20735
Clinton Park 20735
Clinton Vista 20735
Clinton Woods 20735
Clopper 20878
Cloverfields 21666
Clover Hill♦ 21702
Cloverlea 21106
Cloverly 20904
Club of Stedwick 20879
Clubside 20879
Clydesdale Acres 21048
Cobb Island 20625
Cockeysville 21030-31
For specific ZIP Codes call (888) 275-8777, or your local postmaster.
Cohasset 20814
Cohill Estates 21750
Cokesburg 21851
Cokesbury 21904
Cold Spring Estates 20854
Coleman 21678
Colesville 20904-05
For specific ZIP Codes call (888) 275-8777, or your local postmaster.
Colesville Farm Estates 20904
Colesville Gardens 20904
Colesville Manor 20904
Colesville Park 20904
College (Part of Westminster)‡ 21157
College Estates (Part of Frederick)‡ 21702
College Gardens (Part of Rockville) 20850
College Heights Estates 20783
College Park 20740*
 20741†
College Park Woods (Part of College Park) 20740
College View 20902
Colmar Manor 20722
Colonial Acres, *Cecil* 21921
Colonial Acres, *Harford* 21014
Colonial Gardens 21228
Colonial Park, *Baltimore* 21207
Colonial Park, *Washington* 21740
Colonial Village 21208
Colony Heights 21502
Colony Ridge 21113
Colora 21917
Coltons Point 20626
Columbia♦ 21044-46
For specific ZIP Codes call (888) 275-8777, or your local postmaster.
Columbia Beach 20764
Columbia Hills 21043
Columbia Park 20785
Compton 20627
Comus 20842
Concord 21632
Congressional Forest Estates 20817
Connecticut Avenue Estates 20902
Connecticut Avenue Hills 20902
Connecticut Avenue Park 20906
Connecticut Gardens 20902
Conowingo 21918
Conowingo Village 21034
Contee 20708
Cooksville 21723
Cooperstown 21023
Coopstown 21050
Copenhaver 20854
Copperville, *Carroll* 21787
Copperville, *Talbot* 21601
Coral Hills 20743
Corbett, *Baltimore* 21111
Corbett (Part of Hagerstown) 21740
Cordova 21625
Cornersville 21613
Cornfield Harbor 20687
Corriganville 21524
Costen 21851
Cottage City 20722
Country Club Acres 21550
Country Club Estate 21060
Country Club Manor 21060
Country Club Park 21093
Country Club Village 20814
Country Place 20866
Country Road Estates 20754
Courthouse (Part of Rockville)‡ 20850
Courtleigh 21133
Cove 21520
Coventry 21234
Cove Point 20657
Cowentown 21921
Coxby Estates 21037
Cox Creek Acres 21619
Crabtree 21561
Craigtown 21904
Cranberry 21157
Crapo 21626
Creagerstown 21788
Crellin 21550
Cremona 20659
Cresaptown 21505
Crescendo 21676
Cresthaven 20903
Crestleigh 21042
Crestview 20814
Crestview Manor 20735
Crestwood, *Anne Arundel* 21090
Crestwood, *Wicomico* 21804
Crestwood Acres 21040
Creswell 21015
Crisfield 21817
Crisp (Part of Baltimore) 21225
Criswood Manor 21029
Crocheron 21627
Crofton♦ 21114
Cromwood 21234
Croom 20772
Crosby 21661

Crowder 21043
Crownsville♦ 21032
Croydon Park (Part of Rockville) 20850
Crumpton 21628
Crystal Beach 21919
Cub Hill 21234
Cuckhold Creek 20664
Cumberland 21501-05
For specific ZIP Codes call (888) 275-8777, or your local postmaster.
Curtis Bay (Part of Baltimore) 21226
Cypress Creek 21146
Dailsville 21613
Daisy 21797
Dalton 21045
Damascus♦ 20872
Dameron 20628
Dames Quarter 21821
Dam No. 4 21782
Daniel 21797
Daniels Park (Part of College Park) 20740
Danville 21557
Danwood 21804
Darcy Manor 20746
Dares Beach 20678
Dargan 21782
Darlington 21034
Darnestown 20874
Darryl Gardens 21162
Davidsonville 21035
Dawson 26726
Dawsonville 20841
Day 21797
Daysville 21793
Dayton 21036
Deale♦ 20751
Deale Beach 20751
Deal Island 21821
Deanwood Park 20743
Decatur Heights (Part of Bladensburg) 20710
Deep Creek 21012
Deep Creek Lake 21541
Deep Landing Estates 20639
Deerfield, *Harford* 21034
Deerfield, *Montgomery* 20817
Deerfield Run 20708
Deer Harbour 21804
Deer Park, *Garrett* 21550
Deer Park (Part of Gaithersburg) 20877
Deer Park Estates 21048
Deer Park Heights 20748
Deers Head 21801
Defense Heights, *Baltimore* 21222
Defense Heights, *Prince George's* 20784
Delight 21117
Delmar 21875
Delmont 21144
Den Lee Acres 20735
Dennings 21776
Dennis Grove Apartments 20745
Denton 21629
Dentsville 20646
Derwood 20855
Detmold 21539
Detour 21757
Devonshire Forest 21093
Diamond Farms (Part of Gaithersburg) 20878
Dickerson 20842
District Heights 20747*
20753†
Dodge Park♦ 20785
Dogwood Flats 21521
Dogwood Hills 21286
Dominion 21619
Doncaster 20640
Doncaster Village 21234
Donleigh 21046
Donnybrook 21204
Dorceytown 21771
Dorchester Estates 20735
Dorrs Corner 21108
Dorsey 21075
Dorseys Regard 20879
Doubs 21710
Dowell 20629
Downsville 21795
Drayden 20630
Dresden Green 20706
Drexel Woods 21228
Druid (Part of Baltimore)‡ 21217
Drumcliff 20636
Drumeldra Hills 20904
Drum Point 20657
Drury 20711
Drybranch 21161
Dry Run 21722
Dublin 21034
21154
For specific ZIP Codes call (888) 275-8777, or your local postmaster.
Dufief 20878
Dulaney Village 21204
Dulls Corner 21401
Dumbarton 21208
Dumbarton Heights 21208
Dunbrook 21122
Dundalk♦ 21222
Dundalk Shopping Center 21222
Dundalk-Sparrows Point 21222
Dundee Village 21220
Dunkirk 20754
Dunlaney Village 21093
Dunloggin 21042
Dunwood 21085
Dupont Heights 20746
Dynard 20621
Eagle Harbor 20608
Eakles Mills 21756
Earleigh Heights 21146
Earleville 21919
Earlton 21078
East Columbia Park 20785
Eastfield 21222
East Fort Foote Village 20744
East Meadow 20745
East New Market 21631
Easton 21601
Easton Point 21601
Eastover Knolls 20745
East Park Village 21061
Eastpines 20737
Eastpoint 21222
Eastpoint Mall 21224
Eastport (Part of Annapolis)‡ 21403
East Riverdale 20737
East Springbrook 20904
Eastview, *Carroll* 21048
Eastview, *Frederick* 21702
Eastview Estates 21048
Eckhart Mines 21528
Eden 21822
Eder 21921
Edesville 21661
Edgemere 21221
Edgemont, *Frederick* 21702
Edgemont, *Washington* 21783
Edgemoor 20814
Edgewater 21037
Edgewater Beach 21037
Edgewater Village 21040
Edgewood, *Frederick* 21702
Edgewood, *Harford* 21040
Edgewood, *Montgomery* 20814
Edgewood Arsenal 21040
Edgewood Meadows 21040
Edmondson Ridge 21228
Edmonson Heights 21207
Edmonston 20781
Ednor 20905
Ednor Acres 20904
Elberon 20854
Elder Hill 21531
Eldersburg 21784
Eldorado 21659
Elioak 21044
Elk Mills 21920
Elkmore 21921
Elk Neck 21901
Elk Ranch Park 21921
Elkridge♦ 21075
Elkton 21921*
21922†
Elkton Heights (Part of Elkton) 21921
Elktonia 21401
Elkton Landing (Part of Elkton) 21921
Elkwood Estates 21921
Ellerslie 21529
Ellerton 21773
Ellicott City 21041-43
For specific ZIP Codes call (888) 275-8777, or your local postmaster.
Ellicott Mills, *Baltimore* 21228
Ellicott Mills, *Howard*‡ 21043
Elliott 21869
Elmwood 21206
Elvaton Acres 21108
Elvatone Town 21061
Elwood 21643
Emmitsburg 21727
Emmorton 21009
Emory Grove, *Baltimore* 21071
Emory Grove, *Montgomery* 20877
Emory Hills 21048
Engle Mill 21520
Englewood 20785
English Manor 20853
English Village 20814
Enterprise Estates 20721
Enterprise Shopping Center 20706
Epping Forest 21401
Ernstville 21711
Essex♦ 21221
Estonian Estates 20772
Etchison 20882
Eudowood 21204
21286
For specific ZIP Codes call (888) 275-8777, or your local postmaster.
Eutaw Forest 20603
Evanston 20747
Evergreen Estates 21146
Evergreen Hills 21048
Evergreen Overlook 20745
Evergreen Park 21221
Evergreen Valley Estates 21042
Everlea 21655
Evitts Creek 21502
Ewell 21824
Ewingville 21620
Fahrney Keedy Memorial Home 21713
Fairbank 21671
Fairfield, *Carroll* 21157
Fairfield (Part of Baltimore) 21226
Fairfield Knolls 20747
Fairgreen 20772
Fairgreen Acres 21740
Fair Haven 20754
Fairhaven on the Bay 20754
Fair Hill 21921
Fairidge 20879
Fairknoll 20905
Fairland 20904
Fairland Acres 20866
Fairland Heights 20904
Fairlee 21620
Fairmont 21014
Fairmount 21871
Fairmount Heights 20743
Fair Play 21733
Fairview, *Anne Arundel* 21122
Fairview, *Anne Arundel* (mobile home park) 20707
Fairview, *Washington* 21722
Fairview Estates 20904
Fairway 21015
Fairway Hills 20812
Fairway Island 20879
Fallsmont 21047
Fallston♦ 21047
Family Estates 20743
Farmington, *Cecil* 21911
Farmington, *Montgomery* 20815
Farmsbrook 21702
Faulkner 20632
Faulkner Ridge 21044
Fawsett Farms 20854
Feagaville 21702
Federal Hill 21084
Federalsburg 21632
Felicity Cove 20764
Fellowship Forest 21204
Ferdinand Heights 21061
Ferndale 21060
Fernglen Manor 21061
Fernwood, *Montgomery* 20817
Fernwood, *Prince George's* 20737
Fernwood, *Prince George's* (mobile home park) 20743
Fiddlersburg 21742
Figgs Landing 21863
Finksburg 21048
Finzel 21532
Fishing Creek 21634
Fleishman Village 20746
Flickersville 21756
Flintstone 21530
Flohrville 21784
Florence 21797
Flower Valley 20853
Flower Valley Estates 20853
Fontana Village 21237
Font Hill 21042
Font Hill Manor 21042
Forest Estates 20910
Forest Glen 20910
Forest Green 21001
Forest Heights 20745
Forest Hill 21050
Forest Knolls, *Montgomery* 20901
Forest Knolls, *Prince George's* 20744
Forest Lake 21050
Forest Lawn 21014
Forest Manor 20747
Forest Oaks 21784
Forest Park 20705
Forestville 20747
Forestville Estates 20747
Forge Acres 21128
Forge Heights 21128
Fork 21051
Forrest Hall 20659
Fort Foote Estates 20747
Fort Foote Village 20744
Fort George G. Meade 20755
Fort Howard 21052
Fort Sumner 20816
Fort Washington 20744*
20749†
Fort Washington Estates 20744
Fort Washington Forest 20744
Foundry Siding (Part of Westernport) 21562
Fountaindale 21769
Fountain Green 21015
Fountain Green Heights 21015
Fountain Head 21742
Fountain Mills 21754
Fountain Rock (Part of Walkersville) 21793
Fountain Valley 21157
Four Locks 21722
Four Seasons Estates 21113
Four Winds 21204
Fowblesburg 21155
Fowlers Concord 20747
Fox Chapel 20876
Fox Chapel North 20876
Foxhall 20906
Foxhall Estates 21035
Fox Hills 20854
Fox Hills West 20854
Foxley Manor 21620
Fox Rest 20708
Fox Rest South 20708
Foxridge 21078
Fox Run Estates 20735
Foxville 21780
Franklin (Part of Baltimore)‡ 21223
Franklin Manor Beach 20733
Franklin Manor on-the-Bay 20733
Franklin Park 20852
Franklin Square 20744
Franklinville, *Baltimore* 21087
Franklinville, *Frederick* 21788
Frederick 21701-05
For specific ZIP Codes call (888) 275-8777, or your local postmaster.
Frederick Junction 21701
Frederick Shopping Center (Part of Frederick) 21701
Frederick Towne Mall (Part of Frederick) 21702
Frederick Village 21228
Freedom Forest 21784
Freeland 21053
Free State Mall (Part of Bowie) 20715
Frenchtown (Part of Perryville) 21903
Friendly 20744
Friendly Farms 20744
Friends Creek 21727
Friendship, *Anne Arundel* 20758
Friendship, *Frederick* 21791
Friendship, *Worcester* 21811
Friendship Heights‡ 20813
Friendship Park 21740
Friendsville 21531
Frizzelburg 21158
Frostburg 21532
Frostown 21769
Fruitland 21826
Fullerton 21236
Fulton 20759
Fulton Junction (Part of Baltimore) 21217
Funkstown 21734
Furnace Branch 21061
Gaither 21784
Gaithersburg 20877-79
20882-85
20898
For specific ZIP Codes call (888) 275-8777, or your local postmaster.
Galena 21635
Galestown 19973
Galesville 20765
Gallant Green 20601
Gamber 21048
Gambrills 21054
Gannon 21562
Gapland 21736
Garfield 21783
Garland 21061
Garrett Forest 20906
Garrett Park 20896
Garrett Park Estates 20895
Garretts Mill 21758
Garrison♦ 21055
Gatts Corner 21106
Gayfields 20906
George Island Landing 21864
Georgetown, *Anne Arundel* 20794
Georgetown, *Cecil* 21930
Georgetown, *Kent* (mail Chestertown) 21620
Georgetown, *Kent* (mail Georgetown) 21930
Georgetown Estates 20852
Georgetown Village 20812
Georgian Forest 20902
Germantown, *Montgomery* 20874-76
For specific ZIP Codes call (888) 275-8777, or your local postmaster.
Germantown, *Worcester* 21811
Germantown Estates 20874
Germantown Park 20874
Germantown View 20874
Gibson Island 21056
Gibson Manor 21015
Gilmore 21532
Gingerville Manor Estates 21037
Girdletree 21829
Gist 21784
Glade Towne (Part of Walkersville) 21793
Gladstone Acres 21034
Glassmanor 20745
Glazewood Manor (Part of Takoma Park) 20912
Glebe Heights 21037
Glenallen 20902
Glenarden 20706
Glen Arm 21057
Glen Brook 21042
Glenbrook Knolls 20814
Glenbrook Village 20814
Glen Burnie 21060-61
For specific ZIP Codes call (888) 275-8777, or your local postmaster.
Glen Burnie Mall 21061
Glen Burnie Park 21061
Glencoe, *Baltimore* 21152
Glencoe, *Kent* 21645
Glen Cove 20816
Glendale, *Baltimore* 21204
Glendale (Part of Salisbury) 21801
Glen Echo 20812
Glen Echo Heights 20816
Glenelg 21737
Glen Ellen 21286
Glen Elyn 21047
Glen Farms 21921
Glen Gardens 21060

*** Area Zip Code** **† Post Office Boxes** **‡ Postal Station** **♦ Census Designated Place** *Italic Type* **County**

Glen Hills 20850
Glen Isle 21401
Glen Kyle 19711
Glenmar, *Baltimore* 21220
Glenmar, *Howard* 21043
Glen Mar Park 20814
Glen Mary Heights (Part of Elkton) 21921
Glenmont, *Baltimore* 21239
Glenmont, *Montgomery* 20902
Glenmont Park 20906
Glenmore 21061
Glen Morris 21136
Glenn Dale♦ 20769
Glenn Dale Heights 20769
Glenn Heights 21078
Glen Oaks 20854
Glenora Hills (Part of Rockville) 20850
Glen Park 20854
Glen Ridge 20784
Glenside Park 21234
Glenville 21034
Glen Westover 19711
Glen Willows 20743
Glenwood, *Harford* 21014
Glenwood, *Howard* 21738
Glenwood Estates 21738
Glenwood Park 20706
Glover Acres 21157
Glymont 20640
Glyndon 21071
Goddard Space Flight Center 20770
Golden Beach♦ 20659
Golden Hill 21622
Golden Ring 21237
Goldsboro 21636
Golf Club Shores 21811
Golts 21635
Good Acres 21740
Good Hope 20905
Goodwill 21851
Gorman 26720
Gortner 21550
Goshen 20879
Goshen Estates 20879
Gotts 21032
Govans (Part of Baltimore)‡ 21212
Governors Run 20676
Graceham 21788
Graceton 21160
Grahamtown 21532
Granby Woods 20855
Grand Bel Manor 20906
Grandview 21784
Granite 21163
Grantsville 21536
Grasonville♦ 21638
Gratitude 21661
Gray Haven 21222
Gray Manor 21222
Gray Rock 21042
Grayton 20662
Greater Capitol Heights 20743
Great Mills 20634
Green Acres, *Harford* 21085
Green Acres, *Montgomery* 20817
Greenbelt 20768*
20770†
Greenberry Hills 21740
Greenbriar 21713
Greenbrier (Part of Greenbelt) 20770
Greendale Estates 21047
Greenfield 20735
Greenfield Mills 21710
Green Glade 21561
Green Haven 21122
Green Hill 21856
Green Hill Acres 21742
Green Meadows, *Charles* 20640
Green Meadows, *Prince George's* 20782
Greenmount (Part of Hampstead) 21074
Green Ridge, *Allegany* 21530
Green Ridge, *Baltimore* 21093
Greenridge, *Harford* 21015
Greensboro 21639
Greensburg 21783
Green Spring Hills 21085
Greentop Manor 21030
Greentree, *Anne Arundel* 21061
Greentree, *Montgomery* 20879
Green Tree Manor 20817
Greenvale Village 21783
Green Valley♦ 21771
Greenview Knolls 20634
Greenwich Forest 20814
Greenwood Acres 21401
Greenwood Farms 20777
Greenwood Forest 20706
Gregg Neck 21635
Greystone Manor (Part of Hagerstown) 21740
Grimesville 21053
Grove 21655
Grove Hill 21702
Guilford 20794
Guilford Manor 21225
Gum Springs 20868
Gum Springs Farm 20868
Gunners Lake Village 20874
Gunpowder, *Baltimore* 21021
Gunpowder, *Harford* 21010
Gunpowder Estates 21128
Gwenlee Estates 21738
Gwynn 21042
Gwynn Acres 21042
Gwynnbrook 21117
Gwynn Oak (Part of Baltimore) 21207
21244
For specific ZIP Codes call (888) 275-8777, or your local postmaster.
Hack Point 21919
Hacks Point Acre 21919
Hagerstown 21740-48
For specific ZIP Codes call (888) 275-8777, or your local postmaster.
Halethorpe 21075
21227
For specific ZIP Codes call (888) 275-8777, or your local postmaster.
Halfway 21740
Hallett Heights 21863
Halley Estates 20695
Halpine Village 20852
Hambleton Estates 21140
Hamilton (Part of Baltimore)‡ 21214
Hamilton Park (Part of Hagerstown) 21740
Hamlet North 20855
Hammond 20723
Hammondell Heights 21108
Hampden (Part of Baltimore)‡ 21211
Hampshire Knolls 20783
Hampstead 21074
Hampton 21286
Hampton Park (Part of Capitol Heights)‡ 20791
Hance Point 21901
Hancock 21750
Hanesville 21678
Hanover, *Anne Arundel* 21076
Hanover, *Howard* 21076
Hanson Valley View 20748
Hansonville 21702
Harbor View, *Anne Arundel* 21037
Harbor View, *Queen Anne's* 21619
Hardesty Estates 21035
Harewood 21220
Harewood Park 21220
Harford Estates 21050
Harford Farms 21234
Harford Furnace 21015
Harford Hills 21234
Harford Mall (Part of Bel Air) 21014
Harford Park 21234
Harford Square 21040
Harmans 21077
Harmony, *Caroline* 21655
Harmony, *Frederick* 21773
Harmony Grove 21701
Harmony Hall 20744
Harmony Hills 20906
Harness Woods 21403
Harney 21787
Harpers Choice 21044
Harpers Corner 20659
Harpers Mill 21108
Harris Heights 21061
Harrison Ferry 21643
Harrisonville 21133
Harrisville, *Carroll* 21771
Harrisville, *Cecil* 21917
Harundale 21060
Harundale Mall 21061
Harvest Hills 21047
Harwood, *Anne Arundel* 20776
Har Wood, *Howard* 21075
Harwood Estates 20748
Harwood Park 21075
Havenwood Hills 21783
Haverhill 21234
Havre de Grace 21078
Havre de Grace Heights 21078
Hawbottom 21769
Hawkeye 21631
Hayes Landing 21811
Hazelhurst 21561
Hazelmoor 21919
Head of the Creek 21856
Hearn Bailey Farm 21801
Heather Heights 21784
Heather Hill Apartments 20748
Hebbville 21244
Hebron 21830
Helen 20635
Helen Estates 20635
Henderson 21640
Herald Harbor♦ 21032
Herald Square 21244
Hereford 21111
Heritage Harbor 21401
Heritage Hills 21061
Heritage Walk 20852
Hermanville 20653
Hermitage Park 20906
Hernwood Heights 21133
Herrington Manor 21550
Hickman 21629
Hickory 21014
Hickory Hills (Part of Bel Air) 21014
Hickory Ridge 21044
Hicksburg 21631
Hidden Point 21401
High Bridge 20720
High Bridge Estates 20720
Highfield, *Montgomery* 20879
Highfield, *Washington* 21719
Highland, *Frederick* 21773
Highland, *Howard* 20777
Highland Beach 21403
Highland Park, *Prince George's* 20743
Highland Park, *Worcester* 21811
Highlands 20854
Highlands of Olney 20832
Highland Stone 20854
Highlandtown (Part of Baltimore)‡ 21224
High Point, *Anne Arundel* 21122
High Point, *Montgomery* 20814
Highpoint Heights 20705
High Point Manor 21050
High Ridge 20723
High Ridge Park 20723
High View 21771
High-View Estates, *Carroll* 21074
Highview Estates, *Howard* 21042
Highview on the Bay 20779
Hillandale 20903
Hillandale Forest 20907
Hillandale Heights 20903
Hillcrest, *Anne Arundel* 21225
Hill Crest (Part of Takoma Park) 20912
Hillcrest, *Prince George's* 20748
Hillcrest Estates 20748
Hillcrest Heights, *Howard* 20723
Hillcrest Heights, *Prince George's* 20748
Hillcrest Terrace 20748
Hillendale Shopping Center 21204
Hillmead 20817
Hillmeade 20769
Hillmeade Manor 20769
Hillsboro 21641
Hillsborough 20707
Hillside 21157
Hillsmere Estates 21403
Hillsmere Shores♦ 21403
Hills Point 21613
Hill Top 20646
Hillwood Manor 20783
Hobbs 21629
Hoffman 21532
Holabird (Part of Baltimore) 21224
Holbrook 21133
Holiday Acres 21783
Holiday Beach 20732
Holiday Hills 21044
Holiday Park 20906
Holland Cliff Shores 20639
Holland Heights 21801
Hollaway Estates 20772
Hollinsworth Manor (Part of Elkton) 21921
Holly Beach 21221
Holly Gaf. Acres 20636
Holly Hall Terrace 21921
Holly Hill Harbor 21037
Holly Lake Estates 21804
Holly Spring 20747
Holly Tree 20601
Hollywood (Part of College Park) 20740
Hollywood, *St. Mary's* 20636
Hollywood Beach 21915
Hollywood Estates (Part of College Park) 20740
Hollywood Park 20904
Hollywood Shores 20636
Holmehurst 20720
Home Acres 20705
Homecrest 20906
Homewood, *Allegany* 21502
Homewood, *Montgomery* 20895
Honga 21622
Hood's Mill 21723
Hoopersville 21634
Hope Hill 21701
Hopewell 21817
Hopkins Mead 21029
Horizon Run 20877
Houcksville 21074
Howard Heights 21042
Howardville 21208
Hoyes 21531
Hudson 21613
Hughesville♦ 20637
Hungerford Towne (Part of Rockville) 20852
Hunt Club Estates, *Charles* 20601
Hunt Club Estates, *Howard* 21075
Hunt Crest Estates 21286
Hunters Harbor 21122
Hunters Hill 21093
Hunters Ridge 20610
Huntersville 20659
Hunting Hills 20639
Hunting Lodge 21234
Hunting Park 21801
Huntington Terrace 20814
Huntingtown 20639
Huntsmoor 21227
Huntsville 20785
Hunt Valley 21030-31
For specific ZIP Codes call (888) 275-8777, or your local postmaster.
Hunt Valley Mall 21030
Hurlock 21643
Hurry 20621
Hutton 21550
Huyett 21740
Hyattstown 20871
Hyattsville 20780-88
For specific ZIP Codes call (888) 275-8777, or your local postmaster.
Hyde Park, *Baltimore* 21221
Hyde Park, *Wicomico* 21801
Hydes 21082
Hynesboro 20706
Hynson 21632
Idlewild 20764
Idlewylde 21204
Ijamsville 21754
Ilchester 21043
Imperial Gardens 21133
Indian Creek Estates 20622
Indian Head 20640
Indian Head Manor 20616
Indian Head Naval Ordinance Station 20640
Indian Queen Estates 20744
Indian River Estates 20659
Indian Springs, Frederick 21702
Indian Springs, Washington 21711
Indiantown 21863
Ingleside 21644
Inverness 21222
Inverness Forest 20854
Inverness Woods 20854
Iron Hill 19711
Ironshire 21811
Ironsides 20643
Isabella Park 20783
Island Creek 20685
Island View Beach 21221
Issue 20645
Ivy Hills 21043
Ivytown 21601
Jackson 21903
Jacksonville, *Baltimore* 21131
Jacksonville, *Somerset* 21817
Jacktown 21613
Jacobsville 21122
James 21613
Jarrettsville♦ 21084
Jefferson 21755
Jefferson Heights, *Prince George's* 20743
Jefferson Heights, *Washington* 21742
Jennings 21536
Jersey Heights 21801
Jerusalem, *Baltimore* 21087
Jerusalem, *Frederick* 21773
Jerusalem, *Montgomery* 20837
Jessup♦ 20794
Jesterville 21814
Jewell 20754
Johnsontown 21620
Johnsville, *Carroll* 21784
Johnsville, *Frederick* 21791
Jones 21146
Jonestown 21655
Joppa 21085
Joppa Heights 21234
Joppatowne♦ 21085
Joppa View 21128
Josenhans Corner 21221
Joyce Acres 21012
Kalma Ridge 21032
Kalmia 21015
Kalmia Farms 21036
Kalten Acres 21158
Kastle Estates 20735
Kaywood Gardens (Part of Mount Rainier) 20712
Keedysville 21756
Keeler Glade 21531
Kelfer 25434
Kemp Mill Estates 20902
Kemp Mill Farms 20902
Kempton 26292
Kemptown 21770
Ken Gar 20895
Kennedyville 21645
Kensington 20891†
20895*
Kensington Estates 20895
Kensington Heights 20902
Kensington View 20895
Kent Island Estates 21666
Kentland 20785
Kentmore Park 21645
Kentmorr 21666
Kent Village 20785
Kenwood, *Baltimore* 21236
Kenwood, *Montgomery* 20815
Kenwood Beach 20676
Kerby Hills 20744
Kettering♦ 20774
Kettering Estate Park 20774
Keymar 21757
Keysers Ridge 21536
Keystone Manor 20747
Keysville 21757
Kilbirnie Estates 21804
Kilbourn Estates 20748
Kilmarock 20912
Kimberly Gardens 20708
Kings Contrivance 21045
Kings County 21087
Kings Creek Estate 20774
Kingsford 20721
Kings Grove 21529

*** Area Zip Code** **† Post Office Boxes** **‡ Postal Station** **♦ Census Designated Place** *Italic Type* **County**

Place	ZIP
Kings Manor	20695
Kings Park	21233
Kings Ransom	21113
Kings Ridge	21234
Kingston	21871
Kingston Manor	20772
Kingstown♦	21620
Kingsville♦	21087
Kingwood Common	21244
Kirkham	21601
Kirkwood	20782
Kitzmiller	21538
Klej Grange	21851
Knettishall	21204
Knollview	21043
Knollwood, *Baltimore*	21204
Knollwood, *Prince George's*	20783
Knoxville	21758
Ladiesburg	21759
Lakeland, *Anne Arundel*	21146
Lakeland (Part of College Park)	20740
Lake Linganore	21774
Lake Normandy Estates	20854
Lake Roland	21209
Lake Shore	21122
Lakeside Manor	21801
Lakeside Park	21740
Lakeside Terrace	20817
Lakeside Vista	21085
Lakesville	21622
Lakeview, *Howard*	20723
Lakeview, *Montgomery*	20817
Lakewood	21804
Lakewood Estates, *Calvert*	20754
Lakewood Estates, *Montgomery*	20850
Lancaster	20603
Land-O-Lakes	20636
Landon Woods	20817
Landover	20785
Landover Estates	20784
Landover Hills	20789
Landover Knolls	20785
Landover Park (Part of Cheverly)	20785
Lane Beach	20650
Langley Park	20783
Lanham	20703†
	20706*
Lanham Heights	20706
Lanham Woods	20706
Lansdowne	21227
Lantz	21780
Lapidum	21078
La Plata	20646
Lappans	21733
Larchmont Knolls	20895
Largo	20774
Largo/Kettering‡	20775
Largo Knolls	20774
Laurel	20707-09
	20723-26
For specific ZIP Codes call (888) 275-8777, or your local postmaster.	
Laurel Acres	21122
Laurel Brook	21047
Laureldale	21234
Laurel Grove	20659
Laurel Pines	20708
Laurel Shopping Center (Part of Laurel)	20707
Laurel Wood	20708
La Vale♦	21502
Lawndale Acres	21048
Lawsonia♦	21817
Layhill	20906
Layhill Village	20906
Laytonia	20877
Laytonsville	20882
Lees Woods	21014
Legion Avenue (Part of Annapolis)‡	21401
Le Gore	21757
Leisure World‡	20906
Leitersburg	21742
Leon	20711
Leonardtown	20650
Leslie	21901
Level	21078
Lewis Corner	21811
Lewisdale	20782
Lewis Heights	20783
Lewis Spring Manor	20735
Lewistown, *Frederick*	21701
Lewistown, *Talbot*	21625
Lexington Park	20653
Liberty Grove	21918
Liberty Manor	21244
Libertytown, *Frederick*	21762
Libertytown, *Worcester*	21811
Lime Kiln	21701
Linchester	21655
Lincoln Avenue	21740
Lincoln Heights (Part of Salisbury)	21801
Lincoln Manor	21102
Lincoln Park (Part of Rockville)	20850
Lindamoor on the Severn	21401
Linden	20907
Linden Chapel Hills	21036
Lineboro	21088
Linhigh	21236
Linkwood	21835
Linsey Acres	20748
Linsted on the Severn	21146
Linthicum Heights	21090
Linthicum Hills	21090
Linthicum Oaks	21090
Linwood, *Carroll*	21791
Linwood, *Howard*	21043
Linwood Village	21122
Lipins Corner	21122
Lisbon	21765
Little Orleans	21766
Little Washington	20747
Livingston Grove	20607
Llandaff	21601
Lloyds	21613
Loartown	21532
Lochearn	21207
Loch Haven	21234
Loch Hill	21212
Loch Lynn Heights	21550
Loch Raven	21234
Loch Raven Heights	21234
Loch Raven Village	21234
Locust Grove, *Allegany*	21502
Locust Grove, *Kent*	21645
Locust Grove, *Washington*	21779
Locust Grove Beach	20732
Locust Grove Station	21788
Locust Hill Estates	20814
Locust Valley	21769
Lodge Forest	21222
Lonaconing	21539
Londontown	21037
London Woods	20743
Lone Oak	20814
Long Bar Harbor	21009
Long Beach	20685
Long Corner	21771
Longfellow	21043
Longfield Estates	20747
Long Green	21092
Long Meadow	21784
Long Meadow Estates	20814
Long Meadow Shopping Center (Part of Hagerstown)	21740
Long Meadow West	21208
Long Point	21122
Long Reach	21045
Longview Beach	20618
Longwood	20817
Longwoods	21601
Lord	21532
Lord Calvert Estates	20736
Loreley	21162
Loretta Heights	21401
Lothian	20711
Louisville	21048
Lou Mar Estates	21009
Love Point	21666
Loveville	20656
Lower Magothy Beach	21146
Lower Marlboro	20736
Loyola (Part of Baltimore)	21210
Lucas Heights	21502
Luke	21540
Lusby	20657
Lusby Crossroads	21401
Lute	20906
Lutherville	21093
Lutherville-Timonium♦	21093*
	21094†
Lutz Hill	21237
Luxmanor	20852
Lynch	21678
Lynch Point	21222
Lynnbrook, *Anne Arundel*	21225
Lynnbrook, *Charles*	20601
Lynne Acres	21244
Lyons Creek, *Anne Arundel*	20711
Lyons Creek, *Calvert*	20754
Lyons Homes	21222
Mac Alpine	21042
McCahill Estates	20707
McCanns Corner	21154
McComas Beach	21550
McCoole	26726
McDaniel	21647
Mc Daniel City	20603
Mac Donald Farms	20736
McDonogh	21208
Maceys Corner	21146
McHenry	21541
McKaig	21701
McKay Beach	20650
Mc Kendree	20879
McKenney Hills	20910
McKinleyville	21661
McKinstrys Mill	21791
Maddox	20621
Madison	21648
Madonna	21084
Madonna Manor	21084
Magnolia	21085
Magnolia Springs	20784
Magothy Beach	21122
Magothy Park Beach	21122
Mago Vista Beach	21012
Magruder Landing	20613
Main Street (Part of Salisbury)‡	21801
Malcolm	20601
Mall in Columbia, The	21044
Malvern	21204
Manchester	21102
Manchester Estates	20746
Manhattan Woods	21146
Manokin, *Somerset*	21836
Manokin, *Wicomico*	21801
Manor	21111
Manor Lake	20853
Manor Park	20853
Manor View	21057
Manor Woods	20853
Maple Crest, *Baltimore*	21220
Maplecrest, *Carroll*	21157
Maple Park	21801
Maple Plains	21804
Mapleside (Part of Cumberland)	21502
Maple View	21157
Mapleville	21713
Maplewood, *Howard*	21042
Maplewood, *Montgomery*	20814
Maplewood, *Prince George's*	20744
Marbury♦	20658
Mardela Springs	21837
Margate	21060
Mariners	21817
Marion Station	21838
Market Center (Part of Baltimore)‡	21201
Marley	21060
Marley Heights	21061
Marling Farms	21619
Marlow Heights♦	20748
Marlton	20772
Marlywood	21286
Marriottsville	21104
Mars Estates	21221
Marshall Hall	20616
Marshalls Corner	20646
Marston	21776
Martin's Additions	20815
Martinsburg	20842
Martins Woods (Part of New Carrollton)	20706
Marwood	21061
Marydel	21649
Maryland City	20724
Maryland Line	21105
Maryland Park	20743
Maryland Point	20662
Marymount	20814
Maryvale (Part of Rockville)	20850
Marywood	21014
Masons Beach	20751
Mason Springs	20640
Massey	21650
Matapeake Estates	21666
Mattapex	21666
Mattapony (Part of Bladensburg)	20710
Matthews	21601
Maugansville	21767
Mayberry	21158
Maydale	20868
Mayfield, *Anne Arundel*	21113
Mayfield, *Howard*	21043
Mayo	21106
Mays Chapel Village	21093
Meadowbrook (Part of Bowie)	20715
Meadowbrook Estates	20876
Meadowcliff	21057
Meadowland	21093
Meadowood, *Anne Arundel*	21035
Meadowood, *Montgomery*	20904
Meadowvale Manor (Part of Havre de Grace)	21078
Meadowview Park	21921
Mechanicsville	20659
Medford	21776
Melitota	21620
Mellwood Hills	20772
Melody Acres	20622
Melrose	21102
Melson	21875
Merchants (Part of Baltimore)	21201
Merrimack Park	20817
Merritt Heights	21804
Merrymount	21244
Michigan Park Hills	20782
Middleborough	21221
Middlebrook	20876
Middleburg	21757
Middlepoint	21773
Middle River♦	21220
Middlesex	21221
Middlesex Shopping Center	21221
Middleton Valley	20748
Middletown, *Baltimore*	21053
Middletown, *Frederick*	21769
Middletown Heights	21769
Midland	21542
Midlothian	21543
Milford	21207
Milford Park	21117
Milford Ridge	21244
Millbrook (Part of Laurel)	20707
Mill Creek South	20855
Mill Creek Towne	20707
Mill Creek Towne East	20855
Miller	21532
Millers	21102
Millers Island	21219
Millersville	21108
Mill Green	21154
Millington	21651
Mill Point	20621
Mill Point Shores	20621
Millrace	21108
Mill Run	21562
Mills Choice	20879
Millwood	20743
Millwood Towne	20743
Mimosa Cove	20751
Minefield	21154
Mitchell Manor	21550
Mitchellville (Part of Bowie)	20717
Mondawmin/Metro Plaza (Part of Baltimore)	21215
Monie	21853
Monkton	21111
Monrovia	21770
Montego (Part of Ocean City)‡	21842
Montevideo, *Anne Arundel*	21076
Montevideo, *Howard*	20794
Montgomery Knolls	21043
Montgomery Square	20854
Montgomery Village	20886
Montgomery White Oak	20904
Montpelier	20708*
	20709†
Montpelier Woods	20708
Montrose	20852
Monumental	21227
Mooresfield	20759
Morantown	21532
Morgan	21797
Morgantown	20664
Morganza	20660
Morningside	20746
Moscow	21521
Mount Aetna♦	21740
Mountain	21085
Mountaindale	21788
Mountain Lake Park	21550
Mountain View	21157
Mountain View Estates	20878
Mountain Wood	21122
Mount Airy	21771
Mount Briar	21756
Mount Carmel	21122
Mount Clare (Part of Baltimore)	21223
Mount De Sales	21228
Mount Harmony	20736
Mount Hebron	21042
Mount Hermon	21804
Mount Hope (Part of Baltimore)	21215
Mount Lena	21713
Mount Pleasant, *Frederick*	21701
Mount Pleasant, *Washington*	21713
Mount Pleasant, *Wicomico*	21874
Mount Pleasant Beach	21122
Mount Rainier	20712
Mount Savage	21545
Mount Vernon	21853
Mount Victoria	20661
Mountview	21104
Mountville	21701
Mount Washington (Part of Baltimore)‡	21209
Mount Westley	21863
Mount Zion	21649
Mount Zoar	21918
Mousetown	21713
Muirkirk	20705
Mulberry Hills	21401
Murray Hills	20745
Myersdale (Part of Hancock)	21750
Myersville	21773
Nanjemoy	20662
Nanticoke	21840
Narrows	21638
Narrows Park	21502
National	21532
National Naval Medical Center‡	20814
Naval Academy♦	21402
Naylor	20772
Neavitt	21652
Needwood Estates	20855
Neeld Estates	20639
Neelsville	20876
Neilwood	20852
New Addition	21758
Newark	21841
New Birmingham Manor	20866
Newburg	20664
New Carrollton	20784
Newcomb	21653
New Germany	21536
New Hampshire Estates	20783
	20903
For specific ZIP Codes call (888) 275-8777, or your local postmaster.	
New Hampshire Gardens (Part of Takoma Park)	20912
Newhope	21874
New London	21771
New Mark Commons (Part of Rockville)	20850
New Market, *Frederick*	21774
New Market, *St. Mary's*	20622
New Market View	21771
New Midway	21775
New Orchard Estates	20774
Newport	20622
Newport Hills	20895
Newton	21655
Newton Village	20781
Newtown, *Charles*	20646
Newtown, *Kent*	21678
Newtown, *Talbot*	21625

Place	ZIP
New Valley	21918
New Windsor	21776
Nikep	21539
Nob Hill, *Howard*	21042
Nob Hill, *Montgomery*	20903
Nomira Heights (Part of Elkton)	21921
Norbeck	20906
Normandy Heights	21043
Normans	21666
Norris Corner	21009
Norrisville	21161
Northampton, *Baltimore*	21093
Northampton, *Prince George's*	20774
North Barnaby	20745
North Beach	20714
North Beach Park	20714
North Branch	21502
North Brentwood	20722
North Chevy Chase	20815
North College Park (Part of College Park)‡	20740
North Deale	20751
North East	21901
Northeast Heights	21901
North Englewood	20785
Northern (Part of Hagerstown)‡	21740
North Forestville	20747
North Fort Foote Village	20744
North Glade	21561
North Indian Head Estates	20616
North Junction (Part of Hagerstown)	21740
North Laurel	20723
North Laurel Park	20723
North Linthicum	21090
North Ocean City (Part of Ocean City)‡	21842
North Point	21222
North Point Village	21222
North Potomac Vista	20745
Northridge Manor	21740
North Roblee Acres	20772
North Sherwood Forest	20904
Northshire	21222
North Shore	21122
North Springbrook	20904
North Wellham	21061
Northwest Park, *Montgomery* (mail Bethesda)	20814
Northwest Park, *Montgomery & Prince George's* (mail Silver Spring)	20903
Northwood (Part of Baltimore)‡	21239
Northwood Park	20901
Northwood Village	20901
Norwood Corner	20906
Norwood Estates	20905
Notch Cliff	21057
Nottingham	21236
Nottingham Woods	21236
Oak Acres	21701
Oak Court	21401
Oakcrest	20707
Oakcrest Towers	20743
Oakdale	20853
Oak Estates	20622
Oak Forest	21228
Oak Hollow	21122
Oakhurst	20866
Oakington	21078
Oakland, *Baltimore*	21053
Oakland, *Carroll*♦	21784
Oakland, *Garrett*	21550
Oakland, *Prince George's*	20747
Oakland Acres	20622
Oakland Mills‡	21045
Oakland Park	21133
Oakland Terrace	20895
Oaklawn	20744
Oakleigh	21234
Oakleigh Forest	21146
Oakleigh Manor	21234
Oakley	20609
Oaklyn Manor	21085
Oakmont	20814
Oak Orchard	20735
Oak Park, *Baltimore*	21227
Oak Park, *Garrett*	21550
Oak Ridge	21740
Oak Springs	20868
Oak Summit	21234
Oaksville	21853
Oak View	20903
Oakville	20659
Oakwood	21918
Oakwood Knolls	20817
Ocean City	21842*
	21843†
Ocean City Harbor	21842
Ocean Pines♦	21811
Odonton	21113
Odenton Gardens	21113
Odenton Heights	21113
Odenton Park	21113
Odyssey	20736
Oella	21228
Old Country Estates	21146
Olde Colonial Woods	20832
Olde Fort Village	20744
Olde Towne Village (Part of District Heights)	20747
Old Farm	20852
Old Field, *Dorchester*	21622
Oldfield, *Frederick*	21791
Old Field, *Montgomery*	20854
Old Fort Hills	20744
Old Glory Beach	21060
Old Salem Village	20904
Old Severna Park	21146
Oldtown	21555
Olive	21758
Oliver Beach	21220
Olivet	20657
Olivet Hill	21635
Olney	20830†
	20832*
Olney Mills	20832
Olney Square	20832
Orangeville (Part of Baltimore)	21224
Oraville	20659
Orchard Beach	21226
Orchard Hills, *Baltimore*	21093
Orchard Hills, *Washington*	21742
Oregon	21030
Oriole	21853
Otter Point	21009
Overlea	21206
Owen Brown	21045
Owings	20736
Owings Beach	20751
Owings Mills♦	21117
Owings Wood (Part of North Beach)	20714
Oxford	21654
Oxon Hill	20745*
	20750†
Oxon Hill Village	20745
Oxon Run Hills	20748
Oyster Harbor	21401
Padonia	21030
Pagetts Corner	20748
Paint Branch Estates	20904
Paint Branch Farm	20904
Palmer Park♦	20785
Palmers Corner	20744
Palmetto	21853
Paradise	21228
Paradise Beach	21122
Paramount	21742
Paramount Manor	21740
Paris	20736
Parkertown	21811
Parker Wharf	20685
Parkers Creek	20685
Park Hall, *St. Mary's*	20667
Park Hall, *Washington*	21713
Parkhead	21711
Parkhurst Manor	21804
Parkland	20746
Parkland Apartments	20746
Parkland Terrace	20746
Park Mills	21710
Parkridge	20878
Parkside	20814
Parkside Estates	20855
Parkton	21120
Parktowne	21234
Parkview	20735
Parkville♦	21234
Park West	21061
Parkwood	20814
Parole♦	21401
Parsonsburg	21849
Partridge Place	20879
Pasadena	21122*
	21123†
Patapsco	21048
Patterson (Part of Baltimore)‡	21231
Patuxent	21113
Patuxent Beach	20619
Patuxent Manor	21035
Patuxent Naval Air Test Center	20670
Patuxent Palisades	20754
Patuxent Park	20653
Patuxent River	20670
Peach Orchard Heights	20868
Peachwood	20905
Peacock Corners	21651
Pearl	21701
Pectonville	21711
Pendennis Mount	21401
Peninsula General Hospital (Part of Salisbury)‡	21801
Pen Mar	21719
Penn Mary Junction (Part of Baltimore)	21224
Pepper Mill Village	20743
Perry Hall	21128
Perry Hall Estates	21236
Perry Hall Manor	21128
Perry Hall Shopping Center	21128
Perry Hall Village	21128
Perryman♦	21130
Perry Point	21902
Perrys Corner	21638
Perry View	21128
Perryville	21903
Perry Wright	20640
Petersburg	21643
Petersville	21758
Pfeiffer Corners	21045
Pheasant Run	20708
Phoenix	21131
Picketts Corner	21797
Pike (Part of Rockville)	20852
Pikesville	21208
Pilot Town	21918
Pindell	20711
Pine Cliff	21701
Pinecrest (Part of Takoma Park)	20912
Pinedale	21128
Pinefield	20601
Pine Grove	21804
Pine Grove Village	21122
Pine Hill Estates	20601
Pinehurst Estates	20744
Pinehurst on the Bay	21122
Pine Knoll	21157
Pine Knoll Terrace	21804
Pineleigh	21286
Pine Orchard Meadows	21042
Pine Ridge	21234
Pinesburg	21795
Pines on the Severn	21012
Pinewiff Beach	21037
Pinewood Hill	20744
Piney Glen Farms	20854
Piney Grove	21530
Piney Point	20674
Pinto	21556
Pioneer City	21144
Piscataway	20607
Piscataway Bay	20744
Piscataway Estates	20744
Piscataway Hills	20744
Pisgah	20640
Pittsville	21850
Plainfield	21804
Plane Number Four	21771
Pleasant Fields	20874
Pleasant Grove, *Baltimore*	21136
Pleasant Grove, *Frederick*	21771
Pleasant Hill, *Baltimore*	21117
Pleasant Hill, *Cecil*	21921
Pleasant Hills♦	21087
Pleasant Ridge	21797
Pleasant Springs	20613
Pleasant Valley, *Allegany*	21520
Pleasant Valley, *Carroll*	21158
Pleasant Valley, *Washington*	21783
Pleasant View, *Frederick*	21710
Pleasant View, *Howard*	21043
Pleasantville	21061
Pleasant Walk	21773
Plumgar	20876
Plum Point	20639
Pocomoke City	21851
Pointer Ridge (Part of Bowie)	20716
Point Lookout	20687
Point of Rocks	21777
Point of Rocks Estates	21777
Point Pleasant	21060
Pomfret	20675
Pomona	21620
Pomonkey	20640
Ponder Cove	21037
Pondsville	21783
Pooks Hill	20814
Poole	21034
Poolesville	20837
Popes Creek	20664
Poplar Grove	21154
Poplar Hill	20613
Poplar Hill Estates	20735
Poplar Knob	21788
Poplar Springs	21771
Port Covington (Part of Baltimore)	21230
Port Deposit	21904
Porters Park	21221
Porterstown	21756
Port Herman	21915
Port Republic	20676
Port Tobacco	20677
Port Tobacco Riviera	20677
Potomac	20854*
	20859†
Potomac Commons	20854
Potomac Falls Estates	20854
Potomac Green	20854
Potomac Heights, *Charles*♦	20640
Potomac Heights (Part of Hagerstown)	21740
Potomac Hills	20854
Potomac Park	21502
Potomac Ranch	20854
Potomac Shores, *Charles*	20677
Potomac Shores, *St. Mary's*	20650
Potomac View	20664
Potomac View Estates	20854
Potomac Village	20854
Potomac Vista	20745
Potomac Woods (Part of Rockville)	20854
Pot Spring	21093
Powder Mill Estates	20783
Powder Mill Village	20705
Powellville	21852
Powhatan Beach	21122
Powhattan Mill	21207
Prathertown	20879
Presidential Park	20783
Presidential Towers	20783
Presley Manor	20784
Preston	21655
Preston Manor	21009
Price	21656
Priceville	21152
Prince Frederick♦	20678
Princess Anne	21853
Princeton	20746
Principio Furnace	21903
Prophecy	20744
Prospect Knolls	20720
Prospect Walk	21044
Providence, *Baltimore*	21286
Providence, *Cecil*	21921
Public Landing	21863
Pumphrey	21225
Puncheon Landing	21851
Putnam	21050
Putty Hill	21236
Pylesville	21132
Quail Ridge	21075
Quail Run	20879
Quaint Acres	20904
Quaker Neck Landing	21620
Quantico	21856
Queen Anne	21657
Queen Anne Colony	21666
Queens Chapel Manor (Part of Hyattsville)	20782
Queenstown (Part of Mount Rainier)	20712
Queenstown, *Queen Anne's*	21658
Queenswood	20772
Quince Orchard	20878
Quincy Manor	20784
Radiant Valley	20784
Ramblewood Village	20735
Ramgate	20744
Ranchleigh, *Baltimore*	21209
Ranchleigh (Part of Baltimore)	21209
Randalia	21915
Randallstown	21133
Randle Cliff Beach	20732
Randolph Farms	20852
Randolph Hills	20852
Random Heights	21157
Raspeburg (Part of Baltimore)‡	21206
Rawlings	21557
Rawlings Heights	21557
Raynor Heights	21090
Rayville	21120
Red Coat Woods	20854
Reddings Corner	21678
Redford Estates	20744
Red Hill	20640
Redhouse	21550
Redland	20855
Red Point	21901
Reeder Development (Part of Frederick)	21701
Reese	21157
Reese Manor	21048
Regal Estates	20754
Regency Estates	20852
Regent Park	20854
Regent Square (Part of Rockville)	20850
Rehobeth	21857
Reid	21742
Reids Grove	21659
Reisterstown♦	21136
Reisterstown Road Plaza (Part of Baltimore)‡	21270
Relay	21227
Rest Haven	20751
Revell	21012
Revere Park	21234
Reynolds	21539
Rhodesdale	21659
Rhodes Point	21824
Riawakin Acres	21830
Richards Oak	21917
Ricmar	21804
Riderwood	21139
Riderwood Hills	21139
Ridge	20680
Ridge Lake	21042
Ridgeleigh	21234
Ridgely	21660
Ridgeview	21077
Ridgeville (Part of Mount Airy)	21771
Ridgeway	21144
Ridgeway Estates	20743
Ridgley Park	21784
Riding Woods	21122
Riggins Corner	21622
Ringgold	21740
Rio Vista	21663
Ripley	20646
Ripplewood	21244
Rippling Ridge	21061
Rising Sun	21911
Rison	20640
Ritchie	20747
Ritchie Heights	20747
Ritchie Manor	20747
Riva♦	21140
Rivendell	21146
River Bend	20744
River Bend Estates	20744
River Club Estates	21037
Riverdale, *Anne Arundel*	21146
Riverdale, *Prince George's*	20737*
	20738†
Riverdale Heights	20737
Riverdale Hills	20737
River Falls	20854
River Forest	20744
River Meadows	21045
River Ridge Estates	20745
Riverside	20662
River Springs	20609
Riverton	21837
Riverview Manor	21401
Riverview Village (Part of Indian Head)	20640
Riverwood	21035

*** Area Zip Code** **† Post Office Boxes** **‡ Postal Station** **♦ Census Designated Place** *Italic Type* **County**

Place	ZIP
Riviera Beach	21122
Riviera Isle	21122
Robbins	21626
Roberts	21623
Roberts Glen	20854
Robinson	21146
Robinwood	21742
Roblee Acres	20772
Rockawalking Village	21801
Rockaway Beach	21221
Rock Creek Forest	20815
Rock Creek Gardens	20815
Rock Creek Highlands	20895
Rock Creek Hills	20895
Rock Creek Manor	20853
Rock Creek Palisades	20895
Rock Creek Village	20853
Rockcrest (Part of Rockville)	20851
Rockdale	21244
Rock Hall, *Frederick*	21790
Rock Hall, *Kent*	21661
Rock Hill Beach	21122
Rockland, *Howard*	21043
Rockland (Part of Rockville)	20850
Rockland Run	21209
Rock Point	20682
Rock Run	21078
Rockshire (Part of Rockville)	20850
Rockshire Square (Part of Rockville)	20850
Rockshire Village (Part of Rockville)	20850
Rockview Beach	21122
Rockville	20847-53
For specific ZIP Codes call (888) 275-8777, or your local postmaster.	
Rockville Estates (Part of Rockville)	20850
Rockwell	21228
Rocky Gorge Estates	20707
Rocky Ridge	21778
Rocky Springs	21702
Rodgers Forge	21204
Rogers Heights	20781
Rohrersville	21779
Rohrersville Station	21756
Roland Park (Part of Baltimore)‡	21210
Rolling Acres, *Prince George's*	20623
Rolling Acres, *St. Mary's*	20622
Rolling Green	21028
Rolling Hills, *Anne Arundel*	21401
Rolling Hills, *Carroll*	21784
Rolling Knolls	21401
Rolling Ridge, *Carroll*	21157
Rolling Ridge, *Howard*	21043
Rolling Ridge, *Prince George's*	20743
Rolling Terrace	20912
Rolling Terrace Estates	20912
Rollingwood	20815
Rollins Park (Part of Rockville)	20852
Rolphs	21620
Romancoke	21666
Rosaryville Estates	20772
Rosecroft	20748
Rosecroft Park	20744
Rosedale	21237
Rosedale Estates	20744
Rosedale Park	20815
Rose Haven	20714
Rose Hill Estates	20817
Rosemary Hills	20910
Rosemont, *Baltimore*	21225
Rosemont, *Frederick*	21758
Rosemont, *Montgomery*	20877
Rose Valley Estates	20744
Rossville	21237
Round Acres	21047
Round Bay	21146
Round Hill	21702
Roundtop	21750
Rover Mill Estates	21794
Rowlandsville	21918
Roxboro (Part of Rockville)	20850
Royal Beach	21122
Royal Oak, *Talbot*	21662
Royal Oak, *Wicomico*	21856
Rugby Hall	21012

Place	ZIP
Ruhl	21053
Rumbley	21871
Rumsey Island	21085
Running Brook	21044
Rustic Acres	21804
Rusty Acres	20866
Ruthsburg	21617
Rutledge	21047
Ruxton	21286
Ryceville	20659
Sabillasville	21780
Sackertown	21817
St. Andrews Estates	20619
St. Anthony's	21727
St. Aubins Heights (Part of Easton)	21601
St. Augustine	21915
St. Charles♦	20601
St. Charles Town Center‡	20603
St. Clement Shores	20650
St. Denis	21227
St. George Island	20674
St. Georges	21071
St. George's Park	20690
St. Helena	21222
St. Inigoes	20684
St. James, *Washington*	21781
St. James, *Worcester*	21851
St. Jeromes	20628
St. Johns Manor	21042
St. Johns Village	21042
St. Leonard	20685
St. Margarets	21401
St. Margarets Farm	21401
St. Mark's	21758
St. Martins	21811
St. Marys City	20686
St. Michaels	21663
St. Stephen	21853
Salem	21869
Salisbury	21801-04
For specific ZIP Codes call (888) 275-8777, or your local postmaster.	
Salisbury Mall (Part of Salisbury)	21801
Samples Manor	21782
Sams Creek	21776
Sanders Park	21122
Sandgates	20659
San Domingo	21837
Sand Spring	21531
Sandy Acres	21613
Sandy Bottom	21620
Sandy Hook	21758
Sandy Spring	20860
Sandy Spring Estates	20707
Sandy Spring Meadows	20860
Sandyville	21048
Sang Run	21541
Sanmar	21713
Sansbury Park	20747
Santa Fe Acres	21801
Sassafras	21635
Satyr Hill	21234
Saunders Point	21037
Savage	20763
Scaggsville	20723
Scarboro, *Harford*	21154
Scarboro, *Worcester*	21863
Schnaders Shores	21122
Scientists Cliffs	20676
Scotland, *Montgomery*	20854
Scotland, *St. Mary's*	20687
Scotland Beach	20687
Seabrook	20706
Seabrook Acres	20706
Seabrook Park Estates	20706
Seat Pleasant	20743
Sebring	21045
Secretary	21664
Security	21742
Selassie Villa	20764
Selby-on-the-Bay	21037
Selbysport	21531
Sellman	20838
Seneca	20837
Seneca Park	20876
Sequioa	20868
Severn♦	21144
Severna Forest	21146
Severna Park♦	21146
Severn Grove	21401
Severn Heights	21146
Severnside	21401

Place	ZIP
Sewell	21009
Sewells Orchard	21045
Shad Point	21801
Shady Dale	20659
Shady Oaks	20778
Shady Side♦	20764
Shallmar	21538
Shane	21161
Sharewood Acres	20794
Sharonville	21122
Sharon Woods	20879
Sharperville	20601
Sharpsburg	21782
Sharpstown	21661
Sharptown	21861
Shavox	21804
Shawsville	21161
Shawsville Acres	21161
Shelltown	21838
Shervettes Corner	21784
Sherwood	21665
Sherwood Forest, *Anne Arundel*	21405
Sherwood Forest, *Montgomery*	20904
Sherwood Forest, *Prince George's*	20772
Sherwood Manor, *Prince George's*	20720
Sherwood Manor, *Wicomico*	21804
Shetland Hills	21093
Shiloh, *Charles*	20664
Shiloh, *Dorchester*	21643
Shookstown	21702
Shore Acres	21012
Shoreham Beach	21037
Shoreland	21061
Shorewood Estates	21635
Showell	21862
Sierra Manor	21804
Silesia	20744
Sillery Bay	21122
Siloam	21822
Silver Gate Village	21236
Silver Hill	20746
Silver Hill Park	20746
Silver Meadow	21128
Silver Rock (Part of Rockville)	20850
Silver Run	21158
Silver Sands	21060
Silver Spring	20901-11
	20914-18
For specific ZIP Codes call (888) 275-8777, or your local postmaster.	
Silver Valley	20746
Simpsonville	21150
Sinepuxent	21811
Singerly	21916
Skidmore	21401
Skipton	21625
Skyline	20746
Skyline Additions	20746
Sky Valley	21561
Slabtown	21545
Sligo Park Knolls	20901
Smallwood	21157
Smithsburg	21783
Smithville, *Caroline*	21632
Smithville, *Dorchester*	21669
Smoketown	21713
Smugglers Cove	21146
Snowden Manor	21157
Snowden Oaks	20708
Snow Hill	21863
Snow Hill Manor	20708
Snug Harbor, *Anne Arundel*	20764
Snug Harbor, *Worcester*	21811
Snydersburg	21074
	21157
For specific ZIP Codes call (888) 275-8777, or your local postmaster.	
Social Security Administration	21207
Society Hill	20650
Sollers Homes	21222
Sollers Point	21222
Solley Heights	21060
Solomons	20688
Somerset	20815
Sonoma	20814
South (Part of Baltimore)‡	21230
Southampton	20653
South Cheverly Forest	20784

Place	ZIP
South Cumberland (Part of Cumberland)	21502
Southdown Shores	21037
Southeast (Part of Baltimore)‡	21281
Southern Garden Apartments	20032
South Fort Foote Village	20744
South Gate	21061
South Haven	21401
Southland Hills	21204
South Laurel	20708
South Lawn	20745
South Layhill	20906
South Piscataway	20601
South River Park	21037
South Salisbury (Part of Salisbury)	21801
South Tantallon	20744
Southview	20745
South Woodside Park	20910
Sparks	21152
Sparks Glencoe	21152
Sparrows Point	21219
Spaulding Heights	20747
Spence	21863
Spencerville	20868
Spielman	21733
Spoolsville	21769
Springbrook, *Baltimore*	21133
Springbrook, *Montgomery*	20904
Springbrook Forest	20902
Springbrook Manor	20904
Springbrook Village	20904
Springdale, Baltimore	21030
Springdale, *Prince George's*	20706
Springdale Gardens	20706
Springfield	20814
Spring Gap	21560
Spring Garden Estates	21793
Spring Grove	21837
Springhill Acres	21801
Springhill Lake (Part of Greenbelt)	20770
Springlake	20817
Spring Meadow	21084
Spring Mills	21157
Spring Valley	21740
Squires Woods	20744
Stablersville	21161
Stafford	21078
Stanbrook	21222
Stansbury Estates	21220
Stansbury Manor	21220
Starkeys Corner	21623
Starr	21617
Station A (Part of Cumberland)‡	21502
Stemmer's Run	21220
Stepney	21001
Steuart Level	21037
Stevenson	21153
Stevensville♦	21666
Stevensville South♦	21666
Stewartown	20879
Stillmeadows	21144
Still Pond	21667
Stockton	21864
Stonecrest Hill	21043
Stonegate	20905
Stone Haven	21060
Stoneleigh	21212
Stoneybrook Estates	20906
Stony Beach	21226
Stony Run	21076
Stratford	21093
Strathmore At Bel Pre	20906
Strathmore Estates	20906
Stratton Woods	20817
Strawberry Hills Estates	20616
Strawbridge Estates	21784
Strawleigh	21702
Street	21154
Stronghold	20842
Suburban Acres	21804
Suburbia	21060
Sudbrook Park	21202
Sudlersville	21668
Sugarland	20837
Sugarloaf Estates	21710
Suitland	20746*
	20752†
Sullivan Heights	21157
Summerhill, *Anne Arundel*	21032

Place	ZIP
Summerhill (Part of Poolesville)	20837
Summit Farms	21237
Summit Park	21209
Sumner	20816
Sunair (Part of Salisbury)	21801
Sunderland	20689
Sunny Acres	20747
Sunnybrook	21131
Sunnybrook Hills	21131
Sunny Isle of Kent	21666
Sunrise	20744
Sunrise Beach	21032
Sunset Acres	21740
Sunset Beach	21122
Sunset Heights	21801
Sunset Hills	21702
Sunset Knoll	21122
Sunshine	20833
Sunshine Acres	20639
Sun Valley	21060
Surratt Gardens	20735
Susquehanna Hills	21078
Sussex Square	21108
Sutton Acres	20677
Swallow Falls	21550
Swan Creek	21078
Swanton	21561
Sweet Air Manor	21013
Sweetser Heights	21090
Sycamore Acres	20853
Sycamore Heights	21742
Sykesville	21784
Sylmar	21911
Sylvan Grove	21740
Sylvan View	21122
Table Rock	26720
Takoma Park	20912*
	20913†
Tall Timbers	20690
Tammany Manor	21795
Tanager Forest	21108
Taneytown	21787
Tanglewood	21401
Tantallon	20744
Tantallon North	20744
Tantallon on the Potomac	20744
Tantallon Square	20744
Tanterra	20833
Tanyard	21655
Tarquin Village	20735
Taylor Mill Village	21801
Taylors Island	21669
Taylorsville	21771
Taylorville	21811
Temple Heights	20748
Temple Hills	20748*
	20757†
Temple Hills Park	20748
Templeton Estates	20737
Templeton Manor	20737
Templeville	21670
Temple Woods	20744
Terrace Gardens	21012
Terrace View Estates	21225
Texas	21030
Thayerville	21550
The Colony	20874
The Crest of Wickford	20852
The Downs	21401
The Glen	20854
The Hamlet	20815
The Lakes	21030
The Meadows	20736
The Oaks, *Calvert*	20639
The Oaks, *Howard*	21043
Theodore	21911
The Orchards	21043
The Pines	20774
The Points	20879
Thomas	21613
Thomas Choice	20879
Thomas Run	21015
Thomas Town	21629
Thompson Corner	20659
Thompsontown	21631
Thomson Estates	21921
Thornleigh	21139
Thornwood Knoll	20744
Thorwood Park	21234
Thunder Hill	21045
Thurmont	21788
Thurston	20842
Tilden Woods	20852
Tilghman	21671
Tilghmanton	21713
Timber Grove	21117

*** Area Zip Code** **† Post Office Boxes** **‡ Postal Station** **♦ Census Designated Place** *Italic Type* **County**

Timber Ridge, *Anne Arundel* 21076
Timber Ridge, *Carroll* 21157
Timberview 21075
Timonium 21093
Tintop Hill 20650
Tobytown 20854
Todd Village 21048
Toddville 21672
Tolchester Beach 21620
Tollgate 21117
Tompkinsville 20664
Tonytank 21801
Tower Acres 20723
Tower Garden on the Bay 21666
Town Creek 25434
Town Creek Estates 20653
Town Creek Manor 20653
Town Crest 20855
Towne and Country North 21030
Towne Center 20708
Town Point 21915
Townshend 20613
Townsontown Centre 21286
Towson♦ 21204
 21286
For specific ZIP Codes call (888) 275-8777, or your local postmaster.
Towson Estates 21204
Towson Marketplace 21204
Towson Park 21286
Towson Town Center 21204
Tracys Landing 20779
Trappe, *St. Mary's* 20628
Trappe, *Talbot* 21673
Trappe, *Worcester* 21811
Trappe Station 21654
Travilah 20850
Treetops 21122
Trengall Acres 21740
Trent Hall 20659
Trenton 21155
Trescher Heights 21502
Triple Lakes 21502
Troutville 21798
Truman Heights 20748
Tulip Hill, *Frederick* 21702
Tulip Hill, *Montgomery* 20816
Tunis Mills 21601
Turkey Neck 21561
Turkey Point, *Anne Arundel* 21037
Turkey Point, *Baltimore* 21221
Turnbull Estates 21037
Turners Station 21222
Tuscarora 21790
Tuxedo (Part of Cheverly) 20785
Tuxedo Colony 20785
Twinbrook (Part of Rockville) 20851
Twinbrook Estates 20603
Twin Brook Forest (Part of Rockville) 20851
Twinbrook Park (Part of Rockville) 20851
Twin Harbors 21012
Tyaskin 21865
Tydings on the Bay 21401
Tylerton 21866
Tyrone 21158
Ulmsted Acres 21012
Ulmsted Estate 21012
Ulmsted Gardens 21012
Ulmsted Point 21012
Union Bridge 21791
Union Corner 21636
Union Mills 21158
Uniontown 21158
Unionville, *Frederick* 21791
Unionville, *Talbot* 21601
Unionville, *Worcester* 21851
Unity 20833
University City 20783
University Gardens 20782
University Hills 20783
University Park 20784
Upperco 21155
Upper Crossroads 21047
Upper Fairmount 21867
Upper Falls 21156
Upper Ferry 21801
Upper Hill 21867
Upper Homewood 21502
Upper Marlboro 20772-75
For specific ZIP Codes call (888) 275-8777, or your local postmaster.
Urbana 21701
Utica 21788
Vale 21015
Vale Summit 21532
Valley Crest 21093
Valley Lee 20692
Valley Mede 21042
Valley Stream Estates 20866
Valley View, *Howard* 21043
Valley View, *Prince George's* 20744
Valleywood, *Baltimore* 21093
Valleywood, *Wicomico* 21801
Van Bibber 21040
Van Bibber Manor 21040
Van Lear Manor 21795
Venice on the Bay 21122
Venton 21853
Vernon 21161
Victory Villa 21220
Vienna 21869
Viers Mill Village 20906
View More Acres 21701
Villa Cresta 21234
Village of Vanderway 21234
Villages of Montpelier 20708
Villa Heights 20784
Villa Monticello 21723
Villa Nova 21207
Villa Toscano 21122
Villa Verdi 21054
Waggaman Heights 20748
Wakefield, *Baltimore* 21093
Wakefield, *Carroll* 21776
Wakefield Meadows 21014
Walbrook (Part of Baltimore)‡ 21216
Waldon Woods 20735
Waldorf 20601-04
For specific ZIP Codes call (888) 275-8777, or your local postmaster.
Walker Hill 20707
Walker Mill 20743
Walker Mill Estates 20743
Walkersville 21793
Wallington Estates 20747
Wallville 20685
Walnut Hill 20877
Walnut Ridge 21157
Walnut Woods 20852
Walston 21849
Walter Heights 20748
Wango 21804
Warburton Oaks 20744
Wards Chapel 21133
Warfield Estates 21738
Warfieldsburg 21157
Warington Hills (Part of Indian Head) 20640
Warlinda 20646
Warren 21030
Warwick 21912
Washington Grove 20880
Waterbury 21032
Waterloo 21075
Wateroak Point 21122
Watersville 21771
Waterview 21840
Watkins Glen 20854
Waverly (Part of Baltimore)‡ 21218
Wayside 20664
Webster Village 21078
Weems Creek 21401
Weisburg 21161
Welcome 20693
Wellington Estates 20707
Wenona 21821
Wesley 21626
Wesmond (Part of Poolesville) 20837
West Baltimore (Part of Baltimore) 21227
West Beach (Part of Chesapeake Beach) 20732
West Bethesda 20817
Westboro 20814
West Bowie (Part of Bowie)‡ 20719
Westchester, *Baltimore* 21228
Westchester, *Montgomery* 20902
Westchester Estates 20748
Westchester Park (Part of College Park) 20740
West Denton 21629
West Edmondale 21229
West Elkridge 21075
West End (Part of Annapolis) 21401
West End Park (Part of Rockville) 20850
Westerlea 21228
Westernport 21562
Western Shores Estates 20676
West Friendship 21794
Westgate 20816
West Gate Woods 20706
West Hills, *Baltimore* 21207
West Hills, *Frederick* 21702
West Hyattsville (Part of Hyattsville) 20782
Westlake 21801
West Lanham Estates 20784
West Lanham Hills 20784
West Laurel Acres 20707
West Liberty 21161
West Magothy Manor 21012
Westminster, Carroll 21157-58
For specific ZIP Codes call (888) 275-8777, or your local postmaster.
Westminster, *Montgomery* 20852
Westminster South♦ 21157
Westmore (Part of Rockville) 20850
Westmoreland Hills 20816
West Nottingham 21917
West Ocean City 21842
Westover 21871
Westowne 21229
Westphalia Estates 20772
Westphalia Woods 20774
West River 20778
West Severna Park 21146
West Shady Side 20764
West Shore 21106
West Twin River Beach 21220
Westview 21801
Westview Mall 21228
Westview Park 21228
West View Shores 21919
West Vindex 21538
Westwood 20613
Westwood Estates, *Charles* 20601
Westwood Estates, *Prince George's* 20623
Wetipquin 21856
Weverton 21758
Wexford 21012
Whaleyville 21872
Wheaton 20902
Wheaton Crest 20902
Wheaton Forest 20902
Wheaton-Glenmont♦ 20902
Wheaton Hills 20902
Wheaton Plaza Regional Center 20902
Wheaton Woods 20853
Whetstone 20879
Whipporwill Estates 21122
Whiskey Bottom 20723
Whiteburg 21863
White Crystal Beach 21919
Whitefield Knolls 20706
Whitefield Woods 20706
White Flint Mall 20891
White Flint Park 20895
Whiteford 21160
White Hall, *Baltimore* 21161
Whitehall, *Prince George's* 20607
Whitehall Beach 21401
Whitehall Manor 20814
Whitehaven 21856
Whitehouse Heights 20785
White Landing 20613
Whiteleysburg 21639
White Marsh♦ 21162
White Oak 20904
White Oak Manor 20904
White Oak Park 20904
White Oak Shopping Center 20904
White Oak Tower 20904
White Plains♦ 20695
White Point Beach 20650
White Rock 21702
White Sands 20657
Whitesburg 21863
Whiton 21863
Wicomico 20622
Wicomico Beach 20664
Wilburn Estates 20743
Wilde Lake 21044
Wildercroft 20737
Wild Rose Shores 21403
Wild Wood Beach 21221
Wildwood Estates 20735
Wildwood Hills 20817
Wildwood Manor 20817
Wilelinor Estates 21037
Willards 21874
Willerburn Acres 20854
Williamsburg 21643
Williamsburg Estates 20772
Williamsburg Gardens 20854
Williamsburg Village 20832
Williamsbury 21208
Williamsport 21795
Williams Wharf 20685
Williston 21629
Willoughby Beach 21040
Willow Beach Colony 20732
Willowbrook, *Montgomery* 20854
Willowbrook, *Prince George's* 20783
Willow Lake 20708
Wilson 21722
Wilson Hills 20906
Wilson Point 21220
Wiltondale 21204
Wilton Farm Acres 21043
Winchester on the Severn 21401
Winchester Park 21157
Windbrook 20735
Windham Manor, *Montgomery* 20904
Windham Manor, *Wicomico* 21804
Winding Brook Village 21921
Windmere Acres 20763
Windsor 21244
Windsor Estates 21717
Windsor Terrace 21207
Winfield, *Carroll* 21157
Winfield, *Howard* 21044
Winfield Heights 21157
Wingate 21675
Wingates Point 21675
Winsor Hills 20854
Winterest 20854
Wisperren Oaks 21701
Wittman 21676
Wolfsville 21773
 21783
For specific ZIP Codes call (888) 275-8777, or your local postmaster.
Wolverton Park 20735
Woodacres 20816
Woodberry Forest 20748
Woodbine 21797
Woodbrook 21212
Woodburn 20817
Wood Creek 21045
Woodcroft 21234
Woodensburg 21136
Woodfield 20882
Woodford 21044
Woodhaven 20617
Woodhaven Park 20646
Woodland 21532
Woodland Acres 20619
Woodland Point 20664
Woodlands 21133
Woodlane 20748
Woodlark 20784
Woodlawn, *Baltimore* 21207
Woodlawn, *Cecil* 21904
Woodlawn, *Prince George's* 20784
Woodlawn Heights 21061
Woodmont 20815
Woodmoor, *Baltimore* 21207
Woodmoor, *Montgomery* 20901
Woodmoor, *Washington* 21740
Wood Point 21740
Woodsboro 21798
Woods Corner 20748
Woodside 20901
Woodside Park 20901
Woodstock 21163
Woodville 21771
Woolford 21677
Worthington 21043
Worthington Heights 21014
Worton 21678
Wrights Crossing 21532
Wye Mills 21679
Wyngate 20814
Wynne Wood 21227
Yarrowsburg 21758
Yellow Springs 21702
Yorkshire Knolls 20743
Zihlman 21532
Zion 21901
Zittlestown 21713

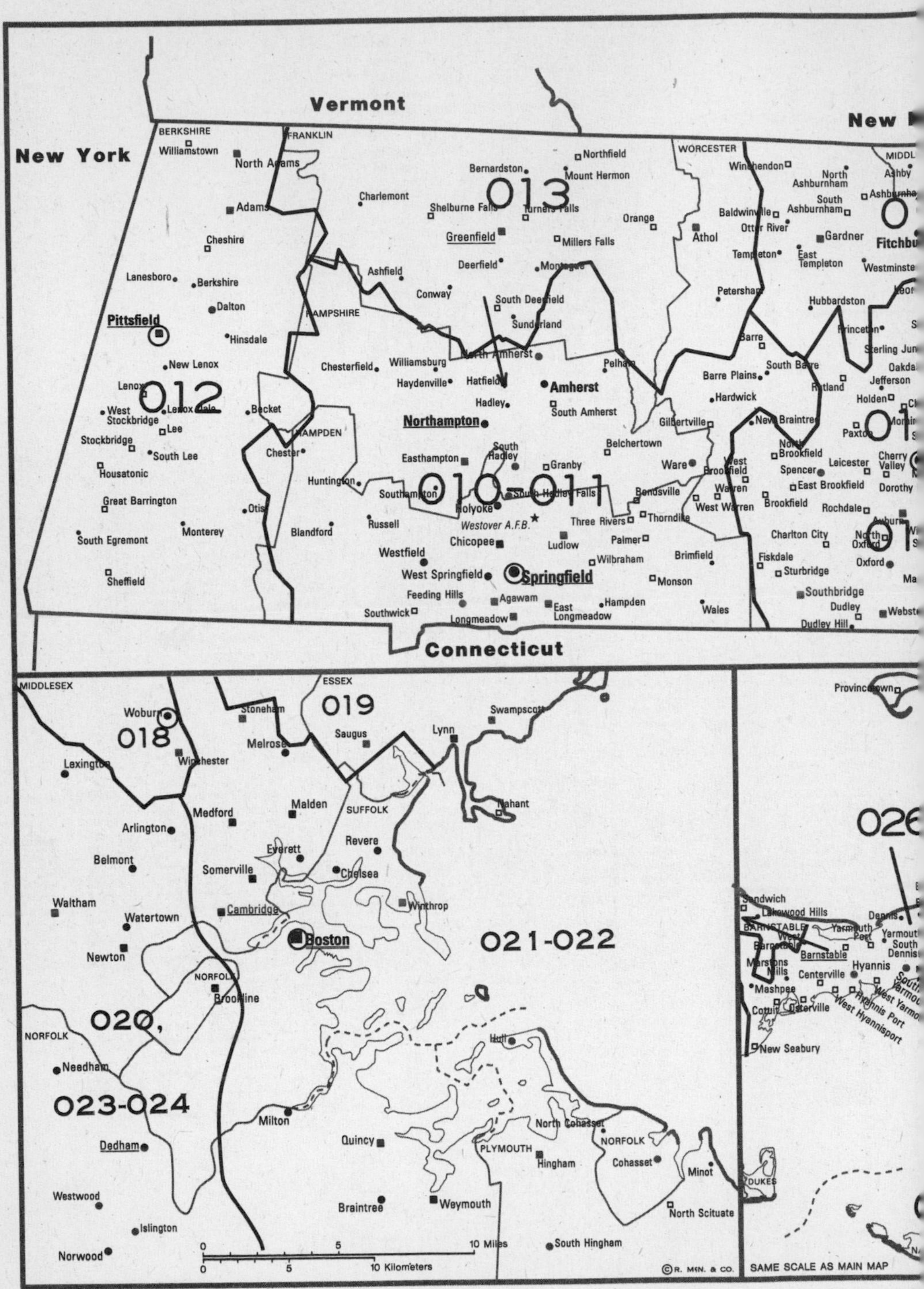

Vermont
New York
Connecticut
BERKSHIRE
FRANKLIN
WORCESTER
HAMPSHIRE
HAMPDEN
013
012
010-011
Williamstown
North Adams
Adams
Cheshire
Lanesboro
Berkshire
Dalton
Pittsfield
Hinsdale
New Lenox
West Stockbridge
Lee
Stockbridge
South Lee
Housatonic
Great Barrington
Monterey
South Egremont
Sheffield
Becket
Otis
Charlemont
Shelburne Falls
Greenfield
Deerfield
Ashfield
Conway
Bernardston
Northfield
Mount Hermon
Millers Falls
Orange
South Deerfield
Sunderland
North Amherst
Amherst
South Amherst
Pelham
Chesterfield
Williamsburg
Haydenville
Hatfield
Hadley
Northampton
Easthampton
South Hadley
Granby
Belchertown
Huntington
Southampton
Holyoke
Westover A.F.B.
Chester
Blandford
Russell
Westfield
Chicopee
Ludlow
Three Rivers
Palmer
Thorndike
Bondsville
Wilbraham
West Springfield
Springfield
Feeding Hills
Agawam
East Longmeadow
Longmeadow
Hampden
Southwick
Monson
Wales
Brimfield
Athol
Ware
Gilbertville
Hardwick
Barre Plains
Barre
South Barre
Petersham
Winchendon
North Ashburnham
South Ashburnham
Baldwinville
Otter River
Templeton
East Templeton
Gardner
Hubbardston
Westminster
Princeton
Rutland
Jefferson
Holden
Paxton
New Braintree
North Brookfield
West Brookfield
Warren
West Warren
Brookfield
East Brookfield
Spencer
Leicester
Cherry Valley
Rochdale
Charlton City
Fiskdale
Sturbridge
Southbridge
Dudley
Dudley Hill
Oxford
North Oxford
Dorothy
MIDDLESEX
ESSEX
SUFFOLK
NORFOLK
PLYMOUTH
018
019
020,
023-024
021-022
Woburn
Winchester
Stoneham
Melrose
Saugus
Lynn
Swampscott
Nahant
Lexington
Medford
Malden
Arlington
Everett
Revere
Belmont
Somerville
Chelsea
Waltham
Watertown
Cambridge
Winthrop
Boston
Newton
Brookline
Needham
Milton
Dedham
Quincy
Hull
North Cohasset
Hingham
Cohasset
Minot
Westwood
Braintree
Weymouth
North Scituate
Islington
Norwood
South Hingham
0 5 10 Miles
0 5 10 Kilometers
©R. McN. & CO.
Provincetown
026
Sandwich
Lakewood Hills
BARNSTABLE
Barnstable
Marstons Mills
Centerville
Hyannis
Mashpee
Cotuit
Osterville
Hyannis Port
West Hyannisport
New Seabury
DUKES
SAME SCALE AS MAIN MAP

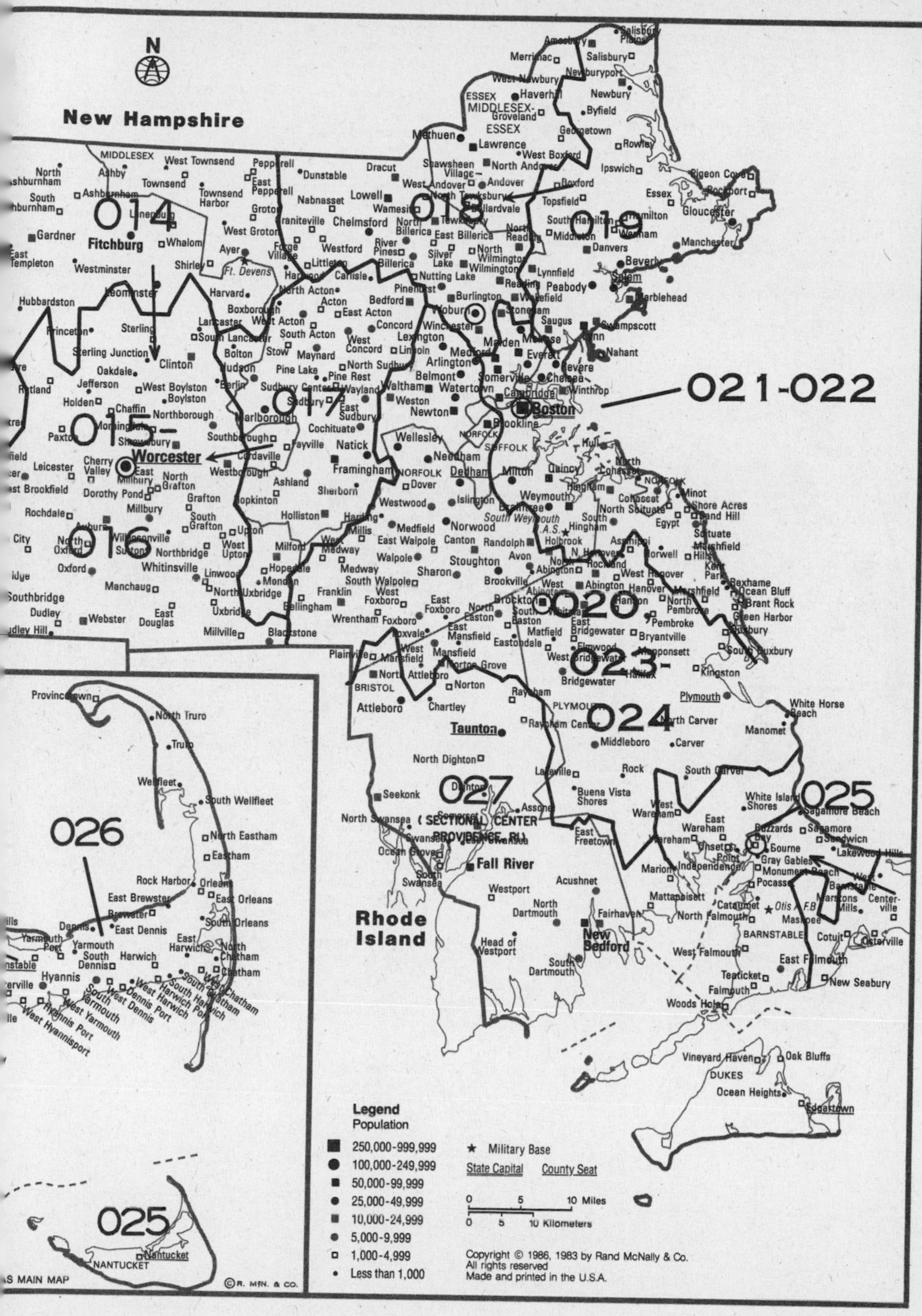
N
New Hampshire
014
Fitchburg
015-
Worcester
016
017
018
019
021-022
Boston
020
023-
024
025
026
027
(SECTIONAL CENTER PROVIDENCE, RI)
Rhode Island
Lowell
Lawrence
Haverhill
Methuen
Gloucester
Salem
Lynn
Cambridge
Quincy
Brockton
Taunton
Fall River
New Bedford
Plymouth
Framingham
Leominster
Gardner
Attleboro
Hyannis
Nantucket
Edgartown
Provincetown
Chatham
Orleans
Falmouth
Vineyard Haven
Oak Bluffs
MIDDLESEX
ESSEX
NORFOLK
SUFFOLK
BRISTOL
PLYMOUTH
BARNSTABLE
DUKES
NANTUCKET
Legend
Population
250,000-999,999
100,000-249,999
50,000-99,999
25,000-49,999
10,000-24,999
5,000-9,999
1,000-4,999
Less than 1,000
★ Military Base
State Capital
County Seat
0 5 10 Miles
0 5 10 Kilometers
Copyright © 1986, 1983 by Rand McNally & Co.
All rights reserved
Made and printed in the U.S.A.
©R. McN. & CO.

Aberdeen (Part of Boston) 02135
Abington♦ 02351
Acapesket 02536
Accord 02018
Acoaxet 02801
Acton 01720
Acton Center 01720
Acushnet♦ 02743
Adams 01220
Adamsdale 02760
Adams Shore (Part of Quincy) 02169
Adamsville 01340
Agawam 01001
Agawam Beach 02571
Agawam Shopping Center (Part of Agawam) 01001
Airport Mail Facility (Part of Boston)‡ 02109
Aldenville (Part of Chicopee) 01013
Alford 01230
Allendale (Part of Pittsfield)‡ 01201
Allendale Shopping Center (Part of Pittsfield) 01201
Allerton‡ 02045
Allston (Part of Boston) 02134
Amesbury 01913
Amesbury Center 01913
Amherst♦ 01002-04
For specific ZIP Codes call (888) 275-8777, or your local postmaster.
Amostown 01089
Amrita 02534
Andover♦ 01810
Annisquam (Part of Gloucester) 01930
Antassawamock Beach 02739
Apponagansett Village 02748
Arlington♦ 02174
02476
For specific ZIP Codes call (888) 275-8777, or your local postmaster.
Arlington Heights 02475
Armory (Part of Springfield) 01101
Arnoldsville 01220
Arsenal Mall (Part of Watertown) 02472
Asbury Grove 01982
Ashburnham 01430
Ashby 01431
Ashdod 02332
Ashfield 01330
Ashland 01721
Ashley Falls 01222
Ashley Heights 02717
Ashmont (Part of Boston) 02124
Assinippi 02339
Assonet 02702
Assonet Bay Shores 02702
Assumption College (Part of Worcester)‡ 01609
Astor (Part of Boston)‡ 02123
Athol 01331
Athol Junction (Part of Springfield) 01101
Atlantic (Part of Quincy) 02169
Attleboro 02703
Attleboro Falls‡ 02763
Auburn 01501
Auburndale (Part of Newton) 02466
Auburn Shopping Mall 01501
Avon 02322
Ayer 01432-33
For specific ZIP Codes call (888) 275-8777, or your local postmaster.
Ayers Village (Part of Haverhill) 01830
Babson Park 02457
Back Bay Annex (Part of Boston)‡ 02115
Bakers Grove 01473
Bakers Island (Part of Salem) 01970
Baldwinville♦ 01436
Ballardvale‡ 01810
Bancroft 01243
Baptist Corner 01370
Barkerville (Part of Pittsfield) 01201
Barnstable 02630
Barre♦ 01005
Barre Plains 01005
Barrowsville 02766
Bass Point 01908
Bass River 02664
Bass Rocks (Part of Gloucester) 01930
Bay State (Part of Northampton) 01062
Baystate West Shopping Center (Part of Springfield) 01103
Bayview, *Bristol* 02748
Bayview (Part of Gloucester) 01930
Beach (Part of Revere) 02151
Beach Bluff 01907
Beachmont (Part of Revere) 02151
Beach Point 02652
Beachwood 01262
Beacon Hill (Part of Boston) 02108
Beaver Brook (Part of Waltham) 02452
Beaver Brook (Part of Worcester) 01602
Beaverdam 01760
Beaverdam 01760
Becket 01223
Becket Center 01011
Bedford 01730
Bedford Springs 01730
Beechwood 02025
Belcher Square 01230
Belchertown♦ 01007
Bellingham 02019
Bell Rock (Part of Malden) 02148
Belmont♦ 02478
Belvidere (Part of Lowell) 01852
Bennetts Corner 02379
Berkley 02779
Berkshire 01224
Berkshire Heights 01230
Berlin 01503
Bernardston 01337
Beverly 01915
Beverly Cove (Part of Beverly) 01915
Beverly Farms (Part of Beverly)‡ 01915
Beverly Junction (Part of Beverly) 01915
Big Pond 01029
Billerica 01821*
01822†
Birch Island 01570
Birds Hill 02492
Blackinton (Part of North Adams) 01247
Black Rock 02025
Blackstone 01504
Blandford 01008
Bleachery (Part of Lowell) 01852
Bleachery (Part of Waltham) 02154
Bliss Corner♦ 02748
Blissville 01364
Bloomingdale (Part of Worcester) 01604
Blue Hills 02186
Blush Hollow 01243
Bolton 01740
Bondsville♦ 01009

Boston

02101-25
02127-28
02133
02163
02199
02201-22
For specific ZIP Codes call (888) 275-8777, or your local postmaster.

Colleges & Universities

Art Institute 02215
Bay State Coll 02116
Berklee Coll of Music 02215
Boston Architectural Ctr 02115
Boston Conservatory 02215
Boston Univ 02215
Emerson Coll 02116
Emmanuel Coll 02115
Massachusetts Coll of Pharmacy & Allied Health Sciences 02115
MGH Institute of Health Professions 02114
New England Coll of Optometry 02115
New England Conservatory of Music 02115
New England School of Law 02116
Northeastern Univ 02115
School of the Museum of Fine Arts 02115
Simmons Coll 02115
Suffolk Univ 02108
Univ of Massachusetts 02125
Wentworth Institute of Technology 02115
Wheelock Coll 02215

Financial Institutions

BankBoston 02110
Boston Safe Deposit & Trust Co 02108
Brown Brothers Harriman & Co 02109
Citizens Bank 02110
Fleet Nat Bank 02211
PNC Bank, New England 02110
State Street Bank & Trust Co 02110
USTrust 02111

Hospitals

Beth Israel Deaconess Med Ctr 02215
Brigham & Women's Hosp 02115
Children's Hosp 02115
Massachusetts General Hosp 02114
New England Med Ctr 02111

Hotels/Motels

Back Bay Hilton 02115
Fairmont Copley Plaza 02116
Four Seasons Hotel 02116
Harborside Hyatt Con Ctr & Hotel 02128
Holiday Inn, Boston Airport 02128
Holiday Inn Select, Government Ctr 02114
Le Meridien 02110
Logan Airport Ramada 02128
Marriott, Copley Place 02116
Marriott, Long Wharf 02109
Omni Parker House 02108
The Park Plaza Hotel & Towers 02116
Radisson 02116
Ritz-Carlton 02117
Sheraton Hotel & Towers 02199
Swissotel 02111
Tremont Hotel 02116
The Westin, Copley Place 02116

Military Installations

Coast Guard Support Ctr 02109
Naval Recruiting Dist, New England 02210
1st Coast Guard Dist 02110

Boston College (Part of Newton) 02467
Boston University (Part of Boston)‡ 02215
Bourne‡ 02532
Bournedale 02532
Boxborough 01719
Boxford♦ 01921
Boylston 01505
Bradford (Part of Haverhill) 01835
Bradstreet 01038
Braintree♦ 02184-85
For specific ZIP Codes call (888) 275-8777, or your local postmaster.
Braintree Highlands 02184
Braleys 02717
Bramanville 01527
Brant Rock 02020
Brayton Point 02725
Brewster♦ 02631
Briarwood Beach 02571
Bridgewater♦ 02324
Brier Neck (Part of Gloucester) 01930
Brigadoon Village 01949
Briggsville 01247
Brighton (Part of Boston) 02135
Brightside (Part of Holyoke) 01040
Brightwood (Part of Springfield)‡ 01107
Brimfield 01010
Brittan Square (Part of Worcester) 01605
Broadway (Part of Malden) 02148
Brockton 02301-05
For specific ZIP Codes call (888) 275-8777, or your local postmaster.
Brookfield 01506
Brookline♦ 02445-46
For specific ZIP Codes call (888) 275-8777, or your local postmaster.
Brookline Hill 02445
Brookline Village 02447
Brooks Place 02379
Brookville 02343
Brownell Corner 02790
Browns Point 01950
Brushwood (Part of Franklin) 02038
Bryantville 02327
Buckland 01338
Buckland Four Corners 01338
Buena Vista Shores 02346
Buffington Corner 02726
Buffumville 01540
Bullardville 01475
Burlington♦ 01803
Burlington Mall 01803
Burncoat (Part of Worcester) 01606
Buzzards Bay♦ 02532
02542
For specific ZIP Codes call (888) 275-8777, or your local postmaster.
Byfield 01922
C (Part of Worcester)‡ 01607
Cabot (Part of Newton) 02458
Cambridge 02138-42
02238
For specific ZIP Codes call (888) 275-8777, or your local postmaster.
Cambridge Galleria (Part of Cambridge) 02141
Campello (Part of Brockton)‡ 02303-04
For specific ZIP Codes call (888) 275-8777, or your local postmaster.
Cambridge Galleria (Part of Cambridge) 02141
Campground Landing 02651
Camp Grounds 01564
Canterbury Estates 02563
Canton 02021
Canton Junction 02021
Cape Cod Mall (Part of Barnstable) 02601
Carletonville (Part of Salem) 01970
Carlisle 01741
Carver 02330
Castle Hill (Part of Salem) 01970
Cataumet 02534
Cathedral (Part of Boston)‡ 02118
Cayenne 01089
Cedar Bushes 02345
Cedarville 02360
Center (Part of Woburn) 01801
Center, *Plymouth*‡ 02360
Centerville (Part of Barnstable) 02632
02634
02636
For specific ZIP Codes call (888) 275-8777, or your local postmaster.
Centerville (Part of Beverly) 01915
Central Village‡ 02790
Centralville (Part of Lowell) 01850
Chadwick Square (Part of Worcester) 01605
Chaffin 01520
Chandler Hill (Part of Worcester) 01609
Chapel Hill Estates 02359
Chappaquiddick Island 02539
Chappaquoit 02574
Charlemont 01339
Charles River Grove 02019
Charles Street (Part of Boston)‡ 02114
Charlestown (Part of Boston) 02129
Charlton 01507
Charlton City 01508
Charlton Depot 01509
Chartley 02712
Chaseville 01571
Chatham♦ 02633
Chelmsford♦ 01824
Chelsea 02150
Cherry Brook 02493
Cherry Valley 01611
Cheshire 01225
Cheshire Harbor 01220
Chester 01011
Chester Center 01011
Chesterfield 01012
Chestnut Hill (Part of Newton) 02467
Chicopee 01013-22
For specific ZIP Codes call (888) 275-8777, or your local postmaster.
Chicopee Center (Part of Chicopee)‡ 01020
Chilmark 02535
Chiltonville 02360
Churchill Landing 02345
Churchill Shores 02346
City Mills 02056
City Point (Part of Boston) 02127
Clarendon Hills (Part of Boston) 02131
Clarksburg (Town) 01247
Clayton 06018
Clematis Brook (Part of Waltham) 02453
Clevelandtown 02539
Clicquot 02054
Clifton 01945
Cliftondale 01906
Clinton♦ 01510
Coburnville 01701
Cochesett 02379
Cochituate‡ 01778
Cohasset 02025
Cohasset Army Ammunition Activity 02043
Coldbrook Springs 01068
Cold Spring 01253
Cole Corner 02043
College Hill (Part of Worcester) 01610
Collinsville 01826
Colonial Park 01570
Colonial Station (Part of Springfield)‡ 01103
Colrain 01340
Coltsville (Part of Pittsfield) 01201
Columbus Park (Part of Worcester) 01603
Cominsville 01542
Concord 01742
Congamond 01077
Conomo 01929
Conway 01341
Cooks Brook Beach 02651
Cooleyville 01355
Coolidge Corner 02445
Copley Place (Part of Boston) 02116
Cordaville♦ 01772
Cotley (Part of Taunton) 02780
Cottage Hill 02152
Cottage Park 02152
Cotuit (Part of Barnstable) 02635
Country View Estates (Part of Franklin) 02038
Court Park 02152
Coury Heights 02743
Cow Yard 02748
Craigville (Part of Barnstable) 02636

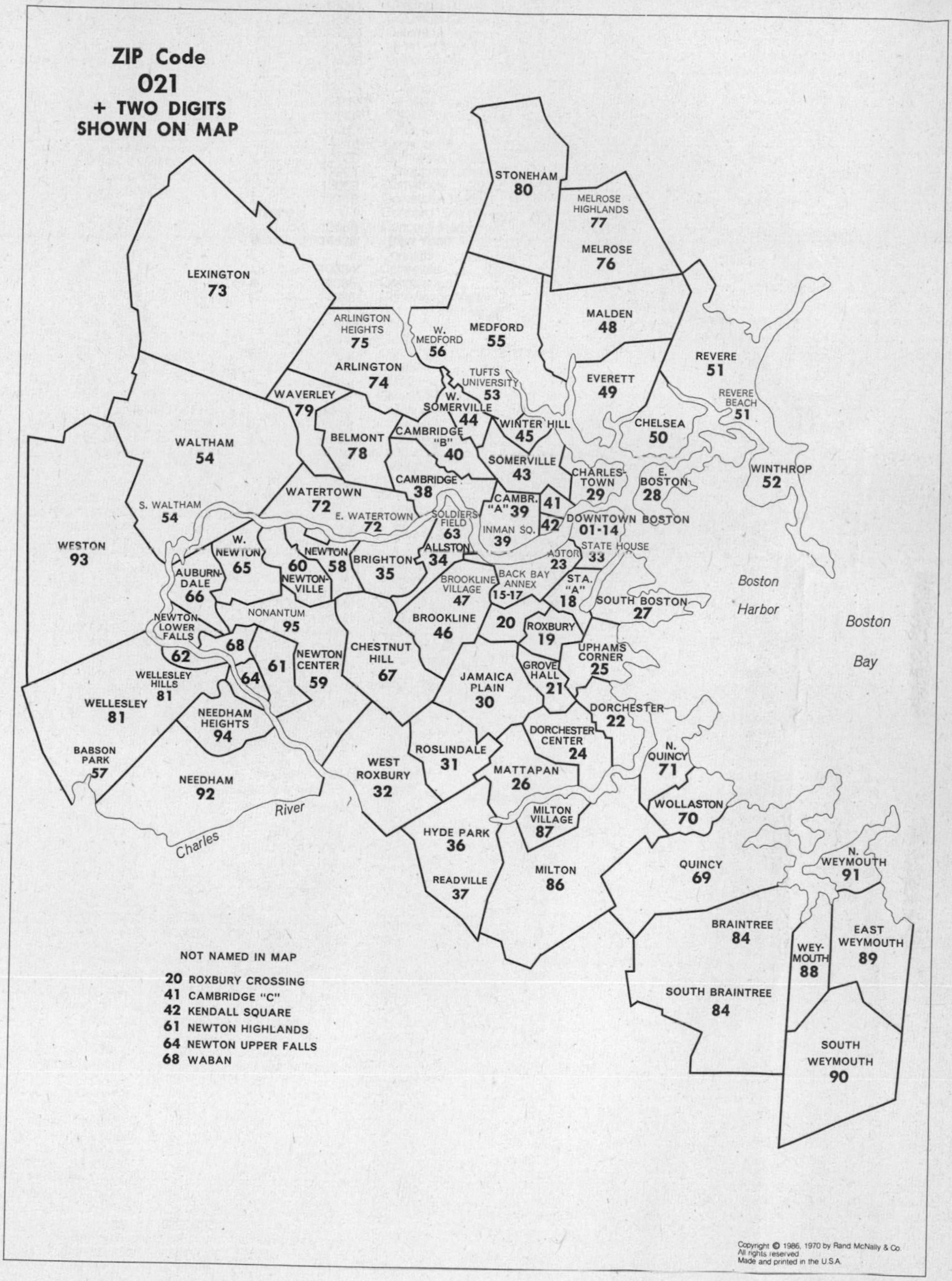

ZIP Code
021
+ TWO DIGITS
SHOWN ON MAP
STONEHAM 80
MELROSE HIGHLANDS 77
MELROSE 76
LEXINGTON 73
ARLINGTON HEIGHTS 75
W. MEDFORD 56
MEDFORD 55
MALDEN 48
ARLINGTON 74
TUFTS UNIVERSITY 53
EVERETT 49
REVERE 51
REVERE BEACH 51
WAVERLEY 79
W. SOMERVILLE 44
WINTER HILL 45
CHELSEA 50
WALTHAM 54
BELMONT 78
CAMBRIDGE "B" 40
SOMERVILLE 43
CHARLES-TOWN 29
E. BOSTON 28
WINTHROP 52
CAMBRIDGE 38
WATERTOWN 72
CAMBR. "A" 39
41
42
S. WALTHAM 54
E. WATERTOWN 72
SOLDIERS FIELD 63
INMAN SQ. 39
DOWNTOWN BOSTON 01-14
WESTON 93
W. NEWTON 65
NEWTON 58
60
BRIGHTON 35
ALLSTON 34
ASTOR 23
STATE HOUSE 33
AUBURN-DALE 66
NEWTON-VILLE
BROOKLINE VILLAGE 47
BACK BAY ANNEX 15-17
STA. "A" 18
Boston Harbor
SOUTH BOSTON 27
NONANTUM 95
BROOKLINE 46
20
ROXBURY 19
Boston Bay
NEWTON LOWER FALLS 62
68
61
NEWTON CENTER 59
CHESTNUT HILL 67
UPHAMS CORNER 25
WELLESLEY HILLS 81
64
JAMAICA PLAIN 30
GROVE HALL 21
WELLESLEY 81
NEEDHAM HEIGHTS 94
DORCHESTER 22
DORCHESTER CENTER 24
BABSON PARK 57
WEST ROXBURY 32
ROSLINDALE 31
N. QUINCY 71
NEEDHAM 92
MATTAPAN 26
WOLLASTON 70
River
Charles
MILTON VILLAGE 87
HYDE PARK 36
QUINCY 69
N. WEYMOUTH 91
READVILLE 37
MILTON 86
BRAINTREE 84
EAST WEYMOUTH 89
WEY-MOUTH 88
NOT NAMED IN MAP
20 ROXBURY CROSSING
41 CAMBRIDGE "C"
42 KENDALL SQUARE
61 NEWTON HIGHLANDS
64 NEWTON UPPER FALLS
68 WABAN
SOUTH BRAINTREE 84
SOUTH WEYMOUTH 90
Copyright © 1986, 1970 by Rand McNally & Co.
All rights reserved
Made and printed in the U.S.A.

Craigville Beach (Part of Barnstable) 02636
Crescent Beach, *Plymouth* 02739
Crescent Beach (Part of Revere) 02151
Crescent Mills 01050
Crooks Corner 02019
Cummaquid 02637
Cummington 01026
Cushman 01002
Cuttyhunk 02713
Dalton 01226*
01227†
Danvers♦ 01923
Danvers Center 01923
Danversport 01923
Dartmouth 02714
Davisville 02536
Dawson 01520
Dedham♦ 02026*
02027†
Dedham Mall 02026
Deerfield 01342
Deer Island (Part of Boston) 02152
Dennis♦ 02638
Dennis Port♦ 02639
Devenscrest 01432
Devereux 01945
Dighton 02715
Dodge 01507
Dorchester Center (Part of Boston) 02121-22
02124-25
For specific ZIP Codes call (888) 275-8777, or your local postmaster.
Dorchester Lower Mills (Part of Boston) 02124
Dorothy Manor 01527
Dorothy Pond 01527
Douglas 01516
Dover♦ 02030
Downtown (Part of Lowell)‡ 01852
Dracut 01826
Drury 01343
Drury Square 01501
Dry Pond 02072
Dudley 01571
Dudley Hill 01570
Dudleyville 01072
Dunstable 01827
Duxbury♦ 02331†
02332*
Dwight 01007
Eagleville 01364
East Acton 01720
East Arlington 02474
02476
For specific ZIP Codes call (888) 275-8777, or your local postmaster.
East Billerica 01821
East Blackstone 01504
East Boston (Part of Boston) 02128
East Boxford 01921
East Braintree 02184
East Brewster 02631
East Bridgewater 02333
East Brimfield 01010
East Brookfield♦ 01515
East Cambridge (Part of Cambridge) 02141
East Carver 02355
East Charlemont 01370
East Chelmsford 01824
East Dedham‡ 02026
East Deerfield 01342
East Dennis♦ 02641
East Douglas♦ 01516
East Fairhaven 02719
East Falmouth♦ 02536
Eastfield Mall (Part of Springfield) 01129
East Forest Park (Part of Springfield) 01108
East Foxboro 02035
East Freetown 02717
East Gloucester (Part of Gloucester) 01930
East Greenfield 01301
Eastham 02642
Easthampton 01027
East Harwich♦ 02645
East Holliston 01746
East Junction (Part of Attleboro) 02703
East Lee 01238
East Leverett 01054
East Longmeadow 01028
East Lynn (Part of Lynn) 01904
East Mansfield 02031
East Marion 02738
East Middleboro 02346
East Millbury 01527
East Milton 02186
East Natick 01760
East Northfield 01360
Easton 02334
Eastondale 02375
East Orleans 02643
East Otis 01029
East Pembroke 02359
East Pepperell♦ 01463
East Princeton 01541
East Sandwich 02537
East Saugus 01906
East Springfield (Part of Springfield) 01101
East Sudbury 01776
East Swansea 02777
East Taunton (Part of Taunton) 02718
East Templeton 01438
East Village 01570
Eastville 02557
East Walpole 02032
East Wareham 02538
East Watertown (Part of Watertown) 02472
East Weymouth 02189
East Windsor 01270
East Woburn (Part of Woburn) 01801
Eddyville 02346
Edgartown 02539
Edgemere 01545
Edgewater Estates 02359
Edgeworth (Part of Malden) 02148
Egleston Square (Part of Boston) 02116
Egremont (Town) 01252
Egypt 02066
Ellisville 02360
Elmdale 01569
Elm Grove 01340
Elm Square 02379
Elmwood (Part of Holyoke) 01040
Elmwood, *Plymouth* 02337
Endicott 02026
Erving 01344
Essex, *Essex*♦ 01929
Essex (Part of Boston)‡ 02112
Everett 02149
Factory Hollow 01002
Fairfield Mall (Part of Chicopee) 01020
Fairhaven 02719
Fairlawn 01545
Fairmount (Part of Boston) 02136
Fairview (Part of Chicopee) 01020
Fall River 02720-24
For specific ZIP Codes call (888) 275-8777, or your local postmaster.
Falmouth♦ 02540*
02541†
Falmouth Cliffs 02574
Falmouth Heights 02540
Farley 01344
Farm Hill 02180
Farnams 01225
Farnumsville 01560
Faulkner (Part of Malden) 02148
Faulkner Hill 01720
Fayville‡ 01745
Federal (Part of Worcester)‡ 01601
Feeding Hills 01030
Felchville 01760
Fellsway (Part of Medford) 02155
Fentonville 01069
Fields Corner (Part of Boston) 02122
Fieldston 02065
Findlen 02026
First Cliff 02066
Fiskdale♦ 01518
Fitchburg 01420
Five Corners 02356
Flint (Part of Fall River)‡ 02723
Flints Corner 01879
Florence (Part of Northampton) 01062
Florida 01247
Fore River (Part of Quincy) 02169
Forestdale♦ 02644
Forestdale Estates 02359
Forest Hills (Part of Boston) 02130
Forest Lake 01069
Forest Park (Part of Bellingham) 02019
Forest Park (Part of Springfield)‡ 01108
Forest River (Part of Salem) 01970
Forge Village‡ 01886
Fort Bellingham 02019
Fort Devens 01432
Fort Heath 02152
Fort Point (Part of Boston)‡ 02205
Foundry Village 01340
Foxboro (Foxborough)♦ 02035
Foxvale 02035
Framingham♦ 01701-05
For specific ZIP Codes call (888) 275-8777, or your local postmaster.
Framingham Centre 01703
Franklin 02038
Franklin Park (Part of Revere) 02151
Freetown (Town) 02702
Fresh Pond (Part of Cambridge) 02138
Freshwater Cove (Part of Gloucester) 01930
Fuller Shores 02346
Furnace Pond Colony 02359
Furnace Village 02334
Gardner 01440
Gay Head 02535
Georgetown 01833
Germantown (Part of Quincy) 02169
Gilbertville 01031
Gill 01376
Gillett Corner 01077
Gleasondale 01775
Glendale 01229
Glen Echo 02072
Glen Grove 01508
Glen Grove Annex 01508
Glenridge 02030
Gloucester 01930*
01931†
Goodrichville 01462
Goshen 01032
Gosnold (Town) 02713
Goss Heights 01050
Goulding Village 01331
Grafton 01519
Granby♦ 01033
Graniteville 01886
Granville 01034
Granville Center 01034
Gray Gables 02532
Great Barrington♦ 01230
Great Brook Valley (Part of Worcester) 01605
Greenbush 02040
Greendale (Part of Worcester)‡ 01606
Greenfield♦ 01301*
01302†
Greenfield Center 01301
Green Harbor 02041
Greenlodge 02026
Green Ridge Park 01226
Greenview Estates 02035
Greenville 01542
Greenwood‡ 01880
Greenwood Manor Estates 02359
Greylock (Part of North Adams) 01247
Griswoldville 01340
Grosvenor Corner (Part of Methuen) 01844
Groton♦ 01450
Grove Hall (Part of Boston) 02121
Groveland 01834
Hadley 01035
Halfway Pond 02360
Halifax 02338
Halifax Beach 02338
Hamilton 01936
Hamilton (Part of Worcester) 01604
Hamilton Beach 02571
Hampden 01036
Hampshire Mall 01035
Hampton Mills 01027
Hancock 01237
Hancock Village 02445
Hanover 02339
Hanover Center 02339
Hanover Street (Part of Boston)‡ 02113
Hanscom Air Force Base 01731
Hanson♦ 02341
Happy Hills 02019
Harbor Beach 02739
Harbor View 02719
Harding 02052
Hardwick 01037
Harrisville 01475
Harrubs Corner 02367
Harthaven 02557
Hartsville 01230
Harvard 01451
Harvard Square (Part of Cambridge)‡ 02138
Harwich♦ 02645
Harwich Port 02646
Harwood‡ 01460
Hastings 02493
Hatchville 02536
Hatfield♦ 01038
Hathorne 01937
Haverhill 01830-32
01835
For specific ZIP Codes call (888) 275-8777, or your local postmaster.
Hawley 01339
Hayden Row 01748
Haydenville 01039
Head of Westport 02790
Heath 01346
Heaven Heights 02717
Hebronville (Part of Attleboro) 02703
Hemlocks 02346
Hickory Hills Lake 01462
Highland (Part of Springfield)‡ 01109
Highland Lake 02056
Highland Park (Part of Holyoke) 01040
Highlands (Part of Holyoke) 01040
Highlands (Part of Lowell)‡ 01851
High Rock Woods 02497
Hillcrest Acres 02790
Hilltop Acres 02346
Hingham 02043
Hingham Center 02043
Hinsdale 01235
Hinsdale Estates 02019
Hixville 02747
Hodges Village 01540
Holbrook♦ 02343
Holden 01520
Holland♦ 01521
Holliston 01746
Holly Woods 02739
Holyoke 01040*
01041†
Holyoke Mall at Ingleside (Part of Holyoke) 01040
Hoosac Tunnel 01367
Hopedale 01747
Hopkinton♦ 01748
Horseneck Beach 02790
Hortonville 02777
Houghs Neck (Part of Quincy) 02169
Houghtonville 01247
Housatonic♦ 01236
Hovey's Corner 01463
Howe 01949
Hubbardston 01452
Huckleberry Corner 02576
Huckleyberry Shores 02346
Hudson♦ 01749
Hull♦ 02045
Humarock 02047
Huntington 01050
Hyannis (Part of Barnstable) 02601
Hyannis Port (Part of Barnstable) 02647
Hyde Park (Part of Boston) 02136
Hyderville 01475
Idlewell 02188
Indian Mound Beach 02532
Indian Orchard (Part of Springfield) 01151
Indian Shore 02346
Ingleside (Part of Holyoke) 01040
Inman Square (Part of Cambridge) 02139
Interlaken 01266
Ipswich♦ 01938
Island Creek 02332
Islington‡ 02090
Jamaica Plain (Part of Boston) 02130
Jefferson 01522
Jefferson Shores 02532
Jeffries Point (Part of Boston) 02128
John Fitzgerald Kennedy (Part of Boston)‡ 02114
John W. Mc Cormack (Part of Boston)‡ 02101-07
02208-09
For specific ZIP Codes call (888) 275-8777, or your local postmaster.
Katama 02539
Kearney Square (Part of Lowell)‡ 01852
Kelly's Corner 01720
Kempton Croft 02747
Kendal Green 02493
Kendall Square (Part of Cambridge)‡ 02142
Kenmore (Part of Boston)‡ 02215
Kent Park 02050
Kenwood 01826
Killdeer Island 01570
Kingsbury Beach 02642
Kings Forest 01921
Kingston♦ 02364
Kinsmans Corner 01983
Knightville 01050
Knollmere 02719
Konkapot 01259
Lagoon Heights 02557
Lake Attitash 01913
Lake Forest Park 01760
Lake Hiawatha 02019
Lake Mattawa 01364
Lake Pleasant 01347
Lakeside, *Bristol* 02790
Lakeside, *Plymouth* 02346
Lakeview (Part of Waltham) 02451
Lake View (Part of Worcester) 01604
Lakeview Heights 02717
Lakeview Terrace (Part of Pittsfield) 01201
Lakeville (Town) 02347
Lakeville♦ 02347
Lakewood (Part of Pittsfield) 01201
Lakewood Hills 02537
Lakewood Park 01473
Lambs Grove 01562
Lancaster 01523
Lanesboro (Lanesborough) 01237
Lanesville (Part of Gloucester)‡ 01930
Lane Village 01430
Larrywaug 01262
Laurel Park (Part of Northampton) 01060
Lawrence 01840-43
For specific ZIP Codes call (888) 275-8777, or your local postmaster.
Le Count Hollow 02663
Lee♦ 01238
Leeds (Part of Northampton) 01053
Leicester 01524
Leino Park 01473
Lenox♦ 01240
Lenox Dale 01242
Leominster 01453
Leverett 01054
Lexington♦ 02420-21
For specific ZIP Codes call (888) 275-8777, or your local postmaster.
Leyden (Town) 01301

Liberty Heights (Part of Springfield) 01104
Liberty Tree Mall 01923
Lincoln 01773
Lincoln Center‡ 01773
Lincoln Mall Station (Part of Worcester)‡ 01605
Lincoln Square (Part of Worcester) 01601
Linden (Part of Malden) 02148
Lindenwood 02180
Linwood 01525
Lithia 01032
Little Acres 02327
Little Harbor Beach 02571
Little Nahant 01908
Little Neck, *Bristol* 02777
Little Neck, *Essex* 01938
Little River (Part of Westfield) 01085
Littleton♦ 01460
Lobsterville 02535
Lockerville 01760
Locks Village 01072
Long Beach 01966
Long Hill Acres 02359
Long Island Hospital (Part of Boston) 02169
Longmeadow♦ 01106
Long Plain 02743
Long Pond Park 01826
Long Pond Village 02360
Longwood 02445
Loudville 01027
Lovell Corners 02188
Lowell 01850-54
For specific ZIP Codes call (888) 275-8777, or your local postmaster.
Lower Mills (Part of Boston) 02126
Lower Village 01775
Ludlow, *Hampden* 01056
Ludlow (Part of Worcester) 01603
Lunenburg♦ 01462
Lynn 01901-05
For specific ZIP Codes call (888) 275-8777, or your local postmaster.
Lynnfield♦ 01940
Lynnhurst 01906
Lyonsville 01340
Madaket 02554
Magnolia (Part of Gloucester)‡ 01930
Mahkeenac Heights 01262
Main Street‡ 02532
Main Street Station (Part of Worcester)‡ 01601
Malden 02148
Manchaug 01526
Manchester 01944
Manleys Corner 02379
Manomet 02345
Manomet Beach 02345
Manomet Bluffs 02345
Mansfield♦ 02048
Maple Park (Part of Methuen) 01844
Maplewood (Part of Malden) 02148
Maplewood, *Worcester* 01536
Mara Vista 02536
Marblehead♦ 01945
Marblehead Neck 01945
Marion♦ 02738
Marlboro 01833
Marlborough 01752
Marshfield♦ 02050
Marshfield Hills♦ 02051
Marstons Mills (Part of Barnstable) 02648
Mashnee Island 02532
Mashpee 02649
Masons Corner 02717
Matfield 02379
Mattapan (Part of Boston) 02126
Mattapoisett♦ 02739
Maynard♦ 01754
Mayo Beach 02667
Medfield♦ 02052
Medford 02153†
02155*
Medway 02053
Meeting House Hill (Part of Boston) 02122

Megansett 02556
Melrose 02176-77
For specific ZIP Codes call (888) 275-8777, or your local postmaster.
Melrose Highlands (Part of Melrose) 02177
Menauhant 02536
Mendon 01756
Menemsha 02552
Merrick 01089
Merrimac 01860
Merrimack College 01845
Merrimacport 01860
Merrymount (Part of Quincy) 02169
Methuen 01844
Methuen Mall (Part of Methuen) 01844
Middleboro♦ 02346
Middleborough (Town) 02346
Middlefield 01243
Middleton 01949
Midland 02019
Mile Oak Center 01095
Milford 01757
Millbury 01527
Millers Falls‡ 01349
Millerville 01504
Millis 02054
Mill River, *Berkshire* 01244
Mill River, *Franklin* 01373
Mill Valley 01002
Millville 01529
Millville Center 01529
Milton♦ 02186
Milton Center 02186
Milton Village 02187
Minot 02055
Miramar 02332
Mirror Lake 02093
Mishaum Point 02748
Mission Hill (Part of Boston)‡ 02120
M.I.T. (Part of Cambridge)‡ 02139
Mittineague 01089
Monomoy 02554
Monponsett 02350
Monroe (Town) 01350
Monroe Bridge 01350
Monson♦ 01057
Montague 01351
Montague City 01376
Montello (Part of Brockton)‡ 02303
02305
For specific ZIP Codes call (888) 275-8777, or your local postmaster.
Monterey 01245
Montgomery 01085
Montserrat (Part of Beverly) 01915
Montville 01255
Monument Beach♦ 02553
Moores Corner 01054
Moores Corners 01564
Morningdale 01505
Morrills 02062
Morseville 01760
Mount Auburn (Part of Watertown) 02472
Mount Bowdoin (Part of Boston) 02121
Mount Hermon 01354
Mount Pleasant (Part of New Bedford)‡ 02745
Mount Saint James (Part of Worcester)‡ 01610
Mount Tom 01027
Mount Washington 12517
Myricks 02718
Mystic Grove 01507
Mystic Wharf (Part of Boston) 02109
Nabnasset‡ 01886
Nahant♦ 01908
Nantucket♦ 02554
02584
For specific ZIP Codes call (888) 275-8777, or your local postmaster.
Nashaquitsa 02535
Natick 01760
Natick Development Center 01760
Natick Laboratories 01760
Natick Mall 01760

Needham♦ 02492
02494
For specific ZIP Codes call (888) 275-8777, or your local postmaster.
Needham Heights 02494
Nelsons Grove 02346
Nelsons Shores 02346
Neponset (Part of Boston) 02122
New Ashford 01237
New Bedford 02740-42
02744-46
For specific ZIP Codes call (888) 275-8777, or your local postmaster.
New Boston 01255
New Braintree 01531
Newbury (Town) 01950
Newbury 01951
Newburyport 01950-51
For specific ZIP Codes call (888) 275-8777, or your local postmaster.
New England Shopping Center 01906
New Harbour Mall (Part of Fall River) 02721
New Lenox 01240
New Marlboro (New Marlborough) 01230
New Salem 01355
New Seabury‡ 02649
Newton 02456
02458-62
02464-65
02495
For specific ZIP Codes call (888) 275-8777, or your local postmaster.
Newton Center (Part of Newton) 02459
Newton Highlands (Part of Newton) 02461
Newton Lower Falls (Part of Newton) 02462
Newton Upper Falls (Part of Newton) 02464
Newtonville (Part of Newton) 02458
02460
For specific ZIP Codes call (888) 275-8777, or your local postmaster.
New Town (Part of Newton) 02456
New Village 01588
Nobscot 01701
Nobska Beach 02571
Nonantum (Part of Newton) 02495
Nonquitt 02748
Noquochoke‡ 02790
Norfolk 02056
North (Part of New Bedford)‡ 02746
North Abington 02351
North Acton 01720
North Adams 01247
North Adams Junction (Part of Pittsfield) 01201
North Agawam (Part of Agawam) 01030
North Amherst♦ 01059
Northampton 01060*
01061†
North Andover 01845
North Andover Center 01845
North Ashburnham 01430
North Attleborough (Town) 02760
North Attleboro♦ 02760-61
02763
For specific ZIP Codes call (888) 275-8777, or your local postmaster.
North Bellingham 02019
North Beverly (Part of Beverly) 01915
North Billerica 01862
North Blandford 01008
Northborough♦ 01532
Northbridge 01534
Northbridge Center 01588
North Brighton (Part of Boston) 02135
North Brookfield♦ 01535
North Cambridge (Part of Cambridge) 02138
North Carver 02355

North Chatham 02650
North Chelmsford 01863
North Chester 01050
North Cohasset 02025
North Dartmouth 02747
North Dartmouth Mall 02747
North Dighton 02764
North Duxbury 02332
North Eastham♦ 02651
North Easton 02356
North Egremont 01252
Northey Point (Part of Salem) 01970
North Fairhaven 02719
North Falmouth♦ 02556
North Farms (Part of Northampton) 01062
Northfield♦ 01360
Northgate Shopping Center (Part of Revere) 02151
North Grafton 01536
North Hadley 01035
North Hancock 01267
North Hanover 02339
North Harwich 02645
North Hatfield 01066
North Lancaster 01523
North Leominster (Part of Leominster) 01453
North Leverett 01054
North Littleton 01460
North Marshfield 02059
North Middleboro 02346
North Milford 01757
North Natick 01760
North New Salem 01364
North Orange 01364
North Otis 01253
North Oxford 01537
North Pembroke♦ 02358
North Pepperell 01463
North Plymouth‡ 02360
North Plympton 02364
North Quincy (Part of Quincy) 02171
North Randolph 02368
North Reading 01864
North Rehoboth 02769
North Rutland 01543
North Salem (Part of Salem) 01970
North Saugus 01906
North Scituate‡ 02060
North Seekonk♦ 02771
Northshore Shopping Center (Part of Peabody) 01960
North Somerville (Part of Somerville) 02143
North Stoughton 02072
North Sudbury 01776
North Swansea 02777
North Tewksbury 01876
North Tisbury 02568
North Truro 02652
North Uxbridge 01538
North Village 01570
North Waltham (Part of Waltham) 02452
North Weymouth 02191
North Wilmington 01887
North Woburn (Part of Woburn) 01801
North Worcester (Part of Worcester) 01606
Norton♦ 02766
Norton Grove 02766
Norwell 02061
Norwich Bridge 01050
Norwood♦ 02062
Norwood Central 02062
Nutting Lake 01865
Oak Bluffs 02557
Oakdale (Part of Holyoke) 01040
Oakdale, *Norfolk* 02026
Oakdale, *Worcester* 01539
Oak Grove (Part of Malden) 02148
Oakham 01068
Oak Island (Part of Revere) 02151
Oakland Vale 01906
O'Briens Corner 01030
Ocean Bluff 02065
Ocean Grove‡ 02777
Ocean Heights 02539
Ocean Spray 02152
Old City 01474
Old Common 01527

Old Furnace 01031
Oldham Pines 02359
Oldham Village 02359
Old Hill (Part of Springfield) 01109
Old Silver Beach 02556
Old Sturbridge Village 01566
Old Town House‡ 01810
Onset♦ 02558
Orange♦ 01364
Orchard Street (Part of New Bedford)‡ 02740
Orient Heights (Part of Boston) 02128
Orleans♦ 02653
Osceola 01254
Osterville (Part of Barnstable) 02655
Otis 01253
Otis Air Force Base 02542
Otter River 01436
Overbrook 02482
Oxford, *Bristol* 02719
Oxford, *Worcester*♦ 01540
Oyster Harbors (Part of Barnstable) 02655
Packard Heights 01331
Padanaram 02748
Pages Beach 01430
Painting Island 02738
Pakachoag 01501
Palmer♦ 01069
Park Street (Part of Medford) 02155
Parkwood Beach 02571
Patuisset 02559
Pawtucketville (Part of Lowell) 01854
Paxton 01612
Payson Park (Part of Watertown) 02472
Peabody 01960*
01961†
Pearl Hill (Part of Fitchburg) 01420
Pelham 01002
Pembroke 02359
Pembroke Heights 02358
Pepperell♦ 01463
Perryville, *Bristol* 02769
Perryville, *Worcester* 01570
Peru 01235
Petersham 01366
Phelps Mills (Part of Peabody) 01960
Phillips Beach 01907
Phillipston 01331
Phillipston Four Corners 01331
Pierceville 02576
Piety Corner (Part of Waltham) 02451
Pigeon Cove‡ 01966
Pilgrim Heights 02652
Pilgrim Pines Estates 02327
Pilgrim Village 02019
Pine Grove (Part of Northampton) 01062
Pilot Grove Hill 01775
Pine Bluffs 02346
Pinefield 01938
Pine Grove (Part of Northampton) 01060
Pine Hill Acres (Part of New Bedford) 02745
Pinehurst♦ 01866
Pinehurst Beach 02571
Pine Island 01951
Pine Island Lake 01027
Pine Lake 01776
Pine Point (Part of Springfield) 01101
Pine Rest 01776
Piney Point Beach 02738
Pingryville 01460
Pittsfield 01201-03
For specific ZIP Codes call (888) 275-8777, or your local postmaster.
Plainfield 01070
Plainville, *Hampshire* 01002
Plainville, *Norfolk* 02762
Pleasant Lake 02645
Plimptonville 02081
Plumbush 01951
Plum Island (Part of Newburyport) 01950
Plummer Corner 01588
Plymouth♦ 02360-62
For specific ZIP Codes call (888) 275-8777, or your local postmaster.

Place	ZIP Code
Plympton	02367
Pocasset♦	02559
Pocomo	02554
Podunk	01515
Point Independence	02532
Point of Pines (Part of Revere)	02151
Point Pleasant	01570
Point Shirley	02152
Polpis	02554
Pomponotto Pines	02333
Ponakin Mill	01523
Pond Hill	01913
Pond Village	02652
Pondville, *Norfolk*	02056
Pondville, *Plymouth*	02532
Pondville, *Worcester*	01501
Ponkapoag	02021
Pontoosuc Gardens (Part of Pittsfield)	01201
Pope Beach	02719
Popponesset Beach	02649
Porter Square (Part of Cambridge)‡	02140
Potoosuc Lake	01237
Pottersville	02726
Pratt Corner	01072
Precinct	02346
Prentice Corner	01588
Prides Crossing (Part of Beverly)	01965
Princeton	01541
Priscilla Beach	02360
Proctor (Part of Peabody)	01960
Provincetown	02657
Provincetown Wharf	02657
Prudential Center (Part of Boston)‡	02199
Putnamville	01923
Quaise	02554
Queen Lake	01331
Quidnet	02554
Quincy	02169-71
	02269
For specific ZIP Codes call (888) 275-8777, or your local postmaster.	
Quincy Adams (Part of Quincy)	02169
Quincy Center (Part of Quincy)	02169
Quincy Point (Part of Quincy)	02169
Quinsigamond Village (Part of Worcester)	01607
Quissett	02540
Rakeville	02019
Randolph♦	02368
Raynham	02767
Raynham Center♦	02768
Reading♦	01867
Readville (Part of Boston)	02137
Redstone Shopping Center	02180
Rehoboth	02769
Renfrew	01220
Reservoir	02445
Revere	02151
Revere Beach (Part of Revere)	02151
Rexhame	02050
Rice Square (Part of Worcester)	01604
Richmond	01254
Richmond Furnace	01254
Rings Island	01950
Rio Vista	01862
Risingdale	01230
Riverdale (Part of Gloucester)‡	01930
Riverdale, *Norfolk*	02026
Riverdale, *Worcester*	01534
Rivermoor	02066
River Pines	01821
Riverside, *Franklin*	01376
Riverside (Part of Haverhill)	01830
Riverside (Part of Holyoke)	01040
Riverside, *Plymouth*	02558
Riverview (Part of Gloucester)	01930
Riverview (Part of Waltham)	02453
Roberts (Part of Waltham)	02453
Rochdale	01542
Rochester	02770
Rock	02346
Rockdale	01236
Rock Harbor	02653
Rockland	02370
Rockport (Town)	01966
Rocks Village (Part of Haverhill)	01830
Rock Valley (Part of Holyoke)	01040
Rockville	02054
Rocky Hill	01757
Rocky Neck (Part of Gloucester)	01930
Rocky Nook Park	02364
Rolling Acres Estates	01886
Roosterville	01255
Roslindale (Part of Boston)	02131
Rowe	01367
Rowley♦	01969
Roxbury‡	02118-20
For specific ZIP Codes call (888) 275-8777, or your local postmaster.	
Royalston	01368
Russell	01071
Russellville	01085
Rutland♦	01543
Saconesset Hills	02540
Sagamore♦	02561
Sagamore Beach	02562
Sagamore Highlands	02562
Salem	01970*
	01971†
Salem Neck (Part of Salem)	01970
Salem State College (Part of Salem)‡	01970
Salisbury (Town)	01950
Salisbury♦	01952
Salisbury Beach	01952
Salisbury Heights (Part of Worcester)	01609
Salisbury Plains	01950
Salters Point	02748
Sandersdale	01550
Sand Hill	02066
Sandisfield	01255
Sandwich♦	02563
Sandy Beach, *Norfolk*	02025
Sandy Beach, *Worcester*	01543
Santuit (Part of Barnstable)	02635
Sassaquin (Part of New Bedford)	02745
Saugus♦	01906
Saugus Center	01906
Saundersville	01560
Savin Hill (Part of Boston)	02125
Savoy	01256
Savoy Center	01256
Saxonville‡	01705
Schoosett	02359
Scituate♦	02066
Scorton Shores	02537
Scott Hill Acres	02019
Searstown Mall (Part of Leominster)	01453
Searsville	01096
Sea View	02050
Second Cliff	02066
Seekonk	02771
Segreganset	02715
Shaker Village	01451
Sharon	02067
Sharon Heights	02067
Shattuckville	01369
Shawkemo	02554
Shawsheen Heights	01810
Shawsheen Village‡	01810
Sheffield	01257
Shelburne	01370
Shelburne Falls♦	01370
Sheldonville	02070
Shell Beach	02739
Shepardville	02762
Sherborn	01770
Sherwood Forest, *Berkshire*	01011
Sherwood Forest, *Bristol*	02743
Shimmo	02554
Shirkshire	01341
Shirley♦	01464
Shirley Center	01464
Shoppers World	01701
Shore Acres, *Bristol*	02748
Shore Acres, *Plymouth*	02066
Shrewsbury	01545
Shutesbury	01072
Siasconset	02564
Siggsville	01220
Silver Beach	02565
Silver Hill	02493
Silver Lake, *Middlesex*	01887
Silver Lake, *Plymouth*	02364
Silver Shell Beach	02719
Silver Spring Beach	02651
Sippewisset	02540
Sixteen Acres (Part of Springfield)	01101
Smith Highlands (Part of Chicopee)	01020
Smiths Ferry (Part of Holyoke)	01040
Smoke Rise Heights	02777
Snug Harbor‡	02332
Soldiers Field (Part of Boston)‡	02163
Solomon Pond Mall (Part of Marlborough)	01752
Somerset♦	02725-26
For specific ZIP Codes call (888) 275-8777, or your local postmaster.	
Somerset Centre	02726
Somerville	02143-45
For specific ZIP Codes call (888) 275-8777, or your local postmaster.	
South (Part of Fall River)‡	02724
South Acton	01720
South Amherst♦	01002
Southampton	01073
South Ashburnham♦	01430
South Ashfield	01330
South Athol	01331
South Attleboro (Part of Attleboro)‡	02703
South Barre	01074
South Bellingham	02019
South Berlin	01503
South Billerica	01730
South Bolton	01740
Southborough	01772
South Boston (Part of Boston)	02127
South Braintree	02184
Southbridge	01550
South Byfield	01922
South Carver	02366
South Charlton	01507
South Chatham	02659
South Chelmsford	01824
South Dartmouth	02748
South Deerfield♦	01373
South Dennis♦	02660
South Duxbury♦	02332
South Easton	02375
South Egremont	01258
South End (Part of Springfield)	01105
Southfield	01259
South Foxboro	02035
South Framingham‡	01704
South Georgetown	01833
South Grafton	01560
South Groveland	01834
South Hadley	01075
South Hadley Falls	01075
South Hamilton	01982
South Hanover	02339
South Harwich	02661
South Hingham	02043
South Lakeville	02346
South Lancaster♦	01561
South Lawrence (Part of Lawrence)	01842
South Lee	01260
South Lowell	01876
South Lynnfield‡	01940
South Mashpee	02649
South Middleboro	02346
South Milford	01747
South Natick	01760
South Orleans	02662
South Peabody (Part of Peabody)	01960
South Pond	02360
South Quincy (Part of Quincy)	02169
South Rehoboth	02769
South Royalston	01331
South Salem (Part of Salem)	01970
South Sandisfield	01255
South Sandwich	02563
South Shore Plaza	02184
South Springfield (Part of Springfield)	01101
South Stoughton	02072
South Sutton	01516
South Swansea	02777
South Truro	02666
South Uxbridge	01569
Southville	01772
South Walpole	02071
South Waltham (Part of Waltham)	02453
South Wareham	02571
South Wellfleet	02663
South Westport	02790
South Weymouth	02190
Southwick	01077
South Williamstown	01267
South Wilmington (Part of Woburn)	01801
South Worthington	01050
South Yarmouth♦	02664
Spencer♦	01562
Spindleville	01747
Springdale, *Norfolk*	02021
Springdale (Part of Holyoke)	01040
Springdale Mall (Part of Springfield)	01101
Springfield	01101-05
	01107-09
	01118-44
	01152
For specific ZIP Codes call (888) 275-8777, or your local postmaster.	
Springfield Plaza (Part of Springfield)	01104
Spring Hill (Part of Somerville)	02143
Squantum (Part of Quincy)	02171
Standish (Part of Taunton)	02780
Staples Shore	02346
State House (Part of Boston)‡	02133
State Line	01266
Sterling	01564
Sterling Junction	01564
Stetson Road	02359
Stevens Corner	01201
Still River	01467
Stockbridge	01262
Stoneham♦	02180
Stoneville, *Franklin*	01344
Stoneville, *Worcester*	01501
Stony Brook	02493
Stoughton	02072
Stoughton Junction	02072
Stow	01775
Sturbridge♦	01566
Sudbury	01776
Sudbury Center	01776
Summer Heights	02021
Summit (Part of Worcester)	01606
Summit Grove	02747
Sunderland, *Franklin*	01375
Sunderland (Part of Worcester)	01604
Sunken Meadow Beach	02651
Sunnyside	01571
Sunset Hill	01008
Surfside	02554
Sutton	01527
Swampscott♦	01907
Swansea	02777
Swansea Center	02777
Swanson Corners	01073
Sweets Corner	01267
Swift River	01026
Symmes Corner	01890
Tafts Corner	01562
Tahanto Beach	02559
Tapleyville	01923
Tarkiln	02332
Tatnuck (Part of Worcester)	01602
Taunton	02718
	02780
For specific ZIP Codes call (888) 275-8777, or your local postmaster.	
Teaticket‡	02536
Templeton	01468
Tewksbury	01876
Texas	01537
The Green	02346
The Marsh	02726
The Plains	01944
The Pines	01866
Thomastown	02346
Thorndike	01079
Three Rivers♦	01080
Thumpertown Beach	02651
Tihonet	02571
Tinkertown	02332
Tinkhamtown	02739
Tisbury (Town)	02568
Tobeys Island	02553
Tolland	01034
Tonset	02653
Topsfield♦	01983
Touisset	02777
Town Crest Village	01225
Town Hall, *Middlesex*	01760
Town Hall, *Plymouth*	02341
Townsend♦	01469
Townsend Harbor	01469
Townsend Hill (Part of Fall River)	02724
Tozier Corner (Part of Methuen)	01844
Truro	02666
Tufts University (Part of Medford)	02153
Tully	01331
Turkey Hill Shores	01543
Turners Falls♦	01349
	01376
For specific ZIP Codes call (888) 275-8777, or your local postmaster.	
Turnpike‡	01545
Tyngsboro	01879
Tyngsborough (Town)	01879
Tyringham	01264
Union Market (Part of Watertown)	02472
Union Point	01570
Unionville (Part of Franklin)	02038
Unionville, *Worcester*	01520
University Park (Part of Worcester)	01605
Uphams Corner (Part of Boston)	02125
Upper Hill (Part of Springfield)	01129
Upton	01568
Uxbridge	01569
Vallersville	02532
Valley View	02019
Van Deusenville	01236
Varnumtown	01826
Victory Hill (Part of Pittsfield)	01201
Village‡	02053
Village Mall, The	02021
Village of Nagog Woods	01718
Vineyard Haven♦	02568
	02573
For specific ZIP Codes call (888) 275-8777, or your local postmaster.	
Vineyard Highlands	02557
Waban (Part of Newton)	02468
Wachusett (Part of Fitchburg)	01420
Wakeby	02563
Wakefield♦	01880
Wakefield Center	01880
Wakefield Junction	01880
Wales	01081
Wallis Street (Part of Peabody)‡	01960
Walnut Hill (Part of Woburn)	01801
Walpole♦	02081
Walpole Mall, The	02032
Waltham	02451-54
For specific ZIP Codes call (888) 275-8777, or your local postmaster.	
Waltham Highlands (Part of Waltham)	02451
Wamesit	01876
Wampun Corner	02093
Wapping	01342
Waquoit‡	02536
Ward Hill (Part of Haverhill)	01835
Ware♦	01082
Wareham♦	02571
Warren♦	01083

*** Area Zip Code** **† Post Office Boxes** **‡ Postal Station** **♦ Census Designated Place** *Italic Type* **County**

Warren Terrace 02359
Warrentown 02346
Warwick...................... 01378
Washington 01223
Watertown 02471*
.... 02472†
Waterville, *Plymouth*.... 02346
Waterville, *Worcester* .. 01475
Watuppa (Part of Fall River) 02721
Wauwinet.................... 02554
Waverley 02479
Wawela Park 01570
Wayland...................... 01778
Wayside Inn 01776
Webster......................01570-71
For specific ZIP Codes call (888) 275-8777, or your local postmaster.
Webster Square (Part of Worcester)‡ 01603
Wedgemere 01890
Weir Village (Part of Taunton) 02780
Wellesley♦ 02481-82
For specific ZIP Codes call (888) 275-8777, or your local postmaster.
Wellesley Farms 02481
Wellesley Fells 02482
Wellesley Hills 02481
Wellfleet...................... 02667
Wellington (Part of Medford) 02155
Wellville 01430
Wendell 01379
Wendell Depot 01380
Wenham, *Essex* 01984
Wenham, *Plymouth* 02355
West Abington 02351
West Acton‡ 01720
West Andover 01810
West Auburn 01501
West Barnstable (Part of Barnstable) 02668
West Becket 01238
West Bedford 01730
West Berlin 01503
West Billerica 01862
Westborough.............. 01581
West Boxford.............. 01885
West Boylston 01583
West Bridgewater 02379
West Brimfield 01069
West Brookfield♦ 01585
West Cambridge (Part of Cambridge) 02138
West Center................ 01236
West Chatham♦.......... 02669
West Chelmsford 01863
Westchester (Part of Worcester) 01605
West Chesterfield........ 01084
West Chop‡ 02573
West Concord‡ 01742
West Cummington 01026
Westdale 02333
West Deerfield 01342
West Dennis♦ 02670
West Dudley 01571
West Duxbury 02332
West Falmouth♦ 02574
West Farms (Part of Northampton) 01062
Westfield 01085*
.... 01086†
West Fitchburg (Part of Fitchburg) 01420
Westford 01886
West Foxboro 02035
Westgate Mall & Plaza (Part of Brockton)...... 02301
Westgate Park (Part of New Bedford) 02745
West Gloucester (Part of Gloucester) 01930
West Granville 01034
West Groton 01472
Westhampton 01027
West Hanover‡ 02339
West Harwich 02671
West Hatfield 01088
West Hawley 01339
West Hingham 02043
West Hyannisport 02672
Westlands 01824
West Leominster (Part of Leominster) 01453
West Leyden 01337
West Lynn (Part of Lynn) 01905
West Manchester........ 01944
West Mansfield 02048
West Medford (Part of Medford) 02156
West Medway 02053
West Millbury 01586
Westminster................ 01473
West Natick 01760
West New Boston 01255
West Newbury 01985
West Newton (Part of Newton) 02165
Weston 02493
West Orange 01364
West Otis.................... 01245
Westover Air Force Base 01022
West Peabody (Part of Peabody)‡ 01960
West Pelham 01002
Westport♦ 02790
Westport Factory........ 02790
Westport Point............ 02791
West Quincy (Part of Quincy) 02169
West Roxbury (Part of Boston) 02132
West Royalston 01331
West Side (Part of Worcester)‡ 01602
West Somerville (Part of Somerville) 02144
West Springfield♦........ 01089*
.... 01090†
West Sterling 01564
West Stockbridge 01266
West Stockbridge Center 01266
West Stoughton.......... 02072
West Sutton................ 01527
West Tatnuck (Part of Worcester)................ 01602
West Tisbury 02575
West Townsend.......... 01474
West Upton 01568
Westview (Part of Franklin).................... 02038
Westville (Part of Taunton) 02780
West Walpole.............. 02081
West Ware.................. 01082
West Wareham♦ 02576
West Warren 01092
West Watertown (Part of Watertown) 02472
West Whately.............. 01039
West Wind Shores 02532
Westwood 02090
West Worthington 01098
West Wrentham.......... 02070
West Yarmouth♦ 02673
Wethersfield................ 02019
Weymouth♦................02188-91
For specific ZIP Codes call (888) 275-8777, or your local postmaster.
Weymouth Heights 02188
Weymouth Landing 02188
Whalom 01420
Whately 01093
Whately (East Whately) 01373
Wheelockville.............. 01569
Wheelwright................ 01094
White City 01747
White City Shopping Center 01545
White Horse Beach 02381
White Island Shores♦.. 02538
White Oaks 01267
White Valley 01005
Whitinsville♦................ 01588
Whitman 02382
Whittenton (Part of Taunton) 02780
Wigginsville (Part of Lowell) 01850
Wilbraham♦................ 01095
Wilkinsonville 01527
Williamsburg 01096
Williamstown♦ 01267
Williamsville, *Berkshire* 01200
Williamsville, *Worcester* 01452
Wilmington♦................ 01887
Wilson (Part of Gloucester) 01930
Winchendon♦ 01475
Winchendon Springs .. 01477
Winchester♦ 01890
Winchester Highlands 01890
Windsor 01270
Winnecunnet 02766
Winnmere 01803
Winslows 02062
Winter Hill (Part of Somerville) 02145
Winthrop♦ 02152
Winthrop Beach.......... 02152
Winthrop Highlands 02152
Woburn 01801*
.... 01888†
Wollaston (Part of Quincy) 02170
Woodland Park 01501
Woods Hole................ 02543
Woods Hole Coast Guard Base 02543
Woodville.................... 01784
Worcester 01601-10
..................................01613-55
For specific ZIP Codes call (888) 275-8777, or your local postmaster.
Worcester Common Fashion Outlet (Part of Worcester).... 01608
Woronoco 01097
Woronoco Heights...... 01097
Worthington................ 01098
Worthington Center 01098
Wrentham 02093
Wyben 01085
Wynnmere 01803
Wyoming (Part of Melrose).................... 02176
Yankee Orchards (Part of Pittsfield) 01201
Yarmouth.................... 02675
Yarmouth Port♦ 02675
Yarmouth Station........ 02675
Yirrell Beach................ 02152
Zoar............................ 01367
Zylonite 01220

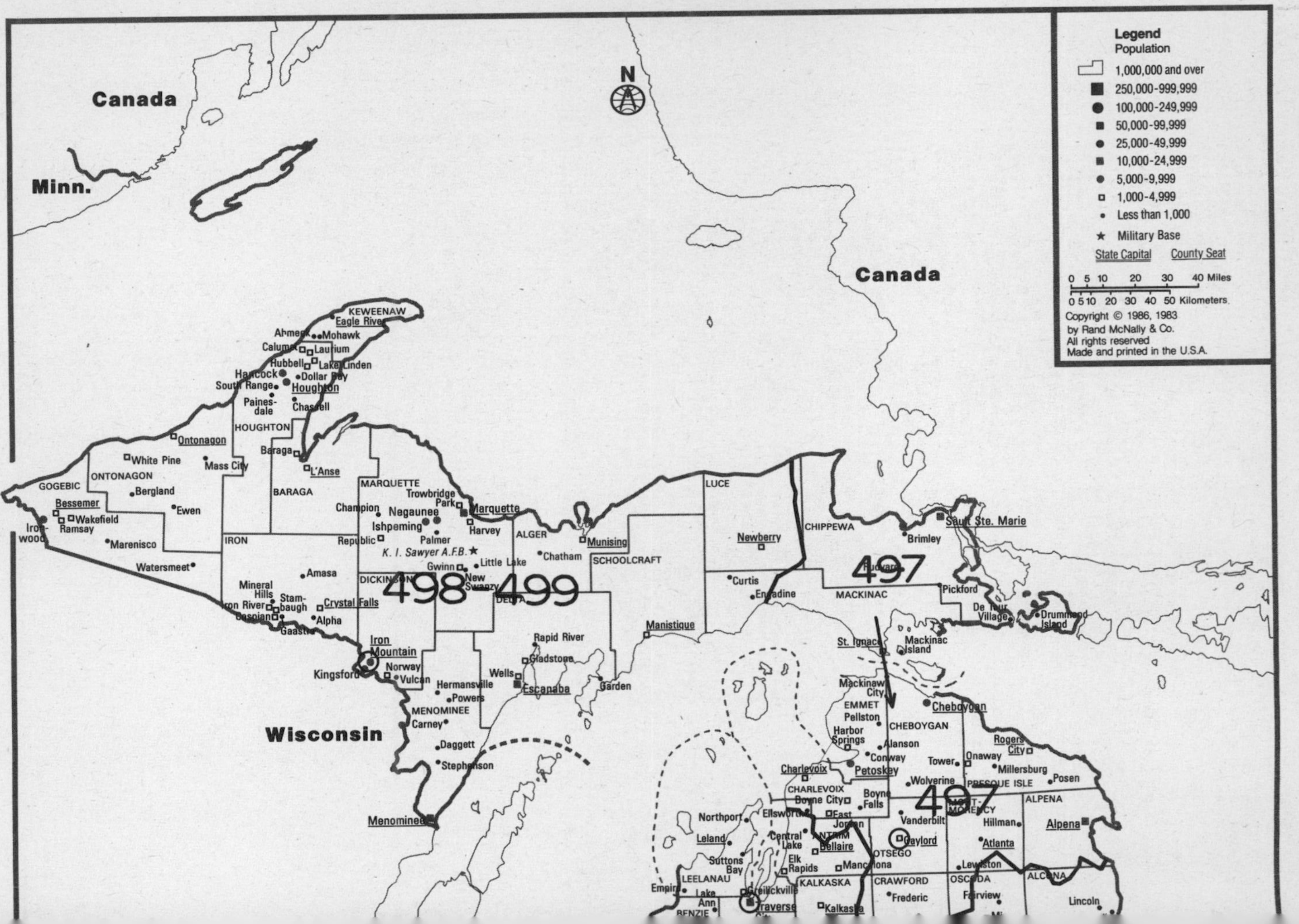
Legend
Population
1,000,000 and over
250,000-999,999
100,000-249,999
50,000-99,999
25,000-49,999
10,000-24,999
5,000-9,999
1,000-4,999
Less than 1,000
Military Base
State Capital
County Seat
0 5 10 20 30 40 Miles
0 5 10 20 30 40 50 Kilometers
Copyright © 1986, 1983
by Rand McNally & Co.
All rights reserved
Made and printed in the U.S.A.
Canada
Minn.
N
Canada
Wisconsin
497
498
499
497
KEWEENAW
HOUGHTON
ONTONAGON
GOGEBIC
BARAGA
IRON
MARQUETTE
DICKINSON
ALGER
SCHOOLCRAFT
LUCE
CHIPPEWA
MACKINAC
MENOMINEE
EMMET
CHEBOYGAN
CHARLEVOIX
PRESQUE ISLE
ALPENA
OTSEGO
KALKASKA
CRAWFORD
LEELANAU
Eagle River
Mohawk
Laurium
Lake Linden
Hubbell
Dollar Bay
Houghton
South Range
Painesdale
Chassell
Ontonagon
White Pine
Mass City
Baraga
L'Anse
Bergland
Bessemer
Wakefield
Ramsay
Ewen
Marenisco
Watersmeet
Trowbridge Park
Marquette
Champion
Negaunee
Ishpeming
Harvey
Palmer
Republic
K. I. Sawyer A.F.B.
Little Lake
Chatham
Munising
Gwinn
Amasa
Mineral Hills
Stambaugh
Crystal Falls
Alpha
Iron Mountain
Kingsford
Norway
Vulcan
Hermansville
Powers
Carney
Daggett
Stephenson
Menominee
Rapid River
Gladstone
Wells
Escanaba
Garden
Manistique
Newberry
Curtis
Brimley
Sault Ste. Marie
Pickford
Mackinac Island
St. Ignace
Mackinaw City
Pellston
Harbor Springs
Alanson
Cheboygan
Rogers City
Onaway
Tower
Millersburg
Posen
Charlevoix
Petoskey
Wolverine
Boyne City
Boyne Falls
Vanderbilt
Hillman
Alpena
Northport
Leland
Central Lake
Bellaire
Gaylord
Atlanta
Suttons Bay
Elk Rapids
Frederic
Lincoln

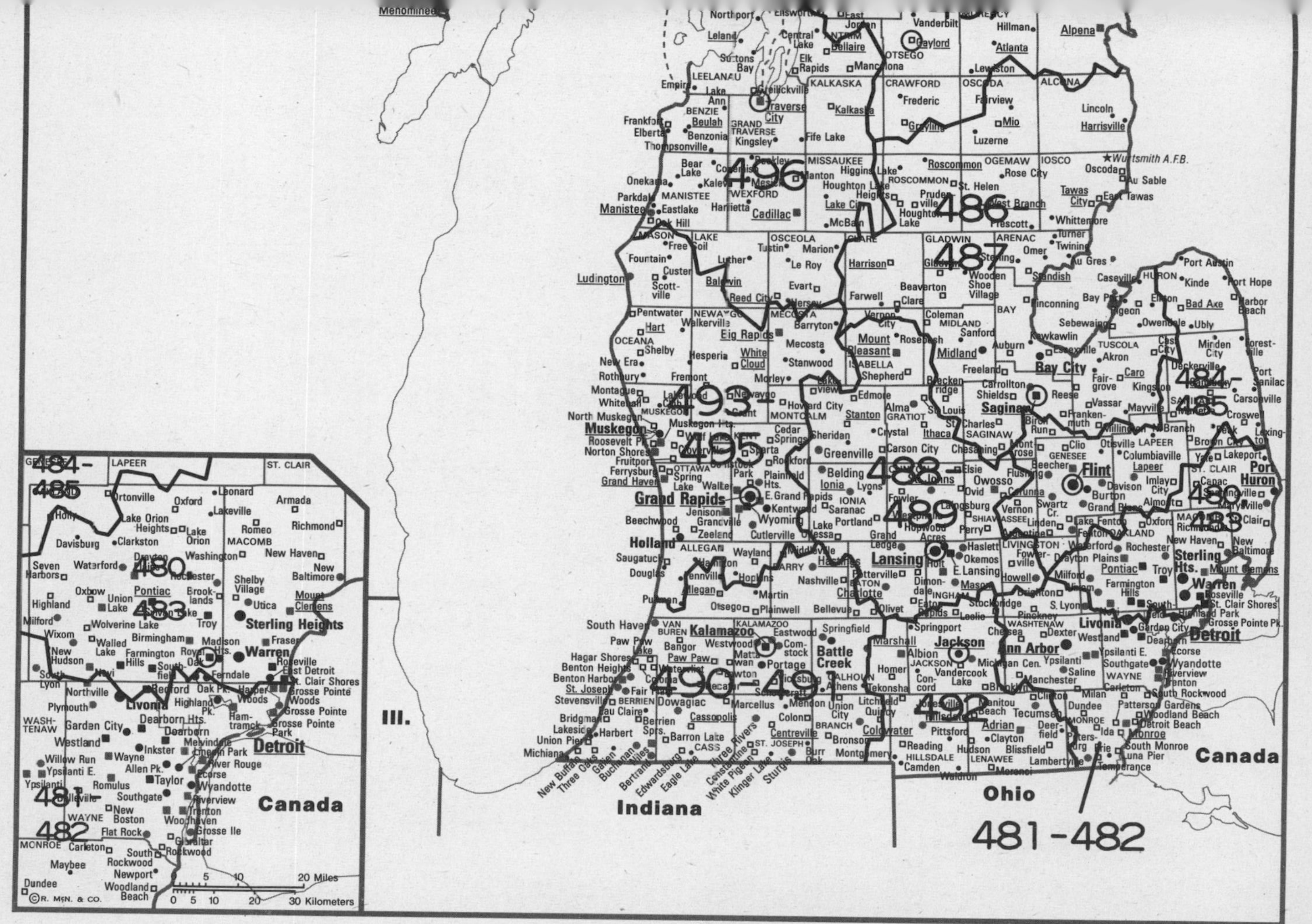

Canada
Ohio
Indiana
Ill.
481-482
484-485
480-483
486
487
488-489
490-491
492
493
495
496
Detroit
Lansing
Flint
Saginaw
Bay City
Grand Rapids
Kalamazoo
Battle Creek
Jackson
Ann Arbor
Muskegon
Holland
Midland
Port Huron
Livonia
Warren
Sterling Hts.
Pontiac
Traverse City
Cadillac
Alpena
Ludington
Manistee
Sterling Heights
20 Miles
30 Kilometers
©R. McN. & CO.

Place	ZIP
A (Part of Bay City)‡	48706
Abscota	49029
Ackerson Lake	49201
Acme	49610
Ada	49301
Adair	48064
Adams, *Arenac* (Twp)	48659
Adams, *Hillsdale* (Twp)	49262
Adams, *Houghton* (Twp)	49963
Adams Park	49097
Adamsville	49112
Addison, *Oakland* (Twp)	48367
Addison, *Lenawee*	49220
Adrian	49221
Advance	49712
Aetna, *Mecosta* (Twp)	49336
Aetna, *Missaukee* (Twp)	48632
Aetna, *Newaygo*	49349
Afton	49705
Agate	49967
Agnew	49460
Ahmeek	49901
Airport Forest	48625
Akron	48701
Alabaster	48763
Alaiedon (Twp)	48854
Alamo	49009
Alanson	49706
Alaska	49302
Alba	49611
Albee (Twp)	48655
Albert (Twp)	49756
Alberta	49946
Albion, *Calhoun*	49224
Albion, *Houghton*	49913
Albright Shores	48612
Alcona (Twp)	48721
Alcona	48740
Alden	49612
Algansee	49082
Alger	48610
Algoma (Twp)	49341
Algonac	48001
Allegan	49010
Allen	49227
Allendale, *Clare*	48625
Allendale, *Ottawa*♦	49401
Allen Park	48101
Allenton	48002
Allenville	49760
Allis (Twp)	49765
Allouez	49805
Allyn	49643
Alma	48801
Almeda Beach	48653
Almena	49079
Almer (Twp)	48723
Almira (Twp)	49630
Almont	48003
Aloha	49721
Alpena	49707
Alpena Junction (Part of Alpena)	49707
Alpha	49902
Alpine	49321
Alston	49958
Alto	49302
Altona	49336
Alverno	49721
Amador	48422
Amasa	49903
Amber (Twp)	49431
Amble	49329
Amboy (Twp)	49232
Anchorville♦	48004
Andersonville	48350
Andrews	49104
Ann Arbor (Twp)	48105
Ann Arbor	48103-09
	48113
For specific ZIP Codes call (888) 275-8777, or your local postmaster.	
Antioch (Twp)	49688
Antoine (Part of Iron Mountain)	49801
Antrim, *Shiawassee* (Twp)	48418
Antrim, *Antrim*	49659
Antwerp (Twp)	49065
Anvil	49911
Aplin Beach	48706
Applegate	48401
Arbela (Twp)	48746
Arborland Consumer Mall (Part of Ann Arbor)	48104
Arbutus Beach	49735
Arcada (Twp)	48801
Arcade (Part of Ann Arbor)‡	48106
Arcadia, *Lapeer* (Twp)	48412
Arcadia, *Manistee*	49613
Arenac	48658
Argentine♦	48451
Argyle	48410
Arlington (Twp)	49013
Armada	48005
Armstrong Corners	49079
Arnheim	49958
Arnold	49819
Artesia Beach	48656
Arthur (Twp)	48617
Arthur Bay	49858
Arvon (Twp)	49962
Ash (Twp)	48117
Ashland (Twp)	49327
Ashland Center	49327
Ashley	48806
Ashmore	48767
Ashton	49655
Askel	49958
Assyria	49021
Athens	49011
Atlanta	49709
Atlantic Mine	49905
Atlas (Twp)	48438
Atlas	48411
Attica	48412
Atwood	49729
Auburn	48611
Auburn Hills	48321†
	48326*
Au Gres	48703
Augusta, *Washtenaw* (Twp)	48191
Augusta, *Kalamazoo*	49012
Aura	49946
Aurelius	48854
Aurora (Part of Ironwood)	49938
Au Sable, *Roscommon* (Twp)	48653
Au Sable, *Iosco*♦	48750
Au Sable River Park	48656
Austin, *Mecosta* (Twp)	49346
Austin, *Sanilac* (Twp)	48475
Austin, *Hillsdale*	49232
Austin, *Marquette*	49841
Austin Center	48475
Austin Lake (Part of Portage)	49081
Au Train	49806
Auvinen Corner	49938
Avalon Beach	48161
Averill	48657
Avery (Twp)	49709
Avoca	48006
Avondale	49631
Azalia	48110
Bach	48759
Backus (Twp)	48656
Backus Beach	48762
Bad Axe	48413
Bagley, *Otsego* (Twp)	49735
Bagley, *Menominee*	49821
Baie de Wasai	49783
Bailey	49303
Bainbridge (Twp)	49022
Bainbridge Center	49022
Bakertown	49107
Baldwin, *Delta* (Twp)	49872
Baldwin, *Iosco* (Twp)	48770
Baldwin, *Lake*	49304
Baltic	49905
Baltimore, *Barry* (Twp)	49058
Baltimore, *Ontonagon*	49912
Bamfields	48737
Banat	49821
Bancroft	48414
Banfield	49017
Bangor, *Bay* (Twp)	48706
Bangor, *Van Buren* (Twp)	49103
Bangor, *Van Buren*	49013
Bankers	49242
Banks (Twp)	49729
Banksons Lake	49065
Bannister	48807
Baraga	49908
Barbeau	49710
Barker Creek	49690
Bark River	49807
Bar Lake	49660
Barnard	49720
Barnes Lake-Millers Lake♦	48421
Baroda	49101
Barron Lake	49120
Barry (Twp)	49060
Barryton	49305
Barton (Twp)	49338
Barton City	48705
Barton Hills	48105
Barton Lake	49097
Base Line Lake	49055
Bass Lake	49449
Batavia	49036
Batavia Center	49036
Bates, *Iron*	49935
Bates, *Grand Traverse*	49690
Bath	48808
Battle Creek	49014-18
For specific ZIP Codes call (888) 275-8777, or your local postmaster.	
Bauer	49426
Baw Beese Lake	49242
Bay (Twp)	49712
Bay City	48706-08
For specific ZIP Codes call (888) 275-8777, or your local postmaster.	
Bay de Noc (Twp)	49878
Bay Mills	49715
Bay Mills Indian Reservation	49715
Bay Port	48720
Bayshore	49711
Bay View	49770
Beach Grove	49858
Beachwood	48654
Beacon	49814
Beacon Hill	49905
Beadle Lake	49014
Beal City♦	48858
Bear Creek (Twp)	49770
Bearinger (Twp)	49759
Bear Lake, *Kalkaska* (Twp)	49646
Bear Lake, *Hillsdale*	49242
Bear Lake, *Manistee*	49614
Beaugrand (Twp)	49721
Beaver, *Bay* (Twp)	48611
Beaver, *Newaygo* (Twp)	49309
Beaver Creek (Twp)	48653
Beaverdam	49464
Beaver Grove	49855
Beaverton	48612
Bedford, *Calhoun* (Twp)	49017
Bedford, *Monroe* (Twp)	48182
Bedford, *Calhoun*	49020
Beebe	48847
Beecher♦	48458
Beechwood, *Iron*	49935
Beechwood, *Ottawa*♦	49423
Belding	48809
Belknap (Twp)	49743
Bell	49707
Bellaire	49615
Belleville	48111*
	48112†
Bellevue	49021
Bell Oak	48892
Belmont	49306
Belsay (Part of Burton)	48503
Belvedere	49720
Belvidere (Twp)	48886
Bendon	49643
Bengal (Twp)	48879
Bennington	48867
Benona (Twp)	49455
Bentheim	49419
Bentley, *Gladwin* (Twp)	48652
Bentley, *Bay*	48613
Bentleys Corners	49245
Benton, *Berrien* (Twp)	49022
Benton, *Cheboygan* (Twp)	49721
Benton, *Eaton* (Twp)	48876
Benton Harbor	49022*
	49023†
Benton Heights♦	49022
Benzonia	49616
Bergland	49910
Berkley	48072
Berlamont	49026
Berlin, *Ionia* (Twp)	48846
Berlin, *Monroe* (Twp)	48166
Berlin, *St. Clair* (Twp)	48002
Berne	48755
Berrien (Twp)	49102
Berrien Center	49102
Berrien Springs	49103
Berryville	49277
Bertrand	49120
Berville	48002
Bessemer (Twp)	49959
Bessemer	49911
Bete Grise	49950
Bethany (Twp)	48880
Bethany Beach	49125
Bethel	49036
Betsy	49945
Betzer	49271
Beulah	49617
Beverly Hills (Part of Negaunee)	49866
Beverly Hills, *Oakland*	48025
Big Bay	49808
Big Creek (Twp)	48647
Biggs Settlement	48647
Big Prairie (Twp)	49349
Big Rapids	49307
Big Rock	49709
Billings (Twp)	48612
Bingham, *Clinton* (Twp)	48879
Bingham, *Huron* (Twp)	48475
Bingham, *Leelanau* (Twp)	49684
Bingham Farms	48025
Birch Beach	48450
Birch Creek	49858
Birch Run	48415
Birchwood, *Berrien*	49115
Birchwood, *Cheboygan*	49721
Birmingham	48009-12
For specific ZIP Codes call (888) 275-8777, or your local postmaster.	
Bismarck (Twp)	49779
Bitely	49309
Black Lake Bluffs	49765
Blackman (Twp)	49202
Black River	48721
Black River Harbor	49938
Blaine, *Benzie* (Twp)	49635
Blaine, *St. Clair*	48032
Blair (Twp)	49684
Blanchard	49310
Blaney Park	49836
Blendon (Twp)	49426
Bliss	49755
Blissfield	49228
Bloomer (Twp)	48811
Bloomfield, *Huron* (Twp)	48468
Bloomfield, *Missaukee* (Twp)	49651
Bloomfield, *Oakland* (Twp)	48302
Bloomfield (Part of Bloomfield Hills)	48304
Bloomfield Glens	48322
Bloomfield Hills	48301-04
For specific ZIP Codes call (888) 275-8777, or your local postmaster.	
Bloomfield Hills North	48302
Bloomfield Township♦	48301-02
For specific ZIP Codes call (888) 275-8777, or your local postmaster.	
Bloomfield Town Square	48302
Bloomfield Village	48301
Bloomingdale	49026
Blue Jacket	49913
Blue Lake, *Kalkaska* (Twp)	49646
Blue Lake, *Muskegon* (Twp)	49461
Blue Water Beach	48450
Bluff Beach	49099
Blumfield (Twp)	48757
Blumfield Corners	48757
Boardman (Twp)	49680
Bohemia (Twp)	49965
Boichott Acres	48906
Bois Blanc (Twp)	49775
Bolles Harbor	48161
Bolton	49707
Bombay	48642
Boon	49618
Bootjack	49945
Borculo	49464
Boston, *Ionia* (Twp)	48881
Boston, *Houghton*	49930
Bostwick Lake	49341
Boulder Park	49720
Bourret (Twp)	48610
Bowens Mills	49333
Bowne (Twp)	49302
Boyne City	49712
Boyne Falls	49713
Boyne Valley (Twp)	49713
Bradley	49311
Brady, *Kalamazoo* (Twp)	49097
Brady, *Saginaw* (Twp)	48649
Brampton	49837
Branch (Twp)	49458
Branch	49402
Brandon (Twp)	48462
Brandywine Lake	49055
Brant	48614
Brassar	49783
Bravo	49408
Breckenridge	48615
Breedsville	49027
Breen (Twp)	49834
Breezy Beach	49099
Breitung (Twp)	49876
Brent Creek	48433
Brethren	49619
Bretton Woods	48917
Brevort	49760
Briarwood (Part of Ann Arbor)	48108
Bridgehampton (Twp)	48419
Bridgeport♦	48722
Bridgeton	49327
Bridgeville	48879
Bridgewater (Twp)	48158
Bridgewater	48115
Bridgman	49106
Brightmoor (Part of Detroit)‡	48223
Brighton	48114
	48116
For specific ZIP Codes call (888) 275-8777, or your local postmaster.	
Briley (Twp)	49709
Brimley	49715
Brinton	48632
Bristol	49688
Britton	49229
Broad Acres	48035
Broadbridge Station	48039
Brockway	48097
Brohman	49312
Bronson	49028
Brookfield, *Huron* (Twp)	48754
Brookfield, *Eaton*	48813
Brooklyn	49230
Brooks (Twp)	49337
Brookside	49412
Brookville	48175
Broomfield (Twp)	49340
Brown (Twp)	49660
Brown City	48416
Brownlee Park♦	49014
Brownstown (Twp)	48134
Brownsville	49031
Brownwood Lake	49079
Bruce, *Chippewa* (Twp)	49783
Bruce, *Macomb* (Twp)	48065
Bruce Crossing	49912
Bruningville	49779
Brunswick	49425
Brutus	49716
Bryant	48737
Buchanan	49107
Buckeye (Twp)	48624
Buckley	49620
Bucks Corners	49449
Buel (Twp)	48422
Buena Vista♦	48601
Bullock Creek	48642
Bumbletown	49805
Bunker Hill	49251
Bunny Run	48362
Burdell (Twp)	49688
Burdickville	49664
Burgess	49720
Burleigh (Twp)	48770
Burleigh Corners	49017
Burlington, *Lapeer* (Twp)	48727
Burlington, *Calhoun*	49029
Burnips	49314
Burns (Twp)	48418
Burnside	48416
Burr Oak	49030
Burt, *Alger* (Twp)	49839
Burt, *Cheboygan* (Twp)	49721

* **Area Zip Code** † **Post Office Boxes** ‡ **Postal Station** ♦ **Census Designated Place** *Italic Type* **County**

Burt, *Saginaw*♦ 48417
Burtchville (Twp) 48059
Burt Lake 49717
Burton, *Genesee* 48509
Burton, *Shiawassee* 48867
Burton-Northeast (Part of Burton) 48509
Burton-Southeast (Part of Burton) 48529
Bushnell (Twp) 48884
Butler 49082
Butman (Twp) 48624
Butterfield (Twp) 48632
Butternut 48811
Byron, *Kent* (Twp) 49315
Byron, *Shiawassee* 48418
Byron Center 49315
C (Part of Grand Rapids)‡ 49506
Cadillac 49601
Cadmus 49221
Cady 48035
Calcite (Part of Rogers City) 49779
Calderwood 49967
Caldwell (Twp) 49651
Caledonia, *Alcona* (Twp) 48762
Caledonia, *Shiawassee* (Twp) 48817
Caledonia, *Kent* 49316
California 49255
Calumet 49913
Calvin (Twp) 49031
Calvin Center 49031
Cambria 49242
Cambridge (Twp) 49265
Cambridge Junction 49230
Camden 49232
Campbell (Twp) 48815
Campbells Corner 48367
Campbells Corners 48661
Canada Corners 49318
Canada Creek Ranch 49709
Canada Shores 49036
Canal Station (Part of Sault Ste. Marie)‡ 49783
Canandaigua 49235
Canfield Beach 49765
Cannon (Twp) 49341
Cannonsburg 49317
Canton (Twp) 48184
Canton 48187-88
For specific ZIP Codes call (888) 275-8777, or your local postmaster.
Capac 48014
Caribou Lake 49725
Carland 48831
Carleton 48117
Carlisle 49508
Carlshend 49885
Carlton (Twp) 49058
Carlton Center 49325
Carmel (Twp) 48813
Carney 49812
Caro 48723
Carp Lake, *Ontonagon* (Twp) 49953
Carp Lake, *Emmet* 49718
Carrollton♦ 48724
Carr Settlement 49402
Carson City 48811
Carsonville 48419
Carter Creek 49643
Cascade 49506
Casco, *Allegan* (Twp) 49090
Casco, *St. Clair* (Twp) 48064
Case (Twp) 49759
Caseville 48725
Cash 48471
Casnovia 49318
Caspian 49915
Cass City 48726
Cassopolis 49031
Castle Park 49423
Castleton (Twp) 49073
Cathro 49707
Cato (Twp) 48850
Cedar, *Osceola* (Twp) 49631
Cedar, *Leelanau* 49621
Cedar Bluff 49090
Cedar Creek, *Muskegon* (Twp) 49457
Cedar Creek, *Wexford* (Twp) 49663
Cedar Creek, *Barry* 49046
Cedar Lake, *Montcalm* 48812
Cedar Lake, *Van Buren* 49067
Cedar River 49813
Cedar Run 49684
Cedar Springs 49319
Cedarville, *Menominee* (Twp) 49813
Cedarville, *Mackinac* 49719
Cement City 49233
Centennial Heights 49913
Center (Twp) 49769
Center Line 48015
Centerville (Twp) 49621
Central 49950
Central Lake 49622
Centreville 49032
Ceresco 49033
Chamberlains 49067
Champion 49814
Chandler, *Charlevoix* (Twp) 49712
Chandler, *Huron* (Twp) 48731
Channing 49815
Chapin 48841
Charleston, *Kalamazoo* (Twp) 49053
Charleston, *Sanilac* 48456
Charlevoix 49720
Charlotte 48813
Charlton (Twp) 49751
Chase 49623
Chassell 49916
Chatham 49816
Chatham Corners (Part of Chatham) 49816
Chauncey 49306
Cheboygan 49721
Chelsea 48118
Cherry Beach 48039
Cherry Bend 49684
Cherry Grove (Twp) 49601
Cherry Hill 48187
Cherry Island (Part of Rockwood) 48173
Cherryland Mall (Part of Traverse City) 49686
Cherry Valley (Twp) 49623
Chesaning 48616
Cheshire (Twp) 49010
Cheshire Center 49010
Chester, *Otsego* (Twp) 49735
Chester, *Ottawa* (Twp) 49403
Chester, *Eaton* 48813
Chesterfield (Twp) 48047
Chesterfield 48051
Chestonia (Twp) 49611
Chicagon Lake 49920
Chicora 49010
Chief Lake 49645
Chikaming (Twp) 49116
China (Twp) 48054
Chippewa, *Chippewa* (Twp) 49790
Chippewa, *Isabella* (Twp) 48858
Chippewa, *Mecosta* (Twp) 49320
Chippewa Lake 49320
Chippewa Vista 49305
Chocolay (Twp) 49855
Christie Lake 49045
49064
For specific ZIP Codes call (888) 275-8777, or your local postmaster.
Christmas 49862
Churchill, *Ogemaw* (Twp) 48661
Churchill (Part of Norton Shores) 49441
Circle Pine Center 49046
Cisco Lake 49969
Clam Lake (Twp) 49601
Clam River 49615
Clam Union (Twp) 48632
Clare 48617
Clarence (Twp) 49224
Clarendon 49245
Clarion 49713
Clark, *Benzie* 49643
Clark, *Mackinac* (Twp) 49719
Clarklake 49234
Clarksburg 49814
Clarkston 48346-48
For specific ZIP Codes call (888) 275-8777, or your local postmaster.
Clarksville 48815
Clawson 48017
Clay (Twp) 48001
Claybanks (Twp) 49452
Clayton, *Arenac* (Twp) 48659
Clayton, *Genesee* (Twp) 48473
Clayton, *Lenawee* 49235
Clear Lake 48661
Clearwater (Twp) 49676
Clement (Twp) 48610
Cleon (Twp) 49625
Cleveland (Twp) 49664
Clifford 48727
Climax 49034
Clinton, *Oscoda* (Twp) 48619
Clinton, *Lenawee* 49236
Clinton, *Macomb*♦ 48035-36
48038
For specific ZIP Codes call (888) 275-8777, or your local postmaster.
Clinton Village 48906
Clio 48420
Cloverdale 49035
Cloverville 49444
Clyde, *Allegan* (Twp) 49408
Clyde, *St. Clair* (Twp) 48049
Clyde, *Oakland* 48357
Coats Grove 49058
Coddes Beach 49765
Cody (Part of Flint)‡ 48507
Coe 48880
Cohoctah 48836
Cohoctah Center 48816
Cold Springs (Twp) 49646
Coldwater, *Isabella* (Twp) 48632
Coldwater, *Branch* 49036
Coleman 48618
Colfax, *Benzie* (Twp) 49683
Colfax, *Huron* (Twp) 48413
Colfax, *Mecosta* (Twp) 49307
Colfax, *Oceana* (Twp) 49459
Colfax, *Wexford* (Twp) 49663
College Park (Part of Detroit)‡ 48221
College Town 48706
Colling 48767
Collins 48851
Coloma 49038
Colon 40040
Columbia, *Jackson* (Twp) 49230
Columbia, *Tuscola* (Twp) 48767
Columbia, *Van Buren* (Twp) 49056
Columbia Corners 48767
Columbiaville 48421
Columbus, *Luce* (Twp) 49853
Columbus, *St. Clair* (Twp) 48063
Colwood 48767
Comins (Twp) 48619
Comins 48621
Commerce (Twp) 48382
Commerce 48387
Comstock 49041
Comstock Northwest♦ 49041
Comstock Park♦ 49321
Concord 49237
Condit 49245
Cone 48160
Conklin 49403
Connorville 49968
Constantine 49042
Convis (Twp) 49017
Conway, *Livingston* (Twp) 48836
Conway, *Emmet* 49722
Cooks 49817
Cooks Corners 48809
Cooper (Twp) 49004
Cooper Center 49004
Coopersville 49404
Copemish 49625
Copenhagen Beach 49854
Copper City 49917
Copper Harbor 49918
Coral 49322
Corey 49093
Corinne 49838
Cornell 49818
Corunna 48817
Corwith (Twp) 49795
Coryell Islands 49719
Cottage Grove 48653
Cottage Park 49724
Cottrellville (Twp) 48039
Court (Part of Kalamazoo)‡ 49007
Courtland (Twp) 49341
Courtland Center (Part of Burton) 48509
Covert 49043
Covington 49919
Cranbrook (Part of Bloomfield Hills) 48303
Crescent Lake Estates 48327
Crisp 49423
Crockery (Twp) 49448
Crofton 49680
Crooked Lake, *Barry* 49046
Crooked Lake, *Livingston* 48116
Crossroads, The (Part of Portage) 49024
Cross Village 49723
Croswell 48422
Croton 49337
Croton Heights 49337
Crump 48634
Crystal, *Oceana* (Twp) 49420
Crystal, *Montcalm* 48818
Crystal Beach 49036
Crystal Falls 49920
Crystal Lake (Twp) 49635
Crystal Valley 49420
Cumber 48475
Cumming (Twp) 48635
Cunard 49847
Curran 48728
Curtis, *Alcona* (Twp) 48737
Curtis, *Mackinac* 49820
Curtisville 48761
Custer, *Antrim* (Twp) 49659
Custer, *Sanilac* (Twp) 48471
Custer, *Mason* 49405
Cutlerville♦ 49508
Dafter 49724
Daggett 49821
Dailey 49031
Dallas (Twp) 48835
Dalton 49445
Damon 48654
Danby (Twp) 48890
Danish Landing 49738
Dansville 48819
Darragh 49646
Davis 48065
Davisburg 48350
Davison 48423
Day (Twp) 48852
Dayton, *Newaygo* (Twp) 49412
Dayton, *Tuscola* (Twp) 48744
Dayton, *Berrien* 49113
Dayton Center 49412
Dearborn 48120-21
48123-24
48126
48128
For specific ZIP Codes call (888) 275-8777, or your local postmaster.
Dearborn Heights 48125
48127
For specific ZIP Codes call (888) 275-8777, or your local postmaster.
Decatur 49045
Decker 48426
Deckerville 48427
Deep River (Twp) 48659
Deerfield, *Isabella* (Twp) 48858
Deerfield, *Lapeer* (Twp) 48421
Deerfield, *Livingston* (Twp) 48451
Deerfield, *Mecosta* (Twp) 49336
Deerfield, *Lenawee* 49238
Deerfield Center, *Isabella* 48858
Deerfield Center, *Livingston* 48451
Deer Park 49868
Deerton 49822
Deford 48729
Dehoco 48175
Deibert 49680
Delano 48703
Delaware (Twp) 48456
Delhi (Twp) 48842
Delray (Part of Detroit) 48217
Delta (Twp) 48917
Delta Mills 48917
Delton 49046
Delwin 48858
Denmark (Twp) 48758
Denton, *Roscommon* (Twp) 48651
Denton, *Wayne* 48111
Denver, *Isabella* (Twp) 48858
Denver, *Newaygo* (Twp) 49421
Derby 49127
Detour (Twp) 49725
De Tour Village 49725

Detroit

48201-17
48219
48221-24
48226-28
48231-35
48238
48242-44
For specific ZIP Codes call (888) 275-8777, or your local postmaster.

Colleges & Universities

Center for Creative Studies-Coll of Art & Design 48202
Detroit Coll of Law 48201
Mary Grove Coll 48221
Sacred Heart Major Seminary/Coll & Theologate 48206
Univ of Detroit Mercy 48219
Wayne State Univ 48202

Financial Institutions

Comerica 48226
First of America 48215
NBD Bank 48226

Hospitals

Children's Hosp of Michigan 48201
Detroit Receiving Hosp & Univ Health Ctr 48201
Grace Hosp 48235
Harper Hosp 48201
Henry Ford Hosp 48202
Hutzel Hosp 48201
John D Dingell VA 48201
Sinai Hosp 48235
St John Hosp & Med Ctr 48236

Hotels/Motels

Crowne Plaza Pontchartrain 48226
Doubletree Downtown 48226
Holiday Inn, Fairlane 48228
Westin 48243

Military Installations

Coast Guard Sta, Belle Isle 48207

Detroit Beach♦ 48162
Detroit River (Part of Detroit) 48222
Devereaux 49224
Devils Lake 49253
De Witt 48820
Dexter (Twp) 48169
Dexter 48130
Diamond Lake 49349
Diamond Shores 49031
Diamond Springs 49419
Dice Corners 48626
Dickson (Twp) 49619
Diffin 49891
Dighton 49688
Dimondale 48821
Diorite 49814
Dixboro 48105
Dodgeville 49921
Dollar Bay 49922
Dollar Settlement 49715
Dollarville 49868
Dolph 49632
Donaldson 49783
Donken 49965
Donoghue Beach 48706
Doriva Beach 49721
Dorr 49323
Doster 49080
Doughertys Corners 49009
Douglas 49406
Douglass (Twp) 48888
Dover, *Lake* (Twp) 49656
Dover, *Lenawee* (Twp) 49235
Dover, *Otsego* (Twp) 49738
Dowagiac 49047
Dowling 49050
Downington 48427
Downtown (Part of Flint)‡ 48502
Downtown (Part of Lansing)‡ 48901†
48924*

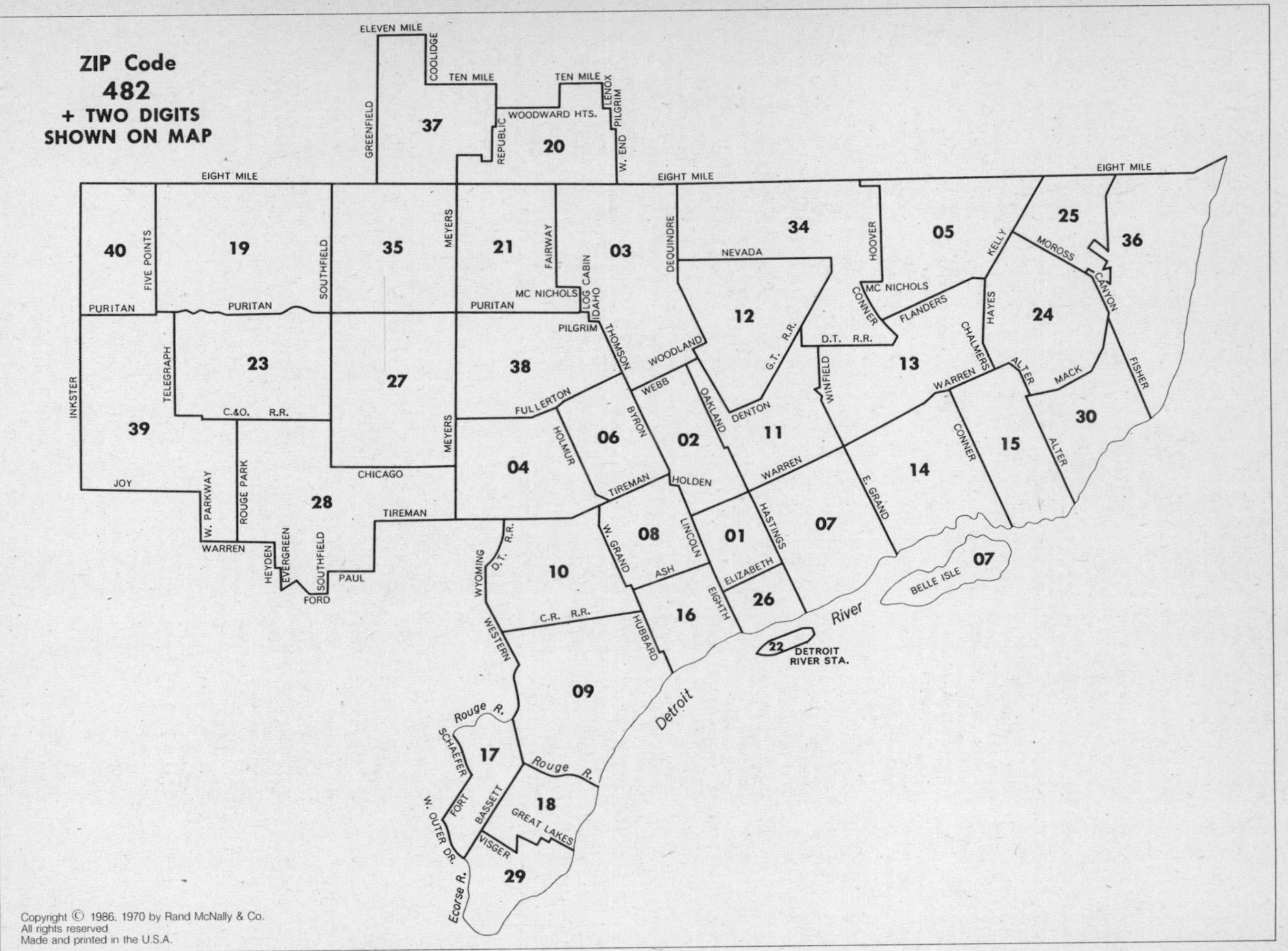
ZIP Code
482
+ TWO DIGITS
SHOWN ON MAP
EIGHT MILE
TEN MILE
ELEVEN MILE
COOLIDGE
GREENFIELD
WOODWARD HTS.
REPUBLIC
LENOX
PILGRIM
W. END
MEYERS
SOUTHFIELD
FIVE POINTS
PURITAN
INKSTER
JOY
TELEGRAPH
W. PARKWAY
WARREN
ROUGE PARK
C.&O. R.R.
HEYDEN
EVERGREEN
FORD
PAUL
TIREMAN
CHICAGO
FAIRWAY
MC NICHOLS
LOG CABIN
IDAHO
THOMSON
PILGRIM
FULLERTON
HOLMUR
BYRON
WEBB
WOODLAND
OAKLAND
DENTON
G.T. R.R.
NEVADA
DEQUINDRE
HOOVER
CONNER
D.T. R.R.
WINFIELD
FLANDERS
HAYES
KELLY
MOROSS
CANYON
FISHER
MACK
ALTER
CHALMERS
E. GRAND
HASTINGS
ELIZABETH
HOLDEN
LINCOLN
EIGHTH
ASH
W. GRAND
HUBBARD
C.R. R.R.
D.T. R.R.
WYOMING
WESTERN
Rouge R.
SCHAEFER
FORT
BASSETT
VISGER
GREAT LAKES
W. OUTER DR.
Ecorse R.
BELLE ISLE
DETROIT RIVER STA.
Detroit River
01 02 03 04 05 06 07 08 09 10 11 12 13 14 15 16 17 18 19 20 21 22 23 24 25 26 27 28 29 30 34 35 36 37 38 39 40
Copyright © 1986, 1970 by Rand McNally & Co.
All rights reserved
Made and printed in the U.S.A.

Place	ZIP
Downtown (Part of Midland)‡	48640
Doyle (Twp)	49840
Drayton Plains	48330
Drenthe	49464
Drummond (Twp)	49726
Drummond Island	49726
Dryburg	49780
Dryden	48428
Dublin	49689
Duck Lake, *Allegan*	49055
Duck Lake, *Calhoun*	49224
Duel	48640
Duffield	48473
Dukes	49885
Duncan (Twp)	48131
Dundee	48131
Dunham Lake	48353
Dunningville	49010
Dunn Location	49920
Duplain (Twp)	48831
Duplain	48879
Durand	48429
Dutton	49316
Dwight (Twp)	48445
Eagle	48822
Eagle Harbor	49950
Eagle Lake, *Cass*	49112
Eagle Lake, *Van Buren*	49079
Eagle Point	49031
Eagle River	49950
Eagles Nest	49858
East Bay (Twp)	49686
Eastbrook Mall (Part of Grand Rapids)	49523
East China (Twp)	48054
East Cooper	49004
East Dayton	48723
Eastgate Shopping Center (Part of Roseville)	48066
East Gilead	49028
East Grand Rapids	49506
East Houghton (Part of Houghton)	49931
East Jordan	49727
East Kingsford	49802
Eastlake	49626
Eastland Center (Part of Harper Woods)‡	48225
East Lansing	48823-26
For specific ZIP Codes call (888) 275-8777, or your local postmaster.	
East Leroy	49051
Eastmanville	49404
Easton, *Ionia* (Twp)	48846
Easton, *Shiawassee*	48867
East Paris (Part of Kentwood)	49508
Eastpointe	48021
Eastport	49627
East Rockwood	48173
East Saugatuck	49419
East Sebewa	48890
East Side (Part of Saginaw)‡	48601
East Tawas	48730
Eastview	48065
Eastwood♦	49001
Eaton (Twp)	48813
Eaton Rapids	48827
Eau Claire	49111
Eben Junction	49825
Echo (Twp)	49622
Eckerman	49728
Eckerman Corner	49728
Eckford	49245
Ecorse	48229
Eden, *Lake* (Twp)	49644
Eden, *Mason* (Twp)	49454
Eden, *Ingham*	48854
Edenville	48620
Edgemont Park♦	48917
Edgerton	49341
Edgewood Beach	49858
Edmore	48829
Edwards (Twp)	48661
Edwardsburg	49112
Edwards Corners	49067
Egelston (Twp)	49442
Eight Point Lake	48632
Elba, *Gratiot* (Twp)	48807
Elba, *Lapeer*	48446
Elberta	49628
Elbridge (Twp)	49459
Eldorado	48653
Elizabeth Lake Estates	48327
Elk, *Lake* (Twp)	49644
Elk, *Sanilac* (Twp)	48466
Elkland (Twp)	48726
Elk Rapids	49629
Elkton	48731
Ellington	48723
Ellis (Twp)	49705
Ellsworth, *Lake* (Twp)	49656
Ellsworth, *Antrim*	49729
Elmdale	48815
Elmer, *Oscoda* (Twp)	48647
Elmer, *Sanilac* (Twp)	48471
Elm Hall	48830
Elmira	49730
Elm River (Twp)	49965
Elmwood, *Leelanau* (Twp)	49684
Elmwood, *Tuscola*	48726
Elo	49958
Eloise (Part of Westland)	48186
Elsie	48831
Elwell	48832
Ely (Twp)	49814
Emerson (Twp)	48615
Emmett, *Calhoun* (Twp)	49014
Emmett, *St. Clair*	48022
Empire	49630
Engadine	49827
Ensign	49878
Ensley (Twp)	49329
Ensley Center	49343
Enterprise (Twp)	49667
Entrican	48888
Epoufette	49762
Epsilon	49770
Erie	48133
Erwin (Twp)	49938
Escanaba	49829
Essex (Twp)	48879
Essexville	48732
Estey	48652
Estral Beach	48166
Eureka, *Montcalm* (Twp)	48838
Eureka, *Clinton*	48833
Evangeline (Twp)	49712
Evans	49319
Evans Lake	49287
Evart	49631
Eveline (Twp)	49727
Everett (Twp)	49349
Evergreen, *Montcalm* (Twp)	48884
Evergreen, *Sanilac* (Twp)	48426
Evergreen Acres	48161
Evergreen Shores	49781
Ewen	49925
Ewing (Twp)	49880
Excelsior (Twp)	49646
Exeter (Twp)	48159
Fabius (Twp)	49093
Factoryville	49066
Fairbanks (Twp)	49817
Fairfax	49040
Fairfield, *Shiawassee* (Twp)	48831
Fairfield, *Lenawee*	49221
Fairgrove	48733
Fairhaven, *Huron* (Twp)	48720
Fair Haven, *St. Clair*♦	48023
Fairlane Town Center (Part of Dearborn)	48126
Fairplain, *Montcalm* (Twp)	48838
Fair Plain, *Berrien*♦	49022
Fairplain Plaza	49022
Fairport	49835
Fairview	48621
Fairview Heights	48197
Faithorn	49892
Fallasberg	49331
Falmouth	49632
Fargo	48006
Farmers Creek	48455
Farmington	48331-36
For specific ZIP Codes call (888) 275-8777, or your local postmaster.	
Farmington Hills	48331-34
For specific ZIP Codes call (888) 275-8777, or your local postmaster.	
Farrandville	48420
Farwell	48622
Fawn River	49091
Fayette, *Hillsdale* (Twp)	49250
Fayette, *Delta*	49835
Federal Building (Part of Saginaw)‡	48606
Felch	49831
Felch Mountain	49801
Fenkell (Part of Detroit)‡	48238
Fennville	49408
Fenton	48430
Fenwick	48834
Ferndale	48220
Ferris (Twp)	48891
Ferry	49455
Ferrysburg	49409
Fibre	49780
Fife Lake	49633
Filer (Twp)	49660
Filer City	49634
Filion	48432
Filmore	49423
Findley	49030
Fisher (Part of Wyoming)	49509
Fisher Building (Part of Detroit)‡	48211
Fisherville	48611
Fitchburg	49285
Five Lakes	48446
Five Points	48867
Flat Rock, *Delta*	49837
Flat Rock, *Wayne*	48134
Flint (Twp)	48532
Flint	48501-07
	48531-32
For specific ZIP Codes call (888) 275-8777, or your local postmaster.	
Florence (Twp)	49042
Florida	49913
Flowerfield	49093
Floyd	48640
Flushing	48433
Flynn (Twp)	48453
Foote Site Village	48750
Ford Lake	49410
Ford River	49829
Forest, *Cheboygan* (Twp)	49792
Forest, *Genesee* (Twp)	48463
Forest, *Missaukee* (Twp)	49651
Forester	48419
Forest Grove	49426
Forest Grove Station	49426
Forest Hill	48801
Forest Hills	49506
Forest Home (Twp)	49615
Forest Lake	49862
Forestville	48434
Fork (Twp)	49305
Forsyth (Twp)	49833
Fort Dearborn‡	48123†
	48124*
Fort Gratiot (Twp)	48059
Fortune Lake	49920
Foster (Twp)	48661
Foster City	49834
Fosters	48415
Fostoria	48435
Fountain	49410
Fountain Park	49266
Four Mile Corner	49868
Fowler	48835
Fowlerville	48836
Fox	49813
Fox Creek (Part of Detroit)‡	48215
Francisco	49240
Frandor Shopping Center (Part of Lansing)‡	48912
Frankenlust (Twp)	48706
Frankenmuth	48734
Frankentrost	48601
Frankfort	49635
Franklin, *Clare* (Twp)	48625
Franklin, *Houghton* (Twp)	49930
Franklin, *Lenawee* (Twp)	49287
Franklin, *Oakland*	48025
Franklin Mine	49930
Fraser, *Bay* (Twp)	48634
Fraser, *Macomb*	48026
Freda	49905
Frederic	49733
Fredonia (Twp)	49068
Freedom, *Cheboygan*	49721
Freedom, *Washtenaw* (Twp)	48158
Freeland♦	48623
Freeman (Twp)	48632
Freeport	49325
Free Soil	49411
Freiburger	48475
Fremont, *Isabella* (Twp)	49310
Fremont, *Saginaw* (Twp)	48655
Fremont, *Sanilac* (Twp)	48097
Fremont, *Tuscola* (Twp)	48744
Fremont, *Newaygo*	49412
French Landing (Part of Romulus)	48174
Frenchtown, *Monroe* (Twp)	48162
Frenchtown (Part of Ishpeming)	49849
French Town, *Oceana*	49449
Friendship (Twp)	49740
Frontier	49239
Frost (Twp)	48625
Frost Corners	48875
Fruitland (Twp)	49461
Fruitport	49415
Fruitport Siding (Part of Norton Shores)	49444
Fulton, *Gratiot* (Twp)	48871
Fulton, *Kalamazoo*	49052
Fulton, *Keweenaw*	49950
Gaastra	49927
Gagetown	48735
Gaines, *Kent* (Twp)	49508
Gaines, *Genesee*	48436
Galesburg	49053
Galien	49113
Ganges	49408
Garden	49835
Garden City	48135*
	48136†
Garden Corners	49817
Gardendale	48059
Gardenville	49783
Gardner	49821
Garfield, *Bay* (Twp)	48634
Garfield, *Clare* (Twp)	49684
Garfield, *Grand Traverse* (Twp)	49684
Garfield, *Kalkaska* (Twp)	49633
Garfield, *Mackinac* (Twp)	49827
Garfield, *Newaygo* (Twp)	49337
Garnet	49762
Garth	49878
Gay	49945
Gaylord	49534†
	49535*
General Post Office (Part of Detroit)‡	48233
Genesee	48437
Geneva, *Midland* (Twp)	48618
Geneva, *Van Buren* (Twp)	49056
Genoa (Twp)	48114
	48116
For specific ZIP Codes call (888) 275-8777, or your local postmaster.	
Georgetown (Twp)	49426
Gera	48734
Germfask	49836
Gerrish (Twp)	48653
Gibraltar	48173
Gibson, *Bay* (Twp)	48613
Gibson, *Allegan*	49423
Gilchrist	49762
Gilead	49028
Gilford	48736
Gilmore, *Benzie* (Twp)	49628
Gilmore, *Isabella* (Twp)	48622
Gingellville	48359
Girard	49036
Gladstone	49837
Gladwin	48624
Glen Arbor	49636
Glencoe Hills Apartments (Part of Ann Arbor)	48108
Glendale	49079
Glendora	49107
Glen Haven	49621
Glenn	49416
Glenn Haven Shores	49090
Glennie	48737
Glenn Shores	49090
Glenside (Part of Norton Shores)	49441
Glenwood	49047
Gobles	49055
Goetzville	49736
Golden (Twp)	49436
Golfcrest	48162
Goodar (Twp)	48761
Goodells	48027
Good Hart	49737
Goodison	48306
Goodland (Twp)	48444
Goodrich	48438
Goodwell (Twp)	49349
Gordon Beach	49129
Gordonville	48640
Gore (Twp)	48468
Gotts Corners	48725
Gould City	49838
Gourley (Twp)	49812
Gowen	49326
Graafschap	49423
Grace	49759
Graham Lake	49014
Grand Beach	49117
Grand Blanc	48439
Grand Haven	49417
Grand Island (Twp)	49862
Grand Junction	49056
Grand Ledge	48837
Grand Marais	49839
Grand Rapids (Twp)	49505
	49525
For specific ZIP Codes call (888) 275-8777, or your local postmaster.	
Grand Rapids	49501-99
For specific ZIP Codes call (888) 275-8777, or your local postmaster.	
Grand River (Part of Detroit)‡	48208
Grand Shelby (Part of Detroit)‡	48216
Grand View	48145
Grand View Acres	48167
Grand View Beach	49749
Grandville	49418*
	49468†
Grant, *Cheboygan* (Twp)	49721
Grant, *Clare* (Twp)	48617
Grant, *Grand Traverse* (Twp)	49643
Grant, *Huron* (Twp)	48726
Grant, *Iosco* (Twp)	48763
Grant, *Keweenaw* (Twp)	49918
Grant, *Mason* (Twp)	49411
Grant, *Mecosta* (Twp)	49307
Grant, *Oceana* (Twp)	49452
Grant, *St. Clair* (Twp)	48032
Grant, *Newaygo*	49327
Grant Center	49307
Grape	48162
Grass Lake, *Gladwin*	48624
Grass Lake, *Jackson*	49240
Gratiot (Part of Detroit)‡	48207
Grattan	48809
Gravel Lake	49065
Grawn	49637
Grayling	49738
Greater Galesburg♦	49053
Great Lake Beach	48450
Great Western (Part of Crystal Falls)	49920
Greeley	49753
Green, *Alpena* (Twp)	49753
Green, *Mecosta* (Twp)	49338
Green, *Ontonagon*	49953
Greenbush, *Clinton* (Twp)	48833
Greenbush, *Alcona*	48738
Greendale (Twp)	48883
Greenfield Village (Part of Dearborn)	48124
Green Lake, *Grand Traverse* (Twp)	49643
Green Lake, *Allegan*	49316
Greenland	49929
Greenleaf (Twp)	48726
Greenmead (Part of Livonia)‡	48153
Green Oak (Twp)	48116
Green River	49659
Green Road (Part of Ann Arbor)‡	48113
Greenville	48838
Greenwood, *Clare* (Twp)	48625
Greenwood, *Oceana* (Twp)	49412

Greenwood, *Oscoda* (Twp) 49756
Greenwood, *St. Clair* (Twp) 48006
Greenwood, *Wexford* (Twp) 49663
Greenwood, *Marquette* 49849
Greenwood, *Ogemaw* 48610
Gregory 48137
Greilickville♦ 49684
Gresham 48813
Grim (Twp) 48652
Grindstone City 48467
Groos 49837
Gros Cap 49781
Grosse Ile♦ 48138
Grosse Pointe (Twp) 48236
Grosse Pointe 48230
48236
For specific ZIP Codes call (888) 275-8777, or your local postmaster.
Grosse Pointe Farms 48230
Grosse Pointe Park 48230
Grosse Pointe Shores 48230
Grosse Pointe Woods 48230
Grosvenor 49228
Grout (Twp) 48624
Groveland (Twp) 48462
Gulliver 49840
Gull Lake 49083
Gunplain (Twp) 49080
Gustin (Twp) 48740
Gwinn♦ 49841
Hadley (Twp) 48455
Hadley 48440
Hagar (Twp) 49038
Hagar Shores♦ 49039
Hagensville 49779
Hagerman Lake 49935
Haight (Twp) 49912
Hale 48739
Halfway Corners 48441
Hamburg 48139
Hamilton, *Clare* (Twp) 48625
Hamilton, *Gratiot* (Twp) 48847
Hamilton, *Van Buren* (Twp) 49045
Hamilton, *Allegan* 49419
Hamlin, *Eaton* (Twp) 48827
Hamlin, *Mason* (Twp) 49431
Hammond Bay 49759
Hampton (Twp) 48732
Hampton Village Centre (Part of Rochester Hills) 48308
Hamtramck 48212
Hancock 49930
Handy (Twp) 48836
Hannah 49649
Hannahville Indian Community 49896
Hanover, *Wexford* (Twp) 49620
Hanover, *Jackson* 49241
Hansen 49858
Harbert 49115
Harbor Beach 48441
Harbor Point 49740
Harbor Springs 49740
Harbor View 49777
Hardwood 49807
Haring (Twp) 49601
Harlan 49625
Harlem 49424
Harper (Part of Detroit)‡ 48213
Harper Woods 48225
Harrietta 49638
Harris 49845
Harrisburg 49451
Harrison, *Macomb* (Twp) 48045
Harrison, *Clare* 48625
Harrison Beach 49854
Harrison Township♦ 48045
Harrisville 48740
Harsens Island 48028
Hart 49420
Hartford 49057
Hartland 48353
Hartwick (Twp) 49631
Harvard 49319
Harvey♦ 49855
Haslett♦ 48840
Hastings 49058
Hotmaker 49036
Hatton (Twp) 48625

Hautala Corner 49938
Hawes (Twp) 48742
Hawkhead 49416
Hawkins 49677
Hawks 49743
Hay (Twp) 48624
Hayes, *Charlevoix* (Twp) 49720
Hayes, *Clare* (Twp) 48625
Hayes, *Otsego* (Twp) 49735
Haynes (Twp) 48742
Hazel 49958
Hazelhurst 49115
Hazel Park 48030
Hazelton (Twp) 48433
Heath (Twp) 49419
Hebron (Twp) 49755
Helena, *Antrim* (Twp) 49612
Helena, *Huron* 48441
Hell 48169
Helmer 49853
Helps 49873
Hemans 48426
Hematite (Twp) 49903
Hemlock♦ 48626
Henderson, *Wexford* (Twp) 49601
Henderson, *Shiawassee* 48841
Hendricks (Twp) 49762
Henrietta (Twp) 49259
Henrietta Station 49259
Herman 49946
Hermansville 49847
Herron 49744
Hersey 49639
Hesperia 49421
Hessel 49745
Hetherton 49751
Hiawatha (Twp) 49854
Hickory Corners 49060
Higgins (Twp) 48653
Higgins Lake 48627
Highland, *Oakland* (Twp) 48356
Highland, *Osceola* (Twp) 49665
Highland, *Oakland* 48356-57
For specific ZIP Codes call (888) 275-8777, or your local postmaster.
Highland Lakes 48167
Highland Park, Kalamazoo 49083
Highland Park, *Wayne* 48203
Highway 49913
Hi Hill Villa 48360
Hill (Twp) 48739
Hillcrest 49938
Hillcrest Orchard 48145
Hilliards 49328
Hillman 49746
Hillsdale 49242
Hinchman 49103
Hinton (Twp) 48850
Hockaday 48624
Hodunk 49094
Holland, *Missaukee* (Twp) 48632
Holland, *Ottawa* (Twp) 49423
Holland, *Ottawa* 49422-24
For specific ZIP Codes call (888) 275-8777, or your local postmaster.
Holloway 49229
Holly 48442
Holmes (Twp) 49821
Holt♦ 48842
Holton 49425
Home, *Montcalm* (Twp) 48829
Home, *Newaygo* (Twp) 49309
Home Acres (Part of Wyoming) 49508
Homer, *Midland* (Twp) 48640
Homer, *Calhoun* 49245
Homestead, *Benzie* (Twp) 49640
Homestead, *Chippewa* 49783
Hongore Bay 49765
Honor 49640
Hooper 49080
Hope, *Barry* (Twp) 49058
Hope, *Midland* 48628
Hopkins 49328
Hopkinsburg 49328
Hopwood Acres 48912

Horton, *Ogemaw* (Twp) 48661
Horton, *Jackson* 49246
Houghton, *Keweenaw* (Twp) 49924
Houghton, *Houghton* 49931
Houghton Lake♦ 48629
Houghton Lake Heights 48630
Houghton Point 48629
Howard (Twp) 49120
Howard City 49329
Howardsville 49067
Howell (Twp) 48843
Howell 48843*
48844†
Hoxeyville 49601
Hubbard Lake 49747
Hubbardston 48845
Hubbell♦ 49934
Hudson, *Charlevoix* (Twp) 49730
Hudson, *Lenawee* (Twp) 49247
Hudson, *Mackinac* (Twp) 49762
Hudson, *Lenawee* 49247
Hudsonville 49426
Hulbert 49748
Humboldt (Twp) 49814
Hume (Twp) 48467
Hunters Creek 48446
Huntington Woods 48070
Huron, *Huron* (Twp) 48467
Huron, *Wayne* (Twp) 48164
Huron City 48467
Huron Gardens 48341
Huronia Heights 48450
Huron Mountain 49808
Hurontown 49931
Hyde 49807
Ida 48140
Idlewild 49642
Imlay (Twp) 48444
Imlay City 48444
Imperial Heights 49861
Ina 49688
Independence (Twp) 48346
Indianfield (Part of Portage) 49081
Indianfields (Twp) 48723
Indian Lake 49047
Indian River 49749
Indiantown 48601
Ingalls 49848
Ingallston 49858
Ingersoll (Twp) 48623
Ingham (Twp) 48819
Ingleside 49755
Inkster 48141
Inland (Twp) 49643
Inland Corners 49643
Interior (Twp) 49967
Interlochen 49643
Inverness (Twp) 49721
Inwood (Twp) 49817
Ionia 48846
Iosco (Twp) 48836
Ira (Twp) 48023
Iron Mountain 49801
Iron River 49935
Irons 49644
Ironton 49720
Ironwood 49938
Irving 49058
Isabella, *Isabella* (Twp) 48878
Isabella, *Delta* 49878
Isabella Indian Reservation 48858
Isadore 49621
Ishpeming 49849
Ithaca 48847
Iva 48626
Ivanrest (Part of Grandville) 49418
Jackson 49201-04
For specific ZIP Codes call (888) 275-8777, or your local postmaster.
Jacobsville 49945
Jam 48637
James (Twp) 48609
Jamestown (Twp) 49426
Jamestown 49427
Jasper, *Midland* (Twp) 48880
Jasper, *Lenawee* 49248
Jeddo 48032
Jefferson, *Cass* (Twp) 49112
Jefferson, *Hillsdale* (Twp) 49266

Jefferson, *Jackson* 49230
Jefferson (Part of Detroit)‡ 48214
Jenison♦ 49428*
49429†
Jennings 49651
Jericho Corners 49090
Jerome, *Midland* (Twp) 48657
Jerome, *Hillsdale* 49249
Jessieville (Part of Ironwood) 49938
Johannesburg 49751
Johnstown (Twp) 49050
Johnswood 49726
Jones 49061
Jonesfield (Twp) 48637
Jonesville 49250
Joppa 49051
Jordan (Twp) 49729
Joyfield, *Benzie* (Twp) 49616
Joyfield (Part of Detroit)‡ 48228
Juddville 48817
Jugville 49349
Juhl 48453
Juniata (Twp) 48768
Juniata 48744
Kaiserville 48137
Kalamazoo (Twp) 49004
Kalamazoo 49001-09
49019
For specific ZIP Codes call (888) 275-8777, or your local postmaster.
Kalamo 49096
Kaleva 49645
Kalkaska 49646
Karlin 49643
Kasson (Twp) 49664
Kawkawlin 48631
Kearney (Twp) 49615
Kearsarge 49942
Keego Harbor 48320
Keeler 49057
Keene (Twp) 48881
Kegomic 49770
Kellogg 49010
Kelloggsville (Part of Kentwood) 49508
Kellys Corners 49451
Kelsey Lake 49031
Kendall 49062
Kenockee (Twp) 48006
Kensington (Part of Detroit)‡ 48224
Kent City 49330
Kenton 49943
Kentwood 49508
Kerby 48817
Kessington 49112
49130
For specific ZIP Codes call (888) 275-8777, or your local postmaster.
Kewadin 49648
Keweenaw Bay 49908
Kibbie Corners 49090
Killarney Beach 48706
Killmaster 48740
Kilmanagh 48759
Kimball 48074
Kincheloe 49788
Kinde 48445
Kinderhook 49036
King Arthur's Court 48906
Kingsford 49802
Kingsley 49649
Kings Mill 48461
Kingston (Twp) 48729
Kingston 48741
Kinneville 48827
Kinross 49752
Kipling 49837
Kiva 49891
Klacking (Twp) 48654
Klinger Lake 49091
49099
For specific ZIP Codes call (888) 275-8777, or your local postmaster.
Klingville 49916
Kneeland 48647
Knollwood Park 49203
Kochville (Twp) 48604
Koehler (Twp) 49705
Koss 49887
Koylton (Twp) 48741
Krakow (Twp) 49776
La Branche 49873

Lacey 49021
Lachine 49753
Lac La Belle 49950
Lacota 49063
Lafayette (Twp) 48662
Lagoon Beach 48706
La Grange 49031
Laing 48472
Laingsburg 48848
Laird (Twp) 49952
Lake, *Benjie* (Twp) 49640
Lake, *Berrien* (Twp) 49106
Lake, *Huron* (Twp) 48725
Lake, *Lake* (Twp) 49304
Lake, *Macomb* (Twp) 48236
Lake, *Menominee* (Twp) 49821
Lake, *Missaukee* (Twp) 49651
Lake, *Roscommon* (Twp) 48629
Lake, *Clare* 48632
Lake Angeline (Part of Ishpeming) 49849
Lake Angelus 48326
Lake Ann 49650
Lake Charter (Twp) 49640
Lake City 49651
Lake Fenton♦ 48430
Lakefield, *Luce* (Twp) 49853
Lakefield, *Saginaw* (Twp) 48637
Lake George 48633
Lakeland 48143
Lake Lansing 48840
Lake Leelanau 49653
Lake Linden 49945
Lake Margrethe 49738
Lake Mine 49948
Lake Nepessing 48446
Lake Odessa 48849
Lake Orion 48359-62
For specific ZIP Codes call (888) 275-8777, or your local postmaster.
Lake Orion Heights 48361†
48362*
Lake Pleasant 48412
Lakeport 48059
Lake Roland 49968
Lakeside, *Berrien* 49116
Lakeside (Part of Port Austin) 48467
Lakeside (Part of Sterling Heights) 48313
Lakeside Landing 48430
Laketon (Twp) 49445
Laketown (Twp) 49423
Lakeview, *Berrien* 49129
Lakeview, *Montcalm* 48850
Lakeview (Part of Battle Creek) 49015
Lakeview Square (Part of Battle Creek) 49015
Lakeville 48366
Lakewood, *Alpena* 49707
Lakewood, *Kalamazoo* 49002
Lakewood (Part of Luna Pier) 48157
Lakewood Club 49457
Lamar (Part of Wyoming) 49509
Lamb 48027
Lambertville♦ 48144
Lamont 49430
Lamotte (Twp) 48426
Lanewood (Part of Chelsea) 48118
Langston 48888
L'Anse 49946
L'Anse Indian Reservation 55401
Lansing (Twp) 48912
Lansing 48901-33
For specific ZIP Codes call (888) 275-8777, or your local postmaster.
Lapeer 48446
Laporte 48623
Larkin (Twp) 48642
Larson Beach 48762
La Salle 48145
La Salle Gardens 48341
Lathrup Village 48076
Laurel Park Place (Part of Livonia) 48152
Laurium 49913
Lawrence 49064
Lawson 49885
Lawton 49065
Layton Corners 48118

*** Area Zip Code** **† Post Office Boxes** **‡ Postal Station** **♦ Census Designated Place** *Italic Type* **County**

Leaton 48858
Leavitt (Twp) 49459
Lebanon (Twp) 48845
Ledyard (Part of Grand Rapids)‡ 49523
Lee, *Allegan* (Twp) 49450
Lee, *Calhoun* (Twp) 49068
Lee, *Midland* (Twp) 48640
Lee Center 49076
Leelanau (Twp) 49670
Leer 49776
Legrand 49705
Leighton (Twp) 49316
Leisure 49090
Leland 49654
Lemon Park 49097
Lennon 48449
Lennon Green Estates 48449
Lenox (Twp) 48048
Leonard 48367
Leoni 49201
Leonidas 49066
Leota 48625
Leroy, *Calhoun* (Twp) 49051
Leroy, *Ingham* (Twp) 48892
Le Roy, *Osceola* 49655
Leroy, *Presque Isle* 49707
Les Cheneaux Club 49719
Leslie 49251
Lesterville 48002
Level Park 49017
Levering 49755
Lewiston 49756
Lewisville 48468
Lexington 48450
Lexington Heights 48450
Liberty, *Jackson* (Twp) 49234
Liberty, *Wexford* (Twp) 49663
Liberty, *Jackson* 49233
Liberty (Part of Ann Arbor)‡ 48107
Lilley (Twp) 49309
Lima (Twp) 48118
Lima Center 48130
Lime Island 49730
Limestone 49816
Lincoln, *Arenac* (Twp) 48658
Lincoln, *Berrien* (Twp) 49127
Lincoln, *Clare* (Twp) 48633
Lincoln, *Huron* (Twp) 48432
Lincoln, *Isabella* (Twp) 48883
Lincoln, *Midland* (Twp) 48640
Lincoln, *Newaygo* (Twp) 49349
Lincoln, *Osceola* (Twp) 49677
Lincoln, *Alcona* 48742
Lincoln Park (Part of Norton Shores) 49441
Lincoln Park, *Wayne* 48146
Linden 48451
Linkville 48755
Linwood, *Bay* 48634
Linwood (Part of Detroit)‡ 48206
Linwood Beach 48634
Lisbon 49403
Liske 49743
Litchfield 49252
Littlefield (Twp) 49706
Little Lake 49833
Little Point Sable 49455
Little Traverse (Twp) 49740
Livernois (Part of Detroit)‡ 48210
Livingston (Twp) 49735
Livonia 48150-54
For specific ZIP Codes call (888) 275-8777, or your local postmaster.
Livonia Mall (Part of Livonia) 48152
Loch Alpine 48103
Locke (Twp) 48895
Lockport (Twp) 49032
Lockwood 49036
Lodi, *Washtenaw* (Twp) 48103
Lodi, *Kalkaska* 49646
Logan, *Mason* (Twp) 49402
Logan, *Ogemaw* (Twp) 48756
London (Twp) 48159
Long Beach 49858
Long Lake, *Grand Traverse* (Twp) 49684
Long Lake, *Clare* 48625
Long Lake, *Ionia* 48865
Long Lake, *Iosco* 48743
Long Lake Shores 48323
Long Point 49721
Long Rapids 49753
Longrie 49887
Loomis 48617
Loretto 49852
Lost Lake Woods 48762
Loud (Twp) 48619
Lovells 49738
Lowell 49331
Loxley 48629
Lucas 49657
Ludington 49431
Lulu 48140
Lum 48412
Luna Pier 48157
Lupton 48635
Luther 49656
Luzerne 48636
Lyndon (Twp) 48118
Lynn (Twp) 48097
Lyon, *Oakland* (Twp) 48167
Lyon, *Roscommon* (Twp) 48653
Lyon Lake 49068
Lyons 48851
Mabel 49690
Macatawa 49434
McBain 49657
McBrides 48852
McCords 49302
McDonald 49013
McFarlands 49880
McGregor 48427
McIntyre Landing 49738
Mackinac Island 49757
Mackinaw (Twp) 49701
Mackinaw City 49701
McKinley, *Emmet* (Twp) 49769
McKinley, *Huron* (Twp) 48755
McKinley, *Oscoda* 48647
McLean 49412
McLeods Corner 49868
McMillan, *Luce* (Twp) 49868
McMillan, *Ontonagon* (Twp) 49925
McMillan, *Luce* 49853
McMillan Corner 49853
Macomb 48042
48044
For specific ZIP Codes call (888) 275-8777, or your local postmaster.
Macomb Mall (Part of Roseville) 48066
Macon 49236
Madison (Twp) 49221
Madison Center (Part of Madison Heights) 48071
Madison Heights 48071
Mancelona 49659
Manchester 48158
Manistee 49660
Manistique 49854
Manitou Beach, *Lenawee* 49253
Manitou Beach, *Presque Isle* 49779
Manlius (Twp) 49408
Manning 49721
Mansfield 49920
Manton 49663
Maple (Part of Dearborn)‡ 48126
Maple City 49664
Maple Forest (Twp) 49738
Maple Grove, *Manistee* (Twp) 49645
Maple Grove, *Saginaw* (Twp) 48460
Maple Grove, *Barry* 49073
Maple Grove Corners 49090
Maple Hill 49339
Maple Lake (Part of Paw Paw) 49079
Maple Rapids 48853
Maple Ridge, *Alpena* (Twp) 49707
Maple Ridge, *Delta* (Twp) 49880
Maple Ridge, *Arenac* 48766
Maple River (Twp) 49716
Mapleton, *Grand Traverse* 49686
Mapleton, *Midland* 48640
Maple Valley, *Montcalm* (Twp) 49347
Maple Valley, *Sanilac* (Twp) 48416
Maple Valley, *Roscommon* 48656
Maplewood 49878
Marathon (Twp) 48421
Marcellus 49067
Marengo 49224
Marenisco 49947
Marilla 49625
Marine City 48039
Marion, *Charlevoix* (Twp) 49720
Marion, *Livingston* (Twp) 48843
Marion, *Saginaw* (Twp) 48614
Marion, *Sanilac* (Twp) 48426
Marion, *Osceola* 49665
Marion Springs 48614
Markey 48629
Marlette 48453
Marne 49435
Marquette, *Mackinac* (Twp) 49774
Marquette, *Marquette* 49855
Marshall 49068
Martin 49070
Martiny (Twp) 49342
Marysville 48040
Mason, *Arenac* (Twp) 48766
Mason, *Cass* (Twp) 49112
Mason, *Houghton* 49930
Mason, *Ingham* 48854
Masonville (Twp) 49878
Mass City 49948
Mastodon (Twp) 49902
Matchwood (Twp) 49925
Matherton 48845
Mathias (Twp) 49891
Mattawan 49071
Matteson 49028
Max Myers Addition 49120
Maxton 49726
Maybee 48159
Mayfield, *Grand Traverse* (Twp) 49649
Mayfield, *Lapeer* (Twp) 48446
Mayfield, *Grand Traverse* 49666
Mayflower 49913
Mayville 48744
Maywood 49878
Meade, *Huron* (Twp) 48432
Meade, *Mason* (Twp) 49411
Meade, *Macomb* 48048
Meads Landing 48629
Mears 49436
Meauwataka 49601
Mecosta (Twp) 49346
Mecosta 49332
Medina 49247
Melbourne 48604
Melita 48659
Mellen (Twp) 49848
Melrose (Twp) 49796
Melstrand 49884
Melvin 48454
Melvindale 48122
Memphis 48041
Mendon 49072
Menominee 49858
Menonaqua Beach 49740
Mentha 49055
Mentor, *Cheboygan* (Twp) 49799
Mentor, *Oscoda* (Twp) 48647
Meredith 48624
Meridian (Twp) 48823
Meridian Mall 48864
Merle Beach 48820
Merrill, *Newaygo* (Twp) 49309
Merrill, *Saginaw* 48637
Merriman 49801
Merritt, *Bay* (Twp) 48747
Merritt, *Missaukee* 49667
Merriweather 49947
Merson 49010
Mesick 49668
Metamora 48455
Metropolitan 49801
Metropolitan Airport‡ 48242-44
For specific ZIP Codes call (888) 275-8777, or your local postmaster.
Metz 49776
Meyer (Twp) 49847
Miami Park 49090
Michelson 48629
Michiana 49117
Michigamme 49861
Michigan Center♦ 49254
Michigan State University (Part of East Lansing) 48824
Michigan State University Residence Halls (Part of East Lansing) 48825
Middlebelt (Part of Romulus) 48174
Middle Branch (Twp) 49665
Middlebury (Twp) 48866
Middleton 48856
Middletown♦ 48817
Middle Village 49737
Middleville 49333
Midland (Twp) 48642
Midland 48640-42
For specific ZIP Codes call (888) 275-8777, or your local postmaster.
Midland Park 49060
Mikado 48745
Milan, *Monroe* (Twp) 48160
Milan, *Washtenaw* 48160
Milford (Twp) 48381
Milford 48380-81
For specific ZIP Codes call (888) 275-8777, or your local postmaster.
Millbrook 49310
Millburg 49022
Millecoquins 49827
Millen (Twp) 48705
Millersburg 49759
Millers Corners 49633
Millett 48917
Milleville Beach 48173
Mill Grove 49010
Millington 48746
Mill Lake 49055
Mills, *Midland* (Twp) 48652
Mills, *Ogemaw* (Twp) 48756
Mills, *Houghton* 49934
Mills, *Sanilac* 48427
Millville 49285
Milnes 49250
Milton, *Antrim* (Twp) 49648
Milton, *Cass* (Twp) 49120
Minards Mill 49269
Minden (Twp) 48456
Minden City 48456
Mineral Hills 49935
Minor Beach 49854
Mio♦ 48647
Missaukee Park 49651
Mitchell (Twp) 48728
Moddersville 48632
Moffatt (Twp) 48610
Mohawk 49950
Moline 49335
Moltke (Twp) 49779
Monitor (Twp) 48706
Monongahela Location 49920
Monroe, *Monroe* (Twp) 48161-62
For specific ZIP Codes call (888) 275-8777, or your local postmaster.
Monroe, *Newaygo* (Twp) 49349
Monroe, *Monroe* 48161-62
For specific ZIP Codes call (888) 275-8777, or your local postmaster.
Monroe Center 49637
Montague 49437
Montcalm (Twp) 48838
Monterey (Twp) 49010
Monterey Center 49010
Montgomery 49255
Montmorency (Twp) 49746
Montrose 48457
Moore (Twp) 48471
Moore Park 49093
Moores Junction 48659
Moorestown 49651
Mooreville 48160
Moorland 49451
Moran (Twp) 49781
Moran 49760
Morenci 49256
Morgan 49073
Morgan Corners 49017
Morley 49336
Morrice 48857
Morseville 48415
Morton (Twp) 49332
Moscow 49257
Mosherville 49258
Mosherville Station 49250
Mottley 49952
Mott Park (Part of Flint)‡ 48504
Mottville 49099
Mound Spring 49091
Mountain Beach 49460
Mount Clemens 48043
Mount Clemens Southeast 48043
Mount Elliott (Part of Detroit)‡ 48234
Mount Forest 48650
Mount Haley (Twp) 48637
Mount Morris 48458
Mount Pleasant, *Allegan* 49090
Mount Pleasant, *Isabella* 48804†
48858*
Mount Vernon 48306
Mueller (Twp) 49840
Muir 48860
Mullet Lake 49761
Mullett (Twp) 49791
Mulliken 48861
Mundy (Twp) 48507
Munger 48747
Munising (Twp) 49895
Munising 49862
Munith 49259
Munro (Twp) 49755
Munson 49256
Muskegon (Twp) 49445
Muskegon 49440-45
For specific ZIP Codes call (888) 275-8777, or your local postmaster.
Muskegon Heights 49444
Muskegon Mall (Part of Muskegon) 49440
Mussey (Twp) 48014
Muttonville (Part of Richmond) 48062
Nadeau 49863
Nagel Corner 49743
Nahma 49864
Napoleon♦ 49261
Nashville 49073
Nathan 49821
National (Part of Crystal Falls) 49920
National City 48748
National Mine 49865
Naubinway 49762
Nazareth (Part of Kalamazoo) 49074
Needmore 48813
Neeley 49080
Negaunee 49866
Nellsville 48629
Nelson, *Kent* (Twp) 49343
Nelson, *Saginaw* 48626
Nessen City 49683
Nester (Twp) 48624
Nestoria 49861
New Allouez 49901
Newark, *Gratiot* (Twp) 48847
Newark, *Oakland* 48442
Newaygo 49337
New Baltimore 48047
48051
For specific ZIP Codes call (888) 275-8777, or your local postmaster.
Newberg (Twp) 49061
Newberry 49868
New Boston 48164
New Bristol Location 49920
New Buffalo 49117
New Era 49446
Newfield (Twp) 49421
New Greenleaf 48726
New Haven, *Gratiot* (Twp) 48889
New Haven, *Shiawassee* (Twp) 48867
New Haven, *Macomb* 48048
48050
For specific ZIP Codes call (888) 275-8777, or your local postmaster.
New Holland 49424
New Hudson 48165
Newkirk (Twp) 49656
New Lothrop 48460
Newport 48166
New Richmond 49408
New Salem 49315
New Swanzy 49841

Place	ZIP
Newton, *Calhoun* (Twp)	49017
Newton, *Mackinac* (Twp)	49838
New Troy	49119
Nicholsville	49067
Niles	49120
Nirvana	49623
Nisula	49952
Noble (Twp)	49028
Noordeloos	49424
Norman (Twp)	49689
North Adams	49262
North Allis (Twp)	49765
North Bay City	48706
North Bell	48815
North Blendon	49426
North Bradley	48618
North Branch	48461
North Dorr	49323
Northeast (Part of Burton)	48509
Northeast (Part of Grand Rapids)‡	49505
	49515
	49525
For specific ZIP Codes call (888) 275-8777, or your local postmaster.	
Northeast (Part of Livonia)‡	48152
North End (Part of Detroit)‡	48202
North Epworth	49431
Northfield (Twp)	48189
Northgate	49505
North Kent Mall	49525
North Lake, *Lapeer*	48464
North Lake, *Marquette*	49849
North Lake, *Van Buren*	49055
North Lakeport	48059
Northland	49869
Northland Shopping Center (Part of Southfield)	48075
North Manitou	49654
North Morenci	49256
North Muskegon	49445
North Paynesville	49912
North Plains (Twp)	48845
Northport	49670
Northport Point	49670
North Shade (Twp)	48856
North Shore	49022
North Shores	48145
Northside (Part of Flint)‡	48505
North Star	48862
North Street	48049
Northview♦	49525
Northville, *Kent*	49525
Northville, *Wayne*	48167
Northville Commons	48167
Northwest (Part of Grand Rapids)‡	49504
Northwestern (Part of Detroit)‡	48204
North Wheeler	48662
Northwood	49004
Norton Shores	49441
Norvell	49263
Norwalk	49660
Norway (Twp)	49892
Norway	49870
Norwich, *Missaukee* (Twp)	49651
Norwich, *Newaygo* (Twp)	49307
Norwood	49720
Nottawa, *Isabella* (Twp)	48858
Nottawa, *St. Joseph*	49075
Novesta (Twp)	48729
Novi (Twp)	48375
Novi	48374-77
For specific ZIP Codes call (888) 275-8777, or your local postmaster.	
Novi Town Center (Part of Novi)	48375
Nunda (Twp)	49799
Nunica	49448
Oakfield (Twp)	48838
Oak Grove, *Livingston*	48863
Oak Grove, *Otsego*	49735
Oak Grove, *Roscommon*	48653
Oak Hill	49660
Oakhurst	48701
Oakland, *Oakland* (Twp)	48363
Oakland, *Allegan*	49419
Oakley	48649
Oak Manor	49120
Oak Park, *Calhoun*	49017
Oak Park, *Oakland*	48237
Oak Shade Park	49230
Oakville	48160
Oakwood, *Oakland*	48371
Oakwood, *St. Joseph*	49099
Oakwood (Part of Melvindale)	48122
Oceola (Twp)	48843
Ocqueoc	49759
Oden	49764
Odessa (Twp)	48849
Odgers Location	49920
Ogden (Twp)	49228
Ogden Center	49228
Ogemaw (Twp)	48661
Ogemaw Springs	48661
Oil City	48883
Okemos♦	48805†
	48864*
Old Mission	49673
Old Redford (Part of Detroit)‡	48219
Olive, *Clinton* (Twp)	48879
Olive, *Ottawa* (Twp)	49460
Olive Center	49424
Olive Hills	49460
Oliver, *Huron* (Twp)	48731
Oliver, *Kalkaska* (Twp)	49646
Olivet	49076
Olson	48640
Omena	49674
Omer	48749
Onaway	49765
Oneida (Twp)	48837
Onekama	49675
Onondaga	49264
Onota	49822
Onsted	49265
Ontonagon	49953
Ontwa (Twp)	49112
Orange, *Ionia* (Twp)	48846
Orange, *Kalkaska* (Twp)	49646
Orangeville	49080
Orchard	49776
Orchard Beach	49721
Orchard Lake	48323-24
For specific ZIP Codes call (888) 275-8777, or your local postmaster.	
Orchard Park (Part of Battle Creek)	49017
Orchard Point	49707
Oregon (Twp)	48446
Orient (Twp)	49679
Orion (Twp)	48360-62
For specific ZIP Codes call (888) 275-8777, or your local postmaster.	
Orleans	48865
Oronoko (Twp)	49103
Ortonville	48462
Osceola, *Osceola* (Twp)	49631
Osceola, *Houghton*	49913
Oscoda♦	48750
	48753
For specific ZIP Codes call (888) 275-8777, or your local postmaster.	
Oshtemo	49077
Osier	49878
Oskar	49931
Osseo	49266
Ossineke (Twp)	49747
Ossineke♦	49766
Otisco (Twp)	48809
Otisville	48463
Otsego	49078
Otsego Lake	49735
Ottawa Beach	49423
Ottawa Center	49404
Ottawa Lake	49267
Otter	49952
Otterburn (Part of Swartz Creek)	48473
Otter Lake	48464
Otto (Twp)	49421
Overisel	49423
Oviatt	49650
Ovid, *Branch* (Twp)	49036
Ovid, *Clinton*	48866
Owasippe	49457
Owendale	48754
Owosso	48867
Owosso Junction (Part of Owosso)	48867
Oxbow	49126
Oxford (Twp)	48371
Oxford	48370-71
For specific ZIP Codes call (888) 275-8777, or your local postmaster.	
Ozark	49760
Paavola	49930
Painesdale	49955
Paint Creek	48191
Palestine	49887
Palisades Park	49043
Palmer	49871
Palms	48465
Palmyra	49268
Palo	48870
Paradise, *Grand Traverse* (Twp)	49649
Paradise, *Chippewa*	49768
Parchment	49004
Paris, *Huron* (Twp)	48470
Paris, *Mecosta*	49338
Parisville	48470
Park, *Ottawa* (Twp)	49423
Park, *St. Joseph* (Twp)	49093
Parkdale	49660
Park Grove (Part of Detroit)‡	48205
Park Lake, *Clinton*	48808
Park Lake, *Osceola*	49665
Park Plaza (Part of Lincoln Park)‡	48146
Park Shore Resort	49031
Parkville	49093
Parma (Twp)	49224
Parma	49269
Parnell	49301
Parshallville	48430
Partello	49076
Patterson Gardens	48161
Patterson Lake	48169
Paulding	49912
Pavilion (Twp)	49088
Paw Paw	49079
Paw Paw Lake♦	49038
Payment	49783
Paynesville	49912
Peacock	49644
Peaine (Twp)	49782
Pearl	49408
Pearl Beach, *Branch*	49036
Pearl Beach, *St. Clair*♦	48001
Pearl Grange	49022
Peck	48466
Pelkie	49958
Pellston	49769
Peninsula (Twp)	49686
Penn	49031
Pennellwood	49103
Pennfield	49017
Penobscot (Part of Detroit)‡	48226-28
For specific ZIP Codes call (888) 275-8777, or your local postmaster.	
Pentland (Twp)	49868
Pentoga	49920
Pentwater	49449
Pequaming	49946
Pere Marquette (Twp)	49431
Perkins	49872
Perrinton	48871
Perronville	49873
Perry	48872
Perry Acres	48360
Perry Lake Heights	48462
Peshawbestown	49682
Peters	48039
Petersburg	49270
Petoskey	49770
Pewabic	49930
Pewamo	48873
Phelps	49720
Phillipsville	49805
Phoenix, *Keweenaw*	49950
Phoenix (Part of Pontiac)‡	48342
Pickford	49774
Pier Cove	49090
Pierport	49614
Pierson	49339
Pigeon	48755
Pinckney	48169
Pinconning	48650
Pine (Twp)	48888
Pine Bluffs	48653
Pine Creek	49051
Pine Grove	49055
Pine River, *Gratiot* (Twp)	48801
Pine River, *Arenac*	48658
Pine Run	48420
Pine Stump Junction	49868
Piney Woods	48625
Pinnebog	48445
Pinora (Twp)	49677
Pioneer (Twp)	49651
Pipestone (Twp)	49111
Pittsburg	48867
Pittsfield	48108
	48197
For specific ZIP Codes call (888) 275-8777, or your local postmaster.	
Pittsford	49271
Plainfield, *Iosco* (Twp)	48739
Plainfield, *Kent* (Twp)	49321
Plainfield, *Livingston*	48137
Plainfield Heights	49525
Plainwell	49080
Platte (Twp)	49640
Pleasant Lake, *Hillsdale*	49266
Pleasant Lake, *Jackson*	49272
Pleasant Lake, *Washtenaw*	48158
Pleasanton (Twp)	49614
Pleasant Plains (Twp)	49304
Pleasant Ridge	48069
Pleasant Valley	48880
Pleasant View	49740
Plymouth (Part of Wakefield)	49968
Plymouth, *Wayne*	48170
Plymouth Township♦	48170
Pogy	49639
Point Au Gres	48703
Pointe Aux Barques	48467
Pointe aux Peaux Farms	48166
Pointe aux Pins	49775
Point Mills	49922
Point Nipigon	49721
Pokagon	49047
Polaski	49776
Polkton (Twp)	49404
Pomona	49625
Pompeii	48874
Ponchartrain Shores	49781
Ponshewaing	49706
Pontiac	48340-43
For specific ZIP Codes call (888) 275-8777, or your local postmaster.	
Portage, *Houghton* (Twp)	49921
Portage, *Mackinac* (Twp)	49820
Portage, *Kalamazoo*	49081
Portage Entry	49916
Portage Lake	48169
Port Austin	48467
Port Austin Air Force Station	48467
Porter, *Cass* (Twp)	49042
Porter, *Midland* (Twp)	48615
Porter, *Van Buren* (Twp)	49065
Port Gypsum (Part of Tawas City)	48763
Port Hope	48468
Port Huron (Twp)	48060
Port Huron	48060*
	48061†
Portland	48875
Port Sanilac	48469
Port Sheldon	49460
Portsmouth (Twp)	48708
Posen	49776
Poseyville	48640
Potters Lake	48423
Potterville	48876
Powell (Twp)	49808
Powers	49874
Prairie Ronde (Twp)	49087
Prairieville (Twp)	49080
Prairieville	49046
Prattville	49271
Prescott	48756
Presque Isle	49777
Princeton	49841
Prosper	49632
Prudenville♦	48651
Pulaski	49241
Pulawski (Twp)	49776
Pullman	49450
Putnam (Twp)	48169
Putney Corners	49635
Quanicassee	48733
Quarry	48720
Quimby	49058
Quincy, *Hougton* (Twp)	49930
Quincy, *Branch*	49082
Quinnesec♦	49876
Rabbit Bay	49945
Rabbits Back	49781
Raber	49736
Raco	49715
Rainy Beach	49765
Raisin (Twp)	49221
Raisinville (Twp)	48161-62
For specific ZIP Codes call (888) 275-8777, or your local postmaster.	
Ralph	49877
Rambaultown	49913
Ramona Park	49740
Ramsay	49959
Ranch Acres	49456
Randall Lake	49036
Randville	49801
Rankin	48473
Ransom	49266
Rapid City	49676
Rapid River, *Kalkaska* (Twp)	49659
Rapid River, *Delta*	49878
Rapson	48413
Rathbone	48615
Ravenna	49451
Ravenswood	48917
Ray, *Macomb* (Twp)	48096
Ray, *Branch*	46737
Ray Center	48096
Raymond Corners	49656
Reading	49274
Readmond (Twp)	49723
Redding (Twp)	48625
Redford♦	48239-40
For specific ZIP Codes call (888) 275-8777, or your local postmaster.	
Redman	48468
Red Oak	49756
Red Park	49660
Redridge	49905
Reed City	49677
Reeder (Twp)	49651
Reeds Lake (Part of East Grand Rapids)	49506
Reeman	49412
Reese	48757
Regional Shopping Center	48043
Remus	49340
Renaissance Center (Part of Detroit)‡	48243
Reno (Twp)	48770
Republic (Twp)	49879
Republic	49879
Rescue	48735
Resort (Twp)	49770
Rexton	49762
Reynolds (Twp)	49329
Rhodes	48652
Rice	49616
Rich (Twp)	48744
Richfield, *Genesee* (Twp)	48423
Richfield, *Roscommon* (Twp)	48656
Richfield Center	48423
Richland, *Missaukee* (Twp)	49657
Richland, *Montcalm* (Twp)	48891
Richland, *Ogemaw* (Twp)	48756
Richland, *Saginaw* (Twp)	48626
Richland, *Kalamazoo*	49083
Richmond, *Macomb* (Twp)	48062
Richmond, *Marquette* (Twp)	49871
Richmond, *Osceola* (Twp)	49677
Richmond, *Macomb*	48062
Richmondville	48427
Richville	48758
Ridgeway	49275
Riga	49276
Riley, *Clinton*	48879
Riley, *St. Clair* (Twp)	48041
Riley Center	48041
Ripley	49930

*** Area Zip Code** **† Post Office Boxes** **‡ Postal Station** **♦ Census Designated Place** *Italic Type* **County**

Riverdale 48877
River Rouge 48218
Riverside, *Missaukee* (Twp) 49657
Riverside, *Berrien* 49084
Riverton (Twp) 49454
Riverview 48192
Rives (Twp) 49277
Rives Junction 49277
Roaring Brook 49740
Roberts Corners 49868
Roberts Landing 48001
Robinson 49460
Rochester 48306-09
For specific ZIP Codes call (888) 275-8777, or your local postmaster.
Rochester Hills 48306-07
48309
For specific ZIP Codes call (888) 275-8777, or your local postmaster.
Rock 49880
Rockford 49341
Rockland 49960
Rock River (Twp) 49825
Rockwood 48173
Rodney 49342
Rogers (Twp) 49779
Rogers City 49779
Roger's Plaza (Part of Wyoming) 49509
Rolland (Twp) 49310
Rolland Center 49310
Rollin 49278
Rome (Twp) 49221
Rome Center 49221
Romeo 48065
Romulus 48174
Ronald (Twp) 48846
Rondo 49799
Roosevelt Park 49441
Roscommon 48653
Rose, *Oakland* (Twp) 48442
Rose, *Ogemaw* (Twp) 48654
Roseburg 48097
Rosebush 48878
Rose Center 48442
Rose City 48654
Rosedale 49783
Rose Island 48759
Rose Lake (Twp) 49655
Roseville 48066
Ross (Twp) 49012
Rothbury 49452
Round Lake, *Emmet* 49740
Round Lake, *Mason* 49410
Rousseau 49948
Rowes Corner 48158
Roxand (Twp) 48837
Royal Oak (Twp) 48220
Royal Oak 48067-68
48073
For specific ZIP Codes call (888) 275-8777, or your local postmaster.
Royal Oak Beach 49721
Royalton (Twp) 49085
Rubicon (Twp) 48468
Ruby 48027
Rudyard 49780
Rumely 49826
Rush (Twp) 48841
Rush Lake 48169
Rusk 49464
Russell Island 48001
Russellville 48423
Rust 49746
Rustford 49336
Ruth 48470
Rutland (Twp) 49058
Sac Bay 49835
Saddle Lake 49056
Saganing 48658
Sage (Twp) 48624
Saginaw (Twp) 48603
Saginaw 48601-09
For specific ZIP Codes call (888) 275-8777, or your local postmaster.
Saginaw Township North♦ 48603
Saginaw Township South♦ 48603
Sagola 49881
St. Anthony 48182
St. Charles 48655
St. Clair 48079
St. Clair Shores 48080-82
For specific ZIP Codes call (888) 275-8777, or your local postmaster.
St. Helen♦ 48656
St. Ignace 49781
St. Jacques 49878
St. James 49782
St. Johns 48879
St. Joseph (Twp) 49022
St. Joseph 49085
St. Louis 48880
St. Marys Lake 49017
St. Nicholas 49880
Salom, *Allegan* (Twp) 49314
Salem, *Washtenaw* (Twp) 48178
Salem, *Washtenaw* 48175
Saline (Twp) 49236
Saline 48176
Salisbury (Part of Ishpeming) 49849
Samaria 48177
Sanborn (Twp) 49766
Sand Beach (Twp) 48441
Sand Creek 49279
Sand Lake, *Iosco* 48748
Sand Lake, *Kent* 49343
Sand River 49822
Sands 49841
Sandstone (Twp) 49201
Sandusky 48471
Sandy Beach 49091
Sanford 48657
Sanilac (Twp) 48469
San Souci Beach 49036
Santiago 48765
Saranac 48881
Sauble (Twp) 49402
Sauble Station 49402
Saugatuck 49453
Sault Ste. Marie 49783
Sault Ste. Marie Air Force Station 49783
Sault Ste. Marie Indian Reservation 49783
Sawyer 49125
Sawyer Lake 49815
Schaffer 49807
Schoolcraft, *Houghton* (Twp) 49934
Schoolcraft, *Kalamazoo* 49087
Schuck Island 48759
Schultz 49058
Scio (Twp) 48130
Sciota (Twp) 48848
Scipio (Twp) 49250
Scottdale 49085
Scott Lake 49927
Scotts 49088
Scottville 49454
Sears 49679
Sears Lincoln Park Shopping Center (Part of Lincoln Park) 48146
Sebewa (Twp) 48875
Sebewaing 48759
Secord (Twp) 48624
Segwun 49331
Seidler 48611
Selfridge Air National Guard Base 48045
Selkirk 48661
Selma (Twp) 49601
Seneca 49280
Seneca Location 49950
Seney 49883
Senter 49922
Seven Harbors 48356
Seven Oaks (Part of Detroit)‡ 48235
Seville (Twp) 48832
Seymour Square (Part of Grand Rapids)‡ 49510
Shabbona 48426
Shady Shores 48635
Shadyside 49266
Shafer Location 49920
Shaftsburg 48882
Shaldas Corner 49664
Shanghai Corners 49111
Sharon, *Kalkaska* 49633
Sharon, *Washtenaw* (Twp) 48158
Sharon Hollow 48158
Sharps Corners 48653
Shawnee Shores 49036
Shelby, *Macomb* (Twp) 48315-18
For specific ZIP Codes call (888) 275-8777, or your local postmaster.
Shelby, *Oceana* 49455
Shelbyville 49344
Sheldon 48111
Shepardsville 48866
Shepherd 48883
Sheridan, *Calhoun* (Twp) 49224
Sheridan, *Clare* (Twp) 48617
Sheridan, *Huron* (Twp) 48413
Sheridan, *Mason* (Twp) 49410
Sheridan, *Mecosta* (Twp) 49305
Sheridan, *Newaygo* (Twp) 49412
Sheridan, *Montcalm* 48884
Sherman, *Gladwin* (Twp) 48624
Sherman, *Huron* (Twp) 48456
Sherman, *Iosco* (Twp) 48748
Sherman, *Isabella* (Twp) 48632
Sherman, *Keweenaw* (Twp) 49945
Sherman, *Mason* (Twp) 49410
Sherman, *Newaygo* (Twp) 49412
Sherman, *Osceola* (Twp) 49688
Sherman, *St. Joseph* (Twp) 49091
Sherman, *Wexford* 49668
Sherman City 48632
Sherwood 49089
Sherwood Corners 48647
Shiawassee (Twp) 48429
Shiawasseetown 48429
Shields♦ 48609
Shiloh 48865
Shingleton 49884
Shoreham 49085
Shore Line Junction (Part of Hancock) 49930
Shorewood Hills 49125
Sibley (Part of Trenton) 48183
Sidnaw 49961
Sidney 48885
Sid Town 48750
Sigel (Twp) 48441
Sigma 49646
Silver City 49953
Silver Creek (Twp) 49047
Silverwood 48760
Simar 49948
Sims (Twp) 48703
Sister Lakes 49047
Sitka 49412
Six Lakes 48886
Skandia 49885
Skanee 49962
Skeels 48624
Skidway Lake♦ 48756
Slagle (Twp) 49638
Slapneck 49816
Sleepy Hollow 49912
Slocum 49451
Smith Corners 49420
Smiths Creek 48074
Smyrna 48887
Snover 48472
Snyderville 48063
Sodus 49126
Sokol Camp 49117
Solon, *Kent* (Twp) 49319
Solon, *Leelanau* 49621
Somerset 49281
Somerset Center 49282
Somerset Collection, The (Part of Troy) 48084
Sonoma 49017
Soo (Twp) 49783
South Airport 49696
South Arm (Twp) 49727
South Blendon 49426
South Boardman 49680
South Branch, *Crawford* (Twp) 48653
South Branch, *Wexford* (Twp) 49601
South Branch, *Ogemaw* 48761
South Butler 49082
Southeast (Part of Burton) 48519
Southfield (Twp) 48009
Southfield 48034
48037
48075-76
48086
For specific ZIP Codes call (888) 275-8777, or your local postmaster.
South Flint Plaza (Part of Flint) 48507
Southgate 48195
Southgate Shopping Center (Part of Southgate) 48192
South Haven 49090
South Ionia 48846
Southland Center (Part of Taylor) 48180
Southland Mall (Part of Portage) 49081
South Lyon 48178
South Manitou 49654
South Monroe 48161
South Monterey 49010
South Range 49963
South Riley 48820
South Rockwood 48179
Spalding 49886
Sparlingville♦ 48074
Sparr 49735
Sparta 49345
Spaulding (Twp) 48655
Speaker (Twp) 48454
Spencer, *Kent* (Twp) 49326
Spencer, *Kalkaska* 49646
Spinks Corners 49022
Spratt 49753
Spring Arbor♦ 49283
Spring Beach 49031
Springdale (Twp) 49683
Springfield, *Kalkaska* (Twp) 49680
Springfield, *Calhoun* 49015
Springfield, *Oakland* 48346
Springfield Place (Part of Battle Creek) 49015
Spring Grove 49416
Spring Lake 49456
Springport 49284
Springvale (Twp) 49770
Springville, *Wexford* (Twp) 49668
Springville, *Lenawee* 49265
Springwells (Part of Detroit)‡ 48209
Spruce 48762
Spurr (Twp) 49861
Stalwart 49736
Stambaugh (Twp) 49935
Stambaugh 49964
Standale (Part of Walker) 49544
Standish 48658
Stannard (Twp) 49912
Stanton, *Houghton* (Twp) 49931
Stanton, *Montcalm* 48888
Stanwood 49346
Star (Twp) 49611
Star City 49651
Star Corners, *Manistee* 49660
Star Corners, *Menominee* 49887
Starville 48039
Steamburg 49242
Stephenson 49887
Sterling 48659
Sterling Heights 48310-14
For specific ZIP Codes call (888) 275-8777, or your local postmaster.
Steuben 49854
Stevensville 49127
Stockbridge 49285
Stonington 49878
Stony Creek 48197
Stony Lake 49455
Stony Point♦ 48166
Strasburg 48161
Strathmoor (Part of Detroit)‡ 48227
Strawberry Point 49456
Stronach 49660
Strongs 49790
Strongs Corners 49790
Stuart Lake 49068
Sturgeon Point 48740
Sturgis 49091
Stutsmanville 49740
Sugar Island (Twp) 49783
Sugar Rapids 48624
Sullivan 49451
Summerfield, *Clare* (Twp) 48625
Summerfield, *Monroe* (Twp) 49270
Summit, *Jackson* (Twp) 49203
Summit, *Mason* (Twp) 49431
Summit City 49649
Summit Heights 48629
Summit Place 48328
Sumner 48889
Sumnerville 49120
Sumpter (Twp) 48111
Sun 49327
Sunfield 48890
Sunrise Heights 49015
Sunset Beach 49230
Superior, *Chippewa* (Twp) 49715
Superior, *Washtenaw* (Twp) 48197
Surrey (Twp) 48622
Suttons Bay 49682
Swains Lake 49237
Swan Creek 48609
Swanson 49821
Swartz Creek 48473
Swedetown 49913
Sweetwater (Twp) 49304
Sylvan, *Osceola* (Twp) 49631
Sylvan, *Washtenaw* (Twp) 48118
Sylvan Center 48118
Sylvan Lake 48320
Sylvester 49332
Tabor 49126
Talbot 49821
Tallmadge 49544
Tallman 49410
Tamarack 49913
Tapiola 49916
Tawas (Twp) 48763
Tawas City 48763*
48764†
Taylor 48180
Taymouth (Twp) 48417
Teapot Dome 49079
Tecumseh 49286
Tekonsha 49092
Teleford (Part of Dearborn Heights)‡ 48128
Tel-Twelve Mall (Part of Southfield) 48034
Temperance♦ 48182
Temple 48625
Texas (Twp) 49009
Texas Corners 49009
The Fingerboard Corner 49705
The Heights 49230
Theodore 49801
Thetford (Twp) 48420
Thomas, *Saginaw* (Twp) 48609
Thomas, *Oakland* 48371
Thomaston 49968
Thompson 49854
Thompsons Heights 49642
Thompsonville 49683
Thornapple (Twp) 49333
Thornville 48455
Three Lakes 49861
Three Mile Lake 49079
Three Oaks 49128
Three Rivers 49093
Thunder Mountain 49038
Tilden (Twp) 49849
Tipton 49287
Tittabawassee (Twp) 48623
Tobacco (Twp) 48612
Tobico Beach 48706
Tobin Location 49920
Tobins Harbor 55605
Toivola 49965
Tompkins 49277
Topaz 49925
Topinabee 49791
Toquin 49057
Torch Lake, *Antrim* (Twp) 49648
Torch Lake, *Houghton* (Twp) 49934
Torch Lake, *Antrim* 49627
Torch River 49676
Towar Gardens 48823
Tower 49792
Tower Hill 49125
Town Corners 49446
Traunik 49891
Traverse Bay 49945
Traverse City 49684-86
For specific ZIP Codes call (888) 275-8777, or your local postmaster.
Tremaine Corners 48846
Trenary 49891
Trent 49303
Trenton 48183

*** Area Zip Code** **† Post Office Boxes** **‡ Postal Station** **♦ Census Designated Place** *Italic Type* **County**

Place	ZIP Code
Trimountain	49905
Trolley‡	48231-35
For specific ZIP Codes call (888) 275-8777, or your local postmaster.	
Trombly	49880
Trout Creek	49967
Trout Lake	49793
Trowbridge, *Allegan* (Twp)	49010
Trowbridge (Part of East Lansing)	48823
Trowbridge Park♦	49855
Troy, *Newaygo* (Twp)	49309
Troy, *Oakland*	48007
	48083-84
	48098-99
For specific ZIP Codes call (888) 275-8777, or your local postmaster.	
Trufant	49347
Turin (Twp)	49880
Turk Lake	48838
Turner	48765
Turner Shores	49116
Tuscarora (Twp)	49749
Tuscola	48769
Tustin	49688
Twelve Corners	49022
Twining	48766
Twin Lake♦	49457
Twin Lakes, *Cass*	49047
Twin Lakes, *Houghton*	49965
Two Rivers	48858
Tyre	48475
Tyrone, *Kent* (Twp)	49330
Tyrone, *Livingston* (Twp)	48430
Tyrone Lake	48430
Ubly	48475
Unadilla	48137
Union, *Branch* (Twp)	49094
Union, *Grand Traverse* (Twp)	49633
Union, *Isabella* (Twp)	48858
Union, *Cass*	49130
Union City	49094
Union Lake	48387
Union Pier	49129
Unionville	48767
Universal Mall (Part of Warren)	48092
Upjohn (Part of Portage)	49081
Upper Peninsula Mail Processing Center	49802
Urbandale (Part of Battle Creek)	49017
Utica	48315-18
For specific ZIP Codes call (888) 275-8777, or your local postmaster.	
Utopia Beach	49858
Valley (Twp)	49010
Valley Center	48416
Valley Farms	48906
Van	49755
Van Buren (Twp)	48111
Vandalia	49095
Vanderbilt	49795
Vandercook Lake♦	49203
Van Meer	49884
Vantown	48892
Vassar	48768
Venice (Twp)	48817
Vergennes (Twp)	49331
Vermontville	49096
Vernon, *Isabella* (Twp)	48617
Vernon, *Shiawassee* (Twp)	48429
Vernon, *Shiawassee*	48476
Vernon City	48617
Verona (Part of Battle Creek)	49017
Verona (Part of Wakefield)	49968
Verona, *Huron*	48413
Verona Park	49017
Vestaburg	48891
Vevay (Twp)	48854
Vickery Landing	49050
Vickeryville	48884
Vicksburg	49097
Victor (Twp)	48848
Victoria	49960
Victory (Twp)	49454
Vienna, *Genesee* (Twp)	48420
Vienna, *Montmorency*	49751
Virginia Park	49423
Vogel Center	49657
Volinia	49045
Volney	49309
Vriesland	49464
Vulcan	49892
Wabaningo	49463
Wacousta	48837
Wadhams	48074
Wagarville	48624
Wainola	49948
Wakefield	49968
Wakelee	49067
Wakeshma (Twp)	49052
Waldenburg	48044
Waldron	49288
Wales	48027
Walhalla	49458
Walker, *Cheboygan* (Twp)	49705
Walker, *Kent*	49504
Walkers Point	49721
Walkerville	49459
Wallace	49893
Walled Lake	48390-91
For specific ZIP Codes call (888) 275-8777, or your local postmaster.	
Wallin	49683
Wall Lake	49046
Walloon Lake	49796
Walnut Lake	48301
Walnut Point	49068
Walters	48346
Walton (Twp)	49076
Waltz	48164
Wardcliff	48823
Warner (Twp)	49730
Warren, *Midland* (Twp)	48618
Warren, *Macomb*	48089-93
For specific ZIP Codes call (888) 275-8777, or your local postmaster.	
Wasepi	49032
Washington, *Gratiot* (Twp)	48806
Washington, *Sanilac* (Twp)	48401
Washington, *Gratiot*	48094-95
For specific ZIP Codes call (888) 275-8777, or your local postmaster.	
Washington Harbor	55605
Washington Heights (Part of Battle Creek)	49017
Waterford♦	48327-29
For specific ZIP Codes call (888) 275-8777, or your local postmaster.	
Waterloo	49240
Watermill Lake	49642
Waters	49797
Watersmeet	49969
Watertown, *Clinton* (Twp)	48820
Watertown, *Tuscola* (Twp)	48435
Watertown, *Sanilac*	48471
Watervale	49613
Watervliet	49098
Watrousville	48768
Watson	49078
Wattles Park	49014
Watton	49970
Waucedah	49892
Waverly, *Cheboygan* (Twp)	49765
Waverly, *Van Buren* (Twp)	49079
Waverly, *Eaton*♦	48917
Wawatam (Twp)	49701
Wawatam Beach (Part of Mackinaw City)	49701
Wayland	49348
Wayne, *Cass* (Twp)	49047
Wayne, *Wayne*	48184
Weadock	49755
Weale	48720
Weare (Twp)	49420
Webber (Twp)	49304
Webberville	48892
Webster (Twp)	48130
Weesaw (Twp)	49128
Weidman♦	48893
Welcome Corners	49058
Weldon (Twp)	49683
Wellington (Twp)	49753
Wells, *Marquette* (Twp)	49818
Wells, *Tuscola* (Twp)	48723
Wells, *Delta*	49894
Wellston	49689
Wellsville	49228
Wenona Beach	48706
Wequetonsing	49740
West Bloomfield	48322-25
For specific ZIP Codes call (888) 275-8777, or your local postmaster.	
West Bloomfield Township♦	48323-24
For specific ZIP Codes call (888) 275-8777, or your local postmaster.	
West Branch, *Dickinson* (Twp)	49877
West Branch, *Marquette* (Twp)	49885
West Branch, *Missaukee* (Twp)	49667
West Branch, *Ogemaw*	48661
Westchester Village	48301
West Ishpeming	49849
Westland	48185-86
For specific ZIP Codes call (888) 275-8777, or your local postmaster.	
Westland Center (Part of Westland)	48185
West Leroy	49051
West Olive	49460
Weston	49289
Westphalia	48894
West Sebewa	48875
West Side (Part of Saginaw)‡	48603
West Traverse (Twp)	49740
Westville	48888
West Willow	48198
West Windsor	48813
Westwood♦	49006
	49009
	49019
For specific ZIP Codes call (888) 275-8777, or your local postmaster.	
Westwood Heights	48504
Wetmore	49895
Wetzel	49659
Wexford (Twp)	49668
Wheatfield (Twp)	48895
Wheatland, *Hillsdale* (Twp)	49220
Wheatland, *Mecosta* (Twp)	49340
Wheatland, *Sanilac* (Twp)	48427
Wheeler	48662
White	49952
White Cloud	49349
Whitefish (Twp)	49728
Whitefish Point	49768
Whiteford (Twp)	49267
Whiteford Center	49267
Whitehall	49461
White Lake	48383-86
For specific ZIP Codes call (888) 275-8777, or your local postmaster.	
White Oak (Twp)	49285
White Pigeon	49099
White Pine	49971
White River (Twp)	49437
White Rock	48441
Whites Beach	48658
White Star	48624
Whitewater (Twp)	49690
Whitmore Lake♦	48189
Whitney (Twp)	48765
Whitneyville	49302
Whittaker	48190
Whittemore	48770
Wickware	48726
Wilber (Twp)	48730
Wilcox (Twp)	49349
Wildwood, *Cheboygan*	49706
Wildwood, *Manistee*	49614
Willard	48611
Williams (Twp)	48611
Williamsburg	49690
Williamsport	49660
Williamston	48895
Williamsville, *Cass*	49095
Williamsville, *Livingston*	48137
Willis	48191
Willow	48164
Wilmot, *Cheboygan* (Twp)	49799
Wilmot, *Tuscola*	48729
Wilson, *Alpena* (Twp)	49707
Wilson, *Charlevoix* (Twp)	49729
Wilson, *Menominee*	49896
Windemere	48917
Windsor (Twp)	48821
Winegars	48624
Winfield (Twp)	48850
Winn	48896
Winona	49965
Winsor (Twp)	48755
Winterfield (Twp)	49665
Winters	49891
Winthrop Junction (Part of Ishpeming)	49849
Wise (Twp)	48618
Wisner (Twp)	48733
Wisner	48701
Witch Lake	49879
Wixom	48393
Wolf Lake, *Jackson*	49201
Wolf Lake, *Muskegon*♦	49442
Wolverine	49799
Wolverine Lake	48390
Wonderland Mall (Part of Livonia)	48150
Woodard Lake	48834
Woodbridge (Twp)	49242
Woodbury	48849
Wooden Shoe Village	48624
Woodhaven	48183
Woodhull (Twp)	48872
Woodland	48897
Woodland Beach♦	48162
Woodland Lake	48114
Woodland Mall (Part of Kentwood)	49512
Woodland Park	49309
Woods	48622
Wood Spur	49953
Woodstock (Twp)	49220
Woodville	49349
Wooster	49412
Worden	48178
Worth, *Sanilac* (Twp)	48422
Worth, *Arenac*	48650
Wright, *Hillsdale* (Twp)	49271
Wright, *Ottawa*	49403
Wyandotte	48192
Wyman	49310
Wyoming	49509
Wyoming Park (Part of Wyoming)	49509
Yale (Part of Bessemer)	49911
Yale, *St. Clair*	48097
Yankee Springs (Twp)	49333
Yates (Twp)	49642
Yellow Jacket	49913
York (Twp)	48160
Yorkville	49083
Ypsilanti (Twp)	48197
Ypsilanti	48197-98
For specific ZIP Codes call (888) 275-8777, or your local postmaster.	
Yuba	49690
Yuma	49668
Zeba	49946
Zeeland	49464
Zilwaukee	48604
Zutphen	49426

*** Area Zip Code** **† Post Office Boxes** **‡ Postal Station** **♦ Census Designated Place** *Italic Type* **County**

Place	ZIP
Ada	56510
Adams	55909
Adolph (Part of Hermantown)	55701
Adrian	56110
Afton	55001
Ah-Gwah-Ching	56430
Aitkin	56431
Akeley	56433
Albany	56307
Alberta	56207
Albert Lea	56007
Albertville	55301
Albion Center	55302
Alborn	55702
Alden	56009
Aldrich	56434
Alexandria	56308
Alida	56676
Allen Junction (Part of Hoyt Lakes)	55750
Alma City	56048
Almelund	55002
Almora	56551
Alpha	56111
Altura	55910
Alvarado	56710
Alvwood	56630
Amboy	56010
Amherst	55922
Amiret	56175
Amor	56515
Andover	55304
Andree	55006
Andyville	55912
Angle Inlet	56711
Angora	55703
Angus	56712
Annandale	55302
Anoka	55303-04
For specific ZIP Codes call (888) 275-8777, or your local postmaster.	
Antlers Park (Part of Lakeville)	55044
Apache Mall (Part of Rochester)	55902
Apache Plaza (Part of St. Anthony)	55421
Appleton	56208
Apple Valley	55124
Arco	56113
Arcturus (Part of Taconite)	55786
Arden Hills	55112
Arendahl	55962
Argonne (Part of Lakeville)	55044
Argyle	56713
Arlington	55307
Armstrong	56009
Arnesen	56673
Arnold♦	55803
Arthyde	56350
Artichoke Lake	56227
Ashby	56309
Ashcreek	56173
Ash Lake	55771
Askov	55704
Aspelund	55946
Assumption	55338
Atkinson	55718
Atwater	56209
Atwood (Part of Edina)	55424
Audubon	56511
Augusta	55318
Aure	56676
Aurora	55705
Austin	55912
Austin Acres	55912
Auto Club (Part of Bloomington)	55420
Automba	55757
Averill	56547
Avoca	56114
Avon	56310
Babbitt	55706
Backus	56435
Badger	56714
Bagley	56621
Baker	56513
Balaton	56115
Bald Eagle	55110
Balkan	55719
Ball Bluff	55752
Ball Club	56636
Balmoral	56515
Bancroft	56007
Barden (Part of Shakopee)	55379
Barnesville	56514
Barnum	55707
Barr	55992
Barrett	56311
Barrows	56401
Barry	56210
Bassett	55602
Basswood	56576
Basswood Grove	55033
Battle Lake	56515
Battle River	56630
Baudette	56623
Baxter	56425
Bay Lake	56444
Bayport	55003
Bayview	56359
Bear Creek (Part of Rochester)‡	55904
Beardsley	56211
Bear River	55723
Bear Valley	55041
Beauford	56065
Beaulieu	56557
Beaver	55910
Beaver Bay	55601
Beaver Creek	56116
Beaver Falls	56270
Bechyn	56283
Becida	56678
Becker	55308
Beckville	55355
Bejou	56516
Belgrade	56312
Bellaire	55110
Bellechester	55027
Belle Creek	55027
Belle Plaine	56011
Belle Prairie	56345
Belleriver	56319
Bellingham	56212
Beltrami	56517
Belvidere Mills	55027
Belview	56214
Bemidji	56601-19
For specific ZIP Codes call (888) 275-8777, or your local postmaster.	
Bena	56626
Benedict	56436
Bennettville	56431
Benson	56215
Bergen	56101
Bergville	56661
Berkey	56586
Bernadotte	56054
Berne	55985
Berner	56644
Berning Mill	55376
Beroun	55063
Bertha	56437
Bethany	55910
Bethel	55005
Big Bend City	56262
Bigelow	56117
Big Falls	56627
Bigfork	56628
Big Island (Part of Orono)	55331
Big Lake	55309
Big Spring	55939
Big Stone City (Part of Ortonville)	56278
Big Woods	56744
Bingham Lake	56118
Birch Beach	56686
Birchdale	56629
Birchwood Village	55110
Bird Island	55310
Biscay	55336
Biwabik	55708
Bixby	55917
Blackberry	55744
Blackduck	56630
Black Hammer	55974
Blaine	55434
	55439
For specific ZIP Codes call (888) 275-8777, or your local postmaster.	
Blakeley	56011
Blomford	55040
Blomkest	56216
Bloom Dale (Part of Bloomington)	55431
Blooming Prairie	55917
Bloomington	55420
	55425
	55431
	55435
	55437-39
For specific ZIP Codes call (888) 275-8777, or your local postmaster.	
Bloomington Ferry (Part of Bloomington)	55438
Blue Earth	56013
Blue Grass	56477
Bluffton	56518
Bock	56313
Bodum	55040
Boisberg	56296
Bois Fort	55772
Bombay	55946
Bonanza Grove	56211
Bongards	55368
Bonnie Glen	55013
Border	56623
Borup	56519
Bovey	55709
Bovey-Coleraine (Part of Bovey)	55709
Bowlus	56314
Bowstring	56631
Boyd	56218
Boy River	56672
Bradford	55040
Braham	55006
Brainerd	56401
Branch	55056
Brandon	56315
Bratsberg	55971
Breckenridge	56520
Breezy Point	56472
Bremen	55957
Brennyville	56329
Brevik	56655
Brewster	56119
Bricelyn	56014
Bridge Court (Part of Anoka)	55303
Bridgeman	56473
Bridgewater	55021
Brimson	55602
Bristol	55939
Britt	55710
Brookdale Shopping Center (Part of Brooklyn Center)	55430
Brooklyn (Part of Hibbing)	55746
Brooklyn Center	55428-30
For specific ZIP Codes call (888) 275-8777, or your local postmaster.	
Brooklyn Park	55428
	55443-45
For specific ZIP Codes call (888) 275-8777, or your local postmaster.	
Brook Park	55007
Brooks	56715
Brookston	55711
Brooten	56316
Browerville	56438
Brownsdale	55918
Browns Valley	56219
Brownsville	55919
Brownton	55312
Bruno	55712
Brunswick	55051
Brush Creek	56014
Brushvale	56520
Buckman	56317
Buffalo	55313
Buffalo Lake	55314
Buhl	55713
Bunde	56222
Burchard	56115
Burnett	55779
Burnsville	55306
	55337
For specific ZIP Codes call (888) 275-8777, or your local postmaster.	
Burnsville Center (Part of Burnsville)	55337
Burr	56220
Burschville (Part of Corcoran)	55357
Burtrum	56318
Bushville	56329
Butler	56567
Butler Quarter (Part of Minneapolis)‡	55403
Butterfield	56120
Butternut	56055
Buyck	55771
Bygland	56721
Byron	55920
Cable	56304
Caledonia	55921
Callaway	56521
Calumet	55716
Cambria	56073
Cambridge	55008
Camden Place (Part of Minneapolis)	55412
Campbell	56522
Camp Lacupolis	55041
Camp Ripley	56345
Canby	56220
Cannon City	55021
Cannon Falls	55009
Cannon Lake	55021
Canton	55922
Canyon	55717
Cardigan Junction (Part of Shoreview)	55112
Caribou	56735
Carimona	55965
Carlisle	56537
Carlos	56319
Carlton	55718
Carmody	55016
Carp	56623
Carver	55315
Cashtown (Part of Ortonville)	56278
Casino	56473
Cass Lake	56633
Castle Danger	55616
Castle Rock	55010
Cazenovia	56164
Cedar	55011
Cedar Beach	55960
Cedar Grove (Part of Eagan)	55111
Cedar Mills	55350
Cedar Riverside (Part of Minneapolis)	55440
Celina	55723
Center City	55012
Centerville, *Anoka*	55038
Centerville, *Winona*	55987
Central	56481
Central Lakes	55734
Ceylon	56121
Chamberlain	56433
Champlin	55316
Chandler	56122
Chanhassen	55317
Charlesville	56583
Chaska	55318
Chatfield	55923
Cherry	55751
Cherry Grove	55975
Chester	55904
Chicago Bay	55606
Chickamaw Beach	56474
Chippewa City	55604
Chisago City	55013
Chisholm	55719
Choice	55954
Chokio	56221
Chowens Corner (Part of Deephaven)	55391
Circle Pines	55014
City (Part of Rochester)‡	55904
City Center (Part of Minneapolis)	55402
Civic Center (Part of Duluth)‡	55802
Clara City	56222
Claremont	55924
Clarissa	56440
Clarkfield	56223
Clarks Grove	56016
Clearbrook	56634
Clear Lake	55319
Clearwater	55320
Clements	56224
Clementson	56623
Cleveland	56017
Cliff (Part of Lilydale)	55118
Clifton	55804
Climax	56523
Clinton	56225
Clinton Falls	55060
Clitherall	56524
Clontarf	56226
Cloquet	55720
Clotho	56347
Cloverdale	55037
Cloverton	55072
Clyde	55979
Coates	55068
Cobden	56085
Cohasset	55721
Coin	56358
Cokato	55321
Colby (Part of Hoyt Lakes)	55750
Cold Spring	56320
Coleraine	55722
Collegeville	56321
Collis	56236
Cologne	55322
Columbia Heights	55421
Comfrey	56019
Commerce (Part of Minneapolis)‡	55415
Como (Part of St. Paul)‡	55108
Comstock	56525
Conception	55945
Concord	55985
Conger	56020
Constance (Part of Andover)	55303
Cook	55723
Cooley	55769
Coon Creek (Part of Coon Rapids)	55433
Coon Lake Beach (Part of East Bethel)	55092
Coon Rapids	55433
	55448
For specific ZIP Codes call (888) 275-8777, or your local postmaster.	
Coopers Corner	55005
Copas	55073
Corcoran	55357
Cordova	56057
Cormorant	56572
Corning	55912
Correll	56227
Corvuso	56228
Cosmos	56228
Cottage Grove	55016
Cotton	55724
Cottonwood	56229
Courtland	56021
Cove	56359
Craigville	56639
Crane Lake	55725
Credit River	55372
Croftville	55604
Cromwell	55726
Crookston	56716
Crosby	56441
Crosby Beach	56444
Crosslake	56442
Crown	55070
Crow River	56243
Crow Wing	56401
Crystal	55422
	55427-29
For specific ZIP Codes call (888) 275-8777, or your local postmaster.	
Crystal Bay (Part of Orono)	55323
Crystal Shopping Center (Part of Crystal)	55428
Culver	55779
Cummingsville	55923
Currie	56123
Cushing	56443
Cusson	55771
Cutler	56431
Cuyuna	56444
Cyrus	56323
Dakota	55925
Dalbo	55017
Dale	56549
Dalton	56324
Danube	56230
Danvers	56231
Darfur	56022
Darling	56345
Darwin	55324
Dassel	55325
Dawson	56232
Day	55006
Dayton (Part of Ramsey)	55303
Dayton, *Hennepin*	55327
Daytons Bluff (Part of St. Paul)‡	55106
Debs	56676
Deephaven	55391

* **Area Zip Code** † **Post Office Boxes** ‡ **Postal Station** ♦ **Census Designated Place** *Italic Type* **County**

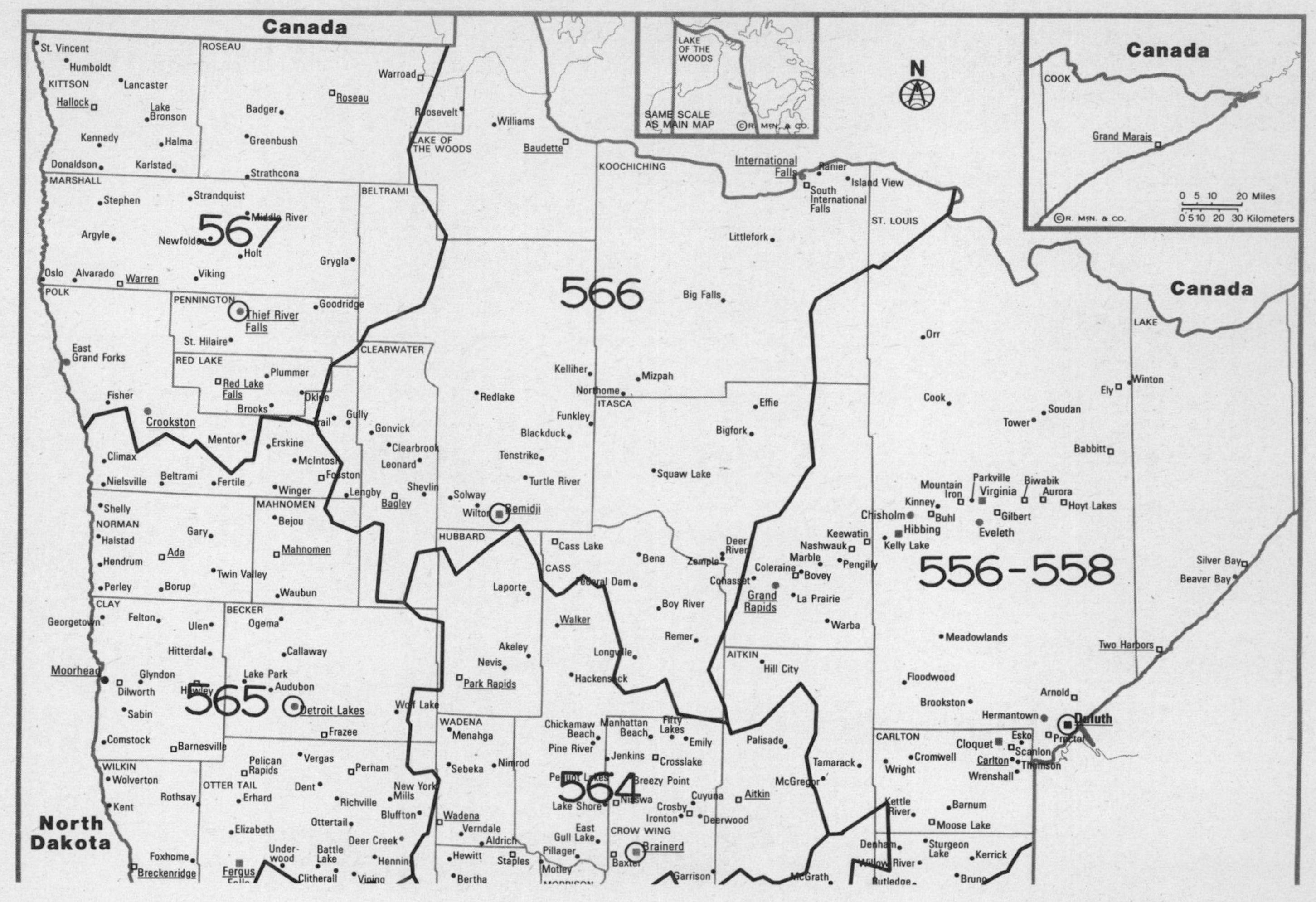
Canada
North Dakota
567
566
565
564
556-558
N
Canada
COOK
Grand Marais
0 5 10 20 Miles
0 5 10 20 30 Kilometers
©R. MSN. & CO.
LAKE OF THE WOODS
SAME SCALE AS MAIN MAP
KITTSON
ROSEAU
MARSHALL
POLK
PENNINGTON
RED LAKE
BELTRAMI
LAKE OF THE WOODS
KOOCHICHING
CLEARWATER
ITASCA
ST. LOUIS
LAKE
HUBBARD
CASS
AITKIN
CARLTON
CROW WING
WADENA
MAHNOMEN
NORMAN
CLAY
BECKER
OTTER TAIL
WILKIN
St. Vincent
Humboldt
Hallock
Lancaster
Lake Bronson
Kennedy
Donaldson
Halma
Karlstad
Stephen
Argyle
Alvarado
Warren
Oslo
Newfolden
Strandquist
Middle River
Holt
Viking
Grygla
Goodridge
Thief River Falls
St. Hilaire
Red Lake Falls
Plummer
Oklee
Brooks
East Grand Forks
Fisher
Crookston
Mentor
Erskine
McIntosh
Fosston
Gully
Trail
Gonvick
Clearbrook
Leonard
Shevlin
Bagley
Lengby
Winger
Fertile
Beltrami
Climax
Nielsville
Shelly
Halstad
Hendrum
Perley
Georgetown
Ada
Gary
Borup
Twin Valley
Mahnomen
Bejou
Waubun
Ogema
Felton
Ulen
Hitterdal
Hawley
Glyndon
Dilworth
Moorhead
Sabin
Comstock
Barnesville
Lake Park
Audubon
Detroit Lakes
Callaway
Frazee
Wolverton
Kent
Rothsay
Foxhome
Breckenridge
Pelican Rapids
Erhard
Elizabeth
Fergus Falls
Underwood
Battle Lake
Clitherall
Vining
Henning
Ottertail
Dent
Vergas
Pernam
Richville
Deer Creek
Bluffton
New York Mills
Wolf Lake
Sebeka
Menahga
Verndale
Wadena
Hewitt
Bertha
Aldrich
Staples
Nimrod
Park Rapids
Nevis
Akeley
Laporte
Walker
Hackensack
Longville
Federal Dam
Cass Lake
Bemidji
Wilton
Solway
Turtle River
Tenstrike
Blackduck
Funkley
Redlake
Kelliher
Northome
Mizpah
Squaw Lake
Bigfork
Effie
Big Falls
Littlefork
International Falls
Ranier
South International Falls
Island View
Baudette
Williams
Roosevelt
Warroad
Roseau
Badger
Greenbush
Strathcona
Orr
Cook
Tower
Soudan
Ely
Winton
Babbitt
Hoyt Lakes
Aurora
Biwabik
Gilbert
Eveleth
Virginia
Parkville
Mountain Iron
Buhl
Kinney
Hibbing
Chisholm
Kelly Lake
Keewatin
Nashwauk
Pengilly
Marble
Bovey
Coleraine
La Prairie
Warba
Grand Rapids
Cohasset
Deer River
Zemple
Bena
Boy River
Remer
Hill City
Palisade
Aitkin
McGregor
Tamarack
Floodwood
Meadowlands
Brookston
Hermantown
Arnold
Duluth
Proctor
Two Harbors
Silver Bay
Beaver Bay
Esko
Cloquet
Scanlon
Thomson
Carlton
Wrenshall
Cromwell
Wright
Barnum
Moose Lake
Kettle River
Sturgeon Lake
Kerrick
Willow River
Rutledge
Denham
McGrath
Garrison
Deerwood
Cuyuna
Crosby
Ironton
Emily
Fifty Lakes
Crosslake
Breezy Point
Jenkins
Manhattan Beach
Pequot Lakes
Nisswa
Brainerd
Baxter
Chickamaw Beach
Pine River
Lake Shore
East Gull Lake
Pillager
Motley

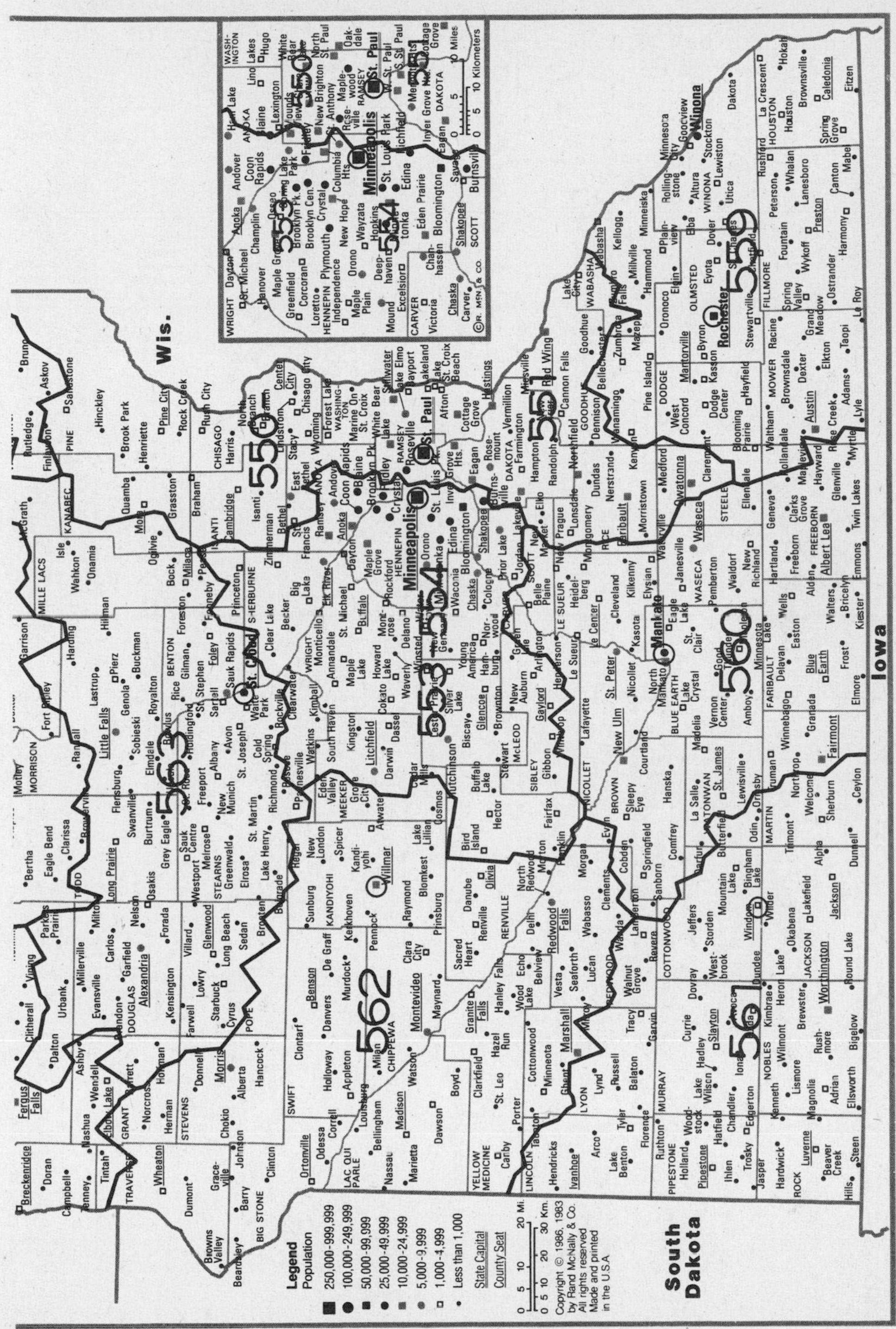
Legend
Population
250,000-999,999
100,000-249,999
50,000-99,999
25,000-49,999
10,000-24,999
5,000-9,999
1,000-4,999
Less than 1,000
State Capital
County Seat
0 5 10 20 Mi.
0 5 10 20 30 Km.
Copyright © 1986, 1983 by Rand McNally & Co. All rights reserved Made and printed in the U.S.A.
Wis.
Iowa
South Dakota
Minneapolis
St. Paul
Rochester
Mankato
St. Cloud
Duluth
0 5 10 Miles
0 5 10 Kilometers
550
551
553
554
559
560
561
562
563

Place	ZIP
Deer Creek	56527
Deer Creek Indian Reservation	56639
Deerfield	55049
Deer River	56636
Deerwood	56444
De Graff	56271
Delano	55328
Delavan	56023
Delft	56101
Delhi	56283
Dell	56013
Dellwood	55110
Denham	55783
Dennison	55018
Dent	56528
Detroit Lakes	56501*
	56502†
Dexter	55926
Diamond Lake (Part of Minneapolis)‡	55419
Dilworth	56529
Dinkytown (Part of Minneapolis)‡	55414
Dodge Center	55927
Donaldson	56720
Donnelly	56235
Dora Lake	56661
Doran	56522
Dorothy	56750
Dorset	56470
Douglas	55960
Douglas Lodge	56460
Dover	55929
Dovray	56125
Downer	56514
Dresbach	55947
Duelm	56329
Duluth	55801-16
For specific ZIP Codes call (888) 275-8777, or your local postmaster.	
Duluth International Airport, 4787th Air Base Group	55814
Dumfries	55981
Dumont	56236
Dundas	55019
Dundee	56131
Dunnell	56127
Dunvilla	56572
Duquette	55729
Duxbury	55072
Eagan	55120-23
For specific ZIP Codes call (888) 275-8777, or your local postmaster.	
Eagle Bend	56446
Eagle Lake	56024
East Beaver Bay	55601
East Bethel	55005
East Chain	56031
East Cottage Grove (Part of Cottage Grove)	55016
Eastern Heights (Part of St. Paul)‡	55119
East Grand Forks	56721
East Gull Lake	56401
East Hastings (Part of Hastings)	55033
East Lake	55760
East Lake Francis Shores	55040
Easton	56025
East Prairieville	55021
Eastside (Part of Minneapolis)‡	55418
East Union	55315
Ebro	56621
Echo	56237
Echols	56081
Eddsville	55310
Eden	55927
Eden Prairie	55344
	55346-47
For specific ZIP Codes call (888) 275-8777, or your local postmaster.	
Eden Prairie Center (Part of Eden Prairie)	55344
Eden Valley	55329
Edgerton	56128
Edgewood	55008
Edina	55410
	55416
	55424
	55435-36
	55439
For specific ZIP Codes call (888) 275-8777, or your local postmaster.	
Effie	56639
Eidswold	55020
Eitzen	55931
Elba	55910
Elbow Lake	56531
Eldes Corner	55810
Eldred	56523
Elgin	55932
Elizabeth	56533
Elkland	55021
Elko	55020
Elk River	55330
Elkton	55933
Ellendale	56026
Ellsworth	56129
Elmdale	56314
Elmer	55765
Elmore	56027
Elmwood (Part of St. Louis Park)‡	55416
Elrosa	56325
Elway (Part of St. Paul)‡	55116
Ely	55731
Ely Lake	55734
Elysian	56028
Embarrass	55732
Emco (Part of Hoyt Lakes)	55750
Emily	56447
Emmaville	56470
Emmons	56029
Empire	55024
Enfield	55362
Englund	56758
Erdahl	56531
Erhard	56534
Ericksonville	56359
Ericsburg	56649
Erie	56725
Erskine	56535
Esden	56444
Esko	55733
Essig	56030
Estes Brook	56357
Etna	55975
Etter	55089
Euclid	56722
Eureka (Part of Shorewood)	55331
Evan	56266
Evansville	56326
Eveleth	55734
Everdell	56520
Evergreen	56544
Excelsior	55331
Eyota	55934
Fairbanks	55602
Fairfax	55332
Fairhaven	55382
Fairmont	56031
Faith	56584
Falcon Heights	55108
Faribault	55021
Farming	56368
Farmington	55024
Farris	56633
Farwell	56327
Federal Dam	56641
Felton	56536
Fergus Falls	56537*
	56538†
Fernando	55385
Fertile	56540
Fifty Lakes	56448
Fillmore	55990
Finland	55603
Finlayson	55735
Fisher	56723
Flensburg	56328
Fletcher	55369
Flintwood Hills (Part of Ramsey)	55303
Flom	56541
Floodwood	55736
Florence	56170
Florenton	55792
Florian	56758
Foley	56329
Fond du Lac Indian Reservation	55720
Forada	56308
Forbes	55738
Fordson (Part of Eagan)	55121
Forest City	55355
Forest Grove	56660
Forest Lake	55025
Forest Mills	55992
Foreston	56330
Fork	56744
Fort Ripley	56449
Fort Snelling	55111
Fosston	56542
Fossum	56584
Fountain	55935
Four Corners	55811
Fourtown	56727
Foxhome	56543
Fox Lake	56181
Franconia	55074
Franklin, *Renville*	55333
Franklin, *St. Louis*	55792
Franklin Avenue (Part of Minneapolis)	55404
Frazee	56544
Freeborn	56032
Freeburg	55921
Freedhem	56345
Freeport	56331
Fremont	55979
French Lake	55302
French River	55804
Fridley	55432
Friesland	55037
Frontenac	55026
Frost	56033
Fulda	56131
Funkley	56630
Garden City	56034
Garfield	56332
Garrison	56450
Garvin	56132
Gary	56545
Gatzke	56724
Gaylord	55334
Gem Lake	55110
Gemmell	56660
Geneva	56035
Genoa, *Olmsted*	55920
Genoa (Part of Eveleth)	55734
Genola	56364
Gentilly	56716
Georgetown	56546
Georgeville	56312
Gheen	55771
Gheen Corner	55771
Ghent	56239
Gibbon	55335
Giese	55735
Gilbert	55741
Gilfillan	56283
Gilman	56333
Gladstone (Part of Maplewood)	55109
Glen	56431
Glencoe	55336
Glendale	55771
Glendorado	55371
Glen Lake (Part of Minnetonka)	55345
Glenville	56036
Glenwood	56334
Glenwood Junction (Part of Golden Valley)	55427
Glory	56431
Gloster (Part of Maplewood)	55109
Gluek	56260
Glyndon	56547
Godahl	56081
Golden Hill	55902
Golden Hills (Part of St. Louis Park)	55416
Golden Valley	55416
	55422
	55426-27
For specific ZIP Codes call (888) 275-8777, or your local postmaster.	
Gonvick	56644
Goodhue	55027
Goodland	55742
Goodridge	56725
Good Thunder	56037
Goodview	55987
Gordon	56036
Gotha	55322
Graceton	56686
Graceville	56240
Granada	56039
Grand Falls	56627
Grand Marais	55604
Grand Meadow	55936
Grand Portage	55605
Grand Portage Indian Reservation	55605
Grand Rapids	55730†
	55744*
Grand View Heights	56573
Grandy	55029
Granger	55939
Granite Falls	56241
Grant	55082
Grass Lake	55006
Grasston	55030
Grattan	56661
Greaney	55771
Greenbush	56726
Greenfield	55357
Green Isle	55338
Greenland	56028
Greenleaf	55355
Greenleafton	55965
Green Valley	56258
Greenwald	56335
Greenwood	55331
Grey Eagle	56336
Grogan	56081
Groningen	55072
Grove City	56243
Grove Lake	56334
Groveland	55391
Grygla	56727
Guckeen	56013
Gully	56646
Gutches Grove	56347
Guthrie	56461
Hackensack	56452
Hackett	56623
Hader	55992
Hadley	56151
Hagan	56262
Hallock	56728
Halma	56729
Halstad	56548
Hamburg	55339
Hamel (Part of Medina)	55340
Hamilton	55975
Ham Lake	55304
Hammond	55991
Hampton	55031
Hancock	56244
Hanley Falls	56245
Hanover	55341
Hanska	56041
Happyland	56653
Harding	56364
Hardwick	56134
Har-Mar Mall (Part of Roseville)	55113
Harmony	55939
Harnell Park	55779
Harris	55032
Hart	55971
Hartland	56042
Hassan	55369
Hassman	56431
Hastings	55033
Hasty	55320
Hatfield	56164
Havana	55060
Hawick	56246
Hawley	56549
Hay Creek	55066
Haydenville	56256
Hayfield	55940
Haypoint	55748
Hayward	56043
Hazel Run	56241
Hazelwood	55057
Heatwole	55350
Hector	55342
Heiberg	56584
Heidelberg	56071
Heinola	56567
Henderson	56044
Hendricks	56136
Hendrum	56550
Henning	56551
Henriette	55036
Henrytown	55939
Herman	56248
Hermantown	55810-11
For specific ZIP Codes call (888) 275-8777, or your local postmaster.	
Heron Lake	56137
Hewitt	56453
Hiawatha Spur (Part of Eagan)	55111
Hibbing	55746*
	55747†
Hidden Creek (Part of Andover)	55303
High Forest	55976
Highland, *Fillmore*	55949
Highland, *Lake*	55616
Highland, *Wright*	55349
Highland (Part of Minneapolis)‡	55411
High Landing	56725
Highland Park (Part of St. Paul)	55116
Hill City	55748
Hillman	56338
Hills	56138
Hilltop	55421
Hillview	56477
Hinckley	55037
Hines	56647
Hitterdal	56552
Hoffman	56339
Hoffmans Corners (Part of Gem Lake)	55110
Hokah	55941
Holdingford	56340
Holland	56139
Hollandale	56045
Holloway	56249
Hollywood	55388
Holmes City	56341
Holt	56738
Holyoke	55749
Homer	55942
Hoot Lake (Part of Fergus Falls)	56537
Hope	56046
Hopkins	55305
	55343
	55345
For specific ZIP Codes call (888) 275-8777, or your local postmaster.	
Hopper (Part of Mountain Iron)	55792
Houston	55943
Hovland	55606
Howard Lake	55349*
	55575†
Hoyt Lakes	55750
Hubbard	56470
Hugo	55038
Humboldt	56731
Huntersville	56464
Huntley	56047
Huot	56750
Husby Spur (Part of Arden Hills)	55112
Hutchinson	55350
Hutton	55939
Hydes Lake	55322
Ideal Corners	56472
Idington	55703
Ihlen	56140
Illgen City	55614
Imogene	56039
Independence, *Hennepin*	55359
Independence, *St. Louis*	55779
Indus	56629
Industrial (Part of St. Paul)‡	55104
Inger	56636
Inguadona	56655
International Falls	56649
Inver Grove Heights	55076-77
For specific ZIP Codes call (888) 275-8777, or your local postmaster.	
Iona	56141
Ironhub	56431
Iron Junction	55751
Ironton	56455
Isabella	55607
Isanti	55040
Island Lake	56667
Island Park (Part of Mound)	55364
Island View	56649
Isle	56342
Ivanhoe	56142
Iverson	55718
Jackson	56143
Jacobson	55752
Jacobs Prairie	56320
Jakeville	56329
Jameson	56649
Janesville	56048
Jarretts	55957
Jasper	56144
Jaynes	56628
Jeffers	56145
Jenkins	56456
Jennie	55325
Jessenland	56044
Jessie Lake	56637
Johnsburg	55909

Johnson 56236
Johnsville (Part of Blaine) 55434
Jonathan (Part of Chaska) 55318
Jordan 55352
Judson 56055
Kabekona 56461
Kabetogama 56669
Kanaranzi 56146
Kandi Mall Shopping Center (Part of Willmar) 56201
Kandiyohi 56251
Karlstad 56732
Kasota 56050
Kasson 55944
Katrine 56444
Keewatin 55753
Kelliher 56650
Kellogg 55746
Kelly Lake (Part of Hibbing) 55746
Kelsey 55724
Kennedy 56733
Kenneth 56147
Kensington 56343
Kent 56553
Kenwood (Part of Duluth) 55811
Kenwood (Part of Minneapolis) 55403
Kenyon 55946
Kerkhoven 56252
Kerr (Part of Hibbing) 55746
Kerrick 55756
Kettle River 55757
Kiester 56051
Kilkenny 56052
Kimball 55353
Kimberly 56431
Kinbrae 56131
Kingsdale 55072
Kings Park 55960
Kingston 55325
Kinmount 55771
Kinney 55758
Kitzville (Part of Hibbing) 55746
Kjellberg Park 55362
Klossner 56073
Knapp 55321
Knife River 55609
Knollwood Mall (Part of St. Louis Park) 55426
Komensky 55350
Kragnes 56560
Kroschel 55037
Lac qui Parle 56265
La Crescent 55947
Lafayette 56054
Lagoona Beach 56278
Lake Benton 56149
Lake Bronson 56734
Lake Center 56511
Lake City 55041
Lake Crystal 56055
Lake Elmo 55042
Lake Eunice 56554
Lakefield 56150
Lake George 56458
Lake Henry 56362
Lake Hubert 56459
Lake Itasca 56460
Lakeland 55043
Lakeland Shores 55043
Lake Lillian 56253
Lake Netta (Part of Ham Lake) 55303
Lake Nichols 55717
Lake Park 56554
Lake Sarah (Part of Greenfield) 55357
Lake Shore 56468
Lake Shore Park (Part of White Bear Lake) 55110
Lakeside, Renville 55314
Lakeside (Part of Duluth)‡ 55804
Lake St. Croix Beach 55043
Lake Street (Part of Minneapolis)‡ 55408
Lakeville 55044
Lake Wilson 56151
Lamberton 56152
Lamoille 55987
Lamson 55325
Lancaster 56735
Landfall 55128
Lanesboro 55949
Langdon (Part of Cottage Grove) 55016
Lansing 55950
Laporte 56461
La Prairie 55744
Larsmont 55616
La Salle 56056
Lastrup 56344
Lauderdale 55108
Lavinia 55746
Lawler 55760
Lawndale 56579
Lax Lake 55614
Leader 56466
Leaf Lake 56551
Leaf Valley 56332
Leavenworth 56085
Le Center 56057
Leech Lake Indian Reservation 56633
Leetonia (Part of Hibbing) 55746
Le Hillier 56001
Lena 55963
Lengby 56651
Lenora 55922
Leonard 56652
Leonidas 55734
Leota 56153
Lerdal 56007
Le Roy 55951
Lester Prairie 55354
Le Sueur 56058
Lewis Lake 55006
Lewiston 55952
Lewisville 56060
Lexington, *Anoka* 55014
Lexington, *Le Sueur* 56057
Libby 55760
Lilydale 55118
Lime Creek 56131
Lincoln 56443
Linden Grove 55723
Lindford 56653
Lindstrom 55045
Lino Lakes 55014
55038
For specific ZIP Codes call (888) 275-8777, or your local postmaster.
Linwood 55005
Lismore 56155
Litchfield 55355
Litomysl 55060
Little Canada 55117
Little Chicago 55057
Little Falls 56345
Littlefork 56653
Little Marais 55614
Little Pine 56431
Little Rock, *Beltrami*♦ 56671
Little Rock, *Morrison* 56373
Little Sauk 56347
Little Swan (Part of Hibbing) 55746
Local 56501
Lockhart 56510
Loman 56654
London 56036
Long Beach 56334
Long Lake 55356
Long Point 56686
Long Prairie 56346†
56347*
Long Siding 55371
Longville 56655
Lonsdale 55046
Loop (Part of Minneapolis)‡ 55402
Loretto 55357
Loring (Part of Minneapolis)‡ 55403
Lost Lake (Part of Plymouth)‡ 55441-42
For specific ZIP Codes call (888) 275-8777, or your local postmaster.
Louisburg 56256
Louriston 56260
Lower Sioux Indian Reservation 56270
Lowry 56349
Lowry Avenue (Part of Minneapolis)‡ 55411-12
For specific ZIP Codes call (888) 275-8777, or your local postmaster.
Lucan 56255
Lude 56686
Lutsen 55612
Luverne 56156
Luxemburg 56301
Lydia 55352
Lyle 55953
Lynd 56157
Lyndale (Part of Independence) 55359
Lynwood (Part of Hibbing) 55746
Mabel 55954
McCauleyville 56553
McGrath 56350
McGregor 55760
McHugh 56501
McIntosh 56556
McKee (Part of Eagan) 55121
McKinley 55741
Madelia 56062
Madison 56256
Madison East (Part of Mankato)‡ 56001
Madison Lake 56063
Mae 56662
Magnolia 56158
Mahkonce 56557
Mahnomen 56557
Mahtomedi 55115
Mahtowa 55707
Maine 56586
Maine Prairie 55353
Makinen 55763
Mall (Part of Fairmont)‡ 56031
Mall of America (Part of Bloomington) 55420
Malmo 56431
Malung 56751
Manannah 56243
Manchester 56064
Manhattan Beach 56442
Manitou 56629
Mankato 56001-06
For specific ZIP Codes call (888) 275-8777, or your local postmaster.
Mansfield 56009
Mantorville 55955
Maple 55387
Maple Bay 56736
Maple Grove 55311
55369
For specific ZIP Codes call (888) 275-8777, or your local postmaster.
Maple Hill 55604
Maple Island 56045
Maple Lake 55358
Maple Plain 55359
Mapleton 56065
Mapleview 55912
Maplewood 55109
55119
For specific ZIP Codes call (888) 275-8777, or your local postmaster.
Maplewood Mall (Part of Maplewood) 55109
Marble 55764
Marcell 56657
Margie 56658
Marietta 56257
Marine on St. Croix 55047
Marion 55904
Markham 55763
Markville 55072
Marshall 56258
Martin Lake 55079
Marty 55353
Marysburg 56063
Marystown 55379
Matawan 56072
Mattson 56728
Mavie 56725
Max 56659
Mayer 55360
Mayhew 56379
Mayhew Lake 56379
Maynard 56260
Mayowood 55902
Mayville 55912
Mazeppa 55956
M&D Junction (Part of White Bear Lake) 55110
Meadowlands 55765*
55780†
Medford 55049
Medicine Lake 55441
Medina 55340
Meire Grove 56352
Melby 56326
Melrose 56352
Melrude 55766
Menahga 56464
Mendota 55150
Mendota Heights 55118
55120
For specific ZIP Codes call (888) 275-8777, or your local postmaster.
Mentor 56736
Meriden 56093
Merrifield 56465
Merton 55060
Mesaba (Part of Hoyt Lakes) 55750
Middle River 56737
Midway, *Becker* 56464
Midway (Part of St. Paul)‡ 55104
Midway (Part of Virginia) 55792
Midway Center (Part of St. Paul) 55104
Miesville 55009
Milaca 56353
Milan 56262
Mille Lacs Indian Reservation 56359
Miller Hill (Part of Duluth) 55811
Miller Hill Mall (Part of Duluth) 55811
Millersburg 55021
Millerville 56315
Millville 55957
Milroy 56263
Miltona 56354
Mineral Center 55605

Minneapolis

55401-70
55480
For specific ZIP Codes call (888) 275-8777, or your local postmaster.

Colleges & Universities

Augsburg Coll 55454
Minneapolis Coll of Art Design 55404
North Central Bible Coll 55404
Univ of Minnesota-Twin Cities 55455
Walden Univ 55401

Financial Institutions

Firstar Bank 55417
USBank, NA 55402

Hospitals

Abbott-Northwestern Hosp 55407
Fairview Riverside Med Ctr 55454
Fairview Southdale Hosp 55435
Hennepin County Med Ctr 55415
Univ of Minnesota Hosp & Clinic 55455
Veterans Affairs Med Ctr 55417

Hotels/Motels

Airport Hilton 55425
Best Western Thunderbird Hotel & Convention Ctr 55425
Doubletree Grand 55425
Hilton & Towers 55403
Holiday Inn, Metrodome 55454
Holiday Inn Select, International Airport 55425
Hyatt Regency, Nicollet Mall 55403
The Marquette 55402
Marriott, City Ctr 55402
Radisson Hotel & Conference Ctr 55441
Radisson Hotel, South 55439
Radisson, Metrodome 55414
Radisson Plaza 55402
Regal 55403
Sheraton, Metrodome 55413
Sofitel 55439

Military Installations

Marine Corps Res Ctr, Twin Cities 55450
934th Mission Support Squadron, Air Res Base 55450

Minnehaha (Part of Minneapolis)‡ 55406
Minneiska 55910
Minneota 56264
Minnesota City 55959
Minnesota Lake 56068
Minnesota Transfer (Part of St. Paul)‡ 55114
Minnetonka 55305
55343
55345
For specific ZIP Codes call (888) 275-8777, or your local postmaster.
Minnetonka Beach 55361
Minnetonka Mills (Part of Minnetonka) 55305
Minnetrista 55364
Minnewawa 55760
Mizpah 56660
Moland 55946
Money Creek 55943
Montevideo 56265
Montgomery 56069
Monticello 55362*
55365†
Montrose 55363
Moorhead 56560*
56561†
Moose Lake 55767
Mora 55051
Morgan 56266
Morgan Park (Part of Duluth)‡ 55808
Morningside (Part of Edina) 55424
Morrill 56329
Morris 56267
Morristown 55052
Morton 56270
Moscow 55912
Motley 56466
Mound 55364
Mound Prairie 55943
Mounds View 55112
Mountain Iron 55768
Mountain Lake 56159
Mount Royal (Part of Duluth)‡ 55803
Munger 55720
Murdock 56271
Murphy City 55603
Muskoda 56547
Myrtle 56036
Nashua 56565
Nashwauk 55769
Nassau 56272
Navarre (Part of Orono) 55392
Naytahwaush♦ 56566
Nebish 56667
Nelson 56355
Nerstrand 55053
Nett Lake 55772
Nett Lake Indian Reservation 55772
Nevis 56467
New Auburn 55366
New Brighton 55112
Newburg 55954
Newfolden 56738
New Germany 55367
New Hartford 55925
New Hope 55427-28
For specific ZIP Codes call (888) 275-8777, or your local postmaster.
Newhouse 55954
New London 56273
New Market 55054
New Munich 56356
Newport 55055
New Prague 56071
New Richland 56072
New Rome 55307
Newry 56045
New Trier 55031
New Ulm 56073
New York Mills 56567
Nickerson 55797
Nicollet 56074
Nicols (Part of Eagan) 55121
Nicolville 55912
Nielsville 56568
Nimrod 56478
Nininger 55033

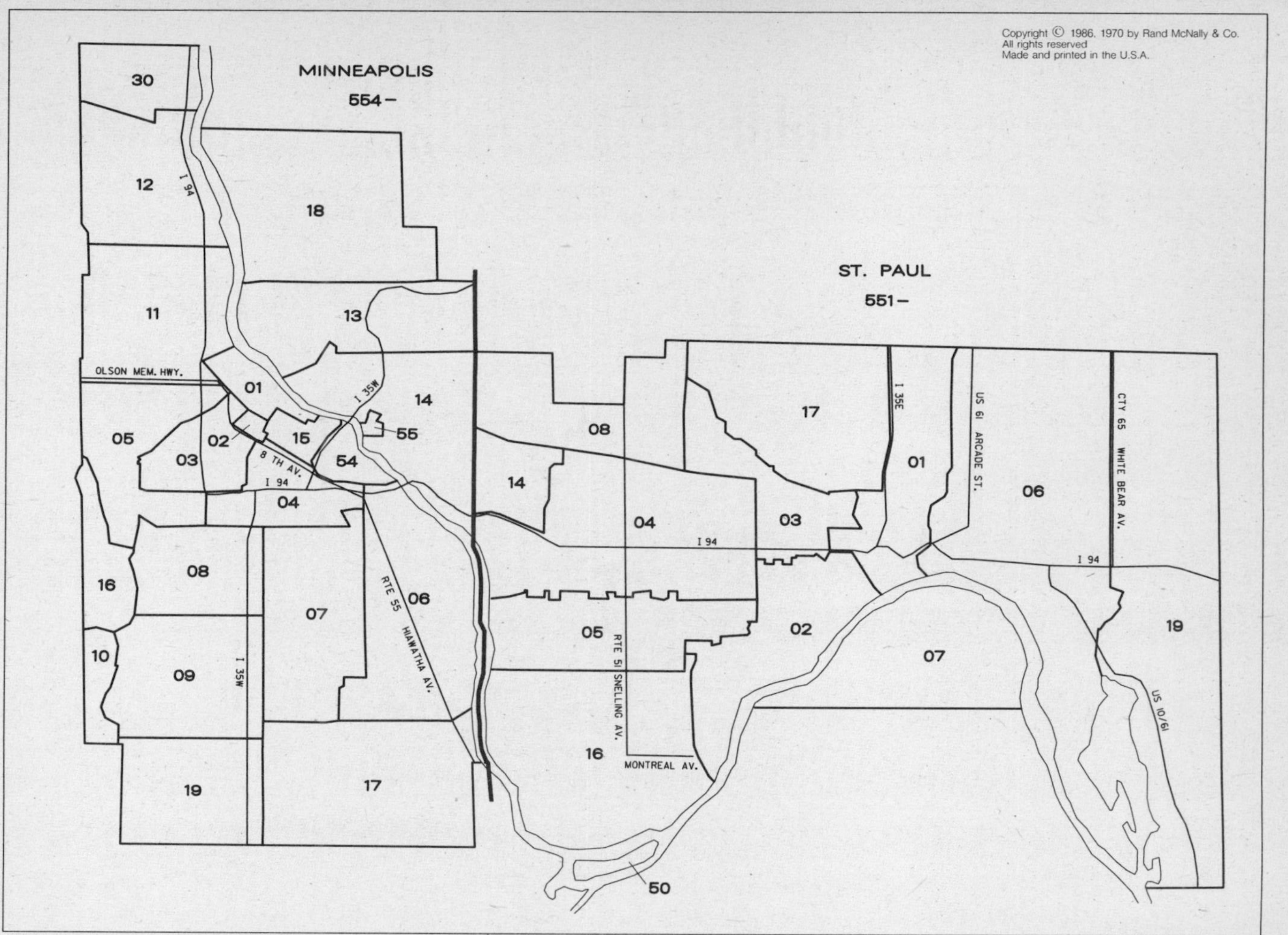
Copyright © 1986, 1970 by Rand McNally & Co.
All rights reserved
Made and printed in the U.S.A.
MINNEAPOLIS
554–
ST. PAUL
551–
I 94
OLSON MEM. HWY.
I 35W
8 TH AV.
RTE 55 HIAWATHA AV.
RTE 51 SNELLING AV.
MONTREAL AV.
I 35E
US 61 ARCADE ST.
CTY 65 WHITE BEAR AV.
US 10/61
30
12
18
11
13
01
14
05
02
15
55
03
54
04
16
08
06
07
10
09
19
17
50

Nisswa 56468
Nodine 55925
Nokomis (Part of Minneapolis)‡ 55417
Nopeming 55810
Norcross 56274
Normandale (Part of Edina)‡ 55439
Norseland 56082
North Benton 56329
North Branch 55056
Northcote 56728
Northdale (Part of Coon Rapids) 55433
North Douglas (Part of Crystal) 55422
Northfield 55057
North Mankato 56002†
56003*
North Oaks 55127
Northome 56661
North Prairie 56314
North Redwood 56283
Northrop 56075
Northside (Part of Albert Lea)‡ 56007
North St. Paul 55109
Northtown Mall (Part of Blaine) 55434
Northwest Terminal (Part of Minneapolis) 55418
Novak's Corner 56329
Norway Lake 56289
Norwood (Part of Norwood Young America) 55368*
55383†
Norwood Young America 55368
55383
55394
55397
For specific ZIP Codes call (888) 275-8777, or your local postmaster.
Nowthon 55000
Noyes 56740
Oak Center 55041
Oakdale 55128
Oak Grove 55011
Oakhill 56347
Oak Island 56741
Oak Knoll (Part of Minnetonka) 55305
Oakland 56076
Oak Park (Part of Blaine) 55434
Oak Park, *Benton* 56357
Oak Park Heights 55082
Oakport♦ 56560
Oak Ridge 55910
Odessa 56276
Odin 56160
Ogema 56569
Ogilvie 56358
Okabena 56161
Oklee 56742
Old Frontenac 55026
Olga 56646
Olivia 56277
Onamia 56359
Onigum 56484
Opole 56340
Opstead 56342
Orchard Lake (Part of Lakeville) 55044
Org 56187
Orleans 56735
Ormsby 56162
Orono 55323
Oronoco 55960
Orr 55771
Orrock 55309
Orth 56661
Ortonville 56278
Osage 56570
Osakis 56360
Oshawa 56082
Oslo, *Dodge* 55940
Oslo, *Marshall* 56744
Oslund 56680
Osseo 55311
55369
For specific ZIP Codes call (888) 275-8777, or your local postmaster.
Oster 55388
Ostrander 55961
Otisco 56093
Otisville 55073
Otrey 56278
Otsego 55301
Ottawa 56058
Otter Creek 55718
Ottertail 56571
Outing 56662
Owatonna 55060
Oxlip 55040
Oylen 56481
Padua 56378
Palisade 56469
Palmdale 55084
Palmers 55804
Palo 55705
Parent 56329
Parkers Prairie 56361
Park Rapids 56470
Park View (Part of Crookston)‡ 56716
Parkville (Part of Mountain Iron) 55768
Payne 55765
Paynesville 56362
Pease 56363
Pelican Rapids 56572
Pelland 56649
Pemberton 56078
Pencer 56751
Pengilly 55775
Pennington 56663
Pennock 56279
Pequaywan Lake 55801
Pequot Lakes 56472
Perham 56573
Perkins 55943
Perley 56574
Petersburg 56143
Peterson 55962
Petran 56043
Phelps 56586
Philbrook 56466
Pickwick 55987
Pierz 56364
Pigeon River 55605
Pike Lake 55811
Pillager 56473
Pillsbury 56382
Pilot Grove 56027
Pilot Mound 55923
Pine Bend (Part of Rosemount) 55068
Pine Bend, *Mahnomen* 56651
Pine Brook 55008
Pine Center 56401
Pine City 55063
Pinecreek 56751
Pine Island 55963
Pine River 56474
Pine Springs 55115
Pineville 55705
Pinewood 56664
Pioneer (Part of St. Paul)‡ 55101
Pipestone 56164
Pitt 56623
Plainview 55964
Plato 55370
Pleasant Grove 55976
Pleasant Lake 56301
Plummer 56748
Plymouth 55441-42
55446-47
For specific ZIP Codes call (888) 275-8777, or your local postmaster.
Point Douglas 55033
Ponemah♦ 56666
Ponsford 56575
Poplar 56479
Popple Creek 56379
Port Cargill (Part of Savage) 55378
Porter 56280
Post Town 55920
Potsdam 55932
Powderhorn (Part of Minneapolis)‡ 55407
Prairie Island Indian Reservation 55089
Prairieville 55021
Pratt 55060
Predmore 55934
Preston 55965
Priam 56282
Princeton 55371
Prinsburg 56281
Prior Lake 55372
Proctor 55810
Prosit 55702
Prosper 55954
Pulaski Lake Shores 55313
Puposky 56667
Quamba 55007
Racine 55967
Radium 56762
Rainy Junction (Part of Virginia) 55792
Ramey 56329
Ramsey, *Anoka* 55303
Ramsey, *Mower* 55912
Randall 56475
Randolph 55065
Ranier 56668
Rapidan 56001
Rassat 55313
Rauch 55771
Ray 56669
Raymond 56282
Reading 56165
Reads Landing 55968
Redby♦ 56670
Redlake♦ 56671
Red Lake Falls 56750
Red Lake Indian Reservation 56671
Red Rock 55605
Red Top 56342
Red Wing 55066
Redwood Falls 56283
Reformatory (Part of St. Cloud) 56301
Regal 56312
Remer 56672
Reno 55919
Renova 55926
Renville 56284
Revere 56166
Rice 56367
Riceford 55954
Rice Street (Part of St. Paul)‡ 55117
Richfield 55423
Richfield Hub Shopping Center (Part of Richfield) 55423
Richmond 56368
Rich Valley (Part of Rosemount) 55075
Richville 56576
Richwood 56577
Ridgedale Shopping Center (Part of Minnetonka) 55343
Ridgeway 55943
Rindal 56540
Riverside (Part of Minneapolis)‡ 55454
Riverside Heights 56013
Riverton 56455
Riverview (Part of St. Paul)‡ 55107
Robbin 58225
Robbinsdale 55422
Robinson 55731
Rochert 56578
Rochester 55901-06
For specific ZIP Codes call (888) 275-8777, or your local postmaster.
Rock Creek 55067
Rock Dell 55920
Rockford 55373
Rockville 56369
Rogers 55374
Rollag 56549
Rollingstone 55969
Rollins 55602
Ronneby 56329
Roosevelt 56673
Roscoe, *Goodhue* 55983
Roscoe, *Stearns* 56371
Roseau 56751
Rose City 56446
Rose Creek 55970
Roseland 56216
Rosemount 55068
Rosen 56212
Rosendale 56243
Roseport (Part of Inver Grove Heights) 55075
Roseville 55113
Rosewood 56701
Ross 56751
Rossburg 56431
Rothsay 56579
Round Lake 56167
Round Prairie 56347
Rowena 56293
Rowland (Part of Eden Prairie) 55344
Royalton 56373
Roy Lake 56557
Ruby Junction (Part of Hibbing) 55746
Rush City 55069
Rushford 55971
Rushford Village 55962
Rushmore 56168
Rush Point 55080
Rush River 56058
Ruskin 55021
Russell 56169
Rustad 56560
Ruthton 56170
Rutledge 55795
Sabin 56580
Sacred Heart 56285
Saga Hill (Part of Orono) 55323
Saginaw 55779
St. Anna 56310
St. Anthony, *Hennepin* 55418
St. Anthony, *Stearns* 56307
St. Augusta 56301
Saint Benedict 56071
St. Bonifacius 55375
St. Charles 55972
St. Clair, *Blue Earth* 56080
St. Clair (Part of St. Paul) 55116
St. Cloud 56301-04
56397-98
For specific ZIP Codes call (888) 275-8777, or your local postmaster.
St. Croix Junction (Part of Hastings) 55033
St. Francis, *Anoka* 55070
St. Francis, *Stearns* 56331
St. George 56073
St. Henry 56057
St. Hilaire 56754
St. James 56081
St. Joseph 56374
St. Killian 56185
St. Leo 56264
St. Louis Park 55426
St. Martin 56376
St. Mary's Point 55043
St. Mathias 56449
St. Michael 55376
St. Nicholas 55389
St. Patrick 56071

St. Paul

55101-29
55164-89
For specific Zip Codes call (888) 275-8777, or your local postmaster.

Colleges & Universities

Bethel Coll 55112
Bethel Theological Seminary 55112
Coll of Saint Catherine 55105
Coll of Visual Arts 55102
Concordia Univ 55104
Hamline Univ 55104
Luther Seminary 55108
Macalester Coll 55105
Metropolitan State Univ 55106
Northwestern Coll 55113
Univ of St Thomas 55105
William Mitchell Coll of Law 55105

Financial Institutions

Firstar Bank, NA 55116
Norwest Bank, NA 55101
USBank, NA 55101

Hospitals

Healtheast St Joseph's Hosp 55102
Regions Hosp 55101
United Hosp 55102

Hotels/Motels

Radisson Hotel 55101
The Saint Paul 55102

Military Installations

Minnesota Air Nat Guard, FB6231, Minneapolis-St.Paul International Airport 55111

St. Paul Park 55071
St. Peter 56082
St. Rosa 56331
St Stephen 56375
St. Thomas 56058
St. Vincent 56755
St. Wendel 56310
Salem Corners 55920
Salol 56756
Sanborn 56083
Sandstone 55072
Santiago 55377
Saratoga 55972
Sargeant 55973
Sartell 56377
Sauk Centre 56378
Sauk Rapids 56379
Saum 56650
Savage 55378
Sawyer 55780
Scandia 55073
Scandia Valley 56443
Scanlon 55720
Schley 56633
Schroeder 55613
Scotts Corner 55718
Seaforth 56287
Searles 56084
Sebeka 56477
Section Thirty 55731
Sedan 56334
Sedil 55068
Seven-Hi Shopping Center (Part of Minnetonka) 55345
Shafer 55074
Shakopee 55379
Shaw 55717
Sheffield Mill (Part of Faribault) 55021
Sheldon 55921
Shelly 56581
Sherack 56722
Sherburn 56171
Sheshebee 55760
Shevlin 56676
Shieldsville 55021
Shooks 56661
Shoreham 56501
Shoreview 55126
Shorewood 55331
Shotley 56650
Shovel Lake 55785
Side Lake 55781
Signal Hills Shopping Center (Part of West St. Paul) 55118
Silica 55746
Silo 55952
Silver Bay 55614
Silver Corners 56367
Silver Creek, *Lake* 55616
Silver Creek, *Wright* 55380
Silverdale 55771
Silver Lake 55381
Simpson 55904
Sioux Valley 51347
Skibo 55750
Skyburg 55946
Skyline 56001
Slayton 56172
Sleepy Eye 56085
Sletten 56556
Smiths Mill 56048
Snellman 56570
Sobieski 56345
Soderville (Part of Ham Lake) 55304
Sogn 55018
Solway 56678
Soudan 55782
South Bend 56001
South Branch 56081
Southdale (Part of Edina) 55435
Southdale Shopping Center (Part of Edina) 55435
South Haven 55382
South International Falls (Part of International Falls) 56679
South Minneapolis (Part of Minneapolis) 55408
South St. Paul 55075
Southtown Center (Part of Bloomington) 55420
Spafford 56187
Spectacle Lake 55008
Spicer 56288
Spring Creek 56223

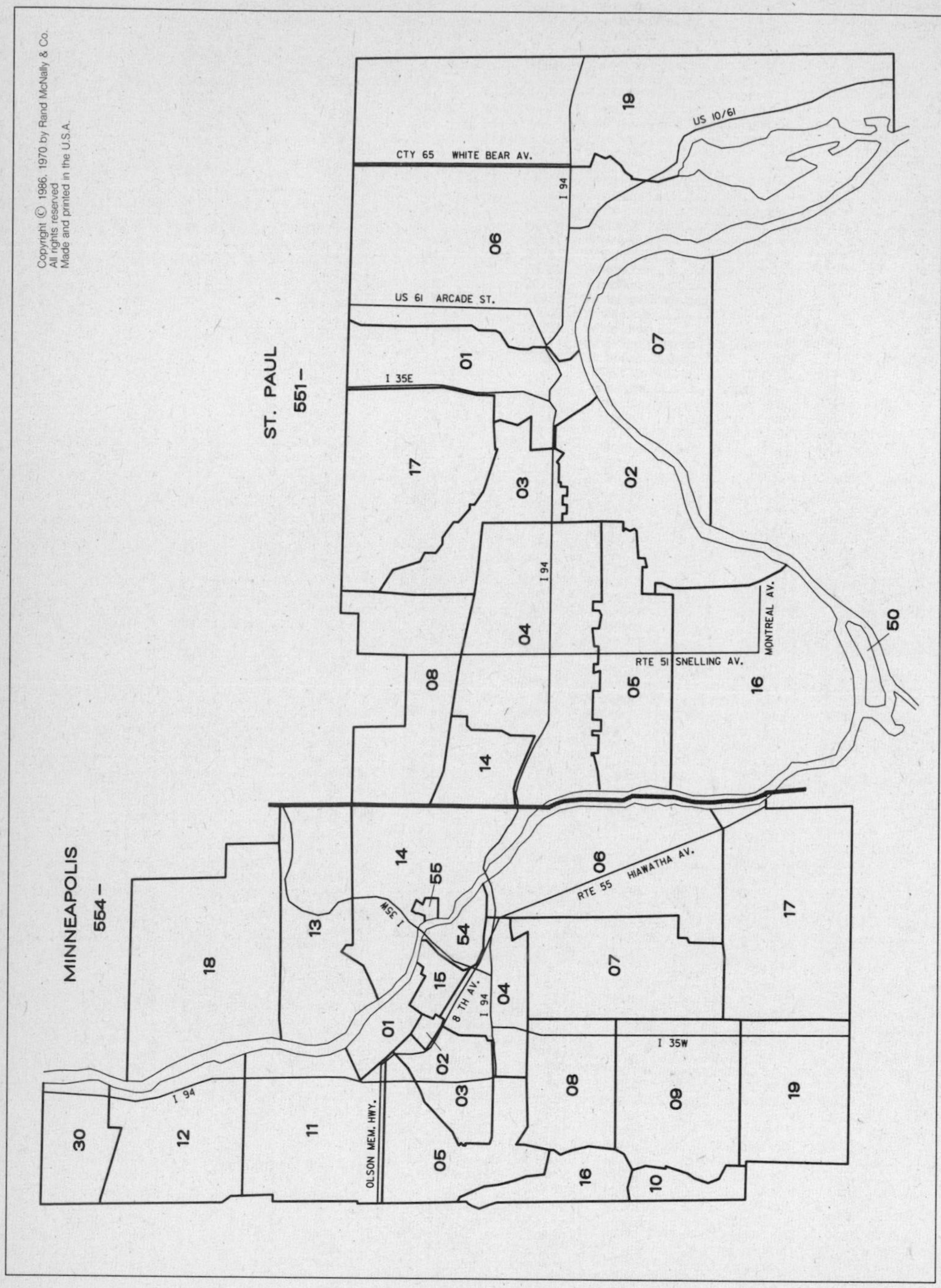
Copyright © 1986, 1970 by Rand McNally & Co.
All rights reserved
Made and printed in the U.S.A.
ST. PAUL
551-
MINNEAPOLIS
554-
CTY 65 WHITE BEAR AV.
US 61 ARCADE ST.
I 35E
I 94
US 10/61
RTE 51 SNELLING AV.
MONTREAL AV.
RTE 55 HIAWATHA AV.
I 35W
8 TH AV.
OLSON MEM. HWY.
I 35W
19
06
01
07
17
03
02
04
08
05
16
14
50
14
55
13
54
15
18
04
06
17
07
01
02
03
05
08
09
19
16
10
11
12
30

Springfield	56087
Spring Grove	55974
Spring Hill	56352
Spring Lake, *Isanti*	55056
Spring Lake, *Itasca*	56680
Spring Lake Park	55432
Spring Park	55384
Springsteel Island	56763
Springvale	55080
Spring Valley	55975
Spruce Center	56354
Squaw Lake	56681
Stacy	55078†
	55079*
Stanchfield	55080
Stanley	55008
Stanton	55018
Staples	56479
Starbuck	56381
Stark	55032
Steele Center	55060
Steelton (Part of Duluth)	55808
Steen	56173
Stephen	56757
Sterling Center	56010
Stewart, *Lake*	55616
Stewart, *McLeod*	55385
Stewartville	55976
Stillwater	55082*
	55083†
Stockholm	55321
Stockton	55988
Storden	56174
Strandquist	56758
Strathcona	56759
Strout	55355
Stubbs Bay (Part of Orono)	55356
Sturgeon	55703
Sturgeon Lake	55783
Sugar Loaf (Part of Winona)	55987
Summit	55917
Sumter	55336
Sunburg	56289
Sundal	56545
Sunfish Lake	55118
Sunrise	55056
Suomi	56636
Svea	56216
Sveadahl	56081
Swanburg	56474
Swan River	55784
Swanville	56382
Swatara	55785
Swift	56682
Swift Falls	56215
Sylvan	56473
Syre	56584
Tabor	56712
Taconite	55786
Taconite Harbor	55613
Talmoon	56637
Tamarack	55787
Taopi	55977
Taunton	56291
Tawney	55954
Taylors Falls	55084
Tenney	56583
Tenstrike	56683
Terrace	56334
Terrebonne	56750
The Arches	55952
Theilman	55945
Thief River Falls	56701
Third Crow Wing Lake	56467
Thompsonburg	56142
Thompson Grove (Part of Cottage Grove)	55016
Thompson Heights (Part of Coon Rapids)	55433
Thompson Heights Shopping Center (Part of Coon Rapids)	55433
Thompson Park (Part of Coon Rapids)	55433
Thompson Riverview Terrace (Part of Coon Rapids)	55433
Thomson	55718
Thor	56431
Thorhult	56727
Tintah	56583
Toad Lake	56544
Tofte	55615
Togo	55723
Toimi	55602
Toivola	55765
Tonka Bay	55331
Tower	55790
Tracy	56175
Traffic (Part of Minneapolis)‡	55403
Trail	56684
Trails End	55604
Traverse	56082
Trimont	56176
Trommald	56441
Trosky	56177
Troy	55972
Truman	56088
Turtle River	56601
Twig	55791
Twin Cities (Part of Richfield)	55111
Twin Lakes	56089
Twin Valley	56584
Two Harbors	55616
Two Inlets	56470
Tyler	56178
Ulen	56585
Underwood	56586
Union Hill	56071
University (Part of Minneapolis)‡	55414
Upper Grey Cloud Island	55016
	55071
For specific ZIP Codes call (888) 275-8777, or your local postmaster.	
Upper Sioux Indian Reservation	56241
Upsala	56384
Uptown (Part of St. Paul)‡	55102
Urbank	56361
Utica	55979
Vadnais Heights	55127
Valley Ridge (Part of Burnsville)	55337
Valley West Shopping Center (Part of Bloomington)	55420
Vasa	55089
Verdi	56164
Vergas	56587
Vermillion	55085
Vermillion Dam	55771
Verndale	56481
Vernon Center	56090
Veseli	55046
Vesta	56292
Victoria	55386
Viking	56760
Village North Shopping Center (Part of Brooklyn Park)	55429
Villard	56385
Vineland♦	56359
Vining	56588
Viola	55934
Virginia	55777†
	55792*
Vista	56093
Wabasha	55981
Wabasso	56293
Wabedo	56655
Waconia	55387
Wacouta	55066
Wadena	56482
Wahkon	56386
Waite Park	56387
Walbo	55008
Waldo	55616
Waldorf	56091
Wales	55616
Walker	56484
Walnut Grove	56180
Walters	56097
Waltham	55982
Wanamingo	55983
Wanda	56294
Wannaska	56761
Warba	55793
Ward Springs	56336
Warman	55051
Warren	56762
Warroad	56763
Warsaw	55087
Waseca	56093
Washington	55975
Wasioja	55927
Waskish	56685
Wastedo	55009
Waterford	55057
Watertown	55388
Waterville	56096
Watkins	55389
Watson	56295
Watts	56662
Waubun	56589
Waverly	55390
Wawina	55736
Wayzata	55391
Wayzata Boulevard (Part of St. Louis Park)	55416
Wealthwood	56431
Weaver	55910
Weber	55056
Webster	55088
Wegdahl	56265
Welch	55089
Welcome	56181
Wells	56097
Weme	56634
Wendell	56590
West Albany	55957
West Albion	55302
West Bloomington‡	55437-38
For specific ZIP Codes call (888) 275-8777, or your local postmaster.	
Westbrook	56183
Westbury	56501
West Concord	55985
West Duluth (Part of Duluth)‡	55807
West Edina (Part of Edina)‡	55436
West End (Part of St. Paul)‡	55102
West Lake Francis Shores	55040
West Lynn	55350
West Newton	55945
West Point	55008
Westport	56385
West Rock	55063
West St. Paul	55118
West Union	56389
West Virginia (Part of Mountain Iron)	55792
Whalan	55949
Wheatland	56069
Wheaton	56296
Wheeler's Point	56623
Whipholt	56484
White Bear Beach	55110
White Bear Lake	55110
White Earth♦	56591
White Earth Indian Reservation	56591
Whiteface	55766
White Rock	55009
Whyte	55616
Wig Wam Bay	56359
Wilbert	56121
Wilder	56101
Wildwood	56661
Wilkinson	56633
Willernie	55090
Williams	56686
Willmar	56201
Willow Creek	56010
Willow River	55795
Wilmington	55921
Wilmont	56185
Wilno	56142
Wilpen (Part of Hibbing)	55746
Wilson	55987
Wilton, *Beltrami*	56687
Wilton, *Waseca*	56093
Windom	56101
Winger	56592
Winnebago, *Faribault*	56098
Winnebago, *Houston*	55921
Winnipeg Junction	56549
Winona	55987
Winsted	55395
Winthrop	55396
Winton	55796
Wirock	56141
Wirt	56688
Withrow	55082
Witoka	55987
Wolf	55751
Wolf Lake	56593
Wolford	56441
Wolverton	56594
Woodbury	55125
	55128-29
For specific ZIP Codes call (888) 275-8777, or your local postmaster.	
Wood Lake	56297
Woodland, *Hennepin*	55391
Woodland, *Kanabec*	56342
Woodland (Part of Duluth)	55803
Woodland Park	56551
Woodland Terrace (Part of Andover)	55303
Woodstock	56186
Worthington	56187
Wrenshall	55797
Wright	55798
Wrightstown	56453
Wyattville	55952
Wykoff	55990
Wylie	56750
Wyman (Part of Hoyt Lakes)	55750
Wyoming	55092
York	55939
Yorktown (Part of Edina)	55435
Young America (Part of Norwood Young American)	55394
	55397
For specific ZIP Codes call (888) 275-8777, or your local postmaster.	
Yucatan	55943
Zemple	56636
Zerkel	56621
Zim	55738
Zimmerman	55398
Zumbra Heights (Part of Victoria)	55386
Zumbro Falls	55991
Zumbrota	55992

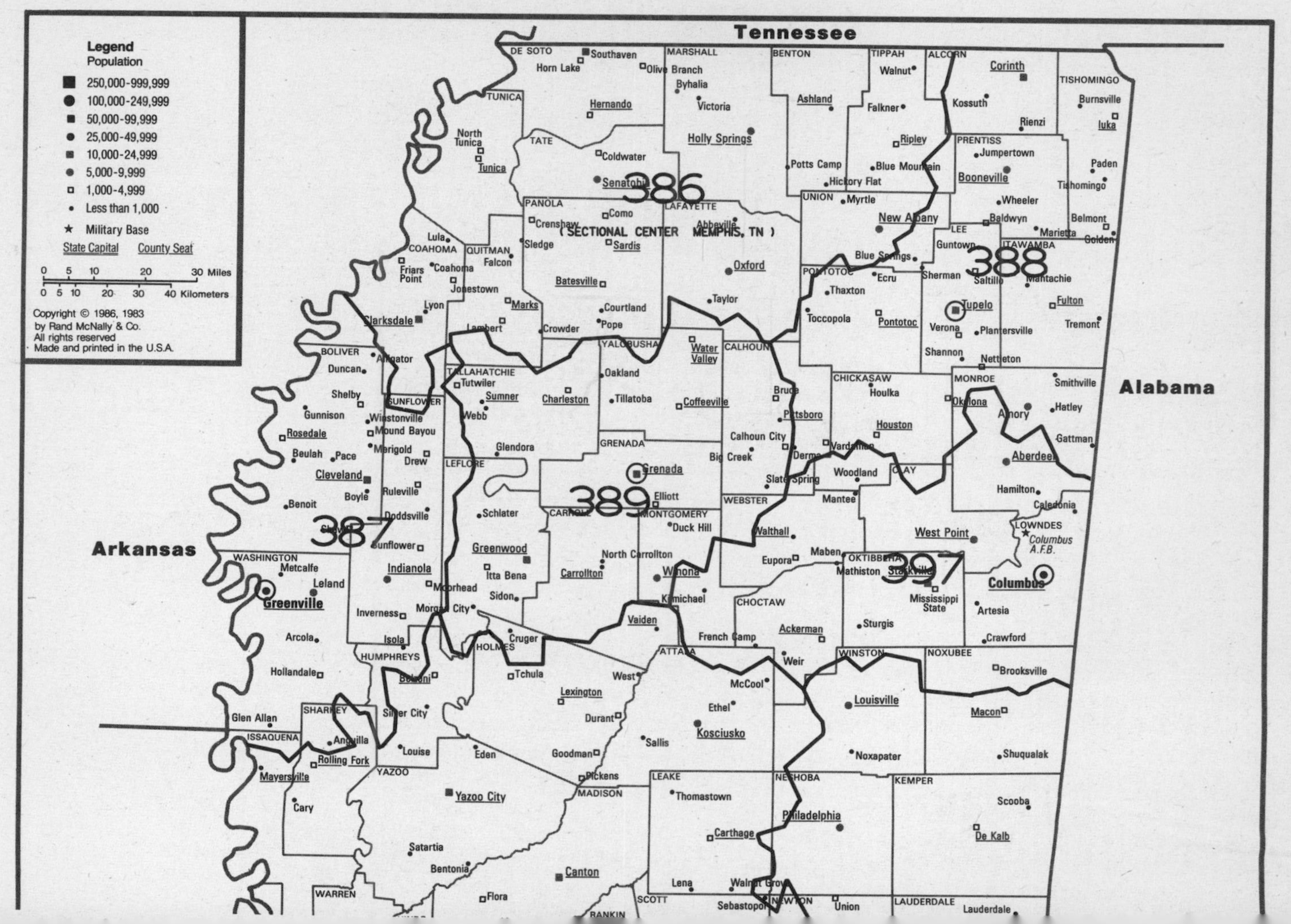
Tennessee
Alabama
Arkansas
386
387
388
389
397
(SECTIONAL CENTER MEMPHIS, TN)
DE SOTO
Southaven
Horn Lake
Olive Branch
Hernando
MARSHALL
Byhalia
Victoria
Holly Springs
BENTON
Ashland
Potts Camp
TIPPAH
Walnut
Falkner
Ripley
Blue Mountain
Hickory Flat
ALCORN
Corinth
Kossuth
Rienzi
TISHOMINGO
Burnsville
Iuka
Paden
Tishomingo
Belmont
Golden
PRENTISS
Jumpertown
Booneville
Wheeler
Baldwyn
Marietta
TUNICA
North Tunica
Tunica
TATE
Coldwater
Senatobia
PANOLA
Crenshaw
Como
Sledge
Sardis
Batesville
LAFAYETTE
Abbeville
Oxford
Taylor
UNION
Myrtle
New Albany
LEE
Guntown
Blue Springs
Sherman
Saltillo
ITAWAMBA
Mantachie
Fulton
Tremont
Tupelo
Verona
Plantersville
Shannon
Nettleton
PONTOTOC
Ecru
Thaxton
Toccopola
Pontotoc
Lula
COAHOMA
Friars Point
Coahoma
QUITMAN
Falcon
Jonestown
Lyon
Clarksdale
Marks
Lambert
Courtland
Pope
Crowder
YALOBUSHA
Water Valley
CALHOUN
BOLIVER
Alligator
Duncan
Shelby
Gunnison
Rosedale
Beulah
Pace
Cleveland
Boyle
Benoit
TALLAHATCHIE
Tutwiler
Sumner
Webb
Charleston
Oakland
Tillatoba
Coffeeville
Bruce
Pittsboro
Calhoun City
Big Creek
Derma
Slate Spring
SUNFLOWER
Winstonville
Mound Bayou
Merigold
Drew
Ruleville
Doddsville
Sunflower
Indianola
Inverness
Glendora
LEFLORE
Schlater
Greenwood
Itta Bena
Moorhead
Sidon
Morgan City
GRENADA
Grenada
Elliott
CARROLL
MONTGOMERY
Duck Hill
North Carrollton
Carrollton
Winona
Kilmichael
Vaiden
CHICKASAW
Houlka
Houston
Vardaman
Woodland
CLAY
Mantee
WEBSTER
Walthall
Eupora
Maben
OKTIBBEHA
Mathiston
Starkville
Mississippi State
Sturgis
MONROE
Okolona
Amory
Smithville
Hatley
Gattman
Aberdeen
Hamilton
Caledonia
LOWNDES
Columbus A.F.B.
West Point
Columbus
Artesia
Crawford
WASHINGTON
Metcalfe
Leland
Greenville
Arcola
Hollandale
Glen Allan
SHARKEY
ISSAQUENA
Anguilla
Rolling Fork
Mayersville
Cary
Isola
HUMPHREYS
Belzoni
Silver City
Louise
YAZOO
Yazoo City
Satartia
Bentonia
Eden
HOLMES
Cruger
Tchula
West
Lexington
Durant
Goodman
Pickens
MADISON
Canton
Flora
CHOCTAW
French Camp
Ackerman
Weir
ATTALA
McCool
Ethel
Kosciusko
Sallis
WINSTON
Louisville
Noxapater
NOXUBEE
Brooksville
Macon
Shuqualak
LEAKE
Thomastown
Carthage
Lena
NESHOBA
Philadelphia
Walnut Grove
KEMPER
Scooba
De Kalb
SCOTT
Sebastopol
NEWTON
Union
LAUDERDALE
Lauderdale
WARREN
RANKIN
Legend
Population
250,000-999,999
100,000-249,999
50,000-99,999
25,000-49,999
10,000-24,999
5,000-9,999
1,000-4,999
Less than 1,000
Military Base
State Capital
County Seat
0 5 10 20 30 Miles
0 5 10 20 30 40 Kilometers
Copyright © 1986, 1983
by Rand McNally & Co.
All rights reserved
Made and printed in the U.S.A.

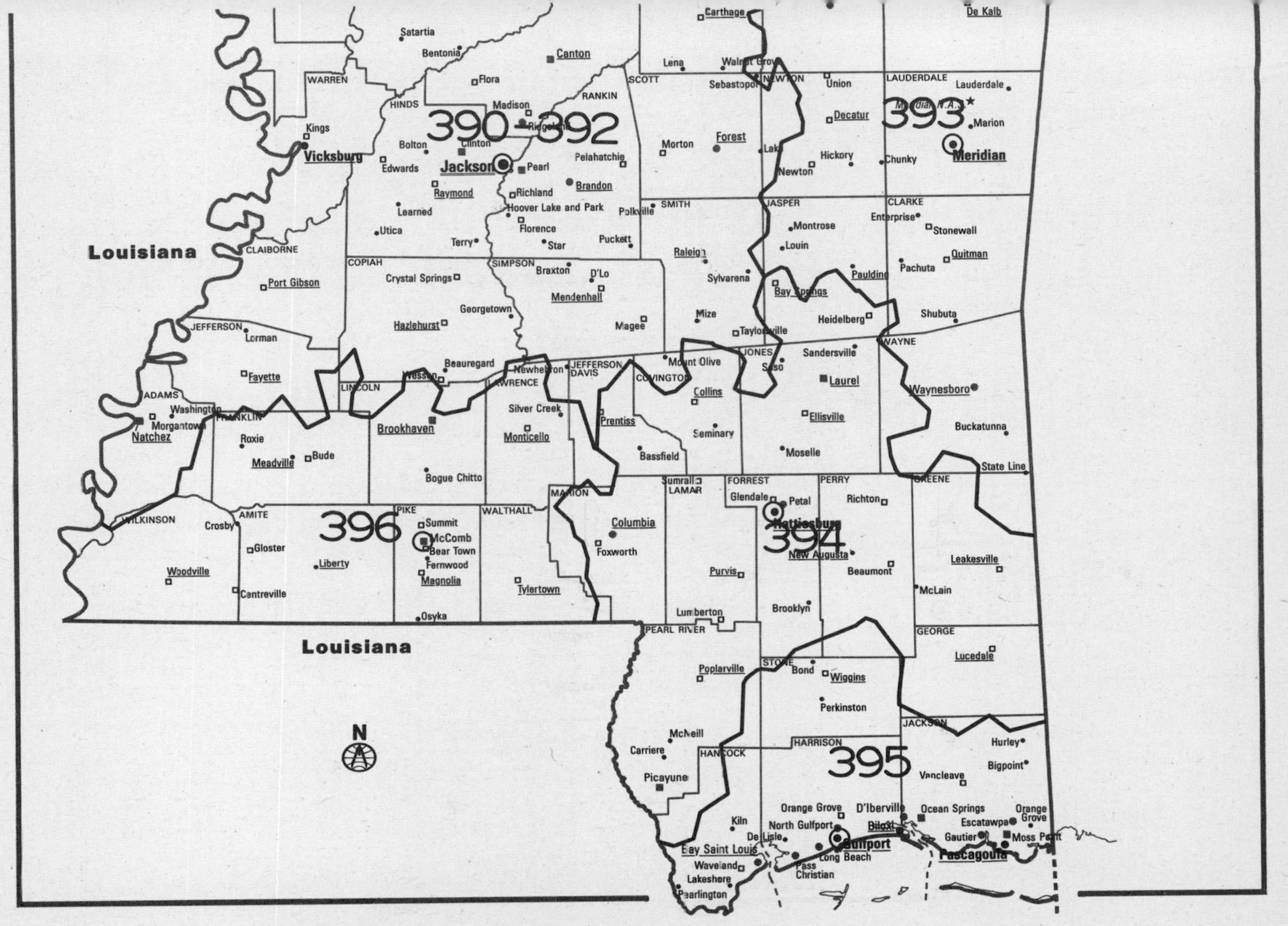
390-392
393
394
395
396
Louisiana
Louisiana
N
De Kalb
Carthage
Canton
Satartia
Bentonia
Flora
Madison
Warren
Hinds
Rankin
Scott
Lena
Sebastopol
Newton
Union
Lauderdale
Lauderdale
Marion
Meridian
Decatur
Hickory
Chunky
Newton
Forest
Morton
Kings
Vicksburg
Bolton
Clinton
Edwards
Jackson
Pearl
Pelahatchie
Brandon
Raymond
Richland
Learned
Hoover Lake and Park
Polkville
Smith
Jasper
Clarke
Enterprise
Stonewall
Montrose
Louin
Utica
Florence
Terry
Star
Puckett
Raleigh
Quitman
Pachuta
Claiborne
Copiah
Simpson
Braxton
D'Lo
Crystal Springs
Mendenhall
Sylvarena
Pauldinq
Port Gibson
Georgetown
Hazlehurst
Magee
Mize
Heidelberg
Shubuta
Jefferson
Lorman
Beauregard
Wesson
Newhebron
Jefferson Davis
Covington
Mount Olive
Jones
Sandersville
Wayne
Fayette
Lincoln
Lawrence
Collins
Laurel
Waynesboro
Adams
Washington
Morgantown
Franklin
Silver Creek
Prentiss
Ellisville
Natchez
Brookhaven
Monticello
Roxie
Seminary
Buckatunna
Meadville
Bude
Bassfield
Moselle
Bogue Chitto
State Line
Marion
Forrest
Perry
Greene
Glendale
Petal
Richton
Wilkinson
Amite
Pike
Walthall
Summit
McComb
Columbia
Crosby
Gloster
Bear Town
Foxworth
New Augusta
Fernwood
Beaumont
Leakesville
Liberty
Woodville
Magnolia
Tylertown
Purvis
McLain
Centreville
Brooklyn
Lumberton
Osyka
Pearl River
George
Lucedale
Poplarville
Stone
Bond
Wiggins
Perkinston
Jackson
McNeill
Hurley
Carriere
Harrison
Hancock
Bigpoint
Vancleave
Picayune
Orange Grove
D'Iberville
Ocean Springs
Orange Grove
Kiln
North Gulfport
Biloxi
Escatawpa
De Lisle
Gulfport
Gautier
Moss Point
Bay Saint Louis
Long Beach
Pascagoula
Waveland
Pass Christian
Lakeshore
Pearlington

A (Part of Hattiesburg)‡ 39406
Abbeville 38601
Abbott 39773
Aberdeen 39730
Ackerman 39735
Acona 39095
Adams 39175
Adaton 39759
Addie 38744
Agricola 39452
A H McCoy Federal Bldg (Part of Jackson)‡ 39269
Airey 39574
Albin 38966
Algoma 38820
Allen 39083
Alligator 38720
Alpine 38849
Altitude 38829
Alva 38925
Amory 38821
Anchor 39776
Anchorage 39194
Anding 39040
Anguilla 38721
Anse 39073
Ansley 39558
Antioch 39443
Apple Ridge (Part of Jackson) 39204
Arcola 38722
Ariel 39638
Arkabutla 38602
Arlington, *Lincoln* 39629
Arlington, *Neshoba* 39350
Arm 39663
Arnold Line 39402
Artesia 39736
Ashland 38603
Askew 38621
Athens 39730
Atlanta 39776
Atway 38635
Auburn, *Lee* 38801
Auburn, *Lincoln* 39666
Austin 38676
Avalon 38912
Avera 39451
Avon 38723
Bailey 39320
Baird 38751
Baker 38652
Bald Hill 38652
Baldwyn 38824
Ballard 39046
Ballardsville 38801
Ballentine 38621
Ball Ground 39156
Baltzer 38732
Banks 38664
Banner 38913
Barlow 39083
Barnes 39051
Barnesville 38109
Barnett 39347
Barr 38668
Barrontown 39465
Bartahatchie 39740
Barth 39470
Barto 39648
Barton, *George* 39452
Barton, *Marshall* 38017
Basic 39330
Basin 39452
Bassfield 39421
Batesville 38606
Batson 39401
Battlefield (Part of Jackson)‡ 39204
Battle Field, *Newton* 39325
Battles 39362
Baugh 38669
Baxter 39338
Baxterville 39455
Bayland 39194
Bay Saint Louis 39520-21
For specific ZIP Codes call (888) 275-8777, or your local postmaster.
Bayside Park 39520
Bay Springs 39422
Beacon Hill 38652
Beans Ferry 38843
Bear Town 39648
Beasley 39755
Beatline 39350
Beatrice 39330
Beatty 39176
Beaumont 39423
Beauregard 39191
Becker 38825
Beech Springs 38866
Beechwood 39645
Beelake 39169
Belden 38826
Belen 38609
Bellefontaine 39737
Belle Isle 39572
Belleville 39462
Bellewood 38754
Bells School 39759
Belmont 38827
Belzoni 39038
Benjoe 39456
Benndale 39456
Benoit 38725
Benson 39437
Bentley 39751
Bent Oak 39701
Benton 39039
Bentonia 39040
Benwood 38922
Berclair 38941
Berwick 39645
Bethany 38849
Betheden 39339
Bethel 39345
Bethlehem, *Marshall* 38659
Bethlehem, *Pontotoc* 38863
Bethsaida 39350
Bett 38618
Beulah, *Bolivar* 38726
Beulah, *Newton* 39337
Beulah Hubbard 39337
Bewelcome 39638
Bexley 39452
Bigbee 38821
Bigbee Valley 39739
Big Creek 38914
Biggersville 38834
Big Level 39573
Bigpoint 39581
Billups 39701
Biloxi 39530-35
For specific ZIP Codes call (888) 275-8777, or your local postmaster.
Binford 39730
Binnsville 39358
Birmingham Ridge 38828
Bissell 38801
Black Bayou Junction 38928
Black Hawk 38923
Blackjack 39759
Blackland 38829
Blackwater, *Kemper* 39326
Blackwater, *Lafayette* 38685
Blaine 38778
Blair 38849
Blakely 39183
Blanton 39159
Bloody Springs 38827
Bloomfield, *Kemper* 39328
Bloomfield, *Neshoba* 39350
Blue Hills 39144
Blue Lake 38737
Blue Mountain 38610
Blue Springs 38828
Bluff Springs, *Kemper* 39328
Bluff Springs, *Panola* 38666
Bobo, *Coahoma* 38614
Bobo, *Quitman* 38646
Boggan Bend 38849
Bogue Chitto, *Kemper*♦ 39350
Bogue Chitto, *Lincoln* 39629
Boice 39367
Bolatusha 39160
Bolivar 38725
Bolton 39041
Bond, *Neshoba* 39350
Bond, *Stone* 39577
Bon Homme 39401
Bonita (Part of Meridian) 39301
Boon 39339
Boone 38614
Booneville 38829
Bothwell 39476
Bounds Crossroads 35582
Bourbon 38756
Bovina 39180
Bowdre 38664
Bowling Green 39063
Bowman 38618
Boyer 38751
Boyette 39160
Boyle 38730
Bradley 39759
Branch 39117
Brandon 39042-43
 39047
For specific ZIP Codes call (888) 275-8777, or your local postmaster.
Branyan 38828
Brasfield 39096
Braxton 39044
Brazil 38963
Brewer, *Clarke* 39355
Brewer, *Lee* 38868
Brewer, *Perry* 39476
Bright 38632
Bristers Store 39641
Brockton (Part of Meridian) 39301
Brody 38603
Brookhaven 39601-03
For specific ZIP Codes call (888) 275-8777, or your local postmaster.
Brookhaven West (Part of Brookhaven)‡ 39603
Brook Hollow 39212
Brooklyn 39425
Brooks 38737
Brooksville 39739
Brownfield 38683
Browning 38930
Brownsville 39041
Brown Town 39452
Brozville 39095
Bruce 38915
Brunswick 39183
Bryant 38922
Buchannan 38863
Buckatunna 39322
Buckhorn 38864
Bude 39630
Buena Vista, *Chickasaw* 38851
Buena Vista, *Tippah* 38663
Buena Vista Lakes 38632
Bunker Hill 39429
Bunkley 39653
Burgess 38655
Burns 39153
Burnside 39350
Burnsville 38833
Burrell 38628
Burtons 38829
Bush 39149
Busy Corner 39638
Butler 39169
Byhalia 38611
Byram‡ 39272
Cadamy 38876
Cadaretta 38929
Caesar 39466
Caile 38754
Cairo 38873
Caledonia 39740
Calhoun, *Jones* 39443
Calhoun, *Newton* 39345
Calhoun City 38916
Calyx 39361
Cambridge 38601
Camden 39045
Cameron 39146
Cameta 39159
Campbell (Part of Ripley) 38663
Canaan 38603
Candlestick (Part of Jackson) 39212
Cannonsburg 39120
Canton 39046
Cardsville 38858
Carlisle 39086
Carlos 39191
Carmack 39176
Carmichael, *Clarke* 39360
Carmichael, *Perry* 39423
Carnes 39455
Carolina 38858
Carpenter 39086
Carriere 39426
Carrollton 38917
Carson 39427
Carter 39194
Carterville (Part of Petal) 39465
Carthage 39051
Cary 39054
Cascilla 38920
Caseyville 39191
Cato 39042
Cayce 38017
Cayuga 39175
Cedarbluff 39741
Cedar Hill, *Madison* 39071
Cedar Hill, *Montgomery* 38925
Cedars 39180
Cedarview 38654
Center, *Attala* 39090
Center, *Union* 38652
Center Hill 39307
Center Ridge, *Newton* 39337
Center Ridge, *Smith* 39168
Center Ridge, *Winston* 39339
Centerville 38855
Central Academy 38606
Centralgrove 38858
Centreville 39631
Chalybeate 38683
Champion Hill 39066
Chapel Hill 39175
Charleston 38921
Chatawa 39632
Chatham 38731
Cheraw 39483
Cherrycreek 38828
Chester 39735
Chesterville 38801
Chicora 39322
Chiwapa 38863
Choctaw, *Bolivar* 38773
Choctaw (Part of Laurel)‡ 39442
Chulahoma 38635
Chunky 39323
Church Hill 39120
Clack 38664
Clara 39324
Claremont 38614
Clarksburg 39117
Clarksdale 38614
Clarkson 39752
Clay 38843
Clayrysville 38663
Clayton 38626
Clayton Village 39759
Claytown 39339
Clem 39474
Cleo 39443
Clermont Harbor 39558
Cleveland, Bolivar 38732-33
For specific ZIP Codes call (888) 275-8777, or your local postmaster.
Cleveland, *Kemper* 39328
Clifton 39074
Cliftonville 39739
Clinton 39056*
 39060†
Cloverdale 39120
Clover Hill 38645
Cloverleaf Mall (Part of Hattiesburg) 39401
Coahoma 38617
Coats 39119
Cobbs 39601
Cobbville 39046
Cockrum 38632
Coffeeville 38922
Cohay 39153
Coila 38923
Colby 39194
Coldwater, *Neshoba* 39350
Coldwater, *Tate* 38618
Coles 39633
College (Part of Columbus)‡ 39701
College Hill 38655
Collins 39428
Collinsville♦ 39325
Colonial (Part of Jackson)‡ 39211
Colony Town 38941
Colsub (Part of Amory) 38821
Columbia 39429
Columbus 39701-05
For specific ZIP Codes call (888) 275-8777, or your local postmaster.
Columbus Air Force Base 39701
Commerce 38664
Como 38619
Concord 38652
Conehatta♦ 39057
Conway 39051
Cooksville 39341
Cooperville 39117
Coosa 39051
Corinth 38834-35
For specific ZIP Codes call (888) 275-8777, or your local postmaster.
Cornersville 38633
Corrona 38849
Cotton Plant 38610
Cottonville 38618
Counts 38614
County Line 39362
Courthouse (Part of Gulfport)‡ 39501
Courtland 38620
Cowart 38921
Coxburg 39095
Coxs Ferry 39041
Coy 39354
Craigside 38930
Craig Springs 39769
Crandall 39355
Crane Creek 39573
Cranfield 39661
Crawford 39743
Crenshaw 38621
Crockett 38668
Crosby 39633
Crossgates (Part of Brandon) 39042
Crossroad 39051
Crossroads, *George* 39452
Crossroads, *Neshoba* 39350
Crossroads, *Pearl River* 39470
Cross Roads, *Rankin* 39145
Cross Roads, *Tishomingo* 38852
Crossroads (Part of Greenville)‡ 38703
Crotts 39437
Crowder 38622
Cruger 38924
Crupp 39194
Crystal Springs 39059
Cuba 38834
Cub Lake 38632
Cuevas 39571
Cumberland 39750
Curtis Station 38606
Cybur 39466
Cynthia 39206
D (Part of Hattiesburg)‡ 39401
Dahomey 38725
Daisy-Vestry 39573
Daleville 39326
Damascus, *Kemper* 39328
Damascus, *Scott* 39189
Dancy 39751
Daniel 39151
Darbun 39643
Darden 38650
Darling 38623
Darlove 38748
Darracott 39730
Darrington 39633
Davenport 38614
Davis 39046
Days 38641
Deans Corner 38641
Deasonville 39179
Decatur 39327
Deemer 39350
Deemer Station 39320
Deep Creek 39425
Deerbrook 39739
Deeson 38740
De Kalb 39328
De Lay 38655
De Lisle 39571
Delta 38621
Delta City 39061
Delta Drive (Part of Jackson)‡ 39213
Delta State University (Part of Cleveland)‡ 38733
Denham 39367
Denmark 38655
Dennis 38838
Dennis Settlement 39092
Dentontown 38916
Dentville 39086
Deovolente 39038
Derby 39470
Derma 38839
De Soto 39360
Deweese 39350
Dexter 39667
Diamondhead♦ 39525
D'Iberville 39532
Dinsmore 39341

* **Area Zip Code** † **Post Office Boxes** ‡ **Postal Station** ♦ **Census Designated Place** *Italic Type* **County**

Divide 39654
Dixie 39401
Dixie Pine 39401
Dixon 39350
D'Lo 39062
Doddsville 38736
Doloroso 39669
Donegal 39669
Doolittle 39345
Dorsey 38843
Doskie 38852
Dossville 39051
Dover, *Neshoba* 39365
Dover, *Yazoo* 39040
Dowdville 39350
Downtown (Part of Gulfport)‡ 39501
Downtown (Part of Jackson)‡ 39201
39205
39207
39215
39225
For specific ZIP Codes call (888) 275-8777, or your local postmaster.
Downtown (Part of Tupelo)‡ 38801
Downtown (Part of Vicksburg)‡ 39181
Drew 38737
Dry Creek 39428
Dubard 38901
Dubbs 38626
Dublin 38739
Duck Hill 38925
Duffee 39337
Dumas 38625
Duncan 38740
Dundee 38626
Dunleith 38756
Durant 39063
Dwiggins 38737
Dwyer 38778
E (Part of Hattiesburg)‡ 39401
Eagle Lake 39183
Earlygrove 38642
East Aberdeen 39730
Eastabuchie 39436
Eastfork 39664
East Heights (Part of Tupelo)‡ 38801
East Hillsboro 39074
Eastlawn (Part of Pascagoula)‡ 39569
East Lincoln 39601
East Moss Point (Part of Moss Point) 39563
Eastport 38852
East Side 39476
East Tupelo (Part of Tupelo) 38801
Eatonville 39401
Ebenezer 39095
Ecru 38841
Eddiceton 39647
Eden 39194
Edgewater Mall (Part of Biloxi) 39532
Edinburg 39051
Edwards 39066
Eggville 38801
Egremont 39159
Egypt, *Chickasaw* 38860
Egypt, *Holmes* 38924
Electric Mills 39358
Elizabeth 38756
Ellard 38915
Elliott 38926
Ellistown 38838
Ellisville 39437
Ellisville Junction 39437
Elsie 38878
Elton (Part of Jackson) 39212
Elwood 39355
Eminence 39479
Emory 39095
Endville 38828
Energy 39301
Enid 38927
Enon 39641
Enondale 39352
Enterprise, *Amite* 39645
Enterprise, *Clarke* 39330
Enterprise, *Lincoln* 39601
Enterprise, *Union* 38650
Enzor 39301
Errata 39443
Erwin 38744
Escatawpa♦ 39552
Eset 39362
Eskridge 38925
Essex 38623
Estes 39339
Estesmill 39051
Estill 38748
Ethel 39067
Etta 38627
Eucutta 39360
Eudora 38632
Eunice 39638
Eupora 39744
Eureka Springs 38620
Evansville, *Tate* 38618
Evansville, *Tunica* 38676
Everett 39114
Evergreen 38843
Expose 39429
Fairfield 38828
Fairground 39350
Fairhaven 38654
Fairhill 39361
Fairlane (Part of Columbus)‡ 39701
Fair Oaks Springs 39601
Fair River 39601
Fairview, *Itawamba* 38847
Fairview, *Sunflower* 38751
Falcon 38628
Falkner 38629
Fame 39744
Fannin 39047
Farmhaven 39046
Farmington 38834
Farrell 38630
Fayette 39069
Fenton 39571
Fentress 39735
Fenwick 39120
Fernwood 39635
Fikestown 39092
Fitler 39159
Fitzhugh 38737
Flora 39071
Florence 39073
Flowerdale (Part of Tupelo) 38801
Floweree 39156
Flowood 39208
Floyd 38603
Fondren (Part of Jackson)‡ 39216
Fontainebleau 39564
Fords Creek 39470
Fordyke 39039
Forest 39074
Forestdale 39365
Forest Grove 39051
Forest Hill (Part of Jackson) 39212
Forkville 39117
Fort Adams 39669
Fort Stephens 39320
Four Corners 39090
Four Mile 39038
Foxworth 39483
Franklin 39661
Frankstown 38824
Freeny 39051
Freerun 39194
Freetrade 39051
Freeze Corner 38632
French Camp 39745
French Store 39073
Friars Point 38631
Friendship, *Lincoln* 39601
Friendship, *Pontotoc* 38841
Frog Island 38801
Frostbridge 39367
Fruitland Park 39577
Fugate 39039
Fulton 38843
Furrs 38863
Futheyville 38901
Gallman 39077
Gandsi 39479
Garden City 39661
Garlandville 39345
Gaston 38865
Gatesville 39059
Gatewood 38922
Gattman 38844
Gault 38655
Gautier 39553
Geeslin Corner 38901
Geeville 38829
Geneill 38756
General Mail Facility (Part of Jackson)‡ 39205
Georgetown 39078
Gholson 39354
Gibson 39730
Gift 38834
Giles 39358
Gill 39051
Gillsburg 39657
Gitano 39168
Glade 39443
Glancy 39083
Glen 38846
Glen Allan 38744
Glendale 39401
Glendora 38928
Glenfield (Part of New Albany) 38652
Glenville 38619
Glenwild 38901
Gloster 39638
Glover 38680
Gluckstadt 39110
Golden 38847
Golden Grove 39365
Goldfield 38737
Gooden Lake 39038
Good Hope, *Leake* 39094
Good Hope, *Neshoba* 39350
Good Hope, *Perry* 39476
Goodman 39079
Goodwater 39366
Goodyear (Part of Picayune) 39466
Gore Springs 38929
Goshen Springs 39047
Goss 39429
Grace 38745
Grady 39744
Graham 38824
Grand Gulf 39150
Grange 39140
Grange Hall 39180
Grapeland 38725
Gravel Hill 38930
Graves 38828
Gravestown 38663
Greenbrier Park 39466
Greenfield 39042
Greenfield Addition (Part of Greenville) 38701
Green Grove 38767
Greenland 39365
Greenville 38701-04
For specific ZIP Codes call (888) 275-8777, or your local postmaster.
Greenville Mall (Part of Greenville) 38701
Greenville North (Part of Greenville) 38701
Greenwood, *Itawamba* 38843
Greenwood, *Leflore* 38930-35
For specific ZIP Codes call (888) 275-8777, or your local postmaster.
Greenwood Springs 38848
Grenada 38901*
38902†
Griffith 39741
Gulde 39042
Gulf Hills Country Club 39564
Gulf Park Estates♦ 39564
Gulfport 39501-07
For specific ZIP Codes call (888) 275-8777, or your local postmaster.
Gum Grove 39169
Gums 38922
Gum Springs 39074
Gunnison 38746
Guntown 38849
Gwin (Part of Tchula) 39169
Gwinville 39140
Hale 39360
Halltown 38849
Hamburg 39661
Hamilton 39746
Hampton 38744
Handle 39339
Handsboro (Part of Gulfport) 39501
Handy Corner 38654
Hard Cash 39038
Hardy 38901
Harleston 39452
Harmontown 38619
Harmony 39355
Harperville 39080
Harriston 39081
Harrisville 39082
Harvey (Part of Petal) 39465
Hathorn 39429
Hatley 38821
Hattiesburg 39401-07
For specific ZIP Codes call (888) 275-8777, or your local postmaster.
Hayes Crossing 38666
Hays 39057
Hazel 39092
Hazlehurst 39083
Heads 38756
Heathman 38751
Hebron, *Jefferson Davis* 39140
Hebron, *Jones* 39168
Heidelberg 39439
Helena 39581
Helm 38756
Henderson's Point (Part of Pass Christian) 39571
Hendrix 39747
Henleyfield 39426
Herbert Springs 39325
Hermanville 39086
Hernando 38632
Hero 39345
Hesterville 39192
Heucks Retreat 39191
Hickory 39332
Hickory Flat 38633
Hideaway Hills 38666
Hidi 39166
Higgins 39482
High Hill 39350
Highlandale 38952
High Point 39339
Hightown 38834
Hillhouse 38720
Hillman 39451
Hillsboro 39087
Hillsdale 39470
Hinchcliff 38646
Hinkle 38865
Hintonville 39423
Hinze 39108
Hiram 38963
Hiwannee 39367
Hobo Station 38829
Hohenlinden 39751
Holcomb 38940
Holcut 38852
Hollandale 38748
Hollis 38878
Holly Bluff 39088
Holly Grove 38954
Holly Ridge 38749
Holly Springs 38634-35
For specific ZIP Codes call (888) 275-8777, or your local postmaster.
Hollywood 38676
Holmesville 39648
Holts Spur 38833
Homewood 39074
Homochitto 39638
Honey Island 39038
Hoover Lake and Park 39073
Hope 39350
Hopedale 39113
Hopewell, *Benton* 38067
Hopewell, *Copiah* 39059
Hopoca 39051
Horn Lake 38637
Horseshoe, *Holmes* 39169
Horse Shoe, *Scott* 39189
Hortontown 38863
Hot Coffee 39428
Houlka 38850
House 39365
Houston 38851
Howard 39095
Howell 39452
Howison 39574
Hoy 39443
Hub 39429
Hubbard 39066
Hudsonville 38635
Humber 38614
Huntsville 39745
Hurley 39555
Hurricane 38863
Hurricane Creek 39301
Hushpuckena 38774
Improve 39429
Increase 39301
Inda 39573
Independence, *Scott* 39117
Independence, *Tate* 38638
Indian Hills 38866
Indianola 38751
Indian Springs 39401
Industrial 39466
Ingomar 38652
Ingrams Mill 38611
Inverness 38753
Isola 38754
Itta Bena 38941
Iuka 38852
Jacinto 38865
Jack 39175
Jackson 39201-98
For specific ZIP Codes call (888) 275-8777, or your local postmaster.
Jackson Mall (Part of Jackson) 39213
Jackson Square (Part of Jackson)‡ 39204
Jackson State University (Part of Jackson)‡ 39217
Jago 38671
Jaketown 39038
James 38748
Jamestown 39483
Janice 39425
Jayess 39641
Jeannette 39120
Jeff Davis 39180
Jefferson 38917
Jeffries 38626
Jenkins 39437
Jericho 38824
Johns 39042
Johnson 39437
Johnston 39666
Jonathan 39451
Jonestown, *Coahoma* 38639
Jonestown, *Yazoo* 39194
Jug Fork 38828
Jumpertown 38829
Junction City 39355
Kalem 39117
Keirn 38024
Kellis Store 39354
Kelona 39366
Kendrick 38834
Keownville 38652
Kewanee 39364
Key Field (Part of Meridian) 39301
Kilmichael 39747
Kiln♦ 39556
King and Anderson 38614
Kings 39183
Kingston 39120
Kinlock 38751
Kipling 39328
Kirby 39661
Kirkville 38843
Kittrell 39423
Klem 39074
Klondike 39320
Knobtown 39362
Knoxo 39667
Knoxville 39661
Kokomo 39643
Kola 39428
Kolola Springs 39740
Kosciusko 39090
Kossuth 38834
Kreole (Part of Moss Point) 39563
Lackey 39730
Lafayette Springs 38655
Lake 39092
Lake Center 38659
Lake City, *Prentiss* 38829
Lake City, *Yazoo* 39194
Lake Como 39422
Lake Cormorant 38641
Lakeland (Part of Richland) 39218
Lake of Hills 38632
Lakeshore 39558
Lake View 38680
Lamar 38642
Lamar Park 39401
Lambert 38643
Lamkin 39166
Lamont 38703
Lampton 39429
Landon (Part of Gulfport) 39503
Langford 39042
Langsdale 39360
Larue 39565
Latimer♦ 39565

Latonia 39452
Lauderdale 39335
Laurel 39440-43
For specific ZIP Codes call (888) 275-8777, or your local postmaster.
Laurelhill 39350
Lawrence 39336
Laws Hill 38685
Leaf 39456
Leakesville 39451
Learned 39154
Lebanon, *Hinds* 39154
Lebanon, *Marshall* 38659
Lee Donald 39366
Leedy 38833
Leesburg 39117
Leesdale 39661
Leeville 39401
Lefleur (Part of Jackson)‡ 39211
Leflore 38940
Leigh Mall (Part of Columbus) 39701
Leland 38756
Lemon 39074
Lena 39094
Lessley 39669
Le Tourneau 39180
Leverett 38920
Lewisburg 38654
Lexie 39667
Lexington 39095
Liberty, *Amite* 39645
Liberty, *Kemper* 39328
Lightsey 39443
Lillian 39074
Linn 38736
Linwood, *Neshoba* 39365
Linwood, *Yazoo* 39179
Little Creek 39423
Little Italy 39092
Little Rock 39337
Little Texas 38676
Little Yazoo 39040
Litton 38773
Lizana 39503
Lobdell 38726
Lobutcha 39108
Loch Leven 39669
Locke Station 38606
Lockhart 39335
Lodi, *Humphreys* 39166
Lodi, *Montgomery* 39767
Lombardy 38774
Long 38756
Long Beach 39560
Longino 39350
Long Lake, *Coahoma* 38617
Long Lake, *Warren* 39183
Longshot 38773
Longtown 38665
Longview, *Oktibbeha* 39759
Longview, *Pontotoc* 38863
Looxahoma 38668
Lorena 39074
Lorenzen 39159
Lorman 39096
Louin 39338
Louise 39097
Louisville 39339
Love 38632
Loyd 38878
Loyd Star 39601
Lucas 39474
Lucedale 39452
Lucern 39365
Lucien 39601
Luckney 39208
Ludlow 39098
Lula 38644
Lumberton 39455
Lurand 38614
Lux 39401
Lyman (Part of Gulfport) 39503
Lynchburg 38109
Lynn Creek 39739
Lynville 39354
Lyon 38645
Maben 39750
McAdams 39107
McBride 39144
McCall Creek 39647
McCallum 39401
McCarley 38943
McComb 39648-49
For specific ZIP Codes call (888) 275-8777, or your local postmaster.

McCondy 38854
McCool 39108
McCrary 39701
McCutcheon 38722
Mc Donald, *Leake* 39094
McDonald, *Neshoba* 39365
Macedonia, *Forrest* 39401
Macedonia, *Lee* 38801
Macedonia, *Union* 38650
Macel 38950
McElveen 39666
McHenry 39561
McLain 39456
McLaurin 39401
McLaurin Heights (Part of Pearl) 39208
McLeod 39341
McMillan 39339
McNair 39069
McNeal 39338
McNeill 39457
Macon 39341
McSwain 39476
McVille 39090
Madden 39109
Madison 39110*
39130†
Madisonville 39046
Magee 39111
Magnolia 39652
Mahned 39462
Main (Part of Meridian)‡ 39302
Malone 38685
Malvina 38769
Mannassa 39355
Mantachie 38855
Mantee 39751
Marcella 39169
Marianna 38635
Marie 38751
Marietta 38856
Marion 39342
Maris Town (Part of Canton) 39046
Markette 38655
Markham 38761
Marks 38646
Mars Hill 39666
Martin 39325
Martin Bluff♦ 39553
Martinsville 39083
Martintown 38652
Martinville 39114
Marydell 39051
Mashulaville 39341
Matherville 39360
Mathiston 39752
Mattson 38758
Maxie 39425
Maybank 39401
Maybell 39437
Mayersville 39113
Mayhew 39753
Mayton 39042
Maywood 38654
Meadville 39653
Mechanicsburg 39040
Meehan 39301
Meeks 38924
Melba 39482
Meltonville 39046
Memphis 38680
Mendenhall 39114
Meridian 39301-07
For specific ZIP Codes call (888) 275-8777, or your local postmaster.
Meridian Naval Air Station 39309
Merigold 38759
Merit 39114
Merrill 39452
Mesa 39667
Metcalfe 38760
Metrocenter (Part of Jackson) 39209
Meyers 39401
Michigan City 38647
Midnight 39115
Midway, *Copiah* 39191
Midway, *Hinds* 39170
Midway, *Leake* 39051
Midway, *Scott* 39074
Midway, *Tishomingo* 38852
Midway, *Yazoo* 39039
Mileston 39169
Millard 39470
Mill Creek, *Jones* 39443
Mill Creek, *Pearl River* 39426

Mill Creek, *Rankin* 39047
Millcreek, *Winston* 39339
Mill Creek Cabin Area 38852
Miller 38654
Millington 39358
Millsaps College (Part of Jackson)‡ 39210
Mill Town (Part of Canton) 39046
Mimms 38606
Mineral Wells 38654
Mingo 38873
Minter City 38944
Missionary 39356
Mississippi Choctaw Indian Reservation 39350
Mississippi City (Part of Gulfport) 39501
Mississippi College (Part of Clinton)‡ 39058
Mississippi State 39762
Mitchell 38663
Mize 39116
Money 38945
Monroe 39653
Monterey 39073
Monte Vista 39744
Montgomery 39191
Monticello 39654
Montpelier 39754
Montrose 39338
Moon 38617
Moores Mill 38838
Mooreville 38857
Moorhead 38761
Morgan City 38946
Morgans 39170
Morgantown, *Adams* 39120
Morgantown, *Marion* 39483
Morgantown, *Oktibbeha* 39769
Morning Star 39066
Morriston 39401
Morton 39117
Moscow 39328
Moselle 39459
Moss 39460
Moss Point 39562-63
For specific ZIP Codes call (888) 275-8777, or your local postmaster.
Mossy Lake 38959
Mound Bayou 38762
Mound City, *Bolivar* 38726
Mound City, *Union* 38828
Mount Carmel 39474
Mount Nebo 39328
Mount Olive, *Covington* 39119
Mount Olive, *Franklin* 39653
Mount Olive, *Jones* 39443
Mount Pleasant, *Itawamba* 38876
Mount Pleasant, *Marshall* 38649
Mount Vernon 38801
Mount Zion 39111
Movella 39452
Muldon 39730
Mullins Store 38655
Murphy 38748
Murry 38663
Muskegon 39092
Myrick 39443
Myrleville 39039
Myrtle 38650
Nancy 39366
Nason 38940
Natchez 39120-22
For specific ZIP Codes call (888) 275-8777, or your local postmaster.
National Cemetery (Part of Vicksburg) 39180
Necaise 39573
Neely 39461
Nellieburg♦ 39307
Nesbit 38651
Neshoba 39365
Nettleton 38858
Nevada 39041
New Albany 38652
New Augusta 39462
New Byram 39212
New Canaan 38603
New Fitler 39159
New Garden 38618
New Harmony 38828
New Hebron 39140
New Hope♦ 39702

Newman 39066
Newmans 39180
Newmans Grove 39154
Newport, *Attala* 39160
Newport, *DeSoto* 38641
New Salem 38843
New Sight 39601
New Site 38859
Newton 39345
New Town 38668
New Wren 39730
Nichols 38959
Nicholson 39463
Nida 39169
Nitta Yuma 38763
Nixon, *Humphreys* 39115
Nixon, *Pontotoc* 38863
Nod 39039
Nola 39665
Norfield 39629
Norfolk 38641
Norris 39074
North (Part of Jackson)‡ 39206
North (Part of Meridian)‡ 39305
North Bay (Part of D'Iberville) 39532
North Bend 39350
North Carrollton 38947
North Crossroads 38852
North Greenville (Part of Greenville) 38701
North Gulfport (Part of Gulfport) 39503
North Haven 38652
North Long Beach (Part of Long Beach) 39560
Northpark Mall (Part of Ridgeland) 39157
North Tunica♦ 38676
Northwest Junior College (Part of Senatobia)‡ 38668
Norton 38663
Noxapater 39346
Oak Bowery 39437
Oak Grove, *Holmes* 39169
Oak Grove, *Jones* 39437
Oak Grove, *Lamar* 39401
Oak Grove, *Perry* 39423
Oakland, *Itawamba* 38843
Oakland, *Pike* 39666
Oakland, *Yalobusha* 38948
Oakley 39154
Oak Ridge 39183
Oak Vale 39656
Obadiah 39320
Ocean Springs 39564-66
For specific ZIP Codes call (888) 275-8777, or your local postmaster.
Ocobla 39350
Ofahoma 39051
Oil City 39040
Okahola 39475
Oklahoma 38917
Okolona 38860
Oktoc 39759
Old Cairo 38829
Old Dominion 38946
Oldenburg 39661
Oldham 38852
Old Hamilton 39746
Old Houlka 38850
Old Red Star 39601
Old Union 38868
Olive Branch 38654
Oloh 39482
Oma 39654
Omega 39169
Onward 39159
Ora 39428
Orange 39347
Orange Grove (Part of Gulfport) 39503
Orange Grove, *Jackson* 39581
Orange Hill 39041
O'Reilly 38730
Orwood 38655
Osborn 39759
Osborne Creek 38829
Osyka 39657
Ovett 39464
Owens Wells 39095
Oxberry 38940
Oxford, *Amite* 39638
Oxford, *Lafayette* 38655
Ozona 39426

Pace 38764
Pachuta 39347
Paden 38873
Palmer 39401
Palmetto 38801
Panther Burn 38765
Parham 38848
Paris 38949
Parks 38652
Parksplace 38619
Pascagoula 39567-69
39581
For specific ZIP Codes call (888) 275-8777, or your local postmaster.
Pascagoula River Estates 39456
Pass Christian 39571
Patosi 39194
Pattison 39144
Paul 38920
Paulding 39348
Paulette 39341
Paynes 38920
Pearl, *Rankin* 39208
Pearl, *Simpson* 39073
Pearl City (Part of Pearl) 39208
Pearlington♦ 39572
Pearl River 39350
Pearson 39208
Pecan 39581
Pecan Grove 39437
Pelahatchie 39145
Penantly 39356
Pendorff 39443
Penns Station 39743
Penton 38664
Peoples 38663
Peoria 39645
Percy 38748
Perdue 39337
Perkinston 39573
Perrytown 39633
Perth 39069
Perthshire 38746
Petal 39465
Peteet 38946
Peyton 39144
Pheba 39755
Philadelphia 39350
Philipp 38950
Phillipstown 38954
Phoenix 39040
Piave 39476
Picayune 39466
Pickens 39146
Pickwick 39483
Pierce Crossroads 39194
Piggtown 39094
Piketown 39074
Pinckneyville 39669
Pinebluff 39751
Pinebur 39429
Pinedale 38627
Pine Flat, *Lafayette* 38965
Pine Flat, *Tishomingo* 38852
Pine Grove, *Benton* 38633
Pine Grove, *Lamar* 39475
Pine Grove, *Lee* 38868
Pine Grove, *Tippah* 38829
Pine Ridge, *Adams* 39120
Pine Ridge, *Lamar* 39475
Pine Springs 39301
Pine Valley 38965
Pineview 39443
Pineville 39074
Piney Woods 39148
Pinola 39149
Pisgah, *Greene* 39452
Pisgah, *Prentiss* 38865
Pisgah, *Rankin* 39047
Pistol Ridge 39455
Pittman 39483
Pittsboro 38951
Plainview (Part of Richland) 39218
Plantersville 38862
Plattsburg 39350
Pleasant Grove 38666
Pleasant Hill, *Copiah* 39668
Pleasant Hill, *DeSoto* 38651
Pleasant Hill, *Union* 38652
Pleasant Ridge, *Jones* 39443
Pleasant Ridge, *Union* 38625
Plum Point 38671
Pluto 39169
Poagville 38618
Pocahontas 39072
Pokal 39140

*** Area Zip Code** **† Post Office Boxes** **‡ Postal Station** **♦ Census Designated Place** *Italic Type* **County**

Place	ZIP
Polfrey	39564
Polkville	39117
Pollock	38751
Pond	39669
Ponta	39301
Pontotoc	38863
Poolville	38650
Pope	38658
Poplar Corners	38680
Poplar Creek	39747
Poplar Springs, *Holmes*	39063
Poplar Springs, *Montgomery*	39747
Poplar Springs, *Newton*	39345
Poplarville	39470
Porterville	39352
Port Gibson	39150
Posey Mound	38623
Post	39325
Potts Camp	38659
Powell	38626
Powers	39443
Prairie	39756
Prairie Point	39341
Prentiss	39474
Presidential Hills (Part of Jackson)	39213
Preston	39354
Pricedale	39666
Prichard	38676
Prince Chapel	39354
Priscilla	38701
Prismatic	39320
Progress, *Jefferson Davis*	39474
Progress, *Perry*	39423
Progress, *Pike*	39648
Prospect	39057
Puckett	39151
Pulaski	39152
Pumpkin Center	38652
Purvis	39475
Pyland	38851
Quentin	39647
Quincy	38848
Quitman	39355
Quito	38941
Quofaloma	39169
Rainey	39459
Raleigh	39153
Ramsey Springs	39573
Randolph	38864
Rankin	39042
Ratliff	38855
Rawls Springs	39401
Raworth	39117
Raymond	39154
Raytown	39046
Red Banks	38661
Redbone	39180
Reddoch	39168
Red Lick	39096
Redstar	39191
Redwater♦	39051
Redwood	39156
Reedtown	39175
Reform	39735
Refuge	38701
Reid	38951
Remus	39051
Rena Lara	38767
Renfroe	39051
Renova	38732
Revive	39045
Rexburg	38756
Rexford	39073
Rhodes	39476
Riceville	39573
Rich	38617
Richardson	39466
Richland, *Holmes*	39079
Richland, *Humphreys*	39166
Richland, *Rankin*	39218
Richmond	38801
Richton	39476
Ridgeland	39157*
	39158†
Rienzi	38865
Ripley	38663
Rising Sun	38954
Riverton (Part of Clarksdale)	38614
Riverview Estates	39456
Robbs	38864
Roberts	39336
Robinson Gin	38632
Robinsonville	38664
Robinwood	39654
Rock Creek	39365
Rock Hill, *Alcorn*	38834
Rock Hill, *Forrest*	39475
Rock Hill, *Oktibbeha*	39759
Rock Hill, *Panola*	38666
Rock Hill, *Rankin*	39042
Rockport	39083
Rocky Springs	39086
Rodney	39096
Roebuck	38954
Rogerslacy	39477
Rolling Fork	39159
Rome	38768
Roseacres	38617
Rosebloom	38920
Rosebud	39189
Rosedale	38769
Rose Hill	39356
Rosella	39654
Rosemary	39170
Rosetta	39633
Rough Edge	38863
Roundaway	38614
Roundlake	38740
Rounsaville	39452
Roxie	39661
Ruby	38950
Rudyard	38617
Ruleville	38771
Runnelstown	39401
Rural Hill	39108
Russell	39301
Russellville	39162
Russum	39096
Ruth	39662
Ryan	38843
Sabino	38646
Sabougla	38916
St. Ann	39051
St. Martin♦	39533
Salem, *Leake*	39189
Salem, *Walthall*	39667
Sallis	39160
Saltillo	38866
Sanatorium	39112
Sandersville	39477
Sand Hill, *Copiah*	39191
Sand Hill, *Greene*	39476
Sand Hill, *Jones*	39437
Sandhill, *Rankin*	39161
Sandpoint	39153
Sandtown	39350
Sandy Hook	39478
Sanford	39479
Sapa	39744
Sarah	38665
Saratoga	39111
Sardis, *Copiah*	39083
Sardis, *Panola*	38666
Sarepta	38864
Sartinsville	39641
Satartia	39162
Saucier	39574
Saukum	39633
Savage	38665
Savannah	39470
Savannah Grove (Part of Meridian)	39301
Savoy	39301
Schamberville	39325
Schlater	38952
Schley	39140
Scobey	38953
Scooba	39358
Scotland	39040
Scott	38772
Sebastopol	39359
Sellers	39573
Sels Prairie	39360
Seminary	39479
Senatobia	38668
Senatobia Lakes	38668
Seneca	39455
Sessums	39759
Seven Springs	39154
Shackleford	39169
Shady Grove, *Copiah*	39083
Shady Grove, *Jones*	39443
Shannon	38868
Sharkey	38921
Sharon, *Jones*	39443
Sharon, *Madison*	39163
Sharpsburg	39146
Shaw	38773
Shelby	38774
Shellmound	38930
Shelton	39459
Sheppard Town	38946
Sherard	38669
Sherman	38869
Sherwood	39752
Sherwood Forest	39042
Shiloh, *Itawamba*	38855
Shiloh, *Rankin*	39145
Shipman	39452
Shivers	39149
Shoccoe	39046
Shoreline Park♦	39576
Shrock	39079
Shubuta	39360
Shucktown	39301
Shuford	38620
Shuqualak	39361
Sibley	39165
Sibleyton	39747
Sidon	38954
Signal	39180
Silver City	39166
Silver Creek	39663
Silver Run	39573
Singleton	39051
Singleton Settlement	39074
Skene	38730
Skuna	38915
Skyline	38801
Slate Spring	38955
Slayden	38642
Sledge	38670
Sloan	39046
Smith, *Covington*	39428
Smith, *Lauderdale*	39364
Smithdale	39664
Smiths	39066
Smithville	38870
Smyrna, *Attala*	39090
Smyrna, *Copiah*	39083
Snell	39301
Snow Lake Shores	38603
Somerville	38944
Sonora	38851
Sontag	39665
Soso	39480
South Amory (Part of Amory)	38821
Southaven	38671
Southern (Part of Hattiesburg)	39401
South McComb (Part of McComb)	39648
Spanish Fort	39088
Sparta	39776
Splinter	38673
Splunge	38848
Spring Cottage	39429
Spring Creek	39350
Springdale	38965
Springdale Lakes	38650
Spring Hill, *Benton*	38647
Springhill, *Jones*	39443
Spring Hill, *Lafayette*	38655
Spring Hill, *Neshoba*	39350
Springville	38863
Stallo	39350
Stampley	39069
Standing Pine♦	39051
Stanton	39120
Star	39167
Starkville	39759-60
For specific ZIP Codes call (888) 275-8777, or your local postmaster.	
State Line	39362
Steele	39074
Steens	39766
Steiner	38773
Stewart	39767
Stokes	39046
Stoneville	38776
Stonewall, *Clarke*	39363
Stonewall, *DeSoto*	38611
Stonewall, *Holmes*	39169
Stovall	38614
Straight Bayou	38721
Stratton	39365
Strayhorn	38665
Strengthford	39443
Strickland	38834
Stringer	39481
Stringtown	38725
Stronghope	39191
Strongs	39730
Sturgis	39769
Sucarnochee	39352
Success	39574
Sumbax	39483
Summerland	39168
Summit	39666
Sumner	38957
Sumrall	39482
Sunflower (Part of Booneville)	38829
Sunflower, *Sunflower*	38778
Sunnycrest	38901
Sunnyside	38944
Sunrise, *Forrest*	39401
Sunrise, *Leake*	39051
Suqualena	39301
Swan Lake	38958
Sweatman	38925
Swiftown	38959
Swiftwater	38701
Sylvarena	39153
Symonds	38769
Tallula	39159
Talowah	39455
Tatum	39638
Taylor	38673
Taylorsville	39168
Tchula	39169
Teasdale	38927
Ted	39338
Teoc	38917
Terry	39170
Thaxton	38871
Theadville	39355
Theo	38683
Thomastown	39171
Thomasville	39073
Thompson	39664
Thompsonville	39059
Thorn	38851
Thornton	39169
Thrashers	38829
Three Rivers	39581
Thyatira	38668
Tibbee	39773
Tibbs	38670
Tie Plant	38960
Tilden	38843
Tillatoba	38961
Tillman	39150
Tilton	39654
Tinsley	39173
Tiplersville	38674
Tippah	38603
Tippo	38962
Tishomingo	38873
Toccopola	38874
Tocowa	38620
Tomnolen	39744
Toomsuba	39364
Topeka	39641
Topisaw	39662
Topton	39301
Touchstone	39044
Tougaloo (Part of Jackson)	39174
Townsend	39352
Tralake	38756
Trapp	39350
Traxler	39111
Trebloc	38875
Tremont	38876
Triangle (Part of Biloxi)‡	39534
Tribbett	38779
Trinity, *DeSoto*	38632
Trinity, *Lowndes*	39743
Troy	38863
Truitt	39146
Tucker♦	39350
Tuckers Crossing	39443
Tula	38675
Tunica	38676
Tupelo	38801-03
For specific ZIP Codes call (888) 275-8777, or your local postmaster.	
Turnbull	39669
Turnerville	39338
Turon	38870
Tuscola	39094
Tutwiler	38963
Twin	39478
Twin Lakes	38680
Tylertown	39667
Tyro	38668
Union, *Jones*	39437
Union, *Lee*	38862
Union, *Newton*	39365
Union, *Simpson*	39149
Union Church	39668
Union Hall	39601
Unity	38849
University (Part of Oxford)	38677
University Medical Center (Part of Jackson)‡	39216
Usrytown	39074
Utica	39175
Utica Junior College	39175
Vaiden	39176
Valewood	38744
Valley	39194
Valley Hill	38917
Valley Park	39177
Value (Part of Brandon)	39042
Van Buren	38858
Vance	38964
Vancleave♦	39565
Van Vleet	38877
Vardaman	38878
Vaughan	39179
Vaughn	39601
Velma	38965
Vernal	39452
Vernon, *Madison*	39339
Vernon, *Winston*	39339
Verona	38879
Vickland	39159
Vicksburg	39180-83
For specific ZIP Codes call (888) 275-8777, or your local postmaster.	
Victoria	38679
Vidalia	39571
Village Fair Mall (Part of Meridian)	39301
Vimville	39301
Virlilia	39046
Vossburg	39366
Waco	38753
Waddell	39741
Wade, *Jackson*	39581
Wade, *Sunflower*	38737
Wahalak	39358
Wakefield	38618
Wakeland	38930
Waldrup	39422
Wallerville	38652
Wallhill	38618
Walls	38680
Walnut, *Quitman*	38964
Walnut, *Tippah*	38683
Walnut Grove, *Coahoma*	38767
Walnut Grove, *Leake*	39189
Walters	39437
Waltersville	39183
Walthall	39771
Wanilla	39654
Wardwell	38878
Warrenton	39180
Warsaw	38611
Washington	39190
Waterford	38685
Water Oak	39367
Water Valley	38965
Watson, *Forrest*	39401
Watson, *Marshall*	38611
Wautubbee	39330
Waveland	39576
Waxhaw	38746
Way	39046
Waynesboro	39367
Wayside	38780
Weathersby	39114
Webb	38966
Weir	39772
Wells (Part of Caledonia)	39740
Wells Town	39455
Wenasoga	38834
Wesson	39191
West, *Holmes*	39192
West (Part of Meridian)‡	39305
West Biloxi (Part of Biloxi)‡	39531
West Days	38641
West Gulfport (Part of Gulfport)	39501
West Hill	39063
West Jackson (Part of Jackson)	39207
Westland (Part of Jackson)‡	39209
West Lincoln	39601
West Marks	38646
West Point	39773
West Poplarville	39470
Westside	39150
West Union	38650
Westville	39114
Wheeler	38880
Whistler	39367
White Apple	39661

* **Area Zip Code** † **Post Office Boxes** ‡ **Postal Station** ♦ **Census Designated Place** *Italic Type* **County**

Whitebluff.................. 39483
White Cap 39638
Whitehead 38928
White Oak 39111
Whites, *Clay*.............. 39773
Whites, *Rankin*........... 39073
Whitesand,
Jefferson Davis 39140
White Sand,
Pearl River 39470
Whites Crossing......... 39577
Whitfield..................... 39464
Whitney 38737
Whitten Town 38663
Whynot 39301
Wickware.................... 39345
Wiggins, *Leake* 39051
Wiggins, *Stone* 39577
Wilco Estates............. 38632
Wildwood 38930
Wilkinson 39669
Willet 38748
Williamsburg 39428
Williamsville, *Attala* 39090
Williamsville, *Neshoba* 39350
Willowood 39212
Willows 39150
Winborn...................... 38633
Winchester.................. 39367
Windsor Park.............. 39564
Wingate (Part of
New Augusta) 39462
Winona 38967
Winstonville 38781
Winterville 38782
Wolf Springs 39301
Woodburn 38751
Woodland, *Chickasaw* 39776
Woodland, *Pontotoc* .. 38863
Woodland Lake 38632
Woodville.................... 39669
Woodwards................ 39367
Woolmarket♦ 39532
Wortham 39574
Wren 39730
Wright 38746
Wyatte 38668
Yazoo City 39194
Yocona 38655
Yokena 39180
Youngs 38922
Zama 39090
Zemuly........................ 39160
Zero 39301
Zetus 39601
Zieglerville 39039
Zion 38863
Zumbro 38732

Place	ZIP
A (Part of Joplin)‡	64804
Aaron	64720
Abesville	65656
Abo	65536
Acorn Corner	63877
Acornridge	63960
Adair	63533
Adrian	64720
Advance	63730
Affton♦	63123
Agency	64401
Aid	63825
Airline Acres	63834
Airport Drive	64801
Akers	65560
Alanthus	64489
Alba	64830
Albany, *Gentry*	64402
Albany, *Ray*	64077
Aldrich	65601
Alexandria	63430
Alfalfa Center	63834
Algonquin (Part of Webster Groves)	63119
Allbright	63655
Allendale	64420
Allenton	63001
Allenville	63740
Alley Spring	65466
All Saints Village	63376
Alma	64001
Almartha	65773
Almon	65732
Alpha	64652
Altamont	64620
Altenburg	63732
Altheim	63141
Alton	65606
Altona	64720
Amazonia	64421
Americus	65069
Amity	64422
Amoret	64722
Amsterdam	64723
Amy	65626
Anabel	63431
Anaconda	63077
Anderson	64831
Annada	63330
Annapolis	63620
Anniston	63820
Anson	52626
Anthonies Mill	65441
Antioch, Clark	63445
Antioch (Part of Kansas City)‡	64119
Antioch Center (Part of Kansas City)	64119
Antonia	63052
Anutt	65540
Apache Flats	65101
Apple Creek	63775
Appleton City	64724
Aquilla	63825
Arab	63787
Arbela	63432
Arbor	63740
Arbor Terrace (Part of Northwoods)	63121
Arbyrd	63821
Arcadia	63621
Archie	64725
Arcola	65603
Ardeola	63730
Arditta	65626
Ardmore	65247
Argo	65441
Argyle	65001
Arkmo	63821
Arkoe	64468
Arley	64060
Arlington	65550
Armstrong	65230
Arnica	65674
Arnold	63010
Aroma	64844
Arroll	65571
Arrowhead Beach (Part of Lake Ozark)	65049
Arrowhead Lake Estates	65326
Arrow Rock	65320
Arthur	64779
Asbury	64832
Ashburn	63433
Asherville	63960
Ash Grove	65604
Ash Hill	63940
Ashland	65010
Ashley	63334
Ashley Creek	65555
Ashton	63453
Aspenhoff	63357
Athens	63465
Atherton	64050
Atlanta	63530
Atlas	64836
Atwater Terrace	63136
Auburn	63343
Aud	65024
Augusta	63332
Aullville	64037
Aurora	65605
Aurora Springs	65026
Austin	64725
Auxvasse	65231
Ava	65608
Avalon	64621
Avenue City	64505
Avert	63825
Avery	65355
Avilla	64833
Avon	63640
Avondale	64117
Axtell	63552
Ayers	65349
Azen	63432
Babbtown	65085
Bachelor	65231
Bacon	65046
Baden (Part of St. Louis)	63147
Baderville	63862
Bado	65689
Bagnell	65026
Bahner	65350
Baker	63846
Bakersfield	65609
Bakersville	63827
Baldwin Park	64080
Ballard	64730
Ballwin	63011
	63021-22
	63024
For specific ZIP Codes call (888) 275-8777, or your local postmaster.	
Bancroft	64642
Banner	63623
Bannister	65786
Bannister Mall (Part of Kansas City)	64137
Bardley	63935
Baring	63531
Barnard	64423
Barnesville	63530
Barnett	65011
Barnhart	63012
Barretts	63122
Barry (Part of Kansas City)	64155
Bartlett	65438
Barwick	64649
Baryties	63626
Bassville	65757
Bates City	64011
Batesville	63932
Battlefield	65619
Battlefield Mall (Part of Springfield)	65804
Baxter	65681
Bay	65041
Baydy Peak	65065
Bayshore (Part of Arnold)	63010
Beach	65632
Beaman	65350
Bean Lake	64484
Bearcreek	65649
Bearfield	65201
Beaufort	63013
Beckville (Part of Piedmont)	63957
Bedford	64643
Bedison	64434
Belews Creek	63050
Belgique	63775
Belgrade	63622
Bellair	65237
Bellamy	64784
Bella Villa	63125
Bell City	63735
Belle	65013
Belle Center	64801
Bellefontaine, *St. Louis*	63017
Bellefontaine, *Washington*	63630
Bellefontaine Neighbors	63137
Bellerive	63121
Bellerive Estates	63141
Belleview	63623
Belleville	64801
Bellflower	63333
Bel-Nor	63133
Bel-Ridge	63133
Belton	64012
Belvidere (Part of Grandview)	64030
Bem	65066
Ben Avis (Part of Ferguson)	63135
Benbow	63440
Benbush	63141
Bendavis	65433
Benjamin	63435
Bennett Springs	65536
Bentley Farms	63026
Benton	63736
Benton City	65232
Benton Park (Part of St. Louis)‡	63104
Bentonville	65355
Berger	63014
Berkeley	63134
Berlin	64463
Bermott	65706
Bernheimer	63357
Bernie	63822
Berryman	65565
Bertrand	63823
Berwick	65723
Bessville	63764
Bethany	64424
Bethel	63434
Bethpage	64867
Beulah, *Madison*	63636
Beulah, *Phelps*	65436
Beverly	64079
Beverly Hills	63121
Bevier	63532
Biblegrove	63531
Biehle	63775
Bigelow	64437
Big Lake	64437
Big Piney	65550
Big River Mills	63628
Bigspring	63363
Billings	65610
Billingsville	65233
Billmore	65690
Birch Tree	65438
Birds Corners	63846
Birds Point	63834
Birdtown	65637
Birmingham	64161
Bismarck	63624
Bixby	65439
Black	63625
Blackburn	65321
Blackjack, *St. Clair*	65785
Black Jack, *St. Louis*	63034
Black Walnut	63301
Blackwater	65322
Blackwell	63626
Blairstown	64726
Bland	65014
Blendville (Part of Joplin)	64801
Blodgett	63824
Blomeyer	63740
Bloomfield	63825
Blooming Rose	65436
Bloomington	63532
Bloomsdale	63627
Blosser	65339
Blue Branch	65355
Blue Eye	65611
Blue Lick	65340
Blue Mound	64638
Blue Ridge	64424
Blue Ridge Mall (Part of Kansas City)	64133
Blue Springs	64013-15
For specific ZIP Codes call (888) 275-8777, or your local postmaster.	
Blue Summit	64126
Blue Vue (Part of Kansas City)	64133
Bluffton	65069
Blythedale	64426
Boaz	65631
Boekerton	63873
Bogard	64622
Bois D'Arc	65612
Bolckow	64427
Boles	63055
Bolivar	65613
Bona	65601
Bonanza	64650
Bongor Lake Estate	65202
Bonne Terre	63628
Bonnots Mill	65016
Boonesboro	65250
Boonville	65233
Boschertown	63301
Bosky Dell (Part of Lanagan)	64831
Boss	65440
Boston	64759
Bosworth	64623
Boulder City	64844
Bourbon	65441
Bowen	65360
Bowers Mill	64848
Bowling Green	63334
Boydsville	65251
Boyer	65667
Boynton	63556
Boys Ranch	65617
Boys Town	65559
Bracken	65706
Bradleyville	65614
Braggadocio	63826
Bragg City	63827
Braley	64477
Branch	65786
Brandon	65360
Brandsville	65688
Branson	65615*
	65616†
Branson West	65737
Brashear	63830
Brasher	63877
Braymer	64624
Brays	65486
Brazeau	63737
Brazil	63664
Brazito	65101
Breckenridge	64625
Breckenridge Hills	63114
Breen Acres (Part of Kansas City)	64152
Brentwood	63144
Brewer	63775
Briar	63931
Brickeys	63627
Bridgeton	63044
Bridgeton Terrace (Part of Bridgeton)	63044
Bridlecroft	64083
Brighton	65617
Brimson	64642
Brinktown	65443
Briscoe	63379
Bristow	64772
Brixey	65618
Broadway (Part of St. Louis)‡	63147
Brock	63555
Bronaugh	64728
Brookdale	63141
Brookfield	64628
Brooking Park	65301
Brookline	65619
Brooklyn	64481
Brooklyn Heights	64836
Broseley	63932
Brownbranch	65608
Brownfield	65556
Browning	64630
Brownington	64740
Browns	65202
Browns Spring	65610
Brownwood	63738
Brumley	65017
Bruner	65620
Brunot	63636
Brunswick	65236
Brushcreek	65536
Brushyknob	65608
Buck Donic	63829
Buckhart	65608
Buckhorn, *Madison*	63655
Buckhorn, *Pulaski*	65583
Bucklin	64631
Buckner	64016
Bucoda	63876
Bucyrus	65444
Buell	63361
Buffalo	65622
Buffington	63846
Bull Creek	65616
Bullion	63501
Bunceton	65237
Bunker	63629
Bunker Hill, *Howard*	65257
Bunker Hill, *Schuyler*	63536
Burbank	63944
Burdett	64720
Burfordville	63739
Burgess	64769
Burke City	63135
Burksville	63469
Burlington Junction	64428
Burnham	65793
Burns	65613
Burr	72478
Burton	65248
Burtville	65336
Butcher	65774
Butler	64730
Butler Hill Estates	63128
Butterfield	65623
Butts	65441
Bynumville	65281
Byrnes Mill	63051
Byron	65013
Cabanne (Part of St. Louis)	63112
Cabool	65689
Caddo	65706
Cadet	63630
Cainsville	64632
Cairo	65239
Caledonia	63631
Calhoun	65323
California	65018
Callao	63534
Calm	63942
Calton Mill	65769
Calumet	63336
Calverton Park	63136
Calwood	65251
Cambridge	65330
Camden	64017
Camden Point	64018
Camdenton	65020
Cameron	64429
Campbell	63933
Campbellton	63068
Camp Clark	64772
Canaan	65014
Canalou	63828
Cane Hill	65635
Caney Creek	63771
Cannon Mines	63630
Canton	63435
Cantwell (Part of Desloge)	63601
Cape Fair	65624
Cape Girardeau	63701-03
For specific ZIP Codes call (888) 275-8777, or your local postmaster.	
Capital Mall (Part of Jefferson City)	65109
Capitol Hill	63136
Caplinger Mills	65607
Cappeln	63365
Capps	65082
Cardwell	63829
Carl Junction	64834
Carlow	64648
Carmack	64402
Carola	63961
Carondelet (Part of St. Louis)	63111
Carr (Part of Florissant)‡	63031
Carrington	65251
Carr Lane	72616
Carrollton	64633
Carsonville	63121
Carterville	64835
Carthage	64836
Caruth	63857
Caruthersville	63830
Carytown	64836
Cascade	63632
Case	65041
Cash	63534
Cassel Addition	65785
Cassidy	65714
Cassville	65625
Castle Point♦	63136
Castle Rock (Part of Joplin)	64801
Castlewood	63021
Catawba	64624
Catawissa	63015
Catherine Place	63645
Cato	65605
Catron	63833
Caulfield	65626
Cave	63379
Cave Hill	65041
Caverna	72739
Cave Spring	65770

*** Area Zip Code** **† Post Office Boxes** **‡ Postal Station** **♦ Census Designated Place** *Italic Type* **County**

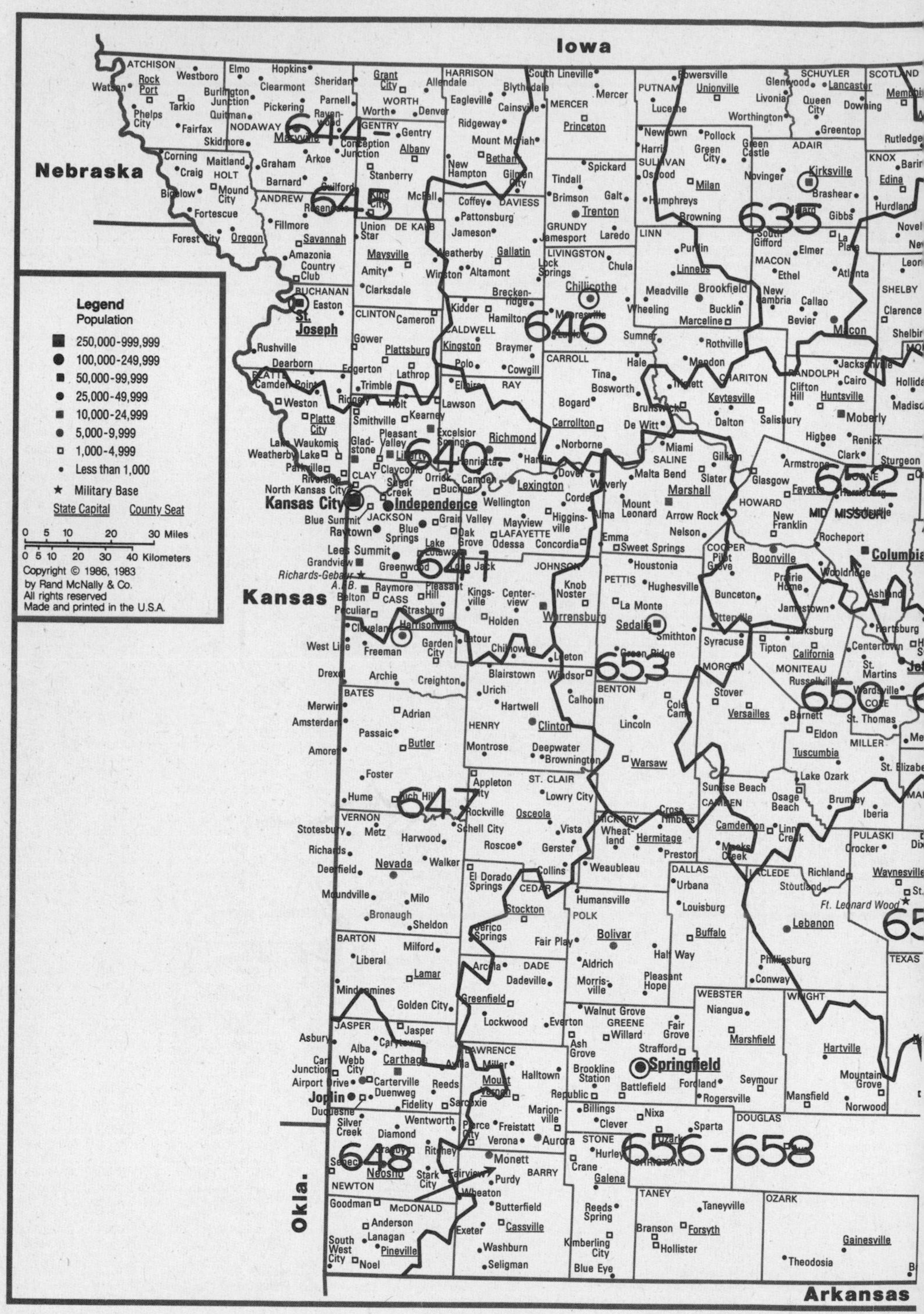
Iowa
Nebraska
Kansas
Okla.
Arkansas
644
645
646
635
640
641
652
653
650
647
648
656-658
Legend
Population
250,000-999,999
100,000-249,999
50,000-99,999
25,000-49,999
10,000-24,999
5,000-9,999
1,000-4,999
Less than 1,000
Military Base
State Capital
County Seat
0 5 10 20 30 Miles
0 5 10 20 30 40 Kilometers
Copyright © 1986, 1983
by Rand McNally & Co.
All rights reserved
Made and printed in the U.S.A.
Kansas City
Independence
St. Joseph
Springfield
Joplin
Columbia
Sedalia
Kirksville

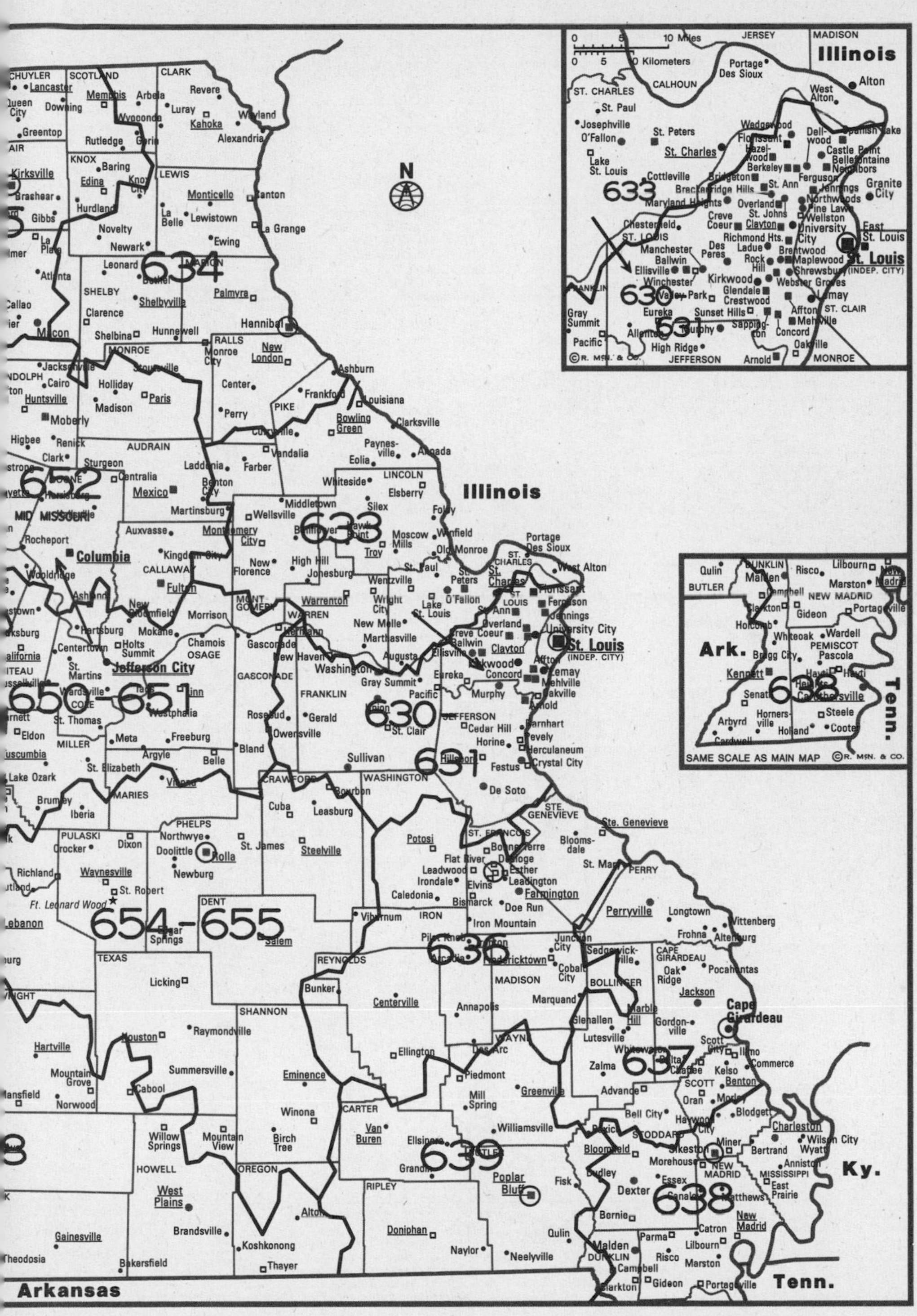
Illinois
Alton
West Alton
St. Charles
St. Peters
St. Paul
Josephville
O'Fallon
Lake St. Louis
Cottleville
633
Maryland Heights
Chesterfield
Creve Coeur
Clayton
Richmond Hts.
Ladue
Des Peres
Manchester
Ballwin
Ellisville
Winchester
Valley Park
Kirkwood
Glendale
Crestwood
Sunset Hills
Eureka
Allenton
Pacific
Gray Summit
High Ridge
Murphy
Arnold
Concord
Affton
Oakville
Lemay
Mehlville
Webster Groves
Shrewsbury
Maplewood
Brentwood
Rock Hill
University City
Wellston
Pine Lawn
Northwoods
Jennings
Ferguson
Overland
St. Ann
St. Johns
Berkeley
Bridgeton
Florissant
Dellwood
Castle Point
Bellefontaine Neighbors
Granite City
East St. Louis
St. Louis (INDEP. CITY)
ST. CLAIR
JEFFERSON
MONROE
CALHOUN
JERSEY
MADISON
Portage Des Sioux
0 5 10 Miles
0 5 10 Kilometers
630
631
Illinois
Hannibal
Palmyra
Monroe City
New London
Ashburn
Louisiana
Bowling Green
Clarksville
Frankford
Vandalia
Farber
Laddonia
Mexico
Centralia
Sturgeon
Columbia
Rocheport
Fulton
Jefferson City
Holts Summit
Chamois
OSAGE
Westphalia
St. Thomas
Eldon
Meta
Freeburg
Argyle
Belle
St. Elizabeth
Lake Ozark
Iberia
MILLER
MARIES
Vienna
Rolla
Newburg
Doolittle
St. James
Steelville
Cuba
Leasburg
Bourbon
Sullivan
Gerald
Owensville
Bland
Rosebud
Washington
Union
St. Clair
Hermann
Warrenton
Wentzville
Troy
Moscow Mills
Winfield
Old Monroe
Foley
Elsberry
Silex
Whiteside
Eolia
Paynesville
Annada
Middletown
Wellsville
Montgomery City
New Florence
High Hill
Jonesburg
Augusta
Marthasville
New Melle
Festus
Hillsboro
Crystal City
Herculaneum
Pevely
Barnhart
Cedar Hill
Horine
De Soto
Potosi
Flat River
Leadwood
Irondale
Caledonia
Bismarck
Farmington
Doe Run
Iron Mountain
Viburnum
IRON
Pilot Knob
Arcadia
Fredericktown
Junction City
Cobalt City
MADISON
Marquand
Annapolis
Centerville
Bunker
REYNOLDS
Ellington
Des Arc
Piedmont
Mill Spring
Greenville
Williamsville
Van Buren
CARTER
Ellsinore
Grandin
639
Poplar Bluff
Fisk
Qulin
Naylor
Neelyville
Doniphan
RIPLEY
Alton
Koshkonong
Thayer
OREGON
Birch Tree
Winona
Eminence
SHANNON
Summersville
Raymondville
Houston
Licking
TEXAS
Cabool
Mountain Grove
Norwood
Hartville
Mansfield
Willow Springs
Mountain View
HOWELL
West Plains
Brandsville
Gainesville
Theodosia
Bakersfield
Salem
DENT
Sugar Springs
654-655
Ft. Leonard Wood
St. Robert
Waynesville
Richland
Crocker
Dixon
PULASKI
PHELPS
Lebanon
Hartville
Ste. Genevieve
Bloomsdale
St. Mary
PERRY
Perryville
Longtown
Wittenberg
Frohna
Altenburg
CAPE GIRARDEAU
Pocahontas
Oak Ridge
Jackson
Cape Girardeau
Gordonville
Scott City
Illmo
Commerce
Kelso
Benton
Chaffee
Delta
Whitewater
637
Zalma
Lutesville
Glenallen
Marble Hill
BOLLINGER
Sedgewickville
Advance
Bell City
SCOTT
Oran
Morley
Blodgett
Charleston
Wilson City
Wyatt
Anniston
Bertrand
MISSISSIPPI
East Prairie
Ky.
Sikeston
Miner
Morehouse
NEW MADRID
STODDARD
Bloomfield
Dudley
Dexter
Essex
638
Matthews
Bernie
Catron
New Madrid
Parma
Lilbourn
Risco
Marston
Malden
DUNKLIN
Campbell
Gideon
Clarkton
Portageville
Tenn.
Arkansas
Kirksville
Memphis
Lancaster
Downing
Greentop
Rutledge
Arbela
Revere
Luray
Kahoka
Wayland
Alexandria
Canton
La Grange
Monticello
Lewistown
La Belle
Ewing
Edina
Baring
Hurdland
Novelty
Newark
Brashear
Gibbs
La Plata
Atlanta
Leonard
634
Bethel
Shelbyville
Clarence
Shelbina
Hunnewell
Macon
SHELBY
LEWIS
KNOX
CLARK
SCOTLAND
RALLS
PIKE
MONROE
Stoutsville
Paris
Holliday
Madison
Cairo
Huntsville
Moberly
Renick
Higbee
Clark
AUDRAIN
Martinsburg
Auxvasse
Kingdom City
CALLAWAY
Mokane
Morrison
New Bloomfield
Hartsburg
Centertown
Ashland
652
650-651
Linn
CRAWFORD
WASHINGTON
FRANKLIN
GASCONADE
WARREN
LINCOLN
JEFFERSON
ST. FRANCOIS
STE. GENEVIEVE
Illinois
Qulin
BUTLER
DUNKLIN
Malden
Campbell
Clarkton
Holcomb
Whiteoak
Bragg City
Kennett
Senath
Arbyrd
Cardwell
Hornersville
Holland
Steele
Cooter
Caruthersville
Hayti
PEMISCOT
Pascola
Wardell
Portageville
Gideon
Marston
Risco
Lilbourn
NEW MADRID
Ark.
Tenn.
SAME SCALE AS MAIN MAP
©R. McN. & CO.

Cawood	64427
Cedar City (Part of Jefferson City)	65022
Cedarcreek	65627
Cedar Gap	65746
Cedar Hill♦	63016
Cedar Hill Lakes	63016
Cedar Lake	65201
Cedar Ridge	65590
Cedar Springs	64744
Cedar Valley	63901
Cedarville	64756
Celt	65764
Center	63436
Center Square (Part of Kansas City)‡	64196
Centertown	65023
Centerview	64019
Centerville	63633
Central (Part of Kansas City)‡	64142
Central City	64801
Centralia	65240
Centropolis (Part of Kansas City)‡	64120
	64125-26
For specific ZIP Codes call (888) 275-8777, or your local postmaster.	
Chadwick	65629
Chaffee	63740
Chain of Rocks	63369
Chain-O-Lakes	65625
Chambersburg	63445
Chamois	65024
Champ	63042
Champion	65717
Champion City	63056
Chandler	64060
Chapel Hill	64011
Chapel Hills	65785
Chapelwood Estates	65301
Chariton	63565
Charity	65644
Charlack	63114
Charles Nagel (Part of St. Louis)‡	63115
Charleston	63834
Charteroak	63833
Cherokee Pass	63645
Cherry Box	63451
Cherry Valley Estates	65804
Cherryville	65446
Chesapeake	65712
Chesterfield	63005-06
	63017
For specific ZIP Codes call (888) 275-8777, or your local postmaster.	
Chestnutridge	65630
Chicopee	63965
Chilhowee	64733
Chillicothe	64601
Chilton	63965
Chitwood (Part of Joplin)	64801
Chouteau (Part of St. Louis)‡	63110
Christian Center	65721
Chula	64635
Circle City	63846
Civic Center (Part of Kansas City)‡	64106
Civil Bend	64670
Clapper	63456
Clara	65483
Clarence	63437
Clark	65243
Clark City	63445
Clarksburg	65025
Clarksdale	64430
Clarkson Valley	63005
Clarksville	63336
Clarkton	63837
Claryville	63775
Claycomo	64119
Claysvill	65039
Clayton	63105
	63124
For specific ZIP Codes call (888) 275-8777, or your local postmaster.	
Clear Creek	65276
Clearmont	64431
Clear Spring	63965
Clear Springs	65793
Clearview	65202
Clearwater	63670
Cleavesville	65014
Clementine	65550
Cleveland	64734
Clever	65631
Cliff Village	64804
Clifton City	65348
Clifton Hill	65244
Climax Springs	65324
Clines Island	63846
Clinton	64735
Cliquot	65640
Clover Bottom	63090
Cloverdale	65590
Clubb	63934
Clyde	64432
Coal	64735
Coal Hill	64744
Coatsville	63535
Cobalt City	63645
Cody	65742
Coffey	64636
Coffeyton	65441
Coffman	63670
Coldspring	65717
Cold Springs	65355
Coldwater	63964
Cole Camp	65325
Coleman	64078
College Mound	65247
Collins	64738
Coloma	64622
Colony	63563
Columbia	65201-05
	65299
For specific ZIP Codes call (888) 275-8777, or your local postmaster.	
Columbia Mall (Part of Columbia)	65203
Columbus	64019
Comet	65646
Commerce	63742
Commerce Tower (Part of Kansas City)‡	64199
Commercial (Part of Springfield)‡	65803
Competition	65470
Conception	64433
Conception Junction	64434
Conclay (Part of Ladue)	63124
Concord, *Callaway*	65231
Concord, *St. Louis*♦	63128
Concord Hill	63357
Concordia	64020
Connelsville	63559
Conran	63838
Converse	64465
Conway	65632
Cook Station	65449
Cool Valley	63135
Cooper Hill	65014
Cooter	63839
Cora	63556
Corder	64021
Cornelia	64093
Corning	64437
Cornwall	63645
Corridon	63633
Corry	65635
Corsicana	65734
Corso	63377
Corticelli	65074
Cosby	64436
Cottage Farm	63050
Cottleville	63338
Cotton Plant	63855
Cottonwood Point	63830
Couch	65690
Country Club, *Andrew*	64505
Country Club (Part of Kansas City)‡	64113
Country Club Estates	65301
Country Club Hills	63136
Country Club Plaza (Part of Kansas City)	64112
Country Lake Woods	63021
Country Life Acres	63131
Countryside (Part of Kansas City)	64152
Courtney (Part of Sugar Creek)	64050
Courtois	65565
Cowgill	64637
Coy	64831
Crabbs	65746
Craig	64437
Crane	65633
Crawford	63555
Creighton	64739
Crescent	63025
Crescent Hill	64720
Crescent Lake (Part of Excelsior Springs)	64024
Crestwood	63126
Crestwood Plaza (Part of Crestwood)	63126
Cretcher	65351
Creve Coeur	63141
Crider	65790
Crites Corner	63937
Crocker	65452
Crockerville	65325
Cross Keys	63033
Cross Keys Shopping Center (Part of Florissant)	63033
Cross Roads, *Douglas*	65608
Cross Roads, *Ozark*	65637
Cross Timbers	65634
Crosstown	63775
Cross Way	65706
Crowder	63801
Crown	65706
Cruise Mill	63626
Crump	63785
Crystal City	63019
Crystal Lake Park	63131
Crystal Lakes	64024
Cuba	65453
Cunningham, *Chariton*	64681
Cunningham, *Pemiscot*	63851
Curdton	63960
Cureall	65790
Currentview	63935
Curryville	63339
Custer	65560
Cyclone	64856
Cyrene	63334
Dadeville	65635
Daisy	63743
Daleview	64446
Dalton	65246
Damascus	64776
Dameron	63343
Damsel (Part of Osage Beach)	65065
Danby	63627
Danforth	63559
Danville	63361
Dardenne	63366
Dardenne Prairie	63366
Darien	65560
Darksville	65259
Darlington	64438
Daugherty	64701
Davis, *Lincoln*	63379
Davis, *St. Francois*	63601
Davisville	65456
Dawn	64638
Dawson	65711
Dawsonville	64428
Dawt	65760
Dayton	64747
Daytown	63653
Dearborn	64439
Decaturville	65536
Deckard-Y	65690
Dederick	64744
Deepwater	64740
Deer	65024
Deerfield	64741
Deering	63840
Deer Land	63857
Deer Park	65201
Deer Ridge	63447
Deer Run	63965
Defiance	63341
Deicke	63025
De Kalb	64440
De Lassus	63640
Delaware	65438
Delbridge	63664
Dell Junction	65355
Dellwood	63136
Delmar	64735
Delmo	63801
Delta	63744
Dennis Acres	64804
Denton, *Johnson*	64040
Denton, *Pemiscot*	63877
Denver	64441
Derby	63601
Derrahs	63473
Des Arc	63636
Desloge	63601
De Soto	63020
Des Peres	63131
Dessa	64850
Detmold	63068
Devils Elbow	65457
De Witt	64639
Dexter	63841
Diamond	64840
Dickens	65759
Diehlstadt	63834
Diggins	65636
Dikeland	64083
Dillard	65456
Dillon	65401
Dissen	63068
Dittmer	63023
Dixie	65063
Dixon	65459
Dockery	64085
Doc Long Estates	65355
Doe Run	63637
Dogwood, *Douglas*	65746
Dogwood, *Mississippi*	63845
Dolly Siding (Part of Bonne Terre)	63628
Dongola	63730
Doniphan	63935
Doolittle	65401
Dora	65637
Dorena	63845
Doss	65560
Dotham	64446
Dove	65536
Dover, *Lafayette*	64022
Dover, *Lewis*	63448
Downing	63536
Drake	65066
Dresden	65301
Drexel	64742
Dripping Spring	65202
Drury	65638
Dudenville	64748
Dudley	63936
Duenweg	64841
Dugginsville	65761
Duke	65461
Duncan	65706
Duncans Bridge	63437
Duncans Point	65324
Dundee	63090
Dunksburg	65351
Dunlap	64683
Dunn, *New Madrid*	63848
Dunn, *Texas*	65711
Dunnegan	65640
Duquesne	64801
Durham	63438
Dutchtown	63745
Dutzow	63342
Dye	64098
Dykes	65444
E (Part of Kansas City)‡	64109
Eagle Rock	65641
Eagleville	64442
Easley	65203
East Bonne Terre	63628
East End	63623
East Hills Mall (Part of St. Joseph)	64506
East Independence (Part of Independence)	64056
East Kirkwood (Part of Kirkwood)	63122
East Leavenworth	64079
East Lynne	64743
East Mexico (Part of Mexico)	65265
Easton	64443
East Prairie	63845
East Purdy	65734
Eastside (Part of St. Joseph)‡	64508
Eastville	65262
Eastwood	63965
Ebenezer	65803
Ebo	63664
Eccles	65261
Echo Valley	65065
Economy	63530
Ectonville	64089
Edgar Springs	65462
Edge Acres	65785
Edgehill	63625
Edgerton	64444
Edgerton Junction	64439
Edgewater Beach	65653
Edgewood	63334
Edina	63537
Edinburg	64683
Edith	65786
Edmonson	65338
Edmundson	63134
Edwards	65326
Egypt Grove	65626
Egypt Mills	63701
El Chaparral	65201
Eldon	65026
El Dorado Springs	64744
Eldridge	65463
Elgin	63434
Elijah	65626
Elk Creek	65464
Elkhead	65753
Elkhorn	64077
Elkhurst	65201
Elkland	65644
Elk Prairie	65401
Elk Springs	64854
Elkton	65650
Ellington	63638
Ellis	64772
Ellis Prairie	65444
Ellisville	63011
Ellsinore	63937
Elm	64061
Elmdale Village (Part of St. John)	63114
Elmer	63538
Elmira	64062
Elmo	64445
Elmont	63080
Elmwood	65321
Elsberry	63343
Elsey	65633
Elston	65101
Elvins (Part of Park Hills)	63601
Elwood	65802
Ely	63461
Emden	63439
Emerald Beach	65658
Emerson	63454
Eminence	65466
Emma	65327
Empire Prairie	64463
Englewood, *Boone*	65010
Englewood (Part of Independence)‡	64052
Enon, *Moniteau*	65074
Enon, *St. Charles*	63385
Enyart	64453
Eolia	63344
Epworth	63469
Erie	64843
Ernestville	64020
Essex	63846
Estes	63359
Esther (Part of Park Hills)	63601
Estill	65274
Ethel	63539
Ethlyn	63369
Etlah	63014
Etna	63432
Etterville	65031
Eudora	65645
Eugene	65032
Eunice	65468
Eureka	63025
Evans	65608
Evansville, *Buchanan*	64507
Evansville, *Monroe*	65270
Eve	64741
Eveningshade	65557
Everett	64725
Eversonville	64688
Everton	65646
Ewing	63440
Excello	65247
Excelsior	65084
Excelsior Estates	64062
Executive Park (Part of Kansas City)‡	64120
Exeter	65647
Fagus	63938
Fairdealing	63939
Fairfax	64446
Fairgrounds (Part of St. Louis)‡	63107
Fair Grove	65648
Fair Haven	64750
Fairleigh (Part of St. Joseph)‡	64506
Fairmont	63474
Fairmount (Part of Independence)	64053
Fair Play	65649
Fairport	64447
Fairview, *Newton*	64842
Fairview, *Taney*	65744
Fairview, *Texas*	65689

*** Area Zip Code** **† Post Office Boxes** **‡ Postal Station** **♦ Census Designated Place** *Italic Type* **County**

Place	ZIP
Fairview Acres (Part of Park Hills)	63601
Fairville	65349
Falcon	65470
Fanchon	65788
Fanning	65453
Farber	63345
Farewell	64487
Farley	64028
Farmer	63339
Farmersville	64683
Farmington	63640
Farrar	63746
Farrenberg	63869
Faucett	64448
Fayette	65248
Fayetteville	64093
Federal (Part of Park Hills)	63601
Fee Fee	63141
Fegley	63501
Femme Osage	63332
Fenton	63026
Ferguson	63135
Fern Ridge	63141
Fernview Estates	63141
Ferrelview	64163
Fertile	63630
Festus	63028
Fidelity	64836
Field (Part of St. Louis)‡	63108
Filley	64744
Fillmore	64449
Finey	64740
Fishermans Lake	63020
Fisk	63940
Flag Springs, *Andrew*	64494
Flag Springs, *Phelps*	65559
Flat	65550
Flat River (Part of Park Hills)	63601
Flatwood	65466
Fleming	64077
Flemington	65650
Fletcher	63030
Flinthill	63346
Flordell Hills	63136
Florence (Part of St. Joseph)	64504
Florence, *Morgan*	65329
Florida	65283
Florissant	63031-34
For specific ZIP Codes call (888) 275-8777, or your local postmaster.	
Floyd	64077
Flucom	63020
Foil	65755
Foley	63347
Folk	65085
Foose	65622
Forbes	64473
Ford City	64463
Fordland	65652
Forest City	64451
Forest Green	65281
Forest Hills	65355
Foristell	63348
Forker	64651
Forkners Hill	65632
Forrest Mill	64859
Forsyth	65653
Fortescue	64437
Fort Henry	65259
Fort Leonard Wood	65473
Fortuna	65034
Fort Zumwalt	63366
Foster	64745
Fountain Grove	64659
Fox Creek	63069
Fox Haven	64083
Foxwood Springs	64083
Frailie	63848
Frankclay	63644
Frankenstein	65016
Frankford	63441
Franklin	65250
Franks	65459
Frazier	64401
Fredericksburg	65061
Fredericktown	63645
Fredville	64850
Freeburg	65035
Freedom, *Camden*	65591
Freedom, *Osage*	65024
Freeman	64746
Freistatt	65654
Fremont	63941
Fremont Hills	65714
French Village	63036
Friedheim	63747
Friendly Valley	63775
Frisbee	63852
Frisco	63846
Fristoe	65355
Frohna	63748
Frontenac	63131
Fruitland, *Cape Girardeau*	63755
Fruitland, *Greene*	65648
Fulton	65251
Gaines	64735
Gainesville	65655
Galena	65656
Galesburg	64855
Gallatin	64640
Galloway (Part of Springfield)	65804
Galmey	65779
Galt	64641
Gamburg	63955
Game	63830
Gamma	63333
Garden City	64747
Gardenview	63033
Garfield	65690
Garland	64735
Garrison	65657
Garwood	63957
Gasconade	65036
Gascondy	65013
Gashland (Part of Kansas City)	64155
Gateway Drive (Part of Joplin)	64801
Gateway South	65201
Gatewood	63942
Gaynor	64475
Gazette	63359
Gentry	64453
Gentryville, *Douglas*	65608
Gentryville, *Gentry*	64402
Georgetown, *Boone*	65203
Georgetown, *Pettis*	65301
Georgia City	64832
Gerald	63037
Germantown	64770
Gerster	64776
Gibbs	63540
Gibson	63847
Gideon	63848
Gilbert	63855
Gilliam	65330
Gilman City	64642
Gilmore	63385
Ginger Blue	64854
Gipsy	63750
Girdner	65608
Gladden	65560
Gladstone	64118-19
For specific ZIP Codes call (888) 275-8777, or your local postmaster.	
Glasgow	65254
Glasgow Village♦	63137
Glenaire	64068
Glenallen	63751
Glencoe	63038
Glendale, *Putnam*	63551
Glendale, *St. Louis*	63122
Glen Echo Park	63121
Glennon	63764
Glennonville	63933
Glen Park	63070
Glensted	65084
Glenstone (Part of Springfield)‡	65804
Glenwood	63541
Glenwood Junction (Part of Glenwood)	63541
Glidewell	65803
Glover	63646
Gobler	63849
Golden	65658
Golden City	64748
Golden Oak (Part of Kansas City)	64117
Goldman	63050
Goldsberry	63539
Gooch Mill	65068
Goodhope	65608
Goodland	63623
Goodman	64843
Goodson	65659
Gordonville	63752
Gorin	63543
Goshen	64673
Gospel Ridge (Part of St. Robert)	65583
Gower	64454
Graff	65660
Graham	64455
Grain Valley	64029
Granby	64844
Grand Center	63534
Grand Falls Plaza	64804
Grandin	63943
Grand Pass	65339
Grandview, *Benton*	65355
Grandview, *Jackson*	64030
Granger	63442
Graniteville	63650
Grant (Part of Grantwood Village)	63123
Grant City	64456
Grantwood Village	63123
Granville	65275
Grassy	63753
Gravelhill	63739
Gravelton	63655
Gravois (Part of St. Louis)‡	63116
Gravois Mills	65037
Grayridge	63850
Grayson	64492
Grays Point	65707
Gray Summit♦	63039
Graysville	63551
Green Acres	64801
Green Bay Terrace	65079
Greenbrier	63730
Greencastle	63544
Green City	63545
Greendale	63133
Greenfield	65661
Green Forest	63901
Green Grove	63559
Green Lawn	63462
Green-Mar	63026
Green Mound Ridge	65669
Green Mountain	65711
Green Oaks	63936
Green Park	63128
Green Ridge	65332
Greensburg	63531
Greenstreet	63013
Greentop	63546
Green Trail	63017
Greenville, *Clay*	64060
Greenville, *Wayne*	63944
Greenwood	64034
Greer	65606
Gregory	63435
Gregory Heights	65202
Gretna	65616
Grimmet	65775
Grisham	63764
Grogan	65464
Grover	63040
Grovespring	65662
Grubville	63041
Guilford	64457
Gumbo	63601
Gunn City	64747
Guthrie	65063
Hagers Grove	63437
Hahatonka	65020
Hahn	63764
Hailey	65605
Hale	64643
Half Rock	64679
Halfway	65663
Halls	64504
Hallsville	65255
Halltown	65664
Hamilton	64644
Hammond	65762
Hams Prairie	65251
Hancock	65452
Handy	63941
Hanley Hills	63133
Hannibal	63401
Hannon	64762
Happy Hollow	63630
Hardeman	65340
Hardenville	65666
Hardin	64035
Harg	65201
Harold	65770
Harper	64776
Harris	64645
Harrisburg	65256
Harrisonville	64701
Harry S. Truman (Part of Independence)‡	64055
Hart	64865
Hartford	63565
Hartsburg	65039
Hartshorn	65479
Hartville	65667
Hartwell	64788
Hartzell	63848
Harvester	63304
Harviell	63945
Harwood	64750
Haseltine	65802
Hassard	63456
Hastain	65326
Hatfield	64458
Hatton	65231
Havenhurst	64856
Hawkeye	65452
Hawk Point	63349
Hayden	65459
Hayes Park (Part of Sibley)	64088
Hayti	63851
Hayti Heights	63851
Hayward	63873
Haywood City	63736
Hazelgreen	65556
Hazel Run	63628
Hazelwood	63042
Heatonville	65707
Hebron	65775
Hecla	64653
Hedge City	63460
Helena	64459
Helm	65459
Heman Park (Part of University City)	63130
Hematite	63047
Hemple	64490
Henderson	65742
Hendrickson	63967
Henley	65040
Henrietta	64036
Henry's Acres	65338
Henry Winfield Wheeler (Part of St. Louis)‡	63101
Herbs	65338
Herculaneum	63048
Hercules	65614
Heritage Hills	64083
Hermann	65041
Hermitage	65668
Hermondale	63877
Hickman Mills (Part of Kansas City)‡	64134
Hickory	65803
Hickory Creek	64683
Hickory Hill	65040
Hiderbrand	63775
Higbee	65257
Higdon	63645
Higginsville	64037
High Gate	65559
High Hill	63350
Highland	63775
Highlandville	65669
Highley Heights (Part of Desloge)	63601
High Point	65042
High Ridge♦	63049
Hilda	65680
Hill City	65625
Hillhouse Addition (Part of Richland)	65556
Hilliard	63901
Hillsboro	63050
Hillsdale	63133
Hill Top	63935
Hinch	65441
Hinton	65202
Hiram	63947
Hitt	63555
Hoberg	65712
Hobson	65560
Hocomo	65626
Hodge	64096
Hoene Spring	63025
Hoffman Junction	63628
Holcomb	63852
Holden	64040
Holiday Shores	65326
Holland	63853
Holliday	65258
Holliday Landing	63944
Hollister	65672*
	65673†
Hollow	63069
Hollywood	63821
Holman	65757
Holmes Park (Part of Kansas City)	64131
Holstein	63357
Holt	64048
Holts Summit	65043
Homestead	64024
Homestown	63879
Honey Creek	65101
Hooker	65550
Hoover	64079
Hope	65061
Hopewell, *Warren*	63357
Hopewell, *Washington*	63660
Hopkins	64461
Horine♦	63070
Hornersville	63855
Hornet	64865
Horton	64751
House Creek	63965
House Springs	63051
Houston	65483
Houstonia	65333
Houston Lake	64152
Howards Ridge	65655
Howardville	63869
Howell	63303
Howes Mill	65560
H. S. Jewell (Part of Springfield)‡	65802
Hudson	64724
Huggins	65484
Hughesville	65334
Hugo	65052
Humansville	65674
Hume	64752
Humphreys	64646
Hunnewell	63443
Hunter	63943
Hunters Mill	63664
Hunters Ridge	65301
Hunterville	63846
Huntingdale	64735
Huntington	63456
Huntleigh	63131
Huntsdale	65203
Huntsville	65259
Hurdland	63547
Hurley	65675
Hurlingen	64443
Huron	65613
Hurricane	63764
Hurricane Deck	65079
Hurryville	63640
Hutton Valley	65793
Iantha	64759
Iatan	64098
Iberia	65486
Iconium	64776
Idalia	63825
Idlewild	63960
Ike	65737
Ilasco	63467
Illmo (Part of Scott City)	63780
Imperial	63052
Independence	64050-58
For specific ZIP Codes call (888) 275-8777, or your local postmaster.	
Independence Center (Part of Independence)	64057
Indian Creek	63456
Indian Ford	65582
Indian Grove	65236
Indian Hills (Part of Kansas City)	64114
Indian Lake	65453
Indian Point	65616
Indian Springs	64783
Ink	65466
Ionia	65335
Irondale	63648
Iron Gates	64801
Iron Mountain	63650
Iron Mountain Lake	63624
Ironton	63650
Irwin	64759
Isabella	65676
Isadora	64456
Ishmael	63664
Island City	64489
Ives	63936
Jack	65560
Jacket	65745
Jacks Fork	65466
Jackson, *Benton*	65355
Jackson, *Cape Girardeau*	63755
Jacksonville	65260
Jadwin	65501
Jake Prairie	65453
James Crews (Part of Kansas City)‡	64127
Jameson	64647
Jamesport	64648

*** Area Zip Code** **† Post Office Boxes** **‡ Postal Station** **♦ Census Designated Place** *Italic Type* **County**

Jamestown 65046
Jamesville 65631
Jane 64856
Japan 63080
Jarvis 63050
Jasper 64755
Jaudon 64012
Jawdea 64083
Jaywye 63873
Jedburg 63021
Jefferson City 65101-10
For specific ZIP Codes call (888) 275-8777, or your local postmaster.
Jefferson Memorial (Part of St. Louis)‡ 63102
Je-Ke-Ki 65326
Jenkins 65605
Jennings 63136
Jerico 65746
Jerico Springs 64756
Jerk Tail 65667
Jerome 65529
Jesse M. Donaldson (Part of Kansas City)‡ 64195
Jewett 63620
J&G Junction (Part of Joplin) 64801
Johnson City 64724
Johnstown, *Bates* 64770
Johnstown (Part of Carterville) 64835
Jonesburg 63351
Joplin 64801-04
For specific ZIP Codes call (888) 275-8777, or your local postmaster.
Jordan 65634
Jordan W Chambers (Part of St. Louis)‡ 63106
Josephville 63385
Judge 65051
Junction City 63645
Junland 63901
Kahoka 63445
Kaiser 65047
Kampville 63301
Kampville Beach 63301
Kampville Court 63301

Kansas City

64101-99
For specific ZIP Codes call (888) 275-8777, or your local postmaster.

Colleges & Universities

Avila Coll 64145
Calvary Bible Coll & The Dogical Seminary 64147
Cleveland Chiropractic Coll of Kansas City 64131
DeVry Institute of Technology 64131
Kansas City Art Institute 64111
Midwestern Baptist Theological Seminary 64118
Nazarene Theological Seminary 64131
Research Coll of Nursing 64132
Rockhurst Coll 64110
Saint Luke's Coll 64111
Saint Paul School of Theology 64127
The Univ of Health Sciences 64124
Univ of Missouri 64110

Financial Institutions

Bank Midwest, NA 64105
Commerce Bank 64106
Mercantile Bank 64106
NationsBank, NA 64105

Hospitals

Baptist Med Ctr 64131
Research Med Ctr 64132
Saint Joseph Health Ctr 64114
Saint Luke's Hosp 64111
Trinity Luthern Hosp 64108
Truman Med Ctr East 64139
Truman Med Ctr West 64108
Veterans Affairs Med Ctr 64128

Hotels/Motels

Adam's Mark 64133
Crowne Plaza 64111
Doubletree 64105
Embassy Suites Country Club Plaza 64111
Hyatt Regency Crown Center 64108
Marriott, Downtown 64105
Marriott, Kansas City Airport 64153
Park Place 64120
Ramada Inn at Benjamin Ranch 64138
The Ritz-Carlton 64112
Sheraton Suites Country Club Plaza 64112
Westin Crown Center 64108

Military Installations

Marine Corps Recruiting Sta 64153
U S Army Corps of Engineers 64106

Karr's 65355
Kaseyville 63534
Kearney 64060
Keener Cave 63967
Keenland 64083
Keethtown 65486
Keightley's Beach 65355
Kellerville 63469
Kelso 63758
Keltner 65720
Kendricktown 64836
Kennett 63857
Kenoma 64759
Keota 63532
Kerr 64429
Kersey Coates (Part of Kansas City) 64105
Ketterman 64790
Kewanee 63860
Keys Summit 63122
Keysville 65565
Keytesville 65261
Kidder 64649
Kiel 63068
Killarney Shores 63650
Kilwinning 63536
Kimberling City 65686
Kimberling Hills (Part of Kimberling City) 65686
Kimble 65542
Kime 63944
Kimmswick 63053
Kinder 63960
Kinderpost 65542
Kinfolks Ridge 63830
King City 64463
Kingdom City 65262
Kingdom of Callaway Estates 63388
Kings Lake 63347
Kings Point 65682
Kingston, *Caldwell* 64650
Kingston, *Washington* 63626
Kingsville 64061
Kingsway Mall (Part of Sikeston) 63801
Kinloch 63140
Kinsey 63627
Kirbyville 65679
Kirksville 63501
Kirkwood 63122
Kirschner (Part of St. Joseph) 64504
Kissee Mills 65680
Kliever 65018
Klondike 64834
Knobby 65326
Knob Lick 63651
Knob Noster 65336
Knobtown (Part of Kansas City) 64138
Knolls 65065
Knorpp 63020
Knox City 63446
Knoxville 64084
Kodiak 64485
Koeltztown 65048
Koenig 65013
Koester Spring 63036
Koshkonong 65692
Krakow 63090
Kurreville 63766
Labadie 63055
La Belle 63447
Lac du Bois 63141
Laclede 64651
La Crosse 63549
Lacyville 64720
Laddonia 63352
La Due, *Henry* 64735
Ladue, *St. Louis* 63124
Laflin 63760
La Forge 63869
Lagonda 63558
La Grange 63448
Laguna Beach (Part of Osage Beach) 65065
Lake Adelle 63016
Lake Annette 64746
Lake Arrowhead 63060
Lake City (Part of Independence) 64016
Lake Contrary 64504
Lake Creek 65325
Lake Forest Estates 63670
Lake Junction (Part of Webster Groves) 63119
Lake Kah-Tan-Da 63775
Lake Lafayette 64076
Lakeland 65026
Lake Lotawana 64086
Lake Mykee Town 65043
Lakenan 63468
Lake of the Woods 65201
Lake Ozark 65049
Lake Sherwood 63357
Lakeshire 63125
Lakeside, *Benton* 65338
Lakeside, *Boone* 65256
Lakeside, *Jasper* 64801
Lakeside, *Miller* 65026
Lake Spring 65532
Lake St. Louis 63367
Lake Tapawingo 64015
Lake Tekakwitha 63069
Lake Timberline 63628
Lake Valle 63020
Lakeview, *Cass* 64083
Lakeview, *Miller* 65026
Lakeview, *Ray* 64035
Lakeview Heights 65338
Lake Viking 64640
Lake Ware 63050
Lake Waukomis 64152
Lake Wauwanoka 63050
Lake Winnebago 64034
Lake Wittona 64683
Lakewood 65201
Lamar 64759
Lamar Heights 64759
Lambert 63736
Lamine 65233
La Monte 65337
Lampe 65681
Lanagan 64847
Lancaster 63548
Lanes Prairie 65013
Langdon 64446
Lanton 65775
La Plata 63549
Laquey 65534
Laredo 64652
Larimore 63138
La Russell 64848
Latham 65050
Lathrop 64465
La Tour 64747
Latty 63664
Laurel Heights (Part of Raytown) 64133
Laurie 65038
La Valle 63833
Lawrenceburg 65646
Lawrenceton 63627
Lawson 64062
Leadington 63601
Lead Mine 65764
Leadwood 63653
Leann 65605
Leasburg 65535
Leawood 64801
Lebanon 65536
Lebeck 64744
Lebo 65775
Lecoma 65540
Leeds (Part of Kansas City)‡ 64129
Leemon 63755
Leeper 63957
Lees Summit 64063-64
64081-82
64086
For specific ZIP Codes call (888) 275-8777, or your local postmaster.
Leesville 64735
Leeton 64761
Leisure Lake 64683
Lemay♦ 63125
Lemons 63565
Lenox 65541
Lentner 63450
Leonard 63451
Leon Mercer Jordan (Part of Kansas City)‡ 64128
Leopold 63760
Leora 63825
Leota 65626
Leslie 63056
Lesterville 63654
Levasy 64066
Levicks Mill 65260
Lewis 64735
Lewis and Clark Village 64484
Lewistown 63452
Lexington 64067
Liberal 64762
Liberty, *Callaway* 65063
Liberty, *Clay* 64068*
54069†
Libertyville 63640
Licking 65542
Liguori 63057
Lilbourn 63862
Lilly 64477
Lincoln 65338
Lindbergh 65202
Linden 65742
Lindley 64652
Lingo 64631
Linkville (Part of Kansas City) 64152
Linn 65051
Linn Creek 65052
Linneus 64653
Lisbon 65254
Lisle 64742
Lithium 63775
Little Blue (Part of Kansas City) 64133
Little Village (Part of Kansas City) 64118
Livonia 63551
Lock Springs 64654
Lockview Estates 65785
Lockwood 65682
Locust Hill 63460
Lodi 63950
Logan 65705
Lohman 65053
Loma Linda 63901
Lonedell 63060
Lone Elm, *Cooper* 65237
Lone Elm, *Jasper* 64801
Lone Hill 63901
Lone Jack 64070
Lone Tree 64701
Long Beach 65616
Long Lane 65590
Longrun 65761
Longtown 63775
Longview (Part of Kansas City)‡ 64138-39
For specific ZIP Codes call (888) 275-8777, or your local postmaster.
Longview, *McDonald* 64861
Longwood 65340
Loose Creek 65054
Loring 65667
Loughboro 63601
Louisburg 65685
Louisiana 63353
Louisville 63334
Lowground 63559
Lowndes 63951
Lowry City 64763
Low Wassie 65588
Lucas 64788
Lucas and Hunt Village 63121
Lucerne 64655
Ludlow 64656
Luebbering 63061
Lulu 65606
Luna 65655
Lupus 65046
Luray 63453
Lutesville (Part of Marble Hill) 63764
Luystown 65016
Lynchburg 65543
Lyon 63068
Mc Allister Springs 65333
McBaine 65203
McBride 63776
McCarty 63830
McClurg 65701
McCord Bend 65656
McCracken 65753
McCurry 64438
McDowell 65769
Macedonia 65401
McFall 64657
McGee 63763
McGirk 65055
McGuire 63837
Machens 63373
McKenna Villa 65326
Mackenzie 63123
McKinley 65705
McKittrick 65056
Macks Camp 65355
Macks Creek 65786
McMullin 63801
McNatt 64867
Macomb 65702
Macon 63552
Madison 65263
Madisonville 63436
Madry 65605
Magnolia 64040
Main City 64742
Maitland 64466
Majorville 65355
Makalu Estates 65065
Malden 63863
Malta Bend 65339
Mammoth 65655
Manchester 63011
Mandeville 64622
Manes 65711
Mano 65625
Mansfield 65704
Many Springs 65606
Mapaville 63065
Maplegrove 64748
Maples 65542
Maplewood, *Cass* 64083
Maplewood, *Pettis* 65301
Maplewood, *St. Louis* 63143
Marble Hill 63764
Marceline 64658
March 65644
Marco 63870
Margona Village (Part of St. John) 63114
Marion 65023
Marionville 65705
Mark Twain Mall (Part of St. Charles) 63301
Marlborough 63123
Marling 63359
Marquand 63655
Marshall 65340
Marshall Junction 65340
Marshfield 65706
Marston 63866
Marthasville 63357
Martin City (Part of Kansas City)‡ 64114
64145-47
64149
For specific ZIP Codes call (888) 275-8777, or your local postmaster.
Martinsburg 65264
Martinstown 63565
Martinsville 64467
Marvel Cave Park 65616
Marvin 65084
Marvin Terrace (Part of St. John) 63114
Maryden 63624
Maryknoll 63369
Maryland Heights 63043
Marys Home 65032
Maryville 64468
Maryville Gardens (Part of St. Louis)‡ 63111
Masters 65649
Matson 63341
Mattese 63129
Matthews 63867
Maud 63437
Maupin 63061
Mayesburg 64788
Mayfield 63662
Maysville 64469
Mayview 64071
Maywood 63454
Meacham Park (Part of Kirkwood) 63122

Place	ZIP
Meadowbrook Acres	64083
Meadowbrook Downs (Part of Overland)	63114
Meadowbrook West	65203
Meadville	64659
Medford	64040
Medill	63445
Medoc	64855
Mehlville♦	63129
Meinert	65682
Melbourne	64642
Melrose	63069
Memphis	63555
Mendon	64660
Mendota	63565
Menfro	63775
Mentor	65742
Meramec Height	63010
Mercer	64661
Mercyville	63538
Merriam Woods	65653
Merritt	65720
Merwin	64723
Mesler	63772
Meta	65058
Metro North Mall (Part of Kansas City)	64155
Metz	64765
Mexico	65265
Miami	65344
Miami Station	64633
Michelles Corner	65444
Micola	63877
Middle Brook	63656
Middle Grove	65263
Middletown	63359
Midland	63559
Midridge	63629
Mid Rivers Mall (Part of St. Peters)	63376
Midvale	65571
Midway, *Andrew*	64427
Midway, *Boone*	65202
Midway, *Lewis*	63452
Mike	64658
Milan	63556
Mildred	65679
Milford	64766
Millard	63501
Millcreek	63645
Miller	65707
Millersburg	65251
Millersville	63766
Mill Grove	64673
Millheim	63775
Mill Spring	63952
Millville	64085
Millwood	63377
Milo	64767
Milton, *Atchison*	64446
Milton, *Randolph*	65270
Mincy	65679
Mindenmines	64769
Mine La Motte	63645
Mineola	63361
Miner	63801
Mineral City	63637
Mineral Point	63660
Mineral Spring	65625
Mineville (Part of Kansas City)	64161
Mingo	63960
Minimum	63620
Minnith	63673
Mint Hill	65024
Mirabile	64671
Missionary Acres	63944
Missouri City	64072
Mitchell	63601
Moberly	65270
Modena	64673
Mokane	65059
Moline Acres	63136
Molino	65265
Monark Springs	64850
Monegaw Springs	64776
Monett	65708
Monkey Run	63467
Monroe City	63456
Montague	65669
Montague Hill	65340
Montevallo	64767
Montgomery City	63361
Monticello	63457
Montier	65546
Montreal	65591
Montrose	64770
Montserrat	65336
Moody	65777
Mooresville	64664
Mora	65345
Morehouse	63868
Morgan	65632
Morgan Heights	64836
Morley	63767
Morrison	65061
Morrisville	65710
Morse Mill	63066
Morton	64085
Mosby	64073
Moscow Mills	63362
Moselle	63084
Mosher	63670
Mound City	64470
Moundville	64771
Mountain	65772
Mountain Grove	65711
Mountain View	65548
Mount Airy	65259
Mount Freedom	63050
Mount Hope	63077
Mount Hulda	65325
Mount Leonard	65339
Mount Moriah	64665
Mount Pleasant	65026
Mount Shira	64854
Mount Sterling	65062
Mount Vernon	65712
Mount Zion, *Douglas*	65608
Mount Zion, *Henry*	64740
Mulberry (Part of Burgess)	66756
Mulberry, *Bates*	64722
Mullendike	64083
Munsell	65466
Murphy♦	63026
Murry	65255
Musicks Ferry	63034
Musselfork	65261
Myrtle	65778
Mystic	63545
Napier	64451
Napoleon	64074
Napton	65340
Nashua (Part of Kansas City)	64155
Nashville	64855
Naylor	63953
Nebo	65470
Neck City	64849
Neelys	63755
Neelyville	63954
Neeper	63445
Neier	63084
Nelson	65347
Nelsonville	63440
Nemo	65724
Neola	65661
Neosho	64850
Netherlands	63851
Nettleton	64644
Nevada	64772
Newark	63458
New Bloomfield	65063
New Boston	63557
Newburg	65550
New Cambria	63558
New Florence	63363
New Frankfort	65349
New Franklin	65274
New Hamburg	63736
New Hampton	64471
New Harmony	63339
New Hartford	63359
New Haven	63068
New Hope, *Dent*	65560
New Hope, *Lincoln*	63343
New Lebanon	65237
New Liberty	65588
New London	63459
New Madrid	63869
New Market	64439
New Melle	63365
New Offenburg	63661
New Piper	64788
New Point	64473
Newport	64759
New Santa Fe (Part of Kansas City)	64145
New Survey	63877
Newtonia	64853
Newtown	64667
New Truxton	63381
New Wells	63732
New Woolam	65066
New York	64644
Niangua	65713
Niangua Junction	65713
Nichols (Part of Springfield)	65802
Nind	63501
Ninnescah Park	64740
Nixa	65714
Noble	65715
Nodaway	64421
Noel	64854
Nona	63332
Norborne	64668
Normandy	63121
Normandy Shopping Center (Part of Northwoods)	63121
Norris	64726
North County	63138
Northeast (Part of Kansas City)‡	64123
Northern Heights (Part of Kansas City)	64152
North Kansas City	64116
Northland Shopping Center (Part of Jennings)	63136
North Lilbourn	63862
Northmoor	64152
North Noel (Part of Noel)	64854
North Park Mall (Part of Joplin)	64801
North Patton	63662
North Salem	63566
North Shores	65355
Northview	65706
North Wardell	63879
Northwest Plaza (Part of St. Ann)	63074
Northwoods	63121
Northwye	65401
Norwood	65717
Norwood Court	63121
Nottinghill	65762
Novelty	63460
Novinger	63559
Nyhart	64730
Nyssa	63932
Oak	64422
Oak Grove, *Franklin*	63080
Oak Grove, *Jackson*	64075
Oak Grove, *Madison*	63645
Oak Grove Heights	65801
Oak Hill	65453
Oakland, *Laclede*	65536
Oakland, *St. Louis*	63122
Oakland Park	64870
Oak Leaf	65065
Oak Ridge	63769
Oaks	64118
Oakside	65548
Oakton	64759
Oakvale	63020
Oakview	64118
Oakville♦	63129
Oakwood, *Clay*	64116
Oakwood (Part of Hannibal)	63401
Oakwood Park	64116
Oates	63625
Ocie	65761
Octa	63876
Odessa	64076
Odin	65667
Oermann	63023
O'Fallon	63366
Ogborn	63640
Oglesville	63961
Ohio	64763
Okete	63379
Olathia	65704
Old Appleton	63770
Old Bland	65014
Olden	65789
Oldfield	65720
Old Fredonia	65355
Oldham	65010
Old Linn Creek	65052
Old Merritt	65720
Old Mines	63630
Old Monroe	63369
Old Orchard (Part of Webster Groves)	63119
Old Post Office (Part of St. Louis)‡	63169
Old Woollam	65066
Olean	65064
Olive, Dallas	65648
Olive (Part of St. Louis)‡	63101
Olivette	63132
Olivewood	64083
Olney	63370
Olympia	64744
Olympian Village	63020
Omaha	63565
Ongo	65753
Opolis	66760
Oran	63771
Orange	65605
Orchard Farm	63301
Orchard Lakes	63141
Orearville	65349
Oregon	64473
Oriole	63701
Orla	65536
Oronogo	64855
Orrick	64077
Orrsburg	64475
Osage	65101
Osage Beach	65065
Osage Bend	65101
Osage Bluff	65101
Osage Hill (Part of Kirkwood)	63122
Osborn	64474
Oscar	65542
Osceola	64776
Osgood	64641
Oskaloosa	64762
Otterville	65348
Otto	63052
Overland	63114
Overton	65233
Owens	65717
Owensville	65066
Owls Bend	65466
Owsley	65332
Oxford	64475
Oxly	63955
Oyer	64744
Ozark	65721
Ozark Beach	65653
Ozark Springs	65583
Ozark View	63122
Pacific	63069
Pack	64854
Pagedale	63133
Painton	63772
Palace	65550
Palisades	63011
Palmer	63664
Palmyra	63461
Palopinto	65338
Papin	63020
Papinsville	64780
Paradise	64089
Paradise Point	65355
Paris	65275
Paris Springs	65646
Parkcrest Village (Part of Springfield)	65807
Parkdale, *Jefferson*	63049
Parkdale (Part of Kansas City)	64152
Parker Lake	63775
Park Forest (Part of Kansas City)	64152
Park Hills	63601
Parkville	64152
Parkway, *Franklin*	63077
Parkway (Part of Kansas City)‡ For specific ZIP Codes call (888) 275-8777, or your local postmaster.	64129-30
Parma	63870
Parnell	64475
Parshley	64862
Pasadena Hills	63121
Pasadena Park	63121
Pascola	63871
Passaic	64777
Patterson	63956
Patton	63662
Patton Junction	63662
Pattonsburg	64670
Paulding	63821
Paulina Hills	63010
Paydown	65582
Paynesville	63336
Peace Valley	65788
Peach Orchard	63848
Peaksville	63465
Pea Ridge	63080
Pearl	65770
Pebble Acres	63141
Peculiar	64078
Peerless Park	63088
Peers	63357
Pendleton	63383
Penermon	63846
Pennsboro	65752
Pennville	63545
Peoria	63622
Pepsin	64844
Perkins	63774
Perrin	64477
Perry	63462
Perryville	63775
Pershing	65061
Peru	64730
Peruque	63301
Petersburg	65250
Petersville	63055
Pevely	63070
Phelps	64848
Phelps City	64482
Phenix	65770
Philadelphia	63463
Phillipsburg	65722
Pickering	64476
Piedmont	63957
Pierce City	65723
Pierpont	65201
Pierre Laclede (Part of St. Louis)‡	63108
Pilot Grove	65276
Pilot Knob	63663
Pinckney	63357
Pine	63935
Pine Cove	65324
Pine Crest	65571
Pine Lawn	63120
Pineville	64856
Piney Park	63077
Pinhook	63845
Pioneer	65734
Piper	64770
Pisgah	65237
Pittsburg	65724
Pittsville	64040
Plad	65764
Plato	65552
Platte City	64079
Platte Woods	64151
Plattin	63028
Plattsburg	64477
Plaza (Part of Kansas City)‡	64112
Plaza Shopping Center (Part of Springfield)	65804
Pleasant Gap	64730
Pleasant Green	65276
Pleasant Grove	65068
Pleasant Hill	64080
Pleasant Hope	65725
Pleasant Ridge, *Barry*	65769
Pleasant Ridge, *Bates*	64780
Pleasant Valley, *Clay*	64068
Pleasant Valley, *Jasper*	64836
Plevna	63464
Plew	64848
Plymouth	64624
Pocahontas	63779
Point Lookout	65726
Point Pleasant	63873
Polk	65727
Pollock	63560
Polo	64671
Pomona	65789
Pom-o-sa Heights	65355
Ponce de Leon	65728
Pond	63038
Ponder	63935
Pondfork	65762
Pontiac	65729
Pony Express (Part of St. Joseph)‡	64503
Poplar	65355
Poplar Bluff	63901*
	63902†
Portage Des Sioux	63373
Portageville	63873
Port Hudson	63068
Portland	65067
Possumwalk	64428
Post Oak	64761
Potosi	63664
Pottersville	65790
Powe	63822
Powell	65730
Powellville	65550
Powersite	65731
Powersville	64672
Poynor	63935
Prairie City	64780
Prairie Hill	65281
Prairie Home	65068
Prairie Lick	65233
Prairie Meadows Estate	65201

* **Area Zip Code** † **Post Office Boxes** ‡ **Postal Station** ♦ **Census Designated Place** *Italic Type* **County**

Place	ZIP
Prathersville, *Boone*	65202
Prathersville, *Clay*	64024
Pratt	63935
Prescott	65483
Preston, *Hickory*	65732
Preston, *Jasper*	64836
Prices Branch	63363
Princeton	64673
Proctor	65037
Prospect Hill (Part of Riverview)	63137
Prosperity	64801
Protem	65733
Providence	63863
Pulaski	63935
Pulaskifield	65708
Pumpkin Center	64423
Purcell	64857
Purdin	64674
Purdy	65734
Pure Air	63559
Purina Farm	63039
Purman	63935
Purvis	65079
Puxico	63960
Pyletown	63841
Pyrmont	65078
Quail Run	65301
Quaker	63664
Quarles	64735
Queen City	63561
Quincy	65735
Quitman	64478
Qulin	63961
Racine	64858
Racket	65355
Racola	63630
Rader, *Maries*	65582
Rader, *Webster*	65713
Ralls	63401
Randles	63740
Randolph	64161
Randolph Springs	65259
Ravanna	64673
Ravena (Part of Pleasant Valley)	64068
Ravena Gardens (Part of Pleasant Valley)	64068
Ravenwood	64479
Raymondville	65555
Raymore	64083
Raytown	64133
Rayville	64084
Rea	64480
Readsville	65067
Rector	65560
Redbird	65014
Red Bridge (Part of Kansas City)	64131
Redford	63665
Redings Mill	64801
Redman	63431
Redmondville	63623
Red Oak	64848
Red Top	65757
Reeds	64859
Reeds Spring	65737
Reform	65077
Regal	64624
Reger	63556
Renick	65278
Rensselaer	63401
Republic	65738
Rescue	64848
Revere	63465
Reynolds	63666
Rhineland	65069
Rhyse	65560
Richards	64778
Richards-Gebaur Air Force Base	64147
Rich Fountain	65035
Rich Hill	64779
Richland	65556
Richmond	64085
Richmond Heights	63117
Richville, *Douglas*	65637
Richville, *Holt*	64473
Richwoods	63071
Ridgedale	65739
Ridgely	64444
Ridgeway	64481
Ridgley	65647
Riggs	65284
Rimby	65663
Ripley (Part of Independence)	64056
Risco	63874
Rise Branch	65324
Ritchey	64844
River Aux Vases	63670
Riverbend	64058
River Bend Estates	63017
Riverdale	65721
Rivermines (Part of Park Hills)	63601
River Roads Mall (Part of Jennings)	63136
Riverside, *Dunklin*	63829
Riverside, *Platte*	64150
Riverside Inn	64854
Riverton	65606
Riverview	63137
Rives	63875
Roach	65787
Roads	64668
Roanoke	65230
Roanridge (Part of Kansas City)	64152
Robbins	64093
Robertson	63042
Robertsville	63072
Robinwood East	63141
Robinwood West	63141
Roby	65557
Rocheport	65279
Rochester	64459
Rockaway Beach	65740
Rockbridge	65741
Rockbridge Estate	65201
Rock Creek	63010
Rock Hill	63124
Rockingham	64035
Rock Port	64482
Rock Springs	63601
Rockview	63740
Rockville	64780
Rocky Comfort	64861
Rocky Mount	65072
Rocky Ridge	63670
Rogersville	65742
Rolla	65401-02
For specific ZIP Codes call (888) 275-8777, or your local postmaster.	
Rolling Hills	64083
Rombauer	63962
Rome	65608
Rondo	65650
Roosterville (Part of Liberty)	64068
Rosati	65559
Roscoe	64781
Rosebud	63091
Rosedale (Part of St. Louis)	63112
Rose Hill	64747
Roseland	65323
Roselle	63650
Rosendale	64483
Rothville	64676
Roubidoux	65444
Round Grove	65707
Round Spring	65466
Rover	65775
Rowena	65240
Royal	65559
Royal Heights (Part of Joplin)	64801
Royal Oak	65606
Ruble	63638
Rucker	65243
Rueter	65744
Running Deer	65065
Rush Hill	65280
Rush Tower	63028
Rushville	64484
Ruskin Heights (Part of Kansas City)	64134
Russ	65536
Russellville, *Cole*	65074
Russellville, *Ray*	64668
Rutledge	63563
Sabula	63620
Saco	63645
Sac Valley Estates	65785
Safe	65559
Sage Hill	65605
Saginaw	64864
St. Albans	63073
St. Ann	63074
St. Anthony	65486
St. Aubert	65024
St. Catharine	64628
St. Charles	63301-04
For specific ZIP Codes call (888) 275-8777, or your local postmaster.	
St. Clair	63077
St. Clement	63334
St. Cloud	65441
St. Elizabeth	65075
St. Francisville	63430
Ste. Genevieve	63670
St. George, *St. Louis*	63125
St. George, *Wright*	65667
St. James	65559
St. John	63114
St. Johns Station (Part of St. John)	63114
St. Joseph	64501-08
For specific ZIP Codes call (888) 275-8777, or your local postmaster.	
St. Joseph Stock Yards (Part of St. Joseph)	64501

St. Louis

Place	ZIP
	63101-88
For specific ZIP Codes call (888) 275-8777, or your local postmaster.	
Colleges & Universities	
Aquinas Institute of Theology	63108
Concordia Seminary	63105
Covenant Theological Seminary	63141
Deaconess Coll of Nursing	63139
Fontbonne Coll	63105
Harris-Stowe State Coll	63103
Jewish Hosp Coll of Nursing & Allied Health	63110
Maryville Univ	63141
Missouri Baptist Coll	63141
Missouri Technical School	63132
Saint Louis Coll of Pharmacy	63110
Saint Louis Univ	63103
Univ of Missouri	63121
Washington Univ	63130
Webster Univ	63119
Financial Institutions	
Commerce Bank, NA	63105
Magna Bank, NA	63101
Mercantile Bank, NA	63101
NationsBank, NA	63101
Hospitals	
Barnes-Jewish Hosp	63110
Children's Hosp	63110
Christian Hosp Northeast	63136
Deaconess Central Hosp	63139
St Anthony's Med Ctr	63128
St Mary's Health Ctr	63117
Veterans Affairs Med Ctr	63125
Hotels/Motels	
Adam's Mark	63102
Frontenac Hilton	63131
Holiday Inn, Clayton Plaza	63105
Holiday Inn, Downtown Riverfront	63102
Holiday Inn Select, Convention Ctr	63101
Holiday Inn, Westport	63146
Hyatt Regency at Union Station	63103
Marriott Pavilion	63102
Regal Riverfront	63102
The Ritz-Carlton	63105
Renaissance	63134
Sheraton Westport Inn	63146
Military Installations	
Coast Guard Industrial Support Ctr	63106
Defense Energy Off	63125
Defense Mapping Agency, Operations Customer Replication Warehouse (FLIP)	63103
Defense Mapping Agency West	63118
U S Army Aviation & Troop Command	63120
U S Army Corps of Engineers	63103
U S Army Publications Distribution Ctr	63114
U S Army Res Personnel Ctr	63132

Place	ZIP
St. Louis Centre (Part of St. Louis)	63102
St. Louis Galleria (Part of Richmond Heights)	63117
St. Luke	65632
St. Martins	65101
St. Mary	63673
St. Patrick	63466
St. Paul	63366
St. Peters	63376
St. Robert	65583
St. Thomas	65076
Salcedo	63801
Salem	65560
Saline	64632
Saline City	65349
Salisbury	65281
Salt Springs	65339
Samford	63877
Sampsel	64601
Sampson	65713
San Antonio	64443
Sandhills	63563
Sandstone	64767
Sandy Hook	65046
Santa Fe	65282
Santa Rosa	64670
Sapp	65203
Sappington♦	63126-28
For specific ZIP Codes call (888) 275-8777, or your local postmaster.	
Saratoga	64854
Sarcoxie	64862
Sarvis Point	65746
Savannah	64485
Saverton	63467
Saxton	64507
Schell City	64783
Schlatitz	63730
Schluersburg	63332
Schofield	65663
Scholten	65605
Schubert	65101
Schuermann Heights (Part of Woodson Terrace)	63114
Schult	63851
Scobeville	63857
Scopus	63764
Scotland	64836
Scotsdale	63051
Scott City	63780
Scotts Corner	63352
Scrivner	65074
Scrub Ridge	63873
Seaton	65560
Sedalia	65301*
	65302†
Sedgewickville	63781
Seligman	65745
Selma	63028
Selmore	65721
Selsa (Part of Independence)	64057
Senate Grove	63014
Senath	63876
Seneca	64865
Sequoita (Part of Springfield)	65804
Sereno	63775
Seymour	65746
Shackelford	65340
Shade	63851
Shady Dell	63901
Shady Grove, *Christian*	65753
Shady Grove, *Pulaski*	65583
Shady Slope	65065
Shamrock	63361
Shannondale, *Chariton*	65281
Shannondale, *Shannon*	65560
Sharon	65349
Shaw	65202
Shawnee Mound	64733
Shawneetown	63755
Shearwood	64648
Sheffield (Part of Kansas City)	64125
Shelbina	63468
Shelby	64674
Shelbyville	63469
Sheldon	64784
Shell Knob	65747
Sheridan	64486
Sherrill	65542
Shibboleth	63630
Shibleys Point	63559
Shirley	63664
Shoal Creek Drive	64801
Shoal Creek Estates	64801
Shook	63963
Short Bend	65560
Shoveltown	63033
Shrewsbury	63119
Sibley	64088
Sigsbee	63434
Sikeston	63801
Silex	63377
Silica	63028
Siloam Springs	65775
Silva	63964
Silver Creek	64801
Silver Dollar City	65616
Silver Lake, *Cass*	64083
Silver Lake, *Perry*	63775
Silver Mine	63645
Simcoe	64861
Simmons	65689
Sinsabaugh	63953
Sitze Store	63753
Skidmore	64487
Slabtown	65542
Slagle	65613
Slater	65349
Sleeper	65536
Sligo	65560
Smallett	65608
Smelter Hill (Part of Joplin)	64801
Smithfield	64834
Smithton	65350
Smithville	64089
Smittle	65662
Smoky Hollow	65560
Sni Mills	64075
Snow Hollow Lake	63656
Snyder	65286
Solo	65564
Souder	65773
Soulard (Part of St. Louis)‡	63157
South Carrollton (Part of Carrollton)	64633
South County Center	63129
Southeast Postal Store (Part of Springfield)	65814
Southeast (Part of Kansas City)‡	64132
Southern Hills	65301
South Fork	65776
Southgate Shopping Center (Part of Springfield)	65804
South Gifford	63549
South Greenfield	65752
South Lee (Part of Lees Summit)	64081
South Liberty (Part of Liberty)	64068
South Lineville	50147
South Mall (Part of Warrensburg)	64093
South Point (Part of Washington)	63090
South Saint Joseph (Part of St. Joseph)	64504
South Shore	63301
South Side (Part of Springfield)‡	65806
South Troost (Part of Kansas City)‡	64131
South Troy	63379
South Van Buren	63965
South Walnut Hills	65301
Southwest (Part of St. Louis)‡	63139
Southwest (Part of Springfield)‡	65817
South West City	64863
Spalding	63401
Spanish Lake♦	63138
Sparta	65753
Speed	65233
Spencerburg	63339
Sperry	63501
Spickard	64679
Splitlog	64843

Spokane 65754
Sprague 64779
Spring Bluff 63080
Spring City 64801
Spring Creek 65461
Springfield 65801-10
65814
65817
For specific ZIP Codes call (888) 275-8777, or your local postmaster.
Spring Fork 65301
Spring Garden 65032
Springhill 64601
Spring Lake 63501
Springtown 63660
Spring Valley, *Camden* 65065
Spring Valley (Part of Noel) 64854
Sprott 63670
Spruce 64730
Spurgeon 64850
Squires 65755
Stahl 63559
Stanberry 64489
Stanhope 65339
Stanton 63079
Star City 65734
Stark 63353
Stark City 64866
Starkenburg 65069
State Line 63877
Steedman 65077
Steele 63877
Steeles 63935
Steelville 65565
Steffenville 63470
Steinmetz 65254
Stella 64867
Stephens, *Boone* 65202
Stephens, *Callaway* 65201
Stet 64680
Stewartsville 64490
Stillings 64079
Stinson 65707
Stockton 65785
Stockton Hills 65785
Stockyards (Part of St. Joseph)‡ 64504
Stockyards (Part of Kansas City)‡ 64101-02
For specific ZIP Codes call (888) 275-8777, or your local postmaster.
Stone Hill 65560
Stoneridge 65737
Stony Dell 65529
Stony Hill 63068
Stotesbury 64752
Stotts City 65756
Stoutland 65567
Stoutsville 65283
Stover 65078
Strafford 65757
Strain 63080
Strasburg 64090
Stringtown, *Butler* 63901
Stringtown, *Cole* 65053
Stringtown, *Jasper* 64834
Strother 65275
Stults 65737
Stultz 65464
Sturdivant 63782
Sturgeon 65284
Sturges 64601
Sublette 63546
Success 65570
Sue City 63549
Sugar Creek 64054
Sugar Lake 64484
Sugartree 64668
Sullivan 63080
Sulphur Springs 63052
Sumach 63852
Summerfield 65013
Summerset Lake 63020
Summersville 65571
Summit Shopping Center (Part of Lees Summit) 64081
Sumner 64681
Sundown 65761
Sunland Hills 63033
Sunlight 63622
Sunny Slope (Part of Kansas City)‡ 64110
Sunnyvale (Part of Joplin) 64801
Sunrise 63855
Sunrise Beach 65079
Sunrise Lake 63020
Sunset Hills 63127
Susanna 65713
Sutherland 65360
Swan 65759
Swart 64771
Swedeborg 65572
Sweden 65608
Sweet Springs 65351
Sweetwater, *Newton* 64850
Sweetwater, *Reynolds* 63638
Swift 63851
Swinton 63730
Swiss 65041
Sycamore 65760
Sycamore Hills 63114
Sycamore Valley 65355
Syenite 63651
Sylvania 65682
Syracuse 65354
Taberville 64780
Table Rock 65616
Taitsville 64671
Tallapoosa 63878
Taneyville 65759
Tanner 63801
Tan Tar Estates 65065
Tanyard 64801
Taos, *Buchanan* 64448
Taos, *Cole* 65101
Tara 63123
Tarkio 64491
Tarrants 63334
Tarsney Lakes 64075
Taskee 63967
Tauria 65737
Taylor 63471
Tea 63091
Teal Bend 65355
Tebbetts 65080
Tecumseh 65760
Tempo 63141
Ten Brook (Part of Arnold) 63010
Tenmile 63552
Ten Mile Corner 64784
Teresita 65573
Terre Du Lac 63628
Terry 63851
Thayer 65791
The Landing 63456
Theodosia 65761
Thomas Hill 65244
Thomasville 65438
Thompson 65285
Thoms 64834
Thornfield 65762
Thorpe 65644
Thox Rock 65550
Thrush 64735
Tiff 63674
Tiffany Springs (Part of Kansas City) 64152
Tiff City 64868
Tiffin 64744
Tightwad 64735
Tillman 63730
Tilsit 63755
Timber 65560
Times Beach 63025
Tina 64682
Tindall 64683
Tinkerville 63857
Tinney Grove 64624
Tin Town 65622
Tipton 65081
Tipton Ford 64801
Tip Top 65355
Toga 63730
Toledo 65755
Tolona 63452
Torch 63953
Toronto 65591
Tower Grove (Part of St. Louis)‡ 63163
Town and Country 63131
Town Pavilion (Part of Kansas City) 64105
Tracy 64079
Trask 65548
Treloar 63378
Trenton 64683
Trimble 64492
Triplett 65286
Troutt 63664
Troy 63379
Truesdail 63383
Truman Corners (Part of Grandview) 64030
Truxton 63381
Tuckahoe 64801
Tucker 63942
Tunas 65764
Turley 65552
Turners 65765
Turnerville 65548
Turney 64493
Turtle 65560
Tuscumbia 65082
Tuxedo Park (Part of Webster Groves) 63119
Twelve Mile 63645
Twin 65355
Twin Bridges, *Douglas* 65775
Twin Bridges, *Laclede* 65536
Twin Oaks 63021
Twin Springs 63079
Tyler 63877
Tyrone 65483
Udall 65766
Ulman 65083
Umber 65785
Umberland 65785
Umber View 65785
Umber View Heights 65785
Union, *Franklin* 63084
Union, *Ray* 64062
Union City 65610
Union Star 64494
Uniontown 63783
Unionville 63565
Unity Village 64064
University City 63130
Uplands Park 63121
Upton 65552
Urbana 65767
Urbandale (Part of Moberly) 65270
Urich 64788
Utica 64686
Vale (Part of Kansas City) 64138
Valles Mines 63087
Valley City 65336
Valley Park 63088
Valley Ridge 63933
Valley View, *Benton* 65355
Valley View, *Ste. Genevieve* 63627
Valley Water Mills 65803
Van 65613
Van Buren 63965
Vance 65713
Vancleve 65058
Vandalia 63382
Vandiver 65265
Vanduser 63784
Vanzant 65768
Vastus 63954
Velda Village 63133
Velda Village Hills 63121
Vera 63334
Verdella 64762
Verona 65769
Verona Hills (Part of Kansas City) 64145
Versailles 65084
Veterans Hospital (Part of Kansas City)‡ 64128
Vibbard 64062
Viburnum 65566
Vichy 65580
Victoria 63020
Vida 65401
Vienna 65582
Vigus 63042
Village of Charlack 63114
Village of Four Seasons 65049
Villa Heights (Part of Joplin) 64801
Villa Ridge♦ 63089
Vineland 63020
Vinita Park 63114
Vinita Terrace 63114
Vinson 63841
Viola 65747
Virgil City 64744
Virginia 64730
Vista 64789
Vulcan 63675
Waco 64869
Wagoner 65785
Wainwright 65043
Wakenda 64687
Waldo (Part of Kansas City) 64114
Waldron 64092
Walker 64790
Wallace 64439
Wall Street 65590
Walnut Grove 65770
Walnut Shade 65771
Wanamaker 65340
Wanda 64866
Wappapello 63966
Wardell 63879
Ward Parkway Center (Part of Kansas City) 64114
Wardsville 65101
Ware 63050
Warren 63456
Warrensburg 64093
Warrenton 63383
Warsaw 65355
Warson Woods 63122
Washburn 65772
Washington 63090
Washington Center 64467
Wasola 65773
Waterloo 64097
Watson 64496
Waverly 64096
Wayland 63472
Wayne 65772
Waynesville 65583
Weatherby 64497
Weatherby Lake 64152
Weaubleau 65774
Webb City 64870
Weber Hill 63051
Webster Groves 63119
Webster Park (Part of Webster Groves) 63119
Wedgewood 63031
Wedgewood Green 63031
Weingarten 63670
Wela 64865
Weldon Spring 63301
Weldon Spring Heights 63301
Wellington 64097
Wellston 63112
Wellston (Part of St. Louis)‡ 63112
Wellsville 63384
Wentworth 64873
Wentzville 63385
Wesco 65586
West Alton 63386
West Aurora 65026
Westboro 64498
Westbrooke 65201
West County Center (Part of Des Peres) 63131
West Ely 63401
West Eminence 65466
West Hermondale 63877
Westlake Village 65301
West Line 64734
Weston 64098
West Park Mall (Part of Cape Girardeau) 63701
Westphalia 65085
West Plains 65775
Westport (Part of Kansas City)‡ 64111
West Quincy 63471
Westview 64850
Westville 64658
Westwood 63131
Wet Glaize 65591
Wheatland 65779
Wheaton 64874
Wheelerville 65605
Wheeling 64688
Whispering Hills 63141
Whispering Pines 65401
Whitakerville 65355
White Branch 65355
White Church 65789
White Cloud 65779
White Hall Fields (Part of Liberty) 64068
Whiteman Air Force Base 65305
Whiteoak 63880
Whiteside 63387
Whitesville 64480
Whitewater 63785
Whiting 63845
Whitman 65286
Wien 63558
Wilbur Park 63123
Wilcox 64468
Wilderness 63941
Wildwood, *Harrison* 64424
Wildwood, *St. Louis* 63038
Wildwood Estates 65804
Wildwood Lake (Part of Raytown) 64133
Wilhelmina 63933
Willard 65781
William M Chick (Part of Kansas City)‡ 64124
Williamsburg 63388
Williamstown 63473
Williamsville 63967
Willmathsville 63546
Willow Brook 64448
Willow Springs 65793
Wilson City 63882
Wilton 65039
Winchester, *Clark* 63435
Winchester, *St. Louis* 63021
Winchester Gap 65536
Windsor 65360
Windsor Springs (Part of Kirkwood) 63122
Windyville 65783
Winfield 63389
Winigan 63566
Winnipeg 65534
Winnwood (Part of Kansas City) 64117
Winnwood Gardens (Part of Kansas City) 64117
Winnwood Lake (Part of Kansas City) 64117
Winona 65588
Winston 64689
Winthrop 64484
Wisdom 65355
Wishart 65710
Withers Mill 63401
Wittenberg 63748
Wolf Island 63881
Womack 63645
Woodbine Heights (Part of Kirkwood) 63122
Woodcliffe 65804
Woodland 63461
Woodland Estates 65301
Woodland Shores 65055
Woodlandville 65279
Woodlawn 65263
Woodridge 63033
Woodruff 64098
Woods Heights 64024
Woodson Terrace 63134
Woodville 65247
Wooldridge 65287
Worland 64752
Worlds of Fun (Part of Kansas City)‡ 64161
Wornall (Part of Kansas City)‡ 64113-14
For specific ZIP Codes call (888) 275-8777, or your local postmaster.
Worth 64499
Wortham 63601
Worthington 63567
Wright City 63390
Wyaconda 63474
Wyatt 63882
Wyatt Park (Part of St. Joseph)‡ 64507
Wyeth 64483
Yacht Club Harbor 65065
Yancy Mills 65401
Yarrow 63501
Yates 65257
Yonkerville 65723
Youngstown 63559
Yount 63775
Yukon 65589
Zalma 63787
Zanoni 65784
Zell 63670
Zion 63645
Zora 65078

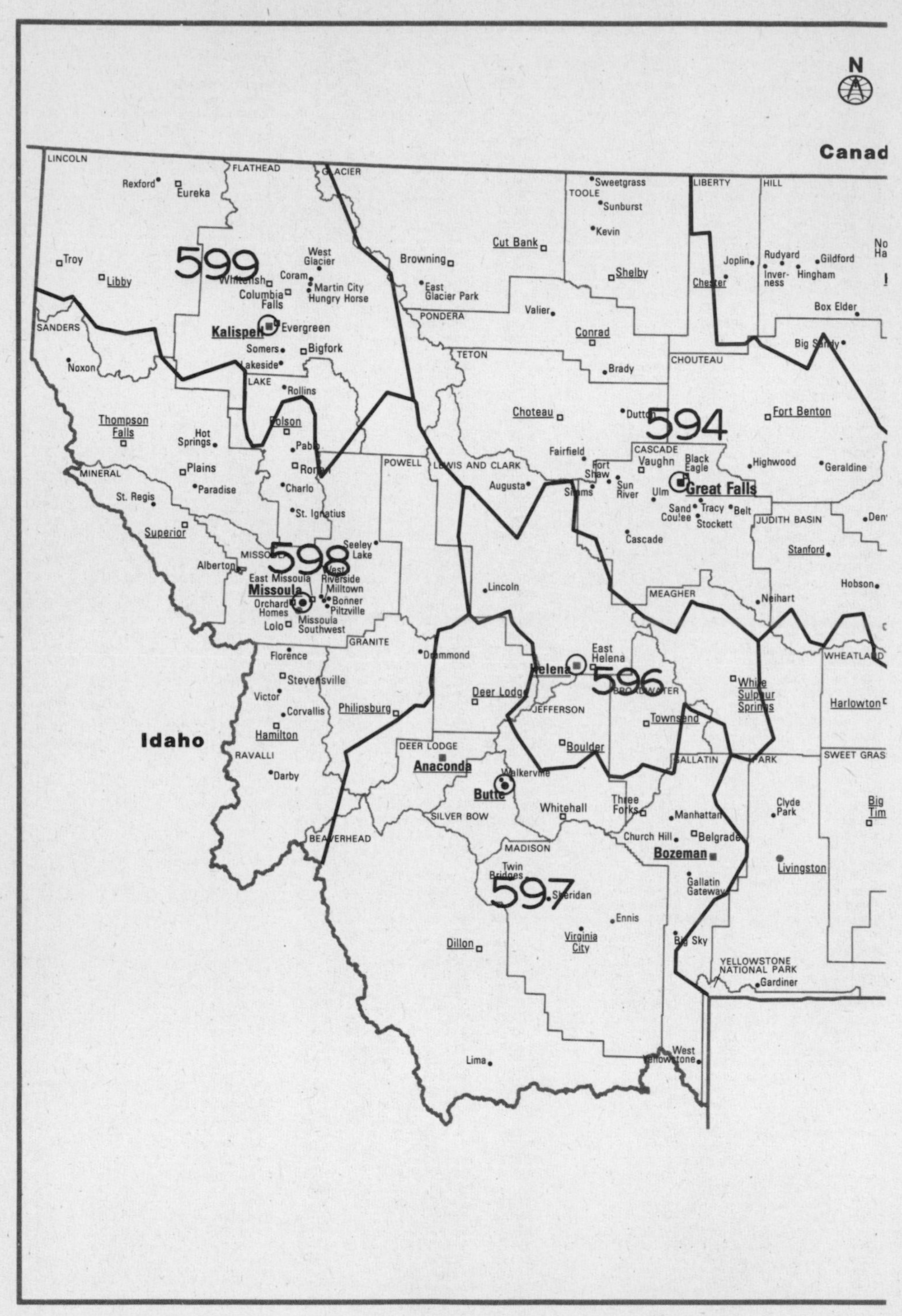

Canad
Idaho
599
598
597
596
594
LINCOLN
FLATHEAD
GLACIER
TOOLE
LIBERTY
HILL
SANDERS
LAKE
PONDERA
TETON
CHOUTEAU
MINERAL
POWELL
LEWIS AND CLARK
CASCADE
JUDITH BASIN
MEAGHER
GRANITE
WHEATLAND
JEFFERSON
BROADWATER
DEER LODGE
RAVALLI
SILVER BOW
GALLATIN
SWEET GRASS
BEAVERHEAD
MADISON
YELLOWSTONE NATIONAL PARK
Rexford
Eureka
Sweetgrass
Sunburst
Kevin
Cut Bank
Shelby
Troy
Libby
West Glacier
Coram
Martin City
Hungry Horse
Columbia Falls
Browning
East Glacier Park
Joplin
Rudyard
Gildford
Inver-ness
Hingham
Chester
Kalispell
Evergreen
Somers
Bigfork
Lakeside
Valier
Conrad
Box Elder
Big Sandy
Noxon
Rollins
Brady
Thompson Falls
Polson
Choteau
Dutton
Fort Benton
Hot Springs
Pablo
Fairfield
Highwood
Geraldine
Plains
Paradise
Ronan
Charlo
Augusta
Fort Shaw
Vaughn
Black Eagle
Great Falls
Sun River
Simms
Ulm
St. Regis
St. Ignatius
Sand Coulee
Tracy
Belt
Stockett
Superior
Cascade
Stanford
Seeley Lake
Alberton
East Missoula
West Riverside
Milltown
Bonner
Piltzville
Missoula
Orchard Homes
Missoula Southwest
Lolo
Lincoln
Hobson
Neihart
Florence
Drummond
East Helena
Helena
Stevensville
Victor
Corvallis
Philipsburg
Deer Lodge
White Sulphur Springs
Harlowton
Townsend
Hamilton
Boulder
Anaconda
Walkerville
Butte
Darby
Clyde Park
Big Timber
Whitehall
Three Forks
Manhattan
Church Hill
Belgrade
Bozeman
Livingston
Twin Bridges
Sheridan
Gallatin Gateway
Ennis
Virginia City
Dillon
Big Sky
Gardiner
West Yellowstone
Lima
N

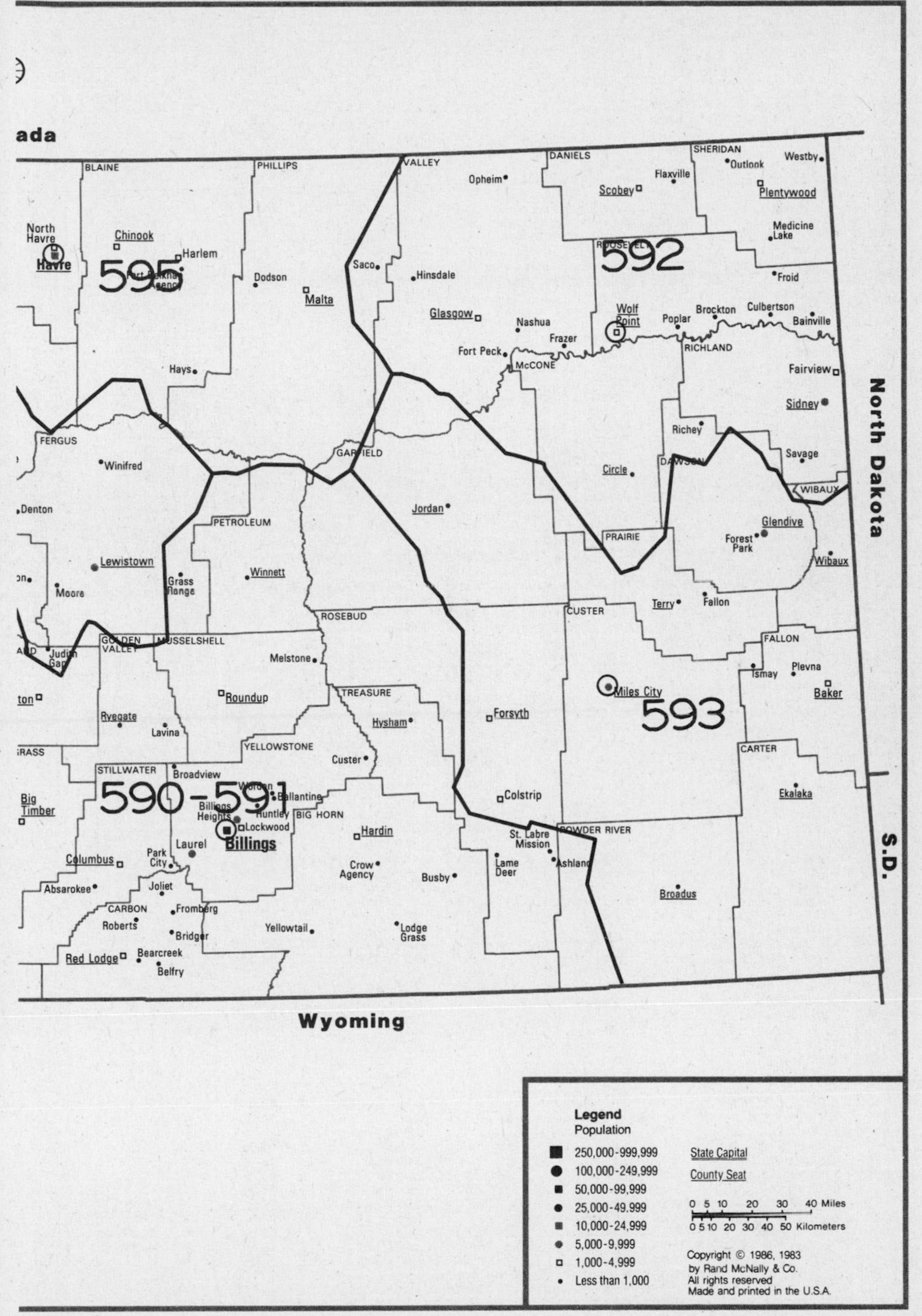

ada
BLAINE
PHILLIPS
VALLEY
DANIELS
SHERIDAN
North Havre
Havre
Chinook
Harlem
595
Dodson
Malta
Saco
Opheim
Hinsdale
Glasgow
Scobey
Flaxville
Outlook
Westby
Plentywood
Medicine Lake
592
Froid
Wolf Point
Poplar
Brockton
Culbertson
Bainville
Nashua
Frazer
Fort Peck
McCONE
RICHLAND
Fairview
Sidney
North Dakota
Hays
FERGUS
Winifred
GARFIELD
Richey
Savage
WIBAUX
Circle
DAWSON
Denton
Jordan
PETROLEUM
Glendive
Forest Park
PRAIRIE
Wibaux
Lewistown
Grass Range
Winnett
Moore
ROSEBUD
CUSTER
Terry
Fallon
GOLDEN VALLEY
MUSSELSHELL
FALLON
Melstone
Ismay
Plevna
Baker
Roundup
TREASURE
Miles City
593
Forsyth
Ryegate
Lavina
Hysham
YELLOWSTONE
CARTER
Custer
STILLWATER
Broadview
590-591
Ballantine
Big Timber
Billings Heights
Huntley
BIG HORN
Colstrip
Ekalaka
Lockwood
Billings
Hardin
St. Labre Mission
POWDER RIVER
S.D.
Laurel
Columbus
Park City
Crow Agency
Lame Deer
Ashland
Busby
Absarokee
Joliet
Broadus
CARBON
Fromberg
Roberts
Bridger
Yellowtail
Lodge Grass
Red Lodge
Bearcreek
Belfry
Wyoming
Legend
Population
250,000-999,999
100,000-249,999
50,000-99,999
25,000-49,999
10,000-24,999
5,000-9,999
1,000-4,999
Less than 1,000
State Capital
County Seat
0 5 10 20 30 40 Miles
0 5 10 20 30 40 50 Kilometers
Copyright © 1986, 1983
by Rand McNally & Co.
All rights reserved
Made and printed in the U.S.A.

Place	ZIP Code
A (Part of Butte)‡	59701
Absarokee♦	59001
Acton	59002
Adel	59421
Agawam	59422
Agency	59831
Alberton	59820
Albion	59311
Alder	59710
Alhambra	59634
Alloy (Part of Butte)	59701
Alpine	59071
Alzada	59311
Amazon	59632
Amsterdam	59741
Anaconda	59711
Anceney	59741
Andes	59218
Angela	59312
Antelope	59211
Apgar	59936
Argenta	59725
Arlee♦	59821
Armington	59412
Ashland♦	59003
Ashuelot	59443
Augusta	59410
Avon	59713
Babb	59411
Bainville	59212
Baker	59313
Ballantine	59006
Bannack	59725
Basin	59631
Bearcreek	59007
Bearmouth	59832
Bear Spring	59430
Beaverton	59261
Beehive	59061
Belfry	59008
Belgrade	59714
Belknap	59874
Belle Creek	59317
Belmont	59046
Belt	59412
Beltower	59324
Benchland	59462
Benteen	59031
Bergum Station East (Part of Helena)‡	59601
Biddle	59314
Big Arm	59910
Bigfork	59911
Bighorn	59010
Big Sandy	59520
Big Sky	59716
Big Timber	59011
Billings	59101-08
For specific ZIP Codes call (888) 275-8777, or your local postmaster.	
Billings Heights	59105
Birch Creek Colony	59486
Birney	59012
Black Eagle	59414
Blackfeet Indian Reservation	59417
Blackfoot	59417
Bloomfield	59315
Blossburg	59728
Bonner	59823
Boulder	59632
Box Elder	59521
Boyd	59013
Boyes	59316
Bozeman	59715
	59719
	59771-73
For specific ZIP Codes call (888) 275-8777, or your local postmaster.	
Bozeman Hot Springs	59715
Brady	59416
Brandenberg	59301
Brandon	59749
Bridger, *Carbon*	59014
Bridger (Part of Bozeman)‡	59722
Broadus	59317
Broadview	59015
Brock Creek	59731
Brockton	59213
Brockway	59214
Brooks	59457
Brown (Part of Anaconda)	59711
Brown Addition	59472
Browning	59417
Brusett	59318
Buffalo	59418
Busby♦	59016
Butte	59701-03
	59750
For specific ZIP Codes call (888) 275-8777, or your local postmaster.	
Buxton (Part of Butte)	59750
Bynum	59419
Camas	59845
Camas Prairie	59859
Cameron	59720
Canyon Creek	59633
Canyon Ferry	59601
Capitol	57724
Cardwell	59721
Carlyle	59353
Carter	59420
Cartersville	59347
Cascade	59421
Castle Rock	59327
Castner Falls	59421
Cat Creek	59087
Centennial (Part of Billings)‡	59108
Centerville, *Cascade*	59472
Centerville (Part of Butte)	59701
Central Park	59714
Champion (Part of Anaconda)	59722
Chapman	59537
Charles M. Russell (Part of Great Falls)‡	59405
Charlo♦	59824
Charlos Heights	59840
Checkerboard	59053
Chester	59522
Chico Hot Springs	59065
Chinook	59523
Choteau	59422
Christina	59451
Church Hill	59741
Circle	59215
Clancy	59634
Clinton	59825
Clyde Park	59018
Coalridge	59219
Coalwood	59351
Cobden	59872
Coffee Creek	59424
Cohagen	59322
Colorado Gulch	59601
Colstrip♦	59323
Columbia Falls	59912
Columbia Gardens (Part of Butte)	59701
Columbia Heights	59912
Columbus	59019
Comanche	59015
Condon	59826
Conner	59827
Conrad	59425
Cooke City	59020
Coram	59913
Corbin	59638
Corvallis	59828
Corwin Springs	59030
Crackerville (Part of Anaconda)	59711
Craig	59648
Crane	59217
Creston	59902
Crow Agency♦	59022
Crow Indian Reservation	59022
Crow Rock	59301
Culbertson	59218
Cushman	59046
Custer	59024
Cut Bank	59427
Dagmar	59219
Danvers	59457
Darby	59829
Dawson (Part of Butte)	59748
Dayton	59914
Dearborn	59648
De Borgia	59830
Decker	59025
Deerfield Colony	59457
Deer Lodge	59722
Del Bonita	59427
Dell	59724
Delphia	59073
Dempsey	59722
Denton	59430
Dentons Point (Part of Anaconda)	59711
Devon	59474
Dewey	59727
Dillon	59725
Divide (Part of Butte)	59727
Dixon	59831
Dodson	59524
Donald (Part of Butte)	59759
Dover	59479
Dovetail	59087
Downtown (Part of Billings)‡	59101
Drummond	59832
Dublin Gulch (Part of Butte)	59701
Dunkirk	59474
Dupuyer	59432
Durant (Part of Butte)	59748
Dutton	59433
Eagleton	59520
East Butte (Part of Butte)	59701
East Glacier Park♦	59434
East Helena	59635
East Missoula (Part of Missoula)	59808
Ekalaka	59324
Elkhorn Hot Springs	59746
Elliston	59728
Elmdale	59213
Elmo	59915
Emigrant	59027
Enid	59243
Ennis	59729
Epsie	59317
Essex	59916
Ethridge	59435
Eureka	59917
Evaro	59808
Evergreen♦	59901
Everson	59430
Fairfield	59436
Fairview	59221
Fallon	59326
Farmington	59422
Feely (Part of Butte)	59727
Ferdig	59466
Fergus	59451
Findon	59053
Finley Point♦	59860
First Creek	59538
First Electronic Combat Range Group - Detachment 17	59501
Fishtail	59028
Flathead Indian Reservation	59831
Flatwillow	59087
Flaxville	59222
Floral Park (Part of Butte)	59701
Florence	59833
Floweree	59440
Forestgrove	59441
Forest Park	59330
Forsyth	59327
Fort Belknap Indian Reservation	59526
Fort Benton	59442
Fortine	59918
Fort Keogh	59301
Fort Kipp	59213
Fort Peck	59223
Fort Peck Indian Reservation	59255
Fort Shaw	59443
Four Buttes	59263
Fourchette	59538
Four Corners	59466
Frazer♦	59225
Frenchtown	59834
Froid	59226
Fromberg	59029
Galata	59444
Galen (Part of Anaconda)	59722
Gallatin Gateway	59730
Gardiner	59030
Garland	59301
Garneill	59445
Garrison	59731
Garryowen	59031
Georgetown (Part of Anaconda)	59711
Geraldine	59446
Geyser	59447
Gibson Flats	59401
Gildford	59525
Gilt Edge	59457
Glacier Colony	59427
Glasgow	59230
Glasgow Air Base	59231
Glen	59732
Glendive	59330
Glentana	59240
Goldcreek	59733
Golden Ridge	59436
Goldstone	59540
Grace (Part of Butte)	59759
Grant	59725
Grantsdale	59835
Grass Range	59032
Great Falls	59401-06
For specific ZIP Codes call (888) 275-8777, or your local postmaster.	
Greenfield	59436
Greenough	59836
Gregson (Part of Butte)	59748
Greycliff	59033
Hackney (Part of Butte)	59748
Half Moon	59912
Hall	59837
Hamilton	59840
Hammond	59332
Hammond Valley	59327
Happyis Inn	59923
Happy Valley	59937
Hardin	59034
Hardy	59421
Harlem	59526
Harlowton	59036
Harrison	59735
Hathaway	59333
Haugan	59842
Havre	59501
Havre North♦	59501
Hays♦	59527
Heart Butte♦	59448
Heath	59457
Hedgesville	59078
Helena	59601-24
For specific ZIP Codes call (888) 275-8777, or your local postmaster.	
Helena Valley Northeast♦	59601
Helena Valley Northwest♦	59601
Helena Valley Southeast♦	59601
Helena Valley West Central♦	59601
Helena West Side♦	59601
Hellgate (Part of Missoula)‡	59808
Helmville	59843
Heron	59844
Herron Park	59501
Hesper	59106
Highwood	59450
Hilger	59451
Hingham	59528
Hinsdale	59241
Hobson	59452
Hodges	59353
Hogeland	59529
Holiday Village (Part of Great Falls)	59405
Holter Dam	59648
Homestead	59242
Hopp	59520
Hot Springs	59845
Howard	59327
Hughesville	59463
Hungry Horse	59919
Huntley	59037
Huson	59846
Hysham	59038
Iliad	59520
Ingomar	59039
Inverness	59530
Ismay	59336
Jackson	59736
Janney (Part of Butte)	59701
Jardine	59030
Jeffers	59729
Jefferson City	59638
Jefferson Island	59721
Jellison Place	59085
Joliet	59041
Joplin	59531
Jordan	59337
Judith Gap	59453
Kalispell	59901-04
For specific ZIP Codes call (888) 275-8777, or your local postmaster.	
Kenilworth	59520
Kevin	59454
Kicking Horse♦	59864
Kila	59920
Kingsbury Colony	59486
Kinsey	59338
Kiowa	59417
Kirby	59016
Klein	59072
Kolin	59451
Kremlin	59532
Lake McDonald	59921
Lakeside	59922
Lakeview	59739
Lambert	59243
Lame Deer♦	59043
Landusky	59524
Larslan	59244
LaSalle	59912
Last Chance (Part of Helena)‡	59601
Laurel	59044
Laurin	59749
Lavina	59046
Lebo	59053
Ledger	59456
Lennep	59053
Lewistown	59457
Libby	59923
Lima	59739
Limestone	59061
Lincoln	59639
Lindsay	59339
Livingston	59047
Lloyd	59535
Lockwood♦	59101
Lodge Grass	59050
Lodge Pole	59524
Logan	59741
Lohman	59523
Lolo♦	59847
Lolo Hot Springs	59847
Loma	59460
Lonepine	59848
Loring	59537
Lost Creek (Part of Anaconda)	59711
Lothair	59461
Lower Sun River (Part of Great Falls)	59401
Lustre	59225
Luther	59068
McAllister	59740
McCabe	59245
McClellans Creek	59635
McGlone Heights (Part of Butte)	59701
McLeod	59052
McQueen (Part of Butte)	59701
Madoc	59222
Maiden	59457
Maiden Rock (Part of Butte)	59743
Malmstrom Air Force Base	59402
Malta	59538
Manchester	59404
Manhattan	59741
Many Glacier Hotel	59411
Marion	59925
Marsh	59326
Martin City	59926
Martinsdale	59053
Marysville	59640
Maudlow	59714
Maxville	59858
Medicine Lake	59247
Medicine Springs	59827
Melrose (Part of Butte)	59743
Melstone	59054
Melville	59055
Mildred	59341
Miles City	59301
Milford Colony	59648
Mill Creek (Part of Anaconda)	59711
Miller Colony	59422
Mill Iron	59324
Milltown	59851
Miner	59027
Missoula	59801-08
For specific ZIP Codes call (888) 275-8777, or your local postmaster.	
Missoula Southwest	59804
Mizpah	59301
Moccasin	59462
Moffit Canyon	59715
Moiese	59824
Molt	59057
Mona	59213
Monarch	59463
Monida	59739
Montague	59442

Place	ZIP
Montana City	59634
Montanapolis Springs	59065
Moore	59464
Morel (Part of Anaconda)	59711
Morgan	59537
Mosby	59058
Moulton	59451
Mount Ellis	59715
Muddy♦	59016
Mullan (Part of Missoula)‡	59808
Musselshell	59059
Myers	59038
Nashua	59248
Navajo	59222
Neihart	59465
Nevada City	59755
New Chicago	59832
Newcomb (Part of Butte)	59701
New Miami Colony	59425
New Rockport Colony	59422
Niarada	59845
Nibbe	59088
Nickwall	59201
Nine Mile	59846
Nissler (Part of Butte)	59701
Nohle	59221
Norris	59745
North Browning♦	59417
Northern Cheyenne Indian Reservation	59043
Northridge Heights (Part of Kalispell)	59901
Noxon	59853
Nye	59061
Oilmont	59466
Olive	59343
Ollie	59313
Olney	59927
Opheim	59250
Opportunity (Part of Anaconda)	59711
Orchard Homes	59804
Ossette	59244
Oswego	59201
Otter	59062
Outlook	59252
Ovando	59854
Pablo♦	59855
Paradise	59856
Park City	59063
Park Grove	59248
Peerless	59253
Pendroy	59467
Perma	59859
Petrolia	59087
Philipsburg	59858
Piegan	59411
Piltzville	59808
Pine Creek	59047
Pinegrove	59808
Pinesdale	59841
Pinnacle	59916
Pioneer (Part of Billings)‡	59102
Pioneer (Part of Butte)	59701
Pioneer Junction	59923
Plains	59859
Pleasant Prairie	59222
Pleasant Valley	59925
Pleasant View	59330
Plentywood	59254
Plevna	59344
Plum Creek	59457
Polaris	59746
Polebridge	59928
Polson	59860
Pompeys Pillar	59064
Pony	59747
Poplar	59255
Portage	59440
Post Creek	59865
Potomac	59823
Powderville	59345
Power	59468
Pray	59065
Proctor	59929
Pryor♦	59066
Quinn (Part of Butte)	59743
Racetrack	59722
Radersburg	59641
Ramsay (Part of Butte)	59748
Rapelje	59067
Rattlesnake (Part of Missoula)	59808
Ravalli	59863
Ravenna	59825
Raymond	59256
Raynesford	59469
Red Bluff	59745
Red Lodge	59068
Redstone	59257
Reedpoint	59069
Regina	59538
Reserve	59258
Rexford	59930
Richey	59259
Richland	59260
Ridgelawn	59270
Ridgway	59332
Rimini	59601
Rimrock Mall (Part of Billings)	59102
Ringling	59642
Rising Sun	59434
Riverside	59840
Rivulet	59820
Roberts	59070
Rocker (Part of Butte)	59701
Rockport Colony	59467
Rock Springs, *Rosebud*	59312
Rock Springs, *Sheridan*	59258
Rockvale	59041
Rocky Boy	59521
Rocky Boys Indian Reservation	59521
Rollins	59931
Ronan	59864
Roosville	59917
Roscoe	59071
Rosebud	59347
Rossfork	59457
Roundup	59072
Roy	59471
Ruby	59710
Rudyard	59540
Ryegate	59074
Saco	59261
Sage Creek	59522
St. Ignatius	59865
St. Labre Mission	59004
St. Marie	59231
St. Mary	59417
St. Peter	59421
St. Regis	59866
St. Xavier	59075
Salmon Prairie	59911
Saltese	59867
Sand Coulee	59472
Sand Creek	59201
Sanders	59038
Sand Springs	59077
Santa Rita	59473
Sapphire Village	59452
Savage	59262
Savoy	59526
Scobey	59263
Seaver Park	59601
Sedan	59086
Seeley Lake	59868
Shawmut	59078
Shelby	59474
Shepherd	59079
Sheridan	59749
Shonkin	59450
Sidney	59270
Silesia	59041
Silver Bow (Part of Butte)	59750
Silver Bow Park (Part of Butte)	59701
Silver Gate	59081
Silver Star	59751
Simms	59477
Simpson	59501
Sipple	59464
Sleeping Buffalo	59261
Smelter Hill	59414
Somers	59932
Sonnette	59348
South Browning♦	59417
Southern Cross (Part of Anaconda)	59711
Southgate Mall (Part of Missoula)	59801
Spring Creek Colony	59457
Springdale	59082
Springdale Colony	59645
Square Butte	59442
Stanford	59479
Stark	59846
Starr School♦	59417
State Capitol (Part of Helena)‡	59601
Staton (Part of Anaconda)	59711
Stemple	59633
Stevensville	59870
Stockett	59480
Stone	59837
Straw	59418
Stryker	59933
Stuart (Part of Anaconda)	59711
Suffolk	59451
Sula	59871
Sumatra	59083
Summit	59434
Summit Valley	59721
Sunburst	59482
Sunnyside (Part of Anaconda)	59711
Sun Prairie, *Cascade*♦	59487
Sun Prairie, *Phillips*	59538
Sun River	59483
Sunset	59836
Superior	59872
Swan Lake	59911
Sweetgrass	59484
Swiftcurrent	59411
Tampico	59230
Tarkio	59872
Teigen	59084
Terry	59349
The Pines	59859
Thompson Falls	59873
Three Forks	59752
Toston	59643
Townsend	59644
Tracy	59472
Trego	59934
Trident	59752
Trout Creek	59874
Troy	59935
Truly	59485
Turah	59825
Turner	59542
Turner Colony	59542
Twin Bridges	59754
Twin Creeks	59823
Twodot	59085
Ulm	59485
Unionville	59601
Utica	59452
Valier	59486
Vandalia	59273
Varney	59729
Vaughn	59487
Victor	59875
Vida	59274
Virgelle	59520
Virginia City	59755
Volborg	59351
Volt	59201
Wagner	59538
Walkerville	59701
Wan-i-gan	59065
Ware	59457
Warmsprings (Part of Anaconda)	59756
Warren	82423
Warrick	59520
Washoe	59007
Waterloo	59759
Wayne	59412
Webster	59313
Weldon	59215
Westby	59275
West Glacier	59936
West Lewistown	59457
West Park Plaza (Part of Billings)	59102
West Riverside	59808
West Valley (Part of Anaconda)	59711
West Yellowstone	59758
Whately	59248
Wheeler	59230
Whitefish	59937
Whitehall	59759
White Haven	59923
Whitepine	59874
White Sulphur Springs	59645
Whitetail	59276
Whitewater	59544
Whitlash	59545
Wibaux	59353
Wickes	59638
Willard	59354
Williamsburg (Part of Butte)	59701
Willow Creek	59760
Wilsall	59086
Windham	59479
Winifred	59489
Winnett	59087
Winston	59647
Wisdom	59761
Wise River	59762
Wolf Creek	59648
Wolf Point	59201
Woods Bay	59911
Woodside	59875
Woodworth	59836
Worden	59088
Wyola	59089
Yaak Valley	59935
Yellowtail	59035
York	59601
Zortman	59546
Zurich	59547

*** Area Zip Code** **† Post Office Boxes** **‡ Postal Station** **♦ Census Designated Place** *Italic Type* **County**

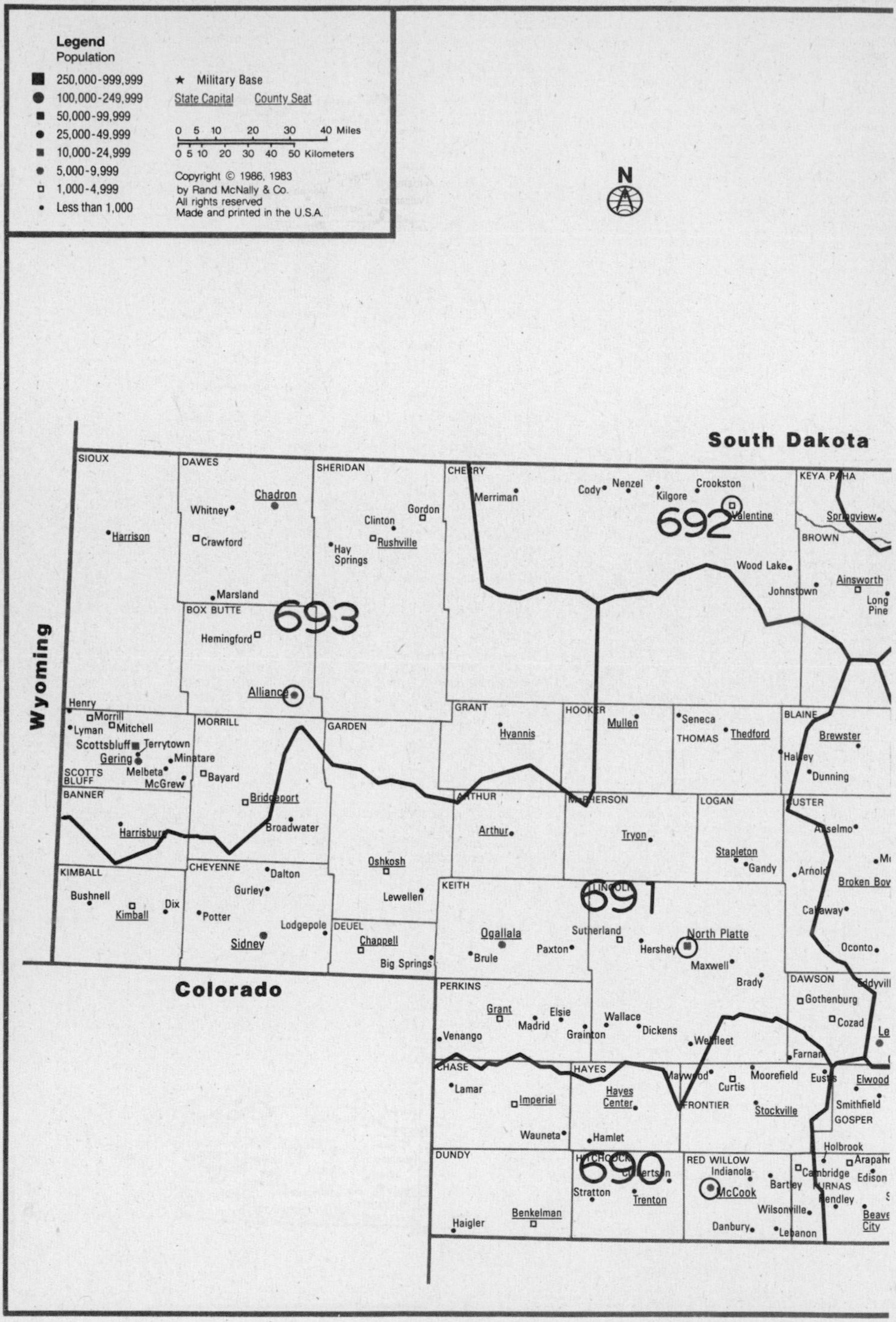

Legend
Population
250,000-999,999
100,000-249,999
50,000-99,999
25,000-49,999
10,000-24,999
5,000-9,999
1,000-4,999
Less than 1,000
★ Military Base
State Capital County Seat
0 5 10 20 30 40 Miles
0 5 10 20 30 40 50 Kilometers

South Dakota
Wyoming
Colorado
SIOUX
Harrison
DAWES
Chadron
Whitney
Crawford
Marsland
SHERIDAN
Gordon
Clinton
Rushville
Hay Springs
CHERRY
Merriman
Cody
Nenzel
Kilgore
Crookston
Valentine
692
KEYA PAHA
Springview
BROWN
Wood Lake
Johnstown
Ainsworth
Long Pine
BOX BUTTE
693
Hemingford
Alliance
Henry
Morrill
Lyman
Mitchell
Scottsbluff
Terrytown
Gering
Minatare
Melbeta
McGrew
SCOTTS BLUFF
MORRILL
Bayard
Bridgeport
Broadwater
GARDEN
Oshkosh
Lewellen
GRANT
Hyannis
HOOKER
Mullen
Seneca
THOMAS
Thedford
BLAINE
Brewster
Halsey
Dunning
BANNER
Harrisburg
ARTHUR
Arthur
McPHERSON
Tryon
LOGAN
Stapleton
Gandy
CUSTER
Anselmo
Arnold
Broken Bow
Callaway
Oconto
KIMBALL
Bushnell
Kimball
Dix
CHEYENNE
Dalton
Gurley
Potter
Lodgepole
Sidney
DEUEL
Chappell
Big Springs
KEITH
Ogallala
Brule
Paxton
Sutherland
LINCOLN
691
Hershey
North Platte
Maxwell
Brady
DAWSON
Gothenburg
Cozad
Eddyville
PERKINS
Grant
Elsie
Madrid
Venango
Grainton
Wallace
Dickens
Wellfleet
Farnam
CHASE
Lamar
Imperial
HAYES
Hayes Center
Maywood
Curtis
Moorefield
Eustis
FRONTIER
Stockville
Elwood
Smithfield
GOSPER
Wauneta
Hamlet
DUNDY
HITCHCOCK
690
Culbertson
Stratton
Trenton
RED WILLOW
Indianola
McCook
Bartley
Cambridge
Arapahoe
FURNAS
Edison
Hendley
Wilsonville
Beaver City
Danbury
Lebanon
Benkelman
Haigler

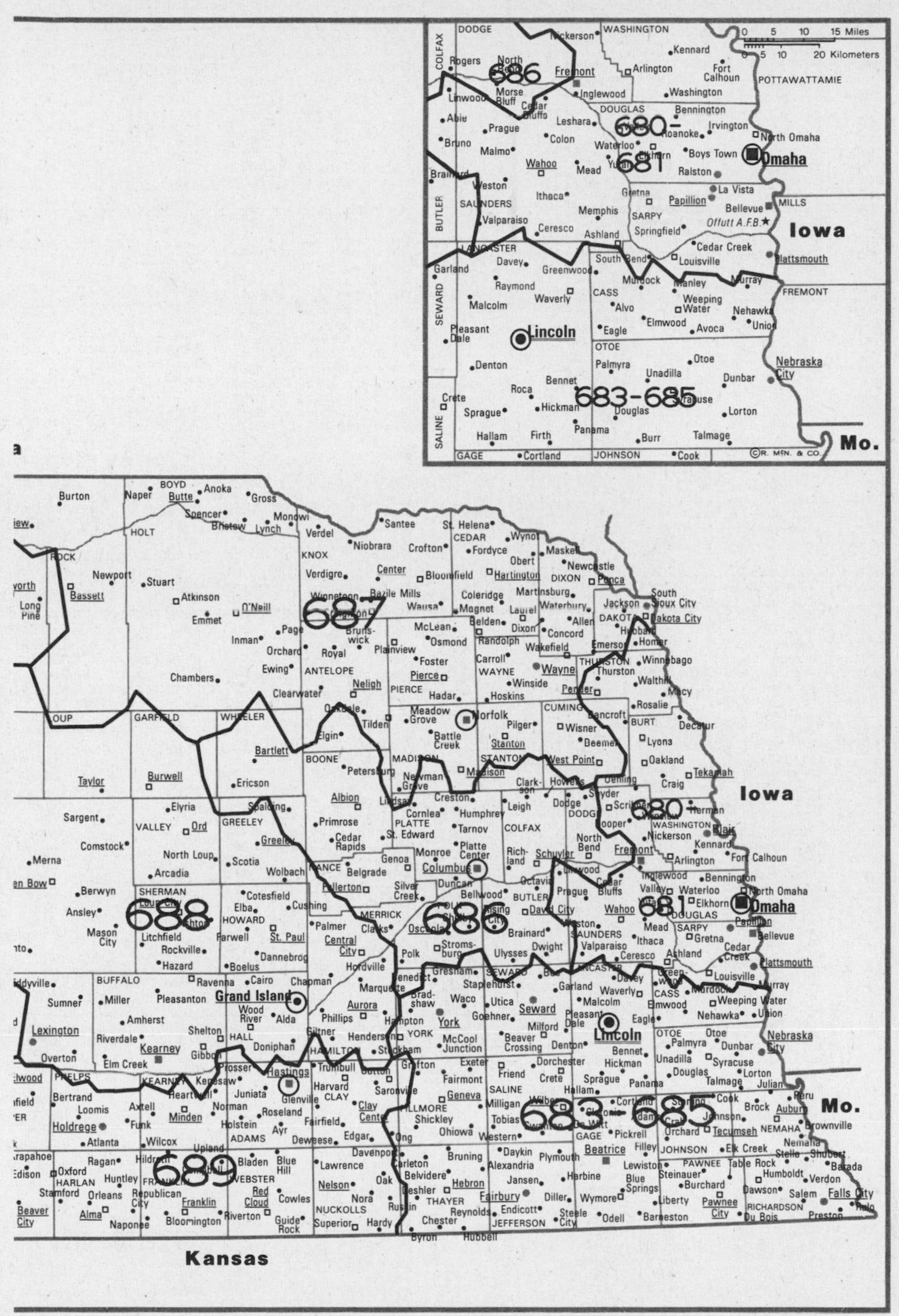
0 5 10 15 Miles
0 5 10 20 Kilometers
DODGE
WASHINGTON
COLFAX
POTTAWATTAMIE
DOUGLAS
SARPY
MILLS
BUTLER
SAUNDERS
LANCASTER
SEWARD
CASS
OTOE
SALINE
GAGE
JOHNSON
FREMONT
Iowa
Mo.
Nickerson
Kennard
Fort Calhoun
Arlington
Rogers
Fremont
Inglewood
Washington
Linwood
Morse Bluff
Cedar Bluffs
Abie
Prague
Leshara
Bennington
Irvington
North Omaha
Bruno
Malmo
Colon
Waterloo
Elkhorn
Boys Town
Omaha
Wahoo
Mead
Ralston
Weston
Ithaca
Gretna
Papillion
La Vista
Bellevue
Valparaiso
Memphis
Springfield
Offutt A.F.B.
Ceresco
Ashland
Cedar Creek
Plattsmouth
Garland
Davey
Greenwood
South Bend
Louisville
Raymond
Waverly
Murdock
Manley
Murray
Malcolm
Alvo
Weeping Water
Nehawka
Union
Pleasant Dale
Lincoln
Eagle
Elmwood
Avoca
Denton
Palmyra
Otoe
Unadilla
Nebraska City
Bennet
Dunbar
Crete
Roca
Hickman
Syracuse
Sprague
Douglas
Lorton
Hallam
Firth
Panama
Burr
Talmage
Cortland
Cook
686
680-681
683-685
©R. McN. & CO.
BOYD
Anoka
Burton
Naper
Butte
Gross
Spencer
Bristow
Lynch
Monowi
Verdel
Santee
St. Helena
HOLT
KNOX
CEDAR
Wynot
Niobrara
Crofton
Fordyce
Maskell
Obert
Newcastle
ROCK
Newport
Stuart
Center
Bloomfield
Hartington
DIXON
Ponca
Bassett
Long Pine
Atkinson
O'Neill
Verdigre
Coleridge
Martinsburg
South Sioux City
Emmet
Bazile Mills
Wausa
Magnet
Laurel
Waterbury
Jackson
Dakota City
Allen
DAKOTA
Inman
Page
Brunswick
Osmond
McLean
Belden
Dixon
Concord
Homer
Orchard
Royal
Plainview
Randolph
Wakefield
Emerson
Ewing
ANTELOPE
Foster
Carroll
Wayne
Winnebago
THURSTON
Chambers
Clearwater
Neligh
PIERCE
Pierce
WAYNE
Winside
Walthill
Hadar
Hoskins
Pender
Rosalie
Macy
Meadow Grove
Norfolk
CUMING
Bancroft
BURT
Decatur
Tilden
Elgin
Oakdale
Pilger
Wisner
Battle Creek
Stanton
Beemer
Lyons
GARFIELD
WHEELER
Bartlett
BOONE
MADISON
STANTON
West Point
Oakland
Petersburg
Newman Grove
Madison
Howells
Tekamah
Taylor
Burwell
Ericson
Craig
Albion
Clarkson
Snyder
Scribner
Elyria
Spalding
Creston
Dodge
Herman
Sargent
VALLEY
Ord
GREELEY
Primrose
Lindsay
Humphrey
Leigh
DODGE
Blair
Cornlea
PLATTE
Tarnov
COLFAX
Hooper
Comstock
Greeley
Cedar Rapids
St. Edward
Platte Center
North Bend
Fort Calhoun
Merna
North Loup
Scotia
Genoa
Monroe
Richland
Schuyler
Arlington
Arcadia
Wolbach
Belgrade
Columbus
Bennington
Berwyn
SHERMAN
Loup City
Cotesfield
Fullerton
Silver Creek
Duncan
Bellwood
BUTLER
Octavia
Prague
Valley
Waterloo
North Omaha
Elkhorn
Omaha
Ansley
Elba
HOWARD
Cushing
MERRICK
Rising City
David City
Wahoo
DOUGLAS
Papillion
Mason City
Litchfield
Farwell
St. Paul
Palmer
Central City
Clarks
Osceola
Shelby
Brainard
Mead
SARPY
Gretna
Bellevue
Rockville
Dannebrog
Polk
Stromsburg
Ulysses
Dwight
SAUNDERS
Ithaca
Valparaiso
Ceresco
Ashland
Cedar Creek
Plattsmouth
Hazard
Boelus
Hordville
Gresham
SEWARD
Louisville
BUFFALO
Ravenna
Cairo
Chapman
Marquette
Benedict
Staplehurst
Garland
Davey
Waverly
CASS
Murdock
Murray
Sumner
Miller
Pleasanton
Grand Island
Aurora
Bradshaw
Waco
Utica
Seward
Malcolm
Elmwood
Weeping Water
Amherst
Wood River
Alda
Phillips
Hampton
York
Goehner
Pleasant Dale
Lincoln
Eagle
Nehawka
Union
Lexington
Riverdale
Shelton
HALL
Giltner
Henderson
YORK
McCool Junction
Milford
Beaver Crossing
OTOE
Otoe
Nebraska City
Overton
Kearney
Gibbon
Doniphan
HAMILTON
Stockham
Denton
Palmyra
Dunbar
Elm Creek
Prosser
Hastings
Trumbull
Sutton
Grafton
Exeter
Dorchester
Bennet
Hickman
Unadilla
Syracuse
PHELPS
KEARNEY
Kenesaw
Glenville
Harvard
CLAY
Fairmont
Friend
Crete
Sprague
Panama
Douglas
Talmage
Lorton
Julian
Bertrand
Heartwell
Juniata
Saronville
Geneva
SALINE
Hallam
Cook
Peru
Loomis
Axtell
Norman
Roseland
Clay Center
FILLMORE
Milligan
Wilber
Cortland
Sterling
Brock
Auburn
Holdrege
Funk
Minden
Holstein
Ayr
Fairfield
Shickley
Tobias
Clatonia
Adams
Johnson
Tecumseh
NEMAHA
Brownville
Atlanta
Wilcox
Upland
ADAMS
Deweese
Edgar
Ohiowa
Western
De Witt
GAGE
Pickrell
Orchard
Ragan
Hildreth
Bladen
Blue Hill
Davenport
Bruning
Daykin
Plymouth
Beatrice
Filley
JOHNSON
Elk Creek
Nemaha
Stella
Shubert
Oxford
HARLAN
Huntley
WEBSTER
Lawrence
Carleton
Belvidere
Alexandria
Harbine
Lewiston
Blue Springs
PAWNEE
Table Rock
Humboldt
Barada
Verdon
Stamford
Orleans
Republican City
Franklin
Red Cloud
Cowles
Nelson
Nora
Oak
Deshler
THAYER
Hebron
Jansen
Fairbury
Diller
Wymore
Steinauer
Burchard
Dawson
Salem
Falls City
Beaver City
Alma
Naponee
Bloomington
Riverton
Guide Rock
NUCKOLLS
Superior
Hardy
Ruskin
Chester
Reynolds
Endicott
JEFFERSON
Steele City
Odell
Barneston
Liberty
Pawnee City
RICHARDSON
Du Bois
Preston
Rulo
Byron
Hubbell
687
688
686
680
681
683-685
689
Iowa
Mo.
Kansas

A (Part of Omaha) 68120
Abie 68001
Adams 68301
Agate 69346
Agnew 68428
Ainsworth 69210
Air Mail Facility (Part of Omaha)‡ 68119
Air Park West (Part of Lincoln) 68524
Akron 68620
Albion 68620
Alda 68810
Alexandria 68303
Allen 68710
Alliance 69301
Alma 68920
Almeria 68879
Aloys 68788
Altona 68787
Alvo 68304
Amelia 68711
Ames 68621
Ames Avenue (Part of Omaha)‡ 68110-11
For specific ZIP Codes call (888) 275-8777, or your local postmaster.
Amherst 68812
Amick Acres 68832
Angora 69331
Angus 68961
Anoka 68722
Anselmo 68813
Ansley 68814
Antioch 69340
Arapahoe 68922
Arcadia 68815
Archer 68816
Arizona 68061
Arlington 68002
Arnold 69120
Arthur 69121
Ashby 69333
Ashland 68003
Ashton 68817
Assumption 68955
Aten 68730
Atkinson 68713
Atlanta 68923
Auburn 68305
Aurora 68818
Autumn Hills (Part of Omaha) 68134
Avoca 68307
Axtell 68924
Ayr 68925
Bancroft 68004
Barada 68355
Barneston 68309
Bartlett 68622
Bartley 69020
Bassett 68714
Battle Creek 68715
Bayard 69334
Bazile Mills 68729
Beacon View 68028
Beatrice 68310
Beaver City 68926
Beaver Crossing 68313
Bee 68314
Beemer 68716
Belden 68717
Belgrade 68623
Bellevue 68005
Bellwood 68624
Belvidere 68315
Benedict 68316
Benkelman 69021
Bennet 68317
Bennington 68007
Benson (Part of Omaha)‡ 68104
Berea 69301
Bertrand 68927
Berwyn 68819
Bethany (Part of Lincoln) 68505
Big Springs 69122
Bingham 69335
Bixby 68979
Bladen 68928
Blair 68008-09
For specific ZIP Codes call (888) 275-8777, or your local postmaster.
Bloomfield 68718
Bloomington 68929
Blue Hill 68930
Blue River Lodge 68333
Blue Springs 68318
Boelus 68820
Boone 68620
Bostwick 68978
Bow Valley 68739
Boys Town 68010
Bradshaw 68319
Brady 69123
Brainard 68626
Brandon 69140
Breslau 68765
Brewster 68821
Bridgeport 69336
Briggs 68122
Bristow 68719
Broadwater 69125
Brock 68320
Broken Bow 68822
Brownlee 69166
Brownson 69162
Brownville 68321
Brule 69127
Bruning 68322
Bruno 68014
Brunswick 68720
Burchard 68323
Burkett (Part of Grand Island)‡ 68801
Burr 68324
Burress 68354
Burton 68778
Burwell 68823
Bushnell 69128
Butte 68722
Byron 68325
Cadams 68978
Cairo 68824
Callaway 68825
Cambridge 69022
Campbell 68932
Carleton 68326
Carroll 68723
Cedar Bluffs 68015
Cedar Creek 68016
Cedar Rapids 68627
Center 68724
Central City 68826
Ceresco 68017
Chadron 69337
Chalco♦ 68046
Chambers 68725
Champion 69023
Chapman 68827
Chappell 69129
Cheneys 68526
Chester 68327
Clarks 68628
Clarkson 68629
Clatonia 68328
Clay Center 68933
Clearwater 68726
Clinton 69343
Cody 69211
Coleridge 68727
College View (Part of Lincoln)‡ 68506
Colon 68018
Colton 69162
Columbus 68601-02
For specific ZIP Codes call (888) 275-8777, or your local postmaster.
Comstock 68828
Concord 68728
Conestoga Mall (Part of Grand Island) 68803
Constance 68730
Cook 68329
Cordova 68330
Cornlea 68642
Cortland 68331
Cotesfield 68835
Cowles 68930
Cozad 69130
Crab Orchard 68332
Craig 68019
Crawford 69339
Creighton 68729
Creston 68631
Crete 68333
Crofton 68730
Crookston 69212
Crossroads Mall (Part of Omaha) 68114
Crowell 68057
Crown Point (Part of Omaha) 68122
Culbertson 69024
Curtis 69025
Cushing 68873
Dakota City 68731
Dalton 69131
Danbury 69026
Dannebrog 68831
Darr 69130
Davenport 68335
Davey 68336
David City 68632
Dawson 68337
Daykin 68338
Debolt (Part of Omaha) 68152
Decatur 68020
Denman 68956
Denton 68339
Deshler 68340
De Soto 68023
Deweese 68934
De Witt 68341
Dickens 69132
Diller 68342
Dix 69133
Dixon 68732
Dodge 68633
Doniphan 68832
Dorchester 68343
Douglas 68344
Downtown (Part of Omaha)‡ 68101
Du Bois 68345
Duff 68772
Dunbar 68346
Duncan 68634
Dunning 68833
Dustin 68713
Dwight 68635
Eagle 68347
Eddyville 68834
Edgar 68935
Edholm 68036
Edison 68936
Elba 68835
Eldorado 68818
Elgin 68636
Eli 69201
Elk City 68064
Elk Creek 68348
Elkhorn 68022
Ellis 68310
Ellsworth 69340
Elm Creek 68836
Elmwood 68349
Elmwood Park (Part of Omaha)‡ 68105-06
For specific ZIP Codes call (888) 275-8777, or your local postmaster.
Elsie 69134
Elsmere 69135
Elwood 68937
Elyria 68837
Emerald 68528
Emerick 68752
Emerson 68733
Emmet 68734
Enders 69027
Endicott 68350
Enola 68701
Ericson 68637
Ericson Lake 68637
Eustis 69028
Ewing 68735
Exeter 68351
Fairbury 68352
Fairfield 68938
Fairmont 68354
Fairview Heights 68138
Falls City 68355
Farnam 69029
Farwell 68838
Filley 68357
Firth 68358
Florence (Part of Omaha)‡ 68112
Fontanelle 68044
Fordyce 68736
Fort Calhoun 68023
Fort Robinson 69339
Foster 68737
Franklin 68939
Fremont 68025*
68026†
Friend 68359
Fullerton 68638
Funk 68940
Gandy 69163
Garland 68360
Garrison 68632
Gates 68822
Gateway Shopping Center (Part of Lincoln) 68505
Geneva 68361
Genoa 68640
Gering 69341
Gibbon 68840
Gilead 68362
Giltner 68841
Gladstone 68352
Glen 69346
Glenover (Part of Beatrice) 68310
Glenvil 68941
Glenwood Park 68847
Goehner 68364
Good Samaritan Village (Part of Hastings) 68901
Gordon 69343
Gothenburg 69138
Grafton 68365
Grainton 69169
Grand Island 68801-03
For specific ZIP Codes call (888) 275-8777, or your local postmaster.
Grand Island Mall (Part of Grand Island) 68801
Grant 69140
Greeley 68842
Green Meadows 68164
Greenwood 68366
Gresham 68367
Gretna 68028
Gross 68719
Grover 68405
Guide Rock 68942
Gurley 69141
Hadar 68738
Haig 69357
Haigler 69030
Hallam 68368
Halsey 69142
Hamlet 69031
Hampton 68843
Hansen 68901
Harbine 68377
Hardy 68943
Harrisburg 69345
Harrison 69346
Hartington 68739
Harvard 68944
Hastings 68901*
68902†
Havelock (Part of Lincoln)‡ 68529
Havens 68628
Hayes Center 69032
Hay Springs 69347
Hazard 68844
Heartwell 68945
Hebron 68370
Hemingford 69348
Henderson 68371
Hendley 68946
Henry 69349
Herman 68029
Hershey 69143
Hickman 68372
Hideaway Acres 68730
Hildreth 68947
Hillerage 69361
Holbrook 68948
Holdrege 68949
Holland 68372
Hollinger 68967
Holmesville 68374
Holstein 68950
Homer 68030
Hooper 68031
Hordville 68846
Hoskins 68740
Howe 68305
Howells 68641
Hubbard 68741
Hubbell 68375
Humboldt 68376
Humphrey 68642
Huntley 68971
Hyannis 69350
Imperial 69033
Imperial Mall (Part of Hastings) 68901
Inavale 68952
Indianola 69034
Indian Village (Part of Lincoln)‡ 68502*
68542†
Inglewood 68025
Inland 68954
Inman 68742
Irvington 68134
Ithaca 68033
Jacinto 69133
Jackson 68743
Jamison 68759
Jansen 68377
Johnson 68378
Johnson Lake 68937
Johnstown 69214
Julian 68378
Juniata 68955
Kearney 68847*
68848†
Keene 68924
Kenesaw 68956
Kennard 68034
Keystone 69144
Kilgore 69216
Kimball 69145
King Lake 68064
Knievels Corner 68735
Kohles Acres 68730
Kramer 68333
Kronborg 68854
Kuesters Lake 68801
Lake Forest Estates 68134
Lakeside 69351
Lamar 69023
Lanham 68415
La Platte 68123
Laurel 68745
La Vista 68128
Lawrence 68957
Lebanon 69036
Lee Valley (Part of Omaha) 68134
Leigh 68643
Lemoyne 69146
Leshara 68035
Lewellen 69147
Lewiston 68380
Lexington 68850
Liberty 68381
Lillian 68822
Lincoln 68501-88
For specific ZIP Codes call (888) 275-8777, or your local postmaster.
Lincoln Crossing (Part of Lincoln) 68524
Lindsay 68644
Lindy 68718
Linoma Beach 68028
Linwood 68036
Lisco 69148
Litchfield 68852
Lodgepole 69149
Loma 68626
Londer 68847
Long Pine 69217
Loomis 68958
Lorenzo 69162
Loretto 68620
Lorton 68382
Louisville 68037
Loup City 68853
Lowell 68840
Lushton 68371
Lyman 69352
Lynch 68746
Lyons 68038
McCook 69001
McCool Junction 68401
McGrew 69353
McLean 68747
Macon 68939
Macy♦ 68039
Madison 68748
Madrid 69150
Magnet 68749
Main Office (Part of Omaha)‡ 68102-03
68108
For specific ZIP Codes call (888) 275-8777, or your local postmaster.
Malcolm 68402
Malmo 68040
Manley 68403
Maple Hills (Part of Omaha) 68134
Mariaville 68759
Marion 69026
Marquette 68854
Marsland 69354
Martell 68404

* Area Zip Code † Post Office Boxes ‡ Postal Station ♦ Census Designated Place *Italic Type* **County**

Martinsburg 68710
.... 68770
For specific ZIP Codes call (888) 275-8777, or your local postmaster.
Mascot 68967
Maskell 68751
Mason City 68855
Max 69037
Maxwell 69151
Maywood 69038
Mead 68041
Meadow Grove 68752
Meadow Oaks 68059
Melbeta 69355
Memphis 68042
Menominee 68736
Merna 68856
Merriman 69218
Milford 68405
Millard (Part of Omaha) 68137
.... 68144
For specific ZIP Codes call (888) 275-8777, or your local postmaster.
Millard Highlands (Part of Omaha)‡ 68137
Miller 68858
Milligan 68406
Mills 68753
Mills Beach 68731
Milton Store 68858
Minatare 69356
Minden 68959
Minersville 68410
Mitchell 69357
Monowi 68746
Monroe 68647
Monterey 68788
Moorefield 69039
Morrill 69358
Morse Bluff 68648
Mount Michael 68022
Mullen 69152
Murdock 68407
Murphy 68865
Murray 68409
Mynard 68048
Naper 68755
Naponee 68960
Nashville 68112
Nebraska City 68410
Nehawka 68413
Neligh 68756
Nelson 68961
Nemaha 68414
Nenzel 69219
Newark 68847
Newcastle 68757
Newman Grove 68758
Newport 68759
Nickerson 68044
Nimburg 68036
Nim City 68337
Niobrara 68760
Nora 68961
Norfolk 68701*
.... 68702†
Norman 68963
North Auburn (Part of Auburn) 68305
North Bend 68649
North Loup 68859
North Oaks 68122
North Omaha (Part of Omaha) 68112
North Platte 69101*
.... 89103†
Northport 69336
North Shore 68776

Northwest (Part of Omaha) 68134
Oak 68964
Oakdale 68761
Oakland 68045
Oakview Mall (Part of Omaha) 68144
Obert 68757
Oconto 68860
Octavia 68632
Odell 68415
Odessa 68861
Offutt Air Force Base 68113
Ogallala 69153
Ohiowa 68416
Old Mill (Part of Omaha) 68134
Olean 68633
Omaha 68101-12
.... 68114-22
.... 68124-27
.... 68130-32
.... 68134-45
.... 68152-64
For specific ZIP Codes call (888) 275-8777, or your local postmaster.
Omaha Indian Reservation 68039
O'Neill 68763
Ong 68452
Orchard 68764
Ord 68862
Orleans 68966
Orum 68008
Osceola 68651
Oshkosh 69154
Osmond 68765
Otoe 68417
Overton 68863
Oxford 68967
Page 68766
Palisade 69040
Palmer 68864
Palmyra 68418
Panama 68419
Papillion 68046
.... 68133
For specific ZIP Codes call (888) 275-8777, or your local postmaster.
Parks 69041
Parkview (Part of Grand Island) 68801
Paul 68410
Pauline 68941
Pawnee City 68420
Paxton 69155
Pender 68047
Peru 68421
Petersburg 68652
Phillips 68865
Pickrell 68422
Pierce 68767
Pilger 68768
Plainview 68769
Platte Center 68653
Plattsmouth 68048
Pleasant Dale 68423
Pleasant Hill 68343
Pleasant Valley 68739
Pleasanton 68866
Plymouth 68424
Polk 68654
Ponca 68770
Potter 69156
Powell 68352
Prague 68050
Prairie Home 68527
Precept 68977
Preston 68355
Primrose 68655

Princeton 68404
Prosser 68883
Purdum 69157
Raeville 68652
Ragan 68969
Ralston 68127
Randolph 68771
Ravenna 68869
Raymond 68428
Red Cloud 68970
Redington 69336
Regency (Part of Omaha) 68114
Republican City 68971
Reynolds 68429
Richfield 68054
Richland 68601
Ringgold 69167
Rising City 68658
Riverdale 68870
Riverside Lakes 68069
Riverside Park 68405
Riverton 68972
Roanoke (Part of Omaha) 68134
Roca 68430
Rockford 68310
Rockville 68871
Rogers 68659
Rokeby 68523
Rosalie 68055
Roscoe 69153
Rose 68772
Roseland 68973
Rosemont 68930
Rosenburg 68644
Round Valley 68822
Royal 68773
Rulo 68431
Rushville 69360
Ruskin 68974
Sac and Fox Indian Reservation 68355
Sacramento 68949
Saddle Creek (Part of Omaha)‡ 68131-32
For specific ZIP Codes call (888) 275-8777, or your local postmaster.
St. Bernard 68644
St. Columbans 68056
St. Edward 68660
St. Helena 68774
St. James 68792
St. Libory 68872
St. Mary 68443
St. Paul 68873
St. Stephens 68957
Salem 68433
Santee 68760
Santee Indian Reservation 68760
Sarben 69155
Sargent 68874
Saronville 68975
Schaupps 68817
Schuyler 68661
Scotia 68875
Scottsbluff 69361*
.... 69363†
Scribner 68057
Seneca 69161
Seward 68434
Seymour Park (Part of Ralston) 68127
Shelby 68662
Shelton 68876
Shickley 68436
Sholes 68771
Shubert 68437
Sidney 69162
Silver Creek 68663

Skyline♦ 68022
Smithfield 68976
Smyrna 68978
Snyder 68664
South Bend 68058
South Minden (Part of Minden) 68959
South Omaha (Part of Omaha)‡ 68107
Southroads Shopping Center (Part of Bellevue) 68005
South Sioux City 68776
South Yankton 57078
Spalding 68665
Sparks 69220
Sparta 68783
Spencer 68777
Spencer Park (Part of Hastings) 68901
Sprague 68438
Springfield 68059
Springview 68778
Stamford 68977
Stanton 68779
Staplehurst 68439
Stapleton 69163
State House (Part of Lincoln)‡ 68509
Steele City 68440
Steinauer 68441
Stella 68442
Sterling 68443
Still Meadow (Part of Omaha) 68122
Stockham 68818
Stockville 69042
Stock Yards (Part of Omaha)‡ 68107
Strang 68444
Stratton 69043
Stromsburg 68666
Stuart 68780
Sumner 68878
Sunnyslope (Part of Omaha) 68134
Sunol 69149
Superior 68978
Surprise 68667
Sutherland 69165
Sutton 68979
Swanton 68445
Swedeburg 68066
Sybrant 68714
Syracuse 68446
Table Rock 68447
Talmage 68448
Tamora 68434
Tarnov 68642
Taylor 68879
Tecumseh 68450
Tekamah 68061
Telbasta 68002
Terrytown 69341
Thayer 68460
Thedford 69166
Thompson 68352
Thurston 68062
Tilden 68781
Tobias 68453
Touhy 68065
Trenton 69044
Trumbull 68980
Tryon 69167
Uehling 68063
Ulysses 68669
Unadilla 68454
Union 68455
University Place (Part of Lincoln)‡ 68504
Upland 68981
Utica 68456

Valentine 69201
Valley 68064
Valparaiso 68065
Venango 69168
Venice 68069
Verdel 68760
Verdigre 68783
Verdon 68457
Vesta 68450
Veterans' Administration Hospital (Part of Omaha) 68105
Villa Springs 68059
Virginia 68458
Vorhees 68620
Wabash 68407
Waco 68460
Wagners Lake 68601
Wahoo 68066
Wakefield 68784
Walkers Valley View 68730
Wallace 69169
Walthill 68067
Walton 68461
Walworth 68874
Wann 68003
Washington 68068
Waterbury 68785
Waterloo 68069
Wauneta 69045
Wausa 68786
Waverly 68462
Wayne 68787
Wayside 69337
Weeping Water 68463
Wee Town 68767
Weissert 68880
Wellfleet 69170
Western 68464
Westerville 68881
West Omaha (Part of Omaha)‡ 68114
Weston 68070
West Point 68788
Westroads (Part of Omaha) 68114
Westwood Plaza (Part of Omaha) 68144
White Clay 69365
Whitman 69366
Whitney 69367
Wilber 68465
Wilcox 68982
Willis 68743
Willow Island 69171
Wilsonville 69046
Winnebago 68071
Winnebago Indian Reservation 68071
Winnetoon 68789
Winside 68790
Winslow 68072
Wisner 68791
Wolbach 68882
Wood Lake 69221
Woodland Park 68701
Wood River 68883
Woods Park (Part of Lincoln)‡ 68503
Worms 68872
Wymore 68466
Wynot 68792
York 68467
Yossem's Paradise Valley (Part of Omaha) 68134
Yutan 68073

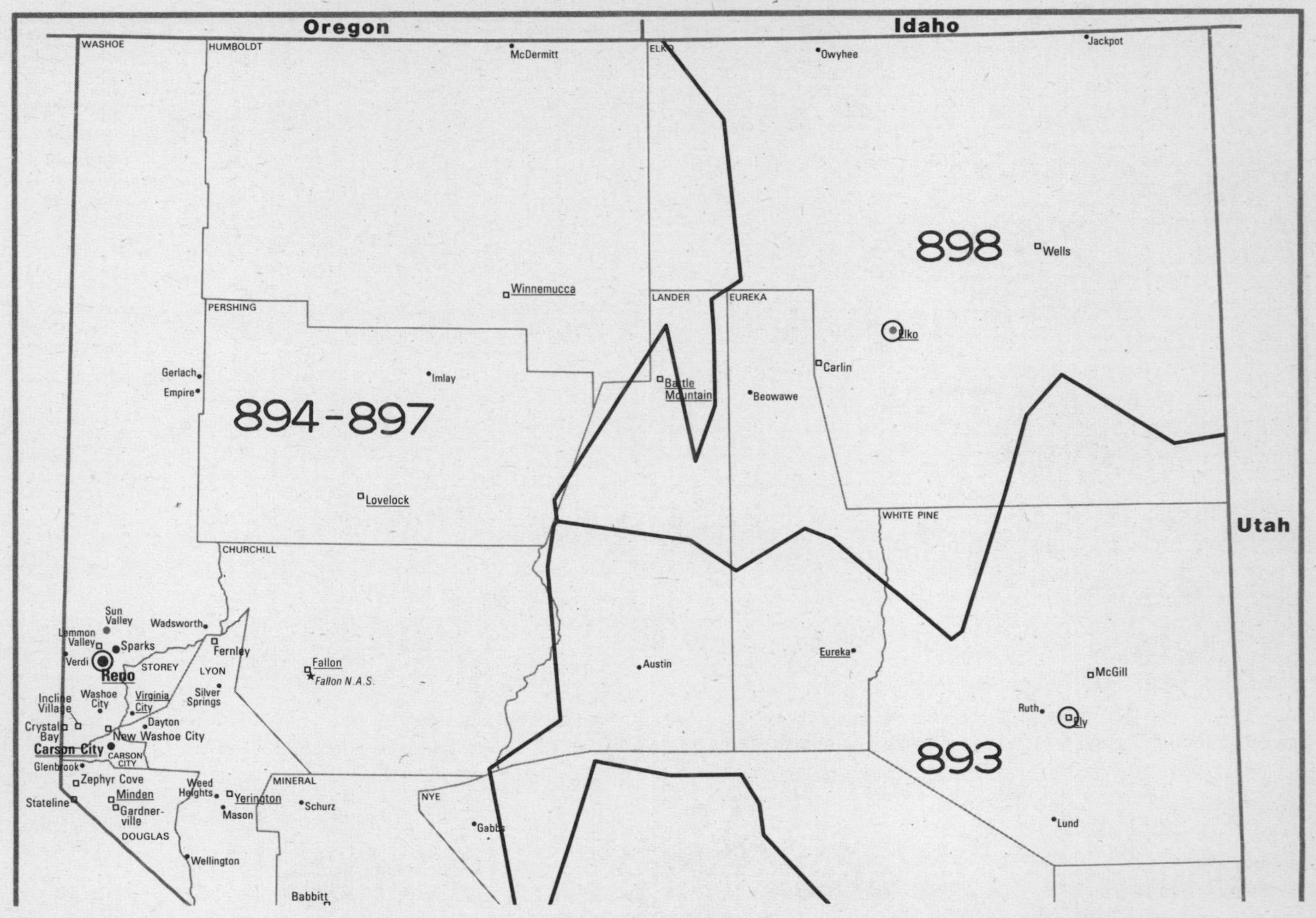

Oregon
Idaho
Utah
WASHOE
HUMBOLDT
McDermitt
ELKO
Owyhee
Jackpot
898
Wells
Winnemucca
PERSHING
LANDER
EUREKA
Elko
Carlin
Gerlach
Empire
Imlay
Battle Mountain
Beowawe
894-897
Lovelock
CHURCHILL
WHITE PINE
Sun Valley
Wadsworth
Lemmon Valley
Sparks
Fernley
Verdi
Reno
STOREY
LYON
Fallon
Fallon N.A.S.
Austin
Eureka
McGill
Incline Village
Washoe City
Virginia City
Silver Springs
Ruth
Ely
Crystal Bay
Dayton
New Washoe City
Carson City
CARSON CITY
893
Glenbrook
Zephyr Cove
Weed Heights
MINERAL
Stateline
Minden
Yerington
Schurz
NYE
Gardnerville
Mason
Gabbs
Lund
DOUGLAS
Wellington
Babbitt

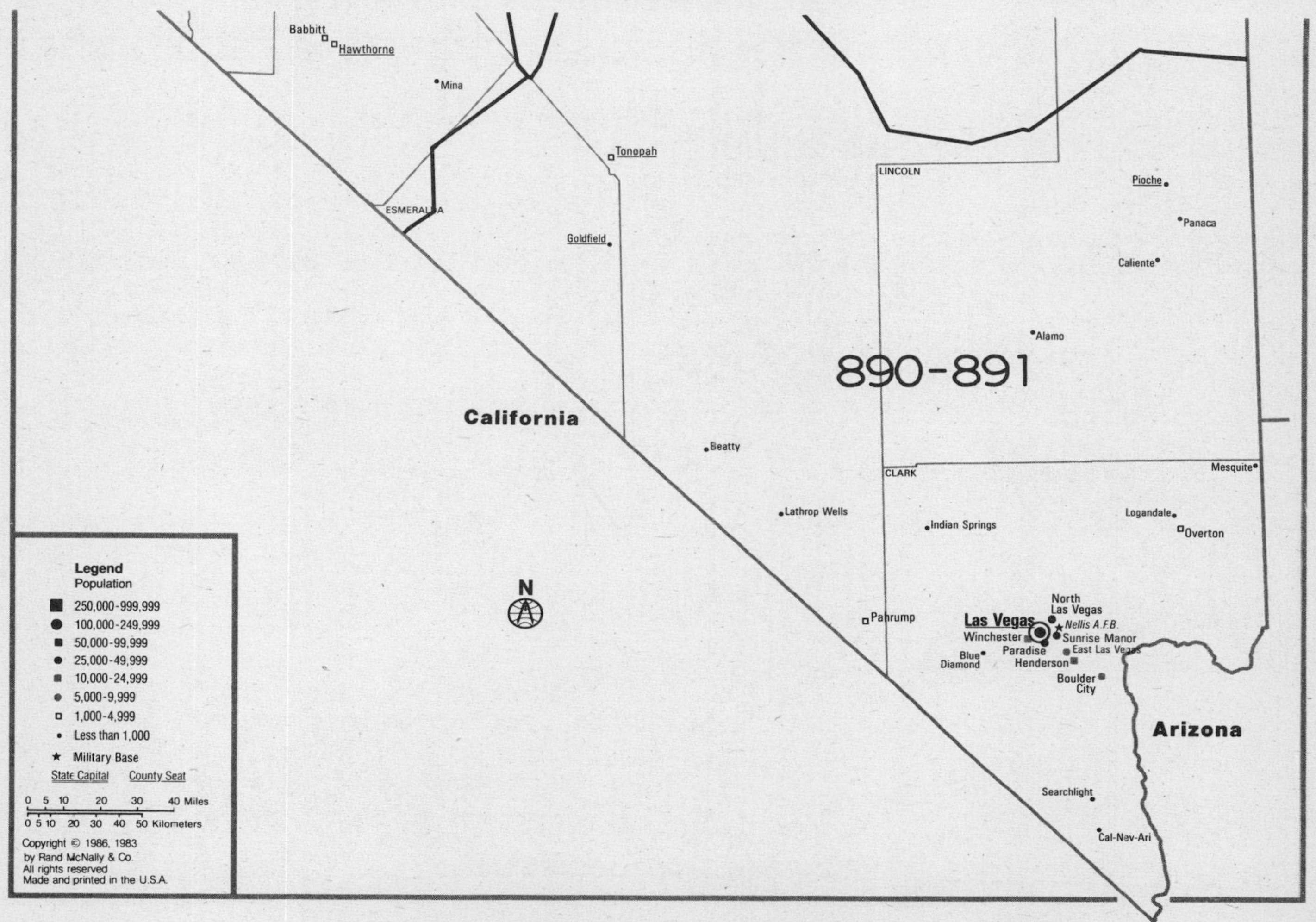
Babbitt
Hawthorne
Mina
Tonopah
ESMERALDA
Goldfield
LINCOLN
Pioche
Panaca
Caliente
Alamo
890-891
California
Beatty
CLARK
Mesquite
Lathrop Wells
Indian Springs
Logandale
Overton
N
Pahrump
North Las Vegas
Las Vegas
Nellis A.F.B.
Winchester
Sunrise Manor
Paradise
East Las Vegas
Blue Diamond
Henderson
Boulder City
Arizona
Searchlight
Cal-Nev-Ari
Legend
Population
250,000-999,999
100,000-249,999
50,000-99,999
25,000-49,999
10,000-24,999
5,000-9,999
1,000-4,999
Less than 1,000
Military Base
State Capital
County Seat
0 5 10 20 30 40 Miles
0 5 10 20 30 40 50 Kilometers

Alamo 89001
Amargosa Valley 89020
Arthur 89833
Ash Springs 89017
Atlanta 89043
Austin 89310
Baker 89311
Basalt 93512
Battle Mountain♦ 89820
Beatty♦ 89003
Belmont 89022
Beowawe 89821
Black Springs 89506
Blue Diamond 89004
Bluffs (Part of Elko) 89801
Bonanza (Part of Las Vegas)‡ 89106*
89127†
Border Town 89506
Boulder City 89005*
89006†
Boulevard Mall, The 89109
Buckeye 89410
Bunkerville 89007
Cactus Springs 89124
Caliente 89008
Cal Nev Ari 89039
Carlin 89822
Carlton Square (Part of North Las Vegas) 89030
Carp 89008
Carson City 89701-03
89705-21
For specific ZIP Codes call (888) 275-8777, or your local postmaster.
Carson Meadows (Part of Carson City) 89701
Carvers 89045
Caselton 89043
Centerville 89410
Chaparral Ridge (Part of Elko) 89801
Charleston 89801
Charleston Park 89108
Cherry Creek 89301
Clover Hills (Part of Elko) 89801
Coaldale 89049
Cobre 89835
Cold Springs 89406
Contact 89825
Cottonwood Cove 89046
Country Lane Estates 89406
Crescent Valley 89821
Crystal 89048
Crystal Bay 89402
Currant 89301
Currie 89301
Dayton 89403
Deep Creek 89801
Deeth 89823
Denio 89404
Dixie Valley 89406
Downtown (Part of Las Vegas)‡ 89101
89125
For specific ZIP Codes call (888) 275-8777, or your local postmaster.
Downtown (Part of Reno)‡ 89501
89504-05
For specific ZIP Codes call (888) 275-8777, or your local postmaster.
Dresslerville 89410
Duck Valley Indian Reservation 89832
Duckwater 89314
Duckwater Indian Reservation 89314
Dunphy 89820
Dyer 89010
East Elko (Part of Elko)‡ 89802
East Ely (Part of Ely) 89315
Eastland Hills (Part of Elko) 89801
East Las Vegas‡ 89112
89121-22
89160
For specific ZIP Codes call (888) 275-8777, or your local postmaster.
Echo Bay 89040
Edgewood 89449
Elburz 89824
Eldorado Lakes 89403
Elgin 89008
Elko 89801-03
89815
For specific ZIP Codes call (888) 275-8777, or your local postmaster.

Elk Point 89448
Ely 89301
Empire 89405
Enterprise♦ 89118
Etna 89008
Eureka 89316
Fallon 89406*
89407†
Fallon Indian Reservation 89406
Fallon Naval Air Station 89496
Federal (Part of Las Vegas)‡ 89101
Fernley 89408
Fish Spring 89410
Flanigan 89506
Fort McDermitt Indian Reservation 89421
Fort Mojave Indian Reservation 92363
Gabbs 89409
Galena (Part of Reno)‡ 89511
Galena Forest Estates 89511
Gardnerville♦ 89410
Gardnerville Ranchos♦ 89410
Garside (Part of Las Vegas)‡ 89102
89107
89126
89146
For specific ZIP Codes call (888) 275-8777, or your local postmaster.
Genoa 89411
Gerlach 89412
Glenbrook 89413
Glendale, *Clark* 89025
Glendale, *Washoe* 89431
Golconda 89414
Golden Valley 89501
Goldfield 89013
Gold Hill 89440
Gold Point 89013
Goodsprings 89019
Goshute Indian Reservation 84034
Greenbrae (Part of Sparks) 89431
Green Valley (Part of Henderson)‡ 89014
Halleck 89824
Hawthorne♦ 89415*
89416†
Hazen 89408
Henderson 89009
89011-12
89014-16
For specific ZIP Codes call (888) 275-8777, or your local postmaster.
Hidden Valley 89502
Highland Estates 89705
Hiko 89017
Horizon Hills 89501
Huffakers (Part of Reno) 89501
Humboldt 89418
Huntridge (Part of Las Vegas)‡ 89104
Imlay 89418
Incline Village 89450-52
For specific ZIP Codes call (888) 275-8777, or your local postmaster.
Indian Hills 89705
Indian Springs♦ 89018
Indian Springs Air Force Auxiliary Field 89018
Ione 89310
Jackpot 89825
Jacks Valley 89705
Jarbidge 89826
Jean 89019
Jiggs 89815
Johnson Lane♦ 89423
Kingston 89310
Lake Mead Base 89191
Lakeridge 89448
Lake Village 89449
Lamoille 89828
Lane 89301

Las Vegas

89101-85
89193-99
For specific ZIP Codes call (888) 275-8777, or your local postmaster.

Colleges & Universities
Univ of Nevada 89154

Financial Institutions
Bank of America, NTSA 89101

Hospitals
Columbia Sunrise Hosp & Med Ctr 89109
Desert Springs Hosp 89119
Univ Med Ctr 89102
Valley Hosp Med Ctr 89106

Hotels/Motels
Bally's 89109
Caesars Palace 89109
Circus Circus Hotel & Casino 89109
Excalibur Hotel & Casino 89109
Flamingo Hilton 89109
Golden Nugget Hotel & Casino 89101
Harrah's 89109
Hilton 89109
Imperial Palace 89109
Luxor Hotel/Casino 89119
MGM Grand Hotel/Casino 89109
The Mirage 89109
Monte Carlo Resort & Casino 89109
New York-New York Hotel & Casino 89109
Riviera Hotel Casino 89109
Sahara Hotel & Casino 89109
Stardust Resort & Casino 89109
Stratosphere 89104
Treasure Island at the Mirage 89109
Tropicana Resort & Casino 89109

Military Installations
Nevada Test Site 89193

Laughlin♦ 89028†
89029*
Lawton 89503
Lee 89815
Lemmon Valley 89506
Lida 89013
Lincoln Park 89413
Lockwood 89434
Logandale 89021
Lovelock 89419
Lower Kingsbury 89449
Lund 89317
Luning 89420
McDermitt♦ 89421
McGill♦ 89318
Majors Place 89301
Manhattan 89022
Mason 89447
Mayberry-Highland Park (Part of Reno) 89501
Meadowood Mall (Part of Reno) 89502
Meadows, The (Part of Las Vegas) 89107
Mercury 89023
Mesquite 89024†
89027*
Metropolis 89835
Midas 89414
Mill City 89418
Mina 89422
Minden♦ 89423
Moapa 89025
Moapa River Indian Reservation 89025
Mogul 89523
Montello 89830
Mottsville 89410
Moundhouse 89706
Mountain City 89831
Mountain Springs 89101
Mountain View Estates (Part of Elko) 89801
Mount Montgomery 93512
Mustang 89434
Naval Ammunition Depot 89415
Nellis Air Force Base 89191
Nelson 89046
New Empire (Part of Carson City) 89701
New Washoe City♦ 89701
Nixon 89424
North Battle Mountain 89820
North 7 Estates (Part of Elko) 89801
North Fork 89801
North Las Vegas 89030-36
For specific ZIP Codes call (888) 275-8777, or your local postmaster.
Northridge (Part of Elko) 89801
North Valley (Part of Reno) 89506
Oasis 89835
Oreana 89419
Orovada 89425
Overton 89040
Owyhee♦ 89832
Pahrump♦ 89041
89048
For specific ZIP Codes call (888) 275-8777, or your local postmaster.
Palomino Valley 89433
Panaca 89042
Panther Valley (Part of Reno) 89501
Paradise Hill 89445
Paradise Valley, *Clark*‡ 89119
Paradise Valley, *Humboldt* 89426
Park Lane Center (Part of Reno) 89502
Park Terrace (Part of Carson City) 89701
Patrick 89434
Peavine (Part of Reno)‡ 89523
Pinenut 89410
Pioche 89043
Pittman (Part of Henderson) 89015
Pleasant Valley 89511
Preston 89301
Pyramid Lake Indian Reservation 89424
Quail Ridge 89403
Rachel 89001
Raleigh Heights (Part of Reno) 89506
Rancho Estates 89410
Rancho Haven 89506
Rancho Vista 89403
Red Rock Estates 89506
Red Rock Vista‡ (Part of Las Vegas) 89108
89129-31
89134
For specific ZIP Codes call (888) 275-8777, or your local postmaster.
Reno 89501-70
For specific ZIP Codes call (888) 275-8777, or your local postmaster.
Reno Park 89506
Rhyolite 89003
Ridgeview Estates 89705
Riverside 89007
River Village 89403
Rixie's 89820
Round Hill Village 89448
Round Mountain 89045
Rowland 83604
Ruby Valley 89833
Ruth 89319
Sagecrest Complex (Part of Elko) 89801
Sage Hills 2 (Part of Elko) 89801
Sandy Valley 89019
San Jacinto 89825
Satalite Hills (Part of Sparks) 89436
Schurz♦ 89427
Scotty's Junction 89013
Searchlight 89046
Shafter 89835
Sheridan 89410
Sheridan Acres 89410
Shoshone 89301
Sierra (Part of Reno)‡ 89506
Silverado Heights 89705
Silver City 89428
Silverpeak 89047
Silver Springs 89429
Skyland 89448
Sloan 89103
Smith 89430
Southgate 89801
South Hills 89501
Spanish Springs Valley 89436
Sparks 89431-32
89434-36
For specific ZIP Codes call (888) 275-8777, or your local postmaster.

Spring Creek♦‡ 89815
Spring Valley‡ 89103
89113
89117
89147
89180
For specific ZIP Codes call (888) 275-8777, or your local postmaster.
Stagecoach 89429
Stanton Park (Part of Carson City) 89701
Stateline, Clark 89019
Stateline, Douglas♦ 89449
Steamboat‡ 89511
Steptoe 89318
Stewart (Part of Carson City) 89701
Stewarts Point 89040
Stillwater 89406
Strip Station‡ 89114
Summerlin (Part of Las Vegas)‡ 89128
89134
89137-38
For specific ZIP Codes call (888) 275-8777, or your local postmaster.
Summit Lake Indian Reservation 89404
Suncrest (Part of Elko) 89801
Sundance Estates (Part of Elko) 89801
Sunrise Manor♦ 89110
Sunset Galleria (Part of Henderson) 89014
Sun Valley‡ 89433
Sutcliffe 89501
Tahoe Village 89449
Te-Moak Indian Reservation 89801
Tempiute 89001
Thomas Creek Estates 89501
Thousand Springs 89835
Timberline Estates (Part of Carson City) 89703
Tonopah♦ 89049
Topaz Junction 89410
Topaz Lake 89410
Topaz Ranch Estates 89444
Tracy-Clark 89434
Tuscarora 89834
Tyrolean Village 89450
Unionville 89418
University, *Clark*‡ 89170
University (Part of Reno)‡ 89507
Upper Kingsbury 89449
Ursine 89043
Valle Verde (Part of Henderson)‡ 89012
Valmy 89438
Verdi 89439
Virginia City 89440
Vista (Part of Sparks) 89436
Vya 96104
Wabuska 89447
Wadsworth♦ 89442
Walker Lake 89415
Walker River Indian Reservation 89427
Warm Springs 89049
Washington (Part of Reno)‡ 89503*
89513†
Washoe City 89701
Washoe Indian Reservation 89410
Washoe Valley 89704
Weed Heights 89447
Wellington 89444
Wells 89835
Westland Mall (Part of Las Vegas) 89102
West Reno (Part of Reno) 89509
West Wendover 89883
Westwood Village 89423
Willow Beach 89005
Winchester♦ 89101
Winnemucca 89445*
89446†
Yerington 89447
Yerington Indian Reservation 89447
Yomba Indian Reservation 89310
Zephyr Cove 89448

* **Area Zip Code** † **Post Office Boxes** ‡ **Postal Station** ♦ **Census Designated Place** *Italic Type* **County**

Place	ZIP Code
Acworth	03601
Albany	03818
Alexandria	03222
Allenstown	03275
Alstead	03602
Alstead Center	03602
Alton	03809
Alton Bay	03810
Amherst	03031
Andover	03216
	03265
For specific ZIP Codes call (888) 275-8777, or your local postmaster.	
Angle Pond	03873
Antrim♦	03440
Arlington Park	03079
Ashland	03217
Ashuelot	03441
Atkinson	03811
Atkinson Heights	03811
Atlantic Heights (Part of Portsmouth)	03801
Auburn	03032
Baboosic Lake	03031
Bagley	03278
Bank	03071
Barnstead	03218
Barrington	03825
Bartlett	03812
Base	03595
Bath	03740
Bay Meetinghouse	03269
Bean Island	03077
Beatties	03590
Beaver Lake	03038
Bedford	03110
Beebe River	03223
Belmont	03220
Bennett Corners	03883
Bennington	03442
Benton	03785
Berlin	03570
Bersum Gardens (Part of Portsmouth)	03801
Bethlehem	03574
Birch Hill	03855
Blackwater (Part of Somersworth)	03878
Blair	03264
Blodgett Landing	03255
Bonds Corner	03458
Boscawen	03303
Boston Harbor (Part of Dover)	03820
Boutin Corner	03785
Bow	03304
Bow Center	03304
Bowkerville	03465
Box Corner	03221
Bradford	03221
Bradford Center	03221
Brentwood	03833
Brentwood Corners	03833
Bretton Woods	03575
Bridgewater	03222
Bristol♦	03222
Broad Acres (Part of Nashua)	03063
Brookfield	03872
Brookhurst	03809
Brookline	03033
Browns Corner	03045
Bungy	03576
Burkehaven	03782
Cable Road	03870
Campton	03223
Campton Hollow	03223
Campton Lower Village	03223
Campton Upper Village	03223
Canaan	03741
Canaan Center	03741
Canaan Street	03741
Candia	03034
Candia Four Corners	03034
Canobie Lake	03079
Canterbury (Town)	03224
Canterbury Center	03224
Carroll	03595
Cascade	03581
Cedar Pond	03588
Cemetery Corners	03862
Center Barnstead	03225
Center Conway	03813
Center Effingham	03814
Center Harbor	03226
Center Haverhill	03774
Center Ossipee	03814
Center Sandwich	03227
Center Strafford	03815
Center Tuftonboro	03816
Central Park (Part of Somersworth)	03878
Charlestown♦	03603
Chases Grove	03838
Chase Village	03281
Chatham	04058
Cheever	03266
Chesham	03455
Chester	03036
Chesterfield	03443
Chichester	03234
Chicks Corner	03227
Chocorua	03817
Christian Hollow	03608
Christian Shore (Part of Portsmouth)	03801
Cilleyville	03265
Claremont	03743
Claremont Junction (Part of Claremont)	03743
Clark Landing	03254
Clarksville (Town)	03592
Clinton Grove	03281
Clinton Village	03440
Coburn	03855
Cold Regions Research and Engineering Laboratory	03755
Cold River	03608
Colebrook	03576
Colletts Grove	03038
Columbia (Town)	03576
Concord	03301-03
For specific ZIP Codes call (888) 275-8777, or your local postmaster.	
Conleys Grove	03038
Contoocook♦	03229
Contoocook Lake	03452
Converseville	03461
Conway♦	03818
Coos Junction	03584
Cornish	03745
Cornish City	03745
Cornish Flat	03746
Cornish Mills	03745
Crawford Notch	03595
Crawfords Purchase (Town)	03595
Cricket Corner	03031
Crockett Corner	03257
Croydon	03773
Croydon Flat	03773
Crystal	03582
Cushman	03598
Dalton	03598
Danbury	03230
Danville	03819
Davisville, *Hillsborough*	03086
Davisville, *Merrimack*	03278
Deerfield	03037
Deerfield Center	03037
Deerfield Parade	03037
Deering	03244
Derry	03038
Derry Village	03038
Dixville (Town)	03576
Dixville Notch	03576
Dorchester	03266
Dorrs Corner	03814
Dover	03820-21
For specific ZIP Codes call (888) 275-8777, or your local postmaster.	
Dover Point (Part of Dover)	03820
Dows Corner	03833
Drewsville	03604
Dublin	03444
Ducks Head	03846
Dummer	03588
Dunbarton (Town)	03301
Dunbarton Center	03301
Durham♦	03824
East Alstead	03602
East Alton	03809
East Andover	03231
East Barrington	03825
East Candia	03040
East Concord (Part of Concord)	03301
East Conway	04037
East Deering	03244
East Derry	03041
East Freedom	03836
East Grafton	03240
East Grantham	03753
East Hampstead	03826
East Haverhill	03780
East Hebron	03232
East Holderness	03217
East Kingston	03827
East Lempster	03605
East Milford	03055
Easton	03580
East Plainfield	03781
East Rindge	03461
East Rochester (Part of Rochester)	03868
East Sandwich	03227
East Sullivan	03445
East Sutton	03278
East Swanzey	03446
East Tilton	03276
East Unity	03773
Eastview	03450
East Wakefield	03830
East Washington	03280
East Westmoreland	03467
East Wilder (Part of Lebanon)	03784
East Wolfeboro	03894
Eaton (Town)	03832
Eaton Center	03832
Effingham	03814
Effingham Falls	03814
Elkins	03233
Ellsworth (Town)	03264
Elmwood, *Hillsborough*	03449
Elmwood, *Merrimack*	03230
Elmwood Corners	03842
Elwyn Park (Part of Portsmouth)	03801
Enfield♦	03748
Enfield Center	03749
Epping♦	03042
Epsom	03234
Errol	03579
Etna	03750
Exeter♦	03833
Exeter Hampton Mobile Village	03833
Exeter Villa	03833
Exeter West	03833
Fabyan	03595
Fairhill Manor	03870
Farmington♦	03835
Fitzwilliam	03447
Fitzwilliam Depot	03447
Fogg Corner	03862
Forest Lake	03470
Fosters Corners	03079
Foundry (Part of Somersworth)	03878
Foyes Corner	03870
Francestown	03043
Franconia	03580
Franklin	03235
Freedom	03836
Fremont	03044
Gardners Grove	03220
Gates Corner (Part of Dover)	03820
Gaza	03269
Georges Mills	03751
Gerrish	03301
Gilford	03246
Gilmans Corner	03777
Gilmanton	03237
Gilmanton Iron Works	03837
Gilsum	03448
Glen	03838
Glencliff	03238
Glendale	03246
Glenmere Village	03824
Global Plaza (Part of Nashua)	03060
Goffs Falls (Part of Manchester)	03103
Goffstown	03045
Gonic (Part of Rochester)	03839
Goodrich Falls	03846
Goose Hollow	03223
Gorham♦	03581
Goshen	03752
Goshen Four Corners	03752
Gossville	03234
Governors Lake	03077
Grafton	03240
Grafton Center	03240
Grange	03584
Granite	03864
Grantham	03753
Grasmere	03045
Great Boars Head	03842
Greenfield	03047
Greenland	03840
Greenville♦	03048
Greenwood Station	03840
Groton	03241
Groveton♦	03582
Guild	03754
Hampstead	03841
Hampton♦	03842-43
For specific ZIP Codes call (888) 275-8777, or your local postmaster.	
Hampton Beach	03842
Hampton Falls	03844
Hancock	03449
Hanover♦	03755
Hanover Center	03755
Happy Corner	03592
Happy Valley	03458
Harrisville	03450
Hart's Location (Town)	03812
Hastings	03257
Haverhill	03765
Hayes (Part of Rochester)	03867
Haynes Corner	03833
Hebron	03241
Hell Hollow	03746
Henniker♦	03242
High Bridge	03071
Hill	03243
Hill Center	03243
Hillsborough♦	03244
Hillsborough Center	03244
Hillsborough Lower Village	03244
Hillsborough Upper Village	03244
Hills Corner	03815
Hinsdale♦	03451
Holderness	03245
Hollis	03049
Hooksett♦	03106
Hopkinton	03229
Horses Corner	03234
Howards Grove	03038
Hudson♦	03051
Hudson Center	03051
Interlaken Park (Part of Laconia)	03246
Intervale	03845
Jackson	03846
Jackson Falls	03846
Jady Hill	03833
Jefferson Highlands	03583
Jaffrey♦	03452
Jaffrey Center	03452
Jefferson	03583
Jones Corner	03461
Kearsarge	03847
Keene	03431
Keewayden	03894
Kelleys Corner	03234
Kellyville	03773
Kelwyn Park	03878
Kensington	03827
Kidderville	03576
Kingston	03848
Laconia	03246*
	03247†
Lakeport (Part of Laconia)	03246
Lancaster♦	03584
Landaff (Town)	03585
Landaff Center	03585
Langdon	03602
Langs Corner	03870
Laskey Corner	03887
Laurel Lake	03447
Lawrence Corner	03054
Leavitts Hill	03037
Lebanon	03756†
	03766*
Lee	03824
Lempster	03605
Lincoln	03251
Lincoln Park (Part of Nashua)	03063
Lisbon♦	03585
Litchfield	03052
Little Boars Head	03862
Little Island Pond	03076
Littleton♦	03561
Lochmere	03252
Lockehaven	03748
Londonderry	03053
Long Sands	03814
Lost Nation	03584
Loudon	03301
Loudon Center	03301
Lower Bartlett	03845
Lower Gilmanton	03263
Lower Village, *Cheshire*	03448
Lower Village, *Merrimack*	03278
Lucas Pond	03261
Lyme (Town)	03768
Lyme	03768
Lyme Center	03769
Lyndeborough	03082
Madbury	03820
Madison	03849
Mall at Rockingham Park, The	03079
Mall of New Hampshire, The (Part of Manchester)	03103
Manchester	03101-05
	03108-09
For specific ZIP Codes call (888) 275-8777, or your local postmaster.	
Maplehaven (Part of Portsmouth)	03801
Maplewood	03574
Marlborough♦	03455
Marlow	03456
Marshall Corner	03833
Marshall Farms	03833
Martin	03106
Mascoma (Part of Lebanon)	03748
Mason	03048
Masons	03590
Massabesic (Part of Manchester)	03104
Meaderboro Corner (Part of Rochester)	03867
Meadowbrook (Part of Portsmouth)	03801
Meadows	03583
Melrose Corner (Part of Rochester)	03868
Melvin Mills	03278
Melvin Village	03850
Meredith♦	03253
Meredith Center	03253
Meriden	03770
Merrill Corners	03855
Merrimack	03054
Merrymeeting Lake	03855
Middleton (Town)	03887
Middleton Corners	03887
Milan	03588
Milford♦	03055
Mill Hollow	03602
Millsfield (Town)	03579
Mill Village, *Cheshire*	03464
Mill Village, *Sullivan*	03781
Millville	03079
Milton	03851
Milton Mills	03852
Mirror Lake	03853
Monroe	03771
Mont Vernon	03057
Moultonborough	03254
Moultonborough Falls	03254
Moultonville	03814
Mountain Lake	03774
Mount Sunapee	03255
Mount Washington	03589
Munsonville	03457
Murray Hill	03243
Nashua	03060-63
For specific ZIP Codes call (888) 275-8777, or your local postmaster.	
Nashua Mall (Part of Nashua)	03063
Nelson	03457
New Boston	03070
New Boston Air Force Tracking Station	03031
Newbury	03255
New Castle	03854
New Durham	03855
Newfields	03856
New Hampton	03256
Newington (Town)	03801
New Ipswich	03071
New London	03257
Newmarket♦	03857
Newport♦	03773
New Rye	03234
Newton	03858
Newton Junction	03859
Noone	03458
North Barnstead	03225

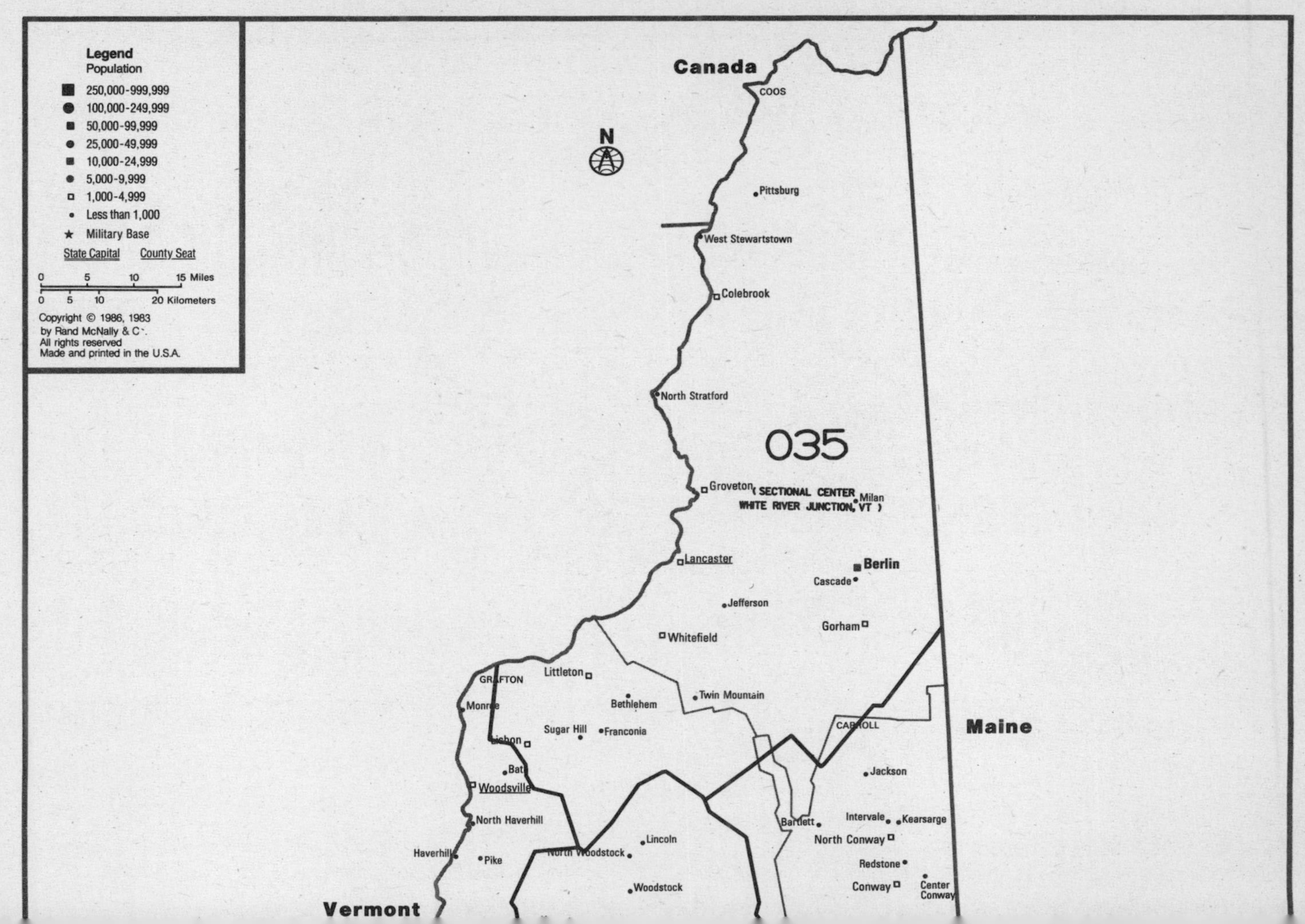
Legend
Population
250,000-999,999
100,000-249,999
50,000-99,999
25,000-49,999
10,000-24,999
5,000-9,999
1,000-4,999
Less than 1,000
Military Base
State Capital
County Seat
0 5 10 15 Miles
0 5 10 20 Kilometers
Copyright © 1986, 1983
by Rand McNally & C-.
All rights reserved
Made and printed in the U.S.A.
Canada
COOS
N
Pittsburg
West Stewartstown
Colebrook
North Stratford
035
Groveton
(SECTIONAL CENTER
WHITE RIVER JUNCTION, VT)
Milan
Lancaster
Berlin
Cascade
Jefferson
Gorham
Whitefield
Littleton
GRAFTON
Twin Mountain
Monroe
Bethlehem
Sugar Hill
Franconia
CARROLL
Maine
Jackson
Woodsville
North Haverhill
Bartlett
Intervale
Kearsarge
North Conway
Lincoln
Haverhill
Pike
North Woodstock
Redstone
Woodstock
Conway
Center Conway
Vermont

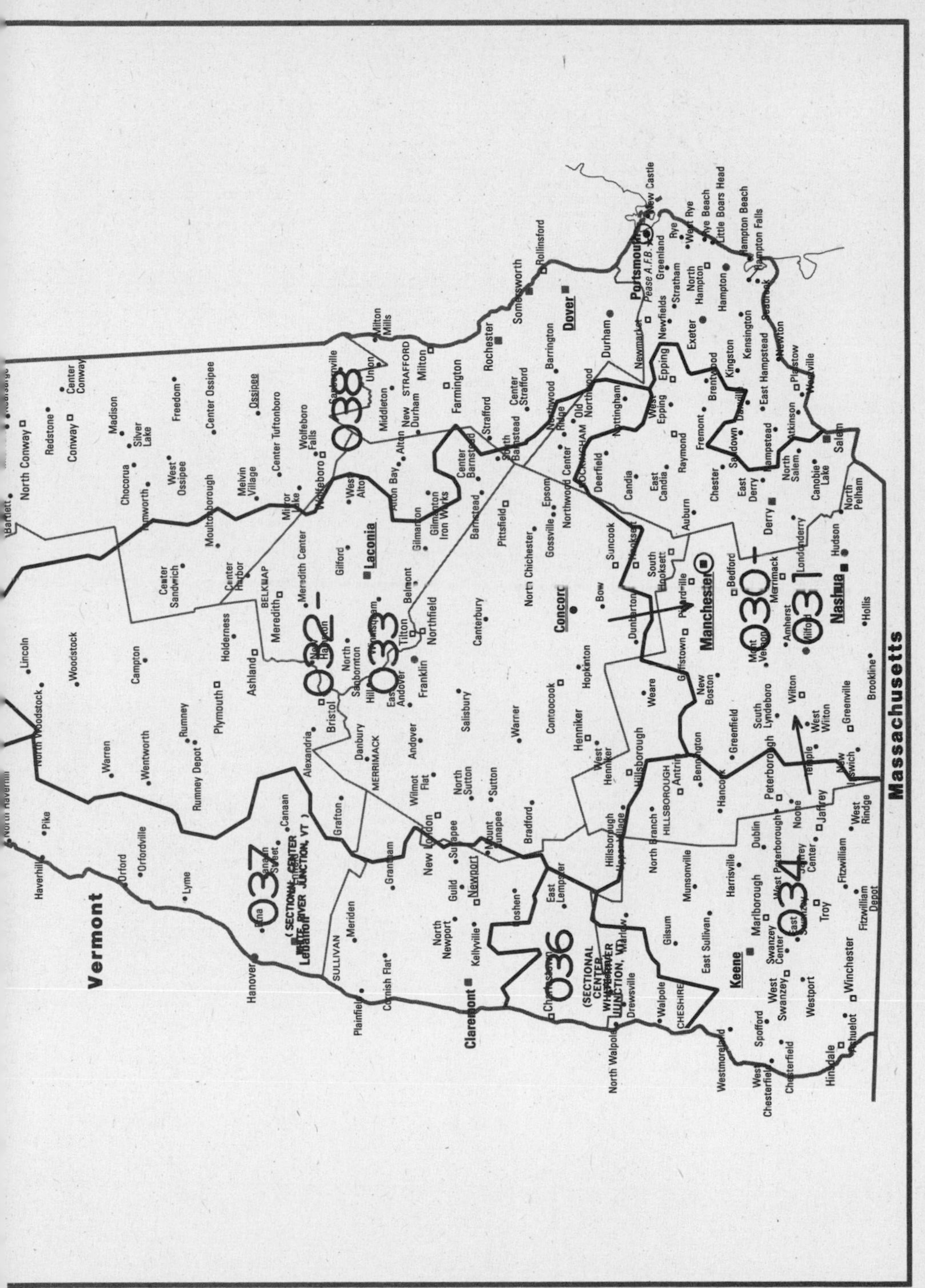
Vermont
Massachusetts
030-
031
032-
033
034
036
037
038
(SECTIONAL CENTER WHITE RIVER JUNCTION, VT)
Concord
Manchester
Nashua
Keene
Laconia
Dover
Portsmouth
Claremont
Lebanon
Hanover
Rochester
Somersworth
Newport
Ossipee
Franklin
Derry
Salem
Exeter
Hampton
Durham
Conway
North Conway
Plymouth
Bristol
Tilton
Meredith
Wolfeboro
Hillsborough
Peterborough
Jaffrey
Milford
Hudson
Londonderry
Merrimack
Bedford
Goffstown
Hooksett
Pittsfield
Barnstead
Farmington
Milton
New London
Canaan
Haverhill
Lincoln
Woodstock
Pease A.F.B.
BELKNAP
MERRIMACK
SULLIVAN
CHESHIRE
HILLSBOROUGH
ROCKINGHAM
STRAFFORD

North Beach 03842
North Branch 03440
North Brookline 03055
North Charlestown 03603
North Chatham 04058
North Chester 03036
North Chichester 03234
North Conway 03860
North Danville 03819
Northfield 03276
North Grantham 03753
North Groton 03266
North Hampton 03862
North Hampton Center 03862
North Haverhill 03774
North Hinsdale 03451
North Littleton 03561
North Londonderry 03053
North Newport 03773
North Pelham 03076
North Pembroke 03275
North Richmond 03470
North Rochester (Part of Rochester) 03867
North Salem 03073
North Sanbornton 03269
North Sandwich 03259
North Stratford 03590
North Sutton 03260
North Swanzey 03431
Northumberland 03582
North Village 03458
North Wakefield 03864
North Walpole 03609
North Weare 03281
North Wilmot 03230
North Wolfeboro 03894
Northwood 03261
Northwood Center 03261
Northwood Narrows 03261
Northwood Ridge 03261
North Woodstock 03262
Nottingham 03290
Noyes Terrace 03079
Nuttings Beach 03222
Onway Lake 03077
Orange 03741
Orford 03777
Orfordville 03777
Ossipee 03864
Ossipee Lake Shores 03814
Ossipee Valley 03814
Pages Corner 03301
Pannaway Manor (Part of Portsmouth) 03801
Parker 03045
Parker Hill 03585
Park Hill 03467
Partridge Lake 03561
Passaconaway 03818
Pearls Corner 03301
Pelham 03076
Pembroke (Town) 03275
Pembroke Hill 03275
Penacook (Part of Concord) 03303
Pendleton Beach (Part of Laconia) 03246
Pequawket 03817
Percy 03582
Perkins Hill 03833
Peterborough 03458
Pheasant Lane Mall (Part of Nashua) 03063
Pickering (Part of Rochester) 03867
Pierce Bridge 03574
Piermont 03779
Pike 03780
Pinardville♦ 03045
Pine Grove Park 03079
Pine River 03814
Pine Valley 03086
Pinkhams (Town) 03581
Pittsburg 03592
Pittsfield♦ 03263
Plaice Cove 03842
Plainfield 03781
Plaistow 03865
Plymouth♦ 03264
Ponemah 03055
Poocham 03814
Portsmouth 03801-04
For specific ZIP Codes call (888) 275-8777, or your local postmaster.
Portsmouth Plains (Part of Portsmouth) 03801
Potter Place 03265
Puckershire (Part of Claremont) 03743
Quaker City 03603
Quincy 03266
Rand 03461
Randolph 03570
Raymond♦ 03077
Redstone 03813
Reed Road Parcel 03873
Reeds Ferry 03054
Richardson 03055
Richmond 03470
Rindge 03461
Rings Corner 03263
Rivercrest 03755
Riverdale 03281
Riverhill (Part of Concord) 03301
Riverside 03874
Riverton 03583
Robinson Corner 03240
Roby 03278
Rochester 03839
03866-68
For specific ZIP Codes call (888) 275-8777, or your local postmaster.
Rockwold 03245
Rollinsford 03869
Roundys Corner 03448
Rowes Corner 03858
Roxbury (Town) 03431
Rumney 03266
Rumney Depot 03266
Ryder Corner 03773
Rye 03870
Rye Beach 03871
Rye North Beach 03870
Sachem Village (Part of Lebanon) 03784
Salem 03079
Salem Depot 03079
Salisbury 03268
Salisbury Heights 03268
Sanbornton 03269
Sanbornville 03872
Sandown 03873
Sandwich 03227
Sawyer Lake 03237
Sawyers (Part of Dover) 03820
Scotland 03470
Seabrook 03874
Seabrook Beach 03874
Seacrest Village (Part of Portsmouth) 03801
Severance 03032
Sharon 03458
Shelburne 03581
Shellcamp 03237
Sherwood Forest 03833
Short Falls 03234
Silver Lake 03875
Smith Colony 03842
Smithtown 03874
Smithville 03071
Snowville 03832
Snumshire 03603
Somersworth 03878
Soo Nipi 03257
South Acworth 03607
South Barnstead 03225
South Brookline 03033
South Charlestown 03603
South Chatham 04037
South Conway 03813
South Cornish 03745
South Danville 03819
South Deerfield 03037
South Effingham 03882
South Hampton 03827
South Hooksett♦ 03106
South Keene (Part of Keene) 03431
South Kingston 03848
South Lee 03824
South Lyndeboro 03082
South Merrimack 03054
South Milford 03055
South Newbury 03272
South Pittsfield 03263
South Seabrook 03874
South Stoddard 03464
South Sutton 03273
South Tamworth 03883
South Weare 03281
South Wolfeboro 03894
Spofford 03462
Spofford Lake 03462
Springfield 03284
Spring Haven 03809
Squag City 03745
Squantum 03452
Stark 03582
Steeplegate Mall (Part of Concord) 03301
Stewartstown 03576
Stewartstown Hollow 03576
Stinson Lake 03274
Stockbridge Corners 03809
Stoddard 03464
Strafford 03884
Strafford Corner 03815
Stratford 03590
Stratham 03885
Sugar Hill 03585
Suissevale 03254
Sullivan 03445
Sunapee 03782
Suncook 03275
Sunrise Lake 03887
Surry 03431
Sutton 03221
Swanzey (Town) 03431
Swanzey Center 03431
Swiftwater 03785
Tamworth 03886
Tavern Village 03281
Temple 03084
The Five Corners 03842
The Glen 03592
The Plains 03276
Thomas 03461
Thornton 03223
Thorntons Ferry 03054
Tilton 03276
Tinkerville, *Coos* 03590
Tinkerville, *Grafton* 03585
Trapshire 03603
Troy 03465
Tuftonboro 03864
Twin Mountain 03595
Union 03887
Union Wharf 03816
Unity 03603
Upper Kidderville 03576
Upper Village 03581
Wadley Falls 03824
Wakefield 03872
Wallis Sands 03870
Walpole 03608
Warner 03278
Warren 03279
Washington 03280
Waterloo 03278
Water Village 03864
Waterville Valley 03215
Wawbeek 03816
Weare 03281
Weare Corner 03874
Webster 03301
Webster Lake (Part of Franklin) 03235
Webster Place (Part of Franklin) 03235
Webster Mill 03263
Weirs Beach (Part of Laconia)‡ 03246
Welshs Corner 03815
Wendell 03782
Wentworth, *Coos* (Town) 03579
Wentworth, *Grafton* 03282
Wentworth Acres (Part of Portsmouth) 03801
Wentworth Terrace 03820
West Alton 03809
West Andover 03265
West Barrington 03825
West Campton 03223
West Canaan‡ 03741
West Center Harbor 03217
West Chesterfield 03466
West Claremont (Part of Claremont) 03743
West Deering 03440
West Dummer 03588
West Epping 03042
West Franklin (Part of Franklin) 03235
West Gonic (Part of Rochester) 03839
West Hampstead 03841
West Henniker 03242
West Hopkinton 03229
West Kingston 03848
West Lebanon (Part of Lebanon) 03784
West Milan 03588
Westmoreland 03467
West Nottingham 03291
West Ossipee 03890
West Peterborough 03468
West Plymouth 03264
Westport 03469
West Rindge 03461
West Rumney 03266
West Rye 03870
West Salisbury 03268
West Springfield 03284
West Stewartstown 03597
West Swanzey♦ 03469
West Thornton 03223
West Unity 03743
Westville 03865
West Wilton 03086
West Windham 03087
Whiteface 03259
Whitefield♦ 03598
Whittier 03886
Willey House 03812
Wilmot 03287
Wilmot Flat 03287
Wilton♦ 03086
Wilton Center 03086
Winchester♦ 03470
Windham 03087
Windham Depot 03087
Windsor (Town) 03244
Winniconic 03885
Winnicut Mills 03885
Winnisquam 03289
Winona 03217
Wolfeboro 03894
Wolfeboro Center 03894
Wolfeboro Falls 03896
Wonalancet 03897
Woodland Park 03054
Woodman 03830
Woodmere 03461
Woodstock 03293
Woodsville♦ 03785

* **Area Zip Code** † **Post Office Boxes** ‡ **Postal Station** ♦ **Census Designated Place** *Italic Type* **County**

Place	ZIP
A (Part of Montclair)‡	07042
A (Part of Plainfield)‡	07063
Aberdeen (Twp)	07747
Abertown	07827
Absecon	08201
Absecon Highlands	08201
Ackors Corner	08534
A Country Place	08701
Adams	08902
Adamston	08723
Adelphia	07710
Afton (Part of Florham Park)	07932
Albion	08009
Albion Place (Part of Clifton)	07013
Aldene (Part of Roselle Park)	07204
Alderbrook Homes (Part of Little Silver)	07739
Aldine	08318
Alexandria (Twp)	08848
Allamuchy	07820
Allendale	07401
Allenhurst	07711
Allentown	08501
Allenwood	08720
Allerton	08833
Allison Acres	07435
Alloway♦	08001
Allwood (Part of Clifton)‡	07012
Almonesson	08096
Alpha	08865
Alphano	07838
Alpine	07620
Amon Heights	08110
Ampere (Part of East Orange)‡	07017
Ancora	08037
Anderson	07865
Andover (Twp)	07860
Andover	07821
Anglesea (Part of North Wildwood)	08260
Annandale♦	08801
Anthony	08826
Applegarth	08512
Apple Hill	08002
Apshawa	07405
Arcola (Part of Paramus)	07652
Ardena	07728
Arlington (Part of Kearny)	07032
Arneys Mount	08068
Arneytown	08501
Arrowhead Lake	07834
Arrowhead Village	08723
Asbury	08802
Asbury Park	07712
Ashland	08043
Atco	08004
Athenia (Part of Clifton)	07013
Atlantic City	08401*
	08404†
Atlantic Highlands	07716
Atlantis	08087
Atsion	08088
Auburn	08085
Audubon	08106
Audubon Park	08106
Augusta	07822
Aura	08028
Avalon	08202
Avenel♦	07001
Avon-by-the-Sea	07717
Avondale	07110
Awosting	07421
B (Part of Long Branch)‡	07740
Babbitt	07047
Bacons Neck	08302
Bakersville	08648
Baldwins Corner	08534
Baleville	07860
Baltusrol	07081
Bamber Lake	08731
Baptistown	08803
Barbertown	08825
Barclay Farm	08034
Bargaintown	08234
Barley Sheaf	08822
Barnegat♦	08005
Barnegat Beach	08758
Barnegat Light	08006
Barnegat Pines	08731
Barnsboro	08080
Barrington	08007
Barry Lakes	07422
Bartles Corner	08822
Bartley	07836
Basking Ridge	07920
Bass River (Twp)	08224
Bates Mill	08037
Batesville	08034
Batsto	08037
Bay Harbor Estates	08723
Bay Head	08742
Bayonne	07002
Bay Point	08311
Bay Shore	08753
Bay Side, *Cumberland*	08302
Bay Side, *Ocean*	08050
Bayview Heights	08753
Bayville	08721
Bayway (Part of Elizabeth)‡	07202
Baywood	08723
Beach Glen	07866
Beach Haven	08008
Beach Haven Crest	08008
Beach Haven Gardens	08008
Beach Haven Heights	08008
Beach Haven Terrace	08008
Beach Haven West♦	08050
Beach View	08005
Beachwood	08722
Beattyestown	07840
Beaufort (Part of Roseland)	07068
Beaver Dam	08070
Beaver Lake	07416
Beaver Run	07419
Beckerville	08733
Beckett♦	08085
Bedminster	07921
Beemerville	07461
Beesleys Point	08223
Belcoville	08330
Belford	07718
Belle Mead	08502
Belleplain	08270
Belleville♦	07109
Bellmawr	08031*
	08099†
Bells Crossing (Part of Glen Gardner)	08826
Bells Lake	08012
Bellview	08077
Belmar	07719
Belvidere	07823
Belwood Park	07109
Bennetts Mills	08527
Bergen (Part of Jersey City)‡	07304
Bergenfield	07621
Bergenline (Part of Union City)‡	07087
Bergen Mall (Part of Paramus)	07652
Bergen Point (Part of Bayonne)‡	07002
Berkeley (Twp)	08721
Berkeley Heights♦	07922
Berkshire Valley	07885
Berlin	08009
Berlin Estates	08009
Berlin Heights (Part of Berlin)	08009
Bernards (Twp)	07920
Bernardsville	07924
Berryland	08094
Bertrand Island (Part of Mount Arlington)	07856
Bethlehem (Twp)	08802
Beverly	08010
Billingsport (Part of Paulsboro)	08066
Birches	08012
Birches West	08071
Birch Hill	07981
Birchwood Lakes	08055
Birchwood Park	08723
Birmingham	08011
Bivalve	08349
Black Horse Center (Part of Audubon)	08106
Blackwells Mills	08873
Blackwood♦	08012
Blackwood Terrace	08096
Blairstown	07825
Blansingburg	08750
Blawenburg	08504
Blenheim	08012
Bloomfield♦	07003
Bloomingdale (Part of Riverdale)	07457
Bloomingdale, *Passaic*	07403
Bloomsbury	08804
Blue Anchor	08037
Blue Bell	08344
Blue Star Shopping Center (Part of Watchung)	07060
Bogota	07603
Bon Air	08110
Bonhamtown	08817
Boonton	07005
Bordentown	08505
Bossert Estates	08505
Bound Brook	08805
Braddock	08037
Bradevelt	07746
Bradley Beach	07720
Bradley Gardens	08807
Bradley Park	07753
Braeburn Heights	08638
Brainards	08865
Brainy Boro (Part of Metuchen)‡	08840
Branchburg (Twp)	08876
Branchville	07826
Brant Beach	08008
Brass Castle	07882
Breton Woods	08723
Brick (Twp)	08723
Brick	08723-24
For specific ZIP Codes call (888) 275-8777, or your local postmaster.	
Brick Church (Part of East Orange)‡	07018
Brick Plaza	08723
Bricksboro	08332
Bridgeboro	08075
Bridgepoint	08502
Bridgeport	08014
Bridgeton	08302
Bridgeton Junction (Part of Bridgeton)	08302
Bridgeville	07823
Bridgewater	08807
Brielle	08730
Brigantine	08203
Brighton Beach	08008
Broad Lane	08094
Broadway	08808
Brookdale‡	07003
Brookfield	08034
Brooklawn	08030
Brookside	07926
Brook Tree	08520
Brook Valley (Part of Kinnelon)	07405
Brookview	08816
Brookville, *Hunterdon*	08559
Brookville, *Ocean*	08005
Brookwood	08527
Brotmanville	08302
Browns Mills♦	08015
Browntown‡	08857
Brunswick Acres	08852
Brunswick Square	08816
Brush Hollow	08055
Buckingham	08759
Buckshutem	08332
Budd Lake♦	07828
Buddtown	08088
Buena	08310
Buena Vista (Twp)	08310
Bulltown	08215
Bunker Hill	08080
Bunnvale	07830
Burleigh	08210
Burlington	08016
Burnt Mills	07921
Bustleton	08016
Butler	07405
Butler Park	07882
Butlers Park	07882
Butterworth Farms	07801
Buttzville	07829
Byram, *Sussex* (Twp)	07821
Byram, *Hunterdon*	08559
Byram Cove (Part of Hopatcong)	07843
Caldwell♦	07006*
	07007†
Caldwell Borough (Twp)	07006
Califon	07830
Cambridge	08075
Cambridge Park	08053
Camden	08101-05
For specific ZIP Codes call (888) 275-8777, or your local postmaster.	
Candlewood	07731
Canterbury at Piscataway	08854
Canton	08079
Cape May	08204
Cape May Coast Guard Training Center	08204
Cape May Court House♦	08210
Cape May Point	08212
Capitol Hill	08010
Cardiff	08234
Carlls Corner	08302
Carlstadt	07072
Carlton Hill (Part of East Rutherford)	07073
Carmel	08332
Carmerville	07719
Carneys Point	08069
Carpenterville	08865
Carriage Pointe	08854
Carteret	07008
Cassville‡	08527
Castle Point (Part of Hoboken)	07030
Cecil	08094
Cedar Beach	08721
Cedar Bonnet Island	08050
Cedar Bridge Manor	08723
Cedar Brook	08018
Cedar Crest Manor	08069
Cedar Glen Homes East	08757
Cedar Glen Lakes♦	08759
Cedar Glen West♦	08733
Cedar Grove, *Cape May*	08210
Cedar Grove, *Essex*♦	07009
Cedar Grove, *Gloucester*	08062
Cedar Grove, *Ocean*	08753
Cedar Heights	08801
Cedar Knolls	07927
Cedar Lake	07834
Cedar Run	08092
Cedarville, *Cumberland*	08311
Cedarville, *Salem*	08098
Cedarwood Park	08723
Centennial Lake	08053
Center Square	08085
Centerton, *Burlington*	08054
Centerton, *Salem*	08318
Centerville, *Hunterdon*	08853
Centerville, *Mercer*	08534
Central (Part of East Orange)‡	07018
Central Park	08070
Centre City	08051
Centre Grove	08332
Chadwick Beach	08735
Chairville	08055
Chambersburg (Part of Trenton)‡	08611
Chambers Corners	08060
Changewater	07831
Chapel Heights	08080
Charleston	08046
Charlotteburg	07435
Chatham	07928
Chatsworth	08019
Cheesequake	08857
Chelsea Heights (Part of Atlantic City)	08401
Cherry Hill (Twp)	08002
Cherry Hill♦	08002-03
	08034
For specific ZIP Codes call (888) 275-8777, or your local postmaster.	
Cherry Hill Estates	08002
Cherry Hill Mall	08002
Cherry Quay	08723
Cherryville	08822
Cherrywood	08012
Chesilhurst	08089
Chester	07930
Chesterfield	08650
Chestnut‡	07083
Chewalla Park	08619
Chews Landing	08012
Chrome (Part of Carteret)	07008
Churchtown	08070
Cinnaminson♦	08077
City of Orange (Twp)	07050
Clark♦	07066
Clarksboro	08020
Clarksburg	08510
Clarks Landing (Part of Point Pleasant)	08742
Clarkstown	08330
Clayton	08312
Claytons Corner	07746
Clayville (Part of Vineland)	08360
Clearbrook Park♦	08512
Clear View Lake	07860
Clearwater	07871
Clementon	08021
Clermont, *Burlington*	08060
Clermont, *Cape May*	08210
Cliff Park (Part of Cliffside Park)‡	07010
Cliffside Park	07010
Cliffwood	07721
Cliffwood Beach♦	07735
Cliffwood Lake	07460
Clifton	07011-15
For specific ZIP Codes call (888) 275-8777, or your local postmaster.	
Clinton, *Hunterdon* (Twp)	08801
Clinton, *Essex*	07004
Clinton, *Hunterdon*	08809
Clinton Hill (Part of Newark)‡	07108
Closter	07624
Cloverhill, *Hunterdon*	08822
Clover Hill, *Monmouth*	07733
Clover Leaf Lakes	08330
Cobbs Corner	07054
Cohansey	08302
Cokesbury	08833
Cold Indian Springs	07712
Cold Spring	08204
Colemans Hollow	07970
Colesville	07461
Collings Lakes♦	08094
Collingswood	08108
Collingwood Park	07727
Collinsville	07960
Cologne	08213
Colonia♦	07067
Colonial Arms	08527
Colonial Manor	08096
Colonial Park	08550
Colonial Terrace	07712
Colts Neck	07722
Columbia	07832
Columbia Lakes	08002
Columbus	08022
Colwick	08002
Commercial (Twp)	08349
Communipaw (Part of Jersey City)	07304
Concordia♦	08512
Conovertown	08201
Constable Hook (Part of Bayonne)	07002
Constable Junction (Part of Bayonne)	07002
Convent Station	07961
Cookstown	08511
Coontown	07060
Cooper Park Village	08002
Copper Hill	08551
Corbin City	08270
Cornish	07823
Cottrell Corners	08857
Country Farms	07733
Country Lake Estates♦	08015
Country Woods	07733
Coytesville (Part of Fort Lee)	07024
Cozy Lake	07438
Cragmere Park	07430
Cramer Hill (Part of Camden)	08105
Cranberry Lake	07821
Cranbury	08512
Cranbury Manor	08512
Cranbury Station	08512
Crandon Lakes♦	07860
Cranford♦	07016
Cranford Junction	07016
Cream Ridge	08514
Crescent Heights	08088
Crescent Park	07480
Cresskill	07626
Crestmere	07435
Crestmoor	07853
Creston	08619
Crestwood Village♦	08759
Cropwell	08053
Cross Keys	08080
Crossroads	08055
Crosswicks	08515
Croton	08822
Crystal Lake (Part of Oakland)	07436
Crystal Lake, *Ocean*	08721
Culvers Lake	07826
Cumberland	08332
Cumberland Mall (Part of Vineland)	08360
Cuthbert Manor	08108
Da Costa (Part of Hammonton)	08037
Danceys Corner	08069
Daretown	08318
Darlington	07430
Darts Mills	08822
Davis	08514
Davis Bridge	07946
Dayton♦	08810
Deacons	08060
Deal	07723
Deal Park	07723
Deans	08852
De Cou Village	08610
Deepwater	08023

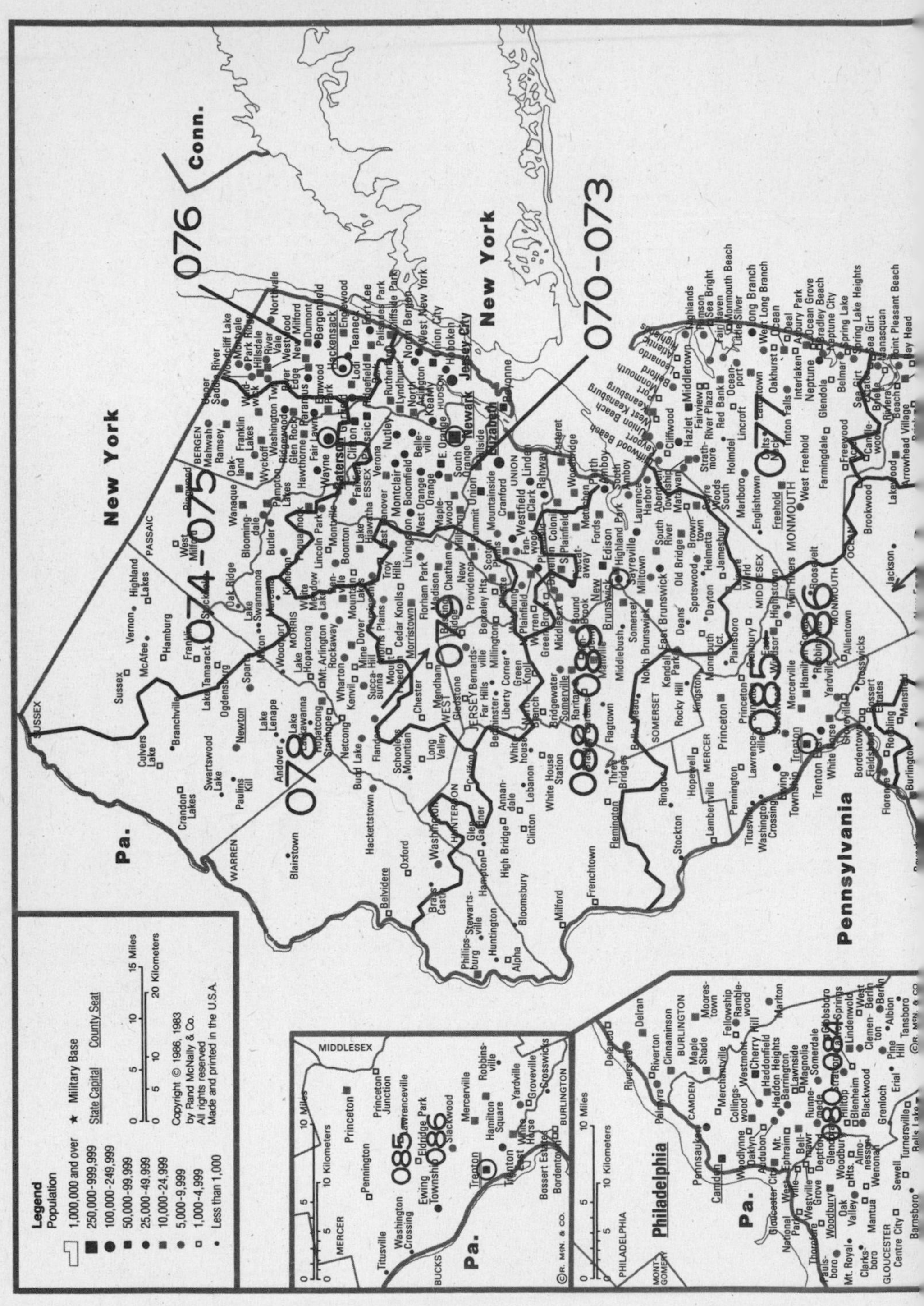

Legend
Population
1,000,000 and over
250,000–999,999
100,000–249,999
50,000–99,999
25,000–49,999
10,000–24,999
5,000–9,999
1,000–4,999
Less than 1,000
★ Military Base
State Capital
County Seat
15 Miles
20 Kilometers
Copyright © 1986, 1983 by Rand McNally & Co.
All rights reserved
Made and printed in the U.S.A.
076
074–075
078
079
070–073
077
088–089
085–086
080–084
New York
Conn.
Pa.
Pennsylvania
Philadelphia
Trenton
Newark
Jersey City
Paterson
Elizabeth

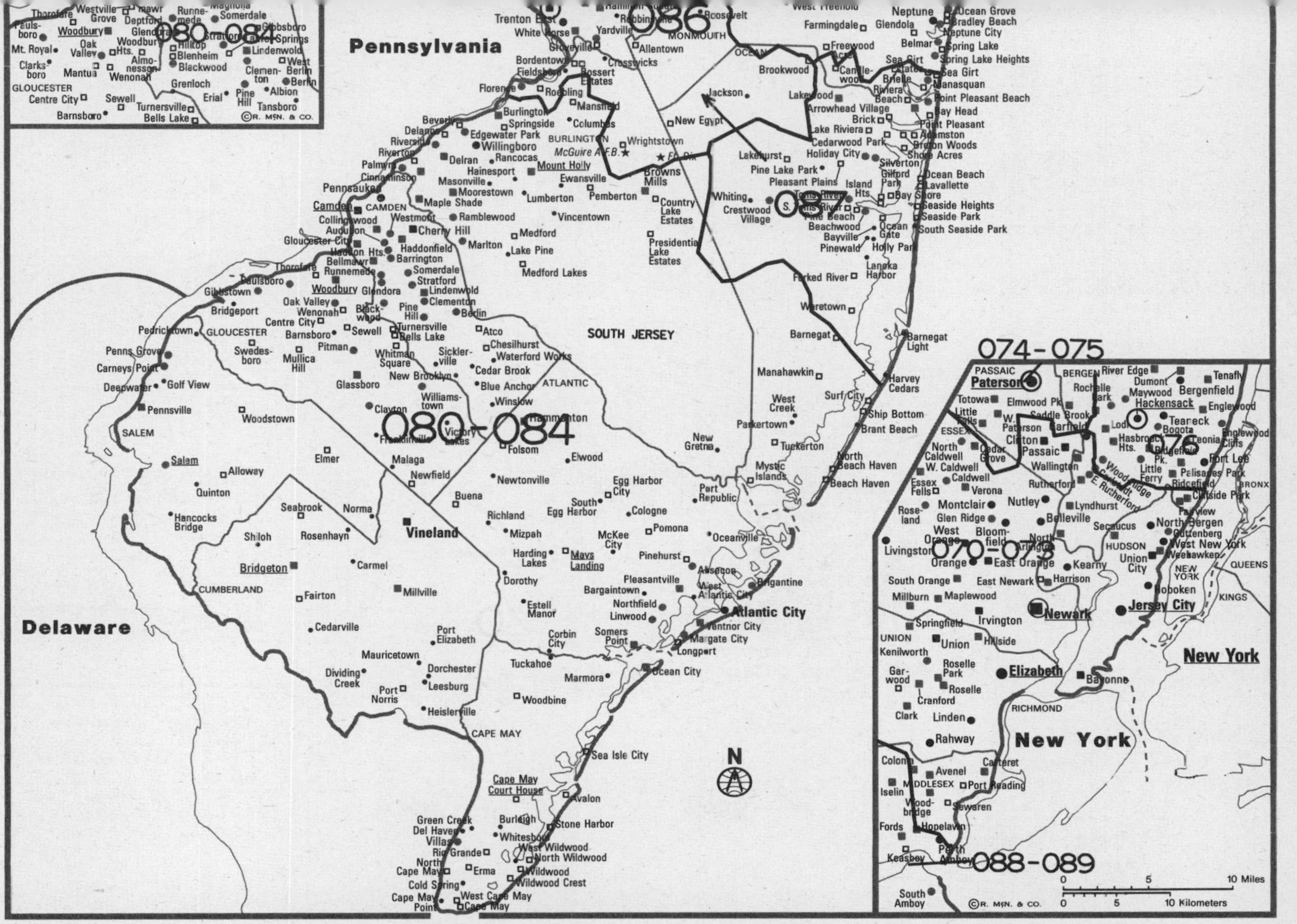
Pennsylvania
Delaware
New York
SOUTH JERSEY
074-075
070-073
088-089
080-084
086
Atlantic City
Vineland
Newark
Jersey City
Elizabeth
Paterson
Hackensack
Camden
Bridgeton
Salem
Woodbury
Cape May Court House
10 Miles
10 Kilometers

Place	ZIP
Deerfield (Twp)	08352
Deerfield	08313
Deerfield Park	08087
Deer Park	08003
Deer Trail Lake	07460
DeKays	07462
Delair	08110
Delanco♦	08075
Delawanna (Part of Clifton)‡	07014
Delaware, *Hunterdon* (Twp)	08559
Delaware, *Warren*	07833
Delaware Gardens	08110
Delaware Park	08865
Del Haven	08251
Delmont	08314
Delran	08075
Delwood	08002
Demarest	07627
Dennis (Twp)	08214
Dennisville	08214
Denville	07834
Deptford	08096
Deptford Mall	08096
Devonshire	08215
Diamond Hill	07840
Dias Creek	08210
Dicktown	08081
Dividing Creek	08315
Doddtown (Part of East Orange)‡	07017
Dorchester	08316
Dorothy	08317
Dover (Twp)	08753
Dover	07801-03
For specific ZIP Codes call (888) 275-8777, or your local postmaster.	
Dover Walk	08753
Downe (Twp)	08315
Downer	08094
Downs Farms	08002
Downtown (Part of Trenton)‡	08608
Drakestown	07840
Dumont	07628
Dunbarton	08004
Dundee (Part of Passaic)‡	07055
Dunellen	08812
Dunhams Corner	08816
Dunham Siding	07047
Dutch Neck	08550
Dutchtown	08802
E (Part of Trenton)‡	08629
Eagleswood (Twp)	08092
Earle	07722
Eastampton (Twp)	08060
East Amwell (Twp)	08551
East Berlin	08009
East Brunswick♦	08816
East Burlington (Part of Burlington)	08016
East Camden (Part of Camden)‡	08105
East Freehold♦	07728
East Greenwich (Twp)	08020
East Hanover♦	07936
East Keansburg‡	07734
East Long Branch (Part of Long Branch)	07740
East Millstone‡	08873
East Newark	07029
East Orange	07017-19
For specific ZIP Codes call (888) 275-8777, or your local postmaster.	
East Pennsauken	08110
East Riverton	08077
East Rutherford	07073
East Side (Part of Bridgeton)‡	08302
East Spotswood	08857
East Trenton Heights	08619
East Vineland	08360
East Windsor	08520
Eatontown	07724
Echelon	08043
Echelon Mall	08043
Edgar	07095
Edgebrook (Part of New Brunswick)	08901
Edgewater	07020
Edgewater Park	08010
Edinburg	08691
Edison (Twp)	08817
Edison♦	08817-20
	08837
	08899
For specific ZIP Codes call (888) 275-8777, or your local postmaster.	
Egg Harbor (Twp)	08234
Egg Harbor City	08215
Eilers Corner	08520
Elberon (Part of Long Branch)‡	07740
Elberon Park	07740
Eldora	08270
Eldridge Park	08638
Eldridges Hill	08098
Elizabeth	07201-02
	07206-08
For specific ZIP Codes call (888) 275-8777, or your local postmaster.	
Elizabethport (Part of Elizabeth)‡	07206
Elk (Twp)	08028
Elks Terrace	08079
Ellisburg‡	08002
Ellisdale	08501
Elm	08037
Elmer	08318
Elmora (Part of Elizabeth)‡	07202
Elmwood Park	07407
Elsinboro (Twp)	08079
Elwood	08217
Emerson	07630
Englewood	07631-32
For specific ZIP Codes call (888) 275-8777, or your local postmaster.	
Englewood Annex (Part of Englewood)‡	07631
Englewood Cliffs	07632
English Creek	08234
Englishtown	07726
Erial‡	08081
Erlton	08002
Erma	08204
Erma Park	08204
Ernston (Part of Sayreville)‡	08859
Erskine (Part of Ringwood)	07456
Erskine Lakes (Part of Ringwood)	07456
Espanong	07849
Essex Fells	07021
Essex Green Mall	07052
Estell Manor	08319
Estelville (Part of Estell Manor)	08319
Etra	08520
Everett	07738
Everittstown	08867
Evesboro	08053
Evesham (Twp)	08053
Ewan	08025
Ewansville	08060
Ewing (Twp)	08618
Ewing Park	08638
Ewingville	08638
Extonville	08620
Fairfield, *Cumberland* (Twp)	08320
Fairfield, *Essex*♦	07004
Fairfield, *Monmouth*	07728
Fair Haven	07704
Fair Lawn	07410
Fairmount, *Hunterdon*	07830
Fairmount, *Morris*	07853
Fairton♦	08320
Fairview, *Bergen*	07022
Fairview, *Burlington* (Delran Twp)	08055
Fairview, *Burlington* (Medford Twp)	08075
Fairview (Part of Camden)	08104
Fairview, *Gloucester*	08080
Fairview, *Hudson*	07047
Fairview, *Monmouth*♦	07701
Fairway Mews (Part of Spring Lake Heights)	07762
Fanwood	07023
Fardale	07430
Far Hills	07931
Farmcrest Acres	07438
Farmersville	07830
Farmingdale	07727
Farmington	08234
Farrington Lake Heights	08850
Fashion Center, The (Part of Paramus)	07652
Fawn Lakes	08050
Fayson Lakes (Part of Kinnelon)	07405
Fellowship	08057
Fenwick	08098
Fernwood	08618
Ferrell	08343
Fieldsboro	08505
Finderne	08807
Finesville	08865
Fishing Creek	08204
Five Corners (Part of Jersey City)‡	07308
Five Points, *Salem*	08067
Five Points, *Sussex*	07860
Flagtown	08821
Flanders	07836
Flanders Valley	07836
Flatbrookville	07832
Flemington	08822
Flemington Junction	08822
Florence, *Burlington*	08518
Florence, *Camden*	08009
Florham Park	07932
Folsom	08037
Fords♦	08863
Forest Grove	08360
Forest Hill, *Camden*	08003
Forest Hill (Part of Newark)	07104
Forest Lake	07821
Forked River	08731
Forked River Beach	08731
Forrest Lake Estates	08328
Fort Dix	08640
Fort Elfsborg	08079
Fortescue	08321
Fort Lee	07024
Fort Mott	08079
Fort Plains	07728
Forty-Fifth Street (Part of Union City)‡	07087
Foster Village (Part of Bergenfield)‡	07621
Foul Rift	07823
Four Bridges	07853
Fox Chase	08088
Fox Hill	07046
Fox Hollow Woods	08003
Francis Mills	08527
Frankford (Twp)	07826
Franklin, *Gloucester* (Twp)	08322
Franklin, *Hunterdon* (Twp)	08867
Franklin, *Warren* (Twp)	08808
Franklin, *Somerset*‡	08873
Franklin, *Sussex*	07416
Franklin Lakes	07417
Franklin Park	08823
Franklinville	08322
Frazier Park	08008
Fredon (Twp)	07860
Free Acres	07922
Freehold	07728
Freewood Acres	07731
Frelinghuysen (Twp)	07825
Frenchtown	08825
Freneau (Part of Matawan)	07747
Fresh Ponds	08816
Friendship (Carneys Point Twp)	08069
Friendship (Upper Pittsgrove Twp)	08318
Fries Mill	08322
Galilee (Part of Monmouth Beach)	07750
Galloway (Twp)	08201
Gandys Beach	08345
Garden City	08012
Gardendale	08079
Gardens of Pleasant Plains	08755
Garden State Plaza (Part of Paramus)	07652
Gardenville	08096
Gardenville Center	08096
Garfield	07026
Garwood	07027
General Lafayette (Part of Jersey City)‡	07309
Georgetown	08022
Georgia	07728
Germania	08215
Germania Gardens	08213
Gibbsboro	08026
Gibbstown♦	08027
Giffordtown	08087
Gilford Park♦	08753
Gillespie (Part of Sayreville)	08872
Gillette	07933
Gilman Lake	08343
Gladstone (Part of Peapack and Gladstone)	07934
Glassboro	08028
Glasser (Part of Hopatcong)	07837
Glen Cove	08721
Glendale	08043
Glendola	07719
Glendora♦	08029
Glen Gardner	08826
Glen Oaks	08021
Glen Ridge	07028
Glen Rock	07452
Glenside	08070
Glenwood	07418
Gloucester (Twp)	08012
Gloucester City	08030
Golf Manor	08069
Golf View	08069
Gordon Lakes	07405
Goshen	08218
Gouldtown	08302
Grandin	08801
Granton Junction	07047
Grasselli (Part of Linden)‡	07036
Gravel Hill	07726
Greater Cross Roads	07921
Great Meadows	07838
Great Notch	07424
Green (Twp)	07821
Green Bank	08215
Greenbriar	08723
Greenbrook	07480
Green Brook	08812
Green Creek	08219
Greendell	07839
Greenfield	08230
Greenfield Heights	08096
Greenfields Village	08096
Green Grove	07712
Greenhaven	08002
Green Hills	08876
Green Island	08753
Green Knoll	08876
Greenland (Part of Magnolia)	08049
Green Pond	07435
Green Pond Junction (Part of Kinnelon)	07405
Greensand	08817
Green Village	07935
Greenville (Part of Jersey City)‡	07305
Greenville, *Ocean*	08701
Greenville, *Salem*	08318
Greenwich, *Gloucester* (Twp)	08027
Greenwich, *Warren* (Twp)	08886
Greenwich, *Cumberland*	08323
Greenwich Pier	08323
Greenwood Park	08071
Grenloch	08032
Grenloch Terrace	08032
Griggstown	08540
Grove‡	07003
Grovers Mill	08550
Groveville	08620
Gum Tree Corner	08302
Guttenberg	07093
Hackensack	07601*
	07602†
Hackettstown	07840
Hacklebarney	07930
Haddon (Twp)	08106
Haddonfield	08033
Haddon Heights	08035
Haddon Hills	08033
Haddon Leigh (Part of Haddonfield)	08033
Haddontowne	08034
Hainesburg	07832
Haines Corner	08690
Hainesport	08036
Hainesville	07826
Haledon	07508*
	07538†
Haledonn	07538
Haleyville	08349
Halsey	07860
Hamburg	07419
Hamden	08801
Hamilton, *Atlantic* (Twp)	08330
Hamilton, *Mercer* (Twp)	08610
Hamilton, *Monmouth*	07753
Hamilton Square	08690
Hammonton	08037
Hampton, *Sussex* (Twp)	07860
Hampton, *Hunterdon*	08827
Hancocks Bridge	08038
Hanover (Twp)	07981
Hanover Neck	07936
Harbourton	08530
Harding (Twp)	07936
Harding Lakes	08330
Hardingville	08343
Hardistonville (Part of Hamburg)	07419
Hardwick (Twp)	07825
Hardyston (Twp)	07460
Harlingen	08502
Harmersville	08079
Harmony, *Monmouth*	07748
Harmony, *Ocean*	08527
Harmony, *Warren*	08865
Harrington Park	07640
Harrison, *Gloucester* (Twp)	08062
Harrison, *Hudson*	07029
Harrisonville, *Gloucester*	08039
Harrisonville, *Salem*	08079
Hartford	08057
Harvey Cedars	08008
Hasbrouck Heights	07604
Haskell (Part of Wanaque)	07420
Haven Beach	08008
Haworth	07641
Hawthorne	07506*
	07507†
Hazelton	07001
Hazen	07823
Hazlet	07730
Head of River (Part of Estell Manor)	08270
Headquarters	08557
Hedding	08505
Heislerville	08324
Helmetta	08828
Hensfoot	08827
Herbertsville	08723
Heritage Village	08053
Hermon	08215
Herwood	08002
Hesstown	08332
Hewitt	07421
Hibernia	07842
Hickory Acres	08520
Hickory Tree	07928
Hickstown	08012
High Bridge	08829
High Crest Lake	07480
Highland Lakes♦	07422
Highland Park (Part of Gloucester City)	08030
Highland Park, *Middlesex*	08904
Highlands	07732
Highlands Beach	08251
High Point (Part of Harvey Cedars)	08008
Highs Beach	08210
Hightstown	08520
Hightstown Heights	08520
Highview	07480
Highview Park	08736
Hillcrest (Part of Paterson)‡	07502
Hillcrest (Part of Trenton)	08618
Hillsborough (Twp)	08853
Hillsborough	08502
Hillsdale	07642
Hillsdale Manor (Part of Hillsdale)	07642
Hillside♦	07205
Hilltop	08012
Hilltop Terrace	08816
Hilltown	07885
Hi-Lo Acres	07435
Hi-Nella	08083
Hoboken	07030
Hoffmans	07830
Ho Ho Kus	07423
Holgate	08008
Holiday Beach	08731
Holiday City	08753
Holiday City at Berkeley	08757
Holiday City South♦	08757
Holiday City West	08757
Holiday Heights♦	08757
Holiday on the Bay	08753
Holland, *Hunterdon*	08848
Holland, *Morris & Sussex*	07460
Holly Park	08721
Holmansville	08527
Holmdel	07733
Holmeson	08510
Homes Mills	08514
Homestead Park	07933
Homestead Run	08755
Hoot Owl Estates	08055
Hopatcong	07843
Hopatcong Heights (Part of Hopatcong)	07843

Hopatcong Hills (Part of Hopatcong) 07843
Hope 07844
Hopelawn 08861
Hopewell, *Cumberland* (Twp) 08302
Hopewell, *Mercer* (Twp) 08560
Hopewell, *Mercer* 08525
Hornerstown 08514
Howell (Twp) 07727
Howell 07731
Hudson City (Part of Jersey City)‡ 07307
Hudson Heights‡ 07047
Hudson Mall (Part of Jersey City) 07304
Hughesville 08848
Hunter's Crossing 08887
Huntsburg 07860
Huntsville 07821
Hunt Tract 08034
Hurdtown 07885
Hurffville 08080
Hutchinson 08865
Hutchinson Mills 08619
Hyson 08527
Idell 08825
Imlaystown 08526
Independence (Twp) 07840
Independence Corner 07461
Indian Lake 07834
Indian Mills 08088
Industrial-Hillside 07205
Interlaken 07712
Interstate Shopping Center (Part of Ramsey) 07446
Iona 08322
Ironbound (Part of Newark)‡ 07105
Ironia 07845
Iron Rock 08109
Irvington♦ 07111
Iselin♦ 08830
Island Heights 08732
Ivystone Farms 08004
Ivywood 08077
Jackson (Part of Jersey City)‡ 07305
Jackson, *Ocean* 08527
Jacksonburg 07825
Jackson Estates 08527
Jacksons Mills 08527
Jacksonville, *Burlington* 08505
Jacksonville (Part of Lincoln Park) 07035
Jacobstown 08562
Jamesburg 08831
Janvier 08322
Jefferson, *Morris* (Twp) 07849
Jefferson, *Gloucester* 08062
Jenkins 08019
Jersey City 07301-11
For specific ZIP Codes call (888) 275-8777, or your local postmaster.
Jerseyville 07728
Jobstown 08041
Johnsonburg 07846
Jones Island 08311
Jordantown 08109
Journal Square (Part of Jersey City)‡ 07306
Juliustown 08042
Jutland 08827
Karrsville 07865
Kay Gardens 08067
Keansburg 07734
Kearny 07032
Keasbey 08832
Kemah Lake 07860
Kendall Park♦ 08824
Kenilworth 07033
Kenvil 07847
Keswick Grove 08759
Keyport 07735
Kingsland 07071
Kingston 08528
Kingston Estates 08034
Kings Woods (Part of Alpine) 07620
Kingwood (Twp) 08825
Kinkora 08505
Kinnelon 07405
Kirbys Mill 08055
Kirkwood 08043
Kitchell Lake 07480
Kittatinny Lake 07826
Klinesville 08822
Knollwood 08002
Knowlton 07832
Kresson 08053
Lacey (Twp) 08731
Lafayette 07848
La Gorce Square 08016
Lake Como (Part of Spring Lake) 07762
Lake Forest 07849
Lake Grinnell 07871
Lake Hiawatha 07034
Lakehurst 08733
Lakehurst Naval Air Station 08733
Lake Iliff 07860
Lake Lackawanna 07874
Lakeland 08012
Lake Lenape 07860
Lake Neepaulin 07461
Lake Nelson 08854
Lake Owassa 07860
Lake Pine 08053
Lakeridge 07747
Lake Riviera 08723
Lake Rogerine (Part of Mount Arlington) 07856
Lake Shawnee 07885
Lakeside 07421
Lakeside Park 08610
Lake Swannanoa 07438
Lake Tamarack 07460
Lake Telemark♦ 07866
Lake Tranquility 07821
Lakeview 08060
Lake Villa Estates 08043
Lake Wallkill 07461
Lakewood♦ 08701
Lambertville 08530
Lambs Terrace 08081
Lamington 07921
Landing 07850
Landisville (Part of Buena) 08326
Land of Pines 07737
Landsdown 08801
Lanes Mills 08701
Lanoka Harbor 08734
Lanson's Corner 08551
Laureldale 08330
Laurel Harbor 08734
Laurel Lake 08332
Laurel Springs 08021
Laurelton 08723
Laurelton Gardens 08723
Laurence Harbor 08879
Lavallette 08735
Lawnside 08045
Lawrence, *Cumberland* (Twp) 08311
Lawrence, *Mercer* (Twp) 08648
Lawrence Brook Manor 08816
Lawrenceville♦ 08648
Layton 07851
Lebanon (Twp) 07830
Lebanon 08833
Lebanon Lake Estates 08015
Ledgewood 07852
Ledgewood Mall 07852
Leeds Point 08220
Leektown 08215
Leesburg 08327
Leisure Knoll♦ 08733
Leisuretowne♦ 08088
Leisure Village♦ 08701
Leisure Village East♦ 08753
Leisure Village West 08733
Lenola 08057
Leonardo♦ 07737
Leonardville 07737
Leonia 07605
Lewisville 08648
Liberty (Twp) 07863
Liberty Corner 07938
Libertyville 07461
Lincoln 08062
Lincoln Park 07035
Lincroft♦ 07738
Linden 07036
Linden Junction (Part of Linden) 07036
Lindenwold 08021
Lindy's Lake 07480
Linvale 08551
Linwood 08221
Little Egg Harbor (Twp) 08087
Little Falls♦ 07424
Little Ferry 07643
Little Rocky Hill 08540
Little Silver 07739
Little Silver Point (Part of Little Silver) 07739
Littleton (Part of Morris Plains) 07950
Little York 08834
Livingston♦ 07039
Livingston Mall 07039
Loch Arbour 07711
Locktown 08822
Locust 07760
Locust Grove 08003
Lodi 07644
Logan (Twp) 08014
Lommasons Glen 07823
London Terrace 08859
Long Beach 08008
Long Beach Park 08008
Long Branch 07740
Long Bridge 07838
Long Hill (Twp) 07946
Long Hill 07928
Longport 08403
Long Valley♦ 07853
Longwood Lake 07438
Lookover Lake 07421
Lopatcong (Twp) 08865
Louden 08004
Loveladies 08008
Lower (Twp) 08204
Lower Alloways Creek (Twp) 08038
Lower Bank 08215
Lower Harmony 08865
Lower Montville 07045
Lower Squankum 07727
Lower Valley (Part of Califon) 07830
Lows Hollow 08886
Lucaston (Part of Lindenwold) 08009
Lumberton 08048
Lumistown 08311
Lyndhurst♦ 07071
Lynn Woodoaks 07067
Lyons 07920
Lyonsville 07005
McAfee 07428
McCoys Corner 07461
Macedonia (Part of Tinton Falls) 07724
McGuire Air Force Base 08641
McKee City 08234
Macopin 07405
Madison 07940
Madison Park 08859
Madisonville 07920
Magnolia, *Atlantic* 08217
Magnolia, *Burlington* 08068
Magnolia, Camden 08049
Mahoneyville 08070
Mahwah 07430
.... 07495
For specific ZIP Codes call (888) 275-8777, or your local postmaster.
Main Avenue (Part of Clifton)‡ 07011
Malaga 08328
Malapardis 07981
Mall at Short Hills, The 07078
Manahawkin♦ 08050
Manalapan 07726
Manasquan 08736
Manasquan Park 08736
Manasquan Shores 08736
Manchester (Twp) 08759
Mandalay 08723
Mannington (Twp) 08079
Mansfield, *Warren* (Twp) 07840
Mansfield, *Burlington* 08022
Mansfield Square 08022
Mantoloking 08738
Mantoloking Estates 08738
Mantoloking Shores 08738
Mantua 08051
Mantua Grove 08061
Mantua Terrace 08051
Manunkachunk 07832
Manville 08835
Maplecrest‡ 07040
Maple Glen 08527
Maple Grange 07462
Maple Meade 08902
Maple Shade♦ 08052
Maple Tree 08753
Maple View 08857
Maplewood♦ 07040
Marcella 07866
Margate City 08402
Marksboro 07825
Marlboro, *Burlington* 08053
Marlboro, *Cumberland* 08302
Marlboro, *Monmouth* 07746
Marlboro Heights 07726
Marlton 08053
Marlton Heights 08098
Marlton Lakes 08004
Marlyn Manor 08242
Marmora 08223
Marshalls Corner 08525
Marshalltown 08079
Marshallville 08270
Martins Beach 08046
Martinsville 08836
Maryland 08527
Masonicus 07430
Masonville 08054
Matawan 07747
Matchaponix 08831
Maurice River (Twp) 08327
Mauricetown 08329
Maxim 08701
Mayetta 08092
Mays Landing♦ 08330
Mayville 08210
Maywood 07607
Meadford Farms 08088
Meadowbrook 08109
Meadowbrook Village 08527
Meadows (Part of Secaucus)‡ 07094
Meadowview‡ 07047
Meadow Village 07009
Mechanicsville (Part of South Amboy) 08879
Mechanicsville, *Monmouth* 07730
Medford 08055
Medford Lakes 08055
Melrose, *Burlington* 08055
Melrose (Part of Sayreville) 08879
Mendham 07945
Menlo Park‡ 08837
Menlo Park Mall 08817
Menlo Park Terrace 08840
Mercerville 08619
Merchantville 08109
Meriden 07005
Metedeconk 08723
Mettler 08873
Metuchen 08840
Meyersville 07933
Miami Beach 08251
Mickleton 08056
Middle (Twp) 08210
Middlebush‡ 08873
Middlesex 08846
Middletown, *Monmouth* 07748
Middletown, *Morris* 07866
Middle Valley 07853
Middleville 07855
Midland Park 07432
Mid State Mall 08816
Midstreams Park 08723
Midtown (Part of Newark)‡ 07102
Milford 08848
Military Ocean Terminal (Part of Bayonne)‡ 07002
Millbridge 08021
Millbrook 07832
Millburn♦ 07041
Millhurst 07728
Millington 07946
Millside Heights 08075
Millstone, *Monmouth* (Twp) 08510
Millstone, *Somerset* 08876
Milltown, *Middlesex* 08850
Milltown, *Morris* 07930
Millville 08332
Milmay 08340
Milton 07438
Mimosa Lake 08053
Mine Brook 07931
Mine Hill 07803
Minotola (Part of Buena) 08341
Mizpah 08342
Money Island 08345
Monitor (Part of West New York)‡ 07093
Monmouth Beach 07750
Monmouth Heights 07746
Monmouth Hills 07732
Monmouth Junction♦ 08852
Monmouth Mall (Part of Eatontown) 07724
Monroe, *Gloucester* (Twp) 08094
Monroe, *Middlesex* (Twp) 08520
Monroe, *Morris* 07981
Monroe, *Sussex* 07871
Monroeville 08343
Montague (Twp) 12771
Montague 07827
Montana 08865
Montclair♦ 07042-43
For specific ZIP Codes call (888) 275-8777, or your local postmaster.
Montclair Heights 07042
Montgomery (Twp) 08558
Montrose 07722
Montvale 07645
Montville 07045
Moonachie 07074
Moorestown 08057
Moosepack Pond 07439
Morehousetown 07039
Morgan (Part of Sayreville) 08879
Morganville 07751
Morris, *Morris* (Twp) 07961
Morris, *Camden* 08110
Morris Beach 08234
Morris Park 08865
Morris Plains 07950
Morris Street (Part of Morristown)‡ 07960
Morristown, *Middlesex* 07747
Morristown, *Morris* 07960-63
For specific ZIP Codes call (888) 275-8777, or your local postmaster.
Morrisville 08110
Morsemere (Part of Ridgefield) 07657
Mountain Lake 07823
Mountain Lakes 07046
Mountainside 07092
Mountain Spring Lakes 07405
Mountain View 07470
Mountainville 08833
Mount Airy 08530
Mount Arlington 07856
Mount Bethel, *Somerset* 07059
Mount Bethel, *Warren* 07865
Mount Ephraim 08059
Mount Fern 07801
Mount Freedom 07970
Mount Hermon 07825
Mount Holly♦ 08060
Mount Hope 07885
Mount Horeb 07059
Mount Joy 08848
Mount Kemble Lake 07960
Mount Laurel 08054
Mount Olive 07828
Mount Pleasant (Part of Woodbine) 08270
Mount Pleasant, *Hunterdon* 08848
Mount Pleasant, *Warren* 07832
Mount Rose 08525
Mount Royal 08061
Mount Salem 07461
Mounts Mills 08831
Mount Tabor 07878
Mount Vernon 07832
Muhlenberg (Part of Plainfield)‡ 07060
Mullica (Twp) 08215
Mullica Hill♦ 08062
Murray Grove 08731
Murray Hill (Part of New Providence) 07974
Myrtle Grove 07860
Mystic Islands‡ 08087
Mystic Shores 08087
National Park 08063
Naughright 07853
Navesink 07752
Navesink Beach (Part of Sea Bright) 07760
Neptune 07753*
.... 07754†
Neptune City 07753
Nesco 08037
Neshanic 08853
Neshanic Station 08853
Netcong 07857
Netcong Heights 07857
Netherwood (Part of Plainfield)‡ 07062
New Albany 08077
New Amsterdam Village 08879
Newark 07101-08
.... 07112-75
For specific ZIP Codes call (888) 275-8777, or your local postmaster.
Newark Heights 07040
Newbakers Corners 07825
New Bedford 07719
Newbolds Corner 08060

*** Area Zip Code** **† Post Office Boxes** **‡ Postal Station** **♦ Census Designated Place** *Italic Type* **County**

Place	ZIP Code
New Bridge (Part of New Milford)	07646
New Brooklyn	08081
New Brunswick	08901
	08903
	08906
For specific ZIP Codes call (888) 275-8777, or your local postmaster.	
New Canton	08501
New Durham, *Hudson*	07047
New Durham, *Middlesex*	08837
New Egypt♦	08533
Newfield	08344
Newfoundland	07435
New Freedom	08009
New Gretna	08224
New Hampton	08827
New Hanover (Twp)	08511
New Lisbon	08064
New Market‡	08854
New Milford	07646
New Monmouth	07748
Newport, *Cumberland*	08345
Newport, *Hunterdon*	08826
Newport Centre (Part of Jersey City)	07310
New Providence	07974
New Russia	07438
New Sharon, *Gloucester*	08080
New Sharon, *Mercer*	08691
Newton	07860
Newtonville	08346
Newtown	08854
Newtown Heights	08816
New Vernon	07976
New Village	08886
Nixon‡	08817
Norma	08347
Normandie (Part of Sea Bright)	07760
Normandy Beach	08739
North (Part of Newark)‡	07104
North Arlington	07031
North Beach	08008
North Beach Haven	08008
North Bergen♦	07047
North Branch	08876
North Branch Depot	08876
North Brunswick♦	08902
North Caldwell	07006
North Cape May♦	08204
North Center‡	07003
North Church	07416
North Church Estates	07416
North Crosswicks	08620
North Dennis	08214
North Edison	08817
North Elizabeth (Part of Elizabeth)‡	07208
Northfield, *Atlantic*	08225
Northfield, *Essex*	07039
North Hackensack (Part of River Edge)‡	07661
North Haledon	07508
North Hanover (Twp)	08562
North Hawthorne (Part of Hawthorne)	07507
North Long Branch (Part of Long Branch)	07740
Northmont (Part of Mount Ephraim)	08059
North Newark (Part of Newark)	07104
North Plainfield	07060
North Port Norris	08349
Northvale	07647
North Vineland (Part of Vineland)	08360
North Wildwood	08260
North Woodbury	08096
Norton	08827
Nortonville	08085
Norwood	07648
Nottingham	08619
Nugentown	08087
Nutley♦	07110
Oak Glen	07731
Oak Hill	07748
Oakhurst♦	07755
Oakland	07436
Oaklyn	08107
Oak Ridge	07438
Oak Ridge Estates	08755
Oak Shades	07747
Oak Tree, *Middlesex*	08817
Oak Tree, *Ocean*	08527
Oak Valley♦	08090
Oakwood Beach	08079
Oakwood Lakes	08055
Oakwood Park (Part of New Providence)	07974
Ocean, *Monmouth* (Twp)	07755
Ocean, *Ocean* (Twp)	08758
Ocean Beach	08735
Ocean City	08226
Ocean Gate	08740
Ocean Grove♦	07756
Ocean Heights (Part of Somers Point)	08244
Oceanport	07757
Ocean View	08230
Oceanville	08231
Ogdensburg	07439
Old Bridge	08857
Old Forge Village	07960
Old Manor	07733
Oldmans (Twp)	08067
Old Milford Estates	07480
Old Tappan	07675
Oldwick	08858
Olivet	08318
Oradell	07649
Orange♦	07050*
	07051†
Orchard View	08016
Ortley Beach	08751
Osage	08043
Osbornsville	08723
Othello	08302
Outcalt	08831
Outwater (Part of Garfield)‡	07026
Overbrook (Part of Lindenwold)	08021
Overbrook, *Essex*‡	07009
Oxford♦	07863
Oyster Creek	08201
Packanack Lake‡	07470
Pahaquarry (Twp)	07832
Palatine	08318
Palermo	08223
Palisade (Part of Fort Lee)‡	07024
Palisades Park	07650
Palmer Square (Part of Princeton)‡	08540
Palmyra	08065
Pamrapo (Part of Bayonne)‡	07002
Pancoast	08310
Panther Lake	07821
Paradise Lakes	08079
Paramus	07652*
	07653†
Paramus Park (Part of Paramus)	07652
Park (Part of Paterson)‡	07513
Park Avenue‡	07087
Parker	07853
Parkertown	08087
Park Ridge	07656
Park Ridge Farms	08505
Park Village	07016
Parkway Pines	08701
Parkway Village	08628
Parlin (Part of Sayreville)	08859
Parry	08077
Parsippany	07054
Parsippany-Troy Hills♦	07005
Parsonville	08505
Passaic	07055
Passaic Park (Part of Passaic)‡	07055
Paterson	07501-05
	07509-10
	07513-33
	07543-44
For specific ZIP Codes call (888) 275-8777, or your local postmaster.	
Patricks Corners	08816
Pattenburg	08802
Paulas Corners	08816
Paulina	07825
Paulins Kill	07860
Paulsboro	08066
Pavonia (Part of Camden)	08105
Peahala Park	08008
Peapack (Part of Peapack & Gladstone)	07977
Peapack and Gladstone	07977
Pebble Beach	08005
Pecks Corner	08079
Pedricktown	08067
Pelican Island	08751
Pellettown	07822
Pemberton (Twp)	08015
Pemberton	08068
Pemberton Heights♦	08068
Penbryn	08009
Penekum	08012
Penn Beach	08070
Pennington	08534
Pennsauken♦	08110
Penns Grove	08069
Penns Neck	08540
Pennsville	08070
Penny Pot (Part of Folsom)	08037
Penton	08079
Penwell	07865
Pequannock	07440
Pequest	07863
Perkintown	08067
Perrineville	08535
Perth Amboy	08861*
	08862†
Petersburg, *Cape May*	08270
Petersburg, *Warren*	07840
Phalanx	07722
Pheasant Run	08077
Philips Mills	07734
Phillipsburg	08865
Phoenix (Part of Sayreville)	08871
Picatinny Arsenal	07806
Pierces Point	08210
Pilesgrove (Twp)	08098
Pine Beach	08741
Pine Brook (Part of Tinton Falls)	07724
Pine Brook, *Morris*	07058
Pine Brook, *Somerset*	08502
Pine Cliff Lake	07480
Pine Grove	08055
Pine Hill	08021
Pinehurst	08201
Pine Lake Park	08753
Pine Ridge at Crestwood♦	08759
Pines Lake	07470
Pine Terrace	08753
Pine Valley	08021
Pinewald	08721
Pinkneyville	07871
Piscataway	08854*
	08855†
Pitman	08071
Pittsgrove (Twp)	08347
Pittstown	08867
Plainfield	07060-63
For specific ZIP Codes call (888) 275-8777, or your local postmaster.	
Plainsboro	08536
Plainville, *Gloucester*	08322
Plainville, *Somerset*	08502
Plaza, *Burlington*‡	08046
Plaza (Part of Secaucus)‡	07094
Plaza at Cherry Hill, The (Part of Cherry Hill)	08034
Plaza Park	08016
Pleasant Gardens	08527
Pleasant Grove, *Morris*	07853
Pleasant Grove, *Ocean*	08527
Pleasant Hill	07876
Pleasant Mills	08037
Pleasant Plains♦	08755
Pleasant Run	08822
Pleasant Valley, *Morris*	07945
Pleasant Valley, *Warren*	07882
Pleasant View	08502
Pleasantville	08232
	08234
For specific ZIP Codes call (888) 275-8777, or your local postmaster.	
Pluckemin	07978
Plumbsock	07461
Plumsted (Twp)	08533
Pohatcong (Twp)	08804
Pointers	08079
Point Pleasant, *Ocean*	08742
Point Pleasant (Part of Hopatcong)	07843
Point Pleasant Beach	08742
Pole Tavern	08318
Polkville	07832
Pomona♦	08240
Pompton Junction (Part of Pompton Lakes)	07442
Pompton Lakes	07442
Pompton Plains	07444
Porchtown	08344
Port-au-Peck (Part of Oceanport)	07757
Port Colden	07882
Port Elizabeth	08348
Portertown	08098
Port Johnson (Part of Bayonne)	07002
Port Monmouth♦	07758
Port Morris	07850
Port Murray	07865
Port Newark (Part of Newark)	07114
Port Norris	08349
Port Reading♦	07064
Port Republic	08241
Port Warren	08886
Possumtown	08854
Potters	08817
Potterstown	08833
Pottersville	07979
Powerville	07005
Prallsville (Part of Stockton)	08559
Preakness‡	07470
Presidential Lakes Estates♦	08015
Prices Switch	07462
Princeton (Twp)	08540
Princeton	08540-43
For specific ZIP Codes call (888) 275-8777, or your local postmaster.	
Princeton Ivy East	08520
Princeton Junction	08550
Prospect Heights	08638
Prospect Park	07508
Prospect Plains	08512
Prospect Point	07849
Prospertown	08514
Pullentown	08501
Quaker Gardens	08619
Quakertown	08868
Quarryville	07461
Quinton	08072
Racoon Island	07849
Radburn (Part of Fair Lawn)	07410
Rahway	07065
Rainbow Lakes	07834
Raines Corner	08069
Ralston	07945
Ramblewood	08054
Ramsey	07446
Ramseysburg	07832
Ramtown	07731
Rancocas	08073
Rancocas Heights	08060
Rancocas Woods	08054
Randolph (Twp)	07869
Raritan, *Hunterdon* (Twp)	08822
Raritan, *Somerset*	08869
Raritan Gardens (Part of New Brunswick)	08902
Raven Rock	08559
Readington	08870
Reaville	08822
Red Bank, *Gloucester*	08063
Red Bank, *Monmouth*	07701
Red Lion, *Burlington*	08088
Red Lion, *Middlesex*	08902
Redshaw Corner	08857
Reeds Beach	08210
Reevytown (Part of Tinton Falls)	07753
Repaupo	08066
Repaupo Station	08085
Retreat	08088
Rhode Hall	08828
Richard Mine	07885
Richfield (Part of Clifton)	07013
Richland	08350
Richwood	08074
Ridgefield	07657
Ridgefield Park	07660
Ridgeway	08733
Ridgewood	07450*
	07451†
Riegel Ridge	08848
Riegelsville	08848
Ringoes	08551
Ringwood	07456
Rio Grande♦	08242
Ritz (Part of Garfield)‡	07026
River Bank	08741
Riverdale	07457
River Edge	07661
Riverfront Plaza (Part of Newark)‡	07102
River Plaza	07701
River Road (Part of Fair Lawn)‡	07410
Riverside♦	08075
Riverside Park	08075
Riverside Square (Part of Hackensack)	07601
River Street (Part of Paterson)‡	07524
Riverton	08076-77
For specific ZIP Codes call (888) 275-8777, or your local postmaster.	
River Vale♦	07675
Riverwood	08755
Riviera Beach	08723
Roadstown	08302
Robbinsville	08691
Robertsville	07751
Robins Estates	08527
Rochelle Park♦	07662-63
For specific ZIP Codes call (888) 275-8777, or your local postmaster.	
Rockaway	07866
Rockaway Neck	07054
Rockaway Valley	07005
Rockleigh	07647
Rockport	07840
Rock Ridge Lake	07834
Rocktown	08551
Rocky Hill	08553
Roebling	08554
Roosevelt	08555
Roosevelt City	08759
Roosevelt Park (Part of Millville)	08332
Rosedale (Part of Hammonton)	08037
Rosedale, *Mercer*	08540
Rose Hill Heights	08865
Roseland	07068
Roselle	07203
Roselle Park	07204
Rosemont, *Hunterdon*	08556
Rosemont, *Mercer*	08619
Rosenhayn♦	08352
Roseville (Part of Newark)‡	07107
Ross Corner	07822
Rossmoor♦	08831
Round Top	07059
Roxburg	08865
Roxbury (Twp)	07876
Rudeville	07419
Rumson	07760
Runnemede	08078
Runyon	08857
Rutgers (Part of New Brunswick)	08901
Rutherford	07070-75
For specific ZIP Codes call (888) 275-8777, or your local postmaster.	
Saddle Brook♦	07663
Saddle River	07458
St. Cloud	07052
Salem	08079
Salem Hill	08701
Salina	08080
Sand Brook	08559
Sand Hills	08852
Sands Point (Part of Oceanport)	07757
Sandyston (Twp)	07851
Sarepta	07823
Saxton Falls	07874
Sayres Neck	08311
Sayreville	08871†
	08872*
Sayre Woods (Part of Sayreville)	08859
Sayre Woods South	08857
Schooleys Mountain	07870
Scobeyville	07722
Scotch Plains♦	07076
Scotts Corner	08536
Scudders Falls	08628
Scullville	08234
Seaboard (Part of Kearny)	07032
Sea Breeze	08302
Sea Bright	07760
Seabrook♦	08302
Sea Girt	08750
Sea Girt Estates	08750
Sea Isle City	08243
Seaside Heights	08751
Seaside Park	08752
Seaview Park	08201
Seaview Square	07712
Seaville	08230
Secaucus	07094*
	07096†
Seeley	08302
Sergeantsville	08557
Seven Stars	08701

Sewaren♦ 07077
Sewell 08080
Shady Lake 07480
Shafto Corners (Part of Tinton Falls) 07727
Shamong (Twp) 08088
Shark River Hills♦ 07753
Sharptown 08098
Shaw Crest 08260
Shaytown 07827
Sheffield‡ 07470
Sherwood on the Green 08096
Shiloh 08353
Shimer Manor 08865
Ship Bottom 08008
Shippenport 07850
Shirley 08318
Shongum 07970
Shore Acres 08723
Shore View 07067
Short Hills 07078
Shrewsbury (Twp) 07724
Shrewsbury (Borough) 07702
Shrewsbury (Upper Freehold Twp) 08501
Sicklerville 08081
Sidney 08867
Siloam 07728
Silver Bay 08753
Silver Beach 08735
Silver Lake 07825
Silver Ridge Park West 08757
Silver Springs 07850
Silverton 08753
Simons Lake 07461
Sim Place 08005
Singac 07424
Sinnickson Landing 08079
Six Points 08302
Skillman 08558
Skyline Lakes (Part of Ringwood) 07465
Slackwoods 08638
Smalleytown 07059
Smithburg 07728
Smiths Mills 07405
Smithville, *Atlantic* 08201
Smithville, *Burlington* 08060
Smoke Rise (Part of Kinnelon) 07405
Snow Hill (Part of Lawnside) 08045
Society Hill♦ 08817
Somerdale 08083
Somerset, *Mercer* 08628
Somerset, *Somerset*♦ 08873*
08875†
Somers Point 08244
Somerville 08876-77
For specific ZIP Codes call (888) 275-8777, or your local postmaster.
South (Part of Newark)‡ 07114
South Amboy 08879
Southampton (Twp) 08088
Southard 07731
South Belmar 07719
South Bound Brook (Part of Middlesex) 08846
South Bound Brook, *Somerset* 08880
South Branch 08876
South Brunswick (Twp) 08852
South Camden (Part of Camden)‡ 08104
South Dennis 08245
South Egg Harbor 08215
South Hackensack 07606
South Harrison (Twp) 08039
South Lakewood 08701
South Livingston‡ 07039
South Mantoloking Beach 08738
South Old Bridge 08857
South Orange♦ 07079
South Orange Village (Twp) 07079
South Paterson (Part of Paterson)‡ 07503
South Pemberton (Part of Pemberton) 08068
South Penns Grove 08069
South Plainfield 07080
South River 08882
South Seaside Park 08752
South Seaville 08246
South Toms River 08757
South Vineland (Part of Vineland)‡ 08360
South Westville (Part of Westville) 08093
Southwind 08527
Southwood 08857
Sparta♦ 07871
Sparta Junction 07871
Sparta Lake 07871
Sperry Springs (Part of Hopatcong) 07843
Spotswood 08884
Spray Beach 08008
Springdale, *Camden* 08002
Springdale, *Somerset* 07059
Springdale, *Sussex* 07860
Springfield, *Burlington* (Twp) 08041
Springfield, *Union*♦ 07081
Spring Lake 07762
Spring Lake Heights 07762
Spring Mills 08848
Springside 08016
Springtown, *Cumberland* 08302
Springtown, *Morris* 07853
Springtown, *Warren* 08865
Springville 08057
Squire Village 08753
Stafford (Twp) 08050
Staffordville 08092
Stanhope 07874
Stanton 08885
Stanton Station 08822
Stanwick 08057
Stanwick Glen 08057
Star Cross 08322
Staten Island Junction 07016
Station A (Part of Linden)‡ 07036
Steelmantown 08270
Steelmanville 08234
Stelton 08837
Stephensburg 07865
Stevens 08016
Stewartsville 08886
Still Valley 08865
Stillwater 07875
Stirling 07980
Stockholm 07460
Stockton 08559
Stone Harbor 08247
Stone House 07946
Stone Tavern 08514
Stonetown (Part of Ringwood) 07465
Stony Hill 07922
Stoutsburg 08525
Stow Creek (Twp) 08302
Stow Creek Landing 08302
Stratford 08084
Strathmere 08248
Strathmore♦ 07747
Styertowne Shopping Center (Part of Clifton) 07012
Suburban 07701
Succasunna 07876
Summerfield 07823
Summit 07901*
07902†
Summit Avenue (Part of Union City)‡ 07087
Sunbury 08068
Sunnyside 08801
Sunrise Beach 08731
Sunset Beach 08012
Sunset Hill Gardens 08540
Surf City 08008
Sussex 07461
Sutton Park 07836
Swainton 08210
Swartswood 07877
Swartswood Lake 07860
Swedesboro 08085
Sweet Briar 07733
Sweetwater 08037
Sykesville 08562
Sylvan Glen 08505
Sylvan Lake 08016
Tabernacle 08088
Tabor 07834
Tanglewood Farms 07733
Tanners Corners 08816
Tansboro 08004
Taunton Lake 08053
Taurus (Part of West New York)‡ 07093
Tavistock 08033
Taylortown 07005
Teaneck♦ 07666
Tenafly 07670
Tennent 07763
Teterboro 07608
Tewksbury (Twp) 08833
The Orchards 08619
Thompsons Beach 08324
Thorofare 08086
Three Bridges 08887
Tierneys Corner 07849
Timber Lakes 08094
Timbuctoo 08060
Tinton Falls 07724
Titusville 08560
Toms River♦ 08753-57
For specific ZIP Codes call (888) 275-8777, or your local postmaster.
Totowa 07511†
07512*
Towaco 07082
Town Bank 08204
Town Center‡ 07052
Town Estates 08016
Townley‡ 07083
Townsbury 07863
Townsends Inlet (Part of Sea Isle City) 08243
Tranquility 07879
Tremley (Part of Linden) 07036
Tremley Point (Part of Linden) 07036
Trenton 08601-91
For specific ZIP Codes call (888) 275-8777, or your local postmaster.
Trenton Gardens 08610
Troy Hills 07054
Tuckahoe 08250
Tuckerton 08087
Turkey Point Corner 08349
Turnersville♦ 08012
Tuttles Corner 07826
Twin Rivers♦ 08520
Tyler Park‡ 07047
Ukrainian Village 08873
Union, *Hunterdon* (Twp) 08802
Union, *Union*♦ 07083
Union Beach 07735
Unionburg 07083
Union Center‡ 07083
Union City 07087
Union Hill 07801
Union Mills 08060
Union Square (Part of Elizabeth)‡ 07201
Uniontown 08865
Union Valley 08512
Union Village 07922
Unionville 08060
United States Army Armament Research, Development and Engineering Center 07806
Upper (Twp) 08250
Upper Deerfield (Twp) 08313
Upper Freehold (Twp) 08501
Upper Greenwood Lake 07421
Upper Mohawk 07871
Upper Montclair‡ 07043
Upper Montvale (Part of Montvale) 07645
Upper Pittsgrove (Twp) 08318
Upper Saddle River 07458
Uptown (Part of Hoboken)‡ 07030
Vail 07832
Vailsburg (Part of Newark)‡ 07106
Valentine 08817
Valley‡ 07470
Vanhiseville 08527
Vasa Home 07840
Vauxhall 07088
Ventnor City 08406
Ventnor Heights (Part of Ventnor City) 08406
Verga 08093
Vernon 07462
Vernoy 07830
Verona♦ 07044
Veterans Affairs Medical Center (Part of East Orange) 07018
Victoria 08344
Victory Gardens 07801
Victory Lakes 08094
Vienna 07880
Vienna Gardens 08213
Villas♦ 08251
Vincentown 08088
Vineland 08360
Voorhees 08043
Voorhees Corner 08822
Vulcanite (Part of Alpha) 08865
Wading River 08215
Waldwick 07463
Wall 07719
Wallington 07057
Wallpack Center 07881
Wallworth Park 08002
Walnford 08501
Walnut Valley 07832
Walpack (Twp) 07881
Wanamassa♦ 07712
Wanaque 07465
Wanaque-Midvale (Part of Wanaque) 07465
Wantage (Twp) 07461
Waretown♦ 08758
Warners (Part of Linden) 07036
Warren 07059
Warren Glen 08804
Warren Grove 08005
Warren Point (Part of Fair Lawn)‡ 07410
Washington, *Bergen* (Twp) 07675
Washington, *Burlington* (Twp) 08215
Washington, *Gloucester* (Twp) 08080
Washington, *Mercer* (Twp) 08691
Washington, *Morris* (Twp) 07853
Washington, *Warren* 07882
Washington Corners 07945
Washington Crossing 08560
Washington Park (Part of Newark)‡ 07102
Washington Street (Part of Hoboken)‡ 07030
Washington Valley 07960
Watchung 07060
Waterford (Twp) 08004
Waterford Works 08089
Waterloo 07874
Watsessing‡ 07003
Wayne♦ 07470*
07474†
Wayne Towne Center 07470
Wayside 07712
Wedgewood 08071
Weehawken♦ 07087
Weekstown 08037
Weequahic (Part of Newark) 07112
Wellington Park 08077
Wellwood (Part of Merchantville) 08109
Wenonah 08090
Wescoatville 08037
West (Part of Newark)‡ 07103
West Allenhurst 07711
Westampton (Twp) 08060
West Amwell (Twp) 08530
West Atco 08004
West Atlantic City 08234
West Belmar♦ 07719
West Berlin 08091
Westboro (Part of Red Bank)‡ 07701
West Caldwell♦ 07006-07
For specific ZIP Codes call (888) 275-8777, or your local postmaster.
West Cape May 08204
West Carteret (Part of Carteret) 07008
West Collingswood 08107
West Collingswood Heights 08059
West Creek 08092
West Deal 07712
West Deptford (Twp) 08086
West End (Part of Long Branch)‡ 07740
West End (Part of Woodbury) 08096
West Englewood‡ 07666
West Farms 07727
Westfield 07090*
07091†
West Freehold♦ 07728
West Grove 07753
West Haddonfield (Part of Haddonfield) 08033
West Hudson (Part of Kearny)‡ 07032
West Keansburg 07734
West Long Branch 07764
West Mahwah 07430
West Mantoloking 08723
West Milford 07480
Westmont 08108
West Moorestown 08057
West New York 07093
Weston (Part of Manville) 08835
Westons Mills (Part of New Brunswick) 08816
West Orange♦ 07052
West Paterson 07424
West Point Island (Part of Lavallette) 08735
West Portal 08802
West Side (Part of Hoboken)‡ 07304
West Side (Part of Jersey City)‡ 07304
West Trenton 08628
West Tuckerton 08087
West View (Part of Ridgefield Park) 07660
West Village 08302
Westville 08093
Westville Grove 08093
West Wildwood 08260
West Windsor (Twp) 08550
Westwood 07675
Weymouth (Twp) 08317
Weymouth 08330
Whale Beach 08248
Wharton 07885
Wheatland 08759
Whippany 07981
White (Twp) 07823
Whitehall 07821
White Horse♦ 08610
Whitehouse 08888
Whitehouse Station♦ 08889
White Meadow Lake♦ 07866
White Rock Lake 07439
Whitesbog 08015
Whitesboro 08252
Whitesville, *Monmouth* 07753
Whitesville, *Ocean* 08527
Whiting 08759
Whitman Park (Part of Camden) 08104
Whitman Square 08012
Wickatunk 07705
Wilburtha 08628
Wildwood 08260
Wildwood Crest 08260
Williamstown♦ 08094
Williamstown Junction 08009
Willingboro♦ 08046
Willowbrook Mall 07470
Willowdale 08003
Willow Grove 08344
Windsor 08561
Winfield 07036
Winslow 08095
Winslow Junction 08095
Wonder Lake 07480
Woodbine 08270
Woodbridge♦ 07095
Woodbridge Center 07095
Woodbridge Oaks 08830
Woodbury 08096
Woodbury Gardens 08096
Woodbury Heights 08097
Woodcliff‡ 07047
Woodcliff Lake 07675
Woodcrest‡ 08003
Woodglen 07830
Woodland (Twp) 08019
Woodland Ridge 07801
Woodlynne 08107
Woodmere 08527
Woodport 07885
Wood-Ridge 07075
Woodruff 08302
Woods Tavern 08876
Woodstock 07438
Woodstown 08098
Woodstream 08053
Woodsville 08525
Woolwich (Twp) 08085
Wortendyke (Part of Midland Park) 07432
Wrights Mill 08343
Wrightstown 08562
Wrightsville, *Burlington* 08077
Wrightsville, *Monmouth* 08501
Wyckoff♦ 07481
Wyckoff Mills 07728
Wyckoffs Mills 08512
Wykertown 07826
Yardville 08620
Yardville Heights 08620
Yellow Frame 07860
Yorktown 08098
Zarephath 08890
Zion 08558

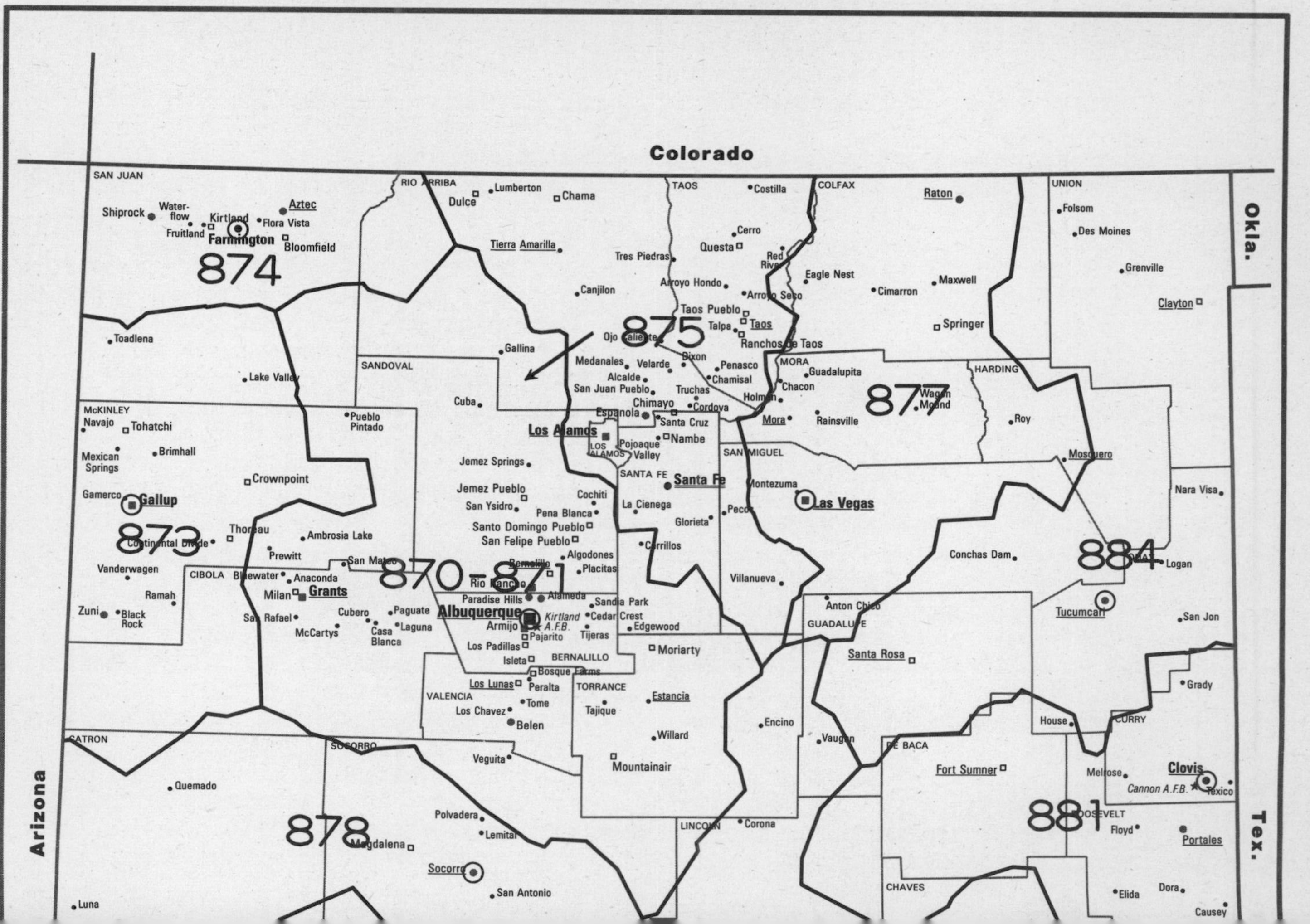

Colorado
Okla.
Tex.
Arizona
874
875
877
873
870-871
878
881
884
SAN JUAN
RIO ARRIBA
TAOS
COLFAX
UNION
HARDING
MORA
SAN MIGUEL
SANTA FE
LOS ALAMOS
SANDOVAL
McKINLEY
CIBOLA
BERNALILLO
VALENCIA
TORRANCE
GUADALUPE
CURRY
CHAVES
LINCOLN
CATRON
Shiprock
Water-flow
Fruitland
Kirtland
Farmington
Flora Vista
Aztec
Bloomfield
Toadlena
Lake Valley
Crownpoint
Navajo
Tohatchi
Mexican Springs
Brimhall
Gallup
Gamerco
Vanderwagen
Ramah
Zuni
Black Rock
Prewitt
Anaconda
Milan
Grants
Ambrosia Lake
McCartys
Cubero
Paguate
Laguna
Casa Blanca
Pueblo Pintado
Dulce
Lumberton
Chama
Tierra Amarilla
Gallina
Cuba
Canjilon
Tres Piedras
Costilla
Cerro
Questa
Arroyo Hondo
Taos
Taos Pueblo
Talpa
Medanales
Velarde
Alcalde
San Juan Pueblo
Chimayo
Santa Cruz
Truchas
Cordova
Penasco
Chamisal
Chacon
Guadalupita
Eagle Nest
Cimarron
Maxwell
Springer
Raton
Folsom
Des Moines
Grenville
Clayton
Roy
Rainsville
Mora
Nara Visa
Logan
San Jon
Conchas Dam
Las Vegas
Glorieta
Santa Fe
Nambe
Pojoaque Valley
La Cienega
Los Alamos
Cochiti
Pena Blanca
Santo Domingo Pueblo
San Felipe Pueblo
Algodones
Placitas
Jemez Springs
Jemez Pueblo
San Ysidro
Paradise Hills
Albuquerque
Kirtland A.F.B.
Armijo
Pajarito
Los Padillas
Isleta
Sandia Park
Cedar Crest
Tijeras
Edgewood
Moriarty
Peralta
Los Lunas
Tome
Los Chavez
Belen
Estancia
Willard
Tajique
Mountainair
Veguita
Villanueva
Santa Rosa
Encino
Corona
Fort Sumner
House
Grady
Clovis
Cannon A.F.B.
Floyd
Portales
Dora
Elida
Causey
Lemitar
Polvadera
San Antonio
Quemado
Luna

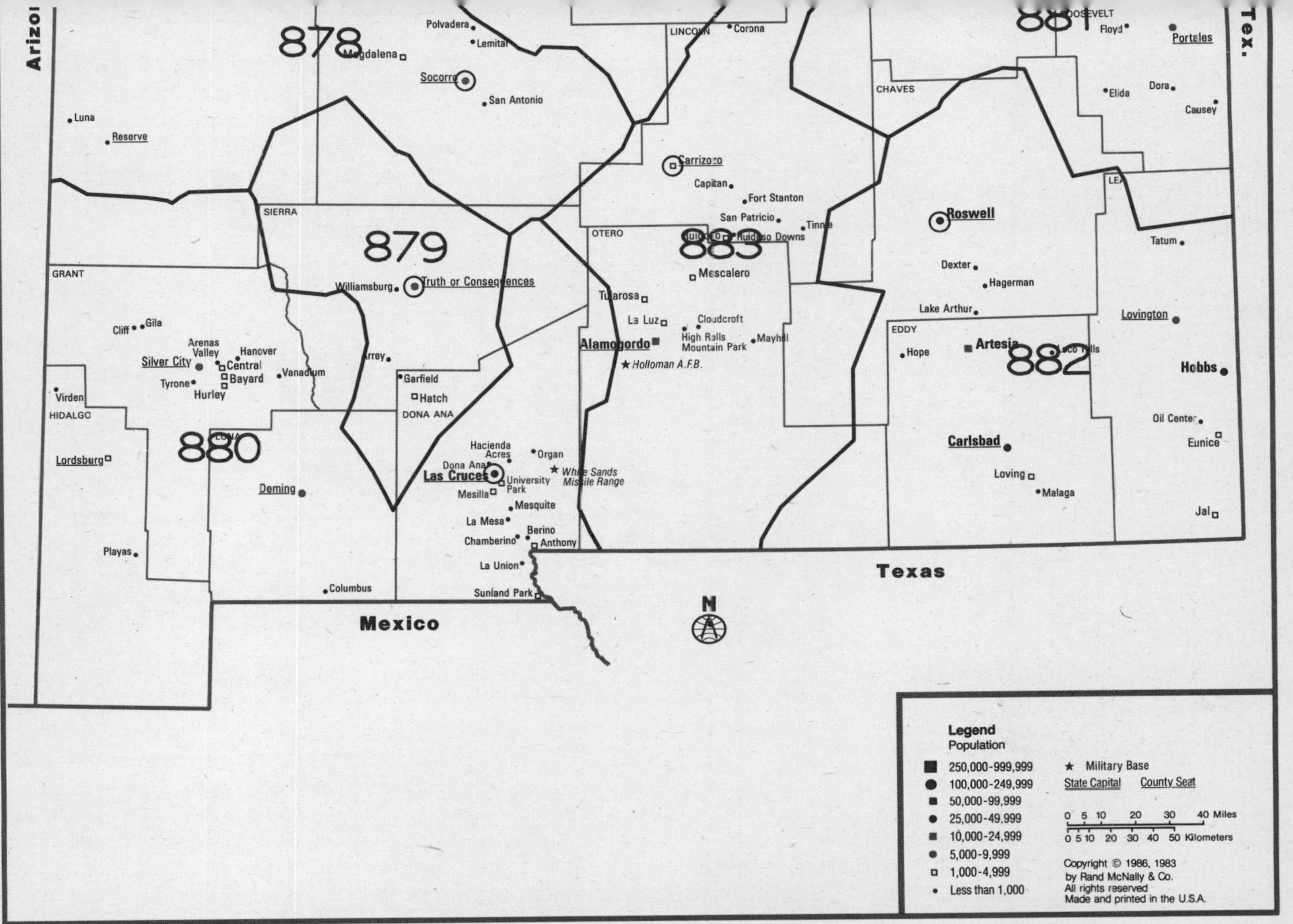
Arizo
Tex.
Texas
Mexico
878
879
880
881
882
883
Polvadera
Lemitar
Magdalena
Socorro
San Antonio
Luna
Reserve
LINCOLN
Corona
ROOSEVELT
Floyd
Portales
CHAVES
Elida
Dora
Causey
Carrizozo
Capitan
Fort Stanton
San Patricio
Tinnie
Ruidoso Downs
LEA
Roswell
Tatum
SIERRA
GRANT
OTERO
Mescalero
Williamsburg
Truth or Consequences
Tularosa
Dexter
Hagerman
Lake Arthur
Lovington
La Luz
Cloudcroft
High Rolls
Mountain Park
Mayhill
Alamogordo
Holloman A.F.B.
EDDY
Hope
Artesia
Hobbs
Cliff
Gila
Arenas
Valley
Silver City
Hanover
Central
Bayard
Vanadium
Tyrone
Hurley
Arrey
Garfield
Hatch
Virden
HIDALGO
DONA ANA
LUNA
Lordsburg
Hacienda
Acres
Organ
Dona Ana
Las Cruces
University
Park
White Sands
Missile Range
Mesilla
Deming
Oil Center
Eunice
Carlsbad
Loving
Malaga
Mesquite
La Mesa
Berino
Chamberino
Anthony
Jal
Playas
La Union
Columbus
Sunland Park
N
Legend
Population
250,000-999,999
100,000-249,999
50,000-99,999
25,000-49,999
10,000-24,999
5,000-9,999
1,000-4,999
Less than 1,000
★ Military Base
State Capital
County Seat
0 5 10 20 30 40 Miles
0 5 10 20 30 40 50 Kilometers
Copyright © 1986, 1983
by Rand McNally & Co.
All rights reserved
Made and printed in the U.S.A.

Abbott 87747
Abeytas 87006
Abiquiu 87510
Abo 87036
Abuelo 87732
Academy (Part of Albuquerque)‡ 87109
87113
87122
87199
For specific ZIP Codes call (888) 275-8777, or your local postmaster.
Acoma 87049
Acoma Indian Reservation 87031
Acomita 87034
Acomita Lake♦ 87034
Adelino 87031
Adobe Acres 87105
Agua Fria 87501
Air Mail Facility (Part of Albuquerque)‡ 87119
Alameda 87114*
87184†
Alamillo 87831
Alamo 87825
Alamogordo 88310*
88311†
Alamo Navajo Indian Reservation 87825
Albert 87733
Albuquerque 87101-16
87118-23
87125-54
87176-99
For specific ZIP Codes call (888) 275-8777, or your local postmaster.
Alcalde♦ 87511
Algodones 87001
Alire 87518
Allison 87301
Alma 88039
Alpine Village 88345
Alto 88312
Amalia 87512
Ambrosia Lake 87020
Amistad 88410
Anaconda 87020
Ancho 88301
Angel Fire 87710
Angostura, *Dona Ana* 87937
Angostura, *Sandoval* 87001
Angostura, *Taos* 87579
Angus 88316
Animas 88020
Animas Valley Mall (Part of Farmington) 87401
Antelope Springs 87032
Anthony♦ 88021
Anton Chico 87711
Apache Creek 87830
Apache Park 88345
Apache Summit 88340
Apodaca 87527
Arabela 88351
Aragon 87820
Arch 88130
Arenas Valley 88022
Arkansas Junction 88240
Armijo 87105
Arrey 87930
Arroyo del Agua 87012
Arroyo Hondo 87513
Arroyo Seco 87514
Artesia 88210*
88211†
Artesia Camp 88347
Atoka 88210
Atrisco (Part of Albuquerque) 87105
Aurora, *Mora* 87734
Aurora, *San Miguel* 87583
Aztec 87410
Bacaville (Part of Belen) 87002
Bard 88411
Barelas (Part of Albuquerque) 87102
Barranca 87510
Bayard 88023
Beaverhead 87943
Becenti 87313
Belen 87002
Bell Ranch 88441
Bellview 88112
Bennett 88252
Bent 88314
Berino 88024
Bernal 87569
Bernalillo 87004
Bernardo 87006
Beulah 87745
Bibo 87014
Biklabito 87420
Bingham 87832
Bisti 87401
Black Forest (Part of Ruidoso) 88345
Black Lake 87734
Black River Village 88220
Black Rock♦ 87327
Blanchard 87569
Blanco 87412
Blanco Trading Post 87413
Bloomfield 87413
Bluewater, *Cibola* 87005
Bluewater, *Lincoln* 88351
Boles 88311
Boles Acres♦ 88311
Bonito 88341
Borica 88435
Bosque 87006
Bosque Farms 87068
Boys Ranch 87002
Brazos 87551
Bread Springs 87301
Brimhall 87310
Broadview 88112
Broadview Acres 87020
Buckeye 88260
Buckhorn 88025
Buena Vista 87712
Bueyeros 88415
Burnham 87401
Butterfield Park 88011
Caballo 87931
Cameron 88120
Campus (Part of Socorro)‡ 87801
Canada de los Alamos 87501
Canjilon 87515
Cannon Air Force Base 88103
Canon, *Sandoval* 87024
Canon, *Taos* 87571
Canoncito (rural), *Bernalillo* 87008
Canoncito (Canoncito Indian Reservation), *Bernalillo* 87026
Canoncito, *Rio Arriba* 87527
Canoncito, *San Miguel* 87745
Canoncito, *Santa Fe* 87505
Canoncito Indian Reservation 87026
Canones 87516
Canon Plaza 87581
Canova 87582
Canyoncito 87535
Capitan 88316
Caprock 88213
Capulin 88414
Carlsbad 88220*
88221†
Carnuel 87123
Carrizo 88345
Carrizozo 88301
Carson 87517
Casa Blanca♦ 87007
Casa Colorada 87002
Causey 88113
Cebolla 87518
Cedar Creek 88345
Cedar Crest 87008
Cedar Grove 87015
Cedar Hill 87410
Cedarvale 87009
Cedro Village 87059
Cerrillos 87010
Cerro 87519
Chacon 87713
Chama 87520
Chamberino 88027
Chamisal♦ 87521
Chamita 87566
Chaparral♦ 88021
Chapelle 87569
Chaperito 87701
Chelwood Park (Part of Albuquerque) 87112
Chical 87031
Chi Chil Tah 87326
Chili 87537
Chilili 87059
Chimayo♦ 87522
Chippeway Park 88317
Chloride 87943
Chupadero 87501
Church Rock 87311
Cimarron 87714
Clapham 88415
Claunch 87011
Clayton 88415
Cleveland 87715
Cliff 88028
Clines Corners 87070
Cloud Country Estates 88339
Cloudcroft 88317
Cloverdale 88020
Clovis 88101*
88102†
Cochiti Indian Reservation 87041
Cochiti Lake 87083
Cochiti Pueblo♦ 87072
Colonias 88435
Columbine 87556
Columbus 88029
Comanche Hill 88201
Conchas Dam 88416
Continental Divide 87312
Contreras 87028
Coolidge 87312
Corazon 87701
Cordillera 87732
Cordova 87523
Corona 88318
Coronado (Part of Santa Fe)‡ 87501*
87502†
Coronado Center (Part of Albuquerque) 87110
Corrales 87048
Coruco 87560
Costilla 87524
Cotton City 88020
Cottonwood (Part of Albuquerque)‡ 87187
Counselor 87018
Country Club Estates, *Bernalillo* 87114
Country Club Estates (Part of Ruidoso) 88345
Country Club Heights (Part of Ruidoso) 88345
Cowles 87573
Coyote 87012
Cree Meadows Heights (Part of Ruidoso) 88345
Crossroads 88114
Crownpoint♦ 87313
Cruzville 87830
Crystal 87328
Cuba 87013
Cubero 87014
Cuchillo 87901
Cuervo 88417
Cundiyo 87522
Cuyamungue♦ 87501
Dahlia 87711
Dalies 87031
Dalton Pass 87313
Datil 87821
Del Norte (Part of Ruidoso) 88345
Deming 88030*
88031†
Derry 87933
Des Moines 88418
DeVargas Station (Part of Santa Fe)‡ 87594
Dexter 88230
Dilia 87724
Dixon 87527
Dog Canyon Estates 88310
Domingo 87052
Dona Ana♦ 88032
Dora 88115
Double Crossing 88338
Downtown (Part of Albuquerque)‡ 87103
Dulce♦ 87528
Dunken 88344
Dunlap 88119
Duran 88301
Dusty 87943
Eagle Nest 87718
East Grand Plains 88201
East Pecos 87552
Edgewood 87015
El Alto 87732
El Ancon 87560
El Cerrito 87583
El Cerro 87031
Eldorado (Part of Albuquerque)‡ 87111
87154
87191
For specific ZIP Codes call (888) 275-8777, or your local postmaster.
Eldorado at Santa Fe♦ 87505
El Duende 87537
Elephant Butte 87935
Elephant Butte Estates 87935
El Gauche 87566
El Guique 87566
El Huerfano Trading Post 87413
Elida 88116
Elizabethtown 87718
Elk 88339
Elkins 88201
Elk Silver 88314
El Llanito 87004
El Llano, *Rio Arriba* 87532
El Llano, *San Miguel* 87701
El Morro 87034
El Oro 87732
El Portero 87522
El Porvenir 87731
El Prado 87529
El Pueblo 87560
El Rancho 87532
El Rancho Loma Linda 87579
El Rincon de los Trujillos 87522
El Rito 87530
El Turquillo 87722
El Vado 87575
El Valle 87521
Embudo 87531
Emplazado 87745
Encinal 87014
Encino 88321
Engele 87935
Ensenada 87575
Escabosa 87059
Escondida 87801
Espanola 87532-33
For specific ZIP Codes call (888) 275-8777, or your local postmaster.
Estaca 87566
Estancia 87016
Eunice 88231
Fairacres 88033
Fairview (Part of Espanola)‡ 87533
Farley 88422
Farmington 87401-02
87499
For specific ZIP Codes call (888) 275-8777, or your local postmaster.
Faywood 88034
Fence Lake 87315
Field 88124
Fierro 88041
Five Points‡ 87105
87121
87195
For specific ZIP Codes call (888) 275-8777, or your local postmaster.
Flora Vista♦ 87415
Florida 87801
Floyd 88118
Flume Canyon (Part of Ruidoso) 88345
Flying H 88339
Folsom 88419
Forest Heights (Part of Ruidoso) 88345
Forest Park 87008
Forrest 88427
Fort Bliss 79916
Fort Stanton 88323
Fort Sumner 88119
Fort Wingate 87316
Fort Wingate Depot Activity 87301
French Corners 87747
Fruitland 87416
Gabaldon 87701
Galisteo 87540
Gallegos 88426
Gallina 87017
Gallina Plaza 87017
Gallinas 87731
Gallup 87301-05
For specific ZIP Codes call (888) 275-8777, or your local postmaster.
Gamerco 87317
Garanbuio 87560
Garfield 87936
Garita 88421
Garrison 88132
Gary 88045
Gascon 87742
Gavilan 87029
Gila 88038
Gila Hot Springs 88061
Gladstone 88422
Glencoe 88324
Glenrio 88434
Glenwood 88039
Glorieta 87535
Gobernador 87412
Golden 87047
Golondrinas 87712
Gonzales Ranch 87560
Grady 88120
Gran Quivira 87036
Grants 87020
Greenfield 88230
Green Meadows (Part of Ruidoso) 88345
Greens Gap 87821
Grenville 88424
Grier 88101
Guachupangue 87532
Guadalupita 87722
Hachita 88040
Hacienda Acres 88011
Hagerman 88232
Hagerman Acres (Part of Carlsbad) 88220
Hanover 88041
Happy Valley 88220
Hatch 87937
Hayden 88410
Hernandez 87537
Highland (Part of Albuquerque)‡ 87108*
87198†
High Lonesome 88201
High Rolls 88325
Hill 88005
Hillburn City 88260
Hillsboro 88042
Hobbies 87059
Hobbs 88240-42
For specific ZIP Codes call (888) 275-8777, or your local postmaster.
Hoffman Town (Part of Albuquerque) 87112
Holloman Air Force Base 88330
Hollywood (Part of Ruidoso)‡ 88345
Holman 87723
Hondo 88336
Hooverville 88416
Hope 88250
Horse Springs 87821
Hospah 87313
Hot Springs 87731
Hot Springs Landing 87935
House 88121
Humble City 88240
Hurley 88043
Hyde Park Estates 87501
Idlewild 87718
Ilfeld 87538
Ima 88417
Indian Hills (Part of Ruidoso) 88345
Isleta♦ 87022
Isleta Indian Reservation 87022
Iyanbito 87316
Jacona 87501
Jaconita♦ 87501
Jal 88252
Jarales 87023
Jemez Indian Reservation 87024
Jemez Pueblo♦ 87024
Jemez Springs 87025
Jicarilla 88301
Jicarilla Apache Indian Reservation 87528
Jordan 88427
Jornada North 88012
Jornada South 88011
Juan Tomas 87059
June Acres 88011
Kenna 88122
Kingston 88042
Kirtland♦ 87417

Place	ZIP
Kirtland Air Force Base	87117
Knowles	88240
La Bolsa	87531
La Cienega♦	87501
La Constancia	87002
La Cueva, *Mora*	87712
La Cueva, *Santa Fe*	87535
La Fraqua	87560
Laguna♦	87026
Laguna Indian Reservation	87026
Lagunita	87560
La Jara	87027
La Joya, *Santa Fe*	87535
La Joya, *Socorro*	87028
La Junta	87531
Lake Arthur	88253
Lake Valley	87313
Lake View Pines	87718
Lakewood	88254
La Ladera	87031
La Loma	87724
La Luz♦	88337
Lama	87556
La Madera, *Rio Arriba*	87539
La Madera, *Sandoval*	87047
La Manga	87701
La Mesa	88044
La Mesilla	87532
Lamy	87540
La Plata	87418
La Puebla	87532
La Puente	87575
Las Collinas	88012
Las Cruces	88001
	88003-06
	88011-12
For specific ZIP Codes call (888) 275-8777, or your local postmaster.	
Las Dispensas	87745
La Senda	87544
Las Mochas	87579
Las Nutrias	87062
Las Palomas	87942
Las Placitas	87530
Las Tablas	87581
Las Tusas	87745
Las Vegas	87701
La Union	88021
La Villita	87511
Ledoux	87732
Lemitar	87823
Lesbia	88401
Levy	87752
Leyba	87560
Lincoln	88338
Lindrith	87029
Lingo	88123
Little Walnut Village	88061
Littlewater	87420
Llano	87543
Llano del Medio	87724
Llano Largo	87561
Llano Quemado	87557
Llaves	87027
Loco Hills	88255
Logan	88426
Lordsburg	88045
Los Alamos, *Los Alamos*♦	87544
Los Alamos, *San Miguel*	87745
Los Candelarias (Part of Albuquerque)	87107
Los Chavez♦	87002
Los Cordovas	87571
Los Duranes (Part of Albuquerque)	87104
Los Febres	87734
Los Griegos (Part of Albuquerque)	87107
Los Hueros	87734
Los Lentes (Part of Los Lunas)	87031
Los Luceros	87511
Los Lunas	87031
Los Montoyas	87701
Los Ojos	87551
Los Pachecos	87522
Los Padillas	87105
Los Pinos	81120
Los Ranchos	87101
Los Ranchos de Albuquerque	87107
Lost Lodge	88317
Los Trujillos	87002
Los Vigiles	87701
Lourdes	87701
Lovato	87560
Loving	88256
Lovington	88260
Lower La Posada	87552
Lower Nutria	87327
Lower Pueblo	87560
Lower Ranchito	87581
Lower Rociada	87742
Lower San Francisco Plaza	87830
Lucero	87736
Lucy	87063
Luis Lopez	87801
Lumberton	87528
Luna	87824
Lybrook	87013
Lyden	87582
McAlister	88427
McCartys	87049
McDonald	88262
McGaffey	87316
Macimiliano Luna	87701
McIntosh	87032
McNew	88220
Madrid	87010
Maes	87701
Magdalena	87825
Malaga	88263
Maljamar	88264
Mangas	87821
Mangas Springs	88061
Manuelitas	87745
Manuelito	87319
Manzano (Part of Albuquerque)‡	87112
	87153
	87192
For specific ZIP Codes call (888) 275-8777, or your local postmaster.	
Manzano, *Torrance*	87036
Mariano Lake	87301
Maxwell	87728
Mayhill	88339
Meadow Lake♦	87031
Medanales	87548
Melrose	88124
Mentmore	87319
Mesa Poleo	87012
Mescalero♦	88340
Mescalero Apache Indian Reservation	88340
Mesilla	88046
Mesilla Park (Part of Las Cruces)	88047
Mesilla Valley Mall (Part of Las Cruces)	88001
Mesita♦	87026
Mesquite	88048
Mexican Springs♦	87320
Miami	87729
Mid Valley Air Park	87031
Midway	88230
Miera	87059
Milagro	88321
Milan	87021
Mills	87730
Milnesand	88125
Mimbres	88049
Mimbres Hot Springs	88041
Mineral Hill	87701
Mission Park	87031
Mogollon	88039
Monero	87528
Monte Aplanado	87732
Monte Verde (Part of Angel Fire)	87710
Montezuma	87731
Montgomery Plaza Mall (Part of Albuquerque)	87110
Monticello	87939
Montoya	88401
Monument	88265
Moqino	87040
Mora	87732
Moriarty	87035
Mosquero	87733
Mountainair	87036
Mountain Park	88325
Mountain View, *Bernalillo*	87105
Mountain View, *Chaves*	88201
Mount Dora	88429
Mule Creek	88051
Nadine	88240
Nageezi	87037
Nambe♦	87501
Nambe Indian Reservation	87501
Nambe Pueblo	87501
Nara Visa	88430
Naschitti♦	87325
Navajo♦	87328
Navajo Dam	87419
Navajo Estates	87375
Navajo Indian Reservation	86515
Navajo Wingate Village	87311
Newcomb♦	87455
Newkirk	88431
New Laguna	87038
New York	87014
Nogal	88341
North Acomita Village♦	87034
North Carmen	87732
North Hurley	88043
North San Ysidro	87538
Nutrias	87575
Ocate	87734
Oil Center	88240
Ojito, *Rio Arriba*	87029
Ojito, *Taos*	87521
Ojitos Frios	87701
Ojo Amarillo♦	87417
Ojo Caliente, *Cibola*	87327
Ojo Caliente, *Taos*	87549
Ojo Feliz	87735
Ojo Sarco	87521
Old Albuquerque (Part of Albuquerque)‡	87104
Old Picacho	88033
Omega	87829
Organ	88052
Orogrande	88342
Oscuro	88301
Otis	88220
Paguate♦	87040
Pajarito, *Bernalillo*	87105
Pajarito, *Santa Fe*	87532
Pajarito Acres	87544
Paradise Hills♦	87114
Park Springs	87701
Pastura	88435
Paxton Springs	87020
Pecos	87552
Pena Blanca♦	87041
Penasco♦	87553
Penasco Blanco	87742
Pendaries	87742
Pep	88126
Peralta♦	87042
Perea	87316
Pescado	87327
Petaca	87554
Philadelphia	87014
Philmont	87714
Picacho	88343
Picuris	87553
Picuris Indian Reservation	87553
Pie Town	87827
Pilar	87571
Pine	87552
Pinedale	87301
Pinehill	87357
Pine View	87579
Pineywoods Estates	88375
Pino (Part of Albuquerque)‡	87114
	87120
For specific ZIP Codes call (888) 275-8777, or your local postmaster.	
Pinon	88344
Pinos Altos	88053
Pinoswells	87063
Pintada	88435
Placita, *Sierra*	87939
Placita, *Taos*	87579
Placitas, *Dona Ana*	87937
Placitas, *Rio Arriba*	87515
Placitas, *Sandoval*♦	87043
Playas	88009
Plaza Blanca	87551
Pleasant Hill	88135
Pleasanton	88039
Pojoaque Indian Reservation	87501
Pojoaque Valley♦	87501
Polvadera	87828
Ponderosa	87044
Ponderosa Heights (Part of Ruidoso)	88345
Ponderosa Pines	87059
Portales	88130
Pot Creek	87571
Potrero	87522
Prairieview	88260
Prewitt	87045
Progresso	87063
Pueblito	87566
Pueblitos	87002
Pueblo of Acoma	87034
Pueblo Pintado	87013
Puerto de Luna	88435
Punta de Agua	87036
Quarris Acres	88317
Quarteles	87532
Quay	88433
Queen	88220
Quemado	87829
Querinda Park	87558
Questa	87556
Radium Springs	88054
Ragland	88433
Rainsville	87736
Ramah	87321
Ramah Navajo Indian Reservation	87327
Ramon	88136
Ranchito	87571
Ranchitos	87532
Rancho Grande Estates	87830
Ranchos de Taos♦	87557
Ranchos Lake Conchas	88431
Ranchvale	88101
Raton	87740
Red Hill	87829
Red River	87558
Redrock, *Grant*	88055
Red Rock, *McKinley*	87420
Regina	87046
Rehoboth	87322
Rencona	87562
Reserve	87830
Ribera	87560
Richard J. Pino Station (Part of Albuquerque)	87193
Rincon	87940
Rinconada	87531
Rincon Montoso	87745
Rio Chiquito	87522
Rio Communities♦	87002
Rio Grande Estates	87002
Rio Lucio	87553
Rio Puerco	87064
Rio Rancho	87124*
	87174†
Rio West Mall (Part of Gallup)	87301
Rito de las Sillas	87064
Riverside, *Eddy*	88210
Riverside, *Grant*	88028
Riverside, *Lincoln*	88201
Road Forks	88045
Robin Hood Park	88339
Rociada	87742
Rock Canyon	87935
Rock Springs	87375
Rodarte	87561
Rodeo	88056
Rodey	87937
Rogers	88132
Romeroville	87701
Rosebud	88410
Roswell	88201*
	88202†
Roswell Mall (Part of Roswell)	88201
Rowe	87562
Roy	87743
Ruidoso	88345*
	88355†
Ruidoso Downs	88346
Rutheron	87551
Sabinal	87006
Sabinoso	87746
Sacramento	88347
St. Vrain	88133
Salem	87941
San Acacia	87831
San Antonio, *Bernalillo*	87008
San Antonio, *San Miguel*	87701
San Antonio, *Socorro*	87832
San Antonio de Padua del Rancho	87501
San Antonito	87047
Sanchez	87746
San Cristobal	87564
Sandia♦	87047
Sandia National Laboratory	87115
Sandia Indian Reservation	87004
Sandia Knolls	87047
Sandia Park	87047
Sandia Pueblo	87004
San Felipe Indian Reservation	87004
San Felipe Pueblo♦	87001
San Fidel	87049
San Francisco	87006
San Francisco Plaza	87830
San Geronimo	87701
San Ignacio, *Guadalupe*	88435
San Ignacio, *San Miguel*	87745
San Ildefonso Indian Reservation	87502
San Ildefonso Pueblo♦	87501
San Jon	88434
San Jose (Part of Albuquerque)	87102
San Jose (Part of Carlsbad)	88220
San Jose, *Rio Arriba*	87537
San Jose, *San Miguel*	87565
San Juan, *Grant*	88041
San Juan, *San Miguel*	87565
San Juan Indian Reservation	87566
San Juan Pueblo	87566
San Lorenzo	88041
San Luis	87013
San Mateo	87020
San Miguel, *Dona Ana*	88058
San Miguel, *Rio Arriba*	81120
San Miguel, *San Miguel*	87560
Sanostee♦	87461
San Pablo	87701
San Patricio	88348
San Pedro	87532
San Rafael, *Cibola*	87051
San Rafael, *San Miguel*	88400
San Sebastian	87505
Santa Ana Indian Reservation	87004
Santa Ana Pueblo♦	87004
Santa Clara	88026
Santa Clara Indian Reservation	87532
Santa Clara Pueblo♦	87532
Santa Cruz	87567
Santa Fe	87501-06
	87592-94
For specific ZIP Codes call (888) 275-8777, or your local postmaster.	
Santa Rosa	88435
Santa Teresa	88008
Santo Domingo Indian Reservation	87052
Santo Domingo Pueblo♦	87052
Santo Nino	87532
	87567
For specific ZIP Codes call (888) 275-8777, or your local postmaster.	
Santo Tomas	88044
San Ysidro	87053
Sapello	87745
Seama♦	87014
Seboyeta	87014
Sedan	88436
Sedillo	87059
Sena	87560
Seneca	88437
Separ	88045
Serafina	87569
Servilleta Plaza	87539
Seton Village	87505
Seven Lakes	87313
Seven Rivers	88254
Seven Springs	87025
Shady Brook	87571
Sheep Springs	87364
Shiprock♦	87420
Sierra Vista	88312
Sierra Vista Estates	87008
Sile	87041
Silver Acres	88061
Silver City	88061*
	88062†
Sipapu	87579
Sixmile Hill	88201
Sixteen Springs	88317
Skyline-Ganipa♦	87034
Smith Lake	87365

Place	ZIP
Socorro	87801
Sofia	88424
Soham	87565
Solano	87746
Sombrillo	87532
South Carmen	87732
South San Ysidro	87538
South Springs Acres	88201
Spencerville	87410
Springer	87747
Springstead	87301
Squirrel Springs	87325
Standing Rock	87313
Stanley	87056
Star Lake	87013
Stead	88415
Sumner Lake State Park	88119
Sunland Park	88063
Sunset	88343
Sunshine	88030
Sunspot	88349
Sun Valley	88312
Taiban	88134
Tajique	87057
Talpa	87557
Taos	87571
Taos Indian Reservation	87571
Taos Pueblo♦	87571
Taos Ski Valley	87525
Tatum	88267
Tecolote	87701
Tecolotito	87711
Tererro	87573
Tesuque♦	87574
Tesuque Indian Reservation	87501
Tesuque Pueblo	87501
Texico	88135
Thomas	88415
Thoreau	87323
Three Rivers	88352
Tierra Amarilla	87575
Tierra Monte	87742
Tijeras	87059
Timberon	88350
Tinian	87013
Tinnie	88351
Tinsley Crossing	88130
Tiptonville	87753
Toadlena	87455
Tocito	87461
Tohatchi♦	87325
Tohlakai	87325
Tolar	88134
Tome	87060
T-O Ranch	87740
Torreon, *Sandoval*	87013
Torreon, *Torrance*	87061
Tortugas	88047
Totavi	87544
Trampas	87576
Trementina	88439
Tres Piedras	87577
Tres Ritos	87579
Truchas	87578
Trujillo	87701
Truth or Consequences	87901
Tse Bonito	87301
Tucumcari	88401
Tularosa	88352
Turley	87412
Twin Forks Estates	88317
Twin Lakes	87301
Two Gray Hills	87325
Two Wells	87326
Tyrone	88065
University (Part of Albuquerque)‡	87196
University (Part of Portales)‡	88130
University Park♦	88003
Upper Anton Chico	87711
Upper Dilia	87724
Upper Nutria	87327
Upper Pueblo	87560
Upper Rociada	87742
Uptown (Part of Albuquerque)‡	87110
	87176
	87190

For specific ZIP Codes call (888) 275-8777, or your local postmaster.

Place	ZIP
Ute Mountain Indian Reservation	81334
Ute Park	87749
Vadito♦	87579
Vado	88072
Valdez	87580
Valencia♦	87031
Vallecitos, *Mora*	87715
Vallecitos, *Rio Arriba*	87581
Vallecitos de los Indios	87025
Valle Escondido	87571
Valmora	87750
Val Verde	87718
Vanadium	88023
Vanderwagen	87326
Vaughn	88353
Veguita	87062
Velarde	87582
Vermejo Park	87740
Via Linda (Part of Santa Fe)‡	87592
Villa Linda Mall (Part of Santa Fe)	87505
Villa Madonna	88312
Villanueva	87583
Virden	85534
Volcano Cliffs (Part of Albuquerque)	87105
Wagon Mound	87752
Walker (Part of Roswell)‡	88201
Waterfall	88317
Waterflow	87421
Watrous	87753
Weed	88354
Westgate Heights (Part of Albuquerque)	87105
West Las Vegas (Part of Las Vegas)	87701
White Horse	87013
White Lakes	87056
White Oaks	88301
White Rock, *Los Alamos*‡	87544
White Rock, *San Juan*	87313
White Sands Missile Range	88002
Whites City	88268
White Signal	88061
Whitetail	88340
Willard	87063
Williams Acres	87301
Williamsburg	87942
Willow Creek	88039
Winrock Center (Part of Albuquerque)	87110
Winston	87943
Wyoming Mall, The (Part of Albuquerque)	87112
Yah-Ta-Hey	87375
Yeso	88136
Youngsville	87064
Zamora	87059
Zia Indian Reservation	87053
Zia Pueblo♦	87053
Zuni♦	87327
Zuni Indian Reservation	87327

A (Part of New York)‡ 11358
Abbotts 14727
Academy (Part of Albany)‡ 12208
Academy, *Ontario* 14424
Accord 12404
Acidalia 12760
Acra 12405
Adams 13605
Adams Basin 14410
Adams Center♦ 13606
Adams Corners 10579
Adams Cove 13634
Adamsville 12827
Addison 14801
Addison Hill 16920
Adelphi (Part of New York)‡ 11238
Aden 12768
Adirondack 12808
Adrian 14823
Afton 13730
Afton Lake 13730
Air Mail Facility (Part of Buffalo) 14241
Airmont 10901
Airmont Heights (Part of Airmont) 10901
Akins Corners 12563
Akron 14001
Alabama 14003

Albany

12201-60
For specific ZIP Codes call (888) 275-8777, or your local postmaster.

Colleges & Universities

Albany Coll of Pharmacy of Union Univ 12208
Albany Law School of Union Univ 12208
Albany Medical Coll 12208
Coll of Saint Rose 12203
Regents Coll, Univ of the State of New York 12203
State Univ of New York 12222

Financial Institutions

Chase Manhattan Bank 12211
Fleet Bank 12207
Key Bank, NA 12207
Marine Midland Bank 12205
OnBank & Trust Co 12207
Trustco Bank, NA 12207

Hospitals

Albany Med Ctr 12208
St Peter's Hosp 12208

Hotels/Motels

The Desmond 12211
Holiday Inn, Turf on Wolf Road 12205
Marriott 12205
Omni 12207

Albany Medical Center (Part of Albany)‡ 12208
Albertson♦ 11507
Albia (Part of Troy) 12180
Albion (Town) 13302
Albion 14411
Alburg 12916
Alcove 12007
Alden 14004
Alden Center 14004
Alden Manor 11003
Alder Bend 12910
Alder Creek 13301
Alexander 14005
Alexander Corners 13650
Alexander Shopping Center (Part of Yonkers) 10710
Alexandria (Town) 13607
Alexandria Bay 13607
Alfred 14802
Alfred Station 14803
Allaben 12480
Allard Corners 12586
Allegany 14706
Allegany Indian Reservation 14081
Allen (Town) 14709
Allen Center 14735
Allens Hill 14469
Allentown, *Allegany* 14707
Allentown, *Saratoga* 12835
Allenwood 11021
Allerton (Part of New York)‡ 10467
Alligerville 12440
Alloway 14489
Alma 14715
Almond (Town) 14804
Almond 14804
Aloquin 14561
Alpine 14805
Alplaus 12008
Alps 12018
Alsen 12414
Altamont, *Franklin* (Town) 12986
Altamont, *Albany* 12009
Altay 14837
Altmar 13302
Alton 14413
Altona♦ 12910
Amagansett 11930
Amawalk 10501
Amber 13110
Amblerville 13843
Amboy, *Oswego* (Town) 13493
Amboy, *Onondaga* 13031
Amboy Center 13493
Amenia♦ 12501
Amenia Union 12501
Ames 13317
Amherst 14221
14225-26
14228
14231
For specific ZIP Codes call (888) 275-8777, or your local postmaster.
Amity, *Allegany* (Town) 14813
Amity, *Orange* 10990
Amity Harbor 11701
Amityville 11701
Amsdell Heights 14075
Amsterdam 12010
Ancram 12502
Ancramdale 12503
Andes 13731
Andover 14806
Andrea Park Estates 10598
Angelica 14709
Angola 14006
Angola on the Lake♦ 14006
Annadale (Part of New York) 10312
Annandale-on-Hudson 12504
Annsville, *Oneida* (Town) 13471
Annsville, *Westchester* 10566
Ansonia (Part of New York)‡ 10023
Antwerp 13608
Apalachin♦ 13732
Apex 13783
Appleton 14008
Apulia 13159
Apulia Station 13020
Aquebogue♦ 11931
Aqueduct 12308
Aquetuck 12143
Arcade 14009
Arcade Junction (Part of Arcade) 14009
Arcadia (Town) 14513
Arcadia Hills 10924
Archdale 12834
Archer Ave (Part of New York)‡ 11435
Archville 10510
Arden 10910
Ardonia 12515
Ardsley 10502
Ardsley-on-Hudson (Part of Irvington) 10503
Argusville 13459
Argyle 12809
Arietta (Town) 12139
Arkport 14807
Arkville 12406
Arkwright (Town) 14718
Arlington, *Dutchess*♦ 12603
Arlington (Part of New York) 10303
Arlyn Oaks 11758
Armonk♦ 10504
Armor 14075
Arnolds Mill 12037
Arrochar (Part of New York) 10305
Arthur Manor (Part of Scarsdale) 10583
Arthursburg 12533
Arverne (Part of New York) 11692
Ashantee 14414
Asharoken 11768
Ashford (Town) 14171
Ashford 14731
Ashford Hollow 14171
Ash Grove 12816
Ashland, *Chemung* (Town) 14894
Ashland, *Greene* 12407
Ashokan 12481
Ashville 14710
Ashville Bay 14710
Ashwood 14098
Aspenwood 12065
Aspinwall Corners 13650
Assembly Point 12845
Association Island 13651
Astoria (Part of New York) 11101-06
For specific ZIP Codes call (888) 275-8777, or your local postmaster.
Athens 12015
Athol 12810
Athol Springs 14010
Atlanta 14808
Atlantic Beach 11509
Atlantique 11706
Attica 14011
Attica Center 14011
Attlebury 12581
Atwater 13081
Atwell 13338
Atwood 12484
Auburn 13021*
13022†
Audubon, *Erie* 14068
Audubon (Part of New York)‡ 10032
Augusta 13425
Aurelius (Town) 13034
Auriesville 12072
Aurora, *Erie* (Town) 14052
Aurora, *Cayuga* 13026
Aurora Tract 13088
Au Sable (Town) 12944
Au Sable Chasm 12911
Au Sable Forks 12912
Austerlitz 12017
Ava 13303
Averill Park♦ 12018
Avoca 14809
Avon 14414
Axeville 14726
Axton Landing 12986
B (Part of New York)‡ 11414
Babcock Hill 13318
Babcock Lake 12138
Babylon 11702
Bacon Hill 12871
Baggs Corner 13601
Bainbridge 13733
Baiting Hollow 11933
Bakers Mills 12811
Bakerstand 14101
Balcom 14138
Balcom Beach 14777
Bald Mountain 12834
Baldwin, *Chemung* (Town) 14861
Baldwin, *Nassau*♦ 11510
Baldwin Harbor♦ 11510
Baldwin Heights (Part of Olean) 14760
Baldwin Place 10505
Baldwin Place Shopping Center 10505
Baldwinsville 13027
Ballina 13035
Ballston (Town) 12019
Ballston Center 12020
Ballston Lake 12019
Ballston Spa 12020
Balltown 14062
Balmat 13642
Balmville♦ 12550
Baltimore 13141
Bangall, *Dutchess* 12506
Bangall, *Onondaga* 13112
Bangor 12966
Bangor Station 12966
Bank Plaza‡ 11566
Barberville 12018
Barbourville 13754
Barcelona 14787
Barclay Heights (Part of Saugerties) 12477
Bardonia♦ 10954
Bardwells Mill 13438
Barker, *Broome* (Town) 13746
Barker, *Niagara* 14012
Barkers Grove 12154
Barkersville 12850
Barkertown 14836
Barnegat 12603
Barnerville 12092
Barnes Corners 13626
Barnes Hole 11930
Barneveld 13304
Barnum Island♦ 11558
Barre (Town) 14411
Barre Center 14411
Barrington (Town) 14837
Barrytown 12507
Barryville 12719
Bartlett 13440
Bartlett Corners 14468
Bartlett Hollow 13775
Barton 13734
Basket 12760
Basom 14013
Batavia (Town) 14020
Batavia 14020*
14021†
Batchellerville 12134
Bates 12469
Bath 14810
Bath Beach (Part of New York)‡ 11214
Bathgate (Part of New York)‡ 10457
Battenville 12834
Battery Park City (Part of New York) 10007
Baxter Estates 11050
Bay (Part of New York)‡ 11235
Bayberry 13088
Bayberry Dunes 11772
Bayberry Park (Part of New Rochelle) 10804
Bayberry Shopping Center 13088
Baychester (Part of New York)‡ 10469
Bay Park 11518
Bay Point 11963
Bayport♦ 11705
Bay Ridge (Part of New York)‡ 11220
Bay Shore♦ 11706
Bay Shores 13110
Bayside (Part of New York) 11361
Bayside Annex (Part of New York)‡ 11361
Bayswater (Part of New York) 11691
Bay Terrace (Part of New York)‡ 11360
Bay View, *Erie* 14075
Bayview, *Suffolk* 11971
Bayville 11709
Baywood♦ 11706
Beach Hampton 11930
Beach Ridge 14120
Beach Shopping Center (Part of Peekskill) 10566
Beachville 14807
Beacon 12508
Beacon Hill 12508
Beantown 14859
Bear Mountain 10911
Bearsville 12409
Beaver Brook 12764
Beaver Dam 12549
Beaverdam Lake-Salisbury Mills♦ 12553
Beaver Dams 14812
Beaver Falls 13305
Beaverkill 12758
Beaver Meadow 13832
Beaver River 13367
Beaver Valley 14812
Beckers Corners 12158
Becks Grove (Part of Rome) 13308
Bedell 12430
Bedford (Part of New York) 11210
Bedford, *Westchester*♦ 10506
Bedford Hills 10507
Bedford Park (Part of New York) 10458
Bedford-Stuyvesant (Part of New York) 11233
Beecher Corners 12442
Beechertown 13697
Beech Hill (Part of Yonkers) 10710
Beechhurst (Part of New York) 11357
Beechmont (Part of New Rochelle) 10804
Beechmont Woods (Part of New Rochelle) 10804
Beechwood (Part of Rochester)‡ 14609
Beekman (Town) 12570
Beekman 12533
Beekman Corners 13459
Beekmantown 12901
Beixedon Estates 11971
Belcher 12865
Belcoda 14546
Belden 13787
Belfast 14711
Belfort 13327
Belfort Heights (Part of New Hempstead) 10977
Belgium 13027
Bellaire (Part of New York) 11429
Belle Harbor (Part of New York) 11694
Belle Isle 13209
Bellerose, *Nassau*‡ 11426
Bellerose (Part of New York) 11001
Bellerose Terrace 11426
Belle Terre 11777
Belleview 14712
Belleville 13611
Bellevue, *Erie* 14225
Bellevue (Part of Schenectady) 12306
Bellevue Gardens 12151
Bellmont (Town) 12917
Bellmont Center 12920
Bellmore♦ 11710
Bellona 14415
Bellona (Gage) 14415
Bellow Corners 14171
Bellport 11713
Bellvale 10912
Bellville 14717
Belmont 14813
Belvidere 14813
Bemis Heights 12170
Bemus Point 14712
Benedict Beach 14464
Bennett Bridge 13302
Bennettsburg 14818
Bennetts Corner 14470
Bennettsville 13733
Bennington 14011
Benson 12134
Bensonhurst (Part of New York) 11223
Benson Mines 13690
Benton (Town) 14527
Benton Center 14527
Berea 12549
Bergen 14416
Bergen Beach (Part of New York) 11234
Bergen Beach, *Seneca* 14847
Bergen Park 11746
Bergholtz 14304
Berkshire, *Fulton* 12078
Berkshire, *Onondaga* 13066
Berkshire, *Tioga* 13736
Berkshire Terrace 10512
Berlin 12022
Berne 12023
Bernhards Bay 13028
Berryville 12068
Berwyn 13084
Best 12018
Bethany 14054
Bethel, *Dutchess* 12567
Bethel, *Sullivan* 12720
Bethel Corners 13111
Bethel Grove 14850
Bethford 14219
Bethlehem (Town) 12054
Bethlehem Center 12077
Bethlehem Heights 12161
Bethpage♦ 11714
Beukendaal 12302
Beverly Inn Corners 13315
Bible School Park (Part of Johnson City) 13737
Bidwell (Part of Buffalo) 14222
Big Brook 13486
Big Flats♦ 14814
Big Fresh Pond 11968
Big Indian 12410
Big Island 10924
Big Moose 13331
Big Tree 14219
Big Wolf Lake 12986
Billings 12510
Billington Bay 13030
Billington Heights♦ 14052
Biltmore Shores 11758
Bingham Mills 12526
Binghamton (Town) 13902
Binghamton 13901-05
For specific ZIP Codes call (888) 275-8777, or your local postmaster.

Conn.
SAME SCALE AS MAIN MAP
©R. McN. & CO.
East Marion
Orient
Greenport
Shelter Island Hts.
Southold
Peconic
Shelter Island
Cutchogue
Mattituck
Noyac
Sag Harbor
Freetown
Amagansett
New Suffolk
SUFFOLK
East Hampton
Bridgehampton
Water Mill
Southampton
Flanders
Shinnecock Hills
Hampton Bays
East Quogue
Westhampton Beach
Rocky Point
Sound Beach
Miller Place
Port Jefferson
Wading River
Selden
Coram
Riverhead
Brentwood
Holbrook
Deer Pk.
NASSAU
Melville
Hicksville
Wyandanch
Amityville
Huntington
East Northport
Smithtown
Hauppauge
Commack
1
2
3
4
5
6
7
Legend
Population
1,000,000 and over
250,000-999,999
100,000-249,999
50,000-99,999
25,000-49,999
10,000-24,999
5,000-9,999
1,000-4,999
Less than 1,000
Military Base
State Capital
County Seat
0 5 10 20 30 Miles
0 5 10 20 30 40 Kilometers
Copyright © 1986, 1983
by Rand McNally & Co.
All rights reserved
Made and printed in the U.S.A.
Canada
Roosevelt Beach
Olcott
Wilson
Barker
Lyndonville
ORLEANS
NIAGARA
Newfane
Ransomville
Youngstown
Lewiston
Colonial Village
Lockport
Middleport
Gasport
Albion
Medina
Holley
Town of Niagara
Niagara Falls
Sanborn
S. Lockport
St. Johnsburg
Sandy Beach
North Tonawanda
Tonawanda
Town of Tonawanda
Kenmore
Amherst
Williamsville
Cheektowaga
Buffalo
Depew
Lancaster
Sloan
W. Seneca
Elma
Lackawanna
Blasdell
Orchard Park
Mount Vernon
Wanakah
Lake View
Derby
Armor
Hamburg
ERIE
East Aurora
Eden
North Boston
Angola on the Lake
Lake Erie Beach
Angola
Boston
Colden
Holland
Farnham
Brant
North Collins
Silver Creek
Collins
Collins Center
Sardinia
Dunkirk
Forestville
Fredonia
Brocton
Portland
CHAUTAUQUA
Lily Dale
Cassadaga
Westfield
South Dayton
Cattaraugus
CATTARAUGUS
Machias
Yorkshire
Delevan
Arcade
Ripley
Mayville
Sinclairville
Cherry Creek
Ellicottville
Franklinville
Maple Springs
Sunset Bay
Sherman
Gerry
Ellington
Little Valley
East Randolph
Randolph
Kill Buck
Salamanca
Findley Lake
Greenhurst
Fluvanna
Falconer
Kennedy
Lakewood
Jamestown
Celoron
Frewsburg
Panama
Clymer
Allegany
Olean
Limestone
Westons Mills
Portville
Hinsdale
GENESEE
Oakfield
Elba
Alden
East Pembroke
Batavia
Corfu
Le Roy
Alexander
Darien Center
Attica
WYOMING
Wyoming
Warsaw
Perry
Silver Springs
Gainesville
Castile
ALLEGANY
Fillmore
Houghton
Rushford
Belfast
Angelica
Cuba
Belmont
Friendship
Scio
Wellsville
Richburg
Bolivar
Stannards
Whitesville
Hamlin
Hilton
MONROE
Brockport
Spencerport
Churchville
North Chili
Chili Center
Gates
Greece
Rochester
Irondequoit
Brighton
Penfield
Fairport
E. Rochester
W. Henrietta
Scottsville
Honeoye Falls
Victor
Caledonia
Pavilion
Avon
York
Lima
Livonia
Geneseo
Hemlock
Leicester
Mount Morris
LIVINGSTON
Nunda
Dansville
Canaseraga
Arkport
Almond
Alfred
Andover
Webster
WAYNE
Walworth
Sodus
North Rose
Marion
Palmyra
Lyons
Newark
Clyde
Savannah
Manchester
Shortsville
Clifton Sprs.
Phelps
Waterloo
Canandaigua
Holcomb
Gorham
Honeoye
ONTARIO
Rushville
YATES
Dresden
Penn Yan
Springwater
Naples
Keuka Park
Wayland
Cohocton
Atlanta
Prattsburg
Dundee
STEUBEN
Avoca
North Hornell
Hornell
Canisteo
Hammondsport
SCHUYLER
Watkins Glen
Burdett
Montour Falls
Odessa
Bath
Savona
CHEMUNG
Horseheads
Breesport
Elmira Hts.
Elmira
West Elmira
Southport
Big Flats
Corning
Gang Mills
South Corning
East Corning
Addison
Woodhull
Pine City
Oswego
Minetto
Fulton
Fair Haven
Hannibal
Red Creek
Wolcott
CAYUGA
Cato
Weedsport
Port Byron
Seneca Falls
Cayuga
Auburn
Union Springs
Aurora
Geneva
SENECA
Seneca Army Depot
Moravia
Interlaken
Lodi
Groton
Jacksonville
TOMPKINS
Cayuga Hts.
Ithaca
Newfield
Van Etten
Spencer
TIOGA
Tioga Cen.
Waverly
Pennsylvania
ORANGE
Greenwood Lake
PASSAIC
Ringwood
N.J.
Wanaque
MORRIS
Pompton Lakes
Wayne
Paterson
ESSEX
Montclair
Bloomfield
W. Orange
Orange
S. Orange
Maplewood
Union
Cranford
Linden
Clark
Rahway
Colonia
MIDDLESEX
Metuchen
Can.
CLINTON
Champlain
Rouses Point
Mooers
Fort Covington
Chateaugay
Burke
Massena
Raymondville
Waddington
Brushton
Malone
Chazy
West Chazy
ST. LAWRENCE
Norfolk
Brasher Falls
Winthrop
Madrid
Norwood
FRANKLIN
Lyon Mountain
Dannemora
Morrisonville
Plattsburgh
Plattsburgh A.F.B.
Cadyville
Ogdensburg
Potsdam
St. Regis Falls
Heuvelton
Parishville
Rensselaer Falls
Canton
Hannawa Falls
Redford
Peru
Morristown
Hermon
Keeseville
Hammond
Richville
Paul Smiths
Gouverneur
Edwards
Wilmington
Au Sable Forks
Willsboro Point
Bloomingdale
Jay
Saranac Lake
Willsboro
Ray Brook
Lake Placid
Lewis
Elizabethtown
Vt.
Alexandria Bay
Redwood
Clayton
Theresa
Antwerp
Newton Falls
Oswegatchie
Star Lake
Tupper Lake
Westport
Cape Vincent
LaFargeville
JEFFERSON
Philadelphia
Harrisville
LEWIS
Three Mile Bay
Chaumont
Evans Mills
Black River
Deferiet
Natural Bridge
Dexter
Calcium
Herrings
Felts Mills
Brownville
Carthage
West Carthage
Watertown
Sackets Harbor
Adams Center
Copenhagen
Castorland
Croghan
HERKIMER
HAMILTON
ESSEX
Mineville
Witherbee
Moriah
Port Henry
Long Lake
Newcomb
Crown Point
Schroon Lake
Ticonderoga
©R. McN. & CO.

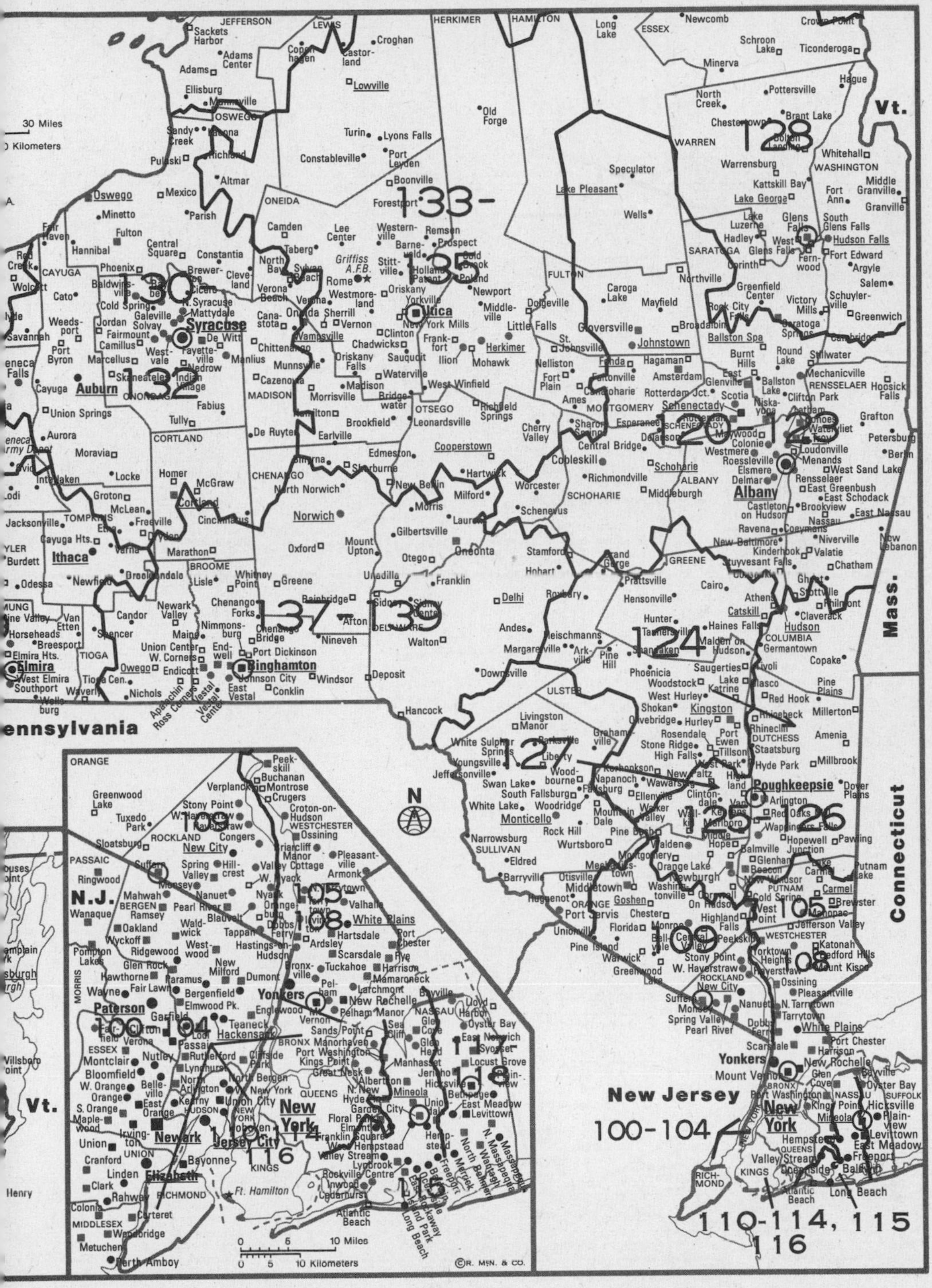

JEFFERSON
LEWIS
HERKIMER
HAMILTON
ESSEX
Sackets Harbor
Adams Center
Adams
Ellisburg
Croghan
Castorland
Copenhagen
Lowville
Old Forge
Long Lake
Newcomb
Schroon Lake
Crown Point
Ticonderoga
Minerva
Hague
North Creek
Pottersville
Brant Lake
Chestertown
Bolton Landing
128
Vt.
30 Miles
Kilometers
OSWEGO
Sandy Creek
Lacona
Turin
Lyons Falls
Pulaski
Richland
Constableville
Port Leyden
Altmar
Boonville
Forestport
133-
Speculator
Lake Pleasant
Wells
WARREN
Warrensburg
Whitehall
WASHINGTON
Kattskill Bay
Lake George
Fort Ann
Middle Granville
Granville
Oswego
Mexico
Parish
Minetto
Fulton
Fair Haven
Hannibal
Central Square
Constantia
ONEIDA
Camden
Lee Center
Western-ville
Remsen
Taberg
Barneveld
Prospect
Griffiss A.F.B.
Rome
Stittville
135
Holland Patent
Cold Brook
Poland
Newport
Glens Falls
South Glens Falls
Hudson Falls
Fort Edward
Argyle
SARATOGA
Lake Luzerne
Hadley
West Glens Falls
Fernwood
Corinth
Salem
CAYUGA
Phoenix
Brewerton
Cleveland
North Bay
Sylvan Beach
Verona Beach
Verona
Oneida
Westmoreland
Oriskany
Yorkville
Utica
Sherrill
Vernon
New York Mills
Middleville
FULTON
Dolgeville
Caroga Lake
Northville
Mayfield
Greenfield Center
Victory Mills
Schuylerville
Greenwich
Wolcott
Cato
Baldwinsville
30
Cold Spring
N. Syracuse
Mattydale
Galeville
Solvay
Syracuse
Jordan
Weedsport
Port Byron
Fairmount
Camillus
Westvale
Fayetteville
De Witt
Manlius
Canastota
Chittenango
Wampsville
Clinton
Chadwicks
Frankfort
Ilion
Mohawk
Herkimer
Little Falls
Gloversville
St. Johnsville
Johnstown
Broadalbin
Rock City Falls
Ballston Spa
Saratoga Springs
Stillwater
Cambridge
Savannah
Marcellus
Skaneateles
132
Nedrow
Indian Village
Munnsville
Cazenovia
Oriskany Falls
Sauquoit
Waterville
West Winfield
Nelliston
Fort Plain
Fonda
Fultonville
Hagaman
Amsterdam
Burnt Hills
Round Lake
Mechanicville
RENSSELAER
Hoosick Falls
Seneca Falls
Cayuga
Auburn
ONONDAGA
Fabius
MADISON
Madison
Morrisville
Bridgewater
Richfield Springs
OTSEGO
Canajoharie
Ames
MONTGOMERY
Rotterdam Jct.
Schenectady
Glenville
East Glenville
Ballston Lake
Scotia
Niskayuna
Clifton Park
Union Springs
Tully
Hamilton
Brookfield
Leonardsville
Cherry Valley
Sharon Springs
Esperance
120-129
Waterford
Troy
Grafton
Petersburg
Berlin
Aurora
CORTLAND
De Ruyter
Earlville
Cooperstown
Central Bridge
Delanson
Maywood
Colonie
Westmere
Roessleville
Loudonville
Menands
Moravia
Edmeston
Sherburne
Smyrna
Cobleskill
Schoharie
West Sand Lake
Interlaken
Locke
Homer
McGraw
CHENANGO
North Norwich
Hartwick
Worcester
Richmondville
ALBANY
Elsmere
Delmar
Albany
Rensselaer
East Greenbush
East Schodack
Groton
Cortland
New Berlin
Milford
SCHOHARIE
Middleburgh
Castleton on Hudson
Brookview
Nassau
East Nassau
Lodi
McLean
Freeville
Cincinnatus
Norwich
Morris
Schenevus
Laurens
Gilbertsville
Ravena
Coeymans
Niverville
New Lebanon
Jacksonville
TOMPKINS
Etna
Dryden
Cayuga Hts.
Varna
Ithaca
Marathon
Oxford
Mount Upton
Otego
Oneonta
Stamford
Grand Gorge
GREENE
New Baltimore
Kinderhook
Valatie
Chatham
Stuyvesant Falls
Burdett
Newfield
Brooktondale
BROOME
Whitney Point
Greene
Unadilla
Franklin
Hobart
Prattsville
Cairo
Coxsackie
Ghent
Odessa
Lisle
Bainbridge
Sidney
Sidney Center
Roxbury
Hensonville
Athens
Stottville
Philmont
Mass.
Van Etten
Candor
Newark Valley
Chenango Forks
137-139
Afton
DELAWARE
Delhi
Hunter
Tannersville
Catskill
Claverack
Horseheads
Spencer
Maine
Nimmonsburg
Chenango Bridge
Nineveh
Andes
Fleischmanns
Haines Falls
Hudson
COLUMBIA
Germantown
Breesport
Elmira Hts.
TIOGA
Union Center
W. Corners
Endwell
Port Dickinson
Walton
Margaretville
Arkville
Pine Hill
124
Palenville
Malden on Hudson
Elmira
West Elmira
Southport
Owego
Endicott
Binghamton
Johnson City
Windsor
Deposit
Downsville
Phoenicia
Saugerties
Tivoli
Copake
Tioga Cen.
Nichols
Waverly
Wellsburg
Apalachin
Ross Corners
Vestal
Vestal Center
East Vestal
Conklin
ULSTER
Woodstock
West Hurley
Lake Katrine
Glasco
Red Hook
Pine Plains
Shokan
Kingston
Millerton
Pennsylvania
Hancock
Livingston Manor
Olivebridge
Hurley
Rhinebeck
Rhinecliff
Rosendale
Port Ewen
DUTCHESS
Amenia
White Sulphur Springs
Parksville
Grahamsville
Stone Ridge
Tillson
Staatsburg
Youngsville
127
Liberty
High Falls
West Park
Hyde Park
Millbrook
Jeffersonville
Swan Lake
Woodbourne
Kerhonkson
Napanoch
New Paltz
Highland
Poughkeepsie
Dover Plains
South Fallsburg
Fallsburg
Wawarsing
Ellenville
Clintondale
Arlington
White Lake
Woodridge
Walker Valley
Red Oaks Mill
Monticello
Mountain Dale
Wallkill
Marlboro
Wappingers Falls
135-26
Narrowsburg
Rock Hill
Pine Bush
Milton
Hopewell Junction
Pawling
SULLIVAN
Wurtsboro
Walden
Hope
Balmville
Eldred
Montgomery
Orange Lake
Newburgh
Glenham
Beacon
Carmel
Putnam Lake
Barryville
Otisville
Middletown
Washingtonville
New Windsor
PUTNAM
Cornwall on Hudson
Cold Spring
Brewster
Huguenot
ORANGE
Goshen
Port Jervis
Chester
Highland Falls
West Point
105
Mahopac
Jefferson Valley
Unionville
Florida
Monroe
Central Valley
Bellvale
109
Peekskill
WESTCHESTER
Katonah
Bedford Hills
Mount Kisco
Pine Island
Warwick
Greenwood Lake
Stony Point
W. Haverstraw
ROCKLAND
New City
Yorktown Heights
Haverstraw
108
Ossining
Pleasantville
Suffern
Monsey
Spring Valley
Pearl River
Nanuet
N. Tarrytown
Tarrytown
White Plains
Dobbs Ferry
Scarsdale
Port Chester
Harrison
Yonkers
Mount Vernon
New Rochelle
Bayville
Glen Cove
Oyster Bay
SUFFOLK
New Jersey
BRONX
Port Washington
NASSAU
Kings Point
Hicksville
100-104
New York
Mineola
Plainview
Levittown
East Meadow
Hempstead
Freeport
Baldwin
QUEENS
Valley Stream
Oceanside
KINGS
RICHMOND
Atlantic Beach
Long Beach
110-114, 115
116
Connecticut

ORANGE
Greenwood Lake
Tuxedo Park
Sloatsburg
ROCKLAND
Stony Point
W. Haverstraw
Haverstraw
Congers
New City
Peekskill
Buchanan
Montrose
Crugers
Verplanck
Croton-on-Hudson
WESTCHESTER
Ossining
Briarcliff Manor
Pleasantville
Valley Cottage
Armonk
PASSAIC
Ringwood
Suffern
Spring Valley
Hillcrest
Monsey
W. Nyack
Nanuet
Nyack
Tarrytown
Valhalla
N.J.
Wanaque
Mahwah
BERGEN
Ramsey
Pearl River
Blauvelt
Orangeburg
Irvington
White Plains
Hartsdale
Port Chester
Oakland
Waldwick
Tappan
Dobbs Ferry
Ardsley
Wyckoff
West wood
Hastings-on-Hudson
Scarsdale
Rye
Pompton Lakes
Ridgewood
Glen Rock
New Milford
Dumont
Bronxville
Tuckahoe
Mamaroneck
Hawthorne
Paramus
Pelham
Larchmont
Bayville
MORRIS
Wayne
Fair Lawn
Bergenfield
Yonkers
New Rochelle
Lloyd Harbor
Paterson
Elmwood Pk.
Englewood
Mt. Vernon
Pelham Manor
NASSAU
Oyster Bay
Garfield
Teaneck
Sands Point
Sea Cliff
Glen Cove
East Norwich
100-104
Clifton
Lodi
Hackensack
BRONX
Manorhaven
Glen Head
Syosset
Little Falls
Verona
Passaic
Rutherford
Port Washington
Kings Point
Great Neck
Manhasset
Jericho
Locust Grove
ESSEX
Montclair
Nutley
Lyndhurst
Cliffside Park
Bloomfield
North Arlington
North Bergen
Hicksville
Plainview
W. Orange
Belleville
Kearny
New York
QUEENS
N. New Hyde Park
Albertson
Mineola
Orange
East Orange
HUDSON
Union City
Garden City
Uniondale
Bethpage
East Meadow
S. Orange
Maplewood
Newark
Hoboken
New York
Floral Park
Elmont
Levittown
Irvington
Jersey City
Franklin Square
Hempstead
Union
UNION
West Hempstead
Valley Stream
Cranford
Bayonne
Lynbrook
Linden
Elizabeth
Rockville Centre
Oceanside
Baldwin
Freeport
Merrick
Wantagh
North Merrick
Massapequa
N. Massapequa
Clark
Rahway
RICHMOND
Ft. Hamilton
Inwood
Cedarhurst
Island Park
Colonia
Carteret
Atlantic Beach
Long Beach
MIDDLESEX
Woodbridge
Metuchen
Perth Amboy
0 5 10 Miles
0 5 10 Kilometers
©R. McN. & CO.

Vt.
Henry
Willsboro Point

Binghamton Plaza (Part of Binghamton) 13901
Bingley 13035
Binnewater 12401
Birchwood Estates 12184
Birdsall 14709
Birmingham Corners 13491
Bishopville 14807
Black Brook 12912
Black Corners 14062
Black Creek 14714
Blackmans Corners 12959
Black River 13612
Black Rock (Part of Buffalo) 14207
Blackwatch Hills 14450
Blakeley 14052
Blasdell 14219
Blauvelt♦ 10913
Bleecker 12078
Blenheim (Town) 12131
Bliss 14024
Bliss Corner 13470
Blockville 14710
Blodgett Mills 13738
Bloomerville 14809
Bloomfield, *Ontario* 14469
Bloomfield (Part of New York) 10314
Bloomingburg 12721
Bloomingdale 12913
Blooming Grove 10914
Bloomington 12411
Bloomville 13739
Blossvale 13308
Blue Mountain 12477
Blue Mountain Lake 12812
Blue Point♦ 11715
Blue Ridge, *Columbia* 12534
Blue Ridge, *Essex* 12855
Blue Stores 12526
Bluff Point 14478
Blythebourne (Part of New York)‡ 11219
Boardmanville (Part of Olean) 14760
Boght Corners 12047
Bohemia♦ 11716
Boiceville 12412
Bolivar 14715
Bolton 12824
Bolton Landing 12814
Bolts Corners 13147
Bombay 12914
Bon Air Heights (Part of Suffern) 10901
Bonney 13464
Bonni Castle 14590
Bonnie Crest (Part of New Rochelle) 10804
Bonny Lee Estates 12184
Boomertown 14710
Boonville 13309
Borden 14801
Border City 14456
Borodino 13152
Borough Hall (Part of New York)‡ 11424
Borough Park (Part of New York) 11219
Boston 14025
Boston Corners 12546
Botanical (Part of New York)‡ 10458
Bouckville 13310
Boughton Hill 14564
Boulevard (Part of New York)‡ 10459
Boulevard Mall 14226
Boultons Beach (Part of Sackets Harbor) 13685
Bouquet 12936
Bournes Beach 14787
Bovina (Town) 13740
Bovina Center 13740
Bowens Corners 13069
Bowerstown 13326
Bowling Green (Part of New York)‡ 10004
Bowmansville 14026
Boylston (Town) 13083
Boylston Center 13083
Boyntonville 12090
Boysen Bay 13039
Braddock Heights 14612
Bradford 14815
Bradley 12754
Braeside 12123
Brainard 12024
Brainards Corners 13315
Brainardsville 12915
Braman Corners 12053
Bramans Corners 12186
Bramanville 12092
Brambler Ridge 14450
Branchport 14418
Brandon (Town) 12966
Brandon Center 12966
Brandreth 12847
Brant 14027
Brantingham 13312
Brant Lake 12815
Brasher (Town) 13613
Brasher Center 13613
Brasher Falls 13613
Brasher Iron Works 13613
Brasie Corners 13642
Breakabeen 12122
Breesport 14816
Breezy Point (Part of New York) 11697
Brentwood♦ 11717
Brevoort (Part of New York)‡ 11216
Brewerton♦ 13029
Brewster 10509
Brewster Heights 10509
Brewster Hill♦ 10509
Briarcliff Manor 10510
Briarwood (Part of New York) 11435
Bridge (Part of Niagara Falls)‡ 14305
Bridgehampton♦ 11932
Bridgeport♦ 13030
Bridgeville 12701
Bridgewater 13313
Brier Hill 13614
Brighton, *Franklin* (Town) 12970
Brighton (Part of New York)‡ 11235
Brighton (Part of Rochester)‡ 14610
Brighton, *Monroe*♦ 14610
Brighton, *Otsego* 13439
Brighton Beach (Part of New York) 11235
Brightside 13436
Brightwaters 11718
Brinckerhoff♦ 12524
Brisben 13830
Briscoe 12783
Bristol 14469
Bristol Center 14424
Bristol Springs 14512
Broadacres 13905
Broadalbin 12025
Broad Channel (Part of New York)‡ 11693
Broadway (Part of New York)‡ 11106
Broadway Mall 11801
Brockport 14420
Brockville 14411
Brocton 14716
Brodhead 12494
Bronx 10401-75
For specific ZIP Codes call (888) 275-8777, or your local postmaster.
Bronxsdale (Part of New York) 10462
Bronxville 10708
Bronxville Heights (Part of Yonkers) 10708
Brookdale 13668
Brookfield 13314
Brookhaven♦ 11719
Brooklyn 11201-56
13775
For specific ZIP Codes call (888) 275-8777, or your local postmaster.
Brooklyn Heights (Part of New York) 11201
Brooks Avenue Station (Part of Rochester) 14624
Brooksburg 12496
Brooks Grove 14510
Brooktondale 14817
Brookview 12033
Brookville 11545
Broome (Town) 12122
Broome Center 12076
Broughton Park 13760
Browns Bridge 13625
Browns Hollow 13317
Brownsville (Part of New York)‡ 11212
Brownsville, *Ontario* 14564
Brownville 13615
Bruceville 12440
Brunswick (Town) 12180
Brushton 12916
Brutus (Town) 13166
Bruynswick 12589
Bryant (Part of New York)‡ 10036
Bryn Mawr Park (Part of Yonkers) 10701
Buchanan 10511
Buckleyville 12037
Bucks Bridge 13660
Buck Settlement 14810
Buckton 13697
Buel 13317
Buellville 13104
Buena Vista 14823

Buffalo

14201-40
For specific ZIP Codes call (888) 275-8777, or your local postmaster.

Colleges & Universities

Canisius Coll 14208
D'Youville Coll 14201
Medaille Coll 14214
State Univ of New York 14214

Financial Institutions

The Chase Manhattan Bank 14203
Citibank 14203
Fleet Bank 14202
Key Bank, NA 14202
Marine Midland Bank 14203

Hospitals

Erie County Med Ctr 14215
General Hosp 14203
Mercy Hosp 14220
Millard Fillmore Health System 14209
Sisters of Charity Hosp 14214
Veterans Affairs Med Ctr 14215

Hotels/Motels

Holiday Inn, Downtown 14202
Hyatt Regency, Downtown 14202

Military Installations

Coast Guard Grp 14203

Buffalo Creek (Part of Buffalo) 14224
Buffalo Junction (Part of Buffalo) 14201
Buffalo Lake (Part of Buffalo) 14222
Bull Hill 13324
Bulls Head (Part of New York) 10314
Bulls Head (Part of Rochester)‡ 14611
Bullville 10915
Bundys 13126
Burden 12526
Burden Lake 12018
Burdett 14818
Burgoyne 12871
Burke 12917
Burke Center 12917
Burlingham 12722
Burlington 13315
Burlington Flats 13315
Burnhams (Part of Cassadaga) 14718
Burns 14807
Burnside 12575
Burns-Whitney Estates 12110
Burnt Hills 12027
Burnwood 13756
Burrs Mills 13601
Burt 14028
Burtonsville 12066
Bushes Landing 13367
Bushnell Basin 14534
Bushnellsville 12480
Bush Terminal (Part of New York)‡ 11232
Bushville, *Genesee* 14020
Bushville, *Sullivan* 12701
Bushwick (Part of New York)‡ 11221
Buskirk 12028
Busti 14701
Butler (Town) 14590
Butler Center 14590
Butlerville 10519
Butterfield (Part of Utica)‡ 13503
Butternut Grove 12776
Butternuts (Town) 13776
Byersville 14517
Byron 14422
C (Part of Buffalo)‡ 14208-09
For specific ZIP Codes call (888) 275-8777, or your local postmaster.
C (Part of New York)‡ 11367
Cabinhill 13752
Cadiz 14737
Cadosia 13783
Cadyville 12918
Cahoonzie 12780
Cairo♦ 12413
Calcium♦ 13616
Calcutta 12064
Caldor Shopping Center (Part of Port Chester) 10573
Caledonia 14423
Calico Colony 12065
Callicoon (Town) 12791
Callicoon 12723
Callicoon Center 12724
Calverton 11933
Cambria (Town) 14094
Cambria Heights (Part of New York)‡ 11411
Cambridge 12816
Camby 12545
Camden 13316
Cameron 14819
Cameron Mills 14820
Camillus 13031
Camillus Plaza 13031
Campbell 14821
Campbell Hall 10916
Camp Hemlock 12721
Camp Hill (Part of Pomona) 10970
Camps Mills 13601
Campville 13760
Camroden 13440
Canaan 12029
Canaan Center 12029
Canada Lake‡ 12032
Canadice 14560
Canajoharie 13317
Canal Street (Part of New York)‡ 10013
Canandaigua (Town) 14424
Canandaigua 14424-25
For specific ZIP Codes call (888) 275-8777, or your local postmaster.
Canarsie (Part of New York)‡ 11236
Canaseraga 14822
Canastota 13032
Canawaugus 14423
Candor 13743
Caneadea 14717
Canisteo 14823
Cannon Corners 12959
Canoe Place 11946
Canoga 13148
Canterbury Hill (Part of Rome) 13440
Canterbury Woods 13116
Canton 13617
Cape Vincent 13618
Capitol (Part of Albany)‡ 12224
Capitol Annex (Part of Albany)‡ 12225
Cardiff 13084
Carle Place♦ 11514
Carle Terrace 12449
Carleys Mills 13076
Carlisle 12031
Carlisle Center 12035
Carlisle Gardens 14094
Carlton 14411
Carman 12303
Carmel♦ 10512
Carmel Park Estates 10512
Carnegie 14075
Caroga (Town) 12032
Caroga Lake 12032
Caroline 14817
Caroline Center 14817
Carousel Center (Part of Syracuse)‡ 13290
Carroll (Town) 14738
Carrollton (Town) 14753
Carrollton 14748
Carson 14823
Carterville 13493
Carthage 13619
Cascade 13118
Case 13084
Casowasco 13118
Cassadaga 14718
Cassville 13318
Castile 14427
Castile Center 14427
Castle Creek 13744
Castle Hill (Part of New York)‡ 10462
Castle Point 12511
Castleton Corners (Part of New York) 10314
Castleton On Hudson 12033
Castorland 13620
Catatonk 13827
Catharine 14869
Cathedral (Part of New York)‡ 10025
Catherineville 13672
Catlin (Town) 14812
Cato 13033
Caton 14830
Catskill 12414
Cattaraugus 14719
Cattaraugus Indian Reservation 14081
Cattown 13337
Caughdenoy 13036
Cayuga 13034
Cayuga Heights 14850
Cayuta 14824
Cayutaville 14805
Caywood 14860
Cazenovia 13035
Cecil Park (Part of Yonkers) 10707
Cedar Cliff 12542
Cedarcrest 14487
Cedar Flats 10980
Cedar Hill 12158
Cedarhurst 11516
Cedar Knolls (Part of Yonkers) 10708
Cedarvale 13215
Cedarville 13357
Celoron 14720
Cementon 12414
Centenary 10956
Center Avenue (Part of East Rockaway) 11518
Center Berlin 12022
Center Brunswick 12180
Centereach♦ 11720
Center Falls 12834
Centerfield 14424
Center Lisle 13797
Center Moriches♦ 11934
Centerport, *Cayuga* 13166
Centerport, *Suffolk* 11721
Center Valley 13320
Centerville, *Allegany* 14029
Centerville, *Delaware* 13756
Center White Creek 12057
Central Bridge 12035
Centralia 14782
Central Islip♦ 11722
Central Nyack 10960
Central Park (Part of Buffalo)‡ 14214-15
For specific ZIP Codes call (888) 275-8777, or your local postmaster.
Central Park Shopping Center (Part of Buffalo) 14214
Central Square 13036
Central Valley♦ 10917
Centre Island 11771
Centre Village 13787
Centuck (Part of Yonkers)‡ 10710
Ceres 14721
Chadwicks 13319
Chaffee 14030
Chamberlain Corners 13660
Chambers 14812
Champion 13619
Champlain 12919
Champlain Park 12901
Chapel Hill Estates 10598
Chapin 14424
Chappaqua 10514
Charleston, *Montgomery* (Town) 12066
Charleston (Part of New York) 10309
Charleston Four Corners 12166
Charlesworth Corners 13339
Charlotte, *Chautauqua* (Town) 14782
Charlotte (Part of Rochester)‡ 14612
Charlotte Center 14782
Charlotteville 12036
Charlton 12019
Charwood Manor 12065
Chase Lake 13343
Chase Mills 13621
Chaseville 12116
Chasm Falls 12953
Chateaugay 12920

Place	ZIP Code
Chatham	12037
Chatham Center	12184
Chaumont	13622
Chautauqua	14722
Chautauqua Mall (Part of Lakewood)	14750
Chazy	12921
Chazy Lake	12935
Chazy Landing	12921
Chedwel	14712
Cheektowaga (Town)	14225
Cheektowaga♦	14225
	14227
For specific ZIP Codes call (888) 275-8777, or your local postmaster.	
Cheektowaga Northwest	14225
Cheektowaga Southwest	14227
Chelsea, *Dutchess*	12512
Chelsea (Part of New York)	10314
Chemung	14825
Chemung Center	14825
Chenango (Town)	13745
Chenango Bridge	13745
Chenango Forks	13746
Chenango Lake	13815
Cheneys Point	14710
Cheningo	13158
Chepachet	13491
Cherokee (Part of New York)‡	10021
Cherry Creek	14723
Cherry Grove	11782
Cherry Lane (Part of Fredonia)	14063
Cherry Plain	12040
Cherrytown	12446
Cherry Valley	13320
Cherry Valley Junction	12043
Cheshire	14424
Chester (Town)	12860
Chester	10918
Chesterfield (Town)	12944
Chester Hill Park (Part of Mount Vernon)	10550
Chestertown	12817
Chestnut Hill	13088
Chestnut Ridge, *Dutchess*	12545
Chestnut Ridge (Part of Lockport)	14094
Chestnut Ridge, *Rockland*	10952
Cheviot	12526
Chichester	12416
Childs	14411
Childwold	12922
Chili (Town)	14428
Chili Center	14624
Chiloway	12776
Chilson	12883
Chinatown (Part of New York)‡	10013
Chipman	13660
Chipmonk	14706
Chippewa Bay	13623
Chittenango	13037
Chittenango Falls	13035
Choconut Center	13905
Church Street (Part of New York)‡	10007
Churchtown	12521
Churchville, *Monroe*	14428
Churchville, *Oneida*	13478
Churubusco	12923
Cicero	13039
Cicero Center	13041
Cincinnatus	13040
Circleville	10919
City Island (Part of New York)‡	10464
Clairemont Farms	13088
Clare (Town)	13684
Claremont Park (Part of New York)‡	10457
Clarence	14031
Clarence Center♦	14032
Clarendon	14429
Clark Heights	12569
Clark Mills♦	13321
Clarksburg	14057
Clarks Chapel	12123
Clarks Corners	14747
Clarks Mills	12834
Clarkson	14430
Clarkstown (Town)	10956
Clarksville, *Allegany* (Town)	14786
Clarksville, *Albany*	12041
Clarkville	12134
Claryville	12725
Clason Point (Part of New York)‡	10473
Claverack	12513
Clay	13041
Clayburg	12981
Clayton	13624
Clayville	13322
Clear Creek	14726
Clearfield	14221
Clemmons	13638
Clemons	12819
Clermont	12526
Cleveland	13042
Cleveland Hill	14225
Cleverdale	12820
Cliff Haven	12901
Clifford	13069
Cliffside	12116
Clifton, *St. Lawrence* (Town)	13666
Clifton, *Monroe*	14428
Clifton (Part of New York)	10304
Clifton Gardens	12065
Clifton Heights	14085
Clifton Knolls	12065
Clifton Park	12065
Clifton Park Center	12065
Clifton Springs	14432
Climax	12042
Clinton, *Clinton* (Town)	12923
Clinton, *Dutchess* (Town)	12514
Clinton, *Oneida*	13323
Clinton Corners	12514
Clintondale♦	12515
Clinton Heights	12144
Clinton Hollow	12578
Clinton Park	12144
Clintonville	12924
Clockville	13043
Clough Corners	13862
Clove, *Dutchess*	12545
Clove, *Schoharie*	12043
Clover Bank	14075
Cloverville	12430
Clyde	14433
Clymer	14724
Cobb	11976
Cobleskill	12043
Cochecton	12726
Cochecton Center	12727
Coeymans	12045
Coeymans Hollow	12046
Coffins Mills	13670
Cohocton	14826
Cohoes	12047
Cokertown	12571
Colchester	13755
Cold Brook, *Herkimer*	13324
Coldbrook, *Schenectady*	12303
Colden	14033
Coldenham	12549
Coldspring, *Cattaraugus* (Town)	14783
Cold Spring, *Putnam*	10516
Cold Spring Harbor♦	11724
Cold Springs, *Onondaga*	13027
Cold Springs, *Steuben*	14810
Cold Spring Terrace	11743
Coldwater	14624
Colemans Mills	13492
Coleman Station	12546
Colesville (Town)	13787
Colgate (Part of Hamilton)‡	13346
Collabar	12549
Collamer	13057
College (Part of New York)‡	10030
College Park	12571
College Point (Part of New York)‡	11356
Colliersville	13747
Collingwood	13084
Collingwood Estates	14174
Collins (Town)	14034
Collins	14034
Collins Center	14035
Collins Landing	13607
Collinsville	13433
Colonial Acres	12077
Colonial Green	12188
Colonial Heights, *Dutchess*	12603
Colonial Heights (Part of Yonkers)	10708
Colonial Park (Part of New York)‡	10039
Colonial Village (Part of Niagara Falls)	14304
Colonie (Town)	12212
Colonie	12205
Colonie Center	12205
Colosse	13131
Colton	13625
Columbia (Town)	13357
Columbia Center	13357
Columbia University (Part of New York)‡	10025
Columbiaville	12050
Columbus	13411
Columbus Circle (Part of New York)‡	10023
Colvin Elmwood (Part of Syracuse)‡	13207
Commack♦	11725
Commack Corners Shopping Center	11725
Comstock	12821
Comstock Tract	13027
Concord, *Erie* (Town)	14141
Concord (Part of New York)	10304
Conesus	14435
Conesville	12076
Conewango	14726
Conewango Valley	14726
Coney Island (Part of New York)‡	11224
Conger Corners	13480
Congers♦	10920
Conifer	12986
Conklin	13748
Conklin Forks	13903
Conklingville	12835
Connelly	12417
Connelly Park	14710
Conquest	13140
Constable	12926
Constableville	13325
Constantia♦	13044
Constantia Center	13028
Continental Village	10567
Cook Corners	13625
Cooksburg	12469
Cooks Falls	12776
Cookville	14036
Cooley	12768
Coolidge Beach	14172
Coonrod (Part of Rome)	13440
Co-op City (Part of New York)‡	10475
Cooper (Part of New York)‡	10003
Coopers Plains	14827
Cooperstown	13326
Cooperstown Junction	12116
Coopersville, *Clinton*	12919
Coopersville, *Livingston*	14517
Copake	12516
Copake Falls	12517
Copake Lake	12521
Copenhagen	13626
Copiague♦	11726
Coram♦	11727
Coram Hill	11763
Corbett	13755
Corbettsville	13749
Cordova (Part of Fredonia)	14063
Coreys	12986
Corfu	14036
Corinth	12822
Cornell (Part of New York)‡	10473
Corning	14830
Corning Manor	14830
Cornwall (Town)	12518
Cornwall on Hudson	12520
Cornwallville	12418
Corona (Part of New York)	11368
Corona-A (Part of New York)‡	11368
Cortland	13045
Cortlandt (Town)	10520
Cortlandville (Town)	13045
Cosmos Heights	13045
Cossayuna	12823
Coss Corners	14810
Cottage	14138
Cottage City	14424
Cottage Park	14750
Cottam Hill	12590
Cottekill	12419
Cottonwood Point	14435
Council Meadows	12027
Country Knolls♦	12019
Country Knolls	12151
Country Knolls South	12065
Country Life Press (Part of Garden City)	11530
Country Ridge Estates	10573
County Line	14098
Cove Neck	11771
Coventry	13778
Coventryville	13733
Covert	14847
Coveytown Corners	12917
Covington	14525
Cowlesville	14037
Coxsackie	12051
Crafts	10512
Cragsmoor	12420
Craigville	10918
Crains Mills	13158
Cranberry Creek	12117
Cranberry Lake	12927
Crandall Corners	12154
Cranes Corners	13340
Cranesville	12010
Cranford (Part of New York)‡	10470
Crary Mills	13617
Craryville	12521
Craterclub	12936
Crawford (Town)	12566
Creek Locks	12411
Crescent	12188
Crescent Beach	14612
Crescent Estates	12065
Crescent Estates North	12065
Crestview Heights	13760
Crestwood (Part of Yonkers)	10710
Crestwood Gardens (Part of Yonkers)	10710
Crittenden	14038
Crocketts	13156
Croghan	13327
Crompond	10517
Cropseyville	12052
Cross Country Shopping Center (Part of Yonkers)	10704
Crossgates Mall	12203
Cross River	10518
Cross Roads Estates	10598
Crotona Park (Part of New York)‡	10460
Croton Falls	10519
Croton Heights	10598
Croton-on-Hudson	10520*
	10521†
Crotonville	10562
Crown Heights♦	12603
Crown Point	12928
Crown Point Center	12928
Crown Village	11762
Crugers	10521
Crum Creek	13452
Crystal Brook	11766
Crystal Dale	13367
Crystal Lake	12147
Cuba	14727
Cuddebackville	12729
Cullen	13439
Culvertown	12785
Cummingsville	14437
Curriers	14009
Curry	12765
Currytown	12166
Curtis, *Herkimer*	13454
Curtis, *Steuben*	14821
Cutchogue	11935
Cutting	14724
Cuyler	13158
Cuyler Hill	13158
Cuylerville	14481
Cypress Hills (Part of New York)‡	11208
D (Part of New York)‡	11423
Dadville	13367
Dag Hammarskjold (Part of New York)‡	10017
Dahlia	12758
Dairyland	12435
Dale	14039
Dalton	14836
Damascus	13865
Danby	14850
Dannemora	12929
Dansville, *Steuben* (Town)	14807
Dansville, *Livingston*	14437
Danube (Town)	13365
Danville	13754
Darien	14040
Darien Center	14040
Darrowsville	12817
Davenport	13750
Davenport Center	13751
Davis Park	11772
Daws	14020
Day (Town)	12835
Day Center	12835
Days Rock	13407
Dayton	14041
Daytonville	13480
Dean	14784
Deansboro	13328
Debruce	12758
Decatur	12197
Deck	13407
Deckertown	12758
Deerfield (Town)	13503
Deerland	12847
Deerpark, *Orange* (Town)	12729
Deer Park, *Suffolk*♦	11729
Deer River	13627
Deferiet	13628
Defreestville	12144
Degrasse	13684
De Kalb	13630
De Kalb Junction	13630
De Lancey	13752
Delanson	12053
Delaware, *Sullivan* (Town)	12723
Delaware (Part of Albany)‡	12209
Delevan	14042
Delhi	13753
Delmar♦	12054
Delphi Falls	13051
Delray	14224
Dempster Beach	13126
Demster	13126
Denmark	13631
Dennies Hollow	12117
Denning	12725
Dennison Corners	13407
Denton	10958
Denver	12421
Depauville	13632
Depew	14043
De Peyster	13633
Deposit	13754
Derby	14047
Dering Harbor	11964
DeRuyter	13052
Deuels Corners	14127
Devereux	14731
Devon	11930
Dewey (Part of Rochester)‡	14613
Dewey Bridge	12827
De Witt♦	13214
Dewittville	14728
Dexter	13634
Dexterville	13069
Diamond Point	12824
Diana (Town)	13648
Dibbletown	13308
Dickersonville	14131
Dickinson, *Broome* (Town)	13905
Dickinson, *Franklin* (Town)	12930
Dickinson Center	12930
Dick Urban	14043
Dimmick Corners	12831
Dineharts	14810
Divine Corners	12759
Dix, *Schuyler* (Town)	14891
Dix, *Oneida*	13440
Dix Hills	11746
Dobbs Ferry	10522
Dodge	14738
Dogtail Corners	12594
Dolgeville	13329
Dongan Hills (Part of New York)	10304
Doraville	13813
Doris Park	13044
Dorloo	12043
Dormansville	12055
Dorwood Park	14131
Douglass	12944
Douglaston (Part of New York)‡	11363
Dover (Town)	12522
Dover Furnace	12522
Dover Plains♦	12522
Downsville	13755
Downtown (Part of Elmira)‡	14901
Downtown (Part of Rochester)‡	14603
Downtown (Part of Syracuse)‡	13201
Doyle	14206
Dreiser Loop (Part of New York)‡	10475
Dresden, *Washington* (Town)	12887
Dresden, *Yates*	14441
Dresden Station	12887
Dresserville	13118
Drews Corner	13694
Dryden (Town)	13053
Dryden	13053
Duane (Town)	12953

Duanesburg 12056
Dublin 14433
Dugway 13131
Dunbar 13865
Dundee 14837
Dunewood 11706
Dunham Hollow 12018
Dunham Manor 13492
Dunkirk 14048
Dunnsville 12009
Dunraven 12455
Dunsbach Ferry 12047
Dunwoodie (Part of Yonkers) 10701
Dunwoody Heights (Part of Yonkers) 10701
Durham 12422
Durhamville 13054
Durkeetown 12828
Durlandville 10924
Dutchess Junction 12508
Dutch Flats 14167
Dutch Hollow 14145
Dutch Meadows 12065
Dutch Settlement 13637
Dwaar Kill 12566
Dyke 14830
Dykemans 10509
Dyker Heights (Part of New York)‡ 11228
Eagle 14009
Eagle Bay 13331
Eagle Bridge 12057
Eagle Center 14024
Eagle Harbor 14411
Eagle Lake 12883
Eagle Mills 12180
Eagle Point 14454
Eagle Valley 10987
Eagle Village 13104
Eagleville 12873
Earlton 12058
Earlville 13332
East (Part of Yonkers)‡ 10704
East Amherst 14051
East Arcade 14009
East Atlantic Beach 11509
East Aurora 14052
East Avon 14414
East Bay 14590
East Beekmantown 12901
East Bend Park 12603
East Berkshire 13736
East Berne 12059
East Bethany 14054
East Bloomfield (Town) 14443
East Bloomfield (Part of Bloomfield) 14443
East Branch 13756
East Brentwood 11717
East Buffalo 14225
East Buskirk 12028
East Campbell 14870
East Cayuga Heights 14850
East Chatham 12060
Eastchester (Town) 10709
Eastchester (Part of New York) 10466
East Chester (Part of Chester) 10918
Eastchester, *Westchester*♦ 10709
East Cobleskill 12157
East Concord 14055
East Corning 14830
East De Kalb 13630
East Durham 12423
East Eden 14057
East Elmhurst (Part of New York) 11369
Eastern Hills Mall 14221
Eastern Parkway (Part of New York) 11213
East Farmingdale‡ 11735
East Fishkill (Town) 12533
East Flatbush (Part of New York) 11203
East Floyd 13354
East Frankfort 13340
East Freetown 13040
East Gaines 14411
East Galway 12850
East Genoa 13092
East Glenville♦ 12302
East Greenbush♦ 12061
East Greenlawn 11731
East Greenwich 12865
East Half Hollow Hills 11746
East Hamilton 13355
East Hampton 11937
East Hampton North♦ 11937
East Hartford 12832
East Hebron 12865
East Herkimer 13350
East Hill 14850
East Hills 11576
East Hillsdale 12529
East Homer 13056
East Hoosick 12090
East Hounsfield 13601
East Huntington 11743
East Irvington 10533
East Islip♦ 11730
East Ithaca♦ 14850
East Jefferson 12093
East Jewett 12424
East Kingston 12401
East Koy 14536
East Lansing 14852
East Leon 14719
East Line 12020
East Marion 11939
East Martinsburg 13367
East Masonville 13839
East Massapequa 11758
East Mattituck 11952
East McDonough 13830
East Meadow♦ 11554
East Meredith 13757
East Middletown♦ 10940
Eastmor 12180
East Moriches♦ 11940
East Nassau 12062
East Neck 11743
East New York (Part of New York)‡ 11207
East Nichols 13812
East Northport♦ 11731
East Norwich♦ 11732
East Olean (Part of Olean) 14760
Easton (Town) 12834
East Otto 14729
East Palermo 13036
East Palmyra 14513
East Park 12538
East Part 13697
East Patchogue 11772
East Pembroke 14056
East Penfield 14450
East Pharsalia 13758
East Pitcairn 13648
East Pittstown 12028
East Poestenkill 12018
Eastport 11941
East Quogue 11942
East Randolph 14730
East Ridge 12741
East Ripley 14775
East River 13045
East Rochester 14445
East Rockaway 11518
East Rodman 13601
East Salamanca (Part of Salamanca) 14779
East Schodack 12063
East Schuyler 13340
East Seneca 14224
East Setauket 11733
East Shelby 14103
East Shoreham♦ 11786
East Side (Part of Binghamton)‡ 13904
East Side (Part of Buffalo)‡ 14206
Eastside, *Suffolk* 11937
East Sidney 13775
East Springfield 13333
East Steamburg 14886
East Stone Arabia 13428
East Syracuse 13057
East Taghkanic 12502
East Tremont (Part of New York) 10460
East Varick 14541
East Vestal 13902
East Victor 14564
East View 10595
East Watertown 13601
East White Plains (Part of Harrison) 10604
East Williamson 14449
East Williston 11596
East Windham 12439
East Windsor 13865
East Winfield 13491
Eastwood (Part of Syracuse)‡ 13206
East Woods 10576
East Worcester 12064
Eaton (Town) 13334
Eaton 13334
Eatons Neck♦ 11768
Eatonville 13365
Eavesport 12490
Ebenezer 14224
Ebenezer Junction 14224
Echota (Part of Niagara Falls) 14302
Eddy 13617
Eddyville, *Cattaraugus* 14755
Eddyville, *Ulster* 12401
Eden♦ 14057
Edenville 10990
Edenwald (Part of New York) 10466
Edgemere (Part of New York) 11690
Edgemont 10583
Edgewater Beach 13308
Edgewater Park 13669
Edgewood, *Greene* 12450
Edgewood, *Suffolk* 11717
Edgewood Garden 13164
Edinburg 12134
Edmeston 13335
Edson 13865
Edwards 13635
Edwards Hill 12811
Edwards Park 12029
Edwardsville 13646
Eggertsville 14226
Egypt 14450
Einstein (Part of New York)‡ 10475
Elayne Meadows 12188
Elba 14058
Elbridge 13060
Eldred 12732
Elizabethtown 12932
Elizaville 12523
Elka Park 12427
Elk Brook 12776
Elk Creek 12155
Elkdale 14779
Ellenburg 12933
Ellenburg Center 12934
Ellenburg Depot 12935
Ellenville 12428
Ellery (Town) 14756
Ellery Center 14712
Ellicott, *Chautauqua* (Town) 14733
Ellicott, *Erie* 14127
Ellicott (Part of Buffalo)‡ 14203-05
For specific ZIP Codes call (888) 275-8777, or your local postmaster.
Ellicottville 14731
Ellington 14732
Ellisburg 13636
Ellis Hollow 14850
Ellistown 14892
Elma♦ 14059
Elm Beach 14521
Elmdale 13642
Elm Grove 13808
Elmhurst, *Chautauqua* 14701
Elmhurst (Part of New York)‡ 11373
Elmhurst-A (Part of New York)‡ 11380
Elmira (Town) 14902
Elmira 14901-25
For specific ZIP Codes call (888) 275-8777, or your local postmaster.
Elmira Heights 14903
Elmira Heights North 14903
Elmont♦ 11003
Elm Park (Part of New York) 10303
Elmsford 10523
Elm Valley 14806
Elmwood (Part of Syracuse)‡ 13207
Elnora 12065
Elpis 13316
Elsmere 12054
Eltingville (Part of New York)‡ 10312
Elton 14042
Elwood♦ 11731
Elwood Farms 11731
Embogcht 12414
Emerson 13140
Emerson Hill (Part of New York) 10304
Emeryville 13642
Eminence 12175
Emmons 13820
Empeyville 13316
Empire State (Part of New York)‡ 10001
Empire State Plaza (Part of Albany)‡ 12220
Endicott 13760-61
13763
For specific ZIP Codes call (888) 275-8777, or your local postmaster.
Endwell♦ 13762
Enfield 14850
Ensenore 13118
Ephratah 13339
Erieville 13061
Erin 14838
Erwins 14870
Escarpment 14092
Esopus 12429
Esperance 12066
Esplanade (Part of New York)‡ 10469
Essex 12936
Etna 13062
Euclid 13041
Evans (Town) 14006
Evans Center 14006
Evans Mills 13637
Exeter (Town) 13315
Exeter Center 13315
F (Part of Buffalo)‡ 14212
Fabius 13063
Factory Village 12020
Factoryville 12928
Fairdale 13074
Fairfield 13406
Fairfield Gardens 12205
Fair Harbor 11706
Fair Haven 13064
Fairlawn Estates 12110
Fairmount 13219
Fairmount Fair Mall 13219
Fair Oaks 10940
Fairport 14450
Fairview, *Allegany* 14060
Fairview, *Westchester* 10603
Fairview, *Wyoming* 14427
Falconer 14733
Falcon Manor 14304
Falconwood 14072
Falls (Part of Niagara Falls)‡ 14303
Fallsburg 12733
Fancher 14452
Fargo 14036
Farleys Point 13160
Farmers Mills 10512
Farmersville (Town) 14060
Farmersville Station 14060
Farmingdale 11735
Farmington 14425
Farmingville♦ 11738
Farnham 14061
Farragut (Part of New York)‡ 11203
Far Rockaway 11601-95
10697
For specific ZIP Codes call (888) 275-8777, or your local postmaster.
Fawn Ridge 13027
Fayette 13065
Fayetteville 13066
Fayville 12025
Federal (Part of Rochester)‡ 14614
Federal Reserve (Part of New York)‡ 10045
Felts Mills 13638
Fenimore 12801
Fenner (Town) 13035
Fenton (Town) 13833
Fentonville 14738
Ferenbaugh 14830
Fergusons Corners 14456
Fergusonville 12155
Ferndale 12734
Fernwood, *Oswego* 13142
Fernwood, *Sullivan* 12760
Ferry Village 14072
Feura Bush 12067
Fieldston (Part of New York)‡ 10463
Filer Corners 13808
Fillmore 14735
Finchville 10940
Findley Lake 14736
Fine 13639
Fineview 13640
Finger Lakes Manor (Part of Canandaigua) 14424
Fink Basin 13365
Finnegans Corners 10924
Fire Island Pines 11782
Firthcliffe♦ 12518
Firthcliffe Heights 12584
Fish Creek, *Lewis* 13325
Fish Creek, *Ulster* 12477
Fish Creek Landing 13308
Fishers 14453
Fishers Island 06390
Fishers Landing 13641
Fisherville 14903
Fish House 12025
Fishkill 12524
Fishkill Plains 12590
Fishs Eddy 13774
Five Corners, *Cayuga* 13071
Five Corners, *Genesee* 14125
Five Corners (Part of Oneida) 13421
Five Corners, *Oneida* 13480
Fivemile Point 13795
Five Points 14456
Five Town Plaza 11598
Flackville 13669
Flanders♦ 11901
Flatbrook 12029
Flatbush (Part of New York)‡ 11226
Flatbush, *Ulster* 12477
Flat Creek, *Montgomery* 13317
Flat Creek, *Schoharie* 12076
Flatlands (Part of New York) 11234
Fleetwood (Part of Mount Vernon)‡ 10552
Fleischmanns 12430
Fleming 13021
Flemingville 13827
Flint 14561
Floral Park 11001-02
11005
For specific ZIP Codes call (888) 275-8777, or your local postmaster.
Florence 13316
Florence Hill 13316
Florida, *Montgomery* (Town) 12010
Florida, *Orange* 10921
Floridaville 13033
Flower Hill 11050
Flowers 13865
Floyd 13440
Flushing 11301-88
For specific ZIP Codes call (888) 275-8777, or your local postmaster.
Fluvanna 14701
Fly Creek 13337
Flying Point 11976
Fly Summit 12834
Folsomdale 14037
Fonda 12068
Foots Corners 14435
Ford Corners 12193
Fordham (Part of New York)‡ 10458
Forest 12935
Forestburgh (Town) 12701
Forestburgh 12777
Forest Glen (Part of Hamburg) 14075
Forest Hills (Part of New York)‡ 11375
Forest Home♦ 14850
Forest Knolls (Part of New Rochelle) 10804
Forest Lawn 14580
Forest Park, *Chautauqua* 14787
Forest Park, *Dutchess* 12572
Forestport 13338
Forestport Station 13338
Forestville 14062
Forge Hollow 13328
Forks 14225
Forsonville 10524
Forsyth 14775
Fort Ann 12827
Fort Covington 12937
Fort Covington Center 12937
Fort Drum 13603
Fort Edward 12828
Fort George (Part of New York)‡ 10040
Fort Herkimer 13407
Fort Hunter, *Albany* 12303
Fort Hunter, *Montgomery* 12069
Fort Jackson 12965
Fort Johnson 12070
Fort Miller 12828
Fort Montgomery♦ 10922
Fort Niagara Beach 14174
Fort Orange (Part of Albany)‡ 12206
Fort Plain 13339
Fort Salonga 11768
Fortsville 12831
Fort Washington (Part of New York)‡ 10032
Foster 13827
Fosterdale 12726
Fosterville 13021

Place	ZIP Code
Foster-Wheeler Junction (Part of Dansville)	14437
Fourth Lake	12846
Fowler	13642
Fowlersville	13433
Fowlerville, *Livingston*	14423
Fowlerville, *Sullivan*	12777
Fox Hill	12134
Fox Hills (Part of New York)	10304
Fox Meadows (Part of Scarsdale)	10583
Frankfort	13340
Frankfort Center	13340
Franklin (Part of Syracuse)	13218
Franklin, *Franklin* (Town)	12913
Franklin, *Delaware*	13775
Franklin D. Roosevelt (Part of New York)‡	10022
Franklin Park	13057
Franklin Springs	13341
Franklin Square♦	11010
Franklinton	12122
Franklinville	14737
Fraser	13753
Fredonia	14063
Freedom	14065
Freedom Plains	12569
Freehold	12431
Freeman	14801
Freeport	11520
Freetown, *Cortland* (Town)	13803
Freetown, *Suffolk*	11937
Freetown Corners	13803
Freeville	13068
Fremont, *Sullivan* (Town)	12736
Fremont, *Steuben*	14807
Fremont Center	12736
Fremont Heights	13057
Fremont Hills	13057
French Creek (Town)	14724
Frenchville	13486
French Woods	13783
Fresh Meadows (Part of New York)‡	11365
Fresh Pond (Part of New York)‡	11385
Frewsburg♦	14738
Freysbush	13339
Friend	14527
Friendship♦	14739
Friends Point	12836
Frontenac	13624
Fruitland	14519
Fruit Valley	13126
Fullerville	13642
Fulmer Valley	14806
Fulton, *Schoharie* (Town)	12122
Fulton, *Oswego*	13069
Fultonham	12071
Fultonville	12072
Furnace Brook	10925
Furnaceville	14519
Furnace Woods	10567
Furniss	13126
Gabriels	12939
Gaines	14411
Gainesville	14066
Galatia	13803
Gale	12973
Galen (Town)	14433
Galeville, *Onondaga*	13088
Galeville, *Ulster*	12589
Gallatin	12567
Galleria at Crystal Run	10940
Galleria of White Plains (Part of White Plains)	10601
Gallupville	12073
Galway	12074
Galway Lake	12025
Ganahgote	12525
Gang Mills♦	14870
Gansevoort	12831
Garbutt	14546
Garden City	11530
	11599
For specific ZIP Codes call (888) 275-8777, or your local postmaster.	
Garden City Park♦	11040
Garden City South♦	11530
Gardenville	14224
Gardiner	12525
Gardiner Manor Mall	11706
Gardiners Bay Estates	11939
Gardnersville	12043
Gardnertown	12550
Garfield	12168
Garland	14420
Garlinghouse	14512
Garnerville (Part of West Haverstraw)	10923
Garnet Lake	12843
Garoga	12095
Garrattsville	13342
Garrison	10524
Garrison Four Corners	10524
Garwoods	14822
Gaskill	13827
Gasport♦	14067
Gates	14624
Gates Center	14611
Gates-North Gates♦	14626
Gay Ridge Estates	10598
Gayville	13044
Geddes (Town)	13209
Gedney (Part of White Plains)‡	10605
Geers Corners	13648
Genegantslet	13778
Genesee (Town)	14754
Genesee Falls (Town)	14536
Geneseo	14454
Geneva	14456
Genoa	13071
Georgetown, *Madison*	13072
	13129
For specific ZIP Codes call (888) 275-8777, or your local postmaster.	
Georgetown, *Monroe*	14450
Georgetown Square (Part of Williamsville)	14221
Georgtown Station	13334
German	13040
German Flatts (Town)	13407
Germantown, *Columbia*	12526
Germantown (Part of Port Jervis)	12771
German Village	14617
Germonds	10956
Gerry	14740
Getman Corners	13407
Getzville	14068
Geyser Crest	12866
Ghent	12075
Gibson (Part of Valley Stream)	11580
Gibson, *Steuben*	14830
Gifford	12056
Gilbert Mills	13135
Gilbertsville	13776
Gilboa	12076
Gilgo Beach	11702
Gilmantown	12190
Glasco♦	12432
Glass Lake	12018
Glen	12072
Glen Aubrey	13777
Glen Castle	13901
Glenclyffe	10524
Glenco Mills	12534
Glen Cove	11542
Glendale, *Lewis*	13343
Glendale, *Westchester*	10562
Glendale (Part of New York)‡	11385
Glendale Manor (Part of Rome)	13440
Glenerie	12477
Glenfield	13343
Glenford	12433
Glenham	12527
Glen Haven, *Monroe*	14617
Glenhaven, *Oneida*	13492
Glen Head♦	11545
Glen Island	12814
Glen Lake	12804
Glenmark	14516
Glenmont	12077
Glenmore, *Essex*	12942
Glenmore, *Oneida*	13471
Glen Oaks (Part of New York)	11004
Glenora	14837
Glen Park	13601
Glenridge	12302
Glens Falls	12801
Glen Spey	12737
Glen Street (Part of Sea Cliff)	11579
Glenville, *Schenectady* (Town)	12302
Glenville, *Westchester*	10591
Glen Wild	12738
Glenwood, *Erie*	14069
Glenwood (Part of Yonkers)	10701
Glenwood Landing♦	11547
Gloversville	12078
Godeffroy	12739
Golden Glow Heights	14905
Goldens Bridge♦	10526
Goodman Street (Part of Rochester)	14607
Goodyears Corners	13081
Goose Bay Estates	11971
Goose Island	12809
Gordon Heights	11727
Gorham	14461
Goshen	10924
Goshen Hills	10924
Gothicville	12197
Goulds	12760
Goulds Mill	13368
Gouverneur	13642
Governors Island (Part of New York)	10004
Gowanda	14070
Gracie, *Cortland*	13045
Gracie (Part of New York)‡	10028
Grafton	12082
Graham Hill	10537
Grahamsville	12740
Granby (Town)	13069
Granby Center	13069
Grand Central (Part of New York)‡	10017
Grand Gorge	12434
Grand Island	14072
Grand Station (Part of New York)‡	11103
Grand View Beach	14612
Grand View Heights	14612
Grand View-on-Hudson	10960
Grandview Park	13640
Grandyle Village	14072
Granger (Town)	14735
Grangerville	12871
Granite	12446
Granite Springs	10527
Graniteville (Part of New York)	10314
Grant	13324
Grant Avenue (Part of Auburn)‡	13021
Grant Hollow	12121
Grant Park	11557
Granville	12832
Grapeville	12042
Graphite	12836
Grasmere (Part of New York)	10304
Grassy Point	10980
Gravesend (Part of New York)‡	11223
Gravesville	13431
Gray	13324
Graymoor	10524
Gray Oaks (Part of Yonkers)	10703
Great Bend	13643
Great Kills (Part of New York)‡	10308
Great Neck	11020-27
For specific ZIP Codes call (888) 275-8777, or your local postmaster.	
Great Neck Estates	11021
Great Neck Plaza	11020
Great River	11739
Great South Bay (Part of Lindenhurst)	11702
Great Valley	14741
Greece♦	14616
	14626
For specific ZIP Codes call (888) 275-8777, or your local postmaster.	
Greeley Square (Part of New York)‡	10001
Green Acres (Part of Fredonia)	14063
Green Acres Mall (Part of Valley Stream)	11581
Green Acres Valley	14226
Greenburgh (Town)	10591
Green Corners	12010
Green Crest	14063
Greendale	12534
Greene	13778
Greenfield (Town)	12833
Greenfield Center	12833
Greenfield Park	12435
Greenhaven (Part of Rye)	10580
Greenhurst	14742
Green Island	12183
Greenlawn♦	11740
Greenpoint (Part of New York)‡	11222
Greenport, *Columbia* (Town)	12534
Greenport, *Suffolk*	11944
Greenport West♦	11944
Green River	12529
Greenvale	11548
Greenville, *Orange* (Town)	12771
Greenville, *Greene*	12083
Greenville, *Steuben*	14826
Greenville, *Westchester*♦	10583
Greenville Center	12083
Greenway (Part of Rome)	13440
Greenwich	12834
Greenwood	14839
Greenwood Lake	10925
Gregorytown	13755
Greig	13345
Greigsville	14533
Greigsville Station	14533
Grenell	13624
Greycourt (Part of Chester)	10918
Greystone‡	10701*
	10702†
Gridleyville	13864
Griffins Mills	14170
Grindstone	13624
Grooms Corners	12148
Groton	13073
Groton City	13073
Grove (Town)	14884
Groveland	14462
Grover	14226
Grover Hills	12956
Grovernor Corners	12035
Groveville	12508
Grymes Hill (Part of New York)	10301
Guilderland	12084
Guilderland Center	12085
Guilford	13780
Guilford Center	13780
Gulfport (Part of New York)	10303
Gulf Summit	13865
Gunther Park (Part of Yonkers)	10708
Gurn Spring	12831
Guymard	12739
Gypsum	14432
Hadley	12835
Hadley Bay	14785
Hagaman	12086
Hagedorns Mills	12074
Hagerman	11713
Hague	12836
Hailesboro	13645
Haines Falls	12436
Halcott (Town)	12430
Halcott Center	12430
Halcottsville	12438
Hales Eddy	13783
Halesite♦	11743
Half Acre	13021
Half Hollow Hills	11746
Halfmoon	12188
Halfway	13060
Haliham Hill	12401
Hall	14463
Hallow	13413
Halls Corners, *Seneca*	14847
Halls Corners, *Wyoming*	14569
Halls Mills	12725
Hallsport	14895
Hallsville	13339
Halsey (Part of New York)‡	11233
Halseys (Part of Plattsburgh)	12901
Halsey Valley	14883
Hambletville	13754
Hamburg, *Erie*	14075
Hamburg, *Greene*	12414
Hamburg-on-the-Lake	14075
Hamden	13782
Hamilton	13346
Hamilton Beach (Part of New York)	11414
Hamilton Center	13346
Hamilton Grange (Part of New York)‡	10031
Hamilton Park (Part of New York)	10309
Hamlet	14138
Hamlin	14464
Hammel (Part of New York)	11693
Hammertown	12567
Hammond	13646
Hammondsport	14840
Hampton	12837
Hampton Bays	11946
Hamptonburgh (Town)	10916
Hampton Manor♦	12144
Hampton Park	11968
Hancock	13783
Handsome Eddy	12719
Hankins	12741
Hannacroix	12087
Hannawa Falls	13647
Hannibal	13074
Hannibal Center	13074
Hanover (Town)	14136
Hanover Center	14136
Harbor Acres (Part of Sands Point)	11050
Harbor Heights Park	11743
Harbor Hills	11023
Harbor Isle	11558
Hardenburgh (Town)	12455
Hardys	14066
Harford	13784
Harford Mills	13835
Harkness	12972
Harlem (Part of New York)	10030
Harlem River (Part of New York)	10454
Harlemville	12075
Harmon Park	12302
Harmony (Town)	14767
Harmony Corners	12020
Harpersfield	13786
Harpursville	13787
Harriet	14223
Harrietstown (Town)	12983
Harriman	10926
Harris	12742
Harrisburg, *Lewis*	13367
Harrisburg, *Warren*	12878
Harris Corners	14145
Harris Hill♦	14221
Harris Hill Manor	14903
Harrison	10528
Harrisville	13648
Harrower	12010
Hartfield	14728
Hartford	12838
Hartland	14067
Hartmans Corners	12009
Hartsdale♦	10530
Harts Hill	13492
Hartson Point	14487
Hartsville (Town)	14843
Hartsville	14843
Hartwick (Town)	13348
Hartwick	13348
Hartwick Seminary	13326
Hartwood	12777
Harvard	13756
Hasbrouck	12788
Haskell Flats	14727
Haskinville	14826
Hastings	13076
Hastings Center	13036
Hastings-on-Hudson	10706
Hatch's Corner	13684
Hauppauge♦	11760
	11788
For specific ZIP Codes call (888) 275-8777, or your local postmaster.	
Haven	12790
Haverstraw	10927
Haviland♦	12538
Hawkeye	12912
Hawkins Corner	13440
Hawkinsville	13309
Hawleys	13856
Hawleyton	13903
Hawthorne♦	10532
Hawthorne Hill	12309
Hawthorne Park	14787
Hawversville	12122
Hay Beach Point	11964
Haydenville	14760
Haynersville	12180
Hayt Corners	14521
Hazel	12758
Head of the Harbor	11780
Heathcote (Part of New Rochelle)	10801
Heathcote (Part of Scarsdale)	10583
Heatherwood North	11733
Heatherwood South	11720
Heath Grove	13110
Heavenly Valley	12466
Hebron (Town)	12832
Hecla	13490
Hector	14841
Hedgesville	14801
Helena	13649
Hell Gate (Part of New York)‡	10029
Hemlock	14466
Hempstead	11550*
	11551†
Hempstead Gardens	11552
Hemstreet Park	12118
Henderson	13650

*** Area Zip Code** **† Post Office Boxes** **‡ Postal Station** **♦ Census Designated Place** *Italic Type* **County**

Place	ZIP
Henderson Harbor	13651
Hendy Creek	14871
Henrietta	14467
Hensonville	12439
Heritage (Part of Schenectady)‡	12303
Heritage Hills	12020
Heritage Knolls	12020
Herkimer	13350
Hermitage, *Steuben*	14810
Hermitage, *Wyoming*	14066
Hermon	13652
Herrick Grove	13622
Herricks♦	11040
Herrings	13619
Hertel (Part of Buffalo)‡	14216
Herthum Heights	13492
Hervey Street	12418
Hessville	13339
Heuvelton	13654
Hewittville	13668
Hewlett♦	11557
Hewlett Bay Park	11557
Hewlett Harbor	11557
Hewlett Neck	11598
Hickeys Corners	12866
Hickorybush	12401
Hickory Grove	13126
Hicks	14859
Hicks Corners	14009
Hicksville♦	11801*
	11802†
Higgins	14065
Higgins Bay	12108
Higginsville	13054
High Bank	12981
High Bridge (Part of New York)‡	10452
High Bridge, *Onondaga*	13066
High Falls	12440
High Flats	13625
Highland, *Sullivan* (Town)	12732
Highland, *Ulster*♦	12528
Highland Falls	10928
Highland Lake	12743
Highland Mills♦	10930
Highland-on-the-Lake	14047
Highlands (Town)	10928
Highlawn (Part of New York)‡	11223
High Mills	12027
Highmount	12441
High View	12721
High Woods	12477
Hiler	14223
Hillburn	10931
Hillcrest, *Allegany*	14717
Hillcrest, *Broome*	13901
Hillcrest, *Rockland*♦	10977
Hiller Heights	13041
Hillis	12603
Hillsboro	13316
Hillsdale	12529
Hillside, *Bronx* (Part of New York)‡	10469
Hillside, *Queens* (Part of New York)	11433
Hillside, *Oneida*	13486
Hillside Lake♦	12590
Hillside Manor	11040
Hillside Park (Part of Johnstown)	12095
Hillview	12144
Hilton	14468
Himrod	14842
Hinckley	13352
Hinckleyville	14559
Hindsburg	14411
Hinmans Corners	13905
Hinmansville	13135
Hinsdale	14743
Hitching Corner	13491
Hoag Corners	12062
Hobart	13788
Hoboken	13411
Hoffmans	12302
Hoffmeister	13353
Hogansburg	13655
Hogtown	12827
Holbrook♦	11741
Holcomb (Part of Bloomfield)	14469
Holcombville	12853
Holiday Manor (Part of Geneva)	14456
Holland♦	14080
Holland Cove	14589
Holland Patent	13354
Holley	14470
Hollis (Part of New York)	11423
Hollowville	12530
Holmes	12531
Holmesville	13843
Holton Beach	14847
Holtsville	11742
Homecrest (Part of New York)‡	11229
Homer	13077
Homer Hill (Part of Olean)	14760
Homestead Park (Part of New Rochelle)	10801
Homestead Village	11727
Homewood	13066
Homewood Park	14225
Honeoye	14471
Honeoye Falls	14472
Honest Hill	14470
Honeywell Corners	12025
Honk Hill	12458
Honnedaga Lake	13338
Hoosick	12089
Hoosick Falls	12090
Hoosick Junction	12133
Hope (Town)	12134
Hope Falls	12134
Hope Farm	12545
Hope Valley	12134
Hopewell (Town)	14424
Hopewell Center	14424
Hopewell Junction♦	12533
Hopkinton	12965
Horace Harding (Part of New York)‡	11362
Horicon (Town)	12815
Hornby	14812
Hornell	14843
Hornellsville (Town)	14807
Horseheads	14844†
	14845*
Horseheads North♦	14845
Horseshoe Hill	10576
Horton	12776
Horton Estates	10587
Hortonville	12745
Houghton♦	14744
Hounsfield (Town)	13685
Houseville	13473
Housons Corners	12122
Howard	14809
Howard Beach (Part of New York)	11414
Howardville	13302
Howells	10932
Howes Cave	12092
Howlett Hill	13031
Hub (Part of New York)‡	10455
Hubbardsville	13355
Hubbardtown	13743
Hudson	12534
Hudson Falls	12839
Hudson Upper (Part of Hudson)	12534
Hughsonville	12537
Huguenot, *Orange*	12746
Huguenot (Part of New York)	10312
Huguenot Park (Part of New Rochelle)	10801
Hulberton	14470
Huletts Landing	12841
Hullsville	13827
Hume	14745
Humphrey (Town)	14741
Humphrey Center	14741
Hungerford Corners	13650
Hunt	14846
Hunt Corners	14433
Hunter	12442
Hunter Lake	12768
Huntersland	12122
Huntington	11743
Huntington Bay	11743
Huntington Beach	11721
Huntington Square	11731
Huntington Station♦	11746
Huntingtonville	13601
Hunts Corners, *Cortland*	13803
Hunts Corners, *Erie*	14031
Hunts Corners, *Sullivan*	12764
Hurd Corners	12564
Hurley♦	12443
Hurleyville	12747
Huron (Town)	14590
Hurricane	13324
Hyde Park, *Dutchess*	12538
Hyde Park, *Otsego*	13326
Hylan Shopping Plaza (Part of New York)	10306
Hyndsville	12043
Idle Hour	11769
Idlewood	14085
Ilion	13357
Inavale	14739
Independence	14806
Index	13326
Indian Castle	13365
Indian Cove	13118
Indian Falls	14036
Indian Kettles	12836
Indian Lake	12842
Indian Neck	11958
Indian Park	10925
Indian River	13327
Indian Springs	13027
Indian Village	13120
Ingham Mills	13365
Ingleside	14512
Ingraham	12992
Inlet	13360
Inman	12989
Interlaken	14847
Interlaken Beach	14847
International Junction	14223
Inwood, Nassau♦	11696
Inwood (Part of New York)	10034
Ionia, *Onondaga*	13112
Ionia, *Ontario*	14475
Ira	13033
Ireland Corners	12525
Irelandville	14891
Irish Settlement	13625
Irishtown	12857
Irona	12910
Irondale, *Dutchess*	12546
Irondale, *Herkimer*	13454
Irondequoit‡	14617
Irondequoit Mall	14622
Irondequoit Manor	14617
Irongate	13088
Ironville	12928
Irving	14081
Irvington	10533
Ischua	14743
Island (Part of New York)‡	10044
Island Cottage Beach	14612
Islandia	11722
Island Park	11558
Isle of San Souci (Part of New Rochelle)	10805
Islip♦	11751
Islip Terrace♦	11752
Italy	14512
Itaska	13862
Ithaca (Town)	14850
Ithaca	14850-53
For specific ZIP Codes call (888) 275-8777, or your local postmaster.	
Ivanhoe	13839
Ives Corner	12018
Ives Hollow	13454
Jackson (Town)	12816
Jacksonburg	13407
Jackson Corners	12571
Jackson Heights (Part of New York)‡	11372
Jackson Summit	12117
Jacksonville, *Onondaga*	13135
Jacksonville, *Tompkins*	14854
Jacks Reef	13112
Jamaica	11401-36
For specific ZIP Codes call (888) 275-8777, or your local postmaster.	
James A Farley (Part of New York)‡	10001
Jamesport	11947
Jamestown	14701*
	14702†
Jamestown West♦	14701
Jamesville	13078
Janesville	12043
Jasper	14855
Java (Town)	14082
Java Center	14082
Java Lake	14009
Java Village	14083
Jay	12941
Jeddo	14103
Jefferson	12093
Jefferson Heights♦	12414
Jefferson Park	13650
Jefferson Valley	10535
Jefferson Valley Mall	10598
Jeffersonville	12748
Jenksville	13736
Jericho, *Clinton*	12910
Jericho, *Nassau*♦	11753
Jericho, *Suffolk*	11937
Jerome Avenue (Part of New York)‡	10468
Jersey Colony	11971
Jerusalem (Town)	14418
Jerusalem Corners	14047
Jewell	13042
Jewel Manor	13088
Jewett	12444
Jewett Center	12442
Jewettville, *Erie*	14170
Jewettville, *Jefferson*	13685
John F. Kennedy Airport (Part of New York)‡	11430
Johnsburg	12843
Johnson	10933
Johnsonburg	14167
Johnson City	13790
Johnson Creek	14067
Johnsonville	12094
Johnstown (Town)	12078
Johnstown	12095
Jones Point	10986
Jonesville	12065
Jordan	13080
Jordanville	13361
Junction Boulevard (Part of New York)‡	11372
Junius (Town)	13165
Kabob	14782
Kaisertown	12549
Kanona	14856
Kaser	10977
Kasoag	13302
Kast Bridge	13350
Katonah	10536
Katsbaan	12477
Kattelville	13901
Kattskill Bay	12844
Kauneonga Lake	12749
Kaydeross Park (Part of Saratoga Springs)	12866
Kayuta Lake	13338
Kecks Center	12095
Keefers Corners	12067
Keene	12942
Keene Valley	12943
Keeney	13158
Keeseville	12924
	12944
For specific ZIP Codes call (888) 275-8777, or your local postmaster.	
Kelleys	12056
Kelloggsville	13118
Kelly Corners, *Chautauqua*	14784
Kelly Corners, *Delaware*	12455
Kelsey	13783
Kendaia	14541
Kendall	14476
Kendall Mills	14470
Kenilworth (Part of Kings Point)	11024
Kenmore	14217
Kennedy	14747
Kenoza Lake	12750
Kensington (Part of Buffalo)	14215
Kensington (Part of New York)‡	11218
Kensington, *Nassau*	11021
Kent, *Putnam* (Town)	10512
Kent, *Orleans*	14477
Kent Cliffs	10512
Kents Corners	13630
Kenwood (Part of Oneida)‡	13421
Kenwood Estates	10512
Kenyonville	14571
Kerhonkson♦	12446
Kerleys Corners	12571
Kernan (Part of Utica)‡	13502
Kerryville	13783
Ketchums Corner	12170
Ketchumville	13736
Keuka	14837
Keuka Park	14478
Kew Gardens (Part of New York)‡	11415
Kew Gardens Hills (Part of New York)	11366
Kiamesha Lake	12751
Kiantone	14701
Kidders	14847
Killawog	13794
Kill Buck	14748
Kimball Stand	14701
Kinderhook	12106
King Ferry	13081
Kings Bridge (Part of New York)‡	10463
Kings Bridge Heights (Part of New York)	10463
Kingsbury	12839
Kings Ferry	13081
Kings Park	11754
Kings Plaza Shopping Center and Marina (Part of New York)	11234
Kings Point	11024
Kings Settlement	13815
Kings Station	12831
Kingston	12401*
	12402†
Kingston Plaza (Part of Kingston)	12401
Kipps	10924
Kirk	13844
Kirkland	13323
Kirkville	13082
Kirkwood	13795
Kirkwood	14826
Kirschnerville	13327
Kiryas Joel	10950
Kisco Park	10549
Kiskatom	12414
Kismet	11706
Kitchawan	10562
Knapp Creek	14760
Knapps Corner	12603
Knappville	13470
Knickerbocker (Part of New York)‡	10002
Knights Creek	14880
Knights Eddy	12780
Knight Settlement	14810
Knowelhurst	12878
Knowlesville	14479
Knox	12107
Knoxboro	13362
Koenig's Point	13021
Kohlertown	12748
Komar Park	12019
Kortright	13739
Kossuth	14715
Kringsbush	13452
Kripplebush	12484
Krumville	12461
Kuckville	14571
Kyserike	12440
Lackawack	12458
Lackawanna	14218
Lacona	13083
Ladentown (Part of Pomona)	10970
LaFargeville	13656
LaFayette	13084
Lafayetteville	12571
La Grange, *Dutchess* (Town)	12540
Lagrange, *Wyoming*	14525
Lagrangeville	12540
La Guardia Airport (Part of New York)‡	11371
Lairdsville	13476
Lake	10990
Lake Bluff	14590
Lake Bonaparte	13648
Lake Carmel♦	10512
Lake Charles	12563
Lake Clear	12945
Lake Como	13045
Lake Delta	13440
Lake Desolation	12850
Lake Erie Beach♦	14006
Lake Gardens	10541
Lake George	12845
Lake Grove	11755
Lake Hill	12448
Lake Huntington	12752
Lake Katonah	10536
Lake Katrine♦	12449
Lake Kitchawan	10590
Lakeland, *Onondaga*	13209
Lakeland, *Suffolk*	11779
Lake Lincolndale	10541
Lake Lucille	10956
Lake Luzerne	12846
Lake Mahopac	10541
Lakemont	14857
Lake Moraine	13346
Lake Muskoday	12776
Lake Osceola	10535
Lake Osiris Colony	12586
Lake Panamoka	11961
Lake Peekskill	10537
Lake Placid	12946
Lake Placid Club Resort (Part of Lake Placid)	12946
Lake Pleasant	12108
Lakeport	13037
Lake Purdy	10578
Lake Ronkonkoma	11779
Lake Ronkonkoma Heights	11779
Lake Secor	10541
Lakeside, *Orange*	10930
Lakeside, *Wayne*	14519
Lakeside Park, *Albany*	12205

*** Area Zip Code** **† Post Office Boxes** **‡ Postal Station** **♦ Census Designated Place** *Italic Type* **County**

Lakeside Park, *Orleans* 14571
Lake Station 10990
Lake Success 11040
Lake Success Shopping Center 11040
Lake Sunnyside 12845
Lake Vanare 12846
Lake View, *Erie* 14085
Lakeview, *Nassau*♦ 11552
Lakeview, *Oswego* 13126
Lakeville, *Livingston* 14480
Lakeville (Part of Lake Success) 11040
Lakewood 14750
Lamberton 14063
Lambs Corner 12083
Lamont 14427
Lamson 13135
Lancaster 14086
Lane (Part of Batavia) 14020
Lanesville 12450
Langdon 13795
Langdon Corners 13617
Langford 14057
Lansing, *Oswego* 13126
Lansing, *Tompkins* 14882
Lansingburg (Part of Troy)‡ 12182
Laona 14063
Lapala 12401
Lapeer (Town) 13803
Laphams Mills 12972
Larchmont 10538
Larchmont North 10538
La Salle (Part of Niagara Falls)‡ 14304
Lassellsville 13452
Lathams Corners 13843
Lattingtown 11560
Laughing Waters 11971
Laurel♦ 11948
Laurel Hollow 11791
Laurelton, *Monroe* 14609
Laurelton (Part of New York) 11413
Laurens 13796
Lava 12764
Lawrence, *St. Lawrence* (Town) 12965
Lawrence, *Nassau* 11559
Lawrence Farms 10514
Lawrence Park (Part of Yonkers) 10708
Lawrenceville 12967
Lawtons 14091
Lawyersville 12043
Lebanon 13332
Lebanon Center 13332
Lebanon Springs 12125
Ledyard (Town) 13026
Ledyard 13081
Lee 13440
Lee Center 13363
Leeds 12451
Leedsville 12501
Leeside 10512
Leesville 13459
Lefever Falls 12472
Lefferts (Part of New York)‡ 11225
Leibhardt 12404
Leicester 14481
LeMarr Estates 12184
Lenox (Town) 13032
Lenox Furnace 13032
Lenox Hill (Part of New York)‡ 10021
Lenox Park 14456
Lent Hill 14826
Leon 14751
Leonardsville 13364
Leonta 13775
Le Ray (Town) 13637
Le Roy 14482
Le Roy Island 14590
Levanna 13026
Levant 14733
Levittown♦ 11756
Lewbeach 12758
Lewis (Town) 13489
Lewis 12950
Lewisboro (Town) 10590
Lewiston 14092
Lewiston Heights (Part of Lewiston) 14092
Lewiston Manor 13224
Lexington 12452
Leyden (Town) 13433
Liberty 12754
Liberty Gardens (Part of Rome) 13440
Libertypole 14437
Lido Beach♦ 11561
Lily Dale 14752
Lima 14485
Lime Lake 14042
Limerick 13657
Lime Rock 14482
Limestone 14753
Limestreet 12414
Lincklaen 13052
Lincoln, *Madison* (Town) 13043
Lincoln, *Wayne* 14502
Lincolndale 10540
Lincoln Park, *Erie* 14222
Lincoln Park (Part of Rochester) 14611
Lincoln Park, *Ulster*♦ 12401
Lincolnshire 13760
Lincolnton (Part of New York)‡ 10037
Lincolnwoods 14094
Lindbergh Court (Part of Colonie) 12204
Linden 14054
Linden Acres 12571
Linden Hill (Part of New York)‡ 11354
Lindenhurst 11757
Lindley 14858
Linlithgo 12526
Linwood 14486
Lisbon 13658
Lisha Kill 12201
Lisle 13797
Litchfield (Town) 13456
Lithgow 12545
Little America 13144
Little Bow 13642
Little Britain 12575
Little Canada 14054
Little Falls (Town) 13407
Little Falls 13365
Little Falls Park (Part of Wappingers Falls) 12590
Little France 13036
Little Genesee 14754
Little Neck (Part of New York) 11363
Little Plains 11731
Little Ram Island 11964
Little Utica 13135
Little Valley 14755
Littleville, *Livingston* 14414
Littleville, *Ontario* 14424
Little York, *Cortland* 13087
Little York, *Orange* 10969
Liverpool 13088-90
For specific ZIP Codes call (888) 275-8777, or your local postmaster.
Livingston 12541
Livingston Manor♦ 12758
Livingstonville 12122
Livonia 14487
Livonia Center 14488
Lloyd (Town) 12528
Lloyd Harbor 11743
Lochada Lake 12719
Loch Muller 12857
Loch Sheldrake 12759
Lock Berlin 14489
Locke 13092
Lockport (Town) 14094
Lockport 14094*
14095†
Locksley Park 14075
Lockwood 14859
Locust Grove, *Lewis* 13309
Locust Grove, *Nassau* 11791
Locust Manor (Part of New York) 11434
Locust Point (Part of New York) 10465
Locust Valley♦ 11560
Lodi 14860
Lodi Center 14860
Lodi Point 14860
Loehmanns Plaza 14618
Logan 14818
Logtown 12771
Lomala 12533
Lombard 14775
Lomond Shore 14476
Lomontville 12401
London Terrace (Part of New York)‡ 10011
Lonelyville 11706
Long Beach 11561
Long Branch 13088
Long Branch Manor 13088
Long Bridge 13153
Long Eddy 12760
Long Island City 11101-09
For specific ZIP Codes call (888) 275-8777, or your local postmaster.
Long Lake 12847
Long Point 14454
Long Ridge Mall 14626
Long View 14710
Loomis 12754
Loomises 14710
Loon Lake 12989
Lordville 13783
Lorenz Park♦ 12534
Lorings 13045
Lorraine 13659
Lost Valley 12010
Loudenville Heights 12211
Loudonville♦ 12211
Louisville 13662
Lounsberry 13812
Lowell 13440
Lower Chateaugay Lake 12920
Lower Cincinnatus 13040
Lower Genegantslet Corner 13778
Lower Melville 11747
Lower Oswegatchie 13670
Lower Rotterdam 12306
Lower South Bay 13041
Lowertown (Part of Lockport) 14094
Low Hampton 05743
Lowman 14861
Lowville 13367
Ludingtonville 12531
Ludlow (Part of Yonkers) 10705
Ludlowville 14882
Lumberland (Town) 12770
Luther 12061
Lutheranville 12064
Lycoming 13093
Lyell (Part of Rochester)‡ 14606
Lykers 12166
Lyme (Town) 13693
Lynbrook 11563
Lyncourt♦ 13208
Lyndon, *Cattaraugus* (Town) 14737
Lyndon, *Onondaga*♦ 13066
Lyndonville 14098
Lynelle Meadows 13088
Lynnwood 12835
Lyon Mountain 12952
Lyons 14489
Lyonsdale 13368
Lyons Falls 13368
Lyonsville 12404
Lysander 13027
Mabbettsville 12545
McClure 13754
McConnellsville 13401
MacDonnell Heights 12603
McDonough 13801
MacDougall 14541
Macedon 14502
Macedon Center 14502
McGraw 13101
Machias 14101
McKeever 13338
Mackey 12076
McKinley 13428
McKownville 12203
McLaughlin Acres 10541
McLean 13102
McMasters Corners 13201
McNalls 14067
Macomb (Town) 13642
McPherson Point 14487
Madison 13402
Madison Park 11731
Madison Square (Part of New York)‡ 10010
Madrid 13660
Madrid Springs 13660
Magnolia 14757
Mahopac♦ 10541
Mahopac Falls 10542
Mahopac Hills 10541
Mahopac Point 10541
Mahopac Ridge 10541
Maidstone Park 11937
Maine 13802
Main Settlement 14770
Main Village (Part of Williamsville) 14226
Malba (Part of New York) 11357
Malden Bridge 12115
Malden on Hudson 12453
Mall‡ 11706
Mall at Greeceridge Center, The 14626
Mall at New Rochelle, The (Part of New Rochelle) 10801
Mallory 13103
Malone 12953
Malta 12020
Malta Ridge 12020
Maltaville 12020
Maltbie Heights 14070
Malverne 11565
Malvic Manor 13088
Mamakating (Town) 12790
Mamakating Park 12790
Mamaroneck 10543
Manchester 14504
Manchester Bridge 12603
Mandana 13152
Manhasset♦ 11030
Manhasset Hills♦ 11040
Manhattan 10001-99
10101-99
10201-82
For specific ZIP Codes call (888) 275-8777, or your local postmaster.
Manhattan Beach (Part of New York) 11235
Manhattan Park (Part of White Plains) 10601
Manhattanville (Part of New York)‡ 10027
Manhattanville College (Part of Harrison)‡ 10577
Manheim (Town) 13329
Manheim Center 13365
Manitou 10524
Manitou Beach 14468
Manlius 13104
Manlius Center 13066
Mannetto Hills 11747
Manning 14470
Mannsville 13661
Mannville 12189
Manny Corners 12010
Manor 13413
Manorhaven 11050
Manorkill 12076
Manorville, *Suffolk*♦ 11949
Manorville, *Ulster* 12477
Mansfield (Town) 14755
Maple Bay 14710
Maple Beach 14454
Maplecrest 12454
Mapledale, *Oneida* 13304
Mapledale, *Ulster* 12406
Maple Grove, *Hamilton* 12134
Maple Grove, *Otsego* 13808
Maple Hill 12401
Maplehurst 14743
Maples 14755
Maple Springs 14756
Mapleton 13021
Mapletown 13317
Maple Valley 13488
Maple View 13107
Maplewood, *Albany* 12189
Maplewood, *Sullivan* 12701
Marathon 13803
Marbletown, *Ulster* 12401
Marbletown, *Wayne* 14513
Marcellus 13108
Marcellus Falls 13108
Marcy (Town) 13503
Marengo 14433
Margaretville 12455
Mariandale (Part of Ossining) 10562
Mariaville 12137
Marietta 13110
Marilla 14102
Marine Hospital (Part of New York) 10301
Mariners Harbor (Part of New York)‡ 10303
Marion 14505
Mariposa 13155
Markhams 14070
Marlboro♦ 12542
Marlborough (Town) 12542
Marshall, *Oneida* (Town) 13328
Marshall, *Allegany* 14711
Marshland Heights 13760
Marshville, *Montgomery* 13317
Marshville, *St. Lawrence* 13652
Martindale Depot 12521
Martinsburg 13404
Martisco 13108
Martville 13111
Maryknoll 10545
Maryland 12116
Marymount (Part of Tarrytown)‡ 10591
Masonville 13804
Maspeth (Part of New York)‡ 11378
Massapequa♦ 11758
Massapequa Park 11762
Massawepie 12986
Massena 13662
Massena Center 13662
Massena Springs (Part of Massena) 13662
Masten Lake 12790
Mastic♦ 11950
Mastic Beach♦ 11951
Matinecock 11560
Matteawan (Part of Beacon) 12508
Mattituck♦ 11952
Mattydale♦ 13211
Maybrook 12543
Mayfair 12302
Mayfield 12117
Mayville 14757
Maywood, *Albany* 12205
Maywood, *Suffolk* 11701
McColloms 12970
Mc Duffie Town 14541
McGrath Point 14888
Meacham 11003
Meadowbrook 12550
Meadowdale 12009
Meadow Hill 12550
Meadow Lane Estates 12184
Meadowmere Park 11598
Meadow Run (Part of Hamburg) 14075
Meads 12498
Meads Creek 14870
Mechanicville 12118
Mecklenburg 14863
Meco 12078
Medford♦ 11763
Medina 14103
Medusa 12120
Medway 12042
Meekerville 13338
Melcourt (Part of New York)‡ 10451
Mellenville 12544
Melody Lake 12701
Melrose (Part of New York) 10456
Melrose, *Rensselaer* 12121
Melrose Park♦ 13021
Melville♦ 11747
Memphis 13112
Menands 12204
Mendon 14506
Mendon Center 14472
Menteth Point 14424
Mentz (Town) 13140
Meredith 13753
Meridale 13806
Meridian 13113
Merillon Avenue (Part of Garden City) 11530
Merrick♦ 11566
Merrickville 13839
Merriewold 12777
Merriewold Lake 10950
Merrifield 13147
Merrill 12955
Merrillsville 13421
Merrilville 12986
Mertensia 14564
Messengerville 13803
Metropolitan (Part of New York)‡ 11206
Mettacahonts 12404
Mews 11507
Mexico 13114
Middle Bridge 13730
Middleburgh 12122
Middlebury (Town) 14591
Middle Falls 12848
Middlefield 13450
Middlefield Center 13320
Middle Granville 12849
Middle Grove 12850
Middle Hope 12550
Middle Island♦ 11953
Middleport, *Madison* 13346
Middleport, *Niagara* 14105
Middlesex 14507
Middletown, *Delaware* (Town) 12455
Middletown, *Orange* 10940-41
For specific ZIP Codes call (888) 275-8777, or your local postmaster.
Middletown Psychiatric Center (Part of Middletown) 10940
Middle Village (Part of New York) 11379
Middleville, *Herkimer* 13406
Middleville, *Suffolk* 11768
Mid-Island Mall 11801

Midland Beach (Part of New York) 10306
Midtown (Part of New York)‡ 10018
Midtown Plaza (Part of Rochester)‡ 14604
Midway 14864
Midwood (Part of New York)‡ 11230
Milan (Town) 12571
Mileses 12741
Milford 13807
Milford Center 13820
Millbrook 12545
Millen Bay 13618
Miller Place♦ 11764
Millers 14098
Millers Mills 13491
Millersport 14051
Millerton 12546
Millertown 12094
Mill Grove 14770
Mill Hook 12404
Mill Neck 11765
Mill Point 12010
Millport 14864
Millsburgh 10933
Mills Mills 14735
Millville 14103
Millwood 10546
Milo (Town) 14527
Milo Center 14527
Milton, *Saratoga* 12020
Milton, *Ulster*♦ 12547
Milton Point (Part of Rye) 10580
Mina 14781
Minaville 12010
Minden 13339
Mindenville 13339
Mineola 11501
Mineral Springs 12043
Minerva 12851
Minetto♦ 13115
Mineville 12956
Minisink (Town) 10998
Minisink Ford 12719
Minoa 13116
Mitchellsville 14810
Model City 14107
Modena 12548
Moffitsville 12981
Mohawk, *Montgomery* (Town) 12068
Mohawk, *Herkimer* 13407
Mohawk Hill 13309
Mohawk Mall 12304
Mohawk View 12110
Mohawk Village 12303
Mohegan Heights (Part of Yonkers) 10708
Mohegan Lake 10547
Mohonk Lake 12561
Moira 12957
Mombaccus 12446
Mongaup 12780
Mongaup Valley 12762
Monroe 10950
Monsey♦ 10952
Monsey Heights 10952
Montague (Town) 13367
Montario Point 13661
Montauk♦ 11954
Montauk Beach 11954
Montclair Colony 11964
Montebello 10901
Monterey 14812
Montezuma 13117
Montgomery 12549
Monticello 12701
Montour (Town) 14865
Montour Falls 14865
Montrose 10548
Montville 13118
Moody 12986
Mooers 12958
Mooers Forks 12959
Moores Mill 12569
Moorhouse Corner 12037
Moose River 13433
Moravia 13118
Moreau (Town) 12801
Morehouse (Town) 13324
Morehouseville 13324
Moreland 14812
Morey Park 12123
Morgan (Part of New York) 10001
Morgan Hill 12401
Morganville 14143
Moriah 12960
Moriah Center 12961
Moriches 11955
Morley 13617
Morningside (Part of New York)‡ 10026
Morris 13808
Morrisania (Part of New York)‡ 10456
Morris Heights (Part of New York)‡ 10453
Morrison Heights 12549
Morrisonville♦ 12962
Morris Park (Part of New York)‡ 10461
Morristown 13664
Morrisville 13408
Morsston 12758
Morton, *Monroe* 14464
Morton, *Orleans* 14508
Mosherville 12074
Mosholu (Part of New York)‡ 10467
Mosquito Point 12468
Mott Haven (Part of New York)‡ 10454
Mott Haven Junction (Part of New York) 10454
Mottville 13119
Mountain Dale 12763
Mountain Lodge 10950
Mountain View, *Franklin* 12969
Mountain View, *Rensselaer* 12180
Mountain View East 10989
Mountainville 10953
Mount Carmel (Part of New York)‡ 10458
Mount Hope, *Orange* 10940
Mount Hope (Part of Hastings-on-Hudson) 10706
Mount Ivy♦ 10970
Mount Kisco 10549
Mount Loretto (Part of New York) 10309
Mount Marion 12456
Mount Merion Park 12456
Mount Morris 14510
Mount Pleasant, *Westchester* (Town) 10591
Mount Pleasant, *Oswego* 13069
Mount Pleasant, *Ulster* 12457
Mount Prosper 12790
Mount Ross 12567
Mount Sinai♦ 11766
Mount Tremper 12457
Mount Upton 13809
Mount Vernon, *Erie* 14075
Mount Vernon, *Westchester* 10550-53
For specific ZIP Codes call (888) 275-8777, or your local postmaster.
Mount View Acres 12184
Mount View Estates 12184
Mount Vision 13810
Moyers Corners 13339
Mt. Riga 12546
Mud Mills 14513
Muitzeskill 12156
Mumford 14511
Mungers Corners 13069
Municipal Building (Part of New York)‡ 11201
Munnsville 13409
Munsey Park 11030
Munsons Corners♦ 13045
Murdochs Crossing 14098
Murdock Woods 10583
Murray 14470
Murray Hill, *New York* (Part of New York)‡ 10016*
… 10156†
Murray Hill, *Queens* (Part of New York) 11354
Murray Hill (Part of Scarsdale) 10583
Murray Isle 13624
Muttontown 11791
Mycenae 13066
Myers 14882
Myers Grove 12739
Nanticoke (Town) 13803
Nanticoke 13802
Nanuet♦ 10954
Nanuet Mall 10954
Napanoch♦ 12458
Napeaque 11930
Naples 14512
Napoli 14755
Narrowsburg 12764
Nashville 14062
Nassau 12123
Nassau Lake 12123
Nassau Mall 11756
Nassau Shores 11758
Natural Bridge 13665
Natural Dam 13642
Naumburg 13620
Nauraushaun 10965
Navarino 13108
Nedrow 13120
Nelliston 13410
Nelson 13035
Nelsonville 10516
Nepera Park (Part of Yonkers) 10710
Neponsit (Part of New York) 11694
Nepperhan (Part of Yonkers) 10703
Neptune (Part of New York)‡ 11224
Nesconset♦ 11767
Neversink 12765
Nevis 12583
New Albion 14719
Newark 14513
Newark Valley 13811
New Baltimore 12124
New Berlin 13411
New Berlin Junction 13733
New Boston 13158
New Bremen 13367
New Brighton (Part of New York) 10310
Newburg 14550
Newburgh (Town) 12550
Newburgh 12550-52
For specific ZIP Codes call (888) 275-8777, or your local postmaster.
New Cassel♦ 11590
New Castle (Town) 10514
New City♦ 10956
New City Park 10956
Newcomb 12852
New Concord 12060
New Dorp (Part of New York)‡ 10306
New Dorp Beach (Part of New York) 10306
New Ebenezer 14224
New Falconwood 14072
Newfane♦ 14108
Newfield♦ 14867
New Hackensack 12590
New Hamburg 12590
New Hampton 10958
New Hartford♦ 13413
New Hartford Shopping Center (Part of New Hartford) 13413
New Haven 13121
New Hempstead 10977
New Hope 13118
New Hudson (Town) 14714
New Hurley 12525
New Hyde Park 11040-42
For specific ZIP Codes call (888) 275-8777, or your local postmaster.
New Ireland 13905
New Kingston 12459
Newkirk (Part of New York)‡ 11226
New Lebanon 12125
New Lebanon Center 12125
New Lisbon 13415
New Lots (Part of New York)‡ 11208
New Market (Part of Niagara Falls)‡ 14301
New Milford 10959
New Oregon 14057
New Paltz 12561
Newport, *Herkimer* 13416
Newport, *Monroe* 14617
Newport, *Onondaga* 13164
New Rochelle 10801-02
… 10804-05
For specific ZIP Codes call (888) 275-8777, or your local postmaster.
New Russia 12964
New Salem, *Albany* 12186
New Salem, *Ulster* 12401
New Scotland 12159
Newsday‡ 11747
New Springville (Part of New York)‡ 10314
New Square 10977
Newstead (Town) 14001
New Suffolk 11956
Newton Falls 13666
Newton Hook 12173
Newtonville 12128
Newtown 11946
New Utrecht (Part of New York) 11204
New Vernon 10940
Newville 13365
New Windsor♦ 12553
New Woodstock 13122

New York

… 10001-99
… 10101-99
… 10201-82
For specific ZIP Codes call (888) 275-8777, or your local postmaster.

Colleges & Universities

Audrey Cohen Coll 10013
Bank Street Coll of Education 10025
Barnard Coll 10027
Boricua Coll 10032
City Univ of N Y, Bernard M Baruch Coll 10010
City Univ of N Y, City Coll 10031
City Univ of N Y, Graduate School & Univ Center 10036
City Univ of N Y, Hunter Coll 10021
City Univ of N Y, John Jay Coll of Criminal Justice 10019
The Coll of Insurance 10007
Columbia Univ in the City of N Y 10027
Cooper Union 10003
Cornell Univ Medical Campus 10021
Fashion Institute of Technology 10001
The Juilliard School 10023
Manhattan School of Music 10027
Marymount Manhattan Coll 10021
Mount Sinai School of Medicine 10029
New School for Social Reasearch 10011
New York Institute of Technology-Manhattan Campus 10023
New York Law School 10013
New York School of Interior Design 10021
New York Univ 10012
Pace Univ 10038
School of Visual Arts 10010
Teachers Coll, Columbia Univ 10027
Touro Coll 10010
Yeshiva Univ 10033

Financial Institutions

Amalgamated Bank 10003
Apple Bank for Svgs 10172
Bank Leumi USA 10017
Bank of New York 10286
Bank of Tokyo-Mitsubishi Trust 10020
Brown Brothers Harriman & Co 10005
The Chase Manhattan Bank 10081
Citibank, NA 10043
Commercial Bank 10022
Depository Trust Co 10041
The Dime Savings Bank 10017
Emigrant Svgs Bank 10017
First Chicago International 10019
Flushing Savings Bank 10003
The Fuji Bank & Trust Co 10048
GreenPoint Bank 10017
IBJ Schroder Bank & Trust Co 10004
Israel Discount Bank 10017
LTCB Trust Co 10006
Manufacturers & Traders Trust Co 10022
Marine Midland Bank 10005
The Merchants Bank 10013
Morgan Guaranty Trust Co 10260
Republic Nat Bank 10018
Safra Nat Bank 10036
The Sanwa Bank Limited 10055

Hospitals

Bellevue Hosp Ctr 10016
Beth Isreal Med Ctr 10128
Lenox Hill Hosp 10021
Memorial Hosp for Cancer & Allied Diseases 10021
Mount Sinai Med Ctr 10029
New York Univ Med Ctr 10016
Presbyterian Hosp 10032
St Luke's-Roosevelt Hosp Ctr 10025
St Vincent's Hosp & Med Ctr 10011

Hotels/Motels

Best Western President 10036
Crowne Plaza Manhattan 10019
Doubletree Guest Suites 10036
Edison 10036
Four Seasons 10022
Grand Hyatt 10017
The Helmsley 10017
Hilton & Towers 10019
Holiday Inn, Manhattan-Soho Downtown 10013
Hotel Pennsylvania 10001
Le Parker Meridien 10019
Loews 10022
Marriott at the World Trade Center 10048
Marriott Marquis 10036
Mayflower 10023
Millennium Broadway 10036
The Millennium Hilton 10007
New Yorker 10001
Palace 10022
Park Central 10019
The Plaza 10019
Quality Lexington 10017
Ramada Milford Plaza 10036
Roosevelt 10017
St Moritz on the Park 10019
Sheraton Hotel & Towers 10019
The Waldorf-Astoria 10022
Wellington 10019

Military Installations

Coast Guard Support Ctr, Governors Island 10004

New York Mills 13417
New York Mills Gardens 13492
Niagara (Town) 14302
Niagara Falls 14301-05
For specific ZIP Codes call (888) 275-8777, or your local postmaster.
Niagara Falls International Airport (AFB 6670) 914 14304
Niagara Square‡ 14201-02
For specific ZIP Codes call (888) 275-8777, or your local postmaster.
Niagara University 14109
Nichols, *Steuben* 14801
Nichols, *Tioga* 13812
Nichols Plaza (Part of Watertown) 13601
Nichols Run 14753
… 14760
For specific ZIP Codes call (888) 275-8777, or your local postmaster.
Nicholville 12965
Niets Crest 14710
Nile 14739
Niles 13152
Nimmonsburg 13901
Nineveh 13813
Nineveh Junction 13730
Niobe 14758
Niskayuna 12309
Nissequogue 11780
Niverville 12130
Noblesboro 13324
Norfolk♦ 13667
Normansville 12054
North (Part of Yonkers)‡ 10703
North Afton 13730
North Almond 14807
North Amityville♦ 11701
Northampton, *Fulton* (Town) 12134
Northampton, *Suffolk* 11901
North Argyle 12809
North Babylon♦ 11703
North Bailey 14226
North Baldwin‡ 11510
North Bangor 12966
North Bay 13123
North Bay Shore♦ 11706

* Area Zip Code † Post Office Boxes ‡ Postal Station ♦ Census Designated Place *Italic Type* **County**

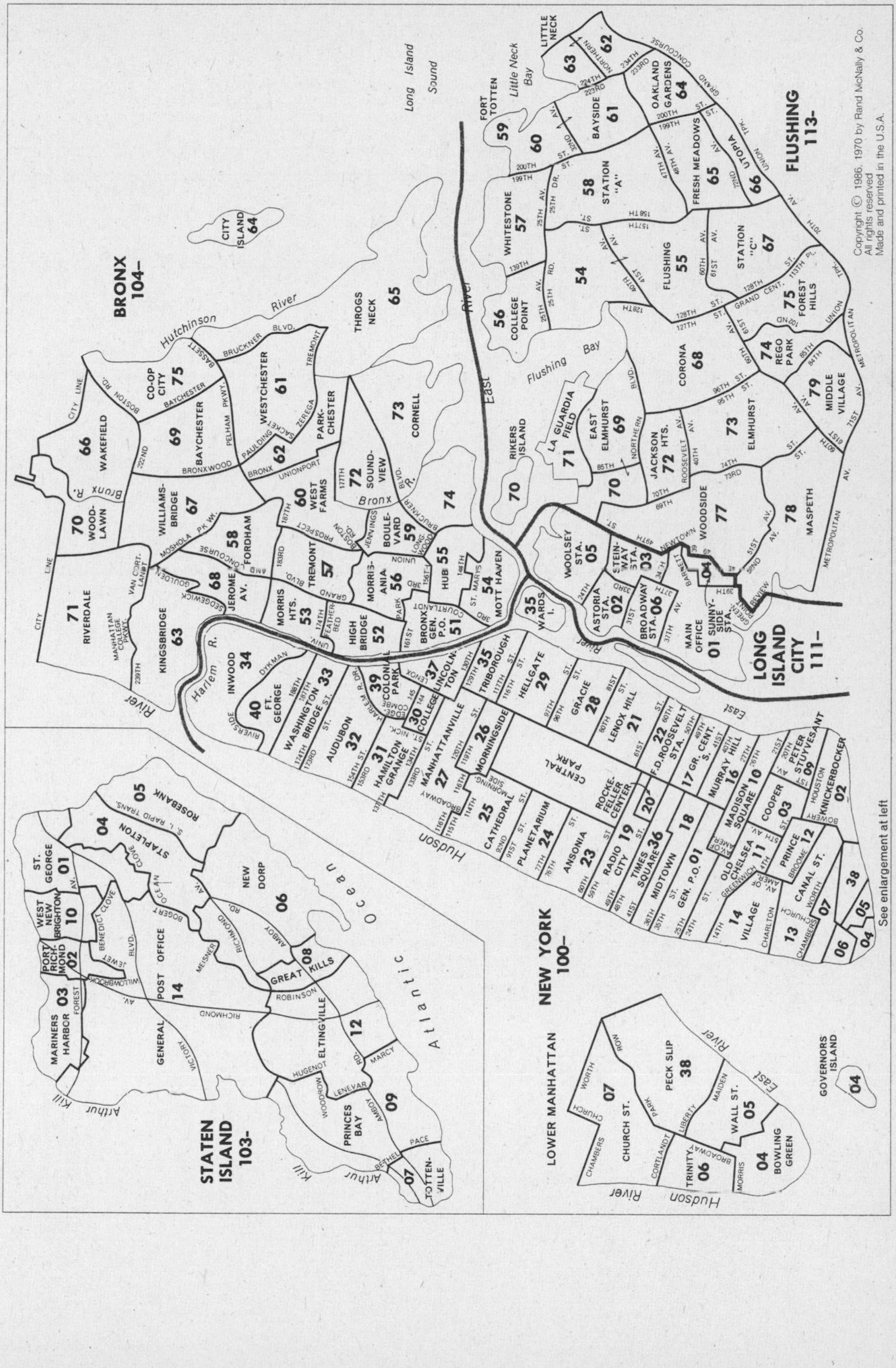

BRONX 104-

CITY ISLAND 64, THROGS NECK 65, WESTCHESTER 61, CO-OP CITY 75, WAKEFIELD 66, BAYCHESTER 69, PARK-CHESTER 62, CORNELL 73, SOUND-VIEW 72, WEST FARMS 60, WILLIAMS-BRIDGE 67, WOOD-LAWN 70, FORDHAM 58, BOULE-VARD 59, 74, TREMONT 57, MORRIS-ANIA 56, HUB 55, MOTT HAVEN 54, RIVERDALE 71, KINGSBRIDGE 63, JEROME AV. 68, MORRIS HTS. 53, HIGH BRIDGE 52, BRONX GEN. P.O. 51

NEW YORK 100-

INWOOD 34, FT. GEORGE 40, WASHINGTON BRIDGE 33, AUDUBON 32, COLONIAL PARK 39, HAMILTON GRANGE 31, COLLEGE 30, LINCOLN-TON 37, MANHATTANVILLE 27, MORNINGSIDE 26, TRIBOROUGH 35, WARDS I. 35, HELLGATE 29, GRACIE 28, LENOX HILL 21, CATHEDRAL 25, PLANETARIUM 24, ANSONIA 23, CENTRAL PARK, ROCKE-FELLER CENTER 20, RADIO CITY 19, TIMES SQUARE 36, F.D. ROOSEVELT STA. 22, GR. CENT. S. 17, MIDTOWN 18, MURRAY HILL 16, GEN. P.O. 01, MADISON SQUARE 10, OLD CHELSEA 11, COOPER 03, PETER STUYVESANT 09, KNICKERBOCKER 02, VILLAGE 14, PRINCE 12, CANAL ST. 13, 07, 38, 05, 06, 04

See enlargement at left

LOWER MANHATTAN

CHURCH ST. 07, PECK SLIP 38, WALL ST. 05, TRINITY 06, BOWLING GREEN 04, GOVERNORS ISLAND 04

LONG ISLAND CITY 111-

WOOLSEY STA. 05, ASTORIA STA. 02, STEIN-WAY STA. 03, BROADWAY STA. 06, MAIN OFFICE 01, SUNNY-SIDE STA. 04

FLUSHING 113-

LITTLE NECK 62, 63, OAKLAND GARDENS 64, BAYSIDE 61, FORT TOTTEN 59, 60, WHITESTONE 57, STATION "A" 58, FRESH MEADOWS 65, UTOPIA 66, COLLEGE POINT 56, 54, FLUSHING 55, STATION "C" 67, FOREST HILLS 75, REGO PARK 74, CORONA 68, MIDDLE VILLAGE 79, RIKERS ISLAND, LA GUARDIA FIELD 71, EAST ELMHURST 69, JACKSON HTS. 72, ELMHURST 73, 70, WOODSIDE 77, MASPETH 78

STATEN ISLAND 103-

ST. GEORGE 01, ROSEBANK 05, STAPLETON 04, WEST NEW BRIGHTON 10, PORT RICHMOND 02, NEW DORP 06, GREAT KILLS 08, MARINERS HARBOR 03, GENERAL POST OFFICE 14, ELTINGVILLE 12, PRINCES BAY 09, TOTTEN-VILLE 07

Long Island Sound, Little Neck Bay, Flushing Bay, East River, Harlem R., Hudson River, Hutchinson River, Bronx R., Atlantic Ocean, Arthur Kill

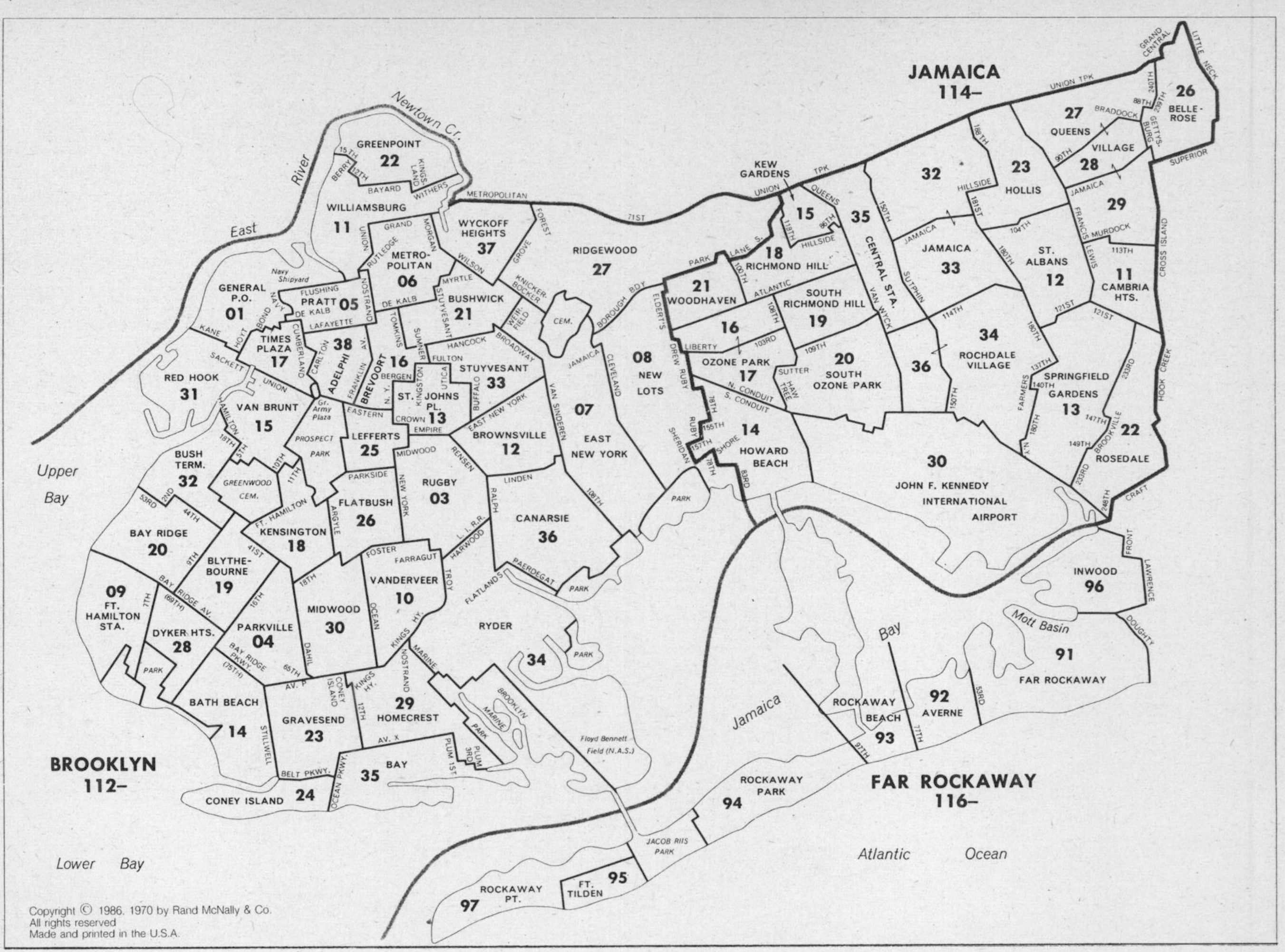
JAMAICA
114–
26 BELLE-ROSE
27 QUEENS
28 VILLAGE
29
11 CAMBRIA HTS.
22 ROSEDALE
13 SPRINGFIELD GARDENS
12 ST. ALBANS
23 HOLLIS
32
33 JAMAICA
34 ROCHDALE VILLAGE
36
35 CENTRAL STA.
19 SOUTH RICHMOND HILL
20 SOUTH OZONE PARK
15
18 RICHMOND HILL
KEW GARDENS
16
17 OZONE PARK
14 HOWARD BEACH
21 WOODHAVEN
30 JOHN F. KENNEDY INTERNATIONAL AIRPORT
96 INWOOD
91 FAR ROCKAWAY
92 AVERNE
93 ROCKAWAY BEACH
94 ROCKAWAY PARK
95 FT. TILDEN
97 ROCKAWAY PT.
FAR ROCKAWAY
116–
Atlantic Ocean
Mott Basin
Jamaica Bay
27 RIDGEWOOD
08 NEW LOTS
07 EAST NEW YORK
36 CANARSIE
34 RYDER
37 WYCKOFF HEIGHTS
21 BUSHWICK
33 STUYVESANT
12 BROWNSVILLE
03 RUGBY
13 ST. JOHNS PL.
16
22 GREENPOINT
11 WILLIAMSBURG
06 METRO-POLITAN
05 PRATT
38 ADELPHI
BREVOORT
25 LEFFERTS
26 FLATBUSH
10 VANDERVEER
29 HOMECREST
35 BAY
30 MIDWOOD
23 GRAVESEND
24 CONEY ISLAND
18 KENSINGTON
04 PARKVILLE
15 VAN BRUNT
17 TIMES PLAZA
01 GENERAL P.O.
31 RED HOOK
32 BUSH TERM.
19 BLYTHE-BOURNE
20 BAY RIDGE
28 DYKER HTS.
14 BATH BEACH
09 FT. HAMILTON STA.
Floyd Bennett Field (N.A.S.)
Newtown Cr.
East River
Upper Bay
Lower Bay
BROOKLYN
112–

Place	ZIP
North Beach (Part of New York)	11369
North Bellmore♦	11710
North Bellport	11713
North Bergen	14416
North Bethlehem	12203
North Blenheim	12131
North Bloomfield	14472
North Boston♦	14110
North Branch	12766
North Bridgewater	13318
North Broadalbin	12025
North Brookfield	13418
North Burke	12917
Northbush	12095
North Cameron	14819
North Castle (Town)	10504
North Centereach	11720
North Chatham	12132
North Chemung	14861
North Chili	14514
North Chittenango	13037
North Clove	12545
North Clymer	14767
North Cohocton	14808
North Collins	14111
North Columbia	13357
North Corners	13658
North Country Shopping Center (Part of Plattsburgh)	12901
North Creek	12853
Northcrest	12065
North Cuba	14727
North Dansville (Town)	14437
North Darien	14036
North East (Town)	12546
Northeast Center	12546
Northeast Henrietta	14534
Northeast Ithaca♦	14850
North Easton	12834
North Elba (Town)	12946
North Evans	14112
North Fair Haven (Part of Fair Haven)	13064
North Fenton	13746
Northfield	13856
North Franklin	13820
North Gage	13502
North Gainesville	14550
Northgate Estates (Part of Rome)	13440
North Germantown	12526
North Granville	12854
North Great River♦	11722
North Greece	14515
North Greenbush (Town)	12198
North Greenwich	12834
North Hannibal	13074
North Harmony (Town)	14785
North Harpersfield	12093
North Hartland	14008
North Haven	11963
North Hebron	12832
North Hempstead (Town)	11040
North Highland	10516
North Hills	11040
North Hillsdale	12529
North Hoosick	12133
North Hornell	14843
North Hudson	12855
North Huron	14590
North Ilion	13340
North Jasper	14819
North Java	14113
North Jay	12941
North Kortright	13739
North Lansing	14852
North Lawrence	12967
North Lindenhurst♦	11757
North Litchfield	13340
North Lynbrook	11563
North Manlius	13082
North Massapequa♦	11758
North Merrick♦	11566
North New Hyde Park♦	11040
North Norwich	13814
North Olean (Part of Olean)	14760
North Pembroke	14020
North Petersburg	12138
North Pharsalia	13844
North Pitcher	13124
North Pole	12946
Northport	11768
North River	12856
North Rockville Centre	11570
North Rose	14516
North Rush	14543
North Russell	13617
North Salem	10560
North Sanford	13754
North Schodack	12061
North Selden	11784
North Settlement	12496
North Shore Beach	11778
North Side (Part of Buffalo)‡	14207
North Spencer	14883
North Stephentown	12168
North Sterling	13156
North Stockholm	13668
North Syracuse	13212
North Tarrytown	10591
North Tonawanda	14120
Northtown Plaza	14226
Northumberland	12871
North Victory	13111
Northview Gardens	14094
Northville, *Fulton*	12134
Northville, *Suffolk*	11901
North Waverly	14892
Northway Mall, The	12205
Northway Plaza	12801
North Western	13486
Northwest Ithaca♦	14850
North White Plains (Part of White Plains)‡	10603
North Wilmurt	13438
North Winfield	13491
North Wolcott	14590
Northwood	12188
North Woodmere	11581
Norton Hill	12083
Norton Summit	14895
Norway	13416
Norwich	13815
Norwich Corners	13456
Norwood	13668
Nostrand (Part of New York)‡	11235
Nottingham Estates	14094
Noxon	12603
Noyack♦	11963
Number Four	13367
Nunda	14517
Nyack	10960
Oak Beach	11702
Oakdale♦	11769
Oakdale Mall (Part of Johnson City)	13790
Oakfield	14125
Oak Hill	12460
Oakland	14517
Oakland Gardens (Part of New York)‡	11364
Oakland Valley	12729
Oak Orchard	14103
Oak Point	13646
Oak Ridge, *Montgomery*	12066
Oakridge, *Onondaga*	13088
Oaks Corners	14518
Oaksville	13337
Oakwood, *Cayuga*	13021
Oakwood (Part of New York)	10306
Oakwood Beach (Part of New York)	10306
Oakwood Heights (Part of New York)	10301
Obernburg	12767
Obi	14727
Occanum	13865
Ocean Bay Park	11706
Ocean Beach	11770
Oceanside♦	11572
Odessa	14869
Ogden (Town)	14559
Ogden Center (Part of Spencerport)	14559
Ogdensburg	13669
O'Hara Corners	12083
Ohio	13324
Ohioville	12561
Oil Springs Indian Reservation	14081
Olcott♦	14126
Old Bethpage♦	11804
Old Brookville	11545
Old Central Bridge	12035
Old Chatham	12136
Old Chelsea (Part of New York)‡	10011
Old Field	11733
Old Field South	11790
Old Forge	13420
Old Mastic	11951
Old Orchard Point	14487
Old Stony Brook	11790
Old Town (Part of New York)	10304
Old Village (Part of Great Neck)‡	11023
Old Westbury	11568
Olean	14760
Olean Center Mall (Part of Olean)	14760
Olive (Town)	12461
Olivebridge	12461
Oliverea	12410
Olmstedville	12857
Omar	13607
Omi	12075
Onativia	13084
Onchiota	12989
Oneida	13421
Oneida Castle	13421
Oneonta (Town)	13861
Oneonta	13820
Onesquethaw	12067
Oniontown	12522
Onleys Station	10940
Onondaga	13215
Onondaga Indian Reservation	13120
Ontario	14519
Ontario Center	14520
Ontario on the Lake	14519
Onteo Beach	14464
Onteora Park	12485
Oot Park	13057
Open Meadows	14710
Oppenheim	13329
Oquaga Lake	13754
Oramel	14711
Oran	13104
Orange (Town)	14812
Orangeburg♦	10962
Orange Lake	12550
Orangeport	14067
Orangetown (Town)	10960
Orangeville (Town)	14569
Orangeville Center	14011
Orchard Knoll	14845
Orchard Park	14127
Orchard Village	13031
Oregon, *Fulton*	13470
Oregon, *Suffolk*	11952
Orient	11957
Orienta (Part of Mamaroneck)	10543
Oriental Park	14712
Orient Point	11957
Oriskany	13424
Oriskany Falls	13425
Orlando	14755
Orleans, *Jefferson* (Town)	13656
Orleans, *Ontario*	14432
Orleans Four Corners	13656
Orwell	13426
Oscawana Lake	10579
Osceola	13316
Ossian (Town)	14437
Ossian Center	14437
Ossining	10562
Oswegatchie (Town)	13654
Oswegatchie	13670
Oswego	13126
Oswego Bitter	13031
Oswego Center	13126
Otego	13825
Otisco	13159
Otisco Valley	13110
Otisville	10963
Otsego (Town)	13337
Otselic	13072
Otter Creek	13343
Otter Lake	13338
Ott Meadows	13088
Otto	14766
Ouaquaga	13826
Overlook, *Dutchess*	12603
Overlook, *Saratoga*	12822
Ovid	14521
Ovington (Part of New York)‡	11220
Owasco	13130
Owego	13827
Owens Mills	14825
Owls Head	12969
Oxbow	13671
Oxford, *Chenango*	13830
Oxford, *Orange*	10918
Oyster Bay♦	11771
Oyster Bay Cove	11771
Ozone Park (Part of New York)	11416
Pacama	12401
Paddlefords	14424
Paddy Hill	13634
Paines Hollow	13407
Painted Post	14870
Palatine (Town)	13428
Palatine Bridge	13428
Palentown	12446
Palenville	12463
Palermo	13069
Palisades	10964
Palmyra	14522
Pamelia (Town)	13637
Pamelia Four Corners	13637
Panama	14767
Panorama	14625
Panther Lake	13028
Pantigo	11937
Paradise Hill	12051
Paradox	12858
Parcells Corner	14062
Paris	13456
Parish	13131
Parishville	13672
Parishville Center	13676
Paris Station	13456
Parkchester (Part of New York)‡	10462
Park Hill, *Onondaga*	13057
Park Hill (Part of Yonkers)	10705
Park of Edgewater (Part of New York)	10465
Parkside (Part of New York)‡	11375
Park Slope (Part of New York)‡	11215
Park Station	14838
Parkston	12758
Parksville	12768
Park Terrace	13903
Parkville (Part of New York)‡	11204
Parkway (Part of New York)‡	10462
Parma (Town)	14468
Parma Center	14468
Parma Corners	14559
Parson Farms	13031
Pastime Park	14456
Pataukunk	12446
Patchin (Part of New York)‡	10011
Patchinville	14572
Patchogue	11772
Patria	12187
Patroon (Part of Albany)‡	12204
Patterson	12563
Pattersonville	12137
Paul Smiths	12970
Pavilion	14525
Pavilion Center	14525
Pawling	12564
Payne Beach	14468
Peabrook	12760
Peach Lake♦	10509
Peakville	13756
Pearl Creek	14591
Pearl River♦	10965
Peas Eddy	13783
Peasleeville	12985
Peat Corners	13036
Pebble Beach	14480
Peck Slip (Part of New York)‡	10038
Peconic♦	11958
Peekskill	10566-67
For specific ZIP Codes call (888) 275-8777, or your local postmaster.	
Pekin	14132
Pelham	10803
Pelham Manor	10803
Pellets Island	10958
Pembroke	14036
Penataquit‡	11706
Pendleton	14094
Pendleton Center	14094
Penfield	14526
Pennellville	13132
Penn Yan	14527
Peoria	14525
Perch River	13601
Perinton (Town)	14450
Perkinsville	14529
Perry	14530
Perry Center	14530
Perry City	14886
Perrysburg	14129
Perrys Mills	12919
Perryville	13032
Persia (Town)	14070
Perth	12010
Peru, *Clinton*♦	12972
Peru, *Onondaga*	13112
Peruville	13073
Peterboro	13134
Petersburgh	12138
Peter Stuyvesant (Part of New York)‡	10009
Peth	14741
Petries Corners	13367
Petrolia	14895
Pharsalia (Town)	13758
Phelps	14532
Philadelphia	13673
Philipse Manor (Part of North Tarrytown)	10591
Philipstown (Town)	10516
Phillipsburg	10940
Phillips Creek	14813
Phillips Mills	14712
Phillipsport	12769
Philmont	12565
Phoenicia	12464
Phoenix	13135
Phoenix Mills	13326
Picketts Corners	12981
Pickettsville	13672
Piercefield	12973
Pierces Corner	13642
Pierceville	13334
Piermont	10968
Pierrepont	13617
Pierrepont Manor	13674
Pierstown	13326
Piffard	14533
Pike	14130
Pike Five Corners	14024
Pilgrim (Part of New York)‡	10461
Pilgrim Corners (Part of Middletown)	10940
Pilgrimport	14489
Pillar Point	13634
Pilot Knob	12844
Pinckney (Town)	13626
Pindars Corners	13860
Pine (Part of Albany)‡	12203
Pine Aire	11706
Pinebrook (Part of New Rochelle)	10804
Pinebrook Heights (Part of New Rochelle)	10804
Pine Bush♦	12566
Pine City	14871
Pine Grove, *Lewis*	13343
Pine Grove, *St. Lawrence*	13658
Pine Grove, *Schoharie*	12122
Pinegrove Park	12205
Pine Hill, *Erie*	14225
Pine Hill, *Oneida*	13471
Pine Hill, *Ulster*	12465
Pinehill Estates	12303
Pinehurst	14085
Pine Island	10969
Pine Knolls	13760
Pine Lake	12032
Pine Meadows	13302
Pine Neck	11963
Pine Plains♦	12567
Pine Ridge Estates	10573
Pinesville	13856
Pine Tavern Corners	14481
Pine Valley, *Chemung*	14872
Pine Valley, *Suffolk*	11901
Pineville	13302
Pinewood Estates	12303
Pine Woods	13310
Pioneer	12020
Piseco‡	12139
Pitcairn	13648
Pitcher	13136
Pitcher Hill	13212
Pittsfield	13411
Pittsford	14534
Pittstown	12094
Place Corners	12431
Plainedge♦	11714
Plainfield (Town)	13491
Plainfield Center	13491
Plainview♦	11803
Plainville	13137
Plandome	11030
Plandome Heights	11030
Plandome Manor	11030
Planetarium (Part of New York)‡	10024
Plato	14171
Platte Clove	12427
Plattekill	12568
Platten	14098
Plattsburgh (Town)	12918
Plattsburgh	12901-03
For specific ZIP Codes call (888) 275-8777, or your local postmaster.	
Plattsburgh Air Force Base	12903
Plattsburgh West♦	12962
Plaza (Part of New York)‡	11101
Pleasantbrook	13320
Pleasantdale	12182
Pleasant Plains, *Dutchess*	12580
Pleasant Plains (Part of New York)	10309

Pleasant Point 13126
Pleasant Ridge 12594
Pleasantside 10567
Pleasant Valley, *Dutchess*♦ 12569
Pleasant Valley, *Oneida* 13480
Pleasant Valley, *Steuben* 14810
Pleasantville 10570-72
For specific ZIP Codes call (888) 275-8777, or your local postmaster.
Plessis 13675
Plymouth 13832
Pocantico Hills 10591
Podunk 14886
Poestenkill♦ 12140
Point Au Rouche 12901
Point Breeze 14477
Point Chautauqua 14728
Point Lookout 11569
Point O'Woods 11706
Point Peninsula 13693
Point Pleasant 14622
Point Rochester 14512
Point Rock 13471
Point Stockholm 14712
Point Vivian 13607
Poland, *Chautauqua* (Town) 14747
Poland, *Herkimer* 13431
Poland Center 14747
Polkville 13101
Pomfret (Town) 14063
Pomona 10970
Pomona Heights (Part of Pomona) 10901
Pomonok (Part of New York)‡ 11365
Pompey 13138
Pompey Center 13104
Ponck Hockie (Part of Kingston) 12401
Pond Eddy 12770
Ponquogue 11946
Poolsburg 12173
Poolville 13332
Poospatuck Indian Reservation 11950
Pope Mills 13654
Poplar Beach 14541
Poplar Ridge 13139
Poquott 11733
Portage 14846
Portageville 14536
Port Authority (Part of New York)‡ 10011
Port Ben 12489
Port Byron 13140
Port Chester 10573
Port Crane 13833
Port Dickinson 13901
Porter (Town) 14131
Porter Center 14131
Porter Corners 12859
Porterville 14052
Port Ewen♦ 12466
Port Gibson 14537
Port Henry 12974
Port Ivory (Part of New York) 10303
Port Jefferson 11777
Port Jefferson Station♦ 11776
Port Jervis 12771
Port Kent 12975
Portland 14769
Portlandville 13834
Port Leyden 13433
Port Morris (Part of New York) 10454
Port Ontario 13142
Port Richmond (Part of New York)‡ 10302
Portville 14770
Port Washington♦ 11050
Port Washington North 11050
Post Corners 12057
Post Creek 14812
Potsdam 13676
Potter 14527
Potter Hollow 12469
Pottersville 12860
Poughkeepsie (Town) 12602
Poughkeepsie 12601-03
For specific ZIP Codes call (888) 275-8777, or your local postmaster.
Poughquag 12570
Pound Ridge 10576
Pratt (Part of New York)‡ 11205
Pratt Corners 13087
Prattsburgh 14873
Pratts Hollow 13409
Prattsville 12468
Preble 13141
Prendergast Point 14757
Presho 14858
Preston 13830
Preston Hollow 12469
Price Corners 14772
Prince (Part of New York)‡ 10012
Princes Bay (Part of New York)‡ 10309
Princetown 12056
Progress 12078
Prospect 13435
Prospect Heights 12144
Prospect Hill 12188
Prospect Park West (Part of New York)‡ 11215
Providence (Town) 12850
Pulaski 13142
Pulteney 14874
Pultneyville 14538
Pulvers 12075
Pulvers Corners 12567
Pumpkin Hill 14422
Pumpkin Hollow 12529
Purchase (Part of Harrison) 10577
Purdys 10578
Purdys Mills 12910
Purling 12470
Putnam (Town) 12861
Putnam Lake♦ 10509
Putnam Station 12861
Putnam Valley 10579
Pyramid Mall Ithaca (Part of Lansing) 14850
Pyrites 13677
Quackenbush Hill 14830
Quackenkill 12052
Quail (Part of Albany) 12206
Quaker Basin 13052
Quaker Hill 12564
Quaker Ridge (Part of New Rochelle) 10801
Quaker Springs 12871
Quaker Street 12053
Quarry Heights 10603
Quarryville 12477
Queechy 12029
Queens 11001-06
11101-06
11301-86
11401-36
11601-97
For specific ZIP Codes call (888) 275-8777, or your local postmaster.
Queensbury (Town) 12801
Queensbury 12804
Queen's Center (Part of New York) 11373
Queens Village (Part of New York)‡ 11428
Quigley Park 14710
Quinneville 13746
Quioque 11978
Quogue 11959
Raceville 05764
Radio City (Part of New York)‡ 10019
Radison 13027
Rainbow Lake 12976
Ralmar Park 12302
Ramapo 10931
Ram Island 11964
Rampasture 11946
Randall 12072
Randallsville 13346
Randelville 10921
Randolph 14772
Ransomville♦ 14131
Rapids♦ 14094
Raquette Lake 13436
Rathbone 14801
Ravena 12143
Ravenwood (Part of Colonie) 12205
Rawson 14727
Ray Brook 12977
Raymertown 12180
Raymondville 13678
Rayville 12136
Reading (Town) 14876
Reading Center 14876
Reber 12996
Red Creek 13143
Redfalls 12468
Redfield 13437
Redford 12978
Red Hook, *Dutchess* 12571
Red Hook (Part of New York)‡ 11231
Red House 14779
Red Mills, *Columbia* 12513
Red Mills, *St. Lawrence* 13669
Red Oaks Mill♦ 12603
Red Rock, *Columbia* 12060
Red Rock, *Onondaga* 13027
Redwood, *Jefferson* 13679
Redwood (Part of Sag Harbor) 11963
Reeds Corner 14437
Reeds Corners 14437
Reeves Park 11901
Rego Park (Part of New York) 11374
Reidsville 12186
Remsen 13438
Remsenburg 11960
Rensselaer 12144
Rensselaer Falls 13680
Rensselaerville 12147
Residence Park (Part of New Rochelle) 10805
Retsof 14539
Rexford 12148
Rexville 14877
Reydon Shores 11971
Reynoldsville 14818
Rheims 14840
Rhinebeck 12572
Rhinecliff 12574
Rhode Island 13155
Ricard 13302
Rice Grove 13110
Riceville, *Cattaraugus* 14171
Riceville, *Fulton* 12078
Richburg 14774
Richfield 13439
Richfield Springs 13439
Richford 13835
Richland 13144
Richmond, *Ontario* (Town) 14471
Richmond, *Richmond* 10301-14
For specific ZIP Codes call (888) 275-8777, or your local postmaster.
Richmond Hill (Part of New York) 11418
Richmond Valley (Part of New York) 10309
Richmondville 12149
Richs Corners 14411
Richville 13681
Riders Mills 12024
Ridge, *Livingston* 14510
Ridge, *Suffolk* 11961
Ridgebury 10973
Ridgelea Heights 14094
Ridge Mills (Part of Rome) 13440
Ridgemont Plaza 14626
Ridgeway 14103
Ridgeway (Part of White Plains) 10601
Ridgewood, *Niagara* 14094
Ridgewood, *Oneida* 13501
Ridgewood (Part of New York) 11385
Ridgewood (Part of Owego) 13827
Rifton 12471
Riga (Town) 14428
Rigney Bluff 14612
Riley Cove 12020
Ringdahl Court (Part of Rome) 13440
Rio 12780
Riparius 12862
Ripley♦ 14775
Rippleton 13035
Risingville 14820
River (Part of Rochester)‡ 14627
Riverdale (Part of New York)‡ 10471
Riverhead♦ 11901
Riverside, *Broome* 13795
Riverside (Part of Buffalo) 14207
Riverside, *Otsego* 13838
Riverside, *Saratoga* 12118
Riverside, *Steuben* 14830
Riverside, *Suffolk*♦ 11901
Riverside Estates 11901
Riverside Mall (Part of Utica) 13502
Riverside Manors 14172
Riverside Park 12401
Riverview 12981
Roanoke 14143
Robbins Rest 11770
Roberts Corner 13650
Rochdale 12603
Rochdale Village (Part of New York)‡ 11434
Rochelle Heights (Part of New Rochelle) 10801
Rochelle Park (Part of New Rochelle) 10801
Rochester, *Ulster* (Town) 12404

Rochester, *Monroe* 14601-92

For specific ZIP Codes call (888) 275-8777, or your local postmaster.

Colleges & Universities

Nazareth Coll 14618
Roberts Wesleyan Coll 14624
Rochester Institute of Technology 14623
Saint Bernard's Institute 14620
St John Fisher Coll 14618
Univ of Rochester 14627

Financial Institutions

The Chase Manhattan Bank 14643
Citibank 14604
Fleet Bank 14638
Key Bank 14614
Manufacturers & Traders Trust Co 14614
Marine Midland 14639
OnBank & Trust Co 14618

Hospitals

General Hosp 14621
Genesee Hosp 14607
Monroe Community Hosp 14620
Strong Memorial Hosp of the Univ of Rochester 14642

Hotels/Motels

Holiday Inn, Henrietta 14623
Holiday Inn, Rochester Airport 14624
Hyatt Regency, Downtown 14604
Marriott, Thruway 14602
Radisson, Rochester Airport 14623

Military Installations

U S Property & Fiscal Off for New York (Warehouse No 2) 14623

Rockaway‡ 11690-91
For specific ZIP Codes call (888) 275-8777, or your local postmaster.
Rockaway Beach (Part of New York)‡ 11693
Rockaway Park (Part of New York)‡ 11694
Rockaway Point (Part of New York)‡ 11697
Rock City, *Cattaraugus* 14760
Rock City, *Dutchess* 12571
Rock City Falls 12863
Rock Cut 13078
Rockdale 13809
Rockefeller Center (Part of New York)‡ 10020
Rock Glen 14550
Rock Hill 12775
Rockhurst 12801
Rockland, *Rockland* 10962
Rockland, *Sullivan* 12776
Rockland Lake 10989
Rock Stream 14878
Rock Tavern 12575
Rockton 12010
Rock Valley 12760
Rockville, *Allegany* 14711
Rockville, *Orange* 10940
Rockville Centre 11570*
11571†
Rockville Lake 14711
Rockwells Mills 13843
Rockwood 12095
Rocky Point, *Clinton* 12901
Rocky Point, *Suffolk*♦ 11778
Rodman 13610†
13682*
Roe Park 10567
Roessleville♦ 12205
Rolling Acres 14559
Rolling Hills 14450
Rolling Meadows 12401
Romanoff 10512
Rombout Ridge 12603
Rome 13440-42
For specific ZIP Codes call (888) 275-8777, or your local postmaster.
Romulus 14541
Rondaxe 13420
Rondout (Part of Kingston) 12401
Ronkonkoma♦ 11779
Roosa Gap 12721
Roosevelt♦ 11575
Roosevelt Beach 14172
Roosevelt Field (Part of Garden City) 11530
Rooseveltown 13683
Root (Town) 12166
Roscoe 12776
Rose 14542
Rosebank (Part of New York)‡ 10305
Roseboom 13450
Rosecrans Park 12123
Rosedale (Part of New York) 11422
Rose Hill 13110
Rosemont Park (Part of Rensselaer) 12144
Rosendale♦ 12472
Roseton 12550
Rosiere 13618
Roslyn 11576
Roslyn Estates 11576
Roslyn Harbor 11576
Roslyn Heights♦ 11577
Rossburg 14776
Ross Corners 13850
Rossie 13646
Rossman 12173
Ross Mill 14733
Rosstown 14871
Rossville (Part of New York) 10309
Rotterdam♦ 12303
Rotterdam Junction 12150
Rotterdam Square Mall (Part of Schenectady) 12306
Round Lake 12151
Roundout Harbor 12466
Round Top 12473
Rouses Point 12979
Roxbury 12474
Roxbury (Part of New York) 11697
Royalton 14067
Ruby 12475
Ruby Corner 13646
Rugby (Part of New York)‡ 11203
Rumsey Ridge 14092
Rural Grove 12166
Rural Hill 13650
Rush 14543
Rushford 14777
Rushford Lake 14717
Rushville 14544
Russell 13684
Russell Gardens 11021
Russia 13431
Rutland (Town) 13638
Rutland Center 13601
Ryder (Part of New York)‡ 11234
Rye (Town) 10573
Rye 10580
Rye Brook 10573
Rye Hills 10573
Sabael 12864
Sabattis 12847
Sabbath Day Point 12874
Sacandaga 12134
Sackets Harbor 13685
Sacketts Lake 12701
Saddle Rock 11023
Saddle Rock Estates 11021
Sagamore 13436
Sagaponack 11962
Sages Cottages 11944
Sagetown 14871
Sag Harbor 11963
Sailors Snug Harbor (Part of New York) 10301
St. Albans (Part of New York) 11412
St. Andrew 12586
St. Armand (Town) 12913
St. Bonaventure♦ 14778
St. Elmo 12548
St. George (Part of New York)‡ 10301
St. Huberts 12943
St. James♦ 11780
St. James Heights 11780
St. Johnsburg 14302
St. Johns Place (Part of New York)‡ 11213

Place	ZIP
St. Johnsville	13452
St. Lawrence Park	13607
St. Mary's Park (Part of New York)	10455
St. Regis Falls	12980
St. Regis Indian Reservation	13655
St. Remy	12401
Saintsville	13082
Salamanca	14779
Salem	12865
Salem Center	10578
Salina, *Onondaga* (Town)	13088
Salina (Part of Syracuse)‡	13208
Salisbury	13365
Salisbury Center	13454
Salisbury Mills	12577
Salmon River	12901
Saltaire	11706
Salt Point	12578
Salt Springville	13320
Sammonsville	12095
Samsondale (Part of West Haverstraw)	10993
Samsonville	12481
Sanborn	14132
Sandford Boulevard (Part of Mount Vernon)‡	10550
Sandfordville	13676
Sand Hill, *Erie*	14001
Sand Hill, *Montgomery*	13339
Sand Hill, *Otsego*	13849
Sand Lake	12153
Sand Ridge♦	13132
Sands Point	11050
Sandusky	14133
Sandy Beach	14072
Sandy Creek	13145
Sandy Harbour Beach	14464
Sanford (Town)	13754
Sangerfield	13455
Sanitaria Springs	13833
San Remo	11754
Santa Clara	12980
Santapoque	11707
Saranac	12981
Saranac Inn	12983
Saranac Lake	12983
Saratoga (Town)	12871
Saratoga Lake	12866
Saratoga Springs	12866
Sardinia	14134
Saugerties	12477
Saugerties South♦	12477
Sauquoit	13456
Savannah	13146
Savona	14879
Sawkill	12401
Sawyers Corners	13021
Saxon Park	11706
Sayville♦	11782
Scarborough (Part of Briarcliff Manor)‡	10510
Scarsdale	10583
Schaghticoke	12154
Schaghticoke Hill	12154
Schenectady	12301-09
	12325
For specific ZIP Codes call (888) 275-8777, or your local postmaster.	
Schenevus	12155
Schermerhorn Corners	14747
Schodack (Town)	12033
Schodack Center	12033
Schodack Landing	12156
Schoharie	12157
Schonowe	12306
Schroeppel (Town)	13135
Schroon (Town)	12870
Schroon Falls	12870
Schroon Lake	12870
Schultzville	12572
Schuluski Estates	12188
Schuyler (Town)	13340
Schuyler Falls	12985
Schuyler Lake	13457
Schuylerville	12871
Scio	14880
Sciota	12992
Scipio (Town)	13147
Scipio Center	13147
Scipioville	13147
Sconondoa	13421
Scotchbush, *Fulton*	13452
Scotch Bush, *Montgomery*	12010
Scotia	12302
Scott	13077
Scottsburg	14545
Scotts Corner	12549
Scottsville	14546
Scranton	14075
Scriba (Town)	13126
Scriba Center	13126
Scribner Corners	13421
Sea Breeze	14617
Sea Cliff	11579
Seaford♦	11783
Seagate (Part of New York)	11224
Seager	12406
Searingtown♦	11507
Searsburg	14886
Sears Corners	10509
Searsville	12549
Seaside (Part of New York)	11694
Seaview	11770
Second Milo	14527
Seeley Creek	14871
Selden♦	11784
Selkirk	12158
Selkirk Beach	13142
Sellecks Corners	13625
Semans Corners	14512
Sempronius	13118
Seneca (Town)	14561
Seneca Army Depot	14541
Seneca Castle	14547
Seneca Falls	13148
Seneca Hill	13126
Seneca Knolls	13209
Seneca Mall, *Erie*	14224
Seneca Mall, *Onondaga*	13088
Seneca Point	14512
Sennett	13021
Sentinel Heights	13078
Setauket	11733
Settlers Hill	10509
Seven Hills	10512
Seventh Day Hollow	13072
Severance	12872
Seward	12043
Shackport	13757
Shadigee	14008
Shady	12409
Shandaken	12480
Shandelee	12758
Shannon Corners	14837
Sharon	13459
Sharon Center	13459
Sharon Springs	13459
Shawangunk (Town)	12589
Shawnee	14132
Sheds	13122
Sheepshead Bay (Part of New York)	11235
Shekomeko	12546
Shelby	14103
Shelby Basin	14103
Shelby Center	14103
Sheldon	14145
Sheldon Center	14145
Sheldrake	14521
Sheldrake Springs	14847
Shelter Island♦	11964
Shelter Island Heights♦	11965
Shenandoah	12533
Shenorock	10587
Shepards Corner	14433
Sherburne	13460
Sheridan	14135
Sheridan Park (Part of Geneva)	14456
Sherman	14781
Sherman Park	10594
Shermerhorn Landing	13646
Sherrill	13461
Sherwood Forest	12065
Sherwood Knolls	13031
Sherwood Park	12144
Shinhopple	13755
Shinnecock Hills♦	11946
Shinnecock Indian Reservation	11968
Shirewood	12065
Shirley♦	11967
Shivers Corners	12061
Shokan	12481
Sholam	12458
Shongo	16923
Shooktown (Part of Lockport)	14094
Shoppingtown Mall	13214
Shore Acres, *Chautauqua*	14712
Shore Acres, *Monroe*	14468
Shore Acres, *Suffolk*	11952
Shore Acres (Part of Mamaroneck)	10543
Shoreham	11786
Shore Haven	14787
Shorelands	14728
Shore Oaks	13126
Shorewood	11721
Shortsville	14548
Short Tract	14735
Shrub Oak	10588
Shumla	14063
Shushan	12873
Shutter Corners	12157
Shutts Corners	12043
Sibleyville	14472
Sidney	13838
Sidney Center	13839
Siena	12211
Sillimans Corners	14030
Siloam	13409
Silver Bay	12874
Silver Beach	11965
Silver Creek	14136
Silver Lake, *Orange*	10940
Silver Lake, *Wyoming*	14549
Silver Lake Village	10940
Silver Springs	14550
Simmons Island (Part of Cohoes)	12047
Simpsonville	12155
Sinclairville	14782
Sissonville	13676
Skaneateles	13152
Skaneateles Falls	13153
Skaneateles Junction	13060
Skerry	12966
Skinnerville	13697
Sky Meadow Farms	10573
Slab City, *Cortland*	13141
Slab City, *St. Lawrence*	13676
Slate Hill	10973
Slaterville Springs	14881
Slateville	12832
Sleepy Hollow Manor (Part of Tarrytown)	10591
Sleightsburg	12401
Slingerlands	12159
Sloan	14225
Sloansville	12160
Sloatsburg	10974
Slyboro	12832
Smallwood	12778
Smartville	13083
Smithboro	13840
Smith Corners	13407
Smithfield, *Madison* (Town)	13134
Smithfield, *Dutchess*	12501
Smith Haven Mall (Part of Lake Grove)	11755
Smiths Basin	12827
Smiths Corner	12120
Smiths Mills	14062
Smithtown (Part of Village of the Branch)	11787
Smithtown, *Suffolk*	11787
Smithtown Branch	11787
Smithtown Pines	11787
Smith Valley	14805
Smithville, *Chenango* (Town)	13778
Smithville, *Jefferson*	13605
Smithville Center	13778
Smithville Flats	13841
Smyrna	13464
Snooks Corners	12010
Snufftown	10924
Snyder	14226
Snyder Crossing	13082
Snyders Corners, *Albany*	12193
Snyders Corners, *Rensselaer*	12198
Snyders Lake	12198
Sodom, *Putnam*	10509
Sodom, *Warren*	12853
Sodus	14551
Sodus Center	14551
Sodus Point	14555
Solon	13040
Solsville	13465
Solvay	13209
Somers	10589
Somerset	14012
Somerset Lake	13783
Somerville	13642
Sonora	14879
Sonyea	14556
Sound Beach♦	11789
Soundview (Part of New York)‡	10472
South (Part of Yonkers)‡	10705
South Addison	14801
South Alabama	14013
South Albion	13302
South Amenia	12592
Southampton	11968*
	11969†
Southampton College	11968
South Amsterdam (Part of Amsterdam)	12010
South Apalachin	13732
South Argyle	12809
South Avon	14414
South Bay	13032
South Bay Shopping Center	11702
South Bay Village	12827
South Beach (Part of New York)	10305
South Bethlehem	12161
South Bloomfield	14469
South Bolivar	14715
South Bombay	12957
South Bradford	14879
South Bristol	14512
South Brookfield	13485
South Brooklyn (Part of New York)	11231
South Buffalo (Part of Buffalo)	14210
South Butler	13154
South Byron	14557
South Cairo	12482
South Cambridge	12028
South Canisteo	14823
South Centereach	11720
South Centerville	10940
South Chili	14546
South Colton	13687
South Columbia	13407
South Corinth	12822
South Corning	14830
South Cortland	13045
South Danby	13864
South Dansville	14807
South Dayton	14138
South Dover	12594
South Durham	12405
Southeast (Town)	10509
Southeast Owasco	13118
South Edmeston	13411
South Edwards	13635
South Erin	14838
South Fallsburg♦	12779
South Farmingdale♦	11735
Southfields	10975
South Floral Park	11001
South Flushing (Part of New York)	11365
Southgate Plaza	14224
South Gilboa	12167
South Glens Falls	12803
South Glenwood Landing	11547
South Granville	12832
South Greece	14626
South Hamilton	13332
South Hannibal	13074
South Hartford	12838
South Hartwick	13810
South Haven	11719
South Hempstead♦	11550
South Highland	10524
South Hill♦	14850
South Holbrook	11741
South Horicon	12815
South Hornell	14843
South Huntington♦	11746
South Ilion	13357
South Jamesport	11970
South Jefferson	12167
South Jewett	12442
South Kortright	13842
South Lake	10512
South Lebanon	13332
South Lima	14558
South Livonia	14487
South Lockport♦	14094
South Millbrook	12545
South New Berlin	13843
South Newstead	14001
South Nyack	10960
Southold♦	11971
South Olean (Part of Olean)	14760
South Onondaga	13120
South Otselic	13155
South Owego	13827
South Oxford	13830
South Ozone Park (Part of New York)	11420
South Park (Part of Buffalo)	14220
South Plainedge	11758
South Plymouth	13844
South Pole (Part of New York)	10090
Southport♦	14904
South Pulteney	14840
South Richmond Hill (Part of New York)	11419
South Ripley	14775
South Russell	13684
South Rutland	13626
South Salem	10590
South Schodack	12162
South Schroon	12870
South Setauket	11733
South Shore Mall	11706
South Side (Part of Buffalo)‡	14220
South Side (Part of Elmira)‡	14904
South Sodus	14489
South St. Johnsville	13339
South Stockton	14782
South Stony Brook	11790
South Trenton	13304
South Utica (Part of Utica)	13501
South Valley, *Cattaraugus* (Town)	14779
South Valley, *Otsego*	13320
South Valley Stream♦	11581
South Vandalia	14706
South Vestal	13850
Southview (Part of Binghamton)‡	13903
Southview Gardens	14094
Southville	13672
South Wales	14139
South Warsaw	14569
South Westbury	11590
South Westerlo	12083
Southwest Oswego	13126
Southwood	13078
South Worcester	12197
Spafford	13077
Sparkill	10976
Sparkle Lake	10598
Sparrow Bush	12780
Sparta, Livingston (Town)	14437
Sparta (Part of Ossining)	10562
Spawn Hollow	12161
Speculator	12164
Speedsville	13736
Speigletown	12182
Spencer	14883
Spencerport	14559
Spencers Corner	12546
Spencer Settlement	13440
Spencertown	12165
Speonk	11972
Split Rock	13031
Spragueville	13642
Sprakers	12166
Spring Brook	14140
Spring Creek (Part of New York)‡	11239
Springfield (Town)	13468
Springfield Center	13468
Springfield Gardens (Part of New York)‡	11413
Spring Glen	12483
Spring Lake	13140
Spring Mills	14897
Springport (Town)	13160
Springs♦	11937
Springtown	12561
Springvale	13815
Spring Valley, *Rockland*	10977
Spring Valley (Part of Ossining)	10562
Springville, *Erie*	14141
Springville, *Suffolk*	11946
Springwater	14560
Springwood Village	12538
Sprout Brook	13317
Spruceton	12492
Spuyten Duyvil (Part of New York)‡	10463
Squiretown	11946
Staatsburg	12580
Stacy Basin	13054
Stadium (Part of New York)‡	10452
Stafford	14143
Stamford	12167
Standish	12952
Stanford (Town)	12581
Stanford Heights	12301
Stanfordville	12581
Stanley	14561
Stanley Manor	13031
Stannards♦	14895
Stanwix (Part of Rome)	13440
Stanwix Heights (Part of Rome)	13440
Stanwood	10549

Place	ZIP Code
Stapleton (Part of New York)‡	10304
Star	12933
Starbuckville	12817
Stark (Town)	13339
Starkey	14837
Starks Knob	12871
Starkville	13339
Star Lake♦	13690
State Bridge	13054
State Line	14775
Staten Island	10301-14
For specific ZIP Codes call (888) 275-8777, or your local postmaster.	
Staten Island Mall (Part of New York)	10314
State University (Part of Old Westbury)‡	11568
Steamburg	14783
Steam Valley	14760
Stears Corners	13659
Steelton	14219
Steinway (Part of New York)‡	11103
Stella	13905
Stella Niagara	14144
Stephens Mills	14843
Stephentown	12168-69
For specific ZIP Codes call (888) 275-8777, or your local postmaster.	
Stephentown Center	12168
Sterling	13156
Sterling Forest	10979
Sterlington	10974
Sterling Valley	13156
Stetsonville	13415
Steuben (Town)	13354
Steuben Valley	13354
Stever Mill	12025
Stewart Air Force Base	12550
	12553
For specific ZIP Codes call (888) 275-8777, or your local postmaster.	
Stewart Manor	11530
Stilesville	13754
Stillman Village	12138
Stillwater, *Chautauqua*	14701
Stillwater, *Putnam*	10541
Stillwater, *Saratoga*	12170
Stillwater Hill	10562
Stirling	11944
Stissing	12581
Stittville	13469
Stockbridge	13409
Stockholm (Town)	13697
Stockholm Center	13697
Stockport, *Columbia*	12534
Stockport, *Delaware*	13783
Stockport Station	12534
Stockton	14784
Stockwell	13480
Stokes	13363
Stone Arabia	13339
Stone Church	14416
Stonedam	16923
Stone Gate	10950
Stone Mills	13656
Stone Ridge, *Montgomery*	12072
Stone Ridge, *Ulster*	12484
Stony Brook	11790
Stony Creek	12878
Stony Creek Estates	12065
Stony Hollow	12401
Stony Point, *Rensselaer*	12033
Stony Point, *Rockland*♦	10980
Stormville	12582
Stottville♦	12172
Stow	14785
Straits Corners	13827
Stratford	13470
Strathmore‡	11030
Streetroad	12883
Strykersville	14145
Stuyvesant	12173
Stuyvesant (Part of New York)‡	11233
Stuyvesant Falls	12174
Suffern	10901
Suffern Park (Part of Airmont)	10901
Sugarbush	12989
Sugar Loaf	10981
Sugartown	14741
Sullivan	13037
Sullivanville	14845
Summerdale	14781
Summerhill	13092
Summerville	14617
Summit	12175
Summit Park	10977
Summit Park Mall (Part of Niagara Falls)	14304
Summitville	12781
Sun	12917
Sundown	12782
Sun Haven (Part of New Rochelle)	10801
Sunmount (Part of Tupper Lake)	12986
Sunny Side, *Chautauqua*	14701
Sunnyside, *Columbia*	12106
Sunnyside (Part of New York)	11104
Sunrise Mall	11758
Sunrise Terrace	13902
Sunset (Part of New York)‡	11220
Sunset Bay	14081
Sunset Beach, *Niagara*	14172
Sunset Beach, *Orleans*	14571
Sunset Manor	13492
Sunset View	14590
S U N Y (Part of Albany)‡	12203
Surprise	12176
Surrey Meadows	10918
Swain	14884
Swan Lake	12783
Swartwood	14889
Swastika	12985
Swazy Acres	12188
Sweden (Town)	14420
Sweden Center	14420
Sweet Meadows	12401
Swenson Drive (Part of Wappingers Falls)	12590
Swifts Mills	14001
Swormville	14051
Sycaway	12180
Sylvan Beach	13157
Sylvan Lake	12533
Syosset♦	11791
Syracuse	13201-10
	13212-90
For specific ZIP Codes call (888) 275-8777, or your local postmaster.	
Taberg	13471
Tabor Corners	14572
Taborton	12153
Taconic Lake	12138
Taghkanic	12502
Talcottville	13309
Talcville	13635
Tallman (Part of Airmont)	10982
Tanglewood Hills	11727
Tannersville	12485
Tappan	10983
Tarrytown	10591
Tarrytown Heights (Part of Tarrytown)	10591
Taunton	13219
Taylor	13040
Taylor Center	13040
Taylorshire	14170
Teall (Part of Syracuse)‡	13217
Teboville	12953
Teed Corners	14481
Teleport (Part of New York)‡	10311
Ten Mile River	12764
Tennanah Lake	12776
Terminal (Part of New York)‡	10301
Terrace Park	13669
Terry's Corners	14067
Terryville♦	11776
Texas	13114
Texas Valley	13803
Thayer Corners	12917
The Bridges	14477
The Forge	12920
The Forks	14030
The Glen	12885
The Hook	12809
The Narrows	14737
Thendara	13472
Theresa	13691
The Terrace	11050
The Vly	12484
Thiells♦	10984
Thomaston	11021
Thompson, *Sullivan* (Town)	12701
Thompson, *Ontario*	14489
Thompson Corners	13316
Thompson Ridge	10985
Thompsons Lake	12059
Thompsonville	12784
Thomson	12834
Thornton	14723
Thornton Grove	13152
Thornton Heights	13152
Thornwood	10594
Thousand Island Park‡	13692
Three Mile Bay	13693
Three Rivers	13041
Throg's Neck (Part of New York)‡	10465
Throop (Town)	13021
Throopsville	13021
Thruway Mall	14225
Thurman (Town)	12885
Thurston	14821
Thurston Road (Part of Rochester)‡	14619
Tiana	11946
Tiana Shores	11942
Ticonderoga	12883
Tillson♦	12486
Tilly Foster	10512
Times Plaza (Part of New York)‡	11217
Times Square (Part of New York)‡	10036
Timothy Heights	12569
Tindall Corners	13490
Tinkertown	14803
Tioga (Town)	13845
Tioga Center	13845
Tioga Terrace	13732
Tiona	13811
Titusville	12603
Tivoli	12583
Toddsville	13326
Toddville	10567
Todt Hill (Part of New York)	10301
Toll Gate Corner	14770
Tomhannock	12185
Tomkins Cove	10986
Tompkins (Town)	13754
Tompkins Corners	14845
Tompkins Square (Part of New York)‡	10009
Tompkinsville (Part of New York)	10301
Tonawanda (Town)	14150
Tonawanda	14150*
	14151†
Tonawanda♦	14223
Tonawanda Indian Reservation	14150
Torrey (Town)	14441
Tottenville (Part of New York)‡	10307
Towerville Corners	14701
Towlesville	14810
Towners	12531
Town Line♦	14086
Town Pump	14559
Townsend	14891
Townsendville	14847
Tracy Creek	13850
Trainsmeadow (Part of New York)‡	11370
Transitown	14221
Travis (Part of New York)	10314
Treadwell	13846
Tremont (Part of New York)‡	10457
Trenton (Town)	13304
Trenton Assembly Park	13304
Trenton Falls	13304
Triangle	13778
Triangle Lake	12122
Tribes Hill♦	12177
Triborough (Part of New York)‡	10035
Triphammer Mall (Part of Lansing)	14852
Tripoli, *Cortland*	13158
Tripoli, *Washington*	12827
Troupsburg	14885
Troutburg	14464
Trout Creek	13847
Trout River	12926
Troy	12180-83
For specific ZIP Codes call (888) 275-8777, or your local postmaster.	
Truesdale Lake	10590
Trumansburg	14886
Trumbulls Corners	14867
Truthville	12854
Truxton	13158
Tuckahoe, *Suffolk*	11968
Tuckahoe, *Westchester*	10707
Tucker Heights	12019
Tucker Terrace	13662
Tully	13159
Tunnel	13848
Tupper Lake	12986
Turin	13473
Turnwood	12758
Tuscan	12197
Tuscarora, *Steuben* (Town)	14801
Tuscarora, *Livingston*	14510
Tuscarora Indian Reservation	14094
Tusten (Town)	12764
Tuthilltown	12525
Tuxedo (Town)	10987
Tuxedo Park	10987
Twilight Park	12436
Twin Lakes Village	10590
Twin Orchards	13850
Tyner	13830
Tyre	13148
Tyrone	14887
Ulster (Town)	12401
Ulster Heights	12428
Ulster Landing	12477
Ulster Park	12487
Ulsterville	12566
Ulysses (Town)	14886
Unadilla	13849
Unadilla Forks	13491
Underwood	12964
Union, *Broome* (Town)	13760
Union (Part of Endicott)‡	13760*
	13763†
Union Center	13760
Uniondale♦	11553
Union Falls	12912
Union Hill	14563
Union Mills	12025
Union Port (Part of New York)	10473
Union Settlement	13167
Union Shopping Center (Part of Endicott)	13760
Union Springs	13160
Union Vale (Town)	12585
Union Valley	13052
Unionville, *Albany*	12054
Unionville, *Ontario*	14532
Unionville, *Orange*	10988
Unionville, *St. Lawrence*	13676
University (Part of Syracuse)‡	13210
University Gardens♦	11020
University Heights (Part of New York)‡	10452
Upper Benson	12134
Upper Brookville	11545
Upper Grand View	10960
Upper Hollowville	12530
Upper Jay	12987
Upper Lisle	13862
Upper Little York	13087
Upper Mongaup	12737
Upper Nyack	10960
Upper Red Hook	12571
Upper St. Regis	12945
Upper Union	12309
Upperville	13464
Upton Lake	12514
Uptonville (Part of Rochester)	14617
Uptown (Part of Kingston)‡	12401
Urbana (Town)	14840
U.S. Cadet Corps‡	10997
Ushers	12151
U.S. Military Academy	10996
Utica	13501-05
For specific ZIP Codes call (888) 275-8777, or your local postmaster.	
Utopia (Part of New York)‡	11366
Vail Mills	12025
Vails Gate♦	12584
Vail's Grove	10509
Valatie	12184
Valcour	12972
Valhalla	10595
Valley Brook	13339
Valley Cottage♦	10989
Valley Falls	12185
Valley Mills	13409
Valley Pond Estates	10536
Valley Stream	11580-82
For specific ZIP Codes call (888) 275-8777, or your local postmaster.	
Valley View Manor (Part of Rome)	13440
Vallonia Springs	13813
Valois	14888
Van Brunt (Part of New York)‡	11215
Van Buren (Town)	13027
Van Buren Bay	14048
Van Buren Point	14166
Van Burenville	10940
Van Cortlandtville	10567
Van Cott (Part of New York)‡	10467
Vandalia	14706
Van Deusenville	13317
Vandever (Part of New York)‡	11210
Van Etten	14889
Van Hornesville	13475
Van Nest (Part of New York)‡	10462
Van Riper Tract	13827
Van Schaick Island (Part of Cohoes)	12047
Van Vleet	14801
Varick (Town)	14541
Varna	14850
Varysburg	14167
Vaughs Corners	12839
Vega	12455
Venice	13147
Venice Center	13147
Verbank	12585
Verbank Village	12585
Verdoy	12110
Vermillion	13114
Vermontville	12989
Vernon	13476
Vernon Center	13477
Vernon Valley	11768
Verona	13478
Verona Beach	13162
Verona Mills	13440
Verplanck	10596
Versailles	14168
Vesper	13159
Vestal	13850*
	13851†
Vestal Center	13850
Vestal Gardens	13850
Veteran, *Chemung* (Town)	14864
Veteran, *Ulster*	12477
Veterans Administration Facility (Part of Batavia)	14020
Veterans Administration Hospital (Part of Buffalo)	14215
Veterans Hospital (Part of Syracuse)	13210
Victor	14564
Victoria	14710
Victory	13033
Victory Mills	12884
Victory Park (Part of New Rochelle)	10804
Vienna	13308
Viewmonte	12526
Village (Part of New York)‡	10014
Village, *Niagara*	14094
Village Green, *Onondaga*♦	13027
Village Green, *Saratoga*	12065
Village of the Branch	11787
Villenova (Town)	14138
Vincent	14424
Vine Valley	14507
Vintonton	12187
Viola♦	10952
Viola Park	10952
Virgil	13045
Vischer Ferry	12148
Vista	06840
Voak	14527
Vollentine	14772
Volney	13069
Volusia	14787
Voorheesville	12186
Vukote	14710
Waccabuc	10597
Waddington	13694
Wadhams	12993
Wadhams Park	13669
Wagners Hollow	13339
Wainscott	11975
Waits	13827
Wakefield (Part of New York)‡	10466
Walden, *Erie*	14225
Walden, *Orange*	12586
Walden Galleria (Part of Buffalo)	14225
Waldos Corners	14009

Wales (Town) 14139
Wales Center 14169
Wales Hollow 14139
Walesville 13492
Walker 14468
Walker Lane 12801
Walker Valley 12588
Wallace 14809
Wallington 14551
Wallins Corner 12010
Wallkill, *Orange* (Town) 10919
Wallkill, *Ulster*♦ 12589
Walloomsac 12090
Wall Street (Part of New York)‡ 10005
Walton 13856
Walton Park 10950
Walt Whitman Mall 11746
Walworth 14568
Wampsville 13163
Wanakah 14075
Wanakena 13695
Wantagh♦ 11793
Wappinger (Town) 12590
Wappingers Falls 12590
Ward (Town) 14880
Wards Island (Part of New York)‡ 10035
Warners 13164
Warnerville 12187
Warren 13439
Warrensburg♦ 12885
Warrens Corners 14094
Warsaw 14569
Warwick 10990
Washington (Town) 12545
Washington Bridge (Part of New York)‡ 10033
Washington Heights (Part of New York) 10033
Washington Heights, *Orange*♦ 10940
Washington Hollow 12545
Washington Lake 12550
Washington Mills 13479
Washingtonville 10992
Wassaic 12592
Waterboro 14747
Waterburg 14886
Waterford 12188
Water Island 11772
Waterloo 13165
Waterman Corners 14728
Water Mill♦ 11976
Waterport 14571
Waterside Park 11768
Watertown (Town) 13601
Watertown 13601-03
For specific ZIP Codes call (888) 275-8777, or your local postmaster.
Watertown Center 13601
Watertown Junction (Part of Watertown) 13601
Watervale 13104
Water Valley 14075
Waterville, *Jefferson* 13659
Waterville, *Oneida* 13480
Watervliet 12189
Watkins Glen 14891
Watson 13367
Watsonville 12122
Wattlesburg 14775
Watts Flats 14710
Wautoma Beach 14468
Wave Crest (Part of New York) 11691
Waverly, *Franklin* (Town) 12980
Waverly, *Tioga* 14892
Wawarsing 12489
Wawayanda (Town) 10973
Wawbeek 12986
Wayland 14572
Wayne, *Steuben* (Town) 14840
Wayne, *Schuyler* 14893
Wayne Center 14489
Webatuck 12594
Webb (Town) 13420
Webbs Crossing 14843
Webbs Mills 14871
Webster 14580
Webster Crossing 14560
Websters Corners 14127
Wedgewood 14891
Weedsport 13166
Wegatchie 13608
Welcome 13810
Wells 12190
Wells Bridge 13859
Wellsburg 14894
Wellsville, *Allegany* 14895
Wellsville, *Montgomery* 12010
Weltonville 13811
Wendelville 14120
Wesley 14070
Wesley Chapel 10901
Wesley Hills 10901
West Almond 14804
West Amboy 13167
West Babylon♦ 11704*
11707†
West Bainbridge 13733
West Bangor 12966
West Barre 14411
West Batavia 14020
West Bellport 11772
West Berne 12023
West Bethany 14054
West Bloomfield 14585
West Branch 13303
Westbrookville 12785
West Burlington 13482
Westbury, *Cayuga* 13143
Westbury, *Nassau* 11590
West Bush 12078
West Cameron 14819
West Camp 12490
West Candor 13743
West Carthage 13619
West Caton 14830
West Charlton 12010
West Chazy 12992
West Chenango 13905
Westchester (Part of New York)‡ 10461
Westchester, The (Part of White Plains) 10602
West Chili 14514
West Clarksville 14786
West Colesville 13904
West Conesville 12076
West Copake 12593
West Corners 13760
West Coxsackie (Part of Coxsackie) 12192
Westdale 13483
West Danby 14883
West Davenport 13860
West Dryden 13068
West Durham 12422
West Eaton 13484
West Edmeston 13485
West Elmira♦ 14905
West Endicott 13760
Westerlea 13031
Westerleigh (Part of New York) 10314
Westerlo 12193
Western (Town) 13486
Western Lights Shopping Center (Part of Syracuse) 13219
Westernville 13486
West Exeter 13491
West Falls 14170
West Farms (Part of New York)‡ 10460
Westfield 14787
Westford 13488
West Fort Ann 12827
West Fort Salonga 11768
West Frankfort 13340
West Fulton 12194
West Gaines 14411
West Galway 12010
Westgate 14624
West Genesee Terrace 13031
West Ghent 12075
West Gilgo Beach 11702
West Glens Falls♦ 12801
West Glenville 12010
West Granville Corners 12832
West Greece 14626
West Greenwood 14839
West Groton 13073
Westhampton♦ 11977
Westhampton Beach 11978
West Harpersfield 13786
West Harrison (Part of Harrison) 10604
West Haverstraw 10993
West Hebron 12865
West Hempstead♦ 11552
West Henrietta 14586
West Hill 12301
West Hills 11743
West Hoosick 12028
West Huntington 11743
West Hurley♦ 12491
West Islip♦ 11795
West Jewett 12444
West Kendall 14476
West Kill 12492
West Latham‡ 12110
West Laurens 13796
West Lebanon 12195
West Lee 13363
West Leyden 13489
West Lowville 13367
West Mahopac 10541
West Martinsburg 13367
Westmere♦ 12203
West Meredith 13757
West Middleburg 12122
West Middlebury 14054
West Milton 12020
Westminster Park 13607
West Monroe 13167
Westmoreland, *Oneida* 13490
Westmoreland, *Suffolk* 11965
West Newark 13811
West New Brighton (Part of New York)‡ 10310
West Newburgh (Part of Newburgh)‡ 12550
West Notch 14715
West Nyack 10994
Weston 14837
West Oneonta 13861
Westons Mills♦ 14788
Westover 13790
West Park 12493
West Pawling 12564
West Perrysburg 14129
West Perth 12010
West Phoenix 13135
West Pierrepont 13617
West Point♦ 10996*
10997†
Westport 12993
West Portland 14787
West Potsdam 13676
West Ridge (Part of Rochester)‡ 14615
West Rush 14543
West Salamanca (Part of Salamanca) 14779
West Sand Lake♦ 12196
West Saugerties 12477
West Sayville♦ 11796
West Schuyler 13502
West Seneca♦ 14224
West Shelby 14103
West Shokan 12494
West Side (Part of Buffalo)‡ 14213
West Side (Part of Elmira)‡ 14905
West Slaterville 14881
West Somerset 14008
West Sparta (Town) 14437
West Stephentown 12168
West Stockholm 13696
West Sweden 14420
West Taghkanic 12502
West Tiana 11946
Westtown 10998
West Turin (Town) 13325
West Union (Town) 14877
West Utica (Part of Utica) 13502
Westvale♦ 13219
West Valley 14171
West Valley Falls (Part of Valley Falls) 12185
Westview (Part of Binghamton)‡ 13905
Westview, *Livingston* 14437
Westville, *Franklin* 12926
Westville, *Otsego* 12155
Westville Center 12926
West Walworth 14502
West Waterford (Part of Waterford) 12188
West Webster 14580
West Windsor 13865
West Winfield 13491
West Yaphank 11980
Wethersfield (Town) 14569
Wethersfield Springs 14569
Wevertown 12886
Whaley Lake 12531
Whallonsburg 12936
Wheatfield (Town) 14150
Wheatland (Town) 14546
Wheatley (Part of Old Westbury) 11568
Wheatley Heights♦ 11798
Wheatville 14013
Wheeler 14810
Wheeler Estates 12019
Wheelerville 12032
Whig Corners 13326
Whippleville 12995
Whippoorwill 10504
White Bay 13650
White Creek 12057
Whitehall 12887
Whitehouse Crossing 12546
White Lake, *Oneida* 13494
White Lake, *Sullivan* 12786
Whitelaw 13032
White Plains 10601-03
10605-10
For specific ZIP Codes call (888) 275-8777, or your local postmaster.
Whiteport 12401
Whitesboro 13492
Whites Store 13843
Whitestone (Part of New York) 11357
Whitestown (Town) 13492
White Sulphur Springs 12787
Whitesville 14897
Whitfield 12404
Whitman 13804
Whitney Country 14450
Whitney Farms 14450
Whitney Highlands 14450
Whitney Point 13862
Wiccopee 12533
Wickham Knolls 10990
Wickham Village 10990
Wilbur (Part of Kingston) 12401
Wildwood 11792
Wileyville 14877
Willard 14588
Willet 13863
Williams Bridge (Part of New York)‡ 10467
Williamsburg (Part of New York)‡ 11211
Williams Grove 13110
Williams Lake 12472
Williamson 14589
Williamstown 13493
Williamsville 14221
Willing (Town) 14895
Williston Park 11596
Willoughby 14741
Willow 12495
Willow Brook, *Chautauqua* 14712
Willowbrook (Part of New York) 10314
Willow Brook Estates 12303
Willow Brook Park 12302
Willowemac 12758
Willow Glen, *Saratoga* 12118
Willow Glen, *Tompkins* 13053
Willow Grove, *Cayuga* 13140
Willow Grove, *Rockland* 10980
Willow Point 13850
Willow Ridge Estates 14226
Willsboro 12996
Willsboro Point 12996
Willseyville 13864
Wilmington 12997
Wilna (Town) 13619
Wilson 14172
Wilton 12866
Winchester, *Erie* 14224
Winchester (Part of Buffalo) 14224
Winderest Park 13031
Windham 12496
Windham Ridge 12496
Winding Ways 13152
Windmill Farms 10504
Windom 14219
Windsor 13865
Windsor Beach 14617
Winebrook Hills 12852
Winfield (Town) 13491
Wingdale 12594
Winona 13659
Winona Lake 12550
Winthrop 13697
Wirt (Town) 14774
Wiscoy 14536
Wisner 10990
Witherbee 12998
Wittenberg 12409
Wolcott 14590
Wolcottsburg 14032
Wolcottsville 14001
Woodberry Hills 13413
Woodbourne 12788
Woodbury, *Orange* (Town) 10930
Woodbury, *Nassau*♦ 11797
Woodbury Falls 10930
Woodcliff Park 11933
Woodgate 13494
Wood Haven (Part of New York) 11421
Woodhull, *Oneida* 13338
Woodhull, *Steuben* 14898
Woodinville 12564
Woodland 12464
Woodland Hills 12065
Woodlands 10607
Woodlawn (Part of New York)‡ 10470
Woodlawn, *Chautauqua* 14710
Woodlawn Beach 14219
Woodmere♦ 11598
Woodridge 12789
Woodrow (Part of New York) 10312
Woodruff Heights 12302
Woodsburgh 11598
Woods Corner 14801
Woods Corners 13815
Woods Falls 12910
Woodside (Part of New York) 11377
Woods Mills 12918
Woodstock♦ 12498
Woodsville 14437
Woodville, *Jefferson* 13650
Woodville, *Ontario* 14512
Woodwinds 13732
Wooglin 14728
Woolsey (Part of New York)‡ 11105
Worcester 12197
Worth 13659
Worthington (Part of White Plains) 10607
Wright (Town) 12073
Wright Park Manor (Part of Rome) 13440
Wrights Corners 14094
Wurtemburg 12572
Wurtsboro 12790
Wurtsboro Hills 12790
Wyandanch♦ 11798
Wyatts 12302
Wycoff Heights (Part of New York)‡ 11237
Wykagyl (Part of New Rochelle)‡ 10804
Wykagyl Park (Part of New Rochelle) 10804
Wynantskill♦ 12198
Wyomanock 12168
Wyoming 14591
Yaddo 12866
Yagerville 12458
Yaleville 13668
Yankee Lake 12790
Yaphank♦ 11980
Yates (Town) 14098
Yates Center 14098
Yatesville 14527
Yonkers 10701-05
10710
For specific ZIP Codes call (888) 275-8777, or your local postmaster.
York 14592
York Corners 14895
Yorkshire♦ 14173
Yorktown 10598
Yorktown Heights 10598
Yorkville (Part of New York)‡ 10128
Yorkville, *Oneida* 13495
Yosts 12068
Young Corners 12010
Young Hickory 14885
Youngstown 14174
Youngstown Estates 14174
Youngsville 12791
Yulan 12792
Zena♦ 12498
Zoar 13682

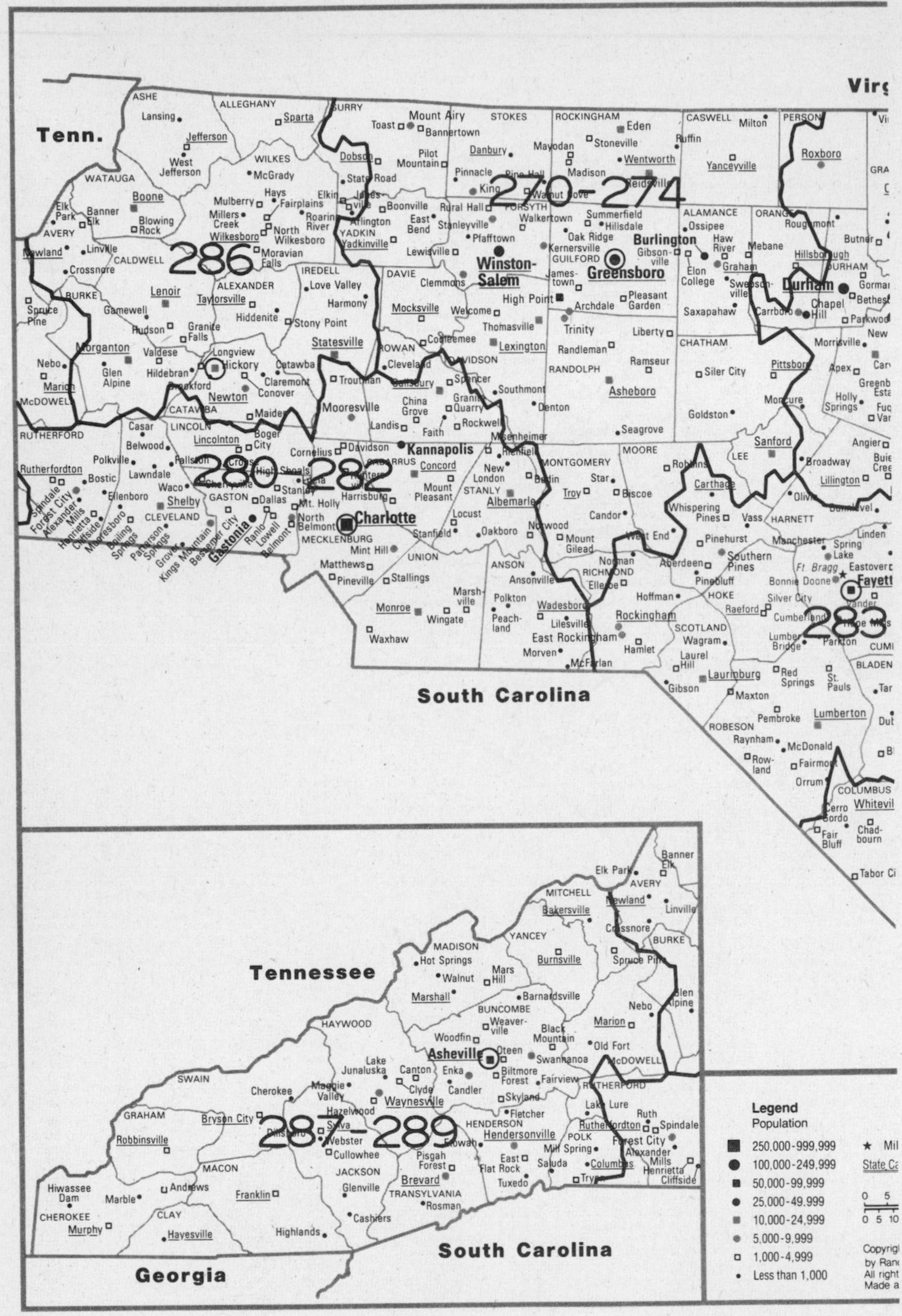

Tenn.
Virg
270-274
286
280-282
283
287-289
South Carolina
Tennessee
Georgia
South Carolina
Winston-Salem
Greensboro
Burlington
Durham
Charlotte
Kannapolis
Gastonia
Asheville
Legend
Population
250,000-999,999
100,000-249,999
50,000-99,999
25,000-49,999
10,000-24,999
5,000-9,999
1,000-4,999
Less than 1,000

rginia

Military Base

e Capital County Seat

5 10 20 30 Miles

10 20 30 40 Kilometers

Aarons Corner 27053
Abbottsburg 28320
Abee 28690
Aberdeen 28315
Abner 27356
Abshers 28635
Academy Street (Part of Cary)‡ 27519
Acme 28456
Acorn Hill 27979
Acorn Woods 28079
Acre 27865
Adako 28645
Addie 28779
Addor 28315
Adoniram 24598
Advance 27006
Advent Crossroads 28601
Afton 27589
Aho 28607
Ahoskie 27910
Ai 27583
Airboro (Part of Goldsboro) 27530
Airlie 27850
Air Mail Facility (Part of Greensboro) 27425
Airport (Part of Charlotte) 28219
Alamance 27201
Alamance Square (Part of Greensboro)‡ 27406
Alarka 28713
Albemarle 28001*
28002†
Albemarle Beach 27970
Albertson 28508
Albrittons 28504
Alert 27589
Alexander 28701
Alexander Mills 28043
Alexis 28006
Alfordsville 28383
Allen 28212
Allendale 28150
Allen Grove 27839
Allen Jay (Part of High Point) 27263
Allens Crossroads 28174
Allens Level 27573
Allensville 27573
All Healing Springs 28681
Alliance 28509
Alligator 27925
Allison 27326
Allreds 27356
Alma 28364
Almond 28702
Alspaugh (Part of Winston-Salem) 27105
Altamahaw 27202
Altamont 28657
Altan 28112
Altapass 28777
Amantha 28679
Amerotron Mill (Part of Red Springs) 28377
Amity 27013
Amity Gardens (Part of Charlotte) 28205
Ammon 28337
Anderson, *Caswell* 27215
Anderson (Part of Kitty Hawk) 27949
Anderson Creek 28323
Anderson Crossroads 27850
Andrews 28901
Angier 27501
Angola 28454
Ansonville 28007
Antioch, *Brunswick* 28422
Antioch, *Hoke* 28377
Antioch, *Madison* 28753
Apex 27502
Appie 27888
Apple Grove 28643
Aquadale 28128
Aquone 28781
Arabia 28376
Arapahoe 28510
Ararat 27007
Arba 28580
Arcadia 27295
Archdale 27263
Archer 27520
Arcola 27589
Arden 28704
Ardmore (Part of Winston-Salem)‡ 27103
Ardulusa 28301
Argura 28783
Arlington 28642
Armour 28456
Arnold 27295
Arran Hills 28304
Arrowhead Beach 27932
Arrowhead Place 28025
Arrowood (Part of Charlotte)‡ 28241
Artesia 28442
Asbury 27330
Ash 28420
Asheboro 27203*
27204†
Asheville 28801-16
For specific ZIP Codes call (888) 275-8777, or your local postmaster.
Asheville Mall, The (Part of Asheville) 28805
Ashford 28752
Ash Hill 27007
Ashland, *Ashe* 28615
Ashland, *Bertie* 27957
Ashland, *Rockingham* 27320
Ashley Heights 28315
Ashton 28425
Ashton Forrest 28304
Ashwood 28571
Askewville 27983
Askin 28527
Atkinson 28421
Atlantic 28511
Atlantic Beach 28512
Auburn 27610
Audubon (Part of Wilmington) 28403
Aulander 27805
Aurelian Springs 27850
Aurora 27806
Austin 28621
Autryville 28318
Avalon Valley 27253
Avent Ferry Road (Part of Raleigh)‡ 27606
Aventon 27891
Averasboro 28334
Avery Creek♦ 28704
Avery Shores 27974
Avon 27915
Axtell 27563
Ayden 28513
Aydlett 27916
Ayersville 27027
Azalea, Buncombe 28805
Azalea (Part of Wilmington)‡ 28403
28406
For specific ZIP Codes call (888) 275-8777, or your local postmaster.
Bachelor 28532
Badin 28009
Bagley 27542
Bahama 27503
Bailey 27807
Bailey Camp 28645
Bailey Town 27052
Baker Rhyne Apartments 28152
Bakers 28110
Bakers Crossroads 27320
Bakersville 28705
Bald Creek 28714
Bald Head Island 28461
Bald Mountain 28714
Baldwin 28694
Baldwin Woods (Part of Whiteville) 28472
Balfour♦ 28791
Ballantree 28803
Ballard 27840
Ballards Crossroad 27834
Ballew Store 28714
Balm 28604
Balsam 28707
Balsam Grove 28708
Baltic 28398
Baltimore 28434
Bamboo 28605
Bandana 28705
Bandy 28609
Banks 27603
Banks Creek 28714
Banner Elk 28604
Bannertown 27030
Banoak 28168
Barber 27013
Barclaysville 27501
Barco 27917
Barham 27587
Barium Springs 28010
Barker Heights♦ 28792
Barkers Creek 28789
Barker Ten Mile♦ 28358
Barnard 28753
Barnardsville 28709
Barnesfield 28570
Barnesville 28319
Barrett 28623
Barriers Mill 28124
Bartlett 27921
Barton College (Part of Wilson)‡ 27893
Bass Crossroads 27882
Basstown 28328
Bat Cave 28710
Batchelor Crossroads 27882
Bath 27808
Baton 28630
28645
For specific ZIP Codes call (888) 275-8777, or your local postmaster.
Battleboro 27809
Battleground (Part of Greensboro)‡ 27438
Batts Crossroads 27889
Bay 27925
Bayboro 28515
Bayleaf 27615
Baynes 27302
Bayshore♦ 28411
Baytree 27613
Bayview 27808
Beach Spring 27944
Beamans Crossroads 28366
Bear Creek, *Chatham* 27207
Bear Creek, *Onslow* 28539
Beard 28301
Bear Grass 27892
Bearpond 27536
Bear Poplar 28125
Bearskin 28328
Bearwallow 28735
Beatties Ford 28216
Beaufort 28516
Beaufort Heights 27889
Beaver Creek 28694
Beaverdam, *Buncombe* 28715
Beaver Dam, *Cleveland* 28152
Beaver Dam, *Columbus* 28431
Beaverdam, *Cumberland* 28382
Beaverdam, *Halifax* 27823
Beaverdam, *Haywood* 28716
Beckwith 27865
Beech 28787
Beech Bottom 28657
Beechbrook (Part of Belmont) 28012
Beech Creek 28622
Beechertown 28781
Beech Mountain 28604
Beechwood Shores 27958
Bee Log 28714
Beesons Crossroads 27284
Belair 28306
Belcross 27921
Belews Creek 27009
Belfast 27530
Belgrade 28555
Belhaven 27810
Bellarthur 27811
Belle Mead 28601
Bellemont 27216
Bell Island 27929
Bells Crossroads 28166
Bells Fork (Part of Jacksonville) 28546
Bells Fork, *Pitt* 27858
Belltown 27565
Bell View 28906
Belmont, *Gaston* 28012
Belmont, *Halifax* 27870
Belva 28753
Belvedere 27834
Belvidere 27919
Belville 28451
Belvoir 27834
Belwood 28090
Benham 28621
Bennett 27208
Benson 27504
Bent Creek♦ 28806
Benton Heights (Part of Monroe) 28110
Bentons Crossroad 28110
Berea 27565
Berkeley (Part of Goldsboro)‡ 27534
Bertha 27965
Bertie (Part of Windsor) 27983
Bessemer (Part of Greensboro) 27405
Bessemer City 28016
Bests 28551
Beta 28779
Bethabara (Part of Winston-Salem)‡ 27106
Bethania 27010
Bethany 27320
Bethany Crossroads 28391
Bethel, *Caswell* 27311
Bethel, *Columbus* 28432
Bethel, *Haywood* 28716
Bethel, *Hoke* 28376
Bethel, *Perquimans* 27944
Bethel, *Pitt* 27812
Bethel Hill 27573
Bethesda, *Davidson* 27295
Bethesda, *Durham* 27703
Bethlehem♦ 28601
Bettie 28516
Beulah, *Hyde* 27875
Beulah, *Polk* 28756
Beulahtown 27542
Beulaville 28518
Beverly Woods (Part of Charlotte) 28210
Bexley (Part of Wilmington) 28412
Biddleville (Part of Charlotte) 28216
Big Cove 28719
Biggs Park (Part of Lumberton) 28358
Big Laurel 28753
Big Lick 28129
Big Pine 28753
Big Ridge, *Carteret* 28570
Big Ridge, *Jackson* 28736
Biltmore (Part of Asheville)‡ 28813
Biltmore Forest 28803
Birchwood 27215
Bird Cage 28431
Birdtown 28719
Biscoe 27209
Bishops Cross 27860
Bixby 27006
Blackburn 28658
Black Creek 27813
Black Jack 27858
Blackman 27524
Black Mountain 28711
Blackwell 27311
Blackwood 27514
Bladenboro 28320
Bladenboro North (Part of Bladenboro) 28320
Bladen Springs 28434
Blaine 27239
Blanch 27212
Blantyre 28768
Blevins Crossroads 28675
Blevins Store 27017
Blizzards Crossroads 28365
Bloomingdale 28369
Blossomtown 28734
Blounts Creek 27814
Blowing Rock 28605
Blue Ridge, *Buncombe* 28711
Blue Ridge, *Henderson* 28792
Blue Ridge Mall (Part of Hendersonville) 28792
Bluff 28743
Boardman 28438
Boat Club Road 28012
Bobbitt 27544
Boddies Millpond 27856
Boger City♦ 28092
Bogue 28570
Boiling Spring Lakes 28461
Boiling Springs, *Cherokee* 28906
Boiling Springs, *Cleveland* 28017
Bolivia 28422
Bolton 28423
Bolyston Creek 28768
Bon Air (Part of Winston-Salem) 27105
Bonaparte Landing 28459
Bonham Heights (Part of Morehead City) 28557
Bonlee 27213
Bonnerton 27806
Bonnetsville 28328
Bonnie Doone 28303
Bonsal 27562
Boomer 28606
Boone 28607
Boones Crossroads 27845
Boone Trail 27552
Boonford 28705
Boonville 27011
Bordeaux (Part of Fayetteville) 28304
Bostian Heights 28023
Bostic 28018
Bostwood Estates 28027
Botany Woods 28805
Bottom 27030
Boulevard (Part of Eden) 27288
Bowdens 28398
Bowditch 28714
Bowmore 28376
Boyds 27837
Boyles Chapel 27021
Bradfords Crossroads 28625
Braggtown (Part of Durham) 27704
Branch Village 27807
Branon 27055
Brantleys Grove 27910
Brasstown 28902
Braswell 28431
Brendletown 28734
Brentwood, *Cumberland* 28304
Brentwood (Part of Raleigh)‡ 27616
27629
For specific ZIP Codes call (888) 275-8777, or your local postmaster.
Brettonwood 28311
Brevard 28712
Briarwood Terrace 28147
Brices Crossroads 28458
Brickhaven 27559
Bricks 27891
Brickton 28732
Bridgersville 27852
Bridgeton 28519
Brief 28107
Briertown 28781
Brigand Bay 27920
Brightwood (Part of Greensboro) 27214
Brindle Town 28655
Brinkleyville, *Hertford* 27910
Brinkleyville, *Lee* 27823
British Acres 27215
Broad Acres 27253
Broad Creek 28570
Broadway 27505
Brocks 28574
Brogden 27577
Brook Cove 27052
Brookdale 28792
Brookford 28601
Brookhaven 27612
Brookland Manor 28792
Brooks Crossroads 27020
Brooksdale 27573
Brookside (Part of Goldsboro) 27530
Brookston 27536
Brook Valley 27858
Browns Summit 27214
Brown Town (Part of Belmont) 28012
Brownwood 28684
Bruce 27834
Brunswick 28424
Brutonville 27229
Bryantown 27869
Bryantville Park 27818
Brynn Marr (Part of Jacksonville)‡ 28546
Bryson City 28713
Buckhead 28423
Buckhorn 27243
Buckhorn Crossroads 27542
Buckland 27937
Bucklesberry 28551
Buckner 28754
Buck Shoals 27020

* Area Zip Code † Post Office Boxes ‡ Postal Station ♦ Census Designated Place *Italic Type* County

Buena Vista 27983
Buffalo Cove 28645
Bug Hill 28455
Buie 28377
Buies Creek♦ 27506
Buladean 28705
Bullhead Crossroads 27807
Bullock 27507
Bunn 27508
Bunnlevel 28323
Bunyan 27889
Burbage Crossroads 27808
Burden 27805
Burgaw 28425
Burgess 27944
Burke Chapel 28601
Burkemont 28655
Burlington 27215-17
For specific ZIP Codes call (888) 275-8777, or your local postmaster.
Burney 28399
Burningtown 28734
Burnsville, *Anson* 28135
Burnsville, *Yancey* 28714
Burnt Mills 27976
Busbee (Part of Asheville) 28803
Bushy Fork 27541
Busick 28714
Butlers Crossroads 28328
Butner♦ 27509
Butters 28320
Buxton 27920
Buzzards Crossroads 27924
Bynum 27228
Cabarrus 28107
Cabin 28572
Cairo 28119
Cajah's Mountain 28630
28638
28645
For specific ZIP Codes call (888) 275-8777, or your local postmaster.
Calabash 28467
Calahaln 27028
Caldwell, *Mecklenburg* 28078
Caldwell, *Orange* 27572
California, *Dare* 27954
California, *Hertford* 27910
California, *Madison* 28754
California, *Pitt* 27828
Callisons 28571
Calvander 27516
Cal-Vel 27573
Calvert 28712
Calvin Heights 28570
Calypso 28325
Camden 27921
Camelot 27529
Cameron 28326
Cameron Village (Part of Raleigh)‡ 27605
Campbell Creek 27806
Camp Glenn (Part of Morehead City) 28557
Camp Leach 27889
Camp Lejeune 28542
28547
For specific ZIP Codes call (888) 275-8777, or your local postmaster.
Camp Lejeune Central 28542
Camp MacKall 28347
Camp Springs 27320
Camp Sutton (Part of Monroe) 28110
Cana 27028
Candler 28715
Candler Heights 28715
Candlewick Estates 27834
Candor 27229
Cane Creek 28167
Cane Mountain 27349
Cane River 28714
Cannon Ferry 27980
Canto 28716
Canton 28716
Cape Carteret 28584
Cape Colony 27932
Cape Fear 27562
Capella 27021
Capelsie 27229
Carbonton 27330
Carlos 28356
Carmel Road (Part of Charlotte)‡ 28226
28247
28270
28277
For specific ZIP Codes call (888) 275-8777, or your local postmaster.
Caroleen 28019
Carolina 27217
Carolina Beach 28428
Carolina Circle Mall (Part of Greensboro)‡ 27405
Carolina East Mall (Part of Greenville) 27834
Carolina Forest 27371
Carolina Mall (Part of Concord) 28025
Carolina Pines 28303
Carolina Place (Part of Charlotte) 28134
Carolina Trace 27330
Carolina Village 28792
Carova Beach 27927
Carpenter 27560
Carpenter Bottom 28657
Carr 27302
Carrboro 27510
Carr Creek 27330
Carroll 28398
Carter Cove 28904
Carters 27938
Cartersville 28466
Carthage 28327
Cartoogechaye 28734
Carvers 28434
Cary 27511-13
27518-19
For specific ZIP Codes call (888) 275-8777, or your local postmaster.
Cary Towne Center (Part of Cary) 27511
Casar 28020
Cashiers 28717
Cason Old Field 28170
Castalia 27816
Castle Hayne♦ 28429
Castoria 27888
Casville 27326
Caswell Beach 28465
Catawba 28609
Catawba Heights 28012
Catawba Mall (Part of Hickory) 28601
Catfish 28609
Catherine Lake 28574
Catherine Square 28518
Cat Square 28168
Ca-Vel (Part of Roxboro) 27573
Cayton 28527
Cedar Creek 28301
Cedar Croft 28025
Cedar Falls 27230
Cedar Fork 28518
Cedar Grove, *Orange* 27231
Cedar Grove, *Randolph* 27203
Cedar Hill, *Anson* 28170
Cedar Hill, *Brunswick* 28451
Cedar Island 28520
Cedar Lodge 27360
Cedar Mountain 28718
Cedar Point 28584
Cedarrock 27816
Cedar Village 28001
Ceffo 27573
Celeste Hinkle 28677
Celo 28714
Celotex 28333
Center, *Davie* 27028
Center, *Yadkin* 27055
Center City (Part of Winston-Salem)‡ 27120
Center Pigeon 28716
Centerview (Part of Kannapolis) 28083
Centerville 27549
Central 28625
Central Falls (Part of Asheboro) 27203
Central Heights 28025
Century (Part of Raleigh)‡ 27601*
27602†
Cerro Gordo 28430
Chadbourn 28431
Chadwick 28573
Chadwick Acres 28460
Chalybeate Springs 27526
Champion 28624
Chantilly, *Camden* 27921
Chantilly (Part of Charlotte) 28205
Chapanoke 27944
Chapel Hill 27514-16
For specific ZIP Codes call (888) 275-8777, or your local postmaster.
Charity 28458
Charles 28677
Charleston 27874
Charlotte 28201-99
28256-99
For specific ZIP Codes call (888) 275-8777, or your local postmaster.
Chatham 27514
Cheeks 27316
Cherokee 28719
Cherokee Indian Reservation 28719
Cherry 27928
Cherryfield 28712
Cherry Grove 28430
Cherry Lane 28627
Cherry Oaks 27858
Cherry Point 28533
Cherry Springs 28762
Cherryville 28021
Chesterfield 28655
Chestnut Dale 28657
Chestnut Grove 27021
Chestnut Hill, *Ashe* 28617
Chestnut Hill, *Henderson* 28735
Chimney Rock 28720
China Grove 28023
China Grove Cotton Mill Village 28023
Chinquapin 28521
Chip, *Craven* 28586
Chip, *Montgomery* 27306
Choco Village 27817
Chocowinity 27817
Chowan Beach, *Chowan* 27932
Chowan Beach, *Hertford* 27855
Chub Lake 27573
Church Crossroads 27871
Church Hill 27551
Churchland 27295
Cid 27292
Cisco 27980
City View (Part of Winston-Salem) 27101
Claremont 28610
Clarendon 28432
Clark 28562
Clarkton 28433
Clarrissa 28705
Clay 27565
Clayroot 28513
Clayton 27520
Clear Creek 28212
Clear Run 28441
Clegg 27560
Clemmons 27012
Clement 28318
Cleveland 27013
Clifdale 28304
Cliffside 28024
Clifton 28693
Climax 27233
Clinchfield 28752
Clingman 28670
Clinton 28328*
28329†
Cloverdale (Part of Garner) 27529
Clover Garden 27217
Cloverleaf 28304
Club Pines 27834
Clyde 28721
Coakley 27886
Coalville 28901
Coats 27521
Coats Crossroads 27504
Cobbs Shop 27326
Cobb Town 27829
Cofield 27922
Cognac 28363
Coinjock 27923
Cokesbury, *Harnett* 27526
Cokesbury, *Vance* 27536
Cold Springs 28025
Cold Water 28025
Cole Park 27514
Cole Park Plaza (Part of Chapel Hill)‡ 27514
Colerain 27924
Coleridge 27316
Colewood Acres 27604
Colfax 27235
Colington 27948
College (Part of Durham)‡ 27708
College Downs 28213
College Lakes 28301
College Park, *Cabarrus* 28075
College Park (Part of Dobbins Heights) 28345
College Park (Part of Greensboro) 27403
Collettsville 28611
Collinstown 24171
Colly 28448
Colon 27330
Colonial Heights (Part of Washington) 27889
Colonial Heights, *Wake* 27603
Colony Park (Part of Durham) 27705
Columbia 27925
Columbia Heights (Part of Winston-Salem) 27107
Columbus 28722
Comfort 28522
Commodore Peninsula 28117
Como 27818
Complex 27239
Concord, *Cabarrus* 28025-27
For specific ZIP Codes call (888) 275-8777, or your local postmaster.
Concord, *Duplin* 28453
Concord, *Person* 27573
Concord, *Rutherford* 28018
Concord, *Sampson* 28328
28382
For specific ZIP Codes call (888) 275-8777, or your local postmaster.
Conetoe 27819
Congleton 27871
Connarista 27805
Connelly Springs 28612
Conover 28613
Conway 27820
Cooksville 28168
Cooktown 28705
Cooleemee 27014
Cool Spring 27013
28677
For specific ZIP Codes call (888) 275-8777, or your local postmaster.
Cool Springs 27330
Cooper Estates 27253
Copeland 27017
Coral Bay 28557
Corapeake 27926
Corbett 27302
Cordova 28330
Core Creek 28516
Core Point 27814
Corinth, *Chatham* 27559
Corinth, *Nash* 27856
Corinth, *Rutherford* 28040
Cornatzer 27028
Cornelius 28031
Corner High 27935
Cornwall 27565
Corolla 27927
Correll Park 28146
Corriher Heights 28023
Costin 28421
Cotswold Mall (Part of Charlotte) 28211
Cottonade 28303
Cotton Grove 27292
Cottonville 28128
Council 28434
Country Club Estates 28472
Country Hills 27529
Country Homes Estates 27258
Courtney 27055
Cove City 28523
Cove Creek 28786
Covington 27306
Cowee 28734
Cox Crossing 27858
Coxs Crossroad 27814
Coxville 28513
Cozart 27522
Crab Point 28557
Crabtree 28721
Crabtree Valley Mall (Part of Raleigh)‡ 27612
Craggy 28804
Cramerton 28032
Cranberry 28657
Cranberry Gap 28657
Crater Park 28213
Creedmoor 27522
Creekside Estates 28016
Creeksville 27820
Cremo 27924
Crescent 28138
Crestmont 28601
Creston 28615
Crestview 27344
Creswell 27928
Cricket♦ 28659
Crisp 27852
Croatan 28560
Crockers Nub 27557
Cross Landing 27925
Cross Mill 28752
Crossnore 28616
Cross Road 27030
Crossroads Plaza (Part of Cary) 27602
Crossway 28352
Crosswinds 27615
Crouse 28033
Crowders 28052
Crowells 27839
Crumpler 28617
Crump Town (Part of Wagram) 28396
Cruso 28716
Crusoe Island 28472
Crutchfield Crossroads 27344
Crystal Park 28306
Culberson 28903
Culbreth 27565
Cullasaja 28734
Cullowhee♦ 28723
Cumberland 28331
Cumnock 27237
Cunningham 27343
Currie 28435
Currituck 27929
Currytown 27295
Cutshalltown 28753
Cycle 27020
Cypress Creek, *Columbus* 28472
Cypress Creek, *Duplin* 28466
Cypress Lake 28348
Dabney 27536
Dalit Town 27886
Dallas 28034
Dalton 27043
Dana 28724
Danbury 27016
Danieltown 28043
Dan River Shores 27016
Dan Valley 27048
Darby 28624
Darden 27846
Dark Ridge 28622
Darlington 27839
Davenport Forks 27970
Davidson 28036
Davidson River 28768
Davie Crossroads 27028
Davis 28524
Davistown, *Edgecombe* 27864
Davistown, *McDowell* 28762
Dawson 28501
Dawson Crossroads 27823
Day Book 28740
Days Crossroads 27839
Deep Creek 28133
Deep Gap 28618
Deep River (Part of High Point) 27265
Deep Run 28525
Deerfield 28607
Deerwood 28532
Dehart 28635
Delco 28436
Delight 28090
Dellview 28021
Dellwood 28786
Delway 28458
Democrat 28787
Dennis 27052
Denny Store 27573

*** Area Zip Code** **† Post Office Boxes** **‡ Postal Station** **♦ Census Designated Place** *Italic Type* **County**

Denton	27239
Denver	28037
Deppe	28555
Derby	28338
Derita (Part of Charlotte)‡	28213
Devonshire	28025
Devotion	27017
Dewey Pier	27925
Dexter	27565
Dickens Park	28570
Dickerson	27565
Diggs	28379
Dillard	27025
Dillsboro	28725
Dilworth (Part of Charlotte)‡	28203
Dixie	27893
Dixon	28445
Dixon Crossroad	28590
Dobbersville	28365
Dobbins Heights	28345
Dobson	27017
Dockery	28635
Dodgetown	27025
Dodsons Crossroads	27278
Dogtown	27886
Dogwood Acres (Part of Asheboro)	27203
Dogwood Acres (Part of Durham)	27704
Dogwood Acres, *Orange*	27516
Dogwood Park	28027
Don Lee Heights	28532
Donnaha	27050
Doolie	28115
Dortches	27801
Dosier	27040
Dothan	29569
Double Shoals	28090
Douglas Crossroads	27889
Dover	28526
Downtown (Part of Asheville)‡	28802
Downtown (Part of Boone)‡	28607
Downtown (Part of Charlotte)‡	28202-04
	28206
	28230-37
For specific ZIP Codes call (888) 275-8777, or your local postmaster.	
Downtown (Part of New Bern)‡	28563
Downtown (Part of Salisbury)‡	28145
Draco	28645
Drake	27809
Drake Park	28304
Draper (Part of Eden)	27288
Draughn	27891
Drewry	27553
Drexel	28619
Druid Hills (Part of Hendersonville)	28791
Drum Hill	27937
Drums Crossroads	28609
Dry Creek	27229
Duan	28658
Duart	28384
Dublin	28332
Duck‡	27949
Dudley	28333
Dudley Heights (Part of Greensboro)	27401
Dudley Shoals	28630
Duff Creek	28464
Duffies	28377
Duke (Part of Durham)‡	27706
Duke Power Village	28120
Dukes	27856
Dulah	28463
Dula Springs	28787
Duncan	27526
Dundarrach	28386
Dunn	28334*
	28335†
Dunn Crossroads	27822
Dunns Rock	28712
Dunns Store	27874
Dunnsview Acres	28146
Dupree Crossroads	27829
Durants Neck	27930
Durham	27701-22
For specific ZIP Codes call (888) 275-8777, or your local postmaster.	
Dutchess Downs	27529
Dysartville	28761
Eagle Mills	27020
Eagle Rock	27523
Eagle's Nest	28570
Eagle Springs	27242
Eagletown	27869
Earl	28038
Earley	27910
Earpsboro	27597
Easonburg	27801
Easons Crossroads	27938
East Arcadia	28456
East Bend	27018
Eastbrook	28146
East Carolina University‡	27834*
	27835†
Eastcrest Ridge	28025
East Durham (Part of Durham)‡	27703
East Fayetteville	28301
East Flat Rock♦	28726
East Franklin (Part of Franklin)	28734
East Lake	27953
Eastland Mall (Part of Charlotte)	28212
East Laport	28723
East Laurinburg	28352
East Lumberton (Part of Lumberton)	28358
East Marion	28752
East Monbo	28677
Easton (Part of Winston-Salem)	27107
Eastover, *Cumberland*♦	28301
Eastover (Part of Charlotte)	28207
Eastridge (Part of Gastonia)‡	28054
Eastridge Mall (Part of Gastonia)	28053
East Rockingham	28379
East Rocky Mount (Part of Rocky Mount)‡	27801
East Side Park (Part of Rockingham)	28379
East Side Park, *Robeson*	28340
East Spencer	28039
East Tabor	28463
Eastway (Part of Charlotte)‡	28205
East Wilmington (Part of Wilmington)	28405
Eastwood	28327
Ebenezer	28906
Echo	28383
Echo Heights	27603
Eck Reece	28642
Eden	27288*
	27289†
Edenhouse	27957
Edenton	27932
Edgar	27350
Edgemont	28611
Edgewood Acres	28016
Edmonds	28623
Edneyville	28727
Edward	27821
Edwards Crossroads, *Alleghany*	28675
Edwards Crossroads, *Nash*	27882
Edwards Crossroads, *Northampton*	27820
Edwards Fork	27874
Efland	27243
Ela	28713
Elams	23845
Elberon	27589
Eldorado	27371
Eleanors Crossroads	27937
Eleazer	27371
Elf	28904
Eli Whitney	27253
Elizabeth (Part of Charlotte)‡	28204
Elizabeth City	27906-09
For specific ZIP Codes call (888) 275-8777, or your local postmaster.	
Elizabeth City Coast Guard Air Station	27909
Elizabeth Heights	27896
Elizabethtown	28337
Elkin	28621
Elk Mountain (Part of Woodfin)	28804
Elk Park	28622
Elk Valley	28604
Ellenboro	28040
Ellendale, *Alexander*	28681
Ellendale, *Wake*	27545
Eller	27107
Ellerbe	28338
Ellerbe Grove	28379
Ellijay	28734
Elliott	28393
Ellis Crossroads	28144
Ellis Store	27983
Elm City	27822
Elm Grove, *Bertie*	27924
Elm Grove, *Lenoir*	28504
Elmore	28352
Elmores Crossroads	28054
Elmwood	28625
Elon College	27244
Embro	27551
Emerald Gardens	28304
Emerald Isle	28594
Emerald Village	27610
Emerson, *Bladen*	28433
Emerson, *Columbus*	28463
Emerywood (Part of High Point)‡	27262
Emit	27557
Emma	28806
Enderly Park (Part of Charlotte)	28208
Endy	28001
Enfield	27823
Engelhard	27824
Englewood (Part of Rocky Mount)‡	27801
English Woods	28025
Enka	28728
Enka Village	28728
Ennice	28623
Eno	27278
Enochville♦	28023
Enola	28655
Enon	27018
Eno Valley (Part of Durham)‡	27712
Enterprise, *Davidson*	27295
Enterprise, *Warren*	27850
Ephesus	27028
Epsom	27536
Erastus	28723
Erect	27341
Ernul	28527
Ervintown	28574
Erwin	28339
Erwin Heights (Part of Thomasville)	27360
Essex	27844
Estatoe	28777
Estelle	27305
Ether	27247
Etowah♦	28729
Eubanks	27516
Eufola	28677
Eure	27935
Eureka	27830
Eureka Springs	28301
Eutaw (Part of Fayetteville)‡	28303
Evansdale	27893
Everetts	27825
Everetts Crossroads	27865
Evergreen, *Beaufort*	27817
Evergreen, *Columbus*	28438
Evergreen Estates	28304
Exum	28420
Exway	27306
Fair Bluff	28439
Fairfield, *Hyde*	27826
Fairfield, *Union*	28103
Fairfield, *Wilson*	27893
Fairfield Harbour	28560
Fair Field Heights	28152
Fairfield Sapphire Valley	28774
Fair Grove	27360
Fairlane	28303
Fairmont	28340
Fairmont Junction	28383
Fairplains♦	28659
Fairport	27544
Fairview, *Buncombe*	28730
Fairview, *Orange*♦	27278
Fairview, *Rockingham*	27288
Fairview, *Union*	28110
Fairview Crossroads	27017
Fairview Park	28636
Fairway Heights	28150
Fairway Hills	28786
Faison	28341
Faisons	27876
Faith	28041
Falcon	28342
Falkland	27827
Fall Creek	27018
Falling Creek	28504
Falling Creek Estates	28601
Falls	27609
Fallston	28042
Far Away Place	28025
Farmer	27203
Farmington	27028
Farmville, *Chatham*	27330
Farmville, *Pitt*	27828
Faro	27883
Farrington	27514
Faust	28754
Fayblock (Part of Fayetteville)	28301
Fayetteville	28301-06
	28309-14
For specific ZIP Codes call (888) 275-8777, or your local postmaster.	
Fayetteville North (Part of Fayetteville)	28311
Fearrington Post	27312
Federal Building (Part of Elizabeth City)‡	27909
Feezor	27292
Feltonville	27502
Ferguson	28624
Ferncliff Estates	28075
Fibreville (Part of Canton)	28716
Fields	28551
Fines Creek	28721
Finger	28124
Fires Creek	28904
First Union (Part of Charlotte)‡	28202
Fisher Park (Part of Greensboro)	27401
Fisher Town	28025
Fitch	27379
Five Forks, *Person*	27573
Five Forks, *Rowan*	28023
Five Forks, *Warren*	27551
Five Point (Part of Raleigh)‡	27608
Five Points, *Beaufort*	27889
Five Points, *Columbus*	28431
Five Points, *Hoke*	28376
Five Points, *Richmond*	28379
Flat Branch, *Gates*	27938
Flat Branch, *Harnett*	27546
Flat Creek	28787
Flat Rock, *Henderson*	28731
Flat Rock, *Stokes*	27043
Flat Rock, *Surry*♦	27030
Flats	28781
Flat Shoals	27019
Flat Springs	28622
Flay	28021
Fleetwood	28626
Fleetwood Acres	28052
Fletcher	28732
Flint Hill, *Montgomery*	27371
Flint Hill, *Randolph*	27350
Flint Hill, *Yadkin*	27018
Florence	28556
Florence Town	27302
Flowes Store	28025
Floytan Crossroads	27536
Folkstone	28445
Fontana Dam	28733
Footsville	27055
Forbes	28705
Forestburg	27944
Forest City	28043
Forest Hills (Part of Fayetteville)	28303
Forest Hills (Part of Wilmington)	28403
Forest Hills (Part of Winston-Salem)	27105
Forest Hills, *Gaston*	28120
Forest Hills, *Rockingham*	27320
Forest Oaks♦	27406
Forest Ridge	28152
Forestville, *Anson*	28091
Forestville, *Wake*	27587
Fork Church	27006
Fort Barnwell	28526
Fort Bragg	28307
Fort Caswell	28465
Fort Junction	28307
Fort Landing	27925
Fort Macon Coast Guard Base	28512
Fort Point	27817
Foscoe	28604
	28607
For specific ZIP Codes call (888) 275-8777, or your local postmaster.	
Foster Creek	28753
Fountain, *Duplin*	28521
Fountain, *Pitt*	27829
Fountain Hill	28133
Fountain Fork	27886
Four Oaks	27524
Four Seasons (Part of Hendersonville)‡	28792
Four Seasons Town Centre (Part of Greensboro)‡	27407
Fourway	28538
Foxcroft East (Part of Charlotte)‡	28226
Fox Fire, *Cumberland*	28303
Foxfire, *Moore*	27281
Foxlair	28570
Foxwood Acres	28025
Francisco	27053
Francis Mill	27805
Francktown	28574
Frank	28657
Franklin, *Macon*	28734*
	28744†
Franklin, *Rowan*	28147
Franklin Grove	28713
Franklin Street (Part of Chapel Hill)‡	27514
Franklinton	27525
Franklinville	27248
Frazier Crossroads	27557
Fraziers Crossroads	27910
Frederick	27817
Freedom (Part of Charlotte)‡	28208
Freedom Mall (Part of Charlotte)	28208
Freeland	28420
Freeman	28423
Fremont	27830
Friendly Acres	28027
Friendly Shopping Center (Part of Greensboro)‡	27404
Friendship, *Cherokee*	28906
Friendship, *Duplin*	28398
Friendship, *Guilford*	27410
Friendship, *Wake*	27502
Friendship, *Yadkin*	27018
Frisco	27936
Frog Island	27909
Frog Level	27834
Frog Pond	28129
Frogsboro	27314
Fruitland	28792
Frying Pan Landing	27925
Fulchers Landing	28460
Fullers	27360
Fulp	27052
Funston	28479
Fuquay Springs (Part of Fuquay-Varina)	27526
Fuquay-Varina	27526
Furches	28644
Furnitureland (Part of High Point)‡	27264
Galatia	27876
Gales Creek	28570
Galloway Crossroads	27858
Gallup Acres	28304
Gamble Hill	28016
Gamewell	28645
Garden Homes (Part of Greensboro)	27408
Gardnerville	28513
Gardner Webb College (Part of Boiling Springs)	28017
Garland	28441
Garner	27529
Garysburg	27831
Gaston	27832
Gastonia	28051-56
For specific ZIP Codes call (888) 275-8777, or your local postmaster.	
Gaston Mall (Part of Gastonia)	28054
Gates	27937
Gates Four	28306
Gatesville	27938

Place	ZIP Code
Gateway	28789
Gatewood	27315
Gause Landing	28469
Gay	28779
Gaylord	27808
Gela	27565
Gentry Store	27573
George	27897
Georgetown, *Buncombe*	28806
Georgetown, *Davidson*	27284
Georgetown, *Lenoir*	28501
Georgeville	28025
Germanton	27019
Germantown	27875
Gerton	28735
Gethsemane	27891
Gibson	28343
Gibsontown	28716
Gibsonville	27249
Giddensville	28341
Gilkey	28139
Gill	27536
Gillburg	27536
Glade Valley	28627
Glady	28715
Glass (Part of Kannapolis)	28081
Glen Alpine	28628
Glen Ayre	28705
Glenbrook	28304
Glencoe	27217
Glen Cove	27909
Glendale Acres (Part of Fayetteville)	28304
Glendale Springs	28629
Glendon	27325
Glenhaven	28304
Glen Lennox (Part of Chapel Hill)	27514
Glenn	27705
Glenola	27263
Glen Raven♦	27215
Glenview	27823
Glenville	28736
Glenwood (Part of Greensboro)	27403
Glenwood, *McDowell*	28737
Glenwood (Part of Rockingham)	28379
Globe	28645
Gloucester	28528
Glovers Crossroads	27924
Gneiss	28734
Goat Neck	27925
Godwin	28344
Golden Forest	27604
Golden Gate (Part of Greensboro)	27405
Gold Hill, *Hoke*	28386
Gold Hill, *Rockingham*	27025
Gold Hill, *Rowan*	28071
Gold Mine	28741
Gold Point	27871
Goldrock	27891
Goldsboro	27530-34
For specific ZIP Codes call (888) 275-8777, or your local postmaster.	
Goldston	27252
Gold Valley Crossroads	27557
Goodsonville	28092
Goose Creek	27974
Gooseneck	28456
Goose Pond	27924
Gordonton	27541
Gordontown	27292
Gorman♦	27704
Goshen, *Granville*	27565
Goshen, *Wilkes*	28697
Governors Island	28713
Grace (Part of Asheville)‡	28814
Grace Chapel	28630
Gradys	28365
Graham	27253
Graingers	28501
Grandin	28645
Grandfather	28646
Grandview	28906
Grandview Heights (Part of Boone)	28607
Grandy	27939
Granite Falls	28630
Granite Quarry	28072
Grantham	27530
Granthams	28560
Grantsboro	28529
Grantville	27203
Grape Creek	28906
Grapevine	28753
Graphite	28762
Grassy Creek, *Ashe*	28631
Grassy Creek, *Mitchell*	28777
Grays Chapel	27248
Gray's Creek	28348
Grayson	28615
Great Neck Landing	28539
Green Acres, *Alamance*	27217
Green Acres, *Gaston*	28012
Green Acres, *Wake*	27603
Green Acres Park	28025
Greenbrier Estates	27603
Greene Cove	28705
Greenevers	28458
Green Farm	27834
Greenfield	27932
Greenhill, *Haywood*	28716
Green Hill, *Rutherford*	28139
Greenlee	28762
Green Level, *Alamance*	27217
Green Level, *Wake*	27502
Greenmountain	28740
Green River	28722
Greensboro	27401-95
For specific ZIP Codes call (888) 275-8777, or your local postmaster.	
Greens Creek	28779
Green Valley, *Ashe*	28615
Green Valley, *Cleveland*	28152
Greenville	27834-36
	27858
For specific ZIP Codes call (888) 275-8777, or your local postmaster.	
Greenwood Homes (Part of Fayetteville)	28303
Gregory	27973
Gregory Crossroads, *Bertie*	27957
Gregory Crossroads, *Onslow*	28574
Greystone	27536
Griffins Crossroads	27312
Grifton	28530
Grimes Crossroads	27009
Grimesdale	28792
Grimesland	27837
Grissettown	28470
Grissom	27522
Grist	28431
Grove Hill	27551
Grovemont	28778
Grove Park (Part of Charlotte)	28215
Grover	28073
Grovestone	28778
Growers Crossroads	27924
Guide	28463
Guideway	28463
Guilford (Part of Greensboro)‡	27409
Guilford College (Part of Greensboro)	27410
Guilford Hills (Part of Greensboro)	27408
Gulf	27256
Gull Rock	27824
Gumberry	27838
Gumbranch	28540
Gum Neck	27925
Gum Springs	27312
Guntertown	28753
Gupton	27549
Gurganus	28454
Guthrie	27284
Guyton	28320
Haddocks Crossroads	28590
Hadley	28518
Hairtown	28302
Half Hell	28422
Half Moon♦	28540
Halifax	27839
Hallsboro	28442
Halls Crossroads	28318
Halls Ferry Junction	28127
Halls Mills	28649
Halls Store	28385
Hallsville	28518
Hamer	27212
Hamilton	27840
Hamilton Crossroads	28103
Hamilton Lakes (Part of Greensboro)	27410
Hamlet	28345
Hampstead	28443
Hamptonville	27020
Hamrick	28714
Hams Crossroads	27837
Hancheys Store	28466
Hancock	27932
Handy	27239
Hanes Mall (Part of Winston-Salom)‡	27103*
	27130†
Hanrahan	28530
Happy Valley, *Buncombe*	28805
Happy Valley, *Caldwell*	28645
	28661
For specific ZIP Codes call (888) 275-8777, or your local postmaster.	
Harbinger	27941
Harbor Island (Part of Wrightsville Beach)	28480
Hardee Crossroads	27504
Hardins	28034
Hare	28627
Hargetts Cross Roads	28574
Harkers Island♦	28531
Harlem Heights	28170
Harlowe	28570
Harmony	28634
Harnett	27546
Harper's Crossroads	27207
Harrells	28444
Harrellsville	27942
Harrelsonville	28472
Harris, *Moore*	28327
Harris, *Rutherford*	28074
Harrisburg	28075
Harrisburg Estates	28075
Harris Crossroads, *Franklin*	27596
Harris Crossroads, *Vance*	27536
Harris Landing	27932
Harrisons Crossroads	27320
Harrisville	27229
Hartman	27016
Hartsease	27886
Harveytown	28501
Hassell	27841
Hastings Corner	27921
Hasty	28352
Hatteras	27943
Havelock	28532
Havelock Station (Part of Havelock)	28532
Haw Branch, *Moore*	27330
Haw Branch, *Onslow*	28574
Haw Creek (Part of Asheville)	28805
Hawfields	27302
Hawk	28705
Haw River	27258
Haws Run	28454
Hayesville	28904
Haymount (Part of Fayetteville)‡	28305
Hayne	28318
Hays♦	28635
Hayti (Part of Durham)	27701
Haywood	27559
Haywood Road (Part of Asheville)‡	28806
Hazelwood	28738
Hazelwood Park	27864
Healing Springs	27239
Heathsville	27823
Heaton	28622
Hebron	27565
Hedrick Grove	27292
Helens Crossroads	28513
Helton	28631
Hemby Acres	28079
Henderson	27536
Hendersonville	28739
	28792-93
For specific ZIP Codes call (888) 275-8777, or your local postmaster.	
Hendrix Estates	28147
Henrico	27842
Henrietta	28076
Henry	28168
Henry River	28602
Hepco	28721
Heritage Hill	27516
Heritage Square (Part of Durham)‡	27707
Heritage Woods	28025
Herrings Crossroads, *Duplin*	28508
Herrings Crossroads, *Greene*	27888
Hertford	27944
Hester	27581
Hesters Store	27541
Hestertown	28358
Hewitt	28781
Hexlena	27805
Hibbs Acres	28570
Hickmans Crossroads	28470
Hickory	28601-03
For specific ZIP Codes call (888) 275-8777, or your local postmaster.	
Hickory Crossroads	27919
Hickory Furniture Mart (Part of Hickory)	28602
Hickory Grove, *Cumberland*	28304
Hickory Grove, *Gaston*	28056
Hickory Grove (Part of Charlotte)	28215
Hickory Hill	28152
Hickory Knoll	28734
Hickory Point	27806
Hickory Rock	27549
Hicks Crossroads, *Mecklenburg*	28078
Hicks Crossroads, *Vance*	27565
Hidden Hut Farms	28147
Hiddenite	28636
Higdonville	28734
Higgins	28714
High Crossroads	27807
Highfalls	27259
High Hampton	28717
Highland Park	28345
Highland Park West (Part of Greensboro)	27407
Highlands	28741
High Point	27260-65
For specific ZIP Codes call (888) 275-8777, or your local postmaster.	
High Rock	27239
High Shoals	28077
Highsmiths	28382
Hightowers	27379
Hildebran	28637
Hillcrest, *Hoke*	28376
Hill Crest, *Moore*	28327
Hilliardston	27856
Hills	28001
Hillsborough	27278
Hills Crossroads	27839
Hillsdale, *Davie*	27006
Hillsdale, *Guilford*	27405
Hillsville	27350
Hilltop (Part of Greensboro)‡	27417
Hilltop, *Lincoln*	28092
Hilltop Acres	28570
Hill View	28580
Hines Crossroad	27834
Hinsons Crossroads	28439
Hiwassee Dam	28906
Hobbsville	27946
Hobbton	28366
Hobgood	27843
Hobucken	28537
Hodges Gap	28607
Hodman	27028
Hoffman	28347
Hog Island	28394
Ho-Ho Village	28570
Holden Beach	28462
Holdens Crossroads	27893
Holiday Island	27944
Holiday Shores	27371
Holland	27526
Hollemans Crossroads	27562
Hollis	28040
Hollister	27844
Holly Grove, *Davidson*	27292
Holly Grove, *Gates*	27926
Holly Hill Mall (Part of Burlington)	27215
Holly Ridge	28445
Holly Spring	27316
Holly Springs, *Macon*	28734
Holly Springs, *Wake*	27540
Hollyville	28515
Hollywood	28304
Hollywood Crossroads	27858
Homestead (Part of Charlotte)	28214
Homestead Heights (Part of Durham)	27704
Honey Hill	28442
Honey Island	28420
Honey Town	28379
Honolulu	28530
Hood Swamp	27534
Hookerton	28538
Hooper Hill	28451
Hoopers Creek	28732
Hootentown	27889
Hopedale	27217
Hope Mills	28348
Hope Valley (Part of Durham)	27707
Hopewell, *Rutherford*	28040
Hopewell, *Wayne*	28365
Hopkins	27597
Horner	27565
Horse Shoe	28742
Hosiery Mill	28170
Hoskins (Part of Charlotte)	28214
Hothouse	28906
Hot Springs	28743
Houston	28112
Houstonville	28634
Howland Parkway	28516
Hubert	28539
Hudson	28638
Hudsons Crossroads	27858
Huffmantown	28574
Hughes	28657
Hugo	28530
Hulls Crossroads	28168
Huntdale	28740
Hunters Bridge	27865
Huntersville	28070†
	28078*
Hunting Creek	28659
Huntley	28385
Huntsboro	27565
Huntsville, *Rockingham*	27025
Huntsville, *Yadkin*	27055
Hurdle Mills	27541
Husk	28639
Hyatt Creek	28786
Hydeland	27885
Hyde Park Estates	28216
Hymans	28562
Icard♦	28666
Icaria	27980
Ida	28351
Idalia	27806
Idlewild, *Ashe*	28694
Idlewild (Part of Charlotte)‡	28212
Idlewild Annex (Part of Charlotte)‡	28227
Ijames Crossroads	27028
Independence (Part of Charlotte)‡	28212
Independence Mall (Part of Wilmington)	28403
Index	28694
Indian Beach	28512
Indian Hills	28789
Indian Springs	28578
Indian Town	27973
Indian Trail	28079
Indian Valley	27217
Inez	27589
Ingalls	28657
Ingleside	27549
Ingold	28446
Institute	28551
Intelligence	27025
Iotla	28734
Iris Gardens	28306
Ironduff	28786
Irongate	28306
Ironhill	28463
Iron Station	28080
Irving Park (Part of Greensboro)	27408
Isenhour	28127
Island View Shores	27808
Isle of Pines	27817
Ita	27823
Ivanhoe	28447
Ivy	28754
Ivy Hills	28786
Jackson	27845
Jackson Hamlet	28315
Jackson Hill	27239
Jackson Line	28713
Jackson Park (Part of Concord)	28027
Jackson Park (Part of Kannapolis)	28081

Jacksons Creek	27239
Jacksons Crossroads	28504
Jackson Springs	27281
Jacksons Store	28518
Jacksontown	27556
Jacksonville	28540-41
	28546
For specific ZIP Codes call (888) 275-8777, or your local postmaster.	
Jacktown	28752
Jakesville	27295
James City	28560
Jamestown	27282
Jamesville	27846
Janeiro	28510
Jarmantown	28574
Jarvisburg	27947
Jason	28551
Jasper	28523
	28562
For specific ZIP Codes call (888) 275-8777, or your local postmaster.	
Jefferson	28640
Jefferson Park	28379
Jenkins Heights (Part of Gastonia)	28052
Jenny Lind	28551
Jericho	27379
Jerome	28399
Jerusalem	27028
Joe	28743
Johns	28352
Johnson Crossroad	27501
Johnsons Corner	27976
Johnsontown, *Davidson*	27360
Johnsontown, *Sampson*	28328
Johnsonville, *Cherokee*	28906
Johnsonville, *Harnett*	28326
Johnstown	28021
Jonas Ridge	28641
Jonathan	28786
Jones	27311
Jonesboro (Part of Sanford)	27330
Jones Chapel	27545
Jonestown	28572
Jonesville	28642
Joppa	27919
Jordan	27576
Joyceton (Part of Hudson)	28638
Joyland (Part of Durham)	27703
Joyners Crossroads	27801
Joynes	28685
Jubilee	27299
Judges Quarter	27885
Jugtown	28715
Julian	27283
Juno	28806
Jupiter	28787
Justice	27882
Kalmia	28777
Kannapolis	28081-83
For specific ZIP Codes call (888) 275-8777, or your local postmaster.	
Kapps Mill	27017
Katesville	27525
Kearney	27549
Keene	27707
Keener	28328
Kelford	27847
Kellersville	28604
Kellogs Fork	27979
Kellum	28546
Kellumtown	28539
Kelly	28448
Kenansville	28349
Kendale Shopping Center (Part of Sanford)	27330
Kenilworth (Part of Asheville)	28805
Kenly	27542
Kenmure	28731
Kennebec	27592
Kennells Beach	28529
Kentwood	28025
Kernersville	27284*
	27285†
Kerr	28444
Kershaw	28571
Keys Crossroads	27946
Kikers	28133
Kilby Island	27808
Kill Devil Hills	27948
Kimesville	27298
King	27021
King Charles (Part of Raleigh)	27610
Kingsboro	27801
Kings Creek	28606
	28645
For specific ZIP Codes call (888) 275-8777, or your local postmaster.	
Kings Crossroads, *Guilford*	27284
Kings Crossroads, *Pitt*	27829
Kings Forest	28147
Kings Mountain	28086
Kingstown	28150
King Whites Fork	27843
Kinston	28501-04
For specific ZIP Codes call (888) 275-8777, or your local postmaster.	
Kinton Fork	27565
Kipling	27543
Kirbys Crossing	27851
Kirkwood (Part of Greensboro)	27408
Kittrell	27544
Kitty Fork	28328
Kitty Hawk	27949
Knightdale	27545
Knob Hill	28379
Knollwood (Part of Southern Pines)	28387
Knotts Island	27950
Kona	28705
Kornbow	28303
Kornegay	28508
Kure Beach	28449
Kyle	28781
Laboratory	28092
Lackey Hill	28713
Lackey Town	28762
Ladonia	27030
Lafayette‡	28304
Lagoon	28448
La Grange, *Cumberland*	28303
La Grange, *Lenoir*	28551
Lake Comfort	27885
Lakecrest	28301
Lakedale (Part of Fayetteville)‡	28306
Lake Daniel (Part of Greensboro)	27408
Lake Ellsworth	27834
Lake Gaston Estates	27551
Lake Glenwood	27858
Lake in the Pine	27371
Lake Junaluska♦	28745
Lake Landing	27824
Lake Lure	28746
Lake Lynn	28306
Lake Montonia	28086
Lakemont Park	28601
Lake Park	28079
Lakeside (Part of Winston-Salem)	27105
Lakeside, Stanly	28001
Lake Toxaway	28747
Lakeview, *Alamance*	27215
Lakeview, *Davidson*	27299
Lakeview, *Moore*	28350
Lakeview Estates, *Alamance*	27215
Lakeview Estates, *Henderson*	28792
Lake View Park	27870
Lake Waccamaw	28450
Lakewood, *Cabarrus*	28025
Lakewood, *Henderson*	28739
Lambert	28163
Lambs Corner	27921
Lamm	27893
Lamms Crossroads	27882
Lancaster Crossroads	27816
Landis	28088
Lane	28356
Langley Store	27801
Lansdowne (Part of Charlotte)	28226
Lansing	28643
Lanvale	28451
Lasker	27845
Last Chance	27824
Latham Town (Part of Greensboro)	27407
Lattimore	28089
Lauada	28713
Laurel	28753
Laurel Hill, *Buncombe*	28715
Laurel Hill, *Scotland*	28351
Laurel Hills	27612
Laurel Park‡	28739
Laurel Springs	28644
Laurinburg	28352*
	28353†
Lawndale, Cleveland	28090
Lawndale (Part of Greensboro)	27408
Lawrence	27886
Lawsonville, *Rockingham*	27320
Lawsonville, *Stokes*	27022
Laytown	28645
Leaksville (Part of Eden)	27288
Leaman	27325
Leasburg	27291
Leatherman	28734
Ledbetter	28379
Ledger	28705
Leechville	27810
Lee Landing	28560
Lee's Ridge	28806
Leewood Acres	28092
Legerwood	28645
Leggett	27886
Leggetts Crossroads	27889
Leicester	28748
Leland	28451
Lemon Springs	28355
Lennon Crossroads	28422
Lennons Crossroads	28438
Lennoxville	28516
Lenoir	28645
Lenoir Mall (Part of Lenoir)	28645
Lenoir Rhyne (Part of Hickory)‡	28601
Letitia	28906
Level Cross, *Randolph*	27317
Level Cross, *Surry*	27017
Levels	27925
Lewis	27565
Lewisburg	28714
Lewiston	27849
Lewisville	27023
Lexington	27292-95
For specific ZIP Codes call (888) 275-8777, or your local postmaster.	
Lexington Plaza (Part of Lexington)‡	27293
Liberia	27589
Liberty, *Cherokee*	37391
Liberty, *Randolph*	27298
Liberty, *Rowan*	28071
Liberty Hill	27306
Liddell	28578
Light Oak♦	28150
Liledown	28681
Lilesville	28091
Lillington	27546
Lilly	27976
Lincolnton	28092*
	28093†
Lindell	27883
Linden	28356
Lindley Mill	27253
Lindley Park (Part of Greensboro)	27403
Lineberry	27233
Linville	28646
Linville Falls	28647
Linwood	27299
Lisbon	28434
Little Creek	28754
Littlefield	28513
Little Horse Creek	28643
Little Mountain	28761
Little Pinecreek	28753
Little Richmond	28621
Little River, *Alexander*	28681
Little River, *Transylvania*	28766
Littles Mill	27306
Little Switzerland	28749
Littleton	27850
Livingstons Quarters	28351
Lizard Lick	27591
Lizzie	28580
Lloyd Crossroads	27942
Loafers Glory	28705
Lobelia	28394
Lochlommond	28304
Locust	28097
Locust Hill	27320
Loftins Crossroads	28504
Logan	28139
Lola	28520
Lomax	28669
Lone Hickory	27055
Long Acres (Part of Jacksonville)	28546
Longcreek	28457
Longisland	28609
Long John Mountain Estates	28791
Longleaf	28570
Long Leaf Park (Part of Wilmington)	28403
Long Pine	28133
Long Point	28555
Long Ridge	28754
Long Shoals	28092
Long Store	27573
Longtown, *Burke*	28761
Longtown, *Yadkin*	27011
Long View, *Bladen*	28448
Long View, *Catawba*‡	28602
Longview, *Cumberland*	28301
Longwood	28452
Longwood Park	28345
Loray	28625
Louisburg	27549
Love Field	28779
Lovejoy	27371
Love Valley	28625
Lowell	28098
Lowes Grove	27713
Lowesville	28164
Lowgap	27024
Lowland	28552
Luart	27546
Lucama	27851
Lucia	28120
Luck	28743
Lumber Bridge	28357
Lumberton	28358-60
For specific ZIP Codes call (888) 275-8777, or your local postmaster.	
Luther	28715
Lyman	28521
Lynchs Corner	27909
Lynn	28750
Lynndale	27858
Lynwood Lakes	27406
Mabel	28698
McAdenville	28101
McAdoo Heights (Part of Greensboro)	27405
McArthur Crossroads	28352
Macclesfield	27852
McConnell	27325
McCray	27215
McCullen	28328
McCullers	27603
Mc Cutcheon Field	28545
McDade	27231
McDaniel	28382
McDonald	28340
Macedonia, *Wake*	27606
Macedonia, *Washington*	27962
McFarlan	28102
MacGee Crossroads	27501
McGehees Mill	27343
McGinnis Crossroads	28722
McGowans Crossroads	27858
McGrady	28649
Machpelah	28080
Mackeys	27970
Macks Village	27526
McLamb Crossroads	28366
McLeansville♦	27301
Maco	28451
Macon	27551
Madison	27025
Maggie Valley	28751
Magnolia (Part of Morganton)‡	28655
Magnolia, *Duplin*	28453
Magnolia, *New Hanover*‡	28402†
	28411*
Maiden	28650
Maine	27028
Main Street (Part of Garner)	27529
Makatoka	28420
Makleyville	27875
Malmo	28451
Malpass Corner	28425
Maltby	28905
Malvern Hills (Part of Asheville)	28806
Mamers	27552
Mamie	27966
Manchester (Part of Spring Lake)	28390
Mandale	27253
Mangum	27306
Manly	28387
Manns Harbor	27953
Manor‡	27103-04
	27114
For specific ZIP Codes call (888) 275-8777, or your local postmaster.	
Mansfield	28557
Mansfield Park	28557
Manson	27553
Manteo	27954
Maple	27956
Maple Cypress	28530
Maple Hill	28454
Maple Springs	28665
Mapleton	27855
Mapleville	27549
Maplewood (Part of Rockingham)	28379
Marble	28905
Maready	28521
Margaret	27549
Margaretsville	27853
Maribel	28515
Marietta	28362
Marion	28752
Mariposa	28164
Marlboro	27828
Marler	27020
Marlwood Acres (Part of Charlotte)	28212
Mar-Mac♦	27530
Mar-Man	28532
Marshall	28753
Marshallberg	28553
Mars Hill	28754
Marshville	28103
Marston	28363
Martel Village (Part of Woodfin)	28804
Martins Creek	28906
Martins Point	27949
Martins Stores	27055
Marvin	28173
Marys Grove	28086
Mashoes	27953
Masons Crossroads	28343
Masontown	28581
Massapoag (Part of Lincolnton)	28092
Mast	28692
Mathews Crossroads	27816
Matkins	27249
Matney	28604
Matthews	28104-06
For specific ZIP Codes call (888) 275-8777, or your local postmaster.	
Maury	28554
Mavaton	27932
Maxton	28364
Mayfair	28304
Mayfield	27326
Mayhew	28117
Mayodan	27027
Maysville	28555
Mazeppa	28115
Meadow, *Johnston*	27504
Meadow, *Stokes*	27052
Meadowbrook	28150
Meadowood	28379
Meadowood Lakes	27302
Meadow Summit (Part of Eden)	27288
Meadow Wood	28304
Meat Camp	28607
Mebane	27302
Medfield	27607
Melanchton	27298
Melrose	28773
Melville	27302
Melvin Hill	28722
Menola	27910
Meredith College (Part of Raleigh)	27601
Merrimon	28516
Merritt	28556
Merry Hill	27957
Merry Oaks	27559
Mesic	28515
Method (Part of Raleigh)‡	27606

Mewborns Crossroads 28504
Micaville 28755
Micro 27555
Middleburg 27556
Middle Fork 28712
Middlesex 27557
Middletown 27824
Midland 28107
Midpine 28086
Midway, *Alexander* 28636
Midway, *Beaufort* 27889
Midway, *Bertie* 27957
Midway, *Brunswick* 28422
Midway (Part of Kannapolis) 28081
Midway, *Richmond* 28379
Midway, *Rockingham* 27320
Midway Park 28544
Midwood (Part of Charlotte) 28205
Milburnie 27604
Mildred 27886
Miles 27302
Milboro 27248
Mill Branch 28420
Millbridge 28147
Millbrook (Part of Raleigh) 27609
Mill Creek, *Ashe* 28684
Mill Creek, *Brunswick* 28479
Mill Creek, *Carteret* 28570
Mill Crossroads 27932
Millennium 27805
Millers Creek♦ 28651
Millersville 28681
Millingport 28001
Mill Neck 27818
Mill Spring 28756
Mills River 28742
Milltown 28771
Milton 27305
Milwaukee 27854
Mimosa Shores 27889
Mineral Springs, *Anson* 28135
Mineral Springs, *Union* 28108
Mingo 28334
Minneapolis 28652
Minnesott Beach 28510
Minnie-Bert 27884
Minpro 28777
Mint Hill‡ 28227
Mintons Store 27897
Mintonsville 27946
Mintz 28382
Minuet (Part of Charlotte)‡ 28209-10
For specific ZIP Codes call (888) 275-8777, or your local postmaster.
Mirror Lake 28741
Misenheimer 28109
Mitchells Fork 27946
Mitchell Village 28557
Mitcheners Crossroads 27525
Mocksville 27028
Moffitt Hill 28762
Mollie 28432
Moltonville 28328
Momeyer 27856
Monbo 28609
Moncure 27559
Monks Crossroads 28366
Monroe 28110-12
For specific ZIP Codes call (888) 275-8777, or your local postmaster.
Monroe Mall (Part of Monroe) 28110
Monroeton 27320
Monroetown 28387
Monroeton 27320
Montague 28435
Montclair 28304
Montezuma 28653
Monticello 27214
Montreat 28757
Montrose 28376
Moores Beach 27810
Mooresboro 28114
Moores School House 27542
Moores Springs 27053
Mooresville 28115
28117
For specific ZIP Codes call (888) 275-8777, or your local postmaster.
Mooresville Junction (Part of Mooresville) 28115
Moravian Falls♦ 28654
Mordecai (Part of Raleigh) 27604
Morehead City 28557
Morgans Corner 27909
Morganton 28655*
28680†
Morgantown 27215
Moriah 27572
Morlan Park (Part of Salisbury) 28146
Morning Star 28716
Morris Landing 28445
Morrisville 27560
Mortimer 28611
Morven 28119
Moss Hill 28504
Mother Vineyard 27954
Motleta 27203
Moulton 27549
Mountain Home♦ 28758
Mountain Island 28120
Mountain Park 28676
Mountain Valley 28790
Mountain View, *Buncombe* 28704
Mountain View, *Catawba*‡ 28601
Mountain View, *Gaston* 28086
Mountain View, *Orange* 27278
Mountain View, *Stokes* 27021
Mount Airy 27030
Mount Carmel 27371
Mount Carmel Acres 28806
Mount Energy 27522
Mount Gilead, *Avery* 28622
Mount Gilead, *Cabarrus* 28025
Mount Gilead, *Montgomery* 27306
Mount Gould 27957
Mount Herman 28638
Mount Holly 28120
Mount Mourne 28123
Mount Olive, *Bladen* 28337
Mount Olive, *Columbus* 28472
Mount Olive, *Hyde* 27810
Mount Olive, *Stokes* 27021
Mount Olive, *Wayne* 28365
Mount Pleasant, *Avery* 28657
Mount Pleasant, *Cabarrus* 28124
Mount Pleasant, *Cherokee* 28906
Mount Pleasant, *Nash* 27807
Mount Pleasant, *Richmond* 28338
Mount Pleasant, *Yadkin* 27011
Mount Sterling 37821
Mount Tabor (Part of Winston-Salem)‡ 27106
Mount Tabor, *Washington* 27928
Mount Tirzah 27583
Mount Ulla 28125
Mount Vernon, *Rowan* 27013
Mount Vernon, *Rutherford* 28139
Mount Vernon Springs 27344
Mount Zion (Part of Greensboro) 27406
Moxley 28635
Moyock 27958
Mt. Mitchell 28083
Mt. Pleasant 27592
Muddy Cross 27946
Mulberry♦ 28659
Murdocksville 28374
Murfreesboro 27855
Murphy, *Cherokee* 28906
Murphy, *Duplin* 28458
Murray Hills 28025
Murrays Mills 28609
Murraysville 28411
Murray Town 28425
Musgraves Crossroads 27863
Myers Park (Part of Charlotte)‡ 28207
Myrick Estates 27850
Myrtle Grove♦ 28403
Nags Head 27959
Nahunta 27863
Nakina 28455
Nantahala 28781
Naples 28760
Nashville 27856
Nathans Creek 28617
28640
For specific ZIP Codes call (888) 275-8777, or your local postmaster.
Naval Hospital 28542
Navassa 28404
Nebo, *McDowell* 28761
Nebo, *Yadkin* 27011
Nebraska 27824
Needmore, *Rowan* 27054
Needmore, *Swain* 28713
Neel Estates 28147
Nelson 27560
Neuse 27661
Neuse Crossroads (Part of Raleigh) 27616
Neuse Forest 28560
New Bern 28560-64
For specific ZIP Codes call (888) 275-8777, or your local postmaster.
Newbold (Part of Fayetteville) 28301
New Bridge (Part of Woodfin) 28804
Newdale 28714
Newell 28126
Newfound 28748
New Haven 28675
New Hill 27562
New Holland 27885
New Hope (Part of Gastonia) 28054
New Hope, *Chatham* 27559
New Hope, *Franklin* 27549
New Hope, *Iredell* 28689
New Hope, *Orange* 27514
New Hope, *Randolph* 27239
New Hope, *Wake*♦ 27616
New Hope, *Wayne* 27534
New Hope, *Wilson* 27896
New House 28150
Newland 28657
New Lands 27925
New Life 28635
New London 28127
New Market 27350
Newport 28570
New River Marine Corps Air Station 28540
New River Plaza (Part of Jacksonville)‡ 28540
New Salem 28103
Newsom 27239
Newton 28658
Newton Grove 28366
Newton Park 27896
Newtons Crossroads 28478
Niagara 28387
Nixons Beach 27932
Nixonton 27909
Nobles Crossroads 28525
Nocarva 27551
Nocho Park (Part of Greensboro) 27406
Norfleet 27874
Norlina 27563
Norman 28367
Norrington Crossroads 27546
North (Part of Winston-Salem)‡ 27105
North Albemarle (Part of Albemarle) 28001
North Asheboro (Part of Asheboro) 27203
North Belmont (Part of Belmont) 28012
North Brevard 28712
North Burlington (Part of Burlington)‡ 27215
North Charlotte (Part of Charlotte)‡ 28225
North Chase (Part of Wilmington) 28405
North Concord (Part of Concord) 28025
North Cooleemee (Part of Cooleemee) 27014
North Cove 28752
North Durham (Part of Durham)‡ 27712
North Elkin 28621
Northgate (Part of Durham)‡ 27701
Northgate Mall (Part of Durham) 27701
North Harbor 28516
North Harlowe 28532
North Henderson (Part of Henderson) 27536
North Hickory♦ 28601
North Hills Mall & Plaza (Part of Raleigh)‡ 27609
27614
27619
For specific ZIP Codes call (888) 275-8777, or your local postmaster.
Northlakes♦ 28630
North Lumberton (Part of Lumberton) 28358
Northmoor 28601
North Point (Part of Winston-Salem) 27106
North Raeford 28376
North Ridge (Part of Raleigh)‡ 27615
North River 28516
North River Corner 28516
North Roxboro (Part of Roxboro)‡ 27573
Northside, *Granville* 27564
Northside (Part of Elm City) 27822
North Topsail Beach 28460
North Tryon (Part of Charlotte)‡ 28213
28215
28256
28262
28269
For specific ZIP Codes call (888) 275-8777, or your local postmaster.
Northview 27330
Northwest 28451
Northwest Cabarrus Woods 28025
North Wilkesboro 28659
North Winston (Part of Winston-Salem) 27105
Northwoods (Part of Jacksonville)‡ 28540
Norton, *Jackson* 28723
Norton, *Macon* 28763
Norwood, *Rockingham* 27320
Norwood, *Stanly* 28128
Norwood Beach 28128
Norwood Hollow 28604
Oakboro 28129
Oak City 27857
Oak Crest (Part of Fayetteville) 28301
Oakdale (Part of Jamestown) 27282
Oak Forest 28803
Oak Grove, *Cleveland* 28086
Oak Grove (Part of Greensboro) 27406
Oak Grove, *Jones* 28573
Oak Grove, *Macon* 28734
Oak Grove, *Surry* 27030
Oak Grove Inn 28576
Oak Hill, *Burke* 28655
Oak Hill, *Caldwell* 28645
Oak Hill, *Granville* 27565
Oak Hollow Mall (Part of High Point) 27262
Oakhurst (Part of Charlotte) 28205
Oak Island 28465
Oakland 28160
Oakley (Part of Asheville) 28803
Oak Park, *Buncombe* 28704
Oak Park, *Cherokee* 28906
Oak Ridge 27310
Oaks, *Craven* 28560
Oaks, *Orange* 27514
Oaksmith Acres 28557
Oakview (Part of High Point) 27265
Oak Villa 27910
Oakville 27589
Oakwillow 27910
Oakwood (Part of Greensboro) 27407
Oakwood Acres 27292
Occoneechee 27278
Ocean 28570
Ocean Isle Beach 28469
Ocracoke 27960
Ogburn (Part of Winston-Salem) 27105
Ogreeta 28906
Oine 27563
Okeewemee 27371
Okisko 27909
Old Bethlehem 27589
Old Dock 28472
Olde Farm 28390
Old Farm 28025
Old Ford 27889
Old Fort 28762
Old Fort Shores 27817
Old Hundred 28351
Old Providence (Part of Charlotte) 28226
Old Sparta 27852
Old Spring Hope 27882
Oldtown (Part of Winston-Salem) 27106
Old Trap 27974
Olin 28660
Olive Branch 28103
Olive Hill 27573
Olivers Crossroads 28658
Olivia 28368
Olympia 28560
Olyphic 28463
Onvil 27306
Ophir 27371
Orange Grove 27278
Orchard Hills 28146
Oregon Hill 27326
Oriental 28571
Ormondsville 28513
Orrum 28369
Osborne 28345
Osceola 27214
Osgood 27330
Osmond 27291
Ossipee 27244
Oswalt 28166
Oteen‡ 28805
Othello 28694
Otto 28763
Otway 28516
Outer Banks (Part of Kill Devil Hills)‡ 27948
Outlaws Bridge 28508
Overhills Park 28390
Oxford 27565
Oxford Park 28610
Oyster Creek Landing 27885
Pacolet Valley 28782
Pactolus 27834
Padgett 28454
Paint Fork 28754
Paint Rock 28743
Pala Alto 28555
Palestine 28001
Palmerville 28127
Palmyra 27859
Pamlico 28571
Pamlico Beach 27810
Pantego 27860
Panther Creek 28721
Paradise East 28570
Paradise Point 28012
Parkersburg 28441
Parkers Fork 27926
Park Road (Part of Charlotte)‡ 28209
Parks Crossroads 27316
Park Spring 27315
Parkstone (Part of Charlotte) 28210
Parkstown 28551
Parkton 28371
Parktown 27589
Parkville 27944
Parkway Forest (Part of Asheville) 28805
Parkwood, *Cabarrus* 28027
Parkwood, *Durham*♦ 27713
Parkwood, *Moore* 28327
Parkwood (Part of Wilson)‡ 27893
Parmele 27861
Parrott Fork 28504
Parsonville 28665
Paschall 27589
Pates 28372
Patetown 27530
Patterson 28661
Patterson Grove 28086
Patterson Springs 28152
Pauls Crossing 28137
Paw Creek (Part of Charlotte) 28130
Paynes Tavern 27573
Peace Haven Estates 27104
Peachland 28133
Peachtree 28906

*** Area Zip Code** **† Post Office Boxes** **‡ Postal Station** **♦ Census Designated Place** *Italic Type* **County**

Peacock Crossing 28431
Pearces 27597
Pea Ridge, *Polk* 28756
Pea Ridge, *Yadkin* 27020
Pecan Grove 27874
Peden 28672
Pee Dee 27306
Pekin 27306
Peletier 28584
Pelham 27311
Pembroke 28372
Pender Crossroad 27822
Penderlea 28478
Pendleton 27862
Penland 28765
Penrose 28766
Pensacola 28714
Perch 27043
Perfection 28523
Perkinsville (Part of Boone) 28607
Perry's Beach 27924
Perrytown 27924
Peru 28460
Petersburg, *Madison* 28753
Petersburg, *Onslow* 28574
Petersville 27295
Pettys Shore 27922
Pfafftown 27040
Philadelphia 27974
Philadelphus 28377
Phillips Cross Roads 28585
Phoenix 28451
Piedmont Heights (Part of Greensboro) 27403
Pierceville 27976
Pigeon Roost 28740
Pike Crossroads 27863
Pike Road 27860
Pikeville 27863
Pilands Crossroads 27922
Pilot, *Davidson* 27360
Pilot, *Franklin* 27597
Pilot Mountain 27041
Pinebluff 28373
Pine Crest 27808
Pinecrest Acres 28301
Pinecroft (Part of Greensboro) 27407
Pine Hall 27042
Pine Haven 27239
Pine Hill, *Hoke* 28315
Pine Hill, *Surry* 27041
Pinehurst 28374
Pinehurst Park 28370
28374
For specific ZIP Codes call (888) 275-8777, or your local postmaster.
Pine Knoll (Part of Hope Mills) 28348
Pine Knoll Shores 28512
Pine Lakes 27030
Pine Level 27568
Pinelog 28472
Pineola 28662
Pine Ridge, *Cabarrus* 28201
Pine Ridge, *Franklin* 27597
Pine Ridge, *Surry* 27030
Pine Ridge, *Washington* 27970
Pinetops 27864
Pinetown 27865
Pine Valley 28409
Pineview 27330
Pineville 28134
Piney Creek 28663
Piney Green, *Onslow* 28544
Piney Green, *Sampson* 28328
Piney Grove, *Brunswick* 28422
Piney Grove, *Orange* 27278
Piney Ridge 28328
Pin Hook 28466
Pink Hill 28572
Pinkney 27830
Pinnacle 27043
Pireway 28463
Pisgah 27203
Pisgah Forest 28768
Pisgah View (Part of Asheville) 28806
Pitt Crossroads 27852
Pittmans Store 27891
Pittsboro 27312
Plainview 28383
Plateau 28658
Plaza (Part of Charlotte)‡ 28299
Plaza (Part of Greensboro)‡ 27429
Plaza (Part of Kingston)‡ 28503
Plaza, The (Part of Greenville) 27858
Pleasant Acres 28301
Pleasant Garden♦ 27313
Pleasant Gardens 28752
Pleasant Grove, *Alamance* 27217
Pleasant Grove, *Buncombe* 28787
Pleasant Grove, *Caswell* 27379
Pleasant Grove, *Duplin* 28365
Pleasant Grove, *Northampton* 27831
Pleasant Grove, *Washington* 27970
Pleasant Hill, *Jones* 28572
Pleasant Hill, *Northampton* 27866
Pleasant Hill, *Wilkes*♦ 28621
Pleasant Plains 27910
Pleasant Ridge 27316
Pleasant View 27925
Pleasantville 27025
Plott Farm Addition 28716
Plumtree 28664
Plyler 28001
Plymouth 27962
Pocomoke 27525
Point Caswell 28421
Point Harbor 27964
Pole Creek 28715
Polks Landing 27514
Polkton 28135
Polkville 28136
Pollocksville 28573
Pomona (Part of Greensboro) 27407
Ponderosa, Cumberland 28303
Ponderosa, *Harnett* 28334
Ponzer 27810
Poole Town 28137
Poor Town 27910
Pope Air Force Base 28308
Poplar 28740
Poplar Branch 27965
Poplar Grove 28341
Poplar Springs 27021
Porter 28128
Portsmouth 27960
Postell 28906
Potecasi 27867
Pot Neck 28551
Potters Curve 28431
Potters Hill 28572
Pottertown 28684
Powell Crossroads 27946
Powells Point 27966
Powells Store 27326
Powellsville 27967
Powhatan 27520
Prentiss 28734
Prestonville 27025
Price 27048
Price Creek 28714
Princeton 27569
Princeville 27886
Proctors Corner 27910
Proctorville 28375
Propst Crossroads 28601
Prospect 28462
Prospect Hill 27314
Prosper 28436
Providence, *Caswell* 27315
Providence, *Granville* 27565
Providence, *McDowell* 28752
Providence, *Mecklenburg* 28104
Providence Square (Part of Charlotte)‡ 28211
Proximity (Part of Greensboro) 27405
Pumpkin Center, *Lincoln* 28092
Pumpkin Center, *Onslow*♦ 28540
Pumpkintown 28779
Pungo 27860
Pungo Shores 27810
Purlear 28665
Purley 27379
Purnell 27587
Purvis 28383
Push 27541
Putnam 28327
Pyatte 28657
Quail Corners (Part of Charlotte)‡ 28210
Quail Ridge, *Craven* 28532
Quail Ridge, *Cumberland* 28306
Quail Ridge, *Lee* 27330
Qualla 28789
Quarry Hill Country Club 27253
Quebec 28747
Queen 27371
Quick 27326
Quinerly 28530
Quinns Store 28518
Quitsna 27983
Rabbit Corner 27909
Radical 28649
Radio Island 28516
Raeford 28376
Raemon 28364
Rainbow Springs 28734
Raleigh 27601-76
For specific ZIP Codes call (888) 275-8777, or your local postmaster.
Rama Woods 28025
Ramseur 27316
Ramseytown 28714
Randleman 27317
Randolph (Part of Charlotte)‡ 28211
Randolph Mall (Part of Asheboro) 27203
Ranger 28906
Rangewood 27603
Rankin (Part of Greensboro) 27405
Ranlo 28054
Ransomville 27810
Ravenswood 28573
Rawls 27526
Rayconda 28304
Raynham 28383
Rebel Acres 27604
Rebel City 28318
Red Banks 28364
Redbug 28442
Red Cross, *Randolph* 27233
Red Cross, *Stanly* 28129
Reddies River 28651
Red Hill, *Bladen* 28433
Red Hill, *Duplin* 28365
Red Hill, *Edgecombe* 27891
Red Hill, *Mitchell* 28705
Redland 27006
Red Oak, *Nash* 27868
Red Oak, *Pitt* 27834
Red Springs 28377
Reeds Cross Roads 27295
Reedy Creek 27295
Reelsboro 28560
Reepsville 28168
Reese 28692
Reeves Ferry 28455
Regal 28906
Regan 28420
Register 28458
Rehoboth 27845
Reidsville 27320-23
For specific ZIP Codes call (888) 275-8777, or your local postmaster.
Relief 28740
Rena 27020
Rennert 28386
Renston 28513
Republican 27983
Rest Haven 27808
Revolution (Part of Greensboro) 27405
Rex (Part of Ranlo) 28054
Rex, *Robeson* 28378
Reynolda (Part of Winston-Salem)‡ 27109
Reynolda Park (Part of Winston-Salem) 27107
Reynolds Crossroads 28328
Reynoldson 27937
Rheasville 27870
Rhems 28562
Rhems Landing 28562
Rhodes 27805
Rhodes-Rhyne 28092
Rhodhiss 28667
Rhodo 28901
Rhoney 28602
Rhyne Crossroads 28425
Riceville 28805
Richardson 28320
Richfield 28137
Richlands 28574
Richmond Hill (Part of Burlington) 27215
Richmond Hill, *Yadkin* 27011
Richmond Mills 28351
Rich Square 27869
Rico 28472
Riddle 27973
Ridgecrest 28770
Ridge Haven 27591
Ridge Run 28025
Ridgeville 27314
Ridgeway 27570
Ridgewood 28379
Riegelwood 28456
Riley 27596
Rimer 28025
Ringwood 27823
River Acres 27889
River Bend 28562
Riverdale 28560
River Hills 27858
Rivermont 28504
River Neck 27925
River Run Plantation 28422
Riverside, *Craven* 28530
Riverside (Part of New Bern) 28562
Riverside, *Yancey* 28714
Riverton 27932
Roanoke Rapids 27870
Roaring Creek 28657
Roaring Gap 28668
Roaring River 28669
Robbins 27325
Robbinsville 28771
Roberdel 28379
Roberdo 27306
Robersonville 27871
Roberta Mill 28027
Robin Hood Forest 27545
Robinson's 28570
Robinwood (Part of Gastonia) 28056
Rock Creek 27349
Rockdale (Part of Belwood) 28090
Rockefeller Estates 28326
Rockfish 28376
Rockford 27011
Rock Hill 28025
Rockingham 28379*
28380†
Rockingham Lake 27320
Rock Ridge 27893
Rockwell 28138
Rockwell Park (Part of Charlotte) 28213
Rocky Cross 27557
Rocky Ford 27544
Rockyhock 27932
Rocky Mount 27801-04
For specific ZIP Codes call (888) 275-8777, or your local postmaster.
Rocky Pass 28761
Rocky Point 28457
Rocky River 28025
Rocky Springs 28636
Rodanthe 27968
Roduco 27969
Rolesville 27571
Rolling Hills 28147
Rollingwood, *Cleveland* 28150
Rollingwood, *Cumberland* 28301
Rominger 28604
Ronda 28670
Rooks 28421
Roper 27970
Rose Bay 27885
Roseboro 28382
Rosebud, *Stokes* 27052
Rosebud, *Wilson* 27822
Rose Hill, *Duplin* 28458
Rose Hill, *Warren* 27553
Roseland, *Columbus* 28432
Roseland, *Lincoln* 28092
Roseland, *Moore* 28315
Rosemary Park 28079
Rosemead 27924
Rosemont (Part of Winston-Salem) 27107
Roseneath 27874
Roseville 27573
Rosewood 27530
Rosin 28366
Rosindale 28434
Roslin 28348
Rosman 28772
Ross Store 27052
Rougemont 27572
Roughedge 28112
Roundtree 28513
Rowan Mill (Part of Salisburg) 28147
Rowes Corner 28560
Rowland 28383
Roxboro 27573
Roxobel 27872
Royal, *Beaufort* 27806
Royal, *Franklin* 27549
Royal Oaks (Part of Kannapolis) 28083
Royal Pines♦ 28704
Royster 28451
Rudd 27214
Ruffin 27326
Rufus 28645
Rural Hall 27045
Ruskin 28399
Russtown 28420
Ruth 28139
Rutherford College 28671
Rutherfordton 28139
Rutherwood 28607
Ryland 27980
Saddletree 28360
Sadler 27320
Safe 28466
St. Helena 28425
St. James 28450
St. John 27805
27910
For specific ZIP Codes call (888) 275-8777, or your local postmaster.
St. Johns, *Chowan* 27932
St. Johns, *Pitt* 28530
St. Lewis 27852
St. Martin 28001
St. Pauls 28384
Salem, *Burke*♦ 28655
Salem, *Lincoln* 28092
Salem, *Nash* 27891
Salem, *Randolph* 27317
Salem, *Surry* 27030
Salem (Part of Winston-Salem)‡ 27108
Salemburg 28385
Salisbury 28144-47
For specific ZIP Codes call (888) 275-8777, or your local postmaster.
Salter Path 28575
Salty Shores 28570
Saluda 28773
Salvo 27972
Samarcand 27242
Samaria 27557
Sanderling 27948
Sand Hill, *Buncombe* 28806
Sandhill, *Pamlico* 28560
Sandhill Acres 27229
Sands 28607
Sandy Bottom 28504
Sandy Bottoms 28352
Sandy Creek 28451
Sandy Cross, *Gates* 27946
Sandy Cross, *Nash* 27856
Sandy Cross, *Rockingham* 27320
Sandy Grove, *Davidson* 27295
Sandy Grove, *Hoke* 28376
Sandymush, *Buncombe* 28753
Sandy Mush, *Rutherford* 28043
Sandy Plain, *Columbus* 28463
Sandy Plain, *Duplin* 28572
Sandy Plains 28782
Sandy Ridge, *Guilford* 27235
Sandy Ridge, *Stokes* 27046
Sanford 27330-31
For specific ZIP Codes call (888) 275-8777, or your local postmaster.
Sans Souci 27983
Santeetlah 28771
Sapona 28301
Sapphire 28774
Saratoga 27873
Sardis Village (Part of Charlotte)‡ 28270
Sarecta 28349
Sarvis Heights 28052

* **Area Zip Code** † **Post Office Boxes** ‡ **Postal Station** ♦ **Census Designated Place** *Italic Type* **County**

Sassers Mill 28526
Satterwhite 27565
Saulston 27530
Saunook 28786
Savannah 28779
Saw 28023
Sawmills 28630
28638
For specific ZIP Codes call (888) 275-8777, or your local postmaster.
Saxapahaw♦ 27340
Sayles Village (Part of Asheville) 28803
Scaly Mountain 28775
Schley 27278
Scholl 28345
Schrams Beach 27810
Scotch Grove 28352
Scotland Neck 27874
Scotsdale, *Cumberland* 28304
Scotsdale (Part of Laurinburg) 28352
Scott Acres 27302
Scott Park (Part of Greensboro) 27401
Scotts, *Iredell* 28699
Scotts, *Wilson* 27851
Scotts Crossroads 27886
Scotts Hill 28411
Scotts Store, *Duplin* 28365
Scotts Store, *Pamlico* 28560
Scottville 28672
Scranton 27875
Scuffleton 28513
Scuppernong 27928
Seaboard 27876
Seabreeze 28409
Seagate♦ 28403
Seagate IV 28516
Seagrove 27341
Sealevel 28577
Seaside 28468
Sedalia 27342
Sedgefield, *Guilford* 27407
Sedgefield (Part of Charlotte)‡ 28203
Sedgefield Lakes 27407
Sedgefield Park 27407
Sedge Garden♦ 27105
Selica 28712
Selma 27576
Selwin 27946
Selwyn Park (Part of Charlotte) 28209
Seminole 27505
Semora 27343
Senia 28657
Seven Devils 28604
Seven Lakes♦ 27376
Seven Paths 27549
Seven Springs 28578
Severn 27877
Seversville (Part of Charlotte) 28208
Sevier 28752
Seward 27040
Seymour Johnson Air Force Base 27531
Shacktown 27055
Shadey Oaks Acres 28150
Shady Banks 27889
Shady Brook (Part of Kannapolis) 28081
Shady Forest 28467
Shady Grove 28501
Shallotte 28459
Shallotte Point 28470
Shallow Well 27330
Shanghai, *Cleveland* 28017
Shanghai, *Sampson* 28458
Shankletown 28025
Shannon 28386
Shannon Plaza (Part of Durham)‡ 27707
27717
For specific ZIP Codes call (888) 275-8777, or your local postmaster.
Sharon, *Camden* 27976
Sharon, *Iredell* 28625
Sharonbrook (Part of Charlotte) 28210
Sharp Point 27829
Sharpsburg 27878
Shatley Springs 28617
Shawboro 27973
Shaw Heights 28303
Sheffield 27028

Shelby 28150-52
For specific ZIP Codes call (888) 275-8777, or your local postmaster.
Shell Rock Landing 28539
Shelmerdine 28513
Shelter Neck 28425
Shelton 27311
Shelton Town 27030
Shepard (Part of Durham)‡ 27707
Shepherds 28115
Sherrills Ford 28673
Sherron Acres (Part of Durham) 27703
Sherwood 28692
Sherwood Forest, *Buncombe* 28778
Sherwood Forest (Part of Asheville) 28805
Sherwood Forest (Part of Winston-Salem) 27104
Sherwood Forest, *Transylvania* 28712
Sherwood Forest, *Wilson* 27896
Sherwood Park 28306
Sherwood Terrace 28712
Sherwood Village (Part of High Point) 27260
Shields Commissary 27874
Shiloh (Part of Asheville) 28803
Shiloh, *Camden* 27974
Shiloh, *Rutherford* 28043
Shine 28580
Shingle Hollow 28139
Shinnville 28115
Shoal 27043
Shoofly 27581
Shooting Creek 28904
Shopton 28210
Short Off 28741
Shotwell 27545
27591
For specific ZIP Codes call (888) 275-8777, or your local postmaster.
Shuffletown 28214
Shulls Mills 28607
Shupings Mill 28138
Sidestown 28025
Sidney, *Beaufort* 27810
Sidney, *Columbus* 28472
Signal Hill Mall (Part of Statesville) 28677
Sign Pine 27980
Siler City 27344
Silk Hope 27344
Siloam 27047
Silver City♦ 28376
Silverdale 28539
Silver Hill, *Davidson* 27295
Silver Hill, *Pamlico* 28560
Silverstone 28698
Silver Valley 27292
Simpson 27879
Sims 27880
Sioux 28740
Sivey Town 28462
Six Forks, *Wake* 27615
Six Forks (Part of Raleigh) 27615
Skibo 28304
Skinnersville 27970
Skyco 27954
Skycrest Village 27604
Skyland 28776
Skyline 28394
Skyway Terrace 28364
Sladesville 27875
Slatestone Hills 27889
Sligo 27958
Sloan 28466
Slocomb 28311
28356
For specific ZIP Codes call (888) 275-8777, or your local postmaster.
Slocum 27824
Small 27806
Small Crossroads 27980
Smallwood (Part of Washington) 27889
Smethport 28694
Smith Creek♦ 28480
Smith Crossing 28442
Smithfield 27577
Smith Grove 27028
Smith's Corner 27921
Smithtown, *Beaufort* 27810

Smithtown, *Perquimans* 27944
Smithtown, *Yadkin* 27018
Smyre 28054
Smyrna 28579
Sneads Ferry♦ 28460
Sneads Grove 28352
Snow Camp 27349
Snowden 27958
Snow Hill, *Chowan* 27980
Snow Hill, *Greene* 28580
Snow Hill, *Sampson* 28382
Snug Harbor 27944
Sodom 28753
Somerset, *Chowan* 27932
Somerset, *Person* 27573
Somerset Hills 27604
Sophia 27350
Soul City 27553
Sound Side (Part of Nags Head) 27959
Sound Side, *Tyrrell* 27925
South Albemarle (Part of Albemarle) 28001
South Aulander 27805
South Belmont (Part of Belmont) 28012
South Creek 27806
Southern Hills 28025
Southern Pines 28387*
28388†
Southern Shores, *Dare* 27949
Southern Shores, *Perquimans* 27944
South Fork (Part of Winston-Salem) 27104
South Gastonia 28052
Southgate 28304
South Henderson♦ 27536
South Hills Elizabethtown 28337
South Hills Mall and Plaza (Part of Cary) 27606
South Hills Outlet Mall (Part of Cary) 27511
South Hominy 28715
South Lexington (Part of Lexington) 27292
South Lumberton (Part of Lumberton) 28358
South Mills 27976
Southmont 27351
Southpark Shopping Center (Part of Charlotte) 28211
Southport 28461
South River 28516
South Rocky Mount (Part of Rocky Mount) 27801
South Rosemary♦ 27870
South Salisbury (Part of Salisbury) 28147
Southside (Part of Hendersonville)‡ 28793
Southside, *Lincoln* 28092
South Square (Part of Durham) 27707
South Tunis 27986
South Wadesboro 28170
South Weldon♦ 27890
Southwest 28540
South Whiteville (Part of Whiteville) 28472
Southwood 28504
Southwood Apartments 28304
Sparta 28675
Spear 28657
Speed 27881
Speedwell 28723
Speights Bridge 27888
Spencer 28159
Spencer Mountain 28056
Spences Corner 27921
Spies 27325
Spindale 28160
Spivey's Corner 28334
Spot 27966
Spout Springs 28326
Spray (Part of Eden) 27288
Spring Creek, *Beaufort* 27806
Spring Creek, *Madison* 28743
Springfield 28635
Springfield Mills 28351
Spring Garden 28562
Spring Hill 27874

Spring Hope 27882
Spring Lake 28390
Spring Road (Part of Hickory)‡ 28601
Spring Valley (Part of Charlotte) 28210
Spring Valley (Part of Greensboro)‡ 27406
Springwood (Part of Belmont) 28052
Spruce Pine 28777
Stackhouse 28753
Stacy 28581
Stag Park 28425
Staley 27355
Stallings‡ 28104*
28106†
Stamey Town 28657
Stanfield 28163
Stanhope 27882
Stanley 28164
Stanleyville♦ 27045
Stantonsburg 27883
Star 27356
Starmount (Part of Charlotte)‡ 28224
Starmount Forest (Part of Greensboro) 27403
Startown (Part of Newton) 28658
State Road 28676
Statesville 28625
28677
28687
For specific ZIP Codes call (888) 275-8777, or your local postmaster.
State University (Part of Raleigh)‡ 27607
Stecoah 28771
Stedman 28391
Steeds 27341
Steen Town 28345
Stella 28582
Stem 27581
Sterling (Part of Charlotte) 28134
Stevens Mill 27533
Stocksville 28787
Stokes 27884
Stokesdale 27357
Stokestown 28513
Stonebridge 27613
Stonehaven (Part of Charlotte) 28211
Stoneville 27048
Stonewall 28583
Stoneybrook 28147
Stoneycrest 28791
Stoney Knob 28787
Stonycreek 27244
Stony Fork 28618
Stony Hill 27587
Stony Knoll 27017
Stony Point♦ 28678
Storys 27935
Stotts Crossroads 27880
Stouts 28110
Stovall 27582
Strabane 28504
Straits 28516
Stratford 28675
Strickland Crossroads 27882
Stubbs 28169
Stumpy Point 27978
Sturdivants 28103
Sturgills 28643
Sugar Grove 28679
Sugar Hill 28752
Sugarloaf Shores 27371
Sugar Mountain 28604
Sugar Town 28135
Suggs Crossroads 27864
Sulphur Springs 27030
Summerfield♦ 27358
Summerhaven 28778
Summer Hill 28303
Summerlins Crossroads 28365
Summit (Part of Greensboro)‡ 27405
Summit, *Halifax* 27850
Summit, *Wilkes* 28665
Sunburst 28716
Sunbury 27979
Sunny Point Military Ocean Terminal (U.S. Army) 28461
Sunnyside, *Burke* 28655
Sunny Side, *Dare* 27954

Sunnyside, *Gaston* 28016
Sunny Side, *Halifax* 27850
Sunnyside (Part of Winston-Salem) 27107
Sunny View 28756
Sunset Beach 28468
Sunset Harbor 28422
Sunset Hills, *Catawba* 28601
Sunset Hills (Part of Greensboro) 27403
Sunset Hills, *Rockingham* 27288
Sunshine 28018
Supply 28462
Surf City 28445
Surl 27583
Sutherlands 28615
Sutton Park (Part of Monroe)‡ 28110
Suttontown 28341
Swain 27970
Swainsville 28152
Swancreek 28642
Swann 27330
Swannanoa 28778
Swanns 27330
Swanquarter 27885
Swansboro 28584
Sweet Gum 28771
Swepsonville♦ 27359
Swindell's Fork 27885
Swiss 28714
Sylva 28779
Tabor City 28463
Talleys Crossing 27284
Tanglewood 28306
Tapoco 28771
Tarawa Terrace 28543
Tarboro 27886
Tar Corner 27976
Tar Heel, *Bladen* 28392
Tarheel, *Gates* 27935
Tar Landing 28540
Tar River 27565
Tarrytown Mall (Part of Rocky Mount) 27804
Tate Street (Part of Greensboro)‡ 27403
Taylor Crossroads 27856
Taylor's Beach 27921
Taylors Bridge 28328
Taylors Corners 28585
Taylors Store, *Bertie* 27957
Taylors Store, *Nash* 27856
Taylorsville 28681
Taylorsville Beach 28681
Taylortown 28374
Teachey 28464
Teer 27516
Temple Point 28532
Temple's 28570
Ten Mile Fork 28573
Terrace Gardens (Part of Hendersonville) 28791
Terra Ceia 27860
Terra Cotta (Part of Greensboro) 27407
Terrell 28682
Texaco Beach 27974
Texana 28906
Texas 27974
Thankful 28606
The Black Cat 28516
The Borough 28435
The Bottom 27924
Thelma 27850
Thomasboro 28470
Thomas Landing 28445
Thomas Valley 28789
Thomasville 27360*
27361†
Three Mile 28657
Thruway Shopping Center (Part of Winston-Salem) 27103
Thurman 28560
Thurmond 28683
Tick Bite 28530
Tillery 27887
Timberlake 27583
Timberlyne (Part of Chapel Hill)‡ 27516
Timber Ridge 28025
Timothy 28334
Tin City 28466
Tiny Oak Fork 27885
Tipton Hill 28740
Toast♦ 27049
Tobaccoville 27050
Tobemory 28384

Todd 28684
Todds Crossroads 27983
Toddy 27828
Toecane 28705
Tolarsville 28384
Toledo 28740
Toluca 28090
Tomahawk 28444
Tomotla 28905
Toms Creek 28752
Topia 28672
Topnot 27379
Topsail Beach 28445
Topton 28781
Town and Country Woods 27030
Town Creek, *Brunswick* 28451
Town Creek, *Wilson* 27822
Town Forest 28791
Town Mountain Estates 28804
Townsville 27584
Trading Ford 28146
Tramway 27330
Tranquility 28081
Trap 27924
Traphill 28685
Travis 27925
Trayton Woods 28025
Tree Haven 28791
Trenholm Woods 28739
Trenton 28585
Trent Woods 28562
Triangle, *Lincoln* 28037
Triangle, *Wake* 27709
Trinity, *Randolph*♦ 27370
Trinity, *Union* 28112
Triple Springs 27573
Triplett 28618
Trotville 27946
Troutman 28166
Troy 27371
Trust 28743
Tryon, *Gaston* 28016
Tryon, *Polk* 28782
Tryon Mall (Part of Charlotte) 28213
Tuckasegee 28783
Tuckerdale 28643
Tungsten 27536
Tunis 27986
Turkey 28393
Turkey Knob 28675
Turlington 28334
Turnersburg 28688
Turners Crossroads 27853
Turnpike 28715
Tuscarora 28562
Tuscarora Beach 27986
Tusk 28579
Tuskeegee 28771
Tusquitee 28904
Tuxedo 28784
Twin Lake (Part of Sunset Beach) 28468
Twin Oaks 28675
Tyner 27980
Tyro 27295
Ulah 27203
Unaka 28906
Union, *Hertford* 27910
Union, *Macon* 28734
Union, *Rutherford* 28139
Union Cross 27107
.... 27284
For specific ZIP Codes call (888) 275-8777, or your local postmaster.
Union Grove 28689
Union Hill 27018
Union Mills 28167
Union Ridge 27215
Unionville 28110
University Estates, *Cumberland* 28301
University Estates, *Rockingham* 27320
University Mall and Plaza (Part of Chapel Hill) 27514
University of North Carolina-Charlotte (Part of Charlotte) 28223
University of North Carolina (Part of Wilmington)‡ 28403*
28407†
University Park (Part of Charlotte)‡ 28297

Upchurch 27502
Upton 28611
.... 28645
For specific ZIP Codes call (888) 275-8777, or your local postmaster.
Upward 28731
Uwharie 27371
Valdese 28690
Vale 28168
Valhalla, *Chowan* 27932
Valhalla, *Polk* 28782
Valle Crucis 28691
Valley 28657
Valley Hill♦ 28739
Valley Hills Mall (Part of Hickory) 28601
Vanceboro 28586
Van Crossroads 28328
Vandemere 28587
Vander♦ 28301
Vannoy 28651
Varnum 28462
Vashti 28636
Vass 28394
Vaughan 27586
Vein Mountain 28752
Venable 28803
Venters 28513
Vernon Park Mall (Part of Kinston) 28504
Verona 28540
Vests 28906
Vicksboro 27536
Vienna 27040
Viewmont (Part of Hickory)‡ 28601
Vilas 28692
Village (Part of Pinehurst) 28370
Villa Heights (Part of Charlotte) 28205
Vinegar Hill 28463
Vineland Park 28306
Vine Swamp 28504
Vinton Woods 28034
Violet 28906
Virgilina 24598
Vista 28443
Vixen 28714
Volunteer 27043
Waccamaw 28420
Waco 28169
Wade 28395
Wade Mills (Part of Wadesboro) 28170
Wadesboro 28170
Wades Point 27810
Wadeville 27306
Wagoner, *Ashe* 28640
Wagoner, *Yadkin* 27020
Wagram 28396
Wake Crossroads 27616
Wakefield 27597
Wake Forest 27587*
.... 27588†
Wakelon 27924
Wakulla 28364
Walkers Crossroads 27587
Walkertown, *Forsyth* 27051
Walkertown, *Harnett* 28356
Wallace 28466
Walla Watta 27865
Wallburg 27373
Walnut 28753
Walnut Cove 27052
Walnut Creek, *Madison* 28753
Walnut Creek, *Wayne* 27534
Walnut Island 27939
Walstonburg 27888
Wananish (Part of Lake Waccamaw) 28450
Wanchese♦ 27981
Warbler 27826
Wards 28431
Wards Corner 28425
Wardville 27979
Warne 28909
Warren Plains 27589
Warrensville 28693
Warrenton 27589
Warrior 28645
Warsaw 28398
Washburn 28017
Washburn Store 28018
Washington 27889
Washington Forks 28560
Washington Park 27889
Watauga 28734

Waterlily 27923
Waterville 37821
Watery Branch 27883
Watha 28471
Watson Crossroads 27542
Watts Crossroads 28025
Waughtown (Part of Winston-Salem)‡ 27107
.... 27117
.... 27127
For specific ZIP Codes call (888) 275-8777, or your local postmaster.
Waverly 28754
Waves 27982
Waxhaw 28173
Waycross 28453
Waynesville 28786
Wayside 28376
Weaversford 28617
Weaverville 28787
Webster 28788
Weddington 28173
Wedgewood Lakes 27958
Weeksville 27909
Wehutty 37391
Welcome♦ 27374
Weldon 27890
Wellons Village (Part of Durham) 27703
Wells 28304
Welmar Heights 28304
Wendell 27591
Wenona 27860
Wentworth 27375
Wesley Chapel 28110
Wesley Heights (Part of Charlotte) 28208
Wesser 28713
West Asheville (Part of Asheville)‡ 28816
West Brook (Part of Kannapolis) 28081
Westbrook Crossroads 28349
Westchester Mall (Part of High Point) 27262
Westcliff 28147
West Concord (Part of Concord) 28027
West Cramerton (Part of Cramerton) 28032
West Durham (Part of Durham)‡ 27705
West Edgecombe 27801
Westend (Part of High Point) 27262
West End, *Moore* 27376
Western Prong 28472
Westerwood (Part of Greensboro) 27403
Westfield 27053
West Gastonia (Part of Gastonia) 28052
Westhaven 27834
West Highlands (Part of Winston-Salem) 27104
West Jefferson 28694
West Lake Hills 28001
West Lumberton (Part of Lumberton) 28358
West Marion♦ 28752
West Market Street (Part of Greensboro)‡ 27402
Westminster 28139
Westmont (Part of Asheboro) 27203
Westmore 27341
West New Bern (Part of New Bern) 28562
Westover, *Wake* 27606
Westover, *Washington* 27962
.... 27970
For specific ZIP Codes call (888) 275-8777, or your local postmaster.
West Philadelphia 27242
Westport♦ 28037
Westridge (Part of Rocky Mount)‡ 27801
West Rockingham 28379
West Rocky Mount (Part of Rocky Mount)‡ 27801
Westry 27801
West Salem (Part of Winston-Salem) 27101
Wests Mill 28734
West Smithfield♦ 27577

West Trade Street (Part of Charlotte) 28202
Westview (Part of Winston-Salem) 27114
Westwood (Part of Laurinburg) 28352
Westwood, *Surry* 27049
West Yanceyville 27379
Wexford 28213
Whalebone (Part of Nags Head) 27959
Whaley 28622
Wharton 27889
Whichard 27884
Whichard Beach 27817
Whispering Pines 28327
Whitakers 27891
White Cross 27516
Whitehall Shores 27921
Whitehead 28695
White Hill 27330
Whitehouse 28167
Whitehurst 27871
Whitehurst Park 28025
White Lake 28337
White Level 27549
White Oak, *Bladen* 28399
White Oak, *Gates* 27935
White Oak (Part of Greensboro) 27405
White Oak, *Halifax* 27823
White Oak, *Nash* 27856
White Oaks Acres 27893
White Oaks Acres West 27893
White Pines 27049
White Plains, *Hyde* 27824
White Plains, *Surry*♦ 27031
Whitepost 27808
Whiterock 28753
White's Beach 27924
Whites Chapel 27292
Whites Crossroads 27924
Whites Fork 27843
White Stocking 28425
Whiteston 27919
White Store 28133
Whiteville 28472
Whitfield Crossroads 28578
Whitley Heights 27520
Whitley's Crossroads 27557
Whitnel (Part of Lenoir) 28645
Whitsett 27377
Whittier 28789
Whitt Town 27573
Whortonville 28556
Whynot 27341
Wilbanks 27822
Wilbar 28651
Wilbon 27526
Wilbourns Store 24598
Wilders Grove (Part of Raleigh) 27604
Wildwood, *Carteret* 28570
Wildwood, *Henderson* 28732
Wilgrove (Part of Charlotte) 28212
Wilkerson Crossroads 27542
Wilkesboro 28697
Wilkes Mall (Part of Wilkesboro) 28697
Wilkinson 27860
Willard 28478
Willeyton 27937
Williams 28472
Williamsboro 27536
Williamsburg, *Iredell* 28634
Williamsburg, *Rockingham* 27320
Williams Crossroads 27603
Williamson Crossroads 28431
Williamston 27892
Willis Landing 28539
Williston 28589
Willits 28779
Wil-Lotta Acres 28025
Willow 27946
Willow Green 28513
Willow Spring 27592
Wilmar 28586
Wil-Mar Park (Part of Concord)‡ 28025
Wilmington 28401-12
For specific ZIP Codes call (888) 275-8777, or your local postmaster.
Wilmington Beach 28428
Wilmore (Part of Charlotte) 28203

Wilmot 28789
Wilshire Park (Part of Asheville) 28806
Wilson 27893-96
For specific ZIP Codes call (888) 275-8777, or your local postmaster.
Wilsons Mills 27593
Wilsonville 27502
Wilton 27525
Wind Blow 27281
Windom 28714
Windsor 27983
Windsors Crossroads 27020
Windy Gap 28659
Winfall 27985
Wing 28705
Wingate 28174
Winnabow 28479
Winstead Crossroads 27822
Winsteadville 27810
Winston-Salem 27101-30
For specific ZIP Codes call (888) 275-8777, or your local postmaster.
Wintergreen 28523
Winter Park 28152
Winterville 28590
Winton 27986
Wise 27594
Wise Forks 28526
Witherspoon Crossroads 28610
Wittys Crossroads 27320
Wolf Creek 37317
Wolf Laurel 28754
Wolf Mountain 28783
Wood 27549
Woodard, *Bertie* 27983
Woodard (Part of Wilson)‡ 27893
Woodburn 28451
Wood Crest 28570
Woodfin 28804
Woodington 28504
Woodland 27897
Woodland Acres 27892
Woodland Hills 28804
Woodlawn, *Alamance* 27302
Woodlawn, *Cleveland* 28150
Woodlawn, *McDowell* 28752
Woodlea 28304
Woodleaf 27054
Woodrow (Part of New Bern) 28560
Woodrow, *Haywood* 28716
Woodrun 27306
Woodsdale 27573
Woodside 28081
Woodside Hills 28715
Woodville (Part of Lewiston Woodville) 27849
Woodville, *Perquimans* 27944
Woodville, *Surry* 27030
Woodworth 27536
Wootens Crossroads, *Columbus* 28433
Wootens Crossroads, *Greene* 27888
Wootens Crossroads, *Lenoir* 28504
Worley 28753
Worthingtons Crossroads 27858
Worthville 27317
Wrightsboro♦ 28401
Wrightsville 28480
Wrightsville Beach 28480
Yadkin 28144
Yadkin Valley 28624
.... 28645
For specific ZIP Codes call (888) 275-8777, or your local postmaster.
Yadkinville 27055
Yamacraw 28435
Yanceyville 27379
Yaupon Beach 28465
Yeatsville 27808
Yellow Creek 28771
Yeopim 27932
Yorick 28399
Yorkmont Park (Part of Charlotte) 28217
Yorkwood 28052
Youngsville 27596
Zebulon 27597
Zephyr 28621
Zionville 28698

*** Area Zip Code** **† Post Office Boxes** **‡ Postal Station** **♦ Census Designated Place** *Italic Type* **County**

Place	ZIP Code
Abercrombie	58001
Absaraka	58002
Acres A-Plenty	58504
Adams	58210
Adrian	58472
Agate	58310
Akra	58220
Alamo	58830
Alexander	58831
Alfred	58454
Alice	58031
Alkabo	58845
Almont	58520
Alpha	58654
Alsen	58311
Ambrose	58833
Amenia	58004
Amidon	58620
Anamoose	58710
Anderson Acres	58504
Aneta	58212
Anselm	58068
Antler	58711
Appam	58830
Apple Creek Country Club	58501
Apple Creek Estates	58558
Apple Valley	58558
Ardoch	58213
Arena	58494
Argusville	58005
Arnegard	58835
Arthur	58006
Arvilla	58214
Ashley	58413
Ashlund Estates	58504
Auburn	58237
Aurelia	58734
Ayr	58007
Backoo	58282
Baker	58386
Baldwin	58521
Balfour	58712
Balta	58313
Dantry	58713
Bar-D Estates	58504
Barks Spur	58331
Barlow	58421
Barney	58008
Bartlett	58344
Barton	58384
Bathgate	58216
Battleground Addition	58703
Battleview	58773
Bayshore	58072
Beach	58621
Belcourt♦	58316
Belden	58784
Belfield	58622
Benedict	58716
Bentley	58562
Berea	58072
Bergen	58792
Berlin	58415
Berthold	58718
Berwick	58788
Beulah	58523
Big Bend	58531
Binford	58416
Bisbee	58317
Bismarck	58501-07
For specific ZIP Codes call (888) 275-8777, or your local postmaster.	
Blabon	58046
Blacktail Lake	58801
Blaisdell	58718
Blanchard	58009
Blue Grass	58563
Bluffview Estates	58504
Bonetraill	58801
Bordulac	58421
Bottineau	58318
Bowbells	58721
Bowdon	58418
Bowesmont	58225
Bowman	58623
Braddock	58524
Brampton	58017
Brantford	58356
Breen's Addition	58501
Breien	58570
Brekke Addition	58701
Bremen	58319
Brentwood Estates	58501
Briardale	58504
Briarwood	58104
Bridgeview Addition	58701
Brinsmade	58320
Brocket	58321
Brookfield Estates	58501
Brooks Addition	58703
Brooktree Park	58042
Buchanan	58420
Bucyrus	58639
Buffalo	58011
Buffalo Springs	58623
Burke Addition	58201
Burlington	58722
Burnstad	58495
Burt	58646
Butte	58723
Buttzville	58054
Buxton	58218
Caledonia	58219
Calio	58352
Calvin	58323
C and L Estates	58504
Cando	58324
Cannon Ball♦	58528
Carbury	58783
Carlsbad	58504
Carolville	58801
Carpio	58725
Carrington	58421
Carson	58529
Cartwright	58838
Cashel	58225
Casselton	58012
Cathay	58422
Cavalier	58220
Cayuga	58013
Center	58530
Chaffee	58014
Charbonneau	58831
Charlson	58763
Chaseley	58423
Chrisan	58104
Christine	58015
Churchs Ferry	58325
Circle K Estates	58501
City View Heights	58504
Cleveland	58424
Clifford	58016
Clyde	58352
Cogswell	58017
Coleharbor	58531
Colfax	58018
Colgan	58844
Colgate	58046
Columbia Mall (Part of Grand Forks)	58201
Columbus	58727
Concrete	58220
Conway	58233
Cooperstown	58425
Corinth	58830
Coteau	58721
Coulee	58734
Country Acres	58047
Country-Side Addition	58201
Courtenay	58426
Crary	58327
Crested Butte Addition	58501
Crete	58040
Crosby	58730
Crown Butte	58554
Crystal	58222
Crystal Springs	58467
Cuba	58072
Cummings	58223
Dahlen	58224
Dakota Boys Ranch	58703
Dakota Square (Part of Minot)	58701
Davenport	58021
Dawson	58428
Dazey	58429
Decker	58601
Deering	58731
De Lamere	58060
Denbigh	58788
Denhoff	58430
Des Lacs	58733
Devils Lake	58301
Devils Lake Sioux Indian Reservation	58335
Dickey	58431
Dickinson	58601*
	58602†
Dodge	58625
Donnybrook	58734
Douglas	58735
Downtown (Part of Bismarck)‡	58501
Doyon	85327
Drake	58736
Drayton	58225
Dresden	58249
Driscoll	58532
Dunn Center	58626
Dunning	58760
Dunseith	58329
Durbin	58059
Dwight	58075
Eagle Bend Estates	58301
East Dunseith♦	58329
East Fairview	59221
Eastside Estates	58701
Eckelson	58432
Eckman	58760
Edgeley	58433
Edinburg	58227
Edmore	58330
Edmunds	58476
Egeland	58331
El Dorado Acres	58601
Eldridge	58401
Elgin	58533
Ellendale	58436
Elliott	58054
Embden	58079
Emerado	58228
Emmet	58540
Emrick	58422
Enderlin	58027
Englevale	58033
Epping	58843
Erie	58029
Erie Junction	58029
Esmond	58332
Everest	58012
Evergreen	58051
Faiman's Sunrise Addition	58504
Fairdale	58229
Fairfield	58627
Fairmount	58030
Falconer Estates	58504
Falkirk	58577
Fallon	58535
Fargo	58102-09
For specific ZIP Codes call (888) 275-8777, or your local postmaster.	
Fessenden	58438
Fillmore	58332
Fingal	58031
Finley	58230
Finley Air Force Station, 785th Radar Squadron	58230
Flasher	58535
Flaxton	58737
Flora	58348
Fonda	58366
Forbes	58439
Fordville	58231
Forest River, *Cass*	58104
Forest River, *Walsh*	58233
Forest River Colony	58231
Forman	58032
Fort Berthold Indian Reservation	58763
Fort Buford	58801
Fort Clark	58530
Fort Ransom	58033
Fort Rice	58554
Fort Totten♦	58335
Fortuna	58844
Fortuna Air Force Station, 780th Radar Squadron	59275
Fort Yates	58538
Four Bears Village♦	58763
Four K's Estates	58501
Foxholm	58718
Fox Island	58504
Fradet	58047
Frazier (Part of Wimbledon)	58492
Fredonia	58440
Fried	58401
Frison	58301
Frontier	58104
Fryburg	58622
Fullerton	58441
Gackle	58442
Galchutt	58075
Galesburg	58035
Gardar	58227
Gardena	58748
Gardner	58036
Garrison	58540
Garske	58382
Gascoyne	58653
Geneseo	58053
Gilby	58235
Gladstone	58630
Glasser	58504
Glasston	58236
Glenburn	58740
Glenfield	58443
Glen Ullin	58631
Glenwood Estates	58501
Glover	58474
Golden Valley	58541
Goldfines Shopping Center (Part of Grand Forks)	58201
Golva	58632
Goodrich	58444
Gorham	58627
Grace City	58445
Grafton	58237
Grandberg	58104
Grand Forks	58201-03
	58206-08
For specific ZIP Codes call (888) 275-8777, or your local postmaster.	
Grand Forks Air Force Base	58204-05
For specific ZIP Codes call (888) 275-8777, or your local postmaster.	
Grandin	58038
Grand Prairie Estates	58501
Grand Rapids	58458
Grandview	58801
Grano	58750
Granville	58741
Grassna	58573
Grassy Butte	58634
Great Bend	58039
Green Acres Estates	58501
Greene	58787
Greenvale	58601
Grenora	58845
Guelph	58474
Guthrie	58736
Gwinner	58040
Hague	58542
Halliday	58636
Hallson	58220
Hamar	58380
Hamberg	58337
Hamilton	58238
Hamlet	58795
Hampden	58338
Hankinson	58041
Hanks	58856
Hanks Corner	58220
Hannaford	58448
Hannah	58239
Hannover	58563
Hansboro	58339
Happy Valley	58701
Harlow	58346
Hartland	58725
Harvey	58341
Harwood	58042
Hastings	58049
Hatton	58240
Havana	58043
Havelock	58647
Hay Creek	58501
Hay Creek Pines	58501
Haynes	58639
Hazelton	58544
Hazen	58545
Heaton	58418
Hebron	58638
Heil	58533
Heimdal	58341
Hensel	58241
Hensler	58530
Heritage Hills Estates	58104
Hesper	58348
Hettinger	58639
Hickson	58047
Hi-Land Heights	58801
Hillcrest Acres	58501
Hillsboro	58045
Holiday Colony	58701
Holmen's	58104
Holmes	58275
Home on the Range for Boys	58654
Honeyford	58235
Hoople	58243
Hope	58046
Horace	58047
Horseshoe Bend	58104
Huff	58554
Hull	58542
Hunter	58048
Hurdsfield	58451
Hutterite Colony	58458
Imperial Manor	58701
Imperial Valley	58504
Inkster	58244
Jamestown	58401*
	58402†
Jessie	58452
Jewett Landing	58072
Jiran	58504
Johnsons Corner	58847
Johnstown	58235
Joliette	58271
Juanita	58443
Jud	58454
Judson	58563
Karlsruhe	58744
Kathryn	58049
Keene	58847
Kelso	58045
Kelvin	58329
Kempton	58267
Kenaston	58746
Kenmare	58746
Kensal	58455
Kief	58747
Killdeer	58640
Kindred	58051
Kings Court	58701
Kintyre	58549
Kirkwood Plaza (Part of Bismarck)	58504
Kloten	58254
KMK Estates	58501
Knox	58343
Kongsberg	58792
Kralicek	58601
Kramer	58748
Kubishta	58601
Kulm	58456
Lake Jessie	58801
Lake Metigoshe	58318
Lake Park	58801
Lake Side Estate	58401
Lake Shure Estates	58102
Lake Tschida	58533
Lake Williams	58470
Lakewood Park	58301
Lakota	58344
Lamoine Addition	58201
Lamoure	58458
Landa	58783
Langdon	58249
Lankin	58250
Lansford	58750
Larimore	58251
Lark	58535
Larson	58727
Lawton	58345
Leal	58479
Leeds	58346
Lefor	58641
Lehigh	58601
Lehr	58460
Leisure World Estates	58504
Leith	58529
Leonard	58052
Leroy	58282
Lewis and Clark Estates	58504
Leyden	58282
Lidgerwood	58053
Lignite	58752
Lincoln	58504
Lincoln Valley	58430
Linha Addition	58703
Linton	58552
Lisbon	58054
Litchville	58461
Little Ponderosa	58703
Livonia	58544
Logan	58701
Loma	58311
Lone Tree	58718
Loraine	58761
Lostwood	58784
Lucca	58027
Ludden	58474
Lunds Valley	58784
Luverne	58056
Lynchburg	58059
Lyons	58554
McCanna	58251
Mcclusky	58463
Mcgregor	58755
Mchenry	58464
Mckenzie	58553
McLeod	58057
McVille	58254
Maddock	58348
Maida	58255
Makoti	58756
Mandan	58554

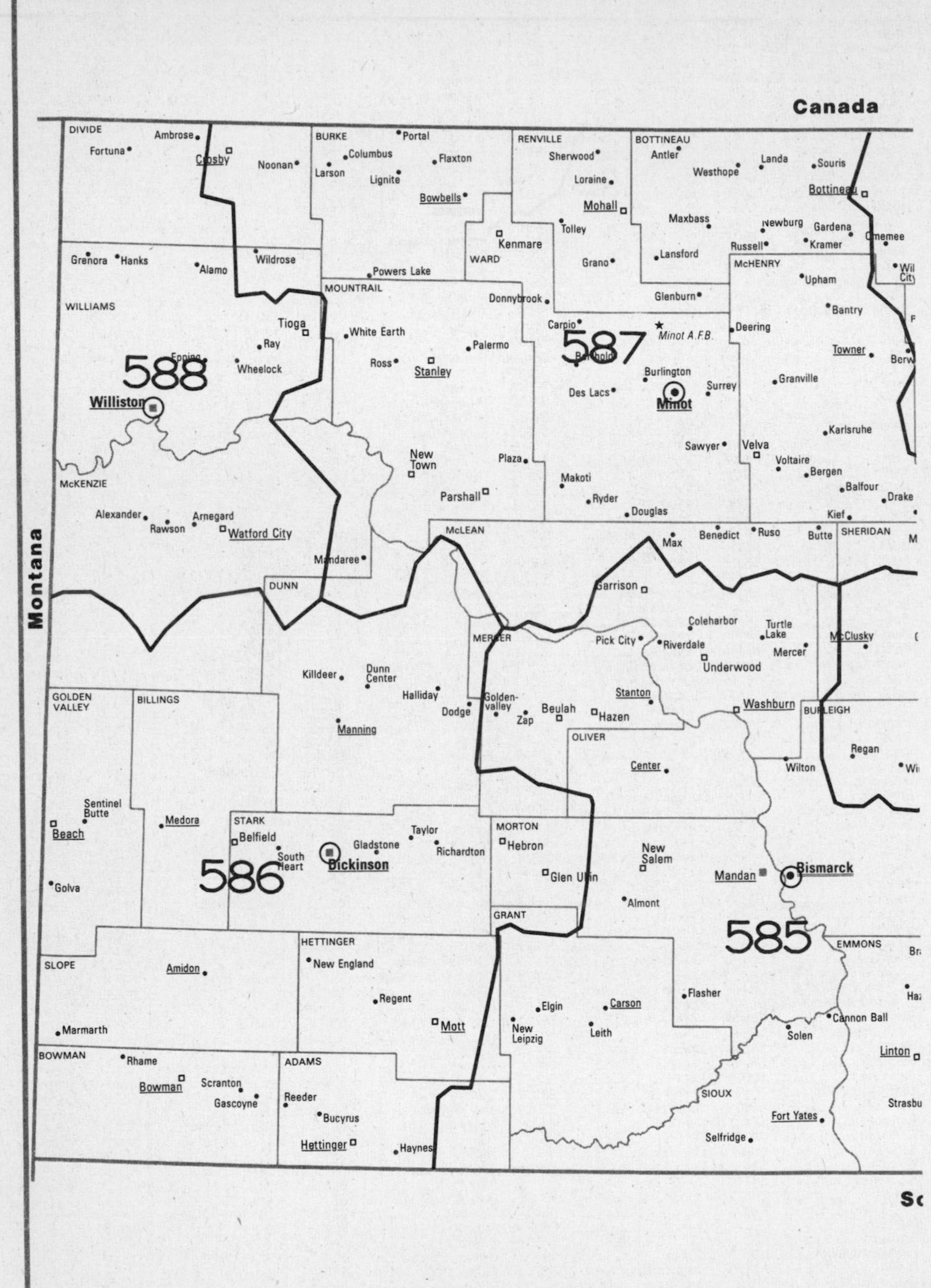
Canada
Montana
588
587
586
585
DIVIDE
Ambrose
Fortuna
Crosby
Noonan
BURKE
Portal
Columbus
Larson
Flaxton
Lignite
Bowbells
RENVILLE
Sherwood
Loraine
Mohall
Tolley
Grano
BOTTINEAU
Antler
Westhope
Landa
Souris
Bottineau
Maxbass
Newburg
Gardena
Russell
Kramer
Omemee
Lansford
Kenmare
WARD
Grenora
Hanks
Alamo
Wildrose
Powers Lake
MOUNTRAIL
WILLIAMS
Tioga
Ray
Wheelock
White Earth
Ross
Stanley
Palermo
Donnybrook
Carpio
Minot A.F.B.
Glenburn
McHENRY
Upham
Bantry
Deering
Towner
Williston
Burlington
Des Lacs
Minot
Surrey
Granville
Karlsruhe
Sawyer
Velva
Voltaire
Bergen
Balfour
Drake
Kief
New Town
Plaza
Parshall
Makoti
Ryder
Douglas
McKENZIE
Alexander
Rawson
Arnegard
Watford City
McLEAN
Max
Benedict
Ruso
Butte
SHERIDAN
Mandaree
DUNN
Garrison
Coleharbor
Turtle Lake
Pick City
Riverdale
Mercer
McClusky
MERCER
Underwood
Killdeer
Dunn Center
Halliday
Dodge
Golden-valley
Zap
Beulah
Hazen
Stanton
Washburn
BURLEIGH
GOLDEN VALLEY
BILLINGS
Manning
OLIVER
Center
Wilton
Regan
Sentinel Butte
Beach
Medora
STARK
Belfield
South Heart
Dickinson
Gladstone
Taylor
Richardton
MORTON
Hebron
Glen Ullin
New Salem
Mandan
Bismarck
Golva
Almont
GRANT
HETTINGER
New England
EMMONS
SLOPE
Amidon
Regent
Flasher
Elgin
Carson
Mott
New Leipzig
Leith
Cannon Ball
Solen
Marmarth
BOWMAN
Rhame
ADAMS
Linton
Bowman
Scranton
Gascoyne
Reeder
Bucyrus
SIOUX
Fort Yates
Hettinger
Haynes
Selfridge

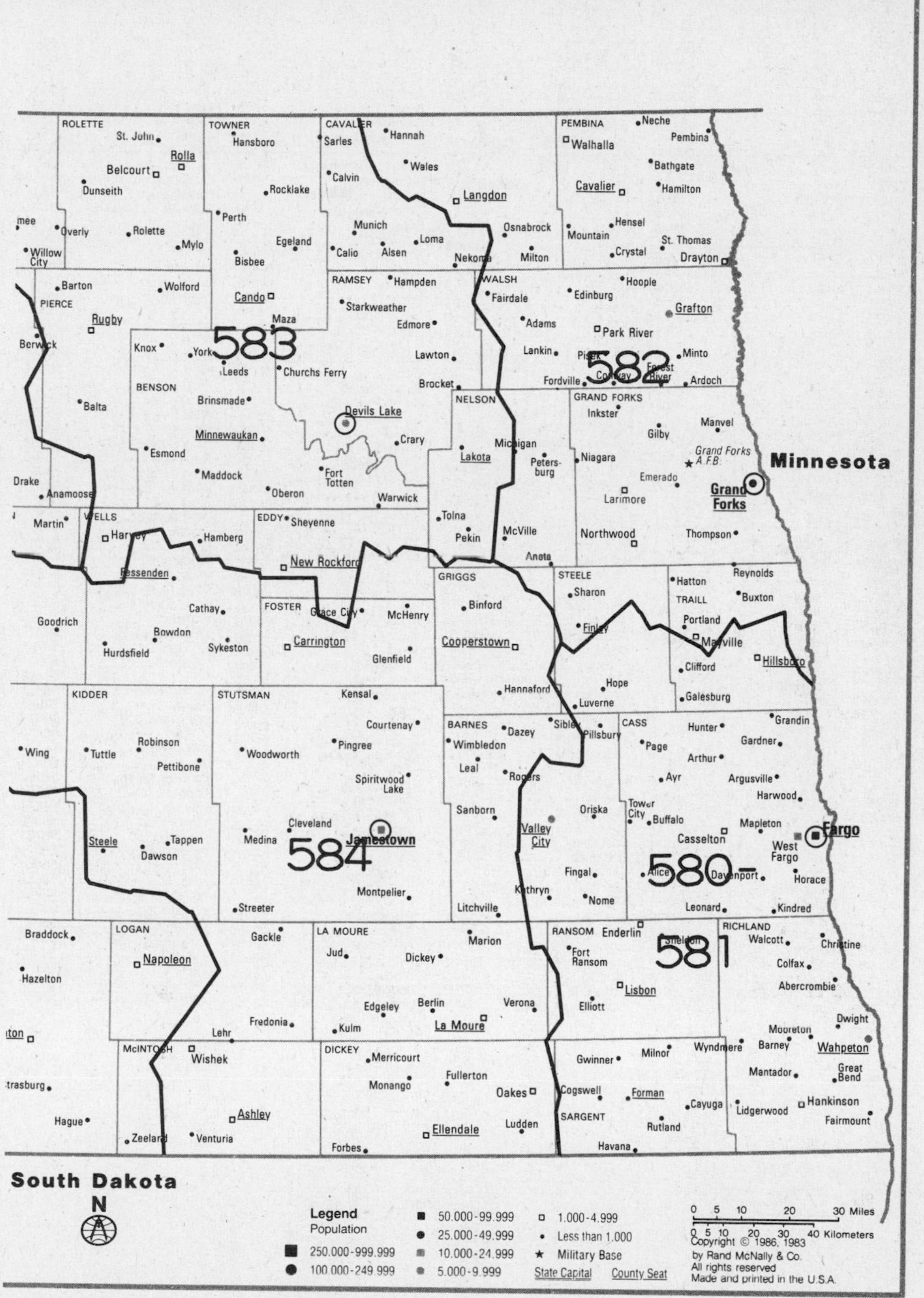
ROLETTE
St. John
Rolla
Belcourt
Dunseith
Overly
Rolette
Willow City
TOWNER
Hansboro
Rocklake
Perth
Egeland
Mylo
Bisbee
Cando
CAVALIER
Sarles
Hannah
Wales
Calvin
Langdon
Munich
Loma
Calio
Alsen
Nekoma
PEMBINA
Neche
Walhalla
Pembina
Bathgate
Cavalier
Hamilton
Osnabrock
Hensel
Mountain
Milton
Crystal
St. Thomas
Drayton
Barton
Wolford
PIERCE
Rugby
RAMSEY
Hampden
Starkweather
Edmore
Lawton
Brocket
WALSH
Fairdale
Edinburg
Hoople
Grafton
Adams
Park River
Lankin
Pisek
Conway
Forest River
Minto
Fordville
Ardoch
Berwick
Knox
York
Maza
583
Leeds
Churchs Ferry
BENSON
Brinsmade
Balta
Minnewaukan
Devils Lake
Esmond
Maddock
Crary
Fort Totten
Oberon
Warwick
NELSON
Lakota
Michigan
Petersburg
GRAND FORKS
Inkster
Niagara
Gilby
Manvel
Grand Forks A.F.B.
Emerado
Larimore
Grand Forks
Minnesota
582
Drake
Anamoose
WELLS
Martin
Harvey
Hamberg
Fessenden
EDDY
Sheyenne
New Rockford
Tolna
Pekin
McVille
Aneta
Northwood
Thompson
Reynolds
Goodrich
Cathay
Bowdon
Hurdsfield
Sykeston
FOSTER
Grace City
McHenry
Carrington
Glenfield
GRIGGS
Binford
Cooperstown
STEELE
Sharon
Finley
Hatton
TRAILL
Buxton
Portland
Mayville
Hillsboro
Clifford
Galesburg
Hope
Hannaford
Luverne
KIDDER
Wing
Tuttle
Robinson
Pettibone
STUTSMAN
Woodworth
Kensal
Courtenay
Pingree
Spiritwood Lake
BARNES
Dazey
Wimbledon
Leal
Rogers
Sibley
Pillsbury
CASS
Page
Hunter
Grandin
Gardner
Arthur
Ayr
Argusville
Harwood
Steele
Tappen
Dawson
Medina
Cleveland
Jamestown
584
Sanborn
Valley City
Oriska
Tower City
Buffalo
Casselton
Mapleton
Fargo
West Fargo
Horace
580-
Fingal
Alice
Davenport
Kathryn
Nome
Montpelier
Streeter
Litchville
Leonard
Kindred
Braddock
LOGAN
Napoleon
Gackle
LA MOURE
Jud
Dickey
Marion
RANSOM
Enderlin
Fort Ransom
Sheldon
581
RICHLAND
Walcott
Christine
Colfax
Abercrombie
Hazelton
Edgeley
Berlin
Verona
Lisbon
Elliott
Fredonia
Kulm
La Moure
Lehr
Mooreton
Dwight
McINTOSH
Wishek
DICKEY
Merricourt
Fullerton
Monango
Oakes
Gwinner
Milnor
Wyndmere
Barney
Wahpeton
Mantador
Great Bend
Cogswell
Forman
Cayuga
Lidgerwood
Hankinson
Fairmount
SARGENT
Ashley
Hague
Zeeland
Venturia
Ellendale
Ludden
Rutland
Forbes
Havana
South Dakota
N
Legend
Population
250.000-999.999
100.000-249.999
50.000-99.999
25.000-49.999
10.000-24.999
5.000-9.999
1.000-4.999
Less than 1.000
Military Base
State Capital
County Seat
0 5 10 20 30 Miles
0 5 10 20 30 40 Kilometers
Copyright © 1986, 1983
by Rand McNally & Co.
All rights reserved
Made and printed in the U.S.A.

Place	ZIP Code
Mandaree♦	58757
Manfred	58341
Manitou	58776
Manning	58642
Mantador	58058
Manvel	58256
Mapes	58344
Mapleton	58059
Marion	58466
Marmarth	58643
Marshall	58644
Martin	58758
Max	58759
Maxbass	58760
Mayville	58257
Maza	58324
Meadowbrook	58701
Meadow View (Part of Bismarck)	58504
Medina	58467
Medora	58645
Mee's Country Home Estates	58558
Mekinock	58258
Melville	58421
Menoken	58558
Mercer	58559
Merricourt	58433
Michigan	58259
Midway Estates	58104
Millarton	58472
Mills	58504
Milnor	58060
Milton	58260
Minnewaukan	58351
Minot (For specific ZIP Codes call (888) 275-8777, or your local postmaster.)	58701-03
Minot Air Force Base (For specific ZIP Codes call (888) 275-8777, or your local postmaster.)	58704-05
Minot Air Force Station, 786th Radar Squadron	58759
Minto	58261
Mirror Lake	58639
Missouri River Estates	58504
Moffit	58560
Mohall	58761
Monango	58436
Montpelier	58472
Mooreton	58061
Mott	58646
Mountain	58262
Mount Carmel	58249
Mouse River Park	58787
Mr. B's	58501
Munich	58352
Murray	58257
Mylo	58353
Nanson	58366
Napoleon	58561
Nash	58237
Neche	58265
Nekoma	58355
Newburg	58762
New England	58647
New Hradec	58601
New Leipzig	58562
Newman	58006
New Rockford	58356
New Salem	58563
New Town	58763
Niagara	58266
Niobe	58746
Nome	58062
Noonan	58765
Norma	58746
North Dakota State University (Part of Fargo)‡	58105
North Forty Estates	58501
Northgate	58737
North Grand Forks	58203
North Lemmon	57638
North River	58102
North Star Acres	58501
Northwood, *Cass*	58102
Northwood, *Grand Forks*	58267
Northwood Estates	58501
Nortonville	58454
Norwich	58768
Oakes	58474
Oak Ridge	58270
Oakwood	58237
Oberon	58357
Olga	58249
Omemee	58384
Oriska	58063
Orr	58244
Orrin	58359
Osnabrock	58269
Overly	58384
Oxbow	58047
Page	58064
Painted Woods	58801
Palermo	58769
Palm Beach	58601
Park Manor (Part of Grand Forks)	58201
Park River	58270
Parshall	58770
Patterson Lake	58601
Pekin	58361
Pembina	58271
Penn	58362
Perth	58363
Petersburg	58272
Pettibone	58475
Picardville	58463
Pick City	58545
Pillsbury	58065
Pingree	58476
Pisek	58273
Pitcher Park	58301
Plaza	58771
Pleasant Lake	58368
Ponderosa	58104
Ponderosa Riverside Village	58501
Porcupine	58569
Portal	58772
Portland	58274
Powell	58201
Powers Lake	58773
Prairie Rose	58104
Prairie View Acres	58501
Price	58530
Prosper	58042
Raleigh	58564
Raub	58779
Raulston	58801
Rawson	58831
Ray	58849
Raymond Lee	58801
Red Willow Lake	58416
Reeder	58649
Regan	58477
Regent	58650
Reile's Acres	58102
Reynolds	58275
Rhame	58651
Richards West (Part of Grand Forks)	58201
Richardton	58652
Ridgeview Acres	58504
Rio Vista Heights	58801
River Bend	58047
Riverdale, *Cass*	58104
Riverdale, *McLean*	58565
Riverside (Part of West Fargo)	58078
River View Acres	58504
Riverview Estates	58102
Riverview Heights	58554
Robinson	58478
Rocklake	58365
Rock Haven	58554
Rogers	58479
Rolette	58366
Rolla	58367
Rolling Meadows	58501
Roseglen	58775
Roshau	58601
Ross	58776
Roth	58783
Round Hill Estates	58104
Rugby	58368
Ruso	58778
Russell	58762
Ruthville	58703
Rutland	58067
Ryder	58779
Sabot's First	58501
St. Anthony	58566
St. Benedict	58047
St. Gertrude	58564
St. John	58369
St. Michael	58370
St. Thomas	58276
Sanborn	58480
Sanish	58763
Sarles	58372
Sawdwood	58270
Sawyer	58781
Scenic East	58801
Schefield	58647
Schmidt	58554
Scranton	58653
Secluded Acres	58504
Selfridge	58568
Selz	58341
Sentinel Butte	58654
Shady Acres	58102
Shamrock Acres	58501
Sharon	58277
Sheldon	58068
Shell Valley♦	58316
Shepard	58425
Sherwood	58782
Sheyenne	58374
Sheyenne Valley Addition	58072
Sheyenne Valley Farm	58102
Shields	58569
Shryock	58801
Sibley	58429
Sibley Island Estates	58504
Silva	58368
Simcoe	58741
Sioux Village	58538
Sisseton Indian Reservation	57262
Skyline Estates	58501
Sleepy Hollow, *Burleigh*	58501
Sleepy Hollow, *Cass*	58047
Solen	58570
Sorenson Addition	58701
Souris	58783
Southam	58327
South Forks Plaza (Part of Grand Forks)	58201
South Heart	58655
South Prairie	58701
Southview	58801
Southview Estates	58601
Spiritwood	58481
Spiritwood Lake	58401
Springbrook	58843
Standing Rock Indian Reservation	58538
Stanley	58784
Stanton	58571
Starkweather	58377
Steele	58482
Sterling	58572
Stirum	58069
Strasburg	58573
Straubville	58017
Streeter	58483
Strong	58301
Sunny	58554
Sunnyside Addition	58104
Sunny Slope	58701
Sunrise Acres	58102
Surrey	58785
Sutton	58484
Swansonville	58504
Sykeston	58486
Taft	58045
Tagus	58718
Talbotts	58701
Tappen	58487
Tatley Meadows	58504
Taylor	58656
Temvik	58552
Thompson	58278
Thorne	58366
Tilden	58351
Timber Lane Place	58504
Tioga	58852
TJ Ranch Estates	58501
Tokio	58379
Tolley	58787
Tolna	58380
Tower City	58071
Town and Country	58801
Town and Country Estates	58504
Town And Country Shopping Center (Part of Minot)	58701
Towner	58788
Trenton	58853
Trestle Valley	58701
Trotters	58621
Turtle Lake	58575
Turtle Mountain Indian Reservation	58316
Tuttle	58488
Twin Butte	58504
Twin Buttes	58636
Tyler	58075
Underwood	58576
Union	58260
University of North Dakota (Part of Grand Forks)‡	58202
Upham	58789
Urbana	58481
Valley City	58072
Velva	58790
Venlo	58057
Venturia	58489
Verona	58490
Veseleyville	58237
Vista South	58504
Vohs Dapplegrey	58801
Voltaire	58792
Voss	58261
Wabek	58771
Wahpeton	58074†
	58075*
Walcott	58077
Wales	58281
Walhalla	58282
Walum	58448
Warren	58021
Warsaw	58261
Warwick	58381
Washburn	58577
Watford City	58854
Weaver	58352
Webster	58382
Welle	58501
Wellsburg	58341
West Acres Estates	58801
West Bonetrail	58801
Westbrook	58047
West Fargo	58078
Westfield	58542
West Heart Estates	58504
Westhope	58793
West Industrial Park	58601
West Jamestown	58401
West Town	58401
West Williston	58801
Westwood on the River	58501
Wheatland	58079
Wheelock	58849
White Earth	58794
White Shield♦	58540
Whitman	58259
Wild Rice	58047
Wildrose	58795
Williston	58801*
	58802†
Williston Park	58801
Willow City	58384
Willow Creek	58078
Wilton	58579
Wimbledon	58492
Windsor	58424
Windsor Green	58104
Wing	58494
Wishek	58495
Wolford	58385
Wolseth	58731
Wood Lake	58379
Woodland	58051
Woods	58052
Woodworth	58496
Wutzke	58501
Wyndmere	58081
York	58386
Ypsilanti	58497
Zahl	58856
Zap	58580
Zeeland	58581

Place	ZIP
A (Part of Cleveland)‡	44102
A (Part of Toledo)‡	43605
Abanaka	45874
Abbottsville	45304
Aberdeen	45101
Academia	43050
Acme	44281
Ada	45810
Adams, *Champaign* (Twp)	43070
Adams, *Clinton* (Twp)	45177
Adams, *Coshocton* (Twp)	43832
Adams, *Darke* (Twp)	45308
Adams, *Defiance* (Twp)	43512
Adams, *Guernsey* (Twp)	43725
Adams, *Monroe* (Twp)	43914
Adams, *Muskingum* (Twp)	43821
Adams, *Seneca* (Twp)	44867
Adams, *Washington* (Twp)	45744
Adams Mills	43821
Adamsville, *Gallia*	45614
Adamsville, *Muskingum*	43802
Adario	44837
Addison	45631
Addyston	45001
Adelphi	43101
Adena	43901
Adrian	44801
Africa	43021
Afton	45103
Aid	45645
Ainger	43543
Air Mail Facility (Part of Columbus)‡	43236
Air Mail Facility (Part of Dayton)‡	45490
Air Material Command‡	45433
Airway‡	45431*
	45437†
Akron	44301-72
For specific ZIP Codes call (888) 275-8777, or your local postmaster.	
Albany	45710
Al Bar Meadows (Part of The Village of Indian Hill)	45243
Albion	44287
Alcony	45373
Alexander (Twp)	45701
Alexanders (Part of Independence)	44131
Alexandersville (Part of West Carrollton)	45449
Alexandria	43001
Alexis Place (Part of Toledo)	43612
Alfred	45723
Alger	45812
Alikanna	43952
Alledonia	43902
Allen, *Darke* (Twp)	45362
Allen, *Hancock* (Twp)	45889
Allen, *Ottawa* (Twp)	43412
Allen, *Union* (Twp)	43070
Allen Center	43040
Allensburg	45133
Allensville	45651
Allentown, *Allen*	45807
Allentown, *Scioto*	45694
Alliance	44601
Alma	45690
Alpha	45301
Alpine Village (Part of Valley Hi)	43360
Alta	44903
Altamont Hills	43938
Altamont Park (Part of Mingo Junction)	43938
Alton	43119
Alvada	44802
Alvordton	43501
Amanda, *Allen* (Twp)	45807
Amanda, *Hancock* (Twp)	45867
Amanda, *Fairfield*	43102
Amberley	45236-37
For specific ZIP Codes call (888) 275-8777, or your local postmaster.	
Amberly	43227
Amboy, *Fulton* (Twp)	43540
Amboy (Part of Conneaut)	44030
Amelia	45102
American (Twp)	45807
Ames (Twp)	45711
Amesville	45711
Amherst	44001
Amity (Part of Deer Park)	45236
Amity, *Knox*	43050
Amity, *Madison*	43064
Amity, *Montgomery*	45309
Amlin	43002
Amlin Heights	45385
Amsden	44803
Amsterdam, *Jefferson*	43903
Amsterdam, *Licking*	43076
Anderson, *Hamilton* (Twp)	45230
Anderson (Part of Cincinnati)	45254-55
For specific ZIP Codes call (888) 275-8777, or your local postmaster.	
Anderson, *Ross*	45601
Anderson Ferry (Part of Cincinnati)	45238
Andersonville	45601
Andis	45645
Andover	44003
Angle	45631
Ankenytown	43019
Anlo	45344
Anna	45302
Annapolis	43910
Ansonia	45303
Antioch	43793
Antiquity	45771
Antrim, *Wyandot* (Twp)	43323
Antrim, *Guernsey*	43773
Antwerp	45813
Apple Creek	44606
Apple Grove	45771
Appleton	43031
Aquilla	44024
Arabia	45659
Arcadia	44804
Arcanum	45304
Archbold	43502
Archer (Twp)	43986
Archers Fork	45767
Arion	45652
Arkoe	45661
Arlington, *Hancock*	45814
Arlington, *Montgomery*	45309
Arlington Heights	45215
Armstrongs Mills	43933
Arnheim	45121
Arnold, *Miami*	45383
Arnold, *Union*	43064
Arrow Head (Part of Xenia)	45385
Artanna	43022
Arthur	43512
Ashland	44805
Ashley	43003
Ashley Corner	45694
Ash Ridge	45121
Ashtabula (Twp)	44004
Ashtabula	44004-05
For specific ZIP Codes call (888) 275-8777, or your local postmaster.	
Ashville	43103
Assumption	43558
Athalia	45669
Athens, *Harrison* (Twp)	43981
Athens, *Athens*	45701
Atlanta	43145
Atlas	43713
Attica	44807
Attica Junction	44807
Atwater	44201
Atwater Center	44201
Auburn, *Crawford* (Twp)	44887
Auburn, *Geauga* (Twp)	44255
Auburn, *Tuscarawas* (Twp)	44681
Auburn, *Butler*	45013
Auburn Center, *Crawford*	44875
Auburn Center, *Geauga*	44022
Auburn Corners	44021
Augersburg	44266
Auglaize, *Allen* (Twp)	45850
Auglaize, *Paulding* (Twp)	43512
Augusta	44607
Ault	43947
Aultman	44630
Aurelius (Twp)	45746
Aurora	44202
Aurora East	44240
Aurora Meadows	44202
Ausdale Ave. (Part of Mansfield)	44906
Austin	45628
Austinburg	44010
Austintown	44515
Austintown Plaza	44515
Austin Village (Part of Warren)	44481
Autumn Acres	45239
Ava	43711
Avalon (Part of Middletown)	45042
Avalon, *Perry*	43107
Avalon Heights (Part of Lebanon)	45036
Avenue at Tower City Center, The (Part of Cleveland)	44113
Avon	44011
Avondale (Part of Cincinnati)‡	45229
Avondale, *Belmont*	43947
Avondale, *Licking*	43076
Avondale, *Logan*	43331
Avondale, *Montgomery*	45404
Avondale, *Muskingum*	43777
Avondale, *Stark*	44708
Avon Lake	44012
Avon Park (Part of Girard)	44420
Axtel	44089
Ayersville	43512
B (Part of Cleveland)‡	44103
B (Part of Dayton)‡	45407
Bachman	45309
Badgertown	43719
Bailey Lakes	44805
Baileys Mills	43713
Bainbridge (Twp)	44023
Bainbridge	45612
Bainbridge Center	44022
Bairdstown	45872
Bakersville	43803
Ballville♦	43420
Baltic	40004
Baltimore	43105
Bangs	43050
Bannock	43972
Bannon	43207
Bantam	45103
Barberton	44203
Bardwell	45154
Barlow	45712
Barnesburg	45239
Barnesville	43713
Barnhill	44663
Barretts Mills	45612
Barrs Mills	44681
Bartles	45659
Bartlett	45713
Bartley Estates	45414
Bartlow (Twp)	43516
Barton	43905
Bartramville	45669
Bascom	44809
Bashan	45743
Bass Lake	44024
Batavia	45103
Batemantown	43019
Batesville	43773
Bath, *Allen* (Twp)	45801
Bath, *Greene* (Twp)	45324
Bath, *Summit*	44210
Battlesburg	44626
Baughman (Twp)	44667
Bay (Twp)	43452
Bayard	44657
Bay Bridge	44870
Bays	43462
Bay View	44870
Bay Village	44140
Bazetta	44410
Beach City	44608
Beachland (Part of Cleveland)‡	44119
Beachwood	44122
Beachwood Place (Part of Beachwood)	44122
Beacon Hill	45241
Beallsville	43716
Beals (Part of Pickerington)	43147
Beamsville	45303
Bear Creek	45657
Bearfield (Twp)	43730
Beartown	44622
Beatty	45506
Beaumont	45701
Beaver, *Mahoning* (Twp)	44408
Beaver, *Noble* (Twp)	43773
Beaver, *Pike* (Twp)	45690
Beaver, *Pike*	45613
Beavercreek (Twp)	45401
Beavercreek	45430-32
	45434
	45440
For specific ZIP Codes call (888) 275-8777, or your local postmaster.	
Beaverdam	45808
Beaver Park (Part of Lorain)	44053
Beavertown (Part of Kettering)	45429
Beavertown, *Washington*	45767
Becker Highlands (Part of Steubenville)	43952
Beckett Ridge♦	45069
Becks Mills	44654
Bedford, *Coshocton* (Twp)	43812
Bedford, *Meigs* (Twp)	45769
Bedford, *Cuyahoga*	44146
Bedford Heights	44128
Beebe	45778
Beechcrest	44240
Beechview Estates (Part of Cincinnati)	45201
Beechwold (Part of Columbus)‡	43214
Beechwood (Part of Wintersville)	43953
Beechwood, *Preble*	45064
Beechwood, *Stark*	44601
Beechwood Trails♦	43062
Belden	44044
Belfast, *Clermont*	45122
Belfast, *Highland*	45133
Belfort	44641
Bellaire	43906
Bellaire Gardens	43302
Bellbrook	45305
Belle Center	43310
Bellefontaine	43311
Bellepoint	43015
Belle Valley	43717
Belle Vernon	44882
Belleview Heights (Part of Chillicothe)	45601
Belleview Heights (Part of New Paris)	45347
Bellevue	44811
Bellview	45305
Bellview Estates	45305
Bellview Heights	43906
Bellville	44813
Belmont, *Allen*	45801
Belmont, *Belmont*	43718
Belmont Meadows (Part of Springfield)	45505
Belmont Park	44420
Belmont Ridge	43983
Belmore	45815
Beloit	44609
Belpre	45714
Belvedere	43952
Bennington, *Licking* (Twp)	43011
Bennington, *Morrow* (Twp)	43334
Bentley (Part of Lowellville)	44436
Bentleyville	44022
Benton, *Hocking* (Twp)	43152
Benton, *Monroe* (Twp)	45767
Benton, *Ottawa* (Twp)	43432
Benton, *Paulding* (Twp)	45880
Benton, *Pike* (Twp)	45690
Benton, *Crawford*	44882
Benton, *Holmes*	44654
Benton Ridge	45816
Bentonville	45105
Berea, *Cuyahoga*	44017
Berea (Part of Middleburg Heights)	44130
Bergholz	43908
Berkey	43504
Berkley Heights (Part of Kettering)	45429
Berkshire	43074
Berlin, *Delaware* (Twp)	43015
Berlin, *Erie* (Twp)	44814
Berlin, *Knox* (Twp)	43019
Berlin, *Mahoning* (Twp)	44401
Berlin, *Holmes*	44610
Berlin Center	44401
Berlin Heights	44814
Berlinville	44814
Bern (Twp)	45770
Berne (Twp)	43155
Bernice	43832
Berryman	45805
Berrysville	45133
Berwick	44853
Bessemer	45764
Bethany	45042
Bethel, *Clark* (Twp)	45344
Bethel, *Miami* (Twp)	45371
Bethel, *Monroe* (Twp)	45745
Bethel, *Clermont*	45106
Bethel, *Pike*	45661
Bethesda	43719
Bethlehem, *Coshocton* (Twp)	43812
Bethlehem, *Stark* (Twp)	44662
Bethlehem, *Richland*	44875
Bettsville	44815
Beulah Beach	44089
Beverly	45715
Beverly Gardens	45431
Bevis	45247
Bexley	43209
Bidwell	45614
Big Island	43302
Biglick (Twp)	44802
Big Plain	43140
Big Prairie	44611
Big Rock	45613
Big Run	45724
Big Spring (Twp)	44853
Big Springs	43347
Birds Run	43749
Birmingham, *Erie*	44816
Birmingham, *Guernsey*	43749
Bishopville	45732
Bismarck	44811
Blachleyville	44691
Black Creek (Twp)	45882
Blackfork	45656
Black Fork Junction	45656
Black Horse	44266
Blacklick	43004
Blacklick Estates♦	43232
Black Run	43830
Blacktop	43700
Bladen	45623
Bladensburg	43005
Blaine	43909
Blainesville	43950
Blairmont	43901
Blakeslee	43505
Blanchard, *Hancock* (Twp)	45816
Blanchard, *Putnam* (Twp)	45875
Blanchard, *Hardin*	45836
Blanches Addition	43062
Blanchester	45107
Blendon (Twp)	43231
Blissfield	43805
Bloom, *Fairfield* (Twp)	43136
Bloom, *Morgan* (Twp)	43756
Bloom, *Scioto* (Twp)	45682
Bloom, *Seneca* (Twp)	44818
Bloom, *Wood* (Twp)	44817
Bloom Center	43318
Bloomdale	44817
Bloomer	45318
Bloomfield, *Jackson* (Twp)	45640
Bloomfield, *Logan* (Twp)	43333
Bloomfield, *Trumbull* (Twp)	44450
Bloomfield, *Columbiana*	43920
Bloomfield, *Morrow*	43011
Bloomfield, *Muskingum*	43762
Bloomfield, *Washington*	45734
Bloomingburg	43106
Bloomingdale	43910
Bloominggrove, *Richland* (Twp)	44878
Blooming Grove, *Morrow*	44833
Bloomington	45169
Bloomingville	44870
Bloom Junction	45682
Bloomville	44818
Blue Ash	45241-42
For specific ZIP Codes call (888) 275-8777, or your local postmaster.	
Blue Ball	45005
Bluebell	43772
Bluebird Beach (Part of Vermilion)	44089
Blue Creek, *Paulding* (Twp)	45886
Blue Creek, *Adams*	45616

*** Area Zip Code** **† Post Office Boxes** **‡ Postal Station** **♦ Census Designated Place** *Italic Type* **County**

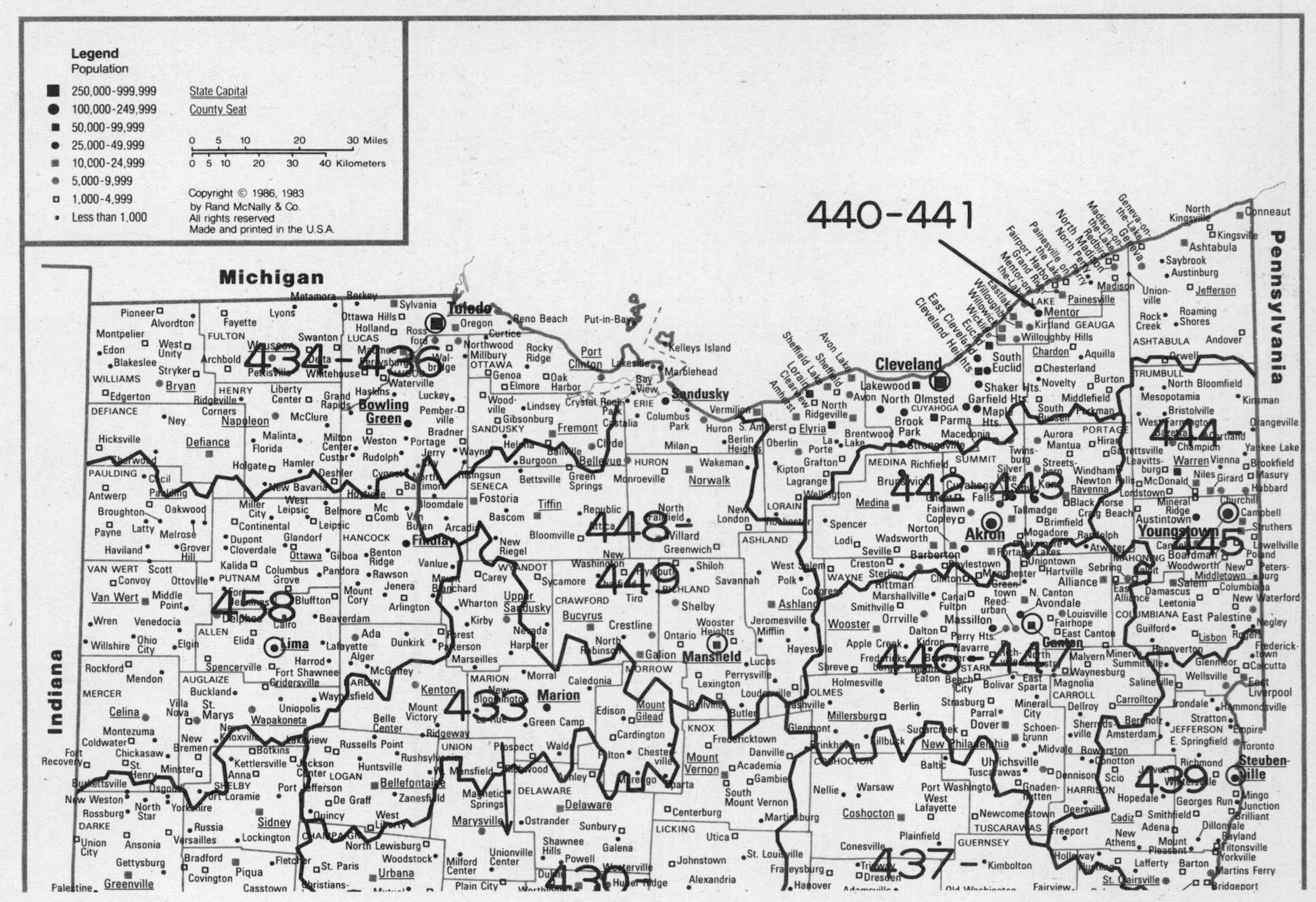
Legend
Population
250,000-999,999
100,000-249,999
50,000-99,999
25,000-49,999
10,000-24,999
5,000-9,999
1,000-4,999
Less than 1,000
State Capital
County Seat
0 5 10 20 30 Miles
0 5 10 20 30 40 Kilometers
Copyright © 1986, 1983
by Rand McNally & Co.
All rights reserved
Made and printed in the U.S.A.
Michigan
Pennsylvania
Indiana
440-441
434-436
444-
445
442-443
446-447
448-
449
458
433
439
437-
Toledo
Cleveland
Akron
Youngstown
Canton
Mansfield
Lima
Marion
Sandusky
Findlay
Bowling Green
Steubenville

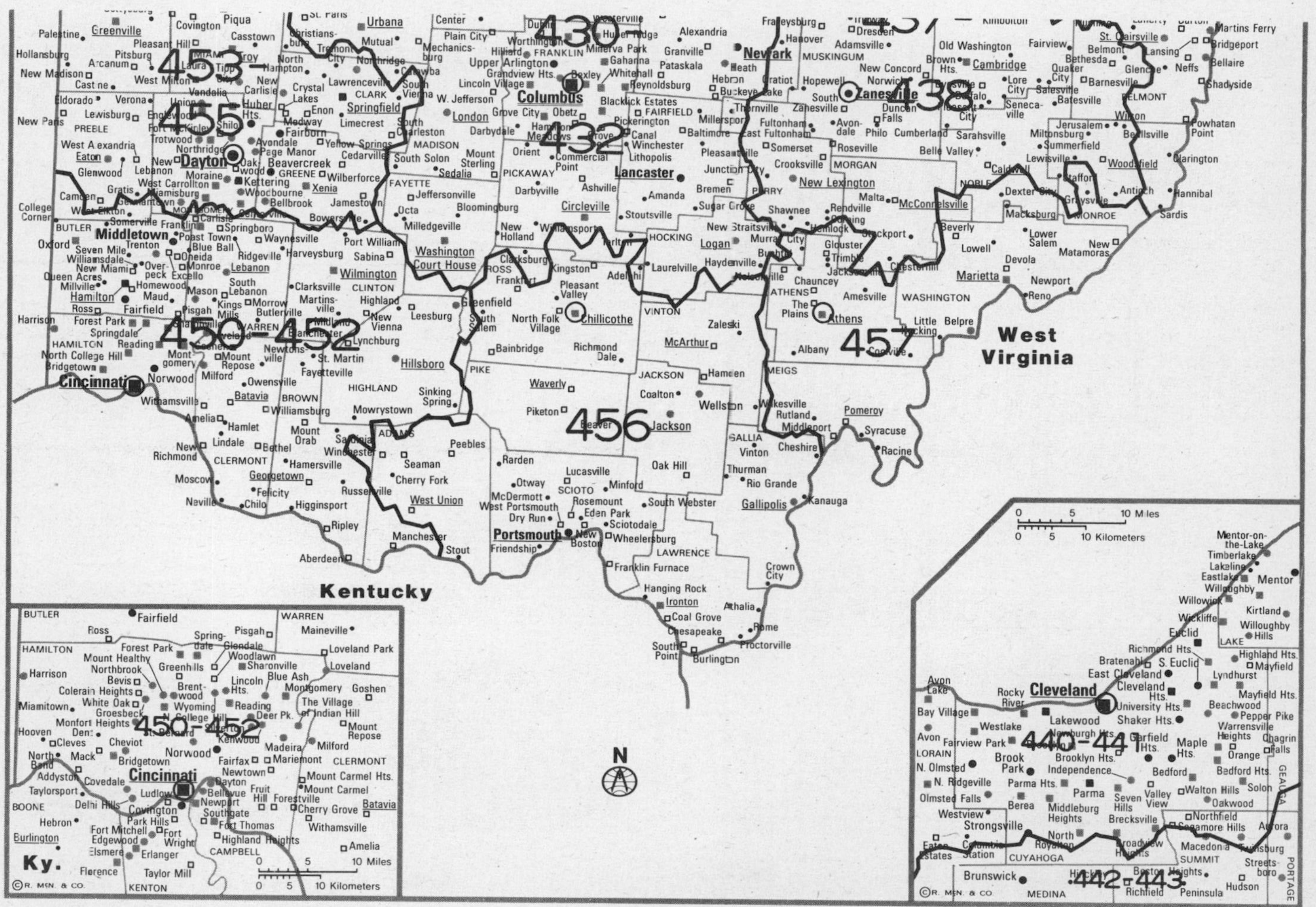

430
432
438
453-
455
450-452
456
457
440-441
442-443
Columbus
Dayton
Cincinnati
Cleveland
Springfield
Middletown
Hamilton
Newark
Zanesville
Lancaster
Chillicothe
Portsmouth
Athens
Marietta
Cambridge
West Virginia
Kentucky
Ky.
N
10 Miles
10 Kilometers
© R. McN. & Co.

Place	ZIP
Blue Rock	43720
Blue Valley Acres	43130
Bluffton	45817
Boardman (Twp)	44512
Boardman♦	44512-13
For specific ZIP Codes call (888) 275-8777, or your local postmaster.	
Boardman Plaza	44512
Bobo	45613
Boden	43762
Bokescreek (Twp)	43358
Bolivar	44612
Bolton	44601
Bond Hill (Part of Cincinnati)	45237
Boneta	44256
Bonn	45788
Bono	43445
Bookwalter	43128
Booth (Part of Oregon)	43618
Booth, *Tuscarawas*	43832
Boston, *Summit* (Twp)	44264
Boston, *Highland*	45133
Boston Heights	44236
Boston Mill	44264
Botkins	45306
Boudes Ferry	45121
Boughtonville	44890
Bourneville	45617
Bowerston	44695
Bowersville	45307
Bowling Green, *Licking* (Twp)	43076
Bowling Green, *Marion* (Twp)	43332
Bowling Green, *Wood*	43402
Bowlusville	43078
Boydsville	43912
Braceville	44444
Braceville Ridge	44444
Bradbury	45760
Bradford	45308
Bradley	43917
Bradner	43406
Bradrick	45619
Brady (Twp)	43570
Brady Lake	44211
Brady Lake Addition	44211
Bradyville	45144
Braffettsville	45347
Brailey	43558
Branch Hill	45140
Brandon	43050
Brandt	45371
Brandywine	44820
Bratenahl	44108
Bratton (Twp)	45660
Brecksville	44141
Brecon	45242
Bremen	43107
Brentwood, *Hamilton*	45231
Brentwood (Part of Mentor)	44060
Brentwood Estates	43953
Brentwood Lake	44044
Brewster	44613
Briarwood Beach	44215
Brice	43109
Brice Road Square (Part of Columbus)	43068
Briceton	45879
Bridgeport, *Belmont*	43912
Bridgeport, *Hardin*	45843
Bridgetown♦	45211
	45248
For specific ZIP Codes call (888) 275-8777, or your local postmaster.	
Bridgeville	43701
Bridgewater (Twp)	43543
Bridgewater Center	43543
Brier Hill (Part of Youngstown)	44510
Brigglesville	43731
Briggs, *Washington*	45714
Briggsdale	43223
Brighton (Part of Cincinnati)	45214
Brighton, *Clark*	45369
Brighton, *Lorain*	44090
Brightwood	44663
Brilliant	43913
Brimfield♦	44240
Brinkhaven	43006
Bristol, *Morgan* (Twp)	43756
Bristol, *Trumbull* (Twp)	44402
Bristol, *Perry*	43764
Bristol Village (Part of Waverly)	45690
Bristolville	44402
Broadacre	43910
Broadview Acres, *Clark*	45504
Broadview Acres, *Muskingum*	43701
Broadview Heights	44147
Broadway	43007
Broadwell	45778
Brock	45380
Brokaw	43787
Brokensword	44820
Brokes	45672
Bronson (Twp)	44857
Brookfield, *Noble* (Twp)	43732
Brookfield, *Trumbull*♦	44403
Brookhill	45224
Brook Hollow	45324
Brooklyn	44144
Brooklyn Heights	44131
Brook Park	44142
Brookside, *Belmont*	43912
Brookside, *Scioto*	45652
Brookside Estates	43085
Brookview	43912
Brookville	45309
Brookwood (Part of Amberley)	45239
Broughton	45879
Brown, *Carroll* (Twp)	44644
Brown, *Darke* (Twp)	45303
Brown, *Delaware* (Twp)	43015
Brown, *Franklin* (Twp)	43026
Brown, *Knox* (Twp)	43014
Brown, *Miami* (Twp)	45317
Brown, *Paulding* (Twp)	45873
Brown, *Vinton* (Twp)	45654
Brown Heights	43725
Brownhelm, *Lorain* (Twp)	44001
Brownhelm (Part of Vermilion)	44089
Brownstown	45171
Brownsville, *Licking*	43721
Brownsville, *Monroe*	45767
Brownsville, *Ross*	45601
Brunersburg	43512
Bruno	43076
Brunswick	44212
Brunswick Hills (Twp)	44280
Brush Creek, *Adams* (Twp)	45650
Brushcreek, *Highland* (Twp)	45172
Brush Creek, *Jefferson* (Twp)	43945
Brush Creek, *Muskingum* (Twp)	43777
Brush Creek, *Scioto* (Twp)	45657
Brush Ridge	43302
Bryan	43506
Buchanan	45690
Buchtel	45716
Buck (Twp)	43326
Buckeye	43701
Buckeye Lake	43008
Buckeye Road (Part of Cleveland)	44102
Buckeyeville	43725
Buckhorn	45694
Buckingham	43730
Buckland	45819
Bucks (Twp)	43824
Buckskin (Twp)	45647
Bucyrus	44820
Buena Vista, *Butler*	45042
Buena Vista, *Fayette*	43160
Buena Vista, *Hocking*	43149
Buena Vista, *Scioto*	45684
Buffalo, *Noble* (Twp)	43772
Buffalo, *Guernsey*	43722
Buford	45110
Bulah	44047
Bulaville	45631
Bunker Hill, *Butler*	45013
Bunker Hill, *Holmes*	44654
Burbank	44214
Burghill	44404
Burgoon	43407
Burkettsville	45310
Burkhart	43754
Burlingham	45776
Burlington, *Licking* (Twp)	43027
Burlington, *Fulton*	43502
Burlington, *Lawrence*♦	45680
Burnetts Corners	44691
Burnet Woods (Part of Cincinnati)‡	45220
Burr Oak	45732
Burr Oaks	43143
Burton	44021
Burton City	44667
Burton Lake	44021
Burton Station	44062
Burtonville	45177
Busch (Part of Columbus)‡	43226
Busenbark (Part of Trenton)	45011
Bushnell	44030
Businessburg	43933
Business Corners	43542
Butler, *Columbiana* (Twp)	44460
Butler, *Darke* (Twp)	45346
Butler, *Knox* (Twp)	43843
Butler, *Mercer* (Twp)	45828
Butler, *Montgomery* (Twp)	45337
Butler, *Richland* (Twp)	44837
Butler, *Richland*	44822
Butlerville	45162
Byers Junction	45692
Byesville	43723
Byhalia	43344
Byington	45646
Byrd (Twp)	45115
Byron	45385
C (Part of Toledo)‡	43607
Cable	43009
Cadiz	43907
Cadiz Junction	43976
Cadmus	45658
Caesars Creek (Twp)	45385
Cain Heights (Part of East Liverpool)	43920
Cairo, *Allen*	45820
Cairo, *Stark*	44721
Calais	43773
Calcutta♦	43920
Caldwell	43724
Caledonia	43314
California, *Clark*	45503
California (Part of Cincinnati)	45228
Calla	44406
Cambridge	43725
Camden, *Lorain* (Twp)	44049
Camden, *Preble*	45311
Cameron	43914
Campbell	44405
Campbellsport	44266
Campbellstown	45320
Camp Creek, *Pike* (Twp)	45671
Camp Creek, *Stark*	44662
Camp Dennison	45111
Camp Ground	43130
Camp Luther (Part of North Kingsville)	44068
Canaan, *Athens* (Twp)	45701
Canaan, *Madison* (Twp)	43064
Canaan, *Morrow* (Twp)	43320
Canaan, *Wayne*	44217
Canaanville	45701
Canal Fulton	44614
Canal Lewisville	43812
Canal Winchester	43110
Candle Lite Estates (Part of Warren)	44484
Canfield	44406
Cannelville	43777
Cannons Creek	45659
Cannons Mills	43920
Canton (Twp)	44701
Canton	44701-35
For specific ZIP Codes call (888) 275-8777, or your local postmaster.	
Canton Centre (Part of Canton)	44708
Canyon Park	44429
Captina	43933
Carbondale	45717
Carbon Hill	43111
Cardinal Lake	44085
Cardington	43315
Carey	43316
Carlisle, *Lorain* (Twp)	44035
Carlisle, *Noble*	43724
Carlisle, *Warren*	45005
Carmel	45133
Caroline	44807
Carpenter	45710
Carriage	45502
Carroll, *Ottawa* (Twp)	43449
Carroll, *Fairfield*	43112
Carrollton	44615
Carrothers	44807
Carryall (Twp)	45813
Carthage, *Athens* (Twp)	45735
Carthage (Part of Cincinnati)	45216
Carthagena	45822
Carysville	45317
Cass, *Hancock* (Twp)	44804
Cass, *Muskingum* (Twp)	43821
Cass, *Richland* (Twp)	44878
Cassell	43725
Cassella	45883
Cassinelli Square (Part of Springdale)	45246
Casstown	45312
Castalia	44824
Castine	45304
Catawba	43010
Catawba Island	43452
Catawba Station	43044
Causeway Manor	44003
Cavallo	43843
Cavett	45891
Caywood	45750
Cecil	45821
Cedarhill	43102
Cedar Mills	45616
Cedar Point (Part of Sandusky)	44870
Cedar Valley	44214
Cedarville	45314
Cedron	45121
Celeryville	44890
Celina	45822
Centenary	45631
Center, *Carroll* (Twp)	44615
Center, *Columbiana* (Twp)	44432
Center, *Mercer* (Twp)	45822
Center, *Monroe* (Twp)	43793
Center, *Morgan* (Twp)	45715
Center, *Noble* (Twp)	43724
Center, *Williams* (Twp)	43506
Center, *Wood* (Twp)	43402
Center, *Guernsey*	43725
Centerburg	43011
Centerfield	45123
Centerpoint	45656
Center Station	45659
Centerton	44890
Center Village	43021
Centerville, *Belmont*	43718
Centerville, *Brown*	45154
Centerville, *Marion*	43342
Centerville, *Montgomery*	45458-59
	45475
For specific ZIP Codes call (888) 275-8777, or your local postmaster.	
Centerville, *Wayne*	44676
Central (Part of Toledo)‡	43603†
	43604*
Central College (Part of Westerville)	43081
Central Point Shopping Center (Part of Columbus)‡	43223
Cessna (Twp)	43326
Ceylon	44839
Chagrin Falls	44022-23
For specific ZIP Codes call (888) 275-8777, or your local postmaster.	
Chagrin Falls Park	44022
Chagrin Harbor (Part of Eastlake)	44094
Chalfants	43739
Chambersburg, *Columbiana*	44657
Chambersburg, *Gallia*	45631
Champion (Twp)	44481
Champion Heights♦	44481
Chandler	43910
Chandlersville	43727
Chapel Hill Shopping Center (Part of Akron)	44310
Chapmans	45692
Chardon	44024
Charity Rotch (Part of Massillon)	44646
Charlestown	44266
Charloe	45873
Charm	44617
Chase	45710
Chasetown	45118
Chaseville	43772
Chaska Beach (Part of Huron)	44839
Chateau Estates	45502
Chateau Ridge (Part of Marion)	43302
Chatfield	44825
Chatham, *Medina* (Twp)	44275
Chatham, *Licking*	43055
Chatham, *Medina*	44256
Chattanooga	45882
Chauncey	45719
Chautauqua	45342
Cherokee	43324
Cherry Fork	45618
Cherry Grove	45245
	45255
For specific ZIP Codes call (888) 275-8777, or your local postmaster.	
Cherry Grove Plaza	45230
Cherry Valley	44003
Chesapeake	45619
Cheshire, *Delaware*	43021
Cheshire, *Gallia*	45620
Chesswood Acres	45239
Chester, *Clinton* (Twp)	45177
Chester, *Geauga* (Twp)	44026
Chester, *Morrow* (Twp)	43338
Chester, *Wayne* (Twp)	44691
Chester, *Meigs*	45720
Chester Center	44026
Chesterfield (Twp)	43567
Chesterhill	43728
Chesterland♦	44026
Chesterville	43317
Cheviot	45211
Cheviot Hills	45502
Chevy Chase	44833
Chickasaw	45826
Chickwan	43901
Chili	43824
Chillicothe	45601
Chillicothe Manor	45601
Chilo	45112
Chipman	45805
Chippewa (Twp)	44230
Chippewa Lake	44215
Chippewa Lake Park	44215
Chocktou Lake♦	43140
Christiansburg	45389
Christopher Columbus (Part of Columbus)‡	43215
Chuckery	43029
Churchill	44505
Churchills (Part of Sylvania)‡	43560
Churchtown	45750

Cincinnati

45201-75

For specific ZIP Codes call (888) 275-8777, or your local postmaster.

Colleges & Universities

Art Academy	45202
Athenaeum of Ohio	45230
Cincinnati Bible Coll & Seminary	45204
Cincinnati Coll of Mortuary Science	45224
Coll of Mount Saint Joseph	45233
God's Bible School & Coll	45210
Union Institute	45206
Univ of Cincinnati	45221
Xavier Univ	45207

Financial Institutions

Bank One, NA	45236
The Fifth Third Bank	45263
The Huntington Nat Bank	45202
KeyBank	45202
PNC Bank, NA	45202
The Provident Bank	45202
Star Bank, NA	45202

Hospitals

Bethesda North Hosp	45242
Bethesda Oak Hosp	45206
Children's Hosp Med Ctr	45229
Christ Hosp	45219
Good Samaritan Hosp	45220
Jewish Hosp	45236
Pauline Warfield Lewis Ctr	45237
Univ Health Alliance	45267
Veterans Affairs Med Ctr	45220

Hotels/Motels

Holiday Inn	45241
Holiday Inn North	45241
Hyatt Regency, Saks Fifth Av	45202

Marriott 45246
Omni Netherland Plaza 45202
Regal 45202
The Westin 45202

Military Installations
Defense Fuel Support Point 45233
U S Army Corps of Engineers, Ohio River Div, Laboratory 45240

Circle Green 43908
Circle Hill, *Athens* 45764
Circle Hill, *Miami* 45308
Circleville 43113
City View Heights 45011
Claiborne 43344
Claibourne (Twp) 43344
Claridon, *Geauga* 44024
Claridon, *Marion* 43314
Clarington 43915
Clark, *Brown* (Twp) 45130
Clark, *Clinton* (Twp) 45146
Clark, *Coshocton* (Twp) 43844
Clark, *Holmes* (Twp) 43804
Clark, *Coshocton* 43812
Clark Corners, *Ashtabula* 44030
Clark Corners (Part of Conneaut) 44030
Clark Corners, *Medina* 44281
Clarksburg, *Belmont* 43960
Clarksburg, *Ross* 43115
Clarksfield 44889
Clarks Lake 43143
Clarkson 44455
Clarkstown 45648
Clarksville, *Clinton* 45113
Clarksville, *Perry* 43748
Clay, *Auglaize* (Twp) 45895
Clay, *Gallia* (Twp) 45631
Clay, *Highland* (Twp) 45171
Clay, *Knox* (Twp) 43080
Clay, *Montgomery* (Twp) 45354
Clay, *Muskingum* (Twp) 43777
Clay, *Ottawa* (Twp) 43430
Clay, *Scioto* (Twp) 45662
Clay, *Tuscarawas* (Twp) 44629
Clay, *Jackson* 45656
Clay Center 43408
Clay Lick 43055
Claysville 43725
Clayton, *Perry* (Twp) 43764
Clayton, *Adams* 45144
Clayton, *Miami* 45318
Clayton, *Montgomery* 45315
Clear Creek, *Ashland* (Twp) 44874
Clearcreek, *Fairfield* (Twp) 43102
Clear Creek, *Warren* (Twp) 45066
Clearport 43130
Clearview, *Athens* 45701
Clearview, *Lorain* 44055
Clearview (Part of Massillon) 44646
Clermontville 45157
Clertoma (Part of Milford) 45150

Cleveland

..... 44101-06
..... 44108-15
..... 44118-21
..... 44124-30
..... 44134-35
..... 44143-44
..... 44181-99
For specific ZIP Codes call (888) 275-8777, or your local postmaster.

Colleges & Universities
Case Western Reserve Univ 44106
Cleveland Institute of Art 44106
Cleveland Institute of Music 44106
Cleveland State Univ 44115
David N Myers Coll 44115
John Carroll Univ 44118
Ohio Coll of Podiatric Medicine 44106
Ursuline Coll 44124

Financial Institutions
Bank One, NA 44114
The Fifth Third Bank of Northeastern Ohio 44114
Firstmerit Bank, NA 44115
The Huntington Natl Bank 44115
KeyBank 44114
Nat City Bank 44114
The Provident Bank 44114
Star Bank, NA 44114

Hospitals
Clinic Hosp 44195
Fairview Hosp 44111
Metrohealth Med Ctr 44109
Mt Sinai Med Ctr 44106
Saint Luke's Med Ctr 44104
St Vincent Charity Hosp 44115
Univ Hosps 44106
Veterans Affairs Med Ctr 44106

Hotels/Motels
Embassy Suites 44114
Holiday Inn, Lakeside City Ctr 44114
Marriott, Airport 44135
Marriott, Key Ctr 44114
Omni International 44106
Renaissance 44113
Sheraton, Airport 44135
Sheraton, City Ctr 44114

Military Installations
NASA Lewis Research Ctr 44135
9th Coast Guard Dist 44199

Cleveland Heights 44118
Cleves 45002
Clifton, *Greene* 45316
Clifton (Part of Cincinnati) 45220
Clifton Farms (Part of Middletown) 45044
Climax 43320
Clinton, *Franklin* (Twp) 43224
Clinton, *Fulton* (Twp) 43567
Clinton, *Knox* (Twp) 43050
Clinton, *Seneca* (Twp) 44883
Clinton, *Shelby* (Twp) 45365
Clinton, *Vinton* (Twp) 45634
Clinton, *Wayne* (Twp) 44676
Clinton, *Summit* 44216
Clintonville (Part of Columbus)‡ 43202
Clipper Mills 45631
Cloverdale 45827
Cloverhill 43764
Cluff 45244
Clyde 43410
Coach Lite Village 43528
Coal, *Jackson* (Twp) 45621
Coal, *Perry* (Twp) 43766
Coalburg 44425
Coal Grove 45638
Coalport (Part of Newcomerstown) 43832
Coal Ridge 43711
Coal Run 45721
Coalton 45621
Coddingville 44256
Coffee Corners 44062
Coitsville (Twp) 44436
Coitsville Center 44505
Colby 43410
Cold Springs 45502
Coldwater 45828
Colebrook 44076
Colerain, *Hamilton* (Twp) 45251
Colerain, *Ross* (Twp) 45644
Colerain, *Belmont* 43916
Colerain Heights 45239
Coles Park 45663
Coletown 45331
College (Twp) 43022
College Corner 45003
College Hill, *Guernsey* 43725
College Hill (Part of Cincinnati) 45224
College Hill Junction (Part of Cincinnati) 45224
College Hills 45324
Collins 44826
Collinsville 45004
Collinwood (Part of Cleveland)‡ 44110
Colonial Hills (Part of Worthington) 43085
Colony Square (Part of Zanesville) 43701
Colton 43510
Columbia, *Hamilton* (Twp) 45243
Columbia, *Lorain* (Twp) 44028
Columbia, *Meigs* (Twp) 45710
Columbia (Part of Massillon) 44646
Columbia, *Tuscarawas* 44622
Columbia, *Williams* 43518
Columbia Center, *Licking* 43062
Columbia Center, *Lorain* 44028
Columbia Hills Corners 44028
Columbiana 44408
Columbia Station 44028

Columbus

..... 43201-40
For specific ZIP Codes call (888) 275-8777, or your local postmaster.

Colleges & Universities
Capital Univ 43209
Columbus Coll of Art & Design 43215
DeVry Institute of Technology 43209
Franklin Univ 43215
Mount Carmel Coll of Nursing 43222
Ohio Dominican Coll 43219
Ohio State Univ 43210
Pontifical Coll Josephinum 43235
Trinity Lutheran Seminary 43209

Financial Institutions
Bank One, NA 43215
The Fifth Third Bank 43215
The Huntington Nat Bank 43215
KeyBank 43215
Nat City Bank 43251
The Provident Bank 43215
Star Bank, NA 43215

Hospitals
Children's Hosp 43205
Doctors Hosp 43201
Grant/Riverside Methodist Hosps 43214
Mount Carmel Health System 43213
Ohio State Univ Med Ctr 43210

Hotels/Motels
Crowne Plaza 43215
Holiday Inn, City Ctr 43215
Holiday Inn East 43232
Holiday Inn, Worthington 43235
Hyatt on Capitol Square at City Ctr 43215
Hyatt Regency at Ohio Ctr 43215
Marriott North 43229
Radisson North 43229
Sheraton Suites 43235

Military Installations
Army Aviation Support Facility No 2, Rickenbacker International Airport 43235
Defense Supply Ctr 43213
Ohio Air Nat Guard, FB6356, Rickenbacker International Airport 43217
U S Property & Fiscal Off for Ohio 43235
U S Property & Fiscal Off for Ohio (Warehouse) 43235

Columbus Circle (Part of Ashland) 44805
Columbus City Center (Part of Columbus) 43215
Columbus Grove 45830
Columbus Mall (Part of Columbus) 43229
Columbus Park 44870
Comet 44216
Commercial Point 43116
Compton Park 45231
Compton Woods (Part of Wyoming) 45215
Conant 45887
Concept 45807
Concord, *Champaign* (Twp) 43072
Concord, *Delaware* (Twp) 43015
Concord, *Fayette* (Twp) 43160
Concord, *Highland* (Twp) 45697
Concord, *Lake* (Twp) 44077
Concord, *Miami* (Twp) 45373
Concord, *Ross* (Twp) 45628
Concord, *Lake* 44060
Concord, *Licking* 43031
Condit 43074
Conesville 43811
Congo 43730
Congress, *Morrow* (Twp) 43338
Congress, *Wayne* 44287
Congress Lake 44632
Conneaut 44030
Conneaut Harbor (Part of Conneaut) 44030
Connett 45764
Connorville 43943
Conotton 44695
Conover 45317
Constitution 45750
Continental 45831
Converse 45887
Convoy 45832
Conway Addition 43731
Cook 43143
Cool Ridge Heights (Part of Mansfield) 44905
Coolville 45723
Coonville 45654
Cooperdale 43821
Coopersville 45657
Copley 44321
Copley Center 44321
Corinth 44417
Cork 44041
Corner 45714
Cornersburg (Part of Youngstown)‡ 44511
Cornerville 45773
Corning 40700
Corryville (Part of Cincinnati)‡ 45219-20
For specific ZIP Codes call (888) 275-8777, or your local postmaster.
Corryville, *Lawrence* 45619
Cortland 44410
Cortsville 45368
Corwin 45068
Coryville 45638
Coshocton 43812
Cottage Grove 44319
Country Acres, *Greene* 45324
Country Acres (Part of Beavercreek) 45430
Country Club Estates (Part of Steubenville) 43952
Country Club Hills 45801
Country Estates 45371
Country Fair Station (Part of Canton)‡ 44708
Cove 45640
Covedale♦ 45238
Coventry (Twp) 44319
Covington 45318
Cozaddale 45122
Crabapple 43950
Craig Beach 44429
Craigton 44676
Cranberry (Twp) 44854
Cranberry Prairie 45883
Crandenbrook 43551
Crane, *Paulding* (Twp) 45821
Crane, *Wyandot* (Twp) 43351
Cranwood (Part of Cleveland)‡ 44128
Crawford, *Coshocton* (Twp) 43804
Crawford, *Wyandot* 43316
Crawford Corners 44254
Cream City (Part of Irondale) 43932
Creola 45622
Crescent 43950
Crescent Gardens 44646
Crescentville (Part of Sharonville) 45241
Crestline 44827
Creston 44217
Crestwood Hills (Part of Vandalia) 45377
Cridersville 45806
Crissey 43528
Cromers 44883
Crooked Tree 45727
Crooksville 43731
Crosby (Twp) 45030
Cross Creek (Twp) 43952-53
For specific ZIP Codes call (888) 275-8777, or your local postmaster.
Crossenville 43107
Crosstown 45176
Crosswick 45068
Croton 43013
Crown City 45623
Crystal Lake 44003
Crystal Lakes♦ 45341
Crystal Rock Park 44870
Crystal Springs 44614
Cuba 45114
Cumberland 43732
Cumminsville (Part of Cincinnati)‡ 45223
Curtice 43412
Custar 43511
Cutler 45724
Cuyahoga Falls 44221-24
For specific ZIP Codes call (888) 275-8777, or your local postmaster.
Cuyahoga Heights 44127
Cygnet 43413
Cynthian (Twp) 45845
Cynthiana 45624
D (Part of Toledo)‡ 43608
Dabel (Part of Dayton)‡ 45420
Dadsville 45381
Dailyville 45690
Dale 43787
Dallas (Twp) 44849
Dallasburg 45140
Dalton 44618
Dalzell 45745
Daman Park 45044
Damascus, *Henry* (Twp) 43534
Damascus, *Mahoning* 44619
Danbury (Twp) 43452
Danville, *Highland* 45133
Danville, *Knox* 43014
Danville, *Meigs* 45741
Darby, *Madison* (Twp) 43064
Darby, *Pickaway* (Twp) 43146
Darby, *Union* (Twp) 43064
Darbydale 43123
Darbyville 43136
Darlington, *Muskingum* 43701
Darlington, *Richland* 44813
Darrowville (Part of Stow) 44224
Darrtown 45056
Dart 45773
Darwin 45769
Davisville 45692
Dawn 45303
Dawson 45333
Day Heights♦ 45150
Dayton 45401-90
For specific ZIP Codes call (888) 275-8777, or your local postmaster.
Dayton View (Part of Dayton)‡ 45406
Dean Dale (Part of Mingo Junction) 43938
Deavertown 43731
Decatur, *Lawrence* (Twp) 45659
Decatur, *Washington* (Twp) 45742
Decatur, *Brown* 45115
Decaturville 45712
Decrow Corners 43031
Dee 44824
Deep Run 43935
Deer Creek, *Madison* (Twp) 43140
Deer Creek, *Pickaway* (Twp) 43164
Deerfield, *Morgan* (Twp) 43758
Deerfield, *Ross* (Twp) 43115
Deerfield, *Warren* (Twp) 45040
Deerfield, *Portage* 44411
Deering 45638
Deer Park 45236
Deersville 44693
Defiance 43512
Defiance Junction (Part of Defiance) 43512
DeForest 44484
De Graff 43318
Dekalb 44887
Delaware, *Defiance* (Twp) 43556
Delaware, *Hancock* (Twp) 45897

Delaware, *Delaware* 43015
Delhi (Part of Cincinnati) 45238
Delhi Hills 45238
Delightful 44470
Delisle 45304
Dellroy 44620
Delmont 43130
Delphi 44890
Delphos 45833
Delta 43515
Denmark, *Ashtabula* (Twp) 44047
Denmark, *Morrow* 43320
Denmark Center 44047
Dennison 44621
Denson 43533
Dent 45248
Denver 45690
Derby 43117
Derwent 43733
Deshler 43516
Deunquat 44882
Devil Town 44691
Devola♦ 45750
Deweyville 45858
Dexter 45741
Dexter City 45727
Deyarmonville 43917
Dialton 45502
Diamond 44412
Dicken 43138
Dilles Bottom 43947
Dillon Falls 43701
Dillonvale, *Hamilton*♦ 45236
Dillonvale, *Jefferson* 43917
Dilworth 44417
Dinsmore (Twp) 45306
Dixie 43782
Dixie Heights (Part of Middletown) 45042
Dixie Heights, *Montgomery* 45414
Dixon, *Preble* (Twp) 45320
Dixon, *Van Wert* 45832
Dixonville 43920
Doanville 45764
Dobbston 45678
Dodds 45036
Dodgeville 44085
Dodson, *Highland* (Twp) 45142
Dodson, *Montgomery* 45309
Dodsonville 45142
Dola 45835
Dolly Varden 45368
Donald L Marrs (Part of Cincinnati)‡ 45258
Doneys (Part of Whitehall) 43213
Donnelsville 45319
Donnersville 43950
Dorcas 45771
Dornbusch 45239
Dorset 44032
Dover, *Athens* (Twp) 45761
Dover, *Fulton* (Twp) 43567
Dover, *Union* (Twp) 43040
Dover, *Tuscarawas* 44622
Dowling 43551
Downtown (Part of Akron)‡ 44308
Doylestown 44230
Drakes 43730
Drakesburg 44288
Dresden 43821
Drexel♦ 45427
Driftwood 44041
Drinkle 43102
Dry Run, *Hamilton*♦ 45244
Dry Run, *Scioto* 45663
Dublin, *Mercer* (Twp) 45882
Dublin, *Franklin* 43016-17
For specific ZIP Codes call (888) 275-8777, or your local postmaster.
Dublin Village Center (Part of Dublin) 43017
Duchouquet (Twp) 45895
Dudley, *Hardin* (Twp) 43326
Dudley, *Noble* 43724
Dueber Station (Part of Canton)‡ 44706
Duffy 43946
Dull 45874
Dumontville 43130
Dunbridge 43414
Duncan Falls 43734
Dundas 45634
Dundee 44624
Dungannon, *Columbiana* 44423
Dungannon, *Noble* 45721
Dunglen 43917
Dunham (Twp) 45784
Dunkinsville 45660
Dunkirk 45836
Dunlap 45239
Dupont 45837
Durbin, *Clark* 45502
Durbin, *Mercer* 45822
Duvall 43137
Dyesville 45769
E (Part of Toledo)‡ 43609
Eagle, *Brown* (Twp) 45171
Eagle, *Hancock* (Twp) 45881
Eagle, *Vinton* (Twp) 43152
Eagle Beach 43452
Eagle City 45504
Eagle Point Colony (Part of Rossford) 43460
Eagleport 43756
Eagleville, *Ashtabula* 44047
Eagleville, *Wood* 44817
East (Twp) 44427
East Akron (Part of Akron)‡ 44305
East Alliance 44601
East Ashtabula (Part of Ashtabula) 44004
East Bass Lake 44024
East Batavia Heights 45103
East Cadiz 43907
East Cambridge (Part of Cambridge) 43725
East Canton 44730
East Carlisle 44035
East Claridon 44033
East Clayton 45764
East Cleveland 44112
East Conesville (Part of Conesville) 43811
East Conneaut (Part of Conneaut) 44030
East Cumminsville (Part of Cincinnati) 45223
East Danville 45133
East End (Part of East Liverpool) 43920
East End (Part of Cincinnati) 45226
East Fairfield 44408
East Fultonham 43735
Eastgate Shopping Center (Part of Mayfield Heights) 44125
East Goshen 44609
East Greenville 44666
Eastlake 44094
Eastland Mall (Part of Columbus)‡ 43232
East Lawn 43447
East Lewistown 44408
East Liberty (Part of Sunbury) 43074
East Liberty, *Logan* 43319
East Liberty, *Summit* 44319
East Liverpool 43920
East Mansfield 44905
East Mecca 44410
East Millersport 43046
East Millfield 45761
East Monroe 45135
East Norwalk 44857
East Norwood (Part of Marietta) 45750
East Norwood (Part of Norwood) 45212
Easton 44270
East Orwell (Part of Orwell) 44076
East Over 45011
East Palestine 44413
East Plains (Part of Middletown) 45044
East Richland 43950
East Rochester 44625
East Side (Part of Youngstown)‡ 44506
East Sparta 44626
East Springfield 43925
East Toledo (Part of Toledo) 43605
East Townsend 44826
East Trumbull 44084
East Union, *Wayne* (Twp) 44606
East Union, *Noble* 43779
East View (Part of Mingo Junction) 43938
Eastview, *Montgomery* 45431
Eastwood 45154
Eastwood Mall (Part of Niles) 44446
Eaton, *Lorain* (Twp) 44035
Eaton, *Preble* 45320
Eaton Estates♦ 44044
Eber 43160
Echo 43940
Echo Glen Lake 44233
Eckmansville 45697
Eden, *Licking* (Twp) 43071
Eden, *Seneca* (Twp) 44845
Eden, *Wyandot* (Twp) 44849
Eden Park (Part of Cincinnati) 45202
Eden Park, *Scioto* 45662
Edenton 45122
Edenville 44849
Edgefield, *Fayette* 43128
Edgefield (Part of Canton) 44709
Edgemont 45216
Edgerton 43517
Edgewater (Part of Lakewood) 44107
Edgewater Beach 43076
Edgewater Park 43232
Edgewood♦ 44004
Edgwood Estates 45805
Edinburg 44272
Edison 43320
Edmunds 45682
Edon 43518
Egypt, *Auglaize* 45865
Egypt, *Belmont* 43713
Eifort 45682
Eileen Gardens 45238
Elba 45746
Elberta Beach (Part of Vermilion) 44089
Eldean 45373
Eldon 43773
Eldorado (Part of Middletown) 45044
Eldorado, *Preble* 45321
Elery 43535
Elgin 45838
Elida 45807
Elizabeth, *Lawrence* (Twp) 45659
Elizabeth, *Miami* (Twp) 45312
Elizabethtown, *Hamilton* 45052
Elizabethtown, *Warren* 45005
Elk, *Noble* (Twp) 45745
Elk, *Vinton* (Twp) 45651
Elkrun (Twp) 44415
Elkton 44415
Ellerton 45342
Ellet (Part of Akron)‡ 44312
Elliot 43728
Elliottville 45701
Ellis 43701
Ellisonville 45638
Elliston 43432
Ellsberry 45101
Ellsworth 44416
Elm Acres 44646
Elm Grove 45661
Elmira 43502
Elmore 43416
Elmville 45133
Elmwood Place 45216
Elroy 45303
Elton 44662
Elyria (Twp) 44035
Elyria 44035-39
For specific ZIP Codes call (888) 275-8777, or your local postmaster.
Emerald, *Paulding* (Twp) 45879
Emerald, *Adams* 45697
Emerson 43917
Emerson Heights (Part of Marietta) 45750
Emery Chapel 45502
Empire 43926
Enchanted Hills 45133
England Station 44805
Englewood 45322
English Woods (Part of Cincinnati) 45225
Enoch (Twp) 43724
Enon 45323
Enterprise, *Hocking* 43138
Enterprise, *Preble* 45381
Epworth 44903
Epworth Heights 45140
Era 43143
Erastus 45822
Erhart 44256
Erie (Twp) 43439
Erieview (Part of Cleveland)‡ 44199
Eris 43078
Erlin 43420
Espyville 43302
Essex 43344
Etna 43018
Euclid 44117
44123
44132
For specific ZIP Codes call (888) 275-8777, or your local postmaster.
Euclid Heights (Part of Middletown) 45044
Euclid Square Mall (Part of Euclid) 44132
Eureka 44408
Evansport 43519
Evanston (Part of Cincinnati) 45207
Evansville 44440
Evendale 45241
Everett 44264
Evergreen, *Gallia* 45614
Evergreen, *Washington* 45750
Ewing 43138
Ewington 45686
Excello 45044
Fairborn 45324
Fairbrondt 44833
Fairdale 43725
Fairfax, *Hamilton* 45227
Fairfax, *Highland* 45133
Fairfield, *Columbiana* (Twp) 44408
Fairfield, *Highland* (Twp) 45135
Fairfield, *Huron* (Twp) 44855
Fairfield, *Madison* (Twp) 43162
Fairfield, *Tuscarawas* (Twp) 44678
Fairfield, *Washington* (Twp) 45724
Fairfield (Part of Fairborn) 45324
Fairfield, *Butler* 45014
Fairfield, *Jefferson* 43944
Fairfield Beach♦ 43076
Fairground Acres 45107
Fairhaven 45003
Fairhope 44641
Fairlawn 44313
44333-34
For specific ZIP Codes call (888) 275-8777, or your local postmaster.
Fairlawn Heights 44484
Fairmount (Part of Cincinnati) 45214
Fair Oaks 45102
Fairplay (Part of Fairfield) 45014
Fairplay, *Jefferson* 43910
Fairpoint 43927
Fairport Harbor 44077
Fairview, *Guernsey & Belmont* 43736
Fairview, *Guernsey* 43772
Fairview, *Highland* 45133
Fairview Heights (Part of Marietta) 45750
Fairview Heights (Part of Toronto) 43964
Fairview Lanes♦ 44870
Fairview Park 44126
Fairway Terrace 45341
Fairway View Estates 45805
Fairwind Acres (Part of Montgomery) 45242
Falls, *Hocking* (Twp) 43138
Falls, *Muskingum* (Twp) 43701
Fallsburg 43822
Fallsbury (Twp) 43822
Fargo 43074
Farmdale 44417
Farmer 43520
Farmers 45146
Farmerstown 43804
Farmersville 45325
Farmington, *Trumbull* (Twp) 44491
Farmington, *Belmont* 43912
Farnham (Part of Conneaut) 44030
Farrington 45373
Fashion Heights 45238
Fawcett 45616
Fayette, *Lawrence* (Twp) 45680
Fayette, *Fulton* 43521
Fayetteville 45118
Fay Gardens 45140
Fearing (Twp) 45788
Feed Springs 44683
Feesburg 45119
Felicity 45120
Fernald 45030
Fernbank (Part of Cincinnati) 45233
Fernell Heights 45244
Fernwood 43952
Ferry, *Erie* 44870
Ferry, *Greene* 45068
Fields Terrace 45619
Filburns Island 45865
Fincastle 45171
Findlater Garden (Part of Cincinnati) 45232
Findlay 45839*
45840†
Findlay Village Mall (Part of Findlay) 45840
Findley Gardens 43964
Fire Brick 45656
Fireside 44811
Firestone Park (Part of Akron)‡ 44301
Fishack 43452
Fitchville 44851
Five Forks 43945
Five Mile 45154
Five Points (Part of Akron)‡ 44302
Five Points (Part of Fairborn) 45324
Five Points, *Mahoning* 44452
Five Points, *Pickaway* 43143
Five Points, *Trumbull* 44404
Five Points, *Warren*♦ 45066
Flatiron, *Perry* 43731
Flat Iron, *Warren* 45005
Flatrock, *Henry* (Twp) 43545
Flat Rock, *Seneca* 44828
Fleatown 43055
Fleetwood Addition 43040
Fleming 45729
Fletcher 45326
Flint (Part of Columbus) 43225
Florence, *Williams* (Twp) 43518
Florence, *Belmont* 43935
Florence, *Erie* 44814
Florence, *Noble* 43724
Florida 43545
Flushing 43977
Fly 45767
Footville 44084
Foraker 45812
Forest 45843
Forestdale 45638
Forest Fair Mall (Part of Forest Park) 45240
Forest Hills 45502
Forest Hills Estates 45230
Forest Park, *Hamilton* 45240
Forest Park (Part of Shiloh)‡ 45405
Forest Park Plaza 45405
Forest View 43952
Forestville♦ 45230
45255
For specific ZIP Codes call (888) 275-8777, or your local postmaster.
Fort Jefferson 45331
Fort Jennings 45844
Fort Loramie 45845
Fort McKinley 45426
Fort Meigs Place 43551
Fort Miami Addition (Part of Maumee) 43537
Fort Recovery 45846
Fort Scott Camps 45030
Fort Seneca 44883
Fort Shawnee 45806
Fort Steuben Mall (Part of Steubenville) 43952
Foster 45039
Fosterville (Part of Youngstown) 44511
Fostoria 44830
Fountain Park 43084
Fowler 44418
Fowlers Mill 44024
Fox, *Carroll* (Twp) 43945
Fox, *Pickaway* 43113
Foxboro Manor (Part of Vandalia) 45377
Foxborough Commons 44870
Fox Chase 43502
Fox Hollow 43542
Frank 44811
Frankfort 45628
Franklin, *Adams* (Twp) 45660
Franklin, *Brown* (Twp) 45121
Franklin, *Clermont* (Twp) 45120

Place	ZIP
Franklin, *Columbiana* (Twp)	43962
Franklin, *Coshocton* (Twp)	43811
Franklin, *Darke* (Twp)	45304
Franklin, *Franklin* (Twp)	43204
	43223
For specific ZIP Codes call (888) 275-8777, or your local postmaster.	
Franklin, *Fulton* (Twp)	43502
Franklin, *Harrison* (Twp)	44699
Franklin, *Jackson* (Twp)	45640
Franklin, *Licking* (Twp)	43055
Franklin, *Mercer* (Twp)	45866
Franklin, *Monroe* (Twp)	43754
Franklin, *Morrow* (Twp)	43338
Franklin, *Portage* (Twp)	44240
Franklin, *Richland* (Twp)	44875
Franklin, *Ross* (Twp)	45601
Franklin, *Shelby* (Twp)	45363
Franklin, *Summit* (Twp)	44216
Franklin, *Tuscarawas* (Twp)	44680
Franklin, *Wayne* (Twp)	44627
Franklin, *Warren*	45005
Franklin Furnace♦	45629
Franklin Park Mall (Part of Toledo)	43623
Franklin Square	44431
Frazeysburg	43822
Frederick, *Miami*	45371
Frederick, *Scioto*	45694
Fredericksburg	44627
Fredericksdale	43779
Fredericktown, *Columbiana*	43920
Fredericktown, *Knox*	43019
Fredonia	43023
Freeburg	44669
Freedom, *Henry* (Twp)	43545
Freedom, *Wood* (Twp)	43450
Freedom, *Portage*	44288
Freeport	43973
Fremont	43420
Frenchtown, *Darke*	45380
Frenchtown, *Seneca*	43316
Fresno	43824
Friendship	45630
Frischkorn Heights	43968
Frontier Park	45239
Frontier Town	44514
Frost	45723
Fruitdale	45123
Fruit Hill♦	45230
Fryburg, *Auglaize*	45895
Fryburg, *Holmes*	44654
Frys Corners	45331
Frytown	45418
Fulda	43724
Fulton, *Fulton* (Twp)	43558
Fulton, *Morrow*	43321
Fultonham	43738
Funk	44691
Fursville	43062
Gabels Corner	43420
Gage	45658
Gageville	44048
Gahanna	43230
Galatea	45872
Galaxy Acres	45239
Galena	43021
Galion	44833
Gallia	45658
Gallipolis	45631
Galloway	43119
Gambier	43022
Ganges	44875
Gano	45241
Garden	45735
Garden Acres, *Clark*	45503
Garden Acres (Part of Steubenville)	43952
Garden City	45694
Garden Hill Top (Part of Cincinnati)	45232
Garden Isle	44254
Garden Terrace (Part of Steubenville)	43952
Garfield	44460
Garfield Heights	44125
Garrettsville	44231
Gaslight Village	45122
Gasper (Twp)	45320
Gates Mills	44040
Gath	45171
Gavers	44432
Geauga Lake (Part of Aurora)	44202
Geeburg	44406
Geneva, *Ashtabula*	44041
Geneva, *Fairfield*	43107
Geneva-on-the-Lake	44041
Genntown	45036
Genoa, *Delaware* (Twp)	43081
Genoa, *Ottawa*	43430
Genung Corners	44057
Georges Run	43938
Georgesville	43123
Georgetown	45121
Gepharts	45694
Gerald	43545
German, *Auglaize* (Twp)	45869
German, *Clark* (Twp)	45504
German, *Fulton* (Twp)	43502
German, *Harrison* (Twp)	43976
German, *Montgomery* (Twp)	45327
Germano	43986
Germantown, *Montgomery*	45327
Germantown, *Washington*	45745
German Village (Part of Columbus)‡	43206
Getaway	45619
Gettysburg, *Darke*	45328
Gettysburg, *Preble*	45347
Geyer	45895
Ghent	44333
Gibisonville	43149
Gibson, *Mercer* (Twp)	45846
Gibson, *Guernsey*	43778
Gibsonburg	43431
Gilbert	43701
Gilboa	45875
Gilead (Twp)	43338
Gillivan	43140
Gilmore	43837
Ginghamsburg	45371
Girard	44420
Girton	43457
Gist Settlement	45159
Givens	45690
Glade	45613
Gladstone	45314
Glandorf	45848
Glasgow, *Columbiana*	43968
Glasgow, *Tuscarawas*	43837
Glass Rock	43739
Glenbrook Acres	45305
Glencoe, *Belmont*	43928
Glencoe, *Hamilton*	45231
Glendale	45246
Glendwell (Part of Steubenville)	43952
Glen Este	45103
Glenford	43739
Glengary Heights	43081
Glen Karn	45332
Glenmary (Part of Fairfield)	45246
Glenmont	44628
Glenmoor♦	43920
Glenmore	45874
Glenns Run	43935
Glen Robbins	43943
Glen Roy	45692
Glenville Bratenahl (Part of Cleveland)‡	44108
Glenwillow	44139
Glenwood	45381
Glenwood Acres	44087
Gloria Glens Park	44215
Glouster	45732
Glynwood	45885
Gnadenhutten	44629
Goes	45387
Golden Corners	44214
Golden Gate Shopping Center (Part of Mayfield Heights)	44124
Goldsboro	45692
Golf Manor	45237
Golfway Acres	45239
Gomer	45809
Good Hope, *Hocking* (Twp)	43149
Good Hope, *Fayette*	43160
Goodland Acres	44688
Goodyear Heights (Part of Akron)	44305
Goose Run	45732
Gordon	45329
Gore	43138
Gorham (Twp)	43521
Goshen, *Auglaize* (Twp)	43331
Goshen, *Belmont* (Twp)	43719
Goshen, *Champaign* (Twp)	43044
Goshen, *Hardin* (Twp)	43326
Goshen, *Mahoning* (Twp)	44460
Goshen, *Clermont*	45122
Goshen, *Tuscarawas*	44663
Gould Park	43230
Goulds	43938
Graceland Shopping Center (Part of Columbus)	43214
Grafton	44044
Grand (Twp)	45843
Grand Prairie (Twp)	43302
Grand Rapids	43522
Grand River	44045
Grandview, *Hamilton*♦	45002
Grandview, *Washington*	45767
Grandview Estates (Part of Delaware)	43015
Grandview Estates, *Marion*	43302
Grandview Heights, *Champaign*	43072
Grandview Heights, *Franklin*	43212
Grandview Homes (Part of Lima)	45804
Grange Hall	43143
Granger	44256
Grants	45843
Granville, *Mercer* (Twp)	45883
Granville, *Licking*	43023
Granville South♦	43023
Grape Grove	45335
Gratiot	43740
Gratis	45330
Graysville	45734
Graytown	43432
Greasy Ridge	45678
Greater State Road Shopping Center (Part of Cuyahoga Falls)	44223
Great Lakes Mall (Part of Mentor)	44060
Great Northern Mall (Part of North Olmsted)	44070
Great Southern Shopping Center (Part of Columbus)	43207
Great Western Shopping Center (Part of Columbus)	43213
Green, *Adams* (Twp)	45684
Green, *Ashland* (Twp)	44842
Green, *Brown* (Twp)	45154
Green, *Clark* (Twp)	45502
Green, *Clinton* (Twp)	45159
Green, *Fayette* (Twp)	45135
Green, *Gallia* (Twp)	45658
Green, *Hamilton* (Twp)	45211
Green, *Harrison* (Twp)	43976
Green, *Hocking* (Twp)	43138
Green, *Mahoning* (Twp)	44406
Green, *Monroe* (Twp)	43793
Green, *Ross* (Twp)	45644
Green, *Scioto* (Twp)	45629
Green, *Shelby* (Twp)	45365
Green, *Wayne* (Twp)	44667
Green, *Summit*	44232
Green Acres	45042
Greenbush, *Brown*	45154
Greenbush, *Preble*	45064
Green Camp	43322
Greencastle	43112
Green Creek (Twp)	43410
Greendale	43138
Greene (Twp)	44450
Greenfield, *Fairfield* (Twp)	43130
Greenfield, *Gallia* (Twp)	45658
Greenfield, *Huron* (Twp)	44855
Greenfield, *Highland*	45123*
	45165†
Greenford	44422
Green Hills, *Greene*	45324
Greenhills, *Hamilton*	45218
Greenland	43115
Greenlex	43302
Green Meadows♦	45323
Greensburg (Twp)	45875
Green Springs	44836
Greens Run	45732
Greens Store	45640
Greentown♦	44630
Greenview	45415
Greenville	45331
Greenwich	44837
Greer	44628
Grelton	43523
Griffith (Part of North Bend)	45052
Griggs	44047
Grimms Bridge	43920
Groton (Twp)	44839
Grove City	43123
Groveport	43125
Grover Hill	45849
Guerne	44691
Guernsey	43749
Guilford, *Medina* (Twp)	44273
Guilford, *Columbiana*	44432
Gunnerville	45335
Gurneyville	45177
Gustavus	44417
Gutman	45895
Guyan (Twp)	45623
Guysville	45735
Gypsum	43433
Hackney	45715
Hagan Addition	43901
Hageman Junction	45036
Hale (Twp)	43340
Hallock	43506
Hallsville	45633
Hambden	44024
Hamburg, *Fairfield*	43130
Hamburg, *Preble*	45321
Hamden	45634
Hamer (Twp)	45133
Hamersville	45130
Hametown (Part of Norton)	44203
Hamilton, *Franklin* (Twp)	43137
	43207
For specific ZIP Codes call (888) 275-8777, or your local postmaster.	
Hamilton, *Jackson* (Twp)	45656
Hamilton, *Lawrence* (Twp)	45638
Hamilton, *Warren* (Twp)	45039
Hamilton, *Butler*	45011-13
	45015-18
For specific ZIP Codes call (888) 275-8777, or your local postmaster.	
Hamilton Meadows	43207
Hamler	43524
Hamlet	45102
Hamley Run	45701
Hammansburg	43413
Hammondsville	43930
Hampton Woods	45502
Hanersville	45631
Hanging Rock	45638
Hanley Village	44904
Hanna Hills	44266
Hannibal	43931
Hanover, *Ashland* (Twp)	44842
Hanover, *Butler* (Twp)	45013
Hanover, *Columbiana* (Twp)	44625
Hanover, *Harrison*	43988
Hanover, *Licking*	43055
Hanoverton	44423
Hanville Corners	44855
Happy Hollow	44626
Harbor (Part of Ashtabula)‡	44004
Harbor Hills♦	43025
Harbor Point	45822
Harbor View	43434
Hardin	45365
Harding (Twp)	43558
Hardy (Twp)	44654
Harewood Acres	45236
Harlan (Twp)	45162
Harlan Park (Part of Middletown)	45042
Harlem	43021
Harlem Springs	44631
Harmar (Part of Marietta)	45750
Harmon	44662
Harmons Landing	45885
Harmony, *Morrow* (Twp)	43315
Harmony, *Clark*	45502
Harper	43311
Harpersfield	44041
Harpster	43323
Harriett, *Guernsey*	43725
Harriett, *Highland*	45133
Harriettsville	45745
Harris, *Ottawa* (Twp)	43416
Harris, *Ross*	45612
Harrisburg, *Franklin*	43126
Harrisburg, *Gallia*	45614
Harrisburg, *Stark*	44641
Harrison, *Carroll* (Twp)	44615
Harrison, *Champaign* (Twp)	43357
Harrison, *Darke* (Twp)	45340
Harrison, *Gallia* (Twp)	45631
Harrison, *Henry* (Twp)	43545
Harrison, *Knox* (Twp)	43022
Harrison, *Licking* (Twp)	43033
Harrison, *Logan* (Twp)	43311
Harrison, *Montgomery* (Twp)	45415
Harrison, *Muskingum* (Twp)	43771
Harrison, *Paulding* (Twp)	45880
Harrison, *Perry* (Twp)	43731
Harrison, *Pickaway* (Twp)	43103
Harrison, *Preble* (Twp)	45338
Harrison, *Ross* (Twp)	45601
Harrison, *Scioto* (Twp)	45653
Harrison, *Van Wert* (Twp)	45891
Harrison, *Vinton* (Twp)	45647
Harrison, *Hamilton*	45030
Harrison Furnace	45662
Harrison Mills	45682
Harrisonville	45769
Harrisville, *Medina* (Twp)	44214
Harrisville, *Harrison*	43974
Harrod	45850
Harshasville	45660
Hartford, *Licking* (Twp)	43013
Hartford, *Trumbull*	44424
Hartland (Twp)	44857
Hartland	44826
Hartland Center	44826
Hartleyville	45732
Hartsgrove	44085
Hartshorn	45734
Hartville	44632
Hartwell (Part of Cincinnati)	45216
Harveysburg	45032
Haskins	43525
Hasting Hill	45662
Hatch	45661
Hatton	43457
Havana	44890
Havens Corners	43004
Havensport	43112
Haven View	45373
Haverhill	45636
Haviland	45851
Hayden	43002
Haydenville	43127
Hayes Colony (Part of Delaware)	43015
Hayes Corners	44062
Hayesville	44838
Haynes	43135
Hazelwood (Part of Blue Ash)	45242
Heath	43056
Heatherdowns (Part of Toledo)‡	43614
Hebbardsville	45701
Hebron	43025
Hecla	45638
Hegemans Landing	45865
Heidelburg Beach	44089
Helena	43435
Helmick	43844
Hemlock	43730
Hemlock Grove	45769
Hempstead (Part of Kettering)	45429
Hendrysburg	43713
Henley	45652
Henrietta (Twp)	44889
Henry (Twp)	45872
Hepburn	43326
Heritage	45805
Heritage Hills	44087
Heritage Park	44212
Hessville	43431
Hickman	43055
Hicksville	43526
Hide-A-Way Hills	43107
Higginsport	45131
Highland, *Defiance* (Twp)	43512
Highland, *Muskingum* (Twp)	43762
Highland, *Highland*	45132
Highland Heights	44124
Highland Hills	44122

Highland Holliday 45133
Highland Park, *Hamilton* 45238
Highland Park, *Mercer* 45822
Highland Park, *Scioto* 45629
Highland Park, *Stark* 44646
Highlands (Part of Springfield) 45503
Highland Terrace 43950
Highlandtown 43945
Highland Trails 45133
Highpoint 45242
High Water 43055
Hill Addition (Part of East Liverpool) 43920
Hill And Hollow (Part of Oxford) 45056
Hillcrest, *Columbiana* 43968
Hillcrest, *Warren* 45036
Hill Crest, *Wayne* 44691
Hillcrest, *Williams* 43543
Hill Grove 45390
Hilliar (Twp) 43011
Hilliard 43026
Hills and Dales (Part of Kettering) 45429
Hills and Dales, *Stark* 44708
Hillsboro, *Highland* 45133
Hillsboro (Part of Mingo Junction) 43938
Hilltop (Part of Columbus)‡ 43204
Hilltop, *Trumbull* 44437
Hilltop Acres (Part of Wyoming) 45215
Hinckley 44233
Hiram 44234
Hiram Rapids 44234
Hiramsburg 43732
Hitchcock 45656
Hoadley 45658
Hoagland 45133
Hoaglin (Twp) 45891
Hobson 45760
Hocking (Twp) 43130
Hockingport 45739
Hoke 45383
Holden 45896
Holgate 43527
Holiday Acres 45236
Holiday Hills 45502
Holiday Lakes 44890
Holiday Valley♦ 45324
Holland 43528
Hollansburg 45332
Hollister 45732
Holloway 43985
Hollowtown 45171
Holman-Stonybrook Shopping Center (Part of Loveland) 45140
Holmes (Twp) 44820
Holmesville 44633
Home Acres, *Butler* 45044
Home Acres, *Miami* 45373
Homedale (Part of Columbus) 43085
Home Orchards (Part of Springfield) 45503
Homer, *Medina* (Twp) 44235
Homer, *Morgan* (Twp) 45732
Homer, *Licking* 43027
Homerville 44235
Homeside 43950
Homeville 44870
Homewood (Part of Hamilton) 45015
Homeworth 44634
Honeytown 44691
Hooker 43130
Hooksburg 43787
Hooring 45766
Hooven 45033
Hopedale 43976
Hopetown 45601
Hopewell, *Licking* (Twp) 43740
Hopewell, *Mercer* (Twp) 45822
Hopewell, *Perry* (Twp) 43739
Hopewell, *Seneca* (Twp) 44809
Hopewell, *Jefferson* 43943
Hopewell, *Muskingum* 43746
Hopkinsville 45039
Horatio 45331
Horns Mill 43130
Hoskinsville 43724
Houck Meadows (Part of Enon) 45502
Houcktown 45814
Houston 45333
Howard 43028
Howenstein 44626
Howland (Twp) 44484
Hoytville 43529
Hubbard 44425
Huber Heights 45424
Huber Ridge♦ 43081
Huber South 45439
Hudson 44236
Hue 45622
Hughes 45042
Hulington 45106
Humboldt 45612
Hume 45806
Hunt 43050
Hunter 43719
Hunterdon 45732
Huntington, *Brown* (Twp) 45101
Huntington, *Gallia* (Twp) 45686
Huntington, *Ross* (Twp) 45601
Huntington, *Lorain* 44090
Huntington Hills 43147
Huntington Park (Part of Aberdeen) 45101
Hunting Valley 44022
Huntsburg 44046
Hunts Corners 44811
Huntsville, *Butler* 45042
Huntsville, *Logan* 43324
Hurford 43901
Huron 44839
Hustead 45502
Hyatts 43065
Hyde Park (Part of Cincinnati)‡ 45208
Hyde Park, *Montgomery* 45429
Hyde Park Plaza (Part of Cincinnati) 45209
Iberia 43325
Idaho 45661
Iler 44830
Ilesboro 43138
Immergrun (Part of Oregon) 43618
Independence, *Washington* (Twp) 45767
Independence, *Cuyahoga* 44131
Independence, *Defiance* 43512
Indian Camp 43725
Indian Knolls (Part of Milford) 45150
Indian Ridge 45231
Indian Springs 45014
Indianview 45147
Ingle Mann (Part of New Paris) 45347
Ingomar 45381
Ink 44883
Ira 44333
Iradale 44313
Irondale, *Jefferson* 43932
Irondale (Part of Dresden) 43821
Ironspot 43777
Ironton 45638
Irvington 45414
Irwin 43029
Island Creek (Twp) 43964
Island View 43331
Isle Saint George 43436
Isleta 43845
Israel (Twp) 45003
Ithaca 45304
Ivorydale (Part of St. Bernard) 45217
Ivorydale Junction (Part of St. Bernard) 45217
Jackson, *Allen* (Twp) 45854
Jackson, *Ashland* (Twp) 44287
Jackson, *Auglaize* (Twp) 45865
Jackson, *Brown* (Twp) 45697
Jackson, *Champaign* (Twp) 45389
Jackson, *Clermont* (Twp) 45145
Jackson, *Coshocton* (Twp) 43812
Jackson, *Crawford* (Twp) 44827
Jackson, *Darke* (Twp) 45390
Jackson, *Franklin* (Twp) 43123
Jackson, *Guernsey* (Twp) 43723
Jackson, *Hancock* (Twp) 45814
Jackson, *Hardin* (Twp) 45843
Jackson, *Highland* (Twp) 45133
Jackson, *Knox* (Twp) 43005
Jackson, *Mahoning* (Twp) 44451
Jackson, *Monroe* (Twp) 45767
Jackson, *Montgomery* (Twp) 45325
Jackson, *Muskingum* (Twp) 43822
Jackson, *Noble* (Twp) 45727
Jackson, *Paulding* (Twp) 45855
Jackson, *Perry* (Twp) 43748
Jackson, *Pickaway* (Twp) 43113
Jackson, *Pike* (Twp) 45690
Jackson, *Preble* (Twp) 45320
Jackson, *Putnam* (Twp) 45844
Jackson, *Richland* (Twp) 44875
Jackson, *Sandusky* (Twp) 43407
Jackson, *Seneca* (Twp) 44830
Jackson, *Shelby* (Twp) 45334
Jackson, *Stark* (Twp) 44646
Jackson, *Union* (Twp) 43344
Jackson, *Van Wert* (Twp) 45863
Jackson, *Vinton* (Twp) 45651
Jackson, *Wood* (Twp) 43529
Jackson, *Wyandot* (Twp) 45843
Jackson, *Jackson* 45640
Jackson Belden (Part of Canton) 44718*
44735†
Jacksonburg 45067
Jackson Center, *Mahoning* 44451
Jackson Center, *Shelby* 45334
Jackson Heights, *Jackson* 45640
Jackson Heights, *Jefferson* 43943
Jackson Lake 45656
Jacksontown 43030
Jacksonville, *Adams* 45660
Jacksonville, *Athens* 45740
Jacksonville, *Clark* 45502
Jacktown 45042
Jacobsburg 43933
Jaite (Part of Brecksville) 44141
Jamestown 45335
Jasper, *Fayette* (Twp) 43128
Jasper, *Pike* 45642
Jasper Mills 43160
Jays 45331
Jefferson, *Adams* (Twp) 45684
Jefferson, *Brown* (Twp) 45168
Jefferson, *Clinton* (Twp) 45148
Jefferson, *Coshocton* (Twp) 43844
Jefferson, *Crawford* (Twp) 44827
Jefferson, *Fayette* (Twp) 43128
Jefferson, *Franklin* (Twp) 43004
Jefferson, *Greene* (Twp) 45335
Jefferson, *Guernsey* (Twp) 43755
Jefferson, *Jackson* (Twp) 45656
Jefferson, *Knox* (Twp) 44628
Jefferson, *Logan* (Twp) 43311
Jefferson, *Madison* (Twp) 43162
Jefferson, *Mercer* (Twp) 45822
Jefferson, *Montgomery* (Twp) 45345
Jefferson, *Muskingum* (Twp) 43821
Jefferson, *Noble* (Twp) 43724
Jefferson, *Preble* (Twp) 45347
Jefferson, *Richland* (Twp) 44813
Jefferson, *Ross* (Twp) 45601
Jefferson, *Scioto* (Twp) 45648
Jefferson, *Tuscarawas* (Twp) 43840
Jefferson, *Williams* (Twp) 43543
Jefferson, *Ashtabula* 44047
Jefferson, *Fairfield* 43112
Jefferson, *Wayne* 44691
Jefferson Estates 43113
Jefferson Heights 43938
Jeffersonville 43128
Jelloway 43014
Jenera 45841
Jenkins Addition 43701
Jennings, *Putnam* (Twp) 45844
Jennings, *Van Wert* (Twp) 45894
Jep 45659
Jericho 45042
Jerome 43064
Jeromesville 44840
Jerry City 43437
Jersey 43062
Jerusalem, *Lucas* (Twp) 43412
Jerusalem, *Monroe* 43747
Jesse C Owens (Part of Cleveland)‡ 44104
Jewell 43530
Jewett 43986
Jobs 45732
Joetown 43758
Johnson (Twp) 43072
Johnsons Corners (Part of Barberton) 44203
Johnston, *Trumbull* 44417
Johnston, *Tuscarawas* 44622
Johnstown 43031
Johnsville (Part of New Lebanon) 45345
Jonesboro, *Clinton* 45146
Jonesboro, *Fayette* 43160
Jonestown 45894
Jordanville 44432
Joy 43728
Joyce Avenue (Part of Columbus) 43219
Jug Run 43917
Jumbo 43326
Jump 43326
Junction 43512
Junction City 43748
Junior Furnace 45629
Justus 44662
Kalida 45853
Kamms (Part of Cleveland)‡ 44111
Kanauga 45631
Kansas 44841
Karen Woods 45502
Kay 45005
Keays (Part of Middletown) 45044
Keene 43828
Keist Manor 43130
Keith 43724
Kelleys Island 43438
Kellogg Corners 44410
Kelloggsville 44030
Kemp 45806
Kendall Heights 44646
Kenmore (Part of Akron)‡ 44314
Kennard 43009
Kennedy Heights (Part of Cincinnati) 45213
Kennonsburg 43773
Keno 45743
Kenridge (Part of Blue Ash) 45242
Kensington 44427
Kensington Park 45305
Kent 44240
44242-43
For specific ZIP Codes call (888) 275-8777, or your local postmaster.
Kenton 43326
Kenwood, *Hamilton*♦ 45236
Kenwood, *Harrison* 43901
Kenwood (Part of Toledo)‡ 43606
Kenwood Heights (Part of Springfield) 45505
Kenwood Knolls 45236
Kenwood Mall 45236
Kenwood Towne Center 45236
Kerr 45643
Kessler 45383
Kettering‡ 45429
Kettlersville 45336
Key 43933
Kidron 44636
Kieferville 45831
Kilbourne 43032
Kile 43064
Kilgore 43988
Killbuck 44637
Kilvert 45778
Kimball 44847
Kimberly 45764
Kimbolton 43749
Kingman 45177
King Mines 43755
Kings Corners 44904
Kings Creek 43078
Kingsdale Center (Part of Columbus) 43221
Kingsgate 45231
Kingsgate Mall (Part of Mansfield) 44901
Kings Mills 45034
Kingston, *Delaware* (Twp) 43074
Kingston, *Ross* 45644
Kingsville 44048
Kingsville On-the-Lake (Part of North Kingsville) 44068
Kingsway 43420
Kinnikinnick 45601
Kinsman, *Belmont* 43950
Kinsman, *Trumbull* 44428
Kiousville 43143
Kipling 43750
Kipton 44049
Kirby 43330
Kirkersville 43033
Kirkpatrick 43302
Kirkwood, *Belmont* (Twp) 43713
Kirkwood, *Shelby* 45365
Kirkwood Heights 43912
Kirtland 44094
Kirtland Hills 44060
Kitchen 45656
Kitts Hill 45645
Kiwanis Lake 44065
Klondike 44410
Knockemstiff 45601
Knollwood (Part of Beavercreek) 45432
Knollwood Village 43113
Knox, *Columbiana* (Twp) 44634
Knox, *Guernsey* (Twp) 43725
Knox, *Holmes* (Twp) 44638
Knox, *Jefferson* (Twp) 43964
Knox, *Vinton* (Twp) 45710
Knoxville 43964
Kolmont 43938
Kossuth 45887
Kunkle 43531
Kyger 45620
La Belle View (Part of Steubenville) 43952
Lacarne 43439
La Croft♦ 43920
Lafayette, *Coshocton* (Twp) 43845
Lafayette, *Allen* 45854
Lafayette, *Madison* 43140
Lafayette, *Medina* 44256
Lafferty 43951
Lagonda (Part of Springfield) 45503
La Grange, *Lawrence* 45638
Lagrange, *Lorain* 44050
Laings 43752
Lake, *Ashland* (Twp) 44628
Lake, *Logan* (Twp) 43311
Lake, *Stark* (Twp) 44720
Lake, *Wood* (Twp) 43447
Lake Cable 44718
Lake Fork 44840
Lakeline 44094
Lake Lorelel 45118
Lake Lucerne 44022
Lake Milton 44429
Lakemore 44250
Lake of the Woods 43021
Lake O'Springs 44718
Lake Seneca 43543
Lakeside (Part of Buckeye Lake) 43008
Lakeside (Part of Middletown) 45042
Lakeside, *Fairfield* 43046
Lakeside, *Ottawa* 43440
Lakeside-Marblehead (Part of Marblehead) 43440
Lake Slagle 44720
Lake Sylvan 45369
Lake View, *Knox* 43019
Lakeview, *Logan* 43331
Lakeview Heights 45690
Lakeville (Part of Conneaut) 44030
Lakeville, *Holmes* 44638

Place	ZIP Code
Lake Waynoka	45171
Lakewood	44107
Lakota Hills	45069
Lamira	43718
Lancaster	43130
Landeck	45833
Landen♦	45040
Langsville	45741
Lanier (Twp)	45381
Lansing	43934
LaPorte	44035
Lapperel	45660
La Rue	43332
Latcha	43447
Latham	45646
Latimer	44428
Lattasburg	44287
Lattaville	45628
Latty (Twp)	45849
Latty	45855
Laura	45337
Laurel, *Hocking* (Twp)	43149
Laurel, *Clermont*	45157
Laurel Creek	44212
Laurel Ridge	44721
Laurelville	43135
Lawco Lake	45659
Lawndale (Part of Massillon)	44646
Lawrence, *Lawrence* (Twp)	45645
Lawrence, *Stark* (Twp)	44614
Lawrence, *Tuscarawas* (Twp)	44612
Lawrence, *Washington* (Twp)	45750
Lawrence, *Lawrence*	45659
Lawrenceville	45502
Lawshe	45660
Layhigh	45013
Layland	44637
Layman	45724
Leaper	45631
Leavittsburg	44430
Leavittsville	44614
Lebanon, *Meigs* (Twp)	45770
Lebanon, *Monroe*	45745
Lebanon, *Warren*	45036
Lecta	45678
Lee, *Athens* (Twp)	45710
Lee, *Carroll* (Twp)	44615
Lee, *Monroe* (Twp)	43946
Lee (Part of Shaker Heights)‡	44120
Leesburg, *Union* (Twp)	43040
Leesburg, *Highland*	45135
Lees Creek	45138
Leesville, *Carroll*	44639
Leesville, *Crawford*	44827
Leetonia	44431
Lehmkuhl Landing	45865
Leipsic	45856
Leipsic Junction (Part of Leipsic)	45856
Leistville	43113
Lemert	44882
Lemon (Twp)	45050
Lemoyne	43441
Lena	45317
Lenox	44047
Leo	45640
Leon	44003
Leonardsburg	43015
Lerado	45176
Leroy (Twp)	44077
Le Sourdsville	45042
Lester	44256
Letart (Twp)	45771
Letart Falls	45771
Levanna	45167
Lewis (Twp)	45121
Lewis Addition	43953
Lewisburg	45338
Lewis Center	43035
Lewistown	43333
Lewisville	43754
Lexington, *Richland*	44904
Lexington, *Stark*	44601
Liberty, *Adams* (Twp)	45693
Liberty, *Butler* (Twp)	45011
Liberty, *Clinton* (Twp)	45177
Liberty, *Crawford* (Twp)	44881
Liberty, *Darke* (Twp)	45352
Liberty, *Delaware* (Twp)	43065
Liberty, *Fairfield* (Twp)	43105
Liberty, *Guernsey* (Twp)	43725
Liberty, *Hancock* (Twp)	45840
Liberty, *Hardin* (Twp)	45810
Liberty, *Henry* (Twp)	43532
Liberty, *Highland* (Twp)	45133
Liberty, *Jackson* (Twp)	45640
Liberty, *Knox* (Twp)	43050
Liberty, *Licking* (Twp)	43031
Liberty, *Logan* (Twp)	43357
Liberty, *Mercer* (Twp)	45882
Liberty, *Putnam* (Twp)	45856
Liberty, *Ross* (Twp)	45647
Liberty, *Seneca* (Twp)	44841
Liberty, *Trumbull* (Twp)	44420
Liberty, *Union* (Twp)	43040
Liberty, *Van Wert* (Twp)	45891
Liberty, *Washington* (Twp)	45745
Liberty, *Wood* (Twp)	43462
Liberty, *Montgomery*	45418
Liberty Center	43532
Liberty Plaza	44505
Lick (Twp)	45640
Licking, *Licking* (Twp)	43076
Licking, *Muskingum* (Twp)	43830
Licking View	43701
Liebs Island	43046
Lightsville	45362
Lilly Chapel	43140
Lima, *Licking* (Twp)	43073
Lima, *Allen*	45801-07
For specific ZIP Codes call (888) 275-8777, or your local postmaster.	
Limaville	44640
Lime City	43551
Limecrest	45502
Limerick	45601
Limestone	43432
Limestone City	45506
Lincoln (Twp)	43321
Lincoln Heights (Part of Steubenville)	43952
Lincoln Heights, *Hamilton*	45215
Lincoln Heights, *Richland*	44903
Lincoln Knolls Plaza (Part of Youngstown)	44505
Lincoln Village♦	43228
Lindair Estates	45502
Lindale	45102
Linden Station (Part of Columbus)‡	43211
Lindentree	44656
Lindenwald (Part of Hamilton)	45015
Lindsey	43442
Lindsley-Gay	44003
Linndale	44135
Linneman	45804
Linnville, *Lawrence*	45696
Linnville, *Licking*	43076
Linton (Twp)	43836
Linwood (Part of Cincinnati)	45226
Linworth	43085
Lippincott	43078
Lisbon, *Clark*	45368
Lisbon, *Columbiana*	44432
Lisman	45659
Litchfield	44253
Lithopolis	43136
Little Farms	43228
Little Hocking	45742
Little Sandusky	43323
Little Walnut	43113
Little Washington	44903
Little York	45414
Liverpool, *Columbiana* (Twp)	43920
Liverpool, *Medina* (Twp)	44280
Livingston (Part of Columbus)‡	43227
Lloydsville	43950
Lock	43011
Lockbourne	43137
Lockington	45356
Lockland	45215
Lock Two	45869
Lockville	43112
Lockwood	44450
Lockwood Corners	44319
Locust Corner	45245
Locust Grove, *Adams*	45660
Locust Grove, *Butler*	45042
Locust Grove, *Mahoning*	44460
Locust Lake	45102
Locust Point	43449
Locust Ridge	45176
Lodi, *Athens* (Twp)	45735
Lodi, *Medina*	44254
Logan, *Auglaize* (Twp)	45887
Logan, *Hocking*	43138
Logan Elm Village♦	43113
Logansville	43318
Logtown	44432
Lombardsville	45652
London, *Madison*	43140
London, *Richland*	44875
Londonderry, *Guernsey*	43973
Londonderry, *Ross*	45647
Long	45331
Long Beach	43449
Long Bottom	45743
Long Lake	44638
Long Run	43917
Longs Crossing	44431
Longstreth	45764
Longview Heights (Part of Athens)	45701
Longvue (Part of Marietta)	45750
Loomis	43718
Lorain	44052-53
	44055
For specific ZIP Codes call (888) 275-8777, or your local postmaster.	
Loramie (Twp)	45363
Lordstown	44481
Lore City	43755
Lostcreek (Twp)	45312
Lost Creek Addition	45804
Lottridge	45723
Louden, *Adams*	45660
Louden, *Tuscarawas*	44622
Loudon, *Carroll* (Twp)	44615
Loudon, *Seneca* (Twp)	44830
Loudonville	44842
Louisville, *Adams*	45660
Louisville, *Stark*	44641
Loveland	45140
Loveland Park♦	45039
	45140
For specific ZIP Codes call (888) 275-8777, or your local postmaster.	
Lovell	43351
Lowell	45744
Lowellville	44436
Lowellville Junction (Part of Lowellville)	44436
Lower Salem	45745
Loyal Oak (Part of Norton)	44203
Lucas	44843
Lucasburg	43723
Lucasville♦	45648
Lucerne	43019
Luckey	43443
Ludington	43730
Ludlow (Twp)	45734
Ludlow Falls	45339
Lugbill Addition (Part of Archbold)	43502
Lumberton	45177
Luray	43025
Lush Addition	43302
Lykens	44818
Lyme (Twp)	44811
Lynchburg, *Columbiana*	44427
Lynchburg, *Highland*	45142
Lyndhurst	44124
Lyndon	45681
Lynn (Twp)	43326
Lynns Corners	44406
Lynx	45650
Lyons	43533
Lyra	45694
Lytle	45068
McArthur, *Logan* (Twp)	43324
McArthur, *Vinton*	45651
McCance	44627
Mc Cappin Mill	45133
McCartyville	45302
McClainville	43906
McClimansville	43143
McClintocksburg	44444
McClure	43534
McComb	45858
McConnelsville	43756
McCracken Corners	44460
McCuneville	43782
McCutchenville	44844
McDermott	45652
McDonald, *Hardin* (Twp)	43326
McDonald, *Trumbull*	44437
McDonaldsville	44720
Macedon	45828
Macedonia	44056
McGill	45880
McGonigle	45013
Mc Gough	43050
McGuffey	45859
McGuffey Heights (Part of Youngstown)	44505
McIntyre	43910
Mack	45248
McKay	44842
McKean (Twp)	43055
McKinley Heights	44446
Mack North♦	45211
Macksburg	45746
Mackstown	43081
McLean (Twp)	45845
McLuney	43731
McMorran	43311
Macon	45697
McZena	44638
Madeira	45243
Madison, *Butler* (Twp)	45042
Madison, *Clark* (Twp)	45368
Madison, *Columbiana* (Twp)	43968
Madison, *Fairfield* (Twp)	43130
Madison, *Fayette* (Twp)	43160
Madison, *Franklin* (Twp)	43125
Madison, *Guernsey* (Twp)	43773
Madison, *Hancock* (Twp)	45814
Madison, *Highland* (Twp)	45123
Madison, *Jackson* (Twp)	45656
Madison, *Licking* (Twp)	43055
Madison, *Montgomery* (Twp)	45426
Madison, *Muskingum* (Twp)	43821
Madison, *Perry* (Twp)	43760
Madison, *Pickaway* (Twp)	43103
Madison, *Richland* (Twp)	44903
Madison, *Sandusky* (Twp)	43435
Madison, *Scioto* (Twp)	45653
Madison, *Vinton* (Twp)	45698
Madison, *Williams* (Twp)	43554
Madison, *Lake*	44057
Madisonburg	44691
Madison Hill	44691
Madison Lake Area	43140
Madison Mills	43143
Madison-on-the-Lake	44057
Madisonville (Part of Cincinnati)	45227
Mad River, *Champaign* (Twp)	43083
Mad River, *Clark* (Twp)	45324
Magnetic Springs	43036
Magnolia	44643
Mahoning	44231
Maineville	45039
Mainsville	43764
Malaga	43757
Malinta	43535
Mall at Fairfield Commons, The (Part of Beavercreek)	45430
Mallet Creek	44256
Malta	43758
Malvern	44644
Manchester, *Morgan* (Twp)	43756
Manchester, *Adams*	45144
Manchester, *Summit*	44216
Mandale	45827
Manhattan (Part of Steubenville)	43952
Manhassett Village (Part of Mason)	45040
Mansfield	44901-07
For specific ZIP Codes call (888) 275-8777, or your local postmaster.	
Mantua	44255
Mantua Center	44255
Mantua Corners	44255
Maple	45130
Maple Corner	45385
Maple Grove, *Geauga*	44231
Maple Grove, *Ross*	45601
Maple Grove, *Seneca*	44883
Maple Heights, *Cuyahoga*	44137
Maple Heights, *Noble*	43724
Maple Lake	43944
Maple Park	45040
Maple Ridge♦	44601
Mapleshade (Part of Gallipolis)	45631
Mapleton	44730
Maple Valley (Part of Akron)‡	44320
Maplewood	45340
Marathon	45145
Marble Cliff	43212
Marble Furnace	45660
Marblehead	43440
Marchand	44720
Marcy	43110
Marengo	43334
Margaretta (Twp)	44824
Maria Stein	45860
Mariemont	45227
Marietta	45750
Marion, *Allen* (Twp)	45833
Marion, *Clinton* (Twp)	45107
Marion, *Fayette* (Twp)	43145
Marion, *Hancock* (Twp)	45840
Marion, *Hardin* (Twp)	45812
Marion, *Henry* (Twp)	43524
Marion, *Hocking* (Twp)	43138
Marion, *Marion* (Twp)	43302
Marion, *Mercer* (Twp)	45883
Marion, *Morgan* (Twp)	43728
Marion, *Noble* (Twp)	43788
Marion, *Pike* (Twp)	45613
Marion, *Marion*	43301†
	43302*
Marion East	43302
Mark (Twp)	43556
Mark Center	43536
Marlain Acres	45231
Marlboro, *Delaware* (Twp)	43015
Marlboro, *Stark*	44601
Marne	43055
Marquis	44406
Marr	43789
Marseilles	43351
Marshall	45133
Marshallville	44645
Martel	43335
Martin	43445
Martinsburg	43037
Martins Ferry	43935
Martinsville	45146
Mary Ann (Twp)	43055
Marygrove	43558
Marysville	43040
Mason, *Lawrence* (Twp)	45696
Mason, *Warren*	45040
Mason Heights (Part of Mason)	45040
Massie (Twp)	45032
Massieville	45601
Massillon	44646-48
For specific ZIP Codes call (888) 275-8777, or your local postmaster.	
Masury	44438
Matville	43146
Maud	45069
Maumee	43537
Maustown	45011
Maximo	44650
Maxville	43748
Mayfield (Part of Middletown)	45044
Mayfield, *Cuyahoga*	44143
Mayfield Heights	44124
Mayflower Village (Part of Massillon)	44647
May Hill	45679
Maynard	43937
Maysville, *Allen*	45810
Maysville, *Wayne*	44606
Mead (Twp)	43947
Meade	45644
Meadowbrook	43701
Meadowbrook Lake (Part of Stow)	44224
Meadow Lawn (Part of Middletown)	45044
Mecca	44410
Mechanic (Twp)	43804
Mechanicsburg, *Champaign*	43044
Mechanicsburg, *Crawford*	44887
Mechanicsburg, *Monroe*	43793
Mechanicsburg, *Wayne*	44691
Mechanicstown	44651
Mechanicsville	44041
Medina (Twp)	44256
Medina	44256*
	44258†
Medway	45341

Place	ZIP
Meeker	43302
Meigs, *Adams* (Twp)	45660
Meigs, *Muskingum* (Twp)	43727
Meigs, *Morgan*	43756
Meigsville (Twp)	43756
Melbern	43506
Melmore	44845
Melrose	45861
Melvin	45177
Memphis	45135
Mendon	45862
Mentor	44060*
	44061†
Mentor Headlands (Part of Mentor)	44060
Mentor-on-the-Lake	44060
Mercer	45862
Mercerville	45631
Mermill	43451
Mesopotamia	44439
Metamora	43540
Metham	43844
Metzger	45601
Mexico	44882
Meyers Lake	44730
Miami, *Clermont* (Twp)	45147
Miami, *Greene* (Twp)	45387
Miami, *Hamilton* (Twp)	45002
Miami, *Logan* (Twp)	43343
Miami, *Montgomery* (Twp)	45342
Miami, *Hamilton*	45041
Miami Heights	45002
Miamisburg	45342*
	45343†
Miami Shores (Part of Moraine)	45439
Miamitown	45041
Miami Township (Part of Centerville)‡	45475
Miami University (Part of Oxford)‡	45056
Miami Valley Center Mall (Part of Piqua)	45356
Miami Villa (Part of Huber Heights)	45424
Miamiville	45147
Michael Manor	45371
Mid City (Part of Dayton)‡	45402
Middle Bass	43446
Middleboro	45152
Middlebourne	43773
Middlebranch	44652
Middleburg, *Jefferson*	43903
Middleburg, *Logan*	43336
Middleburg, *Noble*	43724
Middleburg Heights	44130
Middlebury, *Knox* (Twp)	43019
Middlebury, *Van Wert*	45832
Middlefield	44062
Middle Point	45863
Middleport	45760
Middleton, *Columbiana* (Twp)	44455
Middleton, *Wood* (Twp)	43525
Middleton, *Columbiana*	44408
Middleton, *Jackson*	45692
Middleton Corner	45385
Middletown, *Butler*	45042-44
For specific ZIP Codes call (888) 275-8777, or your local postmaster.	
Middletown, *Champaign*	43009
Middletown, *Crawford*	44833
Midland	45148
Midpark (Part of Parma Heights)	44130
Midtown (Part of Zanesville)‡	43701*
	43702†
Midvale	44653
Midway	43950
Midway Mall (Part of Elyria)	44035
Mifflin, *Franklin* (Twp)	43230
Mifflin, *Pike* (Twp)	45646
Mifflin, *Richland* (Twp)	44843
Mifflin, *Wyandot* (Twp)	43351
Mifflin, *Ashland*	44805
Mifflinville (Part of Columbus)	43224
Milan	44846
Milford, *Butler* (Twp)	45004
Milford, *Defiance* (Twp)	43526
Milford, *Knox* (Twp)	43011
Milford, *Clermont*	45150
Milford Center	43045
Mill (Twp)	44683
Millbrook	44691
Millbury	43447
Mill Creek, *Coshocton* (Twp)	44654
Millcreek, *Union* (Twp)	43040
Mill Creek, *Williams* (Twp)	43501
Milledgeville	43142
Miller, *Knox* (Twp)	43050
Miller, *Lawrence*	45623
Miller City	45864
Millers	45383
Millersburg	44654
Millersport	43046
Miller Station	43976
Millerstown	43072
Millersville	43435
Millertown	43730
Millfield	45761
Milligan	43731
Millport, *Columbiana*	44427
Millport, *Pickaway*	43103
Millville, *Butler*	45013
Millville, *Mahoning*	44460
Millwood, *Guernsey* (Twp)	43773
Millwood, *Knox*	43028
Milton, *Ashland* (Twp)	44805
Milton, *Jackson* (Twp)	45692
Milton, *Mahoning* (Twp)	44429
Milton, *Wayne* (Twp)	44270
Milton, *Wood* (Twp)	43441
Milton Center	43541
Miltonsburg	43793
Miltonville	45042
Mineral	45766
Mineral City	44656
Mineral Ridge♦	44440
Minersville	45769
Minerva	44657
Minerva Park	43231
Mineyahta on-The-Bay	43440
Minford	45653
Mingo	43047
Mingo Junction	43938
Minster	45865
Misco, *Morgan*	43731
Misco, *Perry*	43731
Mishler	44260
Mississinawa (Twp)	45390
Mitiwanga	44839
Mizer Addition	43832
Modest	45122
Modoc	45732
Moffit Heights	44646
Moffitt	45816
Mogadore	44260
Mohawk	43844
Mohawk Lake	44883
Mohican (Twp)	44840
Mohicanville	44840
Moline	43465
Momeneetown (Part of Oregon)	43616
Monclova	43542
Monclova Gardens (Part of Maumee)	43537
Monday Creek (Twp)	43138
Monfort Heights	45239
Monfort Heights East♦	45239
Monfort Heights South♦	45239
Monnette	43302
Monroe, *Adams* (Twp)	45144
Monroe, *Allen* (Twp)	45807
Monroe, *Ashtabula* (Twp)	44030
Monroe, *Carroll* (Twp)	44620
Monroe, *Clermont* (Twp)	45148
Monroe, *Coshocton* (Twp)	43844
Monroe, *Darke* (Twp)	45358
Monroe, *Guernsey* (Twp)	43749
Monroe, *Harrison* (Twp)	44695
Monroe, *Henry* (Twp)	43535
Monroe, *Holmes* (Twp)	44654
Monroe, *Knox* (Twp)	43050
Monroe, *Licking* (Twp)	43031
Monroe, *Logan* (Twp)	43360
Monroe, *Madison* (Twp)	43140
Monroe, *Miami* (Twp)	45371
Monroe, *Muskingum* (Twp)	43762
Monroe, *Perry* (Twp)	43730
Monroe, *Pickaway* (Twp)	43143
Monroe, *Preble* (Twp)	45338
Monroe, *Putnam* (Twp)	45831
Monroe, *Richland* (Twp)	44843
Monroe, *Butler*	45050
Monroe Center	44030
Monroe Mills	43028
Monroeville, *Huron*	44847
Monroeville, *Jefferson*	43945
Monterey, *Putnam* (Twp)	45833
Monterey, *Clermont*	45103
Montezuma	45866
Montgomery, *Ashland* (Twp)	44805
Montgomery, *Marion* (Twp)	43332
Montgomery, *Wood* (Twp)	43466
Montgomery, *Hamilton*	45242
Montgomery Heights (Part of Montgomery)	45242
Monticello	45887
Montpelier	43543
Montra	45302
Montrose	44333
Montville, *Medina* (Twp)	44256
Montville, *Geauga*	44064
Moorefield, *Clark* (Twp)	45502
Moorefield, *Harrison*	43907
Moores Fork	45107
Moores Junction	43731
Mooresville	45601
Moraine	45439
Moreland	44691
Moreland Hills	44022
Morgan, *Ashtabula* (Twp)	44084
Morgan, *Butler* (Twp)	45053
Morgan, *Gallia* (Twp)	45686
Morgan, *Knox* (Twp)	43050
Morgan, *Morgan* (Twp)	43756
Morgan, *Scioto* (Twp)	45648
Morgan Center	45686
Morgandale	44481
Morgan Place (Part of Englewood)	45322
Morgansville	43758
Morgantown, *Mahoning*	44514
Morgantown, *Pike*	45612
Morges	44688
Morning Sun	45311
Morning View Court (Part of Orrville)	44667
Morral	43337
Morris (Twp)	43019
Morris Apartments	45414
Morristown, *Athens*	45761
Morristown, *Belmont*	43759
Morrisville	45146
Morrow	45152
Moscow	45153
Moss Run	45750
Moulton	45895
Moultrie	44657
Moundbuilders (Part of Newark)‡	43055
Moundsville	43724
Mount Adams (Part of Cincinnati)	45202
Mount Air	43085
Mount Airy (Part of Cincinnati)	45224
	45239
For specific ZIP Codes call (888) 275-8777, or your local postmaster.	
Mount Auburn (Part of Cincinnati)	45219
Mount Blanchard	45867
Mount Carmel, *Clermont*♦	45245
Mount Carmel, *Sandusky*	43410
Mount Carmel Heights	45244
Mount Cory	45868
Mount Eaton	44659
Mount Ephraim	43779
Mount Everett (Part of Marietta)	45750
Mount Forest Trails	45244
Mount Gilead	43338
Mount Healthy	45231
Mount Healthy Heights	45231
Mount Holly, *Clermont*	45102
Mount Holly, *Warren*	45068
Mount Hope	44660
Mount Jefferson	45333
Mount Joy	45657
Mount Liberty	43048
Mount Lookout (Part of Cincinnati)	45226
Mount Olive	45106
Mount Orab	45154
Mount Perry	43760
Mount Pisgah	45157
Mount Pleasant, *Hocking*	43138
Mount Pleasant, *Jefferson*	43939
Mount Pleasant, *Sandusky*	44811
Mount Pleasant, *Stark*	44720
Mount Repose♦	45140
Mount Sterling	43143
Mount St. Joseph	45051
Mount Union (Part of Alliance)‡	44601
Mount Vernon	43050
Mount Victory	43340
Mount View	45133
Mountville	45732
Mount Washington (Part of Cincinnati)‡	45230
Mowrystown	45155
Moxahala	43761
Moxahala Park	43701
Mudsock, *Franklin*	43026
Mudsock, *Gallia*	45658
Muhlenberg (Twp)	43146
Mulberry♦	45150
Mule Town	45653
Muncie Hollow	43420
Munroe Falls	44262
Munson (Twp)	44024
Munson Hill	44004
Murdock	45140
Murlin Heights	45414
Murray City	43144
Museville	43720
Muskingum, *Muskingum* (Twp)	43830
Muskingum, *Washington* (Twp)	45744
Mutual	43044
Myersville	44685
Myrtle Brook	45140
Myrtle Village	45140
Naceville	45646
Nankin	44848
Napoleon	43545
Nashport	43830
Nashville, *Darke*	45331
Nashville, *Holmes*	44661
Nashville, *Miami*	45373
National Road	43025
Navarre	44662
Neapolis	43547
Neave (Twp)	45331
Needmore	45833
Neel	45167
Neelysville	43756
Neffs♦	43940
Negley	44441
Nellie	43844
Nelson	44231
Nelsonville	45764
Neptune	45822
Nettle Lake	43543
Nevada	44849
Neville	45156
New Albany, *Franklin*	43054
New Albany, *Mahoning*	44460
New Alexander	44625
New Alexandria	43938
New Antioch	45177
Newark (Twp)	43055
Newark	43055-58
For specific ZIP Codes call (888) 275-8777, or your local postmaster.	
Newark Air Force Station	43057
New Athens	43981
New Baltimore, *Hamilton*	45030
New Baltimore, *Stark*	44601
New Bavaria	43548
New Bedford	43804
Newberry (Twp)	45318
New Bloomington	43341
New Boston	45662
New Bremen	45869
New Buffalo	44406
Newburg (Part of Cleveland)‡	44105
Newburgh Heights	44105
New Burlington	45231
Newbury	44065
New California	43064
New Carlisle	45344
New Castle, *Belmont*	43716
Newcastle, *Coshocton*	43843
New Castle, *Lawrence*	45638
New Cleveland	45875
Newcomerstown	43832
New Concord	43762
New Cumberland	44656
New Dover	43040
Newell	43941
Newell Run	45768
New England	45778
Newfain	45660
New Floodwood	45764
New Franklin	44657
New Garden	44423
New Germany (Part of Beavercreek)	45431
New Guilford	43843
New Hagerstown	44695
New Hampshire	45870
New Harmony	45154
New Harrisburg	44615
New Harrison	45331
New Haven, *Hamilton*	45030
New Haven, *Huron*	44850
New Holland	43145
Newhope, *Brown*	45121
New Hope, *Preble*	45320
New Jasper	45385
New Jerusalem	43311
New Knoxville	45871
New Lebanon	45345
New Lexington, *Perry*	43764
New Lexington, *Preble*	45381
New Liberty	44413
New London	44851
New Lyme	44085
New Madison	45346
Newman	44646
New Market	45133
Newmarket Station (Part of Canton)‡	44701†
	44702*
New Marshfield	45766
New Martinsburg	45123
New Matamoras	45767
New Miami	45011
New Middletown	44442
New Moorefield	45502
New Moscow	43812
New Palestine	45157
New Paris	45347
New Petersburg	45123
New Philadelphia	44663
New Pittsburg	44691
New Pittsburgh	44865
New Plymouth	45654
New Plymouth Heights	45629
Newport, *Madison*	43140
Newport, *Shelby*	45845
Newport, *Tuscarawas*	44683
Newport, *Washington*	45768
New Princeton	43844
New Reading	43783
New Richland	43310
New Richmond	45157
New Riegel	44853
New Rochester	43450
New Rome	43228
New Rumley	43984
New Russia (Twp)	44074
New Salem	43148
New Salisbury	43930
New Somerset	43964
New Springfield	44443
New Stark	45897
New Straitsville	43766
New Strasburg	43102
Newton, *Licking* (Twp)	43055
Newton, *Miami* (Twp)	45339
Newton, *Muskingum* (Twp)	43735
Newton, *Pike* (Twp)	45661
Newton, *Trumbull* (Twp)	44444
Newton Falls	44444
Newtonsville	45158
Newtown, *Hamilton*	45244-45
For specific ZIP Codes call (888) 275-8777, or your local postmaster.	
Newtown, *Jefferson*	43917
Newtowne Mall (Part of New Philadelphia)	44663
New Vienna	45159
Newville	44864
New Washington	44854
New Waterford	44445
New Weston	45348
New Westville	47374
New Winchester	44820
Ney	43549
Nicholsville	45106

Place	ZIP Code
Nile (Twp)	45630
Niles	44446
Nimishillen (Twp)	44641
Nimisila	44216
Nipgen	45612
Noble, *Auglaize* (Twp)	45885
Noble, *Defiance* (Twp)	43512
Noble, *Noble* (Twp)	43724
Normandy Heights	45015
Norris	45383
North (Twp)	43988
North Akron (Part of Akron)	44310
Northampton (Twp)	44221
North Auburn	44887
North Baltimore	45872
North Bend	45052
North Benton, *Mahoning*	44449
North Benton, *Portage*	44449
North Berne	43130
North Bloomfield, *Morrow* (Twp)	44833
North Bloomfield, *Trumbull*	44450
North Brewster (Part of Brewster)	44613
North Bristol	44402
Northbrook	45231
	45251
For specific ZIP Codes call (888) 275-8777, or your local postmaster.	
North Canton	44720
North Clippinger (Part of The Village of Indian Hill)	45243
North College Hill	45231
	45239
For specific ZIP Codes call (888) 275-8777, or your local postmaster.	
North Condit	43074
North Creek	45831
North Dayton, *Darke*	45390
North Dayton (Part of Dayton)‡	45404
Northeast (Part of Columbus)‡	43231
North East Waterworks (Part of Canton)‡	44705
North Eaton	44044
North Fairfield	44855
North Feesburg	45130
Northfield	44067
Northfield Center	44067
North Findlay	45840
North Fork Village♦	45601
North Georgetown	44665
North Greenfield	43358
North Hampton	45349
North Hill (Part of Akron)‡	44310
North Hills Estates	45224
North Houston	45333
North Industry	44707
North Jackson	44451
North Kenova (Part of South Point)	45680
North Kingsville	44068
Northland (Part of Columbus)‡	43229
Northland Mall (Part of Columbus)	43229
North Lawrence	44666
North Lewisburg	43060
North Liberty	44822
North Lima	44452
North Madison	44057
North Monroeville	44847
Northmoor	45315
North Moreland (Part of Portsmouth)	45662
North Mount Vernon	43050
North Olmsted	44070
North Perry	44081
North Randall	44128
North Richmond	44003
Northridge, *Clark*♦	45502
Northridge, *Montgomery*‡	45413†
	45414*
North Ridgeville	44039
North Robinson	44856
North Royalton	44133
North Sagamore Heights	45236
North Salem	43749
North Side (Part of Youngstown)‡	44504
North Star	45350
North Towne Square Mall (Part of Toledo)	43612
North Uniontown	45133
Northup	45658
Northwest, *Williams* (Twp)	43518
Northwest (Part of Columbus)‡	43220
Northwest Plaza (Part of Dayton)	45405
Northwood, *Logan*	43310
Northwood, *Wood*	43619
North Woodbury	44813
North Zanesville♦	43701
Norton, *Delaware*	43356
Norton, *Summit*	44203
Norwalk	44857
Norwich, *Franklin* (Twp)	43026
Norwich, *Huron* (Twp)	44890
Norwich, *Muskingum*	43767
Norwood, *Hamilton*	45212
Norwood (Part of Marietta)	45750
Norwood Heights (Part of Cincinnati)	45212
Nottingham, *Harrison* (Twp)	43907
Nottingham (Part of Cleveland)	44110
Nova	44859
Novelty	44072
Oakdale (Part of Kettering)	45429
Oakdale, *Athens*	45732
Oakdale, *Stark*	44646
Oakfield, *Perry*	43731
Oakfield, *Trumbull*	44450
Oak Grove, *Clark*	45502
Oak Grove, *Washington*	45750
Oak Harbor	43449
Oak Hill	45656
Oakland (Part of Monroe)	45050
Oakland, *Clinton*	45177
Oakland, *Fairfield*	43102
Oakley (Part of Cincinnati)‡	45209
Oakmont	43920
Oak Park	43907
Oak Run (Twp)	43143
Oak Shade	43567
Oakview	45805
Oakwood, *Cuyahoga*	44146
Oakwood, *Montgomery*	45419
Oakwood, *Paulding*	45873
Oberlin	44074
Oberlin Beach	44839
Obetz	43207
Oceola	44860
Oco	43950
O'Connor Landing	43310
Octa	43160
Ogden	45177
Ogontz	44814
Ohio, *Clermont* (Twp)	45157
Ohio, *Gallia* (Twp)	45623
Ohio, *Monroe* (Twp)	43931
Ohio City	45874
Ohio Furnace	45638
Ohio Soldiers and Sailors Home	44870
Okeana	45053
Okolona	43550
Old Towne (Part of Columbus)‡	43205
Old Fort	44861
Old Gore	43138
Old Mill Creek	44212
Old Plymouth Heights	45629
Old Straitsville	43766
Oldtown	45385
Old Washington	43768
Old West End (Part of Toledo)‡	43610
Olena	44857
Olentangy	44820
Olive, *Meigs* (Twp)	45743
Olive, *Noble* (Twp)	43724
Olive Branch	45103
Olive Green, *Delaware*	43074
Olive Green, *Noble*	43724
Oliver (Twp)	45693
Olivesburg	44805
Olivett	43713
Olmsted (Twp)	44138
Olmsted Falls	44138
Olszeski	43917
Omega	45690
Oneida, *Butler*	45042
Oneida, *Carroll*	44644
Ontario	44862
Opperman	43732
Oran	45365
Orange, *Ashland* (Twp)	44805
Orange, *Carroll* (Twp)	44639
Orange, *Delaware* (Twp)	43021
Orange, *Hancock* (Twp)	45817
Orange, *Meigs* (Twp)	45723
Orange, *Shelby* (Twp)	45365
Orange, *Coshocton*	43832
Orange, *Cuyahoga*	44022
Orangeville	44453
Orbiston	45732
Orchard Beach	44089
Orchard Island	43331
Orchard Park Heights	44904
Oregon	43616
	43618
For specific ZIP Codes call (888) 275-8777, or your local postmaster.	
Oregonia	45054
Oreville	43766
Orient	43146
Orland	45654
Orrville	44667
Orwell	44076
Osage	43964
Osgood	45351
Osnaburg (Twp)	44730
Ostrander	43061
Otsego	43762
Ottawa	45875
Ottawa Hills	43606
Otterbein Home	45036
Ottokee	43567
Ottoville	45876
Otway	45657
Outville	43062
Overlook	45431
Overlook Court	43906
Overlook Hills	43953
Overlook Homes	45431
Overpeck	45055
Over The Rhine (Part of Cincinnati)	45210
Overton	44691
Owens Hill	43701
Owensville	45160
Oxford, *Coshocton* (Twp)	43845
Oxford, *Delaware* (Twp)	43003
Oxford, *Erie* (Twp)	44870
Oxford, *Guernsey* (Twp)	43773
Oxford, *Tuscarawas* (Twp)	43832
Oxford, *Butler*	45056
Ozark	43716
Padanaram	44003
Padua	45846
Page Manor	45431
Pagetown	43334
Pageville	45710
Painesville	44077
Painesville on the Lake	44077
Paint, *Fayette* (Twp)	43106
Paint, *Highland* (Twp)	45612
Paint, *Holmes* (Twp)	44690
Paint, *Madison* (Twp)	43140
Paint, *Ross* (Twp)	45612
Paint, *Wayne* (Twp)	44659
Painters Creek	45304
Paintersville	45335
Paint Valley	44654
Palermo	44615
Palestine	45352
Palmer, *Putnam* (Twp)	45831
Palmer, *Washington* (Twp)	43787
Palmyra, *Knox*	43019
Palmyra, *Portage*	44412
Palos	45732
Pancoastburg	43160
Pandora	45877
Pansy	45107
Paradise	44406
Paradise Hill	44805
Paris, *Union* (Twp)	43040
Paris, *Portage*	44266
Paris, *Stark*	44669
Parkdale (Part of Forest Park)	45218
Parkdale (Part of Steubenville)	43952
Parkertown	44824
Park Layne, *Clark*♦	45344
Park Layne, *Montgomery*	45431
Parkman	44080
Park Place (Part of Wyoming)	45215
Park Ridge Acres	45506
Parkview (Part of Fairview Park)	44126
Parkview Heights	45224
Parlett	43907
Parma	44129
Parma Heights	44130
Parmatown Mall (Part of Parma)	44129
Parral	44622
Parrott	43160
Pasadena (Part of Kettering)	45429
Pasco	45365
Pataskala	43062
Patmos	44460
Patriot	45658
Patterson, *Darke* (Twp)	45388
Patterson, *Hardin*	45843
Pattersonville	44657
Pattin Addition (Part of Marietta)	45750
Pattonville	45640
Paulding	45879
Paul Laurence Dunbar (Part of Dayton)‡	45417
Pavonia	44903
Pawnee	44254
Paxton (Twp)	45612
Payne	45880
Peacock Acres	45502
Pearlbrook (Part of Cleveland)‡	44109
Pease (Twp)	43935
Pebble (Twp)	45690
Pedro	45659
Peebles	45660
Pee Pee (Twp)	45690
Pekin, *Carroll*	44657
Pekin, *Jefferson*	43952
Pekin, *Warren*	45036
Pemberton	45353
Pemberville	43450
Penfield (Twp)	44090
Penfield	44052
Peniel	45658
Peninsula	44264
Penn, *Highland* (Twp)	45135
Penn, *Morgan* (Twp)	43787
Pennsville	43770
Penn View	44003
Peoli	43832
Peoria, *Butler*	45056
Peoria, *Union*	43067
Pepper Pike	44124
Perintown	45150
Perkins (Twp)	44870
Perry, *Allen* (Twp)	45806
Perry, *Ashland* (Twp)	44866
Perry, *Brown* (Twp)	45118
Perry, *Carroll* (Twp)	43988
Perry, *Columbiana* (Twp)	44460
Perry, *Coshocton* (Twp)	43843
Perry, *Fayette* (Twp)	45135
Perry, *Franklin* (Twp)	43017
Perry, *Gallia* (Twp)	45658
Perry, *Hocking* (Twp)	43135
Perry, *Lawrence* (Twp)	45638
Perry, *Licking* (Twp)	43055
Perry, *Logan* (Twp)	43319
Perry, *Monroe* (Twp)	43793
Perry, *Montgomery* (Twp)	45309
Perry, *Morrow* (Twp)	44904
Perry, *Muskingum* (Twp)	43701
Perry, *Pickaway* (Twp)	43145
Perry, *Pike* (Twp)	45616
Perry, *Putnam* (Twp)	45837
Perry, *Richland* (Twp)	44813
Perry, *Shelby* (Twp)	45353
Perry, *Stark* (Twp)	44708
Perry, *Tuscarawas* (Twp)	44699
Perry, *Wood* (Twp)	44817
Perry, *Lake*	44081
Perry Addition	45648
Perry Heights♦	44646
Perrysburg (Twp)	43551
Perrysburg	43551*
	43552†
Perrysburg Heights	43551
Perrysville, *Ashland*	44864
Perrysville, *Carroll*	43988
Perryton	43822
Peru, *Huron* (Twp)	44847
Peru, *Morrow* (Twp)	43334
Peru, *Huron*	44857
Petersburg, *Carroll*	44615
Petersburg, *Jackson*	45640
Petersburg, *Mahoning*	44454
Petrea	45640
Petroleum	44438
Pettisville	43553
Pfeiffer Station	43326
Phalanx	44470
Pharisburg	43040
Phillippstown (Part of Columbus)	43201
Phillipsburg	45354
Philo	43771
Philothea	45828
Phoneton	45371
Pickaway (Twp)	43113
Pickerington	43147
Pickrelltown	43357
Piedmont	43983
Pierce (Twp)	45245
Pierpont	44082
Pigeon Creek♦	44321
Pigeon Run	44646
Pike, *Brown* (Twp)	45176
Pike, *Clark* (Twp)	45502
Pike, *Coshocton* (Twp)	43822
Pike, *Fulton* (Twp)	43515
Pike, *Knox* (Twp)	44822
Pike, *Madison* (Twp)	43029
Pike, *Perry* (Twp)	43764
Pike, *Stark* (Twp)	44626
Piketon	45661
Pikeville	45331
Pine Grove	45638
Pinehurst	45750
Pine Valley (Part of Dillonvale)	43917
Piney Fork	43941
Pink	45630
Pinkerman	45682
Pioneer	43554
Piqua	45356
Piqua East Mall (Part of Piqua)	45356
Pisgah	45069
Pitchin	45502
Pitsburg	45358
Pitt (Twp)	43323
Pittlime (Part of Norton)	44203
Pittsburgh Junction	43986
Pittsfield	44090
Placid Meadows	45238
Plain, *Franklin* (Twp)	43081
Plain, *Stark* (Twp)	44708
Plain, *Wayne* (Twp)	44691
Plain, *Wood* (Twp)	43402
Plain City	43064
Plainfield	43836
Plain View	43793
Plankton	44882
Planktown	44878
Plantation Acres	45224
Plants	45771
Plantsville	43728
Plattsburg	45368
Plattsville	45365
Playhouse Square (Part of Cleveland)‡	44115
Pleasant, *Brown* (Twp)	45121
Pleasant, *Clark* (Twp)	43010
Pleasant, *Fairfield* (Twp)	43130
Pleasant, *Franklin* (Twp)	43123
Pleasant, *Hancock* (Twp)	45858
Pleasant, *Hardin* (Twp)	43326
Pleasant, *Henry* (Twp)	43527
Pleasant, *Knox* (Twp)	43050
Pleasant, *Logan* (Twp)	43318
Pleasant, *Madison* (Twp)	43143
Pleasant, *Marion* (Twp)	43302
Pleasant, *Perry* (Twp)	43731
Pleasant, *Putnam* (Twp)	45830
Pleasant, *Seneca* (Twp)	44861
Pleasant, *Van Wert* (Twp)	45891
Pleasant Bend	43548
Pleasant City	43772
Pleasant Corners	43123
Pleasant Grove, *Belmont*	43901
Pleasant Grove, *Muskingum*♦	43701
Pleasant Heights (Part of East Liverpool)	43920
Pleasant Heights (Part of Steubenville)	43952
Pleasant Hill, *Athens*	45701
Pleasant Hill, *Jefferson*	43952

Pleasant Hill, *Miami* 45359
Pleasant Hills 45231
Pleasant Home 44287
Pleasant Lea 43130
Pleasant Plain 45162
Pleasant Ridge (Part of Cincinnati) 45213
Pleasant Run Farm♦ 45240
Pleasant Valley, *Coshocton* 43812
Pleasant Valley, *Pike* 45661
Pleasant Valley, *Ross* 45601
Pleasant Valley, *Vinton* 45601
Pleasant View, *Fayette* 43128
Pleasant View, *Stark* 44705
Pleasantville 43148
Plumwood 43140
Plymouth, *Ashtabula* 44004
Plymouth, *Richland* 44865
Plymouth Center 44004
Poast Town 45042
Point Isabel 45153
Point Place (Part of Toledo)‡ 43611
Point Pleasant 45153
Point Rock 45710
Poland 44514
Poland Center 44436
Polaris (Part of Columbus)‡ 43240
Polk, *Crawford* (Twp) 44833
Polk, *Ashland* 44866
Pomeroy 45769
Pond Run 45684
Poplargrove 45660
Portage, *Hancock* (Twp) 45872
Portage, *Ottawa* (Twp) 43452
Portage, *Wood* 43451
Portage Lakes♦ 44319
Port Clinton 43452
Porter, *Delaware* (Twp) 43074
Porter, *Scioto* (Twp) 45694
Porter, *Gallia* 45614
Porterfield 45714
Portersville 43730
Port Homer 43964
Port Jefferson 45360
Portland 45770
Portsmouth 45662-63
For specific ZIP Codes call (888) 275-8777, or your local postmaster.
Port Union 45015
Port Washington 43837
Port William 45164
Possum Woods 45506
Post Town 45042
Post Town Heights 45042
Potsdam 45361
Pottery Additon 43952
Powell 43065
Powellsville 45629
Powhatan Point 43942
Prairie, *Franklin* (Twp) 43119
Prairie, *Holmes* (Twp) 44633
Prairie Meadows 43812
Pratts Fork 45776
Prattsville 45651
Prentiss 45856
Preston Addition 45648
Price Hill (Part of Cincinnati)‡ 45205
Pricetown, *Highland* 45133
Pricetown, *Trumbull* 44429
Pride 45601
Princeton 45015
Proctor 44266
Proctorville 45669
Prospect 43342
Prout 44870
Providence (Twp) 43504
Provident 43950
Provincial Point 45244
Public Square (Part of Cleveland)‡ 44114
Pulaski 43506
Pulaskiville 43338
Pulse 45118
Pultney (Twp) 43906
Puritas Park (Part of Cleveland)‡ 44135
Purity 43071
Pusheta (Twp) 45895
Put-In-Bay 43456
Putnam Place (Part of Marietta) 45750
Pymatuning Shores 44003
Pyrmont 45309
Pyro 45656
Quaker City 43773
Qualey 45724
Queen Acres 45013
Quincy 43343

Raccoon (Twp) 45685
Racine 45771
Radcliff 45695
Radford Road 45701
Radio Heights 43920
Radnor 43066
Ragersville 44681
Rainsboro 45165
Ra-Mar Estates 45502
Ramsey 43917
Ranchwood 44870
Randall Park Mall (Part of North Randall) 44128
Randolph, *Montgomery* (Twp) 45322
Randolph, *Portage* 44265
Range 43143
Ransom 45381
Rarden 45671
Rathbone, *Delaware* 43015
Rathbone (Part of Marietta) 45750
Rathbone Heights (Part of Marietta) 45750
Ravenna 44266
Ravenna Army Ammunition Plant 44266
Rawson 45881
Ray 45672
Rayland 43943
Raymond 43067
Rays Corners 44047
Reading, *Perry* (Twp) 43783
Reading, *Columbiana* 44634
Reading, *Hamilton* 45215
Recovery (Twp) 45846
Red Bank (Part of Fairfax) 45227
Redbird 44057
Redbush 45742
Red Coach Farm (Part of Centerville) 45429
Redfield 43764
Red Fox 44240
Redhaw 44866
Red Lion 45005
Redoak 45167
Red River 45308
Redtown 45732
Reed (Twp) 44807
Reedsburg 44691
Reedsmills 43910
Reedsville 45772
Reedtown 44807
Reedurban 44710
Reese 43207
Reesville 45166
Reform 43055
Rehoboth 43764
Reily 45056
Reinersville 43756
Reminderville 44202
Remington 45140
Remsen Corners 44256
Rendville 43730
Reno 45773
Reno Beach 43412
Rensselaer Park 45216
Republic 44867
Resaca 43140
Residence Park (Part of Dayton) 45417
Revenge 43130
Reynoldsburg 43068
Reynolds Corner (Part of Toledo)‡ 43615
43617
43635
For specific ZIP Codes call (888) 275-8777, or your local postmaster.
Rialto 45069
Rice, *Sandusky* (Twp) 43420
Rice, *Putnam* 45831
Riceland 44667
Richfield, *Henry* (Twp) 43516
Richfield, *Lucas* (Twp) 43504
Richfield, *Summit* 44286
Richfield Center 43504
Richfield Heights (Part of Richfield) 44286
Rich Hill, *Muskingum* (Twp) 43727
Rich Hill, *Knox* 43011
Richland, *Allen* (Twp) 45817
Richland, *Belmont* (Twp) 43950
Richland, *Clinton* (Twp) 45169
Richland, *Darke* (Twp) 45380
Richland, *Defiance* (Twp) 43512
Richland, *Fairfield* (Twp) 43150

Richland, *Guernsey* (Twp) 43780
Richland, *Holmes* (Twp) 44628
Richland, *Logan* (Twp) 43310
Richland, *Marion* (Twp) 43302
Richland, *Vinton* (Twp) 45651
Richland, *Wyandot* (Twp) 43359
Richland, *Montgomery* 45431
Richland Mall (Part of Ontario) 44906
Richmond, *Ashtabula* (Twp) 44032
Richmond, *Huron* (Twp) 44890
Richmond, *Jefferson* 43944
Richmond Center 44003
Richmond Dale 45673
Richmond Heights 44143
Richmond Mall (Part of Richmond Heights) 44143
Richville 44706
Richwood 43344
Rickard Acres 45005
Ridge, *Van Wert* (Twp) 45891
Ridge, *Wyandot* (Twp) 43316
Ridgefield (Twp) 44847
Ridgeland 45640
Ridgeton 44820
Ridgeville, *Henry* (Twp) 43555
Ridgeville, *Warren* 45036
Ridgeville Corners 43555
Ridgeway 43345
Ridgewood, *Allen* 43701
Ridgewood, *Muskingum* 43821
Ridgewood Heights 45427
Rigrish 45662
Riley, *Putnam* (Twp) 45877
Riley, *Sandusky* (Twp) 43420
Rimer 45830
Rinard Mills 45734
Ringgold, *Morgan* 43758
Ringgold, *Pickaway* 43113
Rio Grande 45674
Ripley, *Holmes* (Twp) 44676
Ripley, *Huron* (Twp) 44837
Ripley, *Brown* 45167
Risingsun 43457
Rittman 44270
River Corners 44275
Riverdale 45661
Riveredge (Twp) 44135
Riverlea 43085
Riverside, *Montgomery* 45424
Riverside (Part of Cincinnati) 45238
Riverside (Part of Sidney) 45365
Riverside Park 44683
River Styx 44256
River Valley Mall (Part of Lancaster) 43130
Riverview, *Belmont* 43906
Riverview, *Washington* 45750
Rix Mills 43762
Roachester 45152
Roads 45640
Roaming Rock Shores 44085
Roaming Shores 44085
Roanoke 44683
Robertsville 44670
Robins 43723
Robtown 43103
Robyville 43901
Rochester 44090
Rochester Place (Part of Northwood) 43618
Rockbridge 43149
Rock Camp, *Columbiana* 44432
Rock Camp, *Lawrence* 45675
Rock Creek 44084
Rockdale 45015
Rockford 45882
Rockhill 43977
Rockland (Part of Belpre) 45714
Rock Mills 43160
Rockport 45830
Rock Way 45504
Rockwood, *Erie* 44824
Rockwood (Part of Chesapeake) 45619
Rocky Fall Estates 45133
Rockyhill 45640
Rocky Point 45502
Rocky Ridge 43458
Rocky River 44116

Rodney 45631
Rogers 44455
Rokeby Lock 43756
Rolandus 45771
Rollersville 43431
Rolling Acres (Part of Akron) 44322
Rolling Mill Park 45044
Rome, *Athens* (Twp) 45723
Rome, *Ashtabula* 44085
Rome, *Lawrence* 45669
Rome, *Richland* 44878
Rome Station 44085
Romohr Acres 45244
Rootstown 44272
Rose (Twp) 44643
Rosedale 43029
Rose Farm 43731
Rose Heights (Part of Steubenville) 43952
Rose Hill 45348
Roseland 44906
Roselawn (Part of Cincinnati)‡ 45237
Roselms 45849
Rosemont 44451
Rosemont Commons (Part of Fairlawn) 44313
Rosemount♦ 45662
Roseville 43777
Rosewood 43070
Roslyn (Part of Kettering) 45429
Ross, *Greene* (Twp) 43153
Ross, *Jefferson* (Twp) 43944
Ross, *Butler*♦ 45061
Rossburg 45362
Rossford 43460
Rossmoyne 45236
Rossville (Part of Hamilton) 45013
Roswell 44663
Round Bottom 43915
Roundhead 43346
Rousculp 45806
Rowsburg 44866
Roxabell 45628
Roxanna 45068
Roxbury 43787
Royalton, *Fulton* (Twp) 43533
Royalton, *Fairfield* 43130
Royersville 45638
Rubyville 45662
Rudolph 43462
Ruggles (Twp) 44851
Ruggles 44837
Ruggles Beach 44839
Rumley, *Harrison* (Twp) 43986
Rumley, *Shelby* 45302
Rural 45120
Ruraldale 43720
Rush, *Champaign* (Twp) 43084
Rush, *Scioto* (Twp) 45652
Rush, *Tuscarawas* (Twp) 44683
Rush Creek, *Fairfield* (Twp) 43107
Rushcreek, *Logan* (Twp) 43347
Rushmore 45844
Rush Run 43943
Rushsylvania 43347
Rushtown 45652
Rushville 43150
Russell, *Geauga* (Twp) 44072
Russell, *Highland* 45133
Russell Center 44072
Russell Heights 43968
Russells 43701
Russells Point 43348
Russellville 45168
Russia, *Lorain* (Twp) 44074
Russia, *Shelby* 45363
Rustic Hills 44256
Rutland 45775
Rye Beach (Part of Huron) 44839
Sabina 45169
Sagamore Hills 44067
Sahara Sands 44646
St. Albans (Twp) 43062
St. Anthony 45846
St. Bernard 45216-17
For specific ZIP Codes call (888) 275-8777, or your local postmaster.
St. Charles 45013
St. Clair, *Butler* (Twp) 45011
St. Clair, *Columbiana* (Twp) 43920
St. Clairsville 43950
St. Henry 45883

St. Joe 43906
St. Johns 45884
St. Joseph, *Williams* (Twp) 43517
St. Joseph, *Mercer* 45846
St. Joseph, *Portage* 44201
St. Louisville 43071
St. Martin 45118
St. Marys 45885
St. Paris 43072
St. Pauls 43103
St. Peters 45846
St. Rosa 45886
St. Sebastian 45826
St. Stephens 44807
St. Wendelin 45883
Salem, *Auglaize* (Twp) 45887
Salem, *Champaign* (Twp) 43078
Salem, *Columbiana* (Twp) 44431
Salem, *Highland* (Twp) 45133
Salem, *Jefferson* (Twp) 43944
Salem, *Meigs* (Twp) 45741
Salem, *Monroe* (Twp) 43915
Salem, *Muskingum* (Twp) 43802
Salem, *Ottawa* (Twp) 43449
Salem, *Shelby* (Twp) 45365
Salem, *Tuscarawas* (Twp) 43832
Salem, *Warren* (Twp) 45152
Salem, *Washington* (Twp) 45745
Salem, *Wyandot* (Twp) 43351
Salem, *Columbiana* 44460
Salem Center 45741
Salem Heights 44460
Salesville 43778
Saline (Twp) 43932
Salineville 43945
Salisbury (Twp) 45769
Saltair 45106
Salt Creek, *Hocking* (Twp) 43135
Salt Creek, *Holmes* (Twp) 44660
Salt Creek, *Muskingum* (Twp) 43727
Salt Creek, *Pickaway* (Twp) 43113
Salt Creek, *Wayne* (Twp) 44627
Saltillo 43777
Salt Lick (Twp) 43782
Salt Rock (Twp) 43337
Salt Run 43943
Samantha 45135
Sand Beach 43449
Sand Hill, *Erie* 44870
Sand Hill, *Scioto* 45694
Sand Hill, *Washington* 45773
Sand Ridge 45761
Sandrun 45764
Sandusky, *Crawford* (Twp) 44887
Sandusky, *Richland* (Twp) 44827
Sandusky, *Sandusky* (Twp) 43420
Sandusky, *Erie* 44870*
44871†
Sandy, *Stark* (Twp) 44688
Sandy, *Tuscarawas* (Twp) 44656
Sandy Beach 45885
Sandy Springs 45684
Sandyville 44671
San Margherita 43204
Santa Fe 45895
Santoy 43730
Sarahsville 43779
Sardinia 45171
Sardis 43946
Savannah 44874
Saville Estates 45431
Savona 45331
Sawyerwood 44312
Saybrook 44004
Saybrook-on-the-Lake 44004
Saylor Park (Part of Cincinnati) 45233
Sayre 43731
Scenic Hills 43162
Schauers Acres 45341
Schley 45768
Schoenbrunn 44663
Schooleys 45601
Schrader 45601
Schumm 45898
Scio 43988
Scioto, *Delaware* (Twp) 43061
Scioto, *Jackson* (Twp) 45640

Scioto, *Pickaway* (Twp) 43103
Scioto, *Pike* (Twp) 45687
Scioto, Ross (Twp) 45601
Sciotodale♦ 45662
Scioto Furnace 45677
Sciotoville (Part of Portsmouth)‡ 45662
Scipio, *Meigs* (Twp) 45710
Scipio, *Seneca* (Twp) 44867
Scipio, *Butler* 45053
Scotch Ridge 43450
Scott, *Adams* (Twp) 45679
Scott, *Brown* (Twp) 45121
Scott, *Marion* (Twp) 43302
Scott, *Sandusky* (Twp) 43435
Scott, *Van Wert* 45886
Scottown 45678
Scotts Crossing 45833
Scotty's Beauty Beach 45822
Scroggsfield 44615
Scrub Ridge 45616
Seal, *Pike* (Twp) 45661
Seal, *Wyandot* 44849
Seaman 45679
Seasons Four 45140
Sebring 44672
Secedar Corners 44425
Sedalia 43151
Sedamsville (Part of Cincinnati) 45233
Seilcrest Acres 45140
Sellers Point 43046
Selma 45368
Seneca, *Monroe* (Twp) 43754
Seneca, *Noble* (Twp) 43779
Seneca, *Seneca* (Twp) 44853
Senecaville 43780
Senior 45152
Sentinel 44032
Seven Hills, *Cuyahoga* 44131
Seven Hills, *Hamilton* 45231
Seven Mile 45062
Seventeen 44629
Severance Town Center (Part of Cleveland Heights) 44118
Seville 44273
Seward 43533
Sewellsville 43713
Shade 45776
Shademore 45244
Shadeville 43137
Shady Bend 43832
Shady Glen 43964
Shady Grove 45324
Shadyside, *Belmont* 43947
Shadyside (Part of East Liverpool) 43920
Shaker Crossing (Part of Kettering) 45429
Shaker Heights 44120
Shalersville (Twp) 44266
Shalersville 44255
Shandon 45063
Shane 43944
Shanesville (Part of Sugarcreek) 44681
Shannon 43821
Sharon, *Franklin* (Twp) 43081
Sharon, *Medina* (Twp) 44274
Sharon, *Richland* (Twp) 44875
Sharon, *Noble* 43724
Sharon Center 44274
Sharon Hills 43085
Sharon Park, *Allen* 45805
Sharon Park, *Butler* 45013
Sharonville 45241
45262
For specific ZIP Codes call (888) 275-8777, or your local postmaster.
Sharon West 44438
Sharpeye 45331
Sharpsburg 45777
Shartz Road 45005
Shauck 43349
Shawnee, *Allen* (Twp) 45805
Shawnee, *Perry* 43782
Shawnee Hills, *Delaware* 43065
Shawnee Hills, *Greene*♦ 45335
Shawnee Meadows 45806
Shawtown 45858
Shawville (Part of North Ridgeville) 44035
Shay 45767
Sheffield, *Ashtabula* (Twp) 44048
Sheffield, *Lorain* 44054
Sheffield Lake 44054
Shelby 44875
Shelby Junction (Part of Shelby) 44875
Shell Beach 43076
Shenandoah 44837
Shepard (Part of Columbus) 43219
Shepherdstown 43950
Sheridan 45680
Sherman, *Huron* (Twp) 44847
Sherman (Part of Mansfield)‡ 44906
Sherman (Part of Norton) 44203
Sherritts 45688
Sherrodsville 44675
Sherwood, *Defiance* 43556
Sherwood, *Hamilton*♦ 45230
Sherwood Park 45805
Shillings Mill 44429
Shiloh, *Clermont* 45122
Shiloh, *Montgomery* 45415
Shiloh, *Richland* 44878
Shinrock 44839
Shore (Part of Euclid) 44123
Shoregate Shopping Center (Part of Willowick) 44095
Short Creek (Twp) 43901
Short Creek 43989
Short North (Part of Columbus)‡ 43201
Shreve 44676
Sidney 45365
Signal 44432
Silica 43560
Silver Creek, *Greene* (Twp) 45335
Silver Creek, *Medina* 44281
Silver Lake 44221
Silverton 45236
Simons 44093
Singing Hills 45440
Sinking Spring 45172
Sitka 45750
Six Corners 43526
Skyline Acres 45231
Skypark 44281
Skyview Acres 43968
Slabtown 45801
Slate Mills 45601
Slaters 43724
Sligo 45177
Slocums 45662
Smith, *Belmont* (Twp) 43718
Smith, *Mahoning* (Twp) 44672
Smith Corners 44515
Smithfield (railroad station) 43943
Smithfield 43948
Smithville, *Wayne* 44677
Smithville, *Wyandot* 43351
Smyrna 43973
Snodes 44609
Snowville 45710
Snyder Terrace (Part of Springfield) 45504
Snyderville 45502
Soaptown 44440
Socialville 45050
Soldiers Home 44870
Solon 44139
Somerdale 44678
Somerford (Twp) 43044
Somers (Twp) 45311
Somerset, *Belmont* (Twp) 43713
Somerset, *Perry* 43783
Somersville 43067
Somerton 43713
Somerville 45064
Sonora 43701
South Amherst 44001
South Arlington (Part of Akron)‡ 44306
South Bay 43019
South Bloomfield, *Morrow* (Twp) 43050
South Bloomfield, *Pickaway* 43103
South Bloomingville 43152
South Boy 43019
Southbrook 45409
South Brooklyn (Part of Cleveland) 44109
South Canal♦ 44444
South Charleston 45368
South Columbus (Part of Columbus)‡ 43207
South Condit 43074
Southdale (Part of Kettering) 45429
Southern Hills (Part of Kettering) 45409
Southern Knoll (Part of Oxford) 45056
Southern Park Mall 44513
South Euclid 44121
South Excello 45042
Southfield Park (Part of Columbus) 43201
Southgate (Part of Springfield) 45506
Southgate Acres 44870
Southgate Shopping Center (Part of Newark) 43056
Southgate U.S.A. (Part of Maple Heights) 44137
South Highlands (Part of Middletown) 45042
South Hill Park 43528
Southington 44470
South Kingman 45177
Southland Shopping Center (Part of Middleburg Heights) 44130
Southland Shopping Center (Part of Toledo) 43614
South Lebanon 45065
South Logan (Part of Logan) 43138
South Lorain (Part of Lorain)‡ 44055
South Madison 44057
South Milford (Part of Milford) 45150
South Moor Shores 45885
South Mount Vernon 43050
South Newbury 44021
South Olive 43724
South Park, *Allen* 45804
South Park (Part of Independence) 44131
South Park (Part of Upper Sandusky) 43351
South Perry 43135
South Plymouth 43160
South Point 45680
Southridge 45505
South Russell 44022
South Salem 45681
South Shore Acres 45885
South Shore Park (Part of Oregon) 43618
South Side (Part of New Philadelphia) 44663
South Side (Part of Youngstown)‡ 44507
South Solon 43153
South Vienna 45369
South Webster 45682
Southwest (Part of Mansfield)‡ 44907
South West Hubbard 44425
Southwood 45805
South Woodbury 43334
Southworth 45833
Southwyck Shopping Center (Part of Toledo) 43614
South Zanesville 43701
Spargursville 45612
Sparta 43350
Speaker's Addition 43952
Speidel 43719
Spencer, *Allen* (Twp) 45887
Spencer, *Guernsey* (Twp) 43732
Spencer, *Lucas* (Twp) 43528
Spencer, *Medina* 44275
Spencerville 45887
Spokane 44402
Spreading Oaks 45701
Spreng 44840
Sprigg (Twp) 45144
Springboro 45066
Springbrook 43464
Springcreek (Twp) 45356
Springdale 45246
Springfield, *Clark* (Twp) 45505
Springfield, *Gallia* (Twp) 45614
Springfield, *Hamilton* (Twp) 45231
Springfield, *Jefferson* (Twp) 43903
Springfield, *Lucas* (Twp) 43528
Springfield, *Mahoning* (Twp) 44442
Springfield, *Muskingum* (Twp) 43701
Springfield, *Richland* (Twp) 44906
Springfield, *Ross* (Twp) 45601
Springfield, *Summit* (Twp) 44312
Springfield, *Williams* (Twp) 43557
Springfield, *Clark* 45501-06
For specific ZIP Codes call (888) 275-8777, or your local postmaster.
Springhills 43318
Spring Meadows 45231
Spring Mill 44903
Spring Mountain 43844
Springvale 45140
Spring Valley (Part of Elyria) 44035
Spring Valley, *Greene* 45370
Spring Valley, *Lucas* 43528
Springville, *Seneca* 43316
Springville, *Wayne* 44676
Springwood 45056
Squirrel Town 45684
Stafford 43786
Standardsburg 44847
Standley 43527
Stanleyville 45788
Stanwood 44662
Starbucktown 45177
Starlight Plaza (Part of Sylvania) 43560
Starr (Twp) 45764
Starr 45654
Starrs Corners 44406
State Road (Part of Cuyahoga Falls)‡ 44223
Staunton, *Fayette* 43160
Staunton, *Miami* 45373
Steam Corners 44904
Steinersville 43942
Stella 45622
Stelvideo 45331
Sterling, *Brown* (Twp) 45154
Sterling, *Wayne* 44276
Sterling Heights 45005
Steuben 44847
Steubenville 43952-53
For specific ZIP Codes call (888) 275-8777, or your local postmaster.
Stewart 45778
Stewartsville 43960
Stillwater 44679
Stillwell 44637
Stiversville 45770
Stock, *Harrison* (Twp) 43988
Stock, *Noble* (Twp) 43724
Stockdale 45683
Stockham 45694
Stockport 43787
Stockton (Part of Fairfield) 45014
Stokes, *Logan* (Twp) 43331
Stokes, *Madison* (Twp) 43153
Stone 43720
Stone Creek 43840
Stonelick 45103
Stony Lake 44615
Stony Ridge 43463
Stonyrill 45005
Storms 45612
Story Place (Part of Chillicothe)‡ 45601
Stout 45684
Stoutsville 43154
Stovertown 43701
Stow 44224
Strasburg 44680
Stratford 43015
Stratton 43961
Streetsboro 44241
Stringtown, *Athens* 45701
Stringtown, *Brown* 45167
Stringtown, *Clermont* 45120
Stringtown, *Muskingum* 43701
Stringtown, *Perry* 43731
Strongs Ridge 44811
Strongsville 44136
44149
For specific ZIP Codes call (888) 275-8777, or your local postmaster.
Struthers 44471
Stryker 43557
Stuart Manor 43952
Suffield 44260
Sugar Bush Knolls 44240
Sugar Creek, *Allen* (Twp) 45807
Sugar Creek, *Greene* (Twp) 45305
Sugar Creek, *Putnam* (Twp) 45830
Sugar Creek, *Stark* (Twp) 44662
Sugar Creek, *Wayne* (Twp) 44618
Sugar Creek, *Athens* 45701
Sugarcreek, *Tuscarawas* 44681
Sugar Grove, *Crawford* 44820
Sugar Grove, *Fairfield* 43155
Sugar Grove, *Jefferson* 43964
Sugar Grove, *Miami* 45318
Sugar Grove, *Scioto* 45663
Sugar Grove Hill 45506
Sugar Ridge 43402
Sugar Tree Ridge 45133
Sugar Valley 45320
Sullivan 44880
Sulphurgrove (Part of Huber Heights) 45424
Sulphur Springs, *Crawford* 44881
Sulphur Springs, *Perry* 43782
Summerfield 43788
Summerford 43140
Summerside 45244
Summerside Estates 45244
Summit, *Monroe* (Twp) 43754
Summit (Part of Cincinnati) 45238
Summit, *Ross* 45601
Summit, *Trumbull* 44420
Summithill 45601
Summit Mall (Part of Fairlawn) 44333
Summit Station♦ 43073
Summitville 43062
Sumner 45720
Sunbury, *Delaware* 43074
Sunbury, *Montgomery* 45327
Sundale 43767
Sunfish (Twp) 45661
Sunny Acres 43952
Sunnyland 45502
Sunny Meade 43725
Sunnyside Beach (Part of Vermilion) 44089
Sunsbury (Twp) 43716
Sunset Beach 44429
Sunset Heights 43912
Sunset Point 44077
Sunshine 45684
Sunshine Park 43952
Sun Valley Estates 45505
Superior (Twp) 43543
Surrey Hill 44484
Sutton (Twp) 45771
Swan (Twp) 45622
Swan Creek (Twp) 43558
Swanders 45369
Swanktown 45309
Swanton, *Lucas* (Twp) 43558
Swanton, *Fulton* 43558
Swickards Additions 43952
Swifton Commons (Part of Cincinnati) 45237
Switzerland (Twp) 43942
Sybene 45680
Sycamore, *Hamilton* (Twp) 45236
45249
For specific ZIP Codes call (888) 275-8777, or your local postmaster.
Sycamore (Part of Cincinnati)‡ 45242
Sycamore, *Wyandot* 44882
Sycamore Valley 43789
Sychar Road 43050
Sylvania 43560
Symmes, *Hamilton* (Twp) 45140
45242
45249
For specific ZIP Codes call (888) 275-8777, or your local postmaster.
Symmes, *Lawrence* (Twp) 45688
Symmes (Part of Fairfield) 45014
Syracuse 45779
Taborville 44022
Tacoma 43713
Taft 45236
Tallmadge 44278

*** Area Zip Code** **† Post Office Boxes** **‡ Postal Station** **♦ Census Designated Place** *Italic Type* **County**

Tama 45822
Tarlton 43156
Tate (Twp) 45106
Tatmans 43730
Tawawa 45365
Taylor, *Union* (Twp) 43344
Taylor (Part of Gahanna) 43230
Taylor Creek (Twp) 43326
Taylorsburg 45315
Taylors Creek 45239
Taylorsville 45133
Taylortown, *Jefferson* 43964
Taylortown, *Richland* 44875
Tedrow 43567
Teegarden 44432
Temperanceville 43713
Ten Hills 45805
Tennyson 45661
Terrace Park 45174
Terre Haute 43078
Terry Acres 45324
Texas, *Crawford* (Twp) 44882
Texas, *Henry* 43532
Thackery 43078
Thatcher 43113
The Avenue 44438
The Bend 43512
The Eastern 43908
Thelma City 44601
The Plains♦ 45780
The Village of Indian Hill 45243
Thompson, *Delaware* (Twp) 43066
Thompson, *Seneca* (Twp) 44828
Thompson, *Geauga* 44086
Thorn (Twp) 43076
Thornville 43076
Thorny Acres 45042
Three Locks 45601
Thrifton 45123
Thurman 45685
Thurston 43157
Tiffany Acres 45502
Tiffin, *Adams* (Twp) 45693
Tiffin, *Defiance* (Twp) 43512
Tiffin, *Seneca* 44883
Tiltonsville 43963
Timberlake 44094
Timberview 43040
Tinny 43435
Tipp City 45371
Tippecanoe 44699
Tipton 45851
Tiro 44887
Tiverton 43006
Toboso 43055
Tod (Twp) 44882
Todds 43728
Toledo 43601-15
43617
43620-99
For specific ZIP Codes call (888) 275-8777, or your local postmaster.
Toledo Dock (Part of Oregon) 43618
Toledo Great Eastern Shopping Center (Part of Northwood) 43616
Toledo Miracle Mile Shopping Center (Part of Toledo) 43613
Tom Corwin 45692
Tomlison Addition 45648
Tontogany 43565
Torch 45781
Toronto 43964
Town and Country Estates 45429
Town and Country Shopping Center (Part of Whitehall) 43213
Townsend, *Huron* (Twp) 44826
Townsend, *Sandusky* (Twp) 43464
Townview 45427
Townwood 45856
Tradersville 43044
Trail 44624
Trail Run 43946
Tranquility 45679
Traschel 43302
Trebein (Part of Beavercreek) 45434
Tremont City 45372
Trenton, *Delaware* (Twp) 43021
Trenton, *Butler* 45067
Triadelphia 43758
Tri-County Mall (Part of Springdale) 45246
Trimble 45782
Trinway 43842
Tri-Village (Part of Columbus)‡ 43212
Trotwood 45426
Trowbridge 43432
Troy, *Ashland* (Twp) 44859
Troy, *Athens* (Twp) 45723
Troy, *Delaware* (Twp) 43015
Troy, *Geauga* (Twp) 44021
Troy, *Morrow* (Twp) 44901
Troy, *Richland* (Twp) 44904
Troy, *Wood* (Twp) 43443
Troy, *Miami* 45373
Truetown 45761
Trumbull 44041
Truro (Twp) 43068
Truro (Part of Columbus) 43068
Tuckaho 44003
Tucson 45601
Tully, *Marion* (Twp) 43314
Tully, *Van Wert* (Twp) 45832
Tunnel 45750
Tunnel Hill 43844
Tuppers Plains 45783
Turpin Hills♦ 45244
Turtle Creek, *Shelby* (Twp) 45365
Turtle Creek, *Warren* (Twp) 45036
Tuscarawas, *Coshocton* (Twp) 43812
Tuscarawas, *Stark* (Twp) 44646
Tuscarawas, *Tuscarawas* 44682
Twain 44212
Twenty Mile Stand 45140
Twightwee 45140
Twin, *Darke* (Twp) 45304
Twin, *Preble* (Twp) 45381
Twin, *Ross* (Twp) 45617
Twin Lakes, *Allen* 45804
Twin Lakes, *Portage* 44240
Twinsburg 44087
Twinsburg Heights 44087
Twin Valley 45662
Two Hundred Ten Row 45701
Tymochtee (Twp) 44882
Tymochtee 43351
Tyndall 43812
Uhrichsville 44683
Union, *Auglaize* (Twp) 45895
Union, *Belmont* (Twp) 43759
Union, *Brown* (Twp) 45167
Union, *Butler* (Twp) 45069
Union, *Carroll* (Twp) 44615
Union, *Champaign* (Twp) 43009
Union, *Clermont* (Twp) 45245
Union, *Clinton* (Twp) 45177
Union, *Fayette* (Twp) 43160
Union, *Hancock* (Twp) 45881
Union, *Highland* (Twp) 45133
Union, *Knox* (Twp) 43014
Union, *Lawrence* (Twp) 45619
Union, *Licking* (Twp) 43025
Union, *Logan* (Twp) 43311
Union, *Madison* (Twp) 43140
Union, *Mercer* (Twp) 45862
Union, *Miami* (Twp) 45383
Union, *Morgan* (Twp) 43758
Union, *Muskingum* (Twp) 43762
Union, *Pike* (Twp) 45648
Union, *Putnam* (Twp) 45844
Union, *Ross* (Twp) 45628
Union, *Scioto* (Twp) 45652
Union, *Tuscarawas* (Twp) 44621
Union, *Union* (Twp) 43045
Union, *Van Wert* (Twp) 45891
Union, *Warren* (Twp) 45036
Union, *Athens* 45766
Union, *Montgomery* 45322
Union City 45390
Union Furnace 43158
Union Landing Siding 45638
Union Plains 45154
Unionport 43966
Union Station 43025
Uniontown, *Belmont* 43950
Uniontown, *Stark*♦ 44685
Unionvale 43907
Unionville, *Ashtabula* 44088
Unionville, *Morgan* 43756
Unionville, *Washington* 45750
Unionville Center 43077
Uniopolis 45888
Unity, *Adams* 45693
Unity, *Columbiana* 44413
University (Part of Columbus)‡ 43210
University Center (Part of Cleveland)‡ 44106
University Heights, *Allen* 45804
University Heights, *Cuyahoga* 44118
University View 43212
Upland Heights 43943
Upper (Twp) 45645
Upper Arlington (Part of Middletown) 45042
Upper Arlington, *Franklin* 43220-21
For specific ZIP Codes call (888) 275-8777, or your local postmaster.
Upper Five Mile 45154
Upper Fox Hollow 45502
Upper Lowell 45744
Upper Sandusky 43351
Urbana 43078
Urbancrest 43123
Utica, *Licking* 43080
Utica, *Warren* 45036
Utopia 45121
Valley, *Guernsey* (Twp) 43772
Valley, *Scioto* (Twp) 45648
Valley, *Columbiana* 44460
Valley City 44280
Valley City Station 44280
Valley Crossing (Part of Columbus) 43207
Valley Forge 44212
Valley Glen 43938
Valley Hi 43360
Valley View, *Cuyahoga* 44131
Valleyview, *Franklin* 43204
Valley View, *Jefferson* 43910
Valley View, *Scioto* 45662
Valley View Estates 44403
Valley View Heights 45244
Valley View Village 43701
Valleywood (Part of Beavercreek) 45430
Vanatta 43055
Van Buren, *Darke* (Twp) 45304
Van Buren, *Hancock* (Twp) 45897
Van Buren, *Putnam* (Twp) 45856
Van Buren, *Shelby* (Twp) 45336
Van Buren, *Hancock* 45889
Vanburen, *Licking* 43055
Vandalia 45377
Vanlue 45890
Van Wert 45891
Vaughnsville 45893
Vega 45685
Venedocia 45894
Venice, *Seneca* (Twp) 44807
Venice (Part of Sandusky)‡ 44870
Venice Heights 44484
Vera Cruz 45118
Vermillion, *Ashland* (Twp) 44805
Vermilion, *Erie* 44089
Vermilion-on-the-Lake (Part of Vermilion) 44089
Vernon, *Clinton* (Twp) 45113
Vernon, *Crawford* (Twp) 44827
Vernon, *Scioto* (Twp) 45694
Vernon, *Lawrence* 45659
Vernon, *Trumbull* 44428
Vernon Heights (Part of Marion) 43302
Vernon Junction 44875
Verona 45378
Versailles 45380
Vesuvius 45659
Veterans Administration (Part of Dayton)‡ 45428
Veto 45714
Vickery 43464
Vicksville 45732
Vionna 44473
Vigo 45601
Viking Village 45244
Villa 45503
Villa Nova 45885
Vincent, *Lorain* 44035
Vincent, *Washington* 45784
Vinton (Twp) 45695
Vinton 45686
Violet (Twp) 43147
Virginia (Twp) 43811
Vo-Ash Lake 44615
Volunteer Bay 44089
Vore Ridge 45780
Wabash, *Darke* (Twp) 45380
Wabash, *Mercer* 45822
Wacker Heights 43130
Waco 44707
Wade 45767
Wadsworth (Twp) 44281
Wadsworth 44281-82
For specific ZIP Codes call (888) 275-8777, or your local postmaster.
Waggoner Place 43551
Wagram 43062
Wahlsburg 45121
Wainwright, *Jackson* 45692
Wainwright, *Tuscarawas* 44663
Waite Hill 44094
Wakatomika 43821
Wakefield, *Darke* 45331
Wakefield, *Pike* 45687
Wakeman 44889
Walbridge 43465
Waldo 43356
Walhonding, *Coshocton* 43843
Walhonding, *Guernsey* 43772
Wallace Heights 43964
Walnut, *Fairfield* (Twp) 43046
Walnut, *Gallia* (Twp) 45658
Walnut, *Pickaway* (Twp) 43103
Walnut Creek 44687
Walnut Grove 43358
Walnut Hills (Part of Cincinnati)‡ 45206
Walnut Hills, *Jackson* 45640
Walnut Hills (Part of Massillon) 44646
Walnutrun 43140
Walton Hills 44146
Wamsley 45657
Wapakoneta 45895
Ward (Twp) 43144
Wardwood Acres 45239
Warner 45745
Warnock 43967
Warren, *Belmont* (Twp) 43713
Warren, *Jefferson* (Twp) 43943
Warren, *Trumbull* (Twp) 44430
Warren, *Tuscarawas* (Twp) 44656
Warren, *Washington* (Twp) 45750
Warren, *Trumbull* 44481-85
For specific ZIP Codes call (888) 275-8777, or your local postmaster.
Warrensburg 43061
Warrensville Heights 44122
Warrenton 43943
Warsaw 43844
Warwick, *Tuscarawas* (Twp) 44663
Warwick (Part of Clinton) 44216
Washington, *Auglaize* (Twp) 45871
Washington, *Belmont* (Twp) 43716
Washington, *Brown* (Twp) 45171
Washington, *Carroll* (Twp) 44615
Washington, *Clermont* (Twp) 45153
Washington, *Clinton* (Twp) 45114
Washington, *Columbiana* (Twp) 43945
Washington, *Coshocton* (Twp) 43842
Washington, *Darke* (Twp) 47390
Washington, *Defiance* (Twp) 43549
Washington, *Franklin* (Twp) 43017
Washington, *Guernsey* (Twp) 43749
Washington, *Hancock* (Twp) 45830
Washington, *Hardin* (Twp) 45835
Washington, *Harrison* (Twp) 44699
Washington, *Henry* (Twp) 43532
Washington, *Highland* (Twp) 45133
Washington, *Hocking* (Twp) 43138
Washington, *Holmes* (Twp) 44638
Washington, *Jackson* (Twp) 45692
Washington, *Lawrence* (Twp) 45656
Washington, *Licking* (Twp) 43080
Washington, *Logan* (Twp) 43348
Washington, *Lucas* (Twp) 43612
Washington, *Mercer* (Twp) 45828
Washington, *Miami* (Twp) 45356
Washington, *Monroe* (Twp) 45734
Washington, *Montgomery* (Twp) 45459
Washington, *Morrow* (Twp) 43338
Washington, *Muskingum* (Twp) 43701
Washington, *Paulding* (Twp) 45859
Washington, *Pickaway* (Twp) 43113
Washington, *Preble* (Twp) 45320
Washington, *Richland* (Twp) 44906
Washington, *Sandusky* (Twp) 43442
Washington, *Scioto* (Twp) 45663
Washington, *Shelby* (Twp) 45365
Washington, *Stark* (Twp) 44601
Washington, *Tuscarawas* (Twp) 43832
Washington, *Union* (Twp) 43344
Washington, *Van Wert* (Twp) 45833
Washington, *Warren* (Twp) 45054
Washington, *Wood* (Twp) 43565
Washington Court House 43160
Washingtonville 44490
Waterford, *Knox* 43019
Waterford, *Washington* 45786
Waterloo, *Athens* (Twp) 45766
Waterloo, *Fairfield* 43136
Waterloo, *Lawrence* 45688
Watertown 45787
Waterville 43566
Watkins 43040
Wattsville 44615
Wauseon 43567
Waverly 45690
Waverly Gables 45690
Way 45734
Wayland 44285
Wayne, *Adams* (Twp) 45618
Wayne, *Auglaize* (Twp) 45896
Wayne, *Belmont* (Twp) 43747
Wayne, *Butler* (Twp) 45042
Wayne, *Champaign* (Twp) 43009
Wayne, *Clermont* (Twp) 45122
Wayne, *Clinton* (Twp) 45138
Wayne, *Columbiana* (Twp) 44432
Wayne, *Darke* (Twp) 45380
Wayne, *Fayette* (Twp) 45123
Wayne, *Jefferson* (Twp) 43910
Wayne, *Knox* (Twp) 43019
Wayne, *Monroe* (Twp) 45734
Wayne, *Muskingum* (Twp) 43701
Wayne, *Noble* (Twp) 43773
Wayne, *Pickaway* (Twp) 43113
Wayne, *Tuscarawas* (Twp) 44624
Wayne, *Warren* (Twp) 45068
Wayne, *Wayne* (Twp) 44691
Wayne, *Ashtabula* 44093
Wayne, *Wood* 43466
Wayne Lakes 45331
Waynesburg, *Crawford* 44887

Place	ZIP
Waynesburg, *Stark*	44688
Waynesfield	45896
Waynesville	45068
Weathersfield (Twp)	44420
Weaver Station	45331
Webb Heights	43947
Webb Summit	43138
Webster, *Wood* (Twp)	43450
Webster, *Darke*	45309
Wegee	43947
Welcome	44637
Weller (Twp)	44903
Wellington	44090
Wellington Park	45231
Wellman	45068
Wells (Twp)	43913
Wellston	45692
Wellsville	43968
Welshfield	44021
Welshtown	45769
Wengerlawn	45309
Wernert (Part of Toledo)‡	43613
Wesley (Twp)	45713
Wesleyan Woods (Part of Delaware)	43015
West (Twp)	44625
West Akron (Part of Akron)‡	44307
West Alexandria	45381
West Andover	44003
West Bass Lake	44024
West Bedford	43844
West Bellaire (Part of Bellaire)	43906
West Berlin	43015
Westboro	45148
West Brookfield (Part of Massillon)	44646
West Carlisle, *Coshocton*	43822
West Carlisle, *Lorain*	44035
West Carrollton	45449
West Charleston	45371
West Chesapeake	45619
West Chester, *Butler*	45069*
	45071†
West Chester, *Tuscarawas*	44699
West Clarksfield	44889
West Conesville (Part of Conesville)	43811
West Covington	45318
West Elkton	45070
West Enon Estates	45323
Westerly Park	45805
Western Hills	45238
Western Hills Plaza (Part of Cincinnati)	45211
Western Reserve Estates	44236
Westerville	43081-82
	43086
For specific ZIP Codes call (888) 275-8777, or your local postmaster.	
West Fairport (Part of Grand River)	44045
West Farmington	44491
Westfield, *Medina* (Twp)	44251
Westfield, *Columbiana*	43920
Westfield, *Morrow*	43003
Westfield Center	44251
West Florence	45320
Westgate Mall (Part of Fairview Park)	44126
Westgate Village Shopping Center (Part of Toledo)	43606
West Hill♦	44403
Westhope	43516
West Independence	44802
West Jefferson, *Madison*	43162
West Jefferson, *Williams*	43543
West Lafayette	43845
Westlake	44145
West Lakeville (Part of Conneaut)	44030
West Lancaster	43128
Westland (Twp)	43725
West Lebanon	44618
West Leipsic	45856
West Liberty, *Crawford*	44887
West Liberty, *Logan*	43357
West Liberty, *Morrow*	43334
West Lodi	44811
West Logan	43138
West Manchester	45382
West Mansfield	43358
West Marietta (Part of Marietta)	45750
West Marysville (Part of Marysville)	43040
West Mecca	44410
West Middletown	45042
West Millgrove	43467
West Milton	45383
Westminster	45850
Westmoor	44833
West Newton	45850
Weston	43569
West Park (Part of Cleveland)‡	44111
West Park (Part of Findlay)	45840
West Park (Part of Massillon)	44646
West Park, *Jefferson*	43952
West Point, *Columbiana*	44492
West Point, *Morrow*	44833
West Portsmouth♦	45663
West Richfield (Part of Richfield)	44286
West Rushville	43163
West Salem	44287
West Side (Part of Youngstown)‡	44509
West Sonora	45338
West Toledo (Part of Toledo)‡	43612
West Union	45693
West Unity	43570
Westview	44028
Westville, *Champaign*	43083
Westville, *Columbiana*	44609
Westville Lake	44609
West Warren (Part of Warren)‡	44485
West Wheeling	43906
West Williamsfield	44093
Westwood (Part of Cincinnati)	45211
Westwood (Part of Steubenville)	43952
Westwood, *Wayne*	44691
Westwood Estates (Part of Steubenville)	43952
West Woodville	45107
West Worthington‡	43234-35
For specific ZIP Codes call (888) 275-8777, or your local postmaster.	
Wetzel	45863
Weymouth	44256
Wharton	43359
Wheat Ridge	45693
Wheelersburg♦	45694
Wheeling, *Belmont* (Twp)	43927
Wheeling, *Guernsey* (Twp)	43749
Whetstone (Twp)	44820
Whigville	43788
Whipple	45788
Whisler	45644
White Cottage	43791
White Eyes (Twp)	43824
White Hall, *Athens*	45701
Whitehall, *Franklin*	43213
Whitehouse	43571
Whiteoak, *Highland* (Twp)	45133
White Oak, *Brown*	45154
Whiteoak, *Fayette*	43143
White Oak, *Hamilton*♦	45239
	45247
For specific ZIP Codes call (888) 275-8777, or your local postmaster.	
White Oak East♦	45239
White Oak Meadows	45239
White Oaks (Part of Steubenville)	43952
White Oak Valley	45121
White Oak West♦	45247
White Pond	44321
White's Landing	43464
White Sulphur	43061
Whitetree (Part of Cincinnati)	45236
Whitewater	45002
Whitfield	45342
Wick	44093
Wickliffe, *Lake*	44092
Wickliffe, *Mahoning*	44515
Widowville	44805
Wiggonsville	45106
Wightmans Grove	43420
Wilberforce♦	45384
Wildare	44410
Wildbrook Acres	45231
Wildwood (Part of Middletown)	45042
Wilgus	45696
Wilkesville	45695
Wilkins Corners	43055
Wilkshire Hills	44612
Willard	44890
Willetsville	45133
Williamsburg	45176
Williams Center	43506
Williams Corner	45103
Williamsdale	45011
Williamsfield	44093
Williamsport, *Columbiana*	44432
Williamsport, *Morrow*	43338
Williamsport, *Pickaway*	43164
Williamstown	45897
Williston	43468
Willoughby	44094-96
For specific ZIP Codes call (888) 275-8777, or your local postmaster.	
Willoughby Hills	44092
Willow (Part of Cleveland)‡	44127
Willow (Part of Cuyahoga Heights)	44125
Willow Brook Heights	44721
Willowcrest	44452
Willowdale Lake	44720
Willowdell	45380
Willow Grove	43906
Willowick	44094
Willow Lakes	43701
Willowville	45103
Willow Wood	45696
Wills (Twp)	43755
Wills Creek	43811
Willshire	45898
Wilmington	45177
Wilmot	44689
Wilshire	45122
Wilshire Heights	45005
Wilson, *Clinton* (Twp)	45169
Wilson, *Monroe*	43716
Wiltondale	45224
Winameg	43515
Winchester, *Adams*	45697
Winchester, *Jackson*	45640
Windfall Heights	44256
Windham	44288
Windor Park (Part of Xenia)	45385
Windsor, *Lawrence* (Twp)	45678
Windsor, *Morgan* (Twp)	43787
Windsor, *Ashtabula*	44099
Windsor, *Richland*	44903
Windsor, *Warren*	45162
Windsor Mills	44099
Windy Acres	45502
Winesburg	44690
Winfield	44622
Wingett Run	45789
Wingston	43462
Winona	44493
Winterdale (Part of Wintersville)	43953
Winterhaven	45305
Winterset	43755
Wintersville	43953
Wintondale	45231
Winton Place (Part of Cincinnati)	45232
Winton Place (Part of St. Bernard)	45216
Winton Terrace (Part of Cincinnati)	45232
Wisterman	45831
Withamsville♦	45245
Wolf	43832
Wolfhurst	43912
Wolf Run	43970
Woodbourne	45459
Woodhaven	45005
Woodington	45331
Woodlawn, *Hamilton*	45215
Woodlawn, *Miami*	45373
Woodlawn Village	45373
Woodmere	44122
Woods	45056
Woodsdale	45067
Woodsfield	43793
Woodside	43406
Woodstock	43084
Woodville, *Clermont*	45122
Woodville, *Sandusky*	43469
Woodville Gardens	43616
Woodville Mall (Part of Northwood)	43619
Woodworth	44512
Woodworth Corners	44473
Wooster	44691
Wooster Heights	44903
Worstville	45880
Worthington, *Richland* (Twp)	44822
Worthington, *Franklin*	43085
Wren	45899
Wright Brothers (Part of Oakwood)‡	45409
Wright-Patterson Air Force Base‡	45433
Wrightsville, *Adams*	45144
Wrightsville, *Franklin*	43123
Wrightview (Part of Fairborn)	45324
Wyandot	44849
Wyoming	45215
Wyoming Meadows	45231
Xenia	45385
Yale, *Ottawa*	43468
Yale, *Portage*	44411
Yankeeburg	45768
Yankee Hills	44403
Yankee Lake	44403
Yankeetown	45130
Yatesville	43106
Yellowbud	45601
Yellow Creek, *Columbiana* (Twp)	43968
Yellow Creek, *Jefferson*	43968
Yellow Springs	45387
Yellowtown	43731
Yelverton	43326
Yoder	45806
York, *Athens* (Twp)	45764
York, *Belmont* (Twp)	43942
York, *Darke* (Twp)	45380
York, *Fulton* (Twp)	43515
York, *Medina* (Twp)	44256
York, *Morgan* (Twp)	43731
York, *Sandusky* (Twp)	44811
York, *Tuscarawas* (Twp)	44663
York, *Union* (Twp)	43067
York, *Van Wert* (Twp)	45874
York, *Jefferson*	43901
York Center	43067
Yorkshire	45388
Yorkshire Estates	43302
Yorkville	43971
Young Hickory	43732
Youngs	45657
Youngs Corners	44256
Youngstown	44501-15
For specific ZIP Codes call (888) 275-8777, or your local postmaster.	
Youngsville	45679
Zahns Corners	45690
Zaleski	45698
Zane (Twp)	43336
Zane Addition	45601
Zanesfield	43360
Zanesville	43701*
	43702†
Zenz City	45846
Zimmer Estates	45431
Zimmerman (Part of Beavercreek)	45434
Ziontown	43076
Zoar, *Tuscarawas*	44697
Zoar, *Warren*	45152
Zoarville	44656
Zone	43521

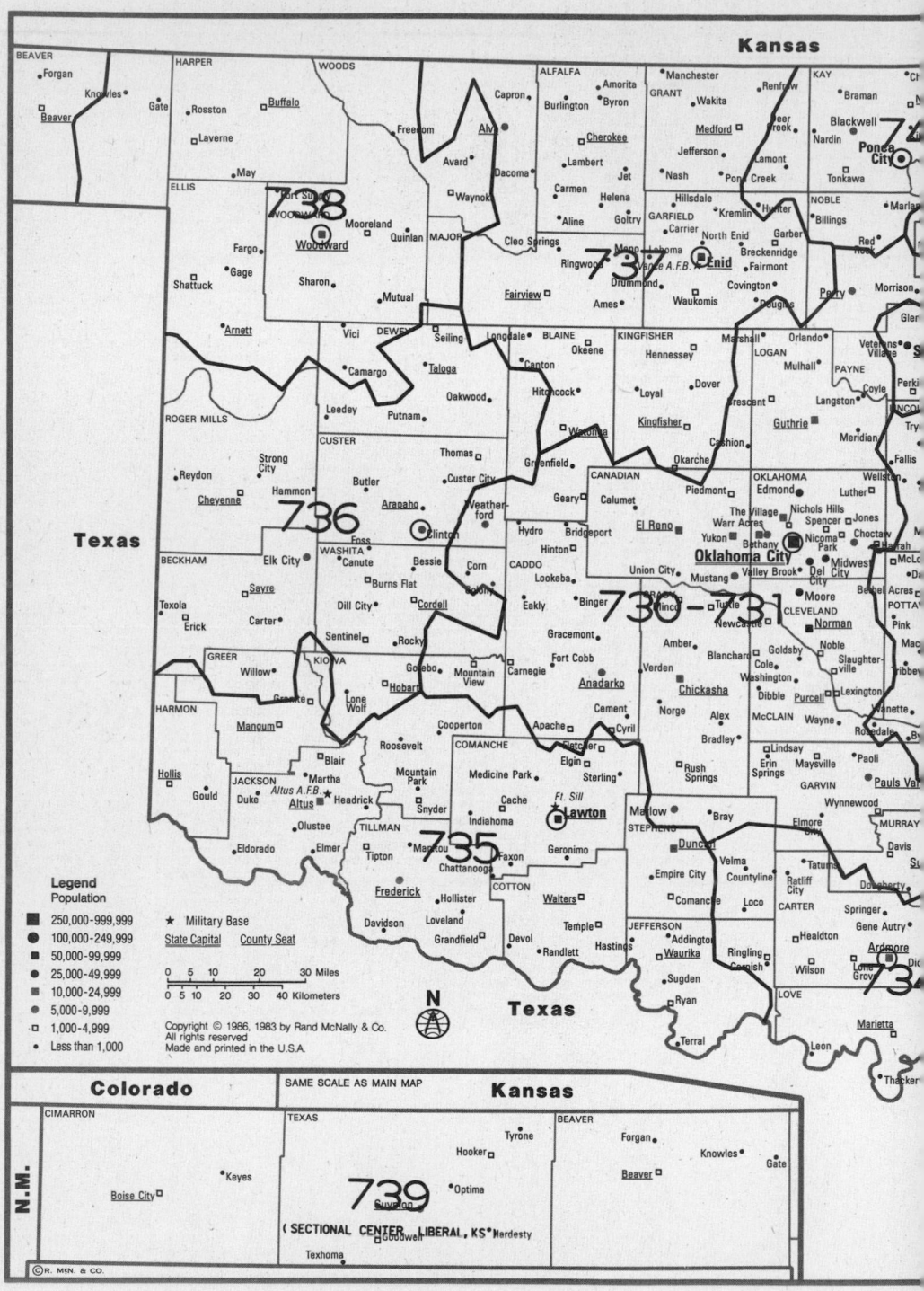

Kansas

Texas

BEAVER
Forgan
Knowles
Beaver
Gate
HARPER
Rosston
Buffalo
Laverne
May
WOODS
Freedom
Alva
Avard
Capron
Dacoma
Waynoka
ALFALFA
Amorita
Byron
Burlington
Cherokee
Lambert
Jet
Carmen
Helena
Aline
Goltry
GRANT
Manchester
Renfrow
Wakita
Deer Creek
Medford
Jefferson
Lamont
Nash
Pond Creek
KAY
Braman
Blackwell
Nardin
Ponca City
Tonkawa
ELLIS
Fort Supply
WOODWARD
Mooreland
Woodward
Quinlan
Fargo
Gage
Shattuck
Sharon
Mutual
MAJOR
Cleo Springs
Ringwood
Fairview
GARFIELD
Hillsdale
Kremlin
Hunter
Carrier
North Enid
Garber
Vance A.F.B.
Enid
Breckenridge
Fairmont
Drummond
Covington
Waukomis
Ames
Douglas
NOBLE
Billings
Red Rock
Perry
Morrison
Arnett
Vici
DEWEY
Seiling
Camargo
Taloga
Leedey
Putnam
Oakwood
ROGER MILLS
Longdale
BLAINE
Okeene
Canton
Hitchcock
Watonga
Greenfield
KINGFISHER
Hennessey
Loyal
Dover
Kingfisher
Cashion
Okarche
Marshall
LOGAN
Orlando
Mulhall
Crescent
Guthrie
PAYNE
Coyle
Langston
Meridian
Reydon
Strong City
Cheyenne
Hammon
CUSTER
Butler
Thomas
Custer City
Arapaho
Weatherford
Clinton
Foss
Hydro
Bridgeport
Hinton
CANADIAN
Calumet
Geary
El Reno
Piedmont
Union City
Mustang
OKLAHOMA
Edmond
The Village
Warr Acres
Nichols Hills
Yukon
Bethany
Spencer
Jones
Nicoma Park
Choctaw
Oklahoma City
Midwest City
Del City
Valley Brook
Luther
Wellston
BECKHAM
Elk City
Sayre
Erick
Texola
Carter
WASHITA
Canute
Burns Flat
Dill City
Cordell
Sentinel
Rocky
Bessie
Corn
Colony
CADDO
Lookeba
Eakly
Binger
Gracemont
Fort Cobb
Carnegie
Anadarko
Cement
Apache
Cyril
GRADY
Minco
Tuttle
Amber
Verden
Chickasha
Norge
Alex
Bradley
Rush Springs
Moore
CLEVELAND
Norman
Newcastle
Blanchard
Goldsby
Noble
Cole
Washington
Dibble
Purcell
Lexington
Slaughterville
McCLAIN
Wayne
GREER
Willow
Granite
Mangum
KIOWA
Lone Wolf
Hobart
Gotebo
Mountain View
Cooperton
Roosevelt
HARMON
Hollis
Gould
JACKSON
Blair
Martha
Duke
Altus A.F.B.
Altus
Headrick
Olustee
Eldorado
Elmer
Mountain Park
Snyder
TILLMAN
Tipton
Manitou
Frederick
Hollister
Davidson
Loveland
Grandfield
COMANCHE
Medicine Park
Elgin
Fletcher
Sterling
Cache
Indiahoma
Ft. Sill
Lawton
Chattanooga
Faxon
Geronimo
COTTON
Walters
Temple
Devol
Randlett
Hastings
STEPHENS
Marlow
Bray
Duncan
Velma
Empire City
Comanche
Countyline
Loco
JEFFERSON
Addington
Waurika
Ringling
Cornish
Sugden
Ryan
Terral
GARVIN
Lindsay
Erin Springs
Maysville
Paoli
Pauls Valley
Wynnewood
Elmore City
CARTER
Ratliff City
Tatums
Springer
Gene Autry
Healdton
Wilson
Ardmore
Lone Grove
LOVE
Marietta
Leon
Thackerville
MURRAY
Davis
Dougherty
Rosedale
Wanette
POTTAWATOMIE
Bethel Acres
Tryon
Fallis
Perkins
Veterans Village
Glencoe
Marland

738
737
736
735
730-731

Legend
Population
250,000-999,999
100,000-249,999
50,000-99,999
25,000-49,999
10,000-24,999
5,000-9,999
1,000-4,999
Less than 1,000

★ Military Base
State Capital
County Seat

0 5 10 20 30 Miles
0 5 10 20 30 40 Kilometers

N

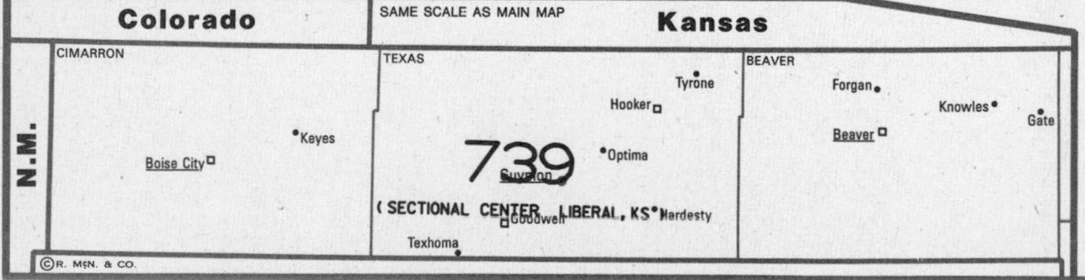

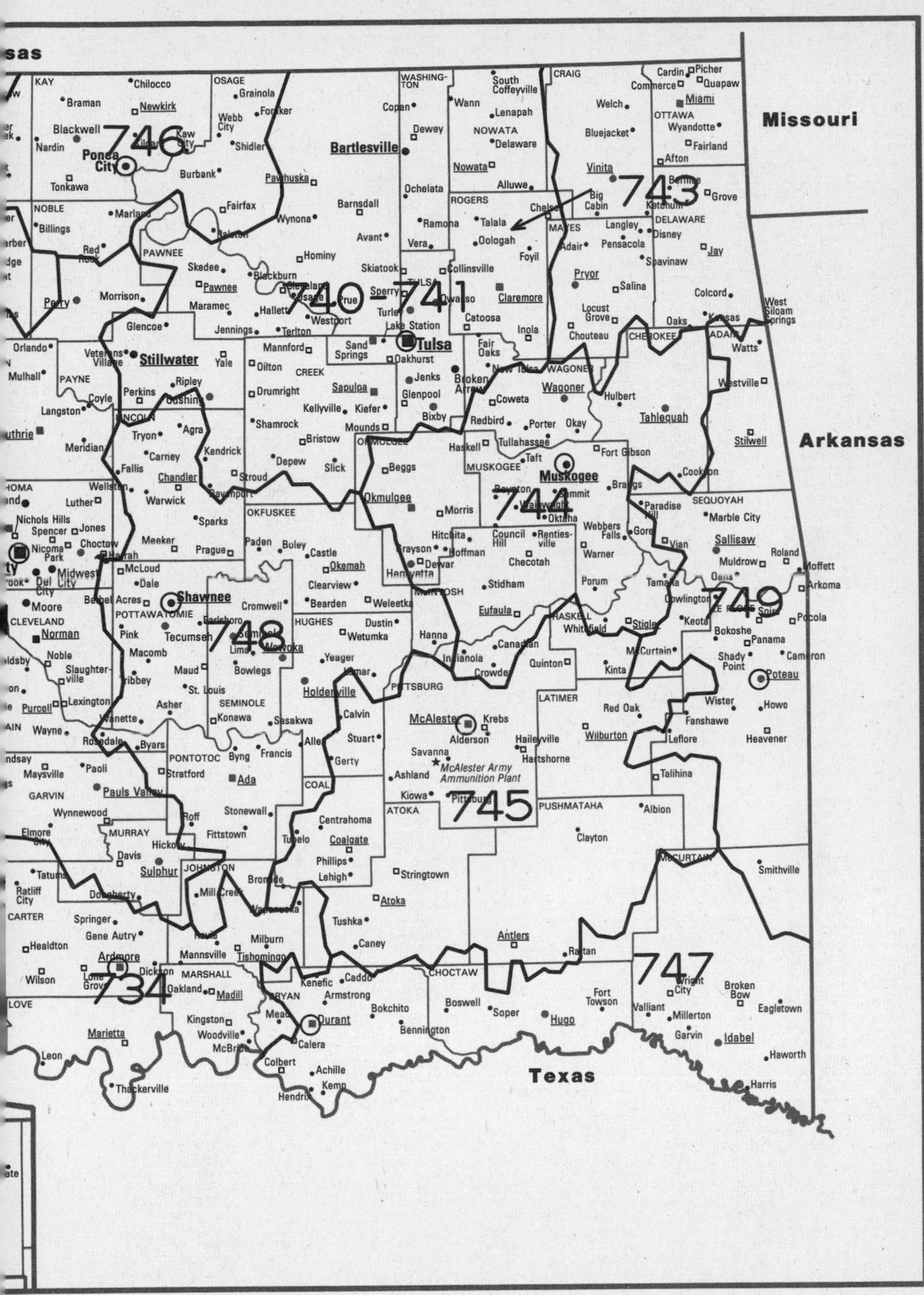
746
743
740-741
744
749
748
745
747
734
Missouri
Arkansas
Texas
KAY
OSAGE
WASHINGTON
NOWATA
CRAIG
OTTAWA
NOBLE
PAWNEE
ROGERS
MAYES
DELAWARE
TULSA
PAYNE
CREEK
WAGONER
CHEROKEE
ADAIR
LINCOLN
OKMULGEE
MUSKOGEE
SEQUOYAH
OKFUSKEE
MCINTOSH
HASKELL
CLEVELAND
POTTAWATOMIE
HUGHES
SEMINOLE
PITTSBURG
LATIMER
GARVIN
PONTOTOC
COAL
ATOKA
PUSHMATAHA
MURRAY
JOHNSTON
MCCURTAIN
CARTER
MARSHALL
CHOCTAW
BRYAN
LOVE
Chilocco
Braman
Newkirk
Blackwell
Nardin
Ponca City
Tonkawa
Grainola
Webb City
Foraker
Shidler
Burbank
Pawhuska
Fairfax
Billings
Red Rock
Wynona
Ralston
Skedee
Pawnee
Blackburn
Hominy
Perry
Morrison
Maramec
Hallett
Cleveland
Osage
Prue
Westport
Jennings
Terlton
Glencoe
Orlando
Stillwater
Yale
Mulhall
Ripley
Cushing
Perkins
Coyle
Langston
Guthrie
Tryon
Agra
Meridian
Carney
Kendrick
Fallis
Chandler
Stroud
Davenport
Wellston
Luther
Warwick
Sparks
Nichols Hills
Spencer
Jones
Nicoma Park
Choctaw
Harrah
Meeker
Prague
Midwest City
Del City
McLoud
Dale
Moore
Bethel Acres
Shawnee
Norman
Tecumseh
Pink
Macomb
Noble
Slaughterville
Tribbey
Maud
Lexington
Purcell
St. Louis
Asher
Wanette
Wayne
Rosedale
Byars
Konawa
Sasakwa
Bowlegs
Seminole
Wewoka
Lima
Earlsboro
Cromwell
Paden
Boley
Castle
Okemah
Clearview
Bearden
Weleetka
Dustin
Wetumka
Yeager
Lamar
Holdenville
Calvin
Allen
Stuart
Gerty
Byng
Francis
Ada
Stratford
Paoli
Maysville
Pauls Valley
Wynnewood
Roff
Stonewall
Fittstown
Elmore City
Davis
Hickory
Sulphur
Tatums
Ratliff City
Dougherty
Mill Creek
Bromide
Wapanucka
Springer
Gene Autry
Ravia
Milburn
Healdton
Ardmore
Mannsville
Tishomingo
Dickson
Lone Grove
Wilson
Oakland
Madill
Kingston
Woodville
McBride
Marietta
Leon
Thackerville
Mead
Durant
Calera
Colbert
Achille
Kemp
Hendrix
Bokchito
Bennington
Kenefic
Caddo
Armstrong
Tushka
Caney
Atoka
Stringtown
Coalgate
Centrahoma
Phillips
Lehigh
Tupelo
Boswell
Soper
Hugo
Fort Towson
Rattan
Antlers
Clayton
Albion
Valliant
Millerton
Garvin
Idabel
Wright City
Broken Bow
Eagletown
Haworth
Harris
Smithville
Kiowa
Pittsburg
Ashland
Savanna
McAlester Army Ammunition Plant
McAlester
Krebs
Alderson
Haileyville
Hartshorne
Wilburton
Red Oak
Talihina
Leflore
Wister
Fanshawe
Heavener
Howe
Poteau
Shady Point
Cameron
Panama
Bokoshe
Keota
Spiro
Pocola
Arkoma
Moffett
Roland
Muldrow
Sallisaw
Marble City
Paradise Hill
Vian
Gore
Tamaha
Cowlington
Stigler
McCurtain
Kinta
Whitefield
Quinton
Canadian
Crowder
Indianola
Hanna
Eufaula
Stidham
Checotah
Council Hill
Rentiesville
Hoffman
Dewar
Henryetta
Grayson
Hitchita
Morris
Okmulgee
Beggs
Slick
Depew
Bristow
Shamrock
Drumright
Oilton
Mannford
Kellyville
Kiefer
Sapulpa
Mounds
Glenpool
Jenks
Bixby
Sand Springs
Tulsa
Oakhurst
Lake Station
Turley
Sperry
Owasso
Catoosa
Broken Arrow
Coweta
Redbird
Porter
Okay
Haskell
Tullahassee
Taft
Muskogee
Boynton
Summit
Wainwright
Oktaha
Braggs
Webbers Falls
Warner
Porum
Fort Gibson
Hulbert
Tahlequah
Cookson
Stilwell
Westville
Watts
West Siloam Springs
Kansas
Oaks
Colcord
Jay
Spavinaw
Salina
Locust Grove
Chouteau
Pryor
Inola
Fair Oaks
New Tulsa
Wagoner
Claremore
Foyil
Oologah
Talala
Collinsville
Skiatook
Ramona
Vera
Avant
Barnsdall
Ochelata
Bartlesville
Dewey
Copan
Wann
South Coffeyville
Lenapah
Delaware
Nowata
Alluwe
Chelsea
Big Cabin
Adair
Pensacola
Langley
Disney
Vinita
Welch
Bluejacket
Ketchum
Bernice
Grove
Cardin
Picher
Quapaw
Commerce
Miami
Wyandotte
Fairland
Afton

Place	ZIP Code
A (Part of Durant)‡	74701*
	74702†
Achille	74720
Acme	73082
Ada	74820*
	74821†
Adair	74330
Adams	73901
Adamson	74547
Addington	73520
Adel	74540
Afton	74331
Agawam	73067
Agra	74824
Ahloso	74820
Ahpeatone	73572
Akins	74955
Albany	74721
Albert	73001
Albion	74521
Alden	73015
Alderson	74522
Aledo	73654
Alex	73002
Alfalfa	73015
Aline	73716
Allen	74825
Allison	74730
Alma	73533
Alpers	73487
Altona	73764
Altus	73521*
	73522†
Alva	73717
Amber	73004
Ames	73718
Amorita	73719
Anadarko	73005
Angus Valley Acres	74063
Antioch	73433
Antlers	74523
Apache	73006
Apperson	74633
Apple	74760
Aqua Park	74435
Arapaho	73620
Arcadia	73007
Arch	74547
Ardmore	73401-03
For specific ZIP Codes call (888) 275-8777, or your local postmaster.	
Arkoma	74901
Arlington	74864
Armstrong	74729
Arnett, *Ellis*	73832
Arnett, *Harmon*	73550
Arpelar	74501
Arrowhead Estates	74425
Arrowhead Mall (Part of Muskogee)	74401
Artillery Village	73503
Asher	74826
Ashland	74570
Atlee	73456
Atoka	74525
	74542
For specific ZIP Codes call (888) 275-8777, or your local postmaster.	
Atwood	74827
Avant	74001
Avard	73717
Avery	74023
Aydelotte	74804
Babbs	73651
Bache	74501
Bacone (Part of Muskogee)	74401
Bailey	73055
Baker	73950
Baldhill	74447
Balko	73931
Ballard	74964
Banner (Part of El Reno)	73036
Banty	74723
Barber	74471
Barnes	73063
Barnsdall	74002
Baron	74960
	74965
For specific ZIP Codes call (888) 275-8777, or your local postmaster.	
Bartlesville	74003-06
For specific ZIP Codes call (888) 275-8777, or your local postmaster.	
Battiest	74722
Baum	73401
Beachton	74957
Bearden	74859
Beaver	73932
Bee	74748
Beggs	74421
Beland	74401
Bell	74960
Bellemont	74864
Bellvue	74010
Belzoni	74523
Bengal	74563
	74566
For specific ZIP Codes call (888) 275-8777, or your local postmaster.	
Bennington	74723
Bentley	74525
Berlin	73662
Bernice	74331
Bessie	73622
Bethany	73008
Bethel, *Comanche*	73501
Bethel, *McCurtain*	74724
Bethel Acres	74801
Big Cabin	74332
Big Cedar	74939
Big Creek	74937
Big Spring	74883
Billings	74630
Binger	73009
Bison	73720
Bixby	74008
Blackburn	74058
Blackgum	74962
Blackwell	74631
Blair	73526
Blanchard	73010
Blanco	74528
Blocker	74529
Blue	74701
Bluejacket	74333
Blue Ridge (Part of Bixby)	74008
Bluff	74759
Boatman	74361
Boehler	74727
Boggy Depot	74525
Bois D'Arc	74601
Boise City	73933
Bokchito	74726
Bokhoma	74740
Bokoshe	74930
Boley	74829
Bond	74426
Boone	73006
Boss	74745
Boswell	74727
Bowden	74066
Bowlegs	74830
Bowlin Spring	74016
Bowring	74009
Box	74962
Boyd	73931
Boynton	74422
Braden	74959
Bradley	73011
Brady	73098
Braggs	74423
Braman	74632
Bray	73012
Breckenridge	73701
Brent	74955
Brentwood (Part of Glenpool)	74033
Briartown	74455
Bridgeport	73047
Briggs	74464
Brinkman	73673
Bristow	74010
Britton (Part of Oklahoma City)‡	73113-14
	73116
	73131
	73151
	73178
For specific ZIP Codes call (888) 275-8777, or your local postmaster.	
Brock	73401
Broken Arrow	74011-14
For specific ZIP Codes call (888) 275-8777, or your local postmaster.	
Broken Bow	74728
Bromide	74530
Brooken	74462
Brookside (Part of Tulsa)‡	74105
Brooksville	74873
Brown	74701
Broxton	73006
Bruner (Part of Tulsa)	74127
Brush Hill	74426
Brushy	74955
Bryans Corner	73931
Bryant	74880
Buffalo, *Harper*	73834
Buffalo, *McCurtain*	74963
Buffalo Valley	74574
Bunch	74931
Burbank	74633
Burlington	73722
Burmah	73659
Burneyville	73430
Burns Flat	73624
Burwell	74754
Bushyhead	74016
Butler	73625
Butner	74884
Byars	74831
Byng	74820
Byron	73722
Cache	73527
Caddo	74729
Cade	74723
Cairo	74538
Calera	74730
Calhoun	74956
Calumet	73014
Calvin	74531
Camargo	73835
Cambria	74545
Cameron	74932
Cameron University (Part of Lawton)‡	73505
Camp Houston	73842
Canadian	74425
Canadian Shores	74501
Caney	74533
Caney Ridge	74471
Canton	73724
Canute	73626
Capitol Hill (Part of Oklahoma City)	73109
Capron	73717
Cardin	74335
Carleton	73772
Carmen	73726
Carnegie	73015
Carney	74832
Carpenter	73644
Carriage Hills (Part of Lawton)	73501
Carrier	73727
Carson	74850
Carter	73627
Cartersville	74941
Cartwright	74731
Cashion	73016
Castle	74833
Catale	74332
Catesby	73843
Catoosa	74015
Cayuga	74344
Cedar Crest	74352
Cedar Lake	73047
Cedar Ridge (Part of Cleveland)	74020
Cedar Valley	73044
Cement	73017
Centennial Station (Part of Edmond)‡	73013
	73083
For specific ZIP Codes call (888) 275-8777, or your local postmaster.	
Center	74820
Center City (Part of Oklahoma City)‡	73101†
	73102*
Center Point	74525
Centerview	74804
Centrahoma	74534
Centralia	74301
Central Mall (Part of Lawton)	73501
Ceres	74651
Cerrogordo	74740
Cestos	73859
Chance	74964
Chandler	74834
Chase	74401
Chattanooga	73528
Checotah	74426
Chelsea	74016
Cherokee	73728
Cherry Tree	74960
Chester	73838
Chewey	74964
Cheyenne	73628
Cheyenne Valley	73737
Chickasha	73018*
	73023†
Chigley	73030
Childers	74027
Chilli	74578
Chilocco	74647
Chimney Hills (Part of Tulsa)‡	74133
	74137
For specific ZIP Codes call (888) 275-8777, or your local postmaster.	
Chitwood	73067
Chloeta	74366
Choctaw	73020
Choska	74429
Chouteau	74337
Christie	74965
Cimarron (Part of Oklahoma City)	73111
Cimarron City	73028
Cisco	74745
Citra	74825
Claremore	74017*
	74018†
Clarita	74535
Clarksville	74454
Clayton	74536
Clayton Lake	74536
Clear Lake	73932
Clearview	74880
Clebit	74728
Clemscot	73437
Cleora	74331
Cleo Springs	73729
Cleveland	74020
Clinton	73601
Clothier (Part of Oklahoma City)	73160
Cloud Chief	73632
Cloudy	74562
Clyde	73759
Coalgate	74538
Coalton	74437
Cobb	74701
Cogar	73059
Colbert	74733
Colcord	74338
Cole	73010
Coleman	73432
College (Part of Stillwater)‡	74074
Collinsville	74021
Colony	73021
Comanche	73529
Commerce	74339
Concho (Part of El Reno)	73022
Connerville	74836
Conser	74937
Cookietown	73562
Cookson	74427
Cooperton	73564
Copan	74022
Corbett	73051
Cordell	73632
Corinne	74735
Corn	73024
Cornish	73456
Corum	73529
Cottonwood	74538
Council Hill	74428
Countyline	73425
Courtney	73456
Cove Acres	73006
Covington	73730
Cowden	73632
Coweta	74429
Cowlington	74941
Cox City	73082
Coyle	73027
Cravens	74563
Crawford	73638
Crekola	74401
Croosoto	74743
Crescent	73028
Criner	73052
Cromwell	74837
Crossbow (Part of Tulsa)‡	74146
Crossroads Mall (Part of Oklahoma City)	73149
Crowder	74430
Crystal	74727
Crystal Lakes	73718
Cumberland	73446
Curt's Shopping Center (Part of Muskogee)	74403
Cushing	74023
Custer City	73639
Cyril	73029
Dacoma	73731
Daisy	74540
Dale	74851
Damon	74578
Dane	73737
Darwin	74523
Davenport	74026
Davidson	73530
Davis	73030
Dawson (Part of Tulsa)	74115
Deer Creek	74636
Degnan	74578
Dela	74523
Delaware	74027
Del City	73115
	73135
	73155
For specific ZIP Codes call (888) 275-8777, or your local postmaster.	
Delhi	73662
Dempsey	73628
Dennis	74301
Depew	74028
Depot	74501
Devol	73531
Dewar	74431
Dewey	74029
Dibble	73031
Dickson	73401
Dighton	74437
Dillard	73463
Dill City	73641
Disney	74340
Dixon	74884
Dodge	74344
Donaldson (Part of Tulsa)‡	74104
Dotyville	74354
Dougherty	73032
Douglas	73733
Dover	73734
Dow	74501
Drake	73086
Driftwood	73728
Drumb	74578
Drummond	73735
Drumright	74030
Duke	73532
Dunbar, *Love*	73448
Dunbar, *Pushmataha*	74557
Duncan	73533-34
	73575
For specific ZIP Codes call (888) 275-8777, or your local postmaster.	
Dunjee Park (Part of Oklahoma City)	73084
Durant	74701*
	74702†
Durham	73642
Durwood (Part of Dickson)	73401
Dustin	74839
Eagle City	73658
Eagletown	74734
Eakly	73033
Earl	73447
Earlsboro	74840
Eastborough	74014
East Jessie	74871
Eastland Mall (Part of Tulsa)	74134
Eastland Shopping Center (Part of Bartlesville)	74003
East Side (Part of Bartlesville)‡	74006
Eastside (Part of Muskogee)	74403
Eastside (Part of Oklahoma City)‡	73104
	73111
	73117
	73121
	73141
For specific ZIP Codes call (888) 275-8777, or your local postmaster.	

Place	ZIP Code
Eastside (Part of Tulsa)‡	74104
	74128-29
	74134
	74169
For specific ZIP Codes call (888) 275-8777, or your local postmaster.	
Eastside (Part of Weatherford)‡	73096
Eddy	74643
Edgewater Park	73006
Edmond	73003
	73013
	73034
	73083
For specific ZIP Codes call (888) 275-8777, or your local postmaster.	
Edna	74010
Eighty Ninth Street (Part of Oklahoma City)‡	73159
Eldon	74464
Eldorado	73537
Elgin	73538
Elk City	73644*
	73648†
Elk Plaza (Part of Duncan)‡	73575
Elmer	73539
Elmore City	73433
Elmwood	73932
El Reno	73036
Emerson Center	73572
Emet	73450
Empire City	73533
Enid	73701-06
For specific ZIP Codes call (888) 275-8777, or your local postmaster.	
Enos	73439
Enterprise	74561
Enville	73448
Eram	74445
Erick	73645
Erin Springs	73052
Estella	74301
Ethel	74523
Etowah	73068
Etta	74471
Eucha	74342
Euchee Creek (Part of Sand Springs)	74063
Eufaula	74432
Eva	73939
Ewing (Part of Clinton)	73601
Fairfax	74637
Fairland	74343
Fairmont	73736
Fair Oaks	74015
Fairview	73737
Falconhead	73430
Falfa	74571
Fallis	74881
Fame	74432
Fanshawe	74935
Fargo	73840
Farley (Part of Oklahoma City)‡	73107*
	73147†
Farmers Hill	74736
Farris	74525
Faxon	73540
Fay	73646
Featherston	74561
Felker	74764
Felt	73937
Fewell	74558
Fillmore	73432
Finley	74543
First National Bank (Part of Oklahoma City)‡	73102
Fisher (Part of Sand Springs)	74063
Fittstown	74842
Fitzhugh	74843
Fleetwood	73569
Fletcher	73541
Floris	73938
Flynn	73107
Folsom	73432
Fontana Shopping Center (Part of Tulsa)‡	74145
	74154-55
For specific ZIP Codes call (888) 275-8777, or your local postmaster.	
Foraker	74652
Forest Hill	74937
Forest Park	73121
Forgan	73938
Forney	74743
Forrester	74937
Fort Cobb	73038
Fort Coffee	74959
Fort Gibson	74434
Fort Reno (Part of El Reno)	73036
Fort Sill	73503
Fort Supply	73841
Fort Towson	74735
Foss	73647
Foster	73434
Four Corners, *Okmulgee*	74437
Four Corners, *Texas*	73939
Fox	73435
Fox Run	74037
Foyil	74031
Francis	74844
Franklin	73026
Frederick	73542
Freedom	73842
French Market (Part of Oklahoma City)‡	73116
Friendship	73521
Frisco	74871
Frogville	74743
Fugate	74569
Gaar Corner	74820
Gage	73843
Gans	74936
Garber	73738
Garden Grove	74804
Gardenview (Part of Bixby)	74008
Garland	74462
Garvin	74736
Gate	73844
Gay	74743
Geary	73040
Gene Autry	73436
Georgetown	74434
Geronimo	73543
Gerty	74531
Gibson	74467
Gideon	74464
Gilcrease (Part of Tulsa)‡	74127
Gilmore	74953
Glencoe	74032
Glendale	74940
Glen Pines (Part of Glenpool)	74033
Glenpool	74033
Glenwood South (Part of Jenks)	74037
Glover	74728
Golden	74737
Goldsby	73093
Goltry	73739
Goodland	74743
Goodwater	74740
Goodwell	73939
Gore	74435
Gotebo	73041
Gould	73544
Gowen	74545
Gracemont	73042
Grady	73569
Graham	73437
Grainola	74652
Grandfield	73546
Grand Lake Towne	74301
Grandview Heights	74403
Granite	73547
Grant	74738
Gray	73931
Gray Horse	74637
Grayson	74437
Greasy	74931
Greenfield	73043
Green Pastures (Part of Oklahoma City)	73084
Green Valley Estates	74962
Greenville	73448
Greenwood	74523
Griggs	73949
Grimes	73628
Grove	74344*
	74345†
Gulftown	74437
Guthrie	73044
Guymon	73942
Gyp	73770
Gypsy	74010
Haileyville	74546
Hall Addition (Part of Sand Springs)	74063
Hallett	74034
Hall Park	73071
Hammon	73650
Hanna	74845
Hanson	74955
Happyland	74820
Harden City	74871
Hardesty	73944
Hardy	74647
Harjo	74873
Harmon	73832
Harmony Star	74017
Harrah	73045
Harris	74740
Harrison	74955
Hartshorne	74547
Haskell	74436
Hastings	73548
Haw Creek	74937
Hawley	73761
Haworth	74740
Hayward	73730
Haywood	74501
Hazel Del	74851
Headrick	73549
Healdton	73438
Heavener	74937
Hefner (Part of Oklahoma City)‡	73142
	73162
	73172
For specific ZIP Codes call (888) 275-8777, or your local postmaster.	
Helena	73741
Hendrix	74741
Hennepin	73444
Hennessey	73742
Henryetta	74437
Heritage Park Mall (Part of Midwest City)	73110
Herring	73650
Hess	73539
Hester	73554
Hewitt (Part of Wilson)	73463
Hext	73645
Hickory	74865
Hicks Addition (Part of Spencer)	73084
Higgins	74545
Highland Park (Part of Tulsa	74107
Hill	74932
Hillsdale	73743
Hill Top	74570
Hinton	73047
Hitchcock	73744
Hitchita	74438
Hobart	73651
Hockerville	74363
Hodgen	74939
Hoffman	74437
Hog Shooter	74006
Holdenville	74848
Holley Creek	74728
Hollis	73550
Hollister	73551
Hollow	74369
Hollywood Corners	73069
Homer	74820
Homestead	73763
Hominy	74035
Honobia	74549
Hontubby	74937
Hooker	73945
Hoot Owl	74365
Hopeton	73746
Horntown	74848
Hough	73942
Howe	74940
Hoyt	74440
Hugo	74743
Hulbert	74441
Hulen	73572
Humphreys	73521
Hunter	74640
Hyde Park (Part of Muskogee)	74403
Hydro	73048
Idabel	74745
Independence	74937
Indiahoma	73552
Indian Meadows	74464
Indianola	74442
Ingalls	74074
Ingersoll	73728
Inola	74036
Iona	73086
Iron Post	74010
Iron Stob Corner	74736
Irving	73565
Isabella	73747
Jackson	74723
Jacktown	74855
Jamestown	74080
Jay	74346
Jefferson	73759
Jenks	74037
Jennings	74038
Jesse	74871
Jet	73749
Jimtown	73430
Johnson	74804
Jollyville	73030
Jones	73049
Joy	73098
Jumbo	74557
Kansas	74347
Katie	73433
Kaw City	74641
Keefeton	74403
Keetonville	74017
Kellond	74523
Kellyville, *Creek*	74039
Kellyville, *Ottawa*	74370
Kemp	74747
Kendalwood (Part of Glenpool)	74033
Kendrick	74079
Kenefic	74748
Kensington Center (Part of Tulsa)	74103
Kent	74759
Kenton	73946
Kenwood	74365
Keota	74941
Ketchum	74349
Keyes	73947
Keys	74451
Kiamichi	74574
Kiefer	74041
Kiersey	74701
Kildare	74604
Kingfisher	73750
Kingston	73439
Kinta	74552
Kiowa	74553
Knowles	73847
Konawa	74849
Kosoma	74557
Krebs	74554
Kremlin	73753
Kulli	74745
Kusa	74437
Lacey	73742
Lafayette	74462
Lahoma	73754
Lake Aluma	73121
Lake Creek	73547
Lake Ellsworth Addition	73006
Lake Hiwasse	73007
Lake Humphreys	73055
Lakeside Village	73538
Lake Station (Part of Sand Springs)	74127
Lake Valley	73041
Lake West	74727
Lamar	74850
Lambert	73728
La Mesa (Part of Enid)‡	73701
Lamont	74643
Lane	74555
Langley	74350
Langston	73050
Lark	73439
Last Chance	74859
Latta	74820
Laverne	73848
Lawrence Creek	74044
Lawton	73501-02
	73505-07
For specific ZIP Codes call (888) 275-8777, or your local postmaster.	
Leach	74364
Lebanon	73440
Leedey	73654
Leflore	74942
Lehigh	74556
Leisure Square (Part of Tulsa)‡	74112
Lenapah	74042
Lenna	74432
Lenora	73667
Lenox	74577
Leon	73441
Leonard	74043
Lequire	74943
Lewisville	74552
Lexington	73051
Liberty, *Bryan*	74741
Liberty, *Sequoyah*	74948
Liberty, *Tulsa*	74101
Lighthouse (Part of Tulsa)‡	74136
Lima	74884
Limestone, *Latimer*	74578
Limestone, *Rogers*	74017
Lincolnville	74363
Lindsay	73052
Little	74868
Little Axe	73069
Little Chief	74637
Little City	73446
Little Ponderosa	67901
Loco	73442
Locust Grove	74352
Lodi	74563
Logan	73848
Lona	74552
Lone Grove	73443
Lone Oak	74948
Lone Wolf	73655
Long	74948
Longdale	73755
Longtown♦	74561
Lookeba	73053
Lookout	73842
Lotsee	74063
Lovedale	73834
Loveland	73553
Lovell	73028
Loving	74937
Lowry	74464
Loyal	73756
Lucien	73757
Lugert	73655
Lula	74825
Luther	73054
Lutie	74578
Lynn Addition	74056
Lyons	74960
McAlester	74501*
	74502†
McAlester Army Ammunition Plant	74501
MacArthur Park (Part of Lawton)	73507
McBride	73439
McCord♦	74637
McCurtain	74944
McKey	74962
McKiddyville	73051
McKnight	73550
McLain	74403
McLoud	74851
McMillan	73446
Macomb	74852
McWillie	73716
Madge	73571
Madill	73446
Maguire (Part of Slaughterville)	73068
Manard	74434
Manchester	73758
Mangum	73554
Manitou	73555
Mannford	74044
Mannsville	73447
Maple	74948
Maramec	74045
Marble City	74945
Marietta	73448
Marland	74644
Marlow	73055
Marshall	73056
Martha	73556
Martin	74403
Martin Luther King (Part of Oklahoma City)‡	73111*
	73136†
Mason	74859
Matoy	74729
Maud	74854
Maxwell	74820
May	73851
Mayfield	73656
Mayhew	74727
May Ridge (Part of Oklahoma City)‡	73119
Maysville	73057
Mazie	74353
Mead	73449
Medford	73759
Medicine Park	73557

*** Area Zip Code** **† Post Office Boxes** **‡ Postal Station** **♦ Census Designated Place** *Italic Type* **County**

Meeker 74855
Meers 73501
Mehan 74074
Mellette 74432
Melvin 74441
Meno 73760
Meridian 73058
Merritt 73644
Messer 74743
Miami 74354*
... 74355†
Micawber 74833
Middleberg 73010
Midland 74723
Midlothian 74834
Midway 74538
Midwest City 73110
... 73130
... 73140
... 73150
For specific ZIP Codes call (888) 275-8777, or your local postmaster.
Milburn 73450
Milfay 74046
Mill Creek 74856
Miller 74557
Millerton 74750
Milo 73458
Milton 74930
Minco 73059
Mocane 73938
Moffett 74946
Monroe 74947
Montclair Addition (Part of Heavener) 74937
Moodys 74444
Moon 74740
Moore 73153
... 73160
... 73165
... 73170
For specific ZIP Codes call (888) 275-8777, or your local postmaster.
Mooreland 73852
Moorewood 73650
Morris 74445
Morrison 73061
Mosley 74338
Mound Grove 74764
Mounds 74047
Mountain Park 73559
Mountain View 73062
Mount Herman 74728
Mount Zion 74736
Mouser 73945
Moyers 74557
Mudsand 74759
Muldrow 74948
Mule Barn (Part of Cleveland) 74101
Mulhall 73063
Murphy 74352
Muse 74949
Muskogee 74401-03
For specific ZIP Codes call (888) 275-8777, or your local postmaster.
Mustang 73064
Mutual 73853
Nani-Chito 74957
Narcissa 74354
Nardin 74646
Nash 73761
Nashoba 74558
Natura 74421
Navina 73044
Nebo 73086
Needmore 73068
Neff 74953
Nelagony 74056
Newalla (Part of Oklahoma City) 74857
New Alluwe 74016
Newby 74010
Newcastle 73065
Newkirk 74647
New Liberty 73662
New Lima 74884
New Oberlin 74727
Newport 73401
New Tulsa 74429
Nichols Hills 73116
Nicoma Park 73066
Nicut 74948
Nida 74748
Niles 73047
Ninnekah 73067
Noble 73068
Nobletown 74884
Non 74531
Norge 73018
Norman 73026
... 73069-72
For specific ZIP Codes call (888) 275-8777, or your local postmaster.
Norris 74563
Northeast (Part of Tulsa)‡ 74112
... 74115-17
... 74158
For specific ZIP Codes call (888) 275-8777, or your local postmaster.
North Enid 73701
North Heights (Part of Bixby) 74008
North McAlester (Part of McAlester)‡ 74501
North Miami 74358
Northside (Part of Tulsa)‡ 74106
... 74110
... 74126
... 74130
... 74148
For specific ZIP Codes call (888) 275-8777, or your local postmaster.
Northwest (Part of Oklahoma City)‡ 73103
... 73106
... 73146
For specific ZIP Codes call (888) 275-8777, or your local postmaster.
Nowata 74048
Nowhere 73038
Nuyaka 74447
Oak Grove, *Murray* 73086
Oak Grove, *Payne* 74030
Oak Hill 74728
Oakhurst♦ 74050
Oakland 73446
Oakman 74820
Oak Park (Part of Bartlesville) 74003
Oaks 74359
Oakwood (Part of Jenks) 74037
Oakwood, *Dewey* 73658
Oakwood Mall (Part of Enid) 73703
Oberlin 74727
Ochelata 74051
Octavia 74957
Ogeechee 74343
Oglesby 74061
Oil Center 74820
Oil City 73463
Oilton 74052
Okarche 73762
Okay 74446
Okeene 73763
Okemah 74859
Okesa 74003
Okfuskee 74859
Oklahoma Baptist University (Part of Shawnee)‡ 74804

Oklahoma City

... 73101-89
For specific ZIP Codes call (888) 275-8777, or your local postmaster.

Colleges & Universities

Mid-America Bible Coll 73170
Oklahoma Christian Univ 73136
Oklahoma City Univ 73106

Financial Institutions

BancFirst 73102
Bank One 73102
NationsBank, NA 73116

Hospitals

Integris Baptist Med Ctr 73112
Integris Southwest Med Ctr 73109
Mercy Health Ctr 73120
Presbyterian Hosp 73104
St Anthony Hosp 73101
Univ Hosp 73104
Veterans Affairs Med Ctr 73104

Hotels/Motels

Clarion 73105
Days Inn, Airport Meridian 73128
Holiday Inn Airport 73108
Marriott 73112
Radisson Inn 73108
The Weston 73102

Military Installations

Defense Distribution Depot 73145
Oklahoma Air Nat Guard, FB6562, Will Rogers World Airport 73179
Tinker Air Force Base/Air Logistics Command 73145
U S Property & Fiscal Off for Oklahoma 73111

Oklahoma State Tech (Part of Okmulgee)‡ 74447
Okmulgee 74447
Oktaha 74450
Oleta 74735
Olive 74030
Olney 74538
Olustee 73560
Omega 73764
Oneta 74012
Oologah 74053
Optima 73945
Ord 74738
Orienta 73737
Orion 73737
Orlando 73073
Orr 73456
Osage (Part of Ponca City)‡ 74604
Osage, *Osage* 74054
Osage Hills Estates (Part of Sand Springs) 74063
Osage Indian Reservation 74056
Oscar 73561
Oswalt 73453
Overbrook 73453
Owasso 74055
Paden 74860
Page 74937
Panama 74951
Panola 74559
Paoli 73074
Paradise Hill 74955
Paradise View 74337
Parker 74538
Park Hill 74451
Parkland 74824
Park Lane (Part of Lawton) 73501
Patterson 74578
Patton 74330
Pauls Valley 73075
Pawhuska 74056
Pawnee 74058
Paw Paw 74948
Payne 73052
Payson 74855
Pearson 74826
Pearsonia 74056
Peckham 74647
Peggs 74452
Pennington Hills Plaza (Part of Bartlesville) 74003
Penn Square Mall (Part of Oklahoma City) 73118
Penn 89th (Part of Oklahoma City)‡ 73139
... 73159
... 73159
... 73169
... 73173
... 73189
For specific ZIP Codes call (888) 275-8777, or your local postmaster.
Pensacola 74301
Peoria 74363
Perkins 74059
Pernell 73076
Perry 73077
Pershing 74002
Petersburg 73456
Petros 74937
Pettit 74451
Pettit Bay 74451
Pharoah 74880
Phillips 74538
Picher 74360
Pickens 74752
Pickett 74820
Piedmont 73078
Pierce 74426
Piney 74960
Pink 74873
Pin Oaks Acres 74337
Pittsburg 74560
Platter 74753
Pleasant Hill 74740
Plunkettville 74963
Pocasset 73079
Pocola 74902
Pollard 74740
Ponca City 74601-04
For specific ZIP Codes call (888) 275-8777, or your local postmaster.
Pond Creek 73766
Pontotoc 74820
Pooleville 73458
Porter 74454
Porter Hill 73538
Porum 74455
Poteau 74953
Powell 73439
Prague 74864
Prattville (Part of Sand Springs) 74063
Preston 74456
Proctor 74457
Prue 74060
Pruitt City 73481
Pryor 74361*
... 74362†
Pumpkin Center, *Comanche* 73501
Pumpkin Center, *Okmulgee* 74445
Purcell 73080
Purdy 73052
Putnam 73659
Pyramid Corners 74333
Quail Creek (Part of Oklahoma City)‡ 73120
Quail Springs Mall (Part of Oklahoma City) 73134
Qualls 74451
Quapaw 74363
Quay 74085
Quinlan 73852
Quinton 74561
Raiford 74432
Ralston 74650
Ramona 74061
Ranchwood Manor (Part of Oklahoma City) 73160
Randlett 73562
Ratliff City 73481
Rattan 74562
Ravia 73455
Reagan 73460
Reck 73463
Redbird 74458
Red Fork (Part of Tulsa) 74107
Red Hill 74941
Red Horse (Part of Midwest City) 73110
Redland 74948
Red Oak 74563
Red Rock 74651
Reed 73554
Regal (Part of Lawton) 73501
Reichert 74937
Remus 74854
... 74873
For specific ZIP Codes call (888) 275-8777, or your local postmaster.
Renfrow 73759
Reno Meridian (Part of Oklahoma City)‡ 73137
Rentiesville 74459
Retrop 73627
Rexroat 73463
Reydon 73660
Reynolds 74553
Rhea 73654
Richards Spur 73538
Richland 73099
Richville 74501
Ringling 73456
Ringold 74754
Ringwood 73768
Ripley 74062
Roberta 74701
Rock Island 74932
Rockwell Plaza (Part of Oklahoma City) 73109
Rocky 73661
Rocky Mountain 74960
Rocky Point 74467
Roff 74865
Roland 74954
Roll 73628
Rolling Meadows (Part of Glenpool) 74033
Roosevelt 73564
Rose 74364
Rosedale 74831
Rosston 73855
Rossville 74881
Roxana 73056
Rubottom 73463
Rufe 74755
Rush Springs 73082
Russell 73554
Russellville 74561
Russett 73447
Ryan 73565
Sacred Heart 74849
Saddle Mountain 73062
Sageeyah 74017
St. Louis 74866
Salem 74437
Salina 74365
Sallisaw 74955
Salt Fork 74640
Sams Point 74501
Sandbluff 74759
Sand Creek 73771
Sand Point 73449
Sand Springs 74063
Sansbois 74552
Santa Fe 73442
... 73491
For specific ZIP Codes call (888) 275-8777, or your local postmaster.
Sapulpa 74066*
... 74067†
Sardis 74536
Sasakwa 74867
Savanna 74565
Sawyer 74756
Sayre 73662
Schlegal 74023
Schoolton 74859
Schulter 74460
Scipio 74501
Scott 73047
Scraper 74464
Scullin 73086
Scullyville 74959
Sedan 73062
Seiling 73663
Selman 73834
Seminole 74818†
... 74868*
Sentinel 73664
Sequoyah 74017
Seward 73044
Shady Grove, *McIntosh* 74426
Shady Grove, *Pawnee* 74112
Shady Grove, *Sequoyah* 74948
Shady Point 74956
Shamrock 74068
Sharon 73857
Shartel (Part of Oklahoma City)‡ 73105
... 73118
... 73154
For specific ZIP Codes call (888) 275-8777, or your local postmaster.
Shattuck 73858
Shawnee 74801-04
For specific ZIP Codes call (888) 275-8777, or your local postmaster.
Shawnee Mall (Part of Shawnee) 74804
Shay 73439
Shepherd Mall (Part of Oklahoma City)‡ 73107
Sheridan (Part of Lawton)‡ 73505

Sheridan (Part of Tulsa)‡ 74133
74135
74153
For specific ZIP Codes call (888) 275-8777, or your local postmaster.
Sherwood 74728
Shidler 74652
Shinewell 74740
Short 74948
Shults 74745
Sickles 73053
Silo 74701
Silver City 74038
Silver Tree (Part of Broken Arrow) 74011
Skedee 74058
Skiatook 74070
Slapout 73848
Slaughterville 73051
Slick 74071
Smith Lee 74723
Smith Village 73115
Smithville 74957
Snow 74567
Snyder 73566
Sobol 74735
Sooner Fashion Mall (Part of Norman)‡ 73072
Soper 74759
Southard 73770
South Coffeyville 74072
South Country Estates (Part of Bixby) 74008
Southeast (Part of Oklahoma City)‡ 73109
73129
73143
For specific ZIP Codes call (888) 275-8777, or your local postmaster.
Southeast (Part of Tulsa)‡ 74145
74147
74155
For specific ZIP Codes call (888) 275-8777, or your local postmaster.
South Heights (Part of Sand Springs) 74063
South Park (Part of Broken Arrow) 74011
Southroads Mall (Part of Tulsa) 74135
Southside‡ 74105
74136-37
74170
For specific ZIP Codes call (888) 275-8777, or your local postmaster.
Southwest (Part of Oklahoma City)‡ 73119
73144
73179
For specific ZIP Codes call (888) 275-8777, or your local postmaster.
Southwood East (Part of Bixby) 74008
Southwood South (Part of Bixby) 74008
Sparks 74869
Spaulding 74848
Spavinaw 74366
Speer 74743
Spelter City 74437
Spencer 73084
Spencerville 74760
Sperry 74073
Spiro 74959
Sportsmen Acres 74361
Springer 73458
Springlake Park (Part of Oklahoma City) 73111
Stafford 73601
Stanley 74536
Stapp 74939
Star 74941
State Capitol (Part of Oklahoma City)‡ 73105*
73152†
Stealy 73095
Stecker 73006
Steedman 74825
Steel Junction 74728
Steen (Part of Enid) 73701
Stella (Part of Oklahoma City) 74857
Sterling 73567
Stidham 74461
Stigler 74462
Stillwater 74074-76
For specific ZIP Codes call (888) 275-8777, or your local postmaster.
Stilwell 74960
Stockyards (Part of Oklahoma City)‡ 73108
Stonebluff 74436
Stones Corner 74429
Stonewall 74871
Stony Point, *Adair* 74960
Stony Point, *Le Flore* 74959
Story 73057
Straight 73942
Strang 74367
Stratford 74872
Stringtown 74569
Strong City 73628
Stroud 74079
Stuart 74570
Sugden 73573
Sullivan Village (Part of Lawton) 73501
Sulphur 73086
Summerfield 74966
Summit 74401
Sumner 73077
Sungate (Part of Lawton) 73501
Sunkist 74727
Sunnybrook Estates 74037
Sunray 73529
Survey Heights 73947
Sweetwater 73666
Swink 74761
Tabler 73018
Tablerville 74734
Taft 74463
Tahlequah 74464*
74465†
Tahona 74932
Tailholt 74471
Talala 74080
Talihina 74571
Tallant 74002
Taloga 73667
Tamaha 74462
Tangier 73801
Tatums 73487
Taylor 73562
Tecumseh 74873
Temple 73568
Teresita 74364
Terlton 74081
Terral 73569
Texanna 74426
Texhoma 73949
Texola 73668
Thackerville 73459
The Meadows (Part of Broken Arrow) 74011
Thirty-Fourth Street (Part of Woodward)‡ 73801
Thirty Ninth Street (Part of Oklahoma City)‡ 73112
Thomas 73669
Ti 74528
Tiajuana 73440
Tiawah 74017
Timber Brook 74014
Timberlane 74020
Tiner 74728
Tipton 73570
Tishomingo 73460
Titanic 74960
Tom 74740
Tonkawa 74653
Topsy 74366
Townwest (Part of Lawton)‡ 73506
Tribbey 74852
Trousdale 74878
Troy 74856
Tryon 74875
Tucker 74959
Tullahassee 74466
Tulsa 74101-70
For specific ZIP Codes call (888) 275-8777, or your local postmaster.
Tulsa Promenade (Part of Tulsa) 74135
Tupelo 74572
Turkey Ford 74344
Turley♦ 74156
Turner 73430
Turpin 73950
Tushka 74525
Tuskahoma 74574
Tuskegee 74010
Tussy 73488
Tuttle 73089
Tuxedo (Part of Bartlesville) 74006
Twin Hills 74447
Twin Oaks 74368
Tyler 73446
Tyrone 73951
Ulan 74442
Ultima Thule 74734
Unger 74727
Union (Part of Norman)‡ 73069
Union (Part of Tulsa) 74012
Union City 73090
Union Valley 74871
University (Part of Enid)‡ 73701
University (Part of Shawnee)‡ 74801
University of Science and Arts (Part of Chickasha)‡ 73018
Uptown Shopping Center (Part of Midwest City) 73110
Utica 74726
Utica Square (Part of Tulsa)‡ 74152
Valley Brook 73149
Valley Park 74017
Valliant 74764
Vamoosa 74849
Vance Air Force Base 73705
Vanoss 74820
Velma 73491
Vera 74082
Verden 73092
Verdigris 74017
Vernon 74845
Vian 74962
Vici 73859
Victoria Pond (Part of Jenks) 74037
Victory 73560
Village 73120
73134
73156
For specific ZIP Codes call (888) 275-8777, or your local postmaster.
Vinco 74059
Vinita 74301
Vinson 73571
Virgil 74756
Vista 74849
Vivian 74432
Wade 74723
Wagoner 74467*
74477†
Wainwright 74468
Wakita 73771
Wallville 73052
Walters 73572
Wanette 74878
Wann 74083
Wapanucka 73461
Ward Springs 74570
Wardville 74576
Warner 74469
Warr Acres 73122-23
73132
For specific ZIP Codes call (888) 275-8777, or your local postmaster.
Warren 73526
Warwick 74834
Washington 73093
Washita 73094
Waterloo 73034
Watonga 73772
Watova 74048
Watson 74963
Watts 74964
Wauhillau 74960
Waukomis 73773
Waurika 73573
Wayne 73095
Waynoka 73860
Weatherford 73096
Weathers 74560
Webb 73835
Webb City 74652
Webbers Falls 74470
Welch 74369
Weleetka 74880
Welling 74471
Wellston 74881
Welty 74833
West Nichols Hills (Part of Oklahoma City) 73116
West Park Mall (Part of Oklahoma City)‡ 73123
Westport 74020
Westside (Part of Muskogee)‡ 74401
Westside (Part of Oklahoma City)‡ 73108
73127-28
For specific ZIP Codes call (888) 275-8777, or your local postmaster.
West Siloam Springs 72761
West Tulsa (Part of Tulsa)‡ 74107
Westville 74965
Wetumka 74883
Wewoka 74884
Wheatland (Part of Oklahoma City) 73097
Wheeless 73933
Whippoorwill 74056
Whispering Creek (Part of Sand Springs) 74063
White Bead 73075
White Eagle 74601
Whitefield 74472
White Oak, *Cherokee* 74451
White Oak, *Craig* 74301
Whitesboro 74577
Whittier (Part of Tulsa)‡ 74120*
74150†
Wichita Mountains Estates 73501
Wilburton 74578
Wildcat Point 74451
Wild Horse 74070
Williams 74932
Willis 73439
Willow 73673
Wilson, *Carter* 73463
Wilson, *Okmulgee* 74437
Winchester 74421
Winganon 74016
Wirt 73438
Wister 74966
Wolco 74002
Wolf 74854
Woodford 73458
Woodland Hills Mall (Part of Tulsa) 74133
Woodland View (Part of Tulsa)‡ 74145
Woodlawn Park 73008
Woods 73020
Woodville 73439
Woodward 73801*
73802†
Woody Chapel 73080
Wright City 74766
Wyandotte 74370
Wybark 74401
Wye 74852
Wynnewood 73098
Wynona 74084
Yale 74085
Yanush 74574
Yarnaby 74741
Yeager 74848
Yewed 73728
Yost Lake 74032
Yuba 74741
Yukon 73085†
73099*
Zafra 74957
Zaneis 73463
Zeb 74464
Zena 74346
Zincville 74363
Zion 74960
Zoe 74939

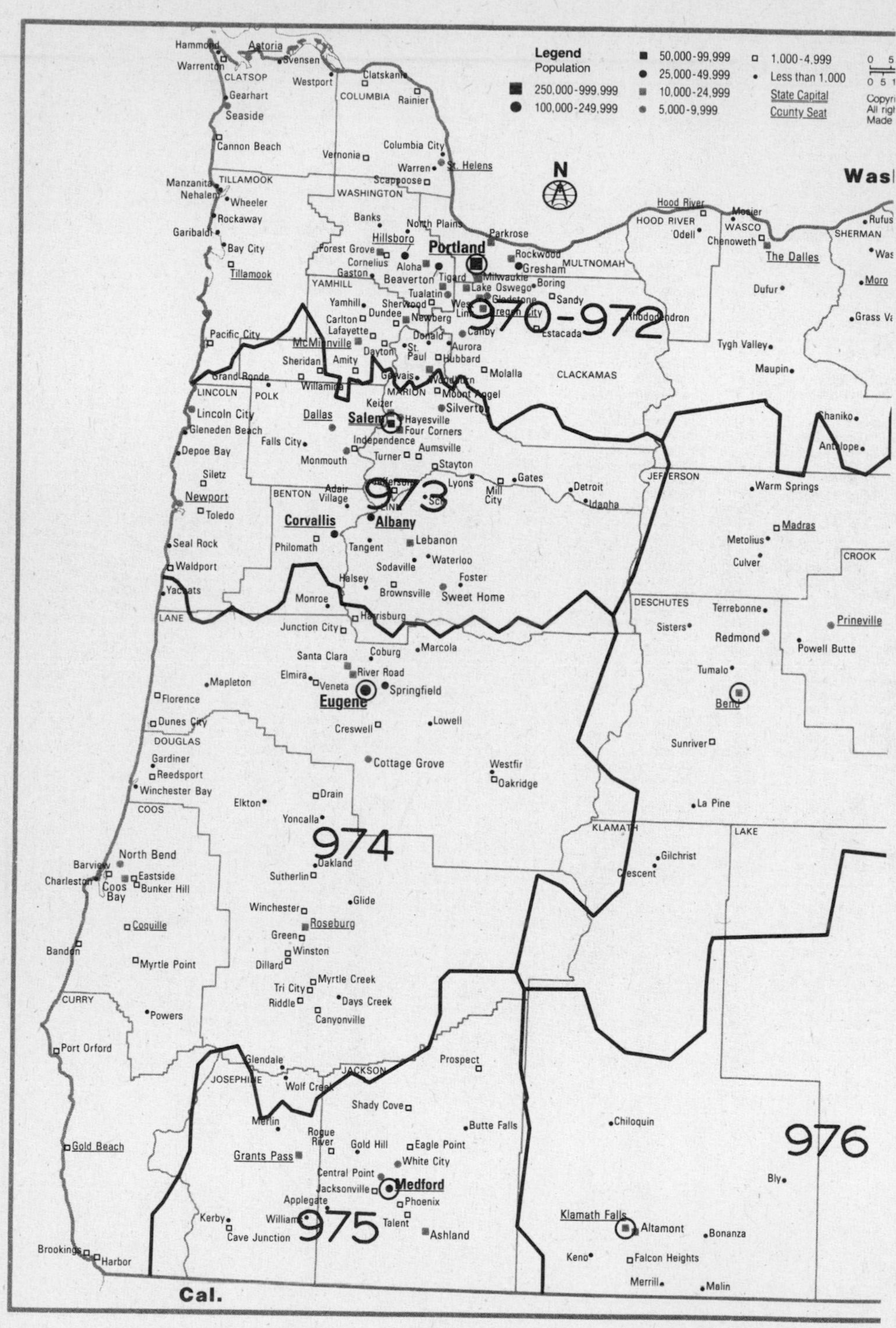
Legend
Population
250,000-999,999
100,000-249,999
50,000-99,999
25,000-49,999
10,000-24,999
5,000-9,999
1,000-4,999
Less than 1,000
State Capital
County Seat
N
Wash
Cal.
970-972
973
974
975
976
CLATSOP
COLUMBIA
TILLAMOOK
WASHINGTON
MULTNOMAH
HOOD RIVER
WASCO
SHERMAN
YAMHILL
CLACKAMAS
POLK
MARION
LINCOLN
BENTON
LINN
JEFFERSON
CROOK
DESCHUTES
LANE
DOUGLAS
COOS
KLAMATH
LAKE
CURRY
JOSEPHINE
JACKSON
Hammond
Astoria
Warrenton
Svensen
Gearhart
Westport
Clatskanie
Rainier
Seaside
Cannon Beach
Vernonia
Columbia City
Warren
St. Helens
Scappoose
Manzanita
Nehalem
Wheeler
Rockaway
Garibaldi
Bay City
Tillamook
Banks
North Plains
Hillsboro
Portland
Parkrose
Rockwood
Gresham
Forest Grove
Cornelius
Aloha
Gaston
Beaverton
Tigard
Milwaukie
Lake Oswego
Boring
Tualatin
Sandy
Yamhill
Sherwood
Dundee
Carlton
Newberg
Lafayette
Canby
Estacada
Hood River
Odell
Mosier
Chenoweth
The Dalles
Rufus
Dufur
Moro
Grass Valley
Tygh Valley
Maupin
Pacific City
McMinnville
Dayton
St. Paul
Aurora
Hubbard
Sheridan
Amity
Molalla
Grand Ronde
Willamina
Gervais
Mount Angel
Keizer
Silverton
Lincoln City
Dallas
Salem
Hayesville
Four Corners
Gleneden Beach
Independence
Aumsville
Falls City
Turner
Depoe Bay
Monmouth
Stayton
Shaniko
Antelope
Siletz
Lyons
Gates
Mill City
Detroit
Idanha
Newport
Adair Village
Toledo
Corvallis
Albany
Warm Springs
Madras
Metolius
Culver
Philomath
Tangent
Lebanon
Seal Rock
Waterloo
Sodaville
Waldport
Halsey
Foster
Brownsville
Sweet Home
Yachats
Monroe
Harrisburg
Terrebonne
Sisters
Redmond
Prineville
Junction City
Marcola
Powell Butte
Coburg
Santa Clara
River Road
Tumalo
Elmira
Veneta
Mapleton
Springfield
Eugene
Bend
Florence
Creswell
Lowell
Dunes City
Sunriver
Gardiner
Cottage Grove
Westfir
Oakridge
Reedsport
Winchester Bay
Drain
Elkton
La Pine
Yoncalla
Oakland
Gilchrist
Crescent
North Bend
Barview
Eastside
Charleston
Coos Bay
Bunker Hill
Sutherlin
Glide
Winchester
Roseburg
Coquille
Green
Winston
Bandon
Myrtle Point
Dillard
Myrtle Creek
Tri City
Riddle
Days Creek
Canyonville
Powers
Port Orford
Glendale
Prospect
Wolf Creek
Shady Cove
Merlin
Butte Falls
Chiloquin
Rogue River
Gold Hill
Eagle Point
White City
Gold Beach
Grants Pass
Central Point
Jacksonville
Medford
Phoenix
Applegate
Bly
Kerby
Talent
Cave Junction
Ashland
Klamath Falls
Altamont
Bonanza
Brookings
Harbor
Keno
Falcon Heights
Merrill
Malin

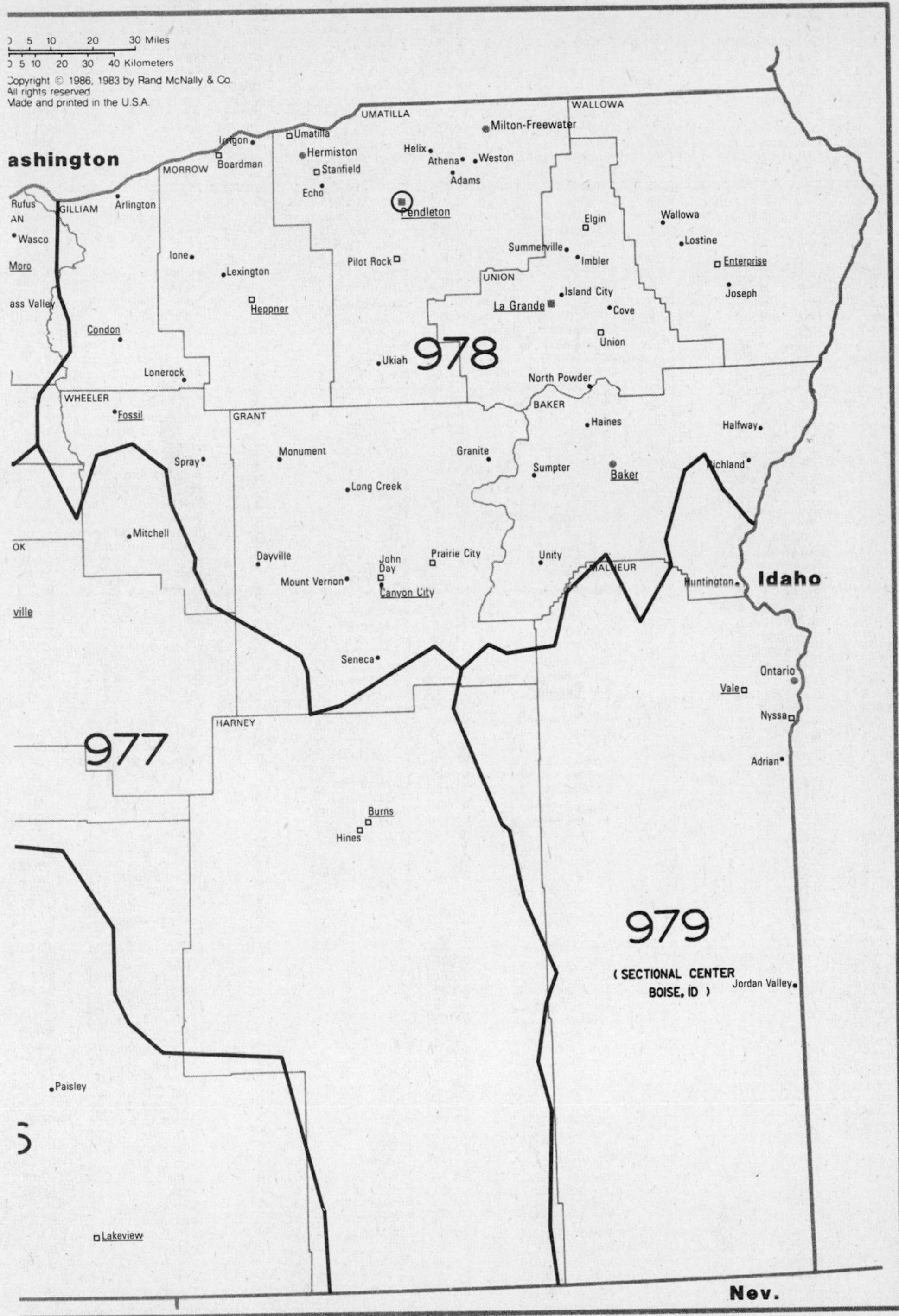

0 5 10 20 30 Miles
0 5 10 20 30 40 Kilometers
Copyright © 1986, 1983 by Rand McNally & Co.
All rights reserved
Made and printed in the U.S.A.
Washington
UMATILLA
WALLOWA
MORROW
GILLIAM
WHEELER
GRANT
UNION
BAKER
MALHEUR
HARNEY
Irrigon
Umatilla
Hermiston
Stanfield
Boardman
Echo
Milton-Freewater
Helix
Athena
Weston
Adams
Pendleton
Rufus
Wasco
Moro
Arlington
Ione
Lexington
Heppner
Condon
Lonerock
Fossil
Pilot Rock
Ukiah
Elgin
Wallowa
Lostine
Enterprise
Joseph
Summerville
Imbler
La Grande
Island City
Cove
Union
North Powder
Haines
Halfway
Richland
Granite
Sumpter
Baker
Monument
Spray
Long Creek
Mitchell
Dayville
John Day
Prairie City
Unity
Mount Vernon
Canyon City
Huntington
Idaho
Seneca
Ontario
Vale
Nyssa
Adrian
Burns
Hines
978
977
979
(SECTIONAL CENTER BOISE, ID)
Jordan Valley
Paisley
Lakeview
Nev.

Acorn Park (Part of Eugene) 97402
Ada 97493
Adair Village 97330
Adams 97810
Adel 97620
Adrian 97901
Agate Beach (Part of Newport) 97365
Agency Lake 97624
Agness 97406
Aims 97019
Airlie 97361
Ajax 97823
Albany 97321
Albany Yard (Part of Albany) 97321
Alder Creek 97055
Aldrich Point 97103
Alfalfa 97701
Alicel 97824
Alkali Lake 97758
Allegany 97407
Allston 97048
Aloha 97006-07
For specific ZIP Codes call (888) 275-8777, or your local postmaster.
Alpine 97456
Alsea 97324
Altamont♦ 97603
Alvadore 97409
Amity 97101
Anchor 97410
Andrews 97720
Anlauf 97428
Annex 83672
Antelope 97001
Apiary 97048
Applegate 97530
Arago 97458
Arch Cape 97102
Arleta (Part of Portland) 97206
Arlington 97812
Arock 97902
Ashland 97520
Ashwood 97711
Astoria 97103
Astoria Coast Guard Base 97103
Athena 97813
Aumsville 97325
Aurora 97002
Austin 97817
Austin Junction 97817
Avon (Part of Rainier) 97048
Azalea 97410
Bakeoven 97037
Baker City 97814
Ballston 97378
Bandon 97411
Banks 97106
Barlow 97013
Barton 97022
Barview, *Coos*♦ 97420
Barview, *Tillamook* 97136
Basque 89421
Bates 97817
Battin 97266
Bay City 97107
Bay Park 97420
Bayshore 97394
Bayside Garden 97131
Bayview 97394
Beatty 97621
Beaver 97108
Beavercreek 97004
Beaver Homes 97048
Beaver Marsh 97731
Beaver Springs 97048
Beaverton 97005-08
97075-76
For specific ZIP Codes call (888) 275-8777, or your local postmaster.
Beaverton Mall (Part of Beaverton) 97005
Belknap Springs 97413
Belleview (Part of Ashland) 97520
Bollovuo 97128
Bellfountain 97456
Bend 97701-09
For specific ZIP Codes call (888) 275-8777, or your local postmaster.
Berlin 97355
Bethany 97123
Bethel Heights 97304

Beulah 97911
Beverly Beach 97365
Biggs 97065
Bingham Springs 97810
Birkenfeld 97016
Blachly 97412
Black Butte Ranch 97759
Blaine 97108
Blalock 97812
Blodgett 97326
Blooming 97113
Blue River 97413
Bly 97622
Boardman 97818
Bolton (Part of West Linn) 97068
Bonanza 97623
Bonneville 97014
Bonny Slope 97229
Boring 97009
Boyd 97021
Boyer 97347
Bradwood 97016
Breitenbush 97342
Brickerville 97453
Bridal Veil 97010
Bridge 97458
Bridgeport, *Baker* 97819
Bridgeport, *Polk* 97338
Brighton 97136
Brightwood 97011
Broadacres 97002
Broadbent 97414
Brockway 97496
Brogan 97903
Brookings 97415
Brooklyn (Part of Portland)‡ 97202*
97242†
Brooks 97305
Brothers 97712
Brownlee 97840
Brownsboro 97524
Brownsmead 97016
Brownsville 97327
Bryant (Part of Lake Oswego) 97035
Buchanan 97720
Buena Vista 97351
Bullrun 97055
Bunker Hill♦ 97420
Burlingame (Part of Portland) 97219
Burlington 97231
Burns 97720
Burnside 97103
Burns Junction 97910
Burns Paiute Indian Reservation 97720
Burnt Woods 97326
Butte Falls 97522
Butteville 97002
Buxton 97109
Cages 97739
Cairo 97914
Calapooya 97386
Camas Valley 97416
Camp Clatsop 97146
Camp Polk 97759
Camp Sherman 97730
Camp Twelve 97391
Campus Station (Part of Corvallis) 97331
Canaan 97054
Canary 97493
Canby 97013
Canemah (Part of Oregon City) 97045
Cannon Beach 97110
Cannon Beach Junction 97138
Canyon City 97820
Canyonville 97417
Cape Meares 97141
Capitol Hill (Part of Portland) 97219
Carlton 97111
Carnation (Part of Forest Grove) 97116
Carpenterville 97415
Carson 97834
Caruo 07045
Carver 97015
Cascade Gorge 97536
Cascade Locks 97014
Cascade Summit 97425
Cascadia 97329
Cave Junction 97523
Cayuse 97821
Cecil 97843

Cedar Dale 97038
Cedar Hills 97225
Cedarhurst Park 97023
Cedar Mill♦ 97229*
97291†
Celilo 97058
Centennial 97236
Central (Part of Portland)‡ 97204*
97240†
Central Point, *Clackamas* 97045
Central Point, *Jackson* 97502
Central Point West 97502
Chapman 97056
Charleston 97420
Charlestown 97838
Chemult 97731
Chenoweth♦ 97058
Cherry Grove 97119
Cherry Heights 97058
Cherryville 97055
Cheshire 97419
Chiloquin 97624
Chitwood 97391
Christmas Valley 97641
Chutes (Part of Portland) 97202
Clackamas♦ 97015
Clackamas Heights (Part of Oregon City) 97045
Clarkes 97004
Clarno 97830
Clatskanie 97016
Clatskanie Heights 97016
Clear Lake 97303
Clifton 97016
Cloverdale, *Deschutes* 97756
Cloverdale, *Lane* 97426
Cloverdale, *Tillamook* 97112
Clow Corner 97338
Coaledo 97420
Coburg 97408
College Hill (Part of Eugene) 97405
Colton 97017
Columbia City 97018
Concord 97222
Condon 97823
Cook (Part of Lake Oswego) 97034
Coos Bay 97420
Cooston 97459
Coquille 97423
Corbett 97019
Cornelius 97113
Cornelius Pass 97231
Coronado Shores 97388
Corvallis 97330-33
97339
For specific ZIP Codes call (888) 275-8777, or your local postmaster.
Cottage Grove 97424
Cottrell 97009
Council Crest (Part of Portland) 97201
Courtrock 97864
Cove 97824
Cove Orchard 97148
Crabtree 97335
Crane 97732
Crater Lake 97604
Crawfordsville 97336
Crescent 97733
Crescent Lake 97425
Crescent Lake Junction 97425
Creston (Part of Portland)‡ 97206*
97286†
Creswell 97426
Crooked River Ranch 97760
Crow 97405
Culp Creek 97427
Culver 97734
Currinsville 97023
Curtin 97428
Cutler City (Part of Lincoln City) 97367
Dairy 97625
Dale 97880
Daloy 07702
Dallas 97338
Damascus 97009
Damascus Heights 97009
Danebo (Part of Eugene) 97402
Danner 97910
Days Creek 97429
Dayton 97114

Dayville 97825
Deadwood 97430
Dee 97031
Deer Island 97054
De Lake (Part of Lincoln City) 97367
Delena 97016
Dellwood 97420
Delmoor 97146
Denmark 97450
Depoe Bay 97341
Deschutes Junction 97701
Detroit 97342
Dever 97321
Dew Valley 97411
Dexter 97431
Diamond 97722
Diamond Lake 97731
Diamond Lake Junction 97731
Dickey Prairie 97038
Dillard 97432
Dilley 97116
Dixie 97907
Dixonville 97470
Dodge 97023
Dodson 97014
Dolph Corner 97338
Donald 97020
Dora 97458
Dorena 97434
Dover 97055
Downing 97016
Downtown (Part of Bend)‡ 97701*
97709†
Drain 97435
Draperville 97321
Drew 97484
Drewsey 97904
Dufur 97021
Dukes Valley 97031
Dundee 97115
Dunes City 97439
Durham 97224
Durkee 97905
Eagle Creek 97022
Eagle Point 97524
East Gardiner 97467
East Lake 97739
East Moreland (Part of Portland) 97202
East Portland‡ 97214-15
97232
For specific ZIP Codes call (888) 275-8777, or your local postmaster.
Eastside (Part of Coos Bay) 97420
Eastwood (Part of Roseburg) 97470
Echo 97826
Echo Dell 97045
Eckman Lake 97394
Eddyville 97343
Elgarose 97470
Elgin 97827
Elk City 97391
Elkhead 97499
Elkhorn 97358
Elk Lake 97701
Elkton 97436
Ellendale 97338
Ellingson Mill 97884
Elliott Prairie 97071
Elmira 97437
Elsie 97138
Elwood 97017
Emerald Heights (Part of Astoria) 97103
Empire (Part of Coos Bay)‡ 97420
Endersby 97058
Englewood 97420
Enterprise 97828
Errol Heights (Part of Portland) 97266
Estacada 97023
Eugene 97401-05
97408
97440
For specific ZIP Codes call (888) 275-8777, or your local postmaster.
Fairfield 97026
Fair Oaks, *Clackamas* 97222
Fairoaks, *Douglas* 97479
Fairview, *Coos* 97423
Fairview, *Multnomah* 97024
Fairview, *Tillamook* 97141

Falcon Heights 97601
Fall Creek 97438
Falls City 97344
Fargo 97002
Faubion 97049
Fayetteville 97377
Fern Corner 97338
Fern Hill, *Clatsop* 97103
Fern Hill, *Columbia* 97048
Ferns 97338
Fields, *Harney* 97710
Fields, *Lane* 97463
Finn Rock 97488
Fir Grove 97404
Fir Villa 97338
Firwood 97055
Fischers Mill 97045
Fishers Corner 97045
Fish Lake Resort 97524
Five Corners 97630
Flora 97828
Floras Lake 97450
Florence 97439
Forest Grove 97116
Forest Park (Part of Portland)‡ 97209-10
For specific ZIP Codes call (888) 275-8777, or your local postmaster.
Forfar 97366
Fort Hill 97396
Fort Klamath 97626
Fort Rock 97735
Fortune Branch 97442
Fossil 97830
Foster 97345
Four Corners, *Jackson* 97502
Four Corners, *Marion*♦ 97301
Fox 97831
Franklin 97448
Freewater (Part of Milton-Freewater) 97862
Frenchglen 97736
Friend 97021
Fruitdale 97526
Fruitvale 97365
Gales Creek 97117
Galice 97532
Garden Home 97223
Gardiner 97441
Gardiner Ridge 97415
Garfield 97023
Garibaldi 97118
Gaston 97119
Gates 97346
Gateway 97741
Gateway Mall (Part of Springfield) 97477
Gaylord 97458
Gazley 97457
Gearhart 97138
George 97023
Gervais 97026
Gibbon 97810
Gilbert (Part of Portland) 97266
Gilchrist 97737
Gillespie Corners 97405
Gilliams 97338
Gladstone 97027
Glasgow 97459
Glenada 97439
Glenbrook 97456
Glen Cullen (Part of Portland) 97201
Glendale 97442
Gleneden Beach 97388
Glengary 97470
Glenmorrie (Part of Lake Oswego) 97034
Glenwood, *Clatsop* 97146
Glenwood, *Lane* 97403
Glenwood, *Washington* 97116
Glide 97443
Globe 97490
Goble 97048
Gold Beach 97444
Gold Hill 97525
Gooseberry 97843
Goshen 97405
Government Camp 97028
Grande Ronde Indian Reservation 97396
Grand Ronde 97347
Grand Ronde Agency 97347
Granite 97877
Grants Pass 97526-28
For specific ZIP Codes call (888) 275-8777, or your local postmaster.

Place	ZIP
Grass Valley	97029
Green♦	97470
Green Acres	97420
Greenberry	97333
Green Hills (Part of Portland)	97221
Greenhorn	97877
Greenleaf	97430
Greenville, *Linn*	97386
Greenville, *Washington*	97116
Greenway (Part of Tigard)	97223
Gresham	97030
	97080
For specific ZIP Codes call (888) 275-8777, or your local postmaster.	
Haines	97833
Halfway	97834
Halsey	97348
Hammond (Part of Warrenton)	97121
Hampton	97712
Happy Valley	97236
Harbor♦	97415
Hardman	97836
Harlan	97343
Harney	97720
Harper	97906
Harriman	97601
Harrisburg	97446
Hauser	97459
Hayesville♦	97303
Hebo	97122
Heceta Beach	97439
Heceta Junction	97439
Helix	97835
Helvetia	97123
Hemlock (Part of Westfir)	97492
Hemlock, *Tillamook*	97112
Henley	97603
Henrice	97045
Heppner	97836
Hereford	97837
Hermiston	97838
Highland	97004
Hildebrand	97623
Hilgard	97850
Hillsboro	97123-24
For specific ZIP Codes call (888) 275-8777, or your local postmaster.	
Hillside (Part of Portland)	97201
Hines	97738
Hobsonville	97107
Holladay Park (Part of Portland)‡	97212
Holland	97523
Holley	97386
Hollywood (Part of Portland)	97212-13
For specific ZIP Codes call (888) 275-8777, or your local postmaster.	
Hollywood (Part of Salem)‡	97303
Homestead, *Baker*	97840
Homestead, *Deschutes*	97702
Hood River	97031
Horton	97412
Hoskins	97326
Hot Lake	97850
Hubbard	97032
Hugo	97526
Hunter Creek	97444
Huntington	97907
Idanha	97350
Idaville	97141
Idleyld Park	97447
Illahe	97406
Illinois Valley	97523
Imbler	97841
Imnaha	97842
Independence	97351
Indian Ford	97759
Indian Village	97720
Inglis	97016
Interlachen	97060
Ione	97843
Ironside	97908
Irrigon	97844
Irving	97402
Irvington (Part of Portland)	97212
Island City	97850
Ivy Station	97103
Izee	97820
Jacksonville	97530
Jamieson	97909
Jantzen Beach Center (Part of Portland)	97217
Jasper	97438
Jeffers Garden	97103
Jefferson	97352
Jennings Lodge♦	97267
Jewell	97138
Jimtown	97834
John Day	97845
Johnson City	97267
Jonesboro	97911
Jordan	97374
Jordan Valley	97910
Joseph	97846
Junction City	97448
Juntura	97911
Kahneeta Hot Springs	97761
Kamela	97801
Kansas City	97116
Keating	97814
Keizer	97303
	97307
For specific ZIP Codes call (888) 275-8777, or your local postmaster.	
Kellogg	97462
Kelso	97009
Kendall	97206
Keno	97627
Kent	97033
Kenton (Part of Portland)‡	97217
Kerby	97531
Kernville	97367
Kimberly	97848
King City	97224
Kingman Kolony	97913
Kings Heights (Part of Portland)	97210
Kingsley Field	97603
Kingston	97383
Kings Valley	97361
Kinton	97007
Kinzua	97830
Kiwanda Beach	97149
Klamath Falls	97601-03
For specific ZIP Codes call (888) 275-8777, or your local postmaster.	
Knappa	97103
Knoll Heights	97702
Lacomb	97355
Ladd Hill	97070
Lafayette	97127
La Grande	97850
Lakecreek	97524
Lake Grove (Part of Lake Oswego)‡	97035
Lake of the Woods	97601
Lake Oswego	97034-35
For specific ZIP Codes call (888) 275-8777, or your local postmaster.	
Lakeside	97449
Lakeview	97630
Lancaster	97448
Lancaster Mall (Part of Salem)	97301
Langell Valley	97623
Langlois	97450
Langrell	97834
La Pine	97739
Larwood	97374
Latham	97424
Latourell Falls	97014
Laurel	97123
Laurel Grove	97411
Laurelhurst (Part of Portland)	97215
Laurelwood	97119
Lawen	97740
Leaburg	97489
Lebanon	97355
Lee's Camp	97141
Leland	97497
Lents (Part of Portland)‡	97266
Leona	97435
Lewisburg	97330
Lexington	97839
Libby	97420
Liberal	97038
Liberty	97386
Lime	97907
Lincoln	97520
Lincoln Beach♦	97341
Lincoln City	97367
Lindbergh	97048
Little Albany	97390
Little Sweden	97346
Lloyd Center (Part of Portland)	97232
Locoda	97016
Logsden	97357
London	97424
Lone Elder	97013
Lonerock	97823
Long Creek	97856
Lookingglass, *Douglas*	97470
Looking Glass, *Union*	97827
Lorane	97451
Lorella	97623
Lostine	97857
Lowell	97452
Lower Logan	97045
Lynch (Part of Portland)	97236
Lyons	97358
McCoy	97371
Mc Dermitt	97910
McEwen	97877
McKee Bridge	97530
Mc Kenzie Bridge	97413
McKinley	97458
Macksburg	97013
McMinnville	97128
McNary (Part of Umatilla)	97882
McNulty	97051
Madras	97741
Malin	97632
Mall 205 (Part of Portland)	97216
Manhattan Beach (Part of Rockaway Beach)	97136
Manning	97125
Manzanita	97130
Mapleton	97453
Marcola	97454
Marion	97359
Marion Forks	97350
Marlene Village	97005
Marquam	97362
Marshland	97016
Martin Manor	97225
Marylhurst	97036
Mason Additions (Part of Prineville)	97754
Maupin	97037
Mayger	97016
May Park	97850
Mayville	97830
Maywood Park	97220
Meacham	97859
Meadowbrook	97038
Meadow View	97448
Meda	97112
Medford	97501
	97504
For specific ZIP Codes call (888) 275-8777, or your local postmaster.	
Medford Center (Part of Medford)	97504
Medical Springs	97814
Mehama	97384
Melrose	97470
Melville	97103
Menlo Park (Part of Portland)	97230
Merlin	97532
Merrill	97633
Metolius	97741
Metzger♦	97223
Midland	97634
Midway, *Multnomah*‡	97233
Midway, *Washington*	97123
Mikkalo	97861
Miles Crossing	97103
Mill City	97360
Millersburg	97321
Millican	97701
Millington	97420
Millwood	97486
Milo	97429
Milton (Part of Milton-Freewater)	97862
Milton-Freewater	97862
Milwaukie	97222
Minam	97827
Mission♦	97801
Mist	97016
Mitchell	97750
Modeville	97351
Modoc Point	97624
Mohawk	97477
Mohawk Junction (Part of Springfield)	97477
Mohler	97131
Molalla	97038
Monitor	97071
Monmouth	97361
Monroe	97456
Montaville (Part of Portland)	97215
Monument	97864
Moody	97391
Morgan	97843
Moro	97039
Mosier	97040
Mountaindale	97113
Mount Angel	97362
Mount Hebron	97801
Mount Hood	97041
Mount Hood-Parkdale	97041
Mount Pleasant (Part of Oregon City)	97045
Mount Vernon	97865
Mulino	97042
Mulloy	97140
Multnomah (Part of Portland)‡	97219*
	97280†
Murphy	97533
Myrick	97810
Myrtle Creek	97457
Myrtle Point	97458
Narrows, *Harney*	97721
Narrows, *Linn*	97386
Nashville	97326
Natal	97064
Neahkahnie	97131
Nedonna	97136
Needy	97013
Nehalem	97131
Nelscott (Part of Lincoln City)	97367
Neotsu	97364
Nesika Beach	97444
Neskowin	97149
Netarts	97143
Newberg	97132
New Bridge	97870
New Era	97013
New Hope	97527
New Idanha	97350
New Pine Creek	97635
Newport	97365
Newton Creek	97470
Nimrod	97488
Ninety One	97013
Nonpareil	97479
North Albany♦	97321
North Bend	97459
North Bend Coast Guard Air Station	97459
North Fork	97467
North Howell	97381
North Plains	97133
North Powder	97867
North Roseburg (Part of Roseburg)	97470
North Santiam	97325
North Umpqua Village	97447
Norway	97460
Norwood	97062
Noti	97461
Nottingham	97702
Nyssa	97913
Nyssa Heights	97913
Oak Grove, *Clackamas*♦	97267-68
For specific ZIP Codes call (888) 275-8777, or your local postmaster.	
Oak Grove, *Hood River*	97031
Oakland	97462
Oakridge	97463
Oak Springs	97037
Oakville	97377
Oakway Mall (Part of Eugene)	97401
O'Brien	97534
Oceanlake (Part of Lincoln City)	97367
Oceanside	97134
Odell	97044
Odessa	97601
Oklahoma Hill	97016
Old Colton	97017
Old Town	97462
Olene	97601
Olex	97812
Olney	97103
Ontario	97914
Ophir	97464
Ordnance	97838
Oregon City	97045
Orenco	97123
Oretech (Part of Klamath Falls)	97601
Oretown	97112
Orient	97030
Orleans	97321
Otis	97368
Otter Rock	97369
Outlook	97045
Owyhee	97913
Oxbow	97840
Pacific City	97135
Page (Part of Albany)	97321
Paisley	97636
Palestine	97321
Paradise Park	97023
Parkdale	97041
Parker	97351
Parkersburg	97411
Park Place (Part of Oregon City)	97045
Parkrose (Part of Portland)‡	97230
Patterson Junction	97844
Paulina	97751
Pedee	97361
Peel	97443
Pendair Heights (Part of Pendleton)	97801
Pendleton	97801
Pendleton Junction (Part of Pendleton)	97801
Peoria	97377
Perry	97850
Perrydale	97101
Philomath	97370
Phoenix	97535
Piedmont (Part of Portland)‡	97211
Pigeon Point	97420
Pike	97148
Pilot Rock	97868
Pine	97834
Pine Grove, *Hood River*	97031
Pine Grove, *Wasco*	97037
Pinehurst	97520
Pine Ridge	97624
Pioneer (Part of Portland)‡	97204
Pistol River	97444
Pittsburg	97064
Plainview, *Deschutes*	97701
Plainview, *Linn*	97377
Pleasant Hill	97455
Pleasant Valley, *Baker*	97814
Pleasant Valley, *Josephine*	97532
Pleasant Valley, *Tillamook*	97141
Plush	97637
Pocahontas	97814
Polk Station	97338
Pondosa	97814
Pony Village (Part of North Bend)‡	97459
Porter Creek	97481

Portland

97201-99

For specific ZIP Codes call (888) 275-8777, or your local postmaster.

Colleges & Universities

Bassist Coll	97201
Concordia Univ	97211
ITT Technical Institute	97218
Lewis & Clark Coll	97219
Multnomah Bible Coll & Biblical Seminary	97220
National Coll of Naturopathic Medicine	97201
Oregon Coll of Oriental Medicine	97216
Oregon Graduate Institute of Science & Technology	97291
Oregon Health Sciences Univ	97201
Pacific Northwest Coll of Art	97205
Portland State Univ	97207
Reed Coll	97202
Univ of Portland	97203
Warner Pacific Coll	97215

Western States Chiropractic Coll 97230

Financial Institutions

Bank of America, NTSA 97204
KeyBank, NA 97204
Pacific One 97204
Union Bank of California 97205
USBank, NA 97204
Washington Mutual Bank 97220
Wells Fargo Bank, NA 97201

Hospitals

Legacy Emanuel Hosp & Health Ctr 97227
Legacy Good Samaritan Hosp & Med Ctr 97210
Oregon Health Science Univ Hosp 97201
Providence Med Ctr 97213
Veterans Affairs Med Ctr 97201

Hotels/Motels

Benson 97205
Doubletree Columbia River 97217
Doubletree Jantzen Beach 97217
Doubletree, Lloyd Ctr 97232
Embassy Suites 97223
Embassy Suites, Downtown 97204
Hilton 97204
Holiday Inn, Portland Airport 97220
Marriott 97201

Military Installations

Oregon Air Nat Guard, FB6371, Portland International Airport 97218
U S Army Corps of Engineers 97208

Portland Heights (Part of Portland) 97201
Port Orford 97465
Post 97752
Powell Butte 97753
Powellhurst 97216
97266
For specific ZIP Codes call (888) 275-8777, or your local postmaster.
Powers 97466
Prairie City 97869
Pratum 97301
Prescott 97048
Princeton 97721
Prineville 97754
Prineville Southeast (Part of Prineville) 97754
Pringle Park Plaza (Part of Salem)‡ 97301*
97308†
Progress 97008
Prospect 97536
Prosper 97411
Quartz Mountain 97630
Quinaby 97303
Quincy 97016
Quines Creek 97442
Rainbow 97413
Rainier 97048
Raleigh Hills♦ 97225
Ramsey 97701
Ramsey Hall 97021
Randolph 97411
Redland 97045
Redmond 97756
Reedsport 97467
Remote 97458
Reston 97470
Rhododendron 97049
Rice Hill 97462
Richardson 97490
Richland 97870
Richmond 97874
Rickreall 97371
Riddle 97469
Rieth 97801
Riley 97758
Ritter 97872
Riverdale (Part of Portland) 97219
Rivergrove 97035
River Road♦ 97404
Riverside, *Linn* 97321
Riverside, *Malheur* 97917
Riverside, *Umatilla* 97801
Riverton 97423
Riverview (Part of Vernonia) 97064
Riverview, *Lane* 97448
Roans Estate 97739
Roaring Springs Ranch 97736
Robinwood (Part of West Linn) 97068
Rockaway Beach 97136
Rock Creek, *Baker* 97833
Rock Creek, *Gilliam* 97812
Rockford 97031
Rockie Four Corners 97375
Rock Point 97525
Rockville 97910
Rockwood 97233
Rocky Point 97601
Rogue River 97537
Rogue Valley Mall (Part of Medford) 97501
Rome 97910
Roseburg 97470
Rose City Park (Part of Portland)‡ 97213
Rose Lodge♦ 97372
Rosemont (Part of West Linn) 97068
Rowena 97058
Roy 97106
Ruch 97530
Rufus 97050
Ruggs 97836
Rural Dell 97032
Russellville (Part of Portland) 97216
Rye Valley 97907
Saginaw 97424
St. Benedict 97373
St. Helens 97051
St. Johns (Part of Portland)‡ 97203
St. Louis 97026
St. Paul 97137
Salem 97301-06
97308-09
For specific ZIP Codes call (888) 275-8777, or your local postmaster.
Salmon Harbor 97467
Salt Creek 97338
Sams Valley 97525
Sand Lake 97112
Sandy 97055
San Marine 97498
Santa Clara♦ 97404
Santiam Terrace 97355
Saunders Lake 97459
Scappoose 97056
Scholls 97123
Scio 97374
Scofield 97109
Scottsburg 97473
Scotts Mills 97375
Seal Rock 97376
Seaside 97138
Seekseequa 97761
Seghers 97119
Sellwood (Part of Portland) 97202
Sellwood Moreland (Part of Portland)‡ 97202*
97282†
Selma 97538
Seneca 97873
Service Creek 97830
Shadowood 97068
Shady Cove 97539
Shady Dell 97038
Shaniko 97057
Shaw 97325
Shedd 97377
Shelburn 97374
Sheridan 97378
Sherwood 97140
Shorewood 97459
Siletz 97380
Siltcoos 97493
Silver Lake 97638
Silverton 97381
Silvies 97720
Simnasho 97761
Sisters 97759
Sitkum 97458
Six Corners (Part of Sherwood) 97140
Sixes 97476
Skelley 97499
Smithfield 97338
Sodaville 97355
Southbeach 97366
Southgate (Part of Portland) 97266
South Junction 97037
South Scappoose 97056
Southside (Part of Eugene)‡ 97405
Spicer 97355
Sprague River 97639
Spray 97874
Springbrook 97132
Springdale 97060
Springfield 97477-78
For specific ZIP Codes call (888) 275-8777, or your local postmaster.
Springwater 97023
Stafford 97068
Staleys Junction 97109
Stanfield 97875
Starkey 97850
Starvout 97410
Stayton 97383
Steamboat 97447
Stewart Lennox Addition (Part of Klamath Falls) 97601
Stimson Mill 97119
Sublimity 97385
Summer Lake 97640
Summer Lake Hot Springs 97636
Summerville 97876
Summit 97326
Sumner 97420
Sumpter 97877
Sunnycrest 97132
Sunnydale 97435
Sunnyside, *Clackamas*♦ 97015
97266
For specific ZIP Codes call (888) 275-8777, or your local postmaster.
Sunnyside, *Umatilla* 97862
Sunny Valley 97497
Sunriver 97707
Sunset (Part of West Linn) 97068
Sunset Beach 97146
Sunset Hills (Part of Seaside) 97138
Suntex Valley 97758
Suplee 97751
Surf Pines 97146
Surprise Valley 97457
Sutherlin 97479
Suver 97361
Suver Junction 97361
Svensen 97103
Swedetown 97016
Sweet Home 97386
Swisshome 97480
Sylvan (Part of Portland) 97221
Table Rock 97501
Taft (Part of Lincoln City) 97367
Takilma 97523
Talbot 97352
Talent 97540
Tallman 97355
Tangent 97389
Taylorville 97016
Telocaset 97883
Tenmile 97481
Terrebonne♦ 97760
Thatcher 97116
The Dalles 97058
Thornhollow 97810
Three Lynx 97023
Thurston (Part of Springfield) 97482
Tide 97480
Tidewater 97390
Tiernan 97453
Tierra Del Mar 97112
Tigard 97223-24
97281
For specific ZIP Codes call (888) 275-8777, or your local postmaster.
Tillamook 97141
Tiller 97484
Tillican 97701
Timber 97144
Timber Grove 97004
Timberline Lodge 97028
Toketee Falls 97447
Toledo 97391
Tollgate 97886
Tolovana Park 97145
Tongue Point Village 97103
Top 97864
Tophill 97109
Town Center (Part of Portland) 97229
Trail 97541
Trask 97141
Treharne 97064
Trent 97431
Triangle Lake 97412
Tri-City♦ 97457
Trout Creek, *Harney* 97710
Trout Creek, *Hood River* 97041
Troutdale 97060
Troy 97828
Tualatin 97062
Tumalo 97701
Turner 97392
Twelve Mile (Part of Gresham) 97030
Twickenham 97750
Twin Rocks 97136
Twomile 97411
Tygh Valley 97063
Ukiah 97880
Umapine 97862
Umatilla 97882
Umatilla Indian Reservation 97801
Umpqua 97486
Union 97883
Union Creek 97536
Union Gap 97462
Union Mills 97042
Union Point 97327
Unionvale 97114
Unity, *Baker* 97884
Unity, *Lane* 97438
University (Part of Eugene)‡ 97403
University (Part of Portland)‡ 97207
Upper Highland 97004
Upper Hood River Valley 97044
Upper Soda 97345
Vale 97918
Valley Falls 97630
Valley Junction 97396
Valley River Center (Part of Eugene) 97401
Valley View 97321
Valsetz 97380
Van 97904
Vaughn 97487
Veneta 97487
Verboort 97116
Vermont Hills (Part of Portland) 97221
Vernonia 97064
Vida 97488
Viola 97023
Vista (Part of Salem)‡ 97302
Waconda 97026
Wagontire 97738
Wagon Trail Ranch 97739
Wakonda Beach 97394
Walden 97424
Waldport 97394
Walker 97426
Wallowa 97885
Wallowa Lake Resort 97846
Walterville 97489
Walton 97490
Wamic 97063
Wapato 97119
Wapinitia 97037
Warm Springs♦ 97761
Warm Springs Indian Reservation 97761
Warren 97053
Warrendale 97014
Warrenton 97146
Wasco 97065
Washington Park Zoo Railway (Part of Portland)‡ 97221
Washington Square (Part of Portland) 97223
Waterloo 97355
Watseco 97136
Weatherby 97905
Wecoma Beach (Part of Lincoln City) 97367
Wedderburn 97491
Welches 97067
Wemme 97067
Westfall 97920
Westfir 97492
West Lake, *Clatsop* 97146
Westlake (Part of Dunes City) 97493
West Linn 97068
West Moreland (Part of Portland) 97206
Weston 97886
Westport 97016
West Portland (Part of Portland) 97219
West Salem (Part of Salem)‡ 97304
West Scio 97374
West Side, *Lake* 97630
West Side (Part of Eugene)‡ 97402
West Slope‡ 97221
97225
97298
For specific ZIP Codes call (888) 275-8777, or your local postmaster.
West Stayton 97325
West St. Helens (Part of St. Helens) 97051
West Union 97123
Wetmore 97830
Weyerhaeuser Townsite 97601
Wheeler 97147
Wheeler Heights (Part of Wheeler) 97147
Whiskey Hill 97032
White City♦ 97503
Whiteson 97101
Wilbur 97494
Wilderville 97543
Wildwood 97049
Wilhoit 97038
Willakenzie (Part of Eugene) 97401
Willamette (Part of West Linn) 97068
Willamette City (Part of Oakridge) 97463
Willamina 97396
Willbridge (Part of Portland) 97210
Williams 97544
Willowcreek 97918
Willowdale 97741
Willsburg Junction (Part of Milwaukie) 97222
Wilson Beach 97141
Wilsonville 97070
Wimer 97537
Winchester 97495
Winchester Bay 97467
Windmaster Corner 97031
Winema Beach 97112
Wingville 97814
Winston 97496
Winterville 97411
Witch Hazel 97123
Wocus 97601
Wolf Creek 97497
Wonder 97543
Woodburn 97071
Woods 97112
Woodson 97016
Woodstock (Part of Portland) 97206
Wood Village 97060
Worden 97601
Wren 97326
Wyeth 97014
Yachats 97498
Yamhill 97148
Yankton 97051
Yaquina 97365
Yoder 97032
Yoncalla 97499
Yonna 97623
Zigzag 97049

*** Area Zip Code** **† Post Office Boxes** **‡ Postal Station** **♦ Census Designated Place** *Italic Type* **County**

Place	ZIP
Aaronsburg	16820
Abbott (Twp)	16922
Abbottstown	17301
Aberdeen	18444
Abington, *Lackawanna* (Twp)	18471
Abington, *Montgomery*	19001
Abrahamsville	12723
Abrams	19406
Academia	17082
Academy Corners	16928
Academy Gardens (Part of Philadelphia)	19114
Acahela	18610
Accomac	17406
Ackermanville	18010
Acme	15610
Acmetonia	15024
Acosta	15520
Adah	15410
Adams, *Butler* (Twp)	16046
Adams, *Cambria* (Twp)	15955
Adams, *Snyder* (Twp)	17813
Adams, *Armstrong*	16028
Adams, *Somerset*	15541
Adamsburg	15611
Adams Corners	16057
Adamsdale	17972
Adams Hill	15642
Adamstown	19501
Adamsville	16110
Addingham	19026
Addison (Twp)	15540
Addison	15411
Adelaide	15425
Admire	17364
Adrian	16210
Adrian Furnace	15801
Advance	15732
Africa	17236
Afton Village	18034
Ahrensville	16301
Aiden Lair	19025
Aiken	16744
Airville	17302
Airydale	17060
Ajax	16323
Akeley	16345
Akersville	15536
Akron	17501
Aladdin	15682
Alameda Park	16001
Alaska	15825
Alba	16910
Albany, *Bradford* (Twp)	18833
Albany, *Berks*	19529
Albany, *Fayette*	15417
Albert	18707
Albidale	19006
Albion, *Erie*	16401
Albion, *Jefferson*	15767
Albrightsville	18210
Alburtis	18011
Alcoa Center	15068
Aldan	19018
Alden	18634
Aldenville	18401
Alderson (Part of Harveys Lake)	18618
Aldham	19460
Aleppo, *Allegheny* (Twp)	15143
Aleppo, *Greene*	15310
Alexander Springs	17004
Alexandria	16611
Alfarata	17841
Alford	18826
Alicia, *Fayette*	15417
Alicia, *Greene*	15338
Alinda	17040
Aline	17853
Aliquippa	15001
Allandale	17011
Allegany (Twp)	16923
Allegheny, *Blair* (Twp)	16635
Allegheny, *Butler* (Twp)	16049
Allegheny, *Cambria* (Twp)	15940
Allegheny, *Somerset* (Twp)	15538
Allegheny, *Venango* (Twp)	16341
Allegheny, *Westmoreland* (Twp)	15613
Allegheny (Part of Pittsburgh)‡	15212
Allegheny Acres	15024
Allegheny Center Mall (Part of Pittsburgh)	15212
Allegheny Furnace (Part of Altoona)	16602
Allegheny Springs	16371
Alleghenyville	19540
Allemans	16639
Allen, *Northampton* (Twp)	18067
Allen, *Cumberland*	17007
Allen Crest	18052
Allen Lane (Part of Philadelphia)	19119
Allenport, *Huntingdon*	17066
Allenport, *Washington*	15412
Allens Mills	15851
Allensville	17002
Allentown	18101-95
For specific ZIP Codes call (888) 275-8777, or your local postmaster.	
Allenvale	15501
Allenwood	17810
Allis Hollow	18837
Allison, *Clinton* (Twp)	17751
Allison, *Fayette*	15413
Allison Heights	15413
Allison Park	15101
Allport, *Cambria*	15714
Allport, *Clearfield*	16821
Almaden	16680
Almedia♦	17815
Almont	18960
Alpha (Part of Wind Gap)	18091
Alpine	17339
Alsace (Twp)	19606
Alsace Manor	19560
Alta Manor (Part of Altoona)	16601
Altamont	17931
Altenwald	17268
Althom	16351
Alton	19380
Alton Park (Part of Allentown)	18103
Altoona	16601-03
For specific ZIP Codes call (888) 275-8777, or your local postmaster.	
Alum Bank	15521
Alum Rock	16373
Aluta	18064
Alverda	15710
Alverton	15612
Amaranth	17267
Amasa	18433
Ambau	17362
Amberson	17210
Ambler	19002
Ambler Highlands	19034
Ambridge	15003
Ambridge Heights	15003
Ambrose	15759
Amend	15401
American Philatelic Society Building (Part of State College)	16803
Amesville	16651
Amity, *Berks* (Twp)	19518
Amity, *Erie* (Twp)	16438
Amity, *Bucks*	18036
Amity, *Washington*	15311
Amity Gardens♦	19518
Amity Hall	17020
Amsbry	16641
Amsterdam	16127
Amwell (Twp)	15301
Analomink	18320
Ancient Oaks♦	18062
Ancient Oaks West	18062
Andalusia	19020
Anderson	17044
Andersonburg	17047
Andersontown	17055
Andreas	18211
Andrews Bridge	17509
Andrews Plan	15001
Andrews Settlement	16923
Angelica	19540
Angels	18445
Angora (Part of Philadelphia)	19143
Anita	15711
Ankeny	15547
Annaline Village	19061
Annin (Twp)	16743
Annisville	16049
Annville♦	17003
Anselma	19425
Ansonia	16901
Ansonville	16656
Antes Fort	17720
Anthony, *Lycoming* (Twp)	17728
Anthony, *Montour* (Twp)	17772
Anthracite (Part of Cornwall)	17016
Antis (Twp)	16617
Antrim, *Franklin* (Twp)	17225
Antrim, *Tioga*	16901
Apolacon (Twp)	18830
Apollo	15613
Apponzoll	18360
Applebachsville	18951
Appletree Hill	19007
Appleville	19380
Applewold	16201
Aquashicola	18012
Aqueduct	17020
Aquetong	18938
Ararat	18465
Arbor	17356
Arbuckle	16438
Arcadia, *Indiana*	15712
Arcadia, *Lancaster*	17563
Archbald	18403
Arch Rock	17059
Arch Spring	16686
Arcola	19420
Ardara	15615
Arden	15301
Ardenheim	16652
Arden Mines	15301
Ardmore♦	19003
Ardmore Manor	19003
Ardmore Park	19003
Ardsley	19038
Arendtsville	17303
Arensberg	15433
Argentine	16040
Argus	18960
Aristes	17920
Arlingham	19031
Arlingham Hills	19031
Arlington, *Allegheny*	15137
Arlington, *Wayne*	18436
Arlington Heights	18360
Arlington Knolls	18052
Armagh, *Mifflin* (Twp)	17063
Armagh, *Indiana*	15920
Armbrust	15616
Armenia (Twp)	16947
Armstrong, *Indiana* (Twp)	15774
Armstrong, *Lycoming* (Twp)	17701
Arndts	18038
Arnold	15068
Arnold City	15012
Arnot	16911
Arnots Addition (Part of St. Clair)	17970
Arona	15617
Aronimink	19026
Arrowhead Lake	18347
Arsenal (Part of Pittsburgh)‡	15201
Artemas	17211
Arundel Village	19044
Arwin Acres	17036
Asaph	16901
Asbury, *Columbia*	17859
Asbury, *Erie*	16509
Ashcom	15537
Asherton	17801
Ashfield	18212
Ashland, *Clarion* (Twp)	16232
Ashland, *Clearfield*	16666
Ashland, *Schuylkill*	17921
Ashley	18706
Ashtola	15963
Ashville	16613
Askam	18706
Aspers	17304
Aspinwall	15215
Aston	19014
Asylum (Twp)	18848
Atco	12764
Atglen	19310
Athens, *Crawford* (Twp)	16404
Athens, *Bradford*	18810
Athol	19519
Atkinsons Mills	17051
Atlantic, *Clearfield*	16651
Atlantic, *Crawford*	16111
Atlantic, *Westmoreland*	15671
Atlas	17851
Atlasburg	15004
Atwood	16249
Auburn, *Susquehanna* (Twp)	18630
Auburn, *Schuylkill*	17922
Auburn Center	18623
Auburn Four Corners	18630
Audenried	18201
Audubon♦	19407
Aughwick	17066
Augustaville	17801
Aultman	15713
Austin	16720
Austinburg	16928
Austinville	16914
Avalon	15202
Avella	15312
Avella Highlands	15312
Avis	17721
Avoca	18641
Avon♦	17042
Avondale	19311
Avondale Knolls	19086
Avon Heights	17042
Avonia♦	16415
Avonmore	15618
Axemann	16823
Ayr (Twp)	17233
Bachmanville	17033
Baden	15005
Baederwood	19046
Bagdad	15656
Baggaley	15650
Baidland♦	15063
Bailey	17074
Baileys Corner	16926
Baileyville	16865
Bainbridge	17502
Bair	17405
Bairdford	15006
Bairdstown	15717
Bakers Summit	16614
Baker Station	19390
Bakerstown	15007
Bakerstown Station	15044
Bakersville	15501
Bala	19004
Bala-Cynwyd	19004
Bala-Cynwyd Shopping Center	19004
Bald Eagle, *Clinton* (Twp)	17751
Bald Eagle, *Blair*	16686
Bald Hill, *Clearfield*	16850
Bald Hill, *Greene*	15349
Baldwin, *Allegheny* (Twp)	15234
Baldwin, *Allegheny*	15227
Baldwin (Part of Eddystone)	19013
Balliettsville	18037
Balls Eddy	18461
Balls Mills	17728
Balltown	16347
Bally	19503
Balsinger	15401
Banbury Crossing	17036
Bando	15501
Banetown	15301
Baney Settlement	16830
Bangor	18013
Banian Junction	16661
Banks, *Carbon* (Twp)	18254
Banks, *Indiana* (Twp)	15742
Banksville (Part of Pittsburgh)	15216
Banner Ridge	15757
Bannerville	17841
Banning	15428
Barbours	17701
Bard	15534
Baresville	17331
Bareville	17540
Barkeyville	16038
Barlow	17325
Barnards	16222
Barnes, *Cambria*	15737
Barnes, *Jefferson*	15825
Barnes, *Warren*	16347
Barnesboro	15714
Barneston	19344
Barnesville	18214
Barnett, *Forest* (Twp)	15828
Barnett, *Jefferson* (Twp)	15860
Barnettstown	16634
Barneytown	17052
Barnitz	17013
Barnsley	19363
Barr (Twp)	15762
Barree (Twp)	16669
Barree	16611
Barren Hill	19444
Barret Plan	15001
Barrett, *Monroe* (Twp)	18342
Barrett, *Clearfield*	16830
Barronvale	15557
Barr Slope	15734
Barrville	17084
Barry (Twp)	17921
Barry Heights (Part of Norristown)	19401
Bart (Twp)	17562
Bart	17503
Barto	19504
Bartonsville	18321
Bartville	17509
Basket	19547
Bassards Corners	18038
Bastress (Twp)	17701
Bath	18014
Bath Addition	19007
Bath Manor	19007
Bauerstown	15209
Baumgardner	17584
Baumstown	19508
Bausman	17504
Bavington	15019
Baxter	15829
Beachdale	15530
Beach Haven	18601
Beach Lake	18405
Beachly	15424
Beadling	15241
Beale (Twp)	17082
Beallsville	15313
Beans Cove	15535
Bear Creek (Twp)	18602
Bear Creek Lake	18229
Bear Creek Village	18602
Bear Gap	17824
Bear Lake	16402
Bear Rocks	15610
Beartown, *Franklin*	17268
Beartown, *Lancaster*	17555
Bear Valley	17866
Beatty	15650
Beaufort Farms	17110
Beaumont	18618
Beaver, *Clarion* (Twp)	16232
Beaver, *Columbia* (Twp)	17815
Beaver, *Crawford* (Twp)	16406
Beaver, *Jefferson* (Twp)	15864
Beaver, *Snyder* (Twp)	17813
Beaver, *Beaver*	15009
Beaver Acres	15136
Beaver Brook	18201
Beaver Center	16435
Beaverdale, *Cambria*	15921
Beaverdale, *Northumberland*	17851
Beaver Dam	16407
Beaver Falls	15010
Beaver Lake	17758
Beaver Meadows	18216
Beaver Springs	17812
	17843
For specific ZIP Codes call (888) 275-8777, or your local postmaster.	
Beavertown, *Blair*	16662
Beavertown, *Snyder*	17813
Beavertown, *York*	17019
Beaver Valley	16640
Beccaria (Twp)	16627
Beccaria	16616
Bechtelsville	19505
Beckersville	19540
Becks	17901
Bedford	15522
Bedminster	18910
Beech Creek	16822
Beecherstown	17307
Beech Flats	17724
Beech Glen	17758
Beech Grove, *Elk*	15822
Beech Grove, *Lycoming*	17771
Beechton	15824
Beechview (Part of Pittsburgh)	15216
Beechwood	15834
Beechwood Park	19014
Beechwoods	15840
Beeman	16946
Beersville	18067
Beesons	15446
Beham	15376
Bela	16049
Belair	17601
Belair Park	17601
Belardley	19007
Belden	15522
Belfast, *Fulton* (Twp)	17238
Belfast, *Northampton*♦	18064
Belfast Junction	18040
Belfry	19401
Belknap	16222
Bell, *Clearfield* (Twp)	15757
Bell, *Jefferson* (Twp)	15767

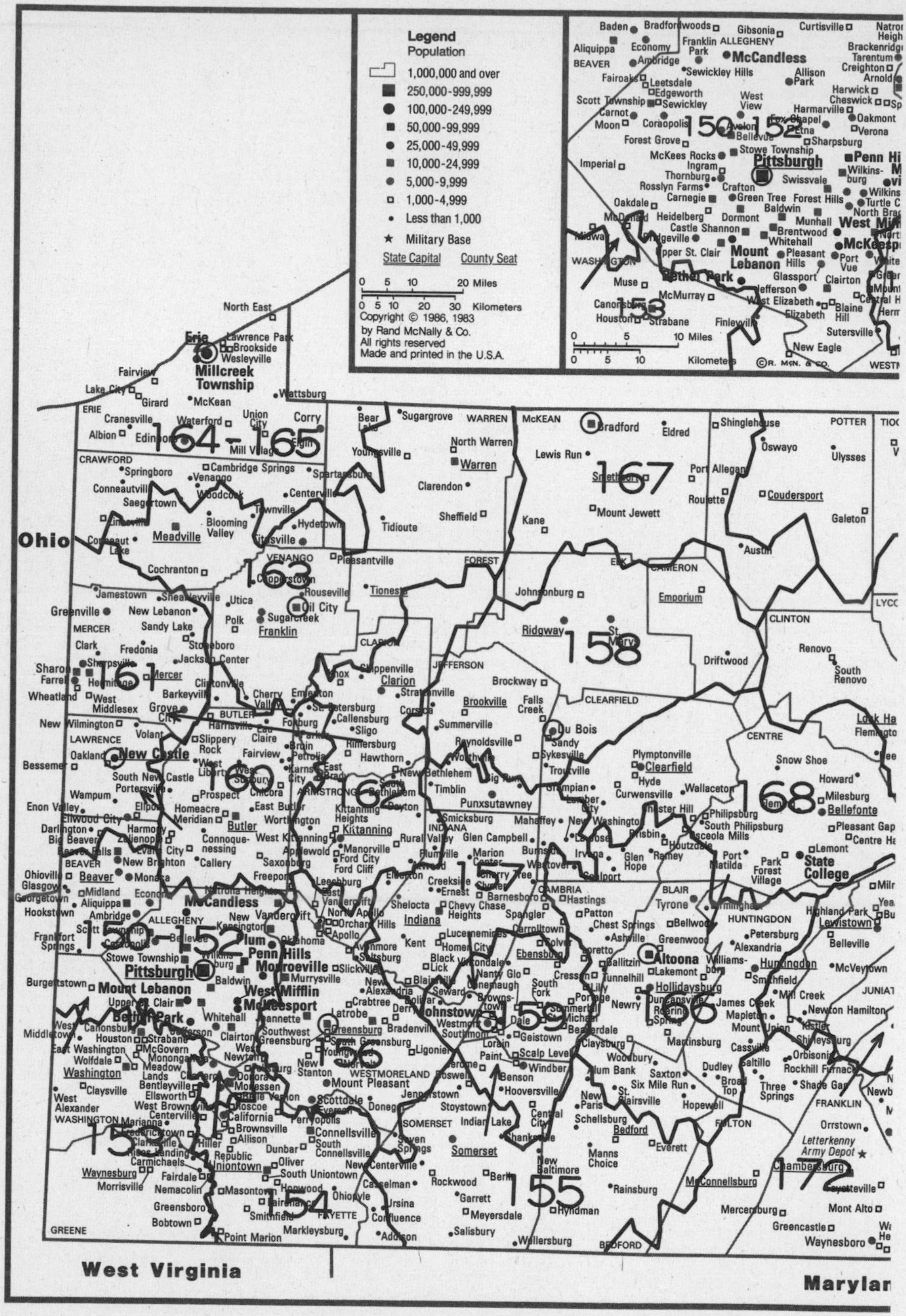

Legend
Population

- 1,000,000 and over
- 250,000-999,999
- 100,000-249,999
- 50,000-99,999
- 25,000-49,999
- 10,000-24,999
- 5,000-9,999
- 1,000-4,999
- Less than 1,000
- ★ Military Base

State Capital County Seat

0 5 10 20 Miles
0 5 10 20 30 Kilometers

Ohio

West Virginia

Marylar

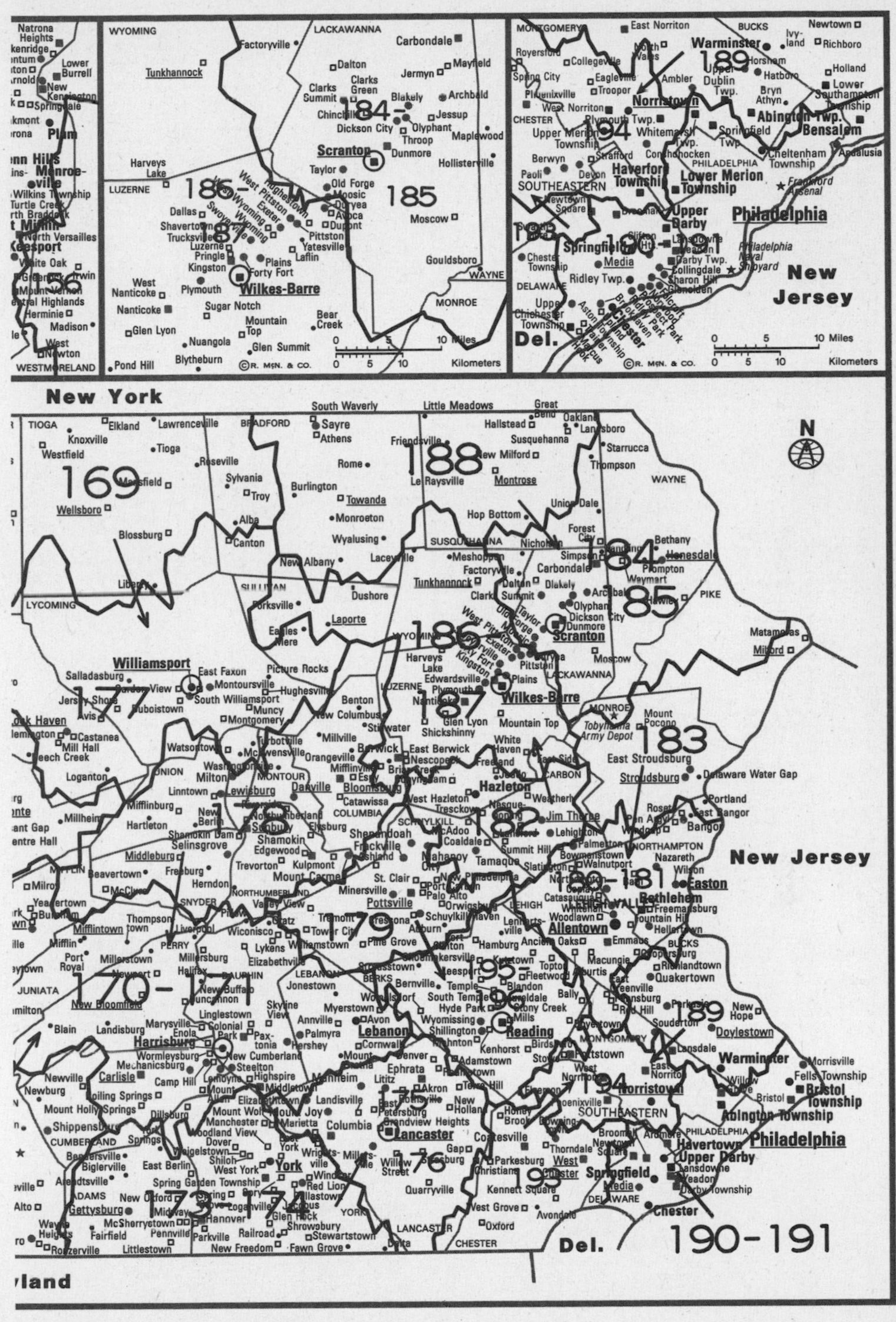

Place	ZIP
Bell, *Westmoreland* (Twp)	15613
Bell Acres	15143
Bella Vista	17754
Belle Bridge (Part of Lincoln)	15037
Bellefield (Part of Pittsburgh)	15213
Bellefonte	16823
Bellegrove	17003
Bellemont	17562
Belle Valley	16509
Belle Vernon	15012
Belleville♦	17004
Bellevue	15202
Bell Mountain (Part of Dickson City)	18508
Bell Point	15613
Bells Camp	16727
Bells Landing	15757
Bells Mills	15767
Belltown, *Elk*	15860
Belltown, *Mifflin*	17841
Bellview	15301
Bellwood	16617
Belmar (Part of Pittsburgh)	15206
Belmar, *Venango*	16323
Belmar Park	16101
Belmont♦	15904
Belmont Corner	18453
Belmont Hills	19020
Belmont Terrace	19406
Belsano	15922
Belsena Mills	16661
Belton	16117
Beltzhoover (Part of Pittsburgh)	15210
Ben Avon, *Allegheny*	15202
Ben Avon, *Indiana*	15701
Ben Avon Heights	15202
Bencetown	15734
Bendersville	17306
Bendertown	17859
Benedicts	17315
Benezett	15821
Benezette (Twp)	15821
Benfer	17812
Benjamin (Part of Perkasie)	18944
Benner (Twp)	16823
Bensalem (Twp)	19020
Bensalem	19020-21
For specific ZIP Codes call (888) 275-8777, or your local postmaster.	
Bens Creek	15938
Benson	15935
Bentley Creek	14894
Bentleyville	15314
Benton, *Columbia* (Twp)	17814
Benton, *Lackawanna* (Twp)	18420
Benton, *Columbia*	17814
Benvenue	17020
Bergey	19438
Berkeley Hills	15237
Berkley	19605
Berkleys Mill	15552
Berkshire Heights (Part of Wyomissing)	19610
Berkshire Mall (Part of Wyomissing)	19610
Berlin, *Wayne* (Twp)	18431
Berlin, *Somerset*	15530
Berlin Junction	17350
Berlinsville	18088
Bermudian	17019
Bern (Twp)	19605
Berne	19526
Bernharts	19605
Bernice	18632
Bernville	19506
Berrysburg	17005
Berrytown	16925
Berwick, *Adams* (Twp)	17316
Berwick, *Columbia*	18603
Berwinsdale	16656
Berwyn	19312
Besco	15322
Bessemer (Part of North Braddock)	15104
Bessemer, *Lawrence*	16112
Bessemer, *Westmoreland*	15666
Best (Part of West Mifflin)	15122
Best Station	18080
Bethany	18431
Bethayres	19006
Bethel, *Armstrong* (Twp)	16226
Bethel, *Delaware* (Twp)	19061
Bethel, *Fulton* (Twp)	17267
Bethel, *Lebanon* (Twp)	17026
Bethel, *Berks*	19507
Bethel, *Mercer*	16159
Bethel, *Westmoreland*	15658
Bethelboro	15401
Bethel Park	15102
Bethesda	17532
Bethlehem, *Northampton* (Twp)	18017
Bethlehem, *Clearfield*	15757
Bethlehem, *Northampton*	18015-20
For specific ZIP Codes call (888) 275-8777, or your local postmaster.	
Bethton	18964
Betula	16749
Betz	16661
Betzwood	19401
Beulah	16661
Beverly Estates	17601
Beverly Heights	17046
Beverly Hills, *Blair*	16601
Beverly Hills, *Delaware*	19082
Beyer	16211
Biddle	15692
Biesecker Gap	17268
Big Beaver	15010
Big Cove Tannery	17212
Biggertown	17774
Bigler (Twp)	16661
Bigler	16825
Biglerville	17307
Big Mine Run	17921
Bigmount	17315
Big Pond	16914
Big Run	15715
Big Shanty	16738
Bimber Corners	16351
Bingen	18015
Bingham, *Potter* (Twp)	16923
Bingham, *McKean*	16726
Bingham Center	16923
Binnstown (Part of Centerville)	15417
Bino	17225
Birchardville	18801
Birchrunville	19421
Birch Valley	19058
Birchwood Lakes	18328
Birdell	19344
Bird in Hand	17505
Birdsboro	19508
Birdville	17052
Birmingham, *Delaware* (Twp)	19317
Birmingham, *Chester*	19380
Birmingham, *Huntingdon*	16686
Bishop	15057
Bitner	15431
Bittersville	17366
Bitumen	17778
Bixler	17047
Black, *Somerset* (Twp)	15557
Black, *Bradford*	18848
Black Ash	16327
Black Bear (Part of St. Lawrence)	19606
Blackburn (Part of Trafford)	15085
Black Creek (Twp)	18246
Black Diamond (Part of Monongahela)	15063
Blackfield	15542
Blackhawk	15010
Blackhorse, *Chester*	19365
Black Horse, *Delaware*	19063
Black Horse, *Montgomery*	19401
Blacklick, *Cambria* (Twp)	15943
Black Lick, *Indiana* (Twp)	15717
Black Lick, *Indiana*	15716
Blacklog	17243
Blackman	18702
Black Ridge	15235
Blackrock	21088
Blacktown	16137
Black Walnut	18623
Blackwell	16938
Blain	17006
Blain City	16627
Blaine (Twp)	15365
Blaine Hill	15037
Blainesburg (Part of West Brownsville)	15417
Blainsport	17569
Blair (Twp)	16635
Blairs Corners	16232
Blairs Mills	17213
Blairsville	15717
Blairtown	15370
Blakely	18447
Blakeslee	18610
Blanchard, *Allegheny*	15084
Blanchard, *Centre*	16826
Blanco	16249
Blandburg	16619
Blandon	19510
Blanket Hill	16201
Blawnox	15238
Bloom (Twp)	16838
Bloomfield, *Bedford* (Twp)	16664
Bloomfield, *Crawford* (Twp)	16438
Bloomfield (Part of Pittsburgh)‡	15224
Bloomingdale (Part of Summit Hill)	18250
Bloomingdale, *Lancaster*	17601
Bloomingdale, *Luzerne*	18655
Blooming Glen	18911
Blooming Grove, *Pike* (Twp)	18464
Blooming Grove, *Pike*	18428
Blooming Grove, *York*	17331
Bloomington, *Clearfield*	16833
Bloomington, *Lackawanna*	18444
Blooming Valley	16335
Bloomsburg	17815
Bloomsdale Gardens	19058
Bloserville	17241
Bloss (Twp)	16911
Blossburg	16912
Blosser Hill	15474
Blossom Hill	17601
Blossom Valley	17601
Blough	15936
Blue Ball	17506
Blue Bell♦	19422
Blue Heron Pond	18328
Blue Hill	17870
Blue Jay	16347
Blue Knob	15946
Blue Ridge	19058
Blue Ridge Summit	17214
Bluff	15341
Blythe (Twp)	17930
Blytheburn	18707
Blythedale	15018
Blythewood	18901
Boaba	18428
Boalsburg♦	16827
Boardman	16863
Bobbys Corners (Part of Hermitage)	16159
Bobtown	15315
Bocktown	15001
Bodines	17722
Boeckel Landing	17302
Boggs, *Armstrong* (Twp)	16259
Boggs, *Centre* (Twp)	16823
Boggs, *Clearfield* (Twp)	16878
Boggsville	16055
Bohemia	18428
Bohrmans Mill	17972
Boiling Springs♦	17007
Bolde Point	18428
Bolivar	15923
Bolivar Run	16701
Boltz	15954
Bon Air, *Cambria*	15902
Bon Air, *Delaware*	19083
Bon Aire	16001
Bondsville	19335
Bonnair	17327
Bonneauville	17325
Bonnie Brook	16001
Bonus	16049
Boone	15926
Booneville	17747
Booths Corner	19061
Boothwyn♦	19061
Boothwyn Highlands	19061
Boot Jack	15853
Boquet	15644
Bordnersville	17038
Borland Manor	15317
Bortondale	19063
Boston	15135
Boston Run	17948
Boswell	15531
Boulevard (Part of Philadelphia)‡	19149
Bourne	18850
Bovard, *Butler*	16020
Bovard, *Westmoreland*	15619
Bowdertown	15724
Bower	15757
Bower Hill, *Allegheny*	15106
Bower Hill, *Washington*	15367
Bowers	19511
Bowie	16133
Bowling Green	19063
Bowman Addition	17331
Bowman Heights	17201
Bowmans	17948
Bowmansdale	17008
Bowmans Store	17329
Bowmanstown	18030
Bowmansville	17507
Bowood	15478
Boyce	15241
Boyds Mills	18443
Boydstown	16025
Boydtown	17872
Boyers	16020
Boyers Junction	19522
Boyertown	19512
Boynton	15532
Brackenridge	15014
Brackney	18812
Bradbury Plan	15001
Braddock, *Allegheny*	15104
Braddock, *Washington*	15301
Braddock Hills	15221
Braden Plan	15322
Bradenville	15620
Bradford, *Clearfield* (Twp)	16881
Bradford, *McKean*	16701
Bradford Hills	19335
Bradford Park (Part of Economy)	15005
Bradfordwoods	15015
Bradley Junction	15931
Bradleytown	16317
Brady, *Butler* (Twp)	16057
Brady, *Clarion* (Twp)	16248
Brady, *Clearfield* (Twp)	15848
Brady, *Huntingdon* (Twp)	17002
Brady, *Lycoming* (Twp)	17752
Brady (Part of Du Bois)‡	15801
Bradys Bend	16028
Braeburn (Part of Lower Burrell)	15068
Braintrim (Twp)	18623
Braman	18417
Bramcote	19464
Branch (Twp)	17901
Branch Dale	17923
Branchton	16021
Branchville	16426
Brandamore	19316
Brandon	16374
Brandonville	17967
Brandt	18847
Brandtsville	17055
Brandy Camp	15822
Brandywine Hills	19380
Brandywine Homes	19320
Brandywine Manor	19343
Brandywine Summit	19342
Brandywine Village	19406
Bratton (Twp)	17044
Brave	15316
Braznell	15442
Breakneck	15425
Brecknock, *Berks* (Twp)	19540
Brecknock, *Lancaster* (Twp)	17517
Breezewood	15533
Breezy Corner	19522
Breinigsville	18031
Brenizer	15717
Brent	16156
Brentwood	15227
Breslau	18702
Bressler	17113
Bretonville	16656
Briarbrook	18707
Briarcliff	19036
Briar Creek	18603
Briar Hill, *Armstrong*	16201
Briar Hill, *Wayne*	18438
Brick Church	16226
Brickerville♦	17543
Brick Tavern	18951
Bridesburg (Part of Philadelphia)‡	19137
Bridgeburg	16210
Bridgeport, *Adams*	17307
Bridgeport, *Carbon*	18661
Bridgeport, *Clearfield*	16833
Bridgeport, *Lancaster*	17602
Bridgeport, *Montgomery*	19405
Bridgeport, *Perry*	17040
Bridgeport, *Westmoreland*	15666
Bridgeton, *Bucks* (Twp)	18972
Bridgeton, *York*	17321
Bridgetown	19047
Bridge Valley	18925
Bridgeville	15017
Bridgewater, *Susquehanna* (Twp)	18801
Bridgewater, *Beaver*	15009
Bridgewater, *Bucks*	19020
Bridgewater Farms	19014
Brier Hill	15415
Briggsville	18635
Brighton (Twp)	15009
Brightwood (Part of Bethel Park)	15102
Brilhart	17404
Brinker	16001
Brinkerton	15601
Brintons	19380
Brisbin	16620
Briscoe Springs	16127
Bristol (Twp)	19021
Bristol	19007
Bristoria	15337
Brittany Farms	18914
Britton Run	16434
Broad Acres	16127
Broad Axe	19002
Broad Ford	15425
Broadlawn Highlands	15241
Broad Street (Part of Hazleton)‡	18201
Broad Top, *Bedford* (Twp)	16679
Broad Top, *Huntingdon*	16621
Broadview	15084
Broadway	18655
Broadway Manor	19007
Brock	15362
Brockport	15823
Brockton	17925
Brockway	15824
Brodbecks	17329
Brodhead	18017
	18020
For specific ZIP Codes call (888) 275-8777, or your local postmaster.	
Brodheadsville♦	18322
Brogue	17309
Brogueville	17322
Brokenstraw (Twp)	16340
Brommerstown	17922
Brookdale, *Cambria*	15942
Brookdale, *Susquehanna*	18822
Brookes Mill	16635
Brookfield (Twp)	16950
Brookhaven	19015
Brookland	16948
Brookline (Part of Pittsburgh)‡	15226
Brookline, *Delaware*	19083
Brooklyn	18813
Brookside, *Cumberland*	17257
Brookside, *Erie*	16510
Brookside, *Lycoming*	17771
Brookside, *Schuylkill*	17963
Brookside, *York*	17315
Brookside Farms	15241
Brookside Villa	18101
Brookston	16347
Brookthorpe Hills	19008
Brookville	15825
Brookwater Park	19426
Broomall♦	19008
Brothersvalley (Twp)	15530
Brotherton	15530
Broughton	15236
Brown, *Lycoming* (Twp)	17727
Brown, *Mifflin* (Twp)	17084
Brownbacks	19475
Browndale	18421
Brownfield	15416
Brown Hill	16403
Browns (Part of Avoca)	18641
Brownsburg	18938
Brownsdale	16053
Browns Mill	17201
Brownstown, *Armstrong*	15630
Brownstown, *Cambria*	15906

Place	ZIP
Brownstown, *Fayette*	15438
Brownstown, *Lancaster*	17508
Brownsville, *Berks*	19565
Brownsville, *Fayette*	15417
Brownsville, *Franklin*	17222
Brownsville, *Schuylkill*	17976
Brownsville Junction	15417
Browntown, *Bradford*	18853
Browntown, *Luzerne*	18640
Bruin	16022
Brunnerville	17543
Brunot Island (Part of Pittsburgh)	15233
Brush Creek (Twp)	15536
Brushtown, *Adams*	17331
Brushtown, *Cumberland*	17241
Brush Valley	15720
Brushville	18847
Bryan, *Armstrong*	16222
Bryan, *Fayette*	15428
Bryan Hill Manor	15701
Bryan Mills	17737
Bryansville	17314
Bryant	15101
Bryn Athyn	19009
Bryn Gweled	18966
Bryn Mawr, *Allegheny*	15241
Bryn Mawr, *Montgomery*♦	19010
Brysonia	17307
Bucher	16661
Buck, *Luzerne* (Twp)	18610
Buck, *Lancaster*	17566
Buckeye	15666
Buck Hill Falls	18323
Buckhorn, *Cambria*	16613
Buckhorn, *Columbia*	17815
Buckingham, *Wayne* (Twp)	18437
Buckingham, *Bucks*	18912
Buckingham Valley	18938
Buckland Valley Farms	18977
Buckman Village (Part of Chester)	19010
Buckmanville	18938
Buck Mountain, *Carbon*	18255
Buck Mountain, *Schuylkill*	18214
Buck Run, *Chester*	19320
Buck Run, *Indiana*	15728
Buck Run, *Schuylkill*	17901
Buckstown	15563
Bucksville	18930
Bucktown	19464
Buck Valley	17267
Buell Corners	16434
Buena Vista, *Allegheny*	15018
Buena Vista, *Butler*	16025
Buena Vista, *Fayette*	15486
Buena Vista, *Franklin*	17268
Buena Vista, *Lancaster*	17527
Buena Vista Springs	17268
Buffalo, *Butler* (Twp)	16055
Buffalo, *Perry* (Twp)	17045
Buffalo, *Union* (Twp)	17837
Buffalo, *Washington* (Twp)	15323
Buffalo, *Washington*	15301
Buffalo Cross Roads	17837
Buffalo Mills	15534
Buffalo Run	16870
Buffalo Springs	17042
Buffalo Valley	16262
Buffington, *Indiana* (Twp)	15961
Buffington, *Fayette*	15468
Buhl (Part of Sharon)‡	16146
Buhls	16033
Bulger	15019
Bullion	16374
Bullis Mills	16731
Bullskin (Twp)	15666
Bully Hill	16323
Bunches	17070
Bungalow Park	18104
Bunker Hill, *Cumberland*	17055
Bunker Hill, *Lebanon*	17046
Bunkertown	17049
Bunola	15020
Burbank	16749
Burd Coleman Village (Part of Cornwall)	17016
Burgettstown	15021
Burholme (Part of Philadelphia)	19111
Burlington (Twp)	18848
Burlington	18814
Burnham	17009
Burning Well	16735
Burnside, *Centre* (Twp)	16845
Burnside, *Clearfield* (Twp)	16692
Burnside, *Clearfield*	15721
Burnside, *Northumberland*	17872
Burnstown	16117
Burnt Cabins	17215
Burnwood	18465
Burrell, *Armstrong* (Twp)	16226
Burrell, *Indiana* (Twp)	15717
Burson Plan	15322
Bursonville	18077
Burtville	16743
Bushkill, *Northampton* (Twp)	18064
Bushkill, *Pike*	18324
Bushkill Center	18064
Bush Patch (Part of Old Forge)	18518
Bustleton (Part of Philadelphia)‡	19115
Bute	15489
Butler, *Adams* (Twp)	17307
Butler, *Butler* (Twp)	16001
Butler, *Luzerne* (Twp)	18222
Butler, *Schuylkill* (Twp)	17921
Butler, *Butler*	16001-03
For specific ZIP Codes call (888) 275-8777, or your local postmaster.	
Butler Junction	16229
Buttonwood, *Luzerne*	18702
Buttonwood, *Lycoming*	17771
Buttonwood Glen	18901
Buttonwood Manor	18901
Butztown	18017
Buyerstown	17535
Buzzingtown	15642
Byberry (Part of Philadelphia)	19116
Bycot	18928
Dyers	19480
Byersdale	15005
Byrnedale	15827
Byrnsville	17927
Byromtown	16239
Bywood	19082
Bywood Heights	19082
Cabot	16023
Cacoossing	19608
Cadis	18837
Cadogan	16212
Caernarvon, *Berks* (Twp)	19543
Caernarvon, *Lancaster* (Twp)	17555
Cains	17527
Cairnbrook	15924
Calder Square (Part of State College)	16805
Caldwell	17745
Caledonia, *Elk*	15868
Caledonia, *Franklin*	17222
California, *Bucks*	18951
California, *Washington*	15419
Calkins	18443
Callapoose	18444
Callensburg	16213
Callery	16024
Callimont	15552
Caln	19320
Calumet	15621
Calvert	17771
Calvert Hills (Part of Altoona)	16601
Calvin	16622
Camargo	17566
Cambra	18611
Cambria (Twp)	15931
Cambria City (Part of Johnstown)	15906
Cambridge, *Crawford* (Twp)	16403
Cambridge, *Chester*	19344
Cambridge Springs	16403
Cameron	15834
Cammal	17723
Camp Akiba	18352
Campbelltown, *Lebanon*♦	17010
Campbelltown, *McKean*	16735
Camp Bnai Brith	18461
Camp Curtin (Part of Harrisburg)	17110
Camp Hill	17001†
	17011*
Camp Hill Shopping Mall (Part of Camp Hill)	17011
Camp Indian Run	19344
Camp Jo-Ann	15668
Camp Perry	16114
Camp Starlight	18461
Camptown	18815
Camp Westmont	18449
Canaan	18472
Canadensis	18325
Canadohta Lake	16438
Canal (Twp)	16314
Canan	16602
Candor	15019
Cannelton	16115
Canoe (Twp)	15772
Canoe Camp	16933
Canoe Creek	16648
Canoe Ridge	15772
Canonsburg	15317
Canton, *Washington* (Twp)	15301
Canton, *Bradford*	17724
Capital City Plaza	17011
Caprivi	17013
Carbon, *Huntingdon* (Twp)	16678
Carbon, *Mercer*	16154
Carbon, *Westmoreland*	15601
Carbon Center	16001
Carbondale	18407
Cardale	15420
Cardiff	15943
Cardington	19082
Carlisle	17013
Carlisle Barracks	17013
Carlisle Springs	17013
Carlson	16735
Carlton	16311
Carlton Heights	17252
Carmichaels	15320
Carnegie	15106
Carnot	15108
Carnwath	16861
Carol Acres	17036
Carpenter Corners	16153
Carpenter Town, *Lackawanna*	18414
Carpentertown, *Westmoreland*	15666
Carriage Hill	19067
Carrick (Part of Pittsburgh)	15210
Carrier (Part of Summerville)	15864
Carroll, *Perry* (Twp)	17090
Carroll, *Washington* (Twp)	15063
Carroll, *York* (Twp)	17019
Carroll, *Clinton*	17747
Carroll Park, *Columbia*	17815
Carroll Park, *Montgomery*	19151
Carrolltown	15722
Carroll Valley	17320
Carson (Part of Pittsburgh)‡	15203
Carsontown	17776
Carson Valley	16635
Carsonville	17032
Carter Camp	16922
Cartwright	15823
Carver Court	19320
Carversville	18913
Carverton	18644
Casanova	16860
Cascade (Twp)	17771
Cashtown	17310
Cass, *Huntingdon* (Twp)	16623
Cass, *Schuylkill* (Twp)	17901
Cassandra	15925
Casselman	15557
Cassville	16623
Castanea♦	17726
Caste Village (Part of Whitehall)	15236
Castle Garden	15832
Castle Rock	19073
Castle Shannon	15234
Castle Valley	18914
Castlewood	16101
Castor (Part of Philadelphia)	19149
Cataract	16871
Catasauqua	18032
Catawissa	17820
Catharine (Twp)	16693
Cavettsville	15085
Ceasetown	18612
Cecil (Twp)	15057
Cecil	15321
Cedarbrook	19095
Cedarbrook Hills	19095
Cedarbrook Mall	19095
Cedar Cliff Manor	17011
Cedar Heights	19428
Cedar Hollow	19355
Cedar Knoll	19320
Cedar Lane	17519
Cedar Ledge	17724
Cedar Ridge	17350
Cedar Run	17727
Cedars	19423
Cedar Springs	17751
Cedar Top	19607
Cedarville	19464
Cementon	18052
Centennial, *Adams*	17331
Centennial, *Centre*	16870
Centennial Hills	18974
Center, *Beaver* (Twp)	15001
Center, *Butler* (Twp)	16001
Center, *Greene* (Twp)	15359
Center, *Indiana* (Twp)	15748
Center (Part of Plum)	15239
Center, *Juniata*	17059
Center, *Perry*	17062
Center Bridge	18938
Center City (Part of Williamsport)‡	17703
Center Hill	16201
Center Mills	17304
Center Moreland	18657
Centerport	19516
Center Road	16424
Center Square	19422
Centertown	16127
Center Union	16652
Center Valley	18034
Centerville, *Bedford*	15522
Centerville, *Bradford*	14894
Centerville, *Crawford*	16404
Centerville, *Lancaster*	17602
Centerville, *Perry*	17045
Centerville, *Washington*	15417
Centerville, *York*	17327
Central (Part of McKeesport)‡	15132
Central (Part of Washington)‡	15301
Central, *Columbia*	17814
Central, *Westmoreland*	15688
Central City (Part of Milesburg)	16853
Central City, *Somerset*	15926
Central Highlands	15037
Centralia	17927
Central Manor	17582
Central Oak Heights	17886
Central Square Greens	19401
Centre, *Berks* (Twp)	19541
Centre, *Perry* (Twp)	17068
Centre, *Snyder* (Twp)	17842
Centre, *Perry*	17047
Centre Hall	16828
Centre Hill	16828
Century	15417
Century III Mall (Part of West Mifflin)	15123
Ceres (Twp)	16748
Cessna	15522
Cetronia	18104
Ceylon	15320
Chadds Ford	19317
Chadville	15401
Chain	17960
Chain Bridge	18940
Chaintown	15428
Chalfant	15112
Chalfont	18914
Chalkhill	15421
Challenge	15823
Chalybeate	15522
Chambersburg	17201
Chambers Hill	17111
Chambers Mill	15301
Chambersville	15723
Champion, *Fayette*	15622
Champion, *Westmoreland*	15622
Chanceford (Twp)	17309
Chandlers Valley	16312
Chaneysville	15535
Chapel	18070
Chapel Downs	15024
Chapel Valley	15001
Chapman, *Clinton* (Twp)	17760
Chapman, *Lehigh*	18106
Chapman, *Northampton*	18014
Chapman, *Snyder*	17864
Chapman Lake	18433
Chapmanville	16354
Charleroi	15022
Charleston, *Tioga* (Twp)	16901
Charleston, *Mercer*	16148
Charlestown, *Chester*	19460
Charlestown, *Franklin*	17236
Charlesville	15522
Charlottsville	16686
Charlton, *Clinton*	17745
Charlton, *Dauphin*	17111
Charmian	17214
Charming Forge	19551
Charteroak	16669
Charter Oaks	16509
Chartiers, *Washington* (Twp)	15342
Chartiers, *Greene*	15322
Chase	18708
Chatham, *Tioga* (Twp)	16935
Chatham, *Chester*	19318
Chatham Park	19083
Chatham Village	19083
Chatwood	19380
Checkerville	16925
Chelsea	19013
Chelten Avenue (Part of Philadelphia)	19144
Cheltenham	19012
Cheltenham Shopping Center	19095
Cheltenham Square	19150
Cherokee Ranch	19560
Cherry, *Butler* (Twp)	16057
Cherry, *Sullivan* (Twp)	18614
Cherry City	15223
Cherry Flats	16917
Cherry Grove, *Huntingdon*	17264
Cherry Grove, *Warren*	16313
Cherryhill, *Indiana* (Twp)	15765
Cherry Hill, *Erie*	16401
Cherry Hill, *Lancaster*	17563
Cherry Hill, *Northampton*	18064
Cherry Hill, *York*	17070
Cherry Lane	15613
Cherry Ridge (Twp)	18431
Cherry Run	17885
Cherrytown	16657
Cherry Tree, *Indiana*	15724
Cherry Tree, *Venango*	16354
Cherry Valley, *Butler*	16373
Cherry Valley, *Washington*	15021
Cherryville, *Northampton*	18035
Cherryville, *Schuylkill*	17966
Chest, *Cambria* (Twp)	16668
Chest, *Clearfield* (Twp)	15753
Chester	19013*
	19016†
Chesterbrook♦	19087
Chesterfield	16627
Chester Heights	19017
Chester Hill	16866
Chester Plaza	19014
Chester Springs	19425
Chester Township♦	19013
Chester Valley Knoll	19355
Chesterville	19350
Chestnut Grove	16838
Chestnuthill, *Monroe* (Twp)	18331
Chestnut Hill, *Erie*	16509
Chestnut Hill, *Lancaster*	17512
Chestnut Hill, *Lehigh*	18036
Chestnut Hill, *Northampton*	18042
Chestnut Hill (Part of Philadelphia)‡	19118
Chestnut Level	17566
Chestnut Ridge, *Fayette*	15422
Chestnut Ridge, *Lancaster*	17603
Chestnut View	17603
Chest Springs	16624
Cheswick	15024
Chevy Chase Heights	15701
Chewton	16157
Cheyney	19319
Chickasaw	16259
Chicora	16025
Childs	18407
Chillisquaque	17850
Chinchilla	18410
Chippewa (Twp)	15010
Choconut (Twp)	18818
Choconut	18812
Christiana	17509
Christian Springs	18064
Christmans	18229

Place	ZIP
Chrome	19362
Chrystal	16748
Church Hill, *Fayette*	15458
Church Hill, *Forest*	16353
Church Hill, *Franklin*	17236
Church Hill, *Mifflin*	17084
Church Hills	17082
Churchill	15235
Churchill Plan	16117
Churchill Valley	15235
Churchtown	17555
Churchville, *Bedford*	16667
Churchville, *Bucks*♦	18966
Churchville, *Clarion*	16255
Circleville	15642
Cisna Run	17047
Cito	17233
City View	17044
Clair Manor	15012
Clairton	15025
Clairton Junction (Part of West Mifflin)	15122
Clamtown	18252
Clappertown	16693
Clapp Farm	16301
Clara (Twp)	16748
Clarence	16829
Clarendon	16313
Clarendon Heights	16313
Claridge	15623
Clarington	15828
Clarion (Twp)	16258
Clarion	16214
Clark	16113
Clark Manor	15001
Clarksburg	15725
Clarks Green	18411
Clarks Mills	16114
Clarks Summit	18411
Clarkstown	17756
Clarksville	15322
Clarksville Hill	15322
Claussville	18069
Clay, *Butler* (Twp)	16061
Clay, *Huntingdon* (Twp)	17264
Clay, *Lancaster* (Twp)	17578
Clay, *Lancaster*	17522
Clay Hill	17201
Claylick	17236
Claypoole Heights	15701
Claysburg♦	16625
Claysville	15323
Clayton	19503
Claytonia	16057
Clearbrook Village	19040
Clearfield, *Butler* (Twp)	16034
Clearfield, *Cambria* (Twp)	16668
Clearfield, *Clearfield*	16830
Clearfield, *Northampton*	18064
Clear Ridge, *Bedford*	15537
Clear Ridge, *Fulton*	17229
Clear Run	15801
Clear Spring	17019
Clearview	17601
Clearview Estates, Beaver	15001
Clearview Estates, *Cumberland*	17011
Clearview Mall	16001
Clearview Manor	18101
Clearville	15535
Cleona	17042
Clermont	16740
Cleveland (Twp)	17820
Cleversburg	17257
Cliff Mine	15108
Clifford, *Snyder*	17870
Clifford, *Susquehanna*	18413
Clifton, *Dauphin*	17057
Clifton, *Lackawanna*	18424
Clifton Heights	19018
Climax, *Armstrong*	16242
Climax, *Clarion*	16242
Climax, *Indiana*	15944
Clinton, *Butler* (Twp)	16059
Clinton, *Lycoming* (Twp)	17752
Clinton, *Venango* (Twp)	16373
Clinton, *Wayne* (Twp)	18472
Clinton, *Wyoming* (Twp)	18419
Clinton, *Allegheny*	15026
Clinton, *Armstrong*	16229
Clinton, *Butler*	16055
Clinton, *Fayette*	15469
Clintondale	17751
Clintonville	16372
Cloe	15767
Clonmell	19390
Clover (Twp)	15829
Clover Creek	16662
Cloverdale Park	18915
Clover Hill	15423
Clover Run	15757
Clune	15727
Cly	17370
Clyde	15944
Clymer, *Tioga* (Twp)	16943
Clymer, *Indiana*	15728
Coal (Twp)	17872
Coal Bluff	15332
Coal Cabin Beach	17314
Coal Castle	17901
Coal Center	15423
Coal City	16374
Coaldale, *Dauphin*	17048
Coaldale, *Schuylkill*	18218
Coal Glen	15824
Coal Hill	16301
Coal Hollow	15846
Coalmont	16678
Coalport (Part of Jim Thorpe)	18229
Coalport, *Clearfield*	16627
Coal Run, *Clearfield*	16666
Coal Run, *Northumberland*	17872
Coal Run, *Somerset*	15552
Coaltown, *Butler*	16057
Coaltown, *Lawrence*	16101
Coal Township (Part of Shamokin)	17866
Coatesville	19320
Cobalt Ridge	19058
Cobblerville	17241
Cobbs Corners	16434
Cobham	16351
Coburn, *Blair*	16601
Coburn, *Centre*	16832
Cocalico	17517
Cochran Acres	15001
Cochrans Mills	16226
Cochranton	16314
Cochranville	19330
Cocolamus	17014
Codorus, *York* (Twp)	17327
Codorus, *York*	17311
Coffeetown, *Lebanon*	17078
Coffeetown, *Lehigh*	18069
Coffeetown, *Northampton*	18042
Cogan House (Twp)	17771
Cogan Station	17728
Cokeburg	15324
Cokeburg Junction	15331
Cold Point	19462
Cold Run	19508
Cold Spring, *Lebanon* (Twp)	17028
Cold Spring, *Wayne*	18431
Cold Spring, *York*	17360
Cold Spring Park	19464
Cold Springs Crossing	19426
Colebrook, *Clinton* (Twp)	17734
Colebrook, *Lebanon*	17042
Colebrookdale	19512
Colegrove	16749
Coleman	15541
Colemanville	17565
Colerain, *Bedford* (Twp)	15522
Colerain, *Lancaster* (Twp)	17536
Colerain, *Huntingdon*	16683
Coles	17948
Colesburg	16915
Coles Creek	17814
Colesville	18015
Coleville, *Centre*	16823
Coleville, *McKean*	16749
Colfax	16652
College (Twp)	16801
College Heights	19605
College Hill (Part of Beaver Falls)	15010
College Manor	18612
College Misericordia	18612
College Park, *Montgomery*	19031
College Park, *Union*	17837
College View Heights	18016
Collegeville	19426
Colley (Twp)	18614
Collier, *Allegheny* (Twp)	15106
Collier, *Fayette*	15401
Collingdale	19023
Collins	17566
Collinsburg	15089
Collinsville	17302
Collinswood Acres	15317
Collomsville	17702
Colmar	18915
Colona (Part of Monaca)	15061
Colonial Crest	17111
Colonial Hills, *Berks*	19608
Colonial Hills, *Mifflin*	17044
Colonial Manor	17603
Colonial Park, *Dauphin*♦	17109
Colonial Park, *Delaware*	19064
Colonial Park, *Lancaster*	17540
Colonial Park, *Northumberland*	17847
Colonial Village, *Chester*	19087
Colonial Village, *Venango*	16301
Colony Park	19608
Columbia, *Bradford* (Twp)	16914
Columbia, *Lancaster*	17512
Columbia Cross Roads	16914
Columbus	16405
Colver♦	15927
Colwyn	19023
Comly	17772
Commerce (Part of Philadelphia)‡	19108
Commodore	15729
Compass	17527
Conashaugh Lake	18337
Concord, *Butler* (Twp)	16025
Concord, *Delaware* (Twp)	19331
Concord, *Erie* (Twp)	16407
Concord, *Franklin*	17217
Concord, *Westmoreland*	15012
Concord Park	19047
Concordville	19331
Conemaugh, *Cambria* (Twp)	15902
Conemaugh, *Indiana* (Twp)	15725
Conemaugh, *Somerset* (Twp)	15935
Conestoga, *Chester*	19520
Conestoga, *Lancaster*	17516
Conestoga Woods	17602
Coneville	16915
Conewago, *Adams* (Twp)	17331
Conewago, *Dauphin* (Twp)	17022
Conewago, *York* (Twp)	17404
Conewago Heights	17345
Conewango (Twp)	16365
Confluence	15424
Congo	19504
Congruity	15601
Conifer	15864
Connaughton	19428
Conneaut, *Crawford* (Twp)	16424
Conneaut, *Erie* (Twp)	16401
Conneaut Lake	16316
Conneaut Lake Park	16316
Conneautville	16406
Connellsville	15425
Connersville	17851
Connerton	17935
Connoquenessing (Twp)	16053
Connoquenessing	16027
Conoy (Twp)	17502
Conrad	16720
Conshohocken	19428
Continental (Part of Philadelphia)‡	19106
Conway	15027
Conyngham, *Columbia* (Twp)	17851
Conyngham, *Luzerne* (Twp)	18655
Conyngham, *Luzerne*	18219
Cook (Twp)	15687
Cooke (Twp)	17241
Cookport	15729
Cooks	16674
Cooksburg	16217
Cookseytown	18707
Cooks Mill	15545
Cooks Run	17778
Coolbaugh (Twp)	18466
Coolbaughs	18324
Coolspring, *Mercer* (Twp)	16137
Coolspring, *Fayette*	15445
Coolspring, *Jefferson*	15730
Cool Valley, *Washington*	15317
Cool Valley, *Westmoreland*	15601
Coon Hunter	17842
Coon Island	15376
Coontown	16735
Cooper, *Clearfield* (Twp)	16839
Cooper, *Montour* (Twp)	17821
Coopersburg	18036
Cooper Settlement	16834
Cooperstown, *Butler*	16059
Cooperstown, *Venango*	16317
Cooperstown, *Westmoreland*	15650
Coopersville	17509
Copella	18014
Copesville	19380
Coplay	18037
Coppersdale (Part of Johnstown)	15906
Coral	15731
Coraopolis	15108
Coraopolis Heights	15108
Corinne	19380
Cork Lane	18640
Corliss (Part of Pittsburgh)‡	15204
Corner Ketch	19335
Corner Store	19460
Corning	18092
Cornish	15478
Cornog	19343
Cornplanter (Twp)	16301
Cornpropst Mills	16652
Cornwall	17016
Cornwall Center (Part of Cornwall)	17016
Corry	16407
Corsica	15829
Cortez	18436
Corwins Corners	16701
Corydon (Twp)	16701
Coryville	16731
Costello	16720
Cosytown	17225
Coterell Lake	18470
Cottage	16669
Cottage Grove	16105
Cottage Hill	16242
Cottageville	18901
Cotton Town	16625
Couchtown	17047
Coudersport	16915
Coulters	15028
Council Crest	18201
Country Club Estates, *Armstrong*	16201
Country Club Estates, *Lancaster*	17601
Country Club Estates, *Montgomery*	19444
Country Club Heights	17601
Country Gardens	17540
Country Hills	15642
Countryside	17011
County Line	18966
County Line Park	18914
Coupon	16629
Court at King of Prussia, The	19406
Courtdale	18704
Courtney	15067
Cove	17020
Covedale	16693
Cove Gap	17236
Coventryville	19464
Coverdale (Part of Bethel Park)	15102
Coveville	18325
Coveytown	18614
Covington, *Clearfield* (Twp)	16836
Covington, *Lackawanna* (Twp)	18424
Covington, *Tioga*	16917
Covode	15767
Cowan	17844
Cowanesque	16918
Cowansburg	15642
Cowanshannock (Twp)	16249
Cowans Village	17224
Cowansville	16218
Cowden	15057
Coxeville	18216
Coy	15748
Coy Junction	15748
Coyleville	16034
Crabapple	15380
Crabtree	15624
Crabtree Hollow	19053
Crackersport	18104
Crafton	15205
Craig	18414
Craigheads	17013
Craigs	17948
Craigs Meadow	18301
Craigsville	16262
Craley	17312
Cramer	15954
Cramer Heights (Part of Latrobe)	15650
Cranberry, *Butler* (Twp)	16066
Cranberry, *Luzerne*	18201
Cranberry, *Venango*	16319
Cranberry Mall	16319
Cranberry Ridge	18201
Cranesville	16410
Crates	16240
Crawford (Twp)	17740
Crawfordtown	15733
Creamery	19430
Creamton	18421
Creekside	15732
Creighton	15030
Crenshaw	15824
Crescent (Twp)	15046
Crescentdale (Part of Wampum)	16157
Crescent Heights	15427
Crescent Lake, *Monroe*	18332
Crescent Lake, *Pike*	18337
Cresco	18326
Cresmont Farms	19335
Cress	17268
Cresson	16630
Cressona	17929
Crestmont, *Clinton*	17745
Crestmont, *Montgomery*	19090
Crestmont Village	15001
Crestview	19040
Crestwood, *Berks*	19606
Crestwood, *Lackawanna*	18444
Creswell	17516
Crete	15701
Criders Corners	16046
Crimson Maple	18837
Croft	16830
Cromby	19460
Cromwell (Twp)	17264
Crookham	15332
Crosby	16724
Cross Creek (Twp)	15312
Cross Creek	15021
Cross Fork	17729
Crossgrove	17841
Crossingville	16412
Cross Keys, *Adams*	17350
Cross Keys, *Blair*	16635
Cross Keys (Part of Doylestown)	18901
Cross Keys, *Juniata*	17021
Crossroads, *Northampton*	18014
Cross Roads, *York*	17322
Crosswicks	19046
Crown	16220
Crown Meadows	15238
Croydon♦	19021
Croydon Acres	19021
Croydon Heights	19021
Croydon Manor	19021
Croyle (Twp)	15956
Crozer Park Gardens (Part of Chester)	19013
Crucible	15325
Crum Creek Manor	19013
Crum Lynne	19022
Crystal	15439
Crystal Lake	18407
Crystal Spring	15536
Crystal Springs	16353
Cuba Mills	17059
Cuddy	15031
Cuddy Hill	15031
Culbertson	17201
Cullen Manor	17888
Culmerville	15084
Culp	16601
Cumberland, *Adams* (Twp)	17325
Cumberland, *Greene* (Twp)	15320
Cumberland Park	17011
Cumberland Valley (Twp)	15522
Cumberland Village	15320
Cumbola	17930
Cummings (Twp)	17776
Cumminstown	17013
Cumru (Twp)	19540
Cupola	19344

Place	ZIP Code
Curley Hill	18901
Curllsville	16221
Curren Terrace (Part of Norristown)	19401
Curry Run	15757
Curryville	16631
Curtin	16841
Curtis Hills	19095
Curtis Park (Part of Sharon Hill)	19079
Curtisville♦	15032
Curwensville	16833
Cush Creek	15712
Cussewago (Twp)	16433
Custards	16314
Custer City	16725
Custis Woods	19038
Cyclone	16726
Cymbria	15714
Cypher	16650
Daggett	16936
Dagus	15846
Daguscahonda	15853
Dagus Mines	15831
Dahoga	15870
Daisytown, *Cambria*	15902
Daisytown, *Washington*	15427
Dale, *Cambria*	15902
Dale, *Clearfield*	16881
Dale Summit	16823
Daleville, *Chester*	19330
Daleville, *Lackawanna*	18424
Dalevue	16801
Daley	15924
Dallas	18612
Dallas City	16701
Dallastown	17313
Dalmatia	17017
Dalton	18414
Damascus	18415
Danboro	18916
Danielsville	18038
Dannersville	18067
Danville	17821
Darby (Twp)	19036
Darby	19023
Darlington, *Beaver*	16115
Darlington, *Delaware*	19063
Darlington, *Westmoreland*	15658
Darlington Corners	19380
Darragh	15625
Darthmouth Farms	17036
Dauberville	19517
Daugherty (Twp)	15066
Dauphin	17018
Davidsburg	17315
Davidson (Twp)	17758
Davidson Heights	15001
Davidsville♦	15928
Davis Grove	19044
Davistown, *Fayette*	15446
Davistown, *Greene*	15349
Dawson	15428
Dawson Manor	19040
Dawson Ridge	15009
Dawson Run	16370
Day	16258
Daylesford	19312
Dayton, *Armstrong*	16222
Dayton, *Dauphin*	17098
Deal	15552
Dean	16636
Deanville	16242
Dearth	15401
Decatur, *Clearfield* (Twp)	16666
Decatur, *Mifflin* (Twp)	17841
Deckard	16314
Deckers Point	15759
Deckertown	18446
Deegan	16020
Deemers Cross Roads	15851
Deemston	15333
Deep Dale East	19058
Deep Dale West	19058
Deep Run	18944
Deep Valley	15352
Deer Creek (Twp)	16145
Deerfield, *Tioga* (Twp)	16928
Deerfield, *Warren* (Twp)	16351
Deer Lake, *Fayette*	15421
Deer Lake, *Schuylkill*	17961
Deer Mt. Lake	18355
Deer Park	18938
Defiance	16633
Degolia	16701
Deiblers Station	17821
Delabole	18072
De Lancey	15733
Delano	18220
Delaware, *Juniata* (Twp)	17094
Delaware, *Mercer* (Twp)	16124
Delaware, *Northumberland* (Twp)	17777
Delaware, *Pike* (Twp)	18328
Delaware Grove	16124
Delaware Run	17777
Delaware Valley College (Part of New Britain)	18901
Delaware Water Gap	18327
Dellville	17020
Delmar (Twp)	16901
Delmont	15626
Delphi	19473
Delps	18038
Delroy	17406
Delta	17314
Delta Manor	18017
Dempseytown	16317
Denbeau Heights (Part of Centerville)	15417
Denbo (Part of Centerville)	15429
Denholm	17059
Denison	15601
Dennison (Twp)	18661
Dennys Corners	16335
Dennys Mill	16023
Dents Run	15832
Denver	17517
Deodate	17022
Deringer	18241
Derrick City	16727
Derrs	17814
Derry, *Dauphin* (Twp)	17033
Derry, *Mifflin* (Twp)	17099
Derry, *Montour* (Twp)	17821
Derry, *Westmoreland*	15627
Derwood Park	19094
Derwyn	19004
Deshon Manor	16001
Desire	15851
Detters Mill	17315
De Turksville	17963
Devault	19432
Devon	19333
Dewart	17730
Dewey Heights	18052
De Young	16728
Diamond	16354
Diamondtown	17851
Diamondville	15728
Dice	17844
Dickerson Run	15430
Dickeys Mountain	17212
Dickinson (Twp)	17065
Dickinson	17241
Dicksonburg	16406
Dickson City	18519
Dieners Hall	17901
Dilliner	15327
Dillinger	18049
Dillingersville	18092
Dillontown	18417
Dillsburg	17019
Dilltown	15929
Dilworthtown	19380
Dime	15690
Dimeling	16830
Dimmsville	17094
Dimock	18816
Dimock Corners	18430
Dingman (Twp)	18337
Dingmans Ferry	18328
Dipple Manor	18201
Distant	16223
District (Twp)	19512
Divide	17814
Dividing Ridge	15530
Dixon	18657
Dixonville	15734
D&M Junction	17019
Doe Run	19320
Dogtown, *Columbia*	17815
Dogtown, *Luzerne*	18655
Dogtown, *Snyder*	17870
Dogwood Acres	18966
Dogwood Hollow	19053
Dolington	18940
Dombach Manor	17601
Donaldson	17981
Donaldsons Crossroads	15317
Donation	16652
Donegal, *Butler* (Twp)	16025
Donegal, *Washington* (Twp)	15323
Donegal, *Westmoreland*	15628
Donegal Heights	17552
Donegal Springs	17552
Donerville	17603
Donnally Mills	17062
Donnelly	15612
Donnellytown	17013
Donohoe	15650
Donora	15033
Dooleyville	17851
Dora, *Greene*	15338
Dora, *Jefferson*	15767
Dormont	15216
Dorneyville	18104
Dornsife	17823
Dorothy	15650
Dorrance	18707
Dorset	17960
Dorseyville	15238
Dott	17267
Dotters Corners	18058
Doubling Gap	17241
Douglass, *Berks* (Twp)	19464
Douglass, *Montgomery* (Twp)	19525
Douglassville	19518
Doutyville	17872
Dover	17315
Down East	19355
Downey	15530
Downieville	16059
Downingtown	19335
Downtown (Part of Erie)‡	16501-02
	16507
	16512
For specific ZIP Codes call (888) 275-8777, or your local postmaster.	
Downtown (Part of Lancaster)‡	17603*
	17608†
Downtown (Part of New Castle)‡	16103
Downtown (Part of Reading)‡	19603
Downtown (Part of Scranton)‡	18501
Downtown (Part of Uniontown)‡	15401
Doylesburg	17219
Doyles Mills	17058
Doylestown	18901
Drake	16156
Drakes Mills	16403
Draketown, *Clinton*	17751
Draketown, *Somerset*	15424
Drane	16666
Draper	16901
Drauckers	15848
Dravosburg	15034
Dreher (Twp)	18445
Drehersville	17961
Drennen (Part of Murrysville)	15068
Dresher	19025
Drexelbrook	19026
Drexel Heights	18067
Drexel Hill♦	19026
Drexel Hills (Part of New Cumberland)	17070
Drexeline Shopping Center	19026
Drexlewood	19610
Drifting	16834
Drifton	18221
Driftwood	15832
Drinker	18444
Dromgold	17090
Druid Hills (Part of Dallas)	18708
Drummond	15823
Drumore (Twp)	17563
Drumore	17518
Drums	18222
Drury Run	17764
Dry Hill	15425
Dry Run	17220
Dry Tavern	15357
Dry Valley Crossroads	17889
Dryville	19539
Dublin, *Fulton* (Twp)	17223
Dublin, *Huntingdon* (Twp)	17239
Dublin, *Bucks*	18917
Dublin Mills	17229
Du Bois	15801
Duboistown	17702
Dudley	16634
Duffield	17201
Duhring	16239
Duke Center	16729
Dumas	15424
Dunbar	15431
Duncan (Twp)	16901
Duncan Circle	15009
Duncannon	17020
Duncansville	16635
Duncott	17901
Dundaff	18407
Dundore	17864
Dungarvin	16877
Dunkard	15327
Dunkelbergers	17872
Dunlevy	15432
Dunlo	15930
Dunmore	18512
Dunningsville	15330
Dunningtown (Part of Murrysville)	15632
Dunns Eddy	16371
Dunnstable (Twp)	17745
Dunnstown♦	17745
Dupont‡	18641
Duquesne	15110
Duquesne Heights (Part of Pittsburgh)	15211
Duquesne Wharf (Part of Duquesne)	15110
Durham	18039
Durham Furnace	18930
Durlach	17522
Durrell	18848
Duryea	18642
Dushore	18614
Dutch Hill, *Clarion*	16049
Dutch Hill, *Fayette*	15450
Dutch Hill (Part of Hermitage)	16148
Dutch Settlement	15946
Dutchtown, *Cambria*	15938
Dutchtown, *Franklin*	17236
Dutton Mill	19380
Dyberry (Twp)	18431
Dysart	16636
Eagle Foundry	16657
Eaglehurst	16505
Eagle Point	19530
Eagle Rock	16301
Eagles Mere	17731
Eagles Mere Park (Part of Eagles Mere)	17731
Eagleville, *Centre*	16826
Eagleville, *Montgomery*♦	19408
Earl, *Berks* (Twp)	19512
Earl, *Lancaster* (Twp)	17557
Earlington	18918
Earlston	15537
Earlville	19519
Earnest	19401
Earnestville	16666
East Allen (Twp)	18067
East Altoona	16601
East Ararat	18470
East Athens	18810
East Bangor‡	18013
East Benton	18414
East Berlin	17316
East Bethlehem (Twp)	15322
East Bradford (Twp)	19380
East Brady	16028
East Branch	16434
East Brandywine (Twp)	19335
East Brook	16101
East Brunswick (Twp)	17960
East Buffalo (Twp)	17837
East Butler	16029
East Caln (Twp)	19341
East Cameron (Twp)	17872
East Canton	17724
East Carnegie (Part of Pittsburgh)	15230
East Carroll (Twp)	15722
East Chillisquaque (Twp)	17847
East Cocalico (Twp)	17517
East Conemaugh	15909
East Connellsville	15425
East Coventry (Twp)	19457
East Deer (Twp)	15030
East Donegal (Twp)	17547
East Drumore (Twp)	17566
East Du Bois (Part of Du Bois)	15801
East Earl	17519
East End (Part of Altoona)	16602
East End (Part of Wilkes-Barre)	18702
East Fairfield (Twp)	16314
East Fallowfield, *Chester* (Twp)	19320
East Fallowfield, *Crawford* (Twp)	16111
East Falls (Part of Philadelphia)‡	19129
East Finley	15377
East Fork (Twp)	16720
East Franklin (Twp)	16201
East Fredericktown	15450
East Freedom	16637
East Germantown (Part of Philadelphia)‡	19138
East Goshen (Twp)	19380
East Greenville	18041
East Hanover, *Dauphin* (Twp)	17028
East Hanover, *Lebanon* (Twp)	17003
East Hempfield (Twp)	17603
East Herrick	18853
East Hickory	16321
East Hills‡	15904
East Honesdale (Part of Honesdale)	18431
East Hopewell (Twp)	17322
East Huntingdon (Twp)	15679
East Kane	16735
East Keating (Twp)	17778
East Kendall	17356
East Kittanning	16201
East Lackawannock (Twp)	16137
East Lampeter (Twp)	17602
Eastland	19362
Eastland Hills, *Franklin*	17268
Eastland Hills, *Lancaster*	17602
Eastland Marketplace	15137
East Lansdowne	19050
East Lawn	18064
Eastlawn Gardens	18064
East Lawrence	16929
East Lemon	18657
East Lenox	18470
East Lewisburg	17847
East Liberty (Part of Pittsburgh)‡	15206
East Mahoning (Twp)	15759
East Manchester (Twp)	17347
East Marianna	15345
East Marlborough (Twp)	19348
East McKeesport	15035
East Mead (Twp)	16335
East Millsboro	15433
East Mines (Part of St. Clair)	17970
Eastmont, *Allegheny*	15235
Eastmont, *York*	17315
East Nantmeal (Twp)	19421
East New Castle	16101
East Newport	17074
East Norriton♦	19401
East Norwegian (Twp)	17901
East Nottingham (Twp)	19363
East Oakmont (Part of Plum)	15239
Easton, *Clarion*	16255
Easton, *Northampton*	18040
	18042-45
For specific ZIP Codes call (888) 275-8777, or your local postmaster.	
East Oreland	19075
East Penn (Twp)	18235
East Pennsboro (Twp)	17025
East Petersburg	17520
East Pike	15701
East Pikeland (Twp)	19460
East Pittsburgh	15112
Eastpoint	17765
East Prospect	17317
East Providence (Twp)	15533
East Riverside	15433
East Rochester	15074
East Rockhill (Twp)	18944
East Run	15759
East Rush	18801
East Salem	17059
East Saxton	16678
East Sharon	16748
East Sharpsburg	16673
East Side	18661
East Smethport	16730
East Smithfield	18817
East Springfield	16411
East St. Clair (Twp)	15559
East Stroudsburg	18301
East Taylor (Twp)	15909
East Texas	18046
East Titusville	16354
East Towanda	18848
Easttown (Twp)	19312
Easttown Woods	19312
East Troy	16947
East Union (Twp)	18248
East Uniontown♦	15401
Eastvale	15010
East Vandergrift	15629

* **Area Zip Code** † **Post Office Boxes** ‡ **Postal Station** ♦ **Census Designated Place** *Italic Type* **County**

Place	ZIP
East View	15370
Eastville	17747
East Vincent (Twp)	19475
East Washington	15301
East Waterford	17021
East Weissport	18235
East Wheatfield (Twp)	15920
East Whiteland (Twp)	19355
Eastwicks (Part of Philadelphia)	19153
East William Penn	17976
Eastwood, *Allegheny*	15235
Eastwood, *Westmoreland*	15601
East Yoe	17356
East York♦	17402
Eaton (Twp)	18657
Eatonville	18657
Eau Claire	16030
Ebenezer	17046
Ebensburg	15931
Eberlys Mill	17011
Ebervale	18223
Echo, *Armstrong*	16222
Echo, *Cambria*	15942
Echo Lake	18301
Echo Valley, *Delaware*	19073
Echo Valley, *Schuylkill*	17981
Eckenrode Mill	16668
Eckley	18255
Eckville	19529
Economy	15005
Eddington	19020
Eddington Gardens	19020
Eddystone	19013
Eddyville	16242
Edelman	18064
Eden, *Lancaster* (Twp)	17566
Eden, *Clearfield*	16836
Eden, *Lancaster*	17601
Edenborn	15458
Edenburg	19526
Edendale	16666
Eden Heights	17601
Edenton	19330
Edenville	17201
Edgebrook (Part of Pittsburgh)	15226
Edgecliff (Part of Lower Burrell)	15068
Edgegrove	17331
Edge Hill	19038
Edgely	19007
Edgemere	18328
Edgemont, *Dauphin*	17109
Edgemont, *Delaware*	19028
Edgemont, *Northampton*	18088
Edgewater Terrace	15650
Edgewood, *Allegheny*	15218
Edgewood, *Indiana*	15701
Edgewood, *Northumberland*♦	17872
Edgewood Grove (Part of Somerset)	15501
Edgewood Park, *Bucks*	19067
Edgewood Park, *Delaware*	19008
Edgeworth	15143
Edgmont (Twp)	19028
Edie	15501
Edinboro	16412
Edinburg	16116
Edison	18901
Edisonville	17579
Edmon	15630
Edwardsville‡	18704
Effort	18330
Egypt, *Clearfield*	16881
Egypt, *Jefferson*	15824
Egypt, *Lehigh*	18052
Egypt Corners	16323
Ehrenfeld	15956
Eichelbergertown	16650
Eidenau	16037
Eighty Four	15330
Ekastown	16055
Elam	19342
Elberta	16601
Elbon	15823
Elbrook	17268
Elco	15434
Elder (Twp)	10040
Elders Ridge	15681
Eldersville	15036
Elderton	15736
El-Do-Lake	18058
Eldora, *Lancaster*	17563
Eldora, *Washington*	15063
Eldorado (Part of Altoona)	16602
Eldorado, *Butler*	16049
Eldred, *Jefferson* (Twp)	15860
Eldred, *Lycoming* (Twp)	17754
Eldred, *Monroe* (Twp)	18058
Eldred, *Schuylkill* (Twp)	17964
Eldred, *Warren* (Twp)	16420
Eldred, *McKean*	16731
Eldredsville	18616
Eleven Mile	16923
Elfinwild	15101
Elgin	16413
Elim♦	15905
Elimsport	17810
Elizabeth, *Allegheny* (Twp)	15018
Elizabeth, *Lancaster* (Twp)	17543
Elizabeth, *Allegheny*	15037
Elizabethtown	17022
Elizabethville	17023
Elk, *Chester* (Twp)	19351
Elk, *Clarion* (Twp)	16232
Elk, *Tioga* (Twp)	16921
Elk, *Warren* (Twp)	16345
Elk City	16232
Elk Creek (Twp)	16401
Elkdale, *Chester*	19352
Elkdale, *Susquehanna*	18470
Elk Grove	17814
Elkins Park	19027
Elk Lake, *Susquehanna*	18801
Elk Lake, *Wayne*	18472
Elkland, *Sullivan* (Twp)	18616
Elkland, *Tioga*	16920
Elk Lick (Twp)	15558
Elk Run Junction (Part of Punxsutawney)	15767
Elkview	19390
Ellen Gowan	17976
Ellenton	17724
Ellerslie	19020
Elliger Park	19034
Elliott (Part of Pittsburgh)	15205
Elliott Heights (Part of Bethlehem)	18015
Elliott Mills	16057
Elliottsburg	17024
Elliottson	17013
Elliottsville	15437
Ellisburg	16923
Ellport	16117
Ellsworth	15331
Ellwood City	16117
Elm	17521
Elmdale	18436
Elmer	16950
Elmhurst	18416
Elmo	16232
Elmora	15737
Elmwood (Part of Philadelphia)	19142
Elmwood, *York*	17403
Elmwood Terrace, *Bucks*	19057
Elmwood Terrace, *Lackawanna*	18444
Elora	16057
Elrama	15038
Elroy	18964
Elstie	16613
Elstonville	17545
Elton	15934
Elverson	19520
Elwood Park	15301
Elwyn	19063
Elwyn Terrace	17545
Elysburg♦	17824
Emanuelsville	18014
Emblem (Part of White Oak)	15131
Embreeville	19320
Emeigh	15738
Emerald	18080
Emerickville	15825
Emigsville	17318
Emilie	19057
Emlenton	16373
Emmaus	18049
Emmaville	15536
Emporium	15834
Emsworth	15202
Endeavor	16322
Enders	17032
Energy	16101
Enfield	19075
Engleside (Part of Lancaster)	17602
Engles Lake	18370
Englesville	19512
Englewood	17931
English Center	17776
Enhaut	17113
Enid	16691
Enlow	15126
Ennisville	16652
Enola♦	17025
Enon	15377
Enon Valley	16120
Enterline	17032
Enterprise, *Mercer*	16127
Enterprise, *Warren*	16354
Entlerville	17241
Entriken	16657
Ephrata	17522
Equinunk	18417
Ercildoun	19320
Erdenheim	19118
Erdman	17048
Erhard	16861
Erie	16501-65
For specific ZIP Codes call (888) 275-8777, or your local postmaster.	
Erie Heights (Part of Erie)	16508
Eriton	15801
Erlen	19126
Erly	17024
Ernest	15739
Erney	17315
Erwinna	18920
Eshbach	19505
Eshcol	17062
Esplen (Part of Pittsburgh)	15204
Espy♦	17815
Espyville	16424
Espyville Station	16424
Essington	19029
Estella	18616
Esterly (Part of St. Lawrence)	19606
Estherton	17110
Etna	15223
Etters	17319
Euclid	16001
Eulalia (Twp)	16915
Eureka	15479
Evansburg♦	19426
Evans City	16033
Evans Falls	18657
Evans Manor	15401
Evanston	15625
Evansville, *Berks*	19522
Evansville, *Columbia*	18603
Evendale	17086
Everett	15537
Evergreen	18833
Evergreen Park	18052
Everhartville	17074
Everson	15631
Ewalt (Part of Pittsburgh)‡	15212
Ewings Mill	15765
Ewingsville	15106
Excelsior	17825
Exchange	17821
Exeter, *Berks* (Twp)	19606
Exeter, *Wyoming* (Twp)	18615
Exeter, *Luzerne*‡	18643
Exmoor	17963
Experiment (Part of Jefferson)	15230
Export	15632
Exton♦	19341
Exton Square Mall	19341
Eyers Grove	17846
Eynon (Part of Archbald)	18403
Factoryville, *Northampton*	18013
Factoryville, *Wyoming*	18419
Faggs Manor	19330
Fagleysville	19525
Fagundus	16351
Fair Acres	17070
Fairbank	15435
Fairbrook	16865
Fairchance	15436
Fairdale, *Greene*	15320
Fairdale, *Susquehanna*	18801
Fairfield, *Crawford* (Twp)	16314
Fairfield, *Lycoming* (Twp)	17754
Fairfield, *Westmoreland* (Twp)	15923
Fairfield, *Adams*	17320
Fairfield, *Erie*	16510
Fairfield, *Washington*	15345
Fair Grounds	15344
Fairhaven Heights	15137
Fairhill, *Bucks*	19440
Fairhill (Part of Philadelphia)‡	19133
Fairhope, *Fayette*	15012
Fairhope, *Somerset*	15538
Fairland	17543
Fairlawn	17728
Fairless	19030
Fairless Hills♦	19030
Fairmont	15642
Fairmount, *Luzerne* (Twp)	17814
Fairmount (Part of Philadelphia)‡	19121
Fairmount, *Lancaster*	17566
Fairmount, *Wayne*	18462
Fairmount City	16224
Fairmount Springs	17814
Fair Oaks, *Allegheny*	15003
Fairoaks, *Montgomery*	19044
Fairplay	17325
Fairview, *Butler* (Twp)	16025
Fairview, *Luzerne* (Twp)	18707
Fairview, *Mercer* (Twp)	16137
Fairview, *York* (Twp)	17070
Fairview (Part of Altoona)	16601
Fairview (Part of Ohioville)	15052
Fairview, *Butler*	16050
Fairview, *Clearfield*	16858
Fairview, *Elk*	15846
Fairview, *Erie*	16415
Fairview, *Franklin*	17268
Fairview, *Jefferson*	15767
Fairview, *Mercer*	16124
Fairview, *Mifflin*	17044
Fairview, *Northumberland*	17872
Fairview Drive	17331
Fairview Heights, *Allegheny*	15238
Fairview Heights, *Berks*	19533
Fairview Heights, *Luzerne*	18707
Fairview Heights, *McKean*	16701
Fairview Hills	18707
Fairview Knolls	18042
Fairview Park, *Chester*	19380
Fairview Park, *Luzerne*	18707
Fairview Park, *York*	17070
Fairview Village	19409
Fairville, *Chester*	19317
Fairville, *Union*	17837
Fairway Park	17603
Fairways of Brookside	18062
Falconcrest	19380
Fall Brook	16939
Fallentimber	16639
Falling Spring, *Franklin*	17201
Falling Spring, *Perry*	17040
Fallowfield (Twp)	15022
Falls, *Bucks* (Twp)	19054
Falls, *Wyoming*	18615
Falls Creek	15840
Fallsdale	18431
Fallsington	19054
Fallston	15066
Falmouth	17502
Fannett (Twp)	17220
Fannettsburg	17221
Faraday Park	19070
Farmbrook	19007
Farmdale	17552
Farmers	17364
Farmers Mills	16875
Farmers Valley, *Bradford*	16947
Farmers Valley, *McKean*	16749
Farmersville, *Lancaster*	17522
Farmersville, *Northampton*	18045
Farming Ridge	19606
Farmington, *Clarion* (Twp)	16233
Farmington, *Tioga* (Twp)	16946
Farmington, *Warren* (Twp)	16345
Farmington, *Berks*	19539
Farmington, *Fayette*	15437
Farmington, *Lehigh*	18103
Farmington Hill	16946
Farquhar Estates	17403
Farragut	17754
Farrandsville	17734
Farrell	16121
Farview	19607
Farwell	17764
Fassett	16925
Faunce	16863
Fawn, *Allegheny* (Twp)	15084
Fawn, *York* (Twp)	17321
Fawn Grove	17321
Faxon	17701
Fayette, *Juniata* (Twp)	17049
Fayette, *Lawrence*	16156
Fayette City	15438
Fayetteville♦	17222
Fayfield	17402
Fay Terrace	16125
Fearnot	17968
Feasterville	19053
Feasterville-Trevose♦	19053
Federal	15071
Federal Reserve (Part of Pittsburgh)‡	15230
Federal Square (Part of Harrisburg)‡	17108
Fell (Twp)	18421
Fellsburg	15012
Fellwick	19034
Felton	17322
Feltonville	19013
Fenelton	16034
Ferguson, *Centre* (Twp)	16801
Ferguson, *Clearfield* (Twp)	15757
Ferguson, *Fayette*	15431
Fergusonville	19007
Fermanagh (Twp)	17059
Fern	16319
Fern Brook	18612
Ferndale, *Bucks*	18921
Ferndale, *Cambria*	15905
Ferndale, *Northumberland*	17872
Ferndale, *Schuylkill*	17985
Fern Glen	18241
Fern Hill	19380
Fernridge	18610
Fern Village	19040
Fernville	17815
Fernway♦	16063
Fernwood, *Clearfield*	16680
Fernwood, *Delaware*	19050
Ferrellton	15563
Fertigs	16364
Fertility	17602
Fetterville	17555
Fiddle Lake	18465
Fiddlers Green	15946
Fidelity (Part of Philadelphia)‡	19109
Fifficktown	15956
Fiketown	15459
Filbert	15435
Fillmore	16823
Finch Hill	18407
Findlay (Twp)	15026
Findley (Twp)	16137
Finland	18073
Finleyville, *Bedford*	16679
Finleyville, *Washington*	15332
Fireside Terrace (Part of York)	17404
Fisher, *Clarion*	16225
Fisher, *Washington*	15063
Fisherdale	17824
Fisher Heights	16001
Fishers Corner	19013
Fishers Ferry	17801
Fishertown, *Bedford*	15539
Fishertown, *Cambria*	15956
Fisherville, *Chester*	19335
Fisherville, *Dauphin*	17032
Fishing Creek (Twp)	17859
Fiske	16639
Fitch Corner	18615
Fitz Henry	15479
Five Corners	16404
Five Forks	17268
Five Points, *Adams*	17350
Five Points, *Beaver*	15001
Five Points, *Berks*	19606
Five Points, *Butler*	16061
Five Points, *Chester*	19348
Five Points, *Clearfield*	15753
Five Points, *Erie*	16509
Five Points, *Indiana*	15732
Five Points, *Luzerne*	18249
Five Points, *Mercer* (mail Jackson Center)	16133
Five Points, *Mercer* (mail Sharpsville)	16150
Five Points, *Northumberland*	17772
Five Points, *Venango*	16342
Five Points, *Westmoreland*	15601
Fivepointville	17517
Fizzleburg	16143

* **Area Zip Code** † **Post Office Boxes** ‡ **Postal Station** ♦ **Census Designated Place** *Italic Type* **County**

Place	ZIP
Flat Rock, *Centre*	16870
Flat Rock, *Fayette*	15459
Flatwoods	15486
Fleetville	18420
Fleetwing Estates	19057
Fleetwood	19522
Fleming	16835
Flemington	17745
Flicksville	18050
Flinton	16640
Flintville	17042
Floradale	17307
Floreffe (Part of Jefferson)	15025
Florence	15021
Florida Park	19073
Florin (Part of Mount Joy)	17552
Flourtown♦	19031
Flourtown Gardens	19031
Flying Hills♦	19607
FM Corners (Part of Hermitage)	16148
Fogelsville	18051
Folcroft	19032
Foleys Siding (Part of Castle Shannon)	15234
Folsom♦	19033
Folstown	18707
Fombell	16123
Font	19335
Fontana	17042
Footedale	15468
Foot of Ten	16635
Forbes Road	15633
Force	15841
Ford City	16226
Ford Cliff	16228
Fordham	15767
Ford View	16226
Fordville	17364
Fordyce	15370
Forest	16879
Forest Castle (Part of Exeter)	18643
Forest City	18421
Forest Grove, *Allegheny*	15108
Forest Grove, *Bucks*	18922
Foresthill, *Union*	17844
Forest Hill, *York*	17356
Forest Hills, *Allegheny*	15221
Forest Hills, *Lancaster*	17540
Forest Inn	18235
Forest Lake	18801
Forest Park (Part of Chalfont)	18914
Forest Park, *Luzerne*	18702
Forestville, *Butler*	16035
Forestville, *Chester*	19390
Forestville, *Schuylkill*	17901
Forge	16686
Forks, *Northampton* (Twp)	18040
Forks, *Sullivan* (Twp)	18614
Forks, *Columbia*	17859
Forks Church	15656
Forkston	18629
Forksville	18616
Forsythia Gate	19056
Fort Allen Plan	15601
Fortenia	18431
Fort Fetter	16648
Fort Hill, *Somerset*	15540
Fort Hill, *Westmoreland*	15687
Fort Hunter	17110
Fort Indiantown Gap	17003
Fort Littleton	17223
Fort Loudon	17224
Fortney	17339
Fort Roberston	17047
Fortuna	18915
Fort Washington♦	19034
Forty Fort	18704
Forward, *Allegheny* (Twp)	15063
Forward, *Butler* (Twp)	16033
Forwardstown	15531
Fossilville	15534
Foster, *Luzerne* (Twp)	18224
Foster, *McKean* (Twp)	16701
Foster, *Schuylkill* (Twp)	17901
Foster, *Indiana*	15681
Foster Brook	16701
Fostoria	16686
Foundryville	18603
Fountain	17938
Fountain Dale	17320
Fountain Hill	18015
Fountain House Corners	16433
Fountain Springs	17921
Fountainville	18923
Fourth Avenue (Part of Pittsburgh)‡	15222
Foustown	17404
Foustwell	15935
Fowler Heights	15701
Fowlersville	18603
Fox, *Elk* (Twp)	15846
Fox, *Sullivan* (Twp)	17724
Foxburg, *Clarion*	16036
Foxburg, *Jefferson*	15767
Fox Chapel	15238
Fox Chase, *Lancaster*	17601
Fox Chase (Part of Philadelphia)‡	19111
Fox Chase Manor	19027
Foxcroft, *Delaware*	19008
Foxcroft, *Montgomery*	19046
Fox Hill, *Franklin*	17268
Fox Hill, *Luzerne*	18702
Fox Run	16046
Foxton Lake	18847
Foxtown	15639
Foxtown Hill	18360
Frackville	17931
Frailey (Twp)	17981
Francis Mine	15021
Franconia	18924
Frankford (Part of Philadelphia)‡	19124
Frankfort Springs	15050
Franklin, *Adams* (Twp)	17307
Franklin, *Beaver* (Twp)	16123
Franklin, *Bradford* (Twp)	18848
Franklin, *Butler* (Twp)	16052
Franklin, *Carbon* (Twp)	18235
Franklin, *Chester* (Twp)	19350
Franklin, *Columbia* (Twp)	17820
Franklin, *Erie* (Twp)	16412
Franklin, *Fayette* (Twp)	15486
Franklin, *Greene* (Twp)	15370
Franklin, *Huntingdon* (Twp)	16865
Franklin, *Luzerne* (Twp)	18640
Franklin, *Lycoming* (Twp)	17742
Franklin, *Snyder* (Twp)	17861
Franklin, *Susquehanna* (Twp)	18801
Franklin, *York* (Twp)	17019
Franklin, *Cambria*	15909
Franklin, *Venango*	16323
Franklin Center, *Delaware*	19063
Franklin Center, *Erie*	16412
Franklindale	18832
Franklin Farms	15301
Franklin Forks	18801
Franklin Hill	18822
Franklin Mills (Part of Philadelphia)	19154
Franklin Park	15143
Franklin Pike Corners	16335
Franklintown	17323
Franklinville	16683
Frankstown	16648
Frazer, *Allegheny* (Twp)	15084
Frazer, *Chester*	19355
Frederick	19435
Fredericksburg, *Armstrong*	16041
Fredericksburg, *Blair*	16625
Fredericksburg, *Crawford*	16335
Fredericksburg, *Lebanon*♦	17026
Fredericksville	19539
Fredericktown	15333
Fredericktown Hill	15333
Fredonia	16124
Freeburg	17827
Freedom, *Adams* (Twp)	17307
Freedom, *Blair* (Twp)	16637
Freedom, *Beaver*	15042
Freehold (Twp)	16402
Freeland	18224
Freemansburg	18017
Freemansburg Heights	18020
Freemansville	19607
Freeport, *Greene* (Twp)	15352
Freeport, *Armstrong*	16229
Freeport, *Erie*	16428
Freeport Junction (Part of Freeport)	16229
French Creek, *Mercer* (Twp)	16311
Frenchcreek, *Venango* (Twp)	16323
Frenchs Corners	16210
Frenchtown	16327
Frenchville	16836
Freysville	17356
Fricks	18927
Fricks Lock	19464
Friedens, *Lehigh*	18080
Friedens, *Somerset*♦	15541
Friedensburg	17933
Friedensville	18015
Friendship Heights	15467
Friendship Village	19320
Friendsville	18818
Friesville	16625
Frisbie	17961
Frisco	16117
Fritztown	19608
Frogtown, *Armstrong*	16028
Frogtown, *Clarion*	16224
Frogtown, *Huntingdon*	16877
Frogtown, *York*	17070
Froman	15332
Frostburg	15740
Frugality	16639
Fruitville, *Lancaster*	17601
Fruitville, *Montgomery*	19473
Frutcheys	18301
Fryburg	16326
Frystown	17067
Fuhrmans Mill	17331
Fulmor Heights	19040
Fulton (Twp)	17563
Fulton Run	15701
Furlong	18925
Furnace Hill, *Fayette*	15431
Furnace Hill, *Mercer*	16159
Furnace Run	16201
Furniss	17563
Gabby Heights	15301
Gabelsville	19512
Gahagen	15926
Gaibleton	15747
Gaines	16921
Galeton	16922
Galilee	18415
Gallagher (Twp)	17745
Gallagherville	19335
Gallatin	15063
Gallery at Market East, The (Part of Philadelphia)	19107
Gallitzin	16641
Galloway (Part of Sugarcreek)	16323
Gamble (Twp)	17771
Ganister	16693
Gans	15439
Gap♦	17527
Gapsville	15533
Garards Fort	15334
Gardeau	16720
Garden City (Part of Monroeville)	15146
Garden City, *Delaware*	19013
Gardendale	19061
Garden Hills	17603
Garden View, *Lycoming*♦	17701
Garden View, *Mifflin*	17084
Gardenville	18926
Gardners	17324
Garfield	19506
Gargol	17337
Garland	16416
Garmantown	15714
Garrett	15542
Garrett Hill	19010
Garretts Run	16201
Garrison	15352
Gas Center	15954
Gaskill (Twp)	15767
Gastonville	15336
Gastown	15774
Gatchellville	17352
Gates	15410
Gatesburg	16877
Gateway Center (Part of Pittsburgh)‡	15222
Gateway Shopping Center (Part of Edwardsville)	18704
Gauff Hill	18015
Gayly	15126
Gaysport (Part of Hollidaysburg)	16648
Gay Street (Part of West Chester)	19380
Gearhartville	16866
Geeseytown	16648
Geiger	15501
Geigertown	19523
Geistown	15904
Gelatt	18825
General Warren Village	19355
Genesee	16923
Geneva	16316
Geneva Hill	15010
Georges (Twp)	15401
George School (Part of Newtown)	18940
Georgetown, *Adams*	17340
Georgetown, *Armstrong*	15656
Georgetown, *Beaver*	15043
Georgetown, *Luzerne*	18702
Georgetown, *Northampton*	18064
Georgeville	15759
German (Twp)	15458
German Corners	18053
Germania	16922
Germans	18235
Germansville	18053
Germantown, *Adams*	17340
Germantown, *Franklin*	17222
Germantown, *Pike*	18428
Germantown (Part of Philadelphia)‡	19144
Germany (Twp)	17340
Geryville	18073
Getty Heights	15701
Gettysburg	17325
Ghennes Heights	15063
Ghent	18850
Giant Oaks	15317
Gibbon Glade	15440
Gibbs Hill	16735
Gibraltar	19508
Gibson, *Cameron* (Twp)	15832
Gibson, *Susquehanna* (Twp)	18842
Gibson, *Susquehanna*	18820
Gibson, *Washington*	15314
Gibsonia	15044
Gibsonton	15012
Gifford	16732
Gilbert	18331
Gilberton	17934
Gilbertsville♦	19525
Gilfoyle	16239
Gillespie	15438
Gillett	16925
Gillingham	16836
Gillintown	16874
Gilmore, *Greene* (Twp)	15352
Gilmore, *Fayette*	15478
Gilmore, *McKean*	16727
Gilmore, *Washington*	15057
Gilpin (Twp)	15656
Ginger Hill	15332
Ginter	16651
Ginther	18252
Gipsy	15741
Girard, *Clearfield* (Twp)	16836
Girard, *Erie*	16417
Girard Avenue (Part of Philadelphia)	19122
Girardville	17935
Girty	15686
Gitts Run	17331
Gladden	15057
Gladden Heights	15057
Glade, *Warren* (Twp)	16365
Glade, *Somerset*	15530
Glade (Part of Warren)	16365
Glade City	15552
Glades	17402
Gladhill	17320
Gladstone (Part of Lansdowne)	19050
Gladwyne	19035
Glasgow, *Beaver*	15059
Glasgow, *Cambria*	16644
Glasgow (Part of Pottstown)	19464
Glass City	16866
Glassmere	15030
Glassport	15045
Glassworks	15338
Glatfelter	17360
Gleason	17724
Gleasonton	17760
Glen Acres	19380
Glen Ashton Farms	19020
Glenburn♦	18414
Glen Campbell	15742
Glen Carbon	17901
Glencoe	15538
Glendale, *Allegheny*	15106
Glendale, *Luzerne*	18641
Glendale Gardens (Part of Glenolden)	19036
Glendale Manor	18701
Glendon, *Northampton*	18042
Glendon, *Schuylkill*	17948
Glen Dower	17901
Glen Eden	16033
Glenfield	15143
Glen Forney	17268
Glen Gormely	15071
Glenhall	19380
Glen Hazel	15870
Glen Hope	16645
Glenhurst (Part of Bryn Athyn)	19009
Gleniron	17845
Glenloch	19380
Glen Lyon♦	18617
Glenmar Gardens	16509
Glen Mawr	17737
Glen Mills	19342
Glenmoore, *Chester*	19343
Glen Moore, *Lancaster*	17601
Glenolden	19036
Glen Oley Farms	19606
Glen Richey	16837
Glen Riddle	19037
Glen Riddle-Lima	19037
Glen Rock	17327
Glen Rose	19320
Glen Roy	19362
Glenruadh	16505
Glen Savage	15538
Glenshaw	15116
Glenside♦	19038
Glenside Gardens	19038
Glenside Heights	19038
Glen Summit	18707
Glenville	17329
Glenwillard	15046
Glenwood (Part of Erie)	16509
Glenwood (Part of Pittsburgh)	15207
Glenwood, *Dauphin*	17109
Glenwood, *Mifflin*	17044
Glenwood, *Susquehanna*	18446
Glenworth	17901
Glosser View	17701
Glyde	15301
Glyndon	16434
Gnatstown	17331
Goat Hill	15301
Godfrey	15656
Goheenville	16259
Gold	16923
Golden Hill	18623
Golden Key Lake	18337
Goldenridge	19057
Golden Rod Farms	16830
Golden Triangle (Part of Pittsburgh)	15222
Goodhope	17055
Good Hope Farms	17055
Good Intent	15323
Goodmans Corners	16364
Goods Corner	15901
Good Spring	17981
Goodtown	15530
Goodville, *Juniata*	17094
Goodville, *Lancaster*	17528
Goodyear	17324
Goosetown	19320
Gordon	17936
Gordonville	17529
Goshen, *Clearfield*	16830
Goshen, *Lancaster*	17563
Goshenville	19380
Gosser Hill	15656
Gottshalls	17872
Gouglersville	19608
Gouldsboro	18424
Gourley	15061
Gowen	18241
Gowen City	17828
Gracedale	18707
Graceton	15748
Graceville	15537
Gracey	17228
Gradwohl Terrace	18020
Gradyville	19039
Grafton	15717
Graham (Twp)	16858
Graham	16866
Grampian	16838
Grampian Hills (Part of Williamsport)	17701
Grand Valley	16420
Grandview (Part of St. Marys)	15857
Grandview, *Armstrong*	16201
Grandview, *Indiana*	15701
Grandview, *Washington*	15063
Grandview Heights	17601
Grandview Park (Part of St. Marys)	15857

Place	ZIP
Grand View Park, *Montgomery*	19426
Grange	15767
Grange Center	16433
Grangeville	17331
Granite	17325
Grant, *Indiana* (Twp)	15759
Grant, *Elk*	15821
Grant City	16051
Grantham	17027
Grantley♦	17403
Grant Street (Part of Pittsburgh)‡	15219
Grantville	17028
Granville, *Bradford* (Twp)	16926
Granville, *Mifflin* (Twp)	17044
Granville, *Mifflin*	17029
Granville Center	16926
Granville Summit	16926
Grapeville	15634
Grassflat	16839
Grassmere Park	17814
Grassy (Part of Olyphant)	18447
Graterford	19426
Gratz	17030
Gratztown	15089
Gravity	18436
Gray, *Greene* (Twp)	15337
Gray, *Clearfield*	16881
Gray, *Somerset*	15544
Graydon	17322
Grays	15717
Grays Landing	15461
Graysville, *Greene*	15337
Graysville, *Huntingdon*	16865
Grazier	15935
Grazierville	16686
Greason	17013
Great Belt	16001
Great Bend (Twp)	18822
Great Bend	18821
Greater Point Marion	15474
Great Southern Shopping Center (Part of Bridgeville)	15017
Greble	17067
Greece City	16025
Greeley	18425
Green, *Forest* (Twp)	16353
Green, *Indiana* (Twp)	15724
Greenawalds	18104
Greenbrae	16201
Green Briar	15825
Greenbrier, *Centre*	16875
Greenbrier, *Dauphin*	17036
Greenbrier, *Northumberland*	17867
Greenbrook	19007
Greenburr	17747
Greencastle	17225
Green Circle	18451
Greencrest Park	16125
Greendale	16735
Greendown Acres	16635
Greene, *Beaver* (Twp)	15050
Greene, *Clinton* (Twp)	17747
Greene, *Erie* (Twp)	16509
Greene, *Franklin* (Twp)	17254
Greene, *Greene* (Twp)	15320
Greene, *Mercer* (Twp)	16134
Greene, *Pike* (Twp)	18426
Greene, *Lancaster*	17518
Greenfield, *Blair* (Twp)	16625
Greenfield, *Erie* (Twp)	16428
Greenfield, *Lackawanna* (Twp)	18407
Greenfield (Part of Pittsburgh)	15207
Greenfield, *Cambria*	16613
Greenfield, *Mercer*	16137
Greenfields, *Berks*	19605
Green Fields, *Dauphin*	17098
Green Garden	15001
Green Grove, *Centre*	16875
Green Grove, *Lackawanna*	18447
Green Hill	19380
Green Hills, *Berks*	19607
Green Hills, *Delaware*	19079
Green Hills, *Washington*	15301
Green Lane	18054
Green Lane Farms	17011
Greenlawn Park	19007
Greenmount	17325
Greenock	15047
Green Park	17031
Green Point	17038
Green Ridge (Part of Scranton)	18509
Green Ridge, *Delaware*	19014
Green Ridge, *Luzerne*	18201
Greenridge, *Westmoreland*	15642
Greensboro	15338
Greensburg	15601
Greens Landing	18810
Greenspring	17241
Green Springs	17331
Greentown	18426
Green Tree, *Allegheny*	15242
Green Tree, *Chester*	19355
Green Valley	15825
Green Village	17201
Greenville, *Somerset* (Twp)	15552
Greenville, *Clearfield*	16838
Greenville, *Mercer*	16125
Greenwald	15670
Greenwich, *Berks* (Twp)	19530
Greenwich, *Cambria*	15714
Greenwood, *Clearfield* (Twp)	15757
Greenwood, *Columbia* (Twp)	17859
Greenwood, *Crawford* (Twp)	16316
Greenwood, *Juniata* (Twp)	17094
Greenwood, *Perry* (Twp)	17062
Greenwood, *Blair*	16602
Greenwood, *Columbia*	17846
Greenwood, *Franklin*	17222
Greenwood Hills	17057
Greenwood Village	16001
Gregg, *Centre* (Twp)	16875
Gregg, *Union* (Twp)	17810
Gregg, *Allegheny*	15071
Gregory (Part of Larksville)	18704
Grenoble	18974
Gresham	16354
Greshville	19512
Gretna	15301
Grey Nuns	19067
Grier City	18214
Griesemersville	19512
Griffiths	16735
Grill	19607
Grimesville	17701
Grimms Crossroads	17356
Grimville	19530
Grindstone	15442
Gringo	15001
Grisemore	15728
Groffdale	17557
Grovania	17821
Grove, *Cameron* (Twp)	15861
Grove, *Chester*	19380
Grove Chapel	15701
Grove City	16127
Grover	17735
Groveton	15108
Grugan (Twp)	17745
Gruversville	18036
Gruvertown	18013
Guenot Settlement	16836
Guernsey	17307
Guffey, *McKean*	16740
Guffey, *Westmoreland*	15642
Guilford (Twp)	17201
Guilford Hills	17201
Guilford Springs	17201
Guitonville	16239
Guldens	17325
Gulich (Twp)	16680
Gulph	19406
Gulph Mills	19428
Gump	15362
Gum Tree	19320
Guth	18104
Guthriesville	19335
Guthsville	18069
Guys Mills	16327
Gwynedd	19436
Gwynedd Square	19446
Gwynedd Valley	19437
Haafsville	18031
Habrenfield Hills	18612
Hackelbernie (Part of Jim Thorpe)	18229
Hackett	15367
Haddenville	15401
Haddock	18201
Hadley	16130
Hagersville	18944
Hahnstown	17522
Hahntown	15642
Haines (Twp)	16882
Haines Acres	17402
Haleeka	17728
Halfmoon (Twp)	16877
Halford Hills	19401
Halfville	17543
Halfway	17042
Halfway House♦	19464
Halifax	17032
Hallam	17406
Hallowell	19044
Halls	17756
Hallstead	18822
Hallston	16057
Hallton	15860
Hallwood	18621
Halsey	16735
Hamburg	19526
Hametown	17327
Hamilton, *Adams* (Twp)	17316
Hamilton, *Franklin* (Twp)	17201
Hamilton, *McKean* (Twp)	16735
Hamilton, *Monroe* (Twp)	18354
Hamilton, *Tioga* (Twp)	16912
Hamilton, *Jefferson*	15744
Hamilton, *Northumberland*	17801
Hamiltonban (Twp)	17325
Hamilton Heights	17201
Hamilton Mall (Part of Allentown)	18101
Hamilton Park	17603
Hamlin, *McKean* (Twp)	16733
Hamlin, *Lebanon*	17026
Hamlin, *Wayne*	18427
Hammersley Fork	17764
Hammett	16510
Hammond	16946
Hammondville	15666
Hamorton	19348
Hampden, *Cumberland* (Twp)	17055
Hampden (Part of Reading)	19604
Hampden Heights (Part of Reading)	19604
Hampshire Heights	15601
Hampton, *Allegheny* (Twp)	15101
Hampton, *Adams*	17350
Hampton Station	16301
Hancock	19539
Haneyville	17745
Hankey Farms	15071
Hanlin	15021
Hannah	16870
Hannahstown	16023
Hannastown	15635
Hannaville	16314
Hann Hill (Part of Hermitage)	16159
Hanover, *Beaver* (Twp)	15050
Hanover, *Lehigh* (Twp)	18103
Hanover, *Luzerne* (Twp)	18702
Hanover, *Washington* (Twp)	15021
Hanover (Part of Nanticoke)	18634
Hanover, *Northampton*	18017
Hanover, *York*	17331
Hanoverdale	17036
Hanover Green	18702
Hanover Heights	19464
Hanover Hills	17036
Hanover Junction	17360
Happy Valley (Part of Exeter)	18643
Harbor	16101
Harborcreek	16421
Harding	18643
Hardy Hill	15431
Harford	18823
Harford Heights	15642
Harkness	16914
Harlan	15829
Harlansburg	16101
Harleigh	18225
Harlem	18062
Harleysville♦	19438
Harmar (Twp)	15024
Harmar Heights	15024
Harmarville	15238
Harmonsburg	16422
Harmonville	19428
Harmony, *Beaver* (Twp)	15003
Harmony, *Forest* (Twp)	16370
Harmony, *Susquehanna* (Twp)	18847
Harmony, *Butler*	16037
Harmony, *Clearfield*	16692
Harmony, *Jefferson*	15767
Harmony Grove	17315
Harmony Hill	19335
Harmony Junction	16037
Harmony Township♦	15003
Harmonyville	19464
Harnedsville	15424
Harpers	18088
Harper Tavern	17003
Harper Village	15001
Harris (Twp)	16827
Harris Acres	16801
Harrisburg	17101-30
For specific ZIP Codes call (888) 275-8777, or your local postmaster.	
Harrison, *Allegheny* (Twp)	15065
Harrison, *Bedford* (Twp)	15534
Harrison, *Potter* (Twp)	16927
Harrison City	15636
Harrison Valley	16927
Harrisonville	17228
Harristown	17562
Harrisville	16038
Harrity	18235
Harrow	18942
Harshaville	15026
Hartfield	16930
Hartleton	17829
Hartley (Twp)	17835
Hartranft	19401
Hartstown	16131
Hartsville	18974
Harveys Lake	18618
Harveyville	18655
Harwick	15049
Harwood	18201
Hasentab's	16635
Hasson Heights	16301
Hastings	16646
Hatboro	19040
Hatfield, *Fayette*	15401
Hatfield, *Montgomery*	19440
Hauto (Part of Nesquehoning)	18240
Haverford, *Delaware* (Twp)	19083
Haverford, *Montgomery*	19041
Havertown	19083
Hawkeye	15683
Hawk Run	16840
Hawksville	17566
Hawley	18428
Hawleywood	18428
Hawstone	17044
Hawthorn	16230
Haycock (Twp)	18951
Haydentown	15478
Hayesville	19363
Hayfield (Twp)	16433
Haymaker	16731
Hays (Part of Pittsburgh)	15230
Hays, *Fayette*	15401
Hays Grove	17241
Hays Mill	15552
Haysville, *Allegheny*	15143
Haysville, *Butler*	16041
Hayti	19320
Hazel Hurst	16733
Hazel Kirk	15063
Hazelwood (Part of Pittsburgh)‡	15207
Hazen, *Beaver*	16123
Hazen, *Jefferson*	15825
Hazle (Twp)	18201
Hazlebrook	18201
Hazleton	18201
Hazle Village (Part of Hazleton)	18201
Hazzard (Part of Monongahela)	15063
Heacock Meadows	19067
Headlee Heights	15334
Heart Lake	18801
Heath (Twp)	15860
Heathville	15864
Hebe	17830
Heberlig	17241
Hebron, *Potter* (Twp)	16915
Hebron, *Lebanon*	17042
Hebron Center	16915
Heckscherville	17901
Hecktown	18020
Hecla	17960
Hector (Twp)	16948
Hegarty Crossroads	16627
Hegins	17938
Heidelberg, *Berks* (Twp)	19567
Heidelberg, *Lebanon* (Twp)	17088
Heidelberg, *Lehigh* (Twp)	18053
Heidelberg, *York* (Twp)	17362
Heidelberg, *Allegheny*	15106
Heidlersburg	17372
Heilmandale	17046
Heilwood	15745
Heise Run	16901
Heistersburg	15433
Helen Furnace	16214
Helen Mills	15823
Helfenstein	17921
Helixville	15559
Hellam (Twp)	17368
Hellertown	18055
Helvetia	15848
Hemlock, *Columbia* (Twp)	17815
Hemlock, *Warren*	16365
Hemlock Grove, *Pike*	18426
Hemlock Grove, *Sullivan*	17758
Hempfield, *Mercer* (Twp)	16125
Hempfield, *Westmoreland* (Twp)	15601
Hempfield Manor	15601
Henderson, *Huntingdon* (Twp)	16652
Henderson, *Jefferson* (Twp)	15767
Henderson, *Clearfield*	16651
Henderson, *Mercer*	16153
Henderson Park	19406
Hendersonville, *Butler*	16046
Hendersonville, *Washington*	15339
Hendricks	18979
Henningsville	18011
Henrietta	16662
Henry Clay (Twp)	15459
Henrys Bend	16301
Henrys Mill	16347
Henryville	18332
Hensel	17566
Hensingerville	18011
Hepburn (Twp)	17728
Hepburn Heights	17728
Hepburnia	16838
Hepburnville	17728
Hephzibah	19320
Hepler	17941
Herbert	15435
Hercules (Part of Stockertown)	18083
Hereford	18056
Heritage Hills	16117
Herman	16039
Herminie	15637
Hermitage	16148
Hermitage Towne Plaza (Part of Hermitage)	16146
Herndon	17830
Hero	15341
Herrick, *Bradford* (Twp)	18853
Herrick, *Susquehanna* (Twp)	18430
Herrick Center	18430
Herrick Corner	18430
Herrickville	18853
Hershey♦	17033
Hershey Heights	17331
Heshbon	15717
Heshbon Park	17701
Hessdale	17560
Hesston	16647
Hetlerville	18635
Hettesheimer Corners	18636
Hiawatha	18462
Hibbs	15443
Hickernell	16435
Hickman	15071
Hickory, *Forest* (Twp)	16322
Hickory, *Lawrence* (Twp)	16105
Hickory, *Washington*	15340
Hickory Corners (Part of Hermitage)	16146
Hickory Corners, *Northumberland*	17017
Hickory Grove	18847
Hickory Heights	16101
Hickoryhill	19363
Hickory Hills	19067
Hickory Run Forest	18229
Hickorytown, *Cumberland*	17013
Hickorytown, *Montgomery*	19401
Hickox	16923
Hicksville	15618

* **Area Zip Code** † **Post Office Boxes** ‡ **Postal Station** ♦ **Census Designated Place** *Italic Type* **County**

Place	ZIP
Hidden Valley, *Montgomery*	19406
Hidden Valley, *Somerset*	15502
Hidden Valley Estates	18062
Higgins Corner	16040
Highcliff	15229
Highfield	16001
High House	15478
Highland, *Adams* (Twp)	17325
Highland, *Chester* (Twp)	19320
Highland, *Clarion* (Twp)	16214
Highland, *Elk* (Twp)	16735
Highland (Part of Big Beaver)	15010
Highland (Part of Pittsburgh)	15206
Highland, *Allegheny*	15237
Highland, *Luzerne*	18224
Highland, *Westmoreland*	15633
Highland Acres	17602
Highland Corners	16735
Highland Meadows	15037
Highland Park, *Bucks*	18960
Highland Park, *Cumberland*	17011
Highland Park, *Delaware*	19082
Highland Park, *Erie*	16506
Highland Park, *Mifflin*	17044
Highland Park, *Northampton*	18042
Highland Woods	18701
High Meadows	19063
Highmount	17406
High Park	19040
High Rock	17302
Highspire	17034
Highville	17516
Hileman Heights (Part of Altoona)	16602
Hillchurch, *Berks*	19512
Hill Church, *Washington*	15317
Hill City	16319
Hillcrest (Part of Bethel Park)	15102
Hillcrest, *Beaver*	15001
Hill Crest, *Fayette*	15425
Hill Crest, *Montgomery*	19126
Hillcrest, *York*	17403
Hillcroft	17403
Hilldale	18702
Hiller♦	15444
Hilliards	16040
Hillman	15767
Hillsboro	15963
Hills Creek Lake	16901
Hillsdale	15746
Hillsgrove	18619
Hillside, *Lehigh*	18069
Hillside, *Luzerne*	18708
Hillside, *Schuylkill*	17901
Hillside, *Westmoreland*	15627
Hillside Junction (Part of Moosic)	18507
Hills Terrace	17948
Hillsview	15658
Hillsville	16132
Hilltop	18951
Hill Top Acres, *Armstrong*	16226
Hilltop Acres (Part of Lancaster)	17603
Hilltown, *Bucks* (Twp)	18911
Hilltown, *Adams*	17307
Hilltown, *Bucks*	18927
Hillville	16041
Hilton	17315
Hines Corners	18449
Hinkle	18947
Hinkletown	17522
Hinkson Corner	19086
Hiyasota	15935
Hoadleys	18431
Hoban Heights	18657
Hobart	17331
Hobble	18660
Hoblitzell	15545
Hockersville	17241
Hoernerstown	17036
Hoffer	17864
Hoffmansville	19435
Hogestown	17055
Hog Island	19029
Hoguetown	16630
Hokendauqua♦	18052
Hokes	17327
Holbrook	15341
Holicong	18928
Holiday Hills	18106
Holiday Park (Part of Plum)	15239
Holiday Pocono	18210
Holland	18966
Hollenback (Twp)	18660
Hollentown	16639
Hollers Hill	18201
Holley Heights	17404
Holliday	16935
Hollidaysburg	16648
Hollinger	17603
Hollisterville	18444
Hollsopple	15935
Hollywood, *Clearfield*	15849
Hollywood, *Luzerne*	18201
Hollywood, *Montgomery*	19027
Hollywood Heights	17403
Holmes	19043
Holmesburg (Part of Philadelphia)‡	19136
Holt	15001
Holtwood	17532
Homans Corner	16678
Home	15747
Homeacre	16001
Home Camp	15856
Homeland	17601
Home Park	18052
Homer (Twp)	16915
Homer City	15748
Homer Gap	16601
Homestead	15120
Homesville	17921
Hometown♦	18252
Homets Ferry	18853
Homeville	19330
Homewood (Part of Pittsburgh)‡	15208
Homewood, *Beaver*	15010
Homewood, *York*	17019
Honeoye	16748
Honesdale	18431
Honey Brook	19344
Honey Creek	17084
Honey Grove	17035
Honey Pot (Part of Nanticoke)	18634
Hooker	16041
Hookstown	15050
Hoover	15458
Hooverhurst	15742
Hooversville	15936
Hop Bottom	18824
Hopeland	17533
Hope Mills	16137
Hopewell, *Beaver* (Twp)	15001
Hopewell, *Cumberland* (Twp)	17240
Hopewell, *Huntingdon* (Twp)	16657
Hopewell, *Washington* (Twp)	15301
Hopewell, *York* (Twp)	17363
Hopewell, *Bedford*	16650
Hopewell, *Chester*	19363
Hoppenville	18073
Hopwood♦	15445
Horatio	15767
Hormtown	15851
Horn Brook	18848
Hornby	16428
Hornerstown (Part of Johnstown)	15902
Horning (Part of Baldwin)	15236
Horseshoe Heights	17602
Horsham♦	19044
Horton (Twp)	15823
Hosensack	18092
Hosensock	18214
Hospital (Part of Norristown)‡	19401
Host	19567
Hostetter	15638
Hottelville	16239
Houserville	16801
Houston	15342
Houston City	18641
Houtzdale	16651
Hovey (Twp)	16049
Howard	16841
Howard Siding	15834
Howe, *Forest* (Twp)	16239
Howe, *Perry* (Twp)	17074
Howe, *Jefferson*	15825
Howellville	19312
Howersville	18088
Howertown	18067
Hoytdale (Part of Big Beaver)	16157
Hoytville	16938
Hublersburg	16823
Hubley (Twp)	17968
Huckenberry	16849
Hudson, *Clearfield*	16866
Hudson, *Luzerne*	18702
Hudsondale	18255
Huefner	16235
Huey	16248
Huffs Church	18011
Hughes Park	19406
Hughestown	18640
Hughesville	17737
Hughs	18621
Hulltown	15428
Hulmeville	19047
Humboldt	18201
Hummelstown	17036
Hummels Wharf♦	17831
Humphreys	15601
Humphreyville	19320
Hungerford (Part of Shrewsbury)	17361
Hungry Hollow	15656
Hunker	15639
Hunlock (Twp)	18621
Hunlock Creek	18621
Hunlock Gardens	18621
Hunter	17872
Hunter Hill	19462
Hunters Run	17324
Hunterstown	17325
Huntersville	17756
Huntingdon	16652
Huntingdon Furnace	16686
Huntingdon Heights	15642
Huntingdon Manor	17540
Huntingdon Valley	19006
Hunting Park (Part of Philadelphia)‡	19140
Huntington, *Adams* (Twp)	17372
Huntington, *Luzerne* (Twp)	18655
Huntington Mills	18622
Huntley	15832
Huntsdale	17013
Huntsville	18612
Husband	15501
Huston, *Blair* (Twp)	16693
Huston, *Centre* (Twp)	16844
Huston, *Clearfield* (Twp)	15849
Huston Run	15332
Hustontown	17229
Hutchins	16740
Hutchinson, *Fayette*	15401
Hutchinson, *Westmoreland*	15640
Hyde♦	16843
Hyde Park (Part of Scranton)	18504
Hyde Park, *Berks*	19605
Hyde Park, *Westmoreland*	15641
Hydetown	16328
Hyde Villa	19605
Hyndman	15545
Hynemansville	18066
Hyner	17738
Icedale	19344
Ickesburg	17037
Idaho	15774
Idamar	15734
Idaville	17337
Idetown (Part of Harveys Lake)	18612
Idlewood (Part of Crafton)	15205
Imler	16655
Imlertown	15522
Immaculata	19345
Imperial	15126
Independence, *Beaver*	15001
Independence, *Snyder*	17864
Independence, *Washington*	15312
Indiana, *Allegheny* (Twp)	15051
Indiana, *Indiana*	15701
Indian Creek, *Bucks*	19057
Indian Creek, *Cumberland*	17055
Indian Crossing	16731
Indian Head, *Erie*	16441
Indian Head, *Fayette*	15446
Indian Hills	16201
Indian King	19380
Indian Lake, *Luzerne*	18661
Indian Lake, *Somerset*	15926
Indianland	18088
Indian Mountain Lake	18210
Indianola	15051
Indian Orchard	18431
Indian Springs Estates	15701
Industry, *Allegheny*	15018
Industry, *Beaver*	15052
Inez	16915
Ingleby	16882
Inglenook	17032
Inglesmith	17211
Ingomar	15237
Ingram	15205
Inkerman	18640
Intercourse	17534
Iola	17846
Iona	17042
Irishtown, *Adams*	17350
Irishtown, *Clearfield*	16838
Irishtown, *McKean*	16738
Irishtown, *Mercer*	16137
Iron Bridge	15666
Iron Springs	17320
Ironton	18037
Ironville, *Blair*	16686
Ironville, *Lancaster*	17512
Irvine	16329
Irving	17963
Irvona	16656
Irwin, *Venango* (Twp)	16038
Irwin, *Westmoreland*	15642
Isabella	15447
Iselin	15681
Iselin Heights	15801
Island Lake	18462
Island Park	17801
Ithan	19085
Iva	17562
Ivarea	16410
Ivyland	18974
Ivy Mills (Part of Chester Heights)	19342
Ivy Ridge (Part of Philadelphia)	19101
Ivywood, *Butler*	16056
Ivywood, *Pike*	18451
Jacks Creek	17044
Jacks Mountain	17320
Jackson, *Butler* (Twp)	16063
Jackson, *Cambria* (Twp)	15909
Jackson, *Columbia* (Twp)	17814
Jackson, *Dauphin* (Twp)	17032
Jackson, *Greene* (Twp)	15341
Jackson, *Huntingdon* (Twp)	16669
Jackson, *Lebanon* (Twp)	17042
Jackson, *Luzerne* (Twp)	18708
Jackson, *Lycoming* (Twp)	17765
Jackson, *Mercer* (Twp)	16133
Jackson, *Monroe* (Twp)	18352
Jackson, *Northumberland* (Twp)	17830
Jackson, *Perry* (Twp)	17006
Jackson, *Snyder* (Twp)	17889
Jackson, *Tioga* (Twp)	16936
Jackson, *Venango* (Twp)	16317
Jackson, *York* (Twp)	17362
Jackson, *Susquehanna*	18825
Jackson Center	16133
Jackson Corner	16652
Jackson Crossing	16365
Jackson Knolls Gardens	16101
Jackson Summit	16936
Jackson Valley	18830
Jacksonville, *Centre*	16841
Jacksonville, *Lehigh*	18066
Jacksonville, *Northampton*	18014
Jacksonwald	19606
Jacksville	16057
Jacktown	15642
Jacktown Acres	15642
Jacobs Creek	15448
Jacobs Mills	17331
Jacobus	17407
Jalappa	19526
James City	16734
James Creek	16657
Jamestown, *Cambria*	15946
Jamestown, *Carbon*	18235
Jamestown, *Mercer*	16134
Jamesville	18014
Jamison, *Bucks*	18929
Jamison, *Fayette*	15401
Jamison, *Forest*	16370
Jamison City	17814
Japan	18224
Jarrettown	19025
Jay (Twp)	15868
Jeanesville	18201
Jeannette	15644
Jeddo	18224
Jednota	17057
Jefferis Crossing	15401
Jefferson, *Berks* (Twp)	19506
Jefferson, *Butler* (Twp)	16056
Jefferson, *Dauphin* (Twp)	17032
Jefferson, *Fayette* (Twp)	15442
Jefferson, *Lackawanna* (Twp)	18436
Jefferson, *Mercer* (Twp)	16148
Jefferson, *Somerset* (Twp)	15501
Jefferson, *Washington* (Twp)	15021
Jefferson, *Allegheny*	15025
Jefferson, *Greene*	15344
Jefferson, *Schuylkill*	17922
Jefferson	15312
Jefferson Center	16056
Jeffersonville	19403
Jenkins (Twp)	18640
Jenkins Corner	17563
Jenkintown	19046
Jenkintown Manor	19027
Jenks (Twp)	16239
Jenner (Twp)	15546
Jenners	15546
Jenners Crossroads	15531
Jennerstown	15547
Jennersville	19390
Jenningsville	18629
Jericho	15861
Jericho Mills	17059
Jermyn	18433
Jerome♦	15937
Jersey Mills	17739
Jersey Shore	17740
Jerseytown	17815
Jerusalem Corners	16341
Jessup, *Susquehanna* (Twp)	18801
Jessup, *Lackawanna*	18434
Jim Thorpe	18229
Jimtown	15501
Joanna	19543
Joanna Heights	19543
Jobs Corners	16936
Joffre	15053
Johnsonburg, *Elk*	15845
Johnsonburg, *Indiana*	15772
Johnsons Corner	19317
Johnstown, *Cambria*	15901-15
For specific ZIP Codes call (888) 275-8777, or your local postmaster.	
Johnstown, *Union*	17844
Johnsville	18974
John Wanamaker (Part of Philadelphia)	19107
Jo Jo	16735
Joliett	17981
Joller	16674
Jollytown	15352
Jonas	18058
Jonathan Point	18210
Jones (Twp)	15870
Jones Mills	15646
Jones Terrace	18042
Jonestown, *Columbia*	17859
Jonestown, *Lebanon*	17038
Jonestown, *Schuylkill*	17901
Jonestown, *Washington*	15022
Jordan, *Clearfield* (Twp)	16656
Jordan, *Lycoming* (Twp)	17774
Jordan, *Northumberland* (Twp)	17830
Jordan, *Lehigh*	18053
Jordan Valley	18053
Josephine	15750
Joyce	16101
Jugtown, *Bucks*	18972
Jugtown, *Franklin*	17268
Julian	16844
Jumonville	15445
Juneau	15751
Junedale	18230
June Meadows	19006
Junewood	19055
Juniata, *Bedford* (Twp)	15550

Juniata, *Blair* (Twp) 16635
Juniata, *Huntingdon* (Twp) 16652
Juniata, *Perry* (Twp) 17074
Juniata (Part of Altoona)‡ 16601
Juniata, *Fayette* 15431
Juniata Gap 16601
Juniata Terrace 17044
Just A Farm 19006
Justus 18411
Kaiserville 18630
Kammerer 15330
Kane 16735
Kanesholm 16735
Kaneville 16301
Kantner 15548
Kantz 17870
Kaolin 19374
Kapp Heights 17857
Karns City 16041
Karthaus 16845
Kaseville 17821
Kasiesville 17236
Kaska 17959
Kasson 16749
Kauffman 17201
Kaybrook Manor 18101
Kaylor 16025
Kaywood 16827
Kearney 16679
Kearsarge 16509
Keating, *McKean* (Twp) 16749
Keating, *Potter* (Twp) 16720
Keating, *Clinton* 17778
Keating Summit 16720
Kecksburg 15666
Kedron Park 19070
Keelersburg 18657
Keelersville 18944
Keeneyville 16935
Keepville 16401
Keewaydin 16836
Keffer 17981
Keifertown 15683
Keisters 16057
Keisterville 15449
Kelayres 18231
Kellersburg 16259
Kellers Church 18944
Kellersville 18360
Kellettville 16353
Kelly, *Union* (Twp) 17837
Kelly, *Armstrong* 16226
Kelly Crossroads 17837
Kelly Point 17837
Kellytown, *Clearfield* 16863
Kellytown, *Tioga* 16933
Kelton 19346
Kemblesville 19347
Kempton 19529
Kendall, *Beaver* 15043
Kendall, *York* 17356
Kendrick 16651
Kenhorst 19607
Kenilworth♦ 19464
Kenmar 17701
Kenmawr 15136
Kennard 16125
Kennedy, *Allegheny* (Twp) 15136
Kennedy, *Tioga* 16901
Kennedy Mill 16051
Kennedy's Corner 15001
Kennells Mills 15545
Kennerdell 16374
Kennett (Twp) 19348
Kennett Square 19348
Kenny Row 15468
Kensington (Part of Philadelphia)‡ 19125
Kensington Heights 17201
Kent 15752
Kenwick Village 17601
Kenwood, *Bucks* 19007
Kenwood, *Indiana* 15728
Kepner 17960
Kepple Hill 15690
Kepples Corner 16025
Kernsville 18069
Kernville (Part of Johnstown) 15901
Kerr 16830
Kerrmoor 16833
Kerrs Corners 16127
Kerrsville 17013
Kerrtown 16335
Kersey 15846
Kesslerville 18064
Keys 17322
Keyser Valley (Part of Scranton) 18504

Keystone (Part of Harrisburg)‡ 17105
Keystone, *Luzerne* 18702
Keystone, *Somerset* 15552
Keystone, *Westmoreland* 15637
Khedive 15320
Kidder (Twp) 18624
Kilbuck, *Allegheny* (Twp) 15143
Kilbuck (Part of Pittsburgh) 15233
Kilgore 16153
Killam Park 18451
Killinger 17061
Kimberton 19442
Kimbles 18428
Kimmel, *Bedford* (Twp) 16655
Kimmel, *Somerset* 15557
Kimmelton 15563
Kim Plan 15642
Kinderhook 17512
Kindts Corner 19555
King 16655
King of Prussia♦ 19406
King of Prussia Plaza 19406
Kingsdale 17340
Kingsessing (Part of Philadelphia)‡ 19143
Kingsley, *Forest* (Twp) 16353
Kingsley, *Susquehanna* 18826
Kings Manor 19406
Kingston, *Luzerne* (Twp) 18708
Kingston, *Luzerne* 18704
Kingston, *Westmoreland* 15650
Kingston-Forty Fort (Part of Kingston) 18704
Kingsville 15864
Kingswood Park 19007
Kingview 15683
Kingwood 15551
Kinlock (Part of Lower Burrell) 15068
Kinney 16923
Kinport 15724
Kintersburg 15728
Kintigh Plan 15601
Kintnersville 18930
Kinzers 17535
Kipps Run 17821
Kirby 15370
Kirbyville 19522
Kirks Bridge 19362
Kirks Mills 19362
Kirkwood 17536
Kirwan Heights 15017
Kiser Corners 16353
Kishacoquillas 17004
Kiskimere 15690
Kiskiminetas (Twp) 15613
Kissel Hill 17543
Kissimmee 17842
Kissingers Mill 16248
Kistler, *Mifflin* 17066
Kistler, *Perry* 17047
Kitches Corners 16125
Kittanning (Twp) 16226
Kittanning 16201
Kittanning (Part of Applewold) 16201
Kittanning Heights 16201
Kladder Station 16648
Klahr 16625
Klecknersville 18014
Kleinfeltersville 17039
Kline (Twp) 18237
Klines Corner 19539
Klines Grove 17801
Klinesville, *Berks* 19534
Klinesville, *Lancaster* 17512
Kline Village (Part of Harrisburg)‡ 17104
Klingerstown 17941
Klondike 16738
Klondyke 17044
Knapp 16901
Knauers 19540
Knauertown 19464
Kneedler 19446
Knepper 17268
Knightsville 17052
Knobsville 17233
Knobville 17063
Knoebel's Grove 17824
Knousetown 17062
Knowltonwood 19065
Knox, *Clarion* (Twp) 16235
Knox, *Clearfield* (Twp) 16863
Knox, *Jefferson* (Twp) 15825
Knox, *Beaver* 16117

Knox, *Clarion* 16232
Knox Dale 15847
Knoxlyn 17325
Knox Run 16858
Knoxville (Part of Pittsburgh) 15210
Knoxville, *Fayette* 15417
Knoxville, *Tioga* 16928
Koonsville 18655
Koppel 16136
Korn Krest 18702
Kossuth 16331
Kralltown 17316
Kratzerville 17870
Krayn 15963
Kreamer 17833
Kregar 15622
Kreidersville 18067
Kremis 16125
Kresgeville 18333
Kreutz Creek 17406
Kricktown 19608
Krings 15904
Krocksville 18104
Krumsville 19534
Kuhn 15501
Kuhnsville 18103
Kuhntown 15341
Kulp 17820
Kulpmont 17834
Kulps Corner 18944
Kulpsville♦ 19443
Kulptown 19518
Kunkle 18612
Kunkletown 18058
Kushequa 16735
Kutztown, *Berks* 19530
Kutztown, *Lebanon* 17067
Kylers Corners 15846
Kylertown 16847
Kyleville 17302
La Anna 18326
La Belle 15450
Laboratory 15301
Labott 17364
Lacey Park 18974
Laceyville 18623
Lack (Twp) 17021
Lackawannock (Twp) 16137
Lackawaxen (Twp) 18425
Lackawaxen 18435
Lacock 15301
Laddsburg 18833
Lafayette 16738
Lafayette College (Part of Easton)‡ 18042
Lafayette Hill 19444
Lafayetteville 16664
Laflin 18705
La Gonda 15301
Lahaska 18931
Lairds Crossing 16262
Lairdsville 17742
La Jose 15753
Lake, *Luzerne* (Twp) 18621
Lake, *Mercer* (Twp) 16153
Lake, *Wayne* (Twp) 18436
Lake Ariel 18436
Lake Carey 18657
Lake City 16423
Lake Como 18437
Lake Donegal 15610
Lake Harmony 18624
Lake Heritage 17325
Lake Idlewild 18470
Lakeland 18436
Lake Lynn 15451
Lake Meade 17316
Lake Monroe 18335
Lakemont 16602
Lake Naomi 18350
Lake Pleasant 16438
Lake Quinn 18472
Lake Sheridan 18446
Lakeside, *Bucks* 19053
Lakeside, *Susquehanna* 18834
Lake Stonycreek 15541
Laketon Heights 15235
Lakeview 18847
Lakeview Heights 17111
Lakeville 18438
Lake Waynewood 18436
Lake Wesauking 18848
Lake Winola 18625
Lakewood, *Erie* 16505
Lakewood, *Wayne* 18439
Lakewood Park 16101
Lake Wynonah♦ 17972
Lamar (Twp) 17751
Lamar 16848
Lamartine 16375
Lamberton 15458
Lambertsville 15563

Lambs Creek 16933
Lamonaville 16239
Lamont 16735
Lamonts Corners (Part of Hermitage) 16150
La Mott 19012
Lampeter 17537
Lanark 18034
Lancaster, *Butler* (Twp) 16037
Lancaster, *Lancaster* (Twp) 17603
Lancaster, *Lancaster* 17601-08
For specific ZIP Codes call (888) 275-8777, or your local postmaster.
Lancaster Avenue (Part of Philadelphia) 19104
Lancaster Junction 17545
Landenberg 19350
Lander 16345
Landingville 17942
Landisburg 17040
Landis Farms 17601
Landis Store 19512
Landis Valley 17604
Landisville 17538
Landreth Manor 19007
Landstreet 15935
Lanesboro 18827
Lanes Mills 15824
Laneville (Part of Freeport) 16229
Langdon 17763
Langdondale 16650
Langeloth 15054
Langhorne 19047
Langhorne Gardens 19047
Langhorne Manor 19047
Langhorne Terrace 19047
Lansdale 19446
Lansdowne 19050
Lansdowne Park Gardens (Part of Collingdale) 19023
Lanse 16849
Lansford 18232
Lantz Corners 16740
Lapidea Hills 19013
La Plume 18440
Laporte (Twp) 17758
Laporte 18626
Larabee 16731
Lardintown 16055
Large (Part of Jefferson) 15025
Larimer, *Somerset* (Twp) 15552
Larimer, *Westmoreland* 15647
Larke 16693
Larksville 18704
Larrys Creek 17740
Larryville 17740
Larue 17327
Lashley 17267
Lathrop (Twp) 18446
Latimore 17372
Latrobe 15650
Lattimer Mines 18234
Laughlin Junction (Part of Pittsburgh) 15207
Laughlintown 15655
Laurel, *Cumberland* 17324
Laurel, *York* 17322
Laurel Bend 19007
Laureldale 19605
Laurel Falls 15552
Laurel Gardens 15229
Laurel Hill, *Fayette* 15431
Laurel Hill (Part of McDonald) 15057
Laurel Lake, *Luzerne* 18707
Laurel Lake, *Susquehanna* 18812
Laurel Mountain 15655
Laurel Park 17845
Laurel Ridge 15009
Laurel Run 18702
Laurelton 17835
Laurelville, *Fayette* 15666
Laurelville, *Lancaster* 17557
Laurys Station 18059
Lausanne (Twp) 18255
Lavansville 15501
Lavelle 17943
Laverock 19118
Lawn 17041
Lawnherst 18045
Lawnton♦ 17111
Lawrence, *Clearfield* (Twp) 16830
Lawrence, *Tioga* (Twp) 16946

Lawrence, *Washington* 15055
Lawrence Park, *Delaware* 19008
Lawrence Park, *Erie*♦ 16511
Lawrenceville (Part of Old Forge) 18642
Lawrenceville (Part of Pittsburgh) 15201
Lawrenceville, *Tioga* 16929
Lawsonham 16248
Lawson Heights♦ 15650
Lawsville Center 18801
Lawton 18828
Layfield 19525
Layton 15473
Leacock (Twp) 17572
Leacock 17540
Leaders Heights 17403
Leaf Park 17603
Leaman Place 17562
Leamersville 16635
Learn Settlement 15729
Leasuresville 16055
Leather Corner Post 18069
Leatherwood 16242
Lebanon, *Wayne* (Twp) 18431
Lebanon, *Lebanon* 17042 ... 17046
For specific ZIP Codes call (888) 275-8777, or your local postmaster.
Lebanon Plaza 17042
Lebanon South♦ 17042
Lebo 17040
Le Boeuf (Twp) 16441
Le Boeuf Gardens 16441
Leck Kill 17836
Leckrone 15454
Lecontes Mills 16850
Lederach 19450
Ledgedale 18463
Lee 18617
Leechburg 15656
Leech Hill 16943
Leedom Estates 19078
Leedom Gardens 19078
Lee Mine 18634
Lee Park 18702
Leeper 16233
Leesburg 16156
Leesburg Station 16156
Lees Cross Roads 17257
Leesport 19533
Leet (Twp) 15143
Leetonia 17727
Leetsdale 15056
Lehigh, *Carbon* (Twp) 18255
Lehigh, *Northampton* (Twp) 18088
Lehigh, *Wayne* (Twp) 18424
Lehigh Furnace 18080
Lehigh Gap, *Carbon* 18071
Lehigh Gap, *Lehigh* 18080
Lehighton 18235
Lehigh University (Part of Bethlehem)‡ 18015
Lehigh Valley General Mail Facility 18001-02
For specific ZIP Codes call (888) 275-8777, or your local postmaster.
Lehigh Valley Mall 18052
Lehman, *Luzerne* (Twp) 18612
Lehman, *Pike* (Twp) 18324
Lehman, *Luzerne* 18627
Lehman, *York* 17362
Leibeyville 17960
Leidy (Twp) 17764
Leinbachs 19605
Leisenring 15455
Leith 15401
Leithsville 18055
Lemasters 17231
Lemon 18657
Lemont 16851
Lemont Furnace 15456
Lemoyne 17043
Lenape 19380
Lenape Heights 16226
Lenhartsville 19534
Lenker Manor 17109
Lenkerville 17061
Lenni 19052
Lenni Heights 19037
Lennox Park (Part of Trainer) 19015
Lenover 19365
Lenox (Twp) 18446
Lenoxville 18441
Lenwood Heights 17236

Leola 17540
Leolyn 17765
Leona 16914
Leopard 19312
Leopard Lakes 19312
Le Raysville 18829
Leroy (Twp) 17724
Leroy 17743
Lester 19029
Letort 17582
Letterkenny (Twp) 17244
Letterkenny Army Depot 17201
Level Corner 17744
Level Green 15085
Levittown♦ 19054-59
For specific ZIP Codes call (888) 275-8777, or your local postmaster.
Levittown Center 19054
Levittown Shopping Center (Part of Tullytown) 19055
Levittown-Tullytown 19007
Lewis, *Lycoming* (Twp) 17771
Lewis, *Northumberland* (Twp) 17772
Lewis, *Union* (Twp) 17880
Lewisberry 17339
Lewisburg 17837
Lewis Run 16738
Lewistown, *Mifflin* 17044
Lewistown, *Schuylkill* 18252
Lewistown Junction 17044
Lewisville, *Chester* 19351
Lewisville, *Indiana* 15725
Lexington 17543
Liberty, *Adams* (Twp) 17320
Liberty, *Bedford* (Twp) 16678
Liberty, *Centre* (Twp) 16841
Liberty, *Mercer* (Twp) 16127
Liberty, *Montour* (Twp) 17821
Liberty, *Susquehanna* (Twp) 18801
Liberty, *Allegheny* 15133
Liberty, *McKean* 16743
Liberty, *Tioga* 16930
Liberty Corners 18848
Liberty Square 17518
Library 15129
Lickdale 17038
Licking (Twp) 16049
Licking Creek (Twp) 17228
Lickingville 16332
Lightner 17404
Light Street 17839
Ligonier 15658
Lilly 15938
Lillyville 16117
Lima♦ 19037
Limehill 18853
Limekiln 19535
Limeport 18060
Limerick 19468
Lime Ridge♦ 17815
Lime Rock 17543
Limestone, *Lycoming* (Twp) 17740
Limestone, *Montour* (Twp) 17821
Limestone, *Union* (Twp) 17844
Limestone, *Warren* (Twp) 16351
Limestone, *Clarion* 16234
Limestoneville 17847
Lime Valley 17584
Limeville 17527
Lincoln, *Bedford* (Twp) 15521
Lincoln, *Huntingdon* (Twp) 16657
Lincoln, *Somerset* (Twp) 15501
Lincoln, *Allegheny* 15037
Lincoln (Part of Ephrata) 17522
Lincoln Acres 15642
Lincoln Beach 15068
Lincoln Colliery 17963
Lincoln Falls 18616
Lincoln Heights (Part of Birdsboro) 19508
Lincoln Heights, *Westmoreland* 15644
Lincoln Hill 15301
Lincoln Park, *Allegheny* 15235
Lincoln Park, *Berks* 19609
Lincoln Park, *Delaware* 19079
Lincoln Place (Part of Pittsburgh) 15207
Lincoln Terrace 18042
Lincolnville 16404
Lincolnway 17404
Linconia 19047
Linden, *Lycoming* 17744
Linden, *Washington* 15317
Linden Hall 16828
Lindenhurst 19067
Linds Crossing 16648
Lindsey (Part of Punxsutawney)‡ 15767
Line Lexington 18932
Line Mountain 17941
Linesville 16424
Linfield 19468
Linglestown♦ 17112
Linhart 15145
Linn 15442
Linntown♦ 17837
Linville Circle (Part of Lancaster) 17602
Linwood♦ 19061
Linwood Park 19061
Linwood Terrace 19061
Lionville 19353
Lippincott 15370
Lisbon 16373
Lisburn 17055
Listie 15549
Listonburg 15424
Litchfield 18810
Lithia Springs 17857
Lithia Valley (Part of Factoryville) 18419
Lititz 17543
Little Beaver (Twp) 16120
Little Britain (Twp) 19363
Little Chicago 15320
Little Cooley 16404
Little Corners 16335
Little Gap 18058
Little Hickory 16353
Little Hope 16428
Little Italy 18956
Little Kansas 17051
Little Mahanoy (Twp) 17823
Little Marsh 16950
Little Meadows 18830
Littlestown 17340
Little Summit 15431
Littletown 15748
Little Washington 19335
Live Easy 15320
Liverpool 17045
Livonia 16872
Llandrilla 19004
Llanfair 15930
Llewellyn 17944
Llewelyn Corners 18602
Lloydell 15921
Lloydesville 15650
Llyswen (Part of Altoona) 16602
Loag 19520
Lobachsville 19547
Lochiel 17837
Lochvale 15742
Locke Mills 17063
Lock Haven 17745
Lockport, *Clinton* 17745
Lockport, *Mifflin* 17044
Lockport, *Westmoreland* 15923
Locksley 19342
Lockview 15022
Locust, *Columbia* (Twp) 17820
Locust, *Indiana* 15771
Locustdale 17945
Locust Gap 17840
Locust Grove, *Centre* 16875
Locust Grove, *York* 17402
Locust Grove Gardens 17402
Locust Hill 15474
Locust Lakes Village 18347
Locust Point 17055
Locust Run 17094
Locust Summit 17840
Locust Valley, *Lehigh* 18036
Locust Valley, *Schuylkill* 18214
Lofty 18201
Logan, *Blair* (Twp) 16601
Logan, *Clinton* (Twp) 17747
Logan, *Huntingdon* (Twp) 16669
Logan, *Indiana* 15742
Logan (Part of Philadelphia)‡ 19141
Logan Mills 17747
Logans Ferry (Part of Plum) 15239
Logans Ferry Heights (Part of Plum) 15239
Logan Square (Part of Norristown) 19401
Loganton 17747
Loganville 17342
Log Pile 15301
London 16127
London Britain (Twp) 19350
Londonderry, *Bedford* (Twp) 15545
Londonderry, *Chester* (Twp) 19330
Londonderry, *Dauphin* (Twp) 17057
London Grove (Twp) 19390
London Grove 19348
Lone Pine 15301
Long Acre Park (Part of Yeadon) 19050
Long Branch 15423
Long Bridge 15658
Longbrook 17758
Longfellow 17044
Longlevel 17368
Long Pond 18334
Long Run 18235
Longs Crossroad 16668
Longsdale 19539
Longsdorf 17241
Longstown 17402
Longswamp 19539
Longview (Part of Bethel Park) 15102
Longwood Gardens 19348
Lookabough Corners 15656
Lookout 18417
Loomis Park 18702
Loop 16648
Lopez 18628
Lorain 15902
Lorane♦ 19606
Lorberry 17963
Lords Valley 18428
Lorenton 16938
Loretto 15940
Loretto Road 15931
Losh's Run 17020
Lost Creek 17946
Lottsville 16402
Loux Corner 18927
Lovedale 15037
Lovejoy 15729
Lovell 16407
Lovelton 18629
Lovely 15521
Lover 15022
Lowber, *Fayette* 15438
Lowber, *Westmoreland* 15660
Lowe Lake 18470
Lower Allen (Twp) 17011
Lower Alsace (Twp) 19606
Lower Askam 18706
Lower Augusta (Twp) 17801
Lower Brownville 17976
Lower Burrell 15068
Lower Chanceford (Twp) 17302
Lower Chichester (Twp) 19061
Lower Frankford (Twp) 17013
Lower Frederick (Twp) 19492
Lower Gwynedd (Twp) 19437
Lower Heidelberg (Twp) 19604
Lower Longswamp 19539
Lower Macungie (Twp) 18062
Lower Mahanoy (Twp) 17017
Lower Makefield (Twp) 19067
Lower Merion (Twp) 19003
Lower Mifflin (Twp) 17241
Lower Milford (Twp) 18036
Lower Moreland (Twp) 19006
Lower Mount Bethel (Twp) 18063
Lower Nazareth (Twp) 18017
Lower Orchard 19058
Lower Oxford (Twp) 19363
Lower Paxton 17109
Lower Peanut 15480
Lower Pottsgrove (Twp) 19464
Lower Providence (Twp) 19401
Lower Sagon 17877
Lower Salford (Twp) 19438
Lower Saucon (Twp) 18015
Lower Southampton (Twp) 19047
Lower Swatara (Twp) 17057
Lower Towamensing (Twp) 18071
Lower Turkeyfoot (Twp) 15424
Lower Tyrone (Twp) 15428
Lower Wheel 15637
Lower Windsor (Twp) 17368
Lower Yoder (Twp) 15905
Lowhill, *Lehigh* (Twp) 18069
Low Hill (Part of Centerville) 15417
Lowville 16442
Loyalhanna (Twp) 15681
Loyalhanna 15661
Loyalhanna Woodlands No. 1 15681
Loyalsock (Twp) 17701
Loyalsockville 17754
Loyalton 17048
Loyalville 18612
Loysburg 16659
Loysville 17047
Lucernemines♦ 15754
Lucinda 16235
Luciusboro 15748
Lucknow 17110
Lucky 17322
Lucon 19473
Lucy Crossing (Part of Glendon) 18042
Lucy Furnace 17066
Ludlow 16333
Ludwigs Corner 19343
Luke Fidler 17872
Lumber (Twp) 15834
Lumber City, *Clearfield* 16833
Lumber City, *Mifflin* 17084
Lumberville 18933
Lundys Lane 16401
Lungerville 17774
Lurgan 17232
Luthersburg 15848
Luthers Mills 18848
Lutzville 15537
Luxor 15662
Luzerne, *Fayette* (Twp) 15417
Luzerne, *Fayette* 15433
Luzerne, *Luzerne* 18709
Lycippus 15650
Lycoming (Twp) 17728
Lykens 17048
Lyleville 16627
Lynch 16347
Lynchville (Part of St. Marys) 15857
Lyndell 19354
Lyndon 17602
Lyndora 16045
Lynn, *Lehigh* (Twp) 19529
Lynn, *Susquehanna* 18844
Lynnewood 19150
Lynnewood Gardens 19012
Lynnport 18066
Lynnville 18066
Lynnwood, *Fayette* 15012
Lynnwood, *Luzerne* 18702
Lyon Station 19536
Lyon Valley 18066
Mable 17921
Mable Hill 15327
McAdoo 18237
McAdoo Heights 18237
McAlevys Fort 16652
McAlisters Crossroads 15086
McAlisterville 17049
MacArthur (Part of Aliquippa)‡ 15001
McCalmont (Twp) 15711
McCandless (Twp) 15237
McCartney 16661
McCauley 16651
McChesneytown 15650
McClarran 15650
McCleary 15050
McClellan 17032
McClellandtown 15458
McClellan Heights 17403
McClintock 16301
McClure, *Fayette* 15666
McClure, *Snyder* 17841
McConnellsburg 17233
Mcconnells Mills 15301
McConnellstown 16660
McCoysville 17058
McCracken 15380
McCrea 17241
Mccullochs Mills 17035
McCullough 15636
McDonald 15057
Macdonaldton 15530
Macedonia, *Bradford* 18848
Macedonia, *Juniata* 17059
McElhattan 17748
McEwensville 17749
Mcgarey 15825
McGees Mills 15757
McGillstown 17003
McGrann 16236
McGregor 16222
McHenry (Twp) 17723
McIlhaney 18322
McIntyre, *Lycoming* (Twp) 17763
McIntyre, *Indiana* 15756
McKean 16426
McKeansburg 17960
McKee 16637
McKee Half Falls 17864
McKeesport 15130-35
For specific ZIP Codes call (888) 275-8777, or your local postmaster.
McKees Rocks 15136
Mackeyville 17750
McKinley 19027
McKinley Hill (Part of Point Marion) 15474
McKinney 17240
McKnight 15237
McKnightstown 17343
McLane 16426
McMurray♦ 15317
McNett (Twp) 17765
McPherron 15753
McSherrystown 17344
Macungie 18062
McVeytown 17051
McVille 16229
Maddensville 17229
Madera 16661
Madison, *Armstrong* (Twp) 16259
Madison, *Clarion* (Twp) 16248
Madison, *Columbia* (Twp) 17846
Madison, *Lackawanna* (Twp) 18444
Madison, *Westmoreland* 15663
Madisonburg 16852
Madisonville 18444
Madley 15534
Magee 16351
Magill Heights 15024
Magnolia Gardens 19007
Magnolia Hill 19007
Mahaffey 15757
Mahanoy (Twp) 17976
Mahanoy City 17948
Mahanoy Plane (Part of Gilberton) 17949
Mahoning, *Armstrong* (Twp) 16242
Mahoning, *Carbon* (Twp) 18235
Mahoning, *Lawrence* (Twp) 16132
Mahoning, *Montour* (Twp) 17821
Mahoning, *Armstrong* 16259
Mahoning Manor 17847
Mahoningtown (Part of New Castle)‡ 16102
Maidencreek (Twp) 19605
Maiden Creek 19510
Main (Twp) 17815
Mainesburg 16932
Mainland 19451
Mainsville 17257
Mainville 17815
Maitland 17044
Maizeville (Part of Gilberton) 17934
Majeriks Corners 16441
Malden Place (Part of Centerville) 15417
Mall at Steamtown, The (Part of Scranton)‡ 18502
Malta 17017
Malvern 19355
Mammoth 15664
Mamont 15632
Manada Gap 17112
Manatawny 19547
Manayunk (Part of Philadelphia)‡ 19127
Manchester, *Wayne* (Twp) 18417
Manchester, *York* (Twp) 17402
Manchester (Part of Pittsburgh) 15233
Manchester, *York* 17345
Mandata 17830
Manhattan 16921
Manheim, *Lancaster* (Twp) 17601
Manheim, *York* (Twp) 17329
Manheim, *Lancaster* 17545
Manifold 15301

Manito	15650
Mann (Twp)	17211
Mannitto	15670
Manns Choice	15550
Mannsville	17024
Manoa	19083
Manor, *Armstrong* (Twp)	16226
Manor, *Lancaster* (Twp)	17603
Manor, *Indiana*	15765
Manor, *Westmoreland*	15665
Manor Hill	16652
Manor Hills (Part of Yeadon)	19050
Manor Ridge	17603
Manorville	16238
Manown	15063
Mansfield	16933
Mansville	15658
Mantz	18252
Maple Beach	19007
Mapledale	16323
Maple Glen, *Montgomery*♦	19002
Maple Glen (Part of Centerville)	15417
Maple Grove, *Berks*	18011
Maple Grove, *Chester*	19363
Maple Grove, *Clarion*	16248
Maple Grove, *Fayette*	15622
Maple Grove Park	19540
Maple Hill, *Lycoming*	17752
Maple Hill, *Montgomery*	19422
Maple Hill, *Schuylkill*	17976
Maple Hills	17319
Maple Hollow	16635
Maplelake	18444
Maple Manor	18201
Maple Ridge	15935
Maple Shade, *Bucks*	19021
Maple Shade, *Venango*	16319
Mapleton Depot	17052
Mapletown	15338
Maplewood	18436
Maplewood Heights	18612
Maplewood Park	19018
Maplewood Terrace	15601
Marble	16334
Marble City	16650
Marble Hall	19444
Marcel Lake Estates	18328
Marchand	15758
Marchwood	19341
Marcus Hook	19061
Marengo	16877
Margaret	16201
Margaretta Furnace	17406
Margo Gardens	19007
Marguerite	15650
Maria	16664
Marianna	15345
Mariann Estates	16254
Mariasville	16373
Marienville	16239
Marietta	17547
Marion, *Beaver* (Twp)	15066
Marion, *Berks* (Twp)	19567
Marion, *Butler* (Twp)	16020
Marion, *Centre* (Twp)	16841
Marion, *Franklin*	17235
Marion Acres	17888
Marion Center	15759
Marion Heights	17832
Marion Hill	15066
Mark Acres	15642
Markelsville	17074
Markes	17236
Market Square (Part of Philadelphia)‡	19118
Market Street (Part of West Chester)‡	19380
Markle	15613
Markleton	15551
Markleysburg	15459
Markton	15764
Markvue Manor	15642
Marlboro	19348
Marlborough (Twp)	18084
Mar Lin	17951
Marple (Twp)	19008
Marron	16833
Mars	16046
Marsh	19520
Marshall (Twp)	15086
Marshall Heights	15716
Marshalls Creek	18335
Marshall Terrace	19061
Marshallton, *Chester*	19380
Marshallton, *Northumberland*♦	17872
Marshbrook	18414
Marshburg	16738
Marsh Hill	17771
Marshlands	16921
Marsh Run	17070
Marshview	18848
Marshwood (Part of Olyphant)	18434
Marsteller	15760
Marstown	17963
Martha Furnace	16870
Martic (Twp)	17565
Martic Forge	17565
Marticville	17565
Martin	15460
Martindale, *Cambria*	15946
Martindale, *Lancaster*	17549
Martinsburg	16662
Martins Corner	19320
Martins Creek	18063
Martinsville	17366
Martzville	18603
Marvel Gardens	19094
Marvindale	16749
Marwood	16023
Mary D	17952
Marysville, *Bedford*	16678
Marysville, *Perry*	17053
Marywood College (Part of Scranton)‡	18509
Mascot	17572
Mason-Dixon	17225
Masontown	15461
Masseyburg	16669
Mastersonville	17545
Mast Hope	18435
Matamoras, *Dauphin*	17032
Matamoras, *Pike*	18336
Mather	15346
Mattawana	17054
Mattey Plan	15012
Matthews Run	16371
Mattie	15537
Mausdale	17821
Maxatawny	19538
Maxwell	15450
Mayberry (Twp)	17821
Mayburg	16347
Mayfair (Part of Philadelphia)	19136
Mayfield	18433
Mayfield East	17405
Mayport	16240
Maysville, *Armstrong*	15618
Maysville, *Mercer*	16125
Maysville, *Northumberland*	17866
Maytown, *Lancaster*♦	17550
Maytown, *York*	17339
Mayville	16105
Maze	17094
Mazeppa	17837
McKimm	16117
Mead (Twp)	16313
Meade Heights	17057
Meadia Heights	17602
Meadowbrook, *Fayette*	15401
Meadowbrook, *Montgomery*	19046
Meadowbrook Manor	19341
Meadow Gap	17243
Meadow Lands	15347
Meadowood♦	16045
Meadowview Estates	17540
Meadville	16335
Mechanicsburg	17055
Mechanics Grove	17566
Mechanicsville, *Bucks*	18934
Mechanicsville, *Clarion*	16214
Mechanicsville, *Lancaster*	17545
Mechanicsville, *Lehigh*	18104
Mechanicsville, *Montour*♦	17821
Mechanicsville, *Schuylkill*	17901
Meckesville	18210
Mecks Corner	17068
Media	19063*
	19065†
Media Annex (Part of Media)	19063
Medix Run	15868
Meeker	18612
Megargee	19320
Mehoopany	18629
Meiser	17842
Meiserville	17853
Melcroft	15462
Mellingertown	15666
Mellwood Manor	15068
Melrose	18847
Melrose Park	19012
Menallen, *Adams* (Twp)	17304
Menallen, *Fayette* (Twp)	15468
Mench	15537
Mendenhall	19357
Mendon	15679
Menges Mills	17346
Menno	17004
Mentcle	15761
Mercer, *Butler* (Twp)	16038
Mercer, *Mercer*	16137
Mercersburg	17236
Mercur	18854
Meredith	16249
Meridian♦	16001
Merion Park	19066
Merion Square	19035
Merion Station	19066
Meriwether Farms	19380
Merlin	19460
Mermaid Estates	19401
Merrian	17851
Merrittstown	15463
Merryall	18853
Mertztown	19539
Merwinsburg	18330
Meshoppen	18630
Messiah College	17027
Messmore	15458
Metal	17224
Metzler	15557
Mexico	17056
Meyersdale	15552
Meyersville	18104
Middleburg, *Luzerne*	18661
Middleburg, *Snyder*	17842
Middlebury (Twp)	16935
Middlebury Center	16935
Middle Churches	15666
Middle City (Part of Philadelphia)‡	19103
Middlecreek, *Snyder* (Twp)	17833
Middlecreek, *Somerset* (Twp)	15557
Middle Creek, *Snyder*	17813
Middle Lancaster	16037
Middle Paxton (Twp)	17018
Middleport	17953
Middlesex, *Butler* (Twp)	16059
Middlesex, *Cumberland*	17013
Middle Smithfield (Twp)	18301
Middle Spring	17257
Middle Taylor (Twp)	15906
Middleton	15757
Middletown, *Bucks* (Twp)	19056
Middletown, *Delaware* (Twp)	19037
Middletown, *Susquehanna* (Twp)	18818
Middletown, *Dauphin*	17057
Middletown, *Huntingdon*	16678
Middletown, *McKean*	16749
Middletown, *Westmoreland*	15601
Middletown Center	18818
Middletown Heights	19063
Midland, *Beaver*	15059
Midland, *Washington*	15342
Midvale	18705
Midvale Manor	19608
Midvalley	17888
Midway, *Adams*♦	17331
Midway, *Lebanon*	17042
Midway, *Washington*	15060
Midway, *Westmoreland*	15601
Mifflin, *Columbia* (Twp)	18631
Mifflin, *Dauphin* (Twp)	17061
Mifflin, *Lycoming* (Twp)	17740
Mifflin, *Juniata*	17058
Mifflinburg	17844
Mifflintown	17059
Mifflinville♦	18631
Milan	18831
Milanville	18443
Mildred	18632
Mile Run	17801
Miles (Twp)	16872
Milesburg	16853
Milford, *Bucks* (Twp)	18968
Milford, *Juniata* (Twp)	17062
Milford, *Pike* (Twp)	18337
Milford, *Pike*	18337
Milford, *Somerset*	15557
Milford Manor	19067
Milford Square	18935
Milfred Terrace	15348
Militia Hill	19034
Millardsville	17067
Millbach	17073
Millbank	15658
Millbourne	19082
Millbrook, *Centre*	16801
Millbrook, *Mercer*	16133
Mill Brook, *Pike*	18426
Millburn	16137
Mill City	18414
Millcreek, *Clarion* (Twp)	16225
Millcreek, *Lebanon* (Twp)	17073
Mill Creek, *Lycoming* (Twp)	17756
Mill Creek, *Mercer* (Twp)	16145
Millcreek, *Erie*	16505-06
	16509
For specific ZIP Codes call (888) 275-8777, or your local postmaster.	
Mill Creek, *Huntingdon*	17060
Mill Creek, *Schuylkill*	17901
Mill Creek Falls	19007
Millcreek Mall	16509
Milledgeville	16311
Miller, *Huntingdon* (Twp)	16652
Miller, *Perry* (Twp)	17094
Miller Heights	18020
Miller Manor	18067
Miller Run	15936
Millersburg	17061
Miller Shaft	15946
Millers Station	16403
Millerstown, *Allegheny*	15084
Millerstown, *Blair*	16662
Millerstown, *Clarion*	16334
Millerstown, *Perry*	17062
Millersville	17551
Millerton	16936
Millertown, *Columbia*	17815
Millertown, *Fayette*	15446
Mill Grove	17820
Mill Hall	17751
Millheim	16854
Milligantown	15068
Millmont	17845
Millport, *Lancaster*	17540
Millport, *Potter*	16748
Millrift	18340
Mill Run, *Blair*	16601
Mill Run, *Clearfield*	15849
Mill Run, *Fayette*	15464
Mills	16937
Millsboro	15348
Millstone (Twp)	15860
Milltown (Part of Sayre)	18840
Milltown, *Allegheny*	15147
Milltown, *Chester*	19380
Millvale	15209
Millview	18616
Mill Village	16427
Millville	17846
Millway	17543
Millwood	15627
Milmont Park	19033
Milnesville	18239
Milnor	17225
Milroy♦	17063
Milton, *Armstrong*	16222
Milton, *Northumberland*	17847
Milton Grove	17552
Milwaukee	18411
Mina	16915
Mineral (Twp)	16342
Mineral Point	15942
Mineral Springs	16855
Miners Mills (Part of Wilkes-Barre)	18705
Miners Village (Part of Cornwall)	17016
Minersville (Part of Johnstown)	15906
Minersville, *Schuylkill*	17954
Minesite (Part of Allentown)	18103
Mingo	19468
Mingoville	16856
Minisink Hills	18341
Minister	16347
Minnequa	17724
Minooka (Part of Scranton)	18507
Miola	16214
Miquon	19452
Miquon Hills	19452
Mission Hill	17601
Mitchell Park (Part of Hatboro)	19040
Mix Run	15832
Mocanaqua	18655
Moc-A-Tek Lake	18436
Mocking Bird Hill	15642
Modena	19358
Moffit Sterling	15327
Mogees	19401
Mohns Hill	19608
Mohnton	19540
Mohrsville	19541
Molino	17961
Molltown	19522
Monaca	15061
Monaghan (Twp)	17404
Monarch	15431
Monessen	15062
Mongul	17257
Moninger	15342
Moniteau	16061
Monocacy Station	19542
Monongahela, *Greene* (Twp)	15338
Monongahela, *Washington*	15063
Monroe, *Bedford* (Twp)	15535
Monroe, *Bradford* (Twp)	18848
Monroe, *Cumberland* (Twp)	17055
Monroe, *Juniata* (Twp)	17086
Monroe, *Snyder* (Twp)	17831
Monroe, *Wyoming* (Twp)	18657
Monroe, *Clarion*	16232
Monroe Heights (Part of Monroeville)	15146
Monroeton	18832
Monroeville	15146
Monroeville Mall (Part of Monroeville)	15146
Mont Alto	17237
Montandon	17850
Mont Clare	19453
Montdale	18447
Montello	19608
Monterey, *Berks*	19530
Monterey, *Franklin*	17214
Monterey, *Lancaster*	17540
Montgomery, *Franklin* (Twp)	17236
Montgomery, *Indiana* (Twp)	15724
Montgomery, *Montgomery* (Twp)	18936
Montgomery, *Lycoming*	17752
Montgomery Ferry	17074
Montgomery Square	18936
Montgomeryville♦	18936
Montmorenci	15853
Montour, *Columbia* (Twp)	17815
Montour, *Allegheny*	15244
Montoursville	17754
Montrose, *Berks*	19607
Montrose, *Susquehanna*	18801
Montrose Hill	15238
Montsera	17013
Monument	16822
Moon	15108
Moon Crest	15108
Moon Run	15136
Moore (Twp)	18014
Mooredale	17013
Mooresburg	17821
Moores Corners	16057
Moorestown	18014
Moorheadville	16428
Moosic	18507
Moosic Lake	18416
Morado (Part of Beaver Falls)	15010
Morann	16663
Moravia	16157
Moravian (Part of Bethlehem)	18018
Mordansville	17815
Morea	17948
Moreland (Twp)	17756
Moreland Farms	19040
Moreland Manor	19040
Morewood	19040
Morgan, *Greene* (Twp)	15344
Morgan, *Allegheny*	15064
Morgan, *Fayette* (rural)	15425
Morgan, *Fayette*	15456
Morgan Hill	15031
Morgans Hill	18042
Morgantown	19543
Morningside (Part of Pittsburgh)	15206

*** Area Zip Code** **† Post Office Boxes** **‡ Postal Station** **♦ Census Designated Place** *Italic Type* **County**

Place	ZIP
Morrellville (Part of Johnstown)	15906
Morris, *Clearfield* (Twp)	16858
Morris, *Greene* (Twp)	15364
Morris, *Huntingdon* (Twp)	16611
Morris, *Washington* (Twp)	15329
Morris, *Tioga*	16938
Morris Crossroads	15451
Morrisdale	16858
Morris Run	16939
Morrisville	19067
Morrows Corner	16210
Morstein	19380
Morton	19070
Mortonville	19320
Morwood	18969
Morysville	19512
Moscow	18444
Moselem	19526
Moselem Springs	19522
Mosgrove	16259
Moshannon, *Cambria*	15938
Moshannon, *Centre*	16859
Mosherville	16925
Mosiertown	16433
Mosserville	18066
Mostoller	15563
Mottarns Mill	15771
Moudy Hill	15946
Moulstown	17331
Mount Aetna	19544
Mountaindale, *Cambria*	16639
Mountain Dale, *Dauphin*	17110
Mountain Grove	17815
Mountainhome♦	18342
Mountain Lake	18848
Mountain Top, *Lancaster*	17555
Mountain Top, *Luzerne*	18707
Mountain Valley Lake	17921
Mount Airy, *Lancaster*	17578
Mount Airy (Part of Philadelphia)‡	19119
Mount Airy Terrace	18708
Mount Allen	17055
Mount Alton	16738
Mount Bethel	18343
Mount Braddock	15465
Mount Carbon	17901
Mount Carmel	17851
Mount Chestnut	16001
Mount Chestnut Springs	16001
Mount Cobb♦	18436
Mount Eagle	16841
Mount Etna	16693
Mount Gretna	17064
Mount Gretna Heights	17064
Mount Holly Springs	17065
Mount Hope, *Adams*	17320
Mount Hope, *Lancaster*	17545
Mount Independence	15456
Mount Jackson	16102
Mount Jewett	16740
Mount Joy, *Adams* (Twp)	17340
Mount Joy, *Lancaster* (Twp)	17022
Mount Joy, *Clearfield*	16830
Mount Joy, *Lancaster*	17552
Mount Joy, *Westmoreland*	15666
Mount Laffee	17901
Mount Laurel	18201
Mount Lebanon♦	15228
Mount Misery	17350
Mount Morris	15349
Mount Nebo, *Allegheny*	15143
Mount Nebo, *Lancaster*	17565
Mount Nebo, *Westmoreland*	15683
Mount Oliver	15210
Mount Patrick	17045
Mount Penn	19606
Mount Pleasant, *Adams* (Twp)	17325
Mount Pleasant, *Columbia* (Twp)	17815
Mount Pleasant, Washington (Twp)	15340
Mount Pleasant, *Wayne* (Twp)	18472
Mount Pleasant, *Adams*	17331
Mount Pleasant, *Berks*	19506
Mount Pleasant, *Delaware*	19087
Mount Pleasant, *Lebanon*	17042
Mount Pleasant, *Mifflin*	17063
Mount Pleasant, *Northampton*	18013
Mount Pleasant, *Northumberland*	17801
Mount Pleasant, *Perry*	17006
Mount Pleasant, *Schuylkill*	17901
Mount Pleasant, *Tioga*	16938
Mount Pleasant, *Westmoreland*	15666
Mount Pleasant, *York*	17019
Mount Pleasant Mills	17853
Mount Pocono	18344
Mountrock, *Cumberland*	17013
Mount Rock, *Franklin*	17257
Mount Royal	17315
Mount Sterling	15461
Mount Tabor	17324
Mount Troy	15212
Mount Union, *Franklin*	17222
Mount Union, *Huntingdon*	17066
Mount Vernon, *Allegheny*	15135
Mount Vernon, *Chester*	19363
Mount Vernon, *Lancaster*	17527
Mount Vernon, *Westmoreland*	15601
Mountville	17554
Mount Washington (Part of Pittsburgh)‡	15211
Mount Wilson	17042
Mount Wolf	17347
Mount Zion, *Cumberland* (Hampden Twp)	17013
Mount Zion, *Cumberland* (South Middleton Twp)	17055
Mount Zion, *Lebanon*	17046
Mount Zion, *Luzerne*	18643
Mount Zion, *Monroe*	18301
Mount Zion, *York*	17402
Moween	15681
Mowersville	17257
Mowry	17921
Moxham (Part of Johnstown)	15902
Moyer	15425
Moylan	19065
Mozart	18925
Mt Pocahontas	18210
Muddy Creek (Twp)	16051
Muddy Creek Forks	17302
Muhlenberg, *Berks* (Twp)	19560
Muhlenberg, *Luzerne*	18621
Muhlenberg Park	19605
Muir	17957
Mullertown	17331
Mumbauersville	18073
Mummasburg	17325
Muncy	17756
Muncy Creek (Twp)	17756
Muncy Valley	17758
Munderf	15825
Mundys Corner	15909
Munhall	15120
Munson	16860
Munster (Twp)	15931
Munster	15940
Murdock	15501
Murrell	17522
Murrinsville	16020
Murry Hill	15317
Murrysville	15668
Muse	15350
Mustard	15037
Mutual	15601
Myersburg	18854
Myerstown, *Cumberland*	17324
Myerstown, *Lebanon*	17067
Mylo Park	15931
Myobeach	18630
Myoma	16046
Myrtle	16748
Mystic Park	16404
Naces Corner	18927
Naceville	18960
Nadine	15147
Naginey	17063
Nansen	16735
Nanticoke	18634
Nantmeal Village	19343
Nanty-Glo	15943
Naomi	15438
Napier (Twp)	15559
Napierville	17522
Narberth	19072
Narbrook Park (Part of Narberth)	19072
Narrows Creek	15801
Narrows Shopping Center (Part of Edwardsville)	18704
Narrowsville	18972
Narvon	17555
Nashua	16101
Nashville, *Indiana*	15771
Nashville, *York*	17362
Nassau Village	19078
Natalie	17851
Natrona	15065
Natrona Heights♦	15065
Nauvoo	16938
Naval Air Development Center	18974
Nazareth	18064
Nealmont	16686
Neason Hill	16335
Neath	18829
Nebo	15622
Nectarine	16038
Ned	15352
Needful	16881
Needmore	17238
Neelyton	17239
Neffs	18065
Neffs Mills	16669
Neffsville	17601*
	17606†
Neiffer	19473
Neiltown	16341
Neiman	17327
Nellie	15486
Nelson (Twp)	16940
Nelson	16940
Nemacolin♦	15351
Nemanie	18451
Nescopeck	18635
Neshaminy	18976
Neshaminy Falls	19047
Neshaminy Hills	19047
Neshaminy Valley	19020
Neshaminy Woods	19047
Neshannock	16105
Neshannock Falls	16156
Nesquehoning	18240
Nether Providence (Twp)	19086
Nether Providence Township♦	19013
Neville (Twp)	15225
Neville Island	15225
New Albany	18833
New Alexandria	15670
New Athens	16248
New Baltimore, *Somerset*	15553
New Baltimore (Part of Hanover)	17331
New Beaver	16141
New Bedford	16140
New Berlin	17855
New Berlinville	19545
Newberry, *York* (Twp)	17370
Newberry (Part of Williamsport)‡	17701
Newberrytown	17319
New Bethlehem	16242
New Bloomfield	17068
Newboro	15435
New Boston	17948
New Bridgeville	17356
New Brighton	15066
New Britain (Twp)	18914
New Britain	18901
New Buena Vista	15550
New Buffalo	17069
Newburg, *Blair*	16601
Newburg, *Cumberland*	17240
Newburg, *Northampton*	18020
Newburg Homes	18045
New Castle, *Schuylkill* (Twp)	17970
New Castle, *Lawrence*	16101-08
For specific ZIP Codes call (888) 275-8777, or your local postmaster.	
New Centerville	15557
Newchester	17350
New Columbia	17856
New Columbus (Part of Nesquehoning)	18240
New Columbus, *Luzerne*	17878
Newcomer	15401
New Cumberland	17070
New Cumberland Army Depot	17070
New Danville	17603
New Derry	15671
New Eagle	15067
Newell	15466
New England	18252
New Enterprise	16664
New Era	18833
Newfield, *Allegheny*	15147
Newfield, *Potter*	16948
New Florence	15944
Newfoundland	18445
New Franklin	17201
New Freedom	17349
New Freeport	15352
New Galena	18914
New Galilee	16141
New Garden (Twp)	19350
New Garden	19374
New Geneva	15467
New Germantown	17071
New Germany	15946
New Grass Manor	18612
New Grenada	16674
New Hamburg	16124
New Hanover	19525
New Hanover Square	19435
Newhard	18080
New Holland	17557
New Hope	18938
New Ireland	16438
New Jerusalem	19522
New Kensington	15068
New Kingstown	17072
Newkirk	18252
New Lebanon	16145
New Lexington	15557
Newlin, *Chester* (Twp)	19380
Newlin, *Columbia*	17820
New London, *Chester*	19360
New London, *Warren*	16351
Newlonsburg (Part of Murrysville)	15668
New Mahoning	18235
Newmanstown♦	17073
Newmansville	16353
New Market	17070
New Milford	18834
New Millport	16861
New Mines	17923
New Oxford	17350
New Paris	15554
New Park	17352
New Philadelphia	17959
Newport, *Luzerne* (Twp)	18634
Newport (Part of New Beaver)	16157
Newport, *Perry*	17074
Newportville	19056
Newportville Terrace	19020
New Providence	17560
New Richmond	16327
New Ringgold	17960
Newry	16665
New Salem, *Armstrong*	16240
New Salem, *Fayette*	15468
New Schaefferstown	19506
New Sewickley (Twp)	15074
New Sheffield	15001
Newside	18080
New Smithville	19530
New Stanton	15672
New Street	17901
New Texas (Part of Plum)	15239
New Texas, *Lancaster*	17563
Newton (Twp)	18411
Newtonburg	15757
Newton Hamilton	17075
Newton Lake	18407
Newtown, *Delaware* (Twp)	19073
Newtown, *Bucks*	18940
New Town, *Centre*	16666
Newtown, *Clearfield*	16878
Newtown, *Greene*	15327
Newtown, *Lancaster*	17512
Newtown, *Lehigh*	18031
Newtown, *Luzerne*	18706
Newtown Grant♦	18940
Newtown Square	19073
New Tripoli	18066
New Vernon	16145
Newville, *Bucks*	18914
Newville, *Cumberland*	17241
Newville, *Lancaster*	17023
New Virginia (Part of Hermitage)	16146
New Washington	15757
New Wilmington	16142
Niagara	18453
Niantic	19504
Nicetown (Part of Philadelphia)‡	19140
Nichola	16262
Nicholson, *Fayette* (Twp)	15461
Nicholson, *Wyoming*	18446
Nickel Mines	17562
Nickleville	16373
Nicklin	16323
Nicktown	15762
Nilan	15474
Niles	16323
Niles Valley	16935
Ninepoints	17509
Nine Row	15927
Nineveh, *Clarion*	16232
Nineveh, *Greene*	15353
Nippenose (Twp)	17720
Nisbet	17759
Nittany	16841
Niverton	15558
Noble	19046
Noblestown	15071
Nockamixon (Twp)	18930
Noll Acres	17055
Nolo	15765
Nook	17058
Nordmont	17758
Normal Square	18235
Normalville	15469
Norristown	19401-04
For specific ZIP Codes call (888) 275-8777, or your local postmaster.	
Norrisville	16406
North Abington (Twp)	18414
Northampton, *Bucks* (Twp)	18954
Northampton, *Somerset* (Twp)	15538
Northampton, *Northampton*	18067
Northampton Hills	18966
North Annville (Twp)	17038
North Apollo	15673
North Bangor	18013
North Barnesboro (Part of Barnesboro)	15714
North Beaver (Twp)	16102
North Belle Vernon	15012
North Bend	17760
North Bessemer	15235
North Bethlehem (Twp)	15360
North Bingham	16941
North Braddock	15104
North Branch (Twp)	18629
Northbrook	19380
Northbrook Hills	17601
North Buffalo (Twp)	16201
North Butler	16001
North Catasauqua	18032
North Centre (Twp)	18603
North Charleroi	15022
North Codorus (Twp)	17362
North Cornwall, *Lebanon* (Twp)	17042
North Cornwall (Part of Cornwall)	17016
North Coventry (Twp)	19464
North East	16428
Northeast Madison (Twp)	17047
North Edinburg	16116
North End (Part of Wilkes-Barre)	18705
Northern Lights Shopping Center (Part of Economy)	15005
North Essington	19029
North Fayette (Twp)	15071
North Fork	16950
North Franklin (Twp)	15301
North Fredericktown	15333
North Freedom	16240
North Hanover Mall (Part of Hanover)	17331
North Heidelberg (Twp)	19506
North Hills, *Montgomery*	19038
North Hills (Part of Milton)	17847
North Hills Village	15237
North Hopewell (Twp)	17322
North Huntingdon (Twp)	15642
North Irwin	15642
North Jackson	18847
North Lebanon (Twp)	17046
North Liberty	16127

North Londonderry (Twp) 17078
North Mahoning (Twp) 15758
North Manheim (Twp) 17901
North Mehoopany 18629
North Middleton (Twp) 17013
Northmoreland (Twp) 18612
North Mountain 17758
North Newton (Twp) 17241
North Oakland 16025
North Orwell 18837
North Philadelphia (Part of Philadelphia)‡ 19132
North Philipsburg 16866
North Pine Grove 16260
North Point, *Bedford* 16679
Northpoint, *Indiana* 15763
North Radcliffe 19007
North Rochester 15074
North Rome 18854
North Scottdale 15683
North Scranton (Part of Scranton)‡ 18508
North Sewickley (Twp) 15010
North Sewickley 16117
North Shenango (Twp) 16424
North Springfield 16430
North Strabane (Twp) 15317
North Towanda 18848
Northumberland 17857
North Union, *Fayette* (Twp) 15401
North Union, *Schuylkill* (Twp) 18241
North Vandergrift 15690
North Versailles♦ 15137
Northview Eatates (Part of Economy) 15005
Northvue 16001
North Wales 19454
North Warren 16365
North Washington, *Butler* 16048
North Washington, *Westmoreland* 15613
Northway Mall 15237
North Weissport 18235
North Whitehall (Twp) 18037
Northwood 16686
North Woodbury (Twp) 16662
Northwood Heights 18045
North York 17404
Norvelt 15674
Norwegian (Twp) 17951
Norwich (Twp) 16724
Norwin Heights 15642
Norwood 19074
Nossville 17213
Nottingham, *Washington* (Twp) 15332
Nottingham, *Bucks* 19020
Nottingham, *Chester* 19362
Nova 17225
Nowrytown 15681
Noxen 18636
Noyes (Twp) 17764
Nuangola 18637
Nuangola Station 18707
Number Five Mine 16137
Number Thirty Seven 15963
Numidia 17858
Nu Mine 16244
Nunnery 17268
Nuremberg 18241
Nutts Corners 16127
Nyesville 17201
Oakbottom 17566
Oakdale, *Allegheny* 15071
Oakdale, *Luzerne* 18224
Oakdale Manor 19067
Oakeola 19036
Oakford 19047
Oak Forest 15370
Oak Grove, *Clearfield* 16858
Oak Grove, *Schuylkill* 17963
Oak Grove, *Westmoreland* 15658
Oak Hall 16827
Oak Hill, *Allegheny* 15145
Oak Hill, *Clearfield* 16845
Oak Hill, *Lancaster* 19362
Oak Hills♦ 16001
Oakhurst (Part of Johnstown) 15906
Oakland, *Butler* (Twp) 16025
Oakland, *Susquehanna* (Twp) 18847
Oakland, *Venango* (Twp) 16317
Oakland (Part of Pittsburgh)‡ 15213
Oakland, *Cambria* 15902
Oakland, *Lawrence*♦ 16101
Oakland, *Mercer* 16137
Oakland, *Susquehanna* 18847
Oakland Hills I 18016
Oakland Mills 17076
Oakland Park 18101
Oak Lane (Part of Philadelphia) 19126
Oaklane Manor 19012
Oakleigh 17111
Oaklyn 17801
Oakmont 15139
Oakmont Villa 17036
Oak Park, *Montgomery* (mobile home park) 19440
Oak Park, *Montgomery* 19446
Oak Park, *Northumberland* 17857
Oak Ridge, *Armstrong* 16245
Oak Ridge, *Clearfield* 16661
Oakryn 17563
Oaks 19456
Oak Shade 17566
Oaktree Hollow 19007
Oakville 17257
Oakwood♦ 16101
Oakwood Park (Part of Laflin) 18702
Obelisk 19492
Oberlin 17113
Oberlin Gardens 17113
Observatory (Part of Pittsburgh)‡ 15214
Odenwelder (Part of West Easton) 18042
Odin 16915
Ogden 19061
Ogdensburg 17765
Ogle, *Somerset* (Twp) 15963
Ogle, *Butler* 16046
Ogletown 15963
Ogontz 19012
Ogontz Campus 19001
O'Hara (Twp) 15238
Ohio (Twp) 15143
Ohiopyle 15470
Ohioview (Part of Industry) 15052
Ohioville 15059
Ohl 15864
Oil City, *Cambria* 15925
Oil City, *Venango* 16301
Oil Creek, *Crawford* (Twp) 16354
Oilcreek, *Venango* (Twp) 16341
Oil Creek (Part of Oil City)‡ 16301
Oklahoma, *Clearfield* 15801
Oklahoma, *Westmoreland* 15613
Okome 17739
Olanta 16863
Old Bethany 15688
Old Boston 18640
Old Clarendon 16313
Old Concord 15329
Old Crabtree 15650
Old Enon 16120
Old Forge 18518
Oldframe 15478
Old Line 17545
Old Lycoming (Twp) 17701
Old Meadow 15683
Old Orchard 18370
Old Port 17082
Old Stanton (Part of New Stanton) 15672
Old Zionsville 18068
Oleopolis 16301
Oley 19547
Oley Furnace 19547
Oliphant Furnace 15401
Oliveburg 15764
Olive Manor (Part of Oil City) 16301
Oliver, *Jefferson* (Twp) 15825
Oliver, *Mifflin* (Twp) 17051
Oliver, *Perry* (Twp) 17074
Oliver, *Fayette* 15472
Olivers Mills (Part of Laurel Run) 18702
Olivet 15618
Olmsted 16915
Olney (Part of Philadelphia) 19120
Olwen Heights 18444
Olyphant 18447
Oneida, *Huntingdon* (Twp) 16652
Oneida, *Butler* 16001
Oneida, *Schuylkill* 18242
Oniontown 16125
Onnalinda 15955
Ono 17077
Ontario 15330
Ontelaunee (Twp) 19605
Opp 17756
Oppermans Corner 19425
Option (Part of Baldwin) 15236
Orange, *Columbia* (Twp) 17859
Orange, *Luzerne* 18612
Orangeville 17859
Orbisonia 17243
Orchard Beach 16428
Orchard Crossing 16686
Orchard Hill 15666
Orchard Hills 15613
Orefield 18069
Oregon, *Wayne* (Twp) 18431
Oregon, *Lancaster* 17540
Oregon Hill 16938
Ore Hill 16673
Oreland♦ 19075
Oreland Gardens 19075
Oreminea 16693
Ore Valley 17403
Oreville 19539
Orient 15420
Oriental 17045
Oriole 17740
Ormrod 18037
Ormsby 16726
Orners Corner 16601
Orrstown 17244
Orrtanna 17353
Orrville 15144
Orson 18449
Orvilla 19440
Orviston 16864
Orwell 18837
Orwigsburg 17961
Orwin 17980
Osborne 15143
Osceola 16942
Osceola Mills 16666
Osgood 16125
Oshanter 16830
Ostend 15757
Osterburg 16667
Osterhout 18657
Oswayo (Twp) 16748
Oswayo 16915
Ottawa 17821
Otter Creek (Twp) 16125
Otto (Twp) 16745
Ottsville 18942
Ott Town 15537
Outcrop 15478
Outlet 18612
Outwood 17963
Oval 17740
Overbrook (Part of Philadelphia)‡ 19151
Overbrook (Part of Pittsburgh) 15226
Overbrook Hills 19151
Overfield (Twp) 18414
Overholt Acres 15642
Overlook, *Lancaster* 17601
Overlook, *Northumberland* 17872
Overlook Heights 16801
Overlook Springs 18049
Overshot 18848
Overton 18833
Overview 17053
Owensdale 15425
Oxbow Meadows 18914
Oxford, *Adams* (Twp) 17350
Oxford, *Chester* 19363
Oxford Valley 19030
Oyster Point 17602
Packer (Twp) 18255
Packerton 18235
Paddytown 15551
Pageville 16401
Paint, *Clarion* (Twp) 16254
Paint, *Somerset* 15963
Paintersville, *Mifflin* 17044
Paintersville (Part of New Stanton) 15639
Paintertown 15642
Paisley 15320
Paletown 18944
Palm 18070
Palmdale 17033
Palmer (Twp) 18045
Palmer Heights♦ 18045
Palmer Park 18045
Palmerton 18071
Palmerton East (Part of Palmerton) 18071
Palmertown 15717
Palmyra, *Pike* (Twp) 18451
Palmyra, *Wayne* (Twp) 18428
Palmyra, *Lebanon* 17078
Palo Alto, *Bedford* 15545
Palo Alto, *Schuylkill* 17901
Palomino Farms 18976
Pancoast 15851
Panic 15851
Panorama Village 16801
Pansy 15864
Pansy Hill 17046
Panther 18445
Paoli 19301
Paper Mills (Part of Bryn Athyn) 19009
Paradise, *Monroe* (Twp) 18326
Paradise, *York* (Twp) 17301
Paradise, *Lancaster*♦ 17562
Paradise, *Schuylkill* 17963
Paradise Falls 18326
Paradise Valley 18326
Pardee 16866
Pardeesville 18201
Pardoe 16137
Pardus 15851
Paris 15021
Park (Part of Vandergrift)‡ 15690
Parkchester 19380
Park City Center (Part of Lancaster) 17601
Park Crest 18214
Parker, *Butler* (Twp) 16049
Parker, *Armstrong* 16049
Parker Ford 19457
Parkers Glen 18458
Parkersville 19380
Parkesburg 19365
Park Forest Village 16803
Park Gate 16117
Park Heights 17331
Parkhill 15945
Park Hills, *Centre* 16803
Park Hills, *York* 17331
Parkland 19047
Park Manor 19607
Park Meadows 15642
Park Place 17948
Parks (Twp) 15690
Parkside 19015
Parkside Courts 18104
Parkside Manor (Part of Parkside) 19015
Parkstown, *Cambria* 15902
Parkstown, *Lawrence* 16101
Parktown Estates 19067
Park View 15215
Parkview Gardens 18052
Park View Heights (Part of Bellefonte) 16823
Parkville 17331
Parkway Center (Part of Green Tree) 15220
Park Way Manor 18104
Parkwood 15774
Parnassus (Part of New Kensington)‡ 15068
Parryville 18244
Parsonville, *Butler* 16050
Parsonville, *Clearfield* 16651
Parvin 17751
Paschall (Part of Philadelphia) 19142
Passer 18036
Patchinville 15724
Patterson (Twp) 15010
Patterson Grove 18655
Patterson Heights 15010
Patterson Hill (Part of Lincoln) 15037
Pattersons Mill 15312
Pattersonville 17967
Patton, *Centre* (Twp) 16803
Patton, *Cambria* 16668
Patton, *Washington* 15301
Pattonville 16226
Paulton 15613
Paupack, *Wayne* (Twp) 18428
Paupack, *Pike* 18451
Paupack Gardens 18451
Pavia 16655
Paxinos 17860
Paxtang 17111
Paxtang Manor 17111
Paxton 17017
Paxtonia♦ 17112
Paxtonville 17861
Peacedale 19363
Peach Bottom, *York* (Twp) 17314
Peach Bottom, *Lancaster* 17563
Peach Bottom Village 17563
Peach Glen 17375
Pealertown 17859
Peanut, *Lawrence* 16116
Peanut, *Westmoreland* 15627
Pearl 16342
Pebble Hill 18901
Pecan 16342
Pechin 15431
Pecks Pond 18328
Peckville (Part of Blakely) 18452
Pemberton 16683
Pen Argyl 18072
Penarth 19004
Penbrook 17103
Penbryn 17765
Pendle Hill 19086
Penfield 15849
Penllyn 19422
Pen Mar 17268
Penn, *Berks* (Twp) 19506
Penn, *Butler* (Twp) 16001
Penn, *Centre* (Twp) 16832
Penn, *Chester* (Twp) 19390
Penn, *Clearfield* (Twp) 16838
Penn, *Cumberland* (Twp) 17257
Penn, *Huntingdon* (Twp) 16647
Penn, *Lancaster* (Twp) 17545
Penn, *Lycoming* (Twp) 17737
Penn, *Perry* (Twp) 17020
Penn, *Snyder* (Twp) 17870
Penn, *Westmoreland* (Twp) 15636
Penn, *York* (Twp) 17331
Penn, *Westmoreland* 15675
Penn Allen 18064
Pennbrook (Part of Lansdale) 19446
Penn Center (Part of Philadelphia) 19102
Penncraft 15433
Penndel 19047
Pennersville 17268
Penn Estates 18301
Pennfield 19007
Penn Five 16666
Penn Forest (Twp) 18210
Penn Glyn (Part of Irwin) 15642
Penn Hall 16875
Penn Heights (Part of Hanover) 17331
Penn Hill 17563
Penn Hills♦ 15235
Penn Hills Shopping Center 15235
Penn Lake Park 18661
Pennline 16424
Penn Pines 19018
Penn Pitt 15338
Penn Rose Park 17601
Penn Run 15765
Pennsburg 18073
Pennsbury (Twp) 19317
Pennsbury Heights 19067
Pennsbury Village 15205
Penns Creek 17862
Pennsdale 17756
Pennside, *Berks* 19606
Pennside, *Erie* 16401
Penns Park 18943
Penn Square Village 19401
Pennsville, *Fayette* 15425
Pennsville, *Northampton* 18067
Penns Woods 15642
Pennsylvania Furnace 16865
Pennvale 17701
Penn Valley 19072
Penn Valley Terrace 19047
Penn Village (Part of Pottstown) 19464
Pennville♦ 17331
Penn Wood 15537
Pennwyn 19607
Penn Wynne♦ 19151
Penobscot 18707
Penowa 15312
Penryn 17564
Pequea (Twp) 17584
Pequea 17565
Percy 15456
Perdix 17020
Perkasie 18944
Perkiomen (Twp) 19426
Perkiomen Heights 18073
Perkiomen Junction 19460
Perkiomen Village 19426

Perkiomenville 18074
Perrine Corners 16153
Perry, *Armstrong* (Twp) 16041
Perry, *Berks* (Twp) 19526
Perry, *Clarion* (Twp) 16049
Perry, *Fayette* (Twp) 15473
Perry, *Greene* (Twp) 15349
Perry, *Jefferson* (Twp) 15767
Perry, *Lawrence* (Twp) 16117
Perry, *Mercer* (Twp) 16130
Perry, *Snyder* (Twp) 17853
Perryopolis 15473
Perry Square (Part of Erie)‡ 16507
Perrysville 15237
Perryville, *Clarion* 16049
Perryville, *Lycoming* 17728
Perryville, *Westmoreland* 15618
Perulack 17021
Peters, *Franklin* (Twp) 17236
Peters, *Washington* (Twp) 15317
Petersburg 16669
Peters Corner 18934
Petersville 18067
Petrolia 16050
Pettis Corners 16335
Pheasant Hill 17601
Pheasant Ridge 18901

Philadelphia

19101-60
For specific ZIP Codes call (888) 275-8777, or your local postmaster.

Colleges & Universities

Alleghany Univ of the Health Sciences 19129
Chestnut Hill Coll 19118
Curtis Institute of Music 19103
Drexel Univ 19104
Holy Family Coll 19114
La Salle Univ 19141
Lutheran Theological Seminary 19119
Moore Coll of Art & Design 19103
Pennsylvania Coll of Optometry 19141
Pennsylvania Coll of Podiatric Medicine 19107
Philadelphia Coll of Osteopathic Medicine 19131
Philadelphia Coll of Pharmacy & Science 19104
Philadelphia Coll of Textiles & Science 19144
Saint Joseph's Univ 19131
Temple Univ 19122
Thomas Jefferson Univ 19107
Univ of Pennsylvania 19104
Westminster Theological Seminary 19118

Financial Institutions

Beneficial Mutual Svgs Bank 19107
Brown Brothers Harriman & Co 19102
Chestnut Hill Bank, Division of Nat Penn Bank 19118
CoreStates Bank, NA 19102
Keystone Bank, NA 19142
PNC Bank, NA 19101

Hospitals

Alleghany Graduate Hosp 19146
Children's Hosp 19104
Frankford Hosp 19124
Hosp of the Univ of Pennsylvania 19104
Methodist Hosp 19148
Nazareth Hosp 19152
Pennsylvania Hosp 19107
Presbyterian Med Ctr 19104
Temple Univ Hosp 19140
Thomas Jefferson Univ Hosp 19107
Veterans Affairs Med Ctr 19104

Hotels/Motels

Adam's Mark 19131
Best Western, Center City 19130
Doubletree 19107
Embassy Suites, Airport 19153
Embassy Suites, Center City 19103
Four Seasons 19103
Holiday Inn, Cityline 19131
Holiday Inn, Independence Mall 19106
Holiday Inn Select, Center City 19103
Marriott 19107
Philadelphia Airport Hilton 19153
Radisson, Philadelphia Airport 19113
The Ritz-Carlton 19103
Sheraton, Society Hill 19106
Sheraton Univ City 19104
Wyndham Franklin Plaza 19103

Military Installations

Coast Guard Grp/Marine Safety Off 19147
Defense Industrial Supply Ctr 19111
Defense Mapping Agency 19120
Defense Personnel Support Ctr 19145
Fort Mifflin Distribution Ctr, U S Army Corps of Engineers 19153
Intra-Fleet Supply Support Operations Team 19112
Naval Inventory Control Point 19120

Philipsburg, *Centre* 16866
Philipsburg (Part of California) 15419
Phillips, *Fayette* 15401
Phillips, *Tioga* 16910
Phillipston 16248
Phillipsville, *Chester* 19320
Phillipsville, *Erie* 16442
Philmont 19006
Philson 15552
Phoenix Park 17901
Phoenixville 19460
Piatt (Twp) 17740
Picture Rocks 17762
Pierce (Part of Jefferson) 15025
Pierceville 17327
Pigeon 16239
Pike, *Berks* (Twp) 19547
Pike, *Bradford* (Twp) 18829
Pike, *Clearfield* (Twp) 16833
Pike, *Potter* (Twp) 16922
Pikeland 19425
Pike Mine 15417
Pikes Creek 18621
Pikes Peak 15765
Piketown 17112
Pikeville 19547
Pilgrim Gardens 19026
Pilgrimham 16232
Pillow 17080
Pilltown 15531
Pine, *Allegheny* (Twp) 15090
Pine, *Armstrong* (Twp) 16259
Pine, *Clearfield* (Twp) 15849
Pine, *Columbia* (Twp) 17846
Pine, *Crawford* (Twp) 16424
Pine, *Indiana* (Twp) 15957
Pine, *Lycoming* (Twp) 16938
Pine, *Mercer* (Twp) 16127
Pine, *Clinton* 17748
Pine Bank 15352
Pine Beach 18428
Pinebrook 17011
Pine City 16254
Pine Creek, *Clinton* (Twp) 17721
Pinecreek, *Jefferson* 15825
Pinecroft 16601
Pinedale (Part of Deer Lake) 17961
Pine Flats 15728
Pine Forge 19548
Pine Glen, *Centre* 16845
Pine Glen, *Mifflin* 17044
Pine Grove, *Schuylkill* (Twp) 17963
Pinegrove, *Venango* (Twp) 16301
Pine Grove, *Warren* (Twp) 16345
Pine Grove, *Perry* 17047
Pine Grove, *Schuylkill* 17963
Pine Grove, *Susquehanna* 18446
Pine Grove Furnace 17324
Pine Grove Mills♦ 16868
Pine Hill, *Armstrong* 16201
Pine Hill, *Schuylkill* 17901
Pine Ridge 19063
Pine Run, *Bucks* 18901
Pine Run, *Lycoming* 17744
Pine Summit 17846
Pine Swamp 19520
Pinetown 17339
Pinetree (Part of Scottdale) 15683
Pine Valley 16405
Pine Valley Estates 18901
Pine View 18707
Pineville, *Bucks* 18946
Pineville, *Warren* 16420
Pinewood 19054
Piney (Twp) 16255
Piney 16214
Piney Fork 15129
Pinola 17257
Pipersville 18947
Pitcairn 15140
Pitman 17964
Pitt Gas 15322
Pittock 15136
Pitts 16901

Pittsburgh

15201-90
For specific ZIP Codes call (888) 275-8777, or your local postmaster.

Colleges & Universities

Carlow Coll 15213
Carnegie Mellon Univ 15213
Chatham Coll 15232
Duquesne Univ 15282
La Roche Coll 15237
Pittsburgh Theological Seminary 15206
Point Park Coll 15222
Univ of Pittsburgh 15620

Financial Institutions

Mellon Bank, NA 15258
Nat City Bank 15222
PNC Bank, NA 15222

Hospitals

Allegheny General Hosp 15212
Children's Hosp 15213
Magee-Womens Hosp 15213
Mercy Hosp 15219
Shadyside Hosp 15232
South Hills Health System 15236
St Clair Hosp 15243
St Francis Med Ctr 15201
UPMC-Passavant Hosp 15237
UPMC, Presbyterian 15213
Veterans Affairs Med Ctr (Highland Dr) 15206
Veterans Affairs Med Ctr 15240
Western Pennsylvania Hosp 15224

Hotels/Motels

Doubletree 15222
Hilton & Towers 15222
Holiday Inn Select, Univ Ctr 15213
Marriott Greentree 15205
Ramada Plaza Suites 15219
Sheraton Station Square 15219
The Westin William Penn 15219

Military Installations

U S Army Corps of Engineers 15222

Pittsburgh Valley 17516
Pittsfield 16340
Pittston (Twp) 18640
Pittston 18640-44
For specific ZIP Codes call (888) 275-8777, or your local postmaster.
Pittston Junction (Part of Wilkes-Barre) 18705
Pittsville 16374
Plainfield, *Northampton* (Twp) 18064
Plainfield, *Cumberland* 17081
Plain Grove (Twp) 16156
Plains♦ 18705
Plainsville 18705
Plainview 17325
Planebrook 19355
Plank 16938
Platea 16417
Plateau Heights 16335
Plattsville 16646
Plaza (Part of Butler)‡ 16001
Plaza Heights (Part of Hanover) 17331
Pleasant (Twp) 16365
Pleasant Acres 17044
Pleasant Corners 18235
Pleasant Gap♦ 16823
Pleasant Grove, *Lancaster* 17563
Pleasant Grove, *Washington* 15323
Pleasant Hall 17246
Pleasant Hill, *Cambria* 15738
Pleasant Hill, *Clearfield* (rural) 16839
Pleasant Hill, *Clearfield* 16866
Pleasant Hill, *Delaware* 19063
Pleasant Hill, *Fayette* 15425
Pleasant Hill, *Indiana* 15701
Pleasant Hill, *Lawrence* 16123
Pleasant Hill, *Lebanon*♦ 17042
Pleasant Hill, *York* 17331
Pleasant Hills, *Allegheny* 15236
Pleasant Hills, *Dauphin* 17112
Pleasant Mount 18453
Pleasant Ridge 17228
Pleasant Union 15552
Pleasant Unity 15676
Pleasant Valley, *Potter* (Twp) 16743
Pleasant Valley (Part of Altoona) 16602
Pleasant Valley, *Bucks* 18951
Pleasant Valley, *Fayette* 15425
Pleasant Valley, *Lancaster* 17604
Pleasant Valley, *Schuylkill* 17963
Pleasant Valley, *Westmoreland* 15642
Pleasant Valley Estates 18058
Pleasant View, *Armstrong* 15690
Pleasant View, *Franklin* 17201
Pleasantview, *Juniata* 17082
Pleasant View, *York* 17356
Pleasantville 16341
Pleasureville 17402
Pleasureville Heights 17402
Plowville 19540
Plum (Twp) 16354
Plum 15239
Plumbridge 19056
Plumbsock 15329
Plumcreek (Twp) 15774
Plumer 16301
Plum Run 17238
Plumsock 19073
Plumstead (Twp) 18923
Plumsteadville 18949
Plumville 16246
Plunketts Creek (Twp) 17701
Plymouth, *Montgomery* (Twp) 19401
Plymouth, *Luzerne* 18651
Plymouth Junction (Part of Larksville) 18651
Plymouth Meeting♦ 19462
Plymouth Meeting Mall 19462
Plymouth Valley 19401
Plymptonville♦ 16830
Pocahontas 15552
Pocono (Twp) 18372
Pocono Country Place 18466
Pocono Farms 18466
Pocono Farms East 18466
Pocono Heights 18301
Pocono Lake 18347
Pocono Lake Preserve 18348
Pocono Manor 18349
Pocono Mt. Lake Forest 18328
Pocono Mtn. Lake Estate 18661
Pocono Park 18360
Pocono Pines♦ 18350
Pocono Summit 18346
Pocono Summit Estates 18346
Pocopson 19366
Pogue 17264
Point, *Northumberland* (Twp) 17857
Point, Bedford 15559
Point Breeze (Part of Philadelphia)‡ 19145
Point Breeze (Part of Pittsburgh) 15208
Point Breeze, *Allegheny* 15147
Point Breeze, *Northumberland* 17872
Point Marion 15474
Point Phillip 18014
Point Pleasant 18950
Point Ridge Farms 17011
Point View 16693
Poland 15327
Polk, *Jefferson* (Twp) 15825
Polk, *Monroe* (Twp) 18333
Polk, *Venango* 16342
Polktown 17268
Polk Valley 18055
Pomeroy 19367
Pomeroy Heights 19320
Pond Bank 17201
Pond Creek 18661
Pond Eddy 12770
Pond Hill 18660
Pont 16401
Poplar Grove, *Fayette* 15425
Poplar Grove, *Lancaster* 17543
Porkey 16347
Portage, *Cameron* (Twp) 15834
Portage, *Potter* (Twp) 16720
Portage, *Cambria* 15946
Port Allegany 16743
Port Ann 17882
Port Barnett 15825
Port Blanchard 18640
Port Carbon 17965
Port Clinton 19549
Porter, *Clarion* (Twp) 16242
Porter, *Clinton* (Twp) 17751
Porter, *Huntingdon* (Twp) 16611
Porter, *Lycoming* (Twp) 17740
Porter, *Pike* (Twp) 18301
Porter, *Schuylkill* (Twp) 17980
Porter, *Jefferson* 15767
Porters Sideling 17354
Portersville 16051
Port Griffith 18640
Port Indian 19401
Port Jenkins 18661
Port Kennedy 19406
Portland 18351
Portland Mills 15853
Port Matilda 16870
Port Providence 19453
Port Royal, *Juniata* 17082
Port Royal, *Westmoreland* 15012
Port Trevorton 17864
Port Vue 15133
Possum Hollow (Part of New Beaver) 16157
Potetown 16673
Potosi 17327
Potter, *Beaver* (Twp) 15061
Potter, *Centre* (Twp) 16828
Potter Brook 16950
Pottersdale 16871
Potters Mills 16875
Potterville 18837
Pottsgrove, *Montgomery*♦ 19464
Potts Grove, *Northumberland* 17865
Pottstown 19464-65
For specific ZIP Codes call (888) 275-8777, or your local postmaster.
Pottstown Landing 19464
Pottsville 17901
Powder Mill Village 15677
Powder Valley 18092
Powell 18832
Powells Valley 17032
Powys 17728
Poyntelle 18454
Prentisvale 16731
Prescott 17042
Prescottville 15851
President 16353
Presidential Heights, *Allegheny* 15237
Presidential Heights, *Franklin* 17201
Presque Isle 16505
Presto 15142
Preston, *Wayne* (Twp) 18455
Preston, *Luzerne* 18706
Preston Hill 17935

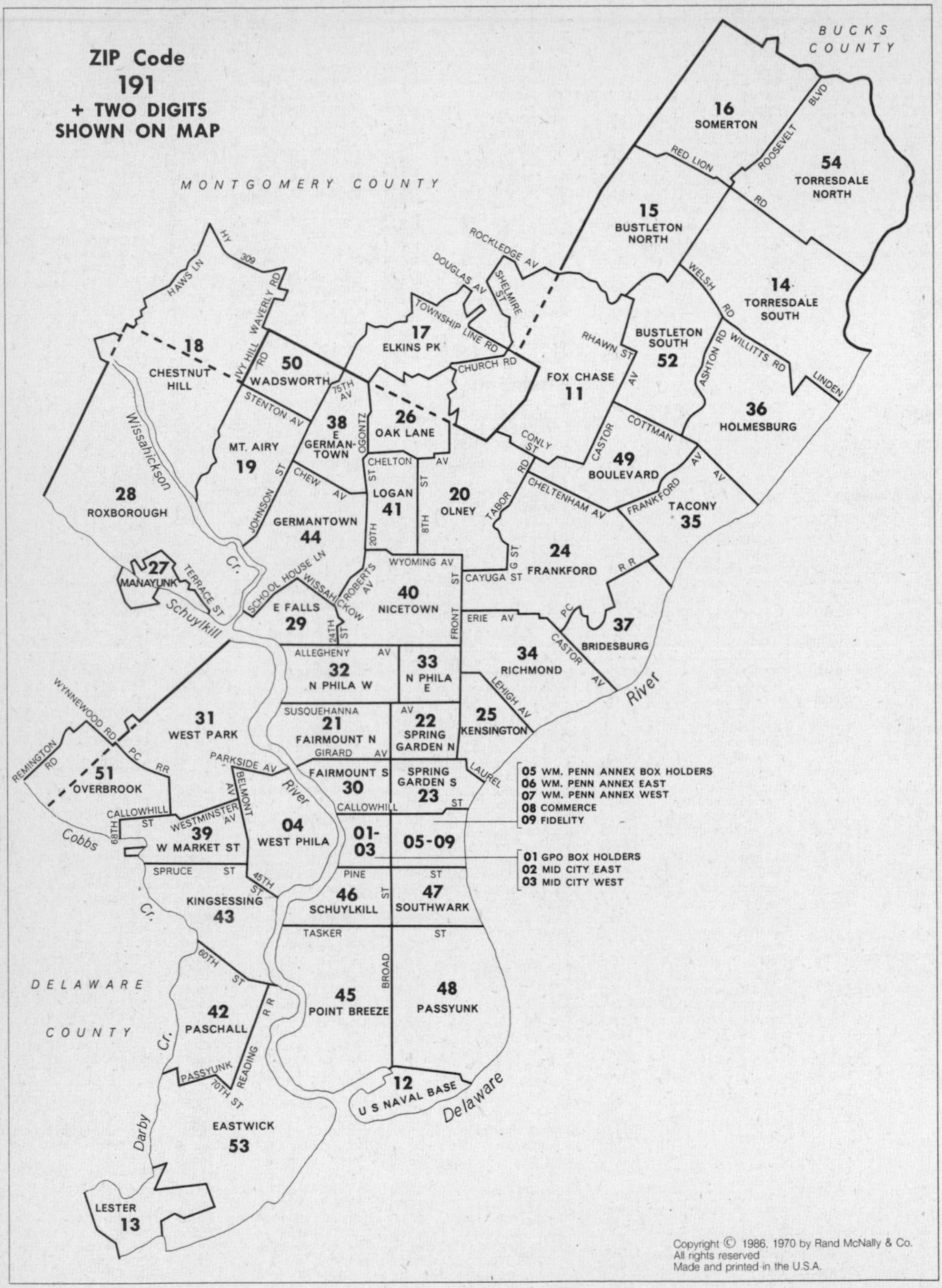

ZIP Code
191
+ TWO DIGITS SHOWN ON MAP

MONTGOMERY COUNTY

BUCKS COUNTY

DELAWARE COUNTY

16 SOMERTON
54 TORRESDALE NORTH
15 BUSTLETON NORTH
14 TORRESDALE SOUTH
52 BUSTLETON SOUTH
17 ELKINS PK
18 CHESTNUT HILL
50 WADSWORTH
11 FOX CHASE
36 HOLMESBURG
26 OAK LANE
38 E GERMAN-TOWN
19 MT. AIRY
49 BOULEVARD
28 ROXBOROUGH
41 LOGAN
20 OLNEY
35 TACONY
44 GERMANTOWN
24 FRANKFORD
27 MANAYUNK
40 NICETOWN
29 E FALLS
37 BRIDESBURG
34 RICHMOND
32 N PHILA W
33 N PHILA E
31 WEST PARK
21 FAIRMOUNT N
22 SPRING GARDEN N
25 KENSINGTON
51 OVERBROOK
30 FAIRMOUNT S
23 SPRING GARDEN S
39 W MARKET ST
04 WEST PHILA
01-03
05-09
46 SCHUYLKILL
47 SOUTHWARK
43 KINGSESSING
45 POINT BREEZE
48 PASSYUNK
42 PASCHALL
12 U S NAVAL BASE
53 EASTWICK
13 LESTER

05 WM. PENN ANNEX BOX HOLDERS
06 WM. PENN ANNEX EAST
07 WM. PENN ANNEX WEST
08 COMMERCE
09 FIDELITY

01 GPO BOX HOLDERS
02 MID CITY EAST
03 MID CITY WEST

Preston Park 18455
Pretoria 15935
Price (Twp) 18301
Priceburg (Part of Dickson City) 18519
Pricedale 15072
Pricetown 19522
Priceville 18417
Primos 19018
Primos-Secane 19018
Primrose, *Schuylkill* 17901
Primrose, *Washington* 15057
Princeton 16101
Pringle 18704
Pritchard 18621
Pritchards Corner 16150
Prittstown 15666
Proctor 17701
Progress♦ 17109
Prompton 18456
Prospect, *Butler* 16052
Prospect (Part of Johnstown) 15901
Prospect Gardens 17602
Prospect Heights 18020
Prospect Park, *Cameron* 15834
Prospect Park, *Delaware* 19076
Prospectville 19002
Prosperity 15329
Providence (Twp) 17560
Providence Downe 19063
Providence Square 19426
Provins Works 15461
Pughtown 19464
Puite 17110
Pulaski, *Beaver* (Twp) 15066
Pulaski, *Lawrence* 16143
Punxsutawney 15767
Purcell 15535
Purchase Line 15729
Puritan, *Cambria* 15946
Puritan, *Fayette* 15458
Putnam (Twp) 16917
Putneyville 16242
Puttstown 16678
Puzzletown 16635
Pyles Mills 16117
Pymatuning (Twp) 16154
Pyrra 16226
Quakake 18245
Quaker Hills (Part of Millersville) 17551
Quaker Lake 18812
Quakertown 18951
Quaker Valley 17307
Quarryville 17566
Quecreek 15555
Queen, *Bedford* 16670
Queen, *Forest* 16351
Queen City 17820
Queens Grant 19067
Queens Run 17745
Queenstown 16041
Quemahoning (Twp) 15563
Quentin 17083
Quicks Bend 18846
Quicktown 18444
Quiggleville 17728
Quincy (Twp) 17268
Quincy 17247
Quincy Hollow 19057
Raccoon (Twp) 15001
Radebaugh 15601
Radnor (Twp) 19087
Rahns 19426
Railroad 17355
Raineytown 15428
Rainsburg 15522
Ralph 15443
Ralpho (Twp) 17872
Ralphton 15563
Ralston 17763
Ramey 16671
Ramona 17067
Ramsay Terrace (Part of Mount Pleasant) 15666
Ramsaytown 15825
Ramsey 17740
Ranavilla 17011
Randolph (Twp) 16327
Rankin 15104
Ranshaw 17866
Ransom (Twp) 18411
Ransom 18653
Rapho (Twp) 17545
Rasler Run 15469
Rasleytown 18072
Rasselas 15870
Rathbun (Part of St. Marys) 15857
Rathmel 15851
Rattigan 16025

Raubsville 18042
Rauchtown 17740
Rauschs 17960
Raven Creek 17814
Raven Run 17946
Ravine 17966
Rawlinsville 17532
Rayburn (Twp) 16201
Raymilton 16342
Raymond 16923
Rayne (Twp) 15747
Raytown 15742
Rea 15312
Reade (Twp) 16619
Reading, *Adams* (Twp) 17350
Reading, *Berks* 19601-12
For specific ZIP Codes call (888) 275-8777, or your local postmaster.
Reading Mines 15563
Reagantown 15679
Reamstown♦ 17567
Reamstown Heights 17567
Rebel Hill 19406
Rebersburg 16872
Rebuck 17867
Rector 15677
Redbank, *Armstrong* (Twp) 16240
Redbank, *Clarion* (Twp) 16224
Red Bank, *Union* 17844
Redbird 15946
Red Bridge 17201
Redclyffe 16239
Red Cross 17823
Redds Mill 15022
Red Gate Farms 18901
Red Hill, *Blair* 16601
Red Hill, *Montgomery* 18076
Redington 18055
Red Lion, *Berks* 18062
Red Lion, *Chester* 19348
Red Lion, *York* 17356
Red Mill 15840
Red Oak 18436
Red Rock, *Luzerne* 17814
Red Rock, *McKean* 16727
Red Rose Gate 19056
Redrun 17517
Redstone (Twp) 15442
Redstone 15438
Reduction 15479
Reeceville 19335
Reed, *Dauphin* (Twp) 17032
Reed, *Northumberland* 17860
Reeder 18938
Reeders 18352
Reeds Gap 17035
Reeds Road 19335
Reedsville♦ 17084
Reels Corners 15926
Reemersville 18426
Reese 16648
Reesedale 16210
Reevesdale 18252
Reflection Lakes 18417
Refton 17568
Regency Park (Part of Plum) 15239
Register 18611
Rehrersburg 19550
Reidsburg 16214
Reiffton♦ 19606
Reightown 16686
Reilly (Twp) 17923
Reillys 16668
Reinerton 17980
Reinholds 17569
Reinoeldville 17046
Reistville 17067
Reitz, *Jefferson* 15824
Reitz, *Somerset* 15924
Relay 17313
Reliance 18964
Rembrant 15728
Renfrew 16053
Rennerdale 15106
Reno (Part of Sugarcreek) 16343
Renovo 17764
Renton (Part of Plum) 15239
Republic 15475
Reserve (Twp) 15212
Reservoir 16648
Retort 16677
Revere 18953
Revloc 15948
Rew 16744
Reward 17062
Rexford 16921
Rexis 15961

Rexmont (Part of Cornwall) 17085
Rextown 18080
Reyburn 18655
Reynolds 18252
Reynoldsdale 15554
Reynolds Heights 16125
Reynoldsville 15851
Rheems♦ 17570
Ribot 16660
Rice (Twp) 18707
Rices Landing 15357
Riceville 16432
Richards Grove 17774
Richardsville 15825
Richboro♦ 18954
Richboro Manor 18954
Richeyville (Part of Centerville) 15358
Richfield 17086
Richhill, *Greene* (Twp) 15380
Rich Hill, *Bucks* 18951
Rich Hill, *Washington* 15347
Richland, *Allegheny* (Twp) 15044
Richland, *Bucks* (Twp) 18951
Richland, *Cambria* (Twp) 15904
Richland, *Clarion* (Twp) 16049
Richland, *Venango* (Twp) 16373
Richland, *Cambria* 16636
Richland, *Lebanon* 17087
Richlandtown 18955
Richmond, *Berks* (Twp) 19530
Richmond, *Crawford* (Twp) 16327
Richmond, *Tioga* (Twp) 16933
Richmond, *Northampton* 18013
Richmond (Part of Philadelphia) 19134
Richmondale 18421
Richmond Furnace 17224
Richvale 17213
Riddlesburg 16672
Riddlewood 19063
Ridgebury (Twp) 16914
Ridge Valley 18960
Ridgeview 17112
Ridgeville 17821
Ridgewood, *Berks* 19508
Ridgewood, *Luzerne* 18705
Ridgewood Farm 19380
Ridgway 15853
Ridley (Twp) 19033
Ridley Farms 19070
Ridley Gardens 19043
Ridley Park, *Cumberland* 17011
Ridley Park, *Delaware* 19078
Riegelsville 18077
Rienze 18853
Rife 17061
Riggles Gap 16601
Riggs 18850
Rillton 15678
Rimer 16259
Rimersburg 16248
Rinely 17363
Ringdale 18614
Ringertown (Part of Murrysville) 15632
Ringgold 15770
Ringing Hill 19464
Ringing Rock Park 19464
Ringtown, *Berks* 19539
Ringtown, *Schuylkill* 17967
Rising Sun 18080
Riterville 16738
Ritzie Village 17112
River Hill 15063
Riverside (Part of Archbald) 18403
Riverside, *Cambria* 15905
Riverside, *Northumberland* 17868
Riverton 18013
River View, *Armstrong* 15690
Riverview, *Clearfield* 16830
River View (Part of New Eagle) 15067
Riverview Acres 18080
Riverview Heights 17011
River View Park 19605
Rixford 16745
Roadside 17268
Roaring Branch 17765
Roaring Brook (Twp) 18444
Roaring Brook Estates 18444
Roaring Creek 17820
Roaring Spring 16673

Robb 15944
Robert Bruce West (Part of Hatboro) 19040
Robertsdale 16674
Robertsville 15767
Robeson (Twp) 19508
Robeson Crossing 19508
Robeson Extension 16693
Robesonia 19551
Robindale Heights 15954
Robin Hood Lakes 18058
Robinson, *Allegheny* (Twp) 15108
Robinson, *Washington* (Twp) 15057
Robinson, *Indiana* 15949
Robinson, *Lawrence* 16132
Rocherty 17042
Rochester 15074
Rochester Mills 15771
Rock 17963
Rockdale, *Crawford* (Twp) 16403
Rockdale, *Bucks* 19007
Rockdale, *Delaware* 19014
Rockdale, *Jefferson* 15840
Rockdale, *Lehigh* 18080
Rockdale Acres 16403
Rockefeller (Twp) 17801
Rock Glen 18246
Rock Hill, *Bucks* 18960
Rockhill, *Lancaster* 17516
Rockhill Furnace 17249
Rockingham 15924
Rock Lake 18453
Rockland, *Berks* (Twp) 19522
Rockland, *Venango* 16374
Rockledge 19111
Rockport 18255
Rockrimmin Ridge 17540
Rock Run 19320
Rockspring 16865
Rockton 15856
Rockton Station 15856
Rocktown 15088
Rockville, *Armstrong* 16226
Rockville, *Cambria* 15956
Rockville, *Chester* 19344
Rockville, *Clarion* 16242
Rockville, *Dauphin* 17110
Rockville, *Juniata* 17059
Rockville, *Mifflin* 17004
Rockville, *Northampton* 18038
Rockwood, *Lebanon* 17046
Rockwood, *Somerset* 15557
Rock Works 15461
Rocky Forest 18623
Rocky Grove (Part of Sugarcreek) 16323
Rocky Hill 19380
Rocky Valley 18036
Roedersville 17963
Rogers Mills 15469
Rogers Stop 15022
Rogerstown 15425
Rogersville 15359
Rogertown 16313
Rohrerstown 17603*
17607†
Rohrsburg 17859
Rolling Glen 19341
Rolling Hills, *Berks* 19607
Rolling Hills, *Lehigh* 18052
Rolling Meadows 15370
Romansville 19320
Romar 15943
Rome, *Bradford* (Twp) 18850
Rome, *Crawford* (Twp) 16354
Rome, *Bradford* 18837
Romney 15446
Ronco 15476
Ronks 17572
Rook (Part of Green Tree) 15220
Roosevelt Mall (Part of Philadelphia) 19149
Roots Crossing 16686
Rosas 12770
Roscoe 15477
Rose (Twp) 15825
Roseann 17063
Rosebud 16627
Roseburg 17074
Rosecrans 17747
Rosedale, *Allegheny* 15147
Rosedale, *Bucks* 18981
Rosedale, *Chester* 19317
Rosedale, *Fayette* 15401
Roseglen 17020
Rosehill (Part of Philadelphia)‡ 19140
Rose Hollow 19067
Rosemont, *Delaware* 19010

Rosemont, *Montgomery* 19010
Rose Point 16101
Roses 16239
Roseto 18013
Rose Valley, *Delaware* 19063
Rose Valley, *Montgomery* 19002
Rose Valley Acres 19063
Roseville, *Jefferson* 15825
Roseville, *Tioga* 16933
Rosewood Gardens 18974
Roslyn, *Chester* 19380
Roslyn, *Montgomery* 19001
Ross, *Allegheny* (Twp) 15237
Ross, *Luzerne* (Twp) 18656
Ross, *Monroe* (Twp) 18353
Ross Common 18353
Rossford 16226
Rossiter 15772
Rossland 18350
Rosslyn Farms 15106
Rossmere 17601
Rossmoyne 17011
Ross Park Mall 15237
Ross Park Malls (Part of Pittsburgh) 15237
Ross Siding 17723
Rosston 16226
Rossville 17358
Rostraver (Twp) 15012
Rote 17751
Rothsville♦ 17543
Rough and Ready 17941
Roulette 16746
Round Knob 16679
Round Top 17325
Roundtown 17404
Rouseville 16344
Rouzerville♦ 17250
Rowes Run 15442
Rowland 18457
Rowland Park 19012
Rowles 15757
Roxborough (Part of Philadelphia) 19128
Roxbury (Part of Johnstown) 15905
Roxbury, *Cumberland* 17055
Roxbury, *Franklin* 17251
Roxbury, *Somerset* 15530
Royal 18446
Royalton 17057
Royer 16693
Royersford 19468
Roystone 16347
Roytown 15501
Rozel Park 18966
Ruble 15478
Ruchsville 18037
Rudytown 17070
Ruff Creek 15329
Ruffs Dale 15679
Ruggles 18636
Rummel 15963
Rummerfield 18853
Rundell 16406
Runville 16823
Rupert 17815
Ruppsville 18106
Rural Ridge 15075
Rural Valley 16249
Ruscombmanor (Twp) 19522
Rush, *Centre* (Twp) 16866
Rush, *Dauphin* (Twp) 17980
Rush, *Northumberland* (Twp) 17821
Rush, *Schuylkill* (Twp) 18252
Rush, *Susquehanna* 18801
Rushland 18956
Rushtown 17821
Rushville 18839
Russell 16345
Russell Hill 18657
Russellton♦ 15076
Russellville, *Chester* 19363
Russellville, *Huntingdon* 16657
Rutan 15341
Rutherford♦ 17111
Rutherford Park 17036
Ruthford 15955
Ruthfred Acres (Part of Bethel Park) 15102
Rutland (Twp) 16933
Rutledge 19070
Rutledgedale 18469
Ryan (Twp) 18214
Ryans Corner 18940
Rydal 19046
Ryde 17051
Rye, *Perry* (Twp) 17053
Rye, *York* 17313
Ryerson Station 15380

*** Area Zip Code** **† Post Office Boxes** **‡ Postal Station** **♦ Census Designated Place** *Italic Type* **County**

Place	ZIP
Ryot	15521
Rywal Park	19020
Sabinsville	16943
Sabula	15801
Sackett	16735
Saco, *Bradford*	18848
Saco, *Lackawanna*	18436
Sacramento	17968
Saddle Brook	18101
Saddlebrook Village I and II	19565
Sadlers Corner	16301
Sadsbury, *Chester* (Twp)	19369
Sadsbury, *Crawford* (Twp)	16316
Sadsbury, *Lancaster* (Twp)	17509
Sadsburyville	19369
Saegersville	18053
Saegertown	16433
Safe Harbor	17516
Sagamore, *Armstrong*	16250
Sagamore, *Fayette*	15446
Sagamore Hills	18101
Saginaw	17347
Sagon	17872
St. Augustine	16636
St. Benedict	15773
St. Boniface	16675
St. Charles	16242
St. Clair, *Westmoreland* (Twp)	15954
St. Clair (Part of Pittsburgh)	15210
St. Clair, *Schuylkill*	17970
St. Clair, *Westmoreland*	15601
St. Clairsville	16667
St. Davids	19087
St. George	16374
St. Johns	18247
St. Joseph	18818
St. Lawrence, *Berks*	19606
St. Lawrence, *Cambria*	16668
St. Leonard	18940
St. Marys	15857
St. Michael	15951
St. Nicholas	17948
St. Paul	15552
St. Peters	19470
St. Petersburg	16054
St. Thomas	17252
St. Vincent Shaft	15650
Salco	15530
Salem, *Clarion* (Twp)	16232
Salem, *Luzerne* (Twp)	18603
Salem, *Wayne* (Twp)	18444
Salem, *Westmoreland* (Twp)	15601
Salem, *Clearfield*	15801
Salem, *Franklin*	17201
Salem, *Mercer*	16125
Salem, *Snyder*	17870
Salem Harbor	19020
Salemville	16664
Salford (Twp)	18969
Salford	18957
Salford Heights	19438
Salfordville	18958
Salida (Part of Baldwin)	15227
Salina	15680
Salisbury, *Lancaster* (Twp)	17535
Salisbury, *Lehigh* (Twp)	18103
Salisbury, *Somerset*	15558
Salisbury Heights	17527
Salix	15952
Salladasburg	17740
Salona	17767
Saltillo	17253
Saltlick (Twp)	15469
Saltsburg	15681
Salunga	17538
Saluvia	17228
Sample Run (Part of Clymer)	15728
Sampson	15063
Sanatoga♦	19464
Sanatoga Park	19464
Sanbourn	16651
Sandbeach	17033
Sand Hill, *Lebanon*♦	17046
Sandhill, *Monroe*	18354
Sand Hill, *Westmoreland*	15666
Sand Patch	15552
Sand Springs	18222
Sandts Eddy	18040
Sandy♦	15801
Sandy Bank	19063
Sandy Creek, *Mercer* (Twp)	16130
Sandycreek, *Venango* (Twp)	16323
Sandy Creek, *Allegheny*	15147
Sandy Hill	19401
Sandy Hollow	16248
Sandy Lake	16145
Sandy Plains	15322
Sandy Ridge	16677
Sandy Ridge Acres	18901
Sandy Run, *Bucks*	19067
Sandy Run, *Greene*	15338
Sandy Run, *Luzerne*	18224
Sandy Shore	18428
Sandy Valley	15851
Sandyville	18324
Sanford	16340
Sankertown	16630
Sarah Furnace	16248
Sardis (Part of Murrysville)	15668
Sartwell	16731
Sarver	16055
Sarverville	16055
Sassamansville	19472
Satterfield	18614
Satterfield Junction	18614
Saucon Acres	18034
Saulsburg	16652
Saville (Twp)	17037
Saville	17074
Sawtown	16301
Sawyer City	16701
Saxonburg	16056
Saxton	16678
Saybrook	16347
Saylorsburg	18353
Sayre	18840
Scalp Level	15963
Scammells Corner	19067
Scandia	16345
Scanlan Hill	15938
Scenery Hill	15360
Schaefferstown	17088
Schellsburg	15559
Schenkel	19464
Schenley	15682
Schenley Heights (Part of Pittsburgh)	15219
Scherersville	18104
Schlusser♦	17013
Schnecksville♦	18078
Schoeneck, *Lancaster*	17578
Schoeneck, *Northampton*	18064
Schoenersville	18103
Schoentown (Part of Port Carbon)	17965
Schofer	19530
Schollard	16137
School Lane	17603
School Lane Hills	17604
School Valley Farms	17520
Schubert	19507
Schultzville, *Berks*	19504
Schultzville, *Lackawanna*	18411
Schuster Heights	16229
Schuyler	17772
Schuylkill, *Chester* (Twp)	19460
Schuylkill, *Schuylkill* (Twp)	17952
Schuylkill (Part of Philadelphia)‡	19146
Schuylkill Haven	17972
Schuylkill Hills	19401
Schwenksville	19473
Sciota	18354
Sconnelltown	19380
Scotch Hill	16233
Scotch Hollow	16666
Scotia (Part of Jefferson)	15025
Scotland	17254
Scotrun	18355
Scott, *Allegheny* (Twp)	15106
Scott, *Columbia* (Twp)	17815
Scott, *Lackawanna* (Twp)	18447
Scott, *Lawrence* (Twp)	16101
Scott, *Wayne* (Twp)	18462
Scott Center	18462
Scottdale	15683
Scott Haven	15083
Scottsville	15001
Scranton	18501-05 18508-15
For specific ZIP Codes call (888) 275-8777, or your local postmaster.	
Scrubgrass (Twp)	16373
Scullton	15557
Scyoc	17021
Seamentown	15729
Seanor	15953
Searights	15401
Sebring	16930
Secane	19018
Seek (Part of Coaldale)	18218
Seelyville	18431
Seemsville	18067
Seger	15627
Seidersville	18015
Seipstown	18031
Seisholtzville	18062
Seitzland	17327
Seitzville	17360
Selea	17264
Selinsgrove	17870
Sellersville	18960
Seltzer	17974
Seminole	16253
Seneca♦	16346
Seneca Valley	15642
Sereno	17846
Sergeant (Twp)	16740
Sergeant	16735
Seven Fields	16046
Seven Hills	18837
Seven Pines	17082
Sevenpoints	17801
Seven Springs	15622
Seven Stars, *Adams*	17325
Seven Stars, *Juniata*	17062
Seven Valleys	17360
Seward	15954
Sewickley, *Westmoreland* (Twp)	15637
Sewickley, *Allegheny*	15143
Sewickley Heights	15143
Sewickley Hills	15143
Seybertown	16028
Seyfert	19508
Shade (Twp)	15926
Shade Gap	17255
Shadeland	16435
Shades Glen	18661
Shade Valley	17213
Shadle	17853
Shado-wood Village	15701
Shady Acres	17834
Shady Grove	17256
Shady Plain	15613
Shadyside (Part of Pittsburgh)‡	15232
Shaffer	15801
Shaffers Corner	15401
Shaffersville	16652
Shaft, *Schuylkill*	17976
Shaft, *Somerset*	15530
Shafton	15642
Shaler (Twp)	15116
Shamokin (Twp)	17860
Shamokin	17872
Shamokin Dam	17876
Shamrock, *Fayette*	15401
Shamrock, *Somerset*	15557
Shamrock Station	19539
Shaner	15642
Shanesville	19512
Shankles (Part of Du Bois)‡	15801
Shanksville	15560
Shankweilers	18069
Shannondale	16240
Shannon Heights	15147
Shanor Heights	16001
Sharon, *Potter* (Twp)	16748
Sharon, *Mercer*	16146
Sharon Center	16748
Sharon Hill	19079
Sharon Park (Part of Sharon Hill)	19079
Sharpsburg, *Allegheny*	15215
Sharpsburg, *Huntingdon*	17002
Sharps Hill	15215
Sharpsville	16150
Sharrertown	15427
Shartlesville	19554
Shavertown, *Delaware*	19061
Shavertown, *Luzerne*	18708
Shawanese (Part of Harveys Lake)	18654
Shaw Mines	15552
Shawmut	15823
Shawnee on Delaware	18356
Shawtown	15642
Shawville	16873
Shay	16226
Sheakleyville	16151
Shearersburg	15613
Sheatown	18634
Sheffield♦	16347
Sheffield Heights	15001
Sheffield Terrace	15001
Sheffield Village	19401
Shehawken	18462
Shellsville	17028
Shelly	18951
Shellytown	16693
Shelocta	15774
Shelvey	15846
Shenandoah	17976
Shenandoah Heights♦	17976
Shenandoah Junction	17949
Shenango, *Lawrence* (Twp)	16101
Shenango, *Mercer* (Twp)	16159
Shenango, *Mercer*	16125
Shenango Valley Mall (Part of Hermitage)	16148
Shenks Ferry	17309
Shepherd Hills	18101
Shepherdstown	17055
Sheppton	18248
Sheraden (Part of Pittsburgh)	15204
Sheridan, *Lebanon*	17073
Sheridan, *Schuylkill*	17980
Sherman	18847
Shermans Dale	17090
Shermansville	16316
Sherrett	16218
Sherwood Acres	15061
Sheshequin (Twp)	18848
Sheshequin	18850
Shetters Grove	17405
Shickshinny	18655
Shieldsburg	15670
Shillington	19607
Shiloh, *Clearfield*	16881
Shiloh, *York*♦	17404
Shiloh East	17405
Shimerville	18049
Shimpstown	17236
Shindle	17841
Shinglehouse	16748
Shingletown	16801
Shintown	17764
Shipmans Eddy	16365
Shippen, *Cameron* (Twp)	15834
Shippen, *Tioga* (Twp)	16901
Shippensburg	17257
Shippenville	16254
Shippingport	15077
Ships Parts Control Center, USN	17055
Shiremanstown	17011
Shirks Corner	19473
Shirley (Twp)	17066
Shirleysburg	17260
Shoaf	15478
Shocks Mills	17547
Shoemaker	15946
Shoemakers, *Monroe*	18301
Shoemakers, *Schuylkill*	17948
Shoemakersville	19555
Shohola	18458
Shope Gardens	17057
Shorbes Hill	17331
Shortsville	16935
Shrader	17084
Shrewsbury, *Lycoming* (Twp)	17737
Shrewsbury, *Sullivan* (Twp)	17758
Shrewsbury, *York* (Twp)	17327
Shrewsbury, *York*	17361
Shumans	17815
Shunk	17768
Sickles Corner	16601
Siddonsburg	17019
Sidman	15955
Siegfried (Part of Northampton)	18067
Sigel	15860
Siglerville	17063
Sigmund	18092
Silkworth	18621
Silvara	18623
Silver Creek	17959
Silverdale	18962
Silver Ford Heights	17066
Silver Lake, *Bucks*	18940
Silver Lake, *Susquehanna*	18812
Silver Lake, *Wayne*	18469
Silver Lake, *York*	17339
Silver Spring, *Cumberland* (Twp)	17055
Silver Spring, *Lancaster*	17575
Silverville	16055
Simmonstown	17527
Simpson	18407
Singersville	17018
Sinking Spring	19608
Sinking Valley	16686
Sinnemahoning	15861
Sinsheim	17362
Sipesville	15561
Siqusca	19376
Sitka	15431
Siverly (Part of Oil City)	16301
Six Mile Run	16679
Six Points	16049
Sixty-Ninth Street Center	19082
Sizerville	15834
Skelp	16601
Skeltontown	16403
Skidmore	16101
Ski Haven Lake Estates	18326
Skinners Eddy	18623
Skippack♦	19474
Skyline Heights	17402
Skyline View♦	17112
Skytop	18357
Sky View	18426
Slab	17302
Slabtown	17268
Slackwater	17551
Slatedale	18079
Slatefield	18038
Slateford	18343
Slate Hill	17314
Slate Lick	16229
Slate Run	17769
Slate Valley	18038
Slateville	19529
Slatington	18080
Slickport	16646
Slickville	15684
Sligo	16255
Slippery Rock, *Lawrence* (Twp)	16101
Slippery Rock, *Butler*	16057
Slippery Rock Park	16057
Slocum (Twp)	18660
Slocum Corners	18660
Slovan	15078
Smallwood (Part of California)	15423
Smethport	16749
Smicksburg	16256
Smiley	15478
Smith, *Washington* (Twp)	15021
Smith, *Indiana*	15717
Smith Bridge	15380
Smithdale	15089
Smithfield, *Bradford* (Twp)	18831
Smithfield, *Monroe* (Twp)	18335
Smithfield, *Fayette*	15478
Smithfield, *Huntingdon*	16652
Smith Gardens	17345
Smithland	16242
Smithmill	16680
Smithport	15742
Smiths	17362
Smiths Corner	18950
Smiths Corners	16374
Smiths Ferry (Part of Ohioville)	15059
Smithton	15479
Smithtown	18947
Smithville	17560
Smock	15480
Smokerun	16681
Smoketown, *Bucks*	18951
Smoketown, *Franklin*	17222
Smoketown, *Lancaster*	17576
Smullton	16872
Smyerstown	15772
Smyrna	17509
Snake Spring (Twp)	15537
Snedekerville	16914
Snively Corners	16232
Snowball Gate	19056
Snowden	15129
Snowdenville	19475
Snow Shoe (Twp)	16829
Snow Shoe	16874
S. N. P. J. (Slovene National Benefit Society)	16120
Snyder, *Blair* (Twp)	16686
Snyder, *Jefferson* (Twp)	15824
Snyder Corner	17356
Snyders	17960
Snydersburg	16235
Snydersville	18360
Snydertown, *Centre*	16841

Snydertown, *Northumberland* 17877
Snydertown, *Westmoreland* 15620
Snyderville 16222
Social Island 17201
Soho (Part of Pittsburgh) 15219
Soldier 15851
Solebury 18963
Somerset, *Washington* (Twp) 15330
Somerset, *Somerset* 15501
Somers Lane 16929
Somerton (Part of Philadelphia)‡ 19116
Somerville 16028
Sonestown 17770
Sonman 15946
Soradoville 17841
Soudersburg 17577
Souderton 18964
Soukesburg 15956
South Abington (Twp) 18410
South Altoona (Part of Altoona) 16602
Southampton, *Bedford* (Twp) 15535
Southampton, *Cumberland* (Twp) 17257
Southampton, *Franklin* (Twp) 17244
Southampton, *Somerset* (Twp) 15552
Southampton, *Bucks* 18966
South Annville (Twp) 17042
South Auburn 18630
South Beaver (Twp) 16115
South Bend (Twp) 15774
South Bend 15686
South Bethlehem 16242
South Bradford 16701
South Buffalo (Twp) 16229
South Canaan (Twp) 18472
South Canaan 18459
South Carnegie 15106
South Centre (Twp) 17815
South Clarksville 15322
South Coatesville 19320
South Connellsville 15425
South Coventry (Twp) 19464
South Creek (Twp) 16925
Southdale 18655
South Duquesne (Part of Duquesne) 15110
Southeastern (Part of Devon) 19397-99
For specific ZIP Codes call (888) 275-8777, or your local postmaster.
South Easton (Part of Easton) 18042
South Eaton 18657
South Enola 17025
South Erie (Part of Erie)‡ 16508
South Fayette (Twp) 15064
South Fork 15956
South Franklin (Twp) 15301
South Gibson 18842
South Greensburg 15601
South Hanover (Twp) 17033
South Heidelberg (Twp) 19565
South Heights 15081
South Hermitage 17555
South Hills (Part of Dormont) 15216
South Hills, *Mifflin* 17044
South Hills Village 15241
South Huntingdon (Twp) 15089
South Lakemont 16602
Southland 4 Seasons Centre (Part of Pleasant Hills) 15236
South Lebanon (Twp) 17042
South Londonderry (Twp) 17010
South Mahoning (Twp) 15747
South Manheim (Twp) 17972
South Media 19063
South Middleton (Twp) 17007
Southmont 15905
South Montrose 18843
South Mountain 17261
South New Castle 16101
South Newton (Twp) 17266
South Park (Twp) 15129
South Philipsburg 16866
South Pottstown 19464
South Pymatuning (Twp) 16150
South Renovo 17764
South Rockwood 15557
South Shenango (Twp) 16134
Southside (Part of Bethlehem)‡ 18015
South Side (Part of Pittsburgh) 15203
South Side (Part of Scranton) 18505
South Side, *Butler* 16001
South Sterling 18460
South Strabane (Twp) 15301
South Tamaqua 18252
South Temple 19560
South Towanda 18848
South Union (Twp) 15401
South Uniontown 15401
South Versailles (Twp) 15028
Southview 15361
Southwark (Part of Philadelphia)‡ 19147
South Waverly 14892
Southwest, *Warren* (Twp) 16354
Southwest, *Westmoreland* 15685
Southwest Greensburg 15601
Southwest Madison (Twp) 17047
South Whitehall (Twp) 18104
South Williamsport 17702
South Woodbury (Twp) 16664
Southwood Hills 17403
Spaces Corners 16201
Spangenberg Lake 18436
Spangler 15775
Spangsville 19512
Sparta, *Crawford* (Twp) 16434
Sparta, *Washington* 15329
Spartansburg 16434
Spears Grove 17021
Speedwell 17543
Speers 15012
Spike Island 10000
Spillway Lake 15473
Spindley City 16641
Spinnerstown 18968
Spinnlers Point 18464
Split Rock 18624
Sporting Hill, *Cumberland* 17055
Sporting Hill, *Lancaster* 17545
Sportsburg 15767
Spraggs 15362
Sprankle Mills 15776
Spring, *Berks* (Twp) 19609
Spring, *Centre* (Twp) 16823
Spring, *Crawford* (Twp) 16435
Spring, *Perry* (Twp) 17040
Spring, *Snyder* (Twp) 17812
Spring Bank 16872
Springboro 16435
Spring Brook (Twp) 18444
Spring Church 15686
Spring City 19475
Spring Creek, *Elk* (Twp) 15853
Spring Creek, *Lehigh* 18011
Spring Creek, *Warren* 16436
Springdale (Twp) 15049
Springdale 15144
Springdell 19320
Springettsbury (Twp) 17402
Springetts Manor-Yorklyn♦ 17402
Springfield, *Bradford* (Twp) 18831
Springfield, *Bucks* (Twp) 18951
Springfield, *Erie* (Twp) 16443
Springfield, *Fayette* (Twp) 15464
Springfield, *Huntingdon* (Twp) 17264
Springfield, *Mercer* (Twp) 16137
Springfield, *Montgomery* (Twp) 19118
Springfield, *York* (Twp) 17327
Springfield, *Bradford* 16914
Springfield, *Cumberland* 17241
Springfield, *Delaware*♦ 19064
Springfield Falls 16137
Springfield Mall 19064
Spring Garden (Part of Mount Pleasant) 15666
Spring Garden (Part of Philadelphia)‡ 19122
Spring Garden, *Bucks* 18940
Spring Garden, *Lancaster* 17535
Spring Garden, *Union* 17810
Spring Garden, *York* 17403
Spring Glen 17978
Spring Grove 17362
Springhill, *Fayette* (Twp) 15478
Springhill, *Greene* (Twp) 15352
Spring Hill (Part of Pittsburgh) 15212
Springhill, *Bradford* 18853
Spring Hill, *Cambria* 15946
Spring Hill, *Delaware* 19018
Springhope 15559
Spring House♦ 19477
Springhouse Farms 18104
Spring Meadow 15554
Spring Meadows 19565
Spring Mill 19428
Spring Mills 16875
Springmont 19609
Spring Mount, *Huntingdon* 16877
Spring Mount, *Montgomery*♦ 19478
Spring Run 17262
Springs 15562
Springtown, *Bucks* 18081
Springtown, *Franklin* 17221
Springtown, *Luzerne* 18707
Springtown, *Northumberland* 17777
Springvale 17356
Spring Valley, *Berks* 19560
Spring Valley, *Bucks* 18901
Spring Valley, *Clearfield* 16878
Spring Valley, *Northampton* 18015
Spring Valley Farms 18901
Springville, *Cumberland* 17007
Springville, *Lancaster* 17535
Springville, *Susquehanna* 10044
Springville 16342
Sproul 16682
Spruce Creek 16683
Spruce Hill 17082
Sprucetown 15474
Spry♦ 17403
Squab Hollow 15846
Square Corner 17325
Squirrel Hill (Part of Pittsburgh)‡ 15217
Stack Town 17502
Stafore Estates 18017
Stahlstown 15687
Stairville 18660
Stalker 12741
Standard (Part of Mount Pleasant) 15666
Standard Shaft 15666
Standing Stone (Twp) 18853
Standing Stone 18854
Stanhope 17963
Stanley 15801
Stanleys Corner 16301
Stanton, *Jefferson* 15825
Stanton, *Luzerne* 15825
Stanton Heights (Part of New Stanton) 15672
Stanton Heights (Part of Pittsburgh) 15201
Stanwood Gardens 19020
Star Brick 16365
Starford 15777
Star Junction 15482
Starkville 18657
Starlight 18461
Starners Station 17324
Starr, *Forest* 16353
Starr, *Warren* 16420
Starrucca 18462
Starview 17347
Starview Heights 17402
State College 16801
16803-05
For specific ZIP Codes call (888) 275-8777, or your local postmaster.
State Hill, *Berks* 19608
State Hill, *Chester* 17527
State Line, *Bedford* 15545
Stateline, *Erie* 16428
State Line, *Franklin* 17263
Station #5 (Part of Millcreek)‡ 16506
Steamburg 16424
Steam Valley 17771
Steel City 18015
Steelstown 17003
Steelton 17113
Steelville 19370
Steene 18472
Steinbachs Corner 18847
Steinsburg 18951
Steinsville 19529
Stemlersville 18235
Sterling, *Wayne* (Twp) 18445
Sterling, *Clearfield* 16651
Sterling, *Wayne* 18463
Sterling Run 15832
Sterlingworth 18104
Sterrettania 16415
Stetlersville 18069
Steuben (Twp) 16404
Stevens, *Bradford* (Twp) 18854
Stevens, *Lancaster* 17578
Stevens Point 18847
Stevenstown 17019
Stevensville 18845
Stewardson (Twp) 17729
Stewart (Twp) 15470
Stewart Run 16341
Stewartstown 17363
Stewartsville 15642
Stickney 16701
Sticks 17329
Stiefler Corner 16670
Stier 18013
Stifflertown 15724
Stiles 18052
Stiles Hill 16943
Still Creek 18252
Stillwater 17878
Stillwater Lake Estates 18346
Stiltz 17327
Stines Corner 18066
Stobo 15061
Stockdale 15483
Stockertown 18083
Stockton 18201
Stockton Number Eight 18201
Stockton Number Seven 18201
Stockton Number Six 18201
Stoddartsville 18610
Stokesdale 16901
Stoneboro 16153
Stone Church 18343
Stone Glen 17018
Stoneham 16313
Stone Hill 17516
Stone House 16258
Stonehurst 19006
Stonerstown 16678
Stonersville 19508
Stonetown 19508
Stonevilla 15601
Stoneybreak 17267
Stonington 17801
Stonybrook 17402
Stonybrook Heights 17402
Stonycreek, *Cambria* (Twp) 15904
Stonycreek, *Somerset* (Twp) 15541
Stony Creek Mills 19606
Stonyfork 16901
Stony Point, *Bucks* 18930
Stony Point, *Crawford* 16316
Stony Point, *Franklin* 17262
Stony Point, *Greene* 15344
Stony Run 19557
Stormstown 16870
Stormville 18360
Stouchsburg 19567
Stoufferstown 17201
Stoughstown 17257
Stover 16686
Stoverdale 17036
Stoverstown 17362
Stowe (Twp) 15136
Stowell 18623
Stoystown 15563
Straban (Twp) 17325
Strabane 15363
Strafford 19087
Strangford 15717
Strasburg (Twp) 17602
Strasburg 17579
Strattanville 16258
Strausstown 19559
Strawberry Ridge 17821
Strawberry Square (Part of Harrisburg) 17101
Strawbridge 17758
Strickersville 19350
Strickhousers 17360
Stricklerstown 17073
Strinestown 17345
Stringtown, *Armstrong* 16226
Stringtown, *Greene* 15320
Strobleton 16353
Strodes Mills 17044
Stronach 16833
Strong 17851
Strongstown 15957
Stroud (Twp) 18360
Stroudsburg 18360
Stroudsburg West 18360
Studa 15312
Stull 18636
Stump Creek 15863
Stumptown 16666
Sturgeon 15082
Sturgis (Part of Archbald) 18447
Suburban Village 19380
Suedburg 17963
Sugarcreek, *Armstrong* (Twp) 16025
Sugarcreek, *Venango* 16323
Sugarcreek (Part of Sugarcreek) 16323
Sugar Grove, *Mercer* (Twp) 16125
Sugar Grove, *Warren* 16350
Sugar Hill 15824
Sugarloaf, *Columbia* (Twp) 17814
Sugarloaf, *Luzerne* (Twp) 18251
Sugarloaf, *Luzerne* 18249
Sugar Notch 18706
Sugar Run 18846
Sugartown 19355
Sullivan (Twp) 16932
Summerdale 17093
Summerhill, *Cambria* (Twp) 15921
Summerhill, *Crawford* (Twp) 16406
Summerhill, *Cambria* 15958
Summer Hill, *Columbia* 18603
Summerhill, *Lancaster* 19362
Summerson 15821
Summersville 18822
Summerville 15864
Summit, *Butler* (Twp) 16001
Summit, *Crawford* (Twp) 16316
Summit, *Erie* (Twp) 16509
Summit, *Potter* (Twp) 16720
Summit, *Somerset* (Twp) 15552
Summit, *Cambria* 16630
Summit, *McKean* 16701
Summit Grove Camp (Part of New Freedom) 17349
Summit Hill 18250
Summit Lawn 18103
Summit Mills 15552
Summit Station 17979
Sumneytown 18084
Sunbrook 16635
Sunbury 17801
Suncliff 15765
Sundale 18920
Sunderlinville 16943
Sunnybrook 19075
Sunnyburn 17302
Sunny Point 18428
Sunnyside (Part of Cleona) 17042
Sunny Side, *Allegheny* 15063
Sunnyside, *Armstrong* 16201
Sunny Side, *Bedford* 16650
Sunnyside, *Lawrence* 16101
Sunnyside, *Northumberland* 17872
Sunrise Lake 18337
Sunset Acres 15701
Sunset Grove 19380
Sunset Hills (Part of Economy) 15042
Sunset Manor 17405
Sunset Pines (Part of Lock Haven) 17745
Sunset Valley 15642
Sunset Village 18451
Sunshine 18655
Sun Valley 18330
Sun Village (Part of Chester) 19013
Sunville 16317
Superior, *Fayette* 15417
Superior, *Westmoreland* 15627
Suplee 19371
Surveyor Mine 16830
Suscon 18641
Susquehanna, *Cambria* (Twp) 15714
Susquehanna, *Dauphin* (Twp) 17109

Susquehanna, *Juniata* (Twp) 17045
Susquehanna, *Lycoming* (Twp) 17701
Susquehanna, *Susquehanna* 18847
Susquehanna Bridge 16830
Susquehanna Trails♦ 17314
Susquehanna Valley Mall 17831
Sutersville 15083
Swales 17049
Swamproot 16127
Swanville 16415
Swart 15364
Swarthmore 19081
Swartzville 17569
Swatara, *Dauphin* (Twp) 17111
Swatara, *Lebanon* (Twp) 17038
Swatara Station 17033
Swede Hill 15601
Swedeland 19401
Sweden (Twp) 16915
Sweden Valley 16915
Swedesburg 19405
Swedetown 16646
Sweeney Plan 15012
Sweeneys Crossroads 15012
Sweet Valley 18656
Swengel 17880
Swiftwater 18370
Swineford (Part of Middleburg) 17842
Swissdale 17745
Swissmont (Part of St. Marys) 15857
Swissvale 15218
Switzer 18066
Swoyersville 18704
Sybertsville 18251
Sycamore 15364
Sygan 15017
Sygan Hill 15017
Sykesville 15865
Sylmar 19362
Sylvan 17236
Sylvan Crest 15061
Sylvan Dell 17702
Sylvan Grove 16858
Sylvan Hills 16648
Sylvania, *Potter* (Twp) 16720
Sylvania, *Bradford* 16945
Sylvis 16692
Syner 17003
Table Rock 17307
Tacony (Part of Philadelphia)‡ 19135
Tafton 18464
Talmage 17580
Talmar 17814
Tamanend 18252
Tamaqua 18252
Tamarack 17764
Tamiment 18371
Tanglewood Lakes 18426
Tanguy 19342
Tank 18249
Tanners Falls 18431
Tannersville 18372
Tannery, *Carbon* 18661
Tannery, *Luzerne* 18661
Tanoma 15728
Tarentum 15084
Tarrs 15688
Tarrtown 16210
Tatamy 18085
Tatesville 15537
Taylor, *Blair* (Twp) 16673
Taylor, *Centre* (Twp) 16686
Taylor, *Fulton* (Twp) 16689
Taylor, *Lawrence* (Twp) 16160
Taylor, *Lackawanna* 18517
Taylor Highlands (Part of Huntingdon) 16652
Tayloria 19363
Taylorstown 15365
Taylorsville 15729
Taylorville 17921
Teagarden Homes 15322
Tearing Run 15748
Teedyuskung Lake 18428
Teepleville 16403
Telescope 16922
Telford 18969
Tell (Twp) 17213
Temple 19560
Templeton 16259
Ten Mile 15311
Tenth Avenue (Part of Bethlehem) 18018
Terminal‡ 19082
Terney Plan 15650
Terrace Acres 18052
Terre Hill 17581
Terry (Twp) 18853
Terrytown 18853
Texas (Twp) 18431
Tharptown 17872
The Hideout 18436
The Meadows 16865
The Pines 17350
The Woodlands 16033
Thieleman Crossroads 16046
Thomas 15330
Thomasdale 15935
Thomas Mills 15935
Thomasville 17364
Thompson, *Fulton* (Twp) 17236
Thompson, *Susquehanna* (Twp) 18462
Thompson, *Susquehanna* 18465
Thompson No. 1, Fayette 15475
Thompson No. 2, Fayette 15468
Thompsontown, *Clearfield* 15753
Thompsontown, *Juniata* 17094
Thompsonville♦ 15317
Thornburg 15205
Thornbury, *Chester* (Twp) 19395
Thornbury, *Delaware* (Twp) 19373
Thorndale♦ 19372
Thorndale Heights 19335
Thornhurst 18424
Thornridge 19054
Thornton 19373
Thornwood 15683
Three Springs 17264
Three Tuns 19002
Throop 18512
Thumptown 16901
Thurston 18657
Tiadaghton 16901
Tidal 16259
Tide 15748
Tidioute 16351
Tiffany 18801
Tilden (Twp) 19526
Tillotson 16438
Timber Lakes 19067
Timberly Heights 16001
Timblin 15778
Timbuck 16738
Time 15337
Tinicum, *Delaware* (Twp) 19029
Tinicum, *Bucks* 18947
Tioga (Twp) 16946
Tioga 16946
Tioga Junction 16946
Tiona 16352
Tionesta 16353
Tippecanoe 15480
Tippery 16301
Tipton♦ 16684
Tire Hill 15959
Titusville 16354
Tivoli 17737
Toboyne (Twp) 17071
Toby, *Clarion* (Twp) 16248
Toby, *Elk* 15846
Toby Farms (Part of Chester) 19015
Tobyhanna (Twp) 18350
Tobyhanna 18466
Tobyhanna Army Depot 18466
Todd, *Fulton* (Twp) 17233
Todd, *Huntingdon* 16685
Toddesville 17325
Toftrees 16803
Toland 17324
Tolna 17349
Tomb 17740
Tompkinsville 18433
Tomstown 17268
Tooley Corners 18444
Topton 19562
Torpedo 16340
Torrance 15779
Torresdale (Part of Philadelphia)‡ 19114
Torresdale Manor 19020
Torrey 18473
Toughkenamon♦ 19374
Towamencin (Twp) 19443
Towamensing (Twp) 18071
Towamensing Trails 18210
Towanda 18848
Tower City 17980
Tower Hill 18914
Tower Hill No. One 15475
Tower Hill No. Two 15417
Towerville 19320
Town Hill 18655
Town Line 18655
Townville 16360
Traces of Lattimore 18328
Trachsville 18071
Trade City 16256
Tradesville 18914
Trafford 15085
Trailwood 18702
Trainer 19013
Transfer 16154
Trappe 19426
Trauger 15650
Traymore 18974
Traymore Manor 18974
Treasure Lake♦ 15801
Tredyffrin (Twp) 19312
Treehaven (Part of Bethel Park)‡ 15102
Trees Mills 15601
Treichlers 18086
Tremont (Twp) 17963
Tremont 17981
Trent 15557
Trenton 17948
Tresckow♦ 18254
Tresslarville 18436
Trevorton♦ 17881
Trevose 19053
Trevose Heights 19047
Trexler 19529
Trexlertown 18087
Trimmer Manor 17405
Trindle Spring 17055
Trinity Park 15301
Tripoli 15927
Triumph (Twp) 16340
Trooper♦ 19401
Trotter 15425
Trout Run 17771
Trouts Corners (Part of Hermitage) 16148
Trouts Crossing 15666
Troutville 15866
Trowbridge 16936
Troxelville 17882
Troy, *Crawford* (Twp) 16404
Troy, *Bradford* 16947
Troy, *Clearfield* 16866
Troy Center 16404
Troy Hill 16201
Truce 17566
Trucksville 18708
Trucksville Gardens 18708
Truemans 16347
Truesdale Terrace 18706
Truittsburg 16224
Truman 15834
Trumbauersville 18970
Trunkeyville 16351
Truxall 15613
Tryonville 16404
Tuckerton 19605
Tullytown 19007
Tulpehocken (Twp) 19550
Tuna 16701
Tunkhannock, *Monroe* (Twp) 18610
Tunkhannock, *Wyoming* 18657
Tunnel 18661
Tunnel Hill 16641
Tunnelton 15681
Turbett (Twp) 17082
Turbot (Twp) 17847
Turbotville 17772
Turkey City 16058
Turkeyfoot, *Franklin* 17201
Turkeyfoot, *Washington* 15332
Turkey Run (Part of Shenandoah) 17976
Turkeytown 15089
Turnersville 16134
Turnip Hole 16373
Turnpike (Part of Shrewsbury) 17361
Turtle Creek 15145
Turtlepoint 16750
Tuscarora, *Bradford* (Twp) 18623
Tuscarora, *Juniata* (Twp) 17035
Tuscarora, *Perry* (Twp) 17062
Tuscarora, *Juniata* 17082
Tuscarora, *Schuylkill*♦ 17982
Tusculam 17257
Tusseyville 16828
Twenty Row 15927
Twilight 15022
Twin Bridge Farm 19380
Twin Bridges 15022
Twin Brooks 17405
Twin Lakes 18458
Twin Oaks, *Adams* 17325
Twin Oaks, *Bucks* 19056
Twin Oaks, *Delaware* 19014
Twin Oaks, *Venango* 16319
Twin Oaks Farms 19014
Twin Rocks 15960
Two Taverns 17325
Tyler 15849
Tylerdale (Part of Washington) 15301
Tyler Hill 18469
Tyler Run-Queens Gate♦ 17403
Tylersburg 16361
Tylersport 18971
Tylersville 17773
Tyre 15126
Tyrone, *Adams* (Twp) 17325
Tyrone, *Perry* (Twp) 17040
Tyrone, *Blair* 16686
Uhlerstown 18972
Uledi 15484
Ulhers 18040
Ulrichtown 17340
Ulster 18850
Ulysses 16948
Unamis 15411
Unicorn 17566
Union, *Adams* (Twp) 17331
Union, *Berks* (Twp) 19508
Union, *Centre* (Twp) 16844
Union, *Clearfield* (Twp) 15856
Union, *Crawford* (Twp) 16335
Union, *Erie* (Twp) 16438
Union, *Fulton* (Twp) 17267
Union, *Huntingdon* (Twp) 17052
Union, *Jefferson* (Twp) 15829
Union, *Lawrence* (Twp) 16101
Union, *Lebanon* (Twp) 17038
Union, *Luzerne* (Twp) 18655
Union, *Mifflin* (Twp) 17004
Union, *Schuylkill* (Twp) 17967
Union, *Snyder* (Twp) 17864
Union, *Tioga* (Twp) 17724
Union, *Union* (Twp) 17889
Union, *Washington* (Twp) 15332
Union, *Lancaster* 17536
Union, *Lancaster* (rural) 17560
Union Center 17724
Union City 16438
Union Dale 18470
Union Deposit 17033
Union Furnace 16686
Union Grove 17519
Union Hill 18235
Union Mills 17004
Union Square 17545
Uniontown, *Fayette* 15401
Uniontown, *Indiana* 15724
Uniontown, *Venango* 16323
Uniontown, *York* 17019
Union Valley, *Lawrence* 16157
Union Valley, *Washington* 15332
Unionville, *Beaver* 15074
Unionville, *Berks* 19518
Unionville, *Butler* 16001
Unionville, *Chester* 19375
Union Water Works 17003
United 15689
Unity, *Westmoreland* (Twp) 15650
Unity (Part of Plum) 15239
Unity House 18373
Unity Junction (Part of Plum) 15239
Unityville 17774
Universal 15235
University City (Part of Philadelphia) 19104
University Heights 18015
University Park (Part of State College) 16802
Upland 19015
Upland Terrace 19004
Upper Allen (Twp) 17055
Upper Augusta (Twp) 17801
Upper Bern (Twp) 19506
Upper Black Eddy 18972
Upper Brownville 17976
Upper Burrell (Twp) 15068
Upper Chichester (Twp) 19061
Upper Darby (Twp) 19082
Upper Darby 19082-83
For specific ZIP Codes call (888) 275-8777, or your local postmaster.
Upper Dublin (Twp) 19034
Upper Exeter 18643
Upper Fairfield (Twp) 17754
Upper Frankford (Twp) 17241
Upper Frederick (Twp) 18074
Upper Gwynedd (Twp) 19454
Upper Hanover (Twp) 18041
Upper Hillville 16248
Upper Lawn 17078
Upper Leacock (Twp) 17540
Upper Lehigh 18224
Upper Macungie (Twp) 18087
Upper Mahanoy (Twp) 17836
Upper Mahantango (Twp) 17941
Upper Makefield (Twp) 18940
Upper Merion (Twp) 19406
Upper Middletown 15480
Upper Mifflin (Twp) 17241
Upper Milford (Twp) 18092
Upper Mill (Part of Mount Holly Springs) 17065
Upper Moreland (Twp) 19090
Upper Mount Bethel (Twp) 18013
Upper Nazareth (Twp) 18064
Upper Orchard 19056
Upper Oxford (Twp) 19363
Upper Paxton (Twp) 17061
Upper Peanut 15480
Upper Pottsgrove (Twp) 19464
Upper Providence, *Delaware* (Twp) 19063
Upper Providence, *Montgomery* (Twp) 19456
Upper Reese 16648
Upper Sagon 17877
Upper Salford (Twp) 18957
Upper Saucon (Twp) 18034
Upper Southampton (Twp) 18966
Upper St. Clair♦ 15241
Upperstrasburg 17265
Upper Tulpehocken (Twp) 19559
Upper Turkeyfoot (Twp) 15557
Upper Two Lick 15701
Upper Tyrone (Twp) 15631
Upper Uwchlan (Twp) 19335
Upper Wheel 15698
Upper Yoder (Twp) 15905
Upton 17225
Uptown (Part of Pittsburgh)‡ 15219
Urban 17830
Urey 15742
Uriah 17324
Ursina 15485
Ursina Junction (Part of Confluence) 15424
Utahville 16627
Utica 16362
Utopia 15613
Uwchlan (Twp) 19341
Uwchlan 19480
Vail 16686
Valemont Heights 15147
Valencia 16059
Valier 15780
Vallamont Hills (Part of Williamsport) 17701
Valley, *Armstrong* (Twp) 16201
Valley, *Chester* (Twp) 19320
Valley, *Montour* (Twp) 17821
Valley Camp (Part of New Kensington) 15068
Valley Falls 19006
Valley Forge 19481-85
For specific ZIP Codes call (888) 275-8777, or your local postmaster.
Valley Forge Estates 19087
Valley Forge Homes 19406
Valley Forge Manor 19460
Valley Furnace 17959
Valley Green Estates 17319
Valley Green Heights 17319
Valley Green West 17319
Valley-Hi 15533
Valley Stream 18707
Valley View, *Centre* 16823
Valley View, *Chester* 19344
Valley View, *Lancaster* 17545
Valley View, *Schuylkill*♦ 17983
Valley View, *York*♦ 17403
Valley View Heights 16226
Van 16319

Van Buren 15329
Vance 15301
Vances Mill 15401
Vanceville 15330
Vanderbilt 15486
Vandergrift 15690
Vandling 18421
Vandyke 17082
Van Emman 15317
Vankirk 15301
Van Meter 15479
Van Ormer 16639
Vanport (Twp) 15009
Van Voorhis 15366
Van Wert 17059
Varden 18436
Vawter 18810
Venango, *Butler* (Twp) 16049
Venango, *Erie* (Twp) 16442
Venango, *Crawford* 16440
Venetia 15367
Venice 15057
Venturetown 16365
Venus 16364
Vera Cruz 18049
Verdilla 17870
Vere Cruz 17569
Vermilion Hill 19054
Vernfield 19438
Vernon, *Crawford* (Twp) 16335
Vernon, *Wyoming* 18657
Vernondale 16505
Vernon Park (Part of Philadelphia) 19144
Verona 15147
Versailles 15132
Vestaburg 15368
Vesta Heights 15333
Veterans Hospital (Part of Pittsburgh)‡ 15240
Veterans Hospital (Part of Wilkes-Barre)‡ 18702
VF Factory Outlet (Part of Wyomissing) 19010
Vicksburg, *Blair* 16648
Vicksburg, *Union* 17883
Victory (Twp) 16342
Victory Heights 16323
Victory Hills 15063
Viewmont Mall (Part of Dickson City) 18519
Village 15241
Village Green 19013
Village Green-Green Ridge♦ 19013
Village of Cross Creek 17402
Village of Olde Hickory 17601
Village of the Four Seasons 18470
Village of Westover 17055
Village Shires♦ 18966
Villa Green 17403
Villa Maria 16155
Villanova 19085
Vinco♦ 15909
Vinemont 17569
Vintage 17562
Vintondale 15961
Violet Hill 17403
Violet Wood 19057
Vira 17044
Virginia Farms 15717
Virginia Hills West 15126
Virginia Mills 17320
Virginville 19564
Voganville 17522
Vogleyville 16001
Volant 16156
Vosburg 18657
Vowinckel 16260
Vulcan 18214
Wadesville 17901
Wadsworth (Part of Philadelphia)‡ 19150
Wagner 17841
Wagnersville 18040
Wagontown 19376
Wahlville 16033
Wahnetah (Part of Jim Thorpe)‡ 18229
Wakena 15681
Walbert 18104
Walcksville 18235
Walden Woods 15126
Walkchalk 16201
Walker, *Centre* (Twp) 16841
Walker, *Huntingdon* (Twp) 16652
Walker, *Juniata* (Twp) 17059
Walker, *Schuylkill* (Twp) 18252
Walkers Mill 15106
Walkertown 15427
Wall 15148
Wallace (Twp) 19343
Wallace Junction (Part of Girard) 16417
Wallaceton 16876
Wallaceville 16354
Wallenpaupack Lake Estates 18436
Waller 17814
Wallingford 19086
Wallis Run 17771
Walls Corners 18414
Wallsville 18414
Walltown 16838
Walmo 16101
Walnut 17082
Walnut Bend 16301
Walnut Bottom 17266
Walnut Gardens 18052
Walnut Grove 17074
Walnut Hill, *Fayette* 15401
Walnut Hill, *Greene* 15327
Walnut Hill, *Montgomery* 19001
Walnutport 18088
Walnuttown 19522
Walsall 15904
Walston 15781
Walston Junction (Part of Punxsutawney) 15767
Walters 18045
Waltersburg 15488
Waltonville 17036
Waltz 15679
Waltz Landing 18428
Wampum 16157
Wanamakers 19529
Wanamie 18634
Wandin 15729
Wanneta 16401
Wapwallopen 18660
Ward, *Tioga* (Twp) 17724
Ward, *Delaware* 19331
Wardville 17062
Warfordsburg 17267
Warminster 18974
Warminster Heights♦ 18974
Warner 15022
Warren, *Bradford* (Twp) 18851
Warren, *Franklin* (Twp) 17236
Warren, *Warren* 16365
Warren Center 18851
Warrendale 15086
Warrensville 17701
Warrington, *York* (Twp) 17019
Warrington, *Bucks* 18976
Warrior Ridge 16669
Warrior Run 18706
Warriors Mark (Twp) 16686
Warriors Mark 16877
Warsaw, *Jefferson* (Twp) 15825
Warsaw (Part of Throop) 18512
Warsaw, *Luzerne* 18702
Warwick, *Bucks* (Twp) 18929
Warwick, *Lancaster* (Twp) 17543
Warwick, *Chester* 19520
Washington, *Armstrong* (Twp) 16218
Washington, *Berks* (Twp) 19512
Washington, *Butler* (Twp) 16061
Washington, *Cambria* (Twp) 15938
Washington, *Clarion* (Twp) 16326
Washington, *Dauphin* (Twp) 17048
Washington, *Erie* (Twp) 16412
Washington, *Fayette* (Twp) 15012
Washington, *Franklin* (Twp) 17268
Washington, *Greene* (Twp) 15370
Washington, *Indiana* (Twp) 15732
Washington, *Jefferson* (Twp) 15840
Washington, *Lawrence* (Twp) 16156
Washington, *Lehigh* (Twp) 18080
Washington, *Lycoming* (Twp) 17810
Washington, *Northampton* (Twp) 18013
Washington, *Northumberland* (Twp) 17867
Washington, *Schuylkill* (Twp) 17963
Washington, *Snyder* (Twp) 17842
Washington, *Westmoreland* (Twp) 15613
Washington, *Wyoming* (Twp) 18657
Washington, *York* (Twp) 17316
Washington, *Cumberland* 17241
Washington, *Washington* 15301
Washington Boro 17582
Washington Crossing 18977
Washington Heights (Part of Lemoyne) 17043
Washington Hill (Part of Pottstown) 19464
Washington Square Gardens 19401
Washingtonville 17884
Wassergass 18055
Waterfall 16689
Waterford, *Erie* 16441
Waterford, *Westmoreland* 15658
Waterford, *York* 17402
Waterloo 17021
Waterloo Mills 19333
Waterman 15748
Waterside 16695
Waterson 16258
Water Street 16611
Waterton 18655
Waterville 17776
Watkins 15775
Watrous 16921
Watrous Corners 18801
Watson, *Lycoming* (Twp) 17740
Watson, *Warren* (Twp) 16351
Watson Farm 16239
Watson Run 16316
Watsontown 17777
Watters 16033
Wattersonville 16218
Watts (Twp) 17020
Wattsburg 16442
Waverly 18471
Wawa (Part of Chester Heights) 19017
Wawaset 19380
Wayland 16335
Waymart 18472
Wayne, *Armstrong* (Twp) 16222
Wayne, *Clinton* (Twp) 17748
Wayne, *Crawford* (Twp) 16314
Wayne, *Dauphin* (Twp) 17032
Wayne, *Erie* (Twp) 16407
Wayne, *Greene* (Twp) 15362
Wayne, *Lawrence* (Twp) 16117
Wayne, *Mifflin* (Twp) 17051
Wayne, *Schuylkill* (Twp) 17933
Wayne, *Delaware* 19087
Waynecastle 17225
Wayne Heights♦ 17268
Waynesboro 17268
Waynesburg 15370
Waynesburg Lakes 15329
Waynesville 17032
Weatherly 18255
Weaverland 17519
Weaversville 18067
Weavertown, *Berks* 19518
Weavertown, *Lancaster* 17505
Weavertown, *Lebanon* 17046
Weavertown, *Washington* 15317
Webster 15087
Webster Mills 17233
Weedville 15868
Wegley 15642
Wehnwood (Part of Altoona) 16601
Weidasville 18078
Weidmanville 17522
Weigelstown♦ 17315
Weikert 17885
Weilersville 18011
Weinel's Crossroads 15656
Weir Lake 18058
Weisel 18944
Weisenberg (Twp) 18066
Weishample 17938
Weissport 18235
Weldbank 16313
Weldon 19006
Wellersburg 15564
Wellington Estates 18901
Welliversville 17815
Wells, *Bradford* (Twp) 16925
Wells, *Fulton* (Twp) 16691
Wellsboro 16901
Wellsboro Junction 16901
Wells Creek 15541
Wells Tannery 16691
Wellsville 17365
Welsh Hill 18470
Welsh Run 17225
Welty 15666
Wendel 15691
Wendover 15601
Wenks 17304
Wentlings Corners 16232
Werleys Corner 18066
Wernersville 19565
Wernersville Heights 19565
Wertz 16693
Wertzville 17055
Wescosville 18106
Wesley 16038
Wesley Chapel 15909
Wesleyville 16510
Wessex Hills 15108
West (Twp) 16669
West Abington (Twp) 18419
West Acres 17837
West Alexander 15376
West Aliquippa (Part of Aliquippa)‡ 15001
West Ambler 19002
West Annville 17003
West Auburn 18623
West Bangor, *Northampton* 18072
West Bangor, *York* 17314
West Beaver (Twp) 17841
West Belt Junction (Part of Pittsburgh) 15230
West Bend 15433
West Berwick (Part of Berwick) 18603
West Bethlehem (Twp) 15345
West Bingham 16923
West Bolivar 15923
West Bowmanstown 18030
West Bradford (Twp) 19335
West Branch, *Potter* (Twp) 16922
West Branch (Part of Barnesboro) 15714
West Brandywine (Twp) 19320
West Bristol 19007
West Brownsville 15417
West Brunswick (Twp) 17961
West Buffalo (Twp) 17844
West Burlington (Twp) 16914
West Burlington 16947
Westbury 15071
West Caln (Twp) 19376
West Cameron 17872
West Carroll (Twp) 15737
West Catasauqua 18052
West Chester 19380-82
For specific ZIP Codes call (888) 275-8777, or your local postmaster.
West Chillisquaque (Twp) 17850
West Clifford 18470
West Cocalico (Twp) 17578
Westcolang 18428
West Conshohocken 19428
West Cornwall (Twp) 17042
West Creek 15834
West Creek Hills 17011
West Cressona (Part of Cressona) 17929
West Damascus 18469
West Decatur 16878
West Deer (Twp) 15044
West Derry 15627
West Donegal (Twp) 17022
West Earl (Twp) 17508
West Easton 18042
West Eldred 16731
West Elizabeth 15088
West Ellwood Junction (Part of Koppel) 16136
West End (Part of Harrisburg) 17102
West End (Part of Pittsburgh) 15220
West End, *Washington* 15301
West Enola 17025
West Fairfield 15944
West Fairview 17025
Westfall (Twp) 18336
West Fallowfield, *Chester* (Twp) 19330
West Fallowfield, *Crawford* (Twp) 16131
West Falls 18615
West Fayetteville 17222
Westfield 16950
Westfield Terrace 17070
West Finley 15377
Westford 16134
West Franklin, *Armstrong* (Twp) 16262
West Franklin, *Bradford* 18832
West Freedom 16049
Westgate Hills 18017
West Goshen (Twp) 19380
West Goshen Hills 19380
West Goshen Park 19380
West Grove 19390
West Hamburg 19526
West Hanover (Twp) 17112
West Hazleton 18201
West Hemlock (Twp) 17821
West Hempfield (Twp) 17601
West Hickory 16370
West Hill 17013
West Hills 17044
West Hills Estates 17701
West Homestead 15120
Westinghouse Village 19029
West Jeannette (Part of Jeannette) 15644
West Jonestown 17038
West Keating (Twp) 16871
West Kittanning 16201
West Lampeter (Twp) 17537
West Lancaster 17603
Westland 15378
West Lawn, *Berks* 19609
West Lawn, *Union* 17837
West Lebanon, *Indiana* 15783
West Lebanon, *Lebanon* 17046
West Leechburg 15656
West Leisenring 15489
West Lenox 18826
West Leroy 17724
West Liberty (Part of Pittsburgh) 15226
West Liberty, *Butler* 16057
West Liberty, *Clearfield* 15801
Westline 16751
West Mahanoy (Twp) 17976
West Mahoning (Twp) 16256
West Manayunk 19151
West Manchester (Twp) 17404
West Manchester Mall (Part of York) 17404
West Manheim (Twp) 17331
West Market (Part of Philadelphia)‡ 19139
West Marlborough (Twp) 19348
West Mayfield 15010
West Mead (Twp) 16335
West Middlesex 16159
West Middletown 15379
West Mifflin 15122-23
For specific ZIP Codes call (888) 275-8777, or your local postmaster.
West Milton 17886
Westminster, *Erie* 16506
Westminster, *Luzerne* 18702
West Monocacy 19518
Westmont, *Cambria* 15905
Westmont, *Lebanon* 17042
West Monterey 16049
Westmont Plan 16201
Westmoreland City 15692
West Moshannon 16651
West Myerstown 17067
West Nanticoke 18634
West Nantmeal (Twp) 19520
West New Kensington 15030
West Newton 15089
West Nicholson 18446
West Norriton♦ 19401
West Nottingham (Twp) 19362
Weston 18256
Weston Place 17976
Westover, *Bucks* 19067
Westover, *Clearfield* 16692
West Overton 15683
Westover Woods 19401
West Park, *Allegheny* 15136

West Park (Part of Philadelphia)‡ 19131
West Pen Argyl 18072
West Penn (Twp) 17960
West Pennsboro (Twp) 17241
West Perry (Twp) 17086
West Philadelphia (Part of Philadelphia)‡ 19104
West Pike 16922
West Pikeland (Twp) 19425
West Pike Run (Twp) 15427
West Pittsburg 16160
West Pittston 18643
West Point, *Cambria* 15942
West Point, *Montgomery* 19486
West Point, *Westmoreland* 15601
Westport 17778
West Pottsgrove 19464
West Providence (Twp) 15537
West Reading 19611
West Renovo 17764
West Ridge 17603
West Rockhill (Twp) 18960
West Sadsbury (Twp) 19365
West Salem (Twp) 16125
West Salisbury 15565
West Scranton (Part of Scranton)‡ 18504
West Shenango (Twp) 16134
Westside (Part of Bethlehem)‡ 18018
West Spring Creek 16407
West Springfield 16443
West St. Clair (Twp) 15521
West Sunbury 16061
West Tarentum (Part of Tarentum) 15084
West Taylor (Twp) 15906
West Telford (Part of Telford) 18969
Westtown 19395
Westtown Acres 19380
West Union 15364
West Valley 16201
West Vandergrift 15690
West View, *Allegheny* 15229
Westview, *Beaver* 15009
Westview Heights 16101
Westville 15824
West Vincent (Twp) 19425
West Warren 13812
West Wayne 19087
West Waynesburg 15370
West Wheatfield (Twp) 15944
West Whiteland (Twp) 19341
West William Penn 17976
West Willow 17583
West Wilmerding 15137
West Winfield 16023
Westwood (Part of Pittsburgh) 15205
Westwood, *Cambria*‡ 15905
Westwood, *Chester* 19320
Westwood Park 19083
West Wyoming 18644
West Wyomissing♦ 19609
West York 17404
West Zollarsville 15345
Wetherills Corner 19460
Wetmore 16735
Wetona 16914
Wexford 15090
Weyant 16655
Wharton, *Fayette* (Twp) 15437
Wharton, *Potter* 16720
Wheatfield (Twp) 17020
Wheatland 16161
Wheatland Hills 17604
Wheat Sheaf 19067
Wheeler 15425
Wheelerville 17724
Whig Hill 16353
Whiskerville 16040
Whitaker 15120
White, *Beaver* (Twp) 15010
White, *Cambria* (Twp) 16639
White, *Indiana* (Twp) 15701
White, *Fayette* 15490
White, *Indiana* 15681
White Bear 19508
White Cottage 15341
White Deer 17887
Whitehall, *Adams* 17340
Whitehall, *Allegheny* 15227
White Hall, *Dauphin* 17110
Whitehall, *Lehigh*♦ 18052
White Hall, *Montour* 17821
Whitehall Mall 18052
Whitehall Park 19401
White Haven 18661
White Hill 17011
White Horse, *Chester* 19073
White Horse, *Lancaster* 17527
White House 15478
Whiteland Crest 19341
Whiteland Farms 19355
Whiteley (Twp) 15370
Whitemarsh (Twp) 19428
Whitemarsh Downs 19075
White Mills 18473
White Oak, *Allegheny* 15131
White Oak, *Lancaster* 17545
White Oak, *Westmoreland* 15068
White Oak Manor 18040
White Oaks 18701
White Pine 17771
Whitesburg 16201
Whites Corner 16927
Whites Crossing 18407
Whites Ferry 18657
Whiteside 16651
Whitesprings 17844
White Squaw Mission 17353
Whitestown 16052
Whites Valley 18453
White Valley (Part of Murrysville) 15632
Whitewood 19057
Whitfield♦ 19609
Whitford Hills 19341
Whitney 15693
Whitney Lake 18428
Whitneyville 16901
Whitpain (Twp) 19422
Whitsett 15473
Wick 16057
Wickerham Manor 15063
Wickerton 19390
Wickham Village 15001
Wickhaven 15492
Wiconisco 17097
Widener College (Part of Chester)‡ 19013
Widnoon 16261
Wiegletown 16101
Wiggans 17948
Wigwam 16731
Wila 17074
Wilawana 18840
Wilber 15563
Wilburton 17888
Wilco Hill 15087
Wilcox 15870
Wild Acres Country Club 18328
Wildcat 16248
Wildwood 15091
Wildwood Terrace 18701
Wiley 17363
Wilgus 15742
Wilkes-Barre (Twp) 18702
Wilkes-Barre 18701-06
18710-73
For specific ZIP Codes call (888) 275-8777, or your local postmaster.
Wilkes Manor 18977
Wilkins (Twp) 15145
Wilkinsburg 15221
Willet 15732
William Penn Annex (Part of Philadelphia)‡ 19106-07
For specific ZIP Codes call (888) 275-8777, or your local postmaster.
William Penn Manor 18020
Williams, *Dauphin* (Twp) 17098
Williams, *Northampton* (Twp) 18042
Williamsburg, *Blair* 16693
Williamsburg, *Clarion* 16214
Williams Grove 17055
Williamson 17270
Williamsport 17701*
17703†
Williamstown, *Dauphin* 17098
Williamstown, *Washington* 16322
Willistown (Twp) 19355
Willopenn 18966
Willowbrook 19061
Willowburn 19085
Willowdale 19348
Willow Grove, *Lawrence* 16101
Willow Grove, *Montgomery*♦ 19090
Willow Grove Naval Air Station 19090
Willow Grove Park 19090
Willow Hill 17271
Willow Lake 17901
Will-O-Wood 19007
Willow Springs, *Columbia* 17815
Willow Springs, *Westmoreland* 15642
Willow Street♦ 17584
Willow View Heights 17584
Wills Creek 15545
Wilmer 19460
Wilmerding 15148
Wilmington, *Lawrence* (Twp) 16105
Wilmington, *Mercer* (Twp) 16142
Wilmore 15962
Wilmore Heights 15958
Wilmot (Twp) 18846
Wilpen 15658
Wilshire Hills, *Lancaster* 17603
Wilshire Hills, *York* 17402
Wilson (Part of Clairton) 15025
Wilson, *Berks* 19608
Wilson, *Northampton* 18042
Wilson Creek 15557
Wilson Heights 18426
Wilsons Corners 19460
Wimmers 18436
Winburne 16879
Windber 15963
Winder Village 19007
Windfall 17724
Wind Gap 18091
Windham, *Bradford* (Twp) 18837
Windham, *Wyoming* (Twp) 18623
Windham Center 18837
Winding Brook Manor 18062
Winding Hill 17055
Winding Hill Heights 17055
Windom 17603
Wind Ridge 15380
Windsor, *Berks* (Twp) 19526
Windsor, *York* (Twp) 17356
Windsor, *York* 17366
Windsor Castle 19526
Windsor Farms 17110
Windsor Park, *Cumberland* 17055
Windsor Park, *York* 17403
Windward Heights 16001
Winfield, *Butler* (Twp) 16023
Winfield, *Union* 17889
Wingate 16823
Wingerton 17268
Winslow (Twp) 15851
Winslow 15767
Winstead 15474
Winterburne 15849
Winterdale 18461
Winterstown 17356
Wintersville 17087
Wireton 15001
Wiscasset 18344
Wishaw 15851
Wismer 18947
Wissahickon Village 19444
Wissingertown 15902
Wissinoming (Part of Philadelphia) 19135
Witinski Villa 18706
Witmer 17585
Wittenberg 15552
Wittmer 15116
Wolf (Twp) 17737
Wolf Creek (Twp) 16127
Wolfdale♦ 15301
Wolfe Store 16872
Wolf Run 16749
Wolfsburg 15522
Wolfs Corners 16353
Wolfs Crossroads 17801
Womelsdorf 19567
Wood (Twp) 16674
Wood 16694
Woodale 18301
Woodbine 17302
Woodbourne♦ 19047
Woodbridgetown 15478
Woodbury, *Blair* (Twp) 16693
Woodbury, *Bedford* 16695
Woodchoppertown 19512
Woodcock 16433
Woodcock Grange 16433
Woodcrest 19380
Wooddale 15425
Woodglen 15442
Woodhaven Estates 15001
Woodhill 18940
Woodland, *Clearfield* 16881
Woodland, *Mifflin* 17084
Woodland Heights 16301
Woodland Park 17701
Woodland View 17402
Woodlawn, *Lancaster* 17603
Woodlawn, *Lehigh* 18104
Woodlawn Park 15001
Woodlyn♦ 19094
Woodlyn Park 19094
Woodrow 15340
Woodruff 15341
Woodside, *Bucks*♦ 19067
Woodside, *Fayette* 15478
Woodside, *Luzerne* 18224
Woods of Sandy Ridge 18901
Woodvale (Part of Johnstown) 15901
Woodvale Heights 15909
Woodville, *Allegheny* 15106
Woodville, *Chester* 19318
Woodward, *Clearfield* (Twp) 16651
Woodward, *Clinton* (Twp) 17745
Woodward, *Lycoming* (Twp) 17744
Woodward, *Centre* 16882
Woodward Acres 15601
Woodycrest 16803
Woolrich 17779
Wopsononock 16636
Worcester 19490
Worden Place (Part of Harveys Lake) 18618
Worleytown 17225
Worman 19518
Wormleysburg 17043
Worth, *Butler* (Twp) 16057
Worth, *Centre* (Twp) 16870
Worth, *Mercer* (Twp) 16133
Worthington 16262
Worthville 15784
Woxall 18979
Wright (Twp) 18707
Wrights 16743
Wrights Corners 16749
Wrightsdale 17563
Wrightstown (Twp) 18980
Wrightstown 18940
Wrightsville, *Warren* 16340
Wrightsville, *York* 17368
Wurtemburg 16117
Wurtemburg Heights 16117
Wyalusing 18853
Wyano 15695
Wyattville (Part of Sugarcreek) 16323
Wycombe 18980
Wydnor 18015
Wyebrooke 19344
Wylandville 15330
Wylie, *Allegheny* 15037
Wylie (Part of Pittsburgh)‡ 15219
Wyncote♦ 19095
Wyncote Hills 19095
Wyncroft 19063
Wyndham Hills 17403
Wyndmoor♦ 19118
Wyndmoor Valley 19075
Wynnewood, *Bucks* 19067
Wynnewood, *Montgomery* 19096
Wynnewood Shopping Center 19096
Wyoming 18644
Wyoming Camp Ground 18643
Wyoming Valley Mall (Part of Wilkes-Barre) 18702
Wyomissing 19610
Wyomissing Hills 19609
Wyomissing Junction (Part of Wyomissing) 19610
Wysox 18854
Yardley 19067
Yardley Farms 19067
Yardley Hunt 19067
Yarnell 16823
Yatesboro 16263
Yatesville, *Luzerne* 18640
Yatesville, *Schuylkill* 17976
Yeadon 19050
Yeagertown♦ 17099
Yellow Creek 16650
Yellow Hammer 16353
Yellow House 19518
Yellowwood 19007
Yerkes 19426
Yocumtown 17319
Yoe 17313
York (Twp) 17403
York 17401-07
For specific ZIP Codes call (888) 275-8777, or your local postmaster.
Yorkana 17402
York County 17402
York Galleria 17402
York Haven 17370
Yorklyn 17402
York Mall 17402
York New Salem 17371
York Road, *Bucks*‡ 18974
York Road, *York* 17331
York Run 15401
Yorkshire 17402
York Springs 17372
Yostville 18444
Young, *Indiana* (Twp) 15725
Young, *Jefferson* (Twp) 15767
Youngdale 17748
Youngsburg 19320
Youngstown, *Fayette* 15456
Youngstown, *Luzerne* 18221
Youngstown, *Westmoreland* 15696
Youngsville, *Northampton* 18038
Youngsville, *Warren* 16371
Youngwood 15697
Yount 15522
Yukon 15698
Zebleys Corner 19061
Zehners 17960
Zelienople 16063
Zerbe, *Northumberland* (Twp) 17881
Zerbe, *Schuylkill* 17981
Zieglerville 19492
Zimmerman 15501
Zion 16823
Zion Grove 17985
Zionhill 18981
Zions View 17404
Zionsville 18092
Zollarsville 15345
Zooks Corner 17602
Zooks Dam 17059
Zora 17320
Zucksville 18040
Zullinger 17272

Abbott Run Valley 02864
Adamsville 02801
Albion 02802
Allendale 02911
Allenton 02852
Alton 02894
Annex (Part of Providence)‡ 02901
Anthony 02816
Apple Blossom (Part of Cranston) 02920
Arcadia 02832
Arctic 02893
Arkwright 02816
Arlington (Part of Cranston) 02920
Arnold Mills 02864
Arnold's Neck (Part of Warwick) 02886
Ashaway♦ 02804
Ashton 02864
Auburn (Part of Cranston) 02910
Austin 02822
Avondale 02891
Barberville 02832
Barrington♦ 02806
Barton's Corner 02818
Bayridge (Part of Warwick) 02818
Bayside (Part of Warwick) 02889
Bay Spring 02806
Bay View (Part of East Providence) 02914
Beach Terrace 02809
Bellefonte (Part of Cranston) 02920
Belleville 02852
Berkeley 02864
Beverage Hill (Part of Pawtucket) 02860
Bishops Heights 02857
Black Plain 02822
Block Island 02807
Bonnet Shores 02882
Boon Lake 02822
Bowdish Lake 02814
Bradford♦ 02808
Branch Village 02896
Brenton Village (Part of Newport) 02840
Bridgeport 02878
Bridgetown 02874
Briggs Beach 02837
Bristol♦ 02809
Bristol Colony 02872
Bristol Ferry 02871
Bristol Highlands 02809
Bristol Narrows 02809
Broadway (Part of Newport)‡ 02840
Brookfield (Part of Cranston) 02920
Brush Neck Cove (Part of Warwick) 02886
Bullocks Point (Part of East Providence) 02914
Burdickville 02808
Burrillville (Town) 02830
Buttonwoods (Part of Warwick) 02886
Canonchet 02832
Carnegie Heights 02865
Carolina 02812
Carpenters Beach 02879
Cedar Grove Estates 02822
Cedar Point 02835
Cedar Tree Point (Part of Warwick) 02886
Centerville, *Kent* 02893
Centerville, *Washington* 02832
Central Falls 02863
Centredale 02911
Charlestown 02813
Charlestown Beach 02813
Chepachet 02814
Chepiwanoxet (Part of Warwick) 02886
Cherry Valley 02814
Cherry Valley Beach 02814
Chopmist 02857
Clarke's Village 02835
Clayville 02815
Clyde 02893
Coasters Harbor (Part of Newport) 02840
Coggeshall 02885
Coles (Part of Warwick) 02889
Columbia Heights 02875
Common Fence Point 02871
Commons 02837
Comstock Gardens (Part of Cranston) 02910
Conanicut Park 02835
Conimicut (Part of Warwick)‡ 02889
Corey's Lane 02871
Coventry 02816
Coventry Center 02816
Cowesett (Part of Warwick) 02886
Cranston 02910
02920-21
For specific ZIP Codes call (888) 275-8777, or your local postmaster.
Crescent Park (Part of East Providence) 02914
Crompton 02893
Cross Mills 02813
Cumberland 02864
Cumberland Hill♦ 02864
Curtis Corners 02883
Darlington (Part of Pawtucket)‡ 02861
Davisville (Part of North Kingstown)‡ 02854
Diamond Hill‡ 02895
Dunns Corners 02891
Durfee Hill 02814
Eagleville 02878
East Greenwich 02818
East Matunuck 02879
East Natick (Part of Warwick) 02893
East Providence 02914
East Providence Wharf (Part of East Providence) 02914
East Side (Part of Providence)‡ 02906
East Warren 02885
Echo Lake 02814
Eden Park (Part of Cranston) 02920
Edgewood (Part of Cranston)‡ 02905
Elmwood (Part of Providence)‡ 02907
Enos (Part of Cranston) 02920
Escoheag 02822
Esmond 02917
Exeter 02822
Fairbanks Corner 02827
Finast (Part of East Providence) 02914
Fiskeville (Part of Cranston) 02823
Fogland Point 02878
Forestdale 02824
Fort Adams (Part of Newport) 02840
Foster 02825
Fox Point (Part of Providence) 02906
Frenchtown 02818
Fruit Hill 02911
Galilee 02882
Garden City (Part of Cranston) 02920
Garden City Center (Part of Cranston) 02920
Gazzaville 02839
Geneva 02911
Georgiaville 02917
Glendale 02826
Glocester (Town) 02814
Goat Island (Part of Newport) 02840
Goulds 02883
Graniteville 02911
Grants Mills 02838
Greene 02827
Green Hill 02879
Greenville♦ 02828
Greenwood (Part of Warwick) 02886
Greystone 02911
Hamilton 02852
Hampden Meadows 02806
Harmony 02829
Harris 02816
Harrisville♦ 02830
Haversham 02891
Highland Beach (Part of Warwick) 02889
Hill's Grove (Part of Warwick) 02886
Hog Island 02809
Homestead 02872
Hope 02831
Hope Valley♦ 02832
Hopkins Hollow 02827
Hopkinton 02833
Horse Neck (Part of Warwick) 02886
Howard (Part of Cranston) 02920
Hoxsie (Part of Warwick) 02889
Hughesdale 02919
Indian Lake Shores 02879
India Point (Part of Providence) 02903
Island Park 02871
Jackson 02823
Jamestown 02835
Jamestown Center 02835
Jamestown Shores 02835
Jerusalem 02879
Johnston 02919
Kent Corner (Part of East Providence) 02914
Kent Heights (Part of East Providence) 02914
Kenyon 02836
Kingston♦ 02881
Knightsville (Part of Cranston) 02920
La Fayette 02852
Lake Bel Air 02896
Lake Mishnock 02817
Lakewood (Part of Warwick) 02888
Langworthy Corner 02891
Laurel Hill 02859
Laurel Park 02885
Leonard Corner (Part of East Providence) 02914
Liberty 02877
Limerock 02865
Lincoln (Town) 02860
Lincoln 02865
Lincoln Park (Part of Warwick) 02888
Lippit 02893
Lippitt Estate 02864
Little Compton 02837
Lockwood Corner (Part of Warwick) 02889
Longmeadow (Part of Warwick) 02889
Lonsdale (Part of Valley Falls) 02864
Lonsdale 02865
Lymansville 02911
Manton (Part of Providence) 02909
Manville 02838
Maple Root Village 02816
Mapleville 02839
Marieville 02904
Matunuck 02879
Mellville 02871
Meshanticut (Part of Cranston) 02920
Millville 02822
Misquamicut‡ 02891
Mohegan 02895
Mohegan Bluffs 02807
Mooresfield 02874
Moosup Valley 02827
Moscow 02832
Mount Pleasant (Part of Providence) 02908
Mount View 02852
Nannaquaket 02878
Narragansett♦ 02882
Narragansett Heights 02878
Nasonville 02895
Natick (Part of Warwick) 02893
Nausauket (Part of Warwick) 02886
Naval Construction Battalion Center 02854
Nayatt 02806
New Harbor 02807
Newport 02840
Newport East♦ 02840
New Shoreham (Town) 02807
Nichols Corner 02818
Nooseneck 02816
North (Part of Providence)‡ 02908
North Foster 02825
North Kingstown (Town) 02852
North Kingstown 02852*
02854†
North Providence♦ 02911
North Quidnessett 02852
North Scituate 02857
North Smithfield (Town) 02896
Norwood (Part of Warwick) 02888
Oakland 02858
Oakland Beach (Part of Warwick) 02886
Oak Lawn (Part of Cranston) 02920
Old Harbor 02807
Olney Arnold Estates (Part of Cranston) 02920
Olneyville (Part of Providence)‡ 02909
Palace Garden (Part of Warwick) 02888
Parcel Post Annex‡ 02891
Pascoag♦ 02859
Pawtucket 02860-62
For specific ZIP Codes call (888) 275-8777, or your local postmaster.
Peace Dale 02883
Pawtuxet 02888
Perryville 02879
Pettaquamscutt Lake Shores 02874
Phenix 02893
Phillipsdale (Part of East Providence) 02914
Pilgrim (Part of Warwick)‡ 02888
Pine Hill 02822
Pleasant View (Part of Pawtucket) 02860
Plum Beach 02874
Plum Point 02874
Poccasett Heights 02871
Point Judith 02882
Pontiac (Part of Warwick) 02886
Popasquash Point 02809
Portsmouth 02871
Potowomut (Part of Warwick) 02818
Potter Hill 02891
Primrose 02896
Print Works (Part of Cranston) 02920

Providence

02901-09
02940
For specific ZIP Codes call (888) 275-8777, or your local postmaster.

Colleges & Universities

Johnson & Wales Univ 02903
Rhode Island Coll 02908
Rhode Island School of Design 02903

Financial Institutions

BankBoston 02903
Citizens Bank 02903
First Nat Bank of New England 02903
Fleet Nat Bank 02903

Hospitals

Miriam Hosp 02906
Rhode Island Hosp 02903

Hotel/Motels

Holiday Inn, Downtown 02903
Marriott 02904
The Westin 02903

Military Installations

U S Property & Fiscal Off for Rhode Island 02906

Prudence Island 02872
Prudence Park 02872
Quidnessett 02852
Quidnick 02816
Quinnville 02865
Quonset Point 02852
Quonochontaug 02813
Rhode Island Mall (Part of Warwick) 02886
Rice City 02827
Rice Plat 02857
Richmond (Town) 02812
River Point 02893
Riverside (Part of East Providence) 02915
River Vue (Part of Warwick) 02889
Rockville 02873
Rocky Point (Part of Warwick) 02889
Rumford (Part of East Providence) 02916
Rumstick Point 02806
Sakonnet 02837
Sandy Point (Part of Warwick) 02818
Sandy Point, *Newport* 02872
Sandy Point, *Washington* 02807
Saunderstown 02874
Saundersville 02857
Saylesville 02865
Scituate (Town) 02857
Shady Harbor 02891
Shannock 02875
Shawomet (Part of Warwick) 02889
Shelter Harbor 02891
Shores Acres 02852
Silver Lake (Part of Providence) 02909
Simmonsville 02919
Slatersville 02876
Slocum 02877
Smithfield (Town) 02917
Smith Hill (Part of Providence) 02908
Sockannosset (Part of Cranston) 02920
South Foster 02825
South Hopkinton 08208
South Kingstown (Town) 02879
South Providence (Part of Providence) 02905
South Warren 02885
Spencer Corner 02818
Spragueville 02828
Spring Green (Part of Warwick) 02888
Spring Grove 02814
Spring Lake Beach 02826
Squantum (Part of East Providence) 02914
Stillwater 02917
Summit 02827
Tarkiln 02895
The Anchorage 02842
The Hummocks 02871
Thornton 02919
Tiverton♦ 02878
Tiverton Four Corners 02878
Tockwotten (Part of Providence) 02903
Tonomy Hill (Part of Newport) 02840
Touisset Highlands 02885
Tuckertown 02879
Tunipus 02837
Union Village 02896
Usquepaug 02892
Valley Falls♦ 02864
Vaughn Hollow 02827
Vernon 02825
Wakefield 02879*
02880†
Walnut Hill (Part of Woonsocket) 02895
Warren 02885
Warren Point 02837
Warwick 02886-89
For specific ZIP Codes call (888) 275-8777, or your local postmaster.
Warwick Mall (Part of Warwick) 02886
Warwick Neck (Part of Warwick)‡ 02889
Washington Park (Part of Cranston) 02905
Watch Hill‡ 02891
Watchmocket Square (Part of East Providence) 02914
Waterford 01504
Waterman Four Corners 02857
Weekapaug‡ 02891
West Barrington 02806
Westcott (Part of Warwick) 02893
Westcott Beach 02814
Westerly♦ 02891
West Glocester 06260
West Greenville 02828
West Greenwich 02817
West Greenwich Center 02817
West Kingston 02892
West Warwick♦ 02893
Weybosset Hill (Part of Providence)‡ 02903
Whipple 02858
White Rock 02891
Wickford Junction 02852
Wildes Corner (Part of Warwick)‡ 02886
Wood Estates 02816
Wood River Junction 02894
Woodville, Providence 02911
Woodville, Washington 02832
Woonsocket 02895
Wyoming 02898
Yorktown Manor 02852

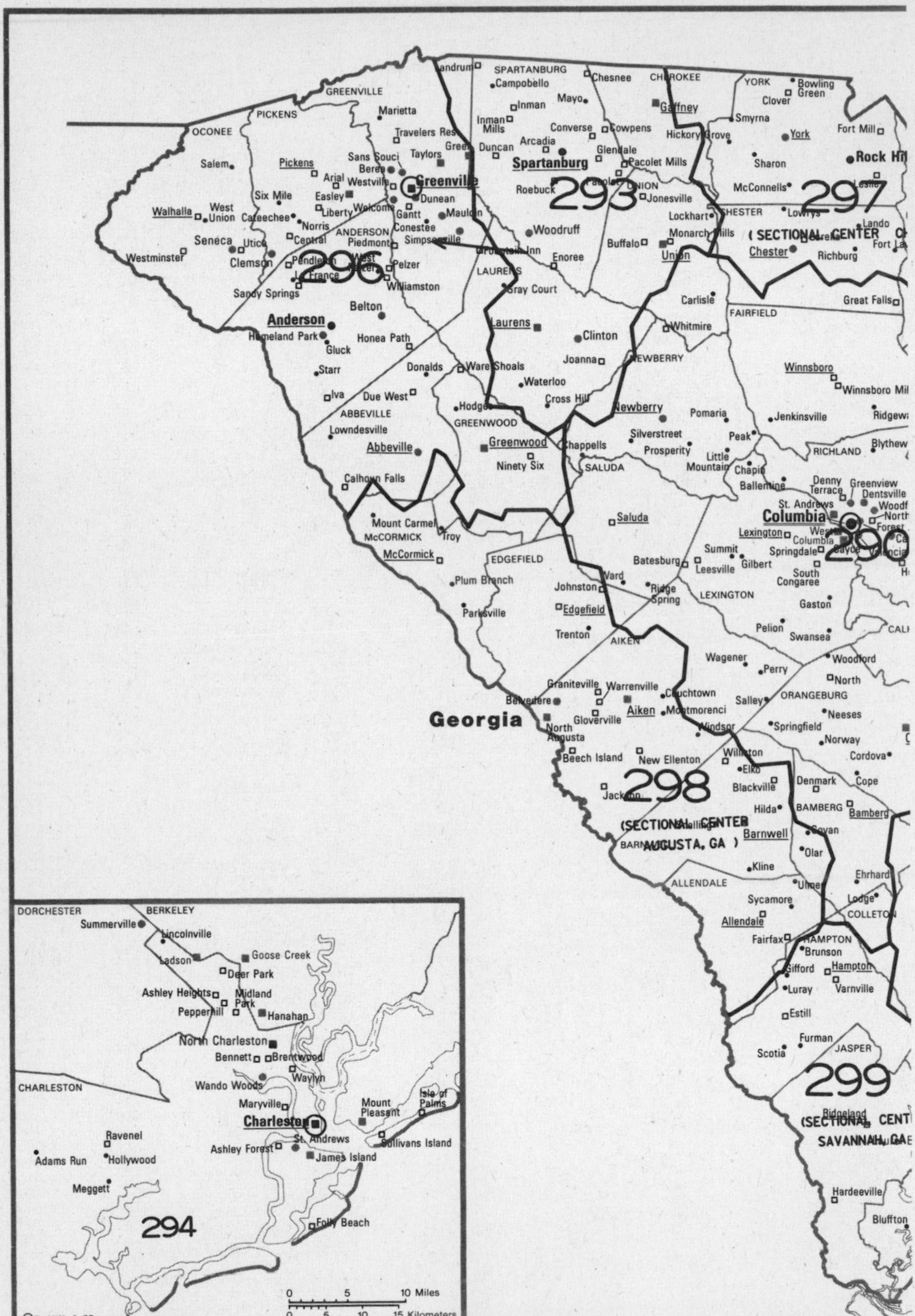

GREENVILLE
PICKENS
OCONEE
SPARTANBURG
CHEROKEE
YORK
UNION
CHESTER
ANDERSON
LAURENS
FAIRFIELD
NEWBERRY
ABBEVILLE
GREENWOOD
RICHLAND
SALUDA
McCORMICK
EDGEFIELD
LEXINGTON
AIKEN
ORANGEBURG
BAMBERG
ALLENDALE
COLLETON
HAMPTON
JASPER
Landrum
Campobello
Chesnee
Gaffney
Bowling Green
Clover
Smyrna
Inman
Mayo
Marietta
Travelers Rest
Inman Mills
Converse
Cowpens
Hickory Grove
York
Fort Mill
Taylors
Duncan
Arcadia
Glendale
Pacolet Mills
Sans Souci
Berea
Spartanburg
Rock Hill
Salem
Pickens
Arial
Westville
Greenville
Roebuck
Pacolet
Jonesville
McConnells
Sharon
Six Mile
Easley
Dunean
Walhalla
West Union
Cateechee
Liberty
Welcome
Gantt
Mauldin
Lockhart
Lowrys
Lando
Norris
Conestee
Monarch Mills
Fort Lawn
Seneca
Utica
Central
Piedmont
Simpsonville
Woodruff
Buffalo
Chester
Richburg
Westminster
Clemson
Pendleton
West Pelzer
Pelzer
Fountain Inn
Enoree
Union
La France
Williamston
Gray Court
Sandy Springs
Carlisle
Great Falls
Belton
Anderson
Laurens
Clinton
Whitmire
Homeland Park
Honea Path
Gluck
Joanna
Winnsboro
Starr
Donalds
Ware Shoals
Waterloo
Winnsboro Mills
Iva
Due West
Cross Hill
Newberry
Pomaria
Jenkinsville
Hodges
Lowndesville
Silverstreet
Peak
Greenwood
Chappells
Prosperity
Little Mountain
Blythewood
Abbeville
Ninety Six
Chapin
Ballentine
Denny Terrace
Greenview
Dentsville
Calhoun Falls
St. Andrews
Columbia
North Forest
Mount Carmel
Saluda
Troy
Lexington
West Columbia
McCormick
Summit
Springdale
Cayce
Batesburg
Leesville
Gilbert
Plum Branch
Ward
South Congaree
Johnston
Ridge Spring
Gaston
Edgefield
Parksville
Pelion
Trenton
Swansea
Wagener
Perry
Woodford
North
Graniteville
Warrenville
Couchtown
Belvedere
Aiken
Montmorenci
Salley
Georgia
Gloverville
North Augusta
Windsor
Springfield
Neeses
Norway
Beech Island
New Ellenton
Williston
Elko
Cordova
Denmark
Cope
Jackson
Blackville
Hilda
Bamberg
Barnwell
Govan
Olar
Kline
Ehrhardt
Ulmer
Sycamore
Lodge
Allendale
Fairfax
Brunson
Gifford
Luray
Varnville
Estill
Furman
Scotia
Ridgeland
Hardeeville
Bluffton
293
296
297
298
299
294
(SECTIONAL CENTER
(SECTIONAL CENTER
AUGUSTA, GA)
DORCHESTER
BERKELEY
CHARLESTON
Summerville
Lincolnville
Ladson
Goose Creek
Deer Park
Ashley Heights
Midland Park
Pepperhill
Hanahan
North Charleston
Bennett
Brentwood
Wando Woods
Waylyn
Maryville
Mount Pleasant
Isle of Palms
Charleston
St. Andrews
Sullivans Island
Ashley Forest
James Island
Ravenel
Adams Run
Hollywood
Meggett
Folly Beach
0 5 10 Miles
0 5 10 15 Kilometers
©R. McN. & CO.

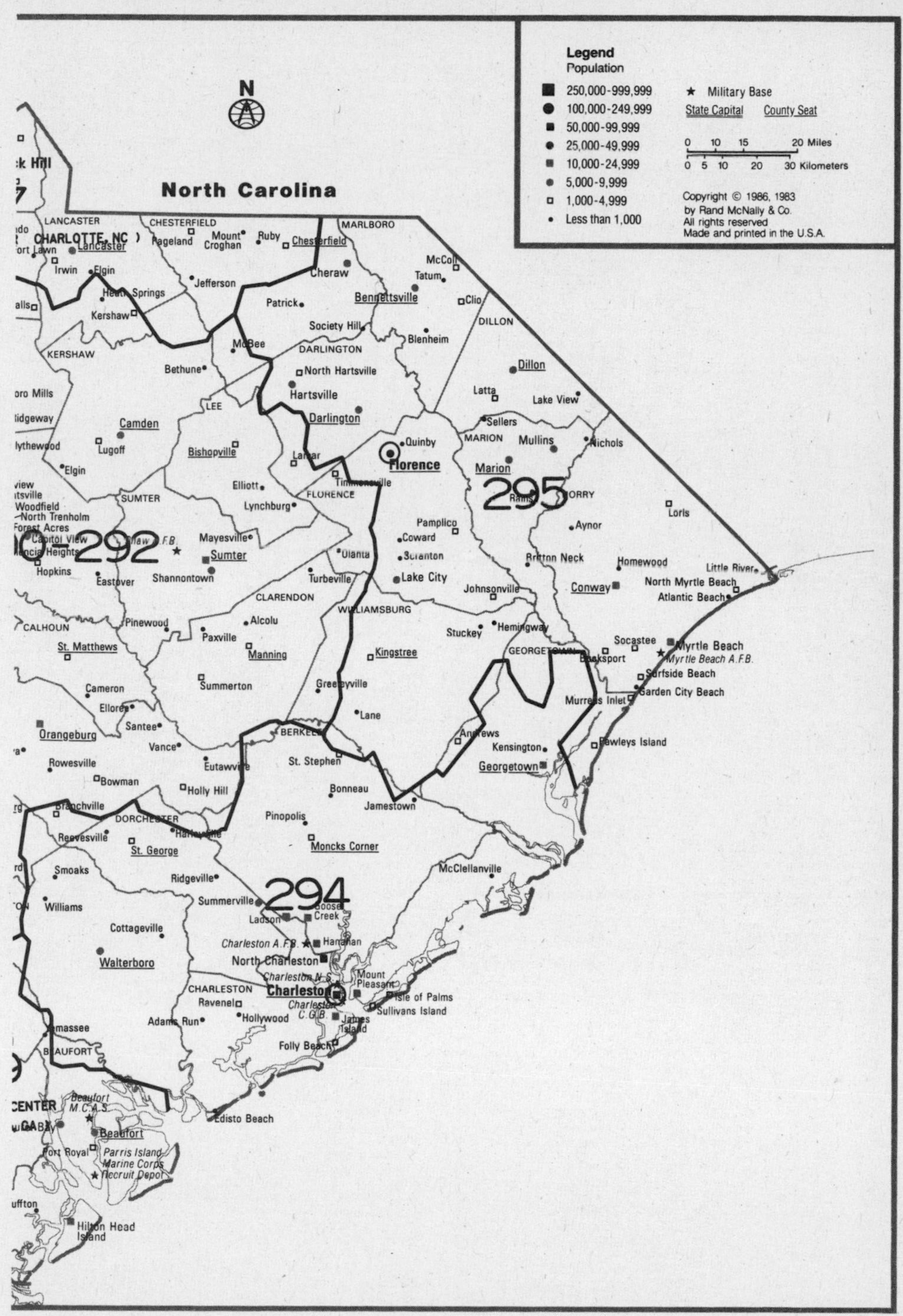
Legend
Population
250,000-999,999
100,000-249,999
50,000-99,999
25,000-49,999
10,000-24,999
5,000-9,999
1,000-4,999
Less than 1,000
Military Base
State Capital
County Seat
0 10 15 20 Miles
0 5 10 20 30 Kilometers
Copyright © 1986, 1983
by Rand McNally & Co.
All rights reserved
Made and printed in the U.S.A.
N
North Carolina
295
292
294
LANCASTER
CHESTERFIELD
MARLBORO
CHARLOTTE, NC
Lancaster
Pageland
Mount Croghan
Ruby
Chesterfield
McColl
Tatum
Cheraw
Irwin
Elgin
Jefferson
Bennettsville
Clio
Kershaw
Patrick
DILLON
Society Hill
Blenheim
KERSHAW
DARLINGTON
North Hartsville
Bethune
Dillon
Hartsville
Latta
Lake View
LEE
Darlington
Sellers
Camden
MARION
Mullins
Nichols
Lugoff
Bishopville
Quinby
Florence
Elgin
Marion
Elliott
FLORENCE
SUMTER
Lynchburg
Loris
Woodfield
North Trenholm
Forest Acres
Aynor
Pamplico
Mayesville
Coward
Sumter
Hopkins
Eastover
Shannontown
Turbeville
Lake City
Homewood
Little River
North Myrtle Beach
Conway
Johnsonville
CLARENDON
Atlantic Beach
WILLIAMSBURG
CALHOUN
Pinewood
Alcolu
Stuckey
Hemingway
Paxville
St. Matthews
Socastee
Manning
Kingstree
Myrtle Beach
Myrtle Beach A.F.B.
Bucksport
Surfside Beach
Summerton
Cameron
Garden City Beach
Elloree
Lane
Santee
Orangeburg
Andrews
Pawleys Island
Vance
Kensington
St. Stephen
Rowesville
Georgetown
Bowman
Holly Hill
Bonneau
Jamestown
Pinopolis
Reevesville
St. George
Moncks Corner
McClellanville
Smoaks
Ridgeville
Williams
Summerville
Ladson
Cottageville
Charleston A.F.B.
North Charleston
Walterboro
Charleston N.S.
CHARLESTON
Mount Pleasant
Charleston
Ravenel
Isle of Palms
Sullivans Island
Charleston C.G.B.
Hollywood
Adams Run
James Island
Folly Beach
Edisto Beach
Beaufort M.C.A.S.
Beaufort
Port Royal
Parris Island Marine Corps Recruit Depot
Hilton Head Island

Abbeville	29620
Abney	29067
Academy Acres	29488
Adamsburg	29379
Adams Run	29426
Adamsville	29570
Adger	29180
Adrian	29526
Aiken	29801-05
For specific ZIP Codes call (888) 275-8777, or your local postmaster.	
Aiken Estates	29803
Aiken Mall (Part of Aiken)	29803
Aiken West	29801
Alcolu	29001
Alcot	29010
Allen	29511
Allendale	29810
Allsbrook	29569
Alvin	29479
Anderson	29621-26
For specific ZIP Codes call (888) 275-8777, or your local postmaster.	
Anderson Mall (Part of Anderson)	29621
Andrews	29510
Angelus	29718
Anne Village	29440
Ansel	29651
Antioch, *Kershaw*	29020
Antioch, *Lancaster*	29720
Antreville	29655
Appleton	29810
Appleton Mills	29625
Aragon Mills (Part of Rock Hill)	29730
Arcadia	29320
Arcadia Lakes	29206
Arial♦	29640
Ariel Crossroads	29574
Arkwright	29301
Arlington	29651
Armenia	29706
Arthurtown	29201
Asbury	29340
Ashepoo	29446
Ashland	29010
Ashleigh	29817
Ashley Forest	29407
Ashley Hall (Part of Charleston)	29401
Ashley Heights	29405
Ashley Junction (Part of North Charleston)	29406
Ashley River (Part of Charleston)‡	29414
	29416
For specific ZIP Codes call (888) 275-8777, or your local postmaster.	
Ashton	29082
Ashwood	29010
Aspen Heights	29646
Atkins	29080
Atlantic Beach	29582
Auburn	29550
Augusta Road (Part of Greenville)‡	29604
Avondale	29407
Awendaw	29429
Aynor	29511
Badham	29471
Baileys Landing	29936
Baker Crossroads	29569
Bald Rock	29379
Baldwin♦	29706
Ballentine	29002
Balltown	29801
Bamberg	29003
Barkersville	29916
Barksdale	29360
Barnes	29655
Barnwell	29812
Barrineau	29560
Bartell Crossroads	29554
Barton	29827
Bascomville	29729
Batesburg (Part of Batesburg-Leesville)	29006
Batesburg-Leesville	29006
Bath	29816
Baton Rouge	29706
Baxter Forks	29569
Bayboro	29569
Bay Shores	29665
Bay Springs	29584
Bay View	29204
Beaufort	29901-06
For specific ZIP Codes call (888) 275-8777, or your local postmaster.	
Beaufort Marine Corps Air Station	29904
Beckhamville	29055
Beech Island	29842
Bel-Clear Heights	29841
Beldoc	29836
Belle Isle Gardens	29440
Belle Meade, *Greenville*	29603
Belle Meade, *Lexington*	29172
Bellinger	29927
Bells	29475
Belmont	29203
Belton	29627
Belvedere, *Aiken*♦	29841
Belvedere, *Richland*	29204
Ben Avon	29302
Bendale (Part of Columbia)	29203
Beneventum	29440
Bennett	29405
Bennettsville	29512
Bent Tree	29678
Berea‡	29610-11
	29617
For specific ZIP Codes call (888) 275-8777, or your local postmaster.	
Berlin	29137
Bethany	29710
Bethera	29430
Bethesda	29584
Bethune	29009
Beufordtown	29453
Beverly Hills	29445
Beverly Woods	29301
Bingham	29565
Birdtown Crossroads	29550
Bishopville	29010
Blackjack	29180
Blacks	29166
Blacksburg	29702
Blackstock	29014
Blackville	29817
Blair	29015
Blakedale	29649
Blenheim	29516
Bloomingvale	29510
Bloomville	29102
Blossom	29583
Blue Heaven	29638
Blue Town	29512
Bluff	29142
Bluff Estates	29209
Bluffton	29910
Blythewood	29016
Bob Jones University (Part of Greenville)	29614
Bob Marina	29163
Boiling Springs‡	29316
Bolentown	29115
Bon Aire	29906
Bon Air Terrace	29150
Bonham	29379
Bonneau	29431
Bonneau Beach	29431
Bonniview Estates	29803
Boones Creek	29676
Bordeaux	29835
Borden	29128
Boulder Bluff	29445
Bounty Land	29672
Bowling Green	29703
Bowman	29018
Bowyer	29059
Boyden Arbor	29206
Boykin, *Kershaw*	29128
Boykin, *Marlboro*	28343
Bradley	29819
Bradleyville	29841
Branchville	29432
Brand	29360
Brandon	29611
Branwood (Part of Greenville)‡	29610
Brasstown	29658
Brattonsville	29726
Brazen Crossroads	29583
Breeze Hill (Part of Burnettown)	29834
Breezewood	29819
Brentwood	29405
Brewerton	29692
Briarcliffe Acres	29572
Briarcreek	29340
Brighton	29922
Brighton Beach	29910
Brightsville	28343
Bristow	29516
Britton	29153
Brittons Neck	29546
Broad Street (Part of Sumter)‡	29150
Broadway Lake	29621
Brock	29691
Brock Circle	29654
Brockington	29556
Brogdon	29150
Brookdale	29115
Brook Forest	29605
Brook Green Park	29501
Brookhaven Estates	29801
Brooklyn	29720
Brooksville	29582
Brownsville, *Dorchester*	29483
Brownsville, *Marlboro*	29516
Brownway	29526
Bruner	29061
Brunson	29911
Brunsons Crossroads	29554
Bryans Crossroads	29590
Buckeye Forest	29377
Buck Hall	29429
Buckingham Landing	29928
Bucksport♦	29526
Bucksville	29526
Buffalo, *McCormick*	29835
Buffalo, *Union*♦	29321
Buford	29720
Buford Crossroads	29720
Bufords Bridge	29843
Bullock Creek	29742
Bunker Hill	29536
Burgess	29576
Burnettown	29834
Burnt Church Crossroads	29474
Burton♦	29902
Bynum	29556
Byrd	29477
Byrds Crossroads	28114
Cades	29518
Caesars Head	28718
Caldwell Street (Part of Rock Hill)‡	29731
Calhoun (Part of Clemson)	29631
Calhoun Falls	29628
Callison	29819
Camden	29020
Cameron	29030
Camp Creek	29720
Camp Croft	29302
Campobello	29322
Campton	29349
Canaan, *Orangeburg*	29038
Canaan, *Spartanburg*	29302
Canadys	29433
Cane Savannah	29154
Canterbury	29673
Capitol (Part of Columbia)‡	29201
	29211
For specific ZIP Codes call (888) 275-8777, or your local postmaster.	
Capitol View	29209
Carlisle	29031
Carmel	29058
Carolina Circle	29488
Caromi Village	29456
Carters Crossroads	29554
Cartersville	29161
Carver Heights	29204
Carvers Bay	29554
Cash	29520
Cashville	29388
Cassatt	29032
Catarrah	29718
Catawba	29704
Cateechee	29667
Catholic Hill	29488
Cave	29810
Cayce	29033
Cedar Grove	29526
Cedar Hill	29835
Cedar Springs	29455
Cedar Terrace	29209
Celriver	29732
Cementon	29059
Centenary	29519
Center Crossroads	29554
Centerville, *Anderson*♦	29621
Centerville, *Dillon*	29565
Central	29630
Central Pacolet	29372
Challedon	29210
Chaparral Ranches	29461
Chapin	29036
Chappells	29037
Charleston	29401-03
	29405-25
For specific ZIP Codes call (888) 275-8777, or your local postmaster.	
Charleston Heights (Part of North Charleston)	29405
Charles Towne Square (Part of North Charleston)	29406
Chartwell	29210
Cheddar	29627
Cheraw	29520
Cherokee	29302
Cherokee Falls	29702
Cherokee Forest	29687
Cherokee Gardens	29672
Cherry Grove Beach (Part of North Myrtle Beach)	29582
Cherry Hill Estates	29906
Cherry Road (Part of Rock Hill)‡	29732
Cherryvale♦	29154
Chesnee	29323
Chester	29706
Chesterfield	29709
Chestnut Hills	29605
Chickasaw Point	29693
Chicora Place (Part of North Charleston)	29405
Choppee	29440
Citadel (Part of Charleston)	29409
Citadel Mall (Part of Charleston)	29407
City View	29611
Claremont	29150
Clarks Hill	29821
Claussen	29505
Clayton	29015
Clearmont	29693
Clear Pond	29003
Clearspring	29681
Clearwater♦	29822
Cleburne	29440
Clemson	29631-33
For specific ZIP Codes call (888) 275-8777, or your local postmaster.	
Cleora	29824
Cleveland	29635
Clifton	29324
Clinton	29325
Clio	29525
Clover	29710
Clubhouse Crossroads, *Dorchester*	29472
Club House Crossroads, *Lexington*	29054
Clyde	29101
Coastal (Part of North Myrtle Beach)‡	29582
	29598
For specific ZIP Codes call (888) 275-8777, or your local postmaster.	
Cochrantown	29526
Cokesbury	29653
Cold Point	29360
Coldstream	29210
College Acres	29803
Colliers	29838
Colonial Heights	29906
Colonial Village	29715
Columbia	29201-92
For specific ZIP Codes call (888) 275-8777, or your local postmaster.	
Columbia Mall	29204
Columbiana Centre (Part of Columbia)	29212
Coneross	29693
Conestee	29636
Congaree	29044
Connecticut Park	29341
Converse	29329
Conway	29526-28
For specific ZIP Codes call (888) 275-8777, or your local postmaster.	
Cooks Crossroads	29644
Cool Branch	29031
Cooley Springs	29323
Cool Spring	29511
Coosaw	29940
Coosawhatchie	29912
Cope	29038
Cordesville	29434
Cordova	29039
Cornwell	29014
Coronaca	29649
Cottageville	29435
Couchtown	29801
Country Club Estates	29730
Country Homes	29646
Courtenay	29672
Coward	29530
Cowpens	29330
Crane Forest	29203
Crescent	29388
Crescent Beach (Part of North Myrtle Beach)	29582
Creston	29030
Crestview	29501
Crocketts Crossroads	29720
Crocketville	29913
Crooks Crossroads	29554
Crosland Park (Part of Aiken)	29801
Cross	29436
Cross Anchor	29331
Crosscreek Mall (Part of Greenwood)	29646
Cross Hill	29332
Cross Keys	29379
Crosswell	29640
Cummings	29944
Cusaac Crossroads	29541
Cypress Crossroads	29069
Cypress Fork	29001
Dacusville	29640
Daisy	29569
Dale	29914
Dalewood	29653
Dalzell	29040
Danwood	29541
Darlington	29532
	29540
For specific ZIP Codes call (888) 275-8777, or your local postmaster.	
Daufuskie Island	29915
Davis Crossroads	29148
Davis Station	29041
Deans	29684
De Bordieu Colony	29440
Deer Park	29405
DeKalb	29175
Delemar Crossroads	29470
Delmar	29070
Delphos	29745
Delta	29178
Denmark	29042
Denny Terrace	29203
Dentsville	29204
Denver	29625
Deweys Hill (Part of North Charleston)	29406
Dillon	29536
Dinkins	29150
Dinkins Mill	29128
Dixiana	29172
Dixie	29720
Dog Bluff	29511
Donalds	29638
Dongola	29526
Dorange	29471
Dorchester	29437
Dorchester Estates	29485
Dorchester Terrace	29405
Douglass	29014
Dovesville	29540
Drake	29516
Drawdy	29488
Drayton, *Charleston*	29407
Drayton, *Spartanburg*	29333
Draytonville	20340
Drexel Lake Hills	29206
Dry Branch	29803
Dubose	29150
Du Bose Crossroads	29153
Du Bose Park	29020
Dudley	29728
Due West	29639
Duford	29581
Dunbar, *Georgetown*	29440
Dunbar, *Marlboro*	29525
Duncan	29334
Dunean♦	29601

Dunes (Part of Myrtle Beach)‡ 29575
.... 29577
For specific ZIP Codes call (888) 275-8777, or your local postmaster.
Dupont 29407
Dusty Bend (Part of Camden)‡ 29020
Dutch Fork‡ 29210*
.... 29212†
Dutchman 29374
Dutch Square 29210
Dutch Village 29063
Dyson 29666
Eadytown 29468
Earle Homes 29624
Earles 29510
Earles Grove 29678
Earlwood Park 29532
Early Branch 29916
Easley 29640-42
For specific ZIP Codes call (888) 275-8777, or your local postmaster.
East Bay (Part of Charleston)‡ 29401
.... 29403
.... 29413
For specific ZIP Codes call (888) 275-8777, or your local postmaster.
East Gaffney♦ 29340
East Gantt 29609
East Greer 29651
East Hartsville 29550
Eastmont 29209
Eastover 29044
East Side Acres 29488
East View 29669
Eau Claire (Part of Columbia)‡ 29203*
.... 29230†
Ebenezer, *Florence* 29501
Ebenezer (Part of Rock Hill) 29732
Eden 29645
Edenwood 29033
Edgefield 29824
Edgemoor 29712
Edgewood (Part of Columbia)‡ 29204*
.... 29240†
Edisto Beach 29438
Edisto Island 29438
Edmund 29073
Effingham 29541
Ehrhardt 29081
Elgin, *Kershaw* 29045
Elgin, *Lancaster*♦ 29720
Elko 29826
Elliott 29046
Elloree 29047
Elmwood Park 29803
Emanuelville 29536
Emerald Place 29646
Emerald Valley 29210
Emory 29138
Enchanted Hills 29672
Enoree 29335
Epworth 29666
Equinox Mill 29625
Estill 29918
Eureka 29847
Eureka Mill♦ 29706
Eutaw Springs 29048
Eutawville 29048
Evans Crossroad 29720
Evergreen 29541
Evergreen Hills 29625
Fairfax 29827
Fairfield (Part of Hilton Head Island)‡ .... 29925†
.... 29928*
Fairfield Terrace 29203
Fair Forest, *Greenwood* 29646
Fairforest, *Spartanburg* 29336
Fairmont 29301
Fair Play 29643
Fairview, *Greenville* 29651
Fairview, *Oconee* 29672
Fairview Crossroads 29070
Farrel Crossroads 29432
Farrow Terrace 29203
Fechtig 29916
Federal (Part of Florence)‡ 29503
Federal (Part of Greenville)‡ 29603

Felderville 29047
Fenwick Hills 29455
Ferndale (Part of North Charleston) 29406
Ferndale, *Spartanburg* 29301
Filbert 29710
Fingerville 29338
Finklea 29569
Finland 29042
Fisher Hill 29520
Five Forks, *Anderson* 29621
Five Forks, *Greenville* 29681
Five Forks, *Pickens* 29657
Five Points, *Oconee* 29693
Five Points (Part of Columbia)‡ 29205*
.... 29250†
Flamingo Acres 29512
Flat Rock 29624
Flat Shoals 29691
Fletcher 29570
Florence 29501-06
For specific ZIP Codes call (888) 275-8777, or your local postmaster.
Floyd Dale 29542
Floyds Crossroads 29581
Folly Beach 29439
Folly Field (Part of Hilton Head Island) 29928
Forest 29437
Forest Acres, *Oconee* 29691
Forest Acres, *Richland*‡ 29206
.... 29260
For specific ZIP Codes call (888) 275-8777, or your local postmaster.
Forest Beach (Part of Hilton Head Island) 29928
Forestbrook♦ 29579
Forest Lake, *Richland* 29206
Forest Lake, *York* 29715
Foreston 29102
Forest Park 29642
Fork 29543
Fork Shoals 29645
Forrest Hills (Part of Latta) 29565
Fort Lawn 29714
Fort Mill 29715*
.... 29716†
Fort Motte 29135
Fountain Inn 29644
Fountain Lake 29048
Four Holes 29115
Four Mile 29464
Fowler 29556
Foxtown 29801
Foxwood Hills 29693
Fraserville 29585
Friarsgate (Part of Irmo) 29063
Friendfield 29591
Friendship 29678
Fripp Island 29920
Fruit Hill 29138
Furman 29921
Gable 29051
Gadsden 29052
Gaffney 29340-42
For specific ZIP Codes call (888) 275-8777, or your local postmaster.
Gaillard Crossroads 29040
Galavon 29536
Galaxy 29209
Galivants Ferry 29544
Gantt 29605
Gapway 29574
Garden City Beach 29576
Gardens Corner 29945
Garnett 29922
Gaston 29053
Gem Lake Estates 29803
Georgetown, *Georgetown* 29440*
.... 29442†
Georgetown, *Pickens* 29640
Gifford 29923
Gilbert 29054
Gillisonville 29936
Givhans 29472
Glass Hill 29526
Glendale 29346
Glenn Springs 29374
Gloverville♦ 29828
Gluck 29624
Glymphville 29126

Godsey 29666
Golden Grove♦ 29673
Golightly 29302
Gooches 29720
Goodwins Crossroads 29325
Goose Creek 29445
Goretown 29569
Gourdin 29564
Govan 29843
Gowensville 29322
Grace 29720
Grahamville, *Horry* 29526
Grahamville, *Jasper* 29936
Gramling 29348
Graniteville 29829
Graves 29440
Gray Court 29645
Grays 29916
Grays Hill 29906
Great Falls 29055
Greeleyville 29056
Green Bay 29450
Greenbriar 29678
Greenbrier 29180
Green Pond, *Colleton* 29446
Green Pond, *Spartanburg* 29388
Green Sea 29545
Greenview 29203
Greenville 29601-17
For specific ZIP Codes call (888) 275-8777, or your local postmaster.
Greenwood 29646-49
For specific ZIP Codes call (888) 275-8777, or your local postmaster.
Greenwood Shores 29666
Greer 29650-52
For specific ZIP Codes call (888) 275-8777, or your local postmaster.
Grenadier 29210
Gresham 29546
Grice Ferry 29574
Grove Park 29501
Grover 29447
Guess 29727
Gurley 29569
Guthries 29726
Hagood 29128
Hamburg (Part of North Augusta) 29841
Hamer 29547
Hammond 29624
Hammond Crossroads 29135
Hampton 29924
Hampton Drive 29488
Hampton Heights 29687
Hampton Park Terrace (Part of Charleston) 29403
Hanahan 29406
Hannah 29583
Hanover Hills 29672
Harbison‡ 29212
Harbour Town (Part of Hilton Head Island)‡ 29928
Hardeeville 29927
Harleyville 29448
Harmony, *Edgefield* 29832
Harmony, *York* 29704
Harmony Hill 29341
Harris 29646
Hartsville 29550*
.... 29551†
Harveytown 29365
Haskell Heights 29203
Hayne 29301
Hayne Junction 29301
Hazelwood Acres 29209
H & B Village (Part of Hampton) 29924
Heatherwood 29640
Heathley Wood (Part of Sumter) 29150
Heath Springs 29058
Hebron 29518
Helena 29108
Hemingway 29554
Hendersonville 29488
Hendricks Corner 29526
Hibernia 29105
Hickory Grove, *Florence* 29501
Hickory Grove, *Horry* 29526
Hickory Grove, *York* 29717
Hickory Hill 29446
Hickory Tavern 29645
High Point 29627

Hilda 29813
Hillcrest (Part of Spartanburg)‡ 29318
Hillcrest Acres (Part of Belton) 29627
Hillcrest Heights (Part of Williamston) 29697
Hillcrest Mall (Part of Spartanburg) 29302
Hilton 29036
Hilton Head Island 29925-26
.... 29928
.... 29938
For specific ZIP Codes call (888) 275-8777, or your local postmaster.
Hobcaw Point 29464
Hodges 29653
Hollands Store 29684
Hollydale 29115
Holly Hill 29059
Holly Springs, *Oconee* 29693
Holly Springs, *Spartanburg* 29349
Hollywood, *Charleston* 29449
Hollywood, *Saluda* 29138
Hollywood Hills 29203
Holmsville 29563
Holtson Crossroads 29006
Homeland Park♦ 29621
Homewood 29526
Homewood Park 29520
Honea Path 29654
Honey Hill 29479
Hoodtown 29742
Hopewell 29717
Hopkins 29061
Horatio 29062
Horeb 29180
Horrel Hill 29061
Horry 29511
Horsegall 29944
Howard 29509
Hudsontown 29477
Huger 29450
Hunley Park (Part of North Charleston) 29404
Huntington Estates 29860
Hyman 29583
Independents 29209
India Hook 29730
Indiantown 29554
Industrial (Part of Rock Hill) 29730
Ingleside 29356
Inman 29349
Inman Mills♦ 29349
Irmo 29063
Irvines Landing 29649
Irwin♦ 29720
Isgett Circle 29520
Islandton 29929
Isle of Palms 29451
Italy 29510
Iva 29655
Jackson 29831
Jacksonboro 29452
Jackson Mill (Part of Wellford) 29385
Jacksonville 29834
Jalapa 29108
James Island‡ 29412
Jamestown, *Berkeley* 29453
Jamestown (Part of Conway) 29526
Jamison 29115
Jedburg 29483
Jefferson 29718
Jenkinsville 29065
Jennys 29827
Jericho 29426
Joanna♦ 29351
Jocassee 29676
Johns Island 29455*
.... 29457†
Johnson City 29301
Johnson Crossroads 29809
Johnsonville 29555
Johnston 29832
Johnstown 29816
Johnsville 29481
Jones Crossroads, *Aiken* 29105
Jones Crossroads, *Lancaster* 29720
Jonesville 29353
Jordan 29102
Jordania 29678
Jordanville 29544
Judson♦ 29611

Judson No. 2 29611
Juniper Bay 29526
Kathwood (Part of West Columbia) 29169
Kelly 29379
Kellytown 29550
Kelton 29353
Kemper 29563
Kensington 29440
Keowee, *Abbeville* 29654
Keowee, *Oconee* 29672
Kershaw 29067
Ketchuptown 29581
Kiawah Island 29455
Kilgore 29335
Killian 29203
Kinards 29355
King Circle 29720
Kingsburg 29555
Kings Creek 29702
Kingstree 29556
Kingswood 29210
Kirkland 29020
Kirksey 29848
Kitchings Mill 29137
Kittredge 29434
Kline 29812
Klondike Crossroads 29526
Kneece 29006
Knightsville 29483
Knollwood Acres 29512
Knox 29706
Ladson♦ 29456
La France 29656
Lake City 29560
Lake Forest, *Greenville* 29606
Lake Forest, *Pickens* 29640
Lake Forest Estates 29860
Lake Lanier 29356
Lakemont 29635
Lake Murray Shores 29070
Lake Shores 29649
Lakeview, *Chester* 29714
Lake View, *Dillon* 29563
Lakewood 29732
Lakewood Manor 29301
Lake Wylie 29710
Lamar 29069
Lambertown 29510
Lambs (Part of North Charleston) 29405
Lancaster 29720*
.... 29721†
Lando 29724
Landrum 29356
Landsford 29704
Lane 29564
Lanford 29335
Langley 29834
Larkin 29377
Lathem (Part of Easley) 29640
Latimer 29628
Latta 29565
Laurel Bay♦ 29906
Laurens 29360
Leawood 29601
Lebanon, *Anderson* 29621
Lebanon, *Fairfield* 29180
Leeds 29031
Leesburg (Part of Columbia)‡ 29909*
.... 29990†
Leesville (Part of Batesburg-Leesville) 29070
Legareville 29455
Lena 29918
Leo 29560
Leslie 29730
Lester 29512
Level Land 29655
Lewis 29706
Lewis Crossroads 29532
Lexington 29071-73
For specific ZIP Codes call (888) 275-8777, or your local postmaster.
Liberty 29657
Liberty Hill (Part of North Charleston) 29406
Liberty Hill, *Kershaw* 29074
Liberty Hill, *McCormick* 29835
Limehouse 29927
Limestone 29118
Lincoln Shire 29203
Lincolnville 29483
Lions Beach 29461
Litchfield Beach 29585
Little Africa 29323

Place	ZIP Code
Little Camden	29201
Little Chicago	29322
Little Eastatoe	29685
Little Mountain	29075
Little River♦	29566
Little Rock	29567
Little Texas	29690
Livingston	29107
Lobeco	29931
Lockhart	29364
Lockhart Junction	29353
Lodge	29082
Lone Star	29030
Long Bay Estates	29030
Long Branch	29853
Longcreek, *Oconee*	29658
Long Creek, *Pickens*	29640
Long Leaf	29488
Long Point	29569
Longs	29568
Longtown	29130
Loris	29569
Lowenstein Mills	29621
Lowndesville	29659
Lowrys	29706
Lucknow	29010
Lugoff♦	29078
Luray	29932
Lydia	29079
Lydia Mills	29325
Lykesland	29061
Lyman	29365
Lynchburg	29080
Lyndhurst	29812
Lynwood	29816
McAlister Square (Part of Greenville)	29607
Mac Arthurs Junction	29638
McBee	29101
McBeth	29431
McClellanville	29458
McColl	29570
McConnells	29726
McCormick	29835
McCormick Crossroads	29536
McCutchen Crossroads	29010
McDonald	29440
Macedonia	29330
McKellar Farms	29646
McKenzie Crossroads	29114
McPhersonville	29916
Maddens	29360
Madison, *Aiken*	29829
Madison, *Oconee*	29693
Magnolia Park	29853
Mallory	29565
Manning	29102
Manning Crossroads	29536
Manville	29010
Maple Crossroads	29526
Maplewood	29340
Marietta	29661
Marion	29571
Marlboro	29512
Mars Bluff	29506
Martin	29836
Maryville, *Charleston*	29407
Maryville (Part of Georgetown)	29440
Masons Crossroads	29621
Mathews (Part of Greenwood)	29646
Mathews Heights	29646
Mauldin	29662
Mayesville	29104
Mayfair	29687
Mayfair Mill (Part of Pickens)	29671
Mayo♦	29368
Mayo Mills	29368
Mayson	29138
Meadowlake	29203
Mechanicsville	29532
Meggett	29449
Melrose	29803
Merchant	29138
Middendorf	29550
Midland Park	29405
Midland Valley	29829
Midway, *Bamberg*	29003
Midway, *Kershaw*	29032
Midway, *Lancaster*	29720
Midway Crossroads	29554
Midway Village	29577
Miley	29933
Mill Creek	29163
Millers Crossroads	29838
Millett	29836
Mill Village (Part of Bennettsville)	29512
Millwood	29556
Millwood Gardens	29150
Milton	29325
Mink Point Plantation	29902
Minturn	29573
Mitchellville	29936
Mitford	29055
Modoc	29838
Monaghan	29617
Monarch Mill♦	29379
Moncks Corner	29461
Monetta	29105
Monroe Crossroads	29512
Montague	29601
Mont Clare	29532
Monticello	29106
Montmorenci	29839
Montrose	29520
Moore	29369
Moores Crossroads	29518
Moreland	29407
Morgan	29927
Morningside	29607
Morris Acres	29455
Moselle	29929
Mountain Brook	29209
Mountain Lakes	29706
Mountain Rest	29664
Mountain View	29316
Mount Carmel	29840
Mount Croghan	29727
Mount Gallagher	29692
Mount Holly	29445
Mount Olive	29581
Mount Pleasant	29464-66
For specific ZIP Codes call (888) 275-8777, or your local postmaster.	
Mount View	29687
Mountville	29370
Mt. Calvary	29536
Mullins	29574
Murphy Estates	29860
Murrells Inlet♦	29576
Myrtle Beach	29572
	29575
	29577-79
	29587
For specific ZIP Codes call (888) 275-8777, or your local postmaster.	
Myrtle Island	29910
Myrtle Square (Part of Myrtle Beach)	29577
Naval Hospital‡	29902
Naval Weapons‡	29445
Naval Weapons Station	29408
Neeses	29107
Nesmith	29580
Nevitt Forest	29621
Newberry	29108
New Cut	29720
New Easley Highway (Part of Greenville)	29611
New Ellenton	29809
New Holland Crossroads	29006
New Hope	29530
Newport	29732
New Prospect	29349
New Road	29945
Newry	29665
Newtonville	29512
New Town	29536
New Zion	29111
Neyles	29488
Nichols	29581
Nicholson Village	29801
Nimmons	29685
Nine Times	29685
Ninety Six	29666
Nixons Crossroads	29566
Nixonville	29526
Nixville	29944
Norris	29667
North	29112
North Aiken (Part of Aiken)	29801
North Anderson (Part of Anderson)‡	29623
North Augusta	29841
	29860-61
For specific ZIP Codes call (888) 275-8777, or your local postmaster.	
North Bridge Terrace (Part of Charleston)	29405
North Charleston	29406
	29410
	29419
For specific ZIP Codes call (888) 275-8777, or your local postmaster.	
North Conway (Part of Conway)	29526
North Forest Beach (Part of Hilton Head Island)	29928
North Gate (part of Myrtle Beach)‡	29577
Northgate, *Cherokee*	29341
Northgate, *Florence*	29501
North Greenwood	29649
North Hartsville♦	29550
Northlake♦	29621
North Litchfield Beach	29585
North Mullins (Part of Mullins)	29574
North Myrtle Beach	29582
	29597-98
For specific ZIP Codes call (888) 275-8777, or your local postmaster.	
North Pacolet	29322
North Santee	29458
North Summerville (Part of Summerville)	29483
North Trenholm	29206
North Winyah Heights (Part of Georgetown)	29440
Northwood Estates	29405
Northwoods Mall (Part of Charleston)	29405
Norway	29113
Oakdale, *Cherokee*	29330
Oak Dale, *Clarendon*	29111
Oakdale, *Florence*	29501
Oakdale, *York*	29730
Oak Grove, *Dillon*	29565
Oak Grove, *Lexington*♦	29073
Oak Hill	29803
Oakland, *Beaufort*	29902
Oakland, *Sumter*♦	29150
Oakland Crossroads	29547
Oakland Mill (Part of Newberry)	29108
Oakley	29461
Oak Ridge	29058
Oaks Crossroads	29142
Oakvale	29673
Oakway	29693
Oakwood	29801
Oatland	29440
Oats	29069
Ocean Drive Beach (Part of North Myrtle Beach)	29582
Ocean Forest (Part of Myrtle Beach)	29577
Oceanview	29412
Oconee Estates	29672
Oconee Station	29691
Ogden	29730
Olanta	29114
Olar	29843
Old House	29936
Old Madison	29693
Olympia	29201
Ora	29360
Orangeburg	29115-18
For specific ZIP Codes call (888) 275-8777, or your local postmaster.	
Orchard Park (Part of Greenville)‡	29615*
	29616†
Orr Mill	29621
Orrville	29621
Orum	29583
Osborn	29426
Osceola	29744
Oswego	29150
Otranto	29405
Outland	29554
Owings	29645
Oyster Point	29412
Pacolet	29372
Pacolet Mills	29373
Pacolet Park (Part of Pacolet Mills)	29373
Padgetts	29481
Pageland	29728
Palmetto	29532
Palmetto Estates	29902
Palmetto Fort	29466
Pamplico	29583
Panola, *Clarendon*	29125
Panola (Part of Greenwood)	29646
Paramount Park	29605
Paris	29609
Parker♦	29611
Parkers Ferry	29426
Parkersville	29585
Park Place‡	29608†
	29609*
Parksville	29844
Parler	29142
Parr	29065
Parris Island Marine Corps Recruit Depot	29905
Parrot Point	29412
Patrick	29584
Pauline	29374
Pawleys Island	29585
Paxville	29102
Peach Valley	29303
Peak	29122
Pecan Terrace	29605
Pecan Way Terrace (Part of Orangeburg)	29115
Pee Dee	29571
Pelham	29651
Pelion	29123
Pelzer	29669
Pendleton	29670
Peniel Crossroads	29161
Pepperhill (Part of North Charleston)	29418
Percival Crossroads	29693
Perry	29124
Philip	29464
Phoenix	29646
Pickens	29671
Pickett Post	29691
Piedmont♦	29673
Piercetown	29697
Pierpont	29414
Pimlico	29461
Pine Grove, *Darlington*	29532
Pine Grove, *Hampton*	29924
Pinehaven (Part of Charleston)‡	29405
	29415
For specific ZIP Codes call (888) 275-8777, or your local postmaster.	
Pinehurst, *Dorchester*	29483
Pinehurst, *Greenwood*	29646
Pine Island	29577
Pineland, *Charleston*	29429
Pineland, *Jasper*	29934
Pineridge, *Darlington*	29101
Pineridge, *Lexington*	29172
Pine Valley	29210
Pineville	29468
Pinewood (Part of Spartanburg)‡	29303*
	29305†
Pinewood, *Sumter*	29125
Pinopolis	29469
Pisgah	29128
Plantation Pines	29180
Plantersville	29440
Playcards	29569
Plaza (Part of Sumter)‡	29150
Pleasantburg (Part of Greenville)‡	29606
Pleasant Grove	29671
Pleasant Hill, *Georgetown*	29554
Pleasant Hill, *Lancaster*	29058
Pleasant Lane	29824
Pleasant Valley	29605
Pleasant View	29569
Plum Branch	29845
Pocotaligo	29945
Poe	29609
Polaris Missile Facility Atlantic	29408
Polk Village	29902
Pomaria	29120
Pontiac	29045
Poovey Farm	29720
Poplar Springs	29369
Port Royal	29935
Port Royal Plantation (Part of Hilton Head Island)	29928
Poston	29555
Powdersville‡	29673
Pregnall	29437
Primus	29720
Princeton	29654
Pritchardville	29910
Promised Land	29819
Prospect Crossroads	29560
Prosperity	29127
Providence	29059
Pumpkintown	29671
Puncheon Creek	29510
Purysburg Landing	29927
Quail Hollow	29169
Quinby	29506
Quinby Estates (Part of Quinby)	29506
Quinby Forest (Part of Quinby)	29501
Rabon Crossroads	29511
Rains	29589
Rantowles	29449
Ravenel	29470
Ravenwood (Part of Forest Acres)	29206
Red Bank♦	29073
Red Bank Landing	29048
Red Bluff Crossroads	29569
Red Hill, *Horry*	29526
Red Hill (rural), *Horry*	29544
Red Hill, *Lee*	29020
Red Top	29455
Reevesville	29471
Rehobeth	29544
Reid Park	29520
Reidville	29375
Rembert	29128
Remount (Part of North Charleston)	29406
Renfrew	29690
Renno	29325
Retreat	29693
Return	29678
Reynold	29817
Rhems	29440
Ribault Park (Part of Beaufort)	29902
Richburg	29729
Rich Hill Crossroads	29058
Richland	29675
Richland Mall (Part of Forest Acres)	29206
Richland Springs	29138
Richmond Hills	29617
Richtex	29180
Ridgecrest	29801
Ridgeland	29936
Ridge Spring	29129
Ridgeville	29472
Ridgeway	29130
Ridgewood, *Charleston*	29456
Ridgewood, *Oconee*	29678
Ridgewood, *Richland*	29203
Rimini	29125
Ringle Heights	29440
Rion	29132
Ritter	29488
Riverdale	29536
River Falls	29661
Riverland	29412
Riverland Terrace	29412
Rivermont	29210
Riverside (Part of Anderson)	29624
Riverside (Part of Ware Shoals)	29692
Riverside, *Greenville*	29611
Riverside, *Lancaster*	29720
Riverside Park	29210
Riverview	29715
Robat	29379
Robbins Circle	29706
Robertville	29922
Robinson	29101
Rock Bluff	29556
Rockbridge	29206
Rock Hill, *Fairfield*	29065
Rock Hill, *York*	29730-34
For specific ZIP Codes call (888) 275-8777, or your local postmaster.	
Rock Hill Galleria (Part of Rock Hill)	29730
Rockton	29180
Rockville	29487
Rocky Bottom	29685
Roddy	29704
Rodman	29706
Roebuck♦	29376
Rogers Fallout	29544
Rosehill Park	29340
Roseida	29906
Rosinville	29477

Round O 29474
Rowell 29704
Rowesville 29133
Ruby 29741
Ruffin 29475
Russellville 29476
St. Andrews, *Charleston*‡ 29407
St. Andrews, *Richland* 29210
St. Charles 29104
St. George 29477
St. Helena Island 29920
St. Julian 29048
St. Matthews 29135
St. Paul 29148
St. Paul Forks 29526
St. Stephen 29479
Salak 29646
Salem, *Florence* 29583
Salem, *Oconee* 29676
Salem Crossroads 29015
Salley 29137
Salters 29590
Saluca 29646
Saluda 29138
Saluda Gardens (Part of West Columbia) 29169
Saluda Terrace (Part of West Columbia) 29169
Samaria 29006
Sampit 29440
Sanders Corner 29062
Sandridge, *Berkeley* 29059
Sand Ridge, *Horry* 29526
Sandwood 29206
Sandy Flat 29687
Sandy Ridge 29666
Sandy Springs 29677
Sans Souci 29609
Sans Souci Heights 29617
Santee 29142
Santee Circle 29461
Santuc 29379
Sardinia 29143
Sardis 29161
Satchel Ford Terrace 29206
Savannah Bluff 29526
Sawyerdale 29112
Saxon♦ 29301
Saylors Crossroads 29627
Scanlonville 29464
Schofield 29843
Schultz Hill (Part of North Augusta) 29841
Scotia 29939
Scottsville 29104
Scranton 29591
Seabrook 29940
Seabrook Island 29455
Sea Pines (Part of Hilton Head Island) 29928
Seaside 29412
Secessionville 29412
Sedalia 29379
Seiglers Crossroads 29801
Seigling 29810
Seivern 29164
Sellers 29592
Selma 29536
Seneca 29672
29678-79
For specific ZIP Codes call (888) 275-8777, or your local postmaster.
Seneca Landing 29678
Seven Mile (Part of North Charleston) 29405
Seven Oaks 29210
Shady Rest (Part of Bennettsville) 29512
Shalimar 29341
Shannon Hill 29010
Shannontown 29150
Sharon 29742
Shaw Air Force Base 29152
Shaw Heights 29152
Sheldon 29941
Shell 29526
Shell Point♦ 29906
Shepard 29032
Sheppard Park 29483
Sherwood Acres 29301
Shiloh, *Oconee* 29678
Shiloh, *Sumter* 29080
Shiloh Estates 29678
Shipyard Plantation (Part of Hilton Head Island) 29928
Shirley 29922
Shoals Junction 29638
Shulerville 29479
Silver 29102
Silver Bluff Estates 29803
Silverstreet 29145
Simpson 29130
Simpsonville 29680-81
For specific ZIP Codes call (888) 275-8777, or your local postmaster.
Singing Pines 29678
Singleton 29135
Six Mile 29682
Six Points 29801
Skyview Terrace 29210
Slansville 29483
Slater 29683
Slighs 29127
Smallwood, *Fairfield* 29130
Smallwood, *Laurens* 29325
Smith 29730
Smithboro 29574
Smith Mills 29554
Smoaks 29481
Smyrna 29743
Snelling 29812
Sniders Crossroads 29475
Snowden 29464
Socastee‡ 29575
29577
29579
For specific ZIP Codes call (888) 275-8777, or your local postmaster.
Society Hill 29593
South Anderson (Part of Anderson)‡ 29624
South Congaree 29172
Southern Meadows 29678
Southern Shops♦ 29303
South Forest Estates 29605
South Greenwood (Part of Greenwood)‡ 29646
South Hartsville 29550
South Hills 29379
South Lynchburg 29080
South Mullins (Part of Mullins) 29574
South Park (Part of Florence)‡ 29504†
29505*
Southside 29505
South Union 29693
Spartanburg 29301-18
For specific ZIP Codes call (888) 275-8777, or your local postmaster.
Spaulding Heights 29501
Spiderweb 29822
Spring Branch 29571
Springdale, *Lancaster* 29720
Springdale, *Lexington* 29170
Springfield, *Orangeburg* 29146
Springfield, *Spartanburg* 29316
Spring Hill, *Lee* 29128
Spring Hill, *Richland* 29177
Springmaid Beach 29577
Spring Mills 29067
Springtown 29481
Spring Valley 29646
Springwood 29204
Stallsville 29485
Stark Terrace 29203
Starmount 29172
Starr 29684
Startex♦ 29377
Stateburg 29150
State College (Part of Orangeburg) 29117
Steedman 29070
Stiefeltown 29851
Stokes 29488
Stokes Bridge 29010
Stomp Springs 29325
Stoneboro 29058
Stoney Hill 29127
Stono 29412
Stover 29014
Stratford Hall 29803
Stratton Capers 29405
Strawberry 29461
Stuart Point 29940
Stuckey 29554
Sullivan's Island 29482
Summer Hill (Part of North Augusta) 29841
Summerton 29148
Summerville 29483-85
For specific ZIP Codes call (888) 275-8777, or your local postmaster.
Summit 29070
Sumter 29150-51
29153-54
For specific ZIP Codes call (888) 275-8777, or your local postmaster.
Sunnyside (Part of Greer) 29651
Sunset 29685
Surfside Beach 29575
Suttons 29510
Swansea 29160
Sweden 29042
Sweetwater, *Aiken* 29860
Sweetwater, *Barnwell* 29812
Switzer 29369
Switzerland 29936
Sycamore 29846
Syracuse 29532
Talatha 29803
Tall Pines 29536
Tamassee 29686
Tanglewood, *Beaufort* 29902
Tanglewood, *Greenville* 29611
Tanglewood, *Oconee* 29672
Tanglewood, *Orangeburg* 29115
Tarboro 29943
Tatum 29594
Taxahaw 29067
Taylors 29687
Tega Cay 29715
Temperance Hill 29571
Ten Mile (Part of Charleston) 29429
Ten Mile, *Charleston* 29464
Terrells Crossroads 29518
Texas 29477
The Farms (Part of Hanahan) 29410
The Groves (Part of Mount Pleasant) 29464
The Meadows 29678
Thor 29123
Three Trees 29412
Tibwin 29458
Tifton 29532
Tigerville 29688
Tillman 29943
Timberlake 29678
Timmonsville 29161
Tirzah 29745
Toddville 29526
Tokeena Crossroads 29678
Toney Creek 29627
Townville 29689
Toxaway (Part of Anderson) 29621
Tradesville 29720
Tranquil Acres 29456
Travelers Rest 29690
Trenton 29847
Triangle (Part of Belton) 29627
Trio 29590
Troy 29848
Tuckertown 29031
Tugtown 29059
Turbeville 29162
Twin Lake Hill 29209
Tyler 29536
Ulmer 29849
Una, *Darlington* 29069
Una, *Spartanburg* 29378
Union 29379
Union Bleachery 29617
Union Crossroads 29111
Unity 28173
University (Part of Columbia)‡ 29208
Utica♦ 29678
Valencia Heights♦ 29205
Valley Falls♦ 29303
Vance 29163
Van Wyck 29744
Varnville 29944
Vaucluse 29850
Verdery 29819
Victor Mills (Part of Greer) 29651
Village Creek 29678
Virginia Acres 29803
Waddell Gardens (Part of Beaufort) 29902
Wadmalaw Island 29487
Wadsworth 29301
Wagener 29164
Walhalla 29691
Wallace 29596
Walnut Grove 29374
Walterboro 29488
Wampee 29568
Wando 29492
Wando Woods 29405
Ward 29166
Ware Place 29669
Ware Shoals 29692
Warren Crossroads 29470
Warrenville 29851
Warsaw 29510
Wateree 29044
Waterford Estates 29440
Waterloo 29384
Watkins Store 29803
Watson Village (Part of Anderson) 29624
Watts Mills♦ 29360
Waverly Mills 29585
Waylyn 29405
Wedgefield 29168
Welcome 29621
Wellford 29385
Wellington Mill 29624
West Andrews (Part of Andrews) 29510
West Columbia 29169-72
For specific ZIP Codes call (888) 275-8777, or your local postmaster.
West Gantt 29605
Westgate (Part of Spartanburg)‡ 29301
Westgate Mall (Part of Spartanburg) 29301
West Marion 29571
Westminster 29693
Westover Acres (Part of West Columbia) 29169
West Pelzer 29669
West Springs 29353
West Union 29696
Westview 29301
Westville, *Greenville* 29611
Westville, *Kershaw* 29175
Whetstone 29664
Whipper Barony (Part of North Charleston) 29405
White Bluff Crossroads 29067
White Hall, *Colleton* 29446
Whitehall, *Greenwood* 29646
Whitehall, *Lexington* 29210
White Oak 29176
White Plains, *Anderson* 29697
White Plains, *Chesterfield* 29718
White Pond 29853
White Rock 29177
White Stone 29386
Whitesville 29461
Whitetown 29845
Whitmire 29178
Whitney 29303
Wilder 29431
Wilkinsville 29340
Wilksburg 29706
Williams 29493
Williams Estate 29720
Williamston 29697
Willington 29835
Williston 29853
Willowbrook 29445
Wilson 29102
Wilson Creek 29646
Wilsons Cross Roads 29532
Windsor 29856
Windsor Estates 29204
Windsor Forest 29501
Windsor Lake Park 29206
Windsor Park 29520
Windsor Plantation 29440
Windwood 29461
Windy Hill 29506
Windy Hill Beach (Part of North Myrtle Beach) 29582
Winnsboro 29180
Winnsboro Mills♦ 29180
Winona 29506
Winthrop College (Part of York)‡ 29730
Wisacky 29010
Wolfton 29112
Woodburn Hills 29301
Woodfield 29206
Woodfields 29605
Woodford 29112
Woodland Hills 29210
Woodrow 29040
Woodruff 29388
Woodside 29610
Woodville 29669
Woodward 29014
Workman 29111
Yarn Mill 29520
Yauhannah 29440
Yeamans Hall (Part of Hanahan) 29410
Yemassee 29945
Yenome 29812
Yonges Island 29449
York 29745
Yorkshire 29209
Yoruba Village 29941
Youngs 29388
Zion 29574

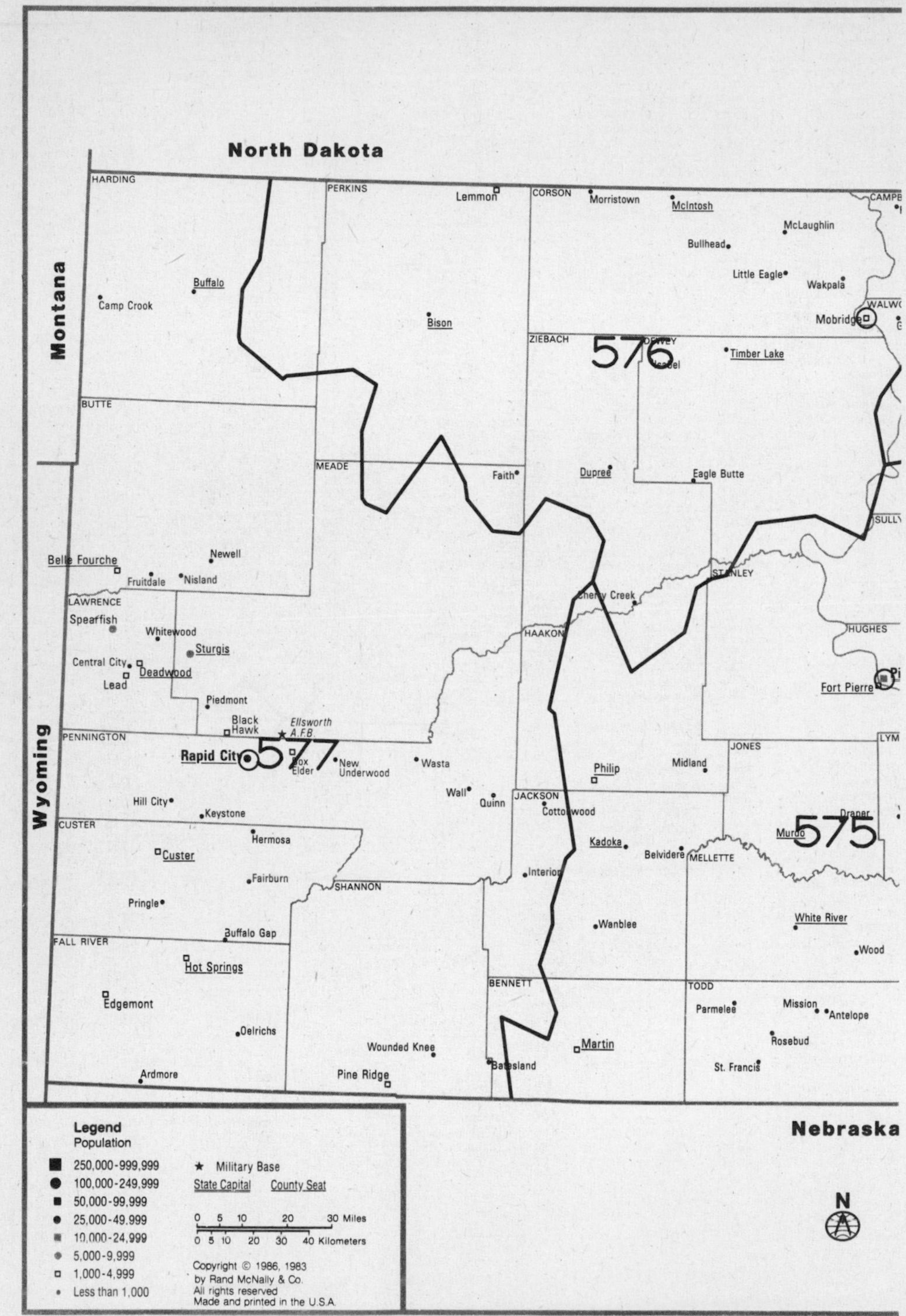

North Dakota
Montana
Wyoming
Nebraska
HARDING
PERKINS
CORSON
ZIEBACH
DEWEY
BUTTE
MEADE
LAWRENCE
PENNINGTON
HAAKON
STANLEY
HUGHES
SULLY
JONES
JACKSON
MELLETTE
CUSTER
SHANNON
FALL RIVER
BENNETT
TODD
Camp Crook
Buffalo
Bison
Lemmon
Morristown
McIntosh
McLaughlin
Bullhead
Little Eagle
Wakpala
Mobridge
Timber Lake
576
Faith
Dupree
Eagle Butte
Belle Fourche
Newell
Fruitdale
Nisland
Cherry Creek
Spearfish
Whitewood
Sturgis
Central City
Deadwood
Lead
Piedmont
Black Hawk
Ellsworth A.F.B.
Rapid City
577
Box Elder
New Underwood
Wasta
Wall
Quinn
Philip
Midland
Fort Pierre
Hill City
Keystone
Cottonwood
Hermosa
Custer
Kadoka
Belvidere
Murdo
575
Draper
Interior
Fairburn
Pringle
Wanblee
White River
Wood
Buffalo Gap
Hot Springs
Edgemont
Parmelee
Mission
Antelope
Oelrichs
Rosebud
Wounded Knee
Martin
Batesland
Ardmore
Pine Ridge
St. Francis
Legend
Population
250,000-999,999
100,000-249,999
50,000-99,999
25,000-49,999
10,000-24,999
5,000-9,999
1,000-4,999
Less than 1,000
Military Base
State Capital
County Seat
0 5 10 20 30 Miles
0 5 10 20 30 40 Kilometers
Copyright © 1986, 1983 by Rand McNally & Co. All rights reserved Made and printed in the U.S.A.
N

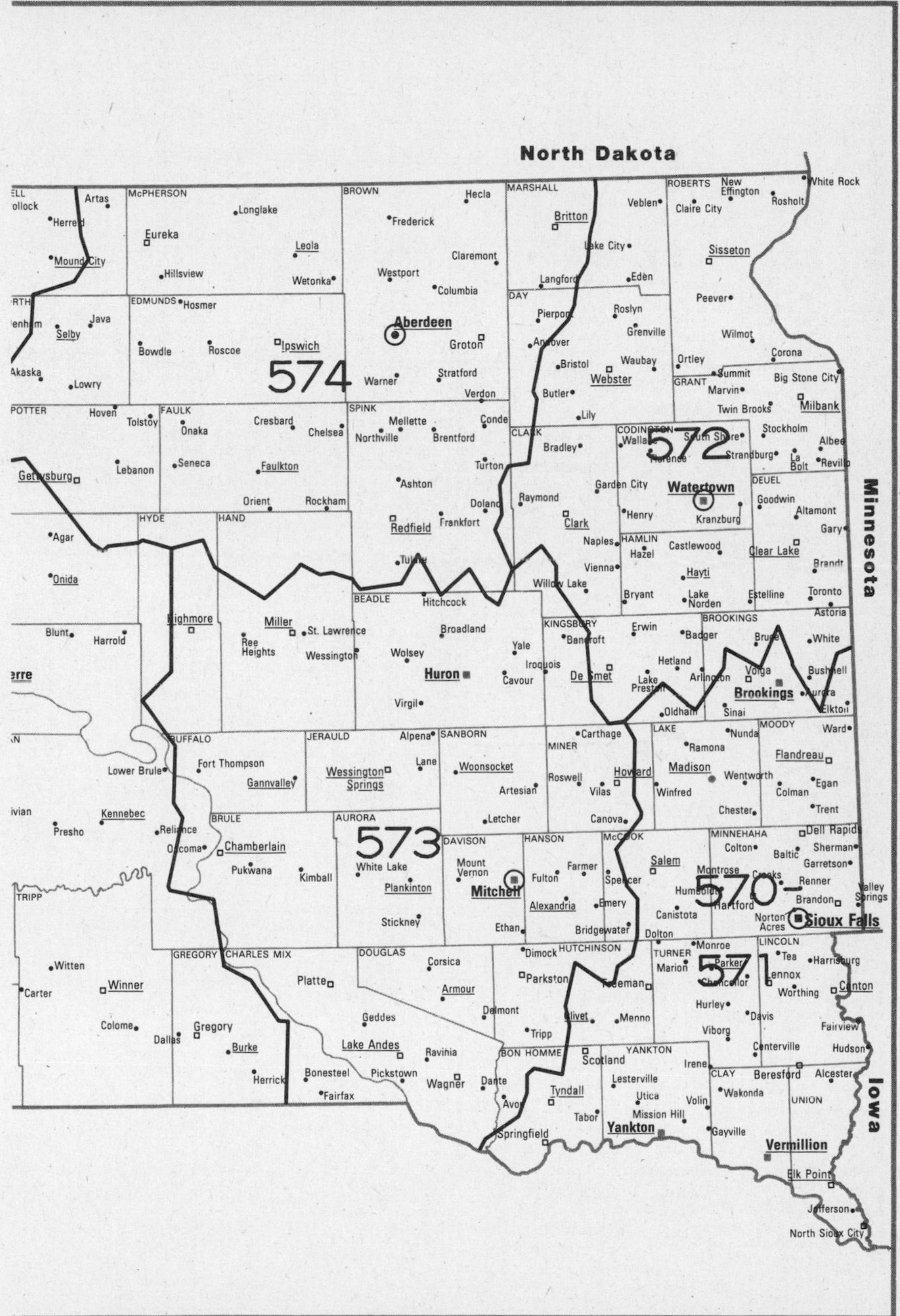
North Dakota
Minnesota
Iowa
574
572
573
570
571
Artas
McPHERSON
Longlake
Eureka
Leola
Hillsview
Wetonka
Mound City
BROWN
Hecla
Frederick
Claremont
Westport
Columbia
Aberdeen
Groton
Stratford
Warner
Verdon
MARSHALL
Britton
Lake City
Langford
Veblen
Eden
ROBERTS
New Effington
Claire City
Rosholt
White Rock
Sisseton
Peever
Wilmot
Corona
EDMUNDS
Hosmer
Selby
Java
Bowdle
Roscoe
Ipswich
Akaska
Lowry
DAY
Roslyn
Grenville
Bristol
Webster
Waubay
Butler
Lily
Ortley
Summit
GRANT
Marvin
Big Stone City
Twin Brooks
Milbank
POTTER
Hoven
Tolstoy
FAULK
Onaka
Cresbard
Chelsea
SPINK
Mellette
Northville
Brentford
Conde
Turton
Ashton
Doland
Redfield
Frankfort
CLARK
Bradley
Garden City
Raymond
Clark
CODINGTON
Watertown
Henry
Kranzburg
Strandburg
Stockholm
Albee
Revillo
DEUEL
Goodwin
Altamont
Gary
Seneca
Lebanon
Faulkton
Gettysburg
Orient
Rockham
Agar
Onida
HYDE
HAND
Highmore
Miller
Ree Heights
St. Lawrence
Wessington
Blunt
Harrold
BEADLE
Hitchcock
Broadland
Yale
Iroquois
Cavour
Wolsey
Huron
Virgil
Naples
Vienna
HAMLIN
Hazel
Castlewood
Hayti
Clear Lake
Brandt
Bryant
Lake Norden
Estelline
Toronto
Astoria
KINGSBURY
Bancroft
Erwin
De Smet
Hetland
Lake Preston
Oldham
BROOKINGS
Badger
Bruce
White
Volga
Brookings
Aurora
Elkton
Sinai
BUFFALO
Fort Thompson
Gannvalley
Lower Brule
JERAULD
Alpena
Lane
Wessington Springs
SANBORN
Woonsocket
Artesian
Letcher
MINER
Carthage
Roswell
Howard
Vilas
Canova
LAKE
Ramona
Madison
Nunda
Wentworth
Winfred
Chester
MOODY
Ward
Flandreau
Egan
Colman
Trent
Kennebec
Presho
Reliance
Oacoma
BRULE
Chamberlain
Pukwana
Kimball
AURORA
White Lake
Plankinton
Stickney
DAVISON
Mount Vernon
Mitchell
Ethan
HANSON
Fulton
Farmer
Alexandria
Emery
McCOOK
Salem
Spencer
Bridgewater
Canistota
Dolton
MINNEHAHA
Colton
Baltic
Dell Rapids
Sherman
Garretson
Montrose
Crooks
Renner
Hartford
Brandon
Valley Springs
Norton Acres
Sioux Falls
TRIPP
Witten
Carter
Winner
Colome
Dallas
GREGORY
Gregory
Burke
Herrick
CHARLES MIX
Platte
Geddes
Lake Andes
Ravinia
Bonesteel
Fairfax
Pickstown
Wagner
DOUGLAS
Corsica
Armour
Delmont
Dimock
HUTCHINSON
Parkston
Tripp
Olivet
Menno
TURNER
Monroe
Marion
Parker
Hurley
Viborg
Davis
LINCOLN
Tea
Harrisburg
Lennox
Worthing
Canton
Fairview
Centerville
Hudson
BON HOMME
Dante
Scotland
Tyndall
Tabor
Springfield
YANKTON
Lesterville
Utica
Mission Hill
Yankton
Irene
Volin
Gayville
CLAY
Wakonda
Beresford
Alcester
UNION
Vermillion
Elk Point
Jefferson
North Sioux City

Place	ZIP Code
Aberdeen	57401*
	57402†
Academy	57369
Agar	57520
Agency Village	57262
Akaska	57420
Albee	57259
Alcester	57001
Alexandria	57311
Allen	57714
Alpena	57312
Altamont	57226
Ames	57362
Amherst	57421
Andover	57422
Antelope♦	57555
Ardmore	57735
Arlington	57212
Arlington Beach	57212
Armour	57313
Arpan	57762
Artas	57437
Artesian	57314
Ashton	57424
Astoria	57213
Athol	57424
Aurora	57002
Aurora Center	57375
Avon	57315
Badger	57214
Baltic	57003
Bancroft	57353
Barnard	57426
Batesland	57716
Bath	57427
Bear Butte	57785
Bear Creek	57636
Belle Fourche	57717
Belvidere	57521
Bemis	57238
Beresford	57004
Bethlehem	57708
Big Bend	57702
Big Springs	57001
Big Stone City	57216
Bijou Hills	57370
Bison	57620
Black Hawk♦	57718
Blacktail	57754
Blumengard Colony	57438
Blunt	57522
Bonesteel	57317
Bon Homme Colony	57063
Bonilla	57348
Bowdle	57428
Box Elder	57719
Bradley	57217
Brandon	57005
Brandt	57218
Brentford	57429
Bridger	57748
Bridgewater	57319
Bristol	57219
Britton	57430
Broadland	57350
Brookings	57006
Brownsville	57754
Bruce	57220
Bryant	57221
Buffalo	57720
Buffalo Gap	57722
Buffalo Ridge	57115
Buffalo Trading Post	57018
Bullhead♦	57621
Burbank	57010
Burke	57523
Bushnell	57276
Butler	57219
Cactus Flat	57567
Camp Crook	57724
Canistota	57012
Canova	57321
Canton	57013
Capa	57552
Caputa	57725
Carpenter	57322
Carter	57526
Carthage	57323
Castle Rock	57760
Castlewood	57223
Cavour	57324
Cedarbutte	57579
Cedar Grove Colony	57369
Center	57058
Center Point	57070
Centerville	57014
Central City	57754
Chamberlain	57325
Chancellor	57015
Chautauqua	57042
Chelsea	57465
Cherry Creek	57622
Chester	57016
Cheyenne Crossing	57754
Cheyenne River Indian Reservation	57625
Claire City	57224
Claremont	57432
Clark	57225
Clark Colony	57258
Clayton	57332
Clearfield	57580
Clear Lake	57226
Cliff Avenue (Part of Sioux Falls)‡	57104
Colman	57017
Colome	57528
Colton	57018
Columbia	57433
Conde	57434
Corn Creek	57560
Corona	57227
Corsica	57328
Corson	57005
Cottonwood	57775
Crandall	57434
Crazy Horse	57730
Creighton	57729
Cresbard	57435
Crocker	57217
Crooks	57020
Crow Creek Indian Reservation	57339
Crow Lake	57382
Custer	57730
Dallas	57529
Dante	57329
Davis	57021
Deadwood	57732
De Grey	57501
Dell Rapids	57022
Delmont	57330
Dempster	57234
Denby	57716
De Smet	57231
Dimock	57331
Dixon	57533
Doland	57436
Dolton	57319
Downtown (Part of Aberdeen)‡	57401
Draper	57531
Dupree	57623
Eagle Butte	57625
East Sioux Falls	57101
Eden	57232
Edgemont	57735
Egan	57024
Elk Point	57025
Elkton	57026
Ellis	57107
Ellsworth Air Force Base	57706
Elmore	57754
Elm Springs	57736
Elm Springs Colony	57334
Emery	57332
Empire	57788
Empire, The (Part of Sioux Falls)	57106
Enning	57737
Epiphany	57321
Erwin	57233
Esmond	57353
Estelline	57234
Ethan	57334
Eureka	57437
Fairburn	57738
Fairfax	57335
Fairpoint	57787
Fairview	57027
Faith	57626
Farmer	57311
Farmingdale	57725
Faulkton	57438
Fedora	57337
Ferney	57439
Firesteel	57628
Flandreau	57028
Flandreau Indian Reservation	57028
Fleetwood (Part of Brandon)	57005
Florence	57235
Forestburg	57314
Fort Pierre	57532
Fort Thompson♦	57339
Frankfort	57440
Franklin	57042
Frederick	57441
Freeman	57029
Froehlich Addition	57104
Fruitdale	57742
Fulton	57340
Galena	57732
Gannvalley	57341
Garden City	57236
Garretson	57030
Gary	57237
Gayville	57031
Geddes	57342
Gettysburg	57442
Glad Valley	57629
Glencross	57630
Glendale Colony	57440
Glenham	57631
Goodwin	57238
Graceville Colony	57076
Greenfield	57010
Green Grass	57625
Greenwood	57380
Gregory	57533
Grenville	57239
Groton	57445
Grover	57201
Hamill	57534
Hammer	57255
Hanna	57754
Harrington	57551
Harrisburg	57032
Harrison	57344
Harrold	57536
Hartford	57033
Hartford Beach	57227
Hayes	57537
Hayti	57241
Hayward Addition	57106
Hazel	57242
Hecla	57446
Henry	57243
Hereford	57785
Hermosa	57744
Herreid	57632
Herrick	57538
Hetland	57244
Hiawatha Beach	57279
Hidden Timber	69201
Highmore	57345
Hill City	57745
Hillhead	57270
Hillside	57328
Hillside Colony	57436
Hillsview	57437
Hisega	57702
Hisle	57577
Hitchcock	57348
Holabird	57540
Holmquist	57274
Hooker	57070
Hoover	57760
Hosmer	57448
Hot Springs	57747
Houghton	57449
Hoven	57450
Howard	57349
Howes	57748
Hub City	57069
Hudson	57034
Huffton	57432
Humboldt	57035
Hurley	57036
Huron	57350
Huron Colony	57350
Ideal	57541
Igloo	57735
Imlay	57780
Interior	57750
Iona	57542
Ipswich	57451
Irene	57037
Iron Lightning	57623
Iroquois	57353
Isabel	57633
James	57445
Java	57452
Jefferson	57038
Johnson Siding	57702
Joubert	57344
Junction City	57010
Junius	57042
Kadoka	57543
Kaylor	57354
Keldron	57634
Kenel	57642
Kennebec	57544
Keyapaha	57580
Keystone	57751
Kidder	57430
Kimball	57355
Kingsburg	57062
Kones Corner	57223
Kranzburg	57245
Kyle♦	57752
La Bolt	57246
Ladner	57720
Lake Andes	57356
Lake Campbell	57006
Lake City	57247
Lake Norden	57248
Lake Preston	57249
Lane	57358
Langford	57454
Lantry	57636
La Plant	57652
Lead	57754
Lebanon	57455
Lemmon	57638
Lennox	57039
Leola	57456
Lesterville	57040
Letcher	57359
Lily	57274
Linden Beach	57227
Littleburg	57555
Little Eagle♦	57639
Lodgepole	57640
Lone Tree	57024
Long Lake	57457
Long Lake Colony	57481
Long Valley	57547
Loomis	57301
Lower Brule♦	57548
Lower Brule Indian Reservation	57548
Lowry	57472
Lucas	57523
Ludlow	57755
Lyons	57041
McCook Lake	57038
McIntosh	57641
McLaughlin	57642
Madison	57042
Madsen Beach	57279
Mahto	57643
Manchester	57353
Manderson	57756
Mansfield	57460
Marcus	57785
Marcy Colony	57366
Marion	57043
Marlow	57270
Martin	57551
Marty♦	57361
Marvin	57251
Maurine	57626
Maxwell Colony	57059
Mayfield	57037
Meadow	57644
Meckling	57044
Mellette	57461
Menno	57045
Midland	57552
Midway	57037
Milbank	57252
Milesville	57553
Millboro	57580
Miller	57362
Miller Dale Colony	57362
Milltown	57366
Mina	57462
Miranda	57438
Mission	57555
Mission Hill	57046
Mission Ridge	57532
Mitchell	57301
Mobridge	57601
Monroe	57047
Montrose	57048
Morningside	57350
Morristown	57645
Mosher	57580
Mound City	57646
Mount Vernon	57363
Mud Butte	57758
Murdo	57559
Mystic	57745
Naples	57271
Nemo	57759
New Effington	57255
Newell	57760
New Holland	57364
New Underwood	57761
Nisland	57762
Nora	57001
Norbeck	57438
Norris	57560
North Eagle Butte♦	57625
North Sioux City	57049
North Spearfish♦	57783
Northville	57465
Norton Acres	57104
Nunda	57050
Oacoma	57365
Oelrichs	57763
Oglala♦	57764
Okaton	57562
Okreek	57563
Ola	57325
Oldham	57051
Olivet	57052
Olsonville	69201
Onaka	57466
Onida	57564
Opal	57765
Oral	57766
Ordway	57433
Orient	57467
Orland	57042
Ortley	57256
Osceola	57353
Owanka	57767
Parade	57647
Parker	57053
Parkston	57366
Parmelee♦	57566
Patricia	57551
Pearl Creek Colony	57353
Pearsons Corner	57070
Pedro	57729
Peever	57257
Peninsula Park	57075
Perkins	57062
Philip	57567
Pickerel	57239
Pickstown	57367
Piedmont	57769
Pierpont	57468
Pierre	57501
Pine Ridge♦	57770
Pine Ridge Indian Reservation	57770
Plainview	57748
Plainview Colony	57451
Plankinton	57368
Plano	57340
Platte	57369
Platte Colony	57369
Pluma	57732
Pollock	57648
Polo	57467
Porcupine♦	57772
Potato Creek	57750
Prairie City	57649
Prairie Village	57042
Presho	57568
Pringle	57773
Promise	57601
Provo	57774
Pukwana	57370
Pumpkin Center	57035
Putney	57445
Quinn	57775
Quinn Table	57790
Ralph	57650
Ramona	57054
Rapid City	57701-03
	57709
For specific Zip Codes call (888) 275-8777, or your local postmaster.	
Rapid Valley♦	57703
Ravinia	57357
Raymond	57258
Red Elm	57623
Redfield	57469
Redig	57776
Redowl	57777
Red Scaffold	57626
Red Shirt	57744
Ree Heights	57371
Reliance	57569
Renner	57055
Reva	57651
Revillo	57259
Richland	57025
Ridgeview	57652
Riverside	57301
Riverside Colony	57350
Rochford	57778
Rockerville	57702
Rockham	57470
Rockport	57311
Roscoe	57471
Rosebud♦	57570
Rosebud Indian Reservation	57570
Rosedale Colony	57301
Rosholt	57260
Roslyn	57261
Roswell	57349

* **Area Zip Code** † **Post Office Boxes** ‡ **Postal Station** ♦ **Census Designated Place** *Italic Type* **County**

Roubaix	57754
Rowena	57056
Rumford	57774
Rumpus Ridge	57012
Running Water	57062
Rushmore Mall (Part of Rapid City)	57701
Rutland	57057
St. Charles	57571
St. Francis	57572
St. Lawrence	57373
St. Onge	57779
Salem	57058
Sanator	57730
Savoy	57754
Scenic	57780
Scotland	57059
Selby	57472
Seneca	57473
Shadehill	57653
Shady Beach	57227
Sharps Corner	57752
Sherman	57030
Silver City	57702
Sinai	57061
Sioux Falls	57101-10
	57116-18
For specific Zip Codes call (888) 275-8777, or your local postmaster.	
Sisseton	57262
Sisseton Indian Reservation	57262
Smiths Park	57075
Smithwick	57782
So Dak Park	57279
Soldier Creek	57555
Sorum	57620
South Shore	57263
Spearfish	57783
Spencer	57374
Spink	57025
Spink Colony	57440
Spring Creek♦	57572
Spring Creek Colony	58439
Springfield	57062
Spring Valley	57036
Spring Valley Colony	57382
Standing Rock Indian Reservation	58538
Stanley Corner	57319
Stephan	57346
Stickney	57375
Stockholm	57264
Stone Bridge	57223
Stoneville	57787
Storla	57359
Strandburg	57265
Stratford	57474
Sturgis	57785
Summit	57266
Sunnyview	57006
Swett	57551
Tabor	57063
Tacoma Park	57433
Tea	57064
Thomas	57241
Thunder Butte	57623
Thunder Hawk	57638
Tilford	57769
Timber Lake	57656
Tolstoy	57475
Toronto	57268
Trail City	57657
Trent	57065
Tripp	57376
Trojan	57754
Troy	57265
Tschetter Colony	57052
Tulare	57476
Turkey Ridge	57036
Turton	57477
Tuthill	57574
Twin Brooks	57269
Two Strike♦	57570
Tyndall	57066
Union Center	57787
Unityville	57058
University (Part of Brookings)‡	57007
Usta	57626
Utica	57067
Vale	57788
Valley Springs	57068
Valley View	57072
Vayland	57381
Veblen	57270
Vedin Corner	57037
Verdon	57434
Vermillion	57069
Vetal	57551
Viborg	57070
Victor	57260
Vienna	57271
Vilas	57349
Villa Trailer Court	57706
Virgil	57379
Vivian	57576
Volga	57071
Volin	57072
Wagner	57380
Wakonda	57073
Wakpala	57658
Wakpamani	57716
Walker	57659
Wall	57790
Wallace	57272
Wanblee♦	57577
Ward	57074
Warner	57479
Wasta	57791
Watauga	57660
Watertown	57201
Waubay	57273
Waverly	57202
Webster	57274
Webster Grove	57106
Wecota	57438
Wentworth	57075
Wessington	57381
Wessington Springs	57382
Western Mall (Part of Sioux Falls)‡	57105*
	57109†
Westerville	57069
Westport	57481
Wetonka	57481
Wewela	57578
White	57276
White Butte	57638
Whitehorse, *Dewey*	57661
White Horse, *Todd*♦	57555
White Lake	57383
White Owl	57792
White River	57579
White Rock	57260
Whitewood	57793
Wicksville	57767
Willow Lake	57278
Wilmot	57279
Winfred	57076
Winner	57580
Witten	57584
Wolf Creek Colony	57052
Wolsey	57384
Wood	57585
Woonsocket	57385
Worthing	57077
Wounded Knee♦	57794
Yale	57386
Yankton	57078
Yankton Indian Reservation	57380
Zell	57469
Zeona	57758

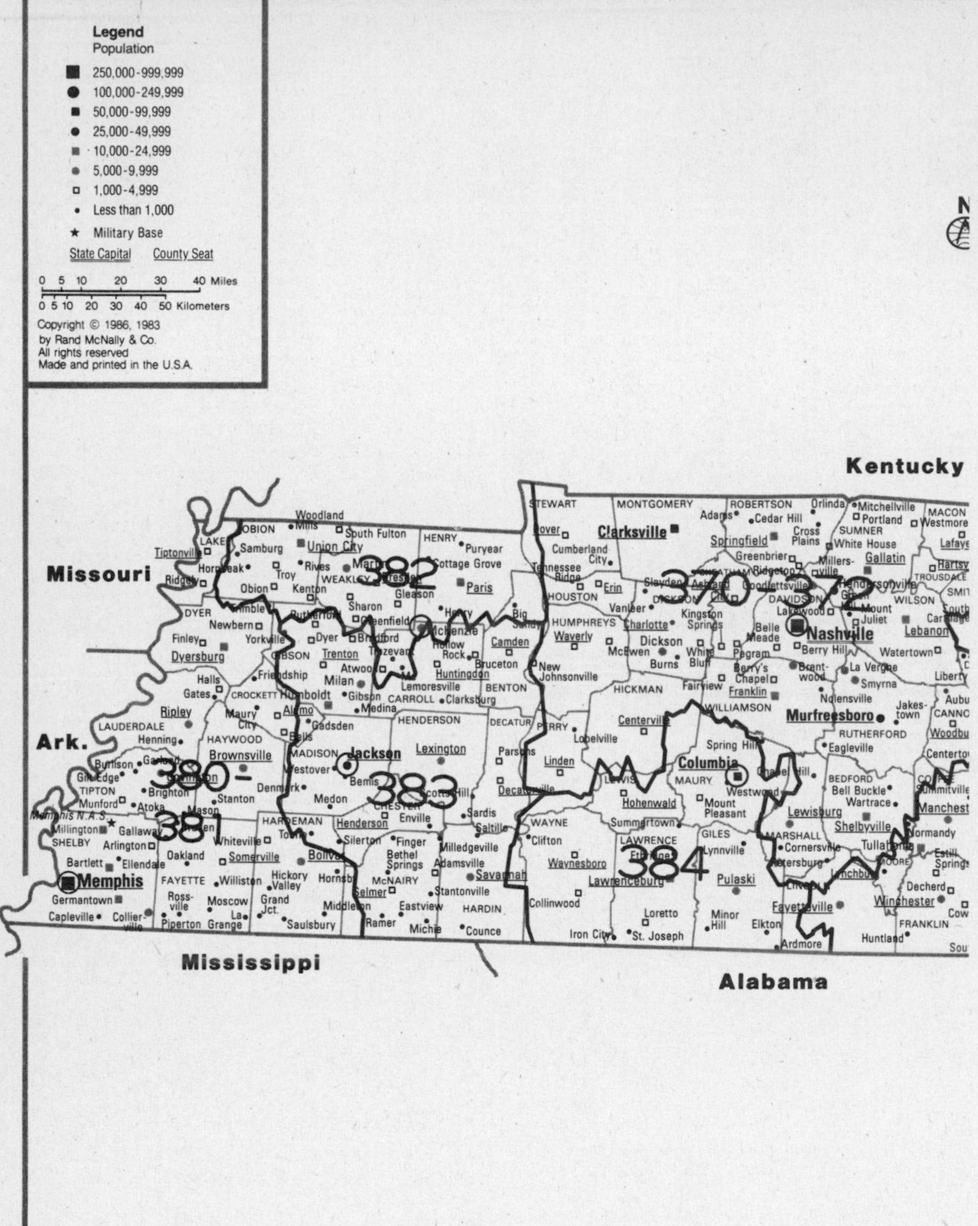
Legend
Population
250,000-999,999
100,000-249,999
50,000-99,999
25,000-49,999
10,000-24,999
5,000-9,999
1,000-4,999
Less than 1,000
Military Base
State Capital
County Seat
0 5 10 20 30 40 Miles
0 5 10 20 30 40 50 Kilometers
Copyright © 1986, 1983
by Rand McNally & Co.
All rights reserved
Made and printed in the U.S.A.
Kentucky
Missouri
Ark.
Mississippi
Alabama
380-
381
382
383
370-372
384
Memphis
Jackson
Nashville
Clarksville
Murfreesboro
Columbia
Dyersburg
Union City
Paris
Brownsville
Lexington
Henderson
Savannah
Lawrenceburg
Pulaski
Fayetteville
Franklin
Lebanon
Gallatin
Springfield
Dickson
Camden
Huntingdon
Trenton
Humboldt
Covington
Somerville
Bolivar
Waverly
Centerville
Hohenwald
Waynesboro
Linden
Lewisburg
Shelbyville
Winchester
Manchester

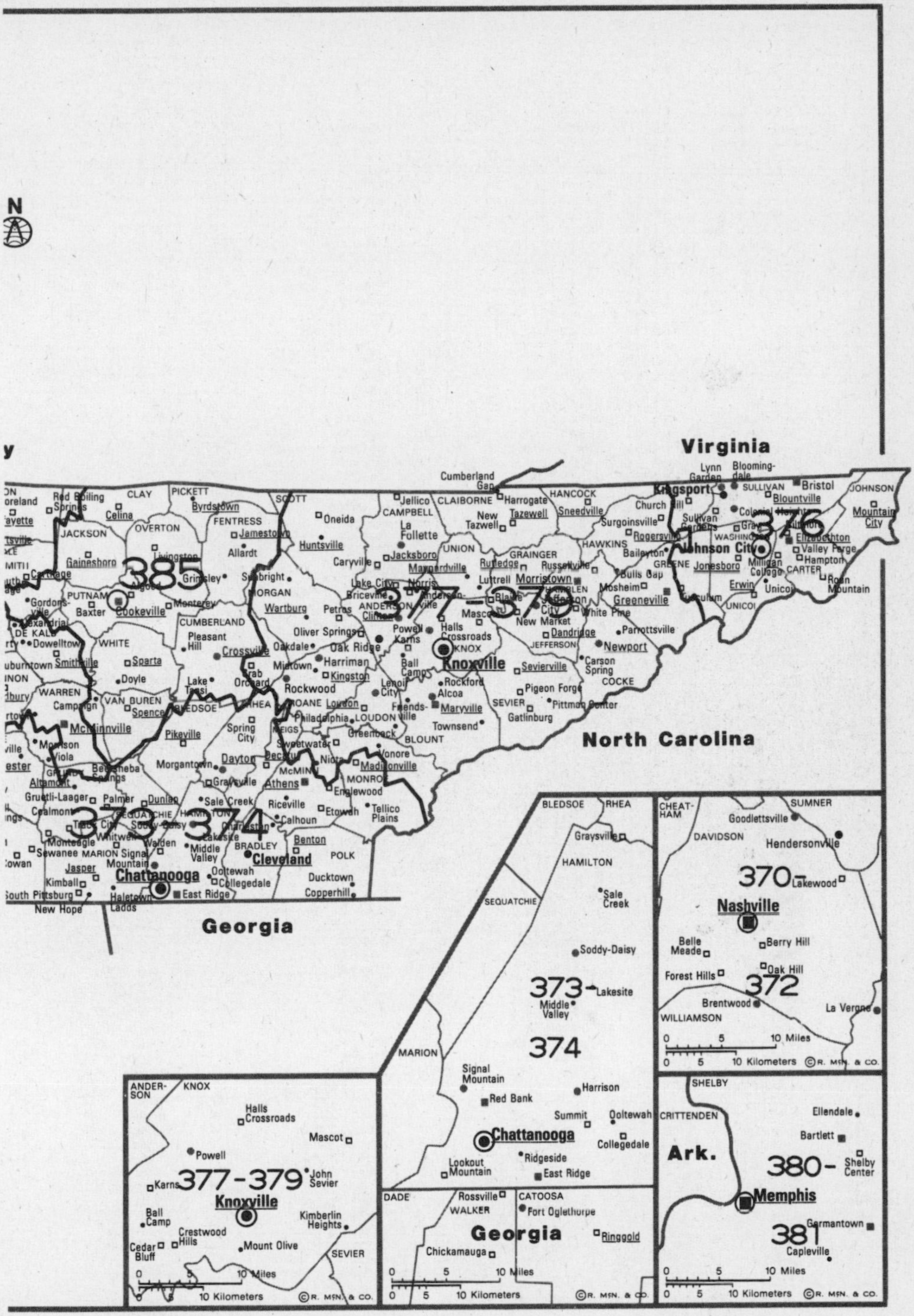

Virginia
North Carolina
Georgia
385
377-379
376
373-374
Kingsport
Bristol
Johnson City
Knoxville
Chattanooga
Cleveland
Cookeville
Crossville
Morristown
Greeneville
Newport
Oak Ridge
Maryville
Sevierville
Gatlinburg
McMinnville
Athens
Dayton

BLEDSOE
RHEA
HAMILTON
SEQUATCHIE
MARION
Graysville
Sale Creek
Soddy-Daisy
373-
Lakesite
Middle Valley
374
Signal Mountain
Red Bank
Harrison
Summit
Ooltewah
Chattanooga
Collegedale
Ridgeside
Lookout Mountain
East Ridge
DADE
Rossville
WALKER
CATOOSA
Fort Oglethorpe
Georgia
Ringgold
Chickamauga
0 5 10 Miles
0 5 10 Kilometers
©R. McN. & CO.

CHEATHAM
SUMNER
Goodlettsville
DAVIDSON
Hendersonville
370-
Lakewood
Nashville
Belle Meade
Berry Hill
Forest Hills
Oak Hill
372
Brentwood
La Vergne
WILLIAMSON
0 5 10 Miles
0 5 10 Kilometers
©R. McN. & CO.

ANDERSON
KNOX
Halls Crossroads
Mascot
Powell
377-379
John Sevier
Karns
Knoxville
Ball Camp
Kimberlin Heights
Crestwood Hills
Cedar Bluff
Mount Olive
SEVIER
0 5 10 Miles
0 5 10 Kilometers
©R. McN. & CO.

SHELBY
CRITTENDEN
Ellendale
Bartlett
Ark.
380-
Shelby Center
Memphis
Germantown
381
Capleville
0 5 10 Miles
0 5 10 Kilometers
©R. McN. & CO.

Acklen (Part of Nashville)‡ 37212
Acton 38357
Adair 38301
Adams 37010
Adams Crossroads 37055
Adamsville 38310
Adolphus 37774
Aetna 37033
Afton 37616
Airport 37110
Airport Estates (Part of Nashville) 37217
Airport Mail Facility (Part of Memphis)‡ 38130
Airport Mail Facility (Part of Nashville)‡ 37217
Akard Addition 37620
Alamo 38001
Alanthus Hill 37879
Albany 37743
Alcoa 37701
Alder Branch 37876
Alder Springs, *Campbell* 37766
Alder Springs, *Union* 37807
Alexander Springs 38456
Alexandria 37012
Algood 38506
Allardt 38504
Allens 38012
Allens Chapel 37166
Allensville 37876
Allisona 37046
Allons 38541
Alloway 37337
Allred 38542
Almaville 37014
Almy 37755
Alpha 37814
Alpha Heights 37814
Alpine 38543
Altamont 37301
Alto 37324
Alton Park (Part of Chattanooga) 37409
Altonville 37857
Alumwell 37857
Alynwick 37804
Amherst (Part of Knoxville) 37931
Amity Heights 37620
Amqui (Part of Nashville) 37115
Anark 38344
Anderson, *Franklin* 37376
Anderson, *Overton* 38574
Anderson Heights 37617
Andersonville 37705
Anes 37091
Angeltown 37022
Anglers Cove 37763
Annadale (Part of Cleveland) 37312
Annadel 37770
Anthony Hill 38460
Antioch, *Davidson* 37011
Antioch, *DeKalb* 37166
Antioch, *Jackson* 38562
Antioch, *Loudon* 37771
Antioch, *Montgomery* 37040
Antioch, *Polk* 37307
Antioch, *Tipton* 38011
Antioch (Part of Nashville) 37011†
37013*
Apison 37302
Appleton 38457
Arcade (Part of Nashville)‡ 37219
Arcadia 37660
Archer 37091
Archville 37369
Arcott 38551
Ardmore 38449
38453
For specific ZIP Codes call (888) 275-8777, or your local postmaster.
Arkland 38487
Arlington (Part of Erin) 37061
Arlington (Part of Knoxville) 37917
Arlington, *Shelby* 38002
Armathwaite 38504
Armona 37804
Armour 38401
Arno 37046
Arnold Air Force Base 37389
Arnold Engineering Development Center 37389
Arnolds Chapel 38544
Arp 38063
Arrington 37014
Arrowhead 37920
Arrowhead Estates 37381
Arthur 37707
Asbury, *Coffee* 37355
Asbury, *Haywood* 38069
Asbury, *Knox* 37914
Asbury, *Lauderdale* 38063
Asbury, *Pickett* 38577
Asbury, *Stewart* 37175
Asbury Estates 37804
Ashburn 37172
Ash Hill 37046
Ashland 38485
Ashland City 37015
Ashport 38063
Ashwood 38401
Asia 37398
Aspen Hill 38478
Athendale 38401
Athens 37303*
37371†
Atkins 37079
Atoka 38004
Atwood 38220
Auburntown 37016
Aulon (Part of Memphis) 38101
Austin Peay State University (Part of Clarksville) 37040
Austin Springs, *Washington* 37601
Austin Springs, *Weakley* 38226
Avoca (Part of Bristol) 37620
Avondale, *Grainger* 37861
Avondale, *Sumner* 37075
Avondale Springs 37861
Ayers 38030
Bacchus 37879
Bacon Gap 37763
Bagdad 37145
Baggettsville 37172
Bailey 38017
Baileyton 37743
Bailey Town 37821
Bain 38320
Bairds Mills 37090
Baker Crossroads 38555
Bakers (Part of Nashville) 37072
Bakers Crossroads 38583
Bakersworks 37029
Bakerton 37150
Bakertown (Part of Lynchburg) 37352
Bakertown (Part of Nashville) 37013
Bakerville 37185
Bakewell 37304
Bald Point 37881
Ball Camp 37921
Ballplay, *Monroe* 37385
Ball Play, *Polk* 37362
Balltown 37331
Baltimore 37843
Baneberry 37890
Bangham 38506
Banner 37738
Banner Hill 37650
Banner Springs 38556
Baptist (Part of Nashville)‡ 37203
Baptist Ridge 38568
Barefoot 37186
Barfield 37129
Bargerton 38351
Barkertown 37365
Barnardsville 37763
Barnes 38573
Barnesville 38483
Barr 38040
Barren Plain 37172
Barretville 38053
Barthelia 37031
Bartlebaugh 37416
Bartlett 38133-35
38184
For specific ZIP Codes call (888) 275-8777, or your local postmaster.
Barton Springs 37813
Bates Hill 37110
Bath Springs 38311
Batley 37716
Battlewood Estates 37064
Baugh 38449
Baugh Spring 37353
Baxter 38544
Bazel Town (Part of Harriman) 37748
Beacon 38363
Beamswitch 38230
Beans Creek 37345
Bean Station 37708
Bear Creek (Part of Oneida) 37892
Beardstown (Part of Lobelville) 37097
Bear Spring 37058
Beartown 37660
Bearwallow 37015
Beasley 37034
Beauty Hill 38315
Beaver 38011
Beaverdam Springs 37147
Beaver Hill 38580
Beaver Ridge 37921
Beckwith 37122
Bedford 37160
Beech 38261
Beech Bluff 38313
Beech Bottom 37083
Beech Fork 37714
Beech Grove, *Anderson* 37769
Beechgrove, *Coffee* 37018
Beech Grove, *Grainger* 37881
Beech Grove, *Hawkins* 37711
Beech Grove, *Trousdale* 37074
Beech Grove, *Weakley* 38230
Beech Hill, *Franklin* 37398
Beech Hill, *Giles* 38478
Beech Hill, *Macon* 37074
Beechnut City 37617
Beech Springs 37764
Beechwood 37020
Beersheba Springs 37305
Bel Air 38261
Bel Aire (Part of Murfreesboro) 37130
Bel Aire (Part of Tullahoma) 37388
Bel-Aire Heights (Part of Winchester) 37398
Belfast 37019
Belinda City♦ 37122
Belk 37166
Bella Mara Estates 37854
Bell Buckle 37020
Bell Campground 37849
Belle Aire (Part of Farragut) 37922
Belle Aire, *White* 38583
Belle Brook Estate (Part of Bristol) 37620
Belle Eagle 38012
Belle Founte 37312
Belle Meade (Part of Maryville) 37801
Belle Meade, *Davidson*‡ 37205
Belleville 37334
Bellevue (Part of Nashville) 37221
Bellevue Center (Part of Nashville) 37221
Bellevue Estates 37331
Bell Mill 37363
Bells 38006
Bellsburg 37036
Bell Town, *Cheatham* 37082
Belltown, *Monroe* 37385
Belltown, *Polk* 37317
Bellview, *Bledsoe* 37367
Bellview, *Lincoln* 37334
Bellwood 37087
Belmont, *Anderson* 37705
Belmont, *Coffee* 37355
Belmont, *Jefferson* 37725
Belmont West 37919
Belvidere 37306
Bemis (Part of Jackson)‡ 38314
Bending Chestnut 37064
Benton 37307
Benton Springs 37307
Berclair (Part of Memphis) 38117
Berea, *Giles* 38478
Berea, *Warren* 38581
Berlin 37091
Berry Hill 37204
Berrys Chapel 37069
Bessie 38079
Bethany 37110
Bethel, *Anderson* 37716
Bethel, *Benton* 38320
Bethel, *Blount* 37882
Bethel, *Carroll* 38344
Bethel, *Cheatham* 37015
Bethel, *DeKalb* 37166
Bethel, *Giles* 38477
Bethel, *Haywood* 38012
Bethel, *Maury* 38482
Bethel, *Perry* 37096
Bethel, *Rutherford* 37129
Bethel Springs 38315
Bethesda, *Greene* 37641
Bethesda, *Williamson* 37046
Bethlehem, *Bedford* 37160
Bethlehem, *Campbell* 37766
Bethlehem, *Hardin* 38310
Bethlehem, *Henry* 38222
Bethlehem, *Monroe* 37354
Bethlehem, *Williamson* 37069
Bethpage 37022
Betsy Willis 37342
Beulah, *Greene* 37810
Beulah, *Union* 37807
Beverly 37918
Bible Hill 38363
Bidwell 37144
Big Boy Junction 38030
Bigbyville 38401
Big Creek, *Hancock* 37869
Big Creek, *Hawkins* 37857
Big Creek, *Monroe* 37354
Big Ivy 38372
Big Lick 38555
Big Mountain 37840
Big Piney 37774
Big Ridge Park 37807
Big Rock 37023
Big Sandy 38221
Big Sinks 37866
Big Spring, *Blount* 37737
Big Spring, *Carter* 37643
Big Spring, *Meigs* 37322
Big Springs, *Hancock* 37731
Big Springs, *Overton* 38570
Big Springs, *Rutherford* 37037
Big Spring Union 37752
Biltmore 37643
Binfield 37804
Bingham 37064
Binghamton (Part of Memphis)‡ 38112
Birchwood 37308
Bird Crossroad 37876
Bird Song 38320
Bishop 38024
Bivens 38472
Black Center (Part of Camden) 38320
Black Creek 37852
Black Fox, *Bradley* 37311
Black Fox, *Grainger* 37888
Black Jack 37355
Blackman 37129
Black Oak 37841
Blackwell 37861
Blaine 37709
Blair 37748
Blair Gap 37660
Blair Lane 37087
Blakeville 37144
Blanche 38488
Blanche Chapel 38449
Blaney Forest (Part of East Ridge) 37412
Blanton Chapel 37355
Bledsoe, *Lincoln* 37144
Bledsoe, *Sumner* 37022
Block City (Part of Mount Carmel) 37642
Blockhouse 37801
Blondy (Part of Hohenwald) 38462
Bloomingdale 37660
Bloomington 38549
Bloomington Heights 37060
Bloomington Springs 38545
Blount Hills 37804
Blountville♦ 37617
Blowing Cave Mill 37876
Blowing Springs 37716
Bluebank 38079
Blue Creek 38472
Bluefields (Part of Nashville) 37214
Blue Goose 38351
Blue Grass 37922
Blue Hill 37110
Blue Ridge (Part of Bristol) 37620
Blue Spring 37643
Blue Springs, *DeKalb* 37166
Blue Springs, *Hamilton* 37341
Blue Springs, *Jefferson* 37871
Bluff City 37618
Bluff Creek 38547
Bluff Springs 37110
Bluhmtown 37166
Blunts Landing 37096
Blythe Ferry 37321
Board Valley 38583
Boatland 38556
Bodenham 38478
Boggs 37861
Bogota 38007
Bohannon Addition (Part of Athens) 37303
Boiling Springs 38544
Bold Spring 37101
Bolivar 38008
38074
For specific ZIP Codes call (888) 275-8777, or your local postmaster.
Bolton 38002
Boma 38544
Bon Air, *Sumner* 37022
Bon Air, *White* 38583
Bon Aqua 37025
Bon Aqua Junction 37098
Bon De Croft 38583
Bone Cave 38581
Bonicord 38024
Bonnertown 38457
Bonny Kate 37920
Bonsack 38554
Bonwood (Part of Jackson) 38301
Boom 38573
Boone 37601
Boones Creek 37615
Booneville 37334
Boonshill 38459
Boothspoint 38030
Bordeaux (Part of Nashville) 37218
Borden Mills (Part of Kingsport) 37660
Boston 37064
Bowen 37861
Bowling 38555
Bowman 38555
Bowmantown 37690
Boxwood Hills 37922
Boyd 37922
Boyd Mill Estates (Part of Franklin) 37064
Boyds Creek 37876
Brace 38483
Brackentown 37148
Bradburn Hill 37745
Bradbury 37763
Braden, *Fayette* 38010
Braden, *Union* 37870
Bradford 38316
Bradley Square (Part of Cleveland) 37312
Bradleytown 38030
Bradshaw, *Giles* 38478
Bradshaw, *Hawkins* 37857
Bradyville 37026
Braemar 37658
Braid Cove 37087
Brainerd (Part of Chattanooga)‡ 37411
Brakebill 37354
Bransford 37022
Bratcher's Crossroads 37110
Brattontown (Part of Lafayette) 37083
Bray 37881
Brayton 37338
Braytown 37710
Brazil 38382
Breckinredge South 37064
Brentlawn (Part of Springfield) 37172
Brentwood, *Hamblen* 37814
Brentwood, *Williamson* 37024
37027
For specific ZIP Codes call (888) 275-8777, or your local postmaster.

Brewer Addition (Part of Athens) 37303
Brewstertown 37852
Briar Thicket 37713
Briarwood 37040
Briceville 37710
Brick Church 38478
Bride 38019
Bridgeport 37821
Bridwell Heights 37617
Bright Hope 37743
Brighton, *Lincoln* 37335
Brighton, *Tipton* 38011
Brims Corner 38001
Bristol 37620-25
For specific ZIP Codes call (888) 275-8777, or your local postmaster.
Britton Ford 38256
Brittontown 37616
Britts Landing 37097
Brittsville 37336
Broad Acres 37849
Broadmoor 38024
Broadview, *Crockett* 38034
Broadview, *Franklin* 37398
Broadway (Part of Nashville)‡ 37202
37203
37218
For specific ZIP Codes call (888) 275-8777, or your local postmaster.
Broadway, *Henderson* 38351
Brockdell 37367
Brockland Acres 37813
Brock's 38230
Brookhaven (Part of Crossville) 38555
Brooks (Part of Hohenwald) 38462
Brookwood 38464
Brotherton 38506
Browder (Part of Jasper) 37347
Brown Crossroads 38469
Brown Ellis 37748
Brownington 37398
Browns 37083
Browns Chapel 37377
Brownsville 38012
Browntown 38578
Brownwood Acres 37064
Broylesville 37681
Bruceton 38317
Bruner Grove 37713
Brunswick 38014
Brush Creek (Part of Dunlap) 37327
Brush Creek, *Smith* 38547
Brush Creek, *Williamson* 37062
Bruton Branch 38365
Bryan Hill (Part of Dayton) 37321
Bryant Station 37091
Bryson 38449
Bryson Mountain 40965
Buchanan 38222
Buck Lodge 37148
Buckner 37166
Bucksnort 37140
Bucktown, *Hardin* 38372
Bucktown, *Loudon* 37771
Buena Vista 38318
Buffalo, *Humphreys* 37078
Buffalo, *Scott* 37756
Buffalo Springs 37861
Buffalo Valley 38548
Bufords 38472
Bugscuffle 37183
Buladeen 37643
Bullards Creek 38562
Bull Creek 37756
Bullet Creek 37369
Bull Run, *Anderson* 37849
Bull Run (Part of Nashville) 37015
Bulls Gap 37711
Bumpus Cove 37650
Bumpus Mills 37028
Buncombe 37617
Bungalow Town 37804
Bunker Hill 38478
Buntontown 37640
Burbank 37687
Burchfield Heights 37830
Burem 37857
Burgen 37026
Burgess 38506
Burke 37367
Burlington (Part of Knoxville)‡ 37914
Burlington Heights (Part of Cleveland) 37312
Burlison 38015
Burnett 38501
Burns 37029
Burnt Church 38372
Burristown 38562
Burrville 37872
Burt 37190
Burton (Part of Rogersville) 37857
Burwood 37179
Busby (Part of Loretto) 38469
Bush Grove 38002
Busselltown 37771
Busseltown 38363
Butler 37640
Butlers Landing 38551
Bybee, *Cocke* 37713
Bybee, *Warren* 37110
Byrdstown 38549
Cabin Row 37171
Cabo 38332
Cades 38358
Cades Cove 37882
Cadet (Part of Franklin) 37064
Cagle 37327
Cain Mill 37860
Cainsville 37085
Cairo, *Crockett* 38001
Cairo, *Sumner* 37066
Cairo Bend 37087
Calderwood 37801
Calfkiller 38574
Calhoun 37309
Calico 37322
Calistia 37049
Callins 38230
Calls 37330
Calvin Estates 38301
Camargo 37334
Cambria 37325
Cambridge 38581
Camden 38320
Camelot (Part of Crossville) 38555
Camelot, *Hawkins* 37857
Camilla Homes 38004
Campaign 38550
Camp Austin 37829
Campbell Army Airfield 42223
Campbell Junction 38555
Campbells 38451
Campbellsville 38478
Camp Creek 37743
Camp Ground, *Fentress* 38553
Camp Ground, *Weakley* 38237
Camp Marymount 37062
Camp Monterey Lake 38574
Camp Nakanawa 38555
Camp Relax 37166
Camps 37869
Camp Ta-Pa-Win-Go 37694
Camp Woodlee 37110
Canadaville 38028
Cane Ridge (Part of Nashville) 37013
Caney Branch 37743
Caney Creek, *Hamblen* 37891
Caney Creek, *Hawkins* 37857
Caney Ford 37748
Caney Spring 37091
Caney Valley 37879
Cantrell 38485
Capitol Hill, *Franklin* 37330
Capitol Hill, *Scott* 37756
Capleville 38118
Caravelle Estates 37122
Cardiff (Part of Rockwood) 37854
Carlisle 37058
Carlock, *Jackson* 38562
Carlock, *McMinn* 37331
Carnegie (Part of Johnson City) 37601
Carpenter Campground 37804
Carr Branch 37825
Carroll 37087
Carroll Reece (Part of Johnson City)‡ 37601
37604
For specific ZIP Codes call (888) 275-8777, or your local postmaster.
Carson Spring 37821
Carter 37643
Carter Chapel 37818
Carters Creek 38401
Carthage 37030
Carthage Junction (Part of Gordonsville) 38567
Cartwright, *Sequatchie* 37397
Cartwright, *Smith* 37145
Caryville 37714
Cash Point 38449
Cassville 38583
Castalian Springs 37031
Castle Heights 37821
Cataska 37385
Cat Corner 38240
Cates 38079
Cates Trailor 37764
Catlettsburg (Part of Sevierville) 37876
Cato 37057
Catons Grove 37722
Catoosa 37770
Cave 38559
Cave Spring 37879
Cedar Bluff 37876
Cedar Bluff Two 37922
Cedar Chapel 38075
Cedar Creek 37743
Cedar Creek Landing 37096
Cedarcrest 37857
Cedarfork, *Claiborne* 37879
Cedar Fork, *Loudon* 37846
Cedar Grove, *Bedford* 37034
Cedar Grove, *Carroll* 38321
Cedar Grove, *Carter* 37601
Cedar Grove, *Henderson* 38371
Cedar Grove, *Humphreys* 37078
Cedar Grove, *Pickett* 38577
Cedar Grove, *Roane* 37763
Cedar Grove, *Rutherford* 37060
Cedar Grove (rural), *Sullivan* 37618
Cedar Grove, *Sullivan* 37660
Cedar Grove, *Wilson* 37087
Cedar Hill, *Putnam* 38544
Cedar Hill, *Robertson* 37032
Cedar Springs 37303
Cedar Valley (Part of Bristol) 37620
Celina 38551
Center, *Crockett* 38337
Center, *Lawrence* 38464
Center, *Monroe* 37385
Center Grove, *Franklin* 37388
Center Grove, *Jackson* 38562
Center Hill, *Cannon* 37190
Center Hill, *Henderson* 38368
Center Hill Loop 38368
Center Point, *Chester* 38332
Center Point, *Giles* 38478
Center Point, *Hardeman* 38042
Center Point, *Lawrence* 38468
Center Point, *Sequatchie* 37327
Center Point, *Stewart* 37058
Center Point, *White* 38587
Center Star 38454
Centersville, *Greene* 37681
Centersville, *Loudon* 37742
Centertown 37110
Centerville, *Hickman* 37033
Centerville, *Wilson* 37087
Central, *Carter*♦ 37601
Central, *Gibson* 38382
Central, *Lauderdale* 38063
Central, *Obion* 38253
Central Heights 37617
Central Point 37861
Central State Psychiactric Hospital (Part of Nashville) 37217
Central View 38587
Cerro Gordo 38372
Chalklevel, *Benton* 38320
Chalk Level, *Hawkins* 37857
Chambers 38261
Champ 37359
Chanceytown 37391
Chandler 37777
Chantay Acres (Part of Columbia) 38401
Chanute 38577
Chapel Hill, *Marshall* 37034
Chapel Hill, *Maury* 38461
Chapman Grove 37763
Chapmans 38478
Chapmansboro 37035
Charity (Part of Lynchburg) 37334
Charles Creek Estates 37110
Charleston, *Bradley* 37310
Charleston, *Tipton* 38069
Charleys Branch 37710
Charlotte 37036
Charlotte Park (Part of Nashville) 37209
Charlton Green (Part of Franklin) 37064
Chaska 37766
Chattanooga 37401-50
For specific ZIP Codes call (888) 275-8777, or your local postmaster.
Cherokee 38380
Cherokee Harshaw 37743
Cherokee Heights 37801
Cherokee Hills (Part of Kingston) 37763
Cherokee Hills (Part of Sevierville) 37862
Cherokee Hills, *Sevier* 37865
Cherry 38041
Cherry Acres (Part of Gruetli-Laager) 37339
Cherrybrook 37912
Cherry Chapel 38372
Cherry Creek 38583
Cherry Grove 38333
Cherry Hill 38582
Cherry Valley 37184
Chesney 37848
Chester Estates (Part of Fairview) 37062
Chesterfield 38351
Chestnut Bluff 38040
Chestnut Glade 38237
Chestnut Grove, *Jefferson* 37725
Chestnut Grove, *Perry* 37096
Chestnut Grove, *Robertson* 37073
Chestnut Grove, *Stewart* 37058
Chestnut Grove, *Sumner* 37148
Chestnut Grove, *Union* 37807
Chestnut Hill, *Cumberland* 38555
Chestnut Hill, *Jefferson* 37725
Chestnut Hill, *Sumner* 37148
Chestnut Mound 38552
Chestnut Orchard 37172
Chestnut Ridge 37641
Chestoa 37650
Chestua 37354
Chestuee 37312
Chewalla 38393
Chic 38030
Chickamauga (Part of Chattanooga)‡ 37421-22
37424
For specific ZIP Codes call (888) 275-8777, or your local postmaster.
Chickasaw Heights (Part of Paris) 38242
Childers Hill 38326
Chilhowee View 37803
China Grove 38233
Chinquapin Grove 37618
Chinubee 38486
Chipman 37022
Chittum 37879
Choptack 37857
Chota 37801
Choto Estates 37922
Choto Hills 37777
Christiana 37037
Christian Bend 37642
Christianburg 37874
Christian Chapel 38343
Christie Hill 37801
Christmasville, *Carroll* 38201
Christmasville, *Haywood* 38012
Chuckey 37641
Church Hill 37642
Churchton 38059
Citico Beach 37885
Clacks Gap 37748
Clairfield 37715
Clark Addition 37804
Clarkrange 38553
Clarksburg 38324
Clarksville 37040-44
For specific ZIP Codes call (888) 275-8777, or your local postmaster.
Clarksville Base 42223
Clarktown 38583
Claxton, *Anderson* 37849
Claxton, *McMinn* 37303
Claybrook 38301
Clay Hill 37892
Claylick 37187
Clayton 38260
Clearbranch 37650
Clear Creek Mill 37332
Clearmont 37110
Clear Springs, *Knox* 37806
Clear Springs, *McMinn* 37309
Clearview 37048
Clearwater 37303
Clements Lake Estates (Part of Fairview) 37062
Clementsville 37150
Cleveland 37311-12
37320
37323
37364
For specific ZIP Codes call (888) 275-8777, or your local postmaster.
Clevenger 37821
Cliff Springs 38574
Clifftops 37356
Cliffwood 38464
Clifton 38425
Clifton Junction 38425
Clifty 38583
Clinton 37716*
37717†
Clopton 38011
Cloud Creek 37857
Clouds 37879
Clouse Hill 37387
Clovercroft 37067
Cloverdale, *Obion* 38240
Cloverdale, *Shelby* 38053
Cloverdale, *White* 38583
Clover Hill, *Blount* 37804
Cloverhill (Part of Nashville) 37214
Cloverport 38381
Club Springs 38560
Coal Chute 37643
Coalfield 37719
Coal Hill, *Morgan* 37872
Coal Hill, *Scott* 37852
Coaling 37036
Coalmont 37313
Coble 37033
Coffee Landing 38310
Coffee Ridge 37650
Cog Hill 37325
Cokercreek 37314
Cold Spring, *Bledsoe* 37367
Cold Spring, *Johnson* 37683
Cold Springs, *Blount* 37886
Cold Springs, *Hawkins* 37873
Coldwater 37334
Colesburg 37055
Coles Ferry 37087
Coles Store 38544
Coletown 37317
College 37367
Collegedale 37315
College Grove 37046
College Grove Estates 37854
College Hill (Part of Dayton) 37321
College Park 37601
College Park Estates 37803
College Square Mall (Part of Morristown) 37813
Colliers Corner 37760
Collierville 38017*
38027†
Collins (Part of Gruetli-Laager) 37365
Collins (Part of Rogersville) 37857
Collinwood 38450
Colonial (Part of Memphis)‡ 38124
Colonial Acres 38225
Colonial Circle 37865
Colonial Heights♦ 37663
Colonial Village (Part of Knoxville) 37920
Columbia 38401*
38402†
Columbia Hill 38574
Columbus Hill 38562

Place	ZIP Code
Comfort	37380
Commerce	37184
Community Acres	37180
Como	38223
Compton	37127
Conasauga	37316
Concord, *Carroll*	38344
Concord, *Gibson*	38382
Concord, *Humphreys*	37185
Concord, *Knox*	37922
Concord, *Rhea*	37332
Concord, *Rutherford*	37153
Conklin	37659
Conner Heights (Part of Pigeon Forge)	37863
Conyersville	38251
Cookeville	38501-03
	38505-06
For specific ZIP Codes call (888) 275-8777, or your local postmaster.	
Coolsprings Galleria (Part of Franklin)	37064
Cool Springs	38259
Cooper	38556
Coopers	38317
Coopertown	37172
Copperhill	37317
Corbin Hill	37840
Cordell	37756
Corders Crossroads	37348
Cordova	38018*
	38088†
Corinth, *Knox*	37918
Corinth, *Sumner*	37148
Cornersville	37047
Coro Lake (Part of Memphis)	38109
Corona	72338
Corryton	37721
Cortner	37360
Cosby	37722
Coster (Part of Knoxville)	37917
Cotham	38382
Cottage Grove	38224
Cottage Home	37095
Cottonport	37322
Cottontown	37048
Cottonwood Estates	37069
Cottonwood Grove	38080
Cotula	37766
Couchville (Part of Nashville)	37214
Coulterville	37373
Counce	38326
Country Club	38008
Country Haven Estates	37179
Country Roads	37064
Countrywood Estates	37064
Countyline (Part of Lynchburg)	37352
County Line, *Sevier*	37865
Courtland	37172
Cove Creek, *Campbell*	37714
Cove Creek, *Carter*	37687
Cove Creek Cascades	37862
Cove Lake Estates (Part of Caryville)	37714
Covington	38019
Cowan	37318
Cowanstown	37640
Coxville	38343
Cozette	38380
Crab Orchard	37723
Crabtree	37687
Crackers Neck	37683
Craggie Hope	37082
Craigfield	37025
Crandull	37688
Cranmore Cove	37321
Cravenstown	38589
Crawfish Valley	38464
Crawford	38554
Creek Store	37810
Creekwood, *Bedford*	37160
Creekwood, *Wilson*	37122
Crenshaw	37920
Crescent	37128
Creson (Part of Fayetteville)	37334
Creston	38555
Crestwood	37763
Crestwood Hills	37918
Crewstown	38464
Crieve Hall (Part of Nashville)	37211
Crippen Gap	37918
Crisp Spring	37357
Crockett	38253
Crockett Mills	38021
Cromwell Crossroads	38450
Cronanville	38079
Crooked Creek	37097
Cross	37617
Cross Anchor	37743
Cross Bridges	38474
Cross Keys	37046
Crossland	42049
Cross Lanes	37186
Cross Plains	37049
Cross Road	37841
Crossroads, *Benton*	38320
Cross Roads, *Cannon*	37190
Crossroads, *Crockett*	38006
Cross Roads, *DeKalb*	37059
Cross Roads, *Dyer*	38034
Cross Roads, *Fentress*	38556
Crossroads, *Hardin*	38372
Cross Roads, *Lawrence* (mail Ethridge)	38456
Crossroads, *Lawrence* (mail Leoma)	38468
Cross Roads, *Macon*	37186
Crossroads, *Shelby*	38017
Cross Roads, *Stewart*	37175
Crossroads, *Wayne*	38450
Crosstown (Part of Memphis)‡	38104
Crossville	38555
	38557-58
For specific ZIP Codes call (888) 275-8777, or your local postmaster.	
Crosswinds	37122
Crowley Store	38230
Crown Point Estates	37122
Crucifer	38345
Crump	38327
Crunk	37073
Crystal	38261
Crystal Springs	37348
Cuba, *Hawkins*	37811
Cuba, *Shelby*	38053
Cuba Landing	37185
Cub Creek	38562
Culleoka	38451
Culpepper	37149
Cumberland City	37050
Cumberland Estates (Part of Knoxville)	37921
Cumberland Furnace	37051
Cumberland Gap	37724
Cumberland Heights, *Grundy*	37313
Cumberland Heights, *Montgomery*	37040
Cumberland Springs	37321
Cumberland View	37757
Cumberland View Estates	37769
Cummings	38583
Cummingsville	38585
Cunningham	37052
Cupp Mill	37825
Curlee	37190
Curve	38063
Cusick	37865
Cuzick	37772
Cypress	38006
Cypress Creek	38222
Cypress Inn	38452
Daisy (Part of Soddy Daisy)	37379
Dale Hollow	38551
Dalewood (Part of Nashville)	37207
Dallas Gardens	37379
Dallas Hills	37379
Dalton Heights (Part of Morristown)	37814
Dancyville	38069
Dandridge	37725
Dante	37921
Darden	38328
Darks Mill	38401
Daugherty Estates	37062
Daus	37327
Davenport	37110
Davidson	38589
Davidson Chapel	38382
Davis Chapel, *Campbell*	37766
Davis Chapel, *Carroll*	38344
Davis Springs	37692
Daylight	37110
Days Crossroads	37083
Daysville	37854
Dayton	37321
Dayton Spur	38555
Deanburg	38366
Deans	37033
DeArmond	37748
Deason	37020
De Busk	37743
Decatur	37322
Decaturville	38329
Decherd	37324
Deep Springs	37725
Deerfield, *Lawrence*	38464
Deerfield, *Williamson*	37064
Deerfield Acres	37620
Deer Lodge	37726
Deermont	37829
Defeated	37030
Defense Depot (Part of Memphis)‡	38114
Delano	37325
Delina	37047
Dellrose	38453
Dellwood	37804
Del Rio	37727
Demory	37766
Denmark	38391
Dennis Cove	37658
Denton	37722
Dentville	37325
Denver, *Cannon*	37149
Denver, *Humphreys*	37054
De Priest Bend (Part of Lobelville)	37097
De Rossett	38583
Detroit	38015
Devonia	37710
Diana	37047
Dibrell	37110
Dickel (Part of Tullahoma)	37388
Dickey Bluff Peninsula	37381
Dickson	37055*
	37056†
Dickson Town	38455
Difficult	37145
Dill	37367
Dilley	37730
Dillton	37127
Disco	37737
Dismal	37095
Disney	37769
Ditty	38506
Dixie	38261
Dixie Lee Junction (Part of Farragut)	37922
Dixon Springs	37057
Dixonville	38053
Doaks Crossroads	37090
Dobson Branch	38501
Dockery	37310
Dodson, *Roane*	37748
Dodson, *White*	38583
Dodson Estates (Part of Nashville)	37076
Dodsons	38472
Doeville	37640
Dog Hill	38034
Dogtown, *Carter*	37643
Dog Town, *Grundy*	37313
Dogtown, *Polk*	37391
Dogwood	37763
Dogwood Heights	37879
Dogwood Shores	37763
Dollar	38318
Donelson (Part of Nashville)‡	37214
Donnel Chapel	37149
Donoho	37030
Doran Addition	37660
Dorton	38555
Dossett	37716
Dotson	37888
Dotsontown	37681
Dotsonville	37191
Doty Chapel	37616
Double Bridges	38040
Double Springs, *McMinn*	37303
Double Springs, *Putnam*	38544
Double Top	38556
Douglas	37064
Douglas Estates	37725
Dover, *Hamblen*	37813
Dover, *Stewart*	37058
Dowelltown	37059
Dowler Heights	37377
Downtown (Part of Chattanooga)‡	37401-03
	37408
For specific ZIP Codes call (888) 275-8777, or your local postmaster.	
Downtown (Part of Cleveland)‡	37311
Downtown (Part of Knoxville)‡	37901
Downtown (Part of Maryville)‡	37801
Doyle	38559
Drapers Crossroads	37083
Dresden	38225
Driftwood (Part of Bristol)	37620
Dripping Springs	37398
Drop	38583
Drummonds	38023
Dry Branch	37869
Dry Creek	37659
Dry Hill, *Johnson*	37640
Dry Hill, *Lauderdale*	38040
Dry Hollow (Part of Kingsport)	37660
Duck Creek	37869
Duck River	38454
Ducktown, *Polk*	37326
Ducktown, *Washington*	37681
Dudney Hill	38562
Due West (Part of Nashville)	37115
Duff	37729
Dukedom	38226
Dulaney	37743
Dull	37036
Dumplin	37820
Dunbar	38311
Duncantown	37330
Dunlap	37327
Duplex	37064
Du Pont	37865
Durhamville	38063
Dutch	37888
Dutch Valley	37716
Dyer	38330
Dyersburg	38024*
	38025†
Dykes Crossroads	38555
Dyllis	37748
Dyson Grove	37640
Eads	38028
Eagan	37730
Eagle Creek	38341
Eagle Furnace	37854
Eagleton Village	37804
Eagleville	37060
Earleyville	37110
East (Part of Memphis)‡	38111
	38114
For specific ZIP Codes call (888) 275-8777, or your local postmaster.	
East (Part of Nashville)‡	37206
East Acres	38053
Eastbrook (Part of Estill Springs)	37330
East Chattanooga (Part of Chattanooga)‡	37406
East Cyruston	37334
East Due West (Part of Nashville)	37115
Easter Seal	37122
East Etowah	37331
East Fork	37876
Eastgate Mall (Part of Chattanooga)	37411
Eastgate Shopping Center (Part of Memphis)	38117
East Jamestown	38556
East Junction (Part of Memphis)	38101
East Lake (Part of Chattanooga)‡	37407
Eastland	38583
East Memphis (Part of Memphis)‡	38111
East Miller's Cove	37886
Eastport	38573
East Ridge	37412
Eastside, *Cannon*	37190
East Side, *Dickson*	37029
East Side (Part of Elizabethton)	37643
Eastside (Part of Kingsport)‡	37664
Eastside, *Warren*	38581
East Springbrook (Part of Alcoa)	37701
East Sweetwater	37874
East Union	38301
Eastview (Part of Greeneville)	37745
Eastview, *McNairy*	38367
East View, *Meigs*	37336
Eastwood (Part of La Vergne)	37086
Eaton	38331
Eaton Crossroad	37771
Eaton Forest	37771
Ebenezer, *Marion*	37347
Ebenezer, *Monroe*	37329
Echo Hills	37743
Eddie Hill	37090
Edenwold (Part of Nashville)	37115
Edgefield (Part of Bristol)	37620
Edgemont, *Cocke*	37821
Edgemont (Part of Bristol)	37620
Edgemoor	37716
Edgewater (Part of Dayton)	37321
Edgewater, *Wilson*	37122
Edgewood, *Dyer*	38059
Edgewood (Part of Kingsport)	37660
Edgewood Acres	37804
Edgewood Heights	37849
Edison	38343
Edith	38063
Edward Grove	38063
Edwards Point	37377
Edwina	37821
Egam	37334
Egypt (Part of Memphis)	38128
Eidson	37731
Elba	38066
Elbethel	37160
Elbridge	38240
Elgin	37732
Elizabeth	38034
Elizabethton	37643*
	37644†
Elkhead	37366
Elkhorn	38242
Elk Mills	37640
Elk Mill Village (Part of Fayetteville)	37334
Elkmont	37738
Elkmont Springs	38449
Elkton	38455
Elk Valley	37847
Ellejoy	37865
Ellendale (Part of Bartlett)	38029
Ellington Park	37064
Ellis Mills	37050
Ellisville	38004
Elm Grove	38015
Elm Springs	37888
Elmwood	38560
Elora	37328
Elverton	37748
Elza	37830
Embreeville	37650
Emerald Acres	37814
Emerts Cove (Part of Pittman Center)	37862
Emery Mill	37367
Emmett	37620
Emory Gap (Part of Harriman)	37748
Emory Heights (Part of Harriman)	37748
Englewood, *McMinn*	37329
Englewood, *Obion*	38260
English Mountain Resort	37876
Enigma	38548
Eno	37055
Enon	37150
Ensor (Part of Baxter)	38544
Enterprise, *Hawkins*	37857
Enterprise, *Maury*	38474
Enville	38332
Epperson	37385
Erasmus	38555
Erie	37846
Erin	37061
Erlanger (Part of Chattanooga)‡	37403

Place	ZIP
Ernestville	37650
Erwin	37650
Essary Springs	38061
Estes Kefauver (Part of Johnson City)‡	37601
Estes Woods	37381
Estill Springs	37330
Ethridge	38456
Etowah	37331
Etter	38549
Eucebia	37865
Eulia	37186
Eureka, *Bradley*	37323
Eureka, *Hardin*	38372
Eureka, *Roane*	37854
Eurekaton	38075
Eva	38333
Evansville	38024
Evensville	37332
Evergreen	37687
Evins Mill	37166
Ewingville (Part of Franklin)	37064
Excell	37040
Executive Estates	38464
Factory	38485
Fair Acres, *Hickman*	37025
Fair Acres (Part of Kingsport)	37660
Fairfield, *Bedford*	37183
Fairfield, *Hickman*	37033
Fairfield, *Sumner*	37186
Fairfield Acres	37814
Fairfield Glade♦	38558
Fair Garden	37876
Fairgrounds (Part of Shelbyville)	37160
Fairlane Estates (Part of Shelbyville)	37160
Fairmont (Part of Bristol)	37620
Fairmount♦	37377
Fairview, *Blount*	37803
Fairview, *Bradley*	37312
Fairview, *Carroll*	38201
Fairview, *Carter*	37658
Fairview, *Clay*	38541
Fairview, *Coffee*	37360
Fairview, *Fentress*	38556
Fairview, *Greene* (mail Afton)	37616
Fairview, *Greene* (mail Mohawk)	37810
Fairview, *Lawrence*	38469
Fair View, *Lincoln*	37334
Fairview, *McMinn*	37303
Fairview, *Macon*	37186
Fairview, *Madison*	38343
Fairview, *Meigs*	37322
Fairview, *Pickett*	38549
Fairview, *Roane*	37763
Fairview, *Scott*	37756
Fairview, *Stewart*	37058
Fairview, *Warren*	37110
Fairview, *Washington*	37659
Fairview, *Wayne*	38463
Fairview, *White*	38583
Fairview, *Williamson*	37062
Fairview Heights, *Jefferson*	37725
Fairview Heights (Part of Fairview)	37062
Fairyland	38555
Faix	38549
Falcon	38375
Fall Branch♦	37656
Fall Creek	37160
Falling Water	37343
Fall River	38468
Falls Mill	37306
Fanchers Mills	38583
Fancy Meadows	37871
Farmers Exchange	38462
Farmers Valley	37096
Farmington, *Marshall*	37091
Farmington, *Williamson*	37064
Farner	37333
Farragut	37922
Farris Chapel	37398
Farrport (Part of Alcoa)	37701
Faulkner Springs	37110
Faxon	38221
Fayette Corners	38075
Fayetteville	37334
Federal Reserve (Part of Nashville)‡	37203
Fellowship	37122
Fernvale	37064
Fernwood	37814
Few Chapel	37101
Fielden Store	37820
Fincastle	37766
Findlay (Part of Sparta)	38583
Finger	38334
Finley	38030
Fisherville	38017
Fishery	37650
Fish Springs	37640
Fisk University (Part of Nashville)‡	37203
Five Points, *Giles*	38478
Five Points, *Lawrence*	38457
Five Points, *Madison*	38366
Five Points, *Rhea*	37321
Flag Branch	37743
Flag Pond	37657
Flat Branch Junction	37387
Flat Creek, *Bedford*	37160
Flat Creek, *Overton*	38570
Flat Gap, *Hancock*	37881
Flatgap, *Jefferson*	37760
Flat Hollow	37870
Flat Rock, *Morgan*	37726
Flat Rock, *Smith*	37090
Flattop	37379
Flatwood (Part of Gilt Edge)	38015
Flatwood, *Warren*	37110
Flatwoods, *Lawrence*	38456
Flatwoods, *Perry*	37096
Flewellyn	37172
Flintville	37335
Flippin	38063
Floraton	37149
Florence	37129
Flourville	37601
Flowertown	37360
Fly	38482
Flynns Lick	38562
Foothills Mall (Part of Maryville)	37804
Forbus	38577
Ford	37772
Ford Chapel	37825
Fordtown (Part of La Follette)	37766
Fordtown, *Sullivan*	37663
Forest Chapel	37186
Forest Grove (Part of Nashville)	37080
Forest Grove, *Meigs*	37322
Forest Hill, *Blount*	37803
Forest Hill (Part of Germantown)	38139
Forest Hills, *Davidson*	37215
Forest Hills (Part of Bristol)	37620
Forest Hills (Part of Knoxville)	37919
Forest Hills (Part of Shelbyville)	37160
Forest Home	37069
Forest Home Farms	37069
Forest Mill	37355
Forge Ridge	37752
Forked Deer	38037
Fork Mountain	37710
Fork of Pike	37095
Fork Ridge	40965
Forrest Park (Part of Tullahoma)	37388
Forsythe (Part of Memphis)	38101
Fort Campbell	42223
Fort Campbell South	42223
Fort Donelson Shores	37058
Fort Henry Mall (Part of Kingsport)	37664
Fort Loudon Estates	37772
Fort Robinson (Part of Kingsport)	37660
Forty Forks	38315
Fosterville	37063
Foundry Hill	38251
Fountain City (Part of Knoxville)‡	37918
	37928
	37938
For specific ZIP Codes call (888) 275-8777, or your local postmaster.	
Fountain Head	37148
Fountain Heights	38401
Fourmile Board Hill	38485
Four Points	37820
Fowler Grove	37713
Fowlkes	38033
Fox Bluff	37015
Fox Branch	37869
Foxfire	38555
Frankewing	38459
Frankfort	37770
Franklin	37064-65
	37067-69
For specific ZIP Codes call (888) 275-8777, or your local postmaster.	
Franklin East	37064
Fraterville	37769
Frayser (Part of Memphis)‡	38127
Fredonia, *Coffee*	37355
Fredonia, *Haywood*	38069
Fredonia, *Montgomery*	37040
Free Communion	38573
Free Hill	38551
Freeland	38222
Free State	38562
Freewill	38358
Fremont	38261
French Broad	37727
Frettin	38052
Friendship, *Bledsoe*	37381
Friendship, *Crockett*	38034
Friendship, *Hamilton*	37341
Friendship, *Hawkins*	37881
Friendship, *Sullivan*	37620
Friends Station	37820
Friendsville	37737
Frisco	37642
Frog Jump, *Crockett*	38040
Frog Jump, *Gibson*	38382
Frog Level	37731
Frog Pond	37083
Front Street (Part of Memphis)‡	38103
Frost Bottom	37840
Fruitland	38343
Fruitvale	38336
Fulton	38041
Gabtown	37656
Gadsden	38337
Gainesboro	38562
Gainsville	38049
Gaitherville	38464
Galaxy Heights (Part of Chattanooga)	37343
Galbraith Springs	37811
Galen	37083
Gallatin	37066
Gallaway	38036
Gandy	38464
Gann	38358
Gapcreek	37643
Gap of the Ridge	37083
Gardner	38237
Garland	38019
Gassaway	37095
Gates	38037
Gath	37110
Gatlinburg	37738
Gattistown	37359
Gause	37035
Gay	37110
General Mail Facility (Part of Knoxville)‡	37950
Gentry	38544
Georgetown, *Gibson*	38382
Georgetown, *Hamilton*	37336
Georgetown, *McMinn*	37370
George W. Lee (Part of Memphis)‡	38126
Georgia Crossing	37398
Germantown (Part of Nashville)	37189
Germantown	38138-39
	38183
For specific ZIP Codes call (888) 275-8777, or your local postmaster.	
Gerren Heights	37367
Gibbs (Part of Union City)	38261
Gibbs Crossroads	37145
Gibson	38338
Gibson Hall	37879
Gibsontown (Part of Kingsport)	37660
Gibson Wells	38343
Gift	38019
Gilbreath	37818
Gilchrist	38310
Gildfield	38002
Gilfield	37686
Gillises Mills	38372
Gilmore	38301
Gilt Edge	38015
Gin House Lake	38011
Gladdice	38562
Glade Creek	38583
Glades, *Morgan*	37726
Glades (Part of Gatlinburg)	37738
Gladeville	37071
Glass	38240
Gleason	38229
Glen	37342
Glen Alice	37854
Glencliff (Part of Nashville)	37211
Glendale (Part of Chattanooga)	37405
Glendale, *Lawrence*	38469
Glendale, *Loudon*	37742
Glendale, *Maury*	38401
Glendale, *Washington*	37681
Glendale Estates	38478
Glen Del Acres	37860
Glenhaven (Part of Fairview)	37062
Glen Mary	37852
Glenmore Estates	37853
Glen Oaks	37122
Glenobey	38556
Glenview (Part of Nashville)‡	37217
Glenwood	37185
Glenwylde	37051
Glimp	38041
Glover	37172
Glover Hill (Part of Jasper)	37347
Glynnwood Lake	38028
Gnat Hill	37355
Goat City	38355
Godwin	38401
Goffton	38501
Goin	37825
Golddust	38063
Goldpoint (Part of Chattanooga)	37343
Goodbars	38581
Goodfield	37322
Good Hope, *Campbell*	37762
Good Hope, *Dyer*	38059
Goodlettsville	37070†
	37072*
Good Luck	38369
Goodspring	38460
Good Springs	37331
Goose Horn	38588
Gooseneck	37705
Gordon (Part of Pulaski)	38478
Gordonsburg	38462
Gordonsville	38563
Gorman	37101
Goshen	37642
Gossburg	37018
Grabal	38358
Graball	37148
Graham	37137
Grammer Estates	37062
Grand Junction	38039
Grand Valley	38067
Grandview, *Greene*	37641
Grandview, *Knox*	37920
Grandview, *Rhea*	37337
Grandview Estates	37764
Grandview Terrace	37620
Granite	37716
Grannys Branch	38221
Grant	38563
Grantsboro	37766
Granville	38564
Grasshopper	37308
Grassland	37064
Grassy Cove	38555
Grassy Creek	37317
Grassy Fork	37753
Grassy Valley	37743
Gratio	38240
Gravel Hill, *McNairy*	38339
Gravel Hill, *Washington*	37681
Gravelly Hill (Part of Jefferson City)	37760
Graveltown	37145
Graveston	37721
Gray♦	37615
Gray Acres	37620
Graysville	37338
Graytown	37033
Graywinds	37122
Green Ack	37840
Green Acres, *Knox*	37921
Green Acres, *Roane*	37763
Green Acres (Part of Kingsport)	37660
Green Acres (Part of Pulaski)	38478
Greenback	37742
Greenbriar	37185
Greenbriar Village (Part of Crossville)	38555
Greenbrier, *Cheatham*	37015
Green Brier, *Pickett*	38549
Greenbrier, *Robertson*	37073
Greenbrier, *Williamson*	37064
Greenbrier Lake	37087
Greeneville	37743-45
For specific ZIP Codes call (888) 275-8777, or your local postmaster.	
Greenfield	38230
Greenfield Bend	38487
Greenfields (Part of Kingsport)	37660
Green Grove	37074
Green Harbor	37138
Greenhaw	37324
Green Hill, *Jefferson*	37725
Green Hill, *Warren*	37110
Green Hill, *Wilson*	37138
Green Hills (Part of Nashville)‡	37215
Greenland	37642
Green Meadow (Part of Alcoa)	37701
Green Meadow, *Bradley*	37311
Green Meadows	38556
Green Pond	38554
Greens Crossroads	37110
Greens Mill	37343
Greentown	37387
Greenvale	37184
Green Valley, *Knox*	37919
Green Valley, *Macon*	37083
Green Valley, *Williamson*	37064
Green Valley, *Wilson*	37122
Green Village (Part of Church Hill)	37642
Greenwood, *Macon*	37150
Greenwood, *Rutherford*	37046
Greenwood, *Washington*	37659
Greenwood, *Wilson*	37087
Greystone	37743
Griffith	37367
Griffith Creek	37397
Grimsley	38565
Grinders	37033
Gruetli (Part of Gruetli-Laager)	37339
Gruetli-Laager	37339
Gudger	37354
Guild	37340
Gulf Park	37919
Gum	37127
Gum Creek	37324
Gum Flat	38006
Gum Spring	37821
Gum Springs	37145
Guntown	37857
Guys	38339
Habersham	37766
Hackberry	37142
Hale	37659
Hales Crossroads	37813
Hales Point	38040
Haley	37183
Half Acre	37166
Halls, *Knox*♦	37918
Halls, *Lauderdale*	38040
Halls Creek	37185
Halls Crossroads	37918
Hallshare Estates	38320
Halls Hill	37118
Halls Mill	37160
Hall Town, *Sumner*	37148
Halltown, *Trousdale*	37074
Hallview Meadows (Part of Fairview)	37062
Hamburg	38376
Hamillville (Part of Chattanooga)	37343
Hamilton Mill	38449
Hamilton Place (Part of Chattanooga)	37421
Hamilton Village (Part of Chattanooga)	37421
Hamlin Town	37715
Hammon Chapel	37683
Hampshire	38461
Hampton	37658
Hamptons Crossroads	38583

Place	ZIP
Hampton Station	37040
Handleyton	37148
Hanging Limb	38554
Happy Hill	38478
Happy Valley	37878
Harbin	37854
Harbison	37721
Harbor Town	38221
Harbour Island	37138
Harbuck	37391
Hardin Estates	37772
Hardsrabble	37190
Hardy	38506
Harmon	37688
Harmony, *Franklin*	37398
Harmony, *Jackson*	38562
Harmony, *Washington*	37659
Harmony Grove	37727
Harmony Hills	37660
Harms	37334
Harpeth	37064
Harpeth Estates	37064
Harpeth Hills	37064
Harpeth Meadows (Part of Franklin)	37064
Harpeth Valley	37187
Harpeth Valley Park (Part of Nashville)	37221
Harrill Hills (Part of Knoxville)	37918
Harriman	37748
Harriman Junction (Part of Harriman)	37748
Harris	38261
Harrisburg	37876
Harrison♦	37341
Harrison Hills	37771
Harrogate	37752
Harrtown	37617
Hartford	37753
Hartmantown	37659
Hartsville	37074
Haskins Chapel	37091
Hatchertown	37862
Hatchie	38392
Havley Springs (Part of Morristown)	37814
Havron Chapel	37347
Hawkinsville	38034
Hawthorne	37160
Haydenburg	38588
Hayes	38583
Hayes Fork	37058
Haynes	38077
Haynesfield (Part of Bristol)	37620
Hays	38057
Haysboro (Part of Nashville)	37216
Haysville	37083
Head of Barren	37825
Heatherwood Hill	37064
Heatoncreek	37687
Hebbertsburg	37723
Hebron	38052
Heiskell	37754
Helena	38556
Helenwood	37755
Heloise	38030
Helton	37012
Helton Springs	37861
Heltonville	37708
Hemlock Hills	37650
Henard Mill	37857
Henardtown	37857
Henderson	38340
Hendersonville	37075*
	37077†
Hendon	37338
Hendron	37920
Henley (Part of Decherd)	37324
Henning	38041
Henrietta	37015
Henry	38231
Henrys Crossroads	37764
Henry Street (Part of Morristown)‡	37814
Henryville	38483
Hensley Chapel	38583
Herbert Domain	37367
Heritage Estates	38555
Heritage Hills	37803
Hermitage (Part of Nashville)	37076
Hermitage Hills (Part of Nashville)	37076
Hermitage Springs	37150
Hermon	37616
Hiawassee	37357
Hickerson Station	37388
Hickey	38582
Hickman	38567
Hickory Bend (Part of Nashville)	37214
Hickory Flat	38321
Hickory Flats, *Henderson*	38368
Hickory Flats, *McNairy*	38310
Hickory Grove, *Franklin*	37345
Hickory Grove, *Gibson*	38382
Hickory Grove, *Sumner*	37031
Hickory Hill (Part of Lynchburg)	37352
Hickory Hill Estates (Part of Tullahoma)	37388
Hickory Hills	37064
Hickory Hollow Mall (Part of Nashville)	37211
Hickory Point	37040
Hickory Star Landing	37807
Hickory Tree	37618
Hickory Valley, *Hardeman*	38042
Hickory Valley, *Union*	37807
Hickory Withe	38043
Hicks Chapel	37397
Hicksville (Part of Jackson)	38301
Hico	38344
Hico Station	38344
Hide-A-Way Hills	38555
Highcliff	37762
Highgate	37064
Highland, *DeKalb*	37166
Highland, *Jackson*	38562
Highland, *Overton*	38570
Highland, *Wayne*	38450
Highland Academy	37148
Highland Acres	37804
Highland Forest (Part of Rockwood)	37854
Highland Heights (Part of Nashville)	37207
Highland Heights, *Giles*	38478
Highland Heights (Part of Memphis)‡	38122
Highland Junction	38589
Highland Manor	37341
Highland Park, *Loudon*	37771
Highland Park (Part of Chattanooga)‡	37404
Highland Park (Part of Kingsport)	37660
Highland Park (Part of La Follette)	37766
Highland Springs	37709
Highlandview	37920
High Point, *Campbell*	37714
High Point, *Scott*	37841
Hilham	38568
Hillcrest (Part of Bluff City)	37618
Hillcrest (Part of Crossville)	38555
Hillcrest (Part of Kingsport)	37660
Hillcrest (Part of Morristown)	37814
Hilldale (Part of Clarksville)‡	37043
Hill Estates (Part of Franklin)	37064
Hilliard	38387
Hillsboro	37342
Hillsboro Acres	37069
Hillsdale	37057
Hillside	38237
Hills View	37370
Hilltop, *Bedford*	37160
Hilltop, *Montgomery*	37040
Hill Top (Part of Johnson City)	37601
Hilltop (Part of Smyrna)	37167
Hill Town	38482
Hillvale	37716
Hillville	38075
Hillwood (Part of Nashville)	37205
Himesville	37160
Hindscreek	37716
Hinds Creek Valley	37807
Hinkle	38371
Hinkledale	38201
Hitchcox	37367
Hiwassee College	37354
Hiwassee Hills	37354
Hixon	37301
Hixson (Part of Chattanooga)	37343
Hobbs Hill	37387
Hodges	37820
Hohenwald	38462
Holiday City (Part of Memphis)‡	38118
Holiday Hills, *Cumberland*	38555
Holiday Hills, *Roane*	37763
Holiday Shores	37028
Holladay, *Benton*	38341
Holladay, *Putnam*	38506
Holland Mill	37616
Hollow Rock	38342
Hollow Springs	37026
Holly Grove, *Haywood*	38006
Holly Grove, *Marshall*	37091
Holly Grove, *Tipton*	38011
Holly Leaf	38220
Holly Springs, *Monroe*	37385
Holly Springs, *Overton*	38570
Hollywood, *Maury*	38451
Hollywood (Part of Memphis)‡	38108
Hollywood Hills	37066
Holston Army Ammunition Plant	37662
Holston Heights (Part of Kingsport)	37660
Holston Hills (Part of Bristol)	37620
Holston Hills (Part of Knoxville)	37914
Holston Terrace	37857
Holston Valley	37620
Holts Corner	37034
Holttown	37821
Holy Hill	37683
Homestead	38555
Honeycutt	37857
Hood Lake (Part of Lawrenceburg)	38464
Hoodoo	37018
Hookers Bend	38361
Hoop	37879
Hoovers Gap	37037
Hopewell, *Bradley*♦	37312
Hopewell, *Carroll*	38348
Hopewell, *Claiborne*	37879
Hopewell, *Gibson*	38389
Hopewell, *Tipton*	38011
Hopewell (Part of Nashville)	37138
Hopewell Springs	37354
Hopper Bluff	37861
Hopson	37687
Hornbeak	38232
Horner	37096
Hornertown	37147
Hornsby	38044
Horn Springs	37087
Horse Creek, *Greene*	37641
Horse Creek, *Sullivan*	37660
Horseshoe	37643
Horseshoe Bend	38560
Horsleys	37074
Housley Addition (Part of Athens)	37303
Houston	38485
Houston Valley	37743
Howard, *Monroe*	37885
Howard, *Sevier*	37865
Howard Chapel	38570
Howard Hill (Part of Kingsport)	37660
Howard Quarter	37879
Howard Springs	38555
Howell, *Lincoln*	37334
Howell, *White*	38583
Howell Hill	37334
Howley	38321
Hubbard	37801
Hubertville	37172
Hudson	38464
Hugarth	38556
Hughes Loop	38358
Hughett	37852
Hughey	37334
Hulan Hollow (Part of Erwin)	37650
Humboldt	38343
Humphrey	37865
Hunter♦	37643
Hunter Hills	37379
Hunters Point	37087
Hunters Ridge	37064
Huntersville	38301
Hunting Creek Farms	37064
Huntingdon	38344
Huntland	37345
Huntsville, *Loudon*	37771
Huntsville, *Scott*	37756
Hurdlow (Part of Lynchburg)	37306
Hurley	38357
Hurley Acres	37813
Huron	38345
Hurricane, *Houston*	37175
Hurricane, *Jackson*	38562
Hurricane, *Wilson*	37090
Hurricane Hill	38063
Hurricane Mills	37078
Hustburg	37134
Hutsell (Part of Athens)	37303
Hygeia Springs	37073
Hyndsver	38237
Iconium	37190
Idaho	38468
Idaville	38004
Ideal Valley	37381
Idlewild, *Gibson*	38346
Idlewild, *McMinn*	37303
Idlewood (Part of Franklin)	37064
Ilemar	37122
Imperial Estates	37921
Independence, *Hancock*	37731
Independence, *Overton*	38573
Independence Estates	37087
India	38242
Indian Bluff	37710
Indian Cave	37709
Indian Creek	37757
Indian Hills	37087
Indian Mound, *DeKalb*	38583
Indian Mound, *Stewart*	37079
Indian Ridge, *Grainger*	37709
Indian Ridge, *Washington*	37601
Indian Springs	37617
Ingleside Hill (Part of Athens)	37303
Inglewood (Part of Nashville)	37216
Inskip (Part of Knoxville)	37912
Interstate Park	37032
Irish Cut	37821
Iron City	38463
Ironsburg	37385
Irving College	37110
Irwinton Shores	37880
Isabella	37317
Isham (Part of Winfield)	37892
Island Home (Part of Knoxville)	37920
Island Park	37618
Isoline	38555
Isom	38461
Ivy	37369
Ivy Bluff	37110
Ivydell	37766
Ivy Point (Part of Nashville)	37072
Ivyton	38543
Jacksboro	37757
Jacks Creek	38347
Jackson	38301-08
	38314
For specific ZIP Codes call (888) 275-8777, or your local postmaster.	
Jackson Heights (Part of Murfreesboro)	37129
Jackson Ridge	37060
Jacksons Chapel	37036
Jackson Square (Part of Oak Ridge)‡	37830
Jacobs Hill	37090
Jakestown	37127
Jamestown, *Fentress*	38556
Jamestown, *Tipton*	38015
Jarrell	38201
Jasper	37347
Jaybird (Part of Newport)	37821
Jaybird, *Hamblen*	37814
Jeannette	38363
Jearoldstown	37641
Jefferson	37166
Jefferson City	37760
Jefferson Estates	37877
Jefferson Springs	37167
Jellico	37762
Jena	37742
Jenkins Hill (Part of Sevierville)	37862
Jenkinsville	38024
Jere Baxter (Part of Nashville)‡	37216
Jernigan Town	37188
Jersey (Part of Chattanooga)	37416
Jessie	37110
Jewell	38225
Jewett	37337
Jimtown	37821
Jockey	37681
Joelton (Part of Nashville)	37080
John Sevier	37914
Johnson City	37601-15
For specific ZIP Codes call (888) 275-8777, or your local postmaster.	
Johnsons	37048
Johnsons Chapel	38583
Johnsons Grove	38006
Johntown	37074
Jones	38006
Jonesborough	37659
Jones Chapel	38549
Jones Cove	37876
Jones Mill	38224
Jones Valley	38482
Jonesville, *Fentress*	38553
Jonesville, *Roane*	37840
Joppa, *Grainger*	37861
Joppa, *White*	38587
Jordonia (Part of Nashville)	37218
Jug Town	37130
Juno	38351
Kagley	37801
Kansas, *Jefferson*	37760
Kansas, *Sumner*	37066
Karns♦	37921
Kaywood (Part of Tullahoma)	37388
Kedron, *Giles*	38477
Kedron, *Maury*	37174
Keefe	38080
Keeling	38069
Keenburg	37643
Keese (Part of Decherd)	37324
Keith Springs	37398
Kellertown	37183
Kelley Town (Part of Oliver Springs)	37840
Kelso	37348
Keltonburg	37166
Kemmer Hill (Part of Spring City)	37381
Kempville	37030
Kendricks Creek	37663
Kennedy Creek	37016
Kenneytown	37745
Kenton	38233
Kepler	37857
Kerrville	38053
Kettle Mills	38461
Key	38583
Key Corner	38040
Keystone (Part of Johnson City)	37601
Killians Chapel (Part of Altamont)	37301
Kilsyth	37766
Kimball	37347
Kimberlin Heights	37920
Kimberly Acres	37122
Kimbrough Crossroad	37890
Kimery	38230
Kimmins	38462
Kimsey	37391
Kin Cove	37122
Kinderhook	38476
Kingfield	37064
Kingsport	37660-65
For specific ZIP Codes call (888) 275-8777, or your local postmaster.	
King Springs (Part of Johnson City)	37601
Kings Ridge (Part of Chattanooga)	37343
Kingston	37763
Kingston Heights	37763
Kingston Hills	37919
Kingston Mill	37160
Kingston Springs	37082
Kingston Woods	37919

*** Area Zip Code** **† Post Office Boxes** **‡ Postal Station** **♦ Census Designated Place** *Italic Type* **County**

Place	ZIP Code
Kinneys	37172
Kinzel Springs	37882
Kirk	38017
Kirkland, *Lincoln*	38488
Kirkland, *Williamson*	37046
Kirkwood	37040
Kite	37857
Kittrell	37149
Kleburne	37174
Klondike	37857
Knapp	37769
Knob Creek, *Lauderdale*	38063
Knob Creek, *Sevier*	37865
Knoxville	37901-50
For specific ZIP Codes call (888) 275-8777, or your local postmaster.	
Knoxville College (Part of Knoxville)‡	37921
Kodak	37764
Kodak Estates	37764
KoKo	38069
Kontika	37087
Kyles Ford	37765
Laager (Part of Gruetli-Laager)	37339
Laconia	38045
Lacy	38052
Lafayette	37083
La Follette	37766
La Grange	38046
Laguardo	37087
Lake City	37769
Lake Colonial Estates	37014
Lake Crest	37663
Lake Drive	38079
Lake Farm Estates	37167
Lake Forest, *Grainger*	37861
Lake Forest (Part of Chattanooga)	37343
Lake Forest (Part of Knoxville)	37920
Lakeharbor	37763
Lake Harbor Estates	37416
Lake Haven	37087
Lake Hills (Part of Tullahoma)	37388
Lakeland	38002
Lakemont	37777
Lakemont Cabin Area	37811
Lakemont Heights (Part of Rockwood)	37854
Lakemoor	37920
Lakemoore (Part of Morristown)	37814
Lake Placid	38340
Lake Road (Part of Fairview)	37062
Lakeshore Estates	37416
Lake Side, *Jefferson*	37890
Lakeside, *Monroe*	37885
Lakeside Estates (Part of Estill Springs)	37330
Lakeside Heights	37890
Lakeside Park	37343
Lakesite	37379
Lake Tansi Village	38555
Lake Tullahoma Estates (Part of Tullahoma)	37388
Lakeview, *Blount*	37777
Lakeview, *Claiborne*	37825
Lakeview, *Roane*	37763
Lakeview, *Robertson*	37172
Lakeview Commercial Park (Part of Franklin)	37064
Lakeview Estates	37777
Lake View Heights (Part of Harriman)	37748
Lakeview Manor	38256
Lakeview Park (Part of Dandridge)	37725
Lakewood	37138
Lakewood Village	37381
Lamar (Part of Memphis)‡	38114
Lamar, *Washington*	37659
Lambert	38068
Lamont	37172
Lamontville	37309
Lancaster	38569
Lancaster Hill	38567
Lancelot Acres	38478
Lancing	37770
Lane	38240
Laneview	38382
Langford Farms	37138
Lanier	37801
Lantana	38555
Lapata	38059
Lascassas	37085
Lassiter Corner	38232
Latham	38225
Laurel, *Anderson*	37716
Laurel, *Sevier*	37876
Laurel Bloomery	37680
Laurel Bluff	37763
Laurel Brook	37321
Laurelburg	38581
Laurel Cove	38581
Laurel Grove	37710
La Vergne	37086
Lavinia	38348
Law	38351
Law Chapel	37801
Lawnville	37763
Lawrenceburg	38464
Lawson Crossroad	37882
Lawton	38375
Leach	38344
Leadvale, *Cocke*	37890
Leadvale, *Jefferson*	37890
Leana	37129
Leapwood	38310
Lea Springs	37709
Leatherwood	38485
Lebanon	37087-90
For specific ZIP Codes call (888) 275-8777, or your local postmaster.	
Ledgemere (Part of Shelbyville)	37160
Lee	37367
Lee College (Part of Cleveland)‡	37311
Leeland	37064
Leemans Corner	37090
Leesburg	37659
Lee Valley	37869
Leeville	37090
Leewood (Part of Memphis)	38101
Leftwich	38401
Legate	37079
Leighs	38019
Leighton	38391
Leinart	37716
Leipers Fork	37064
Lenoir City	37771-72
For specific ZIP Codes call (888) 275-8777, or your local postmaster.	
Lenow	38018
Lenox	38047
Leoma	38468
Leonardtown	37620
Leoni	37190
Lewisburg	37091
Lewis Chapel	37327
Lexie	37306
Lexie Crossroads	37306
Lexington	38351
Liberty, *Benton*	38320
Liberty, *Decatur*	38374
Liberty, *DeKalb*	37095
Liberty, *Franklin*	37398
Liberty, *Giles*	38477
Liberty, *Jackson*	38564
Liberty, *Lincoln*	37334
Liberty, *Morgan*	37887
Liberty, *Sequatchie*	37397
Liberty, *Sumner* (mail Bethpage)	37022
Liberty, *Sumner* (mail Gallatin)	37066
Liberty, *Washington*	37641
Liberty, *Weakley*	38229
Liberty Grove	38469
Liberty Hill, *Giles*	38456
Liberty Hill, *Grainger*	37888
Liberty Hill, *Greene*	37641
Liberty Hill, *McMinn*	37329
Liberty Hill, *Williamson*	37025
Liberty Hill, *Wilson*	37012
Lick Creek, *Benton*	38221
Lick Creek, *Decatur*	38363
Lickskillet	37807
Lickton (Part of Nashville)	37189
Lightfoot	38063
Lillamay	37015
Lillydale	37650
Lily Grove	37825
Limestone	37681
Limestone Cove	37692
Linary	38555
Lincoln	37334
Lincoln Park (Part of Knoxville)	37917
Lincoya Hills (Part of Nashville)	37214
Linden	37096
Lindsay Mill	37769
Link	37037
Linsdale	37325
Linton (Part of Nashville)	37216
Linwood	37090
Lisbon	38052
Little Barren	37825
Littlebrook (Part of Rockford)	37853
Littlecrab	38556
Little Creek	37752
Little Doe	37640
Little Emory	37748
Little Hope, *Rutherford*	37129
Little Hope, *Wayne*	38485
Littlelot	38454
Little Milligan	37640
Little River	37804
Little White Oak	37766
Litton	37367
Litz Manor (Part of Kingsport)	37660
Liverwort	37040
Livesay Mill	37731
Livingston	38570
Lobelville	37097
Locke	38053
Lockertsville	37015
Lockmiller Addition (Part of Athens)	37303
Locust Grove	38059
Locust Mount	37659
Locust Springs	37616
Lodge	37380
Lodi	38486
Logans Lake	38334
Lois (Part of Lynchburg)	37359
Lomax Crossroads	38462
Lone Mountain, *Claiborne*	37825
Lone Mountain, *Scott*	37852
Lone Oak	37377
Lone Oaks (Part of Atoka)	38004
Lone Star	37660
Lonewood	38585
Long Branch (Part of Chattanooga)	37343
Long Branch, *Lawrence*	38464
Long Creek	37843
Long Hollow (Part of La Follette)	37766
Long Island (Part of Kingsport)	37660
Long Rock	38344
Longs Mills (Part of Athens)	37303
Longtown	38049
Longview	37020
Longwood	37064
Lonsdale (Part of Knoxville)	37921
Lookout Mountain	37350
Lookout Valley (Part of Chattanooga)‡	37419
Loon Bay	37028
Loretto	38469
Lorraine	37381
Lost Creek, *Decatur*	38329
Lost Creek, *White*	38583
Lost Mountain	37745
Loudon	37774
Louise	37051
Louisville	37777
Lovejoy	38574
Lovelace	37641
Love Lady	38549
Loveland (Part of Knoxville)	37924
Lovell Heights	37922
Love Station	37650
Lovetown	38474
Lower Mill	37343
Lower Mockeson	38468
Lowland	37778
Lowryville	38372
Luckett	38063
Lucky	37110
Lucy	38053
Luna	37019
Lunns Store	37034
Lupton City (Part of Chattanooga)	37351
Luray	38352
Lusk	37327
Luskville	37309
Luther	37869
Luttrell, *Loudon*	37846
Luttrell, *Union*	37779
Lutts	38471
Lyles	37098
Lynchburg	37352
Lynn Garden	37665
Lynn Point	38316
Lynnville	38472
Lyons View (Part of Knoxville)	37919
McAllister Hill	37317
McAllisters Crossroads	37171
McAnna	38260
McBurg	38459
McCains	38401
McClamerys Stand (Part of Collinwood)	38450
McCloud	37857
McClures Bend	37030
McCoinsville	38562
McConnell	38237
McCullough	38024
Mc Donald	37353
McDonald Hill	37857
Macedonia, *Carroll*	38201
Macedonia, *McMinn*	37329
Macedonia, *Obion*	38233
Macedonia, *White*	38583
McElroy	38559
Mace's Hill	37057
McEwen	37101
McGeetown	37317
McIllwain	38341
McKenzie	38201
McKinley	37601
McKinnon	37175
McLemoresville	38235
McLin's Corner	38034
McMahan (Part of Sevierville)	37862
McMillan	37914
McMinnville	37110*
	37111†
McNairy	38315
Macon	38048
McPheeter Bend	37642
Maddox	38372
Madge	38002
Madie	38080
Madison	37115*
	37116†
Madison College (Part of Nashville)	37115
Madison Hall	38301
Madison Square (Part of Nashville)	37115
Madisonville	37354
Maggart	38560
Magnolia	37175
Magnolia Place (Part of Franklin)	37064
Major	37090
Malesus (Part of Jackson)	38301
Mall at Green Hills, The (Part of Nashville)	37215
Mall at Johnson City, The (Part of Johnson City)	37601
Mall of Memphis, The (Part of Memphis)	38118
Mallory (Part of Memphis)‡	38109
Mallorys (Part of Franklin)	37067
Maloney Heights	37920
Maloneyville	37918
Manchester	33749†
	37355*
Manila	37329
Mankinville	37127
Manlyville	38256
Mansfield	38236
Mansfield Gap	37877
Manson	38556
Maple Grove, *Clay*	38541
Maple Grove, *Macon*	37083
Maple Grove, *Meigs*	37880
Maple Hill	37620
Maplehurst	37618
Maplewood (Part of Nashville)	37216
Marble City (Part of Knoxville)	37919
Marbledale	37914
Marble Hall	37857
Marble Hill, *Blount*	37737
Marble Hill (Part of Lynchburg)	37398
Marble Plains	37398
Marbleton	37692
Marguerite	37814
Marion, *Claiborne*	37715
Marion, *Montgomery*	37051
Markham	38079
Marlborough	38317
Marlow	37716
Marlyn Hills (Part of Bristol)	37620
Marrowbone	37015
Mars Hill, *Lawrence*	38464
Mars Hill, *Rhea*	37381
Martel Estates	37772
Martha	37090
Marthas Chapel	37040
Martha Washington	38553
Martin	38237
Martin Creek, *Hancock*	37879
Martin Creek, *Putnam*	38544
Martin Springs	37380
Marvin	37818
Marys Grove	38488
Maryville	37801-04
For specific ZIP Codes call (888) 275-8777, or your local postmaster.	
Maryville College (Part of Maryville)	37801
Mascot♦	37806
Mason	38049
Mason Grove	38343
Mason Hall	38233
Masseyville	38315
Matheny Grove	38225
Maupin Row (Part of Johnson City)	37601
Maury City	38050
Maxey	38059
Maxwell	37306
Maxwell Chapel	38568
May Acres	37877
Mayhome	37184
Mayland	38555
Maymead	37683
Maynardville	37807
Mayview Heights	37849
McCutchen Heights	38261
Mc Donald	37810
Meacham	38024
Meades Quarry (Part of Knoxville)	37920
Meadorville	37083
Meadow	37742
Meadowbrook, *Blount*	37804
Meadowbrook, *Greene*	37616
Meadow Brook, *Warren*	37110
Meadow Green Acres	37064
Meadow Mead (Part of Paris)	38242
Meadow View, *Hamilton*	37336
Meadowview (Part of Lawrenceburg)	38464
Meadowview Gardens (Part of Harriman)	37748
Meadowwood Acres (Part of Fairview)	37062
Medford	37769
Medina	38355
Medon	38356
Melrose, *Blount*	37886
Melrose (Part of Nashville)	37204
	37220
For specific ZIP Codes call (888) 275-8777, or your local postmaster.	
Melville Hill (Part of Soddy Daisy)	37379
Melvine	37367

Memphis

	38101-37
	38141-82
	38184-90

For specific ZIP Codes call (888) 275-8777, or your local postmaster.

Colleges & Universities

Christian Brothers Univ	38104

* **Area Zip Code** † **Post Office Boxes** ‡ **Postal Station** ♦ **Census Designated Place** *Italic Type* **County**

Crichton Coll 38175
Harding Univ Graduate School of Religion 38117
Lemoyne-Owen Coll 38126
Memphis Coll of Art 38104
Memphis Theological Seminary 38104
Rhodes Coll 38112
Southern Coll of Optometry 38104
Univ of Memphis 38152
Univ of Tennessee 38163

Financial Institutions
First American Nat Bank 38103
First Tennessee Bank, NA 38103
Nat Bank of Commerce 38150
NationsBank, NA 38119
Union Planters Bank, NA 38103

Hospitals
Baptist Memorial Hosp 38146
Methodist Hosp 38104
Regional Med Ctr 38103
St Francis Hosp 38119
Veterans Affairs Med Ctr 38104

Hotels/Motels
Adam's Mark 38120
Crowne Plaza 38103
East Memphis Hilton 38117
Four Points, Airport 38132
Holiday Inn Memphis East/I-240 38119
Holiday Inn, Midtown/Med Ctr 38104
Marriott 38118
The Peabody 38103
Radisson 38103

Military Installations
Defense Distribution Depot 38114
Tennessee Air Nat Guard, FB6422, Memphis International Airport 38118
U S Army Corps of Engineers 38103

Memphis State University (Part of Memphis) 38152
Mendenhall (Part of Memphis) 38117*
38177†
Mengelwood 38047
Mentor 37777
Mercer 38392
Meredith Cave 37766
Merry Oaks (Part of Nashville) 37214
Michie 38357
Middlebrook Heights (Part of Knoxville) 37919
Middleburg, *Hardeman* 38008
Middleburg, *Henderson* 38374
Middle City 38024
Middle Creek 37862
Middle Fork 38345
Middle Settlement 37777
Middleton 38052
Middle Valley 37343
Middle Valley Estates 37343
Midfields 37665
Midland 37020
Midtown 37748
Midtown Heights 37748
Midway, *Cannon* 37026
Midway, *Cocke* 37727
Midway, *Cumberland* 38555
Midway, *DeKalb* 37166
Midway, *Dyer* 38030
Midway, *Franklin* 37375
Midway, *Greene* 37809
Midway, *Johnson* 37640
Midway, *Knox* 37871
Midway, *Obion* 38261
Midway, *Roane* 37763
Midway, *Warren* 37110
Mifflin 38352
Milan 38358
Milan Army Ammunition Plant 38358
Milburnton 37681
Miles Crossroads 37150
Mile Straight (Part of Soddy Daisy) 37379
Milky Way 38478
Mill Brook 37681
Mill Creek, *Anderson* 37705
Mill Creek, *Morgan* 37872
Mill Creek, *Putnam* 38506
Milldale 37172
Milledgeville 38359
Miller's Store 38225
Millersville 37072
Millertown 37914
Millican Grove 37876
Millington 38053-54
38083
For specific ZIP Codes call (888) 275-8777, or your local postmaster.
Millsfield 38024
Mill Spring 37820
Milltown, *Humphreys* 37101
Milltown, *Jackson* 38588
Milltown, *Macon* 37150
Milltown, *Marshall* 37091
Millview 37067
Milo 37381
Milton 37118
Mimms (Part of Nashville) 37211
Mimosa 37334
Mimosa Estates 37777
Mimosa Heights 37777
Mineral Park 37353
Mineral Springs 38574
Mink 38485
Minnick 38240
Minor Hill 38473
Mint 37803
Miser Station 37737
Miston 38056
Mitchell 37148
Mitchellville 37119
Mixie 38342
Moccasin 38485
Mohawk 37810
Mohawk Crossroad 37711
Molino 37334
Mon 37087
Mona 37129
Monoville 37030
Monroe 38573
Montague (Part of Nashville) 37216
Montague, *Rhea* 37321
Monteagle 37356
Monterey 38574
Montezuma 38340
Montgomery Junction 37756
Monticello (Part of Franklin) 37069
Monticello, *Wilson* 37122
Montpier Farms 37069
Montvale 37803
Moodyville 38549
Mooneyham 38585
Moons 38256
Moon Shadows 37341
Mooreland Heights (Part of Knoxville) 37920
Mooresburg 37811
Mooresburg Springs 37811
Moores Chapel 38358
Moores College 38581
Mooresville 37091
Mooretown 37190
Mooring 38079
Morgan Springs 37321
Morganton 37742
Morgantown 37321
Morganville 37397
Morley 37766
Morny (Part of Nashville) 37080
Morris Chapel, *Benton* 38320
Morris Chapel, *Hardin* 38361
Morrison 37357
Morrison City 37665
Morrison Creek 38562
Morristown 37813-16
For specific ZIP Codes call (888) 275-8777, or your local postmaster.
Moscow 38057
Mosheim 37818
Moss 38575
Mossy Grove 37748
Mountain City 37683
Mountain Dale 37650
Mountain Home (Part of Johnson City) 37684
Mountain View (Part of Dayton) 37321
Mountain View, *Scott* 37852
Mountain View Acres (Part of Winchester) 37398
Mount Airy 37327
Mount Ararat 37095
Mount Carmel, *Decatur* 38329
Mount Carmel, *Greene* 37711
Mount Carmel, *Hawkins* 37645
Mount Carmel, *Tipton* 38019
Mount Carmel, *Washington* 37641
Mount Crest 37367
Mount Cumberland 37329
Mount Denson 37172
Mount Gilead, *Henderson* 38321
Mount Gilead, *White* 38583
Mount Harmony, *McMinn* 37826
Mount Harmony, *Monroe* 37385
Mount Helen 38504
Mount Herman, *Bedford* 37160
Mount Herman, *Weakley* 38230
Mount Hope 38485
Mount Horeb 37760
Mount Joy 38474
Mount Juliet 37121†
37122*
Mount Lebanon, *Lawrence* 38464
Mount Lebanon, *Tipton* 38019
Mount Leo (Part of McMinnville) 37110
Mount Moriah 38320
Mount Nebo 38463
Mount Olive, *Grundy* 37110
Mount Olive, *Knox* 37920
Mount Olive, *Marion* 37397
Mount Olive, *Rutherford* 37129
Mount Pelia 38237
Mount Pisgah 38587
Mount Pleasant, *Greene* 37743
Mount Pleasant, *Henry* 38222
Mount Pleasant, *Maury* 38474
Mount Pleasant, *Putnam* 38506
Mount Pleasant, *Scott* 37852
Mount Tabor 37804
Mount Tucker Addition 37617
Mount Union, *Jackson* 38564
Mount Union, *Pickett* 38549
Mount Vernon, *Monroe* 37358
Mount Vernon, *Rutherford* 37153
Mount Vernon, *Sumner* 37022
Mount View (Part of Nashville) 37211
Mount View, *Grundy* 37366
Mount Vinson 38379
Mount Zion, *Cheatham* 37015
Mount Zion, *Monroe* 37885
Mount Zion, *Montgomery* 37051
Mount Zion, *Obion* 38232
Mount Zion, *Warren* 37110
Mourberry 38583
Mowbray 37379
Mt. Carmel 37345
Mt. Lebanon 38329
Mt. Vernon 37388
Mud Creek, *McNairy* 38310
Mud Creek, *Warren* 38581
Muddy Pond 38574
Mudsink 37067
Mulberry 37359
Mulberry Gap 37869
Mulberry Hill 37058
Mulloy 37048
Munford 38058
Murfreesboro 37127-33
For specific ZIP Codes call (888) 275-8777, or your local postmaster.
Murray-Lake Hills (Part of Chattanooga)‡ 37416
Murray Store 37826
Myers (Part of Winchester) 37398
Nameless 38545
Nance 38001
Nance Ferry 37709
Nances Grove 37820
Nankipoo 38040
Napier 38462
Narrows of the Harpeth 37082
Narrow Valley 37861
Nash 38544

Nashville
37201-49
For specific ZIP Codes call (888) 275-8777, or your local postmaster.

Colleges & Universities
Belmont Univ 37212
David Lipscomb Univ 37204
Fisk Univ 37208
Free Will Baptist Bible Coll 37205
ITT Technical Institute 37214
Meharry Medical Coll 37208
Tennessee State Univ 37209
Trevecca Nazarene Univ 37210
Vanderbilt Univ 37240

Financial Institutions
AmSouth Bank 37201
First American Nat Bank 37237
First Tennessee Bank, NA 37219
First Union Nat Bank 37219
Nat Bank of Commerce 37219
NationsBank 37239
SunTrust Bank, NA 37219

Hospitals
Centennial Med Ctr 37203
St Thomas Hosp 37205
Vanderbilt Univ Med Ctr 37232
Veterans Affairs Med Ctr 37212

Hotels/Motels
Clubhouse Inn & Conference Ctr 37203
Crowne Plaza 37219
Doubletree 37219
Embassy Suites Airport 37214
Holiday Inn Select, Opryland/Airport 37214
Holiday Inn Vanderbilt 37203
Loews Vanderbilt Plaza 37203
Marriott 37214
Opryland 37214
Ramada Inn 37214
Regal Maxwell House 37228
Renaissance 37203
Sheraton Music City 37214

Military Installations
Marine Corps Recruiting Sta 37214
Tennessee Air Nat Guard, FB6421, Nashville International Airport 37217
U S Army Corps of Engineers 37202
U S Property & Fiscal Off for Tennessee 37204

Natco (Part of Columbia) 38401
National Cemetery (Part of Memphis) 38122
Natural Bridge 37843
Nauvoo 38024
Neapolis 38401
Neboville 38059
Needmore, *Hamblen* 37891
Needmore, *Maury* 38474
Needmore, *Montgomery* 37079
Needmore, *Wilson* 37138
Needmore (Part of Lewisburg) 37091
Neely 38391
Neely Crossroads 38551
Nelsontown (Part of Kingsport) 37660
Nemo 37887
Nenny 37891
Neptune 37015
Neubert 37920
Neva 37683
Newbern 38059
New Bethel 37331
New Canton 37642
New Castle 38075
Newcomb 37819
New Corinth 37861
New Deal 37048
New Dellrose 38453
New Due West (Part of Nashville) 37115
Newell Station 37865
New Enterprise 38338
New Era 38555
New Harmony, *Bledsoe* 37367
New Harmony, *Macon* 37074
New Haven, *Lawrence* 38464
New Haven, *Scott* 37841
New Herman 37160
New Hope, *Cheatham* 37080
New Hope, *Hancock* 37869
New Hope, *Hardin* 38310
New Hope, *Hawkins* 37857
New Hope, *Houston* 37175
New Hope, *Humphreys* 37101
New Hope, *Jackson* 38568
New Hope, *Lincoln* 37334
New Hope, *McNairy* 38339
New Hope, *Marion* 37380
New Hope, *Roane* 37854
New Hope, *Williamson* 37062
New Hope, *Wilson* 37087
New Johnsonville 37134
New Line 37814
New Loyston 37807
Newmansville 37616
New Market 37820
New Markham 38079
New Middleton 38563
New Midway 37763
Newport 37821*
37822†
New Prospect 38464
New Providence, *Loudon* 37774
New Providence (Part of Clarksville)‡ 37042
New River 37755
New Safford 38328
New Salem, *Hamilton* 37379
New Salem, *Jackson* 38562
New Salem, *Scott* 37841
New Tazewell 37824†
37825*
Newton 38555
New Town, *Marshall* 37047
New Town (Part of Spring Hill) 37174
Newtown, *Polk* 37317
Newtown, *Rutherford* 37153
New Union 37355
New Victory 37659
New Zion, *Carroll* 38344
New Zion, *Macon* 37186
Nickletown 37347
Nicks Creek 37756
Nine Mile 37367
Ninth Model 37357
Niota 37826
Nixon 38372
Noah 37355
Nobles 38242
Nolensville♦ 37135
Nonaburg 37329
Nonaville 37122
Nonconnah (Part of Memphis) 38116
Norene 37136
Norma 37756
Normandy 37360
Norris 37828
North (Part of Memphis)‡ 38107

Place	ZIP
North (Part of Nashville)‡	37208
North Chattanooga (Part of Chattanooga)‡	37405
Northcott	37660
Northcutts Cove, *Grundy*	37110
Northcutt's Cove, *Warren*	37110
Northeast (Part of Nashville)‡	37207
Northern Hills (Part of Chattanooga)	37343
Northgate Mall (Part of Chattanooga)	37415
Northgate Shopping Center (Part of Memphis)	38127
North Glen Estates (Part of Chattanooga)	37343
North Hills (Part of Knoxville)	37917
North Johnson City (Part of Johnson City)	37601
North Knoxville (Part of Knoxville)‡	37917*
	37927†
Northpoint	37874
North Riverside	38462
Northside (Part of Jackson)	38301
North Springs	38588
Norwood (Part of Oliver Springs)	37840
Norwood (Part of Knoxville)‡	37912
Notchy Creek	37354
Nough	37727
Nubia	37186
Nucarbon	38468
Number One (Part of Gallatin)	37066
Nunnelly	37137
Nutbush	38012
Oak City	37865
Oak Court Mall (Part of Memphis)	38117
Oakdale, *Hawkins*	37873
Oakdale, *Macon*	37186
Oakdale, *Morgan*	37829
Oak Dale, *Overton*	38573
Oakdale, *White*	38583
Oakfield	38362
Oak Grove, *Campbell*	37769
Oak Grove, *Carter*	37643
Oak Grove, *Claiborne*	37752
Oak Grove, *Clay*	38575
Oak Grove, *Dickson*	37055
Oak Grove, *Franklin*	37324
Oak Grove, *Giles*	38460
Oak Grove, *Hardin*	38372
Oak Grove, *Henry*	38222
Oak Grove, *Jefferson*	37725
Oak Grove, *Lewis*	38462
Oak Grove, *Madison*	38301
Oak Grove, *Marion*	37397
Oak Grove, *Monroe*	37354
Oak Grove, *Overton* (mail Hilham)	38568
Oak Grove, *Overton* (mail Livingston)	38570
Oak Grove, *Pickett*	38573
Oak Grove, *Polk*	37307
Oak Grove, *Sumner*	37022
Oak Grove, *Tipton*	38019
Oak Grove, *Union*	37866
Oak Grove, *Warren*	37357
Oak Grove, *Washington*♦	37615
Oak Grove, *Weakley*	38237
Oak Grove Heights	37921
Oakhaven (Part of Memphis)	38116
Oak Hill, *Carter*	37658
Oak Hill, *Cocke*	37843
Oak Hill, *Cumberland*	38555
Oak Hill, *Davidson*	37220
Oak Hill, *Overton*	38580
Oak Hill, *Pickett*	38549
Oak Hill, *Washington*	37659
Oak Hill (Part of Bristol)	37620
Oakhurst (Part of Maryville)	37803
Oakland, *Fayette*	38060
Oakland, *Grainger*	37861
Oakland, *Henry*	38242
Oakland, *Jefferson*	37760
Oakland, *Robertson*	37172
Oakland, *Warren*	37110
Oakland, *Washington*	37690
Oakland (Part of Knoxville)	37918
Oaklawn	37166
Oakleigh Estates	37620
Oakley	38541
Oaklyn	38555
Oak Park (Part of Tullahoma)	37388
Oak Plains	37040
Oak Ridge	37830*
	37831†
Oak Ridge Mall (Part of Oak Ridge)	37830
Oak Tree	37062
Oak View	37886
Oakville (Part of Memphis)	38118
Oakwood (Part of Knoxville)	37917
Oakwood, *Montgomery*	37191
Oakwood Estates	37064
Obion	38240
Ocana	37075
Ocoee	37361
O'Connors	38583
Odd Fellows Hall	38478
Officers Chapel	38506
Offutt	37716
Ogden	37321
Okalona	38570
Okolona, *Carter*	37601
Okolona, *Hawkins*	37642
Old Antioch	38562
Old Chihowee	37865
Olde Mill	37343
Oldfort	37362
Old Glory	37804
Old Hickory (Part of Nashville)	37138
Old Hickory Mall (Part of Jackson)	38301
Old Kingsport (Part of Kingsport)	37660
Old Laguardo	37122
Old Lawton	38375
Old Salem	37345
Old Springville	38256
Old Sweetwater	37874
Old Washington	37321
Old Winesap	38555
Old Zion	38583
Olivehill	38475
Oliver Springs	37840
Olivet	38372
One Hundred Oaks Mall (Part of Nashville)	37204
Oneida	37841
Only	37140
Ooltewah	37363
Opossum	38063
Opossum Creek Pines	37379
Oral	37771
Orchard View	37840
Orebank	37664
Ore Spring	38225
Orgains Crossroads	37040
Orlinda	37141
Orme	37380
Orysa	38063
Osage	38242
Osemont Chapel	37190
Ostella	37091
Oswego	37762
Otes	37857
Otter Creek Junction	38555
Ottway	37745
Overall	37127
Overlook	37804
Ovilla	38464
Ovoca	37388
Owens Chapel	37172
Owl City	38079
Owl Hoot	38080
Ozone, *Cumberland*	37842
Ozone, *Overton*	38573
Pactolus	37663
Pailo	37327
Paint Rock	37846
Palestine, *Henderson*	38351
Palestine, *Robertson*	37172
Pall Mall	38577
Palmer	37365
Palmersville	38241
Palmyra	37142
Pandora	37640
Paperville (Part of Bristol)	37620
Paradise Acres	37122
Paragon Mills (Part of Nashville)	37211
Paris	38242
Parkburg	38366
Park City (Part of Knoxville)	37914
Park City, *Lincoln*	37334
Parker	38577
Parkers Crossroads	38388
Park Grove	38464
Park Settlement	37862
Parkshore Estates	37343
Parksville	37307
Parkview	37854
Parkway (Part of Maryville)‡	37801
Parkway Village (Part of Memphis)‡	38118
Parragon	38506
Parrottsville	37843
Parsons	38363
Pasquo (Part of Nashville)	37221
Pate Hill	37818
Patterson	37153
Patterson Crossroads	37752
Pattie Gap	37846
Patty	37325
Paulette	37807
Paw Paw Ridge	38030
Payne Cove	37366
Paynes Store	37022
Peabody	37766
Peak	37716
Peakland	37322
Peanut	37843
Pea Ridge, *DeKalb*	37095
Pea Ridge, *Lawrence*	38464
Pearl City	37334
Peavine	38555
Pebble Hill	38357
Peckerwood Point	38004
Peeled Chestnut	38583
Pegram	37143
Pelham	37366
Penile Hill	37324
Pennine	37381
Pennington Bend (Part of Nashville)	37214
Pennington Chapel	37888
Peppertown	38469
Perrin Hollow	37709
Perryville	38363
Persia	37857
Petersburg, *Hawkins*	37857
Petersburg, *Lincoln*	37144
Peters Landing	38425
Petros	37845
Petway	37015
Peytonsville	37064
Philadelphia, *Jackson*	38545
Philadelphia, *Loudon*	37846
Philadelphia, *Washington*	37641
Philippi	37166
Phillippy	38079
Pickwatina Place (Part of Athens)	37303
Pickwick Dam	38365
Piedmont	37725
Pierce	38257
Pierce Town	37640
Pigeon Forge	37863*
	37868†
Pigeon River Estates (Part of Sevierville)	37862
Pigeon Roost	37185
Pikeville	37367
Pillowville	38201
Pilot Knob	37711
Pilot Mountain	37770
Pine Bluff	37398
Pinebrook Estates	37341
Pine Crest, *Campbell*	37757
Pine Crest, *Carter*♦	37601
Pine Grove, *Greene*	37743
Pine Grove, *Loudon*	37774
Pine Grove, *Rhea*	37381
Pine Grove, *Van Buren*	38585
Pine Grove (Part of Pigeon Forge)	37863
Pine Haven, *Fentress*	38556
Pinehaven, *Shelby*	38053
Pine Hill, *Bradley*	37353
Pine Hill, *Clay*	38575
Pine Hill, *Marion*	37397
Pine Hill, *Scott*	37841
Pine Lake	38002
Pineland	37322
Pine Orchard	37829
Pine Point	38256
Pine Ridge, *Jefferson*	37890
Pine Ridge, *Polk*	37333
Pine Top	37772
Pine Tree Estates	37343
Pineview	37096
Pineville (Part of Morristown)	37814
Pinewood, *Cheatham*	37015
Pinewood, *Hickman*	37137
Piney, *Loudon*	37774
Piney, *Van Buren*	38585
Piney Flats	37686
Piney Grove, *McMinn*	37303
Piney Grove, *Scott*	37892
Piney Grove (Part of Johnson City)	37601
Piney Shores Estates	37381
Pinhook, *Putnam*	38574
Pinhook, *Union*	37807
Pinnacle (Part of Pittman Center)	37876
Pinson	38366
Pioneer	37847
Pipers Chapel	37148
Piperton	38017
Pisgah, *DeKalb*	37166
Pisgah, *Giles*	38478
Pisgah, *Shelby*	38018
Pisgah, *Weakley*	38225
Pittman Center	37862
Plainfield (Part of Maryville)	37804
Plain Grove	38573
Plainview, *Rutherford*	37037
Plainview, *Union*	37779
Plant	37134
Plantation Hills (Part of Knoxville)	37917
Plateau	38555
Pleasant Green	37726
Pleasant Grove, *Bedford*	37160
Pleasant Grove, *Cocke*	37821
Pleasant Grove, *Lincoln*	37334
Pleasant Grove, *Scott*	37892
Pleasant Grove, *Sumner*	37186
Pleasant Grove (Part of Jasper)	37347
Pleasant Hill, *Claiborne*	37870
Pleasant Hill, *Clay*	38541
Pleasant Hill, *Cumberland*	38578
Pleasant Hill, *Greene*	37641
Pleasant Hill, *Hawkins*	37711
Pleasant Hill, *Lauderdale*	38041
Pleasant Hill, *Meigs*	37880
Pleasant Hill, *Obion*	38253
Pleasant Hill, *Polk*	37317
Pleasant Hill, *Rutherford*	37060
Pleasant Hill, *Sevier*	37876
Pleasant Hill, *Weakley*	38237
Pleasant Hill (Part of Lynchburg)	37352
Pleasant Point, *Claiborne*	37825
Pleasant Point, *Lawrence*	38469
Pleasant Ridge, *Cannon*	37190
Pleasant Ridge, *Putnam*	38506
Pleasant Ridge (Part of Knoxville)	37921
Pleasant Shade	37145
Pleasant Valley, *Macon*	37074
Pleasant Valley, *Sumner*	37048
Pleasant Valley, *Washington*	37659
Pleasant View, *Cannon*	37190
Pleasant View, *Cheatham*	37146
Pleasant View, *Claiborne*	37879
Pleasantville	37147
Plunketts Creek	38563
Pocahontas, *Coffee*	37357
Pocahontas, *Hardeman*	38061
Poga	37640
Point Pleasant	37821
Pointview Circle	37122
Polk	38253
Pollard	37061
Pomona, *Cumberland*	38555
Pomona, *Dickson*	37055
Pomona Road	38555
Pond	37055
Ponderosa	37763
Ponderosa Hills	37849
Ponders Gap	37880
Pond Grove	37854
Pond Hill	37303
Pondville	37022
Pope	37096
Poplar	37840
Poplar Corner	38006
Poplar Grove, *Claiborne*	37752
Poplar Grove, *Humphreys*	37101
Poplar Grove, *Lauderdale*	38040
Poplar Grove, *Putnam*	38506
Poplar Hill, *Giles*	38477
Poplar Hill, *McMinn*	37303
Poplar Plaza Shopping Center (Part of Memphis)	38111
Poplar Springs, *Henderson*	38351
Poplar Springs, *Loudon*	37774
Poplar Springs, *Roane*	37763
Poplins Crossroads	37180
Porter Court (Part of Paris)	38242
Porterfield	37118
Porter Gap	38040
Porters Chapel	38474
Porters Creek	38052
Portland	37148
Port Royal	37010
Port Serena	37343
Postelle	37317
Post Oak, *Putnam*	38506
Post Oak, *Roane*	37854
Poteet	38543
Pottsville	38401
Powder Springs	37848
Powell♦	37849
Powell Chapel	38478
Powells Chapel	38044
Powells Crossroads	37397
Powell Valley	37766
Prairie Creek	37379
Prairie Peninsula	37343
Prairie Plains	37342
Prater	37190
Preston Woods (Part of Kingsport)	37660
Price	38041
Price's Switch	38583
Pride	38261
Primm Springs	38476
Princeton (Part of Johnson City)	37601
Proctor City	38079
Prospect, *Blount*	37886
Prospect, *Bradley*	37312
Prospect, *Giles*	38477
Prospect, *Lincoln*	37334
Prospect, *Loudon*	37774
Prospect, *McMinn*	37329
Prosperity, *Macon*	37150
Prosperity, *Wilson*	37016
Protemus	38260
Providence (Part of Nashville)	37211
Providence, *Grundy*	37324
Providence, *Madison*	38301
Providence, *Sumner*	37186
Providence, *Trousdale*	37074
Pruden	37851
Pryor Ridge	37387
Puckett	37153
Pulaski	38478
Pumpkintown	37083
Punch	37030
Puncheon Camp	37888
Purdy	38375
Puryear	38251
Push	38232
Pyburns	38372
Quail Meador	37090
Quebeck	38579
Quincy	38001
Quito	38053

Place	ZIP
Raccoon Valley (Part of Maynardville)	37807
Rader	37743
Rafter	37385
Ragsdale	37355
Raines (Part of Memphis)	38116
Raleigh (Part of Memphis)‡	38128
Raleigh Springs Mall (Part of Memphis)	38128
Rally Hill	38401
Ralston	38237
Ramah	38468
Ramer	38367
Ramsey, *Hancock*	37869
Ramsey, *Knox*	37914
Ramsey, *Wilson*	37087
Randolph	38023
Range	37694
Rankin	37821
Rankin Cove	37347
Rascal Town	38469
Rathburn (Part of Soddy Daisy)	37379
Raus	37388
Raven Branch	37753
Raven Hill	37879
Ravenscroft	38583
Rayon City (Part of Nashville)	37138
Rays Chapel	37034
Raysville	37388
Readyville	37149
Reagan	38368
Rebel Acres (Part of Pulaski)	38478
Rebel Meadows (Part of Franklin)	37069
Red Ash	37714
Red Bank	37415
Red Boiling Springs	37150
Red Hill, *Bradley*	37323
Red Hill, *Claiborne*	37752
Red Hill, *Fentress*	38556
Red Hill, *Lawrence*	38464
Red Hill, *Marion*	37397
Red Hill, *Pickett*	38549
Red Hill, *Weakley*	38225
Red Hill (Part of Manchester)	37355
Red House	37709
Red Row	38474
Redwing Farms	37064
Reeds Lake	38004
Reed Spring	37846
Reedtown	37821
Reesetown	37391
Rehoboth	38024
Reliance	37369
Reubensville	37148
Reverie	72395
Revilo	38468
Rheatown	37641
Rhyan Springs	38573
Rialto	38019
Rice Bend	37657
Riceville	37370
Rich	38472
Rich Acres (Part of Johnson City)	37601
Richard City (Part of South Pittsburg)	37380
Richardson	38023
Richland (Part of Nashville)	37209
Richland, *Grainger*	37709
Richmond	37144
Richview Acres	37865
Richwood	38024
Rickman	38580
Riddleton	37151
Ridenour	37807
Ridgedale (Part of Knoxville)	37931
Ridgedale, *Sullivan*	37620
Ridgefield (Part of Kingsport)	37660
Ridge Lake North (Part of Chattanooga)	37343
Ridgely	38080
Ridgeside	37411
Ridgetop, *Lewis*	38461
Ridgetop, *Robertson*	37152
Ridgeview (Part of Morristown)	37814
Ridgeville (Part of Lynchburg)	37352
Ridgewood	37714
Ridley	38401
Riggs Crossroads	37046
Right	38361
Rim Rock Mesa	38583
Rinnie	38555
Riovista (Part of Elizabethton)	37643
Ripley	38063
Ritchie	37879
Ritta	37918
Riva Lake Camp	37398
Riverdale	37914
Rivergate Mall (Part of Goodlettsville)	37072
River Hill	37650
River Oaks	37341
River Rest	37064
Riversburg	38478
Riverside, *Claiborne*	37879
Riverside, *Sullivan*	37618
Riverside (Part of Memphis)‡	38113
Riverside (Part of Nashville)	37218
Riverton	38556
Riverview, *Claiborne*	37752
Riverview, *Unicoi*	37650
Riverview (Part of Kingsport)	37660
Riverview Estates	37033
Rives	38253
Roan Mountain♦	37687
Roans Creek	37097
Roaring Springs	37616
Robbins, *Pickett*	38549
Robbins, *Scott*	37852
Roberts	38582
Robertson	38315
Robertson Fork	38472
Robinson Crossroads	37921
Robinson Mill	37774
Roby	38332
Rockbridge	37022
Rock City, *Smith*	37030
Rock City, *Sullivan*	37664
Rock Creek (Part of Erwin)	37650
Rockdale	38474
Rockford	37853
Rock Haven	37708
Rock Hill, *Hancock*	37869
Rock Hill, *Henderson*	38351
Rock Hill, *Sullivan*	37694
Rock House	37075
Rock Island	38581
Rockland (Part of Hendersonville)	37075
Rock Ledge Estates	37363
Rock Springs, *Dickson*	37036
Rock Springs, *Dyer*	38024
Rock Springs, *Henderson*	38388
Rock Springs, *Rutherford*	37037
Rock Springs, *Sullivan*	37663
Rock Station	38581
Rockvale	37153
Rockville	37874
Rockwood	37854
Rockwood Hill	37743
Rocky Branch	37886
Rocky Creek	37031
Rocky Fork, *Rutherford*	37167
Rocky Fork, *Unicoi*	37657
Rocky Grove	37722
Rocky Hill (Part of Knoxville)	37919
Rocky Mound	37186
Rocky Point, *Hamblen*	37860
Rocky Point, *Putnam*	38506
Rocky Ridge	38573
Rocky Spring	37354
Rocky Springs	37686
Rocky Valley	37820
Roddy	37381
Roe Junction	37813
Ro Ellen	38024
Rogana	37022
Rogers Creek	37303
Rogers Spring	38052
Rogersville	37857
Rolling Acres, *Jefferson*	37877
Rolling Acres (Part of Fairview)	37062
Rolling Hills, *Hickman*	37025
Rolling Hills, *Unicoi*	37650
Rolling Hills, *Warren*	37110
Rolling Hills (Part of Lewisburg)	37091
Rolling Meadows (Part of Franklin)	37064
Rome	37030
Romeo	37711
Rose Creek	38375
Rosedale	37710
Rose Hill, *Madison*	38301
Rose Hill, *Union*	37807
Rosemark	38053
Rose Valley	37079
Roseville	37183
Roslin	38556
Ross Camp Ground	37642
Rosser	38344
Rossview	37040
Rossville	38066
Rotherwood	37642
Round Pond	37040
Round Rock	37714
Round Top	37012
Routon	38231
Rover	37060
Rowark Cove	37324
Rowland	38581
Royal	37160
Royal Blue	37847
Royal Oak (Part of Manchester)	37355
Royal Oaks (Part of Franklin)	37068
Royal Oaks, *Wilson*	37122
Royer Estates (Part of Murfreesboro)	37130
Rucker	37127
Rudderville	37064
Rudolph	38012
Rugby	37733
Rugby Hills (Part of Memphis)	38127
Rural Hill (Part of Nashville)	37217
Rural Hill, *Wilson*♦	37071
Rural Vale	37385
Russel Fork	37766
Russell Crossroad	37743
Russell Hill	37145
Russellville	37860
Rusty (Part of Fairview)	37062
Rutherford	38369
Rutherford Estates	38401
Ruthton	37620
Ruthville	38237
Rutledge	37861
Rutledge Falls	37355
Rutledge Hill	37342
Ryall Springs	37421
Sadie	37643
Sadlers	37010
Safley	37110
Sagewood Estates	38401
Sailors Rest	37050
St. Andrews	37372
St. Bethlehem (Part of Clarksville)	37155
St. Clair, *Hawkins*	37711
Saint Clair, *Rhea*	37381
St Elmo (Part of Chattanooga)	37409
St. James	37743
St. Joseph	38481
St. Paul	38023
Saint Peters	38012
Sainville	37355
Sale Creek	37373
Salem, *Cocke*	37843
Salem, *Lewis*	37033
Salem, *Montgomery*	37040
Salem, *Tipton*	38004
Salem, *Weakley*	38255
Saltillo	38370
Samburg	38254
Sampson	37367
Sanders	37387
Sandhill	38229
Sandlick	37825
Sand Ridge	38351
Sand Springs	38574
Sand Switch	37375
Sandy	38589
Sandy Hook	38474
Sandy Lane	37385
Sandy Point	38320
Sandy Ridge	37725
Sandy Spring	37032
Sanford	37370
Sanford Hill (Part of Henderson)	38340
Sango	37040
Santa Fe	38482
Saratoga Springs	37367
Sardis	38371
Saulsbury	38067
Saundersville (Part of Hendersonville)	37075
Savannah	38372
Sawdust	38401
Sawyers Mill	38320
Scandlyn	37840
Scarboro (Part of Oak Ridge)	37830
Scattersville	37148
Scenic Point Estates	37777
Scoot Mill	37810
Scottsboro (Part of Nashville)	37218
Scotts Hill	38374
Screamer	38474
Seeber Flats	37710
Selmer	38375
Sengtown	37148
Sentinel Heights (Part of Dayton)	37363
Sequatchie	37374
Sequoia Grove (Part of Cleveland)	37312
Sequoia Hills	37743
Sequoyah Estates (Part of Madisonville)	37354
Sequoyah Hills	37343
Sequoyah Village (Part of Madisonville)	37354
Serles	38052
Settlers Point	37064
Seven Islands	37920
Seven Oaks	37922
Sevier Home	37920
Sevierville	37862
......	37864
......	37876

For specific ZIP Codes call (888) 275-8777, or your local postmaster.

Place	ZIP
Sewanee♦	37375
Sewee	37826
Seymour	37865
Shackle Island	37075
Shacklett	37082
Shades Bridge	38230
Shady Grove, *Coffee*	37357
Shady Grove, *Hamilton*	37379
Shady Grove, *Jackson*	38562
Shady Grove, *Jefferson*	37725
Shady Grove, *Knox*	37922
Shady Grove, *Lincoln*	37335
Shady Grove, *Montgomery*	37040
Shady Grove, *Morgan*	37770
Shady Grove, *Putnam*	38574
Shady Grove, *Trousdale*	37074
Shady Grove, *White*	38587
Shady Grove Shores	37379
Shady Hill	38351
Shady Rest	37110
Shady Valley	37688
Shafter	38230
Shake Rag Hill	38485
Shallowford	37650
Shandy	38008
Shannondale (Part of Knoxville)	37918
Shannon Hills	37343
Sharon	38255
Sharondale (Part of Tullahoma)	37388
Sharp Place	38556
Sharps Chapel	37866
Sharpsville	37130
Shaver Town	38563
Shawanee	37867
Shawnette	38450
Shawtown	38232
Shelby Center (Part of Bartlett)	38134
Shelby Farms (Part of Memphis)	38101
Shelbyville	37160*
......	37162†
Shelbyville Mills	37160
Shell Creek	37687
Shellmound	37347
Shellsford	37110
Shenandoah Heights	37601
Shennendoah	37865
Shepp	38069
Sherrill Heights (Part of Madisonville)	37354
Sherrilltown	37184
Sherwood	37376
Sherwood Estates	37716
Sheybogan	37190
Shiloh, *Bedford*	37183
Shiloh, *Carroll*	38341
Shiloh, *Cumberland*	38555
Shiloh, *Grainger*	37861
Shiloh, *Hardin*	38376
Shiloh, *Hawkins*	37869
Shiloh, *Humphreys*	37101
Shiloh, *Jackson*	38506
Shiloh, *Montgomery*	37051
Shiloh, *Overton*	38554
Shiloh, *Rutherford*	37127
Shiloh, *Sumner*	37066
Shiloh, *Wilson*	37138
Shingleton	37683
Shining Rock	37166
Shipetown	37806
Shipley	38506
Shipps Bend	37033
Shirley	38504
Shirleyton	37397
Shooks Gap	37920
Shop Springs	37184
Shore Acres	37379
Short Creek	37037
Short Mountain	37190
Short Tail Springs	37341
Shouns (Part of Mountain City)	37683
Shubert	38462
Siam	37643
Sidonia	38255
Signal Hills (Part of Chattanooga)	37405
Signal Mountain	37377
Silerton	38377
Silica	37714
Siloam	37186
Silvacola	37617
Silver City	37860
Silver Grove	37618
Silverhill	37087
Silver Point	38582
Silver Ridge (Part of Lenoir City)	37771
Silver Springs	37122
Silvertop	37101
Sims Spring	37160
Singleton, *Bedford*	37160
Singleton, *Blount*	37777
Sinking Cove	37376
Sitka	38358
Sixmile	37803
Skaggston	37806
Skinem	37334
Skinner Crossroad	37810
Skullbone	38316
Skyline	38063
Skyline Park (Part of Signal Mountain)	37377
Slayden	37165
Slick Rock	37852
Slide	37857
Smartt	37378
Smithfield	37385
Smith Fork	38475
Smithland	37348
Smith Mill	37334
Smiths Chapel	37150
Smith Springs (Part of Nashville)	37217
Smithtown, *Bledsoe*	37338
Smithtown, *Marion*	37380
Smithville	37166
Smithwood (Part of Knoxville)	37918
Smoky Junction	37756
Smoky View Estates	37804
Smyrna, *Carroll*	38344
Smyrna, *Pickett*	38549
Smyrna, *Rutherford*	37167
Smyrna, *Warren*	37110
Sneed Forest Estates	37064
Sneed Glen	37064
Sneedville	37869
Snow Hill	37363
Snows Hill	37059
Soddy Daisy	37379*
......	37384†
Solo	38019
Solway	37931
Somerville	38068
South (Part of Chattanooga)‡	37409-10
......	37419

For specific ZIP Codes call (888) 275-8777, or your local postmaster.

*** Area Zip Code** **† Post Office Boxes** **‡ Postal Station** **♦ Census Designated Place** *Italic Type* **County**

South (Part of Nashville)‡ 37210
Southall 37064
South Berlin 37091
South Carthage 37030
South Cleveland♦ 37311
South Clinton (Part of Clinton) 37716
South Columbia (Part of Columbia) 38401
South Covington (Part of Covington) 38019
South Daisy (Part of Soddy Daisy) 37379
South Dyersburg 38024
Southern Hills (Part of Columbia) 38401
South Etowah 37331
South Fulton 38257
Southgate Shopping Center (Part of Memphis) 38109
South Green 37743
South Hall (Part of Alcoa) 37701
South Harriman (Part of Harriman) 37748
South Johnson City (Part of Johnson City) 37601
South Knoxville (Part of Knoxville)‡ 37920
.... 37940
For specific ZIP Codes call (888) 275-8777, or your local postmaster.
Southland Mall (Part of Memphis) 38116
South Liberty 37303
South Pittsburg 37380
Southport 38451
Southside, *Hardin* 38326
Southside, *Montgomery* 37171
South Tunnel 37066
Spain's Hill 37085
Sparkmantown 38559
Sparta 38583
Speedwell 37870
Spencer 38585
Spencer Creek (Part of Franklin) 37064
Spencer Hill 38474
Spencers Mill 37029
Sportman Acres 37122
Spot 37140
Spout Springs 38232
Springbrook (Part of Alcoa) 37701
Springbrook, *Madison* 38301
Spring City 37381
Spring Creek, *Hardeman* 38067
Spring Creek, *McMinn* 37303
Spring Creek, *Madison* 38378
Spring Creek, *Perry* 37096
Spring Creek, *Wilson* 37087
Springdale, *Claiborne* 37879
Springdale, *Sullivan* 37663
Springfield 37172
Spring Hill, *Anderson* 37716
Spring Hill, *Henderson* 38345
Spring Hill, *Maury* 37174
Spring Hill, *White* 38583
Spring Lake 38134
Springmont 37138
Spring Place 37914
Springs Chapel 38553
Springtown 37369
Springvale 37813
Spring View, *Blount* 37801
Springview, *Williamson* 37064
Springville 38256
Spruce Pine 37811
Spurgeon 37615
Squirrel Flat 38556
Staffords Store 38230
Staffordtown 37317
Stainville 37710
Stanfill 37847
Stanley Junction 37841
Stanton 38069
Stantonville 38379
Star Point 38549
State Capitol (Part of Nashville) 37219
State Line 37334
Statesville 37184
State University (Part of Johnson City)‡ 37601

Static 38549
Stayton 37051
Stella 38460
Stephen Holston (Part of Bristol)‡ 37620
Stephens 37840
Stephenson 37342
Steppsville 37110
Sterling Park 37343
Stewart, *Houston* 37175
Stewart, *Warren* 37110
Stewart Chapel 37335
Stinking Creek 37766
Stiversville 38451
Stock Creek 37920
Stockton 38556
Stockton Valley 37774
Stokes 38034
Stone 38562
Stonebrook 37135
Stone River (Part of Nashville) 37076
Stone River Estates (Part of Nashville) 37214
Stones River Homes (Part of Smyrna) 37167
Stonewall 38560
Stoney Fork 37714
Stoney Point 37181
Stony Gap 37869
Stony Point 37873
Strahl 37857
Straight Fork 37847
Strawberry Plains 37871
Striggersville 37857
Stringtown, *Gibson* 38233
Stringtown, *Montgomery* 37191
Stroudsville 37032
Stump Hollow 37381
Suburban Hills, *Knox* 37901
Suburban Hills, *McMinn* 37370
Suck Creek 37405
Sugar Creek, *Jackson* 38562
Sugar Creek, *Johnson* 37683
Sugar Forks (Part of Dandridge) 37725
Sugar Grove, *Bradley* 37323
Sugar Grove, *Roane* 37748
Sugar Grove, *Sumner* 37186
Sugarlimb 37771
Sugar Tree 38380
Suggs Creek 37122
Sullivan Gardens 37663
Sulphur 38570
Sulphura 37148
Sulphur Creek 37147
Sulphur Springs, *Anderson* 37716
Sulphur Springs, *Hamblen* 37814
Sulphur Springs, *Lincoln* 37334
Sulphur Springs, *McNairy* 38375
Sulphur Springs, *Marion* 37397
Sulphur Springs, *Washington* 37659
Sumac 38478
Summer City 37367
Summerfield 37387
Summer Shade 38541
Summertown (Part of Walden) 37377
Summertown, *Lawrence* 38483
Summit, *Hamilton* 37363
Summit, *Hawkins* 37711
Summitville 37382
Sunbright 37872
Sunkist Beach 38079
Sunny Brook (Part of Bristol) 37620
Sunny Hill 38012
Sunny Hills 37620
Sunnyside, *Greene* 37743
Sunnyside, *Hancock* 37869
Sunnyside, *Sullivan* 37617
Sunrise, *Hickman* 37033
Sunrise, *Macon* 37150
Sunset, *Grainger* 37861
Sunset, *Pickett* 38549
Sunset Gap 37722
Sunset Hills (Part of Kingsport) 37660
Sunset Hills (Part of Morristown) 37814
Surgoinsville 37873

Sutherland 24236
Swan (Part of Hohenwald) 38462
Swan Bluff 37033
Swann Chapel 37725
Swannsylvania 37725
Sweet Lips 38340
Sweeton Hill (Part of Coalmont) 37313
Sweetwater, *Lewis* 38462
Sweetwater, *Monroe* 37874
Swift 38372
Sycamore, *Cheatham* 37015
Sycamore (Part of Cookeville) 38501
Sycamore Landing 37185
Sycamore Valley, *Cheatham* 37015
Sycamore Valley, *Macon* 37083
Sykes 38547
Sylvia 37055
Tabernacle, *Haywood* 38012
Tabernacle, *Tipton* 38019
Tabor 38555
Tackett Creek 37766
Taft 38488
Talbott 37877
Tallassee 37878
Talley 37144
Tampico 37861
Tanglewood, *Monroe* 37874
Tanglewood, *Smith* 37030
Tara Estates (Part of Tullahoma) 37388
Tarbett 37853
Tarlton 37110
Tarpley 38478
Tarsus 37142
Tasso 37312
Tate 38344
Tate Springs 37708
Tatesville 37365
Tatumville 38059
Taylor Chapel 37058
Taylor Crossroads 37160
Taylor Hill (Part of Dayton) 37321
Taylor Place 38556
Taylors Crossroads 38573
Taylorsville, *Maury* 38461
Taylorsville, *Wilson* 37087
Taylortown 38459
Tazewell 37879
Teague 38381
Tekoa 37931
Telford 37690
Tellico Hills (Part of Athens) 37303
Tellico Plains 37385
Temperance Hall 37095
Temple Hill 37650
Temple Hills Country Club Estates 37064
Templeton 38059
Templow 37022
Tenchtown 38556
Ten Mile 37880
Ten Mile Center (Part of Knoxville)‡ 37930
Tennemo 38056
Tennessee City 37055
Tennessee Hills (Part of Bristol) 37620
Tennessee Ridge 37178
Tennessee Tech (Part of Cookeville) 38505
Terrace Hills 37122
Terrace View 37381
Terrell 38237
Terry 38321
Terry Creek 37847
Theodore (Part of Hohenwald) 38462
Theta 38401
The Wye 37769
Thick 37034
Thomas 38544
Thomas Addition 37665
Thomas Bridge 37618
Thomasville 37015
Thompsons Station 37179
Thompsons Store 38551
Thorngrove 37871
Thorn Hill 37881
Thornton (Part of Farragut) 37722
Three Churches 38450
Three Oaks 38456
Three Point 38041

Three Points 37918
Three Springs 37860
Throckmorton 37079
Thula 37810
Thurman Addition (Part of Pigeon Forge) 37863
Tibbs 38012
Tidwell 37025
Tiftona (Part of Chattanooga) 37419
Tiger Valley 37658
Tigrett 38070
Tilghman 38233
Timberlake, *Hawkins* 37857
Timberlake, *Henderson* 38351
Timesville 37377
Timothy 38568
Tin Cup 38320
Tinsleys Bottom 38551
Tiprell 37724
Tipton 38071
Tiptonville 38079
Tishamingo 37122
Tobaccoport 37028
Tom Murray (Part of Jackson)‡ 38301
Toone 38381
Top of the World Estates 37878
Topside 37920
Topsy 38485
Toqua 37885
Tottys 38454
Toulon 38063
Towee 37369
Towering Oaks 38464
Town Acres (Part of Greeneville) 37745
Town Creek 37870
Towne Hills (Part of Chattanooga) 37343
Townsend 37882
Trace End Estates 37064
Traceview 37064
Tracy City 37387
Trade 37691
Tradewinds 37122
Trails End 37122
Tranquility 37303
Travisville 38577
Treadway 37881
Trenton 38382
Trent Valley 37869
Trentville 37871
Trevecca College (Part of Nashville) 37210
Trezevant 38258
Tri-Angle 37160
Trigonia 37801
Trimble 38259
Trinity 37067
Triune 37014
Trousdale 37357
Troy 38260
Trundel Crossroad 37865
Tuckahoe 37871
Tuckers Crossroads 37087
Tucker Springs 37353
Tullahoma 37388
Tulu 38357
Tumbling 38201
Tuppertown (Part of Oliver Springs) 37840
Turley 37714
Turners Station 37186
Turnersville 37032
Turnpike 38012
Turtletown 37391
Tusculum (Part of Nashville) 37211
Tusculum, *Greene* 37745
Twin Bridges 37726
Twin Cove 37714
Twin Oak 38544
Twin Oaks 37620
Twinton 38554
Twomey (Part of Centerville) 37033
Tylersville 38030
Tyner Hills (Part of Chattanooga) 37421
Tyson Store 38233
Una (Part of Nashville) 37217
Unaka Springs 37650
Underwood, *Macon* 37083
Underwood, *Sevier* 37764
Unicoi, *Monroe* 37385
Unicoi, *Unicoi* 37692
Union, *Hardin* 38310

Union, *Haywood* 38012
Union, *Morgan* 37840
Union, *Roane* 37763
Union, *Union* 37866
Union, *Warren* 38581
Union Central 38358
Union City 38261
.... 38281
For specific ZIP Codes call (888) 275-8777, or your local postmaster.
Union Grove, *Blount* 37737
Union Grove, *McMinn* 37826
Union Grove, *Meigs* 37322
Union Heights 37813
Union Hill, *Clay* 38575
Union Hill, *Lawrence* 38468
Union Hill, *Sumner* 37066
Union Hill, *Tipton* 38004
Union Hill (Part of Nashville) 37080
Union Ridge 37183
Union Temple 37616
Union Valley 37865
Unionville, *Bedford* 37180
Unionville, *Dyer* 38040
Unitia 37772
University (Part of Knoxville)‡ 37916
University of Tennessee (Part of Martin)‡ 38238
University of the South‡ 37375
Upchurch 37616
Upper Mockeson 38468
Upper Shell Creek 37687
Upper Sinking 37147
Uptonville 38392
Vale 38317
Valleybrook (Part of Chattanooga) 37343
Valley Brook, *Wilson* 37122
Valley Creek 37715
Valley Forge 37643
Valley Hills (Part of Bristol) 37620
Valley View 37716
Van Buren 38042
Vandever 38555
Van Dyke 38242
Van Hill 37857
Vanleer 37181
Vannatta 37160
Vanntown 37335
Vardy 37869
Vasper 37714
Vaughn's Gap (Part of Nashville) 37205
Vaughns Grove 38382
Verdun 37841
Vernon 37137
Vernon Heights 37664
Verona 37091
Verona Hills 37122
Versailles 37153
Vesta 37090
Vestal (Part of Knoxville) 37920
Veterans Administration Center (Part of Murfreesboro) 37129
Veto 38477
Viar 38024
Victoria 37397
Victory 37766
Vildo 38075
Villa Gardens (Part of Knoxville) 37918
Village Green (Part of Farragut) 37922
Vine 37090
Vinegar Hill 37620
Vine Ridge 38554
Viola 37394
Virtue (Part of Farragut) 37922
Vise 38329
Vison Cross Roads 37110
Volunteer Heights (Part of Crossville) 38555
Vonore 37885
Vose (Part of Alcoa) 37701
Waco 38472
Walden 37377
Walden Creek 37862
Waldens Ridge, *Bledsoe* 37381
Waldens Ridge, *Rhea* 37321

Wales 38478
Walkertown, *Greene* 37616
Walkertown, *Hardin* 38372
Walland 37886
Walling 38587
Walnut Acres 37064
Walnut Grove, *Franklin* 37345
Walnut Grove, *Gibson* 38233
Walnut Grove, *Hardin* 38372
Walnut Grove, *Lauderdale* 38063
Walnut Grove, *Meigs* 37322
Walnut Grove, *Sevier* 37876
Walnut Grove, *Sullivan* 37618
Walnut Grove, *Sumner* 37048
Walnut Grove, *Tipton* 38015
Walnut Grove, *Trousdale* 37074
Walnut Hill, *Crockett* 38006
Walnut Hill, *Sullivan* 37620
Walnut Hill (Part of Harriman) 37748
Walnut Log 38261
Walnut Shade 37150
Walter Crossroad 37743
Walterhill♦ 37129
Wa-Ni Village 37861
Ware Branch 37341
Warren 38068
Warrens Bluff 38351
Warrensburg 37818
Wartburg 37887
Wartrace 37183
Warwicktown 37807
Washburn 37888
Washington 37321
Washington College 37681
Washington Heights (Part of Chattanooga) 37406
Watauga 37694
Watauga Flats 37601
Watauga Point (Part of Elizabethton) 37643
Waterstown 37886
Watertown 37184
Water Valley 38487
Waterville 37323
Watkins, *DeKalb* 37166
Watkins, *Tipton* 38019
Watt Heights (Part of Calhoun) 37309
Watts Bar Dam 37395
Watts Bar Estates 37381
Waverly 37185
Wayland Springs 38463
Waynesboro 38485
Wayside 37110
Weakly 38464
Wear Valley 37862
Weaver 37620
Webber City 38456
Webbtown 37083
Webster 37854
Wedgewood Hills 37922
Welch Crossroad 37866
Welchland 38585
Welch's Camp 37714
Well Spring 37870
Wells Station (Part of Memphis) 38122
Wellsville 37801
Wellwood 38006
Wesleyanna 37303
West (Part of Nashville)‡ 37209
West, *Gibson* 38358
West Cyruston 37334
Westel 37854
West Emory 37922
Western Heights 37857
Westfield Estates (Part of Franklin) 37064
West Forest (Part of Knoxville) 37919
West Fork 38543
West Greene (Part of Greeneville)‡ 37743
West Harpeth 37064
Westhaven Village (Part of Knoxville) 37921
West Hills, *Jefferson* 37820
West Hills, *Monroe* 37354
West Hills, *Roane* 37748
West Hills (Part of Knoxville) 37919
West Junction (Part of Memphis) 38101
West Knoxville (Part of Knoxville)‡ 37919*
.... 37939†
West Maryville (Part of Maryville) 37801
West Meade (Part of Nashville) 37205
West Miller Cove 37886
Westmoreland 37186
Westmoreland Heights (Part of Knoxville) 37919
West Nashville (Part of Nashville) 37209
West Oneida (Part of Oneida) 37841
Westover 38301
Westpoint 38486
Westport 38387
West Robbins 37852
West Shiloh 38379
Westside Heights (Part of Tullahoma) 37388
West Springbrook (Part of Alcoa) 37701
West Town Mall (Part of Knoxville) 37919
West Union 38225
West View (Part of Knoxville) 37921
West View, *Washington* 37681
Westview, *Weakley* 38237
West View Acres 37090
West View Park (Part of Kingsport) 37660
Westwood (Part of Columbia) 38401
Westwood Gardens (Part of Jackson) 38301
Westwood Hills 37803
Westwood Homes (Part of Manchester) 37355
Wetmore 37325
Wheel 37160
Wheelerton 38453
Whispering Hills 38261
Whispering Pine 37692
Whitaker 37160
White (Part of Memphis)‡ 38119
White, Warren 37110
White Bluff, *Dickson* 37187
White Bluff, *Trousdale* 37074
White City 37387
White Fern 38313
Whitehaven (Part of Memphis)‡ 38116
Whitehaven Plaza (Part of Memphis) 38116
Whitehead Hills 37687
White Hill, *Robertson* 37072
White Hill, *Van Buren* 38581
White Horn 37711
White House 37188
White Oak, *Campbell* 37766
White Oak, *Morgan* 37829
Whiteoak Crossing 38425
White Oak Flat 37036
White Oaks (Part of Manchester) 37355
White Pine 37890
White Rock 37687
Whitesand 37743
Whitesburg 37891
White Schoolhouse Corners 37840
Whites Creek (Part of Nashville) 37189
White's Creek, *Rhea* 37381
Whiteside 37396
Whiteville 38075
Whitleyville 38588
Whitlock 38242
Whitthorne 38348
Whittle Springs (Part of Knoxville) 37917
Whitway 38358
Whitwell 37397
Widow Town 37876
Wilder 38589
Wilder Chapel 37324
Wildersville 38388
Wild Plum 38555
Wildwood 37804
Wilhite (Part of Cookeville) 38506
Wilkinsville 38004
Willard 37074
Willette 37150
Williams, *Lauderdale* 38063
Williams, *Macon* 37083
Williamsburg 37331
Williams Creek 37841
Williams Crossroads 38544
Williamsport 38487
Williams Springs 37888
Willis 37765
Willis Spring 37362
Williston 38076
Willow Grove, *Bedford* 37360
Willow Grove, *Clay* 38541
Wilmore Estates 37890
Wilson Station 37329
Wilsonville 37821
Winchester 37398
Winchester Springs 37398
Winding Ridge 37072
Windle 38570
Windletown 38554
Windrock 37840
Windrow 37153
Windy City 38343
Windy Hill (Part of Bristol) 37620
Winfield 37892
Wingo 38258
Winklers Crossroads 37150
Winner 37643
Winona 37756
Winton Town 37355
Wirmingham 38573
Withamtown 37022
Witt 37813
Wixtown 37186
Wolf Creek, *Cocke* 37727
Wolf Creek, *DeKalb* 38582
Wolf Creek, *Rhea* 37381
Wolf Hill 37022
Wolf River 38577
Womack, *Sumner* 37066
Womack, *Warren* 37110
Woodbine (Part of Nashville)‡ 37211
Woodbury 37190
Woodcliff 38574
Wooddale 37914
Wooded Acres (Part of Knoxville) 37921
Woodland (Part of Nashville) 37206
Woodland, *Haywood* 38012
Woodland Acres, *Knox* 37919
Woodland Acres, *McMinn* 37309
Woodland Mills 38271
Woodlawn, *Cumberland* 38555
Woodlawn, *Montgomery* 37191
Woodlawn, *Washington* 37659
Woodlawn, *Wayne* 38450
Woodmont (Part of Nashville) 37215
Woodrow 37617
Woodstock 38053
Woods Valley 37051
Woodville, *Chester* 38315
Woodville, *Haywood* 38063
Woody 38555
Wooldridge 37762
Wrigley 37098
Wyatts Chapel 37058
Wyatt Village 37708
Wynn 37766
Wynnburg 38077
Yager 37110
Yankeetown 38583
Yell 37091
Yellow Store 37873
Yett Addition (Part of Sevierville) 37876
Yettland (Part of Sevierville) 37876
Yorkley 38472
Yorktown (Part of Franklin) 37064
Yorkville 38389
Young Bend 37166
Youngs 38301
Youngville 37172
Y Section 37601
Yukon 38488
Yuma 38390
Yum Yum 38068
Zack 38320
Zion Grove 37862
Zion Hill (Part of Surgoinsville) 37857
Zion Hill, *McMinn* 37329

A (Part of Dallas)‡ 75208
A (Part of San Antonio)‡ 78207
Abbott 76621
Aberfoyle 75496
Abernathy 79311
Abilene 79601-06
79608
For specific ZIP Codes call (888) 275-8777, or your local postmaster.
Ables Springs 75161
Abner 75142
Abram 78572
Acala 79839
Ace 77326
Ackerly 79713
Acton 76048
Acuff 79401
Acworth 75426
Adams Gardens 78550
Adams Hill 78245
Adams Oaks 77365
Adamsville 76550
Addicks (Part of Houston) 77079
Addicks Barker (Part of Houston)‡ 77218
Addielou 75412
Addison 75001
Addran 75482
Adell 76088
Ad Hall 76520
Adina 78947
Adkins 78101
Admiral 79504
Adrian 79001
Adsul 75956
Afton 79220
Aggieland (Part of College Station)‡ 77844
Agnes 76082
Agua Dulce 78330
Agua Nueva 78361
Aguilares 78369
Aiken, *Floyd* 79221
Aiken, *Shelby* 75935
Airlawn (Part of Dallas)‡ 75235
75245
For specific ZIP Codes call (888) 275-8777, or your local postmaster.
Airport City 78108
Airport Mail Facility (Part of Houston)‡ 77205
Airville 76501
Alabama and Coushatta Indian Reservation 77351
Alamo 78516
Alamo Alto 79853
Alamo Beach, *Bandera* 78063
Alamo Beach, *Calhoun* 77979
Alamo Heights 78208-09
For specific ZIP Codes call (888) 275-8777, or your local postmaster.
Alamo Ranchettos 79735
Alanreed 79002
Alazan 75961
Alba 75410
Albany 76430
Albert 78671
Albion 75426
Alco 75949
Alderbranch 75801
Aldine 77032
77039
For specific ZIP Codes call (888) 275-8777, or your local postmaster.
Aldine Meadows 77032
Aldine Place 77039
Aledo 76008
Aleman 76531
Alexander 76446
Aley 75143
Alfred 78332
Algerita 76877
Algoa 77511
Alice 78332*
78333†
Alief (Part of Houston) 77411
Allamore 79855
Allen 75002
75013
For specific ZIP Codes call (888) 275-8777, or your local postmaster.
Allendale (Part of Houston) 77017
Allenfarm 77868
Allenhurst 77414
Allens Chapel 75492
Allens Point 75446
Alleyton 78935
Allison 79003
Allmon 79250
Alma 75119
Almeda (Part of Houston)‡ 77045*
77245†
Almeda Mall (Part of Houston) 77075
Almeda Plaza (Part of Houston 77045
Almont 75559
Aloe 77905
Alpine 79830*
79831†
Alsa 75169
Alsdorf 75119
Altair 77412
Alta Loma (Part of Santa Fe) 77510
Alto 75925
Altoga 75069
Alton 78572
Alto Springs 76653
Alum 78160
Alum Creek 78957
Alvarado 76009
Alvin 77511*
77512†
Alvord 76225
Amarillo 79101-89
For specific ZIP Codes call (888) 275-8777, or your local postmaster.
Ambia 75460
Ambrose 75414
Ames, *Coryell* 76528
Ames, *Liberty* 77575
Amherst, *Lamar* 75460
Amherst, *Lamb* 79312
Amigoland Mall (Part of Brownsville) 78520
Ammansville 78945
Amon Carter Boulevard (Part of Fort Worth)‡ 76155
Amy 75432
Anadarko 75667
Anahuac 77514
Anchor 77515
Anchorage 78065
Ander 77963
Anderson 77830
Andice 78628
Andrews 79714
Andrewsville 75683
Angelo State University (Part of San Angelo) 76909
Angleton 77515*
77516†
Angus 75110
Angus Valley (Part of Austin) 78758
Anna 75409
Annarose 78022
Annetta 76008
Annetta North 76087
Annetta South 76008
Anneville 76023
Annona 75550
Anson 79501
Anson Jones (Part of Houston)‡ 77009
Antelope 76389
Anthony 79821
Anthony Harbor 75929
Antioch, *Cass* 75551
Antioch, *Delta* 75432
Antioch, *Henderson* 75758
Antioch, *Houston* 75851
Antioch, *Jasper* 77612
Antioch, *Madison* 75852
Antioch, *Rusk* 75652
Antioch, *Shelby* (mail Center) 75935
Antioch, *Shelby* (mail Timpson) 75975
Anton 79313
Apache Addition (Part of Seguin) 78155
Apache Shores 78734
Apolonia 77830
Apparel Mart (Part of Dallas)‡ 75207*
75258†
Appelt Hill 77964
Appleby 75961
Apple Springs 75926
Aquilla 76622
Aransas Pass 78335†
78336*
Arbala 75482
Arbor 75847
Arbor Oaks (Part of Houston) 77088
Arcadia (Part of Santa Fe) 77517
Arcadia, *Shelby* 75935
Archer City 76351
Arcola 77583
Arden 76901
Argenta 78368
Argo 75558
Argyle 76226
Ariola 77625
Arizona 77367
Arlam 75946
Arledge Ridge 75418
Arlington 76003-07
76010-18
76094
76096
For specific ZIP Codes call (888) 275-8777, or your local postmaster.
Arlington Downs (Part of Arlington) 76010
Arlington Heights (Part of Fort Worth)‡ 76147
Arlington Heights (Part of Houston) 77034
Armstrong 78338
Arneckeville 77954
Arnett, *Coryell* 76528
Arnett, *Hockley* 79336
Arp 75750
Arrowhead Lake 77378
Arrowhead Shores 76048
Arrowhead Village 78130
Arroyo (Part of Harlingen) 78550
Arroyo City 78586
Arsenal (Part of San Antonio)‡ 78283
Art 76820
Artesian Forest 77304
Artesia Wells 78001
Arthur City 75411
Arvana 79331
Asa 76707
Ash, *Henderson* 75751
Ash, *Houston* 75835
Ashby 77465
Asherton 78827
Ashford West (Part of Houston)‡ 77077
Ashland 75640
Ashmore 79342
Ashtola 79226
Ashworth 75142
Asia 75939
Aspermont 79502
Astrodome (Part of Houston)‡ 77025
Astro Hills 78130
Atascocita (Part of Humble) 77346
Atascosa 78002
Ater 76528
Athens 75751
Atlanta 75551
Atlas 75460
Atoy 75785
Atreco (Part of Port Arthur) 77640
Attoyac 75961
Atwell 76437
Aubrey 76227
Auburn 76050
Audobon Park 77396
Augusta 75844
Aurora 76078
Austin 78701-69
For specific ZIP Codes call (888) 275-8777, or your local postmaster.
Austin Lake Estates 78759
Austonio 75835
Austwell 77950
Authon 76088
Autumn Woods 77362
Avalon 76623
Avery 75554
Avinger 75630
Avoca 79503
Avonbell (Part of Amarillo) 79106
Avondale 76179
Avon Park 76708
Axtell 76624
Azle 76020*
76098†
Bacliff♦ 77518
Bagby 75446
Bagwell 75412
Bailey 75413
Baileyboro 79371
Bailey's Prairie 77515
Baileyville 76570
Bainer 79339
Bainville 78119
Baird 79504
Baker 76087
Bakersfield 79752
Balch 79358
Balch Springs 75180
Balcones (Part of Austin)‡ 78759
Balcones Heights 78201
Balcones Village 78750
Bald Hill 75901
Bald Prairie 77856
Baldwin 75661
Ballinger 76821
Balmorhea 79718
Balsora 76426
Bammel 77048
77040
For specific ZIP Codes call (888) 275-8777, or your local postmaster.
Banana Junction 76708
Bancroft (Part of Pinehurst) 77630
Bandera 78003
Bandera Falls 78063
Bangs 76823
Banquete 78339
Barbarosa 78130
Barclay 76656
Bardin Road (Part of Arlington)‡ 76001-02
76018-18
For specific ZIP Codes call (888) 275-8777, or your local postmaster.
Bardwell 75101
Barker 77413
Barksdale 78828
Barnes 75960
Barnhart 76930
Barnum 75939
Barrett♦ 77532
Barrington Oaks (Part of Austin) 78759
Barry 75102
Barstow 79719
Bartlett 76511
Bartley Woods 75492
Barton Creek Square (Part of Austin)‡ 78746
Bartons Chapel 76458
Bartonville 76226
Barwise 79235
Bascom 75705
Basin 79834
Basin Springs 76264
Bassett 75574
Bassett Center (Part of El Paso) 79925
Bastrop 78602
Bastrop Bayou 77515
Bastrop Beach 77515
Bateman 78662
Batesville, *Red River* 75426
Batesville, *Zavala*♦ 78829
Batson 77519
Battle 76664
Baxter 75751
Bay City 77414
Bay Harbor 77554
Baylor University (Part of Waco)‡ 76706
Bay Oaks 77571
Bayou Bend (Part of Houston) 77088
Bayou Chantilly (Part of Dickinson) 77539
Bayou Vista 77563
Bay Plaza (Part of Baytown)‡ 77520
Bayport (Part of Houston) 77058
Bayside 78340
Bayside Terrace 77571
Baytown 77520-22
For specific ZIP Codes call (888) 275-8777, or your local postmaster.
Bayview, *Cameron* 78566
Bay View, *Galveston* 77518
Bayview Estates 76945
Bayway (Part of Baytown)‡ 77520
Baywood (Part of Seabrook) 77586
Bazette 75144
Beach 77301
Beach City 77520
Beacon Hill (Part of San Antonio)‡ 78201
Beadle 77414
Bear Creek‡ 77084
Bear Grass 75846
Beasley 77417
Beattie 76442
Beaukiss 78621
Beaumont 77701-08
77710
77713-26
For specific ZIP Codes call (888) 275-8777, or your local postmaster.
Beaumont Place 77049
Beauxart Gardens 77705
Beaver Dam 75559
Bebe 78603
Becker 75142
Beckville 75631
Becton 79343
Bedford 76021-22
76095
For specific ZIP Codes call (888) 275-8777, or your local postmaster.
Bedias 77831
Bee Cave 78733
Beech Grove 75951
Beechnut (Part of Houston)‡ 77072
Beechwood 75948
Bee House 76525
Beeville 78102*
78104†
Belcherville 76255
Belfalls 76579
Belgrade 75928
Belk 75411
Bellaire 77401*
77402†
Bellaire Addition 75704
Bellaire West (Part of Houston) 77072
Bell Branch 76651
Bellevue 76228
Bellmead 76704-05
76715
For specific ZIP Codes call (888) 275-8777, or your local postmaster.
Bells 75414
Bellview 75410
Bellville 77418
Belmar (Part of Amarillo) 79106
Belmena 76520
Belmont 78604
Belott 75835
Belton 76513
Ben Arnold 76519
Benavides 78341
Ben Bolt 78342
Benbrook 76126
Benchley 77801
Bend 76824
Bending Bough 77373
Ben Franklin 75415
Ben Hur 76664
Benjamin 79505
Bennett 76066
Bennett Estates 77302
Benoit 76882
Bent Tree (Part of Dallas)‡ 75270†
75287*
Bentwood (Part of San Angelo) 76904
Bentwood Acres 75076
Ben Wheeler 75754
Berclair 78107
Berea, *Houston* 75835
Berea, *Marion* 75657
Bergheim 78004
Berlin 77833
Bernardo 78933
Berry Street (Part of Ft. Worth)‡ 76109-10
For specific ZIP Codes call (888) 275-8777, or your local postmaster.
Berryville 75763
Bertram 78605
Bessmay 77612
Best 76932
Bethany 71007
Bethel, *Anderson* 75861
Bethel, *Ellis* 75167
Bethel, *Henderson* 75751
Bethlehem, *Bowie* 75559
Bethlehem, *Collin* 75442
Bethlehem, *Upshur* 75644

* **Area Zip Code** † **Post Office Boxes** ‡ **Postal Station** ♦ **Census Designated Place** *Italic Type* **County**

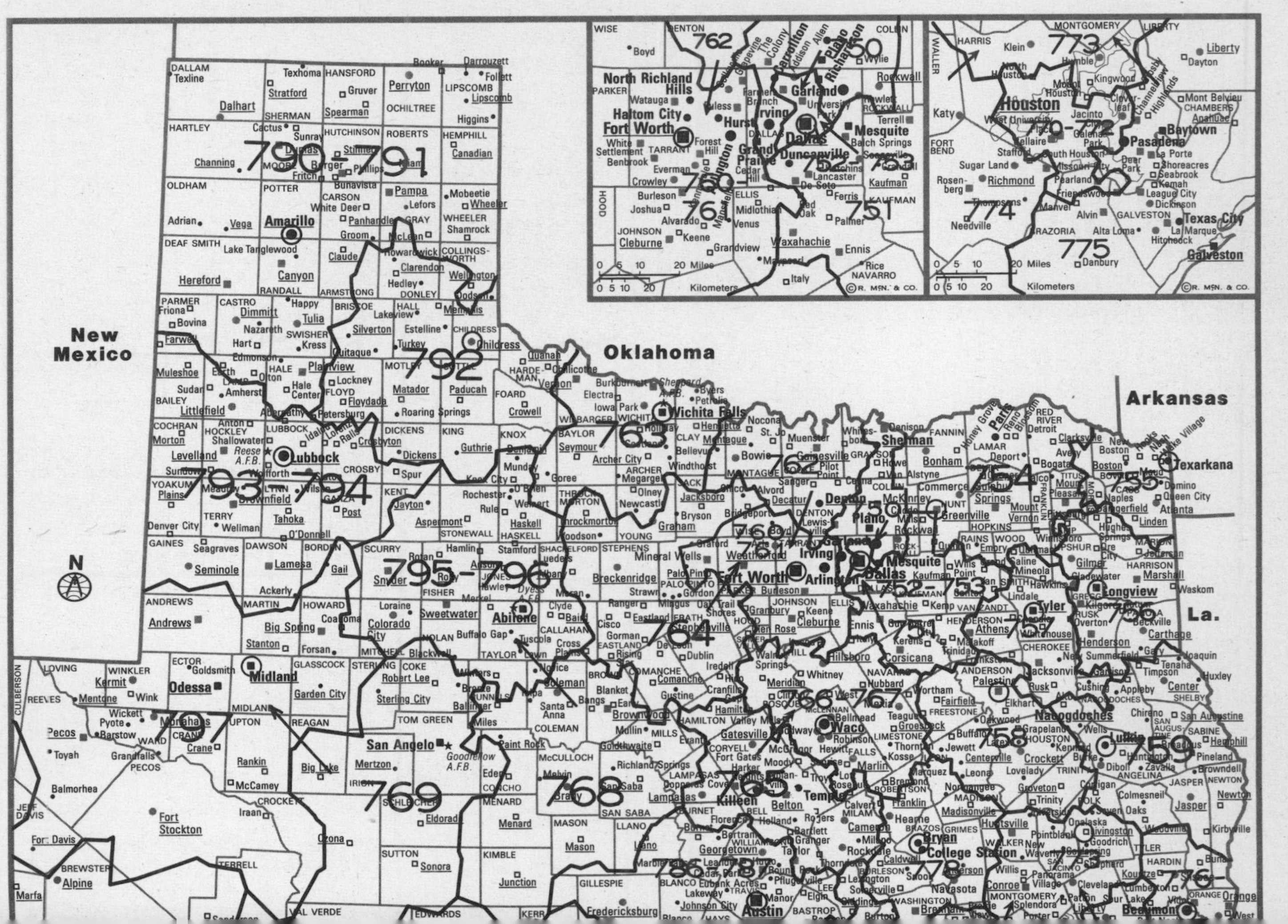

Oklahoma
New Mexico
Arkansas
La.

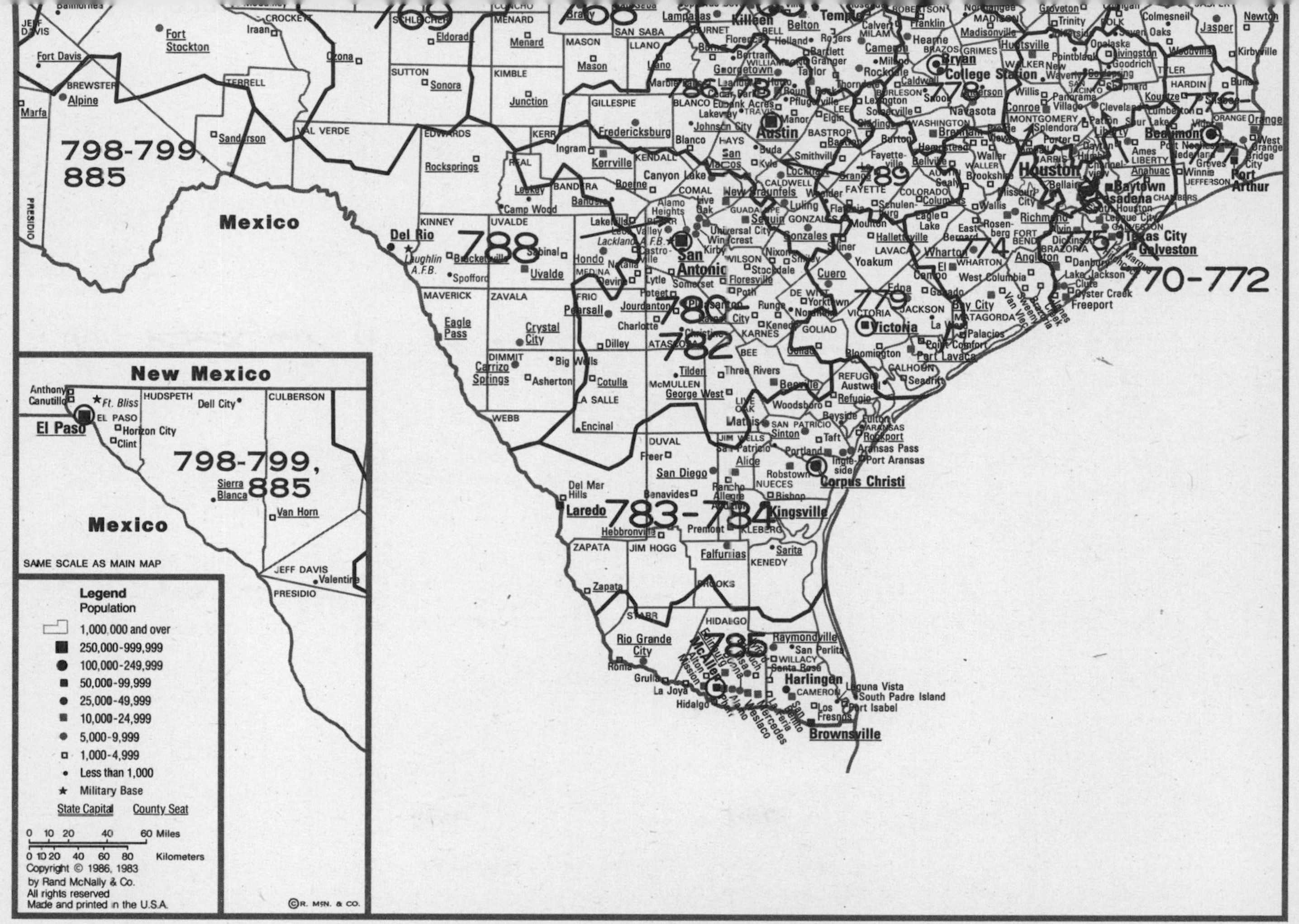
Mexico
New Mexico
SAME SCALE AS MAIN MAP
798-799, 885
798-799, 885
788
780-782
783-784
785
779
774
770-772
El Paso
Del Rio
San Antonio
Austin
Houston
Galveston
Victoria
Corpus Christi
Laredo
Kingsville
Harlingen
Brownsville
Legend
Population
1,000,000 and over
250,000-999,999
100,000-249,999
50,000-99,999
25,000-49,999
10,000-24,999
5,000-9,999
1,000-4,999
Less than 1,000
Military Base
State Capital
County Seat
0 10 20 40 60 Miles
0 10 20 40 60 80 Kilometers
Copyright © 1986, 1983
by Rand McNally & Co.
All rights reserved
Made and printed in the U.S.A.
©R. MSN. & CO.

Place	ZIP
Bethsaida	75551
Bettie	75644
Beulah	75941
Beverly Hills (Part of Dallas)‡	75211
Beverly Hills, *McLennan*	76711
Bevil Oaks	77706
Bevilport	75951
Beyersville	78615
Biardstown	75462
Big Bend National Park	79834
Bigfoot	78005
Big Lake	76932
Big Oaks	75630
Big Sandy	75755
Big Spring	79720*
	79721†
Big Square	79027
Big Thiket	77369
Big Town Regional Mall (Part of Mesquite)	75149
Big Valley Ranchettes	76522
Big Wells	78830
Billington	76624
Biloxi	75928
Binglewood (Part of Houston)	77080
Birch	77879
Birdville (Part of Haltom City)	76117
Birnam Woods	77379
Birome	76673
Birthright	75482
Biry	78016
Bisbee	76063
Bishop	78343
Bivins	75555
Black	79035
Blackfoot	75853
Black Hills	75110
Black Jack, *Cherokee*	75789
Black Jack, *Robertson*	77859
Blackland	75189
Blackoak	75431
Blackwell	79506
Blakeney	75412
Blanchard	77351
Blanco	78606
Blanconia	78102
Blandlake	75972
Blanket	76432
Bleakwood	75956
Bledsoe	79314
Bleiblerville	78931
Blessing	77419
Blevins	76524
Blewett	78801
Blodgett	75686
Bloomburg	75556
Bloomdale	75069
Bloomfield	76258
Blooming Grove	76626
Bloomington♦	77951
Blossom	75416
Blue	78947
Bluebonnet (Part of Austin)‡	78758
Bluegrove	76352
Blue Haven Estates	75169
Blue Lake Estates	78654
Blue Mound	76131
Blue Ridge, *Collin*	75424
Blue Ridge, *Falls*	76661
Blueroan	77434
Bluetown	78592
Blue Water Key	75758
Bluff Dale	76433
Bluff Springs, *Parker*	76020
Bluff Springs, *Travis*	78744
Bluffton	78607
Blum	76627
Blumenthal	78624
Bluntzer	78380
Board	76442
Bob Harris (Part of Pasadena)‡	77506
Bob Lyons (Part of Galveston)‡	77554
Bobo	75974
Bobville	77333
Boca Chica (Part of Brownsville)	78520
Boerne	78006
	78015
For specific ZIP Codes call (888) 275-8777, or your local postmaster.	
Bogata	75417
Bois D'Arc	75801
Boling	77420
Bolivar	76266
Bolton	75686
Bomarton	76380
Bon Ami	75956
Bonanza, *Hill*	76692
Bonanza, *Hopkins*	75420
Bonanza Beach	78611
Bonham	75418
Bonita	76255
Bonnerville	75840
Bonney	77583
Bonnie View	78393
Bono	76031
Bon Wier	75928
Booker	79005
Boonsville	76426
Booth	77469
Boquillas	79834
Borden	78962
Borderland	79932
Bordersville (Part of Houston)	77338
Borger	79007*
	79008†
Bosqueville	76708
Boston (Part of New Boston)	75570
Boswell	77340
Bovina	79009
Bowie	76230
Bowser	76872
Box Church	76642
Boxelder	75550
Boxwood	75683
Boyce	75165
Boyd, *Fannin*	75418
Boyd, *Wise*	76023
Boys Ranch	79010
Boz	75167
Brachfield	75681
Bracken	78266
Brackettville	78832
Brad	76475
Bradfield	75656
Bradford	75853
Bradshaw	79567
Brady, *McCulloch*	76825
Brady, *Shelby*	75935
Braeswood (Part of Houston)	77030
Branch	75407
Branchville	76520
Brandon	76628
Bransford (Part of Colleyville)	76034
Branton	76471
Brashear	75420
Brazoria	77422
Brazos	76472
Brazos Mall (Part of Lake Jackson)	77566
Brazos Point	76652
Breckenridge	76424
Bremond	76629
Brenham	77833*
	77834†
Brentwood Manor	77904
Breslau	77964
Briar	76020
Briarcliff	78669
Briaroaks	76028
Briary	76570
Brice	79226
Bridge Chapel	75455
Bridge City	77611
Bridgeport	76426
Brierwood Bay	75763
Briggs	78608
Bright Star, *Rains*	75410
Bright Star, *Van Zandt*	75169
Briscoe	79011
Bristol	75119
Britton	76063
Broaddus	75929
Broadway, *Crosby*	79243
Broadway (Part of Houston)‡	77207
Broadway, *Lamar*	75460
Broadway Junction	75460
Broadway Square (Part of Tyler)	75703
Brock	76087
Brock Junction	76087
Brogado	79718
Bronco	79355
Bronson	75930
Bronte	76933
Brookeland	75931
Brookesmith	76827
Brook Forest	77357
Brook Glen Addition (Part of La Porte)	77571
Brookhaven (Part of Houston)	77051
Brookhollow (Part of Dallas)‡	75247
Brookshier	76933
Brookshire	77423
Brookside Village	77581
Brookston	75421
Broom City	75839
Broome	76951
Brown College	77880
Browndell	75931
Brownfield	79316
Browning	75705
Brownsboro, *Caldwell*	78644
Brownsboro, *Henderson*	75756
Brownsville	78520-26
For specific ZIP Codes call (888) 275-8777, or your local postmaster.	
Brownwood, *Brown*	76801
	76803-04
For specific ZIP Codes call (888) 275-8777, or your local postmaster.	
Brownwood (Part of Orange)	77630
Broyles	75801
Bruceville (Part of Bruceville-Eddy)	76630
Bruceville-Eddy	76630
Brumley	75686
Brundage	78834
Bruni	78344
Brunswick	75925
Brushie Prairie	76641
Brushy Bend Park	78681
Brushy Creek	75801
Brushy Creek North	78681
Bryan	77801-08
For specific ZIP Codes call (888) 275-8777, or your local postmaster.	
Bryans Mill	75568
Bryson	76427
Buchanan Dam♦	78609
Buchanan Lake Village	78672
Buchel	77954
Buck Creek	75949
Buckeye	77414
Buckholts	76518
Buckhorn, *Austin*	77418
Buckhorn, *Newton*	75928
Buckingham	75080
Buckner	76462
Buda	78610
Buena Vista, *Bexar*	78221
Buena Vista, *Burnet*	78611
Buena Vista, *Shelby*	75975
Buffalo	75831
Buffalo Gap, *Taylor*	79508
Buffalo Gap, *Travis*	78734
Buffalo Springs	76228
Buford	79512
Bugbee Heights	79078
Bug Tussle	75449
Bula	79320
Bullard	75757
Bullock	76470
Bulverde	78163
Buna♦	77612
Bunavista (Part of Borger)	79007
Buncomb	75633
Bunger	76450
Bunker Hill	75486
Bunker Hill Village	77024
Bunyan	76446
Burkburnett	76354
Burke	75941
Burkett	76828
Burkeville	75932
Burleigh	77418
Burleson	76028*
	76097†
Burlington	76519
Burnell	78119
Burnet	78611
Burns, *Bowie*	75561
Burns, *Cooke*	76258
Burr	77488
Burris Crossing	79853
Burrow	75189
Burton	77835
Busby	79543
Bushland	79012
Bushwhacker Peninsula	75147
Bushy	77845
Bustamante	78361
Busterville	79358
Butler, *Bastrop*	78621
Butler, *Freestone*	75855
Byers	76357
Bynum	76631
Byrd	75119
Byrds	76801
C (Part of Dallas)‡	75242
Cabot Kingsmill	79065
Cactus	79013
Caddo	76429
Caddo Mills	75135
Cadiz	78102
Cain City	78624
Calaveras	78114
Caldwell	77836
Caledonia	75946
Calf Creek	76825
Call	75933
Calliham	78007
Callisburg	76240
Call Junction	75933
Calvary	75773
Calvert	77837
Camden	75934
Camelot	78239
Cameron	76520
Camey	75034
Camilla	77331
Camp Air	76856
Campbell	75422
Campbellton	78008
Camp Dallas	75068
Camp Maxey	75473
Campo Alto	78516
Camp Ruby	77351
Camp San Saba	76825
Camp Springs	79526
Camp Stanley	78206
Camp Strake	77301
Campti	75935
Camp Valley	78140
Camp Verde	78010
Camp Wood	78833
Cana	75169
Canada Verde	78114
Canadian	79014
Canal City	77617
Candelaria	79843
Candlelight Oaks (Part of Houston)	77091
Caney	77414
Caney City	75148
Caney Creek Estates	77357
Cannon	75495
Canton	75103
Canutillo♦	79835
Canyon, *Lubbock*	79408
Canyon, *Randall*	79015
Canyon City	78130
Canyon Creek (Part of Richardson)	75080
Canyon Creek Estates	78130
Canyon Lake♦	78130
	78133
For specific ZIP Codes call (888) 275-8777, or your local postmaster.	
Canyon Lake Acres	78130
Canyon Lake Estates	78130
Canyon Lake Forest	78130
Canyon Lake Hills	78130
Canyon Lake Island	78130
Canyon Lake Mobile Home Estates	78130
Canyon Lake Shores	78130
Canyon Lake Village	78130
Canyon Lake Village West	78130
Canyon Springs Resort	78130
Canyon Valley	79356
Canyon View Acres	78163
Capital Plaza (Part of Austin)	78723
Capitol (Part of Austin)‡	78701
Caplen	77617
Capps Corner	76265
Cap Rock	79357
Caprock Shopping Center (Part of Lubbock)	79404
Caps	79606
Caradan	76844
Carancahua	77465
Carbon	76435
Carbondale	75567
Cardinal (Part of Athens)	75751
Carey	79222
Carey Estates (Part of Seabrook)	77586
Carlisle	75862
Carlos	77830
Carl Range (Part of Irving)‡	75015†
	75062*
Carlsbad	76934
Carl's Corner	76645
Carlton	76436
Carmine	78932
Carmona	75939
Caro	75961
Carolina Cove	77367
Carpenter	78101
Carpenters Bluff	75021
Carricitos	78586
Carrizo Springs	78834
Carroll	75771
Carroll Springs	75853
Carrollton	75006-08
	75010-11
For specific ZIP Codes call (888) 275-8777, or your local postmaster.	
Carson	75488
Carta Valley	78840
Carterville	75563
Carthage	75633
Cartwright, *Kaufman*	75142
Cartwright, *Wood*	75494
Casa Piedra	79843
Casa View (Part of Dallas)‡	75228
	75357
For specific ZIP Codes call (888) 275-8777, or your local postmaster.	
Cash	75402
Cason	75636
Cass	75556
Cassie	78611
Castell	76831
Castle Hills	78213
Castlewoods	77039
Castolon	79834
Castroville	78009
Catarina	78836
Cat Spring	78933
Causeway Beach	75143
Cave Creek	78624
Cave Springs	75670
Caviness	75460
Cawthon	77868
Cayote	76689
Cayuga	75832
Cedar Branch, *Henderson*	75147
Cedar Branch, *Houston*	75844
Cedar Creek, *Anderson*	75839
Cedar Creek, *Bastrop*	78612
Cedar Elm (Part of San Antonio)‡	78249
Cedar Grove (Part of Copperas Cove)	76522
Cedar Grove (Part of El Paso)	79915
Cedar Grove, *Cass*	75560
Cedar Grove, *Harris*	77532
Cedar Hill, *Dallas*	75104
	75106
For specific ZIP Codes call (888) 275-8777, or your local postmaster.	
Cedar Hill, *Floyd*	79241
Cedar Hills	78621
Cedar Lake	77414
Cedar Lane	77415
Cedar Mills Resort	76245
Cedar Park	78613
	78630
For specific ZIP Codes call (888) 275-8777, or your local postmaster.	
Cedar Point	77520
Cedar Shores Estates	76671
Cedar Springs, *Falls*	76570
Cedar Springs, *Upshur*	75683
Cedar Valley	78736
Cedarview	75104
Cee Vee	79223
Cego	76524
Cele	78653
Celeste	75423
Celina	75009
Center, *Limestone*	76642
Center, *Shelby*	75935
Center City	76844
Center Grove	75455
Center Line	77879
Center Point, *Camp*	75686
Center Point, *Ellis*	76651
Center Point, *Kerr*	78010
Center Point, *Panola*	75691
Center Point, *Parker*	76087
Center Point, *Titus*	75455
Center Point, *Upshur*	75755
Centerview	75833
Centerville, *Leon*	75833

Centerville, *Trinity* 75845
Central, *Angelina* 75969
Central (Part of Fort Worth)‡ 76102
Central Gardens♦ 77627
Central Heights, *Jefferson* 77627
Central Heights, *Nacogdoches* 75961
Central High 75925
Centralia 75834
Central Mall (Part of Port Arthur) 77640
Central Mall (Part of Texarkana) 75501
Central Park (Part of Houston) 77011
Central Park (Part of San Antonio)‡ 78216
Cestohowa 78113
Chaffee Village 76544
Chalk 79248
Chalk Bluff 76705
Chalk Mountain 76401
Chalybeate 75494
Chambersville 75069
Chambliss 75409
Champion Forest 77303
Chances Store 77839
Chandler 75758
Channelview♦ 77530
Channelwood 77530
Channing 79018
Chaparral Hills 78840
Chaparral Park 78652
Chapman 75652
Chapman Ranch 78347
Chappel 76877
Chappell Hill 77426
Charco 77963
Charleston 75432
Charlie 76306
Charlotte 78011
Chat 76645
Chateau Forest (Part of Houston) 77088
Chateau Woods 77301
Chatfield 75105
Cheapside 77954
Cheek 77705
Cherokee 76832
Cherry Mound 75021
Cherry Spring 78624
Chester 75936
Chesterville 77435
Chico 76431
Chicota 75425
Chief 75142
Chihuahua 78572
Childress 79201
Chillicothe 79225
Chilton 76632
Chimney Corners (Part of Austin)‡ 78731
China 77613
China Grove, *Bexar* 78223
China Grove, *Scurry* 79526
China Spring 76633
Chinati 79843
Chireno 75937
Chisholm (Part of McLendon-Chisholm) 75032
Chita 75862
Choate 78119
Chocolate Bayou 77511
Choice 75935
Chriesman 77838
Christine 78012
Christoval 76935
C H Rouse Estates 77365
Church Hill, *Cherokee* 75766
Church Hill, *Rusk* 75652
Churchill Bridge 77422
Cibolo 78108
Cielo Vista (Part of El Paso) 79925
Cielo Vista Mall (Part of El Paso) 79925
Cienegas Terrace 78840
Circle 79064
Circle Back 79371
Circleville, *Travis* 78736
Circleville, *Williamson* 76574
Cisco 76437
Cistern 78941
Citrus City 78572
Citrus Grove 77465
Civic Center (Part of Houston)‡ 77208
Clairemont 79549
Clairette 76457
Clardy 75468
Clarendon 79226
Clareville 78102
Clark 77327
Clark Station 77979
Clarksville 75426
Clarksville City 75647
Clarkwood (Part of Corpus Christi) 78406
Claude 79019
Clauene 79336
Clawson 75904
Clay 77839
Claydesta Station (Part of Midland)‡ 79710
Clayton, *Jefferson* 77627
Clayton, *Panola* 75637
Claytonville, *Fisher* 79556
Claytonville, *Swisher* 79052
Clear Creek 76544
Clear Lake City (Part of Houston) 77058
Clear Lake Shores 77565
Clear Spring 78130
Clearview 78602
Cleburne 76031*
76033†
Clegg 78022
Clemons 77423
Clemville 77414
Cleveland 77327*
77328†
Clever Creek 75935
Cliffside 79106
Clifton, *Bosque* 76634
Clifton, *Van Zandt* 75169
Climax 75407
Cline 78801
Clint 79836
Clinton, *DeWitt* 77954
Clinton, *Hunt* 75135
Clinton Park (Part of Houston) 77029
Clodine 77469
Close City 79356
Cloverleaf♦ 77015
Club Lake Estates 75708
Clute 77531
Clyde 79510
Coady 77520
Coahoma 79511
Coal Mine (Part of Lytle) 78052
Cobb Creek 75852
Cobb Switch 75161
Cochran 77418
Cockrell Hill 75211
Coffee City 75763
Coffeeville 75683
Coit 76653
Coke 75431
Coldhill 75708
Coldspring 77331
Cole Creek Manor (Part of Houston) 77092
Coleman 76834
Coleman Cove 75929
Colfax 75103
College Country Estates 75020
College Hill 75559
College Mound 75161
Collegeport 77428
College Station 77840-45
For specific ZIP Codes call (888) 275-8777, or your local postmaster.
Colleyville 76034
Collin Creek Mall (Part of Plano) 75075
Collinsville 76233
Colmesneil 75938
Cologne 77905
Colonial (Part of Waco)‡ 76707
Colorado City 79512
Colquitt 75160
Colton 78744
Columbus 78934
Comal 78130
Comanche 76442
Comanche Cove 76048
Comanche Harbor 76048
Combes 78535
Combine 75159
Comfort♦ 78013
Commerce 75428*
75429†
Como 75431
Comstock 78837
Comyn 76444
Concan 78838
Concepcion 78349
Concho 76866
Concord, *Cherokee* 75789
Concord, *Leon* 77850
Concord, *Morris* 75571
Concord, *Rusk* 75681
Concrete 77954
Cone 79357
Conlen 79022
Connor 77864
Conroe 77301-06
77384-85
For specific ZIP Codes call (888) 275-8777, or your local postmaster.
Constitution Village (Part of Sherman) 75495
Content 79519
Converse 78109
Conway 79068
Cooks Point 77836
Cookville 75558
Cool 76088
Cool Crest 78245
Coolidge 76635
Cooper 75432
Cooper Creek 76201
Copano Village 78382
Copeland 75701
Copeville 75121
Coppell 75019
Copperas Cove 76522
Copper Canyon 76226
Corbet 75110
Cordele 77957
Corine 75766
Corinth, *Denton* 76205
Corinth, *Eastland* 76437
Corinth, *Jones* 79553
Corinth, *Leon* 75831
Corinth, *Van Zandt* 75140
Corley 75567
Cornersville 75494
Cornett 75568
Cornudas 79847
Coronado (Part of El Paso)‡ 79912*
79913†
Corpus Christi 78401-80
For specific ZIP Codes call (888) 275-8777, or your local postmaster.
Corral City 76226
Corrigan 75939
Corsicana 75110
75151
For specific ZIP Codes call (888) 275-8777, or your local postmaster.
Corsicana Junction (Part of Corsicana) 75110
Coryell 76689
Cost 78614
Cotton Center, *Fannin* 75418
Cotton Center, *Hale* 79021
Cottondale 76073
Cotton Flat 79701
Cotton Gin 75860
Cotton Mill Spur (Part of Denison) 75020
Cottonwood, *Brazos* 77808
Cottonwood, *Callahan* 79504
Cottonwood, *Falls* 76655
Cottonwood, *Kaufman* 75158
Cottonwood, *Lamar* 75486
Cottonwood, *McLennan* 76691
Cottonwood, *Madison* 77864
Cottonwood Shores 78654
Cotulla 78014
Coughran 78064
Council Creek Village 78611
Country Campus 77340
Country Club Lake Estates 76904
Country Club Terrace (Part of Amarillo) 79106
Country Club Terrace (Part of Victoria) 77904
Country Colony 77372
Country Place Acres 77355
Countryside Plaza (Part of San Antonio)‡ 78216
Country Squire Estates 77630
County Line, *Camp* 75686
County Line, *Hale* 79363
Coupland 78615
Courtney 77868
Cove, *Chambers* 77520
Cove (Part of Orange) 77630
Cove Spring 75766
Covington 76636
Covington Woods (Part of Sugar Land) 77478
Cox 75644
Coyanosa 79730
Coy City 78118
Cozy Corner 78945
Crabb 77469
Crabbs Prairie 77340
Craft 75766
Crafton 76431
Craig 75652
Crandall 75114
Crane 79731
Cranfills Gap 76637
Crawford 76638
Creagleville 75140
Crecy 75845
Creechville 75119
Creedmoor 78747
Creekwood Acres 77375
Creekwood Addition 77372
Crenneland 77650
Crescent 77488
Crescent Heights 75751
Cresson 76035
Cresthaven (Part of San Antonio)‡ 78213
Crestwood (Part of Odessa)‡ 79762
Crestwood, *Marion* 75630
Crestwood Farms 77356
Crews 79567
Crimcrest (Part of Henderson) 75652
Cripple Creek Farms 77355
Cripple Creek Farms West 77362
Cripple Creek North 77355
Crisp 75119
Crockett 75835
Crosby♦ 77532
Crosbyton 79322
Cross, *Grimes* 77861
Cross, *McMullen* 78026
Cross Cut 76801
Crossing (Part of De Soto) 75115
Cross Plains 76443
Crossroads (Part of Balcones Heights)‡ 78201
Crossroads, *Camp* 75686
Cross Roads, *Cass* (mail Hughes Springs) 75656
Crossroads, *Cass* (mail Ganado) 77962
Cross Roads, *Delta* 75432
Cross Roads, *Denton* 76227
Crossroads, *Harrison* 75670
Cross Roads, *Henderson* 75148
Cross Roads, *Milam* 76520
Cross Roads, *Rusk* 75662
Cross Roads, *Van Zandt* 75140
Crossroads of San Antonio (Part of Balcones Heights) 78201
Cross Timber 76028
Croton 79232
Crow 75765
Crowell 79227
Crowley 76036
Cruz Calle 78349
Cryer Creek 76626
Crystal Beach 77650
Crystal City 78839
Crystal Creek Forest 77301
Crystal Lake 75801
Crystal Lakes Estates 77351
Cuadrilla 79836
Cuero 77954
Cullen Mall (Part of Corpus Christi) 78412
Culleoka 75407
Cumby 75433
Cundiff 76458
Cuney 75759
Cunningham 75434
Curtis 75951
Curvitas 78595
Cushing 75760
Cusseta 75566
Cut 75835
Cut and Shoot 77302
Cuthand 75417
Cuthbert 79512
Cyclone 76519
Cypress, *Franklin* 75494
Cypress, *Harris* 77410
77429
77433
For specific ZIP Codes call (888) 275-8777, or your local postmaster.
Cypress Cove 78130
Cypress Creek 78028
Cypress Creek Estates 77429
Cypress Mill 78654
Dabney 78801
Da Costa 77905
Dacus 77356
Daingerfield 75638
Daisetta 77533
Dalby Springs 75559
Dale 78616
Dalhart 79022
Dallardsville 77332

Dallas

75201-99
75301-98
For specific ZIP Codes call (888) 275-8777, or your local postmaster.

Colleges & Universities

Baylor Coll of Dentistry 75246
The Criswell Coll 75246
Dallas Baptist Univ 75211
Dallas Theological Seminary 75204
Parker Coll of Chiropractic 75229
Paul Quinn Coll 75241
Southern Methodist Univ 75275
Univ of Texas Southwestern Med Ctr 75235

Financial Institutions

Bank of America, NA 75201
Bank One, NA 75201
Comerica Bank 75201
Compass Bank 75206
Fidelity Bank 75201
NationsBank, NA 75201

Hospitals

Baylor Univ Med Ctr 75246
Dallas County Hosp Dist-Parkland Memorial Hosp 75235
Dallas Southwest Med Ctr 75230
Methodist Med Ctr 75203
Presbyterian Hosp 75231
St Paul Med Ctr 75235
Veterans Affairs Med Ctr 75216

Hotels/Motels

The Adolphus 75202
Doubletree at Lincoln Centre 75240
Doubletree Campbell Centre 75206
The Fairmont 75201
Harvey 75201
Harvey Hotel, Brookhollow 75247
Hilton, Parkway 75244
Holiday Inn Select, North Dallas 75234
Hyatt Regency 75207
Hyatt Regency, DFW Airport 75261
Inter-Continental 75248
Le Meridien 75201
Marriott Quorum 75240
Omni at Park West 75234
Radisson Central 75206
Radisson Park Central 75251
Ramada Plaza Downtown & Convention Ctr 75247
Renaissance 75207
Sheraton Park Central 75251
The Westin Galleria 75240
Wyndham Anatole 75207

Military Installations

Texas Air Nat Guard, FB6431, Hensley Field 75211
U S Army Corps of Engineers, Southwestern Div 75242

Dallas-Fort Worth Airport (Part of Coppell)‡ 75261
Dalrock 75088-89
For specific ZIP Codes call (888) 275-8777, or your local postmaster.
Dalton 75568
Dalworthington Gardens 76010
Dalys 75844
Dam B 75979
Damon 77430
Danbury 77534
Danciger 77431
Danevang 77432
Danville, *Collin* 75069
Danville, *Gregg* 75662
Daphne 75455
Darco 75670
Darrouzett 79024

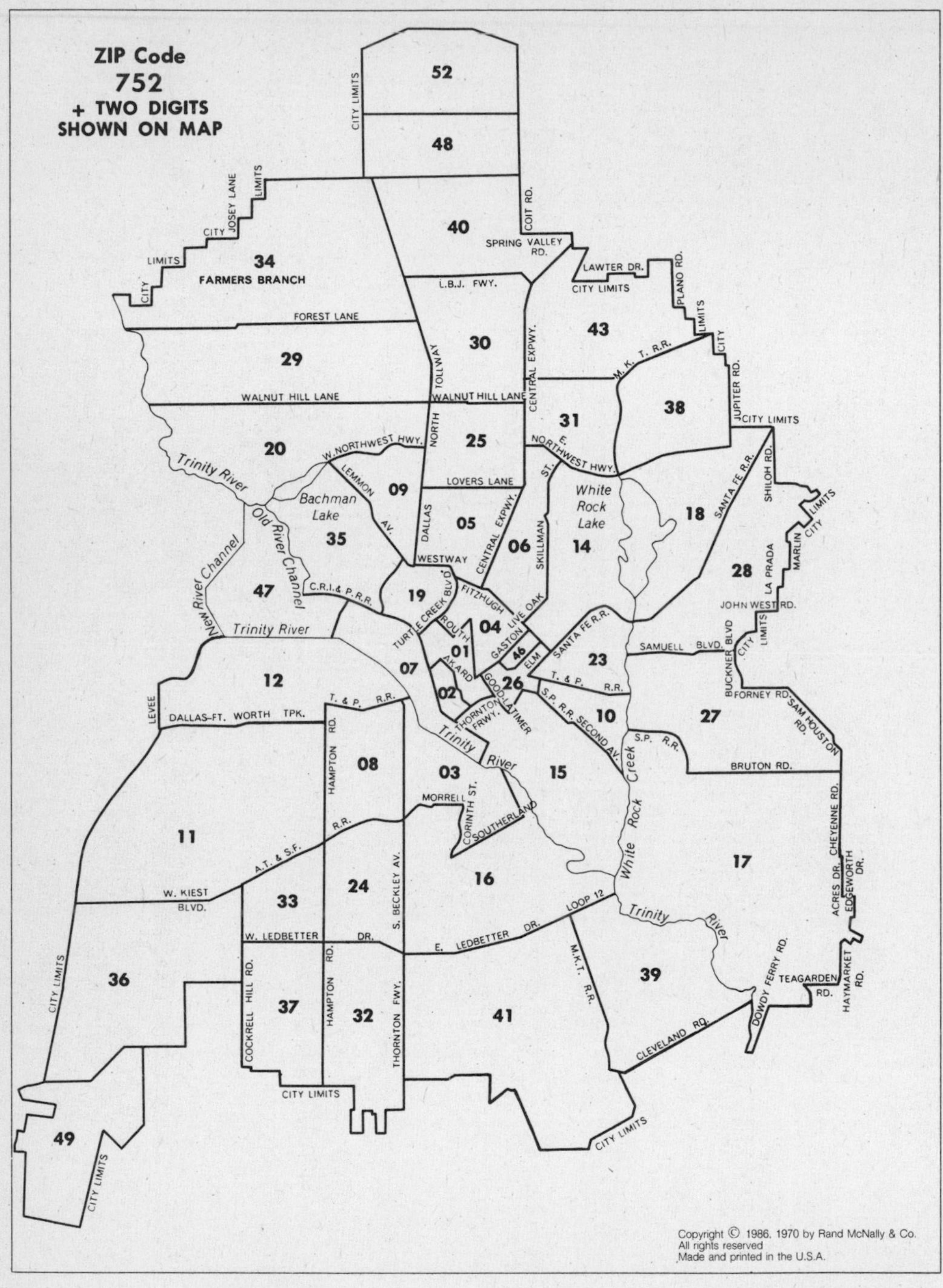
ZIP Code
752
+ TWO DIGITS
SHOWN ON MAP
52
48
40
34
FARMERS BRANCH
29
30
43
38
31
20
25
09
05
06
14
18
28
35
47
19
04
01
46
23
07
12
02
26
10
27
08
03
15
11
17
33
24
16
36
39
37
32
41
49
CITY LIMITS
COIT RD.
SPRING VALLEY RD.
LAWTER DR.
PLANO RD.
JOSEY LANE
FOREST LANE
L.B.J. FWY.
WALNUT HILL LANE
NORTH TOLLWAY
CENTRAL EXPWY.
M. K. T. R.R.
JUPITER RD.
W. NORTHWEST HWY.
E. NORTHWEST HWY.
LOVERS LANE
LEMMON AV.
DALLAS
Trinity River
Old River Channel
New River Channel
Bachman Lake
White Rock Lake
SKILLMAN ST.
SANTA FE R.R.
SHILOH RD.
LA PRADA
MARLIN
WESTWAY
C.R.I.& P. R.R.
TURTLE CREEK BLVD.
FITZHUGH
LIVE OAK
GASTON
ROUTH
ELM
JOHN WEST RD.
SAMUELL BLVD.
BUCKNER BLVD
AKARD
GOOD-LATIMER
THORNTON FRWY.
T. & P. R.R.
S.P. R.R.
SECOND AV.
FORNEY RD.
SAM HOUSTON RD.
LEVEE
DALLAS-FT. WORTH TPK.
HAMPTON RD.
S.P. R.R.
BRUTON RD.
White Rock Creek
MORRELL
CORINTH ST.
SOUTHERLAND
CHEYENNE RD.
A.T. & S.F. R.R.
W. KIEST BLVD.
S. BECKLEY AV.
LOOP 12
ACRES DR.
EDGEWORTH DR.
W. LEDBETTER DR.
E. LEDBETTER DR.
M.K.T. R.R.
DOWDY FERRY RD.
TEAGARDEN RD.
HAYMARKET RD.
COCKRELL HILL RD.
THORNTON FWY.
CLEVELAND RD.

Daugherty	75440
Davenport	75412
Davilla	76523
Davis Prairie	76687
Davisville, *Angelina*	75901
Davisville, *Leon*	75833
Dawn	79025
Dawson	76639
Dayton	77535
Dayton Lakes	77535
Deadwood	75633
Dean, *Clay*	76303
Dean, *Hockley*	79363
Deanville	77852
De Berry	75639
Debora Sue Schatz (Part of Houston)‡	77042
Decatur	76234
Decker, *Nolan*	79506
Decker, *Travis*	78653
Decker Prairie	77355
De Cordova Bend Estates	76049
Deep Water Point Estates	75121
Deer Creek	76365
Deer Haven	78654
Deer Park	77536
Deerwood East	77445
De Kalb	75559
Delba	75452
Delbert L. Atkinson (Part of Pasadena)‡	77505
De Leon	76444
Delhi	78953
Delia	76635
Dell City	79837
Del Mar Hills (Part of Laredo)	78041
Delmita	78536
Del Monte	77627
Delray	75633
Del Rio	78840-43
For specific ZIP Codes call (888) 275-8777, or your local postmaster.	
Delrose	75644
Del Valle	78617
Demi-John Island	77541
Democrat, *Comanche*	76442
Democrat, *Mills*	76442
De Moss (Part of Houston)‡	77036
Denhawken	78160
Denison	75020-21
For specific ZIP Codes call (888) 275-8777, or your local postmaster.	
Denning	75972
Dennis	76439
Denny	76653
Denson Springs	75844
Denton, *Callahan*	79510
Denton, *Denton*	76201-08
For specific ZIP Codes call (888) 275-8777, or your local postmaster.	
Denver City	79323
Denver Harbor (Part of Houston)‡	77020
Deport	75435
Derby	78017
Dermott	79549
Desdemona	76445
Desert	75424
De Soto	75115*
	75123†
Dessau	78753
Detmold	76577
Detroit	75436
Devers	77538
Devils Pocket	77612
Devine	78016
Dew	75860
Dewees	78114
Deweyville♦	77614
Dewville	78140
Dexter	76240
D'Hanis	78850
Dial, *Fannin*	75446
Dial, *Hutchinson*	79007
Dialville	75785
Diamondhead	77356
Diana	75640
Diboll	75941
Dicey	76086
Dickens	79229
Dickinson	77539
Dido	76179
Dies	75979
Dike	75437
Dilley	78017
Dilworth, *Gonzales*	78629
Dilworth, *Red River*	75426
Dime Box	77853
Dimmitt	79027
Dimple	75426
Dinero	78350
Ding Dong	76542
Dinsmore	77488
Direct	75486
Dirgin	75691
Divide	75420
Divot	78017
Dixie, *Grayson*	76273
Dixie, *Jasper*	75951
Dixon	75402
Doans	76384
Dobbin	77333
Dobrowolski	78026
Dodd	79347
Dodd City	75438
Dodge	77334
Dodson	79230
Dogwood	75979
Dogwood City	75762
Dolen	77327
Domino	75572
Donall Estates	78611
Donie	75838
Donna	78537
Don Tol	77420
Doole	76836
Dorchester	75459
Doss	78618
Dot	76524
Dothan	76437
Dotson	75669
Double Bayou	77514
Double Diamond Estates	79036
Double Oak	76226
Doucette	75942
Dougherty	79231
Douglass	75943
Douglassville	75560
Downing	76442
Downsville	76706
Downtown (Part of Amarillo)‡	79105
Downtown (Part of Austin)‡	78767-68
For specific ZIP Codes call (888) 275-8777, or your local postmaster.	
Downtown (Part of Beaumont)‡	77704
Downtown (Part of Brownsville)‡	78522
Downtown (Part of Bryan)‡	77801
Downtown (Part of Corpus Christi)‡	78401-03
	78407-08
For specific ZIP Codes call (888) 275-8777, or your local postmaster.	
Downtown (Part of Dallas)‡	75201-02
	75204
	75221
	75250
	75270
For specific ZIP Codes call (888) 275-8777, or your local postmaster.	
Downtown (Part of El Paso)‡	79901
	79940-55
For specific ZIP Codes call (888) 275-8777, or your local postmaster.	
Downtown (Part of Ft. Worth)‡	76101-02
	76113
For specific ZIP Codes call (888) 275-8777, or your local postmaster.	
Downtown (Part of Freeport)‡	77541
Downtown (Part of Irving)‡	75017†
	75060*
Downtown (Part of Longview)‡	75606
Downtown (Part of Lubbock)‡	79401*
	79408†
Downtown (Part of McAllen)‡	78501*
	78505†
Downtown (Part of San Antonio)‡	78205
	78291-99
For specific ZIP Codes call (888) 275-8777, or your local postmaster.	
Downtown (Part of Tyler)‡	75710
Downtown (Part of Waco)‡	76701
	75703
	75706
	75711
For specific ZIP Codes call (888) 275-8777, or your local postmaster.	
Doyle	76642
Dozier	79079
Drasco	79567
Draw	79373
Dreka	75973
Dresden	75102
Dreyer	77984
Driftwood, *Hays*	78619
Driftwood, *Henderson*	75143
Driners	75937
Dripping Springs	78620
Driscoll	78351
Drop	76247
Dryden	78851
Dubina	78956
Dublin	76446
Dudley	79601
Duffau	76457
Dugas Addition	77611
Dugger	78155
Dumas	79029
Dumont	79232
Dunbar	75440
Duncanville	75116
	75137-38
For specific ZIP Codes call (888) 275-8777, or your local postmaster.	
Dundee	76366
Dunlap	79248
Dunlay	78861
Dunn	79516
Duplex	75447
Durango	76656
Duster	76444
Dye Mound	76265
Dyersdale	77016
	77050
For specific ZIP Codes call (888) 275-8777, or your local postmaster.	
Eagle Lake	77434
Eagle Mountain Acres	76020
Eagle Pass	78852*
	78853†
Earles Camp	79521
Earles Chapel	75764
Early	76802
Earlywine	77833
Earth	79031
East Afton	79220
East Amarillo (Part of Amarillo)	79104
East Arlington (Part of Arlington)‡	76007
East Austin (Part of Austin)‡	78702
East Bernard♦	77435
East Caney	75482
East Center	75140
East Columbia	77486
East Delta	75450
East Donna (Part of Donna)	78537
Easterly	77856
Eastgate	77535
East Glen (Part of El Paso)	79936
East Grand (Part of Dallas)‡	75223
East Hamilton	75973
Easthaven (Part of Houston)	77075
East Houston (Part of Houston)‡	77028
Eastland	76448
East Liberty	75935
East Mayfield (Part of Hemphill)	75948
East Mountain	75644
Easton	75641
East Point	75494
East Ridge (Part of Amarillo)	79107
East Side	75639
East Tawakoni	75453
East Tempe	77351
East Texas (Part of Commerce)‡	75428
Eastvale	75056
East View (Part of Kilgore)	75662
Eastview Terrace	78101
Eastwood (Part of Houston)‡	77023
Eastwood Heights (Part of El Paso)	79925
Eaton	77856
Ebenezer, *Camp*	75686
Ebenezer, *Jasper*	75951
Ebony	76864
Echo, *Coleman*	76834
Echo, *Orange*	77630
Echo Hills	75763
Eckert	78675
Ecleto	78111
Ector	75439
Edcouch	78538
Eddy (Part of Bruceville-Eddy)	76524
Eden	76837
Edgar	77954
Edge	77808
Edgecliff	76134
Edgewater Estates	78368
Edgewood	75117
Edgeworth	76569
Edhube	75418
Edinburg	78539*
	78540†
Edith	76945
Edmonson	79032
Edna	77957
Edna Hill	76446
Edom	75756
Edroy	78352
Egan	76031
Egypt, *Leon*	75833
Egypt, *Montgomery*	77355
Egypt, *Wharton*	77436
Elam (Part of Dallas)	75217
Elam Springs	75755
Elbert	76372
El Calmino	75948
El Campo	77437
El Campo Club	77465
El Campo South	77437
El Cenizo	78043
El Centro (Part of Laredo)‡	78042
El Centro Mall (Part of Pharr)	78577
Eldorado	76936
Eldorado Center	76639
Electra	76360
Electric City	79007
Elevation	76556
El Gato	78516
Elgin	78621
Eliasville	76481
El Indio	78860
El Jardin (Part of Brownsville)	78520
El Jardin Del Mar (Part of Pasadena)	77586
Elk	76624
Elkhart	75839
El Lago	77586
Ellinger	78938
Ellington Air Force Base (Part of Houston)	77209
Elliott, *Robertson*	77859
Elliott, *Wilbarger*	76364
Ellis (Part of Levelland)‡	79338
Elmaton	77440
Elmdale	79601
Elmendorf	78112
Elm Flat	75144
Elm Grove, *Cherokee*	75785
Elm Grove, *Fayette*	78959
Elm Grove, *San Saba*	76872
Elm Grove, *Wharton*	77434
Elm Mott	76640
Elmo	75118
Elmont	75495
Elm Ridge, *Grayson*	75020
Elm Ridge, *Milam*	76520
Elmtown	75801
Elmwood, *Anderson*	75801
Elmwood (Part of Seguin)	78155
Eloise	76680
El Oso	78119
El Paso, *El Paso*	79901-99
	88510-95
For specific ZIP Codes call (888) 275-8777, or your local postmaster.	
El Paso, *Fisher*	79543
El Pinon Estates	75929
El Ranchito	79766
El Rancho Estates	76008
El Refugio	78582
Elroy	78617
Elsa	78543
El Sauz	78582
El Toro	77957
Elwood, *Fannin*	75447
Elwood, *Madison*	75852
Ely	75439
Elysian Fields	75642
Emberson	75486
Emblem	75482
Emerald Valley	78250
Emhouse	75110
Emmett	76641
Emory	75440
Encantada	78586
Enchanted Oaks, *Harris*	77373
Enchanted Oaks, *Henderson*	75147
Enchanted River Estates	78003
Encinal	78019
Encino	78353
Energy	76452
Engle	78956
English	75426
Enloe	75441
Ennis	75119*
	75120†
Enoch	75644
Enochs	79324
Ensign	75119
Enterprise, *Cherokee*	75766
Enterprise, *Van Zandt*	75169
Eola	76937
Eolian	76424
Era	76238
Erath	76708
Erin	75951
Erwin	77830
Escobares♦	78582
Escobas	78361
Eskota	79561
Esmond Estates (Part of Odessa)	79762
Esperanza	79839
Esquire Estates	75147
Esseville	78008
Estacado	79343
Estacado Estates (Part of Amarillo)	79109
Estelline	79233
Estes	78382
Estes Addition	76071
Ethel	76233
Etoile	75944
Etter	79029
Eubank Acres	78753
Eula	79510
Eulalie	75975
Euless	76039-40
For specific ZIP Codes call (888) 275-8777, or your local postmaster.	
Eulogy	76652
Eureka	75110
Eustace	75124
Evadale♦	77615
Evant	76525
Evergreen, *Grimes*	77861
Evergreen, *San Jacinto*	77327
Evergreen Park	77662
Everitt	77327
Everman	76140
Ewell	75644
Exchange Park (Part of Dallas)‡	75245
Eylau	75501
Ezzell	77964
Fabens♦	79838
Fairbanks (Part of Houston)‡	77040-41
For specific ZIP Codes call (888) 275-8777, or your local postmaster.	
Fairchilds	77469
Fairfield	75840
Fairgreen	77039
Fairland	78654
Fairlie	75428
Fairmount	75948
Fairoaks	75838
Fair Oaks Ranch	78015
Fair Park (Part of Dallas)‡	75210
Fair Play	75631
Fairview (Part of Houston)‡	77006
Fairview, *Bailey*	79371
Fairview, *Bosque*	76689
Fairview, *Brazos*	77807
Fairview, *Cass*	75563
Fairview, *Collin*	75002
Fairview, *Gaines*	79360
Fairview, *Howard*	79720
Fairview, *Rusk*	75784
Fairview, *Wilson*	78114

* **Area Zip Code** † **Post Office Boxes** ‡ **Postal Station** ♦ **Census Designated Place** *Italic Type* **County**

Place	ZIP
Fairview, *Wise*	76078
Fairy	76457
Faker	75686
Falcon	78564
Falcon Heights	78545
Falcon Mesa	78076
Falcon Village	78545
Falfurrias	78355
Fallon	76667
Falls City	78113
Fambrough	76424
Famuliner	79346
Fannett	77705
Fannin	77960
Fargo	76384
Farmer	76460
Farmers Branch	75234
Farmers Valley	76384
Farmersville	75442
Farmington	75058
Farnsworth	79033
Farr Addition	79756
Farrar	75838
Farrsville	75977
Farwell	79325
Fashing	78008
Fate	75132
Faught	75462
Faulkner	75416
Fawil	75928
Fayburg	75424
Fayetteville	78940
Faysville	78539
Fedor	78947
Fellowship	75961
Fentress	78622
Ferris	75125
Fetzer	77363
Fiddlers Green	75034
Field Creek	76869
Fieldton	79326
Fife	76825
Files Valley	76055
Fincastle	75763
Fink	75076
Finney, *Hale*	79072
Finney, *King*	79248
First Colony‡	77479
	77496
For specific ZIP Codes call (888) 275-8777, or your local postmaster.	
Fischer	78623
Fisk	76834
Fitze	75946
Fitzhugh	78703
Five Points, *Ellis*	75167
Five Points (Part of El Paso)‡	79903*
	79923†
Flagg	79027
Flamingo Bay (Part of Seabrook)	77586
Flanagan	75691
Flat	76526
Flat Fork	75974
Flatonia	78941
Flat Prairie	77835
Flats	75472
Flatwood	75754
Fleetwood (Part of Houston)	77079
Fletcher	77657
Flint	75762
Flint Creek	76450
Flo	75831
Flomot	79234
Flora	75437
Florence	76527
Florence Hill (Part of Grand Prairie)	75052
Floresville	78114
Florey	79714
Florine (Part of San Antonio)	78209
Flour Bluff‡	78418-19
	78480
For specific ZIP Codes call (888) 275-8777, or your local postmaster.	
Flower Hill	78934
Flower Mound	75022
	75027-28
For specific ZIP Codes call (888) 275-8777, or your local postmaster.	
Floy	78941
Floyd	75401
Floydada	79235
Fluvanna	79517
Flynn	77855
Fodice	75851
Follett	79034
Folley	79255
Fondren (Part of Webster)	77598
Fords Corner	75972
Fordtran	77995
Forest	75925
Forestburg	76239
Forest Chapel	75411
Forest Glade	76667
Forest Grove, *Collin*	75069
Forest Grove, *Henderson*	75758
Forest Heights	77630
Forest Hill (Part of Amarillo)	79107
Forest Hill, *Lamar*	75446
Forest Hill, *Tarrant*	76119
Forest Hill, *Wood*	75783
Forest Hill Estates	76528
Forest Hills (Part of Tyler)	75702
Forest North Estates	78729
Forest Spring	77351
Forney	75126
Forreston	76041
Forsan	79733
Fort Bliss	79916
Fort Clark Springs	78832
Fort Davis	79734
Fort Gates	76528
Fort Hancock	79839
Fort Hood	76544
Fort McKavett	76841
Fort Ringgold (Part of Rio Grande City)	78582
Fort Spunky	76031
Fort Stockton	79735
Fort Worth	76101-16
	76118-26
	76131-79
	76181
	76185
For specific ZIP Codes call (888) 275-8777, or your local postmaster.	
Fort Worth Town Center (Part of Fort Worth)	76115
Forum 303 Mall (Part of Arlington)	76010
Foster, *Fort Bend*	77469
Foster, *Terry*	79316
Foster Hills	75951
Foster Place (Part of Houston)‡	77021
Fosters Store	77836
Fouke	75765
Fountain (Part of Grand Prairie)‡	75050*
	75053†
Fountains on the Lake (Part of Stafford)	77477
Fountain View	77032
Four Corners, *Brazoria*	77422
Four Corners, *Fort Bend*	77469
Four Corners, *Montgomery*	77301
Four Way	79018
Fowlerton	78021
Fox	76088
Fox Landing	75938
Fox Run	77373
Foxwood	77362
Frame Switch	76574
Francis (Part of West Orange)	77630
Francitas	77961
Frankell	76470
Franklin	77856
Frankston	75763
Fred	77616
Fredericksburg	78624
Fredonia, *Gregg*	75662
Fredonia, *Mason*	76842
Fredonia Hill (Part of Nacogdoches)	75961
Freedom (Part of Lubbock)‡	79412
Freedom, *Rains*	75440
Freeneytown	75667
Freeport	77541-42
For specific ZIP Codes call (888) 275-8777, or your local postmaster.	
Freer	78357
Freestone	75838
Freeway Manor (Part of Houston)	77034
Freeway Oaks Estates	77365
Freheit	78130
Frelsburg	78950
French Creek Village (Part of San Antonio)	78240
Frenstat	77836
Fresenius	77656
Fresno	77545
Freyburg	78956
Friday	75845
Friendship, *Jasper*	75966
Friendship, *Lamb*	79371
Friendship, *Leon*	75846
Friendship, *Smith*	75647
Friendship, *Upshur*	75644
Friendship, *Van Zandt*	75140
Friendswood	77546
	77549
For specific ZIP Codes call (888) 275-8777, or your local postmaster.	
Friona	79035
Frisco	75034-35
For specific ZIP Codes call (888) 275-8777, or your local postmaster.	
Fritch	79036
Frog	75161
Frognot	75424
Frontier (Part of Round Rock)	78638
Frontier Lakes	77378
Fronton	78582
Frosa	76678
Frost	76641
Fruitland	76230
Fruitvale	75127
Frydek	77474
Frys Gap	75766
Fulbright	75436
Fuller Springs	75901
Fulshear	77441
Fulton	78358
Fulton Beach (Part of Fulton)	78358
Funston	79501
Furney Richardson	75860
Gail	79738
Gainesville	76240*
	76241†
Galena Park	77547
Galilee	77340
Gallatin	75764
Gallaway	71049
Galle	78638
Galleria (Part of Dallas)	75240
Galleria, The (Part of Houston)	77056
Galveston	77550-54
For specific ZIP Codes call (888) 275-8777, or your local postmaster.	
Galvez Mall (Part of Galveston)	77551
Ganado	77962
Garceno	78582
Garciasville	78547
Garden Acres (Part of Fort Worth)	76028
Garden City, *Glasscock*	79739
Garden City Park (Part of Houston)	77088
Gardendale, *Ector*♦	79758
Gardendale, *La Salle*	78014
Garden Oaks (Part of Houston)‡	77018*
	77206†
Garden Ridge	78266
Garden Valley	75771
Garden Villas	77904
Garfield, *DeWitt*	78164
Garfield, *Travis*	78617
Garland, *Bowie*	75559
Garland, *Dallas*	75040-49
For specific ZIP Codes call (888) 275-8777, or your local postmaster.	
Garland, *Red River*	75550
Garner	76088
Garrett	75119
Garretts Bluff	75411
Garrison	75946
Garth	77520
Garvin	76023
Garwood	77442
Gary	75643
Gasoline	79255
Gastonia	75114
Gatesville	76528
Gatewood	77032
Gause	77857
Gay Hill, *Fayette*	78945
Gay Hill, *Washington*	77833
Gaywood (Part of Houston)	77079
General Mail Facility (Part of Austin)‡	78710
Geneva	75947
Geneva Estates	78736
Genoa (Part of Houston)‡	77034
George	77871
Georges Creek	76031
Georgetown	78626-28
For specific ZIP Codes call (888) 275-8777, or your local postmaster.	
George West	78022
George W. Singer (Part of Lubbock)‡	79424
Georgia	75486
Gerald	76640
Geronimo	78115
Geronimo Forest	78254
Geronimo Village	78253
Gethsemane	75657
Gholson	76705
Gibtown	76486
Giddings	78942
Gilchrist	77617
Gill	75670
Gillett	78116
Gilliland	79227
Gilmer	75644
Gilpin	79370
Ginger	75410
Girard	79518
Girvin	79740
Givens	75462
Gladewater, *Gregg*	75647
Gladewater, *Titus*	75455
Glass	76690
Glaze City	77984
Glazier	79014
Glen Cove, *Coleman*	76834
Glen Cove (Part of League City)	77565
Glencrest (Part of Fort Worth)‡	76119
Glendale	75862
Glenfawn	75760
Glen Flora	77443
Glenn Heights	75115
Glen Rose	76043
Glenwood (Part of Amarillo)	79103
Glenwood, *Upshur*	75644
Glidden	78943
Globe	75486
Glory	75462
Gober	75443
Godley	76044
Gold	78624
Golden	75444
Golden Beach	78643
Golden Oaks	78628
Golden Triangle Mall (Part of Denton)	76206
Goldfinch	78005
Goldsboro	79519
Goldsmith	79741
Goldthwaite	76844
Golfcrest (Part of Houston)	77087
Goliad	77963
Golinda	76655
Gomez	79316
Gonzales	78629
Goober Hill	75973
Goodfellow Air Force Base	76908
Good Hope	77964
Goodland	79371
Goodlett	79252
Goodlow	75144
Goodlow Park	75144
Goodnight, *Armstrong*	79226
Goodnight, *Navarro*	75144
Goodrich	77335
Good Springs	75667
Goodville	76632
Gordon, *Lynn*	79356
Gordon, *Palo Pinto*	76453
Gordonville	76245
Goree	76363
Gorman	76454
Goshen	77340
Gough	75448
Gould	75766
Gouldbusk	76845
Graceton	75644
Graford	76449
Graham, *Garza*	79356
Graham, *Jasper*	75951
Graham, *Young*	76450
Granada Estates	78737
Granbury	76048-49
For specific ZIP Codes call (888) 275-8777, or your local postmaster.	
Grand Bluff	75631
Grandfalls	79742
Grand Prairie	75050-54
For specific ZIP Codes call (888) 275-8777, or your local postmaster.	
Grand Saline	75140
Grand View (Part of El Paso)	79930
Grandview, *Dawson*	79351
Grandview, *Gray*	79039
Grandview, *Johnson*	76050
Grange Hall	75670
Granger	76530
Grangerland	77302
Granite Shoals	78654
Granjeno	78572
Granview Beach	78611
Granville W. Elder (Part of Houston)‡	77013
Grape Creek	76901
Grapeland	75844
Grapetown	78624
Grapevine	76051*
	76099†
Grassland	79356
Graves (Part of Midland)‡	79708
Gray	75657
Grayback	76360
Grayburg	77659
Grays Chapel	75801
Grays Prairie	75158
Graytown	78114
Great Northwest	78250
Great Oaks	78681
Great Southwest (Part of Arlington)‡	76005
Green	78119
Green Acres	77058
Greenbriar (Part of Houston)‡	77098
Green Hill	75455
Green Lake	77979
Green Pastures	78640
Greens Bayou (Part of Houston)	77015
Greens Camp	79521
Greens Creek	76446
Greens North (Part of Houston)‡	77067
Greenspoint Mall (Part of Houston)	77060
Green Valley	76227
Greenview	75420
Greenview Hills (Part of Irving)	75062
Greenview Manor (Part of Houston)	77032
Greenville	75401-04
For specific ZIP Codes call (888) 275-8777, or your local postmaster.	
Greenville Avenue (Part of Dallas)‡	75206
Greenvine	77835
Greenway	78223
Greenway Plaza (Part of Houston)‡	77046
Greenwood, *Hopkins*	75478
Greenwood, *Midland*	79701
Greenwood, *Parker*	76088
Greenwood, *Wise*	76246
Greenwood Acres, *Llano*	78609
Greenwood Acres, *Orange*	77626
Greenwood Forest	78028
Greenwood Village	77093
Greggton (Part of Longview)	75604
Gregory	78359
Gresham	75703
Grey Forest	78023
	78255
For specific ZIP Codes call (888) 275-8777, or your local postmaster.	
Gribble (Part of Farmers Branch)	75234
Grice	75644
Griffin	75789
Griffing (Part of Port Arthur)	77640
Griffing Park (Part of Port Arthur)	77640
Griffith, *Cochran*	79346
Griffith, *Ellis*	76084
Grigsby	75935
Grit, *Mason*	76856
Grit, *Rains*	75410
Groceville	77301
Groesbeck	76642
Groom	79039
Grosvenor	76801
Groves	77619

Groveton 75845
Grow 79248
Gruenau 78164
Gruene 78130
Grulla 78548
Gruver 79040
Guadalupe 77905
Guadalupe Heights 78028
Guajillo 78332
Guerra 78360
Gulf Camp 79756
Gulfgate Mall (Part of Houston) 77087
Gulfway (Part of Corpus Christi)‡ 78412
Gum Springs, *Cass* 75560
Gum Springs, *Harrison* 75601
Gun Barrel City 75147
Gunsight 76437
Gunter, *Grayson* 75058
Gunter, *Wood* 75410
Gussettville 78022
Gustine 76455
Guthrie 79236
Guy 77444
Guys Store 75833
Hacienda Heights (Part of El Paso) 79915
Hackberry (Part of San Antonio)‡ 78210
Hackberry, *Cottle* 79248
Hackberry, *Denton* 75068
Hackberry, *Garza* 79356
Hackberry, *Lavaca* 78956
Hagansport 75487
Hagerman 75090
Hagerville 75847
Hail 75492
Hainesville 75773
Halbert 75973
Hale Center 79041
Halesboro 75417
Halfway 79072
Hall, *Marion* 75657
Hall, *San Saba* 76871
Hallettsville 77964
Halls Bluff 75835
Hallsburg 76705
Halls Store 71007
Hallsville 75650
Halsell 76365
Haltom City 76117
Hamby 79601
Hamilton 76531
Hamlin 79520
Hamon 78629
Hampton 75936
Hamshire 77622
Hancock Oak Hills 78130
Hancock Shopping Center (Part of Austin) 78751
Handley (Part of Fort Worth)‡ 76124
Hankamer 77560
Hannibal 76401
Hanover 76520
Hansford 79081
Happy 79042
Happy Hill 76009
Happy Union 79072
Happy Valley 79566
Harbin 76446
Harbor Grove (Part of Hickory Creek) 75065
Harborlight 75948
Hardin 77561
Hardy 76265
Hare 76574
Hargill 78549
Harker Heights 76542-43
76548
For specific ZIP Codes call (888) 275-8777, or your local postmaster.
Harkeyville 76877
Harlandale (Part of San Antonio)‡ 78214
Harlem 77469
Harleton 75651
Harlingen 78550-53
For specific ZIP Codes call (888) 275-8777, or your local postmaster.
Harmon 75446
Harmony, *Anderson* 75801
Harmony, *Parker* 76087
Harmony, *Rusk* 75684
Harmony Grove 77340
Harmony Hill 75691
Harper 78631
Harriet 76901
Harrisburg (Part of Houston)‡ 77012
Harrisburg, *Jasper* 75951
Harrison 76682
Harrold 76364
Hart 79043
Hartburg 77630
Hart Camp 79339
Hartley 79044
Harts Bluff 75455
Hart Spur (Part of Hurst) 76053
Hartzo 75657
Harvard 75686
Harvest Acres, *Montgomery* 77372
Harvest Acres, *Tom Green* 76905
Harvest Heights 77088
Harvey 77845
Harwood 78632
Haskell 79521
Haslam 75954
Haslet 76052
Hasse 76442
Hatchel 79567
Hatchetville 75437
Havana 78572
Hawkins 75765
Hawkinsville 77414
Hawley 79525
Hawthorne 77358
Hawthorn Place (Part of Houston) 77076
Hayden 75169
Haynesville 76360
Hays 78666
Hazy Hollow 77354
Headlea Estates (Part of Odessa) 79762
Headsville 76653
Heald 79057
Hearne 77859
Heath 75032
Hebbronville♦ 78361
Hebco (Part of San Antonio) 78218
Hebron 75056
Heckville 79329
Hedley 79237
Hedwig Village 77024
Heidelberg 78570
Heidenheimer 76533
Heights (Part of Houston)‡ 77248
Heights (Part of Texas City) 77590
Helena 78118
Helmic 75845
Helotes 78023
Hemphill 75948
Hempstead 77445
Henderson 75652-54
For specific ZIP Codes call (888) 275-8777, or your local postmaster.
Henderson Chapel 76866
Henderson Heights 79763
Henkhaus 77984
Henly 78620
Henning 75946
Henrietta 76365
Henrys Chapel 75789
Hereford 79045
Heritage Northwest 78245
Heritage Oaks 77365
Hermleigh 79526
Herring (Part of San Angelo) 76901
Herty (Part of Lufkin) 75901
Hewitt 76643
Hext 76848
Hickey 75667
Hickory Creek, *Denton* 75065
Hickory Creek, *Hunt* 75423
Hickory Hill 75686
Hickory Hills 77356
Hickory Hollow 75929
Hickston 78959
Hico 76457
Hidalgo 78557
Hidden Echo 77336
Hidden Forest (Part of San Antonio) 78232
Hidden Hill 75065
Hidden Hills Harbor 75147
Hidden Valley (Part of Houston) 77088
Hide-A-Way Lake 75771
Higginbotham 79360
Higgins 79046
Highbank 76680
High Hill 78956
High Island 77623
Highland, *Erath* 76446
Highland, *Johnson* 76031
Highland Acres (Part of Houston) 77088
Highland Acres, *Grayson* 75076
Highland Acres, *Hunt* 75453
Highland Addition, *Parker* 76082
Highland Creek Lakes 78736
Highland Estates (Part of Victoria) 77904
Highland Haven 78654
Highland Hills (Part of Dallas)‡ 75241
Highland Hills (Part of San Antonio)‡ 78223
Highland Mall (Part of Austin) 78752
Highland Park 75205
Highland Range Estates 76901
Highlands♦ 77562
Highland Village 75077
Highland Waters 78003
Highpoint 77093
Highsaw 75763
Hi Ho 77630
Hiland Shores 75076
Hill and Dale Acres 77372
Hill City 76476
Hill Country Village 78232
Hillcrest Village 77511
Hillebrandt 77705
Hillister 77624
Hillje 77455
Hills 78659
Hillsboro 76645
Hillside Estates 75763
Hillside Gardens 77039
Hilltop, *Gillespie* 78624
Hilltop, *Grayson* 75020
Hilltop Acres 78253
Hilltop Lakes 77871
Hilshire Village 77055
Hinckley 75460
Hindes 78026
Hines 76384
Hinkles Ferry 77422
Hiram 75161
Hitchcock 77563
Hitchland 73942
Hoard 75773
Hobbs 79526
Hobson 78117
Hochheim 77967
Hockley 77447
Hodges 79525
Hodgson 75559
Hoen 76691
Hogan Acres 76028
Hogansville 75410
Hogg 77836
Holiday Beach 78382
Holiday Estates 75169
Holiday Harbor 75630
Holiday Hills 75453
Holiday Hills Estates 76424
Holiday Lake Estates 77335
Holiday Lakes 77515
Holiday Oaks 77372
Holland, *Bell* 76534
Holland, *Hardin* 77625
Holland Quarters 75633
Holliday 76366
Hollis 77864
Hollowa Heights (Part of Houston) 77047
Holly 75851
Holly Grove 77351
Holly Springs, *Camp* 75686
Holly Springs, *Jasper* 75951
Holly Springs, *Nacogdoches* 75946
Holly Springs, *Van Zandt* 75754
Holly Terrace 77365
Hollywood Addition 77627
Hollywood Heights 77627
Hollywood Park 78232
Holman 78962
Holt 76872
Homer, *Angelina* 75901
Homer, *Jasper* 75951
Homewood 75951
Hondo 78861
Honea 77356
Honey Grove, *Cass* 75551
Honey Grove, *Fannin* 75446
Honey Island 77625
Hood 76240
Hooks 75561
Hoover 79065
Hoovers Valley 78611
Hope 77995
Hopewell, *Franklin* 75457
Hopewell, *Houston* 75835
Hopewell, *Leon* 75833
Horizon City 79927
Horn Hill 76642
Horseshoe Bay♦ 78654
Horseshoe Bay South 78654
Horseshoe Bay West 78654
Horseshoe Falls 78130
Hortense 77351
Horton, *Delta* 75428
Horton, *Jasper* 75951
Horton, *Panola* 75639
Hostyn 78945
Hot Wells 79851
Houmont Park 77044
Houseman Addition 77662

Houston

77001-99
77101-99
77201-93
For specific ZIP Codes call (888) 275-8777, or your local postmaster.

Colleges & Universities

Baylor Coll of Medicine 77030
Houston Baptist Univ 77074
Houston Graduate School of Theology 77004
Rice Univ 77251
South Texas Coll of Law 77002
Texas Southern Univ 77004
Univ of Houston 77204
Univ of Houston-Clear Lake 77058
Univ of Houston-Downtown 77002
Univ of Saint Thomas 77006
Univ of Texas Health Science Ctr 77225

Financial Institutions

Bank of America, NA 77065
Bank One, NA 77002
Comerica Bank 77020
Compass Bank 77002
Frost Nat Bank 77251
NationsBank, NA 77002

Hospitals

Hermann Hosp 77030
Memorial Hosp-Memorial City 77024
Memorial Hosp-Southwest 77089
Methodist Hosp 77030
St Luke's Episcopal Hosp 77030
Texas Children's Hosp 77030
Univ of Texas M D Anderson Cancer Ctr 77030
Veterans Affairs Med Ctr 77030

Hotels/Motels

Adam's Mark 77042
Crowne Plaza, Galleria Area 77027
Four Seasons 77010
Hobby Airport Hilton 77061
Holiday Inn Intercontinental Airport 77032
Holiday Inn Select 77079
Hyatt Regency Downtown 77002
Lexington Suites 77090
Marriott, Airport 77032
Marriott, JW at Galleria 77056
Marriott, Med Ctr 77030
Marriott North 77060
Marriott Westside 77079
Omni 77056
Post Oak Doubletree 77056
Renaissance 77046
Sheraton, Astrodome 77054
Sheraton, Brookhollow 77092
Westin Galleria 77056
Wyndham Greenspoint 77060

Military Installations

Coast Guard Air Sta 77034
Joint Personal Property Shipping Off 77034
NASA Lyndon B Johnson Space Ctr 77058
Texas Air Nat Guard, FB6433, Ellington Field 77034

Howard 75165
Howardwick 79226
Howe 75459
Howland 75460
Hoxie 76574
Hoyt (Part of Alba) 75410
Hoyte 76520
Hub 79035
Hubbard 76648
Huckabay 76401
Hudson 75904
Hudson Oaks 76087
Huffines 75555
Huffman 77336
Hufsmith 77337
Hughes Springs 75656
Hughey 75662
Hulen Mall (Part of Fort Worth) 76132
Hulen Park (Part of Texas City) 77590
Hull 77564
Humble 77325
77338-39
77345-47
77396
For specific ZIP Codes call (888) 275-8777, or your local postmaster.
Humble Camp 77396
Humble Estates (Part of Houston) 77396
Hungerford 77448
Hunt 78024
Hunter 78130
Hunters Creek Village 77024
Hunters Retreat 77355
Huntington 75949
Huntsville 77340-42
For specific ZIP Codes call (888) 275-8777, or your local postmaster.
Hurnville 76365
Huron 76692
Hurst 76053-54
For specific ZIP Codes call (888) 275-8777, or your local postmaster.
Hurstown 75973
Hurst Springs 76634
Hutchins 75141
Hutto 78634
Huxley 75973
Huxley Bay 75973
Hye 78635
Hylton 79506
Iago 77420
Ida 75491
Idalou 79329
Idyle Hour Acres 78728
Ike 75165
Illinois Bend 76265
Impact 79603
Imperial 79743
Imperial Valley (Part of Houston) 77060
Inadale 79545
Independence 77833
India 75125
Indian Creek 76801
Indian Gap 76531
Indian Harbor Estates 76048
Indian Hill 75977
Indian Hills 78006
Indian Lake, *Cameron* 78586
Indian Lake, *Newton* 77630
Indian Lodge 76652
Indian Oaks, *Henderson* 75163
Indian Oaks, *Waller* 77466
Indianola 77979
Indian Rock 75644
Indian Shores 77532
Indian Springs 77351
Indian Trails (Part of Victoria) 77904
Indian Village 77351
Indian Waters 78003
Indian Woods 77355
Industrial (Part of Dallas)‡ 75207
Industry 78944
Inez♦ 77968
Ingleside 78362
Ingleside Naval Station 78362
Ingleside on the Bay 78362
Ingram 78025
Ingram Park Mall (Part of San Antonio) 78238
Inks Lake Village 78609

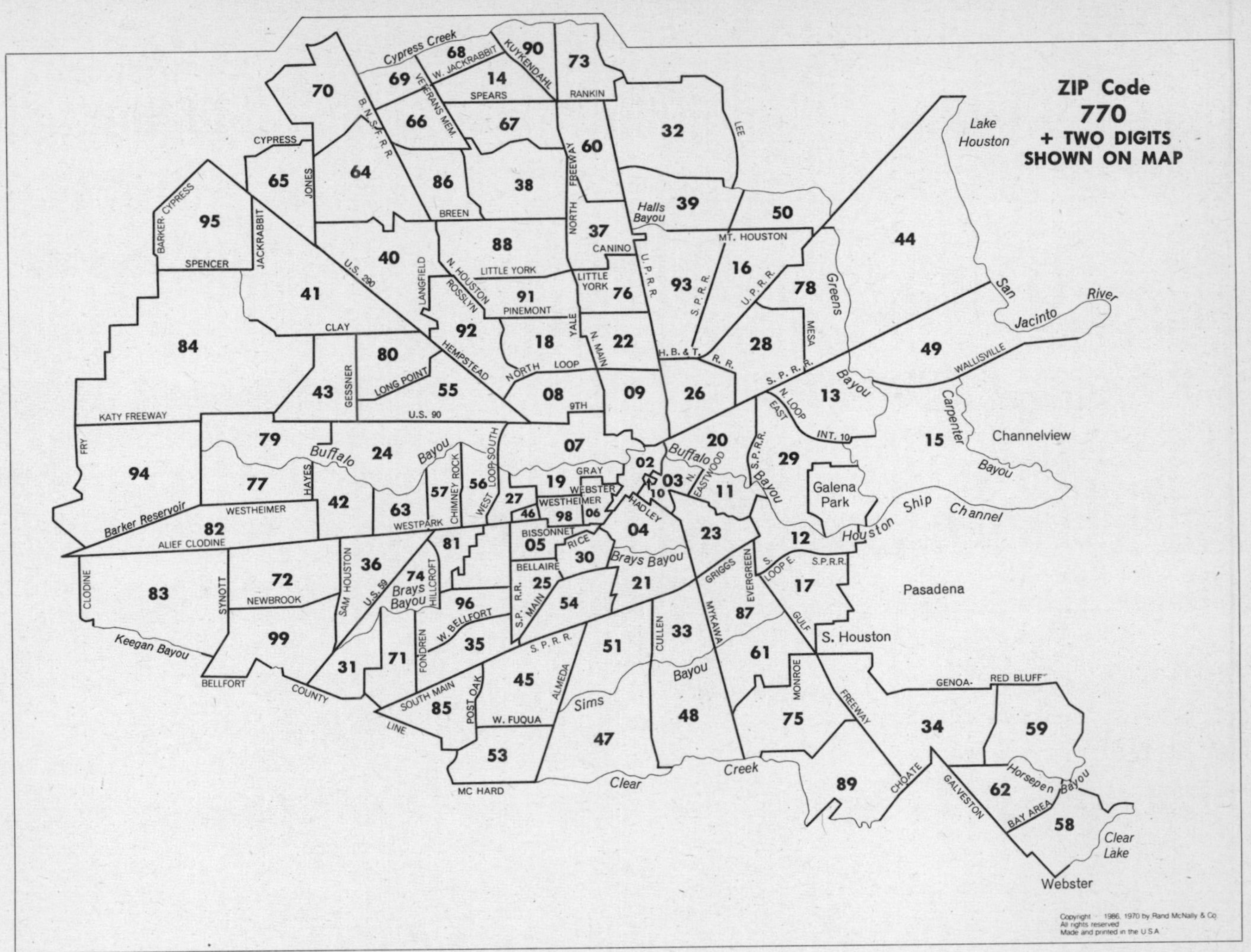
ZIP Code
770
+ TWO DIGITS
SHOWN ON MAP
Lake Houston
San Jacinto River
Channelview
Carpenter Bayou
Houston Ship Channel
Pasadena
Galena Park
S. Houston
Greens Bayou
Halls Bayou
Cypress Creek
Buffalo Bayou
Brays Bayou
Sims Bayou
Clear Creek
Horsepen Bayou
Clear Lake
Webster
Barker Reservoir
Keegan Bayou
70
69
68
90
73
14
66
67
60
32
65
64
86
38
39
50
44
95
40
88
37
93
16
78
41
91
76
92
18
22
28
49
84
80
43
55
08
09
26
13
15
79
24
07
20
29
94
77
42
63
57
56
27
19
02
03
10
11
82
46
98
06
04
23
12
05
30
83
72
36
74
81
25
21
17
96
54
87
99
35
33
51
61
31
71
45
85
48
75
34
59
47
53
89
62
58
CYPRESS
JONES
BARKER-CYPRESS
SPENCER
JACKRABBIT
U.S. 290
CLAY
LANGFIELD
GESSNER
LONG POINT
HEMPSTEAD
U.S. 90
KATY FREEWAY
FRY
HAYES
WESTHEIMER
ALIEF CLODINE
CLODINE
SYNOTT
NEWBROOK
BELLFORT
COUNTY
LINE
B. N. S. F. R. R.
VETERANS MEM.
W. JACKRABBIT
KUYKENDAHL
SPEARS
RANKIN
BREEN
NORTH FREEWAY
LEE
N. HOUSTON ROSSLYN
LITTLE YORK
PINEMONT
YALE
N. MAIN
NORTH LOOP
9TH
CANINO
LITTLE YORK
U. P. R. R.
S. P. R. R.
MT. HOUSTON
U. P. R. R.
MESA
H. B. & T. R. R.
S. P. R. R.
WALLISVILLE
N. LOOP EAST
INT. 10
S.P.R.R.
EASTWOOD
N.
GRAY
WEBSTER
WESTHEIMER
CHIMNEY ROCK
WEST LOOP-SOUTH
WESTPARK
BISSONNET
RICE
BELLAIRE
HADLEY
SAM HOUSTON
U.S. 59
HILLCROFT
FONDREN
W. BELLFORT
S.P. R.R. MAIN
S. P. R. R.
SOUTH MAIN
POST OAK
ALMEDA
W. FUQUA
MC HARD
CULLEN
MYKAWA
GRIGGS
EVERGREEN
S. LOOP E.
S.P.R.R.
GULF FREEWAY
MONROE
GENOA-RED BLUFF
CHOATE
GALVESTON
BAY AREA
Copyright © 1986, 1970 by Rand McNally & Co.
All rights reserved
Made and printed in the U.S.A.

Place	ZIP
Inwood (Part of Dallas)‡	75209
Inwood Forest (Part of Houston)	77088
Iola	77861
Iowa Colony	77583
Iowa Park	76367
Ira	79527
Iraan	79744
Irby	79521
Iredell	76649
Ireland	76538
Irene	76650
Ironton	75766
Irving	75014-17
	75038-39
	75060-63
For specific ZIP Codes call (888) 275-8777, or your local postmaster.	
Irving Mall (Part of Irving)	75062
Irvington (Part of Houston)‡	77022
Island (Part of Galveston)	77550
Island, *Madison*	75852
Italy	76651
Itasca	76055
Ivan	76424
Ivanhoe	75447
Iveys Crossing	79853
Ivy	76854
Izoro	76522
Jacinto City	77029
Jack D Watson (Part of Fort Worth)‡	76161
Jacksboro	76458
Jackson, *Marion*	75657
Jackson, *Shelby*	75954
Jackson, *Van Zandt*	75103
Jacksonville	75766
Jacobia	75401
Jamaica Beach	77554
James	75935
James Griffith (Part of Houston)‡	77080
James Moody (Part of Victoria)‡	77904
Jamestown, *Newton*	75966
Jamestown, *Smith*	75140
Jardin	75428
Jarrell	76537
Jasper	75951
Jasper Heights (Part of Marshall)	75670
Jayton	79528
Jean	76374
Jeddo	78953
Jefferson	75657
Jefferson City Shopping Center (Part of Port Arthur)	77640
Jefferson Heights (Part of San Angelo)	76901
Jenkins	75638
Jennings	75462
Jensen Drive (Part of Houston)‡	77026
Jensens Point	77465
Jericho	79226
Jermyn	76459
Jerrys Quarters	77833
Jersey Village	77040
Jerusalem	77422
Jewett	75846
J. Frank Dobie (Part of San Antonio)‡	78220
Jiba	75142
Joaquin	75954
Joe Pool (Part of Dallas)‡	75244
John Dunlop (Part of Houston)‡	77063
John Foster (Part of Pasadena)‡	77502
Johnson	79316
Johnson City	78636
Johnsons Station (Part of Arlington)	76015
Johnstown	75169
Johnsville	76401
Johntown	75417
Joiner	78945
Joinerville	75658
Joliet	78648
Jolly	76303
Jollyville	78729
Jonah	78626
Jones	75140
Jonesboro	76538
Jones Creek, *Brazoria*	77541
Jones Creek, *Wharton*	77437
Jones Prairie	76520
Jonestown	78645
Jonesville	75659
Joplin	76458
Joppa	78605
Jordan (Part of Amarillo)‡	79159
Josephine	75164
Joshua	76058
Josserand	75845
Jot 'Em Down	75469
Jourdanton	78026
Joy, *Clay*	76365
Joy, *Smith*	75647
Jozye	77864
Juanita Craft (Part of Dallas)‡	75315
	75371
For specific ZIP Codes call (888) 275-8777, or your local postmaster.	
Jubilee Springs	76502
Jud	79544
Judson	75660
Juliff	77583
Julius Melcher (Part of Houston)‡	77027
Jumbo	75669
Junction	76849
Juno	76943
Justiceburg	79330
Justin	76247
Kadane Corner	76360
Kalgary	79370
Kamay	76369
Kamey	77979
Kanawha	75436
Karen	77355
Karnack	75661
Karnes City	78118
Katemcy	76825
Katy	77449-50
	77491-94
For specific ZIP Codes call (888) 275-8777, or your local postmaster.	
Kaufman	75142
Kayare (Part of Harlingen)	78550
Keechi	75831
Keenan	77356
Keene	76059
Keeter	76023
Keith	77861
Keller	76244†
	76248*
Kellerville	79057
Kelly	75409
Kellyville	75657
Kelsey	75644
Kelton	79096
Keltys (Part of Lufkin)‡	75903
Kemah	77565
Kemp	75143
Kempner	76539
Kendalia	78027
Kendleton	77451
Kenedy	78119
Kenefick	77535
Kennard	75847
Kennedale	76060
Kenney	77452
Kensing	75450
Kent	79855
Kentuckytown	75491
Kenwood Place	77039
Kerens	75144
Kermit	79745
Kerrick	79051
Kerrville	78028*
	78029†
Kessler Park (Part of Dallas)	75208
Kevin	77327
Key	79331
Key Ranch Estates	75163
Kickapoo	75763
Kildare	75562
Kildare Junction	75555
Kilgore	75662*
	75663†
Killeen	76540-48
For specific ZIP Codes call (888) 275-8777, or your local postmaster.	
Killeen Mall (Part of Killeen)	76543
Kilowatt (Part of Orange)	77630
Kimball	76652
Kimbro	78653
Kinard Estates	77630
King, *Coryell*	76528
King, *Red River*	75550
King City (Part of Cleveland)	77327
King Ranch	78363
Kingsbury	78638
Kings Cove	78611
Kingsland	78639
Kingsland Estates	78639
Kingsley (Part of Garland)‡	75041
Kings Mill	79065
Kings Point	78073
Kingston	75401
Kings Village	78727
Kingsville	78363*
	78364†
Kingsville Naval Station	78363
Kingswood	75104
Kingtown	75961
Kingwood‡	77339
Kinkler	77964
Kiomatia	75436
Kirby	78219
Kirbyville	75956
Kirkland	79201
Kirkpatrick Addition	75704
Kirtley	78957
Kirvin	75848
Kittrell	75862
Kleberg (Part of Dallas)‡	75253
Klein	77379
Klondike, *Dawson*	79331
Klondike, *Delta*	75448
Klump	77833
Knapp	79527
Knickerbocker	76939
Knippa	78870
Knob Hill	75068
Knollwood	75090
Knott	79748
Knox City	79529
Koerth	77964
Kohrville	77070
Kokomo	76454
Komensky	77975
Kona Kai	77650
Kopernik Shores	78520
Kopperl	76652
Kosciusko	78160
Kosse	76653
Kountze	77625
Kovar	78941
Kress	79052
Kreutzberg	78006
Krugerville	76227
Krum	76249
Kubala Store	78164
Kurten	77862
Kuykendahl Village (Part of Houston)‡	77068
Kyle	78640
Kyote	78005
Labatt	78114
La Blanca	78558
La Casita	78582
Laceola	77864
Lackland Heights	78227
Lackland Terrace (Part of San Antonio)	78227
LaCoste	78039
La Cuchilla (Part of Mission)	78572
Lacy	75845
Lacy-Lakeview	76705
Ladonia	75449
LaFayette	75686
La Feria	78559
Lagarto	78022
La Gloria	78591
Lago	78586
Lago Vista	78645
La Grange	78945
Laguna Heights♦	78578
Laguna Park	76634
Laguna Tres Estates	76049
Laguna Vista	78578
Laguna Vista Estates	75751
La Hacienda Estates	78759
Laird Hill	75666
Lajitas	79852
La Joya	78560
La Junta	76020
Lake Air Center (Part of Waco)	76710
Lake Barbara (Part of Clute)	77531
Lake Bonanza	77356
Lake Bridgeport	76426
Lake Brownwood♦	76801
Lake Chateau Woods	77302
Lake Cherokee	75652
Lake City	78387
Lake Conroe Forrest	77301
Lake Conroe West	77301
Lake Corsicana (Part of Corsicana)	75110
Lake Creek	75450
Lake Creek Estates	77354
Lake Dallas	75065
Lake Forest (Part of Houston)	77078
Lake Gardens	76901
Lake Halbert (Part of Corsicana)	75110
Lake Highlands (Part of Dallas)‡	75238
Lakehills♦	78063
Lake Jackson	77566
Lake Jackson Farms	77566
Lake Kiowa	76240
Lakeland	77302
Lakeland Heights (Part of Grand Prairie)	75050
Lakeland Park	78759
Lake Livingston	77376
Lake Meredith Estates	79036
Lake Pauline	79252
Lake Placid	78155
Lakeport	75603
Lake Ransom Canyon Village	79366
Lake Rolling Wood	77301
Lake Shadows	77532
Lake Shore	76801
Lakeshore Estates	75630
Lakeshore Estates West	75630
Lake Shore Gardens	78368
Lakeside (Part of League City)	77565
Lakeside, *San Patricio*	78368
Lakeside, *Tarrant*	76108
Lakeside Acres	78006
Lakeside Beach	78669
Lakeside City	76308
Lakeside Heights	78639
Lakeside Park	77530
Lakeside Village	76671
Lake Splendora	77372
Lake Tanglewood	79118
Lake Tejas	77071
Lake Thomas	79527
Laketon	79065
Lake Victor	76550
Lakeview (Part of Port Arthur)	77640
Lakeview (Part of San Angelo)	76903
Lakeview (Part of Waco)	76705
Lakeview, *Cherokee*	75766
Lakeview, *Floyd*	79235
Lakeview, *Hall*	79239
Lakeview, *Lynn*	79345
Lakeview, *Orange*	77662
Lakeview, *Swisher*	79088
Lakeview Estates, *Johnson*	76031
Lakeview Estates, *Orange*	77662
Lakeview Estates, *Van Zandt*	75169
Lakeview Hills	78645
Lake View Park	78130
Lakeway	78734
Lake Whitney Estates	76692
Lake Wildwood	77302
Lakewood (Part of Dallas)‡	75214
	75359
For specific ZIP Codes call (888) 275-8777, or your local postmaster.	
Lakewood (Part of Baytown)	77520
Lakewood (Part of Vidor)	77662
Lakewood, *San Augustine*	75929
Lakewood Estates	77304
Lakewood Forest	78639
Lakewood Harbor	76634
Lakewood Heights (Part of Houston)	77336
Lakewood Hills, *Comal*	78130
Lakewood Hills, *Hood*	76049
Lakewood Village	76205
Lake Worth	76135*
	76136†
Lamar	78382
Lamar Park (Part of Corpus Christi)‡	78411
La Marque	77568
Lamar University (Part of Beaumont)‡	77710
Lamasco	75488
Lamesa	79331
Lamkin	76455
Lampasas	76550
Lamplight Village	78758
Lanark	75572
Lancaster	75134
	75146
For specific ZIP Codes call (888) 275-8777, or your local postmaster.	
Lancaster (Part of El Paso)	79907
Landa Park Highlands (Part of New Braunfels)	78130
Lane	75423
Lane City	77453
Lanely	75831
Laneport	76574
Lane Prairie	76058
Laneville	75667
Langtry	78871
Lanham	76538
Lanier	75563
Lannius	75438
Lantana	78586
La Paloma	78586
La Plaza (Part of McAllen)	78503
La Porte	77571*
	77572†
La Pryor♦	78872
La Puerta	78582
Laredo	78040-46
For specific ZIP Codes call (888) 275-8777, or your local postmaster.	
La Reforma	78536
Lariat	79325
Larue	75770
La Salle, *Calhoun*	77979
La Salle, *Jackson*	77969
Lasara	78561
Las Colinas (Part of Irving)‡	75014
Las Milpas	78577
Las Rusias	78586
Lassater	76630
Las Yescas	78586
Latch	75644
Latexo	75849
La Tina	78586
Latium	77835
Latonia	77422
Laughlin Air Force Base	78843
Laureles	78586
Laurel Heights (Part of San Antonio)‡	78212
Lavada	75487
La Vernia	78121
La Villa	78562
Lavon	75166
Lavon Beach Estates	75442
La Ward	77970
Lawn	79530
Lawrence	75160
Lawrence Park (Part of Amarillo)	79109
Lawrence Springs	75140
Lawson	75149
Lazare	79252
Lazbuddie	79053
Leaday	76888
League City	77573*
	77574†
Leagueville	75778
Leakey	78873
Leander	78641
	78645-46
For specific ZIP Codes call (888) 275-8777, or your local postmaster.	
Leary	75501
Leasure Acres	76528
Lebanon	75035
Ledbetter	78946
Ledbetter Hills (Part of Dallas)	75211
Leedale	76569
Leesburg	75451
Leesville	78122
Lefors	79054
Leggett	77350
Legion (Part of Kerrville)‡	78028
Lehman	79346
Leigh	75661
Lela	79079
Lelia Lake	79240
Leming	78050
Lena	78963
Lenorah	79749
Lenz	78118
Leo, *Cooke*	76234
Leo, *Lee*	78947
Leona	75850
Leonard	75452

*** Area Zip Code** **† Post Office Boxes** **‡ Postal Station** **♦ Census Designated Place** *Italic Type* **County**

Leon Junction 76552
Leon Springs 78229
Leon Valley 78238
Leroy 76654
Lesley 79239
Letney Park 75951
Le Tourneau (Part of Longview) 75601
Levelland 79336*
79338†
Leveretts Chapel 75684
Levi 76655
Levita 76528
Lewis Addition 77465
Lewisville 75022
75027-29
75056-57
75067
75077
For specific ZIP Codes call (888) 275-8777, or your local postmaster.
Lexington 78947
Lexington Woods 77373
Liberty, *Hamilton* 76531
Liberty, *Liberty* 77575
Liberty, *Lubbock* 79401
Liberty, *Newton* 75966
Liberty, *Rusk* 75652
Liberty City♦ 75647
Liberty Grove 75098
Liberty Hill, *Houston* 75844
Liberty Hill, *Milam* 76567
Liberty Hill, *Titus* 75455
Liberty Hill, *Williamson* 78642
Liggett (Part of Irving) 75060
Lilac 76577
Lilbert 75760
Lillian 76061
Lily Grove 75961
Lily Island 75934
Lincoln 78948
Lincoln City (Part of Houston) 77088
Lincoln Park 76227
Lindale 75771
Linden 75563
Lindenau 77954
Lindenwood 77630
Lindsay 76250
Lindsay Addition 79772
Lingleville 76461
Link Five (Part of La Porte) 77571
Linkwood Addition 76008
Linn 78563
Linn Flat 75961
Linwood 75925
Lipan 76462
Lipscomb 79056
Lisbon (Part of Dallas) 75216
Lissie 77454
Littig 78621
Little Boy 77662
Little Elm 75068
Littlefield 79339
Little Flock 77879
Little Hope 75494
Little Mexico 79735
Little New York 78629
Little Ridge 75121
Little River 76554
Little Rock 77625
Lively 75143
Live Oak, *Bexar* 78233
Liveoak, *Palo Pinto* 76472
Live Oak Ranchettes 78641
Liverpool 77577
Livingston 77351
Llano 78643
Lobo 79855
Locker 76871
Lockett 76384
Lockettville 79358
Lockhart 78644
Lockhill (Part of San Antonio)‡ 78230*
78278†
Lockney 79241
Locust 75076
Locust Grove 79014
Lodi 75564
Loeb 77657
Loebau 78948
Logan, *Marion* 75657
Logan, *Panola* 71049
Logan Heights (Part of El Paso) 79904
Log Cabin 75148
Log Cabin Estates 75148
Lohn 76852
Loire 78064
Lois 76272
Lolaville 75034
Lolita 77971
Lollipop 75763
Loma 77876
Loma Alta, *McMullen* 78072
Loma Alta, *Val Verde* 78840
Loma Terrace (Part of El Paso) 79907
Loma Vista 78829
Lomax (Part of La Porte) 77571
Lomax, *Howard* 79720
Lometa 76853
London 76854
Lone Camp 76484
Lone Cedar 76626
Lone Elm 75167
Lone Grove 78643
Lone Mountain 75644
Lone Oak, *Bexar* 78101
Lone Oak, *Colorado* 78940
Lone Oak, *Erath* 76446
Lone Oak, *Hunt* 75453
Lone Pine 75801
Lone Star, *Floyd* 79241
Lone Star, *Kaufman* 75142
Lone Star, *Morris* 75668
Lone Star, *Titus* 75558
Long Branch 75669
Longfellow 79848
Longford Place 77630
Long Hollow 77865
Long Lake, *Anderson* 75801
Long Lake, *Montgomery* 77355
Long Mott 77972
Long Point (Part of Houston)‡ 77055
Long Point, *Harrison* 75661
Long Point, *Washington* 77835
Longview 75601-15
For specific ZIP Codes call (888) 275-8777, or your local postmaster.
Longview Heights 75601
Longview Mall (Part of Longview) 75601
Longworth 79543
Lonoke Place 77093
Looneyville 75760
Loop 79342
Lopeno 78564
Lopezville♦ 78589
Loraine 79532
Lorena 76655
Lorenzo 79343
Los Angeles 78014
Los Barreras 78582
Los Campos 78840
Los Ebanos 78565
Los Fresnos 78566
Los Indios 78567
Los Jardines (Part of San Antonio)‡ 78237
Losoya 78221
Los Ricos Pobres 78013
Los Saenz (Part of Roma) 78584
Lost Lakes 77357
Los Velas 78582
Los Ybanez 79331
Lott 76656
Louise 77455
Love Chapel 75656
Lovelace 76645
Lovelady 75851
Lovell Lake 77706
Loving 76460
Lowake 76855
Lowry Crossing 75069
Loyola Beach 78379
Lozano 78568
Lubbock 79401-64
79490-99
For specific ZIP Codes call (888) 275-8777, or your local postmaster.
Lucas 75002
Luckenbach 78624
Lucky Ridge 76023
Lueders 79533
Luella 75090
Lufkin 75901-15
For specific ZIP Codes call (888) 275-8777, or your local postmaster.
Luling 78648
Lull 78539
Lumberton 77657
77711
For specific ZIP Codes call (888) 275-8777, or your local postmaster.
Lums Chapel 79339
Lund 78621
Luther 79720
Lutie 79079
Lydia 75554
Lyford 78569
Lynchburg 77520
Lyndon B. Johnson Space Center 77058
Lynn Grove 77868
Lyons 77863
Lytle 78052
Lytton Springs 78616
Mabank 75147
Mabelle 76380
Mabry 75426
McAdoo 79243
McAllen 78501-05
For specific ZIP Codes call (888) 275-8777, or your local postmaster.
McBeth 77515
McCamey 79752
McCaulley 79534
McClanahan 76661
McCook 78539
McCoy, *Atascosa* 78053
McCoy, *Floyd* 79235
McCoy, *Panola* 75643
McCreless Mall (Part of San Antonio)‡ 78223
McDade 78650
McDade Estates 77304
Macdona 78054
Macedonia, *Austin* 77474
Macedonia, *Bowie* 75501
Macedonia, *Brazoria* 77422
Macedonia, *Liberty* 77327
McElroy 75968
McFaddin 77973
McGalin 77612
McGee Landing 75948
McGregor 76657
McKenzie 75630
McKibben 79081
McKinney 75069-70
For specific ZIP Codes call (888) 275-8777, or your local postmaster.
McKnight 75654
McLean 79057
McLendon (Part of McLendon-Chisholm) 75032
McLendon-Chisholm 75032
McLeod 75565
McMahan 78616
McMillin 76877
McNair 77520
McNair Village 76544
McNary 79839
McNeil, *Caldwell* 78648
McNeil, *Travis* 78651
Macon 75457
McQueeney♦ 78123
Mc Rea Lake 77302
Macune 75972
Macy 77882
Madero 78572
Madisonville 77864
Madras 75426
Magasco 75968
Magic (Part of San Antonio)‡ 78229
78280
For specific ZIP Codes call (888) 275-8777, or your local postmaster.
Magnet 77488
Magnolia 77353-55
For specific ZIP Codes call (888) 275-8777, or your local postmaster.
Magnolia Beach 77979
Magnolia Bend 77302
Magnolia Gardens 77044
Magnolia Hills 77354
Magnolia Park (Part of Houston) 77011-12
For specific ZIP Codes call (888) 275-8777, or your local postmaster.
Magnolia Springs 75956
Magpetco (Part of Port Neches) 77651
Mahl 75961
Mahomet 78605
Mahoney 75482
Main Place (Part of Dallas)‡ 75202*
75250†
Majors 75457
Malakoff 75148
Mallard 76251
Mall Del Norte (Part of Laredo) 78041
Mall of Abilene (Part of Abilene) 79606
Mall of the Mainland (Part of Texas City) 77591
Malone 76660
Malta 75570
Mambrino 76048
Manchaca 78652
Manchester 75412
Manchester (Part of Houston) 77012
Manda 78653
Manheim 78659
Mankin 75163
Mankins 76366
Manor 78653
Mansfield 76063
Manvel 77578
Maple, *Bailey* 79344
Maple, *Red River* 75417
Maple Crest Acres (Part of Vidor) 77662
Maple Springs 75455
Mapleton 75835
Marathon 79842
Marble Falls 78654
78657
For specific ZIP Codes call (888) 275-8777, or your local postmaster.
March Trailer Court 75169
Marfa 79843
Margaret 79227
Marie 76933
Marietta 75566
Marilee 75058
Marion 78124
Markham♦ 77456
Markley 76460
Marlin 76661
Marquez 77865
Marshall 75670-72
For specific ZIP Codes call (888) 275-8777, or your local postmaster.
Marshall Creek 76262
Marshall Ford 78732
Marshall Meadows (Part of San Antonio) 78240
Marshall Springs 75455
Mart 76664
Martindale 78655
Martinez 78219
Martin Luther King (Part of Houston)‡ 77033*
77233†
Martins Mills 75754
Martin Springs 75482
Martinsville 75958
Marvin 75462
Maryneal 79535
Marysville 76252
Mason 76856
Mason Lake Estates 77327
Massey Lake 75861
Masterson 79058
Matador 79244
Matagorda 77457
Mathews 77434
Mathis 78368
Matinburg 75686
Maud 75567
Mauriceville 77626
Maverick 76865
Maxdale 76542
Maxey 75421
Maxwell 78656
May 76857
Maydelle 75772
Mayfair (Part of Houston) 77087
Mayfield, *Hale* 79041
Mayfield, *Hill* 76055
Mayflower, *Newton* 75977
Mayflower, *Rusk* 75691
Mayhill 76205
Maynard 77358
Maypearl 76064
Maysfield 76555
Meador Grove 76557
Meadow 79345
Meadowcreek (Part of San Angelo) 76904
Meadowlakes 78611
Meadowood Acres 78252
Meadows 77477
Mecca 77871
Medical Center (Part of Houston)‡ 77054
Medicine Mound 79252
Medill 75460
Medina 78055
Medio (Part of Houston) 77022
Meeker 77706
Meek Estates 75163
Meeks 76519
Megargel 76370
Megaron (Part of Lubbock)‡ 79423
Melear‡ 76013
76015-17
For specific ZIP Codes call (888) 275-8777, or your local postmaster.
Melissa 75454
Melody Hills (Part of Fort Worth) 76111
Melrose (Part of Kilgore) 75662
Melrose, *Nacogdoches* 75961
Melrose Park (Part of Houston) 77037
Melvin 76858
Memorial City Shopping Center (Part of Houston) 77024
Memorial Park (Part of Houston) 77024
77224
77279
For specific ZIP Codes call (888) 275-8777, or your local postmaster.
Memphis 79245
Menard 76859
Mendoza 78644
Menlow 76621
Mentone 79754
Mentz 78935
Mercedes 78570
Mercer's Gap 76442
Merchandise Mart (Part of Dallas)‡ 75201
Mercury 76872
Mereta 76940
Meridian 76665
Merit 75458
Merkel 79536
Merle 77879
Mertens 76666
Mertzon 76941
Mesa Verde (Part of Amarillo) 79107
Meskill (Part of Texas City)‡ 77590
Mesquite, *Borden* 79351
Mesquite, *Dallas* 75149-50
75180-87
For specific ZIP Codes call (888) 275-8777, or your local postmaster.
Metcalf Gap 76475
Meusebach Creek 78624
Mexia 76667
Mexico 75474
Meyerland Plaza Shopping Center (Part of Houston) 77096
Meyersville 77974
Miami 79059
Mickey 79241
Mico 78056
Midcity 75473
Middleton 75833
Middletowne (Part of Seguin) 78155
Middle Water 79022
Midfield 77458
Midkiff 79755
Mid Lake Village 75948
Midland 79701-12
For specific ZIP Codes call (888) 275-8777, or your local postmaster.
Midland Park Mall (Part of Midland) 79705
Midline 77327
Midlothian 76065
Midway, *Dawson* 79331
Midway, *Fannin* 75418
Midway, *Hill* 76645
Midway, *Jim Wells* 78372
Midway, *Lavaca* 77984
Midway, *Lubbock* 79364
Midway, *Madison* 75852
Midway, *Montgomery* 77327
Midway, *Scurry* 79526
Midway, *Smith* 75792
Midway, *Titus* 75455
Midway, *Upshur* 75644
Midway, *Van Zandt* 75754
Midway Mall (Part of Sherman) 75090
Midyett 75639
Miguel 78005
Milam 75959

Milano 76556
Milburn 76872
Mildred 75110
Mile High 79851
Miles 76861
Milford 76670
Mill Creek 77833
Mill Creek Forest 77355
Miller Grove, *Camp* 75686
Miller Grove, *Hopkins* 75433
Miller's Cove 75455
Millersview 76862
Millett 78014
Millheim 77474
Millican 77866
Millsap 76066
Millsville 78362
Milton 75435
Minden 75680
Mineola 75773
Mineral 78125
Mineral Wells 76067*
... 76068†
Minerva 76567
Mings Chapel 75644
Mingus 76463
Minimaz (Part of Alvin) 77511
Minter 75468
Mirando City 78369
Mission 78572*
... 78573†
Mission Bend♦ 77083
Mission Valley 77905
Missouri City 77459
... 77489
For specific ZIP Codes call (888) 275-8777, or your local postmaster.
Mitchell Avenue (Part of Waco)‡ 76708
Mixon 75789
Mobeetie 79061
Mobile City 75087
Mobile Meadows Park 77600
Mockingbird (Part of Austin)‡ 78745
Moffat 76502
Moffett 75901
Monahans 79756
Monaville 77445
Monkstown 75488
Monroe 75662
Monroe City 77514
Monroe Street (Part of Wichita Falls)‡ 76309
Mont 77964
Montague 76251
Montague Ranch Estates 78003
Montalba 75853
Mont Belvieu 77580
Monte Alto 78538
Montell 78801
Monte Oaks 77357
Monteola 78119
Monterey (Part of Lubbock)‡ 79493
Montgomery 77356
Montgomery Gardens 75708
Monthalia 78614
Monticello 75455
Montopolis (Part of Austin) 78741
Moody 76557
Moonshine Hill 77338
Moore, *Frio* 78057
Moore, *Jasper* 75951
Moore's Chapel 75418
Moores Crossing 78617
Moore Station 75770
Mooreville 76632
Mooring 77801
Morales 77957
Moran 76464
Moravia 78956
Morgan 76671
Morgan Creek 78611
Morgan Mill 76465
Morgan's Point 77571
Morgan's Point Resort 76513
Morningside Heights (Part of El Paso) 79930
Morrill 75925
Morris Ranch 78624
Morse 79062
Morton, *Cochran* 79346
Morton, *Harrison* 75640
Moscow 75960
Mosheim 76689
Moss Bluff 77575
Moss Hill 77575
Mostyn 77354
Moulton 77975
Mound 76558
Mound City 75844
Mountain 76528
Mountain City 78610
Mountain Home 78058
Mountain Peak 76065
Mountain Springs, *Cooke* 76258
Mountain Springs, *Hill* 76645
Mountain Valley Estates 76058
Mountain View (Part of El Paso) 79904
Mount Blanco 79322
Mount Calm 76673
Mount Carmel 76360
Mount Enterprise, *Rusk* 75681
Mount Enterprise, *Wood* 75773
Mount Haven 75766
Mount Houston 77039
... 77050
For specific ZIP Codes call (888) 275-8777, or your local postmaster.
Mount Joy 75441
Mount Lookout 78130
Mount Lucas 78022
Mount Mitchell 75571
Mount Moriah 75571
Mount Olive 77995
Mount Pleasant 75455*
... 75456†
Mount Selman 75757
Mount Sylvan 75771
Mount Union 75956
Mount Vernon 75457
Mozelle 76834
Muddig 75449
Mudville 77801
Muellersville 77833
Muenster 76252
Mulberry 75476
Muldoon 78949
Muleshoe 79047
Mulkey 79027
Mullin 76864
Mullins Prairie 78945
Mumford 77867
Muncy 79241
Munday 76371
Munson 75189
Murchison 75778
Murphy 75094
Murray 76450
Murryhill (Part of Lubbock)‡ 79413
Musgrove 75494
Mustang, *Denton* 76258
Mustang, *Navarro* 75110
Mustang Mott Store 77954
Mustang Ridge 78610
Myra 76253
Myrtle Springs 75169
Naaman (Part of Garland) 75040
Nacalina 75944
Nacogdoches 75961-64
For specific ZIP Codes call (888) 275-8777, or your local postmaster.
Nada 77460
Nadeau (Part of Texas City) 77590
Nancy 75980
Naples 75568
Naruna 76550
Nash, *Bowie* 75569
Nash, *Ellis* 75165
Nassau Bay, *Harris*‡ 77058
Nassau Bay, *Hood* 76049
Nasworthy Hills (Part of San Angelo) 76904
Nat 75760
Natalia 78059
Naval Air (Part of Corpus Christi)‡ 78419
Navarro 75151
Navarro Mills 76679
Navasota 77868-69
For specific ZIP Codes call (888) 275-8777, or your local postmaster.
Navo 76227
Nazareth 79063
Nebgen 78624
Necessity 76424
Nechanitz 78946
Neches 75779
Neches Indian Village 75925
Neches Junction (Part of Port Arthur) 77640
Nederland 77627
Needmore, *Bailey* 79371
Needmore, *Delta* 75448
Needville 77461
Negley 75426
Neinda 79520
Nell 78119
Nelson City 78006
Nelsonville 77418
Nelta 75437
Nemo 76070
Nesbitt, *Harrison* 75670
Nesbitt, *Robertson* 76629
Neuville 75935
Nevada 75173
Newark 76071
New Baden 77870
New Berlin 78121
New Bielau 78962
New Birthright 75482
New Boston 75570
New Braunfels 78130-32
For specific ZIP Codes call (888) 275-8777, or your local postmaster.
New Bremen 78950
Newburg 76442
Newby 75846
New Caney 77357
New Caney Heights 77357
Newcastle 76372
New Chapel Hill 75701
New Clarkson 76570
New Colony 75563
New Corn Hill 76537
New Deal 79350
New Fountain 78861
Newgulf 77462
New Harmony, *Shelby* 75973
New Harmony, *Smith* 75704
Newharp 76239
New Hebron 75685
New Home 79383
New Hope (Part of Sunnyvale) 75149
New Hope, *Cherokee* 75766
New Hope, *Collin* 75069
New Hope, *Henderson* 75756
New Hope, *Jones* 79553
New Hope, *Rusk* 75662
New Hope, *San Jacinto* 77327
New Hope, *Smith* 75703
New Hope, *Wood* 75773
New Katy 78653
Newlin 79245
New London 75682
New Lynn 79381
New Mine 75686
New Moore 79351
Newport, *Clay* 76230
Newport, *Harris* 77532
New Prospect, *Rusk* 75652
New Prospect, *Shelby* 75975
New River Lake Estates 77327
New Salem, *Falls* 76570
New Salem, *Palo Pinto* 76472
New Salem, *Rusk* 75654
Newsome 75451
New Summerfield 75780
New Sweden, *McCulloch* 76825
New Sweden, *Travis* 78653
New Taiton 77437
Newton 75966
New Ulm 78950
New Waverly 77358
New Wehdem 77833
New Willard 77351
New York 75770
Neylandville 75401
Nickel 78629
Nickelberry 75566
Nickel Creek 88220
Niederwald 78640
Nigton 75926
Nimitz (Part of San Antonio)‡ 78216*
... 78279†
Nimrod 76437
Nineveh 75833
Nix 76550
Nixon 78140
Noack 76574
Nobility 75424
Noble 75470
Nockenut 78160
Nocona 76255
Nogalus 75845
Nolan 79537
Nolanville 76559
Nolte 78155
Nome 77629
Nona 77625
Noodle 79536
Noonday 75762
Nopal 78164
Nordheim 78141
Norias 78338
Norman Crossing 76574
Normandy 78877
Normangee 77871
Normanna 78142
Norse 76634
North‡ 75044-45
... 75048
For specific ZIP Codes call (888) 275-8777, or your local postmaster.
North Amarillo (Part of Amarillo)‡ 79117
Northampton 77379
North Austin (Part of Austin)‡ 78751
Northaven (Part of Dallas)‡ 75229
... 75378
For specific ZIP Codes call (888) 275-8777, or your local postmaster.
North Beach (Part of Corpus Christi) 78402
North Bonami 75956
North Branch (Part of Dallas)‡ 75244
North Broadway (Part of San Antonio)‡ 78217
North Caney 75482
North Cedar 75926
North Cleveland 77327
Northcliff 78108
North Concho Lake Estates 76901
Northcrest 76705
Northcrest Estates (Part of Victoria) 77904
Northcross Mall (Part of Austin) 78757
Northeast (Part of Austin)‡ 78752
Northeast Station (Part of Odessa)‡ 79764
Northern Hills 75020
Northfield 79201
Northgate (Part of El Paso)‡ 79914†
... 79924*
Northgate, *Victoria* 77904
North Groesbeck 79252
North Heights (Part of Amarillo) 79107
North Hills Mall (Part of North Richland Hills) 76180
North Houston 77086
North Houston General Mail Facility (Part of Houston)‡ 77315
North Houston Heights 77039
North Lake (Part of Dallas)‡ 75238
Northlake, *Denton* 76247
Northlake Estates 78628
North Line Oaks 77301
Northline Shopping Center (Part of Houston) 77022
Northline Terrace 77037
North Oaks 78753
North Orange Heights 77630
Northpark Center (Part of Dallas)‡ 75225
Northpark Mall (Part of El Paso) 79924
North Port Arthur (Part of Port Arthur)‡ 77642
North Richland Hills 76180*
... 76182†
Northrup 78942
North Rusk (Part of Rusk) 75785
North San Antonio Hills 78253
North Shepherd (Part of Houston)‡ 77088
... 77238
... 77291
For specific ZIP Codes call (888) 275-8777, or your local postmaster.
Northshore Village (Part of Houston) 77015
North Springs 77373
North Star Mall (Part of San Antonio) 78216
Northtown Mall (Part of Dallas) 75234
Northwest (Part of Austin)‡ 78756-57
... 78766
For specific ZIP Codes call (888) 275-8777, or your local postmaster.
Northwest (Part of Dallas)‡ 75220
Northwest Hills 78024
Northwest Mall (Part of Houston) 77292
Northwest Park 77086
Northwood 78758
North Zulch 77872
Norton 76865
Norwood 75972
Notrees 79759
Nottingham Forest 77630
Nottingham Woods 75835
Novice, *Coleman* 79538
Novice, *Lamar* 75462
Novohrad 77975
Noxville 78631
Nugent 79601
Nursery 77976
Oakalla 76542
Oak Canyon 77302
Oak Creek Addition (Part of Grapevine) 76051
Oak Crest Estates 78628
Oak Dale, *Erath* 76401
Oakdale, *Hopkins* 75482
Oak Flat, *Angelina* 75949
Oak Flat, *Nacogdoches* 75760
Oak Flat, *Rusk* 75681
Oak Forest (Part of Austin) 78759
Oak Forest (Part of Houston)‡ 77018
Oak Grove, *Bowie* 75554
Oak Grove, *Camp* 75686
Oak Grove, *Ellis* 75119
Oak Grove, *Kaufman* 75142
Oak Grove, *Tarrant* 76028
Oak Grove, *Wood* 75783
Oak Hill, *Jasper* 75951
Oak Hill, *Johnson* 76031
Oak Hill, *Rusk* 75652
Oak Hill, *Travis*‡ 78735
Oak Hills Acres 77362
Oakhill Station (Part of Austin)‡ 78749
Oakhurst 77359
Oak Island 77514
Oak Lake 76705
Oakland, *Cherokee* 75785
Oakland, *Colorado* 78951
Oakland, *Rusk* 75652
Oakland, *Van Zandt* 75103
Oak Lawn (Part of Dallas)‡ 75219
Oaklawn (Part of Texarkana)‡ 75501
Oak Leaf 75154
Oak Point 75068
Oak Ridge, *Cooke* 76240
Oak Ridge, *Kaufman* 75160
Oak Ridge, *Llano* 78654
Oak Ridge, *Nacogdoches* 75961
Oak Ridge (Part of Weatherford) 76087
Oak Ridge North 77302
Oaks 78119
Oaks North 78260
Oak Terrace 77365
Oak Trail Shores♦ 76048
Oak Valley 75110
Oakview 77611
Oak Village North 78266
Oakville 78060
Oakwilde 77093
Oakwood, *Leon* 75855
Oakwood (Part of Arlington)‡ 76012
Oakwood Village and Westwood Plaza (Part of Abilene) 79603
Oatmeal 78605
O'Brien 79539
Oceanshore 77650
Ocee 76638
Odell 79247
Odell Addition (Part of Grapevine) 76051
Odem 78370
Odessa 79760-69
For specific ZIP Codes call (888) 275-8777, or your local postmaster.
Odom 75147
O'Donnell 79351
Oenaville 76501
O'Farrell 75551
Oglesby 76561

Place	ZIP
Oilla	77630
Oilton	78371
Oklahoma	77355
Oklahoma Flat	79339
Oklahoma Lane	79325
Oklaunion	76373
Okra	76435
Ola	75142
Old Boston	75570
Old Bowling	77865
Old Brazoria (Part of Brazoria)	77422
Old Dime Box	77853
Olden	76466
Oldenburg	78945
Old Ferry	78669
Old Glory	79540
Old Ivy	75847
Old Kinkler	77964
Old Larissa	75757
Old London	75682
Old Mill (Part of Leon Valley)‡	78238
Old Mobeetie (Part of Mobeetie)	79061
Old Moulton	77975
Old Ocean	77463
Old River Lake	77327
Old River Terrace	77530
Old River-Winfree	77520
Olds	75951
Old Sabinetown	75948
Old Salem	75933
Old Union, *Bowie*	75574
Old Union, *Limestone*	76687
Old Union, *Titus*	75455
Old Waverly	77358
Oletha	76687
Olfen	76875
Olin	76457
Olive	77625
Olivia	77979
Olmito	78575
Olmos, *Bee*	78389
Olmos, *Starr*	78582
Olmos Park	78212
Olney	76374
Olton	79064
Omaha	75571
Omen	75789
Onalaska	77360
One Seventy Seven Lake Estates	77356
Onion Creek♦	78747
Opdyke	79336
Opdyke West	79336
Opelika	75778
Oplin	79510
O'Quinn	78945
Ora	75949
Oran	76449
Orange	77630-32
For specific ZIP Codes call (888) 275-8777, or your local postmaster.	
Orangedale	78102
Orangefield	77639
Orange Grove, *Harris*	77039
Orange Grove, *Jim Wells*	78372
Orangeville	75491
Orchard	77464
Ore City	75683
Orient	76901
Orla	79770
Orme (Part of Arlington)	76010
Osage	76528
Oscar	76501
Osceola	76055
Ottine	78658
Otto	76675
Ovalo	79541
Overland Plaza (Part of Arlington)	76003
Overton	75684
Ovilla	75154
Owens, *Brown*	76801
Owens, *Crosby*	79357
Owensville	77856
Owentown	75708
Oyster Creek	77541
Ozona♦	76943
Pacio	75450
Padgett	76374
Padre-Staples Mall (Part of Corpus Christi)	78411
Paducah	79248
Pagoda	75862
Paige	78659
Paint Rock	76866
Pakan	79079
Palacios	77465
Palava	79556
Palestine, *Anderson*	75801*
	75802†
Palestine, *Polk*	75936
Palito Blanco	78332
Palmer	75152
Palmetto (Part of Oakhurst)	77359
Palm Harbor	78382
Palmhurst	78572
Palm Park	78223
Palm Valley	78550
Palmview	78572
Palo Alto	78343
Paloduro	79226
Palo Pinto	76484
Paluxy	76467
Pampa	79065*
	79066†
Pancake	76528
Pandale	76943
Pandora	78143
Panhandle	79068
Panna Maria	78144
Panola	75685
Panorama Estates	75169
Panorama Village	77301
Pantego‡	76094
Panther Creek	77380*
	77393†
Papalote	78387
Paradise	76073
Paradise Bay	75143
Paradise Hills	75929
Paris	75460-62
For specific ZIP Codes call (888) 275-8777, or your local postmaster.	
Park	78945
Park Cities (Part of University Park)	75205
Parkdale (Part of Dallas)‡	75227
Parkdale Mall (Part of Beaumont)	77706
Parkdale Plaza (Part of Corpus Christi)	78411
Parker, *Collin*	75002
Parker, *Johnson*	76050
Parker Point	75980
Park Forest (Part of Dallas)	75240
Park Glen (Part of Houston)	77477
Park Place (Part of Houston)‡	77017
Park Row (Part of Katy)	77449
Parks at Arlington, The (Part of Arlington)	76015
Park Springs	76270
Parkview (Part of Fort Stockton)	79735
Parkview Estates	78155
Parkwood	77612
Parkwood Estates	77032
Parnell	79201
Parvin	75009
Pasadena	77501-08
For specific ZIP Codes call (888) 275-8777, or your local postmaster.	
Pasadena Town Square (Part of Pasadena)	77506
Patilo	76462
Patman	75656
Patrich	75681
Patricia	79331
Patrick, *Dallas*	75125
Patrick, *McLennan*	76708
Patroon	75973
Pattison	77466
Patton	76689
Pattonfield	75644
Patton Park	76544
Patton Village	77372
Pattonville	75468
Pauline	75124
Pauls Store	75973
Pawelekville	78113
Pawnee	78145
Paxton	75954
Paynes Corner	79360
Payne Springs	75124
Payton Colony	78606
Peach Creek	77488
Peach Creek Estates	77372
Peach Tree, *Brazos*	77801
Peachtree, *Jasper*	75951
Peacock	79502
Peadenville	76067
Pearl	76528
Pearland	77581
	77584
	77588
For specific ZIP Codes call (888) 275-8777, or your local postmaster.	
Pearl City	77995
Pear Ridge (Part of Port Arthur)	77640
Pearsall	78061
Pearsons Chapel	75851
Pear Valley	76867
Peaster	76485
Pebble Beach	75121
Pebble Hills (Part of El Paso)‡	79925
Pecan (Part of Del Rio)‡	78840
Pecan Acres, *Orange*	77662
Pecan Acres, *Wise*♦	76071
Pecan Gap	75469
Pecangrove	76528
Pecan Hill	75154
Pecan Lake Area	77835
Pecan Park (Part of Houston)	77087
Pecan Plantation	76048
Pecos	79772
Peeltown	75158
Peerless	75482
Peggy	78062
Pelham	76648
Pelican Bay	76020
Pendleton	76564
Pendleton Harbor	75948
Penelope	76676
Peniel (Part of Greenville)	75401
Penitas	78576
Pennington	75856
Penwell	79776
Peoria	76645
Pep	79353
Percilla	75844
Perezville	78572
Perico	79087
Permian Mall (Part of Odessa)	79762
Pernitas Point	78022
Perrin	76486
Perrin Field	75020
Perrin Heights	75020
Perry	76677
Perry Landing (Part of Jones Creek)	77541
Perryton	79070
Perryville	75494
Pershing (Part of Austin)	78702
Pershing Park	76544
Personville	76642
Pert	75801
Peters	77474
Petersburg	79250
Peterson	77627
Peters Prairie	75426
Petersville	77995
Petrolia	76377
Petronila	78380
Petteway	76629
Pettibone	76520
Pettit	79336
Pettus	78146
Petty, *Lamar*	75470
Petty, *Lynn*	79373
Petty's Chapel	75110
Pflugerville	78660
	78691
For specific ZIP Codes call (888) 275-8777, or your local postmaster.	
Phalba	75147
Pharr	78577
Phelan	78602
Phelps	77340
Phillips	79007
Phillipsburg	77426
Pickens	75751
Pickett	75110
Pickton	75471
Pidcoke	76528
Piedmont, *Grimes*	77830
Piedmont, *Upshur*	75644
Pierce	77467
Pierces Chapel	75766
Piggly Wiggly (Part of Bryan)	77801
Pike	75424
Pilgrim Ridge	77367
Pilgrims Rest	75410
Pilot Grove	75491
Pilot Knob	78744
Pilot Point	76258
Pine	75686
Pine Acres	77357
Pine Branch	75417
Pine Crest	77301
Pine Forest, *Hopkins*	75471
Pine Forest, *Orange*	77662
Pine Grove, *Cherokee*	75766
Pine Grove, *Newton*	75966
Pine Grove (Part of Orange)	77630
Pine Hill, *Cherokee*	75766
Pinehill, *Rusk*	75652
Pinehurst, *Montgomery*♦	77362
Pinehurst, *Orange*	77630
Pine Island	77445
Pine Lake	77356
Pineland	75968
Pine Mills	75773
Pine Park	75948
Pine Prairie	77340
Pine Ridge	77625
Pine Springs, *Culberson*	88220
Pine Springs, *Smith*	75702
Pine Trail Shores	75762
Pine Valley	75941
Pineview	75494
Pinewood (Part of Longview)	75601
Pinewood Estates, *Hardin*♦	77706
Pinewood Estates, *Montgomery*	77372
Pinewood Village (Part of Houston)	77093
Piney	77418
Piney Grove, *Cass*	75551
Piney Grove, *Upshur*	75451
Piney Point, *Montgomery*	77301
Piney Point, *Sabine*	75959
Piney Point Village	77024
Piney Woods	75951
Pinnacle	75644
Pioneer	76471
Pioneer Trails	77302
Pipe Creek	78063
Pirtle	75684
Pisgah	75929
Pitner Junction	75684
Pitts	77338
Pittsburg	75686
Placation Estates	75959
Placedo	77977
Placid	76872
Plains, *Borden*	79351
Plains, *Yoakum*	79355
Plainview, *Denton*	76249
Plainview, *Hale*	79072*
	79073†
Plainview, *Sabine*	75968
Plainview, *Wharton*	77455
Plano	75023-26
	75074-75
	75086
	75093-94
For specific ZIP Codes call (888) 275-8777, or your local postmaster.	
Plantersville	77363
Plaska	79245
Plateau	79855
Pleak	77469
Pleasant Farms	79763
Pleasant Grove (Part of Dallas)‡	75217
Pleasant Grove, *Bowie*	75501
Pleasant Grove, *Falls*	76570
Pleasant Grove, *Upshur*	75755
Pleasant Grove, *Wood*	75494
Pleasant Hill, *Blanco*	78636
Pleasant Hill, *Eastland*	76437
Pleasant Hill, *Nacogdoches*	75946
Pleasant Hill, *Polk*	75939
Pleasant Hill, *Washington*	77833
Pleasanton	78064
Pleasant Point	76009
Pleasant Ridge (Part of Coffee City)	75763
Pleasant Ridge, *Leon*	75833
Pleasant Ridge, *Montague*	76230
Pleasant Ridge, *Panola*	75633
Pleasant Springs	75833
Pleasant Valley (Part of Amarillo)	79108
Pleasant Valley (Part of Sachse)	75040
Pleasant Valley, *Garza*	79356
Pleasant Valley, *Lamb*	79347
Pleasant Valley, *Palo Pinto*	76067
Pleasant Valley, *Wichita*	76305
Pleasant Valley Acres	77355
Pledger, *Fisher*	79543
Pledger, *Matagorda*	77468
Pluck	75939
Plum	78952
Plum Creek	75831
Plum Grove	77327
Plum Ridge	75980
Plymouth Park Shopping Center (Part of Irving)	75061
Poe Prairie	76066
Poesville	76671
Poetry	75161
Point	75472
Point Blank	77364
Point Comfort	77978
Point Enterprise	76667
Point Loma	78368
Point Royal	75758
Point Venture	78641
Polar	79549
Pollok	75969
Polytechnic (Part of Fort Worth)‡	76105
Ponder	76259
Pond Springs	78729
Pone	75667
Ponta	75766
Pontotoc	76869
Poole	75440
Poolville	76487
Porfirio	78580
Port Acres (Part of Port Arthur)	77640
Portairs (Part of Corpus Christi)‡	78405
Port Alto	77979
Port Aransas	78373
Port Arthur	77640-43
For specific ZIP Codes call (888) 275-8777, or your local postmaster.	
Port Bolivar	77650
Porter	77365
Porter Heights♦	77365
Porter Springs	75835
Porterville Timbers	77365
Port Houston (Part of Houston)	77029
Port Isabel	78578
Portland	78374
Port Lavaca	77979
Port Mansfield	78598
Port Neches	77651
Port O'Connor	77982
Porvenir	79854
Posey, *Hopkins*	75482
Posey, *Lubbock*	79364
Possum Kingdom	76449
Post	79356
Post Oak, *Blanco*	78636
Post Oak, *Delta*	75432
Postoak, *Freestone*	75840
Postoak, *Jack*	76230
Postoak, *Lamar*	75416
Post Oak, *Robertson*	76629
Post Oak Bend City	75142
Post Oak Mall (Part of College Station)	77840
Post Oak Point	78950
Poteet	78065
Poth	78147
Potosi	79601
Potters Point	75657
Pottsboro	75076
Pottsville	76565
Powderly	75473
Powell	75153
Powell Point	77451
Poynor	75782
Prade Ranch	78058
Praesel	76567
Praha	78941
Prairie Dell	76571
Prairie Grove, *Angelina*	75941
Prairie Grove, *Limestone*	76667
Prairie Hill, *Limestone*	76678
Prairie Hill, *Washington*	77833
Prairie Lea	78661
Prairie Mountain	78643
Prairie Point	76239
Prairie Valley, *Fayette*	78952
Prairie Valley, *Montague*	76255
Prairie View	77446
Prairieville	75147
Prattville	75432

*** Area Zip Code** † **Post Office Boxes** ‡ **Postal Station** ♦ **Census Designated Place** *Italic Type* **County**

Premont 78375
Presidio 79845*
79846†
Preston (Part of Dallas)‡ 75225
Preston Shores 75076
Prestonwood (Part of Arlington)‡ 76012
Prestonwood (Part of Dallas)‡ 75248
Prestonwood Town Center (Part of Dallas) 75240
Price, *Jefferson* 77627
Price, *Rusk* 75687
Priddy 76870
Primera 78550
Primrose 75754
Princeton 75407
Pringle 79083
Pritchett 75644
Proctor 76468
Proffitt 76372
Progreso 78579
Progreso Lakes 78579
Progress, *Bailey* 79347
Progress, *Palo Pinto* 76067
Promenade (Part of Richardson)‡ 75080
Prospect 75657
Prosper 75078
Providence, *Angelina* 75904
Providence, *Hardin* 77625
Providence, *Polk* 77351
Providence, *Van Zandt* 75140
Provident City 77455
Pruitt, *Cass* 75657
Pruitt, *Van Zandt* 75140
Puckett Place (Part of Amarillo) 79109
Puckett West (Part of Amarillo) 79109
Puerto Rico 78563
Pumphrey 79507
Pumpkin 77358
Pumpkin Center 79331
Pumpville 78851
Punkin Center 76087
Purdon 76679
Purley 75457
Purmela 76566
Pursley 76679
Purves 76446
Putnam 76469
Pyote 79777
Pyron 79545
Quail 79251
Quail Run (Part of Fort Stockton) 79735
Quail Valley 78626
Quanah 79252
Quarry 77833
Queen City 75572
Quemado 78877
Quicksand 75966
Quihi 78861
Quinlan 75474
Quintana 77541
Quitaque 79255
Quite Village 77662
Quitman 75783
Rabb 78380
Rabbit Center 76401
Rabbs 77964
Rabbs Prairie 78945
Rachal 78353
Radium 79501
Ragtown 75411
Rainbow 76077
Rainbow Hills 78227
Raisin 77905
Raleigh 76641
Ralls 79357
Ramah 75974
Rambo 75555
Ramireno 78067
Ramirez 78376
Ranch Harbor Estates 76692
Ranchito 78586
Ranchland (Part of El Paso)‡ 79915*
79926†
Ranchland Acres 79703
Rancho Alegre 78332
Rancho de la Parita 78372
Rancho Viejo, *Cameron* 78520
Rancho Viejo, *Jim Hogg* 78361
Randolph 75475
Randolph Air Force Base 78150
Ranger 76470

Rangerville 78586
Rankin, *Ellis* 75119
Rankin, *Upton* 79778
Ratama 78017
Ratcliff, *Houston* 75858
Ratcliff, *San Augustine* 75972
Ratcliffe 78164
Ratibor 76501
Rattan 75432
Ravenna 75476
Rayburn 77327
Rayburn Hideaway 75937
Rayford 77373
Rayland 76384
Raymondville 78580
Ray Point 78071
Raywood 77582
Reagan 76680
Reagan Wells 78801
Reagor Springs 75165
Realitos 78376
Reata Trails 78628
Redbank 75561
Red Bird Mall (Part of Dallas) 75237
Red Bluff 79770
Red Branch 75855
Redford 79846
Red Gate 78539
Red Hill, *Cass* 75560
Red Hill, *Lamar* 75473
Red Lake 75855
Redland, *Angelina* 75901
75904
For specific ZIP Codes call (888) 275-8777, or your local postmaster.
Redland, *Leon* 75833
Redland, *Van Zandt* 75754
Redlawn 75925
Redlick 75501
Redmond Terrace (Part of College Station) 77840
Red Oak, *Ellis* 75154
Red Oak, *Kaufman* 75142
Red Ranger 76569
Red River Army Depot 75501
Red Rock 78662
Red Springs, *Baylor* 76380
Red Springs, *Bowie* 75501
Red Springs, *Smith* 75701
Red Top 76450
Redtown, *Anderson* 75839
Red Town, *Angelina* 75904
Redwater 75573
Redwood 78666
Reedville 78656
Reese 75766
Reese Air Force Base 79489
Refugio 78377
Regency 76864
Rehburg 77835
Rehobeth 75633
Reilly Springs 75482
Rek Hill 78940
Reklaw 75784
Relampago 78570
Reliance 77801
Remolino 78582
Rendon 76028
Reno, *Lamar* 75462
Reno, *Parker* 76020
Retreat, *Grimes* 77868
Retreat, *Hill* 76627
Retreat, *Navarro* 75110
Retta 76028
Rhea 79035
Rhea Mills 75069
Rhineland 76371
Rhome 76078
Rhonesboro 75494
Ricardo 78363
Rice, *Navarro* 75155
Rice (Part of Tyler) 75701
Rices Crossing 76574
Richards 77873
Richardson 75080-85
For specific ZIP Codes call (888) 275-8777, or your local postmaster.
Richardson Square (Part of Richardson) 75081
Rich Hill (Part of Houston)‡ 77057
Richland (Part of Dallas)‡ 75243*
75374†
Richland, *Navarro* 76681
Richland, *Rains* 75472
Richland Hills 76118
Richland Mall (Part of Waco) 76710

Richland Park (Part of Fort Worth) 76118
Richland Plaza (Part of North Richland Hills) 76118
Richland Springs 76871
Richmond 77406†
77469*
Richwood 77531
Riderville 75633
Ridge, *Mills* 76864
Ridge, *Robertson* 77856
Ridgecrest (Part of Amarillo) 79109
Ridgecrest Addition 77630
Ridgeheights 79701
Ridgemere (Part of Amarillo) 79107
Ridgeway 75482
Ridglea (Part of Fort Worth)‡ 76116
Ridgmar Mall (Part of Fort Worth) 76116
Ridings 75476
Riesel 76682
Rimwick Forrest 77354
Rincon 78582
Ringgold 76261
Rio del Sol 78522
Rio Farms 78538
Rio Frio 78879
Rio Grande City 78582
Rio Hondo 78583
Rio Llano Ranch 78643
Rio Medina 78066
Rio Pecos 79740
Rios 78349
Rio Vista 76093
Rising Star 76471
Rita 77857
River Bend, *Newton* 75932
River Bend, *Sabine* 75948
River Bend (Part of Richland Hills)‡ 76118
River Bend Estates 78003
River Brook 77302
Riverby 75488
Rivercenter (Part of San Antonio) 78205
Riverdrive Mall (Part of Laredo) 78040
River Hill 75633
Riverland 76365
River Oak Lake Estates 78758
River Oaks (Part of Houston)‡ 77019
River Oaks, *Tarrant* 76114
River Oaks Ranch 78063
River Plantation 77302
River Ridge 75951
Riverside (Part of Fort Worth)‡ 76111
Riverside, *Walker* 77367
Riverside Crest (Part of Houston) 77338
Riverside Terrace (Part of Houston) 77021
River Wood Estates 77050
Riviera 78379
Riviera Beach 78379
Roach 75551
Roach Town 75758
Roane 75110
Roanoke 76262
Roans Prairie 77875
Roaring Springs 79256
Robbins 75846
Robert Lee 76945
Robertson 79343
Robinson 76706
Robinson Plaza (Part of Robinson) 76706
Robstown 78380
Roby 79543
Rochelle 76872
Rochester 79544
Rock Creek 76708
Rockdale 76567
Rockett 75165
Rockford 75462
Rock Harbor 76048
Rockhill, *Collin* 75069
Rock Hill, *Jasper* 75951
Rock Hill, *Wood* 75783
Rockhouse 78950
Rock Island, *Colorado* 77470
Rock Island, *Polk* 75939
Rockland 75938
Rockne 78602
Rockport 78381†
78382*
Rock Prairie 77801
Rocksprings 78880

Rockwall 75032
75087
For specific ZIP Codes call (888) 275-8777, or your local postmaster.
Rockwood 76873
Rocky Branch 75638
Rocky Creek Park 77835
Rocky Hill 76661
Rocky Mound 75686
Rocky Point 75440
Rocky Springs, *Angelina* 75949
Rocky Springs, *Tyler* 75938
Roddy 75147
Rodney 76639
Roganville 75956
Rogers 76569
Rogers Hill 76691
Rolling Hills, *Hunt*‡ 75453
Rolling Hills, *Potter* 79108
Rolling Hills, *Waller* 77445
Rolling Hills Shores 76087
Rolling Meadows 75603
Rolling Oaks 75169
Rolling Oaks Mall (Part of San Antonio)‡ 78247
Rollingwood 78746
Roma 78584
Roman Forest 77357
Roman Hills 77356
Romayor 77368
Romero 79022
Romney 76471
Roosevelt, *Kimble* 76874
Roosevelt, *Lubbock* 79401
Ropesville 79358
Rosalie 75417
Rosanky 78953
Roscoe 79545
Rosebud 76570
Rose City 77662
Rosedale 76661
Rose Hill, *Harris* 77375
Rose Hill, *San Jacinto* 77331
Rose Hill, *Wood* 75773
Rose Hill Acres 77657
Rosenberg 77471
Rosenthal 76655
Rosevine 75930
Rosewood 75644
Rosharon 77583
Rosita, *Duval* 78384
Rosita, *Starr* 78582
Ross 76684
Rosser 75157
Rosston 76263
Rossville 78065
Rotan 79546
Round Mountain 78663
Round Prairie 75144
Round Rock 78664
78680-83
For specific ZIP Codes call (888) 275-8777, or your local postmaster.
Round Rock East (Part of Round Rock)‡ 78664
Round Timber 76380
Round Top 78954
Roundup 79313
Rowden 79504
Rowena 76875
Rowlett 75030
75088-89
For specific ZIP Codes call (888) 275-8777, or your local postmaster.
Roxton 75477
Royal Forest 77303
Royal Lane (Part of Dallas)‡ 75230
75251
For specific ZIP Codes call (888) 275-8777, or your local postmaster.
Royal Oaks, *Henderson* 75143
Royal Oaks, *Llano* 78639
Royal Oaks, *Orange* 77626
Royalty 79779
Royalwood 77049
Roy Miller (Part of Corpus Christi)‡ 78465
Roy Royall (Part of Houston)‡ 77016
Royse City 75189
Royston 79543
Rucker 76444
Rugby 75435
Ruidosa 79843
Rule 79547
Rumley 76539
Run 78537

Runaway Bay 76426
Runge 78151
Rural Shade 75144
Rushwood 77067
Rusk 75785
Rustling Oaks (Part of Houston) 77079
Rutersville 78945
Ruth Springs 75163
Ryanville 78377
Rye 77369
Sabanna 76437
Sabathany 76086
Sabinal 78881
Sabine 77640
Sabine Pass 77655
Sabine Sands 75928
Sabinetown 75948
Sachse 75048
Sacul 75788
Saddle and Surrey 77356
Sadler 76264
Sagerton 79548
Saginaw 76179
St. Claire Cove 77650
St. Elmo 75859
St. Francis 79107
St. Francis Village 76036
St. Hedwig 78152
St. Jo 76265
Saint John 78956
Saint John Colony 78616
St. Lawrence 79739
St. Louis (Part of Tyler) 75702
St. Paul, *Brazoria* 77422
St. Paul, *Collin* 75098
St. Paul, *Falls* 76661
St. Paul, *San Patricio* 78387
Salado♦ 76571
Salem, *Bastrop* 78953
Salem, *Milam* 76520
Salem, *Smith* 75789
Salesville 76067
Salineno 78585
Salmon 75839
Salona 76230
Salt Flat 79847
Salt Gap 76836
Saltillo 75478
Sam Houston (Part of Houston)‡ 77002
Sam Houston College (Part of Huntsville)‡ 77341
Samnorwood 79077
Sam Rayburn 75951
Sanaloma Estates 78628
San Angelo 76901-06
For specific ZIP Codes call (888) 275-8777, or your local postmaster.

San Antonio

78201-99
For specific ZIP Codes call (888) 275-8777, or your local postmaster.

Colleges & Universities

Oblate School of Theology 78216
Our Lady of the Lake Univ 78207
St Mary's Univ 78228
Trinity Univ 78212
Univ of Incarnate Word 78209
Univ of Texas 78249

Financial Institutions

Bank of America, NA 78205
Bank One, NA 78205
The Frost Nat Bank 78205
NationsBank, NA 78205
Wells Fargo 78209

Hospitals

Baptist Med Ctr 78205
Brooke Army Med Ctr 78234
Santa Rosa Health Care Corp 78207
South Texas Veterans Healthcare System 78284
Southwest Texas Methodist Hosp 78229
University Health System 78229

Hotels/Motels

Adam's Mark 78205
The Camberley Gunter 78205
Crowne Plaza St Anthony 78205
The Hilton Palacio del Rio 78205
Holiday Inn Market Square 78204
Holiday Inn Northwest 78213

Holiday Inn Riverwalk 78205
Hyatt Regency 78205
Hyatt Regency Hill Country Resort 78251
La Mansion del Rio 78205
Marriott, Plaza Hotel 78205
Marriott River Center 78205
Marriott Riverwalk 78205
The Menger 78205
Radisson, Downtown Market Square 78207
The Wyndham Fairmount 78230

Military Installations

Brooks Air Force Base 78235
Camp Bullis 78234
Defense Distribution Depot 78241
Fort Sam Houston 78234
Joint Personal Property Shipping Off 78216
Kelly Air Force Base 78241
Lackland Air Force Base 78236
Texas Air Nat Guard, FB6432, Kelly Air Force Base 78241

San Augustine 75972
San Benito 78586
San Carlos 78539
Sanco 76945
Sanctuary 76020
Sanderson♦ 79848
Sand Flat, *Rains* 75440
Sandflat, *Smith* 75706
Sand Flat, *Van Zandt* 75140
Sand Hill, *Floyd* 79235
Sand Hill, *Upshur* 75644
Sandia 78383
San Diego 78384
Sandjack 75928
Sand Lake 75119
Sandoval 76574
Sand Ridge, *Houston* 75835
Sand Ridge, *Wharton* 77434
Sand Springs, *Howard* 79720
Sand Springs, *Wood* 75773
Sandusky 76273
Sandy 78665
Sandy Acres 79703
Sandy Corner 77437
Sandy Creek 76556
Sandy Fork 78632
Sandy Harbor 78654
Sandy Hill 77833
Sandy Point 77583
Sandy Ridge 77351
San Elizario♦ 79849
San Felipe 77473
Sanford 79078
Sanford Estates 79036
San Gabriel 76577
San Gabriel Heights 78628
Sanger 76266
San Geromino 78023
San Isidro 78588
San Jacinto (Part of Amarillo)‡ 79106
San Jose 78332
San Juan, *Hidalgo* 78589
San Juan, *Nueces* 78406
San Leanna 78748
San Leon♦ 77539
San Marcos 78666*
...... 78667†
San Patricio 78368
San Pedro 78520
San Perlita 78590
San Saba 76877
Sansom Park 76114
Santa Anna 76878
Santa Catarina 78582
Santa Cruz 78582
Santa Elena 78591
Santa Fe 77510
...... 77517
For specific ZIP Codes call (888) 275-8777, or your local postmaster.
Santa Maria 78592
Santa Monica 78580
Santa Rita (Part of San Angelo) 76901
Santa Rosa 78593
Santo 76472
San Ygnacio 78067
Saragosa 79780
Saratoga 77585
Sarco 77963
Sardis, *Cass* 75656
Sardis, *Ellis* 76065

Sargent 77414
Sarita 78385
Sash 75446
Saspamco 78112
Satin 76685
Satsuma 77041
Sattler 78130
Sauney Stand 77426
Savage 79357
Savoy 75479
Sayers 78602
Scallorn 76853
Scenic Heights 78130
Scenic Hills 78108
Scenic Terrace 78130
Scenic Woods (Part of Houston) 77016
Schattel 78005
Schertz 78154
Schicke Point 77465
Schoolerville 76531
School Land 78140
Schroeder 77963
Schulenburg 78956
Schumannsville 78130
Schwab City 77351
Schwertner 76573
Scissors♦ 78537
Scotland 76379
Scotsdale (Part of El Paso) 79925
Scotsdale (Part of Odessa) 79762
Scott 75169
Scottsville 75688
Scranton 76437
Scrappin Valley 75977
Scroggins 75480
Scurry 75158
Seabrook 77586
Sea Crest Park 77520
Seadrift 77983
Seagoville 75159
Seagraves 79359
Sea Isle 77554
Seale 76687
Sealy 77474
Seaton 76501
Seawillow 78644
Sebastian♦ 78594
Sebastopol 75862
Seco Mines 78852
Security 77327
Sedalia 75495
Segno 77351
Segovia 76849
Seguin 78155*
...... 78156†
Sejita 78376
Selden 76401
Selfs 75446
Selma 78209
Selman City 75689
Seminary Hill (Part of Fort Worth)‡ 76115
Seminole 79360
Senate 76458
Senior 78073
Sequoya Bend 77032
Serbin 78942
Serenada♦ 78628
Serna (Part of San Antonio)‡ 78218
...... 78266
For specific ZIP Codes call (888) 275-8777, or your local postmaster.
Seth Ward♦ 79072
Seven Oaks 77350
Seven Pines 75601
Seven Points 75143
Seven Sisters 78357
Sexton 75972
Sexton City 75684
Seymore 75482
Seymour 76380
Shadow Glen 77530
Shadow Lake Estates 77365
Shadowland 75435
Shadowland Retreat 77365
Shady Acres, *Brazoria* 77422
Shady Acres, *Burnet* 78654
Shady Brook Acres 77355
Shady Grove (Part of Grand Prairie) 75050
Shady Grove, *Angelina* 75941
Shady Grove, *Cherokee* 75785
Shady Grove, *Kerr* 78028
Shady Grove, *Marion* 75657
Shady Grove, *Nacogdoches* 75961
Shady Grove, *Navarro* 76679
Shady Grove, *Panola* 75669

Shady Grove, *Rains* 75440
Shady Grove, *Smith* 75706
Shady Grove, *Upshur* 75755
Shady Hollow 78739
Shady Oaks, *Henderson* 75751
Shady Oaks (Part of Hurst) 76053
Shady Shores, *Denton* 76205
Shady Shores, *Henderson* 75147
Shafter 79850
Shallowater 79363
Shamrock 79079
Shamrock Shores 76801
Shankleville 75932
Shannon 76365
Sharon 75701
Sharp 76518
Sharpstown (Part of Houston)‡ 77036
Sharpstown Center (Part of Houston) 77036
Sharyland (Part of Mission) 78572
Shavano Park 78231
Shaw Bend 76877
Shawnee 75949
Shawnee Shores 75948
Shawnee Shores Estates 75474
Shaws Bend 78934
Sheffield 79781
Shelby 78940
Shelbyville 75973
Sheldon♦ 77049
Shenandoah, *Montgomery* 77301
Shenandoah, *Williamson* 78613
Shep 79566
Shepherd 77371
Shepphard 77612
Shepton 75173
Sher-Den Mall (Part of Sherman) 75090
Sheridan 77475
Sherman 75090-92
For specific ZIP Codes call (888) 275-8777, or your local postmaster.
Sherman-Hansford Plant 79040
Sherman Junction (Part of Denison) 75020
Sherry 75426
Sherwood 76941
Sherwood Forest 78258
Sherwood Place 77093
Sherwood Shores 78654
Shields 76845
Shiloh, *Delta* 75448
Shiloh, *Leon* 75855
Shiloh, *Liberty* 77575
Shiloh, *Limestone* 76667
Shiloh, *Williamson* 76578
Shiner 77984
Shipman Camp 79521
Shirley 75482
Shirley Creek 75937
Shiro 77876
Shive 76531
Shoreacres 77571
Short 75935
Sidney 76474
Sierra Blanca 79851
Siesta Shores, *Travis* 78669
Siesta Shores, *Zapata* 78076
Sikes Senter (Part of Wichita Falls) 76308
Silas 75975
Siloam 75559
Silsbee 77656
Silver 76949
Silver City, *Milam* 76520
Silver City, *Navarro* 76679
Silver City, *Red River* 75426
Silver Creek Village 78611
Silver Creek Village No. 2 78611
Silver Hills 78006
Silver Lake 75140
Silverton 79257
Silver Valley 76834
Simmons 78071
Simms 75574
Simonton 77476
Simpsonville 77465
Simsboro 75860
Sinclair City 75789
Singing Sands 77617
Singletary Sites 75956
Singleton 77831
Sinton 78387

Sipe Springs 76442
Sisterdale 78006
Six Flags Mall (Part of Arlington) 76011
Six Mile 77979
Six Points (Part of Corpus Christi)‡ 78404
Skellytown 79080
Skidmore 78389
Sky Harbor 76048
Slabtown 75462
Slate Shoals 75462
Slaton 79364
Slide 79413
Slidell 76267
Slinger (Part of Lubbock)‡ 79464
Sloan 76877
Slocum 75839
Small 75117
Smeltertown (Part of El Paso) 79927
Smetana 77801
Smiley 78159
Smithfield (Part of North Richland Hills) 76180
Smith Grove 75851
Smith Hill 75561
Smithland 75657
Smith Point 77514
Smiths Bend 76634
Smith Springs 76401
Smithville 78957
Smithwick 78654
Smitty (Part of Athens) 75751
Smyer 79367
Smyrna 75551
Snook 77878
Snow Hill, *Collin* 75442
Snow Hill, *Polk* 75939
Snow Hill, *Upshur* 75683
Snyder 79549*
...... 79550†
Socorro 79927*
...... 79929†
Soda 77351
Soda Springs 76066
Sodville 78387
Solms 78130
Somerset 78069
Somerville 77879
Sonoma (Part of Ennis) 75119
Sonora 76950
Soules Chapel 75644
Sour Lake 77659
South (Part of Garland)‡ 75043
South Amarillo (Part of Amarillo) 79114
South Austin (Part of Austin)‡ 78704
South Bend 76481
South Bosque 76710
South Brice 79226
Southbrook 77060
South Dallas (Part of Dallas)‡ 75215
Southeast (Part of Austin)‡ 78741-44
...... 78760
For specific ZIP Codes call (888) 275-8777, or your local postmaster.
Southeast Crossing (Part of Tyler)‡ 75713
South Elm 76518
South End (Part of Beaumont)‡ 77705*
...... 77725†
Southern Hills (Part of Abilene)‡ 79608
Southern Methodist University (Part of University Park) 75275
South Gale 75021
South Groveton (Part of Groveton) 75845
South Haven 79720
South Houston 77587
Southlake 76092
Southland, *Garza* 79364
Southland, *Wharton* 77437
Southland Hills (Part of San Angelo) 76904
Southmayd 76268
Southmore (Part of Houston)‡ 77004
South Mountain 76528
South Oak Cliff (Part of Dallas)‡ 75216
South Padre Island 78597

South Park Mall (Part of San Antonio) 78224
South Plains 79258
South Plains Mall (Part of Lubbock) 79414
South Post Oak (Part of Houston)‡ 77035
...... 77231
...... 77235
For specific ZIP Codes call (888) 275-8777, or your local postmaster.
South Purmela 76566
Southridge Plaza (Part of Austin)‡ 78745
South San Antonio (Part of San Antonio)‡ 78211
South San Gabriel Ranches 78641
Southside (Part of Corpus Christi)‡ 78413
Southside Estates (Part of Amarillo) 79110
Southside Place 77005
South Sulphur 75496
South Temple (Part of Temple)‡ 76501
South Texas Medical Center (Part of San Antonio)‡ 78229
Southton 78223
South View Estates 78737
Southwestern Baptist Theological Seminary (Part of Fort Worth) 76115
Southwest Freeway (Part of Houston)‡ 77057
Sowells Bluff 75476
Sowers (Part of Irving) 75060
Spade 79369
Spanish Camp 77488
Spanish Fort 76255
Spanish Trail 76048
Sparenberg 79331
Sparks 76534
Speaks 77985
Spearman 79081
Speegleville 76710
Spicewood 78669
Spicewood At Balcones Village 78750
Spicewood Beach 78669
Spillers Store 75850
Spillview Estates 75147
Spinwick Addition (Part of La Porte) 77571
Splawn 76520
Splendora 77372
Splendora Farms 77372
Spofford 78877
Spraberry 79702
Spring 77373
...... 77379-83
...... 77386-93
For specific ZIP Codes call (888) 275-8777, or your local postmaster.
Spring Branch 78070
Spring Creek, *Gillespie* 78624
Spring Creek, *San Saba* 76871
Spring Creek, *Throckmorton* 76370
Spring Creek Acres (Part of Victoria) 77904
Spring Creek Estates 77355
Springdale 75572
Spring Dell 77373
Springfield, *Anderson* 75801
Springfield, *Limestone* 76667
Spring Forest 77373
Spring Hill, *Bowie* 75559
Spring Hill, *Camp* 75686
Spring Hill, *Gregg* 75603
Spring Hill, *Guadalupe* 78155
Spring Hill, *Jasper* 75951
Springhill, *Navarro* 76639
Spring Hills 77373
Springlake 79082
Spring Seat 75846
Spring Shadows (Part of Houston) 77043
...... 77080
For specific ZIP Codes call (888) 275-8777, or your local postmaster.
Springtown 76082
Spring Valley (Part of Dallas)‡ 75240*
...... 75280†
Spring Valley, *Harris* 77055
Spring Valley, *McLennan* 76655

*** Area Zip Code** **† Post Office Boxes** **‡ Postal Station** **♦ Census Designated Place** *Italic Type* **County**

Sprinkle 78754
Spur 79370
Spurger 77660
Stacy 76836
Stafford 77477*
..... 77497†
Stagecoach 77355
Stage Coach Farms 77355
Stage Coach Hills 78255
Stairtown 78648
Staley 77359
Stamford 79553
Stamps 75644
Stanfield 76365
Stanger Springs 75754
Stanton 79782
Staples 78670
Star 76880
Star Harbor 75148
Star Route 79346
Starrville 75792
Startzville 78130
Steeltown (Part of Groves) 77619
Steep Hollow 77801
Stellar 78949
Stephenville 76401
Sterley 79241
Sterling City 76951
Sterlings Island 77367
Sterrett 75165
Stewards Mill 75840
Stewart 75691
Stewart Heights (Part of Baytown) 77520
Stieren 78632
Stilson 77535
Stinnett 79083
Stith 79536
Stockard 75751
Stockdale 78160
Stockman 75975
Stockyards (Part of Fort Worth)‡ 76106
Stoneburg 76230
Stoneham 77868
Stonewall 78671
Stonewall Mall (Part of Corpus Christi)‡ 78409-10
..... 78426
For specific ZIP Codes call (888) 275-8777, or your local postmaster.
Stony 76259
Stout 75494
Stowell♦ 77661
Stranger 76653
Stratford 79084
Stratton 77954
Stratton Ridge 77531
Strawn 76475
Streetman 75859
Strickland 75968
String Prairie 78953
Structure 78621
Stuart Place 78550
Study Butte 79852
Stumptown 75931
Sturdivant 76067
Sturgeon 76273
Styx 75143
Sublett (Part of Arlington) 76063
Sublime 77986
Sudan 79371
Suffolk 75644
Sugar Land 77478-79
..... 77487
..... 77496
For specific ZIP Codes call (888) 275-8777, or your local postmaster.
Sugar Valley 77480
Sullivan City♦ 78595
Sulphur Bluff 75481
Sulphur Springs, *Angelina* 75980
Sulphur Springs, *Hopkins* 75482*
..... 75483†
Sulphur Springs, *Rusk* 75760
Summerall 75147
Summerfield, *Castro* 79085
Summerfield, *Upshur* 75644
Summer Hill 75751
Summit Heights (Part of El Paso)‡ 79930*
..... 79931†
Sumner 75486
Sundown 79372
Sunnyside, *Castro* 79027
Sunnyside (Part of Houston) 77051

Sunny Side, *Waller* 77445
Sunnyslope (Part of Texarkana) 75501
Sunnyvale 75149
Sunray 79086
Sunrise (Part of El Paso)‡ 79904
Sunrise, *Falls* 76661
Sunrise Acres (Part of El Paso) 79904
Sunrise Beach 78643
Sunrise Mall (Part of Brownsville) 78521
Sunrise Mall (Part of Corpus Christi) 78412
Sunset (Part of Lubbock)‡ 79416
Sunset, *Montague* 76270
Sunset Mall (Part of San Angelo) 76904
Sunset Marketown (Part of Amarillo) 79102
Sunset Ridge 77301
Sunset Valley 78745
Sunshine Hill 76360
Sun Valley (Part of El Paso) 79924
Sun Valley, *Lamar* 75462
Surf Oaks (Part of Seabrook) 77586
Surfside Beach 77541
Sutherland Springs 78161
Swamp City 75647
Swan 75706
Swan Lagoon (Part of Nassau Bay) 77058
Swanson Hill 75801
Sweeny 77480
Sweeny Switch 78368
Sweet Home, *Guadalupe* 78155
Sweet Home, *Lavaca* 77987
Sweetwater, *Comanche* 76442
Sweetwater, *Nolan* 79556
Swenson 79502
Swift 75961
Swiss Alp 78956
Swiss Village 78611
Sycamore 75932
Sylvan 75462
Sylvan Beach (Part of La Porte) 77571
Sylvester 79560
Tabor 77801
Tacoma 75633
Tadmor 75847
Taft 78390
Taft Southwest♦ 78390
Tahoka 79373
Talco 75487
Tall Pines 75630
Talpa 76882
Talty 75160
Tamega 78605
Tamina 77302
Tandy Center (Part of Fort Worth)‡ 76102
Tanglewood 78947
Tanglewood Island 76424
Tanglewood Manor 77357
Tankersly 76901
Tarkington Acres 77327
Tarkington Prairie 77327
Tarleton (Part of Stephenville)‡ 76402
Tarpley 78883
Tarrant (Part of Fort Worth) 76039
Tarzan 79783
Tate Springs (Part of Arlington)‡ 76003
Tatum 75691
Tavener 77435
Taylor 76574
Taylor Lake Village 77586
Taylorsville 78662
Taylor Town 75462
Taylorville 75452
Teague 75860
Teaselville 75757
Tecula 75766
Tehuacana 76686
Telegraph 76883
Telephone 75488
Telferner 77988
Telico 75119
Tell 79259
Temple 76501-05
For specific ZIP Codes call (888) 275-8777, or your local postmaster.
Temple Mall (Part of Temple) 76502

Temple Springs 75951
Tenaha 75974
Tennessee 75975
Tennessee Colony 75861
Tennyson 76953
Terlingua 79852
Terrell 75160-61
For specific ZIP Codes call (888) 275-8777, or your local postmaster.
Terrell Hills 78209
Terrell Station 79781
Terrell Wells (Part of San Antonio)‡ 78221
Terrys Chapel 76570
Terryville 77995
Texarkana 75501-05
For specific ZIP Codes call (888) 275-8777, or your local postmaster.
Texas Christian University (Part of Fort Worth) 76119
Texas City 77590-92
For specific ZIP Codes call (888) 275-8777, or your local postmaster.
Texas City Junction (Part of Hitchcock) 77563
Texas City Junction (Part of Texas City) 77590
Texas Lutheran (Part of Seguin)‡ 78155
Texas Woman's University (Part of Denton)‡ 76204
Texhoma 73949
Texline 79087
Texon 76932
Thalia 79227
Thayer 78570
The Bluffs (Part of San Angelo) 76901
The Colony 75056
Thedford 75771
The Grove 76576
The Heights (Part of Alvin) 77511
The Homestead 78736
The Knobbs 78650
Thelma, *Bexar* 78221
Thelma, *Limestone* 76642
The Oaks 78130
Theon 76537
Thermo 75482
The Shores (Part of Amarillo) 79110
The Woodlands♦ 77380
Thicket 77374
Thomas 75644
Thomas Manor (Part of El Paso) 79915
Thomaston 77989
Thompson Heights 75020
Thompsons 77481
Thompsonville 78959
Thornberry 76306
Thorndale 76577
Thornton 76687
Thorntonville 79756
Thorp Spring 76048
Thousand Oaks (Part of San Antonio)‡ 78270
Thrall 76578
Three Leagues 79331
Three Points 78660
Three Rivers 78071
Three Way 76401
Thrifty 76801
Throckmorton 76483
Thurber 76463
Tidwell 75401
Tidwell Prairie 76629
Tierra Linda Ranch 78028
Tigertown 75446
Tiki Island 77554
Tilden 78072
Tilmon 78616
Timber Cove (Part of Taylor Lake Village) 77586
Timberlake 77429
Timberlake Acres 77365
Timber Lake Estates 77380
Timber Ridge, *Bexar* 78251
Timber Ridge, *Montgomery* 77380
Timothy 75105
Timpson 75975
Tin Top 76087
Tioga 76271
Tira 75482
Tivoli 77990
Tivydale 78624

Tobe Hahn (Part of Beaumont)‡ 77706
Toco 75421
Tod (Part of Seabrook) 77586
Todd City 75801
Todd Mission 77363
Togo 78957
Tokio 79376
Tolar 76476
Tolbert 76384
Toledo Village, *Newton* 75932
Toledo Village, *Sabine* 75948
Tolosa 75143
Tomball 77375*
..... 77377†
Tom Bean 75489
Tonkowon Country 78628
Tool 75143
Topsey 76522
Tornillo 79853
Tours 76691
Tow 78672
Town and Country Center (Part of Houston) 77024
Town Bluff 75979
Town East Mall (Part of Mesquite) 75150
Town Oaks (Part of Marshall)‡ 75670
Town West♦ 77478
Toyah 79785
Toyahvale 79786
Tracy 76567
Tradewinds 75143
Trail Lake (Part of Fort Worth)‡ 76162
Travis 76656
Travis Peak 78654
Trawick 75961
Trent 79561
Trenton 75490
Trevat 75845
Tri Cities 75751
Trickham 76878
Tri-Lake Estates 77356
Trimmier Friendship 76542
Trinidad 75163
Trinity 75862
Trinity Park 75098
Trinity River (Part of Fort Worth)‡ 76109
Trophy Club 76262
Tropical Acres 77904
Troup 75789
Trout Creek 75933
Troy 76579
Truby 79525
Truce 76230
Trumbull 75125
Truscott 79227
Tucker 75801
Tuleta 78162
Tulia 79088
Tulip 75447
Tulsita 78119
Tundra 75103
Tunis 77836
Tupelo 75155
Turkey 79261
Turkey Creek (Part of Copperas Cove) 76522
Turlington 75840
Turnersville 76528
Turnertown 75689
Turney 75766
Turtle Bayou 77514
Tuscola 79562
Tuttle Addition 77488
Tuxedo 79553
Twine Cedar Retreat 75948
Twin Shores 77378
Twin Valley Terrace 78073
Twitty 79079
Tye 79563
Tyler 75701-13
For specific ZIP Codes call (888) 275-8777, or your local postmaster.
Tynan 78391
Type 78621
Uhland 78640
Umbarger 79091
Uncertain 75661
Union, *Brazos* 77801
Union, *Franklin* 75478
Union, *Lubbock* 79364
Union, *Scurry* 79549
Union, *Terry* 79316
Union, *Wilson* 78140
Union Academy 75801
Union Bluff 76645

Union Bower (Part of Irving) 75060
Union Center 76471
Union Grove, *Bell* 76513
Union Grove, *Cherokee* 75766
Union Grove, *Upshur* 75647
Union High 76639
Union Hill, *Bosque* 76652
Union Hill, *Henderson* 75756
Union Hill, *Upshur* 75644
Union Springs 75961
Union Valley 75189
Unity 75486
Universal City 78148-50
For specific ZIP Codes call (888) 275-8777, or your local postmaster.
University (Part of Austin)‡ 78712*
..... 78713†
University (Part of Dallas)‡ 75205-06
..... 73372
For specific ZIP Codes call (888) 275-8777, or your local postmaster.
University of Dallas (Part of Irving)‡ 75061
University of Texas at El Paso (Part of El Paso)‡ 79902
University Park (Part of San Antonio)‡ 78228
University Park (Part of Wichita Falls)‡ 76308
University Park, *Dallas* 75205
University Place (Part of Nacogdoches)‡ 75961
Upper Meyersville 78164
Upshaw 75943
Upton 78957
Urbana 77371
Utility (Part of San Antonio) 78219
Utley 78602
Utopia 78884
Uvalde 78801*
..... 78802†
Valdasta 75424
Valentine 79854
Valera 76884
Valle de Oro 79010
Valle Vista Mall (Part of Harlingen) 78552
Valleycreek 75452
Valley Hi (Part of San Antonio)‡ 78227
Valley Lodge (Part of Simonton) 77476
Valley Mills 76689
Valley Spring 76885
Valley View (Part of Waco) 76701
Valley View, *Comal* 78130
Valley View, *Cooke* 76272
Valley View, *Mitchell* 79512
Valley View, *Runnels* 76821
Valley View, *Upshur* 75644
Valley View, *Wichita* 76367
Valley View Center (Part of Dallas) 75240
Valley Wells 78830
Val Verde 76518
Val Verde Park Estates 78840
Van 75790
Van Alstyne 75495
Vance 78828
Vancourt 76955
Vandalia 75426
Vanderbilt 77991
Vanderpool 78885
Vandyke 76442
Vanetia 77865
Van Horn 79855
Van Vleck♦ 77482
Varisco 77801
Vasco 75450
Vashti 76228
Vattmannville 78379
Vaughan 76645
Vealmoor 79720
Veal Station 76082
Vedas Camp 79521
Vega 79092
Venable Village 76544
Ventura 77355
Venus 76084
Vera 76380
Verbena 79356
Verdi 78064
Verhalen 79772
Verhelle 77954

Place	ZIP
Veribest	76886
Vernon	76384*
	76385†
Verona	75424
Veterans Administration (Part of Waco)	76711
Viboras	78361
Vick	76937
Vickery (Part of Dallas)‡	75231*
	75382†
Victoria, *Limestone*	76664
Victoria, *Victoria*	77901-05
For specific ZIP Codes call (888) 275-8777, or your local postmaster.	
Victoria Mall (Part of Victoria)	77904
Victory City	75561
Victory Gardens	77630
Vidauri	78377
Vidor	77662*
	77670†
Vienna	77964
View	79606
Viewpoint	75460
Vigo Park	79088
Vilas	76534
Villa Cavazos	78520
Village Mills	77663
Village Shores	78130
Village Station (Part of Midland)‡	79704
Villa Nueva	78520
Villareales	78582
Vincent	79511
Vineyard	76458
Vinton	79821
Violet	78380
Virginia Point	77554
Vista del Sol (Part of El Paso)	79935
Vista Ridge Mall (Part of Lewisville)	75067
Vistula	75851
Voca	76887
Volente	78641
Von Ormy	78073
Voss	76888
Votaw	77376
Voth (Part of Beaumont)	77709
Vsetin	77964
Waco	76701-11
	76714-98
For specific ZIP Codes call (888) 275-8777, or your local postmaster.	
Wade	78372
Wadsworth	77483
Waelder	78959
Wainwright (Part of San Antonio)‡	78208
Wainwright Heights	76544
Waka	79093
Wake	79243
Wakefield	75939
Wake Village	75501
Walburg	78673
Waldeck	78946
Walden	77356
Walden Place	77093
Waldrip	76852
Walhalla	78954
Walkers Mill	75650
Walker Village	76544
Wall	76957
Wallace	75103
Wallace Chapel	75686
Waller	77484
Wallis	77485
Wallisville	77597
Walnut Bend	76273
Walnut Bend (Part of Houston)	77042
Walnut Creek	77355
Walnut Forest	78753
Walnut Grove, *Collin*	75069
Walnut Grove, *Smith*	75703
Walnut Hill (Part of Dallas)‡	75220
Walnut Hills	77306
Walnut Springs, *Bosque*	76690
Walnut Springs, *Montgomery*	77355
Walston Springs	75801
Walton, *Cass*	71082
Walton, *Van Zandt*	75751
Wamba	75503
Waneta	75844
Waples	76048
Warda	78960
Ward Prairie	75840
Wards Creek	75574
Waring	78074
Warren	77664
Warren City	75647
Warrenton	78961
Warsaw	75142
Washburn	79019
Washington	77880
Waskom	75692
Wastella	79545
Watauga	76148
Water Front Park	78130
Waterloo (Part of Denison)	75020
Waterloo, *Williamson*	76574
Waterman	75935
Waters Bluff	75792
Water Valley	76958
Waterwood, *San Jacinto*	77359
Waterwood, *Walker*	77340
Watkins	75103
Watson	76550
Watson Community (Part of Arlington)‡	76006
Watsonville	76063
Watt	76664
Waxahachie	75165
	75167-68
For specific ZIP Codes call (888) 275-8777, or your local postmaster.	
Wayside	79094
Wealthy	77871
Weatherford	76086-88
For specific ZIP Codes call (888) 275-8777, or your local postmaster.	
Weaver	75478
Webberville	78653
Webbville	76828
Webster, *Harris*	77598
Webster, *Wood*	75494
Weches	75844
Wedgewood‡	76162-63
For specific ZIP Codes call (888) 275-8777, or your local postmaster.	
Weedhaven	77979
Weeping Mary	75925
Weesatche	77993
Weimar	78962
Weinert	76388
Weir	78674
Weirville	75482
Welch	79377
Welch Store	75973
Welcome	78944
Weldon	75851
Welfare	78006
Wellborn	77881
Wellington	79095
Wellman	79378
Wells, *Cherokee*	75976
Wells, *Lynn*	79351
Wellswood	75929
Wentworth	75103
Weser	77963
Weslaco	78596
Weslayan (Part of Houston)‡	77277
Wesley	77833
Wesley Grove	77831
West	76691
West Austin (Part of Austin)‡	78763
West Baytown (Part of Baytown)	77520
West Bluff	77630
Westbrae (Part of Houston)‡	77031
	77215
	77271†
For specific ZIP Codes call (888) 275-8777, or your local postmaster.	
Westbrook	79565
West Camp	79325
Westchase (Part of Houston)‡	77215
Westchester (Part of Grand Prairie)‡	75054
Westcliff	76513
West Cliff Park (Part of Amarillo)	79124
West Columbia	77486
West Delta	75448
Western Hills (Part of Copperas Cove)	76522
Western Plaza Mall (Part of Amarillo)	79101
Westfield, *Harris*‡	77073
Westfield, *Wharton*	77437
Westfield Estates	77093
West Galveston (Part of Jamaica Beach)	77551
Westgate, *Harris*	77429
Westgate (Part of San Angelo)	76901
Westgate Mall (Part of Amarillo)	79160
Westgate Mall (Part of Austin)	78704
Westgate Towne Centre (Part of Abilene)	79605
Westhaven	78130
Westhill Addition	77437
Westhoff	77994
West Lake, *Jasper*	75951
Westlake, *Tarrant*	76248
Westlake (Part of West Lake Hills)‡	78746
West Lake Hills	78746
Westlakes (Part of San Antonio)‡	78245
Westlakes Mercado (Part of San Antonio)	78227
Westlawn	77630
Westminster	75485
West Mountain	75647
West Odessa‡	79764*
	79769†
Weston	75097
West Orange	77630
Westover	76380
Westover Hills	76107
West Payne	77437
Westphalia	76656
West Point, *Fayette*	78963
West Point, *Lynn*	79373
West Sinton	78370
West Tawakoni	75474
West University Place	77005
West Vernon (Part of Vernon)	76384
Westview (Part of Waco)‡	76710
Westville	75862
West Waco (Part of Waco)	76710
Westway♦	79835
Westwood	75951
Westwood Mall (Part of Houston)	77036
Westworth	76114
Wetmore (Part of San Antonio)	78247
Wetsel	75069
Wexford Park	77662
Whaley	75570
Wharton	77488
Whatley	75657
Wheatland	76116
Wheeler	79096
Wheeler Springs	75835
Wheelock	77882
Whispering Oaks (Part of East Tawakoni)	75453
Whispering Oaks (Part of San Antonio)	78230
Whispering Pines, *Montgomery*	77302
Whispering Pines, *Walker*	77358
Whispering Winds	78264
Whisperwood (Part of Lubbock)‡	79416
White City, *San Augustine*	75929
White City, *Wilbarger*	76384
White Deer	79097
Whiteface	79379
Whiteflat	79234
White Hall, *Bell*	76557
White Hall, *Coryell*	76528
White Hall, *Grimes*	77868
Whitehall, *Kaufman*	75147
Whitehouse	75791
Whiteland	76858
White Mound	75090
White Oak, *Gregg*	75693
White Oak, *Montgomery*	77365
White Oak, *Morris*	75571
White Oak, *Titus*	75455
White Oak Valley Estates	77301
White Rock (Part of Dallas)‡	75218
White Rock, *Grayson*	75491
White Rock, *Hunt*	75423
White Rock, *Red River*	75426
White Rock, *Robertson*	76629
White Rock, *San Augustine*	75972
Whitesboro	76273
White Settlement	76108
Whitestar	79234
White Stone (Part of Cedar Park)	78641
Whitetail	78628
Whiteway	76538
Whitewright	75491
Whitharral	79380
Whitman	77833
Whitney	76692
Whitsett	78075
Whitt	76490
Whitton	75103
Whon	76878
Wichita Falls	76301-10
For specific ZIP Codes call (888) 275-8777, or your local postmaster.	
Wichita Valley Farms	76301
Wickett	79788
Wiedeville	77833
Wieland	75402
Wiergate	75977
Wiggins	76691
Wigginsville	77301
Wilcox	77879
Wildcat (Part of Plano)‡	75023
Wilderville	76570
Wild Horse	79855
Wild Hurst	75925
Wildorado	79098
Wild Peach Village♦	77422
Wildwood, *Hardin*	77663
Wildwood, *Walker*	77367
Wilford Hall U.S. Air Force Hospital (Part of San Antonio)	78236
Wilkins	75755
Wilkinson	75455
Willacy County Housing Authority	78580
Willamar	78580
William Beaumont Army Medical Center	79920
William Penn	77833
William Rice (Part of Houston)‡	77005
Williams	76471
Williamsburg (Part of Paris)	75460
Williamsburg, *Lavaca*	77964
William Spear Addition	75704
Willis	77378
Willow Bend (Part of Houston)	77035
Willow City	78675
Willow Grove, *McLennan*	76712
Willow Grove, *Shelby*	75954
Willow Park	76087
Willow Place‡	77070*
	77269†
Willow Point	76426
Willow Springs, *Fayette*	78940
Willow Springs, *Rains*	75440
Willow Springs, *San Jacinto*	77331
Wills Point	75169
Wilmer	75172
Wilmeth	79567
Wilson, *Falls*	76519
Wilson, *Lynn*	79381
Wilson Lake	77351
Wimberley♦	78676
Winchell	76827
Winchester	78945
Windcrest	78239
Windemere	78669
Windmill (Part of Houston)‡	77075
Windom	75492
Windsor Park Mall (Part of San Antonio)	78218
Windthorst	76389
Winedale	77835
Winfield	75493
Winfree, *Chambers*	77535
Winfree, *Orange*	77630
Wingate	79566
Wink	79789
Winkler	75859
Winnie♦	77665
Winningkoff (Part of Lucas)	75069
Winnsboro	75494
Winona	75792
Winter Haven	78839
Winter Hill	75943
Winters	79567
Winwood Mall (Part of Odessa)	79762
Witting	77975
Wixon Valley	77808
Wizard Wells	76458
Woden	75978
Wolfe City	75496
Wolfforth	79382
Womack	76634
Woodbine	76240
Woodbranch	77357
Woodbury	76645
Wood-Canyon Waters	75147
Woodcreek	78676
Woodcreek North	78676
Woodcrest	77301
Woodhaven Estates	77304
Wood Hollow	77365
Woodlake, *Bexar*	78244
Woodlake, *Grayson*	75021
Woodlake, *Trinity*	75865
Woodland, *Bell*	76513
Woodland, *Red River*	75436
Woodland Estates	75948
Woodland Hills, *Henderson*	75143
Woodland Hills, *Hill*	76692
Woodland Lakes	77355
Woodland Shores	75630
Woodlands Mall, The	77380
Woodlawn, *Angelina*	75904
Woodlawn, *Harrison*	75694
Woodlawn Lakes	77355
Woodley	75670
Woodloch	77301
Woodridge Park	78264
Woodrow, *Fort Bend*	77430
Woodrow, *Lubbock*	79401
Woods	75974
Woodsboro	78393
Woods of Shavano (Part of San Antonio)	78249
Woodson	76491
Wood Springs	75701
Woodville	75979
Woodway, *McLennan*	76712
Woodway (Part of Victoria)	77904
Woody Acres	77365
Woosley	75472
World Trade Center (Part of Dallas)‡	75207
Wortham	76693
Worthing	77964
Wright City	75684
Wrightsboro	78677
Wylie, *Collin*	75098
Wylie, *Franklin*	75494
Wylie (Part of Abilene)	79606
Wynnewood Village Shopping Center (Part of Dallas)	75224
Wynnrock Estates	78737
Yancey	78886
Yantis	75497
Yarboro	77868
Yarbrough Plaza (Part of El Paso)	79912
Yard	75861
Yarrelton	76518
Yaupon Cove	77351
Yellowpine	75948
Yoakum	77995
Yorktown	78164
Young	75840
Youngsport	76542
Yowell	75428
Ysleta (Part of El Paso)‡	79907*
	79917†
Zabcikville	76501
Zapata♦	78076
Zavalla	75980
Zephyr	76890
Zionsville	77833
Zippville	78155
Zorn	78666
Zuehl	78124
Zunkerville	78119
Zybach	79011

* **Area Zip Code** † **Post Office Boxes** ‡ **Postal Station** ♦ **Census Designated Place** *Italic Type* **County**

Abraham	84635
Adamsville	84731
Alpine	84004
Alta	84092
Altamont	84001
Alton	84710
Altonah	84002
Amalga	84335
American Fork	84003
Aneth	84510
Angle	84712
Annabella	84711
Antimony	84712
Arcadia	84012
Arsenal (Part of Sunset)	84015
Aspen Acres	84055
Atwood (Part of Murray)	84107
Aurora	84620
Austin	84754
Avon	84328
Axtell	84621
Ballard	84066
Bauer	84071
Bear River City	84301
Beaver	84713
Beaverdam	84306
Belmont Heights (Part of Sandy)	84070
Benjamin	84660
Ben Lomond (Part of Ogden)‡	84404
Bennion (Part of Taylorsville)	84018
	84023
For specific ZIP Codes call (888) 275-8777, or your local postmaster.	
Benson	84335
Beryl	84714
Beryl Junction	84714
Bicknell	84715
Big Water	84741
Bingham Canyon	84006
Birdseye	84629
Blanding	84511
Bloomington	84790
Bluebell	84007
Bluff	84512
Bluffdale	84065
Bonanza	84008
Boneta	84051
Bonnie (Part of Orem)	84057
Bothwell	84337
Boulder	84716
Bountiful	84010*
	84011†
Bowery Haven	84701
Brendel	84540
Brian Head	84719
Bridgeland	84012
Bridgerland Shopping Center (Part of Logan)	84321
Brigham City	84302
Brighton	84121
Brooklyn	84754
Bryce	84764
Bryce Canyon	84717
Bullfrog	84533
Burbank	84751
Burmester	84029
Burrville	84701
Bushnell (Part of Brigham City)	84302
Cache Junction	84304
Cache Valley Mall (Part of Logan)	84321
Caineville	84775
Callao	84034
Call Fort	84302
Cannonville	84718
Carbonville	84501
Castle Dale	84513
Castleton	84532
Castle Valley	84532
Cedar City	84720*
	84721†
Cedar Hills	84062
Cedar Valley	84013
Cedarview	84066
Center Creek	84032
Centerfield	84622
Centerville	84014
Central, *Sevier*	84754
Central, *Washington*	84722
Charleston	84032
Chester	84623
Circleville	84723
Cisco	84515
Clarkston	84305
Clawson	84516
Clear Creek, *Box Elder*	83342
Clear Creek, *Carbon*	84526
Clearfield	84015-16
	84089
For specific ZIP Codes call (888) 275-8777, or your local postmaster.	
Cleveland	84518
Clinton	84015
Clover	84069
Coalville	84017
College Ward	84321
Collinston	84306
Columbia	84520
Columbia Junction (Part of East Carbon)	84520
Copperton	84006
Corinne	84307
Cornish	84308
Cottonwood	84171
Cottonwood Heights	84121
Cove	84320
Crescent (Part of Sandy)	84070
Crossroads Plaza Mall & Tower (Part of Salt Lake City)	84144
Croydon	84018
Cushing (Part of Midvale)	84047
Dammeron Valley	84783
Daniel	84032
Defas Park	84031
Delta	84624
Deseret	84624
Devils Slide	84050
Deweyville	84309
Downtown (Part of Salt Lake City)‡	84101
Draper	84020
Dry Fork	84078
Duchesne	84021
Duck Creek Village	84762
Dugway Proving Ground	84022
Dutch John	84023
East Bay (Part of Provo)‡	84605
East Carbon	84520
Eastland	84535
East Midvale	84047
East Millcreek♦	84117
East Portal	84032
Eastwood Hills	84106
Echo	84024
Eden	84310
Elberta	84626
Elgin	84525
Elk Ridge	84660
Elmo	84521
Elsinore	84724
Elwood	84337
Emery	84522
Emory	84024
Emporium (Part of Park City)‡	84068
Enoch	84720
Enterprise, *Morgan*	84050
Enterprise, *Washington*	84725
Ephraim	84627
Erda	84074
Escalante	84726
Esk Dale	84728
Etna	84313
Eureka	84628
Fairfield	84013
Fairgrounds (Part of Salt Lake City)	84116
Fairview	84629
Family Center at Midvalley, The	84123
Farmington	84025
Farr West	84404
Fashion Place (Part of Murray)	84107
Faust	84080
Fayette	84630
Ferron	84523
Fielding	84311
Fillmore	84631
Fish Lake	84701
Flowell	84631
Foothill (Part of Salt Lake City)‡	84108
Fort Duchesne♦	84026
Fountain Green	84632
Francis	84036
Freedom	84646
Freeport Center (Part of Clearfield)‡	84016
Fremont	84747
Fruita	84775
Fruit Heights	84037
Fruitland	84027
Gandy	84728
Garden City	84028
Garland	84312
Garrison	84728
Genola	84655
Glendale	84729
Glenwood	84730
Goshen	84633
Goshute Indian Reservation	84034
Gouldings Trading Post	86033
Grand Vu	84532
Granger (Part of West Valley City)	84119
Granite♦	84092
Grantsville	84029
Greendale	84023
Green Lake	84023
Green River	84525
Greenville	84731
Greenwich	84732
Grouse Creek	84313
Grover	84773
Gunlock	84733
Gunnison	84634
Gusher	84030
Hailstone	84032
Halchita	84531
Halls Crossing	84533
Hamilton Fort	84720
Hanksville	84734
Hanna	84031
Hardy (Part of Lindon)	84062
Harrisburg Junction	84737
Harrisville	84404
Hatch	84735
Hatton	84637
Hayden	84053
Heber City	84032
Helper	84526
Henefer	84033
Henrieville	84736
Herriman	84065
Hiawatha	84527
Hidden Lake	84055
Highland	84003
Highlands	84050
Hildale	84784
Hill Air Force Base	84056
Hinckley	84635
Hite	84533
Holden	84636
Holiday Park	84055
Holladay	84117
Honeyville	84314
Hooper	84315
Hoovers	84750
Howell	84316
Hoytsville	84017
Hunter (Part of West Valley City)	84120
Huntington	84528
Huntsville	84317
Hurricane	84737
Hyde Park	84318
Hyrum	84319
Ibapah	84034
Indianola	84629
Ioka	84066
Ivins	84738
Jensen	84035
Jerusalem	84646
Joseph	84739
Junction	84740
Kamas	84036
Kanab	84741
Kanarraville	84742
Kanosh	84637
Kaysville	84037
Kearns♦	84118
Keetley	84032
Kelton	84336
Kenilworth	84529
Kimball Junction	84060
Kingston	84743
Koosharem	84744
Lake Point	84074
Lake Powell	84533
Lake Shore	84601
Lakeside Resort	84701
Laketown	84038
Lakeview	84601
Lapoint	84039
Lark	84065
La Sal	84530
La Sal Junction	84530
La Verkin	84745
Lawrence	84528
Layton	84040-41
For specific ZIP Codes call (888) 275-8777, or your local postmaster.	
Layton Hills Mall (Part of Layton)	84041
Leamington	84638
Leeds	84746
Leeton	84066
Lehi	84043
Leland	84660
Levan	84639
Lewiston	84320
Liberty	84310
Lincoln	84074
Lindon	84042
Little Bonanza	84078
Littleton	84050
Loa	84747
Logan	84321-23
	84341
For specific ZIP Codes call (888) 275-8777, or your local postmaster.	
Long Valley Junction	84758
Lund	84720
Lyman	84749
Lynn	83346
Lynndyl	84640
Madsen (Part of Honeyville)	84314
Maeser♦	84078
Magna♦	84044
Mammoth	84601
Manderfield	84713
Manila	84046
Manti	84642
Mantua	84324
Mapleton	84664
Marion	84036
Marriott	84404
Martin	84526
Marysvale	84750
Mayfield	84643
Meadow	84644
Meadowville	84038
Mendon	84325
Mexican Hat	84531
Middleton	84770
Midvale	84047
Midway	84049
Milburn	84629
Milford	84751
Millcreek, *Grand*	84532
Millcreek, *Salt Lake*♦	84109
Mills	84639
Millville	84326
Milton	84050
Minersville	84752
Moab	84532
Modena	84753
Molen	84523
Mona	84645
Monarch	84066
Monroe	84754
Montezuma Creek♦	84534
Monticello	84535
Monti Verdi	84050
Monument Valley	84536
Moore	84523
Morgan	84050
Moroni	84646
Mountain Green	84050
Mountain Home	84051
Mount Carmel	84755
Mount Carmel Junction	84755
Mount Emmons	84001
Mount Ogden (Part of Ogden)‡	84415
Mount Olympus♦	84117
Mount Pleasant	84647
Murray	84107
Myton	84052
Naples	84078
Navajo Indian Reservation	86515
Neola♦	84053
Nephi	84648
Newcastle	84756
New Harmony	84757
Newton	84327
Nibley	84321
North Creek	84713
North Logan	84341
North Ogden	84404
North Salt Lake	84054
Northwest (Part of Salt Lake City)‡	84116
Oak City	84649
Oak Creek	84629
Oakley	84055
Oasis	84650
Ogden	84401-15
For specific ZIP Codes call (888) 275-8777, or your local postmaster.	
Ogden ALC Hardness Test Center	84401
Ogden City Mall (Part of Ogden)	84401
Oljato	86033
Olmstead	84604
Ophir	84071
Orangeville	84537
Orderville	84758
Orem	84057-59
	84097
For specific ZIP Codes call (888) 275-8777, or your local postmaster.	
Ouray	84063
Pallas (Part of Murray)	84107
Palmyra	84660
Panguitch	84759
Paradise	84328
Paragonah	84760
Park City	84060*
	84068†
Park Terrace	84106
Park Valley	84329
Parowan	84761
Partoun	84083
Payson	84651
Penrose	84337
Peoa	84061
Perry	84302
Peruvian Park (Part of Sandy)	84093
Peterson	84050
Pickelville (Part of Garden City)	84028
Pine Mountain	84055
Pine Valley	84781
Pintura	84720
Pioneer (Part of Salt Lake City)‡	84147
Plain City	84404
Pleasant Grove	84062
Pleasant View	84404
Plymouth	84330
Polls	84050
Portage	84331
Portersville	84050
Price	84501
Promontory	84307
Providence	84332
Provo	84601-06
For specific ZIP Codes call (888) 275-8777, or your local postmaster.	
Randlett♦	84063
Randolph	84064
Redmond	84652
Red Rock (Part of St. George)	84790*
	84791†
Red Wash	84078
Redwood (Part of West Valley City)	84119
Richfield	84701
Richmond	84333
Richville	84050
Riverdale	84405
River Heights	84321
Riverside	84334
Riverton	84065
Rockville	84763
Roosevelt	84066
Roper (Part of South Salt Lake)	84115
Rosette	84329

* **Area Zip Code** † **Post Office Boxes** ‡ **Postal Station** ♦ **Census Designated Place** *Italic Type* **County**

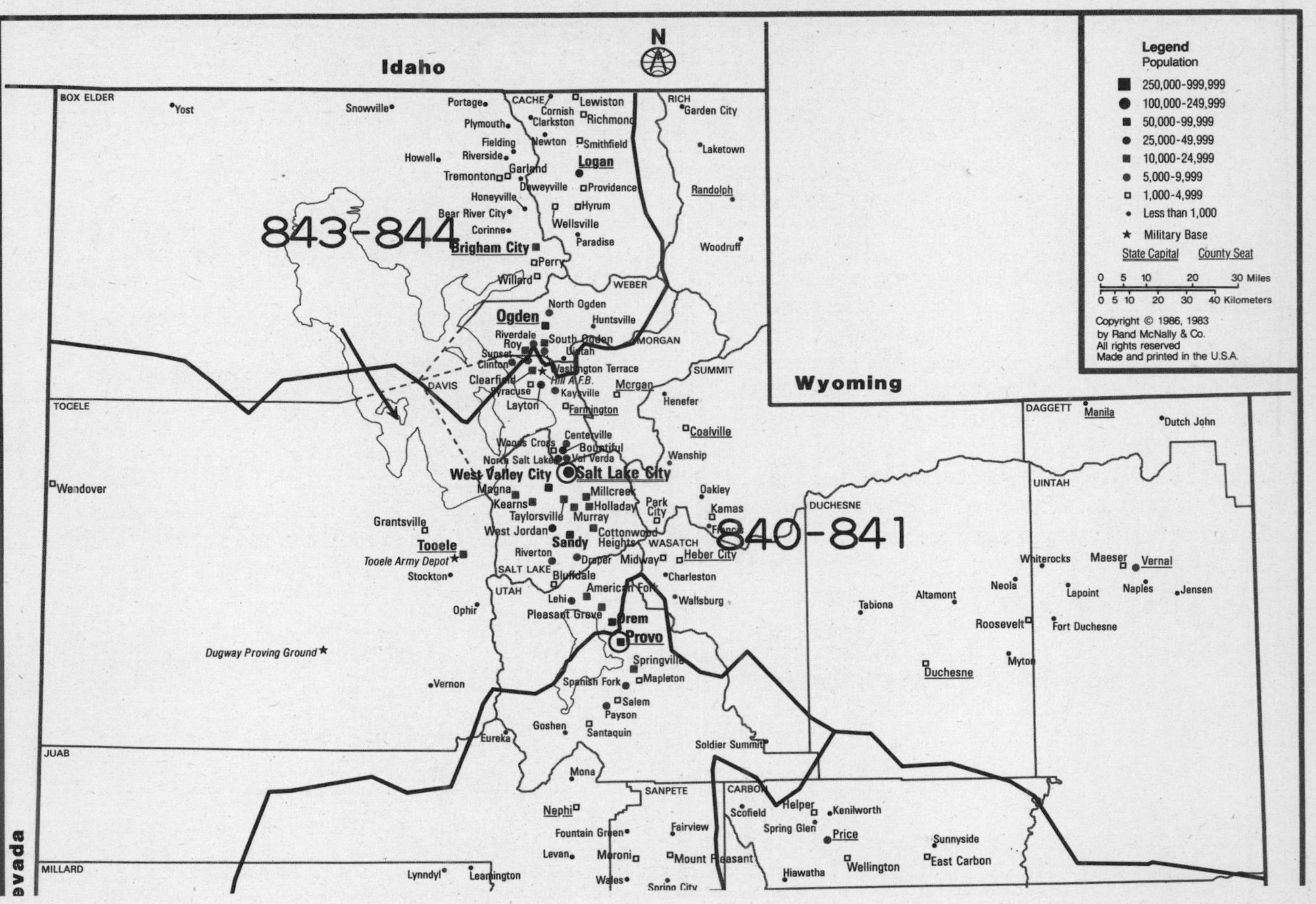
Idaho
N
Wyoming
Legend
Population
250,000-999,999
100,000-249,999
50,000-99,999
25,000-49,999
10,000-24,999
5,000-9,999
1,000-4,999
Less than 1,000
Military Base
State Capital
County Seat
0 5 10 20 30 Miles
0 5 10 20 30 40 Kilometers
Copyright © 1986, 1983
by Rand McNally & Co.
All rights reserved
Made and printed in the U.S.A.
843-844
840-841
BOX ELDER
CACHE
RICH
WEBER
MORGAN
SUMMIT
DAVIS
TOOELE
SALT LAKE
WASATCH
UTAH
DAGGETT
UINTAH
DUCHESNE
JUAB
SANPETE
CARBON
MILLARD
Yost
Snowville
Portage
Plymouth
Fielding
Howell
Riverside
Tremonton
Garland
Honeyville
Bear River City
Corinne
Brigham City
Perry
Willard
Cornish
Clarkston
Newton
Lewiston
Richmond
Smithfield
Logan
Deweyville
Providence
Hyrum
Wellsville
Paradise
Garden City
Laketown
Randolph
Woodruff
Ogden
North Ogden
Huntsville
Riverdale
Roy
Sunset
Clinton
Clearfield
Syracuse
Layton
Kaysville
Hill A.F.B.
Washington Terrace
Morgan
Henefer
Farmington
Coalville
Centerville
Bountiful
Woods Cross
North Salt Lake
Val Verda
Wanship
West Valley City
Salt Lake City
Magna
Kearns
Millcreek
Holladay
Taylorsville
Murray
Park City
Oakley
Kamas
Francis
West Jordan
Sandy
Cottonwood Heights
Riverton
Draper
Midway
Heber City
Bluffdale
Charleston
Wendover
Grantsville
Tooele
Tooele Army Depot
Stockton
Ophir
Dugway Proving Ground
Vernon
Lehi
American Fork
Wallsburg
Pleasant Grove
Orem
Provo
Springville
Spanish Fork
Mapleton
Salem
Payson
Goshen
Santaquin
Eureka
Soldier Summit
Mona
Nephi
Fountain Green
Fairview
Levan
Moroni
Mount Pleasant
Wales
Spring City
Lynndyl
Leamington
Scofield
Helper
Kenilworth
Spring Glen
Price
Wellington
Hiawatha
Sunnyside
East Carbon
Manila
Dutch John
Whiterocks
Maeser
Vernal
Tabiona
Altamont
Neola
Lapoint
Naples
Jensen
Roosevelt
Fort Duchesne
Duchesne
Myton
Nevada

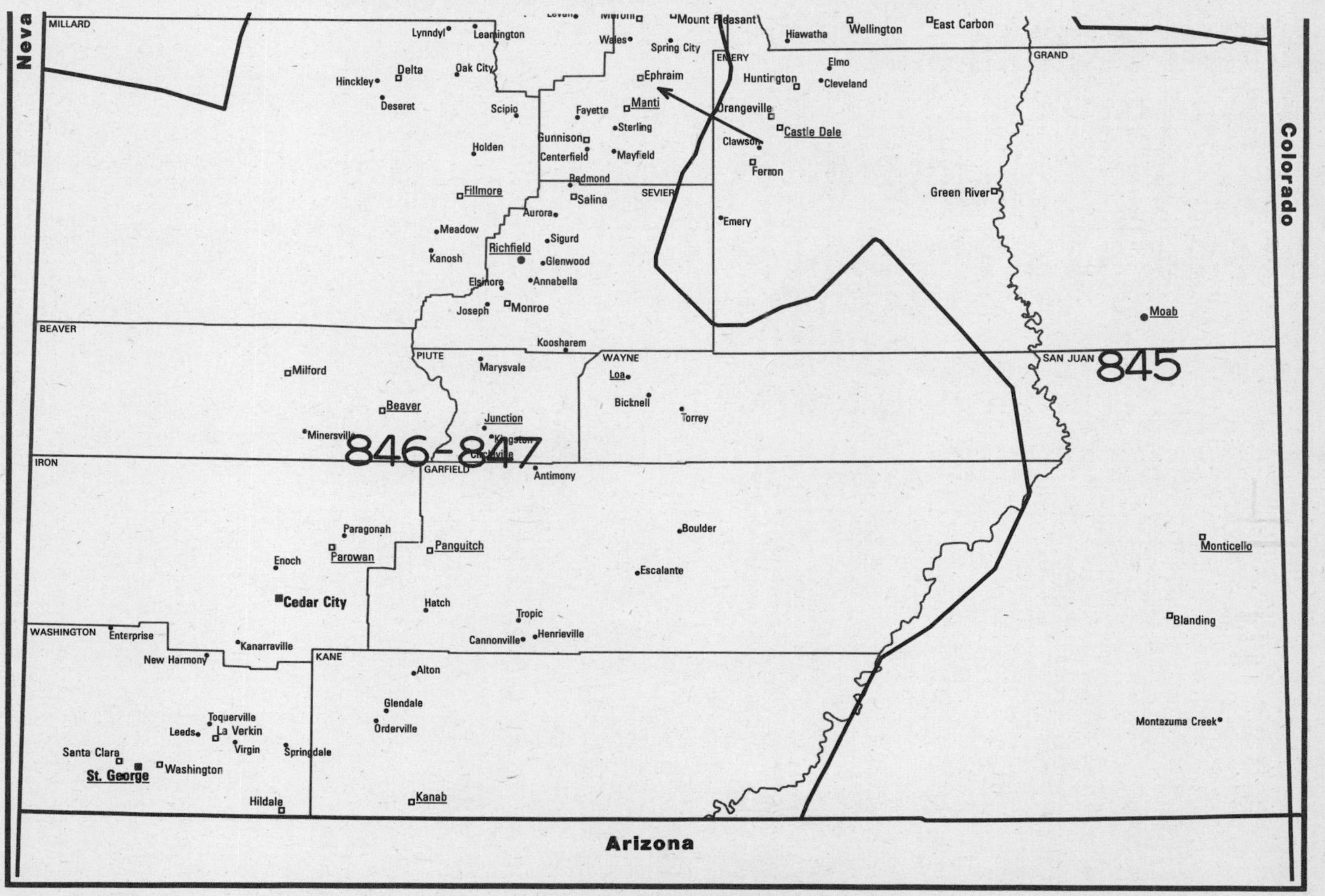
Neva
Colorado
Arizona
845
846-847
MILLARD
BEAVER
IRON
WASHINGTON
KANE
GARFIELD
PIUTE
WAYNE
SEVIER
EMERY
GRAND
SAN JUAN
Lynndyl
Leamington
Wales
Spring City
Mount Pleasant
Hiawatha
Wellington
East Carbon
Delta
Oak City
Hinckley
Deseret
Scipio
Ephraim
Manti
Fayette
Sterling
Huntington
Elmo
Cleveland
Orangeville
Castle Dale
Clawson
Ferron
Holden
Gunnison
Centerfield
Mayfield
Redmond
Salina
Fillmore
Aurora
Emery
Green River
Meadow
Kanosh
Richfield
Sigurd
Glenwood
Elsinore
Annabella
Joseph
Monroe
Moab
Koosharem
Marysvale
Loa
Milford
Bicknell
Torrey
Beaver
Junction
Kingston
Circleville
Minersville
Antimony
Paragonah
Parowan
Panguitch
Boulder
Monticello
Enoch
Escalante
Cedar City
Hatch
Tropic
Cannonville
Henrieville
Blanding
Enterprise
Kanarraville
New Harmony
Alton
Glendale
Orderville
Montezuma Creek
Toquerville
Leeds
La Verkin
Virgin
Springdale
Santa Clara
St. George
Washington
Hildale
Kanab

Round Valley 84038
Roy 84067
Rush Valley 84069
St. George 84770-71
..........84790-91
For specific ZIP Codes call (888) 275-8777, or your local postmaster.
Salem 84653
Salina............. 84654

Salt Lake City

..........84101-80
For specific ZIP Codes call (888) 275-8777, or your local postmaster.

Colleges & Universities

ITT Technical Institute 84123
Univ of Utah............. 84112
Westminster Coll 84105

Financial Institutions

First Security Bank...... 84111
KeyBank 84144
Washington Mutual Bank 84111
Zions First Nat Bank .. 84111

Hospitals

LDS Hosp 84143
Univ of Utah Hosps & Clinics 84132

Hotels/Motels

Best Western Olympus 84101
Doubletree............. 84101
Hilton, Airport............. 84116
Hilton, Salt Lake.......... 84101
Holiday Inn Downtown 84111
Little America Hotel & Towers 84101
Marriott 84101
Wyndham 84101

Military Installations

Stephen A Douglas Armed Forces Res Ctr 84113
Utah Air Nat Guard, FB6441, Salt Lake City International Airport 84116

Samak............. 84036
Sandy 84070
..........84090-94
For specific ZIP Codes call (888) 275-8777, or your local postmaster.
Santa Clara 84765
Santaquin 84655
Scipio 84656
Scofield 84526
Sevier 84766
Sherwood Park (Part of Sandy) 84093
Shivwits 84765
Sigurd 84657
Silver Fork 84121
Silver Reef 84746
Skull Valley Indian Reservation 84029
Slaterville 84404
Smithfield............. 84335
Snowbird............. 84092
Snowville 84336
Snyderville 84098
Soldier Summit 84601
South Jordan............. 84095
South Ogden............. 84403
South Salt Lake 84115
South Weber 84405
Spanish Fork 84660
Spring City............. 84662
Springdale 84767
Springdell............. 84604
Spring Glen 84526
Spring Lake 84651
Springville 84663
Standrod 83342
Stansbury Park♦ 84074
Starr 84645
Sterling 84665
Stockton 84071
Stoddard 84050
Sugar House (Part of Salt Lake City)‡ 84106
Sugarville............. 84624
Summit 84772
Summit Point............. 84535
Sunnyside 84539
Sunset............. 84015
Sutherland............. 84624
Swan Creek............. 84028
Syracuse 84075
Tabiona 84072
Talmage............. 84073
Taylor............. 84401
Taylorsville 84084
..........84118-19
.... 84123
For specific ZIP Codes call (888) 275-8777, or your local postmaster.
Teasdale 84773
Terra 84022
Thatcher 84337
Thompson 84540
Thompsonville 84750
Ticaboo 84533
Tooele 84074
Tooele Army Depot 84074
Toquerville 84774
Torrey 84775
Town (Part of Ogden)‡ 84402
Tremonton............. 84337
Trenton 84338
Tridell............. 84076
Tropic 84776
Trout Creek 84083
Ucolo............. 84535
Uintah 84405
Uintah and Ouray Indian Reservation 84026
Union............. 84047
University (Part of Provo)‡ 84602
University Mall (Part of Orem) 84097
Upalco............. 84007
Upton 84017
Utah State University (Part of Logan)‡ 84322
Utida (Part of Cornish) 84308
Uvada 84753
Val Verda♦............. 84010
Venice 84701
Vermillion 84657
Vernal 84078*
.... 84079†
Vernon............. 84080
Veyo 84782
Vineyard............. 84057
Virgin 84779
Vivian Park............. 84604
Wales 84667
Wallsburg............. 84082
Wanship 84017
Warren............. 84404
Washington 84780
Washington Terrace.... 84403
Wellington 84542
Wellsville 84339
Wendover 84083
West Bountiful 84087
West Haven 84067
West Jordan 84084
.... 84088
For specific ZIP Codes call (888) 275-8777, or your local postmaster.
West Point 84015
West Valley City 84119-20
For specific ZIP Codes call (888) 275-8777, or your local postmaster.
West Warren 84404
West Weber............. 84401
Wheelon 84306
White City♦ 84070
Whiterocks♦ 84085
Wildwood 84604
Willard 84340
Wilson (Part of West Haven) 84401
Woodland 84036
Woodland Hills............. 84653
Woodruff 84086
Woods Cross............. 84087
Yost............. 83342
ZCMI Center (Part of Salt Lake City) 84111
Zion National Park 84767

Place	ZIP
Abnaki	05474
Adamant	05640
Addison	05491
Albany	05820
Albany Center	05845
Alburg	05440
Alburg Center	05440
Alburg Springs	05440
Alfrecha	05759
Alpine Village	05674
Ames Hill	05344
Amsden	05151
Andover (Town)	05143
Arlington	05250
Arnold Bay	05491
Ascutney	05030
Athens	05143
Avalon Beach	05750
Averill	05901
Avery's Gore (Town)	05903
Bailey's Mills	05062
Bakersfield	05441
Baltimore (Town)	05143
Barnard	05031
Barnet	05821
Barnet Center	05821
Barnumtown	05472
Barre (Town)	05678
Barre	05641
Barre Transfer (Part of Montpelier)	05602
Barton	05822
Bartonsville	05143
Basin Harbor	05491
Bayside	05404
Beanville	05060
Beaulieu's Corner	05459
Beebe Plain	05823
Beecher Falls	05902
Bellows Falls	05101
Belmont	05730
Belvidere (Town)	05492
Belvidere Center	05492
Belvidere Corners	05492
Belvidere Junction	05492
Bennington♦	05201
Bennington College (Part of North Bennington)‡	05201
Benson	05731
Benson Landing	05743
Berkshire (Town)	05450
Berkshire	05447
Berlin (Town)	05602
Berlin Corners	05602
Bethel	05032
Bethel Gilead	05060
Binghamville	05444
Birdland	05474
Bliss Pond	05640
Blissville	05764
Bloomfield	03590
Blossoms Corners	05775
Bolton	05676
Bolton Valley	05477
Boltonville	05081
Bomoseen	05732
Bondville	05340
Bordoville	05450
Bowlsville	05742
Bradford	05033
Bragg	05055
Braintree	05060
Braintree Hill	05060
Brandon♦	05733
Brattleboro♦	05301-04
For specific ZIP Codes call (888) 275-8777, or your local postmaster.	
Brattleboro Center	05301
Bread Loaf	05753
Bridgewater	05034
Bridgewater Center	05035
Bridgewater Corners	05035
Bridport	05734
Brighton (Town)	05846
Brimstone Corner	05083
Brimstone Corners	05761
Bristol	05443
Brockways Mills	05143
Brookfield	05036
Brookfield Center	05036
Brookline (Town)	05345
Brookside, *Chittenden*	05494
Brookside, *Windham*	05341
Brooksville	05753
Brownington	05860
Brownington Center	05860
Brownsville	05037
Brunswick (Town)	03590

Place	ZIP
Buck Hollow	05454
Buels (Town)	05487
Burke	05871
Burke Mountain	05832
Burlington	05401-02
	05406
For specific ZIP Codes call (888) 275-8777, or your local postmaster.	
Burnham Hill	05843
Burnham Hollow	05757
Butlers Corners	05452
Butternut Bend	05761
Button Bay	05491
Cabot	05647
Cadys Falls	05661
Calais	05648
Cambridge	05444
Cambridge Junction	05464
Cambridgeport	05141
Canaan	05903
Castleton	05735
Cavendish	05142
Cavendish Center	05142
Cedar Beach	05445
Center Rutland	05736
Centerville, *Lamoille*	05655
Centerville, *Windsor*	05001
Champlain (Part of South Burlington)	05401
Charleston (Town)	05872
Charlotte	05445
Checkerberry	05468
Chelsea	05038
Chelsea West Hill	05041
Chester	05143
Chester Depot	05144
Chimney Corner	05446
Chimney Point	05491
Chipman Lake	05739
Chipmans Point	05760
Chippenhook	05777
Chiselville	05250
Chittenden (Town)	05737
Chittenden	05737
Clarendon	05759
Clarendon Springs	05777
Cleveland Corner	05661
Cloverdale	05489
Colbyville	05676
Colchester	05446*
	05449†
Cold River	05738
Concord	05824
Concord Corner	05824
Copperfield	05079
Corinth	05039
Corinth Center	05039
Corinth Corners	05039
Cornwall	05753
Coventry	05825
Craftsbury	05826
Craftsbury Common	05827
Cream Hill	05734
Crystal Beach	05732
Cuttingsville	05738
Danby	05739
Danby Corners	05739
Danville	05828
Danville Center	05828
Derby (Town)	05829
Derby	05829
Derby Line	05830
Deweys Mills	05059
Dorset	05251
Dover	05341
Downers	05151
Downingville	05443
Dows Crossing	05836
Dowsville	05660
Dummerston	05346
Duxbury	05676
Eagle Point	05855
East Albany	05845
East Alburg	05440
East Arlington	05252
East Barnard	05068
East Barre	05649
East Berkshire	05447
East Bethel	05032
East Braintree	05060
East Brookfield	05036
East Burke	05832
East Cabot	05647
East Calais	05650
East Cambridge	05464
East Charleston	05833
East Charlotte	05445
East Clarendon	05759
East Concord	05906

Place	ZIP
East Corinth	05040
East Craftsbury	05826
East Dorset	05253
East Dover	05341
East Dummerston	05346
East Enosburg	05450
East Fairfield	05448
East Fletcher	05464
East Franklin	05457
East Granville	05669
East Hardwick	05836
East Haven	05837
East Highgate	05459
East Hubbardton	05735
East Jamaica	05343
East Johnson	05656
East Lyndon	05851
East Middlebury	05740
East Monkton	05443
East Montpelier	05651
East Montpelier Center	05602
East Orange	05086
East Peacham	05862
East Pittsford	05701
East Poultney	05741
East Putney	05346
East Randolph	05041
East Richford	05476
East Roxbury	05663
East Rupert	05761
East Ryegate	05042
East Sheldon	05450
East Shoreham	05770
East St. Johnsbury	05838
East Sutton Ridge	05867
East Thetford	05043
East Wallingford	05742
East Warren	05674
Eden	05652
Eden Mills	05653
Egypt	05448
Elmore (Town)	05657
Ely	05045
Enosburg (Town)	05450
Enosburg Center	05450
Enosburg Falls	05450
Essex (Town)	05451
Essex Center	05451
Essex Junction	05452*
	05453†
Ethan Allen Shopping Center (Part of Burlington)	05404
Evansville	05860
Fairfax	05454
Fairfax Falls	05454
Fairfield	05455
Fairfield Station	05455
Fair Haven	05743
Fairlee	05045
Fays Corner	05477
Fayston (Town)	05660
Ferdinand (Town)	05905
Fernville	05733
Ferrisburgh	05456
Fieldsville	05089
Fletcher	05444
Florence	05744
Fonda	05488
Forest Dale	05745
Foxville	05654
Franklin	05457
Freedleyville	05253
Gallup Mills	05858
Garfield	05661
Gassetts	05143
Gaysville	05746
Georgia (Town)	05478
Georgia	05454
Georgia Center	05478
Georgia Plains	05468
Gilman	05904
Glastenbury (Town)	05262
Glover	05839
Goodrich Four Corners	05055
Goose City	05341
Goose Green	05039
Gordon Landing	05458
Goshen	05733
Goulde Mills	05156
Grafton	05146
Grahamville	05149
Granby	05840
Grand Isle	05458
Graniteville	05654
Granville	05747
Green Acres	05477
Green Bay	05046

Place	ZIP
Greenbush	05151
Green River	05301
Greensboro	05841
Greensboro Bend	05842
Greens Corners	05478
Groton	05046
Guildhall	05905
Guilford	05301
Guilford Center	05301
Halifax	05358
Halls Lake	05081
Hammondsville	05062
Hancock	05748
Hanksville	05487
Hardscrabble	05156
Hardwick	05843
Hardwick Center	05843
Hardwick Steet	05836
Harmonyville	05353
Harrisville	05301
Hartford	05047
Hartland	05048
Hartland Four Corners	05049
Harvey	05828
Healdville	05758
Heartwellville	05350
Hectorville	05471
Hewitts Corners	05053
Highgate (Town)	05459
Highgate Center	05459
Highgate Falls	05459
Highgate Springs	05460
Hinesburg, *Chittenden*	05461
Hinesburg, *Windham*	05301
Holden	05763
Holland	05830
Hortonia	05760
Hortonville	05758
Houghtonville	05146
Hubbard Corner	05478
Hubbardton	05732
Huntington	05462
Huntington Center	05462
Huntville	05454
Hutchins	05471
Hyde Park	05655
Hydeville	05750
Indian Point (Part of Newport)	05855
Inwood	05821
Ira	05777
Irasburg	05845
Irasville	05673
Island Pond♦	05846
Isle La Motte	05463
Jacksonville	05342
Jamaica	05343
Jay	05859
Jay Peak	05859
Jeffersonville	05464
Jenneville	05089
Jericho	05465
Jericho Center	05465
Jerusalem	05443
Joes Pond	05873
Johnson	05656
Jonesville	05466
Kansas	05252
Keeler Bay	05486
Kendall	05043
Kendricks Corner	05150
Killington	05751
Kimball	05822
Kirby (Town)	05824
Kirby Corner	05495
Lake Dunmore	05769
Lake Elmore	05657
Lake Fairlee	05045
Lake Hortonia	05743
Lake Morey	05045
Lake Park	05855
Lake Raponda	05363
Lake Rescue	05149
Lake St. Catherine	05764
Lakewood	05488
Landgrove	05148
Lapham Bay	05734
Larrabees Point	05770
Leicester	05733
Leicester Junction	05778
Lemington	03576
Lewis (Town)	05905
Lewiston	05055
Lilliesville	05032
Lincoln	05443
Lindsay Beach	05855
Londonderry	05148
Long Point	05473
Lowell	05847

Place	ZIP
Lower Branch	05060
Lower Cabot	05658
Lower Granville	05747
Lower Plain	05033
Lower Village	05672
Lower Waterford	05848
Lower Websterville	05641
Ludlow	05149
Lunenburg	05906
Lyman‡	05001
Lympus	05032
Lyndon	05849
Lyndon Center	05850
Lyndonville	05851
McIndoe Falls	05050
Mackville	05843
Mad River Glen	05673
Maidstone (Town)	05905
Maidstone Lake	03590
Mallets Bay	05404
Manchester	05254
Manchester Center♦	05255
Manchester Depot	05255
Maple Dell	05156
Maquam	05488
Marlboro	05344
Marshfield	05658
Mary Meyer‡	05353
Mechanicsville	05461
Medburyville	05363
Melville	05478
Mendon	05701
Merrill Corner	05845
Middlebury♦	05753
Middlesex	05602
Middlesex Center	05602
Middletown	05143
Middletown Springs	05757
Mile Point	05491
Miles Pond	05858
Millbrook	05053
Mill Village, *Orange*	05079
Mill Village, *Orleans*	05827
Milton	05468
Miltonboro	05468
Monkton	05469
Monkton Ridge	05473
Montgomery	05470
Montgomery Center	05471
Montpelier	05601†
	05602*
Moretown	05660
Moretown Common	05660
Morgan	05853
Morgan Center	05853
Morristown	05661
Morrisville	05661
Moscow	05662
Mosquitoville	05042
Mount Holly	05758
Mount Snow	05356
Mount Tabor	05739
Nashville	05465
Neshobe Beach	05732
Newark	05871
Newark Hollow	05871
New Boston (Norwich Town)	05772
New Boston (Stockbridge Town)	05055
Newbury	05051
Newbury Center	05081
Newfane	05345
New Haven	05472
New Haven Mills	05443
Newport (Town)	05857
Newport	05855
Newport Center	05857
North Bennington	05257
North Brattleboro‡	05304
North Burlington (Part of Burlington)‡	05401
North Calais	05650
North Cambridge	05464
North Chester	05143
North Clarendon	05759
North Concord	05858
North Danville	05819
North Derby	05855
North Dorset	05253
North Duxbury	05676
North Fairfax	05454
North Fayston	05660
North Ferrisburg	05473
Northfield	05663
Northfield Center	05663
Northfield Falls	05664
North Hartland	05052
North Hero	05474
North Hyde Park	05665

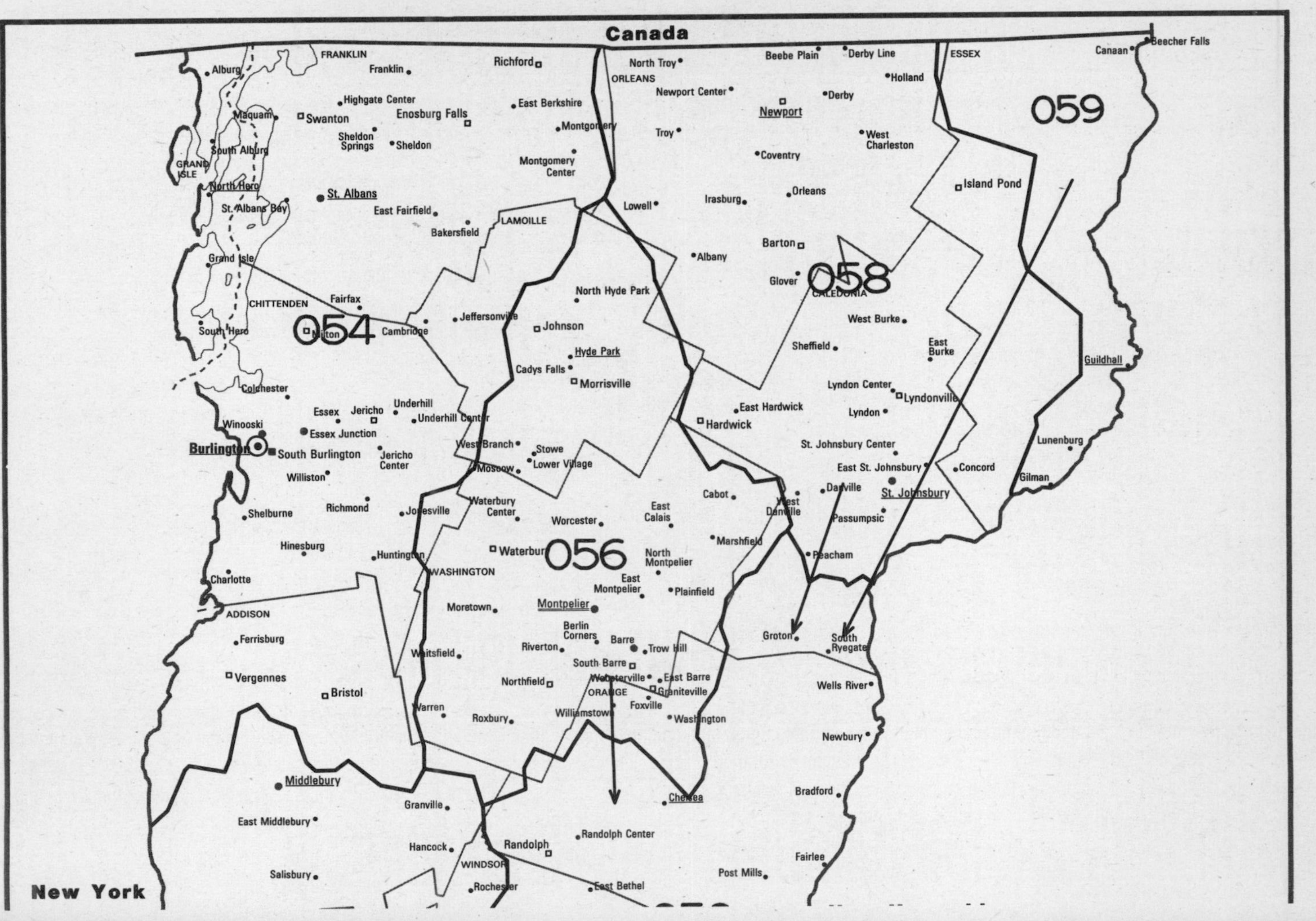

Canada
New York
059
058
056
054
ESSEX
ORLEANS
CALEDONIA
LAMOILLE
FRANKLIN
GRAND ISLE
CHITTENDEN
WASHINGTON
ORANGE
ADDISON
WINDSOR
Beecher Falls
Canaan
Island Pond
Guildhall
Lunenburg
Gilman
Concord
East Burke
Lyndonville
Holland
Derby Line
West Charleston
Derby
Beebe Plain
Newport
Coventry
Orleans
Barton
Glover
West Burke
Sheffield
Lyndon Center
Lyndon
St. Johnsbury Center
East St. Johnsbury
St. Johnsbury
Passumpsic
Danville
Peacham
South Ryegate
Wells River
Newbury
Bradford
Fairlee
Groton
West Danville
Marshfield
Cabot
East Hardwick
Hardwick
Albany
Irasburg
Newport Center
North Troy
Troy
Lowell
North Hyde Park
Hyde Park
Morrisville
Johnson
Cadys Falls
Stowe
Lower Village
Moscow
West Branch
Jeffersonville
Cambridge
Montgomery
Montgomery Center
East Berkshire
Richford
Enosburg Falls
Bakersfield
East Fairfield
Sheldon
Sheldon Springs
Franklin
Highgate Center
Swanton
St. Albans
St. Albans Bay
Maquam
Alburg
South Alburg
North Hero
Grand Isle
South Hero
Fairfax
Milton
Colchester
Winooski
Burlington
South Burlington
Essex
Essex Junction
Jericho
Jericho Center
Underhill
Underhill Center
Williston
Richmond
Shelburne
Hinesburg
Charlotte
Huntington
Jonesville
Waterbury Center
Waterbury
Worcester
East Calais
North Montpelier
Plainfield
East Montpelier
Montpelier
Berlin Corners
Barre
Trow Hill
East Barre
Graniteville
Washington
Chelsea
Foxville
South Barre
Websterville
Williamstown
Riverton
Northfield
Moretown
Waitsfield
Warren
Roxbury
Randolph Center
East Bethel
Randolph
Rochester
Hancock
Granville
Post Mills
Bristol
Vergennes
Ferrisburg
Middlebury
East Middlebury
Salisbury

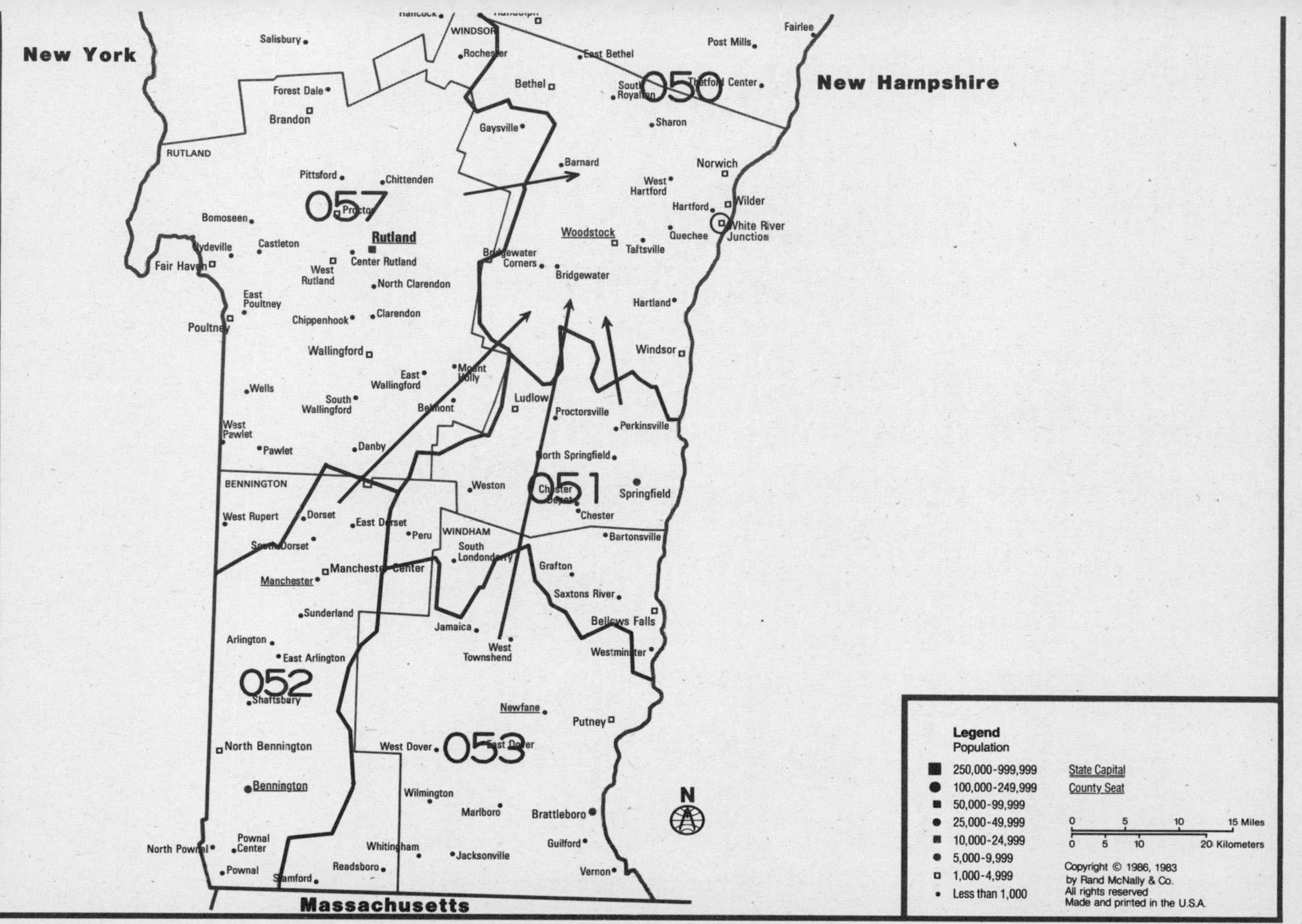
New York
New Hampshire
Massachusetts
050
051
052
053
057
WINDSOR
RUTLAND
WINDHAM
BENNINGTON
Salisbury
Rochester
East Bethel
Post Mills
Fairlee
Forest Dale
Brandon
Bethel
South Royalton
Thetford Center
Sharon
Gaysville
Barnard
Norwich
Pittsford
Chittenden
West Hartford
Hartford
Wilder
Proctor
Bomoseen
White River Junction
Quechee
Woodstock
Taftsville
Hydeville
Castleton
Rutland
Center Rutland
West Rutland
Fair Haven
Bridgewater Corners
Bridgewater
North Clarendon
East Poultney
Hartland
Poultney
Chippenhook
Clarendon
Wallingford
Windsor
Mount Holly
East Wallingford
Wells
South Wallingford
Ludlow
Belmont
Proctorsville
Perkinsville
West Pawlet
Pawlet
Danby
North Springfield
Weston
Chester Depot
Springfield
Chester
West Rupert
Dorset
East Dorset
Peru
Bartonsville
South Dorset
South Londonderry
Grafton
Manchester Center
Manchester
Saxtons River
Sunderland
Bellows Falls
Jamaica
West Townshend
Westminster
Arlington
East Arlington
Shaftsbury
Newfane
Putney
North Bennington
West Dover
East Dover
Bennington
Wilmington
Marlboro
Brattleboro
N
Pownal Center
North Pownal
Whitingham
Jacksonville
Guilford
Pownal
Readsboro
Stamford
Vernon
Legend
Population
250,000-999,999
100,000-249,999
50,000-99,999
25,000-49,999
10,000-24,999
5,000-9,999
1,000-4,999
Less than 1,000
State Capital
County Seat
0 5 10 15 Miles
0 5 10 20 Kilometers
Copyright © 1986, 1983
by Rand McNally & Co.
All rights reserved
Made and printed in the U.S.A.

Place	ZIP Code
North Montpelier	05666
North Orwell	05760
North Pomfret	05053
North Pownal	05260
North Randolph	05041
North Royalton	05068
North Rupert	05761
North Sheldon	05485
North Sherburne	05751
North Shrewsbury	05738
North Springfield	05150
North Thetford	05054
North Troy	05859
North Tunbridge	05077
North Vernon	05354
North Westminster	05101
North Windham	05148
North Wolcott	05680
Norton	05907
Norwich	05055
Norwich University (Part of Northfield)‡	05663
Oakland	05478
Oil City	05072
Old Bennington	05201
Old Church	05060
Orange	05641
Orchard Lane	05156
Orleans	05860
Orwell	05760
Panton	05491
Paper Mill Village	05257
Passumpsic	05861
Pawlet	05761
Peacham	05862
Pearl	05458
Peaseville	05143
Pedden Acres	05156
Pekin	05667
Perkinsville	05151
Peru	05152
Peth	05060
Pierces Corner	05759
Pikes Falls	05343
Pittsfield	05762
Pittsford	05763
Plainfield	05667
Pleasant Valley	05444
Plymouth	05056
Plymouth Kingdom	05149
Plymouth Union	05056
Pomfret	05053
Post Mills	05058
Potash Bay	05491
Potash Point	05491
Pottersville	05680
Poultney	05764
Pownal	05261
Pownal Center	05261
Prindle Corner	05445
Proctor	05765
Proctorsville	05153
Prosper	05091
Putnamville	05602
Putney	05346
Quechee	05059
Queen City Park (Part of South Burlington)	05401
Ralston Corner	05824
Randolph	05060
Randolph Center	05061
Rawsonville	05155
Reading	05062
Reading Center	05062
Readsboro	05350
	05352
For specific ZIP Codes call (888) 275-8777, or your local postmaster.	
Readsboro Falls	05350
Red Village	05851
Reedville	05143
Rhode Island Corner	05477
Rices Mills	05075
Richford	05476
Richmond	05477
Ricker Mills	05046
Ripton	05766
Riverton	05663
Robinson	05767
Rochester	05767
Rockingham	05101
Rockville	05443
Rocky Dale	05443
Round Pond	05069
Roxbury	05669
Roxbury Flat	05669
Royalton	05068
Rupert	05768
Russellville	05738
Russtown	05001
Rutland	05701*
	05702†
Ryegate	05042
St. Albans (Town)	05481
St. Albans	05478
St. Albans Bay	05481
St. Albans Hill	05478
St. Albans Shopping Center (Part of St. Albans)	05478
St. George (Town)	05495
St. Johnsbury♦	05819
St. Johnsbury Center	05863
St. Rocks	05478
Salisbury	05769
Samsonville	05450
Sanderson Corner	05454
Sandgate	05250
Saxtons River	05154
Scottsville	05739
Searsburg	05363
Seymour Lake	05853
Shadow Lake	05839
Shady Rill	05602
Shaftsbury	05262
Shaftsbury Center	05262
Sharon	05065
Shawville	05457
Sheddsville	05089
Sheffield	05866
Sheffield Square	05866
Shelburne	05482
Shelburne Falls	05482
Shelburne Road Section (Part of South Burlington)	05401
Sheldon	05483
Sheldon Junction	05483
Sheldon Springs	05485
Sherburne (Town)	05751
Shoreham	05770
Shoreham Center	05770
Shrewsbury	05738
Simonsville	05143
Simpsonville	05353
Smithville	05149
Smugglers Notch	05464
Sodom	05257
Somerset (Town)	05345
South Albany	05875
South Alburg	05440
South Barre♦	05670
South Burlington	05403
South Cabot	05658
South Cambridge	05464
South Corinth	05039
South Danville	05828
South Dorset	05251
South Duxbury	05660
South End	05739
South Hero	05486
South Lincoln	05443
South Londonderry	05155
South Lunenburg	05906
South Newbury	05051
South Newfane	05351
South Northfield	05663
South Peacham	05821
South Pomfret	05067
South Poultney	05764
South Randolph	05041
South Reading	05153
South Richford	05476
South Royalton	05068
South Ryegate	05069
South Starksboro	05487
South Strafford	05070
South Tunbridge	05068
South Vershire	05079
South Walden	05843
South Wallingford	05773
South Wardsboro	05355
South Washington	05675
South Wheelock	05851
South Windham	05359
South Woodbury	05681
South Woodstock	05071
Spoonerville	05143
Springfield♦	05156
Stamford	05352
Stannard	05842
Starksboro	05487
Stevens Mills	05476
Stevensville	05489
Stockbridge	05772
Stowe	05672
Strafford	05072
Stratton (Town)	05360
Stratton Mountain	05155
Sudbury	05733
Sugarbush Valley	05674
Summer Point	05491
Summit	05758
Sunderland	05250
Sutton	05867
Swanton	05488
Tafts Corner	05495
Taftsville	05073
Talcville	05767
Tarbellville	05742
The Bluffs (Part of Newport)	05855
The Island	05161
Thetford	05074
Thetford Center	05075
Thompsonburg	05148
Thompson's Point	05445
Tinmouth	05773
Topsham	05076
Topsham Four Corners	05040
Townshend	05353
Trow Hill	05641
Troy	05868
Tunbridge	05077
Tyson	05149
Una Bella	05201
Underhill	05489
Underhill Center	05490
Union Village	05043
University Mall (Part of South Burlington)	05403
Upper Graniteville	05654
Vergennes	05491
Vernon	05354
Vershire	05079
Vershire Center	05079
Vershire Heights	05079
Victory (Town)	05858
Waitsfield	05673
Waitsfield Common	05673
Waits River	05086
Walden	05873
Walden Heights	05873
Wallace Pond	05903
Wallingford♦	05773
Waltham (Town)	05491
Wardsboro	05355
Wardsboro Center	05355
Warners (Town)	05903
Warren	05674
Warren's (Town)	05903
Washington	05675
Washington Heights	05657
Waterbury	05676
Waterbury Center	05677
Waterford (Town)	05848
Waterville	05492
Weathersfield (Town)	05151
Weathersfield Bow	05156
Weathersfield Center	05151
Websterville	05678
Wells	05774
Wells River	05081
West Addison	05491
West Arlington	05250
West Barnet	05821
West Berkshire	05450
West Bolton	05465
West Branch	05672
West Brattleboro‡	05301
West Bridgewater	05035
West Bridport	05734
West Brookfield	05060
West Burke	05871
West Castleton	05743
West Charleston	05872
West Corinth	05039
West Cornwall	05753
West Danville	05873
West Dover	05356
West Dummerston	05357
West Enosburg	05450
West Fairlee	05083
West Fairlee Center	05045
Westfield	05874
Westford	05494
West Georgia	05478
West Glover	05875
West Groton	05046
West Halifax	05358
West Hartford	05084
West Haven	05743
West Hill	05450
West Lincoln	05443
West Milton	05468
Westminster	05158
Westminster Station (Part of Westminster)	05159
Westminster West	05346
Westmore	05860
West Newbury	05085
West Norwich	05055
Weston	05161
Weston Priory	05161
West Pawlet	05775
West Rupert	05776
West Rutland	05777
West Salisbury	05769
West Springfield	05156
West Swanton	05488
West Topsham	05086
West Townshend	05359
West Wardsboro	05360
West Waterford	05819
West Windsor (Town)	05037
West Woodstock	05091
Weybridge	05753
Weybridge Hill	05753
Wheelock	05851
White River Junction♦	05001
Whitesville	05142
Whiting	05778
Whitingham	05361
Wilder♦	05088
Williamstown	05679
Williamsville	05362
Williston	05495
Williston Road Section (Part of South Burlington)	05401
Wilmington	05363
Windham	05359
Windsor	05089
Winhall (Town)	05340
Winooski	05404
Winooski Park	05404
Wolcott	05680
Woodbury	05681
Woodford	05201
Woodford Hollow	05201
Woodstock	05091
Worcester	05682
Wrightsville (Part of Montpelier)	05602

Aarons Creek 24598
Abbey Oaks 22180
Abbott 24127
Abilene 23923
Abingdon 24210-12
For specific ZIP Codes call (888) 275-8777, or your local postmaster.
Accomac 23301
Accotink 22060
Accotink Heights 22003
Achilles 23001
Achsah 22727
Acorn 22469
Acredale (Part of Virginia Beach)‡ 23464*
23467†
Acree Acres 23692
Ada 20115
Addison Heights 22202
Aden 22181
Adial 22938
Adkins Store 23140
Adner 23149
Adria 24630
Adsit 23856
Advance Mills 22968
Adwolf♦ 24354
Afton 22920
Agricola 24574
Aiken Summit 24054
Aily 24237
Air Mail Facility (Part of Norfolk)‡ 23519
Airmont 20141
Ajax 24161
Alanthus 22714
Alanton (Part of Virginia Beach) 23450
Albemarle (Part of Norfolk) 23503
Alberene 22959
Alberta 23821
Albin 22603
Alcoma 23921
Aldie 20105
Alexander Corner (Part of Portsmouth) 23707
Alexandria 22301-32
For specific ZIP Codes call (888) 275-8777, or your local postmaster.
Alfonso 22503
Algonquin Park (Part of Norfolk) 23505
Alhambra 22951
Alice Heights 23234
Alleghany 24426
Alleghany Spring 24162
Allen 24226
Allencrest 22207
Allens Creek 24553
Allenslevel 23936
Allentown 23301
Allison Gap 24370
Allisonia 24347
Allmondsville 23061
Allwood 24521
Alma 22851
Almagro (Part of Danville) 24541
Almira (Part of Pound) 24279
Alonzaville 22644
Alpha 23936
Alpine 22003
Alps 22514
Alsop 22553
Altavista 24517
Alto 24483
Alton 24520
Alum Ridge 24091
Alvarado 24211
Amburg 23043
Amelia Court House 23002
Amherst, *Amherst* 24521
Amherst, *Fairfax* 22015
Amissville 20106
Ammon 23822
Amonate 24601
Ampthill 23234
Ampthill Heights (Part of Richmond) 23234
Amsterdam 24175
Andersonville 23911
Andover 24215
Andrew Lewis Place 24153
Angola 23901
Ankum 23868
Annalee Heights 22042
Annandale 22003
Annandale Acres 22003
Annandale Gardens 22003
Annandale Terrace 22003
Annex 24401
Ante 23847
Antioch 24590
Appalachia 24216
Apple Blossom Mall (Part of Winchester) 22601
Apple Grove 23117
Appomattox 24522
Aqua 24435
Aquia Harbor♦ 22554
Aragona Village (Part of Virginia Beach) 23455
Ararat 24053
Arbor Estates (Part of Suffolk) 23434
Arborhill 24401
Arcadia 24066
Arch Mills 24066
Arcola 20107
Arcturus 22308
Ardmore (Part of Fairfax) 22030
Argyle Heights 22405
Ark 23003
Arlington♦ 22201-19
For specific ZIP Codes call (888) 275-8777, or your local postmaster.
Arlington (Part of Hopewell) 23860
Arlington Forest 22203
Arlington Hall‡ 22212
Arlington Heights 22204
Arlington Village 22204
Arlingwood 22207
Armel 22602
Armistead Forest (Part of Portsmouth) 23703
Armstrong 24460
Armstrong Gardens (Part of Hampton) 23669
Aroda 22709
Arrington 22922
Arrowhead (Part of Virginia Beach) 23462
Arthur 24162
Artillery Ridge 22408
Artrip 24225
Arvonia 23004
Asberrys 24377
Ashburn 20146-48
For specific ZIP Codes call (888) 275-8777, or your local postmaster.
Ashby 23040
Ashland 23005
Ashton Heights 22201
Ashville 20115
Ashwood 24445
Aspen 23959
Aspenwall 24528
Assawoman 23302
Atkins♦ 24311
Atlantic, *Accomack* 23303
Atlantic (Part of Virginia Beach)‡ 23458
Atlantic Park (Part of Virginia Beach) 23451
Atlee 23111
Atoka 20115
Attoway 24354
Auburn 20119
Augusta Springs 24411
Aurora Hills 22202
Austinville 24312
Avalon 22473
Avalon Terrace (Part of Virginia Beach) 23462
Averett 24580
Avon 22920
Avondale 23116
Avon Forest 22039
Axtel 24562
Axton 24054
Aylett 23009
Aylor 22727
Azalea Acres (Part of Norfolk) 23518
Azalea Court 23227
Azalea Gardens (Part of Hampton) 23669
Bachelors Hall 24541
Backbay (Part of Virginia Beach)‡ 23457
Bacons Castle 23883
Bacons Fork 23950
Bacova 24412
Bacova Junction 24445
Baden 24228
Bagby 22514
Bagleys Mills 23970
Bailey 24605
Baileys Crossroads 22041
Balcony Falls (Part of Glasgow) 24555
Ballards Crossroads 23315
Ballentine Place (Part of Norfolk) 23509
Balls Hills 22101
Ballston 22203
Ballston Common 22203
Ballsville 23139
Baltimore Corner 23850
Balty 22546
Banco 22711
Bandy 24602
Bane 24134
Banner 24230
Banners Corner 24224
Barbours Creek 24127
Barboursville 22923
Barcroft 22204
Barfoot 24151
Barham 23881
Barhamsville 23011
Barley 23847
Barnesville 23964
Barnett 24266
Barnetts 23030
Barracks Road (Part of Charlottesville)‡ 22903
Barren Ridge 24401
Barren Springs 24313
Barrett Acres (Part of Suffolk) 23434
Bartlett 23314
Bartlick 24256
Bartons Crossroad 24378
Bartonsville 22602
Barytes (Part of Bristol) 24201
Basham 24138
Basic (Part of Waynesboro) 22980
Baskerville 23915
Bassett♦ 24055
Bassett Forks 24055
Bastian 24314
Basye 22810
Batesville 22924
Bath Alum 24460
Battersea (Part of Petersburg) 23803
Battery 22560
Battery Park, *Henrico* 23228
Battery Park, *Isle of Wight* 23304
Battle Beach 23851
Battle Creek 22851
Battlefield Green 22407
Battlefield Park (Part of Petersburg) 23805
Bavon 23138
Bayberry Estates 22485
Bay Colony (Part of Virginia Beach) 23451
Bayford 23354
Bay Island (Part of Virginia Beach) 23451
Bay Lake Beach (Part of Virginia Beach) 23455
Baylake Pines (Part of Virginia Beach) 23455
Baynesville 22520
Bayport 23079
Bayside, *Accomack* 23417
Bayside (Part of Virginia Beach)‡ 23455
23471
For specific ZIP Codes call (888) 275-8777, or your local postmaster.
Bay View 23310
Bayville Park (Part of Virginia Beach) 23455
Baywood 24333
Beach 23838
Beach Grove 22967
Beaconsdale (Part of Newport News) 23607
Bealeton 22712
Beamantown (Part of Big Stone Gap) 24219
Beamon (Part of Suffolk) 23434
Bear Wallow 24622
Beaufont Hills (Part of Richmond) 23225
Beaumont 23014
Beaverdam 23015
Beaverlett 23109
Beazley 22560
Beckham 24538
Bedford 24523
Bee 24217
Beech Fork 23974
Beech Springs 24263
Beechwood 23919
Beechwood Hills, *Arlington* 22207
Beechwood Hills, *Campbell* 24502
Beechwood Manor 23860
Bel Air 22042
Belaire (Part of Norfolk) 23518
Beldor 22827
Belfast Mills 24609
Bellair, *Albemarle* 22903
Bell Air, *Stafford* 22405
Bellamy, *Gloucester* 23017
Bellamy, *Scott* 24251
Bellamy Manor (Part of Virginia Beach) 23464
Bellbluff 23234
Belle Haven, *Accomack* 23306
Belle Haven, *Fairfax* 22307
Belle Haven (Part of Virginia Beach) 23452
Belle Meade, *Fauquier* 22642
Bellemeade (Part of Richmond) 23224
Belle Meadows (Part of Bristol) 24201
Belle View 22307
Belleville (Part of Suffolk) 23435
Bellevue (Part of Richmond) 23227
Bellevue Forest 22207
Bells Cross Road 22553
Bells Cross Roads 23093
Bell Spur, *Carroll* 24120
Bell Spur, *Patrick* 24120
Bells Valley 24439
Bellwood 23234
Bellwood Manor 23234
Belmont, *Loudoun* 20147
Belmont, *Prince William* 22191
Belmont, *Spotsylvania* 22553
Belmont Acres 23234
Belmont Circle 23901
Belmont Farms (Part of Christiansburg) 24073
Belmont Park 22079
Belmont Place (Part of Norfolk) 23505
Belona 23139
Belspring 24058
Belvedere, *Fairfax* 22041
Belvedere (Part of Norfolk) 23504
Belvidere Beach 22405
Belvoir 20115
Bena 23018
Benhams 24202
Ben Hur 24218
Benmoreel (Part of Norfolk) 23505
Bennetts Creek (Part of Suffolk) 23435
Bennetts Harbor (Part of Suffolk) 23434
Bennett Springs 24153
Benns Church 23430
Bensley 23234
Bent Creek 24553
Bent Mountain 24059
Bentonville 22610
Bergton 22811
Berkley (Part of Norfolk)‡ 23523
Berkshire 22207
Berlin 23866
Berryville 22611
Berton 24134
Bestland 22454
Betana Park 20190
Bethany 24312
Bethel, *Fauquier* 20187
Bethel, *Halifax* 24589
Bethel, *Prince William* 22191
Bethel, *Warren* 22630
Bethel Manor (Part of Hampton) 23665
Beulah Church 22560
Beulah Village 23234
Beulahville 23009
Beverley Hills (Part of Alexandria) 22305
Beverly Forest 22150
Beverly Heights (Part of Salem) 24153
Beverly Hills 23229
Beverly Manor 22101
Beverlyville 22539
Big Bethel (Part of Hampton) 23666
Big Fork 23970
Big Island 24526
Big Laurel 24293
Big River 24439
Big Rock 24603
Big Spring 22650
Big Stone Gap 24219
Big Vein 24635
Biltmore 23060
Binns Hall 23030
Birch 24592
Birchett Estate 23875
Birchland Park 24592
Birchleaf 24220
Birch Town 23336
Birchwood Park 23185
Birdneck Acres (Part of Virginia Beach) 23451
Birdsnest 23307
Birmingham 24609
Biscoe 23148
Bishop 24604
Bishops Corner 23938
Blackberry 24055
Black Branch 23924
Black Creek 23851
Blackford 24260
Blacklick 24368
Blackridge 23950
Blacksburg, *Montgomery* 24060-63
For specific ZIP Codes call (888) 275-8777, or your local postmaster.
Blacksburg, *Rockbridge* 24416
Blacksburg, *Washington* 24340
Blackstone 23824
Blackwater, *Lee* 24221
Blackwater (Part of Virginia Beach) 23457
Blackwater Bridge (Part of Virginia Beach) 23457
Blackwells Chapel 24361
Blackwood 24273
Blainville 22835
Blairs 24527
Blakes 23035
Bland 24315
Blandford (Part of Petersburg) 23803
Blanks Store 23030
Blanks Tavern 23030
Bleak 22728
Blevinstown 22030
Bloomfield 20135
Bloomingdale 23228
Blowing Rock 24228
Bloxom 23308
Bluefield 24605
Blue Grass 24413
Bluemont 20135
Blue Mountain 22630
Blue Ridge♦ 24064
Blue Ridge Mountain Estates 22630
Blue Ridge Shores 23093
Bluestone 23927
Blundon Corner 22456
Bocock 24501
Body Camp 24523
Bohannon 23021
Boiling Spring 24426
Boissevain 24606
Bolar 24484
Bolsters Store 23882
Bolton 24266
Bon Air, *Arlington* 22205
Bon Air, *Chesterfield*♦ 23235-36
For specific ZIP Codes call (888) 275-8777, or your local postmaster.
Bonbrook 24065
Bondtown (Part of Coeburn) 24230
Bonny Blue 24282
Bonsack 24012
Boones Mill 24065
Boonesville 22932
Boonsboro 24503
Bordeaux 20190
Boston, *Accomack* 23420
Boston, *Culpeper* 22713

*** Area Zip Code** **† Post Office Boxes** **‡ Postal Station** **♦ Census Designated Place** *Italic Type* **County**

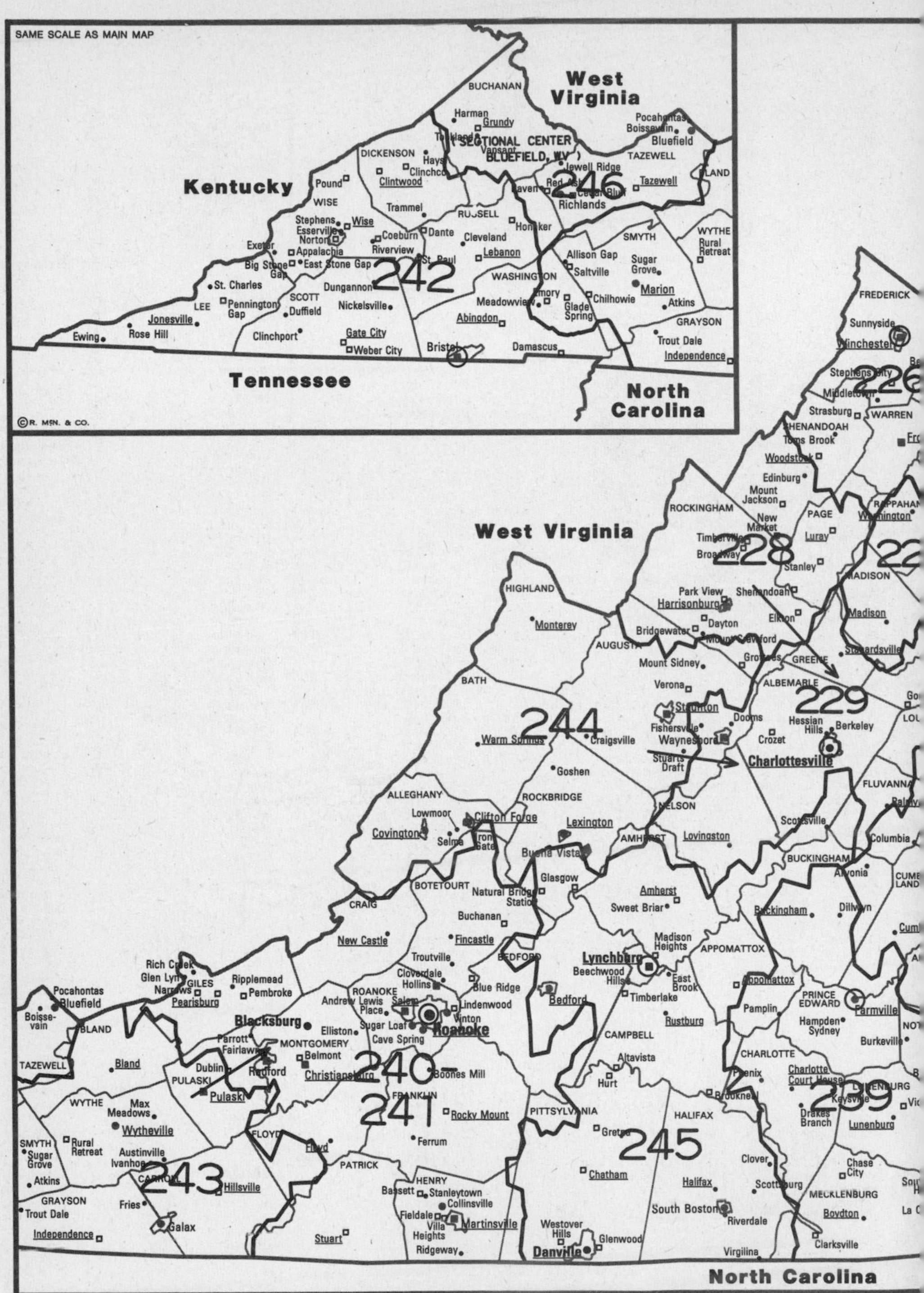
SAME SCALE AS MAIN MAP
West Virginia
Kentucky
Tennessee
North Carolina
BUCHANAN
Harman
Grundy
SECTIONAL CENTER
BLUEFIELD, WV
Pocahontas
Bluefield
TAZEWELL
Jewell Ridge
Tazewell
Richlands
246
DICKENSON
Hays
Clintwood
Pound
WISE
Trammel
RUSSELL
Stephens
Esserville
Wise
Norton
Coeburn
Dante
Cleveland
Lebanon
Riverview
Exeter
Appalachia
Big Stone Gap
East Stone Gap
St. Paul
242
St. Charles
SCOTT
Dungannon
Duffield
Nickelsville
Pennington Gap
LEE
Jonesville
Rose Hill
Ewing
Clinchport
Gate City
Weber City
Bristol
Damascus
Abingdon
Meadowview
Emory
Glade Spring
Chilhowie
WASHINGTON
Allison Gap
Saltville
SMYTH
Sugar Grove
Marion
Atkins
WYTHE
Rural Retreat
GRAYSON
Trout Dale
Independence
©R. McN. & CO.
West Virginia
FREDERICK
Sunnyside
Winchester
Stephens City
Middletown
Strasburg
WARREN
SHENANDOAH
Toms Brook
Woodstock
Edinburg
Mount Jackson
ROCKINGHAM
New Market
PAGE
Luray
Timberville
Broadway
228
Stanley
MADISON
Madison
HIGHLAND
Monterey
Park View
Harrisonburg
Shenandoah
Elkton
Bridgewater
Dayton
AUGUSTA
Mount Sidney
GREENE
BATH
Verona
ALBEMARLE
229
Staunton
Dooms
Hessian Hills
Berkeley
244
Fishersville
Waynesboro
Crozet
Warm Springs
Craigsville
Stuarts Draft
Charlottesville
Goshen
ALLEGHANY
ROCKBRIDGE
FLUVANNA
Lowmoor
Clifton Forge
Lexington
NELSON
Covington
Selma
Iron Gate
Buena Vista
AMHERST
Lovingston
Scottsville
Columbia
BUCKINGHAM
Arvonia
BOTETOURT
Glasgow
Natural Bridge Station
Amherst
Sweet Briar
CRAIG
Buchanan
Buckingham
Dillwyn
New Castle
Fincastle
Madison Heights
APPOMATTOX
Troutville
BEDFORD
Lynchburg
Beechwood Hills
Rich Creek
Glen Lyn
GILES
Narrows
Ripplemead
Pembroke
Pearisburg
Cloverdale
Hollins
Blue Ridge
East Brook
Appomattox
Timberlake
Pocahontas
Bluefield
Boissevain
BLAND
ROANOKE
Andrew Lewis Place
Salem
Lindenwood
Bedford
PRINCE EDWARD
Farmville
Blacksburg
Vinton
Roanoke
Pamplin
Hampden Sydney
Elliston
Sugar Loaf
Cave Spring
Rustburg
CAMPBELL
Burkeville
TAZEWELL
Bland
Parrott
Fairlawn
MONTGOMERY
Belmont
Christiansburg
240
CHARLOTTE
Dublin
Radford
PULASKI
Pulaski
Boones Mill
Altavista
Hurt
Phenix
Charlotte Court House
WYTHE
Max Meadows
Wytheville
FRANKLIN
241
Rocky Mount
PITTSYLVANIA
HALIFAX
239
Keysville
Drakes Branch
Lunenburg
SMYTH
Sugar Grove
Rural Retreat
Austinville
Ivanhoe
FLOYD
Floyd
Ferrum
Gretna
245
Atkins
243
CARROLL
Hillsville
PATRICK
HENRY
Bassett
Stanleytown
Collinsville
Chatham
Halifax
Clover
Scottsburg
Chase City
MECKLENBURG
GRAYSON
Trout Dale
Fries
Galax
Fieldale
Villa Heights
Martinsville
South Boston
Riverdale
Boydton
Independence
Stuart
Ridgeway
Westover Hills
Glenwood
Danville
Virgilina
Clarksville
North Carolina

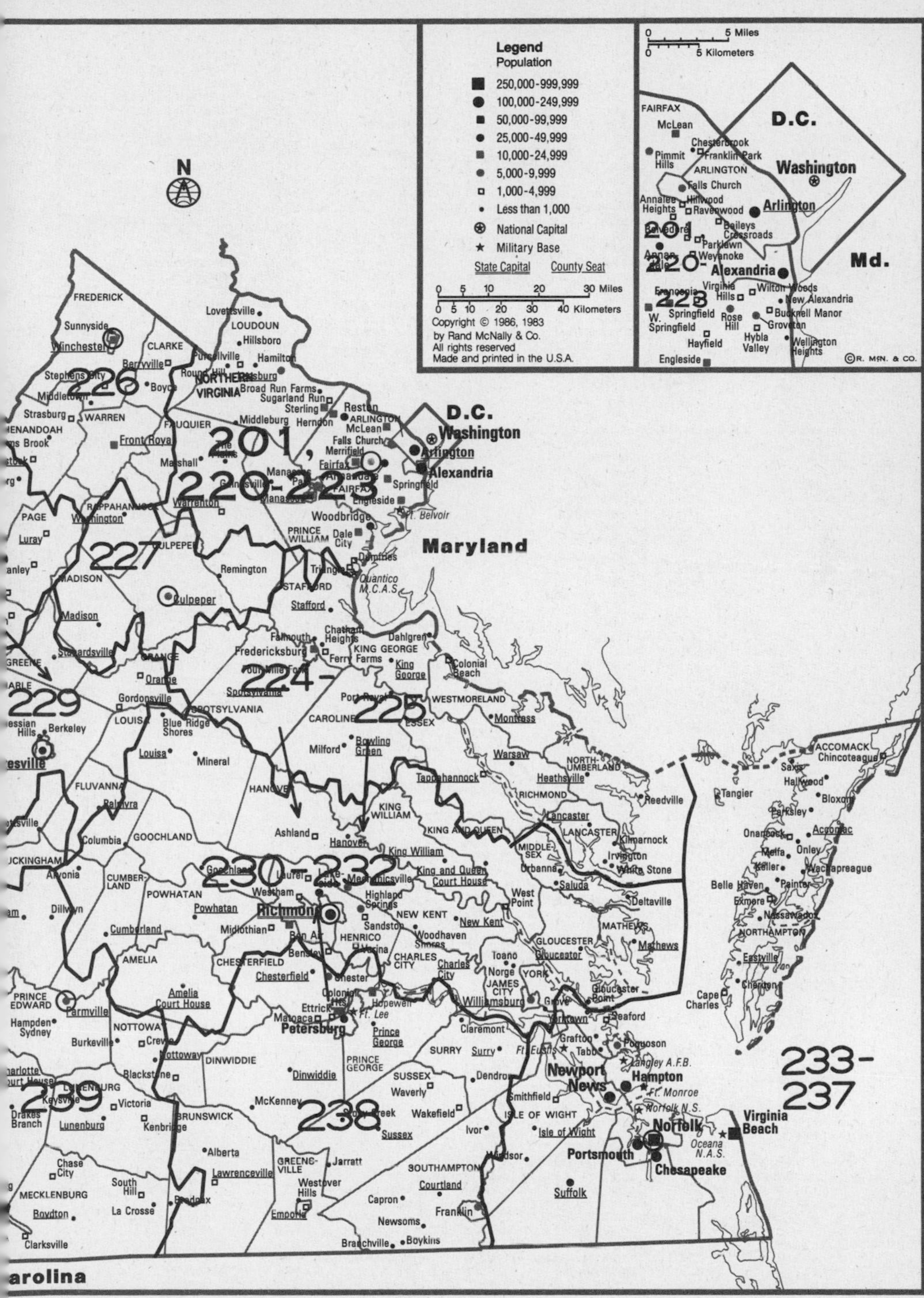
Legend
Population
250,000-999,999
100,000-249,999
50,000-99,999
25,000-49,999
10,000-24,999
5,000-9,999
1,000-4,999
Less than 1,000
National Capital
Military Base
State Capital
County Seat
0 5 10 20 30 Miles
0 5 10 20 30 40 Kilometers
Copyright © 1986, 1983
by Rand McNally & Co.
All rights reserved
Made and printed in the U.S.A.
0 5 Miles
0 5 Kilometers
FAIRFAX
McLean
Chesterbrook
Franklin Park
Pimmit Hills
ARLINGTON
D.C.
Washington
Falls Church
Annalee Heights
Hillwood
Ravenwood
Arlington
Baileys Crossroads
Parklawn
Weyanoke
Alexandria
Md.
Virginia Hills
Wilton Woods
New Alexandria
W. Springfield
Springfield
Rose Hill
Bucknell Manor
Groveton
Hayfield
Hybla Valley
Wellington Heights
Engleside
©R. McN. & CO.
201
220-
223
N
FREDERICK
Sunnyside
Winchester
CLARKE
Berryville
Boyce
Stephens City
Middletown
226
Strasburg
WARREN
Front Royal
FAUQUIER
Marshall
Lovettsville
LOUDOUN
Hillsboro
Hamilton
Purcellville
Round Hill
NORTHERN VIRGINIA
Broad Run Farms
Sugarland Run
Sterling
Herndon
Reston
ARLINGTON
McLean
Falls Church
Merrifield
Fairfax
Middleburg
201,
220-223
D.C.
Washington
Arlington
Alexandria
Springfield
Engleside
Ft. Belvoir
Warrenton
RAPPAHANNOCK
Washington
PAGE
Luray
227
CULPEPER
Culpeper
MADISON
Madison
Remington
PRINCE WILLIAM
Woodbridge
Dale City
Dumfries
Triangle
Quantico M.C.A.S.
Maryland
STAFFORD
Stafford
Falmouth
Chatham Heights
Fredericksburg
Ferry Farms
KING GEORGE
King George
Dahlgren
Colonial Beach
Stanardsville
GREENE
ORANGE
Orange
Gordonsville
229
Berkeley
LOUISA
Louisa
Blue Ridge Shores
Mineral
SPOTSYLVANIA
Spotsylvania
224-
225
CAROLINE
Port Royal
ESSEX
WESTMORELAND
Montross
Milford
Bowling Green
Warsaw
NORTHUMBERLAND
Heathsville
Tappahannock
RICHMOND
Reedville
FLUVANNA
Palmyra
HANOVER
Ashland
Hanover
KING WILLIAM
King William
KING AND QUEEN
King and Queen Court House
Lancaster
LANCASTER
Kilmarnock
Irvington
White Stone
MIDDLESEX
Urbanna
Saluda
Deltaville
Columbia
GOOCHLAND
Goochland
230-232
Mechanicsville
Westham
Highland Springs
Richmond
CUMBERLAND
POWHATAN
Powhatan
Cumberland
Midlothian
Bon Air
Bensley
HENRICO
Sandston
NEW KENT
New Kent
Woodhaven Shores
West Point
Varina
CHARLES CITY
Charles City
Toano
Norge
JAMES CITY
YORK
Williamsburg
GLOUCESTER
Gloucester
MATHEWS
Mathews
Gloucester Point
AMELIA
Amelia Court House
CHESTERFIELD
Chesterfield
Chester
Colonial Hts.
Hopewell
Ft. Lee
Ettrick
Matoaca
Petersburg
Prince George
PRINCE GEORGE
PRINCE EDWARD
Farmville
Hampden-Sydney
NOTTOWAY
Burkeville
Crewe
Nottoway
DINWIDDIE
Dinwiddie
Blackstone
SURRY
Surry
Claremont
SUSSEX
Waverly
Dendron
Sussex
Stony Creek
Wakefield
238
McKenney
LUNENBURG
Keysville
Victoria
Lunenburg
Kenbridge
239
Drakes Branch
BRUNSWICK
Alberta
Lawrenceville
Chase City
GREENSVILLE
Jarratt
Emporia
Westover Hills
South Hill
MECKLENBURG
Boydton
La Crosse
Bracey
Clarksville
SOUTHAMPTON
Courtland
Capron
Newsoms
Franklin
Branchville
Boykins
Ivor
Windsor
ISLE OF WIGHT
Isle of Wight
Smithfield
Suffolk
Ft. Eustis
Yorktown
Grafton
Seaford
Tabb
Poquoson
Langley A.F.B.
Newport News
Hampton
Ft. Monroe
Norfolk N.S.
Norfolk
Portsmouth
Chesapeake
Oceana N.A.S.
Virginia Beach
233-
237
ACCOMACK
Chincoteague
Saxis
Hallwood
Bloxom
Tangier
Parksley
Onancock
Accomac
Melfa
Onley
Keller
Wachapreague
Painter
Belle Haven
Exmore
Nassawadox
NORTHAMPTON
Eastville
Cheriton
Cape Charles
arolina

Place	ZIP
Boston (Part of Suffolk)	23434
Boswells Tavern	22942
Botha	20186
Bottoms Bridge	23150
Boudar Gardens	23228
Boulevard Estates	22031
Bowers Corner	23893
Bowers Hill (Part of Chesapeake)	23321
Bowlers Wharf	22560
Bowling	24263
Bowling Green	22427
Bowling Park (Part of Norfolk)	23504
Bowmans Crossing	22824
Boxley Hills	24012
Boxwood	24054
Boyce	22620
Boyd Tavern	22947
Boydton	23917
Boykins	23827
Boys Home	24426
Bracey	23919
Braddock (Part of Alexandria)	22302
Braddock Heights (Part of Alexandria)	22302
Braddock Hills	22003
Bradford Acres (Part of Virginia Beach)	23455
Bradley Acres	23150
Bradley Forest	20112
Bradshaw	24087
Brambleton (Part of Norfolk)	23504
Branchville	23828
Brand	24401
Brandon	23881
Brandon Heights (Part of Newport News)	23601
Brandon Place (Part of Norfolk)	23513
Brandons Store	23824
Brandon Village	22203
Brandy Creek Estates	23111
Brandy Station	22714
Brattons Bridge	24460
Brays	22560
Brayshore Park	23072
Breaks	24607
Brecon Ridge	22030
Bremo Bluff	23022
Bren Mar Park	22312
Brentsville	22013
Brentwood	20136
Brentwood Forest (Part of Norfolk)	23518
Briarcliff (Part of Vinton)	24179
Briarwood (Part of Bristol)	24201
Briarwood (Part of Portsmouth)	23703
Bridgetown	23405
Bridgewater	22812
Bridle Creek	24348
Briery	23947
Briery Branch	22821
Briggs	22611
Brights	24557
Brightwood	22715
Brilyn Park	22046
Brink	23847
Bristol	24201-03
For specific ZIP Codes call (888) 275-8777, or your local postmaster.	
Bristol Mall (Part of Bristol)	24201
Bristow, *Fairfax*	22003
Bristow, *Prince William*	20136
Britain	20180
Britton Hills Farms	23230
Brittonwood	23234
Broad Bay Colony (Part of Virginia Beach)	23451
Broad Creek (Part of Norfolk)	23502
Broadford	24316
Broad Meadows	23060
Broad Rock (Part of Richmond)	23224
Broad Run	20137
Broad Run Farms	20165
Broadway	22815
Brockroad	22553
Brodnax	23920
Brokenburg	22553
Broken Hill	20155
Brookbury (Part of Richmond)	23234
Brooke	22430
Brookeshire	23181
Brookfield, *Fairfax*	20151
Brookfield, *Stafford*	22405
Brookfield Park (Part of Norfolk)	23503
Brookhaven	22101
Brook Hill	23227
Brookland Estates	22310
Brookland Gardens	23228
Brooklyn	24594
Brookneal	24528
Brook Vale	22503
Brookville (Part of Alexandria)	22304
Brookwood (Part of Virginia Beach)	23452
Brookwood Manor	23141
Brosville	24541
Brown Field (Part of Quantico)	22134
Brown Grove	23005
Brownsburg	24415
Browns Corner	23141
Browns Cove	22932
Browns Store	22473
Brown Town, *Amherst*	24521
Browntown, *Warren*	22610
Broyhill Crest	22003
Broyhill Forest	22207
Broyhill Park	22042
Brucetown	22622
Bruington	23023
Brumley Gap	24210
Bruno	24258
Brunswick	23868
Brush Tavern	24502
Bryan Park	23228
Bryan Parkway	23228
Bryant	22967
Bryants Corner	23847
Bryn Mawr	22101
Buchanan	24066
Buckhall	20111
Buckingham, *Arlington*‡	22203
Buckingham, *Buckingham*	23921
Buckingham, *Chesterfield*	23112
Buckingham Circle	22903
Buckland	20155
Bucknell Heights	22307
Bucknell Manor	22307
Buckner	23024
Buckroe Beach (Part of Hampton)‡	23664
Buckton	22657
Buena	22733
Buena Vista	24416
Buffalo Forge	24555
Buffalo Gap	24479
Buffalo Hill	24521
Buffalo Hills	22044
Buffalo Junction	24529
Buffalo Ridge	24171
Buffalo Springs	24529
Bufford Cross Roads	23847
Bull Run Mountain Estates	20169
Bumpass	23024
Bundy	24265
Bunker Hill	24523
Burdette	23851
Burgess	22432
Burgundy Village	22303
Burke	22009†
	22015*
Burke Heights	22015
Burke Hills	22015
Burkes Garden	24608
Burkes Shop	22580
Burketown	24486
Burkeville	23922
Burks Garden (Part of Tazewell)	24651
Burnam Woods	23168
Burnleys	22923
Burnside Farms	23116
Burnsville	24487
Burnt Chimney	24184
Burnt Store	23950
Burnt Tree	22960
Burr Hill	22433
Burrowsville	23842
Burson Place	24202
Burton (Part of Virginia Beach)	23455
Burtons Shop	24651
Bush Hill	22310
Bush Hill Woods	22310
Bush Mill	24271
Busthead	24609
Bustleburg	24450
Butterworth	23840
Butts Corner	22039
Butylo	22504
Bybee	22963
Byllesby	24350
Bynum Store	23924
Byrdton	22482
Cabin Point	23881
Cadet (Part of Big Stone Gap)	24219
Cady	23069
Caira	23040
Caledonia	23038
Callaghan	24426
Callands	24530
Callao	22435
Callaville	23856
Callaway	24067
Callison	24445
Calno	23069
Calvary	22664
Calverton	20138
Cambria (Part of Christiansburg)‡	24073
Cambridge	23235
Camden Heights (Part of Norfolk)	23502
Camellia Shores (Part of Norfolk)	23518
Camelot	22003
Cameron (Part of Alexandria)	22304
Cameron Station (Part of Alexandria)	22304
Cameron Valley (Part of Alexandria)	22314
Camp	24375
Camp Barrett	22134
Campbell	22947
Camp Creek	24091
Campostella Heights (Part of Norfolk)	23523
Camps Mill (Part of Suffolk)	23434
Camptown	24528
Cana	24317
Candlewax	24260
Cannady	24656
Canova	20112
Canterburg	22655
Canterbury	23229
Canterbury Hills	22901
Canterbury Woods	22003
Canton	24221
Capahosic	23061
Cape Charles	23310
Cape Henry (Part of Virginia Beach)‡	23454
Cape Henry Shores (Part of Virginia Beach)	23451
Cape Story by the Sea (Part of Virginia Beach)	23451
Capeville	23313
Capitol (Part of Richmond)‡	23201-19
For specific ZIP Codes call (888) 275-8777, or your local postmaster.	
Capon Road	22657
Capron	23829
Captain's Cove	23356
Carbo	24225
Cardinal	23025
Cardinal Forest	22152
Cardova	22701
Cardwell	23039
Cardwell Town	24370
Caret	22436
Carfax	24230
Carloover	24445
Carolanne Farms (Part of Virginia Beach)	23462
Caroline Pines	22546
Carriage Hill, *Fairfax*	22181
Carriage Hill (Part of Virginia Beach)	23452
Carrie	24225
Carrollton	23314
Carrsbrook	22901
Carrsville	23315
Carsley	23890
Carson	23830
Carsonville	24348
Carters Mills	24053
Cartersville	23027
Carterton	24266
Carver Court (Part of Hampton)	23669
Carver Gardens	23185
Carysbrook	23055
Casanova	20139
Cascade	24069
Cash	23061
Cash Corner	22942
Cashville	23417
Caskie	24553
Castle Craig	24550
Castle Heights	23917
Castleton	22716
Castlewood	24224
Catalpa	22701
Catawba, *Halifax*	24577
Catawba, *Roanoke*	24070
Catharpin	20143
Catherton (Part of Manassas)	20110
Catlett	20119
Cats Bridge	23420
Cauthornville	23148
Cavalcade	22003
Cavalier Park (Part of Virginia Beach)	23451
Cave Mountain	24579
Cave Spring	24018
Cavetown	22835
Caylor	24248
Cedar Bluff, *Tazewell*	24609
Cedar Bluff, *Washington*	24236
Cedar Branch (Part of Saltville)	24370
Cedar Forest	24569
Cedar Fork	22546
Cedar Green	24401
Cedar Grove, *Halifax*	24520
Cedar Grove, *Mecklenburg*	23970
Cedar Grove, *Northampton*	23310
Cedar Grove Acres (Part of Chesapeake)	23320
Cedarhill	24565
Cedar Lawn	23231
Cedar Level (Part of Hopewell)	23860
Cedar Point	23063
Cedar Springs	24368
Cedarville, *Warren*	22630
Cedarville, *Washington*	24361
Cedon	22580
Celt	22973
Centenary	24590
Center Cross	22437
Center Star	23841
Centerville, *Accomack*	23412
Centerville, *Augusta*	22812
Centerville, *Bedford*	24523
Centerville, *Goochland*	23103
Centerville, *Halifax*	24592
Centerville, *James City*	23188
Centerville, *Louisa*	23117
Central (Part of Richmond)‡	23241
Central Garage	23086
Central Gardens	23223
Central Hill	23487
Centralia	23831
Centralia Gardens	23234
Central Martinsville (Part of Martinsville)‡	24112
Central Plains	22963
Central Point	22514
Centreville	20120-22
For specific ZIP Codes call (888) 275-8777, or your local postmaster.	
Centreville Farms	20120
Ceres	24318
Chadswyck (Part of Chesapeake)	23321
Chalet Woods	20120
Chalk Level	24557
Chamberlain Village	22134
Chamberlayne Farms	23227
Chamberlayne Heights	23227
Chamberlayne North	23227
Chamblissburg	24179
Champlain	22438
Chance	22438
Chancellor	22407
Chancellors Green	22407
Chancellorsville	22553
Chaneys	24565
Chantilly	20151-53
For specific ZIP Codes call (888) 275-8777, or your local postmaster.	
Chantilly Estates	20151
Chapel	24124
Chapel Acres	22153
Chapel Hill (Part of Alexandria)	22302
Chapel Park (Part of Newport News)	23606
Chapel Square	22003
Charity	24185
Charlemont	24526
Charles City	23030
Charlie Hope	23920
Charlotte Court House	23923
Charlottesville	22901-06
	22911
For specific ZIP Codes call (888) 275-8777, or your local postmaster.	
Chase City	23924
Chatham	24531
Chatham Heights	22405
Chatham Hill	24370
Chatmoss	24112
Cheapside	23310
Check	24072
Cheriton	23316
Cherokee Heights (Part of Norfolk)	23518
Cherry Acres (Part of Hampton)	23669
Cherrydale	22207
Cherry Hill, *Charles City*	23030
Cherry Hill, *Dinwiddie*	23872
Cherry Hill, *Prince William*	22026
Chesapeake, *Indep. City*	23320-28
For specific ZIP Codes call (888) 275-8777, or your local postmaster.	
Chesapeake, *Northampton*	23310
Chesapeake Beach, *Northumberland*	22539
Chesapeake Beach (Part of Virginia Beach)	23455
Chesapeake Heights (Part of Hampton)	23664
Chesapeake Manor (Part of Norfolk)	23513
Chesapeake Square (Part of Chesapeake)	23321
Chesconessex	23417
Chesdin Manor	23885
Chesopeian Colony (Part of Virginia Beach)	23452
Chesswood	23234
Chester♦	23831
	23836
For specific ZIP Codes call (888) 275-8777, or your local postmaster.	
Chesterbrook	22101
Chesterbrook Gardens	22101
Chesterbrook Woods	22101
Chester Estates (Part of Bristol)	24201
Chesterfield	23832
	23838
For specific ZIP Codes call (888) 275-8777, or your local postmaster.	
Chesterfield Heights (Part of Norfolk)	23504
Chester Gap	22623
Chestnut Hill, *Fairfax*	22003
Chestnut Hill, *King George*	22485
Chestnut Knob	24112
Chestnut Level	24527
Chestnut Yard	24381
Chewings Corner	22534
Chickahominy Haven	23089
Chickahominy Shores	23089
Childress	24073
Childry	24577
Chilesburg	22546
Chilhowie	24319
Chiltons	22520
Chimney Run	24484
Chincoteague	23336-37
For specific ZIP Codes call (888) 275-8777, or your local postmaster.	
Chinquapin Village (Part of Alexandria)	22302
Chisford	22520

Christchurch 23031
Christensons Corner 23188
Christians 24479
Christiansburg ..... 24068†
..... 24073*
Christie 24598
Chuckatuck (Part of Suffolk)‡ 23432
Chula 23002
Church Hill (Part of Richmond) 23223
Churchill 22043
Churchland (Part of Portsmouth)‡ 23703
Church Road 23833
Church View 23032
Churchville 24421
Cifax 24556
Circlewoods 22031
Cismont 22947
Civic Center (Part of Richmond)‡ 23240
Clam 23308
Clancie 23156
Claraville 22473
Claremont, *Arlington* 22206
Claremont, *Surry* 23899
Clarendon 22201
Claresville 23847
Clarkes Gap 20176
Clarksville, *Mecklenburg* 23927
Clarksville (Part of Glade Spring) 24340
Clarkton 24577
Clary 22657
Claudville 24076
Clay Bank 23061
Claypool Hill♦ 24609
Clays Mill 24589
Clayville 23139
Clear Brook, *Frederick* 22624
Clearbrook, *Roanoke* 24014
Clearfield 22151
Clearfork 24314
Clearview Manor 22101
Clearwater Park 24426
Clell 24631
Clermont Woods 22310
Cleveland 24225
Cliffield 24637
Clifford 24533
Cliffview 24333
Clifton, *Fairfax* 20124
Clifton, *Orange* 22733
Cliftondale 24422
Clifton Forge 24422
Climax 24531
Clinchburg Siding 24361
Clinchco 24226
Clinchport 24244
Clintwood 24228
Clito 24330
Clover, *Halifax* 24534
Clover (Part of Alexandria) 22314
Cloverdale, *Botetourt*♦ 24077
Cloverdale, *Fluvanna* 23022
Clover Hill 22821
Club Court 23227
Cluster Springs 24535
Coalcreek 24333
Coaldan 24641
Coal Kiln 23420
Coal Mine 22657
Coan Stage 22473
Cobbdale (Part of Fairfax) 22030
Cobbs Creek 23035
Cobham 22929
Cobham Park 22572
Cobham Wharf 23883
Cochran 23821
Cody 24577
Coeburn 24230
Coffee 24551
Cohasset 23055
Cohoke 23181
Coke 23072
Colchester 22079
Cold Harbor Farms 23111
Coldwater 23108
Coleman Falls 24536
Coleman Place (Part of Norfolk) 23504
Coles Creek 24151
Coles Point 22442
Coliseum Mall (Part of Hampton) 23666
Colleen 22922
College (Part of Fredericksburg)‡ 22401
..... 22404
For specific ZIP Codes call (888) 275-8777, or your local postmaster.
College Park (Part of Alexandria) 22314
College Park (Part of Staunton) 24401
College Park (Part of Suffolk) 23703
Colley 24220
Collierstown 24450
Collingwood 22308
Collins Crossing 22580
Collinsville♦ 24078
Collinwood 24266
Cologne 23156
Colonial Beach 22443
Colonial Forest 23116
Colonial Heights, *Indep. City* 23834
Colonial Heights, *Washington* 24202
Colonial Heights (Part of Hampton) 23664
Colonial Heights (Part of Norfolk) 23518
Colonial Place (Part of Norfolk) 23508
Colonial Village 22201
Colonial Williamsburg (Part of Williamsburg)‡ 23185
Colosse 23315
Colthurst 22901
Coltons Mill 24523
Columbia 23038
Columbia Forest 22204
Columbia Furnace 22824
Columbia Heights 22204
Columbia Park (Part of Hopewell) 23860
Columbia Pines 22003
Colvin Run 22066
Comans Well 23897
Comers Rock 24326
Comet 23430
Commodore Park (Part of Norfolk) 23503
Commonwealth Acres 23875
Community 22306
Comorn 22405
Compton 22650
Conaway 24603
Concord, *Brunswick* 23876
Concord, *Campbell* 24538
Concord Heights 22401
Conde 20115
Confederate Heights 23222
Conicville 22842
Conners Grove 24380
Conners Valley 24324
Contra 22437
Cookstown 22553
Coolwell 24521
Cooper 23092
Cootes Store 22815
Copper Hill 24079
Copper Valley 24141
Corbin 22446
Corinth 23866
Corn Valley 24260
Cornwall 24416
Coronado (Part of Norfolk) 23513
Cottage Heights (Part of Norfolk) 23504
Cottage Park (Part of Norfolk) 23503
Cottage Road Park (Part of Norfolk) 23505
Coulson 24381
Coulwood 24260
Council 24260
Countis Corner 24202
Country Club Hills, *Arlington* 22207
Country Club Hills (Part of Fairfax) 22030
Country Club Manor 22207
Country Club View 22032
Country Creek 22181
Countryside♦ 20165
Counts 24237
County Line Cross Roads 23923
Court House‡ 22216
Courtland 23837
Courtland Park 22041
Courtney 23060
Cove Colony 22503
Cove Creek, *Bland* 24314
Cove Creek, *Tazewell* 24651
Covesville 22931
Covingston Corner 23047
Covington 24426
Cox's Chapel 24363
Crab Orchard 24230
Crackers Neck, *Scott* 24271
Crackers Neck, *Wise* 24219
Craddockville 23341
Cradock (Part of Portsmouth)‡ 23702
Craigs Mills 24202
Craig Springs 24127
Craigsville 24430
Crandon 24315
Cranes Nest 24230
Craney Island Estates 23111
Creeds (Part of Virginia Beach) 23457
Crescent Hill (Part of Hopewell) 23860
Crescent Hills 22207
Cresthill 22639
Crestview, *Henrico* 23226
Crestview, *Prince Edward* 23901
Crestwood Manor 22003
Crewe 23930
Criders 22820
Criglersville 22727
Crimora 24431
Cripple Creek 24322
Crittenden (Part of Suffolk)‡ 23433
Critz 24082
Croaker 23188
Croatan Beach (Part of Virginia Beach) 23451
Crockett 24323
Crockett Springs 24162
Crofton 24179
Cromwell (Part of Norfolk) 23509
Crooked Oak 24343
Crossbrook 24215
Crosses Corner 23069
Cross Junction 22625
Crosskeys 22841
Crossroads, *Albemarle* 22959
Crossroads, *Halifax* 24577
Crossroads Mall (Part of Roanoke) 24012
Crosswinds 22153
Crouch 22437
Crows 24426
Crozet♦ 22932
Crozier 23039
Crymes Store 23974
Crystal City‡ 22202
Crystal Hill 24539
Crystal Spring Knolls 22207
Cuckoo 23117
Cullen 23934
Culmore 22041
Culpeper 22701
Cumberland 23040
Cummings Heights 24210
Cumnor 23085
Cunningham 22963
Curdsville 23936
Currioman Landing 22520
Currituck Farms 23150
Cuscowilla 23917
Customhouse (Part of Norfolk)‡ 23514
Cypress Chapel (Part of Suffolk) 23434
Cypress Manor 23851
Cypress Point, *James City* 23089
Cypress Point, *Surry* 23899
Dabney Estates 23885
Dabneys 23102
Dahlgren 22448
Dahlia 27866
Dalbys 23310
Dale City♦ 22193
Dalecrest (Part of Alexandria) 22304
Dale Enterprise 22801
Daleville♦ 24083
Damascus 24236
Dam Neck (Part of Virginia Beach)‡ 23461
Dam Neck Corner (Part of Virginia Beach) 23454
Danbury Forest 22151
Dandy 23694
Daniel 22960
Daniel Boone 24251
Danieltown 23821
Danripple 24592
Dante 24237
Danville 24540-43
For specific ZIP Codes call (888) 275-8777, or your local postmaster.
Dare 23692
Darlington Heights 23958
Darnell Town 24265
Darvills 23824
Darwin 24228
Daugherty 23301
Davenport 24239
Davis 24472
Davis Corner (Part of Virginia Beach) 23462
Davis Wharf 23345
Dawley Corner (Part of Virginia Beach) 23457
Dawn 23047
Dayton 22821
Deans (Part of Suffolk) 23435
Deatonville 23083
De Bree (Part of Norfolk)‡ 23517
De Busk Mill 24340
Deel 24656
Deep Bottom 23075
Deep Creek, *Accomack* 23417
Deep Creek (Part of Chesapeake)‡ 23323
Deep Creek (Part of Newport News) 23606
Deep Hole 23336
Deerborne (Part of Richmond) 23234
Deerfield 24432
Deerfield Estates 23832
Deer Park (Part of Manassas) 20110
Deer Park Groove (Part of Newport News) 23607
Deerrock 22938
Defense General Supply Center 23297
De Jarnett 22514
Delaplane 20144
Delaware 23851
Delmar 24236
Del Ray (Part of Alexandria) 22301
Delta (Part of Alexandria) 22304
Deltaville 23043
Delton 24324
Denaro 23002
Denbigh (Part of Newport News)‡ 23602
Denby Park (Part of Norfolk) 23505
Dendron 23839
Denmark 24450
Denniston 24520
Dentons Corner 23921
Derby 24216
Desha 22560
Detrick 22652
Devon Manor (Part of Norfolk) 23503
Devonshire Gardens 22042
Dewey 24279
DeWitt 23840
Dewitt Hospital‡ 22060
Diamond Springs (Part of Virginia Beach) 23455
Diascund 23089
Dickensdale 23230
Dickensonville 24224
Diggs 23045
Diggs Park (Part of Norfolk) 23523
Dillard's Landing 23140
Dillwyn 23936
Dinwiddie 23841
Dinwiddie Gardens 23803
Disputanta 23842
Ditchley 22482
Dixie, *Fluvanna* 23055
Dixie, *Mathews* 23050
Dixie Hill 22030
Dockery 23970
Doe Hill 24433
Dogtown 23063
Dogue 22451
Dogue Creek Village 22060
Dogwood Hill (Part of Staunton) 24401
Dogwood Knoll 23111
Dolphin 23843
Donna Lee Gardens 22046
Dooms♦ 22980
Doran 24612
Dorchester, *Wise* 24273
Dorchester (Part of Richmond) 23234
Dorchester Junction 24273
Dorset Woods 23075
Doswell 23047
Dot 24277
Double Tollgate 22663
Douglas Park (Part of Portsmouth) 23701
Douglass Park 22204
Doveville 22032
Dowden Terrace 22311
Downings 22460
Downtown (Part of Blacksburg)‡ 24063
Downtown (Part of Charlottesville)‡ 22902
Downtown (Part of Leesburg)‡ 20176*
..... 20178†
Downtown (Part of Lynchburg)‡ 24505
Downtown (Part of Manassas)‡ 20110
Downtown (Part of Roanoke)‡ 24001
Doylesville 22932
Drakes Branch 23937
Dranesville 20170
Draper 24324
Drewryville 23844
Drill 24260
Driver (Part of Suffolk)‡ 23435
Drouin Hill 23075
Drum Bay 22469
Dry Branch 24132
Dryburg 24589
Dryden 24243
Dry Fork, *Pittsylvania* 24549
Dry Fork, *Wise* 24230
Drytown 24630
Duane 23009
Dublin 24084
Dudley 24558
Duffield 24244
Dugspur 24325
Dugwell 24151
Duke Gardens (Part of Alexandria) 22304
Dumbarton 23228
Dumfries 22026
Dunavant 22401
Dunbar 24216
Dunbar Gardens (Part of Hampton) 23666
Dunbrooke 22560
Duncan Gap 24293
Duncans Mills 24244
Duncanville 24210
Dundalow (Part of Suffolk)‡ 23434
Dundas 23938
Dunford Town 24602
Dungadin Heights 22630
Dungannon 24245
Dunlop (Part of Colonial Heights) 23834
Dunn Loring 22027
Dunn Loring Woods 22180
Dunnsville 22454
Durrett Town 22920
Dutton 23050
Duty 24217
Dwale 24228
Dwina 24230
Dye 24649
Dyers Store 24112
Dyke 22935
Eads‡ 22202
Eagle Rock 24085
Earlhurst 24426
Earls 23002
Earlysville 22936
East Aberdeen Gardens (Part of Hampton) 23666
East Brook 24501
East End (Part of Richmond)‡ 23223
Eastern Park (Part of Virginia Beach) 23452
East Falls Church 22205
Eastham 22911
East Hampton (Part of Hampton) 23669
East Highland Park 23222

East Hilton (Part of Newport News) 23607
East Lexington 24450
Eastmoreland 23231
East Norton (Part of Norton) 24273
East Norview (Part of Norfolk) 23513
East Ocean View (Part of Norfolk) 23503
Easton Place (Part of Norfolk) 23502
Eastover (Part of Suffolk) 23434
Eastover Gardens 23231
East Point, *Accomack* 23417
East Point, *Rockingham* 22827
East Radford (Part of Radford) 24141
East Stone Gap 24246
East Suffolk Gardens (Part of Suffolk) 23434
Eastville 23347
Eastville Station (Part of Eastville) 23347
Ebenezer 24565
Ebony 23845
Eclipse (Part of Suffolk) 23433
Edge 24554
Edgehill, *King George* 22485
Edgehill, *Southampton* 23851
Edgehill Park 23803
Edgemont (Part of Covington) 24426
Edgemont Park 24210
Edgerton 23868
Edgewater (Part of Norfolk) 23508
Edgewood (Part of Petersburg) 23805
Edinburg 22824
Ednam Forest 22903
Edom 22834
Edsall Park 22151
Edwards Shop 22718
Edwardsville 22456
Effinger 24450
Eggleston 24086
Eheart 22923
Elam 23960
Elberon 23846
Elephant Fork (Part of Suffolk) 23434
Elevon 22438
Elizabeth Park (Part of Norfolk) 23502
Elizabeth River Shores (Part of Virginia Beach) 23464
Elizabeth River Terrace (Part of Virginia Beach) 23464
Elk Creek 24326
Elk Garden 24266
Elk Hill 23063
Elko 23150
Elkrun 22728
Elkton 22827
Elkwood 22718
Ellett 24073
Elliston 24087
Ellisville 23093
Ellsworth (Part of Norfolk) 23505
Elma 22971
Elmhurst (Part of Norfolk) 23513
Elmo 24592
Elmont 23005
Elmwood Estates 22101
El-Nido 22101
Elon 24572
Elsom 23181
Eltham 23181
Elysian Woods 22192
Emmerton 22572
Emory 24327
Emporia 23847
Endicott 24088
Enfield 23106
Engleside♦ 22309
English Hills 23228
Enonville 23936
Eppes Fork 27584
Erica 22520
Esmont 22937
Esnon 23924
Esserville 24273
Estabrook (Part of Norfolk) 23509
Estabrook Park (Part of Norfolk) 23513
Estaline 24430
Estes 22716
Ethel 22572
Ethridge Estates 23805
Etlan 22719
Ettrick♦ 23803
Euclid (Part of Virginia Beach) 23462
Euclid Place (Part of Virginia Beach) 23462
Euclid Terrace (Part of Virginia Beach) 23462
Eureka 23947
Eureka Park (Part of Virginia Beach) 23452
Eustaces Corner 22728
Euwanee Park (Part of Norfolk) 23503
Everets (Part of Suffolk) 23434
Evergreen 23939
Evergreen Hills 24202
Evergreen Shores 23696
Evington 24550
Ewell 23185
Ewing 24248
Exeter 24216
Exmore 23350
Faber 22938
Fagg 24073
Fairchester (Part of Fairfax) 22030
Fair City Mall (Part of Fairfax) 22031
Fairfax 22030-39
For specific ZIP Codes call (888) 275-8777, or your local postmaster.
Fairfax Acres 22030
Fairfax Circle (Part of Fairfax) 22031
Fairfax Forest 22031
Fairfax Station 22039
Fairfax Villa 22030
Fairfax Woods (Part of Fairfax) 22030
Fairfield, *Essex* 22454
Fairfield, *Rockbridge* 24435
Fairhaven 22303
Fair Lakes Center 22033
Fairland 22312
Fairlawn, *Pulaski*♦ 24141
Fairlawn (Part of Covington) 24426
Fairlawn Estates (Part of Norfolk) 23502
Fairlawn Heights 23075
Fairlee 22031
Fair Meadows (Part of Virginia Beach) 23462
Fair Meadows Estates (Part of Virginia Beach) 23462
Fairmont Manor (Part of Norfolk) 23509
Fairmount Park (Part of Norfolk) 23509
Fair Oaks, *Henrico* 23075
Fair Oaks (Part of Fairfax) 22032
Fair Port 22539
Fairview, *Fairfax* 22306
Fairview, *Montgomery* 24149
Fairview, *Northampton* 23310
Fairview, *Scott* 24244
Fairview (Part of Chase City) 23924
Fairview (Part of Fairfax) 22031
Fairview (Part of Luray) 22835
Fairview Beach 22405
Fairview Heights (Part of Clifton Forge) 24422
Fairview Heights (Part of Lexington) 24450
Fairwood 24378
Fairwood Acres 22039
Falconbridge 23234
Falconerville 24521
Falling Creek 23234
Falling Spring 24445
Falls Church 22040-46
For specific ZIP Codes call (888) 275-8777, or your local postmaster.
Falls Hill 22043
Falls Mills 24613
Fallville 24326
Falmouth 22405
Fancy Gap 24328
Fancy Hill 24521
Farmers 22580
Farmers Fork, *Essex* 22509
Farmers Fork, *Richmond* 22572
Farmers Store 24360
Farmingdale (Part of Hopewell) 23860
Farmington, *Albemarle* 22903
Farmington, *Henrico* 23229
Farmville 23901
Farnham 22460
Fauquier Springs 20186
Favonia 24382
Fawcett Gap 22602
Fayette Park 23222
Featherstone 22191
Featherstone Shores 22191
Federal Reserve (Part of Richmond)‡ 23219
Fentress (Part of Chesapeake) 23322
Fentress (Part of Virginia Beach) 23451
Fenwick Park 22042
Fergusonville 23930
Ferncliff 23084
Ferndale Gardens 23803
Ferndale Park 23803
Ferrum♦ 24088
Ferry Farms 22405
Fieldale♦ 24089
Fife 23054
Figsboro 24112
File 22427
Fincastle 24090
Finchley 23927
Fine Creek Mills 23139
Finneywood 23924
First Colony 23185
First Street (Part of Radford)‡ 24141
Fishers Hill 22626
Fishersville 22939
Five Forks, *Amherst* 24521
Five Forks, *Bedford* 24523
Five Forks, *Carroll* 24343
Five Forks, *Dinwiddie* 23833
Five Forks, *Halifax* 24592
Five Forks, *James City* 23185
Five Forks, *Madison* 22960
Five Forks, *Nelson* 24553
Five Forks, *Prince Edward* 23958
Five Forks (Part of Hopewell) 23860
Five Lakes 23141
Five Mile Fork 22407
Five Oaks 24630
Flactem Manor 23805
Flagpond 24221
Flat Gap 24279
Flat Iron 22520
Flatridge 24378
Flat Rock, *Powhatan* 23139
Flatrock, *Russell* 24260
Flat Run 22508
Flat Spur 24237
Flat Top 24230
Flatwood 24312
Flatwoods 24090
Fleeburg 22849
Fleenors 24202
Fleenortown 24263
Fleet (Part of Norfolk) 23511
Fleeton 22539
Flemington 24228
Fletcher 22973
Fletcherville 20186
Flint Hill, *Bedford* 24121
Flint Hill, *Rappahannock* 22627
Flood 24458
Floris 22071
Floyd 24091
Foneswood 22461
Fontaine 24148
Ford 23850
Fordham (Part of Hampton) 23663
Forest 24551
Forest Acres 23805
Forest Hill (Part of Richmond)‡ 23225
Forest Hills (Part of Virginia Beach) 23450
Forest Lake Hills 23116
Forest Park (Part of Hampton) 23666
Forest Park (Part of Norfolk) 23518
Forestville, *Fairfax* 22066
Forestville, *Shenandoah* 22847
Fork Ridge 24639
Forks of Buffalo 24521
Forks of Water 24413
Forksville 23950
Fork Union 23055
Formosa 23962
Fort Belvoir 22060
Fort Blackmore 24250
Fort Chiswell 24360
Fort Defiance 24437
Fortener Addition 24354
Fort Hill, *Henrico* 23226
Fort Hill (Part of Lynchburg)‡ 24502
Fort Lee, *Henrico* 23075
Fort Lee, *Prince George* 23801
Fort Lewis Terrace (Part of Salem) 24153
Fort Mitchell 23941
Fort Myer‡ 22211
Fort Myer Heights 22209
Fort Pickett 23824
Fort Valley 22652
Foster 23056
Fosters Falls 24360
Four Mile Fork 22408
Fourway (Part of Tazewell) 24630
Fox 24348
Foxhall (Part of Norfolk) 23502
Fox Hill (Part of Hampton) 23664
Fox Mill Estates 20170
Foxwells 22578
Fractionville 24210
Fraleytown 24244
Franconia♦ 22310
Franconia Commons 22310
Franklin 23851
Franklin Farms 23805
Franklin Forest 22101
Franklin Heights 24151
Franklin Junction (Part of Suffolk) 23438
Franklin Park 22101
Franks Mill 24401
Franktown 23354
Frederick Hall 23117
Frederick Heights 22602
Fredericksburg, *Indep. City* 22401-08
For specific ZIP Codes call (888) 275-8777, or your local postmaster.
Fredericksburg, *Rockbridge* 24473
Freeman 23856
Freemont 24343
Freeport 23061
Freeshade Corner 23071
Free Union 22940
Fremac (Part of Virginia Beach) 23451
Friendship 24340
Fries 24330
Fringer 24066
Frogtown 20135
Front Royal 22630
22651
For specific ZIP Codes call (888) 275-8777, or your local postmaster.
Frytown 20187
Fugua Farms 23234
Fulks Run 22830
Fulton (Part of Richmond) 23231
Furnace 22827
Furnace Hill 24354
Furnace Mountain 20176
Gainesboro 22603
Gaines Mill Estates 23111
Gainesville 20155*
20156†
Gala 24085
Galax 24333
Gallops Corner (Part of Virginia Beach) 23464
Galts Mill 24572
Gammons Store 23102
Garden City, *Arlington* 22207
Garden City (Part of Hampton) 23661
Garden Wood Park (Part of Virginia Beach) 23455
Gardner 24260
Gardners Crossroads 23117
Garfield Estates 22191
Gargatha 23421
Garland Heights 23234
Garrisonville 22463
Garrisonville Estates 22554
Garysville 23860
Gasburg 23857
Gate City 24251
Gatewood 22534
Gatewood Park (Part of Virginia Beach) 23454
Gaylord 22611
Gaynor Heights 24112
Gayton 23075
Geer 22973
Genito 23139
Genoa 22830
Georges Fork 24228
Georges Mill 20180
Georges Tavern 23063
Georgetown 22842
Georgetown South (Part of Manassas) 20110
Georgetown Village 22191
George Washington (Part of Alexandria)‡ 22305
George Washington Village 22060
Georgian Hamlet 20110
Gether 22514
Getz 22842
Ghent (Part of Norfolk) 23517
Gholsonville 23893
Gibson Station 24248
Gidsville 24521
Gilbert Gardens 23231
Gilmore Mills 24579
Ginter Park (Part of Richmond) 23227
Gladehill 24092
Gladesboro 24343
Glade Spring 24340
Gladstone 24553
Gladys 24554
Glamorgan 24293
Glasgow 24555
Glass 23072
Glebe Point 22432
Gleedsville 20175
Glen Alden 22030
Glen Allen 23058-60
For specific ZIP Codes call (888) 275-8777, or your local postmaster.
Glenbrook Hills 23075
Glencarlyn 22204
Glendale (Part of Newport News) 23607
Glendale Acres 23030
Glen Echo 23223
Glenford 24210
Glen Forest 22041
Glenita 24244
Glen Lyn 24093
Glenmore 24562
Glenns 23149
Glen Oaks 22015
Glenrochie 24211
Glen Rock (Part of Norfolk) 23502
Glen Roy Estates 23061
Glenshellah (Part of Portsmouth) 23707
Glenvar 24153
Glen Wilton 24438
Glenwood (Part of Danville) 24541
Glenwood Farms 23223
Glenwood Park (Part of Norfolk) 23505
Gloucester 23061
Gloucester Banks 23062
Gloucester Courthouse♦ 23061
Gloucester Point 23062
Goblintown 24171
Goddin Hill 23005
Gogginsville 24151
Goldbond 24094
Golddale 22508
Gold Hill 23123
Goldvein 22720
Gonyon 22473
Goochland 23063
Goodall 23192
Goode 24556
Goods Mills 24471
Goodview 24095
Goodwins Ferry 24128
Goose Pimple Junction 24202
Gordonsville 22942

Gore 22637
Goshen 24439
Goshen Cross Road 23015
Gossan Mines 24333
Gouldin 23192
Gowrie Park (Part of Norfolk) 23509
Grady 24530
Grafton 23692
Grafton Village 22405
Grahams Forge 24360
Granby Shores (Part of Norfolk) 23503
Grandin Road (Part of Roanoke)‡ 24015
Grand View (Part of Hampton) 23664
Grangeville 23410
Granite Hills (Part of Richmond) 23225
Granite Springs 22553
Grant 24378
Grant's Field 23803
Granville 23030
Grapefield 24314
Grassland 22733
Grass Ridge 22101
Grassy Creek, *Henry* 24112
Grassy Creek, *Russell* 24224
Gratton 24651
Gravel Hill (Part of Richmond) 23225
Graves Mill 22721
Graves Store 24104
Gray 23897
Graysontown 24141
Gray's Pointe 22033
Graysville 23301
Great Bridge (Part of Chesapeake)‡ 23320*
... 23328†
Great Falls♦ 22066
Great Neck Manor (Part of Virginia Beach) 23450
Green Acres (Part of Fairfax) 22030
Greenbackville 23356
Green Bay 23942
Greenbriar, *Chesterfield* 23831
Greenbriar, *Fairfax* 22033
Greenbrier Mall (Part of Chesapeake) 23320
Greenbush 23357
Green Cove 24236
Greendale, *Henrico* 23228
Greendale, *Washington* 24210
Greendale Manor 23230
Greenes Corner 23024
Greenfield, *Nelson* 22920
Greenfield, *Pittsylvania* 24557
Greenfield, *Washington* 24361
Greenfield Farms (Part of Portsmouth) 23703
Greenlee 24579
Greenmount 22802
Green Oaks (Part of Newport News) 23601
Green Pond 24531
Greens Folly Apartments 24592
Green Spring 22603
Green Springs, *Louisa* 22942
Green Springs, *Washington* 24211
Green Valley (Part of Bristol) 24202
Greenville, *Augusta* 24440
Greenville, *Fauquier* 20181
Greenway Downs 22042
Greenway Hills (Part of Fairfax) 22030
Greenwich, *Prince William* 20181
Greenwich (Part of Virginia Beach) 23462
Greenwood, *Albemarle* 22943
Greenwood, *Henrico* 23060
Greenwood, *Rockingham* 22827
Greenwood (Part of Norfolk) 23513
Greenwood Farms (Part of Hampton) 23666
Gregory Corner 23968
Gressitt 23156
Gretna 24557
Griffinsburg 22701
Griffith 24422
Grimes 22624
Grimsleyville 24639
Grimstead 23064
Grindall Creek 23234
Grit 24563
Grizzard 23879
Groseclose 24368
Grotons 23399
Groton Town 23359
Grottoes 24441
Grove 23185
Grove Hill 22849
Grove Park (Part of Portsmouth) 23707
Groveton 22306
Groveton Heights 22306
Grundy 24614
Guilford, *Accomack* 23308
Guilford, *Fairfax* 22310
Guilford Heights 23899
Guinea 22580
Guinea Mills 23040
Gum Spring 23065
Gum Tree 23005
Gunn Hall Manor (Part of Virginia Beach) 23454
Gunston Heights 22079
Gunston Manor 22079
Gunton Park 24360
Gwathmey 23005
Gwynn 23066
Hacksneck 23358
Haddonfield 24279
Hadensville 23067
Hagans 24263
Hague 22469
Hale Creek 24634
Halemhurst (Part of Fairfax) 22032
Hales Bottom 24605
Halfway 20198
Halifax 24558
Hall Addition 24354
Hallieford 23068
Hallowing Point Estates 22079
Hallsboro 23113
Halls Hill 22207
Hallwood, *Accomack* 23359
Hallwood (Part of Hampton) 23664
Hamburg, *Page* 22835
Hamburg, *Shenandoah* 22824
Hamilton 20158*
... 20159†
Hamiltontown 24273
Hamlin 24224
Hampden Sydney♦ 23943
Hampton 23651-61
... 23663-70
For specific ZIP Codes call (888) 275-8777, or your local postmaster.
Hampton Institute (Part of Hampton)‡ 23668
Hampton Terrace (Part of Hampton) 23669
Hanckel 24361
Handsom 23859
Hanging Rock 24153
Hanover 23069
Hanover Heights 23111
Hansonville 24266
Happy Creek 22630
Harbors of Newport 22191
Harborton 23389
Harbor View 22079
Hardings 22482
Hardware 24590
Hardwood 24245
Hardy 24101
Hardyville 23070
Hare Valley 23350
Harless 24073
Harman, *Buchanan* 24618
Harman, *Tazewell* 24602
Harman Junction 24614
Harmony, *Halifax* 24520
Harmony, *Shenandoah* 22824
Harpersville (Part of Newport News) 23607
Harrell Siding (Part of Suffolk) 23434
Harris Grove 23692
Harrisonburg 22801-02
For specific ZIP Codes call (888) 275-8777, or your local postmaster.
Harriston 24441
Harrisville 22660
Harrowgate 23831
Harryhogan 22435
Hartfield 23071
Harts Shop 23117
Hartwood 22471
Harvey 24219
Hassen Heights (Part of Bristol) 24201
Hatchers 23139
Hat Creek 24528
Hatton 24590
Haven Heights (Part of Virginia Beach) 23462
Hawkinstown 22842
Hawthorne (Part of Norton) 24273
Hayes 23072
Hayfield, *Fairfax* 22315
Hayfield, *Frederick* 22638
Haymarket 20168†
... 20169*
Haynesville 22472
Haysi 24256
Hayters Gap 24210
Haywood 22722
Hazel 24237
Hazel Heights (Part of Bristol) 24201
Head Waters 24442
Healing Springs 24445
Health Science (Part of Richmond)‡ 23219
Healys 23071
Heards 22920
Heathsville 22473
Hebron, *Augusta* 24401
Hebron, *Carroll* 24333
Hebron, *Dinwiddie* 23894
Hechler Village 23223
Heights (Part of Petersburg) 23803
Helmet 23148
Hematite 24426
Hendricks Store 24121
Henry 24102
Henry Clay Heights 23111
Henry Fork 24151
Henrytown (Part of Saltville) 24370
Hepners 22842
Herald 24230
Heritage Court 23228
Heritage Square 22003
Heritage Village 22003
Herman 23967
Hermitage 22980
Hermitage Farms 23228
Hermitage Park 23228
Hermosa 24577
Herndon 20170-72
For specific ZIP Codes call (888) 275-8777, or your local postmaster.
Hessian Hills 22901
Hewlett 22546
Hickory (Part of Chesapeake) 23322
Hickory Flat 24333
Hickory Ground (Part of Chesapeake) 23322
Hickory Grove Acres 20169
Hickory Haven 23103
Hickory Hill 22903
Hickory Junction 24260
Hicks Island 23089
Hicksville 24314
Hiddenbrook 20170
Hideaway Park 22031
Hidenwood (Part of Newport News)‡ 23606
High Knob 22630
Highland 24084
Highland Gardens 23222
Highland Homes 22405
Highland Park, *Arlington* 22205
Highland Park, *Prince William* 20110
Highland Park (Part of Hopewell) 23860
Highland Park (Part of Portsmouth) 23707
Highland Park (Part of Richmond) 23222
Highlands 22201
Highland Springs 23075
High Meadows 24202
High Point (Part of Hopewell) 23860
Hightown, *Highland* 24465
Hightown, *Rockingham* 22834
Highview Park 22207
Hilander Park 24202
Hill 24251
Hillbrook 22003
Hillcrest 23040
Hillcrest Estates 20111
Hillsboro 20132
Hillsdale (Part of Suffolk) 23434
Hillsman Corner 24502
Hillsville 24343
Hill Top (Part of Martinsville) 24112
Hilltop (Part of Suffolk) 23451
Hilltop Manor (Part of Virginia Beach) 23454
Hilltop-Oceana (Part of Virginia Beach)‡ 23454
Hilltown 24330
Hillwood 22042
Hiltons 24258
Hilton Village (Part of Newport News) 23601
Hinesville 24549
Hinnom 22520
Hinton 22831
Hitesburg 24598
Hiwassee 24347
Hixburg 23958
Hoadly 22191
Hobson (Part of Suffolk) 23436
Hockley 23156
Hockman (Part of Bluefield) 24605
Hodges 24554
Hodges Manor (Part of Portsmouth) 23701
Hodgesville 24151
Hoges Chapel 24136
Holcomb Rock 24503
Holdcroft 23030
Holiday Hills (Part of Richmond) 23235
Holiday Point Estates (Part of Suffolk) 23404
Holland (Part of Suffolk)‡ 23437
Hollindale 22306
Hollin Hall 22308
Hollin Hills 22307
Hollins♦ 24019
Hollins College 24020
Holly Brook 24315
Holly Forest 22039
Holly Grove 23024
Holly Hills 23139
Hollymead 22911
Holly Park 22032
Holly Point 23430
Hollywood (Part of Suffolk) 23434
Holman 22853
Holmes Run Acres 22042
Holmes Run Heights 22003
Holmes Run Park 22042
Holston 24210
Holston Mill 24354
Holts Crossing 24554
Home Creek 24614
Homeville 23890
Homewood 22015
Honaker 24260
Honey Branch 24283
Honeyville 22851
Hood 22723
Hopeton 23421
Hopewell, *Indep. City* 23860
Hopewell, *Pittsylvania* 24549
Hopkins 23421
Horizon Hills (Part of Bristol) 24201
Horners 22520
Hornsbyville 23692
Horntown 23395
Horse Gap (Part of Pound) 24279
Horse Head 22473
Horse Pasture♦ 24112
Horsepen 24619
Horsey 23396
Hotchkiss 24460
Hot Springs 24445
Howardsville, *Albemarle* 24562
Howardsville, *Loudoun* 20135
Howellsville 22630
Howertons 22454
Howland 22473
Hubbard Springs 24263
Huckleberry Hills 23805
Huddle 24382
Huddleston 24104
Hudgins 23076
Hudson Crossroads 22842
Hudson Terrace (Part of Newport News) 23607
Huffman 24128
Huffville 24138
Hughes Store 23030
Hull Street (Part of Richmond)‡ 23224
Hume 22639
Hunterdale 23851
Hunters Valley 22181
Huntersville (Part of Norfolk) 23504
Huntersville (Part of Suffolk) 23435
Huntingcreek Hills 23234
Huntington, *Fairfax* 22303
Huntington, *Henrico* 23229
Huntington Heights (Part of Newport News) 23607
Huntly 22640
Hunton 23060
Hunts Village 22032
Hupp 22853
Hurley 24620
Hurricane 24293
Hurt 24563
Huske 23882
Hustle 22476
Hyacinth 22435
Hybla Valley 22306
Hybla Valley Farms 22306
Hyco 24592
Hylas 23146
Hylton Park 23235
Iberis 22503
Ida 22835
Idlewilde (Part of Covington) 24426
Idylwood 22043
Igo 22405
Imboden 24216
Independence 24348
Independent Hill 20112
Index 22485
Indian Field 22572
Indian Gap 24656
Indian Neck 23148
Indian River (Part of Chesapeake)‡ 23325
Indian River Estates (Part of Virginia Beach) 23462
Indian Rock 24066
Indian Run Park 22312
Indian Springs, *Chesterfield* 23234
Indian Springs, *Fairfax* 22312
Indian Valley 24105
Indika 23487
Ingham 22849
Ingleside (Part of Norfolk) 23502
Ingram 24597
Inlet 22701
Inman 24216
Ino 22437
Interior 24094
Intervale 24426
Ira 24620
Irisburg 24054
Irondale 24219
Iron Gate, *Alleghany* 24448
Irongate, *Prince William* 20109
Ironto 24087
Irving 24174
Irvington 22480
Irwin 23063
Isaac 23851
Island Creek 24343
Island Farm 22560
Island Ford 22827
Isle of Wight 23397
Isom 24228
Ivakota 20124
Ivanhoe 24350
Ivondale 22572
Ivor 23866
Ivy 22945
Jacksons Ferry 24312
Jamaica 23079
James River Estates 23238
James Store 23128
Jamesville 23398
Janaf Shopping Center (Part of Norfolk) 23502
Janey 24631
Jarratt 23867
Jasper 24244

Java 24565
Jefferson 23139
Jefferson Manor 22303
Jefferson Mews (Part of Herndon) 22070
Jefferson Park 23860
Jeffersonton 22724
Jefferson Village 22042
Jeffress 23927
Jenkins Bridge 23399
Jenkins Neck 23072
Jennings 23930
Jennings Gap 24421
Jennings Mission 24251
Jennings Store 24244
Jericho, *Carroll* 24381
Jericho (Part of Suffolk) 23434
Jerome 22824
Jersey 22481
Jessup Farms 23234
Jester Gardens (Part of Chesapeake) 23320
Jetersville 23083
Jewell Hollow 22835
Jewell Ridge 24622
Jewell Valley 24622
Johnsontown 23405
Joliff (Part of Chesapeake)‡ 23321
Jolivue♦ 24401
Jollett 22827
Jones 22553
Jonesboro 23824
Jones Corner 22427
Jones Creek (Part of Martinsville) 24112
Jonesville 24263
Jordan Mines 24426
Josephine 24273
Joyce Heights (Part of Fairfax) 22030
Joyner 23829
Justisville 23421
Ka 24245
Karo 22630
Kathmoor 22310
Keats 27553
Kecoughtan (Part of Hampton)‡ 23667
Keeling 24566
Keene 22946
Keene Mill Manor 22152
Keen Mountain 24624
Keezletown 22832
Keith 23009
Keller 23401
Kells Corner 23924
Kelsa 24620
Kemmerer Gem No. 2 24282
Kemp's Place 23231
Kempsville (Part of Virginia Beach) 23462
Kempsville Colony (Part of Virginia Beach) 23464
Kempsville Gardens (Part of Virginia Beach) 23462
Kempsville Heights (Part of Virginia Beach) 23462
Kenbridge 23944
Kendall Acres 23234
Kendall Grove 23347
Kenilworth (Part of Norfolk) 23503
Kennard 22572
Kennelworth (Part of Petersburg) 23803
Kent 24382
Kent Gardens 22101
Kent Park (Part of Norfolk) 23509
Kents Store 23084
Kentuck 24586
Kenwood, *Hanover* 23005
Kenwood (Part of Hopewell) 23860
Keokee 24265
Kerfoot 20114
Kermit 24251
Kerns 24250
Kernstown (Part of Winchester) 22602
Kerrs Creek 24450
Keswick 22947
Keysville 23947
Key West 22911
Kibler 24053
Kidds Fork 22514
Kidd's Store 24590
Kidville 22939
Kiels Gardens 22030
Kiger Hill 24450
Kilby (Part of Suffolk) 23434
Kilby Shores (Part of Suffolk) 23434
Kildare Annex 23230
Kilmarnock 22482
Kilmarnock Wharf 22482
Kimages 23030
Kimballton 24150
Kimberley Hills 23901
Kimberling 24315
Kimberly Acres 23234
Kinderhook 22973
Kindrick 24382
King and Queen Court House 23085
King George 22485
Kingsbury Manor 22980
Kings Corner 23089
Kings Crossroads 23964
Kingsdale 23851
Kings Fork (Part of Suffolk) 23434
Kings Grant (Part of Virginia Beach) 23452
Kings Hill 23231
Kingsland 23234
Kings Park 22151
Kings Park West 22032
Kings Point 23185
Kings Store 24091
Kingston 24550
Kingston Chase 20170
Kingstown 24019
Kingsville 23901
Kingswood 23185
Kingswood Court 23116
Kingtown (Part of Bristol) 24201
King William 23086
Kino 22560
Kinsale 22488
Kiptopeke 23310
Kire 24094
Kirkside 22306
Klotz 24150
Knightly 24437
Knob Hill (Part of Virginia Beach) 23464
Koehler 24112
Koger Executive Center (Part of Norfolk)‡ 23506
Konnarock 24236
Laburnum Manor 23222
Lacey Forest 22205
Lacey Spring 22833
Lackey 23694
La Crosse 23950
Ladd 22980
Ladysmith 22501
Lafayette 24087
Lafayette Boulevard (Part of Norfolk)‡ 23509
Lafayette Park (Part of Norfolk) 23509
Lahore 22567
Lake 22511
Lake Barcroft 22044
Lake Caroline 22546
Lake Crystal Farms 23235
Lake Jackson 20112
Lake Monticello♦ 22963
Lake Of The Woods 22508
Lake Ridge♦ 22192
Lakeside, Henrico 23228
Lakeside (Part of Newport News) 23606
Lakeside (Part of Salem) 24153
Lakeside Heights 23692
Lakeside Hills 23228
Lakeside Village 23038
Lakeview Acres 23901
Lakeville Estates (Part of Virginia Beach) 23464
Lakewood, *Fairfax* 22041
Lakewood, *James City* 23185
Lakewood, *Pittsylvania* 24541
Lakewood (Part of Norfolk) 23509
Lamberts Point (Part of Norfolk) 23508
Lambsburg 24351
Lanahan 24088
Lancaster 22503
Landmark Center (Part of Alexandria) 22304
Landmark Plaza (Part of Alexandria) 22312
Landmark Square (Part of Manassas) 20110
Land of Promise (Part of Virginia Beach) 23457
Land O'Pines 23832
Landtown (Part of Virginia Beach) 23456
Lanes Corner, *Hanover* 23005
Lanes Corner, *Spotsylvania* 22553
Lanesville 23086
Laneview 22504
Lanexa 23089
Langhorne Acres 22031
Langley 22101
Langley Forest 22101
Langley Research Center (Part of Hampton) 23665
Langley View (Part of Hampton) 23669
Lankford Corner 22473
Lantz Mills 22824
Lara 22503
Larchmont, *Arlington* 22201
Larchmont (Part of Norfolk) 23508
Larkspur (Part of Virginia Beach) 23462
Larrys Store 24598
Larwood Acres 24202
Lassiter Courts (Part of Newport News) 23607
Laswell 24360
Latanes 22443
Laurel, *Henrico* 23060
Laurel, *Russell* 24260
Laurel Branch 24091
Laureldale 24236
Laurel Dell 23228
Laurel Fork 24352
Laurel Grove 24594
Laurel Grove Estates 23116
Laurel Hill, *Augusta* 24482
Laurel Hill, *Shenandoah* 22641
Laurel Manor (Part of Virginia Beach) 23451
Laurel Mills 22716
Laurel Oak 23234
Laurel Park, *Henrico* 23228
Laurel Park, *Henry* 24112
Lawndale Farms 23231
Lawrenceville 23868
Lawrenceville Hills 23868
Lawson 23430
Lawson Forest (Part of Virginia Beach) 23455
Lawson's Store, *Mecklenburg* 23924
Lawsons Store, *Russell* 24224
Lawyers 24501
Laymantown♦ 24064
L C Page (Part of Norfolk)‡ 23518
Leaksville 22835
Leatherwood 24112
Lebanon 24266
Lebanon Church 22641
Leck 24230
Leda 24577
Lee 23039
Lee Acres 23875
Lee Boulevard Heights 22044
Leedstown 22443
Lee Forest 22030
Lee Hall (Part of Newport News)‡ 23603
Lee Heights 22207
Lee-Hi Village 22030
Leemaster 24656
Lee Meadows 22032
Lee Mont 23421
Lee Park 23150
Leesburg 20175-78
For specific ZIP Codes call (888) 275-8777, or your local postmaster.
Leesville 24571
Lee Town 24614
Leewood 22151
Lenah 20105
Lennig 24577
Lenox (Part of Norfolk) 23503
Lenox (Part of Virginia Beach) 23451
Leon 22725
Lerty 22520
Lester Manor 23086
Level Run 24563
Lewinsville 22101
Lewinsville Heights 22101
Lewisetta 22511
Lewis Park 22030
Lewiston 23005
Lewisville 22611
Lexington 24450
Liberia Woods (Part of Manassas) 20110
Liberty, *Halifax* 24577
Liberty, *Tazewell* 24651
Lick Fork 24230
Lick Run 24085
Lick Skillet 24370
Lightfoot 23090
Lignum 22726
Lilian 22539
Lilly 22821
Lime Hill 24202
Limeton 22610
Lincoln 20160
Lincolnia, *Fairfax*‡ 22311-12
For specific ZIP Codes call (888) 275-8777, or your local postmaster.
Lincolnia (Part of Alexandria)‡ 22312
Lincolnia Heights 22312
Lincolnia Park 22312
Lincoln Park, *Fairfax* 22030
Lincoln Park (Part of Norfolk) 23513
Lindell 24210
Linden 22642
Lindenwood 24179
Lindsay 22942
Linkhorn (Part of Virginia Beach) 23454
Linkhorn Estates (Part of Virginia Beach) 23454
Linkhorn Shores (Part of Virginia Beach) 23451
Linlier (Part of Virginia Beach) 23451
Linville 22834
Lipps 24273
Lithia 24066
Little Haven (Part of Virginia Beach) 23452
Little Plymouth 23091
Little River Hills (Part of Fairfax) 22031
Little River Pines 22031
Little River Shopping Center 22003
Little Rocky Run 20124
Littleton 23890
Little Vienna Estates 22181
Litwalton 22503
Litz 24340
Lively 22507
Lloyd Place (Part of Suffolk) 23434
Loch Laird (Part of Buena Vista) 24416
Lockhart Flats 24228
Locust Creek 23024
Locust Dale 22948
Locust Grove 22508
Locust Hill, *Middlesex* 23092
Locust Hill, *Wythe* 24360
Locust Mound 23410
Locustville 23404
Lodge 22435
Lodi 24340
Lodore 23002
Lofton 24472
Logan 22553
Loisdale Estates 22150
Lombardy Grove 23970
London Bridge (Part of Virginia Beach) 23454
London Towne 20120
Lone Fountain 24421
Lone Gum 24104
Longbottom (Part of Grundy) 24614
Long Branch 24237
Long Dale, *Alleghany* 24422
Longdale, *Henrico* 23060
Longdale Furnace 24422
Long Island 24569
Long Point (Part of Portsmouth) 23703
Longshop 24060
Long Spur 24084
Longview 23430
Looney's Creek 24614
Loretto 22509
Lorfax Heights 22079
Lorne 22546
Lorraine 23075
Lorton♦ 22079*
22199†
Lost Corner 22663
Lost Forest 23234
Lottsburg 22511
Loudoun Heights 25425
Louisa 23093
Love 22952
Loves Mill 24319
Loves Shop 24558
Lovettsville 20180
Lovingston 22949
Lower Brandon 23881
Lower Elk Creek 24326
Lower Exeter 24216
Lowery Hills 22967
Lowesville 22951
Lowmoor 24457
Lowry 24570
Loxley Place (Part of Portsmouth) 23702
Luck 24565
Lucketts 20176
Lumberton 23890
Lummis (Part of Suffolk) 23434
Lunenburg 23952
Luray 22835
Lurich 24124
Lusters Gate 24060
Luttrellville 22435
Lydia 22973
Lyells 22572
Lynchburg 24501-06
For specific ZIP Codes call (888) 275-8777, or your local postmaster.
Lynch Station 24571
Lyndhurst 22952
Lynhaven (Part of Alexandria) 22305
Lynn Grove 23222
Lynnhaven (Part of Hampton) 23666
Lynnhaven (Part of Virginia Beach) 23450
Lynnhaven Acres (Part of Virginia Beach) 23452
Lynnhaven Colony (Part of Virginia Beach) 23451
Lynnhaven Mall (Part of Virginia Beach) 23452
Lynn Shores (Part of Virginia Beach) 23452
Lynn Spring 24649
Lynnwood, *Rockingham* 24471
Lynnwood (Part of Virginia Beach) 23452
Lynwood 22191
Lyon Park 22201
Lyon Village 22201
Mabe 24244
McAdam 24301
Macanie 22842
McCall Gap 24340
McChesney Heights (Part of Bristol) 24201
McClung 24460
McClure 24269
McConnell 24251
McCoy 24111
McCrady 24370
McDonalds Mill 24060
McDonald's Small Farms 23060
McDowell 24458
Macedonia 23308
Maces Springs 24258
McGaheysville 22840
McHenry 22553
Machipongo 23405
McKendree 24558
McKenney 23872
McKinley 24459
McLean 22101-02
22106
For specific ZIP Codes call (888) 275-8777, or your local postmaster.
McLean Estates 22101
McLean Hamlet 22102
McLean Manor 22101
McMullen 22973
McNeals Corner 22503
Macon 23101
Madison 22727
Madison University (Part of Harrisonburg) 22807
Madison Heights♦ 24572

*** Area Zip Code** **† Post Office Boxes** **‡ Postal Station** **♦ Census Designated Place** *Italic Type* **County**

Madison Manor 22205
Madison Mills 22953
Madison Run 22942
Madisonville 23958
Madrid 22980
Maggie 24127
Magnolia (Part of Suffolk) 23434
Magnolia Gardens (Part of Suffolk) 23434
Maidens 23102
Major 24526
Makemie Park 23442
Malbrook 22044
Malcolm 24202
Malibu (Part of Virginia Beach) 23452
Mallow 24426
Malmaison 24527
Manakin 23103
Manakin Farms 23103
Manakin Sabot 23103
Manassas 20108-13
For specific ZIP Codes call (888) 275-8777, or your local postmaster.
Manassas Park 20111-13
For specific ZIP Codes call (888) 275-8777, or your local postmaster.
Manbur 23150
Manchester Mills 23875
Maness 24282
Mangohick 23069
Mannboro 23105
Manquin 23106
Manry 23888
Mantua 22031
Mantua Hills 22031
Manville 24251
Maple Grove, *Rockbridge* 24450
Maple Grove, *Spotsylvania* 22407
Maple Grove, *Westmoreland* 22443
Maplewood 23002
Mappsburg 23420
Mappsville 23407
Marble Valley 24432
Marcem (Part of Gate City) 24251
Marengo 23950
Margo 22553
Marion 24354
Marion Hill 23231
Marionville 23408
Markham, *Fauquier* 22643
Markham, *Pittsylvania* 24557
Mark Haven Beach 22454
Marksville 22851
Marlan Forest 22307
Marlbank 23692
Marlboro 23224
Marlbrook 24483
Marrowbone Heights 24148
Marshall 20115*
20116†
Marshall Heights 23072
Marsh Run 22712
Marstella Estates 20187
Martha Gap 24256
Martin Siding 23405
Martins Store 22920
Martinsville 24112-15
For specific ZIP Codes call (888) 275-8777, or your local postmaster.
Marumsco Acres 22191
Marumsco Hills 22191
Marumsco Plaza 22191
Marumsco Village 22191
Marumsco Woods 22191
Marvin 24639
Marye 22553
Marysville 24554
Maryus 23107
Mascot 23108
Mason Cove 24153
Mason Creek (Part of Salem) 24153
Massanetta Springs 22801
Massaponax 22407
Massies Mill 22954
Mathews 23109
Matoaca 23803
Mattaponi 23110
Maurertown 22644
Maury Place (Part of Newport News) 23601
Mavisdale 24627
Max Creek 24347
Maxie 24628
Max Meadows 24360
Maxwell 24651
Mayberry 24120
Maybrook 24136
Mayfair Place 23223
Mayfield 23230
Mayfield Farms 23111
Mayflower 24521
Mayo, *Halifax* 24598
Mayo, *Henry* 24165
Maytown (Part of Coeburn) 24230
Meade 22560
Meadowbrook, *Chesterfield* 23234
Meadowbrook (Part of Norfolk) 23505
Meadowbrook Forest (Part of Norfolk) 23518
Meadowcrest (Part of Bristol) 24201
Meadowood 23227
Meadows of Dan 24120
Meadows of Newgate 20121
Meadow View, *Chesterfield* 23234
Meadowview, *Washington* 24361
Meadville 24558
Mears 23409
Mears Station 23409
Mearsville 23409
Mechanicsburg 24315
Mechanicsville, Hanover♦ 23111
23116
For specific ZIP Codes call (888) 275-8777, or your local postmaster.
Mechanicsville, *Rockingham* 22853
Mechums River 22901
Media Park 23231
Meetze 20186-87
For specific ZIP Codes call (888) 275-8777, or your local postmaster.
Meherrin 23954
Melfa 23410
Melrose, *Campbell* 24554
Melrose (Part of Roanoke)‡ 24017
Melrose Gardens 22172
Melton 22942
Memorial Heights 22306
Mendota 24270
Mentow 24104
Meredithville 23873
Meridian Park 22046
Merrimac♦ 24060
Merrimack Park (Part of Norfolk) 23503
Merrimac Shores (Part of Hampton) 23669
Merry Point 22513
Messongo 23399
Metomkin 23421
Mew 24224
Michaux 23139
Midcity Shopping Center (Part of Portsmouth) 23707
Middlebrook 24459
Middleburg 20117*
20118†
Middleridge 22032
Middleton 23228
Middleton Gardens (Part of Salem) 24153
Middletown, *Frederick* 22645
22649
For specific ZIP Codes call (888) 275-8777, or your local postmaster.
Middletown, *Northampton* 23413
Middletowne Farms 23185
Midland 22728
Midlothian 23112-13
For specific ZIP Codes call (888) 275-8777, or your local postmaster.
Midway, *Halifax* 24598
Midway, *Mecklenburg* 23915
Midway, *Tazewell* 24609
Mike 24538
Mila 22473
Milan (Part of Norfolk)‡ 23508
Miles 23025
Milford 22514
Military Circle Center (Part of Norfolk) 23502
Millboro 24460
Millboro Spring 24460
Mill Creek Park 22003
Millenbeck 22503
Miller Park (Part of Lynchburg)‡ 24501
Millers Tavern 23115
Mill Gap 24465
Mill Garden 22553
Milltown 20180
Millwood 22646
Milteer Acres (Part of Suffolk) 23434
Mineral 23117
Mine Run 22508
Minnieville 22193
Minor 22560
Mint Spring 24463
Miona 23415
Miskimon 22473
Mission Home 22940
Mitchells 22729
Mitchelltown 24445
Mobjack 23056
Modern (Part of Hampton) 23666
Modest Town 23412
Moffats Creek 24459
Mogarts Beach 23430
Mollusk 22517
Monaskon 22503
Moneta 24121
Moneys Corner 20170
Monroe 24574
Monroe Gardens (Part of Hampton) 23669
Monroe Hall 22443
Montague 22504
Montclair♦ 22026
Montebello 24464
Monterey 24465
Montevideo 22840
Montezuma 22821
Montezuma Gardens 23223
Montford 22960
Montgomery 24023
Monticello Park (Part of Alexandria) 22305
Monticello Village (Part of Norfolk) 23509
Monticello Woods 22150
Montpelier, *Charles City* 23030
Montpelier, *Hanover* 23192
Montpelier Station 22957
Montrose 23231
Montrose Heights (Part of Richmond)‡ 23231
Montrose Terrace 23231
Montross 22520
Montvale 24122
Montvue 22901
Monument Heights 23226
Moon 23119
Mooreland 23075
Mooreland Farms 23229
Moores Corner 22554
Moorings 23839
Moran 23966
Morattico 22523
Morefield 24283
Morningside Hills 24210
Morning Star 22835
Morrisdale 23831
Morrison (Part of Newport News) 23601
Morrisonville 20180
Morrisville 22712
Morven 23002
Mosby 22042
Mosby Woods (Part of Fairfax) 22030
Moscow 22843
Moseley 23120
Moss Run 24426
Mossy Creek 22812
Motley 24563
Motleys Mill 24531
Motorun 23163
Mountain Falls 22602
Mountain Gap 20175
Mountain Grove 24484
Mountain Hill 24586
Mountain Lake 24136
Mountain Valley 24112
Mountain View, *Giles* 24134
Mountain View, *King George* 22406
Mountain View, *Pulaski* 24084
Mountain View, *Rockbridge* 24416
Mountain View, *Washington* 24211
Mount Airy 24557
Mount Alto 22937
Mount Carmel, *Halifax* 24520
Mount Carmel, *Smyth* 24354
Mountcastle 23140
Mount Clifton 22842
Mount Clinton 22802
Mount Crawford 22841
Mountfair 22932
Mount Garland 23117
Mount Hermon 24541
Mount Heron 24631
Mount Holly 22524
Mount Jackson 22842
Mount Landing 22560
Mount Laurel 24534
Mount Meridian 24441
Mount Nebo 23235
Mount Olive 22660
Mount Pisgah 24467
Mount Pleasant 24521
Mount Pleasant Estates 22405
Mount Sidney 24467
Mount Solon 22843
Mount Vernon Forest 22309
Mount Vernon Park 22309
Mount Vernon Square 22306
Mount Vernon Terrace 22309
Mount Vernon Valley 22309
Mount Vernon Woods 22309
Mountville 20117
Mount Vinco 23921
Mount Williams 22602
Mount Zephyr 22309
Mount Zion 24554
Mouth of Laurel 24609
Mouth of Wilson 24363
Mt. Ararat 23927
Mt. Cross 24540
Mt. View 24354
Mud Fork 24630
Mulch 22460
Munden (Part of Virginia Beach) 23457
Mundy Point 22435
Munson Hill 22041
Murat 24450
Murpheyville 24368
Murphy 24656
Murrayfield 24319
Museville 24531
Mustoe 24468
Mutton Hunk 23421
Myndus 22949
Myrtle (Part of Suffolk) 23434
Nace 24175
Naffs 24065
Nahor 22963
Nain 22603
Namozine Store 23833
Nancy Wrights Corner 22580
Nandua 23420
Nansemond (Part of Suffolk) 23434
Nansemond Shores (Part of Suffolk) 23434
Naola 24574
Narrows 24124
Naruna 24576
Nash Ford 24225
Nasons 22733
Nassawadox 23413
Nathalie 24577
National Airport‡ 20001
National Heights 23231
Natural Bridge 24578
Natural Bridge Station 24579
Natural Well 24445
Naval Base (Part of Norfolk) 23511
Naval Weapons Laboratory 22448
Naval Weapons Station 23691
Navy Annex 20370
Naxera 23061
Naylors Beach 22572
Nealy Ridge 24226
Nebo 24318
Needmore, *Smyth* 24319
Needmore, *Wise* 24273
Neenah 22520
Neersville 20132
Negro Foot 23192
Nellysford 22958
Nelson 24580
Nelson Estates 23231
Nelsonia 23414
Nelson Park 23185
Nesting 23079
Nethers 22740
Nettleridge 24171
New Alexandria 22307
New Baltimore 20187
Newbern 24126
Newberry 20165
New Birchett Estates 23875
New Bohemia 23842
New Canton 23123
New Castle 24127
New Church 23415
Newcomb Hall (Part of Charlottesville) 22904
New Design (Part of Danville) 24541
New Ellett 24060
New Glasgow 24521
New Gosport (Part of Portsmouth) 23702
New Hampden 24413
New Hope, *Augusta* 24469
New Hope, *Charles City* 23030
Newington Station 22153
Newington Woods 22153
New Kent 23124
Newland 22572
New London 24551
New Market 22844
Newmarket Fair (Part of Newport News) 23605
New Point 23125
Newport, *Giles* 24128
Newport, *Page* 22849
Newport News 23601-12
For specific ZIP Codes call (888) 275-8777, or your local postmaster.
New Post 22408
New River 24129
News Ferry 24592
Newsoms 23874
Newstead Farm 23875
New Store 23901
Newton Park (Part of Norfolk) 23523
Newtown, *King and Queen* 23126
Newtown, *Lancaster* 22503
Newtown, *Rockbridge* 24450
Newtown, *Rockingham* 22827
Newville, *Prince George* 23842
Newville, *Sussex* 23890
Nicelytown 24422
Nickelsville 24271
Niday 24124
Nimrod Hall 24460
Ninde 22526
Nineveh 22630
Nokesville 20181*
20182†
Nomini Grove 22572
Nora 24272

Norfolk

23501-41
For specific ZIP Codes call (888) 275-8777, or your local postmaster.

Colleges & Universities

Eastern Virginia Med School 23501
Norfolk State Univ 23504
Old Dominion Univ 23529
Virginia Wesleyan Coll 23502

Financial Institutions

Central Fidelity Nat Bank 23510
First Union Nat Bank 23510

Hospitals

Sentara Leigh Hosp 23502
Sentara Norfolk General Hosp 23507

Hotels/Motels

Airport Hilton 23502
Omni Waterside 23510
Quality Inn Lake Wright 23502
Waterside Marriott 23510

Military Installations

Armed Forces Staff College 23511

Consolidated Personal Property Shipping Off 23511
Defense Distribution Depot 23512
Fleet & Industrial Supply Ctr, Material Operations Dept, Ocean Terminal 23511
Naval Air Station 23511
Naval Amphibious Base, Little Creek 23521
Naval Transportation Support Ctr, Air Terminal 23511
U S Army Corps of Engineers 23510

Norge 23127
Norland 24228
Norman 22701
North, *Arlington*‡ 22207
 22213
For specific ZIP Codes call (888) 275-8777, or your local postmaster.
North, *Mathews* 23128
North Bristol (Part of Bristol) 24201
North Fairlington 22206
Northfields 22901
North Fork 20132
North Gap 24366
North Garden 22959
North Halifax 24577
North Holston 24370
North Jericho (Part of Suffolk) 23434
North Linkhorn Park (Part of Virginia Beach) 23451
North Post‡ 22060
North Rolleston (Part of Norfolk) 23502
North Run Hills 23228
Northside (Part of Richmond)‡ 23222
North Springfield 22151
North Stanton 24577
North Tazewell (Part of Tazewell) 24630
North View 23970
North Virginia Beach (Part of Virginia Beach) 23451
North Weems 22576
North Wellville 23824
Northwest (Part of Chesapeake) 23322
North Woodley 22042
Norton 24273
Nortonsville 22935
Norvello 23917
Norview (Part of Norfolk)‡ 23513
Norwood, *Bedford* 24551
Norwood, *Nelson* 24581
Nottingham, *Scott* 24251
Nottingham (Part of Richmond) 23235
Nottoway 23955
Novelty 24137
Novum 22735
Nurney (Part of Suffolk) 23434
Nurneysville (Part of Suffolk) 23434
Nutbush 23942
Nuttall 23061
Nuttsville 22528
Oakcrest, *Arlington* 22202
Oakcrest (Part of Alexandria) 22302
Oakdale 24450
Oakdale Farms (Part of Norfolk) 23505
Oak Forest 23040
Oak Grove, *Carroll* 24381
Oak Grove, *Loudoun* 20166
Oak Grove, *Spotsylvania* 22407
Oak Grove, *Washington* 24202
Oak Grove, *Westmoreland* 22443
Oak Hall 23416
 23396
For specific ZIP Codes call (888) 275-8777, or your local postmaster.
Oak Hill, *Augusta* 22980
Oak Hill, *Grayson* 24363
Oak Hill, *Henrico* 23223
Oak Hill, *Page* 22650
Oak Hill Estates 23005
Oakhurst (Part of Petersburg) 23805
Oakland (Part of Suffolk) 23432
Oakland Park 23350
Oakleaf Terrace (Part of Norfolk) 23523
Oak Level, *Halifax* 24558
Oaklevel, *Henry* 24055
Oakley 22437
Oakpark 22730
Oak Ridge, *Fairfax* 22180
Oakridge (Part of Suffolk) 23434
Oakridge Estates, *Prince William* 20112
Oakridge Estates (Part of Suffolk) 23434
Oakton 22124
Oak Valley Estates 22181
Oakville 24522
Oakwood, *Arlington* 22213
Oakwood, *Buchanan* 24631
Oakwood, *Fairfax* 22310
Oakwood (Part of Norfolk) 23513
Oakwood Forest 24426
Oatlands 20175
Occoquan 22125
Occupacia 22476
Oceana (Part of Virginia Beach) 23454
Ocean Park (Part of Virginia Beach) 23455
Ocean View (Part of Norfolk)‡ 23503
Ocoonita 24263
Ocran 22578
Oilville 23129
Old Courthouse 22182
Old Creek Estates 22032
Old Dominion 22969
Old Dominion Gardens 22101
Olde Forge 22032
Oldewood 22043
Oldfield (Part of Virginia Beach) 23451
Old Glade Spring 24340
Old Hampton (Part of Hampton)‡ 23669
Oldhams 22529
Old Somerset 22972
Old Tavern 20198
Oldtown 24333
Old Well 23959
Olinger 24219
Olive (Part of Portsmouth)‡ 23701
Omaha 24228
Omega 24592
Onancock 23417
Onemo 23130
Onley 23418
Ontario 23937
Opal 20186-87
For specific ZIP Codes call (888) 275-8777, or your local postmaster.
Opequon 22602
Ophelia 22530
Oranda 22657
Orange 22960
Orange Hunt 22152-53
For specific ZIP Codes call (888) 275-8777, or your local postmaster.
Orapax Farms 23141
Orbit 23487
Orchard Hill 23234
Orchid 23117
Orchid Lake 23065
Ordinary 23131
Oregon Acres (Part of Portsmouth) 23707
Oreton 24219
Oriskany 24130
Orkney Springs 22845
Orlando (Part of Suffolk) 23434
Orlean 20128
Orleans Village 22312
Oronoco 24483
Osaka 24216
Osbornes Chapel 24221
Osborns Gap 24228
Osceola 24211
Osso 22405
Othma 23153
Otter Hill 24523
Otter River 24571
Otterville 24523
Ottobine 22821
Ottoman 22503
Overall 22610
Overbrook (Part of Norfolk) 23513
Overlee Knolls 22205
Owens 22485
Owens Brooke (Part of Manassas) 20110
Owenton 23148
Oxford (Part of Richmond) 23235
Oyster 23419
Oyster Point (Part of Newport News) 23606
Ozeana 22454
Paces 24592
Paeonian Springs 20129
Page 24631
Page Hollow 24370
Paige 22580
Paineville 23083
Paint Bank 24131
Painter 23420
Paint Lick 24637
Palls 23086
Palmer 22578
Palmer Crossroads 27563
Palmer Springs 23917
Palmyra, *Fluvanna* 22963
Palmyra (Part of Suffolk) 23434
Pamlico (Part of Norfolk) 23503
Pamplin 23958
Panoramic Hills 22003
Pardee 24216
Paris 20130
Park (Part of Waynesboro)‡ 22980
Parker 22508
Parkers Shores 22577
Parkfairfax (Part of Alexandria)‡ 22302
Parkglen 22204
Parklawn 22312
Park Lee Place 23234
Park Place (Part of Norfolk) 23508
Parksley 23421
Parkview, *Rockingham* 22802
Parkview (Part of Newport News)‡ 23605
Park View (Part of Portsmouth) 23707
Parkview Hills 22101
Parkwood 22408
Parnassus 24421
Parrott 24132
Parsonage 24224
Partlow 22534
Passapatanzy 22405
Passing 22427
Pastoria 23421
Patna 24487
Patrician Manor (Part of Hampton) 23666
Patrick Henry Heights 23116
Patrick Henry Mall (Part of Newport News) 23607
Patrick Springs 24133
Patterson, *Buchanan* 24631
Patterson, *Wythe* 24343
Pattonsville 24244
Pauls Cross Roads 22560
Paynes Store 22553
Paytes 22553
Peach Bottom 24333
Peaks 23069
Peapatch 24622
Pearisburg 24134
Pearly 24614
Peary 23138
Pedlar Mills 24574
Pedro 22436
Pemberton 23063
Pembroke 24130
Pembroke Mall (Part of Virginia Beach) 23462
Pembroke Manor (Part of Virginia Beach) 23455
Pender 22033
Penderbrook 22033
Pendleton 23117
Penhook 24137
Penn Acres 23235
Penn Daw 22306
Penn Daw Terrace 22307
Pennington Gap 24277
Penn Laird 22846
Penn Lee 24282
Penns Store 24165
Pennsytown (Part of Norfolk) 23513
Penola 22546
Pentagon 20301
Penvir 24124
Peola Mills 22740
Pepper 24141
Perrin 23072
Perrowville 24551
Perryville (Part of Saltville) 24370
Perth 24577
Petersburg 23803-05
For specific ZIP Codes call (888) 275-8777, or your local postmaster.
Peterson Chapel 24244
Petunia 24382
Peytonsburg 24565
Phenix 23959
Philadelphia (Part of Suffolk) 23434
Philbeck Crossroads 23968
Phillip 24202
Phillis 23917
Philomont 20131
Philpott 24055
Phoebus (Part of Hampton)‡ 23663
Piankatank Shores 23071
Pickaway 24597
Pico 24066
Piedmont 24441
Piedmont Mall (Part of Danville) 24540
Pierces Corner 22503
Pierces Shop 22960
Pigeon Hill 22611
Pilgrams Knob 24634
Pilot 24138
Pimmit 22043
Pimmit Hills♦ 22043
Pine 24324
Pineaire (Part of Suffolk) 23434
Pine Chapel Village (Part of Hampton) 23666
Pinecrest 22312
Pinecrest Heights 22003
Pinedale 23229
Pine Grove, *Clarke* 20135
Pine Grove, *Page* 22851
Pine Grove, *Washington* 24270
Pine Grove Court (Part of Hampton) 23669
Pine Grove Terrace (Part of Hampton) 23669
Pine Hill 23116
Pinehurst (Part of Portsmouth) 23703
Pine Ridge, *Fairfax* (mail Annandale) 22003
Pine Ridge, *Fairfax* (mail Fairfax) 22031
Pinero 23061
Pine Springs 22042
Pine Tree 23027
Pinetta 23061
Pineville 22840
Pinewood Lake 22309
Pinewood Lawns 22309
Pinewood Park (Part of Manassas Park) 20111
Pinewood South 22309
Piney Grove 24589
Piney River 22964
Pinners Point (Part of Portsmouth) 23707
Pipers Gap 24333
Pisgah 24651
Pitmans Corner 22576
Pittmantown (Part of Suffolk) 23438
Pittsville 24139
Pizarro 24091
Plain View 23156
Plantersville 23937
Plasterco 24370
Plaza, The (Part of Lynchburg) 24501
Pleasant Gap 24549
Pleasant Grove, *Henry* 24112
Pleasant Grove, *Lunenburg* 23947
Pleasant Grove, *Mecklenburg* 23970
Pleasant Grove Estates 23920
Pleasant Heights 24370
Pleasant Hill (Part of Harrisonburg) 22801
Pleasant Hill (Part of Suffolk) 23434
Pleasant Ridge, *Fairfax* 22003
Pleasant Ridge (Part of Virginia Beach) 23451
Pleasant Shade 23847
Pleasant Valley, *Buckingham* 23936
Pleasant Valley, *Fairfax* 20151
Pleasant Valley, *Rockingham* 22848
Pleasantview 24574
Plum Creek 24340
Plum Point 23181
Plum Tree 23024
Plymouth 23974
Poages Mill 24018
Pocahontas, *Tazewell* 24635
Pocahontas (Part of Petersburg) 23803
Pocket 24282
Poetown (Part of Grundy) 24614
Poff 24091
Pohick Estates 22079
Point Breeze 22454
Point Eastern 22546
Point Pleasant 24315
Pons 23866
Poole Siding 23833
Pope 23829
Poplar Camp 24360
Poplar Cove 23417
Poplar Heights 22046
Poplar Hill, *Fairfax* 22003
Poplar Hill, *Giles* 24134
Poplar Inn 22546
Poplar Springs 23075
Poquoson 23662
Porter 22937
Porters Cross Roads 24382
Port Haywood 23138
Portlock (Part of Chesapeake)‡ 23324
Port Norfolk (Part of Portsmouth) 23707
Port-O-Dumfries 22172
Port Republic 24471
Port Royal 22535
Portside (Part of Portsmouth)‡ 23705
Portsmouth 23701-09
For specific ZIP Codes call (888) 275-8777, or your local postmaster.
Portsmouth Heights (Part of Portsmouth) 23707
Post Oak 22553
Potato Creek 24363
Potomac (Part of Alexandria)‡ 22301
Potomac Beach (Part of Colonial Beach) 22443
Potomac Farms 20147
Potomac Hills 22101
Potomac Mills, *Prince William* 22192
Potomac Mills, *Westmoreland* 22520
Potters Flats 41522
Pound 24279
Pounding Mill 24637
Powcan 23023
Powells Store, *Albemarle* 22937
Powells Store, *Bedford* 24526
Powhatan 23139
Prater 24656
Pratts 22731
Premier 24640
Prentiss Place (Part of Portsmouth) 23707
Preston 24112
Preston Hills 24202
Preston King‡ 22205
Prices Fork 24073
Prices Store 24572
Prilliman 24088
Prince George 23875
Prince George Woods Estates 23875
Princess Anne (Part of Virginia Beach)‡ 23456
Proffit 22911
Prospect 23960

Prospectdale 24134
Providence, *Grayson* 24330
Providence, *Halifax* 24577
Providence Church (Part of Suffolk) 23434
Providence Forge 23140
Providence Park 23222
Provost 23139
Public Fork 23967
Pughsville (Part of Suffolk) 23435
Pulaski 24301
Pumpkin Center 24315
Pungo (Part of Virginia Beach) 23456
Pungoteague 23422
Purcell 24225
Purcellville 20132*
20134†
Purchase 24244
Purdy 23847
Purvis (Part of Suffolk) 23437
Puryear Corner 23927
Putnam 24260
Quail Oaks 23234
Quantico 22134
Quantico Marine Corps Air Station 22134
Quarry 24370
Quebec 24354
Queens Lake 23185
Quicksburg 22847
Quicks Mill 24401
Quinby 23423
Quinque 22965
Quinton 23141
Rabat 24577
Raccoon Ford 22701
Racefield 23168
Radford 24141-43
For specific ZIP Codes call (888) 275-8777, or your local postmaster.
Radford Army Ammunition Plant 24141
Radford University (Part of Radford) 24142
Radiant 22732
Radnor Heights 22209
Ragged Point Beach 22442
Raines Tavern 23901
Rainswood 22473
Raketown 24350
Raleigh Place (Part of Chesapeake) 23320
Raleigh Terrace (Part of Hampton) 23661
Ramoth 22554
Ramsey (Part of Norton) 24273
Randolph 23962
Random Hills 22030
Rangeley 24089
Ransons 23936
Raphine 24472
Rapidan 22733
Rappahannock Academy 22538
Rappahannock Estates 22454
Rappahannock Shores 22454
Rapps Mill 24450
Raven♦ 24639
Ravensworth 22151
Ravensworth Grove 22003
Ravensworth Park 22003
Ravenwood, *Fairfax* 22044
Ravenwood, *Prince William* 20111
Ravenwood Park 22044
Rawhide 24265
Rawley Springs 22831
Rawlings 23876
Raymondale 22042
Raynor 23866
Rayon Terrace (Part of Covington) 24426
Readus 22824
Reams 23803
Reba 24523
Rectortown 20140
Red Apple Orchard 22971
Redart 23076
Red Ash 24640
Red Bank, *Halifax* 24598
Red Bank, *Northampton* 23408
Redd Shop 23901
Red Eye 24531
Red Fox Forest 22003
Red Hill, *Albemarle* 22959
Red Hill, *Charlotte* 24528
Red House 23963
Red Lane 23139
Redlawn 23919
Red Mills 24431
Red Oak 23964
Red Top (Part of Suffolk) 23434
Red Valley 24065
Redwood 24146
Reed Creek 24265
Reedville 22539
Reesedale 24087
Reese Shop 23967
Refuge 22655
Regina 22503
Rehoboth 23974
Rehoboth Church 22482
Reids Ferry (Part of Suffolk) 23434
Reids Grove 22101
Reliance 22649
Remington 22734
Remlik 23175
Remo 22579
Renan 24557
Republican Grove 24585
Rescue 23424
Reservoir Hill (Part of Covington) 24426
Rest 22624
Reston♦ 22090-95
For specific ZIP Codes call (888) 275-8777, or your local postmaster.
Retreat 24151
Reva 22735
Revis 23175
Rexburg 22560
Reynolds Store 22625
Rhoadesville 22542
Rice 23966
Riceville 24565
Richardson 24343
Richardsville 22736
Rich Creek 24147
Richlands 24641

Richmond

23201-98
For specific ZIP Codes call (888) 275-8777, or your local postmaster.

Colleges & Universities

Union Theological Seminary & Presbyterian School of Christian Education 23227
Virginia Commonwealth Univ 23284
Virginia Union Univ 23220

Financial Institutions

Central Fidelity Nat Bank 23219
Crestar Bank 23219
First Union Nat Bank 23261

Hospitals

Bon Secours St Mary's Hosp 23226
Children's Hosp 23220
Chippenham & Johnson-Willis Hosp 23235
Henrico Doctor's Hosp 23229
Hunter Holmes McGuire Veterans Affairs Med Ctr 23249
Med Coll of Virginia Hosps, Virginia Commonwealth Univ 23298

Hotels/Motels

Holiday Inn West Broad 23230
Hyatt 23230
Jefferson 23220
Marriott 23219
Omni 23219

Military Installations

Combined Support Maintenance Shop 23237
Defense Supply Ctr/Defense Distribution Depot 23297
Supply Support Activity, S Gardner Waller Depot 23230

Richmond Beach 22560
Richmond Heights 23231
Rich Neck 22472
Richpatch 24426
Rich Valley 24370
Ridge 23233*
23242†
Ridgecrest 22124
Ridgelea Estates 22031
Ridge View 22310
Ridgeway, *Halifax* 24597
Ridgeway, *Henry* 24148
Ridgeway, *Pittsylvania* 24139
Riggs 24244
Rileyville 22650
Riner 24149
Ringgold 24586
Rio 22901
Ripplemead 24150
Rip Rap 24598
Rivanna 22936
River Bend Estates 20197
Riverdale, *Halifax* 24592
Riverdale, *Southampton* 23851
Riverdale (Part of Hampton)‡ 23666
Riverhill 24333
River Hills 23075
Rivermont, *Augusta* 24477
Rivermont, *Chesterfield* 23836
Rivermont (Part of Covington) 24426
Rivermont (Part of Lynchburg)‡ 24503
Rivermont (Part of Newport News) 23601
River Oaks 22101
River Park (Part of Portsmouth) 23707
River Ridge Mall (Part of Lynchburg) 24502
Rivers Edge 23860
Riverside 24416
Riverside Estates 22309
Riverside Gardens 22308
Riverton (Part of Front Royal)‡ 22630
Riverview, *Wise* 24230
Riverview (Part of Norfolk) 23504
Riverville 24553
Riverwood 22207
Rixeyville 22737
Roanes 23061
Roanoke 24001-38
For specific ZIP Codes call (888) 275-8777, or your local postmaster.
Roaringfork 24216
Roaring Run 24066
Robbins Chapel 24265
Roberts Mill 24375
Robertsons 24523
Robin Ridge 23116
Robinwood 23231
Robley 22460
Robnel (Part of Manassas) 20110
Rochelle 22738
Rockbridge Baths 24473
Rock Castle 23063
Rockfish 22971
Rockland 22630
Rockland Village 20151
Rock Mills 22716
Rock Springs, *Chesterfield* 23234
Rock Springs, *Fauquier* 20187
Rocktown 24202
Rockville 23146
Rocky Bar 22827
Rocky Gap 24366
Rocky Mount 24151
Roda 24216
Rodden 24577
Rodophil 23083
Roebuck 24210
Roetown 24236
Rogers 24073
Roland Park (Part of Norfolk) 23509
Rolling Brook 22192
Rolling Hills 22309
Rolling Meadows 23875
Rolling Valley 22015
Rollins Fork 22544
Rondo 24531
Roosevelt Gardens (Part of Norfolk) 23513
Roseann 24614
Rose Bower 24522
Rosedale 24280
Rose Hill, *Fairfax* 22310
Rose Hill, *Lee* 24281
Roseland 22967
Rosemont, *Fairfax* 22101
Rosemont (Part of Alexandria) 22301
Rosemont (Part of Suffolk) 23434
Rosemont (Part of Virginia Beach) 23452
Roseville 22554
Roslyn Hills 23229
Rosslyn‡ 22209*
22219†
Roth 24631
Rough Creek 23959
Round Bottom 24124
Round Hill 20141*
20142†
Round Top 24293
Roundtree 22042
Rowe 24646
Roxbury, *Charles City* 23140
Roxbury, *Henrico* 23229
Royal City (Part of Grundy)‡ 24614
Royal Court 22003
Ruark 23043
Rubermont 23974
Ruby 22545
Ruckersville 22968
Rudee Inlet (Part of Virginia Beach) 23451
Rue 23421
Ruff 23109
Rugby 24363
Rural Retreat 24368
Rushmere♦ 23430
Rushmere Shores 23430
Russell 24260
Russell Creek 24283
Rustburg 24588
Rustic 23030
Rutherford 22032
Ruther Glen 22546
Ruthland 23228
Ruthville 23147
Ryan 20147
Rye Cove 24244
Sabot 23103
Sadler Heights (Part of Suffolk) 23434
Sago 24137
St. Brides (Part of Chesapeake) 23322
St. Charles 24282
St. Clair 24605
St. Clair Bottom 24319
St. Davids Church 22652
St. Elmo (Part of Alexandria) 22305
St. Joy 23921
St. Just 22567
St. Louis 20117
St. Luke 22664
St. Paul 24283
St. Stephens 20119
St. Stephens Church 23148
Salem, *Culpeper* 22701
Salem, *Indep. City* 24153
Salem Woods 23234
Salisbury 23113
Salona Village 22101
Saltpetre 24085
Saltville 24370
Saluda 23149
Salvia 23148
Samos 23180
Sanburne Park 23150
Sand Bridge (Part of Virginia Beach) 23456
Sandidges 24521
Sands 23874
Sandston 23150
Sandy Bottom (Part of Suffolk) 23432
Sandy Fork 23927
Sandy Hook 23153
Sandy Level 24161
Sandy Point 22579
Sandy River 24054
Sanford 23426
Sangerville 22812
Sanville 24055
Sarah 23130
Saratoga 22153
Saratoga Place (Part of Suffolk) 23434
Saumsville 22644
Saunders (Part of Richmond)‡ 23220
Savage Crossing (Part of Suffolk) 23434
Savageville 23417
Savedge 23881
Saxe 23967
Saxis 23427
Sayersville 24602
Scarborough Neck 23306
Scenic Park (Part of Bristol) 24201
Schley 23154
Schoolfield (Part of Danville)‡ 24541
Schuyler 22969
Scotland 23883
Scott Addition 24210
Scottie Farms 23075
Scottsburg 24589
Scotts Crossroads 23924
Scotts Fork 23002
Scottsville 24590
Scottswood 23851
Scrabble 22749
Scruggs 24121
Seaboard 24641
Seaford 23696
Seaford Shores 23696
Sealston 22547
Seapines (Part of Virginia Beach)‡ 23451
Searcy 23831
Seatack (Part of Virginia Beach) 23451
Seaview 23429
Seawright Spring 24467
Sebrell 23837
Sedalia 24526
Sedgefield (Part of Newport News) 23607
Sedgefield Manor 23228
Sedley 23878
Selden 23061
Selma 24474
Seminary 24219
Seminary Valley (Part of Alexandria) 22304
Senora 22503
Seven Fountains 22652
Seven Mile Ford 24373
Seven Pines 23150
Seven Pines Villa 23150
Severn 23155
Severn Manor 23072
Shacklefords 23156
Shacklefords Fork 23156
Shadow 23163
Shadow Valley (Part of Bristol) 24201
Shadwell 22947
Shady Grove, *Greene* 22940
Shady Grove, *Halifax* 24598
Shady Grove (Part of Abingdon) 24210
Shady Oak 22066
Shadyside 23405
Shanghai 23110
Shannondale 24630
Shannon Hills 24148
Shannon Park 22577
Sharps 22548
Shawnee Land 22602
Shawsville♦ 24162
Shawver Mill 24651
Shea Terrace (Part of Portsmouth) 23707
Sheep Town 24312
Sheffield Court 23235
Sheffield Terrace 24148
Shelby 22727
Shelfar 23117
Shelors Mill 24091
Shelton (Part of Virginia Beach) 23455
Shenandoah, *Page* 22849
Shenandoah (Part of Hopewell) 23860
Shenandoah Farms 22630
Shenandoah Place 23226
Shenandoah Retreat 20135
Shenandoah Shores 22630
Shepherds Hill 24265
Shepherds Store 23038
Sheppards 23901
Sherando 22952
Sherwill 24538
Sherwood Forest 24401
Sheva 24531
Shields 23306
Shiloh, *King George* 22485
Shiloh, *Southampton* 23827

Place	ZIP Code
Shiny Rock	23927
Shipman	22971
Shirley	23030
Shirley Duke (Part of Alexandria)	22304
Shirley Gate Park	22030
Shirlington‡	22206
Shockoe	24531
Shores	22963
Short Lane	23061
Short Pump	23060
Shorts Creek	24312
Shortt Gap	24647
Shoulders Hill (Part of Suffolk)	23435
Shrevewood	22043
Shumansville	22514
Shumate	24124
Siddon	24580
Sigma (Part of Virginia Beach)	23456
Signpine	23061
Sign Post	23395
Siler	22603
Silva	23415
Silver Beach	23398
Silver Springs	22310
Silverwood (Part of Chesapeake)	23320
Simeon	22902
Simmonsville	24127
Simons Corner	22572
Simonsdale (Part of Portsmouth)	23701
Simonson	22460
Simpkins	23310
Simpsons	24072
Sinai	24592
Sinclair Farms (Part of Hampton)	23669
Singers Glen	22850
Sinking Creek	24127
Sinnickson	23395
Sissons Corner	22473
Sixmile Post	24151
Skeetrock	24228
Skeggs	24646
Skinquarter	23120
Skippers	23879
Skipwith	23968
Skipwith Farms, *Henrico*	23229
Skipwith Farms (Part of Williamsburg)	23185
Skyland	22835
Skyland Estates	22642
Skymont (Part of Staunton)	24401
Slabtown	24251
Slate	24614
Slate Mills	22740
Sleepy Hole (Part of Suffolk)	23435
Sleepy Hollow	22042
Sleepy Hollow Estates, *Fairfax*	22044
Sleepy Hollow Estates, *Henrico*	23229
Sleepy Hollow Manor	22044
Sleepy Hollow Run	22003
Sleepy Hollow Woods	22003
Sliders	23936
Sloantown	24244
Smithfield	23430*
	23431†
Smiths Cross Roads	23970
Smoky Ordinary	23868
Snake Creek	24343
Snapp	24340
Snell	22553
Snowden, *Amherst*	24526
Snowden, *Fairfax*	22308
Snowflake	24251
Snow Hill	23156
Snowville	24347
Soles	23050
Solomons Store	23060
Solsburg	22827
Somers	22503
Somerset	22972
Somerton (Part of Suffolk)	23438
Somerville	22739
Sonans	24531
Sorocco (Part of Suffolk)	23434
Soudan	23927
South‡	22204
Southampton (Part of Hampton)	23669
South Anna	23117
South Boston	24592
South Chesconessex	23417
South Clinchfield	24225
Southern Estates	23805
Southern Pine	23803
South Fairlington	22206
South Garden	22959
South Hill	23970
South Jackson	22842
South Martinsville (Part of Martinsville)‡	24112
South Norfolk (Part of Chesapeake)‡	23324
South Plains (Part of Petersburg)	23805
Southport	22191
Southridge	22101
South Roanoke (Part of Roanoke)‡	24014
Southside (Part of Richmond)‡	23224
South Suffolk (Part of Suffolk)	23434
South Woodley	22042
Spainville	23824
Sparkling Springs	22834
Sparta	22552
Speedwell	24374
Speegleville (Part of Hampton)	23666
Spencer	24165
Sperryville	22740
Spitler	22835
Spivey Store	24251
Splash Dam	24256
Spotsylvania	22553
Spottswood	24475
Spout Spring	24593
Springbrook Forest	22003
Spring City	24225
Springcreek	22812
Springdale, *Henrico*	23222
Springdale (Part of Bristol)	24201
Springfield, *Fairfax*	22150-53
For specific ZIP Codes call (888) 275-8777, or your local postmaster.	
Springfield, *Page*	22835
Springfield, *Rockbridge*	24066
Springfield Estates	22150
Springfield Forest	22150
Springfield Mall Regional Shopping Center	22150
Springfield Plaza	22150
Spring Garden, *Pittsylvania*	24527
Spring Garden (Part of Bristol)	24201
Spring Grove	23881
Springhaven Estates	22102
Spring Hill	24401
Spring Meadows	23111
Spring Mills	24538
Springvale	22066
Spring Valley, *Grayson*	24330
Spring Valley, *Stafford*	22405
Springville	24630
Springwood	24066
Sprouses Corner	23936
Stacy	24614
Stafford	22554*
	22555†
Staffordshire	23235
Staffordsville	24167
Stage Junction	23038
Staleys Cross Roads	24368
Stanardsville	22973
Stanley	22851
Stanleytown, *Henry*♦	24168
Stanleytown, *Scott*	24244
Stapleton	24572
Starkey	24018
Starnes	24250
Star Tannery	22654
Statesville	23874
Station Hills	22039
Staunton	24401*
	24402†
Staunton Park (Part of Staunton)	24401
Steeleburg	24609
Steeles Tavern	24476
Steinman	24226
Stella	24133
Stemphleytown	22821
Stephens	24293
Stephens City	22655
Stephenson	22656
Sterling♦	20163-67
For specific ZIP Codes call (888) 275-8777, or your local postmaster.	
Sterling Point (Part of Portsmouth)	23703
Stevensburg	22741
Stevens Creek	24330
Stevensville	23161
Stewart (Part of Richmond)‡	23221
Stewartsburg	24416
Stewartsville	24179
Stickleyville	24244
Stingray Point	23043
Stith	24534
Stockton	24054
Stoddert	23901
Stokesland (Part of Danville)	24541
Stokesville	22843
Stone Bridge	22663
Stone Creek	24277
Stonega	24285
Stone Mountain	24523
Stones Mill	24382
Stone Springs (Part of Harrisonburg)	22801
Stonewall	24538
Stonewall Acres	20110
Stonewall Manor	22180
Stoneybrook	22553
Stony	24245
Stony Battery	24354
Stony Creek	23882
Stony Man	22835
Stony Point	22911
Stony Point Mills	23040
Stony Ridge	24630
Stormont	23149
Story	23837
Stott	23898
Stovall	24577
Stover	24421
Straightstone	24569
Strasburg	22641
	22657
For specific ZIP Codes call (888) 275-8777, or your local postmaster.	
Strasburg Junction	22657
Stratford	22558
Stratford Hills, *Arlington*	22207
Stratford Hills (Part of Richmond)	23225
Stratford Landing	22308
Stratford-on-the-Potomac	22308
Stratford Village	23222
Strathmeade Springs	22003
Strathmore	23022
Stringtown	22611
Stroupes Store	24382
Stuart	24171
Stuarts Draft	24477
Stubbs	22553
Studley	23162
Stukeley Hall Farms	23227
Stumptown, *Loudoun*	20176
Stumptown, *Northampton*	23347
Suburban Apartments	23230
Sudley♦	20109
Sudley Manor	20109
Suffolk	23432-39
For specific ZIP Codes call (888) 275-8777, or your local postmaster.	
Sugar Grove	24375
Sugar Hill	24528
Sugarland Run♦	20164
Sugar Loaf	24018
Suiter	24314
Sulgrave Manor	22309
Sumerduck	22742
Summerdeon	24479
Summit, *Smyth*	24375
Summit, *Spotsylvania*	22408
Sun	24224
Sunbeam	23851
Sunnybank	22539
Sunnybrook	22182
Sunnybrook Estates	20110
Sunnyside, *Cumberland*	23040
Sunnyside, *Frederick*	22603
Sunny View	22309
Sunset Heights	23231
Sunset Hills	20190
Sunset Manor	22312
Sunset Village (Part of Salem)	24153
Supply	22436
Surrey Square	22032
Surry	23883
Susan	23163
Sussex	23884
Sussex Hilton (Part of Newport News)	23605
Sutherland, *Dinwiddie*	23885
Sutherland, *Wise*	24273
Sutherland Manor	23885
Sutherlin	24594
Sutton Place	22031
Sutton Woods	22181
Swansea Manor (Part of Newport News)	23601
Swansonville	24549
Sweet Briar	24595
Sweet Briar Park	23075
Sweet Chalybeate	24426
Sweet Hall	23181
Swift Creek (Part of Colonial Heights)	23834
Swift Run	22827
Switch Back	24445
Swoope	24479
Swords Creek	24649
Sycamore	24557
Sydnorsville	24151
Sylvania Heights	22408
Sylvatus	24343
Syria	22743
Syringa	23169
Tabb	23693
Tabscott	23038
Tacoma	24230
Taft	22578
Talbot Park (Part of Norfolk)	23505
Tall Oaks	22003
Tallysville	23124
Tamworth	23027
Tangier	23440
Tannersville	24377
Tappahannock	22560
Tara	22205
Taro	23934
Tarpon	24228
Tasley	23441
Tatum	22567
Tauxemont	22308
Taylors Store	24184
Taylorstown	20176
Taylors Valley	24236
Taylorsville	23047
Tazewell	24651
Teas	24375
Temperanceville	23442
Temple Hall Estates	23168
Temple Hill (Part of Castlewood)	24224
Templeman	22520
Tenso	24226
Tenth Legion	22815
Terrys Fork	24138
Tetotum	22485
Thaxton	24174
The English Hills	22039
The Hollow	24053
The Knolls	22191
Thelma	22942
The Manors	22192
Theological Seminary (Part of Alexandria)‡	22304
The Plains	20198
The Ridge	23917
Thessalia	24134
The Timbers	22152
The Villas	22191
Thomas Bridge	24354
Thomas Corner (Part of Norfolk)‡	23502
Thomasson Park	22134
Thomas Terrace	24504
Thomastown	24445
Thompson Valley	24651
Thornburg	22565
Thornhill	22960
Thoroughfare	20137
Thoroughgood (Part of Virginia Beach)	23455
Three Forks	24588
Threemile Corner	23117
Three Springs	24202
Three Square, *Goochland*	23063
Three Square, *Louisa*	23024
Threeway	22469
Tibbstown	22942
Tibitha	22539
Ticktown	23301
Tidemill	23072
Tidewater	22572
Tidwells	22520
Tight Squeeze	24531
Tignor	22514
Timberlake	24502
Timberly Heights (Part of Petersburg)	23803
Timber Ridge	24450
Timberville	22853
Timothy Park	22309
Tiny	24220
Tiptop	24630
Tito	24244
Tivis	24256
Toano	23168
Tobaccoville	23139
Todds Tavern	22553
Toga	23936
Tola	23959
Toms Bottom	24256
Toms Brook	22660
Toms Creek	24230
Tookland	24614
Topnot	22657
Topping	23169
Toshes	24139
Totaro	23856
Tower Mall (Part of Portsmouth)	23701
Town and Country Estates	22180
Townsend	23443
Trade Center (Part of Alexandria)‡	22304
Trammel	24289
Trapp	20184
Treemont	23234
Treherneville	23307
Tremont Gardens	22042
Trenholm	23139
Trents Mill	23040
Trevilians	23170
Triangle♦	22172
Trigg	24134
Trinity	24175
Triplet	23868
Troutdale	24378
Troutville	24175
Trower	23480
Troy	22974
Trueblue	22701
Truxillo	23002
Tuckahoe Park	23229
Tuckahoe Village	23229
Tucker Hill	22488
Tuggle	23901
Tunstall	23124
Turbeville	24592
Turnbull	20186
Turners Crossroads	23879
Turner Store	23873
Turnpike (Part of Fairfax)‡	22031
Tuscarora	22454
Twin Pines (Part of Portsmouth)	23703
Twin Poplars	22938
Twin Springs	24271
Twymans Mill	22727
Tye River	22922
Tyler Gardens (Part of Falls Church)	22046
Tyler Park	22042
Tylerton	22405
Tyro	22976
Tysons Corner	22103
Tysons Corner Center	22102
Tysons Green	22182
Union, *Bedford*	24174
Union, *Floyd*	24380
Union Hall	24176
Union Level	23970
Unionville	22567
Unison	20141
United States Marine Reservation	22134
Unity	23898
University (Part of Charlottesville)	22903
University Heights	23229
University of Richmond (Part of Richmond)	23173
Uno	22738
Upper Brandon	23881
Upperville	20184*
	20185†
Upright	22454
Upshaw	23009
Urbanna	23175
Vails Mill	24236
Vale	22124

Place	ZIP Code
Valentine Hills	23228
Valentines	23887
Valley Brook	22042
Valley Creek	24271
Valley Mall (Part of Harrisonburg)	22801
Valley Mills	24479
Valley Ridge	24426
Valley View Mall (Part of Roanoke)	24012
Valleywood	22191
Van Buren Furnace	22644
Vanderpool	24465
Vandola	24541
Vandyke, *Buchanan*	24639
Van Dyke, *Tazewell*	24609
Vannoy Acres	22030
Vannoy Park	20124
Vansant♦	24656
Varina	23231
Varina Grove	23075
Vaucluse	22655
Vaughn	22835
Vawter Corner	23093
Velma	23108
Venia	24260
Vera	24522
Verbena	22827
Verdi	24244
Vernon Hill	24597
Verona♦	24482
Vertain Park	22032
Vesta	24177
Vests Store	23139
Vesuvius	24483
Vicey	24256
Vicker	24073
Vicker Heights	24073
Vicksville	23878
Victoria	23974
Vienna	22180-83
For specific ZIP Codes call (888) 275-8777, or your local postmaster.	
Viers	24256
Viewtown	22746
Village	22570
Villa Heights♦	24112
Villamay	22307
Villamont	24178
Villboro	22580
Vint Hill Farms	20187*
	20188†
Vinton	24179
Virgilina	24598
Virginia Beach	23450-67
	23471
For specific ZIP Codes call (888) 275-8777, or your local postmaster.	
Virginia Center Commons	23060
Virginia City	24283
Virginia Forest (Part of Falls Church)	22046
Virginia Gardens (Part of Norfolk)	23505
Virginia Heights, *Arlington*	22204
Virginia Heights, *Henrico*	23231
Virginia Highlands	22202
Virginia Hills, *Fairfax*	22310
Virginia Hills (Part of Bristol)	24201
Virginia Union University (Part of Richmond)	23220
Vir-Mar Beach	22473
Volens	24577
Volney	24379
Vulcan	22567
Wabun	24153
Wachapreague	23480
Wadesville	22611
Wake	23176
Wakefield, *Sussex*	23888
Wakefield (Part of Alexandria)	22304
Wakefield Chapel	22003
Wakefield Forest	22003
Wake Forest	24060
Wakenva	24237
Waldrop	22942
Walhaven	22310
Walkers	23089
Walker Store	23924
Walkers Well	24531
Walkerton	23177
Wallace	24202
Wallaces Store	23937
Wallops Flight Center	23337
Wallops Island	23337
Walnut Grove	24270
Walnut Hill (Part of Petersburg)‡	23805
Walters	23315
Walters Woods	22044
Walton	24141
Walton Furnace	24360
Walton Park	23112
Waltons Store	24104
Wan	23061
Ward	24620
Wardell	24609
Wards Corner (Part of Norfolk)	23505
Wards Mill	24333
Wardtown	23482
Ware Neck	23178
Wares Crossroads	23117
Wares Wharf	22454
Warfield	23889
Warminster	24599
Warm Springs	24484
Warner	23175
Warren	24590
Warrenton	20186-88
For specific ZIP Codes call (888) 275-8777, or your local postmaster.	
Warren Woods (Part of Fairfax)	22030
Warsaw	22572
Warwick (Part of Newport News)‡	23601
Warwick on the James (Part of Newport News)	23601
Warwick Village (Part of Alexandria)	22305
Washington	22747
Washington Corner	22580
Washington Gardens (Part of Hampton)	23669
Washington National Airport	22201
Washington Park	23847
Watauga	24211
Waterford	20197
Waterlick	22657
Waterloo	22663
Water View, *Middlesex*	23180
Waterview (Part of Portsmouth)	23707
Watson	20175
Wattsville	23483
Waugh	24526
Waverly	23890
Waverly Hills	22207
Waverly Village	22407
Waxpool	20107
Wayland	23235
Waynesboro	22980
Waynewood	22308
Wayside	23030
Weal	24531
Webbtown	22611
Weber City, *Fluvanna*	23022
Weber City, *Scott*	24290
Wedgewood	23229
Weedonville	22485
Weems	22576
Weirwood	23413
Welchs	22580
Welcome	22485
Wellford	22572
Wellington, *Fairfax*	22308
Wellington, *Prince William*	20109
Wellington Heights	22308
West Arlington	22213
West Augusta	24485
West Bottom	23022
Westbourne	23230
Westbriar	23075
Westchester, *Chesterfield*	23235
Westchester, *Fairfax*	22031
Westdale	23229
West Dante	24272
West End Manor	23229
Western (Part of Petersburg)‡	23803
West Falls Church (Part of Falls Church)	22046
Westfield (Part of Bristol)	24201
West Fork	24069
West Fredericksburg (Part of Fredericksburg)	22401
West Galax (Part of Galax)	24333
West Gate of Lomond	20109
West Ghent (Part of Norfolk)	23507
Westgrove	22307
Westham	23229
Westhampton, *Fairfax*	22043
Westhampton (Part of Richmond)‡	23226
Westhaven (Part of Portsmouth)	23707
West Hope	23882
Westland	22578
West Langley	22101
Westlawn	22042
West Leigh	22901
West Lexington (Part of Covington)	24450
West Mclean	22103
Westmoreland, *Albemarle*	22901
Westmoreland, *Westmoreland*	22577
Westmoreland Heights	22043
Westmoreland Park	22046
West Norfolk (Part of Portsmouth)	23703
Westover, *Arlington*	22205
Westover, *Charles City*	23030
Westover Hills, *Augusta*	22980
Westover Hills, *Greensville*	23847
Westover Hills (Part of Danville)	24541
Westover Hills (Part of Richmond)	23225
West Petersburg	23803
West Piney	24382
West Point	23181
West Raven	24639
West Springfield	22152
Wests Store	24577
Westview, *Augusta*	24479
West View, *Goochland*	23063
Westview Hills	22152
West Warm Springs	24484
Westwood	23226
Westwood Estates	24211
Westwood Forest	22182
Westwood Park	22046
Westwood Place	24426
Weyanoke	22312
Weyers Cave	24486
Whaley (Part of Suffolk)	23438
Whaleyville (Part of Suffolk)‡	23438
Wheatfield	22641
Wheatland	22132
Wheeler	24248
Whitacre	22625
White City	23847
White Gate	24134
White Hall, *Albemarle*	22987
Whitehall, *Frederick*	22603
White Head Hall	23828
White Hill	24477
White House	24580
White Marsh	23183
White Mill	24210
White Oak, *Halifax*	24558
White Oak, *Stafford*	22405
White Oaks	22307
White Oak Swamp	23150
White Plains	23893
White Post	22663
White Shop	23086
White Stone	22578
Whitesville	23421
Whitethorne	24060
Whitetop	24292
Whiteville	23040
Whitewood	24657
Whitley	23487
Whitlock	22942
Whitmell	24549
Whittle	24531
Wickford	22310
Wicomico	23184
Wicomico Church	22579
Wide Water	22554
Widewater Beach	22554
Wightman	23924
Wilburdale	22003
Wilda	24477
Wilde Acres	22602
Wilderness	22553
Wilderness Corner	22553
Wildwood, *Fluvanna*	22963
Wildwood, *Henrico*	23227
Wildwood Farms	23842
Wilkinsons Store	23833
Wilkinson Terrace	23234
Willard Park (Part of Norfolk)	23509
Williamsburg	23185-88
For specific ZIP Codes call (888) 275-8777, or your local postmaster.	
Williamsburg Manor	22308
Williams Mill	24251
Williamson Road (Part of Roanoke)‡	24012
Williamsville	24487
Willis	24380
Willisville	20184
Willis Wharf	23486
Willoughby Terrace (Part of Norfolk)	23503
Willow	24521
Willowbrook	23024
Willow Hill	23881
Willow Lakes (Part of Chesapeake)	23320
Willow Lawn	23230
Willow Run	22003
Willow Spring	24266
Willow Woods	22003
Wills Corner	23430
Willston	22044
Wilmington	22963
Wilroy (Part of Suffolk)	23434
Wilsons	23894
Wilson Springs	24473
Wilton Woods	22310
Winchester	22601-04
For specific ZIP Codes call (888) 275-8777, or your local postmaster.	
Windmill Point	22578
Windsor	23487
Windsordale	23229
Windsor Estates	22310
Windsor Farms (Part of Richmond)	23221
Windsor Park	22310
Windsor Place	23075
Windsor Shades	23140
Windy Hill Estates	23111
Winesap	24572
Winfall	24554
Wingina	24599
Winona (Part of Norfolk)	23509
Winslow Hills	22310
Winston	22701
Wintergreen	22958
Winterham	23002
Winterpock	23832
Wirtz	24184
Wise	24293
Wisharts Point	23303
Wistar Farms	23228
Witch Duck (Part of Suffolk)‡	23462*
	23466†
Withams	23488
Wittens Mills	24630
Wolfglade	24333
Wolford	24658
Wolftown	22748
Wolf Trap	24592
Womacks	23923
Wood	24250
Woodberry Forest	22989
Woodberry Hills (Part of Danville)	24541
Woodbridge♦	22191-94
For specific ZIP Codes call (888) 275-8777, or your local postmaster.	
Woodbrook	22901
Woodford	22580
Woodhaven Shores	23141
Woodland Hills	24210
Woodlawn, *Carroll*	24381
Woodlawn (Part of Hopewell)	23860
Woodlawn Manor	22309
Woodlawn Mansion	22060
Woodlawn Park	22309
Woodlawn Terrace, *Fairfax*	22309
Woodlawn Terrace, *Henrico*	23150
Woodlawn Village	22060
Woodlee (Part of Staunton)	24401
Woodley Hills, *Fairfax*	22306
Woodley Hills (Part of Engleside)	22309
Woodman Terrace	23228
Woodmont, *Arlington*	22207
Woodmont, *Chesterfield*	23235
Woodridge	24590
Woodrum (Part of Staunton)‡	24401
Woods Cross Roads	23190
Woodside Estates	22102
Woods Mill	22938
Woodson	22951
Woods Store	24091
Woodstock	22664
Woodville	22749
Woodway	24277
Woolwine	24185
Worlds	24530
Worsham	23901
Worshams	23139
Wren	23959
Wright (Part of Norfolk)‡	23505
Wrights Shop	24572
Wrightsville	22427
Wurno	24301
Wylliesburg	23976
Wyndale	24210
Wythe (Part of Hampton)‡	23661
Wytheville	24382
Yacht Haven Estates	22309
Yale	23897
Yancey Mills	22932
Yanceyville	23093
Yards	24605
Yellow Branch	24550
Yellow Springs	24361
Yellow Sulphur Springs	24073
Yellow Tavern	23060
York Manor	23075
Yorkshire	20111
Yorkshire Acres	20111
Yorkshire Park	20111
York Terrace	23185
Yorktown	23690-93
For specific ZIP Codes call (888) 275-8777, or your local postmaster.	
Yorktown Naval Weapons Station	23691
Yost	24460
Youngers Store	24558
Yuma	24251
Zacata	22581
Zack	24459
Zanoni	23191
Zenda	22802
Zepp	22644
Zion	22942
Zion Crossroads	22942
Ziontown	23075
Zuni	23898

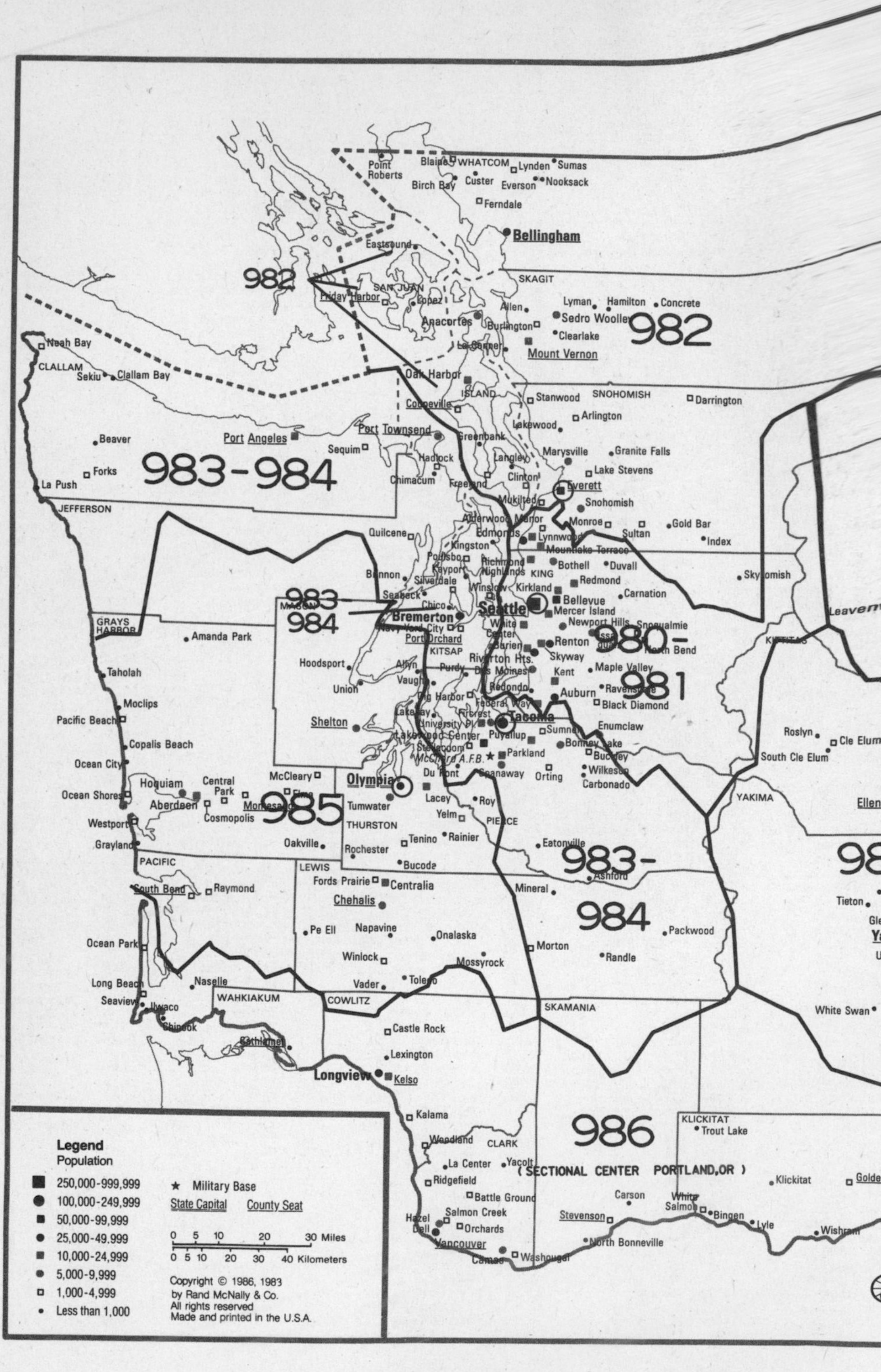

982
Point Roberts
Blaine
WHATCOM
Lynden
Sumas
Birch Bay
Custer
Everson
Nooksack
Ferndale
Bellingham
Eastsound
SAN JUAN
Friday Harbor
Lopez
SKAGIT
Lyman
Hamilton
Concrete
Allen
Sedro Woolley
Anacortes
Burlington
Clearlake
La Conner
Mount Vernon
982
Neah Bay
CLALLAM
Sekiu
Clallam Bay
Oak Harbor
ISLAND
Coupeville
Stanwood
SNOHOMISH
Darrington
Arlington
Lakewood
Port Townsend
Greenbank
Beaver
Port Angeles
Sequim
Marysville
Granite Falls
Hadlock
Langley
Lake Stevens
Forks
983-984
La Push
Chimacum
Freeland
Clinton
Everett
JEFFERSON
Mukilteo
Snohomish
Alderwood Manor
Monroe
Sultan
Gold Bar
Index
Quilcene
Edmonds
Lynnwood
Kingston
Mountlake Terrace
Poulsbo
Richmond Highlands
Bothell
Duvall
Keyport
KING
Brinnon
Silverdale
Redmond
Skykomish
Winslow
Kirkland
Seabeck
983-984
Chico
Seattle
Bellevue
Carnation
MASON
Bremerton
Mercer Island
GRAYS HARBOR
Navy Yard City
White Center
Newport Hills
Snoqualmie
Amanda Park
Port Orchard
Burien
Renton
980-981
North Bend
KITSAP
Riverton Hts.
Skyway
KITTITAS
Hoodsport
Allyn
Purdy
Des Moines
Kent
Maple Valley
Taholah
Vaughn
Union
Redondo
Ravensdale
Gig Harbor
Federal Way
Auburn
Black Diamond
Moclips
Fircrest
Pacific Beach
Lakebay
University Pl.
Tacoma
Enumclaw
Shelton
Lakewood Center
Sumner
Roslyn
Cle Elum
Puyallup
Copalis Beach
Steilacoom
Bonney Lake
McChord A.F.B.
Parkland
Buckley
South Cle Elum
Ocean City
Wilkeson
McCleary
Olympia
Du Pont
Spanaway
Orting
Carbonado
Hoquiam
Central Park
Elma
YAKIMA
Ocean Shores
Aberdeen
Montesano
Lacey
Roy
Cosmopolis
985
Tumwater
Yelm
PIERCE
Westport
THURSTON
Tenino
Rainier
Grayland
Oakville
Rochester
Eatonville
983-984
PACIFIC
Bucoda
Ashford
LEWIS
Fords Prairie
Centralia
South Bend
Raymond
Mineral
Chehalis
Tieton
Pe Ell
Napavine
Packwood
Ocean Park
Onalaska
Morton
Winlock
Randle
Mossyrock
Long Beach
Naselle
Vader
Toledo
Seaview
Ilwaco
WAHKIAKUM
COWLITZ
SKAMANIA
White Swan
Chinook
Castle Rock
Cathlamet
Lexington
Longview
Kelso
Kalama
986
KLICKITAT
Trout Lake
Woodland
CLARK
La Center
Yacolt
(SECTIONAL CENTER PORTLAND, OR)
Klickitat
Ridgefield
Battle Ground
Carson
White Salmon
Bingen
Lyle
Salmon Creek
Stevenson
Hazel Dell
Orchards
Wishram
Vancouver
North Bonneville
Camas
Washougal

Legend
Population

- ■ 250,000-999,999
- ● 100,000-249,999
- ■ 50,000-99,999
- ● 25,000-49,999
- ■ 10,000-24,999
- ● 5,000-9,999
- □ 1,000-4,999
- • Less than 1,000

★ Military Base

State Capital   County Seat

0 5 10 20 30 Miles
0 5 10 20 30 40 Kilometers

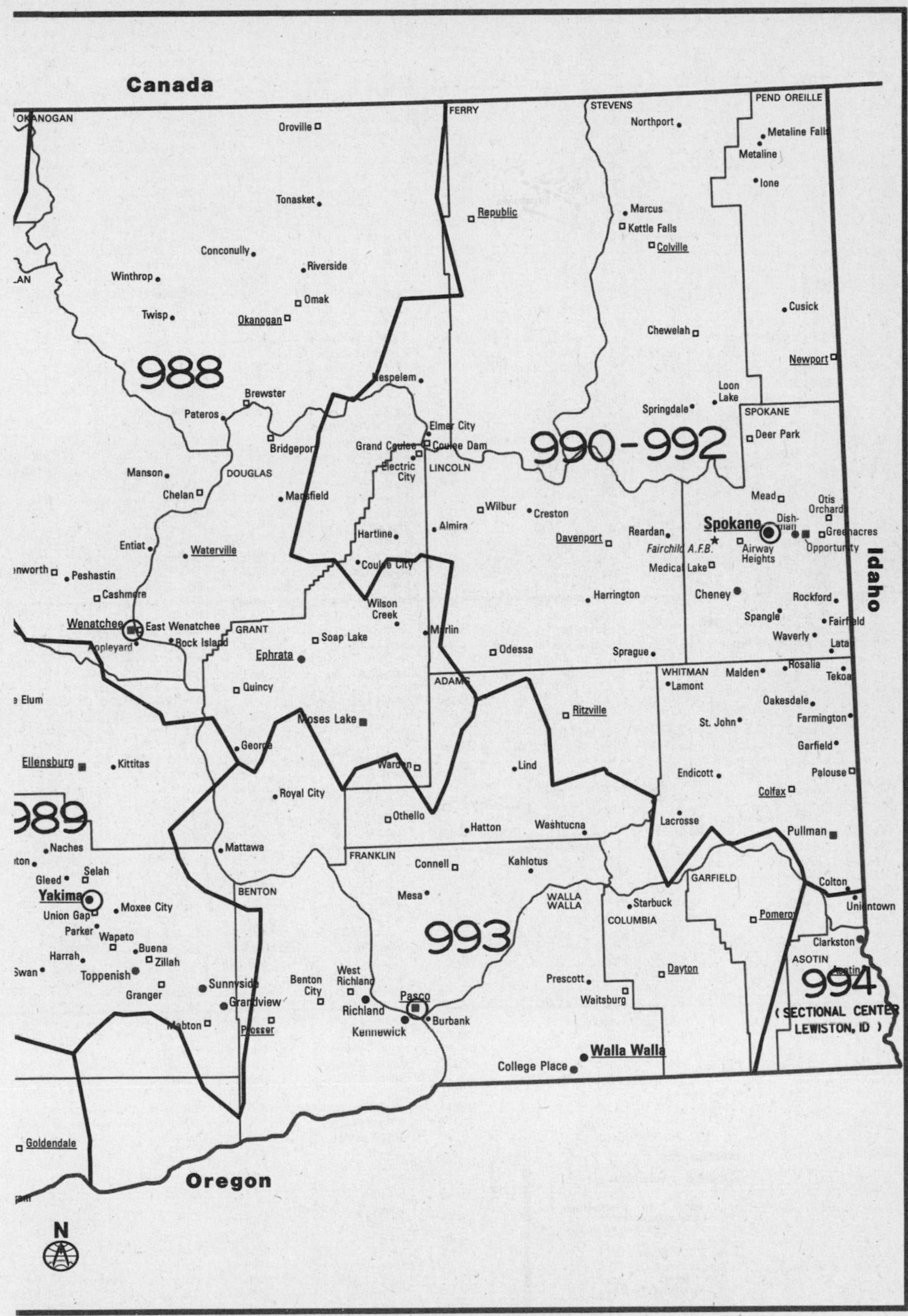
Canada
OKANOGAN
FERRY
STEVENS
PEND OREILLE
Oroville
Northport
Metaline Falls
Metaline
Ione
Tonasket
Republic
Marcus
Kettle Falls
Colville
Conconully
Riverside
Winthrop
Omak
Twisp
Okanogan
Cusick
Chewelah
Newport
988
Nespelem
Brewster
Pateros
Loon Lake
Springdale
SPOKANE
Elmer City
Grand Coulee
Coulee Dam
Bridgeport
990-992
Deer Park
Manson
DOUGLAS
Electric City
LINCOLN
Chelan
Mansfield
Wilbur
Creston
Mead
Otis Orchards
Almira
Hartline
Davenport
Reardan
Spokane
Dishman
Greenacres
Entiat
Waterville
Fairchild A.F.B.
Airway Heights
Opportunity
Peshastin
Coulee City
Medical Lake
Idaho
Cashmere
Harrington
Cheney
Rockford
Wilson Creek
Spangle
Wenatchee
East Wenatchee
GRANT
Marlin
Fairfield
Appleyard
Rock Island
Soap Lake
Waverly
Odessa
Sprague
Latah
Ephrata
Rosalia
WHITMAN
Malden
Tekoa
Lamont
ADAMS
Quincy
Oakesdale
Ritzville
Moses Lake
St. John
Farmington
George
Garfield
Ellensburg
Kittitas
Warden
Lind
Endicott
Palouse
Royal City
Colfax
Othello
Lacrosse
Hatton
Washtucna
Pullman
Naches
Mattawa
FRANKLIN
Connell
Kahlotus
Selah
Gleed
GARFIELD
Colton
Yakima
BENTON
Mesa
WALLA WALLA
Starbuck
Uniontown
Union Gap
Moxee City
COLUMBIA
Pomeroy
Parker
Wapato
993
Clarkston
Buena
ASOTIN
Harrah
Zillah
Asotin
Toppenish
West Richland
Dayton
994
Prescott
Benton City
(SECTIONAL CENTER LEWISTON, ID)
Granger
Sunnyside
Grandview
Pasco
Waitsburg
Richland
Mabton
Burbank
Prosser
Kennewick
Walla Walla
College Place
Goldendale
Oregon
N

Aberdeen 98520
Aberdeen Gardens 98520
Academy 99031
Acme 98220
Adamsview Park 98951
Addy 99101
Adelaide (Part of Federal Way) 98003
Adelma Beach 98368
Admiral's Cove 98239
Adna 98522
Adrian 98851
Aeneas 98855
Agate Bay 98226
Agate Point 98110
Agnew 98362
Ahtanum 98903
Airway Heights 99001
Ajlune 98564
Albion 99102
Alder 98328
Alder Terrace 98926
Alderton 98374
Alderwood 98225
Alderwood Manor‡ 98036
Alexander Beach 98221
Alger 98233
Algona 98001
Allen 98232
Allentown 98178
Allyn 98524
Almira 99103
Aloha 98571
Alpental 98068
Alpha 98570
Altoona 98643
Amanda Park 98526
Amber 99004
Amboy 98601
American Lake 98498
Anacortes 98221
Anatone 99401
Anderson Island 98303
Angle Lake (Part of SeaTac) 98188
Annapolis (Part of Port Orchard) 98366
Appleton 98602
Arbor Heights (Part of Seattle) 98146
Arcadia 98584
Arden 99114
Ardenvoir 98811
Argyle 98250
Ariel 98603
Arletta 98335
Arlington 98223
Arlington Heights 98223
Armar 98270
Arrowhead, *King* 98011
Arrowhead, *Pierce* 98498
Arrowhead Beach 98292
Artic 98537
Artondale 98335
Ashford 98304
Asotin 99402
Auburn 98001-02
.... 98071
.... 98092
For specific ZIP Codes call (888) 275-8777, or your local postmaster.
Auburn Twin Lakes (Part of Federal Way)‡ 98023
Avery 98617
Avon 98273
Ayer 99348
Azwell 98846
Baby Island Heights 98260
Baileysburg 99328
Bainbridge Island 98110
Baker Heights 98273
Ballard (Part of Seattle)‡ 98107
B and G 98201
Bangor 98315
Bangor Submarine Base‡ 98315
Barberton 98665
Baring 98224
Barstow 99141
Basin City 99343
Battle Ground 98604
Battle Point 98110
Bay Center 98527
Bay City 98520
Bayne 98022
Bay Shore 98584
Bay View, *Island* 98260
Bayview, *Skagit* 98273
Bazinet Eddition 98532
Beachcombers Hidden Beach 98253
Beachcrest 98501
Beacon Hill 98632
Beaux Arts Village 98004
Beaver 98305
Beaver Valley 98365
Beckett Point 98368
Belfair 98528
Bellevue 98004-09
.... 98015
For specific ZIP Codes call (888) 275-8777, or your local postmaster.
Bellevue Square (Part of Bellevue) 98004
Bellingham 98225-28
For specific ZIP Codes call (888) 275-8777, or your local postmaster.
Bellis Fair (Part of Bellingham) 98226
Belmont 99104
Belvidere 99116
Bench Drive (Part of Aberdeen) 98520
Benge 99105
Benson Hill 98055
Benton City 99320
Bethel 98366-67
For specific ZIP Codes call (888) 275-8777, or your local postmaster.
Beverly 99321
Beverly Beach 98249
Beverly Park (Part of Everett) 98203
Bickleton 99322
Big Bend 98251
Big Lake 98274
Bingen 98605
Birch Bay♦ 98230
Birchfield 98901
Birdsview 98237
Bissell 99137
Bitter Lake (Part of Seattle)‡ 98133
Biz Point 98221
Black Diamond 98010
Black Lake 99114
Black River (Part of Renton) 98055
Black River, *King* 98178
Black River Junction (Part of Renton) 98055
Blaine 98230*
.... 98231†
Blakely Island 98222
Blanchard 98232
Blewett 98826
Blockhouse 98620
Blue Creek 99109
Blue Lake 99115
Blueslide 99180
Blyn 98382
Boise 98022
Bonneville Spur (Part of Bellingham) 98225
Bonney Lake 98390
Bordeaux 98556
Bossburg 99126
Boston Harbor 98506
Bothell 98011-12
.... 98021
.... 98041
.... 98082
For specific ZIP Codes call (888) 275-8777, or your local postmaster.
Boulevard Park 98188
Bow 98232
.... 98246
For specific ZIP Codes call (888) 275-8777, or your local postmaster.
Bowman Beach 98381
Boyds 99107
Brady 98563
Breidablick 98370
Bremerton 98310-12
.... 98337
For specific ZIP Codes call (888) 275-8777, or your local postmaster.
Brewster 98812
Briarwood 98031
Bridgeport 98813
Brief 98822
Brier 98036
Brinnon 98320
Broadmoor (Part of Seattle) 98112
Broadway (Part of Seattle)‡ 98102
Brookdale 98444
Brooklane Village 98926
Brooklyn 98537
Browns Point 98422
Brownstown 98920
Brownsville 98310
Bruceport 98586
Brush Prairie 98606
Bryant 98223
Bryn Mawr 98178
Buckeye 99005
Buckhorn 98245
Buckley 98321
Bucoda 98530
Buena 98921
Buena Vista 98292
Bunker 98532
Burbank 99323
Burbank Heights 99301
Burien 98146-48
.... 98166-68
For specific ZIP Codes call (888) 275-8777, or your local postmaster.
Burley 98322
Burlington 98233
Burnett 98321
Burton 98013
Bush Point 98249
Butler Acres 98626
Butler Cove 98501
BZ Corner 98672
Cabin Creek 98925
Camaloch 98292
Camano City 98292
Camano Country Club 98292
Camas 98607
Camelot 98001
Campbell's Glen 98236
Camp Murray 98498
Camp Union 98312
Campus (Part of Bellingham)‡ 98225
Canal Tract 98320
Canyon Park (Part of Bothell)‡ 98021
Cape George 98368
Capital Mall (Part of Olympia) 98502
Capitol City Country Club 98501
Capitol Hill (Part of Seattle) 98102
Cap Sante (Part of Anacortes) 98221
Carbonado 98323
Care Free Loop 98331
Carlisle 98536
Carlsborg 98324
Carlton 98814
Carnation 98014
Carrier Annex (Part of Everett)‡ 98204
Carrolls 98609
Carson 98610
Carylon Beach 98501
Cascade Mall 98055
Cascade Park 98683*
.... 98687†
Cascade Terrace 98371
Cascade Valley♦ 98837
Cascade Vista 98058
Cashmere 98815
Castle Rock 98611
Cathan♦ 98270
Cathcart 98296
Cathlamet 98612
Cavelero Beach 98292
Cedardale 98274
Cedar Falls 98045
Cedar Grove 98038
Cedarhome 98292
Cedar Mountain 98055
Cedarview 98390
Cedarville 98568
Cedonia 99137
Center 98376
Centerville 98613
Central (Part of Yakima)‡ 98901
Centralia 98531
Central Park♦ 98520
Central Valley 98370
Ceres 98532
Charleston (Part of Bremerton) 98312
Charleston Beach 98312
Charter Oak 98604
Chattaroy 99003
Chehalis 98532
Chehalis Indian Reservation 98568
Chelan 98816
Chelan Falls 98817
Chelatchie 98601
Cheney 99004
Cherokee Bay Park 98038
Cherry Crest (Part of Bellevue) 98004
Cherry Gardens 98019
Cherry Grove 98604
Cherry Point 98230
Chesaw 98844
Chewelah 99109
Chico 98312
Chimacum 98325
Chinook 98614
Christopher (Part of Auburn) 98002
Chuckanut Village (Part of Bellingham) 98225
Chumstick 98826
Churchlake 98390
Cicero 98223
Cinebar 98533
Cispus 98377
City Center (Part of Bellingham)‡ 98225
Clallam Bay 98326
Claquato 98532
Claremont (Part of Everett)‡ 98201
Clarkston 99403
Clarkston Heights 99403
Clay City 98328
Clayton 99110
Clearbrook 98247
Clear Lake, *Pierce* 98328
Clearlake, *Skagit* 98235
Clear Lake, *Spokane* 99022
Clearview 98296
Clearwater 98331
Cle Elum 98922
Cleveland 99356
Cliffdell 98937
Cline (Part of Springdale) 99173
Clinton♦ 98236
Clipper 98244
Cloverland 99402
Clover Park 98499
Clyde Hill 98004
Coal Creek 98632
Coalfield 98059
Cohasset Beach 98595
Colbert 99005
Colby 98366
Colchester 98366
Coles Corner 98826
Colfax 99111
College (Part of Pullman)‡ 99163
College Place 99324
Colton 99113
Columbia (Part of Seattle)‡ 98118
Columbia Beach 98236
Columbia Center (Part of Kennewick) 99336
Columbia Heights 98632
Columbia Valley Gardens 98632
Colville 99114
Colville Indian Agency 99155
Colville Indian Reservation 99155
Conconully 98819
Concora (Part of Tukwila) 98188
Concrete 98237
Conifer View (Part of Bothell) 98011
Connell 99326
Conway 98238
Cook 98605
Cooper Point 98501
Copalis Beach 98535
Copalis Crossing 98536
Cornwall (Part of Bellingham) 98225
Cosmopolis 98537
Cottage Lake 98072
Cottage Lake Bridle Trail 98033
Cottonwood Beach 98230
Cougar 98616
Coulee City 99115
Coulee Dam 99116
Country Homes♦ 99218
Countryside Beach 98501
Coupeville 98239
Covington 98042
Cowiche 98923
Cozy Nook 99109
Creosote 98110
Crescent Bar 98848
Creston 99117
Crocker 98360
Crockett Lake Estates 98239
Cromwell 98335
Crossroads (Part of Bellevue)‡ 98008
Crown Hill (Part of Seattle) 98117
Crystal Mountain 98022
Crystal Spring 98110
Crystal Springs (Part of University Place) 98466
Crystal Village 98022
Cumberland 98022
Cunningham 99327
Curlew 99118
Curtis 98538
Cushman Dam 98548
Cusick 99119
Custer, *Pierce* 98413
Custer, *Whatcom* 98240
Dabob 98376
Daisy 99167
Dalkena 99156
Dallesport 98617
Danville 99121
Darlington (Part of Everett) 98203
Darrington 98241
Dash Point 98402
Davenport 99122
Day Creek 98284
Day Island 98466
Dayton, *Columbia* 99328
Dayton, *Mason* 98584
Decatur 98221
Deep Creek 99022
Deep River 98638
Deer Harbor 98243
Deer Island 98390
Deer Lake 99148
Deer Park 99006
Delano 99133
Delano Beach 98349
Delphi 98501
Delphi Country Club 98501
Del Ridge 98501
Deming 98244
Denison 99006
Denny Creek 98045
Denny Park 98011
Desert Aire 99344
Des Moines 98188
.... 98198
For specific ZIP Codes call (888) 275-8777, or your local postmaster.
Devereaux Lake 98528
Dewey 98221
Dexter by the Sea 98590
Diablo 98283
Diamond 99111
Diamond Lake 99156
Dieringer 98390
Dines Point 98253
Disautel 98841
Discovery Bay 98368
Dishman♦ 99213
Dixie 99329
Dockton 98070
Dodge 99347
Doe Bay 98279
Dollar's Corner 98604
Donald 98951
Doty 98539
Douglas 98858
Downing 98812
Downtown (Part of Kent)‡ 98032
Downtown (Part of Tacoma)‡ 98401†
.... 98402*
Downtown (Part of Vancouver)‡ 98660
Draper Spring 98619
Driftwood Acres 98940
Driftwood Point 98390
Driftwood Shores 98292

Place	ZIP Code
Dryad	98532
Dryden	98821
Duluth	98642
Dumas Bay-Twin Lakes (Part of Federal Way)	98023
Dungeness	98382
Du Pont	98327
Dusty	99143
Duvall	98019
Duwamish	98188
Eagledale	98110
Eaglemont	98368
Earlington (Part of Renton)	98055
Earlmount (Part of Redmond)	98052
East Aberdeen (Part of Aberdeen)	98520
East Coulee Dam (Part of Coulee Dam)	99116
East Everett	98205
East Farms	99025
Eastgate, *King*♦	98007
Eastgate (Part of Bellevue)‡	98007
Eastgate (Part of Walla Walla)	99362
East Heights	99133
East Hoquiam (Part of Hoquiam)	98550
East Kittitas	98926
Eastmont	98205
East Olympia	98540
Easton	98925
East Port Orchard♦	98366
East Quilcene	98376
East Raymond	98577
East Seattle (Part of Mercer Island)	98040
East Selah	98901
Eastsound	98245
East Spokane	99212
East Stanwood (Part of Stanwood)	98292
East Union (Part of Seattle)‡	98122
Eastview Hills	98204
East Wenatchee	98802
Eatonville	98328
Echo	99114
Echo Lake	98133
Eden	98643
Edgecomb	98223
Edgemoor (Part of Bellingham)	98225
Edgewater (Part of Everett)	98203
Edgewood	98372
Edison	98232
Edmonds	98020
	98026
For specific ZIP Codes call (888) 275-8777, or your local postmaster.	
Edwall	99008
Eglon	98346
Elbe	98330
Elberton	99130
Eldon	98555
Eldorado Hills	98312
Electric City	99123
Elk	99009
Elk Plain	98387
Ellensburg	98926
Ellisford	98855
Ellisport	98070
Ellsworth	98664
Elma	98541
Elmer City	99124
Eltopia	99330
Endicott	99125
Enterprise	99129
Entiat	98822
Enumclaw	98022
Ephrata	98823
Erlands Point	98312
Espanola	99022
Ethel	98542
Etna	98674
Eufaula Heights	98632
Eureka, *Walla Walla*	99348
Eureka (Part of Bellingham)	98225
Evaline	98596
Evans	99126
Everett	98201-08
For specific ZIP Codes call (888) 275-8777, or your local postmaster.	
Everett Mall (Part of Everett)	98208
Evergreen (Part of Tacoma)‡	98411
Evergreen Estates	98501
Evergreen Shores	98501
Everson	98247
Ewan	99127
Factoria‡	98006
Fairchild Air Force Base	99011
Fairfield	99012
Fair Harbor	98546
Fairhaven (Part of Bellingham)‡	98225
Fairmont	98204
Fairview, *Kitsap*	98310
Fairview, *Yakima*	98901
Fairwood, *King*	98058
Fairwood, *Spokane*♦	99218
Fall City♦	98024
Fargher Lake	98675
Farmington	99128
Fawn Lake	98584
Federal (Part of Seattle)‡	98104
Federal Way	98003
	98023
	98063
	98093
For specific ZIP Codes call (888) 275-8777, or your local postmaster.	
Felida♦	98685
Felton Stone Lodge	99026
Ferndale	98248
Fern Hill (Part of Tacoma)‡	98412
Fern Prairie	98607
Fernwood	98367
Fife	98424
Fife Heights	98424
Finley	99337
Fircrest	98466
Fircrest Eddition	98532
Firdale	98577
Firgrove	98204
Fir Tree	98540
Firwood	98371
Fisher	98607
Fish Town	98257
Five Corners♦	98662
Fletcher Bay	98110
Florence	98292
Fobes Hill	98205
Foothill	99217
Forbes	98584
Ford	99013
Fordair	99115
Ford Park	98331
Fords Prairie♦	98531
Forest	98532
Forest Beach	98335
Forest Glen	98501
Forest Hills Addition	99208
Forest Park (Part of Lake Forest Park)	98155
Forks	98331
Fort Lewis	98433
Fort Wright (Part of Spokane)	99204
Foster (Part of Tukwila)	98188
Four Lakes	99014
Fox Island♦	98333
Fragaria	98359
Frances	98577
Frankfort	98638
Frederickson	98446
Freeland♦	98249
Freeman	99015
Fremont (Part of Seattle)	98103
Friday Harbor	98250
Frickon Wye	98541
Fruitland	99129
Fruitvale♦	98902
Furport	99156
Gales Addition	98362
Galvin	98544
Gamblewood	98346
Gardena	99360
Garden City (Part of McCleary)	98557
Gardiner	98382
Garfield	99130
Garland (Part of Spokane)	99205
Gate	98579
Geneva	98226
George	98824
Georgetown (mail Ravensdale)	98051
Georgetown (Part of Seattle)‡	98108
Getchell	98223
Gibraltar	98221
Gifford	99131
Gig Harbor	98329
	98332
	98335
For specific ZIP Codes call (888) 275-8777, or your local postmaster.	
Gilberton	98310
Glacier	98244
Glacier Springs	98244
Gleed	98904
Glen Cove, *Jefferson*	98368
Glencove, *Pierce*	98329
Glendale	98236
Glenoma	98336
Glenrose	99203
Glenwood, *Kitsap*	98367
Glenwood, *Klickitat*	98619
Globe	98554
Gold Bar	98251
Goldendale	98620
Gooseberry Point	98262
Goose Prairie	98929
Gorst	98337
Goss Lake	98260
Govan	99185
Graham	98338
Graham Point	98584
Grand Coulee	99133
Grand Mound	98501
Grandview (Part of Port Angeles)‡	98363
Grandview, *Yakima*	98930
Granger	98932
Granite Falls	98252
Grant Orchards	98851
Grant Road Addition	98802
Granville Grange	98252
Grapeview	98546
Grassmere	98237
Gravelly Lake	98499
Grayland	98547
Grays Harbor City	98550
Grays Landing	99009
Grays River	98621
Greenacres♦	99016
Greenbank	98253
Greenbank Estates	98253
Green Bluff	99003
Green River Gorge	98022
Greens Landing	98816
Greenwater	98022
Greenwater Meadows	98251
Greenwood (Part of Seattle)‡	98103
Greenwood, *Grays Harbor*	98520
Greenwood, *Stevens*	99141
Greenwood, *Whatcom*	98264
Grisdale	98563
Gromore	98903
Grotto	98288
Guemes	98221
Haller Lake (Part of Seattle)	98133
Hamilton	98255
Hansville	98340
Happy Valley (Part of Bellingham)	98225
Harbor Center	98249
Harbor Heights (Part of Gig Harbor)	98338
Harmon Heights	98045
Harper	98366
Harrah	98933
Harrington	99134
Hartford (Part of Lake Stevens)	98258
Hartland	98635
Hartline	99135
Hartstene	98584
Harwood	98908
Hatton	99332
Havillah	98855
Hawk Acres	98501
Hay	99136
Hayford	99224
Haynes Acres	98501
Hays Park (Part of Spokane)‡	99207
Hazel	98223
Hazel Dell	98665
Hazelwood	98055
Heather Downs (Part of Renton)	98055
Heisson	98622
Herron Island	98349
Hidden Valley	98304
Highland, *Asotin*	99403
Highland, *Clark*	98629
Highland, *Snohomish*	98258
Highland Estates	98584
Highland Heights	98571
Highland Park (Part of Seattle)	98106
Highlands (Part of Renton)‡	98056
High Point, *King*	98027
High Point (Part of Seattle)	98126
High Valley	98027
Hilltop	98004
Hillyard (Part of Spokane)‡	99207
	99217
For specific ZIP Codes call (888) 275-8777, or your local postmaster.	
Hintzville	98312
Hobart	98025
Hockinson	98606
Hogans Corner	98550
Hoh Indian Reservation	98331
Hoko	98326
Holcomb	98577
Holden Village	98816
Holiday Valley Estates	98501
Holly	98312
Hollywood	98072
Hollywood Beach	98816
Holman	98644
Holmes Harbor Estates	98253
Home	98349
Home Acres	98205
Home Valley	98648
Honeymoon Vista Bay	98253
Hood	98651
Hoodsport	98548
Hoogdal	98284
Hooper	99333
Hope	98333
Hoquiam	98550
Horseshoe Lake	98367
Houghton (Part of Kirkland)	98033
Humptulips	98552
Hunters	99137
Hunts Point	98004
Huntsville	99328
Husum	98623
Hyak	98068
Illahee (Part of Ocean Shores)	98569
Illahee, *Kitsap*	98310
Ilwaco	98624
Image	98662
Impach	99138
Inchelium♦	99138
Index	98256
Indian Beach	98292
Indianola♦	98342
Indian Village	98221
Inglewood	98011
Inlet Island	98390
Innis Arden	98160
Interbay (Part of Seattle)‡	98119
Intercity	98203
Interlaken	98438
International (Part of Seattle)‡	98104
Ione	99139
Irby	99159
Ireland	98607
Irondale	98339
Iron Springs	98535
Isabella Lake	98584
Island Center	98110
Island Lake	98370
Island View	98381
Issaquah	98027
	98029
For specific ZIP Codes call (888) 275-8777, or your local postmaster.	
Jared	99180
Johnson	99113
Johnson Point	98501
Jordan	98223
Jovita	98372
Joyce	98343
Juanita (Part of Kirkland)	98033
Junction City	98520
Juniper Beach	98292
Kachees Ridge	98925
Kahlotus	99335
Kalama	98625
Kala Point	98368
Kalispel Indian Reservation	99180
Kamilche	98584
Kanaskat	98051
Kangley	98051
Kapowsin	98344
Keller	99140
Kellogg Marsh	98223
Kellys Korner	98501
Kelso	98626
Kendall	98295
Kenmore♦	98028
Kennard Corner	98012
Kennedys Lagoon	98239
Kennewick	99336-38
For specific ZIP Codes call (888) 275-8777, or your local postmaster.	
Kennydale (Part of Renton)	98056
Kenroy	98802
Kent	98031-32
	98035
	98042
	98064
For specific ZIP Codes call (888) 275-8777, or your local postmaster.	
Kettle Falls	99141
Kewa	99138
Key Center	98329
Keyport	98345
Keyport Naval Torpedo Station	98345
Keystone	98849
Kid Valley	98649
Kings Lakeside	98603
Kingston♦	98346
Kiona	99320
Kirkland	98033-34
	98083
For specific ZIP Codes call (888) 275-8777, or your local postmaster.	
Kitsap Lake	98312
Kittitas	98934
Klaber	98538
Klaus	98532
Klickitat	98628
Klipsan Beach	98640
Knab	98591
Knappton	98638
Koontzville	99116
Kooskooskie	99362
Kozy Kamp	98642
Krain	98022
Kruse	98271
Kruse Junction	98271
K Street (Part of Tacoma)	98405*
	98415†
Kummer	98010
Lacamas	98570
La Center	98629
Lacey	98503
	98506
	98509
	98513-16
For specific ZIP Codes call (888) 275-8777, or your local postmaster.	
La Conner	98257
Lacrosse	99143
Lagoon Point	98253
La Grande	98348
Lake Alice	98024
Lakebay	98349
Lake City (Part of Seattle)‡	98125
Lake Crescent	98363
Lakedale	98940
Lake Dolloff	98001
Lake Forest Park‡	98155
Lake Goodwin	98292
Lake Heights	98006
Lake Hills (Part of Bellevue)	98007
Lake Howard	98292
Lake Joy	98014
Lake Kachees	98925
Lake Kathleen	98055
Lake Ki	98223

Lakeland Village (Part of Medical Lake) 99022
Lake Leota 98072
Lake Loma 98271
Lake Louise 98498
Lake Lucerne 98038
Lake Martha 98037
Lake McDonald 98055
Lake Meridian 98042
Lake Pattison 98501
Lake Retreat 98051
Lakeridge 98178
Lake Sawyer 98042
Lakes District♦ 98439
98498-99
For specific ZIP Codes call (888) 275-8777, or your local postmaster.
Lake Shore♦ 98665
98685
For specific ZIP Codes call (888) 275-8777, or your local postmaster.
Lake Stevens 98258
Lakeview 98499
Lakeview Park 98851
Lakeview Terrace 99133
Lake Wilderness 98038
Lakewood 98259
Lakewood Mall (Part of Tacoma) 98402
Lakota (Part of Federal Way) 98003
Lamoine 98858
Lamona 99144
Lamont 99017
Langley 98260
La Push 98350
Larchmont (Part of Tacoma) 98409
Larimers Corner 98296
Latah 99018
Laurel, *Klickitat* 98619
Laurel, *Whatcom* 98225
Laurel Heights (Part of Everett) 98203
Laurelhurst (Part of Seattle) 98105
Laurier 99146
Lawrence (Part of Tacoma)‡ 98409
Lawrence, *Whatcom* 98247
Laws Corner 98672
Lazy C 98320
Leadpoint 99114
Leavenworth 98826
Lebam 98554
Ledgewood Beach 98239
Leland 98376
Lemolo 98370
Lexington 98626
Liberty 98922
Liberty Lake♦ 99019
Liberty Park (Part of Spokane)‡ 99202
Lilliwaup 98555
Lincoln (Part of Poulsbo) 98370
Lincoln, *Lincoln* 99147
Lincoln Station (Part of Tacoma)‡ 98408*
98418†
Lind 99341
Littell 98532
Little Boston 98346
Little Falls 99013
Littlerock 98556
Lochsloy 98258
Lockamas Heights 98607
Locke 99119
Lofall 98370
Lone Lake Shores 98260
Lone Pine 99116
Long Beach 98631
Longbranch 98351
Long Lake, *Kitsap* 98366-67
For specific ZIP Codes call (888) 275-8777, or your local postmaster.
Long Lake, *Lincoln* 99013
Longmire 98397
Long Point Manor 98239
Longview 98632
Longview Junction (Part of Kelso) 98626
Loomis 98827
Loon Lake 99148
Lopez 98261
Lost Creek 99180
Lost Lake 98292
Loveland 98387
Lowden 99360
Lowell (Part of Everett) 98203
Lower Elwha Indian Reservation 98363
Loyal Heights (Part of Seattle) 98117
Lucerne 98816
Lummi Indian Reservation 98226
Lummi Island 98262
Lummi Point 98262
Lyle 98635
Lyman 98263
Lynden 98264
Lynnwood 98036-37
98046
For specific ZIP Codes call (888) 275-8777, or your local postmaster.
Lynwood Center 98110
Mabana 98292
Mabton 98935
McChord Air Force Base 98438
McCleary 98557
McDonald 98837
McGinnis Lake 99116
McGowan 98614
Machias 98290
McKees Beach 98292
Mckenna 98558
McMicken Heights (Part of SeaTac) 98188
McMillin 98360
Madigan Army Medical Center 98431
Madison Park (Part of Seattle) 98112
Madrona Beach 98292
Madrona Point (Part of Bremerton) 98312
Mae 98837
Magnolia (Part of Seattle)‡ 98199
Main Office (Part of Seattle)‡ 98111
Makah Air Force Station 758th Radar Squadron 98357
Makah Indian Reservation 98357
Malaga 98828
Malden 99149
Malo 99150
Malone 98559
Malott 98829
Maltby 98290
Manchester 98353
Manito (Part of Spokane)‡ 99203
Manito Club Estates 99203
Manitou Beach 98061
Manor 98604
Mansfield 98830
Manson 98831
Manzanita 98110
Maple Beach 98281
Maple Falls 98266
Maple Grove 98363
Maple Hills 98031
Maple Valley♦ 98038
Maple Valley Heights 98055
Maplewood (Part of Renton) 98055
Maplewood Heights 98055
Marblemount 98267
Marcus 99151
Marengo 99169
Marietta 98226
Marine Drive (Part of Bremerton) 98312
Marine Hills (Part of Federal Way) 98003
Marine View Estates (Part of Federal Way) 98003
Marketown 98277
Markham 98520
Marlin 98832
Marshall 99020
Martin Luther King Jr Way (Part of Tacoma)‡ 98405
Maryhill 98620
Marys Corner 98532
Marysville 98270-71
For specific ZIP Codes call (888) 275-8777, or your local postmaster.
Matlock 98560
Matneys Spur 99141
Mattawa 99349
Maxwelton 98236
May Creek 98251
Mays Pond 98012
Maytown 98502
Mazama 98833
Mead 99021
Meadow Brook (Part of Snoqualmie) 98065
Meadowbrook, *Yakima* 98903
Meadowdale, *Kitsap* 98310
Meadowdale (Part of Edmonds) 98020
Meadow Glade♦ 98604
Meadow Grange 98274
Medical Lake 99022
Medina 98039
Meeker (Part of Puyallup) 98371
Melbourne 98563
Menlo 98561
Mercer Island 98040
Meredith (Part of Auburn) 98001
Meridian Heights 98042
Merritt 98826
Mesa 99343
Metaline 99152
Metaline Falls 99153
Methow 98834
Metreco 98438
Miami Beach 98380
Mica 99023
Midlakes (Part of Bellevue)‡ 98015
Midland♦ 98404
98444-45
For specific ZIP Codes call (888) 275-8777, or your local postmaster.
Midland Acres (Part of Camas) 98607
Midvale Corner 98236
Midway, *King*‡ 98035
Midway, *Pierce* 98335
Milan 99003
Milco (Part of Kelso) 98626
Miles 99122
Mill A 98605
Mill Creek‡ 98012
Miller River 98288
Millwood 99212
Milton 98354
Mima 98501
Mineral 98355
Minnehaha 98661
Mirror Lake (Part of Federal Way) 98003
Mirrormont♦ 98027
Mission Beach 98271
Misty Meadows 98012
Mobase 98433
Moclips 98562
Mohler 99154
Mold 99115
Molson 98844
Mondovi 99122
Monitor 98836
Monohon 98029
Monroe 98272
Monse 98812
Monta Vista 98499
Montborne 98274
Montesano 98563
Moore 98816
Moorlands 98011
Moran Prairie 99203
Morgan Acres 99217
Morganville (Part of Black Diamond) 98010
Morton 98356
Moses Lake 98837
Moses Lake North♦ 98837
Mossyrock 98564
Mountain Home Park 99328
Mountain View 98274
Mountain View Beach 98292
Mount Baker (Part of Bellingham)‡ 98226
Mount Brook 98672
Mount Hope 99012
Mountlake Terrace 98043
Mount Pleasant 98362
Mount Tahoma Estate 98501
Mount Vernon 98273-74
For specific ZIP Codes call (888) 275-8777, or your local postmaster.
Moxee 98936
Muckleshoot Indian Reservation 98092
Mukilteo 98275
Munson Point 98584
Murdock 98617
Murphy's Corner 98012
Mushroom Corner 98501
Naches 98937
Nahcotta 98637
Nahwatzel Lake 98584
Napavine 98565
Naselle 98638
National 98304
Naval Supply Center Puget Sound 98314
Naval Torpedo Station 98345
Navy Yard City‡ 98312
Neah Bay♦ 98357
Neilton 98566
Nemah 98586
Nespelem 99155
Newaukum 98092
Newcastle‡ 98006
Newhalem 98283
New London 98550
Newman Lake 99025
Newport, *King* 98006
Newport, *Pend Oreille* 99156
Newport Shores (Part of Bellevue) 98004
Newton 98550
Nighthawk 98827
Nile 98937
Nine Mile Falls 99026
Nisqually Indian Community♦ 98513
Nisqually Indian Reservation 98597
Nisson 98550
Nooksack 98276
Nordland 98358
Norma Beach 98020
Norman 98292
Normandy Park 98166
North Beach 98245
North Bend 98045
North Bonneville 98639
North City‡ 98155
North Cove 98547
North Fort Lewis 98434
Northgate (Part of Seattle)‡ 98125
Northgate Shopping Center (Part of Seattle) 98125
North Lake 98001
North Lynnwood 98036
North Marysville 98271
Northport 99157
North Prosser 99350
North Puyallup♦ 98372
Northrup (Part of Bellevue) 98008
Northtown Mall (Part of Spokane) 99207
Northwood 98264
Northwoods 98616
Norwood Village (Part of Bellevue) 98004
Novelty 98019
Nugents Corner 98247
Oakbrook 98497
Oakesdale 99158
Oak Harbor 98277-78
For specific ZIP Codes call (888) 275-8777, or your local postmaster.
Oakland (Part of Tacoma) 98409
Oak Park (Part of Camas) 98607
Oakville 98568
O'Brien (Part of Kent) 98032
Obstruction Pass 98279
Ocean City 98569
Ocean Grove 98571
Ocean Park♦ 98640
Ocean Shores 98569
Ocosta 98520
Odessa 99159
Offutt Lake 98589
Okanogan 98840
Olalla 98359
Olalla Valley 98359
Oldport 98501
Old Tacoma (Part of Tacoma) 98466
Old Willapa 98577
Olga 98279
Olympia 98501-16
For specific ZIP Codes call (888) 275-8777, or your local postmaster.
Olympic View 98383
Olympus Ocean Estates 98571
Omak 98841
Onalaska 98570
Oneida 98643
Onion Creek 99114
Opportunity♦ 99206
Orcas 98280
Orchard Avenue 99211
Orchard Prairie 99217
Orchards 98662
Orient 99160
Orillia (Part of Kent) 98032
Orin 99114
Orondo 98843
Oroville 98844
Orting 98360
Osceola 98022
Oso 98223
Ostrander 98626
Othello 99344
Otis Orchards 99027
Outlook 98938
Overlake (Part of Bellevue)‡ 98007
Oyhut 98550
Oysterville 98641
Ozette 98326
Pacific 98047
Pacific Beach 98571
Packwood 98361
Painted Hills 99206
Palisades 98845
Palmer 98051
Palouse 99161
Panhandle Lake 98584
Paradise Estates 98304
Paradise Inn 98398
Park 98284
Parker 98939
Parkland♦ 98444-46
For specific ZIP Codes call (888) 275-8777, or your local postmaster.
Park Orchard 98031
Park Rapids 99114
Parkwater (Part of Spokane)‡ 99211
Parkway Plaza (Part of Tukwila) 98188
Parkwood♦ 98366
Pasadena Park 99206
Pasco 99301*
99302†
Pataha City 99347
Pateros 98846
Paterson 99345
Peach Acres (Part of University Place) 98465
Pearcot 98801
Pearson 98370
Pe Ell 98572
Pend Orielle Village 99153
Penn Cove Park 98277
Peone 99021
Perrinville (Part of Edmonds)‡ 98026
Peshastin 98847
Picnic Point 98335
Pillar Rock 98643
Pinebrook (Part of Vancouver) 98660
Pine City 99170
Pinecliff 98937
Pinecroft 99214
Pine Glen 98925
Pinehurst (Part of Everett) 98203
Pine Lake 98029
Ping 99347
Pioneer 98642
Pioneer Square (Part of Seattle)‡ 98104
Pipe Lake 98038
Plain 98826
Plaza 99170
Pleasant Harbor 98320
Pleasant Hill 98626
Pleasant Prairie 99217
Pleasant Valley 98665
Plymouth 99346
Pocahontas Bay 99009
Point Roberts 98281

Point White 98110
Pomeroy 99347
Pomona 98901
Pomona Heights 98903
Ponder 98499
Ponderosa Estates 98390
Pontius Park 98021
Portage 98070
Portage Point 98262
Port Angeles 98362-63
For specific ZIP Codes call (888) 275-8777, or your local postmaster.
Port Blakely 98110
Port Discovery 98368
Porter 98541
Port Gamble 98364
Port Gamble Indian Reservation 98346
Port Hadlock♦ 98339
Port Ludlow 98365
Port Madison 98110
Port Madison Indian Reservation 98310
Port Orchard 98366-67
For specific ZIP Codes call (888) 275-8777, or your local postmaster.
Port Stanley 98261
Port Townsend 98368
Possession 98236
Possession Shores 98236
Potlatch 98584
Poulsbo 98370
Poverty Bay (Part of Federal Way) 98003
Prairie 98284
Prairie Center (Part of Coupeville) 98239
Prairie Ridge 98390
Prescott 99348
Preston 98050
Priest Point♦ 98271
Proctor (Part of Tacoma)‡ 98407
Proebstel 98662
Prosser 99350
Prune Hill 98607
Puget Island 98612
Puget Sound Naval Base 98314
Puget Sound Naval Shipyard 98314
Pullman 99163-65
For specific ZIP Codes call (888) 275-8777, or your local postmaster.
Purdy 98332
Puyallup 98371-75
For specific ZIP Codes call (888) 275-8777, or your local postmaster.
Queen Anne (Part of Seattle)‡ 98109
Queensborough 98021
Queets 98331
Quendall (Part of Renton) 98055
Quilcene 98376
Quileute Indian Reservation 98350
Quinault 98575
Quinault Indian Reservation 98587
Quincy 98848
Rainer Valley (Part of Seattle) 98118
Rainier 98576
Rainier Beach (Part of Seattle) 98102
Rainier Terrace 98373
Ralston 99169
Rambler Park 98908
Randle 98377
Raugust 99037
Ravensdale 98051
Raymond 98577
Reardan 99029
Redmond 98052-53
98073
For specific ZIP Codes call (888) 275-8777, or your local postmaster.
Redmond Station (Part of Redmond)‡ 98052
Redondo 98054
Rees Corner 98296
Regal (Part of Spokane)‡ 99208

Reintree 98072
Renton 98055-59
For specific ZIP Codes call (888) 275-8777, or your local postmaster.
Renton Village (Part of Renton) 98055
Republic 99166
Retsil 98378
Rhodesia Beach 98527
Rhododendron Park 98390
Rice 99167
Richland 99352-53
For specific ZIP Codes call (888) 275-8777, or your local postmaster.
Richmond Beach‡ 98160
Richmond Highlands♦ 98133
Ridgecrest 98155
Ridgefield 98642
Ridgetop 98383
Riiho Park 98640
Rimrock 98937
Ritzville 99169
Riverbend 98821
Rivercrest 98204
Riverside, *Okanogan* 98849
Riverside (Part of Spokane)‡ 99201
Riverton Heights‡ 98188
Riverview Hills 99005
Roanoke (Part of Mercer Island) 98040
Robe 98252
Robinswood (Part of Bellevue) 98008
Roche Harbor 98250
Rochester♦ 98579
Rockford 99030
Rock Island 98850
Rockport 98283
Rocky Butte 98812
Rocky Point (Part of Kelso) 98626
Rocky Point, *Island* 98292
Rocky Point, *Kitsap* 98312
Rocky Woods 98387
Rodena Beach 98239
Rollingbay 98061
Rolling Hills 98277
Ronald 98940
Roosevelt, *Klickitat* 99356
Roosevelt, *Snohomish* 98290
Roosevelt Beach 98571
Rosalia 99170
Rosario 98245
Rosario Beach 98221
Rosburg 98643
Rosedale 98335
Rose Hill (Part of Kirkland)‡ 98033
Rose Valley 98626
Rosewood 99208
Roslyn 98941
Roy 98580
Royal Camp 99344
Royal City 99357
Ruby 99119
Ruff 98832
Ruston 98407
Ryderwood 98581
St. Andrews 99115
St. John 99127
99171
For specific ZIP Codes call (888) 275-8777, or your local postmaster.
St. Urbans 98596
Salkum 98582
Salmon Beach (Part of Tacoma) 98424
Salmon Creek 98665
Saltwater 98188
Samish Island 98232
Samish Lake 98226
San de Fuca 98239
Sandy Hook 98236
Sandy Hook Park 98370
Sandy Point 98260
Santiago Beach 98587
Sappho 98305
Sara 98642
Saratoga Beach 98260
Saratoga Heights 98260
Saratoga Shores 98292
Satsop 98583
Sauk River Estates 98283
Sawyer 98951
Scandia 98370
Scatchet Head 98236

Schawana 99321
Schneiders Prairie 98502
Schwarder 98908
Scopa (Part of Renton) 98055
Scott Lake 98501
Sea Acres 98279
Seabeck 98380
Seabold 98110
Sea First (Part of Seattle)‡ 98104
Seahurst (Part of Burien) 98062
Seal Rock 98320
Seamount Estates 98320
SeaTac 98158
Seatac Mall (Part of Federal Way) 98003
Seatons Grove 99116

Seattle

98060
98101-09
98111-99
For specific ZIP Codes call (888) 275-8777, or your local postmaster.

Colleges & Universities

Bastyr Univ 98105
Cornish Coll of the Arts 98102
ITT Technical Institute 98168
Northwest Institute of ACU Puncture & Oriental Medicine 98103
Seattle Pacific Univ 98119
Seattle Univ 98122
Univ of Washington-Seattle 98195

Financial Institutions

Seafirst Bank 98104
Union Bank 98164
U S Bank, NA 98101
Washington Mutual 98118
Wells Fargo 98104

Hospitals

Group Health Cooperative Hosp-Central 98112
Harborview Med Ctr 98104
Northwest Hosp 98133
Providence Seattle Med Ctr 98122
Swedish Med Ctr 98107
Univ of Washington Med Ctr 98195
Virginia Mason Med Ctr 98101

Hotels/Motels

Crowne Plaza 98101
Doubletree Hotel Airport 98188
Four Seasons Olympic 98101
Renaissance Madison 98104
Sheraton Hotel & Towers 98101
The Westin 98101

Military Installations

Coast Guard Integrated Support Command 98134
Headquarters, 124th U S Army Regional Support Command, Fort Lawton 98199
U S Army Corps of Engineers 98124
13th Coast Guard Dist 98134

Seattle Heights (Part of Edmonds) 98036
Seaview 98644
Sedro-Woolley 98284
Sekiu 98381
Selah 98942
Selleck 98051
Sequim 98310-12
98337
For specific ZIP Codes call (888) 275-8777, or your local postmaster.
Sequioa 98031
Seven Bays 99122
Seven Mile 99026

Shadle Garland (Part of Spokane)‡ 99205
99209
For specific ZIP Codes call (888) 275-8777, or your local postmaster.
Shana Park 98501
Shangri-La Shores 98239
Shaw Island 98286
Shawnee 99111
Shelton 98584
Sheridan Beach♦ 98155
Sheridan Park (Part of Bremerton)‡ 98310
Sherwood Forest (Part of Bellevue) 98008
Shine 98365
Shoalwater Indian Reservation 98590
Shore Acres 98335
Shoreline 98133
98155
98160
For specific ZIP Codes call (888) 275-8777, or your local postmaster.
Shorewood 98106
Shorewood Beach 98333
Shrine Beach 98816
Shuwah 98331
Sierra Division 98239
Sifton 98662
Sightly 98649
Silcott 99403
Silvana 98287
Silvana Terraces 98292
Silver Beach (Part of Bellingham) 98225
Silver Brook 98377
Silver Creek 98585
Silverdale 98315
98383
For specific ZIP Codes call (888) 275-8777, or your local postmaster.
Silverlake, *Cowlitz* 98645
Silver Lake, *Snohomish* 98208
Silver Lake, *Spokane* 99022
Similk Beach 98221
Sisco Heights 98223
Skagit City 98273
Skagit Country Club 98233
Skamania 98648
Skamokawa 98647
Skokomish♦ 98584
Skokomish Indian Reservation 98584
Skykomish 98288
Skyway‡ 98178
Sleepy Hollow 98647
Smithville 98635
Smokey Point 98223
Smyrna 99357
Snee Oosh♦ 98257
Snohomish 98290-91
98296
For specific ZIP Codes call (888) 275-8777, or your local postmaster.
Snoqualmie 98065
Snoqualmie Pass 98068
Soap Lake 98851
South Aberdeen (Part of Aberdeen) 98520
South Bay 98501
South Beach, *Kitsap* 98110
South Beach, *Whatcom* 98281
South Bellingham (Part of Bellingham) 98225
South Bend 98586
South Broadway♦ 98902
Southcenter (Part of Tukwila) 98188
South Cle Elum 98943
South Colby 98384
South Elma 98541
Southgate 98499
South Hill Mall (Part of Puyallup) 98373
South Montesano 98563
South Park (Part of Seattle) 98108
South Park Village 98366
South Point 98365
South Prairie 98385
South Seattle (Part of Seattle) 98102

Southshore Mall (Part of Aberdeen) 98520
Southside (Part of Everett)‡ 98208
South Snohomish 98296
South Sound Center (Part of Lacey) 98503
South Tacoma (Part of Tacoma)‡ 98409
South Union 98501
South Wenatchee♦ 98801
Southworth 98386
Spanaway♦ 98387
Spangle 99028
99031
For specific ZIP Codes call (888) 275-8777, or your local postmaster.
Spokane 99201-28
For specific ZIP Codes call (888) 275-8777, or your local postmaster.
Spokane Indian Reservation 99129
Sprague 99032
Spring Creek 98940
Springdale 99173
Spring Glen 98024
Squaxin Island Indian Reservation 98584
Stabler 98610
Stanwood 98292
Starbuck 99359
Star Lake 98001
Startup 98293
Stehekin 98852
Steilacoom 98388
Steptoe 99174
Sterling 98284
Stevenson 98648
Stiebels Corner 98346
Stillwater 98014
Stimson Crossing♦ 98223
Strandell (Part of Everson) 98247
Strategic Weapons Facility Pacific 98315
Stratford 98853
Streeters 98611
Stringtown 98624
Sultan 98294
Sumach 98901
Sumas 98295
Summerwood 99005
Summit 98373
Summit Lake 98501
Summit Park 98221
Sumner 98390
Suncrest 99026
Sundale 99356
Sundins Beach 98292
Sun Island 98925
Sunland Estates 98824
Sunlight Beach 98236
Sunlight Shores 98236
Sunny Bay 98335
Sunnydale (Part of Burien) 98155
Sunnyside, *Snohomish* 98205
Sunnyside, *Yakima* 98944
Sunnyside Beach (Part of Steilacoom) 98388
Sunnyslope, *Chelan*♦ 98801
Sunnyslope, *Kitsap* 98367
Sunrise 98335
Sunrise Point 98292
Sunset 99171
Sunset Bay 99034
Sunset Beach, *Grays Harbor* 98571
Sunset Beach, *Island* 98292
Sunset Beach, *Mason* 98528
Sunset Beach (Part of University Place) 98466
Sunset West, *Lewis* 98532
Sunset West, *Yakima* 98903
Sun Village (Part of Kirkland) 98012
Sunwood Lakes 98501
SuperMall of the Great Northwest (Part of Auburn) 98001
Suquamish♦ 98392
Swan Trail 98205
Swede Hill 98332
Swinomish Indian Reservation 98257
Swofford 98564
Sylvan 98333

Synarep 98849
Tacoma 98401-99
For specific ZIP Codes call (888) 275-8777, or your local postmaster.
Tacoma Junction (Part of Fife) 98424
Tacoma Mall (Part of Tacoma) 98409
Tacoma Point 98390
Tahlequah 98070
Taholah♦ 98587
Tahuya 98588
Tampico 98903
Tanglewilde 98503
Tanglewilde East 98516
Tanner 98045
Teanaway 98922
Tekoa 99033
Telma 98826
Tenino 98589
Terminal Annex (Part of Spokane) 99202
Terminal Finance (Part of Seattle)‡ 98134
Teronda West 98239
Terrace Heights♦ 98901
Terrill Beach 98245
Terry Avenue (Part of Seattle) 98109
Terrys Corner 98292
Thomas 98032
Thompson Place 98516
Thornton 99176
Thorp 98946
Thrashers Corner 98021
Throo Lakes 98290
Three Rivers Mall (Part of Kelso) 98626
Thrift 98338
Tieton 98947
Tiger 99180
Tillicum 98492
Tillicum Beach 98292
Tillicum Siding 98492
Timber Lakes 98584
Timberlane 98042
Tokeland 98590
Toledo 98591
Tonasket 98855
Toppenish 98948
Totem Lake (Part of Kirkland)‡ 98033
Touchet 99360
Toutle 98649
Town and Country♦ 99210
Tracyton♦ 98393
Trafton 98223
Treasure Island 98546
Trend (Part of Kirkland) 98033
Trentwood♦ 99215
Triangle Shopping Mall (Part of Longview) 98632
Tri-Cities (Part of Pasco)‡ 99302
Trinidad 98848
Triton 98555
Trout Lake 98650
Tukwila‡ 98108
Tulalip 98271
Tulalip Indian Reservation 98271
Tumtum 99034
Tumwater 98501
Turner 99328
Turner Corner 98072
Twisp 98856
Tyler 99004
Umtanum 98926
Underwood 98651
Union 98592
Union Gap 98903
Union Mill 98501
Uniontown 99179
University (Part of Seattle)‡ 98105
98145
For specific ZIP Codes call (888) 275-8777, or your local postmaster.
University Place♦ 98464-67
For specific ZIP Codes call (888) 275-8777, or your local postmaster.
University Village (Part of Seattle) 98105
Upper Preston 98027
Uranium City 99013
Urban 98221
Useless Bay Country Club 98260
Usk 99180
Utsalady 98292
Vader 98593
Valley 99181
Valleyford 99036
Valley Mall (Part of Union Gap) 98903
Valley Ridge (Part of SeaTac) 98188
Valley View 98331
Van Asselt (Part of Seattle) 98108
Van Buren 98247
Vancouver 98660-68
98682-87
For specific ZIP Codes call (888) 275-8777, or your local postmaster.
Van Horn 98237
Vantage 98950
Van Zandt 98244
Vashon 98070
Vashon Center 98070
Vashon Heights 98070
Vaughn 98394
Veazie 98002
Venersborg 98604
Venice 98110
Veradale♦ 99037
Verlot 98252
Vesta 98537
Veterans Administration Hospital (Part of Vancouver) 98661
View 98629
View Park 98367
View Ridge (Part of Seattle) 98115
Villa Beach 98303
Vinland 98370
Virginia 98370
Vision Acres 98626
Wabash 98022
Wahkiacus 98670
Waitsburg 99361
Waitts Lake 99181
Waldron 98297
Walla Walla 99362
Wallingford (Part of Seattle)‡ 98103
Wallula 99363
Wallula Junction 99363
Walnut Grove♦ 98662
Wanapum Village 99321
Wapato 98951
Warden 98857
Warm Beach 98292
Warnick 98244
Warren 98335
Washougal 98671
Washtucna 99371
Waterman 98366
Waterville 98858
Wauconda 98859
Waukon 99008
Wauna 98395
Waunch Prairie (Part of Centralia) 98531
Wautauga Beach 98366
Waverly 99039
Wawawai 99113
Wedgwood (Part of Seattle)‡ 98115
Wegoe 98433
Weikel 98902
Welcome 98244
Wellpinit 99040
Wenatchee 98801*
98807†
Wenatchee Heights 98802
West Beach 98245
West Blakely 98110
West Clarkston 99403
West Coulee (Part of Coulee Dam) 99116
Westfair (Part of Federal Way)‡ 98023
Westhaven (Part of Westport) 98595
West Hills (Part of Bremerton) 98312
Westmont Acres 98851
West Park (Part of Bremerton) 98312
West Pasco♦ 99301
Westport 98595
West Port Madison 98110
West Richland 99353
West Seattle (Part of Seattle)‡ 98116
Westside (Part of Olympia)‡ 98502
West Sound 98245
West Tapps 98390
Westward Siding (Part of Tacoma) 98406
West Wenatchee♦ 98802
Westwood (Part of Seattle)‡ 98126
Westwood, *Kitsap* 98110
Wheeler 98837
Whidbey Island Naval Air Station 98278
White Center 98106
White Pass 98937
Whites 98541
White Salmon 98672
White Swan 98952
Whitney Esttes 98532
Whitstran 99350
Wickersham 98220
Wilbur 99185
Wilburton (Part of Bellevue) 98004
Wildcat Lake 98312
Wilderness 98501
Wiley 98908
Wilkeson 98396
Willada 99171
Willapa 98577
Willard 98605
Willow Grove 98632
Wilson Creek 98860
Winchester 98848
Winlock 98596
Winona 99125
Winthrop 98862
Winton 98826
Wishkah 98520
Wishram 98673
Wishram Heights 98673
Withrow 98858
Wollochet 98335
Woodinville 98072
Woodland 98674
Woodland Beach 98292
Woodland Creek 98501
Woodland Park 98603
Woodlawn (Part of Hoquiam) 98550
Woodmont Beach 98032
Woodsmuir 98501
Woodway 98020
Wye Lake 98367
Yacht Haven 98250
Yacolt 98675
Yakima 98901-09
For specific ZIP Codes call (888) 275-8777, or your local postmaster.
Yakima Indian Reservation 98948
Yakima Mall (Part of Yakima) 98901
Yale 98603
Yardley 99202
Yarrow Point 98004
Yelm 98597
Yeomalt 98110
Yesler Terrace (Part of Seattle) 98104
Yokeko Point 98221
Yoman Ferry 98303
Zenith 98188
Zillah 98953

* Area Zip Code † Post Office Boxes ‡ Postal Station ♦ Census Designated Place *Italic Type* County

A (Part of Clarksburg)‡	26301*
	62302†
Aarrons Fork	25071
Abbott	26201
Abney	25847
Abraham	25918
Accoville	25606
Acme	25075
Ada	24701
Adaline	26033
Adamston (Part of Clarksburg)	26301
Adamsville	26431
Adlai	26170
Adolph	26280
Adrian	26210
Advent	25231
Afton	26764
Aggregates	26241
Ajax	25676
Albright	26519
Alderson	24910
Alexander	26218
Algoma	24868
Alice	26342
Alkol	25501
Allendale	26003
Allen Junction	25810
Allensville	25427
Alloy	25002
Alma	26320
Alpena	26254
Alpoca	24716
Alta, *Fayette*	26656
Alta, *Greenbrier*	24901
Alton	26210
Alum Bridge	26321
Alum Creek	25003
Alvon	24986
Alvy	26377
Amandaville	25177
Amboy	26705
Ambrosia	25550
Ameagle	25060
Amelia	25160
Ames Heights	25840
Amherstdale	25607
Amigo	25811
Amma	25005
Anawalt	24808
Andersonville	26033
Andrew	25154
Angel Terrace (Part of Charleston)	25303
Angerona	25241
Anjean	25984
Anmoore	26323
Annamoriah	26141
Ansted	25812
Anthony	24938
Antioch, *Doddridge*	26456
Antioch, *Mineral*	26743
Aplin	25244
Apple Farm	25274
Apple Grove, *McDowell*	24844
Apple Grove, *Mason*	25502
Aracoma	25601
Arborland Acres	25177
Arbovale	24915
Arbuckle	25123
Arbutus Park (Part of Clarksburg)	26301
Archer Heights	26035
Arcola	26206
Ardel	25570
Arden, *Barbour*	26405
Arden, *Berkeley*	25401
Argyle	25654
Arkansas	26801
Arlee	25106
Arlington, *Harrison*	26301
Arlington, *Upshur*	26234
Arnett, *Braxton*	26619
Arnett, *Raleigh*	25007
Arnettsville	26501
Arnoldsburg	25234
Arthur	26816
Arthurdale	26520
Artie	25209
Arvilla	26135
Asbury	24916
Asco	24828
Ashford	25009
Ashland	24810
Ashley	26456
Ashton	25503
Aspinall	26412
Astor	26347
Atenville	25524
Athens	24712
Atwell	24813
Atwood	26167
Auburn	26325
Augusta	26704
Aurora	26705
Austen	26410
Auto	24917
Auvil	26290
Avis (Part of Hinton)	25951
Avon	26411
Avondale, *Doddridge*	26456
Avondale, *McDowell*	24811
Ayers	26136
Bablin	26376
Backus	25976
Bachman	25840
Baden	25123
Baisden, *Logan*	25652
Baisden, *Mingo*	25608
Baker	26801
Baker Heights	25401
Baker Ridge	26505
	26508
For specific ZIP Codes call (888) 275-8777, or your local postmaster.	
Bakerton	25410
Bald Knob	25010
Baldwin	26351
Ballard	24918
Ballengee	24919
Balls Gap	25541
Bancroft	25011
Bandytown	25204
Barboursville	25504
Barboursville Mall	25504
Bardane	25430
Bargers Springs	24935
Barker	26419
Barksdale	25951
Barn	25041
Barnabus	25638
Barrackville	26559
Barren Creek	25045
Barrett	25208
Barrs	25276
Bartley	24813
Bartow	24920
Basin	24726
Basnettsville	26570
Basore	26812
Bass	26836
Baxter	26560
Bayard	26707
Bays Height	25931
Beard Heights	24954
Beards Fork	25173
Bear Mountain Mine	26334
Bearsville	26149
Beartown	24844
Beatrice	26178
Beatysville	26133
Beaver♦	25813
Bebee	26155
Becco	25607
Beckley	25801-02
For specific ZIP Codes call (888) 275-8777, or your local postmaster.	
Beckwith	25814
Bedington	25401
Beebe	25625
Beech Bottom	26030
Beech Creek	25682
Beech Glen	26656
Beechgrove	26415
Beech Hill	25187
Beechwood (Part of Parkersburg)	26104
Beechwood, *Wyoming*	25810
Beelick Knob	25976
Beeson	24714
Belgrove	25248
Belington	26250
Bellburn	25958
Belle	25015
Bellepoint (Part of Hinton)	25951
Belleville	26133
Bellmeade	25550
Bellton	26033
Bellview (Part of Fairmont)‡	26554
Bellwood	25962
Belmont	26134
Belo	25670
Belva	26656
Belvedere Heights	25414
Bemis	26268
Benbush	26292
Ben Dale	26452
Benson	26378
Benson Park	25302
Bens Run	26135
Bentons Ferry	26554
Bentree	25125
Benwood	26031
Benwood Junction (Part of Benwood)	26031
Berea	26327
Bergoo	26298
Berkeley	25401
Berkeley Springs	25411
Berlin	26452
Berryburg	26347
Berry Siding	26621
Berryville	25411
Bertha Hill	26541
Berwind	24815
Beryl	26726
Besoco	25857
Bessemer	25401
Bethany	26032
Bethlehem, *Harrison*	26431
Bethlehem, *Ohio*	26003
Betty Zane	26003
Beverly	26253
Beverly Hills (Part of Fairmont)	26554
Beverly Hills (Part of Huntington)‡	25705
Bias	25670
Bickmore	25019
Big Battle	26426
Bigbend	26136
Big Chimney	25302
Big Creek	25505
Big Four	24853
Big Isaac	26426
Big Moses	26320
Big Mountain (Part of Cedar Grove)	25039
Big Otter	25113
Big Run, *Marion*	26582
Big Run, *Marshall*	26033
Big Run, *Webster*	26217
Big Run, *Wetzel*	26561
Big Sandy	24816
Bigson	25206
Big Springs	26137
Big Sycamore	25111
Billings	25270
Bim	25021
Bingamon	26591
Bingamon Junction	26591
Bingham	25958
Birch River	26610
Birchton	25209
Birds Creek	26410
Bishop	24604
Bismarck	26739
Blackberry City	25678
Black Betsy	25159
Black Bottom	25601
Blackhawk	25306
Blacksville	26521
Black Wolf	24871
Blaine	26717
Blair, *Jefferson*	25432
Blair, *Logan*	25022
Blairton	25401
Blakeley	25160
Blandville	26328
Blaser	26444
Blennerhassett♦	26101
Blocton	25685
Bloomery, *Hampshire*	26817
Bloomery, *Jefferson*	25414
Bloomingrose	25024
Blount	25025
Blue	26149
Blue Creek	25026
Bluefield	24701
Blue Jay	25816
Blue Ridge Acres	25425
Blue Rock	26280
Bluestone	24701
Blue Sulphur	25545
Blue Sulphur Springs	24910
Blueville (Part of Grafton)	26354
Bluewell	24701
Blundon	25071
Boaz	26187
Bob White	25028
Boggs	26206
Bolair	26288
Bolivar	25425
Bolt	25817
Bomont	25030
Bonnie	26619
Bonnivale	26150
Booher	26320
Boomer	25031
Boonesborough (Part of Gauley Bridge)	25057
Booth	26522
Boothsville	26554
Borderland	25665
Borgman	26444
Bottom Creek	24853
Boulder	26201
Bowan Ridge	25701
Bowden	26254
Bowlby	26541
Bowles	25523
Boyer	24915
Bozoo	24963
Bradley, *Boone*	25051
Bradley, *Raleigh*♦	25818
Bradshaw, *Logan*	25652
Bradshaw, *McDowell*	24817
Bragg	25918
Bramwell	24715
Branchland	25506
Brandonville	26525
Brandywine	26802
Braxton	26619
Bream	25071
Breeden	25666
Brenton	24818
Bretz, *Preston*	26524
Bretz, *Tucker*	26287
Brierwood	26101
Brick Church	25514
Bridgeport	26330
Bridgeway	26149
Brink	26582
Bristol	26332
Broaddus (Part of Philippi)	26416
Broad Oaks (Part of Clarksburg)	26301
Brohard	26138
Brookhaven	26505
Brooklyn, *Fayette*	25840
Brooklyn (Part of New Martinsville)	26155
Brooks	25951
Brookside	26705
Brounland	25314
Brown	26448
Brownlow	26354
Brownsburg	24954
Browns Mills	26547
Brownsville	25085
Brownton	26334
Bruceton Mills	26525
Bruno	25611
Brush Fork	24701
Brushy Run	26866
Brydon	26435
Bryson	25865
Bubbling Spring	26865
Buck	25951
Buckeye	24924
Buckhannon	26201
Bud	24716
Buffalo	25033
Buffalo Creek	25530
Buff Lick	25039
Bula	26590
Bulger	25501
Bull Run	26547
Bulltown	26631
Bunker Hill, *Berkeley*	25413
Bunker Hill (Part of South Charleston)	25309
Bunners Ridge	26554
Burchfield	26562
Burlington	26710
Burning Springs	26141
Burnsville	26335
Burnt House	26178
Burnwell	25083
Burton	26562
Butchersville	26452
C (Part of Charleston)‡	25312
C (Part of Clarksburg)‡	26301
Cabell	25871
Cabin Creek	25035
Cabins	26855
Cabot	25181
Cabot Station	26147
Cairo	26337
Caldwell	24925
Caledonia Heights	26836
Calis	26033
Calvert (Part of St. Albans)	25177
Calvin	26660
Cambria, *Harrison*	26386
Cambria, *Nicholas*	25125
Camden	26338
Camden-on-Gauley	26208
Cameo	25565
Cameron	26033
Campbelltown	24954
Camp Creek	25820
Camp Ground	26444
Campus	24827
Canaan	26234
Canaan Heights	26260
Canaan Valley	26260
Canebrake	24815
Canfield, *Braxton*	26601
Canfield, *Randolph*	26241
Cannelton	25036
Canterbury	25676
Canton	26456
Cantwell	26362
Canvas	26662
Canyon	26508
Capehart	25123
Capels	24820
Capitol (Part of Charleston)‡	25311
Capon Bridge	26711
Capon Springs	26823
Carbon	25075
Carbondale	25036
Caretta	24821
Carl	26676
Carlisle	25917
Carlos	24844
Carolina	26563
Carpendale	26753
Carrollton	26238
Carswell	24853
Carter	26218
Cascade	26547
Cashmere	24918
Cass	24927
Cassity	26278
Cassville	26527
Catawba	26554
Cave	26807
Cazy	25028
Cedar Grove, *Kanawha*	25039
Cedar Grove, *Wood*	26101
Cedarville	26611
Center Hill	26143
Center Point	26339
Centerville	25555
Central	26101
Centralia	26612
Central Station	26456
Century	26214
Century No. 2	26238
Ceredo	25507
Ceres	24701
Cham, *Chambers*	25654
Chapel	26624
Chapman, *Braxton*	26412
Chapman, *Webster*	26288
Chapman Addition	26070
Chapmanville	25508
Charleston	25301-02
	25304-06
	25311-89
For specific ZIP Codes call (888) 275-8777, or your local postmaster.	
Charleston Ordnance Center (Part of South Charleston)	25303
Charleston Town Center (Part of Charleston)‡	25389
Charles Town	25414
Charlton Heights (Part of Gauley Bridge)	25040
Charmco	25958
Chatham Hill	26571
Chattaroy♦	25667
Chauncey	25612
Cheat Neck	26508
Chelyan	25035
Cherry Falls	26288
Cherry Grove	26804
Cherry Run	25427
Chesapeake, *Kanawha*	25315
Chesapeake, *Marion*	26554
Chester	26034

*** Area Zip Code** **† Post Office Boxes** **‡ Postal Station** **♦ Census Designated Place** *Italic Type* **County**

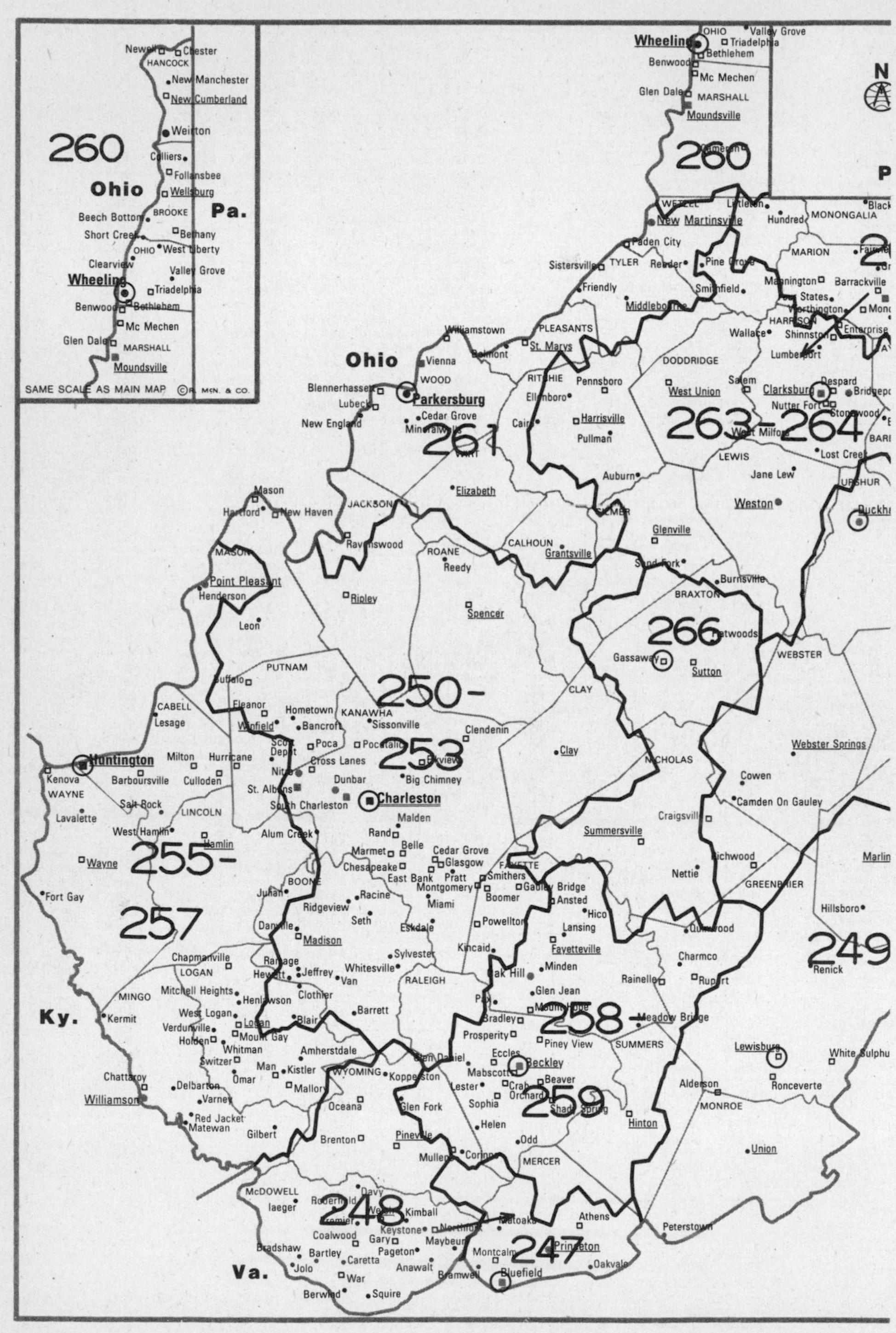
260
Ohio
Pa.
Newell
Chester
HANCOCK
New Manchester
New Cumberland
Weirton
Colliers
Follansbee
Wellsburg
Beech Bottom
BROOKE
Short Creek
Bethany
OHIO
West Liberty
Clearview
Valley Grove
Wheeling
Triadelphia
Benwood
Bethlehem
Mc Mechen
Glen Dale
MARSHALL
Moundsville
SAME SCALE AS MAIN MAP
©R. McN. & CO.
N
Wetzel
New Martinsville
Littleton
Hundred
MONONGALIA
Paden City
Sistersville
TYLER
Reader
Pine Grove
MARION
Friendly
Smithfield
Mannington
Barrackville
Middlebourne
Worthington
HARRISON
Williamstown
PLEASANTS
Wallace
Shinnston
Enterprise
St. Marys
Belmont
Lumberport
Ohio
Vienna
WOOD
RITCHIE
Pennsboro
DODDRIDGE
Salem
Despard
Blennerhassett
Parkersburg
Ellenboro
West Union
Clarksburg
Bridgeport
Lubeck
Nutter Fort
Stonewood
New England
Cedar Grove
Mineralwells
Cairo
Harrisville
Pullman
261
263-264
West Milford
LEWIS
Lost Creek
Auburn
Jane Lew
Elizabeth
Mason
Hartford
New Haven
JACKSON
GILMER
Weston
Glenville
Ravenswood
ROANE
CALHOUN
Grantsville
MASON
Reedy
Sand Fork
Burnsville
Point Pleasant
Henderson
Ripley
Spencer
BRAXTON
Leon
266
Flatwoods
Gassaway
Sutton
WEBSTER
PUTNAM
250-
253
Buffalo
CLAY
CABELL
Eleanor
Hometown
KANAWHA
Lesage
Winfield
Bancroft
Sissonville
Clendenin
Scott Depot
Poca
Pocatalico
Webster Springs
Huntington
Milton
Hurricane
Cross Lanes
Elkview
Clay
Kenova
Barboursville
Culloden
Nitro
NICHOLAS
WAYNE
St. Albans
Dunbar
Big Chimney
Cowen
Salt Rock
LINCOLN
South Charleston
Charleston
Camden On Gauley
Lavalette
Malden
Craigsville
West Hamlin
Alum Creek
Rand
Summersville
Hamlin
255-
257
Marmet
Belle
Cedar Grove
Glasgow
Richwood
Wayne
Chesapeake
Nettie
East Bank
Pratt
FAYETTE
Smithers
BOONE
Montgomery
GREENBRIER
Julian
Gauley Bridge
Fort Gay
Racine
Boomer
Ansted
Hillsboro
Ridgeview
Miami
Hico
Seth
Powellton
Danville
Eskdale
Lansing
Quinwood
Madison
249
Kincaid
Fayetteville
Sylvester
Chapmanville
Renick
Charmco
LOGAN
Ramage
Whitesville
Minden
Hewett
Jeffrey
Oak Hill
Van
RALEIGH
Rainelle
Rupert
MINGO
Mitchell Heights
Clothier
Glen Jean
Henlawson
Mount Hope
Ky.
Kermit
West Logan
Barrett
Pax
258-
Meadow Bridge
Verdunville
Logan
Blair
Bradley
Holden
Mount Gay
Prosperity
Piney View
SUMMERS
Whitman
Lewisburg
White Sulphur
Switzer
Amherstdale
Eccles
Glen Daniel
Beckley
Man
Kistler
Chattaroy
Omar
WYOMING
Mabscott
Beaver
Delbarton
Koppeston
Lester
Crab Orchard
Alderson
Ronceverte
Williamson
Varney
Mallory
259
Oceana
Sophia
Shady Spring
MONROE
Red Jacket
Matewan
Glen Fork
Hinton
Helen
Gilbert
Brenton
Pineville
Odd
Union
Mullens
Corinne
MERCER
MCDOWELL
Davy
Iaeger
Roderfield
248
Welch
Kimball
Matoaka
Athens
Premier
Northfork
Peterstown
Keystone
Coalwood
Gary
Maybeury
Bradshaw
Pageton
Montcalm
247
Princeton
Bartley
Caretta
Anawalt
Va.
Jolo
War
Bramwell
Bluefield
Oakvale
Berwind
Squire

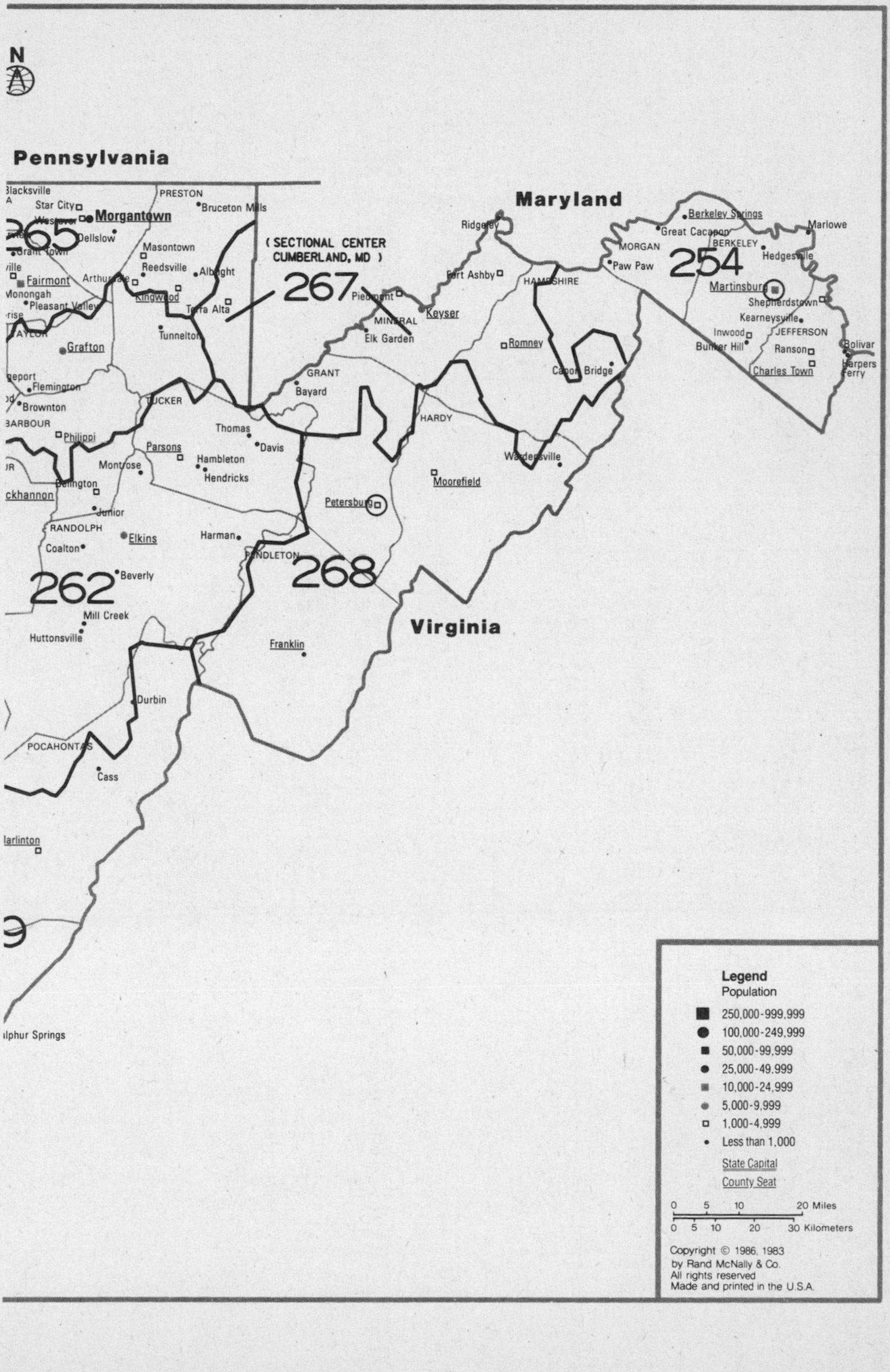

N

Pennsylvania

Maryland

Virginia

Blacksville
Star City
Westover
Morgantown
Dellslow
Grant Town
Fairmont
Monongah
Pleasant Valley
Arthurdale
Kingwood
Terra Alta
Tunnelton
Grafton
Bridgeport
Flemington
Brownton
BARBOUR
Philippi
TAYLOR
PRESTON
Bruceton Mills
Masontown
Reedsville
Albright
TUCKER
Parsons
Thomas
Davis
Hambleton
Hendricks
Montrose
Elkins
Junior
Ellington
Buckhannon
RANDOLPH
Coalton
Beverly
Mill Creek
Huttonsville
Harman
Durbin
POCAHONTAS
Cass
Marlinton
Sulphur Springs

(SECTIONAL CENTER
CUMBERLAND, MD)

265
267
262
268
254

Ridgeley
Fort Ashby
Piedmont
MINERAL
Keyser
Elk Garden
GRANT
Bayard
Petersburg
PENDLETON
Franklin
HARDY
Moorefield
Wardensville
HAMPSHIRE
Romney
Capon Bridge
MORGAN
Paw Paw
Great Cacapon
Berkeley Springs
BERKELEY
Hedgesville
Marlowe
Martinsburg
Shepherdstown
Kearneysville
Inwood
Bunker Hill
JEFFERSON
Ranson
Charles Town
Bolivar
Harpers Ferry

Legend
Population

- 250,000-999,999
- 100,000-249,999
- 50,000-99,999
- 25,000-49,999
- 10,000-24,999
- 5,000-9,999
- 1,000-4,999
- Less than 1,000

State Capital
County Seat

0 5 10 20 Miles
0 5 10 20 30 Kilometers

Place	ZIP Code
Chesterville	26150
Chestnut Hill (Part of Weirton)	26062
Chestnut Ridge	26505
Chiefton	26301
Childs	26155
Chimney Corner	25085
Chloe	25235
Christian	25650
Christy Heights	25526
Churchville	26338
Cicerone	25243
Cinco	25201
Cinderella	25661
Circle View	25801
Circleville	26804
Cirtsville	25801
Cisco	26137
Clarence	25244
Clarksburg	26301*
	26302†
Clay	25043
Clay Junction (Part of Clay)	25043
Claypool, *Logan*	25617
Claypool, *Summers*	25976
Claysville	26743
Clayton	24910
Clear Creek	25044
Clear Fork	24822
Clearview	26003
Clem	26623
Clemtown	26405
Clendenenville	24957
Clendenin	25045
Cleveland	26215
Clifftop	25831
Clifton	25260
Clifton Mills	26525
Clinton, *Boone*	25208
Clinton, *Ohio*	26059
Clintonville	24931
Clio	25045
Clothier	25047
Clouston	26033
Clover, *Cabell*	25823
Clover, *Roane*	25276
Cloverdale	24963
Clover Lick	24927
Coalbottom	25130
Coalburg	25035
Coal City	25823
Coaldale	24724
Coal Fork♦	25306
Coal Mountain	24823
Coalton	26257
Coal Valley	25047
Coalwood	24824
Coburn	26562
Coco	25071
Coketon	26292
Colcord	25048
Cold Stream	26711
Coldwater	26411
Colebank	26405
Coleman	25517
Colfax	26566
Colliers	26035
Collinsdale	25083
Columbia	25118
Combs Addition	25617
Comfort	25049
Conaway	26149
Concord	26410
Condit	26585
Confidence	25168
Conings	26443
Consol No. 9	26571
Cool Ridge	25825
Coopertown	25148
Copen	26615
Copley	26452
Cora	25614
Cordova	24966
Core	26529
Corinne	25826
Corinth	26764
Corley, *Barbour*	26250
Corley, *Braxton*	26621
Corliss	25962
Cornstalk	24901
Cornwallis	26337
Cortland	26260
Corton	25045
Costa	25051
Cottageville	25239
Cottle	26205
Cotton	25045
Cottontown	26562
Countsville	25243
Cove (Part of Weirton)‡	26062
Cove Gap	25534
Covel	24719
Cowen	26206
Coxs Mills	26342
Coxtown (Part of Weston)	26452
Crab Orchard♦	25827
Craig	25962
Craigmoor	26408
Craigsville	26205
Cranberry	25801
Craneco	25630
Cranesville	26764
Crany	24870
Crawford	26343
Crawley	24931
Creamery	24910
Crede	25302
Cremo	26141
Crescent	25136
Cressmont	25043
Creston	26141
Crichton	25981
Crickmer	25831
Crooked Creek	25639
Crosby	25125
Cross Lanes	25313
Crossroads	26589
Crow	25813
Crown, *Logan*	25606
Crown, *Monongalia*	26501
Crown Hill	25067
Crow Summit	26164
Crum	25669
Crumpler	24825
Crystal	24747
Crystal Block	25644
Crystal Lake	26456
Crystal Springs	26241
Cubana	26237
Cucumber	24826
Culloden♦	25510
Cumberland Heights	24701
Cunard	25840
Curtin	26288
Curtisville	26582
Cusicks Crossing	26562
Custer Addition	26301
Cutlips	26619
Cuzzart	26525
Cyclone	24827
Cyrus	25530
Czar	26224
Dabney	25654
Dahmer	26807
Dailey	26259
Daisy	25505
Dakota	26554
Dale	26377
Dallas	26036
Dallison	26180
Dameron	25844
Danese	25831
Daniels♦	25832
Dans Run	26763
Danville	25053
Darkesville	25428
Dartmont	25009
Dartmoor	26250
Davenport	26175
Davin	25617
Davis, *Logan*	25625
Davis, *Tucker*	26260
Davis Creek	25003
Davisville	26142
Davy	24828
Dawes	25054
Dawmont	26301
Dawson	24910
Daybrook	26570
Daysville	26201
Deanville, *Lewis*	26452
Deanville, *Upshur*	26201
Decota	25075
Deep Valley, *Marion*	26582
Deep Valley, *Tyler*	26415
Deep Water	25057
Deer Creek	24927
Deer Run	26807
Deerwalk	26180
Dehue	25654
Delbarton	25670
Dellslow	26531
Delong	26170
Delray	26714
Dempsey	25840
Denver	26444
Denver Heights	26033
Derryhale	25846
Despard	26301
Dessie	26623
Devon	25682
Dewitt	25648
Diamond, *Kanawha*	25015
Diamond, *Logan*	25625
Diana	26217
Dickinson	25015
Dickson	25535
Dille	26617
Dingess	25671
Dink	25113
Divide	25868
Dixie	25059
Doane	25511
Dobra	25183
Dog Patch	25636
Dola	26386
Donaldson	26206
Donwood	25136
Doortown	26288
Dorcas	26847
Dorothy	25060
Dothan	25833
Dott	24736
Douglas, *Calhoun*	25235
Douglas, *Tucker*	26292
Downtown (Part of Huntington)‡	25701
	25716-22
	25724-29
For specific ZIP Codes call (888) 275-8777, or your local postmaster.	
Downtown (Part of Wheeling)†	26003
Drennen	26667
Drews Creek	25140
Droop	24946
Drybranch	25061
Dry Creek	25062
Dryfork	26263
Dry Hill	25801
Duck	25063
Dudeon	25248
Dudley Gap	25541
Duffields	25442
Duffy	26376
Duhring	24747
Dukes	25252
Dunbar	25064
Duncan	25252
Dundon	25043
Dunloup	25880
Dunlow	25511
Dunmore	24934
Dunns	25841
Duo	25984
Dupont City	25015
Durbin	26264
Durgon	26836
Dutchman	26148
Dutch Ridge	25045
Dyer	26206
Eagle	25136
Earling	25632
Earnshaw	26585
East Bank	25067
East Beckley (Part of Beckley)‡	25801
East Dailey	26259
Eastgate	25915
East Kermit	25674
East Kingston	25917
East Lynn	25512
East Nitro (Part of Nitro)	25143
East Oak Hill (Part of Oak Hill)	25901
East Pea Ridge	25705
East Salem	26426
Eastside (Part of Fairmont)‡	26554*
	26555†
East View	26301
East Williamson (Part of Williamson)	25661
Eaton	26180
Eccles	25836
Echo	25570
Eckman	24829
Eden, *Boone*	25024
Eden, *Ohio*	26003
Eden, *Upshur*	26234
Edgarton	25672
Edgemont (Part of Fairmont)	26554
Edgewater Acres (Part of St. Albans)	25177
Edgewood (Part of Charleston)	25302
Edgewood (Part of Clarksburg)	26301
Edgewood (Part of Wheeling)	26003
Edgewood Acres (Part of Charleston)	25302
Edison	24701
Edmond	25837
Edna	26501
Edray	24954
Edwight	25140
Effie	25514
Egeria	25902
Eggleton	25523
Elana	25266
Elbert (Part of Gary)	24830
Eldora	26554
Eleanor	25070
Elgood	24740
Elizabeth	26143
Elk	26271
Elk City	26416
Elk Forest	25311
Elk Garden	26717
Elk Hills	25302
Elkhorn	24831
Elkhurst	25164
Elkins	26241
Elkridge, *Fayette*	25161
Elkridge, *McDowell*	24868
Elk Run Junction	25209
Elkview♦	25071
Elkwater	26273
Ellamore	26267
Ellenboro	26346
Ellison	25969
Elm Grove, *Ohio*	26003
Elm Grove (Part of Wheeling)‡	26003
Elmira	26618
Elm Terrace (Part of Wheeling)	26003
Elmwood, *Mason*	25123
Elmwood, *Wayne*	25570
Eloise	25511
Elton	25965
Emma	25124
Emmett	25650
Emmons	25003
Emoryville	26717
Endicott	26581
Engle	25425
English	24832
Ennis	24887
Enoch	25043
Enon	26651
Enterprise, *Harrison*♦	26568
Enterprise, *Wirt*	26160
Entry Mountain	26807
Epperly	25823
Erbacon	26203
Erie	26301
Erwin	26705
Eskdale	25075
Esty	24966
Etam	26425
Ethel	25076
Euclid	26636
Eunice	25209
Eureka	26134
Evans	25241
Evansdale (Part of Morgantown)	26505
Evansville	26440
Evenwood	26254
Everettville	26533
Evergreen	26218
Evergreen Hills	25239
Everson	26554
Excelsior (Part of War)	24892
Excelsior, *Upshur*	26201
Exchange	26619
Extra	25168
Fairdale	25839
Fairlea♦	24902
Fairmont	26554*
	26555†
Fairmor (Part of Westover)	26501
Fairplain	25271
Fairview, *Marion*	26570
Fairview, *Marshall*	26055
Fairview, *Mason*	25253
Fairview, *Mingo*	25661
Fallen Timber	26437
Falling Rock	25079
Falling Waters	25419
Falls	26833
Falls Mill	26631
Falls Mills	26146
Fallsview	25002
Fanco	25606
Fanny	24834
Fanrock	24834
Far	26167
Farmington	26571
Farnum	26369
Faulkner	26241
Fayette Heights	25840
Fayetteville	25840
Federal (Part of Bluefield)‡	24701
Federal Ridge	26170
Fellowsville	26444
Fenwick	26202
Ferguson	25511
Ferrellsburg	25524
Fetterman (Part of Grafton)	26354
Filbert (Part of Gary)	24830
Finch	26346
Finley	25003
Fireco	25856
Fisher	26818
Fitzpatrick	25801
Five Block	25022
Five Forks, *Calhoun*	26136
Five Forks, *Preston*	26525
Five Forks, *Ritchie*	26362
Fivemile, *Kanawha*	25201
Fivemile, *Mason*	25106
Flaggy Meadow	26501
Flatrock	25123
Flat Top	25841
Flat Top Lake	25843
Flatwoods, *Braxton*	26621
Flatwoods, *Jackson*	26164
Flatwoods, *Kanawha*	25312
Flemington	26347
Flinderation	26332
Flint	26456
Flipping	24747
Floe	25235
Flower	26611
Fola	25019
Follansbee	26037
Folsom	26348
Forest Hill	24935
Forest Hill Estates	25401
Forest Hills (Part of Charleston)	25314
Forest Hills (Part of Wheeling)	26003
Forks of Cacapon	25434
Forks of Coal	25003
Forks of Hurricane	25514
Fort Ashby♦	26719
Fort Branch	25076
Fort Gay	25514
Fort Grand	26533
Fort Hill (Part of Charleston)	25303
Fort Martin	26541
Fort Neal (Part of Parkersburg)	26103
Fort Run	26836
Fort Seybert	26802
Fort Spring	24936
Foster	25081
Fosterville	25181
Four Mile	26562
Four States	26572
Fowlerstown	26070
Frame	25071
Frametown	26623
Francis	26554
Frank	24920
Frankford	24938
Franklin, *Brooke*	26070
Franklin, *Pendleton*	26807
Franklintown	25441
Fraziers Bottom	25082
Freed	26138
Freeman	24724
Freemansburg	26452
Freeport, *Preston*	26764
Freeport, *Wirt*	26180
Freeze Fork	25076
French Creek	26218
Frenchton	26219
Frew	26149
Friars Hill	24938
Friendly	26146
Friendly View	25062
Frogtown	25625
Frost	24954
Frozen Camp	25252
Fry	25524

Fulton (Part of Wheeling) 26003
Gaines 26234
Gallagher 25083
Gallipolis Ferry 25515
Galloway 26349
Galloway Junction 26349
Galmish 26167
Gandeeville 25243
Ganotown 25427
Gap Mills 24941
Gardner 24740
Garfield 25252
Garland 24811
Garretts Bend 25564
Garrison 25209
Garten 25840
Garwood 24726
Gary 24836
Gassaway 26624
Gaston 26452
Gaston Junction (Part of Fairmont) 26554
Gates 24983
Gatewood 25840
Gauley Bridge 25085
Gauley Mills 26208
Gay 25244
Gaymont 25938
Gem 26335
Genoa 25517
Georges Run 26456
Georgetown, *Lewis* 26372
Georgetown, *Marshall* 26033
Georgetown, *Monongalia* 26501
Gerrardstown 25420
Ghent 25843
Giatto 24736
Gilbert 25621
Gilboa 26671
Giles 25054
Gill 25557
Gilliam 24897
Gillman Bottom 25617
Gilman 26241
Gilmer 26350
Gip 26618
Given 25245
Glace 24983
Glade Farms 26525
Glade Springs 25832
Gladesville 26374
Glade View 26206
Gladwin 26241
Glady 26268
Glasgow 25086
Glen 25088
Glen Alum 25651
Glen Dale, *Marshall* 26038
Glendale, *Ritchie* 26337
Glendale Heights 26038
Glen Daniel 25844
Glendon 26623
Glen Easton 26039
Glen Elk (Part of Clarksburg) 26301
Glen Falls 26301
Glen Ferris 25090
Glen Fork 25845
Glengary 25421
Glenhayes 25519
Glen Jean 25846
Glenmore 26241
Glen Morgan 25847
Glenray 24910
Glen Rogers 25848
Glen View 25827
Glenville 26351
Glen White 25849
Glenwood, *Mason* 25520
Glenwood (Part of Wheeling) 26003
Glenwood Park 24701
Glover Gap 26585
Gluck 24817
Godby Heights 25508
Godfrey 24747
Goffs 26362
Golden 26036
Golden Acres 26704
Goldtown 25248
Goodhope 26378
Goodman 25667
Goodwill 24747
Gordon 25093
Gore 26301
Gormania 26720
Gormley 26267
Goshen 26234
Gould, *Clay* 25113
Gould, *Upshur* 26218
Grace 25270
Grafton 26354
Graham Heights 26554
Graham Station 25253
Grand Central Mall (Part of Vienna) 26101
Grandview 25813
Grangeville 26582
Grantsville 26147
Grant Town 26574
Granville 26534
Grape Island 26170
Grassy Meadows 24943
Grave Creek 26041
Graydon 25938
Graysville 26055
Great Cacapon 25422
Green Bank 24944
Green Bottom 25537
Green Castle 26180
Greendale 26656
Green Hill 26155
Greenland, *Grant* 26833
Green Spring 26722
Greenstown 25901
Green Sulphur Springs 25976
Green Valley, *Mercer* 24701
Green Valley, *Nicholas* 25981
Greenview 25053
Greenville 24945
Greenwood, *Boone* 25010
Greenwood, *Doddridge* 26415
Greer, *Mason* 25550
Greer, *Monongalia* 26508
Greggsville (Part of Wheeling) 26003
Greyeagle 25674
Griffithsville 25521
Grimms Landing 25095
Grippe 25314
Grove 26411
Groves 25063
Grubbs Corner 25401
Guardian 26217
Gum Spring 26508
Gunville 25123
Guthrie 25312
Guyandotte (Part of Huntington)‡ 25702
Guyan Estates 25504
Guyan Terrace 25601
Gypsy 26361
Hacker Valley 26222
Haddleton 25130
Hagans 26529
Hager 25506
Hall 26201
Hallburg 25063
Halleck 26508
Halltown 25423
Halo 26206
Hambleton 26269
Hamlin 25523
Hammond 26566
Hampden 25621
Hampton 26201
Hancock 25411
Handley 25102
Hanna 26180
Hannahsville 26290
Hanover 24839
Hansford 25103
Hany 25511
Harding 26250
Hardy 24740
Harlem Heights 25901
Harlin 26456
Harman 26270
Harmony 25243
Harmony Grove 26501
Harper, *Pendleton* 26807
Harper, *Raleigh* 25851
Harper Heights 25801
Harpers Ferry 25425
Harpertown 26241
Harrison 25105
Harrisville 26362
Harters Hill 26591
Hartford 25247
Hartland 25043
Hartmansville 26717
Harts 25524
Harvey 25901
Harveytown (Part of Huntington) 25704
Hastings 26377
Hatcher, *Mercer* 24740
Hatcher (Part of Oceana) 24870
Havaco 24801
Haywood 26366
Haywood Junction 26431
Hazelgreen 26362
Hazelton 26535
Hazelwood 26241
Hazy 25140
Headsville 26710
Heaters 26627
Heatherfield 25443
Heavener Grove 26201
Hebron 26346
Hedgesville 25427
Hedgeview 25637
Heights (Part of Point Pleasant) 25550
Heizer 25159
Helen 25853
Helens Run 26591
Helvetia 26224
Hemlock 26224
Hemphill 24842
Henderson 25106
Hendricks 26271
Henlawson 25624
Henning 24938
Henrietta 26147
Hensley 24843
Hensley Heights 25635
Hepzibah, *Harrison* 26369
Hepzibah, *Taylor* 26330
Hereford 25252
Herndon 24726
Herndon Heights 24726
Hernshaw 25107
Herold 26601
Herring 26547
Hettie 26376
Hetzel 25076
Hewett 25108
Hiawatha 24729
Hickory Chapel 25550
Hico 25854
Highland 26346
Highland Park 26241
Highlawn (Part of St. Albans) 25177
High View 26808
Hildebrand 26501
Hillcrest (Part of Fairmont) 26554
Hilldale 25951
Hillsboro 24946
Hillsdale (Part of Charleston) 25302
Hillsdale, *Monroe* 24976
Hilltop 25855
Hillview, *Cabell* 25702
Hillview, *Marion* 26554
Hillview Terrace 26041
Hilton Village 25962
Hinch 25682
Hines 25967
Hinkleville 26201
Hinton 25951
Hiorra 26410
Hitop 25160
Hix 25951
Hodgesville 26201
Hogsett 25515
Hokes Mill 24970
Holbrook 26456
Holcomb 26261
Holden 25625
Hollygrove 25103
Hollywood 24983
Holton 25411
Homeland 26378
Hometown 25109
Homewood 26452
Hominy Falls 26679
Hoodsville 26588
Hoohoo 25865
Hookersville 26651
Hooverson Heights 26037
Hoover Town 26218
Hopecrest (Part of Morgantown) 26501
Hopeville 26855
Hopewell, *Barbour* 26416
Hopewell, *Fayette* 25938
Hopewell, *Marion* 26554
Hopewell, *Preston* 26525
Hopkins Fork 25181
Horner 26372
Horsepen 24619
Horse Shoe Run 26716
Horton 26296
Hosterman 26264
Hotchkiss 25920
Hoult 26554
Howells Mill 25545
Howesville 26444
Hoy 26704
Hubball 25506
Hubbardstown 25555
Hudson 26519
Huff Junction 25635
Hughart 24931
Hughes 26404
Hugheston 25110
Hugo 25168
Hundred 26575
Hunt 25635
Huntersville 24954
Huntington 25701-79
For specific ZIP Codes call (888) 275-8777, or your local postmaster.
Huntington Mall (Part of Barboursville) 25504
Hur 26151
Hurricane 25526
Hurst 26321
Hutchinson 26591
Huttonsville 26273
Iaeger 24844
Idamay 26576
Ikes Fork 24845
Independence, *Clay* 25125
Independence, *Jackson* 25275
Independence, *Preston* 26374
Indian (Part of St. Albans) 25177
Indian Meadows 25545
Indian Mills 24935
Indore 25111
Industrial 26375
Industry 26152
Ingleside 24740
Ingram Branch 25119
Inkerman 26801
Institute 25112
Intermont 26851
Inwood♦ 25428
Ireland 26376
Irona 26537
Iroquis 25928
Isaban 24846
Island Branch 25320
Isom 25121
Israel 26444
Itmann 24847
Iuka 26149
Ivy 26201
Ivydale 25113
Jacksonburg 26377
Jackson Flats 24873
Jacksons Mill 26452
Jacobs Fork 24884
Jacox 24946
Jakes Run 26529
James Crest Farms 25801
Jamestown 25446
Jane Lew 26378
Janie 25209
Jarrolds Valley (Part of Whitesville) 25209
Jarvisville 26332
Jawood 25811
Jeffrey 25114
Jenkinjones 24848
Jenks 25506
Jenningston 26254
Jere 26546
Jerome Park 26505
Jerrys Run 26133
Jesse 24849
Jimtown 25411
Jimtown, *Randolph* 26257
Job 26270
Jockeycamp Run 26456
Jodie 26674
Joetown 26582
Johnnycake 24844
Johnsontown 25427
Johnstown, *Harrison* 26385
Johnstown, *McDowell* 24884
Joker 26141
Jolo 24850
Jonben 25823
Jones Springs 25427
Jordan 26554
Jordan Run 26833
Josephine 25857
Josephs Mills 26320
Joy 26456
Judson 24910
Judy Gap 26814
Julia 24966
Julian 25529
Jumping Branch 25969
Junction 26824
Junior 26275
Justice 24851
Justice Addition 25601
Kabletown 25414
Kalamazoo 26416
Kanawha 26142
Kanawha City (Part of Charleston)‡ 25304
Kanawha Drive 26351
Kanawha Estates (Part of Charleston) 25304
Kanawha Falls 25115
Kanawha Head 26228
Kanawha Mall (Part of Charleston) 25387
Kansooth 26033
Kasson 26405
Katy 26554
Katy Lick 26301
Kearneysville 25430
Kedron 26201
Keeler Glade 26525
Keenan 24983
Kegley 24731
Keister 24901
Keith 25148
Kelly 25022
Kelly Hill 25045
Kellysville 24732
Kenna 25248
Kenova 25530
Kent 26055
Kentuck 25248
Kera Landing 25262
Kerens 26276
Kermit 25674
Keslers Cross Lanes 26675
Kessler 25984
Kettle 25243
Keyrock 24874
Keyser 26726
Keystone 24852
Kiahsville 25534
Kidwell 26149
Kieffer 24950
Killarm 26554
Killarney 25915
Kilsyth 25859
Kimball 24853
Kimberly 25118
Kincaid 25119
Kincheloe 26378
Kingmont 26578
Kingstown 26561
Kingsville 26257
Kingwood 26537
Kirby 26729
Kirby Addition 24740
Kirbyton 25181
Kirk 25671
Kirt 26203
Kistler 25628
Kitchen 25508
Kitsonville (Part of Weston) 26452
Kline 26866
Klines Gap 26833
Knob Fork 26581
Knobs 24983
Knollwood 25302
Knollwood Estates 25526
Knottsville 26354
Kodol 26186
Kopperston 24854
Kyle 24855
Lacoma 24827
LaFrank (Part of Richwood) 26261
Lahmansville 26731
Lake 25121
Lake Floyd 26332
Lake Ridge 26330
Lamberton 26346
Lanark 25860
Landes 26847
Landgraff 24829
Landisburg 25831
Lando Mines 25670
Landville 25635
Laneville 26263
Lanham 25159
Lansing 25862
Largent 25422

Place	ZIP
Larkmead	26101
Lashmeet	24733
Lauckport (Part of Parkersburg)	26101
Laura Lee Mine	26386
Laurel Branch	24984
Laurel Dale	26743
Laurel Park	26301
Laurel Point	26501
Laurel Valley	26301
Lavalette	25535
Lawn	25976
Lawrenceville (Part of Chester)	26034
Lawton	25864
Layland	25864
Leachtown	26143
Lead Mine	26290
Leadsville	26241
Leander	25912
Leckie	24856
Lee	25880
Leet	25524
Leetown	25430
Leevale	25209
Leewood	25075
Leewood Park	26003
Left Hand	25251
Lego	25857
Lehew	26865
Leivasy	26676
Lenore	25676
Lenox	26519
Leon	25123
Leonard	24966
Leopold	26443
Lerona	25971
Le Roy	25252
Lesage	25537
Leslie	25972
Lester	25865
Letart	25253
Letherbark	25234
Letter Gap	25255
Levels	25431
Lewisburg	24901
Lexington Estates	25526
Liberty, *Harrison*	26301
Liberty, *Putnam*	25124
Lick Creek	25979
Lico	25314
Lightburn	26378
Lila	24808
Lilac Hills	24740
Lillybrook	25857
Lillydale, *Monroe*	24945
Lillydale, *Wyoming*	24822
Lilly Grove	24740
Lillyhaven	24857
Lilly Park	25962
Lima	26377
Limestone, *Marshall*	26041
Limestone, *Mineral*	26726
Limestone Hill	26143
Linden	25259
Lindside	24951
Lindytown	25204
Link	26167
Linn	26384
Linwood	26291
Little	26146
Little Birch	26629
Little Falls	26508
Little Italy	25113
Little Otter	26624
Little Pittsburg	26434
Littlesburg	24701
Littleton	26581
Litwar	24844
Lively	25917
Liverpool	25252
Livingston	25083
Lizemores	25125
Lloydsville	26619
Lobata	25678
Lobelia	24946
Lochgelly	25866
Lockbridge	25976
Lockhart	25275
Lockney	25267
Lockwood	26651
Lodgeville	26330
Logan	25601
Logan Heights	25614
Logansport	26582
Lomax	24899
London	25126
Lonetree	26149
Longacre	25186
Long Branch, *Fayette*	25867
Long Branch, *Wyoming*	24882
Longdale	25253
Lone Oak Park	25177
Longpole	24844
Long Run	26426
Longview	26238
Lookout	25868
Loom	26704
Looneyville	25259
Lorado	25630
Lorentz	26229
Lorton Lick	24701
Lost City	26810
Lost Creek	26385
Lost River	26810
Loudendale	25314
Loudenville	26033
Loudon Heights (Part of Charleston)	25314
Louise	26070
Lovern	24740
Lowdell	26169
Lowell	24962
Lower Belle	25015
Lower Falls	25177
Low Gap	25130
Lowney	25666
Lowsville	26533
Lubeck♦	26101
Lucas	25938
Lucille	26160
Lucretia	26354
Lumberport	26386
Lundale	25631
Lyburn	25632
Lynco	24857
Lynn	25678
Lynn Camp	26039
Lynwinn	25823
Lyonsville	26651
Maben	25870
Mabie	26278
Mabscott	25871
McAlpin	25921
MacArthur♦	25873
McCauley	26801
McClellan	26582
McComas	24747
McConnell	25646
McCorkle	25564
McCreery	25864
McCurdyville	26588
Macdale	26521
Macdonald	25880
McDowell	24810
MacDunn	25161
Mace	26291
Macfarlan	26148
McGee	26354
McGraws	25875
McGuire Park	26452
McIntire	26369
McKeefrey	26041
McKinleyville	26070
Macksville	26884
McMechen	26040
Macomber	26425
McRoss	25962
McWhorter	26385
Madam Creek	25951
Madeline	25811
Madison	25130
Magnolia	25422
Mahan	25083
Maher	25661
Mahone	26362
Maidsville	26541
Maitland	24801
Majorsville	26036
Malcom Spring Heights	25541
Malden	25306
Mallory	25634
Mammoth	25132
Man	25635
M and K Junction (Part of Rowlesburg)	26425
Manheim	26425
Manila	25508
Mannings	25425
Mannington	26582
Manown	26537
Mansfield (Part of Philippi)	26416
Maple Acres	24701
Maple Fork	25880
Maple Lake	26330
Maple Meadow	25865
Maple View	24701
Maplewood	25831
Marfrance	25981
Margaret	26448
Marianna	24818
Marie	24918
Marine	24828
Market	26411
Markwood	26710
Marland Heights (Part of Weirton)	26062
Marlaing Addition	25177
Marlinton	24954
Marlowe	25419
Marmet	25315
Marquess	26444
Marrtown	26101
Marshall	25252
Marshall Terrace	26070
Marshall University (Part of Huntington)‡	25703
Marshville	26332
Martha	25504
Marthatown	25021
Martin	26743
Martinsburg	25401*
	25402†
Martinsburg Mall	25401
Marvel	25812
Marytown	24889
Mason	25260
Masontown	26542
Masonville	26847
Masseyville	25174
Matewan	25678
Matheny	24860
Mathias	26812
Matoaka	24736
Maxine	25049
Maxwell	26170
Maxwell Acres	26041
Maxwelton	24957
Maybeury	24861
Maynor	25801
Maysel	25133
Maysville	26833
Mead	25915
Meadland	26330
Meador	25682
Meadow Bluff	24958
Meadow Bridge	25976
Meadowbrook, *Harrison*	26404
Meadowbrook, *Kanawha*	25311
Meadowbrook (Part of Point Pleasant)	25550
Meadow Creek	25977
Meadowdale	26554
Meadowville	26250
Meadville	26135
Mechanicstown	25414
Mechlenberg Heights	25443
Medina	26164
Medley	26734
Meighen	26039
Melissa	25504
Mellin	26362
Melrose	24712
Melville	25646
Mercers Bottom	25123
Meriden	26416
Merrimac	25661
Metz	26585
Meyerstown	25414
Miami	25134
Micco	25647
Middlebourne	26149
Middle Grave Creek	26041
Middle Run	26623
Middleway	25430
Midkiff	25540
Midland	26241
Midway, *Barbour*	26250
Midway, *Fayette*	25901
Midway, *Mercer*	24701
Midway, *Putnam*	25168
Midway, *Raleigh*	25878
Mifflin	25047
Milam, *Hardy*	26838
Milam, *Wyoming*	25875
Milvuen	25304
Mile Branch	24844
Millard	25276
Millbrook	26711
Mill Creek	26280
Millersville	26554
Millertown	26354
Milliken	25071
Mill Point	24946
Mill Run	26271
Millstone	25261
Milltown	25181
Millville	25432
Millwood	25262
Milo	25235
Milton	25541
Minden	25879
Mineral City	25617
Mineral Wells	26150
Mingo	26294
Minnehaha Springs	24954
Minnie	26155
Minnora	25268
Miracle Run	26570
Missouri Branch	25511
Mitchell Branch	25692
Mitchell Heights	25601
Moatstown	26815
Moatsville	26405
Mobley	26437
Mohawk	24862
Mohegan	24820
Moler Crossroads	25443
Monarch	25039
Monaville	25636
Monclo	25183
Monitor	24976
Monkeytown	26814
Monongah	26554
Montana Mines	26586
Montcalm♦	24737
Montcoal	25140
Monterville	26282
Montgomery	25136
Montgomery Heights	25057
Montpelier (Part of Clarksburg)	26301
Montrose	26283
Moore	26283
Moorefield	26836
Mooresville	26529
Morgan Heights (Part of Westover)	26501
Morgan Hills	25801
Morgansville	26456
Morgantown	26501-08
For specific ZIP Codes call (888) 275-8777, or your local postmaster.	
Morning Star	25276
Morrall Mine	26416
Morristown	26143
Morrisvale	25565
Mossy	25917
Moundsville	26041
Mountain	26407
Mountain Cove	25938
Mountaindale	26525
Mountaineer Mall (Part of Morgantown)	26501
Mountain Mission	25425
Mountain View, *Logan*	25644
Mountain View, *Preston*	26444
Mount Alto	25264
Mount Carbon	25139
Mount Clare	26408
Mount de Chantel (Part of Wheeling)	26003
Mount Echo	26060
Mount Gay	25637
Mount Harmony	26554
Mount Hope, *Fayette*	25880
Mount Hope, *Roane*	25286
Mount Liberty	26416
Mount Lookout	26678
Mount Nebo, *Nicholas*	26679
Mount Nebo, *Preston*	26519
Mount Olive, *Mason*	25503
Mount Olive, *Roane*	25276
Mount Olivet	26003
Mount Pleasant	25446
Mount Storm	26739
Mount Tabor	25801
Mount Vernon, *Preston*	26547
Mount Vernon, *Putnam*	25526
Mountview	25825
Mount Welcome	25286
Mount Zion	26151
Moyers	26815
Mozart (Part of Wheeling)	26003
Mozer	26866
Mud	25565
Muddlety	26651
Mudfork	25235
Mullens	25882
Mullensville	24874
Mullenix Addition	26187
Munday	26152
Murphy	26201
Murphytown	26142
Murraysville	26164
Muses Bottom	26164
Musick	25696
Myra	25544
Myrtle	25670
Nallen	26680
Nancy Run	25276
Naoma	25140
Napier	26631
National	26501
Natrium	26055
Naugatuck	25685
Neal	25530
Nebo, *Clay*	25141
Nebo, *Upshur*	26201
Needmore	26801
Neibert	25632
Nellis	25142
Nelson	25181
Nemours	24738
Neola	24986
Neptune	26164
Nestlow	25512
Nestorville	26405
Nethkin	26726
Nettie	26681
Neville (Part of Beckley)‡	25801
Newark	26143
Newberne	26342
Newburg	26410
New Creek	26743
New Cumberland	26047
Newdale	26155
Newell♦	26050
New England	26181
New Era	25275
Newhall	24866
New Hamlin	25523
New Haven	25265
New Hill, *Marion*	26591
New Hill, *Monongalia*	26527
New Hope	24740
Newlonton	26236
New Manchester	26056
New Martinsville	26155
New Milton	26411
New Richmond	24867
Newton	25266
Newtown, *Fayette*	25901
Newtown, *Mingo*	25686
Newville	26601
Next	26175
Nicolette	26101
Nicut	26636
Nimitz	25978
Nitro	25143
Nitro Park Addition	25143
Nobe	26137
Nolan	25687
Nollville	25401
Normantown	25267
North Berkeley	25411
Northfork	24868
North Hills, *Monongalia*	26505
North Hills, *Wood*	26101
North Matewan	25688
North Mitchell Heights	25601
North Mountain	25427
North Page	25152
North Parkersburg (Part of Parkersburg)	26104
North River Mills	26711
North Spring	24869
North View (Part of Clarksburg)	26301
Norton	26285
Norwood (Part of Fairmont)	26554
Numan	26426
Nuriva (Part of Mullens)	25882
Nursery Gap	25514
Nutter Farm	26137
Nutter Fort	26301
Nutter Fort Stonewood (Part of Nutter Fort)	26301
Nutterville	25981
Oakdale	26582
Oak Flat	26802
Oak Hill	25901
Oakmont, *Mineral*	26717
Oakmont (Part of Wheeling)	26003
Oak Ridge	25840

*** Area Zip Code** **† Post Office Boxes** **‡ Postal Station** **♦ Census Designated Place** *Italic Type* **County**

Oakvale 24739
Oakview Heights 25530
O'Brion 25063
Oceana 24870
Odaville 25275
Odd 25902
Ogden 26184
Ohley 25054
Olcott 25314
Old Arthur 26816
Old Fields 26845
Omar 25638
Omps 25411
Ona 25545
Onego 26886
O'Neil 26301
Oney Gap 24740
Onoto 24954
Opekiska 26501
Oral Lake 26330
Orchard 24918
Orchard Hills 25438
Organ Cave 24970
Orgas 25148
Orient Hill 25958
Orlando 26412
Orleans Cross Roads.. 25422
Orma 25268
Orr 26764
Ortin Heights 25143
Orville 25654
Osage 26543
Osborne 25045
Osbornes Mills 25045
Oscar 24966
O'Toole 24808
Otsego 25882
Ottawa 25149
Otto 25276
Ovapa 25150
Overfield 26416
Owings 26431
Oxford 26456
Packs Branch 25880
Packsville 25209
Pad 25286
Paden City 26159
Page 25152
Pageton 24871
Palace Valley 26224
Palermo 25506
Palestine, *Greenbrier* .. 24910
Palestine, *Wirt* 26160
Pansy 26847
Panther 24872
Paradise 25124
Parchment Valley 25271
Parcoal 26288
Pardee 25630
Parkersburg 26101-04
For specific ZIP Codes call (888) 275-8777, or your local postmaster.
Parkview (Part of Wheeling) 26003
Park View, *Taylor* 26354
Parkway Terrace (Part of St. Albans) 25177
Par Metta Crest 26184
Parsley Bottom 25676
Parsons 26287
Patterson Creek 26753
Paw Paw 25434
Pax 25904
Paynesville 24873
Peach Creek 25639
Pecks Mill 25547
Pecks Run 26201
Peeltree 26238
Peewee 25252
Pemberton 25878
Pence Springs 24962
Peniel 25270
Pennsboro 26415
Pentress 26544
Peora 26431
Pepper 26330
Perkins 26634
Perry 26851
Persinger 26651
Petersburg 26847
Peterson 26423
Peterstown 24963
Petroleum 26161
Pettit Heights 26070
Pettry 24712
Pettry Bottom 25140
Pettus 25209
Pettyville 26101
Peytona 25154

Pharoah 25555
Phico 25508
Philippi 26416
Piatt 25015
Pickaway 24976
Pickens 26230
Pickle Street 26321
Pickshin 25857
Pie 25670
Piedmont, *Mercer* 24736
Piedmont, *Mineral* 26750
Pierce 26292
Pierpont, *Monongalia* .. 26508
Pierpont, *Wyoming* 25870
Pigeon 25164
Pike 26346
Pikeside 25401
Pikeview Acres 25401
Pikeview Acres 25401
Pinch 25156
Pine Bluff 26431
Pine Creek 25625
Pine Grove, *Marion* 26554
Pine Grove, *Wetzel* 26419
Pineknob 25140
Pineville 24874
Piney 26167
Piney View♦ 25906
Pinoak 24733
Pipestem 25979
Pisgah 26525
Pleasant Creek 26416
Pleasant Dale, *Hampshire* 26704
Pleasantdale, *Preston* 26537
Pleasant Hill 26147
Pleasant Home 26133
Pleasant Run 26276
Pleasant Valley, *Hancock* 26062
Pleasant Valley, *Marion* 26554
Pleasant Valley, *Marshall* 26033
Pleasant Valley (Part of Wheeling) 26003
Pleasant View, *Jackson* 26164
Pleasant View, *Lincoln* 25506
Pleasant View, *Marion* 26588
Pleasant View, *Wood* .. 26101
Pleasure Valley 26283
Pliny 25082
Pluto 25951
Poca 25159
Pocatalico 25320
Poe 26675
Point Lick 25306
Point Mills (Part of Valley Grove) 26059
Point Pleasant 25550
Points 25437
Polard 26149
Polemic 26601
Polk Gap 25870
Pondco (Part of Wharton) 25208
Pond Creek 26133
Pond Gap 25160
Pool 26684
Port Amherst 25306
Porters Falls 26162
Porterwood 26283
Porto Rico 26411
Posey 25180
Potomac 16003
Potomac Park 25419
Powell 26554
Powellton 25161
Power 26070
Powhatan 24877
Prairietown 25559
Pratt 25162
Premier 24878
Prenter 25181
Price Hill (Part of Madison) 25130
Price Hill, *Raleigh* 25818
Pricetown, *Lewis* 26452
Pricetown, *Wetzel* 26437
Prichard 25555
Priestly 25003
Prince 25907
Princeton 24740
Princewick 25908
Procious 25164
Proctor 26055
Propstburg 26802
Prospect Valley 26431
Prosperity♦ 25909

Prudence 25840
Pruntytown 26354
Pullman 26421
Pumpkintown 26257
Purgitsville 26852
Puritan Mines 25670
Pursglove 26546
Pursley 26175
Putney 25132
Quaker 25511
Quarrier 25075
Queens 26237
Queen Shoals 25045
Quick 25045
Quiet Dell 26408
Quinland 25205
Quinnimont 25910
Quinwood 25981
Rabbit Hill 26070
Rachel 26587
Racine 25165
Racy 26161
Rada 26852
Radnor 25517
Ragland 25690
Rainelle 25962
Raines Corner 24951
Raleigh 25911
Ramage 25114
Ramp 25985
Ramsey 25912
Rand 25306
Randall 26543
Ranger 25557
Ranson 25438
Raven 26651
Ravencliff 25913
Raven Rock 26170
Ravenswood 26164
Rawl 25691
Rayburn 25550
Raymond City 25159
Raysal 24879
Reader 26167
Ream (Part of Gary) 24836
Reamer 25045
Red Campbell 25076
Red Creek 26289
Red House 25168
Red Jacket♦ 25692
Red Run 26271
Red Spring 25976
Redstar 25914
Red Sulphur Springs .. 24918
Reedson 25442
Reedsville 26547
Reedy 25270
Reedyville 25276
Reeses Mill 26726
Reger 26201
Renick 24966
Renicks Valley 24966
Rensford 25306
Replete 26222
Reynoldsville 26422
Rhodell 25915
Richard 26508
Richardson 25234
Richlands 24901
Richwood 26261
Rider 26385
Ridersville 25411
Ridgedale 26508
Ridge Farms 26588
Ridgeley 26753
Ridgeview, *Boone* 25169
Ridgeview, *Logan* 25637
Ridgeville 26710
Ridgeway 25440
Riffle 26601
Rift 24892
Rig 26836
Rinehart 26448
Ringgold 26508
Rio 26755
Ripley 25271
Ripley Landing 25262
Ripling Waters 25248
Rippon 25441
Rita 25632
Riverbend 25177
Riverdale Acres 25143
Riverlake Estates 25177
Riverside, *Kanawha* 25086
Riverside (Part of Westover) 26501
Riverton 26814
Rivesville 26588
Roach 25504
Roanoke 26423

Roberts 26456
Robertsburg 25123
Robey 26386
Robinette 25607
Robson 25173
Rock 24747
Rock Camp 24951
Rock Castle 25245
Rock Cave 26234
Rock Creek 25174
Rockdale 26070
Rockford 26385
Rock Forge 26508
Rock Gap 25411
Rock Lake 26554
Rock Lake Village (Part of South Charleston) 25309
Rocklick 26033
Rock Oak 26801
Rockport 26169
Rockridge 24873
Rock Run 26456
Rocksdale 25234
Rockton 26623
Rock View 24880
Rockville 25540
Rocky Fork 25312
Rodemer 26764
Roderfield 24881
Rohr 26547
Rolfe 24897
Rollins Branch 24870
Romance 25248
Romines Mills 26385
Romney 26757
Romont 25812
Ronceverte 24970
Ronda 25061
Roneys Point 26059
Rosbys Rock 26041
Rosebud (Part of Clarksburg)‡ 26301*
.... 26302†
Rosebud, *Harrison* 26386
Rosedale, *Fayette* 25901
Rosedale, *Gilmer* 26636
Rosedale, *Monongalia* 26541
Rosemont 26424
Roseville Addition 25177
Rossmore 25636
Rough Run 26866
Round Bottom 26575
Rowlesburg 26425
Roxalana 25259
Ruddle 26807
Rumble 25009
Runa 26679
Rupert 25984
Rush Creek 25276
Rusk 26161
Russelldale 26710
Russellville 26680
Russett 26147
Ruth 25314
Ruthbelle 26519
Ruthdale 25314
Rutherford 26362
Rutledge 25311
Ryanville 26330
Rymer 26582
Sabine 25916
Sabraton (Part of Morgantown)‡ 26505
Sago 26201
St. Albans 25177
St. Clara 26321
St. Cloud 26589
St. George 26290
St. Joe (Part of Albright) 26519
St. Joseph 26055
St. Marys 26170
Salem, *Fayette* 25901
Salem, *Harrison* 26426
Salt Hill 25271
Saltlick Bridge 26627
Saltpetre 25514
Salt Rock 25559
Salt Sulphur Springs .. 24983
Saltwell 26330
Sam Black Church 24931
Sanderson 25045
Sand Fork 26430
Sand Hill, *Marshall* 26003
Sand Hill, *Wood* 26101
Sandlick 24701
Sand Ridge 25274
Sand Run 26201
Sandstone 25985

Sandy 25156
Sandy Huff 24844
Sandy Summit 25252
Sandyville 25275
Sanford 26554
Sanger 25901
Sanoma 26160
Sarah 25559
Sarah Ann 25644
Sardis 26301
Sarton 24983
Sassafras 25287
Sattes (Part of Nitro) 25143
Saulsbury 26150
Saulsville 25876
Saunders 25630
Saxman 26202
Saxon 25180
Scarbro 25917
Scary 25177
Scherr 26726
Schrader 25071
Schultz 26170
Scott Depot 25560
Scrabble 25443
Seaman 25252
Secondcreek 24974
Sedalia 26426
Seebert 24946
Selbyville 26236
Seminole 26361
Seneca 26505
Seneca Rocks 26884
Seng Creek 25209
Servia 25063
Seth 25181
Seven Pines 26582
Shady Brook (Part of Weston) 26452
Shady Spring♦ 25918
Shafer 26290
Shamrock 25614
Shanghai 25427
Shanks 26761
Shannondale 25425
Sharon 25182
Sharon Heights 25621
Sharples 25183
Shegon 25649
Shenandoah Junction 25442
Shepherdstown 25443
Sheridan 25506
Sherman 26173
Sherrard 26003
Sherwood 26456
Shiloh, *Raleigh* 25844
Shiloh, *Tyler* 26146
Shinnston 26431
Shirley 26434
Shively 25508
Shoals 25562
Shock 26638
Short Creek 26058
Short Creek Valley 26003
Short Gap 26726
.... 26753
For specific ZIP Codes call (888) 275-8777, or your local postmaster.
Short Line Junction (Part of Clarksburg) .. 26301
Shrewsbury 25015
Sias 25506
Sidneyville 25271
Sigman 25168
Silver Grove 25425
Silver Hill 26155
Silver Lake 26716
Silverton 26164
Simoda 26814
Simon 24882
Simpson 26435
Sinclair 26405
Sinks Grove 24076
Sir Johns Run 25411
Sissonville 25320
Sistersville 26175
Six 24824
Six Mile 25053
Skeetersville 25442
Skelton 25919
Skygusty 24871
Slab Fork 25920
Slabtown 25621
Slagle 25654
Slanesville 25444
Slate 26143
Slatyfork 26291
Sleepy Creek 25411
Smithburg 26436

Place	ZIP
Smith Crossroads	25411
Smithers	25186
Smithfield	26437
Smithtown	26508
Smithville	26178
Smoke Hole	26866
Smoot	24977
Snider	26537
Snowden	25573
Snow Flake	24936
Snow Hill	25311
Snowshoe	26209
Sod	25564
Sodom	25183
Sophia	25921
South Charleston	25303
South Fork Junction	24883
South Hills (Part of Charleston)	25314
South Hills (Part of Morgantown)	26501
South Madison (Part of Madison)	25130
South Park (Part of Charleston)	25304
South Park, *Lewis*	26378
South Parkersburg (Part of Parkersburg)	26101
Southridge Centre (Part of Charleston)	25309
South Ruffner (Part of Charleston)	25304
Southside	25187
South Side Junction (Part of Thurmond)	25936
South Worthington	26591
Spangler	25160
Spanishburg	25922
Spaulding	25666
Speed	25276
Speedway	24712
Spelter	26438
Spencer	25276
Sprague	25926
Sprattsville	25621
Spread	25043
Sprigg	25561
Spring Creek	24966
Spring Dale, *Fayette*	25986
Springdale, *Ohio*	26003
Springfield	26763
Spring Hill (Part of South Charleston)	25309
Spring Hill Chapel	26301
Springton	24736
Spring Valley	25701
Spruce Valley	25022
Spurlockville	25565
Squire	24884
Stanaford	25927
Standard	25083
Star City	26505
Statler Run	26570
Statts Mills	25279
Stealey (Part of Clarksburg)	26301
Steeles	24844
Steelton (Part of New Martinsville)	26155
Stephenson	25928
Steptown	25674
Stevensburg	26444
Stewart	26101
Stewartstown	26508
Stickney	25140
Stinson	25235
Stirrat	25645
Stohrs Cross Roads	25411
Stollings	25646
Stone Branch	25508
Stonecoal	25674
Stoneville	24834
Stonewall (Part of Charleston)‡	25302
Stonewood	26301
Stonewood Forest (Part of Morgantown)	26501
Stony Bottom	24927
Stony River	26739
Stotesbury	25921
Stotlers Crossroads	25411
Stouts Mills	26430
Stover	25844
Stowe	25607
Strange Creek	26639
Streby	26833
Streeter	25969
Stringtown, *Barbour*	26250
Stringtown, *Marion*	26582
Stringtown, *Roane*	25276
Stumptown	25280
Sugar Camp	26411
Sugar Grove	26815
Sugar Valley, *Pleasants*	26135
Sugar Valley, *Preston*	26525
Sullivan, *Raleigh*	25847
Sullivan, *Randolph*	26241
Sully	26254
Sulphur City	26717
Sulphur Spring	25625
Sumerco	25567
Summerlee	25931
Summers	26456
Summersville	26651
Summit, *Lincoln*	25567
Summit, *Wood*	26101
Summit Park	26301
Summit Point	25446
Sun	25846
Sunbeam	25076
Suncrest (Part of Morgantown)	26505
Suncrest Lake (Part of Morgantown)	26505
Sundial	25140
Sun Flower	25252
Sun Hill	24882
Sunlight	24991
Sunrise	26101
Sunset Acres	26452
Sunset Beach	26508
Sunset Court	25508
Sunshine	26582
Sun Valley (Part of Weirton)	26062
Sun Valley, *Harrison*	26301
Sun Valley, *Kanawha*	25177
Superior	24801
Superior Bottom	25638
Surosa	25678
Surveyor	25932
Sutton	26601
Swandale	25043
Sweeneysburg	25801
Sweet Acres (Part of St. Albans)	25177
Sweetland	25523
Sweet Run	25530
Sweet Springs	24941
Swiss	26690
Switchback	24887
Switzer♦	25647
Sycamore, *Calhoun*	25261
Sycamore, *Harrison*	26301
Sycamore, *Logan*	25625
Sydnor Addition	25694
Sylvester	25193
Table Rock	25813
Tablers	25428
Tacy	26416
Tad	25201
Tague	26623
Talbott	26250
Talcott	24981
Tallmansville	26237
Tamcliff	25621
Tams	25921
Tango	25523
Tanner	26137
Tannery	26836
Taplin	25632
Tappan	26354
Tarico Heights	25413
Tariff	25281
Tate	26623
Tavennersville (Part of Parkersburg)	26101
Taylorville	25670
Teaberry	24901
Teays	25569
Tempa	24910
Ten Mile	26237
Tennerton	26201
Terra Alta	26764
Terry	25864
Tesla	26629
Teter	26238
Teterton	26884
Thacker	25694
Thacker Mines	25694
Thayer	25936
The Mileground	26505
The Y	25275
Thoburn	26554
Thomas	26292
Thompson Heights	25526
Thompson Town	25649
Thornhill	24747
Thornton	26440
Thornwood	24920
Thorpe (Part of Gary)	24888
Three Churches	26757
Threefork Bridge	26374
Three Mile	25071
Thurmond	25936
Thursday	26178
Tichenal	26385
Tidewater	24853
Tilden	25847
Tioga	26691
Tipton	26651
Tolleys	25801
Toll Gate	26415
Tomahawk	25427
Toney	25524
Toney Fork	24870
Topins Grove	26164
Tornado	25202
Trace Junction	25625
Trap Hill	25844
Triadelphia	26059
Tribble	25123
Triplett	25043
Tripp	25669
Triune	26508
Trout	24991
Troy	26443
Troy Town	25649
Trubada	26351
True	25988
Tuckahoe	24986
Tunnelton	26444
Turkey Knob, *Fayette*	25880
Turkey Knob, *Marion*	26591
Turner Douglass	26764
Turnertown	26452
Turtle Creek	25203
Twilight	25204
Twin Branch	24889
Two Lick	26378
Two Mile (Part of Charleston)	25301
Two Run	26160
Tyler	26320
Tyler Heights	25312
Tyler Mountain	25312
Tyrone	26508
Uffington	26508
Uler	25266
Uneeda	25205
Unger	25411
Union	24983
Union Addition	25136
Union City	24844
Union Ridge	25545
Uniontown	26581
United	25075
Upland, *McDowell*	24877
Upland, *Mason*	25503
Upper Addis Run	26362
Upper Glade	26266
Upper Leatherwood	25019
Upper Tract	26866
Upper Whitman	25652
Upton	26570
Ury	25853
Utica	26133
Uvilla	25442
Vadis	26321
Vago	24938
Vale	25976
Valley Bend, *Barbour*	26250
Valley Bend, *Randolph*	26293
Valley Chapel	26452
Valley Fork	25283
Valley Furnace	26405
Valley Grove	26060
Valley Head	26294
Valley Mills (Part of Parkersburg)	26101
Valley Point	26519
Vallscreek	24819
Van	25206
Vanclevesville	25401
Vandalia (Part of Charleston)	25303
Vandalia, *Lewis*	26423
Van Junction	25206
Vanville	25401
Van Voorhis	26508
Varney	25696
Vaucluse	26170
Vaughan	26656
Vegan	26267
Venus (Part of Gary)	24836
Verdunville	25649
Verner	25650
Victor	25938
Victoria	26374
Vienna	26105
Villa	25311
Viola, *Marion*	26554
Viola, *Marshall*	26003
Virginia Heights	25177
Virginia Manor (Part of Morgantown)	26505
Virginville	26035
Viropa	26431
Vivian	24853
Volcano	26180
Volga	26238
Vulcan	25697
Wadestown	26589
Wadeville	26133
Wahoo	26554
Wainville	26206
Waiteville	24984
Waldeck	26452
Walgrove	25071
Walker	26180
Walkersville	26447
Wallace	26448
Wallback	25285
Walnut	25235
Walnut Bottom	26818
Walnut Grove	25414
Walnut Hill	25652
Walton	25286
Wana	26590
Wanda	25076
War	24892
Ward	25039
Warden	25927
Wardensville	26851
War Eagle	24844
Warriormine (Part of War)	24894
Warwood (Part of Wheeling)‡	26003
Washburn	26362
Washington	26181
Washington Lake	26181
Waterloo	25123
Watson (Part of Fairmont)‡	26554
Waverly	26184
Wayne	25570
Wayside	24985
Weaver	26250
Webb	25669
Weberwood (Part of South Charleston)	25303
Webster	26354
Webster Springs	26288
Weircrest (Part of Weirton)	26062
Weirton	26062
Weirton Heights (Part of Weirton)	26062
Welch	24801
Wellford	25045
Wellington Heights	26416
Wellsburg	26070
Wendel	26347
Werner	26250
Werth	26651
Westchester	26554
West Columbia	25287
West Dunbar	25064
West End	26444
West Gilbert (Part of Gilbert)	25621
West Grafton (Part of Grafton)	26354
West Hamlin	25571
West Junction	25206
West Liberty	26074
West Logan	25601
West Milford	26451
Weston	26452
Westover	26501
West Pea Ridge	25705
West Raleigh	25911
West Union	26456
West Van Voorhis	26541
Westview Estates	25526
West Williamson (Part of Williamson)	25661
Weyanoke	24736
Wharncliffe	25651
Wharton	25208
Wheeler	26222
Wheeling	26003
Wheeling Island (Part of Wheeling)	26003
Whipple	25917
Whitby	25823
Whitehall	26554
White Oak, *Raleigh*	25989
White Oak Springs	26764
White Pine	26147
Whites Addition	25653
Whites Creek	25555
White Sulphur Springs	24986
Whitesville	25209
Whitman	25652
Whitman Junction	25652
Whitmer	26296
Whittaker	25083
Wick	26149
Wickham	25871
Widen	25211
Wikel	24945
Wilbur	26320
Wilcoe (Part of Gary)	24895
Wildcat	26376
Wilding	26164
Wiles Hill (Part of Morgantown)	26505
Wiley Ford	26767
Wileyville	26186
Wilkinson	25653
Willard	26431
William	26292
Williamsburg	24991
Williamsburg Colony	25504
Williams Mountain	25181
Williamson	25661
Williamsport	26710
Williamstown	26187
Willis Branch	25880
Willow Bend	24983
Willow Island	26134
Willowton	24740
Wilmore	24844
Wilsie	26641
Wilsonburg	26301
Wilsondale	25699
Wilsontown	26234
Winding Gulf	25823
Windom	24818
Windsor Heights	26075
Windy	26143
Winebrenners Crossroad	25401
Winfield, *Marion*	26554
Winfield, *Putnam*	25213
Wingrove	25917
Winifrede	25214
Winona	25942
Wiseburg	25275
Witcher	25015
Wolfcreek	24993
Wolfe	24751
Wolf Pen	24896
Wolf Run	26033
Wolf Summit	26426
Wood	25123
Woodburn (Part of Morgantown)	26505
Woodland Forest	25213
Woodland Forest	25213
Woodland Park (Part of Parkersburg)	26101
Woodlands	26055
Woodrow	24954
Woodruff	26033
Woodsdale (Part of Wheeling)	26003
Woodville	25572
Woodward Woods (Part of Charleston)	25312
Woosley	24801
Worth	24897
Worthington	26591
Wriston	25840
Wyatt	26463
Wyco	25943
Wymer	26254
Wyoma	25515
Wyoming	24898
Yards	24605
Yates Crossing	25545
Yawkey	25573
Yellow Spring	26865
Yolyn	25654
Youngs Bottom	25071
Youngstown	25840
Yukon	24899
Zela	26651
Zenith	24951
Zigler	26807
Zinnia	26426
Zion	26218

A (Part of Green Bay)‡ 54306
Abbotsford 54405
Abells Corners 53121
Abrams 54101
Ackerville 53086
Ackley (Town) 54409
Ada 53020
Adams, *Adams* (Town) 53934
Adams, *Green* (Town) 53504
Adams, *Jackson* (Town) 54615
Adams, *Adams* 53910
Adams, *Walworth* 53120
Adams Beach 54929
Addison 53002
Adell 53001
Adrian (Town) 54648
Advance 54111
Afton 53501
Agenda (Town) 54514
Ahnapee (Town) 54201
Ainsworth (Town) 54462
Airport Mail Center (Part of Milwaukee)‡ 53237
Akan (Town) 54655
Alaska 54216
Alban (Town) 54473
Albany, *Pepin* (Town) 54755
Albany, *Green* 53502
Albertville 54730
Albion, *Jackson* (Town) 54615
Albion, *Trempealeau* (Town) 54738
Albion, *Dane* 53534
Alden (Town) 54017
Alderley 53066
Algoma, *Winnebago* (Town) 54901
Algoma, *Kewaunee* 54201
Allen 54770
Allens Grove 53114
Allenton 53002
Allenville 54904
Allouez 54301
Alma, *Jackson* (Town) 54611
Alma, *Buffalo* 54610
Alma Center 54611
Almena (Town) 54826
Almena 54805
Almon (Town) 54416
Almond 54909
Alpha 54840
Alto 53919
Altoona 54720
Alvin 54542
Amberg 54102
Amery 54001
Amherst (Town) 54977
Amherst 54406
Amherst Junction 54407
Amnicon (Town) 54874
Amnicon Falls 54874
Anacker 53901
Anderson, *Burnett* (Town) 54840
Anderson, *Iron* (Town) 54565
Angelica 54162
Angelo 54656
Angus 54817
Aniwa (Town) 54414
Aniwa 54408
Annaton 53825
Anson (Town) 54748
Anson 54729
Anston 54301
Anthony 54755
Antigo 54409
Applecreek 54911
Apple River (Town) 54810
Appleton * 54911-15
For specific ZIP Codes call (888) 275-8777, or your local postmaster.
Applewood 53711
Arbor Vitae 54568
Arcade Acres 54971
Arcadia 54612
Arena 53503
Argonne 54511
Argyle 53504
Arkansaw 54721
Arkdale 54613
Arland 54004
Arlington (Town) 53555
Arlington 53911
Armenia (Town) 54646
Armstrong, *Oconto* (Town) 54149
Armstrong, *Fond du Lac* 53079
Armstrong Creek 54103
Arnott 54481
Arpin 54410
Artesia Beach 53049
Arthur, *Chippewa* (Town) 54727
Arthur, *Grant* 53818
Ashford 53010
Ashippun 53003
Ashland (Town) 54846
Ashland 54806
Ash Ridge 54664
Ashton 53562
Ashton Corners 53562
Ashwaubenon 54304
Askeaton 54126
Astico 53925
Athelstane 54104
Athens 54411
Atlanta (Town) 54819
Atlas 54853
Attica 53502
Atwater 53922
Atwood 54460
Auburn, *Chippewa* (Town) 54757
Auburn, *Fond du Lac* (Town) 53040
Auburndale 54412
Auburn Lake 53010
Augusta 54722
Aurora, *Taylor* (Town) 54433
Aurora, *Waushara* (Town) 54923
Aurora, *Florence* 54151
Auroraville 54923
Avalanche 54665
Avalon 53505
Avoca 53506
Avon, *Lafayette* 53530
Avon, *Rock* 53520
Aztalan (Town) 53038
Babcock 54413
Badger Army Ammunition Plant 53913
Bad River Indian Reservation 54806
Bagley, *Oconto* (Town) 54161
Bagley, *Grant* 53801
Baileys Harbor 54202
Bakerville 54449
Baldwin (Town) 54028
Baldwin 54002
Balsam Lake (Town) 54024
Balsam Lake 54810
Bancroft 54921
Bangor (Town) 54653
Bangor 54614
Baraboo (Town) 53951
Baraboo 53913
Barksdale 54806
Barnes (Town) 54873
Barneveld 53507
Barnum 54631
Barre (Town) 54601
Barre Mills 54601
Barron 54812
Barronett, *Washburn* (Town) 54871
Barronett, *Barron* 54813
Barron Junction (Part of Barron) 54812
Bartolme (Town) 54416
Barton (Town) 53090
Barton (Part of West Bend) 53090
Basco 53508
Bashaw, *Washburn* (Town) 54871
Bashaw, *Burnett* 54871
Bass Bay (Part of Muskego) 53150
Bassett 53101
Bass Lake, *Sawyer* (Town) 54843
Bass Lake, *Washburn* (Town) 54875
Basswood 53573
Batavia 53001
Bateman 54729
Bay City 54723
Bayfield 54814
Bay Park Square (Part of Ashwaubenon) 54304
Bay Settlement (Part of Green Bay) 54301
Bay Shore Mall (Part of Glendale) 53217
Bayside 53217
Bayview (Town) 54891
Bay View Saint Francis (Part of Milwaukee)‡ 53207
Beachs Corners 54627
Bear Bluff (Town) 54666
Bear Creek, *Sauk* (Town) 53577
Bear Creek, *Waupaca* (Town) 54922
Bear Creek, *Outagamie* 54922
Bear Lake, *Barron* (Town) 54868
Bear Lake, *Rusk* 54728
Bear Valley 53937
Beaver, *Clark* (Town) 54446
Beaver, *Polk* (Town) 54889
Beaver, *Marinette* 54114
Beaver Brook (Town) 54871
Beaver Dam 53916
Beaver Edge 53916
Beecher 54156
Beecher Lake 54156
Beechwood 53001
Beetown 53802
Beldenville 54003
Belgium 53004
Bell (Town) 54827
Bell Center 54631
Belle Plaine 54166
Belleville 53508
Bellevue 54311
Bell Heights (Part of Appleton) 54911
Bellinger 54771
Bellwood 54820
Belmont, *Lafayette* (Town) 53818
Belmont, *Portage* (Town) 54909
Belmont, *Lafayette* 53510
Beloit (Town) 53511
Beloit 53511*
53512†
Beloit Mall (Part of Beloit) 53511
Belvidere (Town) 54610
Benderville 54301
Benet Lake 53102
Bennett 54873
Benoit 54816
Benton 53803
Bergen, *Marathon* (Town) 54455
Bergen, *Vernon* (Town) 54658
Berlin, *Marathon* (Town) 54401
Berlin, *Green Lake* 54923
Bern (Town) 54411
Berry (Town) 53528
Bethel 54410
Bethesda 53189
Bevent 54440
Big Bend, *Rusk* (Town) 54819
Big Bend, *Waukesha* 53103
Big Falls, *Rusk* (Town) 54848
Big Falls, *Waupaca* 54926
Big Flats (Town) 54613
Big Flats 53934
Big Patch 53818
Big Spring 53965
Billings Park (Part of Superior) 54880
Binghamton 54106
Birch, *Lincoln* (Town) 54442
Birch, *Ashland* 54559
Birch Creek (Town) 54745
Birchwood 54817
Birchwood Lake 53010
Birnamwood 54414
Biron 54494
Black Brook (Town) 54005
Black Creek 54106
Black Earth (Town) 53560
Black Earth 53515
Black Hawk 53588
Black River 53081
Black River Falls 54615
Blackwell 54541
Black Wolf (Town) 54901
Blaine, *Burnett* (Town) 54830
Blaine, *Portage* 54909
Blair 54616
Blanchard (Town) 53516
Blanchardville 53516
Blenker 54415
Bloom (Town) 54639
Bloom City 54617
Bloomer 54724
Bloomfield, *Walworth* (Town) 53128
Bloomfield, *Waushara* (Town) 54965
Bloomingdale 54667
Blooming Grove (Town) 53701
Bloomington (Town) 53810
Bloomington 53804
Bloomville 54435
Blueberry 54854
Blue Mounds (Town) 53572
Blue Mounds 53517
Blue River 53518
Bluff Siding 54629
Bluffview 53913
Boardman 54017
Boaz 53581
Bohners Lake♦ 53105
Bolt 54208
Boltonville 53040
Bonduel 54107
Bone Lake (Town) 54837
Borth 54923
Boscobel 53805
Bosstown 53581
Boulder Junction 54512
Bovina (Town) 54170
Bowers 53121
Bowler 54416
Boyceville 54725
Boyd 54726
Boydtown 53826
Brackett 54742
Bradford (Town) 53505
Bradley, *Lincoln* 54487
Bradley (Part of Milwaukee)‡ 53223-24
For specific ZIP Codes call (888) 275-8777, or your local postmaster.
Branch 54203
Brandon 53919
Branstad 54840
Brant 53014
Brantwood 54513
Braund Addition 54660
Brazeau (Town) 54161
Breed 54174
Briarcrest Estates 53545
Briarton 54162
Briarwood 53575
Brice Prairie♦ 54650
Brickson Park 53558
Bridge Creek (Town) 54722
Bridgeport 53821
Briggsville 53920
Brigham (Town) 53507
Brighton, *Marathon* (Town) 54488
Brighton, *Kenosha* 53139
Brill 54818
Brillion 54110
Bristol, *Dane* (Town) 53590
Bristol, *Kenosha* 53104
Bristow 54665
Brockway (Town) 54615
Brodhead 53520
Brodtville 53801
Brokaw 54417
Brookfield (Town) 53189
Brookfield 53005
53008
53045
For specific ZIP Codes call (888) 275-8777, or your local postmaster.
Brookfield Square (Part of Brookfield) 53005
Brookhaven 54494
Brooklyn, *Green Lake* (Town) 54941
Brooklyn, *Washburn* (Town) 54888
Brooklyn, *Green* 53521
Brooks 53952
Brookside, *Adams* 53910
Brookside, *Oconto* 54101
Brookwood (Part of Madison)‡ 53711
Brothertown 53014
Brown Deer 53209
Browning (Town) 54451
Browns Lake♦ 53105
Brownsville 53006
Browntown 53522
Bruce 54819
Bruemmerville 54201
Brule 54820
Brunswick (Town) 54701
Brushville 54965
Brussels 54204
Bryant 54418
Buchanan (Town) 54911
Buck Creek 53581
Buckhorn Corner 53916
Buckman 54208
Budd 54665
Budsin 54960
Buena Park 53185
Buena Vista, *Portage* (Town) 54467
Buena Vista, *Richland* (Town) 53556
Buena Vista, *Waukesha* 53072
Buffalo, *Buffalo* (Town) 54629
Buffalo, *Marquette* (Town) 53949
Buffalo, *Buffalo* 54622
Buffalo Estates 53949
Bundy 54435
Bunker Hill 53924
Burke 53590
Burkhardt 54016
Burlington 53105
Burnett 53922
Burnett Corners 53922
Burns 54614
Burnside (Town) 54747
Burr Oak 54644
Burton 53820
Busseyville 53534
Butler, *Clark* (Town) 54771
Butler (Part of Wauwatosa) 53213
Butler, *Waukesha* 53007
Butte des Morts 54927
Butternut 54514
Butternut Island 53039
Byrds Creek 53518
Byron (Town) 54618
Byron 53009
Cable 54821
Caddy Vista 53108
Cadiz (Town) 53522
Cadott 54727
Cady (Town) 54027
Cainville 53536
Calamine 53565
Calamus (Town) 53916
Caldwell 53149
Caledonia, *Columbia* (Town) 53901
Caledonia, *Trempealeau* (Town) 54630
Caledonia, *Waupaca* (Town) 54940
Caledonia, *Racine* 53108
Calhoun (Part of New Berlin) 53151
Calumet (Town) 53049
Calumetville 53049
Calvary 53057
Cambria 53923
Cambridge 53523
Cameron, *Wood* (Town) 54449
Cameron, *Barron* 54822
Campbell (Town) 54601
Campbellsport 53010
Camp Douglas 54618
Campia 54868
Camp Lake 53109
Camp Leonard 53558
Canton, *Buffalo* (Town) 54736
Canton, *Barron* 54868
Capitol (Part of Madison)‡ 53703
Capitol Court (Part of Milwaukee) 53216
Carey (Town) 54534
Carlsville 54235
Carlton (Town) 54216
Carnot 54213
Carol Beach Estates 53143
Caroline 54928
Carrollville (Part of Oak Creek) 53154
Carson (Town) 54443
Carter 54566
Cary (Town) 54466
Caryville 54701
Cascade 53011
Casco (Town) 54216
Casco 54205
Casey (Town) 54801
Cashton 54619
Cassel (Town) 54426
Cassian (Town) 54529
Cassville 53806
Castle Rock (Town) 53809
Castle Rock 53569
Caswell (Town) 54511
Cataract 54620
Catawba (Town) 54459
Catawba 54515
Cato 54230
Cavour 54511
Cayuga 54546
Cazenovia 53924
Cecil 54111
Cedar 54559
Cedarburg 53012
Cedar Creek 53095

*** Area Zip Code** **† Post Office Boxes** **‡ Postal Station** **♦ Census Designated Place** *Italic Type* **County**

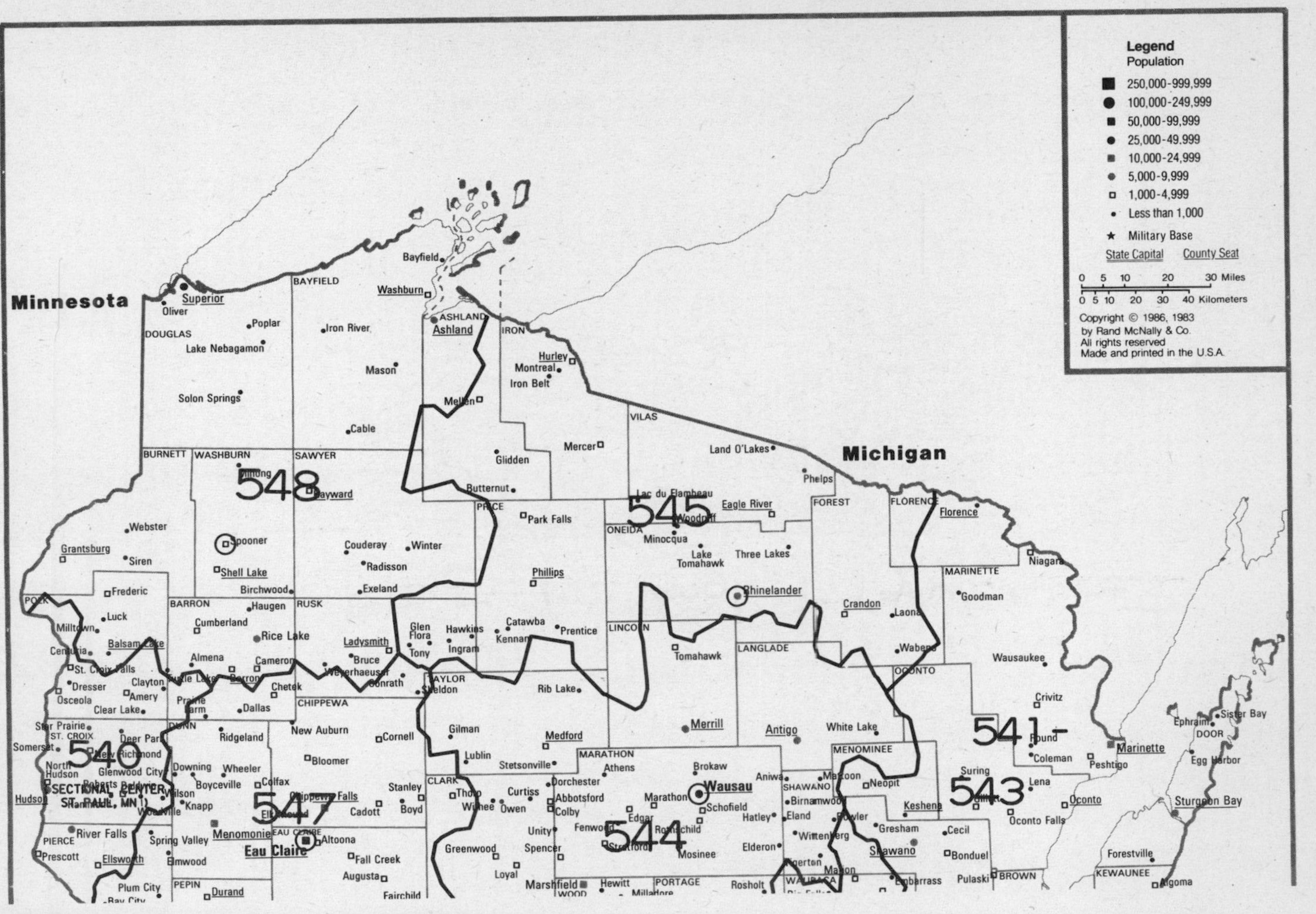

Legend
Population
250,000-999,999
100,000-249,999
50,000-99,999
25,000-49,999
10,000-24,999
5,000-9,999
1,000-4,999
Less than 1,000
Military Base
State Capital
County Seat
0 5 10 20 30 Miles
0 5 10 20 30 40 Kilometers
Copyright © 1986, 1983
by Rand McNally & Co.
All rights reserved
Made and printed in the U.S.A.
Minnesota
Michigan
540
541
543
544
545
547
548
SECTIONAL CENTER ST. PAUL, MN
DOUGLAS
BAYFIELD
ASHLAND
IRON
VILAS
FOREST
FLORENCE
MARINETTE
OCONTO
DOOR
KEWAUNEE
BROWN
SHAWANO
MENOMINEE
LANGLADE
ONEIDA
LINCOLN
MARATHON
PORTAGE
WOOD
TAYLOR
CLARK
PRICE
RUSK
SAWYER
WASHBURN
BURNETT
POLK
BARRON
CHIPPEWA
EAU CLAIRE
DUNN
ST. CROIX
PIERCE
PEPIN
Superior
Oliver
Poplar
Lake Nebagamon
Solon Springs
Iron River
Washburn
Bayfield
Ashland
Mason
Cable
Hayward
Mellen
Hurley
Montreal
Iron Belt
Mercer
Glidden
Butternut
Park Falls
Phillips
Land O'Lakes
Eagle River
Phelps
Three Lakes
Rhinelander
Lac du Flambeau
Woodruff
Minocqua
Lake Tomahawk
Tomahawk
Crandon
Laona
Wabeno
Florence
Goodman
Niagara
Wausaukee
Crivitz
Pound
Coleman
Peshtigo
Marinette
Oconto
Lena
Oconto Falls
Suring
Bonduel
Cecil
Pulaski
Keshena
Neopit
Gresham
Shawano
Embarrass
Wittenberg
Marion
Birnamwood
Eland
Hatley
Elderon
Rosholt
White Lake
Antigo
Aniwa
Merrill
Brokaw
Wausau
Schofield
Rothschild
Mosinee
Marathon
Edgar
Stratford
Athens
Fenwood
Hewitt
Marshfield
Spencer
Unity
Colby
Abbotsford
Dorchester
Stetsonville
Medford
Rib Lake
Prentice
Catawba
Kennan
Hawkins
Ingram
Glen Flora
Tony
Gilman
Lublin
Curtiss
Owen
Withee
Thorp
Loyal
Greenwood
Stanley
Boyd
Cadott
Cornell
Conrath
Ladysmith
Bruce
Weyerhaeuser
Exeland
Radisson
Couderay
Winter
Birchwood
Haugen
Rice Lake
Cameron
Chetek
Dallas
Almena
Cumberland
Shell Lake
Spooner
Webster
Siren
Grantsburg
Frederic
Luck
Balsam Lake
Milltown
Centuria
St. Croix Falls
Dresser
Osceola
Clayton
Amery
Clear Lake
New Auburn
Bloomer
Chippewa Falls
Colfax
Eau Claire
Altoona
Fall Creek
Augusta
Fairchild
Menomonie
Wheeler
Boyceville
Downing
Knapp
Ridgeland
Glenwood City
Deer Park
New Richmond
Star Prairie
Somerset
North Hudson
Hudson
Woodville
Spring Valley
Elmwood
Durand
River Falls
Ellsworth
Prescott
Plum City
Sister Bay
Ephraim
Egg Harbor
Sturgeon Bay
Algoma
Forestville

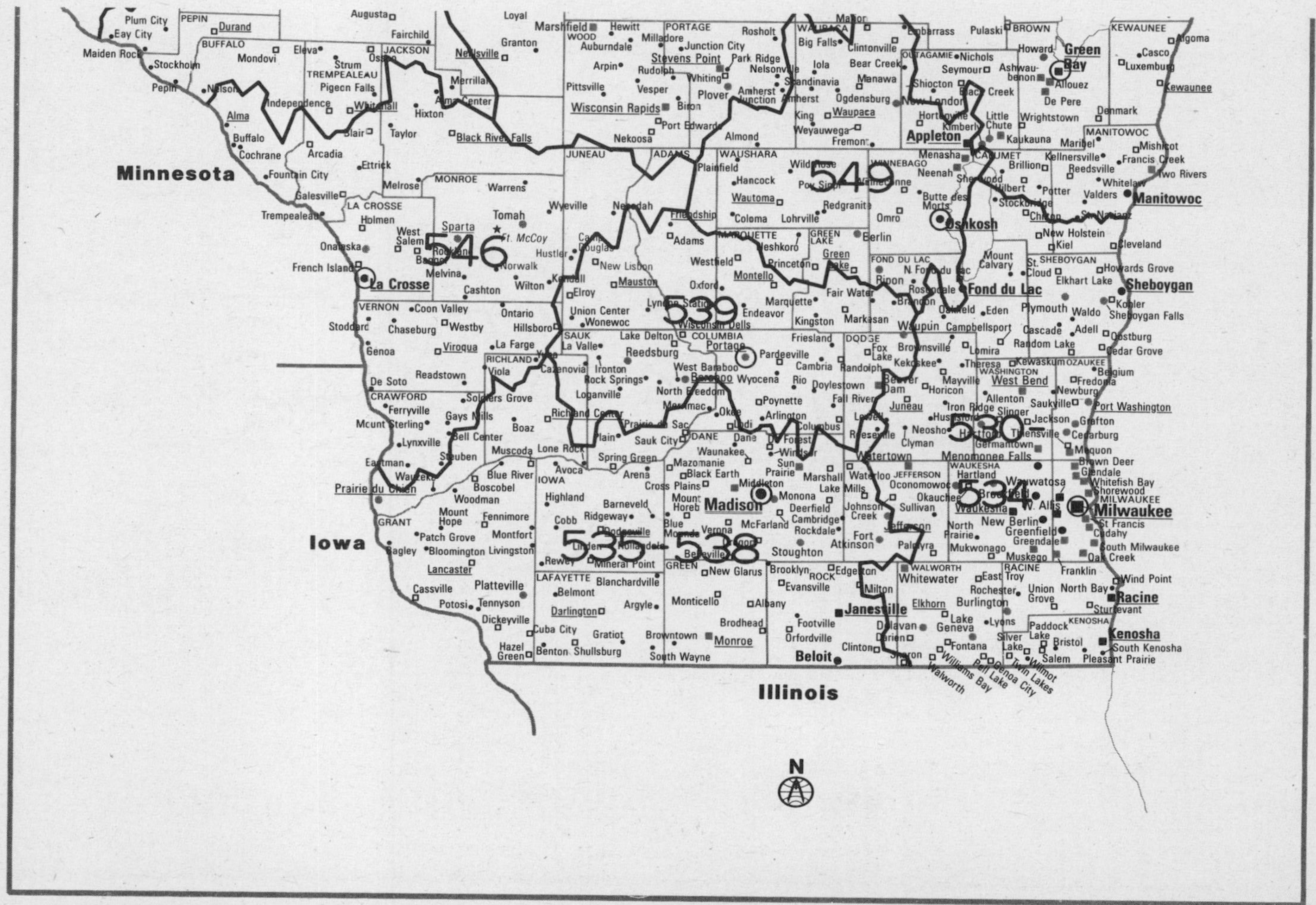
Minnesota
Iowa
Illinois
N
549
539
546
530
534
535
538
Green Bay
Appleton
Oshkosh
Fond du Lac
Sheboygan
Manitowoc
Milwaukee
Racine
Kenosha
Madison
Janesville
Beloit
La Crosse
Stevens Point
Wisconsin Rapids
Portage
Prairie du Chien
Waukesha
West Bend
Watertown
Menomonee Falls
Monroe
Lancaster
Sparta
Tomah
Mauston
Reedsburg
Baraboo
Kewaunee
Two Rivers
Port Washington
Ft. McCoy

Cedar Falls 54751
Cedar Grove 53013
Cedar Lake (Town) 54868
Cedar Rapids (Town) 54526
Center, *Outagamie* (Town) 54911
Center, *Rock* (Town) 53545
Center House 53946
Center Lake Woods 53179
Center Ninety (Part of Onalaska) 54650
Center Valley 54106
Centerville, *Manitowoc* (Town) 53015
Centerville, *Trempealeau* 54630
Central Avenue (Part of Superior) 54880
Central Park (Part of Superior) 54880
Centuria 54824
Chaffey 54836
Chain o' Lakes 54981
Chambers Island 54212
Champion 54229
Chapel Ridge Heights 54301
Charlesburg 53014
Charlestown (Town) 53014
Charlie Bluff 53563
Chase 54171
Chaseburg 54621
Chelsea 54451
Chenequa 53029
Cherokee 54421
Cherrywood 53593
Chester (Town) 53963
Chetek 54728
Chicago Corners 54115
Chicog (Town) 54888
Chili 54420
Chilton 53014
Chimney Rock (Town) 54770
Chippewa (Town) 54514
Chippewa Falls 54729
Chiwaukee 53143
Christiana, *Dane* (Town) 53523
Christiana, *Vernon* (Town) 54667
Christie 54456
Cicero 54165
City Point 54466
Clam Falls 54837
Clam Lake 54517
Clark 54498
Clark Mills 54230
Clarks Point 54986
Clarno 53566
Clay Banks (Town) 54201
Clayton, *Crawford* (Town) 54655
Clayton, *Winnebago* (Town) 54956
Clayton, *Polk* 54004
Clear Creek (Town) 54770
Clearfield (Town) 53950
Clear Lake, *Polk* 54005
Clear Lake, *Rock* 53563
Clearwater Lake 54521
Cleghorn 54738
Cleveland, *Chippewa* (Town) 54732
Cleveland, *Jackson* (Town) 54741
Cleveland, *Marathon* (Town) 54484
Cleveland, *Taylor* (Town) 54433
Cleveland, *Manitowoc* 53015
Clifford 54564
Clifton, *Grant* (Town) 53554
Clifton, *Pierce* (Town) 54022
Clifton, *Monroe* 54618
Clinton, *Barron* (Town) 54805
Clinton, *Vernon* (Town) 54619
Clinton, *Rock* 53525
Clintonville 54929
Clover, *Bayfield* (Town) 54844
Clover, *Manitowoc* 54220
Cloverdale 54646
Cloverland, *Douglas* (Town) 54854
Cloverland, *Vilas* (Town) 54521
Clyde 53506
Clyman (Town) 53039
Clyman 53016
Cobb 53526
Cobban 54732
Cochrane 54622
Coddington 54467
Colburn, *Adams* (Town) 54943
Colburn, *Chippewa* 54726
Colby 54421
Cold Spring 53538
Coleman 54112
Colfax 54730
Colgate 53017
Collins 54207
Coloma 54930
Coloma Corners 54930
Columbia 54456
Columbus 53925
Combined Locks 54113
Commonwealth 54121
Como♦ 53147
Comstock 54826
Concord 53066
Connorsville 54725
Conover 54519
Conrath 54731
Cooks Valley (Town) 54724
Cooksville 53536
Coomer 54837
Coon (Town) 54621
Coon Rock 53503
Coon Valley 54623
Cooperstown (Town) 54227
Cooperstown 54208
Coral City 54773
Corinth 54411
Cormier (Part of Howard) 54301
Cornelia 53818
Cornell 54732
Corning (Town) 54452
Cornucopia 54827
Cottage Grove 53527
Cottonville 53934
Couderay (Town) 54835
Couderay 54828
Country Estates 53105
County Line 54153
Courtland (Town) 53932
Crandon 54520
Cranmoor 54495
Cream 54610
Crescent, *Oneida* (Town) 54501
Crescent, *Chippewa* 54727
Crescent Park 53558
Crestview 53402
Crivitz 54114
Cross (Town) 54629
Cross Lake 60002
Cross Plains 53528
Crystal (Town) 54801
Crystal Lake, *Barron* (Town) 54826
Crystal Lake, *Marquette* (Town) 54960
Crystal Lake Corners 54981
Cuba City 53807
Cudahy 53110
Cumberland 54829
Curran, *Jackson* (Town) 54635
Curran, *Kewaunee* 54208
Curtiss 54422
Cushing 54006
Custer 54423
Cutler (Town) 54618
Cutler 54646
Cylon 54017
Czechville 54629
Dacada 53075
Dairyland 54830
Dakota 54982
Dale 54931
Daleyville 53572
Dallas 54733
Dalton 53926
Danbury 54830
Dancy 54455
Dane (Town) 53555
Dane 53529
Daniels (Town) 54872
Danville 53925
Darboy 54911
Darien (Town) 53115
Darien 53114
Darlington 53530
Davis Corners 53965
Day (Town) 54484
Dayton, *Richland* (Town) 53581
Dayton, *Waupaca* (Town) 54981
Dayton, *Green* 53508
Deansville 53559
Decatur (Town) 53520
Deckers Corner 53012
Decorah Prairie 54630
Dedham 54836
Deerbrook 54424
Deer Creek, *Outagamie* (Town) 54170
Deer Creek, *Taylor* (Town) 54480
Deerfield, *Waushara* (Town) 54943
Deerfield, *Dane* 53531
Deer Park, *Eau Claire* 54742
Deer Park, *St. Croix* 54007
De Forest 53532
Dekorra (Town) 53955
Delafield (Town) 53072
Delafield 53018
Delavan 53115
Delavan Lake♦ 53115
Dell 54667
Dellona (Town) 53965
Dell Prairie (Town) 53965
Dellwood 53927
Delmar (Town) 54726
Delta (Town) 54856
Delton (Town) 53959
Denmark 54208
Denoon (Part of Muskego) 53150
Denzer 53951
De Pere (Town) 54301
De Pere 54115
Deronda 54001
De Soto 54624
Dewey, *Burnett* (Town) 54845
54871
For specific ZIP Codes call (888) 275-8777, or your local postmaster.
Dewey, *Portage* (Town) 54481
Dewey, *Rusk* (Town) 54563
Dewey, *Douglas* 54880
Dewhurst (Town) 54456
Dexter (Town) 54466
Dexterville 54466
Diamond Bluff 54014
Dickeyville 53808
Diefenbach Corners 53086
Dilly 54634
Disco 54615
Dobie 54868
Dodge 54625
Dodges Corners 53149
Dodgeville 53533
Doering 54435
Donald 54433
Dorchester 54425
Doty (Town) 54149
Dotyville 53057
Douglas (Town) 53930
Dousman 53118
Dover, *Buffalo* (Town) 54755
Dover, *Racine* (Town) 53182
Dovre (Town) 54757
Downing 54734
Downing Junction (Part of Downing) 54734
Downsville 54735
Downtown (Part of Green Bay)‡ 54305
Downtown (Part of Oshkosh)‡ 54901
Doyle (Town) 54868
Doylestown 53928
Drammen (Town) 54739
Draper 54896
Dresser 54009
Dr. Martin Luther King, Jr. (Part of Milwaukee)‡ 53212
Drummond 54832
Drywood 54727
Duck Creek (Part of Howard) 54301
Dudley 54435
Dunbar (Town) 54156
Dunbar 54119
Dunbarton 53586
Dundas 54130
Dundee 53010
Dunkirk 53589
Dunn, *Dane* (Town) 53558
Dunn, *Dunn* (Town) 54751
Duplainville 53189
Dupont (Town) 54950
Durand 54736
Durham (Part of Muskego) 53130
Durham Hill (Part of Franklin) 53132
Duvall 54217
Dyckesville 54217
Eagle, *Richland* (Town) 53573
Eagle, *Waukesha* 53119
Eagle Corners 53573
Eagle Lake♦ 53139
Eagle Lake Manor 53139
Eagle Point (Town) 54729
Eagle River 54521
Eagleton 54724
Eagleville 53149
Earl 54875
East Bristol 53925
East Delavan 53115
East Ellsworth (Part of Ellsworth) 54010
East End (Part of Superior)‡ 54880
East Farmington 54020
East Friesland 53956
East Krok 54216
Eastman (Town) 53826
Eastman 54626
Easton, *Marathon* (Town) 54471
Easton, *Adams* 53910
East Side (Part of Madison)‡ 53704
East Towne Mall (Part of Madison) 53704
East Troy 53120
East Waupun 53963
Eastwood 54494
Eaton, *Brown* (Town) 54217
Eaton, *Clark* (Town) 54437
Eaton, *Manitowoc* (Town) 53042
Eau Claire 54701-03
For specific ZIP Codes call (888) 275-8777, or your local postmaster.
Eau Galle (Town) 54028
Eau Galle 54737
Eau Pleine, *Marathon* (Town) 54484
Eau Pleine, *Portage* (Town) 54443
Eden, *Fond du Lac* (Town) 53010
Eden, *Iowa* (Town) 53526
Eden, *Fond du Lac* 53019
Edgar 54426
Edgerton 53534
Edgewater 54834
Edgewood 53072
Edithton Beach 53143
Edmund 53535
Edson 54726
Edwards 53015
Edwards Park (Part of McFarland) 53558
Egg Harbor 54209
Eidsvold 54768
Eileen (Town) 54806
Eisenstein (Town) 54552
Eland 54427
Elba (Town) 53925
Elcho 54428
Elderon (Town) 54440
Elderon 54429
Eldorado 54932
Eleva 54738
Elk (Town) 54555
Elk Creek 54747
Elk Grove 53807
Elkhart Lake 53020
Elkhorn 53121
Elk Mound 54739
Ella 54721
Ellenboro (Town) 53813
Ellington (Town) 54944
Ellis 54481
Ellison Bay 54210
Ellisville 54217
Ellsworth (Town) 54003
Ellsworth 54011
Elm Grove 53122
Elmhurst 54409
Elm Island 53185
Elmore 53010
Elm Tree Corners (Part of Howard) 54301
Elmwood 54740
Elmwood Park 53405
Elmwood Plaza (Part of Racine) 53403
El Paso 54003
Elroy 53929
Elton 54430
Embarrass 54933
Emerald 54012
Emerald Grove 53545
Emery (Town) 54513
Emmet, *Dodge* (Town) 53098
Emmet, *Marathon* (Town) 54426
Empire (Town) 54935
Enchanted Valley Estates 53562
Endeavor 53930
Enterprise 54463
Ephraim 54211
Erdman 53083
Erin, *Washington* (Town) 53027
Erin, *St. Croix* 54017
Erin Prairie (Town) 54002
Esadore Lake 54451
Esdaile 54723
Esofea 54667
Estella (Town) 54732
Ettrick 54627
Eureka, *Polk* (Town) 54024
Eureka, *Winnebago* 54934
Eureka Center 54024
Euren 54205
Evansville 53536
Evergreen, *Langlade* (Town) 54491
Evergreen, *Washburn* (Town) 54801
Excelsior, *Sauk* (Town) 53961
Excelsior, *Richland* 53518
Exeland 54835
Exeter (Town) 53508
Exile 54761
Fahey Heights 53575
Fairbanks (Town) 54486
Fairburn 54923
Fairchild 54741
Fairfield, *Sauk* (Town) 53913
Fairfield, *Rock* 53114
Fairplay 53811
Fairview 54628
Fairview Beach 54901
Fairwater 53931
Fall City 54739
Fall Creek 54742
Fall River 53932
Falun 54840
Fargo 54665
Farmersville 53050
Farmhill 54740
Farmington, *La Crosse* (Town) 54644
Farmington, *Polk* (Town) 54017
Farmington, *Washington* (Town) 53040
Farmington, *Waupaca* (Town) 54981
Farmington, *Jefferson* 53094
Fayette 53530
Fence 54120
Fennimore 53809
Fenwood 54426
Fern (Town) 54121
Ferron Park 54801
Ferryville 54628
Fifield 54524
Fillmore 53021
Finley 54646
Fish Creek 54212
Fisk 54904
Fitchburg 53711
53713
53719
For specific ZIP Codes call (888) 275-8777, or your local postmaster.
Five Corners, *Outagamie* 54911
Five Corners, *Ozaukee* 53012
Five Points 53518
Flambeau, *Price* (Town) 54555
Flambeau, *Rusk* (Town) 54848
Flambeau, *Rusk* 54745
Flintville 54301
Florence 54121
Folsom 54655
Fond du Lac (Town) 54935
Fond du Lac 54935-37
For specific ZIP Codes call (888) 275-8777, or your local postmaster.
Fontana 53125
Fontenoy 54208
Footville 53537
Ford (Town) 54433
Forest, *Fond du Lac* (Town) 54935
Forest, *Richland* (Town) 54664
Forest, *Vernon* (Town) 54639
Forest, *St. Croix* 54012
Forest Junction 54123
Forest Mall (Part of Fond du Lac) 54935
Forestville 54213
Fort Atkinson 53538
Fort McCoy 54656
Fort Winnebago (Town) 53901
Forward 53572

* **Area Zip Code** † **Post Office Boxes** ‡ **Postal Station** ♦ **Census Designated Place** *Italic Type* **County**

Foster, *Clark* (Town) 54493
Foster, *Eau Claire* 54758
Fountain (Town) 53929
Fountain City 54629
Fountain Prairie (Town) 53932
Four Corners, *Burnett* 54837
Four Corners, *Douglas* 54880
Foxboro 54836
Fox Creek 54810
Fox Lake 53933
Fox Point 53217
Fox River 53105
Fox River Mall (Part of Appleton) 54915
Francis Creek 54214
Frankfort, *Marathon* (Town) 54426
Frankfort, *Pepin* (Town) 54721
Franklin, *Kewaunee* (Town) 54216
Franklin, *Manitowoc* (Town) 54230
Franklin, *Sauk* (Town) 53943
Franklin, *Vernon* (Town) 54665
Franklin, *Jackson* 54659
Franklin, *Milwaukee* 53132
Franklin, *Sheboygan* 53073
Franksville 53126
Franzen (Town) 54499
Frazer 54162
Frederic 54837
Fred John (Part of Milwaukee)‡ 53225
Fredonia (Town) 53075
Fredonia 53021
Freedom, *Forest* (Town) 54566
Freedom, *Sauk* (Town) 53951
Freedom, *Outagamie* 54131
Freeman (Town) 54628
Freistadt (Part of Mequon) 53092
Fremont, *Clark* (Town) 54420
Fremont, *Waupaca* 54940
French Island♦ 54601
Frenchville 54627
Friendship, *Fond du Lac* (Town) 54937
Friendship, *Adams* 53934
Friesland 53935
Frog Creek (Town) 54859
Fulton 53534
Fussville (Part of Menomonee Falls) 53051
Gale (Town) 54630
Galesville 54630
Galloway 54432
Garden Valley (Town) 54611
Garden Village 53511
Gardner (Town) 54204
Garfield, *Jackson* (Town) 54758
Garfield, *Polk* (Town) 54001
Garfield, *Portage* 54407
Garnet 53049
Gays Mills 54631
Genesee 53149
Genesee Depot 53127
Geneva (Town) 53121
Genevista 53147
Genoa (Town) 54624
Genoa 54632
Genoa City 53128
Georgetown, *Polk* (Town) 54853
Georgetown, *Price* (Town) 54537
Georgetown, *Grant* 53807
Germania, *Shawano* (Town) 54486
Germania (Part of Montreal) 54550
Germania, *Marquette* 54960
Germantown, *Juneau* (Town) 53948
Germantown, *Washington* (Town) 53076
Germantown, *Washington* 53022
Gibbsville 53070
Gibraltar (Town) 54212
Gibson (Town) 54228
Gilbert 54487
Gile (Part of Montreal) 54525
Gillett 54124
Gillingham 53581
Gills Rock 54210
Gilman, *Pierce* (Town) 54767
Gilman, *Taylor* 54433
Gilmanton 54743
Gingles (Town) 54806
Glasgow 54627
Gleason 54435
Glenbeulah 53023
Glencoe (Town) 54629
Glendale, *Milwaukee* 53211-12
For specific ZIP Codes call (888) 275-8777, or your local postmaster.
Glendale, *Monroe* 54638
Glen Flora 54526
Glen Haven 53810
Glenmore (Town) 54208
Glenwood (Town) 54012
Glenwood City 54013
Glidden 54527
Globe 54456
Goetz (Town) 54727
Goodman 54125
Goodnow 54529
Goodrich (Town) 54451
Goodrich 54411
Gooseville 53075
Gordon, *Ashland* (Town) 54527
Gordon, *Douglas* 54838
Gotham 53540
Grafton 53024
Grand Avenue, The (Part of Milwaukee) 53203
Grand Chute (Town) 54911
Grand Marsh 53936
Grand Rapids (Town) 54494
Grand View 54839
Granite Heights 54401
Grant, *Clark* (Town) 54436
Grant, *Dunn* (Town) 54730
Grant, *Monroe* (Town) 54666
Grant, *Portage* (Town) 54494
Grant, *Rusk* (Town) 54848
Grant, *Shawano* (Town) 54950
Granton 54436
Grantsburg 54840
Gratiot 53541
Gravesville 53014
Green Acres 53121
Green Bay (Town) 54229
Green Bay 54301-24
For specific ZIP Codes call (888) 275-8777, or your local postmaster.
Green Bay Plaza (Part of Green Bay) 54303
Greenbush 53026
Greendale 53129
Greenfield, *La Crosse* (Town) 54623
Greenfield, *Monroe* (Town) 54660
Greenfield, *Sauk* (Town) 53913
Greenfield, *Milwaukee* 53219-21
53228
For specific ZIP Codes call (888) 275-8777, or your local postmaster.
Greenfield Park (Part of Fitchburg) 53711
Green Grove (Town) 54460
Green Lake 54941
Green Lake Terrace 54941
Greenleaf 54126
Greenridge Park 53558
Greenstreet 54227
Green Valley, *Marathon* (Town) 54455
Green Valley, *Shawano* 54127
Greenville 54942
Greenwood, *Taylor* (Town) 54451
Greenwood, *Vernon* (Town) 54634
Greenwood, *Clark* 54437
Gregorville 54201
Grellton 53094
Gresham 54128
Grimms 54230
Grover, *Marinette* (Town) 54157
Grover, *Taylor* (Town) 54451
Grow (Town) 54563
Guenther (Town) 54455
Gull Lake (Town) 54875
Gurney 54559
Hackett (Town) 54555
Hager City 54014
Halder 54455
Hale 54758
Hales Corners 53130
Hallie 54729
Halsey (Town) 54411
Hamburg, *Vernon* (Town) 54621
Hamburg, *Marathon* 54411
Hamilton (Town) 54669
Hammel (Town) 54451
Hammond (Town) 54002
Hammond 54015
Hampden (Town) 53960
Hamples Corners 54911
Hampton (Part of Milwaukee)‡ 53218
Hancock 54943
Haney (Town) 54631
Hannibal 54439
Hanover 53542
Hansen (Town) 54489
Hansonville 54822
Happy Corners 53807
Harbor (Part of Milwaukee)‡ 53204
Harding (Town) 54452
Harmony, *Price* (Town) 54515
Harmony, *Rock* (Town) 53545
Harmony, *Vernon* (Town) 54665
Harmony, *Marinette* 54143
Harmony Grove 53555
Harris (Town) 53949
Harrison, *Calumet* (Town) 54911
Harrison, *Grant* (Town) 53818
Harrison, *Marathon* (Town) 54409
Harrison, *Waupaca* (Town) 54945
Harrison, *Lincoln* 54435
Harrisville 53949
Harshaw 54529
Hartford 53027
Hartland, *Pierce* (Town) 54011
Hartland, *Shawano* (Town) 54107
Hartland, *Waukesha* 53029
Harvey Estates 53589
Hatchville 54751
Hatfield 54754
Hatley 54440
Hauer 54876
Haugen 54841
Haven 53083
Hawkins 54530
Hawthorne 54842
Hayes 54174
Hay River (Town) 54725
Hayton 53014
Hayward 54843
Hazel Green 53811
Hazelhurst 54531
Heafford Junction 54532
Heart Prairie 53190
Hebel 54208
Hebron 53538
Hegg 54627
Helena 53503
Helenville 53137
Helvetia (Town) 54962
Hendren (Town) 54493
Henrietta (Town) 53924
Henrysville 54217
Herbster 54844
Herman, *Dodge* (Town) 53078
Herman, *Shawano* (Town) 54166
Herman, *Sheboygan* (Town) 53085
Herman Center 53050
Herold 54610
Hersey 54027
Hertel 54845
Hewett (Town) 54456
Hewitt, *Marathon* (Town) 54401
Hewitt, *Wood* 54441
Hiawatha Trail Estates 53934
Hickory Corners 54174
Hickory Grove (Town) 53805
Hickory Hill 53593
Hickory Hill Estates 53719
Hickory Meadows 53597
High Bridge 54846
High Cliff 54952
Highland, *Douglas* (Town) 54849
Highland, *Iowa* 53543
Highland Park 53049
Highland Shore 54904
Hika (Part of Cleveland) 53015
Hilbert 54129
Hilbert Junction (Part of Hilbert) 54129
Hiles (Town) 54466
Hiles 54511
Hill (Town) 54459
Hilldale (Part of Madison)‡ 53705
Hilldale Shopping Center (Part of Madison) 53705
Hill Point 53937
Hillsboro (Town) 54638
Hillsboro 54634
Hillsdale 54744
Hillside 53523
Hilltop (Part of Milwaukee)‡ 53205
53233
For specific ZIP Codes call (888) 275-8777, or your local postmaster.
Hines 54874
Hingham 53031
Hintz 54124
Hixon (Town) 54498
Hixton 54635
Hoard (Town) 54422
Hobart (Town) 54303
Hofa Park 54165
Hoffman Corners 54638
Hogarty 54408
Holcombe 54745
Holiday Heights 53934
Holiday Hills 53511
Holland, La Crosse (Town) 54636
Holland, *Sheboygan* (Town) 53070
Holland, *Brown* 54130
Hollandale 53544
Hollister 54491
Holmen 54636
Holton (Town) 54405
Holway (Town) 54451
Holy Cross 53004
Homestead (Town) 54121
Honey Creek, *Sauk* (Town) 53577
Honey Creek, *Walworth* 53138
Honey Lake 53105
Hoopers Mill 53551
Hope 53527
Horicon 53032
Horns Corners 53012
Horse Creek 54026
Hortonia (Town) 54961
Hortonville 54944
Houlton 54082
How (Town) 54174
Howard, *Chippewa* (Town) 54730
Howard, *Brown* 54303
Howards Grove 53083
Hubbard, *Dodge* (Town) 53032
Hubbard, *Rusk* (Town) 54848
Hubbellton 53094
Hub City 53581
Hubertus 53033
Hudson 54016
Hughes (Town) 54820
Hullsburg 53078
Hull, *Marathon* (Town) 54421
Hull, *Portage* (Town) 54481
Humbird 54746
Humboldt (Town) 54217
Humboldt 54229
Hunter (Town) 54843
Hunting 54486
Huntington 54017
Hurley 54534
Huron 54768
Hurricane 53813
Husher 53108
Hustisford (Town) 53039
Hustisford 53034
Hustler 54637
Hutchins (Town) 54414
Hyde 53582
Idlewild 54235
Iduna 54627
Imalone 54819
Independence 54747
Indian Creek 54837
Indianford 53534
Indian Shores 54986
Ingram 54526
Inlet 53115
Ino 54856
Institute 54235
Iola 54945
Irma 54442
Iron Belt 54536
Iron Ridge 53035
Iron River 54847
Ironton (Town) 53959
Ironton 53941
Irving (Town) 54615
Irvington 54751
Isaar 54165
Isabelle (Town) 54723
Island Beach 54901
Island Lake 54757
Island Park 54963
Itasca (Part of Superior) 54880
Ithaca 53581
Ives (Part of Racine) 53404
Ives Grove 53177
Ixonia 53036
Jackson, *Adams* (Town) 53952
Jackson, *Burnett* (Town) 54893
Jackson, *Washington* 53037
Jacksonport 54235
Jacobs (Town) 54527
Jamestown (Town) 53807
Janesville (Town) 53545
Janesville 53545-47
For specific ZIP Codes call (888) 275-8777, or your local postmaster.
Janesville Mall (Part of Janesville) 53545
Jefferson, *Green* (Town) 53550
Jefferson, *Jefferson* (Town) 53137
Jefferson, *Monroe* (Town) 54619
Jefferson, *Vernon* (Town) 54667
Jefferson, *Jefferson* 53549
Jefferson Junction 53549
Jenkynsville 53807
Jennings 54463
Jericho, *Calumet* 53014
Jericho, *Waukesha* 53119
Jewett 54017
Jim Falls 54748
Joel 54001
Johannesburg 54017
John P. Cofrin (Part of Green Bay)‡ 54302*
54308†
Johnsburg 53049
Johnson (Town) 54411
Johnson Creek 53038
Johnsonville 53085
Johnstown, *Polk* (Town) 54889
Johnstown, *Rock* 53505
Johnstown Center 53545
Jonesdale 53565
Jordan, *Green* (Town) 53504
Jordan, *Portage* 54481
Jordan Center 53504
Jordan Lake 53965
Juda 53550
Jump River 54434
Junction City 54443
Juneau, *Dodge* 53039
Juneau (Part of Milwaukee)‡ 53202-03
For specific ZIP Codes call (888) 275-8777, or your local postmaster.
Kaiser 54552
Kansasville 53139
Kaukauna 54130
Keene 54921
Keenville 54901
Kekoskee 53050
Kellner 54494
Kellnersville 54215
Kelly, *Bayfield* (Town) 54856
Kelly, *Marathon* 54476
Kempster 54444
Kendall, *Lafayette* (Town) 53530
Kendall, *Monroe* 54638
Kennan 54537
Kenosha 53140-44
For specific ZIP Codes call (888) 275-8777, or your local postmaster.
Keshena♦ 54135
Keshena Falls 54135
Kettle Moraine Lake 53010
Kewaskum 53040
Kewaunee 54216
Keyeser 53532
Keyesville 53937
Keystone, *Bayfield* (Town) 54806

*** Area Zip Code** **† Post Office Boxes** **‡ Postal Station** **♦ Census Designated Place** *Italic Type* **County**

Keystone, *Chippewa* 54732
Kickapoo (Town) 54652
Kickapoo Center 54664
Kiel 53042
Kieler 53812
Kildare (Town) 53944
Kimball (Town) 54534
Kimberly 54136
King, *Lincoln* (Town) 54487
King, *Waupaca* 54946
Kingsbridge 54241
Kingston, *Green Lake* (Town) 53926
Kingston, *Juneau* (Town) 54641
Kingston, *Green Lake* 53939
Kinnickinnic (Town) 54022
Kirby 54666
Kirchhayn 53012
Klevenville 53572
Klondike 54112
Kloten 53014
Knapp, *Jackson* (Town) 54666
Knapp, *Dunn* 54749
Kneeland 53108
Knellsville 53074
Knight (Town) 54536
Knowles 53048
Knowlton 54455
Knox (Town) 54513
Kodan 54201
Kohler 53044
Kohlsville 53090
Kolberg 54213
Komensky (Town) 54754
Koshkonong, *Jefferson* (Town) 53538
Koshkonong, *Rock* 53538
Kossuth (Town) 54220
Krakow 54137
Kroghville 53594
Krok 54216
Kronenwetter (Town) 54455
Kunesh 54162
Lac Courte Oreilles Indian Reservation 54876
Lac du Flambeau♦ 54538
Lac du Flambeau Indian Reservation 54538
Lac La Belle 53066
La Crosse 54601-03
For specific ZIP Codes call (888) 275-8777, or your local postmaster.
Ladoga 53963
Ladysmith 54848
La Farge 54639
Lafayette, *Chippewa* (Town) 54729
Lafayette, *Monroe* (Town) 54656
Lafayette, *Walworth* (Town) 53121
La Follette (Town) 54872
La Grange, *Monroe* (Town) 54660
La Grange, *Walworth* 53190
Lake, *Marinette* (Town) 54159
Lake, *Price* (Town) 54552
Lake Beulah 53120
Lake Camelot 54475
Lake Church 53004
Lake Como Beach 53147
Lake Delton 53940
Lake Eau Claire 54722
Lake Emily 54407
Lakefield 53024
Lake Five 53017
Lake Geneva 53147
Lake George, *Kenosha* 53104
Lake George, *Oneida* 54501
Lake Hallie 54729
Lake Holcombe (Town) 54745
Lake Ivanhoe 53147
Lake Keesus 53029
Lakeland (Town) 54813
Lake Lorraine 53115
Lake Mills 53551
Lake Nebagamon 54849
Lake Shangrila 60002
Lake Sherwood 54457
Lakeside (Town) 54874
Lake Tomahawk 54539
Laketown (Town) 54006
Lake Wazeecha♦ 54494
Lake Windsor 53598
Lake Wissota♦ 54729
Lakewood 54138
Lamartine 53065
Lamont 53530
Lampson 54888
Lanark (Town) 54981
Lancaster 53813
Land O'Lakes 54540
Landstad 54107
Langes Corners 54208
Langlade (Town) 54465
Langlade 54491
Lannon 53046
Laona 54541
La Pointe 54850
La Prairie (Town) 53545
Lark 54126
Larrabee, *Waupaca* (Town) 54929
Larrabee, *Manitowoc* 54241
Larsen 54947
LaRue 53951
Lasleys Point 54986
Lauderdale 53121
La Valle 53941
LaVerne Dilweg (Part of Green Bay) 54303
Lawrence, *Brown* (Town) 54115
Lawrence, *Rusk* (Town) 54526
Lawrence, *Marquette* 53964
Lawton 54003
Layton Park (Part of Milwaukee)‡ 53215
Lead Mine 53807
Lebanon, *Waupaca* (Town) 54961
Lebanon, *Dodge* 53047
Ledges 53532
Leeds 53571
Leeds Center 53911
Leeman 54170
Leipsig 53916
Leland 53951
Lemington 54835
Lemonweir (Town) 53948
Lena 54139
Lenroot (Town) 54843
Leola (Town) 54921
Leon, *Monroe* (Town) 54646
Leon, *Waushara* (Town) 54965
Leon, *Monroe* 54656
Leonards Point 54904
Leopolis 54948
LeRoy 53048
Leslie 53510
Lessor (Town) 54107
Levis (Town) 54456
Lewis 54851
Lewiston 53965
Leyden 53545
Liberty, *Grant* (Town) 53825
Liberty, *Manitowoc* (Town) 54245
Liberty, *Outagamie* (Town) 54170
Liberty, *Vernon* (Town) 54664
Liberty Grove (Town) 54202
Liberty Pole 54665
Liddell 54729
Lilly Lake 53105
Lily 54491
Lima, *Grant* (Town) 53818
Lima, *Pepin* (Town) 54736
Lima, *Rock* (Town) 53190
Lima, *Sheboygan* (Town) 53085
Lima Center 53190
Lime Ridge 53942
Lincoln, *Adams* (Town) 53964
Lincoln, *Bayfield* (Town) 54856
Lincoln, *Buffalo* (Town) 54610
Lincoln, *Burnett* (Town) 54893
Lincoln, *Eau Claire* (Town) 54722
Lincoln, *Forest* (Town) 54520
Lincoln, *Monroe* (Town) 54666
Lincoln, *Polk* (Town) 54001
Lincoln, *Trempealeau* (Town) 54773
Lincoln, *Vilas* (Town) 54521
Lincoln, *Wood* (Town) 54449
Lincoln, *Kewaunee* 54205
Lind (Town) 54983
Lind Center 54981
Linden (Town) 53565
Linden 53553
Lindina (Town) 53948
Lindsey 54449
Linn (Town) 60034
Linton 53147
Linwood (Town) 54481
Lisbon, *Juneau* (Town) 53950
Lisbon, *Waukesha* (Town) 53089
Little Black 54451
Little Chicago 54448
Little Chute 54140
Little Falls, *Monroe* (Town) 54656
Little Falls, *Polk* 54001
Little Grant (Town) 53813
Little Hope 54981
Little Kohler 53021
Little Prairie 53119
Little Rapids 54115
Little Rice (Town) 54564
Little River (Town) 54153
Little Rose 54484
Little Sturgeon 54235
Little Suamico 54141
Little Wolf (Town) 54949
Livingston 53554
Loddes Mill 53583
Lodi 53555
Loganville 53943
Lohrville 54970
Lombard 54771
Lomira (Town) 53006
Lomira 53048
London 53523
London Square Mall (Part of Eau Claire) 54701
Lone Rock, *Juneau* 54618
Lone Rock, *Richland* 53556
Long Lake, *Washburn* (Town) 54817
Long Lake, *Florence* 54542
Long Lake, *Fond du Lac* 53011
Longwood 54498
Lookout 54755
Loomis 54159
Lorain (Town) 54837
Loretta 54896
Lost Lake 53956
Louisburg 53807
Louis Corners 53042
Lowell (Town) 53579
Lowell 53557
Lower Nemahbin Lake 53066
Lowville (Town) 53955
Loyal 54446
Loyd 53924
Lublin 54447
Lucas (Town) 54751
Luck (Town) 54837
Luck 54853
Ludington 54742
Lugerville 54555
Lund 54769
Lunds 54166
Luxemburg 54217
Lykens 54810
Lymantown 54552
Lyndhurst 54128
Lyndon, *Juneau* (Town) 53944
Lyndon, *Sheboygan* (Town) 53073
Lyndon Station 53944
Lynn 54436
Lynne (Town) 54564
Lynxville 54640
Lyons 53148
McAllister 54177
McCartney 53806
McFarland 53558
Mackford (Town) 53946
McKinley, *Taylor* (Town) 54766
McKinley, *Polk* 54829
Mackville 54911
McMillan (Town) 54449
McNaughton 54543
Madge (Town) 54870
Madison (Town) 53701
Madison 53701-44
For specific ZIP Codes call (888) 275-8777, or your local postmaster.
Madsen 54220
Magenta (Part of Eau Claire) 54701
Magnolia 53536
Maiden Rock 54750
Maine, *Marathon* (Town) 54401
Maine, *Outagamie* (Town) 54170
Mallwood 53534
Malone 53049
Manawa 54949
Manchester, *Jackson* (Town) 54615
Manchester, *Green Lake* 53946
Manitowish 54547
Manitowish Waters 54545
Manitowoc (Town) 54220
Manitowoc 54220*
54221†
Manitowoc Rapids (Part of Manitowoc) 54220
Maple 54854
Maple Bluff 53704
Maple Creek (Town) 54961
Maple Grove, *Barron* (Town) 54744
Maple Grove, *Manitowoc* (Town) 54110
Maple Grove, *Shawano* (Town) 54162
Maple Grove, *Manitowoc* 54230
Maple Heights 53014
Maple Hills 53125
Maplehurst (Town) 54498
Maple Plain (Town) 54829
Mapleton 53066
Maple Valley (Town) 54174
Maplewood 54226
Marathon (Town) 54448
Marathon 54448
Marblehead 53019
Marcellon (Town) 53901
March Rapids 54484
Marengo 54855
Maribel 54227
Marietta (Town) 53805
Marinette 54143
Marion, *Grant* (Town) 53805
Marion, *Juneau* (Town) 53948
Marion, *Waushara* (Town) 54960
Marion, *Waupaca* 54950
Markesan 53946
Marquette (Town) 53946
Marquette 53947
Marshall, *Richland* (Town) 53581
Marshall, *Rusk* (Town) 54731
Marshall, *Dane* 53559
Marshfield, *Fond du Lac* (Town) 53057
Marshfield, *Wood* 54449
Marshland 54629
Martell 54767
Martinsville 53528
Martintown 61089
Marxville 53560
Mary Lake 53597
Marytown 53061
Mason 54856
Mather 54641
Matteson (Town) 54929
Mattoon 54450
Mauston 53948
Maxville 54736
May Corner 54157
Mayfair Mall (Part of Wauwatosa) 53226
Mayfield 53037
Mayville, *Clark* (Town) 54425
Mayville, *Dodge* 53050
Mazomanie 53560
Mead (Town) 54437
Meadowbrook (Town) 54835
Mecan (Town) 53949
Medary (Town) 54650
Medford 54451
Medina, *Dane* (Town) 53559
Medina, *Outagamie* 54951
Meeker (Part of Germantown) 53022
Meeme 53063
Meenon (Town) 54893
Meggers 53061
Mellen 54546
Melnik 54247
Melrose 54642
Melrose Park 54901
Melvina 54619
Memorial Mall (Part of Sheboygan) 53081
Menasha 54952
Menchalville 54230
Menekaunee (Part of Marinette)‡ 54143
Menominee (Town) 54150
Menominee Indian Reservation 54135
Menomonee Falls 53051*
53052†
Menomonie 54751
Menomonie Junction (Part of Menomonie) 54751
Mentor (Town) 54746
Mequon 53097
Mercer 54547
Meridean 54755
Merrill 54452
Merrillan 54754
Merrimac 53561
Merton (Town) 53029
Merton 53056
Meteor (Town) 54835
Metomen (Town) 54971
Metz 54940
Mid-City (Part of Milwaukee)‡ 53208
Middle Inlet 54114
Middle Ridge 54614
Middleton 53562
Middleton Junction 53719
Midway (Part of Allouez) 54301
Midway, *La Crosse* 54650
Mifflin 53580
Mikana 54857
Mikesville 54901
Milan 54411
Milford 53551
Milladore (Town) 54412
Milladore 54454
Millard 53121
Mill Center 54301
Millersville (Part of Howards Grove) 53083
Millhome 53042
Millston 54643
Millstone Heights 53532
Milltown 54858
Millville 53827
Milton, *Buffalo* (Town) 54629
Milton, *Rock* 53563
Milton Junction (Part of Milton) 53563

Milwaukee

53201-34
53237-95
For specific ZIP Codes call (888) 275-8777, or your local postmaster.

Colleges & Universities

Alverno Coll 53234
Cardinal Stritch Coll 53217
Columbia Coll of Nursing 53211
Marquette Univ 53201
Medical Coll of Wisconsin 53226
Milwaukee Institute of Art & Design 53202
Milwaukee School of Engineering 53202
Mount Mary Coll 53222
Univ of Wisconsin 53201
Wisconsin Lutheran Coll 53226

Financial Institutions

Bank One, NA 53202
Firstar Bank, NA 53202
Marshall & Ilsley Bank 53202
Norwest Bank, NA 53202
USBank, NA 53259

Hospitals

Children's Hosp of Wisconsin 53226
Columbia Hosp 53211
Froedtert Memorial Lutheran Hosp 53226
St Francis Hosp 53215
St Joseph's Hosp 53210
St Luke's Med Ctr 53215
St Mary's Hosp 53211
Sinai Samaritan Med Ctr 53233

Hotels/Motels

Grand 53207
Hilton 53203
Hyatt Regency, Downtown 53203
The Pfister 53202

Military Installations

Coast Guard Grp 53207
U S Army Res Ctr Complex 53218
Wisconsin Air Nat Guard, FB6491, General Mitchell International Airport 53207
440th Airlift Wing (AFRES), General Mitchell International Airport 53207

Mindoro 54644
Mineral Point 53565

Place	ZIP
Minnesota Junction	53032
Minocqua	54548
Minong	54859
Mishicot	54228
Mitchell (Town)	53093
Modena	54755
Moeville	54011
Mole Lake	54520
Mole Lake Indian Reservation	54520
Molitor (Town)	54451
Monches	53029
Mondovi	54755
Monico	54501
Monona	53716
Monroe, *Adams* (Town)	54613
Monroe, *Green*	53566
Monroe Center	54613
Montana	54747
Montello	53949
Monterey	53066
Montfort	53569
Monticello, *Lafayette* (Town)	54810
Monticello, *Green*	53570
Montpelier (Town)	54217
Montreal	54550
Montrose (Town)	53508
Moon	54455
Moose Junction	54830
Moquah	54806
Morgan, *Oconto*	54154
Morgan, *Shawano*	54128
Morrison (Town)	54126
Morrison	54126
Morrisonville	53571
Morris Park	53558
Morse (Town)	54546
Morse	54527
Moscow (Town)	53507
Mosel (Town)	53015
Mosinee	54455
Mosling	54124
Moundville (Town)	53930
Mountain	54149
Mount Calvary	53057
Mount Hope	53816
Mount Horeb	53572
Mount Ida	53809
Mount Morris	54982
Mount Pleasant, *Green* (Town)	53502
Mount Pleasant, *Racine* (Town)	53401
Mount Sterling	54645
Mount Tabor	54638
Mount Vernon	53572
Mount Zion	53805
Mukwa (Town)	54961
Mukwonago	53149
Murphy Corner	54130
Murry (Town)	54819
Muscoda	53573
Muskego	53150
Myra	53095
Nabob	53090
Namakagon (Town)	54821
Namur	54204
Naples (Town)	54755
Nasbro	53006
Nasewaupee (Town)	54235
Nashotah	53058
Nashville (Town)	54520
Nasonville	54449
Navarino	54107
Necedah	54646
Neda	53035
Neenah (Town)	54956
Neenah	54956*
	54957†
Neillsville	54456
Nekimi (Town)	54901
Nekoosa	54457
Nelma	49935
Nelson	54756
Nelsonville	54458
Nenno	53002
Neopit♦	54150
Neosho	53059
Nepeuskun (Town)	54971
Neshkoro	54960
Neuern	54217
Neva (Town)	54424
Neva Corners	54424
Newald	54511
New Amsterdam	54636
Newark	53511
New Auburn	54757
New Berlin	53151
Newbold (Town)	54501
Newburg	53060
Newburg Corners	54614
New Centerville	54002
New Chester (Town)	53936
New Denmark (Town)	54208
New Diggings	61075
New Fane	53040
New Franken	54229
New Glarus	53574
New Haven, *Adams* (Town)	53920
New Haven, *Dunn* (Town)	54005
New Holstein (Town)	53061
New Holstein	53061-62
For specific ZIP Codes call (888) 275-8777, or your local postmaster.	
New Hope (Town)	54407
New Lisbon	53950
New London	54961
New Lyme (Town)	54656
New Miner	54646
New Munster	53152
New Odanah	54861
Newport (Town)	53965
New Post♦	54828
New Prospect	53010
New Richmond	54017
New Rome	54457
Newry	54619
Newton, *Marquette* (Town)	53964
Newton, *Manitowoc*	53063
Newton, *Vernon*	54665
Newtonburg	54220
Newville	53534
Niagara (Town)	49870
Niagara	54151
Nichols	54152
Nippersink Manor	53128
Nokomis (Town)	54487
Nora	53531
Norman	54216
Norrie	54414
Norske	54945
North Andover	53810
North Bay, *Door*	54202
North Bay, *Racine*	53402
North Bend	54642
North Branch	54611
North Bristol	53590
North Cape	53126
Northeim	53063
Northfield	54635
North Fond du Lac	54937
North Freedom	53951
North Hudson	54016
North Lake, *Walworth*	53121
North Lake, *Waukesha*	53064
North Lancaster (Town)	53813
Northland	54945
North Leeds	53911
North Lowell	53039
North Menomonie (Part of Menomonie)	54751
North Park	53402
Northport, *Door*	54210
Northport, *Waupaca*	54961
North Prairie	53153
Northridge Mall (Part of Milwaukee)	53223
North Tomah	54660
Northway Mall (Part of Marshfield)	54449
Northwoods Beach	54843
North York	54846
Norton	54730
Norwalk	54648
Norway (Town)	53182
Norway Grove	53532
Norwegian Bay	54940
Norwood (Town)	54409
Nutterville	54401
Nye	54020
Oak Center	53065
Oak Creek	53154
Oakdale	54649
Oakfield	53065
Oak Grove, *Barron* (Town)	54868
Oak Grove, *Pierce* (Town)	54021
Oak Grove, *Dodge*	53039
Oak Hill	53156
Oakland, *Burnett* (Town)	54893
Oakland, *Douglas* (Town)	54874
Oakland	53538
Oakley	53550
Oakridge	53179
Oak Shores	53125
Oakwood (Part of Oak Creek)	53154
Oakwood Mall (Part of Eau Claire)	54703
Oasis (Town)	54966
Oconomowoc (Town)	53069
Oconomowoc	53066
Oconomowoc Lake	53066
Oconto (Town)	54139
Oconto	54153
Oconto Falls	54154
Odanah♦	54861
Ogdensburg	54962
Ogema	54459
Oil City	54648
Ojibwa	54862
Okauchee	53069
Okauchee Lake	53058
Okee	53555
Old Albertville	54730
Old Ashippun	53003
Old Lebanon	53098
Oliver	54880
Olivet	54767
Oma (Town)	54534
Omro (Town)	54901
Omro	54963
Onalaska	54650
Oneida	54155
Oneida Indian Reservation	54155
Ono	54750
Ontario	54651
Oostburg	53070
Orange (Town)	54618
Orange Mill	54618
Oregon	53575
Orfordville	53576
Orienta (Town)	54865
Orihula	54940
Orion	53573
Osborn (Town)	54165
Osceola, *Fond du Lac* (Town)	54010
Osceola, *Polk*	54020
Oshkosh (Town)	54901
Oshkosh	54901-04
For specific ZIP Codes call (888) 275-8777, or your local postmaster.	
Osman	53063
Osseo	54758
Ostrander	54961
Otsego	53925
Ottawa (Town)	53118
Otter Creek, *Dunn* (Town)	54772
Otter Creek, *Eau Claire* (Town)	54722
Oulu (Town)	54847
Ourtown	53085
Owen	54460
Oxbo	54552
Oxford	53952
Pacific (Town)	53954
Packwaukee	53953
Paddock Lake	53168
Padus	54566
Palmyra	53156
Paoli	53508
Pardeeville	53954
Parfreyville	54981
Paris, *Grant* (Town)	53807
Paris, *Kenosha* (Town)	53182
Park Falls	54552
Parkland (Town)	54874
Parklawn (Part of Milwaukee)‡	53216
Park Plaza (Part of Oshkosh)	54902
Park Ridge	54481
Parrish	54435
Patch Grove (Town)	53821
Patch Grove	53817
Patzau	54836
Pearson	54462
Peck (Town)	54424
Pecks Station	53121
Peebles	54935
Peeksville (Town)	54527
Pelican (Town)	54501
Pelican Lake	54463
Pella	54950
Pell Lake♦	53157
Pembine	54156
Pence	54550
Peninsula Center	54202
Pensaukee	54153
Pepin	54759
Peplin	54455
Perkinstown	54451
Perry (Town)	53572
Pershing (Town)	54433
Peru, *Dunn* (Town)	54755
Peru, *Portage*	54407
Peshtigo (Town)	54143
Peshtigo	54157
Petersburg	54631
Petty Acres	53589
Pewaukee	53072
Phantom Lake	53149
Pheasant Branch (Part of Middleton)	53562
Phelps	54554
Phillips	54555
Phipps	54843
Phlox	54464
Piacenza	54486
Pickerel	54465
Pickett	54964
Piehl (Town)	54501
Pierce (Town)	54216
Pigeon (Town)	54773
Pigeon Falls	54760
Pike Lake	54440
Pilsen, *Bayfield* (Town)	54806
Pilsen, *Kewaunee*	54217
Pine Bluff	53528
Pine Creek	54625
Pine Grove, *Portage* (Town)	54921
Pine Grove, *Brown*	54301
Pine Lake, *Oneida* (Town)	54501
Pine Lake, *Iron*	54534
Pine River, *Lincoln* (Town)	54452
Pine River, *Waushara*	54965
Pine Valley (Town)	54456
Pipe	53049
Pipersville	53094
Pittsfield (Town)	54301
Pittsville	54466
Plain	53577
Plainfield	54966
Plainville	53965
Plat	53017
Platteville	53818
Pleasant Prairie	53158
Pleasant Ridge	53533
Pleasant Springs (Town)	53589
Pleasant Valley, *Eau Claire* (Town)	54701
Pleasant Valley, *St. Croix* (Town)	54015
Pleasant Valley, *Vernon*	54658
Pleasant View	54615
Pleasantville	54758
Plover, *Marathon* (Town)	54414
Plover, *Portage*	54467
Plugtown	53805
Plum City	54761
Plum Lake (Town)	54560
Plymouth, *Juneau* (Town)	53929
Plymouth, *Rock* (Town)	53545
Plymouth, *Sheboygan*	53073
Poland	54301
Polar	54418
Polifka Corners	54247
Polk (Town)	53076
Polley	54433
Polonia	54423
Poniatowski	54426
Poplar	54864
Popple Lake	54729
Popple River	54542
Porcupine	54721
Portage	53901
Port Andrew	53518
Port Edwards (Town)	54457
Port Edwards	54469
Porter (Town)	53545
Porterfield	54159
Portland, *Dodge*	53594
Portland, *Monroe*	54619
Port Plaza Mall (Part of Green Bay)	54301
Port Washington	53074
Port Wing	54865
Poskin	54812
Post Lake	54428
Postville	53516
Potawatomi Indian Reservation	54520
Potosi	53820
Potter	54160
Potter Lake♦	53120
Potts Corners	54639
Pound (Town)	54139
Pound	54161
Powell	54547
Powers Lake♦	53159
Poygan (Town)	54963
Poynette	53955
Poy Sippi	54967
Praag	54610
Prairie Corners	53807
Prairie du Chien	53821
Prairie du Sac (Town)	53583
Prairie du Sac	53578
Prairie Farm	54762
Prairie Lake (Town)	54728
Pray	54466
Preble (Part of Green Bay)	54302
Prentice	54556
Prescott	54021
Presque Isle	54557
Preston, *Adams* (Town)	53934
Preston, *Trempealeau* (Town)	54616
Preston, *Grant*	53809
Price, *Langlade* (Town)	54418
Price, *Jackson*	54741
Primrose (Town)	53593
Princeton	54968
Prospect (Part of New Berlin)	53151
Pukwana Beach	53049
Pulaski, *Iowa* (Town)	53506
Pulaski, *Brown*	54162
Pulcifer	54124
Purdy	54665
Quarry	54230
Quincy (Town)	53910
Quincy Details	53934
Quinney	53014
Racine	53401-08
For specific ZIP Codes call (888) 275-8777, or your local postmaster.	
Radisson	54867
Randall, *Kenosha* (Town)	60071
Randall, *Burnett*	54840
Randolph, *Columbia* (Town)	53923
Randolph, *Dodge*	53956
Random Lake	53075
Range	54001
Rankin	54201
Rantoul (Town)	53014
Rattman Heights	53701
Ravenoaks	53575
Rawson (Part of Oak Creek)	53172
Raymond	53126
Readfield	54969
Readstown	54652
Red Banks	54940
Red Cedar (Town)	54751
Red Cliff	54814
Red Cliff Indian Reservation	54806
Redgranite	54970
Red Mound	54624
Red River, *Kewaunee* (Town)	54205
Red River, *Shawano*	54166
Red Springs (Town)	54128
Redville	54498
Reedsburg	53959
Reedsville	54230
Reeseville	53579
Reeve	54004
Regency Mall (Part of Racine)	53406
Reid (Town)	54440
Reighmoor	54963
Remington (Town)	54413
Reseburg (Town)	54437
Reserve	54876
Retreat	54624
Rewey	53580
Rhine	53020
Rhinelander	54501
Rib Falls	54426
Rib Lake	54470
Rib Mountain (Town)	54401
Rice Lake	54868
Richardson	54004
Richfield, *Adams* (Town)	53934
Richfield, *Wood* (Town)	54449
Richfield, *Washington*	53076
Richford	54930
Richland, *Richland* (Town)	53581

*** Area Zip Code** **† Post Office Boxes** **‡ Postal Station** **♦ Census Designated Place** *Italic Type* **County**

Place	ZIP Code
Richland, *Rusk* (Town)	54526
Richland Center	53581
Richmond, *St. Croix* (Town)	54017
Richmond, *Shawano* (Town)	54166
Richmond, *Walworth*	53115
Richwood, *Richland* (Town)	53518
Richwood, *Dodge*	53098
Ridgeland	54763
Ridgeville (Town)	54648
Ridgeway	53582
Rief's Mills	54247
Rietbrock (Town)	54411
Rileys	53593
Rileys Point	54235
Ringle	54471
Rio	53960
Rio Creek	54201
Riplinger	54479
Ripon	54971
Rising Sun	54628
River Falls	54022
River Hills	53209
	53217
For specific ZIP Codes call (888) 275-8777, or your local postmaster.	
Rivermoor	54963
Riverside	53541
Riverview (Town)	54149
Riverwood	54613
River Wood Estates	53589
Roberts	54023
Robinson	53147
Rochester (Town)	53105
Rochester	53167
Rock, *Rock* (Town)	53545
Rock, *Wood* (Town)	54466
Rockbridge	53581
Rock Creek (Town)	54755
Rockdale	53523
Rock Elm	54740
Rock Falls, *Lincoln* (Town)	54442
Rock Falls, *Dunn*	54764
Rockfield	53022
Rock Lake	53179
Rockland, *Brown* (Town)	54115
Rockland, *Manitowoc* (Town)	54207
Rockland, *La Crosse*	54653
Rock Springs	53961
Rockton	54639
Rockville, *Grant*	53820
Rockville, *Manitowoc*	53042
Rockwood	54220
Rocky Run	54481
Rodell	54722
Rogersville	54974
Rolling (Town)	54409
Rolling Acres	53589
Rolling Ground	54655
Rolling Prairie	53039
Rolling View	53589
Romance	54632
Rome, *Adams* (Town)	54457
Rome, *Jefferson*	53178
Roosevelt, *Burnett* (Town)	54813
Roosevelt, *Taylor* (Town)	54447
Roosevelt, *Oneida*	54501
Root River (Part of Milwaukee)	53227
Rose (Town)	54984
Rosecrans	54227
Rose Lawn	54165
Rosemere (Part of Manitowoc)	54220
Rosendale (Town)	54964
Rosendale	54974
Rosholt	54473
Rosiere	54205
Ross, *Forest* (Town)	54511
Ross, *Vernon*	54665
Ross D. Sills	53125
Rostok	54216
Rothschild	54474
Round Lake (Town)	54843
Rowleys Bay	54210
Roxbury	53583
Royalton	54975
Rozellville	54484
Rubicon	53078
Ruby (Town)	54745
Rudolph	54475
Rural	54981
Rushford (Town)	54963
Rush Lake	54971
Rush River (Town)	54002
Rusk, *Burnett* (Town)	54801
Rusk, *Rusk* (Town)	54728
Rusk, *Dunn*	54751
Russell, *Bayfield* (Town)	54814
Russell, *Lincoln* (Town)	54435
Russell, *Sheboygan* (Town)	53079
Russell, *Trempealeau*	54747
Rutland (Town)	53589
Sabin	53581
St. Anna	53061
St. Anthony	53002
St. Cloud	53079
St. Croix Falls (Town)	54824
St. Croix Falls	54024
St. Croix Indian Reservation	54830
St. Francis	53235
Saint George	53085
St. Germain	54558
St. John	54129
St. Joseph, *St. Croix* (Town)	54016
St. Joseph, *Fond du Lac*	53079
St. Joseph, *La Crosse*	54601
St. Kilian	53010
St. Lawrence (Town)	54962
St. Lawrence	53027
St. Marie (Town)	54968
St. Martins (Part of Franklin)	53132
St. Marys	54619
St. Michaels	53040
St. Nazianz	54232
St. Peter	53049
St. Wendel (Part of Cleveland)	53015
Salem, *Pierce* (Town)	54750
Salem, *Kenosha*	53168
Salem Oaks	53168
Salvatorian Center (Part of New Holstein)‡	53062
Sampson, *Chippewa* (Town)	54757
Sampson, *Oconto*	54171
Sanborn (Town)	54861
Sanborn	54806
Sand Bay, *Bayfield*	54814
Sand Bay, *Door*	54235
Sand Creek	54765
Sand Lake, *Burnett* (Town)	54893
Sand Lake, *Sawyer* (Town)	54876
Sandlake, *Polk*	54009
Sand Prairie	53518
Sandusky	53937
Saratoga (Town)	54494
Sarona	54870
Sauk City	53583
Saukville (Town)	53074
Saukville	53080
Saxeville	54976
Saxon	54559
Saylesville, *Dodge*	53078
Saylesville, *Waukesha*	53189
Sayner	54560
Scandinavia	54977
Scarboro	54217
Schleswig (Town)	53042
Schley (Town)	54452
Schnappsville	54411
Schoepke (Town)	54463
Schofield	54476
School Hill	53042
Schraven Circle	54937
Scott, *Brown* (Town)	54229
Scott, *Burnett* (Town)	54893
Scott, *Columbia* (Town)	53923
Scott, *Crawford* (Town)	53518
Scott, *Lincoln* (Town)	54452
Scott, *Monroe* (Town)	54666
Scott, *Sheboygan* (Town)	53001
Sechlerville	54635
Seeleys	54843
Seif (Town)	54456
Seneca, *Green Lake* (Town)	54923
Seneca, *Shawano* (Town)	54978
Seneca, *Wood* (Town)	54494
Seneca, *Crawford*	54654
Sequoia (Part of Milwaukee)‡	53223-24
For specific ZIP Codes call (888) 275-8777, or your local postmaster.	
Sevastopol (Town)	54235
Seven Mile Creek (Town)	53944
Sextonville	53584
Seymour, *Eau Claire* (Town)	54701
Seymour, *Lafayette* (Town)	53586
Seymour, *Outagamie*	54165
Shamrock	54615
Shanagolden	54527
Shantytown	54473
Sharon, *Portage* (Town)	54473
Sharon, *Walworth*	53585
Shawano	54166
Shawano North Beach	54166
Sheboygan (Town)	53081
Sheboygan	53081-83
For specific ZIP Codes call (888) 275-8777, or your local postmaster.	
Sheboygan Falls	53085
Sheil	53575
Shelby (Town)	54601
Sheldon, *Monroe* (Town)	54651
Sheldon, *Rusk*	54766
Shell Lake	54871
Shennington	54618
Shepley	54499
Sheridan, *Dunn* (Town)	54725
Sheridan, *Waupaca*	54981
Sherman, *Clark* (Town)	54479
Sherman, *Dunn* (Town)	54751
Sherman, *Iron* (Town)	54552
Sherman, *Sheboygan* (Town)	53075
Sherman Center	53075
Sherry	54454
Sherwood, *Clark* (Town)	54466
Sherwood, *Calumet*	54169
Shields, *Dodge* (Town)	53098
Shields, *Marquette* (Town)	53949
Shiocton	54170
Shirley	54115
Shopiere	53511
Shoreview	53179
Shorewood	53211
Shorewood Hills	53705
Shortville	54456
Shoto	54241
Shullsburg	53586
Sidney	54456
Sigel, *Chippewa* (Town)	54727
Sigel, *Wood* (Town)	54494
Silica	53049
Silver Cliff (Town)	54104
Silver Creek	53075
Silver Lake, *Kenosha*	53170
Silver Lake, *Walworth*	53121
Silver Lake, *Waushara*	54982
Sinsinawa	53824
Sioux	54891
Sioux Creek (Town)	54728
Siren	54872
Sister Bay	54234
Skanawan (Town)	54442
Slab City	54107
Slabtown	53549
Slades Corner	53105
Slinger	53086
Slovan	54205
Smelser (Town)	53807
Sobieski	54171
Sobieski Corners	54141
Soldiers Grove	54655
Solon Springs	54873
Somers	53171
Somerset (Town)	55082
Somerset	54025
Somo (Town)	54564
Soperton	54566
South Beaver Dam	53916
South Byron	53006
South Chase	54162
South Chippewa (Part of Chippewa Falls)	54729
South Fork (Town)	54530
Southgate Mall (Part of Milwaukee)	53215
South Itasca (Part of Superior)	54880
South Janesville (Part of Janesville)	53545
South Kenosha	53143
South Lancaster (Town)	53813
South Luxemburg (Part of Luxemburg)	54217
South Milwaukee	53172
South Necedah (Part of Necedah)	54646
South Randolph	53956
South Range	54874
Southridge Mall (Part of Greendale)	53129
South Side (Part of Madison)‡	53715*
	53725†
South Wayne	53587
Sparta	54656
Spaulding	54466
Spencer	54479
Spider Lake (Town)	54843
Spirit	54513
Spirit Falls	54564
Split Rock	54486
Spokeville	54479
Spooner	54801
Sprague	54646
Spread Eagle	54121
Spring Bluff	54930
Spring Brook, *Dunn* (Town)	54751
Springbrook, *Washburn*	54875
Springdale (Town)	53593
Springfield, *Dane* (Town)	53528
Springfield, *Jackson* (Town)	54659
Springfield, *Marquette* (Town)	53964
Springfield, *St. Croix* (Town)	54013
Springfield, *Walworth*	53176
Springfield Corners	53529
Spring Green	53588
Spring Grove (Town)	53550
Spring Hill Edition	53589
Spring Lake, *Pierce* (Town)	54767
Spring Lake, *Waushara*	54960
Spring Prairie	53121
Springstead	54552
Springvale, *Columbia* (Town)	53960
Springvale, *Fond du Lac* (Town)	54974
Spring Valley, *Rock* (Town)	53576
Spring Valley, *Manitowoc*	53063
Spring Valley, *Pierce*	54767
Springville, *Adams* (Town)	53965
Springville, *Vernon*	54665
Springwater (Town)	54984
Spruce	54139
Stanbery	54875
Standart	53533
Stanfold (Town)	54812
Stangelville	54208
Stanley, *Barron* (Town)	54822
Stanley, *Chippewa*	54768
Stanton, *Dunn* (Town)	54725
Stanton, *St. Croix* (Town)	54017
Stark (Town)	54639
Starks	54501
Star Lake	54561
Star Prairie (Town)	54025
Star Prairie	54026
Star Valley	54655
Starview Heights	53545
State Line	53142
State Street (Part of Racine)‡	53404
Steffenrud Addition	54656
Stella (Town)	54501
Stephenson (Town)	54114
Stephenson Island (Part of Marinette)	54143
Stephensville	54944
Sterling, *Polk* (Town)	54006
Sterling, *Vernon* (Town)	54624
Stetsonville	54480
Stettin (Town)	54401
Steuben	54657
Stevens Point	54481
Stevenstown	54636
Stiles	54139
Stiles Junction	54139
Stinnett (Town)	54875
Stitzer	53825
Stockbridge (Town)	53014
Stockbridge	53088
Stockbridge Indian Reservation	54416
Stockholm	54769
Stockton	54481
Stoddard	54658
Stonebank	53066
Stone Lake	54876
Stoughton	53589
Strader	54722
Stratford	54484
Strickland (Town)	54895
Strongs Prairie (Town)	54613
Strum	54770
Stubbs (Town)	54819
Sturgeon Bay	54235
Sturtevant	53177
Suamico	54173
Sugar Bush, *Brown*	54217
Sugar Bush, *Outagamie*	54961
Sugar Camp	54501
Sugar Creek (Town)	53121
Sugar Grove	54655
Sugar Island	53098
Sullivan (Town)	53549
Sullivan	53178
Summit, *Douglas* (Town)	54836
Summit, *Juneau* (Town)	53948
Summit, *Langlade* (Town)	54435
Summit, *Waukesha* (Town)	53058
Summit Corners	53066
Summit Lake	54485
Sumner, *Barron* (Town)	54868
Sumner, *Jefferson* (Town)	53538
Sumner, *Trempealeau* (Town)	54758
Sumner, *Barron*	54822
Sumpter (Town)	53951
Sunburst	53701
Sun Prairie (Town)	53559
Sun Prairie	53590
Sunset	54401
Sunset Beach	53916
Superior (Town)	54880
Superior	54880
Superior (Village)	54880
Suring	54174
Sussex	53089
Swiss (Town)	54830
Sylvan	54664
Sylvania	53177
Sylvester (Town)	53550
Symco	54949
Tabor	53404
Taegesville	54401
Taft (Town)	54771
Tainter (Town)	54730
Tamarack	54612
Tarrant	54736
Taus	54230
Taycheedah	54935
Taylor	54659
Teegarden	54751
Tell	54610
Tennyson	53820
Terrace Park	53532
Tess Corners (Part of Muskego)	53130
Teutonia (Part of Milwaukee)‡	53206
Texas (Town)	54401
Theresa (Town)	53050
Theresa	53091
Thiensville	53092
Thiry Daems	54217
Thompson	53027
Thompsonville	53126
Thornapple (Town)	54819
Thornton	54166
Thorp (Town)	54768
Thorp	54771
Three Lakes	54562
Tibbets	53121
Tichigan Lake	53185
Tiffany, *Dunn* (Town)	54725
Tiffany, *Rock*	53511
Tigerton	54486
Tilden	54729
Tilleda	54978
Tipler	49935
Tisch Mills	54240
Token Creek	53532

Tomah 54660
Tomahawk 54487
Tonet 54217
Tony 54563
Towerville 54655
Townsend 54175
Trade Lake 54837
Trade River 54840
Trego 54888
Trempealeau 54661
Trenton, *Dodge* (Town) 53916
Trenton, *Pierce* (Town) 54014
Trenton, *Washington* (Town) 53095
Trevor 53179
Tri City (Part of Oak Creek)‡ 53154
Trimbelle 54011
Tripoli 54564
Tripp (Town) 54847
Troy, *St. Croix* (Town) 54022
Troy, *Sauk* (Town) 53583
Troy, *Walworth* (Town) 53120
Troy, *Walworth* 53121
Troy Center 53120
True (Town) 54526
Truesdell 53142
Truman 53530
Trusler Circle 53575
Tuckaway (Part of Milwaukee) 53221
Tuleta Hills 53946
Tunnel City 54662
Turtle (Town) 53511
Turtle Lake, *Barron* (Town) 54004
Turtle Lake, *Barron* 54889
Turtle Lake, *Walworth* 53115
Tustin 54940
Twelfth Street Junction (Part of Superior) 54880
Twelve Corners 54106
Twenty-Eighth Street Junction (Part of Superior) 54880
Twin Bluffs 53581
Twin Grove 53550
Twin Lakes 53181
Two Creeks 54241
Two Rivers 54241
Ubet 54009
Underhill 54124
Union, *Burnett* (Town) 54830
Union, *Door* (Town) 54204
Union, *Eau Claire* (Town) 54701
Union, *Pierce* (Town) 54750
Union, *Vernon* (Town) 54634
Union, *Waupaca* (Town) 54949
Union, *Grant* 53818
Union, *Rock* 53536
Union Center 53962
Union Church 53126
Union Grove 53182
Unity, *Clark* (Town) 54488
Unity, *Trempealeau* (Town) 54770
Unity, *Marathon* 54488
University (Part of Madison)‡ 53715
Upham (Town) 54485
Upper Third Street (Part of Milwaukee)‡ 53212
Upson 54565
Uptown (Part of Racine) 53403
Urne 54736
Utica, *Crawford* (Town) 54655
Utica, *Winnebago* (Town) 54964
Utica, *Dane* 53523
Utica, *Waukesha* 53066
Valders 54245
Valley 54639
Valley Junction 54660
Valley View Mall (Part of La Crosse) 54601
Valmy 54235
Valton 53968
Van Buskirk 54534
Vance Creek (Town) 54868
Vandenbroek (Town) 54130
Vandyne 54979
Vaudreuil 54615
Veedum 54466
Vermont (Town) 53515
Vernon (Town) 53103
Verona 53593
Vesper 54489
Veterans Administration Hospital (Part of Shorewood Hills)‡ 53705
Victory 54624
Vienna (Town) 53532
Vignes 54235
Vilas, *Langlade* (Town) 54424
Vilas, *Dane* 53527
Villard (Part of Milwaukee)‡ 53209
Vineyard 53575
Vinland (Town) 54901
Viola 54664
Viroqua 54665
Voltz Lake 53179
Wabeno 54566
Wagner (Town) 54177
Waino 54820
Waldo 53093
Waldwick 53565
Wales 53183
Walhain 54217
Walsh 54159
Walworth 53184
Wandawega 53121
Wanderoos 54001
Warner (Town) 54437
Warren, *St. Croix* (Town) 54023
Warren, *Waushara* (Town) 54923
Warrens 54666
Warrentown 54750
Wascott 54890
Washburn, *Clark* (Town) 54456
Washburn, *Bayfield* 54891
Washington, *Door* (Town) 54246
Washington, *Eau Claire* (Town) 54742
Washington, *Green* (Town) 53570
Washington, *La Crosse* (Town) 54619
Washington, *Rusk* (Town) 54819
Washington, *Sauk* (Town) 53937
Washington, *Shawano* (Town) 54107
Washington, *Vilas* (Town) 54521
Washington Island 54246
Waterford 53185
Waterford Woods 53185
Waterloo, *Grant* (Town) 53820
Waterloo, *Jefferson* (Town) 53551
Waterloo, *Jefferson* 53594
Watertown (Town) 53094
Watertown 53094
.... 53098
For specific ZIP Codes call (888) 275-8777, or your local postmaster.
Waterville, *Pepin* (Town) 54721
Waterville, *Waukesha* 53066
Watterstown (Town) 53805
Waubeek (Town) 54736
Waubeesee 53185
Waubeka 53021
Waubesa Heights 53558
Waucousta 53010
Waukau 54980
Waukechon (Town) 54166
Waukesha (Town) 53189
Waukesha 53186-89
For specific ZIP Codes call (888) 275-8777, or your local postmaster.
Waumandee 54622
Waunakee 53597
Waupaca 54981
Waupun, *Fond du Lac* (Town) 53963
Waupun, *Dodge* 53963
Wausau (Town) 54401
Wausau 54401-03
For specific ZIP Codes call (888) 275-8777, or your local postmaster.
Wausau Center (Part of Wausau) 54401
Wausaukee 54177
Wautoma 54982
Wauwatosa 53210
.... 53213
.... 53222
.... 53226
For specific ZIP Codes call (888) 275-8777, or your local postmaster.
Wauzeka 53826
Waverly 54740
Wayne, *Lafayette* (Town) 53587
Wayne, *Washington* 53010
Wayside 54126
Webb Lake 54830
Webster, *Vernon* (Town) 54639
Webster, *Burnett* 54893
Weirgor 54835
Wellington (Town) 54651
Wells (Town) 54656
Wentworth 54874
Werley 53809
Wescott (Town) 54166
West Allis 53214
.... 53227
For specific ZIP Codes call (888) 275-8777, or your local postmaster.
West Baraboo 53913
West Bend 53090
.... 53095
For specific ZIP Codes call (888) 275-8777, or your local postmaster.
West Bloomfield 54983
Westboro 54490
Westby 54667
West De Pere (Part of De Pere) 54115
Western (Part of Milwaukee)‡ 53210
Westfield, *Sauk* (Town) 53943
Westfield, *Marquette* 53964
Westford, *Dodge* (Town) 53916
Westford, *Richland* (Town) 53924
West Jacksonport 54209
West Kewaunee (Town) 54216
West Lima 54639
Westlyn 54494
West Marshland (Town) 54840
West Milwaukee 53215
.... 53234
For specific ZIP Codes call (888) 275-8777, or your local postmaster.
Weston, *Clark* (Town) 54456
Weston, *Marathon* (Town) 54476
Weston, *Dunn* 54751
West Plainfield 54966
West Point (Town) 53555
Westport, *Dane* (Town) 53597
Westport, *Richland* 53518
West Prairie 54665
West Racine (Part of Racine)‡ 53405*
.... 53408†
West Rosendale 54974
West Salem 54669
Westside (Part of Madison)‡ 53711
West Sweden (Town) 54837
West Towne Mall (Part of Madison) 53719
Weyauwega 54983
Weyerhaeuser 54895
Wheatland, *Vernon* (Town) 54624
Wheatland, *Kenosha* 53105
Wheaton (Town) 54739
Wheeler 54772
Whitcomb 54486
White Creek 53965
Whitefish Bay, *Door* 54235
Whitefish Bay, *Milwaukee* 53217
Whitehall 54773
White Lake 54491
Whitelaw 54247
White Oak Springs (Town) 53586
White River (Town) 54855
Whitestown (Town) 54639
Whitewater 53190
Whiting 54481
Whittlesey 54451
Wien (Town) 54426
Wild Rose 54984
Wildwood 54028
Wilkinson (Town) 54895
Willard, *Rusk* (Town) 54731
Willard, *Clark* 54493
Williams Bay 53191
Williamstown (Town) 53032
Willow (Town) 53924
Willow Springs, *Lafayette* (Town) 53565
Willow Springs (Part of Menomonee Falls) 53051
Wilmore Heights 54971
Wilmot 53192
Wilson, *Dunn* (Town) 54733
Wilson, *Lincoln* (Town) 54487
Wilson, *Rusk* (Town) 54817
Wilson, *Sheboygan* (Town) 53081
Wilson, *Eau Claire* 54726
Wilson, *St. Croix* 54027
Wilton 54670
Winchester, *Vilas* 54545
Winchester, *Winnebago* 54947
Wind Lake♦ 53185
Wind Point 53402
Windsor♦ 53598
Windsor Hills 53532
Windsor Prairie 53532
Winfield (Town) 53959
Wingville (Town) 53569
Winnebago 54985
Winnebago Heights 53049
Winnebago Indian Reservation 53965
Winnebago Mission 54615
Winneboujou 54820
Winneconne (Town) 54927
Winneconne 54986
Winter 54896
Wiota 53587
Wisconna (Part of Glendale) 53209
Wisconsin Dells 53965
Wisconsin Rapids 54494-95
For specific ZIP Codes call (888) 275-8777, or your local postmaster.
Withee (Town) 54771
Withee 54498
Wittenberg 54499
Witwen 53583
Wolfcreek 54024
Wolf Lake 53079
Wolf River, *Langlade* (Town) 54491
Wolf River, *Winnebago* (Town) 54940
Wonewoc (Town) 53929
Wonewoc 53968
Wood, *Wood* (Town) 54466
Wood (Part of Milwaukee) 53295
Woodboro 54501
Wooddale 54817
Woodford 53599
Woodhull 54932
Woodland, *Sauk* (Town) 53968
Woodland, *Dodge* 53099
Woodman 53827
Woodmohr (Town) 54724
Wood River (Town) 54840
Woodruff 54568
Woodstock 53581
Woodville, *Calumet* (Town) 54129
Woodville, *St. Croix* 54028
Woodworth 53194
Worcester (Town) 54555
Worden (Town) 54771
Wrightstown (Town) 54115
Wrightstown 54180
Wuertsburg 54411
Wyalusing 53801
Wyeville 54660
Wyocena 53969
Wyoming, *Iowa* (Town) 53588
Wyoming, *Waupaca* (Town) 54945
Yahara Heights 53597
Yellow Lake 54830
York, *Clark* (Town) 54436
York, *Dane* (Town) 53925
York, *Green* (Town) 53516
York, *Jackson* 54758
York Center 53559
Yorkville 53182
Young America 53090
Yuba 54639
Zachow 54182
Zander 54208
Zenda 53195
Zittau 54940

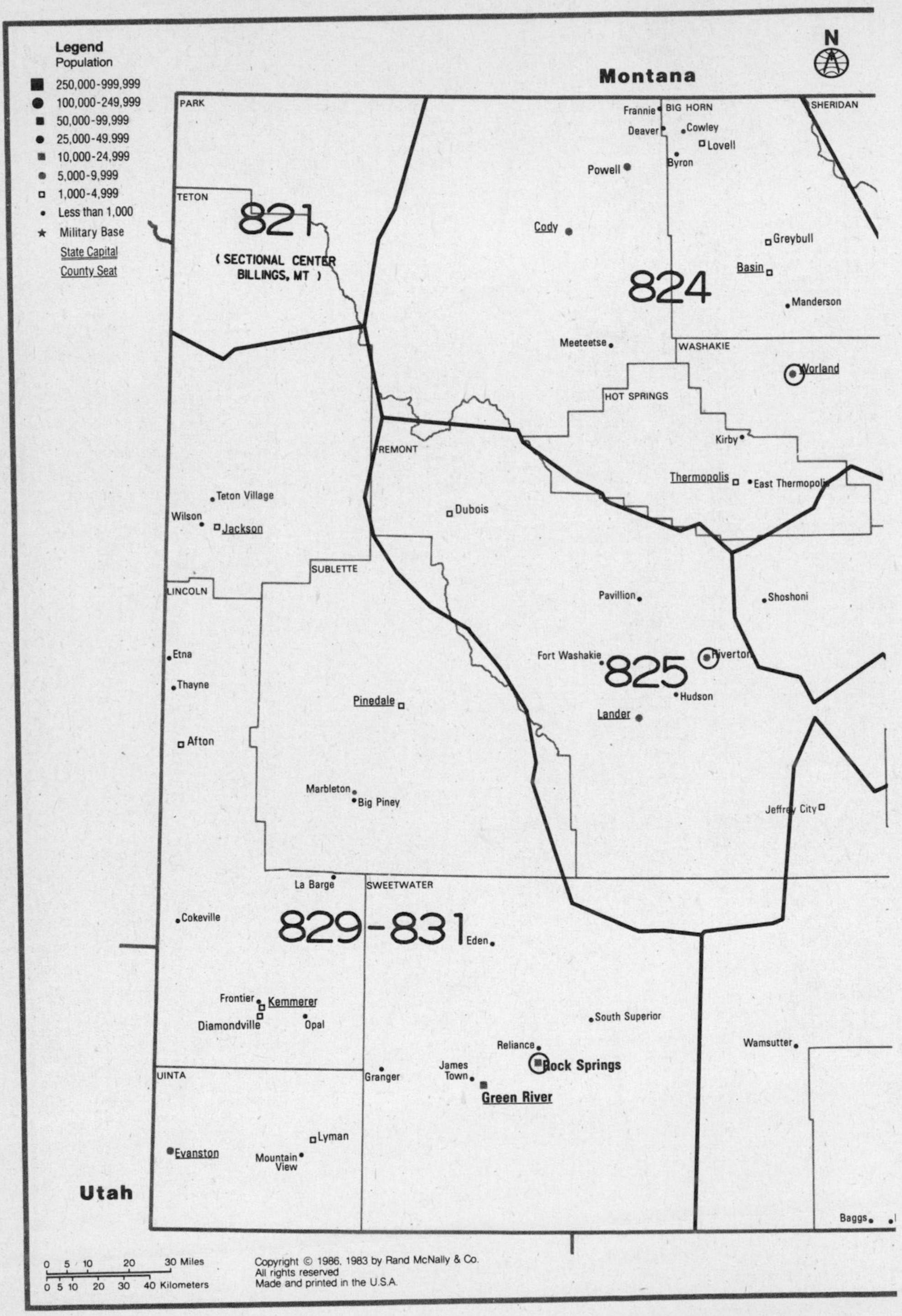
Legend
Population
250,000-999,999
100,000-249,999
50,000-99,999
25,000-49,999
10,000-24,999
5,000-9,999
1,000-4,999
Less than 1,000
Military Base
State Capital
County Seat
Montana
N
PARK
BIG HORN
SHERIDAN
Frannie
Deaver
Cowley
Lovell
Byron
Powell
TETON
821
(SECTIONAL CENTER BILLINGS, MT)
Cody
Greybull
Basin
824
Manderson
Meeteetse
WASHAKIE
Worland
HOT SPRINGS
Kirby
FREMONT
Thermopolis
East Thermopolis
Teton Village
Wilson
Jackson
Dubois
SUBLETTE
LINCOLN
Pavillion
Shoshoni
Etna
Fort Washakie
825
Riverton
Thayne
Hudson
Pinedale
Lander
Afton
Marbleton
Big Piney
Jeffrey City
La Barge
SWEETWATER
Cokeville
829-831
Eden
Frontier
Kemmerer
Diamondville
Opal
South Superior
Wamsutter
Reliance
James Town
Rock Springs
UINTA
Granger
Green River
Lyman
Evanston
Mountain View
Utah
Baggs
0 5 10 20 30 Miles
0 5 10 20 30 40 Kilometers

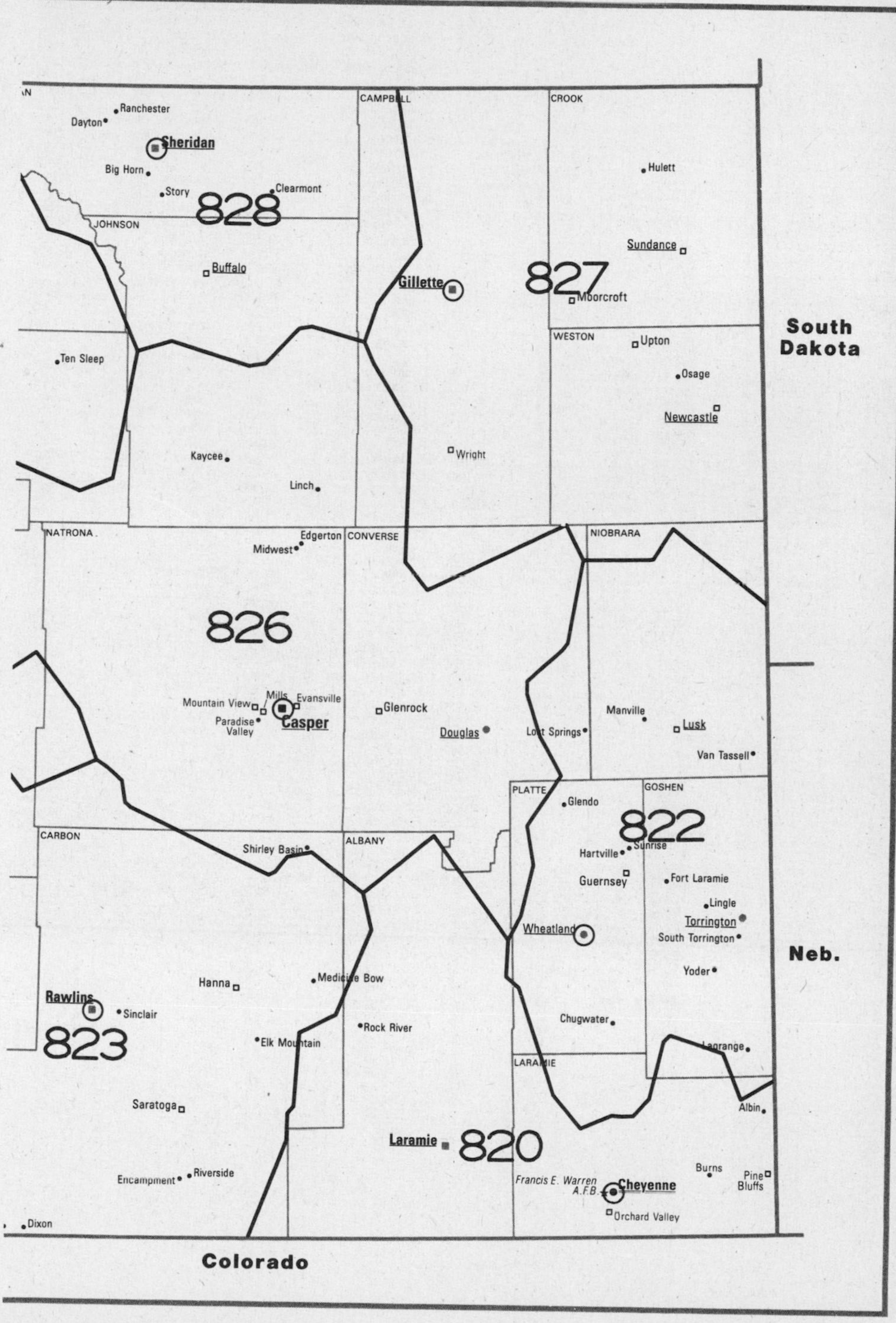
CAMPBELL
CROOK
Ranchester
Dayton
Sheridan
Big Horn
Story
Clearmont
828
JOHNSON
Hulett
Sundance
Buffalo
Gillette
827
Moorcroft
WESTON
Upton
South Dakota
Ten Sleep
Osage
Newcastle
Wright
Kaycee
Linch
NATRONA
Edgerton
Midwest
CONVERSE
NIOBRARA
826
Mountain View
Mills
Evansville
Paradise Valley
Casper
Glenrock
Douglas
Manville
Lusk
Van Tassell
PLATTE
GOSHEN
Glendo
822
CARBON
ALBANY
Shirley Basin
Hartville
Sunrise
Guernsey
Fort Laramie
Lingle
Torrington
Wheatland
South Torrington
Neb.
Yoder
Hanna
Rawlins
Sinclair
823
Rock River
Elk Mountain
Chugwater
LARAMIE
Saratoga
Albin
Laramie
820
Burns
Pine Bluffs
Francis E. Warren A.F.B.
Cheyenne
Encampment
Riverside
Orchard Valley
Dixon
Colorado

Place	ZIP Code
Adkins Valley	82801
Afton	83110
Airport (Part of Cheyenne)‡	82001
Aladdin	82710
Albany	82070
Albin	82050
Alcova	82620
Allendale	82601
Almy	82930
Alpine	83128
Alpine Junction (Part of Alpine)	83128
Alta	83422
Alva	82711
Arapahoe♦	82510
Arminto	82630
Arrow Head Lodge	82836
Arvada	82831
Atlantic City	82520
Auburn	83111
Baggs	82321
Bairoil	82322
Banner	82832
Barnum	82639
Bar Nunn	82601
Basin	82410
Bear Lodge	82836
Beckton	82801
Bedford	83112
Beulah	82712
Big Horn	82833
Big Piney	83113
Bill	82631
Bondurant	82922
Bonneville	82649
Bosler	82051
Bosler Junction	82051
Boulder	82923
Boxelder	82637
Bronx	83115
Brundage Place	82801
Buffalo	82834
Buford	82052
Burlington	82411
Burns	82053
Burntfork	82938
Burris	82512
Byron	82412
Calpet	83123
Canyon‡	82190
Capitol Station (Part of Cheyenne)‡	82001
Carlile	82713
Carpenter	82054
Carter	82937
Casper	82601-09
For specific ZIP Codes call (888) 275-8777, or your local postmaster.	
Centennial	82055
Chatham	82401
Cheyenne	82001-09
For specific ZIP Codes call (888) 275-8777, or your local postmaster.	
Chugwater	82210
Clareton	82701
Clark	59008
Clay	82723
Clearmont	82835
Cody	82414
Cokeville	83114
Colony	57717
Colter Bay	83001
Cora	82925
Cowley	82420
Creston	82301
Creston Junction	82301
Crowheart	82512
Daniel	83115
Dayton	82836
Deaver	82421
Devils Tower	82714
Diamondville	83116
Dixon	82323
Douglas	82633
Downer	82801
Dubois	82513
Dwyer	82201
Eastridge Mall (Part of Casper)	82601
East Thermopolis	82443
Eden	82932
Edgerton	82635
Egbert	82053
Elk Mountain	82324
Elmo (Part of Hanna)	82327
Emblem	82422
Encampment	82325
Esterbrook	82633
Ethete	82520
Etna	83118
Evanston	82930*
	82931†
Evansville	82636
Fairview	83119
Farson	82932
Fishing Bridge	82190
Fontenelle	83101
Fort Bridger	82933
Fort Laramie	82212
Fort Steele	82301
Fort Washakie	82514
Four Corners	82715
Foxpark	82070
Francis E. Warren Air Force Base	82001
Frannie	82423
Freedom	83120
Frontier	83121
Frontier Mall (Part of Cheyenne)	82001
Garland	82435
Garrett	82058
Gas Camp 1	82643
Gillette	82716-18
For specific ZIP Codes call (888) 275-8777, or your local postmaster.	
Glendo	82213
Glenrock	82637
Granger	82934
Granite Canon	82059
Grant Village	82190
Grass Creek	82443
Green River	82935
Greybull	82426
Grover	83122
Guernsey	82214
Halfway	83113
Hamilton Dome	82427
Hanna	82327
Happy Jack Ranchettes	82007
Harriman	82059
Hartville	82215
Hawk Springs	82217
Hiland	82638
Hillsdale	82060
Hilltop (Part of Casper)‡	82609
Hoback Junction	83001
Horse Creek	82061
Hudson	82515
Hulett	82720
Huntley	82218
Hyattville	82428
Iron Mountain	82001
Jackson	83001-02
For specific ZIP Codes call (888) 275-8777, or your local postmaster.	
Jackson Lake Lodge	83013
James Town	82935
Jay Em	82219
Jeffrey City	82310
Jelm	82063
Jenny Lake	83012
Kaycee	82639
Kearny	82832
Keeline	82227
Kelly	83011
Kemmerer	83101
Keystone	82070
Kinnear	82516
Kirby	82430
La Barge	83123
Lagrange	82221
Lake	82190
Lake Creek Resort	82070
Lamont	82301
Lance Creek	82222
Lander	82520
Laramie	82070-71
For specific ZIP Codes call (888) 275-8777, or your local postmaster.	
Leiter	82837
Leo	82327
Linch	82640
Lingle	82223
Little America	82929
Lonetree	82936
Lost Cabin	82642
Lost Springs	82224
Lovell	82431
Lucerne	82443
Lucky MacCamp	82501
Lusk	82225
Lyman	82937
Lysite	82642
McFadden	82083
McKinley	82633
McKinnon	82938
Manderson	82432
Mantua	82435
Manville	82227
Marbleton	83113
Mayoworth	82639
Medicine Bow	82329
Meeteetse	82433
Meriden	82081
Merna	83115
Midvale	82501
Midwest	82643
Midwest Heights	82601
Milford	82520
Mills	82644
Moneta	82601
Moorcroft	82721
Moose	83012
Moran	83013
Morton	82501
Mountain Home	82070
Mountain View, *Natrona*♦	82604
Mountain View, *Uinta*	82936*
	82939†
Muddy Gap	82301
Museum (Part of Cheyenne)‡	82001
Natrona	82646
Newcastle	82701
New Haven	82720
Node	82225
Number One (Part of Cheyenne)‡	82001
O'Donnell Spur	82435
Old Faithful	82190
Opal	83124
Orchard Valley	82007
Orin	82633
Orpha	82633
Osage	82723
Oshoto	82721
Osmond	83110
Otto	82434
Pahaska	82414
Paradise Valley (Part of Casper)	82601
Parkerton	82637
Parkman	82838
Pavillion	82523
Piedmont	82933
Pine Bluffs	82082
Pinedale	82941
Pine Haven	82721
Point of Rocks	82942
Powder River	82648
Powell	82435
Prospector Village	82717
Ralston	82440
Ranchester	82839
Rawhide Village	82717
Rawlins	82301
Recluse	82725
Red Buttes Village	82604
Red Desert	82336
Red Lane	82443
Reliance	82943
Reno (Part of Wright)	82732
Reno Junction (Part of Wright)	82732
Riovista	82935
Riverside	82325
Riverton	82501
Riverview	57735
Robertson	82944
Rock River	82083
Rock Springs	82901-02
For specific ZIP Codes call (888) 275-8777, or your local postmaster.	
Rockypoint	82721
Rolling Hills	82637
Rozet	82727
Ryan Park	82331
Saddlestring	82840
Sand Draw	82501
Saratoga	82331
Savery	82332
Seminoe Dam	82334
Shawnee	82229
Shell	82441
Sheridan	82801
Sheridan Gardens	82801
Shirley Basin	82615
Shoshoni	82649
Sinclair	82334
Slater	82201
Smoot	83126
South Jackson	83001
South Laramie	82070
South Pass City	82520
South Torrington	82240
Spotted Horse	82831
Story	82842
Sundance	82729
Sunrise (Part of Casper)‡	82604
Sunrise, *Platte*	82215
Sunshine	82433
Superior	82945
Sussex	82639
Sweetwater Station	82520
Taylor	82643
Ten Sleep	82442
Teton Village	83025
Thayne	83127
Thermopolis	82443
Three Forks	82301
Tie Siding	82084
Torrington	82240
Tower Junction	82190
Turnerville	83112
Ucross	82835
Ulm	82835
University (Part of Laramie)‡	82071
Upton	82730
Urie	82937
Uva	82201
Valley	82414
Van Tassell	82242
Veteran	82243
Walcott	82335
Wamsutter	82336
Wapiti	82450
Wapiti Valley	82450
Western Hills (Part of Cheyenne)	82001
West Lance Creek	82222
West Laramie	82070
Weston	82731
West Thumb	82190
Wheatland	82201
Willwood	82435
Wilson	83014
Wind River Indian Reservation	82514
Wolf	82844
Woods Landing	82063
Worland	82401
Wright	82732
Wyarno	82845
Wyodak	82718
Yellowstone National Park	82190
Yoder	82244